BUSINESS STATISTICS
OF THE
UNITED STATES

PATTERNS OF ECONOMIC CHANGE

15TH EDITION
2010

BUSINESS
STATISTICS
OF THE
UNITED STATES

PATTERNS OF ECONOMIC CHANGE

15TH EDITION
2010

Edited by Cornelia J. Strawser

Associate Editor
Mary Meghan Ryan

Lanham, Maryland

Published in the United States of America
by Bernan Press, a wholly owned subsidiary of
The Rowman & Littlefield Publishing Group, Inc.
4501 Forbes Boulevard, Suite 200
Lanham, Maryland 20706

Bernan Press
800-865-3457
info@bernan.com
www.bernan.com

ISBN-13: 978-1-59888-414-2

eISBN: 978-1-59888-415-9

ISSN: 1086-8488

CONTENTS

PREFACE

Business Statistics of the United States: Patterns of Economic Change, 15th Edition, 2010 is a basic desk reference for anyone requiring statistics on the U.S. economy. It contains about 3,500 economic time series in all, portraying the period since World War II in comprehensive detail, and, in the case of about 200 key series, the period from 1929 through 1948 as well. The data are predominantly from federal government sources. Of equal importance are the extensive background notes for each chapter, which help users to understand the data, use them appropriately, and, if desired, seek additional information from the source agencies.

The 2010 Edition

U.S. economic statistics change to keep up with a continually changing economy, and the 15th edition of *Business Statistics* provides background and up-to-date, complete historical information incorporating important new features of our comprehensive and complex statistical system. Notably, the 2009 comprehensive revision of the National Income and Product Accounts (NIPAs), released in July 2009, is incorporated throughout this volume, providing consistent new current- and constant-dollar estimates of output, demand, and incomes all the way back to 1929.

- New information has been introduced into all of the NIPA series that measure value, real output, and prices. The complete historical production and price indexes have been rebased to 2005 = 100, and the complete history of constant-dollar GDP has been restated in 2005 dollars.
- The classification of consumer expenditures has been updated to reflect changes in consumer buying patterns since the 1940s, when the original categories were defined. Consumer spending components that were previously measured, and included in total consumer spending but lumped in with unrelated products, have been regrouped into new relevant major product categories, such as recreational goods and vehicles and financial services and insurance.
- Consumption spending by nonprofit organizations, previously included with all other consumer spending, is now identified separately from consumption spending by households.
- A new series on real income, "Personal income excluding current transfer receipts" in constant dollars, has been introduced. Total personal income includes transfer receipts, such as Social Security and unemployment insurance; subtracting the transfer components makes this new series more responsive to the state of the economy. For that reason, it is an important business cycle indicator.

- Restaurant meals have been reclassified from "goods" to "services."
- The treatment of disasters, such as hurricanes, has been changed, so that the direct effects of property destruction are reflected in capital accounts and capital stock measurement but not in incomes from current production or current transfer payments.

Another new development in the U.S. statistical system is the monthly reporting of hours and earnings for all employees on nonfarm payrolls. The monthly report on Employment and Earnings from the Bureau of Labor Statistics now includes hours of work, earnings per hour, and earnings per week for all employees, as well as continuing to report hours and earnings for production or nonsupervisory workers. *Business Statistics* now provides comprehensive historical data under both definitions for all nonfarm industry and for major industry groups.

In addition, because of the importance of U.S. trade and financial relationships with China, a series on the value of the U.S. dollar in terms of the Chinese yuan has been introduced in Chapter 13, International Comparisons. (The value of U.S. goods trade with China is reported in Chapter 7, U.S. Foreign Trade and Finance.)

THE PLAN OF THE BOOK

The history of the U.S. economy is told in major U.S. government sets of statistical data: the national income and product accounts compiled by the Bureau of Economic Analysis (BEA); the data on labor force, employment, hours, earnings, and productivity compiled by the Bureau of Labor Statistics (BLS); the price indexes collected by BLS; and the financial market data compiled primarily by the Board of Governors of the Federal Reserve System (FRB). All of these sets exist in annual and either monthly or quarterly form beginning in 1946, 1947, or 1948, and many are available, at least annually, as far back as 1929.

In Part A, *Business Statistics* presents annual values for major indicators and their significant components back as far as space and availability permit, along with recent quarterly or monthly data. This enables easy calculation of growth rates and more flexible comparisons of recent values with historical data.

However, historical data with a higher frequency than annual are required for many purposes, including comparisons of activity before and after business cycle turning points. For the main series presented in Part A, historical quarterly or monthly data are presented in Part C that go all the way back to the beginning of the postwar period, where available. Part C also includes, for the same series, the annual values back to the end of World War II that had to be dropped from the tables in Part A for space reasons.

In both Part A and Part C, the presentations begin with the national income and product accounts, or NIPAs. The NIPAs comprise a comprehensive, thorough, and internally consistent data set. They measure the value of the total output of the U.S. economy (the gross domestic product, or GDP) and they allocate that value between its quantity, or "real," and price components. They show how the value of aggregate demand is distributed among consumers, business investors, government, and foreign customers; how much of aggregate demand is supplied by imports and how much by domestic production; and how the income generated in domestic production is distributed between labor and capital.

Production estimates covering only the "industrial" sectors of the economy—manufacturing, mining, and utilities—are shown in Chapter 2, after the presentation of the overall NIPAs in Chapter 1.

The distribution of income, median income—the best measure of the economic well-being of the "typical" American—and poverty statistics from a Census household survey are presented in Chapter 3.

Then, more detail from the NIPAs is presented for the components of economic activity. GDP by definition consists of the sum of consumption expenditures, business investment, government purchases of goods and services, and exports minus imports—the elementary economics blackboard equation "GDP = C + I + G + X – M." Chapters on each of these components—consumption, investment, government, and foreign trade—are presented in Part A.

Following these chapters, there are a chapter on prices, two chapters on the compensation of labor and capital inputs and the amount and productivity of labor input, one chapter on energy inputs into production and consumption, and one chapter on money and financial markets.

While GDP is initially defined and measured by adding up its demand categories and subtracting imports, this output is produced in industries—some in the old-line heavy industries such as manufacturing, mining, and utilities, but an increasing share in the huge and heterogeneous group known as "service-providing" industries. Part A gives a number of summary measures of activity classified by industry or industrial sector: industrial production, profits, and employment-related data. Further industry information is provided in the next section of the book.

In Part B, *Business Statistics* first presents a general description of the current system of industrial classification, the North American Industry Classification System (NAICS),

and its differences from its predecessor the Standard Industrial Classification system (SIC). This is followed by a table summarizing the structure of the U.S. economy as specified in NAICS. This table indicates how the NAICS statistical system is organized and shows—very roughly, in some cases—how each NAICS industry relates to the earlier SIC industries. The chapters that follow show GDP, income, employment, hours, and earnings by industry, followed by statistics for key sectors such as petroleum, housing, manufacturing, retail trade, and services.

Part C, Historical Data, contains in Chapter 18 graphs and tables summarizing annual values for important economic aggregates for the years 1929 through 1948, giving information about the enormous changes the economy went through as it experienced the Great Depression and the New Deal, mobilized for and fought World War II, and then demobilized.

In Chapters 19 and 20, postwar annual and quarterly or monthly values for the most important NIPA series and other major indicators complete the record shown in Part A for the period since the end of World War II.

Part D, State and Regional Data, contains annual data by state and region on personal income and employment back to 1958, and annual values and quantity indexes for GDP by state and region back to 1977.

Notes and definitions. Productive use of economic data requires accurate knowledge about the sources and meaning of the data. The notes and definitions for each chapter, shown immediately after that chapter's tables, contain definitions, descriptions of recent data revisions, and references to sources of additional technical information. They also include information about data availability and revision and release schedules, which allows users to readily access the latest current values if they need to keep up with the data month by month or quarter by quarter.

THE HISTORY OF *BUSINESS STATISTICS*

The history of *Business Statistics* began with the publication, many years ago, of the first edition of a volume with the same name and general purpose by the U.S. Department of Commerce's Bureau of Economic Analysis (BEA). After 27 periodic editions, the last of which appeared in 1992, BEA found it necessary, for budgetary and other reasons, to discontinue both the publication and the maintenance of the database from which the publication was derived.

The individual statistical series gathered together here are publicly available. However, the task of gathering them from the numerous different sources within the government and assembling them into one coherent database is impractical for most data users. Even when current data are readily available, obtaining the full historical time series is often time-consuming and difficult. Definitions and other documentation can also be inconvenient to find. Believing that a *Business Statistics* compilation was too valuable to be lost to the public, Bernan Press published the first edition of the present publication, edited by Dr. Courtenay M. Slater, in 1995. The first edition received a warm welcome from users of economic data. Dr. Slater, formerly chief economist of the Department of Commerce, continued to develop *Business Statistics* through four subsequent annual editions. The current editor worked with Dr. Slater on the fourth and fifth editions. In subsequent editions, she has continued in the tradition established by Dr. Slater of ensuring high-quality data while revising and expanding the book's scope to include significant new aspects of the U.S. economy and longer historical background.

Nearly all of the statistical data in this book are from federal government sources and are available in the public domain. Sources are given in the applicable notes and definitions.

The data in this volume meet the publication standards of the federal statistical agencies from which they were obtained. Every effort has been made to select data that are accurate, meaningful, and useful. All statistical data are subject to error arising from sampling variability, reporting errors, incomplete coverage, imputation, and other causes. The responsibility of the editor and publisher of this volume is limited to reasonable care in the reproduction and presentation of data obtained from established sources.

The 2010 edition has been edited by Cornelia J. Strawser, in association with Mary Meghan Ryan, who prepared all the tables and graphs and whose ability and experience have been essential in producing a timely and accurate reference work.

Dr. Strawser is the senior economic consultant to Bernan Press. She edited the seventh through fourteenth editions and was the co-editor of two previous editions of *Business Statistics.* She was co-editor of *Foreign Trade of the United States, 2001,* and also worked on the *Handbook of U.S. Labor Statistics.* She was formerly a senior economist for the U.S. House of Representatives Budget Committee and has also served at the Senate Budget Committee, at the Congressional Budget Office, and on the Federal Reserve Board staff.

The editor assumes full responsibility for the interpretations presented in this volume.

BUSINESS STATISTICS IN THE GREAT RECESSION

This 15th edition of *Business Statistics of the United States* presents data on U.S. economic performance through December 2009—24 months after the beginning of the 11th recession of the postwar period, according to the chronology maintained by the National Bureau of Economic Research (NBER).

Many observers believe that the recession ended around the middle of 2009. Real Gross Domestic Product (GDP) rose in the third and fourth quarters of 2009 and the first of 2010. Among the monthly indicators used by NBER to help determine the turning points of the business cycle, industrial production and real manufacturing and trade sales troughed in June 2009 and have been increasing since then. Real personal income minus transfer payments troughed in October 2009. Payroll employment has been rising since a low point in December 2009.

NBER had not made a determination of this recession's end date at the time this was written. Meeting on April 8, the NBER's Business Cycle Dating Committee issued a statement saying that "Although most indicators have turned up, the committee decided that the determination of the trough date on the basis of current data would be premature. Many indicators are quite preliminary at this time and will be revised in coming months."

But even if the trough is, eventually, placed at what currently appears to be the earliest possible month—June 2009—the 2007–2009 recession will have lasted 18 months and will have been the longest of the postwar period: the two longest previous NBER-designated postwar recessions each lasted 16 months. By some measures—see, for example, the chart of payroll employment that follows—it is more severe than any other postwar recession. It is pointed out in the Annual Report of the President's Council of Economic Advisers that the financial shocks that set off this recession were at least as severe as those that precipitated the Great Depression of the 1930s; indeed, "in 1929, household wealth declined only 3 percent—about one-seventh as much as in 2008." While the current recession does not seem to be following the path of the Great Depression—in part because the policy responses have been markedly different—it does not seem to be inappropriate that it is being called the Great Recession.

This article begins with a general discussion of business cycles in the United States economy, including a chronology of the cycles occurring in the years covered by this volume, and a discussion of the meaning of the term "The Great Depression".

- Following this is an example of the use of monthly data, such as those provided in this book, to track recession and recovery.
- Then, other examples are provided of important analytical techniques for extracting key information from a statistical record and focusing on growth issues.
- Following that section, and illustrating the use of the techniques described, is a comparison of the latest completed cycle of recession, recovery, and growth—between 2000 and 2007—with two previous full cycles.
- A subsequent section deals with measuring the standard of living.

BUSINESS CYCLES IN THE U.S. ECONOMY

The study of economic fluctuations in the United States was pioneered by Wesley C. Mitchell and Arthur F. Burns early in the twentieth century, and was carried on subsequently by other researchers affiliated with the National Bureau of Economic Research (NBER), an independent, nonpartisan research organization. These analysts observed that indicators of the general state of business activity tended to move up and down over periods that were longer than a year and were therefore not accounted for by seasonal variation. Although these periods of expansion and contraction have not been uniform in length, and thus not "cycles" in any strict mathematical sense, their recurrent nature caused them to be called "business cycles." NBER has identified 32 complete (peak-to-peak) business cycles over the period beginning with December 1854.

The first NBER-established business cycle dates, identifying the monthly peaks and troughs in general economic activity, were published in 1929. Currently, the dates are established by the NBER Business Cycle Dating Committee, first formed in 1978. It consists of eight economists who are university professors, associated with research organizations, or both.

Business cycle dates are based on monthly data, and have been identified for periods long before the availability of quarterly data on real gross national product (GDP). Even in the recent period for which such data are available, the NBER identification of a recession does not always coincide with the frequently cited definition of recession as two consecutive quarters of decline in real GDP.

The monthly and quarterly dates of the cycles from before the Great Depression to the latest announced turning point—the December 2007 peak ending the expansion

Table A-1. BUSINESS CYCLE REFERENCE DATES 1927–2007

TROUGH	PEAK
NOVEMBER 1927 (IV)	AUGUST 1929 (III)
MARCH 1933 (I)	MAY 1937 (II)
JUNE 1938 (II)	FEBRUARY 1945 (I)
OCTOBER 1945 (IV)	NOVEMBER 1948 (IV)
OCTOBER 1949 (IV)	JULY 1953 (II)
MAY 1954 (II)	AUGUST 1957 (III)
APRIL 1958 (II)	APRIL 1960 (II)
FEBRUARY 1961 (I)	DECEMBER 1969 (IV)
NOVEMBER 1970 (IV)	NOVEMBER 1973 (IV)
MARCH 1975 (I)	JANUARY 1980 (I)
JULY 1980 (III)	JULY 1981 (III)
NOVEMBER 1982 (IV)	JULY 1990 (III)
MARCH 1991 (I)	MARCH 2001 (I)
NOVEMBER 2001 (IV)	DECEMBER 2007 (IV)

SOURCE: NATIONAL BUREAU OF ECONOMIC RESEARCH, HTTP://WWW.NBER.ORG/CYCLES.

that began in November 2001—are shown in Table A-1 above. Quarterly turning points are identified by Roman numerals. NBER considers that the trough month is both the end of the decline and the beginning of the recovery, based on the concept that the actual turning point was some particular day within that month. Thus, the latest expansion ended in December 2007, and the recession also began in December 2007.

For additional information on NBER and its business cycle studies, see the NBER Web site at <http://www.nber.org/cycles>.

WHAT WAS THE GREAT DEPRESSION?

Note that most of the 1930s, after the March 1933 trough, is identified as a period of expansion by NBER, in apparent conflict with the fact that the entire decade is often considered to be in the "Great Depression." The NBER does not identify "depressions;" the popular usage denotes a prolonged period of idle resources.

People interested in the economics and politics of the 1930s may wish to distinguish, as NBER does, between that part of the period when output and employment declined precipitously—the 43-month collapse from August 1929 through March 1933—and the subsequent period when output and employment, though still far below a likely trend line, were rising most of the time, before accepting at face value statements like "the New Deal failed to end the Depression."

Chapter 18 of *Business Statistics* includes five graphs depicting the economic course of the Depression and World War II periods, accompanied by some explanatory narration. The Notes and Definitions to that chapter discuss the business cycle dates for this period and the important issue of the statistical treatment of work relief employment during the Depression.

TRACKING RECESSIONS: TOTAL PAYROLL EMPLOYMENT

Figure A-1 shows how current data can be tracked month by month in comparison with earlier business cycles. The figure depicts proportional movements in total payroll employment (see Tables 10-7 and 20-4 and the associated Notes and Definitions), beginning with the cycle peak and continuing over the following 29 months.

Many economists would prefer to track cycles monthly using a comprehensive measure of aggregate output, not employment. However, we do not have a satisfactory monthly measure of gross domestic product [GDP]; attempts to estimate it have proved to be volatile, "noisy", and subject to excessive revision.

The reliable and long-established monthly index of industrial production is a narrower measure of output, limited to manufacturing, mining, and utilities. It is presented in Chapter 2 of this volume. Mining and utilities are of little significance in the business cycle process—in fact, short-term variation in the utility sector is mostly influenced by unusual weather conditions. As a result, the cyclical movements of the industrial production index are dominated by the manufacturing sector. Because manufacturing now accounts for only about 10 percent of total nonfarm employment, the industrial production index is limited as a general business cycle gauge, but it is still one of the major indicators monitored by the Business Cycle Dating Committee.

The employment count—covering the entire nonfarm economy, based on a large and long-established sample of large and small businesses, and available shortly after the end of each month—is a widely accepted indicator, more reliable and less subject to revision and excessive random variation than any available broad production measure. It is viewed as "the most reliable comprehensive estimate of employment" by the Business Cycle Dating Committee.

For ease of comparing proportional effects in this graph, the employment totals for each recession period are converted to indexes with the cycle's peak month set at 100. To illustrate, the line labeled "From July 1981" represents employment in each successive month, July 1981 through December 1983, divided by the July 1981 value and multiplied by 100. The line labeled "From December 2007" represents employment in each successive month, December 2007 through a preliminary value for May 2010, divided by the December 2007 value and multiplied by 100.

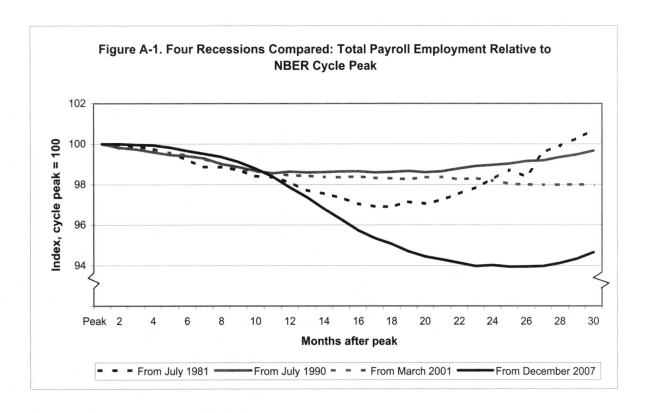

Figure A-1. Four Recessions Compared: Total Payroll Employment Relative to NBER Cycle Peak

Looked at in this way, the similarities among the four recessions in the first 10 months of decline are striking: nearly a year after the peak, employment was down about 1½ percent in each case. Two months later, the four declines no longer looked similar. Employment had leveled off in 1991 and 2002, but lurched sharply downward in winter 2008–2009 as it did in mid-1982. Thus, this recession is comparable in length and severity to, at least, the 1981–1982 recession, rather than to the mild recessions of more recent decades.

Figure A-1 shows that the slide in employment from the July 1981 peak continued for a year and a half and then began a brisk recovery. The 2010 recovery is later, more modest, and in the latest month dependent mainly on temporary government hiring for the 2010 Census.

In comparing the end-of-recession and beginning-of-recovery periods of 1983 and 2009, it should be noted that both periods saw fiscal stimulus enacted, but the monetary conditions are strikingly different. A look at Table 20-6 shows that the federal funds rate (the rate banks charge on overnight loans, set by Federal Reserve open market operations) was 19 percent in July 1981, fell to 13 percent in July 1982, and was 9 percent by July 1983. The Fed had maintained a very tight policy in early 1981 to break the back of inflation, then had plenty of room to reduce rates once the recession was under way.

In contrast, the federal funds rate was already close to zero at the cycle peak in December 2007, and the obstacles to renewed credit flows were not high interest rates but deflation and deteriorating financial balance sheets. These are the conditions that have led some to fear a slide like the one that started in August 1929 and lasted 3 ½ years, similarly fed by deflation and financial institution failures.

As mentioned above, Chapter 18 of this edition of *Business Statistics* includes a statistical picture of the Depression years, as an indication of what today's policymakers are struggling to prevent. Two of today's highest economic officials—Chairman Ben Bernanke of the Federal Reserve Board, and Chairman Christina Romer of the President's Council of Economic Advisers—are respected academic scholars of the Great Depression. The policies they pursue today, including efforts to get credit flowing again that might produce results comparable to the interest rate declines of 1982–83, are undertaken in the light of their knowledge of the failures of the policies of 1929–33. That said, the guidance of history is limited when so many circumstances are different, and much uncertainty remains.

ANALYTICAL TECHNIQUES FOR GROWTH ISSUES

In assessing the performance of an economy over longer periods of time, it is important to use analytical techniques that highlight the most important aspects of the series. In this article and in the graphs and text that accompany nearly every *Business Statistics* data chapter, the editor will frequently make use of three powerful tools: the ratio-scale graph, the calculation of compound annual growth rates, and the use of cyclically comparable years to estimate trends and to separate trend from cyclical behavior. Econometricians use more elaborate methods of statistical analysis to estimate relationships and construct models, but much can be discerned just by using these relatively simple techniques.

Ratio-scale graphs. At the beginning of Chapter 1 (Figure 1-1) is a time series graph of output per capita from 1946 through 2008, drawn on a ratio scale. Output per capita is the constant-dollar value of each year's U.S. gross domestic product (GDP), divided by the size of that year's U.S. population.

The reader will quickly see that equal distances on the vertical scale of this graph do not represent equal differences in 2005-dollar values. However, equal vertical distances do represent equal <u>percent changes</u>. Any upward-sloping straight line plotted on this scale represents a constant percentage rate of growth over the period, and any downward-sloping straight line represents a constant percentage rate of decline.

This ratio-scale graph was produced by the following three steps: (1) The values to be graphed were converted into natural (base e) logarithms. (2) The natural logarithms were graphed. (3) For ease of interpretation, the vertical scale on this graph of the logarithms was re-labeled, replacing the numerical value of the logarithm that was plotted with the numerical value of its antilog—that is, the original value of per capita output.

This technique is only valid for data series that do not include zeroes or negative numbers, for which logarithms do not exist. Because percentage values such as the unemployment rate and percent changes such as the inflation rate are already in percentage terms, and because percent changes may include zero and/or negative values, they are not graphed in this fashion.

Compound annual growth rates. In the text of this article and in the highlights pages that precede and accompany most of the chapters, the editor often uses compound annual growth rates to summarize the history of important economic processes such as economic and demographic growth and inflation.

The compound annual growth rate is the percentage rate which, when compounded annually, would cause a quantity or price "X(t)" observed in a base period "t" to grow (or decline) to a quantity or price "X(t+i)" over a period of "i" years. Using this procedure, growth percentages for different periods spanning different numbers of years can be reduced to a common scale—the annual rate—for comparison. The formula for calculating such a growth rate, "r," is as follows:

$$r = \left(\sqrt[i]{X(t+i)/X(t)} - 1 \right) x100 .$$

When growth rates are functionally related to each other, such as the growth rates for output, hours worked, and output per hour worked (productivity), those rates will be arithmetically consistent as in the following formula, where "o" is the percentage growth rate for output, "h" the rate for hours worked, and "p" the growth rate for output per hour worked:

$$p = \left[[(100+o)/(100+h)] - 1 \right] x100$$

When the percentage growth rates are not very far from zero, relationships of this kind can be approximated or verified by simple addition or subtraction of the relevant percentage rates. For example, the productivity growth rate of 2.2 percent in output per hour at nonfarm business from 1948 to 2000 is approximately the difference between the output growth rate of 3.7 percent and the hours growth rate of 1.5 percent in that period.

Using cyclically comparable end points. For economic processes that have significant business-cycle components, such as output and employment, it is important to use comparable points in the business cycle for estimating underlying growth rates. One commonly used method is to calculate growth rates between years with similar, high rates of resource utilization. The broadest readily available measure of resource utilization is the unemployment rate, which was 3.8 percent in 1948, 4.0 percent in 2000, and 4.6 percent in 2007. (See Table 10-4.) A narrower measure that focuses on capital rather than labor, namely capacity utilization in manufacturing, was 82.5 percent in 1948, 80.1 percent in 2000, and 79.0 percent in 2007. (See Tables 20-1 and 2-3.)

End points that are not comparable: what difference does it make?

An interesting example of non-cyclically-comparable end points can be found in a recent newspaper commentary by Richard W. Rahn in *The Washington Times* (January 27, 2010). He writes that "In the nine quarter-century periods since the American republic was founded in 1789, the one with highest economic growth and job creation was the period from 1983 through 2007." As he shows, the annual average growth rate was 3.33 percent for that period, which he actually is measuring from the year 1982 as a base. However, November 1982 marked the trough of a deep recession, and December 2007 a cycle peak. If GDP growth is measured between the years of the two full cycle peaks nearest to this general time span, 1979 and 2007, it averages 2.96 percent; if it is measured between the two nearest troughs, 1982 and 2009, it averages 2.98 percent. Similarly, growth in payroll employment 1982–2007 averaged 1.73 percent; between 1979 and 2007, 1.53 percent; and between 1982 and 2009, 1.41 percent.

(As will be seen in Table A-2 and the accompanying analysis, that period between 1979 and 2007 includes three full cycles with somewhat different growth rates and other characteristics.)

Comparisons based on other artificial demarcation points such as decades may be subject to similar distortions.

Table A-2. Three Peak-to-Peak Periods Compared

(Number, percent.)

Description	January 1980 to July 1990	July 1990 to March 2001	March 2001 to December 2007
GENERAL DESCRIPTION OF CYCLE			
Length of full cycle, peak to peak, months	126	128	81
Length of expansion phase, months	1 92	120	73
Length of payroll employment expansion	90	116	52
Length of following recession, months	8	8	18 or more
Percent change in real GDP	-1.3	-0.3	-3.8
ECONOMIC MEASUREMENTS OF CYCLE, BASED ON ANNUAL AVERAGES FOR 1979, 1990, 2000, AND 2007			
Real GDP growth (percent change, annual rate, Table 1-2)	2.92	3.40	2.40
Real per capita product and income growth (percent changes, annual rate, Table 1-7):			
Real gross domestic product per capita	1.93	2.16	1.42
Real disposable (after-tax) personal income per capita	2.03	2.06	1.76
Total civilian employment (CPS, Table 10-2):			
Change in jobs, millions	20.0	18.1	9.2
Percent change, annual rate	1.69	1.43	0.93
Nonfarm payroll employment (CES, Table 10-7):			
Change in jobs, millions	19.6	22.3	5.8
Percent change, annual rate	1.80	1.87	0.62
Capital stock growth (percent change, annual rate, in quantity index for the net stock of fixed assets, Table 5-6):			
Private nonresidential	3.02	2.92	2.14
Private residential	2.42	2.46	2.84
Federal government	2.13	-0.32	0.33
State and local government	2.09	2.47	2.49
Productivity growth (percent change, annual rate, output per hour, nonfarm business, Table 9-3)	1.42	2.12	2.63
Growth in real pre-tax compensation and incomes (percent change, annual rate, deflated using CPI-U-RS):			
Employment cost index, all private industry (nonfarm) workers (Tables 9-1, 9-2, and 8-2):			
Total compensation	0.40	0.99	0.75
Wages and salaries	-0.02	0.86	0.31
Median earnings, full-time year-round workers (Table 3-1):			
Men	-0.56	0.52	0.08
Women	1.10	0.82	0.86
Median household income (Table 3-1)	0.45	0.94	-0.09
Gap between productivity growth and real compensation growth rates:			
Total	1.02	1.13	1.88
Caused by deflator difference	0.71	0.68	0.53
Unexplained	0.31	0.45	1.35
Ratio to GDP of credit market debt owed (Tables 12-5 and 1-1):			
Federal and related:			
Beginning of period	0.35	0.67	0.77
End	0.67	0.77	0.89
Nonfederal:			
Beginning of period	1.32	1.70	1.95
End	1.70	1.95	2.67

Sources: National Bureau of Economic Research chronology, except that the incomplete July 1980–July 1981 recovery is ignored; National Income and Product Accounts, Bureau of Labor Statistics data, Census Bureau data, Federal Reserve Flow-of-Funds Accounts.

Note: Credit market debt includes that owed by both financial and nonfinancial entities. "Federal and related" credit market debt includes Treasury securities held by the public (including by the Federal Reserve), budget agency securities and mortgages, debt of government-sponsored enterprises (GSEs), and debt of agency- and GSE-backed mortgage pools.

1 Second phase (Nov. 1982 to July 1990).

In the analysis that follows, the editor will compare the most recent full cycle with the two previous peak-to-peak periods. The analysis will use annual averages, because they are less volatile, and also because it is thereby possible to include, for consistent comparisons, data that are only available annually from the Census Bureau's Current Population Survey of household income and earnings.

The three full cycles are: January 1980 to July 1990 (ignoring the brief and incomplete recovery between July 1980 and July 1981, which left unemployment and production far short of full utilization), July 1990 to March 2001, and March 2001 to December 2007. The measurements of economic developments over those cycles will be based on the high-utilization cyclical peak years 1979, 1990, 2000, and 2007.

It should be noted that the peak-to-peak definition used here includes the recessions themselves as part of the cycle, as well as the subsequent recoveries. The strength and speed of early cyclical recovery has often been related to the depth and speed of the preceding recession. Hence, a comparison of recoveries that began with the cyclical troughs would tend to overestimate the underlying strength of the economy and the sustainable increases in incomes in periods preceded by deep recessions.

COMPARISON OF THE LAST THREE COMPLETED PEAK-TO-PEAK PERIODS

Table A-2 presents a number of comparisons of these last three completed peak-to-peak periods. All of these comparisons use data published in *Business Statistics*, and the annual rates of change are calculated using the formula shown earlier in this article.

To begin with we show measures of the length in months of the cycles—the length of the full cycle and of its expansion phases. Although the recessions at the beginnings of the two later periods here compared were of equal length (8 months) and mildness, the full 2000-2007 cycle was markedly shorter than the 1990-2000 cycle. Also, the actual expansion in employment took longer to get started in the later period, as can be seen by comparing the length of the NBER-designated expansion phase with the length of the expansion in employment.

A further dimension is the "what happened next" question, since performance after a cycle is over can reflect imbalances that grew up during that cycle. For example, some think the Great Depression was shaped by the imbalances in income distribution and the speculative excesses of the 1920s. The relative severity of the recessions of 1973–75 and the early 1980s had to do with the inflationary buildup of the 1960s and 1970s. The recession following December 2007 is already more severe than the one that followed March 2001, and appears to reflect a more pervasive buildup of debt problems.

Turning to the measurements of economic performance in Table A-2, the rates of growth in real GDP per capita, real disposable income per capita, and employment were all slower in the 2000–2007 cycle than in either of the two preceding cycles. Growth in the private nonresidential capital stock—generally considered the part of the capital stock most relevant to growth in economic productivity—was also much slower. Growth in the private residential capital stock was more rapid in the later period, reflecting the housing bubble.

Despite the slower growth in nonresidential capital in the 2000–2007 period, private nonfarm productivity grew faster, perhaps as a delayed result of earlier investment. The faster productivity growth was associated with slower employment growth, as fewer workers were required to produce a given level of output.

Productivity growth is generally welcomed, and even sought as a policy goal, because it has theoretically and historically been associated with growth in real wages. Between the 1980s and the 1990s cycles, this effect seems to be operating: productivity growth speeded up, from 1.42 to 2.12 percent, and real compensation growth, though lower in both periods, speeded up by a comparable amount. In 2000–2007, however, productivity growth speeded up sharply further while real compensation growth slipped back.

There are some valid reasons that growth in hourly worker pay can differ from productivity growth, and these factors are displayed in Table A-2. One is that employers must pay the costs of total compensation, not just wages and salaries. Total compensation includes not only wages and salaries but also employer social insurance taxes and the cost of health, retirement, and other benefits. In recent years, growth in health benefit costs has outpaced hourly wage and salary rates. This can be seen by comparing real growth in the two categories that are shown for the employment cost index, total compensation and wages and salaries. But growth in the index for total compensation still falls far short of productivity growth, and it slows down in the 2000–2007 period even when productivity growth is speeding up.

A second reason for differences between productivity and compensation growth is that the price index used to calculate real compensation—here, a specially-constructed index of consumer prices, the CPI-U-RS (see Chapter 8)—has a somewhat different trend from the productivity price index. The prices of what U.S. workers produce have gone up less than the prices of what they buy, mainly because business sector output includes a greater share of high-tech products—whose prices have decreased dramatically—than the average consumer market basket, whatever measure of consumer prices is used. So even if workers get a constant share of the current-dollar value of output, their earnings lose ground in relative purchasing power. (Economists call this a deterioration in the "terms of trade.") But this deflator difference actually shrank in 2000-2007 compared with the previous cycle periods, and the unexplained difference between productivity growth and compensation growth grew, weakening the case for a link between productivity and worker well-being.

Finally, using data from the Federal Reserve Flow of Funds accounts in Chapter 12, we can look at the ratio of credit market debt to GDP over the course of the cycle. These are comprehensive measures of debt, including that owed by both financial and nonfinancial entities. Both Federal and nonfederal debt grew relative to GDP in all three periods, but the growth in the latest cycle was greater, particularly for nonfederal debt, which started the cycle at twice the annual value of GDP and ended at a ratio of 2.7. This gives some indication of the debt levels now overhanging current levels of spending and activity, measures of which are shown in more detail in Chapter 12.

WHOSE STANDARD OF LIVING?

Some of the measures discussed in the preceding section are averages, such as GDP and personal income per capita and output per hour worked. It is important to note that the average, known technically to statisticians as a "mean," is only one way of describing the central tendency of any set of statistical data, and is not necessarily the method that produces the most representative number.

Most researchers who are interested in the economic well-being of a typical American family or household judge that the best single number to characterize that well-being is the standard of living of the family or household situated at the middle of the income distribution. Half of all families or households have higher incomes and half have lower incomes. This is the measure known as the "median." Medians are not the same as averages or means, and in the case of income distributions, they are invariably lower.

This reason behind this difference is sometimes illustrated by calling up the image of a billionaire walking into a working-class bar. The "average income" (mean income) of each person in the bar would jump, as a billion dollars was added to the numerator of the average and just one unit was added to the denominator. However, the median would be little if at all changed—at most, the addition of one person to the group might mean that the median income moved up from one worker to the next best-paid worker—and this would accord with an accurate perception that the typical person in that bar had not experienced any significant increase in his income. Thus, when a few individuals or households have very high incomes, means are higher than medians and not representative of the typical individual or household.

Furthermore, if over time the incomes of people at the upper end of the distribution increase faster than the incomes of those at the middle and bottom of the distribution (which is what happens when the income distribution becomes more unequal), then the means will also increase more than the medians.

Once a year, as a supplement to the Current Population Survey, the Census Bureau collects data on the incomes of its sample of households. These data are used to produce a report on median incomes, the distribution of incomes, and the poverty rate, providing extensive data on the economic well-being of households and individuals throughout the income distribution. This survey is the source for all of the data in Chapter 3 of *Business Statistics*, including the median earnings and median household income data that are also used to calculate worker earnings and household income growth rates shown in Table A-2. All three of these median measures increase less than the per capita (mean) product and income measures throughout the periods considered, consistent with the continued trend toward income inequality displayed in Tables 3-4 and 3-5.

GENERAL NOTES

These notes provide general information about the data in Tables 1-1 through 21-2. Specific notes with information about data sources, definitions, methodology, revisions, and sources of additional information follow the tables in each chapter.

MAIN DIVISIONS OF THE BOOK

The tables are divided into four main parts:

Part A (Tables 1-1 through 13-8) pertains to the U.S. economy as a whole. Generally, each table presents annual averages as far back as data availability and space permit, and quarterly or monthly values for the most recent year or years. (For the most important series, full quarterly or monthly histories and annual averages back to the beginning of the post-World-War-II period are shown in Part C.) Some chapters present data for the United States only in aggregate, while others—such as the chapters concerning industrial production and capacity utilization (chapter 2), capital expenditures (chapter 5), profits (chapter 9), and employment, hours, and earnings (chapter 10)—also have detail for major industry groups.

Data by industry on industrial production and capacity utilization (Tables 2-2 and 2-3), capital expenditures (Table 5-11), profits (Tables 9-4 through 9-6), and payroll employment, hours, and earnings (Tables 10-7 through 10-16) are classified using the new North American Industry Classification System (NAICS), as far back as such data are made available by the source agencies.

Part B focuses on the individual industries that together produce the gross domestic product (GDP).

Chapter 14 provides an overview of NAICS, presenting the overall structure of the classification system, the definition of each major industry group, and the approximate relationships of each group to the industries in SIC (Standard Industrial Classification), the previous system.

Chapter 15 contains data on GDP, quantity production trends, and factor income by NAICS industry group.

Chapter 16 provides further detail on payroll employment, hours, and earnings classified according to NAICS.

Chapter 17 presents various data sets for key economic sectors. Some of the tables are based on definitions of products, rather than of producing establishments, and are valid for either classification system. This is the case for Tables 17-1, Petroleum and Petroleum Products; 17-2, New Construction; 17-3, Housing Starts and Building Permits, New House Sales, and Prices; and 17-8, Motor Vehicle

Sales and Inventories. Tables 17-4 through 17-7 and 17-9, 17-11, and 17-12, which cover manufacturing and retail and wholesale trade, show data classified according to NAICS. Tables 17-13 and 17-14 present data for services industries classified according to NAICS.

Part C presents further historical detail.

Chapter 18 shows selected data for the years 1929 through 1948. Generally, these are shown on an annual basis only, as many of the series are not available in quarterly or monthly detail. At the beginning of the chapter, graphs with brief narration highlight some of the most important characteristics of the Depression and World War II eras.

Chapters 19 and 20 present quarterly or monthly data back to the earliest postwar year available for major series, along with available annual data back to 1946 that are not shown in Part A.

Part D presents data by state and region, calculated by the Bureau of Economic Analysis. Table 21-1 contains data on GDP and Table 21-2 shows data on personal income, population, and employment.

CHARACTERISTICS OF THE TABLES AND THE DATA

The subtitles or column headings for the data tables normally indicate whether the data are *seasonally adjusted, not seasonally adjusted,* or *at a seasonally adjusted annual rate.* These descriptions refer to the monthly or quarterly data, rather than the annual data. Annual data by definition require no seasonal adjustment. Annual values are normally calculated as totals or averages (as appropriate) of unadjusted data. Such annual values are shown in either or both adjusted or unadjusted data columns.

Seasonal adjustment removes from the time series the average impact of variations that normally occur at about the same time each year, due to occurrences such as weather, holidays, and tax payment dates.

A simplified example of the process of seasonal adjustment, or deseasonalizing, can indicate its importance in the interpretation of economic time series. Statisticians compare actual monthly data for a number of years with "moving average" trends of the monthly data for the 12 months centered on each month's data. For example, they may find that in November, sales values are usually about 95 percent of the moving average, while in December, usual sales values are 110 percent of the average. Suppose that actual November sales in the current year are $100 and December sales are $105. The seasonally adjusted value for November will be $105 ($100/0.95) while the value for December will be $95 ($105/1.10). Thus, an apparent increase in the unadjusted data turns out to be a decrease when adjusted for the usual seasonal pattern.

The statistical method used to achieve the seasonal adjustment may vary from one data set to another. Many of the data are adjusted by a computer method known as X-12-ARIMA, developed by the Census Bureau. A description of the method is found in "New Capabilities and Methods of the X-12-ARIMA Seasonal Adjustment Program," by David F. Findley, Brian C. Monsell, William R. Bell, Mark C. Otto and Bor-Chung Chen (*Journal of Business and Economic Statistics*, April 1998). This article can be downloaded from the Bureau of the Census Web site at <http://www.census.gov>.

Production and sales data presented at *annual rates*—such as NIPA data in dollars, or motor vehicle data in number of units—show values at their annual equivalents: the values that would be registered if the seasonally adjusted rate of activity measured during a particular month or quarter were maintained for a full year. Specifically, seasonally adjusted monthly values are multiplied by 12 and quarterly values by 4 to yield seasonally adjusted annual rates.

Percent changes at seasonally adjusted annual rates for quarterly time periods are calculated using a compound interest formula, by raising the quarter-to-quarter change in a seasonally adjusted series to the fourth power. See the preceding article for an explanation of compound annual growth rates.

Indexes. In many of the most important data sets presented in this volume, aggregate measures of prices and quantities are expressed in the form of indexes. The most basic and familiar form of index, the original Consumer Price Index, begins with a "market basket" of goods and services purchased in a base period. The value weight ascribed to each component of the market basket is moved forward by the observed change in the price of the item selected to represent that component. These weighted component prices—the quantities in the base period repriced in the prices of subsequent periods—are aggregated, divided by the base period aggregate, and multiplied by 100 to provide an index number. An index calculated in this way is known as a *Laspeyres index*. In general, economists believe that Laspeyres price indexes have an upward bias, showing more price increase than if account were taken of consumers' ability to change spending patterns and maintain the same level of satisfaction in response to changing relative prices.

A *Paasche index* is one that uses the weights of the current period. Since the weights in the Paasche index change in each period, Paasche indexes only provide acceptable indications of change relative to the base period. Paasche indexes for two periods neither of which is the base period cannot be correctly compared: for example, a Paasche

price index for a recent period might increase from the period just preceding even if no prices changed between those two periods, because of a change in the composition of output toward prices that had previously increased more from the base period. When the national income and product account (NIPA) measures of real output were Laspeyres measures, using the weights of a single base year, the implicit deflators (current-dollar values divided by constant-dollar values) were Paasche indexes. Just as Laspeyres price indexes are upward-biased, Paasche price indexes are downward-biased because they overestimate consumers' ability to maintain the same level of satisfaction by changing spending patterns.

In recent years, government statisticians—with the aid of elaborate computer programs—have developed measures of real output and prices that minimize bias by using the weights of both periods and updating the weights for each period-to-period comparison. Such measures are described as chained indexes and are used in the NIPAs, the index of industrial production, and an experimental consumer price index. Chained measures are discussed more fully in the notes and definitions for Chapter 1, Chapter 2, and Chapter 8. The "Fisher Ideal" index, the "superlative" index, and the "Tornqvist formula" are all types of chained indexes that use weights for both periods under comparison.

Detail may not sum to totals due to rounding. Since annual data are typically calculated by source agencies as the annual totals or averages of not-seasonally-adjusted data, they therefore will not be precisely equal to the annual totals or averages of monthly seasonally-adjusted data. Also, seasonal adjustment procedures are typically multiplicative rather than additive, which may also prevent seasonally adjusted data from adding or averaging to the annual figure. Percent changes and growth rates may have been calculated using unrounded data and therefore differ from those using the published figures.

The data in this volume are from federal government sources and may be reproduced freely. A list of data sources is shown below.

The tables in this volume incorporate data revisions and corrections released by the source agencies through April 2010.

DATA SOURCES

The source agencies for the data in this volume are listed below. The specific source or sources for each particular data set are identified at the beginning of the notes and definitions for the relevant data pages.

Board of Governors of the Federal Reserve System
20th Street & Constitution Avenue NW
Washington, DC 20551

Data Inquiries and Publication Sales:
Publications Services
Mail Stop 127
Board of Governors of the Federal Reserve System
Washington, DC 20551
Phone: (202) 452-3245

Quarterly Publication:
As of 2006, the *Federal Reserve Bulletin* is available free of charge and only on the Federal Reserve Web site.

URL:
http://www.federalreserve.gov

Census Bureau
U.S. Department of Commerce
4700 Silver Hill Road
Washington, DC 20233

URL:
http://www.census.gov

Ordering Data Products:
Call Center: (301) 763-INFO (4636)

E-mail Questions:
webmaster@census.gov

E-sales:
http://www.census.gov/mp/www/censtore.html

Bureau of Economic Analysis
U.S. Department of Commerce
Washington, DC 20230

Data Inquiries:
Public Information Office
Phone: (202) 606-9900

Monthly Publication:
Survey of Current Business
Available online and by subscription; call (202) 512-1800 or visit **http://bookstore.gpo.gov.**

URL:
http://www.bea.gov

Bureau of Labor Statistics
U.S. Department of Labor
2 Massachusetts Avenue NE
Washington, DC 20212-0001
(202) 691-5200

URL:
http://www.bls.gov

Data Inquiries:
Blsdata_staff@bls.gov

Monthly Publications available online:
Monthly Labor Review
Employment and Earnings
Compensation and Working Conditions
Producer Price Indexes
CPI Detailed Report

Employment and Training Administration
U.S. Department of Labor
200 Constitution Avenue NW
Washington, DC 20210
(877) US2-JOBS

URL:
http://www.doleta.gov
http://www.itsc.state.md.us

Energy Information Administration
U.S. Department of Energy
1000 Independence Avenue SW
Washington, DC 20585

Data Inquiries and Publications:
National Energy Information Center
Phone: (202) 586-8800
E-mail: infoctr@eia.doe.gov

Monthly Publication:
Monthly Energy Review, as of 2007 available only on the EIA Web site, free of charge.

URL:
http://www.eia.doe.gov

Federal Housing Finance Agency
FHFAinfo@FHFA.gov
(202) 414-6921,6922
(202) 414-6376

URL:
http://www.ofheo.gov/hpi

U.S. Department of the Treasury
Office of International Affairs
Treasury International Capital System

URL:
http://www.treas.gov/tic

To order government publications
Superintendent of Documents
Government Printing Office
Washington, DC 20402
(202) 512-1800

URL:
http://bookstore.gpo.gov

PART A

THE U.S. ECONOMY

CHAPTER 1: NATIONAL INCOME AND PRODUCT

Section 1a: Gross Domestic Product: Values, Quantities, and Prices

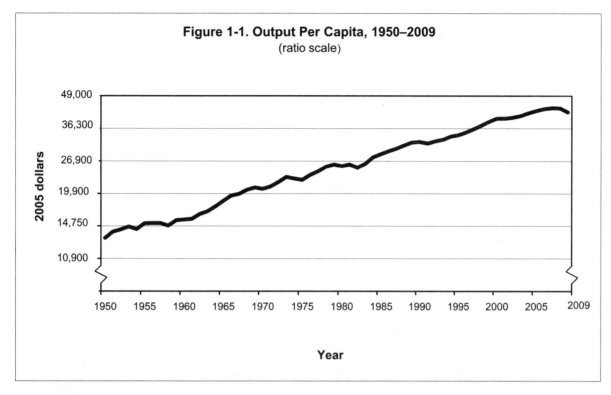

Figure 1-1. Output Per Capita, 1950–2009
(ratio scale)

- Total output of goods and services in the United States (real gross domestic product, or GDP), expressed in constant 2005–value dollars to remove the effect of inflation, rose from $2.00 trillion in 1950 to $13.31 trillion in 2008. This was a nearly seven-fold increase in real value over the 58-year period, with an annual average growth rate of 3.3 percent per year. In 2009, however, real GDP fell 2.4 percent. (Table 1-2)

- Real GDP per capita—the constant-dollar average value of production for each man, woman, and child in the population—rose from $13,225 (2005 dollars) in 1950 to $43,884 in 2007, a growth rate of 2.1 percent per year. Over the next two years, it fell 3.8 percent. This value is charted in Figure 1-1. It is graphed on a "ratio scale," with equal vertical distances signifying equal percent changes. (Table 1-7)

- The figure indicates that growth is not always smooth or uninterrupted. There are times when output levels off or declines, marking the periods identified as recessions in economic activity. According to the National Bureau of Economic Research, the 11th recession of the post-World-War-II period began in December 2007. Although real GDP started to grow again after mid-2009, the Bureau had not yet identified a date for the end of the recession at the time this was written. (Table 1-3)

- Measured in current dollars, the value of GDP has increased even faster, reflecting increases in the average price level. Current-dollar GDP rose from $294 billion in 1950 to over $14 trillion currently. (Table 1-1) The price level in 2009 was more than 7 times that in 1950, reflecting an average inflation rate of 3.5 percent per year. (Table 1-5) Annual changes in the chain-type price index for GDP ranged from inflation of 9 percent or more in 1947, 1974–1975, and 1980–1981 to changes of no more than 1.2 percent in 1949–1950, 1954, 1959, 1961, 1963, 1998, and 2009. Over the last 10 years, inflation averaged 2.4 percent per year. (Table 1-5)

Table 1-1. Gross Domestic Product

(Billions of dollars, quarterly data are at seasonally adjusted annual rates.)   **NIPA Tables 1.1.5, 5.6.5A, 5.6.5B**

Year and quarter	Gross domestic product	Personal consumption expenditures	Gross private domestic investment						Exports and imports of goods and services			Government consumption expenditures and gross investment		
			Total	Fixed investment		Change in private inventories			Net exports	Exports	Imports	Total	Federal	State and local
				Nonresidential	Residential	Farm	Nonfarm							
1950	293.7	192.2	54.1	27.8	20.5	-0.1	5.9		0.7	12.4	11.6	46.7	26.0	20.7
1951	339.3	208.5	60.2	31.8	18.4	1.0	8.9		2.5	17.1	14.6	68.1	45.0	23.0
1952	358.3	219.5	54.0	31.9	18.6	1.4	2.1		1.2	16.5	15.3	83.6	59.1	24.4
1953	379.3	233.1	56.4	35.1	19.4	0.7	1.2		-0.7	15.3	16.0	90.5	64.4	26.1
1954	380.4	240.0	53.8	34.7	21.1	0.2	-2.1		0.4	15.8	15.4	86.1	57.2	28.9
1955	414.7	258.8	69.0	39.0	25.0	-0.6	5.6		0.5	17.7	17.2	86.4	54.9	31.6
1956	437.4	271.7	72.0	44.5	23.6	-1.0	4.9		2.4	21.3	18.9	91.4	56.7	34.7
1957	461.1	286.9	70.5	47.5	22.2	0.1	0.7		4.1	24.0	19.9	99.7	61.3	38.3
1958	467.2	296.2	64.5	42.5	22.3	2.0	-2.3		0.5	20.6	20.0	106.0	63.8	42.2
1959	506.6	317.7	78.5	46.5	28.1	-1.6	5.5		0.4	22.7	22.3	110.0	65.3	44.7
1960	526.4	331.8	78.9	49.4	26.3	0.6	2.7		4.2	27.0	22.8	111.5	64.1	47.5
1961	544.8	342.2	78.2	48.8	26.4	0.9	2.1		4.9	27.6	22.7	119.5	67.9	51.6
1962	585.7	363.3	88.1	53.1	29.0	0.6	5.5		4.1	29.1	25.0	130.1	75.2	54.9
1963	617.8	382.7	93.8	56.0	32.1	0.5	5.1		4.9	31.1	26.1	136.4	76.9	59.5
1964	663.6	411.5	102.1	63.0	34.3	-1.2	6.0		6.9	35.0	28.1	143.2	78.4	64.8
1965	719.1	443.8	118.2	74.8	34.2	0.8	8.4		5.6	37.1	31.5	151.4	80.4	71.0
1966	787.7	480.9	131.3	85.4	32.3	-0.5	14.1		3.9	40.9	37.1	171.6	92.4	79.2
1967	832.4	507.8	128.6	86.4	32.4	0.9	9.0		3.6	43.5	39.9	192.5	104.6	87.9
1968	909.8	558.0	141.2	93.4	38.7	1.4	7.7		1.4	47.9	46.6	209.3	111.3	98.0
1969	984.4	605.1	156.4	104.7	42.6	0.0	9.2		1.4	51.9	50.5	221.4	113.3	108.2
1970	1 038.3	648.3	152.4	109.0	41.4	-0.8	2.8		4.0	59.7	55.8	233.7	113.4	120.3
1971	1 126.8	701.6	178.2	114.1	55.8	1.7	6.6		0.6	63.0	62.3	246.4	113.6	132.8
1972	1 237.9	770.2	207.6	128.8	69.7	0.3	8.8		-3.4	70.8	74.2	263.4	119.6	143.8
1973	1 382.3	852.0	244.5	153.3	75.3	1.5	14.4		4.1	95.3	91.2	281.7	122.5	159.2
1974	1 499.5	932.9	249.4	169.5	66.0	-2.8	16.8		-0.8	126.7	127.5	317.9	134.5	183.4
1975	1 637.7	1 033.8	230.2	173.7	62.7	3.4	-9.6		16.0	138.7	122.7	357.7	149.0	208.7
1976	1 824.6	1 151.3	292.0	192.4	82.5	-0.8	18.0		-1.6	149.5	151.1	383.0	159.7	223.3
1977	2 030.1	1 277.8	361.3	228.7	110.3	4.5	17.8		-23.1	159.4	182.4	414.1	175.4	238.7
1978	2 293.8	1 427.6	438.0	280.6	131.6	1.4	24.4		-25.4	186.9	212.3	453.6	190.9	262.7
1979	2 562.2	1 591.2	492.9	333.9	141.0	3.6	14.4		-22.5	230.1	252.7	500.7	210.6	290.2
1980	2 788.1	1 755.8	479.3	362.4	123.2	-6.1	-0.2		-13.1	280.8	293.8	566.1	243.7	322.4
1981	3 126.8	1 939.5	572.4	420.0	122.6	8.8	21.0		-12.5	305.2	317.8	627.5	280.2	347.3
1982	3 253.2	2 075.5	517.2	426.5	105.7	5.8	-20.7		-20.0	283.2	303.2	680.4	310.8	369.7
1983	3 534.6	2 288.6	564.3	417.2	152.9	-15.4	9.6		-51.7	277.0	328.6	733.4	342.9	390.5
1984	3 930.9	2 501.1	735.6	489.6	180.6	5.7	59.7		-102.7	302.4	405.1	796.9	374.3	422.6
1985	4 217.5	2 717.6	736.2	526.2	188.2	5.8	16.1		-115.2	302.0	417.2	878.9	412.8	466.1
1986	4 460.1	2 896.7	746.5	519.8	220.1	-1.5	8.0		-132.5	320.3	452.9	949.3	438.4	510.9
1987	4 736.4	3 097.0	785.0	524.1	233.7	-6.4	33.6		-145.0	363.8	508.7	999.4	459.5	539.9
1988	5 100.4	3 350.1	821.6	563.8	239.3	-11.9	30.4		-110.1	443.9	554.0	1 038.9	461.6	577.3
1989	5 482.1	3 594.5	874.9	607.7	239.5	0.0	27.7		-87.9	503.1	591.0	1 100.6	481.4	619.2
1990	5 800.5	3 835.5	861.0	622.4	224.0	2.4	12.2		-77.6	552.1	629.7	1 181.7	507.5	674.2
1991	5 992.1	3 980.1	802.9	598.2	205.1	-1.3	0.9		-27.0	596.6	623.5	1 236.1	526.6	709.5
1992	6 342.3	4 236.9	864.8	612.1	236.3	6.3	10.1		-32.8	635.0	667.8	1 273.5	532.9	740.6
1993	6 667.4	4 483.6	953.3	666.6	266.0	-6.2	27.0		-64.4	655.6	720.0	1 294.8	525.0	769.8
1994	7 085.2	4 750.8	1 097.3	731.4	302.1	12.0	51.8		-92.7	720.7	813.4	1 329.8	518.6	811.2
1995	7 414.7	4 987.3	1 144.0	810.0	302.9	-11.1	42.2		-90.7	811.9	902.6	1 374.0	518.8	855.3
1996	7 838.5	5 273.6	1 240.2	875.4	334.1	8.6	22.1		-96.3	867.7	964.0	1 421.0	527.0	894.0
1997	8 332.4	5 570.6	1 388.7	968.6	349.1	3.3	67.7		-101.4	954.4	1 055.8	1 474.4	531.0	943.5
1998	8 793.5	5 918.5	1 510.8	1 061.1	385.9	1.3	62.5		-161.8	953.9	1 115.7	1 526.1	531.0	995.0
1999	9 353.5	6 342.8	1 641.5	1 154.9	425.8	-2.7	63.5		-262.1	989.3	1 251.4	1 631.3	554.9	1 076.3
2000	9 951.5	6 830.4	1 772.2	1 268.7	449.0	-1.4	55.9		-382.1	1 093.2	1 475.3	1 731.0	576.1	1 154.9
2001	10 286.2	7 148.8	1 661.9	1 227.8	472.4	0.0	-38.3		-371.0	1 027.7	1 398.7	1 846.4	611.7	1 234.7
2002	10 642.3	7 439.2	1 647.0	1 125.4	509.5	-2.5	14.5		-427.2	1 003.0	1 430.2	1 983.3	680.6	1 302.7
2003	11 142.1	7 804.0	1 729.7	1 135.7	577.6	0.1	16.3		-504.1	1 041.0	1 545.1	2 112.6	756.5	1 356.1
2004	11 867.8	8 285.1	1 968.6	1 223.0	680.6	8.8	56.1		-618.7	1 180.2	1 798.9	2 232.8	824.6	1 408.2
2005	12 638.4	8 819.0	2 172.2	1 347.3	775.0	0.1	49.8		-722.7	1 305.1	2 027.8	2 369.9	876.3	1 493.6
2006	13 398.9	9 322.7	2 327.2	1 505.3	761.9	-3.6	63.6		-769.3	1 471.0	2 240.3	2 518.4	931.7	1 586.7
2007	14 077.6	9 826.4	2 288.5	1 640.2	629.0	-0.6	20.0		-713.8	1 655.9	2 369.7	2 676.5	976.7	1 699.8
2008	14 441.4	10 129.9	2 136.1	1 693.6	477.2	-7.1	-27.7		-707.8	1 831.1	2 538.9	2 883.2	1 082.6	1 800.6
2009	14 256.3	10 089.1	1 628.8	1 388.8	361.0	-2.4	-118.5		-392.4	1 564.2	1 956.6	2 930.7	1 144.8	1 785.9
2007														
1st quarter	13 795.6	9 658.5	2 267.2	1 574.1	680.0	6.2	6.8		-729.4	1 564.9	2 294.3	2 599.3	942.8	1 656.5
2nd quarter	13 997.2	9 762.5	2 302.0	1 623.5	655.1	-3.9	27.4		-724.8	1 602.1	2 326.9	2 657.4	968.1	1 689.3
3rd quarter	14 179.9	9 865.6	2 311.9	1 665.2	615.6	-2.4	33.4		-698.4	1 685.2	2 383.6	2 700.9	991.4	1 709.5
4th quarter	14 337.9	10 019.2	2 272.9	1 697.9	565.2	-2.5	12.4		-702.5	1 771.6	2 474.0	2 748.3	1 004.3	1 743.9
2008														
1st quarter	14 373.9	10 095.1	2 214.8	1 705.0	518.1	-13.9	5.7		-744.4	1 803.6	2 548.1	2 808.4	1 038.3	1 770.1
2nd quarter	14 497.8	10 194.7	2 164.6	1 719.7	494.2	-3.2	-46.1		-738.7	1 901.5	2 640.2	2 877.1	1 069.5	1 807.6
3rd quarter	14 546.7	10 220.1	2 142.7	1 711.0	468.6	-7.5	-29.4		-757.5	1 913.1	2 670.5	2 941.4	1 108.3	1 833.1
4th quarter	14 347.3	10 009.8	2 022.1	1 638.7	427.8	-3.7	-40.8		-590.5	1 706.2	2 296.7	2 905.9	1 114.3	1 791.7
2009														
1st quarter	14 178.0	9 987.7	1 689.9	1 442.6	374.6	-1.3	-126.1		-378.5	1 509.3	1 887.9	2 879.0	1 106.7	1 772.3
2nd quarter	14 151.2	9 999.3	1 561.5	1 391.8	345.9	0.6	-176.8		-339.1	1 493.7	1 832.8	2 929.4	1 138.3	1 791.2
3rd quarter	14 242.1	10 132.9	1 556.1	1 353.9	358.8	0.0	-156.5		-402.2	1 573.8	1 976.0	2 955.4	1 164.3	1 791.1
4th quarter	14 453.8	10 236.4	1 707.8	1 366.9	364.5	-8.9	-14.7		-449.5	1 680.1	2 129.7	2 959.2	1 170.1	1 789.0

Table 1-2. Real Gross Domestic Product

(Billions of chained [2005] dollars, quarterly data are at seasonally adjusted annual rates.)   **NIPA Tables 1.1.6, 5.6.6A, 5.6.6B**

Year and quarter	Gross domestic product	Personal consumption expenditures	Gross private domestic investment						Exports and imports of goods and services			Government consumption expenditures and gross investment			Residual
			Total	Fixed investment		Change in private inventories			Net exports	Exports	Imports	Total	Federal	State and local	
				Nonresidential	Residential	Farm	Nonfarm								
1950	2 006.0	1 283.3	253.2	. . .	. . .	-0.3	22.8	. . .	54.7	65.8	492.4	. . .	. . .	-11.8
1951	2 161.1	1 303.4	254.0	. . .	. . .	2.1	28.4	. . .	67.1	68.4	672.7	. . .	. . .	-67.7
1952	2 243.9	1 344.6	229.7	. . .	. . .	3.1	7.4	. . .	64.2	74.4	810.0	. . .	. . .	-130.2
1953	2 347.2	1 408.8	240.5	. . .	. . .	2.0	4.5	. . .	59.9	81.4	868.0	. . .	. . .	-148.6
1954	2 332.4	1 438.3	229.3	. . .	. . .	0.5	-7.5	. . .	62.8	77.4	808.9	. . .	. . .	-129.5
1955	2 500.3	1 544.5	285.0	. . .	. . .	-1.9	18.7	. . .	69.5	86.7	779.3	. . .	. . .	-91.3
1956	2 549.7	1 589.7	281.1	. . .	. . .	-3.2	15.6	. . .	80.9	93.7	780.0	. . .	. . .	-88.3
1957	2 601.1	1 629.1	268.9	. . .	. . .	0.4	2.4	. . .	88.0	97.6	814.7	. . .	. . .	-102.0
1958	2 577.6	1 643.3	246.6	. . .	. . .	5.8	-7.7	. . .	76.1	102.3	840.9	. . .	. . .	-127.0
1959	2 762.5	1 736.7	296.6	. . .	. . .	-4.7	19.9	. . .	83.9	113.0	869.5	. . .	. . .	-111.2
1960	2 830.9	1 784.4	296.5	. . .	. . .	1.7	9.9	. . .	98.5	114.5	871.0	. . .	. . .	-105.0
1961	2 896.9	1 821.2	294.6	. . .	. . .	2.5	7.8	. . .	99.0	113.8	914.8	. . .	. . .	-118.9
1962	3 072.4	1 911.2	332.0	. . .	. . .	1.7	20.4	. . .	104.0	126.7	971.1	. . .	. . .	-119.2
1963	3 206.7	1 989.9	354.3	. . .	. . .	1.4	19.0	. . .	111.5	130.1	996.1	. . .	. . .	-115.0
1964	3 392.3	2 108.4	383.5	. . .	. . .	-3.8	21.8	. . .	124.6	137.0	1 018.0	. . .	. . .	-105.2
1965	3 610.1	2 241.8	437.3	. . .	. . .	2.5	30.5	. . .	128.1	151.6	1 048.7	. . .	. . .	-94.2
1966	3 845.3	2 369.0	475.8	. . .	. . .	-1.4	50.2	. . .	137.0	174.1	1 141.1	. . .	. . .	-103.5
1967	3 942.5	2 440.0	454.1	. . .	. . .	2.5	31.5	. . .	140.1	186.8	1 228.7	. . .	. . .	-133.6
1968	4 133.4	2 580.7	480.5	. . .	. . .	4.1	26.5	. . .	151.1	214.7	1 267.2	. . .	. . .	-131.4
1969	4 261.8	2 677.4	508.5	. . .	. . .	0.0	30.9	. . .	158.4	226.9	1 264.3	. . .	. . .	-119.9
1970	4 269.9	2 740.2	475.1	. . .	. . .	-2.4	8.6	. . .	175.5	236.6	1 233.7	. . .	. . .	-118.0
1971	4 413.3	2 844.6	529.3	. . .	. . .	4.1	20.6	. . .	178.4	249.2	1 206.9	. . .	. . .	-96.7
1972	4 647.7	3 019.5	591.9	. . .	. . .	0.4	26.7	. . .	191.8	277.2	1 198.1	. . .	. . .	-76.4
1973	4 917.0	3 169.1	661.3	. . .	. . .	1.8	40.5	. . .	228.0	290.1	1 193.9	. . .	. . .	-45.2
1974	4 889.9	3 142.8	612.6	. . .	. . .	-4.4	39.0	. . .	246.0	283.5	1 224.0	. . .	. . .	-52.0
1975	4 879.5	3 214.1	504.1	. . .	. . .	5.8	-21.4	. . .	244.5	252.0	1 251.6	. . .	. . .	-82.8
1976	5 141.3	3 393.1	605.9	. . .	. . .	-1.6	37.6	. . .	255.1	301.3	1 257.2	. . .	. . .	-68.7
1977	5 377.7	3 535.9	697.4	. . .	. . .	7.2	35.7	. . .	261.3	334.2	1 271.0	. . .	. . .	-53.7
1978	5 677.6	3 691.8	781.5	. . .	. . .	2.1	44.9	. . .	288.8	363.2	1 308.4	. . .	. . .	-29.7
1979	5 855.0	3 779.5	806.4	. . .	. . .	4.2	23.8	. . .	317.5	369.2	1 332.8	. . .	. . .	-12.0
1980	5 839.0	3 766.2	717.9	. . .	. . .	-7.2	-0.4	. . .	351.7	344.7	1 358.8	. . .	. . .	-10.9
1981	5 987.2	3 823.3	782.4	. . .	. . .	10.1	28.2	. . .	356.0	353.8	1 371.2	. . .	. . .	8.1
1982	5 870.9	3 876.7	672.8	. . .	. . .	7.5	-27.4	. . .	328.8	349.3	1 395.3	. . .	. . .	-53.4
1983	6 136.2	4 098.3	735.5	. . .	. . .	-17.4	10.7	. . .	320.3	393.4	1 446.3	. . .	. . .	-70.8
1984	6 577.1	4 315.6	952.1	. . .	. . .	6.3	72.3	. . .	346.4	489.1	1 494.9	. . .	. . .	-42.8
1985	6 849.3	4 540.4	943.3	. . .	. . .	7.0	18.4	. . .	357.0	520.9	1 599.0	. . .	. . .	-69.5
1986	7 086.5	4 724.5	936.9	. . .	. . .	-2.3	10.4	. . .	384.4	565.4	1 696.2	. . .	. . .	-90.1
1987	7 313.3	4 870.3	965.7	. . .	. . .	-9.1	41.1	. . .	425.7	598.9	1 737.1	. . .	. . .	-86.6
1988	7 613.9	5 066.6	988.5	. . .	. . .	-13.1	35.4	. . .	493.9	622.4	1 758.9	. . .	. . .	-71.6
1989	7 885.9	5 209.9	1 028.1	. . .	. . .	0.0	30.8	. . .	550.6	649.8	1 806.8	. . .	. . .	-59.7
1990	8 033.9	5 316.2	993.5	. . .	. . .	2.5	14.0	. . .	600.2	673.0	1 864.0	. . .	. . .	-67.0
1991	8 015.1	5 324.2	912.7	. . .	. . .	-1.8	0.4	. . .	640.0	672.0	1 884.4	. . .	. . .	-74.2
1992	8 287.1	5 505.7	986.7	. . .	. . .	7.1	11.0	. . .	684.0	719.2	1 893.2	. . .	. . .	-63.3
1993	8 523.4	5 701.2	1 074.8	. . .	. . .	-7.5	29.8	. . .	706.4	781.4	1 878.2	. . .	. . .	-55.8
1994	8 870.7	5 918.9	1 220.9	. . .	. . .	13.7	55.9	. . .	768.0	874.6	1 878.0	. . .	. . .	-40.5
1995	9 093.7	6 079.0	1 258.9	792.2	456.1	-13.0	44.3	-98.8	845.7	944.5	1 888.9	704.1	1 183.6	-176.0
1996	9 433.9	6 291.2	1 370.3	866.2	492.5	8.3	23.2	-110.7	916.0	1 026.7	1 907.9	696.0	1 211.1	-154.1
1997	9 854.3	6 523.4	1 540.8	970.8	501.8	3.7	73.6	-139.8	1 025.1	1 165.0	1 943.8	689.1	1 254.3	-118.7
1998	10 283.5	6 865.5	1 695.1	1 087.4	540.4	1.3	62.5	-252.6	1 048.5	1 301.1	1 985.0	681.4	1 303.8	-87.8
1999	10 779.8	7 240.9	1 844.3	1 200.9	574.2	-2.7	63.5	-356.6	1 094.3	1 450.9	2 056.1	694.6	1 361.8	-49.5
2000	11 226.0	7 608.1	1 970.3	1 318.5	580.0	-1.4	55.9	-451.6	1 188.3	1 639.9	2 097.8	698.1	1 400.1	-24.1
2001	11 347.2	7 813.9	1 831.9	1 281.8	583.3	0.0	-38.3	-472.1	1 121.6	1 593.8	2 178.3	726.5	1 452.3	-29.2
2002	11 553.0	8 021.9	1 807.0	1 180.2	613.8	-2.5	14.5	-548.8	1 099.2	1 648.0	2 279.6	779.5	1 500.6	-19.8
2003	11 840.7	8 247.6	1 871.6	1 191.0	664.3	0.1	16.3	-603.9	1 116.8	1 720.7	2 330.5	831.1	1 499.7	-12.1
2004	12 263.8	8 532.7	2 058.2	1 263.0	729.5	8.8	56.1	-688.0	1 222.8	1 910.8	2 362.0	865.0	1 497.1	-3.5
2005	12 638.4	8 819.0	2 172.2	1 347.3	775.0	0.1	49.8	-722.7	1 305.1	2 027.8	2 369.9	876.3	1 493.6	-0.2
2006	12 976.2	9 073.5	2 230.4	1 453.9	718.2	-3.6	63.6	-729.2	1 422.0	2 151.2	2 402.1	894.9	1 507.2	-1.7
2007	13 254.1	9 313.9	2 146.2	1 544.3	585.0	-0.6	20.0	-647.7	1 546.1	2 193.8	2 443.1	906.4	1 536.7	0.3
2008	13 312.2	9 290.9	1 989.4	1 569.7	451.1	-7.1	-27.7	-494.3	1 629.3	2 123.5	2 518.1	975.9	1 543.7	20.0
2009	12 987.4	9 235.1	1 527.6	1 291.0	358.7	-2.4	-118.5	-355.6	1 472.4	1 828.0	2 564.6	1 026.6	1 541.0	18.3
2007														
1st quarter	13 099.9	9 265.1	2 132.6	1 489.6	631.7	5.9	8.3	-705.0	1 485.9	2 190.8	2 409.5	882.8	1 526.5	-3.6
2nd quarter	13 204.0	9 291.5	2 162.2	1 530.3	610.4	-4.4	27.9	-683.4	1 504.8	2 188.1	2 435.4	898.7	1 536.5	0.4
3rd quarter	13 321.1	9 335.6	2 166.5	1 565.8	572.9	-2.6	32.7	-638.4	1 569.9	2 208.3	2 458.9	919.0	1 540.0	2.7
4th quarter	13 391.2	9 363.6	2 123.4	1 591.3	525.0	-2.0	12.5	-564.0	1 624.0	2 188.0	2 468.7	925.1	1 543.7	1.9
2008														
1st quarter	13 366.9	9 349.6	2 082.9	1 598.9	483.2	-12.6	14.5	-550.9	1 623.4	2 174.3	2 484.7	943.4	1 541.9	9.6
2nd quarter	13 415.3	9 351.0	2 026.5	1 604.4	462.9	-1.6	-35.8	-476.0	1 670.4	2 146.5	2 506.9	961.3	1 546.6	17.1
3rd quarter	13 324.6	9 267.7	1 990.7	1 579.2	443.3	-5.0	-24.5	-479.2	1 655.2	2 134.4	2 536.6	991.6	1 547.0	24.7
4th quarter	13 141.9	9 195.3	1 857.7	1 496.1	415.0	-1.9	-35.7	-470.9	1 568.0	2 038.9	2 544.0	1 007.3	1 539.3	28.6
2009														
1st quarter	12 925.4	9 209.2	1 558.5	1 321.2	367.9	0.3	-114.9	-386.5	1 434.5	1 821.0	2 527.2	996.3	1 533.3	23.6
2nd quarter	12 901.5	9 189.0	1 456.7	1 288.4	344.4	2.2	-163.1	-330.4	1 419.5	1 749.8	2 568.6	1 023.5	1 548.0	24.0
3rd quarter	12 973.0	9 252.6	1 474.4	1 269.0	359.6	1.9	-141.4	-357.4	1 478.8	1 836.2	2 585.5	1 043.3	1 545.5	15.5
4th quarter	13 149.5	9 289.5	1 621.0	1 285.5	362.9	-5.9	-13.7	-348.0	1 556.8	1 904.8	2 576.9	1 043.4	1 537.0	10.6

Note: Chained (2005) dollar series are calculated as the product of the chain-type quantity index and the 2005 current-dollar value of the corresponding series, divided by 100. Because the formula for the chain-type quantity indexes uses weights from more than one period, the corresponding chained-dollar estimates are usually not additive. The residual column is the difference between the total and the sum of the most detailed components shown in the Bureau of Economic Analysis (BEA) published data.

. . . = Not available.

Table 1-3. Contributions to Percent Change in Real Gross Domestic Product

(Percent, percentage points.)   NIPA Table 1.1.2

Year and quarter	Percent change at seasonally adjusted annual rate, real GDP	Personal consumption expenditures	Gross private domestic investment				Exports and imports of goods and services			Government consumption expenditures and gross investment		
			Total	Fixed investment		Change in private inventories	Net exports	Exports	Imports	Total	Federal	State and local
				Nonresidential	Residential							
1950	8.7	4.29	5.74	0.86	2.03	2.84	-1.31	-0.66	-0.65	0.02	-0.56	0.58
1951	7.7	1.03	0.05	0.44	-1.14	0.75	0.81	0.98	-0.17	5.84	5.78	0.06
1952	3.8	1.95	-1.65	-0.18	-0.10	-1.37	-0.59	-0.22	-0.37	4.12	4.00	0.11
1953	4.6	2.93	0.70	0.80	0.18	-0.28	-0.70	-0.31	-0.39	1.67	1.33	0.34
1954	-0.6	1.29	-0.69	-0.20	0.42	-0.91	0.40	0.19	0.21	-1.64	-2.24	0.60
1955	7.2	4.63	3.45	1.01	0.90	1.54	-0.04	0.44	-0.48	-0.84	-1.39	0.55
1956	2.0	1.82	-0.23	0.55	-0.49	-0.29	0.37	0.71	-0.33	0.02	-0.23	0.25
1957	2.0	1.54	-0.71	0.16	-0.32	-0.54	0.25	0.43	-0.18	0.94	0.46	0.47
1958	-0.9	0.54	-1.25	-1.12	0.05	-0.18	-0.89	-0.69	-0.20	0.70	-0.01	0.70
1959	7.2	3.61	2.80	0.73	1.21	0.86	0.00	0.45	-0.45	0.76	0.42	0.34
1960	2.5	1.72	0.00	0.52	-0.39	-0.13	0.72	0.78	-0.06	0.04	-0.35	0.39
1961	2.3	1.30	-0.10	-0.06	0.01	-0.05	0.06	0.03	0.03	1.07	0.51	0.56
1962	6.1	3.10	1.81	0.78	0.46	0.57	-0.21	0.25	-0.47	1.36	1.07	0.29
1963	4.4	2.56	1.00	0.50	0.58	-0.08	0.24	0.35	-0.12	0.58	0.01	0.57
1964	5.8	3.69	1.25	1.07	0.30	-0.13	0.36	0.59	-0.23	0.49	-0.17	0.65
1965	6.4	3.91	2.16	1.65	-0.15	0.66	-0.30	0.15	-0.45	0.65	-0.01	0.66
1966	6.5	3.50	1.44	1.29	-0.43	0.58	-0.29	0.36	-0.65	1.87	1.24	0.63
1967	2.5	1.82	-0.76	-0.15	-0.13	-0.49	-0.22	0.12	-0.34	1.68	1.17	0.51
1968	4.8	3.51	0.90	0.46	0.53	-0.10	-0.30	0.41	-0.71	0.73	0.10	0.63
1969	3.1	2.29	0.90	0.78	0.13	0.00	-0.04	0.25	-0.29	-0.05	-0.42	0.37
1970	0.2	1.44	-1.04	-0.06	-0.26	-0.73	0.34	0.56	-0.22	-0.55	-0.86	0.31
1971	3.4	2.37	1.67	0.00	1.10	0.58	-0.19	0.10	-0.29	-0.50	-0.85	0.36
1972	5.3	3.81	1.87	0.93	0.89	0.06	-0.21	0.42	-0.63	-0.16	-0.42	0.26
1973	5.8	3.08	1.96	1.50	-0.04	0.50	0.82	1.12	-0.29	-0.08	-0.41	0.33
1974	-0.6	-0.52	-1.31	0.09	-1.13	-0.27	0.75	0.58	0.18	0.52	0.08	0.44
1975	-0.2	1.40	-2.98	-1.14	-0.57	-1.27	0.89	-0.05	0.94	0.48	0.03	0.45
1976	5.4	3.51	2.84	0.52	0.90	1.41	-1.08	0.37	-1.45	0.10	0.00	0.09
1977	4.6	2.66	2.43	1.19	0.99	0.25	-0.72	0.20	-0.92	0.23	0.19	0.04
1978	5.6	2.77	2.16	1.69	0.35	0.12	0.05	0.82	-0.78	0.60	0.22	0.38
1979	3.1	1.48	0.61	1.23	-0.21	-0.41	0.66	0.82	-0.16	0.37	0.20	0.17
1980	-0.3	-0.22	-2.12	-0.03	-1.17	-0.91	1.68	0.97	0.71	0.38	0.39	-0.01
1981	2.5	0.95	1.55	0.74	-0.35	1.16	-0.15	0.12	-0.27	0.19	0.42	-0.23
1982	-1.9	0.86	-2.55	-0.50	-0.71	-1.34	-0.60	-0.73	0.12	0.35	0.35	0.01
1983	4.5	3.65	1.45	-0.17	1.33	0.29	-1.35	-0.22	-1.13	0.76	0.63	0.13
1984	7.2	3.43	4.63	2.05	0.64	1.95	-1.58	0.63	-2.21	0.70	0.30	0.40
1985	4.1	3.32	-0.17	0.82	0.07	-1.06	-0.42	0.23	-0.65	1.41	0.74	0.67
1986	3.5	2.62	-0.12	-0.36	0.55	-0.32	-0.30	0.54	-0.84	1.27	0.55	0.71
1987	3.2	2.01	0.51	-0.01	0.10	0.42	0.16	0.77	-0.61	0.51	0.35	0.17
1988	4.1	2.64	0.39	0.58	-0.05	-0.14	0.82	1.24	-0.43	0.26	-0.16	0.42
1989	3.6	1.86	0.64	0.61	-0.14	0.17	0.52	0.99	-0.48	0.55	0.14	0.41
1990	1.9	1.34	-0.53	0.05	-0.37	-0.21	0.43	0.81	-0.38	0.64	0.18	0.46
1991	-0.2	0.10	-1.20	-0.57	-0.37	-0.26	0.64	0.63	0.02	0.22	-0.02	0.24
1992	3.4	2.27	1.07	0.31	0.47	0.29	-0.05	0.68	-0.72	0.10	-0.16	0.26
1993	2.9	2.37	1.21	0.83	0.31	0.07	-0.57	0.32	-0.90	-0.16	-0.33	0.17
1994	4.1	2.57	1.94	0.91	0.39	0.63	-0.43	0.85	-1.28	0.00	-0.30	0.30
1995	2.5	1.81	0.48	1.08	-0.14	-0.46	0.11	1.03	-0.92	0.11	-0.20	0.30
1996	3.7	2.35	1.35	1.01	0.33	0.02	-0.15	0.90	-1.04	0.19	-0.08	0.27
1997	4.5	2.48	1.95	1.33	0.08	0.54	-0.32	1.30	-1.62	0.34	-0.07	0.41
1998	4.4	3.50	1.65	1.38	0.32	-0.05	-1.18	0.26	-1.43	0.38	-0.07	0.45
1999	4.8	3.68	1.50	1.24	0.28	-0.02	-0.99	0.47	-1.45	0.63	0.12	0.51
2000	4.1	3.44	1.19	1.20	0.05	-0.05	-0.85	0.91	-1.76	0.36	0.03	0.33
2001	1.1	1.85	-1.24	-0.35	0.03	-0.92	-0.20	-0.61	0.41	0.67	0.24	0.43
2002	1.8	1.85	-0.22	-0.94	0.24	0.48	-0.65	-0.20	-0.46	0.84	0.44	0.40
2003	2.5	1.97	0.55	0.10	0.40	0.06	-0.45	0.15	-0.60	0.42	0.43	-0.01
2004	3.6	2.42	1.55	0.61	0.52	0.42	-0.66	0.89	-1.55	0.26	0.28	-0.02
2005	3.1	2.34	0.92	0.69	0.36	-0.13	-0.27	0.67	-0.94	0.06	0.09	-0.03
2006	2.7	2.01	0.46	0.84	-0.45	0.07	-0.05	0.93	-0.98	0.26	0.15	0.11
2007	2.1	1.84	-0.65	0.70	-1.05	-0.30	0.63	0.96	-0.33	0.32	0.09	0.23
2008	0.4	-0.17	-1.18	0.19	-1.00	-0.37	1.20	0.64	0.56	0.59	0.53	0.06
2009	-2.4	-0.42	-3.45	-2.08	-0.66	-0.71	1.07	-1.18	2.24	0.37	0.39	-0.02
2007												
1st quarter	1.2	2.54	-1.05	0.46	-0.89	-0.61	-0.29	0.39	-0.68	0.00	-0.36	0.36
2nd quarter	3.2	0.81	0.92	1.25	-0.66	0.32	0.66	0.58	0.08	0.82	0.50	0.32
3rd quarter	3.6	1.35	0.14	1.10	-1.14	0.19	1.36	1.99	-0.63	0.75	0.63	0.11
4th quarter	2.1	0.86	-1.29	0.78	-1.44	-0.63	2.24	1.65	0.60	0.31	0.19	0.12
2008												
1st quarter	-0.7	-0.39	-1.20	0.25	-1.24	-0.21	0.36	-0.02	0.38	0.51	0.56	-0.05
2nd quarter	1.5	0.06	-1.66	0.19	-0.60	-1.25	2.35	1.47	0.88	0.71	0.55	0.15
3rd quarter	-2.7	-2.49	-1.04	-0.73	-0.57	0.26	-0.10	-0.48	0.38	0.95	0.93	0.01
4th quarter	-5.4	-2.15	-3.91	-2.47	-0.81	-0.64	0.45	-2.67	3.12	0.24	0.49	-0.25
2009												
1st quarter	-6.4	0.44	-8.98	-5.29	-1.33	-2.36	2.64	-3.95	6.58	-0.52	-0.33	-0.19
2nd quarter	-0.7	-0.62	-3.10	-1.01	-0.67	-1.42	1.65	-0.45	2.09	1.33	0.85	0.48
3rd quarter	2.2	1.96	0.54	-0.59	0.43	0.69	-0.81	1.78	-2.59	0.55	0.62	-0.08
4th quarter	5.6	1.16	4.39	0.51	0.10	3.79	0.27	2.36	-2.09	-0.26	0.01	-0.27

Table 1-4. Chain-Type Quantity Indexes for Gross Domestic Product and Domestic Purchases

(Index numbers, 2005 = 100.)   NIPA Tables 1.1.3, 1.4.3, 2.3.3

Year and quarter	Gross domestic product											Gross domestic purchases
	Gross domestic product, total	Personal consumption expenditures		Private fixed investment			Exports and imports of goods and services		Government consumption expenditures and gross investment			
		Total	Excluding food and energy	Total	Nonresidential	Residential	Exports	Imports	Total	Federal	State and local	
1950	15.9	14.6	12.0	11.4	8.2	24.1	4.2	3.2	20.8	28.4	16.4	15.2
1951	17.1	14.8	12.2	11.0	8.5	20.2	5.1	3.4	28.4	47.2	16.5	16.3
1952	17.8	15.2	12.6	10.7	8.4	19.8	4.9	3.7	34.2	61.4	16.8	17.0
1953	18.6	16.0	13.2	11.5	9.1	20.5	4.6	4.0	36.6	66.3	17.6	17.9
1954	18.5	16.3	13.4	11.7	8.9	22.2	4.8	3.8	34.1	57.6	19.1	17.7
1955	19.8	17.5	14.5	13.2	9.9	25.8	5.3	4.3	32.9	52.4	20.5	19.0
1956	20.2	18.0	14.9	13.2	10.5	23.7	6.2	4.6	32.9	51.5	21.2	19.3
1957	20.6	18.5	15.2	13.1	10.6	22.2	6.7	4.8	34.4	53.3	22.4	19.7
1958	20.4	18.6	15.3	12.2	9.5	22.5	5.8	5.0	35.5	53.3	24.3	19.7
1959	21.9	19.7	16.3	13.9	10.2	28.2	6.4	5.6	36.7	55.0	25.2	21.1
1960	22.4	20.2	16.8	14.0	10.8	26.2	7.6	5.6	36.8	53.5	26.3	21.5
1961	22.9	20.6	17.2	13.9	10.7	26.2	7.6	5.6	38.6	55.7	28.0	22.0
1962	24.3	21.7	18.3	15.2	11.7	28.8	8.0	6.2	41.0	60.5	28.8	23.3
1963	25.4	22.6	19.2	16.4	12.3	32.2	8.5	6.4	42.0	60.5	30.6	24.3
1964	26.8	23.9	20.4	18.0	13.8	34.0	9.6	6.8	43.0	59.7	32.6	25.6
1965	28.6	25.4	21.8	19.8	16.2	33.0	9.8	7.5	44.2	59.7	34.8	27.4
1966	30.4	26.9	23.1	20.9	18.2	30.1	10.5	8.6	48.2	66.3	37.0	29.3
1967	31.2	27.7	23.8	20.5	18.0	29.1	10.7	9.2	51.8	72.9	38.9	30.1
1968	32.7	29.3	25.3	22.0	18.8	33.1	11.6	10.6	53.5	73.5	41.2	31.6
1969	33.7	30.4	26.3	23.3	20.2	34.1	12.1	11.2	53.4	71.0	42.6	32.6
1970	33.8	31.1	26.8	22.8	20.1	32.0	13.4	11.7	52.1	65.7	43.7	32.6
1971	34.9	32.3	28.0	24.6	20.1	40.8	13.7	12.3	50.9	60.7	45.1	33.7
1972	36.8	34.2	30.0	27.5	21.9	48.1	14.7	13.7	50.6	58.2	46.1	35.6
1973	38.9	35.9	31.9	30.0	25.1	47.8	17.5	14.3	50.4	55.8	47.4	37.4
1974	38.7	35.6	31.8	28.2	25.3	37.9	18.8	14.0	51.6	56.2	49.2	36.9
1975	38.6	36.4	32.5	25.1	22.8	33.0	18.7	12.4	52.8	56.4	51.0	36.5
1976	40.7	38.5	34.4	27.6	23.9	40.7	19.6	14.9	53.0	56.4	51.4	38.8
1977	42.6	40.1	36.1	31.6	26.6	49.5	20.0	16.5	53.6	57.6	51.5	40.9
1978	44.9	41.9	38.0	35.4	30.6	52.6	22.1	17.9	55.2	59.1	53.2	43.1
1979	46.3	42.9	39.2	37.4	33.7	50.7	24.3	18.2	56.2	60.5	54.0	44.2
1980	46.2	42.7	39.1	35.0	33.6	40.0	27.0	17.0	57.3	63.4	54.0	43.3
1981	47.4	43.4	40.0	35.8	35.5	36.8	27.3	17.4	57.9	66.4	52.9	44.5
1982	46.4	44.0	40.5	33.2	34.2	30.1	25.2	17.2	58.9	69.0	52.9	43.9
1983	48.6	46.5	43.2	35.7	33.8	42.5	24.5	19.4	61.0	73.6	53.5	46.5
1984	52.0	48.9	45.9	41.7	39.7	48.8	26.6	24.1	63.1	75.8	55.4	50.5
1985	54.2	51.5	48.5	43.9	42.3	49.6	27.4	25.7	67.5	81.8	58.9	52.7
1986	56.1	53.6	50.7	44.4	41.1	55.7	29.4	27.9	71.6	86.4	62.7	54.7
1987	57.9	55.2	52.5	44.6	41.1	56.8	32.6	29.5	73.3	89.5	63.6	56.3
1988	60.2	57.4	54.8	46.1	43.2	56.2	37.8	30.7	74.2	88.0	65.9	58.1
1989	62.4	59.1	56.4	47.5	45.7	54.5	42.2	32.0	76.2	89.4	68.3	59.8
1990	63.6	60.3	57.8	46.5	45.9	49.8	46.0	33.2	78.7	91.2	71.1	60.7
1991	63.4	60.4	57.8	43.5	43.4	45.0	49.0	33.1	79.5	91.0	72.6	60.1
1992	65.6	62.4	60.1	46.1	44.8	51.3	52.4	35.5	79.9	89.4	74.2	62.2
1993	67.4	64.6	62.4	50.0	48.7	55.4	54.1	38.5	79.2	85.8	75.2	64.3
1994	70.2	67.1	65.0	54.7	53.2	60.8	58.8	43.1	79.2	82.6	77.2	67.2
1995	72.0	68.9	66.9	58.2	58.8	58.8	64.8	46.6	79.7	80.4	79.2	68.8
1996	74.6	71.3	69.5	63.4	64.3	63.6	70.2	50.6	80.5	79.4	81.1	71.4
1997	78.0	74.0	72.4	69.3	72.0	64.8	78.6	57.4	82.0	78.6	84.0	74.8
1998	81.4	77.8	76.6	76.8	80.7	69.7	80.3	64.2	83.8	77.8	87.3	78.9
1999	85.3	82.1	81.0	84.0	89.1	74.1	83.8	71.6	86.8	79.3	91.2	83.4
2000	88.8	86.3	85.5	90.2	97.9	74.8	91.0	80.9	88.5	79.7	93.7	87.4
2001	89.8	88.6	88.1	88.5	95.1	75.3	86.0	78.6	91.9	82.9	97.2	88.5
2002	91.4	91.0	90.6	84.7	87.6	79.2	84.2	81.3	96.2	89.0	100.5	90.6
2003	93.7	93.5	93.2	87.5	88.4	85.7	85.6	84.9	98.3	94.8	100.4	93.2
2004	97.0	96.8	96.6	93.9	93.7	94.1	93.7	94.2	99.7	98.7	100.2	96.9
2005	100.0	100.0	100.0	100.0	100.0	100.0	100.0	100.0	100.0	100.0	100.0	100.0
2006	102.7	102.9	103.2	102.3	107.9	92.7	109.0	106.1	101.4	102.1	100.9	102.6
2007	104.9	105.6	106.1	100.2	114.6	75.5	118.5	108.2	103.1	103.4	102.9	104.0
2008	105.3	105.4	106.1	95.1	116.5	58.2	124.8	104.7	106.2	111.4	103.4	103.3
2009	102.8	104.7	105.3	77.7	95.8	46.3	112.8	90.2	108.2	117.2	103.2	99.8
2007												
1st quarter	103.6	105.1	105.4	99.8	110.6	81.5	113.9	108.0	101.7	100.7	102.2	103.3
2nd quarter	104.5	105.4	105.8	100.7	113.6	78.8	115.3	107.9	102.8	102.6	102.9	103.9
3rd quarter	105.4	105.9	106.4	100.6	116.2	73.9	120.3	108.9	103.8	104.9	103.1	104.5
4th quarter	106.0	106.2	106.8	99.6	118.1	67.8	124.4	107.9	104.2	105.6	103.4	104.4
2008												
1st quarter	105.8	106.0	106.6	98.0	118.7	62.4	124.4	107.2	104.8	107.6	103.2	104.2
2nd quarter	106.2	106.0	106.7	97.3	119.1	59.7	128.0	105.8	105.8	109.7	103.6	103.9
3rd quarter	105.4	105.1	106.0	95.2	117.2	57.2	126.8	105.3	107.0	113.2	103.6	103.3
4th quarter	104.0	104.3	105.0	90.0	111.0	53.6	120.2	100.6	107.4	115.0	103.1	101.8
2009												
1st quarter	102.3	104.4	105.1	79.5	98.1	47.5	109.9	89.8	106.6	113.7	102.7	99.6
2nd quarter	102.1	104.2	104.8	76.9	95.6	44.4	108.8	86.3	108.4	116.8	103.6	99.0
3rd quarter	102.6	104.9	105.6	76.6	94.2	46.4	113.3	90.6	109.1	119.1	103.5	99.7
4th quarter	104.0	105.3	105.9	77.6	95.4	46.8	119.3	93.9	108.7	119.1	102.9	101.0

Table 1-5. Chain-Type Price Indexes for Gross Domestic Product and Domestic Purchases

(Index numbers, 2005 = 100.)   NIPA Tables 1.1.4, 1.6.4, 2.3.4

Year and quarter	Gross domestic product												Gross domestic purchases
	Gross domestic product, total	Personal consumption expenditures		Private fixed investment			Exports and imports of goods and services		Government consumption expenditures and gross investment			
		Total	Excluding food and energy	Total	Nonresidential	Residential	Exports	Imports	Total	Federal	State and local	
1950	14.6	15.0	15.0	19.9	25.3	11.0	22.6	17.7	9.5	10.4	8.5	14.4
1951	15.6	16.0	16.0	21.7	27.7	11.8	25.5	21.3	10.1	10.9	9.4	15.4
1952	16.0	16.3	16.3	22.2	28.4	12.1	25.7	20.6	10.3	11.0	9.8	15.7
1953	16.2	16.6	16.6	22.4	28.6	12.2	25.6	19.7	10.4	11.1	10.0	15.9
1954	16.3	16.7	16.8	22.5	28.9	12.3	25.2	20.0	10.7	11.3	10.1	16.0
1955	16.6	16.8	17.0	22.9	29.3	12.5	25.4	19.8	11.1	11.9	10.3	16.3
1956	17.1	17.1	17.4	24.3	31.6	12.8	26.3	20.2	11.7	12.6	11.0	16.8
1957	17.7	17.6	17.9	25.1	33.2	12.9	27.3	20.4	12.2	13.1	11.5	17.4
1958	18.1	18.0	18.3	25.2	33.4	12.8	27.0	19.6	12.6	13.7	11.6	17.8
1959	18.3	18.3	18.7	25.4	33.8	12.9	27.1	19.8	12.7	13.6	11.9	18.0
1960	18.6	18.6	19.0	25.5	34.0	13.0	27.5	19.9	12.8	13.7	12.1	18.2
1961	18.8	18.8	19.3	25.4	33.8	13.0	27.9	19.9	13.1	13.9	12.4	18.4
1962	19.1	19.0	19.5	25.5	33.8	13.0	27.9	19.7	13.4	14.2	12.7	18.7
1963	19.3	19.2	19.8	25.4	33.8	12.9	27.9	20.1	13.7	14.5	13.0	18.9
1964	19.6	19.5	20.1	25.5	34.0	13.0	28.1	20.5	14.1	15.0	13.3	19.2
1965	19.9	19.8	20.3	26.0	34.3	13.4	29.0	20.8	14.4	15.4	13.7	19.5
1966	20.5	20.3	20.8	26.5	34.9	13.9	29.9	21.3	15.0	15.9	14.3	20.1
1967	21.1	20.8	21.4	27.3	35.7	14.3	31.0	21.4	15.7	16.4	15.1	20.6
1968	22.0	21.6	22.4	28.4	37.0	15.1	31.7	21.7	16.5	17.3	15.9	21.5
1969	23.1	22.6	23.4	29.8	38.5	16.1	32.8	22.3	17.5	18.2	17.0	22.6
1970	24.3	23.7	24.5	31.0	40.3	16.7	34.0	23.6	18.9	19.7	18.4	23.8
1971	25.5	24.7	25.7	32.6	42.2	17.6	35.3	25.0	20.4	21.4	19.7	25.0
1972	26.6	25.5	26.5	34.0	43.7	18.7	36.9	26.8	22.0	23.5	20.9	26.1
1973	28.1	26.9	27.5	35.9	45.4	20.4	41.8	31.4	23.6	25.1	22.5	27.6
1974	30.7	29.7	29.7	39.4	49.7	22.5	51.5	45.0	26.0	27.3	25.0	30.5
1975	33.6	32.2	32.2	44.4	56.6	24.5	56.7	48.7	28.6	30.2	27.4	33.3
1976	35.5	34.0	34.1	46.9	59.7	26.1	58.6	50.2	30.5	32.3	29.1	35.2
1977	37.8	36.2	36.3	50.6	63.8	28.8	61.0	54.6	32.6	34.7	31.0	37.6
1978	40.4	38.7	38.7	54.9	68.1	32.3	64.7	58.4	34.7	36.9	33.0	40.3
1979	43.8	42.1	41.6	59.9	73.6	35.9	72.5	68.4	37.6	39.7	36.0	43.8
1980	47.8	46.6	45.4	65.5	80.1	39.8	79.8	85.2	41.7	43.9	40.0	48.4
1981	52.3	50.8	49.3	71.6	87.8	43.0	85.7	89.8	45.8	48.2	44.0	52.9
1982	55.5	53.6	52.5	75.5	92.7	45.3	86.1	86.8	48.8	51.4	46.8	55.9
1983	57.7	55.9	55.2	75.3	91.8	46.4	86.5	83.5	50.7	53.2	48.9	57.8
1984	59.8	58.0	57.5	75.8	91.6	47.7	87.3	82.8	53.3	56.4	51.0	59.9
1985	61.6	59.9	59.7	76.7	92.3	48.9	84.6	80.1	55.0	57.6	53.0	61.6
1986	63.0	61.4	61.9	78.6	93.9	51.0	83.3	80.1	56.0	57.9	54.6	62.9
1987	64.8	63.6	64.3	80.0	94.8	53.1	85.5	84.9	57.5	58.6	56.8	64.9
1988	67.0	66.1	67.1	82.1	96.9	54.9	89.9	89.0	59.1	59.9	58.6	67.2
1989	69.5	69.0	69.9	84.1	98.9	56.7	91.4	91.0	60.9	61.5	60.7	69.7
1990	72.2	72.1	72.8	85.8	100.8	58.0	92.0	93.6	63.4	63.5	63.5	72.5
1991	74.8	74.8	75.7	87.1	102.3	58.8	93.2	92.8	65.6	66.1	65.4	74.9
1992	76.5	77.0	78.2	86.8	101.5	59.5	92.8	92.9	67.3	68.1	66.9	76.7
1993	78.2	78.6	80.1	87.8	101.5	61.9	92.8	92.1	68.9	69.8	68.5	78.3
1994	79.9	80.3	81.8	89.0	102.0	64.1	93.8	93.0	70.8	71.7	70.4	80.0
1995	81.5	82.0	83.7	90.1	102.2	66.4	96.0	95.6	72.8	73.7	72.3	81.7
1996	83.1	83.8	85.3	89.8	101.1	67.8	94.7	93.9	74.5	75.8	73.8	83.2
1997	84.6	85.4	87.0	89.6	99.8	69.6	93.1	90.6	75.9	77.0	75.2	84.4
1998	85.5	86.2	88.2	88.8	97.6	71.4	91.0	85.7	76.9	77.9	76.3	85.0
1999	86.8	87.6	89.6	88.7	96.2	74.2	90.4	86.3	79.3	79.9	79.0	86.3
2000	88.6	89.8	91.1	89.8	96.2	77.4	92.0	90.0	82.5	82.5	82.5	88.5
2001	90.7	91.5	92.7	90.6	95.8	81.0	91.6	87.8	84.8	84.2	85.0	90.1
2002	92.1	92.7	94.3	90.9	95.4	83.0	91.3	86.8	87.0	87.3	86.8	91.4
2003	94.1	94.6	95.8	92.3	95.4	87.0	93.2	89.8	90.7	91.0	90.4	93.6
2004	96.8	97.1	97.8	95.5	96.8	93.3	96.5	94.1	94.5	95.3	94.1	96.4
2005	100.0	100.0	100.0	100.0	100.0	100.0	100.0	100.0	100.0	100.0	100.0	100.0
2006	103.3	102.7	102.3	104.4	103.5	106.1	103.4	104.1	104.8	104.1	105.3	103.4
2007	106.2	105.5	104.7	106.7	106.2	107.5	107.1	108.0	109.6	107.8	110.6	106.4
2008	108.5	109.0	107.2	107.6	107.9	105.8	112.4	119.6	114.5	110.9	116.6	109.8
2009	109.7	109.2	108.9	106.1	107.5	100.7	106.3	107.0	114.3	111.5	115.9	109.8
2007												
1st quarter	105.3	104.3	103.9	106.4	105.7	107.6	105.4	104.7	107.9	106.8	108.5	105.2
2nd quarter	106.0	105.1	104.3	106.6	106.1	107.3	106.5	106.3	109.1	107.7	109.9	106.0
3rd quarter	106.5	105.7	104.9	106.8	106.4	107.5	107.4	107.9	109.9	107.9	111.0	106.6
4th quarter	107.1	107.0	105.7	107.1	106.7	107.7	109.1	113.1	111.3	108.6	113.0	107.8
2008												
1st quarter	107.6	108.0	106.3	106.9	106.6	107.3	111.2	117.2	113.0	110.1	114.8	108.7
2nd quarter	108.1	109.0	107.0	107.2	107.2	106.8	113.9	123.1	114.8	111.3	116.9	109.7
3rd quarter	109.1	110.3	107.7	107.9	108.3	105.8	115.6	125.2	116.0	111.8	118.5	110.9
4th quarter	109.2	108.9	107.9	108.2	109.5	103.2	108.9	112.7	114.2	110.6	116.4	109.8
2009												
1st quarter	109.7	108.4	108.2	107.7	109.2	101.9	105.3	103.7	113.9	111.1	115.6	109.4
2nd quarter	109.7	108.8	108.7	106.5	108.0	100.6	105.3	104.8	114.1	111.2	115.7	109.5
3rd quarter	109.8	109.5	109.0	105.3	106.7	99.9	106.5	107.7	114.3	111.6	115.9	109.9
4th quarter	109.9	110.2	109.5	105.1	106.3	100.5	108.0	111.9	114.8	112.2	116.4	110.4

Table 1-6. Final Sales

(Quarterly dollar data are at seasonally adjusted annual rates.)   NIPA Tables 1.4.4, 1.4.5, 1.4.6

Year and quarter	Final sales of domestic product			Final sales to domestic purchasers		
	Billions of dollars	Billions of chained (2005) dollars	Chain-type price index, 2005 = 100	Billions of dollars	Billions of chained (2005) dollars	Chain-type price index, 2005 = 100
1950	288.0	1 990.7	14.5	287.2	2 021.1	14.2
1951	329.4	2 132.2	15.5	326.8	2 148.1	15.2
1952	354.8	2 245.7	15.8	353.6	2 276.5	15.5
1953	377.4	2 356.4	16.0	378.1	2 405.2	15.7
1954	382.3	2 363.0	16.2	381.9	2 402.2	15.9
1955	409.7	2 496.2	16.4	409.3	2 538.7	16.1
1956	433.5	2 553.3	17.0	431.1	2 587.4	16.7
1957	460.3	2 618.9	17.6	456.2	2 647.9	17.2
1958	467.5	2 600.0	18.0	467.0	2 652.4	17.6
1959	502.7	2 764.0	18.2	502.3	2 819.8	17.8
1960	523.2	2 836.6	18.5	519.0	2 873.5	18.1
1961	541.8	2 904.6	18.7	536.9	2 941.3	18.3
1962	579.6	3 064.9	18.9	575.5	3 111.5	18.5
1963	612.1	3 202.6	19.1	607.2	3 244.7	18.7
1964	658.8	3 393.7	19.4	651.9	3 427.8	19.0
1965	709.9	3 590.7	19.8	704.3	3 639.4	19.4
1966	774.1	3 806.6	20.3	770.2	3 870.9	19.9
1967	822.6	3 923.3	21.0	819.0	3 999.0	20.5
1968	900.8	4 119.4	21.9	899.4	4 211.8	21.4
1969	975.3	4 248.6	23.0	973.8	4 345.7	22.4
1970	1 036.3	4 287.9	24.2	1 032.4	4 370.9	23.6
1971	1 118.6	4 407.4	25.4	1 117.9	4 501.4	24.8
1972	1 228.8	4 640.6	26.5	1 232.2	4 749.2	26.0
1973	1 366.4	4 888.2	28.0	1 362.3	4 962.2	27.5
1974	1 485.5	4 874.1	30.5	1 486.3	4 910.3	30.3
1975	1 644.0	4 926.3	33.4	1 628.0	4 918.9	33.1
1976	1 807.5	5 120.2	35.3	1 809.1	5 167.9	35.0
1977	2 007.8	5 344.9	37.6	2 030.9	5 431.5	37.4
1978	2 268.0	5 639.7	40.2	2 293.3	5 725.2	40.1
1979	2 544.2	5 841.2	43.6	2 566.8	5 889.1	43.6
1980	2 794.5	5 878.7	47.6	2 807.5	5 828.2	48.2
1981	3 097.0	5 959.5	52.0	3 109.6	5 916.7	52.6
1982	3 268.1	5 923.3	55.2	3 288.1	5 916.9	55.6
1983	3 540.4	6 172.9	57.4	3 592.0	6 244.6	57.6
1984	3 865.5	6 495.6	59.6	3 968.2	6 664.0	59.6
1985	4 195.6	6 838.9	61.4	4 310.9	7 035.3	61.3
1986	4 453.5	7 098.7	62.8	4 586.0	7 315.9	62.8
1987	4 709.2	7 296.2	64.6	4 854.2	7 501.6	64.7
1988	5 081.9	7 607.8	66.8	5 192.0	7 752.8	67.0
1989	5 454.5	7 867.5	69.3	5 542.3	7 972.5	69.5
1990	5 786.0	8 032.7	72.0	5 863.6	8 103.2	72.4
1991	5 992.5	8 034.8	74.6	6 019.4	8 053.8	74.8
1992	6 326.0	8 284.3	76.4	6 358.8	8 306.5	76.6
1993	6 646.5	8 515.3	78.1	6 710.9	8 584.5	78.2
1994	7 021.4	8 809.2	79.7	7 114.1	8 914.5	79.8
1995	7 383.5	9 073.2	81.4	7 474.2	9 168.3	81.5
1996	7 807.7	9 412.5	83.0	7 904.0	9 520.4	83.0
1997	8 261.4	9 782.6	84.4	8 362.7	9 920.9	84.3
1998	8 729.8	10 217.1	85.4	8 891.6	10 473.5	84.9
1999	9 292.7	10 715.7	86.7	9 554.7	11 077.0	86.3
2000	9 896.9	11 167.5	88.6	10 279.0	11 623.1	88.4
2001	10 324.5	11 391.7	90.6	10 695.4	11 870.8	90.1
2002	10 630.3	11 543.5	92.1	11 057.5	12 098.4	91.4
2003	11 125.8	11 824.8	94.1	11 629.9	12 433.4	93.5
2004	11 802.8	12 198.2	96.8	12 421.5	12 886.8	96.4
2005	12 588.4	12 588.4	100.0	13 311.2	13 311.2	100.0
2006	13 339.0	12 917.1	103.3	14 108.3	13 646.5	103.4
2007	14 058.3	13 234.3	106.2	14 772.0	13 881.9	106.4
2008	14 476.2	13 341.2	108.5	15 183.9	13 829.8	109.8
2009	14 377.2	13 110.7	109.7	14 769.5	13 458.8	109.7
2007						
1st quarter	13 782.5	13 086.4	105.3	14 511.9	13 791.5	105.2
2nd quarter	13 973.7	13 179.6	106.0	14 698.5	13 863.2	106.0
3rd quarter	14 148.8	13 290.3	106.5	14 847.3	13 928.9	106.6
4th quarter	14 328.0	13 381.1	107.1	15 030.5	13 944.0	107.8
2008						
1st quarter	14 382.1	13 363.5	107.6	15 126.5	13 912.9	108.7
2nd quarter	14 547.2	13 453.5	108.1	15 285.7	13 923.2	109.8
3rd quarter	14 583.7	13 354.3	109.2	15 341.1	13 828.0	110.9
4th quarter	14 391.8	13 193.5	109.1	14 982.3	13 654.9	109.7
2009						
1st quarter	14 305.3	13 055.8	109.6	14 683.9	13 432.7	109.3
2nd quarter	14 327.4	13 077.8	109.6	14 666.5	13 401.4	109.4
3rd quarter	14 398.7	13 127.2	109.7	14 800.9	13 477.2	109.8
4th quarter	14 477.4	13 181.9	109.8	14 926.9	13 524.1	110.4

Table 1-7. Per Capita Product and Income and U.S. Population

(Dollars, except as noted; quarterly data are at seasonally adjusted annual rates.)   **NIPA Table 7.1**

Year and quarter	Current dollars							Chained (2005) dollars						Population (mid-period, thousands)
	Gross domestic product	Personal income	Disposable personal income	Personal consumption expenditures				Gross domestic product	Disposable personal income	Personal consumption expenditures				
				Total	Durable goods	Nondurable goods	Services			Total	Durable goods	Nondurable goods	Services	
1950	1 937	1 509	1 384	1 267	214	556	497	13 225	9 240	8 460	481	2 990	4 912	151 684
1951	2 199	1 672	1 496	1 352	206	603	543	14 007	9 352	8 448	433	2 985	5 114	154 287
1952	2 283	1 753	1 550	1 399	199	621	578	14 296	9 491	8 567	417	3 044	5 253	156 954
1953	2 377	1 828	1 620	1 461	217	628	616	14 710	9 788	8 829	458	3 087	5 385	159 565
1954	2 342	1 812	1 627	1 478	208	628	642	14 363	9 748	8 857	448	3 081	5 476	162 391
1955	2 509	1 912	1 713	1 566	247	645	674	15 128	10 225	9 345	534	3 185	5 651	165 275
1956	2 600	2 018	1 800	1 615	239	666	710	15 157	10 535	9 450	505	3 239	5 819	168 221
1957	2 692	2 093	1 866	1 675	245	686	743	15 187	10 599	9 512	501	3 245	5 913	171 274
1958	2 683	2 119	1 897	1 701	227	701	773	14 802	10 526	9 437	455	3 234	6 004	174 141
1959	2 860	2 215	1 976	1 794	253	721	819	15 596	10 803	9 804	500	3 322	6 196	177 130
1960	2 912	2 275	2 020	1 836	252	727	856	15 661	10 865	9 871	500	3 310	6 309	180 760
1961	2 965	2 334	2 077	1 862	241	733	889	15 766	11 052	9 911	475	3 322	6 435	183 742
1962	3 139	2 446	2 170	1 947	265	748	934	16 466	11 413	10 243	521	3 372	6 636	186 590
1963	3 263	2 533	2 245	2 022	286	760	975	16 940	11 672	10 512	561	3 395	6 819	189 300
1964	3 458	2 680	2 408	2 144	310	796	1 038	17 675	12 342	10 985	605	3 506	7 126	191 927
1965	3 700	2 858	2 562	2 284	342	840	1 102	18 576	12 939	11 535	672	3 636	7 426	194 347
1966	4 007	3 071	2 733	2 446	365	905	1 176	19 559	13 465	12 050	719	3 795	7 705	196 599
1967	4 188	3 261	2 894	2 555	372	931	1 252	19 836	13 904	12 276	722	3 834	7 935	198 752
1968	4 532	3 545	3 112	2 780	423	995	1 362	20 590	14 392	12 856	794	3 957	8 275	200 745
1969	4 856	3 839	3 324	2 985	446	1 057	1 482	21 021	14 706	13 206	816	4 026	8 559	202 736
1970	5 063	4 089	3 586	3 161	439	1 116	1 607	20 820	15 158	13 361	785	4 068	8 792	205 089
1971	5 425	4 348	3 859	3 378	493	1 154	1 731	21 249	15 644	13 696	853	4 093	8 981	207 692
1972	5 897	4 729	4 140	3 669	555	1 226	1 888	22 140	16 228	14 384	949	4 213	9 400	209 924
1973	6 522	5 240	4 615	4 020	616	1 350	2 054	23 200	17 166	14 953	1 038	4 293	9 752	211 939
1974	7 010	5 716	5 010	4 362	609	1 502	2 251	22 861	16 878	14 693	962	4 150	9 847	213 898
1975	7 583	6 180	5 497	4 786	658	1 617	2 512	22 592	17 091	14 881	955	4 145	10 119	215 981
1976	8 366	6 762	5 972	5 279	773	1 732	2 774	23 575	17 600	15 558	1 064	4 300	10 451	218 086
1977	9 216	7 411	6 514	5 801	871	1 854	3 075	24 412	18 025	16 051	1 147	4 354	10 774	220 289
1978	10 303	8 250	7 220	6 413	958	2 022	3 432	25 503	18 670	16 583	1 194	4 464	11 157	222 629
1979	11 382	9 149	7 956	7 069	1 005	2 273	3 790	26 010	18 897	16 790	1 175	4 529	11 371	225 106
1980	12 243	10 107	8 794	7 710	994	2 518	4 198	25 640	18 863	16 538	1 069	4 469	11 413	227 726
1981	13 594	11 227	9 726	8 432	1 061	2 719	4 653	26 030	19 173	16 623	1 069	4 481	11 503	230 008
1982	14 009	11 915	10 390	8 938	1 090	2 783	5 065	25 282	19 406	16 694	1 057	4 484	11 615	232 218
1983	15 084	12 598	11 095	9 766	1 259	2 897	5 611	26 186	19 868	17 489	1 197	4 588	12 113	234 333
1984	16 629	13 828	12 232	10 580	1 447	3 052	6 080	27 823	21 105	18 256	1 356	4 736	12 477	236 394
1985	17 683	14 661	12 911	11 394	1 595	3 175	6 625	28 717	21 571	19 037	1 479	4 836	13 007	238 506
1986	18 531	15 356	13 540	12 036	1 751	3 217	7 068	29 443	22 083	19 630	1 606	4 963	13 272	240 683
1987	19 504	16 160	14 146	12 753	1 820	3 353	7 580	30 115	22 246	20 055	1 622	5 003	13 678	242 843
1988	20 813	17 266	15 206	13 670	1 939	3 519	8 213	31 069	22 997	20 675	1 700	5 089	14 130	245 061
1989	22 160	18 422	16 134	14 530	1 998	3 757	8 774	31 877	23 385	21 060	1 721	5 177	14 421	247 387
1990	23 185	19 373	17 004	15 331	1 987	3 974	9 370	32 112	23 568	21 249	1 694	5 179	14 683	250 181
1991	23 635	19 846	17 532	15 699	1 882	4 024	9 792	31 614	23 453	21 000	1 582	5 095	14 706	253 530
1992	24 686	20 813	18 436	16 491	1 978	4 107	10 406	32 255	23 958	21 430	1 651	5 126	15 029	256 922
1993	25 616	21 393	18 909	17 226	2 119	4 191	10 916	32 747	24 044	21 904	1 751	5 188	15 310	260 282
1994	26 893	22 299	19 678	18 033	2 305	4 325	11 403	33 671	24 517	22 466	1 868	5 326	15 577	263 455
1995	27 813	23 260	20 470	18 708	2 385	4 426	11 898	34 112	24 951	22 803	1 919	5 393	15 785	266 588
1996	29 062	24 439	21 355	19 553	2 507	4 603	12 443	34 977	25 475	23 325	2 039	5 485	16 059	269 714
1997	30 526	25 648	22 255	20 408	2 621	4 731	13 056	36 102	26 061	23 899	2 179	5 579	16 358	272 958
1998	31 843	27 251	23 534	21 432	2 825	4 816	13 791	37 238	27 299	24 861	2 416	5 723	16 881	276 154
1999	33 486	28 321	24 356	22 707	3 069	5 129	14 509	38 592	27 805	25 923	2 699	5 946	17 373	279 328
2000	35 237	30 308	25 944	24 185	3 243	5 465	15 478	39 750	28 899	26 939	2 903	6 072	18 035	282 418
2001	36 049	31 133	26 805	25 054	3 317	5 564	16 173	39 768	29 299	27 385	3 029	6 118	18 290	285 335
2002	36 935	31 444	27 799	25 819	3 443	5 615	16 760	40 096	29 976	27 841	3 228	6 179	18 457	288 133
2003	38 310	32 244	28 805	26 832	3 489	5 888	17 455	40 711	30 442	28 357	3 391	6 346	18 630	290 845
2004	40 435	33 857	30 287	28 228	3 617	6 237	18 374	41 784	31 193	29 072	3 581	6 489	19 004	293 502
2005	42 664	35 398	31 318	29 771	3 732	6 645	19 394	42 664	31 318	29 771	3 732	6 645	19 394	296 229
2006	44 805	37 679	33 157	31 174	3 789	6 984	20 401	43 391	32 271	30 341	3 847	6 767	19 728	299 052
2007	46 611	39 381	34 445	32 535	3 842	7 299	21 394	43 884	32 648	30 838	3 973	6 870	20 001	302 025
2008	47 375	40 149	35 450	33 231	3 593	7 571	22 067	43 671	32 514	30 479	3 760	6 749	19 956	304 831
2009	46 364	39 112	35 526	32 812	3 366	7 221	22 225	42 238	32 519	30 034	3 582	6 625	19 799	307 483
2007														
1st quarter	45 846	38 905	34 055	32 097	3 832	7 156	21 110	43 534	32 668	30 790	3 934	6 880	19 978	300 913
2nd quarter	46 407	39 200	34 287	32 367	3 829	7 239	21 300	43 777	32 633	30 806	3 945	6 850	20 013	301 617
3rd quarter	46 890	39 502	34 540	32 624	3 840	7 292	21 491	44 050	32 684	30 871	3 985	6 868	20 024	302 406
4th quarter	47 294	39 913	34 893	33 049	3 868	7 508	21 672	44 171	32 610	30 886	4 028	6 881	19 988	303 166
2008														
1st quarter	47 312	39 966	34 925	33 228	3 771	7 575	21 882	43 997	32 345	30 774	3 927	6 814	20 036	303 810
2nd quarter	47 620	40 378	36 022	33 486	3 700	7 714	22 072	44 065	33 041	30 715	3 862	6 837	20 012	304 445
3rd quarter	47 666	40 261	35 551	33 489	3 567	7 781	22 141	43 662	32 238	30 368	3 734	6 722	19 898	305 177
4th quarter	46 904	39 993	35 304	32 724	3 334	7 217	22 172	42 963	32 431	30 061	3 520	6 624	19 878	305 890
2009														
1st quarter	46 258	38 998	35 124	32 587	3 345	7 088	22 154	42 172	32 387	30 047	3 547	6 641	19 824	306 496
2nd quarter	46 080	39 234	35 709	32 560	3 294	7 106	22 161	42 011	32 815	29 922	3 490	6 596	19 794	307 101
3rd quarter	46 268	39 001	35 522	32 919	3 415	7 280	22 223	42 146	32 436	30 059	3 647	6 606	19 786	307 815
4th quarter	46 849	39 212	35 747	33 179	3 410	7 407	22 362	42 621	32 440	30 110	3 642	6 656	19 791	308 521

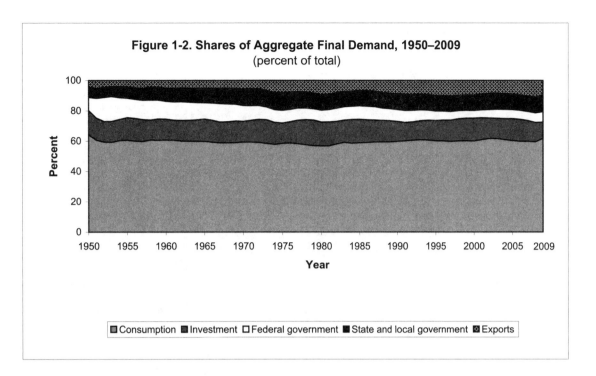

Figure 1-2. Shares of Aggregate Final Demand, 1950–2009
(percent of total)

Legend: ▣ Consumption ■ Investment ☐ Federal government ■ State and local government ▩ Exports

- People often want to know how various sources of demand, especially consumption spending, affect GDP. It is often stated, in discussing such questions, that consumption "accounts for" about 70 percent of GDP. Such statements are based on a NIPA table showing the components of GDP as a percent of total GDP. Such tables indicate that in 2009, personal consumption expenditures (PCE) amounted to 70.8 percent of total GDP, up from a range of 60 to 65 percent earlier in the postwar period. (All such calculations must be made in current dollars, since for reasons stated in the notes and definitions, the 2005-dollar values do not sum to the total GDP.)

- Can this be interpreted as "accounting for" 70.8 percent of GDP? No, because the value of PCE includes imported goods and services—coffee, cocoa, and bananas; crude oil from the Middle East, transformed into gasoline; clothing, cars, and toys manufactured overseas—even the money that U.S. consumers spend when they travel. The import content of PCE doesn't contribute to demand for U.S. GDP, which excludes imports; it contributes to demand for GDP in China and other countries that export to us.

- It is not possible with NIPA data to precisely estimate and subtract out the import content of PCE, and so there is no way to precisely estimate PCE's contribution to GDP. What we can do is calculate PCE and the other sources of aggregate final demand for U.S. output as shares of total final demand; this is shown in Table 1-9 and Figure 1-2. These shares would approximate contributions to GDP if each demand source had about the same percentage "import content" as total GDP.

- Consumption spending has been around 60 percent of final demand ever since 1951. (It was greater in 1946 through 1950, as consumers made up for wartime deprivations.) The shares of exports and state and local government spending have increased to about 10 percent each, while the federal government direct spending share remains below its Korean War highs. (This measure of government spending does not include government financing of medical care and other consumption spending through transfer payment programs such as Social Security and Medicare.) Investment is the most variable share. (Table 1-9)

- The share of imports in the total supply of goods and services in the U.S. market rose from around 4 percent in the 1950s to 15 percent in 2008, falling back to 12 percent in 2009. (Table 1-8)

Table 1-8. Shares of Aggregate Supply

(Billions of dollars, quarterly dollar data are at seasonally adjusted rates, percents.)   NIPA Table 1.1.5

Year and quarter	Aggregate supply (billions of dollars)			Shares of aggregate supply (percent)	
	Total	GDP	Imports	Domestic production (GDP)	Imports
1950	305.3	293.7	11.6	96.2	3.8
1951	353.9	339.3	14.6	95.9	4.1
1952	373.6	358.3	15.3	95.9	4.1
1953	395.3	379.3	16.0	96.0	4.0
1954	395.8	380.4	15.4	96.1	3.9
1955	431.9	414.7	17.2	96.0	4.0
1956	456.3	437.4	18.9	95.9	4.1
1957	481.0	461.1	19.9	95.9	4.1
1958	487.2	467.2	20.0	95.9	4.1
1959	528.9	506.6	22.3	95.8	4.2
1960	549.2	526.4	22.8	95.8	4.2
1961	567.5	544.8	22.7	96.0	4.0
1962	610.7	585.7	25.0	95.9	4.1
1963	643.9	617.8	26.1	95.9	4.1
1964	691.7	663.6	28.1	95.9	4.1
1965	750.6	719.1	31.5	95.8	4.2
1966	824.8	787.7	37.1	95.5	4.5
1967	872.3	832.4	39.9	95.4	4.6
1968	956.4	909.8	46.6	95.1	4.9
1969	1 034.9	984.4	50.5	95.1	4.9
1970	1 094.1	1 038.3	55.8	94.9	5.1
1971	1 189.1	1 126.8	62.3	94.8	5.2
1972	1 312.1	1 237.9	74.2	94.3	5.7
1973	1 473.5	1 382.3	91.2	93.8	6.2
1974	1 627.0	1 499.5	127.5	92.2	7.8
1975	1 760.4	1 637.7	122.7	93.0	7.0
1976	1 975.7	1 824.6	151.1	92.4	7.6
1977	2 212.5	2 030.1	182.4	91.8	8.2
1978	2 506.1	2 293.8	212.3	91.5	8.5
1979	2 814.9	2 562.2	252.7	91.0	9.0
1980	3 081.9	2 788.1	293.8	90.5	9.5
1981	3 444.6	3 126.8	317.8	90.8	9.2
1982	3 556.4	3 253.2	303.2	91.5	8.5
1983	3 863.2	3 534.6	328.6	91.5	8.5
1984	4 336.0	3 930.9	405.1	90.7	9.3
1985	4 634.7	4 217.5	417.2	91.0	9.0
1986	4 913.0	4 460.1	452.9	90.8	9.2
1987	5 245.1	4 736.4	508.7	90.3	9.7
1988	5 654.4	5 100.4	554.0	90.2	9.8
1989	6 073.1	5 482.1	591.0	90.3	9.7
1990	6 430.2	5 800.5	629.7	90.2	9.8
1991	6 615.6	5 992.1	623.5	90.6	9.4
1992	7 010.1	6 342.3	667.8	90.5	9.5
1993	7 387.4	6 667.4	720.0	90.3	9.7
1994	7 898.6	7 085.2	813.4	89.7	10.3
1995	8 317.3	7 414.7	902.6	89.1	10.9
1996	8 802.5	7 838.5	964.0	89.0	11.0
1997	9 388.2	8 332.4	1 055.8	88.8	11.2
1998	9 909.2	8 793.5	1 115.7	88.7	11.3
1999	10 604.9	9 353.5	1 251.4	88.2	11.8
2000	11 426.8	9 951.5	1 475.3	87.1	12.9
2001	11 684.9	10 286.2	1 398.7	88.0	12.0
2002	12 072.5	10 642.3	1 430.2	88.2	11.8
2003	12 687.2	11 142.1	1 545.1	87.8	12.2
2004	13 666.7	11 867.8	1 798.9	86.8	13.2
2005	14 666.2	12 638.4	2 027.8	86.2	13.8
2006	15 639.2	13 398.9	2 240.3	85.7	14.3
2007	16 447.3	14 077.6	2 369.7	85.6	14.4
2008	16 980.3	14 441.4	2 538.9	85.0	15.0
2009	16 212.9	14 256.3	1 956.6	87.9	12.1
2007					
1st quarter	16 089.9	13 795.6	2 294.3	85.7	14.3
2nd quarter	16 324.1	13 997.2	2 326.9	85.7	14.3
3rd quarter	16 563.5	14 179.9	2 383.6	85.6	14.4
4th quarter	16 811.9	14 337.9	2 474.0	85.3	14.7
2008					
1st quarter	16 922.0	14 373.9	2 548.1	84.9	15.1
2nd quarter	17 138.0	14 497.8	2 640.2	84.6	15.4
3rd quarter	17 217.2	14 546.7	2 670.5	84.5	15.5
4th quarter	16 644.0	14 347.3	2 296.7	86.2	13.8
2009					
1st quarter	16 065.9	14 178.0	1 887.9	88.2	11.8
2nd quarter	15 984.0	14 151.2	1 832.8	88.5	11.5
3rd quarter	16 218.1	14 242.1	1 976.0	87.8	12.2
4th quarter	16 583.5	14 453.8	2 129.7	87.2	12.8

Table 1-9. Shares of Aggregate Final Demand

(Billions of dollars, quarterly dollar data are at seasonally adjusted rates, percents.)   **NIPA Table 1.1.5**

| Year and quarter | Aggregate final demand (billions of dollars) | | | | | Government consumption and gross investment | | Shares of aggregate final demand (percent) | | | | | |
	Total	Consumption (PCE)	Nonresidential fixed investment	Residential investment	Exports	Federal	State and local	PCE	Nonresidential investment	Residential investment	Exports	Federal government	State and local government
1950	299.6	192.2	27.8	20.5	12.4	26.0	20.7	64.2	9.3	6.8	4.1	8.7	6.9
1951	343.8	208.5	31.8	18.4	17.1	45.0	23.0	60.6	9.2	5.4	5.0	13.1	6.7
1952	370.0	219.5	31.9	18.6	16.5	59.1	24.4	59.3	8.6	5.0	4.5	16.0	6.6
1953	393.4	233.1	35.1	19.4	15.3	64.4	26.1	59.3	8.9	4.9	3.9	16.4	6.6
1954	397.7	240.0	34.7	21.1	15.8	57.2	28.9	60.3	8.7	5.3	4.0	14.4	7.3
1955	427.0	258.8	39.0	25.0	17.7	54.9	31.6	60.6	9.1	5.9	4.1	12.9	7.4
1956	452.5	271.7	44.5	23.6	21.3	56.7	34.7	60.0	9.8	5.2	4.7	12.5	7.7
1957	480.2	286.9	47.5	22.2	24.0	61.3	38.3	59.7	9.9	4.6	5.0	12.8	8.0
1958	487.6	296.2	42.5	22.3	20.6	63.8	42.2	60.7	8.7	4.6	4.2	13.1	8.7
1959	525.0	317.7	46.5	28.1	22.7	65.3	44.7	60.5	8.9	5.4	4.3	12.4	8.5
1960	546.1	331.8	49.4	26.3	27.0	64.1	47.5	60.8	9.0	4.8	4.9	11.7	8.7
1961	564.5	342.2	48.8	26.4	27.6	67.9	51.6	60.6	8.6	4.7	4.9	12.0	9.1
1962	604.6	363.3	53.1	29.0	29.1	75.2	54.9	60.1	8.8	4.8	4.8	12.4	9.1
1963	638.3	382.7	56.0	32.1	31.1	76.9	59.5	60.0	8.8	5.0	4.9	12.0	9.3
1964	687.0	411.5	63.0	34.3	35.0	78.4	64.8	59.9	9.2	5.0	5.1	11.4	9.4
1965	741.3	443.8	74.8	34.2	37.1	80.4	71.0	59.9	10.1	4.6	5.0	10.8	9.6
1966	811.1	480.9	85.4	32.3	40.9	92.4	79.2	59.3	10.5	4.0	5.0	11.4	9.8
1967	862.6	507.8	86.4	32.4	43.5	104.6	87.9	58.9	10.0	3.8	5.0	12.1	10.2
1968	947.3	558.0	93.4	38.7	47.9	111.3	98.0	58.9	9.9	4.1	5.1	11.7	10.3
1969	1 025.8	605.1	104.7	42.6	51.9	113.3	108.2	59.0	10.2	4.2	5.1	11.0	10.5
1970	1 092.1	648.3	109.0	41.4	59.7	113.4	120.3	59.4	10.0	3.8	5.5	10.4	11.0
1971	1 180.9	701.6	114.1	55.8	63.0	113.6	132.8	59.4	9.7	4.7	5.3	9.6	11.2
1972	1 302.9	770.2	128.8	69.7	70.8	119.6	143.8	59.1	9.9	5.3	5.4	9.2	11.0
1973	1 457.6	852.0	153.3	75.3	95.3	122.5	159.2	58.5	10.5	5.2	6.5	8.4	10.9
1974	1 613.0	932.9	169.5	66.0	126.7	134.5	183.4	57.8	10.5	4.1	7.9	8.3	11.4
1975	1 766.6	1 033.8	173.7	62.7	138.7	149.0	208.7	58.5	9.8	3.5	7.9	8.4	11.8
1976	1 958.7	1 151.3	192.4	82.5	149.5	159.7	223.3	58.8	9.8	4.2	7.6	8.2	11.4
1977	2 190.3	1 277.8	228.7	110.3	159.4	175.4	238.7	58.3	10.4	5.0	7.3	8.0	10.9
1978	2 480.3	1 427.6	280.6	131.6	186.9	190.9	262.7	57.6	11.3	5.3	7.5	7.7	10.6
1979	2 797.0	1 591.2	333.9	141.0	230.1	210.6	290.2	56.9	11.9	5.0	8.2	7.5	10.4
1980	3 088.3	1 755.8	362.4	123.2	280.8	243.7	322.4	56.9	11.7	4.0	9.1	7.9	10.4
1981	3 414.8	1 939.5	420.0	122.6	305.2	280.2	347.3	56.8	12.3	3.6	8.9	8.2	10.2
1982	3 571.4	2 075.5	426.5	105.7	283.2	310.8	369.7	58.1	11.9	3.0	7.9	8.7	10.4
1983	3 869.1	2 288.6	417.2	152.9	277.0	342.9	390.5	59.2	10.8	4.0	7.2	8.9	10.1
1984	4 270.6	2 501.1	489.6	180.6	302.4	374.3	422.6	58.6	11.5	4.2	7.1	8.8	9.9
1985	4 612.9	2 717.6	526.2	188.2	302.0	412.8	466.1	58.9	11.4	4.1	6.5	8.9	10.1
1986	4 906.2	2 896.7	519.8	220.1	320.3	438.4	510.9	59.0	10.6	4.5	6.5	8.9	10.4
1987	5 218.0	3 097.0	524.1	233.7	363.8	459.5	539.9	59.4	10.0	4.5	7.0	8.8	10.3
1988	5 636.0	3 350.1	563.8	239.3	443.9	461.6	577.3	59.4	10.0	4.2	7.9	8.2	10.2
1989	6 045.4	3 594.5	607.7	239.5	503.1	481.4	619.2	59.5	10.1	4.0	8.3	8.0	10.2
1990	6 415.7	3 835.5	622.4	224.0	552.1	507.5	674.2	59.8	9.7	3.5	8.6	7.9	10.5
1991	6 616.1	3 980.1	598.2	205.1	596.6	526.6	709.5	60.2	9.0	3.1	9.0	8.0	10.7
1992	6 993.8	4 236.9	612.1	236.3	635.0	532.9	740.6	60.6	8.8	3.4	9.1	7.6	10.6
1993	7 366.6	4 483.6	666.6	266.0	655.6	525.0	769.8	60.9	9.0	3.6	8.9	7.1	10.4
1994	7 834.8	4 750.8	731.4	302.1	720.7	518.6	811.2	60.6	9.3	3.9	9.2	6.6	10.4
1995	8 286.2	4 987.3	810.0	302.9	811.9	518.8	855.3	60.2	9.8	3.7	9.8	6.3	10.3
1996	8 771.8	5 273.6	875.4	334.1	867.7	527.0	894.0	60.1	10.0	3.8	9.9	6.0	10.2
1997	9 317.2	5 570.6	968.6	349.1	954.4	531.0	943.5	59.8	10.4	3.7	10.2	5.7	10.1
1998	9 845.4	5 918.5	1 061.1	385.9	953.9	531.0	995.0	60.1	10.8	3.9	9.7	5.4	10.1
1999	10 544.0	6 342.8	1 154.9	425.8	989.3	554.9	1 076.3	60.2	11.0	4.0	9.4	5.3	10.2
2000	11 372.3	6 830.4	1 268.7	449.0	1 093.2	576.1	1 154.9	60.1	11.2	3.9	9.6	5.1	10.2
2001	11 723.1	7 148.8	1 227.8	472.4	1 027.7	611.7	1 234.7	61.0	10.5	4.0	8.8	5.2	10.5
2002	12 060.4	7 439.2	1 125.4	509.5	1 003.0	680.6	1 302.7	61.7	9.3	4.2	8.3	5.6	10.8
2003	12 670.9	7 804.0	1 135.7	577.6	1 041.0	756.5	1 356.1	61.6	9.0	4.6	8.2	6.0	10.7
2004	13 601.7	8 285.1	1 223.0	680.6	1 180.2	824.6	1 408.2	60.9	9.0	5.0	8.7	6.1	10.4
2005	14 616.3	8 819.0	1 347.3	775.0	1 305.1	876.3	1 493.6	60.3	9.2	5.3	8.9	6.0	10.2
2006	15 579.3	9 322.7	1 505.3	761.9	1 471.0	931.7	1 586.7	59.8	9.7	4.9	9.4	6.0	10.2
2007	16 428.0	9 826.4	1 640.2	629.0	1 655.9	976.7	1 699.8	59.8	10.0	3.8	10.1	5.9	10.3
2008	17 015.0	10 129.9	1 693.6	477.2	1 831.1	1 082.6	1 800.6	59.5	10.0	2.8	10.8	6.4	10.6
2009	16 333.8	10 089.1	1 388.8	361.0	1 564.2	1 144.8	1 785.9	61.8	8.5	2.2	9.6	7.0	10.9
2007													
1st quarter	16 076.8	9 658.5	1 574.1	680.0	1 564.9	942.8	1 656.5	60.1	9.8	4.2	9.7	5.9	10.3
2nd quarter	16 300.6	9 762.5	1 623.5	655.1	1 602.1	968.1	1 689.3	59.9	10.0	4.0	9.8	5.9	10.4
3rd quarter	16 532.5	9 865.6	1 665.2	615.6	1 685.2	991.4	1 709.5	59.7	10.1	3.7	10.2	6.0	10.3
4th quarter	16 802.1	10 019.2	1 697.9	565.2	1 771.6	1 004.3	1 743.9	59.6	10.1	3.4	10.5	6.0	10.4
2008													
1st quarter	16 930.2	10 095.1	1 705.0	518.1	1 803.6	1 038.3	1 770.1	59.6	10.1	3.1	10.7	6.1	10.5
2nd quarter	17 187.2	10 194.7	1 719.7	494.2	1 901.5	1 069.5	1 807.6	59.3	10.0	2.9	11.1	6.2	10.5
3rd quarter	17 254.2	10 220.1	1 711.0	468.6	1 913.1	1 108.3	1 833.1	59.2	9.9	2.7	11.1	6.4	10.6
4th quarter	16 688.5	10 009.8	1 638.7	427.8	1 706.2	1 114.3	1 791.7	60.0	9.8	2.6	10.2	6.7	10.7
2009													
1st quarter	16 193.2	9 987.7	1 442.6	374.6	1 509.3	1 106.7	1 772.3	61.7	8.9	2.3	9.3	6.8	10.9
2nd quarter	16 160.2	9 999.3	1 391.8	345.9	1 493.7	1 138.3	1 791.2	61.9	8.6	2.1	9.2	7.0	11.1
3rd quarter	16 374.8	10 132.9	1 353.9	358.8	1 573.8	1 164.3	1 791.1	61.9	8.3	2.2	9.6	7.1	10.9
4th quarter	16 607.0	10 236.4	1 366.9	364.5	1 680.1	1 170.1	1 789.0	61.6	8.2	2.2	10.1	7.0	10.8

Section 1b: Income and Value Added

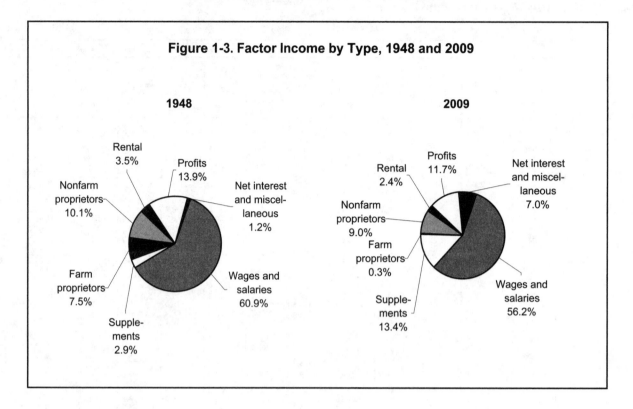

Figure 1-3. Factor Income by Type, 1948 and 2009

- The changing distribution of national income over the postwar period is shown in the figure above, based on data in Tables 1-12 and 19-8. The total income concept whose distribution is shown in this graph is called "net national factor income," formerly known as simply "national income," and is the sum of the income components identified in the graph.

- Although the recession year 2009 is being compared with a high-activity year in 1948, the long-term trends dominate the comparison. The most notable difference between 2009 and the high-activity year 2007 is the fall in the corporate profit share from 13.5 percent in 2007 to 11.7 percent in 2009.

- The share of labor compensation rose from 63.8 percent in 1948 to 69.6 percent in 2009. However, the wage and salary share declined from 60.9 to 56.2 percent. The increase in the total labor share is entirely accounted for by supplements to wages and salaries, which are the costs of fringe benefits—including health insurance—and taxes ("employer contributions") to pay for Social Security and Medicare.

- The farm proprietors' share dropped from 7.5 percent in 1948 to less than 1 percent in 2009, and the share going to nonfarm proprietors declined from 10.1 to 9.0 percent. Proprietors' income includes the return to their labor input as well as to their land and other capital, so it cannot be unequivocally attributed to either capital or labor.

- The share of capital incomes other than proprietors' and rental income—the sum of corporate profits and interest—rose from 15.1 percent in 1948 to 18.7 percent in 2009. In 2009, corporate profits were somewhat lower than in 1948, while net interest and miscellaneous payments were sharply higher, rising from 1.2 percent in 1948 to 7.0 percent in 2009.

Table 1-10. Relation of Gross Domestic Product, Gross and Net National Product, National Income, and Personal Income

(Billions of dollars, quarterly data are at seasonally adjusted annual rates.)   NIPA Table 1.7.5

Year and quarter	Gross domestic product	Plus: Income receipts from the rest of the world	Less: Income payments to the rest of the world	Equals: Gross national product	Less: Consumption of fixed capital									Equals: Net national product
					Total	Private					Government			
						Total	Domestic business			House-holds and institutions	Total	General government	Government enterprises	
							Total	Capital consumption allowances	Less: Capital consumption adjustment					
1950	293.7	2.2	0.7	295.2	29.9	22.0	18.6	14.9	-3.6	3.5	7.9	7.4	0.5	265.2
1951	339.3	2.8	0.9	341.2	33.8	25.2	21.2	17.1	-4.1	4.0	8.6	8.0	0.6	307.4
1952	358.3	2.9	0.9	360.3	36.3	26.7	22.4	18.8	-3.6	4.3	9.5	8.9	0.6	324.0
1953	379.3	2.8	0.9	381.2	38.6	28.2	23.6	20.9	-2.7	4.6	10.4	9.7	0.7	342.6
1954	380.4	3.0	0.9	382.4	40.6	29.5	24.6	22.9	-1.7	4.8	11.1	10.4	0.7	341.9
1955	414.7	3.5	1.1	417.2	42.8	31.1	25.8	25.7	-0.2	5.2	11.7	11.0	0.8	374.4
1956	437.4	3.9	1.1	440.2	47.1	34.3	28.6	27.9	-0.7	5.7	12.8	11.9	0.9	393.1
1957	461.1	4.3	1.2	464.1	50.8	37.2	31.2	30.2	-1.0	6.1	13.6	12.7	0.9	413.3
1958	467.2	3.9	1.2	469.8	53.3	39.4	33.1	31.5	-1.5	6.3	13.9	12.9	1.0	416.5
1959	506.6	4.3	1.5	509.4	55.4	41.0	34.3	33.4	-0.9	6.7	14.5	13.4	1.0	454.0
1960	526.4	4.9	1.8	529.6	56.6	41.6	34.6	35.2	0.5	7.0	15.0	13.9	1.1	473.0
1961	544.8	5.3	1.8	548.3	58.2	42.6	35.4	36.6	1.2	7.2	15.6	14.4	1.2	490.1
1962	585.7	5.9	1.8	589.7	60.6	44.1	36.6	40.9	4.3	7.5	16.5	15.2	1.2	529.2
1963	617.8	6.5	2.1	622.2	63.3	45.9	38.1	43.3	5.3	7.8	17.5	16.1	1.3	558.9
1964	663.6	7.2	2.3	668.6	66.4	48.3	40.0	46.1	6.1	8.3	18.1	16.7	1.4	602.2
1965	719.1	7.9	2.6	724.4	70.7	51.9	42.9	49.4	6.4	8.9	18.9	17.4	1.5	653.7
1966	787.7	8.1	3.0	792.8	76.5	56.5	46.9	53.4	6.5	9.6	20.0	18.3	1.6	716.3
1967	832.4	8.7	3.3	837.8	82.9	61.6	51.2	57.8	6.6	10.4	21.4	19.6	1.8	754.9
1968	909.8	10.1	4.0	915.9	90.4	67.4	56.1	62.6	6.5	11.3	23.0	21.0	2.0	825.5
1969	984.4	11.8	5.7	990.5	99.2	74.5	61.9	68.8	6.9	12.6	24.7	22.5	2.2	891.4
1970	1 038.3	12.8	6.4	1 044.7	108.3	81.7	68.2	73.8	5.7	13.5	26.6	24.1	2.5	936.4
1971	1 126.8	14.0	6.4	1 134.4	117.8	89.5	74.6	79.4	4.8	14.9	28.2	25.5	2.8	1 016.6
1972	1 237.9	16.3	7.7	1 246.4	127.2	97.7	81.2	88.3	7.1	16.5	29.4	26.3	3.1	1 119.3
1973	1 382.3	23.5	10.9	1 394.9	140.8	109.5	90.6	96.8	6.2	18.8	31.3	27.8	3.5	1 254.1
1974	1 499.5	29.8	14.3	1 515.0	163.7	127.8	106.1	107.6	1.5	21.7	35.9	31.6	4.3	1 351.3
1975	1 637.7	28.0	15.0	1 650.7	190.4	150.4	125.8	118.4	-7.3	24.7	39.9	34.9	5.1	1 460.3
1976	1 824.6	32.4	15.5	1 841.4	208.2	165.5	138.5	128.5	-10.0	27.1	42.6	37.1	5.5	1 633.3
1977	2 030.1	37.2	16.9	2 050.4	231.8	186.1	155.5	146.1	-9.3	30.7	45.6	39.6	6.0	1 818.6
1978	2 293.8	46.3	24.7	2 315.3	261.4	212.0	176.4	165.5	-10.9	35.5	49.5	42.8	6.7	2 053.9
1979	2 562.2	68.3	36.4	2 594.2	298.9	244.5	203.5	189.7	-13.8	41.0	54.4	46.9	7.6	2 295.3
1980	2 788.1	79.1	44.9	2 822.3	344.1	282.3	235.4	216.9	-18.5	46.9	61.8	53.0	8.8	2 478.2
1981	3 126.8	92.0	59.1	3 159.8	393.3	323.2	271.2	269.3	-1.9	52.1	70.1	60.1	10.0	2 766.4
1982	3 253.2	101.0	64.5	3 289.7	433.5	356.4	300.7	309.4	8.7	55.8	77.1	66.2	10.9	2 856.2
1983	3 534.6	101.9	64.8	3 571.7	451.1	369.5	311.4	347.9	36.5	58.1	81.6	70.1	11.5	3 120.6
1984	3 930.9	121.9	85.6	3 967.2	474.3	387.5	326.0	393.5	67.5	61.5	86.9	74.7	12.2	3 492.8
1985	4 217.5	112.4	85.9	4 244.0	505.4	412.8	348.0	445.6	97.6	64.8	92.7	79.7	12.9	3 738.6
1986	4 460.1	111.0	93.4	4 477.7	538.5	439.1	369.9	458.5	88.6	69.2	99.4	85.6	13.8	3 939.2
1987	4 736.4	122.8	105.2	4 754.0	571.1	464.5	390.3	475.3	84.9	74.1	106.6	92.0	14.6	4 182.9
1988	5 100.4	151.6	128.3	5 123.8	611.0	497.1	417.6	501.3	83.7	79.5	113.9	98.3	15.6	4 512.8
1989	5 482.1	177.2	151.2	5 508.1	651.5	529.6	444.4	521.3	76.9	85.2	121.8	105.1	16.7	4 856.6
1990	5 800.5	188.5	154.1	5 835.0	691.2	560.4	469.8	521.2	51.4	90.6	130.8	112.9	17.9	5 143.7
1991	5 992.1	168.1	138.2	6 022.0	724.4	585.4	490.6	530.1	39.5	94.8	138.9	120.1	18.8	5 297.6
1992	6 342.3	151.8	122.7	6 371.4	744.4	599.9	500.9	541.3	40.4	99.0	144.5	124.7	19.8	5 627.1
1993	6 667.4	155.2	124.0	6 698.5	778.0	626.4	521.2	567.4	46.2	105.2	151.6	130.5	21.1	5 920.5
1994	7 085.2	184.1	160.0	7 109.2	819.2	661.0	549.4	605.1	55.7	111.5	158.2	135.8	22.4	6 290.1
1995	7 414.7	229.3	199.6	7 444.3	869.5	704.6	586.0	651.1	65.1	118.7	164.8	141.2	23.6	6 574.9
1996	7 838.5	245.8	214.2	7 870.1	912.5	743.4	619.2	697.4	78.2	124.2	169.2	144.5	24.6	6 957.6
1997	8 332.4	279.5	256.1	8 355.8	963.8	789.7	658.5	757.2	98.7	131.2	174.1	148.1	26.0	7 392.0
1998	8 793.5	286.2	268.9	8 810.8	1 020.5	841.6	702.1	810.6	108.5	139.5	179.0	151.9	27.1	7 790.3
1999	9 353.5	319.5	291.7	9 381.3	1 094.4	907.2	756.8	883.8	126.9	150.4	187.2	158.5	28.6	8 286.9
2000	9 951.5	380.5	342.8	9 989.2	1 184.3	986.8	824.3	945.3	121.0	162.5	197.5	166.8	30.7	8 804.9
2001	10 286.2	323.0	271.1	10 338.1	1 256.2	1 051.6	876.5	1 018.8	142.3	175.1	204.6	172.5	32.1	9 081.9
2002	10 642.3	313.5	264.4	10 691.4	1 305.0	1 094.0	908.5	1 110.9	202.4	185.5	210.9	177.3	33.7	9 386.4
2003	11 142.1	353.3	284.6	11 210.8	1 354.1	1 135.9	935.4	1 125.3	189.9	200.5	218.1	182.8	35.4	9 856.8
2004	11 867.8	448.6	357.4	11 959.0	1 432.8	1 200.9	978.7	1 138.8	160.1	222.2	231.9	193.4	38.5	10 526.2
2005	12 638.4	573.0	475.9	12 735.5	1 541.4	1 290.8	1 045.7	965.6	-80.1	245.1	250.6	208.7	41.9	11 194.2
2006	13 398.9	721.1	648.6	13 471.3	1 660.7	1 391.4	1 123.3	1 027.7	-95.6	268.1	269.3	224.7	44.6	11 810.7
2007	14 077.6	861.8	746.0	14 193.3	1 760.0	1 469.6	1 188.5	1 089.7	-98.8	281.1	290.4	242.4	48.1	12 433.3
2008	14 441.4	809.2	667.3	14 583.3	1 847.1	1 536.2	1 252.3	1 340.2	87.8	283.9	310.9	259.5	51.4	12 736.2
2009	14 256.3	589.4	484.5	14 361.2	1 864.0	1 538.8	1 257.7	1 269.6	11.9	281.0	325.2	272.2	53.0	12 497.2
2007														
1st quarter	13 795.6	787.9	724.0	13 859.5	1 726.7	1 443.1	1 164.8	1 083.4	-81.4	278.3	283.7	236.8	46.9	12 132.8
2nd quarter	13 997.2	852.1	776.0	14 073.3	1 749.4	1 461.4	1 180.6	1 085.2	-95.4	280.8	288.0	240.3	47.7	12 324.0
3rd quarter	14 179.9	897.6	759.1	14 318.3	1 771.2	1 478.7	1 196.4	1 090.6	-105.8	282.3	292.5	244.0	48.5	12 547.2
4th quarter	14 337.9	909.4	725.1	14 522.2	1 792.8	1 495.1	1 212.2	1 099.6	-112.7	282.9	297.6	248.3	49.3	12 729.4
2008														
1st quarter	14 373.9	856.3	685.3	14 544.9	1 813.6	1 510.6	1 228.1	1 322.5	94.5	282.6	303.0	252.9	50.1	12 731.2
2nd quarter	14 497.8	840.5	711.6	14 626.6	1 835.6	1 527.0	1 244.1	1 334.6	90.5	282.9	308.5	257.6	50.9	12 791.1
3rd quarter	14 546.7	825.6	664.8	14 707.5	1 858.2	1 544.4	1 260.3	1 346.2	85.9	284.0	313.8	262.0	51.8	12 849.3
4th quarter	14 347.3	714.4	607.4	14 454.3	1 881.0	1 562.6	1 276.8	1 357.3	80.5	285.8	318.4	265.6	52.7	12 573.3
2009														
1st quarter	14 178.0	579.6	479.7	14 277.9	1 883.6	1 561.3	1 277.0	1 267.6	-9.3	284.4	322.3	269.0	53.2	12 394.3
2nd quarter	14 151.2	571.3	478.6	14 243.8	1 864.0	1 540.5	1 259.4	1 270.1	10.6	281.1	323.5	270.4	53.1	12 379.8
3rd quarter	14 242.1	590.6	469.1	14 363.7	1 850.7	1 525.5	1 246.9	1 269.7	22.8	278.6	325.2	272.4	52.8	12 512.9
4th quarter	14 453.8	616.2	510.5	14 559.5	1 857.7	1 527.7	1 247.6	1 271.1	23.5	280.1	330.0	277.1	52.9	12 701.8

Table 1-10. Relation of Gross Domestic Product, Gross and Net National Product, National Income, and Personal Income—Continued

(Billions of dollars, quarterly data are at seasonally adjusted annual rates.)

NIPA Table 1.7.5

Year and quarter	Net national product	Less: Statistical discrepancy	Equals: National income	Less: Corporate profits with IVA and CCAdj	Taxes on production and imports less subsidies	Contributions for government social insurance, domestic	Net interest and miscellaneous payments on assets	Business current transfer payments, net	Current surplus of government enterprises	Wage accruals less disbursements	Plus: Personal income receipts on assets	Personal current transfer receipts	Equals: Personal income	Addendum: Gross national income
1950	265.2	1.4	263.9	35.6	22.4	5.5	3.2	0.9	. . .	0.0	18.6	14.0	228.9	293.8
1951	307.4	3.6	303.8	40.8	24.0	6.6	3.7	1.2	. . .	0.1	19.1	11.4	257.9	337.6
1952	324.0	2.7	321.3	38.8	26.7	6.9	4.1	1.3	. . .	0.0	19.9	11.9	275.2	357.5
1953	342.6	4.0	338.6	39.1	29.0	7.1	4.7	1.2	. . .	-0.1	21.6	12.5	291.7	377.3
1954	341.9	3.1	338.7	38.3	29.0	8.1	5.6	1.0	. . .	0.0	23.2	14.3	294.3	379.3
1955	374.4	2.4	372.0	49.0	31.7	9.1	6.2	1.4	. . .	0.0	25.7	15.7	316.0	414.8
1956	393.1	-1.8	394.9	48.0	33.9	10.0	6.9	1.7	. . .	0.0	28.2	16.8	339.5	442.0
1957	413.3	-0.1	413.3	47.6	35.9	11.4	8.0	1.9	. . .	0.0	30.6	19.5	358.5	464.2
1958	416.5	1.0	415.6	42.5	36.8	11.4	9.5	1.8	. . .	0.0	31.9	23.5	368.9	468.8
1959	454.0	0.5	453.5	53.8	40.0	13.8	9.6	1.8	1.0	0.0	34.6	24.2	392.3	508.9
1960	473.0	-1.0	473.9	53.1	43.4	16.4	10.6	1.9	0.9	0.0	37.9	25.7	411.3	530.5
1961	490.1	-0.6	490.7	54.2	45.0	17.0	12.5	2.0	0.8	0.0	40.1	29.5	428.8	548.9
1962	529.2	0.3	528.9	62.3	48.1	19.1	14.2	2.2	0.9	0.0	44.1	30.4	456.4	589.4
1963	558.9	-0.8	559.7	68.3	51.2	21.7	15.2	2.7	1.4	0.0	47.9	32.2	479.5	623.1
1964	602.2	0.8	601.4	75.5	54.5	22.4	17.4	3.1	1.3	0.0	53.8	33.5	514.3	667.8
1965	653.7	1.5	652.2	86.5	57.7	23.4	19.6	3.6	1.3	0.0	59.4	36.2	555.5	722.9
1966	716.3	6.2	710.1	92.5	59.3	31.3	22.4	3.5	1.0	0.0	64.1	39.6	603.8	786.6
1967	754.9	4.5	750.4	90.2	64.1	34.9	25.5	3.8	0.9	0.0	69.0	48.0	648.1	833.3
1968	825.5	4.3	821.2	97.3	72.2	38.7	27.1	4.3	1.2	0.0	75.2	56.1	711.7	911.6
1969	891.4	2.9	888.5	94.5	79.3	44.1	32.7	4.9	1.0	0.0	84.1	62.3	778.3	987.7
1970	936.4	6.9	929.5	82.5	86.6	46.4	39.1	4.5	0.0	0.0	93.5	74.7	838.6	1 037.8
1971	1 016.6	11.0	1 005.6	96.1	95.8	51.2	43.9	4.3	-0.2	0.6	101.0	88.1	903.1	1 123.4
1972	1 119.3	8.9	1 110.3	111.4	101.3	59.2	47.9	4.9	0.5	0.0	109.6	97.9	992.6	1 237.5
1973	1 254.1	8.0	1 246.1	124.5	112.0	75.5	55.2	6.0	-0.4	-0.1	124.7	112.6	1 110.5	1 386.9
1974	1 351.3	9.8	1 341.5	115.1	121.6	85.2	70.8	7.1	-0.9	-0.5	146.4	133.3	1 222.7	1 505.2
1975	1 460.3	16.3	1 444.0	133.3	130.8	89.3	81.6	9.4	-3.2	0.1	162.2	170.0	1 334.9	1 634.4
1976	1 633.3	23.5	1 609.8	161.6	141.3	101.3	85.5	9.5	-1.8	0.1	178.4	184.0	1 474.7	1 818.0
1977	1 818.6	21.2	1 797.4	191.8	152.6	113.1	101.1	8.5	-2.7	0.1	205.3	194.2	1 632.5	2 029.2
1978	2 053.9	26.1	2 027.9	218.4	162.0	131.3	115.0	10.8	-2.2	0.3	234.8	209.6	1 836.7	2 289.3
1979	2 295.3	47.0	2 248.3	225.4	171.6	152.7	138.9	13.3	-2.9	-0.2	274.7	235.3	2 059.5	2 547.2
1980	2 478.2	45.3	2 433.0	201.4	190.5	166.2	181.8	14.7	-5.1	0.0	338.7	279.5	2 301.5	2 777.0
1981	2 766.4	36.6	2 729.8	223.3	224.2	195.7	232.3	17.9	-5.6	0.1	421.9	318.4	2 582.3	3 123.2
1982	2 856.2	4.8	2 851.4	205.7	225.9	208.9	271.1	20.6	-4.5	0.0	488.4	354.8	2 766.8	3 285.0
1983	3 120.6	49.7	3 070.9	259.8	242.0	226.0	285.3	22.6	-3.2	-0.4	529.6	383.7	2 952.2	3 522.0
1984	3 492.8	31.5	3 461.3	318.6	268.7	257.5	327.1	30.3	-1.9	0.2	607.9	400.1	3 268.9	3 935.6
1985	3 738.6	42.3	3 696.3	332.5	286.8	281.4	341.5	35.2	0.6	-0.2	653.2	424.9	3 496.7	4 201.7
1986	3 939.2	67.7	3 871.5	314.1	298.5	303.4	367.1	36.9	0.9	0.0	694.5	451.0	3 696.0	4 409.9
1987	4 182.9	32.9	4 150.0	367.8	317.3	323.1	366.7	34.1	0.2	0.0	715.8	467.6	3 924.4	4 721.1
1988	4 512.8	-9.5	4 522.3	426.6	345.0	361.5	385.3	33.6	2.6	0.0	767.0	496.5	4 231.2	5 133.3
1989	4 856.6	56.1	4 800.5	425.6	371.4	385.2	434.1	39.2	4.9	0.0	874.8	542.6	4 557.5	5 452.0
1990	5 143.7	84.2	5 059.5	434.4	398.0	410.1	444.2	40.1	1.6	0.1	920.8	594.9	4 846.7	5 750.8
1991	5 297.6	79.7	5 217.9	457.3	429.6	430.2	418.2	39.9	5.7	-0.1	928.6	665.9	5 031.5	5 942.3
1992	5 627.1	110.0	5 517.1	496.2	453.3	455.0	387.7	40.7	8.2	-15.8	909.7	745.8	5 347.3	6 261.5
1993	5 920.5	135.8	5 784.7	543.7	466.4	477.4	364.6	40.5	8.7	6.4	900.5	790.8	5 568.1	6 562.7
1994	6 290.1	108.8	6 181.3	628.2	512.7	508.2	362.2	41.9	9.6	17.6	947.7	826.4	5 874.8	7 000.4
1995	6 574.9	52.5	6 522.3	716.2	523.1	532.8	358.3	45.8	13.1	16.4	1 005.4	878.9	6 200.9	7 391.8
1996	6 957.6	25.9	6 931.7	801.5	545.5	555.1	371.1	53.8	14.4	3.6	1 080.7	924.1	6 591.6	7 844.2
1997	7 392.0	-14.0	7 406.0	884.8	577.8	587.2	407.6	51.3	14.1	-2.9	1 165.5	949.2	7 000.7	8 369.8
1998	7 790.3	-85.3	7 875.6	812.4	603.1	624.7	479.3	65.2	13.3	-0.7	1 269.2	977.9	7 525.4	8 896.1
1999	8 286.9	-71.1	8 358.0	856.3	628.4	661.3	481.4	69.0	14.1	5.2	1 246.8	1 021.6	7 910.8	9 452.4
2000	8 804.9	-134.0	8 938.9	819.2	662.7	705.8	539.3	87.0	9.1	0.0	1 360.7	1 083.0	8 559.4	10 123.2
2001	9 081.9	-103.4	9 185.2	784.2	669.0	733.2	544.4	101.3	4.0	0.0	1 346.0	1 188.1	8 883.3	10 441.4
2002	9 386.4	-22.1	9 408.5	872.2	721.4	751.5	506.4	82.4	6.3	0.0	1 309.6	1 282.1	9 060.1	10 713.5
2003	9 856.8	16.6	9 840.2	977.8	757.7	778.9	504.1	76.1	7.0	15.0	1 312.9	1 341.7	9 378.1	11 194.2
2004	10 526.2	-7.8	10 534.0	1 246.9	817.0	827.3	461.6	81.7	1.2	-15.0	1 408.5	1 415.5	9 937.2	11 966.8
2005	11 194.2	-79.7	11 273.8	1 456.1	869.3	872.7	543.0	95.9	-3.5	5.0	1 542.0	1 508.6	10 485.9	12 815.2
2006	11 810.7	-220.6	12 031.2	1 608.3	935.5	921.8	652.2	83.0	-4.2	1.3	1 829.7	1 605.0	11 268.1	13 691.9
2007	12 433.3	-14.8	12 448.2	1 541.7	974.0	959.3	739.2	102.2	-6.6	-6.3	2 031.5	1 718.0	11 894.1	14 208.2
2008	12 736.2	101.0	12 635.2	1 360.4	993.8	990.6	815.1	118.8	-6.9	-5.0	1 994.4	1 875.9	12 238.6	14 482.3
2009	12 497.2	209.2	12 288.1	1 308.9	964.3	966.9	788.2	134.1	-8.1	5.0	1 792.6	2 104.8	12 026.1	14 152.1
2007														
1st quarter	12 132.8	-121.1	12 253.9	1 535.4	966.0	952.5	690.6	97.8	-8.4	-25.0	1 968.2	1 693.8	11 706.9	13 980.7
2nd quarter	12 324.0	-97.1	12 421.1	1 594.9	966.9	953.7	711.3	99.0	-6.9	0.0	2 022.0	1 699.1	11 823.4	14 170.4
3rd quarter	12 547.2	64.9	12 482.2	1 537.1	976.1	958.6	756.0	105.0	-4.9	0.0	2 065.8	1 725.5	11 945.6	14 253.4
4th quarter	12 729.4	94.0	12 635.4	1 499.4	986.8	972.6	798.9	107.0	-6.0	0.0	2 069.8	1 753.7	12 100.3	14 428.2
2008														
1st quarter	12 731.2	69.8	12 661.5	1 459.7	989.3	985.3	790.7	114.8	-5.6	0.0	2 020.8	1 794.1	12 142.2	14 475.1
2nd quarter	12 791.1	126.7	12 664.4	1 403.7	997.9	988.9	809.0	112.6	-6.3	0.0	1 997.3	1 937.0	12 292.9	14 499.9
3rd quarter	12 849.3	68.3	12 781.0	1 454.6	1 005.7	994.9	806.1	116.0	-6.9	0.0	2 001.4	1 874.3	12 286.6	14 639.2
4th quarter	12 573.3	139.4	12 433.9	1 123.6	982.1	993.3	854.7	131.8	-8.9	-20.0	1 958.1	1 898.0	12 233.5	14 314.9
2009														
1st quarter	12 394.3	185.4	12 208.9	1 182.7	963.2	969.7	826.2	137.9	-10.7	20.0	1 845.5	1 987.3	11 952.7	14 092.5
2nd quarter	12 379.8	161.7	12 218.1	1 226.5	964.6	970.9	784.4	145.4	-8.8	0.0	1 773.4	2 140.3	12 048.8	14 082.1
3rd quarter	12 512.9	253.3	12 259.7	1 358.9	955.4	962.5	759.7	124.8	-6.3	0.0	1 763.1	2 137.5	12 005.2	14 110.4
4th quarter	12 701.8	236.2	12 465.6	1 467.6	973.8	964.7	782.6	128.2	-6.5	0.0	1 788.5	2 153.9	12 097.7	14 323.3

. . . = Not available.

Table 1-11. Gross Domestic Income by Type of Income

(Billions of dollars, quarterly data are at seasonally adjusted annual rates.)   NIPA Tables 1.1.5, 1.10

Year and quarter	Gross domestic income	Compensation of employees, paid			Taxes on production and imports	Less: Subsidies	Net operating surplus					
								Private enterprises				
		Total	Wage and salary accruals	Supplements to wages and salaries			Total	Total	Net interest and miscellaneous payments, domestic industries	Business current transfer payments, net	Proprietors' income with IVA and CCAdj	Rental income of persons with CCAdj
1950	292.4	155.2	147.2	8.0	23.0	0.6	. . .	84.9	3.1	0.9	37.5	9.1
1951	335.7	181.4	171.6	9.8	24.7	0.7	. . .	96.5	3.5	1.2	42.7	10.0
1952	355.6	196.2	185.6	10.5	27.1	0.4	. . .	96.4	4.0	1.3	43.1	11.2
1953	375.4	210.2	199.0	11.2	29.1	0.1	. . .	97.5	4.6	1.2	42.0	12.4
1954	377.2	209.2	197.3	11.9	28.9	-0.1	. . .	98.4	5.4	1.0	42.3	13.4
1955	412.3	225.8	212.2	13.5	31.5	-0.2	. . .	112.1	6.1	1.4	44.3	13.8
1956	439.2	244.6	229.1	15.5	34.2	0.4	. . .	113.6	6.8	1.7	45.9	14.1
1957	461.1	257.6	240.0	17.6	36.6	0.7	. . .	116.7	8.0	1.9	47.8	14.5
1958	466.2	259.6	241.4	18.2	37.7	0.9	. . .	116.5	9.4	1.8	50.2	15.2
1959	506.1	281.1	259.9	21.1	41.1	1.1	129.7	128.7	9.5	1.8	50.3	16.0
1960	527.4	296.6	273.0	23.6	44.5	1.1	130.8	129.9	10.4	1.9	50.7	17.0
1961	545.3	305.4	280.7	24.8	47.0	2.0	136.8	135.9	12.1	2.0	53.2	17.7
1962	585.3	327.2	299.5	27.8	50.4	2.3	149.4	148.5	13.8	2.2	55.3	18.6
1963	618.6	345.3	314.9	30.4	53.4	2.2	158.8	157.5	14.7	2.7	56.5	19.3
1964	662.9	370.7	337.8	32.9	57.3	2.7	171.2	169.9	16.9	3.1	59.4	19.4
1965	717.6	399.5	363.8	35.7	60.7	3.0	189.7	188.3	19.1	3.6	63.9	19.9
1966	781.5	442.6	400.3	42.3	63.2	3.9	203.2	202.2	21.9	3.5	68.2	20.5
1967	827.9	475.1	429.0	46.1	67.9	3.8	205.8	204.9	24.9	3.8	69.8	20.9
1968	905.5	524.3	472.0	52.3	76.4	4.2	218.6	217.4	26.7	4.3	74.2	20.6
1969	981.6	577.6	518.3	59.3	83.9	4.5	225.5	224.4	33.2	4.9	77.5	20.9
1970	1 031.4	617.2	551.5	65.7	91.4	4.8	219.3	219.3	39.9	4.5	78.5	21.1
1971	1 115.8	658.9	584.5	74.4	100.5	4.7	243.3	243.6	44.2	4.3	84.7	22.2
1972	1 228.9	725.1	638.8	86.4	107.9	6.6	275.4	274.9	48.9	4.9	96.0	23.1
1973	1 374.3	811.2	708.8	102.5	117.2	5.2	310.2	310.6	57.5	6.0	113.6	23.9
1974	1 489.6	890.3	772.3	118.0	124.9	3.3	314.1	315.0	72.7	7.1	113.5	24.0
1975	1 621.4	949.2	814.9	134.3	135.3	4.5	351.0	354.3	83.2	9.4	119.6	23.4
1976	1 801.1	1 059.4	899.8	159.6	146.4	5.1	392.3	394.1	85.2	9.5	132.2	22.1
1977	2 008.9	1 180.6	994.2	186.4	159.7	7.1	444.0	446.7	99.8	8.5	146.0	19.6
1978	2 267.7	1 335.6	1 120.7	214.9	170.9	8.9	508.8	511.0	116.2	10.8	167.5	20.9
1979	2 515.3	1 498.4	1 253.4	245.0	180.1	8.5	546.4	549.3	141.5	13.3	181.1	22.6
1980	2 742.9	1 647.7	1 373.5	274.2	200.3	9.8	560.6	565.7	183.0	14.7	173.5	28.5
1981	3 090.3	1 819.8	1 511.5	308.3	235.6	11.5	652.9	658.5	228.9	17.9	181.6	36.5
1982	3 248.4	1 919.8	1 587.7	332.1	240.9	15.0	669.2	673.6	267.0	20.6	174.8	38.1
1983	3 484.9	2 035.7	1 677.7	358.0	263.3	21.3	756.1	759.3	283.1	22.6	190.7	38.2
1984	3 899.4	2 245.7	1 845.1	400.5	289.8	21.1	910.6	912.6	327.1	30.3	233.1	40.0
1985	4 175.2	2 412.0	1 982.8	429.2	308.1	21.4	971.0	970.4	352.8	35.2	246.1	41.9
1986	4 392.3	2 559.4	2 104.1	455.3	323.4	24.9	995.9	995.1	387.2	36.9	262.6	33.8
1987	4 703.5	2 737.0	2 257.6	479.4	347.5	30.3	1 078.1	1 078.0	395.7	34.1	294.2	34.2
1988	5 110.0	2 955.0	2 440.6	514.4	374.5	29.5	1 199.0	1 196.4	418.1	33.6	334.8	40.2
1989	5 426.0	3 132.6	2 584.3	548.3	398.9	27.4	1 270.6	1 265.6	474.0	39.2	351.6	42.4
1990	5 716.3	3 328.6	2 743.5	585.1	425.0	27.0	1 298.6	1 297.0	483.6	40.1	365.1	49.8
1991	5 912.4	3 441.1	2 817.2	623.9	457.1	27.5	1 317.3	1 311.6	462.0	39.9	367.3	61.6
1992	6 232.3	3 634.4	2 960.8	673.6	483.4	30.1	1 400.3	1 392.0	428.7	40.7	414.9	84.6
1993	6 531.6	3 800.4	3 086.4	714.1	503.1	36.7	1 486.7	1 478.0	407.0	40.5	449.6	114.1
1994	6 976.4	4 002.5	3 252.5	750.1	545.2	32.5	1 641.9	1 632.3	412.1	41.9	485.1	142.9
1995	7 362.1	4 199.3	3 438.5	760.8	557.9	34.8	1 770.3	1 757.2	417.5	45.8	516.0	154.6
1996	7 812.5	4 395.5	3 624.1	771.4	580.8	35.2	1 959.0	1 944.7	437.2	53.8	583.7	170.4
1997	8 346.3	4 670.0	3 878.0	792.0	611.6	33.8	2 134.7	2 120.6	487.3	51.3	628.2	176.5
1998	8 878.8	5 027.8	4 185.5	842.3	639.5	36.4	2 227.4	2 214.1	560.2	65.2	687.5	191.5
1999	9 424.6	5 359.2	4 470.4	888.8	673.6	45.2	2 342.6	2 328.5	569.9	69.0	746.8	208.2
2000	10 085.5	5 793.5	4 832.4	961.2	708.6	45.8	2 444.9	2 435.7	642.5	87.0	817.5	215.3
2001	10 389.5	5 984.5	4 957.4	1 027.1	727.7	58.7	2 479.8	2 475.7	656.9	101.3	870.7	232.4
2002	10 664.4	6 116.4	5 002.9	1 113.5	762.8	41.4	2 521.6	2 515.3	609.6	82.4	890.3	218.7
2003	11 125.5	6 388.3	5 160.3	1 228.0	806.8	49.1	2 625.4	2 618.5	595.5	76.1	930.6	204.2
2004	11 875.6	6 699.6	5 416.8	1 282.7	863.4	46.4	2 926.3	2 925.0	569.3	81.7	1 033.8	198.4
2005	12 718.0	7 071.5	5 712.4	1 359.1	930.2	60.9	3 236.0	3 239.4	678.9	95.9	1 069.8	178.2
2006	13 619.5	7 483.6	6 076.8	1 406.9	986.8	51.4	3 539.7	3 544.0	830.1	83.0	1 133.0	146.5
2007	14 092.5	7 863.6	6 409.7	1 453.8	1 028.7	54.8	3 494.9	3 501.5	964.1	102.2	1 096.4	144.9
2008	14 340.4	8 044.8	6 548.2	1 496.6	1 047.3	53.5	3 454.8	3 461.7	1 043.1	118.8	1 106.3	210.4
2009	14 047.1	7 798.6	6 296.2	1 502.5	1 023.9	59.6	3 420.2	3 428.3	988.0	134.1	1 041.0	268.1
2007												
1st quarter	13 916.7	7 764.0	6 325.4	1 438.6	1 015.3	49.2	3 459.9	3 468.3	902.0	97.8	1 094.2	121.1
2nd quarter	14 094.3	7 826.8	6 379.3	1 447.5	1 025.2	58.3	3 551.3	3 558.2	939.2	99.0	1 096.0	140.3
3rd quarter	14 114.9	7 876.7	6 419.7	1 457.1	1 032.2	56.0	3 490.9	3 495.8	980.9	105.0	1 093.2	150.2
4th quarter	14 243.9	7 986.7	6 514.6	1 472.1	1 042.3	55.4	3 477.6	3 483.6	1 034.3	107.0	1 102.1	168.0
2008												
1st quarter	14 304.1	8 024.8	6 540.3	1 484.5	1 042.5	53.1	3 476.3	3 481.9	1 024.7	114.8	1 115.2	179.9
2nd quarter	14 371.1	8 040.0	6 546.5	1 493.5	1 050.8	52.9	3 497.6	3 503.9	1 039.9	112.6	1 111.9	202.8
3rd quarter	14 478.4	8 076.3	6 574.9	1 501.4	1 058.5	52.9	3 538.3	3 545.2	1 035.2	116.0	1 114.4	222.2
4th quarter	14 207.9	8 037.9	6 531.0	1 506.8	1 037.3	55.2	3 307.0	3 315.9	1 072.5	131.8	1 083.6	236.7
2009												
1st quarter	13 992.5	7 833.0	6 335.0	1 498.0	1 018.8	55.5	3 312.7	3 323.4	1 034.8	137.9	1 037.8	245.9
2nd quarter	13 989.5	7 823.0	6 320.2	1 502.8	1 019.6	54.9	3 337.9	3 346.7	986.0	145.4	1 028.0	262.0
3rd quarter	13 988.9	7 758.5	6 256.2	1 502.3	1 023.1	67.7	3 424.3	3 430.6	954.3	124.8	1 037.9	277.9
4th quarter	14 217.6	7 780.1	6 273.3	1 506.8	1 034.1	60.3	3 606.1	3 612.6	977.0	128.2	1 060.3	286.7

. . . = Not available.

Table 1-11. Gross Domestic Income by Type of Income—*Continued*

(Billions of dollars, quarterly data are at seasonally adjusted annual rates.)   **NIPA Tables 1.1.5, 1.10**

Year and quarter	Net operating surplus—*Continued*					Current surplus of government enterprises	Consumption of fixed capital			Statistical discrepancy	Gross domestic product
	Private enterprises—*Continued*										
	Corporate profits with IVA and CCAdj, domestic industries						Total	Private	Government		
	Total	Taxes on corporate income	Profits after tax								
			Total	Net dividends	Undistributed corporate profits						
1950	34.4	17.9	16.4	7.9	8.6	...	29.9	22.0	7.9	1.4	293.7
1951	39.1	22.6	16.5	7.4	9.1	...	33.8	25.2	8.6	3.6	339.3
1952	37.0	19.4	17.6	7.5	10.1	...	36.3	26.7	9.5	2.7	358.3
1953	37.3	20.3	17.0	7.8	9.3	...	38.6	28.2	10.4	4.0	379.3
1954	36.4	17.6	18.7	7.9	10.9	...	40.6	29.5	11.1	3.1	380.4
1955	46.6	22.0	24.6	8.9	15.7	...	42.8	31.1	11.7	2.4	414.7
1956	45.2	22.0	23.2	9.5	13.7	...	47.1	34.3	12.8	-1.8	437.4
1957	44.5	21.4	23.1	9.9	13.3	...	50.8	37.2	13.6	-0.1	461.1
1958	39.9	19.0	21.0	9.8	11.1	...	53.3	39.4	13.9	1.0	467.2
1959	51.1	23.7	27.4	10.7	16.7	1.0	55.4	41.0	14.5	0.5	506.6
1960	50.0	22.8	27.2	11.4	15.8	0.9	56.6	41.6	15.0	-1.0	526.4
1961	50.9	22.9	28.0	11.5	16.5	0.8	58.2	42.6	15.6	-0.6	544.8
1962	58.6	24.1	34.5	12.4	22.1	0.9	60.6	44.1	16.5	0.3	585.7
1963	64.3	26.4	37.9	13.6	24.3	1.4	63.3	45.9	17.5	-0.8	617.8
1964	71.1	28.2	42.9	15.0	27.9	1.3	66.4	48.3	18.1	0.8	663.6
1965	81.8	31.1	50.8	16.9	33.9	1.3	70.7	51.9	18.9	1.5	719.1
1966	88.0	33.9	54.1	17.8	36.3	1.0	76.5	56.5	20.0	6.2	787.7
1967	85.4	32.9	52.5	18.3	34.2	0.9	82.9	61.6	21.4	4.5	832.4
1968	91.6	39.6	52.0	20.2	31.8	1.2	90.4	67.4	23.0	4.3	909.8
1969	87.9	40.0	47.9	20.4	27.5	1.0	99.2	74.5	24.7	2.9	984.4
1970	75.4	34.8	40.6	20.4	20.3	0.0	108.3	81.7	26.6	6.9	1 038.3
1971	88.2	38.2	50.1	20.3	29.7	-0.2	117.8	89.5	28.2	11.0	1 126.8
1972	101.9	42.3	59.6	21.9	37.6	0.5	127.2	97.7	29.4	8.9	1 237.9
1973	109.6	50.0	59.6	23.1	36.5	-0.4	140.8	109.5	31.3	8.0	1 382.3
1974	97.7	52.8	44.9	23.5	21.4	-0.9	163.7	127.8	35.9	9.8	1 499.5
1975	118.7	51.6	67.0	26.4	40.6	-3.2	190.4	150.4	39.9	16.3	1 637.7
1976	145.1	65.3	79.8	30.1	49.7	-1.8	208.2	165.5	42.6	23.5	1 824.6
1977	172.7	74.4	98.3	33.7	64.6	-2.7	231.8	186.1	45.6	21.2	2 030.1
1978	195.6	84.9	110.7	39.6	71.1	-2.2	261.4	212.0	49.5	26.1	2 293.8
1979	190.7	90.0	100.7	41.5	59.2	-2.9	298.9	244.5	54.4	47.0	2 562.2
1980	166.0	87.2	78.8	47.3	31.4	-5.1	344.1	282.3	61.8	45.3	2 788.1
1981	193.6	84.3	109.3	58.3	50.9	-5.6	393.3	323.2	70.1	36.6	3 126.8
1982	173.1	66.5	106.6	61.3	45.3	-4.5	433.5	356.4	77.1	4.8	3 253.2
1983	224.8	80.6	144.1	71.3	72.8	-3.2	451.1	369.5	81.6	49.7	3 534.6
1984	282.0	97.5	184.5	78.5	106.0	-1.9	474.3	387.5	86.9	31.5	3 930.9
1985	294.4	99.4	195.0	85.7	109.3	0.6	505.4	412.8	92.7	42.3	4 217.5
1986	274.7	109.7	165.0	88.3	76.7	0.9	538.5	439.1	99.4	67.7	4 460.1
1987	319.8	130.4	189.4	95.6	93.8	0.2	571.1	464.5	106.6	32.9	4 736.4
1988	369.6	141.6	228.0	98.0	130.0	2.6	611.0	497.1	113.9	-9.5	5 100.4
1989	358.4	146.1	212.4	126.4	86.0	4.9	651.5	529.6	121.8	56.1	5 482.1
1990	358.4	145.4	212.9	144.1	68.8	1.6	691.2	560.4	130.8	84.2	5 800.5
1991	380.8	138.6	242.2	156.4	85.9	5.7	724.4	585.4	138.9	79.7	5 992.1
1992	423.1	148.7	274.4	160.0	114.5	8.2	744.4	599.9	144.5	110.0	6 342.3
1993	466.8	171.0	295.7	182.3	113.4	8.7	778.0	626.4	151.6	135.8	6 667.4
1994	550.3	193.1	357.1	197.6	159.6	9.6	819.2	661.0	158.2	108.8	7 085.2
1995	623.2	217.8	405.4	221.6	183.8	13.1	869.5	704.6	164.8	52.5	7 414.7
1996	699.5	231.5	468.1	257.3	210.7	14.4	912.5	743.4	169.2	25.9	7 838.5
1997	777.3	245.4	531.9	284.0	247.9	14.1	963.8	789.7	174.1	-14.0	8 332.4
1998	709.7	248.4	461.3	309.2	152.1	13.3	1 020.5	841.6	179.0	-85.3	8 793.5
1999	734.8	258.8	476.0	295.7	180.3	14.1	1 094.4	907.2	187.2	-71.1	9 353.5
2000	673.6	265.1	408.5	348.5	60.1	9.1	1 184.3	986.8	197.5	-134.0	9 951.5
2001	614.5	203.3	411.2	330.1	81.1	4.0	1 256.2	1 051.6	204.6	-103.4	10 286.2
2002	714.3	192.3	522.0	351.2	170.8	6.3	1 305.0	1 094.0	210.9	-22.1	10 642.3
2003	812.0	243.8	568.3	392.8	175.5	7.0	1 354.1	1 135.9	218.1	16.6	11 142.1
2004	1 041.9	306.1	735.8	488.0	247.8	1.2	1 432.8	1 200.9	231.9	-7.8	11 867.8
2005	1 216.6	412.4	804.3	296.5	507.8	-3.5	1 541.4	1 290.8	250.6	-79.7	12 638.4
2006	1 351.5	473.3	878.2	626.9	251.3	-4.2	1 660.7	1 391.4	269.3	-220.6	13 398.9
2007	1 193.9	451.5	742.4	641.6	100.8	-6.6	1 760.0	1 469.6	290.4	-14.8	14 077.6
2008	983.2	292.2	691.0	543.3	147.7	-6.9	1 847.1	1 536.2	310.9	101.0	14 441.4
2009	997.1	314.8	682.3	458.9	223.4	-8.1	1 864.0	1 538.8	325.2	209.2	14 256.3
2007											
1st quarter	1 253.2	469.5	783.7	665.2	118.5	-8.4	1 726.7	1 443.1	283.7	-121.1	13 795.6
2nd quarter	1 283.7	466.5	817.2	664.4	152.8	-6.9	1 749.4	1 461.4	288.0	-97.1	13 997.2
3rd quarter	1 166.6	440.0	726.6	636.6	90.0	-4.9	1 771.2	1 478.7	292.5	64.9	14 179.9
4th quarter	1 072.3	430.1	642.2	600.3	41.9	-6.0	1 792.8	1 495.1	297.6	94.0	14 337.9
2008											
1st quarter	1 047.4	323.2	724.2	548.5	175.7	-5.6	1 813.6	1 510.6	303.0	69.8	14 373.9
2nd quarter	1 036.7	317.5	719.2	529.9	189.4	-6.3	1 835.6	1 527.0	308.5	126.7	14 497.8
3rd quarter	1 057.4	304.8	752.6	514.7	237.9	-6.9	1 858.2	1 544.4	313.8	68.3	14 546.7
4th quarter	791.3	223.3	568.0	580.0	-11.9	-8.9	1 881.0	1 562.6	318.4	139.4	14 347.3
2009											
1st quarter	867.0	270.3	596.6	515.3	81.3	-10.7	1 883.6	1 561.3	322.3	185.4	14 178.0
2nd quarter	925.3	305.9	619.4	455.5	163.8	-8.8	1 864.0	1 540.5	323.5	161.7	14 151.2
3rd quarter	1 035.7	321.0	714.7	397.0	317.7	-6.3	1 850.7	1 525.5	325.2	253.3	14 242.1
4th quarter	1 160.4	361.9	798.5	467.6	331.0	-6.5	1 857.7	1 527.7	330.0	236.2	14 453.8

. . . = Not available.

Table 1-12. National Income by Type of Income

(Billions of dollars, quarterly data are at seasonally adjusted annual rates.)   NIPA Tables 1.7.5, 1.12

Year and quarter	National income, total	Compensation of employees							Proprietors' income with IVA and CCAdj			Rental income of persons with CCAdj
		Total	Wage and salary accruals			Supplements to wages and salaries			Total	Farm	Nonfarm	
			Total	Government	Other	Total	Employer contributions for:					
							Employee pension and insurance funds	Government social insurance				
1950	263.9	155.3	147.3	22.6	124.6	8.0	4.7	3.4	37.5	12.9	24.6	9.1
1951	303.8	181.4	171.6	29.2	142.4	9.8	5.7	4.1	42.7	15.3	27.3	10.0
1952	321.3	196.2	185.6	33.4	152.3	10.5	6.4	4.1	43.1	14.3	28.8	11.2
1953	338.6	210.2	199.0	34.3	164.7	11.2	7.0	4.2	42.0	12.2	29.8	12.4
1954	338.7	209.2	197.3	34.9	162.4	11.9	7.3	4.6	42.3	11.7	30.5	13.4
1955	372.0	225.7	212.2	36.6	175.6	13.5	8.4	5.2	44.3	10.7	33.5	13.8
1956	394.9	244.5	229.0	38.8	190.2	15.5	9.8	5.7	45.9	10.6	35.3	14.1
1957	413.3	257.5	240.0	41.0	198.9	17.6	11.2	6.4	47.8	10.6	37.3	14.5
1958	415.6	259.5	241.3	44.1	197.2	18.2	11.9	6.3	50.2	12.4	37.8	15.2
1959	453.5	281.0	259.8	46.1	213.8	21.1	13.3	7.9	50.3	10.0	40.3	16.0
1960	473.9	296.4	272.9	49.2	223.7	23.6	14.3	9.3	50.7	10.6	40.1	17.0
1961	490.7	305.3	280.5	52.5	228.0	24.8	15.2	9.6	53.2	11.2	42.0	17.7
1962	528.9	327.1	299.4	56.3	243.0	27.8	16.6	11.2	55.3	11.2	44.1	18.6
1963	559.7	345.2	314.9	60.0	254.8	30.4	18.0	12.4	56.5	11.0	45.5	19.3
1964	601.4	370.7	337.8	64.9	272.9	32.9	20.3	12.6	59.4	9.8	49.6	19.4
1965	652.2	399.5	363.8	69.9	293.8	35.7	22.7	13.1	63.9	12.0	51.9	19.9
1966	710.1	442.7	400.3	78.4	321.9	42.3	25.5	16.8	68.2	13.0	55.2	20.5
1967	750.4	475.1	429.0	86.5	342.5	46.1	28.1	18.0	69.8	11.6	58.2	20.9
1968	821.2	524.3	472.0	96.7	375.3	52.3	32.4	20.0	74.2	11.7	62.5	20.6
1969	888.5	577.6	518.3	105.6	412.7	59.3	36.5	22.8	77.5	12.8	64.7	20.9
1970	929.5	617.2	551.6	117.2	434.3	65.7	41.8	23.8	78.5	12.9	65.6	21.1
1971	1 005.6	658.9	584.5	126.8	457.8	74.4	47.9	26.4	84.7	13.4	71.3	22.2
1972	1 110.3	725.1	638.8	137.9	500.9	86.4	55.2	31.2	96.0	17.0	79.0	23.1
1973	1 246.1	811.2	708.8	148.8	560.0	102.5	62.7	39.8	113.6	29.1	84.6	23.9
1974	1 341.5	890.2	772.3	160.5	611.8	118.0	73.3	44.7	113.5	23.5	90.0	24.0
1975	1 444.0	949.1	814.8	176.2	638.6	134.3	87.6	46.7	119.6	22.0	97.6	23.4
1976	1 609.8	1 059.3	899.7	188.9	710.8	159.6	105.2	54.4	132.2	17.2	115.0	22.1
1977	1 797.4	1 180.5	994.2	202.6	791.6	186.4	125.3	61.1	146.0	16.0	130.1	19.6
1978	2 027.9	1 335.5	1 120.6	220.0	900.6	214.9	143.4	71.5	167.5	19.9	147.6	20.9
1979	2 248.3	1 498.3	1 253.3	237.1	1 016.2	245.0	162.4	82.6	181.1	22.2	159.0	22.6
1980	2 433.0	1 647.6	1 373.4	261.5	1 112.0	274.2	185.2	88.9	173.5	11.7	161.8	28.5
1981	2 729.8	1 819.7	1 511.4	285.8	1 225.5	308.3	204.7	103.6	181.6	19.0	162.6	36.5
1982	2 851.4	1 919.6	1 587.5	307.5	1 280.0	332.1	222.4	109.8	174.8	13.3	161.5	38.1
1983	3 070.9	2 035.5	1 677.5	324.8	1 352.7	358.0	238.1	119.9	190.7	6.2	184.5	38.2
1984	3 461.3	2 245.4	1 844.9	348.1	1 496.8	400.5	261.5	139.0	233.1	20.9	212.1	40.0
1985	3 696.3	2 411.7	1 982.6	373.9	1 608.7	429.2	281.5	147.7	246.1	21.0	225.1	41.9
1986	3 871.5	2 557.7	2 102.3	397.2	1 705.1	455.3	297.5	157.9	262.6	22.8	239.7	33.8
1987	4 150.0	2 735.6	2 256.3	423.1	1 833.1	479.4	313.1	166.3	294.2	28.9	265.3	34.2
1988	4 522.3	2 954.2	2 439.8	452.0	1 987.7	514.4	329.7	184.6	334.8	26.8	308.0	40.2
1989	4 800.5	3 131.3	2 583.1	481.1	2 101.9	548.3	354.6	193.7	351.6	33.0	318.6	42.4
1990	5 059.5	3 326.3	2 741.2	519.0	2 222.2	585.1	378.6	206.5	365.1	32.2	333.0	49.8
1991	5 217.9	3 438.3	2 814.5	548.8	2 265.7	623.9	408.7	215.1	367.3	27.5	339.8	61.6
1992	5 517.1	3 631.4	2 957.8	572.0	2 385.8	673.6	445.2	228.4	414.9	35.8	379.1	84.6
1993	5 784.7	3 797.1	3 083.0	589.0	2 494.0	714.1	474.4	239.7	449.6	32.0	417.6	114.1
1994	6 181.3	3 998.5	3 248.5	609.5	2 639.0	750.1	495.9	254.1	485.1	35.6	449.5	142.9
1995	6 522.3	4 195.2	3 434.4	629.0	2 805.4	760.8	496.7	264.1	516.0	23.4	492.6	154.6
1996	6 931.7	4 391.4	3 620.0	648.1	2 971.9	771.4	496.6	274.8	583.7	38.4	545.2	170.4
1997	7 406.0	4 665.6	3 873.6	671.8	3 201.8	792.0	502.4	289.6	628.2	32.6	595.6	176.5
1998	7 875.6	5 023.2	4 180.9	701.2	3 479.7	842.3	535.1	307.2	687.5	28.9	658.7	191.5
1999	8 358.0	5 353.9	4 465.2	733.7	3 731.5	888.8	565.4	323.3	746.8	28.5	718.3	208.2
2000	8 938.9	5 788.8	4 827.7	779.7	4 048.0	961.2	615.9	345.2	817.5	29.6	787.8	215.3
2001	9 185.2	5 979.3	4 952.2	821.9	4 130.3	1 027.1	669.1	358.0	870.7	30.5	840.2	232.4
2002	9 408.5	6 110.8	4 997.3	873.1	4 124.2	1 113.5	747.4	366.1	890.3	18.5	871.8	218.7
2003	9 840.2	6 382.6	5 154.6	913.3	4 241.3	1 228.0	845.6	382.4	930.6	36.5	894.1	204.2
2004	10 534.0	6 693.4	5 410.7	952.8	4 457.9	1 282.7	874.6	408.1	1 033.8	49.7	984.1	198.4
2005	11 273.8	7 065.0	5 706.0	991.5	4 714.5	1 359.1	931.6	427.5	1 069.8	43.9	1 025.9	178.2
2006	12 031.2	7 477.0	6 070.1	1 035.2	5 035.0	1 406.9	960.1	446.7	1 133.0	29.3	1 103.6	146.5
2007	12 448.2	7 856.5	6 402.6	1 089.1	5 313.5	1 453.8	993.0	460.8	1 096.4	39.4	1 056.9	144.9
2008	12 635.2	8 037.4	6 540.8	1 141.3	5 399.6	1 496.6	1 023.9	472.7	1 106.3	48.7	1 057.5	210.4
2009	12 288.1	7 791.6	6 289.1	1 182.4	5 106.7	1 502.5	1 043.9	458.5	1 041.0	29.3	1 011.7	268.1
2007												
1st quarter	12 253.9	7 757.2	6 318.6	1 073.2	5 245.3	1 438.6	980.5	458.1	1 094.2	36.7	1 057.5	121.1
2nd quarter	12 421.1	7 819.7	6 372.2	1 084.2	5 288.0	1 447.5	989.4	458.2	1 096.0	35.7	1 060.3	140.3
3rd quarter	12 482.2	7 869.6	6 412.5	1 093.2	5 319.4	1 457.1	996.9	460.2	1 093.2	37.5	1 055.7	150.2
4th quarter	12 635.4	7 979.3	6 507.3	1 105.8	5 401.4	1 472.1	1 005.2	466.9	1 102.1	47.9	1 054.2	168.0
2008												
1st quarter	12 661.5	8 017.5	6 533.0	1 125.3	5 407.7	1 484.5	1 014.0	470.5	1 115.2	57.2	1 057.9	179.9
2nd quarter	12 664.4	8 032.8	6 539.2	1 136.4	5 402.8	1 493.5	1 021.7	471.8	1 111.9	49.4	1 062.5	202.8
3rd quarter	12 781.0	8 069.1	6 567.7	1 148.5	5 419.2	1 501.4	1 026.7	474.7	1 114.4	49.3	1 065.1	222.2
4th quarter	12 433.9	8 030.3	6 523.5	1 154.9	5 368.6	1 506.8	1 033.2	473.6	1 083.6	39.0	1 044.5	236.7
2009												
1st quarter	12 208.9	7 825.8	6 327.8	1 171.8	5 156.0	1 498.0	1 037.8	460.2	1 037.8	27.3	1 010.5	245.9
2nd quarter	12 218.1	7 815.9	6 313.1	1 184.4	5 128.8	1 502.8	1 042.0	460.8	1 028.0	28.9	999.1	262.0
3rd quarter	12 259.7	7 751.5	6 249.2	1 184.8	5 064.3	1 502.3	1 046.1	456.2	1 037.9	25.8	1 012.0	277.9
4th quarter	12 465.6	7 773.1	6 266.3	1 188.6	5 077.8	1 506.8	1 049.8	457.0	1 060.3	35.2	1 025.1	286.7

Table 1-12. National Income by Type of Income—*Continued*

(Billions of dollars, quarterly data are at seasonally adjusted annual rates.)

NIPA Tables 1.7.5, 1.12

| Year and quarter | Corporate profits with IVA and CCAdj | | | | | Net interest and miscellaneous payments | Taxes on production and imports | Less: Subsidies | Business current transfer payments, net | | | Current surplus of government enterprises | Addendum: Net national factor income |
| | Total | Taxes on corporate income | Profits after tax | | | | | | Total 1 | To persons | To government | | |
			Total	Net dividends	Undistributed corporate profits								
1950	35.6	17.9	17.7	8.8	8.9	3.2	23.0	0.6	0.9	0.6	0.3	. . .	240.6
1951	40.8	22.6	18.2	8.6	9.7	3.7	24.7	0.7	1.2	0.9	0.3	. . .	278.6
1952	38.8	19.4	19.4	8.6	10.9	4.1	27.1	0.4	1.3	0.9	0.4	. . .	293.3
1953	39.1	20.3	18.8	8.9	9.9	4.7	29.1	0.1	1.2	0.8	0.4	. . .	308.4
1954	38.3	17.6	20.7	9.3	11.4	5.6	28.9	-0.1	1.0	0.6	0.4	. . .	308.8
1955	49.0	22.0	27.0	10.5	16.5	6.2	31.5	-0.2	1.4	0.9	0.4	. . .	339.0
1956	48.0	22.0	26.0	11.3	14.7	6.9	34.2	0.4	1.7	1.2	0.5	. . .	359.3
1957	47.6	21.4	26.2	11.7	14.5	8.0	36.6	0.7	1.9	1.4	0.5	. . .	375.5
1958	42.5	19.0	23.5	11.6	11.9	9.5	37.7	0.9	1.8	1.2	0.6	. . .	377.0
1959	53.8	23.7	30.1	12.6	17.5	9.6	41.1	1.1	1.8	1.3	0.4	1.0	410.8
1960	53.1	22.8	30.3	13.4	16.9	10.6	44.5	1.1	1.9	1.3	0.5	0.9	427.7
1961	54.2	22.9	31.3	13.9	17.4	12.5	47.0	2.0	2.0	1.4	0.7	0.8	442.9
1962	62.3	24.1	38.3	15.0	23.2	14.2	50.4	2.3	2.2	1.5	0.7	0.9	477.6
1963	68.3	26.4	42.0	16.2	25.7	15.2	53.4	2.2	2.7	1.9	0.8	1.4	504.6
1964	75.5	28.2	47.4	18.2	29.2	17.4	57.3	2.7	3.1	2.2	0.9	1.3	542.4
1965	86.5	31.1	55.5	20.2	35.3	19.6	60.7	3.0	3.6	2.3	1.4	1.3	589.5
1966	92.5	33.9	58.7	20.7	38.0	22.4	63.2	3.9	3.5	2.1	1.4	1.0	646.4
1967	90.2	32.9	57.3	21.5	35.8	25.5	67.9	3.8	3.8	2.3	1.5	0.9	681.6
1968	97.3	39.6	57.6	23.5	34.1	27.1	76.4	4.2	4.3	2.8	1.5	1.2	743.5
1969	94.5	40.0	54.5	24.2	30.3	32.7	83.9	4.5	4.9	3.3	1.6	1.0	803.2
1970	82.5	34.8	47.7	24.3	23.4	39.1	91.4	4.8	4.5	2.9	1.6	0.0	838.4
1971	96.1	38.2	57.9	25.0	32.9	43.9	100.5	4.7	4.3	2.7	1.6	-0.2	905.7
1972	111.4	42.3	69.1	26.8	42.2	47.9	107.9	6.6	4.9	3.1	1.8	0.5	1 003.6
1973	124.5	50.0	74.5	29.9	44.6	55.2	117.2	5.2	6.0	3.9	2.0	-0.4	1 128.5
1974	115.1	52.8	62.3	33.2	29.1	70.8	124.9	3.3	7.1	4.7	2.4	-0.9	1 213.7
1975	133.3	51.6	81.7	33.0	48.7	81.6	135.3	4.5	9.4	6.8	2.6	-3.2	1 307.1
1976	161.6	65.3	96.3	39.0	57.3	85.5	146.4	5.1	9.5	6.7	2.8	-1.8	1 460.8
1977	191.8	74.4	117.4	44.8	72.6	101.1	159.7	7.1	8.5	5.1	3.4	-2.7	1 639.1
1978	218.4	84.9	133.6	50.8	82.8	115.0	170.9	8.9	10.8	6.5	4.4	-2.2	1 857.3
1979	225.4	90.0	135.3	57.5	77.8	138.9	180.1	8.5	13.3	8.2	5.1	-2.9	2 066.3
1980	201.4	87.2	114.2	64.1	50.2	181.8	200.3	9.8	14.7	8.6	6.1	-5.1	2 232.8
1981	223.3	84.3	138.9	73.8	65.2	232.3	235.6	11.5	17.9	11.2	6.7	-5.6	2 493.3
1982	205.7	66.5	139.2	77.7	61.5	271.1	240.9	15.0	20.6	12.4	8.2	-4.5	2 609.4
1983	259.8	80.6	179.2	83.5	95.7	285.3	263.3	21.3	22.6	13.8	8.8	-3.2	2 809.5
1984	318.6	97.5	221.1	90.8	130.3	327.1	289.8	21.1	30.3	19.7	10.6	-1.9	3 164.2
1985	332.5	99.4	233.1	97.6	135.6	341.5	308.1	21.4	35.2	22.3	12.9	0.6	3 373.7
1986	314.1	109.7	204.5	106.2	98.3	367.1	323.4	24.9	36.9	22.9	13.9	0.9	3 535.3
1987	367.8	130.4	237.4	112.3	125.1	366.7	347.5	30.3	34.1	20.2	13.8	0.2	3 798.6
1988	426.6	141.6	285.0	129.9	155.1	385.3	374.5	29.5	33.6	20.6	13.0	2.6	4 141.1
1989	425.6	146.1	279.5	158.0	121.5	434.1	398.9	27.4	39.2	23.2	16.0	4.9	4 385.0
1990	434.4	145.4	289.0	169.1	120.0	444.2	425.0	27.0	40.1	22.2	17.9	1.6	4 619.9
1991	457.3	138.6	318.7	180.7	138.0	418.2	457.1	27.5	39.9	17.6	22.3	5.7	4 742.7
1992	496.2	148.7	347.5	188.0	159.5	387.7	483.4	30.1	40.7	16.3	24.5	8.2	5 014.9
1993	543.7	171.0	372.7	202.9	169.7	364.6	503.1	36.7	40.5	14.1	26.7	8.7	5 269.1
1994	628.2	193.1	435.1	235.7	199.4	362.2	545.2	32.5	41.9	13.3	29.1	9.6	5 617.0
1995	716.2	217.8	498.3	254.4	243.9	358.3	557.9	34.8	45.8	18.7	25.7	13.1	5 940.3
1996	801.5	231.5	570.0	297.7	272.3	371.1	580.8	35.2	53.8	22.9	31.8	14.4	6 318.1
1997	884.8	245.4	639.4	331.2	308.2	407.6	611.6	33.8	51.3	19.4	31.1	14.1	6 762.8
1998	812.4	248.4	564.1	351.5	212.6	479.3	639.5	36.4	65.2	26.0	35.4	13.3	7 194.0
1999	856.3	258.8	597.5	337.4	260.1	481.4	673.6	45.2	69.0	34.0	37.6	14.1	7 646.5
2000	819.2	265.1	554.1	377.9	176.3	539.3	708.6	45.8	87.0	42.4	43.6	9.1	8 180.1
2001	784.2	203.3	580.9	370.9	210.0	544.4	727.7	58.7	101.3	46.8	46.0	4.0	8 410.9
2002	872.2	192.3	679.9	399.3	280.6	506.4	762.8	41.4	82.4	34.2	47.9	6.3	8 598.4
2003	977.8	243.8	734.0	424.9	309.2	504.1	806.8	49.1	76.1	25.7	48.8	7.0	8 999.3
2004	1 246.9	306.1	940.8	550.3	390.5	461.6	863.4	46.4	81.7	16.9	52.5	1.2	9 634.1
2005	1 456.1	412.4	1 043.7	557.3	486.4	543.0	930.2	60.9	95.9	25.8	55.2	-3.5	10 312.2
2006	1 608.3	473.3	1 135.0	704.8	430.3	652.2	986.8	51.4	83.0	21.4	59.6	-4.2	11 017.0
2007	1 541.7	451.5	1 090.2	767.8	322.4	739.2	1 028.7	54.8	102.2	30.2	65.4	-6.6	11 378.6
2008	1 360.4	292.2	1 068.2	689.9	378.3	815.1	1 047.3	53.5	118.8	32.6	78.8	-6.9	11 529.6
2009	1 308.9	314.8	994.1	575.8	418.4	788.2	1 023.9	59.6	134.1	32.7	96.8	-8.1	11 197.8
2007													
1st quarter	1 535.4	469.5	1 065.9	772.6	293.3	690.6	1 015.3	49.2	97.8	27.1	63.0	-8.4	11 198.4
2nd quarter	1 594.9	466.5	1 128.4	778.1	350.3	711.3	1 025.2	58.3	99.0	29.8	63.8	-6.9	11 362.1
3rd quarter	1 537.1	440.0	1 097.1	770.6	326.5	756.0	1 032.2	56.0	105.0	31.6	65.4	-4.9	11 406.1
4th quarter	1 499.4	430.1	1 069.3	749.9	319.4	798.9	1 042.3	55.4	107.0	32.4	69.3	-6.0	11 547.7
2008													
1st quarter	1 459.7	323.2	1 136.4	719.4	417.1	790.7	1 042.5	53.1	114.8	32.6	73.3	-5.6	11 563.0
2nd quarter	1 403.7	317.5	1 086.3	693.7	392.6	809.0	1 050.8	52.9	112.6	32.6	74.6	-6.3	11 560.1
3rd quarter	1 454.6	304.8	1 149.8	676.6	473.2	806.1	1 058.5	52.9	116.0	32.6	76.0	-6.9	11 666.4
4th quarter	1 123.6	223.3	900.4	669.9	230.5	854.7	1 037.3	55.2	131.8	32.7	91.5	-8.9	11 329.0
2009													
1st quarter	1 182.7	270.3	912.4	618.1	294.2	826.2	1 018.8	55.5	137.9	32.5	100.3	-10.7	11 118.5
2nd quarter	1 226.5	305.9	920.6	556.0	364.5	784.4	1 019.6	54.9	145.4	32.7	107.9	-8.8	11 116.9
3rd quarter	1 358.9	321.0	1 037.9	549.9	488.0	759.7	1 023.1	67.7	124.8	32.8	87.5	-6.3	11 185.8
4th quarter	1 467.6	361.9	1 105.7	579.0	526.7	782.6	1 034.1	60.3	128.2	32.9	91.4	-6.5	11 370.2

1 Includes net transfer payments to the rest of the world, not shown separately.
. . . = Not available.

Table 1-13. Gross and Net Value Added of Domestic Corporate Business

(Billions of dollars, quarterly data are at seasonally adjusted annual rates.) NIPA Table 1.14

Year and quarter	Gross value added of corporate business, total	Consumption of fixed capital	Net value added											Gross value added of financial corporate business
			Total	Compensation of employees	Taxes on production and imports less subsidies	Net operating surplus								
						Total	Net interest and miscellaneous payments	Business current transfer payments	Corporate profits with IVA and CCAdj					
									Total	Taxes on corporate income	Profits after tax			
											Total	Net dividends	Undistributed	
1950	160.4	12.0	148.4	98.7	14.8	35.0	-0.1	0.7	34.4	17.9	16.4	7.9	8.6	7.3
1951	183.9	13.6	170.3	114.6	15.9	39.9	-0.2	1.1	39.1	22.6	16.5	7.4	9.1	8.2
1952	192.6	14.5	178.1	123.0	17.3	37.8	-0.2	1.1	37.0	19.4	17.6	7.5	10.1	9.2
1953	206.2	15.4	190.8	134.0	18.5	38.3	0.0	1.0	37.3	20.3	17.0	7.8	9.3	10.2
1954	203.6	16.2	187.5	132.2	17.9	37.3	0.2	0.8	36.4	17.6	18.7	7.9	10.9	10.8
1955	229.5	17.1	212.4	144.6	19.8	48.0	0.2	1.2	46.6	22.0	24.6	8.9	15.7	11.8
1956	245.6	19.2	226.4	158.2	21.5	46.7	0.0	1.5	45.2	22.0	23.2	9.5	13.7	12.9
1957	256.9	21.3	235.7	166.5	22.8	46.4	0.2	1.7	44.5	21.4	23.1	9.9	13.3	13.8
1958	251.8	22.7	229.1	164.0	23.1	42.0	0.6	1.5	39.9	19.0	21.0	9.8	11.1	14.7
1959	281.9	23.7	258.2	180.3	25.6	52.4	-0.2	1.5	51.1	23.7	27.4	10.7	16.7	15.9
1960	293.9	24.0	269.9	190.7	27.8	51.3	-0.2	1.6	50.0	22.8	27.2	11.4	15.8	17.5
1961	302.1	24.6	277.5	195.6	28.9	53.0	0.4	1.8	50.9	22.9	28.0	11.5	16.5	18.4
1962	329.0	25.5	303.5	211.0	31.2	61.3	0.7	2.0	58.6	24.1	34.5	12.4	22.1	19.3
1963	349.5	26.7	322.9	222.7	33.2	67.0	0.4	2.4	64.3	26.4	37.9	13.6	24.3	19.7
1964	377.7	28.2	349.5	239.2	35.6	74.7	0.8	2.9	71.1	28.2	42.9	15.0	27.9	21.6
1965	414.4	30.4	384.0	259.9	37.8	86.3	1.2	3.3	81.8	31.1	50.8	16.9	33.9	23.2
1966	454.1	33.4	420.7	288.5	38.9	93.3	2.3	3.0	88.0	33.9	54.1	17.8	36.3	25.1
1967	479.3	36.8	442.5	308.4	41.4	92.7	4.0	3.3	85.4	32.9	52.5	18.3	34.2	28.1
1968	529.1	40.6	488.5	341.3	47.8	99.4	3.9	3.8	91.6	39.6	52.0	20.2	31.8	31.3
1969	576.7	45.1	531.5	378.6	52.9	100.0	7.8	4.4	87.9	40.0	47.9	20.4	27.5	36.2
1970	597.8	50.0	547.7	400.2	57.0	90.6	11.3	3.9	75.4	34.8	40.6	20.4	20.3	39.4
1971	646.1	54.8	591.3	425.3	62.8	103.2	11.5	3.5	88.2	38.2	50.1	20.3	29.7	43.1
1972	716.7	59.7	657.0	472.5	67.3	117.2	11.3	4.0	101.9	42.3	59.6	21.9	37.6	47.3
1973	802.6	66.9	735.6	533.9	74.1	127.6	13.0	5.0	109.6	50.0	59.6	23.1	36.5	51.8
1974	869.9	78.8	791.0	587.4	78.6	125.0	20.7	6.6	97.7	52.8	44.9	23.5	21.4	60.0
1975	944.4	94.4	850.0	614.9	84.5	150.7	23.4	8.6	118.7	51.6	67.0	26.4	40.6	67.8
1976	1 062.9	104.5	958.4	695.2	91.4	171.7	18.8	7.9	145.1	65.3	79.8	30.1	49.7	73.2
1977	1 205.1	118.0	1 087.1	784.8	100.0	202.3	23.3	6.3	172.7	74.4	98.3	33.7	64.6	85.7
1978	1 376.1	134.2	1 241.9	901.8	108.7	231.3	27.5	8.2	195.6	84.9	110.7	39.6	71.1	103.4
1979	1 529.0	155.1	1 373.9	1 022.0	115.0	236.9	34.9	11.3	190.7	90.0	100.7	41.5	59.2	114.6
1980	1 663.0	179.8	1 483.2	1 120.1	128.6	234.5	55.9	12.6	166.0	87.2	78.8	47.3	31.4	128.5
1981	1 889.0	208.1	1 680.8	1 240.0	154.4	286.4	77.7	15.1	193.6	84.3	109.3	58.3	50.9	146.8
1982	1 967.3	231.4	1 736.0	1 293.8	161.3	280.8	90.0	17.7	173.1	66.5	106.6	61.3	45.3	164.7
1983	2 116.7	240.4	1 876.2	1 367.1	177.4	331.7	86.6	20.3	224.8	80.6	144.1	71.3	72.8	187.6
1984	2 371.3	252.9	2 118.4	1 513.9	195.6	408.9	98.8	28.0	282.0	97.5	184.5	78.5	106.0	209.9
1985	2 526.5	271.7	2 254.8	1 622.4	209.0	423.3	96.9	31.9	294.4	99.4	195.0	85.7	109.3	232.6
1986	2 640.6	289.8	2 350.8	1 720.4	219.6	410.8	106.3	29.9	274.7	109.7	165.0	88.3	76.7	257.4
1987	2 832.6	306.5	2 526.1	1 840.0	233.4	452.7	107.6	25.3	319.8	130.4	189.4	95.6	93.8	281.7
1988	3 065.5	328.8	2 736.7	1 980.4	252.0	504.3	107.8	26.9	369.6	141.6	228.0	98.0	130.0	300.1
1989	3 229.5	350.8	2 878.6	2 088.3	267.5	522.8	130.0	34.4	358.4	146.1	212.4	126.4	86.0	330.3
1990	3 377.0	373.0	3 003.9	2 200.6	284.5	518.9	125.8	34.8	358.4	145.4	212.9	144.1	68.8	341.8
1991	3 467.4	392.1	3 075.3	2 249.4	307.9	518.0	102.6	34.6	380.8	138.6	242.2	156.4	85.9	363.3
1992	3 642.2	402.0	3 240.2	2 375.5	325.9	538.8	80.6	35.1	423.1	148.7	274.4	160.0	114.5	401.1
1993	3 823.2	420.1	3 403.2	2 488.2	342.0	572.9	73.5	32.7	466.8	171.0	295.7	182.3	113.4	424.8
1994	4 110.5	444.9	3 665.7	2 634.8	372.4	658.5	75.0	33.2	550.3	193.1	357.1	197.6	159.6	433.0
1995	4 357.5	476.8	3 880.7	2 776.0	379.1	725.6	64.7	37.7	623.2	217.8	405.4	221.6	183.8	469.5
1996	4 625.0	506.0	4 119.0	2 914.9	390.7	813.4	69.3	44.6	699.5	231.5	468.1	257.3	210.7	505.6
1997	4 978.9	540.9	4 438.1	3 123.9	406.9	907.3	94.8	35.2	777.3	245.4	531.9	284.0	247.9	566.4
1998	5 299.3	578.3	4 720.9	3 396.8	418.4	905.7	142.2	53.8	709.7	248.4	461.3	309.2	152.1	630.9
1999	5 624.5	625.8	4 998.7	3 628.6	441.5	928.6	139.0	54.9	734.8	258.8	476.0	295.7	180.3	669.0
2000	6 016.4	685.1	5 331.4	3 950.7	466.6	914.1	166.6	73.8	673.6	265.1	408.5	348.5	60.1	737.0
2001	6 034.7	730.3	5 304.4	3 986.2	462.6	855.7	154.2	87.0	614.5	203.3	411.2	330.1	81.1	782.2
2002	6 122.7	755.9	5 366.8	3 997.2	492.2	893.9	116.2	63.5	714.3	192.3	522.0	351.2	170.8	815.0
2003	6 360.7	775.5	5 585.2	4 105.5	517.3	962.4	99.4	50.9	812.0	243.8	568.3	392.8	175.5	856.9
2004	6 774.2	809.2	5 965.0	4 265.9	553.7	1 145.4	48.6	54.9	1 041.9	306.1	735.8	488.0	247.8	896.7
2005	7 297.9	862.9	6 435.0	4 498.5	596.7	1 339.8	61.6	61.6	1 216.6	412.4	804.3	296.5	507.8	995.1
2006	7 823.3	925.9	6 897.4	4 743.4	633.7	1 520.3	120.4	48.4	1 351.5	473.3	878.2	626.9	251.3	1 083.0
2007	8 026.0	981.0	7 045.0	4 948.0	655.8	1 441.2	174.8	72.4	1 193.9	451.5	742.4	641.6	100.8	1 055.9
2008	8 112.1	1 036.8	7 075.2	5 005.9	665.4	1 404.0	334.0	86.8	983.2	292.2	691.0	543.3	147.7	1 140.6
2009	7 879.5	1 041.7	6 837.8	4 727.5	645.2	1 465.0	367.9	100.0	997.1	314.8	682.3	458.9	223.4	1 207.3
2007														
1st quarter	7 963.6	960.5	7 003.1	4 893.5	647.2	1 462.4	146.5	62.7	1 253.2	469.5	783.7	665.2	118.5	1 054.2
2nd quarter	8 067.1	974.0	7 093.1	4 927.2	653.4	1 512.5	159.0	69.8	1 283.7	466.5	817.2	664.4	152.8	1 078.4
3rd quarter	8 016.9	987.7	7 029.1	4 950.7	658.0	1 420.4	178.2	75.6	1 166.6	440.0	726.6	636.6	90.0	1 067.2
4th quarter	8 056.3	1 001.6	7 054.7	5 020.7	664.5	1 369.5	215.6	81.6	1 072.3	430.1	642.2	600.3	41.9	1 023.7
2008														
1st quarter	8 090.6	1 015.7	7 075.0	5 019.4	662.7	1 392.8	263.6	81.8	1 047.4	323.2	724.2	548.5	175.7	1 155.8
2nd quarter	8 150.8	1 029.7	7 121.1	5 011.6	668.0	1 441.5	321.3	83.4	1 036.7	317.5	719.2	529.9	189.4	1 176.4
3rd quarter	8 233.0	1 043.9	7 189.1	5 021.8	672.7	1 494.6	352.4	84.9	1 057.4	304.8	752.6	514.7	237.9	1 190.6
4th quarter	7 973.8	1 058.1	6 915.8	4 970.7	658.1	1 287.0	398.8	97.0	791.3	223.3	568.0	580.0	-11.9	1 039.7
2009														
1st quarter	7 839.9	1 058.2	6 781.7	4 781.3	645.8	1 354.5	384.3	103.2	867.0	270.4	596.6	515.3	81.3	1 136.1
2nd quarter	7 844.0	1 043.0	6 801.0	4 749.8	646.3	1 405.0	370.5	109.2	925.3	305.9	619.4	455.5	163.8	1 172.2
3rd quarter	7 838.6	1 032.5	6 806.2	4 686.2	637.3	1 482.7	354.5	92.5	1 035.7	321.0	714.7	397.0	317.7	1 225.1
4th quarter	7 995.3	1 033.1	6 962.2	4 692.7	651.5	1 617.9	362.4	95.1	1 160.4	361.9	798.5	467.6	331.0	1 295.7

Table 1-14. Gross Value Added of Nonfinancial Domestic Corporate Business in Current and Chained Dollars

(Billions of dollars, quarterly data are at seasonally adjusted annual rates.)   NIPA Table 1.14

Year and quarter	Current-dollar gross value added													Gross value added in billions of chained (2005) dollars
	Total	Consumption of fixed capital	Net value added											
			Total	Compensation of employees	Taxes on production and imports less subsidies	Net operating surplus								
						Total	Net interest and miscellaneous payments	Business current transfer payments	Corporate profits with IVA and CCAdj					
									Total	Taxes on corporate income	Profits after tax			
											Total	Net dividends	Undistributed	
1950	153.1	11.5	141.6	94.4	14.4	32.8	0.9	0.6	31.3	16.8	14.5	7.4	7.2	716.1
1951	175.7	13.1	162.6	109.8	15.4	37.4	1.0	0.8	35.6	21.1	14.5	7.0	7.5	756.4
1952	183.4	13.9	169.4	117.8	16.8	34.9	1.2	0.9	32.8	17.7	15.2	7.1	8.1	783.1
1953	195.9	14.8	181.1	128.2	17.9	35.0	1.3	1.0	32.8	18.4	14.4	7.2	7.2	839.7
1954	192.9	15.6	177.3	125.9	17.3	34.0	1.6	0.9	31.6	15.5	16.0	7.4	8.7	830.5
1955	217.7	16.5	201.3	137.9	19.2	44.2	1.6	1.0	41.6	20.1	21.4	8.4	13.0	930.8
1956	232.7	18.5	214.2	150.8	20.8	42.6	1.8	1.1	39.8	19.9	19.8	9.0	10.8	960.2
1957	243.1	20.5	222.6	158.4	22.0	42.2	2.2	1.2	38.8	19.0	19.9	9.2	10.6	972.5
1958	237.1	21.8	215.3	155.2	22.3	37.8	2.8	1.2	33.8	16.1	17.7	9.1	8.6	934.4
1959	266.0	22.7	243.3	170.8	24.4	48.1	2.9	1.3	43.8	20.7	23.1	9.8	13.3	1 040.2
1960	276.4	23.1	253.3	180.4	26.6	46.3	3.2	1.4	41.7	19.1	22.6	10.5	12.1	1 075.0
1961	283.7	23.7	260.1	184.5	27.6	47.9	3.7	1.5	42.7	19.4	23.3	10.6	12.7	1 099.2
1962	309.8	24.5	285.2	199.3	29.9	56.1	4.3	1.7	50.1	20.6	29.5	11.6	17.9	1 193.2
1963	329.9	25.6	304.3	210.1	31.7	62.5	4.7	1.7	56.1	22.8	33.4	12.4	20.9	1 264.9
1964	356.1	27.0	329.0	225.7	33.9	69.5	5.2	2.0	62.4	23.9	38.5	14.0	24.5	1 354.2
1965	391.2	29.1	362.1	245.4	36.0	80.7	5.8	2.2	72.7	27.1	45.5	16.2	29.3	1 466.7
1966	429.0	31.9	397.1	272.9	37.0	87.2	7.0	2.7	77.5	29.5	48.0	16.8	31.2	1 571.9
1967	451.2	35.2	416.0	291.1	39.3	85.6	8.4	2.8	74.4	27.8	46.5	17.3	29.3	1 614.3
1968	497.8	38.7	459.1	321.9	45.5	91.7	9.7	3.1	78.9	33.5	45.4	19.0	26.4	1 719.0
1969	540.5	42.9	497.5	357.1	50.2	90.3	12.7	3.2	74.4	33.3	41.0	19.0	22.0	1 788.5
1970	558.3	47.5	510.8	376.5	54.2	80.1	16.6	3.3	60.2	27.3	32.9	18.3	14.6	1 774.1
1971	603.0	52.0	551.1	399.4	59.5	92.1	17.6	3.7	70.8	30.0	40.8	18.1	22.7	1 847.3
1972	669.4	56.5	613.0	443.9	63.7	105.4	18.6	4.0	82.8	33.8	49.0	19.7	29.3	1 988.5
1973	750.8	63.1	687.6	502.2	70.1	115.4	21.8	4.7	88.9	40.4	48.5	20.8	27.8	2 111.0
1974	809.8	74.2	735.7	552.2	74.4	109.1	27.5	4.1	77.5	42.8	34.6	21.5	13.1	2 077.6
1975	876.7	88.6	788.0	575.5	80.2	132.4	28.4	5.0	98.9	41.9	57.0	24.6	32.5	2 047.1
1976	989.7	97.8	892.0	651.4	86.7	153.9	26.0	7.0	121.0	53.5	67.5	27.8	39.7	2 214.4
1977	1 119.4	110.1	1 009.2	735.3	94.6	179.3	28.5	9.0	141.9	60.6	81.3	30.9	50.4	2 378.5
1978	1 272.7	125.1	1 147.5	845.1	102.7	199.7	33.4	9.5	156.8	67.6	89.2	35.9	53.3	2 534.0
1979	1 414.4	144.3	1 270.2	958.4	108.8	203.0	41.8	9.5	151.8	70.6	81.2	37.6	43.5	2 612.4
1980	1 534.5	166.7	1 367.8	1 047.2	121.5	199.1	54.2	10.2	134.7	68.2	66.5	44.7	21.9	2 584.7
1981	1 742.2	192.4	1 549.8	1 157.6	146.7	245.5	67.2	11.4	166.8	66.0	100.8	52.5	48.3	2 687.9
1982	1 802.6	212.8	1 589.8	1 200.4	152.9	236.5	77.4	8.8	150.2	48.8	101.5	54.1	47.4	2 622.6
1983	1 929.1	219.3	1 709.8	1 263.1	168.0	278.7	77.0	10.5	191.2	61.7	129.5	63.2	66.2	2 746.2
1984	2 161.4	228.8	1 932.6	1 400.0	185.0	347.5	86.0	11.7	249.8	75.9	173.9	67.2	106.7	2 989.4
1985	2 293.9	244.0	2 049.9	1 496.1	196.6	357.2	91.5	16.1	249.6	71.1	178.6	72.0	106.6	3 120.3
1986	2 383.2	258.0	2 125.2	1 575.4	204.6	345.2	98.5	27.3	219.5	76.2	143.2	72.9	70.4	3 197.9
1987	2 551.0	270.0	2 280.9	1 678.4	216.8	385.6	95.9	29.9	259.9	94.2	165.7	76.3	89.4	3 364.7
1988	2 765.4	287.3	2 478.1	1 804.7	233.8	439.6	107.9	27.4	304.3	104.0	200.3	82.2	118.2	3 560.4
1989	2 899.2	303.9	2 595.3	1 905.7	248.2	441.5	133.9	24.0	283.5	101.2	182.3	105.4	77.0	3 618.2
1990	3 035.2	321.0	2 714.2	2 005.5	263.5	445.2	143.1	25.4	276.7	98.5	178.3	118.3	60.0	3 672.6
1991	3 104.1	336.1	2 768.0	2 044.8	285.7	437.5	139.6	26.6	271.3	88.6	182.7	125.5	57.2	3 655.5
1992	3 241.1	344.1	2 897.0	2 152.9	302.5	441.6	114.2	31.3	296.1	94.4	201.7	134.3	67.4	3 768.0
1993	3 398.4	359.0	3 039.3	2 244.0	318.0	477.3	99.8	30.1	347.5	108.0	239.5	149.2	90.3	3 866.5
1994	3 677.6	380.1	3 297.5	2 382.1	347.8	567.5	98.8	35.3	433.5	132.4	301.1	158.0	143.1	4 115.3
1995	3 888.0	408.3	3 479.7	2 511.5	354.2	614.0	112.7	30.7	470.6	140.3	330.3	178.0	152.2	4 309.4
1996	4 119.4	435.1	3 684.4	2 631.3	365.6	687.5	112.1	38.0	537.4	152.9	384.5	197.6	186.9	4 548.0
1997	4 412.5	466.9	3 945.6	2 814.6	381.0	750.0	124.7	39.2	586.2	161.4	424.8	215.9	208.9	4 843.8
1998	4 668.3	499.9	4 168.5	3 049.7	393.1	725.7	146.8	35.2	543.7	158.7	385.1	241.0	144.0	5 123.5
1999	4 955.5	539.3	4 416.3	3 256.5	414.6	745.1	164.5	47.1	533.5	171.4	362.1	224.7	137.4	5 422.5
2000	5 279.4	590.1	4 689.4	3 541.8	439.4	708.2	192.8	47.9	467.5	170.2	297.3	251.3	46.0	5 707.9
2001	5 252.5	632.0	4 620.5	3 559.4	434.5	626.7	197.7	58.9	370.1	111.2	258.8	245.4	13.4	5 604.6
2002	5 307.7	654.5	4 653.1	3 544.2	461.9	647.1	163.7	56.3	427.2	97.1	330.1	254.8	75.3	5 629.3
2003	5 503.7	669.0	4 834.7	3 651.8	484.2	699.2	147.9	65.2	486.1	132.9	353.2	293.4	59.8	5 767.4
2004	5 877.5	695.6	5 181.9	3 786.7	517.7	877.5	134.4	65.5	677.5	187.0	490.6	364.5	126.1	6 040.4
2005	6 302.8	743.0	5 559.8	3 976.3	558.4	1 025.1	148.2	79.3	797.6	271.9	525.8	170.9	354.9	6 302.8
2006	6 740.3	800.9	5 939.4	4 182.3	593.3	1 163.7	164.0	75.8	923.9	307.6	616.2	471.1	145.1	6 536.5
2007	6 970.1	849.4	6 120.6	4 364.2	612.8	1 143.7	228.1	68.6	846.9	299.3	547.6	465.2	82.4	6 649.4
2008	6 971.5	898.4	6 073.0	4 427.9	621.0	1 024.1	242.1	70.4	711.6	237.8	473.8	409.3	64.5	6 675.5
2009	6 672.2	902.0	5 770.2	4 182.9	601.9	985.5	227.4	77.8	680.3	222.1	458.2	361.0	97.3	6 290.6
2007														
1st quarter	6 909.3	831.6	6 077.7	4 314.0	604.8	1 159.0	201.2	70.3	887.5	313.3	574.1	487.7	86.5	6 597.4
2nd quarter	6 988.8	843.4	6 145.4	4 345.1	610.5	1 189.7	223.6	68.4	897.7	305.3	592.4	485.7	106.8	6 649.8
3rd quarter	6 949.7	855.3	6 094.4	4 365.4	614.8	1 114.1	236.6	67.5	810.1	284.4	525.7	459.6	66.1	6 624.9
4th quarter	7 032.6	867.5	6 165.1	4 432.2	620.9	1 112.0	251.2	68.4	792.4	294.2	498.1	428.0	70.1	6 725.5
2008														
1st quarter	6 934.9	879.8	6 055.1	4 429.6	618.5	1 006.9	242.1	68.1	696.7	255.9	440.8	408.8	32.0	6 664.3
2nd quarter	6 974.4	892.2	6 082.2	4 431.6	623.5	1 027.1	246.0	68.3	712.8	263.1	449.7	395.2	54.5	6 735.8
3rd quarter	7 042.4	904.6	6 137.8	4 440.4	627.8	1 069.6	233.3	68.7	767.6	254.5	513.1	383.3	129.7	6 722.6
4th quarter	6 934.1	917.1	6 017.0	4 410.1	614.2	992.7	246.8	76.5	669.4	177.7	491.6	449.9	41.7	6 579.3
2009														
1st quarter	6 703.8	916.7	5 787.1	4 238.5	602.7	945.8	237.4	79.2	629.2	197.9	431.3	373.1	58.1	6 278.8
2nd quarter	6 671.9	903.0	5 768.9	4 194.4	603.1	971.4	229.2	83.2	659.0	217.0	442.1	362.7	79.3	6 269.8
3rd quarter	6 613.6	894.0	5 719.6	4 146.7	593.9	979.0	219.2	73.1	686.6	227.0	459.6	332.7	126.9	6 242.7
4th quarter	6 699.6	894.2	5 805.4	4 152.0	607.7	1 045.7	223.8	75.5	746.4	246.3	500.1	375.3	124.7	6 371.2

Table 1-15. Rates of Return and Related Data for Domestic Nonfinancial Corporations

Year	Rates of return (percent)					Shares of net value added (percent)					Value of produced assets (billions of dollars)	Tax liability as a percent of produced assets	Q3 ratio
	Net operating surplus		Corporate profits		Net interest	Net operating surplus		Corporate profits		Net interest			
	Before tax	After tax	Before tax	After tax		Before tax	After tax	Before tax	After tax				
1960	9.6	5.7	8.7	4.7	0.7	18.4	10.9	16.6	9.1	1.3	487.5	3.9	0.50
1961	9.7	5.8	8.7	4.8	0.7	18.6	11.1	16.6	9.1	1.4	498.3	3.9	0.64
1962	11.1	7.1	9.9	5.9	0.9	19.9	12.7	17.8	10.6	1.5	512.9	4.0	0.61
1963	11.9	7.6	10.6	6.4	0.9	20.7	13.2	18.6	11.1	1.5	530.9	4.3	0.68
1964	12.7	8.3	11.4	7.1	0.9	21.3	14.0	19.1	11.9	1.6	554.8	4.3	0.80
1965	13.8	9.2	12.4	7.8	1.0	22.4	15.0	20.2	12.7	1.6	590.3	4.6	0.88
1966	13.7	9.1	12.2	7.6	1.1	22.0	14.6	19.6	12.2	1.8	640.6	4.6	0.70
1967	12.4	8.4	10.8	6.8	1.2	20.7	14.1	18.0	11.4	2.0	697.6	4.0	0.88
1968	12.2	7.8	10.6	6.1	1.3	20.2	12.9	17.4	10.1	2.1	758.6	4.4	0.99
1969	10.9	6.9	9.0	5.0	1.5	18.2	11.5	15.0	8.4	2.6	831.7	4.0	0.73
1970	8.9	5.9	6.7	3.7	1.8	15.8	10.5	11.9	6.6	3.2	910.1	3.0	0.64
1971	9.4	6.4	7.3	4.3	1.8	16.9	11.5	13.1	7.6	3.2	991.1	3.0	0.70
1972	9.8	6.7	7.7	4.6	1.7	17.2	11.7	13.5	8.0	3.0	1 076.5	3.1	0.81
1973	9.7	6.3	7.5	4.1	1.8	16.8	11.0	13.0	7.1	3.2	1 198.5	3.4	0.52
1974	7.7	4.7	5.4	2.4	1.9	14.8	9.0	10.5	4.7	3.7	1 426.6	3.0	0.19
1975	8.1	5.5	6.1	3.5	1.7	16.9	11.6	12.6	7.3	3.6	1 645.7	2.6	0.35
1976	8.6	5.6	6.8	3.8	1.4	17.3	11.3	13.6	7.6	2.9	1 801.0	3.0	0.41
1977	9.0	5.9	7.1	4.1	1.4	17.7	11.7	14.0	8.0	2.8	1 991.8	3.0	0.31
1978	8.8	5.8	6.9	3.9	1.5	17.2	11.3	13.5	7.6	2.9	2 243.8	3.0	0.29
1979	7.8	5.0	5.8	3.0	1.6	15.8	10.2	11.7	6.2	3.3	2 577.1	2.7	0.30
1980	6.7	4.4	4.5	2.2	1.8	14.4	9.5	9.7	4.8	4.0	2 961.1	2.3	0.36
1981	7.4	5.4	5.0	3.0	2.0	15.9	11.6	10.8	6.5	4.3	3 350.5	2.0	0.28
1982	6.6	5.2	4.2	2.9	2.1	14.9	11.9	9.5	6.5	4.9	3 619.9	1.4	0.30
1983	7.5	5.8	5.2	3.5	2.1	16.4	12.8	11.3	7.7	4.5	3 744.6	1.7	0.34
1984	8.8	6.9	6.3	4.4	2.2	17.9	13.9	12.8	8.9	4.4	3 911.5	1.9	0.30
1985	8.6	6.9	6.0	4.3	2.2	17.2	13.8	12.0	8.5	4.5	4 119.3	1.7	0.39
1986	8.1	6.3	5.2	3.4	2.2	16.2	12.6	10.4	6.8	4.5	4 267.9	1.8	0.47
1987	8.7	6.6	5.9	3.7	2.2	16.9	12.7	11.3	7.2	4.2	4 440.9	2.1	0.45
1988	9.4	7.2	6.5	4.3	2.3	17.8	13.6	12.3	8.1	4.4	4 695.5	2.2	0.48
1989	9.0	7.0	5.7	3.7	2.9	17.2	13.3	10.8	7.0	5.4	4 967.2	2.0	0.59
1990	8.5	6.7	5.3	3.4	2.8	16.4	12.8	10.1	6.5	5.4	5 225.4	1.9	0.56
1991	7.9	6.2	4.9	3.2	2.5	15.4	12.2	9.5	6.3	4.9	5 391.8	1.6	0.79
1992	7.7	6.0	5.3	3.5	2.0	14.8	11.5	10.0	6.8	3.9	5 508.9	1.7	0.93
1993	8.2	6.4	5.9	4.0	1.8	15.5	12.0	11.2	7.6	3.4	5 716.9	1.9	1.00
1994	9.1	6.9	6.9	4.7	1.7	16.7	12.6	12.7	8.6	3.1	6 015.6	2.2	0.92
1995	9.4	7.2	7.1	4.9	1.8	17.3	13.2	13.1	9.0	3.3	6 371.1	2.2	1.12
1996	10.0	7.8	7.8	5.5	1.7	18.3	14.2	14.2	10.1	3.1	6 712.3	2.3	1.21
1997	10.4	8.1	8.1	5.8	1.8	18.7	14.6	14.6	10.5	3.2	7 056.0	2.3	1.41
1998	9.7	7.6	7.3	5.1	2.0	17.2	13.4	12.9	9.1	3.5	7 419.0	2.2	1.53
1999	9.5	7.4	7.0	4.7	2.1	16.8	12.9	12.1	8.3	3.6	7 809.2	2.2	1.84
2000	8.6	6.7	5.8	3.8	2.4	15.2	11.6	10.1	6.5	4.1	8 295.2	2.1	1.35
2001	7.0	5.8	4.1	2.8	2.4	13.2	10.8	7.7	5.3	4.4	8 705.2	1.3	1.11
2002	7.3	6.2	4.8	3.7	1.9	13.8	11.7	9.1	7.0	3.5	8 950.8	1.1	0.74
2003	7.7	6.8	5.7	4.3	1.8	14.5	12.7	10.6	8.1	3.4	9 185.0	1.4	0.93
2004	9.1	7.4	6.8	5.1	1.7	16.7	13.4	12.3	9.2	3.1	9 682.7	1.7	1.04
2005	9.7	7.5	7.9	5.4	1.7	17.9	13.2	13.9	9.5	3.0	10 457.7	2.5	0.87
2006	10.5	...	...	...	...	19.4	...	...	...	...	11 256.7	...	0.86
2007	9.4	...	...	...	...	17.8	...	...	...	...	11 898.4	...	0.82
2008	8.1	...	...	...	...	16.4	...	...	...	...	12 717.1	...	0.40

Note: See notes and definition for explanation.
. . . = Not available.

NOTES AND DEFINITIONS, CHAPTER 1

TABLES 1-1 THROUGH 1-15 AND 19-1 THROUGH 19-11 NATIONAL INCOME AND PRODUCT

SOURCE: U.S. DEPARTMENT OF COMMERCE, BUREAU OF ECONOMIC ANALYSIS (BEA)

All data in these tables are from the national income and product accounts (NIPAs). The data are as published in the 2009 comprehensive NIPA revision, continued through the fourth quarter of 2009 in the estimates released on March 26, 2010.

The changes made in the 2009 revision are described in "Preview of the 2009 Comprehensive Revision of the NIPAs: Changes in Definitions and Presentations," *Survey of Current Business,* March 2009, available at <http://www.bea.gov>.

Definitions and notes on the data:
Basic concepts of total output and income (Tables 1-10 through 1-12)

The NIPAs depict the U.S. economy in several different dimensions. The basic concept, and the measure that is now most frequently cited, is gross domestic product (GDP), which is the market value of all goods and services produced by labor and property located in the United States.

In principle, GDP can be measured by summing the values created by each industry in the economy. However, it can more readily be measured by summing all the final demands for the economy's output. This final-demand approach also has the advantage of depicting the origins of demand for economic production, whether from consumers, businesses, or government.

Since production for the market necessarily generates incomes equal to its value, there is also an income total that corresponds to the production value total. This income can be measured and its distribution among labor, capital, and other income recipients can be depicted.

The structure and relationships of several of these major concepts are illustrated in Table 1-10. The definitions of these concepts are as follows:

Gross domestic product (GDP), the featured measure of the value of U.S. output, is the market value of the goods and services produced by labor and property located in the United States. Market values represent output valued at the prices paid by the final customer, and therefore include taxes on production and imports, such as sales taxes, customs duties, and taxes on property.

The term "gross" in gross domestic product and gross national product is used to indicate that capital consumption allowances (economic depreciation) have not been deducted.

GDP is primarily measured by summing the values of all of the final demands in the economy, net of the demands met by imports. It is the sum of personal consumption expenditures (PCE), gross private domestic investment (including change in private inventories and before deduction of charges for consumption of fixed capital), net exports of goods and services, and government consumption expenditures and gross investment. GDP measured in this way excludes duplication involving "intermediate" purchases of goods and services (goods and services purchased by industries and used in production), the value of which is already included in the value of the final products. Production of any intermediate goods unused in production in the current period is captured in the measurement of inventory change.

In concept, GDP is equal to the sum of the economic value added by (formerly referred to as "gross product originating in") all industries in the United States. This, in turn, also makes it the conceptual equivalent of *gross domestic income (GDI),* a new concept introduced in the 2003 revision. GDI is the sum of the incomes earned in each domestic industry, plus the taxes on production and imports and less the subsidies that account for the difference between output value and factor input value. This derivation is shown in Table 1-11. Since the incomes and taxes can be measured directly, they can be summed to a total that is equivalent to GDP in concept but differs due to imperfections in measurement. The difference between the two is known as the *statistical discrepancy.* It is defined as GDP minus GDI, and is shown in Table 1-11.

Gross national product (GNP) refers to all goods and services produced by labor and property supplied by U.S. residents—whether located in the United States or abroad—expressed at market prices. It is equal to GDP, plus *income receipts from the rest of the world,* less *income payments to the rest of the world. Domestic* production and income refer to the <u>location</u> of the factors of production, with only factors located in the United States included; *national* production and income refer to the <u>ownership</u> of the factors of production, with only factors owned by United States residents included.

Before the comprehensive NIPA revisions that were made in 1991, GNP was the commonly used measure of U.S. production. However, GDP is clearly preferable to GNP when used in conjunction with indicators such as employment, hours worked, and capital utilized—for example, in the calculation of labor and capital productivity—because it is confined to production taking place within the borders of the United States. It is also the measure used by almost all other countries, thus facilitating international comparisons such as those shown in Chapter 13.

The income-side aggregate corresponding to GNP is *gross national income (GNI),* shown as an addendum to Table 1-

10. It consists of gross domestic income plus income receipts from the rest of the world, less income payments to the rest of the world. It is used as the denominator for a national saving-income ratio, presented in Chapter 5. National income is the preferred measure for calculating and comparing saving, since it is the income aggregate from which that saving arises. As with GDP and gross domestic income, the statistical discrepancy indicates the difference between the product-side and income-side measurement of the same concept.

Net national product is the market value, net of depreciation, of goods and services attributable to the labor and property supplied by U.S. residents. It is equal to GNP minus the *consumption of fixed capital (CFC)*. CFC relates only to fixed capital located in the United States. (Investment in that capital is measured by private fixed investment and government gross investment.) As of the 2009 comprehensive revision, CFC represents only the normal using-up of capital in the process of production, and no longer includes extraordinary disaster losses such as those caused by Hurricane Katrina and the 9/11 attacks. These losses are still estimated and used to write down the estimates of the capital stock, but they no longer have negative effects on current income from production.

National income has been redefined and now includes all net incomes (net of the consumption of fixed capital) earned in production. It now includes not only "factor incomes"—net incomes received by labor and capital as a result of their participation in the production process, but also "nonfactor charges"—taxes on production and imports, business transfer payments, and the current surplus of government enterprises, less subsidies. This change has been made to conform with the international guidelines for national accounts, *System of National Accounts (SNA) 1993*. According to *SNA 1993*, these charges cannot be eliminated from the input and output prices.

Since national income now includes the nonfactor charges, it is conceptually equivalent to *net national product* and differs only by the amount of the statistical discrepancy.

The concept formerly known as "national income," which excludes the nonfactor charges, is still included in the accounts as an addendum item, now called "net national factor income." It is shown in Table 1-12 and used as the denominator in Figure 1-3. *Net national factor income* consists of compensation of employees, proprietors' income with inventory valuation and capital consumption adjustments (IVA and CCadj, respectively), rental income of persons with capital consumption adjustment, corporate profits with inventory valuation and capital consumption adjustments, and net interest.

By definition, national income and its components exclude all income from capital gains (increases in the value of owned assets). Such increases have no counterpart on the production side of the accounts. This exclusion is partly accomplished by means of the inventory valuation and capital consumption adjustments, which will be described in the definitions of the components of product and income.

Definitions and notes on the data: Imputation

The term *imputation* will appear from time to time in the following definitions of product and income components. Imputed values are values estimated by BEA statisticians for certain important product and income components that are not explicitly valued in the source data, usually because a market transaction in money terms is not involved. Imputed values appear on both the product and income side of the accounts; they add equal amounts to income and spending, so that no imputed saving is created.

One important example is the imputed rent on owner-occupied housing. The building of such housing is counted as investment, yet in the monetary accounts of the household sector, there is no income from that investment nor any rental paid for it. In the NIPAs, the rent that each such dwelling would earn if rented is estimated and added to both national and personal income (as part of rental income receipts) and to personal consumption expenditures (as part of expenditures on housing services).

Another important example is imputed interest. For example, an individual keeps a monetary balance in a bank or other financial institution. He or she receives either no interest or below-market interest, but receives the institution's services, such as clearing checks and otherwise facilitating payments, with little or no charge. Where is the product generated by the institution's workers and capital? In the NIPAs, the depositor is imputed a market-rate-based interest return on his or her balance, which is then imputed as a service charge received by the institution, and therefore included in the value of the institution's output.

Definitions and notes on the data: Components of product (Tables 1-1 through 1-5)

Personal consumption expenditures (PCE) is goods and services purchased by persons residing in the United States. PCE consists mainly of purchases of new goods and services by individuals from businesses. It includes purchases that are financed by insurance, such as government-provided and private medical insurance. In addition, PCE includes purchases of new goods and services by nonprofit institutions, net purchases of used goods ("net" here indicates purchases of used goods from business less sales of used goods to business) by individuals and nonprofit institutions, and purchases abroad of goods and services by U.S. residents traveling or working in foreign countries. PCE also includes purchases for certain goods and services provided by government agencies. (See the notes and definitions for Chapter 4 for additional information.) In the 2009 revision, new detail has been provided on the allocation of PCE between the household and nonprofit sectors.

Gross private domestic investment consists of gross private fixed investment and change in private inventories.

Private fixed investment consists of both nonresidential and residential fixed investment. The term "residential" refers to the construction and equipping of living quarters for permanent occupancy. Hotels and motels are included in *nonresidential fixed investment*, as described in this section.

Private fixed investment consists of purchases of fixed assets, which are commodities that will be used in a production process for more than one year, including replacements and additions to the capital stock. It is measured "gross," before a deduction for consumption of existing fixed capital. It covers all investment by private businesses and nonprofit institutions in the United States, regardless of whether the investment is owned by U.S. residents. The residential component includes investment in owner-occupied housing; the homeowner is treated equivalently to a business in these investment accounts. (However, when GDP by sector is calculated, owner-occupied housing is no longer included in the business sector. It is allocated to the households and institutions sector.) Private fixed investment does not include purchases of the same types of equipment and structures by government agencies, which are included in government gross investment, nor does it include investment by U.S. residents in other countries.

Nonresidential fixed investment is the total of nonresidential structures and nonresidential equipment and software.

Nonresidential structures consists of new construction, brokers' commissions on sales of structures, and net purchases of used structures by private business and by nonprofit institutions from government agencies (that is, purchases of used structures from government minus sales of used structures to government). New construction also includes hotels and motels and mining exploration, shafts, and wells.

Nonresidential equipment and software consists of private business purchases on capital account of new machinery, equipment, and vehicles; purchases and in-house production of software; dealers' margins on sales of used equipment; and net purchases of used equipment from government agencies, persons, and the rest of the world (that is, purchases of such equipment minus sales of such equipment). It does not include the estimated personal-use portion of equipment purchased for both business and personal use, which is allocated to PCE.

Residential private fixed investment consists of both residential structures and residential producers' durable equipment (including such equipment as appliances owned by landlords and rented to tenants). Investment in structures consists of new units, improvements to existing units, purchases of manufactured homes, brokers' commissions on the sale of residential property, and net purchases of used residential structures from government agencies (that is, purchases of such structures from government minus sales of such structures to government). As noted above, it includes investment in owner-occupied housing.

Change in private inventories is the change in the physical volume of inventories held by businesses, with that <u>change</u> being valued at the average price of the period. It differs from the change in the book value of inventories reported by most businesses; an *inventory valuation adjustment (IVA)* converts book value change using historical cost valuations to the change in physical volume, valued at average replacement cost.

Net exports of goods and services is *exports of goods and services* less *imports of goods and services*. It does not include income payments or receipts or transfer payments to and from the rest of the world.

Government consumption expenditures is the estimated value of the services produced by governments (federal, state, and local) for current consumption. Since these are generally not sold, there is no market valuation and they are priced at the cost of inputs. The input costs consist of the compensation of general government employees; the estimated consumption of general government fixed capital, including software (CFC, or economic depreciation); and the cost of goods and services purchased by government less the value of sales to other sectors. The value of investment in equipment and structures produced by government workers and capital is also subtracted, and is instead included in government investment. Government sales to other sectors consist primarily of receipts of tuition payments for higher education and receipts of charges for medical care.

This definition of government consumption expenditures differs in concept—but not in the amount contributed to GDP—from the treatment in existence before the 2003 revision of the NIPAs. In the current definition, goods and services purchased by government are considered to be intermediate output. In the previous definition, they were considered to be final sales. Since their value is added to the other components to yield total government consumption expenditures, the dollar total contributed to GDP is the same. The only practical difference is that the goods purchased disappear from the goods account and appear in the services account instead. In the industry sector accounts, the value added by government is also unchanged. It continues to be measured as the sum of compensation and CFC, or equivalently as gross government output less the value of goods and services purchased. The new definition increases U.S. conformity with *SNA 1993*.

Gross government investment consists of general government and government enterprise expenditures for fixed assets (structures and equipment and software). Government inventory investment is included in government consumption expenditures.

Definitions and notes on the data:
Real values, quantity and price indexes (Tables 1-2 through 1-7)

Real, or chained (2005) dollar, estimates are estimates from which the effect of price change has been removed. Prior to the 1996 comprehensive revision, constant-dollar measures were obtained by combining real output measures for different goods and services using the relative prices of a single year as weights for the entire time span of the series. In the recent environment of rapid technological change, which has caused the prices of computers and electronic components to decline dramatically relative to other prices, this method distorts the measurement of economic growth and causes excessive revisions of growth rates at each benchmark revision. The current, chained-dollar measure changes the relative price weights each year, as relative prices shift over time. As a result, historical growth rates do not get revised as a result of recent changes in relative prices.

Chained-dollar estimates, although expressed for continuity's sake as if they had occurred according to the prices of a single year (currently 2005), are usually not additive. This means that because of the changes in price weights each year, the chained (2005) dollar components in any given table for any year other than 2005 usually do not add to the chained (2005) dollar total. The amount of the difference for the major components of GDP is called the *residual* and is shown in Table 1-2. In time periods close to the base year, the residual is usually quite small; over longer periods, the differences become much larger. For this reason, BEA no longer publishes chained-dollar estimates prior to 1995, except for selected aggregate series. For the more detailed components of GDP, historical trends and fluctuations in real volumes are represented by *chain-type quantity indexes,* which are presented in Tables 1-4, 4-3, 5-4, 5-6, 6-6, 6-7, 6-11, 6-16, 7-2, 7-3, 15-2, 19-4, and 21-1.

Chain-weighting leads to complexity in estimating the contribution of economic sectors to an overall change in output; it becomes difficult, for someone without access to the complicated statistical methods that BEA uses, to find the correct answers to questions such as "How much is the rise in defense spending contributing to GDP growth?" Because of this, BEA is now calculating and publishing estimates of the arithmetic contribution of each major component to the total change in real GDP. *Business Statistics* reproduces these calculations in Tables 1-3 and 19-3. As will be explained later, these calculations are of limited analytical value because imports are treated as a negative contribution to GDP instead of being subtracted from the demand components that give rise to them. For further information, see J. Steven Landefeld, Brent R. Moulton, and Cindy M. Vojtech, "Chained-Dollar Indexes: Issues, Tips on Their Use, and Upcoming Changes," *Survey of Current Business* (November 2003); and J. Steven Landefeld and Robert P. Parker, "BEA's Chain Indexes, Time Series, and Measures of Long-Term Economic Growth," *Survey of Current Business* (May 1997).

GDP price indexes measure price changes between any two adjacent years (or quarters) for a fixed "market basket" of goods and services consisting of the average quantities purchased in those two years (or quarters). The annual measures are chained together to form an index with prices in 2005 set to equal 100. Using average quantities as weights and changing weights each period eliminates the substitu-

tion bias that arises in more conventional indexes, in which weights are taken from a single base period that usually takes place early in the period under measurement. Generally, using a single, early base period leads to an overstatement of price increase. (The CPI-U and the CPI-W are examples of such conventional indexes, technically known as "Laspeyres" indexes. See the "General Notes" at the beginning of this volume and the notes and definitions for Chapter 8 for further explanation.)

The chain-type formula guarantees that a GDP price index change will differ only trivially from the change in the implicit deflator (ratio of current-dollar to real value, expressed as a percent). Therefore, *Business Statistics* is no longer publishing a separate table of implicit deflators.

Definitions and notes on the data:
Aggregates of sales and purchases (Tables 1-4 through 1-6)

Final sales of domestic product is GDP minus change in private inventories. It is the sum of personal consumption expenditures, gross private domestic fixed investment, government consumption expenditures and gross investment, and net exports of goods and services.

Gross domestic purchases is the market value of goods and services purchased by U.S. residents, regardless of where those goods and services were produced. It is GDP minus net exports (that is, minus exports plus imports) of goods and services; equivalently, it is the sum of personal consumption expenditures, gross private domestic investment, and government consumption expenditures and gross investment. The price index for gross domestic purchases is therefore a measure of price change for goods and services purchased by (rather than produced by) U.S. residents.

Final sales to domestic purchasers is gross domestic purchases minus change in private inventories.

Definitions and notes on the data:
Per capita product and income estimates (Table 1-7)

In Table 1-7, annual and quarterly measures of product, income, and consumption spending are expressed in per capita terms—the aggregate dollar amount divided by the U.S. population. Population data from 1991 forward reflect the results of Census 2000.

National per capita totals, as shown in Table 1-7, are based on definitions of income and population that differ slightly from the sum of the states shown in Table 21-2. See the notes and definitions for Chapter 21 for further explanation.

Definitions and notes on the data:
Shares of aggregate supply and demand (Tables 1-8 and 1-9)

These tables, developed by the editor of *Business Statistics,* are not official NIPA tables. They are components of current-dollar GDP rearranged in order to highlight relationships that are not always apparent in the official presentation of the NIPAs.

Aggregate supply combines the two sources that, between them, supply the goods and services demanded by consumers, businesses, and governments in the U.S. economy—domestic production (GDP) and imports. In this table the user can observe the growing share of imports that satisfy demands in the U.S. marketplace.

Aggregate final demand is the sum of all final demands for goods and services in the U.S. market—consumption spending, fixed investment, exports, and government consumption and investment. It is different from *final sales* (Table 1-6) because imports are not subtracted; in this table, imports are considered a source of supply, not a negative element of demand. It is different from *domestic purchases* (Tables 1-4 through 1-6) because it includes exports, since they are a source of demand for U.S. output.

Table 1-9 provides alternative data on the question of the relative importance of consumption spending and other final demands to the U.S. economy. NIPA statistics on PCE as a percent of GDP are frequently cited, but there is a problem with this, since PCE includes the value of imports while GDP does not.

Definitions and notes on the data:
Components of income (Tables 1-11 and 1-12)

There are now two different presentations of aggregate income for the United States: *gross domestic income* (Table 1-11) and *national income* (Table 1-12). As noted above, domestic income refers to income generated from production within the United States, while national income refers to income received by residents of the United States. This means that some of the income components differ between the two tables. Domestic income payments include payments to the rest of the world from domestic industries. National income payments exclude payments to the rest of the world but include payments received by U.S. residents from the rest of the world. These differences are seen in employee compensation, interest, and corporate profits. Taxes on production and imports, taxes on corporate income, business transfer payments, subsidies, proprietors' income, rental income, and the current surplus of government enterprises are the same in both accounts.

A third income aggregate is *personal income.* The derivation of this well-known statistic from national income is shown in Table 1-10. See Chapter 4 and its notes and definitions for more information.

Compensation of employees is the income accruing to employees as remuneration for their work. It is the sum of wage and salary accruals and supplements to wages and salaries. In the domestic income account, it is called "compensation of employees, paid." It refers to all payments generated by domestic production, including those to workers residing in the "rest of the world." In the national and personal income accounts, it is a different amount labeled "compensation of employees, received"—that is, received by U.S. residents—including from the rest of the world.

Wage and salary accruals consists of the monetary remuneration of employees, including the compensation of corporate officers; corporate directors' fees paid to directors who are also employees of the corporation; commissions, tips, and bonuses; voluntary employee contributions to certain deferred compensation plans, such as 401(k) plans; and receipts-in-kind that represent income. As of the 2003 revision, it also includes judicial fees to jurors and witnesses, compensation of prison inmates, and marriage fees to justices of the peace, all of which were formerly included in "other labor income."

In concept, wage and salary accruals include the value of the exercise by employees of "nonqualified stock options," in which an employee is allowed to buy stock for less than its current market price. (Actual measurement of these values involves a number of problems, particularly in the short run. Such stock options are not included in the monthly wage data from the Bureau of Labor Statistics, which are the main source for current extrapolations of wages and salaries, and are not consistently reported in corporate financial statements. They are, however, generally included in the unemployment insurance wage data that are used to correct the preliminary wage and salary estimates.) Another form of stock option, the "incentive stock option," leads to a capital gain only and is thus not included in the definition of wages and salaries.

Wage and salary accruals include retroactive wage payments for the period in which they were earned, not for the period in which they were paid. In the NIPAs, wages accrued is the appropriate measure for both domestic and national income, since the intent is to measure income associated with production. Wages disbursed is the appropriate measure for personal income, since the latter concept focuses on what individuals receive. The difference, *wage accruals less disbursements,* is shown in Table 1-10. Substantial entries appear for this item in 2003 and 2004 because there were 53 Fridays instead of 52 Fridays in the latter year. As a result, some of the wages disbursed in 2004 were actually accrued in 2003. In 2005, 2006, and 2007, this item reflects unusually large exercises of stock options and financial industry bonuses, paid in the year after they were earned.

Supplements to wages and salaries consists of *employer contributions for employee pension and insurance funds* and *employer contributions for government social insurance.*

Employer contributions for employee pension and insurance funds consists of employer payments (including payments-in-kind) to private pension and profit-sharing plans, private group health and life insurance plans, privately administered workers' compensation plans, government employee retirement plans, and supplemental unemployment benefit plans. This includes the major part of the former category "other labor income." The remainder of "other labor income" has been reclassified as wages and salaries, as noted above.

Employer contributions for government social insurance consists of employer payments under the following federal, state, and local government programs: old-age, survivors, and disability insurance (Social Security); hospital insurance (Medicare); unemployment insurance; railroad retirement; pension benefit guaranty; veterans' life insurance; publicly administered workers' compensation; military medical insurance; and temporary disability insurance.

Taxes on production and imports is included in the gross domestic income account to make it comparable in concept to gross domestic product. It consists of federal excise taxes and customs duties and of state and local sales taxes, property taxes (including residential real estate taxes), motor vehicle license taxes, severance taxes, special assessments, and other taxes. It is equal to the former "indirect business taxes and nontax liabilities" less most of the nontax liabilities, which have now been reclassified as "business transfer payments."

Subsidies (payments by government to business other than purchases of goods and services) are now presented separately from the current surplus of government enterprises, which is presented as a component of net operating surplus. However, for years before 1959, subsidies continue to be presented as net of the current surplus of government enterprises, since detailed data to separate the series for this period are not available.

Net operating surplus is a new aggregate introduced in the 2003 NIPA revision—a grouping of the business income components of the gross domestic income account. It represents the net income accruing to business capital. It is equal to gross domestic income minus compensation of employees, taxes on production and imports less subsidies (that is, the taxes are taken out of income and the subsidies are put in), and consumption of fixed capital (CFC). Net operating surplus consists of the surplus for private enterprises and the current surplus of government enterprises. The net operating surplus of private enterprises comprises net interest and miscellaneous payments, business current transfer payments, proprietors' income, rental income of persons, and corporate profits.

Net interest and miscellaneous payments, domestic industries consists of interest paid by domestic private enterprises and of rents and royalties paid by private enterprises to government, less interest received by domestic private enterprises. Interest received does not include interest received by noninsured pension plans, which are recorded as being directly received by persons in personal income. Both interest categories include monetary and imputed interest. In the *national* account, interest paid to the rest of the world is subtracted from the interest paid by domestic industries and interest received from the rest of the world is added. Interest payments on mortgage and home improvement loans and on home equity loans are included as net interest in the private enterprises account.

It should be noted that net interest does not include interest paid by federal, state, or local governments. In fact, government interest does not enter into the national and domestic

income accounts, though it does appear as a component of personal income. The NIPAs draw a distinction between interest paid by government and that paid by business.

The reasoning behind this distinction is that interest paid by business is one of the income counterparts of the production side of the account. The value of business production (as measured by its output of goods and services) includes the value added by business capital, and interest paid by business to its lenders is part of the total return to business capital.

However, there is no product flow in the accounts that is a counterpart to the payment of interest by government. The output of government does not have a market value. For purposes of GDP measurement, BEA estimates the government contribution to GDP as the sum of government's compensation of employees, purchases of goods and services, and consumption of government fixed capital. (See above, and also the notes and definitions to Chapter 6.) This implies an estimate (described as "conservative" by BEA) that the net return to government capital is zero—that is, that the gross return is just sufficient to pay down the depreciation. Consequently, this assumption generates no income that might correspond to the government's interest payment.

Supporting the distinction between business and government interest payments, it may be noted that most federal government debt was not incurred to finance investment, but rather to finance wars, avoid tax increases and spending cuts during recessions, or stimulate the economy. Some of the largest and most productive government investments—investments for highways—are typically financed by taxes on a pay-as-you-go basis and not by borrowing.

Business current transfer payments, net consists of payments to persons, government, and the rest of the world by private business for which no current services are performed. Net insurance settlements—actual insured losses (or claims payable) less a normal level of losses—are treated as transfer payments. Payments to government consist of federal deposit insurance premiums, fines, regulatory and inspection fees, tobacco settlements, and other miscellaneous payments previously classified as "nontaxes." Taxes paid by domestic corporations to foreign governments, formerly classified as transfer payments, are now counted as taxes on corporate income.

In the NIPAs, capital income other than interest—corporate profits, proprietors' income, and rental income—is converted from the basis usually shown in the books of business and reported to the Internal Revenue Service to a basis that more closely represents income from current production. In the business accounts that provide the source data, depreciation of structures and equipment typically reflects a historical cost basis and a possibly arbitrary service life allowed by law to be used for tax purposes. BEA adjusts these values to reflect the average actual life of the capital goods and the cost of replacing them in the current period's prices. This conversion is done for all three forms of capital income. In addition, corporate and proprietors' incomes also require an adjustment for inventory valuation to exclude any profits or losses that might appear in the books, should the cost of inventory acquisition not be valued in the current period's prices. These two adjustments are called the *capital consumption adjustment (CCAdj)* and the *inventory valuation adjustment (IVA)*. They are described in more detail below.

Proprietors' income with inventory valuation and capital consumption adjustments is the current-production income (including income-in-kind) of sole proprietorships and partnerships and of tax-exempt cooperatives. The imputed net rental income of owner-occupants of farm dwellings is included, but the imputed net rental income of owner-occupants of nonfarm dwellings is included in rental income of persons. Fees paid to outside directors of corporations are included. Proprietors' income excludes dividends and monetary interest received by nonfinancial business and rental incomes received by persons not primarily engaged in the real estate business; these incomes are included in dividends, net interest, and rental income of persons, respectively.

Rental income of persons with capital consumption adjustment is the net current-production income of persons from the rental of real property (except for the income of persons primarily engaged in the real estate business), the imputed net rental income of owner-occupants of nonfarm dwellings, and the royalties received by persons from patents, copyrights, and rights to natural resources. Consistent with the classification of investment in owner-occupied housing as business investment, the homeowner is considered to be paying himself or herself the rental value of the house (classified as PCE for services) and receiving as net income the amount of the rental that remains after paying interest and other costs.

Corporate profits with inventory valuation and capital consumption adjustments (often referred to as "economic profits") is the current-production income, net of economic depreciation, of organizations treated as corporations in the NIPAs. These organizations consist of all entities required to file federal corporate tax returns, including mutual financial institutions and cooperatives subject to federal income tax; private noninsured pension funds; nonprofit institutions that primarily serve business; Federal Reserve Banks, which accrue income stemming from the conduct of monetary policy; and federally sponsored credit agencies. This income is measured as receipts less expenses as defined in federal tax law, except for the following differences: receipts exclude capital gains and dividends received, expenses exclude depletion and capital losses and losses resulting from bad debts, inventory withdrawals are valued at replacement cost, and depreciation is on a consistent accounting basis and is valued at replacement cost.

Since *national* income is defined as the income of U.S. residents, its profits component includes income earned abroad by U.S. corporations and excludes income earned by the rest of the world within the United States.

Taxes on corporate income consists of taxes on corporate income paid to government and to the rest of the world.

Taxes on corporate income paid to government is the sum of federal, state, and local income taxes on all income subject to taxes. This income includes capital gains and other income excluded from profits before tax. These taxes are measured on an accrual basis, net of applicable tax credits.

Taxes on corporate income paid to the rest of the world consists of nonresident taxes, which are those paid by domestic corporations to foreign governments. These taxes were formerly classified as "business transfer payments to the rest of the world."

Profits after tax is total corporate profits with IVA and CCAdj less taxes on corporate income. It consists of dividends and undistributed corporate profits.

Dividends is payments in cash or other assets, excluding those made using corporations' own stock, that are made by corporations to stockholders. In the domestic account, these are payments by domestic industries to stockholders in the United States and abroad; in the national account, these are dividends received by U.S. residents from domestic and foreign industries. The payments are measured net of dividends received by U.S. corporations. Dividends paid to state and local government social insurance funds and general government are included.

Undistributed profits is corporate profits after tax with IVA and CCAdj less dividends.

The *inventory valuation adjustment (IVA)* is the difference between the cost of inventory withdrawals valued at replacement cost and the cost as valued in the source data used to determine profits before tax, which in many cases charge inventories at acquisition cost. It is calculated separately for corporate profits and for nonfarm proprietors' income. Its behavior is determined by price changes, especially for materials. When prices are rising, which has been typical of much of the postwar period, the business-reported value of inventory change will include a capital gains component, which needs to be removed from reported inventory change on the product side in order to correctly measure the change in the volume of inventories, and from reported profits on the income side of the accounts in order to remove the capital gains element. At such times, the IVA will be a negative figure, which is added to reported profits to yield economic profits. Occasionally, falling prices—especially for petroleum and products—will result in a positive IVA. No adjustment is needed for farm proprietors' income, as farm inventories are measured on a current-market-cost basis.

Consumption of fixed capital (CFC) is a charge for the using-up of private and government fixed capital located in the United States. It is not based on the depreciation schedules allowed in tax law, but instead on studies of prices of used equipment and structures in resale markets.

For general government and for nonprofit institutions that primarily serve individuals, CFC on their capital assets is recorded in government consumption expenditures and in personal consumption expenditures, respectively. It is considered to be the value of the current services of the fixed capital assets owned and used by these entities.

Private capital consumption allowances consists of tax-return-based depreciation charges for corporations and nonfarm proprietorships and of historical cost depreciation (calculated by BEA using a geometric pattern of price declines) for farm proprietorships, rental income of persons, and nonprofit institutions.

The *private capital consumption adjustment (CCAdj)* is the difference between private capital consumption allowances and private consumption of fixed capital. The CCAdj has two parts:

The first component of CCAdj converts tax-return-based depreciation to consistent historical cost accounting based on actual service lives of capital. In the postwar period, this has usually been a large positive number, that is, a net addition to profits and subtraction from reported depreciation. This is the case because U.S. tax law typically allows depreciation periods shorter than actual service lives. Tax depreciation was accelerated even further for 2001 through 2004. This component is a reallocation of gross business saving from depreciation to profits; gross saving is unchanged, with exactly offsetting changes in capital consumption and net saving.

The second component is analogous to the IVA: it converts reported business capital consumption allowances from the historical cost basis to a replacement cost basis. It is determined by the price behavior of capital goods. These prices have had an upward drift in the postwar period, which has been much more stable than the changes in materials prices. Hence, this component is consistently negative (serving to reduce economic profits relative to the reported data) but less volatile than the IVA.

In 1982 through 2004, positive values for the first component outweighed negative values for the second, resulting in a net positive CCAdj, an addition to profits. However, when the accelerated depreciation expired in 2005, there was a sharp decline in the consistent-accounting adjustment and it was outweighed by the price adjustment. This led to negative CCAdjs in 2005 through 2007, reducing profits from the reported numbers.

Definitions and notes on the data:
Gross value added of domestic corporate business (Tables 1-13 and 1-14)

Gross value added is the term now used for what was formerly called "gross domestic product originating." It represents the share of the GDP that is produced in the specified sector or industry. Tables 1-13 and 1-14 show the current-dollar value of gross value added for all domestic corporate business and its financial and nonfinancial components. For the total and for nonfinancial corporations, consumption of fixed capital and net value added are shown, as is the allocation of net value added among employee compensation, taxes and transfer payments, and capital income. Constant-dollar values are also shown for nonfinancial corporations.

The data for nonfinancial corporations are often considered to be somewhat sturdier than data for the other sectors of the economy, since they exclude sectors whose outputs are difficult to evaluate—households, institutions, general government, and financial business—as well as excluding all noncorporate business, in which the separate contributions of labor and capital are not readily measured.

Definitions and notes on the data:
Rates of return and related data for domestic nonfinancial corporations (Table 1-15)

Table 1-15 shows various measures of the return to capital in nonfinancial corporate business. The measure of capital is the *value of produced assets,* which is the current-cost value of the net stock of equipment and software and structures and the replacement-cost value of inventories. The basic measure of the total return to capital is the *net operating surplus,* which is the sum of corporate profits, net interest paid, and net business transfer payments; this is shown in Table 1-14. As in that table, corporate profits are adjusted to an economic profits basis by including the inventory valuation and capital consumption adjustments.

Rates of return are total net operating surplus and its major components, before and after corporate taxes, as a percent of the value of produced assets. *Tax liability* is also shown as a percent of produced assets.

Shares of net value added are total net operating surplus and its major components, before and after corporate taxes, as a percent of net value added in nonfinancial domestic corporate business. Net value added, shown in Table 1-14, is the value of the industry's output after deducting the consumption of fixed capital, and is the sum of compensation of employees, the net operating surplus, and taxes on production and imports less subsidies.

A *Q ratio* (often known as "Tobin's Q" for the economist James Tobin, who originally proposed it) is the ratio of the valuation of assets in financial markets to the current-cost value of produced assets. A value of Q above 1 indicates that newly produced physical assets may be purchased more cheaply than the ownership claims to existing assets. Table 1-15 shows the BEA calculation of a ratio termed *Q3*. The numerator is the sum of the market value of outstanding equity and an estimate of the market value of outstanding corporate bonds, minus net liquid assets and land. The denominator is the value of the net stock of produced assets.

The rate of return data do not follow the general NIPA publication and revision schedule. They were presented and described in "Note on the Returns for Domestic Nonfinancial Corporations in 1960–2005," *Survey of Current Business* (May 2006), pp. 6–10. The rate of return for the net operating surplus before tax, the share of net value added, the value of produced assets, and the Q3 ratio were revised and updated in "Returns for Domestic Nonfinancial Business," *Survey of Current Business* (May 2009), pp. 17-21.

Data availability and revisions

Annual data are available beginning with 1929. Quarterly data begin with 1946 for current-dollar values and 1947 for quantity and price measures such as real GDP and the GDP price index. Not all data are available for all time periods.

New data are normally released toward the end of each month. The "advance" estimate of GDP for each calendar quarter is released at the end of the month after the quarter's end. The "second" estimate, including more complete product data and the first estimates of corporate profits, is released at the end of the second month after the quarter's end, and a "third" estimate including still more complete data at the end of the third month. Wage and salary and related income-side components may be revised for previous quarters as well.

At the end of each July, there is an "annual" revision, incorporating more complete data and other improvements, affecting at least the previous 3 years. Every five years, there is a "comprehensive" revision, such as the 2009 revision incorporated in this volume, corresponding with updated statistics from the quinquennial benchmark input-output accounts and incorporating a revision of the base year for constant-price and index numbers.

The most recent data are published each month in the *Survey of Current Business*. Current and historical data may be obtained from the BEA Web site at <http://www.bea.gov> and the STAT-USA subscription Web site at <http://www.stat-usa.gov>.

References

The latest revision is described in "Improved Estimates of the National Income and Product Accounts: Results of the 2009 Comprehensive Revision", *Survey of Current Business,* September 2009. Previous annual and comprehensive revisions are discussed in articles in earlier August issues.

An "Updated Summary of NIPA Methodologies" is published in the November 2009 *Survey of Current Business.* "Measuring the Economy: A Primer on GDP and the National Income and Product Accounts" (September 2007), prepared by the Bureau of Economic Analysis (BEA), contains further references to NIPA concepts, framework, history, estimating methods and source data, and reliability. All of these articles are is available on the BEA Web site at <http://www.bea.gov>.

The treatment of employee stock options is discussed in Carol Moylan, "Treatment of Employee Stock Options in the U.S. National Economic Accounts," available on the BEA Web site at <http://www.bea.gov>.

CHAPTER 2: INDUSTRIAL PRODUCTION AND CAPACITY UTILIZATION

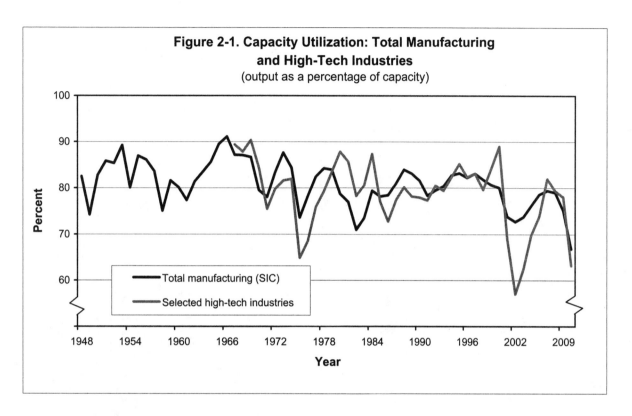

Figure 2-1. Capacity Utilization: Total Manufacturing and High-Tech Industries
(output as a percentage of capacity)

- Manufacturing capacity utilization is a key statistic for the U.S. economy, despite being limited to a sector that by some measures is diminishing in importance. (The Federal Reserve also provides measures of capacity utilization for "total industry"—manufacturing, mining, and utilities. However, mining and utilities are less significant in the context of business cycle analysis, and much of the variation in capacity use by utilities is a result of transitory weather variations, not economic factors.) Manufacturing utilization is an important indicator of inflationary pressure and also measures an important element in the demand for new capital goods. (Tables 2-3 and 20-1)

- Industrial production peaked at 112.3 percent of the 2002 average in January 2008 and fell to a low of 95.8 percent in June 2009—a decline of nearly 15 percent. As of April 2010, the index was up about 7 percent from its low point. (Table 2-1)

- Manufacturing capacity utilization reached a high point of 79.8 percent in January 2006—lower than in previous periods of high activity—and then drifted down during 2006 and 2007, as capacity growth exceeded the increase in output. Then output plunged in 2008–2009, and utilization collapsed to 65.1 percent in June 2009, by far the lowest in the entire postwar period. (Tables 2-3 and 20-1)

- Capacity utilization in the high-tech industries (computers and office equipment, communications equipment, and semiconductors and related electronic components) has been more volatile than in the rest of industry, as seen in Figure 2-1. (Table 2-3)

Table 2-1. Industrial Production Indexes by Market Groups

(Seasonally adjusted, 2002 = 100.)

Year and month	Total industrial production	Final products and nonindustrial supplies							Nondurable consumer goods
		Total	Consumer goods						
			Total	Durable consumer goods					Total
				Total	Automotive products	Home electronics	Appliances, furniture, and carpeting	Miscellaneous durable goods	
1967	39.2	38.5	45.1	31.0	29.8	1.5	44.2	47.3	52.1
1968	41.4	40.4	47.7	34.6	35.5	1.6	47.5	50.4	54.1
1969	43.3	41.9	49.5	36.1	35.8	1.6	50.1	54.5	55.9
1970	41.9	40.6	49.0	33.3	30.1	1.5	49.6	52.7	56.9
1971	42.5	41.2	51.8	37.7	38.4	1.6	52.4	55.5	58.5
1972	46.6	45.0	56.0	42.2	41.4	1.9	61.5	62.3	62.2
1973	50.4	48.4	58.5	45.4	45.0	2.2	66.4	65.1	64.1
1974	50.2	48.2	56.8	41.3	38.9	2.0	60.4	62.9	64.2
1975	45.8	44.9	54.5	37.5	37.5	1.7	51.7	55.8	63.1
1976	49.4	48.1	59.0	42.4	42.7	2.0	58.4	62.1	67.0
1977	53.1	52.0	62.7	47.6	48.3	2.4	65.6	68.8	69.4
1978	56.0	55.1	64.6	48.8	48.0	2.7	69.1	71.0	71.9
1979	57.7	56.9	63.7	47.0	43.2	2.7	69.3	71.6	71.5
1980	56.3	56.2	61.3	40.8	33.3	2.8	64.5	65.6	71.6
1981	57.0	57.3	61.7	41.4	34.3	2.9	63.7	66.6	71.9
1982	54.1	55.9	61.5	39.0	33.3	2.6	57.5	63.0	73.1
1983	55.6	57.4	63.8	43.4	38.7	3.7	63.5	64.8	73.9
1984	60.5	62.2	66.7	48.5	43.2	4.5	70.8	71.7	75.4
1985	61.3	63.8	67.3	48.5	43.2	4.7	70.2	71.7	76.4
1986	61.9	65.1	69.7	51.7	46.4	6.1	73.7	74.1	78.2
1987	65.1	68.3	72.6	54.7	49.5	6.0	77.7	78.7	81.0
1988	68.4	71.7	75.4	57.6	52.1	8.0	78.9	82.2	83.6
1989	69.1	72.4	75.7	59.0	54.2	8.4	79.7	82.7	83.4
1990	69.7	73.3	76.0	57.3	50.8	9.7	77.7	81.9	84.8
1991	68.7	72.2	75.9	54.8	47.4	11.6	72.4	79.0	86.0
1992	70.6	74.0	78.2	60.1	55.5	12.6	76.5	81.6	86.6
1993	72.9	76.3	80.7	65.2	61.3	16.0	80.9	85.2	87.8
1994	76.8	79.7	84.3	71.7	68.7	20.7	86.6	89.9	90.0
1995	80.4	82.9	86.9	75.1	70.8	30.9	86.2	92.5	92.2
1996	84.0	86.1	88.6	78.0	73.0	37.6	87.2	95.6	93.4
1997	90.1	91.8	91.8	83.4	78.5	51.8	91.0	97.8	95.6
1998	95.4	97.1	95.2	89.6	83.7	70.4	97.1	101.2	97.6
1999	99.5	100.0	97.1	96.0	91.7	87.8	100.4	103.5	97.6
2000	103.7	103.5	99.1	99.0	93.7	100.1	103.2	106.3	99.2
2001	100.1	100.8	98.1	94.7	90.8	100.1	98.6	98.6	99.4
2002	100.0	100.0	100.0	100.0	100.0	100.0	100.0	100.0	100.0
2003	101.3	101.2	101.4	103.4	105.6	109.8	99.9	100.1	100.6
2004	103.8	103.4	102.7	104.9	105.2	121.9	103.1	102.2	101.8
2005	107.2	107.4	105.4	105.4	103.0	131.8	105.2	105.1	105.3
2006	109.7	109.8	105.8	104.3	99.5	151.1	101.8	106.7	106.2
2007	111.3	111.1	106.8	104.7	101.5	161.1	96.7	106.5	107.4
2008	108.8	108.2	104.0	94.3	87.7	182.5	84.0	99.9	106.9
2009	98.2	98.8	98.6	78.4	71.2	161.2	68.7	85.3	104.7
2008									
January	112.3	111.7	106.9	102.7	99.4	179.5	91.1	104.5	108.2
February	112.0	111.3	106.7	101.6	98.6	181.9	89.4	103.0	108.2
March	111.6	110.7	105.6	98.7	92.8	184.2	89.1	102.8	107.6
April	111.0	109.9	105.0	96.0	87.6	187.5	88.7	102.3	107.7
May	110.7	109.6	104.7	96.0	87.9	188.8	87.7	102.1	107.3
June	110.4	109.5	104.8	97.1	90.9	185.0	86.9	101.8	107.1
July	110.4	109.2	104.5	97.8	92.4	186.6	86.4	101.6	106.6
August	109.2	107.8	102.7	92.2	83.1	184.2	83.1	100.4	105.9
September	104.8	105.3	101.4	91.5	84.2	182.2	80.1	98.5	104.3
October	106.2	105.7	103.0	89.5	81.5	179.9	78.7	97.1	107.0
November	104.8	104.8	102.0	86.4	79.0	176.7	74.3	94.2	106.7
December	102.4	103.5	100.6	82.6	74.5	174.1	72.3	90.4	106.0
2009									
January	100.1	101.0	98.6	74.6	58.7	176.3	72.2	89.4	105.9
February	99.3	100.0	98.7	76.1	64.2	174.3	70.9	86.6	105.5
March	97.7	98.8	98.3	76.1	66.2	170.1	69.4	84.5	105.0
April	97.2	98.1	97.9	76.2	66.4	165.1	70.2	84.6	104.4
May	96.2	97.0	96.9	74.1	63.5	159.6	69.3	83.4	103.8
June	95.8	96.6	96.3	72.7	61.3	156.2	67.2	83.8	103.5
July	96.9	97.5	97.3	78.8	72.6	153.0	68.1	85.4	102.8
August	98.1	98.4	98.5	80.4	76.9	151.0	66.7	85.0	103.8
September	98.7	98.9	99.4	83.0	81.7	153.5	67.8	84.9	104.3
October	98.9	99.4	100.3	82.1	79.7	156.9	67.8	84.8	105.7
November	99.6	99.6	100.3	83.6	82.0	158.9	68.7	85.5	105.2
December	100.3	100.3	100.9	83.0	81.3	159.0	66.6	85.7	106.2

Table 2-1. Industrial Production Indexes by Market Groups—*Continued*

(Seasonally adjusted, 2002 = 100.)

Year and month	Final products and nonindustrial supplies—*Continued*												
	Consumer goods—*Continued*						Business equipment				Defense and space equipment	Construction supplies	Business supplies
	Nondurable consumer goods—*Continued*					Consumer energy products	Total	Transit	Information processing	Industrial and other			
	Nondurable non-energy consumer goods												
	Total	Foods and tobacco	Clothing	Chemical products	Paper products								
1967	53.7	57.8	163.8	23.9	53.7	43.2	20.4	77.2	1.5	53.9	88.4	49.5	33.8
1968	55.6	59.3	169.8	26.1	53.2	46.2	21.3	86.1	1.6	53.8	88.6	52.1	35.9
1969	57.2	60.9	172.5	27.4	55.0	49.4	22.7	84.9	1.8	57.3	84.3	54.3	38.2
1970	57.7	61.7	167.3	29.8	53.1	52.3	21.9	74.5	1.9	55.3	71.4	52.4	38.4
1971	59.2	63.6	166.5	31.5	54.2	54.8	20.8	72.0	1.8	52.9	64.2	54.1	39.5
1972	63.1	67.1	181.8	34.4	54.6	57.8	23.6	78.5	2.1	60.2	62.4	61.4	43.5
1973	65.2	68.9	185.6	37.0	56.5	58.9	27.4	93.8	2.4	68.5	68.4	66.6	46.2
1974	64.9	69.3	173.4	39.0	55.6	60.4	29.0	91.6	3.0	71.4	70.6	65.0	46.1
1975	63.2	68.1	168.2	37.6	52.4	61.8	25.9	80.5	2.8	62.5	71.2	55.1	42.5
1976	67.3	72.5	177.6	40.9	54.5	65.0	27.6	83.1	3.4	65.1	69.1	59.3	45.3
1977	69.7	73.9	186.7	42.5	59.6	67.5	31.9	98.7	4.4	70.9	61.9	64.6	49.1
1978	72.4	76.7	191.4	45.1	62.6	68.8	36.0	114.6	5.6	75.9	63.0	68.3	51.7
1979	71.5	76.2	180.4	45.2	63.3	70.5	40.5	125.7	7.0	80.6	67.5	70.0	53.5
1980	72.3	77.4	183.7	45.1	64.0	68.0	41.5	118.1	8.8	78.0	80.2	64.8	52.3
1981	72.8	77.7	183.5	45.7	65.7	67.5	42.8	110.1	10.5	77.8	86.9	63.7	53.5
1982	74.2	80.2	183.0	45.8	67.3	68.0	39.1	90.6	11.9	67.3	103.9	57.8	52.9
1983	75.2	80.4	188.2	46.3	70.2	68.5	39.3	89.1	13.7	62.3	96.2	61.9	55.4
1984	76.5	81.4	180.5	47.4	73.8	70.6	45.2	91.7	16.9	71.1	111.4	67.3	60.2
1985	77.7	83.8	180.3	47.8	77.6	70.6	46.9	94.7	18.2	72.0	125.7	69.0	61.8
1986	79.6	85.2	188.4	51.5	78.6	72.0	46.1	86.7	18.3	71.6	142.4	71.3	63.8
1987	82.4	87.1	189.9	55.5	83.2	74.6	49.3	88.4	21.0	74.2	145.4	75.9	67.6
1988	84.7	89.6	186.9	58.8	85.4	78.5	54.4	97.7	23.6	80.6	146.9	77.7	70.1
1989	84.3	89.0	178.2	60.0	85.7	79.0	56.3	102.0	24.4	83.2	147.1	77.4	71.1
1990	86.2	91.5	174.5	62.2	87.3	78.5	58.4	110.3	26.4	82.7	142.0	76.8	72.8
1991	87.1	91.9	173.9	64.4	87.8	80.9	57.4	115.5	26.4	78.3	131.5	72.6	71.8
1992	88.1	93.2	177.5	64.2	88.9	79.8	59.6	111.1	29.8	79.7	122.0	75.7	73.5
1993	88.8	92.4	180.8	65.9	91.0	83.3	62.3	102.5	32.4	85.0	115.3	79.0	75.8
1994	91.2	96.2	184.0	67.3	90.0	84.4	66.0	95.2	36.3	90.8	108.3	84.7	78.8
1995	93.4	98.7	183.1	70.1	90.6	86.6	71.7	91.7	43.3	96.5	105.2	86.7	82.1
1996	94.0	98.3	178.1	73.5	90.2	90.4	78.5	95.2	52.7	99.8	102.0	90.5	85.2
1997	96.8	99.8	177.3	77.7	98.2	89.8	90.3	114.0	66.5	105.9	100.7	95.0	91.3
1998	99.3	102.3	166.8	81.6	102.8	89.8	100.5	136.6	78.8	109.2	105.1	100.1	96.5
1999	98.7	100.4	160.8	82.9	104.9	92.9	106.4	135.7	95.3	106.7	102.2	102.7	100.6
2000	100.1	101.9	153.7	86.0	105.6	95.1	114.7	117.7	116.5	112.9	91.3	105.0	105.2
2001	100.1	101.8	132.4	90.8	103.0	96.2	108.0	112.1	114.9	102.1	100.0	100.1	101.0
2002	100.0	100.0	100.0	100.0	100.0	100.0	100.0	100.0	100.0	100.0	100.0	100.0	100.0
2003	100.6	101.3	94.4	101.9	96.2	100.5	100.0	91.9	105.0	99.6	106.7	99.7	101.7
2004	101.5	102.9	78.5	104.4	96.7	102.9	105.3	97.5	114.9	102.2	104.7	102.0	103.8
2005	104.8	106.3	74.1	109.8	95.8	107.1	112.6	107.4	123.8	107.8	115.8	106.6	107.3
2006	106.4	106.7	68.6	115.6	95.6	105.8	123.2	124.7	141.3	112.6	113.4	109.0	108.5
2007	107.2	109.0	68.8	113.7	95.3	108.4	126.4	121.7	149.4	115.5	117.6	106.9	109.9
2008	106.0	108.6	66.1	111.3	93.0	109.7	125.0	108.2	164.2	111.7	120.6	100.1	106.7
2009	103.0	106.6	57.9	108.8	85.0	109.3	109.6	96.1	152.0	93.6	121.2	82.3	95.8
2008													
January	106.9	108.8	68.7	113.3	94.7	111.9	130.2	125.2	159.8	116.3	122.3	105.0	110.2
February	106.7	108.9	67.8	112.6	94.7	112.2	129.8	123.3	162.2	115.2	120.5	104.0	109.9
March	107.0	109.9	67.2	111.5	95.2	109.6	130.8	122.4	165.2	116.0	120.7	103.3	109.4
April	106.4	109.3	66.7	111.3	93.8	111.4	128.4	118.1	167.2	112.3	120.8	102.1	109.1
May	106.6	109.6	65.2	111.4	93.9	109.4	128.4	117.9	167.5	112.3	120.2	102.2	108.3
June	106.3	108.9	66.3	111.4	94.4	109.5	128.2	119.9	166.5	111.7	121.9	101.7	107.6
July	105.8	108.1	66.6	111.8	92.9	108.8	127.4	119.8	163.7	111.5	120.2	102.4	107.3
August	105.9	108.2	67.7	111.3	93.1	106.3	126.2	113.0	161.7	112.4	120.8	101.2	106.6
September	105.8	108.4	66.7	111.5	91.9	101.0	117.7	74.9	160.1	110.7	118.9	99.1	104.3
October	105.9	109.0	65.4	111.3	90.5	110.5	114.8	64.8	159.7	109.1	120.4	97.8	104.3
November	105.2	108.4	62.9	110.3	90.6	111.4	117.6	86.0	158.1	107.8	120.0	93.6	102.8
December	102.9	105.7	62.0	107.8	90.0	114.9	120.8	113.4	157.1	105.0	119.9	89.1	100.1
2009													
January	102.8	105.6	60.2	108.5	88.2	114.8	115.7	96.9	155.6	102.3	120.5	85.8	98.9
February	103.4	106.6	58.8	109.0	88.9	111.2	113.6	98.4	151.8	99.6	118.4	84.6	97.3
March	103.2	106.6	58.8	109.9	84.5	110.2	110.6	96.6	150.9	95.6	119.2	82.7	95.6
April	102.3	105.6	58.9	108.6	84.2	110.5	108.5	92.7	150.8	93.4	119.0	82.0	95.5
May	102.4	106.9	58.1	107.1	83.2	107.5	106.2	89.8	149.8	90.8	119.7	82.1	94.5
June	102.1	105.8	54.7	108.9	83.0	107.1	105.8	90.2	149.4	90.1	119.8	82.1	94.6
July	101.4	104.7	56.7	108.2	82.6	106.4	107.3	95.9	150.9	90.3	122.0	82.5	94.7
August	103.0	107.1	57.8	108.2	83.9	105.5	108.8	97.6	151.6	92.0	123.1	82.9	94.9
September	103.2	107.2	58.1	108.4	85.1	106.6	108.8	100.4	151.3	91.2	124.8	81.7	95.1
October	103.6	107.9	56.8	108.8	84.5	111.6	109.6	99.8	151.6	92.7	123.6	80.2	95.3
November	104.2	107.8	57.5	110.2	85.9	107.5	109.3	97.6	154.3	91.7	122.6	81.4	95.5
December	103.9	107.6	58.7	109.6	85.4	113.1	110.6	97.0	155.8	93.5	121.4	79.6	97.3

Table 2-1. Industrial Production Indexes by Market Groups—*Continued*

(Seasonally adjusted, 2002 = 100.)

Year and month		Materials										Energy materials
	Total	Non-energy materials										
		Total	Durable				Nondurable					
			Total	Consumer parts	Equipment parts	Other	Total	Textile	Paper	Chemical		
1967	39.1	32.2	25.7	47.6	7.7	58.5	48.2	79.5	49.8	33.7		68.8
1968	41.7	34.6	27.3	53.6	7.8	61.5	53.0	87.8	52.1	39.2		72.0
1969	44.1	36.7	28.7	54.0	8.4	65.5	57.3	90.1	56.5	43.6		75.6
1970	42.6	34.6	26.1	45.3	7.7	61.2	57.7	86.8	56.1	44.6		79.4
1971	43.2	35.2	26.1	50.1	7.7	58.8	60.1	91.0	58.5	47.2		80.1
1972	47.6	39.5	29.6	55.8	8.8	66.6	66.3	95.8	62.5	55.0		83.1
1973	51.9	43.8	33.8	64.8	10.4	73.8	69.6	93.1	67.4	60.6		85.2
1974	51.8	43.7	33.4	57.3	11.0	73.8	70.5	87.0	70.8	62.3		84.8
1975	46.1	37.5	28.0	46.2	9.5	61.7	63.2	85.2	61.5	52.2		84.0
1976	50.1	41.8	31.2	59.1	10.2	66.3	70.0	95.0	67.6	59.8		85.9
1977	53.6	45.2	34.0	64.7	11.5	70.2	75.1	101.3	70.7	66.5		88.6
1978	56.3	48.2	36.7	68.4	12.9	74.8	77.9	91.8	74.2	70.6		89.7
1979	57.8	49.5	37.9	64.6	14.2	76.7	79.4	99.3	77.2	73.5		92.1
1980	55.7	46.6	35.1	49.9	14.6	71.0	76.8	88.6	77.8	68.0		92.8
1981	56.0	46.7	35.2	47.4	15.0	71.1	77.4	94.8	79.3	68.5		93.7
1982	51.7	42.1	30.7	40.3	13.7	60.0	73.3	86.6	79.9	61.4		89.7
1983	53.0	45.0	32.7	49.0	14.0	62.7	78.5	97.2	85.0	67.9		86.9
1984	58.1	50.1	38.0	58.3	16.9	69.5	82.0	88.6	90.3	72.2		92.4
1985	58.0	50.2	38.2	60.6	16.9	69.0	81.3	91.7	89.8	70.9		91.9
1986	57.9	51.1	38.7	60.1	17.2	70.2	83.9	95.5	93.6	74.4		88.2
1987	61.0	54.5	41.4	61.7	18.8	75.2	88.9	107.2	98.2	80.8		90.3
1988	64.4	58.0	44.8	66.8	20.5	80.5	92.2	106.2	101.5	85.7		93.4
1989	64.9	58.4	45.0	63.3	21.2	80.8	93.0	108.5	101.4	86.9		94.3
1990	65.3	58.5	45.1	59.0	22.0	81.2	93.2	103.1	101.8	87.7		96.2
1991	64.3	57.2	43.7	55.8	21.9	77.7	92.2	103.0	99.6	86.5		96.3
1992	66.4	60.0	46.6	62.7	23.1	81.8	94.5	109.0	102.0	88.7		95.4
1993	68.6	62.7	49.7	70.9	24.6	85.0	95.6	113.5	102.0	89.1		95.7
1994	73.1	67.7	55.3	81.9	27.9	91.3	98.4	120.5	105.9	91.9		97.2
1995	77.2	72.4	61.1	85.2	34.1	94.7	99.4	118.4	108.6	92.6		98.7
1996	81.2	76.9	67.5	87.5	41.9	97.6	98.4	115.2	105.1	93.1		100.2
1997	87.8	85.0	76.9	94.2	53.1	102.5	103.1	120.3	106.3	99.8		100.0
1998	93.1	91.4	85.4	97.6	65.4	105.3	104.4	119.3	107.3	100.0		100.4
1999	98.7	98.5	95.0	107.4	80.1	107.0	105.7	116.3	109.2	102.9		99.9
2000	104.0	104.8	104.5	107.7	100.0	108.0	105.5	111.5	108.1	103.6		101.5
2001	99.1	98.7	98.9	95.7	99.4	100.1	98.4	98.6	101.6	95.8		100.3
2002	100.0	100.0	100.0	100.0	100.0	100.0	100.0	100.0	100.0	100.0		100.0
2003	101.3	101.8	103.5	98.7	111.5	99.4	99.0	94.8	96.3	100.6		100.0
2004	104.5	106.4	109.5	98.6	123.6	104.0	101.4	90.5	97.4	107.1		99.6
2005	107.0	110.7	115.4	99.3	138.2	106.6	103.3	93.3	98.0	109.2		98.4
2006	109.5	113.7	119.9	96.9	151.2	109.1	104.1	84.9	98.4	110.9		100.0
2007	111.7	116.0	122.8	93.9	163.7	109.3	105.8	78.8	97.7	115.4		101.8
2008	109.6	111.8	119.5	82.7	170.5	104.8	100.3	70.6	93.3	107.2		103.6
2009	97.6	94.6	94.4	57.4	141.8	82.9	92.8	59.7	81.9	101.4		100.7
2008												
January	113.2	117.1	124.6	90.1	173.3	109.7	106.0	73.8	97.2	115.7		104.2
February	113.1	116.5	124.4	89.5	173.6	109.4	104.8	74.2	95.8	114.5		104.9
March	112.9	116.3	124.0	87.5	175.5	108.8	104.9	73.1	96.4	114.2		104.6
April	112.4	115.6	123.3	85.8	175.0	108.4	104.2	72.3	95.7	113.4		104.6
May	112.1	115.1	122.5	85.3	174.2	107.5	104.1	72.6	97.4	112.7		104.6
June	111.7	114.8	122.9	86.0	174.8	107.6	103.1	70.9	94.7	111.9		104.0
July	111.9	114.4	122.8	86.6	173.8	107.6	102.1	70.6	94.2	110.6		105.2
August	110.9	113.5	121.5	81.2	175.0	107.0	101.8	72.8	94.1	109.1		104.0
September	104.3	107.8	118.9	80.6	172.7	103.7	92.6	70.2	92.1	91.5		96.2
October	106.9	108.2	115.3	77.5	166.9	100.9	97.7	69.4	91.5	103.6		102.3
November	104.7	103.7	110.1	74.0	159.2	96.5	94.1	66.0	87.6	98.2		104.3
December	101.0	98.0	104.0	68.5	152.5	90.8	88.9	61.6	83.2	91.5		104.2
2009												
January	99.0	95.4	98.9	57.4	149.1	87.7	89.2	62.3	81.4	93.5		103.6
February	98.5	95.3	97.0	57.6	146.1	85.5	91.2	58.9	83.2	97.1		102.2
March	96.5	92.7	93.8	55.8	142.9	81.9	89.5	57.4	79.1	95.5		101.3
April	96.2	92.9	92.9	55.9	142.1	80.6	91.0	58.9	78.3	99.8		100.1
May	95.2	92.0	90.4	52.9	137.6	79.3	91.9	58.1	80.5	100.2		99.0
June	94.7	91.7	89.5	50.3	136.5	79.4	92.2	58.4	81.8	101.1		98.0
July	96.4	93.9	93.1	58.3	139.3	81.3	92.8	56.5	82.1	102.9		98.2
August	97.9	95.3	94.2	58.0	140.2	82.9	94.5	58.2	83.2	104.8		99.8
September	98.5	95.9	95.2	60.3	142.0	83.1	94.6	57.2	82.9	105.6		100.5
October	98.3	95.6	95.1	60.3	141.7	83.0	94.1	61.1	81.8	104.2		100.7
November	99.8	97.4	96.3	61.2	141.7	84.8	96.5	65.0	84.7	106.4		101.2
December	100.4	97.3	96.7	60.7	143.0	85.1	95.8	64.2	83.7	106.2		103.8

Table 2-1. Industrial Production Indexes by Market Groups—*Continued*

(Seasonally adjusted, 2002 = 100.)

Year and month	Special aggregates											Total non-energy, excluding high-tech
	Energy						Non-energy					
									Selected high-tech			
	Total	Consumer energy products	Commercial energy products	Oil and gas well drilling	Converted fuels	Primary energy	Total	Total	Computers and office equipment	Communications equipment	Semiconductors and related components	
1967	57.8	43.2	30.8	. . .	57.0	79.7	35.8	0.3	. . .	. . .	. . .	52.9
1968	61.0	46.2	33.4	. . .	61.1	82.0	37.9	0.3	. . .	. . .	. . .	55.8
1969	64.2	49.4	35.1	. . .	65.3	84.8	39.6	0.3	. . .	. . .	. . .	58.1
1970	67.3	52.3	37.8	. . .	68.8	88.9	37.8	0.3	. . .	. . .	. . .	55.4
1971	68.5	54.8	39.7	. . .	70.6	88.2	38.3	0.3	. . .	. . .	. . .	56.4
1972	71.7	57.8	41.9	97.2	75.0	89.6	42.3	0.3	0.1	4.5	0.2	62.0
1973	73.6	58.9	44.2	83.1	77.9	90.7	46.2	0.4	0.1	5.0	0.3	67.4
1974	73.9	60.4	44.2	106.3	76.8	91.1	46.0	0.5	0.2	5.4	0.3	66.6
1975	74.2	61.8	45.9	111.6	74.1	91.9	41.1	0.5	0.2	5.2	0.3	59.4
1976	76.6	65.0	48.2	126.7	78.2	91.9	44.8	0.6	0.3	5.5	0.4	64.4
1977	79.5	67.5	49.9	163.2	81.1	94.6	48.6	0.8	0.4	6.7	0.5	69.3
1978	80.9	68.8	51.4	182.7	80.4	96.8	51.7	1.0	0.6	7.3	0.6	73.1
1979	83.3	70.5	53.7	187.0	83.4	99.0	53.2	1.3	0.8	8.7	0.7	74.4
1980	83.6	68.0	52.9	224.3	81.8	92.7	51.4	1.6	1.2	10.4	0.8	70.9
1981	84.9	67.5	54.2	272.8	80.6	94.7	52.1	1.9	1.6	11.2	0.9	71.1
1982	81.8	68.0	54.9	229.6	74.2	91.8	49.1	2.2	1.9	11.8	1.0	66.2
1983	79.4	68.5	56.0	180.4	74.0	95.8	51.5	2.6	2.7	12.6	1.2	68.7
1984	84.1	70.6	59.1	197.9	78.7	93.5	56.6	3.4	3.9	13.4	1.6	74.6
1985	83.8	70.6	61.2	180.0	78.3	92.9	57.6	3.6	4.6	13.0	1.6	75.7
1986	80.9	72.0	63.0	95.4	75.5	97.0	58.9	3.7	4.9	12.3	1.7	77.4
1987	83.2	74.6	66.3	91.8	79.4	97.7	62.2	4.5	6.3	13.7	2.1	81.0
1988	86.5	78.5	68.5	111.1	83.0	100.4	65.7	5.4	7.7	16.5	2.4	84.6
1989	87.4	79.0	71.1	96.4	86.1	99.7	66.2	5.7	8.1	17.4	2.6	85.0
1990	88.8	78.5	73.1	102.5	86.8	102.4	66.8	6.4	8.7	20.6	3.0	85.1
1991	89.3	80.9	74.1	80.1	86.9	102.5	65.4	6.9	9.0	20.9	3.3	82.8
1992	88.1	79.8	73.7	55.6	88.5	100.0	67.9	8.2	11.3	23.9	4.0	85.0
1993	89.7	83.3	75.9	77.3	90.2	99.1	70.3	9.6	14.0	27.0	4.6	87.3
1994	91.5	84.4	78.9	92.0	91.6	100.8	74.5	12.1	17.4	32.0	6.1	91.1
1995	93.4	86.6	81.7	89.6	92.9	102.3	78.4	16.9	24.3	38.9	9.1	93.4
1996	95.7	90.4	84.2	96.1	94.6	103.8	82.2	24.1	34.4	47.9	13.9	94.9
1997	96.1	89.8	87.7	110.1	96.1	102.6	89.3	35.3	48.8	65.1	21.6	99.6
1998	96.5	89.8	89.2	103.2	97.2	102.5	95.3	49.1	67.2	77.6	32.4	103.2
1999	97.1	92.9	92.7	80.7	98.9	100.5	100.0	70.0	88.2	97.2	51.8	104.5
2000	99.6	95.1	96.5	114.3	101.3	101.7	104.5	98.3	102.8	132.8	79.8	105.3
2001	99.7	96.2	98.1	138.7	97.8	101.6	100.2	101.3	103.8	127.4	86.5	100.1
2002	100.0	100.0	100.0	100.0	100.0	100.0	100.0	100.0	100.0	100.0	100.0	100.0
2003	101.0	100.5	104.8	116.2	100.3	99.8	101.3	120.5	108.2	107.1	134.5	100.0
2004	101.9	102.9	108.6	126.9	102.3	98.3	104.3	137.9	109.4	122.1	162.4	102.1
2005	102.6	107.1	111.4	142.5	103.1	96.3	108.4	158.8	130.2	121.6	197.2	105.4
2006	103.8	105.8	111.8	164.4	102.9	98.6	111.3	189.1	162.0	145.1	230.0	107.0
2007	105.9	108.4	113.9	170.3	107.0	99.5	112.7	213.7	197.4	149.1	264.4	107.6
2008	107.7	109.7	115.7	177.7	106.2	102.2	108.8	238.0	217.0	169.6	292.3	102.9
2009	104.0	109.3	113.1	104.7	101.1	100.0	95.7	204.9	174.9	167.0	235.4	90.7
2008												
January	108.6	111.9	116.9	169.6	110.1	101.7	113.2	237.5	228.1	159.2	294.7	107.3
February	109.2	112.2	118.6	167.6	110.9	102.6	112.6	242.2	232.5	161.9	301.2	106.6
March	108.1	109.6	114.8	171.2	108.9	102.7	112.4	248.1	236.1	167.7	308.3	106.3
April	108.8	111.4	117.1	174.0	108.9	102.7	111.3	251.2	237.5	173.4	309.1	105.0
May	108.2	109.4	115.7	176.8	108.7	102.8	111.1	250.3	234.8	174.4	307.7	104.9
June	108.0	109.5	116.5	179.1	106.2	102.9	110.8	248.4	227.5	173.0	309.6	104.7
July	108.7	108.8	116.9	180.2	104.9	104.8	110.5	246.6	217.9	171.0	314.2	104.4
August	107.0	106.3	114.0	182.7	102.6	104.0	109.4	243.6	209.7	168.9	314.4	103.4
September	100.8	101.0	112.8	189.0	100.7	94.1	105.9	240.0	205.0	169.0	307.8	99.9
October	107.1	110.5	114.9	186.4	104.3	101.1	105.4	228.4	198.9	171.4	277.3	99.7
November	108.6	111.4	115.2	183.2	105.7	103.4	103.0	214.3	190.9	172.6	242.6	97.7
December	109.2	114.9	115.6	172.7	103.8	104.0	99.6	204.9	185.5	172.5	220.5	94.5
2009												
January	108.7	114.8	117.1	154.4	103.7	103.2	96.8	204.2	181.7	175.2	218.0	91.8
February	106.1	111.2	114.1	130.7	101.0	102.4	96.6	199.5	177.2	169.1	215.8	91.7
March	104.8	110.2	113.8	108.3	101.1	101.0	94.9	200.4	173.7	167.6	222.9	90.0
April	104.0	110.5	114.4	97.5	99.7	99.8	94.5	203.6	168.9	169.5	233.1	89.5
May	102.1	107.5	111.5	92.1	99.4	98.3	93.7	199.0	164.9	166.7	226.7	88.8
June	101.3	107.1	111.5	88.4	97.5	97.8	93.4	199.7	165.0	168.6	226.1	88.4
July	101.3	106.4	111.8	88.3	96.8	98.6	94.9	205.5	170.3	165.8	242.1	89.8
August	101.9	105.5	111.0	89.3	99.9	99.4	96.1	206.4	173.2	164.1	244.7	91.0
September	102.9	106.6	112.1	93.8	101.4	99.6	96.6	207.2	177.6	160.0	248.9	91.5
October	104.4	111.6	112.7	96.9	102.1	99.4	96.5	209.7	180.0	163.2	250.0	91.3
November	103.4	107.5	109.9	104.4	102.4	100.0	97.6	210.6	182.1	166.3	246.8	92.4
December	107.6	113.1	117.9	112.2	108.4	100.7	97.3	213.1	184.1	168.5	249.5	92.1

. . . = Not available.

Table 2-2. Industrial Production Indexes by NAICS Industry Groups

(Seasonally adjusted, 2002 = 100.)

Year and month	Total industrial production	Manu-facturing (SIC)	Manufacturing (NAICS) Total	Durable goods manufacturing Total	Wood products	Nonmetallic mineral products	Primary metals	Fabricated metal products	Machinery	Computer and electronic products	Electrical equipment, appliances, and components	Motor vehicles and parts	Aerospace and miscellaneous transport equipment
1967	39.2	36.1	. . .	. . .	. . .	. . .	. . .	. . .	. . .	. . .	. . .	. . .	. . .
1968	41.4	38.1	. . .	. . .	. . .	. . .	. . .	. . .	. . .	. . .	. . .	. . .	. . .
1969	43.3	39.8	. . .	. . .	. . .	. . .	. . .	. . .	. . .	. . .	. . .	. . .	. . .
1970	41.9	38.0	. . .	. . .	. . .	. . .	. . .	. . .	. . .	. . .	. . .	. . .	. . .
1971	42.5	38.6	. . .	. . .	. . .	. . .	. . .	. . .	. . .	. . .	. . .	. . .	. . .
1972	46.6	42.6	41.5	31.4	73.7	74.1	113.7	69.1	68.0	1.4	72.4	44.3	72.4
1973	50.4	46.4	45.3	35.3	71.3	79.5	133.7	76.3	78.5	1.7	81.5	50.7	82.4
1974	50.2	46.3	45.2	35.1	64.8	78.5	137.2	75.0	82.4	1.9	79.6	43.5	83.8
1975	45.8	41.5	40.4	30.5	60.1	70.3	104.7	64.8	71.8	1.7	63.9	38.0	79.6
1976	49.4	45.2	44.2	33.4	67.6	74.3	111.7	69.4	74.9	2.0	72.1	48.5	74.5
1977	53.1	49.1	47.9	36.6	73.0	79.1	112.9	75.3	81.8	2.6	79.5	55.1	75.1
1978	56.0	52.1	50.9	39.5	73.9	84.2	120.7	79.0	88.1	3.1	84.4	57.4	82.8
1979	57.7	53.7	52.5	41.5	71.5	84.1	123.8	82.5	93.0	3.9	87.9	52.6	96.4
1980	56.3	51.8	50.5	39.7	66.2	75.9	107.8	77.8	88.5	4.7	82.6	38.8	95.5
1981	57.0	52.4	51.0	40.1	64.7	72.7	107.9	77.3	87.6	5.4	81.5	37.8	90.4
1982	54.1	49.5	48.1	36.7	58.0	64.3	82.2	69.2	73.3	6.1	73.4	34.1	92.5
1983	55.6	51.9	50.4	38.5	67.3	69.2	84.2	69.8	66.1	7.1	75.9	43.5	88.3
1984	60.5	57.0	55.5	44.0	72.0	74.7	92.3	75.9	77.2	8.7	85.5	52.2	94.2
1985	61.3	57.9	56.3	44.9	72.9	76.1	85.2	77.0	77.4	9.3	84.2	54.2	100.7
1986	61.9	59.2	57.6	45.7	79.2	79.2	83.2	76.5	76.2	9.6	85.7	54.1	105.9
1987	65.1	62.5	60.8	48.4	86.4	83.6	89.7	77.9	77.8	11.0	86.9	56.1	109.8
1988	68.4	65.9	64.3	52.0	86.3	85.3	100.2	81.9	85.7	12.3	91.1	59.9	115.6
1989	69.1	66.4	64.9	52.6	85.0	84.6	97.9	81.3	88.8	12.7	89.7	59.3	122.5
1990	69.7	67.0	65.5	52.8	84.1	83.3	96.7	80.3	86.7	13.8	87.5	55.8	123.0
1991	68.7	65.6	64.3	51.2	78.6	76.7	90.8	76.6	81.4	14.3	82.9	53.3	118.7
1992	70.6	68.0	66.8	53.8	82.9	80.1	93.0	79.0	81.1	16.1	87.9	60.7	109.8
1993	72.9	70.4	69.2	56.8	83.9	81.8	97.5	82.0	87.2	17.7	93.4	67.0	102.3
1994	76.8	74.5	73.6	61.6	88.9	86.4	104.9	89.1	95.5	20.7	100.2	77.0	91.9
1995	80.4	78.5	77.6	66.9	91.0	88.9	106.0	94.6	102.2	26.7	102.5	79.3	87.3
1996	84.0	82.2	81.6	72.8	93.9	94.7	108.6	98.0	105.8	34.5	105.7	79.9	90.7
1997	90.1	89.2	88.5	81.6	96.7	97.8	113.3	102.5	111.6	46.1	109.6	86.1	101.2
1998	95.4	95.1	94.4	90.2	101.1	102.8	115.3	105.8	114.5	59.2	113.6	90.6	117.3
1999	99.5	99.9	99.3	97.8	105.3	103.6	115.1	106.4	112.0	77.2	115.5	100.5	113.1
2000	103.7	104.4	103.9	105.2	103.7	103.6	111.4	110.7	117.7	101.4	121.3	99.9	99.3
2001	100.1	100.1	99.8	100.4	97.1	99.7	99.5	102.6	104.2	103.3	109.3	91.4	105.9
2002	100.0	100.0	100.0	100.0	100.0	100.0	100.0	100.0	100.0	100.0	100.0	100.0	100.0
2003	101.3	101.3	101.6	102.7	100.7	100.5	99.1	98.7	99.7	114.3	97.3	103.5	95.8
2004	103.8	104.3	104.7	107.0	104.4	103.6	110.0	98.9	103.7	129.9	99.0	103.7	94.3
2005	107.2	108.5	109.1	112.8	110.4	108.1	108.0	103.4	110.2	144.5	100.7	103.9	105.0
2006	109.7	111.2	112.1	117.8	110.0	109.9	112.6	109.0	115.5	163.8	101.4	100.2	110.9
2007	111.3	112.7	113.8	120.2	99.2	106.9	110.0	112.1	116.4	176.7	104.8	97.4	121.7
2008	108.8	109.1	110.3	116.3	84.8	100.7	102.4	110.1	109.4	192.8	104.5	83.3	119.3
2009	98.2	96.8	98.1	97.2	66.6	83.3	68.4	90.0	86.3	173.8	92.0	60.0	115.4
2008													
January	112.3	113.4	114.6	121.9	91.5	104.7	113.2	113.6	114.9	191.0	105.7	94.6	127.8
February	112.0	112.8	114.0	121.2	90.5	103.4	111.9	113.5	113.6	194.0	104.6	94.2	125.1
March	111.6	112.7	113.9	121.0	89.9	104.5	110.6	113.6	114.8	197.5	105.8	88.7	125.1
April	111.0	111.7	112.9	119.3	89.0	102.7	109.7	112.6	111.2	199.2	105.7	83.9	124.3
May	110.7	111.5	112.7	118.9	88.2	102.6	107.8	112.1	110.9	199.4	106.1	83.9	123.3
June	110.4	111.0	112.3	119.0	87.3	101.7	107.9	110.5	110.6	199.0	106.3	86.4	125.1
July	110.4	110.8	112.0	119.0	86.7	102.7	110.1	109.8	109.2	198.0	106.2	88.7	123.0
August	109.2	109.7	111.0	117.2	86.1	101.6	108.6	110.2	110.2	196.6	105.4	79.2	122.6
September	104.8	105.7	106.7	113.7	82.8	99.1	102.0	109.2	107.3	194.2	103.4	79.9	103.2
October	106.2	106.0	107.2	110.8	79.0	99.3	93.2	107.3	106.1	188.4	103.5	76.9	99.8
November	104.8	103.6	104.7	108.2	76.8	94.3	81.4	106.0	104.0	180.7	102.7	74.2	109.0
December	102.4	100.6	101.6	105.3	69.7	91.5	71.9	102.4	99.7	176.2	99.1	69.2	123.2
2009													
January	100.1	97.8	98.8	99.9	67.7	86.4	67.3	98.2	96.2	174.9	98.2	51.2	119.3
February	99.3	97.7	98.7	98.7	68.1	84.9	64.5	95.6	94.0	171.6	95.8	55.8	117.8
March	97.7	96.1	97.3	96.4	66.2	81.9	60.7	91.3	88.7	171.4	92.7	56.7	116.8
April	97.2	95.7	96.9	95.7	65.5	82.7	60.3	89.4	86.6	172.5	92.0	56.6	115.0
May	96.2	94.8	96.0	93.7	65.1	81.8	59.2	87.5	83.9	170.3	91.0	52.4	113.4
June	95.8	94.4	95.7	92.9	66.6	82.4	61.1	87.2	82.0	169.6	89.7	49.5	113.9
July	96.9	95.9	97.3	96.3	66.4	85.9	68.0	87.2	82.6	173.3	89.7	61.1	115.8
August	98.1	97.1	98.5	97.4	67.8	85.3	71.7	87.6	83.8	174.5	91.1	63.7	116.2
September	98.7	97.7	99.1	98.4	67.4	84.3	73.3	88.2	82.8	175.1	90.9	68.7	117.0
October	98.9	97.6	99.0	98.2	66.3	81.2	74.1	88.3	84.8	176.0	91.4	67.1	115.2
November	99.6	98.6	100.0	99.2	66.5	83.3	78.4	89.5	84.0	177.5	91.9	68.7	113.2
December	100.3	98.5	99.9	99.3	65.8	79.3	82.0	89.9	86.7	179.2	89.6	68.5	111.7

. . . = Not available.

Table 2-2. Industrial Production Indexes by NAICS Industry Groups—*Continued*

(Seasonally adjusted, 2002 = 100.)

Year and month	Durable goods manufacturing—*Continued*		Manufacturing (NAICS)—*Continued* Nondurable goods manufacturing									Other manu-facturing (non-NAICS)
	Furniture and related products	Miscel-laneous manu-facturing	Total	Food, beverage, and tobacco products	Textile and product mills	Apparel and leather	Paper	Printing and support	Petroleum and coal products	Chemical	Plastics and rubber products	
1967	...	...	...	...	...	...	...	...	...	...	...	...
1968	...	...	...	...	...	...	...	...	...	...	...	...
1969	...	...	...	...	...	...	...	...	...	...	...	...
1970	...	...	...	...	...	...	...	...	...	...	...	...
1971	...	...	...	...	...	...	...	...	...	...	...	...
1972	55.8	42.4	60.9	66.0	86.1	182.9	66.3	51.6	73.9	47.8	34.9	68.3
1973	58.4	43.7	63.8	66.7	85.2	186.1	71.6	54.2	72.6	52.3	39.2	70.5
1974	53.6	42.8	64.1	67.7	78.4	174.5	74.7	52.6	78.3	54.4	38.2	71.0
1975	45.7	39.9	59.4	66.5	75.8	169.8	64.6	49.1	77.2	47.8	32.7	67.5
1976	51.1	43.4	64.9	71.0	84.4	179.0	71.4	52.7	85.5	53.5	36.2	69.6
1977	58.6	47.2	69.3	72.6	92.3	188.1	74.5	57.1	91.6	58.2	42.6	76.3
1978	63.2	48.2	71.8	75.2	92.0	192.5	77.9	60.4	92.5	61.1	44.1	78.9
1979	62.7	48.4	72.2	74.8	91.8	180.3	79.0	62.2	98.8	62.5	43.4	80.6
1980	60.5	45.8	70.0	76.0	88.1	183.9	78.8	62.7	87.5	59.1	38.6	83.4
1981	60.0	47.5	70.6	76.8	86.2	183.7	79.9	64.3	83.5	60.1	40.9	85.4
1982	56.4	48.0	69.6	79.0	79.9	182.5	78.6	69.1	79.8	56.2	40.2	86.4
1983	61.9	48.0	72.8	79.2	90.1	187.7	83.7	74.3	81.1	60.1	43.7	88.8
1984	69.4	52.0	76.2	80.3	92.4	179.2	87.9	80.9	82.9	63.6	50.5	92.8
1985	69.9	52.7	76.6	82.9	89.2	178.8	86.2	84.2	81.7	63.1	52.5	96.5
1986	73.0	53.9	78.8	84.0	92.9	186.3	89.8	88.4	81.2	65.9	54.7	98.4
1987	78.2	58.0	83.0	85.6	102.5	188.2	92.7	94.9	85.1	71.0	60.6	104.1
1988	77.2	63.4	85.8	88.0	101.6	184.7	96.4	98.0	87.7	75.1	63.2	103.6
1989	76.9	64.2	86.3	87.5	103.4	176.5	97.4	98.4	86.8	76.5	65.4	102.1
1990	75.2	67.3	87.7	90.0	99.2	172.4	97.4	102.1	86.9	78.3	67.2	100.9
1991	69.5	68.6	87.4	90.6	97.8	171.2	97.6	98.9	85.7	78.0	66.5	96.8
1992	75.0	71.5	89.6	91.8	103.2	175.7	100.0	104.3	85.3	79.2	71.6	94.8
1993	78.3	75.5	90.9	91.5	107.2	179.2	101.1	104.6	85.8	80.1	76.7	95.5
1994	81.0	76.1	94.0	94.7	113.1	181.3	105.5	105.7	88.2	82.2	83.0	94.7
1995	82.4	79.0	95.7	97.4	112.0	179.9	107.0	107.3	89.8	83.5	85.1	94.7
1996	83.0	82.8	96.0	96.6	109.4	175.6	103.7	108.0	91.9	85.3	87.9	93.8
1997	91.9	84.9	99.5	98.6	115.4	175.1	105.9	110.2	95.0	90.3	93.4	101.7
1998	98.4	89.9	101.0	101.5	114.4	165.1	106.7	111.5	93.2	91.8	96.7	107.8
1999	101.8	91.7	101.7	99.7	114.1	158.0	107.6	112.4	97.1	93.6	101.9	110.9
2000	103.3	96.7	102.2	101.2	111.9	150.8	105.3	113.1	96.9	95.0	102.9	112.6
2001	96.7	95.5	98.9	100.9	100.3	128.2	99.3	106.3	96.4	93.4	96.9	105.7
2002	100.0	100.0	100.0	100.0	100.0	100.0	100.0	100.0	100.0	100.0	100.0	100.0
2003	98.2	103.0	100.1	102.0	96.0	93.3	96.8	96.2	97.9	101.3	100.3	97.1
2004	100.9	103.2	102.0	102.5	94.6	82.0	97.6	96.9	106.0	105.6	101.5	97.9
2005	104.6	109.9	104.8	106.2	96.7	80.4	97.5	99.2	110.1	109.3	102.3	97.6
2006	104.2	113.3	105.7	106.7	88.0	79.1	97.6	99.8	109.7	112.7	102.9	96.6
2007	101.0	118.3	106.7	109.6	81.2	79.3	95.9	100.6	109.1	114.1	104.7	95.3
2008	90.4	117.7	103.6	109.3	72.6	75.9	92.1	93.9	110.0	108.8	99.1	89.9
2009	71.9	113.9	97.8	107.3	60.8	64.9	82.1	80.5	107.4	103.6	84.6	75.7
2008												
January	97.5	119.7	106.6	109.8	76.0	79.1	95.5	98.6	111.2	114.0	103.5	93.9
February	95.9	117.2	106.2	109.7	76.1	78.3	94.0	97.1	111.7	113.2	102.9	93.5
March	95.3	118.8	106.1	110.8	75.4	77.2	94.8	98.0	111.0	112.6	101.9	93.6
April	93.7	117.7	105.8	110.3	74.4	76.5	94.1	96.9	112.4	112.2	100.9	91.8
May	93.4	117.7	105.9	110.3	74.4	75.1	96.2	96.4	112.2	112.1	100.8	90.8
June	92.8	117.4	104.9	109.4	73.3	76.3	94.3	93.4	111.4	111.0	101.2	90.8
July	92.1	117.6	104.5	108.7	73.0	77.0	94.0	91.9	111.5	110.6	101.5	89.3
August	89.1	119.7	104.1	108.9	73.8	77.7	94.2	93.0	110.1	109.7	99.4	88.9
September	87.9	118.2	99.3	108.8	71.9	76.7	91.3	92.3	98.7	101.0	97.7	88.1
October	85.2	117.5	102.7	109.4	71.2	74.6	89.7	91.9	112.0	106.7	96.0	86.9
November	81.6	116.4	100.3	108.8	67.7	71.6	85.9	90.6	109.2	103.2	93.7	86.4
December	79.9	114.5	97.0	106.0	63.6	70.3	81.3	87.4	108.4	98.7	89.4	84.6
2009												
January	79.1	114.6	96.7	106.1	63.9	68.1	80.1	85.3	105.7	99.8	88.2	81.4
February	76.5	112.4	97.7	107.3	61.7	66.8	82.9	82.7	108.7	101.6	86.0	80.4
March	75.1	111.6	96.9	107.3	59.7	66.8	78.9	81.6	108.8	101.3	83.4	76.1
April	72.3	113.0	97.0	106.4	60.3	65.4	78.2	80.1	109.0	102.7	82.9	75.1
May	72.0	112.4	97.1	107.7	59.4	65.4	80.9	79.6	106.9	102.4	82.2	74.4
June	70.8	112.1	97.2	106.3	59.3	61.7	82.5	80.2	108.3	103.1	82.2	74.4
July	71.3	113.0	97.1	105.3	58.2	63.3	82.6	79.9	107.8	103.8	83.2	73.6
August	68.9	114.9	98.3	107.6	59.5	63.9	84.4	80.1	107.3	104.6	83.7	74.0
September	69.6	114.5	98.6	107.5	59.3	63.6	83.7	79.2	108.9	105.7	84.4	74.4
October	69.0	115.1	98.6	108.5	61.5	63.4	81.7	79.3	107.1	105.0	85.4	74.0
November	68.9	117.5	99.7	108.8	63.6	64.1	85.7	78.9	106.7	106.7	86.2	75.3
December	68.7	115.5	99.3	108.4	63.3	65.9	83.9	79.0	103.9	106.8	86.9	75.3

. . . = Not available.

Table 2-2. Industrial Production Indexes by NAICS Industry Groups—*Continued*

(Seasonally adjusted, 2002 = 100.)

Year and month	Mining	Utilities			Selected high-tech industries	Excluding selected high-tech industries	Stage-of-process groups		
		Total	Electric	Natural gas			Crude	Primary and semi-finished	Finished
1967	...	...	...	...	0.3	54.1	...	...	...
1968	...	...	...	...	0.3	57.1	...	...	...
1969	...	...	...	...	0.3	59.5	...	...	...
1970	...	...	...	...	0.3	57.5	...	...	...
1971	...	...	...	...	0.3	58.5	...	...	...
1972	99.4	50.3	40.9	101.9	0.3	63.9	88.3	46.0	40.1
1973	100.0	53.2	44.6	97.5	0.4	68.8	93.0	50.2	43.0
1974	98.5	53.0	44.8	93.9	0.5	68.2	94.2	49.6	42.5
1975	95.9	54.0	46.8	95.6	0.5	62.2	85.5	43.9	40.1
1976	96.7	56.4	49.7	94.6	0.6	66.8	90.4	47.9	44.0
1977	99.1	58.7	52.9	91.4	0.8	71.3	95.3	51.7	47.8
1978	110.8	60.2	54.6	92.2	1.0	74.7	97.1	54.2	50.8
1979	105.8	61.6	55.8	94.6	1.3	76.3	99.7	55.4	51.7
1980	107.8	62.0	56.7	92.6	1.6	73.6	90.6	51.8	50.8
1981	110.9	62.9	58.2	90.5	1.9	74.0	91.9	51.8	51.9
1982	105.0	60.9	56.8	85.0	2.2	69.6	93.4	47.6	51.0
1983	99.0	61.4	58.5	79.6	2.6	70.8	93.6	49.9	53.3
1984	105.9	65.0	61.8	84.5	3.4	76.4	99.8	54.8	58.1
1985	103.7	66.4	64.1	81.0	3.6	77.2	97.2	55.3	59.6
1986	103.9	67.0	65.4	77.0	3.7	77.9	99.6	56.2	61.7
1987	104.8	70.1	68.5	80.6	4.5	81.2	102.8	59.5	64.8
1988	107.5	74.1	72.4	85.5	5.4	84.8	106.2	62.6	68.5
1989	106.2	76.4	74.6	88.6	5.7	85.3	106.3	63.1	69.5
1990	107.8	77.9	76.7	85.6	6.4	85.6	107.9	63.1	70.8
1991	105.4	79.8	78.5	87.9	6.9	83.9	105.1	62.1	70.0
1992	103.1	79.7	78.1	90.4	8.2	85.5	104.2	64.6	71.8
1993	103.0	82.6	80.9	93.8	9.6	87.6	103.0	67.6	73.8
1994	105.4	84.2	82.7	94.4	12.1	91.1	105.2	72.3	76.8
1995	105.3	87.2	85.7	96.9	16.9	93.3	105.6	76.3	80.6
1996	107.1	89.7	87.9	101.5	24.1	94.9	105.3	80.7	83.8
1997	108.9	89.7	88.2	99.5	35.3	98.9	108.1	86.8	90.5
1998	107.2	92.0	91.8	93.1	49.1	101.9	106.2	92.5	96.8
1999	101.6	94.7	94.5	95.7	70.0	103.1	104.2	98.6	99.5
2000	104.2	97.4	97.2	98.6	98.3	104.3	104.6	103.7	103.3
2001	104.8	97.0	96.9	97.2	101.3	100.1	101.7	98.9	101.2
2002	100.0	100.0	100.0	100.0	100.0	100.0	100.0	100.0	100.0
2003	100.2	101.9	102.1	100.9	120.5	100.2	100.2	101.1	101.8
2004	99.6	103.3	104.2	98.8	137.9	102.0	101.5	103.9	104.4
2005	98.3	105.4	107.2	97.1	158.8	104.7	100.8	107.2	109.4
2006	101.5	104.8	107.8	91.3	189.1	106.2	103.6	108.5	113.2
2007	102.1	108.3	110.5	98.1	213.7	107.2	104.6	109.5	116.0
2008	104.2	108.6	110.4	100.5	238.0	104.2	104.5	106.0	113.7
2009	97.4	106.0	107.5	98.9	204.9	94.2	98.5	92.3	105.6
2008									
January	104.2	110.9	112.4	103.8	237.5	107.7	106.6	110.0	117.3
February	105.0	111.4	112.7	104.9	242.2	107.3	106.9	109.8	116.6
March	104.7	108.8	110.5	100.5	248.1	106.8	106.9	109.0	116.6
April	104.9	109.7	111.5	101.3	251.2	106.1	106.7	108.7	115.1
May	104.9	108.2	109.7	100.9	250.3	105.8	106.9	108.0	115.0
June	104.8	109.4	111.8	98.5	248.4	105.6	105.8	107.9	115.1
July	106.9	107.9	110.1	97.6	246.6	105.6	107.3	107.4	114.7
August	106.4	104.3	106.0	95.9	243.6	104.4	106.8	105.9	113.5
September	96.4	105.7	108.0	95.2	240.0	100.2	95.3	102.9	111.4
October	103.5	107.1	108.5	100.2	228.4	101.7	102.7	103.5	110.5
November	105.4	109.1	110.5	102.1	214.3	100.6	102.6	101.0	110.0
December	103.4	111.3	112.7	104.5	204.9	98.4	99.6	98.0	108.8
2009									
January	102.8	111.5	112.3	107.4	204.2	96.1	98.8	95.7	105.9
February	101.3	106.4	108.5	96.4	199.5	95.4	99.0	94.0	106.0
March	98.7	106.1	108.5	95.0	200.4	93.8	96.3	91.9	105.5
April	96.1	106.4	108.5	96.5	203.6	93.3	96.2	91.7	104.4
May	95.1	104.3	107.0	91.7	199.0	92.3	96.4	90.2	103.6
June	93.7	103.8	105.5	95.7	199.7	91.9	96.0	90.0	102.8
July	95.1	102.8	103.9	97.8	205.5	92.9	97.6	90.9	104.3
August	97.0	103.4	104.6	98.5	206.4	94.1	99.5	91.5	105.9
September	96.8	103.9	105.0	99.4	207.2	94.6	100.5	91.9	106.5
October	96.7	106.7	106.3	109.3	209.7	94.8	99.6	92.3	106.8
November	98.6	104.1	106.3	93.4	210.6	95.5	101.0	92.8	107.6
December	97.6	112.0	113.3	105.9	213.1	96.1	100.9	94.1	107.6

. . . = Not available.

Table 2-3. Capacity Utilization by NAICS Industry Groups

(Output as a percentage of capacity, seasonally adjusted.)

Year and month	Total industry	Total manufac- turing (SIC)	Manufacturing (NAICS)										
				Durable goods manufacturing									
			Total	Total	Wood products	Nonmetallic mineral products	Primary metals	Fabricated metal products	Machinery	Computer and electronic products	Electrical equipment, appliances, and compo- nents	Motor vehicles and parts	Aircraft and miscel- laneous transpor- tation equipment
1967	87.0	87.2	...	87.5	...	75.7	85.0	86.4	90.4	...	...	78.9	94.1
1968	87.4	87.1	...	87.3	...	78.5	84.8	87.3	85.1	...	...	90.1	89.6
1969	87.4	86.7	...	87.1	...	79.8	88.2	86.2	86.7	...	...	86.6	84.8
1970	81.3	79.5	...	77.7	...	74.0	79.2	78.5	79.8	...	...	66.2	73.2
1971	79.7	78.0	...	75.5	...	75.7	72.8	78.5	73.9	...	...	78.9	64.3
1972	84.7	83.4	83.4	82.1	92.3	79.8	82.7	85.1	83.0	81.5	89.9	84.2	65.1
1973	88.3	87.6	87.8	88.5	87.6	84.3	94.5	90.9	92.3	85.1	97.7	91.9	73.2
1974	85.1	84.4	84.4	84.6	78.0	81.7	96.5	86.0	91.8	83.1	91.5	76.7	73.9
1975	75.7	73.5	73.4	71.6	70.2	73.0	75.0	72.0	77.6	68.5	70.5	65.6	70.7
1976	79.7	78.2	78.3	76.3	79.4	77.6	78.4	75.5	79.9	71.7	78.8	81.8	66.4
1977	83.4	82.4	82.4	81.2	86.1	82.6	79.1	79.9	85.5	77.7	85.9	89.9	66.8
1978	85.0	84.3	84.2	83.8	84.9	86.3	83.9	80.9	88.5	80.6	88.3	90.7	72.0
1979	85.0	84.0	83.9	84.1	80.2	84.2	85.9	81.7	90.2	83.8	89.5	81.3	81.5
1980	80.7	78.7	78.4	77.6	72.8	75.0	76.2	75.5	83.8	86.7	82.1	59.4	84.6
1981	79.6	77.0	76.6	75.2	70.8	72.2	77.4	73.5	80.8	84.4	79.0	57.3	76.7
1982	73.7	70.9	70.4	66.6	63.3	64.5	55.6	65.4	66.9	80.9	69.7	51.4	69.7
1983	74.9	73.5	73.0	68.7	74.4	70.9	59.2	66.4	60.7	81.9	72.8	67.5	66.1
1984	80.5	79.4	79.0	76.8	79.2	76.3	69.1	73.1	71.1	87.4	82.3	81.6	69.5
1985	79.3	78.2	77.7	75.7	78.8	75.9	66.9	73.8	70.7	80.2	78.9	83.2	72.3
1986	78.6	78.4	78.0	75.3	83.4	78.4	69.6	73.5	70.2	77.4	79.9	78.6	74.0
1987	81.2	81.0	80.5	77.6	86.5	80.9	78.2	75.2	72.0	79.8	82.1	77.4	75.6
1988	84.3	84.0	83.7	82.0	84.8	82.0	88.7	80.0	80.4	81.5	86.9	82.1	79.9
1989	83.7	83.2	83.1	81.6	83.1	81.2	86.7	79.7	84.0	78.8	86.0	79.8	85.2
1990	82.5	81.7	81.5	79.4	81.4	79.6	85.0	77.7	81.6	78.9	83.7	71.2	85.4
1991	79.8	78.4	78.3	75.1	76.4	73.5	79.0	74.1	76.3	77.6	78.9	63.3	83.1
1992	80.4	79.5	79.4	76.9	80.7	77.3	81.2	76.4	75.4	78.9	82.0	71.7	76.9
1993	81.5	80.4	80.3	78.6	81.3	78.9	85.8	77.4	79.5	77.3	86.5	78.5	72.6
1994	83.5	82.7	82.8	81.7	83.8	81.4	91.1	81.9	83.9	79.6	92.0	87.1	66.3
1995	84.0	83.2	83.3	82.5	82.2	81.7	89.9	83.9	85.8	83.2	91.7	84.7	63.8
1996	83.4	82.2	82.3	81.8	81.7	85.4	89.2	83.5	84.9	81.0	90.6	82.1	66.5
1997	84.2	83.2	83.1	82.7	81.1	84.6	89.8	82.6	84.4	81.5	89.3	83.6	73.3
1998	83.0	81.8	81.6	81.2	82.1	84.0	87.4	80.7	81.5	78.3	87.1	80.4	82.4
1999	81.9	80.7	80.4	80.4	82.1	81.0	85.1	78.3	76.8	80.7	84.6	84.2	77.3
2000	81.7	80.1	79.6	80.0	78.2	77.7	82.6	79.3	78.3	84.6	87.1	82.0	66.9
2001	76.1	73.8	73.3	71.4	71.9	72.2	73.7	73.0	68.8	69.3	77.6	72.7	70.7
2002	74.6	72.7	72.2	69.3	74.3	72.3	75.6	71.0	66.8	59.3	73.4	78.3	66.5
2003	75.8	73.7	73.3	70.6	76.9	73.0	74.0	71.5	68.3	63.3	74.6	78.4	63.8
2004	77.9	76.2	75.7	73.5	80.3	74.3	82.9	72.9	72.6	70.2	78.1	76.8	63.4
2005	80.1	78.6	78.3	76.3	84.2	76.3	80.5	75.8	77.5	73.1	81.6	77.0	71.0
2006	80.9	79.4	79.2	77.9	81.8	75.4	83.8	79.5	81.0	78.0	82.5	72.5	75.2
2007	80.6	79.0	78.9	77.2	72.1	71.4	82.4	80.4	80.8	75.3	83.7	71.0	81.6
2008	77.6	75.1	75.0	72.6	61.5	66.8	76.6	77.6	74.7	74.8	81.2	60.8	78.2
2009	70.1	66.8	66.9	60.5	49.6	55.7	51.3	64.1	59.2	64.2	71.1	44.8	75.0
2008													
January	80.5	78.5	78.4	76.8	66.2	69.6	84.8	80.5	79.0	75.8	83.1	69.3	84.6
February	80.2	78.0	77.9	76.1	65.5	68.7	83.8	80.4	78.0	76.5	82.0	69.0	82.6
March	79.8	77.8	77.7	75.8	65.0	69.4	82.8	80.3	78.7	77.4	82.7	64.9	82.5
April	79.2	77.0	76.9	74.6	64.4	68.1	82.1	79.5	76.1	77.8	82.4	61.3	81.7
May	78.9	76.7	76.7	74.3	63.8	68.1	80.7	79.0	75.8	77.5	82.5	61.3	80.9
June	78.7	76.3	76.3	74.2	63.2	67.4	80.7	77.8	75.5	77.1	82.5	63.0	80.2
July	78.6	76.1	76.1	74.1	62.8	68.1	82.3	77.3	74.4	76.5	82.3	64.6	80.4
August	77.6	75.3	75.3	73.0	62.5	67.3	81.2	77.6	75.1	75.8	81.5	57.7	80.1
September	74.5	72.5	72.4	70.7	60.2	65.7	76.2	76.9	73.0	74.6	79.8	58.2	67.3
October	75.4	72.7	72.7	68.8	57.4	65.8	69.7	75.5	72.2	72.2	79.8	56.0	65.0
November	74.4	71.1	71.0	67.2	56.0	62.5	60.8	74.6	70.8	69.0	79.1	54.1	70.9
December	72.7	69.0	68.9	65.4	50.9	60.7	53.7	72.1	67.9	67.0	76.3	50.5	80.1
2009													
January	71.1	67.1	67.0	62.0	49.5	57.4	50.3	69.3	65.5	66.3	75.6	37.5	77.5
February	70.6	67.1	67.0	61.2	49.9	56.4	48.2	67.5	64.0	64.8	73.7	40.9	76.5
March	69.5	66.0	66.1	59.9	48.7	54.5	45.4	64.6	60.5	64.4	71.4	41.7	75.9
April	69.2	65.8	65.9	59.4	48.3	55.1	45.1	63.4	59.1	64.5	70.9	41.8	74.7
May	68.5	65.3	65.4	58.2	48.2	54.6	44.3	62.2	57.3	63.4	70.2	38.8	73.7
June	68.3	65.1	65.2	57.8	49.5	55.1	45.7	62.1	56.1	62.8	69.3	36.8	74.0
July	69.2	66.2	66.4	59.9	49.5	57.5	51.0	62.2	56.6	63.8	69.3	45.7	75.2
August	70.1	67.1	67.3	60.7	50.7	57.2	53.8	62.6	57.6	63.9	70.5	47.8	75.5
September	70.6	67.6	67.8	61.4	50.6	56.6	55.1	63.2	57.0	63.8	70.3	51.8	76.0
October	70.8	67.6	67.9	61.3	49.9	54.6	55.7	63.4	58.5	63.8	70.9	50.8	74.9
November	71.4	68.4	68.7	62.0	50.2	56.1	59.0	64.4	58.0	64.1	71.3	52.2	73.6
December	72.0	68.4	68.6	62.0	49.9	53.5	61.8	64.8	60.0	64.4	69.6	52.3	72.6

. . . = Not available.

Table 2-3. Capacity Utilization by NAICS Industry Groups—Continued

(Output as a percentage of capacity, seasonally adjusted.)

	Manufacturing (NAICS)—Continued											Other manufac- turing (non- NAICS)
Year and month	Durable goods manufacturing —Continued		Nondurable goods manufacturing									
	Furniture and related products	Miscel- laneous manufac- turing	Total	Food, beverage, and tobacco products	Textile and product mills	Apparel and leather	Paper	Printing and support	Petroleum and coal products	Chemical	Plastics and rubber products	
1967	91.9	...	86.3	85.0	...	...	89.7	...	94.9	78.9	88.3	...
1968	91.5	...	86.5	84.8	...	...	89.3	...	95.8	80.1	91.2	...
1969	93.1	...	86.2	85.1	...	...	91.0	...	96.4	79.1	90.4	...
1970	84.6	...	82.2	84.0	...	...	86.1	...	96.7	76.1	79.5	...
1971	85.7	...	81.9	84.0	...	...	86.7	...	95.6	75.4	80.1	...
1972	94.3	80.5	85.3	85.1	89.3	81.8	91.3	92.4	93.6	80.2	88.7	85.8
1973	95.4	79.4	86.6	84.8	86.2	82.0	94.8	94.0	90.4	83.9	92.4	84.7
1974	82.3	74.5	84.2	83.8	76.1	76.2	95.0	88.0	92.8	84.3	84.2	82.8
1975	67.8	67.9	76.0	80.1	72.1	74.6	80.6	79.6	83.6	71.8	70.0	77.2
1976	75.6	72.4	81.0	83.3	80.6	78.0	87.8	82.2	86.0	77.6	77.2	77.5
1977	84.4	77.6	84.2	82.6	88.1	81.8	90.4	86.0	87.6	80.9	88.5	83.3
1978	85.6	79.0	84.9	83.3	87.4	84.1	92.5	87.4	86.5	81.9	88.3	85.0
1979	79.9	78.6	83.6	81.2	87.0	79.0	91.1	86.0	88.8	82.1	83.8	85.7
1980	74.1	73.4	79.5	81.0	82.9	80.2	88.6	83.7	76.1	76.1	73.8	87.1
1981	71.8	75.9	78.8	80.5	80.3	79.0	87.2	81.2	72.8	75.8	76.9	87.5
1982	67.1	73.9	76.3	81.4	74.2	78.2	84.2	82.2	71.3	69.1	73.8	87.4
1983	73.5	70.8	79.5	80.9	83.8	82.1	89.1	86.3	74.4	72.8	80.7	88.1
1984	80.5	76.2	82.4	81.4	85.3	83.4	91.6	89.6	78.6	76.0	90.4	89.5
1985	78.2	74.5	80.8	82.7	80.9	80.2	88.3	85.3	80.1	73.8	86.3	90.3
1986	80.0	74.3	81.9	82.8	83.2	80.9	90.5	85.6	81.8	76.1	84.8	88.9
1987	83.4	77.4	84.8	83.8	90.8	82.6	90.4	89.3	82.5	81.2	89.0	90.7
1988	80.3	81.8	86.1	85.4	88.2	82.9	91.4	89.9	83.2	84.3	88.6	88.6
1989	78.3	79.7	85.0	83.6	88.0	81.0	90.6	88.7	84.2	83.5	86.7	85.3
1990	75.2	79.6	84.4	84.4	83.3	79.7	89.5	88.2	84.7	83.2	83.7	83.8
1991	70.2	78.2	82.4	83.4	81.5	81.1	88.0	83.3	82.8	81.1	78.6	81.0
1992	77.0	76.8	82.7	82.5	85.5	83.4	88.7	85.9	84.9	79.7	81.8	80.0
1993	79.9	77.8	82.6	80.8	87.8	84.6	89.1	85.7	88.0	78.8	86.1	81.2
1994	81.6	77.9	84.3	82.9	90.1	86.0	90.8	85.7	88.7	79.7	90.5	81.1
1995	81.2	80.1	84.3	84.0	87.0	85.5	89.4	85.1	89.5	79.9	88.7	82.0
1996	80.3	81.5	82.9	82.2	83.8	83.0	85.2	83.8	92.1	79.8	87.4	80.7
1997	84.6	79.5	83.6	82.1	85.8	82.2	87.3	82.1	94.1	81.3	88.2	84.9
1998	84.4	79.0	82.2	82.1	82.9	78.0	87.3	80.6	92.0	79.0	86.9	85.6
1999	81.5	77.0	80.3	78.5	81.2	78.0	86.8	78.9	91.1	77.3	86.6	86.1
2000	77.0	77.4	79.1	78.2	78.9	80.1	84.7	78.8	89.3	75.4	82.7	87.9
2001	70.1	72.9	75.8	77.4	71.2	74.7	80.4	76.5	88.2	71.1	76.2	83.4
2002	71.9	74.2	76.3	76.4	73.0	67.3	82.5	73.9	88.5	74.2	78.3	80.8
2003	71.3	75.9	76.9	77.8	72.6	71.6	81.9	72.2	89.2	74.0	79.3	82.0
2004	75.4	74.8	78.6	77.9	74.6	72.4	83.3	74.9	92.3	76.3	82.5	84.5
2005	79.5	77.0	80.6	79.6	78.7	75.8	83.8	78.5	91.5	77.5	84.0	84.4
2006	79.9	76.1	80.7	78.9	74.6	75.7	84.0	78.9	90.1	78.8	83.8	83.0
2007	78.1	75.6	80.8	80.0	72.6	78.0	82.2	79.2	87.7	79.0	84.1	81.3
2008	70.8	71.4	77.7	78.4	68.1	75.4	79.6	74.9	86.4	74.3	77.8	76.0
2009	58.7	67.7	73.9	76.7	60.8	66.7	72.2	67.7	83.8	71.2	67.1	64.1
2008												
January	75.8	74.2	80.2	79.5	69.7	78.3	82.2	77.7	88.2	78.3	82.0	79.8
February	74.6	72.3	79.8	79.2	70.2	77.6	81.0	76.7	88.4	77.7	81.4	79.3
March	74.2	72.9	79.7	79.8	69.8	76.4	81.7	77.5	87.7	77.1	80.4	79.4
April	73.1	72.0	79.4	79.4	69.1	75.8	81.2	76.7	88.6	76.7	79.4	77.8
May	72.9	71.7	79.4	79.2	69.4	74.5	83.0	76.4	88.2	76.6	79.2	76.8
June	72.6	71.2	78.6	78.5	68.7	75.7	81.5	74.3	87.4	75.8	79.3	76.7
July	72.1	71.1	78.3	77.9	68.6	76.5	81.3	73.3	87.4	75.4	79.4	75.4
August	70.0	72.1	77.9	77.9	69.7	77.3	81.6	74.4	86.2	74.8	77.7	75.0
September	69.2	70.9	74.3	77.8	68.3	76.4	79.1	74.0	77.1	68.8	76.4	74.3
October	67.2	70.4	76.8	78.1	67.9	74.5	77.8	74.0	87.5	72.6	75.0	73.3
November	64.6	69.6	75.1	77.7	64.9	71.7	74.6	73.2	85.2	70.3	73.2	72.9
December	63.5	68.3	72.6	75.6	61.3	70.5	70.7	71.0	84.5	67.2	69.9	71.3
2009												
January	63.1	68.3	72.4	75.7	61.9	68.5	69.7	69.6	82.4	68.1	69.0	68.7
February	61.3	66.9	73.2	76.5	60.1	67.4	72.2	67.8	84.6	69.3	67.4	67.8
March	60.4	66.4	72.8	76.5	58.5	67.7	68.9	67.3	84.8	69.1	65.6	64.2
April	58.5	67.2	72.9	75.9	59.4	66.5	68.4	66.4	84.9	70.3	65.3	63.4
May	58.4	66.8	73.2	76.9	58.8	66.8	70.9	66.3	83.3	70.1	64.9	62.9
June	57.8	66.6	73.3	75.9	59.1	63.2	72.4	67.3	84.5	70.7	65.1	63.0
July	58.5	67.2	73.4	75.2	58.4	65.2	72.6	67.4	84.1	71.3	66.1	62.4
August	56.8	68.3	74.4	77.0	60.0	66.0	74.3	68.0	83.7	72.0	66.7	62.8
September	57.6	68.1	74.8	76.9	60.2	66.0	73.9	67.6	85.0	72.8	67.4	63.2
October	57.4	68.5	75.0	77.7	62.7	66.1	72.2	68.2	83.7	72.5	68.5	62.9
November	57.6	69.9	75.9	78.0	65.3	67.2	75.9	68.2	83.4	73.8	69.3	64.1
December	57.7	68.7	75.8	77.8	65.4	69.3	74.5	68.7	81.2	74.0	70.1	64.2

. . . = Not available.

Table 2-3. Capacity Utilization by NAICS Industry Groups—*Continued*

(Output as a percentage of capacity, seasonally adjusted.)

Year and month	Mining	Utilities	Selected high-tech industries				Measures excluding selected high-tech industries		Stage-of-process groups		
			Total	Computers and office equipment	Communications equipment	Semiconductors and related electronic components	Total industry	Manufacturing	Crude	Primary and semi-finished	Finished
1967	81.2	94.5	89.4	. . .	. . .	. . .	86.9	86.8	81.1	85.0	88.2
1968	83.6	95.1	87.8	. . .	. . .	. . .	87.2	87.0	83.4	86.8	87.1
1969	86.7	96.8	90.4	. . .	. . .	. . .	87.1	86.4	85.6	88.1	85.6
1970	89.1	96.3	84.3	. . .	. . .	. . .	81.0	79.3	85.1	81.5	78.2
1971	87.8	94.7	75.4	. . .	. . .	. . .	80.0	78.3	84.3	81.7	75.7
1972	90.7	95.3	79.8	84.6	73.9	84.9	84.9	83.6	88.5	88.2	79.7
1973	91.6	93.3	81.6	81.8	75.1	91.4	88.5	87.9	90.4	92.1	79.7
1974	90.9	86.9	82.0	88.4	73.4	87.4	85.2	84.5	91.1	87.4	83.1
1975	89.0	85.1	64.9	68.8	62.2	64.4	76.1	73.9	83.9	75.1	80.1
1976	89.4	85.5	68.5	76.2	61.9	69.5	80.1	78.7	86.9	80.0	73.5
1977	89.5	86.6	75.9	77.6	72.5	78.2	83.7	82.8	88.9	84.5	76.7
1978	89.6	86.9	79.3	78.6	77.4	82.1	85.2	84.5	88.4	86.2	79.9
1979	91.1	87.0	83.5	78.6	85.6	87.5	85.0	84.0	89.3	86.0	82.1
1980	91.1	85.5	87.8	86.8	91.8	85.3	80.5	78.2	88.9	78.8	81.8
1981	90.8	84.4	85.7	85.4	89.1	83.2	79.4	76.5	89.1	77.3	79.5
1982	84.2	80.2	78.3	70.4	87.0	81.5	73.4	70.5	82.2	70.5	77.6
1983	79.8	79.6	80.6	76.0	85.7	81.7	74.7	73.1	79.8	74.5	73.3
1984	85.7	82.1	87.4	85.4	85.0	91.2	80.1	78.9	85.6	81.1	73.3
1985	84.3	81.8	77.1	76.3	78.0	77.1	79.4	78.3	83.9	79.7	77.4
1986	77.6	81.0	72.7	72.7	74.7	71.3	79.0	78.8	79.3	79.7	76.8
1987	80.3	83.6	77.4	73.7	78.2	79.9	81.4	81.3	83.1	82.8	77.1
1988	84.3	86.6	80.2	76.2	83.8	81.6	84.5	84.3	86.8	85.8	78.7
1989	85.3	86.8	78.2	74.9	79.6	80.0	84.0	83.6	87.3	84.7	81.6
1990	86.9	86.5	77.9	71.4	82.5	80.9	82.8	81.9	88.2	82.7	81.4
1991	85.1	87.8	77.3	74.1	77.9	79.2	79.9	78.5	85.6	79.8	80.6
1992	84.6	86.3	80.5	78.9	79.8	81.4	80.4	79.4	85.6	81.5	78.0
1993	85.9	88.3	79.4	79.8	80.8	78.2	81.6	80.5	85.9	83.5	77.9
1994	87.7	88.4	82.4	76.7	81.7	85.5	83.6	82.7	88.2	86.5	78.0
1995	88.1	89.3	85.3	82.1	78.8	90.0	83.9	83.0	89.0	86.6	79.0
1996	90.4	90.8	82.4	85.8	76.9	84.0	83.5	82.2	88.8	85.8	79.7
1997	91.4	90.3	83.2	82.6	78.0	86.4	84.3	83.1	90.7	86.2	79.2
1998	89.2	92.7	79.6	80.5	83.6	77.0	83.3	82.1	87.7	84.3	80.2
1999	86.1	94.1	84.2	81.4	88.6	82.9	81.7	80.3	86.6	84.2	80.4
2000	90.7	93.8	89.0	77.0	90.5	93.7	81.1	79.1	88.5	84.4	78.3
2001	90.4	89.6	69.0	70.4	67.3	69.9	76.7	74.3	85.3	77.4	77.1
2002	86.1	87.7	57.0	69.7	44.6	61.1	76.1	74.2	82.7	76.6	72.5
2003	88.0	86.0	62.4	75.0	44.4	71.7	76.7	74.7	84.4	77.7	70.7
2004	88.3	84.8	69.7	79.0	52.7	78.1	78.4	76.7	86.1	79.8	71.6
2005	88.6	85.2	73.8	76.3	60.1	81.0	80.5	78.9	86.5	81.7	73.3
2006	90.4	83.4	82.0	76.4	80.3	85.8	80.8	79.2	88.3	81.7	76.0
2007	89.2	85.4	79.3	79.0	78.3	79.9	80.6	79.0	87.8	81.0	77.1
2008	90.1	83.8	78.0	81.9	76.6	77.0	77.5	74.9	86.5	77.3	77.5
2009	84.1	80.2	63.2	66.4	68.7	58.3	70.4	67.0	81.7	67.5	74.1
											68.5
2008											
January	90.6	86.5	79.7	84.5	76.7	79.1	80.5	78.4	88.8	80.6	77.1
February	91.2	86.7	80.7	86.0	77.0	80.2	80.2	77.8	88.9	80.3	76.6
March	90.8	84.5	82.1	87.4	78.7	81.6	79.7	77.5	88.8	79.6	76.3
April	90.9	85.1	82.7	88.3	80.3	81.5	79.1	76.6	88.5	79.4	75.2
May	90.8	83.7	82.2	87.7	79.9	80.9	78.8	76.4	88.6	78.8	75.0
June	90.7	84.4	81.3	85.5	78.3	81.4	78.6	76.1	87.6	78.7	74.9
July	92.3	83.1	80.6	82.5	76.6	82.5	78.5	75.8	88.7	78.3	74.6
August	91.8	80.2	79.4	79.9	74.9	82.6	77.6	75.1	88.3	77.1	73.7
September	83.1	81.2	78.0	78.6	74.2	80.8	74.4	72.2	78.7	74.9	72.2
October	89.2	82.1	74.1	76.6	74.6	72.6	75.5	72.6	84.7	75.4	71.5
November	90.7	83.5	69.3	73.8	74.5	63.4	74.6	71.2	84.7	73.5	71.2
December	89.0	85.1	66.0	72.0	73.9	57.4	73.0	69.1	82.1	71.4	70.3
2009											
January	88.4	85.1	65.4	70.5	74.5	56.5	71.4	67.2	81.5	69.7	68.5
February	87.1	81.1	63.6	68.8	71.3	55.6	70.9	67.2	81.7	68.5	68.6
March	84.9	80.8	63.5	67.3	70.3	57.0	69.8	66.1	79.5	67.1	68.2
April	82.7	80.9	64.1	65.2	70.6	59.2	69.4	65.9	79.5	67.0	67.6
May	81.9	79.2	62.2	63.4	69.0	57.1	68.8	65.4	79.8	65.9	67.0
June	80.7	78.7	61.9	63.0	69.4	56.4	68.5	65.3	79.5	65.8	66.6
July	82.0	77.8	63.2	64.7	67.9	59.8	69.5	66.4	81.0	66.5	67.6
August	83.8	78.2	63.0	65.3	66.8	59.8	70.4	67.3	82.7	67.1	68.7
September	83.8	78.4	62.7	66.6	64.8	60.3	70.9	67.9	83.6	67.5	69.2
October	83.8	80.4	63.0	67.0	65.7	60.0	71.1	67.9	83.0	67.8	69.4
November	85.5	78.3	62.8	67.3	66.6	58.7	71.8	68.7	84.3	68.2	70.0
December	84.8	84.1	63.0	67.7	67.1	58.8	72.3	68.7	84.3	69.3	70.1

. . . = Not available.

NOTES AND DEFINITIONS, CHAPTER 2

TABLES 2-1 THROUGH 2-3 AND 20-1
INDUSTRIAL PRODUCTION AND CAPACITY UTILIZATION

SOURCE: BOARD OF GOVERNORS OF THE FEDERAL RESERVE SYSTEM

The *industrial production index* measures changes in the physical volume or quantity of output of manufacturing, mining, and electric and gas utilities. *Capacity utilization* is calculated by dividing a seasonally adjusted industrial production index for an industry or group of industries by a related index of productive capacity.

Around the 15th day of each month, the Federal Reserve issues estimates of industrial production and capacity utilization for the previous month. The production estimates are in the form of index numbers (currently 2002 = 100) that reflect the monthly levels of total output of the nation's factories, mines, and gas and electric utilities expressed as a percent of the monthly average in the 2002 base year. Capacity estimates are expressed as index numbers, 2002 output = 100 (not 2002 capacity), and capacity utilization is measured by the production index as a percent of the capacity index. Since the bases of those two indexes are the same for each industry, this procedure yields production as a percent of capacity. Monthly estimates are subject to revision in each of the three subsequent months, as well as to annual and comprehensive revisions in subsequent years. Monthly series are seasonally adjusted using the Census X-12-ARIMA program.

Definitions and notes on the data

The index of industrial production measures a large portion of the goods output of the national economy on a monthly basis. That portion, together with construction, has also accounted for the bulk of the variation in output over the course of many historical business cycles. The substantial industrial detail included in the index illuminates structural developments in the economy.

The total industrial production index and the indexes for its major components are constructed from individual industry series (312 series for data from 1997 forward) based on the 2002 North American Industry Classification System (NAICS). See Chapter 14 of this publication for a description of NAICS and a table that outlines its structure.

The Federal Reserve has been able to provide a longer continuous historical series on the NAICS basis than some other government agencies. In a major research effort, the Fed and the Census Bureau's Center for Economic Studies re-coded data from seven Censuses of Manufactures, beginning in 1963, to establish benchmark NAICS data for output, value added, and capacity utilization. The resulting indexes are shown annually for the last 38 years (43 years for aggregate levels) in Tables 2-1 through 2-3.

The Fed's featured indexes for total industry and total manufacturing on the Standard Industrial Classification (SIC) basis do <u>not</u> observe the reclassifications under NAICS of the logging industry to the Agriculture sector and the publishing industry to the Information sector. (The reason cited by the Fed was to avoid "changing the scope or historical continuity of these statistics.") One advantage of the SIC index for capacity utilization is that it is a continuous series back to 1947 (shown in Table 20-1). On the new NAICS basis, production and capacity utilization are shown back to 1972 in Tables 2-2 and 2-3.

The individual series components of the indexes are grouped in two ways: market groups and industry groups.

Market groups. For analyzing market trends and product flows, the individual series are grouped into two major divisions: *final products and nonindustrial supplies* and *materials.* *Final products* consists of products purchased by consumers, businesses, or government for final use. *Nonindustrial supplies* are expected to become inputs in nonindustrial sectors: the two major subgroups are *construction supplies* and *business supplies.* *Materials* comprises industrial output that requires further processing within the industrial sector. This twofold division distinguishes between products that are ready to ship outside the industrial sector and those that will stay within the sector for further processing.

Final products are divided into *consumer goods* and *equipment*, and *equipment* is divided into *business equipment* and *defense and space equipment.* Further subdivisions of each market group are based on type of product and the market destination for the product.

Industry groups are typically groupings by 3-digit NAICS industries and major aggregates of these industries—for example, *durable goods* and *nondurable goods manufacturing*, *mining*, and *utilities*. Indexes are also calculated for *stage-of-process* industry groups—*crude, primary and semifinished*, and *finished* processing. The stage-of-process grouping was a new feature in the 2002 revision, replacing the two narrower and less well-defined "primary processing manufacturing" and "advanced processing manufacturing" groups that were previously published. *Crude processing* consists of logging, much of mining, and certain basic manufacturing activities in the chemical, paper, and metals industries. *Primary and semifinished processing* represents industries that produce materials and parts used as inputs by other industries. *Finished processing* includes industries that produce goods in their finished form for use by consumers, business investment, or government.

The indexes of industrial production are constructed with data from a variety of sources. Current monthly estimates of production are based on measures of physical output where possible and appropriate. For a few high-tech industries, the estimated value of nominal output is deflated by a corresponding price index. For industries in which such direct measurement is not possible on a monthly basis, output is inferred from production-worker hours, adjusted for trends in worker productivity derived from annual and benchmark revisions. (Between the 1960s and 1997, electric power consumption was used as a monthly output indicator for some industries instead of hours. However, the coverage of the electric power consumption survey deteriorated, and in the 2005 revision, the decision was made to resume the use of hours in those industries, beginning with the data for 1997.)

In annual and benchmark revisions, the individual indexes are revised using data from the quinquennial Censuses of Manufactures and Mineral Industries and the Annual Survey of Manufactures and Survey of Plant Capacity, prepared by the Census Bureau; deflators from the Producer Price Indexes and other sources; the *Minerals Yearbook*, prepared by the Department of the Interior; publications from the Department of Energy; and other sources.

The weights used in computing the indexes are based on Census value added—the difference between the value of production and the cost of materials and supplies consumed. (Census value added differs in some respects from the economic concept of industry value added used in the national income and product accounts [NIPAs]. Industry value added as defined in the NIPAs is not available in sufficient detail for the industrial production indexes. See Chapter 15 for data and a description of NIPA value added by major industry group.) Before 1972, a linked-Laspeyres formula is used. Beginning with 1972, the index uses a version of the Fisher-ideal index formula—a chain-weighting system similar to that in the NIPAs. See the "General Notes" article at the front of this book and the notes and definitions for Chapter 1 for more information. Chain-weighting keeps the index from being distorted by the use of obsolete relative prices.

For the purpose of these value-added weights, value added per unit of output is based on data from the Censuses of Manufacturing and Mineral Industries, the Census Bureau's Annual Survey of Manufactures, and revenue and expense data reported by the Department of Energy and the American Gas Association, which are projected into recent years by using changes in relevant Producer Price Indexes.

To separate seasonal movements from cyclical patterns and underlying trends, each component of the index is seasonally adjusted by the Census X-12-ARIMA method.

The index does not cover production on farms, in the construction industry, in transportation, or in various trade and service industries. A number of groups and subgroups include data for individual series not published separately.

Capacity utilization is calculated for the manufacturing, mining, and electric and gas utilities industries. Output is measured by seasonally adjusted indexes of industrial pro-

duction. The capacity indexes attempt to capture the concept of sustainable maximum output, which is defined as the greatest level of output that a plant can maintain within the framework of a realistic work schedule, taking account of normal downtime and assuming sufficient availability of inputs to operate the machinery and equipment in place. The 87 individual industry capacity indexes are based on a variety of data, including capacity data measured in physical units compiled by government agencies and trade associations, Census Bureau surveys of utilization rates and investment, and estimates of growth of the capital stock.

Revisions

Revisions normally occur annually. The revision released on March 27, 2009 is incorporated in this volume, as are subsequent updates through April 2010. The next revision is scheduled for release June 25, 2010.

In the November 2005 revision, the indexes were all rebased from 1997 = 100 to 2002 = 100. A previous comprehensive revision in 1997 moved the reference year from 1987 to 1992 = 100 and introduced annual (instead of quinquennial) updating of the value-added weights for each industry. In the January 2001 revision, recalculation of the value-added weights each month was introduced.

Data availability

Data are available monthly in Federal Reserve release G.17. Current and historical data and background information are available on the Federal Reserve Web site at <http://www.federalreserve.gov>. The total Industrial Production index extends back to 1919.

Chain-weighting makes it difficult for the user to analyze in detail the sources of aggregate output change. An "Explanatory Note," included in each month's index release, provides some assistance for the user, including a reference to a an Internet location with the exact contribution of a monthly change in a component index to the monthly change in the total index.

References

The G.17 release each month contains extensive explanatory material, as well as references for further detail. The 2005 revision is described in "Industrial Production and Capacity Utilization: The 2005 Annual Revision," issued November 7, 2005.

An earlier detailed description of the industrial production index, together with a history of the index, a glossary of terms, and a bibliography is presented in *Industrial Production—1986 Edition*, available from Publication Services, Mail Stop 127, Board of Governors of the Federal Reserve System, Washington, DC 20551.

CHAPTER 3: INCOME DISTRIBUTION AND POVERTY

Section 3a: Household and Family Income

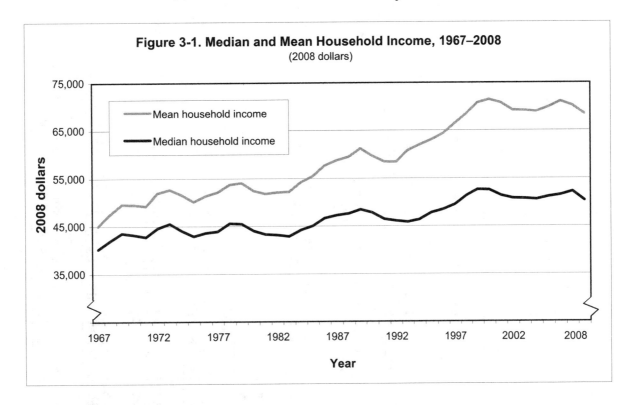

Figure 3-1. Median and Mean Household Income, 1967–2008
(2008 dollars)

- Measured as cash income before taxes, median household income in 2008 was $50,303—down 3.6 percent from the previous year, in constant (2008) dollars, and the lowest since 1997. Measured peak to peak over the latest completed business cycle, from 1999 to 2007, real median household income declined 0.8 percent. In contrast, between the 1969 business cycle peak and 1999, real median household income rose an average 0.6 percent per year. (Table 3-1)

- The Census Bureau also tabulates "mean income," which is the sum of all the reported household incomes divided by the number of households. Mean income is higher than median income when the distribution of income is skewed upward, with very large incomes at the top of the distribution. It rises faster than median income when the income distribution becomes more unequal. (See "Whose Standard of Living?" in the article at the beginning of this book.) Mean household income declined 2.5 percent in 2008, smaller than the drop in median income. Like median income, it failed to increase over the latest complete cycle. (Table 3-1)

- Household income inequality, as measured by the "Gini coefficient," rose in 2008 and remained around the postwar highs first reached in 2001. (Table 3-4)

- The ratio of women's to men's earnings for year-round, full-time workers increased from 0.607 in 1960 to 0.778 in 2007, then fell back slightly in 2008. Men's earnings at the cycle high in 2007 were 3.3 percent below 1973 in real terms, and fell another 1.0 percent in 2008. Women's real earnings in 2007 were up 32.8 percent since 1973, but fell 1.9 percent in 2008. (Table 3-1)

Table 3-1. Median and Mean Household Income and Median Earnings

(2008 dollars.)

Year	Median household income — All races	White — Total	White — Not Hispanic	Black	Asian [1]	Hispanic (any race)	Mean household income, all races	Median earnings of year-round, full-time workers — Male workers	Female workers	Ratio, female to male
1960	...	...	...	...	...	...	...	34 152	20 722	0.607
1961	...	...	...	...	...	...	...	35 242	20 881	0.592
1962	...	...	...	...	...	...	...	35 886	21 280	0.593
1963	...	...	...	...	...	...	...	36 787	21 685	0.589
1964	...	...	...	...	...	...	...	37 647	22 268	0.591
1965	...	...	...	...	...	...	...	38 183	22 881	0.599
1966	...	...	...	...	...	...	...	39 851	22 936	0.576
1967	40 261	41 985	...	24 377	...	...	45 029	40 480	23 391	0.578
1968	41 995	43 726	...	25 784	...	...	47 511	41 567	24 173	0.582
1969	43 557	45 457	...	27 477	...	...	49 554	43 899	25 841	0.589
1970	43 219	45 015	...	27 399	...	...	49 489	44 367	26 340	0.594
1971	42 798	44 766	...	26 443	...	...	49 222	44 557	26 514	0.595
1972	44 632	46 822	47 490	27 330	...	35 334	51 945	46 956	27 169	0.579
1973	45 533	47 720	48 140	28 090	...	35 276	52 658	48 452	27 440	0.566
1974	44 091	46 111	46 505	27 422	...	35 069	51 561	46 713	27 446	0.588
1975	42 936	44 901	45 240	26 955	...	32 257	50 137	46 422	27 305	0.588
1976	43 649	45 723	46 656	27 188	...	32 924	51 342	46 295	27 866	0.602
1977	43 925	46 190	47 106	27 257	...	34 458	52 107	47 336	27 892	0.589
1978	45 625	47 430	48 323	28 503	...	35 748	53 699	47 642	28 319	0.594
1979	45 498	47 704	48 375	28 007	...	36 048	54 047	47 026	28 057	0.597
1980	44 059	46 482	47 306	26 779	...	33 961	52 401	46 303	27 856	0.602
1981	43 328	45 779	46 440	25 689	...	34 755	51 762	46 022	27 261	0.592
1982	43 212	45 238	45 997	25 639	...	32 515	52 077	45 153	27 880	0.617
1983	42 910	44 999	...	25 558	...	32 680	52 188	44 956	28 589	0.636
1984	44 242	46 674	47 643	26 589	...	33 539	54 208	45 827	29 173	0.637
1985	45 069	47 531	48 600	28 279	...	33 328	55 466	46 171	29 815	0.646
1986	46 665	49 061	50 176	28 265	...	34 398	57 653	47 338	30 424	0.643
1987	47 251	49 783	51 152	28 414	58 428	35 058	58 762	47 042	30 661	0.652
1988	47 614	50 335	51 722	28 694	56 432	35 606	59 492	46 619	30 791	0.660
1989	48 463	50 978	52 074	30 317	60 527	36 752	61 228	45 822	31 467	0.687
1990	47 818	49 875	51 015	29 825	61 403	35 660	59 731	44 201	31 655	0.716
1991	46 445	48 670	49 832	28 995	56 193	34 982	58 464	45 358	31 686	0.699
1992	46 063	48 428	50 054	28 199	56 836	33 976	58 399	45 403	32 139	0.708
1993	45 839	48 362	50 142	28 660	56 266	33 580	60 787	44 616	31 909	0.715
1994	46 351	48 885	50 463	30 208	58 157	33 647	61 966	44 325	31 900	0.720
1995	47 803	50 174	52 155	31 414	56 975	32 069	63 041	44 184	31 560	0.714
1996	48 499	50 779	53 001	32 087	59 135	34 033	64 392	43 924	32 399	0.738
1997	49 497	52 128	54 274	33 506	60 523	35 617	66 466	45 041	33 403	0.742
1998	51 295	53 969	55 983	33 442	61 521	37 371	68 404	46 625	34 116	0.732
1999	52 587	54 692	57 059	36 065	65 850	39 730	70 731	47 024	34 005	0.723
2000	52 500	54 908	57 042	37 093	69 713	41 470	71 436	46 576	34 336	0.737
2001	51 356	54 140	56 314	35 840	65 228	40 820	70 790	46 548	35 530	0.763
2002	50 756	...	...	...	...	39 618	69 238	47 189	36 148	0.766
2003	50 711	...	...	...	...	38 629	69 148	47 609	35 968	0.755
2004	50 535	...	...	...	...	39 064	68 923	46 502	35 610	0.766
2005	51 093	...	...	...	...	39 668	69 862	45 644	35 136	0.770
2006	51 473	...	...	...	...	40 346	71 089	45 130	34 722	0.769
2007	52 163	...	...	...	...	40 165	70 207	46 846	36 451	0.778
2008	50 303	...	...	...	...	37 913	68 424	46 367	35 745	0.771
By race										
Race alone										
2002	...	53 960	56 131	34 739	62 984	...	...	...	...	...
2003	...	53 419	55 931	34 705	65 206	...	...	...	...	...
2004	...	53 184	55 751	34 304	65 547	...	...	...	...	...
2005	...	53 550	56 009	34 033	67 380	...	...	...	...	...
2006	...	54 113	55 982	34 139	68 599	...	...	...	...	...
2007	...	54 117	57 030	35 219	68 643	...	...	...	...	...
2008	...	52 312	55 530	34 218	65 637	...	...	...	...	...
Race alone or in combination										
2002	...	...	...	34 920	62 576	...	...	...	...	...
2003	...	...	...	34 756	64 694	...	...	...	...	...
2004	...	...	...	34 464	65 484	...	...	...	...	...
2005	...	...	...	34 139	67 330	...	...	...	...	...
2006	...	...	...	34 313	68 238	...	...	...	...	...
2007	...	...	...	35 401	68 407	...	...	...	...	...
2008	...	...	...	34 345	65 567	...	...	...	...	...

[1]For 1987 through 2001, Asian and Pacific Islander.
. . . = Not available.

Table 3-2. Median Income and Poverty Rates by Race and Hispanic Origin Using 3–Year Moving Averages

(Income in 2008 dollars; percent of population.)

Race and Hispanic origin	Median household income, 2008 dollars						
	2000–2002	2001–2003	2002–2004	2003–2005	2004–2006	2005–2007	2007–2008
All Races	51 537	50 941	50 667	50 780	51 034	51 576	51 313
White alone or in combination	54 287	53 768	53 422	53 292	53 527	53 837	53 443
White alone	54 336	53 840	53 521	53 384	53 616	53 927	53 514
Not Hispanic	56 496	56 125	55 938	55 897	55 914	56 340	56 181
Black alone or in combination	35 951	35 172	34 713	34 453	34 305	34 618	34 686
Black alone	35 891	35 095	34 583	34 347	34 159	34 464	34 525
American Indian and Alaskan Native alone or in combination	39 636	40 658	41 312	41 051	39 903	39 490	39 397
American Indian and Alaskan Native alone	39 119	38 649	37 680	37 091	35 981	36 283	35 570
Asian alone or in combination	65 839	64 166	64 251	65 836	67 017	67 992	67 404
Asian alone	65 975	64 473	64 579	66 044	67 175	68 207	67 626
Native Hawaiian and Other Pacific Islander alone or in combination	. . .	. . .	59 434	59 128	58 599	59 812	59 738
Native Hawaiian and Other Pacific Islander alone	. . .	. . .	58 867	59 913	58 723	58 440	58 142
Hispanic (any race)	40 636	39 689	39 104	39 120	39 693	40 060	39 475

Race and Hispanic origin	Poverty rates						
	2000–2002	2001–2003	2002–2004	2003–2005	2004–2006	2005–2007	2007–2008
All Races	11.7	12.1	12.4	12.6	12.5	12.5	12.7
White alone or in combination	9.9	10.3	10.6	10.7	10.7	10.5	10.8
White alone	9.9	10.2	10.5	10.6	10.6	10.4	10.7
Not Hispanic	7.7	8.0	8.3	8.4	8.4	8.2	8.3
Black alone or in combination	23.0	23.6	24.3	24.6	24.5	24.4	24.4
Black alone	23.1	23.7	24.4	24.7	24.6	24.6	24.5
American Indian and Alaskan Native alone or in combination	21.6	20.0	19.2	19.7	20.9	21.2	21.6
American Indian and Alaskan Native alone	23.1	23.3	24.3	25.3	27.2	26.6	26.7
Asian alone or in combination	10.0	10.7	10.5	10.8	10.3	10.4	10.6
Asian alone	10.1	10.7	10.6	10.9	10.4	10.5	10.8
Native Hawaiian and Other Pacific Islander alone or in combination	. . .	. . .	. . .	. . .	. . .	. . .	. . .
Native Hawaiian and Other Pacific Islander alone	. . .	. . .	. . .	. . .	. . .	. . .	. . .
Hispanic (any race)	21.6	21.9	22.1	22.0	21.4	21.3	21.8

. . . = Not available.

Table 3-3. Median Family Income by Type of Family

(2008 dollars, except as noted.)

Year	All families	Married couples			Male householder [1]	Female householder [1]	4-person families	Average size of family (number of people)
		Total	Wife in paid labor force	Wife not in paid labor force				
1947	25 557	26 215	. . .	. . .	24 756	18 314	27 758	3.64
1948	24 882	25 546	. . .	. . .	25 725	16 114	27 076	3.58
1949	24 561	25 256	30 490	24 173	22 300	16 624	26 703	3.54
1950	25 913	26 904	31 253	25 882	24 320	15 006	28 692	3.54
1951	26 837	27 763	33 509	26 295	24 978	16 063	29 826	3.54
1952	27 641	28 856	34 818	27 087	25 687	15 881	31 073	3.53
1953	29 940	30 851	38 149	29 058	29 030	17 327	. . .	3.59
1954	29 151	30 312	37 328	28 339	28 080	16 048	. . .	3.59
1955	31 044	32 316	39 504	30 397	29 442	17 363	34 564	3.58
1956	33 073	34 408	41 217	32 139	28 832	19 055	36 802	3.60
1957	33 268	34 548	41 139	32 377	30 689	18 510	36 765	3.64
1958	33 165	34 652	40 513	32 487	27 773	17 870	37 064	3.65
1959	35 028	36 612	43 356	34 381	29 829	17 873	39 250	3.67
1960	35 755	37 365	43 899	35 119	30 920	18 883	40 050	3.70
1961	36 124	38 026	45 276	35 223	31 929	18 852	40 545	3.67
1962	37 146	39 060	46 532	35 948	35 618	19 527	42 135	3.68
1963	38 442	40 558	47 916	37 150	35 126	19 753	43 911	3.70
1964	39 868	42 071	49 585	38 466	35 152	20 987	45 445	3.70
1965	41 584	43 425	51 387	39 402	36 749	21 112	46 623	3.69
1966	43 780	45 558	53 742	41 432	37 386	23 308	48 482	3.67
1967	44 713	47 577	56 116	42 898	38 406	24 203	50 693	3.63
1968	46 817	49 594	57 957	44 555	39 707	24 282	53 336	3.60
1969	48 977	51 926	60 379	46 101	43 302	25 036	55 156	3.58
1970	48 825	52 037	60 746	46 040	44 595	25 202	55 258	3.57
1971	48 757	52 100	60 931	46 193	41 348	24 244	55 115	3.53
1972	51 163	54 785	63 963	48 585	47 430	24 587	58 950	3.48
1973	52 199	56 431	65 999	49 457	46 529	25 110	59 385	3.44
1974	50 805	54 825	63 874	48 162	45 906	25 548	58 944	3.42
1975	49 919	54 096	62 720	46 400	47 284	24 903	57 666	3.39
1976	51 466	55 750	64 448	47 932	44 247	24 811	59 576	3.37
1977	51 812	57 013	65 596	48 750	46 987	25 131	60 596	3.33
1978	53 427	58 576	66 962	48 932	48 357	25 856	61 871	3.31
1979	54 138	59 229	68 715	48 939	46 457	27 308	62 223	3.29
1980	52 301	57 570	66 870	47 199	43 584	25 893	60 533	3.27
1981	50 856	56 936	66 436	46 169	45 179	24 896	59 683	3.25
1982	50 200	55 740	65 001	45 628	43 145	24 602	59 168	3.26
1983	50 502	56 061	65 966	44 975	44 882	24 221	59 961	3.24
1984	52 173	58 448	68 427	46 546	46 038	25 270	61 379	3.23
1985	52 926	59 347	69 520	46 859	43 169	26 067	62 547	3.21
1986	55 214	61 487	71 873	48 363	46 787	25 579	65 069	3.19
1987	56 151	63 238	73 885	48 300	45 704	26 621	67 240	3.17
1988	56 299	63 640	74 694	47 605	46 918	26 839	68 296	3.16
1989	57 360	64 627	75 891	48 196	46 687	27 566	68 342	3.17
1990	56 458	63 711	74 701	48 332	46 386	27 040	66 196	3.18
1991	55 407	63 201	74 262	46 366	43 708	25 734	66 379	3.17
1992	54 990	62 984	74 840	45 369	41 462	25 598	66 534	3.19
1993	54 229	63 101	75 131	44 338	38 835	25 594	66 264	3.20
1994	55 715	64 589	76 585	44 788	39 868	26 198	67 538	3.19
1995	56 971	66 020	78 311	45 417	42 587	27 623	69 703	3.20
1996	57 801	67 923	79 776	46 115	43 180	27 208	70 398	3.19
1997	59 613	69 006	81 149	48 188	44 086	28 120	71 359	3.18
1998	61 653	71 471	84 097	49 021	47 069	29 236	73 953	3.18
1999	63 099	73 010	85 903	49 724	48 249	30 705	77 215	3.15
2000	63 430	73 891	86 564	49 989	47 170	32 153	78 356	3.14
2001	62 519	73 377	86 145	49 597	44 499	31 310	76 956	3.15
2002	61 852	73 162	87 136	47 995	45 167	31 624	75 079	3.13
2003	61 671	72 911	88 000	48 141	44 523	31 081	76 203	3.13
2004	61 623	72 525	87 604	48 120	46 006	30 741	75 258	3.13
2005	61 976	72 687	86 858	49 031	45 341	30 047	77 547	3.13
2006	62 372	74 115	88 408	48 863	44 684	30 786	78 399	3.13
2007	63 712	75 378	89 756	49 148	46 062	31 460	78 583	3.15
2008	61 521	72 743	86 621	48 502	43 571	30 129	76 470	3.15

[1]No spouse present.
. . . = Not available.

Table 3-4. Shares of Aggregate Income Received by Each Fifth and Top 5 Percent of Households

Year	Number (thousands)	Share of aggregate income (percent)						Mean household income (2008 dollars)						Gini coefficient
		Lowest fifth	Second fifth	Third fifth	Fourth fifth	Highest fifth	Top 5 percent	Lowest fifth	Second fifth	Third fifth	Fourth fifth	Highest fifth	Top 5 percent	
1967	60 813	4.0	10.8	17.3	24.2	43.6	17.2	9 018	24 986	39 889	55 811	100 440	158 438	0.397
1968	62 214	4.2	11.1	17.6	24.5	42.6	16.3	9 795	26 261	41 654	58 104	100 967	154 363	0.386
1969	63 401	4.1	10.9	17.5	24.5	43.0	16.6	10 031	27 082	43 276	60 618	106 542	163 993	0.391
1970	64 778	4.1	10.8	17.4	24.5	43.3	16.6	9 857	26 701	42 996	60 607	107 295	164 686	0.394
1971	66 676	4.1	10.6	17.3	24.5	43.5	16.7	9 917	26 211	42 500	60 419	107 058	164 206	0.396
1972	68 251	4.1	10.4	17.0	24.5	43.9	17.0	10 508	27 142	44 296	63 594	114 168	176 957	0.401
1973	69 859	4.2	10.4	17.0	24.5	43.9	16.9	10 998	27 652	45 355	65 250	116 747	179 827	0.400
1974	71 163	4.3	10.6	17.0	24.6	43.5	16.5	10 959	27 237	43 894	63 394	112 316	170 720	0.395
1975	72 867	4.3	10.4	17.0	24.7	43.6	16.5	10 585	26 002	42 660	61 988	109 444	166 083	0.397
1976	74 142	4.3	10.3	17.0	24.7	43.7	16.6	10 845	26 552	43 666	63 412	112 232	171 003	0.398
1977	76 030	4.2	10.2	16.9	24.7	44.0	16.8	10 794	26 568	43 948	64 392	114 829	175 664	0.402
1978	77 330	4.2	10.2	16.8	24.7	44.1	16.8	11 161	27 410	45 258	66 299	118 366	180 167	0.402
1979	80 776	4.1	10.2	16.8	24.6	44.2	16.9	11 073	27 540	45 407	66 634	119 584	182 379	0.404
1980	82 368	4.2	10.2	16.8	24.7	44.1	16.5	10 722	26 687	44 037	64 877	115 675	172 863	0.403
1981	83 527	4.1	10.1	16.7	24.8	44.3	16.5	10 454	26 041	43 139	64 305	114 868	170 693	0.406
1982	83 918	4.0	10.0	16.5	24.5	45.0	17.0	10 262	25 967	42 983	63 926	117 245	177 160	0.412
1983	85 407	4.0	9.9	16.4	24.6	45.1	17.0	10 382	26 079	43 117	64 703	118 794	179 486	0.414
1984	86 789	4.0	9.9	16.3	24.6	45.2	17.1	10 729	26 725	44 288	66 682	122 613	185 090	0.415
1985	88 458	3.9	9.8	16.2	24.4	45.6	17.6	10 713	27 149	45 064	67 785	126 619	195 319	0.419
1986	89 479	3.8	9.7	16.2	24.3	46.1	18.0	10 822	27 839	46 587	70 181	132 836	208 096	0.425
1987	91 124	3.8	9.6	16.1	24.3	46.2	18.2	11 118	28 255	47 240	71 404	135 794	213 943	0.426
1988	92 830	3.8	9.6	16.0	24.2	46.3	18.3	11 307	28 537	47 729	72 149	137 741	217 239	0.426
1989	93 347	3.8	9.5	15.8	24.0	46.8	18.9	11 726	29 174	48 495	73 355	143 395	231 676	0.431
1990	94 312	3.8	9.6	15.9	24.0	46.6	18.5	11 444	28 793	47 559	71 706	139 155	221 589	0.428
1991	95 669	3.8	9.6	15.9	24.2	46.5	18.1	11 140	27 982	46 479	70 851	135 864	212 028	0.428
1992	96 426	3.8	9.4	15.8	24.2	46.9	18.6	10 910	27 336	46 056	70 699	136 990	217 428	0.433
1993	97 107	3.6	9.0	15.1	23.5	48.9	21.0	10 798	27 374	45 885	71 309	148 567	254 991	0.454
1994	98 990	3.6	8.9	15.0	23.4	49.1	21.2	11 082	27 618	46 525	72 398	152 203	262 965	0.456
1995	99 627	3.7	9.1	15.2	23.3	48.7	21.0	11 707	28 614	47 845	73 549	153 486	264 895	0.450
1996	101 018	3.6	9.0	15.1	23.3	49.0	21.4	11 745	28 828	48 490	75 049	157 846	274 960	0.455
1997	102 528	3.6	8.9	15.0	23.2	49.4	21.7	11 823	29 557	49 727	77 020	164 205	288 159	0.459
1998	103 874	3.6	9.0	15.0	23.2	49.2	21.4	12 167	30 720	51 403	79 500	168 230	293 224	0.456
1999	106 434	3.6	8.9	14.9	23.2	49.4	21.5	12 812	31 458	52 657	81 955	174 769	303 765	0.458
2000	108 209	3.6	8.9	14.8	23.0	49.8	22.1	12 699	31 709	52 804	82 086	177 878	315 575	0.462
2001	109 297	3.5	8.7	14.6	23.0	50.1	22.4	12 327	30 973	51 843	81 287	177 522	316 764	0.466
2002	111 278	3.5	8.8	14.8	23.3	49.7	21.7	11 956	30 399	51 226	80 577	172 035	300 414	0.462
2003	112 000	3.4	8.7	14.8	23.4	49.8	21.4	11 702	30 061	51 027	80 770	172 181	296 461	0.464
2004	113 343	3.4	8.7	14.7	23.2	50.1	21.8	11 677	29 878	50 623	79 821	172 620	300 807	0.466
2005	114 384	3.4	8.6	14.6	23.0	50.4	22.2	11 751	30 172	51 065	80 318	176 003	310 084	0.469
2006	116 011	3.4	8.6	14.5	22.9	50.5	22.3	12 123	30 730	51 496	81 510	179 586	317 594	0.470
2007	116 783	3.4	8.7	14.8	23.4	49.7	21.2	11 995	30 573	51 888	82 151	174 425	298 226	0.463
2008	117 181	3.4	8.6	14.7	23.3	50.0	21.5	11 656	29 517	50 132	79 760	171 057	294 709	0.466

Table 3-5. Shares of Aggregate Income Received by Each Fifth and Top 5 Percent of Families

Year	Number of families (thousands)	Share of aggregate income (percent)						Mean family income (2008 dollars)						Gini coefficient
		Lowest fifth	Second fifth	Third fifth	Fourth fifth	Highest fifth	Top 5 percent	Lowest fifth	Second fifth	Third fifth	Fourth fifth	Highest fifth	Top 5 percent	
1947	37 237	5.0	11.9	17.0	23.1	43.0	17.5	...	...	...	...	...	...	0.376
1948	38 624	4.9	12.1	17.3	23.2	42.4	17.1	...	...	...	...	...	...	0.371
1949	39 303	4.5	11.9	17.3	23.5	42.7	16.9	...	...	...	...	...	...	0.378
1950	39 929	4.5	12.0	17.4	23.4	42.7	17.3	...	...	...	...	...	...	0.379
1951	40 578	5.0	12.4	17.6	23.4	41.6	16.8	...	...	...	...	...	...	0.363
1952	40 832	4.9	12.3	17.4	23.4	41.9	17.4	...	...	...	...	...	...	0.368
1953	41 202	4.7	12.5	18.0	23.9	40.9	15.7	...	...	...	...	...	...	0.359
1954	41 951	4.5	12.1	17.7	23.9	41.8	16.3	...	...	...	...	...	...	0.371
1955	42 889	4.8	12.3	17.8	23.7	41.3	16.4	...	...	...	...	...	...	0.363
1956	43 497	5.0	12.5	17.9	23.7	41.0	16.1	...	...	...	...	...	...	0.358
1957	43 696	5.1	12.7	18.1	23.8	40.4	15.6	...	...	...	...	...	...	0.351
1958	44 232	5.0	12.5	18.0	23.9	40.6	15.4	...	...	...	...	...	...	0.354
1959	45 111	4.9	12.3	17.9	23.8	41.1	15.9	...	...	...	...	...	...	0.361
1960	45 539	4.8	12.2	17.8	24.0	41.3	15.9	...	...	...	...	...	...	0.364
1961	46 418	4.7	11.9	17.5	23.8	42.2	16.6	...	...	...	...	...	...	0.374
1962	47 059	5.0	12.1	17.6	24.0	41.3	15.7	...	...	...	...	...	...	0.362
1963	47 540	5.0	12.1	17.7	24.0	41.2	15.8	...	...	...	...	...	...	0.362
1964	47 956	5.1	12.0	17.7	24.0	41.2	15.9	...	...	...	...	...	...	0.361
1965	48 509	5.2	12.2	17.8	23.9	40.9	15.5	...	...	...	...	...	...	0.356
1966	49 214	5.6	12.4	17.8	23.8	40.5	15.6	13 630	30 260	43 297	57 962	98 923	151 898	0.349
1967	50 111	5.4	12.2	17.5	23.5	41.4	16.4	13 843	30 955	44 493	59 672	105 366	166 707	0.358
1968	50 823	5.6	12.4	17.7	23.7	40.5	15.6	14 921	32 542	46 492	62 177	106 244	163 779	0.348
1969	51 586	5.6	12.4	17.7	23.7	40.6	15.6	15 395	33 998	48 650	65 171	111 615	171 433	0.349
1970	52 227	5.4	12.2	17.6	23.8	40.9	15.6	15 162	33 525	48 474	65 388	112 442	171 218	0.353
1971	53 296	5.5	12.0	17.6	23.8	41.1	15.7	15 175	33 033	48 331	65 454	112 737	171 895	0.355
1972	54 373	5.5	11.9	17.5	23.9	41.4	15.9	15 838	34 556	50 758	69 315	120 216	184 298	0.359
1973	55 053	5.5	11.9	17.5	24.0	41.1	15.5	16 252	35 202	51 723	70 686	121 278	183 028	0.356
1974	55 698	5.7	12.0	17.6	24.1	40.6	14.8	16 538	34 912	50 970	69 832	117 667	171 630	0.355
1975	56 245	5.6	11.9	17.7	24.2	40.7	14.9	15 890	33 592	49 948	68 389	115 247	169 060	0.357
1976	56 710	5.6	11.9	17.7	24.2	40.7	14.9	16 274	34 441	51 376	70 197	118 147	172 919	0.358
1977	57 215	5.5	11.7	17.6	24.3	40.9	14.9	16 205	34 640	52 097	71 865	121 069	176 499	0.363
1978	57 804	5.4	11.7	17.6	24.2	41.1	15.1	16 434	35 639	53 515	73 732	125 114	183 341	0.363
1979	59 550	5.4	11.6	17.5	24.1	41.4	15.3	16 578	35 843	54 055	74 420	127 646	188 946	0.365
1980	60 309	5.3	11.6	17.6	24.4	41.1	14.6	15 949	34 720	52 450	72 768	122 519	174 171	0.365
1981	61 019	5.3	11.4	17.5	24.6	41.2	14.4	15 453	33 605	51 398	72 163	121 081	169 190	0.369
1982	61 393	5.0	11.3	17.2	24.4	42.2	15.3	14 578	33 077	50 506	71 648	123 804	177 132	0.380
1983	62 015	4.9	11.2	17.2	24.5	42.4	15.3	14 355	33 029	50 818	72 426	125 580	181 062	0.382
1984	62 706	4.8	11.1	17.1	24.5	42.5	15.4	14 845	33 989	52 439	74 988	130 327	188 429	0.383
1985	63 558	4.8	11.0	16.9	24.3	43.1	16.1	15 016	34 458	53 201	76 258	135 523	202 526	0.389
1986	64 491	4.7	10.9	16.9	24.1	43.4	16.5	15 441	35 652	55 233	78 919	142 146	215 858	0.392
1987	65 204	4.6	10.7	16.8	24.0	43.8	17.2	15 424	36 100	56 057	80 228	146 620	229 524	0.393
1988	65 837	4.6	10.7	16.7	24.0	44.0	17.2	15 556	36 227	56 374	80 962	148 551	232 106	0.395
1989	66 090	4.6	10.6	16.5	23.7	44.6	17.9	15 867	36 915	57 349	82 509	155 355	248 866	0.401
1990	66 322	4.6	10.8	16.6	23.8	44.3	17.4	15 703	36 627	56 408	81 121	150 760	236 550	0.396
1991	67 173	4.5	10.7	16.6	24.1	44.2	17.1	15 007	35 621	55 271	80 163	147 277	227 888	0.397
1992	68 216	4.3	10.5	16.5	24.0	44.7	17.6	14 413	34 764	54 921	79 830	148 555	233 890	0.404
1993	68 506	4.1	9.9	15.7	23.3	47.0	20.3	14 290	34 320	54 386	80 621	162 894	281 149	0.429
1994	69 313	4.2	10.0	15.7	23.3	46.9	20.1	14 922	35 305	55 752	82 413	166 085	284 933	0.426
1995	69 597	4.4	10.1	15.8	23.2	46.5	20.0	15 803	36 411	57 007	83 409	167 573	287 390	0.421
1996	70 241	4.2	10.0	15.8	23.1	46.8	20.3	15 561	36 685	58 030	84 792	171 665	297 008	0.425
1997	70 884	4.2	9.9	15.7	23.0	47.2	20.7	16 127	37 789	59 622	87 427	179 615	314 356	0.429
1998	71 551	4.2	9.9	15.7	23.0	47.3	20.7	16 524	38 891	61 554	90 269	185 797	325 197	0.430
1999	73 206	4.3	9.9	15.6	23.0	47.2	20.3	17 197	39 973	63 094	93 125	190 860	329 077	0.429
2000	73 778	4.3	9.8	15.4	22.7	47.7	21.1	17 657	40 371	63 449	93 511	196 195	347 661	0.433
2001	74 340	4.2	9.7	15.4	22.9	47.7	21.0	17 052	39 484	62 678	93 213	194 152	340 903	0.435
2002	75 616	4.2	9.7	15.5	23.0	47.6	20.8	16 776	38 922	62 078	92 329	190 651	333 662	0.434
2003	76 232	4.1	9.6	15.5	23.2	47.6	20.5	16 238	38 511	62 065	93 318	191 197	329 507	0.436
2004	76 866	4.0	9.6	15.4	23.0	47.9	20.9	16 185	38 524	61 830	92 376	192 254	334 936	0.438
2005	77 418	4.0	9.6	15.3	22.9	48.1	21.1	16 286	38 752	62 012	92 748	194 432	340 393	0.440
2006	78 454	4.0	9.5	15.1	22.9	48.5	21.5	16 594	39 265	62 455	94 394	200 109	354 219	0.444
2007	77 908	4.1	9.7	15.6	23.3	47.3	20.1	16 685	39 776	63 805	95 411	193 696	328 784	0.432
2008	78 874	4.0	9.6	15.5	23.1	47.8	20.5	15 906	38 125	61 582	92 160	190 400	326 928	0.438

. . . = Not available.

Table 3-6. Median Household Income by State

(2008 dollars.)

State	1990	1996	1997	1998	1999	2000	2001	2002	2003	2004	2005	2006	2007	2008
United States	47 818	48 499	49 497	51 295	52 587	52 500	51 356	50 756	50 711	50 535	51 093	51 473	52 163	50 303
Alabama	37 300	41 407	42 720	47 840	46 843	44 291	42 760	45 004	43 614	41 752	40 973	40 528	43 834	44 476
Alaska	62 758	72 121	64 195	66 870	66 414	66 074	69 762	63 161	60 684	62 765	61 642	60 248	65 413	63 989
Arizona	46 670	43 231	43 792	48 927	47 805	49 741	51 935	47 554	48 192	49 979	49 900	49 824	49 029	46 914
Arkansas	36 389	37 063	34 993	36 494	38 355	37 130	40 545	38 761	37 464	39 877	40 430	39 573	42 362	39 586
California	53 163	53 035	53 093	53 998	56 377	58 534	57 478	56 774	57 714	56 107	57 080	59 074	57 876	57 014
Colorado	49 080	55 957	57 827	61 471	62 254	60 314	60 074	57 799	58 464	58 003	55 640	59 478	63 490	60 943
Connecticut	62 074	57 554	58 833	61 351	65 376	62 730	64 878	63 895	64 346	62 807	62 683	66 640	66 606	64 682
Delaware	49 193	53 714	57 559	54 689	60 252	62 971	60 324	59 422	57 385	54 770	56 507	55 998	56 687	50 702
District of Columbia	43 744	43 680	42 615	44 103	49 969	51 540	50 068	46 760	52 732	49 529	49 623	51 768	52 734	55 590
Florida	42 615	41 870	43 411	46 050	46 301	48 582	44 294	45 508	45 624	46 205	47 413	48 777	47 554	44 857
Georgia	44 014	44 405	49 039	51 005	50 945	52 389	51 779	51 390	49 681	46 716	50 652	52 694	50 510	46 227
Hawaii	62 156	57 080	54 752	53 857	57 508	64 448	57 693	56 613	60 681	64 109	65 717	64 575	66 482	61 521
Idaho	40 411	47 429	44 680	48 386	46 261	47 025	46 507	45 138	49 604	50 562	48 721	49 350	51 074	47 420
Illinois	51 969	54 049	55 219	56 958	59 867	57 594	56 151	51 116	52 860	52 522	53 378	51 975	54 523	53 254
Indiana	43 003	48 027	52 017	52 411	52 771	51 093	49 107	49 126	49 666	48 250	46 804	48 489	49 276	46 520
Iowa	43 578	45 379	45 187	48 834	53 107	51 251	49 833	49 128	48 447	49 460	51 285	51 393	50 787	50 142
Kansas	47 777	44 526	48 782	48 427	48 261	51 336	50 367	51 007	51 781	46 810	46 351	48 644	50 360	47 877
Kentucky	39 573	44 291	44 744	47 822	43 596	45 342	46 745	45 931	43 998	43 240	40 591	40 475	42 165	41 148
Louisiana	35 780	41 352	44 487	41 863	42 195	38 407	40 525	40 701	39 226	41 524	41 067	38 965	42 900	39 563
Maine	43 859	47 411	43 835	47 014	50 217	46 594	44 526	44 106	43 447	47 110	48 442	48 740	49 734	47 228
Maryland	62 053	60 115	62 444	65 979	67 459	68 185	65 101	67 509	61 243	65 090	66 738	67 990	68 152	63 711
Massachusetts	57 885	53 967	56 208	55 859	56 863	58 455	63 548	59 667	59 652	59 295	61 781	59 086	60 709	60 320
Michigan	47 808	53 600	51 820	55 168	59 556	56 903	54 784	51 122	52 706	48 166	50 659	51 949	51 267	49 788
Minnesota	50 249	56 013	56 932	63 222	60 782	67 830	64 068	65 373	61 839	63 951	59 793	60 027	60 289	54 925
Mississippi	32 224	36 453	38 119	38 414	41 968	42 884	36 680	36 960	38 314	39 616	36 258	37 091	38 711	36 446
Missouri	43 648	46 822	48 892	53 031	53 475	56 385	50 275	51 195	51 231	48 031	47 409	47 605	47 773	46 038
Montana	37 329	39 196	39 073	41 655	40 107	40 981	39 070	41 691	39 929	38 705	41 152	43 895	45 332	42 900
Nebraska	43 888	46 479	46 403	48 034	49 912	52 200	53 038	51 219	51 479	49 910	52 854	51 413	51 063	50 728
Nevada	51 140	52 664	51 970	52 444	53 576	57 211	55 217	53 807	52 896	53 806	53 169	55 831	56 135	54 744
New Hampshire	65 164	53 848	54 837	59 306	59 512	63 673	62 426	66 209	65 051	64 762	62 847	66 177	70 173	66 176
New Jersey	61 857	64 863	64 231	65 728	64 266	63 021	62 962	65 308	65 611	63 006	69 888	72 679	62 833	65 306
New Mexico	39 987	34 279	40 242	41 610	42 092	43 877	40 284	42 436	41 097	45 096	42 954	42 745	46 060	42 102
New York	50 450	48 387	47 882	49 328	51 674	50 942	51 217	50 226	50 091	50 894	52 030	51 495	50 825	50 461
North Carolina	42 047	48 648	47 938	47 276	48 139	47 908	46 411	43 702	43 642	45 866	46 383	42 499	45 185	42 930
North Dakota	40 346	43 003	42 349	39 975	42 207	45 006	43 530	43 325	47 307	44 706	46 533	43 833	49 019	49 631
Ohio	47 930	46 555	48 332	51 348	51 027	53 715	50 817	51 085	50 948	49 077	48 751	49 016	50 986	46 934
Oklahoma	38 941	37 492	41 934	44 491	42 233	40 550	43 306	43 634	42 030	45 155	41 518	41 474	44 877	46 111
Oregon	46 761	48 499	49 820	51 535	52 488	53 136	50 194	50 029	48 745	46 728	48 703	50 288	52 166	51 727
Pennsylvania	46 320	47 688	50 181	51 467	48 791	52 733	52 901	50 862	50 261	50 275	51 064	51 768	50 298	51 402
Rhode Island	51 052	50 540	46 543	53 671	55 201	52 759	55 606	50 766	52 342	54 640	54 576	57 384	56 293	53 241
South Carolina	45 889	47 369	45 828	43 884	47 116	46 974	45 893	45 254	45 047	44 103	44 369	42 306	45 912	42 155
South Dakota	39 239	40 346	39 718	43 250	46 297	45 605	48 246	45 327	46 268	46 857	47 591	48 511	48 202	51 600
Tennessee	36 079	42 073	40 978	44 971	47 194	42 630	43 518	44 318	43 927	43 397	43 461	43 455	42 778	39 702
Texas	45 079	45 192	46 915	47 203	49 992	48 273	49 692	48 051	45 974	47 187	45 684	46 247	47 823	46 490
Utah	48 136	50 611	57 214	58 437	59 506	59 452	57 575	57 281	57 685	57 986	60 453	58 336	55 586	62 537
Vermont	49 663	44 216	46 886	51 938	53 735	49 504	49 612	51 462	50 645	53 949	55 921	55 510	49 211	50 706
Virginia	56 011	53 580	57 458	57 190	59 044	59 612	61 101	59 399	64 133	58 294	57 256	60 996	61 434	61 985
Washington	51 282	50 116	59 605	62 555	58 760	53 169	51 674	54 076	55 617	56 905	55 857	58 438	60 312	56 631
West Virginia	35 352	34 499	36 767	35 227	37 857	36 772	36 087	35 137	38 355	38 041	40 195	41 027	43 708	37 994
Wisconsin	49 045	54 660	52 961	54 516	59 011	56 373	55 148	54 938	54 166	52 129	49 244	55 201	53 247	51 200
Wyoming	47 047	42 296	44 705	46 500	48 132	49 548	48 304	47 589	49 818	51 747	49 319	50 234	50 617	53 337

Section 3b: Poverty

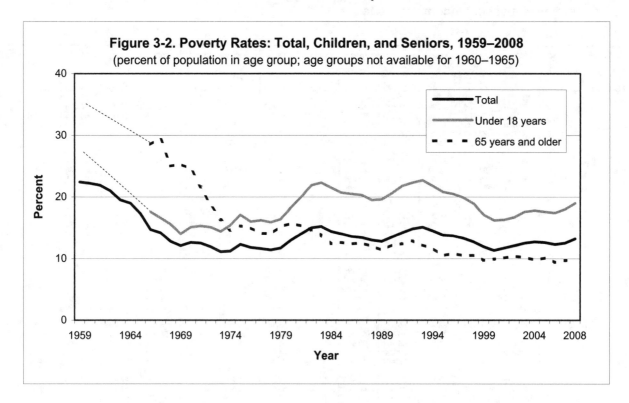

Figure 3-2. Poverty Rates: Total, Children, and Seniors, 1959–2008
(percent of population in age group; age groups not available for 1960–1965)

- The number of Americans with family incomes below the poverty line was 13.2 percent of the population in 2008. The most recent cyclical expansion failed to produce improvement in the poverty rate, which was 12.1 percent in 2002 and 12.5 percent in the peak expansion year of 2007. (Table 3-8)

- The poverty rate rose in 2008 for children under 18 and adults 18 to 64 years old, but was unchanged for people 65 and older. The measured poverty rate for senior citizens (age 65 years and older) has been lower than the rate for adults 18 to 64 in most years since 1993. This is very different from 1959, when the first poverty rate calculations showed more than one-third of all seniors living in poverty, compared with 17 percent of working-age adults. (Table 3-10) Between 1959 and 1974, ad hoc legislative changes raised Social Security benefits by a cumulative 104 percent—exceeding the 69 percent increase in consumer prices—and since then, each year's benefits have been indexed to the rate of change in the Consumer Price Index, Urban Wage Earners and Clerical Workers (CPI-W). (See Chapter 8.) However, the official thresholds do not specifically include medical expenses or account for the disproportionate effect of medical price inflation on senior budgets. (See Chapter 8.) When medical expenses are taken into account, one set of recent Census Bureau estimates indicates that redefining both income and the poverty line would raise the poverty rate of the elderly above the poverty rate of working-age adults. (Table 3-15)

- The poverty rate for children, on the other hand, has always been higher than the average and remains so when the rate is redefined as in Table 3-15. The gap between the official poverty rates for children and for working-age adults has been as high as 10 percentage points (in 1959 and the early 1990s, for example) and as low as 5.3 percentage points (in 1969). (Table 3-10)

- Poverty among Hispanics (who may be of any race) was 23.2 percent in 2008, compared with 8.6 percent for non-Hispanic Whites. Poverty among Blacks was 24.7 percent and poverty among Asians was 11.8 percent. (Table 3-8)

Table 3-7. Weighted Average Poverty Thresholds by Family Size

(Dollars.)

Year	Unrelated individuals			Families of 2 people			Families, all ages								CPI-U, all items (1982–1984 = 100)
	All ages	Under 65 years	65 years and older	All ages	House-holder under 65 years	House-holder 65 years and older	3 people	4 people	5 people	6 people	7 people or more (before 1980)	7 people	8 people	9 people or more	
1959	1 467	1 503	1 397	1 894	1 952	1 761	2 324	2 973	3 506	3 944	4 849	...	...	...	29.2
1960	1 490	1 526	1 418	1 924	1 982	1 788	2 359	3 022	3 560	4 002	4 921	...	...	...	29.6
1961	1 506	1 545	1 433	1 942	2 005	1 808	2 383	3 054	3 597	4 041	4 967	...	...	...	29.9
1962	1 519	1 562	1 451	1 962	2 027	1 828	2 412	3 089	3 639	4 088	5 032	...	...	...	30.3
1963	1 539	1 581	1 470	1 988	2 052	1 850	2 442	3 128	3 685	4 135	5 092	...	...	...	30.6
1964	1 558	1 601	1 488	2 015	2 079	1 875	2 473	3 169	3 732	4 193	5 156	...	...	...	31.0
1965	1 582	1 626	1 512	2 048	2 114	1 906	2 514	3 223	3 797	4 264	5 248	...	...	...	31.5
1966	1 628	1 674	1 556	2 107	2 175	1 961	2 588	3 317	3 908	4 388	5 395	...	...	...	32.5
1967	1 675	1 722	1 600	2 168	2 238	2 017	2 661	3 410	4 019	4 516	5 550	...	...	...	33.4
1968	1 748	1 797	1 667	2 262	2 333	2 102	2 774	3 553	4 188	4 706	5 789	...	...	...	34.8
1969	1 840	1 893	1 757	2 383	2 458	2 215	2 924	3 743	4 415	4 958	6 101	...	...	...	36.7
1970	1 954	2 010	1 861	2 525	2 604	2 348	3 099	3 968	4 680	5 260	6 468	...	...	...	38.8
1971	2 040	2 098	1 940	2 633	2 716	2 448	3 229	4 137	4 880	5 489	6 751	...	...	...	40.5
1972	2 109	2 168	2 005	2 724	2 808	2 530	3 339	4 275	5 044	5 673	6 983	...	...	...	41.8
1973	2 247	2 307	2 130	2 895	2 984	2 688	3 548	4 540	5 358	6 028	7 435	...	...	...	44.4
1974	2 495	2 562	2 364	3 211	3 312	2 982	3 936	5 038	5 950	6 699	8 253	...	...	...	49.3
1975	2 724	2 797	2 581	3 506	3 617	3 257	4 293	5 500	6 499	7 316	9 022	...	...	...	53.8
1976	2 884	2 959	2 730	3 711	3 826	3 445	4 540	5 815	6 876	7 760	9 588	...	...	...	56.9
1977	3 075	3 152	2 906	3 951	4 072	3 666	4 833	6 191	7 320	8 261	10 216	...	...	...	60.6
1978	3 311	3 392	3 127	4 249	4 383	3 944	5 201	6 662	7 880	8 891	11 002	...	...	...	65.2
1979	3 689	3 778	3 479	4 725	4 878	4 390	5 784	7 412	8 775	9 914	12 280	...	...	...	72.6
1980	4 190	4 290	3 949	5 363	5 537	4 983	6 565	8 414	9 966	11 269	13 955	12 761	14 199	16 896	82.4
1981	4 620	4 729	4 359	5 917	6 111	5 498	7 250	9 287	11 007	12 449	...	14 110	15 655	18 572	90.9
1982	4 901	5 019	4 626	6 281	6 487	5 836	7 693	9 862	11 684	13 207	...	15 036	16 719	19 698	96.5
1983	5 061	5 180	4 775	6 483	6 697	6 023	7 938	10 178	12 049	13 630	...	15 500	17 170	20 310	99.6
1984	5 278	5 400	4 979	6 762	6 983	6 282	8 277	10 609	12 566	14 207	...	16 096	17 961	21 247	103.9
1985	5 469	5 593	5 156	6 998	7 231	6 503	8 573	10 989	13 007	14 696	...	16 656	18 512	22 083	107.6
1986	5 572	5 701	5 255	7 138	7 372	6 630	8 737	11 203	13 259	14 986	...	17 049	18 791	22 497	109.6
1987	5 778	5 909	5 447	7 397	7 641	6 872	9 056	11 611	13 737	15 509	...	17 649	19 515	23 105	113.6
1988	6 022	6 155	5 674	7 704	7 958	7 157	9 435	12 092	14 304	16 146	...	18 232	20 253	24 129	118.3
1989	6 310	6 451	5 947	8 076	8 343	7 501	9 885	12 674	14 990	16 921	...	19 162	21 328	25 480	124.0
1990	6 652	6 800	6 268	8 509	8 794	7 905	10 419	13 359	15 792	17 839	...	20 241	22 582	26 848	130.7
1991	6 932	7 086	6 532	8 865	9 165	8 241	10 860	13 924	16 456	18 587	...	21 058	23 582	27 942	136.2
1992	7 143	7 299	6 729	9 137	9 443	8 487	11 186	14 335	16 952	19 137	...	21 594	24 053	28 745	140.3
1993	7 363	7 518	6 930	9 414	9 728	8 740	11 522	14 763	17 449	19 718	...	22 383	24 838	29 529	144.5
1994	7 547	7 710	7 108	9 661	9 976	8 967	11 821	15 141	17 900	20 235	...	22 923	25 427	30 300	148.2
1995	7 763	7 929	7 309	9 933	10 259	9 219	12 158	15 569	18 408	20 804	...	23 552	26 237	31 280	152.4
1996	7 995	8 163	7 525	10 233	10 564	9 491	12 516	16 036	18 952	21 389	...	24 268	27 091	31 971	156.9
1997	8 183	8 350	7 698	10 473	10 805	9 712	12 802	16 400	19 380	21 886	...	24 802	27 593	32 566	160.5
1998	8 316	8 480	7 818	10 634	10 972	9 862	13 003	16 660	19 680	22 228	...	25 257	28 166	33 339	163.0
1999	8 499	8 667	7 990	10 864	11 213	10 075	13 289	17 030	20 128	22 730	...	25 918	28 970	34 436	166.6
2000	8 791	8 959	8 259	11 235	11 589	10 418	13 740	17 604	20 815	23 533	...	26 750	29 701	35 150	172.2
2001	9 039	9 214	8 494	11 569	11 920	10 715	14 128	18 104	21 405	24 195	...	27 517	30 627	36 286	177.1
2002	9 183	9 359	8 628	11 756	12 110	10 885	14 348	18 392	21 744	24 576	...	28 001	30 907	37 062	179.9
2003	9 393	9 573	8 825	12 015	12 384	11 133	14 680	18 810	22 245	25 122	...	28 544	31 589	37 656	184.0
2004	9 646	9 827	9 060	12 335	12 714	11 430	15 066	19 307	22 830	25 787	...	29 233	32 641	39 062	188.9
2005	9 973	10 160	9 367	12 755	13 145	11 815	15 577	19 971	23 613	26 683	...	30 249	33 610	40 288	195.3
2006	10 294	10 488	9 669	13 167	13 569	12 201	16 079	20 614	24 382	27 560	...	31 205	34 774	41 499	201.6
2007	10 590	10 787	9 944	13 540	13 954	12 550	16 530	21 203	25 080	28 323	...	32 233	35 816	42 739	207.3
2008	10 991	11 201	10 326	14 051	14 489	13 030	17 163	22 025	26 049	29 456	...	33 529	37 220	44 346	215.3

. . . = Not available.

Table 3-8. Poverty Status of People by Race and Hispanic Origin

(Thousands of people, percent of population.)

Year	Number of people, all races	Below poverty level											
		All races		White		White, not Hispanic		Black		Asian [1]		Hispanic (any race)	
		Number	Poverty rate (percent)	Number	Poverty rate (percent)	Number	Poverty rate (percent)	Number	Poverty rate (percent)	Number	Poverty rate (percent)	Number	Poverty rate (percent)
1959	176 557	39 490	22.4	28 484	18.1	...	...	9 927	55.1	...	...	...	...
1960	179 503	39 851	22.2	28 309	17.8	...	...	...	...	...	...	...	...
1961	181 277	39 628	21.9	27 890	17.4	...	...	...	...	...	...	...	...
1962	184 276	38 625	21.0	26 672	16.4	...	...	...	...	...	...	...	...
1963	187 258	36 436	19.5	25 238	15.3	...	...	...	...	...	...	...	...
1964	189 710	36 055	19.0	24 957	14.9	...	...	...	...	...	...	...	...
1965	191 413	33 185	17.3	22 496	13.3	...	...	8 867	41.8	...	...	...	...
1966	193 388	28 510	14.7	19 290	11.3	...	...	8 486	39.3	...	...	...	...
1967	195 672	27 769	14.2	18 983	11.0	...	...	7 616	34.7	...	...	...	...
1968	197 628	25 389	12.8	17 395	10.0	...	...	7 095	32.2	...	...	...	...
1969	199 517	24 147	12.1	16 659	9.5	...	...	...	...	...	...	...	...
1970	202 183	25 420	12.6	17 484	9.9	...	...	7 548	33.5	...	...	...	...
1971	204 554	25 559	12.5	17 780	9.9	...	...	7 396	32.5	...	...	...	...
1972	206 004	24 460	11.9	16 203	9.0	12 864	7.5	7 710	33.3	...	...	2 414	22.8
1973	207 621	22 973	11.1	15 142	8.4	13 217	7.7	7 388	31.4	...	...	2 366	21.9
1974	209 362	23 370	11.2	15 736	8.6	...	...	7 182	30.3	...	...	2 575	23.0
1975	210 864	25 877	12.3	17 770	9.7	14 883	8.6	7 545	31.3	...	...	2 991	26.9
1976	212 303	24 975	11.8	16 713	9.1	14 025	8.1	7 595	31.1	...	...	2 783	24.7
1977	213 867	24 720	11.6	16 416	8.9	13 802	8.0	7 726	31.3	...	...	2 700	22.4
1978	215 656	24 497	11.4	16 259	8.7	13 755	7.9	7 625	30.6	...	...	2 607	21.6
1979	222 903	26 072	11.7	17 214	9.0	14 419	8.1	8 050	31.0	...	...	2 921	21.8
1980	225 027	29 272	13.0	19 699	10.2	16 365	9.1	8 579	32.5	...	...	3 491	25.7
1981	227 157	31 822	14.0	21 553	11.1	17 987	9.9	9 173	34.2	...	...	3 713	26.5
1982	229 412	34 398	15.0	23 517	12.0	19 362	10.6	9 697	35.6	...	...	4 301	29.9
1983	231 700	35 303	15.2	23 984	12.1	19 538	10.8	9 882	35.7	...	...	4 633	28.0
1984	233 816	33 700	14.4	22 955	11.5	18 300	10.0	9 490	33.8	...	...	4 806	28.4
1985	236 594	33 064	14.0	22 860	11.4	17 839	9.7	8 926	31.3	...	...	5 236	29.0
1986	238 554	32 370	13.6	22 183	11.0	17 244	9.4	8 983	31.1	...	...	5 117	27.3
1987	240 982	32 221	13.4	21 195	10.4	16 029	8.7	9 520	32.4	1 021	16.1	5 422	28.0
1988	243 530	31 745	13.0	20 715	10.1	15 565	8.4	9 356	31.3	1 117	17.3	5 357	26.7
1989	245 992	31 528	12.8	20 785	10.0	15 599	8.3	9 302	30.7	939	14.1	5 430	26.2
1990	248 644	33 585	13.5	22 326	10.7	16 622	8.8	9 837	31.9	858	12.2	6 006	28.1
1991	251 192	35 708	14.2	23 747	11.3	17 741	9.4	10 242	32.7	996	13.8	6 339	28.7
1992	256 549	38 014	14.8	25 259	11.9	18 202	9.6	10 827	33.4	985	12.7	7 592	29.6
1993	259 278	39 265	15.1	26 226	12.2	18 882	9.9	10 877	33.1	1 134	15.3	8 126	30.6
1994	261 616	38 059	14.5	25 379	11.7	18 110	9.4	10 196	30.6	974	14.6	8 416	30.7
1995	263 733	36 425	13.8	24 423	11.2	16 267	8.5	9 872	29.3	1 411	14.6	8 574	30.3
1996	266 218	36 529	13.7	24 650	11.2	16 462	8.6	9 694	28.4	1 454	14.5	8 697	29.4
1997	268 480	35 574	13.3	24 396	11.0	16 491	8.6	9 116	26.5	1 468	14.0	8 308	27.1
1998	271 059	34 476	12.7	23 454	10.5	15 799	8.2	9 091	26.1	1 360	12.5	8 070	25.6
1999	276 208	32 791	11.9	22 169	9.8	14 735	7.7	8 441	23.6	1 285	10.7	7 876	22.7
2000	278 944	31 581	11.3	21 645	9.5	14 366	7.4	7 982	22.5	1 258	9.9	7 747	21.5
2001	281 475	32 907	11.7	22 739	9.9	15 271	7.8	8 136	22.7	1 275	10.2	7 997	21.4
2002	285 317	34 570	12.1	...	...	...	...	...	...	...	...	8 555	21.8
2003	287 699	35 861	12.5	...	...	...	...	...	...	...	...	9 051	22.5
2004	290 617	37 040	12.7	...	...	...	...	...	...	...	...	9 122	21.9
2005	293 135	36 950	12.6	...	...	...	...	...	...	...	...	9 368	21.8
2006	296 450	36 460	12.3	...	...	...	...	...	...	...	...	9 243	20.6
2007	298 699	37 276	12.5	...	...	...	...	...	...	...	...	9 890	21.5
2008	301 041	39 829	13.2	...	...	...	...	...	...	...	...	10 987	23.2
By race													
Race alone													
2002		...	...	23 466	10.2	15 567	8.0	8 602	24.1	1 161	10.1	...	...
2003		...	...	24 272	10.5	15 902	8.2	8 781	24.4	1 401	11.8	...	...
2004		...	...	25 327	10.8	16 908	8.7	9 014	24.7	1 201	9.8	...	...
2005		...	...	24 872	10.6	16 227	8.3	9 168	24.9	1 402	11.1	...	...
2006		...	...	24 416	10.3	16 013	8.2	9 048	24.3	1 353	10.3	...	...
2007		...	...	25 120	10.5	16 032	8.2	9 237	24.5	1 349	10.2	...	...
2008		...	...	26 990	11.2	17 024	8.6	9 379	24.7	1 576	11.8	...	...
Race alone or in combination													
2002		...	...	24 074	10.3	...	...	8 884	23.9	1 243	10.0	...	...
2003		...	...	24 950	10.6	...	...	9 108	24.3	1 527	11.8	...	...
2004		...	...	26 071	10.9	...	...	9 411	24.7	1 295	9.7	...	...
2005		...	...	25 631	10.7	...	...	9 517	24.7	1 501	10.9	...	...
2006		...	...	25 156	10.4	...	...	9 447	24.2	1 447	10.1	...	...
2007		...	...	25 864	10.6	...	...	9 668	24.4	1 467	10.2	...	...
2008		...	...	27 868	11.3	...	...	9 882	24.6	1 686	11.6	...	...

[1] For 1987 through 2001, Asian and Pacific Islander.

. . . = Not available.

Table 3-9. Poverty Status of Families by Type of Family

(Thousands of families, percent.)

Year	Married couple families				Families with no spouse present						Unrelated individuals	
	Number of families		Poverty rate (percent)		Male householder			Female householder				
						Poverty rate (percent)			Poverty rate (percent)		Below poverty level	Poverty rate
	Total	Total below poverty level	Total	With children under 18 years	Families below poverty level	Total	With children under 18 years	Families below poverty level	Total	With children under 18 years		
1959	39 335	...	...	...	...	...	...	1 916	42.6	59.9	4 928	46.1
1960	39 624	...	...	...	...	...	...	1 955	42.4	56.3	4 926	45.2
1961	40 405	...	...	...	...	...	...	1 954	42.1	56.0	5 119	45.9
1962	40 923	...	...	...	...	...	...	2 034	42.9	59.7	5 002	45.4
1963	41 311	...	...	...	...	...	...	1 972	40.4	55.7	4 938	44.2
1964	41 648	...	...	...	...	...	...	1 822	36.4	49.7	5 143	42.7
1965	42 107	...	...	...	...	...	...	1 916	38.4	52.2	4 827	39.8
1966	42 553	...	...	...	...	...	...	1 721	33.1	47.1	4 701	38.3
1967	43 292	...	...	...	...	...	...	1 774	33.3	44.5	4 998	38.1
1968	43 842	...	...	...	...	...	...	1 755	32.3	44.6	4 694	34.0
1969	44 436	...	...	...	...	...	...	1 827	32.7	44.9	4 972	34.0
1970	44 739	...	...	...	...	...	...	1 952	32.5	43.8	5 090	32.9
1971	45 752	...	...	...	...	...	...	2 100	33.9	44.9	5 154	31.6
1972	46 314	...	...	...	...	...	...	2 158	32.7	44.5	4 883	29.0
1973	46 812	2 482	5.3	...	154	10.7	...	2 193	32.2	43.2	4 674	25.6
1974	47 069	2 474	5.3	6.0	125	8.9	15.4	2 324	32.1	43.7	4 553	24.1
1975	47 318	2 904	6.1	7.2	116	8.0	11.7	2 430	32.5	44.0	5 088	25.1
1976	47 497	2 606	5.5	6.4	162	10.8	15.4	2 543	33.0	44.1	5 344	24.9
1977	47 385	2 524	5.3	6.3	177	11.1	14.8	2 610	31.7	41.8	5 216	22.6
1978	47 692	2 474	5.2	5.9	152	9.2	14.7	2 654	31.4	42.2	5 435	22.1
1979	49 112	2 640	5.4	6.1	176	10.2	15.5	2 645	30.4	39.6	5 743	21.9
1980	49 294	3 032	6.2	7.7	213	11.0	18.0	2 972	32.7	42.9	6 227	22.9
1981	49 630	3 394	6.8	8.7	205	10.3	14.0	3 252	34.6	44.3	6 490	23.4
1982	49 908	3 789	7.6	9.8	290	14.4	20.6	3 434	36.3	47.8	6 458	23.1
1983	50 081	3 815	7.6	10.1	268	13.2	20.2	3 564	36.0	47.1	6 740	23.1
1984	50 350	3 488	6.9	9.4	292	13.1	18.1	3 498	34.5	45.7	6 609	21.8
1985	50 933	3 438	6.7	8.9	311	12.9	17.1	3 474	34.0	45.4	6 725	21.5
1986	51 537	3 123	6.1	8.0	287	11.4	17.8	3 613	34.6	46.0	6 846	21.6
1987	51 675	3 011	5.8	7.7	340	12.0	16.8	3 654	34.2	45.5	6 857	20.8
1988	52 100	2 897	5.6	7.2	336	11.8	18.0	3 642	33.4	44.7	7 070	20.6
1989	52 317	2 931	5.6	7.3	348	12.1	18.1	3 504	32.2	42.8	6 760	19.2
1990	52 147	2 981	5.7	7.8	349	12.0	18.8	3 768	33.4	44.5	7 446	20.7
1991	52 457	3 158	6.0	8.3	392	13.0	19.6	4 161	35.6	47.1	7 773	21.1
1992	53 090	3 385	6.4	8.6	484	15.8	22.5	4 275	35.4	46.2	8 075	21.9
1993	53 181	3 481	6.5	9.0	488	16.8	22.5	4 424	35.6	46.1	8 388	22.1
1994	53 865	3 272	6.1	8.3	549	17.0	22.6	4 232	34.6	44.0	8 287	21.5
1995	53 570	2 982	5.6	7.5	493	14.0	19.7	4 057	32.4	41.5	8 247	20.9
1996	53 604	3 010	5.6	7.5	531	13.8	20.0	4 167	32.6	41.9	8 452	20.8
1997	54 321	2 821	5.2	7.1	507	13.0	18.7	3 995	31.6	41.0	8 687	20.8
1998	54 778	2 879	5.3	6.9	476	12.0	16.6	3 831	29.9	38.7	8 478	19.9
1999	56 290	2 748	4.9	6.4	485	11.8	16.3	3 559	27.8	35.7	8 400	19.1
2000	56 598	2 637	4.7	6.0	485	11.3	15.3	3 278	25.4	33.0	8 653	19.0
2001	56 755	2 760	4.9	6.1	583	13.1	17.7	3 470	26.4	33.6	9 226	19.9
2002	57 327	3 052	5.3	6.8	564	12.1	16.6	3 613	26.5	33.7	9 618	20.4
2003	57 725	3 115	5.4	7.0	636	13.5	19.1	3 856	28.0	35.5	9 713	20.4
2004	57 983	3 216	5.5	7.0	657	13.4	17.1	3 962	28.3	35.9	9 926	20.4
2005	58 189	2 944	5.1	6.5	669	13.0	17.6	4 044	28.7	36.2	10 425	21.1
2006	58 964	2 910	4.9	6.4	671	13.2	17.9	4 087	28.3	36.5	9 977	20.0
2007	58 395	2 849	4.9	6.7	696	13.6	17.5	4 078	28.3	37.0	10 189	19.7
2008	59 137	3 261	5.5	7.5	723	13.8	17.6	4 163	28.7	37.2	10 710	20.8

. . . = Not available.

Table 3-10. Poverty Status of People by Sex and Age

(Thousands of people, percent of population.)

Year	Poverty status of people by sex				Poverty status of people by age					
	Males below poverty level		Females below poverty level		Children under 18 years below poverty level		People 18 to 64 years below poverty level		People 65 years and older below poverty level	
	Number (thousands)	Poverty rate (percent)	Number (thousands)	Poverty rate (percent)	Number (thousands)	Poverty rate (percent)	Number (thousands)	Poverty rate (percent)	Number (thousands)	Poverty rate (percent)
1959	...	...	...	...	17 552	27.3	16 457	17.0	5 481	35.2
1966	12 225	13.0	16 265	16.3	12 389	17.6	11 007	10.5	5 114	28.5
1967	11 813	12.5	15 951	15.8	11 656	16.6	10 725	10.0	5 388	29.5
1968	10 793	11.3	14 578	14.3	10 954	15.6	9 803	9.0	4 632	25.0
1969	10 292	10.6	13 978	13.6	9 691	14.0	9 669	8.7	4 787	25.3
1970	10 879	11.1	14 632	14.0	10 440	15.1	10 187	9.0	4 793	24.6
1971	10 708	10.8	14 841	14.1	10 551	15.3	10 735	9.3	4 273	21.6
1972	10 190	10.2	14 258	13.4	10 284	15.1	10 438	8.8	3 738	18.6
1973	9 642	9.6	13 316	12.5	9 642	14.4	9 977	8.3	3 354	16.3
1974	10 313	10.2	13 881	12.9	10 156	15.4	10 132	8.3	3 085	14.6
1975	10 908	10.7	14 970	13.8	11 104	17.1	11 456	9.2	3 317	15.3
1976	10 373	10.1	14 603	13.4	10 273	16.0	11 389	9.0	3 313	15.0
1977	10 340	10.0	14 381	13.0	10 288	16.2	11 316	8.8	3 177	14.1
1978	10 017	9.6	14 480	13.0	9 931	15.9	11 332	8.7	3 233	14.0
1979	10 535	10.0	14 810	13.2	10 377	16.4	12 014	8.9	3 682	15.2
1980	12 207	11.2	17 065	14.7	11 543	18.3	13 858	10.1	3 871	15.7
1981	13 360	12.1	18 462	15.8	12 505	20.0	15 464	11.1	3 853	15.3
1982	14 842	13.4	19 556	16.5	13 647	21.9	17 000	12.0	3 751	14.6
1983	15 182	13.5	20 084	16.8	13 911	22.3	17 767	12.4	3 625	13.8
1984	14 537	12.8	19 163	15.9	13 420	21.5	16 952	11.7	3 330	12.4
1985	14 140	12.3	18 923	15.6	13 010	20.7	16 598	11.3	3 456	12.6
1986	13 721	11.8	18 649	15.2	12 876	20.5	16 017	10.8	3 477	12.4
1987	14 029	12.0	18 518	15.0	12 843	20.3	15 815	10.6	3 563	12.5
1988	13 599	11.5	18 146	14.5	12 455	19.5	15 809	10.5	3 481	12.0
1989	13 366	11.2	18 162	14.4	12 590	19.6	15 575	10.2	3 363	11.4
1990	14 211	11.7	19 373	15.2	13 431	20.6	16 496	10.7	3 658	12.2
1991	15 082	12.3	20 626	16.0	14 341	21.8	17 586	11.4	3 781	12.4
1992	16 222	12.9	21 792	16.6	15 294	22.3	18 793	11.9	3 928	12.9
1993	16 900	13.3	22 365	16.9	15 727	22.7	19 781	12.4	3 755	12.2
1994	16 316	12.8	21 744	16.3	15 289	21.8	19 107	11.9	3 663	11.7
1995	15 683	12.2	20 742	15.4	14 665	20.8	18 442	11.4	3 318	10.5
1996	15 611	12.0	20 918	15.4	14 463	20.5	18 638	11.4	3 428	10.8
1997	15 187	11.6	20 387	14.9	14 113	19.9	18 085	10.9	3 376	10.5
1998	14 712	11.1	19 764	14.3	13 467	18.9	17 623	10.5	3 386	10.5
1999	14 079	10.4	18 712	13.2	12 280	17.1	17 289	10.1	3 222	9.7
2000	13 536	9.9	18 045	12.6	11 587	16.2	16 671	9.6	3 323	9.9
2001	14 327	10.4	18 580	12.9	11 733	16.3	17 760	10.1	3 414	10.1
2002	15 162	10.9	19 408	13.3	12 133	16.7	18 861	10.6	3 576	10.4
2003	15 783	11.2	20 078	13.7	12 866	17.6	19 443	10.8	3 552	10.2
2004	16 399	11.5	20 641	13.9	13 041	17.8	20 545	11.3	3 453	9.8
2005	15 950	11.1	21 000	14.1	12 896	17.6	20 450	11.1	3 603	10.1
2006	16 000	11.0	20 460	13.6	12 827	17.4	20 239	10.8	3 394	9.4
2007	16 302	11.1	20 973	13.8	13 324	18.0	20 396	10.9	3 556	9.7
2008	17 698	12.0	22 131	14.4	14 068	19.0	22 105	11.7	3 656	9.7

. . . = Not available.

Table 3-11. Poor People Age 16 Years and Older by Work Experience

(Thousands of people, percent of population [poverty rate], percent of total poor people.)

Year	Total number of poor people, 16 years and older	Worked								Did not work		
		Number	Percent of total poor	Worked year-round, full-time			Worked less than year-round or full-time			Number	Poverty rate (percent)	Percent of total poor
				Number	Poverty rate (percent)	Percent of total poor	Number	Poverty rate (percent)	Percent of total poor			
1978	16 914	6 599	39.0	1 309	...	7.7	5 290	...	31.3	10 315	...	61.0
1979	16 803	6 601	39.3	1 394	...	8.3	5 207	...	31.0	10 202	...	60.7
1980	18 892	7 674	40.6	1 644	...	8.7	6 030	...	31.9	11 218	...	59.4
1981	20 571	8 524	41.4	1 881	...	9.1	6 643	...	32.3	12 047	...	58.6
1982	22 100	9 013	40.8	1 999	...	9.0	7 014	...	31.7	13 087	...	59.2
1983	22 741	9 329	41.0	2 064	...	9.1	7 265	...	31.9	13 412	...	59.0
1984	21 541	8 999	41.8	2 076	...	9.6	6 923	...	32.1	12 542	...	58.2
1985	21 243	9 008	42.4	1 972	...	9.3	7 036	...	33.1	12 235	...	57.6
1986	20 688	8 743	42.3	2 007	...	9.7	6 736	...	32.6	11 945	...	57.7
1987	20 546	8 258	40.2	1 821	2.4	8.9	6 436	12.5	31.3	12 288	21.6	59.8
1988	20 323	8 363	41.2	1 929	2.4	9.5	6 434	12.7	31.7	11 959	21.2	58.8
1989	19 952	8 376	42.0	1 908	2.4	9.6	6 468	12.5	32.4	11 576	20.8	58.0
1990	21 242	8 716	41.0	2 076	2.6	9.8	6 639	12.6	31.3	12 526	22.1	59.0
1991	22 530	9 208	40.9	2 103	2.6	9.3	7 105	13.4	31.5	13 323	22.8	59.1
1992	23 951	9 739	40.6	2 211	2.7	9.2	7 529	14.1	31.4	14 212	23.7	59.3
1993	24 832	10 144	40.8	2 408	2.9	9.7	7 737	14.6	31.2	14 688	24.2	59.1
1994	24 108	9 829	40.8	2 520	2.9	10.5	7 309	13.9	30.3	14 279	23.6	59.2
1995	23 077	9 484	41.1	2 418	2.7	10.5	7 066	13.7	30.6	13 593	22.3	58.9
1996	23 472	9 586	40.8	2 263	2.5	9.6	7 322	14.1	31.2	13 886	22.7	59.2
1997	22 753	9 444	41.5	2 345	2.5	10.3	7 098	13.8	31.2	13 310	21.7	58.5
1998	22 256	9 133	41.0	2 804	2.9	12.6	6 330	12.7	28.4	13 122	21.1	59.0
1999	21 762	9 251	42.5	2 559	2.6	11.8	6 692	13.2	30.8	12 511	19.9	57.5
2000	21 080	8 511	40.4	2 439	2.4	11.6	6 072	12.1	28.8	12 569	19.8	59.6
2001	22 245	8 530	38.3	2 567	2.6	11.5	5 964	11.8	26.8	13 715	20.6	61.7
2002	23 601	8 954	37.9	2 635	2.6	11.2	6 318	12.4	26.8	14 647	21.0	62.1
2003	24 266	8 820	36.3	2 636	2.6	10.9	6 183	12.2	25.5	15 446	21.5	63.7
2004	25 256	9 384	37.2	2 891	2.8	11.4	6 493	12.8	25.7	15 871	21.7	62.8
2005	25 381	9 340	36.8	2 894	2.8	11.4	6 446	12.8	25.4	16 041	21.8	63.2
2006	24 896	9 181	36.9	2 906	2.7	11.7	6 275	12.6	25.2	15 715	21.1	63.1
2007	25 297	9 089	35.9	2 768	2.5	10.9	6 320	12.7	25.0	16 208	21.5	64.1
2008	27 216	10 085	37.1	2 754	2.6	10.1	7 331	13.5	26.9	17 131	22.0	62.9

. . . = Not available.

Table 3-12. Poverty Rates by State

(Percent of population.)

State	1990	1996	1997	1998	1999	2000	2001	2002	2003	2004	2005	2006	2007	2008
United States	13.5	13.7	13.3	12.7	11.9	11.3	11.7	12.1	12.5	12.7	12.6	12.3	12.5	13.2
Alabama	19.2	14.0	15.7	14.5	15.2	13.3	15.9	14.5	15.0	16.9	16.7	14.3	14.5	14.3
Alaska	11.4	8.2	8.8	9.4	7.6	7.6	8.5	8.8	9.6	9.1	10.0	8.9	7.6	8.2
Arizona	13.7	20.5	17.2	16.6	12.2	11.7	14.6	13.5	13.5	14.4	15.2	14.4	14.3	18.0
Arkansas	19.6	17.2	19.7	14.7	14.7	16.5	17.8	19.8	17.8	15.1	13.8	17.7	13.8	15.3
California	13.9	16.9	16.6	15.4	14.0	12.7	12.6	13.1	13.1	13.2	13.2	12.2	12.7	14.6
Colorado	13.7	10.6	8.2	9.2	8.5	9.8	8.7	9.8	9.7	10.0	11.4	9.7	9.8	11.0
Connecticut	6.0	11.7	8.6	9.5	7.2	7.7	7.3	8.3	8.1	10.1	9.3	8.0	8.9	8.1
Delaware	6.9	8.6	9.6	10.3	10.4	8.4	6.7	9.1	7.3	9.0	9.2	9.3	9.3	9.6
District of Columbia	21.1	24.1	21.8	22.3	14.7	15.2	18.2	17.0	16.8	17.0	21.3	18.3	18.0	16.5
Florida	14.4	14.2	14.3	13.1	12.4	11.0	12.7	12.6	12.7	11.6	11.1	11.5	12.5	13.1
Georgia	15.8	14.8	14.5	13.5	12.8	12.1	12.9	11.2	11.9	13.0	14.4	12.6	13.6	15.5
Hawaii	11.0	12.1	13.9	10.9	10.8	8.9	11.4	11.3	9.3	8.6	8.6	9.2	7.5	9.9
Idaho	14.9	11.9	14.7	13.0	14.1	12.5	11.5	11.3	10.2	9.9	9.9	9.5	9.9	12.2
Illinois	13.7	12.1	11.2	10.1	9.9	10.7	10.1	12.8	12.6	12.3	11.5	10.6	10.0	12.3
Indiana	13.0	7.5	8.8	9.4	6.7	8.5	8.5	9.1	9.9	11.6	12.6	10.6	11.8	14.3
Iowa	10.4	9.6	9.6	9.1	7.4	8.3	7.4	9.2	8.9	10.9	11.3	10.3	8.9	9.5
Kansas	10.3	11.2	9.7	9.6	12.3	8.0	10.1	10.1	10.8	11.4	12.5	12.8	11.7	12.7
Kentucky	17.3	17.0	15.9	13.5	12.1	12.6	12.6	14.2	14.4	17.8	14.8	16.8	15.5	17.1
Louisiana	23.6	20.5	16.3	19.1	19.2	17.2	16.2	17.5	17.0	16.8	18.3	17.0	16.1	18.2
Maine	13.1	11.2	10.1	10.4	10.6	10.1	10.3	13.4	11.6	11.6	12.6	10.2	10.9	12.0
Maryland	9.9	10.3	8.4	7.2	7.3	7.4	7.2	7.4	8.6	9.9	9.7	8.4	8.8	8.7
Massachusetts	10.7	10.1	12.2	8.7	11.8	9.8	8.9	10.0	10.3	9.3	10.1	12.0	11.2	11.3
Michigan	14.3	11.2	10.3	11.0	9.7	9.9	9.4	11.6	11.4	13.3	12.0	13.3	10.8	13.0
Minnesota	12.0	9.8	9.6	10.3	7.3	5.7	7.4	6.5	7.4	7.0	8.1	8.2	9.3	9.9
Mississippi	25.7	20.6	16.7	17.6	16.2	14.9	19.3	18.4	16.0	18.7	20.1	20.6	22.6	18.1
Missouri	13.4	9.5	11.8	9.8	11.7	9.2	9.7	9.9	10.7	12.2	11.6	11.4	12.8	13.3
Montana	16.3	17.0	15.6	16.6	15.8	14.1	13.3	13.5	15.1	14.2	13.8	13.5	13.0	12.9
Nebraska	10.3	10.2	9.8	12.3	11.0	8.6	9.4	10.6	9.8	9.5	9.5	10.2	9.9	10.6
Nevada	9.8	8.1	11.0	10.6	11.3	8.8	7.1	8.9	10.9	10.9	10.6	9.5	9.7	10.8
New Hampshire	6.3	6.4	9.1	9.8	7.6	4.5	6.5	5.8	5.8	5.5	5.6	5.4	5.8	7.0
New Jersey	9.2	9.2	9.3	8.6	7.8	7.3	8.1	7.9	8.6	8.0	6.8	8.8	8.7	9.2
New Mexico	20.9	25.5	21.2	20.4	20.9	17.5	18.0	17.9	18.1	16.5	17.9	16.9	14.0	19.3
New York	14.3	16.7	16.5	16.7	14.2	13.9	14.2	14.0	14.3	15.0	14.5	14.0	14.5	14.2
North Carolina	13.0	12.2	11.4	14.0	13.8	12.5	12.5	14.3	15.7	14.6	13.1	13.8	15.5	13.9
North Dakota	13.7	11.0	13.6	15.1	13.1	10.4	13.8	11.6	9.7	9.7	11.2	11.4	9.3	11.8
Ohio	11.5	12.7	11.0	11.2	12.0	10.0	10.5	9.8	10.9	11.6	12.3	12.1	12.8	13.7
Oklahoma	15.6	16.6	13.7	14.1	12.8	14.9	15.1	14.1	12.8	10.8	15.6	15.2	13.4	13.6
Oregon	9.2	11.8	11.6	15.0	12.6	10.9	11.8	10.9	12.5	11.8	12.0	11.8	12.8	10.6
Pennsylvania	11.0	11.6	11.2	11.3	9.3	8.6	9.6	9.5	10.5	11.4	11.2	11.3	10.4	11.0
Rhode Island	7.5	11.0	12.7	11.6	10.0	10.2	9.6	11.0	11.5	11.5	12.1	10.5	9.5	12.7
South Carolina	16.2	13.0	13.1	13.7	11.7	11.1	15.1	14.3	12.7	14.9	15.0	11.2	14.1	14.0
South Dakota	13.3	11.8	16.5	10.8	7.7	10.7	8.4	11.5	12.7	13.5	11.8	10.7	9.4	13.1
Tennessee	16.9	15.9	14.3	13.4	11.9	13.5	14.1	14.8	14.0	15.9	14.9	14.9	14.8	15.0
Texas	15.9	16.6	16.7	15.1	15.2	15.5	14.9	15.6	17.0	16.5	16.2	16.4	16.5	15.9
Utah	8.2	7.7	8.9	9.0	5.7	7.6	10.5	9.9	9.1	10.1	9.2	9.3	9.6	7.6
Vermont	10.9	12.6	9.3	9.9	9.6	10.0	9.7	9.9	8.5	7.8	7.6	7.8	9.9	9.0
Virginia	11.1	12.3	12.7	8.8	7.9	8.3	8.0	9.9	10.0	9.4	9.2	8.6	8.6	10.3
Washington	8.9	11.9	9.2	8.9	9.6	10.8	10.7	11.0	12.6	11.4	10.2	8.0	10.2	10.4
West Virginia	18.1	18.5	16.4	17.8	15.7	14.7	16.4	16.8	17.4	14.2	15.4	15.3	14.8	14.5
Wisconsin	9.3	8.8	8.2	8.8	8.6	9.3	7.9	8.6	9.8	12.4	10.2	10.1	11.0	9.8
Wyoming	11.0	11.9	13.5	10.6	11.6	10.8	8.7	9.0	9.8	10.0	10.6	10.0	10.9	10.1

Section 3c: Alternative Measures of Income and Poverty

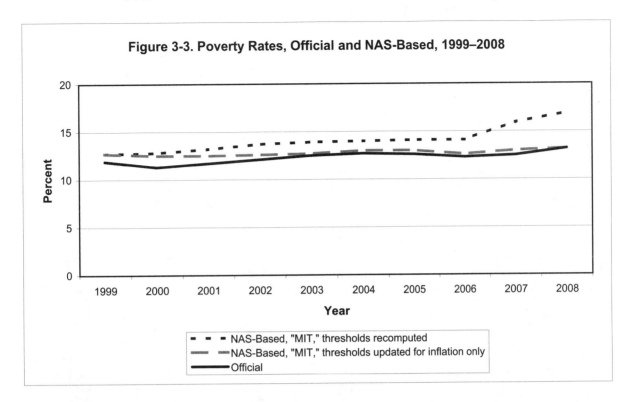

Figure 3-3. Poverty Rates, Official and NAS-Based, 1999–2008

- A special panel of the National Academy of Sciences (NAS) has recommended a complete overhaul of the poverty rate, redefining both needs and resources. For the years 1999 forward, the Census Bureau has calculated experimental poverty measures according to several versions of the NAS recommendations. In Figure 3-3, two of these experimental measures are compared with the official rate. The experimental measures use different approaches to the treatment of medical expenses; the two shown in the graph both use the "MIT" approach, in which medical out-of-pocket expenses are included in the thresholds. Both of the NAS-based measures use more comprehensive and realistic definitions of both needs and resources than the official rate does, and the two shown in the graph both include an adjustment for geographic differences in the cost of living. (Table 3-14)

- The NAS-based thresholds are initially based on needs estimated for the year 1999; in that year, the two experimental measures shown indicated a poverty rate of 12.7 percent, compared with 11.9 percent in the official rate. (Table 3-14)

- One of the NAS-based measures shown above updates the thresholds for inflation only, using the CPI-U, just as is the case with the official series. This measure shows a slight decline in poverty between 1999 and 2006, compared with the increase in the official series, and converges to the level of the official series in 2008. (Table 3-14)

- The other NAS-based measure recomputes the thresholds each year using the percent increase in median expenditures on necessities instead of the percent increase in the CPI. Thus, the thresholds represent a rising standard of living when such spending rises faster than inflation, but would represent a falling standard of living if the median spending were to fall in real terms. In the period in question, median spending on this group of expenditures has been increasing. As a result the poverty rate with recomputed thresholds rises even in a year of economic expansion such as 2000, and diverges even more sharply upward in 2007, compared with the rates that follow the more customary convention of holding the poverty line constant in real terms. (Table 3-14)

Table 3-13. Poverty Rates and Income Distribution Coefficients for People, Based on Alternative Definitions of Income

Year	Definition 1, MI: Money income excluding capital gains (current official measure)			Definition 4: Money income before taxes and cash transfers, plus realized capital gains (losses) and health insurance supplements		
	Poverty rate (percent)		Gini coefficient [2]	Poverty rate (percent)		Gini coefficient
	Official threshold	CPI-U-RS threshold [1]		Official threshold	CPI-U-RS threshold [1]	
1979	11.7	10.6	0.403	18.8	17.8	0.460
1980	13.0	11.5	0.401	20.1	19.0	0.462
1981	14.0	12.2	0.404	21.1	19.8	0.466
1982	15.0	13.2	0.409	22.0	20.6	0.475
1983	15.2	13.7	0.412	21.8	20.6	0.478
1984	14.4	12.8	0.413	20.8	19.5	0.477
1985	14.0	12.5	0.418	20.4	19.1	0.486
1986	13.6	12.2	0.423	19.9	18.7	0.505
1987	13.4	12.1	0.424	19.7	18.7	0.488
1988	13.0	11.7	0.425	19.7	18.5	0.489
1989	12.8	11.3	0.429	19.4	18.1	0.492
1990	13.5	11.9	0.426	19.9	18.7	0.487
1991	14.2	12.4	0.425	21.1	19.7	0.490
1992	14.8	13.1	0.430	22.1	20.6	0.497
1993	15.1	13.4	0.448	22.6	21.1	0.514
1994	14.5	12.6	0.450	22.0	20.3	0.515
1995	13.8	11.7	0.444	21.1	19.5	0.509
1996	13.7	11.6	0.447	20.8	19.1	0.511
1997	13.3	11.3	0.448	20.3	18.7	0.513
1998	12.7	10.6	0.446	19.3	17.4	0.509
1999	11.9	9.9	0.445	18.7	16.9	0.508
2000	11.3	9.7	0.447	18.0	16.5	0.506
2001	11.7	9.9	0.450	18.5	16.9	0.510
2002	12.1	10.1	0.448	19.0	17.4	. . .
2003	12.5	10.5	0.450	19.5	17.8	. . .
2004	12.7	10.8	0.450	20.0	18.3	0.503
2005	12.6	10.8	0.450	19.7	18.1	0.501
2006	12.3	10.5	0.447	18.9	17.3	0.495
2007	12.5	11.0	0.443	19.3	18.0	0.492
2008 [4]	13.2	11.7	0.446	20.8	19.6	0.497

Year	Definition 14, MI - Tx + NC: Income after all taxes and transfers			Definition 15, MI - Tx + NC + HE: Income after all taxes and transfers, plus net imputed return on equity in own home		
	Poverty rate (percent)		Gini coefficient [3]	Poverty rate (percent)		Gini coefficient [3]
	Official threshold	CPI-U-RS threshold [1]		Official threshold	CPI-U-RS threshold [1]	
1979	8.9	7.9	0.359	7.5	6.7	0.352
1980	10.1	8.6	0.354	8.2	7.0	0.347
1981	11.5	9.8	0.358	8.7	7.3	0.350
1982	12.3	10.6	0.366	9.9	8.5	0.359
1983	12.7	11.0	0.374	10.4	9.0	0.368
1984	12.0	10.4	0.378	9.9	8.6	0.372
1985	11.7	10.1	0.385	9.9	8.6	0.381
1986	11.3	9.8	0.409	10.1	8.6	0.404
1987	11.0	9.5	0.382	9.7	8.2	0.380
1988	10.8	9.4	0.385	9.4	8.2	0.384
1989	10.4	8.8	0.389	9.1	7.6	0.387
1990	10.9	9.3	0.382	9.8	8.3	0.381
1991	11.4	9.7	0.380	10.3	8.6	0.379
1992	11.9	10.2	0.385	10.7	9.1	0.381
1993	12.1	10.3	0.398	11.2	9.4	0.395
1994	11.1	9.2	0.400	10.0	8.3	0.395
1995	10.3	8.5	0.394	9.4	7.6	0.388
1996	10.2	8.4	0.398	9.3	7.6	0.392
1997	10.0	8.2	0.403	9.2	7.5	0.397
1998	9.5	7.7	0.405	8.8	7.1	0.399
1999	8.9	7.2	0.408	8.2	6.5	0.402
2000	8.8	7.2	0.410	8.0	6.5	0.402
2001	9.0	7.3	0.412	8.3	6.7	0.407
2002	9.3	7.7	0.394	8.6	7.1	0.388
2003	9.7	7.9	0.394	9.0	7.4	0.390
2004	9.6	7.9	0.404	8.8	7.2	0.398
2005	9.6	8.1	0.402	8.9	7.4	0.398
2006	9.3	7.9	0.405	8.7	7.4	0.400
2007	9.5	8.3	0.403	9.1	7.9	0.399
2008 [4]	9.8	8.4	0.392	9.2	7.9	0.389

[1]Before 1987, threshold based on CPI-U-X1.
[2]Calculated for comparability by same method as the other coefficients in this table; differs from official calculation in Table 3-4.
[3]Earlier years not comparable with 2002 and subsequent years because of a change in tax estimating model.
[4]2008 data do not include estimates of capital gains (losses).
. . . = Not available.

Table 3-14. Official and National Academy of Sciences (NAS)–Based Poverty Rates, 1999–2008

(Percent of population.)

Measurement method	1999	2000	2001	2002 (new tax model)	2003	2004 (revised)	2005	2006	2007	2008
Official measure	11.9	11.3	11.7	12.1	12.5	12.7	12.6	12.3	12.5	13.2
MSI-GA-CPI	12.1	12.0	12.2	12.1	12.3	12.5	12.5	12.2	12.6	12.8
MIT-GA-CPI	12.7	12.5	12.5	12.6	12.7	13.0	13.0	12.6	13.0	13.2
MSI-NGA-CPI	12.2	12.1	12.3	12.3	12.4	12.7	12.6	12.4	12.6	12.8
MIT-NGA-CPI	12.8	12.7	12.7	12.8	12.7	13.1	13.0	12.8	12.9	13.1
MSI-GA-CE	12.1	12.3	12.9	13.2	13.4	13.4	13.3	13.6	15.3	15.8
MIT-GA-CE	12.7	12.8	13.2	13.7	13.9	14.0	14.1	14.1	15.9	16.9
MSI-NGA-CE	12.2	12.5	13.0	13.4	13.5	13.4	13.5	13.7	15.1	15.7
MIT-NGA-CE	12.8	13.0	13.4	13.9	14.1	14.1	14.2	14.2	16.0	17.1

Note: The Census Bureau changed the way it modeled taxes, effective with the revised 2002 estimates. Consequently, comparisons of 2002 and later data with earlier years may be affected.

MSI means "Medical out-of-pocket expenses subtracted from income."
MIT means "Medical out-of-pocket expenses in the thresholds."
GA means "Geographic adjustment (of poverty thresholds)."
NGA means "No geographic adjustment (of poverty thresholds)."
CPI means "Thresholds were adjusted since 1999 using the Consumer Price Index for All Urban Consumers."
CE means "Thresholds were recomputed since 1999 using data from the Consumer Expenditure Survey."

See notes and definitions for further explanation.

Table 3-15. Comparison of NAS-Based and Official Poverty Rates by Selected Characteristics, 2008

(Percent of population.)

Characteristic	Official poverty rate (no geographic adjustment)	NAS-based rate, MIT, CPI adjustment of 1999 thresholds	
		Without geographic adjustment	With geographic adjustment
All People	13.2	13.1	13.2
People in families	11.5	11.2	11.3
Married-couple families	6.7	6.8	7.1
Families with female householder, no husband present	31.4	28.2	27.9
Families with male householder, no wife present	14.2	16.9	16.2
By age			
Under 18 years	19.0	15.4	15.6
18 to 64 years	11.7	12.2	12.4
65 years and older	9.7	13.0	12.8
Race and Hispanic origin			
White alone	11.2	11.6	11.7
Non-Hispanic White alone	8.6	9.2	8.8
Black alone	24.7	21.8	21.0
Non-Hispanic Black alone	24.6	21.7	20.7
Asian alone	11.8	12.0	14.4
Hispanic (any race)	23.2	22.3	24.9
Region			
Northeast	11.6	10.6	13.3
Midwest	12.4	12.0	9.9
South	14.3	14.8	13.2
West	13.5	13.5	16.3

Note: MIT means "Medical out-of-pocket expenses in the thresholds."

NOTES AND DEFINITIONS, CHAPTER 3

TABLES 3-1 THROUGH 3-15
INCOME DISTRIBUTION AND POVERTY

SOURCE: U.S. DEPARTMENT OF COMMERCE, BUREAU OF THE CENSUS

All data in this chapter are derived from the Current Population Survey (CPS), which is also the source of the data on labor force, employment, and unemployment used in Chapter 10. (See the notes and definitions for Tables 10-1 through 10-5.) Early each year, the 60,000 households in this monthly survey are asked additional questions concerning earnings and other income in the previous year. This survey, informally known as the "March Supplement," is now formally known as the Current Population Survey Annual Social and Economic Supplement (CPS-ASEC). It was previously called the Annual Demographic Supplement.

The population represented by the survey is the civilian noninstitutional population of the United States and members of the armed forces in the United States living off post or with their families on post, but excluding all other members of the armed forces. As it is a survey of households, homeless persons are not included.

Definitions: Racial classification and Hispanic origin

In 2002 and all earlier years, the CPS required respondents to report identification with only one race group. Since 2003, the CPS has allowed respondents to choose more than one race group. Income data for 2002 were collected in early 2003; thus, in the data for 2002 and all subsequent years, an individual could report identification with more than one race group. In the 2000 census, about 2.6 percent of people reported identification with more than one race.

Therefore, data from 2002 onward that are classified by race are not strictly comparable with race-classified data for 2001 and earlier years. As alternative approaches to dealing with this problem, the Census Bureau has tabulated two different race concepts for each racial category in a number of cases. In the case of Blacks, for example, this means there is one income measure for "Black alone," consisting of persons who report Black and no other race, and one for "Black alone or in combination," which includes all the "Black alone" reporters plus those who report Black in combination with any other race. The tables in this volume show both the "alone" and the "alone or in combination" values where available.

The race classifications now used in the CPS are *White, Black, Asian, American Indian and Alaska Native,* and *Native Hawaiian and Other Pacific Islander.* (Native Hawaiians and other Pacific Islanders were included in the "Asian" category in the data for 1987 through 2001.) The last two of these five racial groups are too small to provide reliable data for a single year, but in new Census Bureau tables available on the website, household income

and poverty data for all five groups are presented in 2- and 3-year averages. Table 3-2 displays some of these data.

Hispanic origin is a separate question in the survey—not a racial classification—and Hispanics may be of any race. A subgroup of *White non-Hispanic* is shown in some tables. According to the Census Bureau, "Being Hispanic was reported by 13.0 percent of White householders who reported only one race, 2.9 percent of Black householders who reported only one race, and 2.0 percent of Asian householders who reported only one race...Data users should exercise caution when interpreting aggregate results for the Hispanic population or for race groups because these populations consist of many distinct groups that differ in socioeconomic characteristics, culture, and recency of immigration." ("Income, Poverty, and Health Insurance Coverage in the United States: 2008," footnote 3, p. 2)

Definitions: General

Households consists of all persons who occupy a housing unit. A household includes the related family members and all the unrelated persons, if any (such as lodgers, foster children, wards, or employees), who share the housing unit. A person living alone in a housing unit or a group of unrelated persons sharing a housing unit as partners is also counted as a household. The count of households excludes group quarters.

Earnings includes all income from work, including wages, salaries, armed forces pay, commissions, tips, piece-rate payments, and cash bonuses, before deductions such as taxes, bonds, pensions, and union dues. This category also includes net income from nonfarm self-employment and farm self-employment. Wage and salary supplements that are paid directly by the employer, such as the employer share of Social Security taxes and the cost of employer-provided health insurance, are not included.

Income, in the official definition used in the survey, is money income, including *earnings* from work as defined above; unemployment compensation; workers' compensation; Social Security; Supplemental Security Income; cash public assistance (welfare payments); veterans' payments; survivor benefits; disability benefits; pension or retirement income; interest income; dividends (but not capital gains); rents, royalties, and payments from estates or trusts; educational assistance, such as scholarships or grants; child support; alimony; financial assistance from outside of the household; and other cash income regularly received, such as foster child payments, military family allotments, and foreign government pensions. Receipts not counted as income include capital gains or losses, withdrawals of bank deposits, money borrowed, tax refunds, gifts, and lump-sum inheritances or insurance payments.

A *year-round, full-time worker* is a person who worked 35 or more hours per week and 50 or more weeks during the previous calendar year.

CHAPTER 3: INCOME DISTRIBUTION AND POVERTY

A *family* is a group of two or more persons related by birth, marriage, or adoption who reside together.

Unrelated individuals are persons 15 years old and over who are not living with any relatives. The poverty status of unrelated individuals is determined independently of and is not affected by the incomes of other persons with whom they may share a household.

Median income is the amount of income that divides the ranked income distribution into two equal groups, with half having incomes above the median, and half having incomes below the median. The median income for persons is based on persons 15 years old and over with income.

Mean income is the amount obtained by dividing the total aggregate income of a group by the number of units in that group. In this survey, means are higher than medians because of the skewed nature of the income distribution; see the section "Whose standard of living?" in the article at the beginning of this book.

Historical income figures are shown in constant *2008 dollars*. All constant-dollar figures are converted from current-dollar values using the *CPI-U-RS* (the Consumer Price Index, All Urban, Research Series), which measures changes in prices for past periods using the methodologies of the current CPI, and is similar in concept and behavior to the deflators used in the NIPAs for consumer income and spending. See Chapter 8 for CPI-U-RS data and the corresponding notes and definitions.

Definitions: Income distribution

Income distribution is portrayed by dividing the total ranked distribution of families or households into *fifths*, also known as *quintiles,* and also by separately tabulating the top 5 percent (which is included in the highest fifth). The households or families are arrayed from those with the lowest income to those with the highest income, then divided into five groups, with each group containing one-fifth of the total number of households. Within each quintile, incomes are summed and calculated as a share of total income for all quintiles, and are averaged to show the average or mean income within that quintile.

A statistical measure that summarizes the dispersion of income across the entire income distribution is the *Gini coefficient* (also known as Gini ratio, Gini index, or index of income concentration), which can take values ranging from 0 to 1. A Gini value of 1 indicates "perfect" inequality; that is, one household has all the income and the rest have none. A value of 0 indicates "perfect" equality, a situation in which all households have equal income.

There are differences between the Gini coefficients for the official income measure presented in the report's main tables and those presented in Table 3-13. In the latter, the coefficients were recalculated, using a slightly different method, for comparability with the other income definitions.

Definitions: Poverty

The *number of people below poverty level,* or the number of poor people, is the number of people with family or individual incomes below a specified level that is intended to measure the cost of a minimum standard of living. These minimum levels vary by size and composition of family and are known as *poverty thresholds*.

The official poverty thresholds are based on a definition developed in 1964 by Mollie Orshansky of the Social Security Administration. She calculated food budgets for families of various sizes and compositions, using an "economy food plan" developed by the U.S. Department of Agriculture (the cheapest of four plans developed). Reflecting a 1955 Department of Agriculture survey that found that families of three or more persons spent about one-third of their after-tax incomes on food, Orshansky multiplied the costs of the food plan by 3 to arrive at a set of thresholds for poverty income for families of three or larger. For 2-person families, the multiplier was 3.7; for 1-person families, the threshold was 80 percent of the two-person threshold.

These poverty thresholds have been adjusted each year for price increases, using the percent change in the Consumer Price Index for All Urban Consumers (CPI-U).

For more information on the Orshansky thresholds (the description of which has been simplified here), see Gordon Fisher, "The Development of the Orshansky Thresholds and Their Subsequent History as the Official U.S. Poverty Measure" (May 1992), available on the Census Bureau Web site at <http://www.census.gov/hhes/poverty/povmeas/papers/orshansky.html>.

The *poverty rate* for a demographic group is the number of poor people or poor families in that group expressed as a percentage of the total number of people or families in the group.

Average poverty thresholds. The thresholds used to calculate poverty rates vary not only with the size of the family but with the number of children in the family. For example, the threshold for a three-person family in 2007 was $16,218 if there were no children in the family but $16,705 if the family consisted of 1 adult and 2 children. There are 48 different threshold values depending on size of household, number of children, and whether the householder is 65 years old or over (with lower thresholds for the older householders). The full matrix of thresholds is shown in the report referenced below. To give a general sense of the "poverty line," the Census Bureau also publishes the average threshold for each size family, based on the actual mix of family types in that year. These are the values shown in Table 3-7 to represent the history of poverty thresholds. The average value for 3-person families in 2007, as shown in Table 3-7, was $16,530, a weighted average of the values actually used for the 3 different possible family compositions.

A person with *work experience* (Table 3-11) is one who, during the preceding calendar year and on a part-time or full-time basis, did any work for pay or profit or worked without pay on a family-operated farm or business at any time during the year. A *year-round* worker is one who worked for 50 weeks or more during the preceding calendar year. A person is classified as having worked *full time* if he or she worked 35 hours or more per week during a majority of the weeks worked. A *year-round, full-time worker* is a person who worked 35 or more hours per week and 50 or more weeks during the previous calendar year.

Toward better measures of income and poverty

The definition of the official poverty rate is established by the Office of Management of Budget in the Executive Office of the President and has not been substantially changed since 1969. Criticisms of the current definition are legion. In response to these criticisms, the Census Bureau has published extensive research work illustrating the effects of various ways of modifying income definitions and poverty thresholds. Some of the results of this work are published here in Tables 3-13 through 3-15 and explained in the notes and definitions below.

Improving the income concept

One type of criticism accepts the general concept of the Orshansky threshold but recommends making the income definition more realistic by including some or all of the following: capital gains; taxes and tax credits; noncash food, housing, and health benefits provided by government and employers; and the value of homeownership. There is debate about whether it is appropriate to use income data augmented in this way in conjunction with the official thresholds. The original 1964 thresholds made no allowance for health insurance or other health expenses—in effect, they assumed that the poor would get free medical care, or at least that the poverty calculation was not required to allow for medical needs—and because of the imprecision of Orshansky's multiplier it is not clear to what extent they include housing expenses in a way that is comparable with the inclusion of a homeownership component in income. Nevertheless, the Census Bureau has calculated and published income and poverty figures based on broadened income definitions and either the official thresholds or thresholds that are closely related to the official ones. Some of these calculations are presented in Table 3-13 and described below.

Still accepting the validity of the basic Orshansky threshold concept, some critics have also argued that use of the CPI-U in the official measure to update the thresholds each year has overstated the price increase, and that an inflator such as the CPI-U-RS should be used instead. (See the notes and definitions for Chapter 8.) Use of the CPI-U-RS leads to lower poverty thresholds beginning in the late 1970s, when the CPI began to be distorted by housing and other biases subsequently corrected by new methods. Table 3-13 also shows poverty rates using the lower CPI-U-RS thresholds. Use of the CPI-U-RS eliminates a presumed upward bias in the poverty rate relative to the poverty rates

estimated before the bias emerged. This is a bias in the behavior of the time series given the concept of the Orshansky threshold, not necessarily a bias in the current level of poverty, since all the other criticisms of the Orshansky thresholds need to be considered when assessing the general adequacy of today's poverty measurements.

Alternative definitions of income with Orshansky-type poverty thresholds—Table 3-13

The Census Bureau has calculated "alternative" income and poverty measures based on a number of different definitions of income. In many cases, these measures require simulation—use of data from sources other than the CPS to estimate elements of family and individual income and expenses. One system of income definition alternatives, shown in Table 3-13, was used for data through 2003 and has been selectively updated through 2008. The updated data for each year are shown on the website under the category "Detailed poverty tables." This system provides poverty rates including and excluding the effects of government tax and transfer programs, demonstrating the effects of these programs in alleviating poverty.

Table 3-13 shows household income distribution and poverty data according to a system of alternative income definitions that was last used in published reports for 2003 data, issued in June 2005, and has been selectively updated to 2008 on the Website.

Definition 1, also known as "MI," is the official Census Bureau definition of money income described above.

Definition 4 is Definition 1 income minus government cash transfers (Social Security, unemployment compensation, workers' compensation, veterans' payments, railroad retirement, Black Lung payments, government education assistance, Supplemental Security Income, and welfare payments), plus realized capital gains and employers' payments for health insurance coverage. Capital gains and health insurance are not collected in the CPS but are simulated using statistical data from the Internal Revenue Service and the National Medical Care Expenditure Survey. Definition 4 is the closest approach in this set of calculations to a measure of the income generated by the workings of the economy before government interventions in the form of taxes and transfer payments.

Definition 14, also known as "MI – Tx + NC," is income after all government income and earnings tax and transfer interventions. It consists of Definition 4 income minus payroll taxes and federal and state income taxes, plus the Earned Income Credit; plus all of the cash transfers listed above as being subtracted from money income to yield Definition 4; plus the "fungible" value of Medicare and Medicaid (see below for definition); plus the value of regular-price school lunches provided by government; and plus the value of noncash transfers, including food stamps, rent subsidies, and free and reduced-price school lunches. The tax information is not collected in the CPS but is simulated using statistical data from the Internal Revenue Service, Social Security payroll tax formulas, and a model of each state's income tax regulations.

The "fungible" value approach to medical benefits counts such benefits as income only to the extent that they free up resources that would have been spent on medical care. Therefore, if family income is not sufficient to cover the family's basic food and housing requirements, Medicare and Medicaid are treated as having no income value. Data on average Medicare and Medicaid outlays per enrollee are used in the valuation process.

Food stamp values are reported in the March CPS. Estimates of other government subsidy payments use data from the Department of Agriculture (for school lunches) and the 1985 American Housing Survey.

Definition 15 ("MI – Tx + NC + HE") is Definition 14 income plus the net imputed return on equity in owner-occupied housing—the calculated annual benefit of converting one's home equity into an annuity, net of property taxes. This concept can be thought of as measuring the extent to which equity in the home relieves the owner of the need for rental or mortgage payments. Information from the 1987 American Housing Survey is used to assign values of home equity and amounts of property taxes. Since disposable personal income in the national income and product accounts (NIPAs) includes the imputed rent on owner-occupied housing plus most of the cash and in-kind transfers included in Definitions 14 and 15, Definition 15 is the Census Bureau income definition closest to the NIPA concept.

Improving the concepts of income and poverty together

Another type of criticism argues that the official thresholds are no longer relevant to today's needs, and that the concepts of income (or "resources") and of the threshold level that depicts a minimum adequate standard of living need to be rethought together. These critics cite the availability of more up-to-date and detailed information about consumer spending at various income levels. The Consumer Expenditure Survey (CEX), originally designed to provide the weights for the Consumer Price Index, is now conducted annually and provides extensive data on consumer spending patterns. To give just one example of the information available now that was not available to Mollie Orshansky, the CEX indicates that food now accounts for one-sixth, not one-third, of total family expenditures, even among low-income families. (For data and notes on the Consumer Expenditure Survey, see Bernan Press, *Handbook of U.S. Labor Statistics*.)

A special panel of the National Academy of Sciences (NAS) undertook a study that reconsidered both resources and thresholds. The Census Bureau now calculates and publishes poverty rates that have been developed following NAS recommendations, which are presented in Tables 3-14 and 3-15.

Measures based on NAS recommendations—Tables 3-14 and 3-15

The most recent calculations of experimental poverty measures that redefine both income and need are presented in "Alternative Poverty Estimates in the United States: 2003" (see below for complete reference) and updated through 2008 on the Census Bureau Web site at <http://www.census.gov>.

To derive these estimates, a baseline set of poverty thresholds for the year 1999, based on data from the CEX for the years 1997–1999, was developed as follows:

- A reference family type was selected: a 2-adult, 2-child family.
- The definition of necessities for the purpose of the poverty threshold was expenditures on food, clothing, shelter, and utilities (FCSU), augmented by a multiplier of between 1.15 and 1.25 to include other needs such as household and personal supplies. The definition of food includes food away from home. Expenses on shelter include interest (but not principal repayment) for homeowners and rent for renters.
- The numerical estimates were derived as follows: FCSU expenditures for reference families falling between the 30th and 35th percentile of the distribution of expenditures in the CEX, based on 1997–1999 data but expressed in 1999 dollars, were calculated and expanded by the multiplier percentages. The midpoint of these estimates was then selected as the poverty threshold; it turned out to be 96.725 percent of median FCSU expenditures.
- For health care, three different treatments were developed; these treatments are described below.
- Three-parameter equivalence scale adjustments were used to convert the threshold for the reference family to thresholds for other family sizes and compositions, accounting for the differing needs of adults and children and the economies of scale of living in larger families.
- For some of the experimental measures, thresholds were adjusted geographically to reflect differences in the cost of living (in practice, difference in housing costs) in different areas.

The family incomes to be compared with these poverty thresholds were defined and measured to include the effects of all taxes, tax credits, and in-kind benefits such as food stamps, but not the value of homeownership, and to allow for expenses such as child care that are necessary to hold a job.

The 9 measures shown in Table 3-14 are as originally presented in Table B-3 in "Alternative Poverty Estimates in the United States: 2003," and updated in the table "Official and National Academy of Sciences (NAS) Based Poverty Rates: 1999 to 2008," available on the Census Bureau Web site. The following abbreviations are used to define the alternative definitions of poverty that are presented in this table.

- *MSI* indicates that in calculating the poverty rate, medical out-of-pocket expenses are subtracted from family income before comparing that income to the family's threshold.

- *MIT* indicates that poverty thresholds were increased to take the family's potential medical out-of-pocket expenses into account, using the CEX and the 1996 Medical Expenditures Panel Survey, with the amounts depending on family size, age, and health insurance coverage.

- *GA* indicates that the thresholds were adjusted for geographic differences in the cost of living. Measures labeled *NGA* were not.

- *CPI* indicates that the thresholds established for 1999 were updated to succeeding years using the percent change in the CPI-U. This means that the threshold for measures with this indication has been held constant in real (inflation-adjusted) terms since 1999, just as the official threshold has been held constant in real terms— except for bias in the price indexes—since 1964.

- *CE* indicates that the thresholds were updated using the percent change in <u>median</u> FCSU expenditures from the latest available 12 quarters of CEX data. This means that if the actual real FCSU spending of middle-income families rises (or falls), the real standard of living represented by the poverty thresholds will rise (or fall) commensurately.

In Table 3-15, poverty rates for 2008 using one of the NAS-based concepts—adjustment with the CPI, with medical out-of-pocket expenses in the threshold—are shown with and without the geographic adjustment to demonstrate the impact of the new methods and the geographic adjustment.

Notes on the data

The following are the principal changes that may affect year-to-year comparability of all income and poverty data from the CPS.

- Beginning in 1952, the estimates are based on 1950 census population controls. Earlier figures were based on 1940 census population controls.

- Beginning in 1962, 1960 census–based sample design and population controls are fully implemented.

- With 1971 and 1972 data, 1970 census–based sample design and population controls were introduced.

- With 1983–1985 data, 1980 census–based sample design was introduced; 1980 population controls were introduced; and these were extended back to 1979 data.

- With 1993 data, there was a major redesign of the CPS, including the introduction of computer-assisted interviewing. The limits used to "code" reported income amounts were changed, resulting in reporting of higher income values for the highest-income families and, consequently, an exaggerated year-to-year increase in income inequality. (It is possible that this jump actually reflects in one year an increase that had emerged more gradually, so that the distribution measures for 1993 and later years may be properly comparable with data for decades earlier even if they should not be directly compared with 1992.) In addition, 1990 census–based population controls were introduced, and these were extended back to the 1992 data.

- With 1995 data, the 1990 census–based sample design was implemented and the sample was reduced by 7,000 households.

- Data for 2001 implemented population controls based on the 2000 census, which were carried back to 1999. Data from 2000 forward also incorporate results from a 28,000-household sample expansion.

For more information on these and other changes that could affect comparability, see "Current Population Survey Technical Paper 63RV: Design and Methodology" (March 2002) and footnotes to CPS historical income tables, both available on the Census Bureau Web site at <http://www .census.gov/hhes/income>.

Data availability

Data embodying the official definitions of income and poverty are published annually in late summer or early fall by the Census Bureau, as part of a series with the general title *Current Population Reports: Consumer Income, P60.* Most of the data in this chapter were derived from report P60-236RV, "Income, Poverty, and Health Insurance Coverage in the United States: 2008" (September 2009), and from the "Historical Income Tables" and "Historical Poverty Tables" on the Census Web site (see below).

The data in Table 3-13 were first published in two reports, both issued in June 2005: P60-228, "Alternative Income Estimates in the United States: 2003," and P60-227, "Alternative Poverty Estimates in the United States: 2003." Updates available on the website are cited in the table description above. Corrections to the 2006 data on the website were obtained from Census Bureau staff.

The NAS-based data used in Tables 3-14 and 3-15 are posted on the Census Bureau Web site under the titles "Official and National Academy of Sciences (NAS) Based Poverty Rates: 1999 to 2008" and "Alternative Poverty Estimates Based on National Academy of Sciences Recommendations, by Selected Demographic Characteristics and by Region: 2008."

All these reports and related data, including historical tabulations, used in *Business Statistics* are available on the

Census Bureau Web site at <http://www.census.gov>, under the general headings of "Income" and "Poverty."

References

Definitions and descriptions of the concepts and data of the official and alternative series are provided in the source documents listed above and in the references contained therein.

Additional descriptive material on the NAS-based experimental poverty measures is found in the Census report P60-216, "Experimental Poverty Measures: 1999" issued October 2001, available at <http://www.census.gov/prod/2001pubs/p60-216.pdf>; and in Kathleen S. Short and Thesia I. Garner, "A Decade of Experimental Poverty Thresholds 1990 to 2000," (June 27, 2002), available at <http://www.census.gov/hhes/www/povmeas/papers/decade.pdf>.

CHAPTER 4: CONSUMER INCOME AND SPENDING

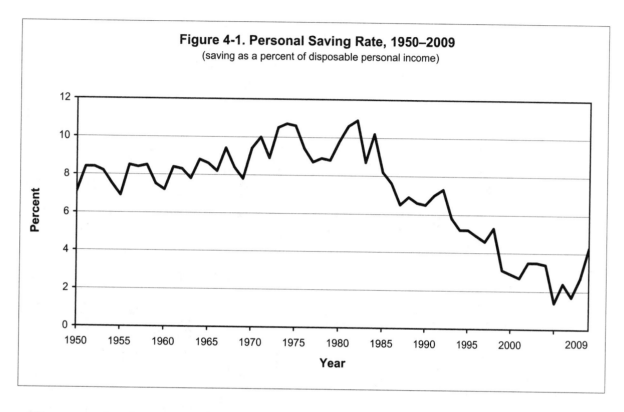

Figure 4-1. Personal Saving Rate, 1950–2009
(saving as a percent of disposable personal income)

- The personal saving rate—saving as a percent of disposable income—averaged 8 to 10 percent for much of the postwar period, but started to trend down around the mid-1980s. From 1999 through 2008, the saving rate ranged between 1.4 and 3.5 percent and averaged 2.7 percent (Table 4-1). According to updated estimates, nonprofit institutions actually dis-saved for much of this period—borrowing and/or spending out of assets—and households saved less, borrowed more, and/or spent more out of assets than in earlier years. (Table 4-6) In 2009, the saving rate rose to 4.3 percent, the highest since 1998, as households reduced their debt levels. (Tables 12-5 and 12-6)

- It should be noted that personal income does not, by definition, include any capital gains. Despite that, taxes on realized capital gains are deducted from personal income to get after-tax income (along with all other income taxes). Capital gains are a source of spending power in addition to current disposable income; they can be, and in recent years have been, converted into cash by asset sales, refinancing, and home equity loans, which contributed to recent low saving rates. (Table 12-10)

- Labor compensation, excluding social insurance contributions, made up 56.7 percent of total personal income in 2009. This was down from 59.4 percent in 2000 and 65.7 percent in 1950. ("Contributions for social insurance," mainly Social Security taxes, are excluded from both the numerator and the denominator of this percentage.) Government social benefits rose from 5.9 percent in 1950 to 12.2 percent in 2000 and 17.2 percent in 2009. It should be noted that "consumption expenditures" in the national income and product accounts includes all spending financed by government health insurance programs such as Medicare and Medicaid, and personal income also includes the amount of that spending, in the government social benefits component. (Table 4-1)

Table 4-1. Personal Income and Its Disposition

(Billions of current dollars, except as noted; quarterly data are at seasonally adjusted annual rates.)   **NIPA Table 2.1**

Year and quarter	Personal income											
					Personal income receipts on assets		Personal current transfer receipts					
								Government social benefits to persons				
	Total	Compensation of employees, received	Proprietors' income with IVA and CCAdj	Rental income of persons with CCAdj	Personal interest income	Personal dividend income	Total	Social Security and Medicare	Government unemployment insurance	Veterans	Family assistance	Other government benefits to persons
1950	228.9	155.3	37.5	9.1	9.7	8.8	13.4	1.0	1.5	7.7	0.6	2.7
1951	257.9	181.4	42.7	10.0	10.5	8.6	10.5	1.9	0.9	4.6	0.6	2.6
1952	275.2	196.2	43.1	11.2	11.3	8.6	11.0	2.2	1.1	4.3	0.5	2.9
1953	291.7	210.3	42.0	12.4	12.7	8.9	11.7	3.0	1.0	4.1	0.5	3.0
1954	294.3	209.2	42.3	13.4	14.0	9.3	13.7	3.6	2.2	4.2	0.6	3.2
1955	316.0	225.9	44.3	13.8	15.2	10.5	14.8	4.9	1.5	4.4	0.6	3.3
1956	339.5	244.5	45.9	14.1	16.9	11.3	15.6	5.7	1.5	4.4	0.6	3.4
1957	358.5	257.5	47.8	14.5	18.9	11.7	18.1	7.3	1.9	4.5	0.7	3.7
1958	368.9	259.5	50.2	15.2	20.3	11.6	22.2	8.5	4.1	4.7	0.8	4.1
1959	392.3	281.0	50.3	16.0	22.0	12.6	22.9	10.2	2.8	4.6	0.9	4.5
1960	411.3	296.4	50.7	17.0	24.5	13.4	24.4	11.1	3.0	4.6	1.0	4.7
1961	428.8	305.3	53.2	17.7	26.2	13.9	28.1	12.6	4.3	5.0	1.1	5.1
1962	456.4	327.1	55.3	18.6	29.1	15.0	28.8	14.3	3.1	4.7	1.3	5.5
1963	479.5	345.2	56.5	19.3	31.7	16.2	30.3	15.2	3.0	4.8	1.4	5.9
1964	514.3	370.7	59.4	19.4	35.6	18.2	31.3	16.0	2.7	4.7	1.5	6.4
1965	555.5	399.5	63.9	19.9	39.2	20.2	33.9	18.1	2.3	4.9	1.7	7.0
1966	603.8	442.7	68.2	20.5	43.4	20.7	37.5	20.8	1.9	4.9	1.9	8.1
1967	648.1	475.1	69.8	20.9	47.5	21.5	45.8	25.8	2.2	5.6	2.3	9.9
1968	711.7	524.3	74.2	20.6	51.6	23.5	53.3	30.5	2.1	5.9	2.8	11.9
1969	778.3	577.6	77.5	20.9	59.9	24.2	59.0	33.1	2.2	6.7	3.5	13.4
1970	838.6	617.2	78.5	21.1	69.2	24.3	71.7	38.6	4.0	7.7	4.8	16.6
1971	903.1	658.3	84.7	22.2	75.9	25.0	85.4	44.7	5.8	8.8	6.2	20.0
1972	992.6	725.1	96.0	23.1	82.8	26.8	94.8	49.8	5.7	9.7	6.9	22.7
1973	1 110.5	811.3	113.6	23.9	94.8	29.9	108.6	60.9	4.4	10.4	7.2	25.7
1974	1 222.7	890.7	113.5	24.0	113.2	33.2	128.6	70.3	6.8	11.8	8.0	31.7
1975	1 334.9	949.0	119.6	23.4	129.3	32.9	163.1	81.5	17.6	14.5	9.3	40.2
1976	1 474.7	1 059.2	132.2	22.1	139.5	39.0	177.3	93.3	15.8	14.4	10.1	43.7
1977	1 632.5	1 180.4	146.0	19.6	160.6	44.7	189.1	105.3	12.7	13.8	10.6	46.7
1978	1 836.7	1 335.2	167.5	20.9	184.0	50.7	203.2	116.9	9.1	13.9	10.8	52.5
1979	2 059.5	1 498.5	181.1	22.6	217.3	57.4	227.1	132.5	9.4	14.4	11.1	59.6
1980	2 301.5	1 647.6	173.5	28.5	274.7	64.0	270.8	154.8	15.7	15.0	12.5	72.8
1981	2 582.3	1 819.6	181.6	36.5	348.3	73.6	307.2	182.1	15.6	16.1	13.1	80.2
1982	2 766.8	1 919.6	174.8	38.1	410.8	77.6	342.4	204.6	25.1	16.4	12.9	83.4
1983	2 952.2	2 036.0	190.7	38.2	446.3	83.3	369.9	222.2	26.2	16.6	13.8	91.0
1984	3 268.9	2 245.2	233.1	40.0	517.2	90.6	380.4	237.8	15.9	16.4	14.5	95.9
1985	3 496.7	2 412.0	246.1	41.9	555.8	97.4	402.6	253.0	15.7	16.7	15.2	102.0
1986	3 696.0	2 557.7	262.6	33.8	588.4	106.0	428.0	268.9	16.3	16.7	16.1	109.9
1987	3 924.4	2 735.6	294.2	34.2	603.6	112.2	447.4	282.6	14.5	16.6	16.4	117.3
1988	4 231.2	2 954.2	334.8	40.2	637.3	129.7	475.9	300.2	13.2	16.9	16.9	128.7
1989	4 557.5	3 131.3	351.6	42.4	717.0	157.8	519.4	325.6	14.3	17.3	17.5	144.8
1990	4 846.7	3 326.2	365.1	49.8	751.9	168.8	572.7	351.8	18.0	17.8	19.2	165.9
1991	5 031.5	3 438.4	367.3	61.6	748.2	180.3	648.2	381.7	26.6	18.3	21.1	200.5
1992	5 347.3	3 647.2	414.9	84.6	722.2	187.6	729.5	414.4	38.9	19.3	22.2	234.6
1993	5 568.1	3 790.6	449.6	114.1	698.1	202.3	776.7	444.7	34.1	20.0	22.8	255.0
1994	5 874.8	3 980.9	485.1	142.9	712.7	235.0	813.1	476.6	23.5	20.1	23.2	269.7
1995	6 200.9	4 178.8	516.0	154.6	751.9	253.4	860.2	508.9	21.4	20.9	22.6	286.4
1996	6 591.6	4 387.5	583.7	170.4	784.4	296.4	901.2	536.9	22.0	21.7	20.3	300.3
1997	7 000.7	4 668.6	628.2	176.5	835.8	329.7	929.8	563.5	19.9	22.6	17.9	306.0
1998	7 525.4	5 023.9	687.5	191.5	919.3	349.8	951.9	574.7	19.5	23.5	17.4	316.8
1999	7 910.8	5 348.8	746.8	208.2	910.9	335.9	987.6	588.6	20.3	24.3	17.9	336.4
2000	8 559.4	5 788.8	817.5	215.3	984.2	376.5	1 040.6	620.5	20.6	25.2	18.4	355.9
2001	8 883.3	5 979.3	870.7	232.4	976.5	369.5	1 141.3	667.7	31.7	26.8	18.1	397.1
2002	9 060.1	6 110.8	890.3	218.7	911.9	397.7	1 247.9	706.1	53.2	29.8	17.7	441.1
2003	9 378.1	6 367.6	930.6	204.2	889.8	423.1	1 316.0	740.4	52.8	32.2	18.4	472.3
2004	9 937.2	6 708.4	1 033.8	198.4	860.2	548.3	1 398.6	790.2	36.0	34.5	18.4	519.6
2005	10 485.9	7 060.0	1 069.8	178.2	987.0	555.0	1 482.7	844.7	31.3	36.8	18.2	551.7
2006	11 268.1	7 475.7	1 133.0	146.5	1 127.5	702.2	1 583.6	943.3	29.9	39.3	18.2	552.9
2007	11 894.1	7 862.7	1 096.4	144.9	1 266.4	765.1	1 687.8	1 003.7	32.3	42.1	18.5	591.2
2008	12 238.8	8 042.4	1 106.3	210.4	1 308.0	686.4	1 843.2	1 070.3	50.6	45.6	18.9	657.9
2009	12 026.1	7 786.6	1 041.0	268.1	1 238.5	554.2	2 072.0	1 156.7	122.0	52.0	19.8	721.6
2007												
1st quarter	11 706.9	7 782.2	1 094.2	121.1	1 198.3	769.9	1 666.7	981.0	31.4	41.0	18.4	595.0
2nd quarter	11 823.4	7 819.7	1 096.0	140.3	1 246.5	775.5	1 669.3	998.2	31.2	42.0	18.4	579.5
3rd quarter	11 945.6	7 869.6	1 093.2	150.2	1 297.9	767.9	1 693.9	1 012.7	32.8	42.2	18.5	587.7
4th quarter	12 100.3	7 979.3	1 102.1	168.0	1 322.8	747.0	1 721.2	1 023.1	33.9	43.0	18.6	602.7
2008												
1st quarter	12 142.2	8 017.5	1 115.2	179.9	1 304.6	716.2	1 761.5	1 049.1	35.7	44.8	18.6	613.3
2nd quarter	12 292.9	8 032.8	1 111.9	202.8	1 306.6	690.7	1 904.4	1 064.5	38.7	45.0	18.8	737.5
3rd quarter	12 286.6	8 069.1	1 114.4	222.2	1 327.8	673.7	1 841.7	1 080.5	57.7	46.1	18.9	638.5
4th quarter	12 233.5	8 050.3	1 083.6	236.7	1 292.9	665.2	1 865.3	1 087.0	70.3	46.5	19.2	642.3
2009												
1st quarter	11 952.7	7 805.8	1 037.8	245.9	1 243.4	602.1	1 954.7	1 128.5	96.2	50.3	19.5	660.4
2nd quarter	12 048.8	7 815.9	1 028.0	262.0	1 241.1	532.3	2 107.7	1 151.1	122.5	50.5	19.7	763.9
3rd quarter	12 005.2	7 751.4	1 037.9	277.9	1 234.9	528.2	2 104.7	1 165.8	135.7	52.0	19.9	731.2
4th quarter	12 097.7	7 773.1	1 060.3	286.7	1 234.4	554.1	2 121.0	1 181.4	133.6	55.1	20.1	730.8

Table 4-1. Personal Income and Its Disposition—Continued

(Billions of current dollars, except as noted; quarterly data are at seasonally adjusted annual rates.)   NIPA Table 2.1

Year and quarter	Personal current transfer receipts—Continued From business, net	Less: Contributions for government social insurance, domestic	Less: Personal current taxes	Equals: Disposable personal income	Total	Personal consumption expenditures	Personal interest payments	Personal current transfer payments Total	To government	To the rest of the world, net	Personal saving Billions of dollars	Percent of disposable personal income	Percent income excluding current transfers	Disposable personal income (chained 2005)
1950	0.6	5.5	18.9	209.9	195.0	192.2	2.0	0.8	0.3	0.4	14.9	7.1	1 434.5	1 401.5
1951	0.9	6.6	27.1	230.8	211.5	208.5	2.2	0.7	0.3	0.4	19.3	8.4	1 540.6	1 442.9
1952	0.9	6.9	32.0	243.2	222.9	219.5	2.6	0.8	0.4	0.4	20.3	8.4	1 612.9	1 489.6
1953	0.8	7.1	33.2	258.4	237.1	233.1	3.2	0.9	0.4	0.5	21.3	8.2	1 687.2	1 561.9
1954	0.6	8.1	30.2	264.1	244.3	240.0	3.4	0.9	0.4	0.5	19.8	7.5	1 677.9	1 583.0
1955	0.9	9.1	32.9	283.1	263.6	258.8	4.0	0.9	0.4	0.4	19.5	6.9	1 792.5	1 690.0
1956	1.2	10.0	36.6	302.9	277.2	271.7	4.6	1.0	0.5	0.5	25.6	8.5	1 887.9	1 772.2
1957	1.4	11.4	38.9	319.7	292.8	286.9	4.9	1.1	0.6	0.5	26.9	8.4	1 925.2	1 815.3
1958	1.2	11.4	38.5	330.4	302.2	296.2	5.0	1.0	0.6	0.4	28.2	8.5	1 916.7	1 833.1
1959	1.3	13.8	42.3	350.1	324.0	317.7	5.5	0.8	0.3	0.5	26.1	7.5	2 012.1	1 913.5
1960	1.3	16.4	46.1	365.2	338.9	331.8	6.2	0.8	0.3	0.5	26.3	7.2	2 073.2	1 963.9
1961	1.4	17.0	47.3	381.6	349.7	342.2	6.5	1.0	0.5	0.5	31.9	8.4	2 125.5	2 030.8
1962	1.5	19.1	51.6	404.9	371.4	363.3	7.0	1.1	0.5	0.6	33.5	8.3	2 240.9	2 129.6
1963	1.9	21.7	54.6	425.0	391.8	382.7	7.9	1.2	0.5	0.7	33.1	7.8	2 325.7	2 209.5
1964	2.2	22.4	52.1	462.3	421.7	411.5	8.9	1.3	0.6	0.7	40.5	8.8	2 463.8	2 368.7
1965	2.3	23.4	57.7	497.8	455.1	443.8	9.9	1.4	0.6	0.8	42.7	8.6	2 623.2	2 514.7
1966	2.1	31.3	66.4	537.4	493.1	480.9	10.7	1.6	0.8	0.8	44.3	8.2	2 779.1	2 647.3
1967	2.3	34.9	73.0	575.1	520.9	507.8	11.1	2.0	1.0	1.0	54.2	9.4	2 883.4	2 763.5
1968	2.8	38.7	87.0	624.7	572.2	558.0	12.2	2.0	1.0	1.0	52.5	8.4	3 032.1	2 889.2
1969	3.3	44.1	104.5	673.8	621.4	605.1	14.0	2.2	1.1	1.1	52.5	7.8	3 168.1	2 981.4
1970	2.9	46.4	103.1	735.5	666.1	648.3	15.2	2.6	1.3	1.3	69.4	9.4	3 228.9	3 108.8
1971	2.7	51.2	101.7	801.4	721.0	701.6	16.6	2.8	1.5	1.4	80.4	10.0	3 304.2	3 249.1
1972	3.1	59.2	123.6	869.0	791.5	770.2	18.1	3.2	1.8	1.4	77.5	8.9	3 507.5	3 406.6
1973	3.9	75.5	132.4	978.1	875.2	852.0	19.8	3.4	1.8	1.6	102.9	10.5	3 712.0	3 638.2
1974	4.7	85.2	151.0	1 071.7	957.5	932.9	21.2	3.4	2.1	1.4	114.2	10.7	3 670.0	3 610.2
1975	6.8	89.3	147.6	1 187.3	1 061.3	1 033.8	23.7	3.8	2.5	1.3	125.9	10.6	3 621.7	3 691.3
1976	6.7	101.3	172.3	1 302.3	1 179.6	1 151.3	23.9	4.4	3.0	1.4	122.8	9.4	3 804.0	3 838.3
1977	5.1	113.1	197.5	1 435.0	1 309.7	1 277.8	27.0	4.8	3.5	1.4	125.3	8.7	3 979.9	3 970.7
1978	6.5	131.3	229.4	1 607.3	1 465.0	1 427.6	31.9	5.4	3.9	1.6	142.4	8.9	4 207.6	4 156.5
1979	8.2	152.7	268.7	1 790.9	1 633.4	1 591.2	36.2	6.0	4.3	1.7	157.5	8.8	4 333.1	4 253.8
1980	8.6	166.2	298.9	2 002.7	1 806.4	1 755.8	43.6	6.9	5.0	2.0	196.3	9.8	4 337.2	4 295.6
1981	11.2	195.7	345.2	2 237.1	2 000.4	1 939.5	49.3	11.5	6.0	5.6	236.7	10.6	4 462.8	4 410.0
1982	12.4	208.9	354.1	2 412.7	2 148.8	2 075.5	59.5	13.8	7.1	6.7	263.9	10.9	4 505.2	4 506.5
1983	13.8	226.0	352.3	2 599.8	2 372.9	2 288.6	69.2	15.1	8.1	7.0	226.9	8.7	4 599.5	4 655.7
1984	19.7	257.5	377.4	2 891.5	2 595.2	2 501.1	77.0	17.1	9.2	7.9	296.3	10.2	4 949.9	4 989.1
1985	22.3	281.4	417.3	3 079.3	2 825.7	2 717.6	89.4	18.8	10.4	8.3	253.6	8.2	5 132.1	5 144.8
1986	22.9	303.4	437.2	3 258.8	3 012.4	2 896.7	94.5	21.1	12.0	9.1	246.5	7.6	5 292.6	5 315.0
1987	20.2	323.1	489.1	3 435.3	3 211.9	3 097.0	91.7	23.2	13.2	10.0	223.4	6.5	5 436.1	5 402.4
1988	20.6	361.5	504.9	3 726.3	3 469.7	3 350.1	94.0	25.6	14.8	10.8	256.6	6.9	5 648.4	5 635.6
1989	23.2	385.2	566.1	3 991.4	3 726.4	3 594.5	103.9	28.0	16.5	11.6	265.0	6.6	5 819.2	5 785.1
1990	22.2	410.1	592.7	4 254.0	3 977.3	3 835.5	111.3	30.6	18.4	12.2	276.7	6.5	5 893.3	5 896.3
1991	17.6	430.2	586.6	4 444.9	4 131.7	3 980.1	115.0	36.7	22.6	14.1	313.2	7.0	5 839.9	5 945.9
1992	16.3	455.0	610.5	4 736.7	4 388.7	4 236.9	111.3	40.5	26.0	14.5	348.1	7.3	5 979.5	6 155.3
1993	14.1	477.4	646.5	4 921.6	4 636.2	4 483.6	107.0	45.6	28.6	17.1	285.4	5.8	6 074.8	6 258.2
1994	13.3	508.2	690.5	5 184.3	4 913.6	4 750.8	113.0	49.8	30.9	18.9	270.7	5.2	6 289.7	6 459.0
1995	18.7	532.8	743.9	5 457.0	5 170.8	4 987.3	130.6	52.9	32.6	20.3	286.3	5.2	6 487.0	6 651.6
1996	22.9	555.1	832.0	5 759.6	5 478.5	5 273.6	147.3	57.6	34.9	22.6	281.1	4.9	6 761.0	6 870.9
1997	19.4	587.2	926.2	6 074.6	5 794.2	5 570.6	159.7	63.9	38.2	25.7	280.4	4.6	7 086.5	7 113.5
1998	26.0	624.7	1 026.4	6 498.9	6 157.5	5 918.5	169.5	69.5	39.9	29.7	341.5	5.3	7 595.0	7 538.8
1999	34.0	661.3	1 107.5	6 803.3	6 595.5	6 342.8	176.5	76.2	44.1	32.2	207.8	3.1	7 864.8	7 766.7
2000	42.4	705.8	1 232.3	7 327.2	7 114.1	6 830.4	200.3	83.4	48.8	34.6	213.1	2.9	8 327.8	8 161.5
2001	46.8	733.2	1 234.8	7 648.5	7 443.5	7 148.8	203.7	91.0	52.9	38.1	204.9	2.7	8 411.1	8 360.1
2002	34.2	751.5	1 050.4	8 009.7	7 727.5	7 439.2	191.3	97.0	56.4	40.6	282.2	3.5	8 387.2	8 637.1
2003	25.7	778.9	1 000.3	8 377.8	8 088.0	7 804.0	182.7	101.3	60.2	41.2	289.8	3.5	8 493.1	8 853.9
2004	16.9	827.3	1 047.8	8 889.4	8 585.7	8 285.1	190.3	110.3	66.7	43.6	303.7	3.4	8 776.4	9 155.1
2005	25.8	872.7	1 208.6	9 277.3	9 149.6	8 819.0	210.8	119.8	71.4	48.4	127.7	1.4	8 977.3	9 277.3
2006	21.4	921.8	1 352.4	9 915.7	9 680.7	9 322.7	230.1	128.0	76.4	51.6	235.0	2.4	9 404.8	9 650.7
2007	30.2	959.3	1 490.9	10 403.1	10 224.3	9 826.4	256.8	141.0	82.3	58.7	178.9	1.7	9 645.4	9 860.6
2008	32.6	990.6	1 432.4	10 806.4	10 520.0	10 129.9	237.7	152.3	87.9	64.5	286.4	2.7	9 504.6	9 911.3
2009	32.7	966.9	1 102.5	10 923.6	10 458.7	10 089.1	213.9	155.7	92.2	63.5	464.9	4.3	9 081.6	9 999.0
2007 1st quarter	27.1	952.5	1 459.5	10 247.4	10 038.3	9 658.5	242.1	137.8	80.0	57.8	209.1	2.0	9 605.4	9 830.2
2nd quarter	29.8	953.7	1 481.8	10 341.7	10 158.2	9 762.5	256.2	139.4	81.5	57.9	183.5	1.8	9 635.9	9 842.7
3rd quarter	31.6	958.6	1 500.7	10 445.0	10 275.6	9 865.6	268.2	141.8	83.1	58.7	169.4	1.6	9 671.1	9 883.9
4th quarter	32.4	972.6	1 521.9	10 578.4	10 425.0	10 019.2	260.7	145.0	84.6	60.4	153.5	1.5	9 669.6	9 886.2
2008 1st quarter	32.6	985.3	1 531.8	10 610.4	10 484.1	10 095.1	239.8	149.2	86.1	63.1	126.3	1.2	9 583.9	9 826.8
2nd quarter	32.6	988.9	1 326.2	10 966.7	10 592.2	10 194.7	243.9	153.6	87.4	66.2	374.4	3.4	9 498.8	10 059.0
3rd quarter	32.6	994.9	1 437.3	10 849.3	10 613.6	10 220.1	238.3	155.2	88.5	66.7	235.7	2.2	9 442.0	9 838.3
4th quarter	32.7	993.3	1 434.3	10 799.1	10 389.9	10 009.8	228.8	151.3	89.5	61.8	409.2	3.8	9 494.4	9 920.4
2009 1st quarter	32.5	969.7	1 187.3	10 765.4	10 362.3	9 987.7	220.4	154.2	90.4	63.8	403.1	3.7	9 188.7	9 926.4
2nd quarter	32.7	970.9	1 082.6	10 966.2	10 370.5	9 999.3	216.7	154.5	91.4	63.1	595.7	5.4	9 100.5	10 077.5
3rd quarter	32.8	962.5	1 071.0	10 934.3	10 502.8	10 132.9	215.5	154.4	92.5	61.9	431.5	3.9	9 010.5	9 984.4
4th quarter	32.9	964.7	1 069.1	11 028.7	10 599.3	10 236.4	203.1	159.8	94.5	65.3	429.3	3.9	9 024.0	10 008.5

Table 4-2. Personal Consumption Expenditures by Major Type of Product

(Billions of dollars, quarterly data are at seasonally adjusted rates.)   NIPA Table 2.3.5

Year and quarter	Personal consumption expenditures, total	Total goods	Goods									
			Durable goods					Nondurable goods				
			Durable goods, total	Motor vehicles and parts	Furnishings and household equipment	Recreational goods and vehicles	Other durable goods	Nondurable goods, total	Food and beverages off-premises	Clothing and footwear	Gasoline and other energy goods	Other nondurable goods
1950	192.2	116.8	32.4	13.7	11.8	4.1	2.9	84.4	41.4	18.9	8.9	15.2
1951	208.5	124.8	31.7	12.1	12.4	4.1	3.2	93.0	46.0	20.5	9.6	16.9
1952	219.5	128.8	31.2	11.4	12.2	4.3	3.4	97.5	48.4	21.2	10.2	17.8
1953	233.1	134.8	34.6	13.8	12.6	4.7	3.5	100.2	49.3	21.3	10.8	18.8
1954	240.0	135.8	33.7	12.7	12.5	4.9	3.6	102.1	50.6	21.4	11.3	18.8
1955	258.8	147.4	40.7	17.7	14.0	5.3	3.7	106.7	52.0	22.4	12.4	19.9
1956	271.7	152.2	40.2	15.7	14.8	5.7	4.0	112.0	54.2	23.4	13.3	21.1
1957	286.9	159.6	42.0	17.5	14.8	5.8	4.0	117.6	57.1	23.6	14.2	22.6
1958	296.2	161.6	39.5	15.0	14.6	5.9	4.1	122.0	59.8	23.9	14.7	23.6
1959	317.7	172.6	44.9	18.8	15.5	6.4	4.2	127.7	61.6	25.4	15.3	25.5
1960	331.8	177.0	45.6	19.6	15.4	6.4	4.3	131.4	62.6	25.9	15.8	27.1
1961	342.2	178.8	44.2	17.7	15.6	6.6	4.3	134.6	63.7	26.6	15.7	28.6
1962	363.3	189.0	49.5	21.4	16.4	6.9	4.7	139.5	64.7	27.9	16.3	30.7
1963	382.7	198.2	54.2	24.2	17.5	7.6	4.9	143.9	65.9	28.6	16.9	32.5
1964	411.5	212.3	59.6	25.8	19.5	8.8	5.5	152.7	69.5	31.1	17.7	34.5
1965	443.8	229.7	66.4	29.6	20.7	10.1	6.0	163.3	74.4	32.7	19.1	37.1
1966	480.9	249.6	71.7	29.9	22.6	12.3	6.9	177.9	80.6	35.8	20.7	40.8
1967	507.8	259.0	74.0	29.6	23.7	13.6	7.1	185.0	82.6	37.5	21.9	43.0
1968	558.0	284.6	84.8	35.4	26.1	15.3	8.0	199.8	88.8	41.3	23.2	46.5
1969	605.1	304.7	90.5	37.4	27.6	16.7	8.7	214.2	95.4	44.3	25.0	49.5
1970	648.3	318.8	90.0	34.5	28.2	17.9	9.4	228.8	103.5	45.5	26.3	53.6
1971	701.6	342.1	102.4	43.2	29.9	19.2	10.1	239.7	107.1	49.0	27.6	55.9
1972	770.2	373.8	116.4	49.4	33.5	22.6	11.0	257.4	114.5	53.5	29.4	60.0
1973	852.0	416.6	130.5	54.4	38.0	25.3	12.9	286.1	126.7	59.2	34.3	65.8
1974	932.9	451.5	130.2	48.2	40.9	26.6	14.5	321.4	143.0	62.4	43.8	72.1
1975	1 033.8	491.3	142.2	52.6	42.6	30.4	16.5	349.2	156.6	66.9	48.0	77.7
1976	1 151.3	546.3	168.6	68.2	47.2	34.2	19.1	377.7	167.3	72.2	53.0	85.2
1977	1 277.8	600.4	192.0	79.8	53.4	37.7	21.1	408.4	179.8	79.3	57.8	91.5
1978	1 427.6	663.6	213.3	89.2	59.0	41.7	23.5	450.2	196.1	89.3	61.5	103.3
1979	1 591.2	737.9	226.3	90.2	65.3	45.8	25.1	511.6	218.4	96.4	80.4	116.5
1980	1 755.8	799.8	226.4	84.4	67.8	46.5	27.6	573.4	239.2	103.0	101.9	129.3
1981	1 939.5	869.4	243.9	93.0	71.5	49.9	29.6	625.4	255.3	113.2	113.4	143.5
1982	2 075.5	899.3	253.0	100.0	71.8	51.3	29.9	646.3	267.1	116.7	108.4	154.0
1983	2 288.6	973.8	295.0	122.9	79.8	58.7	33.7	678.8	277.0	126.4	106.5	168.8
1984	2 501.1	1 063.7	342.2	147.2	88.8	67.8	38.3	721.5	291.1	137.6	108.2	184.6
1985	2 717.6	1 137.6	380.4	170.1	94.6	74.1	41.6	757.2	303.0	146.8	110.5	196.9
1986	2 896.7	1 195.6	421.4	187.5	103.5	83.0	47.5	774.2	316.4	157.2	91.2	209.4
1987	3 097.0	1 256.3	442.0	188.2	109.5	91.8	52.5	814.3	324.3	167.7	96.4	225.9
1988	3 350.1	1 337.3	475.1	202.2	115.2	99.9	57.8	862.3	342.8	178.2	99.9	241.4
1989	3 594.5	1 423.8	494.3	207.8	121.4	103.9	61.3	929.5	365.4	190.4	110.4	263.3
1990	3 835.5	1 491.0	497.1	205.1	120.9	105.6	65.5	994.2	391.2	195.2	124.2	283.6
1991	3 980.1	1 497.4	477.2	185.7	118.8	107.7	64.9	1 020.3	403.0	199.1	121.1	297.1
1992	4 236.9	1 563.3	508.1	204.8	124.3	111.0	68.0	1 055.2	404.5	211.2	125.0	314.5
1993	4 483.6	1 642.3	551.5	224.7	131.4	123.5	72.0	1 090.8	413.5	219.1	126.9	331.4
1994	4 750.8	1 746.6	607.2	249.8	140.5	140.3	76.5	1 139.4	432.1	227.4	129.2	350.6
1995	4 987.3	1 815.5	635.7	255.7	146.7	153.7	79.6	1 179.8	443.7	231.2	133.4	371.4
1996	5 273.6	1 917.7	676.3	273.5	153.5	164.9	84.3	1 241.4	461.9	239.5	144.7	395.2
1997	5 570.6	2 006.8	715.5	293.1	160.5	174.6	87.3	1 291.2	474.8	247.5	147.7	421.3
1998	5 918.5	2 110.0	780.0	320.2	173.6	192.1	94.2	1 330.0	486.5	257.8	133.4	452.3
1999	6 342.8	2 290.0	857.4	350.7	191.2	212.7	102.7	1 432.6	513.6	271.1	148.8	499.2
2000	6 830.4	2 459.1	915.8	363.2	208.1	234.1	110.4	1 543.4	537.5	280.8	188.8	536.2
2001	7 148.8	2 534.0	946.3	383.3	214.9	239.6	108.4	1 587.7	559.7	277.9	183.6	566.5
2002	7 439.2	2 610.0	992.1	401.3	225.9	251.5	113.4	1 617.9	569.6	278.8	174.6	594.9
2003	7 804.0	2 727.4	1 014.8	401.5	233.3	262.6	117.4	1 712.6	593.1	287.0	209.6	622.9
2004	8 285.1	2 892.3	1 061.6	404.7	249.2	284.3	123.4	1 830.7	628.2	300.0	249.9	652.6
2005	8 819.0	3 073.9	1 105.5	409.6	263.9	303.4	128.6	1 968.4	665.0	315.5	304.8	683.0
2006	9 322.7	3 221.7	1 133.0	397.1	276.5	323.4	136.0	2 088.7	698.0	330.1	336.9	723.7
2007	9 826.4	3 365.0	1 160.5	400.3	279.8	337.7	142.7	2 204.5	740.1	341.2	368.0	755.2
2008	10 129.9	3 403.2	1 095.2	342.3	270.1	339.9	142.8	2 308.0	784.3	337.5	413.0	773.2
2009	10 089.1	3 255.2	1 035.0	312.8	253.5	327.9	140.9	2 220.2	790.2	325.8	304.7	799.4
2007												
1st quarter	9 658.5	3 306.3	1 153.0	399.6	281.7	331.8	139.8	2 153.3	727.1	342.7	335.2	748.3
2nd quarter	9 762.5	3 338.2	1 154.9	401.3	279.0	333.0	141.7	2 183.3	732.1	338.8	362.4	750.0
3rd quarter	9 865.6	3 366.6	1 161.4	398.3	279.3	339.5	144.2	2 205.2	742.7	340.1	365.4	756.9
4th quarter	10 019.2	3 448.9	1 172.7	401.9	279.3	346.5	145.0	2 276.2	758.4	343.3	408.8	765.6
2008												
1st quarter	10 095.1	3 447.2	1 145.8	382.7	275.8	342.6	144.7	2 301.4	770.1	341.3	427.8	762.4
2nd quarter	10 194.7	3 474.9	1 126.5	357.5	276.2	347.5	145.2	2 348.4	786.3	344.2	441.9	776.0
3rd quarter	10 220.1	3 463.0	1 088.5	332.7	269.4	342.0	144.3	2 374.5	793.4	338.0	461.4	781.7
4th quarter	10 009.8	3 227.5	1 019.9	296.4	259.1	327.3	137.1	2 207.6	787.5	326.5	321.2	772.5
2009												
1st quarter	9 987.7	3 197.7	1 025.2	300.6	255.7	329.6	139.3	2 172.4	786.5	327.9	271.0	787.0
2nd quarter	9 999.3	3 193.8	1 011.5	299.5	251.3	321.3	139.4	2 182.2	786.3	321.6	279.4	795.0
3rd quarter	10 132.9	3 292.3	1 051.3	331.7	251.6	326.8	141.3	2 241.0	789.4	324.8	324.4	802.3
4th quarter	10 236.4	3 337.1	1 052.0	319.6	255.2	333.8	143.4	2 285.1	798.7	329.0	344.0	813.3

Table 4-2. Personal Consumption Expenditures by Major Type of Product—*Continued*

(Billions of dollars, quarterly data are at seasonally adjusted rates.) **NIPA Table 2.3.5**

| Year and quarter | Services | Household consumption expenditures for services | | | | | | | | Nonprofit institutions serving households (NPISHs) | | |
		Household, total	Housing and utilities	Health care	Transportation services	Recreation services	Food services and accommodations	Financial services and insurance	Other services	Final consumption expenditures	Gross output	Less: receipts from sales of goods and services
1950	75.4	72.9	25.1	6.4	5.4	3.6	12.7	5.6	14.1	2.5	...	...
1951	83.8	81.1	28.1	6.9	6.0	3.8	15.0	6.3	15.1	2.6	...	...
1952	90.7	87.8	31.2	7.6	6.3	4.0	16.0	6.7	16.0	2.9	...	...
1953	98.2	95.2	34.5	8.4	6.8	4.2	16.5	7.8	17.1	3.1	...	...
1954	104.2	100.9	37.4	9.3	6.8	4.5	16.6	8.6	17.8	3.3	...	...
1955	111.4	107.9	40.0	9.9	7.1	4.8	17.0	9.6	19.4	3.5	...	...
1956	119.5	115.6	42.9	10.9	7.6	5.2	17.7	10.4	20.9	3.9	...	...
1957	127.3	123.1	45.9	12.0	8.0	5.2	18.5	11.1	22.4	4.2	...	...
1958	134.6	130.1	49.2	13.4	8.1	5.4	18.7	11.6	23.8	4.5	...	...
1959	145.1	140.0	52.8	14.8	8.7	5.9	19.7	12.5	25.5	5.1	14.1	9.0
1960	154.8	149.5	56.7	16.0	9.2	6.5	20.5	13.6	27.1	5.3	15.1	9.8
1961	163.4	157.9	60.3	17.1	9.6	6.9	21.0	14.8	28.3	5.5	16.0	10.5
1962	174.4	168.7	64.5	19.1	10.1	7.5	22.3	15.4	29.9	5.7	17.2	11.5
1963	184.6	178.6	68.2	21.0	10.6	7.9	23.3	15.9	31.6	6.0	18.6	12.6
1964	199.2	192.5	72.1	24.2	11.4	8.5	24.9	17.7	33.8	6.7	20.5	13.8
1965	214.1	206.9	76.6	26.0	12.1	9.0	27.2	19.4	36.6	7.2	22.3	15.1
1966	231.3	223.5	81.2	28.7	13.1	9.8	29.6	21.3	39.9	7.8	24.6	16.9
1967	248.8	240.4	86.3	31.9	14.3	10.5	31.0	22.8	43.6	8.4	27.4	18.9
1968	273.4	264.0	92.7	36.6	15.9	11.7	34.6	25.8	46.8	9.3	30.9	21.6
1969	300.4	290.4	101.0	42.1	18.0	12.9	37.5	28.5	50.5	10.1	34.6	24.6
1970	329.5	318.4	109.4	47.7	20.0	14.0	41.6	31.1	54.6	11.1	38.7	27.6
1971	359.5	347.2	120.0	53.7	22.4	15.1	43.8	34.1	58.1	12.3	43.4	31.1
1972	396.4	382.8	131.2	59.8	24.5	16.3	48.9	38.3	63.7	13.6	48.2	34.5
1973	435.4	420.7	143.5	67.2	26.1	18.3	54.8	41.5	69.3	14.6	52.7	38.1
1974	481.4	465.0	158.6	76.1	28.5	20.9	60.6	45.9	74.4	16.4	59.7	43.3
1975	542.5	524.4	176.5	89.0	32.0	23.7	68.8	54.0	80.3	18.1	68.2	50.2
1976	604.9	584.9	194.7	101.8	36.2	26.5	77.8	59.3	88.6	20.1	77.4	57.3
1977	677.4	655.6	217.8	115.7	41.4	29.6	85.7	67.8	97.7	21.8	86.3	64.5
1978	764.1	739.6	244.3	131.2	45.2	32.9	97.1	80.6	108.3	24.5	98.1	73.6
1979	853.2	825.4	273.4	148.8	50.7	36.7	110.9	87.6	117.2	27.8	111.0	83.2
1980	956.0	924.1	311.8	171.7	55.4	40.8	121.7	95.6	127.1	31.9	128.0	96.1
1981	1 070.1	1 033.9	352.0	201.9	59.8	47.1	133.9	102.0	137.2	36.3	147.8	111.5
1982	1 176.2	1 136.1	387.0	225.2	61.7	52.5	142.5	116.3	150.9	40.1	165.9	125.8
1983	1 314.8	1 271.9	421.2	253.1	68.9	59.4	153.6	145.9	169.8	42.9	181.4	138.5
1984	1 437.4	1 389.8	458.3	276.5	80.0	66.1	164.9	156.6	187.4	47.6	196.6	149.0
1985	1 580.0	1 529.7	500.7	302.2	90.1	74.0	174.3	180.5	207.9	50.3	211.7	161.4
1986	1 701.1	1 645.8	535.7	330.2	95.0	80.4	186.7	196.7	221.2	55.4	230.1	174.7
1987	1 840.7	1 782.1	571.8	366.0	103.1	87.3	204.4	207.1	242.4	58.5	249.7	191.2
1988	2 012.7	1 946.0	614.5	410.1	114.2	99.2	225.8	219.4	262.8	66.8	279.0	212.2
1989	2 170.7	2 099.0	655.6	451.2	121.8	110.7	242.6	235.7	281.3	71.7	304.9	233.2
1990	2 344.2	2 264.5	696.4	506.2	126.4	121.8	262.7	253.2	297.9	79.6	338.2	258.6
1991	2 482.6	2 398.4	735.5	555.8	123.7	127.2	273.4	282.0	300.9	84.2	367.0	282.8
1992	2 673.6	2 581.3	771.2	612.8	133.6	139.8	286.3	311.8	325.8	92.3	400.8	308.5
1993	2 841.2	2 746.6	814.5	648.8	146.1	153.4	298.6	341.0	344.2	94.6	423.3	328.7
1994	3 004.3	2 901.9	866.5	680.5	161.9	164.7	308.7	349.0	370.7	102.4	444.7	342.3
1995	3 171.7	3 064.6	913.8	719.9	177.9	181.1	316.7	364.7	390.5	107.2	463.4	356.2
1996	3 355.9	3 240.2	961.2	752.1	195.0	195.6	327.4	393.6	415.3	115.7	488.8	373.1
1997	3 563.9	3 451.6	1 009.6	790.9	214.3	208.3	344.6	431.3	452.3	112.2	509.3	397.0
1998	3 808.5	3 677.5	1 065.2	832.0	227.2	220.6	363.0	469.6	499.8	131.0	550.5	419.6
1999	4 052.8	3 907.4	1 125.0	863.6	243.3	238.8	381.6	514.2	540.9	145.4	585.3	439.9
2000	4 371.2	4 205.9	1 198.6	918.4	262.3	255.5	410.1	570.0	591.1	165.4	632.0	466.6
2001	4 614.8	4 428.6	1 287.7	996.6	262.7	263.6	421.2	562.8	634.0	186.2	688.0	501.8
2002	4 829.2	4 624.2	1 334.8	1 082.9	256.7	272.8	438.2	576.2	662.7	205.0	749.7	544.7
2003	5 076.6	4 864.8	1 393.8	1 149.3	263.1	289.5	462.8	601.8	704.6	211.8	785.8	574.0
2004	5 392.8	5 182.8	1 462.2	1 229.7	273.2	312.0	492.9	667.5	745.3	210.0	827.7	617.7
2005	5 745.1	5 531.0	1 582.8	1 316.0	285.9	326.8	525.3	712.6	781.6	214.1	874.6	660.6
2006	6 100.9	5 860.6	1 686.0	1 380.7	297.0	348.8	559.7	752.4	836.0	240.4	933.6	693.3
2007	6 461.4	6 207.9	1 763.1	1 469.6	307.4	371.7	587.9	824.2	884.0	253.5	987.5	734.0
2008	6 726.8	6 448.0	1 843.7	1 554.2	307.8	383.1	608.7	835.6	915.0	278.7	1 049.4	770.7
2009	6 833.9	6 568.5	1 877.2	1 627.0	304.6	382.5	605.6	828.0	943.5	265.4	1 069.6	804.2
2007												
1st quarter	6 352.2	6 103.7	1 741.4	1 442.9	304.7	365.4	575.9	799.3	874.0	248.5	971.7	723.1
2nd quarter	6 424.3	6 179.5	1 755.8	1 458.4	306.4	369.9	583.4	819.5	886.1	244.8	978.2	733.4
3rd quarter	6 499.0	6 242.8	1 770.4	1 475.2	308.7	373.7	592.3	835.3	887.2	256.2	990.1	733.9
4th quarter	6 570.3	6 305.8	1 784.8	1 501.7	309.9	377.9	600.0	842.8	888.7	264.5	1 010.0	745.5
2008												
1st quarter	6 647.9	6 377.5	1 811.9	1 531.6	308.0	380.7	601.8	839.6	903.9	270.4	1 031.3	760.9
2nd quarter	6 719.8	6 446.1	1 838.6	1 551.0	308.3	384.9	610.8	842.1	910.5	273.7	1 044.9	771.2
3rd quarter	6 757.1	6 474.5	1 852.2	1 559.3	309.1	385.9	614.7	837.3	915.9	282.6	1 055.2	772.7
4th quarter	6 782.3	6 494.1	1 872.1	1 574.9	305.7	380.9	607.3	823.5	929.8	288.2	1 066.1	778.0
2009												
1st quarter	6 790.0	6 522.0	1 878.8	1 598.0	301.6	383.4	607.3	816.7	936.0	268.0	1 060.8	792.7
2nd quarter	6 805.6	6 545.9	1 871.1	1 622.6	301.1	381.5	606.0	824.9	938.7	259.7	1 065.8	806.1
3rd quarter	6 840.6	6 575.7	1 872.5	1 633.0	306.3	382.5	603.7	832.4	945.3	264.9	1 070.7	805.8
4th quarter	6 899.3	6 630.3	1 886.4	1 654.5	309.6	382.6	605.2	837.9	954.0	269.0	1 081.1	812.1

. . . = Not available.

Table 4-3. Chain-Type Quantity Indexes for Personal Consumption Expenditures by Major Type of Product

(Index numbers, 2005 = 100.)   NIPA Table 2.3.3

Year and quarter	Personal consumption expenditures, total	Goods										
		Total goods	Durable goods					Nondurable goods				
			Durable goods, total	Motor vehicles and parts	Furnishings and household equipment	Recreational goods and vehicles	Other durable goods	Nondurable goods, total	Food and beverages off-premises	Clothing and footwear	Gasoline and other energy goods	Other nondurable goods
1950	14.6	15.2	6.6	13.3	10.8	0.8	7.5	23.0	36.6	12.7	31.5	14.0
1951	14.8	15.1	6.0	11.2	10.3	0.8	7.7	23.4	36.8	12.6	33.2	14.7
1952	15.2	15.4	5.9	10.1	10.3	0.8	8.3	24.3	37.8	13.3	34.6	15.3
1953	16.0	16.2	6.6	12.5	10.6	0.9	8.5	25.0	39.2	13.4	35.5	16.0
1954	16.3	16.4	6.6	11.9	10.6	1.0	8.8	25.4	40.3	13.4	36.4	15.9
1955	17.5	17.9	8.0	16.4	11.9	1.1	9.4	26.7	42.2	14.1	39.3	16.7
1956	18.0	18.2	7.7	13.9	12.5	1.2	9.9	27.7	43.6	14.4	41.0	17.4
1957	18.5	18.5	7.8	14.6	12.3	1.1	9.9	28.2	44.7	14.3	42.0	18.1
1958	18.6	18.3	7.2	12.1	12.1	1.1	10.1	28.6	44.8	14.5	43.9	18.5
1959	19.7	19.4	8.0	14.4	12.9	1.2	10.4	29.9	46.7	15.2	45.0	19.6
1960	20.2	19.8	8.2	15.3	12.7	1.2	10.4	30.4	47.0	15.4	45.7	20.5
1961	20.7	19.9	7.9	13.7	12.8	1.3	10.7	31.0	47.7	15.7	45.4	21.6
1962	21.7	20.9	8.8	16.3	13.5	1.4	11.6	32.0	48.0	16.4	46.9	23.1
1963	22.6	21.8	9.6	18.3	14.4	1.5	12.1	32.6	48.4	16.7	48.5	24.1
1964	23.9	23.0	10.5	19.4	16.0	1.8	13.1	34.2	50.0	17.9	51.1	25.2
1965	25.4	24.7	11.8	22.4	17.1	2.1	14.4	35.9	52.5	18.7	53.5	26.7
1966	26.9	26.2	12.8	22.8	18.6	2.5	16.6	37.9	54.6	19.9	56.5	28.8
1967	27.7	26.8	13.0	22.3	19.0	2.8	16.8	38.7	55.8	20.1	57.9	29.7
1968	29.3	28.4	14.4	25.7	20.1	3.1	18.4	40.4	58.3	20.9	60.3	30.9
1969	30.4	29.3	15.0	26.7	20.5	3.3	19.1	41.5	59.9	21.3	63.0	31.7
1970	31.1	29.5	14.6	23.9	20.5	3.5	20.0	42.4	61.6	21.0	65.4	32.8
1971	32.3	30.7	16.0	28.5	21.4	3.6	21.0	43.2	62.3	21.9	67.7	32.9
1972	34.2	32.8	18.0	32.5	23.7	4.2	22.1	44.9	63.6	23.5	71.1	34.5
1973	35.9	34.5	19.9	35.6	26.2	4.7	25.1	46.2	62.5	25.2	75.2	36.9
1974	35.6	33.2	18.6	29.7	26.1	4.7	26.4	45.1	61.2	24.7	69.1	36.7
1975	36.4	33.4	18.7	29.6	24.7	5.0	27.9	45.5	62.3	25.3	70.7	35.5
1976	38.5	35.8	21.0	35.6	26.2	5.4	30.7	47.6	65.4	26.5	74.4	37.0
1977	40.1	37.3	22.8	39.3	28.6	5.8	32.4	48.7	66.3	27.9	75.8	37.6
1978	41.9	38.8	24.0	41.1	30.1	6.2	34.2	50.5	66.0	30.8	77.0	40.3
1979	42.9	39.5	23.9	38.6	31.4	6.5	33.8	51.8	67.0	32.6	74.8	42.6
1980	42.7	38.5	22.0	33.7	30.2	6.3	30.9	51.7	67.7	33.6	68.2	43.4
1981	43.4	38.9	22.2	34.4	29.6	6.4	31.4	52.4	67.4	35.8	67.3	44.3
1982	44.0	39.2	22.2	35.4	28.3	6.5	31.4	52.9	68.7	36.4	67.4	44.2
1983	46.5	41.7	25.4	42.2	30.7	7.5	34.2	54.6	70.5	38.9	68.9	45.3
1984	48.9	44.7	29.0	49.1	33.8	8.8	38.1	56.9	71.9	42.1	70.7	47.8
1985	51.5	47.0	31.9	55.4	35.6	9.8	41.0	58.6	74.0	44.0	72.1	49.1
1986	53.6	49.7	35.0	59.5	38.5	11.3	45.7	60.7	75.5	47.2	75.8	50.2
1987	55.2	50.6	35.6	57.1	40.1	12.7	47.3	61.7	75.0	49.0	77.2	52.0
1988	57.5	52.4	37.7	60.4	41.6	13.9	48.9	63.4	77.0	50.4	79.4	53.2
1989	59.1	53.8	38.5	60.2	43.7	14.5	49.5	65.1	78.0	53.1	80.7	55.0
1990	60.3	54.1	38.3	59.3	43.1	14.8	49.8	65.8	79.6	52.7	79.2	56.4
1991	60.4	53.0	36.3	52.2	42.1	15.3	47.6	65.6	79.5	52.8	78.6	56.1
1992	62.4	54.7	38.4	56.5	43.5	16.3	48.6	66.9	79.2	55.6	81.7	57.2
1993	64.6	57.0	41.2	59.7	45.8	18.8	51.0	68.6	79.8	58.0	83.8	59.3
1994	67.1	60.0	44.5	63.4	48.2	21.8	53.4	71.3	82.1	61.2	85.1	62.3
1995	68.9	61.8	46.3	62.4	50.4	24.9	54.6	73.0	82.5	63.7	86.7	64.9
1996	71.3	64.5	49.7	65.4	52.6	28.8	58.2	75.2	83.3	66.8	88.1	67.7
1997	74.0	67.6	53.8	69.8	55.1	33.3	61.1	77.4	84.0	69.0	89.9	71.5
1998	77.8	72.2	60.4	77.2	59.6	39.9	67.2	80.3	85.0	73.2	93.1	75.3
1999	82.1	77.9	68.2	84.3	66.5	48.5	75.2	84.4	88.3	78.0	95.9	80.0
2000	86.3	82.0	74.2	86.9	72.9	56.9	81.8	87.1	90.3	81.8	94.2	84.1
2001	88.6	84.6	78.2	91.4	76.6	62.6	80.1	88.7	91.4	82.6	94.9	86.8
2002	91.0	88.1	84.1	96.2	82.2	70.2	85.4	90.4	91.6	85.1	96.4	89.7
2003	93.5	92.1	89.2	98.9	87.4	78.1	89.8	93.8	93.6	89.8	99.1	93.7
2004	96.8	96.1	95.1	100.4	94.5	88.8	94.6	96.8	96.1	94.2	100.6	97.0
2005	100.0	100.0	100.0	100.0	100.0	100.0	100.0	100.0	100.0	100.0	100.0	100.0
2006	102.9	103.3	104.1	96.8	105.3	113.1	103.7	102.8	103.2	105.1	97.9	103.7
2007	105.6	106.5	108.5	98.2	107.5	126.1	104.6	105.4	105.4	109.6	98.6	106.8
2008	105.4	104.3	103.7	84.8	104.4	132.8	99.6	104.5	105.4	109.3	94.3	106.7
2009	104.7	102.3	99.6	77.4	98.3	135.7	96.6	103.5	104.9	104.6	96.0	105.4
2007												
1st quarter	105.1	105.9	107.1	98.2	107.6	120.9	102.9	105.2	105.4	109.0	98.9	106.3
2nd quarter	105.4	105.9	107.6	98.6	106.6	123.0	104.0	105.0	104.7	108.8	98.8	106.4
3rd quarter	105.9	106.7	109.0	97.8	107.5	127.9	105.8	105.5	105.1	110.1	98.9	107.0
4th quarter	106.2	107.5	110.5	98.3	108.2	132.4	105.6	106.0	106.2	110.7	97.9	107.5
2008												
1st quarter	106.0	106.1	107.9	93.8	106.4	131.8	103.7	105.2	106.5	110.2	96.0	106.1
2nd quarter	106.0	106.0	106.4	88.2	107.1	135.2	100.5	105.7	106.6	112.1	95.1	107.4
3rd quarter	105.1	103.9	103.1	82.5	104.0	134.4	99.8	104.2	105.2	108.8	91.9	107.7
4th quarter	104.3	101.2	97.4	74.7	100.1	130.0	94.4	102.9	103.2	106.3	94.2	105.5
2009												
1st quarter	104.4	101.8	98.3	76.0	98.3	132.9	96.1	103.4	103.4	105.8	96.2	106.1
2nd quarter	104.2	101.0	96.9	74.7	96.3	131.3	95.6	102.9	104.3	103.6	96.4	106.6
3rd quarter	104.9	102.8	101.6	81.8	97.9	136.7	97.1	103.3	105.3	103.5	96.0	104.9
4th quarter	105.3	103.5	101.7	77.2	100.6	141.9	97.6	104.3	106.5	105.4	95.5	106.1

Table 4-3. Chain-Type Quantity Indexes for Personal Consumption Expenditures by Major Type of Product—*Continued*

(Index numbers, 2005 = 100.)

NIPA Table 2.3.3

Year and quarter	Services	Household consumption expenditures for services								Nonprofit institutions serving households (NPISHs)		
		Household, total	Housing and utilities	Health care	Transporta-tion services	Recreation services	Food services and accommo-dations	Financial services and insurance	Other services	Final consumption expenditures	Gross output	Less: receipts from sales of goods and services
1950	13.0	13.6	12.8	9.8	17.0	9.3	22.7	10.0	16.8	3.1	. . .	. . .
1951	13.7	14.5	13.8	10.1	17.6	9.4	24.8	11.2	17.1	3.1	. . .	. . .
1952	14.4	15.1	14.8	10.6	17.8	9.5	25.9	11.2	17.5	3.4	. . .	. . .
1953	15.0	15.7	15.6	11.1	18.3	9.6	26.9	11.7	18.0	3.5	. . .	. . .
1954	15.5	16.3	16.5	12.0	17.7	9.8	26.8	12.5	18.4	3.7	. . .	. . .
1955	16.3	17.1	17.4	12.3	18.3	10.3	27.5	13.5	19.8	3.7	. . .	. . .
1956	17.0	17.9	18.4	13.1	18.8	10.8	28.3	14.2	20.6	4.0	. . .	. . .
1957	17.6	18.6	19.3	13.8	19.1	10.4	28.6	14.6	21.3	4.1	. . .	. . .
1958	18.2	19.1	20.3	14.9	18.8	10.3	28.2	15.1	22.0	4.3	. . .	. . .
1959	19.1	20.1	21.5	16.0	19.6	11.1	28.8	15.4	23.0	4.8	14.9	21.1
1960	19.9	20.8	22.6	16.2	20.2	11.7	29.1	16.0	23.7	5.3	15.5	21.2
1961	20.6	21.6	23.7	16.9	20.5	12.2	29.2	16.8	24.5	5.5	16.2	22.3
1962	21.6	22.6	25.1	18.5	21.2	12.8	30.2	16.8	25.5	5.6	17.1	23.7
1963	22.5	23.6	26.3	19.7	22.2	13.3	31.0	17.4	26.4	5.8	18.0	25.3
1964	23.8	24.9	27.5	21.9	23.4	13.8	32.6	18.6	27.6	6.5	19.4	26.9
1965	25.1	26.3	29.0	22.9	24.6	14.4	34.9	19.9	29.2	6.8	20.5	28.6
1966	26.4	27.6	30.3	24.2	26.0	15.2	36.6	20.5	30.9	7.0	21.9	30.9
1967	27.5	28.7	31.7	25.3	27.4	15.7	36.3	21.6	32.7	7.4	23.3	32.9
1968	28.9	30.3	33.3	27.3	29.1	16.7	38.5	22.7	33.6	7.9	25.0	35.4
1969	30.2	31.6	35.1	29.3	31.1	17.7	39.4	23.0	34.6	8.0	26.3	37.9
1970	31.4	32.9	36.4	30.9	32.1	18.4	40.7	23.8	35.7	8.5	27.6	39.6
1971	32.5	34.0	38.0	33.1	33.5	19.0	40.7	24.7	35.8	8.9	29.5	42.6
1972	34.3	35.9	40.0	35.3	35.4	20.0	43.8	26.2	37.4	9.5	31.3	45.2
1973	36.0	37.7	41.9	37.9	36.0	21.7	46.0	27.7	38.5	9.5	32.2	46.8
1974	36.7	38.5	43.9	39.2	36.2	23.2	45.5	28.3	37.2	9.4	32.5	47.9
1975	38.0	39.9	45.3	41.2	36.7	24.4	47.4	31.0	37.5	9.4	33.8	50.3
1976	39.7	41.6	46.6	43.0	38.5	26.0	50.3	32.7	39.0	9.9	35.5	52.9
1977	41.3	43.4	47.9	45.1	41.3	27.7	51.6	34.8	40.9	10.1	36.9	55.3
1978	43.2	45.4	50.1	47.2	42.3	29.0	53.8	36.5	43.0	10.6	39.0	58.4
1979	44.6	46.8	51.9	48.7	43.5	30.4	55.5	37.6	43.4	11.0	40.1	60.0
1980	45.2	47.5	53.6	50.1	41.0	31.5	55.5	38.1	43.2	11.5	41.3	61.4
1981	46.1	48.2	54.5	52.6	39.4	34.1	56.1	37.8	43.0	12.5	43.0	63.2
1982	47.0	48.9	54.9	52.7	38.6	35.8	56.4	40.8	43.8	14.4	44.8	63.6
1983	49.4	51.3	56.1	54.3	41.5	38.8	58.3	46.6	46.7	16.6	46.4	63.9
1984	51.3	53.2	58.1	55.1	46.3	41.4	59.9	47.1	49.1	19.2	48.0	63.8
1985	54.0	55.9	60.3	56.8	51.2	44.4	60.7	52.1	52.5	20.7	49.7	65.2
1986	55.6	57.3	61.6	58.6	53.4	46.5	62.5	53.7	53.0	23.5	52.2	66.8
1987	57.8	59.6	63.4	61.0	55.6	48.6	65.7	54.0	56.8	25.2	54.2	68.8
1988	60.3	61.9	65.6	63.4	58.8	53.2	69.6	53.9	59.1	29.0	57.2	70.7
1989	62.1	63.5	67.2	64.2	60.1	56.5	71.6	55.9	60.9	33.1	59.3	71.0
1990	63.9	65.1	68.4	66.3	60.1	59.0	74.1	57.2	62.0	39.9	62.8	72.3
1991	64.9	65.8	70.0	67.6	57.2	58.5	74.1	61.0	59.7	45.4	65.1	73.0
1992	67.2	67.8	71.4	69.6	60.1	62.4	76.0	62.7	62.1	54.4	68.6	74.0
1993	69.4	69.8	73.3	70.0	63.5	66.4	77.8	67.9	63.4	58.7	70.3	74.7
1994	71.4	71.8	76.0	70.5	69.6	69.7	79.0	68.3	65.8	63.5	71.8	75.0
1995	73.2	73.6	78.0	72.0	74.8	75.1	79.2	68.7	67.1	66.5	72.8	75.3
1996	75.4	75.6	79.7	73.5	80.9	78.4	79.7	71.3	69.3	70.5	74.7	76.5
1997	77.7	78.2	81.5	75.8	87.0	80.9	81.5	73.7	73.4	65.7	75.9	79.7
1998	81.1	81.6	84.0	78.2	90.7	83.6	83.6	78.4	79.5	71.9	79.7	82.7
1999	84.5	84.8	86.7	79.5	95.7	87.7	85.7	85.0	84.0	77.1	82.4	84.6
2000	88.7	88.9	89.3	82.2	100.1	90.3	89.6	93.4	90.1	83.1	85.6	86.8
2001	90.8	90.9	91.7	86.3	99.2	90.2	89.5	92.7	93.7	89.4	89.8	90.1
2002	92.6	92.4	92.4	91.4	96.5	90.8	90.8	92.4	94.3	97.7	95.0	94.2
2003	94.3	94.0	93.5	93.4	96.8	93.5	94.0	92.3	96.7	102.5	96.5	94.5
2004	97.1	96.9	95.6	96.4	99.1	98.1	96.8	97.1	99.0	102.0	98.4	97.2
2005	100.0	100.0	100.0	100.0	100.0	100.0	100.0	100.0	100.0	100.0	100.0	100.0
2006	102.7	102.4	102.1	101.8	99.7	103.3	103.1	103.2	103.4	110.0	103.0	100.8
2007	105.1	104.8	103.1	104.5	100.9	107.1	104.3	108.4	106.3	114.4	105.7	102.9
2008	105.9	105.2	104.1	107.6	95.8	107.0	103.8	106.6	105.6	124.6	109.4	104.6
2009	106.0	105.4	104.7	110.0	92.2	105.7	100.8	106.2	106.6	120.1	109.6	106.2
2007												
1st quarter	104.6	104.3	102.9	103.7	101.1	106.4	103.8	107.0	106.4	112.6	105.1	102.7
2nd quarter	105.1	104.8	103.0	104.2	101.2	106.8	104.0	109.0	107.0	110.7	105.2	103.4
3rd quarter	105.4	105.0	103.3	104.7	100.9	107.6	104.3	109.3	106.3	114.9	105.6	102.7
4th quarter	105.5	104.9	103.2	105.4	100.2	107.6	104.9	108.1	105.6	119.4	106.9	103.0
2008												
1st quarter	106.0	105.4	103.9	107.1	98.2	107.4	104.2	107.5	106.1	121.7	108.6	104.4
2nd quarter	106.0	105.4	104.1	107.8	96.4	107.8	104.9	107.2	105.4	122.5	109.2	105.0
3rd quarter	105.7	105.0	103.7	107.6	95.2	107.0	104.2	106.4	105.0	125.4	109.4	104.4
4th quarter	105.8	105.0	104.6	108.1	93.3	105.9	102.0	105.3	106.1	128.7	110.3	104.6
2009												
1st quarter	105.8	105.2	104.7	109.0	91.6	106.4	101.6	105.4	106.5	121.2	109.5	105.8
2nd quarter	105.8	105.3	104.4	110.0	91.8	106.0	101.0	106.5	106.5	117.7	109.6	106.8
3rd quarter	106.0	105.5	104.5	110.1	92.7	105.1	100.5	106.9	106.8	119.8	109.4	106.1
4th quarter	106.3	105.7	105.2	110.7	92.9	105.1	100.2	106.2	106.7	121.6	109.8	106.0

. . . = Not available.

Table 4-4. Chain-Type Price Indexes for Personal Consumption Expenditures by Major Type of Product

(Index numbers, 2005 =1000.)   NIPA Table 2.3.4

			Goods									
			Durable goods					Nondurable goods				
Year and quarter	Personal consumption expend- itures, total	Total goods	Durable goods, total	Motor vehicles and parts	Furnishings and household equipment	Recreational goods and vehicles	Other durable goods	Nondurable goods, total	Food and beverages off-premises	Clothing and footwear	Gasoline and other energy goods	Other nondurable goods
1950	15.0	24.9	44.5	25.1	41.2	177.6	30.0	18.6	17.0	47.3	9.2	15.9
1951	16.0	26.9	47.5	26.4	45.4	181.2	31.8	20.2	18.8	51.4	9.5	16.9
1952	16.3	27.2	47.8	27.5	45.0	174.9	31.8	20.4	19.3	50.5	9.7	17.0
1953	16.6	27.1	47.4	27.0	45.1	172.7	31.9	20.3	18.9	50.4	10.0	17.2
1954	16.7	27.0	46.4	26.1	44.9	167.2	31.3	20.4	18.9	50.5	10.2	17.3
1955	16.8	26.8	46.2	26.4	44.5	162.0	30.9	20.3	18.5	50.4	10.3	17.4
1956	17.1	27.3	47.3	27.6	44.9	163.8	31.2	20.6	18.7	51.3	10.6	17.7
1957	17.6	28.1	49.1	29.3	45.6	169.6	31.4	21.2	19.2	52.1	11.1	18.3
1958	18.0	28.8	50.0	30.4	45.5	174.2	31.4	21.7	20.0	52.3	11.0	18.8
1959	18.3	28.9	50.8	31.9	45.6	169.2	31.6	21.7	19.8	52.8	11.1	19.1
1960	18.6	29.1	50.6	31.3	46.0	170.3	31.7	22.0	20.0	53.5	11.3	19.4
1961	18.8	29.3	50.7	31.5	46.1	169.4	31.6	22.1	20.1	53.8	11.4	19.4
1962	19.0	29.4	50.9	32.0	46.1	167.6	31.5	22.2	20.3	54.0	11.4	19.5
1963	19.2	29.6	51.1	32.3	46.1	167.2	31.6	22.4	20.5	54.4	11.4	19.7
1964	19.5	30.0	51.3	32.5	46.1	165.2	32.4	22.7	20.9	54.9	11.3	20.0
1965	19.8	30.3	50.9	32.3	45.9	162.9	32.3	23.1	21.3	55.4	11.7	20.3
1966	20.3	31.0	50.8	32.0	46.2	161.1	32.3	23.8	22.2	57.0	12.0	20.7
1967	20.8	31.5	51.6	32.5	47.3	162.1	33.0	24.3	22.2	59.3	12.4	21.2
1968	21.6	32.6	53.3	33.6	49.1	165.3	33.8	25.2	22.9	62.6	12.6	22.0
1969	22.6	33.9	54.8	34.3	50.9	169.1	35.4	26.2	23.9	66.0	13.0	22.8
1970	23.7	35.2	56.0	35.3	52.0	169.3	36.4	27.4	25.3	68.5	13.2	23.9
1971	24.7	36.2	57.9	37.0	52.9	175.3	37.4	28.2	25.8	70.9	13.4	24.8
1972	25.5	37.1	58.5	37.1	53.7	177.9	38.6	29.1	27.1	72.2	13.6	25.4
1973	26.9	39.4	59.4	37.3	54.9	180.6	39.8	31.4	30.5	74.6	15.0	26.1
1974	29.7	44.3	63.3	39.6	59.4	188.6	42.9	36.2	35.1	80.2	20.8	28.7
1975	32.2	47.8	69.0	43.5	65.3	201.1	46.1	39.0	37.8	83.7	22.3	32.0
1976	34.0	49.7	72.7	46.8	68.1	208.0	48.4	40.3	38.5	86.4	23.4	33.7
1977	36.2	52.4	76.0	49.5	70.7	214.0	50.5	42.6	40.8	90.1	25.0	35.6
1978	38.7	55.6	80.3	53.0	74.2	221.7	53.3	45.3	44.7	91.8	26.2	37.6
1979	42.1	60.8	85.6	57.0	78.9	231.5	57.7	50.2	49.0	93.6	35.3	40.0
1980	46.6	67.6	93.0	61.2	85.3	244.4	69.5	56.3	53.2	97.1	49.0	43.7
1981	50.8	72.7	99.2	65.9	91.6	255.4	73.4	60.7	56.9	100.3	55.3	47.4
1982	53.6	74.7	103.1	69.0	96.3	261.3	74.1	62.1	58.4	101.7	52.7	51.0
1983	55.9	76.0	105.2	71.2	98.5	258.1	76.5	63.1	59.1	103.1	50.7	54.5
1984	58.0	77.4	106.7	73.2	99.7	254.5	78.1	64.4	60.9	103.7	50.2	56.6
1985	59.9	78.7	107.9	74.9	100.8	250.0	78.9	65.7	61.6	105.9	50.3	58.8
1986	61.4	78.3	109.0	77.0	101.9	242.1	80.8	64.8	63.0	105.4	39.5	61.1
1987	63.6	80.8	112.2	80.5	103.5	239.0	86.3	67.0	65.0	108.5	40.9	63.6
1988	66.1	83.0	114.0	81.8	105.0	237.5	91.9	69.1	66.9	112.0	41.2	66.4
1989	69.0	86.2	116.1	84.2	105.3	236.9	96.2	72.6	70.5	113.6	44.9	70.1
1990	72.1	89.7	117.3	84.5	106.4	234.9	102.3	76.7	73.9	117.3	51.4	73.6
1991	74.8	91.9	119.0	86.8	107.0	232.0	106.1	79.0	76.2	119.5	50.6	77.5
1992	77.0	93.0	119.8	88.5	108.2	224.8	108.9	80.1	76.8	120.4	50.2	80.5
1993	78.6	93.8	121.0	92.0	108.8	216.8	109.7	80.8	77.9	119.8	49.7	81.8
1994	80.3	94.7	123.4	96.2	110.5	212.2	111.5	81.2	79.2	117.8	49.8	82.4
1995	82.0	95.6	124.3	100.0	110.3	203.3	113.3	82.1	80.9	115.0	50.5	83.8
1996	83.8	96.7	123.0	102.0	110.6	188.9	112.6	83.9	83.4	113.6	53.9	85.4
1997	85.4	96.6	120.3	102.4	110.5	173.1	111.1	84.8	85.0	113.7	53.9	86.3
1998	86.2	95.1	116.9	101.3	110.4	158.5	109.0	84.2	86.0	111.6	47.0	87.9
1999	87.6	95.6	113.7	101.6	108.9	144.7	106.3	86.3	87.4	110.1	50.9	91.4
2000	89.8	97.5	111.7	102.0	108.1	135.6	104.9	90.0	89.5	108.8	65.8	93.4
2001	91.5	97.4	109.5	102.4	106.3	126.3	105.2	91.0	92.1	106.7	63.5	95.5
2002	92.7	96.4	106.7	101.9	104.1	118.2	103.3	90.9	93.5	103.9	59.4	97.1
2003	94.6	96.4	102.9	99.1	101.2	110.8	101.6	92.8	95.3	101.3	69.4	97.3
2004	97.1	97.9	101.0	98.4	99.9	105.5	101.4	96.1	98.3	100.9	81.5	98.5
2005	100.0	100.0	100.0	100.0	100.0	100.0	100.0	100.0	100.0	100.0	100.0	100.0
2006	102.7	101.5	98.5	100.1	99.5	94.2	101.9	103.2	101.7	99.6	112.9	102.2
2007	105.5	102.8	96.7	99.5	98.7	88.3	106.1	106.3	105.6	98.6	122.4	103.5
2008	109.0	106.2	95.5	98.5	98.0	84.3	111.5	112.2	111.9	97.8	143.7	106.1
2009	109.2	103.5	94.0	98.7	97.7	79.7	113.3	109.0	113.3	98.7	104.1	111.0
2007												
1st quarter	104.3	101.6	97.4	99.3	99.2	90.4	105.7	104.0	103.8	99.6	111.2	103.1
2nd quarter	105.1	102.5	97.1	99.3	99.2	89.2	105.9	105.7	105.2	98.7	120.3	103.2
3rd quarter	105.7	102.6	96.4	99.5	98.5	87.4	106.0	106.2	106.2	97.9	121.2	103.6
4th quarter	107.0	104.4	96.0	99.9	97.8	86.2	106.7	109.1	107.3	98.3	136.9	104.3
2008												
1st quarter	108.0	105.7	96.0	99.6	98.2	85.7	108.5	111.2	108.7	98.1	146.1	105.2
2nd quarter	109.0	106.7	95.8	99.0	97.7	84.7	112.4	112.8	110.9	97.4	152.3	105.7
3rd quarter	110.3	108.5	95.5	98.6	98.2	83.9	112.4	115.8	113.4	98.4	164.6	106.3
4th quarter	108.9	103.8	94.7	96.9	98.1	83.0	112.9	109.0	114.7	97.4	111.7	107.2
2009												
1st quarter	108.4	102.2	94.3	96.7	98.6	81.8	112.7	106.7	114.4	98.2	92.4	108.6
2nd quarter	108.8	102.9	94.4	97.9	98.9	80.7	113.4	107.7	113.3	98.4	95.0	111.3
3rd quarter	109.5	104.2	93.7	99.1	97.4	78.8	113.0	110.2	112.7	99.4	110.8	112.0
4th quarter	110.2	104.9	93.6	101.2	96.1	77.5	114.3	111.3	112.7	98.9	118.1	112.3

Table 4-4. Chain-Type Price Indexes for Personal Consumption Expenditures by Major Type of Product—*Continued*

(Index numbers, 2005 =1000.)   **NIPA Table 2.3.4**

Year and quarter	Services	Services								Nonprofit institutions serving households (NPISHs)		
		Household consumption expenditures for services										
		Household, total	Housing and utilities	Health care	Transporta-tion services	Recreation services	Food services and accommo-dations	Financial services and insurance	Other services	Final consumption expenditures	Gross output	Less: receipts from sales of goods and services
1950	10.1	9.7	12.4	5.0	11.1	12.0	10.7	8.0	10.6	37.2	. . .	. . .
1951	10.6	10.1	12.8	5.2	11.9	12.4	11.5	8.1	11.1	40.4	. . .	. . .
1952	11.0	10.5	13.3	5.4	12.4	12.9	11.8	8.6	11.5	40.4	. . .	. . .
1953	11.4	10.9	13.9	5.7	12.9	13.5	11.7	9.5	12.0	41.2	. . .	. . .
1954	11.7	11.2	14.3	5.9	13.4	14.1	11.8	9.9	12.2	42.2	. . .	. . .
1955	11.9	11.4	14.5	6.1	13.7	14.5	11.8	10.2	12.4	43.3	. . .	. . .
1956	12.2	11.7	14.8	6.3	14.2	15.0	11.9	10.5	12.8	45.3	. . .	. . .
1957	12.6	12.0	15.0	6.6	14.7	15.5	12.3	10.9	13.2	47.3	. . .	. . .
1958	12.9	12.3	15.3	6.8	15.1	16.1	12.6	11.0	13.6	48.6	. . .	. . .
1959	13.2	12.6	15.6	7.0	15.5	16.5	13.1	11.7	14.0	49.5	10.8	6.5
1960	13.6	13.0	15.9	7.5	15.9	17.1	13.4	12.2	14.4	46.3	11.1	7.0
1961	13.8	13.3	16.1	7.7	16.4	17.6	13.7	12.6	14.5	46.7	11.3	7.2
1962	14.1	13.5	16.2	7.9	16.7	18.0	14.0	13.1	14.8	47.4	11.5	7.3
1963	14.3	13.7	16.4	8.1	16.8	18.4	14.3	13.1	15.1	48.2	11.8	7.5
1964	14.6	14.0	16.6	8.4	17.0	18.9	14.5	13.7	15.4	48.4	12.1	7.8
1965	14.8	14.2	16.7	8.6	17.3	19.3	14.8	14.0	15.8	49.7	12.4	8.0
1966	15.3	14.6	16.9	9.0	17.6	19.8	15.4	14.8	16.3	51.6	12.8	8.3
1967	15.8	15.1	17.2	9.6	18.3	20.5	16.3	15.2	16.8	53.2	13.4	8.7
1968	16.5	15.8	17.6	10.2	19.1	21.6	17.1	16.3	17.5	55.3	14.1	9.2
1969	17.3	16.6	18.2	10.9	20.3	22.5	18.1	17.8	18.4	58.7	15.1	9.8
1970	18.3	17.5	19.0	11.7	21.8	23.5	19.5	18.7	19.3	61.3	16.0	10.6
1971	19.3	18.5	19.9	12.3	23.4	24.5	20.5	19.8	20.4	64.6	16.8	11.0
1972	20.1	19.3	20.7	12.9	24.3	25.2	21.3	21.0	21.4	67.3	17.6	11.6
1973	21.1	20.2	21.6	13.5	25.3	26.1	22.7	21.5	22.7	71.6	18.7	12.3
1974	22.9	21.9	22.8	14.8	27.5	27.9	25.3	23.2	25.2	81.9	21.0	13.7
1975	24.8	23.8	24.6	16.4	30.5	29.9	27.6	24.9	27.0	89.5	23.1	15.1
1976	26.6	25.4	26.4	18.0	32.8	31.4	29.4	26.0	28.6	94.3	24.9	16.4
1977	28.6	27.3	28.7	19.5	35.1	32.9	31.6	27.9	30.1	100.7	26.8	17.7
1978	30.8	29.5	30.8	21.1	37.4	34.9	34.3	31.6	31.7	107.4	28.8	19.1
1979	33.4	31.9	33.3	23.2	40.7	37.2	38.0	33.4	34.0	117.9	31.7	21.0
1980	36.8	35.2	36.7	26.0	47.3	40.0	41.7	35.9	37.1	129.1	35.5	23.7
1981	40.6	38.9	40.8	29.2	53.0	42.6	45.5	38.7	40.9	136.0	39.3	26.7
1982	43.7	42.1	44.6	32.5	56.0	44.9	48.1	40.9	44.1	129.7	42.4	30.0
1983	46.4	44.9	47.4	35.4	58.1	46.8	50.1	44.8	46.5	120.7	44.7	32.8
1984	48.9	47.4	49.9	38.1	60.4	48.8	52.4	47.7	48.9	115.9	46.8	35.4
1985	51.1	49.6	52.5	40.4	61.6	51.0	54.6	49.7	50.7	113.6	48.7	37.5
1986	53.4	52.0	55.0	42.8	62.2	52.9	56.9	52.5	53.4	110.2	50.4	39.6
1987	55.4	54.1	57.0	45.6	64.8	55.0	59.2	53.9	54.6	108.4	52.6	42.1
1988	58.1	56.9	59.2	49.1	67.9	57.1	61.7	57.1	56.9	107.5	55.7	45.5
1989	60.8	59.7	61.6	53.4	70.9	59.9	64.5	59.1	59.1	101.1	58.8	49.7
1990	63.8	62.9	64.3	58.0	73.6	63.2	67.5	62.1	61.5	93.2	61.6	54.1
1991	66.6	65.9	66.4	62.5	75.6	66.5	70.2	64.8	64.4	86.7	64.4	58.7
1992	69.2	68.9	68.3	66.9	77.7	68.5	71.7	69.7	67.2	79.3	66.8	63.1
1993	71.3	71.1	70.2	70.4	80.4	70.7	73.1	70.5	69.5	75.3	68.8	66.6
1994	73.2	73.1	72.0	73.3	81.4	72.2	74.4	71.7	72.1	75.3	70.8	69.1
1995	75.4	75.3	74.0	76.0	83.2	73.8	76.1	74.5	74.5	75.3	72.8	71.7
1996	77.5	77.5	76.2	77.8	84.3	76.3	78.2	77.5	76.6	76.7	74.8	73.8
1997	79.8	79.8	78.3	79.3	86.1	78.8	80.5	82.1	78.8	79.9	76.7	75.4
1998	81.7	81.5	80.1	80.8	87.6	80.7	82.7	84.1	80.4	85.1	79.0	76.8
1999	83.5	83.3	82.0	82.6	89.0	83.3	84.8	84.9	82.4	88.1	81.2	78.7
2000	85.8	85.5	84.8	84.9	91.6	86.5	87.2	85.7	83.9	93.0	84.4	81.4
2001	88.4	88.1	88.7	87.8	92.6	89.4	89.6	85.2	86.5	97.3	87.6	84.3
2002	90.8	90.5	91.3	90.1	93.1	91.9	91.8	87.5	89.9	98.1	90.2	87.5
2003	93.7	93.6	94.2	93.5	95.1	94.8	93.8	91.5	93.2	96.6	93.1	91.9
2004	96.7	96.7	96.7	96.9	96.5	97.3	96.9	96.5	96.4	96.2	96.2	96.2
2005	100.0	100.0	100.0	100.0	100.0	100.0	100.0	100.0	100.0	100.0	100.0	100.0
2006	103.4	103.5	104.3	103.0	104.2	103.4	103.4	102.3	103.4	102.1	103.6	104.1
2007	107.0	107.1	108.0	106.8	106.6	106.2	107.3	106.7	106.4	103.5	106.8	107.9
2008	110.6	110.8	111.9	109.7	112.4	109.5	111.6	110.0	110.8	104.5	109.7	111.5
2009	112.3	112.6	113.3	112.4	115.5	110.8	114.3	109.4	113.2	103.3	111.6	114.7
2007												
1st quarter	105.7	105.8	106.9	105.7	105.4	105.1	105.6	104.8	105.1	103.1	105.7	106.6
2nd quarter	106.4	106.6	107.7	106.3	105.8	106.0	106.8	105.5	106.0	103.3	106.4	107.4
3rd quarter	107.3	107.5	108.3	107.1	107.0	106.3	108.1	107.2	106.8	104.2	107.2	108.2
4th quarter	108.4	108.6	109.3	108.2	108.2	107.5	108.9	109.4	107.7	103.5	108.0	109.6
2008												
1st quarter	109.2	109.4	110.2	108.7	109.7	108.4	109.9	109.6	109.0	103.8	108.6	110.3
2nd quarter	110.3	110.5	111.6	109.4	111.8	109.2	110.9	110.3	110.6	104.4	109.4	111.2
3rd quarter	111.3	111.5	112.8	110.1	113.5	110.4	112.3	110.4	111.6	105.3	110.2	112.0
4th quarter	111.5	111.8	113.0	110.7	114.6	110.0	113.3	109.7	112.1	104.6	110.5	112.6
2009												
1st quarter	111.7	112.1	113.4	111.4	115.1	110.3	113.8	108.7	112.5	103.3	110.8	113.5
2nd quarter	112.0	112.3	113.3	112.0	114.6	110.2	114.2	109.1	112.8	103.0	111.2	114.2
3rd quarter	112.3	112.7	113.2	112.7	115.5	111.3	114.4	109.3	113.3	103.3	111.9	115.0
4th quarter	113.0	113.4	113.3	113.6	116.6	111.4	114.9	110.7	114.4	103.3	112.6	115.9

. . . = Not available.

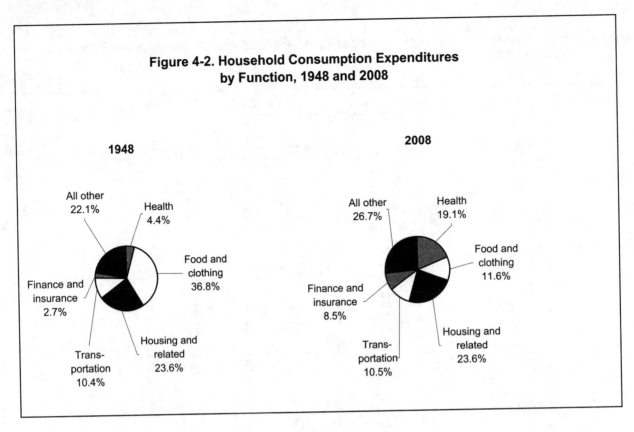

Figure 4-2. Household Consumption Expenditures
by Function, 1948 and 2008

- Household spending on health in 2008 made up 19.1 percent of all household consumption spending—more than four times the percentage in 1948. This includes medical care payments made by government and private insurance on behalf of individuals as well as out-of-pocket consumer payments. (Table 4-5)

- In 2008, much smaller shares were required for food and clothing than in 1948, as seen in the figure. The shares of housing-related spending and transportation were almost exactly the same in the two years. The share of finance and insurance spending tripled, and households also spent a larger share on the remaining category, which includes education, communication, recreation, food services, accommodations, and other miscellaneous goods and services. (Table 4-5)

Table 4-5. Household Consumption Expenditures by Function

(Billions of dollars.)   NIPA Table 2.5.5

Year	Household consumption expenditures, total	Food and beverages off-premises	Clothing, footwear, and related services	Housing, utilities, and fuels	Furnishings, household equipment, and maintenance	Health	Transportation	Communication	Recreation	Education	Food services and accommodations	Financial services and insurance	Other goods and services	Foreign travel and expenditures, net
1939	66.2	15.2	7.7	12.3	5.5	2.8	6.3	0.7	3.6	0.6	4.1	2.3	5.0	0.2
1940	70.2	15.9	8.1	12.8	6.0	3.0	7.0	0.7	3.9	0.6	4.4	2.4	5.3	0.1
1941	80.0	18.2	9.5	13.7	7.1	3.2	8.3	0.8	4.5	0.6	5.3	2.5	6.0	0.1
1942	87.7	21.6	11.8	14.8	7.4	3.6	5.4	1.0	4.9	0.7	6.9	2.6	6.8	0.2
1943	98.4	24.3	14.4	15.5	7.4	4.0	5.4	1.2	5.3	0.8	9.1	2.8	8.0	0.3
1944	107.0	26.0	15.7	16.2	8.0	4.5	5.7	1.3	5.8	0.9	10.9	3.0	8.5	0.6
1945	118.2	28.2	17.6	16.9	8.9	4.8	6.6	1.4	6.5	0.9	12.7	3.2	9.3	1.2
1946	142.3	34.9	19.7	18.8	12.7	5.9	12.1	1.6	9.0	1.0	12.7	3.8	10.3	-0.1
1947	159.9	40.2	20.4	21.2	15.5	6.6	15.4	1.7	9.8	1.2	12.5	4.2	11.1	0.0
1948	172.7	41.8	21.8	23.9	16.8	7.6	18.0	1.9	10.3	1.3	12.6	4.7	11.7	0.3
1949	176.1	40.4	21.1	25.6	16.3	7.9	21.2	2.1	10.6	1.4	12.4	4.9	11.8	0.6
1950	189.8	41.4	21.4	28.4	18.7	8.5	24.6	2.3	11.7	1.5	12.7	5.6	12.2	0.7
1951	205.9	46.0	23.1	31.6	19.7	9.3	24.2	2.6	12.3	1.6	15.0	6.3	13.3	0.9
1952	216.6	48.4	23.9	34.6	19.3	10.1	24.4	2.9	13.0	1.7	16.0	6.7	14.3	1.1
1953	230.0	49.3	24.2	37.9	20.0	11.0	28.0	3.2	13.8	1.8	16.5	7.8	15.0	1.5
1954	236.7	50.6	24.3	40.9	19.9	11.9	27.4	3.3	14.3	1.9	16.6	8.6	15.4	1.5
1955	255.3	52.0	25.4	43.8	22.3	12.8	33.4	3.6	15.4	2.1	17.0	9.6	16.3	1.6
1956	267.8	54.2	26.5	46.8	23.6	14.1	32.7	3.9	16.4	2.4	17.7	10.4	17.5	1.7
1957	282.7	57.1	26.8	50.0	23.9	15.5	35.7	4.3	16.8	2.6	18.5	11.1	18.8	1.7
1958	291.7	59.8	27.1	53.3	24.1	17.1	33.7	4.5	17.3	2.9	18.7	11.6	19.9	1.9
1959	312.6	61.6	28.6	56.9	25.6	18.8	38.8	4.8	18.8	3.1	19.7	12.5	21.4	2.0
1960	326.5	62.6	29.3	60.5	26.2	20.4	40.8	5.2	19.7	3.4	20.5	13.6	22.4	2.1
1961	336.7	63.7	29.9	64.0	26.8	21.8	39.3	5.6	20.5	3.6	21.0	14.8	23.7	2.0
1962	357.6	64.7	31.3	68.2	28.3	24.3	44.1	5.9	22.1	4.0	22.3	15.4	24.9	2.3
1963	376.7	65.9	32.1	72.2	29.8	26.4	47.8	6.4	23.9	4.3	23.3	15.9	26.2	2.5
1964	404.8	69.5	34.7	76.2	32.7	29.8	50.7	6.9	26.3	4.8	24.9	17.7	27.8	2.6
1965	436.6	74.4	36.5	81.0	34.7	32.0	56.5	7.5	28.9	5.5	27.2	19.4	30.2	2.9
1966	473.1	80.6	39.8	85.9	37.8	35.0	59.0	8.1	33.4	6.2	29.6	21.3	33.3	3.1
1967	499.4	82.6	41.7	91.1	39.7	38.4	61.0	8.9	35.8	6.9	31.0	22.8	35.8	3.8
1968	548.7	88.8	45.6	97.4	43.2	43.8	69.8	9.7	39.9	7.7	34.6	25.8	38.6	3.7
1969	595.0	95.4	48.8	105.5	45.4	50.0	75.9	10.7	43.7	8.7	37.5	28.5	41.0	4.0
1970	637.2	103.5	49.9	113.8	46.6	56.8	76.5	11.6	47.0	9.9	41.6	31.1	44.3	4.5
1971	689.3	107.1	53.4	124.5	48.8	63.4	88.7	12.8	50.1	10.9	43.8	34.1	47.0	4.8
1972	756.6	114.5	58.0	136.2	53.5	70.4	98.3	14.4	56.2	11.7	48.9	38.3	51.0	5.2
1973	837.4	126.7	63.7	149.7	59.9	78.7	108.6	16.1	63.0	13.0	54.8	41.5	56.9	4.7
1974	916.5	143.0	66.9	166.3	64.6	88.7	112.8	17.7	68.9	14.2	60.6	45.9	62.2	4.7
1975	1 015.7	156.6	71.4	184.8	67.8	102.7	124.4	20.0	77.1	15.9	68.8	54.0	67.8	4.4
1976	1 131.2	167.3	76.9	204.6	75.0	116.8	147.4	22.4	86.2	17.4	77.8	59.3	76.3	3.8
1977	1 256.0	179.8	84.3	228.7	84.0	131.6	168.1	24.3	94.9	18.8	85.7	67.8	83.8	4.3
1978	1 403.2	196.1	94.6	255.6	93.6	149.4	186.3	27.0	106.3	20.9	97.1	80.6	93.2	4.3
1979	1 563.4	218.4	101.9	287.5	104.3	169.9	207.1	29.4	118.9	22.9	110.9	87.6	100.4	4.1
1980	1 723.9	239.2	108.8	327.0	110.7	195.5	226.5	31.8	127.4	25.4	121.7	95.6	110.7	3.5
1981	1 903.2	255.3	119.1	367.5	118.3	228.9	250.7	36.0	141.6	28.3	133.9	102.0	121.2	0.4
1982	2 035.4	267.1	122.7	401.2	121.0	254.9	255.9	41.1	151.4	31.0	142.5	116.3	127.8	2.5
1983	2 245.7	277.0	132.9	434.5	132.3	287.1	284.9	44.8	169.3	34.3	153.6	145.9	143.4	5.4
1984	2 453.5	291.1	144.7	471.9	147.1	315.2	321.8	48.4	190.0	37.7	164.9	156.6	157.7	6.6
1985	2 667.3	303.0	154.3	514.0	156.0	345.3	357.4	53.1	207.2	41.2	174.3	180.5	173.3	7.7
1986	2 841.4	316.4	165.1	546.8	168.7	378.4	362.6	56.9	225.4	44.5	186.7	196.7	190.0	3.3
1987	3 038.4	324.3	176.4	582.8	176.9	419.9	376.6	60.0	247.0	48.8	204.4	207.1	208.2	6.1
1988	3 283.3	342.8	188.2	625.9	186.6	470.7	404.8	63.1	273.4	54.4	225.8	219.4	225.4	2.8
1989	3 522.8	365.4	201.4	667.3	197.5	519.0	428.3	67.3	295.7	60.6	242.6	235.7	245.7	-3.7
1990	3 755.8	391.2	207.0	709.1	200.6	583.7	442.9	70.1	314.7	66.0	262.7	253.2	262.3	-7.7
1991	3 895.8	403.0	210.4	747.8	199.1	638.4	418.3	73.9	326.3	70.6	273.4	282.0	268.0	-15.2
1992	4 144.5	404.5	223.0	783.3	209.4	700.4	451.3	81.1	346.8	76.4	286.3	311.8	290.1	-20.0
1993	4 389.0	413.5	231.0	826.9	221.9	741.7	485.3	85.8	378.4	81.1	298.6	341.0	304.5	-20.7
1994	4 684.4	432.1	239.7	879.2	238.6	779.9	528.2	93.3	414.0	86.4	308.7	349.0	316.9	-17.5
1995	4 880.1	443.7	244.1	926.8	251.7	826.0	554.1	98.9	449.8	92.3	316.7	364.7	332.7	-21.5
1996	5 157.9	461.9	252.7	975.5	263.7	868.3	598.9	108.3	481.5	99.6	327.4	393.6	350.8	-24.5
1997	5 458.4	474.8	262.0	1 023.1	277.3	919.9	641.8	120.1	509.5	107.1	344.6	431.3	368.4	-21.5
1998	5 787.5	486.5	273.0	1 076.8	296.8	979.7	669.2	130.6	546.0	115.2	363.0	469.6	394.8	-13.7
1999	6 197.4	513.6	287.1	1 137.4	319.7	1 033.3	730.5	144.7	593.6	123.9	381.6	514.2	431.6	-13.8
2000	6 665.0	537.5	297.3	1 214.5	342.5	1 109.6	798.4	162.1	639.9	134.3	410.1	570.0	462.3	-13.3
2001	6 962.6	559.7	294.3	1 303.2	351.1	1 209.4	814.1	171.3	655.7	143.6	421.2	562.8	483.5	-7.4
2002	7 234.2	569.6	295.2	1 349.1	363.5	1 317.1	818.4	177.5	680.9	149.5	438.2	576.2	504.3	-5.1
2003	7 592.2	593.1	302.8	1 410.6	376.5	1 403.8	857.4	181.8	712.5	159.7	462.8	601.8	529.9	-0.5
2004	8 075.1	628.2	315.9	1 480.6	400.4	1 500.6	909.5	187.9	764.6	169.4	492.9	667.5	557.0	0.5
2005	8 604.9	665.0	331.8	1 603.9	423.9	1 601.5	979.3	192.8	807.4	180.7	525.3	712.6	580.9	-0.1
2006	9 082.3	698.0	347.2	1 708.2	445.4	1 688.1	1 008.8	207.8	859.1	192.7	559.7	752.4	611.2	3.7
2007	9 572.9	740.1	359.1	1 787.2	456.2	1 790.4	1 051.6	219.0	906.5	206.8	587.9	824.2	647.1	-3.2
2008	9 851.2	784.3	355.6	1 870.3	449.9	1 878.2	1 036.5	229.0	928.0	220.8	608.7	835.6	667.9	-13.5

Table 4-6. Personal Saving: Households and Nonprofit Institutions Serving Household (NPISHs)

(Billions of dollars, except as noted.)

Year	Personal saving as a percentage of disposable personal income (percent)	Households				Nonprofit Institutions Serving Households (NPISHs)					
		Disposable income	Less: outlays	Equals: household saving		Income	Less: gross output	Plus: receipts from sales	Less: transfer payments	Saving	
				Billions of dollars	Percent of income					Billions of dollars	Percent of income and receipts from sales
1992	7.3	4 710.6	4 378.8	331.8	7.0	131.7	400.8	308.5	23.2	16.3	3.7
1993	5.8	4 896.4	4 625.5	270.9	5.5	135.3	423.3	328.7	26.2	14.5	3.1
1994	5.2	5 157.1	4 898.3	258.8	5.0	142.9	444.7	342.3	28.6	11.9	2.5
1995	5.2	5 423.1	5 152.3	270.8	5.0	151.3	463.4	356.2	28.7	15.5	3.0
1996	4.9	5 726.3	5 466.8	259.5	4.5	170.9	488.8	373.1	33.5	21.6	4.0
1997	4.6	6 039.8	5 799.2	240.6	4.0	188.8	509.3	397.0	36.7	39.9	6.8
1998	5.3	6 473.4	6 154.0	319.4	4.9	196.7	550.5	419.6	43.7	22.1	3.6
1999	3.1	6 776.2	6 596.0	180.1	2.7	221.8	585.3	439.9	48.8	27.6	4.2
2000	2.9	7 298.6	7 117.2	181.4	2.5	248.7	632.0	466.6	51.7	31.7	4.4
2001	2.7	7 630.3	7 421.5	208.9	2.7	241.0	688.0	501.8	58.7	-4.0	-0.5
2002	3.5	7 999.9	7 691.6	308.3	3.9	240.8	749.7	544.7	61.9	-26.1	-3.3
2003	3.5	8 370.9	8 046.7	324.2	3.9	243.0	785.8	574.0	65.6	-34.4	-4.2
2004	3.4	8 882.0	8 569.1	312.9	3.5	270.6	827.7	617.7	69.8	-9.1	-1.0
2005	1.4	9 262.1	9 138.5	123.6	1.3	294.7	874.6	660.6	76.6	4.0	0.4
2006	2.4	9 900.0	9 650.9	249.1	2.5	305.9	933.6	693.3	79.7	-14.2	-1.4
2007	1.7	10 385.6	10 174.6	211.0	2.0	303.6	987.5	734.0	82.2	-32.1	-3.1
2008	2.7	10 793.0	10 447.0	346.0	3.2	306.7	1 049.4	770.7	87.5	-59.6	-5.5

NOTES AND DEFINITIONS, CHAPTER 4

SOURCE: U.S. DEPARTMENT OF COMMERCE, BUREAU OF ECONOMIC ANALYSIS (BEA)

All personal income and personal consumption expenditure series are from the national income and product accounts (NIPAs). All quarterly series are shown at seasonally adjusted annual rates. Current and constant dollar values are in billions of dollars. Indexes of price and quantity are based on the average for the year 2005, which equals 100.

Tables 4-1 through 4-4 cover all income and spending by the personal sector, which includes nonprofit institutions serving households (NPISHs). In a new feature introduced in the 2009 comprehensive revision of the NIPAs, Tables 4-2, 4-3, and 4-4 show the services component of personal consumption expenditures broken down into separate aggregates for "household consumption expenditures for services" and "final consumption expenditures" by NPISHs. The last two tables give further details that are only available annually. Table 4-5 shows a more detailed functional breakdown of household consumption expenditures, not including NPISHs. Table 4-6 show income, spending, and saving data estimated separately for households and NPISHs.

In several cases, the notes and definitions below will refer to *imputations* or *imputed values*. See the notes and definitions to Chapter 1 for an explanation of imputation and the role it plays in national and personal income measurement.

TABLES 4-1 THROUGH 4-4 AND 19-6
SOURCES AND DISPOSITION OF PERSONAL INCOME; PERSONAL CONSUMPTION EXPENDITURES BY MAJOR TYPE OF PRODUCT

Definitions

Personal income is the income received by persons residing in the United States from participation in production, from government and business transfer payments, and from government interest, which is treated similarly to a transfer payment rather than as income from participation in production. *Persons* denotes the total for individuals, *nonprofit institutions that primarily serve households (NPISHs)*, private noninsured welfare funds, and private trust funds. (Income, outlays, and saving excluding NPISHs are referred to as *household* income, outlays, and saving.) All proprietors' income is treated as received by individuals. Life insurance carriers and private noninsured pension funds are not counted as persons, but their saving is credited to persons.

Income from the sale of illegal goods and services is excluded by definition from national and personal income, and the value of purchases of illegal goods and services is not included in personal consumption expenditures.

Personal income is the sum of compensation received by employees, proprietors' income with inventory valuation and capital consumption adjustments (IVA and CCAdj), rental income of persons with capital consumption adjustment, personal receipts on assets, and personal current transfer receipts, less contributions for social insurance.

Personal income differs from national income in that it includes current transfer payments and interest received by persons, regardless of source, while it excludes the following income components: employee and employer contributions for social insurance; business transfer payments, interest payments, and other payments on assets other than to persons; taxes on production and imports less subsidies; the current surplus of government enterprises; and undistributed corporate profits with IVA and CCAdj. The relationships of GDP, gross and net national product, national income, and personal income are displayed in Table 1-10.

Compensation of employees, received is the sum of wage and salary accruals and supplements to wages and salaries, as defined in the *national* income account (see Table 1-12 and the notes and definitions to Chapter 1), minus an adjustment item *wage accruals less disbursements*. By subtracting this adjustment, BEA puts retroactive wage payments back into the quarter <u>in which</u> the wages were received by workers rather than the quarter <u>for which</u> they were paid. This adjustment item is zero in most quarters but appears more frequently in recent years. There are substantial entries in 2003 and 2004 because 53 Friday paydays fell in 2004 instead of the usual 52. In other years there are entries for this item reflecting stock options and financial industry bonuses paid in a year different from the year of the activity with which they are associated. See the notes and definitions to Chapter 1. *Wage accruals less disbursements* is shown in Table 1-10, but is not shown separately in Tables 4-1 or 19-6.

As in *national* income, the *compensation of employees* component of personal income refers to compensation received by residents of the United States, including compensation from the rest of the world, but excludes compensation from domestic industries to workers residing in the rest of the world.

Wage and salary disbursements consists of the monetary remuneration of employees, including the compensation of corporate officers; corporate directors' fees paid to directors who are also employees of the corporation; the value of employee exercise of "nonqualified stock options"; commissions, tips, and bonuses; voluntary employee contributions to certain deferred-compensation plans, such as 401(k) plans; receipts in kind that represent income; and judicial fees to jurors and witnesses, compensation of prison inmates, and marriage fees to justices of the peace, all of which were formerly included in "other labor income."

Supplements to wages and salaries consists of employer contributions to employee pension and insurance funds and to government social insurance funds.

The following two categories, *proprietors' income* and *rental income,* are both measured net of depreciation of the capital (structures and equipment) involved. BEA calculates normal depreciation, based on the estimated life of the capital, and subtracts it from the estimated value of receipts to yield net income.

Proprietors' income with inventory valuation and capital consumption adjustments is the current-production income (including income-in-kind) of sole proprietors and partnerships and of tax-exempt cooperatives. The imputed net rental income of owner-occupants of farm dwellings is included. Dividends and monetary interest received by proprietors of nonfinancial business and rental incomes received by persons not primarily engaged in the real estate business are excluded. These incomes are included in personal income receipts on assets and rental income of persons, respectively. Fees paid to outside directors of corporations are included. The two valuation adjustments are designed to obtain income measures that exclude any element of capital gains: inventory withdrawals are valued at replacement cost, rather than historical cost, and charges for depreciation are on an economically consistent accounting basis and are valued at replacement cost.

Rental income of persons with capital consumption adjustment consists of the net current-production income of persons from the rental of real property (other than the incomes of persons primarily engaged in the real estate business), the imputed net rental income of owner-occupants of nonfarm dwellings, and the royalties received by persons from patents, copyrights, and rights to natural resources. The capital consumption adjustment converts charges for depreciation to an economically consistent accounting basis valued at replacement cost. Rental income is net of interest and other expenses, and hence is affected by changing indebtedness and interest payments on owner-occupied and other housing.

Personal income receipts on assets consists of personal interest income and personal dividend income.

Personal interest income is the interest income (monetary and imputed) of persons from all sources, including interest paid by government to government employee retirement plans as well as government interest paid directly to persons.

Personal dividend income is the dividend income of persons from all sources, excluding capital gains distributions. It equals net dividends paid by corporations (dividends paid by corporations minus dividends received by corporations) less a small amount of corporate dividends received by general government. Dividends received by government employee retirement systems are included in personal dividend income.

Personal current transfer receipts is income payments to persons for which no current services are performed. It consists of government social benefits to persons and net receipts from business.

Government social benefits to persons consists of benefits from the following categories of programs:

- *Social Security and Medicare,* consisting of federal old-age, survivors, disability, and health insurance;

- *Unemployment insurance;*

- *Veterans' benefits;*

- *Family assistance,* which consists of aid to families with dependent children and (beginning in 1996) assistance programs operating under the Personal Responsibility and Work Opportunity Reconciliation Act of 1996;

- *Other government benefits to persons,* which includes pension benefit guaranty, workers' compensation, military medical insurance, temporary disability insurance, food stamps, Black Lung benefits, supplemental security income, public assistance (including Medicaid), educational assistance, and the earned income credit. Government payments to nonprofit institutions, other than for work under research and development contracts, also are included. Payments from government employee retirement plans are not included.

Contributions for government social insurance, domestic, which is subtracted to arrive at personal income, includes payments by U.S. employers, employees, self-employed, and other individuals who participate in the following programs: old-age, survivors, and disability insurance (Social Security); hospital insurance and supplementary medical insurance (Medicare); unemployment insurance; railroad retirement; veterans' life insurance; and temporary disability insurance. Contributions to government employee retirement plans are not included in this item.

In the 2009 comprehensive revision, most transactions between the U.S. government and economic agents in Guam, the U.S. Virgin Islands, American Samoa, Puerto Rico, and the Northern Mariana Islands are treated as government transactions with the rest of the world. Since the NIPAs only cover the 50 states and the District of Columbia, the *domestic* contributions to government social insurance funds are the only ones that need to be subtracted from NIPA payroll data to calculate personal income. The social insurance receipts of governments, shown in Chapter 6, will be somewhat larger than this personal income entry because they will include contributions from residents of those territories and commonwealths.

Personal current taxes is tax payments (net of refunds) by persons residing in the United States that are not chargeable to business expenses, including taxes on income, on realized net capital gains, and on personal property. As of the 1999 revisions, estate and gift taxes are classified as capital transfers and are not included in personal current taxes.

Disposable personal income is personal income minus personal current taxes. It is the income from current production that is available to persons for spending or saving. However, it is not the cash flow available, since it excludes realized capital gains. Disposable personal income in chained (2005) dollars represents the inflation-adjusted value of disposable personal income, using the implicit price deflator for personal consumption expenditures.

Personal income excluding current transfer receipts, also shown in chained (2005) dollars, is an important business cycle indicator, to which particular attention is paid because it is calculated monthly as well as quarterly and annually, and thus can help establish monthly cycle turning point dates. As a pre-income-tax measure which excludes transfer payments received, it is more directly related to the workings of the economy than alternative monthly income indicators such as total or disposable personal income.

Personal outlays is the sum of *personal consumption expenditures* (defined below), *personal interest payments,* and *personal current transfer payments.*

Personal interest payments is nonmortgage interest paid by households. As noted above in the definition of rental income, mortgage interest is subtracted from gross rental or imputed rental receipts of persons to yield a net rental income estimate; hence, it is not included as an interest outlay in this category.

Personal current transfer payments to government includes donations, fees, and fines paid to federal, state, and local governments.

Personal current transfer payments to the rest of the world (net) is personal remittances in cash and in kind to the rest of the world less such remittances from the rest of the world.

Personal saving is derived by subtracting personal outlays from disposable personal income. It is the current net saving of individuals (including proprietors), nonprofit institutions that primarily serve individuals, life insurance carriers, retirement funds (including those of government employees), private noninsured welfare funds, and private trust funds. Conceptually, personal saving may also be viewed as the sum of the net acquisition of financial assets and the change in physical assets less the sum of net borrowing and consumption of fixed capital. In either case, it is defined to exclude both realized and unrealized capital gains.

Note that in the context of national income accounting, the term just defined is *saving,* not "savings." *Saving* refers to a flow of income during a particular time span (such as a year or a quarter) that is not consumed. It is therefore available to finance a commensurate flow of investment during that time span. Strictly defined, "savings" denotes an accumulated stock of monetary funds—possibly the cumulative effects of successive periods of *saving*—available to the owner in asset form, such as in a bank savings account.

Personal consumption expenditures (PCE) is goods and services purchased by persons residing in the United States. Per-

sons are defined as individuals and nonprofit institutions that primarily serve individuals. PCE mostly consists of purchases of new goods and services by individuals from business, including purchases financed by insurance (such as medical insurance). In addition, PCE includes purchases of new goods and services by nonprofit institutions, net purchases of used goods by individuals and nonprofit institutions, and purchases abroad of goods and services by U.S. residents traveling or working in foreign countries. PCE also includes purchases for certain goods and services provided by the government, primarily tuition payments for higher education, charges for medical care, and charges for water and sanitary services. Finally, PCE includes imputed purchases that keep PCE invariant to changes in the way that certain activities are carried out. For example, to take account of the value of the services provided by owner-occupied housing, PCE includes an imputation equal to what (estimated) rent homeowners would pay if they rented their houses from themselves. (See the discussion of imputation in the notes and definitions to Chapter 1.) Actual purchases of residential structures by individuals are classified as gross private domestic investment.

In the 2009 comprehensive revision, the classification system used for breakdowns of PCE was revised, and new calculations were introduced separating the consumption spending of the household sector proper from that of nonprofit institutions serving households.

Goods is the sum of *Durable* and *Nondurable goods.*

The PCE category *Durable goods* now is subdivided into *Motor vehicles and parts, Furnishings and household equipment, Recreational goods and vehicles,* and *Other durable goods.*

Nondurable goods now encompasses *Food and beverages off-premises, Clothing and footwear, Gasoline and other energy goods,* and *Other nondurable goods.* This food and beverages category no longer includes meals and beverages purchased for consumption on the premises, which are now included in services, since they have a high service component and since their prices are much more stable than those of off-premises food and beverages.

Services, total is now subdivided into *Household* consumption of services and *Final consumption expenditures of nonprofit institutions serving households (NPISHs).* The latter is the difference between the *Gross output* of NPISHs and the amounts that they receive from sales of goods and services to households—for example, payments for services of a nonprofit hospital. Such sales of goods and services appear in the appropriate category of household expenditures—for example, *Health* in the case of the hospital services.

The components of *Household services* are *Housing and utilities, Health care, Transportation services, Recreation services, Food services and accommodations* (which includes meals and beverages purchased for consumption on premises, as well as payments for hotels and similar accommodations), *Financial services and insurance,* and *Other services.*

These are the categories used in the quarterly data presented in Tables 4-2, 4-3, and 4-4.

This classification system is not particularly helpful with respect to the objective of spending. For example, the *Health care* component of services does not include drugs and medicines, which are included instead in nondurable goods. For a more precise classification of consumption spending by objective, see Table 4-5, Household Consumption Expenditures by Function, described in more detail below. This classification by type of expenditure is only available on an annual basis.

Data availability

Monthly data are made available in a BEA press release, usually distributed the first business day following the monthly release of the latest quarterly national income and product account (NIPA) estimates. Monthly and quarterly data are subsequently published each month in the BEA's *Survey of Current Business*. Current and historical data are available on the BEA Web site at <http://www.bea.gov>, and may also be obtained from the STAT-USA subscription Web site at <http://www.stat-usa.gov>.

References

The latest revision incorporated in this volume is presented and described in an article on the national income and product accounts in the September 2009 *Survey of Current Business*. Other references can be found in the notes and definitions to Chapter 1. A discussion of monthly estimates of personal income and its disposition appears in the November 1979 edition of the *Survey of Current Business*. Additional and more recent information can be found in the articles listed in the notes and definitions for Chapter 1.

TABLE 4-5
HOUSEHOLD CONSUMPTION EXPENDITURES BY FUNCTION

SOURCE: BUREAU OF ECONOMIC ANALYSIS (BEA)

In this table, also derived from the NIPAs, annual estimates of the current-dollar value of PCE by households—excluding the "final" consumption expenditures of nonprofit institutions serving households (NPISHs); see definition above—are presented by function.

Definitions

Food and beverages includes food and beverages (including alcoholic beverages) purchased for home consumption and food produced and consumed on farms.

Clothing, footwear, and related services includes purchases, rental, cleaning, and repair of clothing and footwear.

Housing, utilities, and fuels includes rents paid for rental housing, imputed rent of owner-occupied dwellings, and purchase of fuels and utility services.

Furnishings, household equipment, and routine household maintenance includes furniture, floor coverings, household textiles, appliances, tableware etc., tools, and other supplies and services.

Health includes drugs, other medical products and equipment, and outpatient, hospital, and nursing home services.

Transportation includes the purchase and operation of motor vehicles and public transportation services.

Communication includes telephone equipment, postal and delivery services, telecommunication services, and Internet access.

Recreation includes video and audio equipment, computers, and related services; sports vehicles and other sports goods and services; memberships and admissions; magazines, newspapers, books, and stationery; pets and related goods and services; photo goods and services; tour services; and legal gambling. (As noted earlier, purchases of goods and services that are illegal and the incomes from such purchases are outside the scope of the national income and product accounts.)

Education includes educational services and books.

Food services and accommodations includes meals and beverages purchased for consumption on the premises, food furnished to employees, and hotel and other accommodations including housing at schools.

Financial services and insurance consists of financial services and life, household, medical care, motor vehicle, and other insurance.

Other goods and services includes personal goods (such as cosmetics, jewelry, and luggage) and services, social services and religious activities, professional and other services, and tobacco.

Foreign travel and expenditures, net consists of foreign travel spending and other expenditures abroad by U.S. residents minus expenditures in the United States by nonresidents. A negative figure indicates that foreigners spent more here than U.S. residents spent abroad. Positive values for this foreign travel category, indicating that U.S. residents spent more abroad than foreigners spent here, appear in the 1980s when the dollar was strong against other major currencies. (The international value of the dollar is shown in Table 13-8.) Negative values in subsequent years resulted from the weakening of the dollar, which discouraged U.S. residents' travel abroad and encouraged tourism by foreigners in the United States. The negative sign does not indicate a drain on GDP—these effects of a weaker dollar are in fact positive for GDP—but rather reflects the fact that the goods and services purchased by foreigners in the United States must be subtracted from the total consumer purchases recorded elsewhere in this table in order to be added to other exports and classified in the category of exports rather than in the consumption spending of U.S. residents.

Data availability and revisions

Data are updated once a year and are available on the BEA Web site at <http://www.bea.gov>.

TABLE 4-6
PERSONAL SAVING: HOUSEHOLDS AND NONPROFIT INSTITUTIONS SERVING HOUSEHOLDS

SOURCE: BUREAU OF ECONOMIC ANALYSIS (BEA)

As noted above, the "personal" sector includes not only households but also "nonprofit institutions serving households" (NPISHs). This category comprises all nonprofit institutions except those that are considered to be serving government and business, such as chambers of commerce and trade associations. Those institutions are included in the business sector instead.

For annual (not quarterly) data beginning with 1992, BEA now compiles and makes available tables showing personal income and its disposition for households and NPISHs separately. Each major type of income and expenditure is estimated separately for the two groups. Household receipts from NPISHs, purchases from NPISHs, and contributions to NPISHs are identified separately instead of being netted out as they are in the quarterly accounts. Selected aggregates for households and NPISHs are shown in Table 4-6.

Data availability and references

These data and the data on income and outlays for the household and nonprofit sectors on which they are based become available about two months after the release of the midyear revision of the NIPAs. They are published in Table 2.9 in the NIPA tables on the BEA Web site at <http://www.bea.gov>. An article from the April 2003 *Survey,* "Income and Outlays of Households and of Nonprofit Institutions Serving Households," can also be found on the BEA Web site.

CHAPTER 5: SAVING AND INVESTMENT; BUSINESS SALES AND INVENTORIES

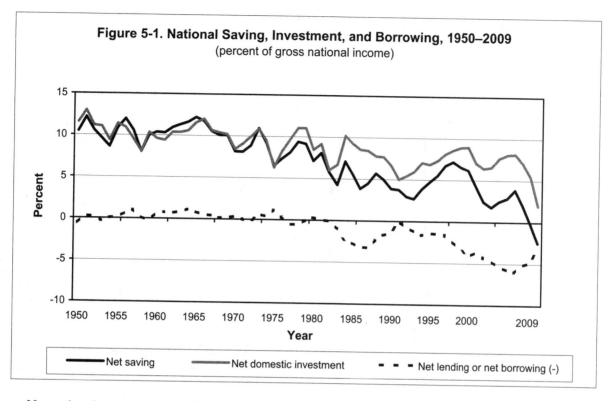

Figure 5-1. National Saving, Investment, and Borrowing, 1950–2009
(percent of gross national income)

- Net national saving—the middle line in Figure 5-1—averaged about 5 percent of gross national income (GNI) in the years 1984 through 2000, which was already lower than the rates seen in the 1950s and 1960s. Net saving is saving by U.S. persons, businesses, and governments, excluding the consumption of fixed capital—that is, saving available for investment over and above the replacement of the existing stock. In the years 2001–2007 the national saving rate fell even more, averaging 2 3/4 percent. In the recession that began at the end of 2007, national saving fell into negative territory for the first time since the depression years 1931 through 1934. (Tables 5-1, 18-1, and 19-9)

- What accounted for the decline in the saving rate in the 2000s? Comparing 2007 with 2000, the biggest factor was the federal government's swing—in a prosperous economy, not in a recession—from a surplus of 1.9 percent of GNI to a deficit of 1.6 percent. A substantial decline in the personal saving rate and a small decline in state and local saving also contributed to the drop, while there was a small increase in corporate profits relative to GNI. (Table 5-1)

- Net domestic investment (gross investment minus consumption of fixed capital) reached rates over 8 percent of GNI in the late 1990s. After the 2001 recession, it recovered to 8 percent in 2005 and 2006, before declining to 2.0 percent in 2009. This was the lowest investment rate in the entire postwar period—indeed, the lowest since net investment was negative (that is, gross investment was less than capital consumption) in the early 1930s. (Tables 5-1, 18-1, and 19-9)

- The excess of investment over saving in the 2000s was financed by a further increase in borrowing overseas (a larger negative entry for the lower line on the graph above), which reached a record 5.9 percent of GNI in 2006, then subsided somewhat as demand for foreign investment funds dwindled in the recession. (Table 5-1)

89

Table 5-1. Saving and Investment

(Billions of dollars, except as noted; quarterly data are at seasonally adjusted annual rates.)   **NIPA Tables 1.7.5, 5.1**

Year and quarter	Total	Net saving Total	Private Total¹	Personal saving	Undistributed corporate profits with IVA and CCAdj	Federal	State and local	Consumption Total	Private Total	Domestic business	Households and institutions	Federal	State and local
1950	60.6	30.7	23.8	14.9	8.9	5.6	1.3	29.9	22.0	18.6	3.5	5.8	2.1
1951	75.1	41.3	29.0	19.3	9.7	9.7	2.6	33.8	25.2	21.2	4.0	6.1	2.6
1952	74.2	37.9	31.2	20.3	10.9	3.7	3.0	36.3	26.7	22.4	4.3	6.8	2.7
1953	75.1	36.5	31.2	21.3	9.9	1.8	3.5	38.6	28.2	23.6	4.6	7.6	2.8
1954	73.4	32.8	31.2	19.8	11.4	-1.7	3.2	40.6	29.5	24.6	4.8	8.2	2.9
1955	88.0	45.2	36.0	19.5	16.5	5.7	3.5	42.8	31.1	25.8	5.2	8.6	3.1
1956	99.4	52.3	40.4	25.6	14.7	7.5	4.4	47.1	34.3	28.6	5.7	9.2	3.5
1957	99.6	48.8	41.3	26.9	14.5	3.3	4.2	50.8	37.2	31.2	6.1	9.7	3.9
1958	90.8	37.5	40.1	28.2	11.9	-5.4	2.9	53.3	39.4	33.1	6.3	9.9	4.0
1959	106.1	50.7	43.6	26.1	17.5	3.3	3.8	55.4	41.0	34.3	6.7	10.2	4.2
1960	111.3	54.7	43.3	26.3	16.9	7.1	4.3	56.6	41.6	34.6	7.0	10.6	4.4
1961	114.3	56.1	49.3	31.9	17.4	2.6	4.3	58.2	42.6	35.4	7.2	10.9	4.7
1962	124.9	64.3	56.7	33.5	23.2	2.4	5.2	60.6	44.1	36.6	7.5	11.5	5.0
1963	133.2	69.8	58.8	33.1	25.7	5.3	5.7	63.3	45.9	38.1	7.8	12.1	5.4
1964	143.4	77.0	69.7	40.5	29.2	0.9	6.4	66.4	48.3	40.0	8.3	12.3	5.7
1965	158.5	87.7	78.0	42.7	35.3	3.2	6.5	70.7	51.9	42.9	8.9	12.6	6.2
1966	168.7	92.3	82.3	44.3	38.0	2.3	7.8	76.5	56.5	46.9	9.6	13.1	6.9
1967	170.6	87.6	89.9	54.2	35.8	-9.3	7.0	82.9	61.6	51.2	10.4	13.9	7.5
1968	182.0	91.6	86.6	52.5	34.1	-2.4	7.5	90.4	67.4	56.1	11.3	14.7	8.3
1969	198.4	99.3	82.7	52.5	30.3	8.6	8.0	99.2	74.5	61.9	12.6	15.4	9.3
1970	192.8	84.5	92.9	69.4	23.4	-15.5	7.1	108.3	81.7	68.2	13.5	16.1	10.6
1971	209.2	91.5	113.7	80.4	32.9	-28.7	6.5	117.8	89.5	74.6	14.9	16.5	11.8
1972	237.3	110.1	119.4	77.5	42.2	-24.9	15.6	127.2	97.7	81.2	16.5	16.6	12.8
1973	292.2	151.4	147.5	102.9	44.6	-11.8	15.7	140.8	109.5	90.6	18.8	17.0	14.3
1974	301.8	138.1	143.3	114.2	29.1	-14.5	9.3	163.7	127.8	106.1	21.7	18.2	17.7
1975	296.9	106.5	174.6	125.9	48.7	-70.6	2.5	190.4	150.4	125.8	24.7	19.7	20.2
1976	342.0	133.8	180.1	122.8	57.3	-53.7	7.4	208.2	165.5	138.5	27.1	21.4	21.3
1977	396.7	164.9	197.9	125.3	72.6	-46.1	13.1	231.8	186.1	155.5	30.7	23.0	22.6
1978	476.3	214.9	225.2	142.4	82.8	-28.9	18.7	261.4	212.0	176.4	35.5	25.0	24.5
1979	533.2	234.3	235.3	157.5	77.8	-14.0	13.0	298.9	244.5	203.5	41.0	27.0	27.5
1980	542.7	198.6	246.5	196.3	50.2	-56.6	8.8	344.1	282.3	235.4	46.9	30.0	31.8
1981	646.1	252.7	301.9	236.7	65.2	-56.8	7.6	393.3	323.2	271.2	52.1	33.8	36.3
1982	621.5	187.9	325.4	263.9	61.5	-135.3	-2.2	433.5	356.4	300.7	55.8	37.6	39.5
1983	602.4	151.3	322.6	226.9	95.7	-176.2	4.9	451.1	369.5	311.4	58.1	40.7	40.9
1984	753.4	279.0	426.5	296.3	130.3	-171.5	23.9	474.3	387.5	326.0	61.5	44.5	42.3
1985	738.4	232.9	389.2	253.6	135.6	-178.6	22.4	505.4	412.8	348.0	64.8	48.0	44.6
1986	709.3	170.8	344.7	246.5	98.3	-194.6	20.7	538.5	439.1	369.9	69.2	51.6	47.8
1987	782.3	211.2	348.5	223.4	125.1	-149.3	12.0	571.1	464.5	390.3	74.1	55.2	51.4
1988	901.5	290.5	411.7	256.6	155.1	-138.4	17.2	611.0	497.1	417.6	79.5	59.1	54.8
1989	924.1	272.7	386.5	265.0	121.5	-133.9	20.1	651.5	529.6	444.4	85.2	63.3	58.5
1990	917.6	226.4	396.7	276.7	120.0	-176.4	6.2	691.2	560.4	469.8	90.6	67.7	63.0
1991	951.3	227.0	451.2	313.2	138.0	-218.4	-5.8	724.4	585.4	490.6	94.8	72.0	66.9
1992	932.3	187.9	491.8	348.1	159.5	-302.5	-1.4	744.4	599.9	500.9	99.0	74.6	69.9
1993	958.4	180.4	461.6	285.4	169.7	-280.2	-0.9	778.0	626.4	521.2	105.2	77.8	73.8
1994	1 094.7	275.5	487.7	270.7	199.4	-220.4	8.2	819.2	661.0	549.4	111.5	80.1	78.1
1995	1 219.0	349.6	546.6	286.3	243.9	-206.2	9.2	869.5	704.6	586.0	118.7	81.7	83.1
1996	1 344.4	431.8	557.1	281.1	272.3	-148.2	23.0	912.5	743.4	619.2	124.2	81.9	87.2
1997	1 525.7	561.9	585.7	280.4	308.2	-60.1	36.3	963.8	789.7	658.5	131.2	82.5	91.6
1998	1 654.4	633.9	553.4	341.5	212.6	33.6	46.9	1 020.5	841.6	702.1	139.5	82.8	96.2
1999	1 708.0	613.6	473.0	207.8	260.1	98.8	41.8	1 094.4	907.2	756.8	150.4	85.0	102.1
2000	1 800.1	615.8	389.4	213.1	176.3	185.2	41.3	1 184.3	986.8	824.3	162.5	87.8	109.7
2001	1 695.7	439.4	414.9	204.9	210.0	40.5	-15.9	1 256.2	1 051.6	876.5	175.1	88.6	116.0
2002	1 560.9	255.9	562.8	282.2	280.6	-252.8	-54.1	1 305.0	1 094.0	908.5	185.5	89.2	121.8
2003	1 552.8	198.7	613.9	289.8	309.2	-376.4	-38.8	1 354.1	1 135.9	935.4	200.5	90.8	127.3
2004	1 724.2	291.4	679.2	303.7	390.5	-379.5	-8.4	1 432.8	1 200.9	978.7	222.2	94.8	137.1
2005	1 903.4	362.0	619.1	127.7	486.4	-283.0	25.9	1 541.4	1 290.8	1 045.7	245.1	100.4	150.1
2006	2 174.4	513.7	666.5	235.0	430.3	-203.8	51.0	1 660.7	1 391.4	1 123.3	268.1	106.6	162.7
2007	2 040.2	280.2	495.0	178.9	322.4	-236.5	21.7	1 760.0	1 469.6	1 188.5	281.1	112.6	177.9
2008	1 824.1	-23.0	659.8	286.4	378.3	-642.6	-40.2	1 847.1	1 536.2	1 252.3	283.9	119.8	191.2
2009	1 508.4	-355.6	888.3	464.9	418.4	-1 224.7	-19.2	1 864.0	1 538.8	1 257.7	281.0	125.6	199.6
2007													
1st quarter	2 036.1	309.3	477.4	209.1	293.3	-200.9	32.8	1 726.7	1 443.1	1 164.8	278.3	110.2	173.4
2nd quarter	2 096.8	347.4	533.8	183.5	350.3	-221.3	34.9	1 749.4	1 461.4	1 180.6	280.8	111.7	176.3
3rd quarter	2 028.7	257.5	495.9	169.4	326.5	-258.8	20.3	1 771.2	1 478.7	1 196.4	282.3	113.2	179.2
4th quarter	1 999.3	206.5	472.9	153.5	319.4	-265.0	-1.3	1 792.8	1 495.1	1 212.2	282.9	115.2	182.4
2008													
1st quarter	1 903.5	89.9	543.4	126.3	417.1	-433.5	-20.1	1 813.6	1 510.6	1 228.1	282.6	117.2	185.8
2nd quarter	1 780.1	-55.5	767.0	374.4	392.6	-796.9	-25.5	1 835.6	1 527.0	1 244.1	282.9	119.6	188.9
3rd quarter	1 842.4	-15.8	709.0	235.7	473.2	-665.7	-59.0	1 858.2	1 544.4	1 260.3	284.0	121.0	192.8
4th quarter	1 770.5	-110.5	619.7	409.2	230.5	-674.1	-56.1	1 881.0	1 562.6	1 276.8	285.8	121.2	197.2
2009													
1st quarter	1 595.3	-288.3	717.4	403.1	294.2	-969.1	-36.6	1 883.6	1 561.3	1 277.0	284.4	122.5	199.8
2nd quarter	1 530.7	-333.3	960.2	595.7	364.5	-1 268.9	-24.6	1 864.0	1 540.5	1 259.4	281.1	124.0	199.5
3rd quarter	1 401.7	-449.0	919.5	431.5	488.0	-1 353.6	-14.9	1 850.7	1 525.5	1 246.9	278.6	126.1	199.1
4th quarter	1 505.9	-351.7	956.0	429.3	526.7	-1 307.2	-0.5	1 857.7	1 527.7	1 247.6	280.1	130.0	200.0

¹Includes wage accruals less disbursements, not shown separately.

Table 5-1. Saving and Investment—*Continued*

(Billions of dollars, except as noted; quarterly data are at seasonally adjusted annual rates.)

NIPA Tables 1.7.5, 5.1

Year and quarter	Gross domestic investment, capital account transactions, and net lending, NIPAs							Net domestic investment	Gross national income	Gross saving as a percent of gross national income	Net saving as a percent of gross national income
	Total	Gross domestic investment			Capital account transactions, net	Net lending or net borrowing (-), NIPAs	Statistical discrepancy				
		Total	Private	Government							
1950	62.0	63.9	54.1	9.8	. . .	-1.8	1.4	33.9	293.8	20.6	10.4
1951	78.7	77.8	60.2	17.6	. . .	0.9	3.6	44.0	337.6	22.2	12.2
1952	76.9	76.3	54.0	22.3	. . .	0.6	2.7	40.0	357.5	20.7	10.6
1953	79.1	80.4	56.4	24.0	. . .	-1.3	4.0	41.8	377.3	19.9	9.7
1954	76.5	76.3	53.8	22.5	. . .	0.2	3.1	35.7	379.3	19.3	8.6
1955	90.4	90.0	69.0	21.0	. . .	0.4	2.4	47.2	414.8	21.2	10.9
1956	97.6	94.9	72.0	22.9	. . .	2.7	-1.8	47.8	442.0	22.5	11.8
1957	99.5	94.8	70.5	24.4	. . .	4.7	-0.1	44.0	464.2	21.5	10.5
1958	91.8	91.0	64.5	26.5	. . .	0.8	1.0	37.7	468.8	19.4	8.0
1959	106.6	107.8	78.5	29.3	. . .	-1.3	0.5	52.4	508.9	20.8	10.0
1960	110.3	107.2	78.9	28.3	. . .	3.2	-1.0	50.6	530.5	21.0	10.3
1961	113.7	109.5	78.2	31.3	. . .	4.2	-0.6	51.3	548.9	20.8	10.2
1962	125.2	121.4	88.1	33.3	. . .	3.8	0.3	60.9	589.4	21.2	10.9
1963	132.3	127.4	93.8	33.6	. . .	4.9	-0.8	64.1	623.1	21.4	10.9
1964	144.2	136.7	102.1	34.6	. . .	7.5	0.8	70.3	667.8	21.5	11.5
1965	160.0	153.8	118.2	35.6	. . .	6.2	1.5	83.1	722.9	21.9	12.1
1966	174.9	171.1	131.3	39.8	. . .	3.8	6.2	94.6	786.6	21.5	11.7
1967	175.1	171.6	128.6	43.0	. . .	3.5	4.5	88.6	833.3	20.5	10.5
1968	186.4	184.8	141.2	43.6	. . .	1.5	4.3	94.4	911.6	20.0	10.1
1969	201.3	199.7	156.4	43.3	. . .	1.6	2.9	100.5	987.7	20.1	10.0
1970	199.7	196.0	152.4	43.6	. . .	3.7	6.9	87.6	1 037.8	18.6	8.1
1971	220.2	219.9	178.2	41.8	. . .	0.3	11.0	102.2	1 123.4	18.6	8.1
1972	246.2	250.2	207.6	42.6	. . .	-4.0	8.9	123.1	1 237.5	19.2	8.9
1973	300.2	291.3	244.5	46.8	. . .	8.9	8.0	150.6	1 386.9	21.1	10.9
1974	311.6	305.7	249.4	56.3	. . .	6.0	9.8	142.0	1 505.2	20.1	9.2
1975	313.2	293.3	230.2	63.1	. . .	19.8	16.3	102.9	1 634.4	18.2	6.5
1976	365.4	358.4	292.0	66.4	. . .	7.1	23.5	150.2	1 818.0	18.8	7.4
1977	417.9	428.8	361.3	67.5	. . .	-10.9	21.2	197.1	2 029.2	19.6	8.1
1978	502.4	515.0	438.0	77.1	. . .	-12.6	26.1	253.6	2 289.3	20.8	9.4
1979	580.2	581.4	492.9	88.5	. . .	-1.2	47.0	282.4	2 547.2	20.9	9.2
1980	588.0	579.5	479.3	100.3	. . .	8.5	45.3	235.4	2 777.0	19.5	7.2
1981	682.6	679.3	572.4	106.9	. . .	3.4	36.6	285.9	3 123.2	20.7	8.1
1982	626.2	629.5	517.2	112.3	-0.1	-3.2	4.8	196.0	3 285.0	18.9	5.7
1983	652.1	687.2	564.3	122.9	-0.1	-35.0	49.7	236.0	3 522.0	17.1	4.3
1984	784.9	875.0	735.6	139.4	-0.1	-89.9	31.5	400.6	3 935.6	19.1	7.1
1985	780.7	895.0	736.2	158.8	-0.2	-114.1	42.3	389.5	4 201.7	17.6	5.5
1986	777.1	919.7	746.5	173.2	-0.2	-142.5	67.7	381.3	4 409.9	16.1	3.9
1987	815.1	969.2	785.0	184.3	-0.2	-153.9	32.9	398.1	4 721.1	16.6	4.5
1988	892.0	1 007.7	821.6	186.1	-0.4	-115.4	-9.5	396.7	5 133.3	17.6	5.7
1989	980.3	1 072.6	874.9	197.7	-0.2	-92.2	56.1	421.2	5 452.0	17.0	5.0
1990	1 001.8	1 076.7	861.0	215.7	6.7	-81.6	84.2	385.5	5 750.8	16.0	3.9
1991	1 031.0	1 023.2	802.9	220.3	4.6	3.2	79.7	298.8	5 942.3	16.0	3.8
1992	1 042.3	1 087.9	864.8	223.1	-0.8	-44.8	110.0	343.5	6 261.5	14.9	3.0
1993	1 094.2	1 172.8	953.3	219.4	1.5	-80.0	135.8	394.8	6 562.7	14.6	2.7
1994	1 203.5	1 318.2	1 097.3	220.9	1.9	-116.6	108.8	499.0	7 000.4	15.6	3.9
1995	1 271.6	1 376.6	1 144.0	232.6	1.1	-106.2	52.5	507.2	7 391.8	16.5	4.7
1996	1 370.3	1 484.4	1 240.2	244.2	0.9	-115.1	25.9	571.9	7 844.2	17.1	5.5
1997	1 511.7	1 641.0	1 388.7	252.4	1.2	-130.6	-14.0	677.2	8 369.8	18.2	6.7
1998	1 569.1	1 773.6	1 510.8	262.9	1.0	-205.5	-85.3	753.1	8 896.1	18.6	7.1
1999	1 637.0	1 928.9	1 641.5	287.4	5.2	-297.1	-71.1	834.5	9 452.4	18.1	6.5
2000	1 666.2	2 076.5	1 772.2	304.3	1.4	-411.7	-134.0	892.2	10 123.2	17.8	6.1
2001	1 592.3	1 984.0	1 661.9	322.0	-11.7	-380.0	-103.4	727.7	10 441.4	16.2	4.2
2002	1 538.9	1 990.4	1 647.0	343.5	1.8	-453.4	-22.1	685.4	10 713.5	14.6	2.4
2003	1 569.4	2 085.5	1 729.7	355.8	3.8	-519.9	16.6	731.4	11 194.2	13.9	1.8
2004	1 716.3	2 340.9	1 968.6	372.4	-1.1	-623.5	-7.8	908.2	11 966.8	14.4	2.4
2005	1 823.7	2 564.2	2 172.2	392.0	-11.1	-729.5	-79.7	1 022.9	12 815.2	14.9	2.8
2006	1 953.8	2 752.2	2 327.2	425.1	4.2	-802.6	-220.6	1 091.6	13 691.9	15.9	3.8
2007	2 025.4	2 750.0	2 288.5	461.6	2.2	-726.8	-14.8	990.0	14 208.2	14.4	2.0
2008	1 925.2	2 632.4	2 136.1	496.3	-0.4	-706.8	101.0	785.3	14 482.3	12.6	-0.2
2009	1 712.5	2 142.6	1 628.8	513.8	3.0	-433.1	209.2	278.6	14 152.1	10.7	-2.5
2007											
1st quarter	1 914.9	2 714.3	2 267.2	447.1	2.5	-801.8	-121.1	987.5	13 980.7	14.6	2.2
2nd quarter	1 999.7	2 762.3	2 302.0	460.2	0.8	-763.3	-97.1	1 012.9	14 170.4	14.8	2.5
3rd quarter	2 093.6	2 778.4	2 311.9	466.6	2.8	-687.6	64.9	1 007.2	14 253.4	14.2	1.8
4th quarter	2 093.3	2 745.2	2 272.9	472.3	2.7	-654.6	94.0	952.4	14 428.2	13.9	1.4
2008											
1st quarter	1 973.2	2 690.7	2 214.8	475.9	2.8	-720.3	69.8	877.1	14 475.1	13.2	0.6
2nd quarter	1 906.8	2 660.2	2 164.6	495.5	3.0	-756.4	126.7	824.6	14 499.9	12.3	-0.4
3rd quarter	1 910.6	2 647.8	2 142.7	505.0	-11.6	-725.5	68.3	789.6	14 639.2	12.6	-0.1
4th quarter	1 909.9	2 530.9	2 022.1	508.9	4.0	-625.1	139.4	650.0	14 314.9	12.4	-0.8
2009											
1st quarter	1 780.8	2 190.3	1 689.9	500.4	3.1	-412.6	185.4	306.7	14 092.5	11.3	-2.0
2nd quarter	1 692.4	2 082.0	1 561.5	520.4	3.0	-392.5	161.7	218.0	14 082.1	10.9	-2.4
3rd quarter	1 654.9	2 080.4	1 556.1	524.3	2.9	-428.4	253.3	229.7	14 110.4	9.9	-3.2
4th quarter	1 742.1	2 217.8	1 707.8	510.0	2.9	-478.6	236.2	360.1	14 323.3	10.5	-2.5

. . . = Not available.

Table 5-2. Gross Private Fixed Investment by Type

(Billions of dollars, quarterly data are at seasonally adjusted annual rates.)   **NIPA Table 5.3.5**

Year and quarter	Total gross private fixed investment	Nonresidential Total	Structures Total	Commercial and health care	Manufacturing	Power and communication	Mining exploration, shafts, and wells	Other nonresidential structures	Equipment and software Total	Information processing equipment and software Total	Computers and peripheral equipment
1950	48.3	27.8	10.0	1.8	1.1	2.8	1.4	2.9	17.8	1.8	. . .
1951	50.3	31.8	12.0	1.9	2.1	3.0	1.7	3.2	19.9	2.1	. . .
1952	50.5	31.9	12.2	1.6	2.3	3.1	2.0	3.3	19.7	2.4	. . .
1953	54.5	35.1	13.6	2.1	2.2	3.6	2.1	3.5	21.5	2.7	. . .
1954	55.8	34.7	13.9	2.6	2.0	3.3	2.3	3.6	20.8	2.4	. . .
1955	64.0	39.0	15.2	3.4	2.3	3.3	2.5	3.7	23.9	2.8	. . .
1956	68.1	44.5	18.2	4.2	3.2	4.1	2.7	4.0	26.3	3.4	. . .
1957	69.7	47.5	19.0	4.1	3.6	4.5	2.6	4.1	28.6	4.0	. . .
1958	64.9	42.5	17.6	4.2	2.4	4.4	2.4	4.2	24.9	3.6	. . .
1959	74.6	46.5	18.1	4.6	2.1	4.3	2.5	4.7	28.4	4.0	0.0
1960	75.7	49.4	19.6	4.8	2.9	4.4	2.3	5.2	29.8	4.9	0.2
1961	75.2	48.8	19.7	5.5	2.8	4.1	2.3	5.0	29.1	5.3	0.3
1962	82.0	53.1	20.8	6.2	2.8	4.1	2.5	5.2	32.3	5.7	0.3
1963	88.1	56.0	21.2	6.1	2.9	4.4	2.3	5.6	34.8	6.5	0.7
1964	97.2	63.0	23.7	6.8	3.6	4.8	2.4	6.2	39.2	7.4	0.9
1965	109.0	74.8	28.3	8.2	5.1	5.4	2.4	7.2	46.5	8.5	1.2
1966	117.7	85.4	31.3	8.3	6.6	6.3	2.5	7.8	54.0	10.7	1.7
1967	118.7	86.4	31.5	8.2	6.0	7.1	2.4	7.8	54.9	11.3	1.9
1968	132.1	93.4	33.6	9.4	6.0	8.3	2.6	7.3	59.9	11.9	1.9
1969	147.3	104.7	37.7	11.7	6.8	8.7	2.8	7.8	67.0	14.6	2.4
1970	150.4	109.0	40.3	12.5	7.0	10.2	2.8	7.8	68.7	16.6	2.7
1971	169.9	114.1	42.7	14.9	6.3	11.0	2.7	7.9	71.5	17.3	2.8
1972	198.5	128.8	47.2	17.6	5.9	12.1	3.1	8.6	81.7	19.5	3.5
1973	228.6	153.3	55.0	19.8	7.9	13.8	3.5	9.9	98.3	23.1	3.5
1974	235.4	169.5	61.2	20.6	10.0	15.1	5.2	10.3	108.2	27.0	3.9
1975	236.5	173.7	61.4	17.7	10.6	15.7	7.4	10.1	112.4	28.5	3.6
1976	274.8	192.4	65.9	18.1	10.1	18.2	8.6	11.0	126.4	32.7	4.4
1977	339.0	228.7	74.6	20.3	11.1	19.3	11.5	12.5	154.1	39.2	5.7
1978	412.2	280.6	93.6	25.3	16.2	21.4	15.4	15.2	187.0	48.7	7.6
1979	474.9	333.9	117.7	33.5	22.0	24.6	19.0	18.5	216.2	58.5	10.2
1980	485.6	362.4	136.2	41.0	20.5	27.3	27.4	20.0	226.2	68.8	12.5
1981	542.6	420.0	167.3	48.3	25.4	30.0	42.5	21.2	252.7	81.5	17.1
1982	532.1	426.5	177.6	55.8	26.1	29.6	44.8	21.3	248.9	88.3	18.9
1983	570.1	417.2	154.3	55.8	19.5	25.8	30.0	23.3	262.9	100.1	23.9
1984	670.2	489.6	177.4	70.6	20.9	26.5	31.3	28.1	312.2	121.5	31.6
1985	714.4	526.2	194.5	84.1	24.1	26.5	27.9	31.8	331.7	130.3	33.7
1986	739.9	519.8	176.5	80.9	21.0	28.3	15.7	30.7	343.3	136.8	33.4
1987	757.8	524.1	174.2	80.8	21.2	25.4	13.1	33.7	349.9	141.2	35.8
1988	803.1	563.8	182.8	86.3	23.2	25.0	15.7	32.5	381.0	154.9	38.0
1989	847.3	607.7	193.7	88.3	28.8	27.5	14.9	34.3	414.0	172.6	43.1
1990	846.4	622.4	202.9	87.5	33.6	26.3	17.9	37.6	419.5	177.2	38.6
1991	803.3	598.2	183.6	68.9	31.4	31.6	18.5	33.2	414.6	182.9	37.7
1992	848.5	612.1	172.6	64.5	29.0	33.9	14.2	31.0	439.6	199.9	44.0
1993	932.5	666.6	177.2	69.4	23.6	33.2	16.6	34.5	489.4	217.6	47.9
1994	1 033.5	731.4	186.8	75.4	28.9	31.2	16.4	34.9	544.6	235.2	52.4
1995	1 112.9	810.0	207.3	83.1	35.5	33.1	15.0	40.6	602.8	263.0	66.1
1996	1 209.4	875.4	224.6	91.5	38.2	29.2	16.8	48.9	650.8	290.1	72.8
1997	1 317.7	968.6	250.3	104.3	37.6	28.8	22.4	57.2	718.3	330.3	81.4
1998	1 447.1	1 061.1	275.1	116.0	40.5	34.2	22.3	62.2	786.0	366.1	87.9
1999	1 580.7	1 154.9	283.9	125.4	35.1	40.4	18.3	64.7	871.0	417.1	97.2
2000	1 717.7	1 268.7	318.1	139.3	37.6	48.1	23.7	69.4	950.5	478.2	103.2
2001	1 700.2	1 227.8	329.7	137.3	37.8	51.1	34.6	68.9	898.1	452.5	87.6
2002	1 634.9	1 125.4	282.8	119.4	22.7	51.0	30.2	59.3	842.7	419.8	79.7
2003	1 713.3	1 135.7	281.9	115.1	21.4	48.1	38.4	58.9	853.8	430.9	77.6
2004	1 903.6	1 223.0	306.7	125.3	23.7	42.8	51.9	62.9	916.4	455.3	80.2
2005	2 122.3	1 347.3	351.8	135.9	29.9	45.2	77.1	63.7	995.6	475.3	78.9
2006	2 267.2	1 505.3	433.7	156.4	35.1	53.3	114.2	74.6	1 071.7	505.2	84.9
2007	2 269.1	1 640.2	535.4	181.9	45.3	74.8	142.5	90.9	1 104.8	537.4	89.2
2008	2 170.8	1 693.6	609.5	185.2	60.8	94.4	165.9	103.3	1 084.1	562.9	86.7
2009	1 749.7	1 388.8	480.0	138.4	75.9	95.4	87.5	82.7	908.8	522.7	75.0
2007											
1st quarter	2 254.1	1 574.1	489.5	173.9	38.0	63.4	134.0	80.2	1 084.6	525.1	88.8
2nd quarter	2 278.6	1 623.5	519.9	180.1	41.0	70.7	139.2	88.9	1 103.5	530.1	86.9
3rd quarter	2 280.8	1 665.2	556.1	185.0	48.9	78.2	149.3	94.8	1 109.1	538.4	88.2
4th quarter	2 263.0	1 697.9	575.9	188.4	53.4	86.9	147.5	99.7	1 122.0	555.8	93.1
2008											
1st quarter	2 223.0	1 705.0	586.3	188.2	53.8	91.9	150.8	101.7	1 118.7	566.3	93.7
2nd quarter	2 214.0	1 719.7	610.6	189.7	57.1	96.5	162.0	105.3	1 109.2	576.2	92.9
3rd quarter	2 179.7	1 711.0	620.4	186.5	61.5	95.9	171.6	104.9	1 090.6	568.8	84.3
4th quarter	2 066.6	1 638.7	620.7	176.3	70.7	93.2	179.2	101.3	1 018.0	540.2	75.8
2009											
1st quarter	1 817.2	1 442.6	533.1	159.2	80.3	90.9	110.7	92.0	909.5	508.3	71.1
2nd quarter	1 737.7	1 391.8	494.8	147.6	84.4	97.9	76.5	88.5	897.0	512.2	72.0
3rd quarter	1 712.6	1 353.9	457.9	130.9	74.3	97.1	76.1	79.4	895.9	519.0	72.5
4th quarter	1 731.4	1 366.9	434.1	116.0	64.6	95.7	86.8	71.0	932.8	551.3	84.6

. . . = Not available.

Table 5-2. Gross Private Fixed Investment by Type—*Continued*

(Billions of dollars, quarterly data are at seasonally adjusted annual rates.)   **NIPA Table 5.3.5**

Year and quarter	Nonresidential—*Continued*					Residential						
	Equipment and software—*Continued*											
	Information processing equipment and software—*Continued*		Industrial equipment	Transportation equipment	Other nonresidential equipment	Total	Residential structures					Residential equipment
							Total	Permanent site			Other residential structures	
	Software [1]	Other information processing						Total	Single family	Multifamily		
1950	...	1.8	4.5	6.4	5.1	20.5	20.2	16.1	...	...	4.0	0.4
1951	...	2.1	5.7	6.6	5.5	18.4	18.1	13.8	...	...	4.3	0.4
1952	...	2.4	5.9	5.7	5.6	18.6	18.2	13.4	...	...	4.9	0.4
1953	...	2.7	6.7	6.6	5.6	19.4	19.0	13.9	...	...	5.1	0.4
1954	...	2.4	7.1	6.0	5.3	21.1	20.7	15.4	...	...	5.3	0.4
1955	...	2.8	7.3	7.5	6.3	25.0	24.6	18.6	...	...	6.0	0.4
1956	...	3.4	8.8	7.4	6.7	23.6	23.1	16.5	...	...	6.6	0.5
1957	...	4.0	9.6	8.3	6.7	22.2	21.7	15.1	...	...	6.6	0.5
1958	...	3.6	8.2	6.1	6.9	22.3	21.9	15.4	13.1	2.3	6.4	0.5
1959	0.0	4.0	8.5	8.3	7.6	28.1	27.5	19.7	16.7	3.0	7.9	0.6
1960	0.1	4.6	9.4	8.5	7.1	26.3	25.8	17.5	14.9	2.6	8.3	0.5
1961	0.2	4.8	8.8	8.0	7.0	26.4	25.9	17.4	14.1	3.3	8.5	0.5
1962	0.2	5.1	9.3	9.8	7.5	29.0	28.4	19.9	15.1	4.8	8.5	0.5
1963	0.4	5.4	10.0	9.4	8.8	32.1	31.5	22.4	16.0	6.4	9.1	0.6
1964	0.5	5.9	11.4	10.6	9.9	34.3	33.6	24.1	17.6	6.4	9.5	0.6
1965	0.7	6.7	13.7	13.2	11.0	34.2	33.5	23.8	17.8	6.0	9.7	0.7
1966	1.0	8.0	16.2	14.5	12.7	32.3	31.6	21.8	16.6	5.2	9.8	0.7
1967	1.2	8.2	16.9	14.3	12.4	32.4	31.6	21.5	16.8	4.7	10.1	0.7
1968	1.3	8.7	17.3	17.6	13.0	38.7	37.9	26.7	19.5	7.2	11.1	0.9
1969	1.8	10.4	19.1	18.9	14.4	42.6	41.6	29.2	19.7	9.5	12.4	1.0
1970	2.3	11.6	20.3	16.2	15.6	41.4	40.2	27.1	17.5	9.5	13.2	1.1
1971	2.4	12.2	19.5	18.4	16.3	55.8	54.5	38.7	25.8	12.9	15.8	1.3
1972	2.8	13.2	21.4	21.8	19.0	69.7	68.1	50.1	32.8	17.2	18.0	1.5
1973	3.2	16.3	26.0	26.6	22.6	75.3	73.6	54.6	35.2	19.4	19.0	1.7
1974	3.9	19.2	30.7	26.3	24.3	66.0	64.1	43.4	29.7	13.7	20.7	1.9
1975	4.8	20.2	31.3	25.2	27.4	62.7	60.8	36.3	29.6	6.7	24.5	1.9
1976	5.2	23.1	34.1	30.0	29.6	82.5	80.4	50.8	43.9	6.9	29.6	2.1
1977	5.5	28.0	39.4	39.3	36.3	110.3	107.9	72.2	62.2	10.0	35.7	2.4
1978	6.3	34.8	47.7	47.3	43.2	131.6	128.9	85.6	72.8	12.8	43.3	2.7
1979	8.1	40.2	56.2	53.6	47.9	141.0	137.8	89.3	72.3	17.0	48.6	3.2
1980	9.8	46.4	60.7	48.4	48.3	123.2	119.8	69.6	52.9	16.7	50.2	3.4
1981	11.8	52.5	65.5	50.6	55.2	122.6	118.9	69.4	52.0	17.5	49.5	3.6
1982	14.0	55.3	62.7	46.8	51.2	105.7	102.0	57.0	41.5	15.5	45.0	3.7
1983	16.4	59.8	58.9	53.5	50.4	152.9	148.6	95.0	72.5	22.4	53.7	4.2
1984	20.4	69.6	68.1	64.4	58.1	180.6	175.9	114.6	86.4	28.2	61.3	4.7
1985	23.8	72.9	72.5	69.0	59.9	188.2	183.1	115.9	87.4	28.5	67.2	5.1
1986	25.6	77.7	75.4	70.5	60.7	220.1	214.6	135.2	104.1	31.0	79.4	5.5
1987	29.0	76.4	76.7	68.1	63.9	233.7	227.9	142.7	117.2	25.5	85.2	5.8
1988	34.2	82.8	84.2	72.9	69.0	239.3	233.2	142.4	120.1	22.3	90.9	6.1
1989	41.9	87.6	93.3	67.9	80.2	239.5	233.4	143.2	120.9	22.3	90.1	6.1
1990	47.6	90.9	92.1	70.0	80.2	224.0	218.0	132.1	112.9	19.3	85.8	6.0
1991	53.7	91.5	89.3	71.5	70.8	205.1	199.4	114.6	99.4	15.1	84.8	5.7
1992	57.9	98.1	93.0	74.7	72.0	236.3	230.4	135.1	122.0	13.1	95.3	5.9
1993	64.3	105.4	102.2	89.4	80.2	266.0	259.9	150.9	140.1	10.8	109.0	6.1
1994	68.3	114.6	113.6	107.7	88.1	302.1	295.9	176.4	162.3	14.1	119.5	6.2
1995	74.6	122.3	129.0	116.1	94.7	302.9	296.5	171.4	153.5	17.9	125.1	6.3
1996	85.5	131.9	136.5	123.2	101.0	334.1	327.7	191.1	170.8	20.3	136.6	6.3
1997	107.5	141.4	140.4	135.5	112.1	349.1	342.8	198.1	175.2	22.9	144.7	6.3
1998	126.0	152.2	147.4	147.1	125.4	385.9	379.2	224.0	199.4	24.6	155.3	6.7
1999	157.3	162.5	149.1	174.4	130.4	425.8	418.5	251.3	223.8	27.4	167.2	7.3
2000	184.5	190.6	162.9	170.8	138.6	449.0	441.2	265.0	236.8	28.3	176.1	7.8
2001	186.6	178.4	151.9	154.2	139.5	472.4	464.4	279.4	249.1	30.3	185.0	8.0
2002	183.0	157.0	141.7	141.6	139.6	509.5	501.3	298.8	265.9	33.0	202.4	8.2
2003	191.3	162.0	142.6	132.9	147.5	577.6	569.1	345.7	310.6	35.1	223.4	8.5
2004	205.7	169.4	142.0	161.1	157.9	680.6	671.4	417.5	377.6	39.9	253.9	9.2
2005	218.0	178.4	159.6	181.7	178.9	775.0	765.2	480.8	433.5	47.3	284.4	9.8
2006	229.8	190.6	178.4	198.2	189.8	761.9	751.6	468.8	416.0	52.8	282.8	10.3
2007	245.6	202.5	193.2	181.7	192.6	629.0	618.6	354.1	305.2	49.0	264.5	10.4
2008	264.1	212.1	193.8	132.3	195.1	477.2	467.2	229.9	185.8	44.2	237.3	10.0
2009	244.2	203.5	150.1	72.5	163.5	361.0	351.7	135.2	105.4	29.8	216.5	9.2
2007												
1st quarter	238.3	197.9	182.1	192.3	185.2	680.0	669.6	393.5	339.8	53.7	276.1	10.4
2nd quarter	242.6	200.6	198.8	183.0	191.6	655.1	644.8	373.5	324.0	49.6	271.2	10.3
3rd quarter	246.7	203.6	199.0	176.5	195.2	615.6	605.3	345.0	298.0	47.0	260.3	10.3
4th quarter	254.8	208.0	192.9	175.1	198.2	565.2	554.8	304.6	259.1	45.5	250.2	10.4
2008												
1st quarter	263.2	209.5	195.3	164.3	192.7	518.1	507.9	265.5	220.5	44.9	242.4	10.2
2nd quarter	268.0	215.3	197.3	143.8	192.0	494.2	484.0	243.3	197.4	45.9	240.7	10.2
3rd quarter	266.4	218.1	194.8	125.9	201.1	468.6	458.7	220.7	176.0	44.7	238.0	10.0
4th quarter	258.7	205.6	187.9	95.3	194.7	427.8	418.3	190.3	149.1	41.1	228.0	9.5
2009												
1st quarter	240.5	196.7	157.8	65.4	178.0	374.6	365.2	149.4	111.8	37.5	215.9	9.4
2nd quarter	240.2	200.1	151.4	70.6	162.7	345.9	336.8	125.8	93.1	32.7	211.1	9.1
3rd quarter	241.4	205.1	146.5	73.2	157.2	358.8	349.6	132.1	105.2	26.9	217.5	9.1
4th quarter	254.6	212.2	144.6	80.9	156.0	364.5	355.3	133.7	111.7	22.1	221.5	9.3

[1] Excludes software "embedded," or bundled, in computers and other equipment.
. . . = Not available.

Table 5-3. Real Gross Private Fixed Investment by Type

(Billions of chained [2005] dollars, quarterly data are at seasonally adjusted annual rates.)   **NIPA Table 5.3.6**

Year and quarter	Total gross private fixed investment	Nonresidential									
		Total	Structures						Equipment and software		
			Total	Commercial and health care	Manufac-turing	Power and communi-cation	Mining exploration, shafts, and wells	Other non-residential structures	Total	Information processing equipment and software	
										Total	Computers and peripheral equipment [1]
1995	1 235.7	792.2	342.0	126.7	51.7	45.4	52.6	59.2	493.0	149.5	. . .
1996	1 346.5	866.2	361.4	136.5	54.4	39.0	56.1	69.6	545.4	179.1	. . .
1997	1 470.8	970.8	387.9	150.8	51.9	37.6	66.0	79.0	620.4	220.8	. . .
1998	1 630.4	1 087.4	407.7	160.2	53.7	44.2	57.7	83.2	710.4	271.1	. . .
1999	1 782.1	1 200.9	408.2	166.1	44.8	52.1	48.8	83.3	810.9	332.0	. . .
2000	1 913.8	1 318.5	440.0	177.2	46.2	60.1	61.0	85.8	895.8	391.9	. . .
2001	1 877.6	1 281.8	433.3	168.6	44.9	62.0	71.9	81.7	866.9	390.2	. . .
2002	1 798.1	1 180.2	356.6	142.8	26.2	60.5	52.6	68.9	830.3	379.3	. . .
2003	1 856.2	1 191.0	343.0	133.8	24.3	55.7	60.0	66.5	851.4	405.0	. . .
2004	1 992.5	1 263.0	346.7	137.1	25.5	46.2	69.9	67.4	917.3	443.1	. . .
2005	2 122.3	1 347.3	351.8	135.9	29.9	45.2	77.1	63.7	995.6	475.3	. . .
2006	2 171.3	1 453.9	384.0	144.2	33.0	48.7	88.3	69.6	1 069.6	514.8	. . .
2007	2 126.3	1 544.3	441.4	158.5	40.4	65.3	97.1	80.8	1 097.0	555.7	. . .
2008	2 018.4	1 569.7	486.8	155.6	50.6	77.3	112.7	89.8	1 068.6	588.8	. . .
2009	1 648.2	1 291.0	390.3	115.2	61.5	76.7	65.9	73.2	890.7	556.7	. . .
1998											
1st quarter	1 561.6	1 041.6	392.0	153.6	54.8	39.1	60.1	78.4	679.6	254.4	. . .
2nd quarter	1 616.0	1 079.7	413.1	161.7	54.4	45.1	59.9	83.8	700.4	265.3	. . .
3rd quarter	1 646.8	1 096.0	413.2	159.7	53.0	48.1	58.6	84.8	714.6	274.0	. . .
4th quarter	1 697.1	1 132.2	412.6	165.9	52.6	44.4	52.3	85.7	747.0	290.6	. . .
1999											
1st quarter	1 728.6	1 158.4	410.9	164.6	49.0	51.3	47.1	84.6	771.3	306.6	. . .
2nd quarter	1 769.0	1 190.9	405.9	166.0	44.8	47.4	50.0	85.4	803.4	329.4	. . .
3rd quarter	1 810.2	1 225.1	405.6	166.7	43.7	53.3	46.7	81.2	834.3	344.6	. . .
4th quarter	1 820.4	1 229.0	410.4	166.9	41.7	56.4	51.5	82.0	834.6	347.6	. . .
2000											
1st quarter	1 873.7	1 274.7	418.4	168.1	43.4	56.7	54.3	84.6	870.7	370.9	. . .
2nd quarter	1 920.8	1 321.7	435.7	175.8	47.4	56.2	60.2	86.2	901.6	389.9	. . .
3rd quarter	1 927.5	1 336.3	452.1	181.5	46.8	63.1	63.3	87.7	903.7	397.0	. . .
4th quarter	1 933.3	1 341.5	454.0	183.3	47.3	64.3	66.1	84.5	907.1	409.7	. . .
2001											
1st quarter	1 921.8	1 328.7	441.5	181.7	50.4	53.5	71.7	79.3	904.2	409.1	. . .
2nd quarter	1 891.7	1 293.8	443.0	175.0	47.5	63.6	73.7	79.0	870.9	392.1	. . .
3rd quarter	1 871.9	1 272.5	445.5	163.3	45.6	63.1	76.5	93.4	849.2	381.7	. . .
4th quarter	1 824.9	1 232.2	403.2	154.3	36.2	67.8	65.6	75.2	843.3	377.7	. . .
2002											
1st quarter	1 808.7	1 203.4	381.4	151.5	30.4	68.9	51.8	71.3	832.9	375.8	. . .
2nd quarter	1 801.5	1 183.9	360.7	144.6	27.2	61.4	50.1	70.8	830.5	379.0	. . .
3rd quarter	1 798.4	1 177.8	344.7	139.5	23.9	55.3	54.5	67.2	837.3	385.9	. . .
4th quarter	1 783.9	1 155.6	339.6	135.6	23.4	56.3	53.9	66.4	820.4	376.8	. . .
2003											
1st quarter	1 784.1	1 150.4	336.2	130.8	22.6	60.7	54.1	64.3	818.3	386.0	. . .
2nd quarter	1 829.7	1 181.4	346.3	132.3	24.7	57.8	60.7	68.2	839.5	391.1	. . .
3rd quarter	1 888.7	1 208.3	345.6	135.6	24.9	53.1	62.6	67.3	865.7	412.5	. . .
4th quarter	1 922.4	1 224.0	343.9	136.6	25.0	51.1	62.7	66.5	882.0	430.4	. . .
2004											
1st quarter	1 918.6	1 214.3	341.9	134.6	24.4	50.3	65.8	65.7	874.4	431.4	. . .
2nd quarter	1 977.7	1 247.0	345.9	139.8	23.7	43.1	70.6	68.4	902.5	438.6	. . .
3rd quarter	2 019.7	1 281.2	349.4	139.5	24.9	44.5	71.7	68.5	932.5	446.7	. . .
4th quarter	2 053.9	1 309.6	349.7	134.6	28.9	47.0	71.4	67.3	959.8	455.6	. . .
2005											
1st quarter	2 079.2	1 321.5	356.0	136.9	30.1	46.5	76.6	65.6	965.6	462.0	. . .
2nd quarter	2 116.0	1 340.8	354.6	136.3	29.2	45.1	81.2	62.8	986.0	471.2	. . .
3rd quarter	2 143.0	1 359.7	347.2	134.5	29.8	44.1	76.1	62.6	1 012.5	481.5	. . .
4th quarter	2 151.0	1 367.3	349.3	136.0	30.4	44.9	74.4	63.9	1 018.2	486.4	. . .
2006											
1st quarter	2 200.2	1 424.9	364.8	139.1	30.9	48.6	80.5	65.7	1 060.7	505.7	. . .
2nd quarter	2 189.9	1 450.3	383.7	143.6	33.2	46.9	89.3	70.0	1 066.3	508.9	. . .
3rd quarter	2 162.2	1 466.0	393.2	147.5	34.8	48.8	90.9	70.7	1 072.0	520.4	. . .
4th quarter	2 132.9	1 474.5	394.6	146.5	32.8	50.3	92.3	72.0	1 079.3	524.1	. . .
2007											
1st quarter	2 118.8	1 489.6	409.2	153.5	34.5	56.1	93.0	71.8	1 078.1	540.2	. . .
2nd quarter	2 137.7	1 530.3	430.7	158.3	37.0	62.2	94.4	79.4	1 095.2	546.9	. . .
3rd quarter	2 135.6	1 565.8	456.8	160.9	43.5	68.0	100.8	84.2	1 101.3	558.2	. . .
4th quarter	2 113.0	1 591.3	469.1	161.3	46.4	74.7	100.2	87.9	1 113.3	577.5	. . .
2008											
1st quarter	2 079.2	1 598.9	476.8	160.6	46.3	78.0	103.5	89.3	1 111.9	591.7	. . .
2nd quarter	2 064.8	1 604.4	493.2	161.1	48.8	80.4	111.0	91.9	1 097.7	601.3	. . .
3rd quarter	2 020.4	1 579.2	493.1	156.6	51.1	77.3	116.0	90.9	1 071.0	594.5	. . .
4th quarter	1 909.3	1 496.1	484.0	144.0	56.2	73.3	120.4	87.2	993.7	567.6	. . .
2009											
1st quarter	1 687.5	1 321.2	419.4	129.2	63.2	71.7	78.0	79.3	887.5	537.5	. . .
2nd quarter	1 631.9	1 288.4	400.0	121.6	67.4	78.3	58.2	77.8	876.5	544.8	. . .
3rd quarter	1 626.7	1 269.0	380.2	111.1	61.8	78.9	59.4	71.4	879.8	554.9	. . .
4th quarter	1 646.6	1 285.5	361.7	99.0	53.5	77.9	68.2	64.3	918.9	589.7	. . .

[1]See notes and definitions.
. . . = Not available.

Table 5-3. Real Gross Private Fixed Investment by Type—*Continued*

(Billions of chained [2005] dollars, quarterly data are at seasonally adjusted annual rates.)   NIPA Table 5.3.6

Year and quarter	Nonresidential—*Continued*					Residential						
	Equipment and software—*Continued*						Residential structures					Residential equipment
	Information processing equipment and software—*Continued*		Industrial equipment	Transportation equipment	Other non-residential equipment	Total	Total	Total	Permanent site			
	Software 2	Other information processing							Total	Single family	Multifamily	Other residential structures
1995	66.9	93.7	145.5	131.5	110.6	456.1	450.1	268.7	240.2	28.3	180.9	5.9
1996	78.5	102.7	150.9	136.8	114.8	492.5	486.8	293.9	262.4	31.3	192.6	5.9
1997	101.7	111.5	154.1	148.2	125.9	501.8	496.3	295.5	261.6	33.7	200.2	5.8
1998	122.8	125.5	160.8	162.0	138.8	540.4	534.5	323.5	290.1	33.4	210.6	6.2
1999	151.5	139.9	161.8	190.3	142.4	574.2	567.5	347.6	311.5	36.0	219.8	6.9
2000	172.4	168.4	175.8	186.2	150.4	580.0	572.6	350.4	315.0	35.4	222.1	7.4
2001	173.7	163.2	162.8	169.6	149.3	583.3	575.6	352.5	315.4	36.9	223.1	7.6
2002	173.4	148.4	151.9	154.2	148.2	613.8	605.9	366.6	327.7	38.9	239.0	7.9
2003	185.6	156.4	151.6	140.4	155.0	664.3	655.9	402.5	362.6	39.9	253.2	8.4
2004	204.6	168.1	147.4	162.3	164.4	729.5	720.1	449.1	406.1	43.0	271.0	9.4
2005	218.0	178.4	159.6	181.7	178.9	775.0	765.2	480.8	433.5	47.3	284.4	9.8
2006	227.1	191.2	172.9	196.5	185.5	718.2	708.1	438.8	391.1	47.6	269.3	10.2
2007	241.5	202.3	180.9	177.4	184.1	585.0	575.0	327.1	283.9	42.8	248.4	10.1
2008	257.0	211.1	174.7	128.9	180.3	451.1	441.5	217.4	179.7	36.4	224.7	9.8
2009	240.6	202.4	133.6	66.1	145.1	358.7	349.6	135.8	108.9	25.6	214.3	9.2
1998												
1st quarter	115.1	122.0	163.4	148.7	136.8	517.5	511.8	306.1	272.0	33.9	205.1	6.0
2nd quarter	119.1	124.5	162.0	155.4	140.7	533.0	527.1	316.4	283.9	32.4	210.3	6.2
3rd quarter	125.0	125.5	158.7	163.8	139.9	549.0	543.0	330.7	297.4	33.3	212.2	6.3
4th quarter	132.2	130.1	159.2	180.2	137.7	562.2	556.0	340.9	307.2	33.8	215.0	6.5
1999												
1st quarter	138.6	132.3	159.0	181.9	142.4	565.5	559.1	344.5	309.6	34.9	214.7	6.6
2nd quarter	148.6	139.0	161.2	187.7	140.3	571.6	564.9	343.9	308.4	35.5	220.8	6.9
3rd quarter	156.9	144.3	163.4	199.3	141.9	576.4	569.4	346.8	309.5	37.2	222.4	7.1
4th quarter	161.9	144.0	163.7	192.2	145.0	583.4	576.4	355.2	318.6	36.5	221.3	7.1
2000												
1st quarter	167.5	159.3	171.5	190.7	149.1	588.0	580.7	359.2	323.9	35.4	221.6	7.3
2nd quarter	172.1	166.2	176.0	193.1	152.5	584.0	576.6	354.8	318.8	36.0	221.8	7.4
3rd quarter	172.5	170.4	179.2	185.4	150.1	573.7	566.3	343.5	309.2	34.4	222.5	7.4
4th quarter	177.7	177.6	176.4	175.5	150.0	574.2	566.6	344.0	308.0	35.9	222.4	7.5
2001												
1st quarter	179.1	172.3	176.8	170.4	152.2	576.8	569.3	348.7	312.1	36.5	220.5	7.5
2nd quarter	175.0	163.7	164.3	171.5	148.0	584.9	577.4	354.9	318.1	36.7	222.4	7.5
3rd quarter	172.9	160.3	157.4	164.5	150.6	588.1	580.5	356.5	319.6	36.8	223.9	7.6
4th quarter	167.7	156.7	152.9	171.8	146.3	583.1	575.2	349.7	311.9	37.7	225.3	7.8
2002												
1st quarter	169.2	149.2	154.2	163.1	144.5	598.7	590.8	355.3	316.6	38.5	235.1	7.9
2nd quarter	173.7	149.6	150.2	155.1	149.6	613.4	605.4	366.6	327.2	39.3	238.5	7.9
3rd quarter	177.6	149.3	152.0	152.7	149.3	616.9	609.1	370.2	331.0	39.1	238.6	7.9
4th quarter	173.2	145.5	151.2	145.9	149.2	626.4	618.4	374.4	335.8	38.6	243.7	7.9
2003												
1st quarter	177.2	148.8	150.4	131.5	151.2	632.4	624.5	382.4	342.9	39.4	242.0	8.0
2nd quarter	179.1	151.8	156.2	142.5	151.5	646.8	638.5	387.5	348.2	39.3	250.8	8.3
3rd quarter	189.4	159.5	152.0	144.0	157.8	679.8	671.1	408.2	367.6	40.6	262.7	8.7
4th quarter	196.6	165.7	148.0	143.7	159.6	698.2	689.3	432.0	391.6	40.4	257.5	8.9
2004												
1st quarter	199.1	166.0	141.9	142.5	158.2	704.5	695.4	434.6	393.9	40.7	260.8	9.1
2nd quarter	200.4	169.9	145.2	156.8	161.7	731.0	721.7	448.9	406.5	42.4	272.8	9.3
3rd quarter	206.6	168.7	149.7	169.0	167.2	738.4	728.9	456.3	412.0	44.3	272.6	9.5
4th quarter	212.5	167.8	152.7	181.1	170.6	744.2	734.5	456.7	412.0	44.7	277.8	9.7
2005												
1st quarter	213.4	174.9	156.2	174.3	173.2	757.7	748.1	469.7	423.9	45.8	278.4	9.6
2nd quarter	218.6	176.3	154.4	180.1	180.3	775.3	765.6	477.6	430.2	47.3	288.1	9.7
3rd quarter	219.9	181.7	160.7	189.7	180.5	783.3	773.5	483.9	435.9	48.1	289.6	9.7
4th quarter	220.1	180.6	167.2	182.7	181.7	783.5	773.5	492.1	444.1	48.0	281.3	10.0
2006												
1st quarter	222.4	192.2	165.1	202.6	187.3	775.2	764.9	490.3	442.4	47.9	274.5	10.3
2nd quarter	224.8	189.8	176.2	194.1	187.0	740.1	730.0	456.9	409.4	47.5	273.0	10.1
3rd quarter	228.5	191.9	174.7	193.7	183.4	697.4	687.3	421.4	374.6	46.8	265.9	10.1
4th quarter	232.8	191.0	175.6	195.5	184.3	660.2	650.2	386.6	338.0	48.2	263.9	10.1
2007												
1st quarter	235.0	198.4	172.4	188.2	178.3	631.7	621.6	362.0	314.0	47.5	260.1	10.2
2nd quarter	238.9	200.3	186.9	178.1	183.7	610.4	600.4	345.9	301.6	43.9	255.0	10.0
3rd quarter	242.6	203.1	185.9	171.8	186.4	572.9	562.9	319.3	277.9	41.0	244.2	10.1
4th quarter	249.6	207.4	178.6	171.5	188.0	525.0	515.0	281.3	242.1	38.7	234.3	10.2
2008												
1st quarter	257.3	209.2	179.3	161.9	182.3	483.2	473.3	246.7	208.6	37.3	227.4	10.1
2nd quarter	260.3	214.2	178.6	141.0	180.9	462.9	453.0	227.8	189.1	37.5	225.9	10.1
3rd quarter	258.3	216.7	173.7	121.7	185.4	443.3	433.7	209.8	171.8	36.6	224.6	9.8
4th quarter	252.2	204.3	167.2	90.9	172.6	415.0	405.8	185.4	149.4	34.3	221.0	9.4
2009												
1st quarter	235.5	195.8	140.8	59.8	157.3	367.9	358.9	146.6	112.9	31.5	212.9	9.2
2nd quarter	236.2	199.1	135.2	62.7	144.0	344.4	335.5	126.5	96.3	28.1	209.5	8.9
3rd quarter	239.2	203.9	130.4	66.0	140.1	359.6	350.5	134.9	110.4	23.6	216.1	9.3
4th quarter	251.5	210.7	128.0	76.1	139.1	362.9	353.5	135.3	116.2	19.1	218.7	9.6

2Excludes software "embedded," or bundled, in computers and other equipment.

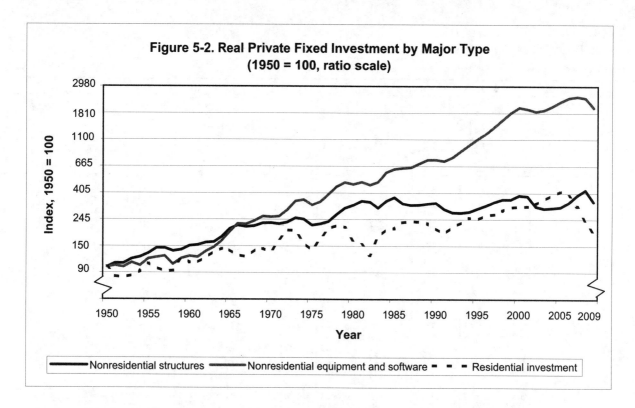

Figure 5-2. Real Private Fixed Investment by Major Type
(1950 = 100, ratio scale)

- Between 1950 and 2006, which was the recent high point for real investment, the quantity of real gross private fixed investment increased ninefold, with an average annual growth rate of 4.0 percent. Every major type of investment grew in real terms between those two years, but as Figure 5-2 indicates, by far the fastest-growing category has been nonresidential equipment and software, which includes computers, other information processing equipment, and computer software. (Table 5-4)

- Between 2006 and 2009, however, investment fell 24 percent in real terms, a collapse unprecedented in the postwar period. Nonresidential structures fell 20 percent, equipment and software 19 percent, and residential investment in 2009 was more than 50 percent below its volume in 2005. Single-family home construction was down 75 percent. (Table 5-4)

Table 5-4. Chain-Type Quantity Indexes for Private Fixed Investment by Type

(Index numbers, 2005 = 100, quarterly data are seasonally adjusted.)   NIPA Table 5.3.3

Year and quarter	Total gross private fixed investment	Nonresidential									
			Structures						Equipment and software		
		Total	Total	Commercial and health care	Manufac-turing	Power and communi-cation	Mining exploration, shafts, and wells	Other non-residential structures	Total	Information processing equipment and software	
										Total	Computers and peripheral equipment
1950	11.4	8.1	32.5	13.8	36.3	55.6	41.0	47.5	4.5	0.1	. . .
1951	10.9	8.5	34.9	13.2	63.9	55.8	43.1	46.5	4.6	0.2	. . .
1952	10.7	8.4	34.8	10.3	68.2	56.3	47.9	46.7	4.5	0.2	. . .
1953	11.5	9.1	37.9	14.1	65.2	61.9	52.4	48.4	4.9	0.2	. . .
1954	11.7	8.9	39.2	17.6	61.0	56.6	57.9	51.0	4.6	0.2	. . .
1955	13.2	9.9	42.0	22.9	66.8	53.8	62.3	51.1	5.2	0.2	. . .
1956	13.2	10.5	46.4	25.9	87.8	62.9	60.3	50.6	5.4	0.2	. . .
1957	13.1	10.6	46.4	24.6	93.1	65.3	56.9	50.6	5.5	0.3	. . .
1958	12.2	9.5	43.9	25.9	64.2	62.8	53.2	52.9	4.7	0.2	. . .
1959	13.9	10.2	44.9	28.1	57.2	60.2	54.6	58.5	5.3	0.3	0.0
1960	14.0	10.8	48.5	29.9	77.6	60.8	51.3	64.9	5.5	0.3	0.0
1961	13.9	10.7	49.2	34.1	75.9	57.0	52.2	63.4	5.4	0.4	0.0
1962	15.2	11.7	51.4	38.0	76.7	57.3	54.8	64.7	6.0	0.4	0.0
1963	16.4	12.3	52.0	36.8	76.9	61.1	51.4	68.5	6.5	0.5	0.0
1964	17.9	13.8	57.4	40.0	92.5	66.6	55.1	75.1	7.4	0.5	0.0
1965	19.8	16.2	66.6	46.9	127.9	73.6	54.4	84.5	8.7	0.6	0.0
1966	20.9	18.2	71.1	45.8	158.9	84.0	51.6	87.6	10.1	0.9	0.0
1967	20.5	18.0	69.3	44.0	139.8	91.9	49.3	85.8	10.0	0.9	0.0
1968	22.0	18.8	70.3	48.2	134.6	102.1	49.6	75.8	10.7	1.0	0.0
1969	23.3	20.2	74.1	55.6	141.6	102.1	51.7	75.2	11.6	1.2	0.0
1970	22.8	20.1	74.3	56.3	136.7	111.7	48.6	70.7	11.5	1.3	0.0
1971	24.6	20.1	73.1	61.5	112.9	112.6	45.0	66.3	11.6	1.4	0.0
1972	27.5	21.9	75.4	67.2	98.6	117.4	48.3	67.0	13.1	1.6	0.0
1973	30.0	25.1	81.5	70.3	122.2	125.0	51.5	72.2	15.5	1.9	0.0
1974	28.2	25.3	79.8	65.9	139.2	117.0	61.3	66.1	15.9	2.2	0.0
1975	25.1	22.8	71.4	51.3	133.5	107.6	71.5	58.3	14.4	2.2	0.0
1976	27.6	23.9	73.1	50.6	123.3	117.3	77.2	61.2	15.3	2.5	0.0
1977	31.6	26.6	76.1	53.3	126.6	115.5	87.2	64.5	17.6	3.0	0.1
1978	35.4	30.6	87.1	60.7	168.8	121.0	99.4	73.3	20.3	3.9	0.1
1979	37.4	33.7	98.1	72.4	207.4	125.6	105.9	80.5	22.0	4.7	0.2
1980	35.0	33.6	103.8	79.6	173.5	126.8	148.8	78.2	21.2	5.5	0.3
1981	35.8	35.5	112.2	86.2	197.0	130.0	173.0	75.7	22.1	6.4	0.5
1982	33.2	34.2	110.3	93.9	190.2	122.8	159.9	71.4	21.0	6.9	0.6
1983	35.7	33.7	98.4	91.1	137.6	105.6	132.4	75.4	22.1	8.0	0.9
1984	41.7	39.7	112.1	110.9	142.3	107.9	150.5	88.3	26.5	10.2	1.5
1985	43.9	42.3	120.1	128.1	159.2	106.7	134.1	97.2	28.2	11.3	1.8
1986	44.4	41.1	106.9	119.0	133.8	113.9	78.6	91.3	28.7	12.2	2.1
1987	44.6	41.1	103.9	114.6	130.4	101.3	76.8	96.8	29.1	13.0	2.7
1988	46.1	43.2	104.5	118.1	137.6	95.5	84.2	90.2	31.3	14.5	3.1
1989	47.5	45.7	106.6	116.6	164.9	99.2	76.2	92.1	33.6	16.5	3.7
1990	46.5	45.9	108.2	112.0	186.7	92.3	88.0	97.8	33.6	17.3	3.7
1991	43.5	43.4	96.2	87.0	172.0	109.6	86.1	84.8	32.7	18.2	4.0
1992	46.1	44.8	90.4	80.8	157.9	116.2	71.2	78.6	35.1	21.0	5.4
1993	50.0	48.7	89.8	84.1	124.0	108.6	82.8	84.8	39.5	23.8	7.0
1994	54.7	53.2	91.4	88.0	146.8	98.4	80.5	83.0	44.2	26.8	8.7
1995	58.2	58.8	97.2	93.2	173.1	100.5	68.3	92.9	49.5	31.5	13.1
1996	63.4	64.3	102.7	100.4	182.0	86.5	72.8	109.2	54.8	37.7	18.9
1997	69.3	72.1	110.3	111.0	173.8	83.3	85.6	123.9	62.3	46.5	27.4
1998	76.8	80.7	115.9	117.9	179.7	97.8	74.9	130.5	71.4	57.0	39.8
1999	84.0	89.1	116.0	122.2	149.9	115.4	63.4	130.7	81.5	69.9	56.6
2000	90.2	97.9	125.1	130.4	154.6	133.1	79.1	134.6	90.0	82.4	68.6
2001	88.5	95.1	123.2	124.0	150.3	137.3	93.3	128.2	87.1	82.1	70.3
2002	84.7	87.6	101.4	105.1	87.7	133.9	68.2	108.2	83.4	79.8	73.7
2003	87.5	88.4	97.5	98.4	81.3	123.3	77.9	104.4	85.5	85.2	80.3
2004	93.9	93.7	98.6	100.9	85.3	102.3	90.6	105.8	92.1	93.2	89.5
2005	100.0	100.0	100.0	100.0	100.0	100.0	100.0	100.0	100.0	100.0	100.0
2006	102.3	107.9	109.2	106.1	110.3	107.8	114.5	109.2	107.4	108.3	123.1
2007	100.2	114.6	125.5	116.6	135.0	144.5	126.0	126.8	110.2	116.9	144.9
2008	95.1	116.5	138.4	114.5	169.3	171.1	146.3	140.9	107.3	123.9	157.0
2009	77.7	95.8	111.0	84.8	205.7	169.9	85.6	114.8	89.5	117.1	148.6
2007											
1st quarter	99.8	110.6	116.3	112.9	115.5	124.3	120.7	112.7	108.3	113.7	137.5
2nd quarter	100.7	113.6	122.4	116.5	123.7	137.7	122.6	124.6	110.0	115.1	138.7
3rd quarter	100.6	116.2	129.9	118.4	145.6	150.6	130.7	132.1	110.6	117.5	145.7
4th quarter	99.6	118.1	133.3	118.6	155.4	165.5	130.0	138.0	111.8	121.5	157.7
2008											
1st quarter	98.0	118.7	135.6	118.1	155.0	172.8	134.3	140.2	111.7	124.5	164.9
2nd quarter	97.3	119.1	140.2	118.6	163.2	178.0	144.0	144.2	110.3	126.5	167.0
3rd quarter	95.2	117.2	140.2	115.2	171.0	171.1	150.6	142.6	107.6	125.1	154.5
4th quarter	90.0	111.0	137.6	106.0	188.0	162.4	156.3	136.8	99.8	119.4	141.7
2009											
1st quarter	79.5	98.1	119.2	95.0	211.3	158.8	101.2	124.4	89.1	113.1	136.2
2nd quarter	76.9	95.6	113.7	89.4	225.7	173.5	75.5	122.1	88.0	114.6	141.6
3rd quarter	76.6	94.2	108.1	81.8	206.9	174.8	77.1	112.0	88.4	116.7	144.9
4th quarter	77.6	95.4	102.8	72.8	179.1	172.6	88.5	100.9	92.3	124.1	171.7

. . . = Not available.

Table 5-4. Chain-Type Quantity Indexes for Private Fixed Investment by Type—*Continued*

(Index numbers, 2005 = 100, quarterly data are seasonally adjusted.) NIPA Table 5.3.3

Year and quarter	Nonresidential—*Continued*					Residential						
	Equipment and software—*Continued*						Residential structures					Residential equipment
	Information processing equipment and software—*Continued*		Industrial equipment	Transportation equipment	Other nonresidential equipment	Total	Total	Permanent site			Other residential structures	
	Software [1]	Other information processing						Total	Single family	Multifamily		
1950	...	2.1	23.7	17.8	19.6	24.1	24.8	33.0	...	...	12.3	6.4
1951	...	2.4	26.6	17.1	19.7	20.1	20.7	26.4	...	...	12.1	5.9
1952	...	2.7	27.7	14.2	19.9	19.8	20.3	24.8	...	...	13.5	5.9
1953	...	3.0	30.5	16.8	19.5	20.5	21.1	25.6	...	...	14.0	6.2
1954	...	2.7	31.4	14.7	18.3	22.2	22.8	28.2	...	...	14.6	6.4
1955	...	3.1	31.2	18.8	21.5	25.8	26.5	33.3	...	...	16.1	7.3
1956	...	3.6	34.4	16.9	22.2	23.7	24.3	28.8	...	...	17.3	8.0
1957	...	4.1	34.9	18.0	21.0	22.2	22.8	26.2	...	...	17.4	8.1
1958	...	3.6	29.1	13.1	21.3	22.5	23.0	26.9	25.1	38.8	17.0	8.6
1959	0.0	3.9	29.5	17.4	22.8	28.2	28.9	34.3	31.9	49.9	20.6	9.9
1960	0.0	4.5	31.8	17.9	21.0	26.2	26.8	30.3	28.2	43.9	21.5	9.2
1961	0.1	4.8	30.1	17.0	20.8	26.2	26.9	30.1	26.8	55.3	21.9	9.3
1962	0.1	5.1	31.6	20.9	22.1	28.8	29.5	34.3	28.5	80.4	22.0	9.8
1963	0.1	5.3	34.2	20.2	25.7	32.1	33.0	38.9	30.5	107.9	23.8	11.0
1964	0.2	5.8	38.6	22.9	28.5	34.0	34.9	41.6	33.4	107.2	24.6	11.8
1965	0.2	6.6	45.5	28.7	31.7	33.0	33.8	39.7	32.7	96.4	24.6	13.1
1966	0.4	7.7	52.4	31.6	35.6	30.1	30.7	34.9	29.1	80.8	24.2	13.4
1967	0.4	7.8	52.6	30.5	33.6	29.1	29.7	33.2	28.5	70.2	24.1	13.8
1968	0.5	8.0	51.5	36.7	34.1	33.1	33.7	39.1	31.3	101.4	25.3	16.4
1969	0.6	9.3	55.0	38.2	36.4	34.1	34.6	40.2	29.8	126.1	25.9	18.7
1970	0.8	10.0	55.8	31.3	37.9	32.0	32.4	36.3	25.9	123.4	26.2	20.4
1971	0.9	10.1	51.2	33.8	37.8	40.8	41.4	49.0	35.9	157.1	29.8	22.9
1972	1.0	10.7	55.2	39.3	42.9	48.1	48.7	59.3	42.7	196.7	32.7	27.4
1973	1.2	13.0	65.3	47.2	50.1	47.8	48.3	59.0	41.7	202.2	31.9	30.8
1974	1.3	14.3	70.3	42.8	49.4	37.9	38.1	42.7	32.0	130.2	31.1	31.4
1975	1.6	13.8	59.6	36.8	45.8	33.0	33.1	32.7	29.2	58.1	33.7	29.2
1976	1.7	15.1	59.9	41.0	46.2	40.7	41.0	42.9	40.7	56.3	38.2	30.8
1977	1.8	18.1	63.5	49.8	51.9	49.5	50.0	55.4	52.3	74.6	41.7	33.7
1978	2.1	21.6	70.6	55.0	57.2	52.6	53.1	57.9	54.0	84.0	45.8	36.6
1979	2.6	24.3	75.7	57.4	58.3	50.7	51.0	54.2	47.9	102.6	46.2	40.1
1980	3.1	26.1	72.4	46.9	52.4	40.0	40.0	38.1	31.5	91.9	43.1	40.2
1981	3.6	27.6	71.3	45.6	53.8	36.7	36.7	35.1	28.6	88.4	39.3	40.1
1982	4.2	27.8	65.1	40.4	46.6	30.1	29.8	27.4	22.0	72.0	33.9	38.6
1983	4.9	29.2	59.9	45.5	44.9	42.5	42.5	44.7	38.1	98.6	39.3	43.0
1984	6.2	33.3	68.6	54.2	50.8	48.8	48.9	52.6	44.3	120.5	43.4	47.7
1985	7.4	34.4	71.8	56.3	51.3	49.6	49.6	51.9	43.9	117.4	46.2	51.5
1986	8.3	35.8	71.4	54.2	50.4	55.7	55.7	57.9	50.2	120.9	52.6	55.7
1987	9.4	34.3	69.6	51.5	51.8	56.8	56.8	58.7	54.3	95.4	54.1	58.0
1988	11.2	36.7	73.1	54.3	54.3	56.2	56.2	56.6	53.6	81.4	55.7	59.9
1989	14.5	38.3	78.2	48.9	60.6	54.5	54.4	55.2	52.1	81.2	53.4	60.2
1990	17.1	39.3	73.7	48.6	58.3	49.8	49.6	49.9	47.3	70.8	49.5	58.4
1991	19.3	39.1	69.0	47.3	49.8	45.0	44.8	42.9	41.5	54.6	47.8	56.2
1992	22.7	41.4	70.3	48.2	49.6	51.3	51.1	50.1	50.4	46.4	53.0	57.9
1993	25.4	44.7	76.2	57.1	54.3	55.5	55.4	53.4	55.2	37.4	58.6	59.0
1994	27.9	48.8	83.0	66.9	58.6	60.8	60.9	59.8	61.0	48.3	62.7	59.4
1995	30.7	52.5	91.1	72.4	61.8	58.9	58.8	55.9	55.4	59.9	63.6	60.2
1996	36.0	57.5	94.5	75.3	64.2	63.6	63.6	61.1	60.5	66.2	67.7	59.9
1997	46.6	62.5	96.5	81.6	70.4	64.8	64.9	61.5	60.3	71.3	70.4	59.4
1998	56.3	70.4	100.7	89.2	77.5	69.7	69.9	67.3	66.9	70.5	74.1	63.8
1999	69.5	78.4	101.4	104.7	79.6	74.1	74.2	72.3	71.9	76.1	77.3	70.8
2000	79.1	94.4	110.1	102.5	84.1	74.8	74.8	72.9	72.7	74.8	78.1	75.8
2001	79.7	91.5	102.0	93.3	83.4	75.3	75.2	73.3	72.8	78.1	78.4	77.7
2002	79.6	83.2	95.1	84.9	82.8	79.2	79.2	76.3	75.6	82.2	84.0	80.8
2003	85.1	87.7	95.0	77.3	86.6	85.7	85.7	83.7	83.6	84.4	89.1	86.3
2004	93.9	94.2	92.3	89.3	91.9	94.1	94.1	93.4	93.7	90.9	95.3	95.7
2005	100.0	100.0	100.0	100.0	100.0	100.0	100.0	100.0	100.0	100.0	100.0	100.0
2006	104.2	107.2	108.3	108.1	103.7	92.7	92.5	91.3	90.2	100.7	94.7	103.8
2007	110.8	113.4	113.3	97.6	102.9	75.5	75.1	68.0	65.5	90.4	87.4	103.6
2008	117.9	118.3	109.4	70.9	100.7	58.2	57.7	45.2	41.5	77.0	79.0	100.5
2009	110.4	113.5	83.7	36.4	81.1	46.3	45.7	28.2	25.1	54.1	75.4	94.4
2007												
1st quarter	107.8	111.2	108.0	103.6	99.6	81.5	81.2	75.3	72.4	100.4	91.5	104.3
2nd quarter	109.6	112.3	117.1	98.0	102.7	78.8	78.5	71.9	69.6	92.8	89.7	102.6
3rd quarter	111.3	113.8	116.4	94.5	104.1	73.9	73.6	66.4	64.1	86.7	85.9	103.3
4th quarter	114.5	116.3	111.9	94.4	105.1	67.7	67.3	58.5	55.8	81.8	82.4	104.0
2008												
1st quarter	118.0	117.3	112.3	89.1	101.8	62.4	61.9	51.3	48.1	78.8	80.0	102.7
2nd quarter	119.4	120.1	111.9	77.6	101.1	59.7	59.2	47.4	43.6	79.3	79.5	103.7
3rd quarter	118.5	121.5	108.8	67.0	103.6	57.2	56.7	43.6	39.6	77.4	79.0	99.9
4th quarter	115.7	114.6	104.7	50.0	96.5	53.5	53.0	38.6	34.5	72.5	77.7	95.6
2009												
1st quarter	108.0	109.8	88.2	32.9	87.9	47.5	46.9	30.5	26.0	66.6	74.9	93.8
2nd quarter	108.4	111.6	84.7	34.5	80.5	44.4	43.9	26.3	22.2	59.5	73.7	91.4
3rd quarter	109.7	114.3	81.7	36.3	78.3	46.4	45.8	28.1	25.5	49.8	76.0	94.6
4th quarter	115.4	118.1	80.2	41.9	77.7	46.8	46.2	28.1	26.8	40.4	76.9	97.8

[1] Excludes software "embedded," or bundled, in computers and other equipment.
. . . = Not available.

Table 5-5. Current-Cost Net Stock of Fixed Assets

(Billions of dollars, year-end estimates.)

Year	Total	Private					Government				Private and government fixed assets			Government, by level	
		Total	Nonresidential			Resi-dential	Total	Nonresidential		Resi-dential	Nonresidential		Resi-dential	Federal	State and local
			Total	Equip-ment and software	Struc-tures			Equip-ment and software	Struc-tures		Equip-ment and software	Struc-tures			
1947	735.6	522.5	254.9	66.6	188.3	267.6	213.1	61.7	145.8	5.6	128.3	334.1	273.2	119.8	93.3
1948	781.1	567.8	279.5	81.3	198.3	288.3	213.3	51.9	156.5	5.0	133.1	354.7	293.2	111.8	101.5
1949	786.5	587.5	284.7	85.4	199.3	302.8	199.0	44.1	149.8	5.2	129.5	349.1	307.9	102.1	96.9
1950	873.0	662.7	322.8	99.6	223.3	339.9	210.2	40.3	163.6	6.4	139.8	386.9	346.3	101.0	109.2
1951	956.7	720.6	351.6	109.7	241.9	369.0	236.1	44.1	184.1	7.9	153.8	426.0	376.9	113.2	122.8
1952	1 011.1	758.2	370.5	115.5	255.0	387.8	252.9	50.5	194.9	7.4	166.0	449.9	395.1	122.7	130.1
1953	1 047.2	788.5	386.3	125.0	261.3	402.2	258.7	57.3	193.5	7.8	182.3	454.9	410.0	130.0	128.8
1954	1 094.2	820.1	396.3	128.7	267.6	423.8	274.1	63.9	199.7	10.5	192.6	467.3	434.3	139.7	134.5
1955	1 189.1	893.3	436.8	141.7	295.0	456.5	295.8	69.4	218.8	7.6	211.2	513.8	464.1	146.5	149.3
1956	1 289.8	961.1	482.5	159.1	323.4	478.6	328.7	74.0	245.8	8.9	233.1	569.2	487.5	159.4	169.3
1957	1 352.4	1 009.6	515.1	173.4	341.7	494.6	342.7	76.1	257.2	9.4	249.5	598.9	504.0	165.3	177.4
1958	1 394.4	1 033.6	524.1	178.8	345.2	509.6	360.8	77.8	272.8	10.2	256.6	618.0	519.8	171.3	189.5
1959	1 448.3	1 077.3	545.6	187.3	358.3	531.7	371.1	82.4	277.6	11.1	269.7	635.9	542.8	175.3	195.7
1960	1 493.9	1 109.2	556.7	193.4	363.2	552.6	384.6	85.2	287.7	11.7	278.6	650.9	564.3	179.5	205.1
1961	1 548.5	1 144.5	571.8	196.9	374.9	572.7	404.0	89.1	302.3	12.5	286.0	677.2	585.3	186.5	217.4
1962	1 616.2	1 186.0	592.2	204.6	387.6	593.8	430.1	96.4	320.3	13.4	301.0	707.9	607.2	197.4	232.7
1963	1 672.8	1 221.9	613.4	213.4	400.0	608.4	450.9	99.1	338.1	13.7	312.5	738.1	622.1	202.9	248.1
1964	1 780.1	1 307.0	649.6	226.5	423.1	657.4	473.2	102.0	356.7	14.6	328.4	779.8	671.9	208.5	264.7
1965	1 896.7	1 393.3	695.2	244.3	451.0	698.0	503.4	104.6	383.6	15.3	348.8	834.5	713.3	215.4	288.0
1966	2 055.3	1 511.4	756.6	272.3	484.3	754.9	543.9	109.3	418.1	16.4	381.6	902.4	771.3	225.7	318.2
1967	2 211.5	1 623.8	817.6	298.5	519.1	806.2	587.7	116.1	454.4	17.3	414.6	973.5	823.4	240.0	347.7
1968	2 427.5	1 789.4	898.7	329.5	569.2	890.7	638.1	120.7	498.0	19.4	450.2	1 067.2	910.1	252.2	385.9
1969	2 644.8	1 942.4	989.5	363.8	625.7	952.9	702.4	124.9	555.9	21.6	488.8	1 181.5	974.5	266.6	435.8
1970	2 879.4	2 097.8	1 089.1	399.6	689.5	1 008.7	781.6	131.0	627.5	23.0	530.7	1 317.0	1 031.8	284.5	497.1
1971	3 179.4	2 332.9	1 199.1	428.3	770.8	1 133.8	846.4	131.9	688.7	25.8	560.2	1 459.5	1 159.7	298.5	547.9
1972	3 495.9	2 573.2	1 305.4	462.0	843.5	1 267.8	922.7	134.1	759.7	28.9	596.0	1 603.1	1 296.7	321.8	600.8
1973	3 961.8	2 924.0	1 471.3	515.2	956.2	1 452.6	1 037.9	136.2	869.0	32.7	651.3	1 825.2	1 485.3	348.6	689.3
1974	4 720.4	3 445.1	1 792.1	635.3	1 156.8	1 653.0	1 275.3	149.5	1 089.2	36.6	784.8	2 246.0	1 689.6	402.1	873.2
1975	5 106.4	3 766.4	1 974.3	727.4	1 246.9	1 792.1	1 340.0	164.5	1 135.4	40.1	891.8	2 382.3	1 832.2	425.5	914.4
1976	5 566.6	4 150.0	2 160.9	805.3	1 355.6	1 989.1	1 416.5	178.5	1 193.3	44.7	983.8	2 548.9	2 033.9	461.3	955.2
1977	6 228.8	4 723.4	2 401.9	904.1	1 497.8	2 321.5	1 505.5	194.9	1 259.1	51.5	1 099.0	2 756.9	2 372.9	484.2	1 021.3
1978	7 051.2	5 404.6	2 727.3	1 033.1	1 694.2	2 677.3	1 646.6	207.9	1 379.2	59.5	1 240.9	3 073.4	2 736.8	522.6	1 124.0
1979	8 130.4	6 255.7	3 147.3	1 199.7	1 947.7	3 108.4	1 874.7	225.0	1 579.0	70.8	1 424.6	3 526.6	3 179.2	581.7	1 293.0
1980	9 264.9	7 118.5	3 613.8	1 392.6	2 221.2	3 504.7	2 146.5	251.4	1 817.4	77.7	1 644.0	4 038.6	3 582.3	645.6	1 500.8
1981	10 216.3	7 858.2	4 088.4	1 553.6	2 534.7	3 769.8	2 358.1	282.7	1 990.3	85.1	1 836.4	4 525.1	3 854.9	694.7	1 663.5
1982	10 777.7	8 288.5	4 348.0	1 646.8	2 701.2	3 940.5	2 489.2	307.6	2 091.4	90.2	1 954.4	4 792.6	4 030.7	733.5	1 755.6
1983	11 127.4	8 579.1	4 479.9	1 702.6	2 777.3	4 099.2	2 548.3	337.3	2 110.3	100.7	2 039.9	4 887.6	4 200.0	769.9	1 778.4
1984	11 726.3	9 077.6	4 746.9	1 796.8	2 950.1	4 330.6	2 648.7	361.3	2 182.9	104.5	2 158.1	5 133.0	4 435.1	809.0	1 839.7
1985	12 339.5	9 575.7	5 012.8	1 903.8	3 108.9	4 563.0	2 763.8	383.6	2 274.5	105.6	2 287.5	5 383.5	4 668.6	840.4	1 923.4
1986	13 112.6	10 178.7	5 250.6	2 010.7	3 239.9	4 928.1	2 933.9	411.7	2 412.6	109.5	2 422.4	5 652.6	5 037.6	883.6	2 050.3
1987	13 869.9	10 780.8	5 534.0	2 112.2	3 421.9	5 246.7	3 089.2	436.4	2 533.4	119.4	2 548.5	5 955.3	5 366.1	918.8	2 170.4
1988	14 709.6	11 461.1	5 888.1	2 238.6	3 649.5	5 573.0	3 248.4	470.7	2 642.7	135.0	2 709.4	6 292.2	5 708.0	975.1	2 273.3
1989	15 545.6	12 120.2	6 240.6	2 374.7	3 865.8	5 879.6	3 425.5	507.9	2 773.4	144.2	2 882.7	6 639.2	6 023.8	1 028.9	2 396.6
1990	16 275.3	12 677.5	6 570.5	2 506.7	4 063.8	6 107.0	3 597.8	550.8	2 898.1	148.9	3 057.5	6 961.9	6 255.9	1 076.8	2 521.0
1991	16 664.6	12 945.1	6 701.8	2 577.7	4 124.1	6 243.2	3 719.6	583.7	2 985.8	150.0	3 161.5	7 109.9	6 393.2	1 120.6	2 599.0
1992	17 377.9	13 495.6	6 909.9	2 650.3	4 259.6	6 585.7	3 882.3	612.9	3 110.6	158.8	3 263.2	7 370.2	6 744.5	1 167.3	2 715.1
1993	18 274.5	14 211.6	7 221.6	2 761.4	4 460.2	6 990.0	4 062.9	637.2	3 255.7	170.0	3 398.5	7 715.9	7 160.0	1 208.7	2 854.2
1994	19 382.2	15 088.8	7 602.8	2 911.5	4 691.3	7 486.0	4 293.4	665.5	3 446.4	181.5	3 577.0	8 137.8	7 667.5	1 259.7	3 033.7
1995	20 324.6	15 820.5	7 999.7	3 099.5	4 900.2	7 820.8	4 504.1	675.2	3 640.8	188.1	3 774.7	8 541.0	8 008.9	1 291.5	3 212.6
1996	21 315.9	16 635.4	8 382.4	3 261.8	5 120.6	8 253.0	4 680.5	675.0	3 809.1	196.4	3 936.8	8 929.7	8 449.4	1 315.0	3 365.5
1997	22 456.6	17 552.7	8 838.4	3 418.1	5 420.3	8 714.4	4 903.9	670.6	4 036.5	196.8	4 088.7	9 456.8	8 911.2	1 339.1	3 564.8
1998	23 732.7	18 627.9	9 342.4	3 607.9	5 734.4	9 285.5	5 104.8	677.8	4 220.3	206.8	4 285.7	9 954.7	9 492.3	1 361.2	3 743.6
1999	25 272.0	19 866.7	9 892.2	3 853.0	6 039.1	9 974.6	5 405.2	699.3	4 486.1	219.8	4 552.4	10 525.2	10 194.4	1 407.4	3 997.8
2000	26 961.2	21 240.5	10 572.8	4 133.6	6 439.2	10 667.7	5 720.7	703.7	4 785.5	231.5	4 837.3	11 224.6	10 899.3	1 435.3	4 285.4
2001	28 565.0	22 585.5	11 124.6	4 281.9	6 842.7	11 460.9	5 979.5	703.8	5 029.2	246.4	4 985.7	11 871.9	11 707.3	1 453.2	4 526.3
2002	30 003.6	23 749.9	11 552.2	4 376.9	7 175.4	12 197.7	6 253.7	716.5	5 277.1	260.1	5 093.3	12 452.5	12 457.8	1 482.6	4 771.1
2003	31 694.9	25 180.6	11 942.8	4 492.4	7 450.4	13 237.7	6 514.3	731.6	5 504.3	278.5	5 224.0	12 954.7	13 516.2	1 517.5	4 996.8
2004	35 010.4	27 746.8	12 922.0	4 697.9	8 224.1	14 824.8	7 263.6	767.4	6 190.2	306.0	5 465.3	14 414.3	15 130.8	1 640.7	5 622.8
2005	38 542.4	30 600.9	14 071.1	4 930.8	9 140.3	16 529.9	7 941.4	802.3	6 804.0	335.0	5 733.1	15 944.3	16 864.9	1 748.5	6 192.9
2006	41 651.6	32 870.9	15 188.9	5 243.0	9 945.9	17 682.0	8 780.8	850.1	7 581.8	348.9	6 093.1	17 527.7	18 030.8	1 866.9	6 913.8
2007	43 386.3	33 928.9	16 024.3	5 509.8	10 514.5	17 904.6	9 457.4	891.3	8 219.8	346.2	6 401.1	18 734.3	18 250.8	1 947.4	7 510.0
2008	43 580.9	34 260.8	17 181.8	5 792.1	11 389.7	17 079.0	9 320.2	959.4	8 027.1	333.6	6 751.6	19 416.7	17 412.6	1 943.2	7 377.0

Table 5-6. Chain-Type Quantity Indexes for Net Stock of Fixed Assets

(Index numbers, 2005 = 100.)

Year	Total	Private					Government				Private and government fixed assets			Government, by level	
		Total	Nonresidential			Residential	Total	Nonresidential		Residential	Nonresidential		Residential	Federal	State and local
			Total	Equipment and software	Structures			Equipment and software	Structures		Equipment and software	Structures			
1947	18.62	16.35	15.77	7.54	23.72	17.06	27.57	46.06	23.76	14.68	12.61	23.77	17.04	69.52	15.17
1948	18.90	17.06	16.46	8.33	24.23	17.80	26.07	36.24	24.00	14.95	12.02	24.16	17.78	61.67	15.47
1949	19.27	17.64	16.96	8.80	24.69	18.46	25.57	31.13	24.48	15.86	11.78	24.64	18.44	57.69	15.97
1950	19.82	18.41	17.54	9.36	25.24	19.44	25.18	26.11	25.10	16.67	11.63	25.22	19.41	53.82	16.59
1951	20.57	19.10	18.15	9.89	25.87	20.20	26.18	27.93	25.88	17.92	12.33	25.91	20.19	56.06	17.21
1952	21.35	19.72	18.69	10.33	26.47	20.92	27.56	31.23	26.82	19.33	13.14	26.66	20.93	60.01	17.85
1953	22.19	20.41	19.32	10.85	27.16	21.67	29.03	34.72	27.82	20.60	14.05	27.48	21.69	64.05	18.56
1954	22.98	21.08	19.86	11.19	27.87	22.50	30.28	36.54	28.96	21.18	14.58	28.38	22.51	66.48	19.46
1955	23.85	21.91	20.54	11.72	28.65	23.48	31.34	37.30	30.11	21.64	15.14	29.32	23.48	67.72	20.46
1956	24.70	22.71	21.29	12.24	29.59	24.34	32.37	38.01	31.25	22.22	15.69	30.34	24.34	68.85	21.46
1957	25.52	23.46	22.03	12.77	30.48	25.12	33.42	38.47	32.43	23.28	16.22	31.35	25.12	69.74	22.55
1958	26.24	24.06	22.48	12.94	31.24	25.88	34.64	39.11	33.76	25.16	16.45	32.35	25.91	71.03	23.76
1959	27.14	24.83	23.02	13.22	32.02	26.93	36.07	40.78	35.08	27.28	16.91	33.36	26.98	73.16	24.98
1960	28.02	25.61	23.67	13.61	32.90	27.85	37.35	41.86	36.40	28.84	17.39	34.42	27.91	74.72	26.19
1961	28.92	26.35	24.27	13.91	33.79	28.76	38.88	43.58	37.84	30.74	17.87	35.54	28.84	76.93	27.51
1962	29.93	27.22	25.01	14.39	34.75	29.77	40.47	45.63	39.28	32.87	18.57	36.71	29.88	79.34	28.87
1963	31.01	28.18	25.80	14.97	35.68	30.95	41.98	46.89	40.87	33.97	19.24	37.92	31.05	80.95	30.37
1964	32.21	29.29	26.80	15.76	36.80	32.19	43.52	47.95	42.53	35.16	20.07	39.27	32.30	82.27	31.98
1965	33.52	30.56	28.14	16.91	38.20	33.37	45.04	48.44	44.31	36.43	21.14	40.83	33.48	83.10	33.71
1966	34.91	31.86	29.70	18.36	39.69	34.37	46.74	49.45	46.19	37.80	22.54	42.49	34.48	84.34	35.57
1967	36.21	33.03	31.08	19.58	41.09	35.30	48.53	50.81	48.08	39.34	23.79	44.10	35.43	85.55	37.53
1968	37.55	34.30	32.49	20.85	42.49	36.41	50.13	51.03	50.00	40.85	24.93	45.72	36.55	85.70	39.58
1969	38.90	35.65	34.02	22.25	44.00	37.55	51.49	50.74	51.71	42.76	26.12	47.32	37.71	85.34	41.45
1970	40.09	36.85	35.38	23.40	45.46	38.57	52.62	50.20	53.17	44.72	27.05	48.78	38.75	84.70	43.10
1971	41.31	38.17	36.61	24.40	46.84	40.01	53.44	48.18	54.57	46.61	27.65	50.16	40.19	83.10	44.64
1972	42.71	39.73	38.02	25.71	48.25	41.74	54.24	46.57	55.85	48.19	28.56	51.52	41.92	81.81	46.05
1973	44.25	41.46	39.79	27.59	49.82	43.44	55.09	45.34	57.08	49.70	30.00	52.94	43.61	80.86	47.44
1974	45.57	42.88	41.40	29.33	51.24	44.62	56.05	45.07	58.26	51.12	31.47	54.25	44.80	80.48	48.79
1975	46.57	43.89	42.49	30.33	52.36	45.55	57.03	45.06	59.39	52.82	32.34	55.37	45.75	80.32	50.08
1976	47.72	45.10	43.63	31.45	53.46	46.84	57.99	45.38	60.46	54.15	33.35	56.45	47.04	80.41	51.30
1977	49.13	46.65	45.05	33.04	54.63	48.55	58.83	45.63	61.40	55.41	34.77	57.52	48.74	80.53	52.37
1978	50.80	48.50	46.92	35.17	56.15	50.37	59.82	45.92	62.52	56.47	36.65	58.87	50.55	80.74	53.60
1979	52.57	50.42	49.05	37.49	58.00	52.07	60.94	46.86	63.68	57.48	38.80	60.43	52.24	81.21	54.92
1980	54.02	51.95	50.94	39.17	60.01	53.22	62.07	47.98	64.81	58.77	40.41	62.06	53.39	81.85	56.21
1981	55.43	53.46	52.95	40.81	62.28	54.19	63.08	49.27	65.74	60.30	42.00	63.76	54.37	82.79	57.24
1982	56.49	54.56	54.49	41.68	64.40	54.81	63.99	50.92	66.48	61.71	42.98	65.29	55.01	83.91	58.09
1983	57.71	55.83	55.79	42.61	65.98	56.04	65.03	53.46	67.19	63.41	44.13	66.50	56.26	85.58	58.93
1984	59.39	57.60	57.79	44.44	68.08	57.58	66.34	56.80	68.08	64.85	46.16	68.08	57.79	87.67	60.01
1985	61.20	59.46	59.95	46.21	70.51	59.11	67.95	61.17	69.15	66.62	48.28	69.93	59.33	90.40	61.29
1986	62.97	61.23	61.66	47.67	72.39	60.95	69.72	65.94	70.34	68.51	50.18	71.51	61.17	93.39	62.69
1987	64.69	62.93	63.20	48.84	74.21	62.82	71.52	70.76	71.59	70.49	51.82	73.09	63.05	96.53	64.11
1988	66.39	64.64	64.82	50.28	75.94	64.63	73.15	74.47	72.85	72.24	53.55	74.62	64.85	98.59	65.61
1989	68.05	66.30	66.50	51.89	77.63	66.28	74.79	78.51	74.08	73.78	55.47	76.11	66.50	100.48	67.18
1990	69.61	67.81	68.08	53.13	79.47	67.71	76.61	82.64	75.50	75.49	57.08	77.76	67.94	102.42	68.95
1991	70.83	68.91	69.13	53.92	80.72	68.87	78.30	85.68	76.97	76.97	58.16	79.10	69.11	103.83	70.72
1992	72.08	70.05	70.11	54.94	81.62	70.20	79.91	88.19	78.42	78.58	59.37	80.25	70.45	105.00	72.46
1993	73.56	71.57	71.50	56.72	82.61	71.84	81.26	89.30	79.80	79.98	61.07	81.41	72.09	105.40	74.09
1994	75.17	73.28	73.14	59.13	83.52	73.64	82.44	89.58	81.13	81.13	63.21	82.50	73.88	105.14	75.70
1995	76.97	75.21	75.23	62.12	84.78	75.40	83.74	89.70	82.63	82.54	65.82	83.86	75.63	104.99	77.43
1996	79.03	77.41	77.64	65.53	86.30	77.39	85.25	89.93	84.36	83.94	68.82	85.47	77.61	105.42	79.26
1997	81.01	79.81	80.44	69.57	88.03	79.38	85.65	89.74	84.82	90.14	72.31	86.65	79.59	100.42	81.26
1998	83.45	82.50	83.63	74.37	89.92	81.60	87.10	90.17	86.43	91.53	76.53	88.42	81.79	99.96	83.30
1999	86.09	85.38	87.05	79.89	91.75	83.97	88.78	91.26	88.22	92.88	81.45	90.23	84.13	99.72	85.57
2000	88.85	88.42	90.77	85.79	93.89	86.35	90.51	92.14	90.10	93.93	86.66	92.26	86.49	99.20	87.96
2001	91.21	90.92	93.45	89.58	95.79	88.70	92.30	92.81	92.08	95.20	90.03	94.19	88.82	98.65	90.45
2002	93.29	93.02	95.07	91.89	96.96	91.23	94.32	94.15	94.22	96.55	92.20	95.78	91.33	98.70	93.05
2003	95.42	95.17	96.50	93.96	97.99	94.03	96.36	95.65	96.37	97.85	94.19	97.29	94.10	98.95	95.62
2004	97.71	97.56	98.15	96.63	99.00	97.06	98.27	97.01	98.39	99.04	96.69	98.74	97.10	99.48	97.93
2005	100.00	100.00	100.00	100.00	100.00	100.00	100.00	100.00	100.00	100.00	100.00	100.00	100.00	100.00	100.00
2006	102.57	102.74	102.46	104.14	101.58	102.98	101.92	103.51	101.80	100.46	104.05	101.67	102.93	100.76	102.24
2007	104.89	105.17	105.28	107.87	103.93	105.06	103.86	106.70	103.67	101.12	107.71	103.81	104.98	101.53	104.50
2008	106.77	107.01	107.83	110.19	106.59	106.24	105.89	111.01	105.51	101.72	110.31	106.13	106.15	103.05	106.66

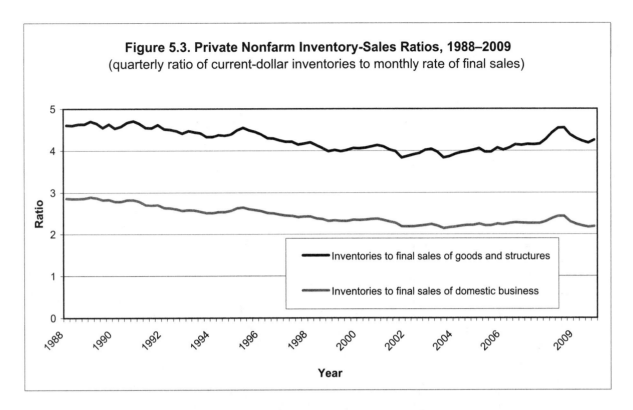

Figure 5.3. Private Nonfarm Inventory-Sales Ratios, 1988–2009
(quarterly ratio of current-dollar inventories to monthly rate of final sales)

- Inventories play a key role in the business cycle, since the change in inventories is a GDP component that although small can be volatile, and even negative. When inventory change is positive, the economy is producing a little more than is sold; when it is negative, production has been reduced below the rate of sales in order to get rid of unwanted stocks. In 2009, inventories were reduced at a rate unprecedented in the postwar period. (Table 1-2)

- Ratios of inventories to sales (I/S ratios) are important cyclical indicators. If sales take an unexpected dip, there can be "involuntary" inventory accumulation. In that case, I/S ratios rise; production then has to be cut back to get back to the desired ratio. Sharply increasing ratios were associated with the 1974–1975 and 1981–1982 recessions. (Table 19-7)

- In 2008 and early 2009, slowdowns and then declines in real final sales (Table 1-6) led to the increases in I/S ratios shown in Table 5-7 and Figure 5-3 above. Very large production cuts and inventory liquidation ensued. Later, in the second half of 2009, sales strengthened, contributing to a reduced rate of inventory liquidation even as I/S ratios stabilized or improved. However, a return to a normal rate of positive inventory growth is likely to require continued growth in the rate of final sales.

Table 5-7. Inventories to Sales Ratios

(Seasonally adjusted, ratio of inventories at end of quarter to monthly rate of sales during the quarter, annual data are for fourth quarter.)

NIPA Tables 5.7.5A, 5.7.5B, 5.7.6A, 5.7.6B

Year and quarter	Ratio, total private inventories to final sales of domestic business		Ratio, nonfarm inventories to final sales of domestic business		Ratio, nonfarm inventories to final sales of goods and structures	
	Current dollars	Chained (2005) dollars	Current dollars	Chained (2005) dollars	Current dollars	Chained (2005) dollars
1950	5.81	3.66	3.04	2.29	3.94	3.96
1951	5.85	3.75	3.15	2.45	4.07	4.23
1952	5.04	3.73	3.08	2.44	4.04	4.22
1953	4.74	3.74	2.88	2.45	3.81	4.21
1954	4.43	3.51	2.95	2.27	3.87	3.93
1955	4.47	3.44	3.03	2.29	4.00	3.93
1956	4.46	3.44	3.01	2.35	4.01	4.06
1957	4.50	3.47	2.90	2.37	3.88	4.13
1958	4.26	3.44	2.90	2.30	3.94	3.99
1959	4.22	3.36	2.89	2.32	3.93	4.07
1960	4.12	3.37	2.81	2.34	3.84	4.09
1961	4.14	3.30	2.82	2.29	3.87	4.02
1962	3.95	3.31	2.78	2.33	3.81	4.10
1963	3.79	3.25	2.75	2.32	3.79	4.06
1964	3.77	3.16	2.72	2.31	3.71	4.06
1965	3.92	3.08	2.92	2.29	4.01	3.98
1966	3.90	3.26	2.99	2.49	4.14	4.37
1967	3.79	3.35	2.90	2.59	4.03	4.55
1968	3.88	3.32	2.98	2.58	4.18	4.55
1969	3.81	3.40	2.96	2.67	4.23	4.75
1970	3.76	3.38	2.88	2.68	4.12	4.82
1971	3.74	3.33	2.77	2.64	3.94	4.74
1972	4.20	3.17	2.98	2.54	4.22	4.52
1973	4.52	3.22	3.54	2.62	5.11	4.66
1974	4.04	3.46	3.16	2.87	4.59	5.24
1975	3.95	3.25	3.19	2.66	4.68	4.87
1976	3.89	3.23	3.16	2.67	4.63	4.91
1977	3.98	3.21	3.15	2.67	4.54	4.86
1978	4.19	3.14	3.34	2.63	4.85	4.71
1979	4.24	3.16	3.44	2.64	5.08	4.74
1980	4.17	3.13	3.49	2.64	5.20	4.80
1981	3.97	3.28	3.30	2.75	5.10	5.02
1982	3.69	3.23	3.08	2.67	4.77	4.98
1983	3.72	2.98	3.16	2.52	4.89	4.63
1984	3.51	3.04	3.01	2.59	4.74	4.71
1985	3.25	2.98	2.82	2.53	4.49	4.64
1986	3.33	2.89	2.90	2.46	4.65	4.52
1987	3.29	2.90	2.86	2.50	4.63	4.61
1988	3.23	2.81	2.83	2.46	4.63	4.54
1989	3.22	2.80	2.82	2.47	4.71	4.55
1990	3.06	2.83	2.70	2.49	4.62	4.65
1991	2.92	2.83	2.56	2.49	4.41	4.73
1992	2.85	2.72	2.51	2.39	4.33	4.52
1993	2.89	2.68	2.56	2.37	4.39	4.46
1994	2.88	2.72	2.58	2.40	4.45	4.46
1995	2.76	2.69	2.47	2.40	4.24	4.45
1996	2.70	2.61	2.42	2.33	4.17	4.27
1997	2.70	2.65	2.42	2.37	4.17	4.31
1998	2.55	2.61	2.32	2.34	3.98	4.21
1999	2.57	2.60	2.35	2.34	4.06	4.22
2000	2.59	2.60	2.37	2.36	4.13	4.25
2001	2.40	2.51	2.19	2.27	3.83	4.09
2002	2.45	2.53	2.22	2.29	4.01	4.21
2003	2.39	2.44	2.16	2.21	3.86	3.99
2004	2.45	2.46	2.22	2.23	4.01	4.04
2005	2.48	2.45	2.25	2.23	4.07	4.02
2006	2.48	2.45	2.27	2.24	4.13	4.06
2007	2.54	2.39	2.31	2.19	4.27	3.98
2008	2.52	2.44	2.30	2.24	4.38	4.15
2009	2.41	2.31	2.19	2.11	4.25	3.94
2007						
1st quarter	2.49	2.43	2.26	2.22	4.15	4.06
2nd quarter	2.48	2.42	2.26	2.22	4.14	4.03
3rd quarter	2.49	2.41	2.26	2.21	4.16	4.01
4th quarter	2.54	2.39	2.31	2.19	4.27	3.98
2008						
1st quarter	2.62	2.41	2.38	2.21	4.43	4.03
2nd quarter	2.69	2.38	2.43	2.18	4.54	3.96
3rd quarter	2.67	2.40	2.43	2.21	4.55	4.02
4th quarter	2.52	2.44	2.30	2.24	4.38	4.15
2009						
1st quarter	2.45	2.44	2.24	2.23	4.29	4.18
2nd quarter	2.41	2.38	2.20	2.18	4.23	4.09
3rd quarter	2.38	2.33	2.17	2.12	4.18	3.97
4th quarter	2.41	2.31	2.19	2.11	4.25	3.94

Table 5-8. Manufacturing and Trade Sales and Inventories

Year and month	Sales, billions of dollars					Inventories, billions of dollars, end of period, seasonally adjusted				Ratios, inventories to sales, seasonally adjusted [1]			
	Not seasonally adjusted, total	Seasonally adjusted				Total	Manufac-turing	Retail trade	Merchant wholesalers	Total	Manufac-turing	Retail trade	Merchant wholesalers
		Total	Manufac-turing	Retail trade	Merchant wholesalers								
1992	6 486.9	6 486.9	2 904.0	1 815.7	1 767.1	837.0	378.7	261.4	196.9	1.57	1.57	1.67	1.31
1993	6 811.0	6 811.0	3 020.5	1 942.2	1 848.2	864.0	379.7	279.5	204.8	1.50	1.50	1.68	1.30
1994	7 323.0	7 323.0	3 238.1	2 110.0	1 974.9	927.3	399.9	305.4	222.0	1.44	1.44	1.66	1.29
1995	7 861.2	7 861.2	3 479.7	2 222.5	2 159.0	986.1	424.8	322.9	238.4	1.44	1.44	1.72	1.29
1996	8 248.2	8 248.2	3 597.2	2 366.7	2 284.3	1 005.5	430.4	334.0	241.1	1.43	1.43	1.67	1.27
1997	8 686.5	8 686.5	3 834.7	2 474.0	2 377.8	1 046.8	443.6	344.6	258.6	1.37	1.37	1.64	1.26
1998	8 914.0	8 914.0	3 899.8	2 587.1	2 427.1	1 078.7	449.1	357.3	272.4	1.39	1.39	1.62	1.31
1999	9 439.6	9 439.6	4 031.9	2 808.6	2 599.2	1 139.0	463.6	385.0	290.3	1.35	1.35	1.59	1.30
2000	10 011.9	10 011.9	4 208.6	2 988.8	2 814.6	1 198.0	481.7	406.9	309.5	1.35	1.35	1.59	1.29
2001	9 823.4	9 823.4	3 970.5	3 067.7	2 785.2	1 120.4	427.7	394.8	297.9	1.38	1.38	1.58	1.32
2002	9 884.6	9 884.6	3 914.7	3 134.3	2 835.5	1 140.9	422.7	416.3	301.9	1.28	1.28	1.55	1.26
2003	10 243.1	10 243.1	4 015.4	3 265.5	2 962.3	1 148.0	408.0	432.4	307.6	1.24	1.24	1.56	1.23
2004	11 079.8	11 079.8	4 309.0	3 474.3	3 296.5	1 239.7	440.3	461.4	338.0	1.19	1.19	1.56	1.18
2005	12 004.4	12 004.4	4 742.1	3 687.4	3 575.0	1 306.6	472.4	471.7	362.5	1.16	1.16	1.51	1.18
2006	12 770.2	12 770.2	5 020.0	3 869.5	3 880.8	1 390.7	510.9	487.5	392.3	1.19	1.19	1.50	1.17
2007	13 226.4	13 226.4	5 081.1	3 994.8	4 150.5	1 446.3	530.0	499.7	416.6	1.23	1.23	1.49	1.16
2008	13 643.8	13 643.8	5 183.1	3 960.0	4 500.7	1 452.1	541.8	483.3	427.0	1.28	1.28	1.52	1.17
2009	11 906.2	11 906.2	4 375.4	3 683.2	3 847.7	1 310.3	494.4	433.0	382.8	1.39	1.39	1.46	1.24
2005													
January	872.8	969.8	381.7	298.2	290.0	1 251.4	446.9	461.9	342.6	1.29	1.17	1.55	1.18
February	888.4	972.5	381.5	300.6	290.4	1 259.6	451.8	463.7	344.1	1.30	1.18	1.54	1.19
March	1 025.2	978.4	388.5	300.7	289.3	1 267.6	455.8	465.7	346.1	1.30	1.17	1.55	1.20
April	979.1	986.6	388.1	305.1	293.5	1 272.8	457.3	466.5	348.9	1.29	1.18	1.53	1.19
May	1 003.0	982.3	388.7	302.0	291.6	1 273.6	457.5	467.0	349.2	1.30	1.18	1.55	1.20
June	1 040.3	992.0	390.3	309.3	292.5	1 271.4	458.3	462.5	350.5	1.28	1.17	1.50	1.20
July	963.3	996.7	387.7	313.7	295.3	1 266.5	461.6	453.6	351.3	1.27	1.19	1.45	1.19
August	1 053.5	1 005.5	397.7	308.7	299.1	1 268.8	460.9	455.9	352.0	1.26	1.16	1.48	1.18
September	1 038.0	1 018.9	404.5	309.1	305.3	1 276.8	462.3	461.3	353.3	1.25	1.14	1.49	1.16
October	1 032.1	1 028.2	405.8	310.6	311.8	1 285.4	466.7	462.5	356.1	1.25	1.15	1.49	1.14
November	1 020.4	1 031.8	409.6	313.6	308.7	1 293.8	468.8	467.2	357.8	1.25	1.14	1.49	1.16
December	1 088.3	1 044.9	418.1	313.5	313.3	1 306.6	472.4	471.7	362.5	1.25	1.13	1.50	1.16
2006													
January	963.3	1 059.3	419.9	323.2	316.2	1 316.1	478.2	474.5	363.4	1.24	1.14	1.47	1.15
February	958.8	1 055.0	417.4	320.3	317.3	1 319.0	478.7	473.6	366.8	1.25	1.15	1.48	1.16
March	1 113.6	1 062.0	422.5	321.4	318.0	1 332.3	483.3	480.3	368.7	1.25	1.14	1.49	1.16
April	1 030.3	1 060.9	418.1	323.4	319.4	1 339.9	488.5	478.7	372.8	1.26	1.17	1.48	1.17
May	1 117.2	1 071.9	427.5	321.3	323.2	1 353.3	492.5	485.1	375.8	1.26	1.15	1.51	1.16
June	1 128.3	1 071.8	425.6	321.2	325.0	1 362.9	496.7	488.1	378.0	1.27	1.17	1.52	1.16
July	1 035.3	1 067.1	416.6	324.0	326.5	1 368.8	500.9	486.9	380.9	1.28	1.20	1.50	1.17
August	1 133.1	1 076.4	423.9	324.1	328.4	1 375.1	503.1	487.8	384.2	1.28	1.19	1.50	1.17
September	1 062.3	1 056.8	410.4	321.9	324.6	1 380.4	507.5	486.7	386.2	1.31	1.24	1.51	1.19
October	1 071.1	1 054.0	406.8	322.7	324.6	1 384.5	509.8	485.9	388.8	1.31	1.25	1.51	1.20
November	1 050.3	1 062.1	410.2	324.3	327.5	1 389.5	510.9	485.0	393.6	1.31	1.25	1.50	1.20
December	1 106.6	1 085.2	421.9	328.4	334.8	1 390.7	510.9	487.5	392.3	1.28	1.21	1.48	1.17
2007													
January	990.2	1 069.0	410.5	327.4	331.1	1 394.2	511.6	489.1	393.5	1.30	1.25	1.49	1.19
February	976.0	1 077.8	414.1	328.8	334.9	1 399.0	512.9	491.0	395.2	1.30	1.24	1.49	1.18
March	1 126.8	1 092.1	421.8	332.0	338.4	1 399.7	513.2	489.4	397.1	1.28	1.22	1.47	1.17
April	1 075.1	1 094.5	423.9	329.5	341.0	1 404.3	516.1	490.7	397.5	1.28	1.22	1.49	1.17
May	1 154.2	1 104.0	427.8	333.8	342.4	1 410.0	518.6	493.0	398.5	1.28	1.21	1.48	1.16
June	1 139.3	1 094.2	422.3	329.7	342.2	1 412.4	518.4	494.9	399.1	1.29	1.23	1.50	1.17
July	1 077.6	1 094.8	423.3	331.0	340.5	1 415.5	518.5	497.2	399.8	1.29	1.22	1.50	1.17
August	1 158.4	1 096.9	422.2	331.7	343.1	1 417.0	517.0	499.3	400.6	1.29	1.22	1.51	1.17
September	1 088.2	1 104.2	420.2	335.2	348.8	1 424.4	521.7	498.3	404.4	1.29	1.24	1.49	1.16
October	1 155.2	1 117.7	425.7	336.8	355.1	1 427.8	522.6	499.0	406.2	1.28	1.23	1.48	1.14
November	1 131.3	1 143.7	435.0	342.8	365.9	1 435.0	525.5	498.5	410.9	1.25	1.21	1.45	1.12
December	1 154.2	1 139.9	435.6	339.1	365.2	1 446.3	530.0	499.7	416.6	1.27	1.22	1.47	1.14
2008													
January	1 071.8	1 156.1	439.9	339.0	377.1	1 463.2	537.1	503.7	422.4	1.27	1.22	1.49	1.12
February	1 073.9	1 143.3	434.3	336.1	373.0	1 472.7	541.5	504.6	426.6	1.29	1.25	1.50	1.14
March	1 160.6	1 156.6	439.3	337.6	379.7	1 474.8	546.0	502.2	426.6	1.28	1.24	1.49	1.12
April	1 170.5	1 171.3	448.7	338.4	384.2	1 484.3	547.7	504.4	432.1	1.27	1.22	1.49	1.12
May	1 218.0	1 177.0	449.7	338.9	388.4	1 488.1	550.2	502.6	435.3	1.26	1.22	1.48	1.12
June	1 229.8	1 187.4	453.0	338.1	396.3	1 495.8	554.7	501.9	439.2	1.26	1.22	1.48	1.11
July	1 201.8	1 185.5	457.1	336.1	392.3	1 510.1	558.3	507.9	443.9	1.27	1.22	1.51	1.13
August	1 192.8	1 160.4	440.9	333.4	386.1	1 511.2	561.2	503.1	446.9	1.30	1.27	1.51	1.16
September	1 155.8	1 134.2	429.2	327.7	377.4	1 506.3	559.1	502.6	444.6	1.33	1.30	1.53	1.18
October	1 133.4	1 090.4	412.9	316.8	360.8	1 495.3	556.0	500.6	438.8	1.37	1.35	1.58	1.22
November	989.3	1 026.9	384.4	307.2	335.3	1 475.8	551.3	490.7	433.9	1.44	1.43	1.60	1.29
December	1 046.1	993.7	373.4	297.6	322.6	1 452.1	541.8	483.3	427.0	1.46	1.45	1.62	1.32
2009													
January	904.2	979.8	363.8	302.3	313.8	1 433.1	535.5	474.3	423.3	1.46	1.47	1.57	1.35
February	890.3	985.2	362.7	304.0	318.5	1 417.4	527.9	470.9	418.5	1.44	1.46	1.55	1.31
March	984.9	969.0	357.2	301.1	310.7	1 399.1	521.5	466.5	411.1	1.44	1.46	1.55	1.32
April	964.3	968.2	357.3	300.1	310.7	1 381.3	515.6	460.0	405.6	1.43	1.44	1.53	1.31
May	979.6	967.8	354.2	301.6	312.1	1 364.1	511.3	452.0	400.8	1.41	1.44	1.50	1.28
June	1 029.6	977.8	360.1	304.7	312.9	1 344.1	505.0	446.6	392.5	1.37	1.40	1.47	1.25
July	995.0	981.8	362.6	304.5	314.7	1 329.2	500.6	442.2	386.3	1.35	1.38	1.45	1.23
August	1 013.8	993.2	362.3	312.9	318.1	1 308.3	496.5	430.6	381.1	1.32	1.37	1.38	1.20
September	1 011.7	994.9	366.9	305.9	322.2	1 303.7	492.6	432.9	378.3	1.31	1.34	1.42	1.17
October	1 031.7	1 006.8	370.3	309.8	326.6	1 307.8	494.4	432.8	380.6	1.30	1.34	1.40	1.17
November	1 004.1	1 030.8	376.0	316.4	338.3	1 314.0	495.3	432.0	386.7	1.27	1.32	1.37	1.14
December	1 096.9	1 041.1	382.7	315.9	342.4	1 310.3	494.4	433.0	382.8	1.26	1.29	1.37	1.12

[1] Annual data are averages of monthly ratios.

Table 5-9. Real Manufacturing and Trade Sales and Inventories

(Billions of chained [2005] dollars, ratios; seasonally adjusted; annual sales figures are averages of seasonally adjusted monthly data.)

NIPA Tables 1BU, 2BU, 3BU

Year and month	Sales, monthly average				Inventories, end of period				Ratios, end-of-period inventories to monthly average sales			
	Total	Manufac-turing	Retail trade	Merchant wholesalers	Total	Manufac-turing	Retail trade	Merchant wholesalers	Total	Manufac-turing	Retail trade	Merchant wholesalers
1997	807.0	365.1	227.9	209.8	1 110.9	490.0	349.5	276.0	1.38	1.34	1.53	1.32
1998	846.1	377.1	241.5	224.7	1 165.0	507.6	364.7	297.3	1.38	1.35	1.51	1.32
1999	893.1	389.1	259.3	242.8	1 225.8	523.8	390.5	315.3	1.37	1.35	1.51	1.30
2000	919.7	393.8	269.3	255.7	1 271.2	531.9	411.1	331.4	1.38	1.35	1.53	1.30
2001	906.6	371.9	275.5	256.4	1 226.2	505.7	400.5	322.6	1.35	1.36	1.45	1.26
2002	919.2	369.8	283.8	263.5	1 246.7	500.5	424.2	323.2	1.36	1.35	1.50	1.23
2003	936.5	370.6	295.2	268.8	1 256.5	492.0	441.5	323.3	1.34	1.33	1.50	1.20
2004	972.0	378.4	308.0	284.7	1 304.9	498.0	465.2	341.7	1.34	1.32	1.51	1.20
2005	1 013.3	395.2	319.6	298.4	1 344.9	519.0	469.8	356.0	1.33	1.31	1.47	1.19
2006	1 041.9	400.0	330.9	311.6	1 387.5	536.0	480.6	370.8	1.33	1.34	1.45	1.19
2007	1 046.0	390.4	338.2	317.8	1 405.8	541.0	486.4	378.2	1.34	1.39	1.44	1.19
2008	1 012.4	367.8	326.9	316.8	1 391.8	537.1	474.6	379.4	1.38	1.46	1.45	1.20
2009	931.0	324.5	312.5	291.3	1 293.9	504.6	449.0	340.4	1.39	1.56	1.44	1.17
2005												
January	1 002.1	390.4	315.4	296.0	1 316.3	503.2	466.8	346.4	1.31	1.29	1.48	1.17
February	999.4	387.0	317.0	294.9	1 322.8	506.3	469.2	347.2	1.32	1.31	1.48	1.18
March	999.5	391.8	316.0	291.3	1 325.7	508.5	468.9	348.4	1.33	1.30	1.48	1.20
April	1 006.9	391.9	319.2	295.9	1 326.7	508.6	467.7	350.4	1.32	1.30	1.47	1.18
May	1 007.6	394.4	317.3	295.8	1 325.7	507.9	467.4	350.3	1.32	1.29	1.47	1.18
June	1 016.6	396.0	324.9	296.0	1 326.5	509.0	466.1	351.4	1.31	1.29	1.44	1.19
July	1 017.6	393.5	327.3	297.2	1 323.1	512.6	458.7	351.9	1.30	1.30	1.40	1.18
August	1 017.2	398.5	319.9	298.9	1 324.8	511.9	461.0	352.0	1.30	1.29	1.44	1.18
September	1 012.7	397.4	314.9	300.1	1 328.8	512.0	464.7	352.1	1.31	1.29	1.48	1.17
October	1 014.7	393.9	317.0	303.7	1 335.9	515.3	467.1	353.5	1.32	1.31	1.47	1.16
November	1 028.9	401.8	323.3	304.2	1 338.5	516.6	468.3	353.6	1.30	1.29	1.45	1.16
December	1 036.0	406.4	323.7	306.5	1 344.9	519.0	469.8	356.0	1.30	1.28	1.45	1.16
2006												
January	1 043.3	405.1	331.6	307.9	1 349.2	522.8	470.4	356.1	1.29	1.29	1.42	1.16
February	1 041.9	403.0	329.2	310.4	1 348.3	521.2	468.1	358.9	1.29	1.29	1.42	1.16
March	1 046.2	406.3	330.3	310.7	1 356.5	523.7	472.7	360.1	1.30	1.29	1.43	1.16
April	1 039.5	401.0	330.6	308.6	1 359.1	526.2	469.6	363.2	1.31	1.31	1.42	1.18
May	1 044.9	406.9	327.9	310.5	1 365.5	527.1	473.2	365.0	1.31	1.30	1.44	1.18
June	1 042.0	403.8	328.1	310.6	1 370.4	529.5	474.8	366.0	1.32	1.31	1.45	1.18
July	1 042.8	401.3	329.6	312.4	1 373.0	531.3	474.3	367.3	1.32	1.32	1.44	1.18
August	1 042.4	401.6	328.4	312.7	1 378.1	532.2	476.8	369.0	1.32	1.33	1.45	1.18
September	1 033.7	392.2	329.3	312.8	1 382.4	534.3	478.3	369.7	1.34	1.36	1.45	1.18
October	1 037.7	391.6	333.1	312.6	1 382.7	535.6	475.6	371.2	1.33	1.37	1.43	1.19
November	1 038.2	390.7	335.0	312.6	1 387.2	536.3	476.3	374.3	1.34	1.37	1.42	1.20
December	1 050.2	396.0	337.5	316.9	1 387.5	536.0	480.6	370.8	1.32	1.35	1.42	1.17
2007												
January	1 039.1	387.5	336.5	315.0	1 385.4	536.2	478.8	370.2	1.33	1.38	1.42	1.18
February	1 039.0	387.6	336.8	314.6	1 387.5	535.8	481.1	370.5	1.34	1.38	1.43	1.18
March	1 044.6	391.0	338.2	316.0	1 386.5	535.2	479.7	371.4	1.33	1.37	1.42	1.18
April	1 044.7	392.9	335.4	317.0	1 388.9	535.8	481.7	371.3	1.33	1.36	1.44	1.17
May	1 050.2	394.2	339.1	317.6	1 390.3	536.8	481.5	371.8	1.32	1.36	1.42	1.17
June	1 043.2	391.0	335.1	317.5	1 391.3	537.2	481.9	372.1	1.33	1.37	1.44	1.17
July	1 049.0	397.9	336.5	315.0	1 395.0	537.5	485.3	372.2	1.33	1.35	1.44	1.18
August	1 047.2	391.9	337.9	318.2	1 396.2	536.4	487.4	372.5	1.33	1.37	1.44	1.17
September	1 047.2	387.9	340.4	319.5	1 401.1	539.0	486.8	375.2	1.34	1.39	1.43	1.17
October	1 051.2	389.9	341.0	320.8	1 402.1	538.1	489.0	375.1	1.33	1.38	1.43	1.17
November	1 052.0	387.2	343.1	322.2	1 403.2	539.3	487.4	376.5	1.33	1.39	1.42	1.17
December	1 044.8	385.6	338.9	320.3	1 405.8	541.0	486.4	378.2	1.35	1.40	1.44	1.18
2008												
January	1 049.9	386.0	337.8	326.2	1 409.6	543.5	486.1	379.6	1.34	1.41	1.44	1.16
February	1 031.5	375.9	334.7	320.6	1 411.9	545.9	485.8	379.8	1.37	1.45	1.45	1.19
March	1 033.9	375.9	335.3	322.2	1 407.7	548.6	482.1	376.4	1.36	1.46	1.44	1.17
April	1 045.1	384.6	336.2	324.1	1 405.8	545.3	481.7	378.2	1.35	1.42	1.43	1.17
May	1 037.4	378.9	335.5	323.0	1 399.8	543.1	479.4	376.6	1.35	1.43	1.43	1.17
June	1 037.2	380.7	331.4	324.5	1 399.2	542.8	478.6	377.2	1.35	1.43	1.44	1.16
July	1 026.5	380.1	327.2	318.5	1 403.8	540.0	484.2	379.5	1.37	1.42	1.48	1.19
August	1 010.7	367.4	326.0	316.3	1 401.2	539.6	479.6	381.4	1.39	1.47	1.47	1.21
September	984.7	353.4	320.2	309.8	1 396.5	535.1	480.0	381.1	1.42	1.51	1.50	1.23
October	975.9	350.5	313.4	310.1	1 396.4	535.5	480.7	379.9	1.43	1.53	1.53	1.23
November	960.8	340.6	315.3	302.8	1 398.1	539.5	477.6	380.5	1.46	1.58	1.51	1.26
December	955.4	339.9	310.1	303.9	1 391.8	537.1	474.6	379.4	1.46	1.58	1.53	1.25
2009												
January	940.9	330.6	314.2	294.0	1 384.0	536.2	467.6	379.5	1.47	1.62	1.49	1.29
February	942.5	330.8	313.2	296.6	1 373.6	532.8	464.6	375.5	1.46	1.61	1.48	1.27
March	932.4	327.3	310.0	292.6	1 364.5	529.9	462.8	371.2	1.46	1.62	1.49	1.27
April	925.6	323.3	309.0	290.5	1 354.4	525.9	461.4	366.6	1.46	1.63	1.49	1.26
May	919.9	318.3	310.4	288.3	1 342.1	523.7	455.1	362.8	1.46	1.65	1.47	1.26
June	915.6	319.2	309.3	283.9	1 325.8	520.0	450.0	355.4	1.45	1.63	1.46	1.25
July	925.7	322.4	309.8	290.6	1 314.8	517.1	447.1	350.3	1.42	1.60	1.44	1.21
August	922.8	317.5	316.6	286.1	1 299.8	513.2	441.2	345.2	1.41	1.62	1.39	1.21
September	924.9	322.3	309.1	290.0	1 292.7	506.2	445.6	340.8	1.40	1.57	1.44	1.18
October	929.3	324.6	312.8	288.9	1 295.4	506.7	447.4	341.3	1.39	1.56	1.43	1.18
November	942.8	326.0	318.5	295.6	1 297.9	506.5	446.6	344.7	1.38	1.55	1.40	1.17
December	949.1	331.2	317.4	298.2	1 293.9	504.6	449.0	340.4	1.36	1.52	1.42	1.14

Table 5-10. Capital Expenditures

(Millions of dollars.)

Capital expenditures	All companies										
	1998	1999	2000	2001	2002	2003	2004	2005	2006	2007	2008
TOTAL	970 897	1 046 952	1 161 029	1 109 004	997 894	975 015	1 042 060	1 144 783	1 309 939	1 354 727	1 371 557
Structures	329 111	320 078	364 407	363 748	358 484	344 641	368 707	401 653	488 701	525 273	562 518
New	284 491	296 496	329 525	335 538	321 191	305 291	324 680	365 938	448 861	480 839	523 079
Used	44 620	23 583	34 882	28 210	37 293	39 350	44 028	35 715	39 840	44 434	39 437
Equipment	641 786	726 874	796 622	745 256	639 410	630 373	673 353	743 130	821 238	829 455	809 041
New	606 210	689 553	750 626	706 617	598 668	579 414	628 591	701 247	777 059	790 407	760 614
Used	35 577	37 321	45 996	38 639	40 741	50 960	44 762	41 884	44 179	39 048	48 427
Not distributed as structures or equipment	0	0	0	0	0	0	0	0	0	0	0
CAPITALIZED COMPUTER SOFTWARE [1]	...	...	...	...	...	...	...	...	...	...	...
Prepackaged	...	...	...	...	...	...	...	...	...	...	...
Vendor-customized	...	...	...	...	...	...	...	...	...	...	...
Internally-developed	...	...	...	...	...	...	...	...	...	...	...
CAPITAL LEASE AND CAPITALIZED INTEREST EXPENSES [1]											
Capital leases	16 533	17 140	19 545	15 529	15 334	15 641	17 996	18 103	24 442	20 210	20 197
Capitalized interest	...	...	...	...	...	...	...	...	...	...	...

Capital expenditures	Companies with employees										
	1998	1999	2000	2001	2002	2003	2004	2005	2006	2007	2008
TOTAL	896 452	974 631	1 089 862	1 052 344	917 490	886 846	953 171	1 062 536	1 217 107	1 270 522	1 295 845
Structures	300 283	293 787	338 120	346 221	325 168	314 021	335 405	368 791	453 893	490 779	531 227
New	260 008	276 094	309 541	323 871	299 941	281 892	300 371	341 223	420 090	457 233	502 051
Used	40 275	17 693	28 579	22 349	25 227	32 128	35 034	27 568	33 802	33 546	29 176
Equipment	596 169	680 843	751 742	706 123	592 321	572 825	617 766	693 745	763 215	779 744	764 618
New	570 397	656 344	718 227	679 090	564 218	540 611	588 110	664 648	734 160	750 353	725 859
Used	25 773	24 499	33 515	27 033	28 103	32 214	29 656	29 096	29 055	29 391	38 759
Not distributed as structures or equipment	0	0	0	0	0	0	0	0	0	0	0
CAPITALIZED COMPUTER SOFTWARE [1]	...	...	...	...	...	49 869	49 868	49 149	58 522	63 116	71 674
Prepackaged	...	...	...	...	...	17 307	17 306	17 630	21 181	21 777	26 218
Vendor-customized	...	...	...	...	...	15 554	15 553	13 876	16 912	17 990	19 277
Internally-developed	...	...	...	...	...	17 008	17 008	17 643	20 433	23 350	26 179
CAPITAL LEASE AND CAPITALIZED INTEREST EXPENSES [1]											
Capital leases	15 631	16 594	19 184	15 500	15 092	15 137	17 526	17 640	23 923	19 432	19 423
Capitalized interest	9 799	9 591	11 423	11 969	...	...	...	...	...	...	...

Capital expenditures	Companies without employees										
	1998	1999	2000	2001	2002	2003	2004	2005	2006	2007	2008
TOTAL	74 445	72 322	71 168	56 660	80 404	88 169	88 889	82 247	92 832	84 205	75 712
Structures	28 828	26 291	26 287	17 527	33 316	30 621	33 302	32 862	34 809	34 494	31 291
New	24 483	20 402	19 984	11 667	21 250	23 399	24 309	24 715	28 771	23 606	21 027
Used	4 345	5 889	6 303	5 860	12 066	7 222	8 993	8 146	6 038	10 888	10 262
Equipment	45 617	46 030	44 880	39 133	47 088	57 549	55 587	49 386	58 023	49 711	44 423
New	35 813	33 209	32 399	27 528	34 450	38 803	40 481	36 598	42 899	40 054	34 754
Used	9 804	12 821	12 481	11 605	12 638	18 746	15 106	12 787	15 124	9 657	9 668
Not distributed as structures or equipment	0	0	0	0	0	0	0	0	0	0	0
CAPITALIZED COMPUTER SOFTWARE [1]	...	...	...	...	...	...	...	...	...	...	...
Prepackaged	...	...	...	...	...	...	...	...	...	...	...
Vendor-customized	...	...	...	...	...	...	...	...	...	...	...
Internally-developed	...	...	...	...	...	...	...	...	...	...	...
CAPITAL LEASE AND CAPITALIZED INTEREST EXPENSES [1]											
Capital leases	902	546	361	29	242	504	469	463	519	778	774
Capitalized interest	...	...	...	...	...	...	...	...	...	...	...

[1]Included in structures and equipment data shown above.
... = Not available.

Table 5-11. Capital Expenditures for Structures and Equipment for Companies with Employees by Major NAICS Industry Sector

(Millions of dollars.)

Year and type of expenditure	Total	Forestry, fishing, and agricultural services (113–115)	Mining (21)	Utilities (22)	Construction (23)	Manufacturing (31–33) Total	Durable goods industries (321, 327, 33)	Nondurable goods industries (31, 322–326)	Wholesale trade (42)	Retail trade (44–45)	Transportation and warehousing (48–49)	Information (51)
1998												
Total expenditures	896 452	854	40 424	36 010	26 867	203 587	117 901	85 685	29 169	57 276	51 287	96 487
Structures, total	300 283	206	26 503	18 574	7 062	39 028	19 406	19 622	7 480	25 105	13 036	24 721
New	260 008	158	24 714	17 771	4 749	37 122	18 449	18 673	6 738	23 104	12 365	24 218
Used	40 275	49	1 789	804	2 313	1 906	957	949	742	2 001	671	503
Equipment, total	596 169	648	13 921	17 436	19 805	164 559	98 496	66 063	21 690	32 171	38 251	71 766
New	570 397	603	12 625	17 266	15 346	159 363	95 571	63 792	20 470	30 359	33 409	70 827
Used	25 773	46	1 296	170	4 458	5 196	2 925	2 271	1 220	1 812	4 842	939
1999												
Total expenditures	974 631	1 716	30 586	42 802	23 110	196 399	117 005	79 394	32 442	64 063	57 299	122 827
Structures, total	293 787	344	17 626	21 241	1 753	33 985	17 320	16 665	7 264	29 494	14 122	34 924
New	276 094	331	17 039	20 784	1 505	32 814	16 581	16 233	6 508	28 670	13 859	33 733
Used	17 693	13	587	457	248	1 171	739	432	756	824	263	1 191
Equipment, total	680 843	1 371	12 960	21 561	21 356	162 414	99 685	62 729	25 179	34 569	43 178	87 903
New	656 344	1 190	12 167	20 545	18 600	157 715	96 434	61 281	23 714	33 567	40 425	85 310
Used	24 499	182	793	1 016	2 756	4 699	3 251	1 448	1 465	1 002	2 752	2 593
2000												
Total expenditures	1 089 862	1 488	42 522	61 302	25 049	214 827	133 786	81 041	33 579	69 791	59 851	160 177
Structures, total	338 120	139	28 620	29 472	2 803	39 434	21 228	18 207	8 923	32 037	13 457	41 502
New	309 541	134	25 500	29 258	2 583	36 643	19 748	16 895	8 364	30 413	13 190	40 062
Used	28 579	5	3 120	214	220	2 791	1 480	1 312	559	1 624	267	1 440
Equipment, total	751 742	1 350	13 902	31 830	22 245	175 393	112 558	62 835	24 656	37 754	46 394	118 675
New	718 227	1 086	12 854	27 937	17 788	169 454	108 703	60 751	23 610	36 428	43 455	117 835
Used	33 515	264	1 048	3 893	4 458	5 939	3 856	2 083	1 046	1 326	2 938	841
2001												
Total expenditures	1 052 344	1 532	51 278	82 823	24 802	192 835	118 875	73 959	29 981	66 917	57 756	144 793
Structures, total	346 221	226	32 678	38 093	3 859	39 815	22 032	17 784	6 932	30 010	16 594	41 742
New	323 871	149	31 825	36 504	3 389	38 001	20 701	17 301	5 357	29 118	14 479	41 384
Used	22 349	77	853	1 588	470	1 814	1 331	483	1 575	892	2 116	358
Equipment, total	706 123	1 306	18 600	44 731	20 943	153 019	96 844	56 176	23 049	36 906	41 161	103 051
New	679 090	1 091	17 567	42 939	17 432	148 397	94 251	54 145	20 757	35 074	38 521	102 410
Used	27 033	215	1 033	1 792	3 511	4 623	2 592	2 030	2 292	1 833	2 640	641
2002												
Total expenditures	917 490	1 910	42 467	65 502	24 773	157 243	84 062	73 181	26 789	59 316	47 124	88 156
Structures, total	325 168	184	30 685	29 893	1 890	32 643	15 133	17 510	5 885	26 286	14 498	33 607
New	299 941	118	29 775	29 008	1 254	31 022	14 396	16 626	5 447	25 051	13 870	33 472
Used	25 227	66	910	886	456	1 622	737	885	438	1 234	628	135
Equipment, total	592 321	1 726	11 783	35 609	23 063	124 600	68 929	55 671	20 904	33 030	32 626	54 550
New	564 218	1 319	10 262	34 816	19 257	118 621	66 112	52 510	18 562	31 157	29 178	54 247
Used	28 103	407	1 520	793	3 806	5 978	2 817	3 161	2 342	1 873	3 447	303
2003												
Total expenditures	886 846	1 894	50 548	54 569	23 159	149 065	80 226	68 839	26 014	65 868	44 460	80 524
Structures, total	314 021	202	36 617	24 841	1 676	31 108	13 330	17 778	5 615	29 675	13 005	30 765
New	281 892	177	35 897	24 580	1 424	29 315	12 631	16 685	4 921	27 393	11 779	30 406
Used	32 128	25	720	261	251	1 793	700	1 093	694	2 282	1 226	358
Equipment, total	572 825	1 692	13 931	29 729	21 484	117 956	66 895	51 061	20 399	36 193	31 454	49 759
New	540 611	1 267	12 135	29 044	16 170	112 102	62 810	49 292	19 457	32 162	26 786	47 857
Used	32 214	425	1 796	685	5 313	5 855	4 086	1 769	942	4 031	4 668	1 902
2004												
Total expenditures	953 171	2 081	51 253	50 409	28 627	156 651	85 119	71 532	32 314	72 170	46 054	83 488
Structures, total	335 405	324	34 564	24 398	4 511	31 823	13 606	18 217	7 133	33 308	13 992	28 636
New	300 371	309	33 583	23 626	4 167	30 016	12 818	17 198	6 555	31 486	13 018	26 253
Used	35 034	15	982	772	345	1 807	788	1 019	578	1 822	975	2 384
Equipment, total	617 766	1 757	16 689	26 011	24 115	124 828	71 513	53 315	25 181	38 862	32 062	54 852
New	588 110	1 507	15 415	25 724	18 939	120 481	68 904	51 576	21 888	36 965	28 472	53 120
Used	29 656	250	1 274	286	5 176	4 347	2 609	1 738	3 293	1 897	3 590	1 732
2005												
Total expenditures	1 062 536	2 702	66 746	58 032	30 072	165 634	92 180	73 455	40 578	73 531	56 926	91 373
Structures, total	368 791	344	46 433	24 186	2 544	34 132	14 735	19 397	9 184	34 119	17 855	31 977
New	341 223	283	45 655	23 485	2 247	32 564	14 033	18 531	8 830	33 360	16 954	31 716
Used	27 568	61	777	701	297	1 569	703	866	355	759	901	262
Equipment, total	693 745	2 358	20 313	33 847	27 528	131 502	77 444	54 058	31 394	39 412	39 072	59 396
New	664 648	2 016	18 495	33 083	22 082	126 387	73 889	52 498	28 224	38 301	34 953	59 071
Used	29 096	341	1 818	764	5 446	5 115	3 555	1 560	3 169	1 111	4 119	325
2006												
Total expenditures	1 217 107	2 672	99 309	69 757	30 257	192 364	106 843	85 521	36 600	86 735	68 021	104 373
Structures, total	453 893	391	68 662	30 587	2 556	41 617	17 515	24 103	10 375	43 188	20 852	31 947
New	420 090	316	67 322	29 294	2 217	39 419	16 243	23 176	9 956	41 985	19 765	31 621
Used	33 802	75	1 340	1 293	338	2 198	1 272	926	419	1 203	1 087	326
Equipment, total	763 215	2 281	30 647	39 170	27 701	150 747	89 328	61 419	26 226	43 547	47 168	72 425
New	734 160	1 846	28 813	37 617	23 276	146 551	86 637	59 914	24 366	41 943	41 258	71 830
Used	29 055	435	1 833	1 553	4 425	4 196	2 692	1 504	1 860	1 604	5 911	595

Note: Detail may not sum to total because of rounding.

Table 5-11. Capital Expenditures for Structures and Equipment for Companies with Employees by Major NAICS Industry Sector—*Continued*

(Millions of dollars.)

Year and type of expenditure	Finance and insurance (52)	Real estate and rental and leasing (53)	Professional, scientific, and technical services (54)	Management of companies and enterprises (55)	Administrative and support and waste management (56)	Educational services (61)	Health care and social assistance (62)	Arts, entertainment, and recreation (71)	Accommodation and food services (72)	Other services, except public administration (81)	Structure and equipment expenditures serving multiple industries
1998											
Total expenditures	118 173	85 184	22 277	1 821	13 110	12 983	47 109	8 994	20 822	20 627	3 392
Structures, total	27 221	36 775	4 886	753	4 288	9 109	23 971	5 045	12 045	13 737	738
New	16 858	24 109	4 572	502	3 745	8 734	21 328	4 838	10 402	13 280	699
Used	10 362	12 666	314	251	543	374	2 643	206	1 643	457	39
Equipment, total	90 952	48 409	17 390	1 068	8 822	3 874	23 138	3 949	8 777	6 890	2 654
New	90 058	46 877	16 868	1 030	8 346	3 825	22 465	3 752	8 005	6 296	2 609
Used	894	1 532	522	38	476	49	672	197	772	594	46
1999											
Total expenditures	130 101	100 629	29 546	6 065	16 227	13 532	51 342	13 355	23 328	16 902	2 359
Structures, total	20 080	33 903	6 780	1 668	2 875	9 767	25 922	8 119	13 431	9 975	516
New	17 918	30 295	6 168	1 509	2 773	9 140	24 159	7 971	11 391	9 033	495
Used	2 162	3 608	613	159	102	627	1 763	148	2 040	941	21
Equipment, total	110 021	66 726	22 766	4 397	13 353	3 766	25 420	5 236	9 897	6 928	1 843
New	109 577	63 555	22 153	4 319	12 323	3 668	24 945	5 125	9 324	6 370	1 752
Used	444	3 171	613	78	1 029	97	475	111	573	558	91
2000											
Total expenditures	133 684	92 456	34 055	5 054	17 506	18 223	52 166	19 125	26 307	21 125	1 572
Structures, total	23 010	24 815	8 141	1 570	4 032	13 699	26 868	12 245	13 873	13 274	206
New	20 298	17 793	7 470	955	3 504	12 965	23 999	11 627	12 879	11 705	200
Used	2 712	7 022	671	615	528	735	2 869	618	993	1 569	6
Equipment, total	110 675	67 641	25 914	3 484	13 475	4 523	25 299	6 880	12 434	7 852	1 366
New	109 678	62 175	24 847	3 403	12 723	4 338	24 407	6 161	11 501	7 192	1 357
Used	997	5 466	1 067	81	752	186	892	719	933	659	10
2001											
Total expenditures	131 105	82 674	30 464	3 035	15 785	17 377	52 932	14 974	21 365	29 006	911
Structures, total	22 744	20 489	7 258	933	3 527	12 852	27 030	8 998	12 248	20 031	163
New	19 571	17 325	6 793	869	3 367	11 860	25 241	8 157	11 402	18 918	162
Used	3 173	3 164	465	64	160	991	1 789	841	846	1 112	0
Equipment, total	108 361	62 185	23 206	2 102	12 258	4 525	25 902	5 976	9 117	8 976	749
New	107 268	60 295	22 330	2 019	11 644	4 238	24 573	5 590	7 921	8 300	725
Used	1 093	1 891	876	83	613	287	1 329	386	1 196	676	24
2002											
Total expenditures	128 444	94 529	25 864	3 430	14 719	19 532	59 311	13 169	22 409	21 269	1 532
Structures, total	24 308	35 579	7 129	933	3 276	14 655	30 291	7 758	12 157	13 261	250
New	19 748	30 227	6 424	913	2 948	13 601	27 273	7 332	10 848	11 363	248
Used	4 739	5 352	706	21	328	1 055	3 018	425	1 309	1 899	2
Equipment, total	103 956	58 949	18 735	2 497	11 443	4 876	29 021	5 412	10 252	8 007	1 282
New	103 421	56 847	18 021	2 481	10 585	4 690	28 196	5 132	9 290	6 858	1 276
Used	535	2 102	714	16	857	186	825	280	962	1 149	6
2003											
Total expenditures	120 787	87 952	24 703	3 298	16 612	16 667	61 151	11 029	21 036	26 035	1 476
Structures, total	26 200	25 028	5 314	925	3 976	11 984	30 996	6 800	10 568	18 518	209
New	17 908	16 446	4 671	869	3 213	11 569	28 885	6 532	9 417	16 288	202
Used	8 292	8 583	643	56	763	415	2 111	268	1 151	2 230	7
Equipment, total	94 587	62 923	19 389	2 373	12 636	4 683	30 155	4 229	10 468	7 517	1 267
New	94 205	61 253	18 675	2 368	11 374	4 569	29 497	4 038	9 684	6 706	1 263
Used	383	1 671	714	5	1 262	114	658	192	783	811	4
2004											
Total expenditures	153 629	91 606	26 688	2 825	17 455	18 919	64 561	12 165	20 641	19 701	1 572
Structures, total	43 919	27 277	6 007	860	2 567	13 728	32 608	7 360	9 860	12 278	321
New	30 216	21 610	5 714	798	2 309	12 781	30 668	7 196	9 126	10 867	307
Used	13 703	5 667	293	62	259	947	1 939	164	734	1 411	13
Equipment, total	109 710	64 329	20 681	1 965	14 888	5 190	31 953	4 804	10 781	7 423	1 252
New	109 244	61 947	20 081	1 931	12 692	4 965	31 280	4 677	10 373	6 788	1 248
Used	466	2 382	600	34	2 196	225	673	128	408	635	3
2005											
Total expenditures	161 389	103 022	33 066	2 809	18 194	17 484	73 825	14 165	30 718	20 105	2 163
Structures, total	39 383	24 791	8 717	857	3 051	12 711	39 089	9 242	17 679	12 036	460
New	31 023	17 341	7 633	795	2 759	11 913	37 493	8 805	16 567	11 350	452
Used	8 360	7 450	1 084	62	292	798	1 597	436	1 112	686	8
Equipment, total	122 005	78 231	24 350	1 951	15 143	4 773	34 736	4 924	13 039	8 069	1 703
New	121 511	76 894	23 887	1 917	13 523	4 597	34 110	4 757	11 950	7 209	1 681
Used	494	1 337	463	34	1 620	176	626	166	1 089	861	22
2006											
Total expenditures	163 069	132 073	30 284	3 306	19 231	22 615	75 296	17 156	36 217	25 959	1 813
Structures, total	41 326	40 794	6 971	875	3 613	17 537	41 197	11 733	22 585	16 621	467
New	34 028	30 240	6 375	799	3 485	16 203	37 765	11 326	21 774	15 754	446
Used	7 298	10 554	596	76	128	1 334	3 433	406	811	866	21
Equipment, total	121 743	91 280	23 313	2 432	15 618	5 078	34 099	5 424	13 632	9 339	1 346
New	121 157	88 957	22 867	2 188	14 932	4 983	33 508	5 121	13 161	8 463	1 322
Used	586	2 323	446	244	686	95	591	303	472	875	24

Note: Detail may not sum to total because of rounding.

Table 5-11. Capital Expenditures for Structures and Equipment for Companies with Employees by Major NAICS Industry Sector—*Continued*

(Millions of dollars.)

Year and type of expenditure	Total	Forestry, fishing, and agricultural services (113–115)	Mining (21)	Utilities (22)	Construction (23)	Manufacturing (31–33)			Wholesale trade (42)	Retail trade (44–45)	Transportation and warehousing (48–49)	Information (51)
						Total	Durable goods industries (321, 327, 33)	Nondurable goods industries (31, 322–326)				
2007												
Total expenditures	1 270 522	2 149	120 681	85 354	36 692	197 298	107 664	89 633	30 776	82 511	67 351	106 084
Structures, total	490 779	469	85 242	40 178	3 529	42 458	17 879	24 579	7 526	41 527	23 712	29 081
New	457 233	320	83 206	37 647	2 704	41 247	17 431	23 816	7 091	40 471	22 808	28 304
Used	33 546	149	2 036	2 531	824	1 211	447	763	436	1 056	904	777
Equipment, total	779 744	1 681	35 440	45 176	33 164	154 840	89 786	65 054	23 250	40 983	43 639	77 003
New	750 353	1 368	33 095	44 107	27 325	150 333	87 020	63 313	21 690	39 668	39 238	76 143
Used	29 391	313	2 344	1 069	5 838	4 507	2 766	1 741	1 560	1 316	4 400	861
2008												
Total expenditures	1 295 845	2 372	149 965	98 268	41 737	211 578	103 339	108 238	33 055	73 251	79 580	103 424
Structures, total	531 227	426	108 303	43 513	11 171	49 293	19 110	30 183	8 683	36 054	29 906	28 907
New	502 051	422	103 695	41 744	10 552	48 103	18 385	29 719	8 194	35 248	29 043	28 614
Used	29 176	4	4 608	1 769	619	1 190	726	464	489	806	863	294
Equipment, total	764 618	1 946	41 662	54 755	30 566	162 285	84 229	78 055	24 372	37 197	49 674	74 517
New	725 859	1 639	37 876	53 087	23 261	156 650	80 767	75 883	22 862	36 394	42 021	73 907
Used	38 759	307	3 786	1 668	7 305	5 635	3 462	2 172	1 510	802	7 653	609

Note: Detail may not sum to total because of rounding.

(Millions of dollars.)

Year and type of expenditure	Finance and insurance (52)	Real estate and rental and leasing (53)	Professional, scientific, and technical services (54)	Management of companies and enterprises (55)	Administrative and support and waste management (56)	Educational services (61)	Health care and social assistance (62)	Arts, entertainment, and recreation (71)	Accommodation and food services (72)	Other services, except public administration (81)	Structure and equipment expenditures serving multiple industries
2007											
Total expenditures	172 894	117 969	31 804	4 542	18 167	23 238	84 160	18 769	38 021	29 680	2 380
Structures, total	45 159	41 222	7 453	1 472	3 859	17 910	45 361	12 589	22 211	19 165	656
New	36 507	34 026	6 944	1 404	3 677	17 322	43 522	11 894	21 226	16 264	650
Used	8 652	7 196	509	69	182	588	1 839	695	984	2 901	6
Equipment, total	127 735	76 747	24 351	3 070	14 308	5 328	38 799	6 180	15 810	10 515	1 725
New	126 763	74 735	23 931	2 943	13 599	5 253	38 258	5 916	14 671	9 593	1 724
Used	972	2 012	420	127	709	75	541	264	1 139	922	1
2008											
Total expenditures	145 366	96 038	32 739	4 561	16 480	27 365	89 964	17 026	40 515	28 580	3 981
Structures, total	35 815	37 182	8 667	1 299	4 074	21 669	49 877	11 515	24 946	18 921	1 006
New	30 435	30 661	8 309	1 241	3 730	20 556	46 975	11 144	24 270	18 114	1 001
Used	5 380	6 521	358	58	344	1 113	2 902	370	675	807	5
Equipment, total	109 551	58 856	24 072	3 263	12 406	5 696	40 087	5 511	15 569	9 659	2 975
New	107 003	57 015	23 280	3 145	11 673	5 640	39 106	5 336	14 008	8 995	2 960
Used	2 548	1 841	792	117	733	56	981	175	1 560	664	16

Note: Detail may not sum to total because of rounding.

NOTES AND DEFINITIONS, CHAPTER 5

TABLES 5-1 THROUGH 5-4 AND 5-7; TABLE 19-9 GROSS SAVING AND INVESTMENT ACCOUNTS; INVENTORIES TO SALES RATIOS

SOURCE: U.S. DEPARTMENT OF COMMERCE, BUREAU OF ECONOMIC ANALYSIS (BEA)

All of the data in these tables are from the National Income and Product Accounts, which are described in the Notes and Definitions to Chapter 1. All quarterly series are shown at seasonally adjusted annual rates. Current and constant dollar values are in billions of dollars. Indexes of quantity are based on the average for the year 2005, set to equal 100.

Definitions: Tables 5-1 and 19-9

Gross saving is saving before the deduction of allowances for the consumption of fixed capital. It represents the amount of saving available to finance gross investment. *Net saving* is gross saving less allowances for fixed capital consumption. It represents the amount of saving available for financing expansion of the capital stock, and comprises net private saving (the sum of personal saving, undistributed corporate profits, and wage accruals less disbursements) and the net saving of federal, state, and local governments.

Personal saving is derived by subtracting personal outlays from disposable personal income. (See Chapter 4 for more information.) It is the current net saving of individuals (including proprietors of unincorporated businesses), nonprofit institutions that primarily serve individuals, life insurance carriers, retirement funds, private noninsured welfare funds, and private trust funds. Conceptually, personal saving may also be viewed as the sum for all persons (including institutions as previously defined) of the net acquisition of financial assets and the change in physical assets, less the sum of net borrowing and consumption of fixed capital. In either case, it is defined to exclude capital gains. That is, it excludes profits on the increase in the value of homes, securities, and other property—whether realized or unrealized—and therefore includes the noncorporate inventory valuation adjustment and the capital consumption adjustment (IVA and CCAdj, respectively). (See notes and definitions to Chapter 1.)

Undistributed profits are corporate profits after tax less dividends, with the corporate IVA and corporate CCAdj. (See notes and definitions for Chapter 1.)

Government net saving was formerly called "current surplus or deficit (-) of general government." (See Chapter 6 for further detail from the government accounts.) Where current receipts of government exceed current expenditures, government has a current surplus (indicated by a positive value) and saving is made available to finance investment by government or other sectors—for example, by the repayment of debt, which can free up funds for private investment. Where current expenditures exceed current receipts, there is a government deficit (indicated by a negative value) and government must borrow, drawing on funds that would otherwise be available for private investment. In these accounts, current expenditures are defined to include a charge for the consumption of fixed capital.

Consumption of fixed capital is an accounting charge for the using-up of private and government fixed capital, including software, located in the United States. It is based on studies of prices of used equipment and structures in resale markets. For general government and nonprofit institutions that primarily serve individuals, consumption of fixed capital is recorded in government consumption expenditures and in personal consumption expenditures (PCE), respectively, as the value of the current services of the fixed capital assets owned and used by these entities. *Private consumption of fixed capital* consists of tax-return-based depreciation charges for corporations and nonfarm proprietorships and historical-cost depreciation (calculated by the Bureau of Economic Analysis [BEA] using a geometric pattern of price declines) for farm proprietorships, rental income of persons, and nonprofit institutions, minus the capital consumption adjustments. (In other words, in the NIPA treatment of saving, the amount of the CCAdj is taken out of book depreciation and added to income and profits—a reallocation from one form of gross saving to another.)

Gross private domestic investment consists of gross private fixed investment and change in private inventories. (See the notes and definitions for Chapter 1.)

Gross government investment consists of federal, state, and local general government and government enterprise expenditures for fixed assets (structures, equipment, and software). Government inventory investment is included in government consumption expenditures. For further detail, see Chapter 6.

Capital account transactions, net are the net cash or in-kind transfers between the United States and the rest of the world that are linked to the acquisition or disposition of assets rather than the purchase or sale of currently-produced goods and services. When positive, it represents a net transfer from the United States to the rest of the world; when negative, it represents a net transfer to the United States from the rest of the world. This is a definitional category that was introduced in the 1999 revision of the NIPAs. Estimates are available only from 1982 forward. With the new treatment of disaster losses and disaster insurance introduced in the 2009 revision, this line will include disaster-related insurance payouts to the rest of the world less what is received from the rest of the world.

Net lending or net borrowing (-), NIPAs is equal to the international balance on current account as measured in the NIPAs (see Chapter 7) less capital account transactions, net. When positive, this represents net investment by the

United States in the rest of the world; when negative, it represents net borrowing by the United States from the rest of the world. For data before 1982, net lending or net borrowing equals the NIPA balance on current account, because estimates of capital account transactions are not available.

By definition, gross national saving must equal the sum of gross domestic investment, capital account transactions, and net international lending (where net international borrowing appears as negative lending). In practice, due to differences in measurement, these two aggregates differ by the *statistical discrepancy* calculated in the product and income accounts. (See Chapter 1.) Gross saving is therefore equal to the sum of gross domestic investment, capital account transactions, and net international lending minus the statistical discrepancy. Where the statistical discrepancy is negative, it means that the sum of measured investment, capital transactions, and net international lending has fallen short of measured saving.

Net domestic investment is gross domestic investment minus consumption of fixed capital.

Gross national income is national income plus the consumption of fixed capital. (See Chapter 1 for further information.) This is a new concept introduced in the 2003 revision. It is conceptually equal to gross national product, but differs by the statistical discrepancy. Gross national income is an appropriate denominator for the national saving ratios. Saving was previously shown as a percentage of gross national product; in the revision, it is instead shown as a percentage of the income-side equivalent of gross national product. Since saving is measured as a residual from income, it is appropriate to involve consistent measurements—and consistent imperfections in those measurements— in both the numerator and the denominator of the fraction.

Definitions: Tables 5-2 through 5-4

Gross private fixed investment comprises both nonresidential and residential fixed investment. It consists of purchases of fixed assets, which are commodities that will be used in a production process for more than one year, including replacements and additions to the capital stock. It is "gross" in the sense that it is measured before a deduction for consumption of fixed capital. It covers all investment by private businesses and nonprofit institutions in the United States, regardless of whether the investment is owned by U.S. residents. It does not include purchases of the same types of equipment and structures by government agencies, which are included in government gross investment, or investment by U.S. residents in other countries.

Gross nonresidential fixed investment consists of structures, equipment, and software that are not related to personal residences.

Nonresidential structures consists of new construction, brokers' commissions on sales of structures, and net purchases (purchases less sales) of used structures by private business and by nonprofit institutions from government agencies. New construction includes hotels, motels, and mining exploration, shafts, and wells.

Other nonresidential structures consists primarily of religious, educational, vocational, lodging, railroads, farm, and amusement and recreational structures, net purchases of used structures, and brokers' commissions on the sale of structures.

Nonresidential equipment and software consists of private business purchases—on capital account—of new machinery, equipment, and vehicles; purchases and in-house production of software; dealers' margins on sales of used equipment; and net purchases (purchases less sales) of used equipment from government agencies, persons, and the rest of the world. (However, it does not include the personal-use portion of equipment purchased for both business and personal use. This is included in PCE.)

Software excludes the value of software "embedded," or bundled, in computers and other equipment, which is instead included in the value of that equipment.

Other information processing includes communication equipment, nonmedical instruments, medical equipment and instruments, photocopy and related equipment, and office and accounting equipment.

Other nonresidential equipment consists primarily of furniture and fixtures, agricultural machinery, construction machinery, mining and oilfield machinery, service industry machinery, and electrical equipment not elsewhere classified.

Residential private fixed investment consists of both *structures* and residential producers' durable *equipment*—that is, equipment owned by landlords and rented to tenants. Investment in *structures* consists of new units, improvements to existing units, manufactured homes, brokers' commissions on the sale of residential property, and net purchases (purchases less sales) of used structures from government agencies.

Other residential structures consists primarily of manufactured homes, improvements, dormitories, net purchases of used structures, and brokers' commissions on the sale of residential structures.

Real gross private investment (Table 5-3) and *chain-type quantity indexes for private fixed investment* (Table 5-4) are defined and explained in the notes and definitions to Chapter 1. The chained-dollar (2005) estimates in Table 5-3 are constructed by applying the changes in the chain-type quantity indexes, as shown in Table 5-4, to the 2005 current-dollar values. Thus, they do not contain any information about time trends that is not already present in the quantity indexes.

As the quantity indexes are chain-weighted at the basic level of aggregation, chained constant-dollar components generally do not add to the chained constant-dollar totals.

For this reason, BEA only makes available year-2005-dollar estimates back to 1995 (except for the very highest levels of aggregation of gross domestic product [GDP]), since the addition problem is less severe for years close to the base year. However, the addition problem is so severe for computers that BEA does not even publish recent year-2005-dollar values for this component. BEA notes that "The quantity index for computers can be used to accurately measure the real growth rate of this component. However, because computers exhibit rapid changes in prices relative to other prices in the economy, the chained-dollar estimates should not be used to measure the component's relative importance or its contribution to the growth rate of more aggregate series." (Footnote to BEA Table 5.3.6, *Survey of Current Business*, available on the BEA Web site at <http://www.bea.gov>.) Accurate estimates of these contributions are shown in BEA Table 5.3.2, which is published in the *Survey of Current Business* and can be found on the BEA Web site.

Definitions: Table 5-7

Inventories to sales ratios. The ratios shown in Table 5-7 are based on the inventory estimates underlying the measurement of inventory change in the NIPAs. They include data and estimates for not only the inventories held in manufacturing and trade (which are shown in the following Tables 5-8 and 5-9), but also stocks held by all other businesses in the U.S. economy.

For the current-dollar ratios, inventories at the end of each quarter are valued in the prices that prevailed at the end of that quarter. For the constant-dollar ratios, they are valued in chained (2005) dollars. In both cases, the inventory-sales ratio is the value of the inventories at the end of the quarter divided by quarterly total sales at monthly rates (quarterly totals divided by 3). In other words, they represent how many months' supply businesses had on hand at the end of the period. This makes them comparable in concept and order of magnitude to the ratios shown in Tables 5-8 and 5-9. Annual ratios are those for the fourth quarter.

Data availability, revisions, and references

See the information on the NIPAs at the end of the notes and definitions to Chapter 1. All current and historical data are available on the BEA Web site at <http://www.bea.gov> or the STAT-USA subscription Web site at <http://www.stat-usa.gov>.

TABLES 5-5 AND 5-6
CURRENT-COST NET STOCK OF FIXED ASSETS; CHAIN-TYPE QUANTITY INDEXES FOR NET STOCK OF FIXED ASSETS

SOURCE: U.S. DEPARTMENT OF COMMERCE, BUREAU OF ECONOMIC ANALYSIS (BEA)

The Bureau of Economic Analysis (BEA) calculates measurements, integrated with the national income and product accounts (NIPAs), of the level of the stock of fixed assets in the U.S. economy, or what is commonly called the "capital stock." (The fixed investment component of the GDP is a flow, or the increment of new capital goods into the capital stock.) Data on consumer stocks of durable goods are also included in the accounts, but are not shown here. Historical data are available back to 1901, with detailed annual estimates of net stocks, depreciation, and investment by type and by NAICS (North American Industry Classification System) industry. This volume of *Business Statistics* presents time series data on the net stock of fixed assets valued in current dollars and also as constant-dollar quantity indexes. Data for 1947 through 2008 are presented in Tables 5-5 and 5-6, and data for 1929 through 1948 are presented in Table 18-3.

Definitions and methods

The definitions of capital stock categories are the same as used in GDP investment categories. (See the notes and definitions to Tables 5-2 through 5-4 for more information.)

The values of fixed capital and depreciation typically reported by businesses are inadequate for economic analysis and are not typically used in these measures. In business reports, capital is generally valued at historical costs—each year's capital acquisition in the prices of the year acquired—and the totals thus represent a mixture of pricing bases. Reported depreciation is generally based on historical cost and on depreciation rates allowable by federal income tax law, rather than on a realistic rate of economic depreciation.

In these data, the *net stock of fixed assets* is measured by a perpetual inventory method. In other words, net stock at any given time is the cumulative value of past gross investment less the cumulative value of past depreciation (measured by "consumption of fixed capital," the component of the NIPAs that is subtracted from GDP in order to yield net domestic product) and also less damages from disasters and war losses that exceed normal depreciation (such as Hurricane Katrina and the terrorist attacks of September 11, 2001).

The initial calculations using this perpetual inventory method are performed in real terms for each type of asset. They are then aggregated to higher levels using an annual-weighted Fisher-type index. (See the definition of *real or chained-dollar estimates* in the notes and definitions for Chapter 1.) This provides the *chain-type quantity indexes* shown in Table 5-6. Growth rates in these indexes measure real growth in the capital stock.

The real values are then converted to a *current-cost* basis to yield the values shown in Table 5-5. They are converted by multiplying the real values by the appropriate price index for the period under consideration. A major use of the current-cost net stock figures is comparison with the value of output in that year; for example, the current-cost net stock of fixed assets for the total economy divided by the current-dollar value of GDP yields a capital-output ratio for the entire economy. Growth rates in current-cost values will reflect both the real growth measured by the quantity indexes and the increase in the value at current prices of the existing stock.

Data availability and references

The latest comprehensive revision was presented and described in "Fixed Assets and Consumer Durable Goods for 1999–2008," *Survey of Current Business* (November 2009). Annual data back to 1925 are available on the BEA Web site at <www.bea.gov/national/FA2004/Index.asp>.

**TABLES 5-8 AND 5-9
MANUFACTURING AND TRADE SALES AND INVENTORIES**

SOURCES: U.S. DEPARTMENT OF COMMERCE, CENSUS BUREAU (CURRENT-DOLLAR SERIES) AND U.S. DEPARTMENT OF COMMERCE, BUREAU OF ECONOMIC ANALYSIS (BEA; CONSTANT-DOLLAR SERIES)

The current-dollar data on which these tables are based bring together summary data from the separate series on manufacturers' shipments, inventories, and orders; merchant wholesalers' sales and inventories; and retail sales and inventories, all of which are included in Part B of this book. Generally, current-dollar inventories are collected on a current cost (or pre-LIFO [last in, first out]) basis. See the notes and definitions for Tables 17-4, 17-5, 17-9, 17-11, and 17-12 for further information about these data.

Based on these current-dollar values and relevant price data, BEA makes estimates of real sales, inventories, and inventory-sales ratios. Note, however, that annual figures for sales are shown as annual totals in Table 5-8 but as averages of the monthly data in Table 5-9. Also note that constant-dollar detail may not add to constant-dollar totals because of the chain-weighting formula; see the discussion of chain-weighted measures in the notes and definitions for Chapter 1.

Inventory values are as of the end of the month or year. In Table 5-8, annual values for monthly current-dollar inventory-sales ratios are averages of seasonally adjusted monthly ratios. However, for the real ratios in Table 5-9, annual figures for inventory-sales ratios are calculated by BEA as year-end (December) inventories divided by the monthly average of sales for the entire year. In all cases, the ratios in these two tables (like those in Table 5-7) represent the number of months' sales on hand as inventory at the end of the reporting period.

Data availability

Sales, inventories, and inventory-sales ratios for manufacturers, merchant wholesalers, and retailers are published monthly by the Census Bureau in a press release entitled "Manufacturing and Trade Inventories and Sales." Recent and historical data are available on the Census Bureau Web site at <http://www.census.gov/mtis/www/mtis.html>. They can also be found by going to the general Census website, <http://www.census.gov>, going to the alphabetical index, finding "Economic Indicators" under "E" and then finding "Manufacturing and trade."

Sales and inventories in constant dollars are available on the BEA Web site at <http://www.bea.gov>. To locate these data on that site, click on "National Economic Accounts." Scroll down to "Supplemental Estimates," click "Underlying Detail Tables," and then click on "List of Underlying Detail Tables." For the most recent data, if there is more than one table with the same title, select the last table listed.

References

For information about the 1996 historical revisions to sales and inventories in constant dollars, see "Real Inventories, Sales, and Inventory-Sales Ratios for Manufacturing and Trade, 1977–95," *Survey of Current Business* (May 1996).

**TABLES 5-10 AND 5-11
ANNUAL CAPITAL EXPENDITURES**

SOURCE: U.S. DEPARTMENT OF COMMERCE, CENSUS BUREAU

These data are from the Census Bureau's Annual Capital Expenditures Survey (ACES). The survey provides detailed information on capital investment in new and used structures and equipment by nonfarm businesses.

The survey is based on a stratified random sample of approximately 46,000 companies with employees and 15,000 non-employer businesses (businesses with an owner but no employees). For companies with employees, the Census Bureau reports data for 132 separate industry categories from the North American Industry Classification System (NAICS); Table 5-11 shows these data for the major NAICS sectors. Total capital expenditures, with no industry detail, are reported for the nonemployer businesses and are shown in Table 5-10, where they can be compared with the totals for companies with employees. The 1999 ACES was the first to use NAICS, providing data for the years 1998 forward on that basis.

Definitions

Capital expenditures include all capitalized costs during the year for both new and used structures and equipment, including software, that were chargeable to fixed asset accounts for which depreciation or amortization accounts are ordinarily maintained. For projects lasting longer than one year, this definition includes gross additions to construction-in-progress accounts, even if the asset was not in use and not yet depreciated. For *capital leases*, the company using the asset (lessee) is asked to include the cost or present value of the leased assets in the year in which the lease was entered. Also included in capital expenditures are capitalized leasehold improvements and capitalized interest charges on loans used to finance capital projects.

Structures consist of the capitalized costs of buildings and other structures and all necessary expenditures to acquire, construct, and prepare the structures. The costs of any machinery and equipment that is integral to or built-in features of the structures are classified as structures. Also included are major additions and alterations to existing structures and capitalized repairs and improvements to buildings.

New structures include new buildings and other structures not previously owned, as well as buildings and other structures that have been previously owned but not used or occupied.

Used structures are buildings and other structures that have been previously owned and occupied.

Equipment includes machinery, furniture and fixtures, computers, and vehicles used in the production and distribution of goods and services. Expenditures for machinery and equipment that is housed in structures and can be removed or replaced without significantly altering the structure are classified as equipment.

New equipment consists of machinery and equipment purchased new, as well as equipment produced in the company for the company's own use.

Used equipment is secondhand machinery and equipment.

Capital leases consist of new assets acquired under capital lease arrangements entered into during the year. Capital leases are defined by the criteria in the Financial Accounting Standards (FASB) Number 13.

Capitalized computer software consists of costs of materials and services directly related to the development or acquisition of software; payroll and payroll-related costs for employees directly associated with software development; and interest cost incurred while developing the software. Capitalized computer software is defined by the criteria in Statement of Position 98-1, Accounting for the Costs of Computer Software Developed or Obtained for Internal Use.

Prepackaged software is purchased off-the-shelf through retailers or other mass-market outlets for internal use by the company and includes the cost of licensing fees and service/maintenance agreements.

Vendor-customized software is externally developed by vendors and customized for the company's use.

Internally-developed software is developed by the company's employees for internal use and includes loaded payroll (salaries, wages, benefits, and bonuses related to all software development activities).

Data availability and references

Current and historical data and references are available on the Census Bureau Web site at <http://www.census.gov/econ/aces>. Preliminary data for 2008 and final revised data for 2007 were posted in February 2010. Around midyear, a more extensive report for 2008 will be available, with data revised from the first preliminary estimates but still subject to further revision in the following year.

CHAPTER 6: GOVERNMENT

Section 6a: Federal Government in the National Income and Product Accounts

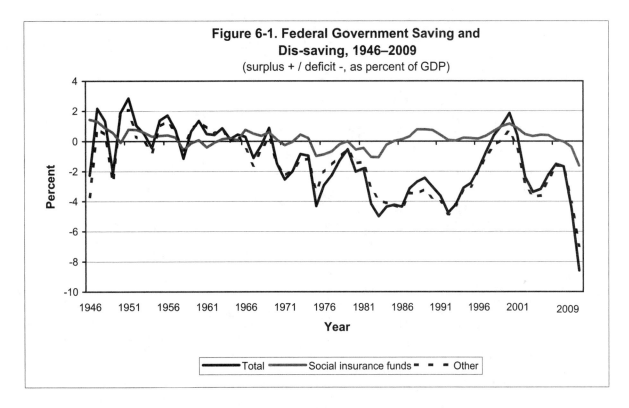

Figure 6-1. Federal Government Saving and Dis-saving, 1946–2009

(surplus + / deficit -, as percent of GDP)

- In the recovery and economic expansion of the 2000s, the federal budget never got back to a surplus such as those achieved in 1999 and 2000. With the onset of the most severe recession of the postwar period beginning in December 2007, deficits grew rapidly as receipts fell while expenditures continued to rise. In calendar 2009, the NIPA budget deficit was 8.6 percent of GDP, including a 1.6 percent deficit in social insurance funds. This was not as great as wartime deficits but exceeded in scale the deficits of the 1930s. (Tables 6-1, 1-1, and 18-6)

- Total federal government current expenditures increased from 17.6 percent of gross domestic product (GDP) in 1953—the peak for Korean War spending— to 24.2 percent of GDP in 2009. The composition of expenditures changed significantly over that period. "Consumption" spending on defense and nondefense programs fell from 72 percent of total spending to 29 percent, while social benefits such as Social Security and Medicare rose from 13 percent to 47 percent. Grants to state and local governments increased from 3 percent to 14 percent. (Tables 6-1 and 1-1)

- Federal government nondefense consumption spending, in real terms (as measured by the quantity index), increased at an annual rate of 2.5 percent from 1953 to 2009. Real federal nondefense gross investment spending rose 3.8 percent per year. (Table 6-6)

- Real defense consumption spending jumped 46 percent in the eight years since 2000, but in 2009 was still only 33 percent (an annual rate of 0.5 percent) above spending in 1953. Real defense investment spending was up 112 percent from 2000, and was up 66 percent (an annual rate of 0.9 percent) from 1953. (Table 6-6)

Table 6-1. Federal Government Current Receipts and Expenditures

(National income and product accounts, calendar years, billions of dollars, quarterly data are at seasonally adjusted annual rates.)

NIPA Table 3.2

				Current receipts										
		Current tax receipts							Contribu-tions for govern-ment social insurance	Income receipts on assets				Current surplus of govern-ment enter-prises
				Taxes on production and imports		Taxes on corporate income		Taxes from the rest of the world					Current transfer receipts	
Year and quarter	Total current receipts	Total tax receipts	Personal current taxes	Excise taxes	Custom duities	Federal Reserve banks	Other corporate taxes			Interest receipts	Dividends	Rents and royalties		
1950	48.8	43.3	17.4	8.2	0.5	0.2	17.0	...	5.3	...	...	...	0.2	...
1951	62.9	56.2	25.4	8.6	0.6	0.3	21.4	...	6.4	...	...	...	0.3	...
1952	65.8	58.9	30.2	9.6	0.6	0.3	18.3	...	6.7	...	...	...	0.3	...
1953	68.6	61.5	31.3	10.1	0.6	0.3	19.1	...	6.8	...	...	...	0.3	...
1954	62.5	54.4	28.1	9.0	0.5	0.3	16.6	...	7.8	...	...	...	0.3	...
1955	71.1	62.0	30.5	9.8	0.7	0.3	20.8	...	8.8	...	...	...	0.3	...
1956	75.8	65.8	33.9	10.2	0.7	0.4	20.5	...	9.6	...	...	...	0.4	...
1957	79.3	67.9	36.0	10.7	0.8	0.5	19.9	...	11.0	...	...	...	0.4	...
1958	76.1	64.6	35.5	10.4	0.8	0.5	17.4	...	11.0	...	...	...	0.4	...
1959	87.0	73.2	38.5	11.2	1.0	0.9	21.6	0.1	13.5	...	...	0.0	0.4	-0.1
1960	93.9	76.5	41.8	12.0	1.1	0.9	20.6	0.1	16.0	1.3	...	0.0	0.4	-0.3
1961	95.5	77.5	42.7	12.1	1.0	0.7	20.8	0.1	16.6	1.4	...	0.1	0.5	-0.5
1962	103.6	83.3	46.5	12.9	1.2	0.8	21.7	0.1	18.6	1.6	...	0.1	0.5	-0.5
1963	111.8	88.6	49.1	13.5	1.2	0.9	23.7	0.2	21.1	1.7	...	0.1	0.6	-0.3
1964	111.8	87.7	46.0	14.1	1.3	1.6	24.6	0.2	21.8	1.7	...	0.1	0.7	-0.3
1965	121.0	95.6	51.1	13.8	1.6	1.3	27.6	0.2	22.7	1.8	...	0.1	1.1	-0.3
1966	138.0	104.7	58.6	12.6	1.9	1.6	29.8	0.2	30.6	2.0	...	0.1	1.2	-0.6
1967	146.9	109.8	64.4	13.3	1.9	1.9	28.1	0.2	34.1	2.3	...	0.2	1.1	-0.6
1968	171.3	129.7	76.4	14.6	2.3	2.5	33.6	0.3	37.9	2.7	...	0.2	1.1	-0.3
1969	192.7	146.0	91.7	15.4	2.4	3.0	33.0	0.4	43.3	2.5	...	0.2	1.1	-0.4
1970	186.1	137.9	88.9	15.6	2.5	3.5	27.1	0.4	45.5	2.8	...	0.2	1.1	-1.5
1971	191.9	138.6	85.8	15.9	3.1	3.4	30.1	0.4	50.3	3.1	...	0.3	1.1	-1.6
1972	220.3	158.2	102.8	15.5	3.0	3.2	33.4	0.4	58.3	3.3	...	0.4	1.3	-1.1
1973	250.8	173.0	109.6	16.5	3.3	4.3	38.9	0.4	74.5	3.4	...	0.4	1.3	-1.8
1974	280.0	192.1	126.5	16.4	3.7	5.6	39.6	0.4	84.1	3.6	...	0.5	1.4	-1.8
1975	277.6	186.8	120.7	16.2	5.9	5.4	38.2	0.5	88.1	4.3	...	0.6	1.5	-3.6
1976	323.0	217.9	141.2	16.8	4.6	5.9	48.7	0.7	99.8	5.2	...	0.7	1.6	-2.2
1977	364.0	247.2	162.2	17.3	5.4	5.9	55.7	0.7	111.1	5.8	...	0.9	2.0	-3.0
1978	424.0	286.6	188.9	18.2	7.1	7.0	64.4	1.0	128.7	7.4	...	1.1	2.7	-2.5
1979	486.9	325.9	224.6	18.2	7.5	9.3	65.1	1.1	149.8	9.2	...	1.5	3.1	-2.6
1980	532.8	355.5	250.0	26.5	7.2	11.7	58.6	1.6	163.6	11.3	...	2.3	3.9	-3.9
1981	619.9	407.7	290.6	41.3	8.6	14.0	51.7	1.5	193.0	14.8	...	3.5	4.1	-3.2
1982	617.4	386.3	295.0	32.3	8.6	15.2	33.8	1.4	206.0	18.3	...	3.8	5.7	-2.9
1983	643.3	393.2	286.2	35.3	9.1	14.2	47.1	1.2	223.1	20.4	...	3.5	6.1	-3.0
1984	710.0	425.2	301.4	35.4	11.9	16.1	59.2	1.3	254.1	22.8	...	3.9	7.4	-3.4
1985	774.4	460.2	336.0	33.9	12.2	17.8	58.5	1.9	277.9	25.7	...	3.5	9.7	-2.6
1986	816.0	479.2	350.0	30.0	13.7	17.8	66.0	1.7	298.9	28.8	...	2.4	8.5	-1.9
1987	896.5	543.6	392.5	30.4	15.5	17.7	85.4	2.0	317.4	25.1	...	2.3	11.0	-3.0
1988	958.5	566.2	402.8	33.4	16.4	17.4	93.8	2.4	354.8	27.4	...	2.0	10.5	-2.3
1989	1 038.0	621.2	451.5	32.3	17.5	21.6	95.6	2.7	378.0	25.9	...	2.1	12.7	-1.7
1990	1 082.8	642.2	470.1	33.4	17.5	23.6	94.5	3.0	402.0	27.0	...	2.6	14.2	-5.3
1991	1 101.9	635.6	461.3	44.9	16.8	20.8	89.2	2.6	420.6	26.3	...	2.8	18.2	-1.6
1992	1 148.0	659.9	475.2	45.0	18.3	16.8	102.0	2.6	444.0	22.2	...	2.6	19.4	0.0
1993	1 224.1	713.0	505.5	46.5	19.8	16.0	122.5	2.7	465.5	22.8	...	2.7	21.3	-1.3
1994	1 322.1	781.4	542.5	57.5	21.4	20.5	136.3	3.1	496.2	20.0	...	2.7	22.8	-0.9
1995	1 407.8	844.6	585.8	55.7	19.8	23.4	155.9	3.9	521.9	20.8	...	2.5	18.4	-0.3
1996	1 526.4	931.9	663.3	53.6	19.2	20.1	170.5	5.2	545.4	22.5	...	4.0	23.8	-1.2
1997	1 656.2	1 030.1	744.2	58.2	19.6	20.7	182.3	5.1	579.4	21.0	...	4.5	21.3	-0.1
1998	1 777.9	1 115.8	825.2	61.1	19.6	26.6	177.7	5.7	617.4	17.3	...	3.9	22.6	0.8
1999	1 895.0	1 195.4	893.0	64.3	19.2	25.4	187.6	5.9	654.8	17.1	...	3.5	23.4	0.8
2000	2 057.1	1 309.6	995.6	66.1	21.1	25.3	194.1	7.3	698.6	19.3	...	5.2	25.7	-1.2
2001	2 020.3	1 249.4	991.8	64.6	20.6	27.1	137.6	7.7	723.3	18.1	...	6.5	27.0	-4.0
2002	1 859.3	1 073.5	828.6	66.9	19.9	24.5	126.0	7.6	739.3	15.4	...	4.8	26.1	0.2
2003	1 885.1	1 070.2	774.2	67.9	21.4	22.0	175.8	9.0	762.8	16.4	...	6.4	25.6	3.7
2004	2 013.9	1 153.8	799.2	71.0	23.3	18.1	232.2	10.0	807.6	16.3	0.1	6.8	29.0	0.3
2005	2 290.1	1 383.7	931.9	73.5	25.3	21.5	319.5	12.1	852.6	16.4	0.2	7.0	33.6	-3.5
2006	2 524.5	1 558.3	1 049.9	72.7	26.7	29.1	366.0	14.0	904.6	18.2	0.3	7.7	38.3	-2.9
2007	2 660.8	1 647.2	1 168.1	65.9	28.8	34.6	335.6	14.2	944.4	21.6	0.2	7.3	42.7	-2.7
2008	2 475.0	1 421.7	1 102.5	62.7	29.2	31.7	180.6	15.0	974.5	19.7	0.6	10.0	52.3	-3.8
2009	2 226.6	1 165.1	829.5	69.5	22.8	44.5	186.5	12.3	950.1	23.9	18.8	5.5	68.1	-4.9
2007														
1st quarter	2 640.1	1 638.3	1 136.8	66.2	28.7	35.0	358.6	13.0	937.3	21.4	0.2	6.7	41.0	-4.8
2nd quarter	2 660.1	1 654.0	1 157.6	66.7	28.1	35.3	352.0	14.2	938.8	22.1	0.2	6.5	41.5	-2.9
3rd quarter	2 659.9	1 644.8	1 177.6	66.4	29.0	34.4	324.1	13.3	943.8	21.9	0.2	7.4	42.6	-0.8
4th quarter	2 682.9	1 651.7	1 200.6	64.3	29.3	33.6	307.7	16.3	957.6	20.8	0.2	8.8	45.8	-2.1
2008														
1st quarter	2 590.7	1 546.0	1 195.3	62.8	29.9	31.9	211.2	14.9	970.0	19.2	0.2	9.9	47.9	-2.5
2nd quarter	2 372.1	1 322.8	984.2	63.6	29.5	27.6	203.6	14.3	973.0	18.9	0.2	12.0	48.4	-3.4
3rd quarter	2 489.5	1 435.2	1 110.1	62.5	29.4	30.7	187.8	14.7	978.5	20.5	0.2	9.9	49.0	-3.9
4th quarter	2 447.8	1 382.9	1 120.2	62.1	28.1	36.5	120.0	15.9	976.4	20.2	1.7	8.1	64.0	-5.4
2009														
1st quarter	2 251.3	1 191.5	900.3	62.2	23.6	25.6	166.4	13.5	953.0	21.9	12.8	6.1	72.7	-6.7
2nd quarter	2 237.0	1 157.4	829.9	70.0	21.6	40.9	182.9	12.1	954.3	23.7	21.0	6.2	79.8	-5.3
3rd quarter	2 188.5	1 138.1	795.8	72.4	21.0	51.2	186.8	10.8	945.7	25.3	19.1	5.1	58.7	-3.5
4th quarter	2 229.8	1 173.6	791.8	73.5	25.0	60.3	209.8	13.1	947.6	24.7	22.4	4.6	61.1	-4.2

. . . = Not available.

Table 6-1. Federal Government Current Receipts and Expenditures—*Continued*

(National income and product accounts, calendar years, billions of dollars, quarterly data are at seasonally adjusted annual rates.)

NIPA Table 3.2

Year and quarter	Total current expenditures	Consumption expenditures	Government social benefits — Benefits to persons	Government social benefits — Benefits to the rest of the world	Other current transfer payments — Grants-in-aid to state and local governments	Other current transfer payments — Payments to the rest of the world	Interest payments — Total	Interest payments — To persons and business	Interest payments — To the rest of the world	Subsidies	Net federal government saving, NIPA (surplus + / deficit -) — Total	Net federal government saving, NIPA (surplus + / deficit -) — Social insurance funds	Net federal government saving, NIPA (surplus + / deficit -) — Other
1950	43.2	22.0	10.2	...	1.9	3.6	4.5	...	0.0	1.0	5.6	-0.3	5.8
1951	53.2	34.4	7.9	...	2.0	3.2	4.6	...	0.0	1.2	9.7	2.6	7.0
1952	62.1	44.2	8.1	...	2.2	2.2	4.6	...	0.1	0.9	3.7	2.7	1.1
1953	66.8	48.3	8.7	...	2.3	2.1	4.7	...	0.1	0.7	1.8	2.1	-0.3
1954	64.2	43.9	10.7	...	2.3	1.9	4.8	...	0.1	0.6	-1.7	1.2	-2.9
1955	65.4	43.9	11.5	...	2.4	2.2	4.8	...	0.1	0.6	5.7	1.5	4.1
1956	68.3	45.0	12.3	...	2.5	2.0	5.2	...	0.2	1.2	7.5	1.7	5.8
1957	76.1	49.5	14.5	...	2.9	2.0	5.7	...	0.2	1.6	3.3	1.1	2.2
1958	81.5	50.9	18.2	...	3.3	2.0	5.4	...	0.1	1.8	-5.4	-2.7	-2.8
1959	83.7	49.9	18.6	...	3.8	4.0	6.3	...	0.3	1.1	3.3	-0.7	3.9
1960	86.8	49.7	19.9	0.2	4.0	3.5	8.4	8.0	0.3	1.1	7.1	0.4	6.7
1961	92.9	51.6	23.1	0.3	4.5	3.5	7.9	7.6	0.3	2.0	2.6	-2.3	4.9
1962	101.2	57.8	23.5	0.3	5.0	3.6	8.6	8.3	0.3	2.3	2.4	-0.6	3.0
1963	106.5	60.8	24.6	0.3	5.6	3.6	9.3	8.9	0.4	2.2	5.3	0.8	4.5
1964	110.9	62.8	25.2	0.3	6.5	3.4	10.0	9.6	0.5	2.7	0.9	1.3	-0.3
1965	117.7	65.7	27.3	0.5	7.2	3.6	10.6	10.1	0.5	3.0	3.2	0.4	2.8
1966	135.7	75.7	29.9	0.5	10.1	4.0	11.6	11.1	0.5	3.9	2.3	6.0	-3.7
1967	156.2	87.0	36.5	0.6	11.7	4.0	12.7	12.1	0.6	3.8	-9.3	4.1	-13.4
1968	173.7	95.3	41.9	0.6	12.7	4.5	14.6	13.9	0.7	4.1	-2.4	3.2	-5.6
1969	184.1	98.3	45.8	0.6	14.6	4.5	15.8	15.0	0.8	4.5	8.6	5.7	2.9
1970	201.6	98.6	55.6	0.7	19.3	4.8	17.7	16.7	1.0	4.8	-15.5	1.0	-16.4
1971	220.6	101.9	66.1	0.8	23.2	6.0	17.9	16.1	1.8	4.6	-28.7	-3.0	-25.7
1972	245.2	107.6	72.9	1.0	31.7	7.2	18.8	16.1	2.7	6.6	-24.9	-0.6	-24.3
1973	262.6	108.8	84.5	1.2	34.8	5.4	22.8	19.0	3.8	5.1	-11.8	5.9	-17.7
1974	294.5	117.9	103.3	1.3	36.3	6.0	26.0	21.7	4.3	3.2	-14.5	3.2	-17.7
1975	348.3	129.5	132.3	2.0	45.1	6.1	28.9	24.4	4.5	4.3	-70.6	-16.3	-54.4
1976	376.7	137.1	143.1	2.5	50.7	4.5	33.8	29.3	4.5	4.9	-53.7	-16.0	-37.6
1977	410.1	150.7	152.1	2.6	56.6	4.2	37.1	31.6	5.5	6.9	-46.1	-14.1	-32.1
1978	452.9	163.3	162.4	2.7	65.5	5.0	45.3	36.7	8.7	8.7	-28.9	-4.7	-24.2
1979	500.9	178.9	182.8	3.0	66.3	5.8	55.7	44.6	11.1	8.2	-14.0	0.0	-13.9
1980	589.5	207.4	219.6	3.5	72.3	7.3	69.7	57.0	12.7	9.4	-56.6	-15.8	-40.8
1981	676.7	238.3	250.1	4.3	72.5	6.7	93.9	76.6	17.3	11.1	-56.8	-14.3	-42.5
1982	752.6	263.3	281.2	4.1	69.5	8.1	111.8	92.5	19.3	14.6	-135.3	-34.4	-100.9
1983	819.5	286.4	303.0	3.6	71.6	8.9	124.6	105.6	19.0	20.9	-176.2	-37.9	-138.4
1984	881.5	309.9	309.2	3.7	76.7	11.2	150.3	129.1	21.2	20.7	-171.5	-9.4	-162.1
1985	953.0	338.3	325.4	4.0	80.9	13.8	169.4	146.3	23.1	21.0	-178.6	0.9	-179.5
1986	1 010.7	358.0	343.7	4.4	87.6	14.2	178.2	153.5	24.6	24.6	-194.6	5.7	-200.3
1987	1 045.9	373.7	356.7	4.3	83.9	12.7	184.6	158.4	26.2	30.0	-149.3	14.5	-163.8
1988	1 096.9	381.7	377.4	4.6	91.6	13.2	199.3	167.6	31.7	29.2	-138.4	39.1	-177.5
1989	1 172.0	398.5	410.1	5.1	98.3	13.5	219.3	181.0	38.4	27.1	-133.9	42.6	-176.6
1990	1 259.2	419.0	445.1	6.2	111.4	13.5	237.5	196.7	40.8	26.6	-176.4	42.4	-218.8
1991	1 320.3	438.3	491.7	6.3	131.6	-25.6	250.9	210.1	40.9	27.1	-218.4	24.7	-243.1
1992	1 450.5	444.1	549.5	6.2	149.1	20.6	251.3	212.2	39.1	29.7	-302.5	5.4	-307.8
1993	1 504.3	441.2	581.5	6.2	164.0	21.7	253.4	214.0	39.4	36.3	-280.2	2.8	-283.1
1994	1 542.5	440.7	606.4	6.8	175.1	19.9	261.3	217.1	44.2	32.2	-220.4	15.4	-235.7
1995	1 614.0	440.1	642.6	6.8	184.2	15.4	290.4	234.8	55.6	34.5	-206.2	15.6	-221.8
1996	1 674.7	446.5	676.9	7.6	191.1	20.4	297.3	230.6	66.6	34.9	-148.2	12.9	-161.2
1997	1 716.3	457.5	702.2	7.9	198.4	17.0	300.0	218.3	81.7	33.4	-60.1	28.9	-89.1
1998	1 744.3	454.6	716.1	8.2	212.6	18.0	298.8	214.7	84.2	35.9	33.6	58.3	-24.7
1999	1 796.2	473.3	735.3	8.5	232.9	18.7	282.7	202.1	80.5	44.8	98.8	92.5	6.3
2000	1 871.9	496.0	769.1	8.7	247.3	22.3	283.3	198.7	84.5	45.3	185.2	114.3	70.9
2001	1 979.8	530.2	836.3	9.4	276.1	18.2	258.6	180.2	78.4	51.1	40.5	88.1	-47.6
2002	2 112.1	590.5	914.9	9.7	304.2	23.3	229.1	154.2	74.9	40.5	-252.8	49.7	-302.5
2003	2 261.5	660.3	962.6	10.1	338.0	28.6	212.9	139.0	73.8	49.0	-376.4	37.6	-413.9
2004	2 393.4	721.4	1 014.3	10.6	349.2	30.9	221.0	138.4	82.5	46.0	-379.5	50.3	-429.7
2005	2 573.1	765.8	1 078.0	11.2	361.2	40.9	255.4	151.5	103.9	60.5	-283.0	49.0	-332.0
2006	2 728.3	811.0	1 180.7	12.4	359.0	34.9	279.2	144.2	135.0	51.0	-203.8	12.4	-216.1
2007	2 897.2	848.8	1 254.2	13.3	378.9	42.2	312.2	147.9	164.3	47.6	-236.5	-4.6	-231.9
2008	3 117.6	934.4	1 388.2	16.0	391.7	44.8	292.0	126.6	165.3	50.6	-642.6	-55.2	-587.4
2009	3 451.3	986.4	1 596.1	15.7	476.6	46.0	272.3	136.0	136.2	58.2	-1 224.7	-231.9	-992.8
2007													
1st quarter	2 841.0	821.1	1 227.3	13.3	375.0	50.7	306.4	150.1	156.2	47.4	-200.9	9.8	-210.7
2nd quarter	2 881.3	839.9	1 246.7	13.4	380.7	31.6	321.3	155.7	165.6	47.7	-221.3	-4.2	-217.0
3rd quarter	2 918.7	860.8	1 263.8	13.3	379.7	37.3	316.6	149.7	166.9	47.3	-258.8	-13.7	-245.1
4th quarter	2 947.9	873.4	1 278.9	13.2	380.3	49.2	304.7	136.1	168.6	48.2	-265.0	-10.2	-254.8
2008													
1st quarter	3 024.2	903.2	1 313.4	13.6	382.5	50.1	312.3	144.4	167.9	49.2	-433.5	-25.6	-407.9
2nd quarter	3 169.0	923.2	1 450.4	22.1	391.8	40.2	291.4	120.1	171.3	49.9	-796.9	-39.8	-757.2
3rd quarter	3 155.2	956.0	1 382.0	14.0	390.0	43.0	319.5	155.3	164.3	50.7	-665.7	-67.9	-597.8
4th quarter	3 121.9	955.4	1 407.0	14.1	402.4	45.9	244.6	86.8	157.8	52.4	-674.1	-87.5	-586.6
2009													
1st quarter	3 220.3	954.2	1 489.1	15.0	437.7	39.5	231.3	85.3	146.0	53.6	-969.1	-177.7	-791.3
2nd quarter	3 505.9	979.1	1 630.2	15.9	497.9	51.7	277.4	138.6	138.8	53.7	-1 268.9	-223.9	-1 045.0
3rd quarter	3 542.1	1 001.2	1 624.6	16.1	483.7	53.7	296.3	164.9	131.4	66.5	-1 353.6	-258.1	-1 095.5
4th quarter	3 537.0	1 011.0	1 640.6	15.9	487.2	39.0	284.1	155.4	128.7	59.1	-1 307.2	-267.8	-1 039.4

. . . = Not available.

Table 6-2. Federal Government Consumption Expenditures and Gross Investment

(National income and product accounts, calendar years, billions of dollars, quarterly data are at seasonally adjusted annual rates.)

NIPA Tables 3.9.5, 3.10.5

Year and quarter	Total	Consumption expenditures					Gross investment						
								National defense			Nondefense		
		Total	Compensation of general government employees	Consumption of general government fixed capital	Intermediate goods and services purchased [1]	Less: Own-account investment and sales to other sectors	Total	Total	Structures	Equipment and software	Total	Structures	Equipment and software
1950	26.0	22.0	11.1	5.7	5.7	0.4	3.9	2.4	0.5	1.9	1.6	1.2	0.4
1951	45.0	34.4	16.6	6.0	12.6	0.9	10.7	9.1	2.0	7.1	1.5	1.1	0.4
1952	59.1	44.2	19.3	6.7	18.7	0.6	15.0	13.4	3.3	10.1	1.6	1.1	0.5
1953	64.4	48.3	19.1	7.5	22.3	0.6	16.1	14.7	3.3	11.4	1.4	1.1	0.3
1954	57.2	43.9	18.3	8.2	18.1	0.7	13.3	12.1	2.7	9.4	1.2	0.9	0.3
1955	54.9	43.9	19.0	8.6	17.7	1.3	10.9	10.1	2.1	8.0	0.9	0.6	0.2
1956	56.7	45.0	19.6	9.1	17.1	0.8	11.6	10.5	2.1	8.4	1.2	0.9	0.3
1957	61.3	49.5	20.2	9.6	20.8	1.3	11.9	10.5	2.3	8.2	1.4	1.1	0.2
1958	63.8	50.9	21.3	9.8	21.1	1.3	12.9	11.3	2.6	8.7	1.6	1.4	0.2
1959	65.3	49.9	21.7	10.1	19.3	1.2	15.4	13.7	2.5	11.2	1.7	1.5	0.2
1960	64.1	49.7	22.6	10.4	17.8	1.1	14.3	12.3	2.2	10.1	2.0	1.7	0.3
1961	67.9	51.6	23.7	10.7	18.2	1.0	16.3	13.9	2.4	11.5	2.4	1.9	0.6
1962	75.2	57.8	25.2	11.3	22.4	1.1	17.4	14.5	2.0	12.5	2.9	2.1	0.8
1963	76.9	60.8	26.5	11.9	23.5	1.2	16.1	12.6	1.6	11.0	3.5	2.3	1.2
1964	78.4	62.8	28.5	12.1	23.3	1.2	15.6	11.5	1.3	10.2	4.2	2.5	1.6
1965	80.4	65.7	30.0	12.4	24.6	1.3	14.7	10.0	1.1	8.9	4.7	2.8	1.9
1966	92.4	75.7	34.3	12.9	30.3	1.7	16.7	11.8	1.3	10.5	4.9	2.8	2.1
1967	104.6	87.0	37.9	13.6	36.8	1.3	17.7	13.5	1.2	12.3	4.2	2.2	1.9
1968	111.3	95.3	41.9	14.4	40.3	1.3	16.0	12.2	1.2	10.9	3.8	2.1	1.7
1969	113.3	98.3	44.9	15.1	39.8	1.4	15.0	11.3	1.5	9.9	3.6	1.9	1.7
1970	113.4	98.6	48.3	15.7	35.9	1.4	14.8	11.1	1.3	9.8	3.8	2.1	1.7
1971	113.6	101.9	51.7	16.1	35.7	1.5	11.7	7.5	1.8	5.7	4.2	2.5	1.7
1972	119.6	107.6	55.4	16.1	38.4	2.3	12.0	7.5	1.8	5.7	4.5	2.7	1.8
1973	122.5	108.8	57.4	16.5	37.7	2.8	13.6	8.7	2.1	6.6	4.9	3.1	1.8
1974	134.5	117.9	62.0	17.5	41.7	3.4	16.6	11.1	2.2	8.9	5.6	3.4	2.2
1975	149.0	129.5	68.4	18.9	45.2	3.0	19.5	13.0	2.3	10.7	6.5	4.1	2.4
1976	159.7	137.1	73.3	20.5	46.2	2.8	22.6	15.3	2.1	13.2	7.3	4.6	2.7
1977	175.4	150.7	79.9	22.1	52.4	3.8	24.7	16.7	2.4	14.4	8.0	5.0	3.0
1978	190.9	163.3	85.8	23.9	58.2	4.5	27.6	17.8	2.5	15.3	9.8	6.1	3.7
1979	210.6	178.9	91.8	25.8	66.9	5.6	31.6	21.4	2.5	18.9	10.2	6.3	4.0
1980	243.7	207.4	102.5	28.7	82.3	6.2	36.3	24.3	3.2	21.1	12.0	7.1	4.9
1981	280.2	238.3	115.1	32.3	97.0	6.2	41.9	28.9	3.2	25.7	13.0	7.7	5.3
1982	310.8	263.3	125.3	35.9	108.2	6.1	47.5	34.7	4.0	30.8	12.7	6.8	6.0
1983	342.9	286.4	132.3	38.9	121.3	6.1	56.4	41.9	4.8	37.1	14.5	6.7	7.8
1984	374.3	309.9	149.4	42.7	124.5	6.7	64.4	48.7	4.9	43.8	15.7	7.0	8.7
1985	412.8	338.3	159.0	46.1	140.2	6.9	74.4	57.5	6.2	51.3	16.9	7.3	9.6
1986	438.4	358.0	163.1	49.5	152.3	6.9	80.4	62.9	6.8	56.1	17.5	8.0	9.5
1987	459.5	373.7	170.3	53.0	158.3	7.9	85.8	66.4	7.7	58.8	19.4	9.0	10.4
1988	461.6	381.7	178.0	56.8	155.8	8.7	79.8	61.3	7.4	53.9	18.6	6.8	11.7
1989	481.4	398.5	185.7	60.7	161.5	9.4	83.0	62.7	6.4	56.3	20.3	6.9	13.4
1990	507.5	419.0	193.9	64.9	170.5	10.3	88.5	65.9	6.1	59.8	22.6	8.0	14.6
1991	526.6	438.3	205.9	69.0	174.8	11.3	88.2	63.4	4.6	58.8	24.8	9.2	15.7
1992	532.9	444.1	210.7	71.3	173.4	11.3	88.8	61.6	5.2	56.3	27.2	10.3	16.9
1993	525.0	441.2	210.9	74.2	167.0	11.0	83.8	55.5	5.3	50.1	28.3	11.2	17.0
1994	518.6	440.7	208.9	76.3	168.6	13.0	77.9	53.0	5.8	47.2	24.9	10.2	14.7
1995	518.8	440.1	205.8	77.8	167.2	10.6	78.6	51.8	6.7	45.1	26.8	10.8	16.0
1996	527.0	446.5	209.7	77.9	170.1	11.1	80.4	51.6	6.3	45.4	28.8	11.3	17.5
1997	531.0	457.5	212.1	77.9	176.6	9.1	73.4	45.3	6.1	39.2	28.1	9.9	18.2
1998	531.0	454.6	214.3	78.0	172.4	10.1	76.4	45.8	5.8	39.9	30.7	10.8	19.9
1999	554.9	473.3	220.6	79.8	181.4	8.5	81.6	48.2	5.4	42.8	33.4	10.7	22.7
2000	576.1	496.0	233.0	82.1	190.7	9.8	80.1	49.2	5.4	43.8	30.9	8.3	22.6
2001	611.7	530.2	242.1	82.8	214.4	9.1	81.5	50.9	5.3	45.6	30.6	8.1	22.5
2002	680.6	590.5	268.4	83.5	248.0	9.4	90.1	57.0	5.8	51.2	33.1	9.9	23.2
2003	756.5	660.3	297.8	85.2	287.2	9.9	96.2	62.8	7.3	55.4	33.5	10.3	23.1
2004	824.6	721.4	323.0	89.0	320.0	10.6	103.3	69.6	7.1	62.4	33.7	9.1	24.6
2005	876.3	765.8	344.4	94.3	340.8	13.7	110.5	74.2	7.5	66.8	36.3	8.3	28.0
2006	931.7	811.0	360.1	100.5	363.2	12.8	120.7	81.0	8.1	72.9	39.7	9.5	30.2
2007	976.7	848.8	379.5	106.3	376.0	12.9	127.9	87.3	10.5	76.8	40.6	11.1	29.5
2008	1 082.6	934.4	402.0	113.2	432.5	13.3	148.2	103.9	12.9	91.0	44.3	11.7	32.5
2009	1 144.8	986.4	439.7	118.9	442.2	14.4	158.4	112.4	16.7	95.7	46.1	13.3	32.7
2007													
1st quarter	942.8	821.1	376.7	104.0	353.2	12.8	121.7	82.5	9.5	73.0	39.3	10.4	28.8
2nd quarter	968.1	839.9	378.7	105.4	368.6	12.7	128.2	87.8	10.9	76.9	40.4	10.9	29.5
3rd quarter	991.4	860.8	380.5	106.9	387.4	14.0	130.7	89.3	10.5	78.8	41.4	11.7	29.7
4th quarter	1 004.3	873.4	382.1	108.8	394.7	12.0	130.9	89.4	10.9	78.5	41.5	11.3	30.2
2008													
1st quarter	1 038.3	903.2	394.5	110.7	410.2	12.2	135.1	93.9	11.5	82.4	41.2	10.4	30.9
2nd quarter	1 069.5	923.2	398.6	113.1	423.9	12.5	146.3	103.2	12.1	91.1	43.1	11.1	32.0
3rd quarter	1 108.3	956.0	404.0	114.5	453.1	15.7	152.4	108.4	13.0	95.3	44.0	12.3	31.7
4th quarter	1 114.3	955.4	410.7	114.5	442.9	12.8	158.9	110.1	14.8	95.3	48.8	13.2	35.6
2009													
1st quarter	1 106.7	954.2	428.0	115.8	424.2	13.8	152.4	107.8	15.8	91.9	44.7	13.2	31.5
2nd quarter	1 138.3	979.1	437.0	117.3	439.1	14.3	159.2	113.5	16.4	97.2	45.7	13.2	32.4
3rd quarter	1 164.3	1 001.2	444.1	119.4	452.5	14.8	163.1	116.5	18.5	98.0	46.6	13.3	33.2
4th quarter	1 170.1	1 011.0	449.9	123.2	452.9	15.0	159.1	111.7	16.2	95.6	47.3	13.7	33.7

[1] Includes general government intermediate inputs for goods and services sold to other sectors and for own-account investment.

Table 6-3. Federal Government Defense and Nondefense Consumption Expenditures by Type

(National income and product accounts, calendar years, billions of dollars, quarterly data are at seasonally adjusted annual rates.)

NIPA Table 3.10.5

Year and quarter	Defense consumption expenditures [1]						Nondefense consumption expenditures [1]					
	Total	Compensation of general government employees	Consumption of general government fixed capital	Intermediate goods and services purchased [2]			Total	Compensation of general government employees	Consumption of general government fixed capital	Intermediate goods and services purchased [2]		
				Durable goods	Nondurable goods	Services				Durable goods	Nondurable goods	Services
1950	17.1	8.0	5.2	1.7	0.9	1.5	4.9	3.1	0.6	0.1	0.5	0.9
1951	30.1	13.5	5.4	4.4	2.3	5.0	4.3	3.1	0.6	0.1	0.1	0.7
1952	38.9	16.1	6.1	8.0	2.8	6.1	5.3	3.2	0.6	0.1	0.5	1.3
1953	41.2	16.0	6.9	9.1	4.2	5.1	7.1	3.1	0.6	0.1	2.4	1.3
1954	37.1	15.4	7.5	6.8	3.2	4.2	6.9	2.9	0.6	0.1	2.2	1.4
1955	36.8	15.8	7.9	6.0	1.7	5.9	7.1	3.2	0.6	0.1	2.5	1.6
1956	38.7	16.1	8.5	6.1	1.7	6.7	6.3	3.5	0.6	0.1	0.8	1.7
1957	43.1	16.5	9.0	6.7	2.2	9.3	6.3	3.7	0.6	0.1	0.8	1.8
1958	44.0	17.0	9.1	7.1	2.1	9.5	6.8	4.3	0.7	0.0	0.7	1.7
1959	40.1	17.3	9.4	5.1	1.8	6.9	9.8	4.4	0.7	0.0	3.3	2.1
1960	41.0	17.7	9.8	4.4	1.9	7.7	8.7	5.0	0.7	0.1	1.1	2.5
1961	42.7	18.3	10.0	3.6	2.3	8.8	9.0	5.4	0.7	0.1	0.4	3.0
1962	46.6	19.4	10.6	4.6	2.9	9.6	11.3	5.8	0.8	0.2	1.5	3.6
1963	48.3	20.1	11.0	4.7	2.7	10.2	12.4	6.4	0.9	0.3	1.2	4.5
1964	48.8	21.6	11.1	4.0	2.9	9.7	14.0	7.0	1.0	0.4	1.1	5.3
1965	50.6	22.6	11.3	4.2	3.2	9.9	15.1	7.4	1.2	0.5	1.1	5.7
1966	59.9	26.3	11.5	6.2	4.7	12.2	15.9	8.0	1.4	0.5	0.4	6.4
1967	69.9	29.3	12.0	6.2	7.3	15.5	17.0	8.6	1.6	0.4	1.2	6.2
1968	77.1	32.4	12.7	7.5	8.4	16.4	18.2	9.5	1.7	0.4	1.9	5.7
1969	78.1	34.7	13.2	6.5	7.6	16.5	20.2	10.1	1.9	0.3	3.0	5.9
1970	76.5	36.6	13.6	6.1	5.4	15.2	22.1	11.7	2.1	0.3	2.0	7.1
1971	77.1	38.2	13.8	4.6	4.4	16.3	24.9	13.4	2.3	0.3	2.1	8.1
1972	79.5	40.5	13.8	5.7	4.7	15.5	28.2	14.8	2.4	0.3	2.4	9.9
1973	79.4	41.4	14.0	5.5	4.3	15.3	29.4	16.0	2.5	0.2	1.9	10.4
1974	84.5	44.1	14.7	5.2	5.2	16.9	33.4	18.0	2.8	0.2	2.6	11.7
1975	90.9	47.9	15.7	6.0	5.1	17.4	38.7	20.5	3.2	0.2	2.8	13.7
1976	95.8	50.3	17.1	5.8	4.5	18.8	41.4	23.1	3.4	0.3	3.5	13.3
1977	104.2	53.6	18.4	8.0	4.5	20.4	46.5	26.3	3.7	0.3	4.4	14.7
1978	112.7	57.5	19.9	9.6	4.9	21.7	50.6	28.3	4.0	0.4	4.9	16.7
1979	123.8	61.7	21.3	11.3	6.2	24.2	55.1	30.1	4.5	0.5	5.2	19.4
1980	143.7	68.6	23.5	12.8	10.0	30.2	63.8	34.0	5.2	0.7	7.4	21.3
1981	167.3	78.8	26.3	16.2	11.8	35.8	71.0	36.3	6.0	0.6	11.2	21.4
1982	191.1	87.4	29.2	19.6	11.5	45.4	72.1	37.9	6.7	0.6	9.1	22.1
1983	208.7	92.4	31.7	25.1	11.3	49.5	77.7	39.9	7.3	0.9	10.6	23.9
1984	232.8	107.5	34.8	27.1	10.4	54.7	77.1	41.8	7.9	0.9	6.4	24.9
1985	253.7	115.3	37.4	29.3	10.0	63.4	84.7	43.6	8.7	1.0	9.5	27.1
1986	267.9	118.8	40.2	31.9	10.2	68.7	90.1	44.3	9.3	1.0	12.4	28.1
1987	283.6	123.5	43.0	33.8	10.3	75.1	90.1	46.8	10.0	1.1	6.9	31.1
1988	293.5	126.9	45.9	33.5	10.6	79.0	88.3	51.1	10.9	1.2	-0.1	31.6
1989	299.4	131.7	49.0	32.0	10.8	78.3	99.1	54.0	11.8	1.3	5.7	33.3
1990	308.0	134.5	52.3	31.6	11.0	81.8	111.0	59.3	12.7	1.5	5.7	38.9
1991	319.7	141.8	55.3	31.0	10.7	84.3	118.6	64.0	13.6	1.6	6.3	41.0
1992	315.2	143.0	57.1	28.4	9.4	81.3	128.9	67.7	14.2	1.7	6.9	45.8
1993	307.5	137.7	59.4	26.4	8.5	79.8	133.7	73.3	14.8	1.7	8.3	42.4
1994	300.8	133.7	61.0	22.9	7.6	81.7	139.9	75.2	15.3	1.6	6.9	47.9
1995	297.0	129.8	61.7	20.9	6.3	81.9	143.2	76.1	16.0	1.5	8.6	47.9
1996	303.2	132.3	61.2	20.8	7.6	85.2	143.4	77.4	16.6	1.7	7.9	46.9
1997	304.5	131.9	60.4	20.9	7.6	87.3	153.0	80.2	17.6	1.7	9.7	49.4
1998	300.3	130.8	59.7	20.9	7.0	85.1	154.3	83.5	18.3	1.7	10.8	46.9
1999	313.0	132.7	60.0	22.2	8.2	92.9	160.3	87.9	19.8	1.8	7.9	48.5
2000	321.8	138.1	60.7	22.1	10.4	93.6	174.2	94.9	21.5	1.8	9.7	53.0
2001	342.0	144.8	60.5	22.3	10.3	107.8	188.1	97.3	22.4	1.9	12.7	59.4
2002	380.7	162.0	60.5	23.2	11.5	127.7	209.8	106.4	23.0	2.3	13.0	70.3
2003	435.2	182.1	61.7	25.7	13.4	156.8	225.1	115.6	23.5	2.2	14.9	74.3
2004	481.2	199.4	64.8	28.8	17.1	175.8	240.2	123.6	24.2	2.4	16.7	79.1
2005	514.8	215.7	68.7	29.5	20.9	185.4	251.0	128.7	25.6	2.8	19.7	82.5
2006	543.9	225.6	73.2	32.8	22.1	196.0	267.1	134.5	27.4	2.9	19.7	89.7
2007	574.9	238.2	77.4	36.1	24.1	205.3	273.9	141.3	28.8	2.9	19.3	88.3
2008	634.0	252.9	82.9	43.1	30.8	229.6	300.4	149.1	30.4	3.2	22.7	103.0
2009	666.6	278.6	87.0	46.7	23.8	236.1	319.7	161.2	32.0	3.4	25.0	107.2
2007												
1st quarter	554.3	235.9	75.6	33.4	22.3	193.7	266.8	140.8	28.3	2.7	17.8	83.2
2nd quarter	568.8	237.4	76.7	35.2	23.7	201.4	271.2	141.2	28.6	2.8	18.9	86.6
3rd quarter	585.1	239.2	77.9	37.4	25.8	211.8	275.6	141.3	29.0	3.0	19.7	89.7
4th quarter	591.4	240.3	79.3	38.3	24.6	214.1	282.1	141.7	29.4	3.0	21.0	93.6
2008												
1st quarter	609.7	247.4	80.9	39.4	27.3	219.8	293.5	147.1	29.9	3.2	22.3	98.2
2nd quarter	622.4	250.3	82.8	42.2	33.1	219.2	300.8	148.3	30.3	3.2	23.0	103.2
3rd quarter	655.2	255.1	83.9	44.7	35.7	241.0	300.7	148.9	30.6	3.2	23.1	105.3
4th quarter	648.8	258.7	83.8	46.0	27.1	238.6	306.6	152.0	30.7	3.3	22.5	105.5
2009												
1st quarter	642.9	269.8	84.6	42.6	21.4	229.8	311.3	158.2	31.3	3.3	24.2	102.8
2nd quarter	662.7	275.7	85.6	46.6	24.6	235.6	316.4	161.3	31.7	3.3	25.5	103.5
3rd quarter	679.3	281.6	87.4	50.0	25.9	240.0	321.9	162.6	32.0	3.4	24.5	108.6
4th quarter	681.7	287.2	90.3	47.6	23.3	238.9	329.3	162.7	32.9	3.6	25.8	113.7

[1] Excludes government sales to other sectors and government own-account investment (construction and software).
[2] Includes general government intermediate inputs for goods and services sold to other sectors and for own-account investment.

Table 6-4. National Defense Consumption Expenditures and Gross Investment: Selected Detail

(National income and product accounts, calendar years, billions of dollars, quarterly data are at seasonally adjusted annual rates.)

NIPA Table 3.11.5

Year and quarter	Compensation of general government employees		Intermediate goods and services purchased [1]							Gross investment			
			Durable goods	Nondurable goods		Services				Equipment and software			
	Military	Civilian	Aircraft	Petroleum products	Ammunition	Research and development	Installation support	Weapons support	Personnel support	Aircraft	Missiles	Ships	Electronics and software
1972	27.0	13.5	2.7	1.8	2.0	5.1	4.4	1.6	1.7	2.6	1.5	1.8	0.8
1973	27.6	13.8	2.4	1.7	1.7	5.3	4.3	1.6	1.5	2.3	1.5	1.6	0.9
1974	29.1	15.0	2.0	2.8	1.4	5.7	4.7	1.8	1.8	2.3	1.7	2.2	1.0
1975	31.1	16.8	2.1	2.9	1.1	5.9	4.9	1.7	2.1	3.6	1.3	2.2	1.2
1976	32.4	17.8	2.0	2.5	0.6	6.4	5.4	1.9	2.3	3.4	1.4	2.4	1.3
1977	34.0	19.7	3.3	2.4	0.8	6.8	6.2	2.1	2.2	3.7	1.2	3.1	1.5
1978	36.2	21.3	3.5	2.5	1.0	7.1	6.3	2.4	2.6	3.7	1.1	3.9	1.8
1979	38.7	22.9	4.8	3.6	1.2	7.7	7.3	2.9	2.7	4.8	1.8	4.3	2.1
1980	43.5	25.1	5.6	6.8	1.4	10.2	8.5	4.4	3.0	6.1	2.3	4.1	2.6
1981	50.5	28.3	7.8	7.7	1.6	12.4	9.3	5.2	4.0	7.5	2.8	5.1	3.2
1982	56.6	30.8	10.2	6.8	2.1	14.1	13.7	6.0	5.8	8.4	3.4	6.2	3.8
1983	59.8	32.7	13.6	6.4	2.5	14.5	15.5	7.3	6.4	10.1	4.6	7.1	4.6
1984	72.8	34.8	14.0	5.9	2.2	16.2	17.0	8.6	6.7	10.9	5.7	8.0	5.6
1985	78.2	37.2	15.4	5.8	1.3	21.7	17.2	9.8	8.4	13.4	6.6	9.0	7.0
1986	80.6	38.1	17.2	3.6	3.6	23.8	18.5	10.4	9.4	17.9	7.9	8.9	7.8
1987	83.7	39.8	18.2	3.9	2.8	27.0	19.1	11.0	10.9	17.6	8.7	8.8	8.7
1988	85.2	41.7	17.9	3.5	3.5	31.5	19.0	9.8	11.4	13.5	7.8	8.6	9.2
1989	87.4	44.3	16.4	4.2	3.1	28.6	19.0	10.3	12.4	12.2	8.8	10.0	9.6
1990	89.1	45.4	14.8	5.3	2.8	26.1	22.1	11.7	13.0	12.0	11.2	10.8	9.9
1991	93.8	48.0	13.6	4.7	2.7	21.9	23.8	10.2	12.7	9.2	10.8	10.2	9.7
1992	93.2	49.8	12.2	3.5	2.6	23.7	23.2	8.5	14.4	8.3	10.6	10.1	9.8
1993	87.0	50.7	10.7	3.2	2.5	26.7	24.8	6.8	12.1	9.3	7.9	8.7	9.9
1994	83.2	50.5	9.2	3.0	1.8	25.6	26.1	7.8	13.8	10.5	5.7	8.1	9.3
1995	80.2	49.5	8.9	2.8	1.2	25.0	25.4	8.2	14.9	9.0	4.7	8.0	8.8
1996	82.9	49.4	8.8	3.4	1.4	27.4	25.9	7.4	15.9	9.2	4.1	6.8	9.0
1997	82.8	49.1	9.4	2.9	1.7	28.2	25.0	8.8	17.2	5.8	2.9	6.1	9.0
1998	82.5	48.2	9.9	2.1	1.9	26.9	23.9	8.5	17.2	5.8	3.3	6.4	9.1
1999	84.3	48.4	10.5	2.6	1.9	27.2	25.0	9.9	21.8	7.0	2.9	6.8	9.7
2000	88.5	49.6	9.8	4.1	1.8	27.0	25.2	10.1	22.2	7.8	2.7	6.6	10.1
2001	94.5	50.3	9.8	4.2	2.1	29.7	27.5	13.3	27.3	8.5	3.3	7.2	9.7
2002	107.6	54.4	9.8	4.6	2.5	36.8	30.5	16.5	33.8	9.4	3.3	8.7	9.9
2003	124.4	57.7	11.2	5.3	2.6	43.1	35.5	21.1	40.5	9.2	3.5	9.5	10.5
2004	135.1	64.3	11.9	7.0	3.6	50.6	35.8	21.5	51.0	11.1	4.1	10.0	11.5
2005	147.0	68.7	10.7	10.1	4.0	53.9	35.3	24.4	55.8	13.5	4.0	9.8	12.6
2006	153.8	71.8	11.0	11.2	4.2	58.0	36.7	25.5	60.8	13.6	4.5	10.5	14.3
2007	162.8	75.4	11.3	12.5	4.1	57.7	36.0	25.4	66.5	12.8	4.3	10.3	16.4
2008	174.3	78.6	12.8	18.0	4.5	62.9	38.9	30.8	79.2	13.9	4.2	11.0	20.5
2009	193.9	84.7	15.4	10.1	4.1	62.4	42.5	30.0	86.2	15.8	4.9	11.1	21.2
2003													
1st quarter	121.4	57.7	9.7	8.0	2.1	35.8	31.9	16.8	34.0	9.4	2.8	8.5	10.3
2nd quarter	125.4	56.8	11.8	5.7	2.7	49.6	34.8	20.9	39.0	9.1	2.9	10.1	10.2
3rd quarter	125.4	57.7	11.4	3.0	2.8	40.2	37.4	24.0	43.7	8.5	3.6	10.1	11.0
4th quarter	125.6	58.6	11.8	4.5	2.9	46.7	37.9	22.7	45.1	9.9	4.7	9.4	10.5
2004													
1st quarter	134.0	62.3	11.3	6.5	3.4	48.1	36.2	21.5	49.1	8.6	3.9	10.0	10.6
2nd quarter	134.4	63.8	11.7	6.8	3.6	51.9	35.1	19.8	49.4	10.0	3.6	9.1	12.0
3rd quarter	134.9	65.7	12.5	9.2	3.8	51.0	37.5	23.5	54.2	11.8	4.4	11.5	11.6
4th quarter	137.2	65.3	12.1	5.7	3.8	51.4	34.5	21.2	51.2	13.8	4.4	9.5	11.8
2005													
1st quarter	148.1	67.8	10.7	6.9	3.7	53.2	33.7	22.8	53.1	12.6	3.1	9.9	11.6
2nd quarter	146.6	68.3	10.7	10.4	4.0	56.8	34.0	22.7	52.4	13.5	4.5	9.5	12.4
3rd quarter	146.5	69.6	10.6	12.2	4.2	55.3	37.6	28.2	60.1	14.0	3.5	10.6	13.5
4th quarter	147.0	68.9	10.9	10.8	4.0	50.5	36.0	23.8	57.7	14.1	4.9	9.2	13.1
2006													
1st quarter	153.5	71.0	10.6	9.9	4.1	58.2	36.0	24.3	60.8	13.0	4.7	9.7	13.5
2nd quarter	153.1	71.7	10.3	11.2	4.1	58.4	37.3	26.8	63.7	15.2	4.7	11.1	13.9
3rd quarter	153.7	71.9	10.8	14.1	4.2	56.0	35.6	23.3	58.7	11.9	3.4	10.6	14.8
4th quarter	154.8	72.7	12.5	9.5	4.4	59.5	37.8	27.8	60.2	14.3	5.3	10.7	14.8
2007													
1st quarter	160.9	75.0	10.1	10.4	4.2	59.3	34.9	23.5	58.9	12.1	5.3	9.8	15.5
2nd quarter	162.1	75.3	10.9	12.3	3.7	58.5	35.6	24.9	63.6	14.1	4.3	10.2	16.2
3rd quarter	164.0	75.2	11.8	13.7	4.4	55.9	37.0	26.9	70.0	13.2	3.9	10.2	17.2
4th quarter	164.3	76.0	12.5	13.5	3.9	57.0	36.3	26.2	73.6	11.7	3.8	11.1	16.9
2008													
1st quarter	169.9	77.5	11.4	14.8	4.5	59.2	36.4	27.7	76.3	10.5	3.8	9.7	19.1
2nd quarter	172.0	78.3	12.4	20.8	4.1	61.2	36.5	27.3	75.2	15.1	4.5	11.0	20.2
3rd quarter	176.0	79.1	13.4	22.7	4.6	61.6	41.8	35.7	84.4	14.9	4.6	11.7	21.3
4th quarter	179.2	79.5	14.0	13.6	4.7	69.5	40.7	32.6	80.7	15.1	4.0	11.7	21.3
2009													
1st quarter	187.8	82.0	14.0	8.6	3.8	61.1	41.2	29.6	82.8	15.0	4.7	10.5	19.8
2nd quarter	192.4	83.3	14.9	10.5	4.3	63.8	42.8	29.9	84.0	17.1	4.9	10.9	21.3
3rd quarter	196.5	85.1	15.7	11.1	4.1	63.0	43.6	31.6	86.8	14.7	5.1	10.9	22.4
4th quarter	198.9	88.3	16.9	10.2	4.3	61.9	42.6	28.8	91.1	16.6	5.1	12.3	21.4

[1] Includes general government intermediate inputs for goods and services sold to other sectors and for own-account investment.

Table 6-5. Federal Government Output, Lending and Borrowing, and Net Investment

(National income and product accounts, calendar years, billions of dollars, quarterly data are at seasonally adjusted annual rates.)

NIPA Tables 3.2, 3.10.5

Year and quarter	Output						Net lending (net borrowing -)							Net investment
	Gross		Value added		Intermediate goods and services purchased [1]		Net saving, current (surplus +, deficit -)	Plus: capital transfer receipts	Minus			Plus: Consumption of fixed capital	Equals: Net lending (borrowing -)	
	Defense	Non-defense	Defense	Non-defense	Defense	Non-defense			Gross investment	Capital transfer payments	Net purchases of non-produced assets			
1950	17.2	5.3	13.1	3.7	4.1	1.6	5.6	0.6	3.9	0.4	...	5.8	...	-1.9
1951	30.6	4.6	18.9	3.7	11.7	0.9	9.7	0.7	10.7	0.4	...	6.1	...	4.6
1952	39.1	5.7	22.2	3.8	16.9	1.9	3.7	0.8	15.0	0.5	...	6.8	...	8.2
1953	41.4	7.5	22.9	3.7	18.5	3.8	1.8	0.9	16.1	0.6	...	7.6	...	8.5
1954	37.3	7.3	23.0	3.5	14.3	3.8	-1.7	0.9	13.3	0.6	...	8.2	...	5.1
1955	37.3	7.9	23.7	3.8	13.6	4.1	5.7	1.0	10.9	0.7	...	8.6	...	2.3
1956	39.1	6.7	24.6	4.1	14.5	2.6	7.5	1.3	11.6	0.8	...	9.2	...	2.4
1957	43.6	7.1	25.5	4.4	18.1	2.7	3.3	1.4	11.9	1.3	...	9.7	...	2.2
1958	44.7	7.4	26.1	5.0	18.6	2.4	-5.4	1.3	12.9	2.3	...	9.9	...	3.0
1959	40.5	10.6	26.7	5.1	13.8	5.5	3.3	1.4	15.4	3.1	...	10.2	...	5.2
1960	41.5	9.3	27.4	5.6	14.0	3.7	7.1	1.8	14.3	2.6	0.5	10.6	2.0	3.7
1961	43.0	9.6	28.3	6.1	14.7	3.5	2.6	2.0	16.3	2.9	0.5	10.9	-4.3	5.4
1962	47.0	11.9	30.0	6.6	17.0	5.3	2.4	2.1	17.4	3.1	0.6	11.5	-5.1	5.9
1963	48.7	13.2	31.1	7.3	17.6	5.9	5.3	2.2	16.1	3.6	0.5	12.1	-0.6	4.0
1964	49.2	14.8	32.7	8.0	16.5	6.8	0.9	2.6	15.6	4.1	0.6	12.3	-4.5	3.3
1965	51.1	15.8	33.8	8.6	17.3	7.3	3.2	2.8	14.7	4.0	0.5	12.6	-0.5	2.1
1966	60.8	16.6	37.8	9.4	23.0	7.2	2.3	3.0	16.7	4.4	0.6	13.1	-3.3	3.6
1967	70.3	17.9	41.4	10.1	29.0	7.8	-9.3	3.1	17.7	4.3	-0.2	13.9	-14.1	3.8
1968	77.3	19.2	45.1	11.3	32.3	8.0	-2.4	3.1	16.0	6.0	-0.9	14.7	-5.7	1.3
1969	78.4	21.3	47.9	12.1	30.5	9.2	8.6	3.6	15.0	5.9	0.1	15.4	6.6	-0.4
1970	76.8	23.2	50.2	13.8	26.6	9.3	-15.5	3.7	14.8	5.3	-0.3	16.1	-15.6	-1.3
1971	77.3	26.1	52.0	15.7	25.3	10.4	-28.7	4.6	11.7	5.9	-0.4	16.5	-24.9	-4.8
1972	80.1	29.8	54.3	17.2	25.8	12.6	-24.9	5.4	12.0	6.1	-0.7	16.6	-20.3	-4.6
1973	80.5	31.2	55.4	18.6	25.1	12.6	-11.8	5.1	13.6	6.0	-3.2	17.0	-6.1	-3.4
1974	86.1	35.2	58.8	20.8	27.3	14.4	-14.5	4.8	16.6	7.9	-5.7	18.2	-10.4	-1.6
1975	92.1	40.4	63.6	23.7	28.5	16.8	-70.6	4.9	19.5	9.7	-0.4	19.7	-74.9	-0.2
1976	96.4	43.6	67.3	26.5	29.1	17.1	-53.7	5.6	22.6	10.6	-2.4	21.4	-57.5	1.2
1977	105.0	49.5	72.0	30.0	32.9	19.5	-46.1	7.2	24.7	11.2	-1.4	23.0	-50.4	1.7
1978	113.6	54.3	77.4	32.3	36.2	22.0	-28.9	5.2	27.6	12.0	-0.6	25.0	-37.7	2.6
1979	124.8	59.7	83.0	34.6	41.8	25.1	-14.0	5.5	31.6	14.5	-2.8	27.0	-24.9	4.6
1980	145.0	68.6	92.0	39.2	52.9	29.4	-56.6	6.5	36.3	16.7	-4.0	30.0	-69.1	6.3
1981	168.9	75.5	105.1	42.3	63.8	33.2	-56.8	6.9	41.9	15.7	-5.5	33.8	-68.2	8.1
1982	193.0	76.4	116.6	44.6	76.4	31.8	-135.3	7.5	47.5	14.7	-3.6	37.6	-148.7	9.9
1983	210.0	82.5	124.1	47.1	85.9	35.4	-176.2	5.8	56.4	15.6	-4.9	40.7	-196.9	15.7
1984	234.5	82.0	142.3	49.8	92.2	32.2	-171.5	6.0	64.4	17.8	-3.9	44.5	-199.2	19.9
1985	255.4	89.8	152.8	52.3	102.7	37.5	-178.6	6.4	74.4	19.6	-1.1	48.0	-217.0	26.4
1986	269.7	95.2	158.9	53.7	110.8	41.5	-194.6	7.0	80.4	20.1	-3.0	51.6	-233.6	28.8
1987	285.7	95.9	166.5	56.8	119.2	39.1	-149.3	7.2	85.8	19.1	-0.4	55.2	-191.5	30.6
1988	295.8	94.7	172.8	62.0	123.1	32.7	-138.4	7.6	79.8	19.8	-0.1	59.1	-171.2	20.7
1989	301.8	106.1	180.7	65.8	121.1	40.3	-133.9	8.9	83.0	20.2	-0.7	63.3	-164.2	19.7
1990	311.2	118.1	186.8	72.0	124.5	46.1	-176.4	11.6	88.5	28.2	-0.7	67.7	-213.1	20.8
1991	323.1	126.6	197.2	77.7	125.9	48.9	-218.4	11.0	88.2	26.5	0.2	72.0	-250.3	16.2
1992	319.2	136.2	200.2	81.8	119.1	54.4	-302.5	11.3	88.8	22.6	0.2	74.6	-328.2	14.2
1993	311.8	140.4	197.1	88.1	114.7	52.3	-280.2	12.9	83.8	24.3	0.2	77.8	-297.8	6.0
1994	306.8	147.0	194.6	90.5	112.2	56.4	-220.4	15.1	77.9	26.0	0.2	80.0	-229.3	-2.2
1995	300.7	150.1	191.5	92.1	109.2	58.0	-206.2	14.9	78.6	27.9	-7.4	81.7	-208.7	-3.1
1996	307.2	150.5	193.5	94.0	113.7	56.4	-148.2	17.5	80.4	28.4	-3.8	81.9	-153.9	-1.5
1997	308.0	158.6	192.2	97.8	115.8	60.8	-60.1	20.6	73.4	29.2	-7.6	82.5	-52.1	-9.1
1998	303.5	161.2	190.4	101.8	113.0	59.4	33.6	25.2	76.4	28.9	-5.8	82.8	42.0	-6.4
1999	316.0	165.8	192.7	107.7	123.3	58.1	98.8	28.8	81.6	36.3	-0.4	85.0	95.0	-3.4
2000	324.9	180.9	198.8	116.3	126.2	64.6	185.2	28.1	80.1	36.6	-0.2	87.8	184.7	-7.7
2001	345.6	193.7	205.2	119.7	140.3	74.0	40.5	28.0	81.5	42.0	-0.7	88.6	34.2	-7.1
2002	384.9	214.9	222.5	129.3	162.4	85.5	-252.8	25.3	90.1	49.2	0.3	89.2	-278.0	0.9
2003	439.7	230.4	243.8	139.1	195.9	91.3	-376.4	22.0	96.2	62.6	-0.2	90.8	-422.2	5.4
2004	485.8	246.2	264.2	147.8	221.6	98.3	-379.5	24.6	103.3	63.5	0.0	94.8	-426.8	8.5
2005	520.2	259.4	284.4	154.4	235.8	105.0	-283.0	25.0	110.5	84.8	-0.5	100.4	-352.4	10.1
2006	549.6	274.2	298.8	161.9	250.9	112.3	-203.8	27.8	120.7	70.5	-13.3	106.6	-247.2	14.1
2007	581.0	280.6	315.6	170.1	265.4	110.5	-236.5	26.5	127.9	82.8	-1.3	112.6	-306.8	15.3
2008	639.3	308.5	335.7	179.4	303.5	129.0	-642.6	28.3	148.2	161.6	-19.2	119.8	-785.1	28.4
2009	672.1	328.7	365.5	193.1	306.6	135.6	-1 224.7	24.8	158.4	223.4	-7.0	125.6	-1 449.1	32.8
2007														
1st quarter	560.9	273.0	311.5	169.2	249.4	103.8	-200.9	25.0	121.7	74.1	-1.3	110.2	-260.1	11.5
2nd quarter	574.4	278.2	314.2	169.9	260.3	108.3	-221.3	26.1	128.2	81.9	-4.3	111.7	-289.2	16.5
3rd quarter	592.1	282.6	317.0	170.3	275.1	112.3	-258.8	26.5	130.7	85.5	2.2	113.2	-337.5	17.5
4th quarter	596.7	288.8	319.7	171.2	277.0	117.6	-265.0	28.3	130.9	89.9	-1.7	115.2	-340.6	15.7
2008														
1st quarter	614.8	300.6	328.3	177.0	286.5	123.6	-433.5	29.1	135.1	87.2	-7.7	117.2	-501.7	17.9
2nd quarter	627.6	308.1	333.2	178.6	294.5	129.5	-796.9	29.8	146.3	90.0	-23.9	119.6	-859.9	26.7
3rd quarter	660.5	311.1	339.0	179.5	321.5	131.6	-665.7	27.6	152.4	105.0	-6.6	121.0	-767.9	31.4
4th quarter	654.1	314.0	342.5	182.7	311.6	131.3	-674.1	26.5	158.9	364.2	-38.4	121.2	-1 011.1	37.7
2009														
1st quarter	648.3	319.7	354.4	189.4	293.9	130.3	-969.1	25.1	152.4	311.2	-26.9	122.5	-1 258.2	29.9
2nd quarter	668.1	325.3	361.3	193.0	306.8	132.3	-1 268.9	25.6	159.2	234.5	-2.6	124.0	-1 510.3	35.2
3rd quarter	684.9	331.1	369.0	194.5	315.9	136.6	-1 353.6	26.1	163.1	162.3	1.8	126.1	-1 528.6	37.0
4th quarter	687.3	338.7	377.5	195.6	309.8	143.1	-1 307.2	22.1	159.1	185.6	-0.4	130.0	-1 499.4	29.1

[1]Includes general government intermediate inputs for goods and services sold to other sectors and for own-account investment.
. . . = Not available.

Table 6-6. Chain-Type Quantity Indexes for Federal Government Defense and Nondefense Consumption Expenditures and Gross Investment

(Seasonally adjusted, 2005 = 100.)   NIPA Tables 3.9.3, 3.10.3

Year and quarter	Defense consumption expenditures [1]						Defense gross investment	Nondefense consumption expenditures [1]						Non-defense gross investment
	Total	Compen-sation of general govern-ment employees	Consump-tion of general govern-ment fixed capital	Intermediate goods and services purchased [2]				Total	Compen-sation of general govern-ment employees	Consump-tion of general govern-ment fixed capital	Intermediate goods and services purchased [2]			
				Durable goods	Non-durable goods	Services					Durable goods	Non-durable goods excluding CCC inventory change	Services	
1950	37.5	86.3	42.5	30.3	40.6	5.0	15.0	22.1	59.4	10.5	7.2	7.8	8.8	19.8
1951	63.8	149.5	41.6	72.7	106.6	14.4	53.3	18.4	54.6	10.7	7.2	13.6	6.5	17.7
1952	82.5	172.1	46.4	128.8	139.3	19.4	77.1	21.7	53.3	10.8	6.6	8.5	11.0	17.2
1953	86.2	168.5	52.0	144.2	223.8	15.6	86.4	28.2	48.9	10.7	6.1	8.5	11.0	15.1
1954	75.1	158.0	55.8	104.9	147.1	13.1	70.4	27.2	46.4	10.7	6.9	8.2	11.9	13.6
1955	70.2	150.0	57.1	89.0	67.6	17.1	56.9	26.7	46.9	10.6	5.7	9.5	12.4	9.8
1956	70.4	146.1	57.5	84.2	66.6	19.3	54.5	23.4	48.0	10.5	5.8	14.7	13.6	12.4
1957	75.2	144.0	57.8	88.1	80.6	25.8	51.6	22.7	49.3	10.5	5.3	20.4	13.3	13.9
1958	73.5	135.6	57.9	91.3	82.1	25.4	55.0	22.7	50.9	10.5	4.2	9.1	12.3	16.5
1959	68.0	131.9	59.1	65.3	68.6	22.8	65.6	32.8	51.0	10.4	3.1	25.0	16.1	16.5
1960	68.8	131.8	60.9	55.5	73.6	25.9	59.1	28.7	55.1	10.3	3.8	19.8	18.8	19.5
1961	70.5	134.5	62.1	45.5	90.8	28.4	65.6	28.4	56.5	10.5	6.9	23.1	22.3	23.5
1962	75.3	140.2	64.0	56.3	115.0	29.8	67.8	34.7	59.5	11.1	11.1	23.0	26.0	27.5
1963	76.2	137.8	65.6	56.8	107.0	32.0	58.6	37.7	63.0	12.3	15.4	25.6	32.6	32.3
1964	74.2	137.7	66.4	48.0	118.1	29.2	53.2	40.4	64.4	13.8	20.0	27.5	37.4	37.1
1965	74.4	137.9	66.3	49.7	127.6	28.9	46.4	42.3	65.7	15.7	25.6	27.6	38.6	42.3
1966	84.9	151.8	66.4	72.4	182.0	34.5	53.7	42.5	68.3	18.0	26.6	32.4	41.9	43.5
1967	96.1	165.2	67.8	71.4	280.0	41.0	60.6	44.4	71.6	19.7	23.3	34.9	38.7	35.4
1968	100.2	167.4	68.9	82.8	320.6	41.7	53.1	44.5	73.3	20.8	18.6	28.1	34.2	30.9
1969	96.3	167.6	68.8	69.1	284.5	39.5	47.0	46.8	74.0	21.6	16.2	35.3	33.4	28.1
1970	87.5	155.4	67.7	61.8	198.0	36.0	42.8	46.6	74.9	22.1	12.9	36.2	37.9	26.6
1971	80.7	143.6	64.9	44.5	161.9	36.0	27.3	48.8	77.4	22.4	12.4	34.4	41.3	27.9
1972	75.8	132.7	61.4	56.9	165.0	32.0	20.4	52.5	79.7	22.5	13.3	38.7	48.9	28.9
1973	70.3	125.8	58.5	52.6	122.6	30.0	23.0	51.9	79.9	22.8	10.5	33.4	49.1	29.7
1974	68.1	123.9	56.7	45.5	105.9	30.4	28.0	54.8	83.9	23.2	9.2	36.7	49.6	30.6
1975	66.4	122.2	55.9	47.2	87.7	28.5	31.1	56.7	85.3	23.7	9.8	27.8	52.3	31.8
1976	65.2	119.7	56.0	42.4	71.6	29.0	33.9	56.6	89.6	24.2	10.5	35.2	46.9	34.1
1977	65.9	118.6	56.2	53.7	66.9	29.4	34.6	59.0	91.6	24.9	12.1	40.2	49.7	35.8
1978	66.6	119.4	56.5	60.0	67.4	29.0	34.4	61.4	93.9	26.1	15.3	47.0	53.4	42.4
1979	67.5	118.5	57.0	64.8	69.5	30.0	39.3	62.5	93.8	27.5	18.4	47.1	57.1	41.4
1980	70.1	119.2	58.1	67.9	75.9	33.8	42.1	65.7	96.4	29.2	21.5	46.4	56.8	44.6
1981	74.1	122.8	59.5	79.2	80.3	37.2	46.4	66.8	93.5	31.0	19.1	77.0	51.7	44.5
1982	79.0	125.6	61.6	86.8	79.9	44.6	52.2	63.9	91.8	32.8	16.4	54.9	49.7	41.3
1983	83.3	127.6	64.5	102.7	83.7	47.2	61.2	66.2	93.1	35.1	25.0	57.5	52.2	46.9
1984	85.8	129.3	68.6	103.8	79.3	50.8	69.9	63.8	93.1	38.1	27.1	60.1	52.7	50.4
1985	91.0	131.8	74.1	111.4	77.9	57.7	84.2	67.5	93.3	41.2	27.7	52.7	55.1	53.8
1986	95.1	132.4	80.4	119.0	98.3	61.0	96.4	69.9	92.0	44.1	28.0	46.5	55.0	55.1
1987	98.6	133.6	86.6	126.4	96.3	64.8	105.3	68.6	93.6	47.0	31.3	53.0	59.9	60.5
1988	99.8	132.0	91.7	130.0	92.8	66.4	97.4	65.1	96.0	49.9	32.7	52.2	59.1	56.6
1989	99.0	131.9	95.8	124.8	89.9	64.3	98.0	70.7	96.5	52.7	35.9	46.3	60.0	60.4
1990	98.4	131.1	99.5	120.3	80.2	64.3	101.0	76.4	101.3	55.9	41.0	49.4	67.9	65.9
1991	98.3	130.6	102.4	114.8	81.7	64.1	95.2	77.2	101.0	59.0	42.2	42.1	69.6	71.3
1992	93.2	123.0	104.1	103.3	75.6	60.4	91.6	81.8	102.8	61.5	45.7	51.6	75.4	78.7
1993	89.5	117.7	104.6	93.9	69.3	58.1	80.4	80.6	102.8	63.7	45.5	57.9	68.0	81.0
1994	85.5	111.6	103.7	80.5	63.1	58.1	74.5	81.4	99.9	65.4	43.2	49.6	75.4	70.6
1995	82.5	105.5	102.2	73.4	51.6	57.0	71.1	80.2	95.9	67.1	42.4	57.4	73.5	74.8
1996	81.3	101.0	100.7	72.8	57.0	58.4	70.5	78.2	93.3	70.0	48.9	51.5	71.0	80.9
1997	80.1	97.4	99.2	73.1	57.4	58.6	63.0	80.9	92.7	73.3	51.9	60.7	73.1	80.0
1998	77.9	94.3	97.6	73.7	59.3	56.1	64.1	80.2	93.8	77.1	52.0	66.4	68.7	88.2
1999	79.2	92.0	96.5	78.3	66.3	60.3	66.4	80.8	94.0	82.5	56.9	47.2	70.2	95.9
2000	78.4	91.4	95.6	77.5	69.6	59.2	67.8	84.6	96.9	87.5	60.7	51.1	74.6	87.3
2001	81.3	92.1	94.9	78.1	71.5	66.1	71.1	89.3	96.9	90.8	65.3	68.0	81.1	86.4
2002	86.6	94.5	94.8	81.3	81.7	76.5	80.4	95.5	98.7	93.6	79.1	73.0	93.7	94.3
2003	94.0	97.9	95.7	89.2	86.3	90.6	88.0	98.5	101.2	95.5	77.5	82.2	96.6	95.4
2004	98.9	99.7	97.5	98.9	99.4	98.3	95.8	99.7	100.2	97.2	86.8	93.0	99.8	95.0
2005	100.0	100.0	100.0	100.0	100.0	100.0	100.0	100.0	100.0	100.0	100.0	100.0	100.0	100.0
2006	100.8	98.5	102.8	108.4	96.4	102.3	107.0	102.6	100.0	104.3	106.8	93.2	105.5	107.8
2007	102.4	98.1	106.2	119.0	99.9	104.0	113.6	101.7	100.6	108.5	108.9	89.3	100.7	109.6
2008	109.1	101.9	110.9	140.9	103.3	112.2	132.5	109.0	104.4	113.3	124.6	100.9	113.5	118.6
2009	114.5	108.9	116.9	151.8	106.3	114.8	143.6	114.2	110.1	119.1	132.9	109.1	118.2	123.7
2007														
1st quarter	100.0	97.8	104.6	109.8	101.0	99.4	108.0	99.5	100.4	106.8	101.9	83.6	96.0	106.0
2nd quarter	101.4	97.4	105.5	116.1	100.1	102.4	114.7	100.4	100.1	107.8	106.2	88.0	98.9	109.0
3rd quarter	104.1	98.5	106.7	123.7	106.6	106.9	115.9	102.3	100.8	109.1	111.9	90.3	102.0	111.6
4th quarter	104.2	98.7	108.0	126.6	91.8	107.3	115.7	104.5	101.2	110.4	115.7	95.1	105.9	111.6
2008														
1st quarter	105.9	99.5	109.6	130.0	96.5	109.2	120.8	106.9	102.5	111.9	120.9	99.1	109.8	110.9
2nd quarter	106.5	100.5	110.7	138.5	101.5	107.4	131.9	109.1	103.8	113.1	124.5	105.8	113.9	115.7
3rd quarter	111.5	102.9	111.5	146.0	106.2	116.5	137.6	108.9	104.7	113.8	124.6	99.0	115.0	117.6
4th quarter	112.4	104.7	111.9	149.3	109.2	115.8	139.9	110.9	106.7	114.2	128.5	99.7	115.4	130.3
2009														
1st quarter	111.0	105.8	113.4	138.6	105.1	112.2	137.5	111.6	108.0	115.9	127.9	108.3	114.2	119.4
2nd quarter	114.3	108.1	115.3	151.7	113.3	115.1	145.3	113.1	110.0	117.7	129.6	112.1	114.7	122.2
3rd quarter	116.5	110.3	117.6	162.5	110.0	116.5	149.1	114.9	111.1	119.7	135.4	106.8	119.4	125.6
4th quarter	116.1	111.4	121.2	154.6	96.0	115.6	142.6	117.3	111.2	123.0	138.5	109.3	124.4	127.6

[1] Excludes government sales to other sectors and government own-account investment (construction and software).
[2] Includes general government intermediate inputs for goods and services sold to other sectors and for own-account investment.

Table 6-7. Chain-Type Quantity Indexes for National Defense Consumption Expenditures and Gross Investment: Selected Detail

(Seasonally adjusted, 2005 = 100.) NIPA Table 3.11.3

| Year and quarter | Compensation of general government employees | | Intermediate goods and services purchased [1] | | | | | | | Gross investment — Equipment and software | | | |
	Military	Civilian	Durable goods Aircraft	Petroleum products	Ammunition	Research and development	Installation support	Weapons support	Personnel support	Aircraft	Missiles	Ships	Electronics and software
1972	131.8	133.5	79.3	317.9	171.7	25.7	51.3	27.1	20.6	24.6	36.1	79.0	5.5
1973	124.3	128.0	66.3	201.2	133.9	25.7	46.8	25.5	16.7	21.6	37.8	66.6	6.1
1974	119.9	131.3	51.5	182.8	91.5	25.5	47.0	27.3	18.9	21.7	41.8	82.2	6.1
1975	117.3	131.3	47.4	153.9	63.7	24.5	44.8	23.7	18.9	32.8	30.5	73.5	7.0
1976	114.5	129.8	39.7	127.5	32.0	25.3	46.0	25.0	18.6	30.7	26.0	75.4	7.4
1977	113.5	128.5	60.7	108.5	43.7	26.2	48.4	24.9	16.4	32.1	20.4	88.0	8.2
1978	112.4	133.0	62.0	107.9	50.5	25.9	45.1	27.1	17.1	30.3	16.7	99.0	10.1
1979	110.6	133.6	77.2	109.8	56.2	26.7	48.2	29.8	16.4	37.9	33.8	101.9	11.1
1980	111.8	133.5	83.8	121.5	56.3	33.0	51.2	40.1	16.1	45.4	48.7	89.6	13.6
1981	115.4	137.2	108.0	119.3	63.6	38.2	52.6	42.9	19.8	52.5	56.5	102.1	16.1
1982	117.4	141.7	126.3	112.3	78.4	41.2	72.0	46.6	27.2	52.8	72.9	119.0	18.6
1983	119.4	143.4	153.7	120.3	91.9	40.7	78.8	54.1	29.0	60.0	92.3	132.3	22.7
1984	120.9	145.8	145.3	120.0	77.8	43.9	84.0	61.7	29.7	64.5	111.0	140.1	28.5
1985	122.7	149.8	156.1	122.0	46.4	58.0	82.4	68.3	36.3	88.0	126.5	154.0	36.5
1986	123.8	148.9	172.7	121.9	124.9	62.2	84.8	71.5	38.5	134.2	160.4	148.7	41.8
1987	125.4	149.4	184.9	125.2	94.8	70.0	84.6	74.0	41.9	154.0	182.5	144.6	47.7
1988	124.4	146.1	191.5	105.5	109.4	82.5	81.0	64.5	39.2	126.5	166.1	137.0	50.5
1989	123.8	147.5	180.6	115.8	91.5	73.6	80.3	65.2	40.0	115.7	190.2	152.1	52.8
1990	124.1	144.1	158.6	114.8	82.5	65.8	88.5	71.5	39.0	106.7	247.0	160.5	54.7
1991	125.5	139.6	141.9	113.4	77.8	54.3	93.7	59.6	35.7	76.8	248.4	144.0	53.9
1992	114.7	138.8	123.8	94.9	73.9	57.2	90.2	47.6	38.5	67.2	245.7	139.1	56.9
1993	108.8	135.0	107.3	91.2	73.4	63.5	95.3	36.8	31.3	72.4	178.4	117.4	57.3
1994	103.6	127.2	91.0	93.9	50.5	59.9	97.5	40.6	34.7	72.3	131.0	105.6	54.8
1995	98.2	119.7	86.8	85.2	32.3	58.4	91.7	42.1	35.8	58.4	110.3	99.4	52.5
1996	94.6	113.5	86.1	86.1	37.9	63.6	92.3	37.2	37.3	56.9	98.8	84.0	56.4
1997	92.1	107.6	92.0	77.3	46.5	63.8	88.9	42.9	39.4	39.5	73.1	74.5	59.2
1998	90.0	102.6	97.6	75.5	52.7	59.9	84.0	41.0	38.5	39.8	82.3	78.8	62.8
1999	88.4	99.0	103.1	83.4	53.6	59.6	86.5	46.9	47.3	41.5	74.7	83.5	69.0
2000	89.2	95.7	96.0	77.0	51.0	57.9	86.3	46.5	46.3	48.3	70.3	79.4	71.4
2001	91.0	94.1	94.7	90.0	58.2	62.7	91.4	54.9	54.9	56.5	88.3	87.1	70.6
2002	94.3	94.8	95.0	103.7	70.8	76.4	98.8	72.5	65.6	65.1	88.2	104.1	74.3
2003	99.5	94.6	106.7	94.4	73.3	86.9	110.0	90.9	76.2	64.6	90.9	112.8	80.4
2004	100.6	97.7	112.0	102.8	96.1	98.2	106.2	90.6	93.7	79.7	103.3	108.5	89.5
2005	100.0	100.0	100.0	100.0	100.0	100.0	100.0	100.0	100.0	100.0	100.0	100.0	100.0
2006	97.7	100.2	99.9	96.1	98.2	103.6	99.8	102.3	105.9	101.6	111.6	98.6	113.8
2007	96.9	100.8	103.7	99.7	92.0	100.2	94.4	99.6	111.7	95.4	105.5	91.8	133.2
2008	101.2	103.4	117.2	101.2	94.2	105.2	98.0	118.3	130.3	100.3	100.5	91.4	168.6
2009	109.0	108.5	140.0	99.2	88.9	103.5	107.7	113.7	139.8	113.1	116.8	97.5	178.1
2003													
1st quarter	97.7	94.9	93.1	131.3	59.4	72.9	100.2	73.1	64.7	65.7	74.2	101.2	78.2
2nd quarter	100.5	93.2	112.9	104.5	76.4	100.3	108.2	90.4	73.8	63.6	75.3	119.5	77.6
3rd quarter	100.1	94.6	108.4	56.8	78.2	80.8	115.7	103.0	82.0	59.4	92.8	119.5	84.2
4th quarter	99.5	95.8	112.5	84.9	79.0	93.4	115.9	97.0	84.3	69.8	121.3	111.0	81.6
2004													
1st quarter	101.1	95.9	107.0	119.2	91.8	94.8	109.1	91.3	90.9	61.4	100.4	113.1	82.7
2nd quarter	100.2	96.5	110.1	102.3	94.6	101.5	104.9	83.9	91.1	71.6	90.9	99.3	92.9
3rd quarter	100.1	99.5	117.7	123.9	99.2	98.4	110.6	98.7	99.3	86.1	111.4	122.0	90.3
4th quarter	101.0	99.1	113.2	65.7	98.8	98.1	100.3	88.6	93.4	99.7	110.5	99.5	92.2
2005													
1st quarter	101.0	99.1	99.9	83.8	94.6	99.9	95.9	94.4	95.8	91.1	79.3	101.0	91.2
2nd quarter	99.8	99.9	99.6	109.5	99.7	105.6	97.0	93.3	94.2	99.6	112.3	97.7	97.8
3rd quarter	99.4	100.7	98.6	111.5	106.3	102.1	106.3	115.3	107.4	104.4	86.8	109.4	106.7
4th quarter	99.7	100.3	102.0	95.2	99.4	92.5	100.9	96.9	102.6	104.9	121.6	92.0	104.4
2006													
1st quarter	97.6	99.6	97.3	91.9	100.7	105.3	99.3	98.4	107.2	97.4	116.5	94.6	107.7
2nd quarter	97.0	99.6	93.0	91.8	97.1	104.5	101.9	107.4	111.4	113.6	115.9	105.1	110.8
3rd quarter	98.2	100.2	97.2	113.2	95.4	99.4	96.1	93.1	101.6	87.4	83.3	97.2	118.3
4th quarter	97.8	101.3	112.0	87.3	99.7	105.0	101.8	110.4	103.6	107.9	130.9	97.5	118.3
2007													
1st quarter	96.7	100.4	91.4	98.2	96.7	104.1	93.1	92.7	100.1	91.8	128.7	89.1	124.4
2nd quarter	96.1	100.2	99.7	102.1	84.6	102.0	93.8	98.3	107.1	107.0	106.4	90.0	130.6
3rd quarter	97.5	100.7	108.4	108.7	100.1	96.8	96.6	105.2	117.2	97.8	95.5	90.1	139.6
4th quarter	97.3	101.8	115.1	89.8	86.6	97.9	94.0	102.2	122.5	85.1	91.3	98.1	138.3
2008													
1st quarter	98.6	101.3	105.3	90.7	98.3	100.4	93.4	107.4	126.9	75.9	90.1	84.3	156.5
2nd quarter	99.4	102.9	113.5	100.7	86.0	102.8	92.2	105.1	124.2	109.0	107.5	90.5	166.0
3rd quarter	102.2	104.5	122.2	106.1	94.4	102.3	104.5	136.3	138.2	107.7	109.5	92.8	175.6
4th quarter	104.6	104.7	127.7	107.4	97.9	115.4	102.1	124.3	131.8	108.4	94.8	97.9	176.2
2009													
1st quarter	106.1	105.0	126.8	104.8	81.9	101.2	105.7	112.2	134.8	107.0	111.2	92.1	165.3
2nd quarter	108.7	106.6	136.0	109.5	92.4	106.1	109.1	113.6	136.4	121.6	116.2	96.7	178.6
3rd quarter	110.7	109.2	142.9	99.2	89.1	104.4	109.4	119.8	140.7	105.0	120.3	95.1	188.1
4th quarter	110.6	113.1	154.4	83.4	92.3	102.2	106.8	109.3	147.5	118.7	119.7	105.9	180.5

[1] Includes general government intermediate inputs for goods and services sold to other sectors and for own-account investment.

Section 6b: State and Local Government in the National Income and Product Accounts

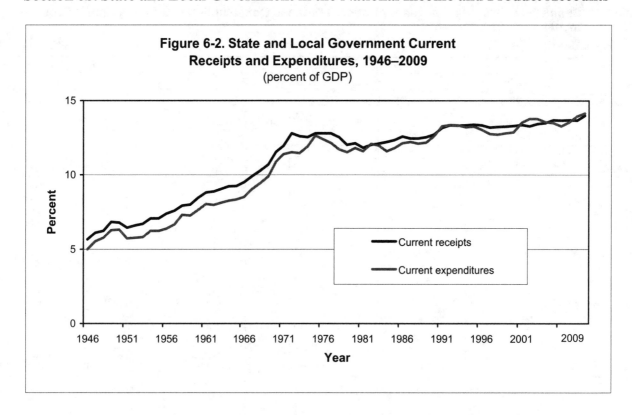

Figure 6-2. State and Local Government Current Receipts and Expenditures, 1946–2009
(percent of GDP)

- Current receipts of state and local governments began to decline in the third quarter of 2008, and their usual small surpluses turned to deficits beginning with the fourth quarter of 2007. Their accounts are estimated to have returned to near-balance by the fourth quarter of 2009, assisted by an increase in federal grants. (Table 6-8)

- Both current receipts and current spending of state and local governments have increased as a share of gross domestic product (GDP) over the postwar period. State and local governments, unlike the federal government, are bound by constraints on deficit spending, and have generally run modest surpluses ("net saving") in their current accounts. (Tables 6-8 and 1-1)

- Despite the net saving usually registered in their current receipts and expenditures accounts, state and local governments on balance have not been suppliers of funds to the capital markets. Though they are constrained against deficits in their annual budgets, these governments can and do borrow—for investment, or just to cover shortfalls in current accounts—by issuing bonds. (Usually, the permission of voters in the state or local jurisdiction is required.) They have usually been net borrowers from the rest of the economy, even before the deficits of the 2000s. This has allowed their net investment usually to exceed the sum of their current surpluses, estimated capital depreciation allowances, and capital transfers (which are mainly federal highway grants). (Table 6-10)

- State and local gross investment rose at an annual rate of 2.7 percent in real terms from 1955 to 2009, compared with 4.8 percent for federal nondefense investment. (Tables 6-6 and 6-11)

Table 6-8. State and Local Government Current Receipts and Expenditures

(National income and product accounts, calendar years, billions of dollars, quarterly data are at seasonally adjusted annual rates.)

NIPA Table 3.3

Year and quarter	Total current receipts		Current receipts									
			Current tax receipts						Contribu-tions for govern-ment social insurance	Income receipts on assets		
		Total tax receipts	Personal current taxes		Taxes on production and imports			Taxes on corporate income				
			Income taxes	Other personal taxes	Sales taxes	Property taxes	Other taxes on prod. and imports			Interest receipts	Dividends	Rents and royalties
1950	20.0	16.5	0.8	0.7	4.8	7.1	2.3	0.8	0.2	0.3	. . .	0.2
1951	21.9	18.1	0.9	0.8	5.4	7.7	2.5	0.9	0.2	0.4	. . .	0.2
1952	23.7	19.7	1.0	0.8	5.8	8.4	2.8	0.8	0.3	0.4	. . .	0.2
1953	25.5	21.1	1.0	0.9	6.3	9.1	3.0	0.8	0.3	0.5	. . .	0.3
1954	26.9	22.2	1.1	1.0	6.5	9.7	3.2	0.8	0.3	0.5	. . .	0.3
1955	29.4	24.4	1.3	1.0	7.1	10.4	3.5	1.0	0.3	0.6	. . .	0.3
1956	32.4	27.0	1.6	1.1	8.0	11.5	3.8	1.0	0.4	0.7	. . .	0.3
1957	35.0	29.0	1.7	1.2	8.6	12.6	3.9	1.0	0.4	0.7	. . .	0.3
1958	37.1	30.6	1.8	1.2	10.0	13.8	2.8	1.0	0.4	0.8	. . .	0.4
1959	40.6	33.8	2.2	1.6	11.1	14.8	2.9	1.2	0.4	0.9	. . .	0.3
1960	44.5	37.0	2.5	1.7	12.2	16.2	3.1	1.2	0.5	1.0	. . .	0.3
1961	48.1	39.7	2.8	1.8	13.0	17.6	3.2	1.3	0.5	1.1	. . .	0.4
1962	52.0	42.8	3.2	1.8	14.0	19.0	3.3	1.5	0.5	1.1	. . .	0.4
1963	56.0	45.8	3.4	2.0	15.0	20.2	3.5	1.7	0.6	1.2	. . .	0.4
1964	61.3	49.8	4.0	2.1	16.5	21.7	3.7	1.8	0.7	1.5	. . .	0.4
1965	66.5	53.9	4.4	2.2	18.2	23.2	3.9	2.0	0.8	1.8	. . .	0.4
1966	74.9	58.8	5.4	2.4	20.0	24.5	4.3	2.2	0.8	2.1	. . .	0.5
1967	82.5	64.0	6.1	2.5	21.4	27.0	4.4	2.6	0.9	2.4	. . .	0.6
1968	93.5	73.4	7.8	2.7	25.1	29.9	4.6	3.3	0.9	2.8	. . .	0.7
1969	105.5	82.5	9.8	3.0	28.6	32.8	4.7	3.6	1.0	3.6	. . .	0.8
1970	120.1	91.3	10.9	3.3	31.6	36.7	5.0	3.7	1.1	4.3	. . .	0.8
1971	134.9	101.7	12.4	3.5	35.4	40.4	5.7	4.3	1.2	4.6	. . .	0.9
1972	158.4	115.6	17.2	3.7	39.8	43.2	6.4	5.3	1.3	4.9	. . .	1.0
1973	174.3	126.3	18.9	4.0	44.1	46.4	7.0	6.0	1.5	6.6	0.0	1.1
1974	188.1	136.0	20.4	4.2	48.2	49.0	7.7	6.7	1.7	8.9	0.0	1.3
1975	209.6	147.4	22.5	4.4	51.7	53.4	8.1	7.3	1.8	9.8	0.0	1.3
1976	233.7	165.7	26.3	4.8	57.8	58.2	9.0	9.6	2.2	9.0	0.0	1.3
1977	259.9	183.7	30.4	5.0	64.0	63.2	9.7	11.4	2.8	10.4	0.0	1.3
1978	287.6	198.2	35.0	5.5	71.0	63.7	10.9	12.1	3.4	13.3	0.1	1.3
1979	308.4	212.0	38.2	5.8	77.3	64.4	12.7	13.6	3.9	18.1	0.1	1.9
1980	338.2	230.0	42.6	6.3	82.9	68.8	15.0	14.5	3.6	23.1	0.1	3.1
1981	370.2	255.8	47.9	6.7	90.7	77.1	17.9	15.4	3.9	28.5	0.1	3.3
1982	391.4	273.2	51.9	7.3	96.2	85.3	18.5	14.0	4.0	33.1	0.2	3.5
1983	428.6	300.9	58.3	7.8	107.7	91.9	19.4	15.9	4.1	37.0	0.2	4.3
1984	480.2	337.3	67.5	8.6	121.0	99.7	21.8	18.8	4.7	42.6	0.2	4.9
1985	521.1	363.7	72.1	9.2	131.1	107.5	23.5	20.2	4.9	49.3	0.2	5.4
1986	561.6	389.5	77.4	9.8	139.9	116.2	23.7	22.7	6.0	52.0	0.2	6.2
1987	590.6	422.1	86.0	10.6	150.3	126.4	24.9	23.9	7.2	52.7	0.2	5.3
1988	635.5	452.8	90.6	11.5	162.4	136.5	25.7	26.0	8.4	55.9	0.2	4.4
1989	687.5	488.0	102.3	12.4	172.3	149.9	26.9	24.2	9.0	61.4	0.2	4.1
1990	738.0	519.1	109.6	13.0	184.3	161.5	28.3	22.5	10.0	64.1	0.2	4.2
1991	789.4	544.3	111.7	13.6	190.7	176.1	28.6	23.6	11.6	63.1	0.3	4.5
1992	846.2	579.8	120.4	14.9	204.3	184.7	31.1	24.4	13.1	59.6	0.5	4.8
1993	888.2	604.7	126.2	14.8	216.4	187.3	33.1	26.9	14.1	56.2	0.6	4.5
1994	944.8	644.2	132.2	15.7	231.4	199.4	35.5	30.0	14.5	58.0	0.8	4.5
1995	991.9	672.1	141.7	16.4	242.7	202.6	37.0	31.7	13.6	63.0	1.0	4.5
1996	1 045.1	709.6	152.3	16.3	256.2	212.4	39.4	33.0	12.5	67.5	1.4	4.6
1997	1 099.5	749.9	164.7	17.3	268.7	223.5	41.6	34.1	10.8	71.9	1.5	4.8
1998	1 164.5	794.9	183.0	18.2	283.9	231.0	43.9	34.9	10.4	75.2	1.6	4.6
1999	1 240.4	840.4	195.5	19.0	301.6	242.8	45.8	35.8	9.8	79.1	1.5	5.1
2000	1 322.6	893.2	217.4	19.4	316.8	254.7	49.8	35.2	10.8	86.7	1.4	6.3
2001	1 374.0	914.3	223.3	19.7	321.8	268.0	52.6	28.9	13.7	82.1	1.4	6.5
2002	1 412.7	928.7	201.3	20.5	331.1	289.4	55.5	30.9	15.9	71.5	1.6	6.6
2003	1 496.3	977.7	204.1	22.1	348.8	306.8	61.9	34.0	20.1	64.6	1.7	7.6
2004	1 601.0	1 059.4	224.7	23.8	370.7	326.7	71.7	41.7	24.1	66.7	2.0	8.5
2005	1 730.4	1 163.1	251.7	25.0	402.2	346.9	82.3	54.9	24.8	76.4	2.1	9.8
2006	1 829.7	1 249.0	276.1	26.4	430.4	370.1	86.9	59.2	21.8	90.9	2.3	10.3
2007	1 927.3	1 313.4	295.5	27.3	446.3	396.3	91.5	56.5	19.8	101.2	2.5	10.5
2008	1 974.2	1 336.3	302.4	27.6	443.9	410.6	100.9	51.0	21.1	100.1	2.9	11.0
2009	1 995.5	1 263.1	245.0	28.0	422.7	421.8	87.0	58.5	21.9	101.8	2.8	11.6
2007												
1st quarter	1 902.3	1 296.8	295.6	27.0	442.3	387.9	90.2	53.8	20.0	99.3	2.4	10.4
2nd quarter	1 923.4	1 309.1	297.0	27.1	446.0	394.3	90.0	54.7	19.7	101.3	2.4	10.4
3rd quarter	1 932.1	1 315.7	295.8	27.3	447.0	399.5	90.3	55.8	19.6	102.3	2.5	10.5
4th quarter	1 951.6	1 331.9	293.6	27.6	449.7	403.5	95.5	61.9	19.9	102.1	2.6	10.6
2008												
1st quarter	1 963.7	1 338.1	309.2	27.2	448.1	406.3	95.4	51.9	20.3	100.8	2.9	10.8
2nd quarter	1 994.2	1 356.9	314.3	27.7	443.8	409.1	104.8	57.2	20.8	100.3	2.8	10.9
3rd quarter	1 987.5	1 351.0	299.4	27.8	447.3	412.0	107.3	57.1	21.4	98.9	2.7	11.0
4th quarter	1 951.4	1 298.9	286.4	27.7	436.3	415.0	95.9	37.7	22.0	100.3	3.1	11.2
2009												
1st quarter	1 961.4	1 272.2	259.2	27.8	429.4	417.7	85.9	52.2	21.8	101.2	3.3	11.3
2nd quarter	1 989.3	1 238.1	224.9	27.8	420.7	420.4	86.9	57.4	21.7	101.5	2.7	11.5
3rd quarter	2 003.6	1 263.5	247.2	28.0	421.2	423.2	85.3	58.6	21.9	102.0	2.6	11.6
4th quarter	2 027.5	1 278.7	248.9	28.4	419.7	426.0	89.9	65.8	22.1	102.6	2.5	11.8

. . . = Not available.

Table 6-8. State and Local Government Current Receipts and Expenditures—*Continued*

(National income and product accounts, calendar years, billions of dollars, quarterly data are at seasonally adjusted annual rates.)

NIPA Table 3.3

Year and quarter	Current receipts—*Continued*				Current surplus of government enterprises	Current expenditures					Net state and local government saving, NIPA (surplus + / deficit -)		
	Current transfer receipts												
	Total	Federal grants-in-aid	From business, net	From persons		Total	Consumption expenditures	Government social benefits to persons	Interest payments	Subsidies	Total	Social insurance funds	Other
1950	2.3	1.9	0.1	0.3	0.4	18.6	14.9	3.2	0.6	...	1.3	0.1	1.2
1951	2.5	2.0	0.1	0.3	0.5	19.4	16.1	2.6	0.6	...	2.6	0.1	2.5
1952	2.6	2.2	0.1	0.3	0.5	20.7	17.1	2.9	0.7	...	3.0	0.1	2.9
1953	2.8	2.3	0.1	0.3	0.6	22.0	18.2	3.0	0.8	...	3.5	0.1	3.4
1954	2.9	2.3	0.2	0.4	0.7	23.7	19.7	3.1	0.9	...	3.2	0.1	3.1
1955	3.0	2.4	0.2	0.4	0.8	25.9	21.6	3.3	1.1	...	3.5	0.1	3.4
1956	3.2	2.5	0.2	0.4	0.9	28.0	23.4	3.3	1.2	...	4.4	0.1	4.3
1957	3.6	2.9	0.2	0.5	0.9	30.8	25.8	3.6	1.4	...	4.2	0.1	4.1
1958	4.1	3.3	0.2	0.5	0.9	34.2	28.6	4.0	1.5	...	2.9	0.0	2.8
1959	4.2	3.8	0.1	0.3	1.1	36.9	30.7	4.3	1.8	0.0	3.8	0.0	3.8
1960	4.5	4.0	0.2	0.3	1.2	40.2	33.5	4.6	2.1	0.0	4.3	0.0	4.3
1961	5.2	4.5	0.2	0.4	1.3	43.8	36.6	5.0	2.2	0.0	4.3	0.0	4.3
1962	5.8	5.0	0.2	0.5	1.4	46.8	39.0	5.3	2.4	0.0	5.2	0.0	5.2
1963	6.4	5.6	0.3	0.5	1.6	50.3	41.9	5.7	2.7	0.0	5.7	0.0	5.7
1964	7.3	6.5	0.3	0.5	1.6	54.9	45.8	6.2	2.9	0.0	6.4	0.0	6.3
1965	8.0	7.2	0.3	0.5	1.7	60.0	50.2	6.7	3.1	0.0	6.5	0.1	6.4
1966	11.1	10.1	0.3	0.7	1.6	67.2	56.1	7.6	3.4	0.0	7.8	0.1	7.6
1967	13.1	11.7	0.5	0.9	1.5	75.5	62.6	9.2	3.7	0.0	7.0	0.1	6.9
1968	14.2	12.7	0.5	1.0	1.5	86.0	70.4	11.4	4.2	0.0	7.5	0.1	7.3
1969	16.2	14.6	0.5	1.1	1.5	97.5	79.8	13.2	4.4	0.0	8.0	0.2	7.8
1970	21.1	19.3	0.6	1.2	1.5	113.0	91.5	16.1	5.3	0.0	7.1	0.2	6.9
1971	25.2	23.2	0.6	1.4	1.4	128.5	102.7	19.3	6.5	0.0	6.5	0.2	6.2
1972	34.0	31.7	0.7	1.7	1.6	142.8	113.2	22.0	7.5	0.1	15.6	0.3	15.4
1973	37.3	34.8	0.9	1.7	1.5	158.6	126.0	24.1	8.5	0.1	15.7	0.3	15.4
1974	39.3	36.3	1.1	2.0	0.9	178.7	143.7	25.3	9.6	0.1	9.3	0.4	9.0
1975	48.7	45.1	1.2	2.4	0.4	207.1	165.1	30.8	11.1	0.2	2.5	0.5	2.0
1976	55.0	50.7	1.4	2.9	0.4	226.3	179.5	34.1	12.5	0.2	7.4	0.6	6.8
1977	61.4	56.6	1.6	3.3	0.3	246.8	195.9	37.0	13.7	0.2	13.1	1.0	12.2
1978	71.1	65.5	1.9	3.7	0.3	268.9	213.2	40.8	14.9	0.2	18.7	1.5	17.2
1979	72.7	66.3	2.2	4.1	-0.3	295.4	233.3	44.3	17.2	0.3	13.0	1.8	11.2
1980	79.5	72.3	2.5	4.7	-1.2	329.4	258.4	51.2	19.4	0.4	8.8	1.3	7.5
1981	81.0	72.5	2.9	5.7	-2.4	362.7	282.3	57.1	22.8	0.4	7.6	1.3	6.3
1982	79.1	69.5	3.2	6.4	-1.6	393.6	304.9	61.2	27.1	0.5	-2.2	1.2	-3.4
1983	82.4	71.6	3.6	7.2	-0.2	423.7	324.1	66.9	32.3	0.4	4.9	1.2	3.7
1984	89.0	76.7	4.2	8.1	1.5	456.2	347.7	71.2	37.0	0.4	23.9	1.4	22.5
1985	94.5	80.9	4.4	9.2	3.2	498.7	381.8	77.3	39.4	0.3	22.4	1.3	21.0
1986	105.0	87.6	6.7	10.6	2.8	540.9	418.1	84.3	38.2	0.3	20.7	1.9	18.9
1987	100.0	83.9	4.9	11.2	3.1	578.6	441.4	90.7	46.2	0.3	12.0	2.2	9.8
1988	109.0	91.6	5.4	12.0	4.8	618.3	471.0	98.5	48.4	0.4	17.2	2.5	14.7
1989	118.1	98.3	6.4	13.4	6.7	667.4	504.5	109.3	53.2	0.4	20.1	2.3	17.8
1990	133.5	111.4	7.1	14.9	6.9	731.8	547.0	127.7	56.8	0.4	6.2	2.0	4.2
1991	158.2	131.6	7.9	18.7	7.3	795.2	577.5	156.5	60.8	0.4	-5.8	2.4	-8.2
1992	180.3	149.1	9.2	21.9	8.3	847.6	606.2	180.0	61.0	0.4	-1.4	3.1	-4.5
1993	198.1	164.0	10.5	23.5	9.9	889.1	634.2	195.2	59.4	0.4	-0.9	4.2	-5.1
1994	212.3	175.1	12.0	25.2	10.5	936.6	668.2	206.7	61.4	0.3	8.2	4.6	3.6
1995	224.2	184.2	13.5	26.5	13.5	982.7	701.3	217.6	63.5	0.3	9.2	4.0	5.1
1996	234.0	191.1	15.2	27.8	15.6	1 022.1	730.2	224.3	67.3	0.3	23.0	2.8	20.2
1997	246.4	198.4	17.7	30.3	14.2	1 063.2	764.5	227.6	70.6	0.4	36.3	1.2	35.1
1998	265.3	212.6	21.6	31.1	12.5	1 117.6	808.6	235.8	72.8	0.4	46.9	1.7	45.2
1999	291.1	232.9	24.0	34.2	13.3	1 198.6	870.6	252.3	75.2	0.4	41.8	1.7	40.1
2000	313.9	247.3	28.6	38.0	10.4	1 281.3	930.6	271.4	78.8	0.5	41.3	2.0	39.3
2001	348.0	276.1	29.8	42.0	8.0	1 389.9	994.2	305.1	83.0	7.7	-15.9	2.6	-18.5
2002	382.3	304.2	32.6	45.6	6.1	1 466.8	1 049.4	333.0	83.5	0.9	-54.1	1.5	-55.6
2003	421.3	338.0	33.8	49.5	3.3	1 535.1	1 096.5	353.4	85.1	0.1	-38.8	3.4	-42.2
2004	439.4	349.2	36.5	53.7	1.0	1 609.3	1 139.1	384.3	85.6	0.4	-8.4	6.9	-15.3
2005	454.3	361.2	36.5	56.5	0.1	1 704.5	1 212.0	404.8	87.3	0.4	25.9	7.4	18.5
2006	456.7	359.0	38.4	59.2	-1.3	1 778.6	1 282.3	402.9	93.0	0.4	51.0	4.7	46.4
2007	483.9	378.9	41.3	63.7	-3.9	1 905.6	1 366.1	433.7	98.7	7.1	21.7	1.9	19.8
2008	506.1	391.7	45.6	68.8	-3.2	2 014.4	1 452.4	455.0	103.9	3.0	-40.2	2.0	-42.2
2009	597.5	476.6	47.9	73.1	-3.2	2 014.6	1 430.5	475.9	106.8	1.4	-19.2	1.9	-21.1
2007													
1st quarter	477.0	375.0	40.2	61.8	-3.6	1 869.5	1 331.2	439.5	97.0	1.9	32.8	2.5	30.2
2nd quarter	484.5	380.7	40.8	63.0	-4.0	1 888.4	1 357.3	422.6	97.8	10.7	34.9	1.9	33.0
3rd quarter	485.6	379.7	41.6	64.3	-4.1	1 911.7	1 373.6	430.2	99.2	8.8	20.3	1.5	18.8
4th quarter	488.4	380.3	42.5	65.6	-3.9	1 952.9	1 402.5	442.4	100.8	7.2	-1.3	1.4	-2.8
2008													
1st quarter	493.9	382.5	44.4	67.0	-3.1	1 983.8	1 429.3	448.2	102.4	4.0	-20.1	1.5	-21.6
2nd quarter	505.4	391.8	45.3	68.3	-2.9	2 019.6	1 458.3	454.0	104.5	2.9	-25.5	1.8	-27.3
3rd quarter	505.5	390.0	46.0	69.4	-3.1	2 046.5	1 480.4	459.7	104.3	2.1	-59.0	2.1	-61.1
4th quarter	519.5	402.4	46.6	70.4	-3.5	2 007.5	1 441.7	458.3	104.7	2.8	-56.1	2.5	-58.5
2009													
1st quarter	555.7	437.7	46.8	71.2	-4.0	1 998.0	1 424.4	465.7	106.0	2.0	-36.6	2.1	-38.7
2nd quarter	617.4	497.9	47.3	72.2	-3.5	2 013.9	1 429.9	477.5	105.4	1.2	-24.6	1.9	-26.5
3rd quarter	604.9	483.7	48.0	73.3	-2.9	2 018.6	1 429.8	480.0	107.5	1.2	-14.9	1.9	-16.8
4th quarter	612.1	487.2	49.4	75.5	-2.3	2 028.0	1 438.1	480.4	108.3	1.2	-0.5	1.8	-2.3

... = Not available.

Table 6-9. State and Local Government Consumption Expenditures and Gross Investment

(National income and product accounts, calendar years, billions of dollars, quarterly data are at seasonally adjusted annual rates.)

NIPA Tables 3.9.5, 3.10.5

Year and quarter	Total	Consumption expenditures [1] Total	Compensation of general government employees	Consumption of general government fixed capital	Intermediate goods and services purchased [2]	Own-account investment	Sales to other sectors Total [3]	Tuition and related educational charges	Health and hospital charges	Gross investment Total	Structures	Equipment and software
1950	20.7	14.9	10.1	1.7	4.9	0.3	1.6	0.1	0.3	5.9	5.4	0.5
1951	23.0	16.1	11.2	2.0	4.9	0.3	1.7	0.1	0.3	7.0	6.4	0.5
1952	24.4	17.1	12.3	2.2	4.9	0.4	1.8	0.2	0.3	7.3	6.7	0.6
1953	26.1	18.2	13.3	2.2	4.9	0.4	1.9	0.2	0.4	7.9	6.7	0.6
1954	28.9	19.7	14.7	2.2	5.2	0.4	2.0	0.2	0.4	9.2	8.5	0.7
1955	31.6	21.6	15.8	2.4	6.0	0.4	2.2	0.2	0.5	10.0	9.3	0.8
1956	34.7	23.4	17.6	2.8	5.9	0.5	2.4	0.2	0.6	11.3	10.4	0.9
1957	38.3	25.8	19.6	3.0	6.4	0.5	2.6	0.3	0.7	12.5	11.5	1.1
1958	42.2	28.6	21.6	3.1	7.5	0.6	3.0	0.3	0.9	13.5	12.5	1.1
1959	44.7	30.7	23.1	3.3	8.3	0.8	3.2	0.4	1.0	13.9	12.8	1.1
1960	47.5	33.5	25.5	3.5	8.9	0.8	3.5	0.4	1.0	13.9	12.7	1.2
1961	51.6	36.6	27.9	3.7	9.7	0.8	3.9	0.5	1.0	15.0	13.8	1.3
1962	54.9	39.0	30.2	3.9	10.1	0.9	4.4	0.6	1.3	15.9	14.5	1.3
1963	59.5	41.9	32.9	4.2	10.8	1.0	4.9	0.7	1.3	17.5	16.0	1.5
1964	64.8	45.8	35.9	4.5	11.9	1.0	5.5	0.8	1.5	19.0	17.2	1.8
1965	71.0	50.2	39.3	4.9	13.4	1.1	6.3	1.0	1.8	20.8	19.0	1.9
1966	79.2	56.1	44.1	5.5	14.9	1.2	7.2	1.2	2.1	23.1	21.0	2.1
1967	87.9	62.6	49.5	6.0	16.5	1.2	8.2	1.4	2.5	25.3	23.0	2.3
1968	98.0	70.4	55.9	6.6	18.7	1.3	9.5	1.6	3.2	27.7	25.2	2.4
1969	108.2	79.8	62.6	7.4	21.8	1.4	10.6	1.9	3.5	28.3	25.6	2.7
1970	120.3	91.5	71.1	8.4	25.4	1.5	11.8	2.4	3.8	28.7	25.8	3.0
1971	132.8	102.7	79.2	9.4	29.2	1.6	13.5	2.9	4.6	30.1	27.0	3.1
1972	143.8	113.2	87.7	10.2	32.2	1.7	15.2	3.2	5.6	30.6	27.1	3.5
1973	159.2	126.0	98.0	11.3	35.4	1.7	17.0	3.7	6.6	33.2	29.1	4.1
1974	183.4	143.7	107.7	14.1	42.7	2.1	18.7	4.0	7.4	39.6	34.7	4.9
1975	208.7	165.1	121.2	15.9	50.7	2.1	20.6	4.3	8.5	43.6	38.1	5.5
1976	223.3	179.5	133.0	16.6	55.2	2.0	23.3	4.7	9.9	43.8	38.1	5.7
1977	238.7	195.9	145.1	17.5	61.1	2.0	25.8	5.2	10.9	42.8	36.9	5.9
1978	262.7	213.2	158.9	18.9	66.9	2.3	29.2	5.8	12.7	49.5	42.8	6.6
1979	290.2	233.3	174.3	21.1	74.3	2.9	33.4	6.4	15.2	56.8	49.0	7.8
1980	322.4	258.4	193.0	24.3	82.0	3.3	37.6	7.2	17.3	64.0	55.1	8.9
1981	347.3	282.3	210.1	27.8	91.6	3.5	43.7	8.3	21.0	65.0	55.4	9.5
1982	369.7	304.9	227.4	30.3	100.6	3.7	49.7	9.4	24.5	64.8	54.2	10.6
1983	390.5	324.1	243.0	31.2	109.6	4.0	55.7	10.7	27.8	66.4	54.2	12.2
1984	422.6	347.7	261.1	32.0	119.0	4.6	59.8	11.7	29.4	75.0	60.5	14.4
1985	466.1	381.8	284.7	33.7	134.0	5.2	65.4	12.8	32.0	84.4	67.6	16.8
1986	510.9	418.1	307.6	36.2	151.6	5.7	71.5	13.9	34.8	92.8	74.2	18.6
1987	539.9	441.4	329.3	39.0	156.2	6.1	76.9	15.0	37.0	98.4	78.8	19.6
1988	577.3	471.0	354.3	41.5	166.0	6.7	84.1	16.6	40.3	106.3	84.8	21.5
1989	619.2	504.5	381.4	44.4	180.2	7.8	93.8	18.4	45.0	114.7	88.7	26.0
1990	674.2	547.0	415.9	48.0	195.2	8.6	103.5	20.3	50.0	127.2	98.5	28.7
1991	709.5	577.5	441.7	51.1	209.4	9.3	115.4	22.7	57.0	132.1	103.2	28.9
1992	740.6	606.2	466.6	53.4	224.9	9.5	129.1	25.5	65.3	134.3	104.2	30.1
1993	769.8	634.2	489.7	56.3	240.6	9.7	142.7	27.5	73.1	135.7	104.5	31.2
1994	811.2	668.2	515.2	59.5	256.8	10.1	153.3	29.4	78.8	143.0	108.7	34.3
1995	855.3	701.3	537.7	63.4	275.8	10.6	165.0	31.2	85.0	154.0	117.3	36.7
1996	894.0	730.2	557.1	66.7	290.6	11.0	173.2	33.0	86.6	163.8	126.8	36.9
1997	943.5	764.5	580.1	70.2	309.6	12.2	183.2	35.5	89.9	178.9	139.5	39.4
1998	995.0	808.6	606.4	73.9	332.8	12.6	191.9	38.0	93.5	186.4	143.6	42.9
1999	1 076.3	870.6	642.5	78.7	364.8	13.5	201.8	40.6	96.7	205.7	159.7	46.1
2000	1 154.9	930.6	679.0	84.7	400.0	14.9	218.2	43.7	104.0	224.3	176.0	48.3
2001	1 234.7	994.2	725.0	89.7	432.5	16.7	236.3	46.2	116.2	240.5	192.3	48.2
2002	1 302.7	1 049.4	765.8	93.8	454.1	17.0	247.3	49.4	120.8	253.3	205.8	47.5
2003	1 356.1	1 096.5	811.7	97.6	464.6	17.2	260.1	53.6	124.8	259.6	211.8	47.8
2004	1 408.2	1 139.1	842.9	104.4	485.2	18.1	275.4	56.9	130.9	269.1	220.2	48.9
2005	1 493.6	1 212.0	883.3	114.4	522.1	19.1	288.7	61.2	132.3	281.6	230.8	50.8
2006	1 586.7	1 282.3	927.1	124.2	556.2	20.5	304.7	65.8	137.8	304.4	249.9	54.5
2007	1 699.6	1 366.1	979.9	136.1	597.5	22.3	325.1	70.8	146.1	333.7	277.2	56.4
2008	1 800.6	1 452.4	1 026.9	146.3	651.5	23.8	348.5	76.2	157.0	348.2	290.9	57.3
2009	1 785.9	1 430.5	1 047.9	153.3	612.3	23.7	359.1	79.9	161.8	355.4	299.6	55.7
2007												
1st quarter	1 656.5	1 331.2	961.0	132.8	575.8	21.6	316.8	68.9	142.6	325.4	269.4	56.0
2nd quarter	1 689.3	1 357.3	974.4	135.0	592.2	22.1	322.1	70.1	144.7	332.0	275.7	56.3
3rd quarter	1 709.5	1 373.6	984.9	137.1	601.3	22.5	327.2	71.3	146.9	335.9	279.4	56.5
4th quarter	1 743.9	1 402.5	999.5	139.6	620.8	23.0	334.3	73.0	150.3	341.4	284.5	56.9
2008												
1st quarter	1 770.1	1 429.3	1 012.3	142.1	640.1	23.2	342.0	74.8	153.8	340.8	283.5	57.3
2nd quarter	1 807.6	1 458.3	1 023.2	144.5	661.6	24.0	347.0	75.9	156.3	349.2	291.5	57.7
3rd quarter	1 833.1	1 480.4	1 033.6	147.5	675.1	24.2	351.6	76.8	158.4	352.7	295.4	57.3
4th quarter	1 791.7	1 441.7	1 038.6	151.1	629.2	23.8	353.4	77.1	159.4	350.0	293.2	56.8
2009												
1st quarter	1 772.3	1 424.4	1 042.8	153.2	607.3	23.5	355.5	78.1	160.4	347.9	292.5	55.4
2nd quarter	1 791.2	1 429.9	1 050.7	153.1	608.2	24.1	357.9	79.3	161.3	361.3	305.8	55.4
3rd quarter	1 791.1	1 429.8	1 048.2	152.9	612.8	24.0	360.1	80.7	162.1	361.3	305.9	55.4
4th quarter	1 789.0	1 438.1	1 050.0	153.8	620.7	23.4	363.1	81.6	163.3	350.9	294.4	56.6

[1] Excludes government sales to other sectors and government own-account investment (construction and software).
[2] Includes general government intermediate inputs for goods and services sold to other sectors and for own-account investment.
[3] Includes components not shown separately.

Table 6-10. State and Local Government Output, Lending and Borrowing, and Net Investment

(National income and product accounts, calendar years, billions of dollars, quarterly data are at seasonally adjusted annual rates.)

NIPA Tables 3.3, 3.10.5

Year and quarter	Output			Net lending (net borrowing -)							Net investment
	Gross	Value added	Intermediate goods and services purchased [1]	Net saving, current (surplus +, deficit -)	Plus: Capital transfer receipts	Minus			Plus: consumption of fixed capital	Equals: Net lending (borrowing -)	
						Gross investment	Capital transfer payments	Net purchases of nonproduced assets			
1950	16.7	11.8	4.9	1.3	0.6	5.9	...	0.3	2.1	-2.1	3.8
1951	18.1	13.2	4.9	2.6	0.7	7.0	...	0.3	2.6	-1.5	4.4
1952	19.3	14.4	4.9	3.0	0.7	7.3	...	0.3	2.7	-1.1	4.6
1953	20.5	15.5	4.9	3.5	0.8	7.9	...	0.3	2.8	-1.1	5.1
1954	22.1	16.9	5.2	3.2	0.8	9.2	...	0.4	2.9	-2.6	6.3
1955	24.2	18.2	6.0	3.5	1.0	10.0	...	0.6	3.1	-3.1	6.9
1956	26.3	20.4	5.9	4.4	1.1	11.3	...	0.7	3.5	-2.9	7.8
1957	29.0	22.6	6.4	4.2	1.6	12.5	...	0.7	3.9	-3.5	8.6
1958	32.2	24.7	7.5	2.9	2.7	13.5	...	0.8	4.0	-4.7	9.5
1959	34.8	26.5	8.3	3.8	3.5	13.9	...	0.8	4.2	-3.2	9.7
1960	37.9	28.9	8.9	4.3	3.0	13.9	...	0.9	4.4	-3.1	9.5
1961	41.3	31.6	9.7	4.3	3.3	15.0	...	1.0	4.7	-3.8	10.3
1962	44.3	34.2	10.1	5.2	3.5	15.9	...	1.1	5.0	-3.2	10.9
1963	47.9	37.1	10.8	5.7	4.1	17.5	...	1.2	5.4	-3.5	12.1
1964	52.3	40.4	11.9	6.4	4.7	19.0	...	1.3	5.7	-3.4	13.3
1965	57.6	44.2	13.4	6.5	4.7	20.8	...	1.3	6.2	-4.6	14.6
1966	64.5	49.6	14.9	7.8	5.1	23.1	...	1.4	6.9	-4.7	16.2
1967	72.0	55.5	16.5	7.0	5.1	25.3	...	1.4	7.5	-7.1	17.8
1968	81.2	62.5	18.7	7.5	6.8	27.7	...	1.4	8.3	-6.4	19.4
1969	91.9	70.0	21.8	8.0	6.8	28.3	...	1.0	9.3	-5.1	19.0
1970	104.9	79.5	25.4	7.1	6.2	28.7	...	1.1	10.6	-6.0	18.1
1971	117.9	88.6	29.2	6.5	7.0	30.1	...	1.6	11.8	-6.4	18.3
1972	130.0	97.9	32.2	15.6	7.3	30.6	...	1.7	12.8	3.4	17.8
1973	144.7	109.3	35.4	15.7	7.3	33.2	...	1.7	14.3	2.4	18.9
1974	164.5	121.8	42.7	9.3	9.2	39.6	...	1.9	17.7	-5.3	21.9
1975	187.9	137.2	50.7	2.5	11.0	43.6	...	1.9	20.2	-11.9	23.4
1976	204.8	149.7	55.2	7.4	12.0	43.8	...	1.7	21.3	-4.9	22.5
1977	223.7	162.6	61.1	13.1	13.1	42.8	...	1.6	22.6	4.5	20.2
1978	244.7	177.8	66.9	18.7	13.7	49.5	...	1.6	24.5	5.8	25.0
1979	269.6	195.4	74.3	13.0	16.2	56.8	...	1.7	27.5	-1.8	29.3
1980	299.3	217.3	82.0	8.8	18.6	64.0	...	1.8	31.8	-6.6	32.2
1981	329.5	237.9	91.6	7.6	17.8	65.0	...	2.0	36.3	-5.3	28.7
1982	358.3	257.7	100.6	-2.2	16.9	64.8	...	2.0	39.5	-12.6	25.3
1983	383.7	274.1	109.6	4.9	18.0	66.4	...	2.2	40.9	-4.9	25.5
1984	412.1	293.1	119.0	23.9	20.1	75.0	...	2.6	42.3	8.8	32.7
1985	452.4	318.4	134.0	22.4	22.0	84.4	...	3.1	44.6	1.5	39.8
1986	495.3	343.7	151.6	20.7	23.0	92.8	...	3.7	47.8	-4.9	45.0
1987	524.4	368.2	156.2	12.0	22.3	98.4	...	4.2	51.4	-16.9	47.0
1988	561.8	395.8	166.0	17.2	23.1	106.3	...	4.3	54.8	-15.5	51.5
1989	606.0	425.8	180.2	20.1	23.4	114.7	0.0	4.9	58.5	-17.5	56.2
1990	659.0	463.9	195.2	6.2	25.0	127.2	0.0	5.7	63.0	-38.8	64.2
1991	702.2	492.8	209.4	-5.8	25.8	132.1	0.0	5.8	66.9	-51.0	65.2
1992	744.8	519.9	224.9	-1.4	26.9	134.3	0.0	5.9	69.9	-44.9	64.4
1993	786.6	546.0	240.6	-0.9	28.2	135.7	0.0	5.9	73.8	-40.5	61.9
1994	831.6	574.7	256.8	8.2	29.9	143.0	0.0	6.2	78.1	-33.0	64.9
1995	876.9	601.2	275.8	9.2	32.4	154.0	0.0	6.6	83.1	-35.9	70.9
1996	914.3	623.7	290.6	23.0	33.8	163.8	0.0	6.0	87.2	-25.7	76.6
1997	959.9	650.3	309.6	36.3	35.2	178.9	0.0	5.8	91.6	-21.7	87.3
1998	1 013.1	680.3	332.8	46.9	35.9	186.4	0.0	7.6	96.2	-15.1	90.2
1999	1 086.0	721.2	364.8	41.8	39.8	205.7	0.0	8.6	102.1	-30.6	103.6
2000	1 163.7	763.7	400.0	41.3	43.8	224.3	0.0	8.6	109.7	-38.1	114.6
2001	1 247.2	814.7	432.5	-15.9	51.2	240.5	0.0	10.1	116.0	-99.3	124.5
2002	1 313.7	859.6	454.1	-54.1	52.4	253.3	0.0	11.2	121.8	-144.4	131.5
2003	1 373.8	909.3	464.6	-38.8	51.5	259.6	0.0	11.4	127.3	-131.1	132.3
2004	1 432.6	947.3	485.2	-8.4	52.0	269.1	4.5	11.4	137.1	-104.2	132.0
2005	1 519.9	997.7	522.1	25.9	56.2	281.6	6.4	10.3	150.1	-66.0	131.5
2006	1 607.5	1 051.3	556.2	51.0	57.4	304.4	0.0	11.1	162.7	-44.3	141.7
2007	1 713.6	1 116.0	597.5	21.7	59.1	333.7	0.0	13.1	177.9	-88.2	155.8
2008	1 824.7	1 173.2	651.5	-40.2	61.7	348.2	0.0	12.9	191.2	-148.4	157.0
2009	1 813.4	1 201.2	612.3	-19.2	63.3	355.4	0.0	13.4	199.6	-125.0	155.8
2007											
1st quarter	1 669.6	1 093.8	575.8	32.8	52.3	325.4	0.0	12.7	173.4	-79.5	152.0
2nd quarter	1 701.5	1 109.3	592.2	34.9	60.0	332.0	0.0	13.1	176.3	-74.0	155.7
3rd quarter	1 723.3	1 122.0	601.3	20.3	63.6	335.9	0.0	13.4	179.2	-86.1	156.7
4th quarter	1 759.8	1 139.0	620.8	-1.3	60.5	341.4	0.0	13.4	182.4	-113.2	159.0
2008											
1st quarter	1 794.5	1 154.4	640.1	-20.1	57.8	340.8	0.0	13.1	185.8	-130.4	155.0
2nd quarter	1 829.3	1 167.7	661.6	-25.5	60.7	349.2	0.0	12.9	188.9	-138.2	160.3
3rd quarter	1 856.2	1 181.1	675.1	-59.0	64.1	352.7	0.0	12.9	192.8	-167.7	159.9
4th quarter	1 819.0	1 189.7	629.2	-56.1	64.1	350.0	0.0	12.9	197.2	-157.6	152.8
2009											
1st quarter	1 803.3	1 196.0	607.3	-36.6	56.3	347.9	0.0	13.1	199.8	-141.5	148.1
2nd quarter	1 812.0	1 203.8	608.2	-24.6	61.4	361.3	0.0	13.2	199.5	-138.2	161.8
3rd quarter	1 813.9	1 201.1	612.8	-14.9	73.8	361.3	0.0	13.5	199.1	-116.8	162.2
4th quarter	1 824.5	1 203.8	620.7	-0.5	61.7	350.9	0.0	13.7	200.0	-103.4	150.9

[1] Includes general government intermediate inputs for goods and services sold to other sectors and for own-account investment.
. . . = Not available.

Table 6-11. Chain-Type Quantity Indexes for State and Local Government Consumption Expenditures and Gross Investment

(Seasonally adjusted, 2005 = 100.)

NIPA Tables 3.9.3, 3.10.3

Year and quarter	Total	State and local government consumption expenditures and gross investment										
		Consumption expenditures [1]								Gross investment		
							Less					
								Sales to other sectors				
		Total	Compensation of general government employees	Consumption of general government fixed capital	Intermediate goods and services purchased [2]	Own-account investment	Total [3]	Tuition and related educational charges	Health and hospital charges	Total	Structures	Equipment and software
1955	20.5	19.1	25.8	12.5	8.6	21.6	11.0	8.0	7.5	24.5	35.1	3.1
1956	21.2	19.8	27.4	13.2	8.2	24.2	11.4	9.1	8.5	25.1	35.6	3.5
1957	22.4	20.9	28.9	14.0	8.6	24.5	12.1	10.5	9.7	26.9	37.7	4.3
1958	24.3	22.5	30.7	14.9	9.9	26.2	13.5	11.9	12.2	29.5	41.8	4.3
1959	25.2	23.5	31.9	15.8	10.6	35.5	14.3	12.8	12.8	30.4	42.9	4.6
1960	26.3	24.8	33.6	16.7	11.2	33.3	14.8	14.2	11.9	30.8	43.1	5.2
1961	28.0	26.2	35.3	17.6	12.0	34.8	15.8	15.5	12.1	33.2	46.7	5.3
1962	28.8	26.9	36.5	18.6	12.4	37.0	17.6	17.5	14.2	34.4	48.2	5.7
1963	30.6	28.2	38.4	19.6	13.3	41.6	19.3	20.0	14.7	37.4	52.2	6.6
1964	32.6	30.1	40.7	20.9	14.5	41.1	21.1	23.4	15.9	40.2	55.6	7.4
1965	34.8	32.1	43.1	22.2	15.9	42.2	23.5	27.2	18.1	43.0	59.6	8.0
1966	37.0	34.0	45.7	23.6	17.2	44.5	25.7	30.8	20.7	45.9	63.3	8.8
1967	38.9	35.6	47.5	25.1	18.6	43.2	28.3	34.3	23.5	48.7	67.4	9.1
1968	41.2	37.9	50.3	26.6	20.4	44.5	31.0	38.6	27.4	50.9	70.4	9.5
1969	42.6	40.3	52.6	28.1	22.7	45.8	32.5	42.5	28.4	48.8	66.7	10.3
1970	43.7	42.7	54.9	29.4	25.0	46.3	34.0	49.5	28.9	45.7	61.7	10.7
1971	45.1	44.8	57.1	30.6	27.3	46.4	37.1	55.7	33.7	44.4	59.7	10.9
1972	46.1	46.5	59.1	31.7	28.9	45.2	39.8	59.2	38.6	43.0	56.7	12.1
1973	47.4	48.1	61.1	32.9	29.9	43.9	41.5	63.8	42.8	43.2	56.3	13.5
1974	49.2	50.3	63.3	34.0	31.5	46.7	41.5	63.6	44.1	43.6	56.1	14.8
1975	51.0	52.8	65.3	35.1	34.1	44.0	41.9	63.7	45.3	43.2	55.7	14.5
1976	51.3	53.5	66.0	36.1	35.0	38.9	44.3	65.8	48.2	42.4	54.7	14.3
1977	51.5	54.6	66.9	37.0	36.1	35.5	45.7	68.4	49.1	39.9	51.1	14.0
1978	53.2	55.7	68.5	37.8	37.0	38.2	47.8	72.2	52.5	43.5	55.9	14.8
1979	54.0	56.0	69.7	38.7	36.9	44.2	50.0	74.2	56.9	45.6	58.3	16.2
1980	54.0	55.9	70.5	39.7	35.7	46.0	50.8	76.7	57.4	45.8	58.0	17.3
1981	52.9	55.7	70.3	40.5	36.0	44.0	53.1	78.3	61.0	41.9	52.4	17.2
1982	52.9	56.5	70.6	41.3	37.6	44.3	54.7	78.2	62.8	39.4	48.1	18.2
1983	53.5	57.1	70.1	42.0	39.9	44.0	56.6	80.7	64.4	39.9	47.5	20.7
1984	55.4	58.2	70.4	43.1	41.7	48.9	56.5	80.6	62.9	44.8	52.8	24.3
1985	58.9	61.3	72.4	44.6	45.9	52.7	58.4	80.6	64.3	49.6	57.9	28.2
1986	62.7	65.1	74.4	46.4	52.0	56.5	60.3	81.2	66.0	53.0	61.5	30.9
1987	63.6	65.9	75.6	48.2	51.9	57.7	61.2	81.8	66.1	54.4	62.8	32.2
1988	65.9	68.1	78.1	50.2	53.2	60.3	62.4	84.3	66.1	57.2	65.6	34.9
1989	68.3	70.4	80.4	52.7	55.3	67.4	64.2	86.9	66.6	60.3	67.0	41.3
1990	71.1	72.6	82.5	55.5	57.0	70.5	65.4	88.8	67.3	65.1	72.0	45.1
1991	72.6	74.1	83.3	58.2	59.6	73.6	67.5	90.3	70.2	66.6	74.4	44.6
1992	74.2	75.8	84.4	60.7	62.5	72.9	70.6	92.0	74.2	67.5	74.7	46.8
1993	75.2	77.3	85.4	63.1	65.6	72.5	74.0	90.9	78.6	66.8	73.0	48.4
1994	77.2	79.3	86.7	65.3	68.8	73.1	76.5	90.9	81.7	68.7	73.5	53.3
1995	79.2	81.1	88.2	67.7	71.4	74.1	79.4	91.3	85.4	71.7	76.0	57.3
1996	81.1	82.6	89.4	70.3	73.2	75.0	80.9	91.5	85.0	75.0	79.9	59.0
1997	84.0	84.8	90.9	73.1	76.7	82.1	83.6	93.6	87.1	80.7	85.3	65.2
1998	87.3	88.3	92.6	76.6	82.7	83.8	86.2	96.2	89.6	83.0	85.1	74.3
1999	91.2	91.5	93.7	80.3	88.5	87.0	88.4	99.0	91.1	89.8	91.4	82.4
2000	93.7	93.5	95.4	84.1	92.0	91.9	92.7	102.4	95.6	94.7	96.3	87.3
2001	97.2	96.8	97.5	87.7	98.1	100.0	97.6	102.9	103.6	99.4	101.7	89.2
2002	100.5	99.9	99.3	91.0	102.5	100.0	98.8	103.0	104.1	102.8	105.8	90.3
2003	100.4	99.6	99.5	94.0	100.6	97.3	98.9	103.1	102.2	103.8	106.4	92.8
2004	100.2	99.6	99.6	97.4	100.2	99.1	99.7	99.9	102.5	102.9	104.6	95.7
2005	100.0	100.0	100.0	100.0	100.0	100.0	100.0	100.0	100.0	100.0	100.0	100.0
2006	100.9	100.7	100.6	102.7	100.6	103.0	100.9	100.9	100.0	101.7	100.3	108.6
2007	102.9	102.5	102.2	105.7	102.9	108.0	103.1	102.1	102.6	104.4	102.7	113.0
2008	103.4	103.3	103.4	108.8	103.4	110.8	105.8	102.6	106.9	103.8	101.7	114.3
2009	103.2	103.1	103.0	111.8	103.1	109.3	105.9	102.3	107.4	103.5	101.9	110.5
2007												
1st quarter	102.2	101.9	101.6	104.6	102.0	106.2	102.0	101.5	101.3	103.3	101.5	111.8
2nd quarter	102.9	102.5	102.2	105.4	102.7	107.6	102.7	101.8	102.1	104.5	102.8	112.5
3rd quarter	103.1	102.7	102.3	106.1	103.3	108.4	103.5	102.2	103.0	104.7	102.9	113.3
4th quarter	103.4	102.9	102.7	106.9	103.4	109.8	104.2	102.9	103.9	105.2	103.3	114.4
2008												
1st quarter	103.2	103.1	103.2	107.7	103.5	109.5	105.4	103.7	105.8	103.8	101.5	115.1
2nd quarter	103.5	103.1	103.4	108.4	103.3	111.8	105.8	103.7	106.7	105.3	103.2	115.5
3rd quarter	103.6	103.3	103.6	109.1	103.3	111.6	106.0	103.5	107.4	104.6	102.6	114.1
4th quarter	103.1	103.4	103.6	109.9	103.4	110.2	105.9	102.9	107.6	101.6	99.4	112.3
2009												
1st quarter	102.7	103.3	103.4	110.6	103.3	108.8	105.8	102.5	107.5	100.0	98.0	109.6
2nd quarter	103.6	103.4	103.3	111.3	103.4	111.2	106.0	102.4	107.4	104.7	103.6	109.7
3rd quarter	103.5	102.8	102.7	112.2	102.9	110.1	105.9	102.3	107.3	106.0	105.0	109.9
4th quarter	102.9	102.8	102.6	113.1	102.7	106.9	105.9	102.2	107.2	103.2	101.2	112.9

[1]Excludes government sales to other sectors and government own-account investment (construction and software).
[2]Includes general government intermediate inputs for goods and services sold to other sectors and for own-account investment.
[3]Includes components not shown separately.

Table 6-12. State Government Current Receipts and Expenditures

(National income and product accounts, calendar years, billions of dollars.)

NIPA Table 3.20

		Current receipts											
			Current tax receipts							Contribu-tions for govern-ment social insurance	Income receipts on assets		
Year	Total [1]	Total	Personal current taxes		Taxes on production and imports				Taxes on corporate income		Total [1]	Interest receipts	Rents and royalties
			Total [1]	Income taxes	Total	Sales taxes	Property taxes	Other					
1959	21.8	16.7	3.1	2.0	12.5	10.0	0.5	2.0	1.1	0.4	0.5	0.3	0.2
1960	23.5	18.1	3.4	2.3	13.5	10.8	0.5	2.2	1.2	0.5	0.5	0.4	0.2
1961	25.2	19.3	3.7	2.5	14.4	11.6	0.5	2.3	1.3	0.5	0.6	0.4	0.2
1962	27.5	21.0	4.0	2.8	15.4	12.6	0.6	2.3	1.5	0.5	0.6	0.4	0.2
1963	29.6	22.4	4.3	3.1	16.4	13.4	0.6	2.4	1.6	0.6	0.6	0.4	0.2
1964	32.3	24.5	4.9	3.6	17.7	14.5	0.6	2.6	1.8	0.7	0.7	0.4	0.2
1965	35.8	26.9	5.4	3.9	19.6	16.1	0.7	2.8	1.9	0.8	0.8	0.5	0.3
1966	42.3	30.2	6.4	4.8	21.7	18.0	0.7	3.0	2.2	0.8	0.9	0.6	0.3
1967	46.5	32.7	7.0	5.3	23.3	19.4	0.7	3.1	2.5	0.9	1.1	0.8	0.3
1968	54.7	38.6	8.8	6.9	26.7	22.8	0.8	3.2	3.1	0.9	1.7	1.4	0.3
1969	62.6	44.0	10.8	8.6	29.9	25.7	0.9	3.3	3.4	1.0	2.1	1.8	0.3
1970	70.1	48.1	12.0	9.6	32.7	28.2	0.9	3.6	3.5	1.1	2.5	2.2	0.3
1971	79.4	53.8	13.4	11.0	36.3	31.4	1.0	3.9	4.0	1.2	2.7	2.3	0.4
1972	96.3	63.5	17.9	15.2	40.7	35.2	1.1	4.4	5.0	1.3	2.9	2.5	0.4
1973	104.5	70.2	19.8	16.8	44.7	38.8	1.2	4.7	5.7	1.5	3.9	3.3	0.5
1974	113.5	75.9	21.1	18.0	48.4	42.0	1.1	5.3	6.3	1.7	5.0	4.4	0.6
1975	127.4	81.9	23.2	19.9	51.8	44.7	1.4	5.6	6.9	1.8	5.6	5.0	0.6
1976	143.4	93.8	27.0	23.4	57.7	49.9	1.5	6.3	9.1	2.2	5.3	4.7	0.6
1977	160.0	105.1	30.9	27.2	63.4	55.0	1.5	6.9	10.8	2.8	6.1	5.4	0.6
1978	179.3	117.4	35.6	31.6	70.3	60.8	1.9	7.6	11.5	3.4	7.4	6.7	0.6
1979	197.3	128.9	38.9	34.6	77.1	65.7	2.3	9.0	12.9	3.9	10.3	9.2	1.1
1980	218.7	140.9	43.7	39.1	83.4	70.0	2.6	10.8	13.7	3.6	13.4	11.2	2.0
1981	239.5	155.6	48.5	43.6	92.7	76.5	2.7	13.6	14.5	3.9	15.6	13.2	2.2
1982	247.9	162.3	52.3	47.0	97.0	80.3	2.8	13.9	13.1	4.0	17.5	15.3	2.1
1983	272.9	180.5	58.9	53.2	106.8	90.0	3.0	13.8	14.9	4.1	19.5	17.2	2.2
1984	308.2	205.4	68.2	61.9	119.7	100.9	3.4	15.5	17.4	4.7	22.4	19.8	2.5
1985	333.1	220.9	73.2	66.1	129.0	109.0	3.5	16.5	18.7	4.9	25.9	23.1	2.6
1986	359.1	234.0	78.3	70.7	134.9	115.8	3.6	15.6	20.7	6.0	27.3	24.5	2.7
1987	380.5	253.7	87.5	79.1	144.3	124.6	3.7	16.0	21.8	7.2	28.3	25.5	2.6
1988	408.8	269.4	90.4	81.5	155.2	135.1	3.8	16.3	23.8	8.4	30.5	27.7	2.7
1989	441.7	288.4	102.4	92.9	163.5	142.3	4.3	17.0	22.4	9.0	32.4	29.8	2.4
1990	476.7	305.6	109.6	99.6	175.4	152.5	4.6	18.3	20.5	10.0	33.9	31.4	2.3
1991	512.4	314.2	111.8	101.4	180.8	157.5	4.9	18.3	21.6	11.6	34.4	31.5	2.6
1992	559.9	338.8	120.6	109.0	195.9	169.7	6.1	20.1	22.2	13.1	33.9	30.8	2.7
1993	594.0	357.1	126.3	114.9	206.3	179.4	5.9	21.0	24.5	14.1	32.5	29.4	2.5
1994	630.6	380.4	132.1	120.2	220.8	191.7	7.0	22.1	27.5	14.5	33.8	30.5	2.5
1995	663.5	401.5	140.9	128.4	231.3	200.5	7.2	23.6	29.2	13.6	36.6	33.1	2.6
1996	696.8	425.9	150.9	138.6	245.0	211.8	8.2	25.0	29.9	12.5	39.3	35.2	2.7
1997	731.2	449.1	162.7	149.7	255.4	221.3	8.1	26.0	31.0	10.8	41.8	37.5	2.7
1998	777.3	480.7	180.4	166.8	268.8	233.3	8.5	27.0	31.6	10.4	43.4	39.3	2.4
1999	828.2	507.9	192.6	178.4	283.0	245.9	9.1	27.9	32.3	9.8	47.1	42.9	2.6
2000	884.1	540.1	213.5	199.2	294.8	255.5	7.8	31.6	31.7	10.8	49.5	44.5	3.6
2001	922.5	546.8	220.1	205.7	300.8	259.9	8.1	32.8	25.9	13.7	47.0	41.9	3.7
2002	940.6	536.4	199.1	184.2	309.6	267.9	7.7	34.0	27.7	15.9	43.0	37.7	3.7
2003	991.8	561.2	201.8	185.8	328.9	282.0	9.1	37.8	30.5	20.1	42.0	35.9	4.4
2004	1 072.2	610.8	221.4	204.4	352.3	300.5	8.3	43.5	37.1	24.1	44.6	37.5	5.1
2005	1 161.8	681.2	246.7	229.2	385.4	325.7	9.0	50.6	49.1	24.8	50.5	42.5	6.0
2006	1 220.0	732.1	271.2	252.9	408.9	346.3	9.7	52.9	52.0	21.8	59.5	50.7	6.4
2007	1 274.7	762.8	290.2	271.5	423.0	357.6	9.9	55.6	49.5	19.8	66.3	57.3	6.5
2008	1 302.7	768.5	296.7	277.9	427.2	353.9	9.6	63.7	44.6	21.1	66.7	57.0	6.9

[1] Includes components not shown separately.

Table 6-12. State Government Current Receipts and Expenditures—*Continued*

(National income and product accounts, calendar years, billions of dollars.)

NIPA Table 3.20

Year	Current receipts—*Continued*					Current expenditures					Net state government saving, NIPA (surplus + / deficit -)		
	Current transfer receipts												
	Total	Federal grants-in-aid	Local grants-in-aid	From business, net	From persons	Total [1]	Consumption expenditures	Government social benefits to persons	Grants-in-aid to local governments	Interest payments	Total	Social insurance funds	Other
1959	3.8	3.4	0.2	0.0	0.1	20.8	8.6	3.6	7.7	0.8	1.0	0.0	1.0
1960	3.9	3.5	0.2	0.0	0.1	22.6	9.3	3.8	8.6	0.9	0.9	0.0	0.9
1961	4.4	4.0	0.3	0.0	0.1	24.5	9.9	4.1	9.4	0.9	0.8	0.0	0.8
1962	4.9	4.4	0.3	0.1	0.2	26.6	10.7	4.4	10.3	1.0	0.9	0.0	0.9
1963	5.4	4.9	0.3	0.1	0.2	28.9	11.6	4.7	11.3	1.1	0.7	0.0	0.6
1964	5.9	5.4	0.3	0.1	0.2	31.4	12.5	5.1	12.4	1.2	0.9	0.0	0.9
1965	6.7	6.1	0.3	0.1	0.3	35.1	13.9	5.5	14.3	1.3	0.6	0.1	0.5
1966	9.6	8.9	0.4	0.1	0.3	40.2	15.6	6.4	16.7	1.4	2.1	0.1	2.0
1967	11.1	10.3	0.5	0.1	0.3	46.4	17.9	7.7	19.1	1.6	0.0	0.1	-0.1
1968	12.6	11.6	0.6	0.1	0.3	53.6	20.2	9.5	22.0	1.8	1.0	0.1	0.9
1969	14.6	13.3	0.8	0.1	0.4	61.4	23.2	10.8	25.4	1.8	1.1	0.2	1.0
1970	17.6	16.2	0.9	0.1	0.4	71.3	26.7	12.9	29.2	2.2	-1.2	0.2	-1.3
1971	21.0	19.4	1.0	0.1	0.4	81.1	29.8	15.3	33.0	2.8	-1.7	0.2	-2.0
1972	27.6	25.8	1.1	0.2	0.5	90.6	32.6	17.5	36.9	3.2	5.8	0.3	5.5
1973	27.9	25.8	1.2	0.2	0.7	101.2	36.5	19.4	41.1	3.6	3.3	0.3	3.0
1974	30.0	27.6	1.3	0.2	0.8	114.3	43.6	19.9	45.9	4.1	-0.8	0.4	-1.1
1975	36.9	33.9	1.7	0.2	1.0	132.4	51.0	24.2	51.4	4.7	-5.0	0.5	-5.4
1976	40.8	37.1	2.3	0.3	1.2	145.1	55.6	26.9	56.2	5.3	-1.8	0.6	-2.4
1977	44.6	40.6	2.4	0.3	1.4	157.5	60.6	29.1	60.7	5.8	2.5	1.0	1.5
1978	49.5	45.2	2.5	0.3	1.5	171.8	64.7	32.0	67.3	6.3	7.5	1.5	6.0
1979	52.4	48.3	2.2	0.4	1.6	191.9	72.0	35.4	75.4	7.3	5.3	1.8	3.6
1980	59.2	54.7	2.3	0.4	1.7	216.5	81.2	41.3	83.8	8.2	2.2	1.3	0.9
1981	62.8	57.7	2.7	0.5	2.0	238.7	89.8	46.7	90.4	9.4	0.8	1.3	-0.5
1982	61.9	56.0	3.1	0.6	2.3	255.9	96.6	51.0	94.5	11.3	-8.0	1.2	-9.2
1983	66.0	58.6	4.2	0.6	2.6	273.7	102.6	55.9	99.0	13.5	-0.8	1.2	-2.0
1984	72.1	63.3	5.0	0.8	3.0	297.3	110.2	59.8	108.7	15.5	10.9	1.4	9.5
1985	76.9	67.3	5.2	0.9	3.6	323.6	118.8	65.2	120.0	16.3	9.5	1.3	8.2
1986	86.7	74.5	5.3	2.8	4.1	343.3	124.4	71.4	128.9	15.0	15.8	1.9	13.9
1987	85.8	74.9	5.5	0.9	4.5	372.6	135.6	77.4	137.8	17.6	7.9	2.2	5.7
1988	93.9	82.1	5.6	1.1	5.2	402.7	146.9	84.4	148.1	18.4	6.1	2.5	3.6
1989	104.6	91.5	5.8	1.3	5.9	436.1	157.9	94.4	159.5	19.2	5.5	2.3	3.2
1990	119.5	104.7	6.2	1.6	6.9	478.6	171.5	111.0	169.4	21.2	-1.9	2.0	-3.9
1991	144.2	124.6	7.6	2.0	10.0	528.1	179.6	137.6	181.9	23.1	-15.7	2.4	-18.0
1992	165.4	141.8	9.0	2.6	12.1	569.8	186.4	159.5	194.8	23.1	-9.9	3.1	-13.0
1993	181.0	155.9	10.1	2.9	12.1	603.8	195.7	173.6	206.0	22.6	-9.8	4.2	-14.0
1994	191.9	165.1	11.0	3.4	12.4	640.5	207.8	184.4	218.9	23.2	-9.9	4.6	-14.5
1995	201.0	173.6	11.1	4.1	12.2	674.2	217.1	194.8	231.6	24.0	-10.7	4.0	-14.8
1996	207.5	178.4	12.0	5.0	12.0	701.5	223.6	202.5	242.4	25.3	-4.7	2.8	-7.5
1997	217.3	184.3	13.5	6.6	13.0	731.9	235.3	206.8	255.1	26.2	-0.7	1.2	-1.9
1998	230.9	194.6	13.3	9.8	13.2	775.6	252.0	214.6	273.3	26.7	1.7	1.7	0.0
1999	251.8	212.7	12.9	11.4	14.9	844.3	280.5	230.3	296.4	27.8	-16.1	1.7	-17.8
2000	272.9	226.7	14.0	15.0	17.2	903.8	297.9	248.4	318.7	29.1	-19.7	2.0	-21.7
2001	304.4	253.6	14.9	16.1	19.8	985.3	319.0	281.0	336.7	31.1	-62.7	2.6	-65.3
2002	334.6	280.3	15.5	17.2	21.5	1 033.8	332.0	307.2	351.9	31.3	-93.2	1.5	-94.7
2003	356.9	301.5	16.4	16.6	22.3	1 068.1	333.5	326.1	366.7	31.3	-76.4	3.4	-79.8
2004	380.4	320.5	17.6	17.7	24.6	1 117.1	339.5	355.2	379.5	32.7	-44.9	6.9	-51.8
2005	392.1	330.2	16.6	18.4	26.9	1 177.7	360.7	373.9	397.8	34.9	-15.9	7.4	-23.3
2006	393.8	332.4	15.0	18.4	28.0	1 218.9	374.4	371.2	423.0	38.3	1.2	4.7	-3.5
2007	414.2	349.1	15.4	19.6	30.0	1 299.6	391.2	400.2	447.1	41.1	-24.9	1.9	-26.8
2008	434.1	363.7	15.8	22.0	32.6	1 360.7	417.7	420.6	462.6	43.4	-58.0	2.0	-60.0

[1]Includes components not shown separately.

Table 6-13. Local Government Current Receipts and Expenditures

(National income and product accounts, calendar years, billions of dollars.)   **NIPA Table 3.21**

Year	Total [1]	Current tax receipts							Taxes on corporate income	Contributions for government social insurance	Income receipts on assets		
		Total	Personal current taxes		Taxes on production and imports						Total [1]	Interest receipts	Rents and royalties
			Total [1]	Income taxes	Total	Sales taxes	Property taxes	Other					
1959	26.9	17.1	0.8	0.2	16.4	1.2	14.3	0.9	0.0	...	0.7	0.5	0.1
1960	29.9	18.8	0.8	0.3	18.0	1.3	15.7	0.9	0.0	...	0.8	0.7	0.1
1961	32.6	20.3	0.9	0.3	19.4	1.4	17.0	1.0	0.0	...	0.9	0.7	0.2
1962	35.2	21.8	1.0	0.3	20.8	1.5	18.4	1.0	0.0	...	1.0	0.8	0.2
1963	38.2	23.4	1.1	0.4	22.3	1.6	19.7	1.0	0.0	...	1.0	0.9	0.2
1964	41.8	25.3	1.2	0.5	24.1	1.9	21.1	1.1	0.0	...	1.3	1.1	0.2
1965	45.5	27.0	1.2	0.5	25.7	2.1	22.5	1.1	0.0	...	1.4	1.2	0.2
1966	49.9	28.5	1.4	0.6	27.1	2.0	23.8	1.3	0.0	...	1.7	1.4	0.3
1967	55.8	31.3	1.6	0.8	29.5	1.9	26.2	1.3	0.2	...	2.0	1.6	0.3
1968	61.7	34.8	1.7	0.9	32.8	2.3	29.1	1.4	0.3	...	1.7	1.4	0.4
1969	69.2	38.4	2.0	1.1	36.1	2.9	31.9	1.4	0.3	...	2.2	1.8	0.4
1970	80.3	43.2	2.3	1.3	40.6	3.5	35.7	1.5	0.2	...	2.6	2.2	0.5
1971	89.8	47.9	2.5	1.5	45.2	4.0	39.5	1.8	0.3	...	2.8	2.3	0.5
1972	100.5	52.0	3.0	2.0	48.8	4.6	42.2	2.0	0.3	...	3.0	2.4	0.6
1973	112.8	56.1	3.0	2.0	52.7	5.2	45.2	2.3	0.3	...	3.9	3.3	0.6
1974	122.6	60.2	3.4	2.3	56.4	6.1	47.9	2.4	0.3	...	5.2	4.5	0.7
1975	136.5	65.5	3.7	2.5	61.4	7.0	51.9	2.5	0.4	...	5.6	4.9	0.7
1976	150.1	71.9	4.1	2.8	67.3	7.9	56.7	2.7	0.5	...	5.1	4.4	0.7
1977	164.5	78.6	4.5	3.2	73.6	9.0	61.7	2.9	0.6	...	5.6	4.9	0.7
1978	179.6	80.8	4.9	3.4	75.3	10.2	61.8	3.3	0.6	...	7.2	6.5	0.7
1979	190.4	83.1	5.1	3.6	77.3	11.5	62.1	3.7	0.6	...	9.8	8.9	0.9
1980	207.6	89.1	5.1	3.5	83.3	12.8	66.2	4.2	0.7	...	12.9	11.8	1.1
1981	226.1	100.2	6.2	4.3	93.0	14.3	74.4	4.3	1.0	...	16.4	15.3	1.1
1982	243.7	110.8	6.9	4.9	103.0	15.9	82.5	4.6	1.0	...	19.2	17.8	1.4
1983	261.7	120.4	7.2	5.1	112.1	17.7	88.9	5.5	1.0	...	21.9	19.8	2.1
1984	288.9	131.9	7.8	5.6	122.7	20.1	96.3	6.3	1.4	...	25.2	22.8	2.4
1985	316.8	142.8	8.2	6.0	133.1	22.1	104.0	7.0	1.5	...	28.9	26.2	2.7
1986	341.0	155.6	8.9	6.8	144.7	24.1	112.6	8.1	2.0	...	31.1	27.5	3.5
1987	358.5	168.5	9.1	6.8	157.3	25.7	122.7	8.9	2.1	...	29.9	27.2	2.7
1988	386.1	183.3	11.7	9.1	169.4	27.2	132.7	9.4	2.3	...	30.0	28.3	1.7
1989	417.1	199.6	12.3	9.4	185.6	30.1	145.6	10.0	1.8	...	33.3	31.6	1.7
1990	443.3	213.6	12.9	10.0	198.7	31.8	157.0	9.9	2.0	...	34.5	32.7	1.8
1991	473.3	230.1	13.5	10.3	214.5	33.2	171.1	10.2	2.1	...	33.6	31.6	1.9
1992	497.1	241.0	14.7	11.4	224.2	34.6	178.6	11.0	2.1	...	30.9	28.8	2.0
1993	517.1	247.7	14.8	11.3	230.5	37.0	181.3	12.1	2.4	...	28.8	26.7	2.1
1994	551.4	263.8	15.9	12.0	245.4	39.7	192.4	13.3	2.5	...	29.5	27.5	2.0
1995	578.9	270.7	17.2	13.3	251.0	42.2	195.3	13.4	2.5	...	31.9	29.9	2.0
1996	611.5	283.7	17.8	13.7	262.9	44.4	204.2	14.4	3.1	...	34.2	32.2	2.0
1997	646.5	300.8	19.3	14.9	278.4	47.4	215.5	15.6	3.1	...	36.4	34.3	2.1
1998	683.8	314.2	20.9	16.2	290.0	50.6	222.5	16.9	3.4	...	38.1	35.9	2.2
1999	731.8	332.5	21.9	17.1	307.1	55.6	233.7	17.8	3.5	...	38.7	36.2	2.5
2000	782.0	353.1	23.2	18.1	326.5	61.3	246.9	18.3	3.5	...	44.8	42.1	2.7
2001	814.6	367.5	22.9	17.6	341.6	61.9	260.0	19.8	3.0	...	43.1	40.3	2.8
2002	851.7	392.3	22.7	17.1	366.4	63.2	281.7	21.5	3.1	...	36.7	33.8	2.9
2003	899.6	416.5	24.4	18.2	388.6	66.8	297.7	24.2	3.5	...	31.9	28.7	3.2
2004	937.2	448.6	27.2	20.3	416.8	70.2	318.4	28.2	4.6	...	32.6	29.2	3.4
2005	995.0	481.9	30.0	22.5	446.0	76.5	337.8	31.7	5.8	...	37.7	33.9	3.8
2006	1 061.5	517.0	31.3	23.1	478.6	84.2	360.3	34.1	7.2	...	44.0	40.1	3.9
2007	1 130.3	550.6	32.6	24.0	511.0	88.6	386.4	35.9	7.0	...	47.9	44.0	3.9
2008	1 165.8	567.8	33.3	24.4	528.1	90.0	401.0	37.2	6.3	...	47.2	43.1	4.1

[1]Includes components not shown separately.
. . . = Not available.

Table 6-13. Local Government Current Receipts and Expenditures—*Continued*

(National income and product accounts, calendar years, billions of dollars.)   **NIPA Table 3.21**

| Year | Current receipts—Continued | | | | | Current expenditures | | | | | Net local government saving, NIPA (surplus + / deficit -) | | |
| | Current transfer receipts | | | | | | | | | | | | |
	Total	Federal grants-in-aid	State grants-in-aid	From business, net	From persons	Total ¹	Consumption expenditures	Government social benefits to persons	Grants-in-aid to state governments	Interest payments	Total	Social insurance funds	Other
1959	8.3	0.4	7.7	0.1	0.1	24.1	22.1	0.7	0.2	1.0	2.8	...	2.8
1960	9.4	0.5	8.6	0.1	0.2	26.4	24.2	0.8	0.2	1.2	3.4	...	3.4
1961	10.4	0.6	9.4	0.2	0.3	29.1	26.6	0.9	0.3	1.3	3.5	...	3.5
1962	11.5	0.6	10.3	0.2	0.3	30.9	28.3	0.9	0.3	1.4	4.3	...	4.3
1963	12.6	0.8	11.3	0.2	0.3	33.2	30.4	1.0	0.3	1.5	5.0	...	5.0
1964	14.0	1.1	12.4	0.2	0.3	36.3	33.3	1.0	0.3	1.7	5.5	...	5.5
1965	15.9	1.1	14.3	0.3	0.3	39.6	36.3	1.1	0.3	1.8	5.9	...	5.9
1966	18.6	1.2	16.7	0.2	0.4	44.2	40.5	1.3	0.4	2.0	5.7	...	5.7
1967	21.6	1.5	19.1	0.4	0.6	48.9	44.7	1.6	0.5	2.1	7.0	...	7.0
1968	24.2	1.1	22.0	0.4	0.7	55.2	50.2	2.0	0.6	2.4	6.5	...	6.5
1969	27.7	1.3	25.4	0.4	0.7	62.4	56.6	2.4	0.8	2.5	6.9	...	6.9
1970	33.6	3.2	29.2	0.4	0.8	72.0	64.9	3.2	0.9	3.1	8.3	...	8.3
1971	38.2	3.8	33.0	0.5	0.9	81.6	72.9	4.0	1.0	3.8	8.2	...	8.2
1972	44.4	5.9	36.9	0.5	1.1	90.6	80.6	4.5	1.1	4.3	9.9	...	9.9
1973	51.8	9.0	41.1	0.7	1.0	100.4	89.5	4.7	1.2	4.9	12.4	...	12.4
1974	56.6	8.7	45.9	0.9	1.1	112.5	100.1	5.4	1.3	5.6	10.1	...	10.1
1975	65.0	11.2	51.4	1.0	1.4	129.1	114.1	6.6	1.7	6.4	7.4	...	7.4
1976	72.6	13.6	56.2	1.1	1.7	140.9	123.9	7.3	2.3	7.2	9.1	...	9.1
1977	79.9	16.0	60.7	1.3	1.9	153.9	135.3	8.0	2.4	7.9	10.6	...	10.6
1978	91.4	20.4	67.3	1.5	2.2	168.5	148.5	8.7	2.5	8.6	11.2	...	11.2
1979	97.8	18.1	75.4	1.8	2.6	182.8	161.3	8.9	2.2	9.9	7.7	...	7.7
1980	106.4	17.6	83.8	2.0	3.0	201.0	177.2	9.9	2.3	11.2	6.6	...	6.6
1981	111.3	14.8	90.4	2.4	3.7	219.4	192.5	10.4	2.7	13.4	6.8	...	6.8
1982	114.8	13.5	94.5	2.7	4.1	237.9	208.2	10.2	3.1	15.8	5.8	...	5.8
1983	119.5	13.0	99.0	3.0	4.5	256.0	221.5	11.0	4.2	18.8	5.7	...	5.7
1984	130.6	13.3	108.7	3.4	5.2	275.9	237.4	11.4	5.0	21.5	13.1	...	13.1
1985	142.7	13.6	120.0	3.5	5.7	304.0	263.0	12.1	5.2	23.0	12.8	...	12.8
1986	152.4	13.2	128.9	3.9	6.5	336.1	293.7	12.9	5.3	23.1	4.9	...	4.9
1987	157.4	9.0	137.8	4.0	6.7	354.4	305.8	13.4	5.5	28.6	4.1	...	4.1
1988	168.8	9.5	148.1	4.3	6.9	375.0	324.1	14.1	5.6	30.0	11.1	...	11.1
1989	178.8	6.8	159.5	5.1	7.5	402.5	346.5	15.0	5.8	34.0	14.6	...	14.6
1990	189.6	6.7	169.4	5.5	8.0	435.3	375.5	16.6	6.2	35.6	8.1	...	8.1
1991	203.5	7.0	181.9	5.9	8.7	463.4	397.9	18.9	7.6	37.7	9.9	...	9.9
1992	218.6	7.4	194.8	6.7	9.8	488.6	419.9	20.5	9.0	37.9	8.5	...	8.5
1993	233.1	8.1	206.0	7.7	11.4	508.3	438.4	21.6	10.1	36.8	8.8	...	8.8
1994	250.3	9.9	218.9	8.6	12.9	533.3	460.4	22.4	11.0	38.2	18.1	...	18.1
1995	265.9	10.6	231.6	9.4	14.3	559.0	484.2	22.9	11.1	39.4	19.9	...	19.9
1996	280.9	12.7	242.4	10.2	15.7	583.8	506.6	21.8	12.0	42.0	27.7	...	27.7
1997	297.6	14.1	255.1	11.1	17.3	609.5	529.3	20.8	13.5	44.5	37.0	...	37.0
1998	321.0	18.0	273.3	11.8	17.9	638.7	556.6	21.1	13.3	46.0	45.2	...	45.2
1999	348.6	20.2	296.4	12.7	19.3	674.0	590.1	22.1	12.9	47.4	57.9	...	57.9
2000	373.7	20.6	318.7	13.5	20.8	721.1	632.8	23.0	14.0	49.7	61.0	...	61.0
2001	395.2	22.5	336.7	13.7	22.3	767.8	675.3	24.0	14.9	51.9	46.8	...	46.8
2002	415.2	23.8	351.9	15.4	24.1	812.6	717.4	25.8	15.5	52.2	39.1	...	39.1
2003	447.5	36.5	366.7	17.2	27.1	862.0	763.0	27.3	16.4	53.8	37.6	...	37.6
2004	456.1	28.7	379.5	18.8	29.1	900.7	799.5	29.1	17.6	52.9	36.6	...	36.6
2005	476.6	31.1	397.8	18.1	29.6	953.2	851.4	30.9	16.6	52.4	41.9	...	41.9
2006	500.9	26.6	423.0	20.0	31.3	1 011.6	907.9	31.7	15.0	54.7	49.9	...	49.9
2007	532.2	29.8	447.1	21.6	33.6	1 083.7	974.9	33.5	15.4	57.6	46.6	...	46.6
2008	550.3	28.0	462.6	23.6	36.2	1 148.0	1 034.7	34.5	15.8	60.5	17.8	...	17.8

¹Includes components not shown separately.
. . . = Not available.

Section 6c: Federal Government Budget Accounts

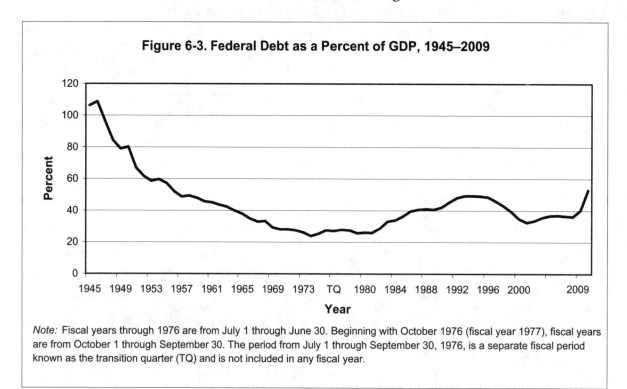

Figure 6-3. Federal Debt as a Percent of GDP, 1945–2009

Note: Fiscal years through 1976 are from July 1 through June 30. Beginning with October 1976 (fiscal year 1977), fiscal years are from October 1 through September 30. The period from July 1 through September 30, 1976, is a separate fiscal period known as the transition quarter (TQ) and is not included in any fiscal year.

- The "debt held by the public" is generally thought to be a more significant measure of the burden of the federal debt on credit markets than the gross debt, because it nets out the intragovernmental debt of the Social Security and other U.S. government trust funds. The ratio of this debt to GDP stabilized in the mid-2000s but rose rapidly by 2009, as the recession reduced revenues and increased spending. The spending increases were a result of both automatic stabilizer programs, such as unemployment insurance, and an unprecedented level of spending for stimulus and financial rescue programs. (Tables 6-14 and 6-15)

- Further increases in the debt ratio are forecast, as a result of an expected slow recovery combined with increased demographic and cost pressures on federal retirement and medical care programs. The forecast ratios are not as high as the level reached at the end of World War II, and it has been argued that rapid economic progress was achieved after that war despite the huge initial debt overhang. But the rapid reduction in the debt/GDP ratio in those years was a result of balanced (on average) budgets—which will be much harder to achieve in coming years—and was helped by some episodes of inflation, which the public might prefer to avoid. (Tables 6-14, 6-15, 8-1 and 20-2)

- From the end of fiscal year 2001 through the end of fiscal year 2009, foreign investors bought 59 percent of the Treasury debt sold to the public to finance the deficits of 2002 through 2009. At the end of 2009, foreign residents held $3.5 trillion of Treasury debt, 46 percent of the $7.5 trillion total debt held by the public. (Table 6-15)

Table 6-14. Federal Government Receipts and Outlays by Fiscal Year [1]

(Budget accounts, millions of dollars.)

Year	Fiscal year GDP	Total receipts, net	Total outlays, net	Budget surplus or deficit (-)			Sources of financing, total		Individual income taxes	Corporate income taxes	Social insurance taxes and contributions		
				Total	On-budget	Off-budget	Borrowing from the public	Other financing			Employment taxes and contributions	Unemployment insurance	Other retirement contributions
1945	221 400	45 159	92 712	-47 553	-48 720	1 167	50 386	-2 833	18 372	15 988	1 592	1 568	291
1946	222 600	39 296	55 232	-15 936	-16 964	1 028	6 679	9 257	16 098	11 883	1 517	1 316	282
1947	233 200	38 514	34 496	4 018	2 861	1 157	-17 522	13 504	17 935	8 615	1 835	1 329	259
1948	256 600	41 560	29 764	11 796	10 548	1 248	-8 069	-3 727	19 315	9 678	2 168	1 343	239
1949	271 300	39 415	38 835	580	-684	1 263	-1 948	1 368	15 552	11 192	2 246	1 205	330
1950	273 100	39 443	42 562	-3 119	-4 702	1 583	4 701	-1 582	15 755	10 449	2 648	1 332	358
1951	320 200	51 616	45 514	6 102	4 259	1 843	-4 697	-1 405	21 616	14 101	3 688	1 609	377
1952	348 700	66 167	67 686	-1 519	-3 383	1 864	432	1 087	27 934	21 226	4 315	1 712	418
1953	372 500	69 608	76 101	-6 493	-8 259	1 766	3 625	2 868	29 816	21 238	4 722	1 675	423
1954	377 000	69 701	70 855	-1 154	-2 831	1 677	6 116	-4 962	29 542	21 101	5 192	1 561	455
1955	395 900	65 451	68 444	-2 993	-4 091	1 098	2 117	876	28 747	17 861	5 981	1 449	431
1956	427 000	74 587	70 640	3 947	2 494	1 452	-4 460	513	32 188	20 880	7 059	1 690	571
1957	450 900	79 990	76 578	3 412	2 639	773	-2 836	-576	35 620	21 167	7 405	1 950	642
1958	460 000	79 636	82 405	-2 769	-3 315	546	7 016	-4 247	34 724	20 074	8 624	1 933	682
1959	490 200	79 249	92 098	-12 849	-12 149	-700	8 365	4 484	36 719	17 309	8 821	2 131	770
1960	518 900	92 492	92 191	301	510	-209	2 139	-2 440	40 715	21 494	11 248	2 667	768
1961	529 900	94 388	97 723	-3 335	-3 766	431	1 517	1 818	41 338	20 954	12 679	2 903	857
1962	567 800	99 676	106 821	-7 146	-5 881	-1 265	9 653	-2 507	45 571	20 523	12 835	3 337	875
1963	599 200	106 560	111 316	-4 756	-3 966	-789	5 968	-1 212	47 588	21 579	14 746	4 112	946
1964	641 500	112 613	118 528	-5 915	-6 546	632	2 871	3 044	48 697	23 493	16 959	3 997	1 007
1965	687 500	116 817	118 228	-1 411	-1 605	194	3 929	-2 518	48 792	25 461	17 358	3 803	1 081
1966	755 800	130 835	134 532	-3 698	-3 068	-630	2 936	762	55 446	30 073	20 662	3 755	1 129
1967	810 000	148 822	157 464	-8 643	-12 620	3 978	2 912	5 731	61 526	33 971	27 823	3 575	1 221
1968	868 400	152 973	178 134	-25 161	-27 742	2 581	22 919	2 242	68 726	28 665	29 224	3 346	1 354
1969	948 100	186 882	183 640	3 242	-507	3 749	-11 437	8 195	87 249	36 678	34 236	3 328	1 451
1970	1 012 700	192 807	195 649	-2 842	-8 694	5 852	5 090	-2 248	90 412	32 829	39 133	3 464	1 765
1971	1 080 000	187 139	210 172	-23 033	-26 052	3 019	19 839	3 194	86 230	26 785	41 699	3 674	1 952
1972	1 176 500	207 309	230 681	-23 373	-26 068	2 695	19 340	4 033	94 737	32 166	46 120	4 357	2 097
1973	1 310 600	230 799	245 707	-14 908	-15 246	338	18 533	-3 625	103 246	36 153	54 876	6 051	2 187
1974	1 438 500	263 224	269 359	-6 135	-7 198	1 063	2 789	3 346	118 952	38 620	65 888	6 837	2 347
1975	1 560 200	279 090	332 332	-53 242	-54 148	906	51 001	2 241	122 386	40 621	75 199	6 771	2 565
1976	1 738 100	298 060	371 792	-73 732	-69 427	-4 306	82 704	-8 972	131 603	41 409	79 901	8 054	2 814
TQ	459 400	81 232	95 975	-14 744	-14 065	-679	18 105	-3 361	38 801	8 460	21 801	2 698	720
1977	1 973 500	355 559	409 218	-53 659	-49 933	-3 726	53 595	64	157 626	54 892	92 199	11 312	2 974
1978	2 217 500	399 561	458 746	-59 185	-55 416	-3 770	58 022	1 163	180 988	59 952	103 881	13 850	3 237
1979	2 501 400	463 302	504 028	-40 726	-39 633	-1 093	33 180	7 546	217 841	65 677	120 058	15 387	3 494
1980	2 724 200	517 112	590 941	-73 830	-73 141	-689	71 617	2 213	244 069	64 600	138 748	15 336	3 719
1981	3 057 000	599 272	678 241	-78 968	-73 859	-5 109	77 487	1 481	285 917	61 137	162 973	15 763	3 984
1982	3 223 700	617 766	745 743	-127 977	-120 593	-7 384	135 165	-7 188	297 744	49 207	180 686	16 600	4 212
1983	3 440 700	600 562	808 364	-207 802	-207 692	-110	212 693	-4 891	288 938	37 022	185 766	18 799	4 429
1984	3 844 400	666 438	851 805	-185 367	-185 269	-98	169 707	15 660	298 415	56 893	209 658	25 138	4 580
1985	4 146 300	734 037	946 344	-212 308	-221 529	9 222	200 285	12 023	334 531	61 331	234 646	25 758	4 759
1986	4 403 900	769 155	990 382	-221 227	-237 915	16 688	233 363	-12 136	348 959	63 143	255 062	24 098	4 742
1987	4 651 400	854 288	1 004 017	-149 730	-168 357	18 627	149 130	600	392 557	83 926	273 028	25 575	4 715
1988	5 008 500	909 238	1 064 416	-155 178	-192 265	37 087	161 863	-6 685	401 181	94 508	305 093	24 584	4 658
1989	5 399 500	991 105	1 143 744	-152 639	-205 393	52 754	139 100	13 539	445 690	103 291	332 859	22 011	4 546
1990	5 734 500	1 031 972	1 253 007	-221 036	-277 626	56 590	220 842	194	466 884	93 507	353 891	21 635	4 522
1991	5 930 500	1 054 996	1 324 234	-269 238	-321 435	52 198	277 441	-8 203	467 827	98 086	370 526	20 922	4 568
1992	6 242 000	1 091 223	1 381 543	-290 321	-340 408	50 087	310 738	-20 417	475 964	100 270	385 491	23 410	4 788
1993	6 587 300	1 154 341	1 409 392	-255 051	-300 398	45 347	248 659	6 392	509 680	117 520	396 939	26 556	4 805
1994	6 976 600	1 258 579	1 461 766	-203 186	-258 840	55 654	184 669	18 517	543 055	140 385	428 810	28 004	4 661
1995	7 341 100	1 351 801	1 515 753	-163 952	-226 367	62 415	171 313	-7 361	590 244	157 004	451 045	28 878	4 550
1996	7 718 300	1 453 055	1 560 486	-107 431	-174 019	66 588	129 695	-22 264	656 417	171 824	476 361	28 584	4 469
1997	8 211 700	1 579 240	1 601 124	-21 884	-103 248	81 364	38 271	-16 387	737 466	182 293	506 751	28 202	4 418
1998	8 663 000	1 721 733	1 652 463	69 270	-29 925	99 195	-51 245	-18 025	828 586	188 677	540 014	27 484	4 333
1999	9 208 400	1 827 459	1 701 849	125 610	1 920	123 690	-88 736	-36 874	879 480	184 680	580 880	26 480	4 473
2000	9 821 000	2 025 198	1 788 957	236 241	86 422	149 819	-222 559	-13 682	1 004 462	207 289	620 451	27 640	4 761
2001	10 225 300	1 991 142	1 862 906	128 236	-32 445	160 681	-90 189	-38 047	994 339	151 075	661 442	27 812	4 713
2002	10 543 900	1 853 149	2 010 907	-157 758	-317 417	159 659	220 812	-63 054	858 345	148 044	668 547	27 619	4 594
2003	10 979 800	1 782 321	2 159 906	-377 585	-538 418	160 833	373 016	4 569	793 699	131 778	674 981	33 366	4 631
2004	11 685 600	1 880 126	2 292 853	-412 727	-567 961	155 234	382 101	30 626	808 959	189 371	689 360	39 453	4 594
2005	12 445 700	2 153 625	2 471 971	-318 346	-493 611	175 265	296 668	21 678	927 222	278 282	747 664	42 002	4 459
2006	13 224 900	2 406 876	2 655 057	-248 181	-434 494	186 313	236 760	11 421	1 043 908	353 915	790 043	43 420	4 358
2007	13 896 000	2 568 001	2 728 702	-160 701	-342 153	181 452	206 157	-45 456	1 163 472	370 243	824 258	41 091	4 258
2008	14 439 000	2 523 999	2 982 554	-458 555	-641 850	183 295	767 921	-309 366	1 145 747	304 346	856 459	39 527	4 169
2009	14 237 200	2 104 995	3 517 681	-1 412 686	-1 549 679	136 993	1 741 657	-328 971	915 308	138 229	848 885	37 889	4 143

[1] Fiscal years through 1976 are from July 1 through June 30. Beginning with October 1976 (fiscal year 1977), fiscal years are from October 1 through September 30. The period from July 1 through September 30, 1976, is a separate fiscal period known as the transition quarter (TQ) and is not included in any fiscal year.

Table 6-14. Federal Government Receipts and Outlays by Fiscal Year [1]—*Continued*

(Budget accounts, millions of dollars.)

Year	Receipts by source—*Continued*					Outlays by function						
				Miscellaneous receipts								
	Excise taxes	Estate and gift taxes	Customs duties and fees	Federal Reserve deposits	All other	National defense	International affairs	General science, space, and technology	Energy	Natural resources and environment	Agriculture	Commerce and housing credit
1945	6 265	637	341	...	105	82 965	1 913	111	25	455	1 635	-2 630
1946	6 998	668	424	...	109	42 681	1 935	34	41	482	610	-1 857
1947	7 211	771	477	15	69	12 808	5 791	5	18	700	814	-923
1948	7 356	890	403	100	68	9 105	4 566	1	292	780	69	306
1949	7 502	780	367	187	54	13 150	6 052	48	341	1 080	1 924	800
1950	7 550	698	407	192	55	13 724	4 673	55	327	1 308	2 049	1 035
1951	8 648	708	609	189	72	23 566	3 647	51	383	1 310	-323	1 228
1952	8 852	818	533	278	81	46 089	2 691	49	474	1 233	176	1 278
1953	9 877	881	596	298	81	52 802	2 119	49	425	1 289	2 253	910
1954	9 945	934	542	341	88	49 266	1 596	46	432	1 007	1 817	-184
1955	9 131	924	585	251	90	42 729	2 223	74	325	940	3 514	92
1956	9 929	1 161	682	287	140	42 523	2 414	79	174	870	3 486	506
1957	10 534	1 365	735	434	139	45 430	3 147	122	240	1 098	2 288	1 424
1958	10 638	1 393	782	664	123	46 815	3 364	141	348	1 407	2 411	930
1959	10 578	1 333	925	491	171	49 015	3 144	294	382	1 632	4 509	1 933
1960	11 676	1 606	1 105	1 093	119	48 130	2 988	599	464	1 559	2 623	1 618
1961	11 860	1 896	982	788	130	49 601	3 184	1 042	510	1 779	2 641	1 203
1962	12 534	2 016	1 142	718	125	52 345	5 639	1 723	604	2 044	3 562	1 424
1963	13 194	2 167	1 205	828	194	53 400	5 308	3 051	530	2 251	4 384	62
1964	13 731	2 394	1 252	947	139	54 757	4 945	4 897	572	2 364	4 609	418
1965	14 570	2 716	1 442	1 372	222	50 620	5 273	5 823	699	2 531	3 954	1 157
1966	13 062	3 066	1 767	1 713	163	58 111	5 580	6 717	612	2 719	2 447	3 245
1967	13 719	2 978	1 901	1 805	302	71 417	5 566	6 233	782	2 869	2 990	3 979
1968	14 079	3 051	2 038	2 091	400	81 926	5 301	5 524	1 037	2 988	4 544	4 280
1969	15 222	3 491	2 319	2 662	247	82 497	4 600	5 020	1 010	2 900	5 826	-119
1970	15 705	3 644	2 430	3 266	158	81 692	4 330	4 511	997	3 065	5 166	2 112
1971	16 614	3 735	2 591	3 533	325	78 872	4 159	4 182	1 035	3 915	4 290	2 366
1972	15 477	5 436	3 287	3 252	380	79 174	4 781	4 175	1 296	4 241	5 227	2 222
1973	16 260	4 917	3 188	3 495	425	76 681	4 149	4 032	1 237	4 775	4 821	931
1974	16 844	5 035	3 334	4 845	523	79 347	5 710	3 980	1 303	5 697	2 194	4 705
1975	16 551	4 611	3 676	5 777	935	86 509	7 097	3 991	2 916	7 346	2 997	9 947
1976	16 963	5 216	4 074	5 451	2 576	89 619	6 433	4 373	4 204	8 184	3 109	7 619
TQ	4 473	1 455	1 212	1 500	111	22 269	2 458	1 162	1 129	2 524	972	931
1977	17 548	7 327	5 150	5 908	623	97 241	6 353	4 736	5 770	10 032	6 734	3 093
1978	18 376	5 285	6 573	6 641	778	104 495	7 482	4 926	7 991	10 983	11 301	6 254
1979	18 745	5 411	7 439	8 327	925	116 342	7 459	5 234	9 179	12 135	11 176	4 686
1980	24 329	6 389	7 174	11 767	981	133 995	12 714	5 831	10 156	13 858	8 774	9 390
1981	40 839	6 787	8 083	12 834	956	157 513	13 104	6 468	15 166	13 568	11 241	8 206
1982	36 311	7 991	8 854	15 186	975	185 309	12 300	7 199	13 527	12 998	15 866	6 256
1983	35 300	6 053	8 655	14 492	1 108	209 903	11 848	7 934	9 353	12 672	22 814	6 681
1984	37 361	6 010	11 370	15 684	1 328	227 411	15 869	8 311	7 073	12 586	13 526	6 959
1985	35 992	6 422	12 079	17 059	1 460	252 743	16 169	8 622	5 608	13 345	25 477	4 337
1986	32 919	6 958	13 327	18 374	1 574	273 373	14 146	8 962	4 690	13 628	31 368	5 058
1987	32 457	7 493	15 085	16 817	2 635	281 996	11 645	9 200	4 072	13 355	26 513	6 434
1988	35 227	7 594	16 198	17 163	3 031	290 360	10 466	10 820	2 296	14 601	17 137	19 163
1989	34 386	8 745	16 334	19 604	3 639	303 555	9 583	12 821	2 705	16 169	16 859	29 709
1990	35 345	11 500	16 707	24 319	3 661	299 321	13 758	14 426	3 341	17 069	11 804	67 599
1991	42 402	11 138	15 949	19 158	4 419	273 285	15 846	16 092	2 436	18 552	15 054	76 270
1992	45 569	11 143	17 359	22 920	4 307	298 346	16 090	16 389	4 499	20 015	15 087	10 918
1993	48 057	12 577	18 802	14 908	4 497	291 084	17 218	17 006	4 319	20 230	20 245	-21 853
1994	55 225	15 225	20 099	18 023	5 094	281 640	17 067	16 189	5 218	21 013	14 914	-4 228
1995	57 484	14 763	19 301	23 378	5 154	272 063	16 429	16 692	4 936	21 900	9 671	-17 808
1996	54 014	17 189	18 670	20 477	5 050	265 748	13 487	16 684	2 839	21 505	9 035	-10 478
1997	56 924	19 845	17 928	19 636	5 777	270 502	15 173	17 136	1 475	21 209	8 889	-14 640
1998	57 673	24 076	18 297	24 540	8 053	268 194	13 054	18 172	1 270	22 283	12 077	1 007
1999	70 414	27 782	18 336	25 917	9 017	274 769	15 239	18 084	911	23 950	22 879	2 641
2000	68 865	29 010	19 914	32 293	10 513	294 363	17 213	18 594	-761	25 010	36 458	3 207
2001	66 232	28 400	19 369	26 124	11 636	304 732	16 485	19 753	9	25 592	26 252	5 731
2002	66 989	26 507	18 602	23 683	10 219	348 456	22 315	20 734	475	29 439	21 965	-407
2003	67 524	21 959	19 862	21 878	12 643	404 744	21 199	20 831	-736	29 674	22 496	727
2004	69 855	24 831	21 083	19 652	12 968	455 833	26 870	23 029	-167	30 706	15 439	5 265
2005	73 094	24 764	23 379	19 297	13 462	495 308	34 565	23 597	429	27 994	26 565	7 566
2006	73 961	27 877	24 810	29 945	14 639	521 827	29 499	23 584	782	33 028	25 969	6 187
2007	65 069	26 044	26 010	32 043	15 513	551 271	28 482	25 525	-860	31 732	17 662	487
2008	67 334	28 844	27 568	33 598	16 407	616 073	28 857	27 731	628	31 825	18 387	27 870
2009	62 483	23 482	22 453	34 318	17 805	661 049	37 529	29 449	4 749	35 574	22 237	291 535

[1]Fiscal years through 1976 are from July 1 through June 30. Beginning with October 1976 (fiscal year 1977), fiscal years are from October 1 through September 30. The period from July 1 through September 30, 1976, is a separate fiscal period known as the transition quarter (TQ) and is not included in any fiscal year.
. . . = Not available.

Table 6-14. Federal Government Receipts and Outlays by Fiscal Year [1]—Continued

(Budget accounts, millions of dollars.)

Year	Outlays by function—Continued										
	Transportation	Community and regional development	Education, employment, and social services	Health	Medicare	Income security	Social Security	Veterans benefits and services	Administration of justice	General government	Net interest
1945	3 654	243	134	211	0	1 137	267	110	178	581	3 112
1946	1 970	200	85	201	0	2 384	358	2 465	176	825	4 111
1947	1 130	302	102	177	0	2 820	466	6 344	176	1 114	4 204
1948	787	78	191	162	0	2 499	558	6 457	170	1 045	4 341
1949	916	-33	178	197	0	3 174	657	6 599	184	824	4 523
1950	967	30	241	268	0	4 097	781	8 834	193	986	4 812
1951	956	47	235	323	0	3 352	1 565	5 526	218	1 097	4 665
1952	1 124	73	339	347	0	3 655	2 063	5 341	267	1 163	4 701
1953	1 264	117	441	336	0	3 823	2 717	4 519	243	1 209	5 156
1954	1 229	100	370	307	0	4 434	3 352	4 613	257	799	4 811
1955	1 246	129	445	291	0	5 071	4 427	4 675	256	651	4 850
1956	1 450	92	591	359	0	4 734	5 478	4 891	302	1 201	5 079
1957	1 662	135	590	479	0	5 427	6 661	5 005	303	1 360	5 354
1958	2 334	169	643	541	0	7 535	8 219	5 350	325	655	5 604
1959	3 655	211	789	685	0	8 239	9 737	5 443	356	926	5 762
1960	4 126	224	968	795	0	7 378	11 602	5 441	366	1 184	6 947
1961	3 987	275	1 063	913	0	9 683	12 474	5 705	400	1 354	6 716
1962	4 290	469	1 241	1 198	0	9 207	14 365	5 619	429	1 049	6 889
1963	4 596	574	1 458	1 451	0	9 311	15 788	5 514	465	1 230	7 740
1964	5 242	933	1 555	1 788	0	9 657	16 620	5 675	489	1 518	8 199
1965	5 763	1 114	2 140	1 791	0	9 469	17 460	5 716	536	1 499	8 591
1966	5 730	1 105	4 363	2 543	64	9 678	20 694	5 916	564	1 603	9 386
1967	5 936	1 108	6 453	3 351	2 748	10 261	21 725	6 735	618	1 719	10 268
1968	6 316	1 382	7 634	4 390	4 649	11 816	23 854	7 032	659	1 757	11 090
1969	6 526	1 552	7 548	5 162	5 695	13 076	27 298	7 631	766	1 939	12 699
1970	7 008	2 392	8 634	5 907	6 213	15 655	30 270	8 669	959	2 320	14 380
1971	8 052	2 917	9 849	6 843	6 622	22 946	35 872	9 768	1 307	2 442	14 841
1972	8 392	3 423	12 529	8 674	7 479	27 650	40 157	10 720	1 684	2 960	15 478
1973	9 066	4 605	12 745	9 356	8 052	28 276	49 090	12 003	2 174	9 774	17 349
1974	9 172	4 229	12 457	10 733	9 639	33 713	55 867	13 374	2 505	10 032	21 449
1975	10 918	4 322	16 022	12 930	12 875	50 176	64 658	16 584	3 028	10 374	23 244
1976	13 739	5 442	18 910	15 734	15 834	60 799	73 899	18 419	3 430	9 706	26 727
TQ	3 358	1 569	5 169	3 924	4 264	14 985	19 763	3 960	918	3 878	6 949
1977	14 829	7 021	21 104	17 302	19 345	61 060	85 061	18 022	3 701	12 791	29 901
1978	15 521	11 841	26 710	18 524	22 768	61 505	93 861	18 961	3 923	11 961	35 458
1979	18 079	10 480	30 223	20 494	26 495	66 376	104 073	19 914	4 286	12 241	42 633
1980	21 329	11 252	31 843	23 169	32 090	86 557	118 547	21 169	4 702	12 975	52 533
1981	23 379	10 568	33 152	26 866	39 149	100 299	139 584	22 973	4 908	11 373	68 766
1982	20 625	8 347	26 612	27 445	46 567	108 155	155 964	23 938	4 842	10 861	85 032
1983	21 334	7 564	26 197	28 641	52 588	123 031	170 724	24 824	5 246	11 181	89 808
1984	23 669	7 673	26 920	30 417	57 540	113 352	178 223	25 575	5 811	11 746	111 102
1985	25 838	7 676	28 592	33 541	65 822	128 979	188 623	26 251	6 426	11 515	129 478
1986	28 113	7 233	29 776	35 933	70 164	120 633	198 757	26 314	6 735	12 491	136 017
1987	26 222	5 049	28 921	39 964	75 120	124 088	207 352	26 729	7 715	7 487	138 611
1988	27 272	5 293	30 931	44 483	78 878	130 377	219 341	29 367	9 397	9 399	151 803
1989	27 608	5 362	35 328	48 380	84 964	137 426	232 542	30 003	9 644	9 316	168 981
1990	29 485	8 531	37 171	57 699	98 102	148 668	248 623	29 034	10 185	10 460	184 347
1991	31 099	6 810	41 235	71 168	104 489	172 462	269 015	31 275	12 486	11 566	194 448
1992	33 332	6 836	42 741	89 486	119 024	199 562	287 584	34 037	14 650	12 881	199 344
1993	35 004	9 146	47 380	99 401	130 552	209 969	304 585	35 642	15 193	12 943	198 713
1994	38 066	10 620	43 286	107 107	144 747	217 166	319 565	37 559	15 516	11 159	202 932
1995	39 350	10 746	51 027	115 399	159 855	223 799	335 846	37 862	16 508	13 799	232 134
1996	39 565	10 741	48 321	119 365	174 225	229 736	349 671	36 956	17 898	11 755	241 053
1997	40 767	11 049	48 975	123 832	190 016	235 032	365 251	39 283	20 617	12 547	243 984
1998	40 343	9 771	50 512	131 425	192 822	237 750	379 215	41 741	23 359	15 544	241 118
1999	42 532	11 865	50 605	141 048	190 447	242 478	390 037	43 155	26 536	15 363	229 755
2000	46 853	10 623	53 764	154 504	197 113	253 724	409 423	46 989	28 499	13 013	222 949
2001	54 447	11 773	57 094	172 233	217 384	269 774	432 958	44 974	30 201	14 358	206 167
2002	61 833	12 981	70 566	196 497	230 855	312 720	455 980	50 929	35 061	16 951	170 949
2003	67 069	18 850	82 587	219 541	249 433	334 632	474 680	56 984	35 340	23 164	153 073
2004	64 627	15 820	87 974	240 122	269 360	333 059	495 548	59 746	45 576	22 338	160 245
2005	67 894	26 262	97 555	250 548	298 638	345 847	523 305	70 120	40 019	16 997	183 986
2006	70 244	54 465	118 482	252 739	329 868	352 477	548 549	69 811	41 016	18 177	226 603
2007	72 905	29 567	91 656	266 382	375 407	365 975	586 153	72 818	41 244	17 425	237 109
2008	77 616	23 952	91 287	280 599	390 758	431 313	617 027	84 653	47 138	20 325	252 757
2009	84 289	27 650	79 746	334 327	430 093	533 224	682 963	95 429	51 549	22 026	186 902

[1] Fiscal years through 1976 are from July 1 through June 30. Beginning with October 1976 (fiscal year 1977), fiscal years are from October 1 through September 30. The period from July 1 through September 30, 1976, is a separate fiscal period known as the transition quarter (TQ) and is not included in any fiscal year.

Table 6-15. Federal Government Debt by Fiscal Year [1]

(Billions of dollars, except as noted.)

Year	Federal government debt held by the public at end of fiscal year		Gross federal debt at end of fiscal year held by:						
	Debt held by the public	Debt/GDP ratio (percent)	Total	Social Security funds	Other U.S. government accounts	Federal Reserve System	Private investors		
							Total	Foreign residents	Domestic investors
1945	235	106.2	260	7	18	22	213	...	...
1946	242	108.7	271	8	21	24	218	...	...
1947	224	96.2	257	9	24	22	202	...	...
1948	216	84.3	252	10	26	21	195	...	...
1949	214	79.0	253	11	27	19	195	...	...
1950	219	80.2	257	13	25	18	201	...	...
1951	214	66.9	255	15	26	23	191	...	...
1952	215	61.6	259	17	28	23	192	...	...
1953	218	58.6	266	18	29	25	194	...	...
1954	224	59.5	271	20	26	25	199	...	...
1955	227	57.2	274	21	27	24	203	...	...
1956	222	52.0	273	23	28	24	198	...	...
1957	219	48.6	272	23	30	23	196	...	...
1958	226	49.2	280	24	29	25	201	...	...
1959	235	47.9	287	23	30	26	209	...	...
1960	237	45.6	291	23	31	27	210	...	...
1961	238	45.0	293	23	31	27	211	...	...
1962	248	43.7	303	22	33	30	218	...	...
1963	254	42.4	310	21	35	32	222	...	...
1964	257	40.0	316	22	37	35	222	...	...
1965	261	37.9	322	22	39	39	222	12	210
1966	264	34.9	328	22	43	42	222	12	210
1967	267	32.9	340	26	48	47	220	11	209
1968	290	33.3	369	28	51	52	237	11	226
1969	278	29.3	366	32	56	54	224	10	214
1970	283	28.0	381	38	60	58	225	14	211
1971	303	28.1	408	41	64	66	238	32	206
1972	322	27.4	436	44	70	71	251	49	202
1973	341	26.0	466	44	81	75	266	59	207
1974	344	23.9	484	46	94	81	263	57	206
1975	395	25.3	542	48	99	85	310	66	244
1976	477	27.5	629	45	107	95	383	70	313
TQ [1]	496	27.0	644	44	105	97	399	75	324
1977	549	27.8	706	40	118	105	444	96	348
1978	607	27.4	777	35	134	115	492	121	371
1979	640	25.6	829	33	156	116	525	120	405
1980	712	26.1	909	32	165	121	591	122	469
1981	789	25.8	995	27	178	124	665	131	534
1982	925	28.7	1 137	19	193	134	790	141	649
1983	1 137	33.1	1 372	32	202	156	982	160	822
1984	1 307	34.0	1 565	32	225	155	1 152	176	976
1985	1 507	36.4	1 817	40	270	170	1 337	223	1 114
1986	1 741	39.5	2 121	46	334	191	1 550	266	1 284
1987	1 890	40.6	2 346	65	391	212	1 678	280	1 398
1988	2 052	41.0	2 601	104	445	229	1 822	346	1 476
1989	2 191	40.6	2 868	157	520	220	1 971	395	1 576
1990	2 412	42.1	3 206	215	580	234	2 177	464	1 713
1991	2 689	45.3	3 598	268	641	259	2 430	506	1 924
1992	3 000	48.1	4 002	319	683	296	2 703	563	2 141
1993	3 248	49.3	4 351	366	737	326	2 923	619	2 304
1994	3 433	49.2	4 643	423	788	355	3 078	682	2 396
1995	3 604	49.1	4 921	483	833	374	3 230	820	2 410
1996	3 734	48.4	5 181	550	898	391	3 343	993	2 350
1997	3 772	45.9	5 369	631	966	425	3 348	1 231	2 117
1998	3 721	43.0	5 478	730	1 027	458	3 263	1 224	2 039
1999	3 632	39.4	5 606	855	1 118	497	3 136	1 281	1 854
2000	3 410	34.7	5 629	1 007	1 212	511	2 898	1 058	1 840
2001	3 320	32.5	5 770	1 170	1 280	534	2 785	1 006	1 780
2002	3 540	33.6	6 198	1 329	1 329	604	2 936	1 201	1 735
2003	3 913	35.6	6 760	1 485	1 362	656	3 257	1 454	1 803
2004	4 296	36.8	7 355	1 635	1 424	700	3 595	1 799	1 797
2005	4 592	36.9	7 905	1 809	1 504	736	3 856	1 931	1 925
2006	4 829	36.5	8 451	1 994	1 628	769	4 060	2 027	2 033
2007	5 035	36.2	8 951	2 181	1 735	780	4 255	2 237	2 018
2008	5 803	40.2	9 986	2 366	1 817	491	5 312	2 800	2 512
2009	7 545	53.0	11 876	2 504	1 827	769	6 776	3 497	3 279

[1]Fiscal years through 1976 are from July 1 through June 30. Beginning with October 1976 (fiscal year 1977), fiscal years are from October 1 through September 30. The period from July 1 through September 30, 1976, is a separate fiscal period known as the transition quarter (TQ) and is not included in any fiscal year.
. . . = Not available.

Section 6d: Government Output and Employment

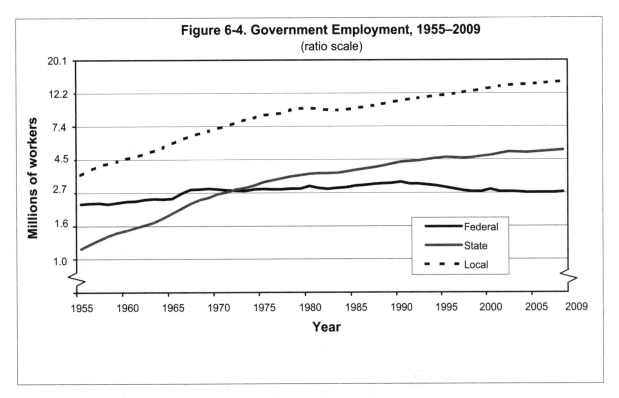

- Since 1955, total reported employment of civilians by all levels of government has increased 221 percent—an annual rate of 2.2 percent per year—and its proportion of total nonfarm payroll employment has risen from 13.8 percent to 17.2 percent. Federal employment rose 23 percent; state government employment rose 343 percent, with half of this increase due to education; and local government rose 309 percent, with 57 percent of this increase due to education. (Tables 6-17, 10-7 and 20-4)

- Reported Department of Defense civilian employment has only increased 3 percent since 2001, even as defense spending has been rising both absolutely and as a percentage of gross domestic product (GDP)(Table 6-14). It should be noted that the figures shown here are for civilian employees only, as compiled by the Bureau of Labor Statistics, and exclude the active-duty armed forces, defense contractors, and employees of the Central Intelligence Agency and the National Security Agency. (Table 6-17 and its notes and definitions)

- Contracting and outsourcing of government spending can be seen in comparisons between government purchases and government value added. The volume of intermediate goods and services purchased for nondefense purposes rose far faster than nondefense value added by government itself (where value added comprises the input of government employees and government-owned capital). For defense, government value added actually declined over that period, while purchases of intermediate goods and services rose 246 percent. (Table 6-16)

- A similar effect is seen at state and local governments, where value added increased 336 percent while goods and services purchased rose 1,140 percent. (Table 6-16)

Table 6-16. Chain-Type Quantity Indexes for Government Output

(Seasonally adjusted, 2005 = 100.)

NIPA Table 3.10.3

Year and quarter	Federal government									State and local government		
	Gross output of general government			Value added			Intermediate goods and services purchased [1]			Gross output of general government	Value added	Intermediate goods and services purchased [1]
	Total	Defense	Nondefense	Total	Defense	Nondefense	Total	Defense	Nondefense			
1950	32.1	37.3	22.9	61.8	72.2	44.9	10.4	12.0	7.9	15.4	19.7	8.0
1951	48.5	64.1	19.2	81.4	103.0	42.0	21.7	31.4	4.7	15.3	20.2	7.4
1952	61.3	81.9	22.5	90.7	117.6	41.2	33.4	47.4	9.0	15.6	20.9	7.2
1953	65.9	85.6	28.8	91.2	119.7	38.3	39.2	51.2	18.1	16.1	21.8	7.2
1954	58.4	74.7	27.9	89.0	117.1	36.6	30.6	37.9	17.8	16.8	22.8	7.5
1955	55.9	70.3	28.9	86.9	113.9	36.9	28.3	33.8	18.9	18.0	23.9	8.6
1956	54.3	70.3	24.1	86.1	112.2	37.6	26.7	34.7	12.4	18.6	25.3	8.2
1957	57.7	75.2	24.4	85.8	111.4	38.4	31.3	41.7	12.4	19.6	26.7	8.6
1958	56.6	73.8	23.9	83.4	107.2	39.5	31.1	42.1	11.1	21.2	28.4	9.9
1959	56.1	67.8	34.1	82.7	106.1	39.6	31.0	34.2	25.5	22.3	29.6	10.6
1960	55.3	68.7	29.7	84.3	107.1	42.3	28.7	34.9	17.4	23.4	31.1	11.2
1961	56.2	70.3	29.5	86.1	109.3	43.3	28.9	35.8	16.4	24.7	32.7	12.0
1962	61.5	75.2	35.5	89.6	113.5	45.7	34.5	40.5	24.0	25.7	33.9	12.4
1963	63.1	75.9	38.8	90.4	113.2	48.6	36.4	41.7	27.1	27.1	35.7	13.3
1964	62.7	74.1	41.1	91.3	113.7	50.3	35.2	38.6	29.6	28.9	37.8	14.5
1965	63.6	74.5	42.8	91.9	113.7	52.0	36.2	39.2	31.1	30.9	40.1	15.9
1966	70.8	85.4	43.1	98.0	121.5	54.8	43.2	51.0	29.6	32.9	42.5	17.2
1967	78.2	95.6	45.3	104.4	129.7	57.8	50.5	61.5	30.9	34.6	44.3	18.6
1968	80.8	99.5	45.5	106.1	131.5	59.5	53.3	66.3	30.0	36.9	47.0	20.4
1969	79.1	95.6	47.8	106.5	131.6	60.3	50.3	60.1	33.0	39.2	49.1	22.7
1970	73.4	87.0	47.6	101.9	124.0	61.2	44.4	51.4	32.0	41.4	51.3	25.0
1971	69.8	80.2	49.7	97.2	115.7	63.0	41.9	46.3	34.2	43.6	53.4	27.3
1972	68.4	75.8	53.9	92.5	107.6	64.7	43.4	45.3	40.2	45.4	55.2	28.9
1973	64.7	70.7	53.1	89.0	102.1	64.9	39.8	40.6	38.6	47.0	57.2	29.9
1974	64.3	68.7	55.9	88.8	100.2	67.9	39.3	38.7	40.9	48.9	59.2	31.5
1975	63.5	66.6	57.5	88.3	98.8	69.1	38.3	36.2	42.8	51.0	61.0	34.1
1976	62.6	65.0	57.8	88.4	97.3	72.3	36.5	34.6	40.5	51.9	61.8	35.0
1977	64.0	65.8	60.6	88.7	96.8	73.9	38.9	36.4	44.2	52.9	62.8	36.1
1978	65.4	66.5	63.4	89.8	97.4	76.0	40.4	37.2	47.4	54.2	64.2	37.0
1979	66.5	67.3	65.0	89.7	97.0	76.5	42.4	38.9	50.0	54.9	65.4	36.9
1980	69.2	70.1	67.6	91.1	97.9	78.9	45.9	42.8	52.5	54.9	66.3	35.7
1981	72.1	74.1	68.1	92.5	100.8	77.5	49.8	47.4	54.7	55.0	66.2	36.0
1982	74.4	79.1	65.0	94.0	103.4	76.9	52.6	53.9	49.6	55.9	66.7	37.6
1983	77.9	83.0	67.7	96.2	105.8	78.6	57.0	58.7	52.9	56.7	66.4	39.9
1984	79.0	85.6	65.5	98.4	108.6	79.7	57.1	61.1	47.8	57.7	66.8	41.7
1985	83.7	90.7	69.2	101.2	112.2	80.9	63.1	67.2	53.7	60.5	68.7	45.9
1986	87.3	94.9	71.7	103.0	114.9	80.8	68.3	72.5	58.4	64.1	70.7	52.0
1987	89.4	98.5	70.7	105.7	117.9	82.9	69.7	76.4	54.5	64.9	72.1	51.9
1988	89.2	99.6	67.6	107.0	118.6	85.5	68.1	77.9	45.9	67.0	74.5	53.2
1989	90.5	98.9	73.2	108.3	119.9	86.8	69.3	75.3	55.8	69.2	76.8	55.3
1990	91.9	98.5	78.5	110.3	120.7	91.2	70.1	73.8	61.9	71.2	79.1	57.0
1991	92.3	98.3	79.9	110.9	121.3	91.9	70.2	72.9	63.9	72.8	80.1	59.6
1992	90.2	93.4	83.7	108.6	116.7	94.0	68.4	67.9	69.4	74.8	81.5	62.5
1993	87.2	89.8	81.9	106.5	113.3	94.5	64.5	64.2	65.3	76.6	82.6	65.6
1994	85.1	86.3	82.7	103.1	108.9	92.6	64.0	61.7	69.1	78.7	84.0	68.8
1995	82.2	82.6	81.4	99.2	104.4	90.0	62.2	58.9	69.4	80.7	85.7	71.4
1996	80.8	81.5	79.4	96.4	100.9	88.6	62.3	60.3	66.6	82.2	87.0	73.2
1997	80.5	80.2	81.2	94.6	97.9	88.9	63.6	60.6	70.2	84.5	88.8	76.7
1998	79.0	77.9	81.2	93.5	95.3	90.6	61.7	58.8	68.1	87.9	90.7	82.7
1999	79.7	79.1	80.9	92.8	93.3	91.9	64.0	63.2	65.9	90.9	92.2	88.5
2000	80.6	78.4	85.0	93.6	92.7	95.2	65.1	62.4	71.0	93.4	94.1	92.0
2001	83.9	81.3	89.0	93.9	92.9	95.8	71.6	68.1	79.4	96.9	96.4	98.1
2002	89.3	86.6	94.6	95.8	94.6	97.9	81.4	77.5	90.0	99.7	98.3	102.5
2003	95.2	94.0	97.6	98.4	97.3	100.2	91.2	90.1	93.7	99.5	98.9	100.6
2004	98.9	98.8	98.9	99.3	99.1	99.7	98.2	98.5	97.7	99.6	99.3	100.2
2005	100.0	100.0	100.0	100.0	100.0	100.0	100.0	100.0	100.0	100.0	100.0	100.0
2006	101.2	100.8	101.9	99.9	99.5	100.7	102.8	102.5	103.6	100.8	100.9	100.6
2007	101.9	102.5	100.8	100.7	100.0	101.9	103.5	105.5	99.2	102.7	102.6	102.9
2008	108.7	108.9	108.3	104.7	104.0	105.9	113.9	114.8	111.8	103.8	104.1	103.4
2009	114.1	114.2	113.8	111.1	110.8	111.5	118.0	118.4	117.1	103.7	104.0	103.1
2007												
1st quarter	99.6	100.1	98.5	100.2	99.5	101.5	98.8	100.9	94.1	102.0	102.0	102.0
2nd quarter	100.9	101.4	99.8	100.0	99.3	101.4	101.9	103.9	97.3	102.6	102.5	102.7
3rd quarter	103.4	104.3	101.5	101.0	100.4	102.2	106.4	109.0	100.5	102.9	102.8	103.3
4th quarter	103.9	104.1	103.5	101.5	100.9	102.7	107.1	108.1	104.7	103.2	103.2	103.4
2008												
1st quarter	105.8	105.7	106.0	102.6	101.9	104.0	110.0	110.5	108.8	103.6	103.7	103.5
2nd quarter	106.9	106.3	108.1	103.7	102.9	105.3	111.1	110.6	112.2	103.7	104.0	103.3
3rd quarter	110.5	111.3	108.9	105.4	104.9	106.2	117.2	119.0	113.0	103.9	104.3	103.3
4th quarter	111.5	112.2	110.1	106.9	106.4	107.9	117.4	119.2	113.4	104.0	104.3	103.4
2009												
1st quarter	110.9	110.8	111.1	108.2	107.6	109.3	114.4	114.7	113.7	103.9	104.2	103.3
2nd quarter	113.6	114.0	112.7	110.3	109.8	111.3	117.9	119.2	114.8	103.9	104.3	103.4
3rd quarter	115.7	116.3	114.5	112.2	112.0	112.5	120.2	121.4	117.4	103.5	103.9	102.9
4th quarter	116.2	115.9	116.8	113.5	113.7	113.1	119.7	118.4	122.4	103.5	103.8	102.7

[1] Includes general government intermediate inputs for goods and services sold to other sectors and for own-account investment.

Table 6-17. Government Employment

(Calendar years, payroll employment in thousands.)

Year and month	Total government employment	Federal			State			Local		
		Total	Department of Defense	Postal Service	Total	Education	State government hospitals	Total	Education	Local government hospitals
1950	6 120	2 023	533	516	. . .	. . .	. . .	. . .	. . .	. . .
1951	6 502	2 415	797	521	. . .	. . .	. . .	. . .	. . .	. . .
1952	6 727	2 539	868	542	. . .	. . .	. . .	. . .	. . .	. . .
1953	6 758	2 418	818	530	. . .	. . .	. . .	. . .	. . .	. . .
1954	6 858	2 295	744	533	. . .	. . .	. . .	. . .	. . .	. . .
1955	7 021	2 295	744	534	1 168	308	. . .	3 558	1 751	. . .
1956	7 386	2 318	749	539	1 249	334	. . .	3 819	1 884	. . .
1957	7 724	2 326	729	555	1 328	363	. . .	4 071	2 026	. . .
1958	7 946	2 298	695	567	1 415	389	. . .	4 232	2 115	. . .
1959	8 192	2 342	699	578	1 484	420	. . .	4 366	2 198	. . .
1960	8 464	2 381	681	591	1 536	448	. . .	4 547	2 314	. . .
1961	8 706	2 391	683	601	1 607	474	. . .	4 708	2 411	. . .
1962	9 004	2 455	697	601	1 669	511	. . .	4 881	2 522	. . .
1963	9 341	2 473	687	603	1 747	557	. . .	5 121	2 674	. . .
1964	9 711	2 463	676	604	1 856	609	. . .	5 392	2 839	. . .
1965	10 191	2 495	679	619	1 996	679	. . .	5 700	3 031	. . .
1966	10 910	2 690	741	686	2 141	775	. . .	6 080	3 297	. . .
1967	11 525	2 852	802	719	2 302	873	. . .	6 371	3 490	. . .
1968	11 972	2 871	801	729	2 442	958	. . .	6 660	3 649	. . .
1969	12 330	2 893	815	737	2 533	1 042	. . .	6 904	3 785	. . .
1970	12 687	2 865	756	741	2 664	1 104	. . .	7 158	3 912	. . .
1971	13 012	2 828	731	731	2 747	1 149	. . .	7 437	4 091	. . .
1972	13 465	2 815	720	703	2 859	1 188	459	7 790	4 262	467
1973	13 862	2 794	696	698	2 923	1 205	472	8 146	4 433	477
1974	14 303	2 858	698	710	3 039	1 267	483	8 407	4 584	483
1975	14 820	2 882	704	699	3 179	1 323	503	8 758	4 722	489
1976	15 001	2 863	693	676	3 273	1 371	518	8 865	4 786	492
1977	15 258	2 859	676	657	3 377	1 385	538	9 023	4 859	494
1978	15 812	2 893	661	660	3 474	1 367	541	9 446	4 958	535
1979	16 068	2 894	649	673	3 541	1 378	538	9 633	4 989	571
1980	16 375	3 000	645	673	3 610	1 398	530	9 765	5 090	604
1981	16 180	2 922	655	675	3 640	1 420	515	9 619	5 095	622
1982	15 982	2 884	690	684	3 640	1 433	494	9 458	5 049	635
1983	16 011	2 915	699	685	3 662	1 450	471	9 434	5 020	644
1984	16 159	2 943	716	706	3 734	1 488	459	9 482	5 076	623
1985	16 533	3 014	738	750	3 832	1 540	449	9 687	5 221	608
1986	16 838	3 044	736	792	3 893	1 561	438	9 901	5 358	601
1987	17 156	3 089	736	815	3 967	1 586	439	10 100	5 469	606
1988	17 540	3 124	719	835	4 076	1 621	446	10 339	5 590	619
1989	17 927	3 136	735	838	4 182	1 668	442	10 609	5 740	632
1990	18 415	3 196	722	825	4 305	1 730	426	10 914	5 902	646
1991	18 545	3 110	702	813	4 355	1 768	417	11 081	5 994	653
1992	18 787	3 111	702	800	4 408	1 799	419	11 267	6 076	665
1993	18 989	3 063	670	793	4 488	1 834	414	11 438	6 206	673
1994	19 275	3 018	657	821	4 576	1 882	407	11 682	6 329	673
1995	19 432	2 949	627	850	4 635	1 919	395	11 849	6 453	669
1996	19 539	2 877	597	867	4 606	1 911	376	12 056	6 592	648
1997	19 664	2 806	588	866	4 582	1 904	360	12 276	6 759	632
1998	19 909	2 772	550	881	4 612	1 922	346	12 525	6 921	630
1999	20 307	2 769	525	890	4 709	1 983	344	12 829	7 120	626
2000	20 790	2 865	510	880	4 786	2 031	343	13 139	7 294	622
2001	21 118	2 764	504	873	4 905	2 113	345	13 449	7 479	628
2002	21 513	2 766	499	842	5 029	2 243	349	13 718	7 654	642
2003	21 583	2 761	486	809	5 002	2 255	348	13 820	7 709	651
2004	21 621	2 730	473	782	4 982	2 238	348	13 909	7 765	656
2005	21 804	2 732	488	774	5 032	2 260	350	14 041	7 856	655
2006	21 974	2 732	493	770	5 075	2 293	357	14 167	7 913	647
2007	22 218	2 734	491	769	5 122	2 318	360	14 362	7 987	654
2008	22 509	2 762	496	747	5 177	2 354	361	14 571	8 084	659
2009	22 549	2 828	519	703	5 180	2 371	360	14 542	8 062	666

. . . = Not available.

NOTES AND DEFINITIONS, CHAPTER 6

TABLES 6-1 THROUGH 6-13 AND 6-16
FEDERAL, STATE, AND LOCAL GOVERNMENT IN THE NATIONAL INCOME AND PRODUCT ACCOUNTS

SOURCE: U.S. DEPARTMENT OF COMMERCE, BUREAU OF ECONOMIC ANALYSIS (BEA)

These data are from the national income and product accounts (NIPAs), as published in the 2009 comprehensive NIPA revision and as updated through March 2010. For general information about the NIPAs and the 2009 revision, see the notes and definitions for Chapter 1.

The framework for the government accounts

In the 2003 revision, a new framework was introduced for government consumption expenditures—federal, state, and local—that explicitly recognizes the services produced by general government. Governments serve several functions in the economy. Three of these functions are recognized in the NIPAs: the production of nonmarket services; the consumption of these services, as the value of services provided to the general public is treated as government consumption expenditures; and the provision of transfer payments. These functions are financed through taxation, through contributions to social insurance funds, and in the world's capital markets.

In the new framework, the value of the government services produced and consumed (most of which are not sold in the market) is measured as the sum of the costs of the three major inputs: compensation of government employees, consumption of fixed capital (CFC), and intermediate goods and services purchased. The purchase from the private sector of goods and services by government, classified as final sales to government before the 2003 revision, was reclassified as intermediate purchases.

The value of government final purchases of consumption expenditures and gross investment, which constitutes the contribution of government demand to the gross domestic product (GDP), was not changed by this reclassification, since the previous definition of that contribution was the sum of compensation, CFC, and goods and services purchased. However, the distribution of GDP by type of product was changed—final sales of goods were reduced by the amount of goods purchased by government, and services were increased by the same amount.

In addition to this change in the conceptual framework, a number of the categories of government receipts and expenditures were redefined to make more precise distinctions. For example, items that used to be called "nontax payments" and included with taxes are now classified as transfer or fee payments and not included in taxes.

Finally, the concept previously known as "current surplus or deficit (-), national income and product accounts" was renamed "net government saving." This recognizes, in part, the role of government in the capital markets. When government runs a current surplus, net government saving is positive and funds are made available (for example, by repayment of outstanding debt) to finance investment—both private-sector capital spending and government investment. When government runs a current deficit, or "dis-saves," it must borrow funds that would otherwise be available to finance investment.

However, this definition of net government saving does not give a complete picture of governments' role in capital markets, because it is based on current receipts and expenditures alone and does not include government investment activity.

In the NIPAs, the capital spending of all levels of government is treated the same way as the accounts treat private investment spending. A depreciation, or more precisely "consumption of fixed capital" (CFC), entry for existing capital is calculated, using estimated replacement costs and realistic depreciation rates. In the government accounts this CFC value is entered as one element of current expenditures and output. Capital spending is excluded from government current expenditures but appears in the account for "net lending or borrowing (-)."

The basic concept expressed in the net lending section of the NIPAs is that when CFC exceeds actual investment expenditures, governments have a positive net cash flow and can lend (or repay debt); if gross investment exceeds CFC, government must borrow to finance the difference, indicating negative net cash flow and requiring borrowing. (As will be seen below in the definitions, capital transfer and purchase accounts also enter into the calculation of net lending.)

The federal *budget* accounts (see Tables 6-14 and 6-15) do not draw a distinction between current and capital spending. The budget accounts of individual state and local governments typically separate capital from current spending and allow capital spending to be financed by borrowing—even when deficit financing of current spending is constitutionally forbidden. However, neither federal nor state and local government budget accounts typically show depreciation as a current expense in the way that is standard to private-sector accounting or in the way adopted in the NIPAs.

Notes on the data

Government receipts and expenditures data are derived from the U.S. government accounts and from Census Bureau censuses and surveys of the finances of state and local governments. However, BEA makes a number of adjustments to the data to convert them from fiscal year to calendar year and quarter bases and to agree with the concepts of national income accounting. Data are converted from the cash basis usually found in financial statements to the timing bases required for the NIPAs. In the NIPAs, receipts from businesses are generally on an accrual basis, purchases of goods and services are recorded when delivered, and receipts from and transfer payments to persons are on a cash basis. The federal receipts and expenditure data from the NIPAs in Table 6-1 therefore differ from the federal receipts and outlay data in Table 6-14. Among other differences, the latter are by fiscal year and are on a modified cash basis.

The NIPA data on government receipts and expenditures record transactions of governments (federal, state, and local) with other U.S. residents and foreigners. Each entry in the government receipts and expenditures account has a corresponding entry elsewhere in the NIPAs. Thus, for example, the sum of personal current taxes received by federal and state and local governments (Tables 6-1 and 6-8) is equal to personal current taxes paid, as shown in personal income (Table 4-1).

Definitions (general)

In the 2003 revision of the NIPAs, several items appear separately that were previously treated as "negative expenditures" and netted against other items on the expenditures side. This grossing-up of the accounts raises both receipts and outlays and has no effect on net saving. Grossing-up has been applied to taxes from the rest of the world, interest receipts (back to 1960 for the federal government and back to 1946 for state and local governments), dividends, and subsidies and the current surplus of government enterprises (back to 1959).

Definitions (current receipts)

Current tax receipts includes personal current taxes, taxes on production and imports, taxes on corporate income and (for the federal government only) taxes from the rest of the world. The category *total tax receipts* does not include *contributions for government social insurance,* which are the taxes levied to finance Social Security, unemployment insurance, and Medicare, and are included in *receipts* in the budget accounts (Table 6-14). Analysts using NIPA data to analyze tax burdens as they are usually understood should add *contributions for government social insurance* to *tax receipts* for this purpose.

Personal current taxes is personal tax payments from residents of the United States that are not chargeable to business expense. Personal taxes consist of taxes on income, including on realized net capital gains, and on personal property. Personal contributions for social insurance are not included in this category. As of the 1999 revisions, estate and gift taxes are classified as capital transfers and are no longer included in personal current taxes. However, estate and gift taxes continue to be included in federal government receipts in Table 6-14.

Taxes on production and imports in the case of the federal government consists of *excise taxes* and *customs duties*. In the case of state and local governments, these taxes include *sales taxes, property taxes* (including residential real estate taxes), and *Other* taxes such as motor vehicle licenses, severance taxes, and special assessments. Before the 2003 revision, these taxes were a component of "indirect business tax and nontax liabilities."

Taxes on corporate income covers federal, state, and local government taxes on all corporate income subject to taxes. This taxable income includes capital gains and other income excluded from NIPA profits. The taxes are measured on an accrual basis, net of applicable tax credits. Federal corporate income tax receipts in the NIPAs include receipts from *Federal Reserve Banks* that represent the return of their surplus earnings. (In the budget accounts in Table 6-14, these are included under "Miscellaneous receipts.")

Contributions for social insurance includes employer and personal contributions for Social Security, Medicare, unemployment insurance, and other government social insurance programs. As of the 1999 revisions, contributions to government employee retirement plans are no longer included in this category; these plans are now treated the same as private pension plans.

Income receipts on assets consists of *interest*, *dividends* and *rents and royalties*.

Interest receipts (1960 to the present for federal government; 1946 to the present for state and local governments) consists of monetary and imputed interest received on loans and investments. In the NIPAs, this no longer includes interest received by government employee retirement plans, which is now credited to personal income. However, such interest received is still deducted from interest paid in the budget accounts that are shown in Table 6-14. Before the indicated years, receipts are deducted from aggregate interest payments in the NIPAs. Hence, they are not shown as receipts, and net interest is presented on the expenditure side. In the federal budget accounts in Table 6-14, net interest (total interest expenditures minus interest receipts) is the interest "expenditure" concept used throughout the period covered.

Current transfer receipts includes receipts in categories other than those specified above from persons and business. In the case of state and local government accounts (Table 6-8), it also includes *federal grants-in-aid,* a component of federal expenditures. Receipts from *business* and *persons* were previously included with income taxes in "tax and nontax payments." They consist of federal deposit insurance premiums and other nontaxes (largely fines and regulatory and inspection fees), state and local fines and other nontaxes (largely donations and tobacco settlements), and net insurance settlements paid to governments as policyholders.

The *current surplus of government enterprises* is the current operating revenue and subsidies received from other levels of government by such enterprises less their current expenses. No deduction is made for depreciation charges or net interest paid. Before 1959, this category of receipts is treated as a deduction from subsidies. In the federal NIPA accounts before 1959, there is no entry shown for the current surplus on the receipts side, and on the expenditure side, there is an entry for subsidies, which is net of the current surplus. (Subsidies are usually a larger amount than the enterprise surplus in the federal accounts.) In the state and local NIPA accounts before 1959, there is an entry for the surplus on the receipts side, which is net of subsidies. (Subsidies are typically smaller than the enterprise surplus in state and local finance.)

Definitions (consumption expenditures, saving, and gross investment)

Government consumption expenditures is expenditures by governments (federal or state and local) on services for current consumption. It includes *compensation of general government employees* (including employer contributions to government employee retirement plans, as of the 1999 revision); an allowance for *consumption of general government fixed capital (CFC)*, including software (depreciation); and *intermediate goods and services purchased.* (See the general discussion above for an explanation.) The estimated value of *own-account investment*—investment goods, including software, produced by government resources and purchased inputs—is subtracted here, and added to *government gross investment. Sales to other sectors*—primarily tuition payments received from individuals for higher education and charges for medical care to individuals—are also deducted.

Government social benefits consists of payments to individuals for which the individuals do not render current services. Examples are Social Security benefits, Medicare, Medicaid, unemployment benefits, and public assistance. Retirement payments to retired government employees from their pension plans are no longer included in this category.

Government social benefits to persons consists of payments to persons residing in the United States (with a corresponding entry of an equal amount in the personal income receipts accounts). Government social benefits to the *rest of the world* appear only in the federal government account, and are transfers, mainly retirement benefits, to former residents of the United States.

Other current transfer payments (federal account only) includes *grants-in-aid to state and local governments* and *grants to the rest of the world*—military and nonmilitary grants to foreign governments.

Federal grants-in-aid comprises net payments from federal to state and local governments that are made to help finance programs such as health (Medicaid), public assis-

tance (the old Aid to Families with Dependent Children and the new Temporary Assistance for Needy Families), and education. Investment grants to state and local governments for highways, transit, air transportation, and water treatment plants are now classified as capital transfers and are no longer included in this category. However, such investment grants continue to be included as federal government outlays in Table 6-14.

Interest payments is monetary interest paid to U.S. and foreign persons and businesses and to foreign governments for public debt and other financial obligations. As noted above, from 1960 forward for the federal government and from 1946 forward for state and local governments, this represents gross total (not net) interest payments. Before those dates in the NIPAs, and throughout the federal budget accounts presented in Table 6-14, net instead of aggregate interest is shown; that is, gross total interest paid less interest received.

Subsidies are monetary grants paid by government to business, including to government enterprises at another level of government. Subsidies no longer include federal maritime construction subsidies, which are now classified as a capital transfer. For years prior to 1959, subsidies continue to be presented net of the *current surplus of government enterprises*, because detailed data to separate the series are not available for this period. See the entry for *current surplus of government enterprises*, described above, for explanation of the pre-1959 treatment of this item in the federal accounts in *Business Statistics*, which differs from the treatment in the state and local accounts.

Net saving, NIPA (surplus+/deficit-), is the sum of current receipts less the sum of current expenditures. This is shown separately for *social insurance funds* (which, in the case of the federal government, include Social Security and other trust funds) and *other* (all other government). As of the 1999 revision, net government saving—particularly that of state and local governments—is measured as being significantly smaller than before that revision, as the net accumulations of government employee retirement plans (not Social Security) are now classified as personal saving rather than in the government sector.

Gross government investment consists of general government and government enterprise expenditures for fixed assets—structures, equipment, and software. The expenditures include the compensation of government employees producing the assets and the purchase of goods and services as intermediate inputs to be incorporated in the assets. Government inventory investment is included in government consumption expenditures.

Capital consumption. Consumption of fixed capital (CFC; economic depreciation) is included in government consumption expenditures as a partial measure of the value of the services of general government fixed assets, including structures, equipment, and software.

Definitions (output, lending and borrowing, and net investment)

In Tables 6-5 and 6-10, current-dollar values of gross output and value added of government are presented, as described in the general discussion above. *Gross output* of government is the sum of the *intermediate goods and services purchased* by government and the value added by government as a producing industry. *Value added* consists of compensation of general government employees and consumption of general government fixed capital. Since this depreciation allowance is the only entry on the product side of the accounts measuring the output associated with such capital, a zero <u>net</u> return on these assets is implicitly assumed.

Gross output minus own-account investment and sales to other sectors (see the previous description) yields *government consumption expenditures*, which represents the contribution of government consumption spending to final demands in GDP.

Net lending (net borrowing -) consists of current *net saving* as defined above, plus the *consumption of fixed capital* (CFC, from the current expenditure account), minus *gross investment*, plus *capital transfer receipts*, and minus *capital transfer payments* and *net purchases of non-produced assets*.

Capital transfer receipts and *payments* include grants between levels of government, or between government and the private sector, associated with acquisition or disposal of assets rather than with current consumption expenditures. Examples are federal grants to state and local government for highways, transit, air transportation, and water treatment plants; federal shipbuilding subsidies and other subsidies to businesses; and lump-sum payments to amortize the unfunded liability of the Uniformed Services Retiree Health Care Fund. Government capital transfer receipts include estate and gift taxes, which are no longer included in personal tax receipts. (Federal estate and gift taxes are shown in Table 6-14 and, although they are reported on a fiscal year basis, are almost identical to the calendar year values for federal capital transfer receipts in Table 6-5.)

Non-produced assets are land and radio spectrum. Unusually large negative entries for net purchases of non-produced assets in recent years result from the negative purchase–that is, the sale–of spectrum.

The values of *net investment* shown in these tables are calculated by the editor, as gross investment minus the consumption of fixed capital.

Definitions (chain-type quantity indexes)

Chain-type quantity indexes represent changes over time in real values, removing the effects of inflation. Indexes for key categories in the government expenditure accounts, as well as for government gross output, value added, and

intermediate goods and services purchased, use the chain formula described in the notes and definitions for Chapter 1 and are expressed as index numbers, with the average for the year 2005 equal to 100.

Data availability

The most recent data are published each month in the *Survey of Current Business*. Current and historical data may be obtained from the BEA Web site at <http://www.bea.gov> and the STAT-USA subscription Web site at <http://www.stat-usa.gov>.

References

See the references regarding the 2009 comprehensive revision of the NIPAs in the notes and definitions for Chapter 1. NIPA concepts and their differences from the budget estimates are discussed in "NIPA Estimates of the Federal Sector and the Federal Budget Estimates," *Survey of Current Business*, March 2007, p. 11.

For information about the classification of government expenditures into current consumption and gross investment, first undertaken in the 1996 comprehensive revisions, see the *Survey of Current Business* article, "Preview of the Comprehensive Revision of the National Income and Product Accounts: Recognition of Government Investment and Incorporation of a New Methodology for Calculating Depreciation" September 1995. Other sources of information about the NIPAs are listed in the notes and definitions for Chapter 1.

TABLES 6-12 AND 6-13
STATE GOVERNMENT CURRENT RECEIPTS AND EXPENDITURES; LOCAL GOVERNMENT CURRENT RECEIPTS AND EXPENDITURES

Source: Bureau of Economic Analysis (BEA)

In the standard presentation of the state and local sector of the national income and product accounts (NIPAs) such as in Tables 6-8 through 6-11 above, state and local governments are combined. Annual measures for aggregate state governments and aggregate local governments are now available on the BEA Web site. These measures are shown in Tables 6-12 and 6-13. The definitions are the same as in the other NIPA tables described above.

Two new categories appear in each table, detailing intergovernmental flows that are consolidated in Table 6-8. State government receipts include not only *federal grants-in-aid* but also *local grants-in-aid*, and state government expenditures include *grants-in-aid to local governments*. Local government receipts include not only *federal grants-in-aid* but also *state grants-in-aid*, and local government expenditures include *grants-in-aid to state governments*. To make room for these columns, the components *current surplus of government enterprises* and *subsidies* are not shown, though they are included in total current receipts and total current expenditures respectively.

These measures are described in "Receipts and Expenditures of State Governments and of Local Governments," *Survey of Current Business*, October 2005. Data back to 1959 are available on the BEA Web site at <http://www.bea.gov>.

TABLE 6-14
FEDERAL GOVERNMENT RECEIPTS AND OUTLAYS BY FISCAL YEAR

SOURCE: U.S. OFFICE OF MANAGEMENT AND BUDGET

These data on federal government receipts and outlays are on a modified cash basis and are from the *Budget of the United States Government: Historical Tables*. The data are by federal fiscal years, which are defined as July 1 through June 30 through 1976 and October 1 through September 30 for 1977 and subsequent years. The period July 1 through September 30, 1976, is a separate fiscal period known as the transition quarter (TQ) and is not included in any fiscal year.

There are numerous differences in both timing and definition between these estimates and the NIPA estimates in Tables 6-1 through 6-7. See the notes and definitions for those tables for the definitional differences that were introduced with the 1999 comprehensive revision of the NIPAs.

Definitions

The definitions for this table are not affected by the 2003 or 1999 changes in the government sectors of the NIPAs.

Table references will be given indicating the source of each item in the *Historical Tables*; for example, "HT Table 1.1."

Receipts consist of gifts and other taxes or other compulsory payments to the government. Other types of payments to the government are netted against outlays. (HT Table 1.1)

Outlays occur when the federal government liquidates an obligation through a cash payment or when interest accrues on public debt issues. Beginning with the data for 1992, outlays include the subsidy cost of direct and guaranteed loans made. Before 1992, the costs and repayments associated with such loans are recorded on a cash basis. As noted previously, various types of nontax receipts are netted against cash outlays. These accounts do not distinguish between investment outlays and current consumption and do not include allowances for depreciation. (HT Table 1.1)

The *total surplus (deficit-)* is receipts minus outlays. (HT Table 1.1)

On-budget and off-budget. By law, two government programs that are included in the federal receipts and outlays totals are "off-budget"—old-age, survivors, and disability insurance (Social Security) and the Postal Service. The former accounts for nearly all of the off-budget activity. The *surplus (deficit-)* not accounted for by these two programs is the on-budget surplus or deficit. (HT Table 1.1)

Sources of financing is the means by which the total deficit is financed or the surplus is distributed. By definition, sources of financing sum to the total deficit or surplus with the sign reversed. The principal source is *borrowing from the public*, shown as a positive number, that is, the increase in the debt held by the public. (Calculated as the change in the debt held by the public as shown in HT Table 7.1.) When there is a budget surplus, as in fiscal years 1998 to 2001, debt can be reduced, indicated by a minus sign in this column. *Other financing* includes drawdown (or buildup, shown here with a minus sign) in Treasury cash balances, seigniorage on coins, direct and guaranteed loan account cash transactions, and miscellaneous other transactions. Large negative "financing" in the two most recent years results from direct loans and asset purchases under TARP and other emergency financial procedures; in other words, the government has borrowed from the public to undertake these loans and asset purchases, but they are not included in budget expenditures or the budget deficit. *Other financing* is calculated by reversing the sign of the surplus/deficit—so that the deficit becomes a positive number—and subtracting the value of borrowing from the public.

Some of the categories of *receipts by source* are self-explanatory. *Employment taxes and contributions* includes taxes for old-age, survivors, and disability insurance (Social Security), hospital insurance (Medicare), and railroad retirement funds. *Other retirement contributions* includes the employee share of payments for retirement pensions, mainly those for federal employees. *Excise taxes* includes federal taxes on alcohol, tobacco, telephone service, and transportation fuels, as well as taxes funding smaller programs such as black lung disability and vaccine injury compensation. *Miscellaneous receipts* includes deposits of earnings by the Federal Reserve system and all other receipts. (HT Tables 2.1, 2.4, and 2.5)

Outlays by function presents outlays according to the major purpose of the spending. Functional classifications cut across departmental and agency lines. Most categories of offsetting receipts are netted against cash outlays in the appropriate function, which explains how recorded outlays in *energy* and *commerce and housing credit* (which, as its name suggests, includes loan programs) can be negative. There is also a category of "undistributed offsetting receipts" (not shown), always with a negative sign, that includes proceeds from the sale or lease of assets and payments from federal agencies to federal retirement funds and the Social Security and Medicare trust funds. Note that *Social Security* is recorded separately from other *income security* outlays, and *Medicare* separately from other *health* outlays. (HT Table 3.1) For further explanation, consult the *Budget of the United States Government*.

In order to provide authoritative comparisons of these budget values with the overall size of the economy, a special calculation of gross domestic product by fiscal year (supplied to the Office of Management and Budget by the BEA) is included in this table. (HT Table 1.2)

Data availability and references

Definitions, budget concepts and historical data are from *Budget of the United States Government for Fiscal Year 2011: Historical Tables*, available on the Office of Management and Budget Web site at <http://www.whitehouse.gov/omb/Budget/historicals>

Similarly defined data for the latest month, the year-ago month, and the current and year-ago fiscal year to date are published in the *Monthly Treasury Statement* prepared by the Financial Management Service, U.S. Department of the Treasury. For those who need up-to-date budget information, this publication is available on the Financial Management Service Web site at <http://www.fms.treas.gov>. As these monthly figures are never revised to agree with the final annual data, they are not published in this volume.

TABLE 6-15
FEDERAL GOVERNMENT DEBT BY FISCAL YEAR

SOURCE: U.S. OFFICE OF MANAGEMENT AND BUDGET

Debt outstanding at the end of each fiscal year is from the *Budget of the United States Government*. Most securities are recorded at sales price plus amortized discount or less amortized premium.

Definitions

Federal government debt held by the public consists of all federal debt held outside the federal government accounts—by individuals, financial institutions (including the Federal Reserve Banks), and foreign individuals, businesses, and central banks. It does not include federal debt held by federal government trust funds such as the Social Security trust fund. The level and change of the ratio of this debt to the value of gross domestic product (GDP) provide proportional measures of the impact of federal borrowing on credit markets. (HT Table 7.1) This measure of debt held by the public is very similar in concept and scope to the total federal government credit market debt outstanding in the flow-of-funds accounts, shown in Business Statistics in Table 12-5; however, it is not identical, being priced somewhat differently, and is shown here in Chapter 6 on a fiscal year rather than calendar year basis.

Gross federal debt—total. This is the total debt owed by the U.S. Treasury. It includes a small amount of matured debt. (HT Table 7.1)

Debt held by Social Security funds is the sum of the end-year trust fund balances for old age and survivors insurance and disability insurance. (HT Table 13.1)

Debt held by other U.S. government accounts is calculated

by subtracting the Social Security debt holdings from the total debt held by federal government accounts, which is shown in HT Table 7.1. It includes the balances in all the other trust funds, including the Medicare funds, federal employee retirement funds, and the highway trust fund.

Debt held by the Federal Reserve System is the total value of Treasury securities held by the 12 Federal Reserve Banks, which are acquired in open market operations that carry out monetary policy. (HT Table 7.1)

Debt held by private investors is calculated by subtracting the Federal Reserve debt from the total debt held by the public.

Debt held by foreign residents is based on surveys by the Treasury Department. (Table 6-7, *Budget of the United States for Fiscal Year 2011: Analytical Perspectives,* p. 69.)

Debt held by domestic investors is calculated by subtracting the foreign debt from the total debt held by private investors.

The "debt subject to statutory limitation," not shown here, is close to the gross federal debt in concept and size, but there are some relatively minor definitional differences specified by law. The debt limit can only be changed by an Act of Congress. For information about the debt subject to limit and other debt subjects, see the latest *Budget of the United States Government: Historical Statistics* and *Analytical Perspectives*.

Data availability and references

For the end-of-fiscal-year data, see *Historical Tables* and *Analytical Perspectives* in the *Budget of the United States Government*, which is available on the OMB Web site at <http://www.whitehouse.gov/omb/Budget>. In the *Analytical Perspectives*, debt analysis and data are included in the "Economic and Budget Analysis" section.

Recent quarterly data, measured on a somewhat different basis, are found in the *Treasury Bulletin* in the chapter on "Ownership of Federal Securities (OFS)," in Tables OFS-1 and OFS-2. The *Treasury Bulletin* can be accessed on the Internet at <http://www.fms.treas.gov/bulletin>. Holdings by Social Security funds are also available in the *Bulletin* in the chapter on "Federal Debt," Table FD-3. The Disability Fund is listed separately from the Old-Age and Survivors Fund.

TABLE 6-17
GOVERNMENT EMPLOYMENT

SOURCE: U.S. DEPARTMENT OF LABOR, BUREAU OF LABOR STATISTICS (SEE NOTES AND DEFINITIONS FOR TABLE 10-7).

Government payroll employment includes federal, state, and local activities such as legislative, executive, and judicial functions, as well as all government-owned and government-operated business enterprises, establishments, and institutions (arsenals, navy yards, hospitals, etc.), and government force account construction. The figures relate to civilian employment only. The Bureau of Labor Statistics (BLS) considers regular full-time teachers (private and governmental) to be employed during the summer vacation period, regardless of whether they are specifically paid in those months.

Employment in federal government establishments reflects employee counts as of the pay period containing the 12th of the month. Federal government employment excludes employees of the Central Intelligence Agency and the National Security Agency.

CHAPTER 7: U.S. FOREIGN TRADE AND FINANCE

Section 7a: Foreign Transactions in the National Income and Product Accounts

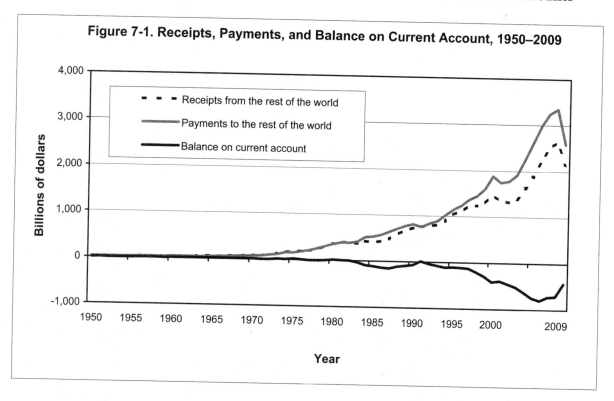

Figure 7-1. Receipts, Payments, and Balance on Current Account, 1950–2009

- For much of the early postwar period, U.S. current receipts from the rest of the world (exports and income receipts) and current payments to the rest of the world (imports, income payments, and net tax and transfer payments) were in rough balance. In most years through 1981, there was a surplus of receipts over payments—a positive balance on current account—that enabled the United States to invest in the economies of the rest of the world. (Table 7-1)

- However, beginning in 1983, large current-account deficits emerged, requiring net capital inflows from abroad to finance them. The only current-account surplus since then occurred in 1991, when payments from other countries financed most of the cost of the first Gulf War. (Table 7-1)

- U.S. current-account deficits typically diminish somewhat during recessions, as receipts hold up somewhat better than payments. The year 2009 was no exception. Payments plunged $764 billion while receipts dropped $487 billion, so the NIPA deficit on current account shrank from $707 billion in 2008 to $430 billion in 2009. (Table 7-1)

- The NIPA current-account deficit of $430 billion in 2009 comprised a deficit of $537 billion on goods, a surplus of $145 billion on services, net income receipts of $105 billion, and net payments of $143 billion in taxes and transfer payments. (Table 7-1)

- Looking at quarterly data on the real volume flows of goods and services in U.S. trade, the quantity index for exports of goods and services reached a high point in the second quarter of 2008 and fell 15 percent over the next year. The second half of 2009 saw a 9.7 percent recovery. Imports of goods and services, also in real terms, peaked earlier—in the third quarter of 2007—and plunged 21 percent between then and the second quarter of 2009. In the second half of 2009, imports recovered 8.9 percent. (Table 7-2)

Table 7-1. Foreign Transactions in the National Income and Product Accounts

(Billions of dollars, quarterly data are at seasonally adjusted annual rates.)   **NIPA Table 4.1**

Year and quarter	Current receipts from the rest of the world					Current payments to the rest of the world					Current taxes and transfer payments, net	Balance on current account, NIPAs	Net lending or net borrowing (-), NIPAs
	Total	Exports of goods and services			Income receipts	Total	Imports of goods and services			Income payments			
		Goods¹		Services¹			Goods¹		Services¹				
		Durable	Nondurable				Durable	Nondurable					
1950	14.5	5.1	5.1	2.1	2.2	16.4	3.0	6.1	2.5	0.7	4.0	-1.8	-1.8
1951	19.9	6.6	7.6	2.9	2.8	19.0	3.8	7.4	3.4	0.9	3.5	0.9	0.9
1952	19.3	6.9	6.5	3.0	2.9	18.7	4.1	6.7	4.5	0.9	2.6	0.6	0.6
1953	18.2	6.9	5.5	2.9	2.8	19.5	4.1	6.9	5.0	0.9	2.5	-1.3	-1.3
1954	18.9	7.1	5.8	2.9	3.0	18.7	3.6	6.7	5.1	0.9	2.3	0.2	0.2
1955	21.2	8.2	6.2	3.3	3.5	20.8	4.5	7.1	5.7	1.1	2.6	0.4	0.4
1956	25.2	9.8	7.8	3.7	3.9	22.5	5.2	7.6	6.1	1.1	2.5	2.7	2.7
1957	28.3	10.9	8.6	4.5	4.3	23.6	5.3	8.0	6.7	1.2	2.4	4.7	4.7
1958	24.4	9.0	7.4	4.1	3.9	23.6	5.0	8.0	7.1	1.2	2.4	0.8	0.8
1959	27.0	8.9	7.5	6.3	4.3	28.3	6.6	8.7	7.0	1.5	4.4	-1.3	-1.3
1960	31.9	11.3	9.2	6.6	4.9	28.8	6.4	8.9	7.6	1.8	4.1	3.2	3.2
1961	32.9	11.5	9.4	6.7	5.3	28.7	6.0	9.0	7.6	1.8	4.2	4.2	4.2
1962	35.0	12.0	9.7	7.4	5.9	31.2	6.9	9.9	8.1	1.8	4.4	3.8	3.8
1963	37.6	12.7	10.7	7.7	6.5	32.7	7.4	10.3	8.4	2.1	4.5	4.9	4.9
1964	42.3	14.7	12.0	8.3	7.2	34.8	8.4	11.0	8.7	2.3	4.4	7.5	7.5
1965	45.0	15.8	12.0	9.4	7.9	38.9	10.4	11.8	9.3	2.6	4.7	6.2	6.2
1966	49.0	17.5	13.2	10.2	8.1	45.2	13.3	13.1	10.7	3.0	5.1	3.8	3.8
1967	52.1	18.4	13.7	11.3	8.7	48.7	14.5	13.2	12.2	3.3	5.5	3.5	3.5
1968	58.0	21.0	14.3	12.6	10.1	56.5	18.8	15.1	12.6	4.0	5.9	1.5	1.5
1969	63.7	23.7	14.6	13.7	11.8	62.1	20.8	16.1	13.7	5.7	5.9	1.6	1.6
1970	72.5	27.1	17.4	15.2	12.8	68.8	22.8	18.1	14.9	6.4	6.6	3.7	3.7
1971	77.0	27.5	18.0	17.4	14.0	76.7	26.6	19.9	15.8	6.4	7.9	0.3	0.3
1972	87.1	31.0	20.8	19.0	16.3	91.2	33.3	23.6	17.3	7.7	9.2	-4.0	-4.0
1973	118.8	41.4	32.6	21.3	23.5	109.9	40.8	31.0	19.3	10.9	7.9	8.9	8.9
1974	156.5	56.5	44.5	25.7	29.8	150.5	50.3	54.2	22.9	14.3	8.7	6.0	6.0
1975	166.7	63.8	45.8	29.1	28.0	146.9	45.6	53.4	23.7	15.0	9.1	19.8	19.8
1976	181.9	69.0	48.7	31.7	32.4	174.8	56.8	67.8	26.5	15.5	8.1	7.1	7.1
1977	196.6	72.0	51.6	35.7	37.2	207.5	69.2	83.4	29.8	16.9	8.1	-10.9	-10.9
1978	233.1	85.3	60.1	41.5	46.3	245.8	89.0	88.4	34.8	24.7	8.8	-12.6	-12.6
1979	298.5	108.0	76.0	46.1	68.3	299.6	100.4	112.3	39.9	36.4	10.6	-1.2	-1.2
1980	359.9	133.3	92.5	55.0	79.1	351.4	111.9	136.6	45.3	44.9	12.6	8.5	8.5
1981	397.3	140.1	99.0	66.1	92.0	393.9	126.0	141.8	49.9	59.1	17.0	3.4	3.4
1982	384.2	124.7	90.3	68.2	101.0	387.5	125.1	125.4	52.6	64.5	19.8	-3.3	-3.2
1983	378.9	120.4	86.9	69.7	101.9	413.9	147.3	125.4	56.0	64.8	20.5	-35.1	-35.0
1984	424.2	132.4	93.2	76.7	121.9	514.3	192.4	143.9	68.8	85.6	23.6	-90.1	-89.9
1985	414.5	137.2	85.0	79.8	112.4	528.8	204.2	139.1	73.9	85.9	25.7	-114.3	-114.1
1986	431.3	142.6	83.4	94.3	111.0	574.0	238.8	131.2	82.9	93.4	27.8	-142.7	-142.5
1987	486.6	162.9	94.6	106.2	122.8	640.7	264.2	150.6	93.9	105.2	26.8	-154.1	-153.9
1988	595.5	208.8	117.0	118.1	151.6	711.2	294.8	157.3	101.9	128.3	29.0	-115.7	-115.4
1989	680.3	239.8	129.5	133.8	177.2	772.7	310.3	174.5	106.2	151.2	30.4	-92.4	-92.2
1990	740.6	262.0	134.7	155.5	188.5	815.6	314.5	193.5	121.7	154.1	31.7	-74.9	-81.6
1991	764.7	282.3	141.3	173.0	168.1	756.9	315.5	185.2	122.8	138.2	-4.9	7.9	3.2
1992	786.8	300.5	147.4	187.0	151.8	832.4	346.7	198.2	122.9	122.7	41.9	-45.6	-44.8
1993	810.8	314.0	146.0	195.7	155.2	889.4	386.4	206.4	127.2	124.0	45.4	-78.6	-80.0
1994	904.8	349.6	160.4	210.6	184.1	1 019.5	454.0	222.8	136.6	160.0	46.1	-114.7	-116.6
1995	1 041.1	394.0	189.3	228.6	229.3	1 146.2	510.8	246.7	145.1	199.6	44.1	-105.1	-106.2
1996	1 113.5	421.1	197.2	249.3	245.8	1 227.6	533.4	274.1	156.5	214.2	49.5	-114.1	-115.1
1997	1 233.9	482.3	205.4	266.7	279.5	1 363.3	588.5	297.1	170.1	256.1	51.4	-129.3	-130.6
1998	1 240.1	486.6	194.3	273.0	286.2	1 444.6	637.7	293.0	184.9	268.9	60.0	-204.5	-205.5
1999	1 308.8	503.3	193.9	292.1	319.5	1 600.7	716.7	331.0	203.7	291.7	57.6	-291.9	-297.1
2000	1 473.7	569.2	215.1	308.9	380.5	1 884.1	823.6	422.9	228.8	342.8	66.1	-410.4	-411.7
2001	1 350.8	521.1	210.1	296.5	323.0	1 742.4	758.3	413.4	227.0	271.1	72.6	-391.6	-380.0
2002	1 316.5	488.5	211.8	302.7	313.5	1 768.1	774.5	419.3	236.3	264.4	73.5	-451.6	-453.4
2003	1 394.4	497.3	229.5	314.2	353.3	1 910.5	806.6	482.6	255.9	284.6	80.7	-516.1	-519.9
2004	1 628.8	561.2	255.8	363.2	448.6	2 253.4	936.3	565.4	297.3	357.4	97.1	-624.6	-623.5
2005	1 878.1	624.9	281.2	399.0	573.0	2 618.6	1 025.4	682.6	319.8	475.9	115.0	-740.5	-729.5
2006	2 192.1	709.1	315.3	446.6	721.1	2 990.5	1 130.2	754.7	355.4	648.6	101.5	-798.4	-802.6
2007	2 517.7	776.8	362.6	516.5	861.8	3 242.4	1 175.1	812.5	382.1	746.0	126.6	-724.7	-726.8
2008	2 640.3	822.8	444.1	564.2	809.2	3 347.6	1 160.9	965.5	412.4	667.3	141.4	-707.2	-706.8
2009	2 153.7	664.6	373.7	525.9	589.4	2 583.8	892.6	682.8	381.2	484.5	142.7	-430.1	-433.1
2007													
1st quarter	2 352.8	747.0	334.5	483.4	787.9	3 152.2	1 166.4	760.5	367.4	724.0	133.9	-799.3	-801.8
2nd quarter	2 454.2	759.0	350.4	492.7	852.1	3 216.8	1 158.0	793.1	375.8	776.0	113.9	-762.6	-763.3
3rd quarter	2 582.8	785.4	371.1	528.6	897.6	3 267.6	1 183.7	810.1	389.8	759.1	124.8	-684.8	-687.6
4th quarter	2 681.0	816.0	394.4	561.2	909.4	3 332.9	1 192.5	886.4	395.2	725.1	133.8	-651.9	-654.6
2008													
1st quarter	2 660.0	819.2	428.1	556.3	856.3	3 377.4	1 187.6	955.5	404.9	685.3	144.0	-717.4	-720.3
2nd quarter	2 742.0	852.8	473.4	575.3	840.5	3 495.3	1 206.4	1 020.4	413.4	711.6	143.6	-753.3	-756.4
3rd quarter	2 738.6	856.6	481.8	574.6	825.6	3 475.8	1 187.7	1 055.6	427.2	664.8	140.4	-737.1	-725.5
4th quarter	2 420.7	762.7	393.0	550.5	714.4	3 041.7	1 062.1	830.4	404.2	607.4	137.5	-621.0	-625.1
2009													
1st quarter	2 089.0	644.7	344.8	519.8	579.6	2 498.5	862.5	645.8	379.6	479.7	130.9	-409.5	-412.6
2nd quarter	2 065.0	617.0	361.1	515.6	571.3	2 454.5	820.9	640.2	371.7	478.6	143.0	-389.5	-392.5
3rd quarter	2 164.4	664.2	381.1	528.5	590.6	2 589.8	895.3	697.5	383.1	469.1	144.8	-425.5	-428.4
4th quarter	2 296.3	732.7	407.9	539.6	616.2	2 772.0	991.6	747.7	390.3	510.5	131.8	-475.7	-478.6

¹Exports and imports of certain goods, primarily military equipment purchased and sold by the federal government, are included in services. Beginning with 1986, repairs and alterations of equipment are reclassified from goods to services.

Table 7-2. Chain-Type Quantity Indexes for Exports and Imports of Goods and Services

(Index numbers, 2005 = 100; quarterly indexes are seasonally adjusted.)

NIPA Table 4.2.3

Year and quarter	Exports of goods and services					Imports of goods and services				
	Total	Goods [1]			Services [1]	Total	Goods [1]			Services [1]
		Total	Durable	Nondurable			Total	Durable	Nondurable	
1967	10.74	9.93	6.99	19.04	12.93	9.21	7.47	4.06	16.43	19.96
1968	11.58	10.71	7.65	20.15	13.93	10.59	9.02	5.17	18.61	20.32
1969	12.14	11.27	8.27	20.34	14.44	11.19	9.51	5.53	19.30	21.60
1970	13.45	12.56	9.05	23.32	15.73	11.67	9.88	5.68	20.35	22.72
1971	13.67	12.51	8.98	23.35	16.94	12.29	10.71	6.25	21.61	22.08
1972	14.70	13.86	9.92	25.96	16.84	13.67	12.17	7.19	24.14	23.01
1973	17.47	17.04	12.36	31.34	18.03	14.31	13.03	7.66	26.03	22.24
1974	18.85	18.39	14.27	31.06	19.43	13.98	12.67	7.69	24.41	22.21
1975	18.73	17.96	13.98	30.23	20.63	12.43	11.07	6.28	22.65	21.25
1976	19.55	18.82	14.17	33.14	21.24	14.86	13.57	7.70	27.79	22.71
1977	20.02	19.06	14.14	34.30	22.61	16.48	15.23	8.71	30.95	23.85
1978	22.13	21.19	15.77	37.98	24.50	17.91	16.59	10.07	31.96	25.55
1979	24.33	23.70	17.95	41.40	25.25	18.21	16.88	10.30	32.33	25.90
1980	26.95	26.52	20.02	46.57	26.83	17.00	15.62	10.38	27.83	25.32
1981	27.28	26.23	19.30	47.79	29.68	17.45	15.95	11.24	27.00	26.78
1982	25.19	23.86	16.77	46.34	28.86	17.23	15.54	11.37	25.42	28.21
1983	24.54	23.18	16.43	44.48	28.38	19.40	17.66	13.70	27.08	30.48
1984	26.55	25.01	18.20	46.24	30.91	24.12	21.93	18.23	30.84	38.13
1985	27.35	25.93	19.67	45.03	31.28	25.69	23.30	20.06	31.21	41.03
1986	29.45	27.26	20.81	46.83	35.82	27.88	25.69	21.92	34.89	41.49
1987	32.62	30.29	23.76	49.63	39.39	29.53	26.88	22.89	36.65	46.38
1988	37.84	35.99	29.48	54.70	42.94	30.69	27.97	23.84	38.05	47.95
1989	42.19	40.28	33.63	59.13	47.38	32.05	29.17	24.90	39.60	50.28
1990	45.99	43.67	37.23	61.61	52.37	33.19	30.02	25.55	40.93	53.56
1991	49.04	46.69	40.00	65.20	55.51	33.14	30.16	25.69	41.05	52.17
1992	52.41	50.18	43.18	69.46	58.50	35.47	33.00	28.39	44.19	50.77
1993	54.13	51.81	45.43	68.97	60.44	38.53	36.30	31.75	47.16	52.12
1994	58.85	56.85	50.93	72.23	64.28	43.13	41.15	37.00	50.66	54.90
1995	64.81	63.51	58.19	76.88	68.32	46.58	44.86	41.24	52.74	56.56
1996	70.19	69.11	64.89	79.45	73.10	50.63	49.06	45.66	56.28	59.51
1997	78.55	79.04	76.61	84.60	77.44	57.45	56.13	53.19	62.13	64.69
1998	80.34	80.81	79.09	84.47	79.30	64.17	62.78	60.20	67.81	71.72
1999	83.85	83.88	82.87	85.63	83.86	71.55	70.61	68.96	73.27	76.57
2000	91.05	93.18	93.56	91.20	86.10	80.87	80.09	79.47	80.46	84.96
2001	85.95	87.41	85.77	90.74	82.53	78.60	77.53	74.56	82.65	84.29
2002	84.22	84.27	80.91	92.13	84.12	81.27	80.41	77.68	85.00	85.84
2003	85.57	85.77	82.34	93.81	85.11	84.86	84.36	81.01	90.13	87.47
2004	93.70	93.03	91.37	96.77	95.24	94.23	93.66	92.16	96.07	97.25
2005	100.00	100.00	100.00	100.00	100.00	100.00	100.00	100.00	100.00	100.00
2006	108.96	109.42	110.73	106.54	107.94	106.09	105.90	108.77	101.74	107.06
2007	118.47	117.51	119.89	112.41	120.64	108.19	107.71	111.16	102.75	110.75
2008	124.84	124.44	125.47	121.85	125.76	104.72	103.47	106.22	99.40	111.48
2009	112.82	109.27	104.45	118.32	120.66	90.15	86.88	84.03	90.02	107.46
2004										
1st quarter	91.74	90.94	89.03	95.29	93.59	90.24	89.37	86.80	93.64	94.79
2nd quarter	93.18	92.45	91.06	95.63	94.83	93.85	93.26	91.60	95.94	96.95
3rd quarter	93.87	93.62	92.37	96.44	94.43	95.21	94.78	93.74	96.39	97.53
4th quarter	96.01	95.09	93.04	99.74	98.10	97.63	97.23	96.51	98.33	99.74
2005										
1st quarter	97.79	97.04	95.53	100.39	99.51	98.19	98.07	97.21	99.42	98.82
2nd quarter	99.88	100.22	99.00	102.92	99.09	99.27	99.23	99.07	99.47	99.44
3rd quarter	99.91	99.96	100.46	98.82	99.80	99.87	99.90	100.29	99.29	99.73
4th quarter	102.42	102.78	105.01	97.87	101.60	102.67	102.79	103.43	101.82	102.01
2006										
1st quarter	106.42	107.09	108.55	103.86	104.90	104.61	104.38	107.59	99.79	105.89
2nd quarter	108.20	109.02	110.13	106.59	106.34	105.77	105.67	108.16	102.06	106.36
3rd quarter	108.35	109.07	110.17	106.65	106.73	107.04	107.10	108.92	104.40	106.72
4th quarter	112.88	112.49	114.06	109.06	113.77	106.92	106.48	110.43	100.73	109.28
2007										
1st quarter	113.86	113.31	115.46	108.67	115.09	108.04	107.79	111.33	102.63	109.38
2nd quarter	115.30	115.05	117.15	110.49	115.87	107.91	107.53	110.00	103.86	109.95
3rd quarter	120.29	119.08	121.38	114.11	123.05	108.90	108.28	111.60	103.48	112.25
4th quarter	124.44	122.61	125.57	116.36	128.57	107.90	107.24	111.72	101.03	111.44
2008										
1st quarter	124.40	123.87	125.35	120.41	125.59	107.23	106.29	110.41	100.60	112.25
2nd quarter	128.00	128.02	129.36	124.82	127.97	105.85	105.04	109.45	99.08	110.21
3rd quarter	126.83	127.45	129.15	123.65	125.43	105.26	104.05	107.05	99.64	111.85
4th quarter	120.15	118.41	118.01	118.50	124.05	100.55	98.52	97.98	98.26	111.61
2009										
1st quarter	109.92	105.52	101.99	111.96	119.62	89.80	86.33	81.47	92.21	108.24
2nd quarter	108.77	103.82	97.85	115.22	119.65	86.29	82.52	77.83	88.20	106.16
3rd quarter	113.32	109.70	104.31	119.90	121.29	90.55	87.27	84.22	90.59	107.96
4th quarter	119.29	118.04	113.67	126.19	122.08	93.93	91.40	92.59	89.07	107.46

[1] Exports and imports of certain goods, primarily military equipment purchased and sold by the federal government, are included in services. Beginning with 1986, repairs and alterations of equipment are reclassified from goods to services.

Table 7-3. Chain-Type Price Indexes for Exports and Imports of Goods and Services

(Index numbers, 2005 = 100; quarterly indexes are seasonally adjusted.)   NIPA Table 4.2.4

Year and quarter	Exports of goods and services					Imports of goods and services				
	Total	Goods [1]			Services [1]	Total	Goods [1]			Services [1]
		Total	Durable	Nondurable			Total	Durable	Nondurable	
1967	31.02	35.77	42.21	25.66	21.89	21.36	21.75	34.93	11.79	19.04
1968	31.70	36.33	43.91	25.18	22.76	21.69	22.04	35.50	11.90	19.41
1969	32.77	37.45	45.83	25.48	23.71	22.25	22.67	36.63	12.19	19.81
1970	34.03	39.14	47.96	26.57	24.16	23.57	24.21	39.11	13.02	20.51
1971	35.28	40.19	49.07	27.43	25.75	25.02	25.45	41.49	13.52	22.37
1972	36.93	41.26	50.06	28.42	28.36	26.77	27.40	45.14	14.35	23.48
1973	41.78	47.88	53.54	36.94	29.68	31.42	32.29	51.97	17.47	27.16
1974	51.48	60.60	63.32	50.98	33.11	44.96	48.32	63.85	32.53	32.30
1975	56.74	67.35	73.07	53.90	35.33	48.70	52.37	70.86	34.52	34.92
1976	58.60	69.08	77.97	52.29	37.47	50.17	53.77	72.00	35.75	36.50
1977	60.99	71.59	81.53	53.51	39.58	54.59	58.69	77.49	39.50	39.09
1978	64.70	75.72	86.55	56.30	42.45	58.44	62.61	86.27	40.52	42.65
1979	72.49	85.71	96.33	65.29	45.75	68.43	73.83	95.15	50.91	48.16
1980	79.84	93.96	106.61	70.60	51.38	85.24	93.16	105.20	71.92	55.89
1981	85.74	100.59	116.21	73.65	55.85	89.82	98.34	109.36	76.92	58.32
1982	86.14	99.44	118.97	69.31	59.23	86.79	94.37	107.35	72.26	58.36
1983	86.48	98.71	117.29	69.47	61.55	83.54	90.42	104.86	67.82	57.40
1984	87.28	99.57	116.40	71.71	62.23	82.82	89.80	102.94	68.35	56.42
1985	84.61	94.59	111.69	67.11	63.93	80.10	86.27	99.28	65.31	56.35
1986	83.34	91.49	109.67	63.31	66.01	80.10	84.34	106.26	55.09	62.45
1987	85.45	93.85	109.73	67.79	67.59	84.95	90.35	112.59	60.20	63.34
1988	89.88	99.90	113.34	76.06	68.94	89.01	94.65	120.59	60.58	66.42
1989	91.37	101.20	114.12	77.91	70.78	90.96	97.30	121.54	64.57	66.07
1990	91.99	100.24	112.62	77.72	74.41	93.56	99.09	120.04	69.27	71.02
1991	93.21	100.13	112.94	77.05	78.13	92.78	97.22	119.76	66.09	73.61
1992	92.83	98.53	111.37	75.48	80.13	92.86	96.69	119.12	65.72	75.67
1993	92.81	97.97	110.61	75.25	81.14	92.14	95.60	118.68	64.10	76.31
1994	93.84	99.02	109.85	78.99	82.14	93.01	96.30	119.69	64.41	77.81
1995	96.00	101.37	108.37	87.54	83.87	95.56	98.87	120.79	68.52	80.24
1996	94.73	98.75	103.87	88.26	85.49	93.89	96.36	113.94	71.34	82.23
1997	93.10	96.02	100.75	86.32	86.34	90.63	92.38	107.91	70.06	82.23
1998	90.97	92.99	98.45	81.79	86.29	85.75	86.80	103.32	63.31	80.63
1999	90.41	91.73	97.19	80.53	87.31	86.25	86.87	101.35	66.19	83.19
2000	92.00	92.90	97.37	83.87	89.92	89.96	91.13	101.08	77.00	84.21
2001	91.63	92.32	97.24	82.33	90.04	87.76	88.48	99.20	73.27	84.22
2002	91.25	91.72	96.64	81.73	90.20	86.78	86.93	97.25	72.27	86.09
2003	93.22	93.52	96.66	86.99	92.53	89.80	89.48	97.11	78.45	91.47
2004	96.52	96.93	98.29	93.98	95.60	94.14	93.87	99.08	86.21	95.57
2005	100.00	100.00	100.00	100.00	100.00	100.00	100.00	100.00	100.00	100.00
2006	103.45	103.33	102.49	105.23	103.72	104.14	104.21	101.34	108.67	103.81
2007	107.10	107.02	103.70	114.70	107.31	108.02	108.05	103.10	115.84	107.86
2008	112.39	112.37	104.96	129.59	112.45	119.56	120.32	106.59	142.30	115.68
2009	106.25	104.92	101.83	112.36	109.22	107.04	106.17	103.58	111.24	110.91
2004										
1st quarter	95.13	95.54	97.28	91.82	94.21	92.12	91.82	98.23	82.48	93.70
2nd quarter	96.30	96.86	98.00	94.40	95.04	93.42	93.15	99.10	84.41	94.81
3rd quarter	96.78	97.17	98.59	94.09	95.91	94.39	94.04	99.35	86.20	96.19
4th quarter	97.86	98.13	99.30	95.62	97.23	96.65	96.48	99.64	91.76	97.59
2005										
1st quarter	98.93	99.15	99.86	97.60	98.43	97.47	97.29	100.19	92.92	98.41
2nd quarter	99.63	99.78	99.95	99.38	99.27	98.83	98.67	100.27	96.23	99.68
3rd quarter	100.34	100.20	99.92	100.79	100.67	100.86	100.84	99.73	102.49	101.01
4th quarter	101.10	100.88	100.27	102.24	101.62	102.84	103.20	99.81	108.35	100.91
2006										
1st quarter	101.83	101.54	101.11	102.51	102.49	103.24	103.39	100.18	108.34	102.45
2nd quarter	103.13	102.92	102.21	104.50	103.61	104.32	104.42	101.09	109.61	103.82
3rd quarter	104.40	104.31	103.06	107.13	104.60	105.12	105.24	101.93	110.43	104.51
4th quarter	104.44	104.55	103.56	106.78	104.19	103.89	103.78	102.15	106.29	104.46
2007										
1st quarter	105.36	105.36	103.54	109.53	105.35	104.71	104.64	102.19	108.50	105.04
2nd quarter	106.52	106.45	103.68	112.86	106.66	106.33	106.22	102.67	111.80	106.89
3rd quarter	107.40	107.24	103.56	115.77	107.75	107.94	107.80	103.45	114.60	108.62
4th quarter	109.14	109.01	104.01	120.66	109.46	113.09	113.52	104.10	128.48	110.90
2008										
1st quarter	111.16	111.20	104.61	126.57	111.06	117.23	118.11	104.91	139.14	112.80
2nd quarter	113.89	114.43	105.54	135.02	112.69	123.07	124.22	107.51	150.90	117.28
3rd quarter	115.64	116.01	106.19	138.72	114.81	125.20	126.36	108.22	155.27	119.42
4th quarter	108.87	107.82	103.48	118.07	111.22	112.73	112.59	105.73	123.88	113.24
2009										
1st quarter	105.27	103.59	101.20	109.65	108.91	103.75	102.40	103.27	102.65	109.66
2nd quarter	105.28	104.08	100.96	111.57	108.00	104.82	103.78	102.88	106.38	109.47
3rd quarter	106.47	105.26	101.95	113.15	109.20	107.69	106.97	103.70	112.86	110.95
4th quarter	107.98	106.74	103.20	115.09	110.76	111.89	111.54	104.46	123.05	113.56

[1]Exports and imports of certain goods, primarily military equipment purchased and sold by the federal government, are included in services. Beginning with 1986, repairs and alterations of equipment are reclassified from goods to services.

Table 7-4. Exports and Imports of Selected NIPA Types of Product

(Billions of dollars, quarterly data are at seasonally adjusted annual rates.)   NIPA Table 4.2.5

Year and quarter	Exports							Imports							
	Goods					Services		Goods						Services	
	Foods, feeds, and beverages	Industrial supplies and materials	Capital goods, except auto-motive	Auto-motive vehicles, engines, and parts	Consumer goods, except auto-motive	Travel	Other private services (financial, profes-sional, etc.)	Foods, feeds, and beverages	Industrial supplies and materials, except petroleum and products	Petroleum and products	Capital goods, except auto-motive	Auto-motive vehicles, engines, and parts	Consumer goods, except auto-motive	Travel	Other private services (financial, profes-sional, etc.)
1967	5.0	10.0	9.9	2.8	2.1	1.6	0.7	4.6	9.9	2.1	2.5	2.4	4.2	3.2	0.4
1968	4.8	11.0	11.1	3.5	2.3	1.8	0.8	5.3	12.0	2.4	2.8	4.0	5.4	3.0	0.5
1969	4.7	11.7	12.4	3.9	2.6	2.0	0.9	5.2	11.7	2.6	3.4	5.1	6.5	3.4	0.6
1970	5.9	13.8	14.7	3.9	2.8	2.3	1.0	6.1	12.2	2.9	4.0	5.7	7.4	4.0	0.6
1971	6.1	12.6	15.4	4.7	2.9	2.5	1.3	6.4	13.6	3.7	4.3	7.6	8.4	4.4	0.7
1972	7.5	13.9	16.9	5.5	3.6	2.8	1.5	7.3	16.0	4.7	5.9	9.0	11.1	5.0	0.8
1973	15.2	19.7	22.0	7.0	4.8	3.4	1.7	9.1	19.2	8.4	8.3	10.7	12.9	5.5	0.9
1974	18.6	29.9	30.9	8.8	6.4	4.0	3.0	10.6	27.0	26.6	9.8	12.4	14.4	6.0	1.9
1975	19.2	29.3	36.6	10.8	6.6	4.7	3.7	9.6	23.6	27.0	10.2	12.1	13.2	6.4	2.3
1976	19.8	31.6	39.1	12.2	8.0	5.7	4.5	11.5	28.5	34.6	12.3	16.8	17.2	6.9	2.9
1977	19.7	33.2	39.8	13.5	8.9	6.2	4.9	14.0	33.4	45.0	14.0	19.4	21.8	7.5	3.2
1978	25.7	38.4	47.5	15.2	11.4	7.2	6.2	15.8	39.3	42.6	19.3	25.0	29.4	8.5	3.9
1979	30.5	53.3	60.2	17.9	14.0	8.4	7.3	18.0	45.0	60.4	24.6	26.6	31.3	9.4	4.6
1980	36.3	68.0	76.3	17.4	17.8	10.6	8.6	18.6	47.3	79.5	31.6	28.3	34.3	10.4	5.1
1981	38.8	65.7	84.2	19.7	17.7	12.9	13.2	18.6	52.0	78.4	37.1	31.0	38.4	11.5	6.3
1982	32.2	61.8	76.5	17.2	16.1	12.4	16.9	17.5	45.4	62.0	38.4	34.3	39.7	12.4	7.4
1983	32.1	57.1	71.7	18.5	14.9	10.9	17.6	18.8	51.1	55.1	43.7	43.0	47.3	13.2	7.3
1984	32.2	61.9	77.0	22.4	15.1	17.2	18.6	21.9	62.6	58.1	60.4	56.5	61.1	22.9	8.2
1985	24.6	59.4	79.3	24.9	14.6	17.8	19.4	21.8	59.2	51.4	61.3	64.9	66.3	24.6	9.4
1986	23.5	59.0	82.8	25.1	16.7	20.4	28.3	24.4	62.5	34.3	72.0	78.1	79.4	25.9	13.8
1987	25.2	67.4	92.7	27.6	20.3	23.6	29.6	24.8	66.1	42.9	85.1	85.2	88.8	29.3	17.3
1988	33.8	84.2	119.1	33.4	27.0	29.4	31.4	24.9	76.6	39.6	102.2	87.9	96.4	32.1	18.4
1989	36.3	95.4	136.9	35.1	35.9	36.2	37.0	24.9	78.8	50.9	112.3	87.4	103.6	33.4	19.9
1990	35.1	101.9	153.0	36.2	43.5	43.0	40.6	26.4	78.2	62.3	116.4	88.2	105.0	37.4	23.3
1991	35.7	106.2	166.6	39.9	46.6	48.4	48.1	26.2	75.7	51.7	121.1	85.5	107.7	35.3	26.8
1992	40.3	105.2	176.4	46.9	51.2	54.7	50.3	27.6	82.4	51.6	134.8	91.5	122.4	38.6	25.4
1993	40.5	102.9	182.7	51.6	54.5	57.9	53.5	27.9	88.7	51.5	153.2	102.1	133.7	40.7	27.8
1994	42.4	115.4	205.7	57.5	59.7	58.4	60.8	31.0	105.0	51.3	185.0	118.1	145.9	43.8	31.6
1995	50.8	141.0	234.4	61.4	64.2	63.4	65.0	33.2	119.6	56.0	222.1	123.7	159.7	44.9	35.2
1996	56.0	141.3	254.0	64.4	69.3	69.8	73.3	35.7	124.6	72.7	228.4	128.7	172.5	48.1	39.7
1997	52.0	153.0	295.8	73.4	77.0	73.4	83.9	39.7	134.7	71.8	253.6	139.4	195.2	52.1	43.2
1998	46.8	143.3	299.8	72.5	79.4	71.3	91.8	41.3	142.2	50.9	269.8	148.6	218.5	56.5	47.6
1999	46.0	142.4	311.2	75.3	80.9	74.8	103.9	43.6	148.3	67.8	295.7	179.0	243.5	59.0	55.5
2000	47.9	166.6	357.0	80.4	89.4	82.4	107.9	46.0	173.6	120.3	347.0	195.9	284.2	64.7	60.5
2001	49.4	155.3	321.7	75.4	88.3	71.9	113.9	46.6	165.8	103.6	298.4	189.8	286.5	60.2	66.0
2002	49.6	153.5	290.4	78.9	84.4	66.6	122.2	49.7	159.6	103.5	283.9	203.7	310.7	58.7	72.6
2003	55.0	168.3	293.7	80.6	89.9	64.4	131.6	55.8	175.7	133.1	296.4	210.1	337.7	57.4	79.8
2004	56.6	199.5	327.5	89.2	103.2	74.5	149.3	62.1	226.4	180.5	344.5	228.2	377.1	65.8	90.3
2005	59.0	227.5	358.4	98.4	115.3	81.8	160.0	68.1	266.0	251.9	380.7	239.4	411.5	69.0	97.8
2006	66.0	267.3	404.0	107.3	129.1	85.8	186.0	74.9	291.4	302.4	420.0	256.6	446.1	72.1	125.5
2007	84.3	303.1	433.0	121.3	146.0	97.1	220.1	81.7	295.7	331.0	446.0	259.2	478.2	76.4	141.7
2008	108.3	369.4	457.7	121.5	161.3	110.1	233.5	89.0	316.5	453.3	455.2	233.8	484.7	79.7	153.3
2009	93.9	282.6	390.9	81.9	150.1	94.9	232.1	81.8	194.5	253.5	369.6	160.5	431.0	73.6	156.2
2004															
1st quarter	56.9	187.7	320.9	83.8	97.7	71.5	144.9	59.8	197.5	160.8	324.9	221.1	359.1	63.4	86.7
2nd quarter	56.0	196.4	326.2	87.7	102.7	74.7	147.3	62.5	223.1	166.5	341.1	229.6	379.8	65.8	88.4
3rd quarter	55.0	201.3	330.2	92.1	104.2	74.8	147.2	61.8	238.4	177.9	351.0	230.2	376.5	66.4	89.3
4th quarter	58.3	212.5	332.9	93.2	108.4	77.3	157.7	64.4	246.7	216.6	361.0	231.8	393.2	67.3	96.6
2005															
1st quarter	57.3	220.8	342.1	95.0	111.6	79.7	158.2	65.1	254.1	214.2	364.3	231.7	408.9	68.8	91.8
2nd quarter	60.5	230.9	358.1	95.5	114.2	83.7	153.4	67.5	256.5	230.1	382.7	234.5	413.2	70.0	95.7
3rd quarter	58.1	228.2	357.3	98.8	116.0	81.6	159.1	68.9	258.8	266.7	382.9	240.2	409.0	68.6	99.3
4th quarter	59.9	230.2	376.1	104.4	119.4	82.1	169.5	70.9	294.7	296.4	393.1	251.4	415.0	68.5	104.5
2006															
1st quarter	61.9	250.1	391.6	106.7	123.9	83.2	179.4	73.6	288.0	291.4	407.7	256.6	430.6	70.5	120.5
2nd quarter	64.5	267.8	403.2	105.6	127.0	85.0	181.8	73.1	288.5	312.9	416.2	256.5	437.3	71.8	124.6
3rd quarter	67.8	271.6	403.8	106.6	129.6	86.4	183.1	75.3	300.0	331.8	426.0	251.6	449.7	72.1	126.0
4th quarter	69.7	279.7	417.6	110.2	135.8	88.6	199.7	77.8	289.1	273.7	429.9	261.8	466.9	74.0	130.8
2007															
1st quarter	73.6	280.9	419.4	115.5	141.2	87.2	207.5	80.0	288.1	281.8	440.0	255.2	482.2	74.1	134.8
2nd quarter	77.9	296.6	421.5	119.6	143.2	92.1	213.8	80.0	299.8	311.2	439.5	252.5	473.4	75.2	138.0
3rd quarter	88.9	307.4	439.4	122.5	147.9	101.2	226.8	82.8	299.4	329.2	448.4	265.4	471.0	77.1	142.6
4th quarter	96.7	327.5	451.7	127.4	151.5	107.7	232.2	83.9	295.3	401.7	456.2	263.9	486.2	79.1	147.7
2008															
1st quarter	108.4	353.6	454.6	124.4	157.8	108.3	229.4	86.2	308.7	450.3	461.2	254.8	487.7	80.9	148.5
2nd quarter	116.2	397.4	467.7	124.8	163.7	112.0	236.8	89.7	329.4	497.7	469.8	248.2	496.5	80.4	153.3
3rd quarter	115.4	411.2	472.3	127.5	167.5	115.3	235.8	91.3	344.0	523.4	462.1	232.6	495.5	79.4	157.3
4th quarter	93.4	315.4	436.1	109.1	156.1	104.7	232.1	88.7	283.9	341.8	427.6	199.4	459.3	78.2	154.0
2009															
1st quarter	86.6	253.5	393.8	70.2	146.0	95.4	228.1	81.7	208.4	208.9	367.1	129.4	425.6	74.5	152.2
2nd quarter	94.7	262.5	373.1	66.7	144.2	91.3	229.0	81.5	174.4	227.8	346.1	126.8	421.0	70.9	154.3
3rd quarter	92.3	296.3	382.2	86.4	150.0	95.6	233.3	81.0	185.5	275.5	364.6	178.0	425.2	74.5	158.4
4th quarter	102.3	318.0	414.6	104.4	160.3	97.3	238.0	83.0	209.9	301.7	400.7	207.9	452.0	74.4	160.1

Table 7-5. Chain-Type Quantity Indexes for Exports and Imports of Selected NIPA Types of Product

(Index numbers, 2005 = 100; quarterly indexes are seasonally adjusted.)   **NIPA Table 4.2.3**

	Exports							Imports						
	Goods					Services		Goods						Services	
Year and quarter	Foods, feeds, and beverages	Industrial supplies and materials	Capital goods, except auto-motive	Auto-motive vehicles, engines, and parts	Consumer goods, except auto-motive	Travel	Other private services (financial, profes-sional, etc.)	Foods, feeds, and beverages	Industrial supplies and materials, except petroleum and products	Petroleum and products	Capital goods, except auto-motive	Auto-motive vehicles, engines, and parts	Consumer goods, except auto-motive	Travel	Other private services (financial, profes-sional, etc.)
1967	26.08	21.44	3.94	14.60	6.16	10.98	1.84	27.20	19.47	16.55	0.64	7.11	4.04	20.07	1.24
1968	25.67	24.39	4.06	17.99	6.70	11.35	1.91	30.86	23.18	19.06	0.73	11.06	5.10	18.19	1.40
1969	25.13	25.51	4.30	19.44	7.17	12.39	2.09	29.25	21.93	21.26	0.86	13.51	6.02	19.73	1.56
1970	30.33	28.56	4.81	19.00	7.60	13.37	2.24	31.24	22.16	22.97	0.89	13.82	6.47	22.76	1.64
1971	29.53	25.82	5.03	21.53	7.62	13.95	2.60	32.25	24.16	26.27	0.88	16.86	6.81	22.74	1.81
1972	34.85	27.50	5.50	24.16	8.91	14.99	2.90	34.33	26.51	32.08	1.13	18.26	8.30	24.60	1.86
1973	45.12	33.83	6.99	28.37	10.87	17.22	3.16	35.21	26.68	45.57	1.39	18.84	8.51	23.20	2.08
1974	40.44	34.82	8.72	31.65	13.52	18.74	5.16	32.57	25.99	43.87	1.49	20.02	7.66	20.83	4.19
1975	42.78	30.46	8.86	33.32	12.46	20.26	5.99	28.81	21.89	43.15	1.41	15.88	5.94	20.09	4.73
1976	48.54	32.90	8.74	34.84	14.05	23.08	6.93	32.79	26.66	52.03	1.71	21.05	7.66	21.37	5.69
1977	48.50	33.17	8.60	35.09	15.20	23.13	7.14	32.46	28.69	62.59	1.83	22.30	9.26	22.02	5.96
1978	59.92	36.66	9.81	36.03	17.55	24.85	8.46	36.45	31.41	59.18	2.36	24.13	11.37	22.75	6.96
1979	63.56	41.98	11.78	36.26	18.45	26.63	9.43	37.41	30.18	59.86	2.88	23.33	11.46	22.19	7.89
1980	71.65	47.64	13.75	30.53	22.36	29.75	10.07	32.56	26.34	48.34	3.40	23.11	11.54	22.17	8.05
1981	73.16	44.44	13.80	30.18	21.44	32.84	14.40	33.88	28.59	42.36	4.00	22.37	12.64	23.45	9.48
1982	68.73	43.09	12.21	24.73	19.30	29.28	17.37	34.53	25.92	36.43	4.36	23.94	13.21	27.79	10.75
1983	65.70	41.00	11.77	25.59	17.65	24.72	17.16	37.48	30.78	36.05	5.27	29.31	15.90	31.49	10.07
1984	63.93	43.10	13.04	30.20	17.56	36.87	17.40	42.46	38.17	38.08	7.88	37.65	20.07	57.55	11.29
1985	55.33	43.35	14.33	32.86	17.04	36.50	17.37	44.30	38.39	35.76	8.88	42.19	21.91	63.52	12.58
1986	57.08	45.28	15.63	32.32	18.85	40.73	24.60	45.34	40.43	44.21	10.08	45.67	24.27	59.05	17.99
1987	61.09	46.41	18.05	34.83	22.17	44.94	24.66	46.48	40.03	46.18	11.50	46.87	25.06	70.02	20.57
1988	67.13	52.32	22.95	41.35	28.32	54.22	25.81	44.63	40.47	51.08	13.26	45.69	25.43	71.95	21.96
1989	69.83	58.19	26.62	42.50	36.31	64.81	29.83	45.64	39.55	55.23	15.00	44.53	26.61	74.14	25.62
1990	72.04	61.62	30.80	42.56	42.60	73.10	31.36	47.38	40.17	55.82	16.20	44.59	26.14	79.21	27.78
1991	73.42	65.80	33.70	45.65	44.14	77.45	35.69	45.24	39.43	55.62	17.42	41.58	26.59	71.73	30.92
1992	83.22	67.03	36.91	52.62	47.54	85.92	36.32	47.76	43.34	58.13	20.18	43.71	29.36	73.85	28.98
1993	82.80	65.25	39.33	57.37	49.94	90.13	37.86	48.32	47.02	63.68	23.55	48.04	31.79	77.47	30.75
1994	83.66	68.64	45.39	63.42	54.57	90.57	42.46	49.43	54.02	67.99	28.88	53.86	34.45	80.22	34.67
1995	92.41	74.05	54.08	66.84	57.84	97.11	44.47	50.67	56.56	66.76	35.54	54.79	37.16	80.85	38.16
1996	90.94	77.81	62.68	69.31	61.69	104.44	49.14	55.73	59.78	72.39	41.77	56.65	40.01	84.02	41.80
1997	91.51	84.59	76.83	78.46	68.04	107.42	55.56	61.38	64.71	75.38	52.42	61.23	45.83	91.27	44.84
1998	90.58	83.66	80.10	77.39	70.10	103.17	60.83	65.87	71.86	80.58	60.29	65.19	52.00	103.17	50.10
1999	93.22	84.39	84.53	79.83	71.72	105.37	70.10	71.98	75.35	81.23	69.11	77.95	58.38	105.17	58.55
2000	98.65	92.66	97.41	84.53	78.89	110.86	72.45	76.91	80.44	85.73	83.01	84.73	68.60	117.09	65.14
2001	101.35	88.95	87.78	79.09	78.25	96.20	76.80	80.43	77.66	88.25	73.55	82.15	69.72	111.52	71.47
2002	99.31	89.22	80.16	82.35	75.11	89.86	82.48	84.67	79.88	86.18	72.36	87.93	76.42	104.66	76.05
2003	101.00	91.48	82.05	83.52	79.60	85.09	87.31	91.23	81.15	91.94	76.54	90.20	83.24	95.40	82.08
2004	94.74	97.42	91.67	91.68	90.55	95.22	96.53	96.50	93.77	98.03	89.93	96.30	92.47	101.80	92.69
2005	100.00	100.00	100.00	100.00	100.00	100.00	100.00	100.00	100.00	100.00	100.00	100.00	100.00	100.00	100.00
2006	107.95	107.51	111.91	107.69	110.56	100.49	112.03	106.06	104.27	98.12	111.11	106.76	108.00	100.58	121.42
2007	117.37	113.42	120.29	120.35	122.45	109.77	128.30	107.40	100.18	95.90	117.51	106.77	114.21	98.53	133.58
2008	125.21	126.13	126.46	119.08	132.47	119.01	132.46	105.98	92.72	93.16	118.15	93.89	112.95	96.89	140.31
2009	121.46	117.08	109.29	79.89	122.99	107.19	132.06	100.68	69.84	85.19	96.84	63.99	100.79	98.19	139.98
2004															
1st quarter	94.25	96.26	90.18	86.57	86.01	92.77	94.90	95.18	85.95	98.36	84.24	93.97	88.03	101.52	89.82
2nd quarter	87.79	97.75	91.32	90.23	90.30	95.89	95.54	97.32	93.11	95.77	88.99	97.18	93.07	102.77	90.88
3rd quarter	94.11	97.11	92.35	94.57	91.17	95.27	94.81	96.09	97.58	96.59	91.87	97.00	92.47	101.77	90.73
4th quarter	102.82	98.57	92.84	95.35	94.72	96.95	100.90	97.41	98.43	101.39	94.64	97.06	96.32	101.15	99.35
2005															
1st quarter	99.15	99.62	95.33	96.85	96.88	99.30	99.82	96.95	99.25	99.49	95.30	96.95	99.26	102.34	94.40
2nd quarter	102.10	102.60	99.76	97.19	99.02	103.67	96.31	98.84	98.88	98.90	99.93	98.22	100.28	100.15	98.07
3rd quarter	97.35	99.97	99.64	100.31	100.68	98.92	99.05	101.55	98.32	98.87	100.76	100.24	99.45	97.40	101.30
4th quarter	101.40	97.82	105.26	105.65	103.42	98.12	104.83	102.65	103.55	102.74	104.01	104.80	101.01	100.11	106.24
2006															
1st quarter	104.46	104.60	109.23	107.73	107.06	98.56	109.25	105.68	104.33	96.93	107.97	107.23	104.58	100.87	118.56
2nd quarter	108.75	107.97	111.92	106.15	109.04	99.25	109.97	104.85	104.46	98.11	110.27	106.87	106.21	100.90	121.14
3rd quarter	110.12	106.60	111.59	106.72	110.40	100.04	109.44	106.01	106.31	103.14	112.64	104.46	108.68	99.41	120.84
4th quarter	108.48	110.89	114.91	110.15	115.74	104.12	119.45	107.70	101.99	94.30	113.58	108.50	112.53	101.13	125.15
2007															
1st quarter	108.27	109.75	115.95	115.04	119.52	101.19	122.35	108.72	100.02	94.50	116.36	105.64	115.66	100.23	128.97
2nd quarter	113.08	111.70	117.18	118.84	120.30	104.81	125.37	106.71	101.46	97.80	116.42	104.37	113.48	97.99	130.98
3rd quarter	123.70	114.19	122.32	121.56	123.84	113.86	131.87	107.75	102.07	96.95	117.82	109.38	112.30	98.27	137.21
4th quarter	124.41	118.03	125.70	125.96	126.14	119.23	133.60	106.43	97.15	94.33	119.42	107.67	115.43	97.62	137.17
2008															
1st quarter	127.03	123.09	126.42	122.65	130.51	118.08	130.64	106.02	95.07	93.98	120.95	102.87	114.74	97.35	137.95
2nd quarter	128.20	129.94	129.32	122.45	134.21	120.44	134.53	105.59	92.95	91.72	121.54	99.72	115.32	92.81	140.17
3rd quarter	125.63	130.06	130.18	124.82	136.96	121.32	132.59	105.18	94.81	92.33	119.17	93.16	114.79	92.96	142.13
4th quarter	119.97	121.42	119.92	106.39	128.19	116.22	132.09	107.13	88.05	94.62	110.95	79.79	106.96	104.41	141.00
2009															
1st quarter	113.44	109.20	110.36	68.36	119.78	108.77	130.73	101.03	73.45	90.62	95.96	51.77	99.45	101.38	138.20
2nd quarter	119.58	111.95	104.74	65.09	118.96	104.62	131.27	100.62	64.79	85.18	90.79	50.80	98.48	94.92	139.13
3rd quarter	119.51	121.54	106.96	84.40	122.55	107.33	132.52	100.36	68.42	86.28	95.56	70.91	99.57	98.68	141.06
4th quarter	133.32	125.62	115.10	101.73	130.67	108.05	133.71	100.72	72.70	78.69	105.05	82.47	105.64	97.78	141.52

Section 7b: U.S. International Transactions Accounts

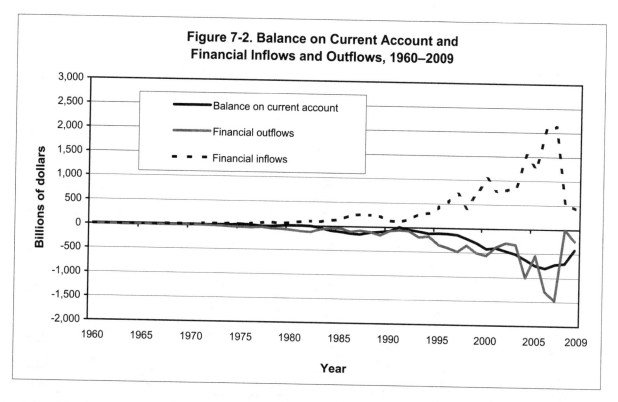

Figure 7-2. Balance on Current Account and Financial Inflows and Outflows, 1960–2009

- The U.S. current-account international balance is also recorded in the International Transactions Accounts (ITAs). The definitional differences between this balance and the balance in the NIPAs are minor, and the trends in the two measures are similar. The ITAs measure the current account surplus or deficit (commonly known as the "balance of payments") and directly measure the financial flows required to finance it. (Table 7-6)

- Figure 7-2 above shows the current-account balance since 1960, culminating in a $420 billion deficit in 2009, and the corresponding estimated financial flows. U.S. net investment in assets abroad contributed a further outflow, amounting to $237 billion, in 2009. Financing the sum of these was a much-reduced financial inflow, that is a net increase in foreign-owned assets in the United States, estimated at $435 billion. The net of the estimated financial flows does not equal the current-account balance because of a small capital transactions item and a huge $225 billion ITA statistical discrepancy. (Table 7-6)

- The large variations during 2008 and 2009 in many types of financial flows, and the startling size of the statistical discrepancy, are evidence of an extreme amount of international financial turbulence, some of which has apparently failed to register in our statistical system. (Table 7-6)

- Before the 1980s, the United States was a net creditor with respect to the rest of the world. In other words, the value of the stock of U.S.-owned assets abroad exceeded the value of foreign-owned assets in the United States. Since then, the persistent net financial inflows associated with current-account deficits have cumulated, resulting in a growing net debtor status, with the value of foreign-owned assets in the United States exceeding the value of U.S.-owned assets abroad by $3.5 trillion as of the end of 2008. (Table 7-8)

Table 7-6. U.S. International Transactions

(Millions of dollars, seasonally adjusted.)

Year and quarter	Current account — Exports of goods and services and income receipts									Compensation of employees
					Income receipts	Income receipts on U.S.-owned assets abroad				
	Total	Exports of goods and services	Exports of goods	Exports of services	Total	Total	Direct investment receipts	Other private receipts	U.S. government receipts	
1960	30 556	25 940	19 650	6 290	4 616	4 616	3 621	646	349	. . .
1961	31 402	26 403	20 108	6 295	4 999	4 999	3 823	793	383	. . .
1962	33 340	27 722	20 781	6 941	5 618	5 618	4 241	904	473	. . .
1963	35 776	29 620	22 272	7 348	6 157	6 157	4 636	1 022	499	. . .
1964	40 165	33 341	25 501	7 840	6 824	6 824	5 106	1 256	462	. . .
1965	42 722	35 285	26 461	8 824	7 437	7 437	5 506	1 421	510	. . .
1966	46 454	38 926	29 310	9 616	7 528	7 528	5 260	1 669	599	. . .
1967	49 353	41 333	30 666	10 667	8 021	8 021	5 603	1 781	636	. . .
1968	54 911	45 543	33 626	11 917	9 367	9 367	6 591	2 021	756	. . .
1969	60 132	49 220	36 414	12 806	10 913	10 913	7 649	2 338	925	. . .
1970	68 387	56 640	42 469	14 171	11 748	11 748	8 169	2 671	907	. . .
1971	72 384	59 677	43 319	16 358	12 707	12 707	9 160	2 641	906	. . .
1972	81 986	67 222	49 381	17 841	14 765	14 765	10 949	2 949	866	. . .
1973	113 050	91 242	71 410	19 832	21 808	21 808	16 542	4 330	936	. . .
1974	148 484	120 897	98 306	22 591	27 587	27 587	19 157	7 356	1 074	. . .
1975	157 936	132 585	107 088	25 497	25 351	25 351	16 595	7 644	1 112	. . .
1976	172 090	142 716	114 745	27 971	29 375	29 375	18 999	9 043	1 332	. . .
1977	184 655	152 301	120 816	31 485	32 354	32 354	19 673	11 057	1 625	. . .
1978	220 516	178 428	142 075	36 353	42 088	42 088	25 458	14 788	1 843	. . .
1979	287 965	224 131	184 439	39 692	63 834	63 834	38 183	23 356	2 295	. . .
1980	344 440	271 834	224 250	47 584	72 606	72 606	37 146	32 898	2 562	. . .
1981	380 928	294 398	237 044	57 354	86 529	86 529	32 549	50 300	3 680	. . .
1982	366 983	275 236	211 157	64 079	91 747	91 747	29 469	58 160	4 118	. . .
1983	356 106	266 106	201 799	64 307	90 000	90 000	31 750	53 418	4 832	. . .
1984	399 913	291 094	219 926	71 168	108 819	108 819	35 325	68 267	5 227	. . .
1985	387 612	289 070	215 915	73 155	98 542	98 542	35 410	57 633	5 499	908
1986	407 098	310 033	223 344	86 689	97 064	96 156	36 938	52 806	6 413	994
1987	457 053	348 869	250 208	98 661	108 184	107 190	46 288	55 592	5 311	995
1988	567 862	431 149	320 230	110 919	136 713	135 718	58 445	70 571	6 703	1 017
1989	648 290	487 003	359 916	127 087	161 287	160 270	61 981	92 638	5 651	1 172
1990	706 975	535 233	387 401	147 832	171 742	170 570	65 973	94 072	10 525	1 290
1991	727 557	578 343	414 083	164 260	149 214	147 924	58 718	81 186	8 019	1 796
1992	750 648	616 883	439 631	177 252	133 766	131 970	57 538	67 316	7 115	1 820
1993	778 921	642 863	456 943	185 920	136 057	134 237	67 245	61 865	5 126	1 943
1994	869 775	703 254	502 859	200 395	166 521	164 578	77 344	83 106	4 128	2 179
1995	1 004 631	794 387	575 204	219 183	210 244	208 065	95 260	108 092	4 713	2 181
1996	1 077 731	851 602	612 113	239 489	226 129	223 948	102 505	116 852	4 591	2 270
1997	1 191 257	934 453	678 366	256 087	256 804	254 534	115 323	135 652	3 559	2 437
1998	1 194 993	933 174	670 416	262 758	261 819	259 382	103 963	151 818	3 601	2 748
1999	1 259 809	965 884	683 965	281 919	293 925	291 177	131 626	156 354	3 197	2 835
2000	1 421 515	1 070 597	771 994	298 603	350 918	348 083	151 839	192 398	3 846	2 879
2001	1 295 692	1 004 895	718 711	286 184	290 797	287 918	128 665	155 692	3 561	2 811
2002	1 258 411	977 469	685 170	292 299	280 942	278 131	145 590	129 238	3 303	2 813
2003	1 340 647	1 020 191	715 848	304 342	320 456	317 643	186 417	126 529	4 697	2 822
2004	1 572 971	1 159 233	806 161	353 072	413 739	410 917	250 606	157 313	2 998	2 890
2005	1 816 723	1 281 460	892 337	389 122	535 263	532 373	294 538	235 120	2 715	2 883
2006	2 133 905	1 451 684	1 015 812	435 873	682 221	679 338	324 816	352 122	2 400	2 971
2007	2 462 099	1 643 168	1 138 384	504 784	818 931	815 960	363 247	450 480	2 233	3 044
2008	2 591 233	1 826 596	1 276 994	549 602	764 637	761 593	370 747	385 940	4 906	2 956
2009	2 115 929	1 554 718	1 045 543	509 175	561 211	558 256	301 842	251 623	4 790	
2006										
1st quarter	503 350	348 137	243 445	104 692	155 212	154 489	77 601	76 298	590	723
2nd quarter	528 763	359 303	252 086	107 217	169 459	168 732	81 748	86 397	587	727
3rd quarter	540 184	364 612	255 925	108 687	175 572	174 859	81 997	92 268	594	713
4th quarter	561 608	379 631	264 355	115 276	181 978	181 258	83 470	97 159	629	720
2007										
1st quarter	574 689	387 708	269 538	118 170	186 981	186 249	83 011	102 679	559	731
2nd quarter	600 300	397 988	277 655	120 333	202 312	201 575	88 628	112 373	574	737
3rd quarter	631 854	418 349	289 160	129 189	213 505	212 760	92 993	119 221	546	745
4th quarter	655 255	439 123	302 031	137 092	216 132	215 376	98 615	116 207	554	757
2008										
1st quarter	654 217	451 290	315 637	135 653	202 927	202 163	98 426	103 024	713	764
2nd quarter	671 886	473 090	332 876	140 214	198 796	198 028	100 538	96 756	735	767
3rd quarter	673 383	478 064	337 912	140 152	195 319	194 554	96 047	97 196	1 311	765
4th quarter	591 747	424 151	290 569	133 583	167 596	166 847	75 736	88 964	2 147	749
2009										
1st quarter	507 291	372 024	249 108	122 917	135 267	134 526	63 079	68 995	2 452	741
2nd quarter	506 204	371 217	245 868	125 349	134 987	134 249	71 476	61 673	1 100	738
3rd quarter	535 114	392 800	263 645	129 155	142 315	141 584	80 810	60 021	753	731
4th quarter	567 322	418 679	286 923	131 756	148 642	147 896	86 477	60 934	485	746

. . . = Not available.

Table 7-6. U.S. International Transactions—*Continued*

(Millions of dollars, seasonally adjusted.)

Year and quarter	Current account—*Continued*									
	Imports of goods and services and income payments [1]									
		Imports of goods and services	Imports of goods	Imports of services	Income payments					Compensation of employees
	Total				Total	Income payments on foreign-owned assets in the U.S.				
						Total	Direct investment payments	Other private payments	U.S. government payments	
1960	-23 670	-22 432	-14 758	-7 674	-1 238	-1 238	-394	-511	-332	. . .
1961	-23 453	-22 208	-14 537	-7 671	-1 245	-1 245	-432	-535	-278	. . .
1962	-25 676	-24 352	-16 260	-8 092	-1 324	-1 324	-399	-586	-339	. . .
1963	-26 970	-25 410	-17 048	-8 362	-1 560	-1 560	-459	-701	-401	. . .
1964	-29 102	-27 319	-18 700	-8 619	-1 783	-1 783	-529	-802	-453	. . .
1965	-32 708	-30 621	-21 510	-9 111	-2 088	-2 088	-657	-942	-489	. . .
1966	-38 468	-35 987	-25 493	-10 494	-2 481	-2 481	-711	-1 221	-549	. . .
1967	-41 476	-38 729	-26 866	-11 863	-2 747	-2 747	-821	-1 328	-598	. . .
1968	-48 671	-45 293	-32 991	-12 302	-3 378	-3 378	-876	-1 800	-702	. . .
1969	-53 998	-49 129	-35 807	-13 322	-4 869	-4 869	-848	-3 244	-777	. . .
1970	-59 901	-54 386	-39 866	-14 520	-5 515	-5 515	-875	-3 617	-1 024	. . .
1971	-66 414	-60 979	-45 579	-15 400	-5 435	-5 435	-1 164	-2 428	-1 844	. . .
1972	-79 237	-72 665	-55 797	-16 868	-6 572	-6 572	-1 284	-2 604	-2 684	. . .
1973	-98 997	-89 342	-70 499	-18 843	-9 655	-9 655	-1 610	-4 209	-3 836	. . .
1974	-137 274	-125 190	-103 811	-21 379	-12 084	-12 084	-1 331	-6 491	-4 262	. . .
1975	-132 745	-120 181	-98 185	-21 996	-12 564	-12 564	-2 234	-5 788	-4 542	. . .
1976	-162 109	-148 798	-124 228	-24 570	-13 311	-13 311	-3 110	-5 681	-4 520	. . .
1977	-193 764	-179 547	-151 907	-27 640	-14 217	-14 217	-2 834	-5 841	-5 542	. . .
1978	-229 870	-208 191	-176 002	-32 189	-21 680	-21 680	-4 211	-8 795	-8 674	. . .
1979	-281 657	-248 696	-212 007	-36 689	-32 961	-32 961	-6 357	-15 481	-11 122	. . .
1980	-333 774	-291 241	-249 750	-41 491	-42 532	-42 532	-8 635	-21 214	-12 684	. . .
1981	-364 196	-310 570	-265 067	-45 503	-53 626	-53 626	-6 898	-29 415	-17 313	. . .
1982	-355 975	-299 391	-247 642	-51 749	-56 583	-56 583	-2 114	-35 187	-19 282	. . .
1983	-377 488	-323 874	-268 901	-54 973	-53 614	-53 614	-4 120	-30 501	-18 993	. . .
1984	-473 923	-400 166	-332 418	-67 748	-73 756	-73 756	-8 443	-44 158	-21 155	. . .
1985	-483 769	-410 950	-338 088	-72 862	-72 819	-72 819	-6 945	-42 745	-23 129	. . .
1986	-530 142	-448 572	-368 425	-80 147	-81 571	-78 893	-6 856	-47 412	-24 625	-2 678
1987	-594 443	-500 552	-409 765	-90 787	-93 891	-91 553	-7 676	-57 659	-26 218	-2 338
1988	-663 741	-545 715	-447 189	-98 526	-118 026	-116 179	-12 150	-72 314	-31 715	-1 847
1989	-721 607	-580 144	-477 665	-102 479	-141 463	-139 177	-7 045	-93 768	-38 364	-2 286
1990	-759 290	-616 097	-498 438	-117 659	-143 192	-139 728	-3 450	-95 508	-40 770	-3 464
1991	-734 564	-609 479	-491 020	-118 459	-125 085	-121 059	2 265	-82 452	-40 872	-4 026
1992	-765 626	-656 094	-536 528	-119 566	-109 531	-104 779	-2 189	-63 509	-39 081	-4 752
1993	-823 914	-713 174	-589 394	-123 780	-110 741	-105 609	-7 943	-58 290	-39 376	-5 132
1994	-951 122	-801 747	-668 690	-133 057	-149 375	-143 423	-22 150	-77 081	-44 192	-5 952
1995	-1 080 124	-890 771	-749 374	-141 397	-189 353	-183 090	-30 318	-97 149	-55 623	-6 263
1996	-1 159 478	-955 667	-803 113	-152 554	-203 811	-197 511	-33 093	-97 800	-66 618	-6 300
1997	-1 286 921	-1 042 726	-876 794	-165 932	-244 195	-237 529	-42 950	-112 878	-81 701	-6 666
1998	-1 356 868	-1 099 314	-918 637	-180 677	-257 554	-250 560	-38 418	-127 988	-84 154	-6 994
1999	-1 511 011	-1 230 974	-1 031 784	-199 190	-280 037	-272 082	-53 437	-138 120	-80 525	-7 955
2000	-1 780 296	-1 450 432	-1 226 684	-223 748	-329 864	-322 345	-56 910	-180 918	-84 517	-7 519
2001	-1 629 475	-1 370 400	-1 148 609	-221 791	-259 075	-250 989	-12 783	-159 825	-78 381	-8 086
2002	-1 652 615	-1 399 071	-1 168 002	-231 069	-253 544	-245 164	-43 244	-127 012	-74 908	-8 380
2003	-1 790 372	-1 515 225	-1 264 860	-250 365	-275 147	-266 635	-73 750	-119 051	-73 834	-8 512
2004	-2 115 739	-1 769 220	-1 477 996	-291 224	-346 519	-337 556	-99 754	-155 266	-82 536	-8 963
2005	-2 459 633	-1 996 728	-1 683 188	-313 540	-462 905	-453 615	-121 333	-228 408	-103 874	-9 290
2006	-2 846 179	-2 212 043	-1 863 072	-348 972	-634 136	-624 646	-150 770	-338 897	-134 979	-9 490
2007	-3 072 675	-2 344 590	-1 969 375	-375 215	-728 085	-718 019	-126 532	-427 159	-164 328	-10 066
2008	-3 168 938	-2 522 532	-2 117 245	-405 287	-646 406	-636 043	-120 862	-349 871	-165 310	-10 364
2009	-2 405 555	-1 933 347	-1 562 588	-370 759	-472 208	-462 163	-95 045	-235 015	-132 103	-10 045
2006										
1st quarter	-681 005	-539 759	-454 618	-85 141	-141 245	-138 888	-34 122	-74 281	-30 485	-2 357
2nd quarter	-707 132	-550 475	-463 797	-86 679	-156 657	-154 306	-37 942	-83 444	-32 920	-2 351
3rd quarter	-730 097	-563 902	-476 361	-87 542	-166 195	-163 849	-41 212	-88 005	-34 632	-2 346
4th quarter	-727 946	-557 906	-468 296	-89 610	-170 039	-167 603	-37 494	-93 167	-36 942	-2 436
2007										
1st quarter	-742 980	-565 746	-475 571	-90 175	-177 234	-174 806	-36 336	-99 414	-39 056	-2 428
2nd quarter	-765 079	-575 548	-483 294	-92 253	-189 531	-187 016	-37 525	-108 090	-41 401	-2 515
3rd quarter	-774 912	-589 814	-494 075	-95 739	-185 098	-182 574	-29 809	-111 051	-41 714	-2 524
4th quarter	-789 703	-613 483	-516 435	-97 048	-176 220	-173 623	-22 862	-108 604	-42 157	-2 597
2008										
1st quarter	-800 185	-633 943	-534 482	-99 461	-166 241	-163 652	-27 269	-94 416	-41 967	-2 590
2nd quarter	-828 458	-655 937	-554 372	-101 565	-172 521	-169 951	-40 071	-87 061	-42 819	-2 571
3rd quarter	-825 200	-664 006	-559 002	-105 004	-161 194	-158 618	-29 050	-88 504	-41 064	-2 576
4th quarter	-715 096	-568 646	-469 389	-99 257	-146 450	-143 823	-24 473	-79 890	-39 460	-2 627
2009										
1st quarter	-581 287	-464 244	-373 107	-91 137	-117 044	-114 496	-11 965	-66 038	-36 493	-2 548
2nd quarter	-570 691	-452 293	-361 318	-90 975	-118 399	-115 911	-23 834	-58 782	-33 295	-2 488
3rd quarter	-602 438	-489 183	-395 746	-93 437	-113 255	-110 757	-24 045	-55 223	-31 489	-2 498
4th quarter	-651 138	-527 627	-432 418	-95 209	-123 511	-121 000	-35 202	-54 972	-30 826	-2 510

[1]A minus sign indicates imports of goods and services or payments of incomes.
. . . = Not available.

Table 7-6. U.S. International Transactions—*Continued*

(Millions of dollars, seasonally adjusted.)

Year and quarter	Current account—*Continued*				Capital account transactions, net [2]	Financial account						
	Unilateral current transfers, net [2]					U.S.-owned assets abroad, net, excluding financial derivatives [2]						
	Total	U.S. government		Private remittances and other transfers		Total	U.S. official reserve assets, net					
		Grants	Pensions and other transfers				Total	Gold	Special drawing rights	Reserve position in the IMF	Foreign currencies
1960	-4 062	-3 367	-273	-423	. . .	-4 099	2 145	1 703	0	442	0
1961	-4 127	-3 320	-373	-434	. . .	-5 538	607	857	0	-135	-115
1962	-4 277	-3 453	-347	-477	. . .	-4 174	1 535	890	0	626	19
1963	-4 392	-3 479	-339	-575	. . .	-7 270	378	461	0	29	-112
1964	-4 240	-3 227	-399	-614	. . .	-9 560	171	125	0	266	-220
1965	-4 583	-3 444	-463	-677	. . .	-5 716	1 225	1 665	0	-94	-346
1966	-4 955	-3 802	-499	-655	. . .	-7 321	570	571	0	537	-538
1967	-5 294	-3 844	-571	-879	. . .	-9 757	53	1 170	0	-94	-1 023
1968	-5 629	-4 256	-537	-836	. . .	-10 977	-870	1 173	0	-870	-1 173
1969	-5 735	-4 259	-537	-939	. . .	-11 585	-1 179	-967	0	-1 034	822
1970	-6 156	-4 449	-611	-1 096	. . .	-9 337	2 481	787	-851	389	2 156
1971	-7 402	-5 589	-696	-1 117	. . .	-12 475	2 349	866	-249	1 350	382
1972	-8 544	-6 665	-770	-1 109	. . .	-14 497	-4	547	-703	153	-1
1973	-6 913	-4 748	-915	-1 250	. . .	-22 874	158	0	9	-33	182
1974	-9 249	-7 293	-939	-1 017	. . .	-34 745	-1 467	0	-172	-1 265	-30
1975	-7 075	-5 101	-1 068	-906	. . .	-39 703	-849	0	-66	-466	-317
1976	-5 686	-3 519	-1 250	-917	. . .	-51 269	-2 558	0	-78	-2 212	-268
1977	-5 226	-2 990	-1 378	-859	. . .	-34 785	-375	-118	-121	-294	158
1978	-5 788	-3 412	-1 532	-844	. . .	-61 130	732	-65	1 249	4 231	-4 683
1979	-6 593	-4 015	-1 658	-920	. . .	-66 054	-1 133	-65	-1 136	-189	257
1980	-8 349	-5 486	-1 818	-1 044	. . .	-86 967	-8 155	0	-16	-1 667	-6 472
1981	-11 702	-5 145	-2 041	-4 516	. . .	-114 147	-5 175	*	-1 823	-2 491	-861
1982	-16 544	-6 087	-2 251	-8 207	199	-127 882	-4 965	0	-1 371	-2 552	-1 041
1983	-17 310	-6 469	-2 207	-8 635	209	-66 373	-1 196	0	-66	-4 434	3 304
1984	-20 335	-8 696	-2 159	-9 479	235	-40 376	-3 131	0	-979	-995	-1 156
1985	-21 998	-11 268	-2 138	-8 593	315	-44 752	-3 858	0	-897	908	-3 869
1986	-24 132	-11 883	-2 372	-9 877	301	-111 723	312	0	-246	1 501	-942
1987	-23 265	-10 309	-2 409	-10 548	365	-79 296	9 149	0	-509	2 070	7 588
1988	-25 274	-10 537	-2 709	-12 028	493	-106 573	-3 912	0	127	1 025	-5 064
1989	-26 169	-10 860	-2 775	-12 534	336	-175 383	-25 293	0	-535	471	-25 229
1990	-26 654	-10 359	-3 224	-13 070	-6 579	-81 234	-2 158	0	-192	731	-2 697
1991	9 904	29 193	-3 775	-15 514	-4 479	-64 389	5 763	0	-176	-366	6 307
1992	-36 636	-16 320	-4 043	-16 273	978	-74 410	3 901	0	2 316	-2 692	4 277
1993	-39 811	-17 035	-4 104	-18 672	-1 299	-200 551	-1 379	0	-537	-43	-798
1994	-40 265	-14 978	-4 556	-20 731	-1 723	-178 937	5 346	0	-441	494	5 293
1995	-38 074	-11 190	-3 451	-23 433	-927	-352 264	-9 742	0	-808	-2 466	-6 468
1996	-43 017	-15 401	-4 466	-23 150	-735	-413 409	6 668	0	370	-1 280	7 578
1997	-45 062	-12 472	-4 191	-28 399	-1 027	-485 475	-1 010	0	-350	-3 575	2 915
1998	-53 187	-13 270	-4 305	-35 612	-766	-353 829	-6 783	0	-147	-5 119	-1 517
1999	-50 428	-13 774	-4 406	-32 248	-4 939	-504 062	8 747	0	10	5 484	3 253
2000	-58 645	-16 714	-4 705	-37 226	-1 010	-560 523	-290	0	-722	2 308	-1 876
2001	-64 487	-11 517	-5 798	-47 172	11 922	-382 616	-4 911	0	-630	-3 600	-681
2002	-64 948	-17 097	-5 125	-42 726	-1 470	-294 646	-3 681	0	-475	-2 632	-574
2003	-71 794	-22 173	-5 341	-44 280	-3 480	-325 424	1 523	0	601	1 494	-572
2004	-88 362	-23 823	-6 264	-58 275	1 323	-1 000 870	2 805	0	-398	3 826	-623
2005	-105 772	-33 647	-6 303	-65 822	11 344	-546 631	14 096	0	4 511	10 200	-615
2006	-91 273	-27 733	-6 508	-57 032	-3 906	-1 285 729	2 374	0	-223	3 331	-734
2007	-115 996	-34 437	-7 323	-74 236	-1 895	-1 472 126	-122	0	-154	1 021	-989
2008	-128 363	-36 003	-8 390	-83 970	953	-106	-4 848	0	-106	-3 473	-1 269
2009	-130 243	-40 930	-9 359	-79 955	-2 859	-237 454	-52 256	0	-48 230	-3 357	-669
2006											
1st quarter	-20 995	-5 742	-1 614	-13 639	-1 721	-387 689	513	0	-67	729	-149
2nd quarter	-23 708	-7 407	-1 627	-14 674	-1 017	-223 953	-560	0	-51	-351	-158
3rd quarter	-24 876	-7 939	-1 620	-15 317	-539	-295 389	1 006	0	-54	1 275	-215
4th quarter	-21 693	-6 645	-1 647	-13 401	-629	-378 698	1 415	0	-51	1 678	-212
2007											
1st quarter	-30 807	-10 747	-1 805	-18 255	-549	-485 867	-72	0	-43	212	-241
2nd quarter	-25 752	-5 930	-1 834	-17 988	-124	-545 158	26	0	-39	294	-229
3rd quarter	-28 557	-7 366	-1 837	-19 354	-625	-192 530	-54	0	-37	230	-247
4th quarter	-30 883	-10 394	-1 849	-18 640	-597	-248 571	-22	0	-35	285	-272
2008											
1st quarter	-33 330	-10 335	-2 082	-20 913	-637	-251 501	-276	0	-29	112	-359
2nd quarter	-31 147	-7 893	-2 097	-21 157	-682	107 343	-1 267	0	-22	-955	-290
3rd quarter	-32 361	-8 568	-2 100	-21 693	2 967	29 322	-179	0	-30	256	-405
4th quarter	-31 527	-9 207	-2 113	-20 207	-695	114 730	-3 126	0	-25	-2 886	-215
2009											
1st quarter	-30 185	-8 342	-2 300	-19 543	-710	94 092	-982	0	-15	-754	-213
2nd quarter	-33 256	-10 841	-2 342	-20 074	-719	36 762	-3 632	0	-8	-3 485	-139
3rd quarter	-35 025	-12 743	-2 353	-19 929	-718	-269 192	-49 021	0	-47 720	-1 098	-203
4th quarter	-31 777	-9 004	-2 364	-20 408	-713	-99 116	1 379	0	-487	1 980	-114

[2]A minus sign indicates increases in U.S. official assets or financial outflows.
. . . = Not available.
* = Less than $500,000 (+/-).

Table 7-6. U.S. International Transactions—*Continued*

(Millions of dollars, seasonally adjusted.)

Year and quarter	Financial account—*Continued*								
	U.S.-owned assets abroad, net, excluding financial derivatives ³—*Continued*								
	U.S. government assets other than official reserve assets, net				U.S. private assets, net				
								U.S. claims	
	Total	U.S. credits and other long-term assets	Repayments on U.S. credits and other long-term assets	U.S. foreign currency holdings and short-term assets, net	Total	Direct investment	Foreign securities	On unaffiliated foreigners reported by U.S. banks and securities brokers	Reported by U.S. banks, and securities brokers
1960	-1 100	-1 214	642	-528	-5 144	-2 940	-663	-394	-1 148
1961	-910	-1 928	1 279	-261	-5 235	-2 653	-762	-558	-1 261
1962	-1 085	-2 128	1 288	-245	-4 623	-2 851	-969	-354	-450
1963	-1 662	-2 204	988	-447	-5 986	-3 483	-1 105	157	-1 556
1964	-1 680	-2 382	720	-19	-8 050	-3 760	-677	-1 108	-2 505
1965	-1 605	-2 463	874	-16	-5 336	-5 011	-759	341	93
1966	-1 543	-2 513	1 235	-265	-6 347	-5 418	-720	-442	233
1967	-2 423	-3 638	1 005	209	-7 386	-4 805	-1 308	-779	-495
1968	-2 274	-3 722	1 386	62	-7 833	-5 295	-1 569	-1 203	233
1969	-2 200	-3 489	1 200	89	-8 206	-5 960	-1 549	-126	-570
1970	-1 589	-3 293	1 721	-16	-10 229	-7 590	-1 076	-596	-967
1971	-1 884	-4 181	2 115	182	-12 940	-7 618	-1 113	-1 229	-2 980
1972	-1 568	-3 819	2 086	165	-12 925	-7 747	-618	-1 054	-3 506
1973	-2 644	-4 638	2 596	-602	-20 388	-11 353	-671	-2 383	-5 980
1974	366	-5 001	4 826	541	-33 643	-9 052	-1 854	-3 221	-19 516
1975	-3 474	-5 941	2 475	-9	-35 380	-14 244	-6 247	-1 357	-13 532
1976	-4 214	-6 943	2 596	133	-44 498	-11 949	-8 885	-2 296	-21 368
1977	-3 693	-6 445	2 719	33	-30 717	-11 890	-5 460	-1 940	-11 427
1978	-4 660	-7 470	2 941	-131	-57 202	-16 056	-3 626	-3 853	-33 667
1979	-3 746	-7 697	3 926	25	-61 176	-25 222	-4 726	-5 014	-26 213
1980	-5 162	-9 860	4 456	242	-73 651	-19 222	-3 568	-4 023	-46 838
1981	-5 097	-9 674	4 413	164	-103 875	-9 624	-5 699	-4 377	-84 175
1982	-6 131	-10 063	4 292	-360	-116 786	-4 556	-7 983	6 823	-111 070
1983	-5 006	-9 967	5 012	-51	-60 172	-12 528	-6 762	-10 954	-29 928
1984	-5 489	-9 599	4 490	-379	-31 757	-16 407	-4 756	533	-11 127
1985	-2 821	-7 657	4 719	117	-38 074	-18 927	-7 481	-10 342	-1 323
1986	-2 022	-9 084	6 089	973	-110 014	-23 995	-4 271	-21 773	-59 975
1987	1 006	-6 506	7 625	-113	-89 450	-35 034	-5 251	-7 046	-42 119
1988	2 967	-7 680	10 370	277	-105 628	-22 528	-7 980	-21 193	-53 927
1989	1 233	-5 608	6 725	115	-151 323	-43 447	-22 070	-27 646	-58 160
1990	2 317	-8 410	10 856	-130	-81 393	-37 183	-28 765	-27 824	12 379
1991	2 923	-12 880	16 777	-974	-73 075	-37 889	-45 673	11 097	-610
1992	-1 667	-7 408	5 807	-66	-76 644	-48 266	-49 166	-387	21 175
1993	-351	-6 311	6 270	-310	-198 823	-83 951	-146 253	766	30 615
1994	-390	-5 383	5 088	-95	-183 893	-80 167	-63 190	-36 336	-4 200
1995	-984	-4 859	4 125	-250	-341 538	-98 750	-122 394	-45 286	-75 108
1996	-989	-5 025	3 930	106	-419 088	-91 885	-149 315	-86 333	-91 555
1997	68	-5 417	5 438	47	-484 533	-104 803	-116 852	-121 760	-141 118
1998	-422	-4 678	4 111	145	-346 624	-142 644	-130 204	-38 204	-35 572
1999	2 750	-6 175	9 559	-634	-515 559	-224 934	-122 236	-97 704	-70 685
2000	-941	-5 182	4 265	-24	-559 292	-159 212	-127 908	-138 790	-133 382
2001	-486	-4 431	3 873	72	-377 219	-142 349	-90 644	-8 520	-135 706
2002	345	-5 251	5 701	-105	-291 310	-154 460	-48 568	-50 022	-38 260
2003	537	-7 279	7 981	-165	-327 484	-149 564	-146 722	-18 184	-13 014
2004	1 710	-3 044	4 716	38	-1 005 385	-316 223	-170 549	-152 566	-366 047
2005	5 539	-2 255	5 603	2 191	-566 266	-36 235	-251 199	-71 207	-207 625
2006	5 346	-2 992	8 329	9	-1 293 449	-244 922	-365 129	-181 299	-502 099
2007	-22 273	-2 475	4 104	-23 902	-1 449 731	-398 597	-366 524	-40 517	-644 093
2008	-529 615	-2 202	2 354	-529 766	534 357	-332 012	60 761	372 229	433 379
2009	541 776	-3 768	2 117	543 426	-726 974	-220 972	-221 539	135 836	-420 299
2006									
1st quarter	1 049	-1 517	2 558	8	-389 251	-58 801	-75 689	-41 792	-212 969
2nd quarter	1 765	-376	2 147	-6	-225 158	-35 160	-80 203	-48 226	-61 569
3rd quarter	1 570	-592	2 170	-8	-297 965	-72 149	-72 552	-57 478	-95 786
4th quarter	962	-507	1 454	15	-381 075	-78 812	-136 685	-33 803	-131 775
2007									
1st quarter	445	-608	1 091	-38	-486 240	-99 975	-122 024	-42 947	-221 294
2nd quarter	-596	-1 405	687	122	-544 588	-94 415	-107 064	-133 201	-209 908
3rd quarter	623	-182	780	25	-193 099	-65 800	-113 826	75 747	-89 220
4th quarter	-22 744	-279	1 546	-24 011	-225 805	-138 408	-23 610	59 884	-123 671
2008									
1st quarter	3 268	-179	490	2 957	-254 493	-89 792	-47 870	116 232	-233 063
2nd quarter	-41 592	-1 106	497	-40 983	150 202	-103 619	-40 566	64 906	229 481
3rd quarter	-225 997	-475	695	-226 217	255 498	-54 115	79 182	87 352	143 079
4th quarter	-265 293	-442	672	-265 523	383 150	-84 486	70 015	103 739	293 882
2009									
1st quarter	244 102	-240	484	243 858	-149 028	-40 903	-36 201	17 477	-89 401
2nd quarter	193 750	-1 947	432	195 265	-153 356	-48 078	-92 589	14 519	-27 208
3rd quarter	57 736	-616	534	57 818	-277 907	-68 537	-46 967	81 700	-244 103
4th quarter	46 187	-965	667	46 485	-146 682	-63 453	-45 782	22 140	-59 587

³A minus sign indicates increases in U.S. official assets or financial outflows.

Table 7-6. U.S. International Transactions—*Continued*

(Millions of dollars, seasonally adjusted.)

Year and quarter	Financial account—*Continued*												
	Foreign-owned assets in the United States, net, excluding financial derivatives [4]												
	Foreign official assets in the United States, net							Other foreign assets in the United States, net				
	Total	Total	U.S. government securities			Other U.S. govern-ment liabilities	U.S. liabilities reported by U.S. banks and securities brokers	Other foreign official assets	Total	Direct investment	U.S. Treasury securities	U.S. securities other than Treasury securities	U.S. currency
			Total	U.S. Treasury securities	Other								
1960	2 294	1 473	655	655	0	215	603	0	821	315	-364	282	...
1961	2 705	765	233	233	0	25	508	0	1 939	311	151	324	...
1962	1 911	1 270	1 409	1 410	-1	152	-291	0	641	346	-66	134	...
1963	3 217	1 986	816	803	12	429	742	0	1 231	231	-149	287	...
1964	3 643	1 660	432	434	-2	298	930	0	1 983	322	-146	-85	...
1965	742	134	-141	-134	-7	65	210	0	607	415	-131	-358	...
1966	3 661	-672	-1 527	-1 548	21	113	742	0	4 333	425	-356	906	...
1967	7 379	3 451	2 261	2 222	39	83	1 106	0	3 928	698	-135	1 016	...
1968	9 928	-774	-769	-798	29	-15	10	0	10 703	807	136	4 414	...
1969	12 702	-1 301	-2 343	-2 269	-74	251	792	0	14 002	1 263	-68	3 130	...
1970	7 226	7 775	9 439	9 411	28	411	-2 075	0	-550	1 464	81	2 189	...
1971	23 687	27 596	26 570	26 578	-8	207	819	0	-3 909	367	-24	2 289	...
1972	22 171	11 185	8 470	8 213	257	892	1 638	185	10 986	949	-39	4 507	...
1973	18 388	6 026	641	59	582	936	4 126	323	12 362	2 800	-216	4 041	...
1974	35 227	10 546	4 172	3 270	902	301	5 818	254	24 682	4 760	697	378	986
1975	16 870	7 027	5 563	4 658	905	1 517	-2 158	2 104	9 843	2 603	2 590	2 503	1 200
1976	37 839	17 693	9 892	9 319	573	4 627	969	2 205	20 147	4 347	2 783	1 284	1 321
1977	52 770	36 816	32 538	30 230	2 308	1 400	773	2 105	15 954	3 728	534	2 437	1 451
1978	66 275	33 678	24 221	23 555	666	2 476	5 551	1 430	32 597	7 897	2 178	2 254	2 239
1979	40 693	-12 526	-21 972	-22 435	463	1 099	7 213	1 135	53 218	11 877	4 060	1 351	1 702
1980	62 037	16 649	11 895	9 708	2 187	1 767	-159	3 145	45 388	16 918	2 645	5 457	2 773
1981	85 684	6 053	6 322	5 019	1 303	755	-3 670	2 646	79 631	25 195	2 927	6 905	1 559
1982	95 056	3 593	5 085	5 779	-694	605	-1 747	-350	91 464	12 635	7 027	6 085	2 467
1983	87 399	5 845	6 496	6 972	-476	602	545	-1 798	81 554	10 372	8 689	8 164	4 105
1984	116 048	3 140	4 703	4 690	13	739	555	-2 857	112 908	24 468	23 001	12 568	2 396
1985	144 231	-1 119	-1 139	-838	-301	844	645	-1 469	145 349	19 742	20 433	50 962	3 316
1986	228 330	35 648	33 150	34 364	-1 214	2 195	1 187	-884	192 681	35 420	3 809	70 969	2 421
1987	247 100	45 387	44 802	43 238	1 564	-2 326	3 918	-1 007	201 713	58 470	-7 643	42 120	3 866
1988	244 833	39 758	43 050	41 741	1 309	-467	-319	-2 506	205 075	57 735	20 239	26 353	4 111
1989	222 777	8 503	1 532	149	1 383	160	4 976	1 835	214 274	68 274	29 618	38 767	3 749
1990	139 357	33 910	30 243	29 576	667	1 868	3 385	-1 586	105 447	48 494	-2 534	1 592	16 586
1991	108 221	17 388	16 147	14 846	1 301	1 367	-1 484	1 359	90 833	23 171	18 826	35 144	12 813
1992	168 349	40 477	22 403	18 454	3 949	2 191	16 571	-688	127 872	19 823	37 131	30 043	11 086
1993	279 758	71 753	53 014	48 952	4 062	1 313	14 841	2 585	208 005	51 363	24 381	80 092	16 618
1994	303 174	39 583	36 827	30 750	6 077	1 564	3 665	-2 473	263 591	46 121	34 274	56 971	20 585
1995	435 102	109 880	72 712	68 977	3 735	-105	34 008	3 265	325 222	57 776	91 544	77 249	8 840
1996	547 585	126 724	120 679	115 671	5 008	-982	5 704	1 323	421 161	86 502	147 022	103 272	14 151
1997	704 452	19 036	-2 161	-6 690	4 529	-881	22 286	-208	685 416	105 603	130 435	161 409	22 425
1998	420 794	-19 903	-3 589	-9 921	6 332	-3 326	-9 501	-3 487	440 697	179 045	28 581	156 315	13 847
1999	742 210	43 543	32 527	12 177	20 350	-2 863	12 964	915	698 667	289 444	-44 497	298 834	24 407
2000	1 038 224	42 758	35 710	-5 199	40 909	-1 825	5 746	3 127	995 466	321 274	-69 983	459 989	-3 357
2001	782 870	28 059	54 620	33 700	20 920	-2 309	-29 978	5 726	754 811	167 021	-14 378	393 885	23 794
2002	795 161	115 945	90 971	60 466	30 505	137	21 221	3 616	679 216	84 372	100 403	283 299	18 861
2003	858 303	278 069	224 874	184 931	39 943	-723	48 643	5 275	580 234	63 750	91 455	220 705	10 591
2004	1 533 201	397 755	314 941	273 279	41 662	-134	69 245	13 703	1 135 446	145 966	93 608	381 493	13 301
2005	1 247 347	259 268	213 334	112 841	100 493	-421	26 260	20 095	988 079	112 638	132 300	450 386	8 447
2006	2 065 169	487 939	428 401	208 564	219 837	2 816	22 365	34 357	1 577 230	243 151	-58 229	683 245	2 227
2007	2 129 460	480 949	269 897	98 432	171 465	5 342	109 019	96 691	1 648 511	275 758	66 807	605 652	-10 675
2008	534 071	487 021	543 498	477 652	65 846	8 626	-153 443	88 340	47 050	319 737	196 619	-126 737	29 187
2009	435 236	447 575	451 108	490 125	-39 017	58 461	-71 588	9 594	-12 339	152 086	37 620	-6 614	12 632
2006													
1st quarter	545 648	130 427	117 579	65 573	52 006	-45	2 394	10 499	415 221	44 357	-25 919	167 589	35
2nd quarter	407 652	127 303	71 299	26 391	44 908	760	43 366	11 878	280 349	65 611	-24 024	139 681	-2 345
3rd quarter	525 441	121 843	121 907	60 641	61 266	913	-7 871	6 894	403 598	55 495	-21 593	197 877	-2 321
4th quarter	586 428	108 366	117 616	55 959	61 657	1 188	-15 524	5 086	478 062	77 688	13 307	178 098	6 858
2007													
1st quarter	700 961	165 837	121 922	40 619	81 303	366	32 614	10 935	535 124	21 016	42 127	183 460	-6 165
2nd quarter	737 457	88 331	61 531	1 500	60 031	-69	15 575	11 294	649 126	83 683	-13 467	310 303	-1 635
3rd quarter	278 424	47 674	12 420	-5 602	18 022	913	8 870	25 471	230 750	97 944	16 865	-9 829	655
4th quarter	412 618	179 107	74 024	61 915	12 109	4 132	51 960	48 991	233 511	73 115	21 282	121 718	-3 530
2008													
1st quarter	426 058	208 646	185 239	106 005	79 234	1 645	-24 173	45 935	217 412	59 473	16 127	-15 179	-6 750
2nd quarter	2 003	178 826	169 365	76 220	93 145	2 439	-29 697	36 719	-176 823	100 706	18 947	19 983	230
3rd quarter	117 897	115 573	105 920	116 479	-10 559	1 642	9 797	-1 786	2 324	62 755	80 049	-102 512	5 845
4th quarter	-11 888	-16 024	82 974	178 948	-95 974	2 900	-109 370	7 472	4 136	96 802	81 496	-29 029	29 862
2009													
1st quarter	-67 583	70 892	118 565	118 309	256	2 720	-51 891	1 498	-138 475	24 025	53 716	-55 992	11 816
2nd quarter	14 648	124 299	120 661	123 713	-3 052	1 228	-732	3 142	-109 651	37 009	-22 755	13 917	-1 935
3rd quarter	343 388	123 786	94 067	123 675	-29 608	53 304	-27 188	3 603	219 602	47 472	-8 896	28 732	4 179
4th quarter	144 782	128 598	117 815	124 428	-6 613	1 209	8 223	1 351	16 184	43 579	15 555	6 729	-1 428

[4] A minus sign indicates financial outflows or a decrease in foreign official assets in the United States.
. . . = Not available.

Table 7-6. U.S. International Transactions—*Continued*

(Millions of dollars, seasonally adjusted.)

Year and quarter	Foreign-owned assets in the United States, net⁴—*Cont.* Other foreign assets in the United States, net—*Cont.* U.S. liabilities To unaffiliated foreigners reported by U.S. nonbanking concerns	Reported by U.S. banks and securities brokers	Financial derivatives, net	Statistical discrepancy ⁵ Total	Seasonal adjustment discrepancy	Balance on goods	Balance on services	Balance on goods and services	Balance on income	Balance on goods, services, and income	Unilateral current transfers, net	Balance on current account
1960	-90	678	...	-1 019	0	4 892	-1 385	3 508	3 379	6 887	-4 062	2 824
1961	226	928	...	-989	0	5 571	-1 376	4 195	3 755	7 950	-4 127	3 822
1962	-110	336	...	-1 124	0	4 521	-1 151	3 370	4 294	7 664	-4 277	3 387
1963	-37	898	...	-360	0	5 224	-1 014	4 210	4 596	8 806	-4 392	4 414
1964	75	1 818	...	-907	0	6 801	-779	6 022	5 041	11 063	-4 240	6 823
1965	178	503	...	-457	0	4 951	-287	4 664	5 350	10 014	-4 583	5 431
1966	476	2 882	...	629	0	3 817	-877	2 940	5 047	7 987	-4 955	3 031
1967	584	1 765	...	-205	0	3 800	-1 196	2 604	5 274	7 878	-5 294	2 583
1968	1 475	3 871	...	438	0	635	-385	250	5 990	6 240	-5 629	611
1969	792	8 886	...	-1 516	0	607	-516	91	6 044	6 135	-5 735	399
1970	2 014	-6 298	...	-219	0	2 603	-349	2 254	6 233	8 487	-6 156	2 331
1971	369	-6 911	...	-9 779	0	-2 260	957	-1 303	7 272	5 969	-7 402	-1 433
1972	815	4 754	...	-1 879	0	-6 416	973	-5 443	8 192	2 749	-8 544	-5 795
1973	1 035	4 702	...	-2 654	0	911	989	1 900	12 153	14 053	-6 913	7 140
1974	1 844	16 017	...	-2 444	0	-5 505	1 213	-4 292	15 503	11 211	-9 249	1 962
1975	319	628	...	4 717	0	8 903	3 501	12 404	12 787	25 191	-7 075	18 116
1976	-578	10 990	...	9 134	0	-9 483	3 401	-6 082	16 063	9 981	-5 686	4 295
1977	1 086	6 719	...	-3 650	0	-31 091	3 845	-27 246	18 137	-9 109	-5 226	-14 335
1978	1 889	16 141	...	9 997	0	-33 927	4 164	-29 763	20 408	-9 355	-5 788	-15 143
1979	1 621	32 607	...	25 647	0	-27 568	3 003	-24 565	30 873	6 308	-6 593	-285
1980	6 852	10 743	...	22 613	0	-25 500	6 093	-19 407	30 073	10 666	-8 349	2 317
1981	917	42 128	...	23 433	0	-28 023	11 852	-16 172	32 903	16 731	-11 702	5 030
1982	-2 383	65 633	...	38 163	0	-36 485	12 329	-24 156	35 164	11 008	-16 544	-5 536
1983	-118	50 342	...	17 457	0	-67 102	9 335	-57 767	36 386	-21 381	-17 310	-38 691
1984	16 626	33 849	...	18 437	0	-112 492	3 419	-109 073	35 063	-74 010	-20 335	-94 344
1985	9 851	41 045	...	18 362	0	-122 173	294	-121 880	25 723	-96 157	-21 998	-118 155
1986	3 325	76 737	...	30 269	0	-145 081	6 543	-138 538	15 494	-123 044	-24 132	-147 177
1987	18 363	86 537	...	-7 514	0	-159 557	7 874	-151 684	14 293	-137 391	-23 265	-160 655
1988	32 893	63 744	...	-17 600	0	-126 959	12 393	-114 566	18 687	-95 879	-25 274	-121 153
1989	22 086	51 780	...	51 756	0	-117 749	24 607	-93 142	19 824	-73 318	-26 169	-99 486
1990	45 133	-3 824	...	27 425	0	-111 037	30 173	-80 864	28 550	-52 314	-26 654	-78 968
1991	-3 115	3 994	...	-42 252	0	-76 937	45 802	-31 136	24 131	-7 005	9 904	2 897
1992	13 573	16 216	...	-43 304	0	-96 897	57 685	-39 212	24 234	-14 978	-36 636	-51 613
1993	10 489	25 063	...	6 898	0	-132 451	62 141	-70 311	25 316	-44 995	-39 811	-84 805
1994	1 302	104 338	...	-902	0	-165 831	67 338	-98 493	17 146	-81 347	-40 265	-121 612
1995	59 637	30 176	...	31 656	0	-174 170	77 786	-96 384	20 891	-75 493	-38 074	-113 567
1996	53 736	16 478	...	-8 977	0	-191 000	86 935	-104 065	22 318	-81 747	-43 017	-124 764
1997	116 518	149 026	...	-77 224	0	-198 428	90 155	-108 273	12 609	-95 664	-45 062	-140 726
1998	23 140	39 769	...	148 863	0	-248 221	82 081	-166 140	4 265	-161 875	-53 187	-215 062
1999	76 247	54 232	...	68 421	0	-347 819	82 729	-265 090	13 888	-251 202	-50 428	-301 630
2000	170 672	116 971	...	-59 265	0	-454 690	74 855	-379 835	21 054	-358 781	-58 645	-417 426
2001	66 110	118 379	...	-13 906	0	-429 898	64 393	-365 505	31 722	-333 783	-64 487	-398 270
2002	95 871	96 410	...	-39 894	0	-482 831	61 230	-421 601	27 398	-394 203	-64 948	-459 151
2003	96 526	97 207	...	-7 880	0	-549 012	53 977	-495 034	45 309	-449 725	-71 794	-521 519
2004	165 872	335 206	...	97 476	0	-671 835	61 848	-609 987	67 219	-542 768	-88 362	-631 130
2005	69 572	214 736	...	36 623	0	-790 851	75 582	-715 268	72 358	-642 910	-105 772	-748 683
2006	244 793	462 043	29 710	-1 698	0	-847 260	86 901	-760 359	48 085	-712 274	-91 273	-803 547
2007	201 681	509 288	6 222	64 912	0	-830 992	129 569	-701 422	90 845	-610 577	-115 996	-726 573
2008	-45 167	-326 589	-28 905	200 055	0	-840 252	144 316	-695 936	118 231	-577 705	-128 363	-706 068
2009	26 965	-235 028	...	224 946	0	-517 045	138 416	-378 628	89 003	-289 625	-130 243	-419 868
2006												
1st quarter	66 064	163 095	1 633	40 780	9 315	-211 173	19 551	-191 622	13 967	-177 655	-20 995	-198 651
2nd quarter	59 820	41 606	14 090	5 305	-2 443	-211 710	20 538	-191 172	12 802	-178 370	-23 708	-202 078
3rd quarter	69 975	104 165	15 134	-29 858	-19 305	-220 435	21 145	-199 290	9 377	-189 913	-24 876	-214 789
4th quarter	48 934	153 177	-1 147	-17 924	12 434	-203 941	25 666	-178 276	11 938	-166 338	-21 693	-188 031
2007												
1st quarter	91 302	203 384	14 795	-30 242	10 399	-206 033	27 995	-178 038	9 747	-168 291	-30 807	-199 098
2nd quarter	127 498	142 744	-1 007	-637	-528	-205 639	28 079	-177 560	12 781	-164 779	-25 752	-190 531
3rd quarter	75 447	49 668	5 942	80 403	-23 938	-204 915	33 450	-171 465	28 407	-143 058	-28 557	-171 614
4th quarter	-92 566	113 492	-13 508	15 388	14 066	-214 404	40 044	-174 360	39 912	-134 448	-30 883	-165 330
2008												
1st quarter	73 211	90 530	-7 966	13 344	14 659	-218 846	36 192	-182 653	36 686	-145 967	-33 330	-179 298
2nd quarter	-54 996	-261 693	-2 355	81 410	-3 037	-221 496	38 649	-182 847	26 274	-156 573	-31 147	-187 719
3rd quarter	76 442	-120 255	-4 075	38 067	-25 884	-221 090	35 148	-185 942	34 125	-151 817	-32 361	-184 178
4th quarter	-139 824	-35 171	-14 509	67 236	14 264	-178 820	34 326	-144 495	21 146	-123 349	-31 527	-154 875
2009												
1st quarter	-8 270	-163 770	8 407	69 976	10 770	-123 999	31 780	-92 219	18 223	-73 996	-30 185	-104 182
2nd quarter	43 003	-178 890	11 265	35 787	-1 441	-115 450	34 374	-81 076	16 589	-64 487	-33 256	-97 743
3rd quarter	13 880	134 235	11 496	17 373	-21 440	-132 101	35 717	-96 383	29 060	-67 323	-35 025	-102 348
4th quarter	-21 648	-26 603	...	70 640	12 108	-145 495	36 547	-108 948	25 132	-83 816	-31 777	-115 593

⁴A minus sign indicates financial outflows or a decrease in foreign official assets in the United States.
⁵Sum of credits and debits with the sign reversed.
. . . = Not available.

Table 7-7. Foreigners' Transactions in Long-Term Securities with U.S. Residents

(Billions of dollars, not seasonally adjusted.)

Year and month	Gross purchases from U.S. residents	Gross sales to U.S. residents	Transactions in U.S. domestic securities between foreigners and U.S. residents							
			Net purchases							
			Total	Private					Official	
				Total	Treasury bonds and notes	Government agency bonds	Corporate bonds	Equities	Total	Treasury bonds and notes
1977	60.7	30.1	30.6	...	...	...	...	...	...	...
1978	60.5	51.1	9.4	3.6	1.0	0.6	0.3	1.7	5.8	3.7
1979	72.9	67.2	5.7	2.5	1.2	0.1	0.2	1.1	3.2	1.7
1980	106.9	91.1	15.8	6.6	1.0	0.4	0.9	4.3	9.2	3.9
1981	126.5	100.5	26.0	10.2	3.3	0.3	1.9	4.8	15.6	11.7
1982	159.5	136.8	22.7	9.2	2.8	0.3	2.5	3.6	13.5	14.6
1983	223.4	211.7	11.7	13.2	4.6	0.5	1.7	6.4	-1.5	0.8
1984	335.5	304.0	31.5	33.8	21.0	1.2	12.5	-0.9	-2.4	0.5
1985	667.2	588.9	78.3	71.9	21.1	4.6	41.4	4.8	6.3	8.1
1986	1 355.4	1 266.9	88.5	76.4	5.2	8.2	45.1	18.0	12.1	14.2
1987	1 692.1	1 623.0	69.1	37.5	-5.5	3.5	22.7	16.8	31.7	31.1
1988	1 827.9	1 753.1	74.8	49.4	22.2	5.4	21.3	0.4	25.4	26.6
1989	2 431.7	2 335.2	96.5	66.5	27.4	13.7	17.5	7.9	30.0	26.8
1990	2 111.2	2 092.4	18.8	-3.6	-5.3	5.6	9.8	-13.7	22.5	23.3
1991	2 382.1	2 324.0	58.1	54.3	18.7	8.9	16.5	10.1	3.8	1.2
1992	2 677.8	2 604.6	73.2	63.1	32.4	14.3	20.0	-3.7	10.1	6.9
1993	3 212.5	3 101.4	111.1	103.2	22.2	31.4	29.9	19.6	7.9	1.3
1994	3 351.1	3 210.7	140.4	94.9	37.0	15.6	38.0	4.3	45.4	41.8
1995	3 737.6	3 505.7	231.9	185.3	94.5	25.0	57.6	8.2	46.5	39.6
1996	4 667.6	4 297.4	370.2	278.1	146.4	36.7	82.2	12.7	92.1	85.8
1997	6 573.3	6 185.3	388.0	339.7	140.2	45.3	82.8	71.3	48.3	44.0
1998	7 633.5	7 355.7	277.8	270.8	44.9	50.5	121.7	53.7	6.9	4.1
1999	7 483.5	7 133.3	350.2	338.8	-0.1	71.9	158.8	108.2	11.4	-9.9
2000	8 684.1	8 226.3	457.8	420.1	-47.7	111.9	182.1	173.8	37.7	-6.3
2001	10 261.8	9 740.9	520.8	494.2	15.0	146.6	218.2	114.4	26.7	3.5
2002	13 022.9	12 475.4	547.6	508.3	112.8	166.6	176.7	52.2	39.3	7.1
2003	13 526.0	12 806.1	719.9	585.0	159.7	129.9	260.3	35.0	134.9	103.8
2004	15 178.9	14 262.4	916.5	680.9	150.9	205.7	298.0	26.2	235.6	201.1
2005	17 157.5	16 145.9	1 011.6	891.1	269.4	187.6	353.1	81.0	120.4	68.7
2006	21 077.1	19 933.9	1 143.2	946.6	125.9	193.8	482.2	144.6	196.6	69.6
2007	29 730.6	28 724.8	1 005.8	818.1	195.0	99.9	342.8	180.4	187.8	3.0
2008	30 702.0	30 290.3	411.7	308.3	238.4	-7.5	59.2	18.1	103.4	76.6
2009	20 481.6	19 842.5	639.1	513.6	379.5	31.4	-38.4	141.2	125.5	159.1
2007										
January	1 833.6	1 709.3	124.3	112.3	21.0	21.2	47.2	23.0	12.0	-4.9
February	2 047.6	1 962.5	85.1	72.5	15.5	0.7	44.1	12.2	12.6	2.2
March	2 719.3	2 617.4	101.9	81.1	29.7	-1.0	43.3	9.1	20.8	1.4
April	2 028.9	1 931.0	97.8	72.5	-8.9	22.4	30.7	28.3	25.3	9.4
May	2 429.8	2 259.7	170.1	158.6	27.2	14.3	74.4	42.7	11.5	-4.6
June	2 624.8	2 501.1	123.8	96.0	17.9	23.6	26.3	28.2	27.8	6.4
July	2 473.7	2 448.5	25.2	20.8	-2.4	1.2	3.7	18.4	4.4	-6.9
August	3 335.3	3 373.0	-37.7	-13.5	25.2	4.3	-3.9	-39.0	-24.2	-29.7
September	2 339.1	2 284.8	54.3	26.0	9.9	2.3	11.3	2.5	28.3	14.4
October	2 683.2	2 550.2	133.0	111.2	50.9	4.8	25.5	29.9	21.8	4.0
November	2 901.8	2 837.7	64.1	52.4	19.4	17.5	11.2	4.3	11.8	0.4
December	2 313.6	2 249.7	63.9	28.1	-10.6	-11.3	29.1	21.0	35.8	11.0
2008										
January	3 132.1	3 058.4	73.8	21.0	0.7	16.4	-0.6	4.5	52.8	36.1
February	2 913.1	2 846.0	67.1	60.4	15.8	32.4	14.9	-2.7	6.7	-3.6
March	3 066.5	2 992.7	73.8	25.4	23.0	0.2	-8.8	11.0	48.4	28.0
April	2 584.6	2 482.4	102.2	61.0	54.3	1.2	17.5	-12.0	41.3	22.3
May	2 599.2	2 496.1	103.1	86.7	5.5	14.5	50.8	15.9	16.4	-3.7
June	2 794.1	2 733.8	60.2	45.4	26.9	20.2	0.6	-2.3	14.9	1.1
July	2 819.5	2 837.5	-18.0	-13.1	23.9	-25.9	-4.3	-6.8	-4.9	10.1
August	2 163.9	2 169.4	-5.5	4.8	28.0	-11.0	-12.6	0.4	-10.2	4.8
September	3 081.8	3 054.1	27.7	32.5	15.2	13.2	-7.3	11.5	-4.8	4.9
October	2 491.9	2 528.5	-36.6	-19.4	34.0	-33.5	-13.8	-6.1	-17.2	-1.1
November	1 562.0	1 621.3	-59.3	-22.2	0.4	-10.6	-15.3	3.3	-37.1	-26.2
December	1 493.2	1 470.2	23.1	25.9	10.7	-24.4	38.1	1.5	-2.8	3.9
2009										
January	1 337.4	1 346.7	-9.3	-0.7	12.9	-7.7	-7.7	1.8	-8.6	-1.9
February	1 457.0	1 434.5	22.6	27.6	23.7	5.3	3.0	-4.3	-5.1	-2.0
March	1 757.8	1 696.1	61.7	35.5	26.2	-12.9	8.2	14.0	26.2	29.0
April	1 485.4	1 451.2	34.1	18.2	24.8	1.1	-10.8	3.0	16.0	17.1
May	1 548.3	1 539.0	9.3	32.6	-0.8	13.7	1.8	18.0	-23.4	-21.8
June	2 040.7	1 915.3	125.4	107.0	78.0	13.7	-2.4	17.7	18.4	22.5
July	1 649.6	1 603.8	45.8	33.9	15.5	2.7	-9.6	25.2	11.9	15.7
August	1 744.0	1 704.8	39.2	27.6	14.9	6.2	-5.5	12.1	11.6	13.2
September	1 815.1	1 758.9	56.2	45.4	25.7	6.7	-2.5	15.4	10.9	19.0
October	1 992.4	1 949.3	43.0	28.4	23.9	-3.9	-1.4	9.7	14.6	15.0
November	1 895.3	1 766.4	128.9	95.6	86.7	3.5	-4.3	9.7	33.3	31.2
December	1 758.8	1 676.6	82.2	62.6	48.0	3.0	-7.2	18.8	19.6	22.0

. . . = Not available.

Table 7-7. Foreigners' Transactions in Long-Term Securities with U.S. Residents—*Continued*

(Billions of dollars, not seasonally adjusted.)

Year and month	Transactions in U.S. domestic securities between foreigners and U.S. residents—*Continued*			Transactions in foreign securities between foreigners and U.S. residents					Net long-term securities transactions	Other acquisitions of long-term securities, net	Net foreign acquisition of long-term securities
	Net purchases—*Continued* Official—*Continued*			Gross purchases from U.S. residents	Gross sales to U.S. residents	Net purchases [1]				
	Government agency bonds	Corporate bonds	Equities			Total	Bonds	Equities			
1977	. . .	. . .	. . .	10.3	15.8	-5.5	-5.1	-0.4	25.1	. . .	. . .
1978	0.7	0.7	0.7	14.8	18.5	-3.7	-4.2	0.5	5.7	. . .	. . .
1979	0.5	0.4	0.6	17.3	22.1	-4.8	-4.0	-0.8	0.9	0.1	1.0
1980	2.2	2.0	1.1	25.0	28.1	-3.1	-1.0	-2.1	12.7	-1.6	11.0
1981	1.3	1.6	1.0	26.9	32.6	-5.7	-5.5	-0.2	20.3	-5.2	15.0
1982	-0.7	-0.7	0.3	34.3	42.3	-8.0	-6.6	-1.3	14.7	-5.4	9.3
1983	-0.5	-0.8	-1.0	49.6	56.6	-7.0	-3.2	-3.8	4.7	-3.2	1.5
1984	0.0	-0.8	-2.1	70.8	75.9	-5.1	-3.9	-1.1	26.4	-1.5	24.9
1985	-0.3	-1.6	0.1	102.1	110.0	-7.9	-4.0	-3.9	70.4	-2.3	68.1
1986	-1.2	-1.6	0.7	216.1	221.7	-5.6	-3.7	-1.9	82.9	-2.3	80.8
1987	1.6	-0.4	-0.6	294.5	301.4	-6.9	-8.0	1.1	62.2	-1.0	61.3
1988	1.3	-0.1	-2.4	293.9	303.3	-9.4	-7.4	-2.0	65.4	0.2	65.6
1989	1.4	-0.2	2.0	344.6	363.2	-18.6	-5.5	-13.1	77.9	0.0	78.0
1990	0.7	-0.1	-1.4	437.7	468.9	-31.2	-21.9	-9.2	-12.4	3.9	-8.5
1991	1.3	0.4	0.9	450.9	497.7	-46.8	-14.8	-32.0	11.3	0.4	11.7
1992	3.9	0.8	-1.5	663.6	711.5	-47.9	-15.6	-32.3	25.3	-0.3	25.0
1993	4.0	0.6	2.0	991.4	1 134.5	-143.1	-80.4	-62.7	-32.0	1.1	-30.8
1994	6.1	0.0	-2.5	1 234.5	1 291.8	-57.3	-9.2	-48.1	83.1	0.5	83.5
1995	3.7	0.2	3.0	1 235.1	1 333.8	-98.7	-48.4	-50.3	133.2	0.4	133.6
1996	5.0	1.5	-0.2	1 564.4	1 675.0	-110.6	-51.4	-59.3	259.6	-0.5	259.1
1997	4.5	1.5	-1.7	2 207.7	2 296.8	-89.1	-48.1	-40.9	298.9	0.0	298.9
1998	6.3	0.2	-3.7	2 257.8	2 269.0	-11.2	-17.3	6.2	266.6	0.1	266.7
1999	20.4	1.5	-0.6	1 975.6	1 965.6	10.0	-5.7	15.6	360.2	0.0	360.2
2000	40.9	2.0	1.1	2 761.1	2 778.3	-17.1	-4.1	-13.1	440.7	-59.8	380.8
2001	17.4	3.8	2.0	2 557.8	2 577.4	-19.6	30.5	-50.1	501.2	-41.5	459.8
2002	28.6	5.6	-2.0	2 640.0	2 613.0	27.0	28.5	-1.5	574.6	-39.3	535.2
2003	25.9	5.4	-0.3	2 761.8	2 818.4	-56.5	32.0	-88.6	663.3	-138.9	524.5
2004	20.8	11.5	2.2	3 123.1	3 276.0	-152.8	-67.9	-85.0	763.6	-38.8	724.8
2005	31.6	19.1	1.0	3 700.0	3 872.4	-172.4	-45.1	-127.3	839.2	-143.0	696.2
2006	92.6	28.6	5.8	5 515.9	5 766.8	-250.9	-144.5	-106.5	892.3	-174.6	717.7
2007	119.1	50.6	15.1	8 187.6	8 416.8	-229.2	-133.9	-95.3	776.6	-235.1	541.4
2008	-31.6	35.0	23.4	7 709.2	7 622.4	86.9	66.4	20.4	498.5	-198.1	300.4
2009	-42.9	-2.3	11.7	5 122.3	5 319.9	-197.6	-138.2	-59.3	441.5	-199.1	242.5
2007											
January	15.1	2.4	-0.6	548.8	561.8	-13.0	-0.5	-12.4	111.4	-18.9	92.4
February	4.5	5.6	0.3	587.6	606.2	-18.6	-4.1	-14.5	66.5	-20.8	45.8
March	16.1	2.9	0.4	697.2	739.9	-42.8	-32.7	-10.0	59.1	-17.9	41.3
April	13.7	2.9	-0.7	624.2	638.3	-14.0	-11.0	-3.0	83.8	-13.1	70.7
May	12.8	4.0	-0.7	735.1	769.4	-34.4	-21.8	-12.6	135.8	-19.7	116.1
June	16.0	3.7	1.7	721.7	736.8	-15.1	-6.7	-8.4	108.6	-20.2	88.4
July	7.5	1.0	2.8	743.8	757.9	-14.1	0.8	-14.9	11.2	-29.2	-18.0
August	4.1	3.0	-1.6	826.3	861.4	-35.1	-22.4	-12.8	-72.9	-20.5	-93.4
September	9.2	4.6	0.1	560.5	600.9	-40.4	-19.1	-21.3	13.9	-24.8	-10.9
October	10.0	7.4	0.4	811.1	815.1	-4.0	-9.1	5.0	128.9	-19.7	109.2
November	6.0	4.9	0.5	731.7	713.8	17.9	8.3	9.6	82.1	-16.7	65.3
December	4.1	8.2	12.5	599.6	615.3	-15.7	-15.7	0.0	48.2	-13.7	34.5
2008											
January	-0.6	3.9	13.3	771.4	792.9	-21.5	-19.2	-2.3	52.2	-17.7	34.5
February	1.2	4.4	4.8	645.8	698.4	-52.5	3.9	-18.3	52.8	-18.2	34.6
March	15.9	4.1	0.4	416.9	755.6	-338.8	-0.2	-2.9	70.7	-20.3	50.4
April	11.0	7.5	0.4	357.2	689.5	-332.3	9.6	-0.2	111.6	-21.1	90.5
May	11.0	9.1	0.0	684.0	705.5	-21.5	-10.2	-18.1	74.9	-22.7	52.2
June	9.1	4.1	0.5	752.5	700.3	52.2	-12.7	1.6	49.1	-16.6	32.5
July	-16.2	0.2	1.1	698.9	687.9	10.9	15.5	16.9	14.5	-14.7	-0.3
August	-13.1	-0.5	-1.4	677.3	565.5	111.7	17.4	2.9	14.5	-13.2	1.6
September	-8.7	-1.2	0.0	689.2	678.6	10.6	33.9	-2.5	59.1	-13.2	45.9
October	-16.7	0.7	-0.1	720.4	618.3	102.1	5.9	21.7	-9.1	-14.3	-23.4
November	-11.7	-0.9	1.6	585.7	385.4	200.4	10.2	21.3	-27.8	-12.1	-39.9
December	-12.9	3.5	2.6	710.0	344.5	365.5	12.2	0.5	35.8	-13.6	22.2
2009											
January	-7.9	0.3	1.0	350.6	374.4	-23.8	-26.9	3.1	-33.1	-16.5	-49.6
February	-3.2	0.0	0.1	314.9	313.4	1.5	-0.1	1.6	24.1	-17.1	6.9
March	-2.7	-0.9	0.7	380.3	381.2	-0.9	-0.3	-0.6	60.8	-20.3	40.5
April	-3.5	1.4	0.9	381.9	404.6	-22.7	-13.8	-8.9	11.4	-21.2	-9.7
May	-0.6	-0.9	-0.1	400.0	426.9	-26.9	-16.1	-10.8	-17.6	-19.2	-36.8
June	-5.8	-0.4	2.2	485.3	518.7	-33.4	-19.5	-13.9	92.0	-21.6	70.3
July	-7.2	-1.2	4.6	438.5	466.9	-28.4	-14.2	-14.2	17.4	-19.9	-2.5
August	-1.6	-0.1	0.2	389.8	392.6	-2.9	10.0	-12.9	36.4	-16.1	20.3
September	-8.3	0.0	0.2	490.2	505.2	-15.0	-15.5	0.5	41.2	-13.5	27.7
October	-1.5	0.5	0.6	555.4	579.1	-23.7	-19.4	-4.3	19.3	-12.2	7.1
November	2.4	-0.3	0.0	482.4	484.9	-2.5	-5.1	2.6	126.4	-13.9	112.5
December	-3.0	-0.7	1.3	453.0	471.9	-18.9	-17.4	-1.5	63.3	-13.0	50.3

[1](-) indicates net U.S. acquisitions of foreign securities.
. . . = Not available.

Table 7-8. International Investment Position of the United States at Year-End

(Millions of dollars.)

Year	U.S. net international investment position	U.S.-owned assets abroad									
		Total	Financial derivatives	Official reserve assets	Other U.S. government assets	Direct investment		Foreign bonds	Foreign corporate stocks	U.S. nonbank claims	U.S. bank claims
						Current cost	Market value				
1976	165 374	456 964	. . .	44 094	44 978	222 283	. . .	34 704	9 453	20 317	81 135
1977	172 395	512 278	. . .	53 376	48 567	246 078	. . .	39 329	10 110	22 256	92 562
1978	208 052	621 227	. . .	69 450	53 187	285 005	. . .	42 148	11 236	29 385	130 816
1979	319 836	786 701	. . .	143 260	58 851	336 301	. . .	41 966	14 803	34 491	157 029
1980	365 502	929 806	. . .	171 412	65 573	388 072	. . .	43 524	18 930	38 429	203 866
1981	346 088	1 001 667	. . .	124 568	70 893	407 804	. . .	45 675	16 467	42 752	293 508
1982	336 778	1 108 436	. . .	143 445	76 903	374 059	226 638	56 604	17 442	35 405	404 578
1983	307 534	1 210 974	. . .	123 110	81 664	355 643	274 342	58 569	26 154	131 329	434 505
1984	171 550	1 204 900	. . .	105 040	86 945	348 342	270 574	62 810	25 994	130 138	445 631
1985	67 121	1 287 396	. . .	117 930	89 792	371 036	386 352	75 020	44 383	141 872	447 363
1986	-21 766	1 469 396	. . .	139 875	91 850	404 818	530 074	85 724	72 399	167 392	507 338
1987	-63 968	1 646 527	. . .	162 370	90 681	478 062	590 246	93 889	94 700	177 368	549 457
1988	-160 865	1 829 665	. . .	144 179	87 892	513 761	692 461	104 187	128 662	197 757	653 227
1989	-239 793	2 070 868	. . .	168 714	86 643	553 093	832 460	116 949	197 345	234 307	713 817
1990	-223 405	2 178 978	. . .	174 664	84 344	616 655	731 762	144 717	197 596	265 315	695 687
1991	-284 746	2 286 456	. . .	159 223	81 422	643 364	827 537	176 774	278 976	256 295	690 402
1992	-404 284	2 331 696	. . .	147 435	83 022	663 830	798 630	200 817	314 266	254 303	668 023
1993	-277 730	2 753 648	. . .	164 945	83 382	723 526	1 061 299	309 666	543 862	242 022	686 245
1994	-291 305	2 987 118	. . .	163 394	83 908	786 565	1 114 582	310 391	626 762	322 980	693 118
1995	-422 911	3 486 272	. . .	176 061	85 064	885 506	1 363 792	413 310	790 615	367 567	768 149
1996	-456 293	4 032 307	. . .	160 739	86 123	989 810	1 608 340	481 411	1 006 135	450 578	857 511
1997	-779 563	4 567 906	. . .	134 836	86 198	1 068 063	1 879 285	543 396	1 207 787	545 524	982 102
1998	-851 464	5 095 546	. . .	146 006	86 768	1 196 021	2 279 601	594 400	1 474 983	588 322	1 009 046
1999	-724 343	5 974 394	. . .	136 418	84 227	1 414 355	2 839 639	548 233	2 003 716	704 517	1 082 928
2000	-1 330 630	6 238 785	. . .	128 400	85 168	1 531 607	2 694 014	572 692	1 852 842	836 559	1 231 517
2001	-1 868 875	6 308 681	. . .	129 961	85 654	1 693 131	2 314 934	557 062	1 612 673	839 303	1 390 897
2002	-2 037 970	6 649 079	. . .	158 602	85 309	1 867 043	2 022 588	702 742	1 373 980	901 946	1 559 457
2003	-2 086 513	7 638 086	. . .	183 577	84 772	2 054 464	2 729 126	868 948	2 079 422	594 004	1 772 899
2004	-2 245 417	9 340 634	. . .	189 591	83 062	2 498 494	3 362 796	984 978	2 560 418	793 556	2 230 535
2005	-1 925 146	11 961 552	1 190 029	188 043	77 523	2 651 721	3 637 996	1 011 554	3 317 705	1 018 462	2 506 515
2006	-2 184 282	14 428 137	1 238 995	219 853	72 189	2 948 172	4 470 343	1 275 515	4 328 960	1 184 073	3 160 380
2007	-2 139 916	18 278 842	2 559 332	277 211	94 471	3 451 482	5 227 962	1 587 089	5 247 990	1 239 718	3 821 549
2008	-3 469 246	19 888 158	6 624 549	293 732	624 100	3 698 784	3 071 189	1 392 903	2 851 408	991 920	3 410 762

Year	Foreign-owned assets in the United States									
	Total	Financial derivatives	Foreign official assets	Direct investment in the United States		U.S. Treasury securities	Corporate and other bonds	Corporate stocks	U.S. currency	U.S. nonbank liabilities	U.S. bank liabilities
				Current cost	Market value						
1976	291 590	. . .	104 445	47 528	. . .	7 028	11 964	42 949	11 250	12 961	53 465
1977	339 883	. . .	140 867	55 413	. . .	7 562	11 456	39 779	12 701	11 921	60 184
1978	413 175	. . .	173 057	68 976	. . .	8 910	11 457	42 097	14 940	16 019	77 719
1979	466 865	. . .	159 852	88 579	. . .	14 210	10 269	48 318	16 642	18 669	110 326
1980	564 304	. . .	176 062	127 105	. . .	16 113	9 545	64 569	19 415	30 426	121 069
1981	655 579	. . .	180 425	164 623	. . .	18 505	10 694	64 391	20 974	30 606	165 361
1982	771 658	. . .	189 109	184 842	130 428	25 758	16 709	76 279	23 441	27 532	227 988
1983	903 440	. . .	194 468	193 708	153 318	33 846	17 454	96 357	27 546	61 731	278 330
1984	1 033 350	. . .	199 678	223 538	172 377	62 121	32 421	96 056	29 942	77 415	312 179
1985	1 220 275	. . .	202 482	247 223	219 996	87 954	82 290	125 578	33 258	86 993	354 497
1986	1 491 162	. . .	241 226	284 701	272 966	96 078	140 863	168 940	35 679	90 703	432 972
1987	1 710 495	. . .	283 058	334 552	316 200	82 588	166 089	175 643	39 545	110 187	518 833
1988	1 990 530	. . .	322 036	401 766	391 530	100 877	191 314	200 978	43 656	144 548	585 355
1989	2 310 661	. . .	341 746	467 886	534 734	166 541	231 673	251 191	47 405	167 093	637 126
1990	2 402 383	. . .	373 293	505 346	539 601	152 452	238 903	221 741	63 991	213 406	633 251
1991	2 571 202	. . .	398 538	533 404	669 137	170 295	274 156	271 872	76 804	208 908	637 245
1992	2 735 980	. . .	437 263	540 270	696 177	197 739	299 287	300 160	87 890	220 666	652 705
1993	3 031 378	. . .	509 422	593 313	768 398	221 501	355 822	340 627	104 508	229 038	677 147
1994	3 278 423	. . .	535 227	617 982	757 853	235 684	368 077	371 618	125 093	239 817	784 925
1995	3 909 183	. . .	682 873	680 066	1 005 726	326 995	459 080	510 769	133 933	300 424	815 043
1996	4 488 600	. . .	820 823	745 619	1 229 118	433 903	539 308	625 805	148 084	346 810	828 248
1997	5 347 469	. . .	873 716	824 136	1 637 408	538 137	618 837	893 888	170 509	459 407	968 839
1998	5 947 010	. . .	896 174	920 044	2 179 035	543 323	724 619	1 178 824	184 356	485 675	1 013 995
1999	6 698 737	. . .	951 088	1 101 709	2 798 193	440 685	825 175	1 526 116	208 763	578 046	1 067 155
2000	7 569 415	. . .	1 030 708	1 421 017	2 783 235	381 630	1 068 566	1 554 448	205 406	738 904	1 168 736
2001	8 177 556	. . .	1 109 072	1 518 473	2 560 294	375 059	1 343 071	1 478 301	229 200	798 314	1 326 066
2002	8 687 049	. . .	1 250 977	1 499 952	2 021 817	473 503	1 530 982	1 248 085	248 061	897 335	1 538 154
2003	9 724 599	. . .	1 562 564	1 580 994	2 454 877	527 223	1 710 787	1 712 069	258 652	450 884	1 921 426
2004	11 586 051	. . .	2 011 899	1 742 716	2 717 383	561 610	2 035 149	1 960 357	271 953	600 161	2 402 206
2005	13 886 698	1 132 114	2 306 292	1 905 979	2 817 970	643 793	2 243 135	2 109 863	280 400	658 177	2 606 945
2006	16 612 419	1 179 159	2 825 628	2 154 062	3 293 053	567 861	2 824 871	2 547 468	282 627	799 471	3 431 272
2007	20 418 758	2 487 860	3 403 995	2 450 132	3 593 291	639 715	3 289 077	2 900 990	271 952	1 000 430	3 974 607
2008	23 357 404	6 464 967	3 871 362	2 646 847	2 556 882	884 965	2 865 903	1 837 626	301 139	873 227	3 611 368

Note: See notes and definitions.

. . . = Not available.

Section 7c: Exports and Imports

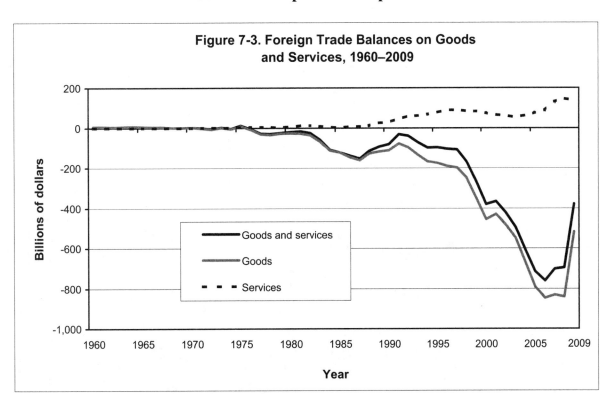

Figure 7-3. Foreign Trade Balances on Goods and Services, 1960–2009

- U.S. imports of goods and services exceeded exports by $760 billion in 2006, setting yet another new record. Between 2006 and 2008, as the economy weakened, aggregate values of both exports and imports continued to increase, but the dollar increase in imports was somewhat smaller than that for exports and the trade deficit was diminished. In 2009, both export and import values fell, but imports fell more and the trade deficit contracted to $379 billion, the smallest since 2001. (Table 7-9)

- In 2009, declines were recorded in all major categories of goods exports and imports, but were less severe for advanced technology products. (Tables 7-10 and 7-11)

- Canada and Mexico are the principal trading partners of the United States, with relations governed by the North American Free Trade Agreement (NAFTA). In 2009, U.S. exports to those two countries brought in $334 billion, compared with $221 billion in exports to the European Union and $211 billion in exports to China, Japan, and the newly industrialized countries of Asia (the NICS—Hong Kong, South Korea, Singapore, and Taiwan). (Table 7-13)

- U.S. imports from Canada and Mexico in 2009 amounted to $401 billion, more than the $281 billion imported from the European Union but somewhat less than the $479 billion from China, Japan, and the Asian NICS. (Table 7-14)

- The value of imports from China, which grew by an average 23 percent <u>per year</u> from 2001 to 2006, slowed to a 12 percent increase in 2007 and a 5 percent rise in 2008, and actually declined 12 percent in 2009. (Table 7-14)

- For U.S. services trade, "other private services" is the largest single category among both exports and imports. This includes such activities as education, financial services, and many other types of business and professional services. The United States had a surplus of $79 billion on "other private services" in 2009, little changed from 2008 but about double what it was in 1997, which accounted for more than half of the total surplus on services. (Tables 7-9, 7-15 and 7-16)

Table 7-9. U.S. Exports and Imports of Goods and Services

(Balance of payments basis; millions of dollars, seasonally adjusted.)

Year and month	Goods and services			Goods			Services		
	Exports	Imports	Balance	Exports	Imports	Balance	Exports	Imports	Balance
1970	56 640	54 386	2 254	42 469	39 866	2 603	14 171	14 520	-349
1971	59 677	60 979	-1 302	43 319	45 579	-2 260	16 358	15 400	958
1972	67 222	72 665	-5 443	49 381	55 797	-6 416	17 841	16 868	973
1973	91 242	89 342	1 900	71 410	70 499	911	19 832	18 843	989
1974	120 897	125 190	-4 293	98 306	103 811	-5 505	22 591	21 379	1 212
1975	132 585	120 181	12 404	107 088	98 185	8 903	25 497	21 996	3 501
1976	142 716	148 798	-6 082	114 745	124 228	-9 483	27 971	24 570	3 401
1977	152 301	179 547	-27 246	120 816	151 907	-31 091	31 485	27 640	3 845
1978	178 428	208 191	-29 763	142 075	176 002	-33 927	36 353	32 189	4 164
1979	224 131	248 696	-24 565	184 439	212 007	-27 568	39 692	36 689	3 003
1980	271 834	291 241	-19 407	224 250	249 750	-25 500	47 584	41 491	6 093
1981	294 398	310 570	-16 172	237 044	265 067	-28 023	57 354	45 503	11 851
1982	275 236	299 391	-24 156	211 157	247 642	-36 485	64 079	51 749	12 329
1983	266 106	323 874	-57 767	201 799	268 901	-67 102	64 307	54 973	9 335
1984	291 094	400 166	-109 072	219 926	332 418	-112 492	71 168	67 748	3 420
1985	289 070	410 950	-121 880	215 915	338 088	-122 173	73 155	72 862	294
1986	310 033	448 572	-138 538	223 344	368 425	-145 081	86 689	80 147	6 543
1987	348 869	500 552	-151 684	250 208	409 765	-159 557	98 661	90 787	7 874
1988	431 149	545 715	-114 566	320 230	447 189	-126 959	110 919	98 526	12 393
1989	487 003	580 144	-93 141	359 916	477 665	-117 749	127 087	102 479	24 607
1990	535 233	616 097	-80 864	387 401	498 438	-111 037	147 832	117 659	30 173
1991	578 344	609 479	-31 135	414 083	491 020	-76 937	164 261	118 459	45 802
1992	616 882	656 094	-39 212	439 631	536 528	-96 897	177 251	119 566	57 685
1993	642 863	713 174	-70 311	456 943	589 394	-132 451	185 920	123 780	62 141
1994	703 254	801 747	-98 493	502 859	668 690	-165 831	200 395	133 057	67 338
1995	794 387	890 771	-96 384	575 204	749 374	-174 170	219 183	141 397	77 786
1996	851 602	955 667	-104 065	612 113	803 113	-191 000	239 489	152 554	86 935
1997	934 453	1 042 726	-108 273	678 366	876 794	-198 428	256 087	165 932	90 155
1998	933 174	1 099 314	-166 140	670 416	918 637	-248 221	262 758	180 677	82 081
1999	965 884	1 230 974	-265 090	683 965	1 031 784	-347 819	281 919	199 190	82 729
2000	1 070 597	1 450 432	-379 835	771 994	1 226 684	-454 690	298 603	223 748	74 855
2001	1 004 896	1 370 400	-365 505	718 711	1 148 609	-429 898	286 184	221 791	64 393
2002	977 470	1 399 071	-421 601	685 170	1 168 002	-482 831	292 299	231 069	61 230
2003	1 020 190	1 515 225	-495 035	715 848	1 264 860	-549 012	304 342	250 365	53 977
2004	1 159 233	1 769 220	-609 987	806 161	1 477 996	-671 835	353 072	291 224	61 848
2005	1 281 459	1 996 728	-715 269	892 337	1 683 188	-790 851	389 122	313 540	75 582
2006	1 451 685	2 212 044	-760 359	1 015 812	1 863 072	-847 260	435 873	348 972	86 901
2007	1 643 168	2 344 590	-701 423	1 138 384	1 969 375	-830 992	504 784	375 215	129 569
2008	1 826 596	2 522 532	-695 937	1 276 994	2 117 245	-840 252	549 602	405 287	144 315
2009	1 554 718	1 933 347	-378 629	1 045 543	1 562 588	-517 045	509 175	370 759	138 416
2007									
January	128 898	187 486	-58 588	89 826	157 568	-67 743	39 072	29 918	9 154
February	127 259	185 079	-57 819	88 225	155 106	-66 881	39 035	29 972	9 062
March	131 551	193 181	-61 630	91 488	162 897	-71 409	40 063	30 285	9 779
April	130 491	190 176	-59 685	91 037	159 746	-68 710	39 455	30 430	9 025
May	132 926	192 092	-59 166	92 717	161 260	-68 543	40 209	30 832	9 377
June	134 571	193 280	-58 709	93 901	162 288	-68 387	40 670	30 992	9 678
July	137 322	195 189	-57 868	95 152	163 447	-68 295	42 170	31 742	10 427
August	140 004	196 276	-56 272	96 532	164 167	-67 635	43 472	32 109	11 362
September	141 024	198 349	-57 325	97 476	166 461	-68 985	43 548	31 888	11 660
October	144 344	201 371	-57 027	99 028	169 038	-70 010	45 315	32 332	12 983
November	146 562	206 084	-59 522	100 560	173 690	-73 130	46 002	32 394	13 608
December	148 217	206 028	-57 810	102 443	173 707	-71 263	45 774	32 321	13 453
2008									
January	149 272	210 758	-61 486	103 776	177 698	-73 922	45 497	33 060	12 437
February	151 618	213 366	-61 749	106 795	180 144	-73 349	44 822	33 222	11 600
March	150 400	209 819	-59 420	105 066	176 640	-71 574	45 334	33 179	12 155
April	154 832	216 973	-62 141	108 969	183 536	-74 567	45 863	33 437	12 426
May	156 631	217 158	-60 528	109 523	183 232	-73 709	47 108	33 926	13 182
June	161 628	221 805	-60 177	114 384	187 603	-73 220	47 244	34 202	13 043
July	164 427	229 318	-64 891	117 227	194 475	-77 248	47 201	34 843	12 357
August	161 653	222 565	-60 913	114 661	186 840	-72 179	46 992	35 725	11 267
September	151 984	212 124	-60 140	106 025	177 687	-71 662	45 960	34 437	11 523
October	149 708	209 097	-59 389	103 831	175 224	-71 393	45 877	33 873	12 004
November	141 525	184 772	-43 247	97 545	151 813	-54 269	43 980	32 959	11 021
December	132 919	174 777	-41 858	89 193	142 352	-53 159	43 726	32 425	11 301
2009									
January	123 944	160 846	-36 901	82 355	129 945	-47 589	41 589	30 901	10 688
February	125 233	151 736	-26 504	84 267	121 468	-37 200	40 965	30 269	10 697
March	122 845	151 660	-28 816	82 485	121 695	-39 210	40 360	29 966	10 394
April	121 653	150 093	-28 440	79 914	119 824	-39 910	41 739	30 269	11 470
May	123 447	149 210	-25 763	81 991	119 210	-37 219	41 456	30 000	11 455
June	126 115	152 990	-26 876	83 963	122 284	-38 321	42 152	30 706	11 446
July	129 450	160 616	-31 165	86 676	129 419	-42 742	42 774	31 197	11 577
August	129 862	159 800	-29 938	86 758	128 745	-41 988	43 105	31 055	12 050
September	133 487	168 767	-35 281	90 211	137 582	-47 371	43 276	31 186	12 090
October	137 150	170 083	-32 933	93 382	138 547	-45 165	43 768	31 536	12 232
November	138 378	174 492	-36 114	94 461	142 881	-48 421	43 917	31 611	12 307
December	143 151	183 053	-39 902	99 081	150 990	-51 909	44 070	32 063	12 007

Table 7-10. U.S. Exports of Goods by End-Use and Advanced Technology Categories

(Census basis, except as noted; billions of dollars; seasonally adjusted, except as noted.)

Year and month	Total exports of goods			Principal end-use category							Advanced technology products [1]
	Total, balance of payments basis	Net adjustments	Total, Census basis	Foods, feeds, and beverages	Industrial supplies and materials		Capital goods, except automotive	Automotive vehicles, engines, and parts	Consumer goods, except automotive	Other goods	
					Total	Petroleum and products					
1980	224.25	3.55	220.70	36.28	72.09	3.57	76.28	17.44	17.75	. . .	. . .
1981	237.04	3.31	233.74	38.84	70.19	4.56	84.17	19.69	17.70	. . .	. . .
1982	211.16	-1.12	212.28	32.20	64.05	6.87	76.50	17.23	16.13	. . .	. . .
1983	201.80	0.09	201.71	32.09	58.94	5.59	71.66	18.46	14.93	. . .	. . .
1984	219.93	1.18	218.74	32.20	64.12	5.43	77.01	22.42	15.09	. . .	. . .
1985	215.92	3.29	212.62	24.57	61.16	5.71	79.32	24.95	14.59	. . .	. . .
1986	223.34	-3.13	226.47	23.52	64.72	4.43	82.82	25.10	16.73	. . .	. . .
1987	250.21	-3.70	253.90	25.23	70.05	4.63	92.71	27.58	20.31	. . .	. . .
1988	320.23	-3.11	323.34	33.77	90.02	4.48	119.10	33.40	26.98	. . .	. . .
1989	359.92	-3.08	363.00	36.34	98.36	6.46	136.94	35.05	36.01	. . .	. . .
1990	387.40	-5.57	392.97	35.18	105.55	8.36	153.07	36.07	43.60	20.73	. . .
1991	414.08	-7.77	421.85	35.79	109.69	8.40	166.72	39.72	46.65	23.66	. . .
1992	439.63	-8.54	448.17	40.34	109.59	7.62	176.50	46.71	51.31	24.39	. . .
1993	456.94	-7.92	464.86	40.59	111.89	7.49	182.85	51.35	54.56	23.89	. . .
1994	502.86	-9.77	512.63	41.96	121.55	6.97	205.82	57.31	59.86	26.50	. . .
1995	575.20	-9.54	584.74	50.47	146.37	8.10	234.46	61.26	64.31	28.72	. . .
1996	612.11	-12.96	625.08	55.53	147.98	9.63	253.99	64.24	70.11	33.85	. . .
1997	678.37	-10.82	689.18	51.51	158.32	10.42	295.87	73.30	77.96	33.51	. . .
1998	670.42	-11.72	682.14	46.40	148.31	8.08	299.87	72.39	80.29	35.44	. . .
1999	683.97	-11.83	695.80	45.98	147.52	8.62	310.79	75.26	80.92	35.32	. . .
2000	771.99	-9.92	781.92	47.87	172.62	12.01	356.93	80.36	89.38	34.77	227.39
2001	718.71	-10.39	729.10	49.41	160.10	10.64	321.71	75.44	88.33	34.11	199.63
2002	682.42	-10.68	693.10	49.62	156.81	10.34	290.44	78.94	84.36	32.94	178.57
2003	713.42	-11.36	724.77	55.03	173.04	12.69	293.67	80.63	89.91	32.49	180.21
2004	807.52	-11.26	818.78	56.57	203.96	17.08	331.56	89.21	103.08	34.40	201.42
2005	894.63	-11.35	905.98	58.96	233.05	22.66	363.32	98.41	115.29	36.96	216.06
2006	1 015.81	-10.16	1 025.97	65.96	276.04	31.57	404.03	107.26	129.08	43.59	252.71
2007	1 138.38	-9.82	1 148.20	84.26	316.38	37.76	433.02	121.26	145.98	47.30	264.88
2008	1 276.99	-10.45	1 287.44	108.35	388.03	67.18	457.66	121.45	161.29	50.66	270.13
2009	1 045.54	-11.32	1 056.86	93.97	296.32	49.22	390.41	81.63	150.03	44.50	244.73
2006											
January	79.97	-0.59	80.56	5.18	20.97	2.02	31.99	8.96	10.15	3.29	18.31
February	80.87	-0.67	81.54	5.02	21.05	2.09	32.76	8.99	10.28	3.44	18.46
March	82.61	-0.69	83.30	5.27	22.44	2.41	33.14	8.73	10.55	3.18	22.83
April	82.56	-0.63	83.19	5.17	22.52	2.83	33.32	8.72	10.28	3.19	19.80
May	83.81	-0.78	84.59	5.42	23.13	2.58	33.37	8.66	10.69	3.31	19.94
June	85.71	-0.72	86.43	5.53	23.49	2.64	34.10	9.01	10.79	3.50	22.25
July	83.57	-0.76	84.33	5.48	22.83	2.76	32.98	8.82	10.72	3.50	19.58
August	85.78	-0.94	86.72	5.79	23.27	2.55	33.75	9.10	11.01	3.80	21.33
September	86.58	-0.93	87.51	5.68	24.18	3.62	34.22	8.72	10.66	4.06	22.02
October	87.29	-0.98	88.26	5.81	24.12	3.00	34.45	8.74	11.16	3.98	22.30
November	88.24	-1.32	89.57	5.66	24.10	2.68	35.05	9.09	11.39	4.28	22.93
December	88.83	-1.16	89.98	5.96	23.96	2.41	34.89	9.73	11.39	4.05	22.97
2007											
January	89.83	-0.93	90.76	6.14	23.95	2.62	35.70	9.29	11.71	3.97	20.40
February	88.23	-0.67	88.89	6.18	23.84	2.46	34.17	9.38	11.56	3.76	18.76
March	91.49	-1.01	92.50	6.08	25.06	2.58	34.99	10.21	12.04	4.12	23.66
April	91.04	-0.99	92.03	6.47	25.48	2.68	34.18	9.99	11.99	3.93	20.17
May	92.72	-0.86	93.57	6.42	25.84	2.77	35.61	9.94	12.09	3.69	21.77
June	93.90	-0.82	94.72	6.59	26.96	3.22	35.59	9.97	11.74	3.87	23.44
July	95.15	-0.83	95.98	6.74	26.20	3.19	36.74	10.30	12.12	3.89	21.27
August	96.53	-0.87	97.40	7.39	27.12	3.17	36.62	10.09	12.31	3.87	22.57
September	97.48	-0.55	98.02	8.09	27.09	3.19	36.49	10.24	12.55	3.55	22.16
October	99.03	-0.63	99.65	7.83	27.49	3.25	37.22	10.46	12.46	4.20	24.04
November	100.56	-1.03	101.59	8.18	28.20	4.28	37.39	10.93	12.45	4.44	22.65
December	102.44	-0.65	103.09	8.17	29.17	4.35	38.31	10.46	12.97	4.01	24.00
2008											
January	103.78	-0.89	104.67	8.74	30.04	4.39	38.19	10.42	13.29	3.99	21.73
February	106.80	-1.15	107.94	8.99	32.21	5.30	38.07	10.86	13.42	4.40	21.37
March	105.07	-0.73	105.80	9.36	32.30	4.87	37.38	9.83	12.76	4.17	23.94
April	108.97	-0.79	109.76	9.55	33.14	4.97	39.14	10.21	13.46	4.26	22.87
May	109.52	-0.61	110.14	9.47	34.24	5.96	38.40	10.23	13.47	4.33	23.23
June	114.38	-0.75	115.14	10.03	36.72	7.97	39.38	10.75	13.99	4.27	24.22
July	117.23	-0.93	118.16	9.96	37.85	7.87	40.08	11.47	14.56	4.24	22.93
August	114.66	-1.22	115.88	9.90	37.00	8.13	40.38	10.25	13.86	4.50	24.08
September	106.03	-0.61	106.64	9.01	32.36	4.78	37.62	10.15	13.47	4.03	21.90
October	103.83	-0.93	104.76	8.35	31.41	4.91	37.54	9.99	13.30	4.17	22.24
November	97.55	-0.98	98.52	7.89	27.57	4.37	36.36	9.20	13.18	4.32	20.39
December	89.19	-0.86	90.05	7.12	23.19	3.66	35.12	8.08	12.55	3.99	21.23
2009											
January	82.36	-0.72	83.07	7.15	22.18	3.40	33.13	5.55	11.38	3.68	18.73
February	84.27	-0.83	85.10	7.15	22.22	3.06	33.30	5.94	12.75	3.73	18.93
March	82.49	-1.06	83.55	7.35	22.39	3.12	31.89	5.97	12.34	3.61	20.73
April	79.91	-0.77	80.68	7.64	21.14	3.05	30.83	5.81	11.87	3.40	18.68
May	81.99	-0.99	82.98	7.89	23.18	4.07	30.94	5.37	12.09	3.51	19.19
June	83.96	-0.97	84.94	8.14	24.35	4.32	31.38	5.44	12.06	3.56	20.73
July	86.68	-1.05	87.73	7.76	24.77	4.50	32.13	6.77	12.44	3.86	19.98
August	86.76	-0.73	87.49	7.86	25.71	4.54	30.82	7.27	12.29	3.54	18.52
September	90.21	-0.77	90.98	7.46	27.11	4.95	32.46	7.49	12.75	3.70	20.50
October	93.38	-1.35	94.74	7.69	27.54	5.00	33.68	7.90	13.74	4.19	23.70
November	94.46	-0.95	95.41	8.97	27.05	4.58	34.04	8.62	13.02	3.72	21.02
December	99.08	-1.13	100.21	8.92	28.68	4.64	35.81	9.50	13.30	4.00	24.01

[1]Not seasonally adjusted.
. . . = Not available.

Table 7-11. U.S. Imports of Goods by End-Use and Advanced Technology Categories

(Census basis, except as noted; billions of dollars; seasonally adjusted, except as noted.)

Year and month	Total, balance of payments basis	Net adjustments	Total, Census basis	Foods, feeds, and beverages	Industrial supplies and materials Total	Petroleum and products	Capital goods, except automotive	Automotive vehicles, engines, and parts	Consumer goods, except automotive	Other goods	Advanced technology products [1]
1980	249.75	4.23	245.52	18.55	124.96	...	30.72	28.13	34.22	...	...
1981	265.07	3.76	261.31	18.53	131.10	...	36.86	30.80	38.30	...	...
1982	247.64	3.70	243.94	17.47	107.82	...	38.22	34.26	39.66	...	...
1983	268.90	7.18	261.72	18.56	105.63	...	42.61	42.04	46.59	...	...
1984	332.42	1.91	330.51	21.92	122.72	...	60.15	56.77	61.19	...	...
1985	338.09	1.71	336.38	21.89	112.48	...	60.81	65.21	66.43	...	...
1986	368.43	2.75	365.67	24.40	101.37	...	71.86	78.25	79.43	...	...
1987	409.77	3.48	406.28	24.81	110.67	...	84.77	85.17	88.82	...	...
1988	447.19	5.26	441.93	24.93	118.06	...	101.79	87.95	96.42	...	...
1989	477.37	3.72	473.65	25.08	132.40	...	112.45	87.38	102.26	...	...
1990	498.34	2.36	495.98	26.65	143.41	62.16	116.04	87.69	105.29	16.09	...
1991	490.98	2.53	488.45	26.21	131.38	51.78	120.80	84.94	107.78	15.94	...
1992	536.46	3.80	532.66	27.61	138.64	51.60	134.25	91.79	122.66	17.71	...
1993	589.44	8.78	580.66	27.87	145.61	51.50	152.37	102.42	134.02	18.39	...
1994	668.59	5.33	663.26	27.87	145.61	51.28	152.37	102.42	134.02	18.39	...
1995	749.57	6.03	743.54	33.18	181.85	56.16	221.43	123.80	159.91	23.39	...
1996	803.33	8.04	796.77	35.74	204.43	72.75	228.07	128.95	172.00	26.11	...
1997	876.37	6.66	869.70	39.69	213.77	71.77	253.28	139.81	193.81	29.34	...
1998	917.18	5.28	911.90	41.24	200.14	50.90	269.56	149.05	216.52	35.39	...
1999	1 029.99	5.37	1 024.62	43.60	221.39	67.81	295.72	178.96	241.91	43.04	...
2000	1 224.42	6.40	1 218.02	45.98	298.98	120.28	347.03	195.88	281.83	48.33	222.08
2001	1 145.90	4.90	1 141.00	46.64	273.87	103.59	297.99	189.78	284.29	48.42	195.18
2002	1 164.72	3.35	1 161.37	49.69	267.69	103.51	283.32	203.74	307.84	49.08	195.15
2003	1 260.72	3.60	1 257.12	55.83	313.82	133.10	295.87	210.14	333.88	47.59	207.03
2004	1 477.09	7.39	1 469.70	62.14	412.83	180.46	343.49	228.20	372.94	50.11	238.28
2005	1 681.78	8.33	1 673.46	68.09	523.77	251.86	379.33	239.45	407.24	55.57	290.76
2006	1 861.38	7.44	1 853.94	74.94	601.99	302.43	418.26	256.63	442.64	59.49	290.76
2007	1 969.38	12.41	1 956.96	81.68	634.75	330.98	444.49	258.92	474.89	62.23	326.81
2008	2 117.25	13.61	2 103.64	89.00	779.48	453.28	453.74	233.76	481.64	66.01	331.18
2009	1 562.55	4.46	1 558.09	81.59	461.11	253.54	369.28	159.98	428.41	57.72	300.68
2006											
January	152.97	0.70	152.27	6.13	50.44	25.20	33.79	22.06	34.94	4.91	21.65
February	149.74	0.57	149.17	5.92	49.63	25.41	32.72	21.38	34.75	4.76	19.80
March	150.58	0.67	149.91	6.26	46.78	22.69	34.46	21.01	36.53	4.86	25.35
April	152.00	0.56	151.44	6.16	48.86	24.07	34.47	21.38	35.69	4.89	21.52
May	156.07	0.59	155.48	6.06	52.34	27.60	34.70	21.27	36.24	4.88	23.09
June	156.95	0.57	156.38	6.11	51.71	26.76	34.69	21.86	37.01	5.00	24.53
July	158.28	0.63	157.65	6.16	53.58	28.11	35.28	20.82	36.89	4.92	24.15
August	160.99	0.70	160.29	6.38	54.88	28.70	35.69	21.07	37.34	4.94	24.92
September	158.63	0.61	158.03	6.35	52.12	26.48	35.60	21.04	37.91	5.01	26.20
October	153.60	0.66	152.94	6.45	46.99	22.13	35.57	20.79	37.96	5.18	27.24
November	153.98	0.63	153.35	6.43	46.68	21.95	35.65	21.07	38.47	5.05	27.21
December	157.60	0.57	157.03	6.53	47.99	23.33	35.65	22.87	38.90	5.09	25.11
2007											
January	157.57	0.66	156.91	6.52	48.74	24.67	36.10	21.13	38.50	4.94	25.37
February	155.11	0.55	154.56	6.56	45.60	21.35	36.45	21.19	40.04	5.13	23.46
March	162.90	1.54	161.36	6.78	49.81	24.77	36.32	21.87	40.51	5.06	27.34
April	159.75	1.34	158.41	6.62	50.54	25.21	36.07	21.35	39.24	4.98	25.22
May	161.26	1.28	159.98	6.72	52.04	26.38	36.67	20.73	39.43	5.17	25.36
June	162.29	0.76	161.53	6.76	52.83	26.55	37.19	21.43	39.49	5.21	27.63
July	163.45	1.21	162.24	6.88	53.55	27.24	37.23	22.23	39.06	5.27	27.12
August	164.17	1.16	163.01	6.96	53.48	27.65	37.28	21.93	39.23	5.27	27.90
September	166.46	1.22	165.25	6.96	53.51	28.13	37.91	22.08	39.38	5.28	28.07
October	169.04	1.00	168.04	6.92	55.14	29.98	37.70	22.17	39.98	5.30	31.77
November	173.69	0.79	172.90	7.10	59.20	33.94	37.85	22.10	40.31	5.47	30.02
December	173.71	0.92	172.78	6.91	60.31	35.12	37.71	20.72	39.73	5.17	27.56
2008											
January	177.70	0.95	176.75	7.17	65.37	39.55	37.89	21.23	39.76	5.34	25.71
February	180.14	1.86	178.29	7.20	63.68	36.90	38.57	22.31	41.23	5.30	25.38
March	176.64	1.73	174.91	7.18	63.50	36.11	38.39	20.16	40.13	5.56	28.07
April	183.54	1.74	181.79	7.42	68.01	40.01	39.09	21.21	40.45	5.62	28.64
May	183.23	0.89	182.34	7.58	67.98	39.69	39.37	20.39	41.51	5.52	27.82
June	187.60	0.92	186.68	7.44	73.22	44.71	38.54	20.46	41.44	5.59	28.96
July	194.48	1.17	193.30	7.52	79.90	49.71	38.74	20.27	40.97	5.91	30.37
August	186.84	0.78	186.06	7.75	73.41	43.67	38.00	19.32	41.95	5.63	28.11
September	177.69	1.52	176.17	7.56	65.89	37.46	38.45	18.56	40.09	5.61	29.35
October	175.22	0.86	174.37	7.65	66.08	38.69	37.21	17.92	40.06	5.45	29.75
November	151.81	0.77	151.05	7.37	48.85	24.19	35.37	16.71	37.36	5.39	24.81
December	142.35	0.42	141.94	7.17	43.59	22.57	34.14	15.23	36.70	5.11	24.22
2009											
January	129.95	0.42	129.53	6.89	38.43	18.34	31.91	11.45	36.13	4.73	20.70
February	121.47	0.35	121.12	6.70	34.28	16.25	30.14	10.19	34.57	5.25	20.38
March	121.70	0.43	121.27	6.78	34.47	17.67	29.57	10.58	35.13	4.74	23.38
April	119.82	0.41	119.42	6.71	33.68	17.99	28.66	10.42	35.52	4.42	23.40
May	119.21	0.31	118.90	6.77	33.03	17.38	28.93	10.11	35.48	4.59	22.76
June	122.29	0.25	122.04	6.84	36.92	21.61	28.87	11.03	33.71	4.66	25.35
July	129.42	0.25	129.17	6.81	38.30	22.32	30.11	13.39	35.41	5.15	26.56
August	128.75	0.43	128.31	6.70	37.46	21.11	30.07	14.67	34.82	4.60	24.14
September	137.58	0.37	137.22	6.69	42.83	25.48	30.93	16.30	35.36	5.11	26.49
October	138.55	0.47	138.08	6.90	41.02	22.79	31.96	16.87	36.58	4.75	29.27
November	142.88	0.42	142.47	6.74	43.16	24.49	33.29	16.68	37.86	4.74	29.32
December	150.94	0.36	150.58	7.06	47.53	28.11	34.86	18.30	37.85	4.99	28.94

[1] Not seasonally adjusted.
. . . = Not available.

Table 7-12. U.S. Exports and Imports of Goods by Principal End-Use Category in Constant Dollars

(Census basis; billions of 2005 chain-weighted dollars, except as noted; seasonally adjusted.)

Year and month	Exports							Imports						
	Total	Foods, feeds, and beverages	Industrial supplies and materials	Capital goods, except auto-motive	Auto-motive vehicles, engines, and parts	Consumer goods, except automotive	Other goods	Total	Foods, feeds, and beverages	Industrial supplies and materials	Capital goods, except auto-motive	Auto-motive vehicles, engines, and parts	Consumer goods, except automotive	Other goods
1986 [1]	227.20	22.30	57.30	75.80	21.70	...	...	365.40	24.40	101.30	71.80	78.20	79.40	...
1987 [1]	254.10	24.30	66.70	86.20	24.60	...	...	406.20	24.80	111.00	84.50	85.00	88.70	...
1988 [1]	322.40	32.30	85.10	109.20	29.30	...	...	441.00	24.80	118.30	101.40	87.70	95.90	...
1989 [1]	363.80	37.20	99.30	138.80	34.80	...	...	473.20	25.10	132.30	113.30	86.10	102.90	...
1990 [1]	393.60	35.10	104.40	152.70	37.40	39.22	18.70	495.30	26.60	146.20	116.40	87.30	105.70	14.46
1991 [1]	421.70	35.70	109.70	166.70	40.00	40.42	21.11	488.50	26.50	131.60	120.70	85.70	108.00	14.15
1992 [1]	448.20	40.30	109.10	175.90	47.00	43.60	21.71	532.70	27.60	138.60	134.30	91.80	122.70	15.46
1993 [1]	471.17	40.19	111.08	190.02	51.93	54.03	23.91	591.45	28.03	151.26	160.16	100.73	132.92	18.35
1994 [1]	522.29	40.43	114.17	225.76	56.54	58.97	26.41	675.05	29.52	168.80	199.56	112.13	144.22	20.82
1994	521.77	51.62	159.70	163.25	62.39	64.22	31.59	685.20	32.84	308.25	110.72	129.08	143.22	23.08
1995	575.21	56.97	170.50	189.60	66.04	67.94	32.45	744.43	33.68	317.29	133.51	131.29	154.16	24.37
1996	636.17	55.14	180.96	225.06	68.73	72.92	37.88	822.10	37.29	336.62	161.05	135.77	165.10	27.20
1997	721.10	54.99	195.82	275.71	77.55	80.09	37.62	936.26	40.87	359.83	201.66	146.78	187.97	30.77
1998	738.13	54.65	195.08	287.90	75.69	83.21	40.74	1 046.57	43.98	394.41	231.31	155.95	213.10	37.92
1999	761.86	56.52	196.50	303.48	78.38	83.80	40.71	1 172.56	48.02	400.70	265.32	186.26	239.28	46.28
2000	845.83	59.67	216.20	351.19	82.88	91.98	39.19	1 328.09	51.14	425.69	318.36	202.50	281.45	51.18
2001	793.55	61.25	206.47	316.74	77.49	90.95	38.49	1 284.06	53.12	423.59	281.01	196.28	286.09	51.67
2002	756.18	59.90	203.13	288.31	80.76	87.14	37.02	1 331.20	56.66	427.34	275.34	210.10	312.59	53.27
2003	775.35	60.94	211.92	293.76	82.08	91.90	35.49	1 400.71	61.89	444.41	290.86	215.53	339.49	50.71
2004	841.49	56.26	226.28	328.37	90.15	104.62	35.91	1 564.30	65.71	500.25	341.32	230.48	376.53	51.85
2005	901.08	58.96	233.05	358.43	98.41	115.29	36.96	1 673.46	68.09	523.77	379.33	239.45	407.24	55.57
2006	990.96	63.32	250.92	402.18	106.13	126.76	41.64	1 769.76	72.08	523.06	422.07	255.47	439.95	57.93
2007	1 068.11	67.32	268.01	431.49	118.74	139.85	42.94	1 802.82	72.79	507.77	447.41	255.47	464.72	58.91
2008	1 139.59	71.23	300.38	453.57	117.63	151.23	43.27	1 742.53	70.85	484.15	450.68	225.02	459.29	59.06
2009	984.30	69.67	267.86	383.85	78.68	139.91	39.95	1 465.98	65.75	406.23	369.29	152.94	409.88	53.74
2006														
January	79.40	5.13	19.96	32.10	8.92	10.07	3.22	148.32	5.91	45.96	34.22	22.14	35.09	4.85
February	80.28	5.02	19.95	32.84	8.94	10.19	3.36	144.65	5.85	44.76	33.22	21.16	34.76	4.75
March	81.87	5.28	21.15	33.19	8.67	10.47	3.10	147.34	6.19	43.73	35.06	20.85	36.75	4.79
April	81.14	5.21	20.77	33.26	8.65	10.16	3.08	145.54	6.12	43.05	34.79	21.18	35.71	4.73
May	81.68	5.42	20.73	33.26	8.59	10.53	3.17	146.20	5.86	43.71	34.94	21.07	35.87	4.72
June	83.14	5.37	20.96	33.99	8.92	10.60	3.34	146.31	5.90	42.48	34.86	21.67	36.78	4.83
July	80.76	5.21	20.26	32.81	8.71	10.48	3.32	145.95	5.99	42.96	35.42	20.53	36.41	4.75
August	82.67	5.46	20.40	33.55	8.99	10.75	3.58	148.58	6.02	44.13	35.83	21.00	36.85	4.78
September	83.71	5.40	21.52	33.91	8.60	10.39	3.84	148.82	5.97	44.06	35.74	20.97	37.33	4.79
October	84.86	5.47	21.92	34.11	8.61	10.90	3.79	147.93	6.09	42.87	35.80	20.81	37.45	5.08
November	85.71	5.10	21.80	34.68	8.96	11.12	4.05	148.82	6.08	42.44	36.13	21.15	38.37	4.89
December	85.75	5.26	21.51	34.49	9.58	11.11	3.82	151.30	6.10	42.90	36.07	22.95	38.58	4.98
2007														
January	86.24	5.41	21.50	35.17	9.13	11.33	3.72	151.09	6.06	44.51	36.59	21.07	38.18	4.79
February	84.15	5.26	21.05	33.95	9.22	11.20	3.49	149.00	6.06	41.01	37.11	20.66	39.52	5.00
March	87.13	5.06	21.79	34.88	10.02	11.65	3.80	154.03	6.32	44.49	36.94	21.45	40.14	4.83
April	86.30	5.42	21.83	34.08	9.80	11.53	3.60	148.86	6.02	42.44	36.47	20.88	38.61	4.66
May	87.47	5.40	22.01	35.54	9.74	11.44	3.37	148.58	6.01	42.35	36.79	20.49	38.33	4.84
June	88.30	5.41	22.84	35.44	9.77	11.26	3.52	149.30	6.03	41.80	37.39	21.05	38.59	4.85
July	89.37	5.51	22.10	36.64	10.08	11.60	3.53	148.60	6.09	41.18	37.20	21.76	37.96	4.92
August	90.64	5.97	22.88	36.57	9.88	11.78	3.51	148.96	6.12	41.49	37.23	21.72	37.86	5.00
September	90.80	6.25	22.78	36.47	10.03	12.01	3.20	150.85	6.05	42.18	37.90	21.94	38.28	4.95
October	91.64	5.81	22.85	37.18	10.21	11.90	3.75	151.16	5.93	42.10	37.75	22.12	38.73	5.03
November	92.47	6.00	22.78	37.32	10.67	11.85	3.92	151.80	6.14	41.90	37.95	21.81	39.46	5.13
December	93.61	5.81	23.61	38.25	10.20	12.31	3.53	150.58	5.97	42.35	38.09	20.52	39.06	4.91
2008														
January	94.26	5.90	24.10	38.04	10.15	12.60	3.47	152.69	5.99	44.50	37.96	20.56	38.44	4.92
February	96.48	5.82	25.59	37.86	10.57	12.70	3.80	153.08	6.05	42.78	38.60	21.59	39.70	4.84
March	92.83	5.81	24.55	37.19	9.55	12.00	3.53	146.85	5.87	40.45	38.36	19.47	38.44	5.02
April	96.20	6.10	25.03	38.81	9.89	12.64	3.60	148.90	5.96	40.95	38.81	20.43	38.54	5.01
May	96.19	6.04	25.63	38.07	9.91	12.62	3.64	145.53	6.03	38.35	38.98	19.64	39.49	4.89
June	99.85	6.23	27.08	39.05	10.43	13.09	3.56	145.18	5.80	38.72	38.20	19.69	39.36	4.91
July	100.03	5.81	26.52	39.65	11.11	13.60	3.44	147.59	5.80	40.55	38.30	19.48	38.85	5.14
August	100.37	6.41	27.02	39.93	9.92	12.93	3.74	144.54	5.90	38.96	37.55	18.52	39.76	4.93
September	93.18	5.81	24.28	37.27	9.82	12.55	3.39	141.10	5.83	37.72	38.05	17.82	38.03	4.96
October	93.29	5.84	24.66	37.04	9.62	12.36	3.57	145.45	5.97	42.06	36.82	17.15	38.02	4.86
November	91.24	5.86	24.05	35.96	8.86	12.36	3.86	136.56	6.00	38.58	35.13	16.04	35.62	4.90
December	85.69	5.61	21.88	34.70	7.79	11.80	3.67	135.06	5.65	40.55	33.94	14.63	35.04	4.68
2009														
January	78.37	5.29	20.92	32.63	5.34	10.60	3.35	127.44	5.42	40.02	31.68	10.97	34.46	4.36
February	80.49	5.37	21.09	32.79	5.73	11.83	3.41	119.87	5.47	36.00	30.03	9.77	33.00	4.87
March	79.85	5.72	21.60	31.46	5.75	11.59	3.33	120.13	5.58	35.88	29.65	10.16	33.66	4.44
April	76.54	5.71	20.08	30.40	5.60	11.21	3.11	116.66	5.42	33.53	28.68	10.03	34.02	4.15
May	78.08	5.71	21.68	30.51	5.18	11.37	3.19	114.22	5.46	31.01	28.97	9.71	33.95	4.30
June	78.69	5.64	21.98	30.96	5.24	11.29	3.18	114.38	5.51	31.84	28.09	10.58	32.26	4.36
July	81.85	5.66	22.56	31.68	6.54	11.59	3.47	120.64	5.59	32.51	30.18	12.83	33.91	4.83
August	80.72	5.74	22.62	30.35	7.02	11.43	3.14	118.47	5.42	30.71	30.12	14.02	33.35	4.30
September	84.18	5.68	23.88	31.89	7.22	11.85	3.30	125.65	5.38	34.23	30.98	15.56	33.86	4.77
October	87.63	5.94	24.16	33.06	7.61	12.76	3.73	126.05	5.52	32.60	32.01	16.05	34.98	4.41
November	87.03	6.68	23.12	33.19	8.30	12.07	3.27	127.89	5.38	32.51	33.27	15.87	36.22	4.37
December	90.86	6.53	24.16	34.92	9.15	12.32	3.49	134.58	5.61	35.38	34.79	17.39	36.22	4.58

[1]Data on the 2005 chain-weighted dollar basis are only available from 1994 forward. To provide more historical range, values in 1992 dollars are shown for the years 1986–1994.
. . . = Not available.

Table 7-13. U.S. Exports of Goods by Selected Regions and Countries

(Census f.a.s. basis; millions of dollars, not seasonally adjusted.)

Year and month	Total, all countries	Selected regions [1]					Selected countries				
		European Union, 15 countries	European Union	Euro area	Asian NICS	OPEC	Brazil	Canada	China	Japan	Mexico
1972	...	...	...	...	...	...	1 243	13 070	...	4 963	1 982
1973	...	...	...	...	...	...	1 916	16 146	...	8 313	2 937
1974	...	28 268	...	...	...	6 723	3 088	21 281	807	10 679	4 855
1975	...	22 862	...	...	...	10 767	3 056	22 948	304	9 563	5 141
1976	...	25 406	...	...	...	12 566	2 809	25 677	135	10 145	4 990
1977	...	26 476	...	...	...	14 019	2 490	27 738	171	10 529	4 806
1978	...	32 051	...	...	...	16 655	2 981	30 540	824	12 885	6 680
1979	...	42 582	...	...	...	15 051	3 442	37 599	1 724	17 581	9 847
1980	...	53 679	...	...	...	17 759	4 344	40 331	3 755	20 790	15 145
1981	...	52 363	...	...	...	21 533	3 798	44 602	3 603	21 823	17 789
1982	...	47 932	...	...	...	22 863	3 423	37 887	2 912	20 966	11 817
1983	201 708	44 311	...	...	...	16 905	2 557	43 345	2 173	21 894	9 082
1984	218 743	46 976	...	...	...	14 387	2 640	51 777	3 004	23 575	11 992
1985	212 621	48 994	...	...	16 918	12 480	3 140	53 287	3 856	22 631	13 635
1986	226 471	53 154	...	...	18 289	10 844	3 885	55 512	3 106	26 882	12 392
1987	253 904	60 575	...	...	23 548	11 058	4 040	59 814	3 497	28 249	14 582
1988	323 335	75 755	...	...	34 816	13 994	4 267	71 622	5 021	37 725	20 628
1989	363 836	86 331	...	...	38 404	13 196	4 804	78 809	5 755	44 494	24 982
1990	392 924	98 027	...	...	40 741	13 679	5 062	83 866	4 807	48 585	28 375
1991	421 764	103 123	...	...	45 628	19 054	6 148	85 150	6 278	48 125	33 277
1992	448 161	102 958	...	...	48 592	21 960	5 751	90 594	7 418	47 813	40 592
1993	465 090	96 973	...	...	52 502	19 500	6 058	100 444	8 763	47 892	41 581
1994	512 626	102 818	...	...	59 595	17 868	8 102	114 439	9 282	53 488	50 844
1995	584 742	123 671	...	...	74 234	19 533	11 439	127 226	11 754	64 343	46 292
1996	625 075	127 710	...	...	75 768	22 275	12 718	134 210	11 993	67 607	56 792
1997	689 182	140 773	...	...	78 225	25 526	15 915	151 767	12 862	65 549	71 388
1998	682 138	149 035	...	...	63 269	25 154	15 142	156 603	14 241	57 831	78 773
1999	695 797	151 814	...	...	70 989	20 166	13 203	166 600	13 111	57 466	86 909
2000	781 918	165 065	...	116 212	84 624	19 078	15 321	178 941	16 185	64 924	111 349
2001	729 100	158 768	...	112 903	71 982	20 053	15 880	163 424	19 182	57 452	101 297
2002	693 103	143 691	...	105 838	69 770	18 812	12 376	160 923	22 128	51 449	97 470
2003	724 771	151 731	...	113 132	71 601	17 279	11 211	169 924	28 368	52 004	97 412
2004	818 775	168 572	172 622	127 158	82 997	22 256	13 886	189 880	34 428	53 568	110 731
2005	905 978	...	186 437	137 497	86 003	31 641	15 372	211 899	41 192	54 681	120 248
2006	1 036 635	...	213 996	155 735	96 496	38 658	18 887	230 656	53 673	58 459	133 722
2007	1 162 479	...	247 242	180 232	105 751	48 485	24 172	248 888	62 937	61 160	135 918
2008	1 287 442	...	271 810	199 986	108 947	64 880	32 299	261 150	69 732	65 142	151 220
2009	1 056 895	...	220 776	162 158	90 469	49 783	26 175	204 700	69 576	51 180	128 998
2007											
January	85 918	...	19 577	14 609	8 015	2 968	2 176	17 804	4 390	4 889	10 684
February	84 921	...	19 247	13 954	7 583	2 890	1 540	18 335	4 533	4 718	9 980
March	100 512	...	23 003	16 448	8 910	4 067	1 833	22 007	5 425	5 631	11 494
April	91 665	...	20 168	14 440	8 602	3 408	1 815	20 220	4 704	5 035	10 893
May	97 902	...	21 141	14 905	8 382	3 507	1 833	21 793	5 129	5 126	11 956
June	99 122	...	20 763	15 043	9 589	3 870	1 868	21 768	5 562	5 191	11 561
July	91 857	...	18 877	13 733	8 668	3 823	2 027	18 772	4 666	4 810	11 189
August	101 143	...	20 257	15 026	9 136	4 422	2 143	21 379	5 553	5 060	12 283
September	98 068	...	20 724	15 397	8 683	4 104	2 139	21 055	5 312	5 066	11 365
October	106 563	...	21 801	16 080	9 458	4 633	2 244	23 300	5 533	5 334	12 330
November	103 363	...	20 934	15 165	8 894	4 937	2 060	22 652	5 582	5 098	12 127
December	101 448	...	20 751	15 432	9 831	5 855	2 494	19 806	6 549	5 203	10 057
2008											
January	98 677	...	21 151	15 291	8 711	4 377	2 270	20 486	5 557	4 951	11 991
February	104 740	...	23 431	16 994	9 082	4 556	2 228	21 256	5 698	5 524	11 962
March	110 932	...	23 595	17 515	10 149	4 540	2 409	22 978	6 294	5 627	11 793
April	109 857	...	23 664	17 129	9 595	5 088	2 453	23 464	5 651	5 431	12 493
May	112 627	...	23 797	17 452	9 908	4 805	2 610	24 387	6 276	6 025	12 298
June	116 787	...	24 834	18 058	10 645	5 238	2 800	23 741	6 188	5 752	13 383
July	114 522	...	23 664	17 486	9 887	5 261	2 938	22 325	6 235	5 601	13 801
August	116 418	...	23 598	17 410	9 524	6 564	3 718	22 076	6 201	5 908	13 750
September	106 072	...	20 826	15 466	9 114	5 735	2 921	22 294	5 258	5 434	12 789
October	111 239	...	22 862	16 824	8 716	6 469	3 018	22 059	6 083	5 339	14 876
November	97 085	...	20 659	15 634	7 192	6 222	2 605	19 172	5 181	5 058	11 945
December	88 486	...	19 729	14 728	6 424	6 026	2 329	16 912	5 111	4 493	10 141
2009											
January	78 379	...	17 652	12 919	5 939	3 931	2 121	14 730	4 178	3 987	9 791
February	80 503	...	18 704	13 905	6 015	4 325	1 845	15 505	4 678	4 211	9 277
March	87 796	...	19 798	14 200	6 884	4 950	1 960	16 863	5 570	4 456	10 020
April	80 969	...	17 844	13 293	6 569	4 081	1 851	16 146	5 165	3 853	9 580
May	83 761	...	17 923	13 587	7 154	3 773	2 007	16 167	5 248	4 250	9 398
June	86 860	...	18 682	13 463	7 360	3 762	2 092	16 829	5 549	4 004	10 569
July	85 737	...	17 090	12 269	7 714	3 526	2 243	16 443	5 274	4 142	11 151
August	87 429	...	16 677	12 062	7 845	3 688	2 339	17 690	5 553	4 040	11 072
September	91 418	...	18 120	13 345	8 467	4 037	2 340	18 407	5 814	4 427	11 591
October	100 285	...	20 584	15 227	9 122	4 499	2 587	19 064	6 857	4 647	12 738
November	94 541	...	18 712	13 860	8 140	4 399	2 286	18 538	7 326	4 234	12 014
December	99 192	...	18 990	14 028	9 263	4 812	2 505	18 317	8 363	4 930	11 797

[1]See notes and definitions for definitions of regions.
... = Not available.

Table 7-14. U.S. Imports of Goods by Selected Regions and Countries

(Census Customs basis; millions of dollars, not seasonally adjusted.)

Year and month	Total, all countries	Selected regions [1]					Selected countries				
		European Union, 15 countries	European Union	Euro area	Asian NICS	OPEC	Brazil	Canada	China	Japan	Mexico
1972	...	...	...	...	...	...	942	14 927	...	9 064	1 632
1973	...	...	...	...	...	...	1 189	17 715	...	9 676	2 306
1974	...	19 035	...	...	...	...	1 700	21 924	...	12 338	3 390
1975	...	16 610	...	...	...	...	1 464	21 747	...	11 268	3 059
1976	...	17 848	...	...	...	...	1 737	26 237	...	15 504	3 598
1977	...	22 087	...	...	...	...	2 241	29 599	...	18 550	4 694
1978	...	29 009	...	...	...	...	2 826	33 525	...	24 458	6 094
1979	...	33 295	...	...	...	...	3 118	38 046	...	26 248	8 800
1980	...	35 958	...	...	...	...	3 715	41 455	...	30 701	12 520
1981	...	41 624	...	...	...	...	4 475	46 414	...	37 612	13 765
1982	...	42 509	...	...	...	...	4 285	46 477	...	37 744	15 566
1983	261 723	43 892	...	...	...	...	4 946	52 130	...	41 183	16 776
1984	330 510	57 360	...	...	...	...	7 621	66 478	...	57 135	18 020
1985	336 383	67 822	...	...	...	22 800	7 526	69 006	3 862	68 783	19 132
1986	365 672	75 736	...	...	...	19 750	6 813	68 253	4 771	81 911	17 302
1987	406 283	81 188	...	...	...	23 953	7 865	71 085	6 294	84 575	20 271
1988	441 926	84 939	...	...	...	22 962	9 294	81 398	8 511	89 519	23 260
1989	473 647	85 153	...	...	...	30 601	8 410	87 953	11 989	93 586	27 162
1990	495 980	91 868	...	...	...	38 017	7 976	91 372	15 224	89 655	30 172
1991	488 452	86 481	...	...	59 277	32 644	6 717	91 064	18 969	91 511	31 130
1992	532 663	93 993	...	...	62 384	33 200	7 609	98 630	25 728	97 414	35 211
1993	580 658	97 941	...	...	64 572	31 739	7 479	111 216	31 540	107 246	39 917
1994	663 256	110 875	...	...	71 388	31 685	8 683	128 406	38 787	119 156	49 494
1995	743 543	131 871	...	...	82 008	35 197	8 830	145 349	45 543	123 479	61 684
1996	795 289	142 947	...	...	82 770	44 285	8 773	155 893	51 513	115 187	74 297
1997	869 704	157 528	...	...	86 164	44 025	9 626	168 201	62 558	121 663	85 938
1998	911 896	176 380	...	...	85 961	33 925	10 102	173 256	71 169	121 845	94 629
1999	1 024 618	195 227	...	...	95 102	41 978	11 314	198 711	81 788	130 864	109 721
2000	1 218 022	220 019	...	163 520	111 438	67 090	13 853	230 838	100 018	146 479	135 926
2001	1 140 999	220 057	...	166 373	93 202	59 754	14 466	216 268	102 278	126 473	131 338
2002	1 161 366	225 771	...	172 573	91 850	53 245	15 781	209 088	125 193	121 429	134 616
2003	1 257 121	244 826	...	187 204	92 818	68 344	17 910	221 595	152 436	118 037	138 060
2004	1 469 704	272 439	281 959	209 606	105 476	94 105	21 160	256 360	196 682	129 805	155 902
2005	1 673 455	298 879	308 776	228 881	102 609	124 940	24 436	290 384	243 470	138 004	170 109
2006	1 853 938	319 590	330 482	246 667	109 730	145 370	26 367	302 438	287 774	148 181	198 253
2007	1 956 962	...	354 409	266 074	111 260	173 818	25 644	317 057	321 443	145 463	210 714
2008	2 103 641	...	367 617	277 658	106 764	242 579	30 453	339 491	337 773	139 262	215 942
2009	1 558 085	...	281 320	212 013	86 835	111 631	20 074	224 911	296 402	95 949	176 537
2007											
January	150 833	...	26 094	19 645	9 544	11 589	2 046	25 115	25 641	11 406	15 373
February	139 793	...	25 379	19 135	8 276	9 337	1 645	23 679	23 039	11 825	15 143
March	161 363	...	31 284	23 693	9 330	12 058	2 223	27 238	22 723	12 884	18 191
April	156 584	...	29 325	22 017	9 061	12 615	2 195	26 084	24 242	12 548	16 255
May	163 324	...	29 714	22 013	9 832	13 951	2 038	26 920	25 291	11 122	18 019
June	164 462	...	30 373	22 758	9 246	13 195	2 203	27 837	27 071	11 827	17 977
July	166 765	...	31 396	23 621	9 776	13 987	2 254	24 610	28 601	12 769	16 897
August	170 766	...	30 193	22 976	9 273	15 135	2 387	26 903	28 425	11 976	19 115
September	162 772	...	27 175	20 078	8 828	14 626	2 213	26 391	29 419	11 404	17 810
October	182 044	...	33 777	25 323	9 705	15 134	2 439	28 714	31 555	13 472	19 856
November	175 663	...	31 182	23 316	9 843	16 418	1 939	28 011	29 781	12 450	19 356
December	162 594	...	28 517	21 500	8 546	17 608	2 063	25 556	25 657	11 781	16 722
2008											
January	168 350	...	27 758	20 867	9 410	20 302	2 284	27 359	26 193	11 709	17 055
February	165 070	...	30 473	23 073	8 553	17 617	2 047	27 499	24 096	12 542	17 675
March	171 194	...	31 692	24 206	8 967	18 816	2 345	29 968	22 440	13 016	17 707
April	182 115	...	32 752	25 030	9 267	20 936	2 383	31 233	25 952	13 045	19 365
May	182 956	...	32 658	24 300	9 173	22 902	2 649	30 271	27 635	11 244	18 837
June	190 117	...	33 388	25 329	8 666	24 145	3 155	31 285	27 931	12 144	19 180
July	202 614	...	34 823	26 291	9 821	29 249	3 022	32 208	31 247	12 029	19 238
August	189 875	...	29 707	22 150	8 855	26 231	2 565	29 994	31 824	11 137	19 523
September	180 189	...	29 150	21 589	9 232	18 787	2 851	29 654	33 079	11 008	17 926
October	185 882	...	32 068	24 175	9 441	20 430	3 086	27 707	34 032	11 476	19 696
November	147 515	...	26 550	20 314	8 046	11 948	2 225	22 603	28 265	10 108	15 472
December	137 763	...	26 599	20 335	7 333	11 217	1 843	19 710	25 080	9 804	14 269
2009											
January	122 226	...	21 128	16 284	7 563	7 963	1 789	17 275	24 748	8 289	12 475
February	109 279	...	22 045	16 273	5 982	6 409	1 335	17 420	18 875	6 417	12 372
March	121 004	...	24 221	18 687	7 036	7 313	1 617	17 630	21 188	7 062	13 930
April	118 933	...	23 188	17 454	6 813	7 632	1 397	17 349	21 919	7 071	13 697
May	116 713	...	20 693	15 682	6 891	7 840	1 544	16 707	22 732	6 164	13 340
June	126 998	...	23 192	17 532	6 999	9 623	1 793	18 355	23 979	7 708	13 996
July	135 347	...	25 048	18 990	7 430	10 474	1 926	18 517	25 691	8 029	14 085
August	131 224	...	22 115	16 378	7 195	10 056	1 610	19 169	25 785	8 377	15 022
September	140 998	...	23 662	17 442	7 717	11 909	1 761	19 938	27 915	8 557	16 150
October	146 793	...	25 500	18 986	7 843	10 343	1 639	21 155	29 521	9 070	17 292
November	142 935	...	25 130	18 823	7 665	10 481	1 817	20 056	27 550	9 666	17 153
December	145 636	...	25 399	19 480	7 703	11 589	1 845	21 321	26 501	9 539	17 026

[1]See notes and definitions for definitions of regions.
. . . = Not available.

Table 7-15. U.S. Exports of Services

(Balance of payments basis, millions of dollars, seasonally adjusted.)

Year and month	Total	Travel	Passenger fares	Other transportation	Royalties and license fees	Other private services (financial, professional, etc.)	Transfers under U.S. military sales contracts [1]	U.S. government miscellaneous services
1960	6 290	919	175	1 607	837	570	2 030	153
1961	6 295	947	183	1 620	906	607	1 867	164
1962	6 941	957	191	1 764	1 056	585	2 193	195
1963	7 348	1 015	205	1 898	1 162	613	2 219	236
1964	7 840	1 207	241	2 076	1 314	651	2 086	265
1965	8 824	1 380	271	2 175	1 534	714	2 465	285
1966	9 616	1 590	317	2 333	1 516	814	2 721	326
1967	10 667	1 646	371	2 426	1 747	951	3 191	336
1968	11 917	1 775	411	2 548	1 867	1 024	3 939	353
1969	12 806	2 043	450	2 652	2 019	1 160	4 138	343
1970	14 171	2 331	544	3 125	2 331	1 294	4 214	332
1971	16 358	2 534	615	3 299	2 545	1 546	5 472	347
1972	17 841	2 817	699	3 579	2 770	1 764	5 856	357
1973	19 832	3 412	975	4 465	3 225	1 985	5 369	401
1974	22 591	4 032	1 104	5 697	3 821	2 321	5 197	419
1975	25 497	4 697	1 039	5 840	4 300	2 920	6 256	446
1976	27 971	5 742	1 229	6 747	4 353	3 584	5 826	489
1977	31 485	6 150	1 366	7 090	4 920	3 848	7 554	557
1978	36 353	7 183	1 603	8 136	5 885	4 717	8 209	620
1979	39 692	8 441	2 156	9 971	6 184	5 439	6 981	520
1980	47 584	10 588	2 591	11 618	7 085	6 276	9 029	398
1981	57 354	12 913	3 111	12 560	7 284	10 250	10 720	517
1982	64 079	12 393	3 174	12 317	5 603	17 444	12 572	576
1983	64 307	10 947	3 610	12 590	5 778	18 192	12 524	666
1984	71 168	17 177	4 067	13 809	6 177	19 255	9 969	714
1985	73 155	17 762	4 411	14 674	6 678	20 035	8 718	878
1986	86 689	20 385	5 582	15 438	8 113	28 027	8 549	595
1987	98 661	23 563	7 003	17 027	10 174	29 263	11 106	526
1988	110 919	29 434	8 976	19 311	12 139	31 111	9 284	664
1989	127 087	36 205	10 657	20 526	13 818	36 729	8 564	587
1990	147 832	43 007	15 298	22 042	16 634	40 251	9 932	668
1991	164 261	48 385	15 854	22 631	17 819	47 748	11 135	690
1992	177 252	54 742	16 618	21 531	20 841	50 292	12 387	841
1993	185 920	57 875	16 528	21 958	21 695	53 510	13 471	883
1994	200 395	58 417	16 997	23 754	26 712	60 841	12 787	887
1995	219 183	63 395	18 909	26 081	30 289	65 048	14 643	818
1996	239 489	69 809	20 422	26 074	32 470	73 340	16 446	928
1997	256 087	73 426	20 868	27 006	33 228	83 929	16 675	955
1998	262 758	71 325	20 098	25 604	35 626	91 774	17 405	926
1999	281 919	74 801	19 785	26 916	39 670	103 934	15 928	885
2000	298 603	82 400	20 687	29 803	43 233	107 904	13 790	786
2001	286 184	71 893	17 926	28 442	40 696	113 857	12 539	831
2002	292 299	66 605	17 046	29 195	44 508	122 207	11 943	795
2003	302 681	64 348	15 693	31 512	46 988	130 561	12 769	810
2004	349 734	74 546	18 851	36 957	54 490	148 149	15 781	959
2005	389 122	81 799	20 970	41 281	64 395	160 051	19 539	1 087
2006	433 905	85 720	22 036	46 323	72 191	189 050	17 430	1 155
2007	504 784	97 050	25 636	51 550	83 824	220 077	25 436	1 212
2008	549 602	110 090	31 623	58 945	91 599	233 529	22 571	1 245
2009	509 175	94 194	26 878	44 935	84 418	231 336	26 051	1 364
2008								
January	45 497	8 855	2 481	4 870	7 535	19 174	2 481	101
February	44 822	8 920	2 461	4 841	7 533	18 971	1 997	99
March	45 334	9 297	2 580	4 830	7 565	19 214	1 748	99
April	45 863	8 930	2 492	5 098	7 709	19 568	1 964	102
May	47 108	9 621	2 637	5 219	7 746	19 753	2 029	102
June	47 244	9 454	2 821	5 284	7 757	19 887	1 938	103
July	47 201	9 786	2 780	5 299	7 718	19 770	1 745	103
August	46 992	9 795	2 844	5 287	7 693	19 529	1 741	104
September	45 960	9 254	2 630	5 035	7 659	19 641	1 634	106
October	45 877	9 165	2 650	4 646	7 700	19 799	1 809	108
November	43 980	8 415	2 564	4 351	7 585	19 213	1 743	109
December	43 726	8 598	2 682	4 185	7 400	19 008	1 743	109
2009								
January	41 589	8 093	2 520	3 659	6 708	18 695	1 810	104
February	40 965	7 881	2 367	3 618	6 690	18 471	1 834	104
March	40 360	7 480	2 227	3 500	6 676	18 580	1 793	104
April	41 739	7 693	2 324	3 563	6 886	18 917	2 250	106
May	41 456	7 506	2 116	3 512	6 947	19 030	2 239	106
June	42 152	7 567	2 189	3 563	6 995	19 244	2 487	107
July	42 774	7 792	2 153	3 682	7 131	19 422	2 479	115
August	43 105	8 004	2 202	3 734	7 200	19 529	2 316	119
September	43 276	7 986	2 154	3 825	7 254	19 655	2 281	121
October	43 768	8 103	2 195	3 960	7 276	19 877	2 233	124
November	43 917	7 994	2 180	4 192	7 311	19 905	2 209	126
December	44 070	8 095	2 250	4 128	7 343	20 007	2 120	127

[1]Contains goods that cannot be separately identified.

Table 7-16. U.S. Imports of Services

(Balance of payments basis, millions of dollars, seasonally adjusted.)

Year and month	Total	Travel	Passenger fares	Other transportation	Royalties and license fees	Other private services (financial, professional, etc.)	Direct defense expenditures [1]	U.S. government miscellaneous services
1960	7 674	1 750	513	1 402	74	593	3 087	254
1961	7 671	1 785	506	1 437	89	588	2 998	268
1962	8 092	1 939	567	1 558	100	528	3 105	296
1963	8 362	2 114	612	1 701	112	493	2 961	370
1964	8 619	2 211	642	1 817	127	527	2 880	415
1965	9 111	2 438	717	1 951	135	461	2 952	457
1966	10 494	2 657	753	2 161	140	506	3 764	513
1967	11 863	3 207	829	2 157	166	565	4 378	561
1968	12 302	3 030	885	2 367	186	668	4 535	631
1969	13 322	3 373	1 080	2 455	221	751	4 856	586
1970	14 520	3 980	1 215	2 843	224	827	4 855	576
1971	15 400	4 373	1 290	3 130	241	956	4 819	592
1972	16 868	5 042	1 596	3 520	294	1 043	4 784	589
1973	18 843	5 526	1 790	4 694	385	1 180	4 629	640
1974	21 379	5 980	2 095	5 942	346	1 262	5 032	722
1975	21 996	6 417	2 263	5 708	472	1 551	4 795	789
1976	24 570	6 856	2 568	6 852	482	2 006	4 895	911
1977	27 640	7 451	2 748	7 972	504	2 190	5 823	951
1978	32 189	8 475	2 896	9 124	671	2 573	7 352	1 099
1979	36 689	9 413	3 184	10 906	831	2 822	8 294	1 239
1980	41 491	10 397	3 607	11 790	724	2 909	10 851	1 214
1981	45 503	11 479	4 487	12 474	650	3 562	11 564	1 287
1982	51 749	12 394	4 772	11 710	795	8 159	12 460	1 460
1983	54 973	13 149	6 003	12 222	943	8 001	13 087	1 568
1984	67 748	22 913	5 735	14 843	1 168	9 040	12 516	1 534
1985	72 862	24 558	6 444	15 643	1 170	10 203	13 108	1 735
1986	80 147	25 913	6 505	17 766	1 401	13 146	13 730	1 686
1987	90 787	29 310	7 283	19 010	1 857	16 485	14 950	1 893
1988	98 526	32 114	7 729	20 891	2 601	17 667	15 604	1 921
1989	102 479	33 416	8 249	22 172	2 528	18 930	15 313	1 871
1990	117 659	37 349	10 531	24 966	3 135	22 229	17 531	1 919
1991	118 459	35 322	10 012	24 975	4 035	25 590	16 409	2 116
1992	119 566	38 552	10 603	23 767	5 161	25 386	13 835	2 263
1993	123 779	40 713	11 410	24 524	5 032	27 760	12 086	2 255
1994	133 057	43 782	13 062	26 019	5 852	31 565	10 217	2 560
1995	141 397	44 916	14 663	27 034	6 919	35 199	10 043	2 623
1996	152 554	48 078	15 809	27 403	7 837	39 679	11 061	2 687
1997	165 932	52 051	18 138	28 959	9 161	43 154	11 707	2 762
1998	180 677	56 483	19 971	30 363	11 235	47 591	12 185	2 849
1999	199 190	58 963	21 315	34 139	13 107	55 510	13 335	2 821
2000	223 748	64 705	24 274	41 425	16 468	60 520	13 473	2 883
2001	221 791	60 200	22 633	38 682	16 538	66 021	14 835	2 882
2002	231 069	58 715	19 969	38 407	19 353	72 604	19 101	2 920
2003	250 276	57 444	20 957	44 705	19 033	79 710	25 296	3 131
2004	292 247	65 750	24 718	54 161	23 274	91 267	29 299	3 778
2005	313 540	68 970	26 149	61 937	24 612	97 818	30 075	3 979
2006	348 918	72 104	27 501	65 262	23 777	125 221	31 032	4 021
2007	375 215	76 354	28 437	67 100	24 656	141 664	32 820	4 184
2008	405 287	79 743	32 597	72 143	26 616	153 267	36 452	4 469
2009	370 759	73 077	25 996	54 688	23 858	152 574	35 677	4 889
2008								
January	33 060	6 756	2 621	5 963	2 110	12 342	2 908	360
February	33 222	6 737	2 636	6 067	2 147	12 354	2 921	361
March	33 179	6 742	2 611	5 927	2 171	12 426	2 940	362
April	33 437	6 625	2 591	6 081	2 162	12 675	2 943	361
May	33 926	6 769	2 669	6 192	2 178	12 766	2 988	364
June	34 202	6 715	2 769	6 223	2 198	12 875	3 055	367
July	34 843	6 644	2 828	6 375	2 273	13 095	3 255	372
August	35 725	6 707	2 778	6 317	3 156	13 108	3 282	377
September	34 437	6 497	2 737	6 232	2 215	13 129	3 247	381
October	33 873	6 537	2 816	6 009	2 079	13 002	3 040	390
November	32 959	6 514	2 830	5 461	2 001	12 800	2 964	389
December	32 425	6 500	2 711	5 297	1 928	12 696	2 909	385
2009								
January	30 901	6 246	2 413	4 798	1 916	12 322	2 838	368
February	30 269	6 226	2 346	4 527	1 892	12 101	2 810	367
March	29 966	6 044	2 189	4 573	1 881	12 103	2 806	370
April	30 269	5 989	2 032	4 366	2 009	12 580	2 903	391
May	30 000	5 600	1 980	4 270	2 048	12 762	2 944	396
June	30 706	5 877	2 083	4 336	2 076	12 951	2 984	399
July	31 197	6 125	2 148	4 606	1 990	12 877	3 050	402
August	31 055	6 262	2 125	4 344	1 981	12 855	3 077	411
September	31 186	6 173	2 077	4 508	1 984	12 934	3 088	422
October	31 536	6 175	2 156	4 664	2 013	13 020	3 060	447
November	31 611	6 120	2 186	4 748	2 027	13 015	3 058	456
December	32 063	6 240	2 261	4 947	2 041	13 054	3 059	461

[1]Contains goods that cannot be separately identified.

Table 7-17. U.S. Export and Import Price Indexes by End-Use Category

(2000 = 100, not seasonally adjusted.)

Year and month	Exports			Imports		
	All commodities	Agricultural	Nonagricultural	All commodities	Petroleum [1]	Nonpetroleum
1990	95.5	105.1	94.4	94.0	75.5	97.1
1991	96.3	103.4	95.4	94.2	67.3	98.7
1992	96.3	102.5	95.7	94.9	62.9	100.0
1993	96.9	104.4	96.2	94.6	57.7	100.6
1994	98.9	109.4	98.0	96.2	54.3	103.2
1995	103.9	119.0	102.5	100.6	59.8	107.2
1996	104.5	132.6	101.6	101.6	71.1	106.4
1997	103.1	120.6	101.3	99.1	66.0	104.1
1998	99.7	108.8	98.8	93.1	44.8	100.4
1999	98.4	101.1	98.2	93.9	60.1	99.0
2000	100.0	100.0	100.0	100.0	100.0	100.0
2001	99.2	101.2	99.0	96.5	82.8	98.5
2002	98.2	103.2	97.8	94.1	85.3	96.2
2003	99.7	112.3	98.8	96.9	103.2	97.3
2004	103.6	123.4	102.1	102.3	134.6	99.8
2005	106.9	121.0	105.9	110.0	185.1	102.5
2006	110.7	125.8	109.6	115.4	223.3	104.2
2007	116.1	150.9	113.6	120.2	249.1	107.0
2008	123.1	183.5	118.8	134.1	343.2	112.7
2009	117.4	160.0	114.3	118.6	219.9	108.0
2005						
January	105.6	116.1	104.9	104.6	141.2	101.6
February	105.7	115.5	105.0	105.5	148.4	101.7
March	106.4	119.9	105.4	107.8	168.3	102.0
April	106.9	120.3	106.0	108.8	174.4	102.4
May	106.7	122.7	105.5	107.9	166.7	102.2
June	106.7	123.9	105.4	109.2	181.5	102.0
July	106.8	123.9	105.5	110.5	195.5	101.8
August	106.6	123.2	105.4	112.1	209.9	101.9
September	107.5	121.5	106.5	114.4	224.4	102.8
October	108.3	121.9	107.3	114.5	217.5	103.8
November	107.6	121.6	106.6	112.3	197.1	103.7
December	107.7	121.0	106.8	112.3	196.6	103.7
2006						
January	108.5	121.7	107.6	113.7	208.1	104.0
February	108.6	120.8	107.8	112.8	206.0	103.3
March	108.8	120.7	108.0	112.7	207.2	103.0
April	109.6	120.2	108.8	115.1	230.7	103.1
May	110.4	120.9	109.6	117.2	245.4	103.8
June	111.2	124.1	110.3	117.3	242.6	104.2
July	111.6	126.5	110.5	118.2	251.3	104.2
August	112.1	127.7	111.0	118.8	253.7	104.7
September	111.7	127.1	110.6	116.2	225.9	104.8
October	111.4	128.4	110.1	113.3	202.5	104.2
November	111.8	134.1	110.2	113.8	199.2	105.2
December	112.5	137.3	110.7	115.1	207.1	105.7
2007						
January	113.0	138.1	111.2	113.7	193.5	105.6
February	113.9	142.0	111.9	114.1	196.8	105.6
March	114.7	145.0	112.6	115.9	213.6	105.9
April	115.2	142.9	113.2	117.5	228.2	106.2
May	115.5	142.8	113.6	118.6	234.3	106.8
June	116.0	146.7	113.8	120.0	245.6	107.1
July	116.1	149.0	113.7	121.5	260.3	107.2
August	116.3	150.5	113.8	121.1	256.4	107.2
September	116.7	156.8	113.8	121.8	264.4	107.1
October	117.6	162.8	114.4	123.6	277.7	107.7
November	118.7	165.0	115.4	127.5	312.2	108.5
December	119.3	169.3	115.7	127.3	306.7	108.9
2008						
January	120.7	177.5	116.6	129.2	319.6	109.7
February	121.8	185.6	117.3	129.5	315.6	110.4
March	123.8	194.3	118.8	133.5	347.5	111.6
April	124.4	190.5	119.6	137.3	375.8	113.1
May	124.8	190.8	120.1	141.2	412.2	113.9
June	126.1	195.2	121.2	145.5	450.3	114.9
July	128.0	208.2	122.3	147.5	465.0	115.6
August	125.9	188.2	121.5	143.0	419.5	115.1
September	124.9	188.3	120.4	137.8	371.5	114.0
October	122.3	172.5	118.7	129.6	288.9	113.0
November	118.4	160.6	115.4	120.0	201.6	111.1
December	115.8	150.8	113.2	114.5	150.8	109.9
2009						
January	116.6	159.7	113.5	113.0	143.8	109.0
February	116.3	157.0	113.3	113.0	151.6	108.2
March	115.5	151.6	112.9	113.6	168.5	107.3
April	116.1	157.2	113.1	114.8	185.5	107.1
May	116.6	162.8	113.4	116.8	206.1	107.3
June	117.8	169.7	114.1	120.0	241.5	107.4
July	117.4	161.3	114.2	119.3	235.8	107.2
August	118.1	161.6	115.0	121.1	253.7	107.6
September	117.9	156.9	115.1	121.3	252.2	107.9
October	117.9	155.8	115.2	122.3	258.3	108.4
November	118.9	161.8	115.8	124.1	272.2	109.1
December	119.7	164.7	116.5	124.4	269.3	109.7

[1] Petroleum and petroleum products.

NOTES AND DEFINITIONS, CHAPTER 7

This chapter presents data from two different data systems on international flows of goods, services, income payments, and financial transactions as they affect the U.S. economy. Tables 7-1 through 7-5 present data on the value, quantities, and prices of foreign transactions in the national income and product accounts (NIPAs). Tables 7-6 through 7-8 show foreign transactions and investment positions as depicted in the U.S. international transactions accounts (ITAs). Both sets of accounts are prepared by the Bureau of Economic Analysis (BEA) and draw on the same original source data. The Census Bureau source data for goods and services are presented in somewhat greater detail in Tables 7-9 through 7-16. Table 7-17 shows selected summary values for export and import price indexes compiled by the Bureau of Labor Statistics (BLS).

Further detail on U.S. foreign trade in goods and services by region, country, state, metropolitan area, product, and industry is published by Bernan online. For information, see: Diane Werneke. *United States Foreign Trade Highlights: Trends in the Global Market* (2nd edition). (Lanham, MD: Bernan Press, 2007. Bernan Press e-book.)

Due to a few differences in concept, scope, and definitions, the aggregate values of international transactions in the NIPAs (shown in Tables 7-1 and 7-4) are not exactly equal to the values for similar concepts in the ITAs or the Census values that serve as their sources, shown in Tables 7-6 through 7-16. The principal sources of differences are as follows:

- The NIPAs cover only the 50 states and the District of Columbia. The ITAs include the U.S. territories and Puerto Rico as part of the U.S. economy.
- Gold is treated differently.
- Services without payment by financial intermediaries except life insurance carriers (imputed interest) is treated differently.

A reconciliation of the two sets of international accounts is published regularly as part of the NIPAs. As of the time of writing, the most up-to-date reconciliation was Reconciliation Table 1, "Relation of Net Exports of Goods and Services and Net Receipts of Income in the NIPAs to Balance on Goods and Services and Income in the ITAs," which can be found in the *Survey of Current Business*, January 2010, page D-88.

In addition, certain conventions of presentation differ between the two sets of international accounts. In the NIPAs (Tables 7-1 through 7-5) and in Census tables of exports and imports of goods and services (Tables 7-9 through 7-16), values of imports are shown as positive values, even though they are in fact subtracted in the calculation of gross domestic product (GDP). In the ITA balance of payments (Table 7-6), however, values of imports of goods and services and of all other transactions that result in a payment to the rest of the world—income payments to

foreigners, net transfers to foreigners, and net acquisition of assets from abroad—are presented with a minus sign.

TABLES 7-1 AND 7-4
FOREIGN TRANSACTIONS IN THE NATIONAL INCOME AND PRODUCT ACCOUNTS

Source: U.S. Department of Commerce, Bureau of Economic Analysis

See the notes and definitions to Chapter 1 for an overview of the national income and product accounts (NIPAs).

In the 2003 comprehensive revision, the NIPA foreign transactions account was split into two accounts—the current account and the capital account. (This change had already been made in the ITAs.) Most international transactions fall into the current account, but occasionally there are substantial flows in the capital account when major already-existing assets are transferred. An example of this is the U.S. government's transfer of the Panama Canal to the Republic of Panama in 1999.

Definitions

In accordance with the split between current and capital account, there are now two NIPA measures of the balance of international transactions.

The *balance on current account, national income and product accounts* is *current receipts from the rest of the world* minus *current payments to the rest of the world*. A negative value indicates that current payments exceed current receipts.

Net lending or net borrowing (-), national income and product accounts is equal to the balance on current account less capital account transactions with the rest of the world (net). Capital account transactions with the rest of the world (net) is not shown separately in Table 7-1 (for space reasons) but can be calculated from that table as the difference between net lending/borrowing and the current account balance. (A similar measure, a component of the ITAs, is shown explicitly in Table 7-6.) Capital account transactions with the rest of the world are cash or in-kind transfers linked to the acquisition or disposition of an existing, nonproduced, nonfinancial asset. In contrast, the current account is limited to flows associated with current production of goods and services.

Net lending or net borrowing provides an indirect measure of the net acquisition of foreign assets by U.S. residents less the net acquisition of U.S. assets by foreign residents. These asset flows are measured directly in the ITAs. See Table 7-6 and its notes and definitions for a more extensive discussion of the relationship between the balances on current and capital account and international asset flows.

Current receipts from the rest of the world is *exports of goods and services* plus *income receipts*.

Current payments to the rest of the world is *imports of goods and services* plus *income payments* plus *current taxes and transfer payments (net)*.

Exports and imports of goods and services. Goods, in general, are products that can be stored or inventoried. *Services*, in general, are products that cannot be stored and are consumed at the place and time of their purchase. Goods imports include expenditures abroad by U.S. residents, except for travel. Services include foreign travel by U.S. residents, expenditures in the United States by foreign travelers, and exports and imports of certain goods—primarily military equipment purchased and sold by the federal government. See the following paragraph for the definition of *travel*.

Table 7-4 shows values for selected components of total goods and services; the components shown will not add to the total because of omitted items. In the case of goods, a miscellaneous "other" category is not shown. In the case of services, only two components are shown in this table. One is *travel*, which does not include passenger fares but includes as exports spending by foreign tourists in the United States, and includes as imports all other spending abroad by tourists from the United States. The other component shown here is a category called *other private services*, which includes the professional and financial services (for example, computer services) that have accounted for a large part of the long-term growth in the service category. The remaining components of total services are transfers under U.S. military agency sales contracts; passenger fares; other transportation; royalties and license fees; and a miscellaneous, smaller *other* category. They are shown separately in Tables 7-15 and 7-16.

Income receipts and payments. Income receipts—receipts from abroad of factor (labor or capital) income by U.S. residents—are analogous to exports and are combined with them to yield total *current receipts from the rest of the world. Income payments* by U.S. entities of factor income to entities abroad are analogous to imports.

Current taxes and transfer payments (net) consists of net payments between the United States and abroad that do not involve payment for the services of the labor or capital factors of production, purchase of currently-produced goods and services, or transfer of an existing asset. It includes net flows from persons, government, and business. The types of payments included are personal remittances from U.S. residents to the rest of the world, net of remittances from foreigners to U.S. residents; government grants; and transfer payments from businesses. Only the net payment to the rest of the world is shown. It usually appears in these accounts as a positive value, with transfers from the United States to abroad exceeding the reverse flow. An exception came in 1991, when U.S. allies in the Gulf War reimbursed the United States for the cost of the war. This resulted in net payments to the United States from the rest of the world and appears as a negative entry in the net transfer payments column of the NIPA accounts. (Note that these signs are reversed in the ITAs, because of the differing measurement conventions described above.)

TABLES 7-2, 7-3 AND 7-5
CHAIN-TYPE QUANTITY AND PRICE INDEXES FOR NIPA FOREIGN TRANSACTIONS

These indexes represent the separation of the current-dollar values in Tables 7-1 and 7-4 into their real quantity and price trends components. (See the notes and definitions to Chapter 1 for a general explanation of chained-dollar estimates of real output and prices.) As those notes explain, quantity indexes are shown instead of constant-dollar estimates, because BEA no longer publishes its real output estimates before 1995 in any detail in the constant-dollar form. Therefore, quantity indexes are the only comprehensive source of information about longer-term trends in real volumes.

TABLES 7-6 AND 19-10
U.S. INTERNATIONAL TRANSACTIONS

SOURCE: U.S. DEPARTMENT OF COMMERCE, BUREAU OF ECONOMIC ANALYSIS

The U.S. international transactions accounts (ITAs), or "balance of payments accounts," provide a comprehensive view of economic and financial transactions between the United States and foreign countries, measured in current dollars only—unlike the NIPAs, in which price and quantity trends are also estimated. Direct measurement of the values of financial asset flows further distinguishes this set of accounts from the NIPAs.

The ITAs are subdivided into three sets of accounts, with each comprising credit and debit items. In concept, all of these items together provide a complete accounting for U.S. international transactions and should therefore sum to zero. In practice, there are substantial discrepancies due to measurement problems. See the definitions below for an explanation of the *statistical discrepancy* in these accounts, which is different from the measure of the same name in the NIPAs.

The *balance on current account* is the most frequently quoted statistic from these accounts, and is often, but imprecisely, called the "trade balance." (See the definitions below for the correct definitions of "trade balance" and "merchandise trade balance," both of which differ from the current account balance.) The current account includes exports and imports of goods and of travel, transportation, and other services; receipts and payments of income between U.S. and foreign residents; and foreign aid and other current transfers. The *financial account* covers most international flows of private and official capital, including direct investment. The *capital account*, which is small relative to the other two accounts, includes certain transactions in existing assets.

More detailed data on exports and imports of goods and services as measured in these accounts are shown in Tables 7-9 through 7-16.

Definitions

Unlike the practice in the NIPA accounts, each category of transaction in the ITAs is presented either as a *credit,* with an implicit plus sign, or as a *debit*, with a clearly marked minus sign. The signs indicate the direction of the ultimate impact on the overall balance.

Credits (+): The following items are treated as credits in the international transactions accounts: exports of goods and services and income receipts; unilateral current transfers to the United States; capital account transactions receipts; and financial inflows, which are increases in foreign-owned assets (U.S. liabilities) and decreases in U.S.-owned assets (U.S. claims). Credits represent payments of funds to U.S. entities, whether earned (as with exports), received as gifts, received in payment for assets, or received in exchange for a claim, such as a stock, bond, or loan agreement, on a U.S. entity.

Debits (-): The following items are treated as debits in the international transactions accounts, indicated by minus signs in the data cells: imports of goods and services and income payments; unilateral current transfers to foreigners; capital accounts transactions payments; financial outflows, which are decreases in foreign-owned assets (U.S. liabilities) and increases in U.S.-owned assets (U.S. claims). Debits represent requirements for U.S. entities to make payments to foreigners, whether for imports, as gifts, or as payments for the acquisition of real or financial assets.

This convention of credits and debits is used only in the ITAs in Table 7-6 and the long-term flow data in Table 7-7 (see below). In Table 7-6, import values all have a negative sign. Import values are shown without negative signs both in the NIPA tables (Tables 7-1 and 7-4) and in the detailed tables from the Census Bureau on exports and imports of goods and services (Tables 7-9 through 7-16).

The *balance on goods* is the excess of exports of goods over imports of goods—the algebraic sum of the two, in ITA transactions accounting. A minus sign indicates an excess of imports over exports. A similar concept, which appears in monthly trade reports, is called the "merchandise trade balance."

The *balance on services* is the excess of service exports over service imports. A minus sign indicates an excess of imports over exports.

The *balance on goods and services* is the sum of the balance on goods and the balance on services. This concept is accurately described as the "balance of trade."

The *balance on income* is the excess of income receipts from abroad over income payments to foreigners. A minus sign indicates an excess of payments over receipts.

The *balance on goods, services, and income* is the excess of exports of goods and services and income receipts over

imports of goods and services and income payments. It is equal to the sum of the balance on goods and services and the balance on income. A minus sign indicates an excess of imports and payments over exports and receipts.

Unilateral current transfers, net is equal to unilateral transfers to the United States minus transfers from the United States. This category includes U.S. government grants, pensions, and other transfers, and private remittances and other transfers. In the July 2009 revision, insurance payments for extraordinary disaster losses were shifted from this account to the *capital account*.

The *balance on current account* is equal to the sum of the balance on goods, services, and income and the net balance on unilateral transfers. It is the featured measure of the U.S. balance of payments.

The *capital account* covers net capital transfers and the acquisition and disposal of nonproduced nonfinancial assets. The major types of *capital transfers* are debt forgiveness and assets that accompany immigrants. *Nonproduced nonfinancial assets* include rights to natural resources, patents, copyrights, trademarks, franchises, and leases. In the July 2009 revision, insurance payments for extraordinary disaster losses such as those caused by major hurricanes and the 2001 terror attack were shifted to the capital account from the current unilateral transfers account.

The *financial account* includes all other inflows and outflows of capital, or changes in U.S.-owned assets abroad and foreign-owned assets in the United States, including official reserve assets, direct investment, securities, currency, and bank deposits. Most of the categories are self-explanatory.

U.S. government assets other than official reserve assets, net and its component *U.S. foreign currency holdings and short-term assets, net* include the initiation and reversal of large swap positions under temporary reciprocal currency arrangements between the U.S. Federal Reserve System and foreign central banks, undertaken in order to deal with the international financial crisis in late 2008. The accounts indicate creation of a half-trillion dollars' worth of swaps in 2008 (because a minus sign in these accounts indicates increases in U.S. official assets) and the reversal of about the same amount in 2009.

Direct investment financial flows are those associated with the acquisition of a significant interest (10 percent or more) in a business enterprise in one country by a resident of another country.

U.S. claims reported by U.S. banks and securities brokers, a component of *U.S. private assets, net*. Beginning with 2003, these entries include securities brokers' claims on their foreign affiliates. Prior to 2003, such claims are included in the claims of nonbanking concerns.

U.S. liabilities reported by U.S. banks and securities brokers, components of *Foreign official assets in the United States, net* and *Other foreign assets in the United States, net.* Beginning with 2003, these entries include securities brokers' liabilities to their foreign affiliates. Prior to 2003, such liabilities are included in the liabilities of nonbanking concerns.

Foreign official assets in the United States. U.S. Treasury securities includes bills, certificates, marketable bonds and notes, and nonmarketable convertible and nonconvertible bonds and notes. *Other U.S. government securities* consists of U.S. Treasury and Export-Import Bank obligations, not included elsewhere, and of debt securities of U.S. government corporations and agencies. *Other U.S. government liabilities* primarily includes U.S. government liabilities to foreign official authorities associated with military agency sales contracts and other transactions arranged with or through foreign official agencies. *Other foreign official assets* consists of official investments in U.S. corporate stocks and in debt securities of private corporations and state and local governments.

In concept, the balance on current account is exactly offset by the net financial and capital inflow or outflow. For example, a U.S. current account deficit results in more dollars held by foreigners, which <u>must</u> be reflected in additional claims on the United States held by foreigners, whether in the form of U.S. currency, dollar bank accounts, securities, loans, or other forms of ownership or obligation. However, because of different and incomplete data sources, the measured financial and capital accounts do not exactly offset the measured current account. The *statistical discrepancy* in the U.S. international accounts—the sum of all credits and debits, with the sign reversed—measures the amount by which the measured net financial and capital flow would have to be augmented (or diminished, in the case of a negative discrepancy) to exactly offset the current account balance. In the quarterly accounts, a part of this discrepancy, the *seasonal adjustment discrepancy*, results from separate seasonal adjustments of the components of the accounts. The statistical discrepancy in the international accounts is not the same as the statistical discrepancy in the national income and product accounts, which arises from measurement differences between domestic output and domestic income.

Notes on the data

There are "breaks" (discontinuities) in the historical series for several of the components of the balance of payments accounts. See Technical Notes in the June 1989–1990, 1992–1995, and July 1996–2007 issues of the *Survey of Current Business.*

Exports and imports of goods in the international transactions account excludes both exports of goods under U.S. military agency sales contracts identified in Census Bureau export documents and imports of goods under direct defense expenditures identified in import documents. They also reflect various other adjustments (for valuation, coverage, and timing) of Census Bureau statistics to a balance-

of-payments basis. See the notes and definitions to Tables 7-9 through 7-16 for further information.

Services includes some goods, mainly military equipment (included in transfers under military agency sales contracts); major equipment, other materials, supplies, and petroleum products purchased abroad by U.S. military agencies (included in direct defense expenditures abroad); and fuels purchased by airline and steamship operators (included in other transportation).

U.S. government grants includes transfers of goods and services under U.S. military grant programs. The positive value in 1991 reflects net grants to the United States from other countries.

Beginning in 1982, *private remittances and other transfers* includes taxes paid by U.S. private residents to foreign governments and taxes paid by private nonresidents to the U.S. government.

At the present time, all U.S. Treasury-owned *gold* is held in the United States.

Repayments on U.S. credits and other long-term assets includes sales of foreign obligations to foreigners. The data for 1974 include extraordinary U.S. government transactions with India, as described in "Special U.S. Government Transactions," *Survey of Current Business,* June 1974, page 27.

Beginning with the data for 1982, *direct investment income payments* and the reinvested earnings component of *direct investment* financial flows are measured on a current-cost (replacement-cost) basis after adjustment to reported depreciation, depletion, and expensed exploration and development costs. For prior years, depreciation is valued in terms of the historical cost of assets and reflects a mix of prices for the various years in which capital investments were made. See *Survey of Current Business,* July 1999, pages 65–67, and *Survey of Current Business*, June 1992, pages 72ff.

The *U.S. Treasury securities* component of *other foreign assets in the United States* includes foreign-currency denominated notes sold to private residents abroad for 1978 through 1983.

Estimates of *U.S. currency flows abroad* were introduced for the first time as part of the July 1997 revisions. Data for 1974 and subsequent years were affected (see *Survey of Current Business*, July 1997). Beginning with the 1998 revisions, currency flows are published separately from U.S. Treasury securities.

Financial derivatives, net are estimated for the first time for 2006. (Previously, they were partly measured in other financial flow components and in part contributed to the statistical discrepancy.) They are reported on a net basis only, indicating net receipts (financial inflows) of $29.7 billion in 2006 and $6.2 billion in 2007, an outflow of $28.9 billion in

2008, and inflows of $31.2 billion in the first three quarters of 2009. See "References," below, for more explanation.

Data availability

Quarterly estimates are reported in a press release around the middle of the third month of each quarter, available on the BEA Web site at <http://www.bea.gov> The data published here were released on March 18, 2010, presenting data for the fourth quarter and year 2009 and revisions of earlier data. Complete historical data are available on the BEA Web site at <http://www.bea.gov/>.

A comprehensive revision of the ITAs is scheduled for June 2010.

References

Discussions of the impact of changes in methodology and incorporation of new data sources when they occur are found in July issues (the June issues for 1995 and earlier years) of the *Survey of Current Business*, with the most recent such article entitled "Annual Revision of the U.S. International Accounts" (July 2009). A similarly titled article in the July 2007 *Survey* includes an extensive discussion of the new data on financial derivatives and their role in the ITA financial account and investment position data.

The Balance of Payments of the United States: Concepts, Data Sources, and Estimating Procedures (May 1990), available on the BEA Web site or from the National Technical Information Service (Accession No. PB 90-268715), describes the methodology in detail and provides a list of data sources.

TABLE 7-7
FOREIGNERS' TRANSACTIONS IN LONG-TERM SECURITIES WITH U.S. RESIDENTS

SOURCE: U.S. DEPARTMENT OF THE TREASURY

Some of the transactions that go into the ITA financial account are collected monthly. Since December 2003, these transactions have been reported by the Treasury Department in a monthly press release. They are presented in Table 7-7.

These data cover transactions in long-term securities, measured at market value plus or minus commissions and fees, between foreigners and U.S. residents. They have more reporting gaps than the more comprehensive quarterly current account data in Table 7-6. These monthly data do not include direct investment, currency flows, changes in bank accounts, or transactions in short-term securities. They may be distorted by inappropriate reporting of repurchases and securities lending transactions. The data are more timely but less detailed than other information sources and are not

reliable for country-by-country detail. They are based on a reporting panel of some 250 banks, securities dealers, and other enterprises with cross-border transactions of at least $50 million. This survey was designed to provide timely information for the balance of payments accounts, and its use for other applications—particularly those involving country detail—is less appropriate.

Definitions and notes on the data

U.S. residents includes any individual, corporation, or organization located in the United States (including branches, subsidiaries, and affiliates of foreign entities located in the United States) and any corporation incorporated in the United States, even if it has no physical presence in the country.

Gross purchases minus *gross sales* equals *net purchases*. As in the ITAs in Table 7-6, positive values for net purchases of U.S. securities by foreigners indicate capital inflows from foreigners to U.S. residents (and increased liabilities to foreigners on the part of the U.S. residents). Negative values for net purchases of foreign securities from U.S. residents indicate a capital outflow from U.S. residents to foreigners (and increased liabilities to U.S. residents on the part of foreigners). The algebraic sum of the two net purchases components gives *net long-term securities transactions*. When positive, this indicates that the net capital inflows on U.S. securities exceed the net U.S. acquisitions of foreign securities.

Other acquisitions of long-term securities, net consists of estimated foreign acquisitions of U.S. equity through stock swaps, plus the increase in nonmarketable treasury bonds and notes issued to official institutions and other residents of foreign countries, minus estimated unrecorded principal payments to foreigners on domestic corporate and agency asset-backed securities, minus estimated U.S. acquisitions of foreign equity through stock swaps.

Net foreign acquisition of long-term securities is the sum of *net long-term securities transactions* and *other acquisitions of long-term securities*.

Revisions

The monthly and annual data are revised frequently, when quarterly and annual benchmark data become available. The June release usually includes the final results from an annual survey of foreign holding of U.S. securities.

Data availability and references

Data for the latest month and recent historical data are published in a press release available around the middle of the second following month. The press release, supporting descriptions, references, and other relevant information concerning the Treasury International Capital System (TIC) can be found online at <http://www.treas.gov/tic>.

TABLE 7-8
INTERNATIONAL INVESTMENT POSITION OF THE UNITED STATES

SOURCE: U.S. DEPARTMENT OF COMMERCE, BUREAU OF ECONOMIC ANALYSIS

The data presented in Tables 7-1 through 7-7 all represent <u>flows</u> of goods, services, and money over the designated time periods. Table 7-8, in contrast, is a measure of <u>stocks</u>, or total holdings of money and other claims. The data on the international investment position of the United States measure the extent to which the United States and its residents hold claims of ownership on foreigners or are creditors of foreigners; the extent to which foreigners, including foreign governments, hold claims of ownership on assets located in the United States or are creditors of U.S. residents and entities; and the net difference between the two amounts. This difference measures the amount by which the United States is a net creditor of the rest of the world or a net debtor to the rest of the world. A position of net U.S. indebtedness is represented by a minus sign in the net international investment position.

Changes in the net investment position can arise in two principal ways:

• The first way is through inflows or outflows of capital. A net inflow of capital increases U.S. indebtedness to foreigners, while a net outflow increases foreigners' indebtedness to the United States. A deficit in the U.S. international current account requires an equivalent inflow of foreign capital, while a surplus would require an equivalent outflow of U.S. capital; see notes for Table 7-6 for further explanation.

• The second way is through valuation adjustments, which are of several kinds: changes in market prices of assets; changes in exchange rates, which can cause revaluation of foreign-currency-denominated assets; and miscellaneous other adjustments due to changes in coverage, statistical discrepancies, and the like.

Two new features were introduced into the investment position accounts with the 2007 revision. First, only one version of the net position is now published, the one in which direct investment is measured at current cost. (See definitions below.) However, alternative measures of direct investment measured at market prices are also published, so that the user can calculate the position with market valuation of direct investment. Second, for the years 2005 forward, assets and the net position include financial derivatives, which introduces a break in the series. The values for financial derivatives are shown separately so that the user can eliminate them from the calculation if desired. The net value of derivatives amounted to $160 billion at the end of 2008. Without including derivatives, the U.S. international investment position would have been net indebtedness of $3.63 trillion instead of the net indebtedness of $3.47 trillion shown in Table 7-8.

Definitions: direct investment, current cost, and market value

Direct investment occurs when an individual or business in one country (the parent) obtains a lasting interest in, and a degree of influence over the management of, a business enterprise in another country (the affiliate). The U.S. data define this degree of interest to be ownership of at least 10 percent of the voting securities of an incorporated business enterprise or the equivalent interest in an unincorporated business enterprise.

When direct investment positions are valued at the historical costs carried on the books of the affiliated companies, much of the investment will reflect the price levels of earlier time periods. Therefore, before calculating the overall U.S. position, BEA re-estimates the <u>aggregate</u> direct investment totals using two alternative valuation bases. <u>Detailed</u> direct investment data by country and industry are available only on a historical cost basis.

At *current cost*, the portion of the direct investment position representing the parents' shares of their affiliates' tangible assets (property, plant, equipment, and inventories) is revalued to replacement cost in today's money, using a perpetual inventory model, appropriate price indexes, and appropriate depreciation allowances. (The same methodology is used for the U.S. stock of fixed assets; see the notes and definitions to Tables 5-5 and 5-6 for further information.) This is an adjustment made to the asset side of the balance sheet and reflects prices of tangible assets only.

The *market value* method revalues the owners' equity portion of the direct investment positions using general country indexes of stock market prices. This adjustment is made on the liability and owner's equity side of the balance sheet. Stock price changes reflect changes not only in the value of tangible assets, but also in the value of intangible assets and in the outlook for a country or industry.

Market values are more volatile than current cost, reflecting the nature of stock markets and the additional uncertainties concerning the intangibles included in the valuation. Typically, the total market value of direct investment is greater than the current replacement cost, though by varying proportions. However, in a few years (such as 1982 through 1984) aggregate market values fell below the estimated replacement cost.

Definitions: net international investment position

U.S. net international investment position is defined as the value of *U.S.-owned assets abroad* minus the value of *foreign-owned assets in the United States.*

U.S.-owned assets abroad is the sum of *financial derivatives, official reserve assets, other U.S. government assets, direct investment at current cost, foreign bonds, foreign corporate stocks, U.S. nonblank claims,* and *U.S. bank claims.*

As a component of U.S.-owned assets, the *financial derivatives* category is the sum of derivatives positions with a positive "fair value" to U.S. residents. The fair value of a derivatives contract is the amount for which the contract could be exchanged between willing parties. A derivatives contract between a U.S. and a foreign resident with a positive fair value represents the amount that the foreign resident would have to pay to the U.S. resident if the contract was terminated.

U.S. official reserve assets includes gold, valued at the current market price; special drawing rights; the U.S. reserve position in the International Monetary Fund; and official holdings of foreign currencies.

Other U.S. government assets includes other U.S. government claims on foreigners and holdings of foreign currency and short-term assets.

U.S. nonbank claims includes U.S. claims on affiliated foreigners reported by U.S. nonbanking concerns.

U.S. bank claims consists of claims on foreigners, such as loans and commercial paper, held by U.S. banks and not reported elsewhere in the accounts.

Foreign-owned assets in the United States includes *financial derivatives, foreign official assets, direct investment in the United States at current cost, U.S. Treasury securities, U.S. currency, corporate and other bonds, corporate stocks, U.S. nonbank liabilities,* and *U.S. bank liabilities.*

As a component of foreign-owned assets in the United States, *financial derivatives* consists of derivatives positions with a negative "fair value" to U.S. residents. A contract with a negative fair value represents the amount that the U.S. resident would have to pay to the foreign resident if the contract was terminated.

Foreign official assets includes foreign government holdings of claims on the United States, including U.S. government securities and other liabilities and deposits held by such governments in U.S. banks.

Foreign-owned assets in the United States, other than official assets, also include *U.S. Treasury securities, U.S. currency, corporate and other bonds, corporate stocks, U.S. liabilities (to foreigners) reported by U.S. nonbanking concerns,* and *U.S. bank liabilities to foreigners* (such as deposits).

Data availability

The annual (year-end) data, along with revisions for earlier years and a descriptive article, are presented each year in the July issue of the *Survey of Current Business.* The articles and the data are available on the BEA Web site at <http://www.bea.gov>.

References

The estimates shown here were published and described in "The International Investment Position of the United States at Yearend 2008" in the July 2009 *Survey of Current Business.* A comparable article in the July 2007 *Survey* includes extensive data and discussion of the new coverage of financial derivatives. For background on the valuation of direct investment and other components, see "Valuation of the U.S. Net International Investment Position," *Survey of Current Business,* May 1991. Also see the references for Table 7-6.

TABLES 7-9 THROUGH 7-16
EXPORTS AND IMPORTS OF GOODS AND SERVICES

SOURCES: U.S. DEPARTMENT OF COMMERCE, CENSUS BUREAU AND BUREAU OF ECONOMIC ANALYSIS

These tables present the source data used to build up the aggregate measures of goods and services flows shown in Tables 7-1 through 7-6. These data are compiled and published monthly, making trends evident before the publication of the quarterly aggregate estimates. They also provide more detail than the quarterly aggregates.

Monthly and annual data on exports and imports of *goods* are compiled by the Census Bureau from documents collected by the U.S. Customs Service. The Bureau of Economic Analysis (BEA) makes certain adjustments to these data (as described below) to place the estimates on a *balance of payments* basis—a basis consistent with the national and international accounts.

Data on exports and imports of *services* are prepared by BEA from a variety of sources. Monthly data on services are available from January 1992. Annual and quarterly data for earlier years are available as part of the international transactions accounts. Current data on goods and services are available each month in a joint Census Bureau-BEA press release.

In the case of some of the detailed breakdowns of exports and imports, such as by end-use categories, monthly data may not sum exactly to annual totals. This is due to later revisions, which are made only to annual data and are not allocated to monthly data. Also, the constant-dollar figures expressed in 2005 dollars are now calculated using chain weights. Therefore, the 2005-dollar detail will not add to the 2005-dollar totals.

In addition, monthly and annual data on exports and imports of goods for individual countries and various country groupings do not reflect subsequent revisions of annual total data. These country data are compiled by the Census Bureau for all countries, although this volume includes only a selection of the most significant countries and areas. The full set of data can be accessed on the Census Web site at <http://www.census.gov>.

Definitions: Goods

Goods: Census basis. The Census basis goods data are compiled from documents collected by the U.S. Customs Service. They reflect the movement of goods between foreign countries and the 50 states, the District of Columbia, Puerto Rico, the U.S. Virgin Islands, and U.S. Foreign Trade Zones. They include government and nongovernment shipments of goods, and exclude shipments between the United States and its territories and possessions; transactions with U.S. military, diplomatic, and consular installations abroad; U.S. goods returned to the United States by its armed forces; personal and household effects of travelers; and in-transit shipments. The general import values reflect the total arrival of merchandise from foreign countries that immediately enters consumption channels, warehouses, or Foreign Trade Zones.

For *imports*, the value reported is the U.S. Customs Service appraised value of merchandise (generally, the price paid for merchandise for export to the United States). Import duties, freight, insurance, and other charges incurred in bringing merchandise to the United States are excluded.

Exports are valued at the f.a.s. (free alongside ship) value of merchandise at the U.S. port of export, based on the transaction price including inland freight, insurance, and other charges incurred in placing the merchandise alongside the carrier at the U.S. port of exportation.

Goods: balance of payments (BOP) basis. Goods on a Census basis are adjusted by BEA to goods on a BOP basis to bring the data in line with the concepts and definitions used to prepare the international and national accounts. In general, the adjustments include changes in ownership that occur without goods passing into or out of the customs territory of the United States. These adjustments are necessary to supplement coverage of the Census basis data, to eliminate duplication of transactions recorded elsewhere in the international accounts, and to value transactions according to a standard definition.

The *export* adjustments include the following: (1) The deduction of *U.S. military sales contracts*. The Census Bureau has included these contracts in the goods data, but BEA includes them in the service category "Transfers Under U.S. Military Sales Contracts." BEA's source material for these contracts is more comprehensive but does not distinguish between goods and services. (2) The addition of *private gift parcels* mailed to foreigners by individuals through the U.S. Postal Service. Only commercial shipments are covered in Census goods exports. (3) The addition to *nonmonetary gold exports* of gold purchased by foreign official agencies from private dealers in the United States and held at the Federal Reserve Bank of New York. The Census data include only gold that leaves the customs territory. (4) *Smaller adjustments* includes deductions for repairs of goods, exposed motion picture film, and military grant aid, and additions for sales of fish in U.S. territorial waters, exports of electricity to Mexico, and vessels and oil rigs that change ownership without export documents being filed.

The *import* adjustments include the following: (1) On *inland freight in Canada*, the customs value for imports for certain Canadian goods is the point of origin in Canada. BEA makes an addition for the inland freight charges of transporting these Canadian goods to the U.S. border. (2) An addition is made to *nonmonetary gold imports* for gold sold by foreign official agencies to private purchasers out of stock held at the Federal Reserve Bank of New York. The Census Bureau data include only gold that enters the customs territory. (3) A deduction is made for *imports by U.S. military agencies*. The Census Bureau has included these contracts in the goods data, but BEA includes them in the service category "Direct Defense Expenditures." BEA's source material is more comprehensive but does not distinguish between goods and services. (4) *Smaller adjustments* includes deductions for repairs of goods and for exposed motion picture film and additions for imported electricity from Mexico, conversion of vessels for commercial use, and repairs to U.S. vessels abroad.

Definitions: Services

The statistics are estimates of service transactions between foreign countries and the 50 states, the District of Columbia, Puerto Rico, the U.S. Virgin Islands, and other U.S. territories and possessions. Transactions with U.S. military, diplomatic, and consular installations abroad are excluded because they are considered to be part of the U.S. economy. Services are shown in the broad categories described below. For six of these categories, the definitions are the same for imports and exports. For the seventh, the export category is "Transfers under U.S. Military Sales Contracts," while for imports, the category is "Direct Defense Expenditures."

Travel includes purchases of services and goods by U.S. travelers abroad and by foreign visitors to the United States. A traveler is defined as a person who stays for a period of less than one year in a country where the person is not a resident. Included are expenditures for food, lodging, recreation, gifts, and other items incidental to a foreign visit. Not included are the international costs of the travel itself, which are covered in *passenger fares* (see below).

Passenger fares consists of fares paid by residents of one country to residents in other countries. Receipts consist of fares received by U.S. carriers from foreign residents for travel between the United States and foreign countries and between two foreign points. Payments consist of fares paid by U.S. residents to foreign carriers for travel between the United States and foreign countries.

Break in series: travel and passenger fares. Beginning with data for 1984, these items incorporate results from a survey administered by the U.S. Travel and Tourism Administration. See *Survey of Current Business*, June 1989, pages 57ff.

Other transportation includes charges for the transportation of goods by ocean, air, waterway, pipeline, and rail carriers to and from the United States. Included are freight charges, operating expenses that transportation companies incur in foreign ports, and payments for vessel charter and aircraft and freight car rentals. (*Break in series*: Estimates of freight charges for the transportation of goods by truck between the United States and Canada are included in the data beginning with 1986. Reliable estimates for earlier years are not available. See *Survey of Current Business*, June 1994, pages 70ff.)

Royalties and license fees consists of transactions with foreign residents involving intangible assets and proprietary rights, such as the use of patents, techniques, processes, formulas, designs, know-how, trademarks, copyrights, franchises, and manufacturing rights. The term *royalties* generally refers to payments for the utilization of copyrights or trademarks, and the term *license fees* generally refers to payments for the use of patents or industrial processes.

Other private services includes transactions with "affiliated" foreigners for which no identification by type is available and transactions with unaffiliated foreigners.

The term "affiliated" refers to a direct investment relationship, which exists when a U.S. person has ownership or control (directly or indirectly) of 10 percent or more of a foreign business enterprise, or when a foreign person has a similar interest in a U.S. enterprise.

Transactions with "unaffiliated" foreigners in this "other private services" category consist of education services, financial services, insurance services, telecommunications services, and business, professional, and technical services. Included in the last group are advertising services; computer and data processing services; database and other information services; research, development, and testing services; management, consulting, and public relations services; legal services; construction, engineering, architectural, and mining services; industrial engineering services; installation, maintenance, and repair of equipment; and other services, including medical services and film and tape rental.

The insurance component of "other private services" was measured before the July 2003 revision as premiums less actual losses paid or recovered. Furthermore, catastrophic losses were entered immediately when the loss occurred, rather than when the insurance claim was actually paid out. This led to sharp swings for any month in which catastrophic losses occurred, such as Hurricane Katrina in August 2005 or the September 11, 2001, terror attacks. In the accounts as revised in July 2003 and presented here, insurance services are now measured as premiums less "normal" losses. Normal losses consist of a measure of expected regularly occurring losses based on six years of past experience plus an additional allowance for catastrophic loss. Catastrophic losses, when they occur, are added in equal increments to the estimate of regularly occurring losses over the 20 years following the occurrence. As adoption of this methodology introduces a difference between actual and normal losses, an amount equal to the difference is entered in the international accounts as a capital account transaction.

BEA conducts surveys of international transactions in financial services and "selected services" (largely business, professional, and technical services). Beginning with data for 1986, *other private services* includes estimates of business, professional, and technical services from the BEA surveys of selected services. (See *Survey of Current Business*, June 1989, pages 57ff.)

Breaks in series: royalties and license fees and other private services. These items are presented on a gross basis beginning in 1982. The definition of exports is revised to exclude U.S. parents' payments to foreign affiliates and to include U.S. affiliates' receipts from foreign parents. The definition of imports is revised to include U.S. parents' payments to foreign affiliates and to exclude U.S. affiliates' receipts from foreign parents.

Transfers under U.S. military sales contracts (exports only) includes exports of goods and services in which U.S. government military agencies participate. This category includes both goods, such as equipment, and services, such as repair services and training, that cannot be separately identified. Transfers of goods and services under U.S. military grant programs are included.

Direct defense expenditures (imports only) consists of expenditures incurred by U.S. military agencies abroad, including expenditures by U.S. personnel, payments of wages to foreign residents, construction expenditures, payments for foreign contractual services, and procurement of foreign goods. Included are both goods and services that cannot be separately identified.

U.S. government miscellaneous services includes transactions of U.S. government nonmilitary agencies with foreign residents. Most of these transactions involve the provision of services to, or purchases of services from, foreigners. Transfers of some goods are also included.

Services estimates are based on quarterly, annual, and benchmark surveys and partial information generated from monthly reports. Service transactions are estimated at market prices. Estimates are seasonally adjusted when statistically significant seasonal patterns are present.

Definitions: Area groupings

The Census trade statistics for groups of countries present "groups as they were at the time of reporting", which means that as multinational organizations such as the European Union expand, the statistics for trade with that group include the added country only beginning with the year it entered the group. The European Union was expanded from 15 to 25 nations on May 1, 2004, and data for that year are available for both the new and the old group; to provide historical perspective, they are both shown here, along with the historical data back to 1974 for the original group.

The *European Union* now includes Austria, Belgium, Bulgaria, Cyprus, Czech Republic, Denmark, Estonia, Finland, France, Germany, Greece, Hungary, Ireland, Italy, Latvia, Lithuania, Luxembourg, Malta, the Netherlands, Poland, Portugal, Romania, Slovakia, Slovenia, Spain, Sweden, and the United Kingdom.

The *Euro area* in 2009 included Austria, Belgium, Cyprus, Finland, France, Germany, Greece, Ireland, Italy, Luxembourg, Malta, the Netherlands, Portugal, Slovakia, Slovenia, and Spain. See the notes and definitions to Table 13-8 for further information about the euro.

The *Asian Newly Industrialized Countries (NICS)* includes Hong Kong SAR, South Korea, Singapore, and Taiwan.

The *Organization of Petroleum Exporting Countries (OPEC)* currently consists of Algeria, Angola, Ecuador, Iran, Iraq, Kuwait, Libya, Nigeria, Qatar, Saudi Arabia, the United Arab Emirates, and Venezuela. Indonesia is no longer a member as of January 2009.

Notes on the data

U.S./Canada data exchange and substitution. The data for U.S. exports to Canada are derived from import data compiled by Canada. The use of Canada's import data to produce U.S. export data requires several alignments in order to compare the two series.

- *Coverage*: Canadian imports are based on country of origin. U.S. goods shipped from a third country are included, but U.S. exports exclude these foreign shipments. U.S. export coverage also excludes certain Canadian postal shipments.
- *Valuation*: Canadian imports are valued at their point of origin in the United States. However, U.S. exports are valued at the port of exit in the United States and include inland freight charges, making the U.S. export value slightly larger. Canada requires inland freight to be reported.
- *Reexports*: U.S. exports include re-exports of foreign goods. Again, the aggregate U.S. export figure is slightly larger.
- *Exchange Rate*: Average monthly exchange rates are applied to convert the published data to U.S. currency.

End-use categories and seasonal adjustment of trade in goods. Goods are initially classified under the Harmonized System, which describes and measures the characteristics of goods traded. Combining trade into approximately 140 export and 140 import end-use categories makes it possible to examine goods according to their principal uses. These categories are used as the basis for computing the seasonal and working-day adjusted data. Adjusted data are then summed to the six end-use aggregates for publication.

The seasonal adjustment procedure is based on a model that estimates the monthly movements as percentages above or below the general level of each end-use commodity series (unlike other methods that redistribute the actual series values over the calendar year). Imports of petroleum and petroleum products are adjusted for the length of the month.

Data availability

Data are released monthly in a joint Census Bureau-BEA press release (FT-900), which is published about six weeks after the end of the month to which the data pertain. The release and historical data are available on the Census Bureau Web site at <http://www.census.gov/foreign-trade/www/>.

Revisions

Data for recent years are normally revised annually. In some cases, revisions to annual totals are not distributed to monthly data; therefore, monthly data may not sum to the revised total shown. Data on trade in services may be subject to extensive revision as part of BEA's annual revision of the international transactions accounts (ITAs), usually released in July.

References

Discussion of the impact of changes in methodology and incorporation of new data sources are found in the discussions of annual revisions of the ITAs in the July issues of BEA's *Survey of Current Business*. The most recent pertinent article is "Annual Revision of the U.S. International Accounts" (July 2009).

TABLE 7-17
EXPORT AND IMPORT PRICE INDEXES

SOURCE: U.S. DEPARTMENT OF LABOR, BUREAU OF LABOR STATISTICS

The International Price Program of the Bureau of Labor Statistics (BLS) collects price data for nonmilitary goods traded between the United States and the rest of the world and for selected transportation services in international markets. BLS aggregates the goods price data into export and import price indexes. Summary values of these price indexes for goods are presented in *Business Statistics*. For product and locality detail on international prices for both goods and services, see the *Handbook of U.S. Labor Statistics*, also published by Bernan Press.

Definitions

The *export* price index provides a measure of price change for all goods sold by U.S. residents (businesses and individuals located within the geographic boundaries of the United States, whether or not owned by U.S. citizens) to foreign buyers.

The *import* price index provides a measure of price change for goods purchased from other countries by U.S. residents.

Notes on the data

Published index series use a base year of 2000 = 100 whenever possible.

The product universe for both the import and export indexes includes raw materials, agricultural products, and manufactures. Price data are primarily collected by mail questionnaire, and directly from the exporter or importer in all but a few cases.

To the greatest extent possible, the data refer to prices at the U.S. border for exports and at either the foreign border or the U.S. border for imports. For nearly all products, the prices refer to transactions completed during the first week of the month and represent the actual price for which the product was bought or sold, including discounts, allowances, and rebates.

For the export price indexes, the preferred pricing basis is f.a.s. (free alongside ship) U.S. port of exportation. Where necessary, adjustments are made to reported prices to place them on this basis. An attempt is made to collect two prices for imports: f.o.b. (free on board) at the port of exportation and c.i.f. (cost, insurance, and freight) at the U.S. port of importation. Adjustments are made to account for changes in product characteristics in order to obtain a pure measure of price change.

The indexes are weighted indexes of the Laspeyres type. (See "General Notes" at the beginning of this volume for further explanation.) The values assigned to each weight category are based on trade value figures compiled by the Census Bureau. They are reweighted annually, with a two-year lag (as concurrent value data are not available) in revisions.

The merchandise price indexes are published using three different classification systems: the Harmonized System, the Bureau of Economic Analysis End-Use System, and the Standard International Trade Classification (SITC) system. The aggregate indexes shown here are from the End-Use System.

Data availability

Indexes are published monthly in a press release and a more detailed report. Indexes are published for detailed product categories, as well as for all commodities. Aggregate import indexes by country or region of origin also are available, as are indexes for selected categories of internationally traded services. Additional information is available from the Division of International Prices in the Bureau of Labor Statistics. Complete historical data are available on the BLS Web site at <http://www.bls.gov>.

References

The indexes are described in "BLS to Produce Monthly Indexes of Export and Import Prices," *Monthly Labor Review* (December 1988), and Chapter 15, "International Price Indexes," *BLS Handbook of Methods* Bulletin 2490 (April 1997).

CHAPTER 8: PRICES

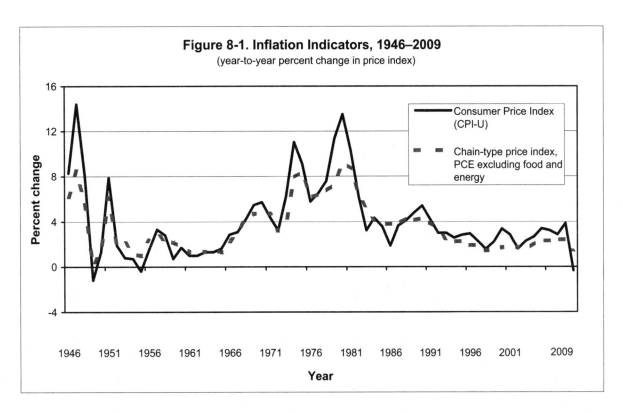

Figure 8-1. Inflation Indicators, 1946–2009
(year-to-year percent change in price index)

- Figure 8-1 shows annual rates of change in the Consumer Price Index for All Urban Consumers (CPI-U), the most widely used measure of the general price level. It also shows changes in the chain-type price index for personal consumption expenditures (PCE) excluding food and energy, which provides one widely used measure of the "core" or underlying rate of inflation. (Tables 8-1, 8-2, 8-3, 19-5, and 20-2)

- The all-items CPI dropped 0.4 percent in 2009—the first year-to-year deflation registered since 1955. A deep, widespread recession brought consumer energy prices down 18 percent. (Table 8-1)

- The core PCE inflation rate fell 0.9 percentage point to 1.5 percent, the lowest since 2003. (Table 8-3)

- From 1965 to 2009, commodity prices in the CPI-U rose at an average rate of 3.6 percent per year, but service prices increased at an average annual rate of 5.3 percent. (Table 8-1)

- The Producer Price Index (PPI) measures prices at the point of production, rather than at the consumer level. The most widely used product of the PPI system—the PPI for Finished Goods—only covers commodities, whereas the CPI covers both commodities and services. For these reasons, the PPI for Finished Goods fluctuates more (both up and down) than the aggregate CPI-U, but has a less inflationary trend. In 2009, the total PPI for finished goods declined 2.5 percent, its energy component dropped 17.6 percent, and finished goods excluding foods and energy rose 2.6 percent. (Table 8-4)

- The PPI data set also includes prices for intermediate materials, supplies, and components and crude materials for further processing. Intermediate materials prices fluctuate more than those of finished goods, and crude materials prices fluctuate most of all. Crude energy materials prices plunged 43 percent in 2009. (Table 8-4)

Table 8-1. Consumer Price Indexes, All Urban Consumers (CPI-U)

(1982–1984 = 100, seasonally adjusted [preliminary], except as noted.)

| Year and month | All items | | | Food and beverages | | | | | | | | | | |
| | Not seasonally adjusted | Seasonally adjusted | | Total | Total food | Food at home | | | | | | | Food away from home [1] | Alcoholic beverages |
		Index	Percent change from previous period			Total	Cereals and bakery products	Meats, poultry, fish, and eggs	Dairy and related products	Fruits and vegetables	Non-alcoholic beverages	Other food at home		
1965	31.5	31.5	1.6	. . .	32.2	33.5	31.9	. . .	36.0	32.6	23.4	. . .	28.4	44.6
1966	32.4	32.4	2.9	. . .	33.8	35.2	33.3	. . .	38.3	33.3	23.3	. . .	29.7	45.4
1967	33.4	33.4	3.1	35.0	34.1	35.1	34.0	38.0	40.0	33.3	23.1	29.3	31.3	46.4
1968	34.8	34.8	4.2	36.2	35.3	36.3	34.2	39.1	41.3	35.9	23.5	29.8	32.9	48.0
1969	36.7	36.7	5.5	38.1	37.1	38.0	35.2	42.6	42.7	36.4	24.2	30.7	34.9	49.7
1970	38.8	38.8	5.7	40.1	39.2	39.9	37.1	44.6	44.7	37.8	27.1	32.9	37.5	52.1
1971	40.5	40.5	4.4	41.4	40.4	40.9	38.8	44.1	46.1	39.7	28.1	34.3	39.4	54.2
1972	41.8	41.8	3.2	43.1	42.1	42.7	39.0	48.0	46.8	41.6	28.0	34.6	41.0	55.4
1973	44.4	44.4	6.2	48.8	48.2	49.7	43.5	60.9	51.2	47.4	30.1	36.7	44.2	56.8
1974	49.3	49.3	11.0	55.5	55.1	57.1	56.5	62.2	60.7	55.2	35.9	47.8	49.8	61.1
1975	53.8	53.8	9.1	60.2	59.8	61.8	62.9	67.0	62.6	56.9	41.3	55.4	54.5	65.9
1976	56.9	56.9	5.8	62.1	61.6	63.1	61.5	68.0	67.7	58.4	49.4	56.4	58.2	68.1
1977	60.6	60.6	6.5	65.8	65.5	66.8	62.5	67.4	69.5	63.8	74.4	68.4	62.6	70.0
1978	65.2	65.2	7.6	72.2	72.0	73.8	68.1	77.6	74.2	70.9	78.7	73.6	68.3	74.1
1979	72.6	72.6	11.3	79.9	79.9	81.8	74.9	89.0	82.8	76.6	82.6	79.0	75.9	79.9
1980	82.4	82.4	13.5	86.7	86.8	88.4	83.9	92.0	90.9	82.1	91.4	88.4	83.4	86.4
1981	90.9	90.9	10.3	93.5	93.6	94.8	92.3	96.0	97.4	92.0	95.3	94.9	90.9	92.5
1982	96.5	96.5	6.2	97.3	97.4	98.1	96.5	99.6	98.8	97.0	97.9	97.3	95.8	96.7
1983	99.6	99.6	3.2	99.5	99.4	99.1	99.6	99.2	100.0	99.8	99.8	99.5	100.0	100.4
1984	103.9	103.9	4.3	103.2	103.2	102.8	103.9	101.3	101.3	105.7	102.3	103.1	104.2	103.0
1985	107.6	107.6	3.6	105.6	105.6	104.3	107.9	100.1	103.2	108.4	104.3	105.7	108.3	106.4
1986	109.6	109.6	1.9	109.1	109.0	107.3	110.9	104.5	103.3	109.4	110.4	109.4	112.5	111.1
1987	113.6	113.6	3.6	113.5	113.5	111.9	114.8	110.5	105.9	119.1	107.5	110.5	117.0	114.1
1988	118.3	118.3	4.1	118.2	118.2	116.6	122.1	114.3	108.4	128.1	107.5	113.1	121.8	118.6
1989	124.0	124.0	4.8	124.9	125.1	124.2	132.4	121.3	115.6	138.0	111.3	119.1	127.4	123.5
1990	130.7	130.7	5.4	132.1	132.4	132.3	140.0	130.0	126.5	149.0	113.5	123.4	133.4	129.3
1991	136.2	136.2	4.2	136.8	136.3	135.8	145.8	132.6	125.1	155.8	114.1	127.3	137.9	142.8
1992	140.3	140.3	3.0	138.7	137.9	136.8	151.5	130.9	128.5	155.4	114.3	128.8	140.7	147.3
1993	144.5	144.5	3.0	141.6	140.9	140.1	156.6	135.5	129.4	159.0	114.6	130.5	143.2	149.6
1994	148.2	148.2	2.6	144.9	144.3	144.1	163.0	137.2	131.7	165.0	123.2	135.6	145.7	151.5
1995	152.4	152.4	2.8	148.9	148.4	148.8	167.5	138.8	132.8	177.7	131.7	140.8	149.0	153.9
1996	156.9	156.9	3.0	153.7	153.3	154.3	174.0	144.8	142.1	183.9	128.6	142.9	152.7	158.5
1997	160.5	160.5	2.3	157.7	157.3	158.1	177.6	148.5	145.5	187.5	133.4	147.3	157.0	162.8
1998	163.0	163.0	1.6	161.1	160.7	161.1	181.1	147.3	150.8	198.2	133.0	150.8	161.1	165.7
1999	166.6	166.6	2.2	164.6	164.1	164.2	185.0	147.9	159.6	203.1	134.3	153.5	165.1	169.7
2000	172.2	172.2	3.4	168.4	167.8	167.9	188.3	154.5	160.7	204.6	137.8	155.6	169.0	174.7
2001	177.1	177.1	2.8	173.6	173.1	173.4	193.8	161.3	167.1	212.2	139.2	159.6	173.9	179.3
2002	179.9	179.9	1.6	176.8	176.2	175.6	198.0	162.1	168.1	220.9	139.2	160.8	178.3	183.6
2003	184.0	184.0	2.3	180.5	180.0	179.4	202.8	169.3	167.9	225.9	139.8	162.6	182.1	187.2
2004	188.9	188.9	2.7	186.6	186.2	186.2	206.0	181.7	180.2	232.7	140.4	164.9	187.5	192.1
2005	195.3	195.3	3.4	191.2	190.7	189.8	209.0	184.7	182.4	241.4	144.4	167.0	193.4	195.9
2006	201.6	201.6	3.2	195.7	195.2	193.1	212.8	186.6	181.4	252.9	147.4	169.6	199.4	200.7
2007	207.3	207.3	2.8	203.3	202.9	201.2	222.1	195.6	194.8	262.6	153.4	173.3	206.7	207.0
2008	215.3	215.3	3.8	214.2	214.1	214.1	244.9	204.7	210.4	278.9	160.0	184.2	215.8	214.5
2009	214.5	214.5	-0.4	218.2	218.0	215.1	252.6	203.8	197.0	272.9	163.0	191.2	223.3	220.8
2008														
January	211.1	212.5	0.4	208.4	208.1	207.1	229.8	199.9	206.9	270.7	156.8	176.5	211.1	210.6
February	211.7	212.9	0.2	209.2	208.9	207.9	233.5	200.0	208.2	268.9	156.8	177.9	211.9	211.6
March	213.5	213.7	0.4	209.7	209.4	208.3	236.4	199.8	206.2	269.6	157.3	178.4	212.5	211.8
April	214.8	214.0	0.2	211.4	211.2	211.0	239.4	201.5	207.7	274.3	159.9	181.3	213.1	213.2
May	216.6	215.0	0.5	212.1	212.0	211.7	243.2	201.9	207.8	275.3	158.4	182.2	214.0	213.4
June	218.8	217.0	0.9	213.5	213.4	213.4	244.4	203.3	209.1	281.6	158.7	183.1	215.0	213.8
July	220.0	218.6	0.7	215.4	215.4	215.9	248.3	205.2	214.0	285.0	159.7	184.9	216.4	214.5
August	219.1	218.6	0.0	216.6	216.6	217.6	248.8	207.2	214.7	290.0	160.1	186.2	217.1	215.3
September	218.8	218.7	0.0	217.7	217.7	218.7	251.4	208.7	213.5	288.7	161.6	188.0	218.2	216.3
October	216.6	216.9	-0.8	218.6	218.6	219.4	253.2	210.3	212.7	284.2	163.5	189.3	219.3	217.0
November	212.4	213.3	-1.7	219.0	219.0	219.5	254.3	209.2	213.1	282.4	163.8	190.6	220.0	217.8
December	210.2	211.6	-0.8	219.2	219.1	219.2	255.7	208.7	210.8	277.8	164.0	191.8	220.7	218.7
2009														
January	211.1	212.2	0.3	219.3	219.2	218.9	255.7	208.5	209.6	274.3	163.8	192.9	221.3	219.2
February	212.2	213.0	0.4	219.1	219.0	218.0	254.3	208.4	204.5	275.4	163.2	192.4	222.0	219.1
March	212.7	212.7	-0.1	218.8	218.7	217.2	253.9	206.5	199.7	275.8	164.8	192.4	222.2	219.4
April	213.2	212.7	0.0	218.4	218.3	215.9	252.1	206.5	197.1	275.8	163.1	190.8	222.9	219.4
May	213.9	212.9	0.1	218.0	217.7	214.9	251.6	204.7	196.1	273.0	162.8	190.6	223.0	219.9
June	215.7	214.5	0.7	218.1	217.8	215.0	251.6	204.4	194.2	276.1	163.0	190.6	223.2	220.4
July	215.4	214.5	0.0	217.6	217.3	213.9	251.4	201.7	193.1	275.4	162.4	190.1	223.3	221.0
August	215.8	215.4	0.4	217.8	217.5	214.0	251.0	202.6	192.4	273.4	163.0	190.5	223.7	221.2
September	216.0	215.8	0.2	217.7	217.3	213.3	251.7	200.6	193.4	270.1	163.0	190.6	224.0	221.7
October	216.2	216.4	0.3	217.8	217.4	213.3	251.8	200.1	195.4	268.3	162.6	191.2	224.2	222.2
November	216.3	217.3	0.4	218.0	217.5	213.3	252.2	200.8	193.9	268.6	162.1	190.9	224.6	222.7
December	215.9	217.5	0.1	218.4	217.9	213.9	253.6	200.8	194.8	269.4	162.5	191.5	224.8	222.8

[1] Not seasonally adjusted.
. . . = Not available.

Table 8-1. Consumer Price Indexes, All Urban Consumers (CPI-U)—*Continued*

(1982–1984 = 100, seasonally adjusted [preliminary], except as noted.)

Year and month	Total	Housing Shelter Total	Rent of shelter [2]	Rent of primary residence	Lodging away from home [3]	Owners' equivalent rent of primary residence [2]	Tenants' and household insur-ance [1,3]	Fuels and utilities Total	Fuel oil and other fuels	Gas (piped) and electricity	Water and sewer and trash collection services [3]	Household furnishings and operations Total	Household oper-ations [1,3]
1965	...	27.0	...	40.9	...	...	...	26.6	14.6	23.5	...	...	...
1966	...	27.8	...	41.5	...	...	...	26.7	15.0	23.6	...	42.0	...
1967	30.8	28.8	...	42.2	...	...	...	27.1	15.5	23.7	...	43.6	...
1968	32.0	30.1	...	43.3	...	...	...	27.4	16.0	23.9	...	45.2	...
1969	34.0	32.6	...	44.7	...	...	...	28.0	16.3	24.3	...		...
1970	36.4	35.5	...	46.5	...	...	...	29.1	17.0	25.4	...	46.8	...
1971	38.0	37.0	...	48.7	...	...	...	31.1	18.2	27.1	...	48.6	...
1972	39.4	38.7	...	50.4	...	...	...	32.5	18.3	28.5	...	49.7	...
1973	41.2	40.5	...	52.5	...	...	...	34.3	21.1	29.9	...	51.1	...
1974	45.8	44.4	...	55.2	...	...	...	40.7	33.2	34.5	...	56.8	...
1975	50.7	48.8	...	58.0	...	...	...	45.4	36.4	40.1	...	63.4	...
1976	53.8	51.5	...	61.1	...	...	...	49.4	38.8	44.7	...	67.3	...
1977	57.4	54.9	...	64.8	...	...	...	54.7	43.9	50.5	...	70.4	...
1978	62.4	60.5	...	69.3	...	...	...	58.5	46.2	55.0	...	74.7	...
1979	70.1	68.9	...	74.3	...	...	...	64.8	62.4	61.0	...	79.9	...
1980	81.1	81.0	...	80.9	...	...	...	75.4	86.1	71.4	...	86.3	...
1981	90.4	90.5	...	87.9	...	...	...	86.4	104.6	81.9	...	93.0	...
1982	96.9	96.9	...	94.6	...	...	...	94.9	103.4	93.2	...	98.0	...
1983	99.5	99.1	102.7	100.1	...	102.5	...	100.2	97.2	101.5	...	100.2	...
1984	103.6	104.0	107.7	105.3	...	107.3	...	104.8	99.4	105.4	...	101.9	...
1985	107.7	109.8	113.9	111.8	...	113.2	...	106.5	95.9	107.1	...	103.8	...
1986	110.9	115.8	120.2	118.3	...	119.4	...	104.1	77.6	105.7	...	105.2	...
1987	114.2	121.3	125.9	123.1	...	124.8	...	103.0	77.9	103.8	...	107.1	...
1988	118.5	127.1	132.0	127.8	...	131.1	...	104.4	78.1	104.6	...	109.4	...
1989	123.0	132.8	138.0	132.8	...	137.4	...	107.8	81.7	107.5	...	111.2	...
1990	128.5	140.0	145.5	138.4	...	144.8	...	111.6	99.3	109.3	...	113.3	...
1991	133.6	146.3	152.1	143.3	...	150.4	...	115.3	94.6	112.6	...	116.0	...
1992	137.5	151.2	157.3	146.9	...	155.5	...	117.8	90.7	114.8	...	118.0	...
1993	141.2	155.7	162.0	150.3	...	160.5	...	121.3	90.3	118.5	...	119.3	...
1994	144.8	160.5	167.0	154.0	...	165.8	...	122.8	88.8	119.2	...	121.0	...
1995	148.5	165.7	172.4	157.8	...	171.3	...	123.7	88.1	119.2	...	123.0	...
1996	152.8	171.0	178.0	162.0	...	176.8	...	127.5	99.2	122.1	...	124.7	...
1997	156.8	176.3	183.4	166.7	...	181.9	...	130.8	99.8	125.1	...	125.4	...
1998	160.4	182.1	189.6	172.1	109.0	187.8	99.8	128.5	90.0	121.2	101.6	126.6	101.5
1999	163.9	187.3	195.0	177.5	112.3	192.9	101.3	128.8	91.4	120.9	104.0	126.7	104.5
2000	169.6	193.4	201.3	183.9	117.5	198.7	103.7	137.9	129.7	128.0	106.5	128.2	110.5
2001	176.4	200.6	208.9	192.1	118.6	206.3	106.2	150.2	129.3	142.4	109.6	129.1	115.6
2002	180.3	208.1	216.7	199.7	118.3	214.7	108.7	143.6	115.5	134.4	113.0	128.3	119.0
2003	184.8	213.1	221.9	205.5	119.3	219.9	114.8	154.5	139.5	145.0	117.2	126.1	121.8
2004	189.5	218.8	227.9	211.0	125.9	224.9	116.2	161.9	160.5	150.6	124.0	125.5	125.0
2005	195.7	224.4	233.7	217.3	130.3	230.2	117.6	179.0	208.6	166.5	130.3	126.1	130.3
2006	203.2	232.1	241.9	225.1	136.0	238.2	116.5	194.7	234.9	182.1	136.8	127.0	136.6
2007	209.6	240.6	250.8	234.7	142.8	246.2	117.0	200.6	251.5	186.3	143.7	126.9	140.6
2008	216.3	246.7	257.2	243.3	143.7	252.4	118.8	220.0	334.4	202.2	152.1	127.8	147.5
2009	217.1	249.4	259.9	248.8	134.2	256.6	121.5	210.7	239.8	193.6	161.1	128.7	150.3
2008													
January	213.0	244.6	255.2	239.6	146.1	250.0	117.4	207.0	318.2	188.6	148.0	126.5	142.8
February	213.5	244.8	255.2	240.1	144.9	250.4	117.6	209.4	320.0	191.2	148.6	126.6	143.5
March	214.3	245.2	255.6	240.7	144.6	250.9	117.7	212.7	334.1	194.3	149.1	127.2	145.0
April	214.9	245.4	255.9	241.5	142.4	251.4	118.4	216.6	341.7	198.3	149.6	127.1	145.8
May	215.8	245.9	256.3	242.0	144.0	251.7	118.4	221.1	356.0	202.9	150.4	127.4	147.0
June	216.8	246.7	257.0	242.9	144.5	252.3	119.1	225.0	376.1	206.2	151.1	127.4	148.0
July	218.0	247.1	257.5	243.7	144.5	252.7	118.8	231.8	382.1	213.8	152.1	127.9	148.3
August	218.0	247.3	257.7	244.4	143.6	253.1	118.6	229.8	357.7	212.2	153.8	128.2	149.2
September	217.8	247.9	258.4	245.1	144.3	253.5	119.9	224.3	344.6	206.2	154.2	128.8	150.2
October	217.8	248.1	258.6	245.8	142.6	253.9	119.9	223.2	323.4	205.6	155.6	128.8	150.1
November	217.6	248.5	259.1	246.5	141.5	254.5	120.2	219.9	287.5	203.5	156.2	128.7	150.0
December	217.6	248.5	259.3	246.9	140.6	254.7	120.0	219.1	263.2	203.7	156.6	128.9	150.7
2009													
January	217.6	248.9	259.8	247.7	139.1	255.3	120.4	217.5	256.2	202.1	157.0	128.8	150.4
February	217.6	248.9	259.5	248.1	136.6	255.7	120.7	217.3	251.5	202.0	157.1	129.0	150.2
March	217.3	248.9	259.3	248.5	133.3	256.3	120.7	214.3	232.2	199.3	157.8	129.4	150.9
April	217.2	249.3	259.9	248.9	134.0	256.3	120.7	210.7	227.4	195.0	158.8	129.4	150.8
May	217.1	249.7	260.2	249.2	134.1	257.0	120.7	207.9	220.3	191.7	159.8	129.4	149.5
June	217.0	249.9	260.3	249.4	134.5	257.1	121.1	206.3	224.7	189.4	160.4	129.4	150.0
July	216.6	249.4	259.8	249.3	131.7	257.1	121.3	206.0	222.3	188.8	161.4	129.3	150.0
August	216.7	249.7	260.0	249.3	132.4	257.3	121.8	206.8	231.0	188.8	162.8	128.5	150.5
September	216.8	249.7	260.2	249.1	134.3	256.9	122.2	207.2	233.5	189.0	163.4	128.5	150.4
October	217.0	249.7	260.3	248.9	134.9	256.9	122.2	209.6	247.5	190.7	164.7	127.8	150.2
November	216.9	249.1	259.8	248.7	132.8	256.6	122.2	212.7	265.5	193.4	165.0	127.4	150.1
December	217.0	249.2	260.0	248.6	133.4	256.5	123.8	212.8	269.9	193.1	165.5	127.5	150.2

[1]Not seasonally adjusted.
[2]December 1982 = 100.
[3]December 1997 = 100.
. . . = Not available.

Table 8-1. Consumer Price Indexes, All Urban Consumers (CPI-U)—*Continued*

(1982–1984 = 100, seasonally adjusted [preliminary], except as noted.)

Year and month	Apparel					Transportation							Motor vehicle parts and equip-ment [1]	Motor vehicle mainte-nance and repair
							Private transportation							
								New and used motor vehicles			Motor fuel			
	Total	Men's and boys' apparel	Women's and girls' apparel	Infants' and toddlers' apparel	Footwear	Total	Total	Total [3]	New vehicles	Used cars and trucks [1]	Total	Gasoline (all types)		
1965	47.8	49.9	58.1	35.1	43.4	31.9	32.5	...	49.8	29.8	25.1	25.1	...	28.7
1966	49.0	51.2	59.2	35.4	46.0	32.3	32.9	...	48.9	29.0	25.6	25.6	...	29.2
1967	51.0	53.1	61.9	35.8	48.2	33.3	33.8	...	49.3	29.9	26.4	26.4	...	30.4
1968	53.7	56.1	65.6	37.3	50.8	34.3	34.8	...	50.7	...	26.8	26.8	...	32.1
1969	56.8	59.7	69.2	38.4	53.9	35.7	36.0	...	51.5	30.9	27.6	27.7	...	34.1
1970	59.2	62.2	71.8	39.2	56.8	37.5	37.5	...	53.1	31.2	27.9	27.9	...	36.6
1971	61.1	63.9	74.4	40.0	58.6	39.5	39.4	...	55.3	33.0	28.1	28.1	...	39.3
1972	62.3	64.7	76.2	41.1	60.3	39.9	39.7	...	54.8	33.1	28.4	28.4	...	41.1
1973	64.6	67.1	78.8	42.5	62.8	41.2	41.0	...	54.8	35.2	31.2	31.2	...	43.2
1974	69.4	72.4	83.5	54.2	66.6	45.8	46.2	...	58.0	36.7	42.2	42.2	...	47.6
1975	72.5	75.5	85.5	64.5	69.6	50.1	50.6	...	63.0	43.8	45.1	45.1	...	53.7
1976	75.2	78.1	87.9	68.0	72.3	55.1	55.6	...	67.0	50.3	47.0	47.0	...	57.6
1977	78.6	81.7	90.6	74.6	75.7	59.0	59.7	...	70.5	54.7	49.7	49.7	...	61.9
1978	81.4	83.5	92.4	77.4	79.0	61.7	62.5	...	75.9	55.8	51.8	51.8	77.6	67.0
1979	84.9	85.4	94.0	79.0	85.3	70.5	71.7	...	81.9	60.2	70.1	70.2	85.1	73.7
1980	90.9	89.4	96.0	85.5	91.8	83.1	84.2	...	88.5	62.3	97.4	97.5	95.3	81.5
1981	95.3	94.2	97.5	92.9	96.7	93.2	93.8	...	93.9	76.9	108.5	108.5	101.0	89.2
1982	97.8	97.6	98.5	96.3	99.1	97.0	97.1	...	97.5	88.8	102.8	102.8	103.6	96.0
1983	100.2	100.3	100.2	101.1	99.8	99.3	99.3	...	99.9	98.7	99.4	99.4	100.7	100.3
1984	102.1	102.1	101.3	102.6	101.1	103.7	103.6	...	102.6	112.5	97.9	97.8	95.6	103.8
1985	105.0	105.0	104.9	107.2	102.3	106.4	106.2	...	106.1	113.7	98.7	98.6	95.9	106.8
1986	105.9	106.2	104.0	111.8	101.9	102.3	101.2	...	110.6	108.8	77.1	77.0	95.4	110.3
1987	110.6	109.1	110.4	112.1	105.1	105.4	104.2	...	114.4	113.1	80.2	80.1	96.1	114.8
1988	115.4	113.4	114.9	116.4	109.9	108.7	107.6	...	116.5	118.0	80.9	80.8	97.9	119.7
1989	118.6	117.0	116.4	119.1	114.4	114.1	112.9	...	119.2	120.4	88.5	88.5	100.2	124.9
1990	124.1	120.4	122.6	125.8	117.4	120.5	118.8	...	121.4	117.6	101.2	101.0	100.9	130.1
1991	128.7	124.2	127.6	128.9	120.9	123.8	121.9	...	126.0	118.1	99.4	99.2	102.2	136.0
1992	131.9	126.5	130.4	129.3	125.0	126.5	124.6	...	129.2	123.2	99.0	99.0	103.1	141.3
1993	133.7	127.5	132.6	127.1	125.9	130.4	127.5	91.8	132.7	133.9	98.0	97.7	101.6	145.9
1994	133.4	126.4	130.9	128.1	126.0	134.3	131.4	95.5	137.6	141.7	98.5	98.2	101.4	150.2
1995	132.0	126.2	126.9	127.2	125.4	139.1	136.3	99.4	141.0	156.5	100.0	99.8	102.1	154.0
1996	131.7	127.7	124.7	129.7	126.6	143.0	140.0	101.0	143.7	157.0	106.3	105.9	102.2	158.4
1997	132.9	130.1	126.1	129.0	127.6	144.3	141.0	100.5	144.3	151.1	106.2	105.8	101.9	162.7
1998	133.0	131.8	126.0	126.1	128.0	141.6	137.9	100.1	143.4	150.6	92.2	91.6	101.1	167.1
1999	131.3	131.1	123.3	129.0	125.7	144.4	140.5	100.1	142.9	152.0	100.7	100.1	100.5	171.9
2000	129.6	129.7	121.5	130.6	123.8	153.3	149.1	100.8	142.8	155.8	129.3	128.6	101.8	177.3
2001	127.3	125.7	119.3	129.2	123.0	154.3	150.0	101.3	142.1	158.7	124.7	124.0	104.8	183.5
2002	124.0	121.7	115.8	126.4	121.4	152.9	148.8	99.2	140.0	152.0	116.6	116.0	106.9	190.2
2003	120.9	118.0	113.1	122.1	119.6	157.6	153.6	96.5	137.9	142.9	135.8	135.1	107.8	195.6
2004	120.4	117.5	113.0	118.5	119.3	163.1	159.4	94.2	137.1	133.3	160.4	159.7	108.7	200.2
2005	119.5	116.1	110.8	116.7	122.6	173.9	170.2	95.6	137.9	139.4	195.7	194.7	111.9	206.9
2006	119.5	114.1	110.7	116.5	123.5	180.9	177.0	95.6	137.6	140.0	221.0	219.9	117.3	215.6
2007	119.0	112.4	110.3	113.9	122.4	184.7	180.8	94.3	136.3	135.7	239.1	238.0	121.6	223.0
2008	118.9	113.0	107.5	113.8	124.2	195.5	191.0	93.3	134.2	134.0	279.7	277.5	128.7	233.9
2009	120.1	113.6	108.1	114.5	126.9	179.3	174.8	93.5	135.6	127.0	202.0	201.6	134.1	243.3
2008														
January	119.7	113.1	110.4	115.6	123.1	195.5	191.6	94.5	135.7	138.3	281.4	280.1	124.3	227.7
February	119.0	114.0	107.9	115.0	123.3	195.6	191.7	94.4	135.3	138.3	281.9	280.5	125.2	228.7
March	118.1	113.3	106.2	114.0	123.2	197.3	193.2	94.2	135.1	138.0	287.9	285.8	126.3	229.8
April	118.5	113.5	106.2	114.3	124.2	195.7	191.5	94.0	134.9	137.2	281.2	278.7	126.0	230.5
May	118.4	113.9	105.9	113.6	124.2	197.9	193.5	93.8	134.8	136.5	289.3	287.1	126.8	231.7
June	118.4	113.2	106.2	113.3	124.5	204.2	199.7	93.8	135.0	135.5	314.5	312.3	127.8	233.2
July	119.5	113.2	107.9	113.0	125.8	207.1	202.5	93.7	135.2	134.5	325.8	322.7	129.1	234.8
August	120.0	113.3	109.6	112.0	124.1	205.2	200.4	93.3	134.3	133.4	317.7	315.5	130.3	236.1
September	119.6	112.8	108.9	113.5	123.9	204.9	200.3	92.6	133.4	131.7	318.8	317.2	131.0	237.1
October	118.8	112.6	107.1	113.5	124.1	195.0	190.4	92.2	132.8	129.5	278.2	276.1	131.9	238.2
November	118.9	112.1	107.3	113.9	125.0	176.1	170.9	91.6	132.2	127.7	197.9	195.2	132.9	239.0
December	118.2	111.5	106.2	113.5	124.5	167.4	162.0	91.3	131.8	126.9	160.7	157.5	133.1	239.4
2009														
January	118.5	113.2	106.5	114.0	124.3	169.5	164.4	91.5	132.1	125.9	169.2	166.8	133.4	241.1
February	120.0	116.3	107.4	112.8	125.2	172.8	168.1	92.0	133.2	123.8	182.0	180.7	134.1	241.7
March	119.7	116.0	106.6	113.5	125.5	170.9	166.3	92.0	134.0	121.7	173.9	173.5	134.5	242.1
April	119.5	114.1	106.8	115.0	126.0	170.3	165.7	92.4	134.6	121.6	169.4	168.7	134.6	242.6
May	119.3	114.6	106.7	113.1	126.2	171.6	167.2	92.8	135.3	122.8	173.9	174.0	134.3	242.5
June	120.2	114.0	108.4	115.7	126.4	178.8	174.8	93.2	136.2	123.9	203.7	204.1	134.3	242.7
July	120.9	113.3	109.7	114.8	127.8	179.2	174.9	93.5	136.8	123.8	202.9	202.5	133.7	243.0
August	120.8	113.9	109.4	116.2	127.5	183.3	179.1	93.2	135.0	126.2	220.8	221.0	133.5	243.5
September	120.9	113.0	109.7	116.4	127.6	184.8	180.4	93.6	135.6	128.2	223.3	223.1	133.4	244.5
October	120.5	112.3	109.0	114.6	127.9	187.3	182.9	95.2	137.8	132.5	226.9	226.7	133.7	245.4
November	120.1	111.5	108.1	114.2	128.8	191.6	187.0	96.0	138.7	135.1	241.0	241.2	134.2	245.5
December	120.5	111.3	109.1	113.6	128.9	192.4	187.7	96.3	138.3	138.5	242.1	241.7	134.8	245.4

[1] Not seasonally adjusted.
[3] December 1997 = 100.
. . . = Not available.

Table 8-1. Consumer Price Indexes, All Urban Consumers (CPI-U)—*Continued*

(1982–1984 = 100, seasonally adjusted [preliminary], except as noted.)

Year and month	Transportation—Continued		Medical care		Medical care services			Recreation		Education and communication	Education		
	Public transportation	Transportation services	Medical care, total	Medical care commodities	Total	Professional services	Hospital and related services	Total[3]	Video and audio[3]	Total[3]	Total[3]	Educational books and supplies	Tuition, other school fees, and childcare
1965	25.2	30.3	25.2	45.0	22.7	...	...	...	...	...	...	...	...
1966	26.1	31.6	26.3	45.1	23.9	...	...	...	...	...	...	...	...
1967	27.4	32.6	28.2	44.9	26.0	30.9	...	...	...	...	...	33.7	...
1968	28.7	33.9	29.9	45.0	27.9	32.5	...	...	...	...	...	35.4	...
1969	30.9	36.3	31.9	45.4	30.2	34.7	...	...	...	...	...	37.4	...
1970	35.2	40.2	34.0	46.5	32.3	37.0	...	...	...	...	...	38.8	...
1971	37.8	43.4	36.1	47.3	34.7	39.4	...	...	...	...	...	41.4	...
1972	39.3	44.4	37.3	47.4	35.9	40.8	...	...	...	...	...	44.2	...
1973	39.7	44.7	38.8	47.5	37.5	42.2	...	...	...	...	...	45.6	...
1974	40.6	46.3	42.4	49.2	41.4	45.8	...	...	...	...	...	47.2	...
1975	43.5	49.8	47.5	53.3	46.6	50.8	...	...	...	...	...	50.3	...
1976	47.8	56.9	52.0	56.5	51.3	55.5	...	...	...	...	...	53.7	...
1977	50.0	61.5	57.0	60.2	56.4	60.0	...	...	...	...	...	56.9	...
1978	51.5	64.4	61.8	64.4	61.2	64.5	55.1	...	...	...	...	61.6	59.8
1979	54.9	69.5	67.5	69.0	67.2	70.1	61.0	...	...	...	...	65.7	64.7
1980	69.0	79.2	74.9	75.4	74.8	77.9	69.2	...	...	...	...	71.4	71.2
1981	85.6	88.6	82.9	83.7	82.8	85.9	79.1	...	...	...	...	80.3	79.9
1982	94.9	96.1	92.5	92.3	92.6	93.2	90.3	...	...	...	...	91.0	90.5
1983	99.5	99.1	100.6	100.2	100.7	99.8	100.5	...	...	...	...	100.3	99.7
1984	105.7	104.8	106.8	107.5	106.7	107.0	109.2	...	...	...	...	108.7	109.8
1985	110.5	110.0	113.5	115.2	113.2	113.5	116.1	...	...	...	...	118.2	119.7
1986	117.0	116.3	122.0	122.8	121.9	120.8	123.1	...	...	...	...	128.1	129.6
1987	121.1	121.9	130.1	131.0	130.0	128.8	131.6	...	...	...	...	138.1	140.0
1988	123.3	128.0	138.6	139.9	138.3	137.5	143.9	...	...	...	...	148.1	151.0
1989	129.5	135.6	149.3	150.8	148.9	146.4	160.5	...	...	...	...	158.0	162.7
1990	142.6	144.2	162.8	163.4	162.7	156.1	178.0	...	...	...	...	171.3	175.7
1991	148.9	151.2	177.0	176.8	177.1	165.7	196.1	...	...	...	...	180.3	191.4
1992	151.4	155.7	190.1	188.1	190.5	175.8	214.0	...	...	...	...	190.3	208.5
1993	167.0	162.9	201.4	195.0	202.9	184.7	231.9	90.7	96.5	85.5	78.4	197.6	225.3
1994	172.0	168.6	211.0	200.7	213.4	192.5	245.6	92.7	95.4	88.8	83.3	205.5	239.8
1995	175.9	175.9	220.5	204.5	224.2	201.0	257.8	94.5	95.1	92.2	88.0	214.4	253.8
1996	181.9	180.5	228.2	210.4	232.4	208.3	269.5	97.4	96.6	95.3	92.7	226.9	267.1
1997	186.7	185.0	234.6	215.3	239.1	215.4	278.4	99.6	99.4	98.4	97.3	238.4	280.4
1998	190.3	187.9	242.1	221.8	246.8	222.2	287.5	101.1	101.1	100.3	102.1	250.8	294.2
1999	197.7	190.7	250.6	230.7	255.1	229.2	299.5	102.0	100.7	101.2	107.0	261.7	308.4
2000	209.6	196.1	260.8	238.1	266.0	237.7	317.3	103.3	101.0	102.5	112.5	279.9	324.0
2001	210.6	201.9	272.8	247.6	278.8	246.5	338.3	104.9	101.5	105.2	118.5	295.9	341.1
2002	207.4	209.1	285.6	256.4	292.9	253.9	367.8	106.2	102.8	107.9	126.0	317.6	362.1
2003	209.3	216.3	297.1	262.8	306.0	261.2	394.8	107.5	103.6	109.8	134.4	335.4	386.7
2004	209.1	220.6	310.1	269.3	321.3	271.5	417.9	108.6	104.2	111.6	143.7	351.0	414.3
2005	217.3	225.7	323.2	276.0	336.7	281.7	439.9	109.4	104.2	113.7	152.7	365.6	440.9
2006	226.6	230.8	336.2	285.9	350.6	289.3	468.1	110.9	104.6	116.8	162.1	388.9	468.1
2007	230.0	233.7	351.1	290.0	369.3	300.8	498.9	111.4	102.9	119.6	171.4	420.4	494.1
2008	250.5	244.1	364.1	296.0	384.9	311.0	534.0	113.3	102.6	123.6	181.3	450.2	522.1
2009	236.3	251.0	375.6	305.1	397.3	319.4	567.9	114.4	101.3	127.4	190.9	482.1	549.0
2008													
January	239.0	238.0	360.5	295.2	380.3	307.0	522.1	112.3	103.3	121.5	176.7	436.3	509.2
February	238.9	238.4	361.0	295.7	380.7	307.3	524.1	112.4	103.1	121.8	177.5	437.3	511.4
March	244.6	240.0	361.8	296.9	381.3	307.7	525.8	112.6	103.2	122.1	178.2	438.5	513.6
April	244.8	240.6	362.3	296.3	382.3	308.3	528.3	112.6	102.9	122.6	179.2	442.3	516.4
May	250.9	242.6	362.8	294.6	383.8	310.1	530.5	112.8	102.5	123.0	180.0	444.6	518.6
June	258.4	245.0	363.7	295.3	384.8	311.0	532.8	112.9	102.4	123.6	180.8	446.6	521.0
July	261.5	246.3	364.1	294.9	385.4	311.7	534.7	113.3	102.3	124.2	181.6	448.5	523.3
August	263.3	247.9	364.8	295.2	386.4	312.4	537.6	113.8	102.6	124.5	182.7	458.2	525.9
September	260.7	248.2	365.8	295.8	387.6	313.2	540.4	114.0	102.7	124.6	183.4	460.0	527.8
October	252.7	247.6	366.4	296.2	388.2	313.6	542.4	114.2	102.2	124.9	184.3	461.2	530.3
November	246.9	246.9	367.3	297.6	388.8	314.5	543.1	114.2	102.1	125.2	184.9	463.0	532.3
December	243.4	246.9	368.3	298.8	389.7	315.1	545.9	114.0	102.2	125.6	185.8	465.3	534.9
2009													
January	239.1	247.6	369.9	299.9	391.5	316.1	550.0	114.0	101.7	125.9	186.4	466.8	536.6
February	234.6	248.6	371.2	301.7	392.5	316.3	554.3	114.5	101.6	126.2	187.2	468.1	539.0
March	232.3	248.4	371.9	302.5	393.2	316.4	557.6	114.5	101.6	126.5	188.1	470.7	541.5
April	230.5	249.2	373.3	303.4	394.7	316.7	562.8	114.0	101.7	126.8	188.9	472.7	543.9
May	228.2	248.9	374.4	304.4	395.9	318.5	563.6	114.0	101.5	127.2	190.0	474.6	546.9
June	227.0	248.7	375.2	304.8	396.8	319.3	565.7	114.6	101.9	127.4	190.7	480.5	548.7
July	231.4	249.9	375.9	304.4	397.9	319.8	569.5	114.6	101.7	127.8	191.7	486.3	551.2
August	234.4	251.5	376.9	306.0	398.7	320.3	572.4	114.7	101.5	128.0	192.7	489.3	554.0
September	239.3	253.1	378.6	308.0	400.2	321.4	575.8	114.6	100.8	128.1	192.7	490.7	554.0
October	241.4	254.3	379.2	308.8	400.8	322.1	577.1	114.2	100.2	128.3	193.3	491.7	555.7
November	247.7	255.8	380.3	308.9	402.3	322.6	581.6	113.9	100.5	128.2	193.8	496.0	556.8
December	251.2	256.7	380.7	308.7	403.0	323.0	584.5	113.5	100.4	128.5	194.5	497.4	559.0

[3]December 1997 = 100.
. . . = Not available.

Table 8-1. Consumer Price Indexes, All Urban Consumers (CPI-U)—*Continued*

(1982–1984 = 100, seasonally adjusted [preliminary], except as noted.)

Year and month	Education and communication—Continued					Other goods and services					Commodity and service groups of CPI-U		Energy
	Communication					Total	Tobacco and smoking products [1]	Personal care			Commodities	Services	
	Total [3]	Information and information processing						Total	Personal care products [1]	Personal care services [1]			
		Total [1,3]	Telephone services [1,3]	Information technology, hardware, and services									
				Total [1,4]	Personal computers and peripheral equipment [1,5]								
1965	...	...	...	...	...	...	32.6	36.6	38.4	34.8	35.2	26.6	22.9
1966	...	...	...	...	...	...	34.2	37.3	38.0	36.4	36.1	27.6	23.3
1967	...	...	...	...	...	35.1	35.5	38.4	38.6	38.1	36.8	28.8	23.8
1968	...	...	...	...	...	36.9	37.8	40.0	39.8	40.1	38.1	30.3	24.2
1969	...	...	...	...	...	38.7	39.8	42.0	41.6	42.2	39.9	32.4	24.8
1970	...	...	...	...	...	40.9	43.1	43.5	42.7	44.2	41.7	35.0	25.5
1971	...	...	...	...	...	42.9	44.9	44.9	44.0	45.7	43.2	37.0	26.5
1972	...	...	...	...	...	44.7	47.4	46.0	45.2	46.8	44.5	38.4	27.2
1973	...	...	...	...	...	46.4	48.7	48.1	46.4	49.7	47.8	40.1	29.4
1974	...	...	...	...	...	49.8	51.1	52.8	51.5	53.9	53.5	43.8	38.1
1975	...	...	...	...	...	53.9	54.7	57.9	58.0	57.7	58.2	48.0	42.1
1976	...	...	...	...	...	57.0	57.0	61.7	61.3	61.9	60.7	52.0	45.1
1977	...	...	...	...	...	60.4	59.8	65.7	64.7	66.4	64.2	56.0	49.4
1978	...	...	...	...	...	64.3	63.0	69.9	68.2	71.3	68.8	60.8	52.5
1979	...	...	...	...	...	68.9	66.8	75.2	72.9	77.2	76.6	67.5	65.7
1980	...	...	...	...	...	75.2	72.0	81.9	79.6	83.7	86.0	77.9	86.0
1981	...	...	...	...	...	82.6	77.8	89.1	87.8	90.2	93.2	88.1	97.7
1982	...	...	...	...	...	91.1	86.5	95.4	95.1	95.7	97.0	96.0	99.2
1983	...	...	...	...	...	101.1	103.4	100.3	100.7	100.0	99.8	99.4	99.9
1984	...	...	...	...	...	107.9	110.1	104.3	104.2	104.4	103.2	104.6	100.9
1985	...	...	...	...	...	114.5	116.7	108.3	107.6	108.9	105.4	109.9	101.6
1986	...	...	...	...	...	121.4	124.7	111.9	111.3	112.5	104.4	115.4	88.2
1987	...	...	...	...	...	128.5	133.6	115.1	113.9	116.2	107.7	120.2	88.6
1988	...	...	...	...	...	137.0	145.8	119.4	118.1	120.7	111.5	125.7	89.3
1989	...	...	...	96.3	...	147.7	164.4	125.0	123.2	126.8	116.7	131.9	94.3
1990	...	...	...	93.5	...	159.0	181.5	130.4	128.2	132.8	122.8	139.2	102.1
1991	...	...	...	88.6	...	171.6	202.7	134.9	132.8	137.0	126.6	146.3	102.5
1992	...	...	...	83.7	...	183.3	219.8	138.3	136.5	140.0	129.1	152.0	103.0
1993	96.7	97.7	...	78.8	...	192.9	228.4	141.5	139.0	144.0	131.5	157.9	104.2
1994	97.6	98.6	...	72.0	...	198.5	220.0	144.6	141.5	147.9	133.8	163.1	104.6
1995	98.8	98.7	...	63.8	...	206.9	225.7	147.1	143.1	151.5	136.4	168.7	105.2
1996	99.6	99.5	...	57.2	...	215.4	232.8	150.1	144.3	156.6	139.9	174.1	110.1
1997	100.3	100.4	...	50.1	...	224.8	243.7	152.7	144.2	162.4	141.8	179.4	111.5
1998	98.7	98.5	100.7	39.9	875.1	237.7	274.8	156.7	148.3	166.0	141.9	184.2	102.9
1999	96.0	95.5	100.1	30.5	598.7	258.3	355.8	161.1	151.8	171.4	144.4	188.8	106.6
2000	93.6	92.8	98.5	25.9	459.0	271.1	394.9	165.6	153.7	178.1	149.2	195.3	124.6
2001	93.3	92.3	99.3	21.3	330.1	282.6	425.2	170.5	155.1	184.3	150.7	203.4	129.3
2002	92.3	90.8	99.7	18.3	248.4	293.2	461.5	174.7	154.7	188.4	149.7	209.8	121.7
2003	89.7	87.8	98.3	16.1	196.9	298.7	469.0	178.0	153.5	193.2	151.2	216.5	136.5
2004	86.7	84.6	95.8	14.8	171.2	304.7	478.0	181.7	153.9	197.6	154.7	222.8	151.4
2005	84.7	82.6	94.9	13.6	143.2	313.4	502.8	185.6	154.4	203.9	160.2	230.1	177.1
2006	84.1	81.7	95.8	12.5	120.9	321.7	519.9	190.2	155.8	209.7	164.0	238.9	196.9
2007	83.4	80.7	98.2	10.6	108.4	333.3	554.2	195.6	158.3	216.6	167.5	246.8	207.7
2008	84.2	81.4	100.5	10.1	94.9	345.4	588.7	201.3	159.3	223.7	174.8	255.5	236.7
2009	85.0	81.9	102.4	9.7	82.3	368.6	730.3	204.6	162.6	227.6	169.7	259.2	193.1
2008													
January	83.4	80.6	98.9	10.2	101.0	339.3	572.7	198.3	158.2	219.9	173.3	251.3	230.7
February	83.4	80.6	98.8	10.3	100.5	340.1	575.2	198.7	157.7	220.8	173.6	251.8	232.2
March	83.5	80.8	99.0	10.2	100.4	341.5	574.9	199.7	158.4	222.8	174.3	252.7	236.9
April	83.7	80.9	99.5	10.2	98.9	342.8	576.4	200.6	159.4	222.8	174.2	253.5	235.8
May	83.9	81.1	99.9	10.1	97.0	344.1	581.2	201.0	158.8	223.6	175.1	254.7	242.1
June	84.4	81.5	100.7	10.1	95.7	345.5	589.9	201.3	158.9	223.5	177.8	255.9	256.2
July	84.8	82.0	101.3	10.1	94.7	347.0	596.8	201.7	159.0	223.7	179.7	257.2	265.3
August	84.7	81.8	101.3	10.0	92.9	347.7	597.4	202.2	159.3	224.2	179.1	257.6	260.1
September	84.5	81.6	101.3	9.9	90.8	348.4	597.6	202.7	159.6	224.6	179.3	257.6	257.4
October	84.5	81.7	101.4	9.9	89.9	349.3	599.7	203.1	159.8	225.6	175.7	257.7	237.3
November	84.6	81.7	101.5	9.9	89.0	349.4	599.8	203.2	161.0	226.2	168.5	257.8	197.1
December	84.7	81.9	101.7	9.9	88.5	349.5	602.6	203.0	161.4	226.3	164.9	258.1	178.8
2009													
January	84.9	82.0	101.9	9.9	88.5	350.5	607.4	203.3	162.6	225.7	165.8	258.4	181.9
February	84.9	82.1	101.9	9.9	87.7	351.1	611.5	203.3	162.5	225.9	167.2	258.7	187.9
March	84.9	82.0	102.0	9.9	86.2	360.8	679.1	203.8	162.7	228.0	166.7	258.6	182.3
April	85.0	82.1	102.1	9.9	85.7	370.0	742.4	204.5	163.8	227.9	166.6	258.6	177.9
May	85.0	82.0	102.3	9.8	84.4	369.2	740.3	204.1	163.1	227.6	167.0	258.6	178.3
June	85.0	81.9	102.2	9.7	83.5	370.2	746.3	204.2	162.3	227.6	169.9	258.8	191.6
July	85.1	82.0	102.6	9.6	80.8	373.1	762.9	204.7	162.9	227.3	169.9	258.8	190.9
August	84.9	81.8	102.7	9.5	78.6	373.4	763.6	204.9	162.5	227.6	171.2	259.3	199.7
September	85.0	82.0	103.0	9.5	78.0	374.4	771.1	204.9	162.4	228.3	171.7	259.6	201.0
October	85.1	82.0	102.9	9.5	78.2	375.4	773.8	205.4	162.3	228.5	172.5	260.0	203.9
November	84.8	81.7	102.5	9.5	78.1	377.1	781.5	205.8	161.8	228.4	174.0	260.2	212.3
December	84.8	81.7	102.7	9.4	78.0	377.6	783.8	206.1	162.3	228.3	174.4	260.4	212.8

[1] Not seasonally adjusted.
[3] December 1997 = 100.
[4] December 1988 = 100.
[5] December 2007 = 100.
. . . = Not available.

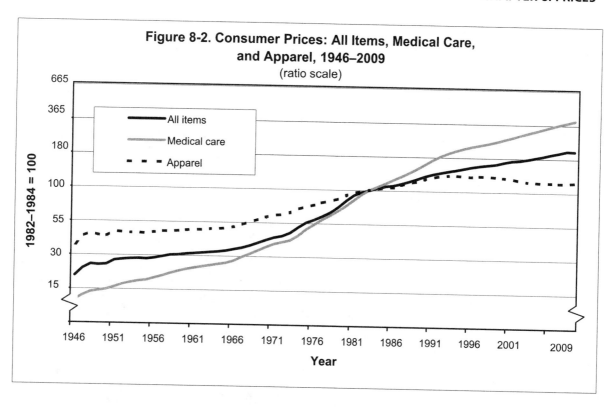

Figure 8-2. Consumer Prices: All Items, Medical Care, and Apparel, 1946–2009
(ratio scale)

- Figure 8-2 charts two components of the Consumer Price Index for All Urban Consumers (CPI-U) along with the all-items total. Since all three indexes have the base years 1982–1984, they converge around 100 in those years. However, over the entire postwar period, the trends of the two components are very different. (Tables 8-1 and 20-2)

- Apparel has been one of the areas most subject to international competition, and the apparel index shows far less growth than the overall average of prices.

- Medical care, on the other hand, has little price competition from producers in other countries. It is often paid for by third-party insurers, both government and private, rather than directly by consumers. Furthermore, it is characterized by trend growth in demand, due to rising income and expectations and to technological progress. All of these economic factors cause medical care prices to rise faster than the general price level.

- Medical care has arguably been overstated in the CPI due to the difficulties of making quality adjustments. Quality adjustments have been much improved in recent years, although such improvements are not retroactively introduced into the official CPIs. But even since 1997, when a major improvement was introduced into the hospital cost component of the CPI, measured medical care prices have increased at a 4.0 percent annual rate, while the total CPI rose at a 2.4 percent average annual rate. (Table 8-1)

- Medical care spending accounts for a greater proportion of out-of-pocket spending by senior citizens than for the public in general. (This is true even though the Consumer Expenditure Survey, which determines the weights for the CPIs, does not include payments for seniors' medical care by Medicare, Medicaid, or private insurance companies.) For this reason, when the CPI is re-weighted to reflect the out-of-pocket spending patterns of persons age 62 years and over, from 1983 to 2009 the resulting "CPI-E" rises an average of 0.2 percentage points per year more rapidly than the CPI-U, and 0.3 percentage points more than the CPI-W. The CPI-W, despite the fact that its market basket excludes all retirees, is the index actually used to escalate Social Security payments. (Table 8-3)

Table 8-2. Alternative Measures of Total and Core Consumer Prices: Index Levels

(Various bases; monthly data seasonally adjusted, except as noted.)

Year and month	CPIs, all items						CPIs, all items less food and energy			Chain-type price indexes for personal consumption expenditures (PCE), 2005 = 100		Excluding food and energy	
	CPI-U, 1982–1984 = 100	CPI-W, 1982–1984 = 100	CPI-U-X1, 1982–1984 = 100	CPI-E, Dec. 1982 = 100, not seasonally adjusted	CPI-U-RS, Dec. 1977 = 100, not seasonally adjusted	C-CPI-U, Dec. 1999 = 100, not seasonally adjusted	CPI-U, 1982–1984 = 100	CPI-U-RS, Dec. 1977 = 100, not seasonally adjusted	C-CPI-U, Dec. 1999 = 100, not seasonally adjusted	PCE, total	PCE, market-based	PCE, total	PCE, market-based
1960	29.6	29.8	32.2	...	...	...	30.6	...	...	18.6	...	19.0	...
1961	29.9	30.1	32.5	...	...	...	31.0	...	...	18.8	...	19.3	...
1962	30.2	30.4	32.8	...	...	...	31.4	...	...	19.0	...	19.5	...
1963	30.6	30.8	33.3	...	...	...	31.8	...	...	19.2	...	19.8	...
1964	31.0	31.2	33.7	...	...	...	32.3	...	...	19.5	...	20.1	...
1965	31.5	31.7	34.2	...	...	...	32.7	...	...	19.8	...	20.3	...
1966	32.4	32.6	35.2	...	...	...	33.5	...	...	20.3	...	20.8	...
1967	33.4	33.6	36.3	...	...	...	34.7	...	...	20.8	...	21.4	...
1968	34.8	35.0	37.7	...	...	...	36.3	...	...	21.6	...	22.4	...
1969	36.7	36.9	39.4	...	...	...	38.4	...	...	22.6	...	23.4	...
1970	38.8	39.0	41.3	...	...	...	40.8	...	...	23.7	...	24.5	...
1971	40.5	40.7	43.1	...	...	...	42.7	...	...	24.7	...	25.7	...
1972	41.8	42.1	44.4	...	...	...	44.0	...	...	25.5	...	26.5	...
1973	44.4	44.7	47.2	...	...	...	45.6	...	...	26.9	...	27.5	...
1974	49.3	49.6	51.9	...	...	...	49.4	...	...	29.7	...	29.7	...
1975	53.8	54.1	56.2	...	...	...	53.9	...	...	32.2	...	32.2	...
1976	56.9	57.2	59.4	...	...	...	57.4	...	...	34.0	...	34.1	...
1977	60.6	60.9	63.2	...	...	...	61.0	...	...	36.2	...	36.3	...
1978	65.2	65.6	67.5	...	104.4	...	65.5	103.6	...	38.7	...	38.7	...
1979	72.6	73.1	74.0	...	114.4	...	71.9	111.0	...	42.1	...	41.6	...
1980	82.4	82.9	82.3	...	127.1	...	80.8	120.9	...	46.6	...	45.4	...
1981	90.9	91.4	90.1	...	139.2	...	89.2	132.2	...	50.8	...	49.3	...
1982	96.5	96.9	95.6	...	147.6	...	95.8	142.4	...	53.6	...	52.5	...
1983	99.6	99.8	99.6	102.1	153.9	...	99.6	150.4	...	55.9	...	55.2	...
1984	103.9	103.3	103.9	106.5	160.2	...	104.6	157.9	...	58.0	...	57.5	...
1985	107.6	106.9	107.6	110.5	165.7	...	109.1	164.8	...	59.9	...	59.7	...
1986	109.6	108.6	109.6	113.3	168.7	...	113.5	171.4	...	61.4	...	61.9	...
1987	113.6	112.5	113.6	117.7	174.4	...	118.2	178.1	...	63.6	64.5	64.3	65.5
1988	118.3	117.0	118.3	122.7	180.8	...	123.4	185.2	...	66.1	67.0	67.1	68.3
1989	124.0	122.6	124.0	128.9	188.6	...	129.0	192.6	...	69.0	70.1	69.9	71.3
1990	130.7	129.0	130.7	136.6	198.0	...	135.5	201.4	...	72.1	73.5	72.8	74.6
1991	136.2	134.3	136.2	143.0	205.1	...	142.1	209.9	...	74.8	76.4	75.7	77.7
1992	140.3	138.2	140.3	147.6	210.3	...	147.3	216.4	...	77.0	78.5	78.2	80.3
1993	144.5	142.1	144.5	152.2	215.5	...	152.2	222.5	...	78.6	80.4	80.1	82.4
1994	148.2	145.6	148.2	156.6	220.1	...	156.5	227.7	...	80.3	82.0	81.8	84.1
1995	152.4	149.8	152.4	161.2	225.4	...	161.2	233.4	...	82.0	83.6	83.7	85.9
1996	156.9	154.1	156.9	166.1	231.4	...	165.6	239.1	...	83.8	85.3	85.3	87.3
1997	160.5	157.6	160.5	170.1	236.4	...	169.5	244.4	...	85.4	86.5	87.0	88.6
1998	163.0	159.7	163.0	173.2	239.7	...	173.4	249.7	...	86.2	87.1	88.2	89.6
1999	166.6	163.2	166.6	177.3	244.7	...	177.0	254.8	...	87.6	88.3	89.6	90.7
2000	172.2	168.9	172.2	183.5	252.9	102.0	181.3	260.8	101.4	89.8	90.4	91.1	92.1
2001	177.1	173.5	177.1	189.2	260.0	104.3	186.1	267.8	103.5	91.5	92.1	92.7	93.7
2002	179.9	175.9	179.9	192.7	264.2	105.6	190.5	273.9	105.4	92.7	93.2	94.3	95.1
2003	184.0	179.8	184.0	197.4	270.1	107.8	193.2	277.9	106.6	94.6	95.0	95.8	96.4
2004	188.9	184.5	188.9	203.3	277.4	110.5	196.6	282.9	108.4	97.1	97.2	97.8	98.1
2005	195.3	191.0	195.3	210.4	286.7	113.7	200.9	289.0	110.4	100.0	100.0	100.0	100.0
2006	201.6	197.1	201.6	217.3	296.1	117.0	205.9	296.2	112.9	102.7	102.8	102.3	102.2
2007	207.3	202.8	207.3	223.8	304.5	120.0	210.7	303.1	115.0	105.5	105.3	104.7	104.4
2008	215.3	211.1	215.3	232.4	316.2	124.4	215.6	310.1	117.3	109.0	109.0	107.2	106.8
2009	214.5	209.6	214.5	231.9	315.0	[1]124.4	219.2	315.4	[1]119.1	109.2	109.3	108.9	108.8
2008													
January	212.2	208.0	212.2	227.9	310.0	121.9	213.7	306.6	116.0	107.7	107.6	106.2	105.7
February	212.7	208.5	212.7	228.7	310.9	122.3	213.9	307.6	116.4	107.9	107.8	106.3	105.9
March	213.5	209.4	213.5	230.7	313.6	123.3	214.3	309.1	116.9	108.3	108.2	106.5	106.1
April	214.1	210.0	214.1	231.8	315.5	124.1	214.5	309.4	117.0	108.5	108.4	106.7	106.3
May	215.3	211.1	215.3	233.5	318.1	125.2	214.9	309.5	117.1	108.9	108.8	107.0	106.5
June	217.3	213.3	217.3	235.8	321.3	126.3	215.5	310.1	117.2	109.6	109.6	107.2	106.7
July	219.1	215.3	219.1	237.2	323.0	126.9	216.2	310.8	117.5	110.2	110.2	107.5	107.0
August	218.8	215.0	218.8	236.2	321.7	126.6	216.5	311.4	117.8	110.2	110.2	107.7	107.2
September	218.8	215.1	218.8	235.5	321.3	126.6	216.8	311.9	118.1	110.4	110.4	107.8	107.4
October	216.8	212.6	216.8	233.5	318.0	125.5	216.8	312.2	118.2	109.9	109.9	107.9	107.6
November	212.9	207.7	212.9	229.8	311.9	123.0	216.9	311.7	118.0	108.6	108.5	107.9	107.6
December	211.3	205.8	211.3	227.8	308.7	121.6	216.9	310.9	117.6	108.1	107.9	107.9	107.7
2009													
January	212.0	206.6	212.0	228.9	310.1	[1]122.2	217.2	311.7	[1]117.9	108.3	108.2	108.0	107.9
February	212.9	207.6	212.9	229.9	311.6	[1]122.9	217.7	313.1	[1]118.4	108.6	108.6	108.2	108.2
March	212.6	207.3	212.6	230.5	312.4	[1]123.1	218.1	314.5	[1]118.9	108.5	108.5	108.3	108.3
April	212.8	207.5	212.8	230.8	313.1	[1]123.5	218.6	315.2	[1]119.1	108.6	108.6	108.6	108.6
May	213.1	207.8	213.1	231.2	314.0	[1]124.0	218.9	315.2	[1]119.1	108.6	108.6	108.7	108.7
June	214.6	209.6	214.6	233.0	316.7	[1]125.2	219.3	315.4	[1]119.1	109.2	109.3	108.9	108.9
July	214.8	209.9	214.8	232.9	316.2	[1]124.9	219.5	315.5	[1]119.1	109.2	109.3	108.9	108.9
August	215.6	210.9	215.6	233.1	316.9	[1]125.2	219.7	315.9	[1]119.2	109.6	109.7	109.0	109.1
September	215.9	211.4	215.9	232.9	317.1	[1]125.2	220.0	316.7	[1]119.5	109.7	109.8	109.1	109.2
October	216.4	211.9	216.4	233.2	317.5	[1]125.4	220.5	317.5	[1]119.8	110.0	110.0	109.4	109.4
November	216.9	212.4	216.9	233.1	317.7	[1]125.4	220.5	317.0	[1]119.5	110.2	110.2	109.5	109.4
December	217.2	212.9	217.2	232.8	317.1	[1]125.2	220.8	316.5	[1]119.3	110.4	110.3	109.6	109.5

[1] Interim values.
. . . = Not available.

Table 8-3. Alternative Measures of Total and Core Consumer Prices: Inflation Rates

(Percent changes from year earlier, except as noted; monthly data seasonally adjusted, except as noted.)

Year and month	CPIs, all items						CPIs, all items less food and energy			Chain-type price indexes for personal consumption expenditures (PCE), 2000 = 100			
										PCE, total	PCE, market-based	Excluding food and energy	
	CPI-U, 1982–1984 = 100	CPI-W, 1982–1984 = 100	CPI-U-X1, 1982–1984 = 100	CPI-E, Dec. 1982 = 100, not seasonally adjusted	CPI-U-RS, Dec. 1977 = 100, not seasonally adjusted	C-CPI-U, Dec. 1999 = 100, not seasonally adjusted	CPI-U, 1982–1984 = 100	CPI-U-RS, Dec. 1977 = 100, not seasonally adjusted	C-CPI-U, Dec. 1999 = 100, not seasonally adjusted			PCE, total	PCE, market-based
1960	1.7	1.7	1.9	...	...	...	1.3	...	...	1.6	...	1.7	...
1961	1.0	1.0	0.9	...	...	...	1.3	...	...	1.0	...	1.3	...
1962	1.0	1.0	0.9	...	...	...	1.3	...	...	1.2	...	1.4	...
1963	1.3	1.3	1.5	...	...	...	1.3	...	...	1.2	...	1.3	...
1964	1.3	1.3	1.2	...	...	...	1.6	...	...	1.5	...	1.5	...
1965	1.6	1.6	1.5	...	...	...	1.2	...	...	1.4	...	1.3	...
1966	2.9	2.8	2.8	...	...	...	2.4	...	...	2.5	...	2.3	...
1967	3.1	3.0	3.0	...	...	...	3.6	...	...	2.5	...	3.1	...
1968	4.2	4.0	3.7	...	...	...	4.6	...	...	3.9	...	4.3	...
1969	5.5	5.1	4.3	...	...	...	5.8	...	...	4.5	...	4.7	...
1970	5.7	5.4	4.6	...	...	...	6.3	...	...	4.7	...	4.7	...
1971	4.4	4.2	4.2	...	...	...	4.7	...	...	4.2	...	4.7	...
1972	3.2	3.3	2.9	...	...	...	3.0	...	...	3.4	...	3.2	...
1973	6.2	5.8	5.9	...	...	...	3.6	...	...	5.4	...	3.8	...
1974	11.0	9.9	9.1	...	...	...	8.3	...	...	10.4	...	7.9	...
1975	9.1	8.3	7.7	...	...	...	9.1	...	...	8.4	...	8.4	...
1976	5.8	5.4	5.4	...	...	...	6.5	...	...	5.5	...	6.1	...
1977	6.5	6.1	6.0	...	...	...	6.3	...	...	6.5	...	6.4	...
1978	7.6	7.2	6.4	...	...	...	7.4	...	...	7.0	...	6.7	...
1979	11.3	10.3	8.8	...	9.6	...	9.8	7.1	...	8.9	...	7.3	...
1980	13.5	11.8	10.1	...	11.1	...	12.4	8.9	...	10.7	...	9.2	...
1981	10.3	9.3	8.7	...	9.5	...	10.4	9.3	...	8.9	...	8.7	...
1982	6.2	5.7	5.8	...	6.0	...	7.4	7.7	...	5.5	...	6.5	...
1983	3.2	2.9	4.0	...	4.3	...	4.0	5.6	...	4.3	...	5.2	...
1984	4.3	3.4	4.1	4.1	4.1	...	5.0	5.0	...	3.8	...	4.2	...
1985	3.6	3.4	3.4	3.6	3.4	...	4.3	4.4	...	3.3	...	3.8	...
1986	1.9	1.6	1.8	2.5	1.8	...	4.0	4.0	...	2.4	...	3.8	...
1987	3.6	3.5	3.5	3.7	3.4	...	4.1	4.0	...	3.6	...	3.8	...
1988	4.1	3.8	4.0	4.1	3.7	...	4.4	3.9	...	4.0	...	4.3	...
1989	4.8	4.6	4.6	4.8	4.3	...	4.5	4.0	...	4.3	...	4.1	...
1990	5.4	5.0	5.1	5.7	5.0	...	5.0	4.6	...	4.6	...	4.3	...
1991	4.2	3.9	4.0	4.5	3.6	...	4.9	4.2	...	3.6	...	3.9	...
1992	3.0	2.8	2.9	3.1	2.5	...	3.7	3.1	...	2.9	...	3.4	...
1993	3.0	2.7	2.9	3.1	2.5	...	3.3	2.8	...	2.2	...	2.4	...
1994	2.6	2.4	2.5	2.8	2.1	...	2.8	2.3	...	2.1	...	2.2	...
1995	2.8	2.8	2.8	2.8	2.4	...	3.0	2.5	...	2.2	...	2.3	...
1996	3.0	2.8	2.9	3.0	2.7	...	2.7	2.4	...	2.2	...	1.9	...
1997	2.3	2.2	2.2	2.4	2.2	...	2.4	2.2	...	1.9	...	1.9	...
1998	1.6	1.3	1.5	1.8	1.4	...	2.3	2.2	...	1.0	...	1.4	...
1999	2.2	2.1	2.2	2.3	2.1	...	2.1	2.0	...	1.6	0.6	1.5	1.1
2000	3.4	3.4	3.3	3.4	3.4	...	2.4	2.4	...	2.5	1.4	1.7	1.2
2001	2.8	2.7	2.8	3.0	2.8	2.3	2.6	2.7	2.1	1.9	1.9	1.8	1.5
2002	1.6	1.4	1.6	1.8	1.6	1.2	2.4	2.3	1.8	1.4	1.1	1.7	1.8
2003	2.3	2.2	2.2	2.4	2.2	2.1	1.4	1.5	1.1	2.0	2.0	1.5	1.5
2004	2.7	2.5	2.6	2.9	2.7	2.5	1.8	1.8	1.7	2.6	2.4	2.1	1.4
2005	3.4	3.4	3.3	3.4	3.4	2.9	2.2	2.2	1.8	3.0	2.8	2.3	2.0
2006	3.2	3.1	3.1	3.2	3.3	2.9	2.5	2.5	2.3	2.7	2.8	2.3	2.2
2007	2.8	2.8	2.8	2.9	2.8	2.5	2.3	2.3	1.8	2.7	2.5	2.4	2.1
2008	3.8	3.9	3.7	3.7	3.8	3.7	2.3	2.3	2.0	3.3	3.4	2.4	2.3
2009	-0.4	-0.7	-0.4	-0.2	-0.4	[1]-0.1	1.7	1.7	[1]1.5	0.2	0.3	1.5	1.9
Percent change, annual rate:													
1978–2009	3.9	3.8	3.8	...	3.6	...	4.0	3.7	...	3.4	...	3.4	...
1983–2009	3.0	2.9	3.0	3.2	2.8	...	3.1	2.9	...	2.6	...	2.6	...
2000–2009	2.5	2.4	2.5	2.6	2.5	2.2	2.1	2.1	1.8	2.2	2.1	2.0	1.9
2009													
January	-0.1	-0.7	-0.1	0.4	0.0	[1]0.2	1.7	1.7	[1]1.6	0.5	0.6	1.7	2.1
February	0.1	-0.4	0.1	0.5	0.2	[1]0.5	1.8	1.8	[1]1.7	0.6	0.7	1.8	2.1
March	-0.4	-1.0	-0.4	-0.1	-0.4	[1]-0.1	1.8	1.7	[1]1.7	0.2	0.4	1.7	2.1
April	-0.6	-1.2	-0.6	-0.4	-0.8	[1]-0.5	1.9	1.9	[1]1.7	0.1	0.2	1.7	2.2
May	-1.0	-1.6	-1.0	-1.0	-1.3	[1]-0.9	1.8	1.8	[1]1.7	-0.3	-0.1	1.6	2.1
June	-1.3	-1.8	-1.3	-1.2	-1.4	[1]-0.9	1.7	1.7	[1]1.6	-0.4	-0.2	1.5	2.0
July	-2.0	-2.5	-2.0	-1.8	-2.1	[1]-1.6	1.6	1.5	[1]1.3	-0.9	-0.8	1.3	1.8
August	-1.5	-1.9	-1.5	-1.3	-1.5	[1]-1.1	1.4	1.4	[1]1.2	-0.6	-0.5	1.3	1.7
September	-1.3	-1.7	-1.3	-1.1	-1.3	[1]-1.0	1.5	1.5	[1]1.2	-0.6	-0.5	1.2	1.6
October	-0.2	-0.3	-0.2	-0.1	-0.2	[1]-0.1	1.7	1.7	[1]1.3	0.1	0.1	1.4	1.7
November	1.8	2.3	1.8	1.5	1.9	[1]2.0	1.7	1.7	[1]1.3	1.5	1.6	1.5	1.7
December	2.8	3.5	2.8	2.2	2.7	[1]3.0	1.8	1.8	[1]1.4	2.1	2.2	1.6	1.6

[1] Interim values.
. . . = Not available.

Table 8-4. Producer Price Indexes and Purchasing Power of the Dollar

(1982 = 100, seasonally adjusted.)

Year and month	Finished goods		Finished consumer goods				Finished consumer goods, except foods			Capital equipment		
				Finished consumer foods								
	Total	Percent change from previous period	Total	Total	Crude	Processed	Total	Durable goods	Nondurable goods less foods	Total	Manufacturing industries	Nonmanufacturing industries
1960	33.4	0.9	33.6	35.5	39.8	35.2	33.5	43.8	28.4	32.8	30.2	34.8
1961	33.4	0.0	33.6	35.4	38.0	35.3	33.4	43.6	28.4	32.9	30.3	34.8
1962	33.5	0.3	33.7	35.7	38.4	35.6	33.4	43.4	28.4	33.0	30.5	34.9
1963	33.4	-0.3	33.5	35.3	37.8	35.2	33.4	43.1	28.5	33.1	30.6	34.8
1964	33.5	0.3	33.6	35.4	38.9	35.2	33.3	43.3	28.4	33.4	31.0	35.1
1965	34.1	1.8	34.2	36.8	39.0	36.8	33.6	43.2	28.8	33.8	31.5	35.4
1966	35.2	3.2	35.4	39.2	41.5	39.2	34.1	43.4	29.3	34.6	32.5	36.0
1967	35.6	1.1	35.6	38.5	39.6	38.8	34.7	44.1	30.0	35.8	33.8	37.0
1968	36.6	2.8	36.5	40.0	42.5	40.0	35.5	45.1	30.6	37.0	35.0	38.2
1969	38.0	3.8	37.9	42.4	45.9	42.3	36.3	45.9	31.5	38.3	36.2	39.5
1970	39.3	3.4	39.1	43.8	46.0	43.9	37.4	47.2	32.5	40.1	38.1	41.3
1971	40.5	3.1	40.2	44.5	45.8	44.7	38.7	48.9	33.5	41.7	39.6	43.0
1972	41.8	3.2	41.5	46.9	48.0	47.2	39.4	50.0	34.1	42.8	40.5	44.2
1973	45.6	9.1	46.0	56.5	63.6	55.8	41.2	50.9	36.1	44.2	42.2	45.3
1974	52.6	15.4	53.1	64.4	71.6	63.9	48.2	55.5	44.0	50.5	48.8	51.2
1975	58.2	10.6	58.2	69.8	71.7	70.3	53.2	61.0	48.9	58.2	56.5	58.9
1976	60.8	4.5	60.4	69.6	76.7	69.0	56.5	63.7	52.4	62.1	60.3	62.9
1977	64.7	6.4	64.3	73.3	79.5	72.7	60.6	67.4	56.8	66.1	64.5	66.8
1978	69.8	7.9	69.4	79.9	85.8	79.4	64.9	73.6	60.0	71.3	70.1	71.8
1979	77.6	11.2	77.5	87.3	92.3	86.8	73.5	80.8	69.3	77.5	77.1	77.7
1980	88.0	13.4	88.6	92.4	93.9	92.3	87.1	91.0	85.1	85.8	86.0	85.7
1981	96.1	9.2	96.6	97.8	104.4	97.2	96.1	96.4	95.8	94.6	94.9	94.4
1982	100.0	4.1	100.0	100.0	100.0	100.0	100.0	100.0	100.0	100.0	100.0	100.0
1983	101.6	1.6	101.3	101.0	102.4	100.9	101.2	102.8	100.5	102.8	102.3	103.0
1984	103.7	2.1	103.3	105.4	111.4	104.9	102.2	104.5	101.1	105.2	104.9	105.4
1985	104.7	1.0	103.8	104.6	102.9	104.8	103.3	106.5	101.7	107.5	107.4	107.6
1986	103.2	-1.4	101.4	107.3	105.6	107.4	98.5	108.9	93.3	109.7	109.7	109.7
1987	105.4	2.1	103.6	109.5	107.1	109.6	100.7	111.5	94.9	111.7	111.8	111.6
1988	108.0	2.5	106.2	112.6	109.8	112.7	103.1	113.8	97.3	114.3	115.5	113.9
1989	113.6	5.2	112.1	118.7	119.6	118.6	108.9	117.6	103.8	118.8	120.3	118.2
1990	119.2	4.9	118.2	124.4	123.0	124.4	115.3	120.4	111.5	122.9	124.5	122.2
1991	121.7	2.1	120.5	124.1	119.3	124.4	118.7	123.9	115.0	126.7	127.8	126.3
1992	123.2	1.2	121.7	123.3	107.6	124.4	120.8	125.7	117.3	129.1	129.3	129.0
1993	124.7	1.2	123.0	125.7	114.4	126.5	121.7	128.0	117.6	131.4	131.2	131.4
1994	125.5	0.6	123.3	126.8	111.3	127.9	121.6	130.9	116.2	134.1	133.2	134.3
1995	127.9	1.9	125.6	129.0	118.8	129.8	124.0	132.7	118.8	136.7	135.8	137.0
1996	131.3	2.7	129.5	133.6	129.2	133.8	127.6	134.2	123.3	138.3	137.2	138.6
1997	131.8	0.4	130.2	134.5	126.6	135.1	128.2	133.7	124.3	138.2	137.7	138.4
1998	130.7	-0.8	128.9	134.3	127.2	134.8	126.4	132.9	122.2	137.6	137.9	137.4
1999	133.0	1.8	132.0	135.1	125.5	135.9	130.5	133.0	127.9	137.6	138.5	137.3
2000	138.0	3.8	138.2	137.2	123.5	138.3	138.4	133.9	138.7	138.8	139.5	138.6
2001	140.7	2.0	141.5	141.3	127.7	142.4	141.4	134.0	142.8	139.7	140.4	139.4
2002	138.9	-1.3	139.4	140.1	128.5	141.0	138.8	133.0	139.8	139.1	140.0	138.7
2003	143.3	3.2	145.3	145.9	130.0	147.2	144.7	133.1	148.4	139.5	139.9	139.3
2004	148.5	3.6	151.7	152.7	138.2	153.9	150.9	135.0	156.6	141.4	142.4	141.0
2005	155.7	4.8	160.4	155.7	140.2	156.9	161.9	136.6	172.0	144.6	146.0	144.1
2006	160.4	3.0	166.0	156.7	151.3	157.1	169.2	136.9	182.6	146.9	149.2	145.9
2007	166.6	3.9	173.5	167.0	170.2	166.7	175.6	138.3	191.7	149.5	152.5	148.3
2008	177.1	6.3	186.3	178.3	175.5	178.6	189.1	141.2	210.5	153.8	157.3	152.5
2009[1]	172.6	-2.5	179.2	175.5	157.8	177.3	179.6	144.3	194.3	156.8	159.3	155.8
2008												
January	173.3	1.0	181.9	174.7	197.5	172.3	184.3	139.5	203.8	151.1	154.4	149.8
February	173.9	0.3	182.5	173.8	180.4	173.0	185.5	139.8	205.4	151.7	155.1	150.3
March	175.8	1.1	185.1	176.0	194.2	174.0	188.3	139.8	209.6	151.8	155.2	150.5
April	176.5	0.4	185.7	176.1	184.9	175.1	189.1	140.6	210.4	152.6	156.0	151.3
May	178.8	1.3	188.7	177.6	179.3	177.2	192.7	140.8	215.8	153.0	156.5	151.7
June	181.5	1.5	192.4	179.8	189.4	178.7	197.0	140.5	222.4	153.2	156.8	151.8
July	183.7	1.2	195.0	180.9	173.5	181.4	200.2	141.0	227.1	154.2	158.1	152.7
August	181.9	-1.0	192.4	181.4	168.4	182.5	196.3	141.7	220.7	154.8	158.7	153.3
September	182.0	0.1	192.3	181.6	173.9	182.2	196.1	142.1	220.2	155.3	159.2	153.8
October	177.3	-2.6	185.5	181.4	177.1	181.7	186.6	143.3	205.2	156.4	159.8	155.0
November	172.3	-2.8	178.7	180.5	176.9	180.6	177.5	143.2	191.4	156.4	159.6	155.2
December	169.4	-1.7	174.6	178.0	157.1	179.8	172.6	143.7	183.7	156.9	159.8	155.7
2009												
January	171.2	1.1	176.9	178.1	168.8	178.6	175.7	143.6	188.5	157.1	159.8	156.0
February	170.9	-0.2	176.5	175.4	156.5	177.0	176.1	143.9	188.9	157.0	159.4	156.0
March	169.6	-0.8	174.8	174.0	155.3	175.6	174.2	143.9	186.0	157.0	159.4	155.9
April	170.6	0.6	176.1	176.7	172.4	176.7	175.1	144.4	187.2	157.0	159.5	155.9
May	170.6	0.0	176.3	174.2	141.3	177.4	176.1	144.5	188.6	156.8	159.4	155.7
June	173.7	1.8	180.4	176.0	161.7	177.1	181.0	145.4	195.5	157.2	159.4	156.3
July	171.6	-1.2	177.5	173.7	150.4	175.8	177.9	144.7	191.2	157.0	159.3	156.0
August	174.1	1.5	180.9	174.3	153.4	176.1	182.2	145.4	197.3	157.5	159.6	156.6
September	173.3	-0.5	179.9	174.3	150.0	176.5	180.9	144.7	195.6	157.2	159.4	156.2
October	173.6	0.2	180.7	176.5	172.3	176.5	181.2	143.3	196.9	156.3	159.0	155.2
November[1]	176.6	1.7	184.7	177.7	175.7	177.4	186.1	144.3	203.6	157.0	159.4	156.0
December[1]	177.3	0.4	185.7	180.0	181.6	179.3	186.7	144.1	204.6	156.9	159.3	155.9

[1]Data are preliminary.

Table 8-4. Producer Price Indexes and Purchasing Power of the Dollar—*Continued*

(1982 = 100, seasonally adjusted.)

| Year and month | Total | Materials and components for manufacturing | | | | | Materials and components for construction | Processed fuels and lubricants | | | Containers, nonreturnable | Supplies | |
		Total	Materials for food manufacturing	Materials for nondurable manufacturing	Materials for durable manufacturing	Components for manufacturing		Total	Manufacturing industries	Nonmanufacturing industries		Total	Manufacturing industries
1960	30.8	33.3	35.7	35.9	30.4	34.0	32.7	16.6	19.7	14.6	33.4	33.3	36.2
1961	30.6	32.9	36.9	35.1	30.0	33.7	32.2	16.8	19.9	14.8	33.2	33.7	35.8
1962	30.6	32.7	36.1	34.9	30.0	33.4	32.1	16.7	19.9	14.7	33.6	34.5	36.0
1963	30.7	32.7	37.9	34.6	30.0	33.4	32.2	16.6	19.8	14.5	33.2	35.0	35.8
1964	30.8	33.1	37.3	34.8	30.6	33.7	32.5	16.2	19.4	14.1	32.9	34.7	35.9
1965	31.2	33.6	38.3	35.2	31.2	34.2	32.8	16.5	19.6	14.4	33.5	35.0	36.1
1966	32.0	34.3	40.0	35.4	31.8	35.4	33.6	16.8	19.9	14.7	34.5	36.5	37.1
1967	32.2	34.5	39.2	35.2	32.3	36.5	34.0	16.9	20.1	14.8	35.0	36.8	37.6
1968	33.0	35.3	39.8	35.6	33.4	37.3	35.7	16.5	19.8	14.2	35.9	37.1	38.7
1969	34.1	36.5	42.0	36.0	35.2	38.5	37.7	16.6	20.0	14.4	37.2	37.8	39.8
1970	35.4	38.0	44.3	36.5	37.0	40.6	38.3	17.7	21.5	15.2	39.0	39.7	41.4
1971	36.8	38.9	45.7	37.0	38.1	41.9	40.8	19.5	23.6	16.6	40.8	40.8	42.5
1972	38.2	40.4	47.0	38.5	39.9	42.9	43.0	20.1	24.5	16.9	42.7	42.5	43.3
1973	42.4	44.1	57.2	42.6	43.1	44.3	46.5	22.2	26.4	19.4	45.2	51.7	45.6
1974	52.5	56.0	82.0	54.6	55.4	51.1	55.0	33.6	35.5	32.7	53.3	56.8	53.3
1975	58.0	61.7	82.1	61.4	60.8	57.8	60.1	39.4	41.9	38.0	60.0	61.8	59.4
1976	60.9	64.0	70.6	64.8	64.8	60.8	64.1	42.3	44.8	41.1	63.1	65.8	62.6
1977	64.9	67.4	71.9	66.8	70.2	64.5	69.3	47.7	51.0	46.2	65.9	69.3	66.6
1978	69.5	72.0	81.0	69.2	76.2	69.2	76.5	49.9	53.7	48.1	71.0	72.9	71.2
1979	78.4	80.9	89.9	78.3	87.3	75.8	84.2	61.6	64.3	60.4	79.4	80.2	78.1
1980	90.3	91.7	103.7	91.2	97.1	84.6	91.3	85.0	85.5	84.7	89.1	89.9	87.2
1981	98.6	98.7	102.1	100.5	100.7	94.7	97.9	100.6	100.2	101.0	96.7	96.9	95.2
1982	100.0	100.0	100.0	100.0	100.0	100.0	100.0	100.0	100.0	100.0	100.0	100.0	100.0
1983	100.6	101.2	101.3	98.5	103.0	102.4	102.8	95.4	96.2	94.9	100.4	101.8	101.5
1984	103.1	104.1	106.3	102.1	104.9	105.0	105.6	95.7	97.1	94.6	105.9	104.1	105.0
1985	102.7	103.3	101.5	100.5	103.3	106.4	107.3	92.8	93.8	92.0	109.0	104.4	107.3
1986	99.1	102.2	98.4	98.1	101.2	107.5	108.1	72.7	75.1	71.2	110.3	105.6	108.3
1987	101.5	105.3	100.8	102.2	106.2	108.8	109.8	73.3	75.9	71.7	114.5	107.7	110.0
1988	107.1	113.2	106.0	112.9	118.7	112.3	116.1	71.2	73.3	69.9	120.1	113.7	114.8
1989	112.0	118.1	112.7	118.5	123.6	116.4	121.3	76.4	78.3	75.3	125.4	118.1	119.8
1990	114.5	118.7	117.9	118.0	120.7	119.0	122.9	85.9	87.3	85.0	127.7	119.4	122.1
1991	114.4	118.1	115.3	116.7	117.2	121.0	124.5	85.3	88.4	83.4	128.1	121.4	124.4
1992	114.7	117.9	113.9	115.4	117.2	122.0	126.5	84.5	87.5	82.6	127.7	122.7	125.9
1993	116.2	118.9	115.6	115.5	119.1	123.0	132.0	84.7	88.1	82.6	126.4	125.0	128.5
1994	118.5	122.1	118.5	119.2	125.2	124.3	136.6	83.1	86.1	81.1	129.7	127.0	130.7
1995	124.9	130.4	119.5	135.1	135.6	126.5	142.1	84.2	87.1	82.3	148.8	132.1	137.0
1996	125.7	128.6	125.3	130.5	131.3	126.9	143.6	90.0	92.4	88.4	141.1	135.9	138.7
1997	125.6	128.3	123.2	129.6	132.8	126.4	146.5	89.3	92.0	87.6	136.0	135.9	139.4
1998	123.0	126.1	123.2	126.7	128.0	125.9	146.8	81.1	85.8	78.1	140.8	134.8	140.6
1999	123.2	124.6	120.8	124.9	125.1	125.7	148.9	84.6	87.9	82.5	142.5	134.2	140.7
2000	129.2	128.1	119.2	132.6	129.0	126.2	150.7	102.0	100.9	102.3	151.6	136.9	143.5
2001	129.7	127.4	124.3	131.8	125.1	126.4	150.6	104.5	105.7	103.5	153.1	138.7	145.4
2002	127.8	126.1	123.2	129.2	124.7	126.1	151.3	96.3	98.7	94.8	152.1	138.9	144.7
2003	133.7	129.7	134.4	137.2	127.9	125.9	153.6	112.6	116.0	110.5	153.7	141.5	146.5
2004	142.6	137.9	145.0	147.8	146.6	127.4	166.4	124.3	125.1	123.8	159.3	146.7	149.2
2005	154.0	146.0	146.0	163.2	158.3	129.9	176.6	150.0	148.6	150.9	167.1	151.9	155.7
2006	164.0	155.9	146.2	175.0	180.5	134.5	188.4	162.8	158.1	165.7	175.0	157.0	161.1
2007	170.7	162.4	161.4	184.0	189.8	136.3	192.5	173.9	172.6	175.0	180.3	161.7	162.9
2008	188.3	177.2	180.4	214.3	203.3	140.3	205.4	206.2	199.4	209.6	191.8	173.8	170.5
2009[1]	172.6	162.8	165.1	191.9	169.0	141.0	202.9	162.3	166.0	161.2	195.8	172.2	168.1
2008													
January	179.1	168.6	173.9	199.6	190.0	137.4	194.6	194.3	184.9	198.9	184.8	166.8	166.4
February	180.9	170.3	176.8	201.7	193.6	137.8	195.8	196.9	186.0	202.2	185.5	168.1	166.9
March	185.1	173.2	179.8	206.2	200.7	137.9	197.3	208.4	196.2	214.3	186.0	169.8	167.6
April	187.0	175.6	180.0	209.7	205.9	138.6	200.2	209.6	196.4	215.8	187.2	171.1	168.5
May	191.7	179.1	181.7	216.0	212.1	139.4	203.3	221.3	205.2	228.8	188.0	172.7	169.1
June	195.5	182.4	184.3	223.0	215.6	140.0	206.5	229.2	209.2	238.4	189.6	174.2	170.2
July	200.8	187.3	186.4	234.9	219.1	141.3	209.7	238.5	219.6	247.2	192.1	177.5	171.9
August	197.8	188.7	186.5	238.9	218.9	141.9	212.9	216.8	208.0	221.3	195.2	178.3	173.0
September	196.8	186.8	184.6	235.0	214.4	142.3	214.0	215.3	206.9	219.6	198.1	178.7	173.7
October	188.3	180.5	179.6	222.7	202.3	142.5	212.4	189.9	187.2	191.9	198.7	176.8	173.5
November	179.2	171.3	176.2	201.0	190.3	142.3	210.5	167.7	166.3	169.0	198.5	175.5	173.3
December	172.1	164.0	171.7	185.4	179.0	141.9	208.4	152.2	155.5	151.5	197.8	173.8	172.7
2009													
January	172.1	162.8	167.5	187.0	173.3	141.7	207.2	156.4	158.6	156.2	200.3	172.9	171.1
February	170.7	161.2	164.3	185.8	168.8	141.4	204.9	154.9	157.6	154.4	199.3	172.2	169.2
March	168.4	159.6	163.1	182.6	166.3	141.2	204.2	147.9	152.8	146.6	198.4	171.7	168.8
April	168.6	159.0	163.9	182.7	163.5	140.7	203.3	150.9	154.5	150.1	197.8	171.8	168.5
May	169.4	160.1	165.1	187.6	162.3	140.7	202.8	152.7	156.1	152.0	196.6	171.8	167.9
June	171.3	160.9	164.9	190.3	162.9	140.6	202.0	159.9	160.8	160.2	195.9	172.3	167.5
July	170.4	161.5	162.5	192.1	164.5	140.6	201.9	155.7	157.2	155.7	194.7	171.4	167.1
August	173.3	163.8	163.2	196.8	168.8	140.7	201.5	165.1	163.4	166.4	193.7	171.4	167.0
September	173.3	164.9	163.8	197.3	173.0	140.8	202.1	162.1	161.5	162.9	193.4	171.7	167.4
October	174.0	165.2	164.2	196.9	174.4	141.1	202.1	164.5	163.8	165.5	192.8	171.7	167.3
November[1]	176.4	166.6	166.2	201.1	175.2	140.9	201.7	172.9	170.6	174.4	192.5	172.0	167.2
December[1]	177.4	167.7	169.0	203.1	176.8	141.1	202.6	174.0	172.6	175.2	192.6	172.9	167.5

[1]Data are preliminary.

Table 8-4. Producer Price Indexes and Purchasing Power of the Dollar—*Continued*

(1982 = 100, seasonally adjusted.)

Year and month	Intermediate materials, supplies, and components—*Continued* Supplies—*Continued* Nonmanufacturing industries Total	Feeds	Other supplies	Crude materials for further processing Total	Foodstuffs and feedstuffs	Crude nonfood materials Total	Crude nonfood materials except fuel [2] Total [2]	Manu-facturing [2]	Construc-tion	Crude fuel [3] Total	Manu-facturing industries	Nonmanu-facturing industries
1960	32.1	37.2	33.2	30.4	38.4	. . .	26.9	26.3	35.9	10.5	9.0	11.8
1961	32.9	40.9	32.9	30.2	37.9	. . .	27.2	26.6	35.9	10.5	9.0	11.8
1962	33.8	43.6	33.2	30.5	38.6	. . .	27.1	26.5	36.1	10.4	8.9	11.8
1963	34.6	45.9	33.2	29.9	37.5	. . .	26.7	26.1	36.0	10.5	9.0	11.9
1964	34.1	45.0	32.9	29.6	36.6	. . .	27.2	26.6	35.9	10.5	9.0	11.9
1965	34.5	45.9	33.0	31.1	39.2	. . .	27.7	27.2	36.1	10.6	9.0	11.9
1966	36.2	50.0	33.8	33.1	42.7	. . .	28.3	27.8	36.3	10.9	9.3	12.3
1967	36.3	48.3	34.5	31.3	40.3	21.1	26.5	25.8	37.0	11.3	9.7	12.8
1968	36.4	46.5	35.4	31.8	40.9	21.6	27.1	26.3	38.4	11.5	9.9	13.1
1969	36.9	46.4	36.0	33.9	44.1	22.5	28.4	27.6	39.8	12.0	10.2	13.8
1970	38.9	49.9	37.6	35.2	45.2	23.8	29.1	28.3	42.1	13.8	11.3	16.6
1971	39.9	50.4	38.9	36.0	46.1	24.7	29.4	28.4	44.1	15.7	12.6	19.3
1972	42.0	56.1	39.8	39.9	51.5	27.0	32.3	31.5	45.0	16.8	13.5	20.6
1973	54.7	97.3	42.7	54.5	72.6	34.3	42.9	42.7	46.2	18.6	14.8	22.9
1974	58.4	90.2	50.5	61.4	76.4	44.1	54.5	55.0	50.0	24.8	19.1	31.8
1975	62.9	84.0	58.9	61.6	77.4	43.7	50.0	49.7	55.9	30.6	24.4	38.0
1976	67.3	95.1	62.0	63.4	76.8	48.2	54.9	54.7	59.6	34.5	29.0	40.5
1977	70.7	99.3	65.2	65.5	77.5	51.7	56.3	56.0	63.1	42.0	37.2	47.4
1978	73.8	95.5	69.7	73.4	87.3	57.5	61.9	61.5	68.7	48.2	43.1	53.8
1979	81.2	106.9	76.3	85.9	100.0	69.6	75.5	75.6	76.6	57.3	53.1	62.0
1980	91.1	110.6	87.5	95.3	104.6	84.6	91.8	92.3	87.9	69.4	66.7	72.5
1981	97.8	111.3	95.4	103.0	103.9	101.8	109.8	110.9	96.8	84.8	83.6	86.2
1982	100.0	100.0	100.0	100.0	100.0	100.0	100.0	100.0	100.0	100.0	100.0	100.0
1983	102.0	109.1	101.0	101.3	101.8	100.7	98.8	98.6	100.1	105.1	105.8	104.4
1984	103.7	104.2	103.7	103.5	104.7	102.2	101.0	100.8	103.1	105.1	105.6	104.6
1985	103.0	86.6	105.3	95.8	94.8	96.9	94.3	93.1	105.7	102.7	102.7	102.5
1986	104.2	90.5	106.2	87.7	93.2	81.6	76.0	72.6	106.5	92.2	91.1	93.6
1987	106.6	94.6	108.3	93.7	96.2	87.9	88.5	84.7	114.8	84.1	82.1	86.3
1988	113.2	115.0	112.7	96.0	106.1	85.5	85.9	81.5	126.5	82.1	80.1	84.5
1989	117.2	114.4	117.5	103.1	111.2	93.4	95.8	91.0	136.9	85.3	83.9	87.0
1990	118.0	102.8	120.2	108.9	113.1	101.5	107.3	102.5	145.2	84.8	82.9	87.0
1991	119.9	101.3	122.5	101.2	105.5	94.6	97.5	92.2	147.5	82.9	82.3	84.1
1992	121.1	103.0	123.7	100.4	105.1	93.5	94.2	87.9	162.1	84.0	83.1	85.2
1993	123.2	105.4	125.8	102.4	108.4	94.7	94.1	85.6	193.6	87.1	85.9	88.6
1994	125.1	105.8	127.9	101.8	106.5	94.8	97.0	88.3	199.1	82.4	81.7	83.6
1995	129.5	103.4	133.2	102.7	105.8	96.8	105.8	97.3	201.7	72.1	72.5	72.9
1996	134.4	133.1	134.6	113.8	121.5	104.5	105.7	97.6	195.7	92.6	90.7	94.3
1997	134.1	129.1	134.8	111.1	112.2	106.4	103.5	95.0	201.4	101.3	98.4	103.3
1998	132.2	100.2	136.2	96.8	103.9	88.4	84.5	76.7	196.0	86.7	84.8	88.5
1999	131.4	89.2	136.5	98.2	98.7	94.3	91.1	83.0	195.7	91.2	90.0	92.9
2000	134.1	94.6	138.8	120.6	100.2	130.4	118.0	108.7	193.4	136.9	136.9	139.3
2001	135.8	96.8	140.5	121.0	106.1	126.8	101.5	93.2	181.7	151.4	150.2	154.2
2002	136.3	98.1	140.9	108.1	99.5	111.4	101.0	92.5	181.4	117.3	113.4	119.8
2003	139.0	106.6	143.1	135.3	113.5	148.2	116.9	107.5	180.8	185.7	176.4	189.9
2004	144.9	119.1	148.4	159.0	127.0	179.2	149.2	137.7	191.8	211.4	200.5	216.2
2005	149.7	107.4	154.9	182.2	122.7	223.4	176.7	163.4	199.3	279.7	263.9	286.3
2006	154.7	110.9	160.1	184.8	119.3	230.6	210.0	194.5	201.1	241.5	229.2	247.0
2007	160.1	138.4	163.2	207.1	146.7	246.3	238.7	221.6	201.7	236.8	224.9	242.2
2008	173.2	182.4	173.4	251.8	163.4	313.9	308.5	287.3	199.0	298.3	283.5	305.0
2009[1]	171.4	170.6	173.0	175.0	134.4	197.1	211.0	196.9	200.4	165.6	184.6	168.3
2008												
January	165.5	165.0	166.9	236.3	164.8	283.8	288.2	268.1	198.7	253.7	240.9	259.3
February	167.0	170.2	167.9	245.3	166.1	299.7	295.5	275.0	197.6	283.0	268.0	289.5
March	169.0	178.2	169.3	261.3	169.0	327.1	324.4	302.1	200.4	305.9	289.2	312.9
April	170.3	178.6	170.7	273.6	168.0	351.6	349.1	325.4	199.1	327.9	310.7	335.3
May	172.1	183.4	172.2	289.5	168.0	381.7	371.9	346.8	199.8	368.4	348.2	376.8
June	173.7	184.3	174.0	296.1	169.8	392.6	382.9	357.1	200.9	378.1	357.3	386.8
July	177.4	201.6	176.2	309.4	172.9	414.8	398.4	371.7	199.7	410.1	387.2	419.6
August	178.2	201.8	177.0	273.5	168.9	350.4	357.7	333.4	200.4	309.8	294.6	316.7
September	178.4	197.7	177.7	254.5	168.4	314.9	324.3	302.0	200.0	273.5	261.2	279.5
October	176.2	182.1	177.0	213.9	151.4	254.7	253.6	235.5	200.3	236.4	227.0	241.4
November	174.5	175.5	175.8	185.0	147.0	204.1	193.1	178.7	196.4	206.8	199.7	211.0
December	172.6	166.9	174.7	174.0	137.7	192.6	164.7	152.0	196.1	225.5	217.0	230.3
2009												
January	171.8	165.9	173.9	171.2	138.7	186.4	160.3	147.7	196.9	216.8	212.6	221.2
February	171.3	167.0	173.2	160.7	134.3	170.9	160.5	147.9	197.4	178.1	190.7	181.2
March	170.9	164.8	172.9	159.7	131.7	171.6	175.5	162.4	198.4	156.8	178.0	159.2
April	170.9	166.0	172.9	163.5	137.1	173.5	182.1	168.8	199.2	151.3	175.6	153.5
May	171.1	171.1	172.6	168.7	136.7	183.6	201.5	187.7	199.6	146.7	168.8	148.9
June	171.6	181.1	172.4	175.9	134.9	198.8	223.8	209.5	200.2	150.1	171.0	152.4
July	170.7	171.6	172.2	170.1	128.5	194.1	209.8	195.8	199.8	159.6	178.5	162.1
August	170.7	170.9	172.2	177.8	129.3	207.9	234.5	220.0	199.6	156.3	175.5	158.7
September	171.0	171.9	172.6	173.9	127.9	201.8	236.8	222.1	200.8	138.2	165.0	140.0
October	171.0	170.0	172.7	186.1	135.4	217.4	246.5	231.6	199.4	161.9	180.4	164.4
November[1]	171.4	171.4	173.0	193.9	136.7	230.8	253.5	238.4	200.2	183.8	195.8	187.0
December[1]	172.3	176.0	173.6	195.4	141.1	229.4	245.5	230.6	201.2	192.3	202.0	195.8

[1] Data are preliminary.
[2] Includes crude petroleum.
[3] Excludes crude petroleum.
. . . = Not available.

Table 8-4. Producer Price Indexes and Purchasing Power of the Dollar—*Continued*

(1982 = 100, seasonally adjusted.)

		Finished goods excluding:			Finished consumer goods excluding:		Intermediate materials					Crude materials		
Year and month	Finished energy goods	Foods	Energy	Foods and energy	Energy	Foods and energy	Intermediate foods and feeds	Intermediate energy goods	Intermediate materials less:			Crude energy materials [2]	Crude materials less energy	Crude nonfood materials less energy [3]
									Foods and feeds	Energy	Foods and energy			
1960	...	...	...	...	...	...	...	...	30.7	...	...	...	...	...
1961	...	...	...	...	...	...	...	...	30.3	...	...	...	...	...
1962	...	...	...	...	...	...	...	...	30.2	...	...	...	...	...
1963	...	...	...	...	...	...	...	...	30.1	...	...	...	...	...
1964	...	...	...	...	...	...	...	...	30.3	...	...	...	...	...
1965	...	...	...	...	...	...	...	...	30.7	...	...	...	...	...
1966	...	...	...	...	...	...	...	...	31.3	...	...	...	...	...
1967	...	35.0	...	...	...	...	41.8	...	31.7	...	...	...	...	...
1968	...	35.9	...	...	...	...	41.5	...	32.5	...	...	...	...	...
1969	...	36.9	...	...	...	...	42.9	...	33.6	...	...	...	...	...
1970	...	38.2	...	...	...	...	45.6	...	34.8	...	...	...	...	...
1971	...	39.6	...	...	...	...	46.7	...	36.2	...	...	...	...	...
1972	...	40.4	...	...	...	...	49.5	...	37.7	...	...	...	...	...
1973	...	42.0	...	48.1	...	50.4	70.3	...	40.6	...	44.3	...	...	70.8
1974	26.2	48.8	...	53.6	58.7	55.5	83.6	33.1	50.5	56.2	54.0	27.8	78.4	83.3
1975	30.7	54.7	62.4	59.7	63.9	60.6	81.6	38.7	56.6	61.7	60.2	33.3	75.9	69.3
1976	34.3	58.1	64.8	63.1	65.7	63.7	77.4	41.5	60.0	64.7	63.8	35.3	77.6	80.2
1977	39.7	62.2	68.6	66.9	69.4	67.3	79.6	46.8	64.1	68.5	67.6	40.4	78.1	79.8
1978	42.3	66.7	74.0	71.9	74.9	72.2	84.8	49.1	68.6	73.4	72.5	45.2	87.5	87.8
1979	57.1	74.6	80.7	78.3	81.7	78.8	94.5	61.1	77.4	81.7	80.7	54.9	101.5	106.2
1980	85.2	86.7	88.4	87.1	89.3	87.8	105.5	84.9	89.4	91.4	90.3	73.1	106.5	113.1
1981	101.5	95.6	95.4	94.6	95.7	94.6	104.6	100.5	98.2	98.2	97.7	97.7	105.7	111.7
1982	100.0	100.0	100.0	100.0	100.0	100.0	100.0	100.0	100.0	100.0	100.0	100.0	100.0	100.0
1983	95.2	101.8	102.5	103.0	102.4	103.1	103.6	95.3	100.5	101.7	101.6	98.7	102.6	105.3
1984	91.2	103.2	105.5	105.5	105.6	105.7	105.7	95.5	103.0	104.6	104.7	98.0	106.3	111.7
1985	87.6	104.6	107.2	108.1	107.0	108.4	97.3	92.6	103.0	104.7	105.2	93.3	97.0	104.9
1986	63.0	101.9	109.7	110.6	109.7	111.1	96.2	72.6	99.3	104.5	104.9	71.8	95.4	103.1
1987	61.8	104.0	112.3	113.3	112.5	114.2	99.2	73.0	101.7	107.3	107.8	75.0	100.9	115.7
1988	59.8	106.5	115.8	117.0	116.3	118.5	109.5	70.9	106.9	114.6	115.2	67.7	112.6	133.0
1989	65.7	111.8	121.2	122.1	122.1	124.0	113.8	76.1	111.9	119.5	120.2	75.9	117.7	137.9
1990	75.0	117.4	126.0	126.6	127.2	128.8	113.3	85.5	114.5	120.4	120.9	85.9	118.6	136.3
1991	78.1	120.9	129.1	131.1	130.0	133.7	111.1	85.1	114.6	120.8	121.4	80.4	110.9	128.2
1992	77.8	123.1	131.1	134.2	131.8	137.3	110.7	84.3	114.9	121.3	122.0	78.8	110.7	128.4
1993	78.0	124.4	132.9	135.8	133.5	138.5	112.7	84.6	116.4	123.2	123.8	76.7	116.3	140.2
1994	77.0	125.1	134.2	137.1	134.2	139.0	114.8	83.0	118.7	126.3	127.1	72.1	119.3	156.2
1995	78.1	127.5	136.9	140.0	136.9	141.9	114.8	84.1	125.5	134.0	135.2	69.4	123.5	173.6
1996	83.2	130.5	139.6	142.0	140.1	144.3	128.1	89.8	125.6	133.6	134.0	85.0	130.0	155.8
1997	83.4	130.9	140.2	142.4	141.0	145.1	125.4	89.0	125.7	133.7	134.2	87.3	123.5	156.5
1998	75.1	129.5	141.1	143.7	142.5	147.7	116.2	80.8	123.4	132.4	133.5	68.6	113.6	142.1
1999	78.8	132.3	143.0	146.1	145.2	151.7	111.1	84.3	123.9	131.7	133.1	78.5	107.9	135.2
2000	94.1	138.1	144.9	148.0	147.4	154.0	111.7	101.7	130.1	135.0	136.6	122.1	111.7	145.2
2001	96.7	140.4	147.6	150.0	150.8	156.9	115.9	104.1	130.5	135.1	136.4	122.3	112.2	130.7
2002	88.8	138.3	147.3	150.2	150.8	157.6	115.5	95.9	128.5	134.5	135.3	102.0	108.7	135.7
2003	102.0	142.4	149.0	150.5	153.1	157.9	125.9	111.9	134.2	137.7	138.5	147.2	123.4	152.5
2004	113.0	147.2	152.4	152.7	157.2	160.3	137.1	123.2	143.0	145.8	146.5	174.6	144.0	193.0
2005	132.6	155.5	155.9	156.4	160.8	164.3	133.8	149.2	155.1	153.3	154.6	234.0	143.5	202.4
2006	145.9	161.0	157.9	158.7	162.7	166.7	135.2	162.8	165.4	162.1	163.8	226.9	152.3	244.5
2007	156.3	166.2	162.8	161.7	168.7	170.0	154.4	174.6	171.5	167.6	168.4	232.8	182.6	282.6
2008	178.7	176.6	169.8	167.2	176.9	176.4	181.6	208.1	188.7	180.9	180.9	309.4	205.4	324.4
2009[1]	147.2	171.2	172.3	171.5	179.2	181.6	165.9	162.8	173.1	172.8	173.4	176.3	164.8	248.6
2008														
January	172.2	172.6	166.5	164.1	173.4	172.9	170.8	196.0	179.7	172.4	172.6	273.5	203.2	308.1
February	173.8	173.6	166.8	164.9	173.6	173.9	174.5	199.2	181.3	173.8	173.8	291.4	206.8	319.9
March	179.8	175.4	167.6	165.1	174.6	174.2	179.3	210.8	185.5	176.1	175.9	324.9	211.8	332.0
April	180.6	176.2	168.2	165.9	175.2	175.0	179.6	211.2	187.5	178.4	178.4	345.4	218.5	366.0
May	188.3	178.8	169.0	166.4	176.1	175.6	182.4	222.8	192.3	181.3	181.3	385.7	219.9	371.8
June	198.2	181.7	169.7	166.6	177.1	175.7	184.4	231.5	196.2	183.8	183.8	400.2	221.6	373.4
July	204.4	184.1	170.8	167.6	178.2	176.8	191.8	242.3	201.4	187.7	187.5	426.4	227.0	386.3
August	193.6	181.7	171.4	168.4	178.9	177.7	191.9	223.1	198.2	188.8	188.6	339.3	221.5	375.7
September	191.9	181.8	172.0	169.1	179.4	178.4	189.2	218.5	197.4	188.8	188.8	304.0	213.1	339.6
October	167.4	175.8	172.7	170.1	180.0	179.5	180.5	193.6	188.8	184.5	184.8	244.9	185.6	278.8
November	145.4	169.8	172.5	170.2	179.7	179.6	176.0	166.4	179.5	180.0	180.4	195.5	170.6	226.6
December	133.2	166.8	172.2	170.6	179.0	180.0	170.1	148.7	172.3	175.7	176.1	182.1	162.1	222.7
2009														
January	139.7	168.8	172.5	171.0	179.4	180.5	166.8	155.2	172.6	174.1	174.7	172.8	163.6	225.6
February	140.0	169.1	172.0	171.2	178.7	180.8	165.1	153.4	171.2	172.8	173.5	151.6	159.7	224.5
March	134.7	167.8	172.0	171.5	178.6	181.4	163.7	145.5	168.8	171.9	172.7	152.4	157.0	221.7
April	136.6	168.4	172.6	171.6	179.6	181.6	164.6	149.0	169.0	171.2	171.9	154.2	161.7	223.0
May	139.0	169.0	172.0	171.5	178.8	181.6	166.3	153.6	169.7	171.1	171.6	163.7	163.4	232.8
June	149.5	172.4	172.8	172.0	179.8	182.2	168.2	160.8	171.6	171.6	172.0	180.9	163.5	239.9
July	142.8	170.3	172.1	171.8	178.9	182.1	164.6	157.0	171.0	171.6	172.3	172.8	159.6	246.6
August	151.7	173.2	172.7	172.3	179.4	182.6	165.1	167.5	174.1	172.5	173.3	184.2	164.2	264.9
September	149.0	172.3	172.5	172.1	179.2	182.4	165.7	164.2	174.1	173.4	174.2	173.7	164.2	270.3
October	150.8	172.2	172.4	171.3	179.6	181.6	165.5	166.5	174.8	173.6	174.4	193.5	171.4	274.6
November[1]	160.3	175.6	173.3	172.1	180.6	182.6	167.1	175.3	177.2	174.3	175.0	212.1	172.2	273.5
December[1]	161.4	175.9	173.8	172.1	181.5	182.7	170.1	176.2	178.1	175.3	175.8	206.2	178.5	285.9

[1]Data are preliminary.
[2]Includes crude petroleum.
[3]Excludes crude petroleum.
. . . = Not available.

Table 8-4. Producer Price Indexes and Purchasing Power of the Dollar—*Continued*

(1982 = 100, except as noted; not seasonally adjusted.)

Year and month	Finished goods							Intermediate materials, supplies, and components	Crude materials for further processing	Purchasing power of the dollar	
	Total	Finished consumer goods					Capital equipment			Producer prices for finished goods (1982–1984 = $1.00)	Consumer prices (CPI-U, 1982–1984 = $1.00)
		Total	Foods	Finished consumer goods except foods							
				Total	Durable goods	Nondurable goods less foods					
1960	33.4	33.6	35.5	33.5	43.8	28.4	32.8	30.8	30.4	3.047	3.373
1961	33.4	33.6	35.4	33.4	43.6	28.4	32.9	30.6	30.2	3.047	3.340
1962	33.5	33.7	35.7	33.4	43.4	28.4	33.0	30.6	30.5	3.038	3.304
1963	33.4	33.5	35.3	33.4	43.1	28.5	33.1	30.7	29.9	3.047	3.265
1964	33.5	33.6	35.4	33.3	43.3	28.4	33.4	30.8	29.6	3.038	3.220
1965	34.1	34.2	36.8	33.6	43.2	28.8	33.8	31.2	31.1	2.984	3.166
1966	35.2	35.4	39.2	34.1	43.4	29.3	34.6	32.0	33.1	2.891	3.080
1967	35.6	35.6	38.5	34.7	44.1	30.0	35.8	32.2	31.3	2.859	2.993
1968	36.6	36.5	40.0	35.5	45.1	30.6	37.0	33.0	31.8	2.781	2.873
1969	38.0	37.9	42.4	36.3	45.9	31.5	38.3	34.1	33.9	2.678	2.726
1970	39.3	39.1	43.8	37.4	47.2	32.5	40.1	35.4	35.2	2.589	2.574
1971	40.5	40.2	44.5	38.7	48.9	33.5	41.7	36.8	36.0	2.513	2.466
1972	41.8	41.5	46.9	39.4	50.0	34.1	42.8	38.2	39.9	2.435	2.391
1973	45.6	46.0	56.5	41.2	50.9	36.1	44.2	42.4	54.5	2.232	2.251
1974	52.6	53.1	64.4	48.2	55.5	44.0	50.5	52.5	61.4	1.935	2.029
1975	58.2	58.2	69.8	53.2	61.0	48.9	58.2	58.0	61.6	1.749	1.859
1976	60.8	60.4	69.6	56.5	63.7	52.4	62.1	60.9	63.4	1.674	1.757
1977	64.7	64.3	73.3	60.6	67.4	56.8	66.1	64.9	65.5	1.573	1.649
1978	69.8	69.4	79.9	64.9	73.6	60.0	71.3	69.5	73.4	1.458	1.532
1979	77.6	77.5	87.3	73.5	80.8	69.3	77.5	78.4	85.9	1.311	1.380
1980	88.0	88.6	92.4	87.1	91.0	85.1	85.8	90.3	95.3	1.156	1.215
1981	96.1	96.6	97.8	96.1	96.4	95.8	94.6	98.6	103.0	1.059	1.098
1982	100.0	100.0	100.0	100.0	100.0	100.0	100.0	100.0	100.0	1.018	1.035
1983	101.6	101.3	101.0	101.2	102.8	100.5	102.8	100.6	101.3	1.002	1.003
1984	103.7	103.3	105.4	102.2	104.5	101.1	105.2	103.1	103.5	0.981	0.961
1985	104.7	103.8	104.6	103.3	106.5	101.7	107.5	102.7	95.8	0.972	0.928
1986	103.2	101.4	107.3	98.5	108.9	93.3	109.7	99.1	87.7	0.986	0.913
1987	105.4	103.6	109.5	100.7	111.5	94.9	111.7	101.5	93.7	0.966	0.880
1988	108.0	106.2	112.6	103.1	113.8	97.3	114.3	107.1	96.0	0.942	0.846
1989	113.6	112.1	118.7	108.9	117.6	103.8	118.8	112.0	103.1	0.896	0.807
1990	119.2	118.2	124.4	115.3	120.4	111.5	122.9	114.5	108.9	0.854	0.766
1991	121.7	120.5	124.1	118.7	123.9	115.0	126.7	114.4	101.2	0.836	0.734
1992	123.2	121.7	123.3	120.8	125.7	117.3	129.1	114.7	100.4	0.826	0.713
1993	124.7	123.0	125.7	121.7	128.0	117.6	131.4	116.2	102.4	0.816	0.692
1994	125.5	123.3	126.8	121.6	130.9	116.2	134.1	118.5	101.8	0.811	0.675
1995	127.9	125.6	129.0	124.0	132.7	118.8	136.7	124.9	102.7	0.796	0.656
1996	131.3	129.5	133.6	127.6	134.2	123.3	138.3	125.7	113.8	0.775	0.638
1997	131.8	130.2	134.5	128.2	133.7	124.3	138.2	125.6	111.1	0.772	0.623
1998	130.7	128.9	134.3	126.4	132.9	122.2	137.6	123.0	96.8	0.779	0.614
1999	133.0	132.0	135.1	130.5	133.0	127.9	137.6	123.2	98.2	0.765	0.600
2000	138.0	138.2	137.2	138.4	133.9	138.7	138.8	129.2	120.6	0.737	0.581
2001	140.7	141.5	141.3	141.4	134.0	142.8	139.7	129.7	121.0	0.723	0.565
2002	138.9	139.4	140.1	138.8	133.0	139.8	139.1	127.8	108.1	0.733	0.556
2003	143.3	145.3	145.9	144.7	133.1	148.4	139.5	133.7	135.3	0.710	0.544
2004	148.5	151.7	152.7	150.9	135.0	156.6	141.4	142.6	159.0	0.685	0.530
2005	155.7	160.4	155.7	161.9	136.6	172.0	144.6	154.0	182.2	0.654	0.512
2006	160.4	166.0	156.7	169.2	136.9	182.6	146.9	164.0	184.8	0.634	0.496
2007	166.6	173.5	167.0	175.6	138.3	191.7	149.5	170.7	207.1	0.611	0.482
2008	177.1	186.3	178.3	189.1	141.2	210.5	153.8	188.3	251.8	0.575	0.465
2009[1]	172.6	179.2	175.5	179.6	144.3	194.3	156.8	172.6	175.0	0.590	0.466
2008											
January	172.0	180.1	174.5	181.9	140.1	200.3	151.4	177.8	235.5	0.592	0.474
February	172.3	180.4	173.6	182.7	140.2	201.4	151.8	179.1	245.5	0.591	0.472
March	175.1	184.2	176.0	187.1	139.9	208.2	151.8	184.5	262.1	0.581	0.468
April	176.5	185.8	175.5	189.6	140.5	211.7	152.4	187.3	274.6	0.577	0.465
May	179.8	190.3	177.6	195.0	140.3	220.0	152.7	192.8	293.1	0.566	0.462
June	182.4	193.8	180.0	199.0	139.7	226.4	152.7	197.2	301.2	0.558	0.457
July	185.1	197.2	181.0	203.4	139.6	233.1	153.3	203.1	313.3	0.550	0.455
August	182.2	193.2	181.3	197.5	140.2	223.9	153.9	199.4	274.6	0.559	0.456
September	182.2	193.0	181.5	197.2	140.3	223.4	154.3	198.6	254.2	0.559	0.457
October	177.4	185.5	180.7	187.0	144.8	205.4	157.0	189.0	212.0	0.574	0.462
November	172.0	178.2	179.8	177.0	144.2	190.6	156.9	179.2	183.3	0.592	0.471
December	168.8	173.7	177.7	171.5	144.4	182.1	157.2	171.6	172.6	0.603	0.476
2009											
January	170.4	175.8	177.7	174.4	144.3	186.5	157.4	171.4	170.2	0.597	0.474
February	169.9	175.2	175.0	174.5	144.3	186.6	157.2	169.7	160.7	0.599	0.471
March	169.1	174.2	173.8	173.5	144.1	185.2	156.9	168.0	160.1	0.602	0.470
April	170.3	176.0	175.9	175.2	144.4	187.7	156.8	168.6	163.9	0.598	0.469
May	171.1	177.3	174.0	177.5	144.2	191.2	156.3	170.2	171.5	0.595	0.468
June	174.3	181.7	176.1	182.7	144.7	198.7	156.6	172.7	179.8	0.584	0.464
July	172.4	179.2	173.5	180.2	143.3	195.7	155.9	172.3	172.9	0.590	0.464
August	174.2	181.6	173.9	183.3	143.8	200.1	156.4	174.8	178.4	0.584	0.463
September	173.2	180.4	173.9	181.6	142.9	198.1	155.9	174.7	173.5	0.588	0.463
October	173.8	180.8	175.6	181.6	144.8	197.1	157.0	174.5	184.0	0.586	0.463
November[1]	176.2	183.9	176.8	185.3	145.6	202.2	157.6	176.3	192.0	0.578	0.462
December[1]	176.2	184.1	179.7	184.6	144.9	201.4	157.2	176.7	193.8	0.578	0.463

[1]Data are preliminary.

Table 8-5. Producer Price Indexes by Major Commodity Groups

(1982 = 100, not seasonally adjusted.)

Year and month	All commodities	Farm products	Processed foods and feeds	Industrial commodities Total	Textile products and apparel	Hides, leather, and related products	Fuels and related products and power	Chemicals and allied products	Rubber and plastics products	Lumber and wood products	Pulp, paper, and allied products	Metals and metal products	Machinery and metal equipment	Furniture and household durables	Nonmetallic mineral products	Transportation equipment	Miscellaneous products
1950	27.3	44.0	33.2	25.0	50.2	32.9	12.6	30.4	35.6	31.4	25.7	22.0	22.6	40.9	23.5	. . .	28.6
1951	30.4	51.2	36.9	27.6	56.0	37.7	13.0	34.8	43.7	34.1	30.5	24.5	25.3	44.4	25.0	. . .	30.3
1952	29.6	48.4	36.4	26.9	50.5	30.5	13.0	33.0	39.6	33.2	29.7	24.5	25.3	43.5	25.0	. . .	30.2
1953	29.2	43.8	34.8	27.2	49.3	31.0	13.4	33.4	36.9	33.1	29.6	25.3	25.9	44.4	26.0	. . .	31.0
1954	29.3	43.2	35.4	27.2	48.2	29.5	13.2	33.8	37.5	32.5	29.6	25.5	26.3	44.9	26.6	. . .	31.3
1955	29.3	40.5	33.8	27.8	48.2	29.4	13.2	33.7	42.4	34.1	30.4	27.2	27.2	45.1	27.3	. . .	31.3
1956	30.3	40.0	33.8	29.1	48.2	31.2	13.6	33.9	43.0	34.6	32.4	29.6	29.3	46.3	28.5	. . .	31.7
1957	31.2	41.1	34.8	29.9	48.3	31.2	14.3	34.6	42.8	32.8	33.0	30.2	31.4	47.5	29.6	. . .	32.6
1958	31.6	42.9	36.5	30.0	47.4	31.6	13.7	34.9	42.8	32.5	33.4	30.0	32.1	47.9	29.9	. . .	33.3
1959	31.7	40.2	35.6	30.5	48.1	35.9	13.7	34.8	42.6	34.7	33.7	30.6	32.8	48.0	30.3	. . .	33.4
1960	31.7	40.1	35.6	30.5	48.6	34.6	13.9	34.8	42.7	33.5	34.0	30.6	33.0	47.8	30.4	. . .	33.6
1961	31.6	39.7	36.2	30.4	47.8	34.9	14.0	34.5	41.1	32.0	33.0	30.5	33.0	47.5	30.5	. . .	33.7
1962	31.7	40.4	36.5	30.4	48.2	35.3	14.0	33.9	39.9	32.2	33.4	30.2	33.0	47.2	30.5	. . .	33.9
1963	31.6	39.6	36.8	30.3	48.2	34.3	13.9	33.5	40.1	32.8	33.1	30.3	33.1	46.9	30.3	. . .	34.2
1964	31.6	39.0	36.7	30.5	48.5	34.4	13.5	33.6	39.6	33.5	33.0	31.1	33.3	47.1	30.4	. . .	34.4
1965	32.3	40.7	38.0	30.9	48.8	35.9	13.8	33.9	39.7	33.7	33.3	32.0	33.7	46.8	30.4	. . .	34.7
1966	33.3	43.7	40.2	31.5	48.9	39.4	14.1	34.0	40.5	35.2	34.2	32.8	34.7	47.4	30.7	. . .	35.3
1967	33.4	41.3	39.8	32.0	48.9	38.1	14.4	34.2	41.4	35.1	34.6	33.2	35.9	48.3	31.2	. . .	36.2
1968	34.2	42.3	40.6	32.8	50.7	39.3	14.3	34.1	42.8	39.8	35.0	34.0	37.0	49.7	32.4	. . .	37.0
1969	35.6	45.0	42.7	33.9	51.8	41.5	14.6	34.2	43.6	44.0	36.0	36.0	38.2	50.7	33.6	40.4	38.1
1970	36.9	45.8	44.6	35.2	52.4	42.0	15.3	35.0	44.9	39.9	37.5	38.7	40.0	51.9	35.3	41.9	39.8
1971	38.1	46.6	45.5	36.5	53.3	43.4	16.6	35.6	45.2	44.7	38.1	39.4	41.4	53.1	38.2	44.2	40.8
1972	39.8	51.6	48.0	37.8	55.5	50.0	17.1	35.6	45.3	50.7	39.3	40.9	42.3	53.8	39.4	45.5	41.5
1973	45.0	72.7	58.9	40.3	60.5	54.5	19.4	37.6	46.6	62.2	42.3	44.0	43.7	55.7	40.7	46.1	43.3
1974	53.5	77.4	68.0	49.2	68.0	55.2	30.1	50.2	56.4	64.5	52.5	57.0	50.0	61.8	47.8	50.3	48.1
1975	58.4	77.0	72.6	54.9	67.4	56.5	35.4	62.0	62.2	62.1	59.0	61.5	57.9	67.5	54.4	56.7	53.4
1976	61.1	78.8	70.8	58.4	72.4	63.9	38.3	64.0	66.0	72.2	62.1	65.0	61.3	70.3	58.2	60.5	55.6
1977	64.9	79.4	74.0	62.5	75.3	68.3	43.6	65.9	69.4	83.0	64.6	69.3	65.2	73.2	62.6	64.6	59.4
1978	69.9	87.7	80.6	67.0	78.1	76.1	46.5	68.0	72.4	96.9	67.7	75.3	70.3	77.5	69.6	69.5	66.7
1979	78.7	99.6	88.5	75.7	82.5	96.1	58.9	76.0	80.5	105.5	75.9	86.0	76.7	82.8	77.6	75.3	75.5
1980	89.8	102.9	95.9	88.0	89.7	94.7	82.8	89.0	90.1	101.5	86.3	95.0	86.0	90.7	88.4	82.9	93.6
1981	98.0	105.2	98.9	97.4	97.6	99.3	100.2	98.4	96.4	102.8	94.8	99.6	94.4	95.9	96.7	94.3	96.1
1982	100.0	100.0	100.0	100.0	100.0	100.0	100.0	100.0	100.0	100.0	100.0	100.0	100.0	100.0	100.0	100.0	100.0
1983	101.3	102.4	101.8	101.1	100.3	103.2	95.9	100.3	100.8	107.9	103.3	101.8	102.7	103.4	101.6	102.8	104.8
1984	103.7	105.5	105.4	103.3	102.7	109.0	94.8	102.9	102.3	108.0	110.3	104.8	105.1	105.7	105.4	105.2	107.0
1985	103.2	95.1	103.5	103.7	102.9	108.9	91.4	103.7	101.9	106.6	113.3	104.4	107.2	107.1	108.6	107.9	109.4
1986	100.2	92.9	105.4	100.0	103.2	113.0	69.8	102.6	101.9	107.2	116.1	103.2	108.8	108.2	110.0	110.5	111.6
1987	102.8	95.5	107.9	102.6	105.1	120.4	70.2	106.4	103.0	112.8	121.8	107.1	110.4	109.9	110.0	112.5	114.9
1988	106.9	104.9	112.7	106.3	109.2	131.4	66.7	116.3	109.3	118.9	130.4	118.7	113.2	113.1	111.2	114.3	120.2
1989	112.2	110.9	117.8	111.6	112.3	136.3	72.9	123.0	112.6	126.7	137.8	124.1	117.4	116.9	112.6	117.7	126.5
1990	116.3	112.2	121.9	115.8	115.0	141.7	82.3	123.6	113.6	129.7	141.2	122.9	120.7	119.2	114.7	121.5	134.2
1991	116.5	105.7	121.9	116.5	116.3	138.9	81.2	125.6	115.1	132.1	142.9	120.2	123.0	121.2	117.2	126.4	140.8
1992	117.2	103.6	122.1	117.4	117.8	140.4	80.4	125.9	115.1	146.6	145.2	119.2	123.4	122.2	117.3	130.4	145.3
1993	118.9	107.1	124.0	119.0	118.0	143.7	80.0	128.2	116.0	174.0	147.3	119.2	124.0	123.7	120.0	133.7	145.4
1994	120.4	106.3	125.5	120.7	118.3	148.5	77.8	132.1	117.6	180.0	152.5	124.8	125.1	126.1	124.2	137.2	141.9
1995	124.7	107.4	127.0	125.5	120.8	153.7	78.0	142.5	124.3	178.1	172.2	134.5	126.6	128.2	129.0	139.7	145.4
1996	127.7	122.4	133.3	127.3	122.4	150.5	85.8	142.1	123.8	176.1	168.7	131.0	126.5	130.4	131.0	141.7	147.7
1997	127.6	112.9	134.0	127.7	122.6	154.2	86.1	143.6	123.2	183.8	167.9	131.8	125.9	130.8	133.2	141.6	150.9
1998	124.4	104.6	131.6	124.8	122.9	148.0	75.3	143.9	122.6	179.1	171.7	127.8	124.9	131.3	135.4	141.2	156.0
1999	125.5	98.4	131.1	126.5	121.1	146.0	80.5	144.2	122.5	183.6	174.1	124.6	124.3	131.7	138.9	141.8	166.6
2000	132.7	99.5	133.1	134.8	121.4	151.5	103.5	151.0	125.5	178.2	183.7	128.1	124.0	132.6	142.5	143.8	170.2
2001	134.2	103.8	137.3	135.7	121.3	158.4	105.3	151.8	127.2	174.4	184.8	125.4	123.7	133.2	144.3	145.2	181.3
2002	131.1	99.0	136.2	132.4	119.9	157.6	93.2	151.9	126.8	173.3	185.9	125.9	122.9	133.5	146.2	144.6	182.4
2003	138.1	111.5	143.4	139.1	119.8	162.3	112.9	161.8	130.1	177.4	190.0	129.2	121.9	133.9	148.2	145.7	179.6
2004	146.7	123.3	151.2	147.6	121.0	164.5	126.9	174.4	133.8	195.6	195.7	149.6	122.1	135.1	153.2	148.6	183.2
2005	157.4	118.5	153.1	160.2	122.8	165.4	156.4	192.0	143.8	196.5	202.6	160.8	123.7	139.4	164.2	151.0	195.1
2006	164.7	117.0	153.8	168.8	124.5	168.4	166.7	205.8	153.8	194.4	209.8	181.6	126.2	142.6	179.9	152.6	205.6
2007	172.6	143.4	165.1	175.1	125.8	173.6	177.6	214.8	155.0	192.4	216.9	193.5	127.3	144.7	186.2	155.0	210.3
2008	189.6	161.3	180.5	192.3	128.9	173.1	214.6	245.5	165.9	191.3	226.8	213.0	129.7	148.9	197.1	158.6	216.6
2009[1]	173.0	134.5	176.2	174.9	129.5	156.7	158.9	229.7	165.1	183.0	225.5	186.9	131.3	153.1	202.4	162.2	217.4
2009																	
January	171.2	136.4	176.8	172.6	130.2	157.0	148.5	226.8	167.5	185.3	228.0	187.0	131.4	152.9	205.8	162.8	218.0
February	169.3	132.8	175.5	170.8	129.9	157.0	143.6	226.5	165.3	183.5	227.0	183.9	131.3	153.3	203.8	162.7	219.0
March	168.1	130.6	174.4	169.5	129.4	157.9	140.2	225.8	164.9	181.7	226.7	181.7	131.5	153.3	203.9	162.2	220.0
April	169.1	136.8	175.5	170.3	129.7	153.6	144.8	225.2	164.5	181.2	225.8	179.9	131.3	153.4	203.7	162.3	217.9
May	170.8	137.8	177.4	172.0	129.1	153.8	152.2	225.8	163.9	180.9	224.8	180.5	131.3	153.3	203.4	161.8	216.6
June	174.1	142.1	177.9	175.5	129.6	151.9	165.0	227.8	163.7	180.8	224.5	181.7	131.1	153.1	202.5	162.3	216.4
July	172.5	131.6	176.2	174.6	129.1	153.1	160.7	230.0	163.9	182.8	224.0	183.5	131.2	153.1	202.1	160.9	216.2
August	175.0	130.1	175.9	177.7	129.4	155.2	169.6	231.1	164.5	183.0	224.4	189.1	131.2	152.6	201.2	161.6	215.9
September	174.1	126.8	175.8	176.9	129.5	158.9	164.9	232.0	165.5	183.7	224.9	192.1	131.2	153.1	201.4	160.7	216.8
October	175.2	133.2	175.3	177.8	129.4	162.0	166.8	231.7	165.8	182.7	224.9	193.3	131.2	153.1	200.6	162.9	216.9
November[1]	177.7	135.6	175.9	180.5	129.5	159.2	175.8	234.5	165.6	184.4	225.0	193.3	131.3	153.2	200.6	163.4	217.5
December[1]	178.1	141.1	177.7	180.4	129.6	162.2	173.3	237.1	166.1	184.9	225.1	196.0	131.4	153.2	200.6	162.8	217.9

[1]Data are preliminary.
. . . = Not available.

Table 8-6. Producer Price Indexes for the Net Output of Selected NAICS Industry Groups

(Various index bases, not seasonally adjusted.)

Year and month	Mining		Manufacturing (Dec. 1984 = 100)									
	Total (Dec. 1984 = 100)	Oil and gas extraction (Dec. 1985 = 100)	Total	Food manufacturing	Leather and products	Petroleum and coal products	Chemicals	Plastics and rubber products	Nonmetallic mineral products	Primary metals	Fabricated metal products	Furniture and related products
1990	81.8	82.7	114.5	116.2	122.6	91.4	121.0	111.3	110.0	116.5	115.1	119.1
1991	78.4	77.9	115.9	116.5	124.8	83.1	124.4	113.7	112.3	113.1	116.6	121.6
1992	76.9	76.5	117.4	116.9	127.0	80.3	125.8	114.2	112.8	111.7	117.2	122.9
1993	76.4	76.2	119.1	118.7	129.0	77.6	127.2	115.4	115.4	111.4	118.2	125.4
1994	73.3	71.1	120.7	120.1	130.6	74.8	130.0	117.1	119.6	117.0	120.3	129.7
1995	71.0	66.6	124.2	121.7	134.1	77.2	143.4	123.3	124.3	128.2	124.8	133.3
1996	84.4	84.8	127.1	127.1	134.7	87.4	145.8	123.1	125.8	123.7	126.2	136.2
1997	86.1	87.5	127.5	127.9	137.1	85.6	147.1	122.8	127.4	124.7	127.6	138.2
1998	70.8	68.3	126.2	126.3	137.1	66.3	148.7	122.1	129.3	120.9	128.7	139.7
1999	78.0	78.5	128.3	126.3	136.5	76.8	149.7	122.2	132.6	115.8	129.1	141.3
2000	113.5	126.8	133.5	128.5	137.9	112.8	156.7	124.6	134.7	119.8	130.3	143.3
2001	114.3	127.5	134.6	132.8	141.3	105.3	158.4	125.9	136.0	116.1	131.0	145.1
2002	96.6	107.0	133.7	132.0	141.1	98.8	157.3	125.5	137.1	116.2	131.7	146.3
2003	131.3	160.1	137.1	137.4	142.8	122.0	164.6	128.4	138.0	118.4	132.9	147.4
2004	153.4	192.7	142.9	144.3	143.6	149.9	172.8	131.7	142.7	142.8	141.3	151.5
2005	201.0	262.0	150.8	146.1	144.5	200.4	187.3	141.2	152.0	156.3	149.5	157.8
2006	208.7	252.5	156.9	146.8	146.6	235.5	196.8	149.7	163.4	179.3	155.7	162.5
2007	220.1	267.1	162.9	158.6	149.7	260.3	203.3	150.6	166.8	190.5	162.3	165.7
2008	274.7	347.5	175.8	173.8	153.5	329.2	228.2	161.3	170.9	211.9	174.4	171.7
2009[1]	178.6	187.5	167.1	169.5	153.8	218.7	224.8	161.2	173.9	172.5	175.0	176.8
2009												
January	173.4	180.3	164.7	170.1	154.3	178.6	226.7	163.4	176.1	177.6	178.9	176.1
February	159.0	154.1	163.9	168.7	154.7	176.4	225.1	161.6	176.0	173.3	177.7	177.0
March	159.1	154.1	162.9	167.6	154.7	168.0	224.6	161.2	175.3	169.5	177.0	176.8
April	160.5	157.0	164.2	168.6	153.9	186.2	223.6	160.9	175.1	164.7	175.5	176.7
May	166.0	168.6	165.8	170.5	153.9	206.5	222.8	160.6	174.5	162.8	175.0	176.9
June	180.2	192.2	168.4	171.4	153.6	238.1	222.4	160.3	174.2	163.8	174.4	176.8
July	173.0	179.9	167.1	169.7	153.2	225.9	224.1	160.3	173.9	165.4	173.9	177.0
August	182.8	194.8	169.4	169.7	154.0	251.6	224.0	160.4	173.4	172.5	173.8	176.2
September	177.2	186.6	168.6	169.5	154.0	241.5	225.1	161.3	173.1	177.8	174.0	176.6
October	192.3	210.8	168.9	168.3	153.3	240.8	225.0	161.5	172.3	180.7	174.1	176.7
November[1]	209.4	236.2	170.7	168.9	152.8	258.8	225.6	161.3	172.2	179.7	173.5	176.8
December[1]	207.4	233.5	170.7	170.8	152.9	253.8	227.7	161.6	172.0	181.8	173.8	176.7

Year and month	Transportation and warehousing					Health care and social assistance			Other services industries (Dec. 1996 = 100)			
	Air transportation (Dec. 1992 = 100)	Rail transportation (Dec. 1996 = 100)	Pipeline transportation (June 1986 = 100)		Postal service (June 1989 = 100)	Offices of physicians (Dec. 1996 = 100)	Home health care (Dec. 1996 = 100)	Hospitals (Dec. 1992 = 100)	Legal services	Architectural, engineering, and related services	Employment services	Accommodation
			Crude oil	Refined petr. products								
1990	...	...	94.2	100.8	100.0	...	...	...	...	...	...	...
1991	...	...	94.4	101.1	117.9	...	...	...	...	...	...	...
1992	...	...	94.8	101.2	119.8	...	...	...	...	...	...	...
1993	105.6	...	95.0	101.3	119.8	...	...	102.5	...	...	...	...
1994	108.5	...	102.5	103.4	119.8	...	...	106.2	...	...	...	...
1995	113.7	...	113.4	104.6	132.2	...	...	110.0	...	...	...	...
1996	121.1	...	104.7	104.3	132.3	...	...	112.6	...	...	...	...
1997	125.3	100.5	96.0	105.3	132.3	101.0	103.3	113.6	102.5	102.2	101.0	104.2
1998	124.5	101.7	96.8	104.8	132.3	103.2	106.2	114.4	106.1	105.1	103.2	108.1
1999	130.8	101.3	95.5	104.9	135.3	105.5	107.1	116.4	108.7	108.5	105.2	112.7
2000	147.7	102.6	101.0	105.3	135.2	107.3	111.1	119.4	112.5	111.8	107.3	116.2
2001	157.2	104.5	111.1	108.5	143.4	110.4	114.0	123.0	117.9	115.9	108.2	121.3
2002	157.8	106.6	112.3	111.0	150.2	110.3	116.6	127.5	121.7	121.1	108.9	121.3
2003	162.1	108.8	111.1	112.7	155.0	112.1	117.0	134.9	125.6	124.3	111.4	122.0
2004	162.3	113.4	115.2	116.0	155.0	114.3	119.8	141.5	131.8	126.8	113.9	125.2
2005	171.0	125.2	125.5	120.3	155.0	116.4	121.1	146.9	138.5	129.2	116.3	131.9
2006	180.4	135.9	135.3	123.8	164.7	117.5	121.8	153.3	145.2	134.4	119.2	136.7
2007	183.7	140.9	138.9	131.7	171.9	122.3	124.0	158.6	153.6	140.0	121.7	142.9
2008	203.8	157.3	152.0	139.2	178.9	123.6	126.1	163.4	161.6	141.0	123.2	146.0
2009[1]	188.2	148.5	156.4	147.3	185.0	126.5	128.0	167.9	166.2	142.9	123.4	141.1
2009												
January	198.4	149.5	157.8	143.1	180.5	125.6	127.2	166.5	164.8	142.9	123.8	140.6
February	190.5	147.6	157.8	143.1	181.6	125.6	127.6	166.8	165.5	142.9	124.0	139.9
March	187.6	146.2	154.8	143.3	181.6	125.9	127.7	167.0	166.0	142.8	123.6	141.3
April	187.2	146.0	156.3	142.9	181.6	125.9	127.7	166.9	166.2	143.0	123.9	141.5
May	179.5	146.0	148.7	142.2	186.8	126.3	127.7	167.2	166.3	143.0	123.5	141.0
June	182.2	147.0	148.7	142.2	186.8	126.5	127.5	167.3	166.3	143.0	123.6	143.7
July	185.5	147.6	158.5	151.1	186.8	126.8	127.9	167.5	166.4	143.0	123.7	146.0
August	189.6	149.9	158.7	151.4	186.8	126.8	128.2	168.4	166.5	142.9	123.6	144.9
September	184.5	150.0	158.6	151.3	186.8	126.8	128.4	168.3	166.6	142.9	123.3	140.9
October	188.5	150.3	158.6	152.0	186.8	127.4	128.8	171.2	166.6	142.8	123.2	141.8
November[1]	191.3	150.9	158.8	152.4	186.8	127.0	128.9	168.7	166.7	142.8	122.7	138.9
December[1]	195.4	150.9	158.8	152.4	186.8	127.1	129.0	171.0	166.9	142.8	122.8	136.8

[1]Data are preliminary.
. . . = Not available.

NOTES AND DEFINITIONS, CHAPTER 8

TABLES 8-1 THROUGH 8-3 AND 20-2
CONSUMER PRICE INDEXES

SOURCES: U.S. DEPARTMENT OF LABOR, BUREAU OF LABOR STATISTICS (BLS) AND U.S. DEPARTMENT OF COMMERCE, BUREAU OF ECONOMIC ANALYSIS (BEA)

The Consumer Price Index (CPI), which is compiled by the Bureau of Labor Statistics (BLS), was originally conceived as a statistical measure of the average change in the cost to consumers of a market basket of goods and services purchased by urban wage earners and clerical workers. In 1978, its scope was broadened to also provide a measure of the change in the cost of the average market basket for all urban consumers. There was still a demand for a wage-earner index, so both versions have been calculated and published since then. The most commonly cited measure in this system is the Consumer Price Index for All Urban Consumers (CPI-U). The wage-earner alternative, used for calculating cost of living adjustments in many government programs, including Social Security, and in wage contracts, is called the Consumer Price Index for Urban Wage Earners and Clerical Workers (CPI-W). Both are presented by the BLS back to 1919; however, the movements (percent changes) in the two indexes before 1978 are identical and are based on the wage-earner market basket.

These CPIs have typically been called "cost-of-living" indexes, even though the original fixed market basket concept does not correspond to economists' definition of a cost-of- living index. In recent years, the concept measured in practice in the CPI has developed into something intended to be closer to the theoretical definition of a cost-of-living index—that is, the cost of maintaining a constant standard of living or level of satisfaction rather than the cost of a fixed market basket. In addition, a new variation of the CPI—the Chained Consumer Price Index for All Urban Consumers (C-CPI-U)—is intended to provide an even closer approximation of a cost-of-living index.

The reference base for the total BLS Consumer Price Index and most of its components is currently 1982–1984 = 100. However, new products that have been introduced into the index since January 1982 are shown on later reference bases, as is the entire C-CPI-U.

Price indexes for personal consumption expenditures (PCE) are calculated and published by the Bureau of Economic Analysis (BEA) as a part of the national income and product accounts (NIPAs). (See Chapters 1 and 4 and their notes and definitions.) The reference base for these indexes is the average in the NIPA base year, 2005. These indexes differ in a number of other respects from the CPIs, and are often emphasized by the Federal Reserve in its analyses of the nation's economy. NIPA data are also available monthly; four important NIPA aggregate price indexes are shown in Tables 8-2 and 8-3 for convenient comparison with the CPIs. See the definitions for those tables for more information.

The CPI-U and the CPI-W

All of the BLS consumer price indexes in Table 8-1 are components of the *CPI-U*. This index uses the consumption patterns for all urban consumers, who comprised about 87 percent of the population in the 1993–1995 period.

A slightly different index that is widely used for adjusting wages and government benefits is the *CPI-W*, of which the all-items total is shown in Tables 8-2 and 8-3. It represents the buying habits of only urban wage earners and clerical workers, who comprised about 32 percent of the population in the 1993–1995 period. The weights are derived from the same Consumer Expenditure Surveys (CES) used for the CPI-U weights, and are changed on the same schedule. However, they include only consumers from the specified categories instead of all urban consumers.

Beginning with January 2010, the weights in both indexes are based on consumer expenditures in the 2007–2008 period. From January 2008 to December 2009, the weights represented expenditures in the 2005–2006 period. From January 2006 to December 2007, the weights represented expenditures in the 2003–2004 period. From January 2004 to December 2005, the weights represented expenditures in the 2001–2002 period. From January 2002 to December 2003, the weights represented consumer expenditures in the 1999–2000 period. Between January 1998 and December 2001, weights from the 1993–1995 period were used. The weights will continue to be updated at two-year intervals, with new weights introduced in the January indexes of each even-numbered year. Previously, new weights were introduced only at the time of a major revision, which translated into a lag of a decade or more.

Specifically, the CPI weights for 1964 through 1977 were derived from reported expenditures of a sample of wage-earner and clerical-worker families and individuals in 1960–1961 and adjusted for price changes between the survey dates and 1963. Weights for the 1978–1986 period were derived from a survey undertaken during the 1972–1974 period and adjusted for price change between the survey dates and December 1977. For 1987 through 1997, the spending patterns reflected in the CPI were derived from a survey undertaken during the 1982–1984 period. The reported expenditures were adjusted for price change between the survey dates and December 1986.

The CPI was overhauled and updated in the latest major revision, which took effect in January 1998. In addition, new products and improved methods are regularly introduced into the index, usually in January.

The latest change in methods was the introduction of a geometric mean formula for calculating many of the basic components of the index. Beginning with the index for January 1999, this formula is used for categories comprising approximately 61 percent of total consumer spending. The new formula allows for the possibility that some consumers may react to changing relative prices within a category by substituting items whose relative prices have declined for products whose relative prices have risen, while maintaining their overall level of satisfaction. The geometric mean formula is not used for categories in which consumer substitution in the short term is not feasible, notably housing rent, utilities, and hospital services.

The CPI-U was introduced in 1978. Before that time, only CPI-W data were available. The movements of the CPI-U before 1978 are therefore based on the changes in the CPI-W. However, the index levels are different because the two indexes differed in the 1982–1984 base period.

Because the official CPI-U and CPI-W are so widely used in "escalation"—the calculation of cost-of-living adjustments for wages and other private contracts, and for government payments and tax parameters—these price indexes are not retrospectively revised to incorporate new information and methods. (An exception is occasionally made for outright error, which happened in September 2000 and affected the data for January through August of that year.) Instead, the new information and methods of calculation are introduced in the current index and affect future index changes only. In Tables 8-2 and 8-3, special CPI and PCE indexes that are subject to retrospective revision are presented. These indexes can be used by researchers to provide more consistent historical information.

Notes on the CPI data

The CPI is based on prices of food, clothing, shelter, fuel, utilities, transportation, medical care, and other goods and services that people buy for day-to-day living. The quantity and quality of these priced items are kept essentially constant between revisions to ensure that only price changes will be measured. All taxes directly associated with the purchase and use of these items, such as sales and property taxes, are included in the index; the effects of income and payroll tax changes are not included.

Data are collected from about 23,000 retail establishments and about 50,000 housing units in 87 urban areas across the country. These data are used to develop the U.S. city average.

Periodic major revisions of the indexes update the content and weights of the market basket of goods and services; update the statistical sample of urban areas, outlets, and unique items used in calculating the CPI; and improve the statistical methods used. In addition, retail outlets and items are resampled on a rotating 5-year basis. Adjustments for changing quality are made at times of major product changes, such as the annual auto model changeover. Other methodological changes are introduced from time to time.

The CES provides the weights—that is, the relative importance—used to combine the individual price changes into subtotals and totals. This survey is composed of two separate surveys: an interview survey and a diary survey, both of which are conducted by the Census Bureau for BLS. Each expenditure reported in the two surveys is classified into a series of detailed categories, which are then combined into expenditure classes and ultimately into major expenditure groups. CPI data as of 1998 are grouped into eight such categories: (1) food and beverages, (2) housing, (3) apparel, (4) transportation, (5) medical care, (6) recreation, (7) education and communication, and (8) other goods and services.

Seasonally adjusted national CPI indexes are published for selected series for which there is a significant seasonal pattern of price change. The factors currently in use were derived by the X-12-ARIMA seasonal adjustment method. Some series with extreme or sharp movements are seasonally adjusted using X-12-ARIMA Intervention Analysis Seasonal Adjustment. Seasonally adjusted indexes and seasonal factors for the preceding five years are updated annually based on data through the previous December. Due to these revisions, BLS advises against the use of seasonally adjusted data for escalation. Detailed descriptions of seasonal adjustment procedures are available upon request from BLS.

CPI Definitions

Definitions of the major CPI groupings were modified beginning with the data for January 1998. These modifications were carried back to 1993. The following definitions are the current definitions currently used for the CPI components.

The *food and beverage index* includes both food at home and food away from home (restaurant meals and other food bought and eaten away from home).

The *housing index* measures changes in rental costs and expenses connected with the acquisition and operation of a home. The CPI-U, beginning with data for January 1983, and the CPI-W, beginning with data for January 1985, reflect a change in the methodology used to compute the homeownership component. A rental equivalence measure replaced an asset-price approach, which included purchase prices and interest costs. The intent of the change was to separate shelter costs from the investment component of homeownership, so that the index would only reflect the cost of the shelter services provided by owner-occupied homes. In addition to measures of the cost of shelter, the housing category includes insurance, fuel, utilities, and household furnishings and operations.

The *apparel index* includes the purchase of apparel and footwear.

The *private transportation index* includes prices paid by urban consumers for such items as new and used automobiles and other vehicles, gasoline, motor oil, tires, repairs and maintenance, insurance, registration fees, driver's licenses, parking fees, and the like. Auto finance charges, like mortgage interest payments, are considered to be a cost of asset acquisition, not of current consumption. Therefore, they are no longer included in the CPI. City bus, streetcar, subway, taxicab, intercity bus, airplane, and railroad coach fares are some of the components of the *public transportation index*.

The *medical care index* includes prices for professional medical services, hospital and related services, prescription and nonprescription drugs, and other medical care commodities. The weight for the portion of health insurance premiums that is used to cover the costs of these medical goods and services is distributed among the items; the weight for the portion of health insurance costs attributable to administrative expenses and profits of insurance providers constitutes a separate health insurance item. Effective with the January 1997 data, the method of calculating the hospital cost component was changed from the pricing of individual commodities and services to a more comprehensive cost-of-treatment approach.

Recreation includes components formerly listed in housing, apparel, entertainment, and "other goods and services."

Education and communication is a new group including components formerly categorized in housing and "other goods and services," such as telephone services and computers.

Other goods and services now includes tobacco, personal care, and miscellaneous.

Alternative price measures in Tables 8-2 and 8-3

Table 8-2 shows the all-items CPI-U and CPI-W, along with a number of other indexes that various analysts of price trends have preferred as measures of the price level. Table 8-3 shows the inflation rates (percent changes in price levels) implied by each of the indexes in Table 8-2.

As food and energy prices are volatile and frequently determined by forces separate from monetary aggregate demand pressures, many analysts prefer an index of prices excluding those components. Indexes *excluding food and energy* are known as *core* indexes, and inflation rates calculated from them are known as *core inflation rates*.

The *CPI-U-X1* is a special experimental version of the CPI that researchers have used to provide a more historically consistent series. As explained above, the official CPI-U treated homeownership on an asset-price basis until January 1983. It then changed to a rental equivalence method. The CPI-U-X1 incorporates a rental equivalence approach to homeowners' costs for the years 1967–1982 as well. It is rebased to the December 1982 value of the CPI-U (1982–1984 = 100); thus, it is identical to the CPI-U in December 1982 and all subsequent periods, as can be seen in Table 8-2. For this reason, it is not updated or published in the CPI news release or on the BLS Web site.

The *CPI-E* is an experimental re-weighting of components of the CPI-U to represent price change for the goods and services purchased by Americans age 62 years and over, who accounted for 16.5 percent of the total number of urban consumer units in the 2001–2002 CES.

The CPI-E is not an ideal measure of price change for older Americans. Because the sample is small, the sampling error in the weights is greater than the error in the all-urban index. The products and outlets sampled are those characteristic of the general urban population rather than older residents. In addition, senior discounts are not included in the prices collected. Such discounts are included—appropriately—in the weights, which are based on the expenditures reported by the older consumers' households, and are thus only a problem if they do not move proportionately to general prices.

The *CPI-U-RS* is a "research series" CPI that retroactively incorporates estimates of the effects of most of the methodological changes implemented since 1978, including the rental equivalence method, new or improved quality adjustments, and improvement of formulas to eliminate bias and allow for some consumer substitution within categories. This index is calculated from 1977 onward. Its reference base is December 1977 = 100. Thus, although it generally shows less <u>increase</u> than the official index, its current <u>levels</u> are considerably higher because the earlier reference base period had lower prices. Unlike the official CPIs and the CPI-U-X1, its historical values will be revised each time a significant change is made in the calculation of the current index. This index is not seasonally adjusted and is not included in the CPI news release. It is available on the BLS Web site, along with an explanation and background material. The CPI-U-RS is used by BLS in the calculation of historical trends in real compensation per hour in its Productivity and Costs system; see Table 9-3 and its notes and definitions. It is also now used by the Census Bureau to convert household incomes into constant dollars, as seen in Chapter 3.

The *C-CPI-U* (Chained Consumer Price Index for All Urban Consumers) is a new, supplemental index that has been published in the monthly CPI news release since August 2002. It is available only from December 1999 to date and is calculated with the base December 1999 = 100; it is not seasonally adjusted. It is designed to be a still-closer approximation to a true cost-of-living index than the CPI-U and the CPI-W, in that it assumes that consumers substitute between as well as within categories as relative prices change, in order to maintain a fixed basket of "consumer satisfaction."

The C-CPI-U is technically a "superlative" index, using a method known as the "Tornqvist formula" to incorporate the composition of consumer spending in the current period as well as in the earlier base period. (All of the other Consumer Price Indexes use a "Laspeyres" formula; see the General Notes at the beginning of this volume.) As it requires consumer expenditure data for the current as well as the earlier period, its final version can only be calculated after the expenditure data become available—about two years before the current period—and is approximated in more recent periods by making more extensive use of the geometric mean formula (see above). With the release of January 2010 data, the indexes for 2008 were revised to their final form, and the initial indexes for 2009 were revised to "interim" levels.

Personal consumption expenditure (PCE) chain-type price indexes are calculated by the Bureau of Economic Analysis (BEA) in the framework of the national income and product accounts (NIPAs). (See the notes and definitions for Chapters 1 and 4.) The scope of NIPA PCE is broader than the scope of the CPI. PCE includes the rural as well as the urban population and also covers the consumption spending of nonprofit entities. The CPI includes only consumer out-of-pocket cash spending, whereas PCE includes some imputed services and includes expenditures financed by government and private insurance, particularly in the medical care area. For this reason, there is a large difference between the relatively small weight of medical care spending in the CPI and the markedly greater percentage of PCE that is accounted for by total medical care spending. Housing, on the other hand, has a somewhat smaller weight in PCE while all non-housing components have a higher weight. It is believed that the CES tends to report housing expenditures accurately and somewhat underestimate other spending, which suggests that the weight of housing relative to all other products may be overestimated in the CPI but measured more correctly in the PCE price index.

PCE chain-type indexes use the expenditure weights of both the earlier and the later period to determine the aggregate price change between the two periods. (See the notes and definitions for Chapter 1, as well as the General Notes on index number formulas.) Thus, they are subject to revision as improved data on the composition of consumption spending become available, and in this respect resemble the C-CPI-U.

For a large share of PCE, the price movements for basic individual spending categories are determined by CPI components. The differences between the rates of change in the aggregate CPI and PCE indexes are largely the result of the different weights, but also reflect some alternative methodologies and the previously mentioned differences in scope.

Market-based PCE indexes are based on household expenditures for which there are observable price measures. They exclude most implicit prices (for example, the services furnished without payment by financial intermediaries) and they exclude items not deflated by a detailed component of either the Consumer Price Index (CPI) or the Producer Price Index (PPI). This means that the price observations that make up these new aggregate measures are all based on observed market transactions, making them "market-based price indexes." The imputed rent for owner-occupied housing is included in the market-based price index, since it is based on observed rentals of comparable homes. Household insurance premiums are also included in the market-based index, since they are deflated by the CPI for

tenants' and household insurance. Excluded are services furnished without payment by financial intermediaries, most insurance purchases, expenses of NPISHs (nonprofit institutions serving households), gambling, margins on used light motor vehicles, and expenditures by U.S. residents working and traveling abroad. Also excluded are medical, hospitalization, and income loss insurance; expense of handling life insurance; motor vehicle insurance; and workers' compensation.

The *inflation rates* shown in Table 8-3 are percent changes in the price indexes introduced in Table 8-2. For annual indexes, the rate is the percent change from the previous year. For monthly indexes, the rate is the percent change from the same month a year earlier. To give an indication of the longer-run implications of these different price indicators, comparisons of compound annual inflation rates, calculated by the editor, are also shown for the 1978–2009, 1983–2009, and 2000–2009 periods, using the growth rate formula presented in the article at the beginning of this volume.

Data availability and references

The CPI-U, CPI-W, and C-CPI-U are initially issued in a press release two to three weeks after the end of the month for which the data were collected. This release and detailed and complete current and historical data on the CPI and its variants and components, along with extensive documentation, are available on the BLS Web site at <http://www.bls.gov/cpi>. Seasonal factors and seasonally adjusted indexes are revised once a year with the issuance of the January index.

Information available on the BLS Web site includes "Common Misconceptions about the Consumer Price Index: Questions and Answers;" another fact sheet on frequently asked questions; a fact sheet on seasonal adjustment; Chapter 17 of the *BLS Handbook of Methods*, entitled "The Consumer Price Index"; a section entitled "Note on Chained Consumer Price Index for All Urban Consumers"; and a number of explanatory CPI fact sheets on specific subjects.

As previously indicated, the CPI-U-X1 is not currently published because its recent values are identical to the CPI-U. The CPI-E is presented in articles in the CPI section of the BLS Web site, the most recent of which is "Experimental Consumer Price Index for Americans 62 Years of Age and Older, 1998–2005"; recent values are available by request from BLS. The CPI-U-RS is updated each month in a report entitled "CPI Research Series Using Current Methods" on the site. In both cases, the reports describe the indexes and provide references.

The monthly PCE indexes are included in the personal income report issued by BEA, which is published near the end of the following month. These indexes are revised month-by-month to reflect new information and annually to reflect the annual and quinquennial benchmarking of the

NIPAs. The complete historical record can be found on the BEA Web site at <http://www.bea.gov> in the Personal Income and Outlays section of the NIPA tables, in tables entitled "Price Indexes for Personal Consumption Expenditures by Major Type of Product."

Two special editions of the *Monthly Labor Review* were devoted to CPI issues. The December 1996 issue describes the subsequently implemented 1997 and 1998 revisions in a series of articles, and the December 1993 issue, entitled *The Anatomy of Price Change*, includes the following articles: "The Consumer Price Index: Underlying Concepts and Caveats"; "Basic Components of the CPI: Estimation of Price Changes"; "The Commodity Substitution Effect in CPI Data, 1982–1991"; and "Quality Adjustment of Price Indexes."

The new formula for calculating basic components is described in "Incorporating a Geometric Mean Formula into the CPI," *Monthly Labor Review* (October 1998). For a detailed discussion of the treatment of homeownership, see "Changing the Homeownership Component of the Consumer Price Index to Rental Equivalence," *CPI Detailed Report* (January 1983).

For a comprehensive professional review of CPI concepts and methodology, see Charles Schultze and Christopher Mackie, ed., *At What Price? Conceptualizing and Measuring Cost-of-Living and Price Indexes* (Washington, DC: National Academy Press, 2001). Earlier references include: "Using Survey Data to Assess Bias in the Consumer Price Index," *Monthly Labor Review* (April 1998); Joel Popkin, "Improving the CPI: The Record and Suggested Next Steps," *Business Economics*, Vol. XXXII, No. 3 (July 1997), pages 42–47; *Measurement Issues in the Consumer Price Index* (Bureau of Labor Statistics, U.S. Department of Labor, June 1997); *Toward a More Accurate Measure of the Cost of Living* (Final Report to the Senate Finance Committee from the Advisory Commission to Study the Consumer Price Index, December 4, 1996)—also known as the "Boskin Commission" report; and *Government Price Statistics* (U.S. Congress Joint Economic Committee, 87th Congress, 1st Session, January 24, 1961)—also known as the "Stigler Committee" report.

For an explanation of the differences between the CPI-U and the PCE index, see Clinton P. McCully, Brian C. Moyer, and Kenneth J. Stewart, "Comparing the Consumer Price Index and the Personal Consumption Expenditures Price Index," *Survey of Current Business*, November 2007, pp. 26-33.

TABLES 8-4 THROUGH 8-6 AND 20-2 PRODUCER PRICE INDEXES

SOURCE: U.S. DEPARTMENT OF LABOR, BUREAU OF LABOR STATISTICS (BLS)

Producer Price Indexes (PPI) measure average changes in prices received by domestic producers. The prices of indi-vidual commodities are organized into three different, separate systems: stage of processing, commodity group, and industry. Most of the indexes currently are published on a base of 1982 = 100. However, there are a number of exceptions for products and industries introduced into the index system since 1982. In this book, alternative base periods are identified in the column headings for the individual series.

Table 8-4 presents price indexes for commodities by stage of processing. Table 8-5 presents data by major commodity groups; these are the groupings that have the longest continuous history. In recent years, the major commodity groups—particularly the totals for all commodities and industrial commodities—have been de-emphasized, as they aggregate successive stages of processing and thus often exaggerate price trends. This effect was particularly acute in the energy price crisis of the early 1970s. To avoid this problem, the stage-of-processing groups were introduced in 1978. However, the individual commodity groups (for example, textile products and apparel) provide a much longer historical perspective on individual industrial sectors than the current industry groupings, and are presented here for that reason.

Table 8-6 presents PPIs for the net output of selected industry groups. As the coverage of the PPI is expanded, indexes for additional industries are frequently introduced, and new industries may only go back to December of the most recent year. This volume includes only those industry groupings with 13 years or more of historical data.

Definitions

The *stage-of-processing* PPI indexes (Table 8-4) organize commodities by class of buyer and degree of fabrication. These have been the featured measures since 1978. The three major indexes are: (1) *finished goods*, or commodities that will not undergo further processing and are ready for sale to the ultimate user (such as automobiles, meats, apparel, and machine tools, and also unprocessed foods such as eggs and fresh vegetables, that are ready for the consumer); (2) *intermediate materials, supplies, and components*, or commodities that have been processed but require further processing before they become finished goods (such as steel mill products, cotton yarns, lumber, and flour), as well as physically complete goods that are purchased by business firms as inputs for their operations (such as diesel fuel and paper boxes); and (3) *crude materials* for further processing, or products entering the market for the first time that have not been manufactured or fabricated and are not sold directly to consumers (such as ores, scrap metals, crude petroleum, raw cotton, and livestock).

PPIs for the *net output* of industries and their products (Table 8-6) are grouped according to the North American Industry Classification System (NAICS). For each industry, they include both measures of price change for the products "primary" to that industry (products made primarily but not necessarily exclusively by that industry), and measures of changes in prices received by establishments classified in the industry for products or services chiefly made in some other industry. Thus, they are designed to be compatible with other economic time series organized by industry, such as data on shipments, employment, wages, and productivity.

Notes on the data

The probability sample used for calculating the PPI provides more than 100,000 price quotations per month, selected to represent the movement of prices of all commodities produced in the manufacturing; agriculture, forestry, and fishing; mining; and gas, electricity, and public utility sectors.

In addition, new PPIs are gradually being introduced for the products and services produced by industries in the construction, transportation, trade, finance, and services sectors. These are only used for industry indexes and are not incorporated in the commodity indexes or the commodity by stage of processing indexes.

To the greatest extent possible, prices used in calculating the PPI represent prices received by domestic producers in the first important commercial transaction for each commodity. These indexes attempt to measure only price changes (changes in receipts per unit of measurement not influenced by changes in quality, quantity sold, terms of sale, or level of distribution). Most quotations are the selling prices of selected manufacturers or other producers, although a few prices are those quoted on organized exchanges or markets. Transaction prices are sought instead of list or book prices.

Price data are generally collected monthly, primarily by mail questionnaire. Most prices are obtained directly from producing companies on a voluntary and confidential basis. Prices are generally reported for the Tuesday of the week containing the 13th day of the month.

The name "Producer Price Index" became effective with the release of March 1978 data and replaced the term "Wholesale Price Index." The change was made to more accurately reflect the coverage of the data. At the same time, there was a shift in analytical emphasis from the All Commodities Index and other traditional commodity grouping indexes (as shown in Table 8-5) to the Finished Goods Index and other stage-of-processing indexes.

The BLS revises the PPI weighting structure when data from economic censuses become available. Beginning with data for January 2007, the weights used to construct the PPI reflect 2002 shipments values as measured by the 2002 Economic Censuses. Data for 2002 through 2006 use 1997 shipments values. Data for 1996 through 2001 reflect 1992 shipments values; 1992 through 1995 reflect 1987 shipments values; 1987 through 1991 reflect 1982 values; 1976 through 1986 reflect 1972 values; and 1967 through 1975 reflect 1963 values.

BLS has been working for a number of years on a comprehensive overhaul of the theory, methodology, and procedures used to construct the PPI. One aspect of this overhaul was the previously mentioned shift in emphasis to the stage-of-processing measures, which began in 1978. Other changes phased in since 1978 include the replacement of judgment sampling with probability sampling techniques; expansion to systematic coverage of the net output of virtually all industries in the mining and manufacturing sectors; introduction of measures for selected services industries, including retail trade; a shift from a commodity to an industry orientation; and the exclusion of imports from, and the inclusion of exports in, the survey universe.

The commodity components of the stage-of-processing indexes, in addition to being available in unadjusted form, are also adjusted for seasonal variation using the X-12-ARIMA method. Since January 1988, BLS has also used X-12-ARIMA Intervention Analysis Seasonal Adjustment for a small number of series to remove unusual values that might distort seasonal patterns before calculating the seasonal adjustment factors. Seasonal factors for the PPI are revised annually to take into account the most recent 12 months of data. Seasonally adjusted data for the previous 5 years are subject to these annual revisions. The industry net output indexes are not seasonally adjusted.

Data availability and references

The indexes are initially issued in a press release two to three weeks after the end of the month for which the data were collected. Data are subsequently published in greater detail in a monthly BLS publication, *PPI Detailed Report*. Each month, data for the fourth previous month (both unadjusted and seasonally adjusted) are revised to reflect late reports and corrections.

The press release, the *PPI Detailed Report*, detailed and complete current and historical data, and extensive documentation are available at <http://www.bls.gov/ppi>. The items available on this Web site include Chapter 14 of the *BLS Handbook of Methods*, "Producer Price Indexes"; a selection of *Monthly Labor Review* articles on the PPI; and fact sheets on a number of issues and index components.

TABLE 8-4
PURCHASING POWER OF THE DOLLAR

SOURCE: U.S. DEPARTMENT OF LABOR, BUREAU OF LABOR STATISTICS (BLS); CALCULATIONS BY THE EDITOR

The purchasing power of the dollar measures changes in the quantity of goods and services a dollar will buy at a particular date compared with a selected base date. It must be defined in terms of the following: (1) the specific commodities and services that are to be purchased with the dollar; (2) the market level (producer, retail, etc.) at which they are purchased; and (3) the dates for which the comparison is to be made. Thus, the purchasing power of the dollar for a selected period, compared with another period, may be measured in terms of a single commodity or a large group of commodities (such as all goods and services purchased by consumers at retail or all finished commodities sold in primary markets).

Broad price indexes calculated by BLS that have been used to measure the purchasing power of the dollar in the United States include: (1) the Producer Price Index (PPI) for Finished Goods, which relates to prices received by the producers of finished commodities at the primary market level; and (2) two versions of the Consumer Price Index (the CPI-U and CPI-W), which measure average changes in retail prices of goods and services. These indexes are described above in the sections of the notes and definitions pertaining to the Producer Price Index and the Consumer Price Index, respectively.

The purchasing power of the dollar is computed by dividing the price index number for the base period by the price index number for the comparison date and expressing the result in dollars and cents. The base period is the period in which the price index equals 100; the purchasing power in that base period is therefore $1.00. In this book, 1982–1984 is used as the base period for both purchasing power measures.

Purchasing power estimates in terms of both the CPI-U and the CPI-W are calculated by BLS and published in the CPI press release. The CPI-U version is shown here. The comparable purchasing power in terms of the finished goods PPI is calculated by the editor of *Business Statistics* after rebasing the index from its published 1982 base to 1982–1984 = 100. In all cases, the purchasing power measure is based on indexes not adjusted for seasonal variation.

CHAPTER 9: EMPLOYMENT COSTS, PRODUCTIVITY, AND PROFITS

Section 9a: Employment Cost Indexes

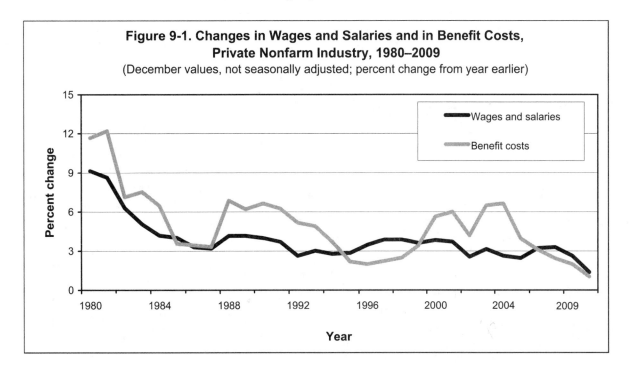

Figure 9-1. Changes in Wages and Salaries and in Benefit Costs, Private Nonfarm Industry, 1980–2009
(December values, not seasonally adjusted; percent change from year earlier)

- Through 2005, benefit costs in private nonfarm industry usually rose faster than wages and salaries, driven by the rising costs of medical benefits. The late 1990s were an exception, and so have been the latest four years. In 2009, both increased by the smallest amount ever recorded in this survey, which has been collected since 1979. (Tables 9-1 and 9-2)

- Between December 2001 and December 2009, total private nonfarm compensation per hour (wages, salaries, and benefits combined) as measured in the ECI—which holds the composition of employment constant in order to isolate increases in compensation for individual workers and excludes stock options—rose at an average annual rate of 3.0 percent. (Table 9-1) The consumer price index for all urban consumers (CPI-U) rose at a 2.4 percent annual rate from 2001 to 2009 (Table 8-1), implying an increase in real worker compensation of about 0.6 percent per year.

- Real worker compensation is said to track worker productivity—but over the same 8-year period, the output per hour of nonfarm industry workers rose 2.7 percent per year (Table 9-3), exceeding the rate of real compensation increase by 2.1 percentage points. Of this gap, 0.4 percentage points reflects a difference between the CPI and the price index used in calculating productivity, leaving a real gap between productivity growth and compensation growth of 1.7 percentage points per year. (Tables 9-3 and 8-1)

Table 9-1. Employment Cost Indexes, NAICS Basis

(December 2005 [not seasonally adjusted] = 100; annual values are for December, not seasonally adjusted; quarterly values, seasonally adjusted, except as noted.)

Year and month	All civilian workers [1]	State and local government workers	Private industry workers											Union [2]	Non-union [2]
			All private industry workers	Excluding incentive paid occupations [2]	By occupational group					By industry				
					Management, professional, and related	Sales and office	Natural resources, construction, and maintenance	Production, transportation, and material moving	Service occupations [3]	Goods-producing industries		Service-providing		
										Total	Manufacturing			
TOTAL COMPENSATION														
2001	87.1	86.2	87.3	. . .	87.4	86.9	86.6	87.4	89.4	86.0	85.5	87.8	84.8	87.8
2002	90.0	89.7	90.0	. . .	89.7	89.8	89.7	90.3	92.0	89.0	88.7	90.4	88.2	90.3
2003	93.5	92.8	93.6	. . .	93.8	93.1	93.3	93.6	95.0	92.6	92.4	94.0	92.3	93.9
2004	97.0	96.1	97.2	. . .	97.1	96.8	97.1	97.8	97.7	96.9	96.9	97.3	97.3	97.2
2005	100.0	100.0	100.0	100.0	100.0	100.0	100.0	100.0	100.0	100.0	100.0	100.0	100.0	100.0
2006	103.3	104.1	103.2	103.2	103.5	102.9	103.6	102.3	103.1	102.5	101.8	103.4	103.0	103.2
2007	106.7	108.4	106.3	106.4	106.8	106.1	106.7	104.5	107.0	105.0	103.8	106.7	105.1	106.5
2008	109.5	111.6	108.9	109.5	109.9	107.9	109.6	106.9	109.8	107.5	105.9	109.4	108.0	109.1
2009	111.1	114.3	110.2	110.9	110.7	109.2	111.2	108.9	111.8	108.6	107.0	110.8	111.1	110.1
2001														
March	84.7	83.6	85.0	. . .	. . .	. . .	. . .	. . .	. . .	84.0	83.7	85.3	82.0	85.5
June	85.5	84.5	85.8	. . .	. . .	. . .	. . .	. . .	. . .	84.7	84.4	86.1	82.9	86.3
September	86.4	85.5	86.7	. . .	. . .	. . .	. . .	. . .	. . .	85.4	84.9	87.1	83.7	87.2
December	87.2	86.1	87.5	. . .	. . .	. . .	. . .	. . .	. . .	86.2	85.8	87.9	84.8	87.8
2002														
March	87.9	86.8	88.2	. . .	88.2	87.8	87.6	88.5	90.3	87.1	86.8	88.6	85.7	88.7
June	88.8	87.5	89.1	. . .	89.0	88.9	88.6	89.1	90.7	87.7	87.5	89.6	86.5	89.6
September	89.5	88.7	89.6	. . .	89.4	89.3	89.3	89.8	91.6	88.2	88.0	90.1	87.5	90.0
December	90.1	89.6	90.2	. . .	90.0	90.1	90.2	90.5	92.1	89.2	89.0	90.5	88.2	90.3
2003														
March	91.2	90.4	91.4	. . .	91.5	90.9	91.0	91.6	93.0	90.6	90.6	91.7	89.5	91.8
June	92.0	91.3	92.2	. . .	92.2	91.7	92.0	92.4	93.5	91.4	91.3	92.4	90.7	92.5
September	92.9	92.0	93.2	. . .	93.2	92.8	92.8	93.2	94.4	92.1	92.0	93.5	91.6	93.5
December	93.6	92.7	93.8	. . .	94.1	93.4	93.7	93.7	95.1	92.8	92.6	94.1	92.3	93.9
2004														
March	94.6	93.5	94.9	. . .	94.7	94.5	95.0	95.4	95.9	94.5	94.6	95.0	94.5	95.0
June	95.5	94.4	95.8	. . .	95.5	95.5	95.9	96.5	96.7	95.4	95.6	96.0	95.9	95.9
September	96.4	95.1	96.7	. . .	96.4	96.5	96.4	97.4	97.2	96.4	96.7	96.8	96.7	96.7
December	97.1	95.9	97.3	. . .	97.4	97.0	97.3	97.9	97.8	97.1	97.1	97.4	97.3	97.2
2005														
March	98.0	97.0	98.2	. . .	98.4	97.9	98.0	98.5	98.4	98.0	98.2	98.3	97.9	98.3
June	98.6	97.8	98.8	. . .	99.0	98.4	98.7	99.0	99.0	98.9	99.0	98.8	98.8	98.9
September	99.3	98.7	99.5	. . .	99.6	99.2	99.4	99.7	99.6	99.7	99.7	99.4	99.6	99.5
December	100.1	99.8	100.2	100.0	100.3	100.2	100.2	100.1	100.1	100.2	100.2	100.2	100.0	100.0
2006														
March	100.7	100.5	100.8	100.9	101.0	100.6	100.9	100.4	100.8	100.3	100.0	100.9	100.5	100.9
June	101.6	101.5	101.6	101.7	101.8	101.5	102.0	101.1	101.5	101.2	100.9	101.7	101.8	101.7
September	102.5	102.8	102.5	102.5	102.9	102.2	102.9	101.7	102.3	101.9	101.4	102.7	102.4	102.6
December	103.4	103.9	103.3	103.2	103.8	103.1	103.7	102.4	103.1	102.6	102.0	103.6	103.0	103.2
2007														
March	104.2	105.1	104.0	104.0	104.5	103.8	104.1	102.5	104.5	102.9	101.9	104.3	102.7	104.2
June	105.1	106.2	104.8	105.0	105.4	104.5	104.8	103.3	105.2	103.7	102.8	105.1	103.9	105.1
September	105.9	107.2	105.6	105.8	106.3	105.2	105.8	103.9	106.4	104.3	103.1	106.0	104.4	105.9
December	106.8	108.2	106.5	106.4	107.1	106.2	106.8	104.6	107.1	105.2	103.9	106.9	105.1	106.5
2008														
March	107.6	109.0	107.2	107.6	108.0	106.8	107.7	105.5	107.8	106.1	104.6	107.6	105.9	107.5
June	108.3	109.9	107.9	108.3	108.8	107.4	108.2	106.0	108.7	106.6	105.1	108.4	106.7	108.3
September	109.0	110.8	108.6	109.0	109.5	107.8	109.0	106.5	109.4	107.2	105.6	109.1	107.4	108.9
December	109.6	111.5	109.1	109.5	110.2	108.0	109.7	106.9	109.8	107.7	106.0	109.6	108.0	109.1
2009														
March	109.9	112.4	109.3	110.0	110.3	108.1	110.0	107.7	110.7	108.0	106.4	109.8	109.1	109.4
June	110.3	113.5	109.5	110.2	110.4	108.1	110.2	108.0	110.9	108.1	106.6	110.0	109.8	109.6
September	110.7	113.5	110.0	110.6	110.6	108.8	110.7	108.6	111.7	108.3	106.8	110.5	110.5	109.9
December	111.2	114.1	110.4	110.9	111.1	109.3	111.3	109.0	111.9	108.8	107.2	111.0	111.1	110.1

[1] Excludes farm workers, private household workers, and federal government employees.
[2] Not seasonally adjusted.
[3] Wages and salaries not seasonally adjusted.
. . . = Not available.

Table 9-1. Employment Cost Indexes, NAICS Basis—*Continued*

(December 2005 [not seasonally adjusted] = 100; annual values are for December, not seasonally adjusted; quarterly values, seasonally adjusted, except as noted.)

Year and month	All civilian workers [1]	State and local government workers	All private industry workers	Excluding incentive paid occupations [2]	Management, professional, and related	Sales and office	Natural resources, construction, and maintenance	Production, transportation, and material moving	Service occupations [3]	Goods-producing industries Total	Goods-producing industries Manufacturing	Service-providing	Union [2]	Non-union [2]
WAGES AND SALARIES														
2001	89.9	90.2	89.9	...	89.5	89.1	90.0	91.0	91.7	90.0	90.2	89.8	89.6	89.9
2002	92.4	93.0	92.2	...	91.7	91.7	92.6	93.3	93.9	92.6	92.8	92.1	92.6	92.2
2003	95.1	95.0	95.1	...	95.3	94.3	95.2	95.4	96.1	94.9	95.1	95.2	94.9	95.1
2004	97.5	97.0	97.6	...	97.8	97.2	97.5	97.8	97.9	97.2	97.4	97.7	97.6	97.6
2005	100.0	100.0	100.0	100.0	100.0	100.0	100.0	100.0	100.0	100.0	100.0	100.0	100.0	100.0
2006	103.2	103.5	103.2	103.2	103.6	103.0	103.4	102.4	102.9	102.9	102.3	103.3	102.3	103.3
2007	106.7	107.1	106.6	106.7	107.2	106.2	107.1	105.0	107.1	106.0	104.9	106.8	104.7	106.9
2008	109.6	110.4	109.4	110.1	110.5	108.0	110.5	107.8	110.1	109.0	107.7	109.6	108.1	109.6
2009	111.2	112.6	110.9	111.6	111.5	109.4	112.0	109.6	112.3	110.0	108.9	111.1	110.9	110.9
2001														
March	87.6	87.6	87.6	...	...	...	...	...	89.7	87.9	88.2	87.4	86.5	87.7
June	88.4	88.4	88.4	...	...	...	...	...	90.2	88.7	89.0	88.3	87.4	88.6
September	89.2	89.4	89.2	...	...	...	...	...	90.6	89.3	89.5	89.1	88.3	89.3
December	90.0	90.0	90.0	...	...	...	...	...	91.7	90.1	90.3	90.0	89.6	89.9
2002														
March	90.7	90.5	90.7	...	90.4	90.1	90.7	91.9	92.5	90.8	91.2	90.7	90.2	90.8
June	91.5	91.2	91.6	...	91.2	91.1	91.6	92.4	92.8	91.3	91.7	91.6	91.1	91.7
September	92.0	92.1	92.0	...	91.5	91.3	92.2	92.8	93.4	91.8	92.2	92.0	91.9	92.0
December	92.4	92.8	92.3	...	91.9	92.0	92.8	93.3	93.9	92.7	93.0	92.2	92.6	92.2
2003														
March	93.3	93.5	93.3	...	93.3	92.5	93.4	94.1	94.5	93.3	93.8	93.2	93.0	93.3
June	93.9	94.1	93.8	...	93.9	93.2	94.0	94.6	94.8	94.0	94.4	93.8	93.8	94.0
September	94.6	94.4	94.7	...	94.8	94.1	94.6	95.1	95.6	94.5	94.8	94.7	94.4	94.9
December	95.1	94.9	95.2	...	95.4	94.5	95.3	95.4	96.1	95.0	95.3	95.2	94.9	95.1
2004														
March	95.7	95.5	95.7	...	95.9	95.2	95.9	96.0	96.4	95.6	95.7	95.8	95.6	95.8
June	96.3	96.0	96.4	...	96.4	96.0	96.5	96.7	96.9	96.2	96.4	96.5	96.4	96.5
September	97.0	96.3	97.2	...	97.2	97.0	97.0	97.6	97.4	97.2	97.4	97.2	97.1	97.3
December	97.5	96.9	97.7	...	98.0	97.3	97.6	97.9	97.9	97.4	97.6	97.8	97.6	97.6
2005														
March	98.2	97.6	98.3	...	98.6	98.0	98.0	98.4	98.6	97.9	98.2	98.4	97.9	98.3
June	98.7	98.3	98.8	...	99.1	98.4	98.6	98.9	99.0	98.6	98.8	98.8	98.7	98.9
September	99.3	98.8	99.4	...	99.5	99.2	99.3	99.5	99.6	99.4	99.6	99.4	99.5	99.5
December	100.1	99.8	100.1	...	100.2	100.1	100.1	100.1	100.0	100.2	100.2	100.1	100.0	100.0
2006														
March	100.7	100.4	100.8	100.8	101.0	100.6	100.8	100.6	100.6	100.7	100.6	100.8	100.3	100.8
June	101.5	101.2	101.6	101.7	101.9	101.5	101.8	101.1	101.3	101.7	101.6	101.6	101.2	101.8
September	102.5	102.4	102.5	102.5	102.9	102.2	102.7	101.7	102.0	102.2	101.8	102.6	101.7	102.7
December	103.3	103.3	103.3	103.2	103.8	103.1	103.5	102.5	102.9	103.1	102.5	103.4	102.3	103.3
2007														
March	104.3	104.2	104.3	104.3	104.9	103.9	104.3	103.2	104.6	103.9	103.2	104.4	102.8	104.5
June	105.0	105.0	105.0	105.2	105.7	104.6	105.0	103.8	105.3	104.6	103.8	105.2	103.7	105.3
September	105.9	106.0	105.9	106.1	106.6	105.2	106.1	104.4	106.5	105.4	104.4	106.1	104.4	106.2
December	106.8	106.9	106.7	106.7	107.4	106.3	107.1	105.1	107.1	106.2	105.1	106.9	104.7	106.9
2008														
March	107.6	107.8	107.6	107.9	108.4	106.8	108.2	106.0	107.9	107.1	105.9	107.7	105.5	107.9
June	108.4	108.7	108.4	108.7	109.2	107.5	108.9	106.7	108.8	107.8	106.6	108.5	106.7	108.7
September	109.2	109.7	109.1	109.5	110.0	107.9	109.7	107.4	109.7	108.5	107.3	109.2	107.4	109.4
December	109.7	110.2	109.6	110.1	110.8	108.1	110.6	107.9	110.1	109.2	107.9	109.7	108.1	109.6
2009														
March	110.0	111.0	109.8	110.6	110.9	108.1	110.7	108.3	111.0	109.3	108.1	110.0	108.8	110.0
June	110.4	112.1	110.0	110.8	111.1	108.2	111.0	108.7	111.2	109.4	108.3	110.2	109.6	110.2
September	110.8	112.0	110.5	111.3	111.3	108.9	111.5	109.3	112.1	109.8	108.6	110.7	110.2	110.6
December	111.3	112.4	111.0	111.6	111.9	109.5	112.1	109.8	112.3	110.3	109.1	111.3	110.9	110.9

[1] Excludes farm workers, private household workers, and federal government employees.
[2] Not seasonally adjusted.
[3] Wages and salaries not seasonally adjusted.
. . . = Not available.

Table 9-1. Employment Cost Indexes, NAICS Basis—*Continued*

(December 2005 [not seasonally adjusted] = 100; annual values are for December, not seasonally adjusted; quarterly values, seasonally adjusted, except as noted.)

Year and month	All civilian workers [1]	State and local government workers	All private industry workers	Excluding incentive paid occupations [2]	By occupational group					By industry		Service-providing	Union [2]	Non-union [2]
					Management, professional, and related	Sales and office	Natural resources, construction, and maintenance	Production, transportation, and material moving	Service occupations [3]	Goods-producing industries				
										Total	Manufacturing			
TOTAL BENEFITS														
2001	80.6	78.1	81.3	...	82.0	81.1	79.8	80.7	82.5	78.5	77.2	82.4	77.3	82.2
2002	84.3	83.0	84.7	...	84.7	84.7	84.1	84.5	86.5	82.3	81.3	85.8	81.2	85.5
2003	89.7	88.2	90.2	...	90.1	90.0	89.8	90.2	91.7	88.2	87.3	91.0	88.1	90.6
2004	95.7	94.1	96.2	...	95.4	95.8	96.4	97.7	97.0	96.3	96.0	96.1	96.8	96.0
2005	100.0	100.0	100.0	...	100.0	100.0	100.0	100.0	100.0	100.0	100.0	100.0	100.0	100.0
2006	103.6	105.2	103.1	...	103.4	102.9	104.0	102.0	103.6	101.7	100.8	103.7	104.2	102.9
2007	106.8	111.0	105.6	...	106.0	106.0	105.9	103.7	106.7	103.2	101.7	106.6	105.8	105.6
2008	109.1	114.2	107.7	...	108.5	107.8	107.7	105.1	108.8	104.7	102.5	108.9	107.8	107.6
2009	110.7	117.9	108.8	...	108.8	108.7	109.5	107.4	110.5	105.8	103.6	109.9	111.4	108.2
2001														
March	78.0	75.2	78.8	...	...	...	...	...	...	76.5	75.4	79.7	74.8	79.9
June	78.8	76.3	79.5	...	...	...	...	...	...	77.0	75.8	80.5	75.7	80.5
September	79.9	77.4	80.6	...	...	...	...	...	...	77.8	76.4	81.7	76.6	81.6
December	80.8	78.0	81.5	...	...	...	...	...	...	78.7	77.4	82.6	77.3	82.2
2002														
March	81.5	78.8	82.3	...	82.7	81.8	81.2	81.8	83.5	79.9	78.8	83.2	78.6	83.2
June	82.5	79.9	83.3	...	83.7	83.2	82.1	82.7	84.4	80.6	79.7	84.4	79.3	84.3
September	83.5	81.4	84.1	...	84.2	84.2	83.3	83.7	86.0	81.2	80.3	85.2	80.5	84.9
December	84.6	82.9	85.0	...	85.2	85.1	84.6	84.8	86.8	82.5	81.5	86.0	81.2	85.5
2003														
March	86.3	84.1	87.0	...	87.1	86.6	86.0	86.7	88.5	85.2	84.7	87.7	83.9	87.8
June	87.5	85.4	88.1	...	88.0	88.0	87.6	88.1	89.4	86.5	85.7	88.8	85.7	88.8
September	88.9	86.9	89.4	...	89.5	89.3	88.7	89.4	90.8	87.5	86.8	90.2	87.2	89.9
December	90.0	88.0	90.5	...	90.7	90.4	90.3	90.4	92.0	88.4	87.5	91.4	88.1	90.6
2004														
March	92.1	89.5	92.9	...	91.9	92.5	92.9	94.4	94.3	92.4	92.7	93.0	92.8	93.0
June	93.7	91.1	94.4	...	93.4	94.2	94.5	96.0	95.9	93.8	94.1	94.6	95.0	94.5
September	94.8	92.5	95.4	...	94.5	95.2	95.4	97.1	96.7	95.0	95.4	95.5	96.0	95.2
December	95.9	93.9	96.5	...	95.9	96.1	96.9	98.0	97.3	96.5	96.1	96.5	96.8	96.0
2005														
March	97.5	95.6	98.0	...	97.9	97.5	98.0	98.6	98.0	98.2	98.2	97.9	98.0	98.2
June	98.4	96.8	98.8	...	98.8	98.3	98.9	99.2	98.8	99.5	99.4	98.6	98.9	99.0
September	99.4	98.4	99.7	...	99.8	99.4	99.7	100.0	99.5	100.3	100.1	99.4	99.8	99.6
December	100.2	99.8	100.3	...	100.5	100.2	100.4	100.1	100.3	100.2	100.1	100.3	100.0	100.0
2006														
March	100.8	100.8	100.8	...	101.0	100.7	101.2	100.1	101.3	99.5	98.9	101.3	100.8	101.0
June	101.7	102.0	101.6	...	101.7	101.4	102.4	100.9	102.1	100.3	99.7	102.1	102.7	101.5
September	102.7	103.5	102.5	...	102.8	102.1	103.5	101.6	103.0	101.2	100.6	103.0	103.4	102.3
December	103.7	105.1	103.4	...	103.9	103.0	104.2	102.1	103.8	101.8	100.9	104.0	104.2	102.9
2007														
March	104.0	107.1	103.1	...	103.5	103.3	103.5	101.2	104.1	101.0	99.5	104.0	102.4	103.4
June	105.2	108.7	104.2	...	104.8	104.2	104.5	102.4	105.0	102.1	100.9	105.0	104.1	104.3
September	106.0	109.7	104.9	...	105.5	105.2	105.3	102.8	106.0	102.4	100.8	106.0	104.3	105.1
December	106.9	110.9	105.9	...	106.4	106.0	106.1	103.7	106.9	103.4	101.7	106.9	105.8	105.6
2008														
March	107.5	111.5	106.5	...	107.1	106.6	106.7	104.4	107.5	104.0	102.3	107.4	106.6	106.5
June	108.1	112.5	106.9	...	107.8	107.0	106.7	104.5	108.3	104.3	102.2	108.0	106.6	107.1
September	108.7	113.2	107.5	...	108.5	107.5	107.4	104.8	108.7	104.5	102.4	108.7	107.2	107.6
December	109.2	114.0	107.9	...	108.9	107.8	107.8	105.0	109.0	104.9	102.6	109.1	107.8	107.6
2009														
March	109.7	115.3	108.1	...	108.6	108.1	108.4	106.4	109.6	105.4	103.4	109.2	109.5	107.9
June	110.0	116.5	108.3	...	108.7	108.0	108.5	106.8	109.8	105.6	103.6	109.3	110.3	108.0
September	110.4	116.8	108.6	...	108.9	108.5	109.2	107.2	110.4	105.6	103.4	109.8	110.9	108.2
December	110.9	117.8	109.0	...	109.2	108.7	109.6	107.4	110.7	106.0	103.7	110.2	111.4	108.2

[1] Excludes farm workers, private household workers, and federal government employees.
[2] Not seasonally adjusted.
[3] Wages and salaries not seasonally adjusted.
. . . = Not available.

Table 9-2. Employment Cost Indexes, SIC Basis

(Not seasonally adjusted, December 2005 = 100; annual values are for December.)

Columns, in order: Year | All civilian workers [1,2] | State and local government workers [2] | All private industry workers [2] | Private industry workers excluding sales occupations | **By occupational group:** Production and nonsupervisory occupations | White-collar occupations | Blue-collar occupations | Service occupations [2] | **Goods-producing industries:** Total [2] | Construction [2] | Manufacturing [2] | **Service-providing industries:** Total [2] | Transportation and utilities | Wholesale trade | Retail trade | Finance, insurance, and real estate [2] | Services

Year	All civ. [1,2]	State & local govt [2]	All priv. ind. [2]	Priv. excl. sales	Prod. & nonsup.	White-collar	Blue-collar	Service occ. [2]	Goods Total [2]	Construction [2]	Manufac- turing [2]	Serv. Total [2]	Transp. & utilities	Wholesale trade	Retail trade	Finance, ins., real estate [2]	Services
TOTAL COMPENSATION																	
1979	...	...	32.8	32.5	...	31.2	35.0	33.9	33.7	...	33.1	32.0	...	...	...	...	...
1980	...	...	35.9	35.9	...	34.2	38.5	37.1	37.0	...	36.4	35.1	...	...	...	...	...
1981	39.0	36.8	39.5	39.4	40.1	37.6	42.2	40.5	40.7	...	40.0	38.6	...	...	...	...	...
1982	41.5	39.4	42.0	42.0	42.8	40.1	44.7	43.9	43.2	...	42.4	41.1	...	...	...	...	...
1983	43.9	41.8	44.4	44.4	45.2	42.7	47.0	46.3	45.3	...	44.6	43.8	...	...	...	...	...
1984	46.2	44.6	46.6	46.7	47.3	44.8	49.0	49.4	47.4	...	46.9	46.0	...	...	...	...	...
1985	48.2	47.1	48.4	48.3	49.1	47.0	50.5	50.9	49.0	50.8	48.4	48.1	50.6	...	52.4	44.7	46.1
1986	49.9	49.6	49.9	49.9	50.5	48.6	51.9	52.4	50.5	52.3	50.0	49.6	51.8	48.5	53.5	46.1	48.1
1987	51.7	51.8	51.6	51.7	52.2	50.4	53.5	53.7	52.1	54.2	51.5	51.4	53.3	50.4	54.8	47.0	50.5
1988	54.2	54.7	54.1	54.1	54.8	52.9	55.9	56.5	54.4	56.5	53.8	54.0	54.9	52.5	58.0	50.0	53.5
1989	56.9	58.1	56.7	56.5	57.6	55.7	58.2	59.0	56.7	59.0	56.3	56.8	56.9	57.1	59.9	52.7	56.4
1990	59.7	61.5	59.3	59.3	60.1	58.4	60.7	61.8	59.4	60.9	59.1	59.4	59.1	58.2	62.5	54.9	59.9
1991	62.3	63.7	61.9	62.0	62.7	61.0	63.4	64.7	62.1	63.3	61.9	61.9	61.7	60.7	65.2	57.2	62.5
1992	64.4	66.0	64.1	64.2	64.9	63.1	65.6	65.6	64.5	65.6	64.3	63.9	63.9	62.5	66.9	57.9	65.2
1993	66.7	67.9	66.4	66.6	67.3	65.4	68.1	68.8	67.0	67.1	66.9	66.2	66.1	64.4	68.9	60.5	67.5
1994	68.7	69.9	68.5	68.6	69.2	67.5	70.0	70.8	69.0	69.6	69.0	68.1	68.7	66.4	70.8	61.8	69.4
1995	70.6	72.0	70.2	70.4	71.0	69.4	71.7	72.1	70.7	71.1	70.8	70.0	71.2	69.4	72.3	64.0	70.9
1996	72.6	73.9	72.4	72.4	73.1	71.7	73.6	74.2	72.7	72.9	72.9	72.3	73.4	71.5	75.1	65.5	73.1
1997	75.0	75.6	74.9	74.9	75.4	74.4	75.5	77.2	74.5	74.8	74.6	75.1	75.5	73.8	77.7	69.9	75.9
1998	77.6	77.8	77.5	77.2	78.1	77.3	77.6	79.4	76.5	77.4	76.6	78.0	78.4	78.0	80.0	74.1	78.2
1999	80.2	80.5	80.2	80.0	80.4	79.9	80.2	82.1	79.1	79.9	79.2	80.6	80.1	81.1	83.0	77.1	80.9
2000	83.6	82.9	83.6	83.6	84.0	83.6	83.6	85.3	82.6	84.6	82.3	84.2	83.5	84.4	86.4	81.0	84.5
2001	87.0	86.4	87.1	87.0	87.4	87.1	86.7	89.1	85.7	88.2	85.3	87.8	87.5	87.2	90.3	83.9	88.3
2002	90.0	89.9	90.0	89.9	90.2	89.9	89.8	92.0	88.9	91.0	88.5	90.5	91.0	91.1	91.9	87.6	90.7
2003	93.5	92.9	93.6	93.6	93.6	93.6	93.4	94.9	92.4	94.1	92.2	94.2	94.0	94.0	94.9	94.1	94.0
2004	96.9	96.1	97.1	97.2	97.2	96.9	97.5	97.7	96.8	96.4	96.7	97.3	97.6	96.5	97.1	96.7	97.5
2005	100.0	100.0	100.0	100.0	100.0	100.0	100.0	100.0	100.0	100.0	100.0	100.0	100.0	100.0	100.0	100.0	100.0
WAGES AND SALARIES																	
1979	...	...	36.1	36.1	36.8	34.1	39.4	37.9	38.2	41.4	37.5	34.9	39.1	33.7	39.7	32.8	31.7
1980	...	...	39.4	39.3	40.3	37.1	43.1	41.0	41.8	45.0	41.0	38.0	43.5	37.1	42.5	35.2	34.5
1981	42.3	40.1	42.8	42.9	43.9	40.4	46.8	44.4	45.4	49.0	44.5	41.4	47.1	40.0	45.6	38.8	38.1
1982	45.0	42.7	45.5	45.6	46.7	43.1	49.4	48.2	48.0	51.5	47.0	44.2	50.5	42.5	47.6	40.0	39.7
1983	47.3	45.0	47.8	47.9	48.9	45.7	51.3	50.4	49.9	53.0	49.0	46.7	53.0	45.1	49.5	41.3	41.2
1984	49.4	47.7	49.8	50.1	50.8	47.6	53.1	53.5	51.8	53.7	51.2	48.7	54.8	47.6	52.0	44.3	43.9
1985	51.5	50.3	51.8	51.9	52.9	50.0	55.0	54.8	53.6	55.3	53.0	51.0	56.9	49.7	54.5	47.9	48.4
1986	53.3	53.0	53.5	53.6	54.3	51.7	56.4	56.2	55.3	56.7	54.8	52.5	57.9	51.5	55.7	49.2	50.3
1987	55.2	55.2	55.2	55.5	56.0	53.6	58.1	57.6	57.1	58.6	56.6	54.3	59.1	53.6	57.2	49.8	53.0
1988	57.5	57.9	57.5	57.5	58.4	56.1	59.9	60.1	58.9	60.7	58.3	56.9	60.6	55.6	60.1	52.9	55.6
1989	60.1	61.0	59.9	59.8	61.0	58.7	62.0	62.3	61.2	62.8	60.6	59.5	62.2	60.7	62.0	55.7	58.3
1990	62.6	64.2	62.3	62.4	63.2	61.2	64.2	64.8	63.4	64.1	63.1	61.8	64.3	61.2	64.2	57.6	61.6
1991	64.9	66.4	64.6	64.7	65.4	63.5	66.4	67.4	65.8	66.0	65.6	64.1	66.6	63.6	66.6	59.6	63.8
1992	66.6	68.4	66.5	66.5	67.2	65.2	68.1	68.8	67.6	67.3	67.6	65.7	68.7	65.5	68.2	59.5	66.0
1993	68.7	70.2	68.3	68.5	69.2	67.4	70.0	70.3	69.6	68.6	69.7	67.8	70.9	67.1	70.2	62.1	68.0
1994	70.6	72.4	70.2	70.5	71.1	69.3	72.0	72.4	71.7	70.8	71.8	69.6	73.5	69.1	71.9	62.8	70.0
1995	72.7	74.7	72.2	72.5	73.0	71.3	74.1	74.0	73.7	72.5	73.9	71.7	76.0	72.4	73.6	65.1	71.7
1996	75.1	76.8	74.7	74.9	75.5	73.8	76.3	76.6	76.0	74.6	76.3	74.2	78.1	74.7	76.8	67.2	74.2
1997	77.9	78.9	77.6	77.7	78.3	77.0	78.8	79.9	78.3	77.1	78.6	77.4	80.7	77.0	79.7	71.8	77.5
1998	80.8	81.3	80.6	80.4	81.4	80.3	81.3	82.4	81.1	79.9	81.3	80.5	83.0	81.5	82.2	76.9	80.1
1999	83.6	84.2	83.5	83.4	83.8	83.1	84.0	85.1	83.8	82.5	84.1	83.4	84.8	84.5	85.2	79.8	83.0
2000	86.7	87.0	86.7	86.7	87.1	86.4	87.1	88.3	87.1	86.9	87.1	86.6	87.5	87.4	88.6	83.4	86.3
2001	90.0	90.2	90.0	90.0	90.4	89.6	90.5	91.8	90.2	90.4	90.2	89.9	91.7	89.3	91.9	85.8	90.0
2002	92.6	93.1	92.4	92.5	92.6	92.0	93.0	94.1	92.9	92.8	93.0	92.3	94.7	92.8	93.2	89.4	92.0
2003	95.2	95.0	95.2	95.4	95.1	95.2	95.2	96.2	95.1	95.1	95.2	95.3	96.2	95.3	95.5	95.9	94.8
2004	97.5	97.0	97.5	97.8	97.5	97.5	97.6	97.9	97.4	97.0	97.5	97.7	98.6	96.6	97.2	97.7	97.8
2005	100.0	100.0	100.0	100.0	100.0	100.0	100.0	100.0	100.0	100.0	100.0	100.0	100.0	100.0	100.0	100.0	100.0

[1] Excludes farm workers, private household workers, and federal government employees.
[2] Roughly continuous and comparable with new NAICS-based series. See notes and definitions for more information.
... = Not available.

Table 9-2. Employment Cost Indexes, SIC Basis—*Continued*

(Not seasonally adjusted, December 2005 = 100; annual values are for December.)

Year	All civilian workers [1,2]	State and local government workers [2]	Private industry workers															
			All private industry workers [2]	Private industry workers excluding sales occupations	By occupational group				By industry division								
					Production and nonsupervisory occupations	White-collar occupations	Blue-collar occupations	Service occupations [2]	Goods-producing industries			Service-providing industries					
									Total [2]	Construction [2]	Manufacturing [2]	Total [2]	Transportation and utilities	Wholesale trade	Retail trade	Finance, insurance, and real estate [2]	Services
TOTAL BENEFITS																	
1979	...	...	25.7	...	...	24.7	27.4	...	26.0	...	25.8	25.4	...	...	...	...	...
1980	...	...	28.7	...	...	27.7	30.4	...	28.8	...	28.5	28.6	...	...	...	...	...
1981	31.8	...	32.2	...	...	31.1	34.0	...	32.4	...	32.1	31.9	...	...	...	...	...
1982	34.2	...	34.5	...	...	33.3	36.5	...	34.8	...	34.4	34.1	...	...	...	...	...
1983	36.8	...	37.1	...	...	35.8	39.1	...	37.2	...	36.9	36.8	...	...	...	...	...
1984	39.3	...	39.5	...	...	38.3	41.4	...	39.6	...	39.3	39.4	...	...	...	...	...
1985	40.8	...	40.9	...	...	40.0	42.5	41.2	40.8	...	40.4	40.9	...	...	...	...	...
1986	42.4	...	42.3	...	...	41.4	43.8	42.9	42.0	...	41.6	42.5	...	...	...	...	...
1987	44.0	...	43.7	...	...	42.9	45.3	43.9	43.2	...	42.7	44.2	...	...	...	...	...
1988	47.0	...	46.7	...	...	45.6	48.6	47.4	46.3	...	46.0	47.1	...	...	...	...	...
1989	50.1	52.2	49.6	...	...	48.6	51.2	50.5	48.8	...	48.7	50.2	...	...	...	...	...
1990	53.5	55.8	52.9	...	...	52.0	54.4	53.8	52.3	...	52.1	53.4	...	...	...	...	...
1991	56.5	58.0	56.2	...	...	55.2	57.8	57.7	55.5	...	55.2	56.7	...	...	...	...	...
1992	59.5	61.1	59.1	...	...	57.8	61.0	61.0	58.7	...	58.3	59.4	...	...	...	...	...
1993	62.2	62.9	62.0	...	...	60.5	64.4	64.4	62.0	...	61.8	62.0	...	...	...	...	...
1994	64.4	64.6	64.3	...	...	63.2	66.2	66.0	64.1	...	63.9	64.4	...	...	...	...	...
1995	65.8	66.3	65.7	...	...	64.8	67.2	66.6	65.2	...	65.0	66.0	...	...	...	...	...
1996	67.1	67.8	67.0	...	...	66.2	68.4	67.3	66.4	...	66.5	67.3	...	...	...	...	...
1997	68.5	68.6	68.5	...	...	68.0	69.4	69.6	67.3	...	67.4	69.2	...	...	...	...	...
1998	70.3	70.7	70.2	...	...	69.9	70.7	70.9	68.1	...	67.9	71.4	...	...	...	...	...
1999	72.6	72.7	72.6	...	...	72.3	73.0	73.4	70.5	...	70.3	73.8	...	...	...	...	...
2000	76.2	74.4	76.7	...	...	76.5	76.9	76.6	74.3	...	73.6	78.1	...	...	...	...	...
2001	80.2	78.5	80.6	...	...	81.1	79.5	81.3	77.3	...	76.3	82.5	...	...	...	...	...
2002	84.2	83.3	84.4	...	...	84.6	83.8	85.7	81.3	...	80.4	86.1	...	...	...	...	...
2003	89.5	88.4	89.8	...	...	89.7	89.8	91.3	87.4	...	86.7	91.2	...	...	...	...	...
2004	95.7	94.3	96.0	...	...	95.3	97.3	97.1	95.7	...	95.3	96.2	...	...	...	...	...
2005	100.0	100.0	100.0	...	...	100.0	100.0	100.0	100.0	...	100.0	100.0	...	...	...	...	...

[1]Excludes farm workers, private household workers, and federal government employees.
[2]Roughly continuous and comparable with new NAICS-based series. See notes and definitions for more information.
. . . = Not available.

Section 9b: Productivity and Related Data

Figure 9-2. Change in Labor Productivity, Nonfarm Business, 1948–2009

- As Figure 9-2 demonstrates, the rate of change in U.S. nonfarm labor productivity has often been quite variable from year to year. Up through the 1980s, productivity tended to decline (growth rates were less than zero) in recession years but rebound sharply in recovery. One explanation of this was that firms expected that declines in demand would be temporary, and therefore held on to their experienced workers in order to be prepared for the recovery. (Tables 9-3 and 19-11)

- On average, measuring between cyclically high growth years, productivity grew at a 2.8 percent annual rate from 1948 to 1973. Productivity growth slowed between 1973 and 1989, averaging just 1.3 percent. From 1989 to 2009, however, productivity growth speeded up to an average of 2.4 percent per year. (Tables 9-3 and 19-11)

- In the 1990s and 2000s, growth rates were still variable but no longer declined in recession years—in fact, in the recession year 2009 when output plunged 3.6 percent, firms reduced labor input 7.1 percent and productivity grew 3.8 percent. This suggests that declines in demand are no longer regarded as temporary. (Table 9-3)

- The productivity accounts for nonfinancial corporations allow us to identify separately the cost pressures and profits trends in this sector. From 2000 to 2008, unit labor costs rose at an annual rate of only 0.8 percent, as a 3.2 percent rate of rise in compensation per hour was largely offset by a 2.4 percent rate of productivity growth. Unit non-labor costs (depreciation, interest, and indirect taxes) rose at a 2.7 percent rate. Unit profits rose at a 3.4 percent annual rate. (Table 9-3)

Table 9-3. Productivity and Related Data

(1992 = 100, seasonally adjusted.)

Year and quarter	Business sector								Nonfarm business sector							
	Output per hour of all persons	Output	Hours of all persons	Compen-sation per hour	Real compen-sation per hour	Unit labor costs	Unit nonlabor payments	Implicit price deflator	Output per hour of all persons	Output	Hours of all persons	Compen-sation per hour	Real compen-sation per hour	Unit labor costs	Unit nonlabor payments	Implicit price deflator
1950	37.4	23.4	62.6	8.3	44.8	22.1	21.5	21.9	42.0	22.9	54.7	8.9	48.0	21.1	20.8	21.0
1951	38.5	24.9	64.6	9.1	45.5	23.5	23.7	23.6	43.1	24.7	57.2	9.6	48.3	22.3	22.4	22.4
1952	39.6	25.7	64.8	9.6	47.4	24.3	23.1	23.8	43.9	25.4	57.9	10.2	50.0	23.2	22.3	22.8
1953	41.1	26.9	65.6	10.2	50.0	24.9	22.5	24.0	44.9	26.6	59.3	10.7	52.4	23.9	22.2	23.3
1954	41.9	26.6	63.4	10.6	51.3	25.2	22.4	24.1	45.7	26.2	57.3	11.1	53.7	24.2	22.2	23.5
1955	43.7	28.7	65.8	10.8	52.8	24.8	23.9	24.5	47.7	28.4	59.6	11.5	55.9	24.1	23.6	23.9
1956	43.8	29.2	66.8	11.5	55.4	26.4	23.4	25.3	47.3	28.9	61.1	12.2	58.4	25.7	23.0	24.7
1957	45.1	29.7	65.8	12.3	57.1	27.2	24.1	26.1	48.5	29.5	60.7	12.9	59.8	26.5	23.8	25.5
1958	46.4	29.2	62.9	12.8	58.0	27.6	24.6	26.5	49.6	28.9	58.2	13.4	60.5	27.0	24.0	25.9
1959	48.2	31.6	65.5	13.4	60.0	27.7	25.1	26.7	51.5	31.4	60.9	13.9	62.4	27.0	24.9	26.2
1960	49.1	32.2	65.6	13.9	61.4	28.4	24.7	27.0	52.1	31.9	61.2	14.5	64.0	27.8	24.2	26.5
1961	50.8	32.8	64.6	14.5	63.2	28.5	25.1	27.2	53.7	32.5	60.6	15.0	65.5	27.9	24.7	26.7
1962	53.1	34.9	65.8	15.1	65.3	28.4	25.9	27.5	56.2	34.8	61.9	15.6	67.4	27.7	25.7	27.0
1963	55.2	36.5	66.2	15.6	66.8	28.3	26.5	27.7	58.1	36.4	62.6	16.1	68.8	27.7	26.2	27.2
1964	57.0	38.9	68.1	16.2	68.4	28.5	27.2	28.0	59.8	38.8	64.9	16.6	70.0	27.8	27.1	27.5
1965	59.1	41.6	70.4	16.8	69.8	28.5	28.3	28.4	61.7	41.6	67.4	17.2	71.2	27.8	28.0	27.9
1966	61.5	44.4	72.3	18.0	72.4	29.2	28.9	29.1	63.9	44.6	69.8	18.2	73.3	28.5	28.6	28.5
1967	62.8	45.3	72.1	19.0	74.3	30.2	29.4	29.9	65.0	45.3	69.7	19.3	75.3	29.6	29.1	29.4
1968	65.0	47.5	73.2	20.5	77.0	31.6	30.3	31.1	67.2	47.7	71.0	20.8	77.9	30.9	30.1	30.6
1969	65.3	49.0	75.0	22.0	78.1	33.6	30.7	32.5	67.3	49.2	73.0	22.2	78.9	32.9	30.3	32.0
1970	66.6	49.0	73.5	23.6	79.6	35.5	31.3	33.9	68.3	49.1	71.9	23.8	80.0	34.8	31.0	33.4
1971	69.3	50.8	73.3	25.1	81.0	36.2	33.9	35.4	71.1	51.0	71.7	25.3	81.5	35.6	33.5	34.8
1972	71.6	54.1	75.6	26.7	83.5	37.3	35.4	36.6	73.4	54.4	74.0	26.9	84.1	36.7	34.7	35.9
1973	73.7	57.9	78.5	29.0	85.2	39.3	37.3	38.5	75.7	58.3	77.0	29.1	85.6	38.4	35.1	37.2
1974	72.5	57.0	78.7	31.8	84.1	43.8	39.7	42.3	74.5	57.5	77.2	31.9	84.6	42.9	37.9	41.0
1975	75.1	56.5	75.3	35.0	85.0	46.6	46.0	46.4	76.6	56.6	73.9	35.2	85.4	45.9	44.6	45.4
1976	77.5	60.2	77.8	38.0	87.3	49.1	48.4	48.8	79.1	60.5	76.5	38.1	87.5	48.2	47.5	47.9
1977	78.8	63.6	80.7	41.1	88.5	52.1	51.2	51.8	80.4	63.9	79.5	41.2	88.9	51.3	50.4	51.0
1978	79.6	67.6	84.9	44.6	89.9	56.0	54.5	55.4	81.4	68.1	83.7	44.9	90.4	55.1	53.1	54.4
1979	79.6	69.8	87.7	48.9	89.9	61.4	58.0	60.1	81.1	70.2	86.6	49.1	90.2	60.5	56.3	59.0
1980	79.4	69.1	87.0	54.1	89.5	68.1	61.2	65.6	80.9	69.5	85.9	54.3	89.9	67.2	60.4	64.7
1981	81.1	71.0	87.6	59.2	89.5	73.1	69.1	71.6	82.0	71.0	86.6	59.6	90.0	72.7	67.8	70.9
1982	80.4	68.8	85.6	63.5	90.5	79.0	70.1	75.7	81.1	68.7	84.7	63.8	90.9	78.7	69.4	75.3
1983	83.3	72.5	87.1	66.1	90.3	79.4	76.4	78.3	84.7	73.1	86.3	66.5	90.9	78.5	76.2	77.7
1984	85.5	78.8	92.2	68.9	90.5	80.6	80.4	80.5	86.4	79.1	91.6	69.2	90.9	80.1	79.5	79.9
1985	87.5	82.5	94.3	72.1	91.6	82.5	82.4	82.4	87.8	82.5	94.0	72.3	91.8	82.3	81.9	82.2
1986	90.0	85.6	95.1	75.8	94.5	84.3	82.9	83.8	90.5	85.7	94.7	76.1	94.9	84.1	82.7	83.6
1987	90.3	88.4	97.9	78.6	94.8	87.1	83.7	85.8	90.8	88.6	97.6	78.8	95.1	86.8	83.4	85.6
1988	91.6	92.2	100.6	82.7	96.2	90.3	85.6	88.5	92.3	92.6	100.4	82.8	96.3	89.7	85.5	88.2
1989	92.6	95.6	103.3	84.9	94.7	91.7	91.9	91.8	93.0	95.9	103.1	84.9	94.7	91.3	91.5	91.4
1990	94.5	97.1	102.7	90.3	96.0	95.6	94.1	95.0	94.7	97.3	102.7	90.2	95.8	95.2	93.9	94.7
1991	96.0	96.2	100.2	95.0	97.4	98.9	96.7	98.1	96.2	96.4	100.2	94.9	97.3	98.7	96.9	98.1
1992	100.0	100.0	100.0	100.0	100.0	100.0	100.0	100.0	100.0	100.0	100.0	100.0	100.0	100.0	100.0	100.0
1993	100.5	103.2	102.7	102.2	99.8	101.7	102.4	102.0	100.6	103.5	102.9	102.0	99.6	101.4	102.9	102.0
1994	101.4	108.3	106.8	103.8	99.2	102.3	106.1	103.7	101.6	108.3	106.6	103.8	99.2	102.2	106.6	103.8
1995	101.5	111.3	109.7	105.9	98.8	104.4	107.6	105.6	102.0	111.8	109.6	106.0	98.9	103.9	108.7	105.7
1996	104.4	116.4	111.5	109.5	99.5	104.9	111.3	107.3	104.6	116.7	111.5	109.5	99.5	104.6	111.4	107.1
1997	106.3	122.4	115.2	113.1	100.6	106.4	113.3	109.0	106.2	122.6	115.4	112.9	100.4	106.3	114.0	109.1
1998	109.4	128.6	117.5	120.0	105.3	109.6	109.8	109.7	109.4	128.9	117.9	119.7	105.0	109.4	110.9	110.0
1999	113.3	135.7	119.8	125.4	107.8	110.7	110.5	110.6	113.0	136.1	120.5	124.8	107.3	110.5	112.0	111.0
2000	117.2	141.9	121.0	134.6	111.9	114.8	108.9	112.6	116.8	142.2	121.7	134.1	111.5	114.8	110.5	113.2
2001	120.7	143.0	118.4	140.9	114.0	116.7	111.0	114.6	120.2	143.4	119.3	140.1	113.3	116.5	112.6	115.1
2002	126.2	145.8	115.6	145.3	115.6	115.1	116.1	115.5	125.7	146.2	116.3	144.5	115.0	115.0	118.1	116.1
2003	131.0	150.3	114.7	152.3	118.6	116.2	118.7	117.1	130.3	150.6	115.5	151.4	117.9	116.2	120.1	117.6
2004	134.9	156.5	116.1	157.6	119.5	116.9	125.8	120.2	134.0	156.8	117.0	156.6	118.7	116.8	126.7	120.4
2005	137.2	161.8	118.0	163.8	120.2	119.5	131.9	124.1	136.2	162.0	118.9	162.8	119.4	119.5	133.6	124.7
2006	138.5	166.8	120.4	170.1	120.8	122.8	135.9	127.7	137.5	167.1	121.5	169.0	120.0	122.9	138.0	128.5
2007	141.0	170.5	120.9	177.3	122.4	125.7	140.0	131.0	140.1	171.0	122.1	176.1	121.6	125.7	141.4	131.5
2008	144.0	170.5	118.4	182.5	121.4	126.8	143.6	133.0	142.9	170.7	119.4	181.4	120.7	126.9	144.7	133.5
2009	149.4	164.5	110.1	186.0	124.2	124.5	150.8	134.3	148.3	164.6	110.9	185.0	123.5	124.7	153.2	135.2
2007																
1st quarter	139.0	168.4	121.1	175.2	122.7	126.0	136.7	130.0	138.3	168.8	122.1	174.3	122.1	126.0	138.2	130.5
2nd quarter	140.0	169.8	121.3	176.3	122.2	125.9	139.4	130.9	139.0	170.3	122.5	174.9	121.3	125.8	141.0	131.4
3rd quarter	142.0	171.4	120.7	177.7	122.5	125.1	141.9	131.4	141.0	172.0	122.0	176.2	121.5	125.0	143.3	131.7
4th quarter	142.8	172.3	120.6	179.9	122.3	126.0	141.9	131.9	142.0	172.8	121.7	178.8	121.5	125.9	142.9	132.2
2008																
1st quarter	142.8	171.7	120.3	180.3	121.2	126.3	141.7	132.1	141.8	172.0	121.3	179.3	120.5	126.4	142.5	132.3
2nd quarter	143.8	172.2	119.8	181.0	120.3	125.8	143.8	132.5	142.8	172.6	120.8	179.7	119.5	125.9	144.9	132.9
3rd quarter	144.3	170.6	118.2	183.6	120.3	127.2	145.3	134.0	143.2	170.8	119.3	182.4	119.5	127.4	146.5	134.4
4th quarter	145.0	167.4	115.4	185.4	124.1	127.8	143.4	133.6	144.0	167.5	116.3	184.4	123.5	128.1	145.1	134.3
2009																
1st quarter	145.3	163.6	112.6	183.5	123.6	126.2	148.0	134.3	144.3	163.7	113.4	182.5	122.9	126.4	150.3	135.2
2nd quarter	148.0	163.2	110.3	186.8	125.4	126.2	147.7	134.2	147.0	163.2	111.1	185.9	124.8	126.4	150.0	135.1
3rd quarter	150.9	164.1	108.7	186.8	124.3	123.8	151.9	134.3	149.8	164.1	109.6	185.7	123.6	124.0	154.6	135.2
4th quarter	153.6	167.1	108.8	187.1	123.4	121.8	155.3	134.3	152.3	167.2	109.7	186.0	122.7	122.1	157.5	135.1

Table 9-3. Productivity and Related Data—*Continued*

(1992 = 100, seasonally adjusted.)

Year and quarter	Nonfinancial corporations										Manufacturing					
	Output per hour of all employees	Output	Employee hours	Compensation per hour	Real compensation per hour	Unit costs			Unit profits	Implicit price deflator	Output per hour of all persons	Output	Hours of all persons	Compensation per hour	Real compensation per hour	Unit labor costs
						Total	Labor costs	Nonlabor costs								
1950	...	...	...	...	...	...	...	...	...	...	...	...	...	...	...	...
1951	...	...	...	...	...	...	...	...	...	...	...	...	...	...	...	...
1952	...	...	...	...	...	...	...	...	...	...	...	...	...	...	...	...
1953	...	...	...	...	...	...	...	...	...	...	...	...	...	...	...	...
1954	...	...	...	...	...	...	...	...	...	...	...	...	...	...	...	...
1955	...	...	...	...	...	...	...	...	...	...	...	...	...	...	...	...
1956	...	...	...	...	...	...	...	...	...	...	...	...	...	...	...	...
1957	...	...	...	...	...	...	...	...	...	...	...	...	...	...	...	...
1958	51.6	24.8	48.0	15.0	67.8	27.8	29.1	24.5	46.0	29.5	...	...	...	...	...	...
1959	54.2	27.6	50.9	15.6	69.9	27.3	28.7	23.5	53.6	29.7	...	...	...	...	...	...
1960	55.1	28.5	51.7	16.2	71.5	27.9	29.4	24.0	49.4	29.9	...	...	...	...	...	...
1961	56.9	29.2	51.3	16.7	73.0	28.1	29.4	24.4	49.5	30.0	...	...	...	...	...	...
1962	59.4	31.7	53.3	17.4	75.1	27.8	29.2	24.1	53.4	30.2	...	...	...	...	...	...
1963	61.6	33.6	54.5	17.9	76.4	27.7	29.1	23.9	56.5	30.3	...	...	...	...	...	...
1964	62.6	35.9	57.5	18.2	76.9	27.7	29.2	23.9	58.6	30.6	...	...	...	...	...	...
1965	64.1	38.9	60.7	18.8	77.8	27.8	29.3	23.7	63.0	31.0	...	...	...	...	...	...
1966	65.3	41.7	63.9	19.8	79.9	28.6	30.4	23.8	62.7	31.7	...	...	...	...	...	...
1967	66.3	42.8	64.6	20.9	81.9	29.9	31.6	25.3	58.6	32.5	...	...	...	...	...	...
1968	68.7	45.6	66.4	22.5	84.5	31.2	32.8	26.8	58.4	33.7	...	...	...	...	...	...
1969	68.8	47.5	69.0	24.1	85.6	33.3	34.9	29.0	52.9	35.1	...	...	...	...	...	...
1970	69.3	47.1	67.9	25.7	86.7	35.9	37.1	32.6	43.2	36.6	...	...	...	...	...	...
1971	72.3	49.0	67.8	27.3	88.2	36.9	37.8	34.2	48.8	38.0	...	...	...	...	...	...
1972	73.8	52.8	71.6	28.8	90.0	37.7	39.1	34.1	53.0	39.1	...	...	...	...	...	...
1973	74.5	56.0	75.2	31.0	91.3	40.1	41.6	36.0	53.6	41.3	...	...	...	...	...	...
1974	73.0	55.1	75.5	34.0	90.0	45.1	46.5	41.3	47.5	45.3	...	...	...	...	...	...
1975	75.8	54.3	71.7	37.3	90.6	48.6	49.2	47.0	61.5	49.8	...	...	...	...	...	...
1976	78.4	58.8	75.0	40.3	92.6	50.2	51.5	46.7	69.5	52.0	...	...	...	...	...	...
1977	80.5	63.1	78.4	43.5	93.9	52.6	54.1	48.4	75.9	54.7	...	...	...	...	...	...
1978	81.5	67.3	82.5	47.6	95.9	56.3	58.4	50.8	78.7	58.4	...	...	...	...	...	...
1979	80.8	69.3	85.8	51.9	95.4	61.8	64.2	55.4	73.9	62.9	...	...	...	...	...	...
1980	80.5	68.6	85.2	57.1	94.5	69.3	70.9	64.9	66.3	69.0	...	...	...	...	...	...
1981	82.6	71.3	86.4	62.2	94.0	75.0	75.4	73.9	79.0	75.4	...	...	...	...	...	...
1982	82.8	69.6	84.1	66.3	94.5	80.6	80.1	82.0	72.9	79.9	...	...	...	...	...	...
1983	85.4	72.9	85.3	68.8	94.0	81.0	80.5	82.2	88.6	81.7	...	...	...	...	...	...
1984	87.4	79.3	90.8	71.6	94.0	81.8	82.0	81.4	106.4	84.1	...	...	...	...	...	...
1985	89.2	82.8	92.9	74.8	95.0	83.8	83.9	83.6	101.8	85.5	...	...	...	...	...	...
1986	91.1	84.9	93.2	78.6	97.9	86.6	86.2	87.5	87.3	86.6	...	...	...	...	...	...
1987	93.0	89.3	96.1	81.2	97.9	87.1	87.3	86.6	98.3	88.1	89.1	92.4	103.8	80.6	97.2	90.5
1988	95.4	94.5	99.1	84.6	98.4	88.4	88.7	87.7	108.8	90.3	90.9	97.2	106.9	83.5	97.1	91.8
1989	94.0	96.0	102.2	86.7	96.6	92.5	92.2	93.3	99.7	93.2	91.9	98.8	107.6	86.0	95.9	93.6
1990	95.1	97.5	102.5	90.8	96.5	96.1	95.6	97.5	95.9	96.1	93.9	98.5	104.9	90.1	95.7	96.0
1991	97.4	97.0	99.6	95.4	97.8	99.2	97.9	102.6	94.4	98.7	96.3	96.8	100.5	95.5	97.9	99.1
1992	100.0	100.0	100.0	100.0	100.0	100.0	100.0	100.0	100.0	100.0	100.0	100.0	100.0	100.0	100.0	100.0
1993	100.2	102.6	102.4	101.8	99.3	101.0	101.6	99.3	114.4	102.2	102.6	103.9	101.3	102.3	100.0	99.7
1994	102.3	109.2	106.8	103.6	99.0	100.9	101.3	99.6	134.0	103.9	106.2	110.1	103.7	104.8	100.1	98.7
1995	103.4	114.4	110.6	105.4	98.4	101.5	102.0	100.0	139.0	104.9	111.0	115.9	104.4	106.5	99.3	95.9
1996	107.2	120.7	112.6	108.5	98.6	100.8	101.3	99.4	150.4	105.3	115.0	119.8	104.2	108.3	98.4	94.1
1997	110.0	128.6	116.9	111.9	99.5	101.1	101.7	99.4	154.0	105.9	121.3	128.7	106.0	110.9	98.7	91.4
1998	113.8	136.0	119.5	118.6	104.0	103.0	104.2	99.8	135.1	105.9	127.9	135.3	105.8	117.8	103.4	92.1
1999	117.8	143.9	122.2	123.8	106.4	104.3	105.1	102.2	125.2	106.2	133.7	140.4	105.1	123.0	105.7	92.0
2000	122.4	151.5	123.8	132.9	110.5	107.9	108.6	105.8	104.2	107.5	139.1	144.2	103.7	132.5	110.2	95.3
2001	123.5	148.7	120.4	137.3	111.0	111.5	111.2	112.3	84.0	109.0	141.2	136.9	96.9	137.5	111.2	97.4
2002	127.9	149.4	116.8	140.9	112.2	110.9	110.2	112.9	96.6	109.6	151.0	136.0	90.1	145.1	115.5	96.1
2003	133.0	153.1	115.1	147.3	114.7	111.3	110.8	112.7	107.3	110.9	160.4	137.3	85.6	156.7	122.0	97.7
2004	137.5	160.3	116.6	150.9	114.4	110.1	109.7	111.3	142.7	113.1	164.0	139.7	85.2	157.9	119.7	96.3
2005	141.0	167.3	118.6	155.7	114.2	111.8	110.4	115.4	161.1	116.3	171.9	144.8	84.3	163.2	119.7	94.9
2006	143.1	173.5	121.2	160.2	113.8	113.8	112.0	118.9	179.9	119.9	173.8	147.5	84.9	166.4	118.2	95.8
2007	144.5	176.5	122.1	166.0	114.6	117.8	114.9	125.8	162.1	121.9	179.2	149.5	83.4	173.5	119.9	96.9
2008	147.6	177.2	120.0	171.4	114.0	120.0	116.1	130.5	135.7	121.4	181.0	144.9	80.1	179.0	119.0	98.9
2009	...	...	...	...	...	...	...	...	...	...	184.2	128.9	70.0	186.9	124.7	101.5
2007																
1st quarter	143.6	175.1	122.0	164.3	115.1	116.8	114.4	123.1	171.2	121.8	176.8	148.0	83.7	172.7	121.0	97.7
2nd quarter	144.3	176.5	122.3	165.0	114.4	117.2	114.4	124.9	171.8	122.2	177.6	149.3	84.1	172.2	119.4	97.0
3rd quarter	144.0	175.8	122.1	166.1	114.5	119.0	115.3	127.4	155.6	122.0	180.1	150.3	83.4	172.9	119.2	96.0
4th quarter	146.2	178.5	122.1	168.6	114.6	119.0	115.3	127.9	149.9	121.6	182.3	150.4	82.5	176.3	119.9	96.7
2008																
1st quarter	145.0	176.9	122.0	168.7	113.4	120.0	116.3	129.1	133.0	121.0	182.7	149.9	82.1	175.6	118.0	96.1
2nd quarter	147.3	178.8	121.3	169.7	112.8	118.9	115.1	129.2	134.7	120.4	180.9	148.0	81.8	176.1	117.1	97.4
3rd quarter	149.1	178.4	119.7	172.4	112.9	119.4	115.6	129.8	145.3	121.8	180.7	144.4	79.9	179.2	117.4	99.2
4th quarter	149.2	174.6	117.0	175.0	117.2	121.8	117.3	134.1	129.5	122.5	179.5	137.2	76.5	185.4	124.1	103.3
2009																
1st quarter	146.6	166.6	113.7	173.2	116.6	123.8	118.1	139.1	127.5	124.1	178.2	129.1	72.4	185.0	124.6	103.8
2nd quarter	149.9	166.4	111.0	175.4	117.8	122.7	117.1	138.0	133.8	123.7	181.1	126.4	69.8	187.8	126.1	103.7
3rd quarter	151.3	165.7	109.5	175.9	117.0	121.5	116.3	135.7	140.0	123.2	187.4	129.1	68.9	187.4	124.7	100.0
4th quarter	...	...	...	...	...	...	...	...	...	...	190.4	130.9	68.7	187.3	123.6	98.4

. . . = Not available.

Section 9c: Returns and Profits by Industry

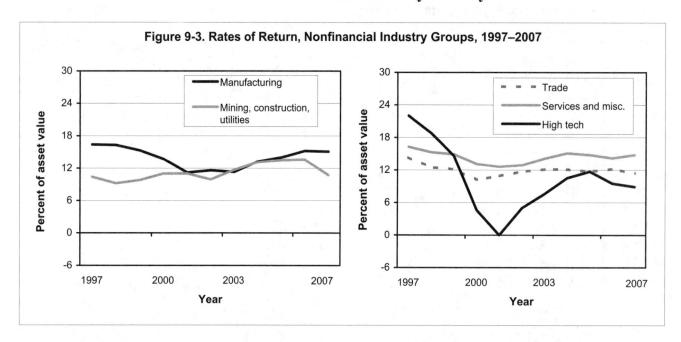

Figure 9-3. Rates of Return, Nonfinancial Industry Groups, 1997–2007

- Corporate profits reached a high point in 1997 and began to decline well before the business cycle peak in early 2001. However, by 2003, aggregate profits measures recovered to surpass their 1997 highs, and they continued to increase through 2006. Measuring between the high points for profits, profits of domestic industries as a share of gross domestic income increased from 9.3 percent in 1997 to 9.9 percent in 2006. But profits plunged 27 percent from 2006 to 2008, before beginning to recover in 2009. (Table 1-11)

- Rates of return on physical capital in nonfinancial industry groups are shown in Figure 9-3. The rate of return is the net operating surplus—the sum of corporate profits, net interest, transfer payments, and proprietors' income—as a percentage of the value of the net stock of capital plus inventories. The net operating surplus is a more comprehensive measure of the return to capital than corporate profits. As the figure indicates, rates of return generally declined from 1997 through 2001. Among the nonfinancial industry groups, only the mining, construction, and utilities group was above its 1997 rate as of 2006. (Table 9-4)

- The high-tech or "ICT-producing" industries—a small group of industries, one of which is a component of manufacturing and the rest of which are components of the services and miscellaneous group ("other" in BEA terminology)—had a more extreme swing, going from a 22 percent rate of return in 1997 to a loss in 2001, then only recovering to 11.7 percent in 2005. (Table 9-4)

- Comparable rate of return data are not available for financial industries, presumably because of greater difficulty in identifying and measuring the capital base. Aggregate profits of financial industries (leaving out the Federal Reserve System) rose an average 15.2 percent per year from 1998 to 2006, much faster than aggregate profits of nonfinancial industries, which rose at a 10.8 percent rate. Financial profits declined faster than nonfinancial profits from 2006 to 2008, but for the full 11-year period from 1998 to 2009, the rate of financial profits growth at 7.0 percent per year still outstripped the 4.7 percent rate for nonfinancial profits. (Tables 9-5 and 9-6)

Table 9-4. Rates of Return and Related Data for Major Nonfinancial Industry Groups, NAICS Basis

Year	Nonfinancial corporations	Nonfinancial industries					
		Total	Mining, construction, and utilities	Manufacturing	Wholesale and retail trade	Other industries [1]	ICT-producing industries [2]
NET OPERATING SURPLUS (Billions of dollars)							
1997	736.3	1 278.1	164.0	320.1	202.9	591.1	71.3
1998	717.4	1 257.5	151.7	331.3	188.1	586.4	65.8
1999	742.7	1 288.5	166.7	322.4	192.4	607.0	55.4
2000	716.5	1 243.7	194.5	300.2	174.2	574.9	19.2
2001	611.8	1 243.9	208.5	251.1	192.5	591.8	-3.2
2002	650.8	1 301.6	197.5	261.5	210.4	632.3	22.5
2003	709.2	1 435.7	240.4	255.1	225.3	714.9	33.8
2004	879.9	1 646.6	291.9	306.0	240.9	807.8	47.3
2005	1 013.5	1 784.7	341.4	342.2	250.2	850.9	54.7
2006	1 180.3	1 938.2	388.4	390.4	280.3	879.2	46.4
2007	1 115.5	1 987.6	328.8	404.8	279.5	974.5	45.6
2008	1 031.0	...	...	...	...	...	...
PRODUCED ASSETS, AVERAGE OF YEAR-END VALUES (Billions of dollars)							
1997	7 056.0	8 580.9	1 584.2	1 951.6	1 422.5	3 622.8	323.7
1998	7 419.0	9 011.4	1 649.8	2 030.7	1 500.7	3 830.3	349.3
1999	7 809.2	9 483.3	1 694.8	2 112.6	1 595.2	4 080.8	378.5
2000	8 295.2	10 074.4	1 776.0	2 195.8	1 702.5	4 400.3	417.5
2001	8 705.2	10 587.0	1 897.3	2 236.9	1 762.6	4 690.2	448.8
2002	8 950.8	10 919.2	1 985.8	2 247.2	1 801.0	4 885.2	451.8
2003	9 185.0	11 252.7	2 057.6	2 255.9	1 867.4	5 071.8	445.3
2004	9 682.7	11 896.2	2 231.8	2 314.1	1 985.6	5 364.1	452.2
2005	10 457.7	12 891.3	2 537.2	2 437.6	2 141.7	5 768.7	468.6
2006	11 256.7	13 930.6	2 854.3	2 566.5	2 300.6	6 203.8	489.4
2007	11 898.4	14 805.0	3 078.6	2 684.6	2 453.8	6 588.1	512.0
2008	12 717.1	...	...	...	...	...	...
RATES OF RETURN (Percent)							
1997	10.4	14.9	10.4	16.4	14.3	16.3	22.0
1998	9.7	14.0	9.2	16.3	12.5	15.3	18.8
1999	9.5	13.6	9.8	15.3	12.1	14.9	14.6
2000	8.6	12.3	11.0	13.7	10.2	13.1	4.6
2001	7.0	11.7	11.0	11.2	10.9	12.6	-0.7
2002	7.3	11.9	9.9	11.6	11.7	12.9	5.0
2003	7.7	12.8	11.7	11.3	12.1	14.1	7.6
2004	9.1	13.8	13.1	13.2	12.1	15.1	10.5
2005	9.7	13.8	13.5	14.0	11.7	14.8	11.7
2006	10.5	13.9	13.6	15.2	12.2	14.2	9.5
2007	9.4	13.4	10.7	15.1	11.4	14.8	8.9
2008	8.1	...	...	...	...	...	...
NET OPERATING SURPLUS AS A SHARE OF NET VALUE ADDED (Percent)							
1997	18.7	20.2	32.1	28.1	19.7	16.2	22.7
1998	17.2	22.0	28.8	27.8	17.5	20.1	18.9
1999	16.8	21.3	29.2	26.5	16.9	19.4	14.5
2000	15.2	19.5	30.6	23.8	14.8	17.4	4.6
2001	13.2	19.3	31.2	21.5	15.8	17.4	-0.9
2002	13.8	19.7	29.4	22.2	16.8	18.0	6.2
2003	14.5	20.7	32.9	21.4	17.3	19.3	9.2
2004	16.7	22.2	35.9	24.3	17.6	20.3	12.3
2005	17.9	22.6	37.7	26.3	17.3	20.0	13.2
2006	19.4	22.9	38.8	27.4	18.1	19.6	10.6
2007	17.8	22.7	33.8	28.6	18.2	20.2	10.1
2008	16.4	...	...	...	...	...	...

[1]Consists of agriculture, forestry, fishing and hunting; transportation and warehousing; information; rental and leasing services and lessors of intangible assets; professional, scientific, and technical services; administrative and waste management services; educational services; health care and social assistance; arts, entertainment, and recreation; accommodation and food services; and "other services, except government."
[2]Information-communication-technology (ICT) producing industries consists of computer and electronic products; publishing industries (includes software); information and data processing services; and computer systems design and related services. Computer and electronic products are included in manufacturing; the other ICT-producing industries are included in "other" industries.
. . . = Not available.

Table 9-5. Corporate Profits with Inventory Valuation Adjustment by Industry Group, NAICS Basis

NIPA Table 6.16D

(Billions of dollars, quarterly data are at seasonally adjusted annual rates.)

Year and quarter	Total	Domestic industries												
		Financial			Nonfinancial								
		Total	Federal Reserve banks	Other financial	Total	Utilities	Manufacturing						
							Total	Durable goods					
								Fabricated metal products	Machinery	Computer and electronic products	Electrical equipment, appliances, and components	Motor vehicles, bodies and trailers, and parts	Other durable goods
1998	738.6	635.9	25.6	133.9	476.4	33.5	155.8	16.4	15.3	4.2	6.2	6.4	34.2
1999	776.6	655.0	26.7	162.6	465.7	33.7	148.8	16.4	11.7	-6.8	6.4	7.7	35.9
2000	755.7	610.0	31.2	158.4	420.4	25.6	143.9	15.8	7.7	4.2	5.9	-0.7	27.1
2001	720.8	551.1	28.9	199.1	323.1	25.2	49.7	9.8	2.0	-48.6	1.9	-8.9	16.8
2002	762.8	604.9	23.5	241.7	339.7	12.3	47.7	9.1	1.4	-34.4	0.0	-4.5	20.7
2003	892.2	726.4	20.1	291.8	414.6	12.4	69.4	8.0	1.0	-14.7	2.2	-11.7	10.8
2004	1 195.1	990.1	20.0	342.3	627.8	19.4	154.1	12.2	7.1	-4.3	0.6	-6.8	31.9
2005	1 609.5	1 370.0	26.6	417.0	926.4	29.8	247.2	18.1	14.5	9.0	-1.4	1.1	54.2
2006	1 784.7	1 527.8	33.8	414.1	1 079.9	54.4	304.5	18.7	19.2	17.4	11.5	-6.8	58.9
2007	1 730.4	1 382.6	37.7	330.1	1 014.9	49.1	278.6	21.3	19.8	11.2	-1.1	-16.4	61.3
2008	1 424.5	1 047.3	35.7	243.2	768.4	40.1	175.5	17.6	16.1	4.7	-4.1	-47.5	43.9
2009	1 436.7	1 124.9	50.1	281.1	793.7	54.1	136.0	13.4	11.0	3.6	-8.5	-28.4	23.8
2007													
1st quarter	1 705.4	1 423.2	38.2	346.0	1 039.0	51.3	288.9	19.1	20.0	17.0	3.5	-15.1	61.4
2nd quarter	1 779.1	1 467.9	38.5	367.7	1 061.7	46.6	316.0	20.6	21.0	10.5	-2.1	-8.7	59.3
3rd quarter	1 732.9	1 362.4	37.5	340.6	984.2	47.3	244.0	22.5	19.3	11.6	-4.5	-24.9	60.9
4th quarter	1 704.1	1 277.0	36.5	266.0	974.5	51.2	265.7	23.0	19.0	5.5	-1.4	-17.0	63.7
2008													
1st quarter	1 512.9	1 100.6	35.9	321.1	743.6	33.1	187.6	18.5	17.1	14.5	-3.6	-35.3	49.8
2nd quarter	1 463.8	1 096.8	31.1	299.7	766.0	43.1	160.1	14.9	13.1	2.0	-2.0	-55.7	47.4
3rd quarter	1 522.2	1 125.0	34.6	262.9	827.5	43.5	205.7	17.7	14.6	0.1	-2.6	-45.4	56.2
4th quarter	1 199.3	866.9	41.1	89.2	736.6	40.8	148.6	19.2	19.6	2.2	-8.4	-53.4	22.3
2009													
1st quarter	1 327.6	1 011.9	28.8	225.1	758.0	53.6	121.6	19.3	12.8	3.2	-6.3	-54.8	33.9
2nd quarter	1 355.1	1 053.9	46.1	234.6	773.3	53.4	132.3	13.7	10.4	3.9	-9.1	-38.5	31.5
3rd quarter	1 477.8	1 154.6	57.6	304.8	792.2	61.5	129.7	10.9	8.1	3.1	-9.6	-16.6	10.8
4th quarter	1 586.3	1 279.2	67.9	359.9	851.4	47.8	160.5	10.0	12.7	4.2	-9.0	-3.7	18.9

Year and quarter	Domestic industries—Continued										Rest of the world, net
	Nonfinancial—Continued										
	Manufacturing—Continued										
	Nondurable goods					Wholesale trade	Retail trade	Transportation and warehousing	Information	Other nonfinancial	
	Total	Food and beverage and tobacco products	Petroleum and coal products	Chemical products	Other nondurable goods						
1998	73.1	22.1	5.3	25.0	20.7	52.8	67.3	21.3	21.9	123.7	102.8
1999	77.6	30.9	2.2	22.8	21.7	54.8	65.7	16.5	12.5	133.6	121.5
2000	83.9	26.0	27.6	13.8	16.5	58.7	60.7	15.2	-15.5	131.8	145.6
2001	76.6	28.2	29.7	11.6	7.1	51.3	72.6	1.2	-24.4	147.4	169.7
2002	55.4	25.3	1.3	17.8	11.0	49.1	81.6	-0.1	-3.8	153.0	157.9
2003	73.8	24.0	23.5	18.9	7.4	54.8	88.9	7.4	4.9	176.7	165.8
2004	113.4	24.3	49.1	24.7	15.3	75.6	93.4	14.4	45.6	225.2	205.0
2005	151.7	27.3	79.4	25.7	19.3	92.2	122.6	29.0	81.3	324.3	239.4
2006	185.7	32.5	76.6	52.5	24.0	103.7	133.2	42.1	92.4	349.6	256.8
2007	182.6	30.2	77.8	51.9	22.7	102.2	121.6	30.0	90.3	343.0	347.8
2008	144.9	33.7	66.5	31.3	13.3	75.1	78.2	11.4	84.7	303.4	377.2
2009	121.1	33.1	21.4	35.9	30.7	87.9	91.2	5.9	108.9	309.7	311.8
2007											
1st quarter	183.0	28.2	78.0	52.4	24.3	107.9	127.9	32.9	90.5	339.6	282.2
2nd quarter	215.4	33.5	110.9	50.2	20.8	117.0	137.2	33.0	77.5	334.4	311.2
3rd quarter	159.1	29.3	64.8	42.6	22.5	107.9	118.7	30.9	93.9	341.5	370.5
4th quarter	172.9	29.8	57.5	62.4	23.2	76.0	102.4	23.4	99.4	356.4	427.1
2008											
1st quarter	126.6	29.2	64.5	16.4	16.6	46.6	75.6	12.9	91.6	296.3	412.3
2nd quarter	140.5	37.1	42.5	48.2	12.7	56.6	80.2	11.9	101.8	312.1	367.0
3rd quarter	165.2	37.3	79.3	39.1	9.5	85.8	77.1	9.2	81.9	324.4	397.2
4th quarter	147.1	31.3	79.7	21.7	14.4	111.5	79.7	11.5	63.6	280.8	332.4
2009											
1st quarter	113.6	34.7	29.4	29.6	19.8	94.0	83.1	6.7	95.4	303.6	315.8
2nd quarter	120.4	33.1	15.2	39.4	32.8	87.5	95.1	1.3	99.4	304.2	301.2
3rd quarter	122.9	35.1	15.8	37.4	34.5	80.6	98.8	4.8	107.0	309.9	323.2
4th quarter	127.6	29.4	25.3	37.3	35.7	89.5	87.8	10.8	133.9	321.0	307.1

Table 9-6. Corporate Profits with Inventory Valuation Adjustment by Industry Group, SIC Basis

(Billions of dollars, quarterly data are at seasonally adjusted rates.)

NIPA Tables 6.16B, 6.16C

Column groups: **Domestic industries** = Financial + Nonfinancial. **Financial** = Total, Federal Reserve banks, Other financial. **Nonfinancial** = Total, Manufacturing. **Manufacturing** = Total, Durable goods. **Durable goods** = Primary metal industries, Fabricated metal products, Industrial machinery and equipment, Electronic and other electric equipment, Motor vehicles and equipment, Other durable goods.

Classification basis, year, and quarter	Total	Financial: Total	Financial: Federal Reserve banks	Financial: Other financial	Nonfinancial: Total	Mfg: Total	Durable: Primary metal industries	Durable: Fabricated metal products	Durable: Industrial machinery and equipment	Durable: Electronic and other electric equipment	Durable: Motor vehicles and equipment	Durable: Other durable goods
1972 SIC Basis												
1948	33.7	32.5	0.2	2.5	29.7	17.5	1.6	0.8	1.3	0.6	1.4	1.8
1949	31.5	30.3	0.2	3.1	27.0	16.2	1.5	0.7	1.3	0.8	2.1	1.7
1950	38.3	37.0	0.2	3.1	33.7	21.0	2.3	1.1	1.6	1.2	3.1	2.6
1951	43.6	41.8	0.3	3.4	38.1	24.7	3.1	1.3	2.3	1.3	2.4	2.8
1952	41.2	39.3	0.3	4.1	34.9	21.7	1.9	1.0	2.3	1.5	2.4	2.6
1953	40.7	38.9	0.4	4.4	34.0	22.0	2.5	1.0	1.9	1.4	2.6	2.6
1954	39.0	37.1	0.3	4.8	32.0	19.9	1.7	0.9	1.7	1.2	2.1	2.9
1955	48.1	45.8	0.3	5.0	40.5	26.1	2.9	1.1	1.7	1.1	4.1	3.5
1956	47.8	44.9	0.5	5.2	39.3	24.8	3.0	1.1	2.1	1.2	2.2	3.1
1957	47.5	44.4	0.6	5.4	38.5	24.1	3.1	1.1	2.0	1.5	2.6	3.1
1958	42.7	40.2	0.6	5.9	33.7	19.5	1.9	0.9	1.5	1.3	0.9	3.1
1959	53.5	50.8	0.7	6.9	43.2	26.5	2.3	1.1	2.2	1.7	3.0	3.5
1960	51.5	48.3	0.9	7.5	39.9	23.8	2.0	0.8	1.8	1.3	3.0	2.7
1961	51.8	48.5	0.8	7.6	40.2	23.4	1.6	1.0	1.9	1.3	2.5	2.9
1962	57.0	53.3	0.9	7.7	44.7	26.3	1.6	1.2	2.4	1.5	4.0	3.4
1963	62.1	58.1	1.0	7.3	49.8	29.7	2.0	1.3	2.6	1.6	4.9	4.0
1964	68.6	64.1	1.1	7.6	55.4	32.6	2.5	1.5	3.3	1.7	4.6	4.4
1965	78.9	74.2	1.3	8.0	64.9	39.8	3.1	2.1	4.0	2.7	6.2	5.2
1966	84.6	80.1	1.7	9.1	69.3	42.6	3.6	2.4	4.6	3.0	5.2	5.2
1967	82.0	77.2	2.0	9.2	66.0	39.2	2.7	2.5	4.2	3.0	4.0	4.9
1968	88.8	83.2	2.5	10.3	70.4	41.9	1.9	2.3	4.2	2.9	5.5	5.6
1969	85.5	78.9	3.1	10.5	65.3	37.3	1.4	2.0	3.8	2.3	4.8	4.9
1970	74.4	67.3	3.5	11.9	52.0	27.5	0.8	1.1	3.1	1.3	1.3	2.9
1971	88.3	80.4	3.3	14.3	62.8	35.1	0.8	1.5	3.1	2.0	5.2	4.1
1972	101.2	91.7	3.3	15.8	72.6	41.9	1.7	2.2	4.5	2.9	6.0	5.6
1973	115.3	100.4	4.5	16.0	79.9	47.2	2.3	2.7	4.9	3.2	5.9	6.2
1974	109.5	92.1	5.7	14.5	71.9	41.4	5.0	1.8	3.3	0.6	0.7	4.0
1975	135.0	120.4	5.6	14.6	100.2	55.2	2.8	3.3	5.1	2.6	2.3	4.7
1976	165.6	149.0	5.9	19.1	124.1	71.3	2.1	3.9	6.9	3.8	7.4	7.3
1977	194.7	175.6	6.1	25.8	143.7	79.3	1.0	4.5	8.6	5.9	9.4	8.5
1978	222.4	199.6	7.6	31.9	160.0	90.5	3.6	5.0	10.7	6.7	9.0	10.5
1979	231.8	197.2	9.4	30.9	156.8	89.6	3.5	5.3	9.5	5.6	4.7	8.5
1980	211.4	175.9	11.8	22.2	141.9	78.3	2.7	4.4	8.0	5.2	-4.3	2.7
1981	219.1	189.4	14.4	14.7	160.3	91.1	3.1	4.5	9.0	5.2	0.3	-2.6
1982	191.0	158.5	15.2	10.8	132.4	67.1	-4.7	2.7	3.1	1.7	0.0	2.1
1983	226.5	191.4	14.6	20.9	155.9	76.2	-4.9	3.1	4.0	3.5	5.3	8.4
1984	264.6	228.1	16.4	18.0	193.7	91.8	-0.4	4.7	6.0	5.1	9.2	14.6
1985	257.5	219.4	16.3	29.5	173.5	84.3	-0.9	4.9	5.7	2.6	7.4	10.1
1986	253.0	213.5	15.5	41.2	156.8	57.9	0.9	5.2	0.8	2.7	4.6	12.1
1987	301.4	253.4	15.7	44.1	193.5	86.3	2.6	5.5	5.4	5.9	3.7	17.6
1987 SIC Basis												
1987	301.4	253.4	15.7	44.1	193.5	86.3	2.6	5.5	5.4	5.9	3.7	17.6
1988	363.9	306.9	17.6	51.1	238.2	121.2	6.0	6.5	11.1	7.7	6.2	16.5
1989	367.4	300.3	20.2	57.8	222.3	110.9	6.4	6.4	12.2	9.3	2.7	14.2
1990	396.6	320.5	21.4	73.0	226.1	113.1	3.5	6.0	11.8	8.5	-1.9	15.9
1991	427.9	351.4	20.3	103.9	227.3	98.0	1.5	5.3	5.7	10.0	-5.4	17.3
1992	458.3	385.2	17.8	111.9	255.4	99.5	0.0	6.2	7.5	10.4	-1.0	17.4
1993	513.1	436.1	16.2	120.6	299.3	115.6	0.4	7.4	7.5	15.2	6.0	19.4
1994	564.6	487.6	18.1	101.8	367.7	147.0	2.3	11.1	9.1	22.8	7.8	21.3
1995	656.0	563.2	22.5	139.7	401.0	173.7	7.1	11.8	14.8	21.5	0.0	25.8
1996	736.1	634.2	22.1	150.5	461.6	188.8	5.6	14.5	16.9	20.1	4.2	29.2
1997	812.3	701.4	23.8	169.2	508.4	209.0	6.3	17.0	16.7	25.3	4.8	33.0
1998	738.5	635.5	25.2	140.7	469.6	173.5	6.5	16.4	19.5	8.9	5.9	30.1
1999	776.8	655.3	26.3	170.1	458.9	175.2	2.4	16.2	12.4	5.3	7.3	35.3
2000	759.3	613.6	30.8	173.0	409.8	166.3	1.2	15.4	16.3	4.7	-1.5	28.8
1998												
1st quarter	752.0	643.1	25.0	147.9	470.2	178.5	6.9	14.9	14.4	12.2	6.4	28.8
2nd quarter	732.5	626.3	25.2	136.4	464.7	170.1	6.2	16.7	19.5	8.3	3.5	27.4
3rd quarter	743.5	647.3	25.4	136.9	485.0	176.6	6.1	18.5	20.4	6.6	4.5	31.3
4th quarter	725.9	625.3	25.1	141.8	458.4	168.8	6.8	15.7	23.7	8.3	9.3	32.9
1999												
1st quarter	771.3	657.3	24.9	163.0	469.5	175.0	3.8	15.9	9.8	4.3	8.9	33.9
2nd quarter	773.2	656.5	25.5	157.8	473.2	182.5	3.1	15.7	12.8	4.9	6.1	37.8
3rd quarter	766.8	648.3	26.2	175.3	446.8	174.2	1.5	16.2	12.3	6.9	7.3	34.3
4th quarter	796.1	659.1	28.6	184.5	446.0	169.1	1.2	17.1	14.7	4.9	6.7	35.3
2000												
1st quarter	766.8	635.7	30.0	179.5	426.2	172.6	2.1	18.8	12.6	2.5	1.2	33.3
2nd quarter	773.5	634.9	30.5	164.5	440.0	186.1	2.0	16.2	16.1	8.7	0.3	33.7
3rd quarter	756.3	611.7	31.1	171.1	409.5	164.9	0.5	15.2	16.1	3.4	-2.4	27.3
4th quarter	740.7	572.1	31.7	176.8	363.6	141.6	0.3	11.3	18.1	4.1	-5.2	21.0

Table 9-6. Corporate Profits with Inventory Valuation Adjustment by Industry Group, SIC Basis
—Continued

(Billions of dollars, quarterly data are at seasonally adjusted rates.)   **NIPA Tables 6.16B, 6.16C**

	Domestic industries—Continued												Rest of the world
	Nonfinancial—Continued												
	Manufacturing—Continued					Transportation and public utilities							
Classification basis, year, and quarter	Nondurable goods									Wholesale trade	Retail trade	Other nonfinancial	
	Total	Food and kindred products	Chemicals and allied products	Petroleum and coal products	Other nondurable goods	Total	Transportation	Communications	Electric, gas, and sanitary services				
1972 SIC Basis													
1948	10.0	1.9	1.7	2.8	3.7	3.0	1.5	0.4	1.1	2.4	3.2	3.5	1.3
1949	8.1	1.6	1.8	1.9	2.8	3.0	1.2	0.5	1.4	1.9	2.8	3.1	1.1
1950	9.0	1.6	2.3	2.3	2.7	4.1	1.9	0.7	1.5	2.1	3.0	3.5	1.3
1951	11.4	1.4	2.8	2.8	4.4	4.7	1.9	1.0	1.8	2.6	2.6	3.6	1.7
1952	10.0	1.8	2.3	2.3	3.6	5.0	1.9	1.1	2.0	2.3	2.7	3.3	1.9
1953	10.0	1.8	2.2	2.7	3.3	5.0	1.6	1.2	2.2	1.8	2.3	3.0	1.8
1954	9.5	1.6	2.2	2.8	2.9	4.7	1.0	1.3	2.4	1.7	2.3	3.3	2.0
1955	11.8	2.2	3.0	3.0	3.6	5.7	1.5	1.7	2.5	2.4	2.9	3.5	2.4
1956	12.0	1.8	2.8	3.3	4.1	5.9	1.4	1.8	2.7	2.2	2.6	3.9	2.8
1957	10.8	1.8	2.8	2.6	3.6	5.9	1.1	2.0	2.7	2.2	2.6	3.8	3.1
1958	10.2	2.1	2.5	2.1	3.4	5.9	0.9	2.3	2.7	2.2	2.6	3.5	2.5
1959	12.9	2.5	3.5	2.6	4.3	7.1	1.1	2.8	3.1	2.9	3.3	3.4	2.7
1960	12.2	2.2	3.1	2.6	4.2	7.5	0.9	3.0	3.6	2.5	2.8	3.3	3.1
1961	12.1	2.4	3.3	2.3	4.2	7.9	1.0	3.2	3.7	2.5	3.0	3.4	3.3
1962	12.3	2.4	3.2	2.2	4.4	8.5	1.0	3.6	3.9	2.8	3.4	3.6	3.8
1963	13.3	2.7	3.7	2.2	4.7	9.5	1.4	3.9	4.2	2.8	3.6	4.1	4.1
1964	14.5	2.7	4.1	2.4	5.3	10.2	1.6	4.0	4.6	3.4	4.5	4.7	4.5
1965	16.5	2.9	4.6	2.9	6.1	11.0	2.1	4.3	4.6	3.8	4.9	5.4	4.7
1966	18.6	3.3	4.9	3.4	6.9	12.0	2.3	4.8	4.9	4.0	4.9	5.9	4.5
1967	18.0	3.3	4.3	4.0	6.4	10.9	1.3	4.8	4.8	4.1	5.7	6.1	4.8
1968	19.4	3.2	5.3	3.8	7.1	11.0	1.0	5.1	4.9	4.6	6.4	6.6	5.6
1969	18.1	3.1	4.6	3.4	7.0	10.7	0.7	5.4	4.6	4.9	6.4	6.1	6.6
1970	17.0	3.2	3.9	3.7	6.1	8.3	-0.1	4.8	3.6	4.4	6.0	5.8	7.1
1971	18.5	3.6	4.5	3.8	6.6	8.9	0.7	4.1	4.1	5.2	7.2	6.4	7.9
1972	19.2	3.0	5.3	3.3	7.6	9.5	1.5	3.9	4.0	6.9	7.4	7.0	9.5
1973	22.0	2.5	6.2	5.4	7.9	9.1	1.3	4.3	3.4	8.2	6.6	8.7	14.9
1974	26.1	2.6	5.3	10.9	7.3	7.6	2.0	4.1	1.5	11.5	2.3	9.1	17.5
1975	34.5	8.6	6.4	10.1	9.5	11.0	1.0	4.3	5.7	13.8	8.2	12.0	14.6
1976	39.9	7.1	8.2	13.5	11.1	15.3	3.0	5.7	6.5	12.9	10.5	14.0	16.5
1977	41.4	6.9	7.8	13.1	13.6	18.6	3.7	6.6	8.3	15.6	12.4	17.8	19.1
1978	45.1	6.2	8.3	15.8	14.8	21.8	4.1	8.6	9.1	15.6	12.3	19.8	22.9
1979	52.5	5.8	7.2	24.8	14.7	17.0	3.5	7.5	6.0	18.8	9.8	21.6	34.6
1980	59.5	6.1	5.7	34.7	13.1	18.4	2.7	7.7	8.0	17.2	6.2	21.8	35.5
1981	71.6	9.2	8.0	40.0	14.5	20.3	1.7	8.6	10.0	22.4	9.9	16.7	29.7
1982	62.1	7.3	5.1	34.7	15.0	23.1	-0.1	8.6	14.6	19.6	13.4	9.2	32.6
1983	56.7	6.3	7.4	23.9	19.1	29.5	3.2	9.9	16.4	21.0	18.7	10.4	35.1
1984	52.6	6.8	8.2	17.6	20.1	40.1	6.1	12.8	21.3	29.5	21.1	11.1	36.6
1985	54.6	8.8	6.6	18.7	20.5	33.8	1.8	14.2	17.8	23.9	22.2	9.2	38.1
1986	31.7	7.5	7.5	-4.7	21.3	35.8	3.4	17.6	14.7	24.1	23.5	15.5	39.5
1987	45.6	11.4	14.4	-1.5	21.3	41.9	3.4	19.4	19.1	18.6	23.4	23.4	48.0
1987 SIC Basis													
1987	45.6	11.4	14.4	-1.5	21.3	41.9	3.4	19.4	19.1	18.6	23.4	23.4	48.0
1988	67.1	12.0	18.6	12.7	23.7	48.4	7.9	19.5	21.1	20.1	20.3	28.3	57.0
1989	59.7	11.1	18.2	6.5	23.9	43.3	1.3	18.2	23.9	21.8	20.8	25.5	67.1
1990	69.2	14.3	16.8	16.4	21.7	44.2	-0.4	20.1	24.5	19.2	20.7	29.0	76.1
1991	63.6	18.1	16.2	7.3	22.0	53.3	2.3	23.5	27.5	21.7	26.7	27.5	76.5
1992	59.0	18.2	16.0	-0.9	25.6	58.4	2.3	27.7	28.4	25.1	32.6	39.7	73.1
1993	59.7	16.4	15.9	2.7	24.7	69.5	7.0	32.9	29.6	26.3	39.1	48.9	76.9
1994	72.6	19.9	23.2	1.2	28.3	83.2	10.5	36.7	36.1	30.9	46.2	60.4	77.1
1995	92.8	27.1	27.9	7.1	30.6	85.8	11.5	33.6	40.8	27.3	43.1	71.2	92.8
1996	98.2	22.1	26.4	15.0	34.7	91.3	15.7	35.0	40.7	39.8	51.9	89.7	101.9
1997	105.9	24.6	32.3	17.3	31.7	84.2	19.0	25.5	39.7	47.6	64.2	103.4	110.9
1998	86.2	21.9	26.5	6.7	31.1	78.9	21.6	21.4	35.8	52.3	73.4	91.5	103.0
1999	96.4	28.1	25.2	4.3	38.9	56.8	15.8	4.6	36.3	52.6	74.6	99.7	121.5
2000	101.5	25.7	16.0	29.1	30.7	43.8	15.2	1.3	27.3	56.9	70.1	72.8	145.7
1998													
1st quarter	94.9	23.6	30.5	9.4	31.3	76.8	20.6	22.1	34.1	50.2	71.3	93.4	108.8
2nd quarter	88.5	24.6	22.9	8.9	32.1	81.0	21.5	24.0	35.5	52.6	72.5	88.6	106.2
3rd quarter	89.2	25.8	24.9	7.3	31.3	86.7	24.2	25.1	37.4	57.5	73.8	90.4	96.2
4th quarter	72.0	13.6	27.6	1.3	29.6	71.0	20.3	14.5	36.3	48.8	76.0	93.8	100.5
1999													
1st quarter	98.5	28.5	31.8	0.6	37.6	62.6	16.8	9.2	36.6	54.8	79.4	97.7	113.9
2nd quarter	102.1	28.6	31.8	4.0	37.7	52.1	16.0	3.4	32.8	53.1	79.0	106.6	116.6
3rd quarter	95.8	27.0	22.1	8.2	38.5	52.5	13.5	1.3	37.6	49.3	69.6	101.2	118.5
4th quarter	89.1	28.2	14.9	4.4	41.6	59.9	17.0	4.5	38.4	53.3	70.5	93.2	137.0
2000													
1st quarter	102.1	28.3	20.0	15.3	38.6	47.5	14.7	-0.3	33.0	52.4	75.5	78.3	131.1
2nd quarter	109.2	25.4	17.4	33.8	32.7	42.4	19.4	-3.4	26.4	63.2	70.8	77.4	138.5
3rd quarter	102.8	28.2	13.3	33.9	27.4	43.2	15.7	0.4	27.1	62.9	70.3	68.3	144.6
4th quarter	91.9	21.0	13.2	33.4	24.3	42.2	11.2	8.4	22.6	48.9	63.9	67.0	168.6

NOTES AND DEFINITIONS, CHAPTER 9

General note on data on compensation per hour

This chapter includes two data series with similar names—the Employment Cost Index for total compensation and the index of compensation per hour—that often display different behavior. Both are compiled and published by the Bureau of Labor Statistics (BLS), but the definitions, sources, and methods of compilation are different. Users should be aware of these differences and of the consequent differences in the appropriate uses and interpretations for each of the two series.

The *Employment Cost Index (ECI)* (Tables 9-1 and 9-2) measures changes in hourly compensation for "all civilian workers", which is not quite as broad as it sounds, as it excludes federal government workers, farm workers, and private household workers. Indexes are also published for subgroups including state and local workers, "all private industry" (again excluding farm and private household workers), and a number of industry and occupational subgroups.

The ECI is calculated and published separately for *total compensation* and for the two major components of hourly compensation, *wages and salaries* and the employer cost of employee *benefits*. It is constructed by analogy with the Consumer Price Index (CPI); that is, it holds the composition of employment constant in order to isolate hourly compensation trends that take place for individual occupations, which are then aggregated, using relative importance weights. The ECI is based on a sample survey and may be revised from time to time, due to updated classification, weighting, and seasonal adjustments. However, it is not subject to major benchmark revision of the underlying wage, salary, and benefit rate observations. By design, it excludes any representation of employee stock options. As it is based on a sample survey, the ECI is measured "from the bottom up," aggregating from individual employers' reports to higher levels. The ECI is frequently and appropriately used as the best available measure of the general trend of wages and of the extent of inflationary pressure exerted on prices by labor costs.

The *compensation per hour* component of the report on "Productivity and Costs" (Table 9-3) is calculated and published for total compensation in total business, nonfarm business, nonfinancial corporations, and manufacturing. The nonfarm business category is similar in scope to the "all private industry" category in the ECI. The measures in Table 9-3, however, are compiled "from the top down," starting with aggregate estimates of compensation and hours, then dividing the former by the latter. Compensation per hour is affected by changes in the composition of employment. If the composition of employment shifts toward higher-paid employees and/or industries, compensation per hour will rise even if there is no increase in hourly compensation for any individual worker.

In addition, *compensation per hour* includes the value of exercised stock options as expensed by companies. Also included are other transitory payments, many of which may be of little relevance to the typical worker or to ongoing production costs. These values are not reported immediately. Instead, they are incorporated when later, more comprehensive reports are received. This process can lead to dramatic revisions in compensation per hour and in the unit labor costs index, which is based on compensation. For example, the fourth-quarter 2004 increase in compensation per hour in nonfarm business was initially reported at an annual rate of 3.1 percent. Four months later, the reported rate for the same time period was 10.2 percent. The rate of increase from a year earlier was revised from 3.6 to 5.9 percent. According to then-Federal Reserve Chairman Alan Greenspan, in testimony before the Joint Economic Committee on June 9, 2005, this reflected "a large but apparently transitory surge in bonuses and the proceeds of stock option exercises," not a potentially inflationary acceleration in the rate of labor compensation increase. More recently, it was reported in August 2009 that "first-quarter unit labor costs were revised to negative 2.7% from positive 3%." (*Wall Street Journal,* August 12, 2009, p. A2.)

These characteristics suggest that *compensation per hour* should not be considered a reliable or appropriate indicator of wage or compensation trends for typical workers. It is useful in conjunction with the productivity series, because aggregate productivity is subject to the same composition shifts—higher-productivity industries also tend to have higher-paid employees. Hence, the measure of *unit labor costs* (derived by dividing compensation per hour by output per hour in this system) is not distorted when the composition of output shifts toward higher-productivity industries. The shift affects the numerator and denominator of the ratio similarly. However, both compensation and unit labor costs can still be distorted by transitory payments, such as those discussed above.

There are other, probably less important differences between the two measures. Compensation per hour refers to the entire quarter, while the ECI is observed in the terminal month of each quarter. Tips and other forms of compensation not provided by employers are included in hourly compensation but not in the ECI. The ECI excludes persons working for token wages, business owners and others who set their own wage, and family workers who do not earn a market wage; all of these workers are included in the productivity and cost accounts. Hourly compensation excludes employees of nonprofit institutions serving individuals—about 10 percent of private workers (mostly in education and medical care) who are within the scope of the ECI. Hourly compensation measures include an estimate for the unincorporated self-employed, who are assumed to earn the same hourly compensation as other employees in the sector. Implicitly, unpaid family workers also are included in the hourly compensation measures with the assumption that their hourly compensation is zero. Both of these groups are also excluded from the ECI.

TABLES 9-1 AND 9-2
EMPLOYMENT COST INDEXES

SOURCE: U.S. DEPARTMENT OF LABOR, BUREAU OF LABOR STATISTICS (BLS)

The Employment Cost Index (ECI) is a quarterly measure of the change in the cost of labor, independent of the influence of employment shifts among occupations and industries. It uses a fixed market basket of labor—similar in concept to the Consumer Price Index's fixed market basket of goods and services—to measure changes over time in employer costs of employing labor. Data are quarterly in all cases and are reported for the final month of each quarter. These measures are expressed as indexes, with the not-seasonally-adjusted value for December 2005 set at 100.

Care should be used in comparing the ECI with other data sets. The "all private industry" category in the ECI excludes farm and household workers (it is sometimes, and more precisely, called "private nonfarm industry"), and the "all civilian workers" category excludes federal government, farm, and household workers, all of whom fall outside the scope of the ECI survey.

The data for 1979 through 2005, which are presented in Table 9-2 and are the official ECI measures for that time period, were based on the 1987 Standard Industrial Classification (SIC) and 1990 Occupational Classification System (OCS).

Currently the ECI is compiled based on the 2007 North American Industry Classification System (NAICS) and the 2000 Standard Occupational Classification Manual (SOC). These data, along with comparable data for 2001 through 2005, are shown in Table 9-1.

For certain broad categories shown in this volume—indicated by footnote 2 in Table 9-2—the old SIC categories are roughly comparable and continuous with the data for 2006 and subsequent years. (However, they differ slightly on overlap dates, and should be "linked" if a continuous time series is desired; see the article at the beginning of this volume.) Many of the new industry and occupational categories are not continuous with the old series shown here, and some of the old categories are not being continued because BLS finds them obsolete and no longer meaningful.

Definitions

Total compensation comprises wages, salaries, and the employer's costs for employee benefits. Excluded from wages and salaries and employee benefits are the value of stock option exercises and items such as payment-in-kind, free room and board, and tips.

Wages and salaries consists of straight-time earnings per hour before payroll deductions, including production bonuses, incentive earnings, commissions, and cost-of-living adjustments. These wage rates exclude premium pay for overtime

and for work on weekends and holidays, shift differentials, and nonproduction bonuses such as lump-sum payments provided in lieu of wage increases. According to BLS, wages and salaries are about 70 percent of total compensation.

Benefits includes the cost to employers for paid leave—vacations, holidays, sick leave, and other leave; for supplemental pay—premium pay for work in addition to the regular work schedule (such as overtime, weekends, and holidays), shift differentials, and nonproduction bonuses (such as referral bonuses and lump-sum payments provided in lieu of wage increases); for insurance benefits—life, health, short-term disability, and long-term disability; for retirement and savings benefits—defined benefit and defined contribution plans; and for legally required benefits—Social Security, Medicare, federal and state unemployment insurance, and workers' compensation. Severance pay and supplemental unemployment benefit (SUB) plans are included in the data through December 2005 but were dropped beginning with the March 2006 data. The combined cost of these two benefits accounted for less than one-tenth of one percent of compensation, and according to BLS, dropping these benefits has had virtually no impact on the index. According to BLS, benefit costs are about 30 percent of total compensation.

Civilian workers are private industry workers, as defined below, and workers in state and local government. Federal workers are not included.

Private industry workers are paid workers in private industry excluding farms and private households. To be included in the ECI, employees in occupations must receive cash payments from the establishment for services performed and the establishment must pay the employer's portion of Medicare taxes on that individual's wages. Major exclusions from the survey are the self-employed, individuals who set their own pay (for example, proprietors, owners, major stockholders, and partners in unincorporated firms), volunteers, unpaid workers, family members being paid token wages, individuals receiving long-term disability compensation, and U.S. citizens working overseas.

Private industry workers excluding incentive paid occupations is a new category introduced in the 2006 revision to eliminate the quarter-to-quarter variability related to the way workers are paid. (The category *private industry workers excluding sales occupations* was intended to serve a similar purpose in the previous SIC-based classification system, but was much less accurate in separately identifying workers with highly variable compensation.)

Goods-producing industries include mining, construction, and manufacturing.

Service-providing industries include the following NAICS industries: wholesale trade; retail trade; transportation and warehousing; utilities; information; finance and insurance; real estate and rental and leasing; professional, scientific, and technical services; management of companies and enterprises; administrative and support and waste management and remediation services; education services; health care and social assistance; arts, entertainment, and recreation; accommodation and food services; and other services, except public administration.

Notes on the data

Employee benefit costs are calculated as cents per hour worked.

The March 2010 data were collected from probability samples of approximately 63,300 occupational observations in about 13,300 sample establishments in private industry, and approximately 11,600 occupations within about 1,800 establishments in state and local governments. The private industry sample is rotated over approximately five years. The state and local government sample is replaced less frequently; the latest sample was introduced in September 2007.

Currently, the sample establishments are classified in industry categories based on the NAICS. Within an establishment, specific job categories are selected and classified into approximately 800 occupational classifications according to the SOC. Similar procedures were followed under the previous classification systems. Data are collected each quarter for the pay periods including the 12th day of March, June, September, and December.

Aggregate indexes are calculated using fixed employment weights. Beginning with March 2006, ECI weights are based on fixed employment counts for 2002 from the BLS Occupational Employment Statistics survey. ECI measures were based on 1990 employment counts from March 1995 through December 2005 and 1980 census employment counts from June 1986 through December 1994. Prior to June 1986, they were based on 1970 census employment counts. Use of fixed weights ensures that changes in the indexes reflect only changes in hourly compensation, not employment shifts among industries or occupations with different levels of wages and compensation. This feature distinguishes the ECI from other compensation series such as average hourly earnings (see Table 10-11 and its notes and definitions) and the compensation per hour component of the productivity series (see Table 9-3 and its notes and definitions, and the general note above), each of which is affected by such employment shifts.

Data availability

Data for wages and salaries for the private nonfarm economy are available beginning with the data for 1975; data for compensation begin with the 1980 data. The series for state and local government and for the civilian nonfarm economy begin with the 1981 data. All series are available on the BLS Web site at <http://www.bls.gov>.

Wage and salary change and compensation cost change data also are available by major occupational and industry groups, as well as by region and collective bargaining status. Infor-

mation on wage and salary change is available from 1975 to the present for most of these series. Compensation cost change data are available from 1980 to the present for most series. For 10 occupational and industry series, benefit cost change data are available from the early 1980s to the present. For state and local governments and the civilian economy (state and local governments plus private industry), wage and salary change and compensation cost change data are available for major occupational and industry series. BLS provides data for all these series from June 1981 to the present.

Updates are available about four weeks after the end of the reference quarter. Reference quarters end in March, June, September, and December.

References

Explanatory notes, including references, are included in a Technical Note in each quarter's ECI news release, and can be found on the BLS Web site, in the PDF version of the release. More detailed information on the ECI is available from Chapter 8, "National compensation measures," (www.bls.gov/opub/hom/pdf/homch8.pdf) from the BLS Handbook of Methods, and several articles published in the *Monthly Labor Review* and *Compensation and Working Conditions*. The articles and other descriptive pieces are available at www.bls.gov/ect/#publications, by calling (202) 691-6199, or sending e-mail to NCSinfo@bls.gov.

TABLES 9-3 AND 19-11
PRODUCTIVITY AND RELATED DATA

SOURCE: U.S. DEPARTMENT OF LABOR, BUREAU OF LABOR STATISTICS (BLS)

Productivity measures relate real physical output to real input. They encompass a family of measures that includes single-factor input measures, such as output per unit of labor input or output per unit of capital input, as well as measures of multifactor productivity—that is, output per unit of combined labor and capital inputs. The indexes published in this book are indexes of labor productivity expressed in terms of output per hour of labor input. (A larger group of BLS productivity measures can be found in Bernan Press's *Handbook of U.S. Labor Statistics*.) Data are provided here for four sectors of the economy: business, nonfarm business, the nonfinancial corporate sector, and manufacturing. All data are presented as indexes with a base of 1992 = 100.

Definitions

Output per hour of all persons (labor productivity) is the value of goods and services in constant prices produced per hour of labor input. By definition, nonfinancial corporations include no self-employed persons. Productivity in this sector is expressed as *output per hour of all employees*.

Compensation per hour is the wages and salaries of employees, plus employers' contributions for social insurance and private benefit plans, plus wages, salaries, and supplementary payments for the self-employed—the sum of these divided by hours at work. Included in compensation is the value of exercised stock options that companies report as a charge against earnings. Stock option values are reported with a delay; consequently, recent values are estimated based on extrapolation. They are revised to actual values when the data become available; sometimes the revisions are very large. The labor compensation of proprietors cannot be explicitly identified and must be estimated. This is done by assuming that proprietors have the same hourly compensation as employees in the same sector. The quarterly labor productivity and cost measures do not contain estimates of compensation for unpaid family workers.

Real compensation per hour is compensation per hour deflated by the CPI-U for recent quarters and the Consumer Price Index Research Series (CPI-U-RS) for the period 1978 through 2008. Changes in the Consumer Price Index for Urban Wage Earners and Clerical Workers (CPI-W) are used for data before 1978, as there was no CPI-U for that period. See the Notes and Definitions to Chapter 8 for explanation of the CPI-U, the CPI-W, and the CPI-U-RS.

Unit labor costs are the current-dollar labor costs expended in the production of a unit of output. They are derived by dividing compensation by output.

Unit nonlabor payments include profits, depreciation, interest, rental income of persons, and indirect taxes per unit of output. They are computed by subtracting current-dollar compensation of all persons from current-dollar value of output and dividing by output.

Unit nonlabor costs are available for nonfinancial corporations only. They contain all the components of unit nonlabor payments except unit profits (and rental income of persons, which is zero by definition for nonfinancial corporations).

Unit profits, the other component of unit nonlabor payments, are also only available for nonfinancial corporations.

Hours of all persons consists of the total hours at work (employment multiplied by the average workweek) of payroll workers, self-employed persons, and unpaid family workers. For the nonfinancial corporations data, there are no self-employed persons; the data represent *employee hours.*

Notes on the data

Output for the business sector is equal to constant-dollar gross domestic product minus: the rental value of owner-occupied dwellings, the output of nonprofit institutions, the output of paid employees of private households, and general government output. The measures are derived from national income and product account (NIPA) data supplied by the U.S. Department of Commerce's Bureau of Economic Analysis (BEA). For manufacturing, BLS produces annual estimates of sectoral output. Quarterly manufacturing output indexes derived from the Federal Reserve Board of Governors' monthly indexes of industrial production (see Chapter 2) are adjusted to these annual measures by the BLS, and are also used to project the quarterly values in the current period.

Nonfinancial corporate output excludes unincorporated businesses and financial corporations from business sector output and accounted for approximately 50 percent of the value of GDP in 2005. Unit profits and unit nonlabor costs can be calculated separately for this sector and are shown in this table.

Compensation and hours data are developed from BLS and BEA data. The primary source for hours and employment is BLS's Current Employment Statistics (CES) program (see the notes and definitions for Tables 10-7 through 10-16). Other data sources are the Current Population Survey (CPS) and the National Compensation Survey (NCS). Weekly paid hours are adjusted to hours at work using the NCS. For paid employees, hours at work differ from hours paid, in that they exclude paid vacation and holidays, paid sick leave, and other paid personal or administrative leave.

Although the labor productivity measures relate output to labor input, they do not measure the contribution of labor or any other specific factor of production. Instead, they reflect the joint effect of many influences, including changes in technology; capital investment; level of output; utilization of capacity, energy, and materials; the organization of production; managerial skill; and the characteristics and efforts of the work force.

Revisions

Data for recent years are revised frequently to take account of revisions in the output and labor input measures that underlie the estimates. Customarily, all revisions to source data are reflected in the release following the source data revision. Data in this volume were released March 4, 2010, and reflect the midyear 2009 revisions to the NIPAs and all revisions in labor input and compensation available up to that release date, including the annual benchmark revision of the CES and updated seasonal factors.

Data availability

Series are available quarterly and annually. Quarterly measures are based entirely on seasonally adjusted data. For some detailed manufacturing series (not shown here), only annual averages are available. Productivity indexes are published early in the second and third months of each quarter, reflecting new data for preceding quarters. Complete historical data are available on the BLS Web site at <http://www.bls.gov>.

BLS also publishes productivity estimates for a number of individual industries. A release entitled "Productivity and

Costs by Industry" is available on the BLS Web site at <http://www.bls.gov>.

References

Further information is available in the Technical Notes and footnotes on the most current monthly release, available on the Web site, and from the following sources: Chapter 10, "Productivity Measures: Business Sector and Major Subsectors," *BLS Handbook of Methods*—Bulletin 2490 (April 1997) and the following *Monthly Labor Review* articles: "Alternative Measures of Supervisory Employee Hours and Productivity Growth" (April 2004); "Possible Measurement Bias in Aggregate Productivity Growth" (February 1999); "Improvements to the Quarterly Productivity Measures" (October 1995); "Hours of Work: A New Base for BLS Productivity Statistics" (February 1990); and "New Sector Definitions for Productivity Series" (October 1976).

TABLE 9-4
RATES OF RETURN AND RELATED DATA FOR MAJOR NONFINANCIAL INDUSTRY GROUPS

SOURCE: U.S. DEPARTMENT OF COMMERCE, BUREAU OF ECONOMIC ANALYSIS

This table presents data on the net operating surplus and rate of return for five major nonfinancial industry groups from 1997 through 2007, based on the NAICS. The industry groups include both corporations and proprietors. Therefore, their data differ from the data for nonfinancial corporations alone, which are available through 2008 and shown for comparison purposes in the first column of this table. (Nonfinancial corporation rates of return and related data for 1960 through 2008 can also be found in Table 1-15.)

Definitions

Net operating surplus for the nonfinancial industries includes corporate profits, net interest, business current transfer payments, and proprietors' income (mainly the income of unincorporated self-employed workers).

Produced assets is the average of the end-year values for the current and previous year of the net stock of capital plus inventories, valued at current cost.

Rate of return is net operating surplus as a percent of the average value of produced assets at the beginning and end of the year.

Share of net value added is the net operating surplus as a percent of total value added in the industry. Value added is the portion of total national gross domestic product (GDP) produced in the industry and includes the net operating surplus, compensation of employees, taxes on production and imports less subsidies, and consumption of fixed capital.

Data availability, revisions, and references

These data were presented for the first time and described in "Returns for Domestic Nonfinancial Business," *Survey of Current Business,* May 2007, pp. 6-10. The data were revised and updated in the May 2009 *Survey of Current Business.*

TABLE 9-5 AND 9-6
CORPORATE PROFITS WITH INVENTORY VALUATION ADJUSTMENT BY INDUSTRY GROUP

SOURCE: U.S. DEPARTMENT OF COMMERCE, BUREAU OF ECONOMIC ANALYSIS

These profits measures are derived from the NIPAs. See the notes and definitions to Chapter 1 for definitions, data availability, and references. Note that this industry breakdown of profits incorporates the inventory valuation adjustment (IVA), which eliminates any capital gain element in profits arising from changes in the prices at which inventories are valued, but does not incorporate the capital consumption adjustment (CCAdj), which adjusts historical costs of fixed capital to replacement costs and uses actual rather than tax-based service lives. This is because the CCAdj is calculated by BEA at an aggregate level, whereas the IVA is calculated at an industry level.

Beginning with 1998, data are compiled on the NAICS basis, as shown in Table 9-5. Data for earlier years based on the December 2003 revision—including an overlap for the years 1998 through 2000—are based on the older Standard Industrial Classification system (SIC) and are shown back to 1948 in Table 9-6 on that basis; these have not been revised and are as shown in previous years' *Business Statistics.* See Chapter 14 for an outline and discussion of NAICS and its relation to SIC.

CHAPTER 10: EMPLOYMENT, HOURS, AND EARNINGS

Section 10a: Labor Force, Employment, and Unemployment

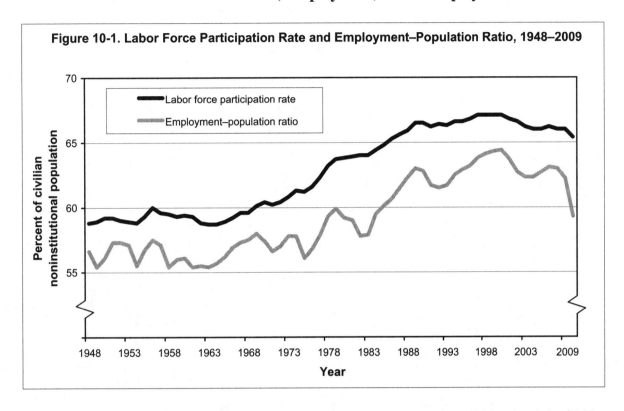

Figure 10-1. Labor Force Participation Rate and Employment–Population Ratio, 1948–2009

- From a high point in January 2008 to a low in December 2009, 8.3 million Americans lost jobs. (Table 20-3A) The employment/population ratio, charted in Figure 10-1 above, registered the steepest plunge of the postwar period. (Tables 10-3 and 20-3)

- Since December 2009, which is the latest observation included in *Business Statistics,* employment has increased each month through April—the latest month available as this was written—and in April there were 1.9 million more employed than in December 2009 (using the December 2009 figure in Table 20-3A which is based on population controls consistent with the current estimates).

- The labor force participation rate, already in a downtrend since the late 1990s, declined more rapidly through 2009, as some workers found searching for a job to be futile. (Tables 10-1 and 20-3)

- As employment growth resumed in early 2010, workers began to re-enter the labor force, and the participation rate rose from 64.6 percent in December 2009 to 65.2 percent in April 2010.

Table 10-1. Civilian Population and Labor Force [1]

(Thousands of persons, 16 years of age and over; percent.)

Year and month	Civilian noninstitutional population	Not seasonally adjusted — Civilian labor force			Seasonally adjusted — Civilian labor force (thousands)				Participation rate (percent) [2]			
		Total	Employed	Unemployed	Total	Men, 20 years and over	Women, 20 years and over	Both sexes, 16 to 19 years	Total	Men, 20 years and over	Women, 20 years and over	Both sexes, 16 to 19 years
1965	126 513	74 455	71 088	3 366	74 455	44 857	23 686	5 910	58.9	83.9	39.4	45.7
1966	128 058	75 770	72 895	2 875	75 770	44 788	24 431	6 558	59.2	83.6	40.1	48.2
1967	129 874	77 347	74 372	2 975	77 347	45 354	25 475	6 521	59.6	83.4	41.1	48.4
1968	132 028	78 737	75 920	2 817	78 737	45 852	26 266	6 619	59.6	83.1	41.6	48.3
1969	134 335	80 734	77 902	2 832	80 734	46 351	27 413	6 970	60.1	82.8	42.7	49.4
1970	137 085	82 771	78 678	4 093	82 771	47 220	28 301	7 249	60.4	82.6	43.3	49.9
1971	140 216	84 382	79 367	5 016	84 382	48 009	28 904	7 470	60.2	82.1	43.3	49.7
1972	144 126	87 034	82 153	4 882	87 034	49 079	29 901	8 054	60.4	81.6	43.7	51.9
1973	147 096	89 429	85 064	4 365	89 429	49 932	30 991	8 507	60.8	81.3	44.4	53.7
1974	150 120	91 949	86 794	5 156	91 949	50 879	32 201	8 871	61.3	81.0	45.3	54.8
1975	153 153	93 775	85 846	7 929	93 775	51 494	33 410	8 870	61.2	80.3	46.0	54.0
1976	156 150	96 158	88 752	7 406	96 158	52 288	34 814	9 056	61.6	79.8	47.0	54.5
1977	159 033	99 009	92 017	6 991	99 009	53 348	36 310	9 351	62.3	79.7	48.1	56.0
1978	161 910	102 251	96 048	6 202	102 251	54 471	38 128	9 652	63.2	79.8	49.6	57.8
1979	164 863	104 962	98 824	6 137	104 962	55 615	39 708	9 638	63.7	79.8	50.6	57.9
1980	167 745	106 940	99 303	7 637	106 940	56 455	41 106	9 378	63.8	79.4	51.3	56.7
1981	170 130	108 670	100 397	8 273	108 670	57 197	42 485	8 988	63.9	79.0	52.1	55.4
1982	172 271	110 204	99 526	10 678	110 204	57 980	43 699	8 526	64.0	78.7	52.7	54.1
1983	174 215	111 550	100 834	10 717	111 550	58 744	44 636	8 171	64.0	78.5	53.1	53.5
1984	176 383	113 544	105 005	8 539	113 544	59 701	45 900	7 943	64.4	78.3	53.7	53.9
1985	178 206	115 461	107 150	8 312	115 461	60 277	47 283	7 901	64.8	78.1	54.7	54.5
1986	180 587	117 834	109 597	8 237	117 834	61 320	48 589	7 926	65.3	78.1	55.5	54.7
1987	182 753	119 865	112 440	7 425	119 865	62 095	49 783	7 988	65.6	78.0	56.2	54.7
1988	184 613	121 669	114 968	6 701	121 669	62 768	50 870	8 031	65.9	77.9	56.8	55.3
1989	186 393	123 869	117 342	6 528	123 869	63 704	52 212	7 954	66.5	78.1	57.7	55.9
1990	189 164	125 840	118 793	7 047	125 840	64 916	53 131	7 792	66.5	78.2	58.0	53.7
1991	190 925	126 346	117 718	8 628	126 346	65 374	53 708	7 265	66.2	77.7	57.9	51.6
1992	192 805	128 105	118 492	9 613	128 105	66 213	54 796	7 096	66.4	77.7	58.5	51.3
1993	194 838	129 200	120 259	8 940	129 200	66 642	55 388	7 170	66.3	77.3	58.5	51.5
1994	196 814	131 056	123 060	7 996	131 056	66 921	56 655	7 481	66.6	76.8	59.3	52.7
1995	198 584	132 304	124 900	7 404	132 304	67 324	57 215	7 765	66.6	76.7	59.4	53.5
1996	200 591	133 943	126 708	7 236	133 943	68 044	58 094	7 806	66.8	76.8	59.9	52.3
1997	203 133	136 297	129 558	6 739	136 297	69 166	59 198	7 932	67.1	77.0	60.5	51.6
1998	205 220	137 673	131 463	6 210	137 673	69 715	59 702	8 256	67.1	76.8	60.4	52.8
1999	207 753	139 368	133 488	5 880	139 368	70 194	60 840	8 333	67.1	76.7	60.7	52.0
2000	212 577	142 583	136 891	5 692	142 583	72 010	62 301	8 271	67.1	76.7	60.6	52.0
2001	215 092	143 734	136 933	6 801	143 734	72 816	63 016	7 902	66.8	76.5	60.6	49.6
2002	217 570	144 863	136 485	8 378	144 863	73 630	63 648	7 585	66.6	76.3	60.5	47.4
2003	221 168	146 510	137 736	8 774	146 510	74 623	64 716	7 170	66.2	75.9	60.6	44.5
2004	223 357	147 401	139 252	8 149	147 401	75 364	64 923	7 114	66.0	75.8	60.3	43.9
2005	226 082	149 320	141 730	7 591	149 320	76 443	65 714	7 164	66.0	75.8	60.4	43.7
2006	228 815	151 428	144 427	7 001	151 428	77 562	66 585	7 281	66.2	75.9	60.5	43.7
2007	231 867	153 124	146 047	7 078	153 124	78 596	67 516	7 012	66.0	75.9	60.6	41.3
2008	233 788	154 287	145 362	8 924	154 287	79 047	68 382	6 858	66.0	75.7	60.9	40.2
2009	235 801	154 142	139 877	14 265	154 142	78 897	68 856	6 390	65.4	74.8	60.8	37.5
2008												
January	232 616	152 828	144 607	8 221	154 048	78 965	68 070	7 013	66.2	76.0	60.9	41.2
February	232 809	152 503	144 550	7 953	153 600	78 880	67 912	6 808	66.0	75.9	60.7	40.0
March	232 995	153 135	145 108	8 027	153 966	78 955	68 180	6 830	66.1	75.9	60.9	40.1
April	233 198	153 208	145 921	7 287	153 936	78 871	68 081	6 985	66.0	75.7	60.8	41.0
May	233 405	154 003	145 927	8 076	154 420	78 897	68 340	7 183	66.2	75.7	61.0	42.1
June	233 627	155 582	146 649	8 933	154 327	79 037	68 393	6 898	66.1	75.7	61.0	40.4
July	233 864	156 300	146 867	9 433	154 410	79 242	68 247	6 920	66.0	75.8	60.8	40.5
August	234 107	155 387	145 909	9 479	154 696	79 238	68 633	6 825	66.1	75.7	61.1	39.9
September	234 360	154 509	145 310	9 199	154 590	79 344	68 403	6 843	66.0	75.8	60.8	40.0
October	234 612	155 012	145 543	9 469	154 849	79 308	68 726	6 815	66.0	75.6	61.0	39.8
November	234 828	154 624	144 609	10 015	154 524	79 203	68 733	6 589	65.8	75.4	61.0	38.5
December	235 035	154 349	143 350	10 999	154 587	79 108	68 904	6 575	65.8	75.3	61.1	38.4
2009												
January	234 739	153 445	140 436	13 009	154 140	78 769	68 793	6 578	65.7	75.1	61.0	38.5
February	234 913	153 804	140 105	13 699	154 401	78 859	68 914	6 628	65.7	75.1	61.1	38.8
March	235 086	153 728	139 833	13 895	154 164	78 680	68 972	6 512	65.6	74.9	61.1	38.1
April	235 271	153 834	140 586	13 248	154 718	79 106	69 105	6 507	65.8	75.2	61.2	38.1
May	235 452	154 336	140 363	13 973	154 956	79 339	69 060	6 557	65.8	75.3	61.1	38.4
June	235 655	155 921	140 826	15 095	154 759	79 246	68 984	6 529	65.7	75.2	60.9	38.3
July	235 870	156 255	141 055	15 201	154 351	78 984	68 910	6 457	65.4	74.8	60.8	37.9
August	236 087	154 897	140 074	14 823	154 426	79 196	68 847	6 383	65.4	75.0	60.7	37.5
September	236 322	153 617	139 079	14 538	153 927	78 977	68 686	6 264	65.1	74.7	60.5	36.8
October	236 550	153 635	139 088	14 547	153 854	79 024	68 687	6 143	65.0	74.6	60.4	36.1
November	236 743	153 539	139 132	14 407	153 720	78 901	68 742	6 077	64.9	74.4	60.4	35.8
December	236 924	152 693	137 953	14 740	153 059	78 402	68 620	6 037	64.6	73.9	60.3	35.6

[1]Changes in survey design, population estimates, and methodology in 1994 and several other years affect year-to-year comparisons. See notes and definitions for more information.
[2]Labor force as a percent of the demographic group's civilian noninstitutional population.

Table 10-2. Civilian Employment [1]

(Thousands of persons, 16 years of age and over; seasonally adjusted, except as noted.)

Year and month	Total	By age and sex			Agricultural	By class of worker						
		Men, 20 years and over	Women, 20 years and over	Both sexes, 16 to 19 years		Nonagricultural industries					Self-employed	Unpaid family workers [2]
						Total	Wage and salary					
							Total	Government	Private industries			
									Private households [2]	Other private industries		
1965	71 088	43 422	22 630	5 036	4 361	66 726	60 031	9 608	. . .	. . .	6 097	600
1966	72 895	43 668	23 510	5 721	3 979	68 915	62 362	10 323	. . .	. . .	5 991	564
1967	74 372	44 294	24 397	5 682	3 844	70 527	64 848	11 146	. . .	. . .	5 174	505
1968	75 920	44 859	25 281	5 781	3 817	72 103	66 519	11 590	. . .	. . .	5 102	485
1969	77 902	45 388	26 397	6 117	3 606	74 296	68 528	12 025	. . .	. . .	5 252	517
1970	78 678	45 581	26 952	6 144	3 463	75 215	69 491	12 431	. . .	. . .	5 221	502
1971	79 367	45 912	27 246	6 208	3 394	75 972	70 120	12 799	. . .	. . .	5 327	522
1972	82 153	47 130	28 276	6 746	3 484	78 669	72 785	13 393	. . .	. . .	5 365	519
1973	85 064	48 310	29 484	7 271	3 470	81 594	75 580	13 655	. . .	. . .	5 474	540
1974	86 794	48 922	30 424	7 448	3 515	83 279	77 094	14 124	. . .	. . .	5 697	489
1975	85 846	48 018	30 726	7 104	3 408	82 438	76 249	14 675	. . .	. . .	5 705	483
1976	88 752	49 190	32 226	7 336	3 331	85 421	79 175	15 132	. . .	. . .	5 783	464
1977	92 017	50 555	33 775	7 688	3 283	88 734	82 121	15 361	. . .	. . .	6 114	498
1978	96 048	52 143	35 836	8 070	3 387	92 661	85 753	15 525	. . .	. . .	6 429	479
1979	98 824	53 308	37 434	8 083	3 347	95 477	88 222	15 635	. . .	. . .	6 791	463
1980	99 303	53 101	38 492	7 710	3 364	95 938	88 525	15 912	. . .	. . .	7 000	413
1981	100 397	53 582	39 590	7 225	3 368	97 030	89 543	15 689	. . .	. . .	7 097	390
1982	99 526	52 891	40 086	6 549	3 401	96 125	88 462	15 516	. . .	. . .	7 262	401
1983	100 834	53 487	41 004	6 342	3 383	97 450	89 500	15 537	. . .	. . .	7 575	376
1984	105 005	55 769	42 793	6 444	3 321	101 685	93 565	15 770	. . .	. . .	7 785	335
1985	107 150	56 562	44 154	6 434	3 179	103 971	95 871	16 031	. . .	. . .	7 811	289
1986	109 597	57 569	45 556	6 472	3 163	106 434	98 299	16 342	. . .	. . .	7 881	255
1987	112 440	58 726	47 074	6 640	3 208	109 232	100 771	16 800	. . .	. . .	8 201	260
1988	114 968	59 781	48 383	6 805	3 169	111 800	103 021	17 114	. . .	. . .	8 519	260
1989	117 342	60 837	49 745	6 759	3 199	114 142	105 259	17 469	. . .	. . .	8 605	279
1990	118 793	61 678	50 535	6 581	3 223	115 570	106 598	17 769	. . .	. . .	8 719	253
1991	117 718	61 178	50 634	5 906	3 269	114 449	105 373	17 934	. . .	. . .	8 851	226
1992	118 492	61 496	51 328	5 669	3 247	115 245	106 437	18 136	. . .	. . .	8 575	233
1993	120 259	62 355	52 099	5 805	3 115	117 144	107 966	18 579	. . .	. . .	8 959	218
1994	123 060	63 294	53 606	6 161	3 409	119 651	110 517	18 293	. . .	. . .	9 003	131
1995	124 900	64 085	54 396	6 419	3 440	121 460	112 448	18 362	. . .	. . .	8 902	110
1996	126 708	64 897	55 311	6 500	3 443	123 264	114 171	18 217	. . .	. . .	8 971	122
1997	129 558	66 284	56 613	6 661	3 399	126 159	116 983	18 131	. . .	. . .	9 056	120
1998	131 463	67 135	57 278	7 051	3 378	128 085	119 019	18 383	. . .	. . .	8 962	103
1999	133 488	67 761	58 555	7 172	3 281	130 207	121 323	18 903	. . .	. . .	8 790	95
2000	136 891	69 634	60 067	7 189	2 464	134 427	125 114	19 248	718	105 148	9 205	108
2001	136 933	69 776	60 417	6 740	2 299	134 635	125 407	19 335	694	105 378	9 121	107
2002	136 485	69 734	60 420	6 332	2 311	134 174	125 156	19 636	757	104 764	8 923	95
2003	137 736	70 415	61 402	5 919	2 275	135 461	126 015	19 634	764	105 616	9 344	101
2004	139 252	71 572	61 773	5 907	2 232	137 020	127 463	19 983	779	106 701	9 467	90
2005	141 730	73 050	62 702	5 978	2 197	139 532	129 931	20 357	812	108 761	9 509	93
2006	144 427	74 431	63 834	6 162	2 206	142 221	132 449	20 337	803	111 309	9 685	87
2007	146 047	75 337	64 799	5 911	2 095	143 952	134 283	21 003	813	112 467	9 557	112
2008	145 362	74 750	65 039	5 573	2 168	143 194	133 882	21 258	805	111 819	9 219	93
2009	139 877	71 341	63 699	4 837	2 103	137 775	128 713	21 178	783	106 752	8 995	66
2008												
January	146 421	75 477	65 181	5 763	2 205	144 146	134 776	20 979	787	113 001	9 288	76
February	146 165	75 439	65 041	5 685	2 202	143 965	134 376	21 246	763	112 358	9 422	100
March	146 173	75 306	65 127	5 740	2 190	143 976	134 585	21 301	744	112 558	9 233	99
April	146 306	75 232	65 178	5 896	2 122	144 129	134 667	21 313	780	112 571	9 343	125
May	146 023	75 044	65 152	5 827	2 125	143 888	134 394	21 236	774	112 381	9 362	132
June	145 768	75 000	65 178	5 590	2 126	143 639	134 153	21 176	862	112 178	9 388	120
July	145 515	74 964	65 067	5 483	2 141	143 422	133 880	21 062	873	111 939	9 503	106
August	145 187	74 698	64 956	5 533	2 148	143 045	133 707	21 275	799	111 703	9 265	84
September	145 021	74 480	65 015	5 526	2 207	142 793	133 551	21 216	820	111 526	9 152	81
October	144 677	74 241	65 003	5 433	2 192	142 576	133 593	21 503	840	111 207	8 930	69
November	143 907	73 850	64 806	5 251	2 195	141 742	132 825	21 389	836	110 543	8 825	65
December	143 188	73 237	64 744	5 207	2 185	140 975	132 022	21 393	782	109 816	8 915	62
2009												
January	142 221	72 625	64 391	5 205	2 147	140 014	131 132	21 225	749	109 140	8 827	41
February	141 687	72 266	64 238	5 183	2 148	139 559	130 454	21 185	719	108 535	8 978	53
March	140 854	71 667	64 110	5 077	2 051	138 830	129 544	20 894	738	107 927	9 190	57
April	140 902	71 665	64 147	5 089	2 143	138 762	129 672	21 196	716	107 742	9 034	54
May	140 438	71 552	63 847	5 039	2 166	138 287	129 240	21 240	779	107 212	8 985	63
June	140 038	71 354	63 741	4 943	2 154	137 825	128 866	21 474	908	106 563	8 898	83
July	139 817	71 255	63 685	4 877	2 138	137 629	128 849	21 330	923	106 631	8 793	68
August	139 433	71 142	63 552	4 740	2 095	137 285	128 168	21 124	859	106 273	9 032	71
September	138 768	70 861	63 280	4 627	2 009	136 752	127 650	20 978	790	105 885	9 009	83
October	138 242	70 662	63 133	4 448	2 041	136 311	127 312	21 161	702	105 401	8 960	67
November	138 381	70 662	63 269	4 450	2 086	136 357	127 160	21 233	776	105 097	9 111	72
December	137 792	70 391	62 998	4 403	2 056	135 717	126 539	21 110	736	104 666	9 135	83

[1]Changes in survey design, population estimates, and methodology in 1994 and several other years affect year-to-year comparisons. See notes and definitions for more information.
[2]Not seasonally adjusted.
. . . = Not available.

Table 10-3. Civilian Employment and Unemployment [1]

(Thousands of persons; percent; seasonally adjusted.)

Year and month	Employment-population ratio, percent				Multiple jobholders		Employed and at work part time		Unemployment (thousands)				
	Total	Men, 20 years and over	Women, 20 years and over	Both sexes, 16 to 19 years	Total (thousands)	Percent of total employed	Economic reasons	Non-economic reasons	Total	Long-term[2]	Men, 20 years and over	Women, 20 years and over	Both sexes, 16 to 19 years
1965	56.2	81.2	37.6	38.9	...	...	2 209	8 466	3 366	755	1 435	1 056	874
1966	56.9	81.5	38.6	42.1	...	...	1 960	8 112	2 875	526	1 120	921	837
1967	57.3	81.5	39.3	42.2	...	...	2 163	8 701	2 975	448	1 060	1 078	839
1968	57.5	81.3	40.0	42.2	...	...	1 970	9 075	2 817	412	993	985	838
1969	58.0	81.1	41.1	43.4	...	...	2 056	9 652	2 832	375	963	1 015	853
1970	57.4	79.7	41.2	42.3	...	...	2 446	9 999	4 093	663	1 638	1 349	1 106
1971	56.6	78.5	40.9	41.3	...	...	2 688	10 152	5 016	1 187	2 097	1 658	1 262
1972	57.0	78.4	41.3	43.5	...	...	2 648	10 612	4 882	1 167	1 948	1 625	1 308
1973	57.8	78.6	42.2	45.9	...	...	2 554	10 972	4 365	826	1 624	1 507	1 235
1974	57.8	77.9	42.8	46.0	...	...	2 988	11 153	5 156	955	1 957	1 777	1 422
1975	56.1	74.8	42.3	43.3	...	...	3 804	11 228	7 929	2 505	3 476	2 684	1 767
1976	56.8	75.1	43.5	44.2	...	...	3 607	11 607	7 406	2 366	3 098	2 588	1 719
1977	57.9	75.6	44.8	46.1	...	...	3 608	12 120	6 991	1 942	2 794	2 535	1 663
1978	59.3	76.4	46.6	48.3	...	...	3 516	12 650	6 202	1 414	2 328	2 292	1 583
1979	59.9	76.5	47.7	48.5	...	...	3 577	12 893	6 137	1 241	2 308	2 276	1 555
1980	59.2	74.6	48.1	46.6	...	...	4 321	13 067	7 637	1 871	3 353	2 615	1 669
1981	59.0	74.0	48.6	44.6	...	...	4 768	13 025	8 273	2 285	3 615	2 895	1 763
1982	57.8	71.8	48.4	41.5	...	...	6 170	12 953	10 678	3 485	5 089	3 613	1 977
1983	57.9	71.4	48.8	41.5	...	...	6 266	12 911	10 717	4 210	5 257	3 632	1 829
1984	59.5	73.2	50.1	43.7	...	...	5 744	13 169	8 539	2 737	3 932	3 107	1 499
1985	60.1	73.3	51.0	44.4	...	...	5 590	13 489	8 312	2 305	3 715	3 129	1 468
1986	60.7	73.3	52.0	44.6	...	...	5 588	13 935	8 237	2 232	3 751	3 032	1 454
1987	61.5	73.8	53.1	45.5	...	...	5 401	14 395	7 425	1 983	3 369	2 709	1 347
1988	62.3	74.2	54.0	46.8	...	...	5 206	14 963	6 701	1 610	2 987	2 487	1 226
1989	63.0	74.5	54.9	47.5	...	...	4 894	15 393	6 528	1 375	2 867	2 467	1 194
1990	62.8	74.3	55.2	45.3	...	...	5 204	15 341	7 047	1 525	3 239	2 596	1 212
1991	61.7	72.7	54.6	42.0	...	...	6 161	15 172	8 628	2 357	4 195	3 074	1 359
1992	61.5	72.1	54.8	41.0	...	...	6 520	14 918	9 613	3 408	4 717	3 469	1 427
1993	61.7	72.3	55.0	41.7	...	...	6 481	15 240	8 940	3 094	4 287	3 288	1 365
1994	62.5	72.6	56.2	43.4	7 260	5.9	4 625	17 638	7 996	2 860	3 627	3 049	1 320
1995	62.9	73.0	56.5	44.2	7 693	6.2	4 473	17 734	7 404	2 363	3 239	2 819	1 346
1996	63.2	73.2	57.0	43.5	7 832	6.2	4 315	17 770	7 236	2 316	3 146	2 783	1 306
1997	63.8	73.7	57.8	43.4	7 955	6.1	4 068	18 149	6 739	2 062	2 882	2 585	1 271
1998	64.1	73.9	58.0	45.1	7 926	6.0	3 665	18 530	6 210	1 637	2 580	2 424	1 205
1999	64.3	74.0	58.5	44.7	7 802	5.8	3 357	18 758	5 880	1 480	2 433	2 285	1 162
2000	64.4	74.2	58.4	45.2	7 604	5.6	3 227	18 814	5 692	1 318	2 376	2 235	1 081
2001	63.7	73.3	58.1	42.3	7 357	5.4	3 715	18 790	6 801	1 752	3 040	2 599	1 162
2002	62.7	72.3	57.5	39.6	7 291	5.3	4 213	18 843	8 378	2 904	3 896	3 228	1 253
2003	62.3	71.7	57.5	36.8	7 315	5.3	4 701	19 014	8 774	3 378	4 209	3 314	1 251
2004	62.3	71.9	57.4	36.4	7 473	5.4	4 567	19 380	8 149	3 072	3 791	3 150	1 208
2005	62.7	72.4	57.6	36.5	7 546	5.3	4 350	19 491	7 591	2 619	3 392	3 013	1 186
2006	63.1	72.9	58.0	36.9	7 576	5.2	4 162	19 591	7 001	2 266	3 131	2 751	1 119
2007	63.0	72.8	58.2	34.8	7 655	5.2	4 401	19 756	7 078	2 303	3 259	2 718	1 101
2008	62.2	71.6	57.9	32.6	7 620	5.2	5 875	19 343	8 924	3 188	4 297	3 342	1 285
2009	59.3	67.6	56.2	28.4	7 271	5.2	8 913	18 710	14 265	7 272	7 555	5 157	1 552
2008													
January	62.9	72.7	58.3	33.9	7 606	5.2	4 776	19 620	7 628	2 540	3 489	2 889	1 251
February	62.8	72.6	58.2	33.4	7 564	5.2	4 846	19 376	7 435	2 419	3 441	2 871	1 123
March	62.7	72.4	58.2	33.7	7 394	5.1	4 880	19 445	7 793	2 472	3 649	3 054	1 091
April	62.7	72.2	58.2	34.6	7 601	5.2	5 216	19 638	7 631	2 668	3 639	2 903	1 089
May	62.6	72.0	58.1	34.1	7 702	5.3	5 256	19 432	8 397	2 773	3 853	3 187	1 357
June	62.4	71.9	58.1	32.7	7 813	5.4	5 491	19 467	8 560	2 911	4 037	3 215	1 308
July	62.2	71.7	57.9	32.1	7 710	5.3	5 854	19 250	8 895	3 107	4 278	3 180	1 437
August	62.0	71.4	57.8	32.4	8 060	5.6	5 883	19 662	9 509	3 430	4 540	3 677	1 292
September	61.9	71.1	57.8	32.3	7 651	5.3	6 317	19 275	9 569	3 627	4 864	3 388	1 318
October	61.7	70.8	57.7	31.8	7 589	5.2	6 834	19 004	10 172	4 040	5 067	3 723	1 382
November	61.3	70.3	57.5	30.7	7 375	5.1	7 389	18 965	10 617	3 990	5 353	3 926	1 338
December	60.9	69.7	57.4	30.4	7 433	5.2	8 090	18 964	11 400	4 599	5 871	4 160	1 368
2009													
January	60.6	69.2	57.1	30.4	7 476	5.3	7 897	18 879	11 919	4 762	6 144	4 402	1 373
February	60.3	68.8	56.9	30.3	7 617	5.4	8 672	18 861	12 714	5 369	6 593	4 676	1 445
March	59.9	68.2	56.8	29.7	7 609	5.4	9 023	18 829	13 310	5 815	7 013	4 863	1 435
April	59.9	68.1	56.8	29.8	7 731	5.5	8 888	18 976	13 816	6 296	7 441	4 957	1 418
May	59.6	68.0	56.5	29.5	7 301	5.2	9 048	18 848	14 518	7 013	7 787	5 213	1 518
June	59.4	67.7	56.3	29.0	7 174	5.1	8 962	18 715	14 721	7 844	7 892	5 243	1 586
July	59.3	67.5	56.2	28.6	7 247	5.2	8 808	18 993	14 534	7 819	7 728	5 225	1 581
August	59.1	67.3	56.0	27.8	7 079	5.1	9 077	18 768	14 993	7 849	8 055	5 295	1 643
September	58.7	67.0	55.7	27.2	7 047	5.1	9 158	18 590	15 159	8 405	8 116	5 406	1 637
October	58.4	66.7	55.6	26.1	7 017	5.1	9 240	18 632	15 612	8 804	8 362	5 554	1 696
November	58.5	66.7	55.6	26.2	7 060	5.1	9 225	18 354	15 340	8 976	8 239	5 473	1 627
December	58.2	66.3	55.3	25.9	6 910	5.0	9 165	18 364	15 267	8 969	8 011	5 622	1 634

[1]Changes in survey design, population estimates, and methodology in 1994 and several other years affect year-to-year comparisons. See notes and definitions for more information.
[2]Fifteen weeks and over.
. . . = Not available.

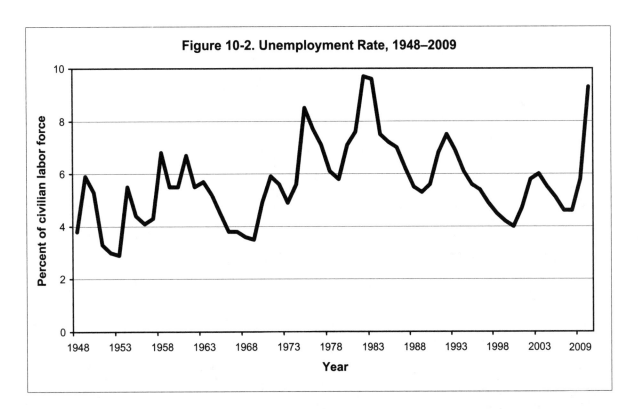

Figure 10-2. Unemployment Rate, 1948–2009

- The unemployment rate peaked at 10.1 percent in October 2009. This was below the postwar record of 10.8 percent, set in November and December 1982. Yet the 1982 employment losses were proportionately less than those of 2008–2009. The difference is in labor force behavior. In 1982, the labor force actually increased despite job losses, which raised the unemployment rate, in contrast to the substantial withdrawal from the labor force that occurred in 2008–2009 and kept the unemployment rate below what it would have been had more unemployed workers remained in the labor force as they did in 1982. (Tables 10-1, 10-3, 10-4, and 20-3)

- In early 2010, workers reentered the labor force by almost the same numbers as the growth in employment. As a result, the unemployment rate in April 2010 was 9.9 percent, not significantly different from the December 2009 rate of 10.0 percent, despite the rapid rate of job growth.

Table 10-4. Unemployment Rates [1]

(Unemployment as a percent of the civilian labor force in group; seasonally adjusted, except as noted.)

Year and month	All civilian workers	By age and sex			By race				Hispanic or Latino ethnicity	By marital status		
		Men, 20 years and over	Women, 20 years and over	Both sexes, 16 to 19 years	White	Black and other	Black or African American	Asian [2]		Married men, spouse present	Married women, spouse present	Women who maintain families [2]
1965	4.5	3.2	4.5	14.8	4.1	8.1	...	...	...	2.4	4.5	...
1966	3.8	2.5	3.8	12.8	3.4	7.3	...	...	...	1.9	3.7	...
1967	3.8	2.3	4.2	12.9	3.4	7.4	...	...	...	1.8	4.5	4.9
1968	3.6	2.2	3.8	12.7	3.2	6.7	...	...	...	1.6	3.9	4.4
1969	3.5	2.1	3.7	12.2	3.1	6.4	...	...	...	1.5	3.9	4.4
1970	4.9	3.5	4.8	15.3	4.5	8.2	...	...	...	2.6	4.9	5.4
1971	5.9	4.4	5.7	16.9	5.4	9.9	...	...	...	3.2	5.7	7.3
1972	5.6	4.0	5.4	16.2	5.1	10.0	10.4	...	...	2.8	5.4	7.2
1973	4.9	3.3	4.9	14.5	4.3	9.0	9.4	...	7.5	2.3	4.7	7.1
1974	5.6	3.8	5.5	16.0	5.0	9.9	10.5	...	8.1	2.7	5.3	7.0
1975	8.5	6.8	8.0	19.9	7.8	13.8	14.8	...	12.2	5.1	7.9	10.0
1976	7.7	5.9	7.4	19.0	7.0	13.1	14.0	...	11.5	4.2	7.1	10.1
1977	7.1	5.2	7.0	17.8	6.2	13.1	14.0	...	10.1	3.6	6.5	9.4
1978	6.1	4.3	6.0	16.4	5.2	11.9	12.8	...	9.1	2.8	5.5	8.5
1979	5.8	4.2	5.7	16.1	5.1	11.3	12.3	...	8.3	2.8	5.1	8.3
1980	7.1	5.9	6.4	17.8	6.3	13.1	14.3	...	10.1	4.2	5.8	9.2
1981	7.6	6.3	6.8	19.6	6.7	14.2	15.6	...	10.4	4.3	6.0	10.4
1982	9.7	8.8	8.3	23.2	8.6	17.3	18.9	...	13.8	6.5	7.4	11.7
1983	9.6	8.9	8.1	22.4	8.4	17.8	19.5	...	13.7	6.5	7.0	12.2
1984	7.5	6.6	6.8	18.9	6.5	14.4	15.9	...	10.7	4.6	5.7	10.3
1985	7.2	6.2	6.6	18.6	6.2	13.7	15.1	...	10.5	4.3	5.6	10.4
1986	7.0	6.1	6.2	18.3	6.0	13.1	14.5	...	10.6	4.4	5.2	9.8
1987	6.2	5.4	5.4	16.9	5.3	11.6	13.0	...	8.8	3.9	4.3	9.2
1988	5.5	4.8	4.9	15.3	4.7	10.4	11.7	...	8.2	3.3	3.9	8.1
1989	5.3	4.5	4.7	15.0	4.5	10.0	11.4	...	8.0	3.0	3.7	8.1
1990	5.6	5.0	4.9	15.5	4.8	10.1	11.4	...	8.2	3.4	3.8	8.3
1991	6.8	6.4	5.7	18.7	6.1	11.1	12.5	...	10.0	4.4	4.5	9.3
1992	7.5	7.1	6.3	20.1	6.6	12.7	14.2	...	11.6	5.1	5.0	10.0
1993	6.9	6.4	5.9	19.0	6.1	11.7	13.0	...	10.8	4.4	4.6	9.7
1994	6.1	5.4	5.4	17.6	5.3	10.5	11.5	...	9.9	3.7	4.1	8.9
1995	5.6	4.8	4.9	17.3	4.9	9.6	10.4	...	9.3	3.3	3.9	8.0
1996	5.4	4.6	4.8	16.7	4.7	9.3	10.5	...	8.9	3.0	3.6	8.2
1997	4.9	4.2	4.4	16.0	4.2	8.8	10.0	...	7.7	2.7	3.1	8.1
1998	4.5	3.7	4.1	14.6	3.9	7.8	8.9	...	7.2	2.4	2.9	7.2
1999	4.2	3.5	3.8	13.9	3.7	7.0	8.0	...	6.4	2.2	2.7	6.4
2000	4.0	3.3	3.6	13.1	3.5	6.7	7.6	3.6	5.7	2.0	2.7	5.9
2001	4.7	4.2	4.1	14.7	4.2	7.7	8.6	4.5	6.6	2.7	3.1	6.6
2002	5.8	5.3	5.1	16.5	5.1	9.2	10.2	5.9	7.5	3.6	3.7	8.0
2003	6.0	5.6	5.1	17.5	5.2	...	10.8	6.0	7.7	3.8	3.7	8.5
2004	5.5	5.0	4.9	17.0	4.8	...	10.4	4.4	7.0	3.1	3.5	8.0
2005	5.1	4.4	4.6	16.6	4.4	...	10.0	4.0	6.0	2.8	3.3	7.8
2006	4.6	4.0	4.1	15.4	4.0	...	8.9	3.0	5.2	2.4	2.9	7.1
2007	4.6	4.1	4.0	15.7	4.1	...	8.3	3.2	5.6	2.5	2.8	6.5
2008	5.8	5.4	4.9	18.7	5.2	...	10.1	4.0	7.6	3.4	3.6	8.0
2009	9.3	9.6	7.5	24.3	8.5	...	14.8	7.3	12.1	6.6	5.5	11.5
2008												
January	5.0	4.4	4.2	17.8	4.4	...	9.2	3.2	6.4	2.7	3.1	7.0
February	4.8	4.4	4.2	16.5	4.4	...	8.3	3.0	6.2	2.7	3.0	6.7
March	5.1	4.6	4.5	16.0	4.5	...	9.1	3.6	6.9	2.9	3.2	7.1
April	5.0	4.6	4.3	15.6	4.4	...	8.6	3.2	6.9	2.8	2.9	6.8
May	5.4	4.9	4.7	18.9	4.8	...	9.6	3.8	6.9	2.9	3.1	6.9
June	5.5	5.1	4.7	19.0	5.0	...	9.4	4.5	7.7	3.0	3.4	7.9
July	5.8	5.4	4.7	20.8	5.2	...	9.9	4.0	7.5	3.3	3.4	8.5
August	6.1	5.7	5.4	18.9	5.5	...	10.8	4.4	8.0	3.6	3.9	9.6
September	6.2	6.1	5.0	19.3	5.5	...	11.4	3.8	8.0	3.9	3.5	8.2
October	6.6	6.4	5.4	20.3	6.0	...	11.3	3.8	8.9	4.1	4.2	8.8
November	6.9	6.8	5.7	20.3	6.3	...	11.5	4.8	8.8	4.3	4.4	9.3
December	7.4	7.4	6.0	20.8	6.7	...	12.1	5.1	9.4	4.6	4.6	9.5
2009												
January	7.7	7.8	6.4	20.9	7.0	...	12.8	6.2	9.9	5.1	4.8	10.3
February	8.2	8.4	6.8	21.8	7.5	...	13.5	6.9	11.0	5.6	5.2	10.3
March	8.6	8.9	7.1	22.0	8.0	...	13.5	6.4	11.6	6.0	5.5	10.8
April	8.9	9.4	7.2	21.8	8.1	...	15.0	6.6	11.4	6.3	5.5	10.0
May	9.4	9.8	7.5	23.2	8.6	...	15.0	6.7	12.7	6.7	5.6	11.0
June	9.5	10.0	7.6	24.3	8.7	...	14.8	8.2	12.3	6.9	5.6	11.7
July	9.4	9.8	7.6	24.5	8.7	...	14.7	8.3	12.4	6.9	5.5	12.6
August	9.7	10.2	7.7	25.7	8.9	...	15.2	7.5	13.0	7.1	5.5	12.2
September	9.8	10.3	7.9	26.1	9.1	...	15.5	7.4	12.7	7.3	5.8	11.6
October	10.1	10.6	8.1	27.6	9.4	...	15.7	7.5	13.1	7.5	5.9	12.9
November	10.0	10.4	8.0	26.8	9.3	...	15.6	7.3	12.7	7.5	5.7	11.4
December	10.0	10.2	8.2	27.1	9.0	...	16.2	8.4	12.9	7.3	5.8	13.0

[1]Changes in survey design, population estimates, and methodology in 1994 and several other years affect year-to-year comparisons. See notes and definitions for more information.
[2]Not seasonally adjusted.
. . . = Not available.

Table 10-5. Unemployment Rates and Related Data [1]

(Seasonally adjusted.)

Year and month	Unemployment rates by reason for unemployment (percent of total civilian labor force)					Duration of unemployment		Alternative measures of labor utilization		
	Total	Job losers and persons who completed temporary jobs	Job leavers	Reentrants	New entrants	Average (mean) weeks unemployed	Median weeks unemployed	Including discouraged workers (U-4)	Including all marginally attached workers (U-5)	Including marginally attached and underemployed (U-6)
1965	4.5	. . .	. . .	. . .	. . .	11.8	. . .	. . .	. . .	. . .
1966	3.8	. . .	. . .	. . .	. . .	10.4	. . .	. . .	. . .	. . .
1967	3.8	1.6	0.6	1.2	0.5	8.7	2.3	. . .	. . .	. . .
1968	3.6	1.4	0.5	1.2	0.5	8.4	4.5	. . .	. . .	. . .
1969	3.5	1.3	0.5	1.2	0.5	7.8	4.4	. . .	. . .	. . .
1970	4.9	2.2	0.7	1.5	0.6	8.6	4.9	. . .	. . .	. . .
1971	5.9	2.8	0.7	1.7	0.7	11.3	6.3	. . .	. . .	. . .
1972	5.6	2.4	0.7	1.7	0.8	12.0	6.2	. . .	. . .	. . .
1973	4.9	1.9	0.8	1.5	0.7	10.0	5.2	. . .	. . .	. . .
1974	5.6	2.4	0.8	1.6	0.7	9.8	5.2	. . .	. . .	. . .
1975	8.5	4.7	0.9	2.0	0.9	14.2	8.4	. . .	. . .	. . .
1976	7.7	3.8	0.9	2.0	0.9	15.8	8.2	. . .	. . .	. . .
1977	7.1	3.2	0.9	2.0	1.0	14.3	7.0	. . .	. . .	. . .
1978	6.1	2.5	0.9	1.8	0.9	11.9	5.9	. . .	. . .	. . .
1979	5.8	2.5	0.8	1.7	0.8	10.8	5.4	. . .	. . .	. . .
1980	7.1	3.7	0.8	1.8	0.8	11.9	6.5	. . .	. . .	. . .
1981	7.6	3.9	0.8	1.9	0.9	13.7	6.9	. . .	. . .	. . .
1982	9.7	5.7	0.8	2.2	1.1	15.6	8.7	. . .	. . .	. . .
1983	9.6	5.6	0.7	2.2	1.1	20.0	10.1	. . .	. . .	. . .
1984	7.5	3.9	0.7	1.9	1.0	18.2	7.9	. . .	. . .	. . .
1985	7.2	3.6	0.8	2.0	0.9	15.6	6.8	. . .	. . .	. . .
1986	7.0	3.4	0.9	1.8	0.9	15.0	6.9	. . .	. . .	. . .
1987	6.2	3.0	0.8	1.6	0.8	14.5	6.5	. . .	. . .	. . .
1988	5.5	2.5	0.8	1.5	0.7	13.5	5.9	. . .	. . .	. . .
1989	5.3	2.4	0.8	1.5	0.5	11.9	4.8	. . .	. . .	. . .
1990	5.6	2.7	0.8	1.5	0.5	12.0	5.3	. . .	. . .	. . .
1991	6.8	3.7	0.8	1.7	0.6	13.7	6.8	. . .	. . .	. . .
1992	7.5	4.2	0.8	1.8	0.7	17.7	8.7	. . .	. . .	. . .
1993	6.9	3.8	0.8	1.7	0.7	18.0	8.3	. . .	. . .	. . .
1994	6.1	2.9	0.6	2.1	0.5	18.8	9.2	6.5	7.4	10.9
1995	5.6	2.6	0.6	1.9	0.4	16.6	8.3	5.9	6.7	10.1
1996	5.4	2.5	0.6	1.9	0.4	16.7	8.3	5.7	6.5	9.7
1997	4.9	2.2	0.6	1.7	0.4	15.8	8.0	5.2	5.9	8.9
1998	4.5	2.1	0.5	1.5	0.4	14.5	6.7	4.7	5.4	8.0
1999	4.2	1.9	0.6	1.4	0.3	13.4	6.4	4.4	5.0	7.4
2000	4.0	1.8	0.5	1.4	0.3	12.6	5.9	4.2	4.8	7.0
2001	4.7	2.4	0.6	1.4	0.3	13.1	6.8	4.9	5.6	8.1
2002	5.8	3.2	0.6	1.6	0.4	16.6	9.1	6.0	6.7	9.6
2003	6.0	3.3	0.6	1.7	0.4	19.2	10.1	6.3	7.0	10.1
2004	5.5	2.8	0.6	1.6	0.5	19.6	9.8	5.8	6.5	9.6
2005	5.1	2.5	0.6	1.6	0.4	18.4	8.9	5.4	6.1	8.9
2006	4.6	2.2	0.5	1.5	0.4	16.8	8.3	4.9	5.5	8.2
2007	4.6	2.3	0.5	1.4	0.4	16.8	8.5	4.9	5.5	8.3
2008	5.8	3.1	0.6	1.6	0.5	17.9	9.4	6.1	6.8	10.5
2009	9.3	5.9	0.6	2.1	0.7	24.4	15.1	9.7	10.5	16.2
2008										
January	5.0	2.5	0.5	1.4	0.4	17.5	9.0	5.2	6.0	9.1
February	4.8	2.5	0.5	1.4	0.4	16.9	8.6	5.1	5.8	8.9
March	5.1	2.7	0.5	1.4	0.5	16.4	8.4	5.3	5.9	9.0
April	5.0	2.6	0.6	1.4	0.4	17.0	9.3	5.2	5.8	9.2
May	5.4	2.7	0.6	1.6	0.5	16.8	8.1	5.7	6.3	9.7
June	5.5	2.8	0.6	1.6	0.5	17.4	9.4	5.8	6.5	10.0
July	5.8	3.0	0.6	1.8	0.5	17.1	9.7	6.0	6.7	10.5
August	6.1	3.2	0.7	1.7	0.5	17.7	9.4	6.4	7.1	10.9
September	6.2	3.4	0.6	1.7	0.5	18.6	10.2	6.5	7.2	11.2
October	6.6	3.7	0.6	1.7	0.5	19.8	10.5	6.9	7.5	11.9
November	6.9	4.1	0.6	1.7	0.5	18.7	9.9	7.2	8.0	12.8
December	7.4	4.4	0.7	1.8	0.5	19.6	10.7	7.8	8.5	13.7
2009										
January	7.7	4.7	0.6	1.8	0.5	19.9	10.6	8.2	9.0	14.0
February	8.2	5.1	0.5	1.9	0.7	20.0	11.4	8.7	9.4	15.0
March	8.6	5.5	0.6	2.0	0.6	20.8	11.9	9.0	9.9	15.6
April	8.9	5.7	0.6	2.0	0.6	21.8	13.1	9.4	10.1	15.8
May	9.4	6.1	0.6	2.1	0.6	22.9	14.9	9.8	10.6	16.4
June	9.5	6.2	0.5	2.1	0.6	24.4	18.2	10.0	10.8	16.5
July	9.4	6.2	0.6	2.1	0.6	25.3	15.9	9.9	10.7	16.4
August	9.7	6.4	0.5	2.1	0.7	25.2	15.5	10.1	11.0	16.8
September	9.8	6.6	0.6	2.1	0.7	26.5	17.8	10.3	11.1	17.0
October	10.1	6.7	0.6	2.2	0.7	27.2	19.0	10.6	11.5	17.4
November	10.0	6.5	0.6	2.1	0.8	28.6	20.2	10.5	11.3	17.2
December	10.0	6.3	0.6	2.2	0.8	29.1	20.5	10.5	11.4	17.3

[1]Changes in survey design, population estimates, and methodology in 1994 and several other years affect year-to-year comparisons. See notes and definitions for more information.
. . . = Not available.

Table 10-6. Insured Unemployment

(Averages of weekly data; thousands of persons, except as noted.)

Year and month	State programs, seasonally adjusted			Federal programs, not seasonally adjusted					
	Initial claims	Insured unemployment	Insured unemployment rate (percent) [1]	Initial claims		Persons claiming benefits			
				Federal employees	Newly discharged veterans	Federal employees	Newly discharged veterans	Railroad retirement	Extended benefits
1967	227	1 206	...	...	...	...	...	...	...
1968	197	1 088	...	...	...	...	...	...	...
1969	196	1 092	...	...	...	...	...	...	...
1970	297	1 848	...	...	...	...	...	...	...
1971	296	2 152	4.1	...	...	...	...	...	...
1972	263	1 844	3.5	...	...	...	...	...	...
1973	244	1 629	2.7	...	...	...	...	...	...
1974	352	2 278	3.5	...	...	...	...	...	...
1975	474	3 965	6.0	...	...	...	...	...	...
1976	383	2 978	4.5	...	...	...	...	...	...
1977	374	2 644	3.9	...	...	...	...	...	...
1978	341	2 337	3.3	...	...	...	...	...	...
1979	383	2 428	3.0	...	...	...	...	...	...
1980	488	3 365	3.9	...	...	...	...	...	...
1981	451	3 032	3.5	...	...	...	...	...	...
1982	586	4 094	4.7	...	...	...	...	...	...
1983	441	3 337	3.9	...	...	...	...	...	...
1984	374	2 452	2.8	...	...	...	...	...	...
1985	392	2 584	2.9	...	...	...	...	...	...
1986	378	2 632	2.8	2.13	2.52	20.24	17.11	...	...
1987	325	2 273	2.4	2.19	2.57	21.29	17.71	...	9.51
1988	309	2 075	2.1	2.32	2.74	22.91	18.13	13.28	1.17
1989	330	2 174	2.1	2.14	2.31	22.17	15.09	10.37	0.61
1990	385	2 539	2.4	2.45	2.54	23.89	18.43	10.56	2.36
1991	447	3 338	3.2	2.55	2.93	30.50	22.12	10.73	32.16
1992	409	3 208	3.1	2.75	4.95	32.10	60.25	8.77	4.61
1993	344	2 768	2.6	2.55	3.94	32.06	54.90	7.40	7.59
1994	340	2 667	2.5	2.54	3.02	32.21	37.65	6.21	31.09
1995	359	2 590	2.4	4.57	2.51	31.68	29.78	5.48	14.27
1996	352	2 552	2.3	7.33	2.13	29.84	24.30	5.40	5.53
1997	322	2 300	2.0	2.01	1.75	23.58	19.66	4.00	5.35
1998	317	2 213	1.9	1.64	1.41	19.60	15.68	3.19	6.43
1999	298	2 186	1.8	1.48	1.18	16.85	14.25	3.24	3.05
2000	299	2 112	1.7	1.73	1.05	18.60	12.54	3.92	0.58
2001	406	3 016	2.4	1.47	1.15	18.57	13.98	...	0.57
2002	404	3 570	2.8	1.46	1.22	17.54	16.07	...	10.79
2003	402	3 532	2.8	1.56	1.46	18.22	19.68	...	22.30
2004	342	2 930	2.3	1.50	1.89	18.14	26.90	...	4.22
2005	331	2 660	2.1	1.46	2.03	16.92	27.58	...	1.69
2006	312	2 456	1.9	1.34	1.96	15.51	26.37	...	1.38
2007	321	1 697	1.9	1.29	1.67	14.90	22.80	...	0.00
2008	419	3 340	2.5	1.25	1.64	14.53	22.16	...	3.43
2009	572	5 809	4.4	1.62	2.03	20.03	30.41	...	380.75
2007									
January	319	2 517	1.9	1.71	1.91	19.46	25.88	...	0.00
February	320	2 563	2.0	1.02	1.70	17.87	24.52	...	0.01
March	306	2 504	1.9	0.98	1.67	15.75	23.47	...	0.00
April	320	2 486	1.9	0.87	1.52	13.19	22.50	...	0.00
May	305	2 444	1.9	0.99	1.52	11.06	21.45	...	0.00
June	317	2 478	1.9	1.43	1.62	11.49	20.97	...	0.00
July	314	2 546	1.9	1.27	1.74	14.03	21.38	...	0.00
August	323	2 561	1.9	1.16	1.86	14.20	21.45	...	0.00
September	315	2 554	1.9	1.34	1.83	14.05	22.12	...	0.00
October	331	2 580	2.0	1.38	1.79	14.97	22.76	...	0.00
November	336	2 627	2.0	1.66	1.54	15.36	23.44	...	0.00
December	346	2 716	2.1	1.63	1.42	17.51	23.82	...	0.00
2008									
January	340	2 789	2.1	1.51	2.37	18.89	24.23	...	0.00
February	343	2 835	2.1	0.93	1.46	16.92	23.08	...	0.00
March	358	2 887	2.2	0.84	1.42	14.91	22.20	...	0.00
April	360	2 942	2.2	0.93	1.42	12.50	21.19	...	0.00
May	369	2 999	2.2	1.01	1.38	10.95	19.93	...	0.00
June	388	3 054	2.3	1.36	1.50	11.41	19.28	...	1.16
July	399	3 183	2.4	1.31	1.65	13.32	20.60	...	1.59
August	439	3 397	2.5	1.06	1.70	13.74	21.40	...	1.36
September	469	3 557	2.7	1.23	1.74	13.46	22.24	...	1.50
October	479	3 763	2.8	1.46	1.70	14.12	22.93	...	10.10
November	523	4 123	3.1	1.81	1.71	15.70	23.99	...	21.31
December	554	4 536	3.4	1.67	1.67	19.12	25.16	...	1.96
2009									
January	573	4 852	3.6	1.82	2.26	20.79	27.39	...	9.65
February	632	5 273	3.9	1.19	1.93	19.65	28.35	...	3.61
March	643	5 701	4.3	1.08	1.76	18.74	28.72	...	21.24
April	627	6 119	4.6	1.15	1.74	16.93	28.69	...	99.72
May	616	6 479	4.9	1.60	1.72	15.57	28.10	...	375.72
June	605	6 511	4.9	1.67	1.99	17.17	28.37	...	578.38
July	563	6 167	4.7	1.69	2.07	19.13	29.87	...	639.11
August	565	6 089	4.6	1.50	2.17	20.13	30.40	...	710.44
September	547	6 044	4.6	1.49	2.28	19.96	30.84	...	636.06
October	527	5 815	4.4	2.18	2.46	22.09	33.37	...	576.85
November	492	5 489	4.2	2.11	2.01	24.50	35.43	...	533.73
December	474	5 164	3.9	1.75	1.82	26.14	36.02	...	346.57

[1] Insured unemployed as a percent of employment covered by state programs.
. . . = Not available.

Section 10b: Payroll Employment, Hours, and Earnings

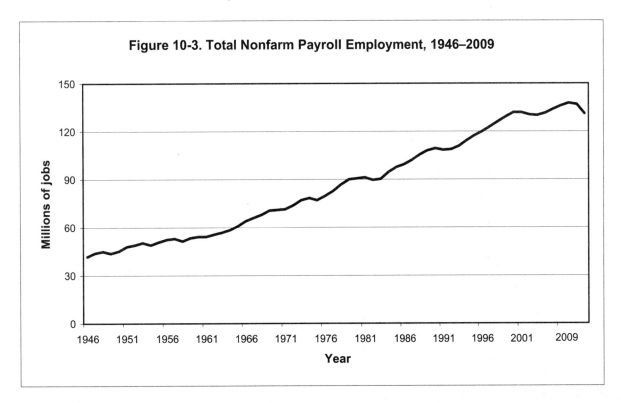

Figure 10-3. Total Nonfarm Payroll Employment, 1946–2009

- The 2001–2007 economic expansion ended in December 2007, according to the National Bureau of Economic Research. Nonfarm payroll employment peaked in the same month and plunged 6.1 percent, a postwar record, between then and December 2009. The total number of jobs lost by this measure was 8.4 million. (Tables 10-7 and 20-4)

- Preliminary data for April 2010 indicate a job gain of 573,000 since the December 2009 low—much less than the household survey featured in the previous section. The differences between these two employment surveys are discussed in the Notes and Definitions to this chapter. Among other differences, the payroll survey for current months is subject to revision when the more complete "benchmark" employment data become available.

- Based on annual average data, payroll employment grew by 5.8 million jobs between the 2000 and 2007 business cycle high points, an average growth rate of 0.6 percent per year during the latest completed cycle. The previous business cycle lasted 10 years between high points, from 1990 to 2000. During that period, 22.3 million jobs were added to U.S. nonfarm payrolls, for an annual average growth rate of 1.9 percent per year. (Table 10-7)

- The diffusion index shows the percentage of industries in which employment is higher than six months earlier. Diffusion indexes measure the extent to which expansion and contraction spread throughout the economy; indexes below 50 percent indicate recession. This index reached a low of 11.9 percent in April 2009—lower than the lowest points reached in any of the previous four recessions (1980, 1981–1982, 1990–1991, and 2001), and thus indicating the most widespread and pervasive decline in 30 years or more. (Table 10-7)

Table 10-7. Nonfarm Payroll Employment by NAICS Supersector

(Thousands; seasonally adjusted, except as noted.)

Year and month	Total	Private							Service-providing				
		Total	Goods-producing						Total	Private			
			Total	Mining and logging	Construc-tion	Manufacturing				Total	Trade, transportation, and utilities		
						Total	Durable	Nondurable			Total	Wholesale trade	Retail trade
1965	60 874	50 683	20 595	694	3 284	16 617	9 973	6 644	40 279	30 089	12 139	2 967	6 262
1966	64 020	53 110	21 740	690	3 371	17 680	10 803	6 878	42 280	31 370	12 611	3 080	6 530
1967	65 931	54 406	21 882	679	3 305	17 897	10 952	6 945	44 049	32 524	12 950	3 158	6 711
1968	68 023	56 050	22 292	671	3 410	18 211	11 137	7 074	45 731	33 759	13 334	3 236	6 977
1969	70 512	58 181	22 893	683	3 637	18 573	11 396	7 177	47 619	35 288	13 853	3 344	7 295
1970	71 006	58 318	22 179	677	3 654	17 848	10 762	7 086	48 827	36 139	14 144	3 418	7 463
1971	71 335	58 323	21 602	658	3 770	17 174	10 229	6 944	49 734	36 721	14 318	3 424	7 657
1972	73 798	60 333	22 299	672	3 957	17 669	10 630	7 039	51 499	38 034	14 788	3 547	8 038
1973	76 912	63 050	23 450	693	4 167	18 589	11 414	7 176	53 462	39 600	15 349	3 688	8 371
1974	78 389	64 086	23 364	755	4 095	18 514	11 432	7 082	55 025	40 721	15 693	3 823	8 536
1975	77 069	62 250	21 318	802	3 608	16 909	10 266	6 643	55 751	40 932	15 606	3 810	8 600
1976	79 502	64 501	22 025	832	3 662	17 531	10 640	6 891	57 477	42 476	16 128	3 920	8 966
1977	82 593	67 334	22 972	865	3 940	18 167	11 132	7 035	59 620	44 362	16 765	4 055	9 359
1978	86 826	71 014	24 156	902	4 322	18 932	11 770	7 162	62 670	46 858	17 658	4 280	9 879
1979	89 932	73 864	24 997	1 008	4 562	19 426	12 220	7 206	64 935	48 868	18 303	4 485	10 180
1980	90 528	74 154	24 263	1 077	4 454	18 733	11 679	7 054	66 265	49 891	18 413	4 557	10 244
1981	91 289	75 109	24 118	1 180	4 304	18 634	11 611	7 023	67 172	50 991	18 604	4 634	10 364
1982	89 677	73 695	22 550	1 163	4 024	17 363	10 610	6 753	67 127	51 145	18 457	4 575	10 372
1983	90 280	74 269	22 110	997	4 065	17 048	10 326	6 722	68 171	52 160	18 668	4 559	10 635
1984	94 530	78 371	23 435	1 014	4 501	17 920	11 050	6 870	71 095	54 936	19 653	4 788	11 223
1985	97 511	80 978	23 585	974	4 793	17 819	11 034	6 784	73 926	57 393	20 379	4 915	11 733
1986	99 474	82 636	23 318	829	4 937	17 552	10 795	6 757	76 156	59 318	20 795	4 935	12 078
1987	102 088	84 932	23 470	771	5 090	17 609	10 767	6 842	78 618	61 462	21 302	5 003	12 419
1988	105 345	87 806	23 909	770	5 233	17 906	10 969	6 938	81 436	63 897	21 974	5 153	12 808
1989	108 014	90 087	24 045	750	5 309	17 985	11 004	6 981	83 969	66 042	22 510	5 284	13 108
1990	109 487	91 072	23 723	765	5 263	17 695	10 737	6 958	85 764	67 349	22 666	5 268	13 182
1991	108 375	89 829	22 588	739	4 780	17 068	10 220	6 848	85 787	67 241	22 281	5 185	12 896
1992	108 726	89 940	22 095	689	4 608	16 799	9 946	6 853	86 631	67 845	22 125	5 110	12 828
1993	110 844	91 855	22 219	666	4 779	16 774	9 901	6 872	88 625	69 636	22 378	5 093	13 021
1994	114 291	95 016	22 774	659	5 095	17 020	10 132	6 889	91 517	72 242	23 128	5 247	13 491
1995	117 298	97 865	23 156	641	5 274	17 241	10 373	6 868	94 142	74 710	23 834	5 433	13 897
1996	119 708	100 169	23 409	637	5 536	17 237	10 486	6 751	96 299	76 760	24 239	5 522	14 143
1997	122 776	103 113	23 886	654	5 813	17 419	10 705	6 714	98 890	79 227	24 700	5 664	14 389
1998	125 930	106 021	24 354	645	6 149	17 560	10 911	6 649	101 576	81 667	25 186	5 795	14 609
1999	128 993	108 686	24 465	598	6 545	17 322	10 831	6 491	104 528	84 221	25 771	5 893	14 970
2000	131 785	110 995	24 649	599	6 787	17 263	10 877	6 386	107 136	86 346	26 225	5 933	15 280
2001	131 826	110 708	23 873	606	6 826	16 441	10 336	6 105	107 952	86 834	25 983	5 773	15 239
2002	130 341	108 828	22 557	583	6 716	15 259	9 485	5 774	107 784	86 271	25 497	5 652	15 025
2003	129 999	108 416	21 816	572	6 735	14 510	8 964	5 546	108 183	86 600	25 287	5 608	14 917
2004	131 435	109 814	21 882	591	6 976	14 315	8 925	5 390	109 553	87 932	25 533	5 663	15 058
2005	133 703	111 899	22 190	628	7 336	14 226	8 956	5 271	111 513	89 709	25 959	5 764	15 280
2006	136 086	114 113	22 531	684	7 691	14 155	8 981	5 174	113 556	91 582	26 276	5 905	15 353
2007	137 598	115 380	22 233	724	7 630	13 879	8 808	5 071	115 366	93 147	26 630	6 015	15 520
2008	136 790	114 281	21 334	767	7 162	13 406	8 463	4 943	115 456	92 947	26 293	5 943	15 283
2009	130 920	108 371	18 620	700	6 037	11 883	7 309	4 574	112 300	89 751	24 949	5 625	14 528
2008													
January	137 941	115 562	21 932	744	7 467	13 721	8 690	5 031	116 009	93 630	26 699	6 031	15 564
February	137 891	115 477	21 877	747	7 439	13 691	8 671	5 020	116 014	93 600	26 656	6 022	15 529
March	137 858	115 419	21 815	755	7 406	13 654	8 642	5 012	116 043	93 604	26 641	6 015	15 518
April	137 709	115 258	21 707	756	7 347	13 604	8 601	5 003	116 002	93 551	26 558	5 995	15 451
May	137 478	115 005	21 626	763	7 286	13 577	8 587	4 990	115 852	93 379	26 465	5 981	15 384
June	137 285	114 775	21 511	767	7 216	13 528	8 559	4 969	115 774	93 264	26 406	5 969	15 347
July	137 075	114 518	21 392	772	7 164	13 456	8 509	4 947	115 683	93 126	26 340	5 947	15 305
August	136 741	114 171	21 254	779	7 112	13 363	8 433	4 930	115 487	92 917	26 238	5 927	15 239
September	136 283	113 715	21 092	782	7 040	13 270	8 368	4 902	115 191	92 623	26 110	5 913	15 160
October	135 729	113 168	20 856	779	6 948	13 129	8 262	4 867	114 873	92 312	25 978	5 878	15 080
November	135 001	112 434	20 573	775	6 799	12 999	8 166	4 833	114 428	91 861	25 792	5 839	14 963
December	134 328	111 767	20 294	768	6 704	12 822	8 042	4 780	114 034	91 473	25 619	5 796	14 863
2009													
January	133 549	110 961	19 855	761	6 551	12 543	7 820	4 723	113 694	91 106	25 475	5 760	14 792
February	132 823	110 254	19 559	747	6 435	12 377	7 702	4 675	113 264	90 695	25 330	5 710	14 723
March	132 070	109 510	19 233	728	6 293	12 212	7 580	4 632	112 837	90 277	25 174	5 672	14 635
April	131 542	108 861	18 956	714	6 179	12 063	7 450	4 613	112 586	89 905	25 052	5 642	14 592
May	131 155	108 527	18 731	700	6 120	11 911	7 326	4 585	112 424	89 796	24 997	5 626	14 570
June	130 640	108 075	18 503	692	6 029	11 782	7 222	4 560	112 137	89 572	24 943	5 613	14 546
July	130 294	107 778	18 375	687	5 949	11 739	7 197	4 542	111 919	89 403	24 845	5 597	14 492
August	130 082	107 563	18 245	678	5 885	11 682	7 151	4 531	111 837	89 318	24 819	5 588	14 477
September	129 857	107 377	18 124	676	5 814	11 634	7 112	4 522	111 733	89 253	24 754	5 580	14 429
October	129 633	107 115	17 993	669	5 747	11 577	7 070	4 507	111 640	89 122	24 670	5 575	14 366
November	129 697	107 190	17 960	676	5 732	11 552	7 047	4 505	111 737	89 230	24 678	5 568	14 375
December	129 588	107 107	17 906	676	5 696	11 534	7 036	4 498	111 682	89 201	24 653	5 564	14 360

Table 10-7. Nonfarm Payroll Employment by NAICS Supersector—*Continued*

(Thousands; seasonally adjusted, except as noted.)

Year and month	Information	Financial activities	Professional and business services	Education and health services	Leisure and hospitality	Other services	Government Total	Federal Total	Federal Department of Defense [1]	State Total	State Education	Local Total	Local Education	Diffusion index, 6-month span, private nonfarm [2]
1965	1 824	2 878	4 306	3 587	3 951	1 404	10 191	2 495	679	1 996	679	5 700	3 031	. . .
1966	1 908	2 961	4 517	3 770	4 127	1 475	10 910	2 690	741	2 141	775	6 080	3 297	. . .
1967	1 955	3 087	4 720	3 986	4 269	1 558	11 525	2 852	802	2 302	873	6 371	3 490	. . .
1968	1 991	3 234	4 918	4 191	4 453	1 638	11 972	2 871	801	2 442	958	6 660	3 649	. . .
1969	2 048	3 404	5 156	4 428	4 670	1 731	12 330	2 893	815	2 533	1 042	6 904	3 785	. . .
1970	2 041	3 532	5 267	4 577	4 789	1 789	12 687	2 865	756	2 664	1 104	7 158	3 912	
1971	2 009	3 651	5 328	4 675	4 914	1 827	13 012	2 828	731	2 747	1 149	7 437	4 091	
1972	2 056	3 784	5 523	4 863	5 121	1 900	13 465	2 815	720	2 859	1 188	7 790	4 262	
1973	2 135	3 920	5 774	5 092	5 341	1 990	13 862	2 794	696	2 923	1 205	8 146	4 433	
1974	2 160	4 023	5 974	5 322	5 471	2 078	14 303	2 858	698	3 039	1 267	8 407	4 584	. . .
1975	2 061	4 047	6 034	5 497	5 544	2 144	14 820	2 882	704	3 179	1 323	8 758	4 722	
1976	2 111	4 155	6 287	5 756	5 794	2 244	15 001	2 863	693	3 273	1 371	8 865	4 786	. . .
1977	2 185	4 348	6 587	6 052	6 065	2 359	15 258	2 859	676	3 377	1 385	9 023	4 859	77.5
1978	2 287	4 599	6 972	6 427	6 411	2 505	15 812	2 893	661	3 474	1 367	9 446	4 958	75.6
1979	2 375	4 843	7 312	6 767	6 631	2 637	16 068	2 894	649	3 541	1 378	9 633	4 989	57.7
1980	2 361	5 025	7 544	7 072	6 721	2 755	16 375	3 000	645	3 610	1 398	9 765	5 090	61.2
1981	2 382	5 163	7 782	7 357	6 840	2 865	16 180	2 922	655	3 640	1 420	9 619	5 095	39.0
1982	2 317	5 209	7 848	7 515	6 874	2 924	15 982	2 884	690	3 640	1 433	9 458	5 049	34.8
1983	2 253	5 334	8 039	7 766	7 078	3 021	16 011	2 915	699	3 662	1 450	9 434	5 020	78.2
1984	2 398	5 553	8 464	8 193	7 489	3 186	16 159	2 943	716	3 734	1 488	9 482	5 076	64.9
1985	2 437	5 815	8 871	8 657	7 869	3 366	16 533	3 014	738	3 832	1 540	9 687	5 221	59.5
1986	2 445	6 128	9 211	9 061	8 156	3 523	16 838	3 044	736	3 893	1 561	9 901	5 358	62.4
1987	2 507	6 385	9 608	9 515	8 446	3 699	17 156	3 089	736	3 967	1 586	10 100	5 469	73.5
1988	2 585	6 500	10 090	10 063	8 778	3 907	17 540	3 124	719	4 076	1 621	10 339	5 590	66.3
1989	2 622	6 562	10 555	10 616	9 062	4 116	17 927	3 136	735	4 182	1 668	10 609	5 740	54.6
1990	2 688	6 614	10 848	10 984	9 288	4 261	18 415	3 196	722	4 305	1 730	10 914	5 902	36.7
1991	2 677	6 558	10 714	11 506	9 256	4 249	18 545	3 110	702	4 355	1 768	11 081	5 994	44.6
1992	2 641	6 540	10 970	11 891	9 437	4 240	18 787	3 111	702	4 408	1 799	11 267	6 076	62.6
1993	2 668	6 709	11 495	12 303	9 732	4 350	18 989	3 063	670	4 488	1 834	11 438	6 206	72.5
1994	2 738	6 867	12 174	12 807	10 100	4 428	19 275	3 018	657	4 576	1 882	11 682	6 329	80.9
1995	2 843	6 827	12 844	13 289	10 501	4 572	19 432	2 949	627	4 635	1 919	11 849	6 453	68.6
1996	2 940	6 969	13 462	13 683	10 777	4 690	19 539	2 877	597	4 606	1 911	12 056	6 592	77.9
1997	3 084	7 178	14 335	14 087	11 018	4 825	19 664	2 806	588	4 582	1 904	12 276	6 759	80.3
1998	3 218	7 462	15 147	14 446	11 232	4 976	19 909	2 772	550	4 612	1 922	12 525	6 921	69.3
1999	3 419	7 648	15 957	14 798	11 543	5 087	20 307	2 769	525	4 709	1 983	12 829	7 120	69.5
2000	3 630	7 687	16 666	15 109	11 862	5 168	20 790	2 865	510	4 786	2 031	13 139	7 294	58.2
2001	3 629	7 808	16 476	15 645	12 036	5 258	21 118	2 764	504	4 905	2 113	13 449	7 479	32.7
2002	3 395	7 847	15 976	16 199	11 986	5 372	21 513	2 766	499	5 029	2 243	13 718	7 654	36.6
2003	3 188	7 977	15 987	16 588	12 173	5 401	21 583	2 761	486	5 002	2 255	13 820	7 709	40.0
2004	3 118	8 031	16 394	16 953	12 493	5 409	21 621	2 730	473	4 982	2 238	13 909	7 765	60.0
2005	3 061	8 153	16 954	17 372	12 816	5 395	21 804	2 732	488	5 032	2 260	14 041	7 856	62.5
2006	3 038	8 328	17 566	17 826	13 110	5 438	21 974	2 732	493	5 075	2 293	14 167	7 913	58.2
2007	3 032	8 301	17 942	18 322	13 427	5 494	22 218	2 734	491	5 122	2 318	14 362	7 987	56.3
2008	2 984	8 145	17 735	18 838	13 436	5 515	22 509	2 762	496	5 177	2 354	14 571	8 084	28.1
2009	2 807	7 758	16 580	19 191	13 102	5 364	22 549	2 828	519	5 180	2 371	14 542	8 062	20.4
2008														
January	3 021	8 218	18 046	18 597	13 527	5 522	22 379	2 739	488	5 141	2 323	14 499	8 054	49.1
February	3 020	8 208	18 007	18 645	13 532	5 532	22 414	2 746	487	5 150	2 331	14 518	8 065	50.6
March	3 018	8 208	17 960	18 696	13 542	5 539	22 439	2 750	487	5 154	2 336	14 535	8 067	51.7
April	3 011	8 202	17 955	18 755	13 529	5 541	22 451	2 757	488	5 160	2 339	14 534	8 058	49.6
May	3 008	8 193	17 889	18 796	13 492	5 536	22 473	2 760	491	5 163	2 341	14 550	8 071	43.9
June	3 001	8 176	17 841	18 837	13 479	5 524	22 510	2 761	496	5 175	2 351	14 574	8 084	39.2
July	2 988	8 161	17 780	18 883	13 452	5 522	22 557	2 763	500	5 195	2 368	14 599	8 110	36.1
August	2 977	8 143	17 687	18 935	13 425	5 512	22 570	2 766	501	5 203	2 374	14 601	8 105	31.6
September	2 965	8 110	17 603	18 944	13 382	5 509	22 568	2 770	498	5 197	2 378	14 601	8 101	28.1
October	2 954	8 073	17 492	18 956	13 346	5 513	22 561	2 774	503	5 190	2 363	14 597	8 090	26.4
November	2 934	8 029	17 341	18 998	13 288	5 479	22 567	2 777	504	5 193	2 367	14 597	8 087	23.0
December	2 908	8 000	17 220	19 033	13 248	5 445	22 561	2 777	505	5 192	2 367	14 592	8 085	21.4
2009														
January	2 888	7 945	17 091	19 069	13 209	5 429	22 588	2 803	504	5 197	2 376	14 588	8 087	17.5
February	2 873	7 894	16 920	19 085	13 183	5 410	22 569	2 792	504	5 188	2 369	14 589	8 091	13.2
March	2 861	7 852	16 774	19 095	13 137	5 384	22 560	2 797	505	5 183	2 365	14 580	8 092	12.1
April	2 837	7 805	16 636	19 099	13 103	5 373	22 681	2 919	507	5 184	2 368	14 578	8 094	11.9
May	2 812	7 773	16 585	19 137	13 126	5 366	22 628	2 865	512	5 189	2 373	14 574	8 087	12.5
June	2 797	7 742	16 453	19 165	13 105	5 367	22 565	2 810	520	5 177	2 366	14 578	8 094	13.4
July	2 785	7 719	16 405	19 186	13 101	5 362	22 516	2 816	525	5 154	2 352	14 546	8 049	13.2
August	2 776	7 695	16 371	19 221	13 083	5 353	22 519	2 815	526	5 172	2 367	14 532	8 034	15.8
September	2 777	7 683	16 349	19 247	13 099	5 344	22 480	2 818	524	5 173	2 366	14 489	8 013	20.4
October	2 774	7 664	16 360	19 282	13 045	5 327	22 518	2 836	530	5 182	2 379	14 500	8 041	20.4
November	2 762	7 666	16 466	19 313	13 024	5 321	22 507	2 833	533	5 172	2 378	14 502	8 054	21.0
December	2 748	7 657	16 488	19 350	12 991	5 314	22 481	2 824	535	5 178	2 384	14 479	8 040	24.7

[1]Not seasonally adjusted.
[2]See notes and definitions for explanation. September value used to represent year.
. . . = Not available.

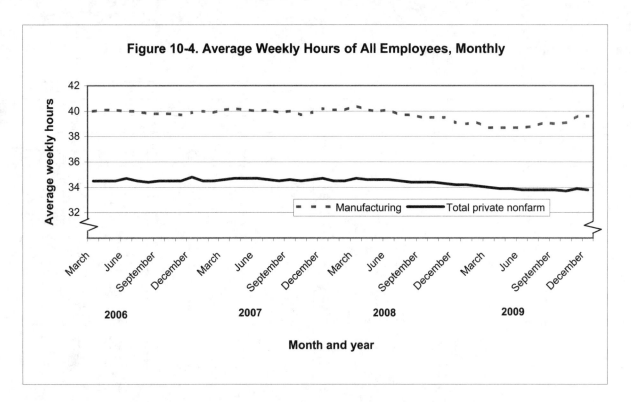

Figure 10-4. Average Weekly Hours of All Employees, Monthly

- The Bureau of Labor Statistics is now collecting and publishing hours and earnings for all nonfarm payroll employees, as well as the hours and earnings for production or nonsupervisory workers that have been collected for many years. The newer, more comprehensive series are available beginning with March 2006. The new monthly data on the length of the workweek for all nonfarm payroll employees and for manufacturing are shown in Figure 10-4. (Table 10-8)

- Differences in order of magnitude between all employees and the older series are not great—perhaps not surprising considering that production or nonsupervisory workers account for about four-fifths of all employees. For manufacturing, the all-employee workweek is somewhat shorter than the production worker workweek; in that industry, production workers characteristically work overtime—averaging 3.3 hours in 2007—and apparently nonproduction workers don't. But for the total nonfarm average, this relation is reversed; the all-employee average workweek is longer than that of nonsupervisory workers, reflecting the prevalence of part-time nonsupervisory jobs in many important industries such as retail trade and many service industries, while evidently supervisors tend to work full time. (Tables 10-8 and 10-13)

- Firms experiencing increases in demand are likely to meet that demand, at first, by having their existing employees work longer hours. If the demand increase is sustained, they become more likely to hire more people. This is the basis for the long-time reputation of the workweek as a leading indicator for employment. As Figure 10-4 demonstrates, the workweek at manufacturing—the most cyclical sector—has been trending upward since June 2009. In May 2010, according to preliminary data, it reached 40.5 percent—the highest yet seen in the short reporting history of this series. The workweek for all private nonfarm industry began to edge up in November 2009 and reached 34.2 hours in May 2010, the highest since January 2009.

Table 10-8. Average Weekly Hours of All Employees on Private Nonfarm Payrolls by NAICS Supersector

(Hours per week, seasonally adjusted.)

Year and month	Total private	Mining and logging	Construc-tion	Manufacturing Average weekly hours	Manufacturing Overtime hours	Trade, transportation, and utilities Total	Wholesale trade	Retail trade	Informa-tion	Financial activities	Profes-sional and business services	Education and health services	Leisure and hospitality	Other services
2007	34.6	44.0	38.0	40.0	3.3	34.6	38.1	31.7	36.1	36.6	35.4	33.5	26.1	32.9
2008	34.5	43.7	37.8	39.8	3.0	34.4	38.4	31.4	36.5	36.5	35.2	33.7	25.9	32.9
2009	33.9	42.1	37.2	39.0	2.3	34.1	37.9	31.3	36.5	36.6	35.0	33.0	25.6	31.6
2006														
January	...	...	...	...	...	...	...	...	...	...	...	...	...	...
February	...	...	...	...	...	...	...	...	...	...	...	...	...	...
March	34.5	42.7	37.7	40.0	3.6	34.0	37.8	31.1	36.3	36.7	35.2	33.4	26.2	33.3
April	34.5	42.9	37.5	40.1	3.6	34.1	37.6	31.3	36.5	36.7	35.2	33.5	26.2	33.3
May	34.5	42.8	37.8	40.1	3.5	34.1	37.5	31.4	36.5	36.7	35.1	33.5	26.3	33.2
June	34.7	42.9	37.9	40.0	3.4	34.3	37.8	31.6	36.5	36.8	35.5	33.5	26.3	33.4
July	34.5	43.2	37.6	40.0	3.3	34.3	37.8	31.5	36.5	36.6	35.3	33.4	26.1	33.2
August	34.4	42.6	37.6	39.8	3.2	34.2	37.7	31.5	36.5	36.5	35.1	33.3	26.1	33.0
September	34.5	42.6	37.8	39.8	3.2	34.3	37.8	31.5	36.3	36.7	35.5	33.4	26.1	33.0
October	34.5	42.3	38.3	39.8	3.0	34.4	37.7	31.7	36.2	36.6	35.1	33.3	26.1	32.9
November	34.5	41.8	37.9	39.7	3.1	34.4	37.8	31.7	36.1	36.6	35.4	33.3	26.3	32.8
December	34.8	42.7	38.8	39.9	3.2	34.8	37.9	32.3	36.0	36.7	35.7	33.4	26.5	32.8
2007														
January	34.5	42.5	37.9	40.0	3.2	34.3	37.4	31.7	36.0	36.5	35.2	33.2	26.3	32.6
February	34.5	43.0	37.4	39.9	3.2	34.2	37.7	31.4	36.1	36.5	35.7	33.2	26.2	32.7
March	34.6	43.3	38.1	40.1	3.4	34.5	38.2	31.7	36.1	36.5	35.5	33.5	26.2	33.0
April	34.7	44.7	37.9	40.2	3.3	34.6	38.2	31.8	36.0	36.5	35.5	33.7	26.2	33.1
May	34.7	44.3	38.3	40.1	3.3	34.5	38.1	31.7	35.9	36.4	35.4	33.7	26.2	33.0
June	34.7	44.2	38.1	40.0	3.4	34.8	38.2	32.0	36.0	36.7	35.5	33.6	26.2	33.1
July	34.6	44.3	37.8	40.1	3.2	34.6	38.3	31.8	36.1	36.5	35.4	33.6	26.0	32.9
August	34.5	43.7	37.5	39.9	3.2	34.5	38.2	31.7	36.1	36.5	35.4	33.5	25.9	32.7
September	34.6	44.7	38.3	40.0	3.2	34.5	38.1	31.6	36.0	36.5	35.5	33.5	25.9	32.7
October	34.5	44.2	38.4	39.7	3.1	34.5	38.1	31.7	36.1	36.5	35.3	33.5	25.9	32.7
November	34.6	43.8	38.3	39.9	3.2	34.5	38.2	31.7	36.2	36.5	35.4	33.5	26.1	32.7
December	34.7	44.1	38.5	40.2	3.3	34.7	38.3	31.9	36.4	36.6	35.5	33.5	26.2	32.6
2008														
January	34.5	43.7	38.2	40.1	3.3	34.5	38.1	31.6	36.5	36.4	35.2	33.4	26.1	32.5
February	34.5	43.8	38.0	40.1	3.3	34.4	38.2	31.5	36.5	36.5	35.4	33.5	26.1	32.7
March	34.7	44.9	38.3	40.4	3.3	34.6	38.4	31.6	36.6	36.5	35.3	33.8	26.2	33.1
April	34.6	43.2	38.1	40.1	3.3	34.6	38.4	31.6	36.7	36.5	35.3	33.9	26.1	33.2
May	34.6	43.7	37.8	40.0	3.1	34.5	38.4	31.5	36.5	36.7	35.2	33.9	26.1	33.0
June	34.6	43.8	38.0	40.1	3.0	34.6	38.5	31.6	36.4	36.6	35.2	33.8	26.0	32.9
July	34.5	43.4	37.6	39.7	2.9	34.5	38.7	31.5	36.5	36.5	35.2	33.8	25.8	32.8
August	34.4	43.3	37.5	39.7	2.9	34.5	38.7	31.4	36.6	36.6	35.3	33.7	25.7	32.9
September	34.4	43.0	37.7	39.5	2.8	34.4	38.5	31.3	36.7	36.5	35.3	33.6	25.7	32.9
October	34.4	43.9	37.8	39.5	2.7	34.4	38.4	31.3	36.8	36.5	35.3	33.6	25.7	32.7
November	34.3	44.3	37.5	39.5	2.5	34.3	38.3	31.3	36.7	36.5	35.2	33.6	25.8	32.6
December	34.2	43.1	37.4	39.1	2.4	34.3	38.3	31.2	36.5	36.5	35.2	33.5	25.7	32.6
2009														
January	34.2	43.5	37.5	39.0	2.3	34.3	38.2	31.3	36.5	36.6	35.1	33.4	25.7	32.5
February	34.1	42.9	37.5	39.1	2.3	34.3	38.2	31.3	36.4	36.5	35.1	33.3	25.7	32.3
March	34.0	42.4	37.3	38.7	2.1	34.3	38.0	31.4	36.3	36.5	35.1	33.3	25.7	31.9
April	33.9	42.2	37.4	38.7	2.1	34.2	37.9	31.3	36.4	36.5	35.0	33.3	25.7	31.9
May	33.9	41.8	37.4	38.7	2.2	34.2	37.9	31.3	36.5	36.5	35.0	33.1	25.6	31.7
June	33.8	41.7	37.2	38.7	2.2	34.1	37.8	31.2	36.4	36.4	35.0	33.0	25.6	31.6
July	33.8	41.8	37.4	38.8	2.2	34.1	37.8	31.3	36.4	36.5	34.9	32.9	25.5	31.5
August	33.8	42.5	37.2	39.1	2.3	34.1	37.8	31.3	36.5	36.5	34.9	32.9	25.6	31.5
September	33.8	41.8	37.0	39.0	2.4	34.1	37.7	31.4	36.6	36.6	34.9	32.9	25.6	31.5
October	33.7	41.6	36.7	39.1	2.5	34.1	37.7	31.3	36.6	36.6	34.9	32.8	25.5	31.4
November	33.9	42.2	37.2	39.6	2.6	34.0	37.7	31.2	36.5	36.6	34.9	32.7	25.4	31.3
December	33.8	42.1	36.9	39.6	2.7	34.0	37.6	31.2	36.5	36.7	35.1	32.7	25.5	31.3

. . . = Not available.

Table 10-9. Indexes of Aggregate Weekly Hours of All Employees on Private Nonfarm Payrolls by NAICS Supersector

(2007 = 100, seasonally adjusted.)

Year and month	Total private	Mining and logging	Construction	Manu-facturing	Trade, transportation, and utilities			Information	Financial activities	Profes-sional and business services	Education and health services	Leisure and hospitality	Other services
					Total	Wholesale trade	Retail trade						
2007	100.0	100.0	100.0	100.0	100.0	100.0	100.0	100.0	100.0	100.0	100.0	100.0	100.0
2008	98.7	105.2	93.3	96.0	98.4	99.6	97.5	99.6	98.0	98.2	103.2	99.1	100.4
2009	92.1	92.7	77.3	83.4	92.6	93.0	92.2	93.6	93.5	91.4	103.0	95.6	94.1
2006													
January	...	...	...	...	...	...	...	...	...	...	...	...	...
February	...	...	...	...	...	...	...	...	...	...	...	...	...
March	98.4	89.6	99.9	102.3	96.9	96.9	97.1	101.2	100.6	96.6	96.3	97.5	100.1
April	98.5	91.5	99.8	102.7	97.2	96.6	97.6	101.5	100.8	96.7	96.8	97.7	100.1
May	98.5	91.7	100.5	102.5	97.2	96.5	97.7	101.3	100.9	96.7	96.9	97.9	99.9
June	99.2	92.5	100.6	102.3	97.8	97.3	98.4	101.2	100.9	98.2	96.9	98.0	100.5
July	98.8	93.7	99.9	102.1	97.9	97.5	98.1	101.0	100.4	97.9	96.8	97.8	99.9
August	98.6	92.8	100.1	101.4	97.7	97.4	98.1	101.0	100.2	97.6	96.8	97.9	99.3
September	98.9	92.9	100.5	101.1	98.1	97.8	98.1	100.0	101.0	98.7	97.4	97.9	99.6
October	98.9	92.9	101.4	100.7	98.5	97.5	98.9	100.0	100.6	97.6	97.3	98.2	99.5
November	99.1	91.9	100.2	100.2	98.7	98.0	99.1	99.7	100.7	98.8	97.6	99.4	99.2
December	100.1	94.5	102.8	100.5	100.0	98.6	101.0	99.7	101.0	99.8	98.1	100.5	99.3
2007													
January	99.4	94.2	100.8	100.8	98.7	97.4	99.4	99.5	100.4	98.7	97.6	99.9	98.7
February	99.5	96.1	98.4	100.5	98.6	98.4	98.7	100.0	100.4	100.3	97.8	99.7	99.2
March	99.9	97.3	101.2	100.8	99.7	99.8	100.0	99.8	100.3	99.9	99.0	99.9	100.3
April	100.3	101.3	100.5	100.9	100.1	100.1	100.2	99.8	100.1	100.0	99.9	100.0	100.7
May	100.4	100.6	101.4	100.6	99.9	99.9	100.0	99.7	99.9	99.9	100.1	100.2	100.5
June	100.4	100.8	101.0	100.1	100.7	100.4	100.8	99.9	100.6	100.2	100.1	100.4	100.9
July	100.2	101.6	99.8	100.3	100.2	100.8	100.2	100.1	100.1	100.0	100.3	99.6	100.3
August	99.8	100.0	98.3	99.3	99.9	100.5	99.9	99.9	99.8	100.0	100.3	99.2	99.6
September	100.0	102.1	100.0	99.2	99.9	100.2	99.5	99.7	99.4	100.2	100.6	99.5	99.5
October	99.8	101.1	100.0	98.2	99.9	100.3	99.8	99.8	99.3	99.9	100.8	99.7	99.6
November	100.2	101.2	99.5	98.7	100.2	100.7	100.2	100.0	99.0	100.2	101.0	100.8	99.8
December	100.5	102.4	99.4	99.3	100.7	100.9	100.8	100.5	99.2	100.8	101.2	101.2	99.6
2008													
January	99.9	102.2	98.3	99.0	100.1	100.3	99.9	100.7	98.6	99.9	101.1	100.7	99.4
February	99.8	102.8	97.4	98.8	99.7	100.4	99.3	100.7	98.7	100.3	101.7	100.8	100.2
March	100.4	106.5	97.8	99.2	100.2	100.8	99.6	100.9	98.7	99.7	102.9	101.2	101.6
April	99.9	102.6	96.5	98.1	99.9	100.4	99.2	100.9	98.6	99.7	103.5	100.8	101.9
May	99.7	104.8	94.9	97.7	99.2	100.2	98.4	100.3	99.1	99.0	103.7	100.5	101.2
June	99.5	105.6	94.5	97.6	99.3	100.3	98.5	99.8	98.6	98.8	103.6	100.0	100.7
July	99.0	105.3	92.8	96.1	98.8	100.4	97.9	99.6	98.2	98.4	103.9	99.0	100.4
August	98.4	106.0	91.9	95.4	98.4	100.1	97.2	99.5	98.2	98.2	103.9	98.4	100.5
September	98.0	105.7	91.5	94.3	97.6	99.3	96.4	99.4	97.5	97.7	103.6	98.1	100.4
October	97.6	107.5	90.5	93.3	97.1	98.5	95.8	99.3	97.1	97.1	103.7	98.2	99.9
November	96.6	107.9	87.9	92.4	96.1	97.6	95.1	98.3	96.6	96.0	103.9	97.8	99.0
December	95.8	104.0	86.4	90.2	95.5	96.9	94.2	96.9	96.2	95.3	103.8	97.1	98.3
2009													
January	95.1	104.0	84.7	88.0	95.0	96.0	94.0	96.3	95.8	94.4	103.7	96.9	97.8
February	94.2	100.7	83.2	87.1	94.4	95.2	93.6	95.5	94.9	93.4	103.4	96.7	96.8
March	93.3	97.0	80.9	85.0	93.8	94.0	93.3	94.8	94.4	92.6	103.5	96.3	95.2
April	92.5	94.7	79.6	84.0	93.1	93.3	92.8	94.3	93.9	91.6	102.9	95.7	94.4
May	92.2	91.9	78.9	82.9	92.9	93.0	92.6	93.7	93.5	91.3	102.8	95.9	93.9
June	91.5	90.7	77.3	82.0	92.4	92.6	92.2	93.0	92.9	90.6	102.6	95.4	93.7
July	91.3	90.2	76.7	81.9	92.1	92.3	92.1	92.6	92.8	90.0	102.7	95.3	93.6
August	91.1	90.5	75.4	82.2	92.0	92.2	92.0	92.5	92.5	89.9	102.9	95.6	93.4
September	90.9	88.8	74.1	81.6	91.7	91.8	92.0	92.8	92.7	89.7	102.7	95.3	93.0
October	90.5	87.4	72.7	81.4	91.4	91.7	91.3	92.7	92.4	89.8	102.6	94.5	92.4
November	91.1	89.6	73.5	82.3	91.2	91.6	91.1	92.1	92.7	90.9	102.8	94.8	92.3
December	90.7	89.4	72.4	82.2	91.1	91.3	91.0	91.6	92.6	91.0	103.0	94.9	92.2

. . . = Not available.

Table 10-10. Average Hourly Earnings of All Employees on Private Nonfarm Payrolls by NAICS Supersector

(Dollars, seasonally adjusted.)

Year and month	Total private	Mining and logging	Construc-tion	Manu-facturing	Trade, transportation, and utilities			Information	Financial activities	Profes-sional and business services	Education and health services	Leisure and hospitality	Other services
					Total	Wholesale trade	Retail trade						
2007	20.97	24.91	23.02	21.50	18.58	23.96	15.13	28.09	25.62	24.68	21.35	12.39	17.62
2008	21.62	26.20	23.96	22.16	18.93	24.37	15.21	28.66	26.16	25.82	22.12	12.77	18.17
2009	22.21	27.30	24.84	23.03	19.34	25.42	15.40	29.38	26.48	27.02	22.41	12.96	19.52
2006													
January	. . .	. . .	. . .	. . .	. . .	. . .	. . .	. . .	. . .	. . .	. . .	. . .	. . .
February	. . .	. . .	. . .	. . .	. . .	. . .	. . .	. . .	. . .	. . .	. . .	. . .	. . .
March	20.07	22.63	21.81	20.64	18.25	22.96	15.25	27.15	24.10	23.31	20.40	11.48	17.06
April	20.15	23.49	22.05	20.87	18.25	23.01	15.19	27.15	24.24	23.34	20.39	11.57	17.02
May	20.14	23.45	22.01	20.71	18.23	23.02	15.17	26.99	24.31	23.36	20.43	11.66	17.08
June	20.21	23.70	22.22	20.78	18.34	23.17	15.28	27.11	24.37	23.39	20.44	11.68	17.14
July	20.30	23.86	22.31	20.98	18.34	23.16	15.22	27.12	24.66	23.46	20.53	11.74	17.20
August	20.32	23.61	22.25	20.96	18.25	23.19	15.07	27.15	24.87	23.64	20.56	11.77	17.25
September	20.42	24.04	22.44	21.03	18.34	23.59	15.05	27.43	24.84	23.84	20.56	11.82	17.36
October	20.49	24.60	22.52	21.24	18.38	23.61	15.14	27.39	24.88	23.96	20.52	11.94	17.46
November	20.50	24.60	22.48	21.11	18.40	23.65	15.16	27.29	25.07	24.01	20.52	11.97	17.55
December	20.55	24.56	22.48	21.27	18.41	23.80	15.14	27.52	25.11	24.09	20.52	11.99	17.65
2007													
January	20.60	24.61	22.58	21.23	18.38	23.59	15.12	27.91	25.15	24.22	20.62	12.08	17.68
February	20.65	24.94	22.68	21.22	18.40	23.52	15.11	28.14	25.32	24.30	20.59	12.15	17.55
March	20.80	24.69	22.68	21.22	18.47	23.76	15.11	28.36	25.47	24.36	21.40	12.18	17.34
April	20.85	25.02	22.83	21.44	18.46	23.79	15.07	28.35	25.50	24.45	21.34	12.27	17.25
May	20.89	24.97	22.96	21.42	18.48	23.86	15.08	28.08	25.54	24.58	21.37	12.36	17.33
June	20.99	25.13	23.02	21.50	18.63	24.11	15.19	28.02	25.64	24.71	21.40	12.41	17.51
July	21.05	24.98	23.12	21.61	18.64	24.09	15.13	27.99	25.74	24.74	21.47	12.50	17.67
August	21.04	24.84	23.09	21.62	18.54	23.92	15.02	28.04	25.78	24.77	21.50	12.48	17.72
September	21.13	25.07	23.27	21.71	18.65	24.11	15.09	28.25	25.76	24.82	21.62	12.50	17.77
October	21.14	25.06	23.18	21.62	18.75	24.19	15.22	28.17	25.72	24.91	21.56	12.54	17.85
November	21.17	24.57	23.30	21.66	18.78	24.25	15.23	28.10	25.78	25.00	21.60	12.57	17.92
December	21.23	25.08	23.40	21.77	18.76	24.25	15.16	28.17	25.88	25.06	21.63	12.70	17.98
2008													
January	21.25	25.40	23.41	21.74	18.71	24.05	15.11	28.33	25.97	25.13	21.72	12.64	18.00
February	21.29	24.92	23.54	21.76	18.73	23.99	15.15	28.52	26.06	25.22	21.67	12.70	17.94
March	21.43	26.25	23.56	21.91	18.82	24.14	15.22	28.70	26.15	25.30	22.14	12.74	17.85
April	21.43	25.13	23.63	21.87	18.85	24.17	15.25	28.68	26.18	25.42	22.03	12.75	17.84
May	21.52	25.39	23.82	22.04	18.90	24.24	15.25	28.49	26.17	25.59	22.10	12.78	17.94
June	21.60	25.85	23.87	22.19	19.01	24.46	15.27	28.47	26.17	25.73	22.08	12.79	18.10
July	21.66	26.50	23.99	22.15	19.02	24.57	15.23	28.64	26.21	25.85	22.16	12.79	18.23
August	21.74	26.90	24.17	22.23	19.00	24.47	15.20	28.82	26.30	25.99	22.24	12.83	18.27
September	21.80	26.83	24.28	22.30	19.02	24.47	15.22	28.85	26.35	26.10	22.34	12.85	18.32
October	21.84	26.66	24.31	22.50	19.04	24.51	15.26	28.70	26.25	26.31	22.26	12.82	18.43
November	21.93	27.11	24.43	22.63	19.08	24.60	15.28	28.73	26.21	26.53	22.34	12.84	18.55
December	21.96	27.23	24.51	22.59	19.11	24.69	15.29	28.76	26.24	26.62	22.38	12.82	18.65
2009													
January	22.01	27.14	24.60	22.77	19.14	24.82	15.31	28.75	26.25	26.70	22.40	12.85	18.78
February	22.05	27.41	24.62	22.92	19.18	24.91	15.34	28.80	26.27	26.80	22.38	12.86	18.93
March	22.08	27.51	24.76	22.94	19.19	25.01	15.33	28.82	26.28	26.92	22.31	12.88	19.11
April	22.11	27.38	24.78	22.96	19.24	25.13	15.36	28.95	26.32	26.99	22.31	12.88	19.31
May	22.14	27.70	24.76	23.02	19.28	25.24	15.38	29.19	26.40	26.97	22.35	12.86	19.42
June	22.16	27.42	24.83	23.02	19.29	25.32	15.39	29.30	26.43	27.00	22.36	12.91	19.50
July	22.20	27.16	24.86	23.06	19.33	25.50	15.41	29.46	26.44	27.10	22.39	12.94	19.60
August	22.28	27.52	24.92	23.14	19.41	25.64	15.45	29.58	26.48	27.20	22.45	13.00	19.70
September	22.30	27.41	24.94	23.16	19.44	25.73	15.47	29.58	26.58	27.18	22.46	13.05	19.82
October	22.35	27.38	25.08	23.15	19.50	25.84	15.46	29.70	26.69	27.13	22.52	13.10	19.95
November	22.39	26.84	25.07	23.16	19.52	25.86	15.46	29.94	26.77	27.11	22.53	13.14	20.02
December	22.38	26.97	25.03	23.10	19.53	25.91	15.47	30.03	26.83	27.09	22.55	13.10	20.04

. . . = Not available.

Table 10-11. Average Weekly Earnings of All Employees on Private Nonfarm Payrolls by NAICS Supersector

(Dollars, seasonally adjusted.)

Year and month	Total private	Mining and logging	Construc-tion	Manu-facturing	Trade, transportation, and utilities			Information	Financial activities	Profes-sional and business services	Education and health services	Leisure and hospitality	Other services
					Total	Wholesale trade	Retail trade						
2007	725.22	1 094.85	875.28	861.22	641.97	913.00	479.91	1 014.38	936.56	874.68	715.84	323.54	578.84
2008	744.80	1 144.59	905.68	882.19	651.96	936.17	477.87	1 047.50	954.82	909.23	745.03	330.32	597.13
2009	753.02	1 150.38	923.11	898.19	660.41	963.49	481.24	1 073.14	968.64	946.84	739.19	331.47	617.72
2006													
January	...	...	...	...	...	...	...	...	...	...	...	...	...
February	...	...	...	...	...	...	...	...	...	...	...	...	...
March	692.42	966.30	822.24	825.60	620.50	867.89	474.28	985.55	884.47	820.51	681.36	300.78	568.10
April	695.18	1 007.72	826.88	836.89	622.33	865.18	475.45	990.98	889.61	821.57	683.07	303.13	566.77
May	694.83	1 003.66	831.98	830.47	621.64	863.25	476.34	985.14	892.18	819.94	684.41	306.66	567.06
June	701.29	1 016.73	842.14	831.20	629.06	875.83	482.85	989.52	896.82	830.35	684.74	307.18	572.48
July	700.35	1 030.75	838.86	839.20	629.06	875.45	479.43	989.88	902.56	828.14	685.70	306.41	571.04
August	699.01	1 005.79	836.60	834.21	624.15	874.26	474.71	990.98	907.76	829.76	684.65	307.20	569.25
September	704.49	1 024.10	848.23	836.99	629.06	891.70	474.08	995.71	911.63	846.32	686.70	308.50	572.88
October	706.91	1 040.58	862.52	845.35	632.27	890.10	479.94	991.52	910.61	841.00	683.32	311.63	574.43
November	707.25	1 028.28	851.99	838.07	632.96	893.97	480.57	985.17	917.56	849.95	683.32	314.81	575.64
December	715.14	1 048.71	872.22	848.67	640.67	902.02	489.02	990.72	921.54	860.01	685.37	317.74	578.92
2007													
January	710.70	1 045.93	855.78	849.20	630.43	882.27	479.30	1 004.76	917.98	852.54	684.58	317.70	576.37
February	712.43	1 072.42	848.23	846.68	629.28	886.70	474.45	1 015.85	924.18	867.51	683.59	318.33	573.89
March	719.68	1 069.08	864.11	850.92	637.22	907.63	478.99	1 023.80	929.66	864.78	716.90	319.12	572.22
April	723.50	1 118.39	865.26	861.89	638.72	908.78	479.23	1 020.60	930.75	867.98	719.16	321.47	570.98
May	724.88	1 106.17	879.37	858.94	637.56	909.07	478.04	1 008.07	929.66	870.13	720.17	323.83	571.89
June	728.35	1 110.75	877.06	860.00	648.32	921.00	486.08	1 008.72	940.99	877.21	719.04	325.14	579.58
July	728.33	1 106.61	873.94	866.56	644.94	922.65	481.13	1 010.44	939.51	875.80	721.39	325.00	581.34
August	725.88	1 085.51	865.88	862.64	639.63	913.74	476.13	1 012.24	940.97	876.86	720.25	323.23	579.44
September	731.10	1 120.63	891.24	868.40	643.43	918.59	476.84	1 017.00	940.24	881.11	724.27	323.75	581.08
October	729.33	1 107.65	890.11	858.31	646.88	921.64	482.47	1 016.94	938.78	879.32	722.26	324.79	583.70
November	732.48	1 076.17	892.39	864.23	647.91	926.35	482.79	1 017.22	940.97	885.00	723.60	328.08	585.98
December	736.68	1 106.03	900.90	875.15	650.97	928.78	483.60	1 025.39	947.21	889.63	724.61	332.74	586.15
2008													
January	733.13	1 109.98	894.26	871.77	645.50	916.31	477.48	1 034.05	945.31	884.58	725.45	329.90	585.00
February	734.51	1 091.50	894.52	872.58	644.31	916.42	477.23	1 040.98	951.19	892.79	725.95	331.47	586.64
March	743.62	1 178.63	902.35	885.16	651.17	926.98	480.95	1 050.42	954.48	893.09	748.33	333.79	590.84
April	741.48	1 085.62	900.30	876.99	652.21	928.13	481.90	1 052.56	955.57	897.33	746.82	332.78	592.29
May	744.59	1 109.54	900.40	881.60	652.05	930.82	480.38	1 039.89	960.44	900.77	749.19	333.56	592.02
June	747.36	1 132.23	907.06	889.82	657.75	941.71	482.53	1 036.31	957.82	905.70	746.30	332.54	595.49
July	747.27	1 150.10	902.02	879.36	656.19	950.86	479.75	1 045.36	956.67	909.92	749.01	329.98	597.94
August	747.86	1 164.77	906.38	882.53	655.50	946.99	477.28	1 054.81	962.58	917.45	749.49	329.73	601.08
September	749.92	1 153.69	915.36	880.85	654.29	942.10	476.39	1 058.80	961.78	921.33	750.62	330.25	602.73
October	751.30	1 170.37	918.92	888.75	654.98	941.18	477.64	1 056.16	958.13	928.74	747.94	330.76	602.66
November	752.20	1 200.97	916.13	893.89	654.44	942.18	478.26	1 054.39	956.67	933.86	750.62	331.27	604.73
December	751.03	1 173.61	916.67	883.27	655.47	945.63	477.05	1 049.74	957.76	937.02	749.73	329.47	607.99
2009													
January	752.74	1 180.59	922.50	888.03	656.50	948.12	479.20	1 049.38	960.75	937.17	748.16	330.25	610.35
February	751.91	1 175.89	923.25	896.17	657.87	951.56	480.14	1 048.32	958.86	940.68	745.25	330.50	611.44
March	750.72	1 166.42	923.55	887.78	658.22	950.38	481.36	1 046.17	959.22	944.89	742.92	331.02	609.61
April	749.53	1 155.44	926.77	888.55	658.01	952.43	480.77	1 053.78	960.68	944.65	738.46	329.73	612.13
May	750.55	1 157.86	926.02	890.87	659.38	956.60	481.39	1 065.44	963.60	943.95	737.55	329.22	613.67
June	749.01	1 143.41	923.68	890.87	657.79	957.10	480.17	1 066.52	962.05	945.00	735.64	329.21	614.25
July	750.36	1 135.29	929.76	894.73	659.15	963.90	482.33	1 072.34	965.06	945.79	736.63	329.97	617.40
August	753.06	1 169.60	927.02	904.77	661.88	969.19	483.59	1 079.67	966.52	949.28	738.61	332.80	620.55
September	753.74	1 145.74	922.78	903.24	662.90	970.02	485.76	1 082.63	972.83	948.58	736.69	332.78	622.35
October	753.20	1 139.01	920.44	905.17	664.95	974.17	483.90	1 087.02	976.85	946.84	736.40	332.74	624.44
November	759.02	1 132.65	932.60	917.14	663.68	974.92	482.35	1 092.81	982.46	951.56	736.73	335.07	626.63
December	756.44	1 135.44	923.61	914.76	664.02	974.22	482.66	1 096.10	984.66	950.86	737.39	335.36	627.25

. . . = Not available.

Table 10-12. Production or Nonsupervisory Workers on Private Nonfarm Payrolls by NAICS Supersector

(Thousands, seasonally adjusted.)

Year and month	Total private	Mining and logging	Construction	Manufacturing	Trade, transportation, and utilities			Information	Financial activities	Professional and business services	Education and health services	Leisure and hospitality	Other services
					Total	Wholesale trade	Retail trade						
1965	42 302	523	2 906	12 905	10 702	. . .	. . .	1 268	2 434	3 515	3 443	3 443	1 161
1966	44 292	517	2 977	13 703	11 095	. . .	. . .	1 334	2 492	3 715	3 623	3 607	1 230
1967	45 185	501	2 903	13 714	11 369	. . .	. . .	1 365	2 585	3 890	3 818	3 734	1 306
1968	46 519	491	2 986	13 908	11 688	. . .	. . .	1 394	2 700	4 067	4 008	3 898	1 379
1969	48 246	501	3 177	14 147	12 152	. . .	. . .	1 438	2 841	4 252	4 196	4 089	1 452
1970	48 180	496	3 158	13 490	12 388	. . .	. . .	1 422	2 922	4 321	4 305	4 185	1 494
1971	48 151	474	3 238	13 034	12 502	. . .	. . .	1 392	2 978	4 354	4 372	4 286	1 521
1972	49 971	494	3 425	13 497	12 954	2 920	7 257	1 437	3 066	4 518	4 531	4 467	1 583
1973	52 235	502	3 576	14 227	13 437	3 041	7 551	1 504	3 164	4 748	4 747	4 664	1 666
1974	52 846	550	3 469	14 040	13 700	3 148	7 673	1 516	3 217	4 907	4 941	4 766	1 740
1975	51 010	581	2 990	12 576	13 578	3 121	7 714	1 416	3 227	4 939	5 088	4 821	1 795
1976	52 916	606	2 999	13 127	14 038	3 212	8 048	1 459	3 300	5 153	5 309	5 046	1 880
1977	55 207	636	3 209	13 591	14 579	3 323	8 396	1 514	3 452	5 404	5 561	5 284	1 978
1978	58 188	658	3 544	14 150	15 329	3 509	8 861	1 586	3 645	5 717	5 874	5 588	2 099
1979	60 403	737	3 760	14 458	15 843	3 667	9 113	1 650	3 825	5 993	6 157	5 772	2 209
1980	60 372	785	3 623	13 667	15 907	3 708	9 158	1 626	3 957	6 197	6 442	5 850	2 318
1981	60 960	861	3 469	13 492	16 004	3 753	9 238	1 633	4 052	6 396	6 694	5 944	2 414
1982	59 465	834	3 208	12 315	15 821	3 662	9 254	1 564	4 055	6 421	6 812	5 976	2 458
1983	60 005	698	3 240	12 121	15 999	3 639	9 494	1 502	4 128	6 581	7 032	6 161	2 542
1984	63 316	714	3 614	12 821	16 797	3 821	9 964	1 631	4 289	6 918	7 368	6 491	2 672
1985	65 436	686	3 868	12 648	17 427	3 935	10 399	1 660	4 476	7 258	7 770	6 817	2 827
1986	66 802	577	3 984	12 449	17 769	3 941	10 704	1 663	4 698	7 532	8 107	7 066	2 957
1987	68 700	541	4 088	12 537	18 196	3 989	10 986	1 717	4 861	7 859	8 488	7 310	3 104
1988	71 029	545	4 199	12 765	18 771	4 132	11 306	1 775	4 894	8 256	8 956	7 587	3 280
1989	72 927	526	4 257	12 805	19 230	4 235	11 565	1 807	4 931	8 648	9 432	7 833	3 459
1990	73 684	538	4 115	12 669	19 032	4 198	11 308	1 866	4 973	8 889	9 748	8 299	3 555
1991	72 520	515	3 674	12 164	18 640	4 122	11 008	1 871	4 911	8 748	10 212	8 247	3 539
1992	72 786	478	3 546	12 020	18 506	4 071	10 931	1 871	4 908	8 971	10 555	8 406	3 526
1993	74 591	462	3 704	12 070	18 752	4 072	11 104	1 896	5 057	9 451	10 908	8 667	3 623
1994	77 382	461	3 973	12 361	19 392	4 196	11 502	1 928	5 183	10 078	11 338	8 979	3 689
1995	79 845	458	4 113	12 567	19 984	4 361	11 841	2 007	5 165	10 645	11 765	9 330	3 812
1996	81 773	461	4 325	12 532	20 325	4 423	12 057	2 096	5 279	11 161	12 123	9 565	3 907
1997	84 158	479	4 546	12 673	20 698	4 523	12 274	2 181	5 415	11 896	12 478	9 780	4 013
1998	86 316	473	4 807	12 729	21 059	4 605	12 440	2 217	5 605	12 566	12 791	9 947	4 124
1999	88 430	438	5 105	12 524	21 576	4 673	12 772	2 351	5 728	13 184	13 089	10 216	4 219
2000	90 336	446	5 295	12 428	21 965	4 686	13 040	2 502	5 737	13 790	13 362	10 516	4 296
2001	89 983	457	5 332	11 677	21 709	4 555	12 952	2 531	5 810	13 588	13 846	10 662	4 373
2002	88 393	436	5 196	10 768	21 337	4 474	12 774	2 398	5 872	13 049	14 311	10 576	4 449
2003	87 658	420	5 123	10 189	21 078	4 396	12 655	2 347	5 967	12 911	14 532	10 666	4 426
2004	88 937	440	5 309	10 072	21 319	4 444	12 788	2 371	5 989	13 287	14 771	10 955	4 425
2005	91 135	473	5 611	10 060	21 830	4 584	13 030	2 386	6 090	13 854	15 129	11 263	4 438
2006	93 451	519	5 903	10 137	22 166	4 724	13 110	2 399	6 281	14 446	15 539	11 568	4 494
2007	94 903	547	5 883	9 975	22 546	4 851	13 317	2 403	6 326	14 784	15 999	11 861	4 578
2008	94 270	574	5 521	9 629	22 337	4 822	13 134	2 388	6 269	14 585	16 488	11 873	4 606
2009	89 271	514	4 583	8 350	21 149	4 536	12 475	2 243	5 999	13 525	16 839	11 583	4 486
2008													
January	95 342	560	5 774	9 909	22 688	4 892	13 383	2 416	6 302	14 884	16 264	11 938	4 607
February	95 261	562	5 738	9 882	22 654	4 890	13 347	2 415	6 300	14 843	16 307	11 942	4 618
March	95 262	567	5 728	9 863	22 661	4 893	13 351	2 413	6 305	14 788	16 357	11 953	4 627
April	95 115	567	5 662	9 810	22 583	4 874	13 286	2 407	6 306	14 796	16 403	11 954	4 627
May	94 909	568	5 619	9 791	22 510	4 864	13 231	2 406	6 298	14 727	16 445	11 922	4 623
June	94 703	571	5 563	9 740	22 442	4 850	13 193	2 400	6 293	14 685	16 485	11 914	4 610
July	94 483	574	5 517	9 676	22 384	4 830	13 157	2 391	6 284	14 632	16 531	11 887	4 607
August	94 196	585	5 486	9 592	22 284	4 812	13 098	2 383	6 275	14 539	16 583	11 865	4 604
September	93 815	588	5 422	9 503	22 173	4 790	13 026	2 375	6 255	14 476	16 589	11 833	4 601
October	93 345	585	5 354	9 367	22 059	4 761	12 957	2 370	6 237	14 356	16 600	11 801	4 616
November	92 686	583	5 222	9 265	21 874	4 730	12 846	2 353	6 200	14 218	16 646	11 751	4 574
December	92 138	575	5 136	9 112	21 750	4 695	12 769	2 333	6 174	14 114	16 680	11 714	4 550
2009													
January	91 458	573	5 026	8 882	21 623	4 656	12 714	2 310	6 136	13 963	16 728	11 684	4 533
February	90 847	561	4 930	8 734	21 501	4 619	12 653	2 301	6 101	13 807	16 739	11 655	4 518
March	90 247	543	4 806	8 593	21 392	4 587	12 594	2 292	6 069	13 688	16 750	11 614	4 500
April	89 676	529	4 703	8 478	21 270	4 557	12 543	2 273	6 029	13 574	16 750	11 577	4 493
May	89 401	516	4 643	8 349	21 215	4 542	12 525	2 252	6 007	13 520	16 791	11 618	4 490
June	88 984	510	4 563	8 244	21 147	4 526	12 493	2 237	5 982	13 406	16 817	11 587	4 491
July	88 760	503	4 493	8 230	21 056	4 511	12 441	2 226	5 969	13 371	16 839	11 584	4 489
August	88 575	493	4 435	8 192	21 020	4 502	12 417	2 218	5 950	13 346	16 873	11 568	4 480
September	88 418	491	4 384	8 166	20 952	4 493	12 372	2 217	5 939	13 324	16 893	11 584	4 468
October	88 194	486	4 338	8 124	20 869	4 484	12 314	2 213	5 926	13 336	16 924	11 521	4 457
November	88 302	491	4 337	8 108	20 876	4 481	12 329	2 200	5 932	13 446	16 945	11 516	4 451
December	88 239	490	4 307	8 089	20 876	4 471	12 329	2 192	5 937	13 463	16 971	11 464	4 450

. . . = Not available.

Table 10-13. Average Weekly Hours of Production or Nonsupervisory Workers on Private Nonfarm Payrolls by NAICS Supersector

(Hours per week, seasonally adjusted.)

Year and month	Total private	Mining and logging	Construction	Manufacturing Average weekly hours	Manufacturing Overtime hours	Trade, transportation, and utilities Total	Trade, transportation, and utilities Wholesale trade	Trade, transportation, and utilities Retail trade	Information	Financial activities	Professional and business services	Education and health services	Leisure and hospitality	Other services
1965	38.6	43.7	37.9	41.2	3.6	39.6	. . .	. . .	38.3	37.1	37.3	35.2	32.5	36.1
1966	38.5	44.1	38.1	41.4	3.9	39.1	. . .	. . .	38.3	37.2	37.0	34.9	31.9	35.8
1967	37.9	43.9	38.1	40.6	3.3	38.5	. . .	. . .	37.6	36.9	36.6	34.5	31.3	35.4
1968	37.7	44.0	37.8	40.7	3.5	38.2	. . .	. . .	37.6	36.8	36.3	34.1	30.8	35.0
1969	37.5	44.3	38.4	40.6	3.6	37.9	. . .	. . .	37.6	36.9	36.3	34.1	30.4	35.0
1970	37.0	43.9	37.8	39.8	2.9	37.6	. . .	. . .	37.2	36.6	35.9	33.8	30.0	34.7
1971	36.8	43.7	37.6	39.9	2.9	37.4	. . .	. . .	37.0	36.4	35.5	33.3	29.9	34.2
1972	36.9	44.0	37.0	40.6	3.4	37.4	39.8	35.1	37.3	36.4	35.5	33.3	29.7	34.2
1973	36.9	43.8	37.2	40.7	3.8	37.2	39.6	34.8	37.3	36.4	35.5	33.3	29.4	34.1
1974	36.4	43.7	37.1	40.0	3.2	36.8	39.2	34.3	37.0	36.3	35.3	33.1	29.1	33.9
1975	36.0	43.7	36.9	39.5	2.6	36.4	39.1	34.0	36.6	36.2	35.1	33.0	28.8	33.8
1976	36.1	44.2	37.3	40.1	3.1	36.3	39.1	33.8	36.7	36.2	34.9	32.7	28.5	33.6
1977	35.9	44.7	37.0	40.3	3.4	36.0	39.2	33.3	36.8	36.2	34.7	32.5	28.1	33.4
1978	35.8	44.9	37.3	40.4	3.6	35.6	39.2	32.7	36.8	36.1	34.6	32.3	27.7	33.2
1979	35.6	44.7	37.5	40.2	3.3	35.4	39.2	32.4	36.6	35.9	34.4	32.2	27.4	33.0
1980	35.2	44.9	37.5	39.7	2.8	35.0	38.8	31.9	36.3	36.0	34.3	32.1	27.0	33.0
1981	35.2	45.1	37.4	39.8	2.8	34.9	38.9	31.9	36.3	36.0	34.3	32.1	26.9	33.0
1982	34.7	44.1	37.2	38.9	2.3	34.6	38.7	31.7	35.8	36.0	34.2	32.1	26.8	33.0
1983	34.9	43.9	37.6	40.1	2.9	34.6	38.8	31.6	36.2	35.9	34.4	32.1	26.8	33.0
1984	35.1	44.6	38.2	40.7	3.4	34.7	38.9	31.6	36.6	36.2	34.3	32.0	26.7	32.9
1985	34.9	44.6	38.2	40.5	3.3	34.4	38.8	31.2	36.5	36.1	34.2	31.9	26.4	32.8
1986	34.7	43.6	37.9	40.7	3.4	34.1	38.7	31.0	36.4	36.1	34.3	32.0	26.2	32.9
1987	34.7	43.5	38.2	40.9	3.7	34.1	38.5	31.0	36.5	36.0	34.3	32.0	26.3	32.8
1988	34.6	43.3	38.2	41.0	3.8	33.8	38.5	30.9	36.1	35.6	34.2	32.0	26.3	32.9
1989	34.5	44.1	38.3	40.9	3.8	33.8	38.4	30.7	36.1	35.6	34.2	32.0	26.1	32.9
1990	34.3	45.0	38.3	40.5	3.9	33.7	38.4	30.6	35.8	35.5	34.2	31.9	26.0	32.8
1991	34.1	45.3	38.1	40.4	3.8	33.7	38.4	30.4	35.6	35.5	34.0	31.9	25.6	32.7
1992	34.2	44.6	38.0	40.7	4.0	33.8	38.5	30.7	35.8	35.6	34.0	32.0	25.7	32.6
1993	34.3	44.9	38.4	41.1	4.4	34.1	38.5	30.7	36.0	35.5	34.0	32.0	25.9	32.6
1994	34.5	45.3	38.8	41.7	5.0	34.3	38.8	30.9	36.0	35.5	34.1	32.0	26.0	32.7
1995	34.3	45.3	38.8	41.3	4.7	34.1	38.6	30.8	36.0	35.5	34.0	32.0	25.9	32.6
1996	34.3	46.0	38.9	41.3	4.8	34.1	38.6	30.7	36.4	35.5	34.1	31.9	25.9	32.5
1997	34.5	46.2	38.9	41.7	5.1	34.3	38.8	30.9	36.3	35.7	34.3	32.2	26.0	32.7
1998	34.5	44.9	38.8	41.4	4.9	34.2	38.6	30.9	36.6	36.0	34.3	32.2	26.2	32.6
1999	34.3	44.2	39.0	41.4	4.9	33.9	38.6	30.8	36.7	35.8	34.4	32.1	26.1	32.5
2000	34.3	44.4	39.2	41.3	4.7	33.8	38.8	30.7	36.8	35.9	34.5	32.2	26.1	32.5
2001	34.0	44.6	38.7	40.3	4.0	33.5	38.4	30.7	36.9	35.8	34.2	32.3	25.8	32.3
2002	33.9	43.2	38.4	40.5	4.2	33.6	38.0	30.9	36.5	35.6	34.2	32.4	25.8	32.0
2003	33.7	43.6	38.4	40.4	4.2	33.6	37.9	30.9	36.2	35.5	34.1	32.3	25.6	31.4
2004	33.7	44.5	38.3	40.8	4.6	33.5	37.8	30.7	36.3	35.5	34.2	32.4	25.7	31.0
2005	33.8	45.6	38.6	40.7	4.6	33.4	37.7	30.6	36.5	35.9	34.2	32.6	25.7	30.9
2006	33.9	45.6	39.0	41.1	4.4	33.4	38.0	30.5	36.6	35.7	34.6	32.5	25.7	30.9
2007	33.9	45.9	39.0	41.2	4.2	33.3	38.2	30.2	36.5	35.9	34.8	32.6	25.5	30.9
2008	33.6	45.1	38.5	40.8	3.7	33.2	38.2	30.0	36.7	35.8	34.8	32.5	25.2	30.8
2009	33.1	43.3	37.6	39.8	2.9	32.9	37.6	29.9	36.6	36.1	34.7	32.3	24.8	30.5
2008														
January	33.7	45.5	38.8	41.1	4.1	33.3	38.3	30.2	36.2	35.7	34.6	32.6	25.3	30.7
February	33.7	45.6	38.8	41.2	4.1	33.3	38.2	30.2	36.2	35.7	34.7	32.6	25.3	30.8
March	33.8	46.3	38.9	41.3	4.1	33.4	38.4	30.2	36.5	35.8	34.8	32.6	25.3	30.9
April	33.8	45.1	38.9	41.2	4.0	33.3	38.3	30.2	36.6	35.9	34.8	32.6	25.4	30.8
May	33.7	44.8	38.5	41.0	3.9	33.2	38.3	30.0	36.6	35.9	34.9	32.7	25.3	30.8
June	33.7	44.9	38.7	41.0	3.9	33.2	38.3	30.0	36.8	35.9	34.9	32.6	25.3	30.8
July	33.6	45.0	38.7	40.9	3.7	33.1	38.5	29.9	36.8	35.8	34.8	32.5	25.2	30.8
August	33.7	45.1	38.7	40.8	3.6	33.2	38.3	30.0	36.8	36.1	34.9	32.6	25.2	30.9
September	33.5	44.4	38.4	40.4	3.5	33.2	38.1	30.1	36.9	36.0	34.8	32.4	25.1	30.8
October	33.5	44.8	38.5	40.3	3.4	33.0	38.2	29.8	36.9	36.0	34.9	32.5	25.1	30.8
November	33.4	45.1	37.7	40.2	3.2	32.9	38.1	29.8	36.9	36.0	34.9	32.4	25.0	30.7
December	33.3	44.2	38.0	39.8	2.9	32.9	37.8	29.8	37.0	35.9	34.8	32.4	25.0	30.6
2009														
January	33.3	44.2	37.9	39.8	2.8	32.9	38.1	29.7	37.1	36.2	34.9	32.4	24.8	30.7
February	33.2	44.0	38.0	39.5	2.7	32.9	37.9	29.8	36.8	36.1	34.8	32.2	24.9	30.6
March	33.1	43.4	37.6	39.4	2.6	32.7	37.7	29.7	36.7	36.1	34.6	32.3	24.8	30.5
April	33.1	43.1	37.5	39.6	2.8	32.8	37.7	29.8	36.5	36.0	34.7	32.3	24.8	30.5
May	33.1	43.3	37.6	39.5	2.8	32.9	37.6	29.9	36.6	36.0	34.7	32.2	24.7	30.4
June	33.0	43.2	37.5	39.5	2.8	32.8	37.6	29.8	36.5	35.9	34.6	32.2	24.7	30.4
July	33.1	42.9	37.8	39.9	3.0	32.9	37.4	29.9	36.5	35.9	34.6	32.2	24.7	30.4
August	33.1	43.3	38.0	40.0	3.0	32.8	37.5	29.8	36.5	36.1	34.7	32.2	24.7	30.5
September	33.1	43.1	37.4	39.9	3.0	32.8	37.4	29.8	36.4	36.0	34.7	32.2	24.8	30.5
October	33.0	42.8	36.9	40.0	3.2	32.9	37.4	29.9	36.4	36.0	34.6	32.2	24.6	30.5
November	33.2	43.0	37.8	40.5	3.4	33.0	37.6	30.0	36.7	36.1	34.8	32.2	24.9	30.5
December	33.2	43.4	37.5	40.5	3.4	32.9	37.6	30.0	36.5	35.9	34.8	32.3	24.8	30.5

. . . = Not available.

Table 10-14. Indexes of Aggregate Weekly Hours of Production or Nonsupervisory Workers on Private Nonfarm Payrolls by NAICS Supersector

(2002 = 100, seasonally adjusted.)

| Year and month | Total private | Mining and logging | Construc-tion | Manu-facturing | Trade, transportation, and utilities | | | Information | Financial activities | Profes-sional and business services | Education and health services | Leisure and hospitality | Other services |
					Total	Wholesale trade	Retail trade						
1965	54.6	121.6	55.2	122.0	59.0	. . .	. . .	55.5	43.3	29.4	26.2	41.0	29.4
1966	56.9	121.1	56.8	130.1	60.5	. . .	. . .	58.3	44.3	30.8	27.3	42.2	30.9
1967	57.2	117.0	55.4	127.8	61.1	. . .	. . .	58.6	45.7	31.9	28.4	42.9	32.4
1968	58.5	114.9	56.5	130.1	62.2	. . .	. . .	59.9	47.6	33.1	29.5	44.1	33.9
1969	60.5	118.1	61.0	131.9	64.3	. . .	. . .	61.7	50.2	34.6	30.9	45.6	35.6
1970	59.5	115.7	59.8	123.3	64.9	. . .	. . .	60.4	51.1	34.7	31.3	46.1	36.3
1971	59.1	109.9	61.0	119.2	65.1	. . .	. . .	58.7	51.9	34.7	31.4	46.9	36.5
1972	61.6	115.6	63.4	125.7	67.5	68.4	64.4	61.1	53.4	36.0	32.6	48.6	37.9
1973	64.3	117.0	66.7	132.9	69.6	71.0	66.4	64.1	55.1	37.8	34.1	50.3	39.9
1974	64.3	127.7	64.5	128.9	70.2	72.7	66.7	64.0	55.8	38.8	35.3	50.8	41.4
1975	61.3	134.9	55.2	113.9	68.9	71.8	66.4	59.1	55.9	38.9	36.2	50.9	42.6
1976	63.8	142.4	56.0	120.8	70.9	73.9	68.8	61.1	57.1	40.3	37.5	52.8	44.3
1977	66.3	151.1	59.4	125.8	73.1	76.7	70.7	63.5	59.7	42.1	39.0	54.4	46.3
1978	69.5	156.9	66.2	131.2	76.1	81.0	73.4	66.6	63.0	44.3	40.9	56.6	48.8
1979	71.8	175.2	70.6	133.3	78.3	84.6	74.7	69.0	65.8	46.3	42.7	57.9	51.2
1980	71.0	187.2	68.0	124.4	77.6	84.8	74.0	67.4	68.1	47.7	44.6	57.9	53.6
1981	71.6	206.2	64.9	123.1	78.0	86.0	74.5	67.6	69.8	49.2	46.3	58.7	55.8
1982	69.0	195.5	59.7	109.9	76.4	83.4	74.2	64.0	69.8	49.2	47.1	58.7	56.8
1983	70.0	162.8	61.0	111.6	77.2	83.3	76.0	62.1	70.9	50.7	48.8	60.5	58.9
1984	74.3	169.3	69.1	119.6	81.2	87.5	79.8	68.0	74.2	53.2	50.9	63.6	61.7
1985	76.2	162.7	73.9	117.5	83.5	89.9	82.2	69.1	77.3	55.6	53.5	66.1	65.1
1986	77.5	133.5	75.5	116.3	84.5	89.8	83.9	69.1	81.2	57.8	55.9	68.0	68.2
1987	79.7	125.2	78.1	117.8	86.5	90.5	86.3	71.4	83.7	60.3	58.5	70.5	71.5
1988	82.1	125.6	80.4	120.2	88.6	93.6	88.5	73.1	83.4	63.3	61.8	73.0	75.7
1989	84.1	123.2	81.7	120.3	90.5	95.9	90.0	74.4	83.9	66.3	65.2	74.9	79.8
1990	84.4	128.6	78.8	117.7	89.5	94.9	87.5	76.2	84.5	68.0	67.2	78.9	81.8
1991	82.6	123.8	70.1	112.8	87.4	93.3	84.8	76.1	83.3	66.7	70.2	77.3	81.2
1992	83.1	113.3	67.5	112.4	87.3	92.4	85.1	76.5	83.5	68.4	72.9	79.3	80.6
1993	85.5	110.3	71.3	113.9	89.0	92.4	86.3	78.0	85.9	71.9	75.4	82.2	82.8
1994	89.2	111.0	77.3	118.3	92.7	95.8	89.8	79.2	88.0	77.0	78.3	85.6	84.5
1995	91.6	110.2	79.9	119.0	95.1	99.2	92.3	82.5	87.8	81.2	81.2	88.5	87.1
1996	93.8	112.7	84.3	118.8	96.6	100.7	93.7	87.0	89.8	85.2	83.4	90.8	89.1
1997	97.1	117.6	88.6	121.4	98.8	103.4	95.9	90.4	92.6	91.5	86.7	93.4	91.9
1998	99.4	112.8	93.4	121.0	100.3	104.8	97.2	92.6	96.5	96.7	88.9	95.5	94.3
1999	101.5	102.9	99.7	118.9	101.9	106.2	99.5	98.5	98.0	101.7	90.6	97.9	96.3
2000	103.6	105.1	104.0	117.7	103.5	107.1	101.3	105.0	98.5	106.6	92.8	100.6	97.8
2001	102.1	108.3	103.2	108.1	101.5	102.9	100.5	106.6	99.5	104.0	96.6	100.7	99.1
2002	100.0	100.0	100.0	100.0	100.0	100.0	100.0	100.0	100.0	100.0	100.0	100.0	100.0
2003	98.7	97.4	98.4	94.5	98.6	98.0	98.9	97.0	101.5	98.7	101.4	100.1	97.5
2004	100.2	104.0	101.7	94.3	99.6	98.9	99.4	98.3	101.9	101.8	103.3	103.0	96.1
2005	102.8	114.7	108.3	93.9	101.6	101.8	100.8	99.4	104.7	106.3	106.4	106.3	96.2
2006	105.8	125.8	115.3	95.6	103.3	105.7	101.1	100.2	107.4	112.1	109.0	108.9	97.5
2007	107.3	133.5	114.8	94.4	104.8	109.2	101.8	100.2	108.7	115.3	112.5	110.9	99.4
2008	105.9	137.6	106.5	90.2	103.3	108.6	99.8	100.0	107.5	113.9	115.7	109.7	99.5
2009	98.8	118.3	86.3	76.3	96.9	100.5	94.3	93.8	103.5	105.2	117.2	105.4	96.1
2008													
January	107.4	135.4	112.2	93.5	105.3	110.3	102.3	99.8	107.7	115.4	114.4	110.7	99.2
February	107.3	136.2	111.5	93.4	105.2	110.0	102.0	99.8	107.6	115.4	114.7	110.7	99.8
March	107.6	139.5	111.6	93.5	105.5	110.6	102.1	100.5	108.0	115.3	115.0	110.8	100.3
April	107.4	135.9	110.3	92.8	104.8	109.9	101.6	100.6	108.3	115.4	115.4	111.3	100.0
May	106.9	135.2	108.3	92.1	104.2	109.7	100.5	100.5	108.2	115.2	116.0	110.6	99.9
June	106.6	136.2	107.8	91.7	103.9	109.4	100.2	100.8	108.1	114.9	115.9	110.5	99.6
July	106.1	137.3	106.9	90.8	103.3	109.5	99.6	100.4	107.7	114.1	115.9	109.8	99.5
August	106.1	140.2	106.3	89.8	103.1	108.5	99.5	100.1	108.4	113.7	116.6	109.6	99.8
September	105.0	138.7	104.2	88.1	102.6	107.5	99.2	100.0	107.8	112.9	115.9	108.9	99.4
October	104.5	139.3	103.2	86.6	101.5	107.1	97.7	99.8	107.4	112.3	116.4	108.6	99.7
November	103.4	139.7	98.6	85.5	100.3	106.1	96.9	99.1	106.8	111.2	116.3	107.7	98.5
December	102.5	135.1	97.7	83.2	99.8	104.5	96.3	98.5	106.1	110.1	116.6	107.3	97.7
2009													
January	101.8	134.6	95.4	81.1	99.2	104.5	95.6	97.8	106.3	109.2	116.9	106.2	97.6
February	100.8	131.2	93.8	79.2	98.6	103.1	95.4	96.7	105.4	107.7	116.3	106.4	97.0
March	99.8	125.2	90.5	77.7	97.5	101.8	94.7	96.0	104.8	106.1	116.7	105.6	96.3
April	99.2	121.2	88.3	77.1	97.3	101.2	94.6	94.7	103.9	105.6	116.7	105.2	96.1
May	98.9	118.7	87.4	75.7	97.3	100.6	94.8	94.1	103.5	105.1	117.0	105.6	96.1
June	98.1	117.1	85.7	74.7	96.7	100.2	94.2	93.2	102.8	104.0	116.8	104.9	95.8
July	98.2	114.7	85.0	75.4	96.6	99.4	94.2	92.8	102.5	103.7	117.0	104.9	95.7
August	98.0	113.4	84.4	75.2	96.1	99.4	93.7	92.4	102.8	103.8	117.2	104.7	95.9
September	97.8	112.5	82.1	74.8	95.8	99.0	93.3	92.1	102.3	103.6	117.3	105.3	95.6
October	97.2	110.5	80.1	74.6	95.7	98.8	93.2	92.0	102.1	103.4	117.6	103.9	95.4
November	97.9	112.2	82.1	75.4	96.0	99.2	93.6	92.2	102.5	104.9	117.7	105.1	95.2
December	97.9	113.0	80.9	75.2	95.7	99.0	93.6	91.3	102.0	105.0	118.2	104.2	95.2

. . . = Not available.

Table 10-15. Average Hourly Earnings of Production or Nonsupervisory Workers on Private Nonfarm Payrolls by NAICS Supersector

(Dollars, seasonally adjusted.)

Year and month	Total private	Mining and logging	Construction	Manufacturing	Trade, transportation, and utilities			Information	Financial activities	Professional and business services	Education and health services	Leisure and hospitality	Other services
					Total	Wholesale trade	Retail trade						
1965	2.63	2.87	3.23	2.49	2.94	...	...	4.47	2.38	3.28	2.12	1.17	1.25
1966	2.73	3.00	3.41	2.60	3.04	...	...	4.56	2.47	3.39	2.23	1.26	1.37
1967	2.85	3.14	3.63	2.71	3.15	...	...	4.68	2.58	3.51	2.36	1.37	1.49
1968	3.02	3.30	3.92	2.89	3.32	...	...	4.85	2.75	3.65	2.49	1.53	1.62
1969	3.22	3.54	4.30	3.07	3.48	...	...	5.05	2.92	3.84	2.68	1.69	1.81
1970	3.40	3.77	4.74	3.23	3.65	...	...	5.25	3.07	4.04	2.88	1.82	2.01
1971	3.63	3.99	5.17	3.45	3.86	...	...	5.53	3.23	4.26	3.11	1.95	2.24
1972	3.90	4.28	5.55	3.70	4.23	4.58	3.52	5.87	3.37	4.50	3.33	2.08	2.46
1973	4.14	4.59	5.89	3.97	4.45	4.80	3.69	6.17	3.55	4.72	3.54	2.20	2.67
1974	4.43	5.09	6.29	4.31	4.74	5.11	3.92	6.52	3.80	5.01	3.82	2.40	2.95
1975	4.73	5.68	6.78	4.71	5.02	5.45	4.14	6.92	4.08	5.29	4.09	2.58	3.21
1976	5.06	6.19	7.17	5.09	5.31	5.75	4.36	7.37	4.30	5.60	4.39	2.78	3.51
1977	5.44	6.70	7.56	5.55	5.67	6.12	4.65	7.84	4.58	5.95	4.72	3.03	3.84
1978	5.88	7.44	8.11	6.05	6.10	6.61	5.00	8.34	4.93	6.32	5.07	3.33	4.19
1979	6.34	8.20	8.71	6.57	6.55	7.12	5.34	8.86	5.31	6.71	5.44	3.63	4.56
1980	6.85	8.97	9.37	7.15	7.04	7.68	5.71	9.47	5.82	7.22	5.93	3.98	5.05
1981	7.44	9.89	10.24	7.86	7.55	8.28	6.09	10.21	6.34	7.80	6.49	4.36	5.61
1982	7.87	10.64	11.04	8.36	7.91	8.81	6.34	10.76	6.82	8.30	7.00	4.63	6.11
1983	8.20	11.14	11.36	8.70	8.23	9.27	6.60	11.18	7.32	8.70	7.39	4.89	6.51
1984	8.49	11.54	11.56	9.05	8.45	9.61	6.73	11.50	7.65	8.98	7.67	4.99	6.79
1985	8.74	11.87	11.75	9.40	8.60	9.88	6.83	11.81	7.97	9.28	7.98	5.10	7.10
1986	8.93	12.14	11.92	9.59	8.74	10.07	6.93	12.08	8.37	9.55	8.25	5.20	7.38
1987	9.14	12.17	12.15	9.77	8.92	10.32	7.02	12.36	8.73	9.85	8.57	5.30	7.69
1988	9.44	12.45	12.52	10.05	9.15	10.71	7.23	12.63	9.07	10.22	8.96	5.50	8.08
1989	9.80	12.91	12.98	10.35	9.46	11.12	7.46	12.99	9.54	10.69	9.46	5.76	8.58
1990	10.20	13.40	13.42	10.78	9.83	11.58	7.71	13.40	9.99	11.14	10.00	6.02	9.08
1991	10.52	13.82	13.65	11.13	10.08	11.95	7.89	13.90	10.42	11.50	10.49	6.22	9.39
1992	10.77	14.09	13.81	11.40	10.30	12.21	8.12	14.29	10.86	11.78	10.87	6.36	9.66
1993	11.05	14.12	14.04	11.70	10.55	12.57	8.36	14.86	11.36	11.96	11.21	6.48	9.90
1994	11.34	14.41	14.38	12.04	10.80	12.93	8.61	15.32	11.82	12.15	11.50	6.62	10.18
1995	11.65	14.78	14.73	12.34	11.10	13.34	8.85	15.68	12.28	12.53	11.80	6.79	10.51
1996	12.04	15.10	15.11	12.75	11.46	13.80	9.21	16.30	12.71	13.00	12.17	6.99	10.85
1997	12.51	15.57	15.67	13.14	11.90	14.41	9.59	17.14	13.22	13.57	12.56	7.32	11.29
1998	13.01	16.20	16.23	13.45	12.39	15.07	10.05	17.67	13.93	14.27	13.00	7.67	11.79
1999	13.49	16.33	16.80	13.85	12.82	15.62	10.45	18.40	14.47	14.85	13.44	7.96	12.26
2000	14.02	16.55	17.48	14.32	13.31	16.28	10.86	19.07	14.98	15.52	13.95	8.32	12.73
2001	14.54	17.00	18.00	14.76	13.70	16.77	11.29	19.80	15.59	16.33	14.64	8.57	13.27
2002	14.97	17.19	18.52	15.29	14.02	16.98	11.67	20.20	16.17	16.81	15.21	8.81	13.72
2003	15.37	17.56	18.95	15.74	14.34	17.36	11.90	21.01	17.14	17.21	15.64	9.00	13.84
2004	15.69	18.07	19.23	16.14	14.58	17.65	12.08	21.40	17.52	17.48	16.15	9.15	13.98
2005	16.13	18.72	19.46	16.56	14.92	18.16	12.36	22.06	17.95	18.08	16.71	9.38	14.34
2006	16.76	19.90	20.02	16.81	15.39	18.91	12.57	23.23	18.80	19.13	17.38	9.75	14.77
2007	17.43	20.97	20.95	17.26	15.78	19.59	12.75	23.96	19.64	20.15	18.11	10.41	15.42
2008	18.08	22.50	21.87	17.75	16.16	20.13	12.87	24.78	20.28	21.18	18.87	10.84	16.09
2009	18.62	23.29	22.67	18.23	16.50	20.85	13.02	25.45	20.83	22.35	19.49	11.11	16.59
2008													
January	17.76	21.73	21.37	17.51	15.98	19.98	12.77	24.42	19.99	20.58	18.57	10.67	15.75
February	17.82	21.83	21.48	17.57	16.03	20.01	12.80	24.49	20.05	20.67	18.60	10.74	15.83
March	17.89	22.13	21.57	17.64	16.07	20.04	12.83	24.53	20.11	20.76	18.71	10.75	15.95
April	17.93	21.71	21.62	17.64	16.09	20.04	12.85	24.57	20.19	20.89	18.72	10.81	16.00
May	18.00	21.73	21.71	17.69	16.14	20.04	12.88	24.68	20.24	20.98	18.80	10.84	16.05
June	18.06	22.06	21.79	17.76	16.17	20.07	12.88	24.76	20.26	21.08	18.84	10.86	16.11
July	18.12	22.60	21.86	17.82	16.19	20.15	12.89	24.90	20.31	21.19	18.91	10.88	16.17
August	18.19	23.11	22.05	17.79	16.24	20.28	12.90	24.93	20.39	21.35	18.95	10.90	16.19
September	18.22	23.24	22.16	17.80	16.21	20.21	12.89	24.92	20.45	21.42	19.02	10.91	16.21
October	18.28	23.16	22.14	17.95	16.24	20.23	12.88	25.00	20.44	21.60	19.05	10.94	16.23
November	18.32	23.29	22.30	17.95	16.28	20.26	12.91	25.00	20.44	21.75	19.10	10.90	16.27
December	18.39	23.28	22.44	17.97	16.29	20.30	12.91	25.00	20.55	21.92	19.17	10.94	16.30
2009													
January	18.43	23.18	22.43	18.01	16.36	20.39	12.95	24.99	20.56	21.99	19.18	10.98	16.36
February	18.47	23.15	22.46	18.09	16.38	20.50	12.94	25.13	20.59	22.11	19.25	10.99	16.39
March	18.52	23.27	22.61	18.14	16.40	20.57	12.95	25.33	20.66	22.21	19.28	11.00	16.43
April	18.53	23.34	22.58	18.15	16.42	20.70	12.95	25.30	20.66	22.24	19.39	11.01	16.45
May	18.55	23.33	22.63	18.15	16.45	20.86	12.96	25.45	20.79	22.23	19.40	11.01	16.50
June	18.57	23.33	22.62	18.17	16.41	20.78	12.96	25.48	20.83	22.30	19.45	11.07	16.51
July	18.62	23.31	22.69	18.26	16.44	20.86	12.96	25.48	20.79	22.39	19.51	11.12	16.57
August	18.69	23.27	22.70	18.31	16.54	20.98	13.04	25.67	20.90	22.45	19.55	11.16	16.65
September	18.71	23.29	22.54	18.39	16.56	21.03	13.07	25.54	20.94	22.53	19.61	11.24	16.71
October	18.78	23.45	22.91	18.41	16.59	21.08	13.05	25.69	21.03	22.52	19.70	11.23	16.78
November	18.80	23.28	22.89	18.38	16.65	21.16	13.12	25.68	21.07	22.50	19.73	11.28	16.81
December	18.85	23.47	22.95	18.38	16.73	21.35	13.16	25.64	21.11	22.58	19.76	11.27	16.85

. . . = Not available.

Table 10-16. Average Weekly Earnings of Production or Nonsupervisory Workers on Private Nonfarm Payrolls by NAICS Supersector

(Dollars, seasonally adjusted.)

Year and month	Total private	Mining and logging	Construc-tion	Manu-facturing	Trade, transportation, and utilities			Information	Financial activities	Profes-sional and business services	Education and health services	Leisure and hospitality	Other services
					Total	Wholesale trade	Retail trade						
1965	101.52	125.42	122.42	102.59	116.42	. . .	. . .	171.20	88.30	122.34	74.62	38.03	45.13
1966	105.11	132.30	129.92	107.64	118.86	. . .	. . .	174.65	91.88	125.43	77.83	40.19	49.05
1967	108.02	137.85	138.30	110.03	121.28	. . .	. . .	175.97	95.20	128.47	81.42	42.88	52.75
1968	113.85	145.20	148.18	117.62	126.82	. . .	. . .	182.36	101.20	132.50	84.91	47.12	56.70
1969	120.75	156.82	165.12	124.64	131.89	. . .	. . .	189.88	107.75	139.39	91.39	51.38	63.35
1970	125.80	165.50	179.17	128.55	137.24	. . .	. . .	195.30	112.36	145.04	97.34	54.60	69.75
1971	133.58	174.36	194.39	137.66	144.36	. . .	. . .	204.61	117.57	151.23	103.56	58.31	76.61
1972	143.91	188.32	205.35	150.22	158.20	182.28	123.55	218.95	122.67	159.75	110.89	61.78	84.13
1973	152.77	201.04	219.11	161.58	165.54	190.08	128.41	230.14	129.22	167.56	117.88	64.68	91.05
1974	161.25	222.43	233.36	172.40	174.43	200.31	134.46	241.24	137.94	176.85	126.44	69.84	100.01
1975	170.28	248.22	250.18	186.05	182.73	213.10	140.76	253.27	147.70	185.68	134.97	74.30	108.50
1976	182.67	273.60	267.44	204.11	192.75	224.83	147.37	270.48	155.66	195.44	143.55	79.23	117.94
1977	195.30	299.49	279.72	223.67	204.12	239.90	154.85	288.51	165.80	206.47	153.40	85.14	128.26
1978	210.50	334.06	302.50	244.42	217.16	259.11	163.50	306.91	177.97	218.67	163.76	92.24	139.11
1979	225.70	366.54	326.63	264.11	231.87	279.10	173.02	324.28	190.63	230.82	175.17	99.46	150.48
1980	241.12	402.75	351.38	283.86	246.40	297.98	182.15	343.76	209.52	247.65	190.35	107.46	166.65
1981	261.89	446.04	382.98	312.83	263.50	322.09	194.27	370.62	228.24	267.54	208.33	117.28	185.13
1982	273.09	469.22	410.69	325.20	273.69	340.95	200.98	385.21	245.52	283.86	224.70	124.08	201.63
1983	286.18	489.05	427.14	348.87	284.76	359.68	208.56	404.72	262.79	299.28	237.22	131.05	214.83
1984	298.00	514.68	441.59	368.34	293.22	373.83	212.67	420.90	276.93	308.01	245.44	133.23	223.39
1985	305.03	529.40	448.85	380.70	295.84	383.34	213.10	431.07	287.72	317.38	254.56	134.64	232.88
1986	309.87	529.30	451.77	390.31	298.03	389.71	214.83	439.71	302.16	327.57	264.00	136.24	242.80
1987	317.16	529.40	464.13	399.59	304.17	397.32	217.62	451.14	314.28	337.86	274.24	139.39	252.23
1988	326.62	539.09	478.26	412.05	309.27	412.34	223.41	455.94	322.89	349.52	286.72	144.65	265.83
1989	338.10	569.33	497.13	423.32	319.75	427.01	229.02	468.94	339.62	365.60	302.72	150.34	282.28
1990	349.75	602.54	513.43	436.16	331.55	444.48	235.62	479.50	354.66	380.52	319.27	156.32	297.91
1991	358.51	625.42	520.41	449.73	339.19	459.27	240.15	495.17	369.57	391.09	334.55	159.15	306.91
1992	368.25	629.02	525.13	464.43	348.68	470.41	249.63	512.20	386.01	400.64	348.29	163.70	315.08
1993	378.91	634.77	539.81	480.83	359.33	484.46	256.89	535.19	403.02	406.20	359.08	167.56	322.69
1994	391.22	653.14	558.53	502.05	370.38	501.17	265.77	551.21	419.20	414.16	368.14	172.33	332.44
1995	400.07	670.32	571.57	509.26	378.79	515.14	272.56	564.92	436.12	426.44	377.73	175.74	342.36
1996	413.28	695.07	588.48	526.55	390.64	533.29	282.76	592.72	451.49	442.81	388.27	180.98	352.62
1997	431.86	720.11	609.48	548.22	407.54	559.39	295.97	622.37	472.37	465.51	404.65	190.52	368.63
1998	448.56	727.28	629.75	557.12	423.30	582.21	310.34	646.34	500.98	490.00	418.82	200.82	384.25
1999	463.15	721.74	655.11	573.14	434.31	602.77	321.63	675.47	517.57	510.99	431.35	208.05	398.77
2000	481.01	734.92	685.78	590.77	449.88	631.40	333.38	700.86	537.37	535.07	449.29	217.20	413.41
2001	493.79	757.92	695.89	595.19	459.53	643.45	346.16	730.88	557.92	557.84	473.39	220.73	428.64
2002	506.75	741.97	711.82	618.75	471.27	644.38	360.81	737.77	575.54	574.66	492.74	227.17	439.76
2003	518.06	765.94	726.83	635.99	481.14	657.29	367.15	760.45	609.08	587.02	505.69	230.42	434.41
2004	529.09	803.82	735.55	658.49	488.42	667.09	371.13	777.25	622.87	597.56	523.78	234.86	433.04
2005	544.33	853.71	750.22	673.30	498.43	685.00	377.58	805.08	644.99	618.87	544.59	241.36	443.37
2006	567.87	907.95	781.21	691.02	514.34	718.63	383.02	850.42	672.21	662.27	564.94	250.34	456.50
2007	590.04	962.64	816.66	711.56	526.07	748.94	385.11	874.65	705.13	700.82	590.09	265.52	477.06
2008	607.95	1 014.69	842.61	724.46	536.06	769.62	386.21	908.99	727.07	737.70	613.73	273.39	495.57
2009	617.11	1 007.85	852.45	725.87	542.36	784.75	388.72	931.93	751.21	775.81	628.56	275.80	506.28
2008													
January	598.51	988.72	829.16	719.66	532.13	765.23	385.65	884.00	713.64	712.07	605.38	269.95	483.53
February	600.53	995.45	833.42	723.88	533.80	764.38	386.56	886.54	715.79	717.25	606.36	271.72	487.56
March	604.68	1 024.62	839.07	728.53	536.74	769.54	387.47	895.35	719.94	722.45	609.95	271.98	492.86
April	606.03	979.12	841.02	726.77	535.80	767.53	388.07	899.26	724.82	726.97	610.27	274.57	492.80
May	606.60	973.50	835.84	725.29	535.85	767.53	386.40	903.29	726.62	732.20	614.76	274.25	494.34
June	608.62	990.49	843.27	728.16	536.84	768.68	386.40	911.17	727.33	735.69	614.18	274.76	496.19
July	608.83	1 017.00	845.98	728.84	535.89	775.78	385.41	916.32	727.10	737.41	614.58	274.18	498.04
August	613.00	1 042.26	853.34	725.83	539.17	776.72	387.00	917.42	736.08	745.12	617.77	274.68	500.27
September	610.37	1 031.86	850.94	719.12	538.17	770.00	387.99	919.55	736.20	745.42	616.25	273.84	499.27
October	612.38	1 037.57	852.39	723.39	535.92	772.79	383.82	922.50	735.84	753.84	619.13	274.59	499.88
November	611.89	1 050.38	840.71	721.59	535.61	771.91	384.72	922.50	735.84	759.08	618.84	272.50	499.49
December	612.39	1 028.98	852.72	715.21	535.94	767.34	384.72	925.00	737.75	762.82	621.11	273.50	498.78
2009													
January	613.72	1 024.56	850.10	716.80	538.24	776.86	384.62	927.13	744.27	767.45	621.43	272.30	502.25
February	613.20	1 018.60	853.48	714.56	538.90	776.95	385.61	924.78	743.30	769.43	619.85	273.65	501.53
March	613.01	1 009.92	850.14	714.72	536.28	775.49	384.62	929.61	745.83	768.47	622.74	272.80	501.12
April	613.34	1 005.95	846.75	718.74	538.58	780.39	385.91	923.45	743.76	771.73	626.30	273.05	501.73
May	614.01	1 010.19	850.89	716.93	541.21	784.34	387.50	931.47	748.44	771.38	626.62	273.05	503.25
June	612.81	1 007.86	848.25	717.72	538.25	781.33	386.21	930.02	747.80	771.58	626.29	273.43	501.90
July	616.32	1 000.00	857.68	728.57	540.88	780.16	387.50	930.02	746.36	774.69	628.22	274.66	503.73
August	618.64	1 007.59	862.60	732.40	542.51	786.75	388.59	936.96	754.49	779.02	629.51	275.65	507.83
September	619.30	1 003.80	843.00	733.76	543.17	786.52	389.49	929.66	753.84	781.79	631.44	278.75	509.66
October	619.74	1 003.66	845.38	736.40	545.81	788.39	390.20	935.12	757.08	779.19	634.34	276.26	511.79
November	624.16	1 001.04	865.24	744.39	549.45	795.62	393.60	942.46	760.63	783.00	635.31	280.87	512.71
December	625.82	1 018.60	860.63	744.39	550.42	802.76	394.80	935.86	757.85	785.78	638.25	279.50	513.93

. . . = Not available.

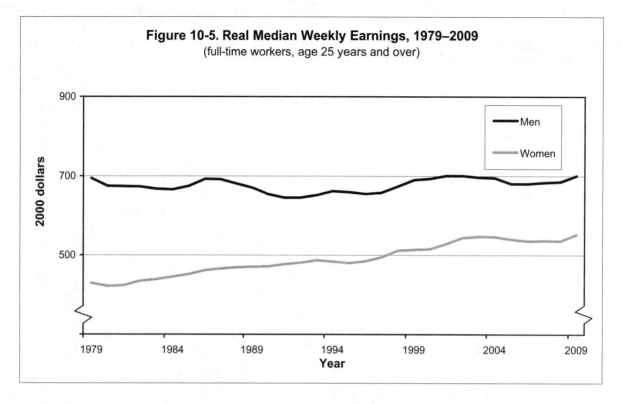

Figure 10-5. Real Median Weekly Earnings, 1979–2009
(full-time workers, age 25 years and over)

- "Median usual weekly earnings of full-time wage and salary workers," as shown in Table 10-17, are derived quarterly from the Current Population Survey, not from the payroll survey that provides the weekly earnings shown in Tables 10-11 and 10-16. That is, they are collected from individual households in the CPS sample, providing better approximations of the paychecks of typical breadwinners than the payroll data on average weekly earnings (AWE). (See the Notes and Definitions to this chapter.)

- The 2009 median earnings of all full-time workers in Table 10-17 are significantly higher than AWE for production or nonsupervisory workers as shown in Table 10-16, because part-time jobs are included in the latter measure. But this effect is outweighed by the inclusion of high-earning supervisors and executives when comparing the median earnings with AWE for all employees in Table 10-11; the latter figure, at $753, is higher than the median of $739. (Tables 10-11, 10-16, and 10-17)

- Focusing on workers 25 and over, women's earnings were moving closer to men's over most of the period covered in this survey, rising from 61.8 percent in 1979 to a high of 79.4 percent in 2005. Since then the ratio has edged down slightly, and the median female full-time worker earned 78.7 cents for every dollar earned by the median male worker in 2009. (Table 10-17)

- As Figure 10-5 shows, typical workers age 25 and over of both sexes lost ground in real terms in most recent years, until consumer prices declined in 2009 and boosted their real earnings. But even with that boost, the median man's real earnings in 2009 were only up at a 0.1 percent annual rate since 2000, and the median woman's only up 0.8 percent. (Table 10-17)

- In contrast, business productivity growth over that 9-year period was 2.7 percent per year. While the difference between deflators and the cost of nonwage benefits absorbs 0.9 percentage point per year of that productivity growth, that still leaves a productivity gain of 1.8 percent per year that might have been reflected in the median worker's wages. (Tables 8-2, 9-1, 9-2 and 9-3)

- Men's real earnings have been essentially stagnant for the entire 30 years, while women's earnings have increased 28.7 percent, or 0.8 percent per year. Again, the growth in these medians, especially for men, fall short of what might have been expected from the 2.1 percent rate of increase in productivity over those 30 years, even after deducting about 1.0 percentage point for deflator and benefits effects. (Tables 10-17, 8-2, 9-1, 9-2, and 9-3)

Table 10-17. Median Usual Weekly Earnings of Full-Time Wage and Salary Workers

(Current dollars, except as noted; not seasonally adjusted.)

Year and quarter	Total, 16 years and over	Men, 16 years and over Total	16 to 24 years	25 years and over Current dollars	2000 dollars [1]	Women, 16 years and over Total	16 to 24 years	25 years and over Current dollars	2000 dollars [1]	White	Black or African American	Asian	Hispanic or Latino ethnicity
1979	240	291	196	314	694	182	154	194	429	247	198	...	...
1980	261	312	208	339	675	201	167	212	422	268	212	...	...
1981	283	339	218	371	674	219	180	233	423	290	234	...	...
1982	302	364	224	393	673	238	191	254	435	309	245	...	...
1983	313	378	223	406	667	252	197	267	439	319	261	...	...
1984	326	391	231	422	666	265	203	282	445	336	269	...	...
1985	343	406	240	442	675	277	210	296	452	355	277	...	...
1986	358	419	245	462	693	290	218	308	462	370	291	...	277
1987	373	433	257	477	692	303	226	321	465	383	301	...	284
1988	385	449	261	487	681	315	235	335	469	394	314	...	290
1989	399	468	271	500	670	328	246	351	471	409	319	...	298
1990	412	481	282	512	654	346	254	369	471	424	329	...	304
1991	426	493	285	523	645	366	266	387	477	442	348	...	312
1992	440	501	284	536	645	380	267	400	481	458	357	...	322
1993	459	510	288	555	651	393	273	415	487	475	369	...	331
1994	467	522	294	576	662	399	276	421	484	484	371	...	324
1995	479	538	303	588	660	406	275	428	480	494	383	...	329
1996	490	557	307	599	655	418	284	444	485	506	387	...	339
1997	503	579	317	615	658	431	292	462	494	519	400	...	351
1998	523	598	334	639	674	456	305	485	512	545	426	...	370
1999	549	618	356	668	690	473	324	497	514	573	445	...	385
2000	576	641	375	693	693	493	344	516	516	590	474	615	399
2001	596	670	391	720	700	512	353	543	528	610	491	639	417
2002	608	679	391	732	701	529	367	568	544	623	498	658	424
2003	620	695	398	744	697	552	371	584	547	636	514	693	440
2004	638	713	400	762	695	573	375	599	546	657	525	708	456
2005	651	722	409	771	680	585	381	612	540	672	520	753	471
2006	671	743	418	797	681	600	395	627	536	690	554	784	486
2007	695	766	443	823	684	614	409	646	537	716	569	830	503
2008	722	798	461	857	685	638	420	670	536	742	589	861	529
2009	739	819	458	873	701	657	424	687	552	757	601	880	541
2001													
1st quarter	589	659	385	708	694	509	356	533	522	605	482	612	408
2nd quarter	592	664	391	715	694	511	348	541	525	606	495	637	419
3rd quarter	596	676	392	729	706	507	349	540	523	610	490	666	421
4th quarter	606	681	398	726	706	522	358	556	540	620	498	649	419
2002													
1st quarter	611	682	405	730	707	530	375	568	550	624	512	653	426
2nd quarter	605	677	398	732	701	520	355	559	535	622	500	648	420
3rd quarter	603	671	376	729	695	527	360	570	544	620	484	665	420
4th quarter	613	686	390	737	700	542	384	576	547	630	495	667	435
2003													
1st quarter	620	695	396	741	697	551	384	581	547	636	516	718	447
2nd quarter	616	692	391	743	697	547	366	582	546	631	509	678	430
3rd quarter	618	689	396	742	692	550	366	585	546	633	509	692	444
4th quarter	625	704	409	750	700	561	372	588	549	646	522	680	441
2004													
1st quarter	634	711	410	757	700	567	387	592	547	652	521	712	450
2nd quarter	639	714	397	763	696	572	370	601	548	655	536	720	451
3rd quarter	632	704	400	759	689	571	371	602	547	651	531	701	458
4th quarter	647	722	396	768	693	578	371	603	544	671	519	698	467
2005													
1st quarter	653	729	401	775	696	586	380	610	547	677	513	738	470
2nd quarter	643	713	407	762	675	580	374	608	538	663	518	743	473
3rd quarter	649	716	407	768	672	585	379	615	538	667	520	761	462
4th quarter	659	731	418	778	677	588	389	614	534	682	533	767	479
2006													
1st quarter	668	744	417	793	686	600	388	624	540	688	560	766	487
2nd quarter	659	731	421	783	667	593	395	619	527	678	534	765	485
3rd quarter	675	749	409	808	684	599	393	629	532	692	555	798	485
4th quarter	682	749	429	800	683	609	403	638	545	702	569	809	489
2007													
1st quarter	693	759	451	811	686	615	414	646	546	714	561	798	502
2nd quarter	690	763	436	819	679	607	404	635	527	713	562	827	503
3rd quarter	695	767	430	831	687	616	398	654	541	713	578	842	502
4th quarter	700	774	459	831	682	618	421	649	533	722	574	856	507
2008													
1st quarter	719	790	466	848	688	637	419	666	541	742	582	842	520
2nd quarter	719	800	469	862	685	634	415	668	531	738	591	855	537
3rd quarter	720	796	446	857	673	631	406	666	523	739	589	854	529
4th quarter	728	807	462	859	694	650	449	679	549	748	593	889	535
2009													
1st quarter	738	823	461	879	714	649	448	679	552	758	577	869	545
2nd quarter	734	815	450	872	701	652	413	679	546	754	592	909	547
3rd quarter	738	812	448	870	695	657	415	691	552	753	607	877	527
4th quarter	748	825	476	871	694	670	436	700	558	763	629	877	547

[1]Converted to 2000 dollars by the editor using CPI-U-RS. See notes and definitions.
. . . = Not available.

NOTES AND DEFINITIONS, CHAPTER 10

General note on employment data

This chapter includes two different data sets that measure employment. Both are compiled and published by the Bureau of Labor Statistics (BLS), but each set has different characteristics. Users should be aware of these dissimilarities and the consequent differences in the appropriate uses and interpretations of data from the two systems.

One set of employment estimates comes from the Current Population Survey (CPS), a large sample survey of approximately 60,000 U.S. households. The numbers in the sample are expanded to match the latest estimates of the total U.S. population. These are the most comprehensive estimates in their scope—that is, in the universe that they are designed to measure. These estimates represent all civilian workers, including the following groups that are excluded by definition from the other set of estimates: all farm workers, household workers (domestic servants), nonagricultural, nonincorporated self-employed workers, and nonagricultural unpaid family workers.

However, official CPS data are characterized by periodic discontinuities, which occur when new benchmarks for Census measures of the total population are introduced. These updates take place in a single month—usually January—and the official data for previous months are typically not modified to provide a smooth transition. Therefore, shorter-term comparisons (for a year or two or for a business cycle phase) will be misleading if such a discontinuity is included in the period. A recent example will illustrate. Beginning with January 2010, the estimates for civilian noninstitutional population, civilian labor force, and employment were all adjusted downward by about 250,000 persons. The reported seasonally adjusted change in employment from December 2009 to January 2010 was an increase of 541,000. If there had been no population control adjustment, the increase in employment would have been 784,000. Such discontinuities occur throughout the history of the series.

For users who would like to examine monthly CPS data in which these discontinuities have been smoothed, BLS now provides unofficial smoothed estimates of total labor force and total employment from January 1990 through December 2009 on its Web site, <http://www.bls.gov>. In this edition of *Business Statistics*, these two series are included in Table 20-3A in Chapter 20, Selected Historical Data.

The CPS is a count of persons employed, rather than a count of jobs. A person is counted as employed in this data set only once, no matter how many jobs he or she may hold. The CPS count is limited to persons 16 years of age and over.

The second set of employment estimates—the payroll survey—comes from a very large sample survey of 150,000 business and government employers at approximately 390,000 establishments, the Current Employment Statistics (CES) survey. It is benchmarked annually to a survey of all employers. Benchmark data are introduced with a smooth adjustment back to the previous benchmark, thus preserving the continuity of the series and making it more appropriate for measurement of employment change over a year or two, a business cycle, or other short- to medium-length periods. This sample is much larger than the CPS sample, and consequently the threshold of statistical significance for changes is lower. The minimum size of the over-the-month change required to be statistically significant is 101,000 jobs in the payroll survey, versus 436,000 persons in the household survey.

Over the latest 11 years, benchmark revisions to payroll survey employment have ranged in magnitude from an upward revision of 0.6 percent, in 2006, to the latest benchmark which reduced the seasonally adjusted level of payroll employment in March 2009 by 902,000 persons, or 0.7 percent. Revisions of 0.1 or 0.2 percent in either direction are more frequent, but larger ones occur in particularly strong or particularly weak labor markets.

The scope of the CES survey is wage and salary workers on nonfarm payrolls, and it is a count of jobs. Thus, a person with more than one nonfarm wage or salary job is counted as employed in each job. Workers are not classified by age; as a result, there may be some workers younger than 16 years old in the job count.

Persons with a job but not at work (absent due to bad weather, work stoppages, personal reasons, and the like) are included in the household survey. However, they are excluded from the payroll survey if on leave without pay for the entire payroll period.

In addition to the differences in definitions and scope between the two series, there are also differences in sample design, collection methodology, and the sampling variability inherent in the surveys.

The payroll survey provides the most reliable and detailed information on the breakdown of employment by industry (for example, the data shown in Table 16-1). In addition, it provides data on weekly hours and hourly and weekly earnings.

The CPS employment estimates provide information not collected in the CES on the breakdown of employment by demographic characteristics, such as age, race, and Hispanic ethnicity; by education levels; and by occupation. A few of these breakdowns are shown in *Business Statistics*. Many more breakdowns, in richer detail, can be found in the *Handbook of U.S. Labor Statistics*, also published by Bernan Press.

The differences between these two employment measures are discussed in an article on the BLS Web site, "Employment from the BLS household and payroll surveys: summary of recent trends," which is updated monthly along with the release of the monthly data, and can be found at <http://www.bls.gov/web/ces_cps_trends>. Further information can be found in an article by Mary Bowler and Teresa L. Morisi entitled "Understanding the employment measures from the CPS and CES survey" in *Monthly Labor Review,* February 2006, available on the BLS Web site http://www.bls.gov.

TABLES 10-1 THROUGH 10-5 AND 20-3
LABOR FORCE, EMPLOYMENT, AND UNEMPLOYMENT

SOURCE: U.S. DEPARTMENT OF LABOR, BUREAU OF LABOR STATISTICS (BLS)

Labor force, employment, and unemployment data are derived from the Current Population Survey (CPS), a sample survey of households conducted each month by the Census Bureau for the Bureau of Labor Statistics (BLS). The data pertain to the U.S. civilian noninstitutional population age 16 years and over.

Due to changes in questionnaire design and survey methodology, data for 1994 and subsequent years are not fully comparable with data for 1993 and earlier years. Additionally, discontinuities in the reported number of persons in the population, and consequently in the estimated numbers of employed and unemployed persons and the number of persons in the labor force, are introduced whenever periodic updates are made to U.S. population estimates.

For example, population controls based on Census 2000 were introduced beginning with the data for January 2000. These data are therefore not comparable with data for December 1999 and earlier. Data for 1990 through 1999 incorporate 1990 census–based population controls and are not comparable with the preceding years. An additional large population adjustment was introduced in January 2004, making the data from that time forward not comparable with data for December 2003 and earlier; further adjustments have been made in each subsequent January and other discontinuities have been introduced in various earlier years, usually with January data. See "Notes on the Data," below, for additional information.

For the most part, these population adjustments distort comparisons involving the numbers of persons in the population, labor force, and employment. They generally have negligible effects on the percentages that comprise the most important features of the CPS: the unemployment rates, the labor force participation rates, and the employment-population ratios.

BLS now makes available unofficial smoothed data for the total number of persons in the civilian labor force and the number of persons employed for 1990 through 2009, which introduce the population adjustments gradually within the period shown. These data are shown in Table 20-3A.

Beginning with the data for January 2000, data classified by industry and occupation use the 2002 North American Industry Classification System (NAICS—see Chapter 14 for more information) and the 2000 Standard Occupational Classification System. This creates breaks in the time series between December 1999 and January 2000 for occupational and industry data at all levels of aggregation. Since the recent history is so short, most industry and occupation data have been dropped from *Business Statistics* in favor of other important and economically meaningful data for which a longer consistent history can be supplied. However, detailed employment data by occupation and industry can be found in Bernan Press's *Handbook of U.S. Labor Statistics.*

Race and ethnic origin

Data for two broad racial categories were made available beginning in 1954: *White* and *Black and other.* The latter included Asians and all other "nonwhite" races, and was discontinued after 2002. Data for *Blacks* only are available beginning with 1972; this category is now called *Black or African American.* Data for *Asians* are shown beginning with 2000. Persons in the remaining race categories—American Indian or Alaska Native, Native Hawaiian or Other Pacific Islanders, and persons who selected more than one race category beginning in 2003 (see below)—are included in the estimates of total employment and unemployment, but are not shown separately because their numbers are too small to yield quality estimates.

Hispanic or Latino ethnicity, previously labeled *Hispanic origin,* is not a racial category and is established in a survey question separate from the question about race. Persons of Hispanic or Latino ethnicity may be of any race.

In January 2003, changes that affected classification by race and Hispanic ethnicity were introduced. These changes caused discontinuities in race and ethnic group data between December 2002 and January 2003.

Individuals in the sample are now asked whether they are of Hispanic ethnicity before being asked about their race. Prior to 2003, individuals were asked their ethnic origin after they were asked about their race. Furthermore, respondents are now asked directly if they are Spanish, Hispanic, or Latino. Previously, they were identified based on their or their ancestors' country of origin.

Individuals in the sample are now allowed to choose more than one race category. Before 2003, they were required to select a single primary race. This change had no impact on the size of the overall civilian noninstitutional population and labor force. It did reduce the population and labor force levels of Whites and Blacks beginning in January 2003, as individuals who reported more than one race are now excluded from those groups.

BLS has estimated, based on a special survey, that these changes reduced the population and labor force levels for

Whites by about 950,000 and 730,000 persons, respectively, and for Blacks by about 320,000 and 240,000 persons, respectively, while having little or no impact on either of their unemployment rates. The changes did not affect the size of the Hispanic population or labor force, but they did cause an increase of about half a percentage point in the Hispanic unemployment rate.

Definitions

The employment status of the civilian population is surveyed each month with respect to a specific week in midmonth—not for the entire month. This is known as the "reference week." For a precise definition and explanation of the reference week, see Notes on the Data, which follows these definitions.

The *civilian noninstitutional population* comprises all civilians 16 years of age and over who are not inmates of penal or mental institutions, sanitariums, or homes for the aged, infirm, or needy.

Civilian employment includes those civilians who (1) worked for pay or profit at any time during the week that includes the 12th day of the month (the reference week), or who worked for 15 hours or more as an unpaid worker in a family-operated enterprise; or (2) were temporarily absent from regular jobs because of vacation, illness, industrial dispute, bad weather, or similar reasons. Each employed person is counted only once; those who hold more than one job are counted as being in the job at which they worked the greatest number of hours during the reference week.

Unemployed persons are all civilians who were not employed (according to the above definition) during the reference week, but who were available for work—except for temporary illness—and who had made specific efforts to find employment sometime during the previous four weeks. Persons who did not look for work because they were on layoff are also counted as unemployed.

The *civilian labor force* comprises all civilians classified as employed or unemployed.

Civilians 16 years of age and over in the noninstitutional population who are not classified as employed or unemployed are defined as *not in the labor force*. This group includes those engaged in own-home housework; in school; unable to work because of long-term illness, retirement, or age; seasonal workers for whom the reference week fell in an "off" season (if not qualifying as unemployed by looking for a job); persons who became discouraged and gave up the search for work; and the voluntarily idle. Also included are those doing only incidental work (less than 15 hours) in a family-operated business during the reference week.

The civilian *labor force participation rate* represents the percentage of the civilian noninstitutional population (age 16 years and over) that is in the civilian labor force.

The *employment-population ratio* represents the percentage of the civilian noninstitutional population (age 16 years and over) that is employed. This is traditionally called a "ratio," although it is traditionally expressed as a percent and therefore would be more appropriately called a "rate," as is the case with the labor force participation rate.

Employment is shown by *class of worker,* including a breakdown of total employment into *agricultural* and *nonagricultural* industries. Employment in *nonagricultural industries* includes *wage and salary workers,* the *self-employed,* and *unpaid family workers.*

Wage and salary workers receive wages, salaries, commissions, tips, and/or pay- in-kind. This category includes owners of self-owned incorporated businesses.

Self-employed workers are those who work for profit or for fees in their own business, profession, trade, or farm. This category includes only the unincorporated; those whose businesses are incorporated are considered wage and salary workers since they are paid employees of a corporation, even if they are the corporation's president and sole employee.

Wage and salary employment comprises *government* and *private industry* wage and salary workers. Domestic workers and other employees of *private households,* who are not included in the payroll employment series, are shown separately from *all other private industries.* The series for *government* and *other private industries* wage and salary workers are the closest in scope to similar categories in the payroll employment series.

Multiple jobholders are employed persons who, during the reference week, either had two or more jobs as a wage and salary worker, were self-employed and also held a wage and salary job, or worked as an unpaid family worker and also held a wage and salary job. Excluded are self-employed persons with multiple businesses and persons with multiple jobs as unpaid family workers. Multiple jobholders are counted as being in the job at which they worked the greatest number of hours during the reference week.

Employed and at work part time excludes employed persons who were absent from their jobs during the entire reference week for reasons such as vacation, illness, or industrial dispute.

At work part time for economic reasons ("involuntary" part time) refers to individuals who worked 1 to 34 hours during the reference week because of slack work, unfavorable business conditions, an inability to find full-time work, or seasonal declines in demand. To be included in this category, workers must also indicate that they want and are available for full-time work.

At work part time for noneconomic reasons ("voluntary" part time) refers to persons who usually work part time and were at work for 1 to 34 hours during the reference week for reasons such as illness, other medical limitations, family obligations, education, retirement, Social Security limits on earnings, or working in an industry where the workweek is less than 35 hours. It also includes respondents who gave an economic reason but were not available for, or did not want, full-time work. At work part time for noneconomic reasons excludes persons who usually work full time, but who worked only 1 to 34 hours during the reference week for reasons such as holidays, illnesses, and bad weather.

The *long-term unemployed* are persons currently unemployed (searching or on layoff) who have been unemployed for 15 consecutive weeks or longer. If a person ceases to look for work for two weeks or more, or becomes temporarily employed, the continuity of long-term unemployment is broken. If he or she starts searching for work or is laid off again, the monthly CPS will record the length of his or her unemployment from the time the search recommenced or since the latest layoff.

The civilian *unemployment rate* is the number of unemployed as a percentage of the civilian labor force. The unemployment rates for groups within the civilian population (such as males age 20 years and over) are the number of unemployed in a group as a percent of that group's labor force.

Unemployment rates by reason provides a breakdown of the total unemployment rate. Each unemployed person is classified into one of four groups.

Job losers and persons who completed temporary jobs includes persons on temporary layoff, permanent job losers, and persons who completed temporary jobs and began looking for work after those jobs ended. These three categories are shown separately without seasonal adjustment in the BLS's "Employment Situation" news release and on its Web site. They are combined, under the title shown here, for the purpose of seasonal adjustment. This is the category of unemployment that responds most strongly to the business cycle.

Job leavers terminated their employment voluntarily and immediately began looking for work.

Reentrants are persons who previously worked, but were out of the labor force prior to beginning their current job search.

New entrants are persons searching for a first job who have never worked.

Each of these categories is expressed as a proportion of the entire civilian labor force, so that the sum of the four rates equals the unemployment rate for all civilian workers (except for possible discrepancies due to rounding or separate seasonal adjustment).

Median and average weeks unemployed are summary measures of the length of time that persons classified as unem-

ployed have been looking for work. For persons on layoff, the duration represents the number of full weeks of the layoff. The *average (mean)* number of weeks is computed by aggregating all the weeks of unemployment experienced by all unemployed persons during their current spell of unemployment and dividing by the number of unemployed. The *median* number of weeks unemployed is the number of weeks of unemployment experienced by the person at the midpoint of the distribution of all unemployed persons, as ranked by duration of unemployment.

Alternative measures of labor underutilization are calculated by BLS and published in the monthly Employment Situation release. They measure alternative concepts of unused working capacity, and are numbered "U-1" through "U-6" in order of increasing breadth of the definition of underutilization.

"U-1" is persons unemployed 15 weeks or longer, as a percent of the civilian labor force. It is not shown in *Business Statistics*.

"U-2" is job losers and persons who completed temporary jobs, as a percent of the civilian labor force; it is shown in *Business Statistics* in the second column of Table 10-5.

"U-3" is the official rate, described above and shown in the first columns of Tables 10-4 and 10-5.

"U-4" through "U-6" are shown in the last three columns of Table 10-5. They are based on additional labor force status questions, now included in the CPS survey, that were introduced beginning in 1994. U-4 and U-5 are increasingly broader rates of unemployment, while U-6 can be described as an "unemployment and underemployment rate."

"U-4" adds discouraged workers to unemployment and the labor force. Discouraged workers are persons not in the officially defined labor force who have given a job-market-related reason for not looking currently for a job—for example, they have not looked for a job because they believed that no jobs were available.

"U-5" adds both discouraged workers and all other "marginally attached" workers to unemployment and the labor force. "Marginally attached" workers are all persons who currently are neither working nor looking for work but indicate that they want and are available for a job and have looked for work some time in the recent past.

"U-6" adds persons employed part time for economic reasons, as shown in Table 10-3, to the number of persons counted as unemployed in "U-5", with the same labor force definition as in "U-5." Recently this statistic, measuring combined unemployment and underemployment, has been cited in press reports on the employment situation.

For more information, see "BLS introduced new range of alternative unemployment measures" in the October 1995 issue of the *Monthly Labor Review.*

Notes on the data

The CPS data are collected by trained interviewers from about 60,000 sample households selected to represent the U.S. civilian noninstitutional population. Sample size was about 60,000 households from mid-1989 to mid-1995, but was reduced for budgetary reasons in two stages to about 50,000 households, beginning in January 1996. This sample size was maintained from 1996 through 2000. The sample size was increased back to 60,000 households, beginning with the data for July 2001, as part of a plan to meet the requirements of the State Children's Health Insurance Program legislation. The CPS provides data for other data series in addition to the BLS employment status data, such as household income and poverty (see Chapter 3) and health insurance.

The employment status data are based on the activity or status reported for the calendar week, Sunday through Saturday, that includes the 12th day of the month (the reference week). Households are interviewed in the week following the reference week. Sample households are phased in and out of the sample on a rotating basis. Consequently, three-fourths of the sample is the same for any two consecutive months. One-half of the sample is the same as the sample in the same month a year earlier.

Data relating to 1994 and subsequent years are not strictly comparable with data for 1993 and earlier years because of a major redesign of the survey questionnaire and collection methodology. The redesign includes new and revised questions for the classification of individuals as employed or unemployed, the collection of new data on multiple job-holding, a change in the definition of discouraged workers, and the implementation of a more completely automated data collection.

The 1994 redesign of the CPS was the most extensive since 1967. However, there are many other significant periods of year-to-year noncomparability in the labor force data. These typically result from the introduction of new decennial census data into the CPS estimation procedures, expansions of the sample, or other improvements made to increase the reliability of the estimates. Each change introduces a new discontinuity, usually between December of the previous year and January of the newly altered year. The discontinuities are usually minor or negligible with respect to figures expressed as nationwide percentages (such as the unemployment rate or the labor force participation rate), but can be significant with respect to levels (such as labor force and employment in thousands of persons). A list of the dates of the major discontinuities follows, with BLS estimates of their quantitative impact on the national totals. (There are likely to be larger impacts on population subgroups.) The discontinuities occur in January unless otherwise indicated. Note that some of the changes caused adjustments that were carried back to an earlier year.

- 1953: 1950 census data introduced. Labor force and employment were raised by about 350,000.

- 1960: Alaska and Hawaii included. The labor force was increased by about 300,000, mainly in nonagricultural employment.
- 1962: 1960 census data introduced. Labor force and employment were reduced by about 200,000.
- 1972: 1970 census data introduced. Labor force and employment were raised by about 300,000.
- March 1973: Further 1970 census data were introduced, reducing White labor force and employment by about 150,000 and raising Black and other labor force and employment by approximately 210,000.
- July 1975: Adjustment for Vietnamese refugee inflow, raising total and Black and other population by 76,000.
- 1978: Sample expansion and revised estimation procedures increased labor force and employment by about 250,000.
- 1982: Change in estimation procedures introduced. To avoid major breaks, many series were reestimated back to 1970. This did not smooth the breaks occurring between 1972 and 1979.
- 1986, with revisions carried back to 1980: Adjustment for better estimates of immigration, raising labor force by nearly 400,000 and employment by 350,000, mainly among Hispanics.
- 1994: 1990 census data introduced and carried back to 1990, when employment was increased by about 880,000 and the unemployment rate was raised by about 0.1 percentage point.
- 1997: New estimates of immigration and emigration, raising labor force and employment by about 300,000, again mainly among Hispanics.
- 1998: New population estimates and estimation procedures, reducing labor force and employment by around 250,000.
- 1999: New information on immigration, raising labor force and employment by around 60,000, but lowering Hispanic employment by about 200,000.
- 2000: Census 2000 data introduced, using the 2002 NAICS and the 2000 Standard Occupational Classification System. The labor force was increased by about 1.6 million in January 2000, growing to around 2.5 million by December 2002.
- 2003: Further population estimates introduced (based on an annual population update and therefore not carried back to 2000), raising the labor force by 614,000.
- 2004: Population controls updated to reflect revised migration estimates, reducing labor force and employment by around 400,000, mostly among Hispanics.
- 2005: Updated migration and vital statistics data decreased labor force and employment by around 45,000.
- 2006: Updated migration and vital statistics data decreased labor force and employment by about 125,000.
- 2007: Updated migration and vital statistics data increased labor force and employment by about 150,000.
- 2008: Updated migration and vital statistics data decreased labor force by 637,000 and employment by 598,000.
- 2009: Updated migration adjustments, new vital statistics data, and methodological changes decreased labor force by 449,000 and employment by 407,000.

- 2010: Updated information on migration, vital statistics, and other data and methodological changes decreased labor force by 249,000 and employment by 243,000.

For further information on these changes, see the BLS publications *Employment and Earnings* for February of each year. The most recent information is posted on <http://www.bls.gov/cps> under "Publications and Other Documentation."

The monthly labor force, employment, and unemployment data are seasonally adjusted by the X-12-ARIMA method. All seasonally adjusted civilian labor force and unemployment rate statistics, as well as major employment and unemployment estimates, are computed by aggregating independently adjusted series. For example, the seasonally adjusted level of total unemployment is the sum of the seasonally adjusted levels of unemployment for the four age/sex groups (men and women age 16 to 19 years, and men and women age 20 years and over). Seasonally adjusted employment is the sum of the seasonally adjusted levels of employment for the same four groups. The seasonally adjusted civilian labor force is the sum of all eight components. Finally, the seasonally adjusted civilian worker unemployment rate is calculated by taking total seasonally adjusted unemployment as a percent of the total seasonally adjusted civilian labor force.

To minimize subsequent revisions, BLS uses a concurrent technique which estimates factors for the latest month using the most recent data. Then, seasonal adjustment factors are fully revised at the end of each year to reflect recent experience. The revisions also affect the preceding four years. An article describing the seasonal adjustment methodology for the household survey data is available at http://www.bls.gov/cps/cpsrs2010.pdf.

Breakdowns other than the basic age/sex classification described above—such as the employment data by class of worker in Table 10-2—will not necessarily add to totals because of independent seasonal adjustment.

Data availability

Data for each month are usually released on the first Friday of the following month in the "Employment Situation" press release, which also includes data from the establishment survey (Tables 10-7 through 10-16 and Chapter 16). The press release and data are available on the BLS Web site at <http://www.bls.gov>. Data are subsequently published in the BLS monthly periodical *Employment and Earnings*, which contains detailed explanatory notes. The last paper issue of *Employment and Earnings* was for April 2007; subsequent issues are available on the BLS Web site. Selected data are published each month in the *Monthly Labor Review*, also available online at the BLS Web site, which also features frequent articles analyzing developments in the labor force, employment, and unemployment.

Monthly and annual data are available beginning with 1948. Historical unadjusted data are published in *Labor Force*

Statistics Derived from the Current Population Survey (BLS Bulletin 2307). Historical seasonally adjusted data are available from BLS upon request. Complete historical data are available on the BLS Web site at <http://www.bls.gov/cps>.

Seasonal adjustment factors are revised each year for the five previous years, with the release of December data in early January. New population controls are introduced with the release of January data in early February.

References

Comprehensive descriptive material can be found at <http://www.bls.gov/cps> under the "Publications and Other Documentation" section. Historical background on the CPS, as well as a description of the 1994 redesign, can be found in three articles from the September 1993 edition of *Monthly Labor Review*: "Why Is It Necessary to Change?"; "Redesigning the Questionnaire"; and "Evaluating Changes in the Estimates." The redesign is also described in the February 1994 issue of *Employment and Earnings*. See also Chapter 1, "Labor Force Data Derived from the Current Population Survey," *BLS Handbook of Methods*, Bulletin 2490 (April 1997).

TABLE 20-3A
LABOR FORCE AND EMPLOYMENT ESTIMATES SMOOTHED FOR POPULATION ADJUSTMENTS

SOURCE: U.S. DEPARTMENT OF LABOR, BUREAU OF LABOR STATISTICS

This table presents seasonally adjusted monthly estimates of total civilian labor force and total civilian employment in which discontinuities caused by the introduction of new population controls in the official series—as described above—have been smoothed. They are taken from "Labor Force and Employment Estimates Smoothed for Population Adjustments, 1990–2009," posted on February 5, 2010 <http://www.bls.gov/cps/cpspopsm.pdf>. The method of smoothing is described in Marisa L. Di Natale, "Creating Comparability in CPS Employment Series," on the BLS Web site at <http://www.bls.gov/cps/cpscomp.pdf>. BLS notes that these series do not match the official estimates in BLS publications, which are also the data shown in all other tables in this volume.

TABLE 10-6
INSURED UNEMPLOYMENT

SOURCE: U.S. DEPARTMENT OF LABOR, EMPLOYMENT AND TRAINING ADMINISTRATION

Definitions

State programs of unemployment insurance cover operations of regular programs under state unemployment insurance laws. In 1976, the law was amended to extend coverage to include virtually all state and local government employees, as well as many agricultural and domestic workers. (This took effect on January 1, 1978.)

Benefits under state programs are financed by taxes levied by the states on employers.

Federal programs are those directly financed by the federal government. They include unemployment benefits for *federal employees* (Unemployment Compensation for Federal Employees, or UCFE), *newly discharged veterans* (Unemployment Compensation for Ex-Service Members, or UCX), *railroad retirement*, and *extended benefits*, which are sometimes enacted by Congress in times of widespread or protracted unemployment.

UCX pays benefits, based on service, to veterans who were on active duty and honorably separated. In the case of both UCFE and UCX, state laws determine the benefit amounts, number of weeks benefits can be paid, and other eligibility conditions.

An *initial claim* is the first claim in a benefit year filed by a worker after losing his or her job, or the first claim filed at the beginning of a subsequent period of unemployment in the same benefit year. The initial claim establishes the starting date for any insured unemployment that may result if the claimant is unemployed for one week or longer. Transitional claims (filed by claimants as they start a new benefit year in a continuing spell of unemployment) are excluded; therefore, these data more closely represent instances of new unemployment and are widely followed as a leading indicator of job market conditions.

Insured unemployment and *persons claiming benefits* both describe the average number of persons receiving benefits in the indicated month or year.

The *insured unemployment rate* for state programs is the level of insured unemployment as a percentage of employment covered by state programs.

Monthly averages in this book are averages, calculated by the editor, of the weekly data published by the Employment and Training Administration. Annual data are averages of the monthly data.

Data availability

Data are published in weekly press releases from the Employment and Training Administration. These releases are available on their Web site at <http://www.doleta.gov> under "Labor Market Data." Historical data on weekly claims are available at the Department of Labor's Information Technology Support Center at <http://www.itsc.state.md.us>.

TABLES 10-7, 10-12, 16-1, 16-2, AND 20-4 NONFARM PAYROLL EMPLOYMENT

SOURCE: U.S. DEPARTMENT OF LABOR, BUREAU OF LABOR STATISTICS (BLS)

These nonfarm employment data, as well as the hours and earnings data in Tables 10-8 through 10-11, 10-13 through 10-16, 16-3 through 16-6, and 20-4, are compiled from payroll records. Information is reported monthly on a voluntary basis to BLS and its cooperating state agencies by a large sample of establishments, representing all industries except farming. These data, formally known as the Current Employment Statistics (CES) survey, are often referred to as the "establishment data" or the "payroll data." They are also known as the BLS-790 survey.

The survey, originally based on a stratified quota sample, has been replaced on a phased-in basis by a stratified probability sample. The new sampling procedure went into effect for wholesale trade in June 2000; for mining, construction, and manufacturing in June 2001; and for retail trade, transportation and public utilities, and finance, insurance, and real estate in June 2002. The phase-in was completed in June 2003, upon its extension to the service industries. The phase-in schedule was slightly different for the state and area series.

The sample has always been very large. Currently, it includes approximately 160,000 businesses and government agencies covering about 390,000 individual worksites, which account for about one-third of total benchmark employment of payroll workers. The sample is drawn from a sampling frame of over 8 million unemployment insurance tax accounts.

With the release of January 2008 data on February 1, 2008, the CES National Nonfarm Payroll series was updated to the 2007 North American Industry Classification System (NAICS) from the 2002 NAICS basis. For further details on the 2007 NAICS update, visit the CES NAICS web page. The previous revision to CES industry classification was the June 2003 replacement of the 1987 Standard Industrial Classification (SIC) with 2002 NAICS. Information on the SIC to NAICS conversion can be found at CES NAICS conversion web page.

BLS has reconstructed historical time series to conform with NAICS, to ensure that all published series have a NAICS-based history extending back to at least January 1990. NAICS-based history extends back to January 1939 for total nonfarm and other high-level aggregates. For more detailed series, the starting date for NAICS data varies depending on the extent of the definitional changes between the old Standard Industrial Classification (SIC) and NAICS.

Definitions

An *establishment* is an economic unit, such as a factory, store, or professional office, that produces goods or services at a single location and is engaged in one type of economic activity.

Employment comprises all persons who received pay (including holiday and sick pay) for any part of the payroll period that includes the 12th day of the month. The definition of the payroll period for each reporting respondent is that used by the employer; it could be weekly, biweekly, monthly, or other. Included are all full-time and part-time workers in nonfarm establishments, including salaried officers of corporations. Persons holding more than one job are counted in each establishment that reports them. Not covered are proprietors, the self-employed, unpaid volunteer and family workers, farm workers, domestic workers in households, and military personnel. Employees of the Central Intelligence Agency, the Defense Intelligence Agency, the National Geospatial-Intelligence Agency, and the National Security Agency are not included.

Persons on an establishment payroll who are on paid sick leave (when pay is received directly from the employer), on paid holiday or vacation, or who work during a portion of the pay period despite being unemployed or on strike during the rest of the period, are counted as employed. Not counted as employed are persons who are laid off, on leave without pay, on strike for the entire period, or hired but not paid during the period.

Intermittent workers are counted if they performed any service during the month. BLS considers regular full-time teachers (private and government) to be employed during the summer vacation period, regardless of whether they are specifically paid during those months.

The *government* division includes federal, state, and local activities such as legislative, executive, and judicial functions, as well as the U.S. Postal Service and all government-owned and government-operated business enterprises, establishments, and institutions (arsenals, navy yards, hospitals, state-owned utilities, etc.), and government force account construction. However, as indicated earlier, members of the armed forces and employees of certain national-security-related agencies are not included.

The monthly *diffusion index of employment change*, currently based on 271 private nonfarm NAICS industries, represents the percentage of those industries in which the seasonally adjusted level of employment in that month was higher than six months earlier, plus one-half of the percentage of industries with unchanged employment. Therefore, the diffusion index reported for September represents the change from March to September. *Business Statistics* uses the September value to represent the year as a whole, since it spans the year's midpoint. Diffusion indexes measure the dispersion of economic gains and losses, with values below 50 percent associated with recessions. The current NAICS-based series begins with January 1991. For October 1976 through December 1990, an earlier series is available based on 347 SIC industries (there are more industries using the older classification system because in SIC manufacturing industries were represented in greater detail). September values from this series are used here to represent the years 1977 through 1990.

Production or nonsupervisory workers include all *production and related workers* in mining and manufacturing; *construction workers* in construction; and *nonsupervisory*

workers in transportation, communication, electric, gas, and sanitary services; wholesale and retail trade; finance, insurance, and real estate; and services. These groups account for about four-fifths of the total employment on private nonagricultural payrolls.

Production and related workers include working supervisors and all nonsupervisory workers (including group leaders and trainees) engaged in fabricating, processing, assembling, inspecting, receiving, storing, handling, packing, warehousing, shipping, trucking, hauling, maintenance, repair, janitorial, guard services, product development, auxiliary production for plant's own use (such as a power plant), record keeping, and other services closely associated with these production operations.

Construction workers include the following employees in the construction division of the NAICS: working supervisors, qualified craft workers, mechanics, apprentices, laborers, and the like, who are engaged in new work, alterations, demolition, repair, maintenance, and other tasks, whether working at the site of construction or working in shops or yards at jobs (such as precutting and preassembling) ordinarily performed by members of the construction trades.

Nonsupervisory employees include employees (not above the working supervisory level) such as office and clerical workers, repairers, salespersons, operators, drivers, physicians, lawyers, accountants, nurses, social workers, research aides, teachers, drafters, photographers, beauticians, musicians, restaurant workers, custodial workers, attendants, line installers and repairers, laborers, janitors, guards, and other employees at similar occupational levels whose services are closely associated with those of the employees listed.

Notes on the data

Benchmark adjustments. The establishment survey data are adjusted annually to comprehensive counts of employment, called "benchmarks." Benchmark information on employment by industry is compiled by state agencies from reports of establishments covered under state unemployment insurance laws; these form an annual compilation of administrative data known as the ES-202. These tabulations cover about 97 percent of all employees on nonfarm payrolls. Benchmark data for the residual are obtained from alternate sources, primarily from Railroad Retirement Board records and the Census Bureau's *County Business Patterns*. The latest benchmark adjustment, which is incorporated into the data in this volume, reduced the seasonally adjusted employment level in the benchmark month March 2009 by 902,000 jobs—an unusually large 0.7 percent.

The estimates for the benchmark month are compared with new benchmark levels for each industry. If revisions are necessary, the monthly series of estimates between benchmark periods are adjusted by graduated amounts between the new benchmark and the preceding one ("wedged back"), and the new benchmark level for each industry is then carried forward month by month based on the sample.

More specifically, the month-to-month changes for each estimation cell are based on changes in a matched sample for that cell, plus an estimate of net business births and deaths. The matched sample for each pair of months consists of establishments that have reported data for both months (which automatically excludes establishments that have gone out of business by the second month). Since new businesses are not immediately incorporated into the sample, a model-based estimate of net business births and deaths in that estimating cell is added. The model-based estimate is based on past benchmark revisions.

Not-seasonally-adjusted data for all months since the last benchmark to which the series has been adjusted are subject to revision.

Beginning in 1959, the data include Alaska and Hawaii. This inclusion resulted in an increase of 212,000 (0.4 percent) in total nonfarm employment for the March 1959 benchmark month.

Seasonal adjustment. The seasonal movements that recur periodically—such as warm and cold weather, holidays, and vacations—are generally the largest single component of month-to-month changes in employment. After adjusting the data to remove such seasonal variation, the basic trends are more evident. BLS uses X-12-ARIMA software to produce the seasonal factors and perform concurrent seasonal adjustment, using the most recent 10 years of data. New factors are developed each month adding the most current data.

For most series, a special procedure called REGARIMA (regression with autocorrelated errors) is used before calculating the seasonal factors; this adjusts for the length of the interval (which can be either four or five weeks) between the survey weeks. REGARIMA has also been used to isolate extreme weather effects that distorted the measurement of seasonal patterns in the construction industry, and to identify variations in local government employment due to the presence or absence of election poll workers.

Seasonal adjustment factors are directly applied to the component levels. Seasonally adjusted totals for employment series are then obtained by aggregating the seasonally adjusted components directly, while hours and earnings series represent weighted averages of the seasonally adjusted component series. Seasonally adjusted data are not published for a small number of series characterized by small seasonal components relative to their trend and/or irregular components. However, these series are used in aggregating to broader seasonally adjusted levels.

Revisions of the seasonally adjusted data, usually for the most recent five-year period, are made once a year coincident with the benchmark revisions. This means that these revisions typically extend back farther than the benchmark revisions.

Data availability

Employment data by industry division are available beginning with 1919. Data for each month usually are released on the first Friday of the following month in a press release that also contains data from the household survey (Tables 10-1 through 10-5). Data are subsequently published in the BLS monthly periodical *Employment and Earnings*, which features detailed explanatory notes. Selected data are published each month in the *Monthly Labor Review*, which frequently contains articles analyzing developments in the labor force, employment, and unemployment. *Employment and Earnings*, the *Monthly Labor Review*, press releases, and complete historical data are available on the BLS Web site at <http://www.bls.gov>.

Benchmark revisions and revised seasonally adjusted data for recent years are made each year with the release of January data in early February. Before 2004, the benchmark revisions were not made until June; the acceleration is due to earlier availability of the benchmark UI (ES-202) data.

References

References can be found at <http://www.bls.gov/ces> under the headings "Special Notices," "Benchmark Information," and "Technical Notes." Extensive changes incorporated in June 2003 are described in "Recent Changes in the National Current Employment Statistics Survey," the *Monthly Labor Review*, June 2003; and in the "Explanatory Notes" in any subsequent issue of *Employment and Earnings*. The latest benchmark revision is discussed in an article available on the BLS Web site. See also Chapter 2, "Employment, Hours, and Earnings from the Establishment Survey," *BLS Handbook of Methods*, Bulletin 2490 (April 1997).

TABLES 10-8, 10-9, 10-13, 10-14, 16-3, 16-6, AND 20-4 AVERAGE HOURS PER WEEK; AGGREGATE EMPLOYEE HOURS

SOURCE: U.S. DEPARTMENT OF LABOR, BUREAU OF LABOR STATISTICS (BLS)

See the notes and definitions to Tables 10-7 and 10-12 for an overall description of the "establishment" or "payroll" survey that is the source of hours data.

Hours and earnings have been reported for production or nonsupervisory workers, as defined above, since the inception of the CES. Beginning with data for March 2006, such data have also been collected for all payroll employees. With sufficient history for calculation of seasonal adjustment factors, BLS began publishing all-employee hours and earnings in February 2010, and these new data are presented in new *Business Statistics* Tables 10-8 through 10-11.

Definitions

Average weekly hours represents the average hours paid per worker during the pay period that includes the 12th of the month. Included are hours paid for holidays and vacations, as well as those paid for sick leave when pay is received directly from the firm.

Average weekly hours are different from standard or scheduled hours. Factors such as unpaid absenteeism, labor turnover, part-time work, and work stoppages can cause average weekly hours to be lower than scheduled hours of work for an establishment.

Average weekly hours pertain to jobs, not to persons; thus, a person with half-time jobs in two different establishments is represented in this series as two jobs that have 20-hour workweeks, not as one person with a 40-hour workweek.

Overtime hours represent the portion of average weekly hours worked in excess of regular hours, for which overtime premiums were paid. Weekend and holiday hours are included only if overtime premiums were paid. Hours for which only shift differential, hazard, incentive, or other similar types of premiums were paid are excluded.

Aggregate hours provide measures of changes over time in labor input to the industry, in index-number form. The indexes are obtained by multiplying seasonally adjusted employment by seasonally adjusted average weekly hours, dividing the resulting series by their monthly averages for a base period, and multiplying the results by 100, so that the annual average for the base period equals 100. For total private, goods-producing, service-providing, and major industry divisions, the indexes are obtained by summing the seasonally adjusted aggregate weekly employee hours for the component industries, dividing by the monthly average for the base period, and multiplying by 100. For the series covering production or nonsupervisory workers, the base period is 2002; for the all-employee series, the base period is 2007.

Notes on the data

Benchmark adjustments. Independent benchmarks are not available for the hours and earnings series. At the time of the annual adjustment of the employment series to new benchmarks, the levels of hours and earnings may be affected by the revised employment weights (which are used in computing the industry averages for hours and earnings), as well as by the changes in seasonal adjustment factors introduced with the benchmark revision.

Method of computing industry series. "Average weekly hours" for individual industries are computed by dividing worker hours (reported by establishments classified in each industry) by the number of workers reported for the same establishments. Estimates for divisions and major industry groups are averages (weighted by employment) of the figures for component industries.

Seasonal adjustment. Hours and earnings series are seasonally adjusted by applying factors directly to the corresponding unadjusted series. Data for some industries are not seasonally adjusted because the seasonal component is small relative to the trend-cycle and/or irregular components. Consequently, they cannot be separated with sufficient precision.

Special adjustments are made to average weekly hours to account for the presence or absence of religious holidays in the April survey reference period and the occasional occurrence of Labor Day in the September reference period. In addition, REGARIMA modeling is used prior to seasonal adjustment to correct for reporting and processing errors associated with the number of weekdays in a month (rather than to correct for the 4- and 5-week effect, which is less significant for hours than it is for employment). This is of particular importance for average weekly hours in the service-providing industries other than retail trade. For this reason, BLS advises that calculations of over-the-year changes (for example, the change for the current month from a year earlier) should use seasonally adjusted data, since the actual not-seasonally-adjusted monthly data may be distorted.

Data availability

See data availability for Tables 10-7 and 10-12.

References

See references for Tables 10-7 and 10-12.

TABLES 10-10, 10-11, 10-15, 10-16, 16-4, 16-5, AND 20-4 HOURLY AND WEEKLY EARNINGS

SOURCE: U.S. DEPARTMENT OF LABOR, BUREAU OF LABOR STATISTICS (BLS)

See the notes and definitions to Tables 10-7 and 10-12 for an overall description of the "establishment" or "payroll" survey that is the source of these earnings data.

Hours and earnings have been reported for production or nonsupervisory workers, as defined above, since the inception of the CES. Beginning with data for March 2006, such data have also been collected for all payroll employees. With sufficient history for calculation of seasonal adjustment factors, BLS began publishing all-employee hours and earnings in February 2010, and these new data are presented in new *Business Statistics* Tables 10-8 through 10-11.

Definitions

Earnings are the payments that workers receive during the survey period (before deductions for taxes and other items), including premium pay for overtime or late-shift work but excluding irregular bonuses and other special payments. After being previously excluded, tips were asked to be reported beginning in September 2005. This made little difference in most industries, and BLS asserts that many respondents had already been including tips. In two industries, full-service restaurants and cafeterias, there was a substantial difference, and the historical earnings data for those industries have been reconstructed to reflect the new higher level of earnings. These effects can be seen beginning with the data for 1974.

Notes on the data

The hours and earnings series are based on reports of gross payroll and corresponding paid hours for full- and part-time workers who received pay for any part of the pay period that included the 12th of the month.

Total payrolls are before deductions, such as for the employee share of old-age and unemployment insurance, group insurance, withholding taxes, bonds, and union dues. The payroll figures also include pay for overtime, holidays, vacations, and sick leave (paid directly by the employer for the period reported). Excluded from the payroll figures are fringe benefits (health and other types of insurance and contributions to retirement, paid by the employer, and the employer share of payroll taxes), bonuses (unless earned and paid regularly each pay period), other pay not earned in the pay period reported (retroactive pay), and the value of free rent, fuel, meals, or other payment-in-kind.

Average hourly earnings data reflect not only changes in basic hourly and incentive wage rates, but also such variable factors as premium pay for overtime and late-shift work and changes in output of workers paid on an incentive basis. Shifts in the volume of employment between relatively high-paid and low-paid work also affect the general average of hourly earnings.

Averages of hourly earnings should not be confused with wage rates, which represent the rates stipulated for a given unit of work or time, while earnings refer to the actual return to the worker for a stated period of time. The earnings series do not represent total labor cost to the employer because of the inclusion of tips and the exclusion of irregular bonuses, retroactive items, the cost of employer-provided benefits, and payroll taxes paid by employers.

Average weekly earnings are not the amounts available to workers for spending, since they do not reflect deductions such as income taxes and Social Security taxes. It should also be noted that they represent earnings per job, not per worker (since a worker may have more than one job) and not per family (since a family may have more than one worker). A person with two half-time jobs will be reflected as two earners with low weekly earnings rather than as one person with the total earnings from his or her two jobs.

Method of computing industry series. Average hourly earnings are obtained by dividing the reported total worker payroll by total worker hours. Estimates for both hours and hourly earnings for nonfarm divisions and major industry

groups are employment-weighted averages of the figures for component industries.

Average weekly earnings are computed by multiplying average hourly earnings by average weekly hours. In addition to the factors mentioned above, which exert varying influences upon average hourly earnings, average weekly earnings are affected by changes in the length of the workweek, part-time work, work stoppages, labor turnover, and absenteeism. Persistent long-term uptrends in the proportion of part-time workers in retail trade and many of the service industries have reduced average workweeks (as measured here), and have similarly affected the average weekly earnings series.

Benchmark adjustments. Independent benchmarks are not available for the hours and earnings series. At the time of the annual adjustment of the employment series to new benchmarks, the levels of hours and earnings may be affected by the revised employment weights (which are used in computing the industry averages for hours and earnings), as well as by the changes in seasonal adjustment factors that were also introduced with the benchmark revision.

Seasonal adjustment. Hours and earnings series are seasonally adjusted by applying factors directly to the corresponding unadjusted series; seasonally adjusted average weekly earnings are the product of seasonally adjusted hourly earnings and weekly hours.

REGARIMA modeling is used to correct for reporting and processing errors associated with variations in the number of weekdays in a month (rather than for the 4- and 5-week effect, which is less significant for earnings than for employment). This is of particular importance for average hourly earnings in wholesale trade, financial activities, professional and business services, and other services. For this reason, BLS advises that calculations of over-the-year changes, for example the change for the current month from a year earlier, should use seasonally adjusted data, since the actual not seasonally adjusted monthly data may be distorted.

Data availability

See data availability for Tables 10-7 and 10-12.

References

See references for Tables 10-7 and 10-12.

TABLE 10-17
MEDIAN USUAL WEEKLY EARNINGS OF FULL-TIME WAGE AND SALARY WORKERS

SOURCE: U.S. DEPARTMENT OF LABOR, BUREAU OF LABOR STATISTICS

These data are from the Current Population Survey, which was described in the notes to Tables 10-1 through 10-5.

Because they are earnings per worker, not per job, and are limited to full-time workers, the data are not distorted by the increasing proportion of part-time workers, as the CES earnings data are.

Definitions

Full-time wage and salary workers are those who receive wages, salaries, commissions, tips, pay in kind, or piece rates, and usually work 35 hours or more per week at their sole or principal job. Both private-sector and public-sector employees are included. All self-employed persons are excluded (even those whose businesses are incorporated). The number of full-time wage and salary workers was about 103.5 million in the first quarter of 2006; these workers made up 73 percent of total civilian employment.

Usual weekly earnings are earnings before taxes and other deductions and include any overtime pay, commissions, or tips usually received. In the case of multiple jobholders they refer to the main job. The wording of the question was changed in January 1994 to better deal with persons who found it easier to report earnings on other than a weekly basis. Such reports are then converted to the weekly equivalent. According to BLS, "the term 'usual' is as perceived by the respondent. If the respondent asks for a definition of usual, interviewers are instructed to define the term as more than half the weeks worked during the past 4 or 5 months."

The *median* is the amount that divides a given earnings distribution into two equal groups, one having earnings above the median and the other having earnings below the median.

2000 dollars. For men 25 and older and women 25 and older, median usual weekly earnings are shown on both a current-dollar and a constant-dollar basis. The editor has converted the current-dollar figures to 2000 dollars using the CPI-U-RS, which is shown and described in Chapter 8. The CPI-U-RS was chosen because it is the deflator used by the Census Bureau to convert household income and earnings to constant dollars and by the Bureau of Labor Statistics to convert compensation per hour to constant dollars. It corrects historical values of the CPI to be consistent with current CPI methodology.

Race and ethnicity. See the notes to Tables 10-1 through 10-5 for the definitions of these categories.

Data availability

These data become available about 3 weeks after the end of each quarter in the "Usual Weekly Earnings of Wage and Salary Workers" press release, available on the BLS Web site at <http://www.bls.gov/cps>. Recent data are available at that location. Also available are greater detail by demographic and age groups, by occupation, by union status, and by education; distributional data, by deciles and quartiles; and earnings for part-time workers. Also available are earnings in 1982 dollars using the CPI-U. Historical data are available upon request from BLS by telephone at (202) 691-6378.

CHAPTER 11: ENERGY

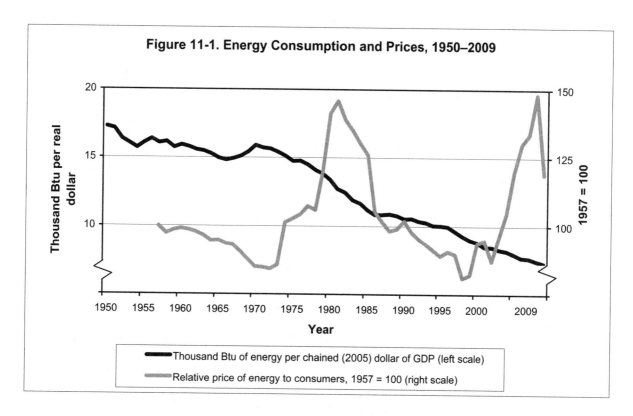

Figure 11-1. Energy Consumption and Prices, 1950–2009

- U.S. energy consumption has nearly tripled since 1950, but real gross domestic product (GDP) is more than six times what it was in that year. Consequently, there has been a downward trend in energy use per dollar of real GDP, which can also be described as an increase in the energy efficiency of national production. (Table 11-2 and Figure 11-1) This trend may seem surprising in light of increases in motor vehicle use, air conditioning, air travel, and other consumer uses of energy. Evidently, these increases are more than offset by factors such as the rising share of services and high-tech goods in GDP and the declining relative importance of energy-intensive materials production processes such as primary metals production.

- As Figure 11-1 also indicates, there have been dramatic ups and downs in relative energy prices—measured as the ratio of the CPI for energy to the total CPI—over the last half-century, including in 2009, when worldwide recession hit energy and other commodity prices much more than the overall price level. (Tables 8-1 and 20-2) Sharp upswings in relative prices do appear to have some effect, though a much-dampened one, on the rate of decline in the energy/GDP trend. (Table 11-2)

- Consumption of petroleum and natural gas per dollar of real GDP rose between 1950 and the early 1970s, but has declined 61 percent since then. Use of other forms of energy per real dollar leveled off during the 1970s and 1980s but then resumed its decline, and is down 63 percent over the entire post-war period. (Table 11-2)

- Net imports supplied 24 percent of total U.S. energy consumption in 2009, compared with 17 percent in 1973 and 1 percent in 1955. Nuclear power, nonexistent in 1955, supplied 9 percent in 2009; renewable energy sources, which provided 4 percent in 1955, accounted for 8 percent in 2009, with the remaining 59 percent accounted for by domestic fossil fuel production. (Table 11-1)

Table 11-1. Energy Supply and Consumption

(Quadrillion Btu.)

Year and month	Imports	Exports	Production, by source								Consumption, by end-use sector			
			Total	Fossil fuels					Nuclear electric power	Renew-able energy, total	Total	Residential and commercial	Industrial	Transport-ation
				Total	Coal	Natural gas	Crude oil	Natural gas plant liquids						
1955	2.790	2.286	40.148	37.365	12.370	9.345	14.410	1.240	0.000	. . .	40.208	11.185	19.472	9.551
1956	3.207	2.945	42.622	39.771	13.306	10.002	15.180	1.283	0.000	. . .	41.754	11.698	20.196	9.860
1957	3.529	3.439	42.983	40.133	13.061	10.605	15.178	1.289	0.000	. . .	41.787	11.686	20.205	9.897
1958	3.884	2.050	40.133	37.216	10.783	10.942	14.204	1.287	0.002	. . .	41.645	12.333	19.307	10.005
1959	4.076	1.534	41.949	39.046	10.778	11.952	14.933	1.383	0.002	. . .	43.466	12.800	20.316	10.349
1960	4.188	1.477	42.804	39.869	10.817	12.656	14.935	1.461	0.006	. . .	45.087	13.667	20.823	10.597
1961	4.437	1.377	43.280	40.307	10.447	13.105	15.206	1.549	0.020	. . .	45.739	14.032	20.937	10.770
1962	4.994	1.473	44.877	41.733	10.901	13.717	15.522	1.593	0.026	. . .	47.828	14.839	21.768	11.221
1963	5.087	1.835	47.174	44.037	11.849	14.513	15.966	1.709	0.038	. . .	49.646	15.261	22.730	11.655
1964	5.447	1.815	49.056	45.789	12.524	15.298	16.164	1.803	0.040	. . .	51.817	15.730	24.090	11.998
1965	5.892	1.829	50.676	47.234	13.055	15.775	16.521	1.883	0.043	. . .	54.017	16.509	25.075	12.434
1966	6.146	1.829	53.534	50.036	13.468	17.011	17.561	1.996	0.064	. . .	57.017	17.517	26.397	13.102
1967	6.159	2.115	56.379	52.596	13.825	17.943	18.651	2.177	0.088	. . .	58.908	18.541	26.616	13.752
1968	6.905	1.998	58.225	54.306	13.609	19.068	19.308	2.321	0.142	. . .	62.419	19.665	27.888	14.866
1969	7.676	2.126	60.541	56.285	13.863	20.446	19.556	2.420	0.154	. . .	65.621	21.000	29.114	15.506
1970	8.342	2.632	63.501	59.186	14.607	21.666	20.401	2.512	0.239	. . .	67.844	22.105	29.641	16.098
1971	9.535	2.151	62.723	58.043	13.186	22.280	20.033	2.544	0.413	. . .	69.289	22.959	29.601	16.729
1972	11.387	2.118	63.920	58.939	14.092	22.208	20.041	2.598	0.584	. . .	72.704	24.036	30.953	17.716
1973	14.613	2.033	63.585	58.241	13.992	22.187	19.493	2.569	0.910	4.433	75.708	24.437	32.653	18.612
1974	14.304	2.203	62.372	56.331	14.074	21.210	18.575	2.471	1.272	4.769	73.991	24.046	31.819	18.119
1975	14.032	2.323	61.357	54.733	14.989	19.640	17.729	2.374	1.900	4.723	71.999	24.308	29.447	18.244
1976	16.760	2.172	61.602	54.723	15.654	19.480	17.261	2.327	2.111	4.768	76.012	25.476	31.430	19.099
1977	19.948	2.052	62.052	55.101	15.755	19.565	17.453	2.327	2.702	4.249	78.000	25.866	32.307	19.820
1978	19.106	1.920	63.137	55.074	14.910	19.485	18.433	2.245	3.024	5.039	79.986	26.637	32.733	20.615
1979	19.459	2.855	65.948	58.006	17.540	20.076	18.103	2.286	2.776	5.166	80.903	26.469	33.962	20.471
1980	15.796	3.695	67.232	59.008	18.598	19.908	18.248	2.254	2.739	5.485	78.122	26.350	32.077	19.696
1981	13.719	4.307	67.014	58.529	18.377	19.699	18.146	2.307	3.008	5.477	76.168	25.897	30.756	19.512
1982	11.861	4.608	66.623	57.458	18.639	18.319	18.308	2.191	3.131	6.034	73.153	26.405	27.656	19.087
1983	11.751	3.693	64.180	54.416	17.247	16.593	18.391	2.184	3.203	6.561	73.038	26.380	27.481	19.174
1984	12.470	3.786	68.924	58.849	19.719	18.008	18.848	2.274	3.553	6.522	76.714	27.434	29.624	19.653
1985	11.780	4.196	67.799	57.539	19.325	16.980	18.992	2.241	4.076	6.185	76.491	27.532	28.876	20.086
1986	14.151	4.021	67.178	56.575	19.509	16.541	18.375	2.149	4.380	6.223	76.756	27.633	28.332	20.788
1987	15.398	3.812	67.659	57.167	20.141	17.136	17.674	2.215	4.754	5.739	79.173	28.265	29.442	21.468
1988	17.295	4.366	69.030	57.875	20.738	17.599	17.278	2.260	5.587	5.568	82.819	29.762	30.737	22.317
1989	18.766	4.661	69.476	57.483	21.360	17.847	16.116	2.158	5.602	6.391	84.944	31.061	31.397	22.477
1990	18.817	4.752	70.870	58.560	22.488	18.326	15.571	2.175	6.104	6.206	84.651	30.348	31.894	22.419
1991	18.334	5.141	70.531	57.872	21.636	18.229	15.700	2.306	6.422	6.237	84.606	31.003	31.486	22.117
1992	19.372	4.937	70.126	57.655	21.694	18.375	15.222	2.363	6.479	5.992	85.955	30.881	32.660	22.414
1993	21.272	4.258	68.494	55.822	20.336	18.584	14.494	2.408	6.410	6.261	87.601	32.125	32.720	22.757
1994	22.389	4.061	70.891	58.044	22.202	19.348	14.102	2.391	6.694	6.153	89.257	32.292	33.606	23.364
1995	22.260	4.511	71.316	57.540	22.130	19.082	13.886	2.442	7.075	6.701	91.169	33.276	34.045	23.846
1996	23.701	4.633	72.639	58.387	22.790	19.344	13.722	2.530	7.087	7.165	94.172	34.744	34.988	24.437
1997	25.215	4.514	72.631	58.857	23.310	19.394	13.658	2.495	6.597	7.177	94.761	34.720	35.287	24.749
1998	26.580	4.299	73.037	59.314	24.045	19.613	13.235	2.420	7.068	6.655	95.178	35.000	34.926	25.255
1999	27.252	3.715	71.903	57.614	23.295	19.341	12.451	2.528	7.610	6.678	96.812	36.004	34.854	25.948
2000	28.972	4.006	71.485	57.366	22.735	19.662	12.358	2.611	7.862	6.257	98.970	37.664	34.756	26.548
2001	30.156	3.770	71.883	58.541	23.547	20.166	12.281	2.547	8.029	5.312	96.316	37.245	32.803	26.275
2002	29.407	3.668	70.931	56.894	22.732	19.439	12.163	2.559	8.145	5.892	97.853	38.242	32.762	26.844
2003	31.060	4.054	70.197	56.099	22.094	19.633	12.026	2.346	7.959	6.139	98.131	38.527	32.612	26.994
2004	33.543	4.433	70.352	55.895	22.852	19.074	11.503	2.466	8.222	6.235	100.310	38.832	33.592	27.895
2005	34.709	4.561	69.592	55.038	23.185	18.556	10.962	2.334	8.161	6.393	100.440	39.565	32.528	28.352
2006	34.673	4.868	71.018	55.968	23.790	19.022	10.801	2.356	8.215	6.834	99.850	38.495	32.527	28.829
2007	34.685	5.448	71.669	56.447	23.493	19.825	10.721	2.409	8.455	6.767	101.580	39.913	32.560	29.118
2008	32.951	7.016	73.465	57.613	23.851	20.833	10.508	2.419	8.427	7.425	99.446	40.052	31.354	28.039
2009	29.766	6.931	73.223	57.040	21.578	21.680	11.241	2.541	8.349	7.833	94.660	39.391	28.242	27.035
2008														
January	2.947	0.537	6.230	4.872	2.008	1.741	0.917	0.210	0.740	0.618	9.491	4.296	2.858	2.336
February	2.600	0.528	5.845	4.604	1.904	1.640	0.862	0.200	0.680	0.561	8.724	3.901	2.649	2.174
March	2.759	0.608	6.192	4.891	1.970	1.779	0.926	0.220	0.680	0.624	8.658	3.558	2.715	2.387
April	2.774	0.591	6.013	4.788	1.979	1.709	0.890	0.210	0.600	0.626	7.882	2.928	2.598	2.359
May	2.742	0.622	6.248	4.883	1.969	1.780	0.917	0.220	0.680	0.688	7.948	2.810	2.694	2.447
June	2.766	0.622	6.090	4.661	1.839	1.731	0.887	0.200	0.740	0.694	8.087	3.137	2.607	2.343
July	2.816	0.606	6.423	4.981	2.019	1.825	0.923	0.210	0.780	0.665	8.467	3.398	2.634	2.431
August	2.836	0.584	6.325	4.948	2.044	1.815	0.880	0.210	0.760	0.618	8.274	3.258	2.594	2.420
September	2.443	0.516	5.665	4.413	2.022	1.539	0.684	0.170	0.700	0.551	7.378	2.843	2.347	2.188
October	2.825	0.589	6.126	4.897	2.123	1.733	0.840	0.200	0.660	0.572	7.826	2.797	2.648	2.384
November	2.689	0.593	5.980	4.745	1.942	1.735	0.874	0.190	0.660	0.572	7.862	3.086	2.534	2.242
December	2.756	0.619	6.329	4.932	2.032	1.806	0.909	0.180	0.760	0.636	8.848	4.041	2.474	2.329
2009														
January	2.842	0.593	6.360	4.929	1.944	1.845	0.943	0.200	0.770	0.656	9.186	4.446	2.503	2.237
February	2.396	0.501	5.740	4.505	1.794	1.684	0.843	0.190	0.670	0.564	7.904	3.648	2.236	2.025
March	2.669	0.557	6.290	4.941	1.921	1.861	0.948	0.210	0.700	0.645	8.105	3.463	2.358	2.289
April	2.490	0.506	5.987	4.698	1.788	1.796	0.910	0.200	0.620	0.668	7.369	2.910	2.222	2.239
May	2.458	0.534	6.114	4.718	1.711	1.837	0.950	0.220	0.680	0.712	7.350	2.792	2.268	2.289
June	2.452	0.564	6.109	4.679	1.781	1.785	0.902	0.210	0.730	0.702	7.578	3.019	2.266	2.291
July	2.591	0.617	6.229	4.808	1.823	1.828	0.941	0.220	0.760	0.659	7.904	3.229	2.318	2.354
August	2.457	0.594	6.209	4.821	1.812	1.841	0.950	0.220	0.760	0.633	7.989	3.253	2.375	2.358
September	2.448	0.598	5.946	4.675	1.769	1.744	0.947	0.210	0.690	0.584	7.293	2.808	2.305	2.181
October	2.312	0.645	6.060	4.811	1.772	1.840	0.975	0.220	0.610	0.642	7.542	2.827	2.418	2.300
November	2.309	0.596	5.958	4.682	1.724	1.789	0.951	0.220	0.620	0.658	7.522	2.938	2.414	2.172
December	2.342	0.626	6.221	4.773	1.738	1.832	0.982	0.220	0.740	0.708	8.917	4.059	2.558	2.300

. . . = Not available.

Table 11-2. Energy Consumption Per Dollar of Real Gross Domestic Product

Year	Energy consumption (quadrillion Btu)			Gross domestic product (billions of chained [2005] dollars)	Energy consumption per real dollar of GDP (thousand Btu per chained [2005] dollar)		
	Total	Petroleum and natural gas	Other energy		Total	Petroleum and natural gas	Other energy
1950	34.616	19.284	15.332	2 006.0	17.26	9.61	7.64
1951	36.974	21.477	15.497	2 161.1	17.11	9.94	7.17
1952	36.748	22.505	14.243	2 243.9	16.38	10.03	6.35
1953	37.664	23.462	14.202	2 347.2	16.05	10.00	6.05
1954	36.639	24.169	12.470	2 332.4	15.71	10.36	5.35
1955	40.208	26.253	13.955	2 500.3	16.08	10.50	5.58
1956	41.754	27.551	14.203	2 549.7	16.38	10.81	5.57
1957	41.787	28.122	13.665	2 601.1	16.07	10.81	5.25
1958	41.645	29.190	12.455	2 577.6	16.16	11.32	4.83
1959	43.466	31.040	12.426	2 762.5	15.73	11.24	4.50
1960	45.087	32.305	12.782	2 830.9	15.93	11.41	4.52
1961	45.739	33.143	12.596	2 896.9	15.79	11.44	4.35
1962	47.828	34.780	13.048	3 072.4	15.57	11.32	4.25
1963	49.646	36.104	13.542	3 206.7	15.48	11.26	4.22
1964	51.817	37.589	14.228	3 392.3	15.27	11.08	4.19
1965	54.017	39.014	15.003	3 610.1	14.96	10.81	4.16
1966	57.017	41.396	15.621	3 845.3	14.83	10.77	4.06
1967	58.908	43.228	15.680	3 942.5	14.94	10.96	3.98
1968	62.419	46.189	16.230	4 133.4	15.10	11.17	3.93
1969	65.621	49.016	16.605	4 261.8	15.40	11.50	3.90
1970	67.844	51.315	16.529	4 269.9	15.89	12.02	3.87
1971	69.289	53.030	16.259	4 413.3	15.70	12.02	3.68
1972	72.704	55.645	17.059	4 647.7	15.64	11.97	3.67
1973	75.708	57.352	18.356	4 917.0	15.40	11.66	3.73
1974	73.991	55.187	18.804	4 889.9	15.13	11.29	3.85
1975	71.999	52.678	19.321	4 879.5	14.76	10.80	3.96
1976	76.012	55.520	20.492	5 141.3	14.78	10.80	3.99
1977	78.000	57.053	20.947	5 377.7	14.50	10.61	3.90
1978	79.986	57.966	22.021	5 677.6	14.09	10.21	3.88
1979	80.903	57.789	23.114	5 855.0	13.82	9.87	3.95
1980	78.122	54.438	23.684	5 839.0	13.38	9.32	4.06
1981	76.168	51.678	24.490	5 987.2	12.72	8.63	4.09
1982	73.153	48.588	24.565	5 870.9	12.46	8.28	4.18
1983	73.038	47.275	25.763	6 136.2	11.90	7.70	4.20
1984	76.714	49.445	27.269	6 577.1	11.66	7.52	4.15
1985	76.491	48.626	27.865	6 849.3	11.17	7.10	4.07
1986	76.756	48.787	27.969	7 086.5	10.83	6.88	3.95
1987	79.173	50.505	28.668	7 313.3	10.83	6.91	3.92
1988	82.819	52.670	30.149	7 613.9	10.88	6.92	3.96
1989	84.944	53.813	31.131	7 885.9	10.77	6.82	3.95
1990	84.651	53.156	31.496	8 033.9	10.54	6.62	3.92
1991	84.606	52.878	31.728	8 015.1	10.56	6.60	3.96
1992	85.955	54.240	31.715	8 287.1	10.37	6.55	3.83
1993	87.601	54.973	32.629	8 523.4	10.28	6.45	3.83
1994	89.257	56.289	32.968	8 870.7	10.06	6.35	3.72
1995	91.169	57.107	34.062	9 093.7	10.03	6.28	3.75
1996	94.172	58.757	35.415	9 433.9	9.98	6.23	3.75
1997	94.761	59.382	35.380	9 854.3	9.62	6.03	3.59
1998	95.178	59.646	35.532	10 283.5	9.26	5.80	3.46
1999	96.812	60.746	36.066	10 779.8	8.98	5.64	3.35
2000	98.970	62.088	36.882	11 226.0	8.82	5.53	3.29
2001	96.316	60.958	35.358	11 347.2	8.49	5.37	3.12
2002	97.853	61.784	36.070	11 553.0	8.47	5.35	3.12
2003	98.198	61.705	36.493	11 840.7	8.29	5.21	3.08
2004	100.336	63.224	37.112	12 263.8	8.18	5.15	3.03
2005	100.467	62.974	37.492	12 638.4	7.95	4.98	2.97
2006	99.850	62.179	37.671	12 976.2	7.69	4.79	2.90
2007	101.565	63.448	38.117	13 254.1	7.66	4.79	2.88
2008	99.481	61.093	38.388	13 312.2	7.47	4.59	2.88
2009	94.892	58.659	36.233	12 987.4	7.29	4.52	2.77

NOTES AND DEFINITIONS, CHAPTER 11

TABLES 11-1 AND 11-2
ENERGY SUPPLY AND CONSUMPTION

SOURCES: U.S. DEPARTMENT OF ENERGY, ENERGY INFORMATION ADMINISTRATION; U.S. DEPARTMENT OF COMMERCE, BUREAU OF ECONOMIC ANALYSIS

Definitions

The *British thermal unit (Btu)* is a measure used to combine data for different energy sources into a consistent aggregate. It is the amount of energy required to raise the temperature of 1 pound of water 1 degree Fahrenheit when the water is near a temperature of 39.2 degrees Fahrenheit. To illustrate one of the factors used to convert volumes to Btu, conventional motor gasoline has a heat content of 5.253 million Btu per barrel. For further information, see the Energy Information Administration's *Monthly Energy Review*, Appendix A.

Production: Crude oil includes lease condensates.

Renewable energy, total includes conventional hydroelectric power, geothermal, solar thermal and photovoltaic, wind, and biomass. Hydroelectric power includes conventional electrical utility and industrial generation. Biomass includes wood, waste, and alcohol fuels (ethanol blended into motor gasoline).

The sum of domestic energy *production* and net imports of energy (*imports* minus *exports*) does not exactly equal domestic energy *consumption*. The difference is attributed to inventory changes; losses and gains in conversion, transportation, and distribution; the addition of blending compounds; shipments of anthracite to U.S. armed forces in Europe; and adjustments to account for discrepancies between reporting systems.

Consumption by end-use sector is based on total, not net, consumption. Components may not add to totals because of different sector-specific conversion factors.

References and notes on the data

These data are published each month in Tables 1.1, 1.2, 1.7, and 2.1 in the *Monthly Energy Review*. Annual data before 1973 are published in the *Annual Energy Review*. These two publications are no longer published in printed form but are available on the EIA Web site at <http://www.eia.doe.gov/emeu/mer> along with all current and historical data. The real gross domestic product (GDP) data used to calculate energy consumption per dollar of real GDP are from the Bureau of Economic Analysis; see Table 1-2 and the applicable notes and definitions in this volume of *Business Statistics*.

CHAPTER 12: MONEY, INTEREST, ASSETS, LIABILITIES, AND ASSET PRICES

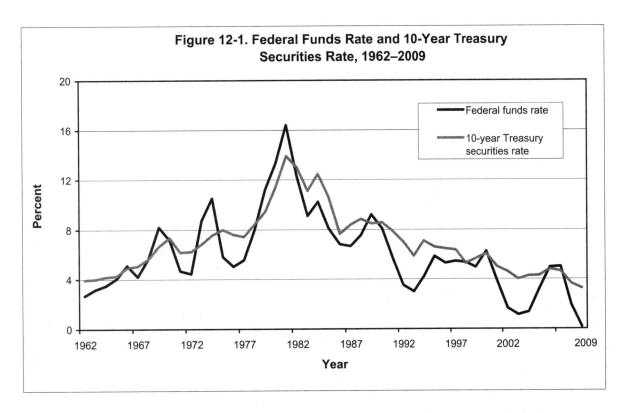

Figure 12-1. Federal Funds Rate and 10-Year Treasury Securities Rate, 1962–2009

- As the recession deepened, the Federal Reserve brought short-term interest rates lower than at any time since the Great Depression, World War II, and its aftermath. The federal funds rate—shown in Figure 12-1—was held at 0.2 percent throughout 2009. "Real" fed funds rates (subtracting out current underlying inflation rates) have been negative since early 2008. The rate on short-term Treasury bills was equally low. (Tables 12-9, 20-6, and 18-3)

- Longer-term rates have also declined dramatically. The rate on Treasury 10-year securities, the ultimate in safe longer-term investments, is also shown in Figure 12-1. It reached a low of 2.42 percent in December 2008, rising back to 3.59 percent by the end of 2009; still, despite the huge volume of federal borrowing in 2009 (see Tables 6-1, 6-14 and 12-5), this interest rate was lower than at any time since 1958. (Tables 12-9 and 20-6)

- The rate spread between Aaa-rated and Baa-rated corporate bonds, representing a market evaluation of risk, was more than 3 percentage points (300 "basis points") in December 2008. This exceeded the previous record postwar spreads seen in 1982. At the end of 2009, the spread had contracted back to about 1 percentage point. (Table 12-9)

- Looking at the easing in quantitative terms, the Federal Reserve added $1.3 trillion to its balance sheet in 2008 and maintained the end-of-2008 level during 2009. The size of the monetary base doubled during 2008 and grew 22 percent further during 2009. (Table 12-3) But with financial institutions reluctant to lend and thereby create deposits, the money supply grew more tamely; M1 grew 16 percent during 2008 and 6 percent during 2009; M2, 10 and 4 percent. (Table 12-1)

Table 12-1. Money Stock Measures and Components of M1

(Billions of dollars, monthly data are averages of daily figures, annual data are for December.)

Year and month	Not seasonally adjusted		Seasonally adjusted					Other checkable deposits		
	M1	M2	M1	M2	Currency	Traveler's checks	Demand deposits	At commercial banks	At thrift institutions	Total
1960	144.5	315.3	140.7	312.4	28.7	0.3	111.6	0.0	0.0	0.0
1961	149.2	338.5	145.2	335.5	29.3	0.4	115.5	0.0	0.0	0.0
1962	151.9	365.8	147.8	362.7	30.3	0.4	117.1	0.0	0.0	0.0
1963	157.5	396.4	153.3	393.2	32.2	0.4	120.6	0.0	0.1	0.1
1964	164.9	428.3	160.3	424.7	33.9	0.5	125.8	0.0	0.1	0.1
1965	172.6	463.1	167.8	459.2	36.0	0.5	131.3	0.0	0.1	0.1
1966	176.9	483.7	172.0	480.2	38.0	0.6	133.4	0.0	0.1	0.1
1967	188.4	528.0	183.3	524.8	40.0	0.6	142.5	0.0	0.1	0.1
1968	202.8	569.7	197.4	566.8	43.0	0.7	153.6	0.0	0.1	0.1
1969	209.4	590.1	203.9	587.9	45.7	0.8	157.3	0.0	0.1	0.2
1970	220.1	627.8	214.4	626.5	48.6	0.9	164.7	0.0	0.1	0.1
1971	234.5	711.2	228.3	710.3	52.0	1.0	175.1	0.0	0.2	0.2
1972	256.1	803.1	249.2	802.3	56.2	1.2	191.6	0.0	0.2	0.2
1973	270.2	856.5	262.9	855.5	60.8	1.4	200.3	0.0	0.3	0.3
1974	281.8	903.5	274.2	902.1	67.0	1.7	205.1	0.2	0.4	0.4
1975	295.3	1 017.8	287.1	1 016.2	72.8	2.1	211.3	0.4	0.5	0.9
1976	314.5	1 153.5	306.2	1 152.0	79.5	2.6	221.5	1.3	1.4	2.7
1977	340.0	1 273.0	330.9	1 270.3	87.4	2.9	236.4	1.8	2.3	4.2
1978	367.9	1 370.8	357.3	1 366.0	96.0	3.3	249.5	5.3	3.1	8.5
1979	393.2	1 479.0	381.8	1 473.7	104.8	3.5	256.6	12.7	4.2	16.8
1980	419.5	1 604.8	408.5	1 599.8	115.3	3.9	261.2	20.8	7.3	28.1
1981	447.0	1 760.3	436.7	1 755.5	122.5	4.1	231.4	63.0	15.6	78.7
1982	485.8	1 917.2	474.8	1 909.3	132.5	4.1	234.1	80.5	23.6	104.1
1983	533.3	2 136.2	521.4	2 125.7	146.2	4.7	238.5	97.3	34.8	132.1
1984	564.6	2 320.9	551.6	2 308.8	156.1	5.0	243.4	104.7	42.4	147.1
1985	633.3	2 506.6	619.8	2 494.6	167.7	5.6	266.9	124.7	54.9	179.5
1986	739.8	2 744.3	724.7	2 731.6	180.4	6.1	302.9	161.0	74.2	235.2
1987	765.4	2 842.9	750.2	2 831.0	196.7	6.6	287.7	178.2	81.0	259.2
1988	803.1	3 006.5	786.7	2 994.1	212.0	7.0	287.1	192.5	88.1	280.6
1989	810.6	3 171.6	792.9	3 158.5	222.3	6.9	278.6	197.4	87.7	285.1
1990	842.7	3 290.4	824.7	3 277.0	246.5	7.7	276.8	208.7	85.0	293.7
1991	915.6	3 391.5	897.0	3 377.3	267.1	7.7	289.6	241.6	90.9	332.5
1992	1 045.6	3 446.2	1 024.9	3 429.7	292.1	8.2	340.0	280.8	103.8	384.6
1993	1 153.3	3 500.4	1 129.6	3 479.9	321.6	8.0	385.4	302.6	112.0	414.6
1994	1 174.5	3 515.9	1 150.6	3 494.6	354.5	8.6	383.6	297.4	106.6	404.0
1995	1 152.7	3 660.9	1 127.5	3 637.4	372.8	9.0	389.0	249.0	107.6	356.6
1996	1 105.8	3 835.9	1 081.6	3 815.8	394.7	8.8	402.3	172.1	103.8	275.9
1997	1 097.5	4 050.3	1 072.8	4 029.7	425.4	8.4	393.8	148.3	96.9	245.2
1998	1 121.2	4 394.2	1 095.8	4 372.2	460.5	8.5	376.7	143.9	106.1	250.0
1999	1 148.2	4 657.9	1 122.7	4 630.5	517.9	8.6	352.9	139.7	103.7	243.3
2000	1 111.7	4 943.3	1 087.7	4 912.6	531.2	8.3	309.9	133.2	105.2	238.4
2001	1 208.3	5 462.7	1 182.2	5 427.8	581.1	8.0	335.7	142.0	115.4	257.4
2002	1 245.1	5 806.9	1 220.4	5 776.6	626.3	7.8	306.8	154.3	125.3	279.6
2003	1 332.0	6 093.1	1 306.9	6 065.5	662.5	7.7	326.4	175.2	135.0	310.3
2004	1 401.3	6 435.6	1 377.1	6 407.1	697.7	7.5	343.5	187.0	141.3	328.3
2005	1 396.5	6 695.5	1 375.3	6 671.6	724.1	7.2	325.0	180.9	138.2	319.1
2006	1 387.3	7 094.5	1 367.9	7 071.7	749.6	6.7	305.3	177.7	128.6	306.3
2007	1 394.4	7 522.2	1 375.8	7 501.4	759.8	6.3	301.9	174.4	133.5	307.8
2008	1 618.7	8 249.3	1 594.7	8 239.7	815.3	5.5	459.7	180.2	134.1	314.3
2009	1 721.6	8 549.7	1 696.4	8 543.9	862.2	5.1	443.4	234.1	151.5	385.7
2008										
January	1 375.5	7 521.1	1 381.1	7 534.3	757.2	6.2	306.7	175.6	135.4	311.0
February	1 365.3	7 605.2	1 387.0	7 623.6	757.0	6.2	310.8	177.2	135.9	313.0
March	1 400.7	7 744.7	1 389.7	7 684.3	759.1	6.2	311.8	177.5	135.1	312.6
April	1 406.4	7 794.9	1 392.1	7 709.3	758.8	6.1	314.4	177.3	135.5	312.8
May	1 396.2	7 733.5	1 391.5	7 732.8	762.7	6.2	309.1	175.2	138.2	313.4
June	1 407.0	7 755.5	1 398.1	7 745.2	768.4	6.1	311.7	176.3	135.7	312.0
July	1 417.4	7 770.5	1 415.1	7 797.0	774.9	5.9	320.8	175.8	137.7	313.5
August	1 400.9	7 767.2	1 400.0	7 785.0	776.7	5.9	311.5	170.1	135.9	306.0
September	1 441.0	7 845.4	1 459.5	7 892.0	781.1	5.8	359.6	175.7	137.3	313.0
October	1 461.9	7 957.6	1 472.7	8 007.1	796.6	5.7	360.2	175.2	135.0	310.2
November	1 513.1	8 046.1	1 518.1	8 058.7	806.3	5.6	399.6	171.5	135.1	306.6
December	1 618.7	8 249.3	1 594.7	8 239.7	815.3	5.5	459.7	180.2	134.1	314.3
2009										
January	1 565.6	8 295.0	1 573.8	8 300.7	827.2	5.5	428.4	177.0	135.7	312.7
February	1 535.6	8 320.5	1 562.0	8 338.4	836.8	5.5	397.3	182.2	140.3	322.4
March	1 577.3	8 452.9	1 564.2	8 390.4	842.9	5.4	390.5	184.5	141.0	325.5
April	1 608.4	8 447.2	1 592.7	8 342.5	847.8	5.3	406.2	191.6	141.6	333.3
May	1 598.3	8 425.8	1 593.0	8 415.4	849.2	5.3	401.9	195.1	141.5	336.6
June	1 652.9	8 447.1	1 641.0	8 442.1	852.3	5.2	434.0	210.4	139.1	349.5
July	1 654.9	8 418.4	1 649.9	8 437.7	854.2	5.1	435.7	215.2	139.8	354.9
August	1 649.3	8 393.2	1 648.3	8 414.5	857.7	5.1	426.9	219.1	139.5	358.6
September	1 640.0	8 399.2	1 660.9	8 455.2	861.4	5.1	430.4	222.3	141.7	364.0
October	1 660.3	8 429.9	1 674.6	8 487.8	862.6	5.1	432.6	226.3	148.0	374.3
November	1 680.8	8 505.4	1 687.6	8 522.7	861.8	5.1	435.5	236.5	148.7	385.1
December	1 721.6	8 549.7	1 696.4	8 543.9	862.2	5.1	443.4	234.1	151.5	385.7

Table 12-2. Components of Non-M1 M2

(Billions of dollars, seasonally adjusted; monthly data are averages of daily figures, annual data are for December.)

Year and month	Savings deposits			Small-denomination time deposits			Retail money funds	Total non-M1 M2	Memorandum: Institutional money funds
	At commercial banks	At thrift institutions	Total	At commercial banks	At thrift institutions	Total			
1960	58.3	100.8	159.1	9.7	2.8	12.5	0.0	171.7	0.0
1961	64.2	111.3	175.5	11.1	3.7	14.8	0.0	190.3	0.0
1962	71.3	123.4	194.8	15.5	4.6	20.1	0.0	214.9	0.0
1963	76.8	137.6	214.4	19.9	5.7	25.5	0.0	240.0	0.0
1964	82.9	152.4	235.2	22.4	6.8	29.2	0.0	264.4	0.0
1965	92.4	164.5	256.9	26.7	7.8	34.5	0.0	291.3	0.0
1966	89.9	163.3	253.1	38.7	16.3	55.0	0.0	308.1	0.0
1967	94.1	169.6	263.7	50.7	27.1	77.8	0.0	341.5	0.0
1968	96.1	172.8	268.9	63.5	37.1	100.5	0.0	369.4	0.0
1969	93.8	169.8	263.7	71.6	48.8	120.4	0.0	384.0	0.0
1970	98.6	162.3	261.0	79.3	71.9	151.2	0.0	412.1	0.0
1971	112.8	179.4	292.2	94.7	95.1	189.7	0.0	481.9	0.0
1972	124.8	196.6	321.4	108.2	123.5	231.6	0.0	553.0	0.0
1973	128.0	198.7	326.8	116.8	149.0	265.8	0.1	592.6	0.0
1974	136.8	201.8	338.6	123.1	164.8	287.9	1.4	627.9	0.2
1975	161.2	227.6	388.9	142.3	195.5	337.9	2.4	729.1	0.5
1976	201.8	251.4	453.2	155.5	235.2	390.7	1.8	845.8	0.6
1977	218.8	273.4	492.2	167.5	278.0	445.5	1.8	939.4	1.0
1978	216.5	265.4	481.9	185.1	335.8	521.0	5.8	1 008.7	3.5
1979	195.0	228.8	423.8	235.5	398.7	634.3	33.9	1 092.0	10.4
1980	185.7	214.5	400.3	286.2	442.3	728.5	62.5	1 191.3	16.0
1981	159.0	184.9	343.9	347.7	475.4	823.1	151.7	1 318.8	38.2
1982	190.1	210.0	400.1	379.9	471.0	850.9	183.4	1 434.4	48.8
1983	363.2	321.7	684.9	350.9	433.1	784.1	135.3	1 604.3	40.9
1984	389.3	315.4	704.7	387.9	500.9	888.8	163.8	1 757.2	63.7
1985	456.6	358.6	815.3	386.4	499.3	885.7	173.8	1 874.8	66.7
1986	533.5	407.4	940.9	369.4	489.0	858.4	207.6	2 006.9	87.3
1987	534.8	402.6	937.4	391.7	529.3	921.0	222.3	2 080.8	94.4
1988	542.4	383.9	926.4	451.2	585.9	1 037.1	243.9	2 207.3	94.5
1989	541.1	352.6	893.7	533.8	617.6	1 151.3	320.6	2 365.6	112.2
1990	581.3	341.6	922.9	610.7	562.6	1 173.3	356.2	2 452.3	141.3
1991	664.8	379.6	1 044.5	602.2	463.1	1 065.3	370.6	2 480.4	190.5
1992	754.2	433.1	1 187.2	508.1	359.7	867.7	349.8	2 404.7	216.0
1993	785.3	434.0	1 219.3	467.9	313.6	781.5	349.5	2 350.3	220.7
1994	752.8	398.5	1 151.3	503.6	313.9	817.5	375.2	2 344.0	216.6
1995	774.8	361.0	1 135.9	575.8	356.5	932.4	441.7	2 509.9	270.9
1996	906.4	368.9	1 275.2	594.2	353.7	947.9	511.0	2 734.2	332.5
1997	1 023.2	378.9	1 402.1	625.5	342.2	967.6	587.1	2 956.9	406.6
1998	1 188.7	416.6	1 605.3	626.4	324.9	951.3	719.9	3 276.5	559.5
1999	1 288.2	451.0	1 739.2	636.9	318.3	955.2	813.4	3 507.8	664.9
2000	1 424.4	454.0	1 878.4	700.8	345.3	1 046.0	900.4	3 824.8	820.3
2001	1 738.5	570.7	2 309.2	636.1	338.5	974.6	961.8	4 245.6	1 222.9
2002	2 060.0	713.6	2 773.6	591.3	303.5	894.7	887.8	4 556.1	1 275.8
2003	2 338.1	824.8	3 162.9	541.8	276.1	817.9	777.8	4 758.6	1 135.5
2004	2 631.7	875.5	3 507.2	551.4	276.3	827.7	695.1	5 030.1	1 087.7
2005	2 775.9	829.0	3 604.9	645.2	346.8	992.0	699.3	5 296.3	1 158.8
2006	2 913.7	784.0	3 697.8	778.8	425.0	1 203.7	802.3	5 703.8	1 365.5
2007	3 047.4	828.8	3 876.2	856.2	416.5	1 272.7	976.7	6 125.6	1 922.0
2008	3 339.2	772.7	4 112.0	1 074.2	378.5	1 452.7	1 080.3	6 645.0	2 412.4
2009	4 007.2	840.5	4 847.7	852.2	318.7	1 171.0	828.8	6 847.4	2 218.8
2008									
January	3 043.2	833.5	3 876.7	858.9	420.7	1 279.6	996.9	6 153.2	1 941.4
February	3 076.5	838.3	3 914.9	863.4	422.2	1 285.6	1 036.1	6 236.6	2 068.0
March	3 113.0	852.9	3 965.8	859.2	418.8	1 278.0	1 050.8	6 294.6	2 138.0
April	3 112.6	856.6	3 969.2	858.0	419.3	1 277.3	1 070.7	6 317.2	2 180.4
May	3 121.5	882.2	4 003.7	859.6	417.0	1 276.6	1 061.0	6 341.3	2 207.7
June	3 121.4	896.6	4 018.0	862.9	411.3	1 274.1	1 054.9	6 347.1	2 238.6
July	3 134.2	903.1	4 037.3	878.4	406.8	1 285.2	1 059.3	6 381.9	2 254.1
August	3 126.5	892.0	4 018.5	903.9	408.7	1 312.6	1 053.8	6 384.9	2 278.1
September	3 180.8	864.3	4 045.2	932.0	404.3	1 336.3	1 051.1	6 432.5	2 240.2
October	3 263.3	786.7	4 050.0	1 024.6	372.5	1 397.1	1 087.3	6 534.4	2 233.1
November	3 260.5	771.2	4 031.8	1 052.6	377.8	1 430.4	1 078.5	6 540.6	2 341.2
December	3 339.2	772.7	4 112.0	1 074.2	378.5	1 452.7	1 080.3	6 645.0	2 412.4
2009									
January	3 428.8	778.5	4 207.3	1 065.9	379.7	1 445.6	1 074.0	6 726.9	2 475.1
February	3 495.1	789.8	4 284.8	1 056.1	381.6	1 437.7	1 053.9	6 776.4	2 497.8
March	3 552.1	804.0	4 356.1	1 042.7	382.4	1 425.0	1 045.0	6 826.2	2 504.9
April	3 520.9	805.4	4 326.4	1 028.0	377.0	1 405.0	1 018.5	6 749.9	2 516.3
May	3 621.3	817.2	4 438.4	1 021.5	362.9	1 384.4	999.5	6 822.4	2 530.3
June	3 640.9	825.9	4 466.9	1 003.2	358.4	1 361.6	972.7	6 801.1	2 512.6
July	3 671.9	834.6	4 506.6	980.6	353.5	1 334.1	947.2	6 787.8	2 492.1
August	3 715.6	830.5	4 546.0	962.1	342.3	1 304.4	915.7	6 766.2	2 446.4
September	3 789.7	842.7	4 632.3	935.8	332.9	1 268.7	893.2	6 794.3	2 405.6
October	3 861.3	854.8	4 716.1	902.3	328.2	1 230.4	866.7	6 813.2	2 338.0
November	3 952.3	834.6	4 787.0	877.4	322.0	1 199.4	848.7	6 835.1	2 280.3
December	4 007.2	840.5	4 847.7	852.2	318.7	1 171.0	828.8	6 847.4	2 218.8

Table 12-3. Aggregate Reserves, Monetary Base, and FR Balance Sheet

(Millions of dollars; reserves and monetary base adjusted for seasonality and changes in reserve requirements, except as noted; annual data are for December.)

Year and month	Reserves					Monetary base	Federal Reserve balance sheet: total assets
	Total	Nonborrowed	Nonborrowed plus extended credit [1]	Required	Excess reserves, not seasonally adjusted		
1960	11 247	11 172	11 172	10 503	743	40 977	. . .
1961	11 499	11 366	11 366	10 915	584	41 853	. . .
1962	11 604	11 344	11 344	11 033	572	42 957	. . .
1963	11 730	11 397	11 397	11 239	490	45 003	. . .
1964	12 011	11 747	11 747	11 605	406	47 161	. . .
1965	12 316	11 872	11 872	11 892	423	49 620	. . .
1966	12 223	11 690	11 690	11 884	339	51 565	. . .
1967	13 180	12 952	12 952	12 805	375	54 579	. . .
1968	13 767	13 021	13 021	13 341	426	58 357	. . .
1969	14 168	13 049	13 049	13 882	286	61 569	. . .
1970	14 558	14 225	14 225	14 309	249	65 013	. . .
1971	15 230	15 104	15 104	15 049	182	69 108	. . .
1972	16 645	15 595	15 595	16 361	284	75 167	. . .
1973	17 021	15 723	15 723	16 717	304	81 073	. . .
1974	17 550	16 823	16 970	17 292	258	87 535	. . .
1975	17 822	17 692	17 704	17 556	266	93 887	. . .
1976	18 388	18 335	18 335	18 115	274	101 515	. . .
1977	18 990	18 420	18 420	18 800	190	110 324	. . .
1978	19 753	18 885	18 885	19 521	232	120 445	. . .
1979	20 720	19 248	19 248	20 279	442	131 143	. . .
1980	22 015	20 325	20 328	21 501	514	142 004	. . .
1981	22 443	21 807	21 956	22 124	319	149 021	. . .
1982	23 600	22 966	23 152	23 100	500	160 127	. . .
1983	25 367	24 593	24 595	24 806	561	175 467	. . .
1984	26 913	23 727	26 331	26 078	835	187 252	. . .
1985	31 569	30 250	30 749	30 505	1 063	203 555	. . .
1986	38 840	38 014	38 317	37 667	1 173	223 416	. . .
1987	38 913	38 135	38 618	37 893	1 019	239 829	. . .
1988	40 453	38 738	39 982	39 392	1 061	256 897	. . .
1989	40 486	40 221	40 241	39 545	941	267 774	. . .
1990	41 766	41 440	41 463	40 101	1 665	293 278	. . .
1991	45 516	45 324	45 325	44 526	990	317 543	. . .
1992	54 421	54 298	54 298	53 267	1 154	350 882	. . .
1993	60 566	60 484	60 484	59 497	1 069	386 586	. . .
1994	59 466	59 257	59 257	58 295	1 171	418 313	. . .
1995	56 483	56 226	56 226	55 193	1 290	434 610	. . .
1996	50 185	50 030	50 030	48 766	1 418	452 088	. . .
1997	46 875	46 551	46 551	45 189	1 687	479 996	. . .
1998	45 172	45 055	45 055	43 659	1 512	513 954	. . .
1999	42 173	41 852	41 852	40 879	1 294	593 740	. . .
2000	38 724	38 515	38 515	37 399	1 325	584 984	. . .
2001	41 428	41 361	41 361	39 785	1 643	635 567	. . .
2002	40 339	40 259	40 259	38 331	2 008	681 648	. . .
2003	42 630	42 585	. . .	41 583	1 047	720 391	. . .
2004	46 540	46 477	. . .	44 631	1 909	759 378	. . .
2005	45 088	44 919	. . .	43 188	1 900	787 578	. . .
2006	43 219	43 028	. . .	41 357	1 862	812 410	. . .
2007	43 214	27 783	. . .	41 429	1 784	824 373	893 758
2008	820 304	166 739	. . .	52 972	767 332	1 654 067	2 240 946
2009	1 138 597	968 670	. . .	63 187	1 075 410	2 017 692	2 237 258
2008							
January	42 288	-3 371	. . .	40 641	1 647	820 299	902 846
February	43 396	-16 761	. . .	41 782	1 614	820 953	896 359
March	45 118	-49 405	. . .	42 474	2 644	824 824	895 768
April	44 789	-90 621	. . .	43 052	1 737	823 692	889 693
May	45 707	-110 074	. . .	43 869	1 837	827 434	905 552
June	45 673	-125 605	. . .	43 449	2 224	833 058	894 137
July	45 273	-120 391	. . .	43 361	1 912	839 686	919 992
August	46 257	-121 822	. . .	44 382	1 875	843 235	911 475
September	103 583	-186 523	. . .	44 101	59 482	905 224	1 213 323
October	315 457	-332 862	. . .	48 299	267 159	1 130 443	1 970 680
November	609 304	-89 481	. . .	50 484	558 821	1 435 012	2 107 651
December	820 304	166 739	. . .	52 972	767 332	1 654 067	2 240 946
2009							
January	856 991	293 495	. . .	58 812	798 179	1 702 464	1 928 549
February	699 934	117 437	. . .	56 486	643 448	1 555 038	1 917 581
March	779 496	167 385	. . .	54 891	724 604	1 640 731	2 073 227
April	881 019	322 825	. . .	56 657	824 361	1 747 297	2 068 149
May	900 865	375 417	. . .	56 798	844 067	1 768 831	2 081 659
June	809 196	370 473	. . .	57 841	751 355	1 679 686	2 027 327
July	794 994	428 033	. . .	62 015	732 979	1 666 475	2 003 053
August	828 466	497 017	. . .	62 639	765 827	1 703 378	2 078 153
September	922 473	615 646	. . .	62 408	860 065	1 800 960	2 144 157
October	1 056 405	791 347	. . .	61 673	994 732	1 936 564	2 164 673
November	1 140 488	923 181	. . .	63 200	1 077 288	2 018 817	2 209 567
December	1 138 597	968 670	. . .	63 187	1 075 410	2 017 692	2 237 258

[1]Extended credit program discontinued January 9, 2003. See notes and definitions for more information.
. . . = Not available.

Table 12-4. Commercial Banks: Bank Credit and Selected Liabilities

(All commercial banks in the United States, billions of dollars, seasonally adjusted, annual data are for December.)

Year and month	Bank credit Total	Securities in bank credit Total	U.S. Treasury and agency securities	Other securities	Loans and leases in bank credit Total	Commercial and industrial	Real estate Total	Revolving home equity	Other residential	Commercial
1955	151.0	76.5	64.4	12.1	74.5	26.7	19.5	. . .	. . .	. . .
1956	156.2	72.7	60.8	11.9	83.5	32.5	21.2	. . .	. . .	. . .
1957	160.6	72.9	60.0	12.9	87.7	33.9	21.5	. . .	. . .	. . .
1958	182.9	84.1	69.2	14.8	98.9	34.9	24.5	. . .	. . .	. . .
1959	189.2	76.2	61.2	15.0	113.1	39.3	27.5	. . .	. . .	. . .
1960	197.1	78.3	63.1	15.2	118.9	42.1	28.1	. . .	. . .	. . .
1961	213.3	86.8	69.4	17.4	126.4	43.8	29.5	. . .	. . .	. . .
1962	232.0	90.8	69.9	20.9	141.1	47.4	33.3	. . .	. . .	. . .
1963	252.0	91.4	66.8	24.6	160.6	52.2	38.1	. . .	. . .	. . .
1964	272.5	93.7	66.2	27.4	178.9	58.3	42.5	. . .	. . .	. . .
1965	300.5	95.1	63.9	31.2	205.4	69.2	47.8	. . .	. . .	. . .
1966	319.5	96.8	61.5	35.4	222.6	79.0	52.5	. . .	. . .	. . .
1967	352.2	111.1	71.5	39.6	241.1	86.1	56.8	. . .	. . .	. . .
1968	391.8	121.6	74.8	46.8	270.2	96.2	63.3	. . .	. . .	. . .
1969	401.6	112.1	65.1	46.9	289.5	106.6	68.4	. . .	. . .	. . .
1970	435.8	129.3	74.5	54.8	306.5	111.4	71.3	. . .	. . .	. . .
1971	488.9	147.3	81.5	65.8	341.5	117.8	80.0	. . .	. . .	. . .
1972	561.8	159.7	86.9	72.8	402.0	133.1	96.9	. . .	. . .	. . .
1973	643.1	166.9	90.1	76.8	476.2	161.2	117.0	. . .	. . .	. . .
1974	707.5	172.1	88.2	83.9	535.4	191.3	129.8	. . .	. . .	. . .
1975	737.8	204.9	118.1	86.8	532.9	183.4	134.1	. . .	. . .	. . .
1976	798.6	226.7	137.5	89.1	571.9	185.2	148.5	. . .	. . .	. . .
1977	885.6	234.3	137.5	96.8	651.3	204.7	175.1	. . .	. . .	. . .
1978	1 003.8	240.3	138.4	101.9	763.5	237.2	210.5	. . .	. . .	. . .
1979	1 119.0	258.6	146.7	111.9	860.4	279.7	241.6	. . .	. . .	. . .
1980	1 217.7	294.2	172.1	122.0	923.6	312.0	262.2	. . .	. . .	. . .
1981	1 298.4	307.4	180.4	127.0	991.0	350.2	283.5	. . .	. . .	. . .
1982	1 398.2	334.4	203.0	131.3	1 063.8	392.0	299.6	. . .	. . .	. . .
1983	1 550.0	398.6	260.9	137.7	1 151.4	413.8	330.2	. . .	. . .	. . .
1984	1 715.6	401.2	260.2	141.0	1 314.4	473.2	376.0	. . .	. . .	. . .
1985	1 876.8	439.9	263.7	176.2	1 436.9	499.0	421.7	. . .	. . .	. . .
1986	2 071.5	498.0	309.4	188.5	1 573.6	539.1	490.1	. . .	. . .	. . .
1987	2 220.8	525.0	335.3	189.7	1 695.8	564.8	585.3	30.1	. . .	. . .
1988	2 394.8	548.3	359.2	189.0	1 846.5	604.4	662.7	40.4	. . .	. . .
1989	2 558.7	569.7	400.3	169.4	1 989.0	636.4	760.1	50.4	. . .	. . .
1990	2 696.1	618.0	458.7	159.2	2 078.1	639.1	841.4	61.9	. . .	. . .
1991	2 805.7	726.8	559.6	167.2	2 078.9	616.9	868.3	70.2	. . .	. . .
1992	2 906.4	824.0	658.6	165.4	2 082.4	597.0	887.1	73.4	. . .	. . .
1993	3 062.7	896.2	724.0	172.2	2 166.5	584.1	928.6	72.7	. . .	. . .
1994	3 235.2	893.5	714.1	179.4	2 341.7	643.6	987.2	74.8	. . .	. . .
1995	3 463.8	895.4	694.3	201.1	2 568.4	715.2	1 061.3	78.8	. . .	. . .
1996	3 634.9	895.6	694.6	200.9	2 739.3	778.5	1 121.5	85.5	. . .	. . .
1997	3 958.4	989.6	748.2	241.4	2 968.8	845.3	1 219.6	98.2	. . .	. . .
1998	4 364.9	1 095.7	790.8	304.9	3 269.2	938.8	1 310.4	97.0	. . .	. . .
1999	4 621.3	1 163.2	805.6	357.7	3 458.1	1 000.3	1 458.4	100.6	. . .	. . .
2000	5 029.4	1 195.9	781.1	414.9	3 833.5	1 087.1	1 637.9	129.7	. . .	. . .
2001	5 216.3	1 329.4	838.1	491.3	3 886.9	1 023.9	1 758.4	153.4	. . .	. . .
2002	5 643.5	1 517.6	1 002.9	514.7	4 125.9	962.0	2 009.6	212.8	. . .	. . .
2003	6 005.5	1 647.0	1 086.4	560.5	4 358.6	899.6	2 208.1	278.7	. . .	. . .
2004	6 576.1	1 744.7	1 143.9	600.7	4 831.4	927.5	2 548.5	395.3	1 076.8	1 076.4
2005	7 291.3	1 856.1	1 133.8	722.4	5 435.2	1 055.6	2 920.2	443.1	1 209.1	1 268.0
2006	8 075.3	1 992.3	1 185.9	806.4	6 083.0	1 201.3	3 360.7	467.4	1 438.5	1 454.8
2007	8 877.8	2 105.0	1 107.7	997.3	6 772.8	1 444.2	3 591.8	484.4	1 523.9	1 583.6
2008	9 352.7	2 100.4	1 238.5	861.9	7 252.3	1 618.3	3 816.3	588.7	1 502.2	1 725.4
2009	9 013.3	2 331.1	1 438.0	893.1	6 682.2	1 317.5	3 783.9	602.5	1 535.3	1 646.2
2008										
January	8 947.3	2 075.4	1 092.0	983.4	6 871.9	1 474.2	3 617.0	488.2	1 530.2	1 598.6
February	8 998.9	2 077.9	1 091.7	986.2	6 921.0	1 496.4	3 643.0	492.7	1 537.0	1 613.2
March	9 054.0	2 073.3	1 101.7	971.5	6 980.8	1 528.6	3 670.2	497.9	1 544.6	1 627.6
April	8 995.8	2 059.9	1 098.4	961.5	6 935.9	1 536.8	3 657.4	503.3	1 519.5	1 634.6
May	9 012.9	2 066.3	1 106.7	959.6	6 946.5	1 541.6	3 647.9	508.7	1 496.1	1 643.2
June	9 002.4	2 073.4	1 120.1	953.3	6 929.0	1 555.1	3 634.1	514.7	1 465.0	1 654.4
July	9 028.7	2 069.3	1 121.6	947.6	6 959.4	1 568.5	3 623.5	521.2	1 442.2	1 660.1
August	9 032.8	2 046.8	1 131.7	915.0	6 986.0	1 577.8	3 626.0	526.0	1 436.6	1 663.5
September	9 165.3	2 075.7	1 151.1	924.6	7 089.6	1 594.5	3 661.6	539.3	1 448.3	1 674.0
October	9 499.1	2 200.1	1 220.3	979.8	7 299.0	1 642.0	3 818.7	577.9	1 522.7	1 718.1
November	9 389.3	2 147.0	1 254.6	892.4	7 242.3	1 635.9	3 819.4	582.6	1 515.0	1 721.8
December	9 352.7	2 100.4	1 238.5	861.9	7 252.3	1 618.3	3 816.3	588.7	1 502.2	1 725.4
2009										
January	9 331.4	2 153.7	1 270.8	883.0	7 177.7	1 601.2	3 801.0	594.0	1 486.3	1 720.8
February	9 352.1	2 170.1	1 261.2	908.8	7 182.0	1 584.7	3 826.7	597.2	1 508.4	1 721.0
March	9 311.8	2 188.6	1 271.5	917.1	7 123.1	1 561.8	3 829.3	601.6	1 507.0	1 720.6
April	9 258.2	2 180.4	1 260.3	920.1	7 077.9	1 541.6	3 841.1	605.3	1 520.3	1 715.6
May	9 315.2	2 199.2	1 259.5	939.7	7 115.9	1 521.3	3 879.6	612.5	1 554.6	1 712.5
June	9 279.3	2 236.3	1 294.7	941.6	7 043.0	1 489.8	3 859.3	610.0	1 544.9	1 704.4
July	9 195.6	2 267.1	1 341.2	925.9	6 928.4	1 451.3	3 830.6	606.8	1 528.4	1 695.3
August	9 153.6	2 297.9	1 379.1	918.7	6 855.7	1 421.0	3 810.1	605.8	1 516.3	1 688.0
September	9 062.8	2 305.1	1 395.9	909.2	6 757.7	1 387.4	3 761.5	603.0	1 480.9	1 677.7
October	8 977.3	2 294.9	1 389.8	905.1	6 682.4	1 355.0	3 734.9	600.7	1 470.5	1 663.7
November	9 045.6	2 304.5	1 402.8	901.6	6 741.1	1 339.8	3 804.2	604.3	1 542.0	1 657.9
December	9 013.3	2 331.1	1 438.0	893.1	6 682.2	1 317.5	3 783.9	602.5	1 535.3	1 646.2

. . . = Not available.

Table 12-4. Commercial Banks: Bank Credit and Selected Liabilities—*Continued*

(All commercial banks in the United States, billions of dollars, seasonally adjusted, annual data are for December.)

Year and month	Bank credit				Selected liabilities			
	Loans and leases in bank credit					Borrowings		
		Consumer loans			Deposits	From banks in the United States	From banks in the United States	From others
	Total	Credit cards and other revolving plans	Other consumer loans	Other loans and leases				
1955	17.1	...	...	11.2	...	...	...	...
1956	18.9	...	...	10.9	...	...	...	...
1957	19.8	...	...	12.5	...	...	...	...
1958	20.4	...	...	19.0	...	...	...	...
1959	24.1	...	...	22.2	...	...	...	...
1960	26.3	...	...	22.4	...	...	...	...
1961	27.6	...	...	25.5	...	...	...	...
1962	30.2	...	...	30.2	...	...	...	...
1963	34.2	...	...	36.2	...	...	...	...
1964	39.5	...	...	38.5	...	...	...	...
1965	45.0	...	...	43.4	...	...	...	...
1966	47.8	...	...	43.4	...	...	...	...
1967	51.2	...	...	46.9	...	...	...	...
1968	57.7	...	...	53.0	...	...	...	...
1969	62.5	...	...	52.0	...	...	...	...
1970	65.2	...	...	58.6	...	...	...	...
1971	73.2	...	...	70.6	...	...	...	...
1972	85.3	...	...	86.8	...	...	...	...
1973	98.4	...	...	99.7	663.7	14.9	...	...
1974	102.1	...	...	112.2	731.4	19.5	...	...
1975	104.3	...	...	111.1	768.0	20.5	...	...
1976	115.8	...	...	122.3	825.9	22.4	...	...
1977	138.0	...	...	133.5	910.9	29.0	...	...
1978	164.4	...	...	151.4	1 003.6	53.3	...	...
1979	183.8	...	...	155.3	1 068.3	176.0	...	...
1980	178.7	...	...	170.7	1 180.3	211.4	...	...
1981	182.1	...	...	175.0	1 243.5	254.6	...	...
1982	187.9	...	...	184.4	1 360.6	280.2	...	...
1983	212.9	...	...	194.5	1 473.5	280.3	...	...
1984	253.8	...	...	211.4	1 606.4	314.5	...	...
1985	290.9	...	...	225.3	1 754.8	340.4	...	...
1986	314.6	...	...	229.6	1 918.5	385.8	...	...
1987	327.2	...	...	218.6	1 981.3	404.4	...	...
1988	355.4	...	...	224.0	2 112.8	454.1	...	...
1989	373.7	...	...	218.8	2 240.3	511.9	...	...
1990	375.8	...	...	221.9	2 334.8	522.9	...	...
1991	363.7	...	...	230.1	2 465.6	463.9	...	...
1992	354.7	...	...	243.5	2 497.7	462.5	...	...
1993	386.2	...	...	267.6	2 534.4	494.9	...	...
1994	443.7	...	...	267.2	2 533.4	580.3	...	...
1995	484.4	...	...	307.5	2 651.8	643.4	...	...
1996	505.6	...	...	333.8	2 832.9	683.1	296.4	386.7
1997	498.6	...	...	405.2	3 080.3	810.2	300.4	509.8
1998	495.9	...	...	524.2	3 294.0	949.0	315.4	633.6
1999	485.6	...	...	513.8	3 475.9	1 082.7	343.1	739.6
2000	532.0	204.7	327.3	576.5	3 724.7	1 173.7	376.9	796.8
2001	549.4	217.6	331.7	555.1	4 078.1	1 171.6	405.0	766.6
2002	578.9	223.1	355.7	575.4	4 351.2	1 322.9	421.4	901.5
2003	635.5	251.9	383.6	615.4	4 626.2	1 370.6	391.1	979.5
2004	685.6	292.0	393.5	669.8	5 150.9	1 485.0	398.4	1 086.6
2005	697.0	298.3	398.7	762.3	5 592.0	1 645.7	371.8	1 273.9
2006	731.2	307.7	423.6	789.8	6 094.5	1 877.7	410.2	1 467.5
2007	792.2	336.0	456.3	944.6	6 668.0	2 143.4	481.1	1 662.3
2008	859.7	369.3	490.4	958.0	7 234.1	2 477.3	388.9	2 088.4
2009	829.4	331.4	497.9	751.4	7 697.8	1 916.9	266.7	1 650.2
2008								
January	791.2	330.4	460.8	989.5	6 711.3	2 140.9	471.9	1 669.0
February	794.8	330.4	464.5	986.9	6 785.3	2 168.4	470.1	1 698.3
March	800.7	331.6	469.1	981.3	6 837.8	2 188.3	464.1	1 724.2
April	805.9	332.2	473.6	935.8	6 826.5	2 194.5	459.0	1 735.5
May	809.3	331.7	477.6	947.7	6 838.5	2 216.4	470.2	1 746.2
June	814.1	333.1	481.0	925.8	6 868.1	2 215.9	465.0	1 751.0
July	824.2	337.6	486.6	943.1	6 882.0	2 249.7	467.6	1 782.2
August	829.6	342.1	487.5	952.6	6 898.2	2 260.9	464.1	1 796.8
September	833.9	347.4	486.5	999.6	7 109.3	2 323.2	471.3	1 851.9
October	850.4	364.3	486.1	988.0	7 179.1	2 583.1	446.9	2 136.2
November	856.2	369.7	486.5	930.9	7 113.8	2 588.7	408.0	2 180.7
December	859.7	369.3	490.4	958.0	7 234.1	2 477.3	388.9	2 088.4
2009								
January	869.7	376.6	493.1	905.7	7 294.6	2 414.7	422.6	1 992.1
February	881.7	386.1	495.7	889.0	7 279.1	2 438.4	424.9	2 013.5
March	872.8	378.8	494.1	859.3	7 302.5	2 435.2	428.4	2 006.8
April	861.3	369.4	491.9	833.9	7 317.9	2 392.3	431.9	1 960.4
May	859.4	363.1	496.3	855.6	7 454.0	2 387.6	428.7	1 958.8
June	856.8	360.9	495.9	837.1	7 521.1	2 322.9	424.3	1 898.6
July	852.4	359.8	492.5	794.3	7 510.1	2 216.9	381.5	1 835.5
August	849.7	356.3	493.5	775.0	7 552.8	2 138.0	341.0	1 796.9
September	846.4	350.9	495.4	762.4	7 592.9	2 034.9	335.6	1 699.2
October	843.5	347.1	496.4	749.0	7 637.5	1 981.9	317.6	1 664.3
November	838.7	342.0	496.6	758.4	7 681.9	1 949.9	285.5	1 664.4
December	829.4	331.4	497.9	751.4	7 697.8	1 916.9	266.7	1 650.2

. . . = Not available.

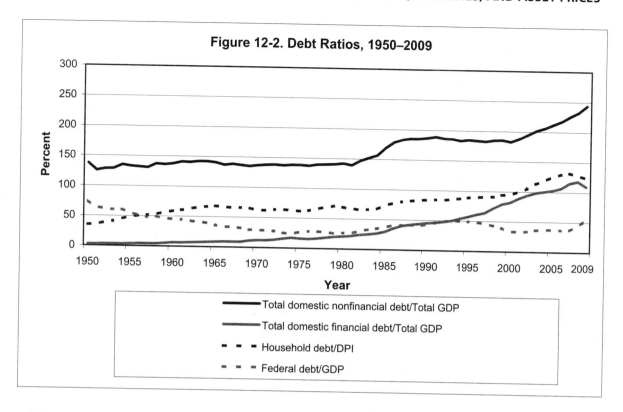

Figure 12-2. Debt Ratios, 1950–2009

Legend:
— Total domestic nonfinancial debt/Total GDP
— Total domestic financial debt/Total GDP
- - - Household debt/DPI
- - - Federal debt/GDP

- Unsustainable debt growth was the source of the credit crisis and economic decline in 2007–2009. Traditionally, analysts have focused on the debt of nonfinancial sectors. Among the major nonfinancial divisions of the economy, the most striking expansion in debt relative to income occurred in the household sector. Household debt in 1984 was no higher, relative to income, than it had been in 1964—but then it began a rapid and uninterrupted expansion. In 2001, debt rose above 100 percent of the annual rate of income, and it reached 132 percent at the end of 2007. Household debt leveled off in 2008 and declined through 2009; by the end of 2009, the ratio to DPI was down to 124 percent. (Table 12-5)

- During this period, financial sector debt—much of it reflecting the securitization of nonfinancial sector debt, especially mortgages, in other words debt built upon other debt—grew more rapidly than nonfinancial sector debt. Between 1985 and 2007, financial sector debt rose from 30 percent to 115 percent of GDP, while total nonfinancial sector debt only grew from 169 to 225 percent. For much of this period, the debt of federal government-related financial entities—government-sponsored enterprises (GSEs) such as "Fannie Mae" and "Freddie Mac" and mortgage pools backed by federal agencies and GSEs— and the debt of private financial sectors both rose rapidly. From 2003 to 2007, there was accelerated growth in the private segment. In 2009, total financial debt actually dropped, especially the private segment, and the ratio to GDP retreated to 110. (Tables 1-1 and 12-5)

- Debt of the federal government itself—that is, Treasury securities issued to fund budget deficits—contributed little, on balance, to the rising trend of aggregate debt—until the recession struck in 2008, revenues fell, and spending rose because of both recession-sensitive programs like unemployment insurance and new moves to stabilize credit markets and the economy. (Tables 12-5, 6-1 and 6-15)

Table 12-5. Credit Market Debt Outstanding, by Borrower and Lender

(Billions of dollars, except as noted; end of period; not seasonally adjusted.)

Year and quarter	Total	Domestic financial sectors			Domestic nonfinancial sectors										
					Total		Federal government			Households		Nonfinancial business			
													Corporate		
		Total	Federal govern-ment-related	Private	Billions of dollars	Percent of GDP	Total	Treasury securities	Budget agency securities and mortgages	Billions of dollars	Percent of DPI	Total	Total	Percent of sector value added	
1950	425.3	8.5	1.9	6.6	402.8	137.1	216.5	216.1	0.4	72.9	34.7	92.1	70.3	45.9	
1951	449.5	9.6	2.1	7.5	425.3	125.3	216.1	215.8	0.2	81.8	35.4	103.9	78.7	44.8	
1952	484.9	11.1	2.2	8.9	458.7	128.0	221.4	220.8	0.6	93.9	38.6	112.6	84.9	46.3	
1953	516.9	12.7	2.2	10.5	488.0	128.7	228.4	226.2	2.3	106.1	41.1	117.7	89.1	45.5	
1954	542.0	12.3	2.1	10.1	513.2	134.9	230.8	228.5	2.3	117.4	44.5	123.9	92.6	48.0	
1955	582.3	15.3	3.2	12.1	550.5	132.7	230.0	228.4	1.6	138.0	48.7	136.4	101.2	46.5	
1956	611.8	17.9	4.0	13.9	576.5	131.8	224.1	222.8	1.4	152.9	50.5	149.1	110.8	47.6	
1957	643.0	20.8	5.1	15.7	603.5	130.9	221.9	220.1	1.8	165.3	51.7	161.3	120.5	49.5	
1958	682.0	21.0	5.2	15.8	640.2	137.0	231.1	229.0	2.1	176.1	53.3	172.3	127.6	53.8	
1959	739.0	27.7	7.5	20.2	689.9	136.2	238.0	236.2	1.8	198.1	56.6	187.1	136.3	51.2	
1960	780.5	32.5	8.1	24.4	724.7	137.7	236.0	234.0	1.9	215.6	59.0	201.0	145.2	52.5	
1961	828.8	34.9	8.9	26.0	768.4	141.0	243.2	240.7	2.5	232.3	60.9	215.2	152.7	53.8	
1962	888.4	39.4	10.5	28.9	821.4	140.2	250.0	246.8	3.3	254.3	62.8	233.3	163.1	52.6	
1963	954.5	46.6	12.0	34.6	877.0	142.0	253.8	250.7	3.2	281.2	66.2	252.8	173.7	52.7	
1964	1 028.8	53.0	12.7	40.3	940.9	141.8	259.9	255.9	4.0	310.3	67.1	275.0	187.5	52.7	
1965	1 107.3	61.9	15.1	46.8	1 008.0	140.2	261.5	257.0	4.5	338.7	68.0	304.6	207.6	53.1	
1966	1 187.8	72.9	20.3	52.5	1 075.5	136.5	265.1	259.3	5.8	361.2	67.2	339.1	232.1	54.1	
1967	1 268.4	73.6	20.4	53.2	1 151.5	138.3	278.1	268.2	9.9	380.4	66.1	375.6	258.1	57.2	
1968	1 373.4	84.0	24.4	59.6	1 243.3	136.7	290.6	277.6	13.0	412.8	66.1	413.8	285.1	57.3	
1969	1 491.2	111.5	33.8	77.7	1 330.4	135.1	287.4	276.8	10.6	442.7	65.7	462.0	317.8	58.8	
1970	1 600.0	127.8	43.6	84.1	1 420.2	136.8	299.5	289.9	9.6	457.1	62.1	513.3	362.1	64.9	
1971	1 750.7	138.9	49.5	89.3	1 555.2	138.0	324.4	315.9	8.5	499.4	62.3	564.7	390.6	64.8	
1972	1 935.1	162.8	57.9	104.8	1 711.2	138.2	339.4	330.1	9.3	555.4	63.9	635.7	429.9	64.2	
1973	2 172.7	209.8	77.9	131.9	1 895.5	137.1	346.3	336.7	9.6	624.9	63.9	729.5	495.6	66.0	
1974	2 409.5	258.3	98.6	159.7	2 069.9	138.0	358.2	348.8	9.4	680.3	63.5	823.2	551.6	68.1	
1975	2 619.1	260.4	108.9	151.6	2 261.8	138.1	443.9	434.9	8.9	734.3	61.8	864.2	571.3	65.2	
1976	2 904.9	283.9	123.1	160.8	2 505.3	137.3	513.1	503.7	9.3	818.9	62.9	935.5	612.1	61.8	
1977	3 293.0	337.8	145.5	192.3	2 826.6	139.2	569.4	560.9	8.4	946.7	66.0	1 054.3	687.1	61.4	
1978	3 779.4	412.5	182.6	229.9	3 211.2	140.0	621.9	614.9	7.0	1 105.4	68.8	1 188.4	761.4	59.8	
1979	4 276.4	504.9	231.8	273.1	3 603.0	140.6	657.7	652.1	5.6	1 276.1	71.3	1 347.0	843.8	59.7	
1980	4 725.1	578.1	276.6	301.5	3 953.5	141.8	735.0	730.0	5.0	1 396.0	69.7	1 478.1	910.2	59.3	
1981	5 258.0	682.4	324.0	358.3	4 361.7	139.5	820.5	815.9	4.5	1 507.2	67.4	1 662.0	1 027.3	59.0	
1982	5 769.6	778.1	388.9	389.2	4 783.4	147.0	981.8	978.1	3.7	1 576.4	65.3	1 811.4	1 117.4	62.0	
1983	6 466.1	882.7	456.6	426.1	5 359.2	151.6	1 167.0	1 163.4	3.6	1 732.0	66.6	1 999.1	1 230.4	63.8	
1984	7 431.5	1 052.4	531.2	521.2	6 146.2	156.4	1 364.2	1 360.8	3.4	1 943.3	67.2	2 325.1	1 438.3	66.5	
1985	8 622.9	1 257.3	631.7	625.6	7 123.1	168.9	1 589.9	1 586.6	3.3	2 277.8	74.0	2 577.5	1 617.8	70.5	
1986	9 811.7	1 593.6	810.3	783.3	7 966.3	178.6	1 805.9	1 802.2	3.6	2 537.3	77.9	2 871.0	1 840.0	77.2	
1987	10 824.6	1 895.5	977.6	917.9	8 670.1	183.1	1 949.8	1 944.6	5.2	2 755.1	80.2	3 122.6	2 033.8	79.7	
1988	11 866.2	2 145.8	1 098.4	1 047.4	9 450.7	185.3	2 104.9	2 082.3	22.6	3 043.6	81.7	3 409.2	2 233.4	80.8	
1989	12 839.2	2 399.3	1 247.8	1 151.4	10 152.1	185.2	2 251.2	2 227.0	24.2	3 319.0	83.2	3 641.5	2 409.4	83.1	
1990	13 766.8	2 613.6	1 418.4	1 195.2	10 834.9	186.8	2 498.1	2 465.8	32.4	3 580.9	84.2	3 768.5	2 542.5	83.8	
1991	14 421.3	2 769.6	1 564.2	1 205.4	11 301.4	188.6	2 776.4	2 757.8	18.6	3 769.7	84.8	3 676.7	2 487.2	80.1	
1992	15 213.0	3 024.1	1 720.4	1 303.6	11 816.5	186.3	3 080.3	3 061.6	18.8	3 970.4	83.8	3 670.6	2 511.8	77.5	
1993	16 180.6	3 321.0	1 885.7	1 435.3	12 391.4	185.9	3 336.5	3 309.9	26.6	4 210.3	85.5	3 691.5	2 553.6	75.1	
1994	17 207.8	3 791.1	2 173.4	1 617.7	12 973.6	183.1	3 492.3	3 465.6	26.7	4 531.8	87.4	3 842.0	2 688.5	73.1	
1995	18 468.6	4 233.5	2 377.7	1 855.8	13 667.5	184.3	3 636.7	3 608.5	28.2	4 841.2	88.7	4 142.8	2 941.5	75.7	
1996	19 804.5	4 747.5	2 609.2	2 138.3	14 399.8	183.7	3 781.7	3 755.1	26.6	5 177.0	89.9	4 415.0	3 140.3	76.2	
1997	21 235.9	5 301.4	2 822.8	2 478.6	15 210.8	182.6	3 804.8	3 778.3	26.5	5 477.6	90.2	4 851.5	3 471.6	78.7	
1998	23 327.7	6 328.2	3 294.4	3 033.8	16 216.4	184.4	3 752.2	3 723.7	28.5	5 903.4	90.8	5 417.1	3 853.4	82.5	
1999	25 389.3	7 349.4	3 887.7	3 461.7	17 291.6	184.9	3 681.0	3 652.7	28.3	6 396.0	94.0	6 033.7	4 270.9	86.2	
2000	27 138.3	8 157.8	4 319.7	3 838.1	18 166.1	182.5	3 385.1	3 357.8	27.3	6 987.3	95.4	6 595.8	4 633.6	87.8	
2001	29 319.6	9 155.9	4 962.3	4 193.6	19 298.3	187.6	3 379.5	3 352.7	26.8	7 659.3	100.1	6 956.1	4 825.8	91.9	
2002	31 832.3	10 042.5	5 509.0	4 533.5	20 716.9	194.7	3 637.0	3 609.8	27.3	8 484.3	105.9	7 147.7	4 859.4	91.6	
2003	34 623.6	10 937.6	5 932.7	5 004.8	22 432.7	201.3	4 033.1	4 008.2	24.9	9 487.4	113.2	7 343.8	4 976.5	90.4	
2004	37 799.0	11 926.2	6 050.9	5 875.3	24 434.0	205.9	4 395.0	4 370.7	24.3	10 548.5	118.7	7 808.0	5 179.8	88.1	
2005	41 267.1	12 989.4	6 134.1	6 855.2	26 763.8	211.8	4 701.9	4 678.0	23.8	11 716.3	126.3	8 491.2	5 514.1	87.5	
2006	45 329.5	14 280.4	6 465.1	7 815.3	29 166.4	217.7	4 885.3	4 861.7	23.5	12 889.7	130.0	9 383.3	5 983.4	88.8	
2007	50 044.5	16 204.0	7 373.7	8 830.3	31 714.1	225.3	5 122.3	5 099.2	23.1	13 747.8	132.2	10 644.8	6 775.5	97.2	
2008	52 524.9	17 083.7	8 142.7	8 941.0	33 576.8	232.5	6 361.5	6 338.2	23.3	13 772.9	127.5	11 188.8	7 119.0	102.1	
2009	52 416.7	15 651.3	8 089.3	7 562.1	34 702.2	243.4	7 805.4	7 781.9	23.5	13 536.0	123.9	10 998.7	7 229.2	108.3	
2007															
1st quarter	46 504.3	14 776.8	6 596.6	8 180.2	29 804.1	216.0	5 037.4	5 014.3	23.2	13 062.6	127.5	9 638.4	6 123.6	88.6	
2nd quarter	47 528.2	15 167.9	6 758.2	8 409.7	30 356.7	216.9	4 927.2	4 904.0	23.2	13 310.9	128.7	9 992.9	6 358.4	91.0	
3rd quarter	48 860.6	15 794.9	7 065.9	8 729.0	31 054.7	219.0	5 032.9	5 010.0	23.0	13 550.9	129.7	10 320.8	6 571.9	94.6	
4th quarter	50 044.5	16 204.0	7 373.7	8 830.3	31 714.1	221.2	5 122.3	5 099.2	23.1	13 747.8	130.0	10 644.8	6 775.5	96.3	
2008															
1st quarter	50 812.6	16 415.9	7 539.5	8 876.4	32 194.7	224.0	5 322.6	5 299.1	23.5	13 805.9	130.1	10 842.9	6 887.0	99.3	
2nd quarter	51 272.7	16 670.9	7 861.6	8 809.4	32 374.1	223.3	5 274.1	5 250.6	23.5	13 816.3	126.0	11 044.1	7 027.7	100.8	
3rd quarter	52 082.5	16 946.5	8 044.6	8 901.9	33 038.3	227.1	5 800.6	5 777.5	23.1	13 845.9	127.6	11 146.1	7 090.9	100.7	
4th quarter	52 524.9	17 083.7	8 142.7	8 941.0	33 576.8	234.0	6 361.5	6 338.2	23.3	13 772.9	127.5	11 188.8	7 119.0	102.7	
2009															
1st quarter	52 882.7	16 986.4	8 160.1	8 826.3	33 999.9	239.8	6 826.9	6 804.4	22.5	13 682.8	127.1	11 207.2	7 187.1	107.2	
2nd quarter	52 686.7	16 455.6	8 121.4	8 334.2	34 280.3	242.2	7 165.3	7 143.1	22.3	13 635.2	124.3	11 168.8	7 221.1	108.2	
3rd quarter	52 549.1	15 998.0	8 100.2	7 897.8	34 530.9	242.5	7 544.0	7 520.8	23.2	13 590.4	124.3	11 069.0	7 215.0	109.1	
4th quarter	52 416.7	15 651.3	8 089.3	7 562.1	34 702.2	240.1	7 805.4	7 781.9	23.5	13 536.0	122.7	10 998.7	7 229.2	107.9	

Table 12-5. Credit Market Debt Outstanding, by Borrower and Lender—*Continued*

(Billions of dollars, except as noted; end of period; not seasonally adjusted.)

Year and quarter	Credit market debt outstanding owed by:—*Continued*				Credit market assets held by:									
	Domestic nonfinancial sectors—*Continued*			Foreign credit market debt held in United States		Selected government-related sectors							Selected domestic financial sectors	
	Nonfinancial business—*Continued*		State and local governments		Total	Total	Federal government	Government-sponsored enterprises	Federally related mortgage pools	State and local governments	State and local retirement funds	Federal government retirement funds	Total, selected sectors	Monetary authority
	Nonfarm noncorporate	Farm												
1950	12.3	9.5	21.2	14.0	425.3	33.2	16.0	3.1	0.0	9.4	4.7	0.0	262.9	20.7
1951	14.3	10.8	23.6	14.7	449.5	36.3	17.2	3.5	0.0	10.1	5.4	0.0	281.4	23.6
1952	16.1	11.6	30.8	15.1	484.9	40.6	18.8	3.6	0.1	11.7	6.4	0.0	303.8	24.1
1953	17.1	11.5	35.8	16.3	516.9	44.9	20.8	3.7	0.1	12.6	7.7	0.0	323.5	25.3
1954	18.9	12.3	41.1	16.6	542.0	47.3	20.5	4.0	0.1	13.5	9.2	0.0	347.0	25.0
1955	21.5	13.7	46.1	16.6	582.3	51.4	21.1	5.0	0.1	14.7	10.5	0.0	369.8	24.4
1956	23.7	14.6	50.4	17.4	611.8	55.6	21.8	6.0	0.1	15.9	11.7	0.0	391.3	24.7
1957	25.2	15.6	55.0	18.8	643.0	59.1	22.4	7.3	0.2	15.9	13.3	0.0	411.7	23.8
1958	27.7	17.0	60.7	20.8	682.0	62.8	23.9	7.7	0.2	16.1	15.0	0.0	445.4	26.3
1959	31.9	18.9	66.7	21.4	739.0	70.1	25.7	9.9	0.2	17.5	16.8	0.0	472.5	26.7
1960	35.8	20.0	72.2	23.2	780.5	76.0	26.7	11.1	0.2	19.1	18.9	0.0	504.1	27.0
1961	41.0	21.6	77.8	25.5	828.8	82.0	28.4	12.1	0.3	20.1	21.1	0.0	542.9	28.8
1962	46.4	23.9	83.8	27.5	888.4	89.4	30.4	13.7	0.4	21.7	23.2	0.0	589.2	30.5
1963	52.6	26.4	89.2	30.8	954.5	96.6	31.9	15.3	0.5	23.3	25.6	0.0	640.7	33.7
1964	58.5	29.0	95.6	35.0	1 028.8	104.7	34.7	16.0	0.6	25.0	28.3	0.0	698.1	36.6
1965	64.7	32.3	103.2	37.5	1 107.3	115.5	37.6	18.3	0.9	27.5	31.3	0.0	761.4	40.6
1966	71.5	35.5	110.0	39.5	1 187.8	129.8	42.7	23.3	1.3	27.5	34.9	0.0	807.8	43.7
1967	78.7	38.8	117.4	43.3	1 268.4	138.5	47.3	23.3	2.0	27.6	38.3	0.0	873.4	49.1
1968	87.1	41.6	126.1	46.1	1 373.4	154.4	52.3	26.5	2.5	31.4	41.6	0.0	947.0	53.0
1969	99.6	44.6	138.3	49.2	1 491.2	175.6	55.4	35.1	3.2	36.4	45.5	0.0	1 004.5	57.2
1970	103.6	47.6	150.3	52.1	1 600.0	191.5	58.2	43.9	4.8	35.1	49.6	0.0	1 078.8	62.2
1971	122.6	51.6	166.7	56.6	1 750.7	201.1	60.3	45.0	9.5	33.4	52.9	0.0	1 190.5	69.6
1972	149.0	56.8	180.7	61.1	1 935.1	223.0	62.2	49.0	14.4	40.1	57.4	0.0	1 336.4	71.2
1973	168.5	65.4	194.8	67.4	2 172.7	260.2	64.9	64.4	18.0	49.8	63.1	0.0	1 503.9	80.5
1974	198.4	73.3	208.2	81.2	2 409.5	304.7	72.2	85.3	21.5	56.4	69.4	0.0	1 641.7	85.3
1975	210.7	82.1	219.4	96.9	2 619.1	347.5	87.1	89.8	28.5	63.8	78.3	0.0	1 773.4	93.5
1976	231.2	92.2	237.8	115.7	2 904.9	398.6	93.7	94.5	40.7	82.0	87.7	0.0	1 968.8	100.3
1977	261.3	105.9	256.2	128.6	3 293.0	471.6	103.6	101.4	56.8	110.6	99.2	0.0	2 227.8	108.9
1978	304.8	122.2	295.6	155.7	3 779.4	582.6	120.6	128.1	70.4	147.5	116.0	0.0	2 526.1	117.4
1979	357.5	145.7	322.2	168.5	4 276.4	696.0	141.4	158.1	94.8	175.2	126.6	0.0	2 841.3	124.5
1980	406.4	161.5	344.4	193.4	4 725.1	804.5	165.5	184.5	114.0	193.4	147.2	0.0	3 108.5	128.0
1981	456.8	177.8	372.1	214.0	5 258.0	931.1	189.9	217.7	129.0	225.6	169.0	0.0	3 415.5	136.9
1982	509.5	184.5	413.8	208.1	5 769.6	1 058.9	205.8	233.7	178.5	250.1	190.7	0.0	3 658.8	144.5
1983	580.3	188.4	461.1	224.1	6 466.1	1 177.7	215.3	236.4	244.8	282.4	198.8	0.0	4 065.9	159.2
1984	698.8	187.9	513.6	232.8	7 431.5	1 339.7	232.6	265.9	289.0	319.0	233.2	0.0	4 638.1	167.6
1985	798.0	161.7	677.9	242.5	8 622.9	1 618.0	251.2	291.0	367.9	455.6	252.4	0.0	5 219.7	186.0
1986	886.0	144.9	752.1	251.9	9 811.7	1 920.0	258.0	307.6	531.6	525.8	297.1	0.0	5 939.5	205.5
1987	956.3	132.4	842.6	259.0	10 824.6	2 156.6	242.8	330.9	669.4	583.6	328.8	1.1	6 487.7	226.5
1988	1 054.2	121.6	893.0	269.8	11 866.2	2 298.7	217.4	364.2	745.3	616.8	350.5	2.7	7 033.3	240.6
1989	1 109.4	122.7	940.4	287.9	12 839.2	2 489.2	209.4	359.9	869.5	664.1	381.5	4.9	7 478.7	233.3
1990	1 101.8	124.1	987.4	318.2	13 766.8	2 749.6	243.1	373.9	1 019.9	703.4	402.0	7.4	7 846.3	241.4
1991	1 066.4	123.1	1 078.6	350.4	14 421.3	2 961.6	251.0	388.9	1 156.5	750.6	404.6	10.0	8 119.8	272.5
1992	1 035.4	123.4	1 095.1	372.4	15 213.0	3 176.3	239.0	458.1	1 272.0	752.3	441.8	13.1	8 500.8	300.4
1993	1 012.7	125.3	1 153.0	468.2	16 180.6	3 400.7	227.5	546.7	1 356.8	784.9	468.6	16.2	9 106.1	336.7
1994	1 024.6	128.8	1 107.5	443.1	17 207.8	3 590.9	222.1	667.9	1 472.4	729.9	478.7	19.9	9 589.3	368.2
1995	1 069.9	131.4	1 046.7	567.6	18 468.6	3 702.7	197.6	762.8	1 570.7	638.6	509.8	23.3	10 325.2	380.8
1996	1 139.2	135.5	1 026.2	657.2	19 804.5	3 916.0	201.6	833.8	1 711.7	604.8	538.4	25.6	10 936.8	393.1
1997	1 237.1	142.8	1 076.9	723.6	21 235.9	4 204.3	213.1	934.2	1 826.3	605.0	598.3	27.5	11 780.6	431.4
1998	1 412.7	150.9	1 143.8	783.2	23 327.7	4 895.5	218.8	1 251.5	2 019.0	714.6	661.5	30.2	12 957.5	452.5
1999	1 608.6	154.2	1 181.0	748.2	25 389.3	5 645.2	256.3	1 538.8	2 293.5	816.5	707.0	33.1	14 093.9	478.1
2000	1 806.0	156.1	1 197.9	814.5	27 138.3	6 216.5	263.1	1 794.4	2 493.2	887.3	743.2	35.1	15 011.5	511.8
2001	1 967.8	162.6	1 303.4	865.4	29 319.6	6 913.3	267.0	2 099.1	2 831.8	981.2	689.4	44.8	16 160.6	551.7
2002	2 118.6	169.7	1 448.0	1 072.8	31 832.3	7 520.4	275.0	2 323.2	3 158.6	1 067.4	638.7	57.6	17 466.1	629.4
2003	2 210.2	157.1	1 568.5	1 253.3	34 623.6	8 014.8	272.4	2 564.2	3 331.5	1 125.6	657.5	63.6	18 826.9	666.7
2004	2 455.3	172.9	1 682.6	1 438.8	37 799.0	8 204.0	274.7	2 613.0	3 374.6	1 198.1	675.3	68.2	20 528.0	717.8
2005	2 786.9	190.1	1 854.5	1 513.9	41 267.1	8 481.1	273.8	2 543.9	3 541.9	1 352.0	693.4	76.0	22 579.6	744.2
2006	3 195.6	204.3	2 008.2	1 882.6	45 329.5	9 088.1	279.9	2 590.5	3 837.3	1 470.6	825.4	84.3	24 738.7	778.9
2007	3 650.3	218.9	2 199.3	2 126.3	50 044.5	10 043.4	286.5	2 829.5	4 463.5	1 512.0	855.6	96.1	26 751.2	740.6
2008	3 850.5	219.4	2 253.5	1 864.4	52 524.9	10 724.5	373.1	3 033.6	4 960.8	1 385.6	851.1	120.3	27 811.3	986.0
2009	3 544.7	224.8	2 362.2	2 063.1	52 416.7	11 092.9	696.6	2 704.1	5 383.0	1 345.9	835.4	127.8	27 220.7	1 987.7
2007														
1st quarter	3 309.5	205.3	2 065.7	1 923.4	46 504.3	9 206.5	284.6	2 558.4	3 952.1	1 501.9	821.5	88.1	25 166.3	780.9
2nd quarter	3 424.5	210.0	2 125.7	2 003.5	47 528.2	9 420.9	285.4	2 596.7	4 073.4	1 550.1	826.4	88.9	25 766.1	790.5
3rd quarter	3 535.0	213.9	2 150.0	2 011.1	48 860.6	9 752.2	287.5	2 758.9	4 241.9	1 528.2	842.4	93.3	26 334.9	779.6
4th quarter	3 650.3	218.9	2 199.3	2 126.3	50 044.5	10 043.4	286.5	2 829.5	4 463.5	1 512.0	855.6	96.1	26 751.2	740.6
2008														
1st quarter	3 747.0	208.9	2 223.4	2 201.9	50 812.6	10 253.0	291.8	2 914.0	4 601.4	1 482.2	857.4	106.1	27 124.4	631.0
2nd quarter	3 796.7	219.6	2 239.6	2 227.7	51 272.7	10 490.2	296.8	3 014.5	4 759.5	1 455.3	856.0	108.1	27 111.9	509.1
3rd quarter	3 839.4	215.9	2 245.6	2 097.7	52 082.5	10 637.7	305.9	3 048.2	4 891.9	1 422.3	854.2	115.1	27 399.6	780.9
4th quarter	3 850.5	219.4	2 253.5	1 864.4	52 524.9	10 724.5	373.1	3 033.6	4 960.8	1 385.6	851.1	120.3	27 811.3	986.0
2009														
1st quarter	3 801.5	218.6	2 283.0	1 896.4	52 882.7	10 823.1	457.4	2 973.2	5 041.8	1 381.8	844.4	124.5	27 635.7	1 168.1
2nd quarter	3 726.3	221.3	2 311.0	1 950.8	52 686.7	10 962.8	553.2	2 900.7	5 173.3	1 370.3	840.6	124.7	27 622.7	1 469.5
3rd quarter	3 632.0	221.9	2 327.5	2 020.2	52 549.1	11 056.2	638.1	2 803.6	5 299.7	1 353.0	836.0	125.8	27 365.1	1 776.6
4th quarter	3 544.7	224.8	2 362.2	2 063.1	52 416.7	11 092.9	696.6	2 704.1	5 383.0	1 345.9	835.4	127.8	27 220.7	1 987.7

Table 12-5. Credit Market Debt Outstanding, by Borrower and Lender—*Continued*

(Billions of dollars, except as noted; end of period; not seasonally adjusted.)

Year and quarter	Credit market assets held by:—*Continued*												
	Selected domestic financial sectors—*Continued*										House-holds	Foreign holdings in United States	All other financial and non-financial sectors
	Com-mercial banks	Savings institutions	Credit unions	Life insurance companies	Property-casualty insurance companies	Private pension funds	Money market mutual funds	Mutual funds	Asset-backed security issuers	Finance companies			
1950	125.6	36.7	0.7	57.9	7.2	5.3	0.0	0.4	0.0	8.2	96.2	4.8	28.2
1951	132.8	39.5	0.8	61.6	7.8	6.0	0.0	0.5	0.0	8.7	96.9	4.9	30.0
1952	141.4	44.1	1.1	65.9	8.7	7.2	0.0	0.5	0.0	10.8	104.6	5.1	30.7
1953	145.2	49.5	1.4	70.6	9.9	8.5	0.0	0.5	0.0	12.5	109.6	5.8	33.1
1954	154.9	55.5	1.6	75.4	10.8	9.8	0.0	0.7	0.0	13.2	109.5	6.4	31.9
1955	159.2	63.2	2.0	80.5	11.5	11.2	0.0	0.8	0.0	17.0	117.6	6.7	36.8
1956	164.8	70.2	2.4	85.6	11.9	12.7	0.0	1.1	0.0	18.0	124.9	7.3	32.7
1957	170.1	77.0	2.9	90.5	12.6	14.5	0.0	1.2	0.0	19.3	131.9	7.5	32.8
1958	185.0	85.5	3.1	95.5	13.4	16.2	0.0	1.5	0.0	19.0	132.7	7.5	33.5
1959	189.7	95.1	3.8	100.5	14.6	17.9	0.0	1.8	0.0	22.4	142.8	11.7	41.9
1960	199.7	104.2	4.5	105.6	15.5	19.7	0.0	2.0	0.0	25.9	150.9	12.6	36.8
1961	215.9	115.3	4.9	110.9	16.5	21.2	0.0	2.4	0.0	27.0	154.9	13.1	35.9
1962	235.2	128.3	5.6	116.9	18.0	22.9	0.0	2.6	0.0	29.2	158.2	14.8	36.7
1963	252.8	144.5	6.3	123.3	18.7	24.8	0.0	2.8	0.0	33.7	159.8	15.9	41.5
1964	276.1	160.2	7.2	130.3	19.5	27.2	0.0	3.2	0.0	37.9	166.2	16.9	42.9
1965	305.1	173.5	8.2	137.8	20.6	29.1	0.0	3.9	0.0	42.7	170.0	17.4	43.0
1966	323.1	181.7	9.4	145.9	22.0	31.9	0.0	5.1	0.0	44.9	190.0	17.3	42.9
1967	359.8	195.0	10.2	153.3	23.5	32.8	0.0	4.3	0.0	45.5	195.2	20.0	41.3
1968	398.7	208.9	11.7	160.7	25.4	33.8	0.0	4.1	0.0	50.6	203.5	22.6	45.9
1969	418.3	221.5	13.8	167.6	27.0	34.6	0.0	5.1	0.0	59.2	241.4	23.2	46.6
1970	455.3	236.8	15.2	174.6	30.9	36.6	0.0	5.7	0.0	61.5	242.4	35.0	52.3
1971	506.5	271.7	17.2	182.8	34.6	35.0	0.0	5.5	0.0	67.6	233.2	62.8	63.0
1972	575.7	314.5	20.1	192.5	38.3	40.5	0.0	6.0	0.0	77.5	230.0	73.2	72.5
1973	662.4	348.0	23.7	204.8	41.8	46.8	0.0	6.6	0.0	89.4	254.7	74.7	79.2
1974	737.5	369.7	26.4	217.7	46.4	55.6	0.8	7.4	0.0	94.8	299.5	79.8	83.8
1975	768.8	415.2	31.7	234.6	53.7	71.2	1.5	8.0	0.0	95.0	320.7	88.3	89.2
1976	833.2	477.5	38.4	258.3	66.2	77.8	2.1	8.4	0.0	106.6	331.3	99.4	106.9
1977	924.6	548.1	45.6	285.8	83.7	88.2	1.9	12.3	0.0	128.6	358.4	135.4	99.7
1978	1 052.6	614.4	52.0	318.9	100.2	98.7	5.1	12.5	0.0	154.2	406.7	161.3	102.7
1979	1 181.8	671.9	53.8	352.0	113.7	120.8	24.9	14.5	0.0	183.4	486.1	149.7	103.3
1980	1 289.9	722.7	53.0	385.1	123.5	151.4	42.0	17.1	0.0	195.8	521.0	169.7	121.3
1981	1 398.2	748.7	55.0	419.8	132.0	178.6	107.5	20.2	0.0	218.6	546.6	197.0	167.9
1982	1 482.9	756.7	57.3	463.2	137.0	225.4	137.6	25.4	0.0	228.9	612.8	240.0	199.3
1983	1 626.1	879.5	69.4	513.8	138.6	267.5	119.7	34.9	3.0	254.0	705.9	263.3	253.3
1984	1 800.1	1 018.6	85.0	570.1	150.3	305.9	164.1	53.9	19.8	302.5	811.4	340.4	301.9
1985	1 989.5	1 097.6	98.4	646.6	176.5	329.0	178.2	129.9	34.8	353.2	970.9	419.9	394.3
1986	2 187.6	1 191.0	113.9	734.5	219.2	333.6	213.1	259.9	71.4	409.9	1 004.5	536.4	411.3
1987	2 323.0	1 310.3	131.3	823.1	258.6	347.2	215.0	291.1	113.2	448.3	1 180.1	586.5	413.7
1988	2 479.5	1 409.3	148.8	927.2	287.9	369.2	225.5	304.5	147.6	493.3	1 386.6	689.1	458.6
1989	2 647.4	1 316.0	156.0	1 028.3	317.5	420.8	293.7	327.2	201.1	537.3	1 483.8	815.8	571.8
1990	2 772.5	1 176.5	166.6	1 134.5	344.0	464.3	371.3	360.1	250.3	564.8	1 745.9	881.7	543.3
1991	2 853.3	1 013.2	179.4	1 218.9	376.6	489.7	403.9	440.2	299.5	572.5	1 829.0	909.6	601.4
1992	2 948.6	937.4	197.1	1 304.4	389.4	515.7	408.6	566.4	357.9	575.0	1 891.4	983.1	661.3
1993	3 090.8	914.1	218.7	1 415.5	422.7	551.9	429.0	725.9	437.8	563.1	1 892.1	1 095.0	686.8
1994	3 254.3	920.8	246.8	1 487.5	446.4	591.5	459.0	718.8	501.0	595.1	2 206.7	1 162.8	658.2
1995	3 520.1	913.3	263.0	1 587.5	468.7	608.4	545.5	771.3	612.0	654.6	2 235.1	1 464.8	740.8
1996	3 707.7	933.2	288.5	1 657.0	491.2	602.3	634.3	820.2	712.2	697.1	2 416.2	1 795.6	739.9
1997	4 031.9	928.5	305.3	1 751.1	515.3	646.8	721.9	901.1	826.5	720.8	2 393.4	2 035.6	822.1
1998	4 336.1	965.5	324.2	1 828.0	521.1	639.7	970.5	1 028.4	1 078.8	812.8	2 445.0	2 202.0	827.6
1999	4 648.3	1 032.6	351.7	1 886.0	518.2	746.9	1 155.3	1 076.8	1 253.3	946.6	2 574.3	2 196.1	879.7
2000	5 019.8	1 088.8	379.7	1 943.9	509.4	621.9	1 317.5	1 103.1	1 413.6	1 101.9	2 464.6	2 451.1	994.7
2001	5 226.0	1 133.5	421.2	2 074.8	518.4	587.0	1 584.9	1 229.7	1 662.6	1 170.7	2 362.4	2 850.2	1 033.1
2002	5 630.8	1 166.9	465.4	2 307.8	558.3	581.7	1 567.1	1 368.4	1 897.8	1 292.5	2 507.3	3 303.0	1 035.5
2003	6 010.9	1 294.2	516.6	2 488.3	625.2	653.5	1 471.3	1 506.4	2 125.0	1 468.7	2 741.2	3 836.1	1 204.6
2004	6 621.2	1 417.7	556.4	2 661.4	698.8	654.6	1 346.3	1 623.0	2 554.8	1 675.9	3 027.3	4 634.7	1 405.0
2005	7 278.4	1 617.1	592.6	2 765.4	765.8	699.9	1 340.8	1 747.1	3 287.7	1 740.6	3 362.8	5 191.3	1 652.3
2006	8 040.5	1 533.2	622.7	2 806.1	813.5	758.3	1 560.8	1 932.0	4 081.2	1 811.6	3 478.2	6 200.1	1 824.4
2007	8 781.6	1 596.1	657.9	2 888.6	839.8	860.7	1 936.4	2 203.1	4 418.0	1 828.2	4 081.8	7 272.5	1 895.6
2008	9 425.1	1 320.0	697.9	2 899.2	823.5	951.4	2 675.0	2 276.4	4 000.9	1 755.9	4 034.2	7 597.5	2 357.4
2009	9 004.5	1 079.2	724.4	3 025.9	857.2	975.9	2 031.2	2 652.2	3 332.9	1 549.5	4 203.4	7 816.9	2 082.8
2007													
1st quarter	8 048.8	1 588.3	629.2	2 831.3	821.7	789.4	1 623.9	2 005.4	4 241.1	1 806.4	3 657.4	6 532.6	1 941.5
2nd quarter	8 239.0	1 605.5	641.0	2 855.4	830.4	817.9	1 686.1	2 093.5	4 399.8	1 807.0	3 613.3	6 828.6	1 899.3
3rd quarter	8 490.3	1 639.6	652.6	2 882.4	838.9	835.4	1 789.5	2 141.6	4 453.1	1 831.9	3 912.3	6 928.9	1 932.4
4th quarter	8 781.6	1 596.1	657.9	2 888.6	839.8	860.7	1 936.4	2 203.1	4 418.0	1 828.2	4 081.8	7 272.5	1 895.6
2008													
1st quarter	8 904.8	1 610.8	665.0	2 916.1	836.6	875.6	2 237.5	2 256.7	4 343.3	1 846.9	4 056.9	7 402.4	1 976.0
2nd quarter	8 972.2	1 618.1	684.7	2 928.4	835.0	896.2	2 232.8	2 356.6	4 243.7	1 835.1	4 112.2	7 579.6	1 978.9
3rd quarter	9 394.9	1 336.5	697.0	2 910.6	826.4	914.4	2 232.0	2 340.9	4 149.1	1 816.9	4 227.9	7 606.2	2 211.1
4th quarter	9 425.1	1 320.0	697.9	2 899.2	823.5	951.4	2 675.0	2 276.4	4 000.9	1 755.9	4 034.2	7 597.5	2 357.4
2009													
1st quarter	9 297.3	1 311.5	698.6	2 946.9	823.8	963.0	2 575.2	2 319.9	3 827.9	1 703.4	4 510.2	7 673.8	2 239.9
2nd quarter	9 278.3	1 212.2	717.0	2 963.2	835.3	964.4	2 418.1	2 436.0	3 651.1	1 651.1	4 195.4	7 720.0	2 185.9
3rd quarter	9 025.8	1 188.2	725.9	3 002.5	846.4	972.8	2 163.8	2 540.0	3 512.7	1 610.4	4 312.0	7 736.3	2 079.5
4th quarter	9 004.5	1 079.2	724.4	3 025.9	857.2	975.9	2 031.2	2 652.2	3 332.9	1 549.5	4 203.4	7 816.9	2 082.8

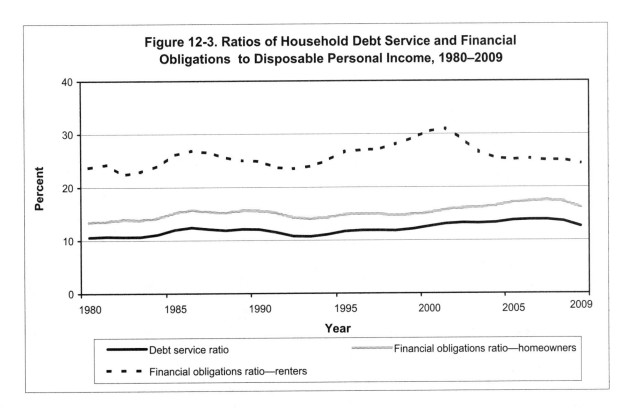

Figure 12-3. Ratios of Household Debt Service and Financial Obligations to Disposable Personal Income, 1980–2009

- The Federal Reserve calculates aggregate household debt service (payments of principal and interest) and total financial obligations as a percentage of aggregate disposable personal income (DPI) for the period 1980 to the present. These measures provide supplements to the ratio of the total level of household debt to DPI (shown in Figure 12-2 and Table 12-5), and are important because lengthening maturities and lower interest rates can mitigate much of the burden of a high level of debt. Unlike the debt/income ratio, the debt service ratio leveled off between 2002 and 2004, reflecting the decline in interest rates. However, the debt service ratio rose to a new record high of 13.9 percent in 2006 and remained there until the first quarter of 2008. Since then it has dropped back to 12.6 percent at the end of 2009, the lowest since 2000. (Table 12-6)

- Financial obligations ratios are higher than the debt service ratio. They are calculated separately for homeowners and renters and include all debt service, rental payments on primary residences, property taxes, homeowners' insurance, and automobile lease payments. The financial obligations ratio for homeowners stood at a record 17.6 percent of income through the first quarter of 2008, but has dropped back to 16.1 percent since then. (Table 12-6)

- Reflecting the lower average incomes of the renters' group, the financial obligations ratio for renters is about double the ratio for homeowners. But the renters' ratio peaked in 2001. It then declined rapidly in the early 2000s and continues to edge down. (Table 12-6)

- Additional evidence of the trend toward more debt is seen in the ratio of aggregate household debt to aggregate household financial and tangible assets, which rose from around 10 percent in 1960 to 21.9 percent in early 2009. (Table 12-6) Narrowing the comparison to mortgage debt alone, home mortgage debt as a percent of the value of real estate has increased from a range of 30 to 35 percent that prevailed from 1960 through 1987 to 70 percent in the first quarter of 2009, and declined somewhat to 65 percent by the end of 2009. In other words, homeowners as a group now have only 35 percent equity in their homes, compared with the nearly 70 percent that they had as recently as 1982. (Table 12-7)

Table 12-6. Household Assets, Liabilities, Net Worth, Financial Obligations, and Delinquency Rates

(Billions of dollars, except as noted; end of period; not seasonally adjusted, except as noted.)

Year and quarter	Financial assets of the household sector [1]													
	Total [2]	Checkable deposits and currency	Time and savings deposits	Money market fund shares	U.S. savings bonds	Other Treasury securities	Agency- and GSE-backed securities	Municipal securities	Corporate and foreign bonds	Mortgages	Corporate equities	Mutual fund shares	Security credit	Life insurance reserves
1950	736.1	57.2	67.1	0.0	49.6	16.9	0.1	5.5	6.0	17.6	129.8	3.3	1.0	55.0
1951	801.1	61.3	71.9	0.0	49.1	16.3	0.1	5.7	6.3	18.6	152.1	3.5	0.9	57.8
1952	830.1	63.4	79.3	0.0	49.2	18.2	0.0	11.0	6.0	19.2	151.0	3.9	0.7	60.7
1953	847.8	64.6	87.5	0.0	49.4	18.7	0.2	13.9	6.0	20.2	145.8	4.1	0.7	63.6
1954	926.1	66.3	96.6	0.0	50.0	16.1	0.1	16.0	4.9	21.4	198.8	6.1	1.0	66.3
1955	1 015.3	67.3	105.1	0.0	50.2	18.6	0.6	19.2	5.0	22.7	248.2	7.8	0.9	69.3
1956	1 083.9	69.1	114.4	0.0	50.1	20.1	1.0	21.9	6.1	24.3	271.0	9.0	0.9	72.7
1957	1 096.4	68.1	126.2	0.0	48.2	23.3	1.5	23.9	7.2	26.2	244.5	8.7	0.9	75.5
1958	1 224.5	70.5	139.9	0.0	47.7	20.9	0.8	24.6	7.9	28.8	322.3	13.2	1.2	78.5
1959	1 300.2	72.8	151.1	0.0	45.9	25.7	2.3	28.4	8.2	30.7	357.3	15.8	1.0	82.0
1960	1 348.4	74.5	163.0	0.0	45.6	26.6	1.0	31.0	10.6	33.5	359.8	17.0	1.1	85.2
1961	1 492.6	73.4	181.1	0.0	46.4	25.5	0.6	32.5	10.8	36.8	443.2	22.9	1.2	88.6
1962	1 534.6	73.0	206.9	0.0	47.0	26.8	0.2	32.1	10.2	39.0	431.2	20.9	1.2	92.4
1963	1 633.1	77.7	232.9	0.0	48.1	24.7	0.0	32.1	10.1	40.5	469.9	24.8	1.2	96.6
1964	1 787.4	80.4	258.8	0.0	49.1	24.5	0.2	34.9	10.3	42.0	544.1	28.4	1.7	101.1
1965	1 953.7	87.0	286.3	0.0	49.7	25.1	1.1	36.5	10.6	42.6	616.1	34.4	2.5	105.9
1966	1 976.3	89.4	305.0	0.0	50.2	28.8	5.9	41.2	11.1	44.6	548.3	33.9	2.7	110.6
1967	2 226.3	99.9	339.9	0.0	51.2	27.8	6.3	38.2	15.1	46.5	682.1	43.0	4.9	115.5
1968	2 490.3	109.2	370.2	0.0	51.9	29.9	6.1	36.5	18.0	49.0	815.3	49.5	7.0	120.3
1969	2 435.2	107.7	379.4	0.0	51.8	41.4	11.3	47.2	22.0	49.1	667.4	45.6	5.2	125.4
1970	2 526.7	114.9	420.9	0.0	52.1	31.0	15.9	47.1	29.7	50.0	650.2	44.5	4.4	130.7
1971	2 812.8	128.3	485.8	0.0	54.4	19.8	14.6	46.0	37.4	47.3	743.7	53.0	4.9	137.1
1972	3 220.2	139.9	557.2	0.0	57.7	19.7	8.9	47.7	38.5	48.2	921.4	56.4	5.0	143.9
1973	3 228.1	147.7	618.7	0.0	60.4	28.1	8.3	55.1	41.5	47.2	693.9	43.7	4.9	151.3
1974	3 203.0	152.5	673.7	2.4	63.3	32.9	13.7	62.2	54.4	50.5	445.0	31.8	3.9	158.4
1975	3 664.3	153.3	751.3	3.7	67.4	44.4	7.6	66.8	64.3	50.4	584.6	38.7	4.5	168.6
1976	4 149.3	163.8	852.5	3.4	72.0	30.7	11.7	72.9	74.3	52.8	731.6	41.4	5.7	177.8
1977	4 427.8	178.3	955.2	3.2	76.8	27.8	8.4	78.8	79.8	55.3	631.3	40.4	5.7	187.8
1978	4 958.6	192.9	1 054.2	8.9	80.7	29.6	9.9	104.2	73.6	62.4	640.0	41.1	8.5	199.4
1979	5 684.5	211.7	1 124.1	39.5	79.9	76.0	12.5	123.6	66.6	71.6	768.1	44.8	10.4	210.3
1980	6 561.3	227.2	1 242.6	64.4	72.5	101.3	18.6	130.1	59.0	87.2	1 010.4	52.1	16.2	220.6
1981	6 952.8	271.0	1 311.3	154.6	68.2	100.6	14.2	160.3	60.0	101.4	905.2	52.6	14.7	230.1
1982	7 540.5	286.7	1 417.7	188.1	68.3	117.4	13.4	201.1	53.0	110.9	966.3	65.1	17.8	238.0
1983	8 316.0	294.1	1 631.6	154.7	71.5	161.3	14.5	246.7	57.0	111.2	1 088.6	98.0	20.6	246.7
1984	8 826.9	308.6	1 857.5	199.2	74.5	205.9	27.7	290.4	44.7	102.5	1 008.7	117.5	21.6	252.8
1985	9 963.6	323.7	1 989.5	204.6	79.8	206.0	23.4	395.1	94.7	115.5	1 229.5	213.8	35.1	264.3
1986	11 081.7	439.6	2 079.5	243.4	93.3	181.1	23.3	410.9	127.8	111.9	1 494.0	378.7	44.0	282.6
1987	11 738.4	443.2	2 200.9	264.6	101.1	210.8	32.1	516.6	144.6	119.5	1 462.6	424.5	39.1	309.5
1988	12 873.1	441.4	2 380.0	282.7	109.6	288.1	52.4	586.0	135.1	121.8	1 757.1	439.1	40.9	335.7
1989	14 198.4	443.5	2 459.1	360.9	117.7	281.3	74.8	613.3	178.1	130.7	2 147.5	513.0	53.2	365.3
1990	14 570.2	432.8	2 489.6	390.6	126.2	382.4	117.3	647.7	237.6	140.9	1 961.4	511.5	62.4	391.7
1991	16 123.6	484.8	2 411.4	407.7	138.1	401.4	115.5	701.8	270.9	142.7	2 759.2	645.0	87.0	418.6
1992	16 967.1	596.1	2 303.7	365.5	157.3	475.0	114.4	672.2	283.2	136.8	3 094.2	799.4	76.2	447.7
1993	18 242.8	644.5	2 190.9	363.5	171.9	506.1	58.3	640.8	320.6	129.4	3 437.0	1 098.0	102.3	484.8
1994	18 918.4	614.5	2 164.2	373.1	179.9	695.5	187.6	594.1	359.4	120.5	3 294.2	1 096.6	109.0	520.3
1995	21 520.3	561.9	2 299.7	472.4	185.0	648.6	216.4	533.4	466.5	113.3	4 434.2	1 253.0	127.6	566.2
1996	23 416.0	494.7	2 440.7	527.9	187.0	707.2	332.8	493.0	514.6	105.8	4 712.2	1 561.5	162.9	610.6
1997	26 726.4	448.1	2 577.3	602.3	186.5	616.6	389.7	497.6	526.9	98.7	6 144.1	1 948.8	215.5	665.0
1998	30 200.7	463.8	2 673.0	706.6	186.6	552.8	441.7	498.7	590.5	94.3	7 648.7	2 351.8	276.7	718.3
1999	34 773.9	417.7	2 775.0	816.1	186.4	628.0	541.8	528.1	503.0	101.6	10 049.8	2 894.9	323.9	783.9
2000	33 401.8	335.1	3 032.9	959.8	184.8	400.1	594.0	531.2	552.0	103.4	8 204.6	2 704.2	412.4	819.1
2001	32 165.5	407.3	3 306.7	1 113.2	190.3	253.4	407.3	580.8	731.2	108.7	6 783.5	2 614.6	454.3	880.0
2002	30 230.9	414.5	3 617.1	1 071.7	194.9	90.4	247.6	678.4	1 094.4	116.6	5 121.4	2 218.4	412.7	920.9
2003	35 305.7	399.1	3 937.9	960.2	203.8	235.0	371.0	703.7	1 026.3	120.9	6 749.9	2 903.4	475.4	1 013.2
2004	39 262.9	359.8	4 426.8	904.1	204.4	327.8	390.0	742.4	1 141.7	131.3	7 483.9	3 417.4	578.3	1 060.4
2005	43 348.5	232.2	4 913.9	949.2	205.1	302.5	488.2	820.9	1 299.5	139.4	7 993.0	3 839.3	575.3	1 082.6
2006	48 133.6	189.2	5 400.4	1 114.5	202.4	230.9	402.6	871.8	1 522.7	122.1	9 493.5	4 387.6	655.7	1 163.7
2007	50 758.5	110.0	5 888.5	1 346.7	196.4	61.5	682.2	896.8	1 988.1	110.5	5 881.0	3 444.9	742.7	1 179.8
2008	41 707.2	211.2	6 049.7	1 580.0	194.0	69.9	701.1	936.8	1 988.1	110.5	7 698.4	4 416.6	668.1	1 249.7
2009	45 114.6	251.1	6 129.7	1 319.8	191.2	604.0	35.0	997.8	2 235.9	102.6	7 698.4	4 416.6	668.1	1 249.7
2007														
1st quarter	49 202.7	197.3	5 610.1	1 105.5	200.3	229.6	450.2	887.5	1 640.2	118.4	9 843.2	4 562.5	690.1	1 172.7
2nd quarter	50 624.8	149.3	5 653.7	1 159.2	198.6	175.8	517.7	912.8	1 553.6	114.3	10 169.7	4 843.0	745.3	1 191.1
3rd quarter	51 312.8	68.9	5 780.6	1 239.7	197.1	206.1	632.2	900.8	1 737.4	111.5	10 125.1	4 949.9	757.8	1 199.6
4th quarter	50 758.5	110.0	5 888.5	1 346.7	196.4	61.5	682.2	896.8	2 011.1	109.1	9 465.0	4 832.0	866.4	1 201.5
2008														
1st quarter	48 969.2	8.0	6 051.8	1 457.9	195.3	136.8	641.6	883.6	1 977.7	107.2	8 776.5	4 575.2	984.5	1 187.2
2nd quarter	48 259.0	23.3	5 953.6	1 393.6	194.9	190.1	659.0	894.4	1 974.7	114.5	8 462.4	4 663.9	992.1	1 196.4
3rd quarter	46 094.7	-18.7	6 112.6	1 445.2	194.2	234.4	829.1	909.7	1 899.9	112.3	7 436.5	4 107.5	998.6	1 197.7
4th quarter	41 707.2	211.2	6 049.7	1 580.0	194.0	69.9	701.1	936.8	1 988.1	110.5	5 881.0	3 444.9	742.7	1 179.8
2009														
1st quarter	40 207.8	200.3	6 100.7	1 547.1	193.9	374.8	486.1	946.7	2 366.0	108.9	5 162.1	3 264.7	666.9	1 181.1
2nd quarter	41 963.3	262.5	6 037.4	1 474.6	193.5	390.8	190.1	964.5	2 315.1	107.1	6 242.9	3 728.2	658.2	1 211.2
3rd quarter	44 437.8	222.8	6 049.4	1 347.6	192.4	543.1	185.0	971.4	2 279.8	104.8	7 412.5	4 168.4	672.6	1 242.9
4th quarter	45 114.6	251.1	6 129.7	1 319.8	191.2	604.0	35.0	997.8	2 235.9	102.6	7 698.4	4 416.6	668.1	1 249.7

[1]Includes nonprofit organizations.
[2]Includes components not shown separately.

Table 12-6. Household Assets, Liabilities, Net Worth, Financial Obligations, and Delinquency Rates —Continued

(Billions of dollars, except as noted; end of period; not seasonally adjusted, except as noted.)

Year and quarter	Financial assets of the household sector [1] —Continued		Tangible assets of the household sector		Debt as a percent of total assets [1]	Total liabilities [1]	Net worth [1]	Ratios to disposable personal income (percent, seasonally adjusted)				Consumer credit card accounts held at banks (percent, seasonally adjusted)	
	Pension fund reserves	Equity in non-corporate business	Total [1]	Household real estate [3]				Household debt service	Household financial obligations			Delinquency rate	Charge-off rate
									Total	Home-owners	Renters		
1950	23.2	294.6	387.2	243.3	6.5	76.3	1 046.9	...	...	...	...	...	...
1951	26.8	320.6	430.7	270.9	6.6	85.3	1 146.6	...	...	...	...	...	...
1952	33.5	322.3	463.8	294.8	7.3	97.6	1 196.2	...	...	...	...	...	...
1953	38.5	322.1	493.2	315.1	7.9	110.4	1 230.6	...	...	...	...	...	...
1954	43.9	325.8	520.7	337.6	8.1	122.6	1 324.1	...	...	...	...	...	...
1955	52.0	334.9	565.3	367.4	8.7	143.9	1 436.7	...	...	...	...	...	...
1956	58.2	351.2	607.8	394.3	9.0	159.2	1 532.6	...	...	...	...	...	...
1957	64.6	363.1	643.4	417.2	9.5	171.6	1 568.3	...	...	...	...	...	...
1958	74.9	378.0	669.9	438.4	9.3	183.6	1 710.8	...	...	...	...	...	...
1959	85.0	378.7	705.4	463.6	9.9	206.1	1 799.5	...	...	...	...	...	...
1960	93.9	388.6	737.1	486.9	10.3	223.8	1 861.7	...	...	...	...	...	...
1961	107.2	405.2	769.1	511.1	10.3	241.9	2 019.8	...	...	...	...	...	...
1962	113.7	421.4	802.9	533.2	10.9	264.0	2 073.4	...	...	...	...	...	...
1963	128.0	425.9	838.3	553.2	11.4	292.9	2 178.5	...	...	...	...	...	...
1964	144.8	444.9	883.1	579.8	11.6	322.1	2 348.5	...	...	...	...	...	...
1965	162.0	470.9	929.7	605.6	11.7	351.5	2 531.8	...	...	...	...	...	...
1966	172.5	504.1	1 004.5	649.0	12.1	374.7	2 606.1	...	...	...	...	...	...
1967	195.6	528.6	1 072.7	685.7	11.5	397.8	2 901.2	...	...	...	...	...	...
1968	218.7	572.9	1 198.8	768.2	11.2	433.8	3 255.3	...	...	...	...	...	...
1969	230.9	606.4	1 306.2	832.4	11.8	461.4	3 280.0	...	...	...	...	...	...
1970	253.7	636.5	1 387.9	874.5	11.7	475.6	3 439.0	...	...	...	...	...	...
1971	293.5	702.3	1 514.8	957.2	11.5	521.6	3 806.0	...	...	...	...	...	...
1972	349.3	782.9	1 710.9	1 098.6	11.3	582.6	4 348.4	...	...	...	...	...	...
1973	358.5	917.7	1 939.3	1 251.4	12.1	649.1	4 518.2	...	...	...	...	...	...
1974	367.5	1 028.3	2 059.7	1 261.1	12.9	704.8	4 557.8	...	...	...	...	...	...
1975	467.0	1 127.9	2 281.5	1 413.7	12.4	760.9	5 184.9	...	...	...	...	...	...
1976	534.5	1 257.4	2 537.6	1 590.0	12.2	850.5	5 836.4	...	...	...	...	...	...
1977	589.9	1 420.3	2 941.3	1 886.8	12.8	981.6	6 387.4	...	...	...	...	...	...
1978	691.4	1 651.1	3 401.6	2 210.9	13.2	1 144.7	7 215.5	...	...	...	...	...	...
1979	801.1	1 916.3	3 954.1	2 603.3	13.2	1 317.8	8 320.8	...	...	...	...	...	...
1980	969.7	2 157.8	4 441.6	2 943.2	12.7	1 447.5	9 555.4	10.6	15.5	13.4	23.8	...	...
1981	1 063.5	2 315.6	4 906.0	3 293.0	12.7	1 559.7	10 299.0	10.7	15.7	13.6	24.3	...	...
1982	1 289.1	2 360.2	5 136.2	3 447.4	12.4	1 633.3	11 043.3	10.6	15.7	13.9	22.4	...	...
1983	1 535.8	2 420.6	5 398.2	3 606.7	12.6	1 800.3	11 913.9	10.7	15.7	13.8	22.9	...	...
1984	1 707.5	2 419.8	6 052.9	4 126.7	13.1	2 011.4	12 868.4	11.1	16.2	14.1	24.1	...	...
1985	2 088.6	2 489.2	6 769.1	4 699.8	13.6	2 368.0	14 364.7	12.0	17.4	15.2	26.1	...	2.98
1986	2 326.8	2 612.2	7 405.2	5 149.6	13.7	2 635.2	15 851.7	12.4	17.9	15.7	26.9	...	3.42
1987	2 504.8	2 703.6	8 023.8	5 599.9	13.9	2 843.3	16 919.0	12.1	17.6	15.4	26.5	...	3.26
1988	2 738.3	2 843.8	8 742.8	6 119.4	14.1	3 143.9	18 472.0	11.9	17.2	15.2	25.6	...	3.22
1989	3 169.0	2 957.4	9 439.4	6 641.1	14.0	3 435.4	20 202.4	12.1	17.5	15.6	25.0	...	3.27
1990	3 310.3	3 006.7	9 717.8	6 802.2	14.7	3 702.9	20 585.1	12.0	17.5	15.6	24.9	...	3.84
1991	3 830.6	2 971.3	9 935.4	6 981.3	14.5	3 916.7	22 142.3	11.5	17.0	15.2	23.8	5.30	4.66
1992	4 139.4	2 955.0	10 244.8	7 257.9	14.6	4 121.7	23 090.1	10.8	16.2	14.2	23.5	4.69	4.54
1993	4 617.5	3 100.4	10 607.3	7 505.7	14.6	4 390.8	24 459.3	10.7	16.1	14.0	23.9	3.90	3.35
1994	4 898.3	3 311.9	11 040.5	7 770.4	15.1	4 716.9	25 242.0	11.1	16.4	14.3	25.0	3.27	3.07
1995	5 725.1	3 493.4	11 464.5	8 054.3	14.7	5 038.4	27 946.3	11.7	17.1	14.8	26.7	3.93	3.93
1996	6 386.7	3 728.3	11 993.2	8 431.6	14.6	5 398.8	30 010.3	11.9	17.2	15.0	27.0	4.59	4.63
1997	7 360.7	3 982.5	12 626.3	8 864.7	13.9	5 745.4	33 607.2	11.9	17.2	15.0	27.1	4.78	5.48
1998	8 265.4	4 252.8	13 692.3	9 691.9	13.4	6 200.1	37 692.8	11.8	17.0	14.7	28.1	4.70	5.14
1999	9 264.1	4 460.8	14 887.6	10 643.3	12.9	6 774.2	42 887.2	12.1	17.3	14.9	29.2	4.51	4.45
2000	9 171.3	4 870.8	16 704.3	12 136.6	13.9	7 376.7	42 729.5	12.6	17.7	15.1	30.4	4.56	4.49
2001	8 764.3	5 032.7	18 320.8	13 572.9	15.2	8 007.6	42 478.7	13.1	18.3	15.7	31.0	4.69	6.22
2002	8 189.4	5 262.6	19 918.4	14 919.4	16.6	8 804.4	41 344.8	13.2	18.2	16.0	28.9	4.85	5.42
2003	9 718.9	5 852.3	21 666.6	16 394.8	16.7	9 847.6	47 124.7	13.2	17.9	16.2	26.6	4.44	5.90
2004	10 635.5	6 758.2	24 631.1	18 981.9	16.5	11 008.2	52 885.8	13.3	17.9	16.4	25.4	4.04	4.57
2005	11 373.7	8 358.0	28 388.4	22 084.5	16.3	12 157.4	59 579.5	13.8	18.4	17.1	25.2	3.54	5.99
2006	12 696.2	8 843.4	29 735.3	22 943.5	16.6	13 404.5	64 464.4	13.9	18.6	17.3	25.4	3.96	4.03
2007	13 375.9	8 797.5	28 036.9	20 978.0	17.4	14 311.7	64 483.7	13.9	18.8	17.5	25.0	4.62	4.20
2008	10 431.9	7 325.5	23 891.4	17 039.2	21.0	14 195.0	51 403.5	13.6	18.6	17.2	25.1	5.68	6.37
2009	11 806.2	6 538.2	23 062.9	16 575.1	19.9	14 001.3	54 176.2	12.6	17.5	16.1	24.4	6.40	9.50
2007													
1st quarter	12 857.4	8 784.2	29 374.6	22 490.8	16.6	13 568.4	65 008.9	13.8	18.7	17.4	25.1	3.99	3.88
2nd quarter	13 388.3	8 958.9	29 199.3	22 164.2	16.7	13 875.4	65 948.6	13.9	18.7	17.4	25.3	3.99	3.80
3rd quarter	13 538.1	8 969.8	28 652.3	21 591.7	16.9	14 082.0	65 883.1	13.9	18.8	17.5	25.2	4.40	4.13
4th quarter	13 375.9	8 797.5	28 036.9	20 978.0	17.4	14 311.7	64 483.7	13.9	18.8	17.5	25.0	4.62	4.20
2008													
1st quarter	12 564.6	8 507.3	27 007.1	19 938.7	18.2	14 414.7	61 561.6	13.9	18.9	17.6	25.1	4.78	4.63
2nd quarter	12 471.0	8 190.0	26 073.2	19 068.5	18.6	14 355.6	59 976.6	13.5	18.3	17.0	24.5	4.85	5.41
3rd quarter	11 824.2	7 949.9	25 178.0	18 165.9	19.4	14 499.7	56 772.9	13.6	18.5	17.2	25.0	4.80	5.68
4th quarter	10 431.9	7 325.5	23 891.4	17 039.2	21.0	14 195.0	51 403.5	13.6	18.6	17.2	25.1	5.68	6.37
2009													
1st quarter	9 896.2	6 859.4	22 389.8	15 685.7	21.9	14 075.6	48 522.0	13.5	18.4	17.0	25.2	6.54	7.56
2nd quarter	10 617.6	6 718.7	22 789.5	16 189.1	21.1	14 041.8	50 711.0	13.0	18.0	16.6	24.6	6.68	9.68
3rd quarter	11 446.1	6 740.3	23 082.5	16 537.2	20.1	14 026.9	53 493.5	12.9	17.9	16.4	24.7	6.49	10.17
4th quarter	11 806.2	6 538.2	23 062.9	16 575.1	19.9	14 001.3	54 176.2	12.6	17.5	16.1	24.4	6.40	9.50

[1]Includes nonprofit organizations.
[3]Excludes nonprofit organizations.
... = Not available.

Table 12-7. Mortgage Debt Outstanding

(Billions of dollars, except as noted; end of period; not seasonally adjusted.)

Year and quarter	Total	By type of property					By type of holder							
		Home		Multi-family residences	Commercial	Farm	Commercial banks	Savings institutions	Life insurance companies	Federal and related agencies	Mortgage pools or trusts			Other
		Billions of dollars	Percent of value of real estate								Total 1	Federally related agencies	ABS issuers	
1950	73	45	18	9	12	6	14	22	16	3	0	0	0	19
1951	83	52	19	11	13	7	15	25	19	3	0	0	0	20
1952	92	58	20	11	14	7	16	29	21	4	0	0	0	21
1953	101	66	21	12	16	8	17	34	23	5	0	0	0	22
1954	114	75	22	13	17	8	19	40	26	5	0	0	0	24
1955	130	88	24	13	19	9	21	48	29	5	0	0	0	26
1956	144	99	25	14	22	10	23	55	33	6	0	0	0	28
1957	157	107	26	15	24	10	23	60	35	7	0	0	0	30
1958	172	117	27	17	27	11	26	68	37	8	0	0	0	34
1959	191	130	28	19	30	12	28	77	39	10	0	0	0	37
1960	208	141	29	21	33	13	29	86	42	11	0	0	0	40
1961	229	154	30	24	37	14	30	96	44	12	0	0	0	46
1962	252	168	32	27	42	15	34	109	47	12	0	0	0	49
1963	279	185	33	30	47	17	39	125	51	11	1	1	0	53
1964	307	202	35	35	51	19	44	140	55	12	1	1	0	56
1965	334	219	36	38	56	21	50	153	60	13	1	1	0	59
1966	358	233	36	41	61	23	54	160	65	16	1	1	0	61
1967	382	246	36	45	66	25	59	170	68	19	2	2	0	65
1968	411	263	34	48	73	27	65	182	70	23	3	3	0	69
1969	440	279	33	53	79	29	71	194	72	28	3	3	0	72
1970	469	292	33	60	87	30	73	205	74	34	5	5	0	78
1971	518	318	33	70	97	32	83	231	75	37	10	10	0	82
1972	590	357	33	83	114	35	99	268	77	40	14	14	0	91
1973	666	400	32	93	134	40	119	300	81	47	18	18	0	101
1974	728	435	35	100	148	45	132	321	86	61	21	21	0	107
1975	786	474	34	101	161	50	136	351	89	73	29	29	0	108
1976	870	535	34	106	174	55	151	398	92	76	41	41	0	113
1977	999	628	33	114	193	64	179	459	97	84	57	57	0	123
1978	1 151	738	33	125	215	73	214	517	106	100	70	70	0	143
1979	1 317	856	33	135	239	87	245	565	118	121	95	95	0	172
1980	1 458	958	33	143	260	97	263	594	131	143	114	114	0	213
1981	1 579	1 030	31	142	300	107	284	612	138	160	129	129	0	256
1982	1 661	1 070	31	146	334	111	301	576	142	177	179	179	0	286
1983	1 850	1 186	33	161	389	114	331	627	151	188	245	245	0	309
1984	2 092	1 321	32	186	472	112	381	710	157	202	300	289	11	342
1985	2 368	1 526	32	206	542	94	431	766	172	213	392	368	25	394
1986	2 655	1 729	34	239	602	84	505	785	194	202	549	532	18	420
1987	2 956	1 928	34	258	694	76	595	824	212	189	701	669	31	435
1988	3 273	2 162	35	275	766	71	677	888	233	192	786	745	40	497
1989	3 526	2 369	36	287	801	69	771	873	254	198	922	870	53	509
1990	3 781	2 606	38	287	820	68	849	802	268	239	1 086	1 020	66	537
1991	3 932	2 774	40	284	806	67	881	705	260	266	1 270	1 156	113	551
1992	4 043	2 942	41	271	763	68	901	628	242	286	1 440	1 272	168	547
1993	4 175	3 101	41	268	738	68	948	598	224	326	1 561	1 357	204	517
1994	4 339	3 278	42	268	723	70	1 013	596	216	316	1 697	1 472	225	502
1995	4 525	3 445	43	274	734	72	1 090	597	213	308	1 812	1 571	242	505
1996	4 793	3 668	44	286	764	74	1 145	628	208	294	1 989	1 712	278	527
1997	5 105	3 903	44	298	826	79	1 245	632	207	285	2 166	1 826	339	570
1998	5 590	4 259	44	331	916	83	1 337	644	214	292	2 487	2 019	468	617
1999	6 196	4 683	44	372	1 053	87	1 495	668	231	320	2 832	2 294	539	649
2000	6 753	5 107	42	402	1 160	85	1 660	723	236	340	3 098	2 493	604	696
2001	7 461	5 659	42	444	1 269	89	1 790	758	243	372	3 557	2 832	725	741
2002	8 361	6 413	43	483	1 370	95	2 058	781	250	432	3 995	3 159	836	845
2003	9 365	7 222	44	563	1 497	83	2 256	871	261	694	4 341	3 331	1 009	943
2004	10 628	8 247	43	616	1 669	96	2 596	1 057	273	703	4 818	3 375	1 444	1 180
2005	12 067	9 356	42	687	1 919	105	2 958	1 153	285	665	5 684	3 542	2 131	1 321
2006	13 464	10 416	45	742	2 199	108	3 403	1 077	304	687	6 603	3 837	2 766	1 390
2007	14 533	11 111	53	843	2 466	113	3 644	1 094	326	725	7 411	4 464	2 948	1 332
2008	14 612	11 000	65	903	2 579	130	3 841	861	342	797	7 554	4 961	2 593	1 216
2009	14 307	10 786	65	897	2 485	138	3 819	633	330	805	7 599	5 383	2 216	1 121
2007														
1st quarter	13 735	10 625	47	760	2 241	109	3 386	1 116	306	693	6 848	3 952	2 896	1 385
2nd quarter	14 051	10 834	49	784	2 323	110	3 472	1 112	312	701	7 086	4 073	3 012	1 368
3rd quarter	14 313	10 984	51	810	2 407	112	3 525	1 146	317	711	7 250	4 242	3 008	1 362
4th quarter	14 533	11 111	53	843	2 466	113	3 644	1 094	326	725	7 411	4 464	2 948	1 332
2008														
1st quarter	14 667	11 179	56	861	2 510	117	3 685	1 112	331	742	7 482	4 601	2 880	1 316
2nd quarter	14 704	11 158	59	879	2 547	121	3 661	1 116	336	757	7 544	4 759	2 784	1 290
3rd quarter	14 683	11 103	61	895	2 559	126	3 853	884	341	758	7 585	4 892	2 693	1 261
4th quarter	14 612	11 000	65	903	2 579	130	3 841	861	342	797	7 554	4 961	2 593	1 216
2009														
1st quarter	14 597	10 987	70	906	2 572	132	3 853	850	339	816	7 544	5 042	2 502	1 196
2nd quarter	14 538	10 936	68	910	2 558	134	3 898	752	335	807	7 573	5 173	2 400	1 173
3rd quarter	14 421	10 844	66	908	2 532	136	3 795	726	332	811	7 607	5 300	2 308	1 149
4th quarter	14 307	10 786	65	897	2 485	138	3 819	633	330	805	7 599	5 383	2 216	1 121

1Outstanding principal balances of mortgage-backed securities issued or guaranteed by the holder indicated.

Table 12-8. Consumer Credit

(Outstanding at end of period, billions of dollars.)

Year and month	Seasonally adjusted			Not seasonally adjusted							
	Total	By major credit type		Total	By major holder						
		Revolving	Non-revolving		Commercial banks	Finance companies [1]	Credit unions	Federal government [1]	Savings institutions	Nonfinancial businesses	Securitized pools [2]
1960	60.0	. . .	60.0	61.2	26.4	15.4	3.4	0.0	2.4	13.5	0.0
1961	62.2	. . .	62.2	63.4	27.9	15.5	3.6	0.0	2.9	13.6	0.0
1962	68.1	. . .	68.1	69.3	30.6	17.3	4.1	0.0	3.0	14.3	0.0
1963	76.6	. . .	76.6	77.9	34.7	19.6	4.5	0.0	3.6	15.5	0.0
1964	86.0	. . .	86.0	87.4	39.8	21.6	5.4	0.0	3.7	16.8	0.0
1965	96.0	. . .	96.0	97.5	45.2	23.9	6.5	0.0	3.9	18.1	0.0
1966	101.8	. . .	101.8	103.4	48.2	24.8	7.5	0.0	4.0	19.0	0.0
1967	106.8	. . .	106.8	108.6	51.7	24.6	8.3	0.0	4.1	19.9	0.0
1968	117.4	2.0	115.4	119.3	58.5	26.1	9.7	0.0	4.3	20.8	0.0
1969	127.2	3.6	123.6	129.2	63.4	27.8	11.7	0.0	4.4	21.9	0.0
1970	131.6	5.0	126.6	133.7	65.6	27.6	13.0	0.0	4.4	23.0	0.0
1971	146.9	8.2	138.7	149.2	74.3	29.2	14.8	0.0	4.7	26.2	0.0
1972	166.2	9.4	156.8	168.8	87.0	31.9	17.0	0.0	5.1	27.8	0.0
1973	190.1	11.3	178.7	193.0	99.6	35.4	19.6	0.0	8.5	29.8	0.0
1974	198.9	13.2	185.7	201.9	103.0	36.1	21.9	0.0	9.1	31.8	0.0
1975	204.0	14.5	189.5	207.0	106.1	32.6	25.7	0.0	10.1	32.6	0.0
1976	225.7	16.5	209.2	229.0	118.0	33.7	31.2	0.0	10.8	35.2	0.0
1977	260.6	37.4	223.1	264.9	140.3	37.3	37.6	0.5	11.8	37.4	0.0
1978	306.1	45.7	260.4	311.3	166.5	44.4	45.2	0.9	13.1	41.2	0.0
1979	348.6	53.6	295.0	354.6	185.7	55.4	47.4	1.5	20.0	44.6	0.0
1980	351.9	55.0	297.0	358.0	180.2	62.2	44.1	2.6	22.7	46.2	0.0
1981	371.3	60.9	310.4	377.9	184.2	70.1	46.7	4.8	24.0	48.1	0.0
1982	389.8	66.3	323.5	396.7	190.9	75.3	48.8	6.4	26.6	48.7	0.0
1983	437.1	79.0	358.0	444.9	213.7	83.3	56.1	4.6	31.5	55.7	0.0
1984	517.3	100.4	416.9	526.6	258.8	89.9	67.9	5.6	44.2	60.2	0.0
1985	599.7	124.5	475.2	610.6	297.2	111.7	74.0	6.8	57.6	63.3	0.0
1986	654.8	141.1	513.7	666.4	320.2	134.0	77.1	8.2	62.9	64.0	0.0
1987	686.3	160.9	525.5	698.6	334.1	140.0	81.0	10.0	65.3	68.1	0.0
1988	731.9	184.6	547.3	745.2	360.8	144.7	88.3	13.2	66.8	71.4	0.0
1989	794.6	211.2	583.4	809.3	383.3	138.9	91.7	16.0	62.5	69.6	47.3
1990	808.2	238.6	569.6	824.4	382.0	133.4	91.6	19.2	49.6	71.9	76.7
1991	798.0	263.8	534.3	815.6	370.2	121.6	90.3	21.1	42.2	67.3	103.0
1992	806.1	278.4	527.7	824.8	362.9	118.1	91.7	24.2	37.4	70.3	120.3
1993	865.7	309.9	555.7	886.2	395.7	116.1	101.6	27.2	37.9	77.2	130.5
1994	997.3	365.6	631.7	1 021.2	458.8	134.4	119.6	37.2	38.5	86.6	146.1
1995	1 140.7	443.9	696.8	1 168.2	502.3	152.1	131.9	43.5	40.1	85.1	213.1
1996	1 253.4	507.5	745.9	1 273.9	527.5	154.9	144.1	51.4	44.7	77.7	273.5
1997	1 324.8	540.0	784.8	1 344.2	515.1	167.5	152.4	57.2	47.2	84.4	320.5
1998	1 421.0	581.4	839.6	1 441.3	512.0	183.3	155.4	64.9	52.4	79.3	393.9
1999	1 531.1	610.7	920.4	1 553.6	507.8	201.6	167.9	81.8	61.7	76.1	456.7
2000	1 716.5	683.5	1 033.0	1 741.3	551.1	234.4	184.4	96.7	64.8	81.5	528.4
2001	1 866.2	715.2	1 151.0	1 891.8	568.4	280.0	189.6	111.9	71.1	73.1	597.8
2002	1 970.8	750.9	1 219.9	1 997.0	602.6	307.5	195.7	117.3	68.7	74.8	630.4
2003	2 076.6	768.2	1 308.4	2 102.9	669.4	393.0	205.9	102.9	77.9	59.1	594.8
2004	2 192.1	799.8	1 392.3	2 220.1	704.3	492.3	215.4	86.1	91.3	59.2	571.5
2005	2 291.7	830.5	1 461.2	2 320.6	707.0	516.5	228.6	89.8	109.1	59.6	609.9
2006	2 385.7	872.2	1 513.5	2 416.0	741.2	534.4	234.5	91.7	95.5	57.6	661.1
2007	2 522.8	942.9	1 579.9	2 555.3	804.1	584.1	235.7	98.4	90.8	58.6	683.7
2008	2 561.1	958.1	1 602.9	2 594.1	878.6	575.8	236.2	111.0	86.3	59.8	646.4
2009	2 448.8	866.1	1 582.7	2 478.8	855.4	487.8	237.2	186.0	77.5	57.2	577.7
2008											
January	2 531.1	949.1	1 582.0	2 553.4	808.7	579.5	233.9	102.4	89.7	57.0	682.3
February	2 540.3	953.6	1 586.7	2 537.5	800.0	577.0	232.0	103.1	88.6	55.9	681.0
March	2 552.1	959.3	1 592.8	2 533.5	796.3	580.7	230.1	103.5	87.5	55.3	680.0
April	2 563.3	962.2	1 601.1	2 545.0	807.4	583.9	231.1	103.9	88.3	55.2	675.2
May	2 563.9	961.7	1 602.3	2 547.7	807.9	584.5	231.7	104.2	89.2	55.5	674.8
June	2 574.7	967.5	1 607.1	2 556.0	813.0	581.8	231.1	104.6	90.0	55.5	680.0
July	2 582.0	974.0	1 608.0	2 566.7	820.3	586.5	233.5	105.3	89.7	55.7	675.6
August	2 576.6	975.6	1 601.1	2 581.4	832.9	592.4	235.5	106.5	89.4	56.2	668.4
September	2 578.9	975.7	1 603.2	2 588.6	841.1	596.3	236.1	106.9	79.3	56.2	669.7
October	2 575.6	971.5	1 604.1	2 580.7	850.7	585.8	236.6	108.6	82.5	56.4	660.2
November	2 565.2	964.7	1 600.6	2 579.8	863.2	580.7	236.9	109.6	83.1	57.3	649.0
December	2 561.1	958.1	1 602.9	2 594.1	878.6	575.8	236.2	111.0	86.3	59.8	646.4
2009											
January	2 563.7	956.3	1 607.4	2 586.3	893.4	556.2	236.5	118.0	84.2	58.3	639.7
February	2 550.7	943.6	1 607.1	2 547.9	879.1	548.4	235.1	119.8	82.2	56.7	626.7
March	2 536.3	935.1	1 601.1	2 517.9	850.7	546.8	233.3	122.7	80.0	55.0	629.3
April	2 521.6	926.8	1 594.8	2 503.8	843.8	540.1	233.2	125.9	78.7	54.4	627.5
May	2 514.6	917.4	1 597.1	2 498.7	853.4	532.5	234.0	128.8	77.3	54.5	618.2
June	2 506.1	912.6	1 593.5	2 487.9	837.8	526.5	234.6	135.4	75.9	53.8	623.8
July	2 497.8	911.9	1 585.9	2 483.2	832.5	522.3	237.4	139.1	76.6	53.6	621.6
August	2 495.3	903.8	1 591.5	2 500.2	840.4	526.3	240.9	148.0	77.4	53.8	613.4
September	2 486.9	895.9	1 591.0	2 496.7	832.7	520.7	240.3	157.8	78.1	53.0	614.1
October	2 479.7	889.2	1 590.5	2 485.0	837.3	500.4	237.9	182.3	77.9	53.3	595.8
November	2 456.3	875.5	1 580.8	2 470.0	847.5	490.9	237.0	183.7	77.7	54.4	578.7
December	2 448.8	866.1	1 582.7	2 478.8	855.4	487.8	237.2	186.0	77.5	57.2	577.7

[1]Student Loan Marketing Association (Sallie Mae) included in federal government sector until end of 2004, and in finance companies since then.
[2]Outstanding balances of pools upon which securities have been issued; these balances are no longer carried on the balance sheets of the loan originators.
. . . = Not available.

Table 12-9. Selected Interest Rates and Bond Yields

(Percent per annum; interest rates are nominal [not adjusted for inflation], except as noted.)

Year and month	Short-term rates								Inflation: percent change from year earlier in PCE chain-type price index excluding food and energy	Real federal funds rate (nominal rate minus inflation)	Interest rate swaps	
	Federal funds	Federal Reserve discount rate ¹	Eurodollar deposits, 1-month	U.S. Treasury bills, secondary market, 3-month	U.S. Treasury bills, secondary market, 6-month	Commercial paper, 3-month ²	CDs (secondary market), 3-month	Bank prime rate			1-year	30-year
1960	3.21	3.36	...	2.87	3.20	...	...	4.82	1.79	1.42	...	...
1961	1.95	3.53	...	2.35	2.59	...	...	4.50	1.25	0.70	...	...
1962	2.71	3.00	...	2.77	2.90	...	...	4.50	1.37	1.34	...	...
1963	3.18	3.00	...	3.16	3.26	...	...	4.50	1.30	1.88	...	...
1964	3.50	3.23	...	3.55	3.68	...	3.92	4.50	1.53	1.97	...	...
1965	4.07	3.55	...	3.95	4.05	...	4.36	4.54	1.26	2.81	...	...
1966	5.11	4.04	...	4.86	5.06	...	5.45	5.63	2.26	2.85	...	...
1967	4.22	4.50	...	4.29	4.61	...	4.99	5.63	3.06	1.16	...	...
1968	5.66	4.19	...	5.34	5.47	...	5.82	6.31	4.29	1.37	...	...
1969	8.21	5.17	...	6.67	6.86	...	7.23	7.96	4.69	3.52	...	...
1970	7.17	5.87	...	6.39	6.51	...	7.55	7.91	4.69	2.48	...	...
1971	4.67	5.95	6.40	4.33	4.52	5.25	5.00	5.73	4.71	-0.04	...	...
1972	4.44	4.88	5.00	4.06	4.47	4.66	4.66	5.25	3.23	1.21	...	...
1973	8.74	4.50	9.19	7.04	7.20	8.21	9.30	8.03	3.82	4.92	...	...
1974	10.51	6.45	10.79	7.85	7.95	10.05	10.29	10.81	7.93	2.58	...	...
1975	5.82	7.83	6.35	5.79	6.10	6.26	6.44	7.86	8.38	-2.56	...	...
1976	5.05	6.25	5.26	4.98	5.26	5.24	5.27	6.84	6.08	-1.03	...	...
1977	5.54	5.50	5.75	5.26	5.52	5.54	5.63	6.83	6.42	-0.88	...	...
1978	7.94	5.46	8.33	7.18	7.58	7.93	8.21	9.06	6.69	1.25	...	...
1979	11.20	7.46	11.66	10.05	10.04	10.95	11.20	12.67	7.28	3.92	...	...
1980	13.35	10.29	13.77	11.39	11.32	12.61	13.02	15.26	9.16	4.19	...	...
1981	16.39	11.77	16.72	14.04	13.81	15.34	15.93	18.87	8.74	7.65	...	...
1982	12.24	13.42	12.74	10.60	11.06	11.90	12.27	14.85	6.45	5.79	...	...
1983	9.09	11.01	9.38	8.62	8.74	8.88	9.07	10.79	5.18	3.91	...	...
1984	10.23	8.50	10.45	9.54	9.78	10.12	10.39	12.04	4.15	6.08	...	...
1985	8.10	8.80	8.12	7.47	7.65	7.95	8.04	9.93	3.79	4.31	...	...
1986	6.80	7.69	6.78	5.97	6.02	6.49	6.51	8.33	3.77	3.03	...	...
1987	6.66	6.32	6.88	5.78	6.03	6.82	6.87	8.21	3.80	2.86	...	...
1988	7.57	5.66	7.69	6.67	6.91	7.66	7.73	9.32	4.34	3.23	...	...
1989	9.21	6.20	9.16	8.11	8.03	8.99	9.09	10.87	4.13	5.08	...	...
1990	8.10	6.93	8.15	7.50	7.46	8.06	8.15	10.01	4.27	3.83	...	...
1991	5.69	6.98	5.81	5.38	5.44	5.87	5.83	8.46	3.89	1.80	...	...
1992	3.52	5.45	3.62	3.43	3.54	3.75	3.68	6.25	3.36	0.16	...	...
1993	3.02	3.25	3.07	3.00	3.12	3.22	3.17	6.00	2.37	0.65	...	...
1994	4.21	3.00	4.34	4.25	4.64	4.66	4.63	7.15	2.21	2.00	...	...
1995	5.83	3.60	5.86	5.49	5.56	5.93	5.92	8.83	2.30	3.53	...	...
1996	5.30	5.21	5.32	5.01	5.08	5.41	5.39	8.27	1.94	3.36	...	...
1997	5.46	5.02	5.52	5.06	5.18	5.49	5.62	8.44	1.92	3.54	...	...
1998	5.35	5.00	5.45	4.78	4.83	5.34	5.47	8.35	1.45	3.90	...	...
1999	4.97	4.92	5.15	4.64	4.75	5.18	5.33	8.00	1.49	3.48	...	...
2000	6.24	4.62	6.33	5.82	5.90	6.31	6.46	9.23	1.74	4.50	6.73	6.93
2001	3.88	5.73	3.81	3.40	3.34	3.65	3.71	6.91	1.79	2.09	3.87	6.20
2002	1.67	3.40	1.71	1.61	1.68	1.69	1.73	4.67	1.73	-0.06	2.21	5.80
2003	1.13	1.17	1.14	1.01	1.05	1.11	1.15	4.12	1.53	-0.40	1.36	5.24
2004	1.35	2.34	1.43	1.37	1.58	1.41	1.57	4.34	2.09	-0.74	2.13	5.38
2005	3.22	4.19	3.33	3.15	3.39	3.42	3.51	6.19	2.26	0.96	4.04	5.03
2006	4.97	5.96	5.09	4.73	4.81	5.10	5.16	7.96	2.29	2.68	5.33	5.44
2007	5.02	5.86	5.28	4.36	4.44	4.92	5.27	8.05	2.35	2.67	5.09	5.45
2008	1.92	2.39	3.03	1.37	1.62	2.13	2.97	5.09	2.40	-0.48	2.75	4.57
2009	0.16	0.50	0.61	0.15	0.28	0.26	0.55	3.25	1.54	-1.38	0.90	3.87
2008												
January	3.94	4.48	3.93	2.75	2.75	3.70	3.84	6.98	2.41	1.53	3.33	4.82
February	2.98	3.50	3.17	2.12	2.04	3.03	3.06	6.00	2.31	0.67	2.69	4.99
March	2.61	3.04	2.87	1.26	1.48	2.70	2.79	5.66	2.41	0.20	2.41	4.78
April	2.28	2.49	2.97	1.29	1.55	2.72	2.85	5.24	2.47	-0.19	2.71	4.80
May	1.98	2.25	2.63	1.73	1.82	2.61	2.66	5.00	2.56	-0.58	2.88	4.92
June	2.00	2.25	2.66	1.86	2.13	2.70	2.76	5.00	2.62	-0.62	3.22	5.12
July	2.01	2.25	2.65	1.63	1.93	2.72	2.79	5.00	2.68	-0.67	3.09	5.02
August	2.00	2.25	2.61	1.72	1.92	2.76	2.79	5.00	2.65	-0.65	3.03	4.95
September	1.81	2.25	4.01	1.13	1.61	2.91	3.59	5.00	2.53	-0.72	3.03	4.65
October	0.97	1.81	4.93	0.67	1.20	3.19	4.32	4.56	2.26	-1.29	2.86	4.30
November	0.39	1.25	2.08	0.19	0.73	1.54	2.36	4.00	2.05	-1.66	2.11	3.83
December	0.16	0.86	1.75	0.03	0.26	1.09	1.77	3.61	1.80	-1.64	1.62	2.69
2009												
January	0.15	0.50	0.89	0.13	0.30	1.10	1.02	3.25	1.74	-1.59	1.15	2.96
February	0.22	0.50	0.77	0.30	0.45	0.67	1.16	3.25	1.78	-1.56	1.33	3.31
March	0.18	0.50	0.98	0.21	0.42	0.62	1.07	3.25	1.67	-1.49	1.36	3.34
April	0.15	0.50	0.94	0.16	0.35	0.48	0.89	3.25	1.74	-1.59	1.19	3.41
May	0.18	0.50	0.71	0.18	0.30	0.37	0.57	3.25	1.61	-1.43	0.94	3.84
June	0.21	0.50	0.65	0.18	0.31	0.36	0.39	3.25	1.52	-1.31	0.95	4.34
July	0.16	0.50	0.56	0.18	0.27	0.33	0.35	3.25	1.34	-1.18	0.78	4.21
August	0.16	0.50	0.46	0.17	0.26	0.29	0.30	3.25	1.27	-1.11	0.77	4.28
September	0.15	0.50	0.40	0.12	0.21	0.23	0.25	3.25	1.22	-1.07	0.61	4.07
October	0.12	0.50	0.35	0.07	0.16	0.22	0.24	3.25	1.44	-1.32	0.62	4.08
November	0.12	0.50	0.30	0.05	0.15	0.19	0.21	3.25	1.51	-1.39	0.50	4.19
December	0.12	0.50	0.32	0.05	0.17	0.20	0.22	3.25	1.60	-1.48	0.57	4.35

¹Federal Reserve Bank of New York. Through 2002, represents the rate for adjustment credit. Beginning in 2003, represents the rate for primary credit. See notes and definitions for more information.
²Prior to September 1997, this series represents both nonfinancial and financial commercial paper rates. Beginning September 1997, rates for financial companies only are shown. See notes and definitions for more information.
. . . = Not available.

Table 12-9. Selected Interest Rates and Bond Yields—*Continued*

(Percent per annum; interest rates are nominal [not adjusted for inflation], except as noted.)

Year and month	U.S. Treasury securities, constant maturities								Bond yields			Fixed-rate first mortgages
	Nominal yields					Inflation-indexed yields			Domestic corporate (Moody's)		State and local bonds (Bond Buyer)	
	1-year	5-year	10-year	20-year	30-year	5-year	20-year	Long-term average	Aaa	Baa		
1960	...	...	...	...	...	...	...	...	4.41	5.19	3.52	...
1961	...	...	...	...	...	...	...	...	4.35	5.08	3.45	...
1962	3.10	3.70	3.95	...	...	...	...	...	4.33	5.02	3.15	...
1963	3.36	3.83	4.00	...	...	...	...	...	4.26	4.86	3.17	...
1964	3.85	4.07	4.19	...	...	...	...	...	4.41	4.83	3.21	...
1965	4.15	4.25	4.28	...	...	...	...	...	4.49	4.87	3.26	...
1966	5.20	5.11	4.93	...	...	...	...	...	5.13	5.67	3.81	...
1967	4.88	5.10	5.07	...	...	...	...	...	5.51	6.23	3.94	...
1968	5.69	5.70	5.64	...	...	...	...	...	6.18	6.94	4.45	...
1969	7.12	6.93	6.67	...	...	...	...	...	7.03	7.81	5.72	...
1970	6.90	7.38	7.35	...	...	...	...	...	8.04	9.11	6.33	...
1971	4.89	5.99	6.16	...	...	...	...	...	7.39	8.56	5.47	...
1972	4.95	5.98	6.21	...	...	...	...	...	7.21	8.16	5.26	7.38
1973	7.32	6.87	6.85	...	...	...	...	...	7.44	8.24	5.19	8.04
1974	8.20	7.82	7.56	...	...	...	...	...	8.57	9.50	6.17	9.19
1975	6.78	7.78	7.99	...	...	...	...	...	8.83	10.61	7.05	9.04
1976	5.88	7.18	7.61	...	...	...	...	...	8.43	9.75	6.64	8.86
1977	6.08	6.99	7.42	...	7.75	...	...	...	8.02	8.97	5.68	8.84
1978	8.34	8.32	8.41	...	8.49	...	...	...	8.73	9.49	6.02	9.63
1979	10.65	9.51	9.43	...	9.28	...	...	...	9.63	10.69	6.52	11.19
1980	12.00	11.45	11.43	...	11.27	...	...	...	11.94	13.67	8.59	13.77
1981	14.80	14.25	13.92	...	13.45	...	...	...	14.17	16.04	11.33	16.63
1982	12.27	13.01	13.01	...	12.76	...	...	...	13.79	16.11	11.66	16.08
1983	9.58	10.79	11.10	...	11.18	...	...	...	12.04	13.55	9.51	13.23
1984	10.91	12.26	12.46	...	12.41	...	...	...	12.71	14.19	10.10	13.87
1985	8.42	10.12	10.62	...	10.79	...	...	...	11.37	12.72	9.10	12.42
1986	6.45	7.30	7.67	...	7.78	...	...	...	9.02	10.39	7.32	10.18
1987	6.77	7.94	8.39	...	8.59	...	...	...	9.38	10.58	7.64	10.20
1988	7.65	8.48	8.85	...	8.96	...	...	...	9.71	10.83	7.68	10.34
1989	8.53	8.50	8.49	...	8.45	...	...	...	9.26	10.18	7.23	10.32
1990	7.89	8.37	8.55	...	8.61	...	...	...	9.32	10.36	7.27	10.13
1991	5.86	7.37	7.86	...	8.14	...	...	...	8.77	9.80	6.92	9.25
1992	3.89	6.19	7.01	...	7.67	...	...	...	8.14	8.98	6.44	8.40
1993	3.43	5.14	5.87	6.29	6.59	...	...	...	7.22	7.93	5.60	7.33
1994	5.32	6.69	7.09	7.49	7.37	...	...	...	7.97	8.63	6.18	8.35
1995	5.94	6.38	6.57	6.95	6.88	...	...	...	7.59	8.20	5.95	7.95
1996	5.52	6.18	6.44	6.83	6.71	...	...	...	7.37	8.05	5.76	7.80
1997	5.63	6.22	6.35	6.69	6.61	...	...	...	7.27	7.87	5.52	7.60
1998	5.05	5.15	5.26	5.72	5.58	...	...	...	6.53	7.22	5.09	6.94
1999	5.08	5.55	5.65	6.20	5.87	...	...	...	7.05	7.88	5.43	7.43
2000	6.11	6.16	6.03	6.23	5.94	...	...	...	7.62	8.37	5.71	8.06
2001	3.49	4.56	5.02	5.63	5.49	...	...	...	7.08	7.95	5.15	6.97
2002	2.00	3.82	4.61	5.43	5.43	...	...	...	6.49	7.80	5.04	6.54
2003	1.24	2.97	4.01	4.96	...	1.27	...	2.54	5.66	6.76	4.75	5.82
2004	1.89	3.43	4.27	5.04	...	1.04	2.14	2.21	5.63	6.39	4.68	5.84
2005	3.62	4.05	4.29	4.64	...	1.50	1.97	1.94	5.23	6.06	4.40	5.86
2006	4.94	4.75	4.80	5.00	4.91	2.28	2.31	2.27	5.59	6.48	4.40	6.41
2007	4.53	4.43	4.63	4.91	4.84	2.15	2.36	2.34	5.56	6.48	4.40	6.34
2008	1.83	2.80	3.66	4.36	4.28	1.30	2.18	2.20	5.63	7.44	4.86	6.04
2009	0.47	2.20	3.26	4.11	4.08	1.06	2.21	2.24	5.31	7.29	4.62	5.04
2008												
January	2.71	2.98	3.74	4.35	4.33	0.86	1.81	1.80	5.33	6.54	4.27	5.76
February	2.05	2.78	3.74	4.49	4.52	0.65	1.87	1.87	5.53	6.82	4.64	5.92
March	1.54	2.48	3.51	4.36	4.39	0.23	1.76	1.76	5.51	6.89	4.93	5.97
April	1.74	2.84	3.68	4.44	4.44	0.62	1.91	1.90	5.55	6.97	4.70	5.92
May	2.06	3.15	3.88	4.60	4.60	0.79	2.00	2.00	5.57	6.93	4.58	6.04
June	2.42	3.49	4.10	4.74	4.69	0.97	2.19	2.20	5.68	7.07	4.69	6.32
July	2.28	3.30	4.01	4.62	4.57	0.84	2.09	2.08	5.67	7.16	4.68	6.43
August	2.18	3.14	3.89	4.53	4.50	1.15	2.15	2.13	5.64	7.15	4.69	6.48
September	1.91	2.88	3.69	4.32	4.27	1.55	2.25	2.25	5.65	7.31	4.86	6.04
October	1.42	2.73	3.81	4.45	4.17	2.75	2.87	2.92	6.28	8.88	5.50	6.20
November	1.07	2.29	3.53	4.27	4.00	3.69	3.00	3.09	6.12	9.21	5.23	6.09
December	0.49	1.52	2.42	3.18	2.87	1.76	2.32	2.43	5.05	8.43	5.56	5.33
2009												
January	0.44	1.60	2.52	3.46	3.13	1.59	2.46	2.51	5.05	8.14	5.07	5.06
February	0.62	1.87	2.87	3.83	3.59	1.29	2.31	2.38	5.27	8.08	4.90	5.13
March	0.64	1.82	2.82	3.78	3.64	1.23	2.26	2.32	5.50	8.42	4.99	5.00
April	0.55	1.86	2.93	3.84	3.76	1.11	2.22	2.28	5.39	8.39	4.78	4.81
May	0.50	2.13	3.29	4.22	4.23	1.07	2.36	2.39	5.54	8.06	4.56	4.86
June	0.51	2.71	3.72	4.51	4.52	1.18	2.36	2.38	5.61	7.50	4.81	5.42
July	0.48	2.46	3.56	4.38	4.41	1.18	2.31	2.31	5.41	7.09	4.72	5.22
August	0.46	2.57	3.59	4.33	4.37	1.29	2.22	2.25	5.26	6.58	4.60	5.19
September	0.40	2.37	3.40	4.14	4.19	1.03	2.13	2.15	5.13	6.31	4.24	5.06
October	0.37	2.33	3.39	4.16	4.19	0.83	2.04	2.03	5.15	6.29	4.20	4.95
November	0.31	2.23	3.40	4.24	4.31	0.48	1.90	1.87	5.19	6.32	4.37	4.88
December	0.37	2.34	3.59	4.40	4.49	0.43	1.99	1.97	5.26	6.37	4.21	4.93

. . . = Not available.

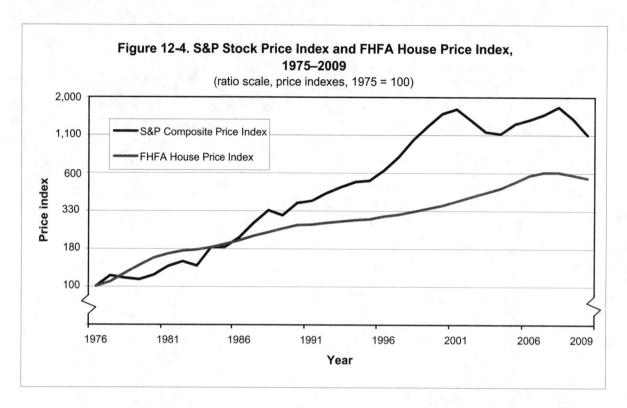

Figure 12-4. S&P Stock Price Index and FHFA House Price Index, 1975–2009
(ratio scale, price indexes, 1975 = 100)

- The rise in prices of existing homes sold and refinanced, as measured by the total Federal Housing Finance Agency (FHFA) House Price Index, ended in 2007, having already slowed from an annual rate of 11 percent in 2005. From the end of 2007 through the end of 2009, prices for this broad category of housing declined 8.7 percent. A separate FHFA index for purchases only, excluding refinancings, has declined 9.4 percent. See the notes and definitions for the limitations of both of these indexes. The total index is shown in Figure 12-4 because it has the longest history. (Table 12-10)

- The long-terms gains in housing prices have been no match for those in the prices of common stocks. This is demonstrated in Figure 12-4 above, where the house price index is compared with the S&P 500 stock index. Neither set of numbers is graphed as published: instead, both are rebased to 1975 =100 so that their growth since then can be directly compared. Over the 34 years, house prices rose at an average 5.2 percent annual rate, while the index of stock prices, though more volatile than home prices, rose at a 7.3 percent rate. (This price increase comparison does not take account of tax considerations, stock dividends, or the value of shelter provided by the owner-occupied home. Past history is no guarantee of future results.) (Table 12-10)

Table 12-10. Common Stock Prices and Yields; Existing House Prices

Year and month	Stock price indexes			Yields based on Standard and Poor's composite (percent)		FHFA House Price Indexes			
						House Price Index (purchases and refinance)		Purchase-Only Index	
	Dow Jones industrials (30 stocks)	Standard and Poor's composite (500 stocks) (1941–1943 = 10)	Nasdaq composite (Feb. 5, 1971 = 100)	Dividend-price ratio	Earnings-price ratio	Level at end of period (1980:I = 100)	Appreciation from same quarter one year earlier (percent)	Level at end of period (1991:I = 100)	Appreciation from same quarter one year earlier (percent)
1955	442.72	40.49	...	4.08	7.95	...	...	...	...
1956	493.01	46.62	...	4.09	7.55	...	...	...	...
1957	475.71	44.38	...	4.35	7.89	...	...	...	...
1958	491.66	46.24	...	3.97	6.23	...	...	...	...
1959	632.12	57.38	...	3.23	5.78	...	...	...	...
1960	618.04	55.85	...	3.47	5.90	...	...	...	...
1961	691.55	66.27	...	2.98	4.62	...	...	...	...
1962	639.76	62.38	...	3.37	5.82	...	...	...	...
1963	714.81	69.87	...	3.17	5.50	...	...	...	...
1964	834.05	81.37	...	3.01	5.32	...	...	...	...
1965	910.88	88.17	...	3.00	5.59	...	...	...	...
1966	873.60	85.26	...	3.40	6.63	...	...	...	...
1967	879.12	91.93	...	3.20	5.73	...	...	...	...
1968	906.00	98.70	...	3.07	5.67	...	...	...	...
1969	876.72	97.84	...	3.24	6.08	...	...	...	...
1970	753.19	83.22	...	3.83	6.45	...	...	...	...
1971	884.76	98.29	107.44	3.14	5.41	...	...	...	...
1972	950.71	109.20	128.52	2.84	5.50	...	...	...	...
1973	923.88	107.43	109.90	3.06	7.12	...	...	...	...
1974	759.37	82.85	76.29	4.47	11.59	...	...	...	...
1975	802.49	86.16	77.20	4.31	9.15	62.52		...	...
1976	974.92	102.01	89.90	3.77	8.90	67.32	7.68	...	...
1977	894.63	98.20	98.71	4.62	10.79	76.88	14.20	...	...
1978	820.23	96.02	117.53	5.28	12.03	87.47	13.77	...	...
1979	844.40	103.01	136.57	5.47	13.46	98.36	12.45	...	...
1980	891.41	118.78	168.61	5.26	12.66	104.91	6.66	...	...
1981	932.92	128.05	203.18	5.20	11.96	109.85	4.71	...	...
1982	884.36	119.71	188.97	5.81	11.60	111.68	1.67	...	...
1983	1 190.34	160.41	285.43	4.40	8.03	116.27	4.11	...	...
1984	1 178.48	160.46	248.88	4.64	10.02	122.22	5.12	...	...
1985	1 328.23	186.84	290.19	4.25	8.12	129.57	6.01	...	...
1986	1 792.76	236.34	366.96	3.49	6.09	139.21	7.44	...	...
1987	2 275.99	286.83	402.57	3.08	5.48	147.36	5.85	...	...
1988	2 060.82	265.79	374.43	3.64	8.01	156.02	5.88	...	...
1989	2 508.91	322.84	437.81	3.45	7.42	165.24	5.91	...	...
1990	2 678.94	334.59	409.17	3.61	6.47	166.19	0.57	...	...
1991	2 929.33	376.18	491.69	3.24	4.79	171.06	2.93	101.14	...
1992	3 284.29	415.74	599.26	2.99	4.22	174.85	2.22	103.82	2.65
1993	3 522.06	451.41	715.16	2.78	4.46	179.09	2.42	106.73	2.80
1994	3 793.77	460.42	751.65	2.82	5.83	181.45	1.32	109.85	2.92
1995	4 493.76	541.72	925.19	2.56	6.09	189.82	4.61	112.82	2.70
1996	5 742.89	670.50	1 164.96	2.19	5.24	194.99	2.72	116.26	3.05
1997	7 441.15	873.43	1 469.49	1.77	4.57	203.97	4.61	120.24	3.42
1998	8 625.52	1 085.50	1 794.91	1.49	3.46	214.09	4.96	126.96	5.59
1999	10 464.88	1 327.33	2 728.15	1.25	3.17	224.58	4.90	134.63	6.04
2000	10 734.90	1 427.22	3 783.67	1.15	3.63	240.83	7.24	143.93	6.91
2001	10 189.13	1 194.18	2 035.00	1.32	2.95	258.38	7.29	153.69	6.78
2002	9 226.43	993.94	1 539.73	1.61	2.92	276.13	6.87	165.42	7.63
2003	8 993.59	965.23	1 647.17	1.77	3.84	295.40	6.98	177.93	7.56
2004	10 317.39	1 130.65	1 986.53	1.72	4.89	326.35	10.48	194.42	9.27
2005	10 547.67	1 207.23	2 099.32	1.83	5.36	362.86	11.19	212.41	9.25
2006	11 408.67	1 310.46	2 263.41	1.87	5.78	380.49	4.86	219.89	3.52
2007	13 169.98	1 477.19	2 578.47	1.86	5.29	380.35	-0.04	217.25	-1.20
2008	11 252.62	1 220.04	2 161.65	2.37	3.54	364.13	-4.26	199.37	-8.23
2009	8 876.15	948.05	1 845.38	2.40	1.86	347.17	-4.66	196.87	-1.25
2008									
January	12 538.12	1 378.76	2 418.09	2.06	...	...	...	...	...
February	12 419.57	1 354.87	2 325.83	2.10					
March	12 193.88	1 316.94	2 254.82	2.17	4.57	380.12	-0.67	213.08	-3.60
April	12 656.63	1 370.47	2 368.10	2.09	...	...	...	...	...
May	12 812.48	1 403.22	2 483.24	2.07					
June	12 056.67	1 341.25	2 427.45	2.15	4.01	373.00	-2.51	212.30	-5.26
July	11 322.38	1 257.33	2 278.14	2.27	...	...	...	...	...
August	11 530.75	1 281.47	2 389.27	2.23					
September	11 114.08	1 217.01	2 205.20	2.36	3.94	364.19	-4.05	207.71	-6.55
October	9 176.71	968.80	1 730.32	2.83	...	...	...	...	...
November	8 614.55	883.04	1 542.70	3.11					
December	8 595.56	877.56	1 525.89	3.00	1.65	364.13	-4.45	199.37	-8.23
2009									
January	8 396.20	865.58	1 537.20	3.01	...	...	...	...	...
February	7 690.50	805.23	1 485.98	3.07					
March	7 235.47	757.13	1 432.23	2.92	0.86	367.02	-3.45	198.03	-7.06
April	7 992.12	848.15	1 641.15	2.60	...	...	...	...	...
May	8 398.37	902.41	1 726.08	2.41					
June	8 593.00	926.12	1 826.99	2.35	0.82	358.18	-3.97	199.70	-5.93
July	8 679.75	935.82	1 873.84	2.31	...	...	...	...	...
August	9 375.06	1 009.72	1 997.51	2.12					
September	9 634.97	1 044.55	2 084.75	2.06	1.19	349.72	-3.97	199.81	-3.80
October	9 857.34	1 067.66	2 122.85	2.02	...	...	...	...	...
November	10 227.55	1 088.07	2 143.53	1.99					
December	10 433.44	1 110.38	2 220.60	1.95	4.57	347.17	-4.66	196.87	-1.25

. . . = Not available.

NOTES AND DEFINITIONS, CHAPTER 12

Most of the data in this chapter are found on the Federal Reserve Board Web site, <http://www.federalreserve.gov>. Current releases and most historical data are found at that site by selecting Economic Research & Data/Statistical Releases and Historical Data and then selecting the appropriate report. This is the location for all data not otherwise specified.

TABLES 12-1, 12-2, AND 20-5B
MONEY STOCK MEASURES AND COMPONENTS

SOURCE: BOARD OF GOVERNORS OF THE FEDERAL RESERVE SYSTEM

Estimates of two monetary aggregates (M1 and M2) and the components of these measures are published weekly. The monthly data are averages of daily figures.

The Federal Reserve Board ceased publication of the M3 aggregate on March 23, 2006. Weekly publication was also discontinued for the following components of M3: large-denomination time deposits, repurchase agreements (RPs), and Eurodollars. The Board continues to publish institutional money market mutual funds as a memorandum item in this release. Measures of large-denomination time deposits continue to be published in the flow of funds accounts (Z.1 release) and in the H.8 release weekly for commercial banks.

The Board stated that "M3 does not appear to convey any additional information about economic activity that is not already embodied in M2 and has not played a role in the monetary policy process for many years. Consequently, the Board judged that the costs of collecting the underlying data and publishing M3 outweigh the benefits." ("Discontinuance of M3," H.6, Money Stock Measures [November 10, 2005, revised March 9, 2006]. [Accessed November 6, 2006.]

Definitions

M1 consists of (1) currency, (2) traveler's checks of non-bank issuers, (3) demand deposits, and (4) other checkable deposits.

M2 consists of M1 plus savings deposits (including money market deposit accounts), small-denomination time deposits, and balances in retail money market mutual funds.

Currency consists of currency outside the U.S. Treasury, the Federal Reserve Banks, and the vaults of depository institutions.

Traveler's checks is the outstanding amount of U.S. dollar-denominated traveler's checks of nonbank issuers. Traveler's checks issued by depository institutions are included in demand deposits.

Demand deposits consists of demand deposits at domestically chartered commercial banks, U.S. branches and agencies of foreign banks, and Edge Act corporations (excluding those amounts held by depository institutions, the U.S. government, and foreign banks and official institutions) less cash items in the process of collection and Federal Reserve float. A "demand deposit" is a deposit that the depositor has a right to withdraw at any time without prior notice to the depository institution—most commonly, a checking account. "Federal Reserve float" is Federal Reserve credit that appears on the books of the depository institution of both the check writer and the check receiver while a check is being processed. This amount and cash items in the process of collection are subtracted to avoid double counting of deposits, so that they will not be counted both at the bank in which the check is deposited and at the bank on which the check is drawn.

Other checkable deposits at commercial banks consists of negotiable order of withdrawal (NOW) and automatic transfer service (ATS) balances at domestically chartered commercial banks, U.S. branches and agencies of foreign banks, and Edge Act corporations.

Other checkable deposits at thrift institutions consists of NOW and ATS balances at thrift institutions, credit union share draft balances, and demand deposits at thrift institutions.

Savings deposits includes money market deposit accounts and other savings deposits at *commercial banks* and *thrift institutions*.

Small time deposits are deposits issued at *commercial banks* and *thrift institutions* in amounts less than $100,000. All Individual Retirement Account (IRA) and Keogh account balances at commercial banks and thrift institutions are subtracted from small time deposits.

Retail money funds exclude IRA and Keogh account balances at money market mutual funds.

Institutional money funds are included in the money stock report for informational purposes. They are not part of M1 or M2.

Notes on the data

Seasonal adjustment. Seasonally adjusted M1 is calculated by summing currency, traveler's checks, demand deposits, and other checkable deposits (each seasonally adjusted separately). Seasonally adjusted M2 is computed by adjusting each of its non-M1 components and then adding this result to seasonally adjusted M1.

Revisions. Money stock measures are revised frequently and have a benchmark and seasonal factor review in the middle of the year; this review typically extends back a number of years. The monetary aggregates were redefined in major revisions introduced in 1980.

Data availability

Estimates are released weekly in Federal Reserve Statistical Release H.6, "Money Stock Measures." Current and historical data are available on the Federal Reserve Web site.

References

Board of Governors of the Federal Reserve System, *The Federal Reserve System: Purposes and Functions,* available online at <http://www.federalreserve.gov> in the category "About the Fed/Features," includes a chapter discussing monetary policy and the monetary aggregates and a glossary of terms as an appendix.

An explanation of the 1980 redefinition of the monetary aggregates is found in the *Federal Reserve Bulletin* for February 1980.

TABLES 12-3 AND 20-5B
AGGREGATE RESERVES, MONETARY BASE, AND FR BALANCE SHEET

SOURCE: BOARD OF GOVERNORS OF THE FEDERAL RESERVE SYSTEM

The data on reserves and the monetary base presented here are in millions of dollars, seasonally adjusted (with one exception), and adjusted for changes in reserve requirements ("break-adjusted") in order to provide a consistent gauge of the effect of Federal Reserve open-market operations. Break adjustment is required because an observed increase in reserves will not represent an easing in monetary conditions if it is simply equal to the increase in reserves required by the Federal Reserve. Therefore, the mandated increases and decreases are deducted to provide the break-adjusted series. Monthly data are averages of daily figures. Annual data are for December.

The series "Federal Reserve balance sheet: total assets" was introduced in the 14th edition of *Business Statistics*. It demonstrates the extent to which the Federal Reserve has, beginning in 2007, undertaken "quantitative easing"—direct purchases of financial assets—in addition to conventional easing, which has consisted of reducing short-term interest rates to near zero. The balance sheet data are accessed on a different part of the Federal Reserve Web site—"Monetary Policy" instead of "Economic Research and Data"—which features an extensive explanation and discussion of the meaning and importance of this indicator. The balance sheet is reported in millions of dollars for each Wednesday, and is shown here with the last Wednesday of the month representing the month and the last Wednesday of December representing the year. These values are not adjusted for seasonal variation.

Definitions

Total reserves consists of reserve balances with the Federal Reserve Banks plus vault cash used to satisfy reserve requirements. Seasonally adjusted, break-adjusted total reserves equal seasonally adjusted, break-adjusted required reserves plus unadjusted excess reserves.

Seasonally adjusted, break-adjusted *nonborrowed reserves* equal seasonally adjusted, break-adjusted total reserves less unadjusted total borrowings of depository institutions from the Federal Reserve.

Extended credit consisted of borrowing at the discount window under the terms and conditions established for the extended credit program to help depository institutions deal with sustained liquidity pressures. Since there was not the same need to repay such borrowing promptly as there was with traditional short-term adjustment credit, the money market impact of extended credit was similar to that of nonborrowed reserves. The extended credit program was significant in the 1980s but used infrequently in subsequent years. It ended with the 2002 revision of the discount window program, effective January 9, 2003. See the explanation of the discount rate in the notes and definitions for Table 12-9.

To adjust *required reserves* for discontinuities due to regulatory changes in reserve requirements, a multiplicative procedure is used to estimate what required reserves would have been in past periods, had current reserve requirements been in effect. Break-adjusted required reserves include required reserves against transactions deposits and personal time and savings deposits (but not reservable nondeposit liabilities).

Excess reserves, not seasonally adjusted equals unadjusted total reserves less unadjusted required reserves.

The seasonally adjusted, break-adjusted *monetary base* consists of (1) seasonally adjusted, break-adjusted total reserves; plus (2) the seasonally adjusted currency component of the money stock; plus (3) the seasonally adjusted, break-adjusted difference between current vault cash and the amount applied to satisfy current reserve requirements for all quarterly reporters on the "Report of Transaction Accounts, Other Deposits and Vault Cash" and for all weekly reporters whose vault cash exceeds their required reserves.

Federal Reserve balance sheet: total assets is total assets from the Consolidated Statement of Condition of All Federal Reserve Banks, which is reported each Wednesday. The last Wednesday of the month is used to represent the month, and the last Wednesday in December is used to represent the year. Currently, the principal components of total assets are Treasury, federal agency, and mortgage-backed securities. Other types of assets representing Federal Reserve credit extension, some of which have varied during the course of the crisis, have been repurchase agreements; term auction credit; portfolio holdings of various limited liability companies (LLCs) set up to manage assets taken over from other institutions; liquidity swaps with foreign central banks; and other loans, including traditional loans to member commercial banks made at the discount rate (see the definitions for Table 12-9). Total assets are equal to the sum of Federal Reserve liabilities and capital. The principal components of liabilities are Federal Reserve notes and the deposits of member banks representing their reserves.

Revisions

The data on reserves and the monetary base are revised annually around midyear to reflect the result of annual reviews of seasonal factors and break factors. The Federal Reserve balance sheet is not subject to revision.

Data availability

Reserve and monetary base data are released weekly in Federal Reserve Release H.3, "Aggregate Reserves of Depository Institutions and the Monetary Base." Current and historical data are available on the Federal Reserve Web site.

The Federal Reserve balance sheet appears each week in the H.4.1 release, Factors Affecting Reserve Balances, released each Thursday at 4:30 p.m., and available on the Federal Reserve Web site under Economic Research and Data/Statistical Releases and Historical Data. However, to obtain the full historical data for total assets, the user must go to Monetary policy/Credit and liquidity programs and the balance sheet/Recent balance sheet trends/Total assets/View as table/All/Copy data. Other explanatory material, including a monthly report on changes in these programs, is available at the Monetary policy location.

TABLE 12-4
COMMERCIAL BANKS: BANK CREDIT AND SELECTED LIABILITIES

SOURCE: BOARD OF GOVERNORS OF THE FEDERAL RESERVE SYSTEM.

Definitions and notes on the data

This table presents selected balance sheet items (not a complete balance sheet with total assets and liabilities) for all commercial banks in the United States. This category covers the following types of institutions in the 50 states and the District of Columbia: domestically chartered commercial banks that report weekly (large domestic), other domestically chartered commercial banks (small domestic), branches and agencies of foreign banks, and Edge Act and Agreement corporations (foreign related institutions). International Banking Facilities are excluded.

Data are collected weekly for Wednesday values, and monthly data are pro rata averages of Wednesday values. Annual data represent December figures.

Data are complete for large domestic banks. Data for other institutions are estimated on the basis of weekly samples and end-of-quarter condition reports. Data are adjusted for breaks caused by the reclassifications of assets and liabilities.

Data before 1988 are based on previous versions of this survey—the G.7 release, "Loans and Securities at Commercial Banks," and the G.10 release, "Major Nondeposit Funds of Commercial Banks."

Most of the categories of credit and liabilities are self-explanatory.

U.S. Treasury and agency securities includes liabilities of the U.S. Treasury, liabilities of U.S. government agencies, and liabilities of U.S. government-sponsored enterprises.

Loans and leases in bank credit excludes various forms of credit extended to other commercial banks in the United States.

Security loans, previously shown as a separate category under "Loans and leases in bank credit", are now included in *Other loans and leases.*"

Allowances for loan and lease losses, interbank loans, cash assets, trading assets including derivatives, and other assets are not components of bank credit and are omitted from Table 12-4. Interbank loans include loans made to commercial banks, reverse RPs with commercial banks, and federal funds sold to commercial banks.

Selected liabilities show *deposits* and *borrowings.* Other components of total liabilities, "trading liabilities" and "other liabilities," are omitted.

Revisions

Data are revised annually around midyear to reflect new benchmark information and revised seasonal factors.

Data availability

Federal Reserve Statistical Release H.8, "Assets and Liabilities of Commercial Banks in the United States," is issued each Friday around 4:30 p.m. (EST). Current and historical data are available on the Federal Reserve Web site.

TABLE 12-5
CREDIT MARKET DEBT OUTSTANDING, BY BORROWER AND LENDER

SOURCE: BOARD OF GOVERNORS OF THE FEDERAL RESERVE SYSTEM

The flow of funds accounts, compiled quarterly by the Federal Reserve Board, supplement the national income and product accounts (NIPAs) by providing a comprehensive and detailed accounting of financial transactions with a balance sheet for each financial and nonfinancial sector of the economy. Table 12-5 is taken from these accounts. It shows the *credit market debt outstanding owed* by the major sectors in the economy, and it shows the major lending sectors in the credit markets under *credit market assets held.* One purpose of these statistics is to show the comparative growth of the various lending sectors.

Aggregates of these data can include multiple layers of financial intermediation, such as banks making advances to finance companies that subsequently lend to households. Adding bank data to finance company data involves duplication of such debt. In macroeconomic analysis, the most widely used flow of funds measure is the total debt of domestic nonfinancial sectors. By eliminating the financial sectors, this measure has little duplication due to financial intermediation. The Federal Reserve uses this along with the monetary aggregates as an indicator of monetary conditions.

Definitions and notes on the data

Quarterly data on debt outstanding are shown on an end-of-period basis, not adjusted for seasonal variation or for "breaks" or discontinuities in the series. Due to these discontinuities, caution should be used in interpreting changes in debt levels. Break-adjusted values of changes, representing best estimates of actual fund flows, can be found in the quarterly flow of funds report, along with a suggested method for calculating percentage changes.

The data on credit market debt exclude corporate equities and mutual fund shares. However, these values of these instruments held by households and nonprofits appear as assets in the household sector accounts in Table 12-6.

Data for the current and several preceding years are revised each year to reflect revisions in source data, including the NIPAs; the revisions are issued about a month after the release of the annual NIPA revisions.

Sectors owing debt

Domestic financial sectors

Federal government-related sectors include government-sponsored enterprises (GSEs) such as Fannie Mae (originally the Federal National Mortgage Association), Freddie Mac (originally the Federal Home Loan Mortgage Corporation), and Ginnie Mae (originally the Government National Mortgage Association); agency and GSE-backed mortgage pools; and the monetary authority (Federal Reserve). However, the Federal Reserve usually owes no credit market debt.

The *private* sector includes commercial banks and bank holding companies, savings institutions, credit unions, life insurance companies, asset-backed securities (ABS) issuers, brokers and dealers, finance and mortgage companies, REITs (real estate investment trusts), and funding corporations.

Domestic nonfinancial sectors

Federal government consists of all federal government agencies and funds included in the unified budget. However, the District of Columbia government is included in the state and local sector.

Treasury securities as shown here excludes securities issued by the Treasury but held by agencies within the U.S. government (e.g., in the Social Security trust funds). In this respect, it corresponds to the "Federal debt" shown in Table 6-15, except that the latter table uses a fiscal-year basis rather than a calendar-year basis. Federal government debt as shown here is smaller than the official total public debt and the "debt subject to limit." Both of those include the securities held by U.S. government agencies. The value shown here is considered to be a more accurate measure of the effect of government borrowing in relation to the economy and credit markets than those obtained from the larger aggregates.

Budget agency securities and mortgages are those issued by government-owned corporations and agencies, such as the Export-Import Bank, that issue securities individually. There are no mortgages currently included in the debt of agencies.

Households also includes personal trusts, nonprofit organizations, and domestic hedge funds.

State and local governments represent operating funds only. State and local government retirement funds are included in the financial sector.

Foreign credit market debt held in the United States shows the foreign credit market debt owed to U.S. residents. This debt is included along with the debt of domestic financial and nonfinancial sectors in total credit market debt outstanding.

Percentage measures

Table 12-5 includes three measures of relative debt burdens, calculated by the editor.

Domestic nonfinancial debt as a percent of GDP is the total debt owed by domestic nonfinancial sectors as a percent of the current-dollar value of total Gross Domestic Product. (Table 1-1)

Household debt as a percent of DPI is the value of debt owed by households as a percent of the current-dollar value of disposable personal income. (Table 4-1)

Corporate nonfinancial business debt as a percent of sector value added is the total debt owed by domestic corporate nonfinancial business as a percent of the current-dollar gross value added of domestic corporate nonfinancial business. (Table 1-13)

For the annual ratios, debt outstanding at the end of the year is taken as a percent of the product or income data for the full preceding year. For the quarterly ratios, the debt outstanding at the end of the quarter is taken as a percent of the annual rate of the product or income flow for that quarter. This means that the end-year ratios will almost inevitably be higher than the corresponding end-quarter ratios and should therefore not be compared with them.

Credit market assets held by sector

Selected government-related sectors

This grouping includes two nonfinancial and four financial sectors. The nonfinancial sectors are the *federal government*, as reflected in the U.S. Budget accounts, and the operations of *state and local governments,* including the District of Columbia. *State and local employee retirement funds* and *federal government retirement funds* are shown separately and considered to be financial sectors. The other two government-related financial sectors are *government-sponsored enterprises (GSEs)* and *federally related mortgage pools.*

Government-sponsored enterprises (GSEs) are financial institutions that provide credit to housing, agriculture, and other specific areas of the economy, such as Federal Home Loan Banks, Fannie Mae, and Freddie Mac (see above for explanation of the latter two terms).

Federally related mortgage pools are entities established for bookkeeping purposes that record the issuance of pooled securities representing an interest in mortgages backed by federal agencies and GSEs. Rather than being composed of a group of institutions, the sector is made up of a set of contractual arrangements in regard to pooled mortgages.

Selected domestic financial sectors

This grouping includes major financial sectors, such as *commercial banks, savings institutions,* and *credit unions*. The *monetary authority* (the Federal Reserve) has been put in this group because it is sometimes included in banking sector totals. Other important financial sectors are *life insurance companies, property-casualty insurance companies,* and *private pension funds*. Additional private financial sectors are *money market mutual funds*, which issue shares and invest in short-term liquid assets; *mutual funds*, whose investments are not restricted to the short-term area; *asset-backed security (ABS) issuers*, which issue debt obligations that are backed by pooled assets, a financial procedure similar to that of federally related mortgage pools; and *finance companies*, which provide credit to businesses and individuals.

Private domestic nonfinancial sectors

Households were the dominant private domestic nonfinancial lenders in earlier years, but lending by domestic households has now been surpassed by *foreign holdings* of assets representing claims on U.S. entities.

A number of lending sectors of smaller importance are included in the category "*All other financial and nonfi-*

nancial." One of those is nonfinancial business, a sector that is important on the borrowing side but not on the lending side. The financial sectors included in this total are closed-end funds, exchange-traded funds, real estate investment trusts (REITs), brokers and dealers, and funding corporations.

Data availability

Debt estimates are released quarterly, about nine weeks following the end of the quarter. The data can be found in Federal Reserve Statistical Release Z.1, "Flow of Funds of the United States," available on the Federal Reserve Web site. The data in Table 12-5 are found in Tables L.1 and L.2 of that release. Current and historical data are also available on the same Federal Reserve Web site.

References

A *Guide to the Flow of Funds Accounts* can be ordered; ordering information is available on the Federal Reserve Web site along with the Z.1 release. Individual table descriptions can be accessed at the same location. The *Federal Reserve Bulletin* for July 2001 includes an article entitled "The U.S. Flow of Funds Accounts and Their Uses." To access *Bulletin* articles on the Federal Reserve Web site, select Economic Research & Data/ Federal Reserve Bulletin and select the year.

TABLE 12-6
HOUSEHOLD ASSETS, LIABILITIES, NET WORTH, FINANCIAL OBLIGATIONS, AND DELINQUENCY RATES

SOURCE: BOARD OF GOVERNORS OF THE FEDERAL RESERVE SYSTEM

The quarterly data on household sector assets, liabilities, and net worth are also obtained from the Federal Reserve Board's flow of funds accounts, which are described above. These data appear in Table B.100 of the Z.1 statistical release, also cited above.

The household credit ratios and rates are also compiled by the Federal Reserve. The household debt service ratio relates required debt service (interest and principal) payments to disposable personal income (DPI). The financial obligations ratios include not only required debt payments, but also rental payments, automobile lease payments, homeowners' insurance, and property taxes. They are also expressed as a percentage of DPI. Unlike the debt service ratio, the financial obligations ratios are not distorted by the trend toward debt-financed homeownership in preference to rental or the trend toward auto leasing in preference to loan financing.

The delinquency and charge-off rates relate delinquent (past due 30 days or more) and charged-off consumer credit card credit at commercial banks to total bank holdings of that type of credit.

Definitions and notes on the data

Quarterly data on holdings of *financial assets* are shown on an end-of-period basis, not adjusted for seasonal variations. Data for the current and preceding years are revised annually to reflect revisions in source data.

> It is important to note that for most categories in this reporting system, the values for the household sector are calculated as residuals. That is, starting with a known total (such as total Treasury securities outstanding), the amounts in that category reported or estimated to be held by other sectors are subtracted and the remainder is assigned to the household sector. This means that any error in one of the other sectors causes an equal and opposite error in the household sector.
>
> It should also be noted that the Flow of Funds "household" balance sheet includes nonprofit organizations, personal trusts, farm households, and domestic hedge funds. Household sector assets exclude holdings by unincorporated businesses.

The table shows total household ownership of *checkable deposits and currency, time and savings deposits, money market fund shares, U.S. savings bonds, other Treasury securities, agency- and GSE-backed securities, municipal securities, corporate and foreign bonds, mortgages, corporate equities* (at market value), *mutual fund shares* (with equities at market value and other assets at book value), *security credit, life insurance reserves, pension fund reserves,* and *equity in noncorporate business.* Note that the reserves of life insurance companies and pension funds, though held by institutions, are counted here as assets of the household sector. *Pension fund reserves* includes insurance and pension fund reserves of federal, state, and local government employee funds—but not the Social Security system—as well as private industry funds. Bank personal trusts were formerly included as a type of household financial asset. However, in the latest revision of the flow of funds accounts, the various assets in these trusts were instead included in the appropriate categories, such as bonds, equities, and so forth. Included in total *financial assets,* but not shown separately, are foreign deposits, open market paper, and claims on insurance companies, such as unearned premium reserves of other insurance companies and health insurance reserves of life insurance companies.

Tangible assets complete the asset side of the household balance sheet. Tangible assets comprise equipment and software owned by nonprofit organizations, real estate, and consumer durable goods. *Household real estate* includes farm homes, mobile homes, second homes not rented, vacant homes for sale, vacant land, and owner-occupied housing. It is valued at market value, while equipment, software, and consumer durables are valued at replacement (current) cost.

Debt as a percent of total assets is calculated by the editor as household credit market debt outstanding, from Table 12-5, as a percent of the total of tangible and financial assets in this table. It covers both households and nonprofit organizations, as defined above.

Total liabilities consists of household credit market debt, as shown in Table 12-5, plus security credit, trade payables of nonprofit organizations, and deferred and unpaid life insurance premiums.

Net worth is the sum of the value of financial and tangible assets minus total liabilities.

The *household debt-service* and *financial obligations ratios* are estimated on a quarterly basis by the Federal Reserve based on aggregate and consumer survey data. They are seasonally adjusted, unlike almost all of the other data in Table 12-6. Fourth-quarter values are shown to represent the calendar year. The denominator for the aggregate ratio is disposable personal income (DPI) from the NIPAs. (See Chapter 4.) The allocation of the NIPA data between *renters* and *homeowners* is estimated by the Federal Reserve based on data from its triennial Survey of Consumer Finances and the Census Bureau's Current Population Survey (CPS). (For more information on the CPS, see the notes and definitions to Chapters 3 and 10.)

Debt service payments are the minimum required monthly payments of principal and interest on mortgage debt (including home equity loans), revolving credit (credit card debt), and auto, student, mobile home, recreational vehicle, marine, and personal loans.

The *financial obligations ratios* include, in addition to debt service, rental payments on primary residences, property taxes, homeowners' insurance, and automobile lease payments.

Delinquency and *charge-off rates of credit card accounts held at banks* are compiled from the quarterly FFIEC (Federal Financial Institutions Examination Council)

Consolidated Reports of Condition and Income (FFIEC 031 through 034) and pertain to all insured U.S.-chartered commercial banks. The *delinquency rate* concerns loans past due 30 days or more and still accruing interest as well as those in nonaccrual status, measured as a percentage of end-of-period loans. The *charge-off rate* is the value of net charge-offs (loans removed from the books and charged against loss reserves, minus recoveries) as a percentage of average loans outstanding over the quarter, annualized.

Data availability

Household balance sheet estimates are released quarterly, about nine weeks following the end of a quarter, in the Federal Reserve Statistical Release Z.1, "Flow of Funds Accounts of the United States." Further information on data availability is given in the notes to Table 12-5, a table which is also based on the flow of funds accounts.

The revised debt service ratio and the new financial obligations ratios are described in "Recent Changes to a Measure of U.S. Household Debt Service," *Federal Reserve Bulletin,* October 2003. The data are estimated by the Federal Reserve about three months after the end of each quarter. Current and historical data and articles from the *Bulletin* are available on the Federal Reserve Web site by selecting Economic Research and Data and either Statistical Releases and Historical Data or Federal Reserve Bulletin, then selecting the year.

Delinquency and charge-off rates of credit card accounts held at banks are also available on the Federal Reserve Web site, listed under "Charge-off and Delinquency Rates on Loans at Commercial Banks." Rates are posted approximately 60 days after the end of the quarter.

TABLE 12-7
MORTGAGE DEBT OUTSTANDING

SOURCE: BOARD OF GOVERNORS OF THE FEDERAL RESERVE SYSTEM

These data are also published in the Federal Reserve's Statistical Release Z.1, "Flow of Funds Accounts," Table L.217. They are based on reports from various government and private organizations.

Definitions and notes on the data

By type of property

Home mortgages includes home equity loans; these are also shown separately in the flow of funds accounts.

Multifamily residences refers to mortgages on structures of five or more units.

By type of holder

Federal and related agencies shows mortgages held directly by the federal government and GSEs (see notes and definitions for Table 12-5 above).

Mortgage pools or trusts show mortgages that were refinanced by their holders through the issuance of mortgage-backed securities. They are shown in two columns: refinancings by *federally related agencies*—mainly the GSEs Fannie Mae, Freddie Mac, and Ginnie Mae (see above)—and refinancings by private conduits (these are referred to as *ABS issuers* in the flow of funds accounts, which stands for issuers of asset-backed securities).

Other holders encompasses a variety of groups, including finance companies, individuals, state and local governments, credit unions, and others.

Home mortgage debt as a percentage of the value of real estate is calculated by the editor, using total home mortgage debt as a percentage of the value of household real estate, which is shown in Table 12-6.

Data availability

Mortgage debt data are compiled quarterly about nine weeks following the end of the quarter in Federal Reserve Statistical Release Z.1, "Flow of Funds Accounts of the United States." The release and current and historical data are available on the Federal Reserve Web site.

TABLE 12-8
CONSUMER CREDIT

SOURCE: BOARD OF GOVERNORS OF THE FEDERAL RESERVE SYSTEM

The consumer credit series cover most short- and intermediate-term credit extended to individuals through regular business channels, excluding loans secured by real estate (such as first and second mortgages and home equity credit). In October 2003, the scope of this survey was expanded to incorporate student loans extended by the federal government and by SLM Holding Corporation (SLM), the parent company of Sallie Mae (Student Loan Marketing Association). The historical data have been revised back to 1977 to reflect this inclusion.

The failure to include home equity credit is an important limitation of this data set. The household debt series presented in Table 12-5 are more comprehensive, comprising both mortgage and consumer debt.

Consumer credit is categorized by major types of credit and by major holders.

Definitions and notes on the data

The major types of consumer credit are *revolving* and *nonrevolving*. *Revolving credit* includes credit arising from purchases on credit card plans of retail stores and banks, cash advances and check credit plans of banks, and some overdraft credit arrangements. *Nonrevolving credit* includes automobile loans, mobile home loans, and all other loans not included in revolving credit, such as loans for education, boats, trailers, or vacations. These loans may be secured or unsecured.

Debt secured by real estate (including first liens, junior liens, and home equity loans) is excluded. Credit extended to governmental agencies and nonprofit or charitable organizations, as well as credit extended to business or to individuals exclusively for business purposes, is excluded.

Categories of *holders* include *commercial banks, finance companies, credit unions, federal government, savings institutions, nonfinancial businesses*, and *pools of securitized assets*. The Student Loan Marketing Association (Sallie Mae) is included in "Federal government" until the end of

2004, at which time it became fully privatized. Beginning with the end of 2004, Sallie Mae is included in "Finance companies." Retailers and gasoline companies are included in the nonfinancial businesses category. *Pools of securitized assets* comprises the outstanding balances of pools upon which securities have been issued; these balances are no longer carried on the balance sheets of the loan originators.

The consumer credit series are benchmarked to comprehensive data that periodically become available. Current monthly estimates are brought forward from the latest benchmarks in accordance with weighted changes indicated by sample data. Classifications are made on a "holder" basis. Thus, installment paper sold by retail outlets is included in the figures for the banks and finance companies that purchased the paper.

The amount of outstanding credit represents the sum of the balances in the installment receivable accounts of financial institutions and retail outlets at the end of each month.

The estimates of the amount of credit outstanding include any finance and insurance charges included as part of the installment contract. Unearned income on loans is included in some cases when lenders cannot separate the components.

The seasonally-adjusted data are adjusted for differences in the number of trading days and for seasonal influences.

Data availability

Current data are available monthly in the Federal Reserve Statistical Release G.19, "Consumer Credit," available along with all current and historical data on the Federal Reserve Web site. In the autumn of each year there is a revision of several years of past data reflecting benchmarking and seasonal factor review.

TABLES 12-9, 12-10 AND 20-6
INTEREST RATES, BOND YIELDS, STOCK PRICES AND YIELDS, AND EXISTING HOUSE PRICES

SOURCES: BOARD OF GOVERNORS OF THE FEDERAL RESERVE SYSTEM; BUREAU OF ECONOMIC ANALYSIS; MOODY'S INVESTORS SERVICE; THE BOND BUYER; DOW JONES, INC.; STANDARD AND POOR'S CORPORATION; NEW YORK STOCK EXCHANGE; FEDERAL HOUSING FINANCE AGENCY (FHFA), PREVIOUSLY OFHEO (OFFICE OF FEDERAL HOUSING ENTERPRISE OVERSIGHT)

Definitions and notes on the data

Interest rates and bond yields are percents per year and are averages of business day figures, except as noted. With four exceptions, they are nominal rates or yields not adjusted for inflation.

The daily effective *federal funds rate* is a weighted average of rates on trades through New York brokers. Monthly fig-

ures include each calendar day in the month. Annualized figures use a 360-day year.

The *Federal Reserve discount rate* is the rate for discount window borrowing at the Federal Reserve Bank of New York. Monthly figures include each calendar day in the month. Annualized figures use a 360-day year.

Beginning in January 2003, the rules governing the discount window programs were revised. "Adjustment credit," which had been extended at a below-market rate (as can be seen in the average discount rates from 1978 through 2002 shown in Table 12-9, which are below the federal funds rate), was replaced by a new type of credit called "primary credit." Primary credit is available for very short terms as a backup source of liquidity to depository institutions in generally sound financial condition, as judged by the lending Federal Reserve Bank. Primary credit is extended at a rate above the federal funds rate, eliminating the incentive for institutions to exploit the spread of money market rates over the discount rate.

Through December 2002, Table 12-9 displays the adjustment credit rate. Beginning in February 2003, the new primary credit rate is shown. The rule change, and the change in discount rates shown, did not entail a change in the stance of monetary policy at that time. The overall stance of monetary policy is consistently measured by the level of the federal funds rate.

The *Eurodollar deposits* rate shown is the bid rate at about 9:30 a.m. (EST) for 1-month Eurodollar deposits. Annualized figures use a 360-day year.

The *U.S. Treasury bills, 3-month rate* and the *U.S. Treasury bills, 6-month rate* are the yields on these securities based on their prices as traded in the secondary market. The rates are quoted on a discount basis. Annualized figures use a 360-day year.

Commercial paper, 3-month rates are interpolated from data on certain commercial paper trades settled by the Depository Trust Company. This company is a clearinghouse and custodian for nearly all domestic commercial paper activity. The trades, which are on a discount basis, represent sales of commercial paper by dealers or direct issuers. Annualized figures use a 360-day year. Prior to September 1997, the series represented both nonfinancial and financial commercial paper. Since September 1997, rates have been reported separately for nonfinancial and financial companies; only rates for financial companies are shown here. This introduces a slight discontinuity in this series between August and September 1997.

CDs (secondary market), 3-month rates are averages of dealer offering rates on nationally traded certificates of deposit. Annualized figures use a 360-day year.

The *bank prime rate* is one of several base rates used by banks to price short-term business loans. It is the rate posted by a majority of the top 25 (by amount of assets in domestic offices) insured U.S.-chartered commercial banks. Monthly figures include each calendar day in the month. Annualized figures use a 360-day year. Before 1949, the data are not on the Federal Reserve Web site but have been reproduced from the Federal Reserve publication *Banking and Monetary Statistics, 1941-1970,* Washington: Board of Governors of the Federal Reserve System, 1976. In that volume, the prime rate is described as "the rate that banks charge their most creditworthy business customers on short-term loans", as posted by the largest banks.

The *inflation* column shown here, calculated by the editor, is the rate of change in the PCE chain-type price index, excluding food and energy. For monthly entries, it is the change from the same month a year earlier. This price index is calculated by the Bureau of Economic Analysis (BEA) and shown in Table 8-2. The inflation rate is shown along with other rates in Table 8-3; see the notes and definitions for that table.

Real federal funds rate. There is no directly observable real short-term rate, but it can be approximated by subtracting some measure of the current inflation rate from the nominal rate. For Table 12-9, the editor has selected one widely-followed measure—the rate of change in the core PCE (personal consumption expenditures, excluding food and energy) chain price index, shown in the previous column of the table—and calculated a "real" federal funds rate by subtracting the core inflation rate from the nominal rate. In the annual data, the inflation rate is the percentage change in the price index from the previous year; in the monthly data, it is the percentage change from the same month a year earlier. As noted in Chapter 8, which includes and defines several different measures of inflation, other price indexes could be used as inflation indicators.

Interest rate swaps. An interest rate swap is a type of financial market derivative in which two parties, known as "counterparties," exchange two streams of cash flows. The rates shown here are the results of transactions in which streams of fixed-rate interest flows are exchanged for streams of floating-rate interest flows. The rates shown are the fixed interest rates which are exchanged for floating-rate flows paying the three-month LIBOR (London Interbank Offered Rate, a rate at which highly-rated banks can borrow short-term). They are International Swaps and Derivatives Association (ISDA ®) mid-market par swap rates, collected at 11 a.m. EST by Garban Intercapital plc and published on Reuters Page ISDAFIX ®1. ISDAFIX is a registered service mark of ISDA. Reprinted by the Federal Reserve from Reuters Limited.

U.S. Treasury securities, constant maturities. The rates shown for 1-year, 5-year, 10-year, 20-year, and 30-year securities are yields on actively traded issues adjusted to constant maturi-

ties. Yields on Treasury securities at "constant maturity" are interpolated by the Treasury Department from the daily yield curve. This curve, which relates the yield on a security to its time to maturity, is based on the closing market bid yields on actively traded Treasury securities in the over-the-counter market. These market yields are calculated from composites of quotations reported by U.S. Government securities dealers to the Federal Reserve Bank of New York. The constant maturity yield values are read from the yield curve at fixed maturities. For example, this method provides a yield for a 10-year maturity, even if no outstanding security has exactly 10 years remaining to maturity. The 30-year series was discontinued as of February 2002, because the Treasury Department was no longer issuing such bonds at that time. However, issuance of 30-year bonds was resumed in 2005 as an additional means of financing rising deficits, and the 30-year interest rate series resumes in 2006.[1] The current 20-year series begins with 1993 and is not comparable with an earlier 20-year series. For further information, see the historical data series on the Federal Reserve Web site.

Inflation-indexed yields. In recent years, the Treasury Department has issued Treasury Inflation-Protected Securities (TIPS), which are marketable long-term bonds whose redemption value is increased by the change in the CPI-U from the date of purchase. (See notes and definitions to Chapter 8.) The purchaser of these bonds, unlike with ordinary securities, is guaranteed that the real value of his or her principal will remain intact. He or she need not make his or her own estimate of future inflation in order to make a rational bid. Therefore, the observed purchase price represents a real rate of interest that purchasers and sellers are mutually willing to accept. Inflation-indexed yields are shown here for 5 and 20 years (adjusted to constant maturities by the Treasury) and for the long-term average, which is the unweighted average of the bid yields for all TIPS with remaining terms to maturity over 10 years.

Domestic corporate bond yields, Aaa and Baa. The rates shown are for general obligation bonds based on Thursday figures, and are provided by Moody's Investors Service and republished by the Federal Reserve. The Aaa rates through December 6, 2001 are averages of Aaa utility and Aaa industrial bond rates. As of December 7, 2001, these rates are averages of Aaa industrial bonds only.

The *state and local bond yields* are the Bond Buyer index as republished by the Federal Reserve. The index is based on 20 state and local government general obligation bonds of mixed quality maturing in 20 years or less. Quotes are as of the Thursday of each week. These rates have typically in the past been lower than those on U.S. Treasury or private long-term bonds because the interest on them is exempt from U.S. income taxes, but the most recent data display different patterns because of changing assessments of credit risks relative to Treasury securities.

[1] From February 18, 2002, to February 9, 2006, the U.S. Treasury published a factor for adjusting the daily nominal 20-year constant maturity in order to estimate a 30-year nominal rate. The historical adjustment factor can be found at www.treas.gov/offices/domestic-finance/debt-management/interest-rate/ltcompositeindex_historical.shtml.

The *fixed-rate first mortgage* rates are primary market contract interest rates on commitments for fixed-rate conventional 30-year first mortgages. The rates are obtained by the Federal Reserve from the Federal Home Loan Mortgage Corporation (FHLMC, or Freddie Mac).

Stock price indexes and yields. The *Dow Jones industrial average* is an average price of 30 stocks compiled by Dow Jones, Inc. The *Standard and Poor's composite* is an index of the prices of 500 stocks that are weighted by the volume of shares outstanding, accounting for about 90 percent of New York Stock Exchange value, with a base of 1941–1943 = 10, compiled by Standard and Poor's Corporation. (Before February 1957, these data are based on a conversion of an earlier 90-stock index.) The *dividend-price ratio* is compiled by Standard and Poor's, covering the 500 stocks in the S&P index. It represents aggregate cash dividends (based on the latest known annual rate) divided by aggregate market value based on Wednesday closing prices. The *earnings/price ratio* measures earnings (after taxes) for four quarters, ending with the indicated quarter, as a ratio to stock prices for the last day of that quarter. Monthly data are averages of weekly figures; annual data are averages of monthly or quarterly figures. The *Nasdaq composite index* is an average price of over 5,000 stocks traded on the Nasdaq exchange.

FHFA (formerly OFHEO) House Price Indexes. The value of single-family owner-occupied houses has been an increasingly important element in household wealth and credit expansion and the subsequent collapse. The Federal Housing Finance Agency (FHFA), a government agency charged with regulation of the government-sponsored mortgage finance institutions Fannie Mae and Freddie Mac and the 12 Federal Home Loan Banks, uses data from those institutions to compile quarterly House Price Indexes of the value of existing single-family homes. Not included are condominiums, cooperatives, multi-unit properties, and planned unit developments. These indexes were developed by the predecessor agency, the Office of Federal Housing Enterprise Oversight (OFHEO), and have been published since the fourth quarter of 1995.

The data come from all properties for which a conventional, "conforming" mortgage has been purchased or securitized by Fannie Mae or Freddie Mac since January 1975. (Conventional mortgages are those not insured or guaranteed by the FHA, VA, or other federal government entities. A conforming mortgage is one no larger than the maximum that the insuring institution will insure. The limit has increased over time and has been $417,000 since the beginning of 2006. Loan limits for mortgages originated in the latter half of 2007 through Dec. 31, 2008, were raised to as much as $729,750 in high-cost areas in the continental United States. Legislation generally extended those limits for 2009-originated mortgages, and the limits for 2010 originations were further extended for certain places.) Every new mortgage transaction that can be matched against a previous transaction for that property yields a rate of price change over the period between the two transactions, which enters into the calculation of the index. This data set is very large, with about 32 million repeat transactions over the 32-year span. Due to the size of this data set, the index can be calculated not only for the United States as a whole but also for regions, states, metropolitan statistical areas (MSAs) and metropolitan divisions (subdivisions of MSAs). The index is computed using a modified version of the Case-Shiller geometric weighted repeat-sales procedure.

In addition, FHFA now publishes a Purchase-Only Index for the house purchase subgroup of new mortgage transactions, excluding refinancing transactions. This index is based on 4.7 million transactions over the latest 16 years. While this is still a very large statistical base, it is subject to somewhat greater revision and is less reliable for smaller geographical areas.

The FHFA price indexes are subject to revision for preceding quarters and years, because each new transaction, when reported, affects the rate of price change since the last time that the property involved in the new transaction changed hands or was refinanced.

Seasonally adjusted data are also available for the purchase-only indexes. Seasonal price patterns appear to have some significance, especially for regional indexes. The seasonally adjusted indexes are not shown here because the year-over-change, calculated from not-seasonally-adjusted data, is the main focus of attention in these data.

The FHFA indexes do not come from a random sample of house prices, and users need to consider possible sources of bias. Expensive houses are under-represented in general because the transactions are limited to conforming mortgages. This is important if the price trends for expensive houses are different. It is also suspected that houses that are refinanced may be those that have appreciated in price more than other houses. In fact, although the new purchase-only indexes sometimes show significantly different appreciation rates quarter by quarter, their longer-term trends are quite similar. Between the end of 1991 and the end of 2007, total house prices rose 122 percent while purchased houses rose 115 percent. Since then the total index declined 8.7 percent while the prices of purchased houses fell 9.4 percent.

New privately-developed house price indexes are now receiving regular media attention, and even provide the basis for a futures contract trading on the Chicago Mercantile Exchange. Standard & Poor's now issues S&P/Case-Shiller® Home Price Indexes each month. They cover resales only for houses at all price ranges, based on information obtained from county assessor and recorder offices. They are value-weighted, meaning that price trends for more expensive homes have greater influence on changes in the index. The FHFA index weights price trends equally for all properties. S&P/Case-Shiller data are only collected for 20 major metropolitan statistical areas. Series description and data can be found at <http://www.homeprice.standardandpoors.com>.

Data availability and references

Interest rates and bond yields are published weekly in the Federal Reserve's H.15 release, "Selected Interest Rates"; the release and current and historical data are available on the Federal Reserve Web site. The starting dates for individual interest rate series vary; some date back to 1911, and many begin in the 1950s and 1960s. See the notes and definitions to Chapters 18 and 20 for sources for data for earlier years not available on the Web site.

Stock market data are published monthly in *Economic Indicators*, and annually in *Economic Report of the President*, available online at <http://www.gpo.gov/fdsys>. Some historical interest rate data that are not available on the Federal Reserve Web site were also taken from the *Economic Report of the President*.

The FHFA house price indexes for the United States as a whole, regions, states, and metropolitan and sub-metropolitan groups are published every 3 months, approximately 2 months after the end of the previous quarter. The release and supporting data and explanatory material are available at <http://www.fhfa.gov>.

The OFHEO (now (FHFA) and other price indexes for houses are discussed and compared in Jordan Rappaport, "Comparing Aggregate Housing Price Measures," *Business Economics*, October 2007, pp. 55-65.

CHAPTER 13: INTERNATIONAL COMPARISONS

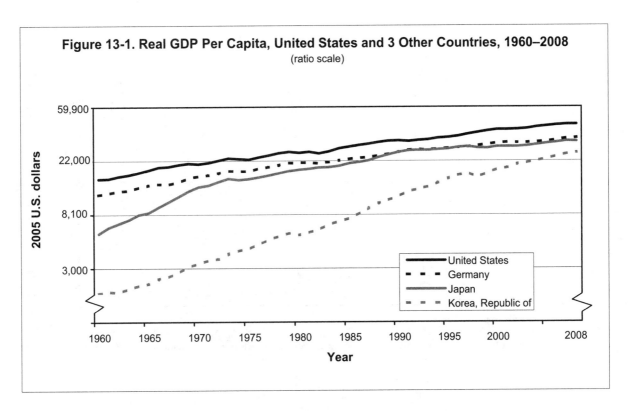

Figure 13-1. Real GDP Per Capita, United States and 3 Other Countries, 1960–2008
(ratio scale)

- In the United States, gross domestic product (GDP) per capita grew at an annual rate of 2.1 percent between 1960 and 2008. The major industrial nations with the next-highest average levels of living in 1960 grew at similar rates of 2.0 to 2.4 percent. Industrial nations that were further behind in 1960—Italy, Japan, and Korea—grew at faster rates: 2.6 percent, 3.6 percent, and 5.6 percent, respectively. The growth paths of the United States, Germany, Japan, and Korea are compared in Figure 13-1. (Table 13-2)

- In France, Germany, Italy, Japan, and the United Kingdom, the growth rate in GDP per employed person—a measure of labor productivity—was very similar to the growth rate in GDP per capita. In other words, growth in productivity and in potential living standards was the same. In contrast, growth in GDP per employee was significantly less than per capita output growth in the United States and the other countries shown. In these countries, a significant fraction of the growth in GDP per capita was obtained from putting a larger proportion of the population to work, instead of from greater efficiency. The growth rates in output per employee in the United States, Australia, and Canada were 1.3 to 1.6 percent, significantly lower than in the other countries shown. (Tables 13-2 and 13-3)

- In 2008, inflation in the 10 countries shown in Table 13-4 ranged from 1.3 percent in Japan to 4.3 percent in Australia. (Table 13-4)

- The portion of the civilian working-age population employed is markedly lower in France, Germany, and Italy than in the Netherlands and the English-speaking countries, with Japan in between. (Table 13-6)

Table 13-1. International Comparisons: Growth Rates in Real Gross Domestic Product (GDP)

(Percent change at annual rate.)

Area and country	1991–2000	2001	2002	2003	2004	2005	2006	2007	2008	2009 [1]	2010 [1]
World	3.1	2.3	2.9	3.6	4.9	4.5	5.1	5.2	3.0	-0.8	3.9
Advanced economies	2.8	1.4	1.7	1.9	3.2	2.6	3.0	2.7	0.5	-3.2	2.1
United States	3.4	1.1	1.8	2.5	3.6	3.1	2.7	2.1	0.4	-2.5	2.7
Japan	1.2	0.2	0.3	1.4	2.7	1.9	2.0	2.3	-1.2	-5.3	1.7
United Kingdom	2.5	2.5	2.1	2.8	3.0	2.2	2.9	2.6	0.5	-4.8	1.3
Canada	2.9	1.8	2.9	1.9	3.1	3.0	2.9	2.5	0.4	-2.6	2.6
Euro area [2]	. . .	1.9	0.9	0.8	2.2	1.7	2.9	2.7	0.6	-3.9	1.0
Germany	2.1	1.2	0.0	-0.2	1.2	0.7	3.2	2.5	1.2	-4.8	1.5
France	2.0	1.8	1.1	1.1	2.3	1.9	2.4	2.3	0.3	-2.3	1.4
Italy	1.6	1.8	0.5	0.0	1.5	0.7	2.0	1.6	-1.0	-4.8	1.0
Spain	2.9	3.6	2.7	3.1	3.3	3.6	4.0	3.6	0.9	-3.6	-0.6
Memorandum:											
Newly industrialized Asian economies [3]	6.1	1.2	5.6	3.1	5.9	4.7	5.6	5.7	1.7	-1.2	4.8
Emerging and developing economies	3.6	3.8	4.8	6.2	7.5	7.1	7.9	8.3	6.1	2.1	6.0
Regional groups:											
Africa	2.4	4.9	6.5	5.4	6.7	5.7	6.1	6.3	5.2	1.9	4.3
Central and eastern Europe	2.0	0.2	4.4	4.8	7.3	6.0	6.6	5.5	3.1	-4.3	2.0
Commonwealth of Independent States [4]	. . .	6.1	5.2	7.8	8.2	6.7	8.4	8.6	5.5	-7.5	3.8
Russia	. . .	5.1	4.7	7.3	7.2	6.4	7.7	8.1	5.6	-9.0	3.6
Developing Asia	7.4	5.8	6.9	8.2	8.6	9.0	9.8	10.6	7.9	6.5	8.4
China	10.4	8.3	9.1	10.0	10.1	10.4	11.6	13.0	9.6	8.7	10.0
India	5.6	3.9	4.6	6.9	7.9	9.2	9.8	9.4	7.3	5.6	7.7
Middle East	4.0	2.5	3.8	6.9	5.9	5.5	5.8	6.2	5.3	2.2	4.5
Western Hemisphere	3.3	0.7	0.6	2.2	6.0	4.7	5.7	5.7	4.2	-2.3	3.7
Brazil	2.5	1.3	2.7	1.1	5.7	3.2	4.0	5.7	5.1	-0.4	4.7
Mexico	3.5	-0.2	0.8	1.7	4.0	3.2	5.1	3.3	1.3	-6.8	4.0

[1]All figures are forecasts as published by the International Monetary Fund.
[2]Euro area consists of: Austria, Belgium, Cyprus, Finland, France, Germany, Greece, Ireland, Italy, Luxembourg, Malta, Netherlands, Portugal, Slovac Republic, Slovenia, and Spain.
[3]Includes Hong Kong SAR (Special Administrative Region of China), Korea (Republic of), Singapore, and Taiwan Province of China.
[4]Includes Mongolia, which is not a member of the Commonwealth of Independent States, but is included for reasons of geography and similarities in economic structure.
. . . = Not available.

Table 13-2. International Comparisons: Real Gross Domestic Product (GDP) Per Capita

(2005 U.S. dollars.)

Year	United States	Australia	Canada	France	Germany [1]	Italy	Japan	Korea, Republic of	Netherlands	Spain	United Kingdom
1960	15 644	13 268	13 016	9 531	11 702	8 369	5 698	1 877	12 344	. . .	12 382
1961	15 749	12 853	13 158	9 899	12 082	8 996	6 375	1 929	12 534	. . .	12 566
1962	16 448	13 343	13 819	10 389	12 498	9 490	6 858	1 914	12 891	. . .	12 587
1963	16 922	13 864	14 284	10 855	12 726	9 949	7 385	2 032	13 135	. . .	13 046
1964	17 660	14 494	14 925	11 439	13 438	10 144	8 124	2 171	14 075	8 878	13 668
1965	18 560	14 899	15 590	11 885	14 001	10 387	8 409	2 238	14 619	9 332	13 880
1966	19 543	15 067	16 319	12 406	14 263	10 924	9 287	2 448	14 832	9 902	14 071
1967	19 818	15 817	16 496	12 915	14 186	11 623	10 197	2 533	15 442	10 209	14 335
1968	20 567	16 412	17 036	13 386	14 905	12 306	11 284	2 755	16 310	10 773	14 868
1969	20 994	17 171	17 639	14 232	15 866	12 983	12 484	3 066	17 220	11 596	15 109
1970	20 789	17 935	17 921	14 967	16 505	13 600	13 488	3 263	18 055	11 943	15 400
1971	21 218	17 815	18 117	15 601	16 834	13 783	13 889	3 463	18 603	12 333	15 640
1972	22 104	17 913	18 884	16 182	17 439	14 211	14 849	3 550	19 064	13 179	16 162
1973	23 155	18 443	19 953	17 105	18 180	15 121	15 820	3 908	19 940	14 049	17 287
1974	22 827	18 442	20 403	17 755	18 193	15 848	15 418	4 117	20 466	14 706	17 056
1975	22 563	18 625	20 474	17 501	18 031	15 425	15 701	4 290	20 291	14 652	16 953
1976	23 536	19 109	21 256	18 200	19 083	16 441	16 158	4 668	21 021	14 961	17 402
1977	24 376	19 225	21 736	18 762	19 667	16 791	16 710	5 055	21 422	15 174	17 824
1978	25 462	19 421	22 371	19 420	20 281	17 273	17 434	5 442	21 869	15 194	18 403
1979	25 978	20 013	22 993	20 019	21 127	18 250	18 237	5 723	22 158	15 089	18 876
1980	25 621	20 341	23 190	20 253	21 262	18 837	18 606	5 551	22 274	15 204	18 453
1981	26 005	20 859	23 708	20 325	21 243	18 973	19 015	5 802	21 946	15 097	18 200
1982	25 259	20 506	22 758	20 696	21 058	19 038	19 405	6 131	21 576	15 204	18 603
1983	26 163	20 136	23 146	20 831	21 504	19 253	19 584	6 693	21 936	15 400	19 269
1984	27 798	21 141	24 261	21 039	22 199	19 870	20 066	7 146	22 522	15 611	19 751
1985	28 690	22 063	25 190	21 293	22 705	20 420	20 956	7 557	22 999	15 915	20 409
1986	29 416	22 204	25 545	21 705	23 222	21 003	21 468	8 277	23 512	16 383	21 180
1987	30 139	22 831	26 281	22 125	23 561	21 671	22 177	9 106	23 807	17 250	22 099
1988	31 101	23 371	27 232	23 011	24 290	22 569	23 580	9 977	24 467	18 088	23 165
1989	31 899	24 039	27 446	23 829	24 922	23 316	24 735	10 545	25 400	18 925	23 627
1990	32 135	24 033	27 086	24 327	25 847	23 775	25 936	11 398	26 284	19 611	23 745
1991	31 657	23 465	26 205	24 453	26 804	24 116	26 699	12 345	26 709	20 064	23 332
1992	32 278	23 652	26 121	24 667	27 193	24 293	26 858	12 936	26 960	20 184	23 307
1993	32 713	24 344	26 438	24 338	26 781	24 062	26 844	13 590	27 107	19 914	23 771
1994	33 618	25 272	27 405	24 787	27 410	24 575	27 070	14 603	27 744	20 333	24 725
1995	34 055	25 875	27 884	25 222	27 847	25 269	27 534	15 782	28 462	20 845	25 406
1996	34 906	26 579	28 039	25 415	28 043	25 539	28 225	16 726	29 307	21 300	26 075
1997	36 042	27 390	28 935	25 894	28 495	26 003	28 600	17 341	30 402	22 066	26 868
1998	37 112	28 436	29 871	26 704	29 081	26 360	27 944	16 036	31 402	22 971	27 760
1999	38 323	29 391	31 267	27 463	29 645	26 742	27 862	17 433	32 652	23 868	28 622
2000	39 292	30 019	32 598	28 344	30 559	27 717	28 600	18 755	33 698	24 792	29 641
2001	39 187	30 221	32 824	28 663	30 881	28 203	28 565	19 331	34 088	25 282	30 254
2002	39 432	31 134	33 405	28 750	30 828	28 242	28 602	20 598	33 894	25 475	30 779
2003	40 050	31 658	33 708	28 860	30 747	28 018	28 959	21 070	33 849	25 848	31 522
2004	41 137	32 505	34 420	29 358	31 125	28 168	29 732	21 961	34 493	26 267	32 235
2005	41 961	32 964	35 075	29 692	31 380	28 144	30 312	22 783	35 111	26 754	32 684
2006	42 725	33 417	35 798	30 148	32 347	28 554	30 929	23 884	36 243	27 456	33 418
2007	43 170	34 119	36 377	30 667	33 184	28 789	31 652	25 021	37 415	28 010	34 209
2008	43 250	34 254	36 123	30 624	33 663	28 245	31 446	25 498	38 035	27 747	34 356

[1]Before 1991, data are based on growth in West Germany alone.

. . . = Not available.

Table 13-3. International Comparisons: Real Gross Domestic Product (GDP) Per Employed Person

(2005 U.S. dollars.)

Year	United States	Australia	Canada	France	Germany [1]	Italy	Japan	Korea, Republic of	Netherlands	Spain	United Kingdom
1960	41 409	32 804	37 322	22 247	23 481	20 079	11 429	. . .	30 834	. . .	26 862
1961	42 356	32 527	37 918	23 358	24 231	21 589	12 616	. . .	31 272	. . .	27 202
1962	44 141	33 584	39 453	24 969	25 273	22 995	13 544	. . .	31 976	. . .	27 365
1963	45 439	34 583	40 605	26 341	25 922	24 695	14 610	7 324	32 587	. . .	28 479
1964	47 048	35 649	41 754	27 750	27 625	25 474	16 006	7 891	34 779	. . .	29 645
1965	48 869	36 206	42 844	29 023	28 940	26 965	16 656	7 919	36 313	. . .	30 005
1966	50 543	35 718	43 900	30 334	29 839	29 053	17 975	8 656	37 042	. . .	30 517
1967	50 615	37 243	43 809	31 762	30 749	30 755	19 564	8 848	39 126	. . .	31 633
1968	51 965	38 360	45 030	33 277	32 398	32 785	21 485	9 376	41 363	. . .	33 118
1969	52 282	39 979	45 854	35 149	34 282	35 036	23 821	10 417	43 452	. . .	33 806
1970	52 079	40 934	46 685	36 820	35 558	36 726	25 974	10 939	45 580	. . .	34 660
1971	53 621	41 570	47 439	38 587	36 497	37 381	26 924	11 449	47 266	29 451	35 413
1972	54 846	41 868	48 558	40 158	37 898	38 861	29 038	11 461	49 365	31 463	36 599
1973	56 155	42 532	49 424	42 220	39 275	41 049	30 677	12 180	52 030	33 068	38 638
1974	54 847	42 734	49 151	43 734	39 835	42 645	30 429	12 507	53 303	34 799	38 046
1975	55 360	43 784	49 141	43 693	40 422	41 721	31 448	12 945	53 717	35 695	37 962
1976	56 469	44 941	50 682	45 278	42 801	44 246	32 432	13 482	55 805	37 282	39 191
1977	57 033	44 986	51 544	46 512	43 956	45 240	33 455	14 367	56 033	38 590	40 093
1978	57 746	45 904	51 999	48 118	44 907	46 552	34 878	14 999	56 987	40 148	41 180
1979	57 949	47 002	51 729	49 565	46 029	48 783	36 417	15 793	57 136	41 094	41 862
1980	57 537	47 028	51 345	50 270	45 775	49 738	37 188	15 466	56 140	42 634	41 159
1981	58 333	47 982	51 640	50 928	45 869	50 198	37 989	16 021	55 395	43 623	41 688
1982	57 674	48 008	51 804	52 104	45 986	50 303	38 723	16 769	54 992	44 549	43 416
1983	59 503	48 649	52 832	52 890	47 470	50 727	38 760	18 414	57 184	45 496	45 320
1984	61 286	50 179	54 534	54 012	48 728	52 367	39 834	20 011	58 205	47 367	45 556
1985	62 557	51 480	55 541	55 139	49 349	53 327	41 633	20 600	58 060	48 969	46 611
1986	63 304	50 431	55 191	56 281	49 817	54 478	42 646	22 001	58 748	49 417	48 187
1987	63 812	51 503	55 924	57 244	50 190	56 088	44 090	23 175	59 826	49 774	49 412
1988	65 035	51 643	56 981	59 335	51 656	57 820	46 532	24 859	60 162	50 539	50 257
1989	66 009	51 798	57 187	60 783	52 760	59 374	48 283	25 491	61 550	51 126	50 114
1990	66 465	51 623	56 905	61 897	54 160	59 643	49 961	27 017	62 085	51 118	50 280
1991	66 975	52 222	56 705	62 458	55 511	59 445	50 606	28 661	61 961	51 797	50 921
1992	68 845	53 551	57 775	63 681	57 584	60 342	50 527	29 770	61 755	53 016	52 238
1993	69 748	55 409	58 847	63 923	57 889	61 457	50 461	31 227	62 604	54 002	53 916
1994	70 982	56 391	60 434	65 244	59 489	63 831	50 962	32 844	64 004	55 550	55 807
1995	71 756	56 250	61 045	66 039	60 477	65 766	51 890	34 861	64 109	56 016	56 842
1996	73 400	57 790	61 480	66 522	61 246	66 109	53 094	36 516	64 962	56 558	57 951
1997	75 059	59 657	62 767	67 713	62 409	67 137	53 554	37 564	65 651	57 081	58 829
1998	77 086	61 340	63 768	69 035	62 924	67 411	53 082	37 228	66 282	57 393	60 339
1999	79 326	63 099	65 618	69 902	63 332	67 664	53 747	40 051	67 566	58 014	61 580
2000	80 222	63 606	67 389	70 738	64 163	68 829	55 630	41 673	68 390	58 890	63 258
2001	80 777	64 216	67 755	70 791	64 674	68 693	56 157	42 438	67 943	59 155	64 289
2002	82 285	65 686	68 073	71 076	65 038	67 845	57 200	44 247	67 177	59 448	65 143
2003	83 520	66 089	67 757	71 758	65 517	66 832	58 199	45 549	67 785	59 421	66 337
2004	85 624	67 309	68 674	73 452	66 045	67 558	59 667	46 770	69 439	59 306	67 456
2005	86 641	67 058	69 676	74 431	66 605	67 612	60 591	47 985	70 825	59 065	68 163
2006	87 437	67 563	70 470	75 342	68 146	67 662	61 557	49 827	71 874	58 956	69 500
2007	88 238	68 328	70 746	76 063	68 644	67 875	62 763	51 741	72 582	59 242	71 130
2008	89 626	68 198	69 991	75 989	68 547	66 959	62 578	52 568	72 995	60 283	71 121

[1]Before 1991, data are based on growth in West Germany alone.
. . . = Not available.

Table 13-4. International Comparisons: Consumer Price Indexes

(1982–1984 = 100.)

Year	United States		Australia		Canada		France		Germany[1]		Italy		Japan		Netherlands		Spain		United Kingdom	
	Index	Percent change	Index	Percent change	Index	Percent change	Index	Percent change	Index	Percent change	Index	Percent change	Index	Percent change	Index	Percent change	Index	Percent change	Index	Percent change
1950	24.1	...	12.6	...	21.6	...	11.2	...	34.0	...		...	...	...	21.0	...	5.5	...	9.8	...
1951	26.0	7.9	15.1	19.8	23.8	10.2	13.1	17.0	36.6	7.6		...	...	...	23.1	10.0	6.0	9.1	10.7	9.2
1952	26.5	1.9	17.7	17.2	24.5	2.9	14.7	12.2	37.3	1.9		...	...	...	23.1	0.0	5.9	-1.7	11.7	9.3
1953	26.7	0.8	18.4	4.0	24.2	-1.2	14.5	-1.4	36.7	-1.6	10.3	...	...	...	23.1	0.0	6.0	1.7	12.1	3.4
1954	26.9	0.7	18.6	1.1	24.4	0.8	14.4	-0.7	36.8	0.3	10.6	2.9	...	...	24.0	3.9	6.1	1.7	12.3	1.7
1955	26.8	-0.4	19.0	2.2	24.4	0.0	14.6	1.4	37.3	1.4	10.9	2.8	...	...	24.5	2.1	6.3	3.3	12.8	4.1
1956	27.2	1.5	20.1	5.8	24.7	1.2	14.9	2.1	38.4	2.9	11.2	2.8	...	...	24.9	1.6	6.7	6.3	13.5	5.5
1957	28.1	3.3	20.6	2.5	25.6	3.6	15.3	2.7	39.1	1.8	11.4	1.8	...	...	26.5	6.4	7.4	10.4	14.0	3.7
1958	28.9	2.8	20.9	1.5	26.3	2.7	17.6	15.0	40.0	2.3	11.7	2.6	...	...	27.0	1.9	8.4	13.5	14.4	2.9
1959	29.1	0.7	21.3	1.9	26.4	0.4	18.7	6.2	40.3	0.7	11.7	0.0	...	...	27.2	0.7	9.0	7.1	14.5	0.7
1960	29.6	1.7	22.1	3.8	26.8	1.5	19.4	3.7	40.9	1.5	11.9	1.7	...	...	27.9	2.6	9.1	1.1	14.6	0.7
1961	29.9	1.0	22.6	2.3	27.1	1.1	20.0	3.1	42.0	2.7	12.2	2.5	...	...	28.4	1.8	9.2	1.1	15.1	3.4
1962	30.2	1.0	22.6	0.0	27.5	1.5	21.0	5.0	43.1	2.6	12.7	4.1	...	...	28.9	1.8	9.7	5.4	15.8	4.6
1963	30.6	1.3	22.7	0.4	27.8	1.1	22.0	4.8	44.4	3.0	13.7	7.9	...	...	30.0	3.8	10.6	9.3	16.1	1.9
1964	31.0	1.3	23.2	2.2	28.3	1.8	22.7	3.2	45.5	2.5	14.5	5.8	...	...	31.7	5.7	11.3	6.6	16.6	3.1
1965	31.5	1.6	24.1	3.9	29.0	2.5	23.3	2.6	46.9	3.1	15.2	4.8	...	...	33.3	5.0	12.8	13.3	17.4	4.8
1966	32.4	2.9	24.9	3.3	30.2	4.1	23.9	2.6	48.5	3.4	15.5	2.0	...	...	35.3	6.0	13.6	6.2	18.1	4.0
1967	33.4	3.1	25.7	3.2	31.3	3.6	24.6	2.9	49.4	1.9	16.1	3.9	...	...	36.4	3.1	14.5	6.6	18.6	2.8
1968	34.8	4.2	26.4	2.7	32.5	3.8	25.7	4.5	50.2	1.6	16.3	1.2	...	...	37.7	3.6	15.2	4.8	19.4	4.3
1969	36.7	5.5	27.2	3.0	34.0	4.6	27.3	6.2	51.1	1.8	16.7	2.5	...	...	40.5	7.4	15.5	2.0	20.5	5.7
1970	38.8	5.7	28.2	3.7	35.1	3.2	28.8	5.5	52.9	3.5	17.5	4.8	38.4	...	42.3	4.4	16.4	5.8	21.8	6.3
1971	40.5	4.4	29.8	5.7	36.1	2.8	30.3	5.2	55.7	5.3	18.4	5.1	40.9	6.5	45.5	7.6	17.7	7.9	23.8	9.2
1972	41.8	3.2	31.7	6.4	37.8	4.7	32.2	6.3	58.7	5.4	19.4	5.4	42.9	4.9	49.1	7.9	19.2	8.5	25.5	7.1
1973	44.4	6.2	34.6	9.1	40.8	7.9	34.6	7.5	62.8	7.0	21.6	11.3	47.9	11.7	53.0	7.9	21.4	11.5	27.8	9.0
1974	49.3	11.0	39.9	15.3	45.3	11.0	39.3	13.6	67.2	7.0	25.7	19.0	59.0	23.2	58.1	9.6	24.8	15.9	32.3	16.2
1975	53.8	9.1	45.9	15.0	50.1	10.6	43.9	11.7	71.2	6.0	30.0	16.7	65.9	11.7	64.0	10.2	29.0	16.9	40.1	24.1
1976	56.9	5.8	52.0	13.3	53.7	7.2	48.2	9.8	74.2	4.2	35.1	17.0	72.2	9.6	69.6	8.7	34.1	17.6	46.8	16.7
1977	60.6	6.5	58.5	12.5	58.1	8.2	52.7	9.3	77.0	3.8	41.0	16.8	78.1	8.2	74.3	6.8	42.4	24.3	54.2	15.8
1978	65.2	7.6	63.1	7.9	63.2	8.8	57.5	9.1	79.1	2.7	46.0	12.2	81.4	4.2	77.3	4.0	50.8	19.8	58.7	8.3
1979	72.6	11.3	68.8	9.0	69.1	9.3	63.6	10.6	82.3	4.0	52.8	14.8	84.3	3.6	80.6	4.3	58.8	15.7	66.6	13.5
1980	82.4	13.5	75.8	10.2	76.0	10.0	72.3	13.7	86.8	5.5	64.0	21.2	91.0	7.9	85.8	6.5	67.9	15.5	78.5	17.9
1981	90.9	10.3	83.1	9.6	85.5	12.5	82.0	13.4	92.2	6.2	75.4	17.8	95.3	4.7	91.6	6.8	77.8	14.6	87.9	12.0
1982	96.5	6.2	92.5	11.3	94.9	11.0	91.6	11.7	97.1	5.3	87.8	16.4	98.1	2.9	97.1	6.0	89.0	14.4	95.4	8.5
1983	99.6	3.2	101.8	10.1	100.4	5.8	100.5	9.7	100.2	3.2	100.7	14.7	99.8	1.7	99.8	2.8	99.9	12.2	99.8	4.6
1984	103.9	4.3	105.8	3.9	104.7	4.3	107.9	7.4	102.7	2.5	111.5	10.7	102.1	2.3	103.1	3.3	111.1	11.2	104.8	5.0
1985	107.6	3.6	112.9	6.7	108.9	4.0	114.2	5.8	104.8	2.0	121.8	9.2	104.2	2.1	105.4	2.2	120.9	8.8	111.1	6.0
1986	109.6	1.9	123.2	9.1	113.4	4.1	117.2	2.6	104.7	-0.1	129.0	5.9	104.8	0.6	105.6	0.2	131.6	8.9	114.9	3.4
1987	113.6	3.6	133.6	8.4	118.4	4.4	120.9	3.2	104.9	0.2	135.1	4.7	104.9	0.1	105.1	-0.5	138.5	5.2	119.7	4.2
1988	118.3	4.1	143.3	7.3	123.0	3.9	124.2	2.7	106.2	1.2	141.9	5.0	104.9	0.1	105.8	0.7	145.2	4.8	125.6	4.9
1989	124.0	4.8	154.1	7.5	129.3	5.1	128.6	3.5	109.2	2.8	150.8	6.3	108.0	2.3	107.0	1.1	155.0	6.7	135.4	7.8
1990	130.7	5.4	165.3	7.3	135.5	4.8	133.0	3.4	112.1	2.7	160.5	6.4	111.3	3.1	109.6	2.4	165.4	6.7	148.2	9.5
1991	136.2	4.2	170.7	3.3	143.1	5.6	137.3	3.2	116.3	3.7	170.6	6.3	115.1	3.4	113.8	3.8	175.2	5.9	156.9	5.9
1992	140.3	3.0	172.4	1.0	145.2	1.5	140.5	2.3	122.3	5.2	179.5	5.2	117.0	1.7	118.1	3.8	185.6	5.9	162.7	3.7
1993	144.5	3.0	175.5	1.8	147.9	1.9	143.5	2.1	127.6	4.3	187.8	4.6	118.5	1.3	120.5	2.0	194.1	4.6	165.3	1.6
1994	148.2	2.6	178.8	1.9	148.1	0.1	145.8	1.6	131.2	2.8	195.5	4.1	119.2	0.6	123.8	2.7	203.3	4.7	169.3	2.4
1995	152.4	2.8	187.1	4.6	151.4	2.2	148.4	1.8	133.4	1.7	205.8	5.3	119.1	-0.1	126.0	1.8	212.8	4.7	175.2	3.5
1996	156.9	3.0	192.0	2.6	153.6	1.5	151.3	2.0	135.3	1.4	214.0	4.0	119.2	0.1	128.7	2.1	220.3	3.5	179.4	2.4
1997	160.5	2.3	192.5	0.3	156.2	1.7	153.2	1.3	137.9	1.9	218.3	2.0	121.5	1.9	131.5	2.2	224.7	2.0	185.1	3.2
1998	163.0	1.6	194.1	0.8	157.8	1.0	154.3	0.7	139.3	1.0	222.6	2.0	122.2	0.6	134.1	2.0	228.8	1.8	191.4	3.4
1999	166.6	2.2	197.0	1.5	160.5	1.7	155.0	0.5	140.0	0.5	226.3	1.7	121.8	-0.3	137.0	2.2	234.1	2.3	194.3	1.5
2000	172.2	3.4	205.8	4.5	164.9	2.7	157.7	1.7	142.0	1.4	232.1	2.6	120.9	-0.7	140.2	2.3	242.1	3.4	200.1	3.0
2001	177.1	2.8	214.8	4.4	169.0	2.5	160.3	1.6	144.8	2.0	238.5	2.8	120.1	-0.7	146.1	4.2	250.8	3.6	203.6	1.7
2002	179.9	1.6	221.2	3.0	172.8	2.2	163.4	1.9	146.9	1.5	244.5	2.5	119.0	-0.9	150.9	3.3	259.7	3.5	207.0	1.7
2003	184.0	2.3	227.4	2.8	177.6	2.8	166.8	2.1	148.5	1.1	251.0	2.7	118.7	-0.3	154.0	2.1	267.6	3.0	213.0	2.9
2004	188.9	2.7	232.7	2.3	180.9	1.9	170.3	2.1	150.9	1.6	256.6	2.2	118.7	0.0	156.0	1.3	275.7	3.0	219.4	3.0
2005	195.3	3.4	238.9	2.7	184.9	2.2	173.4	1.8	153.2	1.5	261.6	1.9	118.3	-0.3	158.6	1.7	285.0	3.4	225.6	2.8
2006	201.6	3.2	247.4	3.6	188.5	1.9	176.2	1.6	155.7	1.6	267.1	2.1	118.7	0.3	160.4	1.1	295.0	3.5	232.8	3.2
2007	207.3	2.8	253.1	2.3	192.7	2.2	178.9	1.5	159.2	2.2	272.0	1.8	118.7	0.0	163.0	1.6	303.3	2.8	242.7	4.3
2008	215.3	3.9	264.1	4.3	197.2	2.3	183.9	2.8	163.3	2.6	281.1	3.3	120.3	1.3	167.1	2.5	315.6	4.1	252.4	4.0

[1]Data prior to 1991 are for West Germany only.
. . . = Not available.

Table 13-5. International Comparisons: Civilian Working Age Population

(Approximating U.S. concepts, thousands of persons.)

Year	United States	Australia	Canada	France	Germany [1]	Italy	Japan	Netherlands	United Kingdom
1960	117 245	. . .	11 494	31 369	43 436	37 130	64 990	. . .	38 952
1961	118 771	. . .	11 708	31 596	43 647	37 358	65 820	. . .	39 287
1962	120 153	. . .	11 940	32 319	43 972	37 815	67 330	. . .	39 804
1963	122 416	. . .	12 179	33 166	44 232	38 083	69 170	. . .	40 036
1964	124 485	7 668	12 453	33 717	44 525	38 515	71 000	. . .	40 281
1965	126 513	7 830	12 755	34 219	44 909	38 724	72 650	. . .	40 481
1966	128 058	8 023	13 083	34 606	45 174	39 276	74 090	. . .	40 631
1967	129 874	8 208	13 444	34 995	45 111	39 456	75 340	. . .	40 779
1968	132 028	8 403	13 805	35 362	45 163	39 833	76 550	. . .	40 874
1969	134 335	8 612	14 162	35 742	45 570	39 781	77 580	. . .	41 006
1970	137 085	8 819	14 528	36 151	46 094	40 279	78 620	. . .	41 101
1971	140 216	9 036	14 872	36 578	46 687	40 385	79 560	. . .	40 397
1972	144 126	9 238	15 186	36 965	47 100	40 780	80 470	. . .	40 564
1973	147 096	9 425	15 526	37 352	47 594	41 186	82 150	9 750	40 741
1974	150 120	9 614	15 924	37 711	47 904	41 745	83 170	9 885	40 912
1975	153 153	9 763	16 323	38 020	48 018	42 131	84 190	9 803	41 103
1976	156 150	9 957	16 582	38 330	48 128	42 312	85 160	9 960	41 331
1977	159 033	10 136	16 964	38 679	48 418	42 529	86 070	10 103	41 608
1978	161 910	10 406	17 302	39 008	48 788	43 000	87 020	10 256	41 904
1979	164 863	10 575	17 663	39 371	49 255	43 436	88 000	10 415	42 228
1980	167 745	10 778	18 032	39 750	49 849	43 860	89 080	10 588	42 570
1981	170 130	10 994	18 398	40 125	50 344	44 184	89 930	10 744	42 868
1982	172 271	11 204	18 716	40 476	50 714	44 847	90 920	10 871	43 083
1983	174 215	11 401	18 981	40 828	50 928	45 457	92 080	10 996	43 327
1984	176 383	11 602	19 220	41 165	51 112	45 853	93 230	11 131	43 596
1985	178 206	11 826	19 459	41 500	51 261	46 174	94 400	11 271	43 863
1986	180 587	12 074	19 715	41 846	51 467	46 628	95 630	11 403	44 087
1987	182 753	12 323	19 985	42 217	51 643	46 986	96 950	11 561	44 296
1988	184 613	12 593	20 257	42 605	51 893	47 778	98 240	11 667	44 456
1989	186 393	12 823	20 540	43 008	52 279	47 660	99 490	11 766	44 602
1990	189 164	13 051	20 852	43 343	53 135	48 016	100 660	11 865	44 705
1991	190 925	13 227	21 176	43 623	66 487	48 044	101 750	11 979	44 793
1992	192 805	13 391	21 459	43 892	67 083	48 203	102 590	12 077	44 848
1993	194 838	13 561	21 731	44 138	67 709	47 130	103 470	12 162	44 887
1994	196 814	13 729	21 994	44 377	68 022	47 430	104 200	12 246	44 960
1995	198 584	13 936	22 274	44 609	68 240	47 702	104 860	12 319	45 104
1996	200 591	14 117	22 575	44 856	68 498	47 909	105 470	12 387	45 266
1997	203 133	14 321	22 866	45 147	68 797	48 096	106 370	12 455	45 432
1998	205 220	14 525	23 130	45 446	68 914	48 277	107 040	12 538	45 610
1999	207 753	14 698	23 390	45 771	69 187	48 388	107 590	12 614	45 828
2000	212 577	14 902	23 692	46 129	69 365	48 567	108 120	12 703	46 085
2001	215 092	15 140	24 033	46 522	69 599	48 750	108 620	12 803	46 395
2002	217 570	15 390	24 395	46 910	69 900	48 894	109 030	12 892	46 680
2003	221 168	15 611	24 714	47 279	70 160	48 896	109 380	12 962	46 975
2004	223 357	15 802	25 046	47 621	70 431	49 080	109 660	13 019	47 339
2005	226 082	16 099	25 381	47 959	70 705	49 606	109 830	13 075	47 766
2006	228 815	16 368	25 760	48 280	70 844	49 913	109 960	13 128	48 166
2007	231 867	16 654	26 134	48 579	70 925	50 301	110 190	13 190	48 569
2008	233 788	16 895	26 507	48 888	70 982	50 704	110 270	13 245	48 962

[1] Data prior to 1991 are for West Germany only.
. . . = Not available.

Table 13-6. International Comparisons: Civilian Employment-Population Ratios

(Approximating U.S. concepts. Civilian employment as a percent of civilian working-age population.)

Year	United States	Australia	Canada	France	Germany [1]	Italy	Japan	Netherlands	United Kingdom
1960	56.1	. . .	52.6	58.6	59.2	54.0	66.7	. . .	60.6
1961	55.4	. . .	52.4	58.2	59.6	54.0	66.8	. . .	60.8
1962	55.5	. . .	52.8	57.1	59.3	53.2	66.0	. . .	60.4
1963	55.4	. . .	53.0	56.6	59.2	51.9	64.9	. . .	60.2
1964	55.7	58.6	53.7	56.9	58.8	51.1	64.1	. . .	60.7
1965	56.2	59.1	54.4	56.4	58.5	49.6	63.6	. . .	61.0
1966	56.9	59.6	55.4	56.4	58.0	48.1	63.7	. . .	60.9
1967	57.3	60.0	55.4	56.2	56.3	48.5	64.0	. . .	60.0
1968	57.5	60.1	55.0	55.5	56.2	47.9	64.1	. . .	59.6
1969	58.0	60.2	55.3	55.9	56.6	47.6	63.9	. . .	59.5
1970	57.4	61.1	54.5	56.1	56.6	47.4	63.8	. . .	59.2
1971	56.6	61.0	54.5	55.8	56.2	47.1	63.4	. . .	60.2
1972	57.0	60.6	54.9	55.6	55.8	45.9	62.9	. . .	60.1
1973	57.8	61.2	56.4	55.8	55.9	45.8	63.2	51.8	60.8
1974	57.8	61.3	57.3	55.8	54.8	46.2	62.2	51.6	60.7
1975	56.1	60.1	56.9	54.9	53.2	46.0	61.2	51.7	60.2
1976	56.8	59.7	58.2	54.9	52.8	46.1	61.1	51.2	59.5
1977	57.9	59.2	57.9	54.9	52.5	46.2	61.3	51.6	59.2
1978	59.3	58.0	58.5	54.7	52.6	45.9	61.3	51.3	59.1
1979	59.9	57.8	59.8	54.3	52.9	45.9	61.4	51.4	59.3
1980	59.2	58.3	60.3	53.9	53.1	46.0	61.3	52.1	58.5
1981	59.0	58.4	60.8	53.2	52.5	45.9	61.2	51.7	56.6
1982	57.8	57.3	58.0	52.8	51.6	45.1	61.2	50.8	55.2
1983	57.9	55.3	57.6	52.4	50.6	44.7	61.4	49.3	54.5
1984	59.5	56.0	58.3	51.5	50.5	44.5	61.0	49.3	55.3
1985	60.1	56.6	59.2	50.9	50.8	44.4	60.6	50.1	55.7
1986	60.7	57.8	60.2	50.8	51.3	44.2	60.4	50.3	55.7
1987	61.5	58.0	61.2	50.5	51.5	43.8	60.1	49.8	56.6
1988	62.3	58.9	62.2	50.5	51.6	43.7	60.4	50.7	58.3
1989	63.0	60.3	62.7	50.8	52.0	43.6	60.8	51.4	59.6
1990	62.8	60.4	62.2	50.9	52.6	43.9	61.3	52.7	59.8
1991	61.7	58.2	60.2	50.7	55.5	44.5	61.8	53.6	58.1
1992	61.5	57.2	58.9	50.1	54.2	44.0	62.0	54.3	56.6
1993	61.7	56.8	58.5	49.2	53.2	43.6	61.7	53.9	56.1
1994	62.5	57.8	59.0	49.0	52.6	42.5	61.3	54.0	56.4
1995	62.9	59.2	59.3	49.2	52.4	42.0	60.9	55.4	57.0
1996	63.2	59.3	59.1	49.1	52.0	42.0	60.9	56.2	57.3
1997	63.8	59.0	59.6	49.1	51.6	41.9	61.0	57.7	58.1
1998	64.1	59.3	60.4	49.7	52.3	42.2	60.2	59.1	58.5
1999	64.3	59.6	61.3	50.4	52.1	42.6	59.4	60.3	59.0
2000	64.4	60.3	62.0	51.4	52.2	43.2	59.0	61.5	59.4
2001	63.7	60.0	61.9	51.9	52.2	43.8	58.4	62.6	59.5
2002	62.7	60.2	62.4	51.8	51.5	44.3	57.5	62.9	59.6
2003	62.3	60.8	63.1	51.5	50.8	44.9	57.1	62.2	59.8
2004	62.3	61.1	63.3	51.1	50.6	45.1	57.1	61.8	60.0
2005	62.7	62.1	63.4	51.1	51.2	44.9	57.3	61.6	60.0
2006	63.1	62.6	63.6	51.2	52.2	45.5	57.5	62.5	60.1
2007	63.0	63.3	64.2	51.6	53.3	45.6	57.6	63.7	60.0
2008	62.2	63.8	64.2	52.1	54.2	45.6	57.4	64.5	59.9

[1] Data prior to 1991 are for West Germany only.
. . . = Not available.

Table 13-7. International Comparisons: Civilian Unemployment Rates

(Approximating U.S. concepts. Civilian unemployment as a percent of civilian labor force.)

Year	United States	Australia	Canada	France	Germany [1]	Italy	Japan	Netherlands	United Kingdom
1960	5.5	1.6	6.5	1.5	1.1	3.7	1.7	. . .	2.2
1961	6.7	3.0	6.7	1.2	0.6	3.2	1.5	. . .	2.0
1962	5.5	2.9	5.5	1.4	0.6	2.8	1.3	. . .	2.7
1963	5.7	2.3	5.2	1.6	0.5	2.4	1.3	. . .	3.3
1964	5.2	1.4	4.4	1.2	0.4	2.7	1.2	. . .	2.5
1965	4.5	1.3	3.6	1.6	0.3	3.5	1.2	. . .	2.1
1966	3.8	1.6	3.3	1.6	0.3	3.7	1.4	. . .	2.3
1967	3.8	1.9	3.8	2.1	1.3	3.4	1.3	. . .	3.3
1968	3.6	1.8	4.5	2.7	1.1	3.5	1.2	. . .	3.2
1969	3.5	1.8	4.4	2.3	0.6	3.5	1.1	. . .	3.1
1970	4.9	1.7	5.7	2.5	0.5	3.2	1.2	. . .	3.1
1971	5.9	1.9	6.2	2.8	0.6	3.3	1.3	. . .	4.2
1972	5.6	2.6	6.2	2.9	0.7	3.8	1.4	. . .	4.4
1973	4.9	2.3	5.6	2.8	0.7	3.7	1.3	3.1	3.7
1974	5.6	2.7	5.3	2.9	1.6	3.1	1.4	3.6	3.7
1975	8.5	4.9	6.9	3.7	3.4	3.4	1.9	5.1	4.5
1976	7.7	4.8	6.9	4.1	3.4	3.9	2.0	5.4	5.4
1977	7.1	5.6	7.8	4.5	3.4	4.1	2.0	4.9	5.6
1978	6.1	6.3	8.1	4.7	3.3	4.1	2.3	5.1	5.5
1979	5.8	6.3	7.3	5.3	2.9	4.4	2.1	5.1	5.4
1980	7.1	6.1	7.3	5.7	2.8	4.4	2.0	6.0	6.9
1981	7.6	5.8	7.3	6.7	4.0	4.9	2.2	8.9	9.7
1982	9.7	7.2	10.7	7.3	5.6	5.4	2.4	10.2	10.8
1983	9.6	10.0	11.6	7.6	6.9	5.9	2.7	11.4	11.5
1984	7.5	9.0	10.9	8.9	7.1	5.9	2.8	11.5	11.8
1985	7.2	8.3	10.2	9.4	7.2	6.0	2.7	9.6	11.4
1986	7.0	7.9	9.3	9.5	6.6	7.5	2.8	10.0	11.4
1987	6.2	7.9	8.4	9.6	6.3	7.9	2.9	9.8	10.5
1988	5.5	7.0	7.4	9.2	6.3	7.9	2.5	9.3	8.6
1989	5.3	6.0	7.1	8.6	5.7	7.8	2.3	8.4	7.3
1990	5.6	6.7	7.7	8.3	5.0	7.0	2.1	7.6	7.1
1991	6.8	9.3	9.8	8.5	5.6	6.9	2.1	7.1	8.9
1992	7.5	10.5	10.6	9.4	6.7	7.3	2.2	6.8	10.0
1993	6.9	10.6	10.8	10.5	8.0	9.8	2.5	6.3	10.4
1994	6.1	9.4	9.6	11.1	8.5	10.7	2.9	6.9	9.5
1995	5.6	8.2	8.6	10.5	8.2	11.3	3.2	7.1	8.7
1996	5.4	8.2	8.8	11.1	9.0	11.3	3.4	6.6	8.1
1997	4.9	8.3	8.4	11.1	9.9	11.4	3.4	5.6	7.0
1998	4.5	7.7	7.7	10.6	9.3	11.5	4.1	4.4	6.3
1999	4.2	6.9	7.0	10.2	8.5	11.0	4.7	3.5	6.0
2000	4.0	6.3	6.1	8.7	7.8	10.2	4.8	3.0	5.5
2001	4.7	6.8	6.5	7.9	7.9	9.2	5.1	2.3	5.1
2002	5.8	6.4	7.0	8.1	8.6	8.7	5.4	2.8	5.2
2003	6.0	5.9	6.9	8.6	9.3	8.5	5.3	3.7	5.0
2004	5.5	5.4	6.4	9.0	10.3	8.1	4.8	4.6	4.8
2005	5.1	5.0	6.0	9.0	11.2	7.8	4.5	4.8	4.9
2006	4.6	4.8	5.5	9.0	10.4	6.9	4.2	3.9	5.5
2007	4.6	4.4	5.3	8.1	8.7	6.2	3.9	3.2	5.4
2008	5.8	4.2	5.3	7.5	7.5	6.8	4.0	2.8	5.7

[1]Data prior to 1991 are for West Germany only.
. . . = Not available.

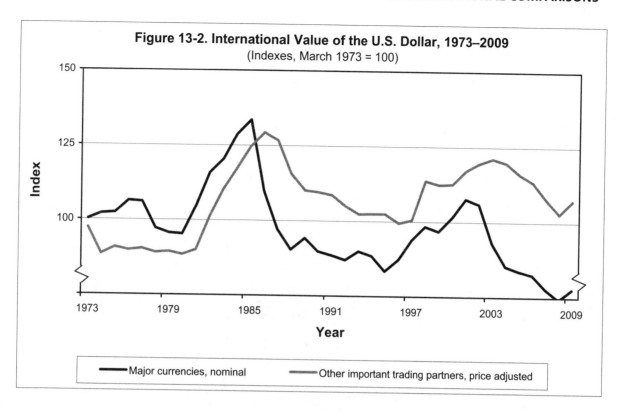

Figure 13-2. International Value of the U.S. Dollar, 1973–2009
(Indexes, March 1973 = 100)

- Aggregate indexes of the value of the dollar based on annual averages, such as the two shown in the above figure, obscure the dramatic shorter-term developments in currency values that occurred when financial crisis struck in the autumn of 2008 and then gradually subsided over the course of 2009. Against European and Canadian currencies, the dollar rose sharply in late 2008, but by December 2009 it had fallen back closer to pre-crisis levels—only to soar again in early 2010 in response to the Greek budget crisis. Against the yen, however, the predominant movement was downward, and the December 2009 value of the dollar in yen was 16 percent below the September 2008 level. (Table 13-8)

- Figure 13-2 above displays two indexes of the dollar's value. One is relative to a weighted average of seven major currencies—the euro, the British pound, the Canadian dollar, the Japanese yen, the Swiss franc, the Australian dollar, and the Swedish krona. These are all major industrial countries whose currencies are freely traded on world markets. Measured against these major currencies in terms of annual averages, the dollar depreciated 31 percent from 2001 to 2008, comparable to the 32 percent drop from 1985 to 1988. Dollar depreciation seems unsurprising in light of the large current-account deficits detailed in Chapter 7. (Table 13-8 and Chapter 7)

- However, the major-currency index is not relevant to the emerging-market currencies ("Other important trading partners" or OITP) that account for much of the U.S. trade deficit. Many emerging-market countries, especially China, are able to control the international values of their currencies (through, for example, direct capital controls) and keep their currencies from appreciating relative to the dollar to maintain their competitiveness in the U.S. market. In 2008 the Chinese allowed some yuan appreciation, as can be seen in Table 13-8. Overall, there was a 12 percent decline in the price-adjusted OITP index from 2001 to 2008. (Table 13-8)

Table 13-8. Foreign Exchange Rates

(Not seasonally adjusted.)

Year and month	Foreign currency per U.S. dollar							Trade-weighted exchange indexes of value of U.S. dollar					
								Nominal				Price-adjusted	
	Canada, dollar	China (P.R.), yuan (renminbi)	EMU members, euro	Germany, mark	Japan, yen	Switzerland, franc	United Kingdom, pound	G-10 countries (March 1973 = 100)	Broad (January 1997 = 100)	Major currencies (March 1973 = 100)	Other important trading partners (January 1997 = 100)	Broad (March 1973 = 100)	Other important trading partners (March 1973 = 100)
1971	1.0099	...	...	3.4673	346.62	4.1171	0.4092	117.81	...	...	...	...	...
1972	0.9908	...	...	3.1889	303.11	3.8186	0.4005	109.07	...	...	...	...	...
1973	1.0002	...	...	2.6719	271.40	3.1688	0.4084	99.14	31.70	100.23	2.03	98.94	...
1974	0.9781	...	...	2.5873	291.94	2.9805	0.4277	101.41	32.58	102.05	2.14	95.50	97.35
1975	1.0173	...	...	2.4614	296.77	2.5839	0.4521	98.50	33.68	102.39	2.39	94.45	88.60
1976	0.9861	...	...	2.5184	296.48	2.5002	0.5567	105.63	35.83	106.42	2.70	94.53	90.83
1977	1.0635	...	...	2.3225	268.38	2.4065	0.5733	103.35	36.88	106.08	3.02	92.90	89.86
1978	1.1408	...	...	2.0089	210.46	1.7907	0.5214	92.39	35.09	97.21	3.18	87.33	90.40
1979	1.1716	...	...	1.8331	219.21	1.6644	0.4720	88.07	35.36	95.60	3.40	88.44	89.09
1980	1.1694	...	...	1.8183	226.58	1.6772	0.4304	87.39	36.35	95.35	3.75	89.78	89.47
1981	1.1989	...	...	2.2606	220.45	1.9675	0.4978	103.26	40.34	104.67	4.27	96.61	88.48
1982	1.2339	...	...	2.4281	249.05	2.0319	0.5727	116.50	46.83	115.76	5.52	106.12	90.08
1983	1.2326	...	...	2.5545	237.45	2.1007	0.6601	125.32	52.81	120.45	7.44	110.60	101.05
1984	1.2952	...	...	2.8483	237.59	2.3500	0.7521	138.34	60.11	128.75	9.78	117.94	110.35
1985	1.3659	...	...	2.9443	238.47	2.4552	0.7792	143.24	67.16	133.60	13.14	122.76	117.16
1986	1.3898	...	...	2.1711	168.50	1.7979	0.6821	112.27	62.35	109.86	16.49	107.43	124.68
1987	1.3261	...	...	1.7976	144.63	1.4918	0.6117	96.95	60.42	97.16	19.92	98.69	129.40
1988	1.2309	...	...	1.7561	128.14	1.4643	0.5621	92.75	60.92	90.41	24.07	92.10	126.68
1989	1.1841	...	...	1.8792	138.00	1.6369	0.6111	98.52	66.90	94.24	29.61	93.83	115.64
1990	1.1670	...	...	1.6159	144.82	1.3901	0.5630	89.05	71.41	89.87	40.10	91.25	110.11
1991	1.1460	...	...	1.6585	134.51	1.4356	0.5667	89.73	74.35	88.52	46.69	89.71	109.62
1992	1.2088	...	...	1.5624	126.75	1.4064	0.5699	86.64	76.91	87.02	53.13	87.81	108.64
1993	1.2902	5.7795	...	1.6537	111.21	1.4781	0.6662	93.17	83.78	89.92	63.37	89.16	105.03
1994	1.3659	8.6397	...	1.6219	102.19	1.3667	0.6531	91.32	90.87	88.42	80.54	88.99	102.39
1995	1.3727	8.3700	...	1.4331	94.11	1.1812	0.6337	84.30	92.65	83.46	92.51	86.54	102.40
1996	1.3637	8.3389	...	1.5049	108.81	1.2361	0.6410	87.34	97.46	87.24	98.24	88.54	99.46
1997	1.3849	8.3193	...	1.7339	121.06	1.4514	0.6106	96.35	104.43	93.92	104.64	93.26	100.51
1998	1.4836	8.3008	...	1.7593	130.99	1.4506	0.6034	98.82	115.89	98.41	125.89	101.23	113.67
1999	1.4858	8.2783	0.9387	1.8359	113.73	1.5045	0.6184	...	116.04	96.84	129.20	100.60	112.39
2000	1.4855	8.2784	1.0864	...	107.80	1.6904	0.6611	...	119.45	101.57	129.84	104.46	112.57
2001	1.5487	8.2770	1.1180	...	121.57	1.6891	0.6948	...	125.93	107.65	135.91	110.46	117.08
2002	1.5704	8.2771	1.0612	...	125.22	1.5567	0.6667	...	126.67	106.01	140.36	110.60	119.53
2003	1.4008	8.2772	0.8851	...	115.94	1.3450	0.6124	...	119.11	93.01	143.52	103.89	121.11
2004	1.3017	8.2768	0.8049	...	108.15	1.2428	0.5458	...	113.63	85.36	143.38	99.27	119.75
2005	1.2115	8.1936	0.8033	...	110.11	1.2459	0.5493	...	110.71	83.72	138.89	97.65	116.08
2006	1.1340	7.9723	0.7960	...	116.31	1.2532	0.5425	...	108.52	82.48	135.38	96.54	113.40
2007	1.0734	7.6058	0.7293	...	117.76	1.1999	0.4995	...	103.40	77.87	130.28	91.92	107.78
2008	1.0660	6.9477	0.6791	...	103.39	1.0816	0.5392	...	99.83	74.41	127.23	88.19	102.75
2009	1.1412	6.8307	0.7176	...	93.68	1.0860	0.6385	...	105.87	77.76	136.68	91.76	107.25
2007													
January	1.1763	7.7876	0.7696	...	120.45	1.2431	0.5105	...	107.59	82.37	133.18	94.68	109.73
February	1.1710	7.7502	0.7645	...	120.50	1.2393	0.5105	...	107.23	82.07	132.77	94.48	109.31
March	1.1682	7.7369	0.7549	...	117.26	1.2178	0.5135	...	106.67	81.23	132.80	94.74	110.32
April	1.1350	7.7247	0.7400	...	118.93	1.2124	0.5030	...	105.30	79.87	131.64	93.98	109.94
May	1.0951	7.6773	0.7398	...	120.77	1.2211	0.5040	...	104.40	79.20	130.48	93.63	109.42
June	1.0651	7.6333	0.7451	...	122.69	1.2330	0.5033	...	104.12	78.93	130.23	93.47	109.16
July	1.0502	7.5757	0.7285	...	121.41	1.2069	0.4913	...	102.77	77.51	129.26	91.94	107.68
August	1.0579	7.5734	0.7339	...	116.73	1.2027	0.4973	...	103.33	77.51	130.72	91.94	107.87
September	1.0267	7.5210	0.7189	...	115.04	1.1852	0.4954	...	101.93	75.91	129.94	90.61	106.95
October	0.9754	7.5019	0.7026	...	115.87	1.1741	0.4890	...	99.80	73.93	127.98	88.52	104.92
November	0.9672	7.4210	0.6811	...	111.07	1.1233	0.4831	...	98.37	72.20	127.40	87.38	104.49
December	1.0021	7.3682	0.6869	...	112.45	1.1402	0.4960	...	99.27	73.69	126.99	87.68	103.57
2008													
January	1.0099	7.2405	0.6790	...	107.82	1.1006	0.5076	...	98.48	73.06	126.08	86.99	102.50
February	0.9986	7.1644	0.6776	...	107.03	1.0890	0.5090	...	97.67	72.57	124.83	85.86	100.42
March	1.0029	7.0722	0.6443	...	100.76	1.0126	0.4996	...	95.77	70.32	123.96	84.76	100.46
April	1.0137	6.9997	0.6348	...	102.68	1.0138	0.5046	...	95.48	70.47	122.91	84.74	99.75
May	0.9993	6.9725	0.6429	...	104.36	1.0448	0.5089	...	95.83	70.75	123.33	85.45	100.72
June	1.0166	6.8993	0.6426	...	106.92	1.0371	0.5085	...	96.09	71.42	122.78	86.11	100.81
July	1.0130	6.8355	0.6346	...	106.85	1.0283	0.5028	...	95.40	70.91	121.89	85.58	100.11
August	1.0535	6.8462	0.6687	...	109.36	1.0841	0.5301	...	97.93	74.09	122.94	87.43	100.43
September	1.0582	6.8307	0.6973	...	106.57	1.1102	0.5564	...	100.30	75.51	126.53	89.23	102.89
October	1.1847	6.8358	0.7538	...	99.97	1.1429	0.5930	...	106.95	80.42	135.09	94.13	108.26
November	1.2171	6.8281	0.7847	...	96.97	1.1910	0.6524	...	109.63	82.74	137.95	94.88	108.54
December	1.2337	6.8539	0.7401	...	91.28	1.1404	0.6732	...	108.47	80.69	138.51	93.11	108.06
2009													
January	1.2248	6.8360	0.7551	...	90.12	1.1267	0.6915	...	109.10	81.01	139.54	93.89	108.73
February	1.2452	6.8363	0.7814	...	92.92	1.1639	0.6933	...	111.82	83.11	142.87	96.48	111.68
March	1.2645	6.8360	0.7663	...	97.86	1.1555	0.7057	...	112.45	83.84	143.24	97.24	112.14
April	1.2242	6.8306	0.7576	...	98.92	1.1481	0.6797	...	109.67	82.28	138.74	95.10	108.84
May	1.1528	6.8235	0.7328	...	96.64	1.1076	0.6486	...	106.49	78.89	136.20	92.53	107.21
June	1.1264	6.8334	0.7136	...	96.61	1.0809	0.6109	...	105.07	77.02	135.78	92.09	107.90
July	1.1229	6.8317	0.7096	...	94.37	1.0780	0.6106	...	104.63	76.45	135.65	91.56	107.43
August	1.0872	6.8323	0.7010	...	94.90	1.0683	0.6049	...	103.30	75.18	134.42	90.29	106.27
September	1.0816	6.8277	0.6861	...	91.27	1.0391	0.6126	...	103.13	74.63	134.95	89.40	105.92
October	1.0547	6.8267	0.6747	...	90.37	1.0213	0.6168	...	101.78	73.56	133.36	87.94	104.30
November	1.0593	6.8271	0.6708	...	89.27	1.0131	0.6024	...	101.29	73.15	132.81	87.34	103.72
December	1.0537	6.8275	0.6859	...	89.95	1.0301	0.6163	...	101.75	73.98	132.55	87.32	102.82

... = Not available.

NOTES AND DEFINITIONS, CHAPTER 13

TABLE 13-1
INTERNATIONAL COMPARISONS: GROWTH RATES IN REAL GROSS DOMESTIC PRODUCT

SOURCE: ECONOMIC REPORT OF THE PRESIDENT, ANNUAL REPORT OF THE COUNCIL OF ECONOMIC ADVISERS, FEBRUARY 2010

Table 13-1 is reprinted from the 2010 *Annual Report of the U.S. Council of Economic Advisers*, where it appears as Table B-112. It is based on data from the Department of Commerce's Bureau of Economic Analysis (BEA) and the International Monetary Fund.

TABLE 13-2 AND 13-3
INTERNATIONAL COMPARISONS: REAL GROSS DOMESTIC PRODUCT PER CAPITA, REAL GROSS DOMESTIC PRODUCT PER EMPLOYED PERSON

SOURCE: U.S. DEPARTMENT OF LABOR, BUREAU OF LABOR STATISTICS (BLS)

Definitions and notes on the data

Real gross domestic product (GDP) per capita can be taken as a rough measure of potential economic welfare; that is, the potential standard of living available to each of a country's residents. Because income distributions are typically "skewed," GDP per capita (which is an average or "mean") should not be taken as a representation of the standard of living actually enjoyed by a typical ("median") individual. See the subsection entitled "Whose standard of living?" in the article at the beginning of this volume.

Real gross domestic product per employed person is a rough measure of productivity (ignoring any differences in hours worked by employees).

The GDP, population, and employment measures for each country come from the country's own national accounts and population sources. Not all countries use annual chain-weighted methods such as those incorporated in U.S. GDP. (See notes and definitions to Chapter 1.) Some of the employment and population figures have been recalculated for greater comparability by BLS. GDP figures are converted from national currency values to U.S. dollar equivalents using purchasing power parities (PPPs) published by the OECD (Organisation for Economic Co-operation and Development) in the OECD-Eurostat PPP Program.

PPPs are currency conversion rates that allow output in different currency units to be expressed in a common unit of value (in this case, U.S. dollars). They are preferable to international market exchange rates for this purpose. According to BLS, "At best, market exchange rates represent only the relative prices of goods and services that are traded internationally, not the relative value of total domestic output, which also consists of goods, and particularly services, that are not traded internationally, or which are isolated from the effects of foreign trade. Market exchange rates also are affected by... currency traders' views of the stability of governments in various countries, relative interest rates among countries, and other incentives for holding financial assets in one currency rather than another."

Measuring PPPs is difficult and subject to error, and BLS emphasizes that statistics using PPPs should be used with caution: "The per capita GDPs of most OECD countries fall within a relatively narrow range, and changes in rankings can occur as a result of relatively minor adjustments to PPP estimates."

In addition to the 11 countries shown here, BLS also calculates and publishes similar data for Austria, Belgium, Denmark, Norway, Sweden, and Singapore. In the latest report, referenced below, there are also data, graphs, and discussion on hours worked, GDP per hour worked and gross national income per capita.

References

These data and related information are contained in Department of Labor, Bureau of Labor Statistics, Division of International Labor Comparisons, "International comparisons of gross domestic product per capita and per employed person, 17 countries, 1960–2008" (July 28, 2009), available online at <http://www.bls.gov/ilc>.

TABLE 13-4
INTERNATIONAL COMPARISONS: CONSUMER PRICE INDEXES

SOURCE: U.S. DEPARTMENT OF LABOR, BUREAU OF LABOR STATISTICS

Notes on the data

These data are prepared by the BLS Division of Foreign Labor Statistics, based on national consumer price indexes as published by each country. The update presented here was issued May 8, 2009. The data are not adjusted for comparability across countries. National differences exist with respect to population coverage, frequency of market basket weight changes, and treatment of homeowner costs. For some countries, BLS publishes indexes for all households and for workers' households; in such cases, *Business Statistics* shows the all-households index.

BLS links published indexes together to form historical series and rebases the foreign indexes to the U.S. base 1982–1984 = 100.

Percent changes have been calculated by the editors and may differ from changes published elsewhere due to rounding differences.

References

For a description of the U.S. index, see the notes and definitions for Table 8-1.

The indexes for the other countries are presented and described in "Consumer Price Indexes, Sixteen Countries, 1950–2008" (May 8, 2009), available at <http://www.bls.gov/ilc>. In addition to the 10 countries shown here, price indexes for Austria, Belgium, Denmark, Norway, Sweden, and Switzerland are also presented and described.

TABLES 13-5 THROUGH 13-7
INTERNATIONAL COMPARISONS: WORKING–AGE POPULATION, EMPLOYMENT-POPULATION RATIOS, AND UNEMPLOYMENT RATES

SOURCE: U.S. DEPARTMENT OF LABOR, BUREAU OF LABOR STATISTICS

Notes on the data

Current and historical data on working-age population, labor force, employment, and unemployment for 10 industrial countries are collected and adjusted by BLS to approximate U.S. concepts and definitions. (For the U.S. concepts and definitions, see the notes and definitions for Tables 10-1 through 10-5.) Nine of those countries are shown in Tables 13-5 through 13-7; the tenth is Sweden. The German data are for the former West Germany through 1990, and for unified Germany from 1991 to the present. Adding the former East Germany raised the 1991 unemployment rate from 4.3 percent (for West Germany alone) to 5.6 percent for unified Germany.

It should be noted that there is also a set of employment-population ratios, quite different from the ones shown here, published by BLS in the report for "Comparative Real Gross Domestic Product Per Capita" that is referenced above in the notes for Tables 13-2 and 13-3. The ratios in that report are for employment divided by the total resident population (including children). The ratios shown and described here are for employment divided by the working-age population.

Historically, there were large differences between published and BLS-adjusted unemployment rates; however, in recent years, the two unemployment rate series have nearly converged for most countries. Major differences between the country's own official unemployment rates and those adjusted by BLS remain for Canada, Germany, the Netherlands, and Sweden.

There are many qualifications to the adjustments for comparability. Many of the adjusted measures still use a lower age limit than the U.S. limit of 16 years, if the age at which compulsory schooling ends in that country is lower than 16. Currently, however, no country's age limit is lower than 15 years. In Japan and Germany, the institutional population is included. In some countries where the customary significance of layoffs is different, workers on layoff are counted as employed, although in the United States they are considered unemployed. In addition, each country except Japan has some break in historical continuity because of methodological change. The source document includes documentation of each country's series breaks and deviations from exact comparability.

Data availability and references

In addition to the series shown here, BLS calculates and publishes comparative labor force participation rates, employment-population ratios, and unemployment rates by sex; employment by sex and by economic sector; and unemployment rates by age. Data for 1960 through 1969 are from the BLS report "International comparisons of annual labor force statistics: 10 countries, 1960–2007" (October 21, 2008). The data for 1970 through 2008 are from BLS, Division of International Labor Comparisons, "International comparisons of annual labor force statistics: 10 countries, 1970–2008" (October 1, 2009). This report and monthly updates to unemployment rates are available on the International Labor Comparisons Web site at <http://www.bls.gov/ilc>.

TABLE 13-8
FOREIGN EXCHANGE RATES

SOURCE: BOARD OF GOVERNORS OF THE FEDERAL RESERVE SYSTEM

Definitions and notes on the data

This table shows measures of the U.S. dollar relative to the currencies of some important individual countries and also relative to average values for major groups of countries. In *Business Statistics*, all of these measures are defined as the foreign currency price of the U.S. dollar. When the measure is relatively high, the dollar is relatively strong—but less competitive (in the sense of price competition)—and the other currency or group of currencies named in the measure is relatively weak and more competitive.

For consistency, this definition is used in *Business Statistics* even in the case of currencies that are commonly quoted in the financial press and elsewhere as dollars per foreign currency unit instead of foreign currency units per dollar. Notably, this is the case for the euro and for the British pound. Where *Business Statistics* shows the December 2009 value of the dollar as 0.6859 euros, the more usual statement—and the one found on the Federal Reserve release used as a source for this information—is that in December 2009, the euro was worth $1.4579 (1 divided by 0.6859). Where *Business Statistics* shows the December 2009 value of the dollar as 0.6163 British pounds, the more usual statement is that the pound was worth $1.6226. The Canadian dollar is also sometimes quoted relative to the U.S. dollar, rather than as shown here and in documents from the Federal Reserve.

(This definition of the dollar's value is the most useful for economic analysis from the U.S. point of view and for foreign tourists in the United States. For American tourists overseas, it is easier to use the inverse of this measure, the value of the other currency; for example, the traveler in Paris can more easily translate prices into dollars by multiplying by the dollar value of the euro than by dividing by the euro value of the dollar.)

The foreign exchange rates shown are averages of the daily noon buying rates in New York City for cable transfers payable in foreign currencies. Annual figures are averages of monthly data.

The introduction of the euro in January 1999 as the common currency for 11 European countries—Austria, Belgium, Finland, France, Germany, Ireland, Italy, Luxembourg, Netherlands, Portugal, and Spain—marked a major change in the international currency system, and the use of the euro subsequently spread to five more countries. Greece entered the European Monetary Union (EMU) in January 2001 and Slovenia entered in January 2007. Cyprus and Malta joined in January 2008 and the Slovak Republic in January 2009. The euro is also the national currency in Monaco, the Vatican City and San Marino, and is the de facto currency in Andorra, Kosovo, and Montenegro. The values of the currencies of these countries no longer fluctuate relative to each other, but the value of the euro still fluctuates relative to the dollar and to currencies for countries outside the EMU. The currency and coins of the individual countries continued to circulate from 1999 through the end of 2001, but in January 2002, new euro currency and coins were introduced, replacing the currency and coins of the individual countries. Once a country has entered the monetary union, its values relative to the <u>dollar</u> will continue to fluctuate—but only due to fluctuations in the value of the euro relative to the dollar.

There is no fully satisfactory historical equivalent to the euro. For comparisons over time, the Federal Reserve Board uses a "restated German mark," derived simply by dividing each historical value of the mark by the euro conversion factor, 1.95583. The G-10 dollar index described below includes five of the currencies that later merged into the euro, but also includes the currencies of Canada, Japan, the United Kingdom, Switzerland, and Sweden.

Trade-weighted indexes of the value of the dollar against groups of foreign currencies also appear in this table. In each case, weighted averages of the individual currency values of the dollar are set at 100 in a base period. The weights are based on goods trade only and exclude trade in services. Base periods differ for different indexes.

The first four columns show the more familiar type of foreign exchange indexes, which use *nominal* values of each currency. The last two columns are *price-adjusted* (indexes of "real" exchange rates), aggregating values of the dollar in terms of each currency that have been adjusted for inflation, using each country's consumer price index.

Where any currency has had an episode of hyperinflation with consequent huge depreciation in terms of the dollar, the nominal index will not reflect the actual competitiveness of the dollar in terms of that currency over the longer term. As there have been hyperinflations in some of the countries making up the broad index and its "other important trading partners" component (see below), price-adjusted indexes are also shown for those two groupings in the final two columns.

The *G-10 Index (March 1973 = 100).* This measure is an index of the exchange value of the U.S. dollar in terms of the weighted average currencies of the G-10 ("Other industrialized") countries, which are Belgium, Canada, France, Germany, Italy, Japan, the Netherlands, Sweden, Switzerland, and the United Kingdom. Unlike the three indexes that follow, the weights in this index—which represented "multilateral" (world market) trade shares—were fixed. The Federal Reserve stopped calculating this index as of December 1998.

The three newer indexes, introduced in December 1998, use weights that focus more directly on U.S. competitiveness and that change as trade flows shift. Each country's weight is based on an average of the country's share of U.S. imports, the country's share of U.S. exports, and the country's share of exports that go to other countries that are large importers of U.S. goods. The weights are updated each year; the latest weights were introduced on January 2, 2007, with the previous weights having been in effect from December 15, 2005 to December 29, 2006. The index formula uses geometric averaging.

The *broad index (January 1997 = 100).* The new overall index includes currencies of all economies that have a share of U.S. non-oil goods imports or goods exports of at least 0.5 percent. These economies encompass the euro area and 25 other countries. The list of currencies is updated each year, though no changes have been made in the list of included countries. These countries are then classified in either the major currency index or the other important trading partners as outlined below.

The *major currency index (March 1973 = 100).* This index serves purposes similar to those of the discontinued G-10 index, and its level and movements are similar. It is a measure of the competitiveness of U.S. products in the major industrial countries and a gauge of financial pressure on the dollar. The index includes countries whose currencies are traded in deep and relatively liquid financial markets and circulate widely outside the country of issue. These are also countries for which information on short and long-term interest rates is readily available. As of January 2007, this index includes the currencies of the euro countries, Canada, Japan, the United Kingdom, Switzerland, Australia, and Sweden. This list has not changed since the introduction of the new indexes in 1998.

The *other important trading partners (OITP) index (January 1997 = 100).* This index captures the competitiveness of U.S. products in key emerging markets in Latin America,

Asia, the Middle East, and Eastern Europe, whose currencies do not circulate widely outside the country of issue. Hyperinflations and large depreciations for some of these countries have led to a persistent upward trend in the nominal version of this index. Hence, the nominal OITP index is mainly useful for analysis of short-term developments, and the price-adjusted index is shown to give a more appropriate measure of longer-term competitiveness. As of January 2007, this index includes Mexico, China, Taiwan, South Korea, Singapore, Hong Kong, Malaysia, Brazil, Thailand, Philippines, Indonesia, India, Israel, Saudi Arabia, Russia, Argentina, Venezuela, Chile, and Colombia.

Data availability and references

Current press releases, historical data, and information on weights and methods for exchange rates and exchange rate indexes are available on the Federal Reserve Web site at <http://www.federalreserve.gov/releases/>. The dollar value indexes are described in the article "Indexes of the Foreign Exchange Value of the Dollar," *Federal Reserve Bulletin* (Winter 2005), available via a link in the "Currency Weights" area of the Federal Reserve Web site.

Additional information on exchange rates can be found on the Federal Reserve Bank of St. Louis Web site at <http://www.stls.frb.org/fred/data/exchange.html>.

PART B

INDUSTRY PROFILES

CHAPTER 14: INDUSTRY DEFINITION AND STRUCTURE

THE STRUCTURE OF U.S. INDUSTRY: AN INTRODUCTION TO THE NORTH AMERICAN INDUSTRY CLASSIFICATION SYSTEM (NAICS)

This volume of *Business Statistics* incorporates data based on the new North American Industry Classification System (NAICS) for all of the major government statistical series that use classification by industry and have incorporated the new classification system.

Industry data collection is important because demands for goods and services are channeled into demands for labor and capital through the industries responsible for producing the requested goods and services. NAICS delineates industries that are better defined in relation to today's demands. It also groups together industries that are more closely related to each other by technology. Notable examples of these new features of NAICS include the more detailed data available on service industries, the more rational grouping of the Computer and electronic product manufacturing subsector, and the creation of the Information sector.

The editor has prepared a table of NAICS industry definitions to use as a guide to the contents of the new categories, which shows the NAICS two-digit industry sectors and their component three-digit subsectors. The table follows this introduction and precedes the chapters of statistical tables. Parenthetical listings of the component activities are shown in places where the short NAICS sector titles are not sufficiently self-explanatory.

For the user needing information as to how the new classifications do (and do not) relate to the old Standard Industrial Classification System (SIC), a column showing a rough match between the 2002 NAICS and the 1987 SIC has been added to the table. It must be emphasized that this match is approximate, not exact, and does not reflect every aspect of the change in the classification systems. However, this column indicates just how thoroughly some SIC industries have been mixed and rematched; it therefore explains why it has been difficult for the statistical agencies to produce longer spans of historical data on the new basis.

As a further illustration, the reader will note frequent references in this table to parts of SIC industries that have been parceled out among different NAICS industries. In some cases, the editor has included, in parentheses, the part of the old SIC industry contained in the new NAICS industry. See the entry of new NAICS subsector 711, Performing arts and spectator sports, for an example. This subsector now contains dinner theaters, which used to be included in eating places (a subdivision of retail trade in the old system).

NAICS industries are groupings of producing units—not of products as such—and are grouped according to similarity of production processes. This is done in order to collect consistent data on inputs and outputs, which are then used to measure important concepts, such as productivity and input-output parameters. Emphasis on the production process helps to explain a number of ways in which the NAICS differs from the SIC.

Manufacturing activities at retail locations, such as bakeries, have been classified separately from retail activity and put into the Food manufacturing industry.

Central administrative offices of companies have a new sector of their own, Management of companies and enterprises (sector 55). For example, the headquarters office of a food-producing corporation is considered part of the new sector instead of part of the Food manufacturing industry.

Reproduction of packaged software, classified as a business service in the SIC, is now classified in sector 334, Computer and electronic product manufacturing, as a manufacturing process.

Electronic markets and agents and brokers, formerly undifferentiated components of wholesale trade industries, have a sector of their own (425).

Retail trade in NAICS (sectors 44 and 45) now includes establishments such as office supply stores, computer and software stores, building materials dealers, plumbing supply stores, and electrical supply stores, that display merchandise and use mass-media advertising to sell to individuals as well as to businesses, and that were formerly classified in wholesale trade.

References

The NAICS is explained and laid out in *North American Industry Classification System: United States, 2007*, from the

Executive Office of the President, Office of Management and Budget. This presents the second five-year updating of the system, which was first introduced in 1997. Changes introduced in these updatings have been minor and have not affected the definitions of industries presented in *Business Statistics*.

More precise information on differences between NAICS and SIC can be found in *North American Industry Classification System: United States, 1997*, from the Executive Office of the President, Office of Management and Budget (which contains matches between the 1997 NAICS and the 1987 SIC); and *North American Industry Classification System: United States, 2002* (which contains matches that show the relatively few changes from the 1997 NAICS to the 2002 NAICS).

The 2002 and 2007 edition of these volumes are available from Bernan Press. These volumes fully describe the development and application of the new classification system and are the sources for the material presented in this volume. Information is also available on the NAICS Web site at <http://www.census.gov/naics>. Additional background information can also be found in Bernan Press's *Business Statistics of the United States: 2002* (8th edition), pp. xxiv–xxviii.

Table 14-1. NAICS Industry Definitions, with Rough Derivation from SIC

NAICS code	NAICS 2-digit industry sector and 3-digit industry subsector	Roughly corresponding major component SIC industry group or industry
11	**AGRICULTURE, FORESTRY, FISHING, AND HUNTING**	Division A – Agriculture, forestry, and fishing; 241 – Logging
111	Crop production	
112	Animal production	
113	Forestry and logging	
114	Fishing, hunting, and trapping	
115	Agriculture and forestry support activities	
21	**MINING**	Division B – Mining
211	Oil and gas extraction	
212	Mining, except oil and gas (includes coal mining, mining for ores, and mining and quarrying of nonmetallic minerals)	
213	Support activities for mining (includes oil and gas well drilling and other support activities)	
22	**UTILITIES**	49 – Electric, gas, and sanitary services (with some exclusions)
221	Utilities (includes electric power generation, transmission, and distribution; natural gas distribution; and water, sewage, irrigation, steam, and air-conditioning systems)	
23	**CONSTRUCTION**	Division C – Construction
236	Construction of buildings	
237	Heavy and civil engineering construction	
238	Specialty trade contractors	
31-33	**MANUFACTURING**	Division D – Manufacturing (excluding 241 – Logging; 271, 272, 273, and 274 – Publishing; and with other exclusions and inclusions)
311	Food manufacturing	20 – Food and kindred products (excluding 208 – Beverages)
312	Beverage and tobacco product manufacturing	208 – Beverages; 21 – Tobacco products
313	Textile mills	221-4, 226, 228 – Yarns, fabrics, and finishing

Table 14-1.   NAICS Industry Definitions, with Rough Derivation from SIC—*Continued*

NAICS code	NAICS 2-digit industry sector and 3-digit industry subsector	Roughly corresponding major component SIC industry group or industry
314	Textile product mills (including household and miscellaneous products)	227 – Carpets and rugs; 229 – Miscellaneous textile products
315	Apparel manufacturing	23 – Apparel; 225 – Knitting mills
316	Leather and allied product manufacturing	31 – Leather and leather products
321	Wood product manufacturing	24 – Lumber and wood products (excluding 241 – Logging)
322	Paper manufacturing	26 – Paper and allied products
323	Printing and related support activities, including quick and instant	275-9 – Commercial printing and miscellaneous printing and trade services
324	Petroleum and coal products manufacturing (includes refineries, asphalt, oil and grease, and coke manufacturing)	29 – Petroleum and coal products
325	Chemical manufacturing (includes basic organic and inorganic chemicals; plastics materials; synthetic fibers and rubber; agricultural chemicals; pharmaceuticals and medicine; paint, adhesives, cleaning, and toilet preparations; and ink, explosives, and miscellaneous)	28 – Chemicals and allied products
326	Plastics and rubber products	30 – Rubber and miscellaneous plastics products
327	Nonmetallic mineral product manufacturing (includes pottery; plumbing fixtures; bricks and structural clay products; glass and products; cement and concrete; and lime, gypsum, and stone products)	32 – Stone, clay, and glass products
331	Primary metal manufacturing (primary and secondary ferrous and nonferrous metals; rolling, drawing, and extruding; and foundries)	33 – Primary metal industries
332	Fabricated metal product manufacturing (includes forging and stamping, cutlery, hardware, structural metal work, boilers, containers, machine shops, valves, fixtures, bearings, metal testing, small arms, ordnance, and ammunition)	34 – Fabricated metal products
333	Machinery manufacturing (includes machinery for agriculture, construction, mining, manufacturing, commercial, and service industries; metalworking machinery; turbine and power transmission; pumps and compressors; elevators and material handling; cranes; and miscellaneous general purpose machinery)	Parts of 35 – Industrial machinery and equipment, 36 – Electronic and other electric equipment, and 38 – Instruments and related products
334	Computer and electronic product manufacturing (includes electronic computers and equipment; communications equipment; audio and video equipment; semiconductors and other electronic components; electromedical equipment; navigation, measuring, and controlling instruments; reproducing software; and media manufacturing and reproducing)	Parts of 357 – Computer and office equipment, 36 – Electronic and other electric equipment, 38 – Instruments and related products, 73 – Business services, and 78 – Motion picture services
335	Electrical equipment and appliance manufacturing (includes electrical lighting, household appliances, electrical equipment, batteries, and wire and cable manufacturing)	Parts of 36 – Electronic and other electric equipment, and 335 – Nonferrous wire drawing
336	Transportation equipment manufacturing (includes motor vehicles and parts, truck trailers, aerospace products and parts, railroad rolling stock, ship and boat building and repairing, motorcycles, bicycles, military armored vehicles, and parts)	37 – Transportation equipment
337	Furniture and related product manufacturing	25 – Furniture and fixtures; parts of other industries
339	Miscellaneous manufacturing (includes medical equipment and supplies, jewelry, silverware, sporting goods, toys, games, office supplies, art supplies, burial caskets, and other goods)	Parts of 38 – Instruments, 39 – Miscellaneous, 25 – Furniture, and other industries

Table 14-1.   NAICS Industry Definitions, with Rough Derivation from SIC—*Continued*

NAICS code	NAICS 2-digit industry sector and 3-digit industry subsector	Roughly corresponding major component SIC industry group or industry
42	**WHOLESALE TRADE**	
423	Merchant wholesalers, durable goods	Parts of 50 – Wholesale trade—durable goods, and other industries
424	Merchant wholesalers, nondurable goods	Parts of 51 – Wholesale trade—nondurable goods, and other industries
425	Electronic markets and agents and brokers	Parts of 50 and 51 – Wholesale trade
44-45	**RETAIL TRADE**	
441	Motor vehicle and parts dealers	Parts of 55 – Automotive dealers and service stations, wholesale trade, and other industries
442	Furniture and home furnishings stores	Parts of 57 – Furniture and home furnishing stores, wholesale trade, and other industries
443	Electronics and appliance stores	5722 – Household appliance stores; 5734 – Computer and software stores; 5946 – Camera and photo supply stores; and parts of wholesale trade and other industries
444	Building material and garden supply stores	52 – Retail building materials and garden supplies, and parts of wholesale trade
445	Food and beverage stores	54 – Food stores, and 5921 – Liquor stores
446	Health and personal care stores	5912 – Drug stores and proprietary stores; and parts of wholesale trade, food stores, and miscellaneous stores
447	Gasoline stations (including stations with convenience stores)	Parts of 55 – Automotive dealers and service stations, and 54 – Food stores
448	Clothing and clothing accessories stores	56 – Apparel and accessory stores; 5944 – Jewelry stores; and 5948 – Luggage and leather goods stores
451	Sporting goods, hobby, book, and music stores	Parts of 59 – Miscellaneous retail, 57 – Furniture and home furnishing stores, and other industries
452	General merchandise stores (includes department stores, warehouse clubs, superstores, and other general merchandise)	53 – General merchandise, and parts of other retail
453	Miscellaneous store retailers (includes florists and office supply and stationery, gift, used merchandise, pet, manufactured and mobile home, tobacco, and miscellaneous other store retailers)	Parts of 59 – Miscellaneous retail, and other industries
454	Nonstore retailers (includes electronic shopping and auctions, mail order, vending machines, fuel, and other direct selling)	Parts of 59 – Miscellaneous retail, and 517 – Wholesale petroleum
48-49	**TRANSPORTATION AND WAREHOUSING**	
481	Air transportation	Parts of 45 – Transportation by air
482	Rail transportation	Parts of 40 – Railroad transportation
483	Water transportation	Parts of 44 – Water transportation
484	Truck transportation	Parts of 42 – Trucking and warehousing
485	Transit and ground passenger transportation	Parts of 41 – Local and suburban transportation

Table 14-1.   NAICS Industry Definitions, with Rough Derivation from SIC—*Continued*

NAICS code	NAICS 2-digit industry sector and 3-digit industry subsector	Roughly corresponding major component SIC industry group or industry
486	Pipeline transportation	46 – Pipelines, except natural gas; and parts of 492 – Gas production and distribution
487	Scenic and sightseeing transportation	Parts of 41 – Local and suburban, 44 – Water, 45 – Air, 47 – Transportation services, and 7999 – Amusement and recreation n.e.c.
488	Support activities for transportation	Parts of industries in transportation, communications, manufacturing, government (air traffic control), and services
491	Postal service	4311 – U.S. Postal Service, and part of 7389 – Business services n.e.c.
492	Couriers and messengers	4513 – Air couriers, and 4215 – Courier services except air
493	Warehousing and storage	Parts of 422 – Public warehousing and storage
51	**INFORMATION**	
511	Publishing industries, except Internet	
5111	Newspaper, book, and directory publishers	Parts of 271 – Newspapers, 272 – Periodicals, 273 – Books, 274 – Miscellaneous publishing, 277 – Greeting cards, and 733 – Mailing, reproduction, and stenographic services
5112	Software publishers	Part of 7372 – Prepackaged software
512	Motion picture and sound recording industries (includes music books and sheet music)	781 – Motion picture production and services; 783 – Motion picture theaters; and parts of 782 – Motion picture distribution and services, and other manufacturing and service industries
515	Broadcasting, except Internet	483 – Radio and television broadcasting; and part of 484 – Cable and other pay TV services
516	Internet publishing and broadcasting	Parts of publishing and service industries
517	Telecommunications	Parts of 481 – Telephone communications, 482 – Telegraph and other communications, and 484 – Cable and other pay TV services
518	ISPs, search portals, and data processing	7374 – Data processing and preparation; 7375 – Information retrieval services; and parts of other service industries
519	Other information services (includes news syndicates, libraries, archives, and other information services)	8231 – Libraries; and parts of other service industries
52	**FINANCE AND INSURANCE**	
521	Monetary authorities—central bank	6011 – Federal Reserve Banks
522	Credit intermediation and related activities (includes commercial banking, savings institutions, credit unions, credit card issuing, sales financing, consumer lending, real estate credit, trade financing, loan brokers, and processing and clearing)	Parts of 60 – Depository institutions, and 61 – Nondepository institutions
523	Securities, commodity contracts, and investments	62 – Security and commodity brokers, and parts of 60 – Depository institutions, 61 – Nondepository institutions, 63 – Insurance carriers, and 67 – Holding and other investment offices
524	Insurance carriers and related activities	64 – Insurance agents, brokers, and service; and parts of 63 – Insurance carriers
525	Funds, trusts, and other financial vehicles	672 – Investment offices; 6798 – Real estate investment trusts; and parts of 63 – Insurance carriers, and 673 – Trusts

n.e.c. = Not elsewhere classified.

Table 14-1. NAICS Industry Definitions, with Rough Derivation from SIC—*Continued*

NAICS code	NAICS 2-digit industry sector and 3-digit industry subsector	Roughly corresponding major component SIC industry group or industry
53	**REAL ESTATE AND RENTAL AND LEASING**	
531	Real estate	Parts of 65 – Real estate, and 4225 – General warehousing and storage (mini-warehouses and self-storage units)
532	Rental and leasing services	7352 – Medical equipment rental; 7377 – Computer rental and leasing; 751 – Automotive rentals, no drivers; 7841 – Video tape rental; and parts of 4499 – Water transportation n.e.c., 4741 – Rental of railroad cars, 7299 – Miscellaneous personal services n.e.c., 735 – Miscellaneous equipment rental, 7922 – Theatrical producers and services, and 7999 – Amusement and recreation n.e.c.
533	Lessors of nonfinancial intangible assets (except copyrighted)	6794 – Patent owners and lessors, and part of 6792 – Oil royalty traders
54	**PROFESSIONAL AND TECHNICAL SERVICES** (includes legal, accounting, bookkeeping, architectural, engineering, design, computer design and programming, management and other consulting, scientific research and development, advertising and public relations, market research, polling, and other services)	741 – Veterinary services; 6541 – Title abstract offices, 731 – Advertising, 7221 – Photographic studios, portrait, 7921 – Tax return preparation, 7336 – Commercial art and graphic design, 7361 – Employment agencies, 7371 – Computer programming; 7373 – Computer systems design, 7376 – Computer facilities management, 8111 – Legal services, 871 – Engineering and architectural services, 873 – Research and testing; and parts of mining, 37 – Aircraft and guided missiles, 73 – Business services, 87 – Engineering and management services, and other industries
55	**MANAGEMENT OF COMPANIES AND ENTERPRISES**	671 – Holding companies, and establishments classified as auxiliaries in producing industries
56	**ADMINISTRATIVE AND WASTE SERVICES**	
561	Administrative and support services (includes office administrative, employment placement, temporary help, telephone call centers, collection agencies, credit bureaus, court reporting, travel arrangement, investigation and security, services to buildings, and other support services)	782 – Lawn and garden services, 783 – Ornamental shrub and tree services, 4724 – Travel agencies, 4725 – Tour operators, 7217 – Carpet and upholstery cleaning, 732 – Credit reporting and collection, 7338 – Secretarial and court reporting, 734 – Services to buildings, 7363 – Help supply services, 7381 – Detective and armored car services, 7382 – Security systems, 8744 – Facilities support, and parts of 458 – Airfields, 472 – Passenger transportation arrangement, 495 – Sanitary services, 729 – Miscellaneous personal services, 73, Business services, 769 – Miscellaneous repair shops, 7819 – Services allied to motion pictures, 79 – Amusement and recreation services, 86 – Membership organizations, and 8741 – Management services
562	Waste management and remediation services	4953 – Refuse systems, and parts of 1799 – Special trade contractors, 4212 – Local trucking, 4959 – Sanitary services, 735 – Miscellaneous equipment rental and leasing (portable toilet rental), and 769 – Miscellaneous repair shops
61	**EDUCATIONAL SERVICES**	82 – Educational services, except 823 – Libraries; and parts of 7231 – Beauty shops, 7241 – Barber shops, 7911 – Dance studios, 7999 – Amusement and recreation n.e.c., and 8748 – Business consulting n.e.c. (educational testing services)
62	**HEALTH CARE AND SOCIAL ASSISTANCE**	
621	Ambulatory health care services	Offices and clinics for: 801 – Doctors, 802 – Dentists, 803 – Osteopaths, and 804 – Other health practicioners, 8071 – Medical laboratories, 8082 – Home health care services, 4119 – Ambulances; 4522 – Air ambulances, and parts of 809 – Health and allied services n.e.c.
622	Hospitals	806 – Hospitals
623	Nursing and residential care facilities	805 – Nursing and personal care facilities, and 836 – Residential care
624	Social assistance	8322 – Individual and family services, except parole and probation offices; 8331 – Job training; and 8351 – Child day care services

n.e.c. = Not elsewhere classified.

Table 14-1.   NAICS Industry Definitions, with Rough Derivation from SIC—*Continued*

NAICS code	NAICS 2-digit industry sector and 3-digit industry subsector	Roughly corresponding major component SIC industry group or industry
71	**ARTS, ENTERTAINMENT, AND RECREATION**	
711	Performing arts and spectator sports	7929 – Bands and other entertainment groups; 7941 – Professional sports clubs and promoters; 7948 – Racing; parts of 5812 – Eating places (dinner theaters) and 6512 – Building operators (stadium and arena owners); and agents, artists, writers, performers, correspondents, taxidermists, and antique restorers, previously classified as part of 738 – Miscellaneous business services; 76 – Miscellaneous repair services; 7819 – Motion picture services; 7999 – Amusement and recreation n.e.c.; and 8999 – Membership organizations, n.e.c.
712	Museums, historical sites, zoos, and parks	84 – Museums and botanical and zoological gardens; and part of 7999 – Amusement and recreation n.e.c. (caverns and miscellaneous commercial parks)
713	Amusements, gambling, and recreation	4493 – Marinas, 793 – Bowling centers, 7991 – Physical fitness facilities, 7992 – Public golf courses, 7995 – Coin operated amusments, 7996 – Amusement parks, 7997 – Membership sports and recreation clubs, and parts of 7911 – Dance studios, and 7999 – Amusement and recreation n.e.c.
72	**ACCOMMODATION AND FOOD SERVICES**	
721	Accommodation (includes hotels, motels, bed-and-breakfast inns, RV parks, camps, and rooming and boarding houses)	70 – Hotels and other lodging places
722	Food services and drinking places	5812 – Eating places (other than dinner theaters), 5813 – Drinking places, and parts of 4789 – Transportation services n.e.c. (contract dining car operations), 5641 – Retail bakeries, and 5963 – Direct selling (mobile food wagons)
81	**OTHER SERVICES, EXCEPT PUBLIC ADMINISTRATION**	
811	Repair and maintenance	753 – Automotive repair shops (other than tire retreading); 7542 – Carwashes; 7631 – Watch, clock, and jewelery repair; 7692 – Welding repair; and parts of 3732 – Boat repair, 7219 – Clothing alteration and repair, 7251 – Shoe repair, 7378 – Computer repair, 7549 – auto window tinting, 7622 – Radio and TV repair, 7623 – Refrigeration repair, 7629 – Electrical repair n.e.c., 7641 – Reupholstery and furniture repair, 7694 – Armature (rewinding), and 7699 – Repair services n.e.c.
812	Personal and laundry services	6553 – Cemetery subdividers and developers; 7211 – Power laundries; 7212 – Garment pressing and cleaners' agents; 7213 – Linen supply; 7215 – Coin-operated laundries and cleaning; 7216 – Drycleaning, except rugs; 7218 – Industrial launderers; 7261 – Funeral service and crematories; 7384 – Photofinishing laboratories; 7521 – Auto parking; and parts of 0752 – Pet care, 6531 – Real estate agents and managers (cemetery management), 7219 – Diaper and miscellaneous services, 7231 – Beauty shops, 7241 – Barber shops, 7251 – Shoe shine parlors, and 7389 – Business services n.e.c. (apparel pressing for the trade, bail bonding)
813	Membership associations and organizations	6732 – Educational, religious and charitable trusts; 8399 – Social services n.e.c. (voluntary health organizations, human rights organizations, environment, conservation, and wildlife, and other grant making, giving, and social advocacy organizations); 8611 – Business associations; 8621 – Professional organizations; 8631 – Labor organizations; 8651 – Political organizations; 8661 – Religious organizations; and parts of 6531 – Real estate agents and managers (condominium associations), 8641 – Civic and social organizations (all except tribal governments), and 8699 – Membership organizations n.e.c. (all except motor travel clubs)
814	Private households	8811 – Private households

n.e.c. = Not elsewhere classified.

Table 14-1. NAICS Industry Definitions, with Rough Derivation from SIC—*Continued*

NAICS code	NAICS 2-digit industry sector and 3-digit industry subsector	Roughly corresponding major component SIC industry group or industry
92	**PUBLIC ADMINISTRATION**	
921	Executive, legislative, and general government	91 – Executive, legislative, and general; 9311 – Finance, taxation, and monetary policy; and part of 8641 – Civic and social associations (tribal governments)
922	Justice, public order, and safety activities	92 – Justice, public order, and safety; and part of 8322 – Individual and family services (parole and probation)
923	Administration of human resource programs	94 – Administration of human resources
924	Administration of environmental programs	951 – Environmental quality
925	Community and housing program administration	953 – Housing and urban development
926	Administration of economic programs	9611 – Administration of general economic programs; 9631 – Regulation and administration of utilities; 9641 – Regulation of agricultural marketing; 9651 – Miscellaneous commercial regulation; and parts of 9621 – Regulation and administration of transportation (all except air traffic control)
927	Space research and technology	9661 – Space research and technology
928	National security and international affairs	97 – National security and international affairs

CHAPTER 15: PRODUCT AND INCOME BY INDUSTRY

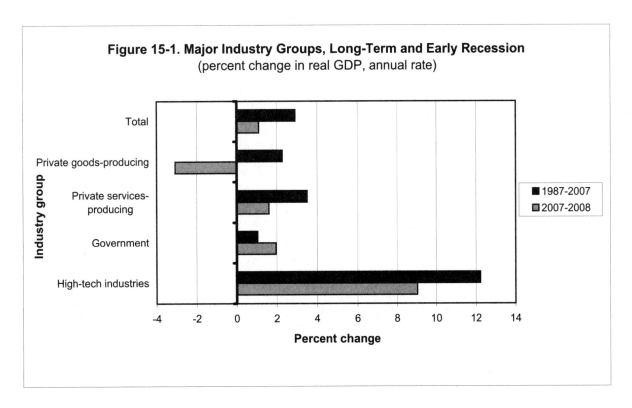

Figure 15-1. Major Industry Groups, Long-Term and Early Recession
(percent change in real GDP, annual rate)

- Between 1987 and 2007, total real gross domestic product (GDP) rose at an average annual rate of 2.9 percent. The goods-producing sector grew at a 2.3 percent rate, while private service-producing industries grew at a 3.5 percent rate. The high-tech sector (information-communications-technology- producing industries), which accounted for just 3.3 percent of total GDP in 1987, grew at a 12.2 percent annual rate over the subsequent 20 years, but still only accounts for 3.7 percent of total GDP. (Tables 15-1 and 15-2)

- Only the early stage of the recession that began in December 2007 is displayed here, because estimates for 2009 were not yet available when this volume was being prepared. Overall, real GDP still showed growth from 2007 to 2008 on an annual average basis, but output plunged 3.1 percent in the goods-producing industries. Services-producing industries grew more slowly than their 1987–2007 average, as did the high-tech sector. (Table 15-2) In Chapter 16 that follows, employment figures through 2009 for these same industry groupings are shown.

- Table 15-3 can be used to assess the share of each industry group in total domestic factor income and the shares paid to employees and accruing to land and capital in each private industry. In 2007, the highest labor share was in education (91 percent), and labor shares exceeding 70 percent were also found in construction, durable goods manufacturing, retail trade, management, administrative and waste management (which includes temporary help), health care and social assistance, accommodation and food services, and other services. The high-tech grouping also falls into this labor-intensive category.

Table 15-1. Gross Domestic Product (Value Added) by NAICS Industry Group

(Billions of dollars.)

Year	Total gross domestic product	Private industries												
		Total	Agriculture, forestry, fishing, and hunting	Mining	Utilities	Construction	Manufacturing		Wholesale trade	Retail trade	Transportation and warehousing	Information	Finance and insurance	Real estate and rental and leasing
							Durable goods	Nondurable goods						
1947	244.2	213.7	19.9	5.7	3.3	9.0	31.7	30.8	15.5	22.9	14.6	6.2	5.7	19.8
1948	269.2	239.2	23.2	7.6	3.7	11.2	35.8	34.2	17.1	24.3	16.1	6.9	6.5	21.6
1949	267.3	235.9	18.6	6.5	4.3	11.3	35.4	33.0	16.6	24.7	15.6	7.4	7.3	23.2
1950	293.8	262.2	19.9	7.6	4.7	12.9	43.5	35.9	18.6	25.8	17.3	8.0	7.9	25.5
1951	339.3	300.4	23.0	8.4	5.4	15.4	53.2	41.4	21.3	28.2	19.6	8.9	9.0	28.4
1952	358.3	313.8	22.1	8.2	5.9	16.6	56.3	42.0	21.5	29.7	20.3	9.6	10.0	31.0
1953	379.4	332.8	20.1	8.6	6.5	17.2	63.4	44.0	22.0	30.6	21.1	10.5	11.2	34.0
1954	380.4	332.1	19.6	8.7	7.2	17.4	58.4	43.2	22.3	31.2	19.6	10.7	12.0	36.9
1955	414.8	363.8	18.8	9.9	7.8	18.6	67.5	47.5	25.1	33.2	21.4	11.6	13.0	39.9
1956	437.5	383.1	18.6	10.7	8.3	20.5	69.7	49.6	27.0	34.4	22.4	12.4	14.0	42.4
1957	461.1	403.0	18.4	10.8	9.0	21.5	74.1	50.2	28.5	36.4	23.3	13.2	15.1	45.3
1958	467.2	405.4	20.6	9.9	9.6	21.2	66.6	50.8	29.2	37.1	22.1	13.8	16.3	48.5
1959	506.6	441.4	19.0	9.7	10.6	23.0	77.2	54.8	33.5	40.4	23.2	15.2	17.5	51.9
1960	526.4	457.1	19.9	10.0	11.5	23.4	77.7	55.7	34.9	41.3	23.4	16.0	18.9	55.5
1961	544.7	471.2	20.1	10.1	12.2	24.4	77.0	57.0	36.0	42.4	23.6	16.9	20.0	59.1
1962	585.6	506.8	20.4	10.2	12.9	26.2	86.9	60.4	38.5	45.5	25.1	18.1	20.5	63.7
1963	617.7	533.2	20.5	10.5	13.5	28.0	92.6	63.1	40.0	47.5	26.0	19.5	21.3	67.7
1964	663.6	572.9	19.6	10.8	14.4	30.7	100.1	67.1	43.2	52.2	27.5	21.2	23.4	72.0
1965	719.1	622.2	22.5	11.0	15.0	33.7	112.5	72.3	46.6	55.9	29.8	22.9	25.5	76.7
1966	787.8	680.2	23.5	11.7	16.1	37.1	125.4	79.4	51.1	60.3	32.4	25.1	28.1	81.8
1967	832.6	714.2	22.9	11.9	16.9	38.7	128.0	81.5	54.1	64.7	33.1	26.9	31.3	86.8
1968	910.0	778.3	23.7	12.7	18.4	42.4	139.2	89.0	59.4	71.4	35.7	29.2	35.1	93.5
1969	984.6	840.8	26.4	13.3	19.7	47.3	146.2	93.0	64.1	77.4	38.0	32.2	39.7	101.6
1970	1 038.5	880.2	27.3	14.9	21.0	50.2	139.2	96.3	68.0	82.8	40.1	35.0	42.9	109.1
1971	1 127.1	954.8	29.4	15.0	23.8	55.2	147.1	101.9	73.8	90.5	44.1	38.1	47.3	121.7
1972	1 238.3	1 051.0	34.4	15.8	26.1	61.0	164.1	109.6	82.0	98.1	48.4	42.6	51.5	133.4
1973	1 382.7	1 180.5	52.3	18.9	28.0	69.1	185.4	117.3	92.2	107.9	53.4	47.0	55.3	147.9
1974	1 500.0	1 277.3	50.1	29.3	29.2	74.0	192.5	125.7	104.7	113.4	58.5	50.9	62.9	160.5
1975	1 638.3	1 391.5	51.4	33.8	37.1	74.8	198.5	138.6	114.6	127.3	59.4	56.5	71.6	176.6
1976	1 825.3	1 556.2	50.2	37.5	41.5	85.5	230.2	156.5	122.7	144.0	68.8	63.5	78.3	193.8
1977	2 030.9	1 739.4	51.3	43.4	45.9	94.2	265.0	173.6	134.9	158.5	76.2	71.1	92.3	211.7
1978	2 294.7	1 977.0	59.8	49.5	50.4	111.5	303.4	186.5	153.4	177.6	86.7	81.4	109.7	237.7
1979	2 563.3	2 217.7	70.6	58.4	51.9	127.0	331.1	212.7	175.8	193.2	96.6	90.3	121.6	268.7
1980	2 789.5	2 405.8	62.0	91.3	60.0	130.3	333.9	222.7	188.7	200.9	102.3	99.0	136.8	305.6
1981	3 128.4	2 702.5	75.4	122.9	70.7	131.8	370.4	246.1	208.3	221.0	109.9	112.7	154.5	343.9
1982	3 255.0	2 792.6	71.3	120.0	81.7	128.8	353.4	249.8	207.9	229.9	105.9	123.6	167.6	372.3
1983	3 536.7	3 043.5	57.1	103.1	91.6	139.8	379.3	273.8	222.9	261.6	117.8	140.0	190.5	414.2
1984	3 933.2	3 395.1	77.1	107.2	102.3	164.4	443.5	280.5	249.4	293.6	131.4	147.1	209.3	460.9
1985	4 220.3	3 637.0	77.1	105.4	109.2	184.6	449.2	291.1	268.3	318.7	136.3	162.9	225.9	503.8
1986	4 462.8	3 842.9	74.2	68.9	114.4	207.7	459.3	306.7	278.5	336.6	145.6	173.1	255.7	539.4
1987	4 739.5	4 080.4	79.8	71.5	123.0	218.2	483.8	327.5	285.3	349.9	151.1	185.0	274.4	565.9
1988	5 103.8	4 399.1	80.2	71.4	122.8	232.7	519.0	357.9	318.1	366.0	161.1	194.0	295.8	614.3
1989	5 484.4	4 732.3	92.8	76.0	135.9	244.8	543.2	384.1	337.4	389.0	164.1	210.4	316.2	659.2
1990	5 803.1	4 997.8	96.7	84.9	142.9	248.5	542.7	404.7	347.7	398.8	169.4	225.1	340.1	702.0
1991	5 995.9	5 138.7	89.2	76.0	152.5	230.2	540.9	416.6	360.5	405.5	178.2	235.2	376.5	727.1
1992	6 337.7	5 440.4	99.6	71.3	157.4	232.5	562.8	433.8	378.9	430.0	186.6	250.9	407.5	769.8
1993	6 657.4	5 729.3	93.1	72.1	165.3	248.3	593.1	446.8	401.2	458.0	201.0	272.6	437.8	803.7
1994	7 072.2	6 110.5	105.6	73.6	174.6	274.4	647.7	471.1	442.7	493.3	218.0	294.0	450.1	847.7
1995	7 397.6	6 407.2	93.1	74.1	181.5	287.0	677.2	500.0	457.0	514.9	226.3	307.6	490.9	892.1
1996	7 816.9	6 795.2	113.8	87.5	183.3	311.7	706.5	502.9	489.1	543.8	235.2	335.7	530.7	940.0
1997	8 304.3	7 247.5	110.7	92.6	179.6	337.6	755.5	524.3	521.2	574.2	253.7	347.8	595.5	997.8
1998	8 747.0	7 652.5	102.4	74.8	180.8	374.4	806.9	537.0	542.9	598.6	273.7	381.6	641.1	1 043.5
1999	9 268.4	8 127.2	93.8	85.4	185.4	406.6	820.4	552.7	577.7	635.5	287.4	439.3	679.8	1 118.6
2000	9 817.0	8 614.3	98.0	121.3	189.3	435.9	865.3	560.9	591.7	662.4	301.6	458.3	740.5	1 190.5
2001	10 128.0	8 869.7	97.9	118.7	202.3	469.5	778.9	562.5	607.1	691.6	296.9	476.9	782.6	1 276.6
2002	10 469.6	9 131.2	95.4	106.5	207.3	482.3	774.8	577.9	615.4	719.6	304.6	483.0	822.7	1 319.2
2003	10 960.8	9 542.3	114.4	143.3	220.0	496.2	771.8	587.5	637.0	751.5	316.6	489.1	864.6	1 380.0
2004	11 685.9	10 194.3	142.2	171.3	240.3	539.2	807.5	620.4	686.7	776.9	344.6	530.6	907.9	1 470.9
2005	12 421.9	10 853.1	133.3	223.8	239.5	605.4	845.1	635.5	722.4	824.7	364.7	557.8	989.5	1 538.5
2006	13 178.4	11 529.3	121.6	262.4	272.7	646.0	899.4	678.0	773.2	866.5	387.4	559.6	1 060.9	1 624.8
2007	13 807.5	12 064.6	167.9	275.0	281.4	610.8	922.0	694.9	805.3	892.5	407.2	586.3	1 091.4	1 719.8
2008	14 264.6	12 424.6	157.7	325.3	306.0	581.5	914.7	723.0	818.8	885.5	414.9	622.0	1 064.9	1 783.5

Table 15-1. Gross Domestic Product (Value Added) by NAICS Industry Group—*Continued*

(Billions of dollars.)

Year	Professional, scientific, and technical services	Management of companies and enterprises	Administrative and waste management services	Educational services	Health care and social assistance	Arts, entertainment, and recreation	Accommodation and food services	Other services except government	Government — Total government	Federal	State and local	Private goods-producing industries	Private services-producing industries	Information-communications-technology-producing industries[1]
1947	3.6	4.0	1.4	0.8	3.8	1.5	6.3	7.2	30.4	20.4	10.0	97.1	116.6	...
1948	4.0	4.5	1.5	0.9	4.3	1.6	6.6	7.6	30.0	18.5	11.5	112.0	127.2	...
1949	4.2	4.5	1.6	1.0	4.5	1.6	6.8	7.8	31.3	18.7	12.6	104.9	131.1	...
1950	4.7	5.0	1.8	1.1	4.9	1.7	7.1	8.3	31.6	18.2	13.4	119.8	142.4	...
1951	5.4	5.8	2.1	1.1	5.5	1.8	7.7	9.0	38.9	23.9	15.0	141.3	159.1	...
1952	5.9	6.1	2.3	1.2	6.0	1.9	8.1	9.3	44.5	28.0	16.5	145.2	168.7	...
1953	6.5	6.5	2.6	1.2	6.6	2.1	8.3	9.8	46.6	28.8	17.8	153.3	179.5	...
1954	6.9	6.4	2.7	1.3	6.8	2.1	8.5	10.1	48.3	28.9	19.3	147.3	184.8	...
1955	7.6	7.1	3.0	1.5	8.1	2.3	9.0	11.0	50.9	30.0	20.9	162.4	201.5	...
1956	8.4	7.4	3.3	1.6	8.5	2.4	9.4	12.0	54.3	31.1	23.2	169.1	214.0	...
1957	9.3	7.8	3.6	1.8	9.4	2.5	10.0	12.7	58.1	32.6	25.5	175.0	228.0	...
1958	9.7	7.7	3.9	1.9	10.3	2.7	10.1	13.2	61.8	34.0	27.8	169.2	236.2	...
1959	10.9	8.6	4.3	2.1	11.5	3.0	11.0	14.1	65.2	35.1	30.1	183.7	257.6	...
1960	11.4	8.8	4.6	2.3	12.1	3.3	11.2	15.1	69.4	36.4	32.9	186.7	270.3	...
1961	12.4	9.0	4.9	2.6	12.8	3.5	11.6	15.8	73.6	37.8	35.7	188.6	282.6	...
1962	13.5	9.8	5.3	2.9	14.0	3.6	12.4	16.7	78.8	40.2	38.6	204.1	302.7	...
1963	14.5	10.2	5.8	3.2	15.0	3.9	13.1	17.4	84.6	42.6	42.0	214.6	318.6	...
1964	16.0	11.0	6.3	3.5	16.6	4.2	14.3	18.6	90.7	45.1	45.6	228.4	344.5	...
1965	17.6	11.9	7.0	3.9	18.0	4.5	15.5	19.5	96.9	47.2	49.7	251.9	370.3	...
1966	20.0	13.1	7.8	4.5	20.2	4.7	16.8	21.2	107.5	52.2	55.3	277.1	403.2	...
1967	21.8	13.8	8.4	4.9	23.1	4.9	18.2	22.5	118.4	56.9	61.5	282.9	431.2	...
1968	23.6	15.1	9.1	5.5	26.0	5.3	20.0	24.1	131.7	62.6	69.1	306.9	471.3	...
1969	26.2	16.1	10.2	6.4	29.7	5.5	21.8	25.9	143.8	66.8	77.1	326.2	514.5	...
1970	28.6	16.6	11.0	7.3	33.6	6.0	23.5	27.0	158.4	71.2	87.2	327.9	552.3	...
1971	31.1	17.8	11.9	8.2	37.2	6.4	25.5	28.9	172.3	75.5	96.9	348.7	606.1	...
1972	34.8	19.4	13.3	9.3	41.8	6.8	27.8	30.8	187.3	80.5	106.8	384.8	666.1	...
1973	40.0	21.4	15.3	10.2	47.0	7.8	30.6	33.4	202.2	83.0	119.2	443.0	737.5	...
1974	44.0	23.3	17.3	10.8	53.5	8.6	32.3	35.8	222.6	90.4	132.2	471.7	805.6	...
1975	48.6	25.6	18.7	11.8	62.5	9.5	36.2	38.4	246.9	98.2	148.7	497.2	894.3	...
1976	54.5	29.0	21.6	12.2	71.8	10.7	41.2	42.8	269.1	107.4	161.7	559.8	996.4	...
1977	64.5	32.7	25.5	12.7	81.1	12.8	45.9	46.1	291.5	116.2	175.4	627.5	1 111.9	...
1978	74.8	37.0	30.0	13.9	92.5	14.2	53.7	53.2	317.7	125.9	191.8	710.6	1 266.4	...
1979	88.0	40.6	35.4	15.3	105.2	16.0	61.1	58.2	345.7	135.6	210.1	799.7	1 417.9	...
1980	102.0	44.6	39.8	17.5	122.3	17.4	66.1	62.6	383.7	150.7	233.0	840.2	1 565.6	...
1981	117.5	49.9	45.8	19.1	140.8	19.4	74.1	68.5	425.9	171.4	254.5	946.6	1 755.9	...
1982	130.0	52.1	48.8	20.7	157.2	20.4	80.5	70.7	462.4	186.2	276.2	923.3	1 869.3	...
1983	147.9	58.5	56.1	23.7	174.6	22.8	89.2	79.2	493.1	197.6	295.6	953.1	2 090.5	...
1984	170.6	66.7	66.5	26.0	188.0	24.1	97.0	89.3	538.1	220.0	318.1	1 072.7	2 322.3	...
1985	193.1	72.9	74.8	27.9	203.4	27.9	106.4	98.0	583.3	236.2	347.1	1 107.4	2 529.5	...
1986	216.7	78.8	83.3	29.6	222.4	29.7	115.1	107.2	620.0	245.2	374.8	1 116.7	2 726.1	...
1987	238.6	81.3	94.1	32.7	253.7	31.6	120.5	112.3	659.1	257.8	401.3	1 180.8	2 899.5	157.9
1988	273.0	87.0	106.3	34.7	274.4	33.8	132.1	124.4	704.7	272.3	432.4	1 261.3	3 137.8	174.0
1989	305.9	92.6	119.5	37.6	309.4	39.1	141.1	133.9	752.0	286.5	465.6	1 341.0	3 391.4	186.4
1990	338.3	98.2	133.3	40.0	346.7	45.5	149.8	142.6	805.3	299.4	505.9	1 377.4	3 620.4	195.8
1991	341.8	103.8	133.7	44.1	380.7	47.9	154.3	144.2	857.2	321.4	535.8	1 352.8	3 785.9	204.2
1992	369.9	110.0	146.7	47.4	416.1	54.8	161.4	153.0	897.3	333.2	564.1	1 400.0	4 040.5	216.5
1993	386.8	116.2	156.1	50.1	437.9	55.5	170.0	163.7	928.1	335.5	592.6	1 453.4	4 275.9	228.4
1994	405.1	123.4	169.9	53.2	457.9	56.9	178.1	173.2	961.8	339.2	622.6	1 572.4	4 538.0	255.4
1995	428.0	127.7	187.4	56.0	477.4	62.4	185.9	180.9	990.4	338.7	651.7	1 631.4	4 775.8	275.3
1996	467.5	134.7	207.8	58.8	493.7	66.6	197.8	188.1	1 021.6	343.7	678.0	1 722.4	5 072.8	306.5
1997	518.1	145.7	232.7	62.2	510.8	74.0	215.8	197.4	1 056.8	349.3	707.5	1 820.8	5 426.8	347.7
1998	565.3	156.8	254.0	67.6	533.9	76.8	229.1	211.1	1 094.5	352.9	741.6	1 895.4	5 757.1	385.0
1999	613.9	170.5	280.1	72.8	561.7	83.8	244.0	217.8	1 141.2	361.9	779.4	1 958.9	6 168.3	425.9
2000	675.1	183.4	282.4	79.2	599.2	88.7	261.4	229.1	1 202.7	378.7	823.9	2 081.5	6 532.8	465.8
2001	698.8	177.6	289.4	85.1	654.2	95.7	265.8	241.5	1 258.3	385.7	872.6	2 027.5	6 842.2	424.2
2002	705.2	183.8	300.0	93.3	706.3	102.4	279.1	252.5	1 338.4	417.3	921.1	2 036.9	7 094.3	416.6
2003	733.1	195.5	320.3	100.1	757.2	107.2	291.7	265.3	1 418.4	448.6	969.8	2 113.3	7 429.1	421.2
2004	792.7	210.1	335.3	108.3	808.0	113.7	313.7	273.9	1 491.6	479.4	1 012.3	2 280.6	7 913.7	440.5
2005	859.4	236.2	368.3	113.6	856.1	118.1	333.6	287.5	1 568.8	501.9	1 066.9	2 443.2	8 409.9	473.6
2006	930.6	246.9	388.9	121.1	904.8	126.9	358.0	299.5	1 649.1	527.6	1 121.5	2 607.4	8 921.8	496.5
2007	1 007.8	271.3	415.1	129.5	957.4	133.8	379.5	315.6	1 742.9	554.0	1 188.9	2 670.6	9 394.0	516.0
2008	1 095.6	283.8	426.5	138.3	1 019.7	140.1	396.2	326.8	1 840.0	586.6	1 253.4	2 702.2	9 722.4	535.7

[1]Consists of computer and electronic products manufacturing; publishing, including software; information and data processing services; and computer systems design and related services.
. . . = Not available.

Table 15-2. Chain-Type Quantity Indexes for Value Added by NAICS Industry Group

(2000 = 100.)

Year	Total gross domestic product	Private industries												
		Total	Agriculture, forestry, fishing, and hunting	Mining	Utilities	Construc-tion	Manufacturing		Wholesale trade	Retail trade	Transpor-tation and ware-housing	Information	Finance and insurance	Real estate and rental and leasing
							Durable goods	Nondurable goods						
1947	16.0	15.0	25.2	49.6	8.8	35.1	12.2	20.7	8.7	14.2	22.6	5.8	12.0	11.9
1948	16.7	15.7	28.9	50.7	9.8	40.7	12.9	22.2	8.9	14.4	21.8	6.2	12.1	12.3
1949	16.7	15.6	27.6	44.3	11.1	40.9	12.1	22.0	9.0	15.1	19.5	6.5	12.6	12.9
1950	18.1	17.0	29.1	49.7	12.0	45.6	14.4	24.1	10.0	16.4	21.2	6.6	13.0	13.8
1951	19.5	18.2	27.6	54.5	14.0	50.9	16.5	25.7	10.3	16.6	23.8	7.1	14.0	14.6
1952	20.3	18.8	29.0	53.0	15.0	53.0	17.4	25.9	10.7	17.0	23.0	7.3	14.7	15.6
1953	21.2	19.7	30.3	54.7	16.2	55.0	19.0	26.9	11.0	17.7	23.2	7.8	15.3	16.5
1954	21.0	19.4	31.3	52.8	17.8	57.0	17.0	26.5	11.1	17.8	21.7	7.9	15.6	17.4
1955	22.5	21.0	32.1	59.4	18.6	60.7	19.2	28.4	12.2	19.2	23.9	8.4	17.1	18.5
1956	23.0	21.4	32.1	61.5	19.8	64.1	18.7	29.0	12.7	19.3	24.5	8.7	18.1	19.3
1957	23.4	21.9	30.8	61.1	21.3	64.3	19.0	29.3	13.0	19.7	24.4	9.1	19.0	20.3
1958	23.2	21.5	31.8	56.1	22.2	66.8	16.4	29.3	13.2	19.7	22.4	9.3	18.7	21.3
1959	24.9	23.3	31.8	58.1	24.2	72.4	18.7	31.9	15.0	20.9	23.7	9.9	19.0	22.8
1960	25.5	23.8	33.3	59.4	25.9	73.2	18.7	32.0	15.6	21.2	24.0	10.3	20.0	24.1
1961	26.1	24.3	33.6	59.9	27.3	74.3	18.4	32.7	16.1	21.2	24.0	10.7	21.0	25.3
1962	27.7	25.8	33.0	61.6	28.8	77.9	20.6	34.8	17.1	22.6	25.3	11.4	21.6	26.9
1963	28.9	27.2	34.3	64.3	30.2	80.0	22.3	37.5	17.8	23.3	26.7	12.2	22.1	28.1
1964	30.5	28.8	33.6	66.6	32.4	84.1	24.3	39.4	18.9	24.9	27.7	13.1	23.2	29.4
1965	32.5	30.8	35.8	69.5	33.8	87.7	27.2	41.9	20.4	26.4	30.1	14.0	23.8	31.1
1966	34.6	32.7	34.7	73.7	36.2	88.6	29.8	45.0	21.7	27.8	32.9	15.2	24.6	32.5
1967	35.5	33.3	37.2	74.6	38.1	86.7	29.7	44.5	22.7	28.1	32.7	16.1	26.0	33.5
1968	37.2	34.9	36.2	76.9	41.5	86.2	31.2	47.4	24.2	29.5	34.3	17.1	27.3	35.2
1969	38.4	36.0	37.3	79.2	44.0	83.2	31.9	48.9	25.2	29.7	35.5	18.5	29.9	37.2
1970	38.4	35.9	38.3	82.2	45.5	76.4	29.1	48.4	25.9	30.2	35.0	19.7	30.8	38.1
1971	39.7	37.1	40.2	80.2	49.0	74.2	29.5	50.6	27.4	31.5	35.6	20.5	31.4	40.7
1972	41.8	39.4	40.7	79.8	50.1	75.2	32.4	54.5	29.5	33.5	38.4	22.0	33.1	43.1
1973	44.2	42.0	40.4	82.5	56.1	78.0	36.3	58.6	30.5	35.5	40.9	23.5	35.0	45.1
1974	44.0	41.6	39.5	79.0	57.1	75.2	35.1	55.0	30.2	34.0	41.3	24.3	37.8	46.9
1975	43.9	41.5	45.9	80.3	60.8	68.1	31.6	53.7	30.9	34.2	38.5	25.2	40.3	48.9
1976	46.3	43.9	44.6	80.1	60.2	73.1	34.9	59.6	32.0	36.9	41.7	26.5	40.4	50.7
1977	48.4	46.1	46.4	86.3	59.9	74.1	37.7	64.0	33.6	38.4	43.5	28.5	41.0	51.4
1978	51.1	48.8	45.1	88.9	59.6	78.4	40.2	66.1	37.1	40.7	45.7	31.5	44.8	53.9
1979	52.7	50.6	48.6	79.7	54.7	81.2	40.8	70.3	39.9	40.7	48.3	34.2	46.5	57.1
1980	52.6	50.3	47.5	90.0	52.0	74.6	38.5	67.2	39.8	38.9	47.2	36.4	49.8	59.1
1981	53.9	51.7	59.7	90.3	51.7	67.9	39.6	72.3	42.1	40.0	46.2	38.3	51.2	60.2
1982	52.9	50.4	63.0	86.3	50.7	59.5	35.6	69.9	42.1	40.0	43.9	38.2	52.6	60.1
1983	55.2	52.8	43.3	81.2	52.7	62.8	38.0	76.7	43.8	44.1	49.5	41.0	52.4	62.9
1984	59.2	56.8	57.1	88.8	57.3	72.2	44.0	76.5	47.1	48.3	52.1	40.7	54.2	65.9
1985	61.7	59.4	69.6	93.1	60.9	79.0	45.2	78.7	49.5	51.2	52.7	42.0	54.1	68.3
1986	63.8	61.1	68.6	87.5	64.4	81.8	45.6	77.5	54.5	54.2	53.0	42.7	56.1	69.0
1987	66.0	63.4	71.5	91.7	72.3	82.4	48.9	83.6	53.1	52.1	55.7	45.8	60.2	69.8
1988	68.7	66.3	64.7	100.0	70.6	85.4	52.8	85.4	56.4	56.5	58.0	47.6	62.4	72.8
1989	71.1	68.7	71.1	97.1	79.0	87.6	53.7	86.1	58.6	58.8	59.5	51.2	63.4	74.9
1990	72.5	69.9	74.7	96.2	84.4	86.5	53.0	85.4	57.3	59.8	62.3	53.4	65.2	76.3
1991	72.3	69.8	75.4	97.6	85.3	79.1	51.5	85.8	59.4	59.5	65.1	54.4	67.4	76.9
1992	74.7	72.4	83.1	95.7	85.4	80.0	52.7	89.7	65.0	63.0	68.8	57.6	67.3	79.9
1993	76.7	74.3	72.8	97.0	85.8	82.0	55.2	92.9	67.1	65.4	72.0	61.4	70.3	81.3
1994	79.8	77.8	84.6	105.3	89.5	86.6	60.2	98.4	71.3	69.8	77.8	65.2	70.5	83.8
1995	81.8	79.7	73.1	105.7	93.8	86.3	65.2	97.8	70.8	73.0	80.5	68.0	72.9	86.0
1996	84.8	83.2	80.0	98.9	95.4	90.7	69.1	98.4	77.3	79.4	84.6	72.7	74.9	88.2
1997	88.7	87.4	88.3	102.5	91.2	93.3	75.3	100.4	85.6	86.0	88.4	74.6	80.1	91.2
1998	92.4	91.7	86.3	101.7	90.5	97.1	84.4	99.8	95.4	90.4	91.5	82.3	85.7	93.1
1999	96.5	96.2	89.2	104.3	94.7	99.4	89.6	101.3	100.4	95.7	95.3	95.5	91.6	97.2
2000	100.0	100.0	100.0	100.0	100.0	100.0	100.0	100.0	100.0	100.0	100.0	100.0	100.0	100.0
2001	100.8	100.9	93.7	94.7	95.1	100.2	94.0	95.0	107.0	107.0	97.4	104.0	104.4	103.5
2002	102.4	102.4	98.8	88.7	99.1	98.2	95.7	99.1	108.1	109.3	99.5	106.3	106.7	103.6
2003	104.9	105.1	106.2	87.9	106.0	96.2	98.2	98.3	110.4	113.6	101.5	109.4	110.5	105.4
2004	108.7	109.2	113.3	88.8	112.1	96.4	103.9	103.5	112.6	116.5	110.8	122.2	111.6	109.7
2005	111.9	113.1	122.9	85.4	105.4	96.0	109.6	98.3	116.3	126.9	115.3	132.9	120.2	111.9
2006	115.1	116.6	116.4	91.8	106.6	92.0	118.5	100.4	117.0	134.0	117.6	136.5	127.7	115.0
2007	117.4	119.0	124.5	91.8	107.9	81.8	124.2	100.8	118.0	140.1	120.6	147.5	127.8	118.8
2008	118.7	119.7	123.9	91.1	109.9	77.2	122.6	96.2	116.2	139.4	116.1	155.2	123.9	120.9

Table 15-2. Chain-Type Quantity Indexes for Value Added by NAICS Industry Group—*Continued*

(2000 = 100.)

Year	Professional, scientific, and technical services	Management of companies and enterprises	Administrative and waste management services	Educational services	Health care and social assistance	Arts, entertainment, and recreation	Accommodation and food services	Other services except government	Total government	Federal	State and local	Private goods-producing industries	Private services-producing industries	Information-communications-technology-producing industries[1]
1947	8.8	18.7	6.4	19.4	10.8	15.8	20.0	41.1	35.4	67.7	20.6	19.7	12.8	...
1948	8.9	19.4	6.5	22.4	11.3	15.5	20.1	42.0	34.1	63.5	21.0	21.4	13.1	...
1949	8.9	19.2	6.6	23.0	11.7	15.3	20.6	41.8	34.0	61.2	22.0	20.5	13.3	...
1950	9.3	21.0	7.2	23.2	12.3	15.4	22.0	42.9	34.4	61.3	22.6	23.0	14.2	...
1951	9.8	22.5	7.5	23.3	12.8	16.2	22.2	43.4	40.6	79.7	23.1	25.0	15.0	...
1952	10.1	23.4	7.9	23.1	13.5	16.1	22.7	43.2	43.8	88.7	23.7	25.8	15.4	...
1953	10.4	24.6	8.2	23.6	14.2	16.5	23.6	43.7	44.6	89.1	24.6	27.4	16.1	...
1954	10.5	23.9	8.2	23.9	15.1	16.5	23.7	43.2	44.4	86.8	25.4	26.2	16.2	...
1955	11.0	25.9	8.8	24.8	15.5	17.1	25.3	46.1	44.6	85.1	26.4	28.6	17.5	...
1956	11.3	26.3	9.3	25.2	16.1	17.8	25.6	47.8	45.4	84.2	27.9	28.7	18.0	...
1957	12.2	26.8	9.9	27.1	17.1	18.1	26.5	49.2	46.3	84.1	29.3	28.8	18.7	...
1958	12.5	25.9	10.4	28.4	18.4	18.5	26.3	50.4	46.8	82.1	30.8	27.3	18.9	...
1959	13.5	28.4	11.2	29.1	19.5	19.8	27.7	52.0	47.5	81.6	32.2	29.8	20.2	...
1960	13.6	28.9	11.6	30.3	20.3	20.8	28.2	54.1	49.2	83.4	33.9	30.1	20.9	...
1961	14.4	29.3	12.3	31.9	21.2	21.5	28.1	55.3	50.9	85.2	35.5	30.2	21.5	...
1962	15.1	31.4	12.9	33.7	23.0	22.0	30.0	56.7	52.8	88.6	36.7	32.4	22.8	...
1963	15.9	33.3	13.5	35.1	24.4	22.9	31.2	57.7	54.4	89.5	38.7	34.6	23.8	...
1964	16.8	35.2	14.4	36.3	27.2	24.1	33.1	59.8	56.4	90.8	40.9	36.7	25.2	...
1965	17.8	38.0	15.4	38.8	28.3	24.6	35.3	61.3	58.5	92.2	43.3	39.8	26.7	...
1966	19.5	40.9	16.8	41.2	29.9	24.9	37.0	64.2	62.1	98.6	45.7	42.4	28.3	...
1967	20.5	41.3	17.2	43.4	31.1	25.1	38.0	65.7	65.2	104.6	47.4	42.3	29.2	...
1968	21.3	43.6	18.1	45.2	33.2	25.8	39.3	66.4	67.9	107.2	50.1	43.9	30.7	...
1969	22.4	45.0	19.4	46.9	35.8	25.4	39.8	67.2	69.6	107.6	52.3	44.7	32.0	...
1970	23.1	44.5	19.8	49.0	38.0	26.1	40.8	66.4	69.7	103.0	54.4	42.5	32.8	...
1971	23.5	46.1	20.1	51.8	40.5	26.6	42.2	66.8	69.9	99.0	56.5	43.2	34.3	...
1972	25.0	49.4	21.8	52.5	42.9	27.4	44.7	69.0	70.2	95.5	58.5	46.1	36.4	...
1973	27.0	53.5	23.5	53.5	45.9	30.3	47.3	70.7	70.4	91.7	60.6	49.7	38.5	...
1974	27.7	50.6	24.8	55.5	47.8	30.8	45.7	68.4	72.3	92.5	62.9	47.6	38.9	...
1975	27.2	49.8	23.7	56.8	51.1	31.5	45.9	68.2	73.1	91.1	64.9	45.5	39.7	...
1976	28.4	53.9	25.0	57.4	53.8	33.8	49.5	71.0	74.3	92.8	65.8	49.1	41.5	...
1977	31.1	57.6	27.2	57.8	57.8	38.2	52.0	71.2	75.0	92.8	66.8	52.3	43.3	...
1978	33.8	60.7	30.0	60.4	60.6	40.1	56.0	75.1	76.7	94.9	68.4	54.6	46.2	...
1979	36.6	61.4	32.9	60.6	63.5	42.4	57.1	75.7	77.7	94.9	69.9	56.1	48.1	...
1980	38.4	60.3	34.2	62.7	67.4	43.7	55.2	74.4	79.0	96.6	71.0	53.9	48.8	...
1981	39.9	59.5	35.3	61.7	69.3	46.2	56.7	72.3	79.3	97.6	70.9	55.8	49.9	...
1982	39.9	59.9	34.3	61.9	69.8	46.4	58.6	69.1	79.5	97.1	71.4	52.0	49.8	...
1983	42.0	65.2	37.2	66.8	71.7	49.1	63.2	72.5	80.2	99.5	71.3	53.4	52.6	...
1984	45.9	72.5	42.4	70.0	72.6	49.5	66.2	77.5	81.0	101.1	71.8	59.5	55.7	...
1985	49.7	77.1	46.0	71.5	73.8	55.6	69.5	80.9	83.2	103.5	73.8	62.6	58.1	...
1986	53.7	82.1	49.8	71.9	75.5	56.9	73.7	82.9	85.1	105.0	76.0	62.5	60.6	...
1987	56.5	83.7	54.9	75.7	80.8	58.3	72.0	84.2	86.8	107.3	77.3	66.2	62.3	16.8
1988	61.4	86.6	58.8	75.6	81.2	60.3	75.1	89.0	88.8	108.2	79.9	69.1	65.2	18.8
1989	65.8	89.5	63.8	77.3	84.8	66.4	76.2	92.2	91.0	109.8	82.4	70.4	68.0	20.4
1990	69.0	92.2	67.5	77.5	88.2	73.3	76.9	94.4	93.2	111.9	84.6	69.9	69.9	21.6
1991	66.4	91.8	65.0	80.9	90.3	73.4	74.5	91.3	93.7	111.9	85.3	68.2	70.3	22.3
1992	68.7	91.8	68.2	83.5	92.8	81.9	75.8	92.5	94.1	111.2	86.3	70.3	73.1	24.2
1993	69.6	92.0	70.9	85.8	93.0	81.0	78.1	95.2	94.1	108.7	87.3	72.1	75.0	26.4
1994	70.8	94.2	75.6	87.7	93.0	80.6	80.6	98.6	94.4	106.8	88.7	77.8	77.7	30.9
1995	71.7	93.5	81.8	90.1	93.9	85.9	82.8	99.7	94.3	102.2	90.6	79.6	79.8	36.9
1996	75.7	97.5	88.6	90.5	94.6	88.2	86.3	99.1	94.8	100.3	92.2	82.6	83.4	44.3
1997	80.4	103.1	95.6	92.3	95.1	95.0	88.8	99.3	95.9	99.7	94.1	87.2	87.4	53.8
1998	86.8	100.4	99.5	95.4	95.6	95.5	92.8	101.9	96.9	99.2	95.9	91.9	91.6	68.3
1999	92.4	101.2	105.1	97.3	97.3	99.1	96.1	100.2	98.0	98.5	97.8	95.4	96.4	83.7
2000	100.0	100.0	100.0	100.0	100.0	100.0	100.0	100.0	100.0	100.0	100.0	100.0	100.0	100.0
2001	100.6	98.1	97.2	99.8	103.6	103.1	98.0	98.3	100.8	98.4	101.9	95.7	102.6	99.6
2002	99.1	101.1	98.4	102.4	108.2	106.8	99.1	98.7	102.5	100.3	103.5	96.9	104.1	99.6
2003	103.0	103.9	104.7	106.1	113.1	108.8	102.5	100.6	103.8	102.8	104.2	97.4	107.5	108.9
2004	111.1	98.9	105.8	108.2	117.0	112.1	106.8	100.8	104.3	103.7	104.5	101.3	111.7	121.3
2005	117.3	101.4	113.7	107.9	120.8	113.0	109.5	102.8	105.0	104.0	105.4	101.9	116.6	136.4
2006	124.0	100.0	114.8	109.8	124.9	117.6	113.0	102.4	105.5	103.8	106.3	104.6	120.4	149.2
2007	132.8	97.8	117.2	113.3	127.3	119.8	114.9	102.8	106.9	104.5	108.1	103.9	123.9	168.5
2008	144.3	98.0	118.6	117.3	133.2	122.2	116.7	103.0	109.0	107.6	109.7	100.7	125.9	183.7

[1]Consists of computer and electronic products manufacturing; publishing, including software; information and data processing services; and computer systems design and related services.

. . . = Not available.

Table 15-3. Gross Domestic Factor Income by NAICS Industry Group

(Billions of current dollars.)

NAICS industry	1998	1999	2000	2001	2002	2003	2004	2005	2006	2007
Gross domestic factor income, total	8 142.5	8 638.6	9 152.4	9 454.6	9 745.2	10 201.5	10 866.7	11 553.0	12 251.9	12 844.4
Compensation of employees	5 023.9	5 362.3	5 787.3	5 947.2	6 096.6	6 331.1	6 662.5	7 037.2	7 440.4	7 819.4
Gross operating surplus	3 118.6	3 276.3	3 365.1	3 507.4	3 648.6	3 870.4	4 204.2	4 515.8	4 811.5	5 025.0
Private industries	7 037.0	7 486.2	7 939.2	8 185.2	8 393.7	8 769.1	9 360.4	9 969.3	10 587.5	11 085.6
Compensation of employees	4 107.7	4 407.0	4 776.4	4 882.4	4 957.6	5 118.7	5 382.2	5 692.4	6 035.3	6 342.0
Gross operating surplus	2 929.3	3 079.2	3 162.8	3 302.8	3 436.1	3 650.4	3 978.2	4 276.9	4 552.2	4 743.6
Agriculture, forestry, fishing, and hunting	107.9	106.8	112.1	110.6	99.2	123.5	148.0	148.6	128.1	170.5
Compensation of employees	31.2	33.0	34.6	36.1	36.4	36.1	38.7	39.6	40.3	42.4
Gross operating surplus	76.7	73.8	77.5	74.5	62.8	87.4	109.3	109.0	87.8	128.1
Mining	63.8	74.6	108.2	104.5	93.8	128.6	154.7	204.4	240.9	251.8
Compensation of employees	34.6	33.4	36.0	38.8	37.7	39.4	44.0	49.4	57.6	64.2
Gross operating surplus	29.2	41.2	72.2	65.7	56.1	89.2	110.7	155.0	183.3	187.6
Utilities	152.0	155.5	158.4	176.5	172.6	182.8	200.9	197.8	228.5	235.2
Compensation of employees	41.2	42.6	46.3	48.4	51.2	51.8	57.4	55.7	56.1	59.8
Gross operating surplus	110.8	112.9	112.1	128.1	121.4	131.0	143.5	142.1	172.4	175.4
Construction	370.0	401.8	430.9	464.3	476.5	489.9	532.2	597.6	637.9	603.0
Compensation of employees	254.3	282.8	309.2	327.6	332.7	341.0	356.3	390.7	424.2	442.8
Gross operating surplus	115.7	119.0	121.7	136.7	143.8	148.9	175.9	206.9	213.7	160.2
Durable goods manufacturing	794.2	807.5	851.7	764.9	760.0	756.2	790.6	827.1	880.3	901.7
Compensation of employees	546.2	570.4	621.2	584.2	570.8	583.6	588.4	598.0	628.5	641.2
Gross operating surplus	248.0	237.1	230.5	180.7	189.2	172.6	202.2	229.1	251.8	260.5
Nondurable goods manufacturing	512.4	527.7	533.8	534.7	548.2	556.8	588.8	601.2	642.4	657.9
Compensation of employees	279.1	283.8	297.6	292.6	303.5	305.0	314.3	310.8	325.1	328.2
Gross operating surplus	233.3	243.9	236.2	242.1	244.7	251.8	274.5	290.4	317.3	329.7
Wholesale trade	416.1	446.4	456.3	471.8	477.5	492.7	532.0	559.2	603.2	630.4
Compensation of employees	291.0	313.9	328.6	334.1	333.4	344.8	363.2	387.1	413.3	438.2
Gross operating surplus	125.1	132.5	127.7	137.7	144.1	147.9	168.8	172.1	189.9	192.2
Retail trade	474.4	502.6	522.0	549.0	572.6	596.5	612.1	646.5	677.5	696.8
Compensation of employees	342.3	368.2	396.6	410.5	422.3	432.6	446.4	466.0	481.4	496.0
Gross operating surplus	132.1	134.4	125.4	138.5	150.3	163.9	165.7	180.5	196.1	200.8
Transportation and warehousing	259.6	272.5	285.6	287.1	288.7	302.4	327.2	345.3	367.2	385.4
Compensation of employees	174.9	186.1	199.3	203.5	204.1	204.1	222.2	229.0	237.3	249.1
Gross operating surplus	84.7	86.4	86.3	83.6	84.6	98.3	105.0	116.3	129.9	136.3
Information	349.9	405.1	421.9	439.9	445.0	450.4	490.1	515.8	517.9	545.2
Compensation of employees	185.6	217.5	248.0	244.4	227.9	225.6	231.6	236.9	247.1	258.4
Gross operating surplus	164.3	187.6	173.9	195.5	217.1	224.8	258.5	278.9	270.8	286.8
Finance and insurance	613.3	650.7	710.4	751.2	789.2	827.9	866.6	945.7	1 015.3	1 044.1
Compensation of employees	344.5	370.7	409.3	437.0	448.0	472.3	508.1	546.4	587.6	617.1
Gross operating surplus	268.8	280.0	301.1	314.2	341.2	355.6	358.5	399.3	427.7	427.0
Real estate and rental and leasing	904.7	972.2	1 036.0	1 111.4	1 139.8	1 189.0	1 265.9	1 320.9	1 392.4	1 481.1
Compensation of employees	66.2	70.7	77.4	81.3	84.1	87.7	94.4	102.4	110.0	113.7
Gross operating surplus	838.5	901.5	958.6	1 030.1	1 055.7	1 101.3	1 171.5	1 218.5	1 282.4	1 367.4
Professional, scientific, and technical services	555.9	603.8	664.2	687.5	693.3	720.6	779.2	844.6	914.9	991.5
Compensation of employees	378.3	422.0	486.9	499.6	489.1	497.4	526.4	579.1	629.9	679.5
Gross operating surplus	177.6	181.8	177.3	187.9	204.2	223.2	252.8	265.5	285.0	312.0
Management of companies and enterprises	153.8	167.3	179.9	174.5	180.7	192.3	206.6	232.4	243.0	266.9
Compensation of employees	127.5	136.1	147.4	139.9	139.5	148.2	162.6	180.7	188.6	206.6
Gross operating surplus	26.3	31.2	32.5	34.6	41.2	44.1	44.0	51.7	54.4	60.3
Administrative and waste management services	247.7	273.3	274.8	281.7	292.0	312.0	326.5	359.0	378.9	404.7
Compensation of employees	193.9	213.1	211.7	217.0	222.9	232.9	242.2	265.6	284.1	301.8
Gross operating surplus	53.8	60.2	63.1	64.7	69.1	79.1	84.3	93.4	94.8	102.9
Educational services	66.6	71.8	78.2	83.9	92.0	98.8	106.9	112.0	119.5	127.7
Compensation of employees	61.2	65.9	72.0	78.1	85.5	90.9	96.9	101.9	108.1	115.8
Gross operating surplus	5.4	5.9	6.2	5.8	6.5	7.9	10.0	10.1	11.4	11.9
Health care and social assistance	527.3	554.7	591.9	646.4	697.8	748.0	798.1	845.1	892.8	944.7
Compensation of employees	425.9	447.1	478.8	516.2	553.8	590.9	628.0	672.2	709.5	753.6
Gross operating surplus	101.4	107.6	113.1	130.2	144.0	157.1	170.1	172.9	183.3	191.1
Arts, entertainment, and recreation	69.1	75.1	79.7	86.2	92.5	96.6	102.4	106.2	114.0	119.6
Compensation of employees	44.5	48.4	53.6	56.9	59.9	63.1	67.1	69.1	73.5	77.3
Gross operating surplus	24.6	26.7	26.1	29.3	32.6	33.5	35.3	37.1	40.5	42.3
Accommodation and food services	201.2	214.0	229.5	233.7	246.2	256.6	276.6	293.1	314.9	334.7
Compensation of employees	143.7	152.8	164.7	170.6	177.8	186.8	199.6	211.3	224.6	236.9
Gross operating surplus	57.5	61.2	64.8	63.1	68.4	69.8	77.0	81.8	90.3	97.8
Other services, except government	197.2	203.0	213.5	225.5	235.7	247.6	255.0	266.8	277.7	293.0
Compensation of employees	141.5	148.5	157.2	165.6	176.7	184.6	194.4	200.4	208.5	219.7
Gross operating surplus	55.7	54.5	56.3	59.9	59.0	63.0	60.6	66.4	69.2	73.3
Government	1 105.5	1 152.3	1 213.1	1 269.3	1 351.5	1 432.3	1 506.2	1 583.6	1 664.4	1 758.8
Compensation of employees	916.2	955.3	1 010.8	1 064.8	1 139.0	1 212.4	1 280.3	1 344.7	1 405.1	1 477.3
Gross operating surplus	189.3	197.0	202.3	204.5	212.5	219.9	225.9	238.9	259.3	281.5
Addenda:										
Private goods-producing industries	1 848.3	1 918.3	2 036.8	1 979.0	1 978.0	2 055.0	2 214.4	2 378.8	2 529.7	2 584.9
Compensation of employees	1 145.4	1 203.4	1 298.7	1 279.3	1 281.2	1 305.1	1 341.7	1 388.5	1 475.8	1 518.8
Gross operating surplus	702.9	714.9	738.1	699.7	696.8	749.9	872.7	990.3	1 053.9	1 066.1
Private services-producing industries	5 188.7	5 567.9	5 902.5	6 206.2	6 415.8	6 714.2	7 146.1	7 590.5	8 057.9	8 500.7
Compensation of employees	2 962.3	3 203.6	3 477.8	3 603.1	3 676.4	3 813.6	4 040.5	4 303.9	4 559.6	4 823.3
Gross operating surplus	2 226.4	2 364.3	2 424.7	2 603.1	2 739.4	2 900.6	3 105.6	3 286.6	3 498.3	3 677.4
Information-communications-technology-producing industries [1]	378.5	418.9	458.1	416.3	408.5	412.7	431.3	463.9	486.1	505.0
Compensation of employees	275.2	320.3	388.8	364.1	330.2	323.5	327.9	351.0	380.4	396.6
Gross operating surplus	103.3	98.6	69.3	52.2	78.3	89.2	103.4	112.9	105.7	108.4

[1]Consists of computer and electronic products manufacturing; publishing, including software; information and data processing services; and computer systems design and related services.

NOTES AND DEFINITIONS, CHAPTER 15

TABLES 15-1 THROUGH 15-3
GROSS DOMESTIC PRODUCT (VALUE ADDED) AND GROSS FACTOR INCOME BY INDUSTRY

SOURCE: U.S. DEPARTMENT OF COMMERCE, BUREAU OF ECONOMIC ANALYSIS (BEA)

In the introduction to the notes and definitions for Chapter 1, it was observed that gross domestic product (GDP), while primarily measured as the sum of final demands for goods and services, is also the sum of the values created by each industry in the economy. In this chapter, selected data are presented from the industry accounts in the national income and product accounts (NIPAs). The industry accounts measure the contribution of each major industry to GDP. They are only calculated on an annual basis; no quarterly data are available.

In recent years, estimates of GDP by industry have been prepared using a methodology integrated with annual input-output accounts in order to produce estimates of gross industry output, industry input, and the difference between the two—industry value added—with greater consistency and timeliness than was previously possible. The current integrated industry accounts also include a wealth of related information too extensive for inclusion here, such as quantity and price indexes for gross output and intermediate inputs, cost per unit of real value added allocated to the three components of value added, and components of domestic supply (domestic output, imports, exports, and inventory change).

The estimates of GDP by NAICS industry have been extended back to 1947, using approximations of current methods in earlier years when the source data were less comprehensive. Table 15-1 presents current-dollar GDP for NAICS industry groups. Table 15-2 presents indexes of real value added for each industry group.

In Table 15-3, the editor presents a measure derived from the components of current-dollar value added as published by BEA. This measure, "gross domestic factor income," enables users to obtain a clearer picture of the quantitative impact of each industry on the economy and of the shares of capital and labor in each industry.

The 2004 revision incorporated a change in terminology. An industry's contribution to total GDP, formerly referred to as "gross product originating" (GPO) or "gross product by industry," is now called "value added." This is consistent with the use of the term "value added" in most economic writing. However, it should not be confused with a concept known as "Census value added," which is used in U.S. censuses and surveys of manufactures. Census value added is calculated at the individual establishment level and does not exclude purchased business services. This means that census value added is not a true measure of economic value added.

Definitions and notes on the data

An industry's *gross domestic product (value added)*, formerly *GPO*, is equal to the market value of its gross output (which consists of the value, including taxes, of sales or receipts and other operating income plus the value of inventory change) minus the value of its intermediate inputs (energy, raw materials, semifinished goods, and services that are purchased from domestic industries or from foreign sources).

In concept, this is also equal to the sum of *compensation of employees, taxes on production and imports less subsidies,* and *gross operating surplus.* (See Chapter 1 and its notes and definitions for more information.)

Compensation of employees consists of wage and salary accruals and supplements to wages and salaries. This approximates the labor share of production, subject to the note below about proprietors' income.

Taxes on production and imports less subsidies. Although this is shown in BEA source data as a single net line item, it represents two separate components.

Taxes on production and imports are included in the market value of the goods and services sold to final consumers and therefore in the consumer valuation of those goods. Since they are not part of the payments to the labor and capital inputs in the producing industries, they must be <u>added</u> to the sum of the returns to those inputs in order to account for the total value to consumers. Taxes that fall into this classification include property taxes, sales and excise taxes, and Customs duties.

BEA allocates these taxes to the industry level at which they are assessed by law. Most sales taxes are considered by BEA to be part of the value added by retail trade. Some sales taxes, most fuel taxes, and all customs duties are allocated by BEA to wholesale trade. Residential real property taxes, including those on owner-occupied dwellings, are allocated by BEA to the real estate industry.

Subsidies to business by government are included in the labor and/or capital payments made by that industry. Since they are payments to the industry in addition to the market values paid by consumers, they are *subtracted* from the values of the labor and capital inputs to make them consistent with the market values as defined in value added. The role of subsidies is obvious in the source data for the agricultural sector, where the net "taxes on production and imports less subsidies" has a negative sign: farm subsidies more than offset this industry's taxes on production and imports, which mainly consist of property taxes, since sales, excise, and import taxes are not levied on farms.

For private sector businesses, *gross operating surplus* consists of business income (corporate profits before tax, proprietors' income, and rental income of persons), net interest and miscellaneous payments, business current transfer payments (net), and capital consumption allowances. For government, households, and institutions, it consists of consumption of fixed capital and (for government) government enterprises' current surplus. This approximates the share of the value of production ascribable to capital and land as measured in the NIPAs accounts; however, as BEA notes, "an unknown portion [of proprietors' income] reflects the labor contribution of proprietors." (*Survey of Current Business*, June 2004, p. 27, footnote 7.) Another aspect to be noted is that gross operating surplus includes the return to owner-occupied housing in the real estate sector. Because there is in the NIPAs no employee compensation attributed to owner-occupied housing, the capital share in that industry as measured by gross operating surplus is very large.

Quantity indexes for value added. Measures of the constant-dollar change in each industry's gross output minus its intermediate input use are calculated by BEA, using a Fisher index-number formula which incorporates weights from two adjacent years. The changes for successive years are chained together in indexes, with the value for the year 2000 set at 100. The indexes are multiplied by the 2000 current-dollar to provide estimates of value added in "chained 2000 dollars," but because the actual weights used change from year to year, components in chained 2000 dollars typically do not add up to total GDP in 2000 dollars—and do not contain any information not already summarized in the indexes. For that reason, only the indexes are published here. At the time this chapter was compiled, these measures had not been updated consistent with the 2009 comprehensive revision of the NIPAs, so these measures are still on the 2000 base.

Gross domestic factor income (not a category published as such in the NIPAs) is calculated by the editor as value added minus "taxes on production and imports less subsidies." The effect of this procedure is to take out the specified taxes, and to leave in the subsidies embedded in the employee compensation and gross operating surplus components. The editor believes that this provides a valuable alternative basis for assessing the importance of different industries in the economy and the shares of labor and capital in each industry's output.

The editor's reasoning is based on the facts that more than half of these taxes are sales, excise, and import taxes, and the assignment of these taxes to industries is economically arbitrary. BEA assigns them to the industry with the legal liability to pay, not to the entity bearing the major incidence

of the tax. Yet economists have demonstrated that most of the burdens of sales and excise taxes and import duties are not borne by the factors in the legally liable industry; instead, they are passed on to consumers. In addition, because the wholesale and retail trade industries are classified as "services-producing," BEA's allocation of those taxes has a very peculiar result: taxes on goods are represented as paid by "service" industries. The process adopted instead by the editor in Table 15-3, which excludes these taxes and focuses on "gross domestic factor income," has the effect (for example) of keeping the wholesale trade industry from appearing to be both larger and more heavily taxed than it really is.

Private goods-producing industries consists of agriculture, forestry, fishing, and hunting; mining; construction; and manufacturing.

Private services-producing industries consists of utilities; wholesale trade; retail trade; transportation and warehousing; information; finance, insurance, real estate, rental, and leasing; professional and business services; educational services, health care, and social assistance; arts, entertainment, recreation, accommodation, and food services; and other services, except government.

Information-communications-technology-producing industries is a category that cuts across the goods and services framework, consisting of computer and electronic products manufacturing; publishing industries (which includes software) from the information sector; information and data processing services; and computer systems design and related services.

Data availability and references

The industry estimates shown here are those published in "Annual Industry Accounts: Revised Statistics for 2005–2007" in the December 2008 *Survey of Current Business*. Information on concepts, methodology, and previous references can be found in that article.

The data for 2008 are advance estimates, with considerably less detail and using approximations of the detailed methods, published late in April 2009, and not including estimates of the data in Table 15-3. Revised estimates for 2008 and advance estimates for 2009 were scheduled for publication in late May 2010, too late for inclusion in this volume.

All data and *Survey of Current Business* articles are available on the BEA Web site at <http://www.bea.gov>. Click on "Annual Industry Accounts." For the tables, click on "Interactive Tables" under "Gross Domestic Product (GDP) by Industry."

CHAPTER 16: EMPLOYMENT, HOURS, AND EARNINGS BY NAICS INDUSTRY

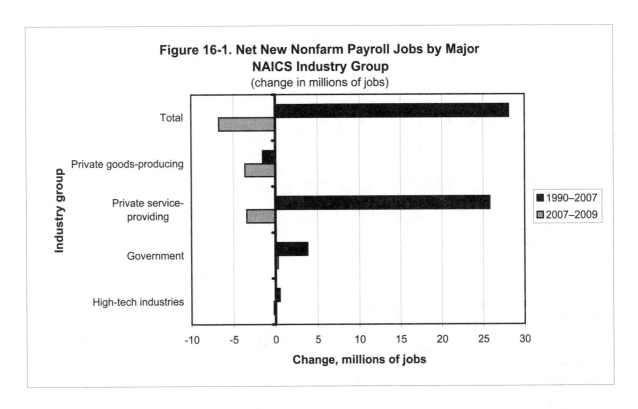

Figure 16-1. Net New Nonfarm Payroll Jobs by Major NAICS Industry Group

(change in millions of jobs)

- From 1990 to the year of the business cycle peak in 2007, U.S. nonfarm employers added a net total of 28.1 million jobs. Over the following two years, 6.7 million jobs were lost based on annual averages; all job gains since 2000 were erased. In the two years of recession, jobs were lost in both the goods and services industries, including the small high-tech sectors, and gains in government employment were slight. (Table 16-1)

- In 2009, the main industries that still had significantly more jobs than in 2000 were in education, health care, and social assistance. Lasting gains could also be found in oil and gas extraction, coal mining, some retail and some transportation industries, some financial sectors (despite steep drops since 2007), some professional and business services, and management. Manufacturing lost 5.4 million jobs over those nine years, and even temporary help services were down by 800,000—a 31 percent decline. (Table 16-1)

- The average workweek for production and nonsupervisory workers fell in most industries from 2007 to 2009. (Table 16-3)

- Average hourly earnings for production or nonsupervisory workers in 2009 ranged from just over $11 in the leisure and hospitality sector to nearly $30 in petroleum and coal products manufacturing and utilities. (Table 16-4)

Table 16-1. Nonfarm Employment by NAICS Sector and Industry

(Wage and salary workers on nonfarm payrolls, thousands.)

Industry	1990	1991	1992	1993	1994	1995	1996	1997	1998	1999
TOTAL NONFARM	109 487	108 375	108 726	110 844	114 291	117 298	119 708	122 776	125 930	128 993
Total Private	91 072	89 829	89 940	91 855	95 016	97 865	100 169	103 113	106 021	108 686
Goods-Producing	23 723	22 588	22 095	22 219	22 774	23 156	23 409	23 886	24 354	24 465
Mining and logging	765	739	689	666	659	641	637	654	645	598
Logging	84.6	78.7	78.7	81.0	82.0	82.5	80.7	82.1	80.0	80.8
Mining	680.1	660.5	609.8	584.9	576.5	558.1	556.4	571.3	564.7	517.4
Oil and gas extraction	190.2	191.0	182.2	170.9	162.4	151.7	146.9	144.1	140.8	131.2
Mining, except oil and gas [1]	302.2	285.1	271.8	250.9	255.2	252.4	249.4	249.5	243.1	234.5
Coal mining	136.0	125.6	117.5	100.2	103.5	96.7	90.5	89.4	85.3	78.6
Support activities for mining	187.6	184.5	155.7	163.1	158.8	154.0	160.1	177.7	180.8	151.7
Construction	5 263	4 780	4 608	4 779	5 095	5 274	5 536	5 813	6 149	6 545
Construction of buildings	1 413.0	1 252.9	1 187.3	1 227.4	1 300.8	1 325.4	1 380.2	1 435.4	1 508.8	1 586.3
Heavy and civil engineering	813.0	759.1	734.2	738.4	761.7	774.7	800.1	824.9	865.3	908.7
Specialty trade contractors	3 037.3	2 768.4	2 686.0	2 813.6	3 032.5	3 174.1	3 355.1	3 552.6	3 775.1	4 049.6
Manufacturing	17 695	17 068	16 799	16 774	17 020	17 241	17 237	17 419	17 560	17 322
Durable goods	10 737	10 220	9 946	9 901	10 132	10 373	10 486	10 705	10 911	10 831
Wood products	540.6	498.5	501.9	524.1	560.6	573.7	582.8	595.4	609.2	620.3
Nonmetallic mineral products	528.4	494.7	487.3	491.1	505.3	513.1	517.3	525.7	535.3	540.8
Primary metals	688.6	656.1	630.3	618.4	630.4	641.7	639.3	638.8	641.5	625.0
Fabricated metal products	1 610.0	1 541.3	1 497.2	1 509.5	1 565.3	1 623.4	1 647.5	1 695.8	1 739.5	1 728.4
Machinery	1 409.8	1 347.9	1 311.2	1 330.9	1 381.4	1 442.3	1 468.9	1 495.9	1 514.1	1 468.3
Computer and electronic products [1]	1 902.5	1 809.3	1 707.3	1 655.9	1 651.1	1 688.4	1 746.6	1 803.3	1 830.9	1 780.5
Computer and peripheral equipment	367.4	348.6	328.5	305.7	297.7	295.6	304.6	316.7	322.1	310.1
Communications equipment	223.0	212.5	202.0	202.6	210.0	224.3	228.9	235.0	237.4	228.7
Semiconductors and electronic components	574.0	546.6	519.4	519.4	535.4	571.0	606.6	639.8	649.8	630.5
Electronic instruments	634.8	598.0	556.2	525.3	501.4	490.5	497.8	502.8	509.2	498.3
Electrical equipment and appliances	633.1	597.7	579.4	575.8	588.5	592.8	591.0	586.3	591.6	588.0
Transportation equipment [1]	2 134.5	2 029.3	1 978.1	1 915.0	1 937.4	1 978.5	1 975.1	2 027.6	2 078.4	2 088.6
Motor vehicles and parts	1 054.2	1 017.6	1 047.0	1 077.8	1 168.5	1 241.5	1 240.3	1 253.9	1 271.5	1 312.5
Furniture and related products	604.0	563.6	565.5	578.1	602.8	609.4	606.5	617.8	643.9	667.6
Miscellaneous manufacturing	685.7	681.8	687.7	702.5	709.0	709.7	710.7	718.2	726.8	724.0
Nondurable goods	6 958	6 848	6 853	6 872	6 889	6 868	6 751	6 714	6 649	6 491
Food manufacturing	1 507.3	1 515.2	1 518.3	1 534.6	1 539.2	1 560.0	1 562.0	1 557.9	1 554.9	1 549.8
Beverage and tobacco products	217.7	214.7	208.5	207.1	204.6	202.6	204.4	206.3	208.9	208.3
Textile mills	491.8	479.9	479.0	478.7	477.6	468.5	443.2	436.2	424.5	397.1
Textile product mills	235.6	225.1	228.0	232.6	242.9	242.1	237.1	236.4	234.7	232.4
Apparel	902.8	876.9	879.3	857.3	831.9	791.1	722.3	680.8	621.4	540.5
Leather and allied products	133.2	124.4	120.8	118.1	113.9	104.9	94.2	89.5	82.9	74.9
Paper and paper products	647.2	638.5	639.6	639.7	639.4	639.5	631.4	630.6	624.9	615.6
Printing and related support activities	808.6	792.3	780.2	785.2	802.2	817.3	815.8	821.1	827.9	814.6
Petroleum and coal products	152.8	154.8	152.3	146.2	144.0	140.4	137.3	136.0	134.5	127.8
Chemicals	1 035.7	1 024.1	1 028.9	1 024.9	1 004.7	987.9	984.5	986.8	992.6	982.5
Plastics and rubber products	824.8	802.1	817.9	847.8	888.1	913.7	918.7	932.7	941.4	947.0
Service-Providing	85 764	85 787	86 631	88 625	91 517	94 142	96 299	98 890	101 576	104 528
Private Service-Providing	67 349	67 241	67 845	69 636	72 242	74 710	76 760	79 227	81 667	84 221
Trade, transportation, and utilities	22 666	22 281	22 125	22 378	23 128	23 834	24 239	24 700	25 186	25 771
Wholesale trade	5 268.4	5 185.3	5 109.7	5 093.2	5 247.3	5 433.1	5 522.0	5 663.9	5 795.2	5 892.5
Durable goods	2 833.7	2 766.6	2 698.8	2 687.0	2 786.0	2 908.8	2 977.8	3 071.9	3 162.4	3 219.6
Nondurable goods	1 900.2	1 891.3	1 891.5	1 888.3	1 927.0	1 969.3	1 977.5	2 007.9	2 032.7	2 061.1
Electronic markets, agents, and brokers	534.5	527.4	519.4	517.9	534.4	555.0	566.7	584.1	600.1	611.8

[1] Includes other industries, not shown separately.

Table 16-1. Nonfarm Employment by NAICS Sector and Industry—*Continued*

(Wage and salary workers on nonfarm payrolls, thousands.)

Industry	2000	2001	2002	2003	2004	2005	2006	2007	2008	2009
TOTAL NONFARM	131 785	131 826	130 341	129 999	131 435	133 703	136 086	137 598	136 790	130 920
Total Private	110 995	110 708	108 828	108 416	109 814	111 899	114 113	115 380	114 281	108 371
Goods-Producing	24 649	23 873	22 557	21 816	21 882	22 190	22 531	22 233	21 334	18 620
Mining and logging	599	606	583	572	591	628	684	724	767	700
Logging	79.0	73.5	70.4	69.4	67.6	65.2	64.4	60.1	56.6	49.8
Mining	520.2	532.5	512.2	502.7	523.0	562.2	619.7	663.8	709.8	650.0
Oil and gas extraction	124.9	123.7	121.9	120.2	123.4	125.7	134.5	146.2	160.5	161.6
Mining, except oil and gas [1]	224.8	218.7	210.6	202.7	205.1	212.8	220.3	223.4	226.0	211.6
Coal mining	72.2	74.3	74.4	70.0	70.6	73.9	78.0	77.2	81.2	82.2
Support activities for mining	170.6	190.1	179.8	179.8	194.6	223.7	264.9	294.3	323.4	276.7
Construction	6 787	6 826	6 716	6 735	6 976	7 336	7 691	7 630	7 162	6 037
Construction of buildings	1 632.5	1 588.9	1 574.8	1 575.8	1 630.0	1 711.9	1 804.9	1 774.2	1 641.7	1 365.6
Heavy and civil engineering	937.0	953.0	930.6	903.1	907.4	951.2	985.1	1 005.4	964.5	846.9
Specialty trade contractors	4 217.0	4 283.9	4 210.4	4 255.7	4 438.6	4 673.1	4 901.1	4 850.2	4 555.8	3 824.4
Manufacturing	17 263	16 441	15 259	14 510	14 315	14 226	14 155	13 879	13 406	11 883
Durable goods	10 877	10 336	9 485	8 964	8 925	8 956	8 981	8 808	8 463	7 309
Wood products	613.0	574.1	554.9	537.6	549.6	559.2	558.8	515.3	456.0	360.7
Nonmetallic mineral products	554.2	544.5	516.0	494.2	505.5	505.3	509.6	500.5	465.0	397.4
Primary metals	621.8	570.9	509.4	477.4	466.8	466.0	464.0	455.8	442.0	364.7
Fabricated metal products	1 752.6	1 676.4	1 548.5	1 478.9	1 497.1	1 522.0	1 553.1	1 562.8	1 527.5	1 317.5
Machinery	1 457.0	1 370.6	1 231.8	1 151.6	1 145.2	1 165.5	1 183.2	1 187.1	1 187.6	1 029.3
Computer and electronic products [1]	1 820.0	1 748.8	1 507.2	1 355.2	1 322.8	1 316.4	1 307.5	1 272.5	1 244.2	1 136.3
Computer and peripheral equipment	301.9	286.2	250.0	224.0	210.0	205.1	196.2	186.2	183.2	166.0
Communications equipment	238.6	225.4	179.0	149.2	143.0	141.4	136.2	128.1	127.3	121.4
Semiconductors and electronic components	676.3	645.4	524.5	461.1	454.1	452.0	457.9	447.5	431.8	377.0
Electronic instruments	487.7	483.6	456.8	435.4	436.9	441.0	444.5	443.2	441.0	421.3
Electrical equipment and appliances	590.9	556.9	496.5	459.6	445.1	433.5	432.7	429.4	424.3	376.7
Transportation equipment [1]	2 057.1	1 939.1	1 830.0	1 775.1	1 766.7	1 772.3	1 768.9	1 711.9	1 608.0	1 353.0
Motor vehicles and parts	1 313.6	1 212.9	1 151.2	1 125.3	1 112.8	1 096.7	1 070.0	994.2	875.5	666.4
Furniture and related products	682.5	645.1	606.9	575.7	576.1	568.2	560.1	531.1	479.6	385.7
Miscellaneous manufacturing	728.0	709.5	683.3	658.3	650.6	647.2	643.7	641.7	628.9	587.0
Nondurable goods	6 386	6 105	5 774	5 546	5 390	5 271	5 174	5 071	4 943	4 574
Food manufacturing	1 553.1	1 551.2	1 525.7	1 517.5	1 493.7	1 477.6	1 479.4	1 484.1	1 480.9	1 459.0
Beverage and tobacco products	207.0	209.0	207.4	199.6	194.6	191.9	194.2	198.2	198.4	187.7
Textile mills	378.2	332.9	290.9	261.3	236.9	217.6	195.0	169.7	151.2	125.6
Textile product mills	229.6	217.0	204.2	187.7	183.2	176.4	166.7	157.7	147.2	126.6
Apparel	483.5	415.2	350.0	303.9	278.0	250.5	232.4	214.6	199.0	169.6
Leather and allied products	68.8	58.0	50.2	44.5	41.8	39.6	36.8	33.8	33.1	29.4
Paper and paper products	604.7	577.6	546.6	516.2	495.5	484.2	470.5	458.2	444.9	407.4
Printing and related support activities	806.8	768.4	706.6	680.5	662.6	646.3	634.4	622.1	594.1	523.8
Petroleum and coal products	123.2	121.1	118.1	114.3	111.7	112.1	113.2	114.5	117.4	115.3
Chemicals	980.4	959.0	927.5	906.1	887.0	872.1	865.9	860.9	847.1	802.8
Plastics and rubber products	950.9	896.2	846.8	814.3	804.7	802.3	785.5	757.2	729.4	627.4
Service-Providing	107 136	107 952	107 784	108 183	109 553	111 513	113 556	115 366	115 456	112 300
Private Service-Providing	86 346	86 834	86 271	86 600	87 932	89 709	91 582	93 147	92 947	89 751
Trade, transportation, and utilities	26 225	25 983	25 497	25 287	25 533	25 959	26 276	26 630	26 293	24 949
Wholesale trade	5 933.2	5 772.7	5 652.3	5 607.5	5 662.9	5 764.4	5 904.5	6 015.2	5 942.7	5 625.3
Durable goods	3 250.7	3 130.4	3 007.9	2 940.6	2 950.5	2 999.2	3 074.8	3 121.5	3 052.0	2 827.0
Nondurable goods	2 064.8	2 031.3	2 015.0	2 004.6	2 010.0	2 022.4	2 041.3	2 062.2	2 047.7	1 980.0
Electronic markets, agents, and brokers	617.7	611.1	629.4	662.2	702.4	742.8	788.5	831.5	842.9	818.4

[1]Includes other industries, not shown separately.

Table 16-1. Nonfarm Employment by NAICS Sector and Industry—*Continued*

(Wage and salary workers on nonfarm payrolls, thousands.)

Industry	1990	1991	1992	1993	1994	1995	1996	1997	1998	1999
Retail trade	13 182	12 896	12 828	13 021	13 491	13 897	14 143	14 389	14 609	14 970
Motor vehicle and parts dealers [1]	1 494.4	1 435.1	1 428.1	1 475.3	1 564.7	1 627.1	1 685.6	1 723.4	1 740.9	1 796.6
Automobile dealers	983.3	938.3	934.8	970.4	1 031.8	1 071.6	1 113.0	1 134.5	1 142.0	1 179.7
Furniture and home furnishings stores	431.5	412.8	410.3	418.6	441.6	461.2	474.2	484.7	499.1	524.4
Electronics and appliance stores	382.3	381.1	378.1	386.9	417.0	448.7	470.2	494.0	510.2	542.2
Building material and garden supply stores	890.9	863.0	872.1	891.9	946.2	981.8	1 007.2	1 043.1	1 062.3	1 101.0
Food and beverage stores	2 778.8	2 767.9	2 743.9	2 774.8	2 825.0	2 879.8	2 927.8	2 956.9	2 965.7	2 984.5
Health and personal care stores	792.0	788.5	780.2	778.6	797.0	811.9	826.4	853.3	876.0	898.2
Gasoline stations	910.2	889.1	876.4	881.2	902.3	922.3	946.4	956.2	961.3	943.5
Clothing and clothing accessories stores	1 313.0	1 275.8	1 249.1	1 259.9	1 261.7	1 246.3	1 220.6	1 235.9	1 268.6	1 306.6
Sporting goods, hobby, book, and music stores	532.0	527.7	534.4	545.2	577.6	605.8	614.0	626.2	635.4	664.3
General merchandise stores [1]	2 499.8	2 416.7	2 414.2	2 450.2	2 541.0	2 635.4	2 657.3	2 657.6	2 686.5	2 751.8
Department stores	1 493.9	1 440.8	1 445.2	1 486.8	1 560.4	1 629.8	1 645.0	1 653.5	1 679.2	1 709.2
Miscellaneous store retailers	738.2	734.7	736.8	752.9	795.7	841.1	874.3	913.2	950.3	985.5
Nonstore retailers	419.2	403.7	404.5	404.9	421.2	435.4	438.5	444.5	453.0	471.6
Transportation and warehousing	3 475.6	3 462.8	3 461.8	3 553.8	3 701.0	3 837.8	3 935.3	4 026.5	4 168.0	4 300.3
Air transportation	529.2	525.4	519.6	516.6	511.2	510.9	525.7	542.0	562.7	586.3
Rail transportation	271.8	255.6	248.1	242.2	234.6	232.5	225.2	221.0	225.0	228.8
Water transportation	56.8	57.4	56.7	52.8	52.3	50.8	51.0	50.7	50.5	51.7
Truck transportation	1 122.4	1 104.6	1 107.4	1 154.8	1 206.2	1 249.1	1 282.4	1 308.2	1 354.4	1 391.5
Transit and ground passenger transportation	274.2	283.9	287.9	299.9	316.6	327.9	339.1	349.6	362.7	371.0
Pipeline transportation	59.8	60.7	60.1	58.7	57.0	53.6	51.4	49.7	48.1	46.9
Scenic and sightseeing transportation	15.7	16.5	17.7	19.3	21.3	22.0	23.2	24.5	25.4	26.1
Support activities for transportation	364.1	376.6	369.9	381.8	404.7	430.4	445.8	473.4	496.8	518.1
Couriers and messengers	375.0	378.9	388.8	414.3	466.2	516.8	539.9	546.0	568.2	585.9
Warehousing and storage	406.6	403.2	405.6	413.4	431.0	443.8	451.8	461.5	474.2	494.1
Utilities	740.0	736.1	726.0	710.7	689.3	666.2	639.6	620.9	613.4	608.5
Information	2 688	2 677	2 641	2 668	2 738	2 843	2 940	3 084	3 218	3 419
Publishing industries, except Internet	870.6	863.4	854.2	873.1	891.0	910.7	927.2	955.5	982.3	1 004.8
Motion picture and sound recording industries	254.6	258.9	254.3	259.6	278.4	311.1	334.7	353.0	369.5	384.4
Broadcasting, except Internet	283.8	281.2	279.7	284.0	290.1	298.1	309.1	313.0	321.2	329.4
Telecommunications	1 008.5	999.9	972.9	969.5	989.5	1 009.3	1 038.1	1 108.0	1 167.4	1 270.8
Data processing, hosting, and related services	211.4	212.8	219.6	223.4	226.9	242.6	252.0	268.4	282.8	307.1
Other information services	59.3	61.2	60.5	58.1	62.5	71.8	79.0	85.5	95.3	121.9
Internet publishing and broadcasting	29.4	28.3	28.2	28.7	29.7	33.7	39.6	45.4	53.9	78.1
Financial activities	6 614	6 558	6 540	6 709	6 867	6 827	6 969	7 178	7 462	7 648
Finance and insurance	4 976.4	4 935.1	4 912.4	5 033.0	5 132.5	5 069.0	5 151.4	5 302.1	5 528.6	5 664.9
Monetary authorities–central bank	24.0	24.2	23.7	23.4	23.4	23.0	22.8	22.1	21.7	22.6
Credit intermediation and related activities [1]	2 424.8	2 352.4	2 317.3	2 360.7	2 375.7	2 314.4	2 368.2	2 433.6	2 531.9	2 591.0
Depository credit intermediation [1]	1 908.5	1 830.7	1 769.0	1 760.5	1 736.7	1 700.2	1 691.4	1 696.6	1 708.9	1 709.7
Commercial banking	1 361.8	1 333.7	1 302.8	1 308.7	1 297.4	1 281.7	1 275.1	1 277.9	1 286.0	1 281.2
Securities, commodity contracts, investments	457.9	455.0	475.7	507.9	553.4	562.2	589.6	636.1	692.2	737.3
Insurance carriers and related activities	2 016.1	2 048.2	2 039.5	2 082.5	2 118.8	2 108.2	2 108.0	2 143.6	2 209.4	2 236.1
Funds, trusts, and other financial vehicles	53.5	55.3	56.2	58.5	61.2	61.2	62.8	66.8	73.4	78.0
Real estate and rental and leasing	1 637.1	1 623.0	1 627.7	1 676.3	1 734.2	1 758.1	1 817.1	1 875.9	1 933.7	1 982.5
Real estate	1 109.0	1 109.8	1 116.7	1 148.6	1 185.9	1 181.7	1 208.6	1 243.8	1 277.7	1 302.6
Rental and leasing services	514.2	499.4	496.4	511.0	529.9	557.4	587.7	609.5	630.8	653.1
Lessors of nonfinancial intangible assets	13.9	13.9	14.6	16.7	18.4	19.0	20.8	22.6	25.3	26.8

[1] Includes other industries, not shown separately.

Table 16-1. Nonfarm Employment by NAICS Sector and Industry—*Continued*

(Wage and salary workers on nonfarm payrolls, thousands.)

Industry	2000	2001	2002	2003	2004	2005	2006	2007	2008	2009
Retail trade	15 280	15 239	15 025	14 917	15 058	15 280	15 353	15 520	15 283	14 528
Motor vehicle and parts dealers [1]	1 846.9	1 854.6	1 879.4	1 882.9	1 902.3	1 918.6	1 909.7	1 908.3	1 831.2	1 640.0
Automobile dealers	1 216.5	1 225.1	1 252.8	1 254.4	1 257.3	1 261.4	1 246.7	1 242.2	1 176.7	1 021.8
Furniture and home furnishings stores ...	543.5	541.2	538.7	547.3	563.4	576.1	586.9	574.6	531.1	450.0
Electronics and appliance stores	564.4	554.5	525.3	512.2	516.2	535.8	541.1	549.4	540.5	487.1
Building material and garden supply stores ...	1 142.1	1 151.8	1 176.5	1 185.0	1 227.1	1 276.1	1 324.1	1 309.3	1 248.0	1 162.6
Food and beverage stores	2 993.0	2 950.5	2 881.6	2 838.4	2 821.6	2 817.8	2 821.1	2 843.6	2 862.0	2 829.0
Health and personal care stores	927.6	951.5	938.8	938.1	941.1	953.7	961.1	993.1	1 002.8	984.2
Gasoline stations	935.7	925.3	895.9	882.0	875.6	871.1	864.1	861.5	842.4	827.0
Clothing and clothing accessories stores ...	1 321.6	1 321.1	1 312.5	1 304.5	1 364.3	1 414.6	1 450.9	1 500.0	1 468.0	1 368.9
Sporting goods, hobby, book, and music stores ...	685.7	679.2	661.3	646.5	641.3	647.0	645.5	656.3	651.0	616.4
General merchandise stores [1]	2 819.8	2 842.2	2 812.0	2 822.4	2 863.1	2 934.3	2 935.0	3 020.6	3 025.6	2 956.1
Department stores	1 755.0	1 768.3	1 684.0	1 620.6	1 605.3	1 595.1	1 557.2	1 591.5	1 540.5	1 471.2
Miscellaneous store retailers	1 007.1	993.3	959.5	930.7	913.5	899.9	881.0	865.4	842.5	784.6
Nonstore retailers	492.4	473.5	443.7	427.3	428.8	434.6	432.8	437.9	438.0	421.8
Transportation and warehousing	4 410.3	4 372.0	4 223.6	4 185.4	4 248.6	4 360.9	4 469.6	4 540.9	4 508.3	4 235.3
Air transportation	614.4	615.3	563.5	528.3	514.5	500.8	487.0	491.8	490.7	459.7
Rail transportation	231.7	226.7	217.8	217.7	225.7	227.8	225.5	233.7	231.0	219.4
Water transportation	56.0	54.0	52.6	54.5	56.4	60.6	62.7	65.5	67.1	63.7
Truck transportation	1 405.8	1 386.8	1 339.3	1 325.6	1 351.7	1 397.6	1 435.8	1 439.2	1 389.0	1 265.9
Transit and ground passenger transportation ...	372.1	374.8	380.8	382.2	384.9	389.2	399.3	412.1	423.3	419.3
Pipeline transportation	46.0	45.4	41.7	40.2	38.4	37.8	38.7	39.9	41.7	41.7
Scenic and sightseeing transportation ...	27.5	29.1	25.6	26.6	27.2	28.8	27.5	28.6	28.0	27.8
Support activities for transportation ...	537.4	539.2	524.7	520.3	535.1	552.2	570.6	584.2	592.0	549.0
Couriers and messengers	605.0	587.0	560.9	561.7	556.6	571.4	582.4	580.7	573.4	547.1
Warehousing and storage	514.4	513.8	516.7	528.3	558.1	594.7	638.1	665.2	672.1	641.6
Utilities	601.3	599.4	596.2	577.0	563.8	554.0	548.5	553.4	558.9	561.1
Information	3 630	3 629	3 395	3 188	3 118	3 061	3 038	3 032	2 984	2 807
Publishing industries, except Internet ...	1 035.0	1 020.7	964.1	924.8	909.1	904.1	902.4	901.2	880.4	796.4
Motion picture and sound recording industries ...	382.6	376.8	387.9	376.2	385.0	377.5	375.7	380.6	371.3	350.4
Broadcasting, except Internet	343.5	344.6	334.1	324.3	325.0	327.7	328.3	325.2	318.7	301.0
Telecommunications	1 396.6	1 423.9	1 280.9	1 166.8	1 115.1	1 071.3	1 047.6	1 030.6	1 019.4	974.8
Data processing, hosting, and related services ...	315.7	316.8	303.9	280.0	267.1	262.5	263.2	267.8	260.3	250.0
Other information services	157.1	146.5	123.6	115.9	116.9	117.7	120.8	126.3	133.5	134.5
Internet publishing and broadcasting ...	110.8	100.4	76.3	67.2	66.1	67.2	69.1	72.9	80.6	82.6
Financial activities	7 687	7 808	7 847	7 977	8 031	8 153	8 328	8 301	8 145	7 758
Finance and insurance	5 676.7	5 769.2	5 813.6	5 919.1	5 945.3	6 018.9	6 156.0	6 132.0	6 014.9	5 762.7
Monetary authorities–central bank ...	22.8	23.0	23.4	22.6	21.8	20.8	21.2	21.6	22.4	21.1
Credit intermediation and related activities [1] ...	2 547.8	2 597.7	2 686.0	2 792.4	2 817.0	2 869.0	2 924.9	2 866.3	2 732.7	2 597.3
Depository credit intermediation [1] ...	1 681.2	1 701.2	1 733.0	1 748.5	1 751.5	1 769.2	1 802.0	1 823.5	1 815.2	1 760.5
Commercial banking	1 250.5	1 258.4	1 278.1	1 280.1	1 280.8	1 296.0	1 322.9	1 351.4	1 357.5	1 318.8
Securities, commodity contracts, investments ...	804.5	830.5	789.4	757.7	766.1	786.1	818.3	848.6	864.2	809.7
Insurance carriers and related activities ...	2 220.6	2 233.7	2 233.2	2 266.0	2 258.6	2 259.3	2 303.7	2 306.8	2 305.2	2 246.7
Funds, trusts, and other financial vehicles ...	81.1	84.4	81.7	80.4	81.7	83.7	87.9	88.7	90.5	87.8
Real estate and rental and leasing	2 010.6	2 038.4	2 033.3	2 057.5	2 085.5	2 133.5	2 172.5	2 169.1	2 129.6	1 995.3
Real estate	1 316.0	1 343.4	1 356.6	1 387.1	1 418.7	1 460.8	1 499.0	1 500.4	1 485.0	1 416.7
Rental and leasing services	666.8	666.3	649.1	643.1	641.1	645.8	645.5	640.3	616.9	552.4
Lessors of nonfinancial intangible assets ...	27.8	28.7	27.6	27.3	25.7	26.9	28.1	28.4	27.7	26.3

[1]Includes other industries, not shown separately.

Table 16-1. Nonfarm Employment by NAICS Sector and Industry—*Continued*

(Wage and salary workers on nonfarm payrolls, thousands.)

Industry	1990	1991	1992	1993	1994	1995	1996	1997	1998	1999
Professional and business services	10 848	10 714	10 970	11 495	12 174	12 844	13 462	14 335	15 147	15 957
Professional and technical services [1]	4 538.2	4 509.2	4 575.6	4 689.1	4 823.3	5 078.4	5 312.7	5 628.8	5 992.3	6 345.4
Legal services	943.6	946.0	949.8	963.9	965.6	959.2	968.4	987.5	1 021.1	1 051.4
Accounting and bookkeeping services	664.1	655.4	657.8	654.2	670.1	706.3	729.8	761.2	802.0	837.6
Architectural and engineering services	941.5	906.2	901.8	922.7	952.0	997.1	1 024.5	1 063.4	1 114.8	1 168.1
Computer systems design and related services	409.7	419.9	444.9	484.8	531.4	611.2	701.4	826.7	974.9	1 132.9
Management and technical consulting services	305.1	314.3	340.2	366.2	396.5	451.8	492.7	541.7	590.4	619.0
Management of companies and enterprises	1 667.4	1 638.1	1 623.4	1 640.1	1 665.9	1 685.8	1 702.7	1 729.7	1 756.1	1 773.8
Administrative and waste services	4 642.8	4 566.6	4 770.5	5 165.6	5 684.4	6 079.7	6 446.5	6 976.6	7 398.0	7 837.5
Administrative and support services [1]	4 413.3	4 334.3	4 533.8	4 917.0	5 423.7	5 806.4	6 164.5	6 686.0	7 098.7	7 527.0
Employment services [1]	1 512.1	1 466.0	1 610.4	1 884.3	2 246.8	2 448.1	2 625.3	2 953.9	3 245.8	3 581.6
Temporary help services	1 155.8	1 123.3	1 212.5	1 388.8	1 632.2	1 743.8	1 849.0	2 059.7	2 245.2	2 469.6
Business support services	504.6	503.3	524.5	549.0	574.4	629.8	678.3	733.9	772.2	780.5
Services to buildings and dwellings	1 174.6	1 150.9	1 159.7	1 197.9	1 267.2	1 302.4	1 361.5	1 424.1	1 460.0	1 534.7
Waste management and remediation services	229.4	232.4	236.7	248.6	260.7	273.3	282.0	290.5	299.3	310.5
Education and health services	10 984	11 506	11 891	12 303	12 807	13 289	13 683	14 087	14 446	14 798
Educational services	1 688.0	1 736.6	1 713.1	1 755.4	1 894.9	2 010.2	2 077.6	2 155.0	2 232.9	2 320.4
Health care and social assistance	9 295.8	9 769.8	10 178.0	10 548.1	10 911.7	11 278.4	11 604.9	11 932.2	12 213.5	12 477.1
Health care	8 210.7	8 617.7	8 954.8	9 253.6	9 529.7	9 808.9	10 092.6	10 358.0	10 540.9	10 690.9
Ambulatory health care services [1]	2 841.6	3 028.4	3 199.9	3 385.5	3 578.8	3 767.5	3 939.9	4 093.0	4 161.2	4 226.6
Offices of physicians	1 278.0	1 345.2	1 401.1	1 442.0	1 480.9	1 540.4	1 603.8	1 660.5	1 723.6	1 786.6
Outpatient care centers	260.5	271.4	286.5	303.1	314.5	328.8	340.2	352.1	363.3	375.4
Home health care services	287.5	340.7	393.4	463.8	553.2	621.8	667.2	702.8	659.5	629.6
Hospitals	3 512.6	3 617.3	3 711.4	3 740.0	3 724.0	3 733.7	3 772.8	3 821.6	3 892.4	3 935.5
Nursing and residential care facilities [1]	1 856.4	1 972.0	2 043.5	2 128.1	2 227.0	2 307.7	2 379.9	2 443.4	2 487.3	2 528.8
Nursing care facilities	1 169.8	1 240.2	1 273.4	1 319.3	1 377.1	1 413.0	1 448.4	1 474.6	1 489.3	1 501.0
Social assistance [1]	1 085.1	1 152.2	1 223.3	1 294.4	1 381.9	1 469.5	1 512.3	1 574.2	1 672.6	1 786.2
Child day care services	387.8	413.2	446.5	468.9	510.0	557.1	559.2	570.4	615.1	673.7
Leisure and hospitality	9 288	9 256	9 437	9 732	10 100	10 501	10 777	11 018	11 232	11 543
Arts, entertainment, and recreation	1 132.0	1 177.0	1 236.3	1 301.9	1 375.6	1 459.4	1 522.1	1 599.9	1 645.2	1 709.1
Performing arts and spectator sports	272.7	282.7	289.5	286.8	296.1	307.7	328.6	349.6	350.0	361.1
Museums, historical sites, zoos, and parks	68.0	71.0	75.0	78.3	81.8	83.9	88.9	93.8	97.4	103.1
Amusements, gambling, and recreation	791.3	823.4	871.8	936.8	997.7	1 067.8	1 104.5	1 156.5	1 197.9	1 244.9
Accommodation and food services	8 155.6	8 078.9	8 200.5	8 430.4	8 724.1	9 041.6	9 254.3	9 417.9	9 586.2	9 833.7
Accommodation	1 616.0	1 574.3	1 561.5	1 580.5	1 615.3	1 652.5	1 698.9	1 729.5	1 773.5	1 831.7
Food services and drinking places	6 539.6	6 504.6	6 639.0	6 849.9	7 108.7	7 389.1	7 555.4	7 688.5	7 812.7	8 002.0
Other services	4 261	4 249	4 240	4 350	4 428	4 572	4 690	4 825	4 976	5 087
Repair and maintenance	1 009.0	960.0	964.0	998.0	1 023.5	1 078.9	1 135.5	1 169.3	1 189.2	1 222.0
Personal and laundry services	1 119.9	1 109.2	1 098.9	1 116.0	1 120.3	1 143.9	1 165.7	1 180.4	1 205.6	1 220.3
Membership associations and organizations	2 132.2	2 179.5	2 177.1	2 236.4	2 284.5	2 348.9	2 389.1	2 474.9	2 581.3	2 644.4
Government	18 415	18 545	18 787	18 989	19 275	19 432	19 539	19 664	19 909	20 307
Federal	3 196	3 110	3 111	3 063	3 018	2 949	2 877	2 806	2 772	2 769
Federal, except U.S. Postal Service	2 370.5	2 296.2	2 310.7	2 269.4	2 197.2	2 098.8	2 009.8	1 940.2	1 891.3	1 879.5
U.S. Postal Service	825.1	813.2	800.0	793.2	820.6	849.9	867.2	866.0	880.5	889.7
State government	4 305	4 355	4 408	4 488	4 576	4 635	4 606	4 582	4 612	4 709
State government education	1 729.9	1 767.6	1 798.6	1 834.1	1 881.9	1 919.0	1 910.7	1 904.0	1 922.2	1 983.2
State government, excluding education	2 574.6	2 587.3	2 609.7	2 653.8	2 693.6	2 715.5	2 695.1	2 677.9	2 690.2	2 725.6
Local government	10 914	11 081	11 267	11 438	11 682	11 849	12 056	12 276	12 525	12 829
Local government education	5 902.1	5 994.1	6 075.9	6 206.3	6 329.4	6 453.1	6 592.3	6 758.5	6 920.9	7 120.4
Local government, excluding education	5 012.4	5 086.9	5 191.6	5 231.9	5 352.2	5 396.0	5 464.1	5 516.9	5 603.9	5 708.6

[1]Includes other industries, not shown separately.

Table 16-1. Nonfarm Employment by NAICS Sector and Industry—*Continued*

(Wage and salary workers on nonfarm payrolls, thousands.)

Industry	2000	2001	2002	2003	2004	2005	2006	2007	2008	2009
Professional and business services	16 666	16 476	15 976	15 987	16 394	16 954	17 566	17 942	17 735	16 580
Professional and technical services [1]	6 701.7	6 871.1	6 648.8	6 602.7	6 747.1	7 024.6	7 356.7	7 659.5	7 799.4	7 508.5
Legal services	1 065.7	1 091.3	1 115.3	1 142.1	1 163.1	1 168.0	1 173.2	1 175.4	1 161.5	1 122.4
Accounting and bookkeeping services	866.4	872.2	837.3	815.3	805.9	849.3	889.0	935.9	951.0	920.4
Architectural and engineering services	1 237.9	1 274.7	1 246.1	1 226.9	1 258.2	1 310.9	1 385.7	1 432.2	1 439.4	1 324.6
Computer systems design and related services	1 254.3	1 297.8	1 152.8	1 116.6	1 148.6	1 195.2	1 284.6	1 372.1	1 439.6	1 426.3
Management and technical consulting services	672.7	715.1	707.7	718.0	763.0	824.2	886.4	952.7	1 002.0	992.5
Management of companies and enterprises	1 796.0	1 779.0	1 705.4	1 687.2	1 724.4	1 758.9	1 810.9	1 866.4	1 904.5	1 856.0
Administrative and waste services	8 168.3	7 826.0	7 621.9	7 696.8	7 922.9	8 170.2	8 398.3	8 416.3	8 031.5	7 214.9
Administrative and support services [1]	7 855.4	7 508.7	7 303.6	7 374.7	7 594.4	7 832.5	8 050.2	8 061.3	7 674.7	6 864.3
Employment services [1]	3 849.3	3 468.2	3 273.2	3 326.4	3 455.5	3 606.9	3 680.9	3 545.9	3 133.0	2 497.6
Temporary help services	2 635.6	2 337.7	2 193.7	2 224.2	2 387.2	2 549.4	2 637.4	2 597.4	2 348.4	1 827.7
Business support services	786.7	779.7	756.6	749.7	757.8	766.4	792.9	817.4	832.3	816.8
Services to buildings and dwellings	1 570.5	1 606.2	1 606.1	1 636.1	1 693.7	1 737.5	1 801.4	1 849.5	1 839.8	1 748.5
Waste management and remediation services	312.9	317.3	318.3	322.1	328.6	337.6	348.1	355.0	356.8	350.7
Education and health services	15 109	15 645	16 199	16 588	16 953	17 372	17 826	18 322	18 838	19 191
Educational services	2 390.4	2 510.6	2 642.8	2 695.1	2 762.5	2 835.8	2 900.9	2 941.4	3 039.7	3 089.9
Health care and social assistance	12 718.0	13 134.0	13 555.7	13 892.6	14 190.2	14 536.3	14 925.3	15 380.2	15 798.3	16 100.8
Health care	10 857.8	11 188.1	11 536.0	11 817.1	12 055.3	12 313.9	12 601.8	12 946.8	13 289.9	13 535.6
Ambulatory health care services [1]	4 320.3	4 461.5	4 633.2	4 786.4	4 952.3	5 113.5	5 285.8	5 473.5	5 646.6	5 777.3
Offices of physicians	1 839.9	1 911.2	1 967.8	2 002.5	2 047.8	2 093.5	2 147.8	2 201.6	2 252.6	2 279.8
Outpatient care centers	386.4	399.7	413.0	426.8	450.5	473.2	492.6	512.0	533.3	543.0
Home health care services	633.3	638.6	679.8	732.6	776.6	821.0	865.6	913.8	961.4	1 023.9
Hospitals	3 954.3	4 050.9	4 159.6	4 244.6	4 284.7	4 345.4	4 423.4	4 515.0	4 627.3	4 677.1
Nursing and residential care facilities [1]	2 583.2	2 675.8	2 743.3	2 786.2	2 818.4	2 855.0	2 892.5	2 958.3	3 016.1	3 081.2
Nursing care facilities	1 513.6	1 546.8	1 573.2	1 579.8	1 576.9	1 577.4	1 581.4	1 602.6	1 618.7	1 643.9
Social assistance [1]	1 860.2	1 945.9	2 019.7	2 075.4	2 134.8	2 222.3	2 323.5	2 433.4	2 508.4	2 565.2
Child day care services	695.8	714.6	744.1	755.3	764.7	789.7	818.3	850.4	859.4	857.0
Leisure and hospitality	11 862	12 036	11 986	12 173	12 493	12 816	13 110	13 427	13 436	13 102
Arts, entertainment, and recreation	1 787.9	1 824.4	1 782.6	1 812.9	1 849.6	1 892.3	1 928.5	1 969.2	1 970.1	1 914.5
Performing arts and spectator sports	381.8	382.3	363.7	371.7	367.5	376.3	398.5	405.0	405.7	397.2
Museums, historical sites, zoos, and parks	110.4	115.0	114.0	114.7	118.3	120.7	123.8	130.3	131.6	129.9
Amusements, gambling, and recreation	1 295.7	1 327.1	1 305.0	1 326.5	1 363.8	1 395.3	1 406.3	1 433.9	1 432.8	1 387.4
Accommodation and food services	10 073.5	10 211.3	10 203.2	10 359.8	10 643.2	10 923.0	11 181.1	11 457.4	11 466.3	11 187.5
Accommodation	1 884.4	1 852.2	1 778.6	1 775.4	1 789.5	1 818.6	1 832.1	1 866.9	1 868.7	1 759.7
Food services and drinking places	8 189.1	8 359.1	8 424.6	8 584.4	8 853.7	9 104.4	9 349.0	9 590.4	9 597.5	9 427.8
Other services	5 168	5 258	5 372	5 401	5 409	5 395	5 438	5 494	5 515	5 364
Repair and maintenance	1 241.5	1 256.5	1 246.9	1 233.6	1 228.8	1 236.0	1 248.5	1 253.4	1 227.0	1 153.7
Personal and laundry services	1 242.9	1 255.0	1 257.2	1 263.5	1 272.9	1 276.6	1 288.4	1 309.7	1 322.6	1 282.3
Membership associations and organizations	2 683.3	2 746.4	2 867.8	2 903.6	2 907.5	2 882.2	2 901.2	2 931.1	2 965.7	2 927.6
Government	20 790	21 118	21 513	21 583	21 621	21 804	21 974	22 218	22 509	22 549
Federal	2 865	2 764	2 766	2 761	2 730	2 732	2 732	2 734	2 762	2 828
Federal, except U.S. Postal Service	1 984.8	1 891.0	1 923.8	1 952.4	1 947.5	1 957.3	1 962.6	1 964.7	2 014.4	2 124.2
U.S. Postal Service	879.7	873.0	842.4	808.6	782.1	774.2	769.7	769.1	747.4	703.2
State government	4 786	4 905	5 029	5 002	4 982	5 032	5 075	5 122	5 177	5 180
State government education	2 030.6	2 112.9	2 242.8	2 254.7	2 238.1	2 259.9	2 292.5	2 317.5	2 354.4	2 370.5
State government, excluding education	2 755.9	2 791.8	2 786.3	2 747.6	2 743.9	2 771.6	2 782.0	2 804.3	2 822.5	2 809.2
Local government	13 139	13 449	13 718	13 820	13 909	14 041	14 167	14 362	14 571	14 542
Local government education	7 293.9	7 479.3	7 654.4	7 709.4	7 765.2	7 856.1	7 913.0	7 986.8	8 083.9	8 062.1
Local government, excluding education	5 844.6	5 970.0	6 063.2	6 110.2	6 144.1	6 184.6	6 253.8	6 375.5	6 486.5	6 479.8

[1]Includes other industries, not shown separately.

Table 16-2. Production or Nonsupervisory Workers on Private Nonfarm Payrolls by NAICS Industry

(Wage and salary workers on nonfarm payrolls, thousands.)

Industry	1990	1991	1992	1993	1994	1995	1996	1997	1998	1999
Total Private	73 684	72 520	72 786	74 591	77 382	79 845	81 773	84 158	86 316	88 430
Goods-Producing	17 322	16 352	16 043	16 236	16 795	17 137	17 318	17 698	18 008	18 067
Mining and logging	538	515	478	462	461	458	461	479	473	438
Construction	4 115	3 674	3 546	3 704	3 973	4 113	4 325	4 546	4 807	5 105
Manufacturing	12 669	12 164	12 020	12 070	12 361	12 567	12 532	12 673	12 729	12 524
Durable goods	7 397	7 001	6 853	6 880	7 134	7 352	7 426	7 599	7 721	7 651
Wood products	449.9	412.8	417.0	436.8	468.7	477.5	484.9	496.6	507.9	514.4
Nonmetallic mineral products	413.2	384.1	378.4	380.7	392.3	399.7	404.8	412.5	420.6	426.0
Primary metals	525.1	496.9	479.0	473.3	487.4	500.3	500.3	501.6	505.3	491.9
Fabricated metal products	1 190.1	1 131.6	1 101.0	1 116.9	1 172.0	1 223.0	1 241.6	1 285.3	1 319.6	1 304.9
Machinery	938.9	884.9	857.7	875.5	922.5	969.9	984.5	1 006.9	1 016.1	978.4
Computer and electronic products	980.2	925.6	876.0	856.4	864.0	890.3	915.3	951.1	964.7	932.9
Electrical equipment and appliances	465.2	435.6	425.0	421.8	434.7	438.4	433.9	427.7	431.8	433.2
Transportation equipment [1]	1 473.4	1 406.4	1 389.0	1 367.1	1 415.6	1 472.2	1 481.0	1 521.9	1 530.2	1 526.5
Motor vehicles and parts	869.5	840.1	868.0	896.4	978.4	1 048.9	1 052.4	1 062.4	1 050.2	1 075.8
Furniture and related products	476.9	441.7	445.0	456.0	477.4	481.7	479.7	491.5	513.9	534.3
Miscellaneous manufacturing	484.2	481.2	486.0	495.1	499.0	499.1	500.1	503.4	511.0	508.9
Nondurable goods	5 272	5 163	5 167	5 191	5 227	5 214	5 106	5 075	5 008	4 872
Food manufacturing	1 165.0	1 174.2	1 182.0	1 195.3	1 200.4	1 221.0	1 227.7	1 227.7	1 227.6	1 228.7
Beverage and tobacco products	117.2	116.9	116.2	117.6	118.2	117.3	120.1	121.4	122.5	120.1
Textile mills	417.9	407.2	406.0	403.9	403.3	393.2	371.7	367.1	357.2	333.7
Textile product mills	194.9	185.0	187.0	191.0	199.0	197.9	192.5	192.6	189.7	186.8
Apparel	805.2	781.0	785.3	764.2	740.1	697.9	631.1	593.7	534.0	458.3
Leather and allied products	116.6	107.5	104.4	101.4	97.2	88.5	78.5	73.6	67.0	59.9
Paper and paper products	493.2	488.4	489.9	490.9	492.8	493.8	487.5	488.7	484.1	474.0
Printing and related support activities	597.6	581.7	573.6	579.7	591.4	599.1	594.0	597.0	598.4	585.1
Petroleum and coal products	97.5	97.4	96.8	93.0	90.9	88.8	87.2	87.8	87.1	84.6
Chemicals	620.3	599.7	586.2	590.1	595.6	598.4	595.1	593.3	600.6	595.2
Plastics and rubber products	646.7	623.9	638.9	663.8	698.5	718.7	720.3	731.7	739.3	746.0
Private Service-Providing	56 362	56 168	56 743	58 355	60 587	62 708	64 455	66 460	68 308	70 363
Trade, transportation, and utilities	19 032	18 640	18 506	18 752	19 392	19 984	20 325	20 698	21 059	21 576
Wholesale trade	4 198.3	4 122.0	4 070.7	4 072.2	4 196.4	4 360.8	4 423.2	4 523.2	4 605.0	4 673.1
Retail trade	11 308.4	11 007.9	10 931.4	11 104.0	11 502.1	11 841.0	12 056.7	12 273.6	12 439.8	12 771.5
Transportation and warehousing	2 940.8	2 928.4	2 934.3	3 019.4	3 152.8	3 260.2	3 339.3	3 406.8	3 521.6	3 641.9
Utilities	584.9	581.5	569.5	556.5	540.9	521.8	505.5	493.8	492.2	489.2
Information	1 866	1 871	1 871	1 896	1 928	2 007	2 096	2 181	2 217	2 351
Financial activities	4 973	4 911	4 908	5 057	5 183	5 165	5 279	5 415	5 605	5 728
Professional and business services	8 889	8 748	8 971	9 451	10 078	10 645	11 161	11 896	12 566	13 184
Education and health services	9 748	10 212	10 555	10 908	11 338	11 765	12 123	12 478	12 791	13 089
Leisure and hospitality	8 299	8 247	8 406	8 667	8 979	9 330	9 565	9 780	9 947	10 216
Other services	3 555	3 539	3 526	3 623	3 689	3 812	3 907	4 013	4 124	4 219

[1]Includes other industries, not shown separately.

Table 16-2. Production or Nonsupervisory Workers on Private Nonfarm Payrolls by NAICS Industry —Continued

(Wage and salary workers on nonfarm payrolls, thousands.)

Industry	2000	2001	2002	2003	2004	2005	2006	2007	2008	2009
Total Private	90 336	89 983	88 393	87 658	88 937	91 135	93 451	94 903	94 270	89 271
Goods-Producing	18 169	17 466	16 400	15 732	15 821	16 145	16 559	16 405	15 724	13 447
Mining and logging	446	457	436	420	440	473	519	547	574	514
Construction	5 295	5 332	5 196	5 123	5 309	5 611	5 903	5 883	5 521	4 583
Manufacturing	12 428	11 677	10 768	10 189	10 072	10 060	10 137	9 975	9 629	8 350
Durable goods	7 659	7 164	6 530	6 152	6 140	6 220	6 355	6 250	5 975	5 008
Wood products	505.6	468.3	448.7	433.0	443.9	453.0	449.9	405.7	356.2	278.4
Nonmetallic mineral products	439.5	427.1	398.8	374.7	387.8	387.0	391.2	383.6	363.4	305.3
Primary metals	490.0	446.9	396.2	370.3	363.7	362.7	362.6	357.5	347.7	274.5
Fabricated metal products	1 325.8	1 253.5	1 147.0	1 092.5	1 108.6	1 129.3	1 161.8	1 170.9	1 142.9	965.3
Machinery	961.4	890.7	786.9	732.3	729.7	748.9	769.8	774.0	771.7	641.4
Computer and electronic products	949.3	875.8	744.1	672.7	655.8	700.1	755.6	743.8	730.0	653.9
Electrical equipment and appliances	433.1	402.2	351.9	319.5	307.2	300.1	302.9	305.2	305.3	268.3
Transportation equipment [1]	1 497.8	1 398.7	1 310.2	1 269.3	1 265.2	1 276.8	1 303.7	1 274.5	1 177.2	951.7
Motor vehicles and parts	1 073.0	986.8	931.0	906.3	902.9	893.7	872.7	804.2	695.5	511.6
Furniture and related products	546.2	510.9	476.7	446.0	445.7	437.1	434.2	410.4	365.4	285.5
Miscellaneous manufacturing	509.8	489.8	469.2	442.1	432.2	424.4	423.4	424.6	415.6	383.9
Nondurable goods	4 769	4 513	4 238	4 037	3 932	3 841	3 782	3 725	3 653	3 341
Food manufacturing	1 227.9	1 221.3	1 202.3	1 192.5	1 177.8	1 170.0	1 172.2	1 183.5	1 183.9	1 163.1
Beverage and tobacco products	116.9	115.6	119.5	106.4	106.5	111.5	114.6	118.1	111.8	111.7
Textile mills	315.2	275.8	242.2	216.9	193.9	174.2	157.8	137.3	122.0	99.6
Textile product mills	183.4	173.7	162.0	148.3	147.1	143.0	134.9	123.2	115.3	98.5
Apparel	403.8	341.4	286.0	241.5	218.6	192.7	182.0	173.4	163.3	134.0
Leather and allied products	55.4	46.8	40.0	34.9	32.7	30.9	28.6	27.3	27.5	24.3
Paper and paper products	467.5	446.3	421.4	392.7	373.7	365.2	357.4	350.5	343.7	313.3
Printing and related support activities	575.7	544.4	492.6	471.2	459.5	447.3	446.6	442.6	424.5	370.7
Petroleum and coal products	83.1	80.9	78.0	74.4	76.7	75.4	72.2	72.6	77.1	69.7
Chemicals	587.7	562.2	531.9	524.9	520.2	510.0	507.7	504.4	512.5	478.0
Plastics and rubber products	752.6	704.4	661.9	633.4	625.6	620.4	607.6	592.3	571.5	478.4
Private Service-Providing	72 167	72 517	71 993	71 926	73 116	74 990	76 893	78 498	78 546	75 823
Trade, transportation, and utilities	21 965	21 709	21 337	21 078	21 319	21 830	22 166	22 546	22 337	21 149
Wholesale trade	4 686.4	4 555.1	4 473.5	4 395.9	4 443.5	4 583.6	4 724.3	4 850.9	4 822.1	4 536.3
Retail trade	13 039.8	12 952.3	12 774.0	12 654.9	12 788.1	13 029.6	13 110.2	13 317.1	13 134.0	12 475.0
Transportation and warehousing	3 753.2	3 718.2	3 611.3	3 563.1	3 637.1	3 774.0	3 889.1	3 934.6	3 930.7	3 686.8
Utilities	485.1	482.8	478.4	463.7	449.9	443.0	442.6	443.5	450.4	450.5
Information	2 502	2 531	2 398	2 347	2 371	2 386	2 399	2 403	2 388	2 243
Financial activities	5 737	5 810	5 872	5 967	5 989	6 090	6 281	6 326	6 269	5 999
Professional and business services	13 790	13 588	13 049	12 911	13 287	13 854	14 446	14 784	14 585	13 525
Education and health services	13 362	13 846	14 311	14 532	14 771	15 129	15 539	15 999	16 488	16 839
Leisure and hospitality	10 516	10 662	10 576	10 666	10 955	11 263	11 568	11 861	11 873	11 583
Other services	4 296	4 373	4 449	4 426	4 425	4 438	4 494	4 578	4 606	4 486

[1]Includes other industries, not shown separately.

Table 16-3. Average Weekly Hours of Production or Nonsupervisory Workers on Private Nonfarm Payrolls by NAICS Industry

(Hours.)

Industry	1990	1991	1992	1993	1994	1995	1996	1997	1998	1999
Total Private	34.3	34.1	34.2	34.3	34.5	34.3	34.3	34.5	34.5	34.3
Goods-Producing	40.1	40.1	40.2	40.6	41.1	40.8	40.8	41.1	40.8	40.8
Mining and logging	45.0	45.3	44.6	44.9	45.3	45.3	46.0	46.2	44.9	44.2
Construction	38.3	38.1	38.0	38.4	38.8	38.8	38.9	38.9	38.8	39.0
Manufacturing	40.5	40.4	40.7	41.1	41.7	41.3	41.3	41.7	41.4	41.4
Overtime hours	3.9	3.8	4.0	4.4	5.0	4.7	4.8	5.1	4.9	4.9
Durable goods	41.1	40.9	41.3	41.9	42.6	42.1	42.1	42.6	42.1	41.9
Overtime hours	3.9	3.7	3.9	4.5	5.3	5.0	5.0	5.4	5.0	5.0
Wood products	40.4	40.2	40.9	41.2	41.7	41.0	41.2	41.4	41.4	41.3
Nonmetallic mineral products	40.9	40.5	41.0	41.5	42.2	41.8	42.0	41.9	42.2	42.1
Primary metals	42.1	41.5	42.4	43.1	44.1	43.4	43.6	44.3	43.5	43.8
Fabricated metal products	41.0	40.8	41.2	41.6	42.3	41.9	41.9	42.3	41.9	41.7
Machinery	42.1	41.9	42.4	43.2	43.9	43.5	43.3	44.0	43.1	42.3
Computer and electronic products	41.3	40.9	41.4	41.8	42.2	42.2	41.9	42.5	41.9	41.5
Electrical equipment and appliances	41.2	41.4	41.8	42.4	43.0	41.9	42.1	42.1	41.8	41.8
Transportation equipment	42.0	41.9	41.9	43.0	44.3	43.7	43.8	44.2	43.2	43.6
Motor vehicles and parts	41.4	41.5	41.6	43.3	44.8	43.8	43.8	43.9	42.6	43.8
Furniture and related products	38.0	37.8	38.7	39.0	39.3	38.5	38.2	39.1	39.4	39.3
Miscellaneous manufacturing	39.0	39.1	39.3	39.2	39.4	39.2	39.1	39.7	39.2	39.3
Nondurable goods	39.6	39.7	40.0	40.1	40.5	40.1	40.1	40.5	40.5	40.4
Overtime hours	3.9	4.0	4.2	4.3	4.6	4.3	4.4	4.7	4.6	4.6
Food manufacturing	39.3	39.2	39.2	39.3	39.8	39.6	39.5	39.8	40.1	40.2
Beverage and tobacco products	38.9	38.8	38.7	38.3	39.3	39.3	39.7	40.0	40.3	41.0
Textile mills	40.2	40.7	41.3	41.6	41.9	40.9	40.8	41.6	41.0	41.0
Textile product mills	38.5	38.6	38.7	39.2	39.4	38.6	38.7	39.2	39.2	39.1
Apparel	34.7	35.4	35.6	35.5	35.7	35.3	35.2	35.6	35.6	35.4
Leather and allied products	37.4	37.6	37.9	38.4	38.2	37.7	37.8	38.2	37.4	37.2
Paper and paper products	43.6	43.6	43.8	43.8	44.2	43.4	43.5	43.9	43.6	43.6
Printing and related support activities	38.7	38.6	39.0	39.2	39.6	39.1	39.1	39.5	39.3	39.1
Petroleum and coal products	44.4	43.9	43.6	44.0	44.3	43.7	43.7	43.1	43.6	42.6
Chemicals	42.8	43.1	43.3	43.2	43.4	43.3	43.3	43.4	43.2	42.7
Plastics and rubber products	40.6	40.5	41.2	41.4	41.8	41.1	41.0	41.4	41.3	41.3
Private Service-Providing	32.5	32.4	32.5	32.5	32.7	32.6	32.6	32.8	32.8	32.7
Trade, transportation, and utilities	33.7	33.7	33.8	34.1	34.3	34.1	34.1	34.3	34.2	33.9
Wholesale trade	38.4	38.4	38.5	38.5	38.8	38.6	38.6	38.8	38.6	38.6
Retail trade	30.6	30.4	30.7	30.7	30.9	30.8	30.7	30.9	30.9	30.8
Transportation and warehousing	37.7	37.4	37.4	38.9	39.5	38.9	39.1	39.4	38.7	37.6
Utilities	41.5	41.5	41.7	42.1	42.3	42.3	42.0	42.0	42.0	42.0
Information	35.8	35.6	35.8	36.0	36.0	36.0	36.4	36.3	36.6	36.7
Financial activities	35.5	35.5	35.6	35.5	35.5	35.5	35.5	35.7	36.0	35.8
Professional and business services	34.2	34.0	34.0	34.0	34.1	34.0	34.1	34.3	34.3	34.4
Education and health services	31.9	31.9	32.0	32.0	32.0	32.0	31.9	32.2	32.2	32.1
Leisure and hospitality	26.0	25.6	25.7	25.9	26.0	25.9	25.9	26.0	26.2	26.1
Other services	32.8	32.7	32.6	32.6	32.7	32.6	32.5	32.7	32.6	32.5

Table 16-3. Average Weekly Hours of Production or Nonsupervisory Workers on Private Nonfarm Payrolls by NAICS Industry—*Continued*

(Hours.)

Industry	2000	2001	2002	2003	2004	2005	2006	2007	2008	2009
Total Private	34.3	34.0	33.9	33.7	33.7	33.8	33.9	33.9	33.6	33.1
Goods-Producing	40.7	39.9	39.9	39.8	40.0	40.1	40.5	40.6	40.2	39.2
Mining and logging	44.4	44.6	43.2	43.6	44.5	45.6	45.6	45.9	45.1	43.3
Construction	39.2	38.7	38.4	38.4	38.3	38.6	39.0	39.0	38.5	37.6
Manufacturing	41.3	40.3	40.5	40.4	40.8	40.7	41.1	41.2	40.8	39.8
Overtime hours	4.7	4.0	4.2	4.2	4.6	4.6	4.4	4.2	3.7	2.9
Durable goods	41.8	40.6	40.8	40.8	41.3	41.1	41.4	41.5	41.1	39.9
Overtime hours	4.8	3.9	4.2	4.3	4.7	4.6	4.4	4.2	3.7	2.7
Wood products	41.0	40.2	39.9	40.4	40.7	40.0	39.8	39.4	38.6	37.4
Nonmetallic mineral products	41.6	41.6	42.0	42.2	42.4	42.2	43.0	42.3	42.1	40.9
Primary metals	44.2	42.4	42.4	42.3	43.1	43.1	43.6	42.9	42.2	40.7
Fabricated metal products	41.9	40.6	40.6	40.7	41.1	41.0	41.4	41.6	41.3	39.4
Machinery	42.3	40.9	40.5	40.8	42.0	42.1	42.4	42.6	42.3	40.1
Computer and electronic products	41.4	39.8	39.7	40.4	40.4	40.0	40.5	40.6	41.0	40.4
Electrical equipment and appliances	41.6	39.8	40.1	40.6	40.7	40.6	41.0	41.2	40.9	39.3
Transportation equipment	43.3	41.9	42.5	41.9	42.5	42.4	42.7	42.8	41.9	41.2
Motor vehicles and parts	43.4	41.6	42.6	42.0	42.6	42.3	42.2	42.3	41.4	40.1
Furniture and related products	39.2	38.3	39.2	38.9	39.5	39.2	38.8	39.2	38.1	37.7
Miscellaneous manufacturing	39.0	38.8	38.6	38.4	38.5	38.7	38.7	38.9	38.9	38.5
Nondurable goods	40.3	39.9	40.0	39.8	40.0	39.9	40.6	40.8	40.4	39.8
Overtime hours	4.5	4.1	4.2	4.1	4.4	4.4	4.4	4.1	3.7	3.2
Food manufacturing	40.1	39.6	39.6	39.3	39.3	39.0	40.1	40.7	40.5	40.0
Beverage and tobacco products	42.0	40.9	39.4	39.1	39.2	40.1	40.8	40.7	38.8	35.7
Textile mills	41.4	40.0	40.6	39.1	40.1	40.3	40.6	40.3	38.7	37.7
Textile product mills	38.7	38.4	39.0	39.3	38.7	38.9	39.8	39.7	38.6	37.9
Apparel	35.7	36.0	36.7	35.6	36.1	35.8	36.5	37.2	36.4	36.0
Leather and allied products	37.5	36.4	37.5	39.3	38.4	38.4	38.9	38.2	37.6	33.6
Paper and paper products	42.8	42.1	41.9	41.5	42.1	42.5	42.9	43.1	42.9	41.8
Printing and related support activities	39.2	38.7	38.4	38.2	38.4	38.4	39.2	39.1	38.3	38.0
Petroleum and coal products	42.7	43.8	43.0	44.5	44.9	45.5	45.0	44.1	44.6	43.4
Chemicals	42.2	41.9	42.3	42.4	42.8	42.3	42.5	41.9	41.5	41.4
Plastics and rubber products	40.8	40.0	40.6	40.4	40.4	40.0	40.6	41.3	41.0	40.2
Private Service-Providing	32.7	32.5	32.5	32.3	32.3	32.4	32.5	32.4	32.3	32.1
Trade, transportation, and utilities	33.8	33.5	33.6	33.6	33.5	33.4	33.4	33.3	33.2	32.9
Wholesale trade	38.8	38.4	38.0	37.9	37.8	37.7	38.0	38.2	38.2	37.6
Retail trade	30.7	30.7	30.9	30.9	30.7	30.6	30.5	30.2	30.0	29.9
Transportation and warehousing	37.4	36.7	36.8	36.8	37.2	37.0	36.9	37.0	36.4	36.0
Utilities	42.0	41.4	40.9	41.1	40.9	41.1	41.4	42.4	42.7	42.1
Information	36.8	36.9	36.5	36.2	36.3	36.5	36.6	36.5	36.7	36.6
Financial activities	35.9	35.8	35.6	35.5	35.5	35.9	35.7	35.9	35.8	36.1
Professional and business services	34.5	34.2	34.2	34.1	34.2	34.2	34.6	34.8	34.8	34.7
Education and health services	32.2	32.3	32.4	32.3	32.4	32.6	32.5	32.6	32.5	32.3
Leisure and hospitality	26.1	25.8	25.8	25.6	25.7	25.7	25.7	25.5	25.2	24.8
Other services	32.5	32.3	32.0	31.4	31.0	30.9	30.9	30.9	30.8	30.5

Table 16-4. Average Hourly Earnings of Production or Nonsupervisory Workers on Private Nonfarm Payrolls by NAICS Industry

(Dollars.)

Industry	1990	1991	1992	1993	1994	1995	1996	1997	1998	1999
Total Private	10.20	10.52	10.77	11.05	11.34	11.65	12.04	12.51	13.01	13.49
Goods-Producing	11.46	11.76	11.99	12.28	12.63	12.96	13.38	13.82	14.23	14.71
Mining and logging	13.40	13.82	14.09	14.12	14.41	14.78	15.10	15.57	16.20	16.33
Construction	13.42	13.65	13.81	14.04	14.38	14.73	15.11	15.67	16.23	16.80
Manufacturing	10.78	11.13	11.40	11.70	12.04	12.34	12.75	13.14	13.45	13.85
Excluding overtime [1]	10.28	10.63	10.86	11.10	11.36	11.68	12.05	12.37	12.70	13.08
Durable goods	11.40	11.81	12.09	12.41	12.78	13.05	13.45	13.83	14.07	14.46
Wood products	8.82	9.03	9.24	9.41	9.66	9.92	10.24	10.52	10.85	11.18
Nonmetallic mineral products	11.11	11.34	11.57	11.83	12.11	12.38	12.80	13.17	13.59	13.97
Primary metals	12.97	13.37	13.72	14.08	14.47	14.75	15.12	15.39	15.66	16.00
Fabricated metal products	10.64	10.97	11.16	11.40	11.64	11.91	12.26	12.64	12.97	13.34
Machinery	11.73	12.12	12.40	12.72	12.94	13.13	13.49	13.94	14.23	14.77
Computer and electronic products	10.89	11.35	11.64	11.95	12.19	12.29	12.75	13.24	13.85	14.37
Electrical equipment and appliances	10.00	10.30	10.50	10.65	10.94	11.25	11.80	12.24	12.51	12.90
Transportation equipment	14.44	15.12	15.59	16.21	16.93	17.21	17.66	17.99	17.91	18.24
Motor vehicles and parts	15.00	15.67	15.92	16.56	17.38	17.72	18.14	18.43	18.21	18.49
Furniture and related products	8.53	8.74	9.01	9.25	9.52	9.75	10.09	10.50	10.88	11.28
Miscellaneous manufacturing	8.87	9.15	9.43	9.64	9.90	10.23	10.59	10.88	11.17	11.55
Nondurable goods	9.87	10.18	10.45	10.70	10.96	11.30	11.68	12.04	12.45	12.85
Food manufacturing	9.04	9.32	9.59	9.82	10.00	10.27	10.50	10.77	11.09	11.40
Beverage and tobacco products	13.24	13.65	14.07	14.30	14.97	15.40	15.73	16.00	16.03	16.54
Textile mills	8.17	8.49	8.82	9.12	9.35	9.63	9.88	10.22	10.58	10.90
Textile product mills	7.37	7.60	7.85	8.09	8.29	8.60	8.95	9.30	9.61	10.04
Apparel	6.22	6.43	6.60	6.74	6.95	7.22	7.45	7.76	8.05	8.35
Leather and allied products	7.18	7.43	7.68	7.88	8.23	8.50	8.94	9.31	9.68	9.93
Paper and paper products	12.06	12.45	12.78	13.13	13.49	13.94	14.38	14.76	15.20	15.58
Printing and related support activities	11.11	11.32	11.53	11.67	11.89	12.08	12.41	12.78	13.20	13.67
Petroleum and coal products	17.00	17.90	18.83	19.43	19.96	20.24	20.18	21.10	21.75	22.22
Chemicals	12.85	13.30	13.70	13.97	14.33	14.86	15.37	15.78	16.23	16.40
Plastics and rubber products	9.76	10.07	10.35	10.55	10.66	10.86	11.17	11.48	11.79	12.25
Private Service-Providing	9.72	10.07	10.35	10.62	10.89	11.21	11.59	12.07	12.61	13.09
Trade, transportation, and utilities	9.83	10.08	10.30	10.55	10.80	11.10	11.46	11.90	12.39	12.82
Wholesale trade	11.58	11.95	12.21	12.57	12.93	13.34	13.80	14.41	15.07	15.62
Retail trade	7.71	7.89	8.12	8.36	8.61	8.85	9.21	9.59	10.05	10.45
Transportation and warehousing	12.50	12.61	12.77	12.71	12.84	13.18	13.45	13.78	14.12	14.55
Utilities	16.14	16.70	17.17	17.95	18.66	19.19	19.78	20.59	21.48	22.03
Information	13.40	13.90	14.29	14.86	15.32	15.68	16.30	17.14	17.67	18.40
Financial activities	9.99	10.42	10.86	11.36	11.82	12.28	12.71	13.22	13.93	14.47
Professional and business services	11.14	11.50	11.78	11.96	12.15	12.53	13.00	13.57	14.27	14.85
Education and health services	10.00	10.49	10.87	11.21	11.50	11.80	12.17	12.56	13.00	13.44
Leisure and hospitality	6.02	6.22	6.36	6.48	6.62	6.79	6.99	7.32	7.67	7.96
Other services	9.08	9.39	9.66	9.90	10.18	10.51	10.85	11.29	11.79	12.26

[1]Derived by assuming that overtime hours are paid at the rate of time and one-half.

Table 16-4. Average Hourly Earnings of Production or Nonsupervisory Workers on Private Nonfarm Payrolls by NAICS Industry—*Continued*

(Dollars.)

Industry	2000	2001	2002	2003	2004	2005	2006	2007	2008	2009
Total Private	14.02	14.54	14.97	15.37	15.69	16.13	16.76	17.43	18.08	18.62
Goods-Producing	15.27	15.78	16.33	16.80	17.19	17.60	18.02	18.67	19.33	19.90
Mining and logging	16.55	17.00	17.19	17.56	18.07	18.72	19.90	20.97	22.50	23.29
Construction	17.48	18.00	18.52	18.95	19.23	19.46	20.02	20.95	21.87	22.67
Manufacturing	14.32	14.76	15.29	15.74	16.14	16.56	16.81	17.26	17.75	18.23
Excluding overtime [1]	13.55	14.06	14.54	14.96	15.29	15.68	15.96	16.43	16.97	17.58
Durable goods	14.92	15.38	16.02	16.45	16.82	17.33	17.68	18.20	18.70	19.35
Wood products	11.63	11.99	12.33	12.71	13.03	13.16	13.39	13.68	14.19	14.93
Nonmetallic mineral products	14.53	14.86	15.40	15.76	16.25	16.61	16.59	16.93	16.90	17.28
Primary metals	16.64	17.06	17.68	18.13	18.57	18.94	19.36	19.66	20.19	20.08
Fabricated metal products	13.77	14.19	14.68	15.01	15.31	15.80	16.17	16.53	16.99	17.49
Machinery	15.21	15.48	15.92	16.29	16.67	17.02	17.20	17.72	17.97	18.38
Computer and electronic products	14.73	15.42	16.20	16.69	17.27	18.39	18.94	19.94	21.04	21.88
Electrical equipment and appliances	13.23	13.78	13.98	14.36	14.90	15.24	15.53	15.93	15.78	16.27
Transportation equipment	18.89	19.48	20.63	21.22	21.48	22.09	22.41	23.04	23.85	24.93
Motor vehicles and parts	19.11	19.66	21.09	21.68	21.71	22.26	22.14	22.00	22.21	21.80
Furniture and related products	11.73	12.14	12.62	12.99	13.16	13.45	13.80	14.32	14.54	15.04
Miscellaneous manufacturing	11.93	12.45	12.91	13.30	13.84	14.07	14.36	14.66	15.20	16.13
Nondurable goods	13.31	13.75	14.15	14.63	15.05	15.27	15.33	15.67	16.15	16.56
Food manufacturing	11.77	12.18	12.55	12.80	12.98	13.04	13.13	13.55	14.01	14.40
Beverage and tobacco products	17.40	17.67	17.73	17.96	19.14	18.76	18.18	18.54	19.35	20.49
Textile mills	11.23	11.40	11.73	11.99	12.13	12.38	12.55	13.00	13.58	13.71
Textile product mills	10.31	10.49	10.85	11.15	11.31	11.61	11.86	11.78	11.73	11.44
Apparel	8.61	8.83	9.11	9.58	9.77	10.26	10.65	11.05	11.40	11.37
Leather and allied products	10.35	10.69	11.00	11.66	11.63	11.50	11.44	12.04	12.96	13.90
Paper and paper products	15.91	16.38	16.85	17.33	17.91	17.99	18.01	18.44	18.89	19.28
Printing and related support activities	14.09	14.48	14.93	15.37	15.71	15.74	15.80	16.15	16.75	16.75
Petroleum and coal products	22.80	22.90	23.04	23.63	24.39	24.47	24.11	25.21	27.41	29.63
Chemicals	17.09	17.57	17.97	18.50	19.17	19.67	19.60	19.55	19.50	20.30
Plastics and rubber products	12.70	13.21	13.55	14.18	14.59	14.80	14.97	15.39	15.85	16.01
Private Service-Providing	13.62	14.18	14.59	14.99	15.29	15.74	16.42	17.11	17.77	18.35
Trade, transportation, and utilities	13.31	13.70	14.02	14.34	14.58	14.92	15.39	15.78	16.16	16.50
Wholesale trade	16.28	16.77	16.98	17.36	17.65	18.16	18.91	19.59	20.13	20.85
Retail trade	10.86	11.29	11.67	11.90	12.08	12.36	12.57	12.75	12.87	13.02
Transportation and warehousing	15.05	15.33	15.76	16.25	16.52	16.70	17.28	17.72	18.41	18.80
Utilities	22.75	23.58	23.96	24.77	25.61	26.68	27.40	27.88	28.83	29.56
Information	19.07	19.80	20.20	21.01	21.40	22.06	23.23	23.96	24.78	25.45
Financial activities	14.98	15.59	16.17	17.14	17.52	17.95	18.80	19.64	20.28	20.83
Professional and business services	15.52	16.33	16.81	17.21	17.48	18.08	19.13	20.15	21.18	22.35
Education and health services	13.95	14.64	15.21	15.64	16.15	16.71	17.38	18.11	18.87	19.49
Leisure and hospitality	8.32	8.57	8.81	9.00	9.15	9.38	9.75	10.41	10.84	11.11
Other services	12.73	13.27	13.72	13.84	13.98	14.34	14.77	15.42	16.09	16.59

[1]Derived by assuming that overtime hours are paid at the rate of time and one-half.

Table 16-5. Average Weekly Earnings of Production or Nonsupervisory Workers on Private Nonfarm Payrolls by NAICS Industry

(Dollars.)

Industry	1990	1991	1992	1993	1994	1995	1996	1997	1998	1999
Total Private	349.75	358.51	368.25	378.91	391.22	400.07	413.28	431.86	448.56	463.15
Goods-Producing	459.55	471.32	482.58	498.82	519.58	528.62	546.48	568.43	580.99	599.99
Mining and logging	602.54	625.42	629.02	634.77	653.14	670.32	695.07	720.11	727.28	721.74
Construction	513.43	520.41	525.13	539.81	558.53	571.57	588.48	609.48	629.75	655.11
Manufacturing	436.16	449.73	464.43	480.83	502.05	509.26	526.55	548.22	557.12	573.14
Durable goods	468.43	483.28	499.60	519.81	544.52	549.49	566.53	589.06	591.77	606.55
Wood products	356.38	362.69	377.76	387.34	402.86	406.51	422.32	435.74	449.78	461.61
Nonmetallic mineral products	453.91	459.21	474.46	490.73	510.92	517.69	538.03	551.70	573.00	587.42
Primary metals	545.36	555.34	581.45	606.49	637.73	639.70	658.81	681.52	681.68	700.93
Fabricated metal products	436.12	447.98	459.64	474.21	492.07	498.48	513.57	534.48	543.20	555.86
Machinery	493.22	507.79	525.26	549.73	567.90	571.04	584.59	613.31	613.69	625.19
Computer and electronic products	449.96	464.25	482.09	499.09	514.78	518.26	534.39	562.80	579.90	596.49
Electrical equipment and appliances	412.42	426.81	439.04	451.44	470.24	471.72	496.69	515.77	522.54	538.98
Transportation equipment	606.71	633.69	652.68	697.18	750.26	751.78	773.51	795.60	774.42	795.73
Motor vehicles and parts	621.68	650.36	662.82	717.68	779.29	776.41	794.09	808.28	775.56	809.31
Furniture and related products	324.30	330.65	348.22	360.82	374.03	375.13	385.75	410.45	428.66	443.61
Miscellaneous manufacturing	345.86	358.31	370.56	378.14	389.79	400.96	414.03	431.77	437.83	454.20
Nondurable goods	390.73	404.17	417.95	429.15	443.88	452.77	467.88	487.04	504.02	519.95
Food manufacturing	355.61	364.90	375.72	386.04	398.50	406.75	414.70	428.58	444.81	458.63
Beverage and tobacco products	515.73	530.09	544.25	547.60	588.39	605.00	624.82	639.69	646.26	679.06
Textile mills	328.11	345.48	364.45	379.74	391.64	394.17	403.08	425.53	434.15	447.38
Textile product mills	283.66	293.45	303.69	317.63	326.47	332.30	346.80	364.16	376.16	392.41
Apparel	215.97	227.82	235.29	239.59	248.42	255.12	261.95	276.01	286.26	295.68
Leather and allied products	268.32	279.41	291.11	302.85	314.18	319.98	337.86	355.63	361.87	369.80
Paper and paper products	525.71	542.26	560.27	575.49	596.19	604.74	625.38	647.55	662.20	679.24
Printing and related support activities	429.93	437.00	450.02	457.91	470.74	472.37	484.99	504.46	518.32	534.15
Petroleum and coal products	754.13	786.05	821.72	855.36	883.81	883.68	881.24	908.50	949.28	947.60
Chemicals	550.25	573.27	593.17	603.67	622.50	644.37	666.10	685.39	700.70	700.55
Plastics and rubber products	396.22	408.28	426.60	436.82	445.90	445.88	458.29	474.94	487.04	505.42
Private Service-Providing	316.03	325.90	336.08	345.65	355.63	364.80	377.37	395.51	413.50	427.98
Trade, transportation, and utilities	331.55	339.19	348.68	359.33	370.38	378.79	390.64	407.54	423.30	434.31
Wholesale trade	444.48	459.27	470.41	484.46	501.17	515.14	533.29	559.39	582.21	602.77
Retail trade	235.62	240.15	249.63	256.89	265.77	272.56	282.76	295.97	310.34	321.63
Transportation and warehousing	471.72	471.12	478.02	494.36	507.27	513.37	525.64	542.55	546.86	547.97
Utilities	670.40	693.40	716.36	756.35	789.98	811.52	830.74	865.26	902.94	924.59
Information	479.50	495.17	512.20	535.19	551.21	564.92	592.72	622.37	646.34	675.47
Financial activities	354.66	369.57	386.01	403.02	419.20	436.12	451.49	472.37	500.98	517.57
Professional and business services	380.52	391.09	400.64	406.20	414.16	426.44	442.81	465.51	490.00	510.99
Education and health services	319.27	334.55	348.29	359.08	368.14	377.73	388.27	404.65	418.82	431.35
Leisure and hospitality	156.32	159.15	163.70	167.56	172.33	175.74	180.98	190.52	200.82	208.05
Other services	297.91	306.91	315.08	322.69	332.44	342.36	352.62	368.63	384.25	398.77

Table 16-5. Average Weekly Earnings of Production or Nonsupervisory Workers on Private Nonfarm Payrolls by NAICS Industry—*Continued*

(Dollars.)

Industry	2000	2001	2002	2003	2004	2005	2006	2007	2008	2009
Total Private	481.01	493.79	506.75	518.06	529.09	544.33	567.87	590.04	607.95	617.11
Goods-Producing	621.86	630.01	651.61	669.13	688.13	705.31	730.16	757.34	776.66	779.83
Mining and logging	734.92	757.92	741.97	765.94	803.82	853.71	907.95	962.64	1 014.69	1 007.85
Construction	685.78	695.89	711.82	726.83	735.55	750.22	781.21	816.66	842.61	852.45
Manufacturing	590.77	595.19	618.75	635.99	658.49	673.30	691.02	711.56	724.46	725.87
Durable goods	624.22	624.47	652.94	671.21	694.06	712.95	732.00	754.77	767.95	771.03
Wood products	477.13	481.36	492.00	514.10	530.16	526.62	533.11	539.34	547.53	559.05
Nonmetallic mineral products	604.87	618.91	646.87	664.92	688.30	700.64	712.67	716.78	711.11	706.16
Primary metals	734.79	723.82	749.32	767.45	799.77	815.90	843.63	843.26	851.29	816.93
Fabricated metal products	576.68	576.60	596.38	610.37	628.80	647.34	668.98	687.20	701.57	689.35
Machinery	643.81	632.56	645.38	664.48	699.42	716.42	728.84	754.19	759.94	737.88
Computer and electronic products	609.73	613.22	642.90	674.72	697.86	735.75	766.96	808.80	861.58	883.07
Electrical equipment and appliances	550.48	548.03	560.33	583.27	607.00	618.88	637.04	656.46	645.60	639.50
Transportation equipment	817.52	816.90	877.66	889.03	912.56	937.78	957.65	986.79	1 000.67	1 026.61
Motor vehicles and parts	828.73	818.68	898.54	910.02	924.72	940.64	934.41	930.51	920.57	874.15
Furniture and related products	459.95	464.69	494.17	505.47	519.72	527.43	535.90	560.84	553.93	566.48
Miscellaneous manufacturing	464.86	483.04	498.84	510.62	533.30	545.04	555.90	569.99	591.95	620.78
Nondurable goods	536.82	548.41	566.72	582.61	602.53	609.24	621.97	639.99	652.22	658.36
Food manufacturing	472.06	481.67	496.94	502.92	509.52	508.55	525.99	551.32	566.91	575.89
Beverage and tobacco products	730.35	721.68	698.39	702.45	751.20	751.54	741.34	755.22	750.25	731.37
Textile mills	464.51	456.64	476.52	469.33	486.68	498.47	509.39	524.40	525.00	517.15
Textile product mills	399.13	402.47	423.08	438.58	438.08	451.14	472.24	467.77	453.10	433.13
Apparel	307.69	317.74	334.24	340.95	352.21	366.71	389.17	411.39	415.14	408.92
Leather and allied products	388.46	388.83	412.99	457.83	446.66	441.96	445.47	459.50	486.58	466.73
Paper and paper products	681.34	690.06	705.62	719.73	754.14	764.04	772.39	795.58	809.57	805.86
Printing and related support activities	552.15	560.89	573.05	587.58	603.97	604.73	618.92	632.02	642.50	635.72
Petroleum and coal products	973.53	1 003.34	990.88	1 052.32	1 095.00	1 114.51	1 085.50	1 112.73	1 222.07	1 285.64
Chemicals	721.87	735.42	759.53	784.07	819.66	831.76	833.51	819.54	809.29	841.33
Plastics and rubber products	517.84	528.73	550.03	572.32	590.06	591.71	608.41	635.63	648.98	643.81
Private Service-Providing	445.74	461.08	473.80	484.68	494.22	509.58	532.78	554.89	574.35	588.07
Trade, transportation, and utilities	449.88	459.53	471.27	481.14	488.42	498.43	514.34	526.07	536.06	542.36
Wholesale trade	631.40	643.45	644.38	657.29	667.09	685.00	718.63	748.94	769.62	784.75
Retail trade	333.38	346.16	360.81	367.15	371.13	377.58	383.02	385.11	386.21	388.72
Transportation and warehousing	562.31	562.70	579.88	598.41	614.96	618.58	636.97	654.95	670.37	677.44
Utilities	955.66	977.18	979.09	1 017.27	1 048.44	1 095.90	1 135.34	1 182.65	1 230.69	1 243.76
Information	700.86	730.88	737.77	760.45	777.25	805.08	850.42	874.65	908.99	931.93
Financial activities	537.37	557.92	575.54	609.08	622.87	644.99	672.21	705.13	727.07	751.21
Professional and business services	535.07	557.84	574.66	587.02	597.56	618.87	662.27	700.82	737.70	775.81
Education and health services	449.29	473.39	492.74	505.69	523.78	544.59	564.94	590.09	613.73	628.56
Leisure and hospitality	217.20	220.73	227.17	230.42	234.86	241.36	250.34	265.52	273.39	275.80
Other services	413.41	428.64	439.76	434.41	433.04	443.37	456.50	477.06	495.57	506.28

Table 16-6. Indexes of Aggregate Weekly Hours of Production or Nonsupervisory Workers on Private Nonfarm Payrolls by NAICS Industry

(2002 = 100.)

Industry	1990	1991	1992	1993	1994	1995	1996	1997	1998	1999
Total Private	84.4	82.6	83.1	85.5	89.2	91.6	93.8	97.1	99.4	101.5
Goods-Producing	106.1	100.1	98.7	100.8	105.6	106.8	108.1	111.2	112.3	112.6
Mining and logging	128.6	123.8	113.3	110.3	111.0	110.2	112.7	117.6	112.8	102.9
Construction	78.8	70.1	67.5	71.3	77.3	79.9	84.3	88.6	93.4	99.7
Manufacturing	117.7	112.8	112.4	113.9	118.3	119.0	118.8	121.4	121.0	118.9
Durable goods	114.2	107.6	106.4	108.2	114.2	116.3	117.5	121.6	122.0	120.5
Wood products	101.5	92.6	95.2	100.5	109.1	109.3	111.6	114.8	117.5	118.6
Nonmetallic mineral products	100.8	92.8	92.6	94.3	98.8	99.7	101.5	103.1	105.8	106.9
Primary metals	131.5	122.9	120.8	121.5	128.0	129.3	129.9	132.3	131.1	128.4
Fabricated metal products	104.7	99.1	97.3	99.7	106.3	109.9	111.6	116.6	118.6	116.7
Machinery	123.8	116.2	113.9	118.6	126.9	132.2	133.7	138.9	137.3	129.8
Computer and electronic products	137.1	128.1	122.9	121.1	123.5	127.1	129.9	136.8	136.7	131.1
Electrical equipment and appliances	136.0	127.9	125.9	126.8	132.4	130.3	129.4	127.7	127.8	128.3
Transportation equipment	111.1	105.8	104.3	105.5	112.5	115.4	116.4	120.7	118.7	119.5
Motor vehicles and parts	90.9	87.9	91.1	97.9	110.6	115.9	116.1	117.5	112.8	118.7
Furniture and related products	97.1	89.5	92.1	95.3	100.5	99.2	98.3	102.9	108.4	112.6
Miscellaneous manufacturing	104.2	103.9	105.3	107.0	108.4	107.9	107.8	110.1	110.4	110.3
Nondurable goods	123.0	120.8	121.7	122.7	124.7	123.1	120.5	120.9	119.4	116.1
Food manufacturing	96.2	96.6	97.3	98.7	100.5	101.6	101.8	102.6	103.4	103.8
Beverage and tobacco products	96.9	96.4	95.4	95.6	98.7	97.9	101.4	103.1	104.9	104.7
Textile mills	170.4	168.4	170.3	170.8	171.6	163.5	154.1	155.2	148.9	139.1
Textile product mills	118.8	113.1	114.8	118.7	124.0	121.0	118.0	119.4	117.6	115.5
Apparel	266.6	263.6	266.8	258.8	252.0	235.0	211.5	201.3	181.0	154.6
Leather and allied products	290.0	268.9	263.5	259.1	246.9	221.8	197.5	187.1	166.6	148.3
Paper and paper products	121.8	120.6	121.7	121.9	123.5	121.4	120.1	121.5	119.5	117.1
Printing and related support activities	122.3	118.7	118.4	120.3	123.8	123.9	122.8	124.6	124.3	120.9
Petroleum and coal products	128.9	127.5	126.0	122.0	120.0	115.5	113.5	112.7	113.4	107.6
Chemicals	118.2	115.0	112.9	113.4	115.1	115.4	114.7	114.7	115.4	113.1
Plastics and rubber products	97.7	94.1	98.0	102.3	108.7	109.8	110.0	112.7	113.7	114.6
Private Service-Providing	78.3	77.8	78.8	81.2	84.6	87.3	89.7	93.1	95.8	98.4
Trade, transportation, and utilities	89.5	87.4	87.3	89.0	92.7	95.1	96.6	98.8	100.3	101.9
Wholesale trade	94.9	93.3	92.4	92.4	95.8	99.2	100.7	103.4	104.8	106.2
Retail trade	87.5	84.8	85.1	86.3	89.8	92.3	93.7	95.9	97.2	99.5
Transportation and warehousing	83.5	82.3	82.7	88.4	93.7	95.6	98.2	101.0	102.6	103.2
Utilities	124.3	123.5	121.6	119.9	117.1	112.9	108.6	106.1	105.8	105.0
Information	76.2	76.1	76.5	78.0	79.2	82.5	87.0	90.4	92.6	98.5
Financial activities	84.5	83.3	83.5	85.9	88.0	87.8	89.8	92.6	96.5	98.0
Professional and business services	68.0	66.7	68.4	71.9	77.0	81.2	85.2	91.5	96.7	101.7
Education and health services	67.2	70.2	72.9	75.4	78.3	81.2	83.4	86.7	88.9	90.6
Leisure and hospitality	78.9	77.3	79.3	82.2	85.6	88.5	90.8	93.4	95.5	97.9
Other services	81.8	81.2	80.6	82.8	84.5	87.1	89.1	91.9	94.3	96.3

Table 16-6. Indexes of Aggregate Weekly Hours of Production or Nonsupervisory Workers on Private Nonfarm Payrolls by NAICS Industry—*Continued*

(2002 = 100.)

Industry	2000	2001	2002	2003	2004	2005	2006	2007	2008	2009
Total Private	103.6	102.1	100.0	98.7	100.2	102.8	105.8	107.3	105.9	98.8
Goods-Producing	113.1	106.6	100.0	95.7	96.8	98.9	102.5	101.7	96.5	80.5
Mining and logging	105.1	108.3	100.0	97.4	104.0	114.7	125.8	133.5	137.6	118.3
Construction	104.0	103.2	100.0	98.4	101.7	108.3	115.3	114.8	106.5	86.3
Manufacturing	117.7	108.1	100.0	94.5	94.3	93.9	95.6	94.4	90.2	76.3
Durable goods	120.3	109.3	100.0	94.3	95.2	96.1	98.9	97.4	92.2	75.0
Wood products	115.8	105.0	100.0	97.8	100.9	101.3	100.0	89.3	76.8	58.2
Nonmetallic mineral products	109.1	106.1	100.0	94.3	98.0	97.4	100.3	96.9	91.3	74.4
Primary metals	128.9	113.0	100.0	93.4	93.3	93.1	94.1	91.4	87.4	66.5
Fabricated metal products	119.1	109.3	100.0	95.3	97.7	99.3	103.1	104.5	101.3	81.6
Machinery	127.5	114.1	100.0	93.6	96.0	98.8	102.2	103.2	102.3	80.7
Computer and electronic products	133.0	117.9	100.0	92.1	89.7	94.8	103.6	102.1	101.2	89.4
Electrical equipment and appliances	127.7	113.4	100.0	92.0	88.7	86.4	88.0	89.1	88.5	74.8
Transportation equipment	116.3	105.3	100.0	95.4	96.4	97.3	99.9	98.0	88.6	70.3
Motor vehicles and parts	117.3	103.6	100.0	95.9	97.0	95.2	92.9	85.8	72.7	51.7
Furniture and related products	114.7	104.7	100.0	93.0	94.3	91.8	90.3	86.1	74.6	57.6
Miscellaneous manufacturing	109.6	104.8	100.0	93.6	91.8	90.6	90.4	91.0	89.2	81.5
Nondurable goods	113.3	106.0	100.0	94.7	92.7	90.3	90.4	89.6	86.9	78.3
Food manufacturing	103.5	101.5	100.0	98.4	97.1	95.8	98.6	101.2	100.7	97.7
Beverage and tobacco products	104.2	100.3	100.0	88.4	88.8	94.8	99.3	102.2	92.0	84.7
Textile mills	132.4	112.2	100.0	86.3	79.0	71.3	65.1	56.3	47.9	38.2
Textile product mills	112.4	105.5	100.0	92.4	90.2	88.0	85.0	77.5	70.5	59.0
Apparel	137.6	117.1	100.0	82.0	75.1	65.7	63.4	61.5	56.7	45.9
Leather and allied products	138.4	113.3	100.0	91.3	83.6	79.0	74.1	69.3	68.8	54.2
Paper and paper products	113.4	106.6	100.0	92.4	89.2	87.9	86.9	85.7	83.5	74.2
Printing and related support activities	119.4	111.5	100.0	95.3	93.4	90.9	92.5	91.6	86.1	74.4
Petroleum and coal products	105.8	105.6	100.0	98.7	102.6	102.4	96.9	95.6	102.4	90.1
Chemicals	110.4	104.7	100.0	99.0	99.0	95.9	96.1	94.1	94.6	88.1
Plastics and rubber products	114.3	104.9	100.0	95.2	94.2	92.4	91.9	91.1	87.1	71.6
Private Service-Providing	101.0	100.8	100.0	99.5	101.1	103.8	106.7	108.9	108.6	103.9
Trade, transportation, and utilities	103.5	101.5	100.0	98.6	99.6	101.6	103.3	104.8	103.3	96.9
Wholesale trade	107.1	102.9	100.0	98.0	98.9	101.8	105.7	109.2	108.6	100.5
Retail trade	101.3	100.5	100.0	98.9	99.4	100.8	101.1	101.8	99.8	94.3
Transportation and warehousing	105.6	102.7	100.0	98.8	101.9	105.2	107.9	109.4	107.7	100.0
Utilities	104.2	102.4	100.0	97.4	94.2	93.1	93.8	96.2	98.3	97.0
Information	105.0	106.6	100.0	97.0	98.3	99.4	100.2	100.2	100.0	93.8
Financial activities	98.5	99.5	100.0	101.5	101.9	104.7	107.4	108.7	107.5	103.5
Professional and business services	106.6	104.0	100.0	98.7	101.8	106.3	112.1	115.3	113.9	105.2
Education and health services	92.8	96.6	100.0	101.4	103.3	106.4	109.0	112.5	115.7	117.2
Leisure and hospitality	100.6	100.7	100.0	100.1	103.0	106.3	108.9	110.9	109.7	105.4
Other services	97.8	99.1	100.0	97.5	96.1	96.2	97.5	99.4	99.5	96.1

NOTES AND DEFINITIONS, CHAPTER 16

TABLES 16-1 THROUGH 16-6
EMPLOYMENT, HOURS, AND EARNINGS BY NAICS INDUSTRY

SOURCE: U.S. DEPARTMENT OF LABOR, BUREAU OF LABOR STATISTICS

See the notes and definitions for Tables 10-7 and 10-12 through 10-16 regarding definitions of *employment, production or nonsupervisory workers, average weekly hours, overtime hours, average hourly earnings, average weekly earnings*, and the *indexes of aggregate weekly hours*. Availability and reference information is also provided in those notes and definitions.

CHAPTER 17: KEY SECTOR STATISTICS

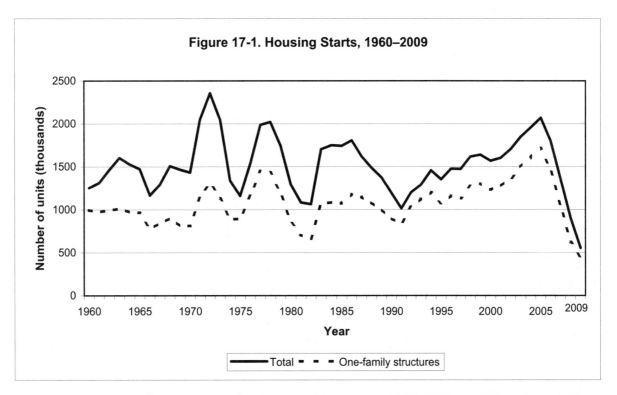

Figure 17-1. Housing Starts, 1960–2009

- The housing sector was the source of the boom and bust cycle of 2001–2009. In 2005, as shown in Figure 17-1, 2.1 million housing units were started, the highest since 1972. Of those, 1.7 million were one-family homes, an all-time record. By 2009, however, both total and single-family starts had plunged to the lowest levels of their 50-year history. (Table 17-3)

- The source of this dramatic swing in real activity was an unsustainable speculative "bubble" in the prices of new and existing homes. Home prices began to fall in 2007 and remain at reduced levels, as can be seen in Table 17-3, Table 12-10, and Figure 12-4. The price bubble encouraged excessive growth in home mortgage debt, which is now weighing heavily on household incomes and net worth, as can be seen in Tables 12-5 through 12-7.

- New orders for nondefense capital goods at U.S. manufacturing firms plunged 40 percent between December 2007 and their lowest point in April 2009. Even excluding the volatile aircraft sector, they were down 27 percent. Both of these important advance indicators of capital spending had regained 14 percent as of December 2009. (Table 17-6)

- Sales of cars and light trucks were 10.3 million in 2009, down 39 percent from their recent high in 2005, and comparable with the 1982 recession. (Table 17-8)

- Service industries were affected later and less. Revenues of the information industry continued to increase through the third quarter of 2008, and fell back quite modestly in the following two quarters. Professional, scientific, and technical services were still trending down at the end of 2009 but were only 5 percent below their high in 2008:3. Administrative services fell 7 percent from 2008:2 to 2009:2; the employment services component, which includes temporary help, was down 11 percent from 2008:1 through 2009:2. The increase in hospital revenues was uninterrupted. (Table 17-13)

- As a percentage of the total supply of petroleum and products (domestic crude oil and natural gas liquids production plus net imports), net imports have increased from 10.4 percent in 1955 to 57.4 percent in 2009. (Table 17-1)

- Sales by electronic shopping and mail order grew from 1.9 percent of total retail sales in 1992 to 6.4 percent in 2009. (Table 17-9) E-commerce alone grew from 0.6 percent of total retail sales at the end of 1999 to 4.1 percent at the end of 2009. (Table 17-10)

Table 17-1. Petroleum and Petroleum Products—Prices, Imports, Domestic Production, and Stocks

(Not seasonally adjusted.)

Year and month	Crude oil futures price (dollars per barrel) Current dollars	Crude oil futures price (dollars per barrel) 2005 dollars	Imports Total energy-related petroleum products (thousands of barrels)	Imports Crude petroleum Thousands of barrels Total	Imports Crude petroleum Thousands of barrels Average per day	Imports Crude petroleum Unit price (dollars per barrel)	Supply Petroleum and products Exports	Supply Petroleum and products Imports	Supply Petroleum and products Net imports	Supply Domestic production Crude oil	Supply Domestic production Natural gas plant liquids	Stocks Crude oil and petroleum products	Stocks Crude petroleum Total	Stocks Crude petroleum Strategic petroleum reserve
1955	...	...	...	...	...	...	368	1 248	880	6 807	771	715	266	...
1956	...	...	...	...	...	...	430	1 436	1 006	7 151	800	780	266	...
1957	...	...	...	...	...	...	568	1 574	1 006	7 170	808	841	282	...
1958	...	...	...	...	...	...	276	1 700	1 424	6 710	808	789	263	...
1959	...	...	...	...	...	...	211	1 780	1 569	7 054	879	809	257	...
1960	...	...	...	...	...	...	202	1 815	1 613	7 035	929	785	240	...
1961	...	...	...	...	...	...	174	1 917	1 743	7 183	991	825	245	...
1962	...	...	...	...	...	...	168	2 082	1 914	7 332	1 021	834	252	...
1963	...	...	...	...	...	...	208	2 123	1 915	7 542	1 098	836	237	...
1964	...	...	...	...	...	...	202	2 259	2 057	7 614	1 154	839	230	...
1965	...	...	...	...	...	...	187	2 468	2 281	7 804	1 210	836	220	...
1966	...	...	...	...	...	...	198	2 573	2 375	8 295	1 284	874	238	...
1967	...	...	...	...	...	...	307	2 537	2 230	8 810	1 409	944	249	...
1968	...	...	...	...	...	...	231	2 840	2 609	9 096	1 504	1 000	272	...
1969	...	...	...	...	...	...	233	3 166	2 933	9 238	1 590	980	265	...
1970	...	...	...	...	...	...	259	3 419	3 160	9 637	1 660	1 018	276	...
1971	...	...	...	...	...	...	224	3 926	3 702	9 463	1 693	1 044	260	...
1972	...	...	...	...	...	...	222	4 741	4 519	9 441	1 744	959	246	...
1973	...	...	...	1 392 970	3 816	3.30	231	6 256	6 025	9 208	1 738	1 008	242	...
1974	...	...	...	1 367 081	3 745	11.17	221	6 112	5 892	8 774	1 688	1 074	265	...
1975	...	...	...	1 584 730	4 342	11.59	209	6 056	5 846	8 375	1 633	1 133	271	...
1976	...	...	...	2 050 424	5 618	12.43	223	7 313	7 090	8 132	1 604	1 112	285	...
1977	...	...	...	2 519 806	6 904	13.33	243	8 807	8 565	8 245	1 618	1 312	348	7
1978	...	...	...	2 392 350	6 554	13.43	362	8 363	8 002	8 707	1 567	1 278	376	67
1979	...	...	...	2 467 315	6 760	18.68	471	8 456	7 985	8 552	1 584	1 341	430	91
1980	...	...	...	1 977 247	5 417	31.36	544	6 909	6 365	8 597	1 573	1 392	466	108
1981	...	...	...	1 763 072	4 830	35.13	595	5 996	5 401	8 572	1 609	1 484	594	230
1982	...	...	...	1 420 753	3 892	33.39	815	5 113	4 298	8 649	1 550	1 430	644	294
1983	30.66	54.83	...	1 293 819	3 545	29.51	739	5 051	4 312	8 688	1 559	1 454	723	379
1984	29.44	50.73	...	1 319 683	3 616	27.68	722	5 437	4 715	8 879	1 630	1 556	796	451
1985	27.89	46.53	...	1 260 856	3 454	26.20	781	5 067	4 286	8 971	1 609	1 519	814	493
1986	15.05	24.51	...	1 634 567	4 478	13.90	785	6 224	5 439	8 680	1 551	1 593	843	512
1987	19.15	30.12	...	1 744 977	4 781	16.80	764	6 678	5 914	8 349	1 595	1 607	890	541
1988	15.96	24.14	...	1 887 860	5 172	13.69	815	7 402	6 587	8 140	1 625	1 597	890	560
1989	19.58	28.38	...	2 146 552	5 881	16.49	859	8 061	7 202	7 613	1 546	1 581	921	580
1990	24.50	33.96	...	2 216 604	6 073	19.75	857	8 018	7 161	7 355	1 559	1 621	908	586
1991	21.50	28.76	2 828 953	2 146 064	5 880	17.46	1 001	7 627	6 626	7 417	1 659	1 617	893	569
1992	20.58	26.74	2 947 582	2 294 570	6 269	16.80	950	7 888	6 938	7 171	1 697	1 592	893	575
1993	18.48	23.50	3 257 008	2 543 374	6 968	15.13	1 003	8 620	7 618	6 847	1 736	1 647	922	587
1994	17.19	21.42	3 416 045	2 704 196	7 409	14.23	942	8 996	8 054	6 662	1 727	1 653	929	592
1995	18.40	22.43	3 361 882	2 767 312	7 582	15.81	949	8 835	7 886	6 560	1 762	1 563	895	592
1996	22.03	26.28	3 622 385	2 893 647	7 906	18.98	981	9 478	8 498	6 465	1 830	1 507	850	566
1997	20.61	24.13	3 802 574	3 069 430	8 409	17.67	1 003	10 162	9 158	6 452	1 817	1 560	868	563
1998	14.40	16.70	4 088 027	3 242 711	8 884	11.49	945	10 708	9 764	6 252	1 759	1 647	895	571
1999	19.30	22.03	4 081 181	3 228 092	8 844	15.76	940	10 852	9 912	5 881	1 850	1 493	852	567
2000	30.26	33.71	4 314 825	3 399 239	9 288	26.44	1 040	11 459	10 419	5 822	1 911	1 468	826	541
2001	25.95	28.36	4 475 026	3 471 067	9 510	21.40	971	11 871	10 900	5 801	1 868	1 586	862	550
2002	26.15	28.20	4 337 075	3 418 022	9 364	22.61	984	11 530	10 546	5 746	1 880	1 548	877	599
2003	30.99	32.75	4 654 638	3 676 005	10 071	26.98	1 027	12 264	11 238	5 681	1 719	1 568	907	638
2004	41.47	42.71	4 917 591	3 820 979	10 440	34.48	1 048	13 145	12 097	5 419	1 809	1 645	961	676
2005	56.70	56.70	5 004 339	3 754 671	10 287	46.81	1 165	13 714	12 549	5 178	1 717	1 698	1 008	685
2006	66.25	64.48	4 880 734	3 734 226	10 231	58.01	1 317	13 707	12 390	5 102	1 739	1 720	1 001	689
2007	72.41	68.63	4 807 811	3 690 568	10 111	64.28	1 433	13 468	12 036	5 064	1 783	1 665	983	697
2008	99.75	91.49	4 613 444	3 590 628	9 810	95.22	1 802	12 915	11 114	4 950	1 784	1 737	1 028	702
2009	62.09	56.84	4 263 292	3 311 883	9 074	56.92	2 026	11 726	9 700	5 310	1 886	1 776	1 052	727
2009														
January	41.92	38.72	404 658	300 137	9 682	39.81	1 927	13 173	11 246	5 246	1 721	1 762	1 057	704
February	39.26	36.15	335 912	254 874	8 789	39.22	1 822	12 190	10 369	5 191	1 792	1 770	1 060	706
March	48.06	44.30	377 470	289 693	9 345	41.36	1 838	12 474	10 636	5 270	1 850	1 795	1 079	713
April	49.95	46.01	367 943	292 601	9 753	46.60	1 900	11 973	10 073	5 228	1 851	1 812	1 089	719
May	59.21	54.50	338 081	261 888	8 448	51.21	2 015	11 596	9 581	5 283	1 934	1 829	1 084	722
June	69.70	63.81	369 963	280 424	9 347	59.17	1 963	11 902	9 939	5 183	1 901	1 839	1 073	724
July	64.29	58.85	377 218	296 274	9 557	62.48	2 348	12 053	9 704	5 233	1 884	1 842	1 071	724
August	71.14	64.91	338 539	268 429	8 659	64.75	2 119	11 243	9 124	5 286	1 896	1 828	1 061	724
September	69.47	63.33	361 956	286 217	9 541	68.17	2 105	11 721	9 616	5 444	1 941	1 845	1 060	725
October	75.82	68.93	329 245	258 829	8 349	67.39	2 223	10 856	8 633	5 422	1 953	1 822	1 058	725
November	78.15	70.92	314 238	245 448	8 182	72.54	2 029	11 080	9 051	5 466	1 970	1 814	1 063	726
December	74.60	67.59	348 069	277 069	8 938	73.20	1 996	10 487	8 490	5 460	1 937	1 776	1 052	727

... = Not available.

Table 17-2. New Construction Put in Place

(Billions of dollars, monthly data are at seasonally adjusted annual rates.)

Year and month	Total	Private											
		Total [1]	Residential	Office	Commercial		Health care	Educational	Amuse-ment and recreation	Transpor-tation	Commu-nication	Power	Manu-facturing
					Total [1]	Multi-retail							
1975	152.6	109.3	51.6	...	...	...	...	...	...	...	...	...	...
1976	172.1	128.2	68.3	...	...	...	...	...	...	...	...	...	...
1977	200.5	157.4	92.0	...	...	...	...	...	...	...	...	...	...
1978	239.9	189.7	109.8	...	...	...	...	...	...	...	...	...	...
1979	272.9	216.2	116.4	...	...	...	...	...	...	...	...	...	...
1980	273.9	210.3	100.4	...	...	...	...	...	...	...	...	...	...
1981	289.1	224.4	99.2	...	...	...	...	...	...	...	...	...	...
1982	279.3	216.3	84.7	...	...	...	...	...	...	...	...	...	...
1983	311.9	248.4	125.8	...	...	...	...	...	...	...	...	...	...
1984	370.2	300.0	155.0	...	...	...	...	...	...	...	...	...	...
1985	403.4	325.6	160.5	...	...	...	...	...	...	...	...	...	...
1986	433.5	348.9	190.7	...	...	...	...	...	...	...	...	...	...
1987	446.6	356.0	199.7	...	...	...	...	...	...	...	...	...	...
1988	462.0	367.3	204.5	...	...	...	...	...	...	...	...	...	...
1989	477.5	379.3	204.3	...	...	...	...	...	...	...	...	...	...
1990	476.8	369.3	191.1	...	...	...	...	...	...	...	...	...	...
1991	432.6	322.5	166.3	...	...	...	...	...	...	...	...	...	...
1992	463.7	347.8	199.4	...	...	...	...	...	...	...	...	...	...
1993	485.5	358.2	208.2	20.0	34.4	11.5	14.9	4.8	4.6	4.7	9.8	23.6	23.4
1994	531.9	401.5	241.0	20.4	39.6	12.2	15.4	5.0	5.1	4.7	10.1	21.0	28.8
1995	548.7	408.7	228.1	23.0	44.1	12.0	15.3	5.7	5.9	4.8	11.1	22.0	35.4
1996	599.7	453.0	257.5	26.5	49.4	13.3	15.4	7.0	7.0	5.8	11.8	17.4	38.1
1997	631.9	478.4	264.7	32.8	53.1	12.2	17.4	8.8	8.5	6.2	12.5	16.4	37.6
1998	688.5	533.7	296.3	40.4	55.7	13.3	17.7	9.8	8.6	7.3	12.5	21.7	40.5
1999	744.6	575.5	326.3	45.1	59.4	15.2	18.4	9.8	9.6	6.5	18.4	22.0	35.1
2000	802.8	621.4	346.1	52.4	64.1	14.9	19.5	11.7	8.8	6.9	18.8	29.3	37.6
2001	840.2	638.3	364.4	49.7	63.6	16.4	19.5	12.8	7.8	7.1	19.6	31.5	37.8
2002	847.9	634.4	396.7	35.3	59.0	15.6	22.4	13.1	7.5	6.8	18.4	32.6	22.7
2003	891.5	675.4	446.0	30.6	57.5	15.4	24.2	13.4	7.8	6.6	14.5	33.6	21.4
2004	991.6	771.4	532.9	32.9	63.2	18.8	26.3	12.7	8.4	6.8	15.5	27.4	23.7
2005	1 102.7	868.5	611.9	37.3	66.6	22.8	28.5	12.8	7.5	7.1	18.8	26.3	29.9
2006	1 167.6	912.2	613.7	45.7	73.4	29.2	32.0	13.8	9.3	8.7	22.2	31.2	35.1
2007	1 150.7	861.6	493.2	53.8	85.9	34.8	35.6	16.7	10.2	9.0	27.5	47.4	45.3
2008	1 072.1	766.2	350.1	57.1	81.5	32.2	39.1	18.6	10.3	9.9	25.5	68.7	60.8
2009	935.6	619.3	251.4	40.3	53.7	20.8	36.8	16.6	7.7	9.1	20.2	76.7	74.1
2007													
January	1 149.7	869.6	549.6	51.8	77.9	30.8	34.6	15.0	9.0	7.7	23.8	33.3	37.0
February	1 156.1	881.1	548.6	51.2	80.4	31.6	35.3	15.4	8.7	8.2	26.6	37.5	38.5
March	1 165.8	887.4	548.6	53.6	80.9	33.5	35.0	15.0	9.8	8.6	26.8	38.4	37.7
April	1 159.1	877.4	532.2	51.5	83.5	33.6	35.0	15.8	9.6	9.0	25.7	39.6	40.7
May	1 167.2	877.8	520.7	52.7	87.6	37.0	35.0	16.0	9.9	8.6	27.6	43.9	39.7
June	1 163.6	875.5	509.3	52.4	88.1	35.2	34.8	16.9	10.0	9.2	28.1	47.5	42.0
July	1 152.9	864.0	494.5	51.8	86.7	33.6	35.1	17.5	10.4	9.1	26.9	47.8	46.4
August	1 157.0	863.5	482.5	54.5	88.7	34.9	35.9	17.5	11.0	9.6	28.5	51.6	45.4
September	1 161.5	864.1	472.3	55.6	88.6	36.2	36.4	17.5	10.6	9.4	28.7	50.8	54.1
October	1 149.4	853.5	447.8	56.8	88.9	35.8	36.7	17.7	10.9	9.5	28.7	58.0	55.7
November	1 124.6	825.7	426.5	57.0	88.6	37.3	36.5	17.6	11.3	9.6	28.1	58.8	49.4
December	1 106.9	810.2	410.3	56.6	85.8	35.3	36.3	17.7	11.0	9.4	29.5	58.0	54.2
2008													
January	1 095.5	802.8	396.6	57.9	88.1	35.7	36.2	18.4	10.8	9.9	29.2	61.2	52.9
February	1 092.1	797.6	385.8	58.0	88.2	34.7	37.0	18.1	10.7	10.7	28.6	63.7	54.3
March	1 095.2	791.0	383.1	56.6	85.1	32.3	37.4	17.9	10.7	10.4	29.5	62.9	53.6
April	1 091.1	787.7	373.4	57.3	87.5	33.6	38.1	18.3	10.5	9.8	27.2	64.7	55.3
May	1 090.7	786.2	363.5	57.0	85.2	32.6	38.7	18.2	11.2	9.2	29.6	70.0	57.1
June	1 075.6	769.5	351.7	57.5	84.0	33.4	39.5	18.6	10.5	9.3	25.8	67.6	58.4
July	1 070.2	759.8	339.9	57.9	82.8	32.9	40.3	19.1	10.4	9.7	25.0	71.3	57.3
August	1 066.1	756.4	340.2	58.0	79.9	31.9	39.3	19.0	10.2	9.8	22.7	70.2	61.1
September	1 081.2	773.6	350.4	58.4	77.9	30.4	39.9	19.2	9.9	10.1	23.4	72.7	65.8
October	1 064.1	754.1	327.7	56.5	76.5	30.8	40.2	19.3	10.2	10.0	22.0	74.9	71.0
November	1 037.3	726.8	310.5	55.8	73.5	30.1	40.9	18.7	9.5	9.9	22.0	70.7	70.6
December	1 002.1	696.6	292.3	51.6	71.0	28.3	40.4	18.3	9.2	10.0	21.9	71.1	70.2
2009													
January	974.3	673.8	278.8	49.0	66.7	25.9	37.4	17.9	8.9	8.9	21.1	69.9	77.3
February	970.4	660.9	260.8	48.4	66.5	26.6	38.6	17.8	9.4	8.5	19.9	71.9	81.3
March	966.7	650.4	248.9	48.1	65.0	25.0	38.4	17.8	9.3	8.7	19.9	72.7	82.0
April	971.4	654.1	252.7	43.7	62.1	25.0	38.9	17.4	8.8	9.4	21.1	77.2	84.1
May	958.3	639.8	241.4	44.1	58.8	23.2	38.5	17.6	8.5	9.8	21.1	78.7	85.4
June	945.1	619.5	237.0	42.1	53.5	21.8	39.9	17.0	8.2	9.4	20.0	78.8	78.6
July	934.2	608.4	237.3	40.0	51.8	20.4	37.8	16.2	7.9	9.4	20.0	78.7	77.6
August	925.5	605.2	244.7	39.3	48.8	19.2	37.2	16.8	7.3	9.1	20.0	78.6	72.6
September	910.5	590.5	243.2	35.3	48.0	18.1	35.0	16.3	6.6	9.0	20.3	79.6	67.9
October	923.9	606.6	271.8	34.6	44.0	16.9	35.4	15.5	6.4	8.9	19.5	75.7	67.8
November	900.8	590.6	265.0	32.1	44.0	16.2	33.0	14.9	5.9	8.6	19.6	77.9	63.9
December	869.9	569.6	253.8	31.5	44.5	16.0	32.7	14.5	5.6	8.5	20.1	77.4	56.8

[1]Includes categories not shown separately.
. . . = Not available.

Table 17-2. New Construction Put in Place—*Continued*

(Billions of dollars, monthly data are at seasonally adjusted annual rates.)

Year and month	Total	Public													Federal
			State and local												
		Total [1]	Residential	Office	Health care	Educa-tional	Public safety	Amuse-ment and recreation	Transpor-tation	Power	Highway and street	Sewage and waste disposal	Water supply		
1975	43.3	37.2	...	...	...	...	...	...	...	...	...	...	...		6.1
1976	44.0	37.2	...	...	...	...	...	...	...	...	...	...	...		6.8
1977	43.1	36.0	...	...	...	...	...	...	...	...	...	...	...		7.1
1978	50.1	42.0	...	...	...	...	...	...	...	...	...	...	...		8.1
1979	56.6	48.1	...	...	...	...	...	...	...	...	...	...	...		8.6
1980	63.6	54.0	...	...	...	...	...	...	...	...	...	...	...		9.6
1981	64.7	54.3	...	...	...	...	...	...	...	...	...	...	...		10.4
1982	63.1	53.1	...	...	...	...	...	...	...	...	...	...	...		10.0
1983	63.5	52.9	...	...	...	...	...	...	...	...	...	...	...		10.6
1984	70.2	59.0	...	...	...	...	...	...	...	...	...	...	...		11.2
1985	77.8	65.8	...	...	...	...	...	...	...	...	...	...	...		12.0
1986	84.6	72.2	...	...	...	...	...	...	...	...	...	...	...		12.4
1987	90.6	76.6	...	...	...	...	...	...	...	...	...	...	...		14.1
1988	94.7	82.5	...	...	...	...	...	...	...	...	...	...	...		12.3
1989	98.2	86.0	...	...	...	...	...	...	...	...	...	...	...		12.2
1990	107.5	95.4	...	...	...	...	...	...	...	...	...	...	...		12.1
1991	110.1	97.3	...	...	...	...	...	...	...	...	...	...	...		12.8
1992	115.8	101.5													14.4
1993	127.4	112.9	3.4	2.8	2.3	24.2	4.6	4.3	9.8	7.4	34.5	11.2	6.4		14.4
1994	130.4	116.0	4.2	3.0	2.4	25.3	4.5	4.7	9.2	5.1	37.3	12.0	6.4		14.4
1995	140.0	124.3	4.5	3.3	2.6	27.5	5.0	5.1	9.6	5.7	38.6	13.0	7.3		15.8
1996	146.7	131.4	3.7	3.6	2.8	31.0	5.5	5.0	10.4	4.8	40.6	13.6	7.7		15.3
1997	153.4	139.4	3.3	3.8	2.9	34.3	5.6	5.7	10.3	4.4	44.4	13.1	8.1		14.1
1998	154.8	140.5	3.2	3.7	2.3	35.1	6.1	6.2	10.5	2.8	45.4	13.2	8.9		14.3
1999	169.1	155.1	3.2	3.6	2.5	39.8	6.2	7.2	11.4	2.9	51.0	14.5	9.6		14.0
2000	181.3	167.2	3.0	4.5	2.8	46.8	5.9	7.6	13.0	5.5	51.6	14.0	9.5		14.2
2001	201.9	186.8	3.5	5.6	2.9	52.8	6.1	9.1	15.9	5.3	56.4	14.2	11.4		15.1
2002	213.4	196.9	3.8	6.3	3.5	59.5	6.0	9.2	17.3	3.8	56.7	15.3	11.7		16.6
2003	216.1	198.2	3.7	6.1	4.0	59.3	5.8	8.4	16.5	6.8	56.3	15.6	11.7		17.9
2004	220.2	201.8	4.1	6.0	5.0	59.7	5.5	7.8	16.4	7.0	57.4	17.1	12.0		18.3
2005	234.2	216.9	4.0	5.2	5.1	65.8	6.0	7.3	16.3	8.3	63.2	18.3	13.5		17.3
2006	255.4	237.8	4.3	5.6	5.6	69.8	6.6	9.4	17.7	7.8	71.0	21.5	14.3		17.6
2007	289.1	268.5	5.1	7.2	7.0	78.4	8.4	10.7	21.1	11.4	75.5	23.3	15.0		20.6
2008	306.0	282.1	4.8	8.4	7.1	83.8	9.6	10.8	21.8	10.6	80.8	23.8	15.8		21.4
2009	316.3	288.5	6.0	9.2	7.1	83.8	9.4	10.6	24.3	10.9	83.7	23.9	15.1		27.0
2007															
January	280.1	259.2	4.5	5.9	6.3	73.4	7.8	10.3	19.3	11.1	77.6	23.2	14.8		20.9
February	275.1	255.9	4.6	6.1	6.3	71.9	7.7	9.9	19.1	10.9	75.5	24.0	15.2		19.1
March	278.4	259.6	4.9	7.2	6.6	74.0	8.2	10.2	18.6	12.5	74.8	22.1	15.7		18.8
April	281.7	262.8	5.3	6.6	6.8	76.3	8.1	10.4	19.6	12.1	74.6	23.0	15.7		18.9
May	289.4	268.9	5.3	7.3	7.2	78.5	8.3	11.2	20.6	11.7	74.8	23.0	16.0		20.5
June	288.1	266.9	5.5	7.1	7.0	79.6	8.5	10.0	20.6	10.5	74.5	22.9	15.4		21.1
July	288.8	267.6	5.4	7.3	7.2	79.8	8.7	11.2	22.6	11.5	71.2	22.8	14.5		21.3
August	293.4	271.1	5.5	7.8	7.6	79.7	8.6	11.3	21.8	10.2	75.1	23.1	15.0		22.3
September	297.3	276.2	5.1	7.4	7.1	80.0	8.8	11.4	22.2	11.9	76.9	24.2	15.3		21.1
October	295.9	275.4	5.1	8.2	7.6	79.8	8.4	10.8	22.9	11.2	76.3	24.1	15.0		20.6
November	298.9	277.9	4.9	7.9	7.4	83.0	9.1	10.4	22.4	11.7	77.7	23.9	14.1		21.0
December	296.7	276.1	4.9	7.9	7.0	82.1	8.9	10.5	22.2	12.8	77.3	23.7	13.5		20.6
2008															
January	292.7	271.3	4.7	7.3	6.9	81.9	9.3	10.7	21.4	11.5	76.0	23.3	12.9		21.4
February	294.5	272.8	4.5	7.8	6.9	79.2	9.3	10.8	22.1	11.8	76.4	23.6	15.3		21.7
March	304.2	283.1	4.4	8.0	7.3	82.6	9.7	10.9	22.0	11.9	82.4	23.5	15.0		21.1
April	303.4	280.7	4.4	8.1	7.0	83.4	9.4	11.0	21.5	11.2	81.7	23.4	14.8		22.7
May	304.5	281.6	4.7	8.3	7.1	85.4	9.8	11.2	21.5	11.3	78.2	23.4	16.1		22.8
June	306.1	283.4	4.9	8.7	6.8	85.3	9.6	10.9	22.4	11.3	78.6	23.4	16.7		22.7
July	310.4	285.5	5.1	8.9	7.2	85.1	9.7	10.6	22.7	10.3	80.2	23.9	17.2		24.9
August	309.7	284.9	5.0	8.5	7.3	85.8	9.6	10.6	22.2	10.4	81.8	23.2	16.0		24.8
September	307.6	283.9	5.2	8.8	7.1	83.7	9.8	11.0	21.9	10.0	82.5	23.9	16.1		23.6
October	310.0	285.1	5.3	8.7	7.2	83.8	9.9	10.8	22.4	9.6	82.5	24.6	16.1		25.0
November	310.5	284.3	5.0	8.7	7.0	83.9	10.0	10.7	21.8	9.8	82.1	24.7	16.7		26.2
December	305.6	277.3	4.8	9.3	6.9	81.7	9.6	10.7	20.7	8.4	80.0	24.7	16.4		28.3
2009															
January	300.4	273.4	5.2	9.0	6.9	83.8	9.1	10.2	20.8	8.3	78.4	23.4	14.6		27.0
February	309.5	282.1	5.5	9.3	7.2	85.7	9.4	10.5	20.7	10.1	80.6	23.3	15.4		27.5
March	316.3	289.1	5.4	9.2	7.3	89.4	9.6	10.4	21.1	11.9	78.6	26.1	15.4		27.2
April	317.2	291.7	5.7	9.7	7.1	88.8	10.0	10.7	21.8	13.7	79.5	25.0	15.4		25.5
May	318.5	291.5	5.8	8.8	7.7	87.9	10.2	10.6	22.9	12.8	80.6	24.5	15.0		27.0
June	325.6	296.5	6.4	9.1	7.7	88.5	10.1	11.1	23.8	12.3	83.6	23.7	15.6		29.1
July	325.8	295.9	6.7	9.3	7.3	86.7	9.5	10.9	26.4	10.9	84.5	23.1	15.9		29.9
August	320.4	292.7	6.3	9.2	6.9	84.1	9.2	10.7	26.2	12.1	84.9	23.4	15.2		27.7
September	320.0	292.3	6.4	9.3	7.2	80.7	9.2	10.8	26.9	11.0	87.4	23.8	15.0		27.7
October	317.3	287.7	6.1	9.4	6.9	79.3	8.9	10.8	25.7	9.6	88.7	23.2	14.6		29.6
November	310.1	280.5	6.1	9.3	6.5	77.4	8.9	10.2	25.3	8.9	83.4	24.6	15.4		29.6
December	300.2	274.3	6.5	9.1	6.6	75.9	9.1	9.7	24.8	8.3	81.1	24.3	14.8		25.9

[1] Includes categories not shown separately.
. . . = Not available.

Table 17-3. Housing Starts and Building Permits; New House Sales and Prices

Year and month	Started (not seasonally adjusted) Total [1]	One-family structures	Five units or more	Seasonally adjusted annual rate — Started Total [1]	One-family structures	Five units or more	Authorized by building permits [2] Total [1]	One-family structures	Five units or more	Shipments of manufac-tured homes (thousands, seasonally adjusted annual rate)	Sold (thousands, annual rate)	For sale, end-of-period (thousands)	Median sales price (dollars)	Price index (2005 = 100)
1975	1 160	892	204	1 160	892	204	939	676	200	213	549	316	39 300	22.1
1976	1 538	1 162	289	1 538	1 162	289	1 296	894	310	246	646	358	44 200	24.0
1977	1 987	1 451	414	1 987	1 451	414	1 690	1 126	443	266	819	408	48 800	27.0
1978	2 020	1 433	462	2 020	1 433	462	1 801	1 183	487	276	817	419	55 700	30.9
1979	1 745	1 194	429	1 745	1 194	429	1 552	982	445	277	709	402	62 900	35.3
1980	1 292	852	331	1 292	852	331	1 191	710	366	222	545	342	64 600	38.9
1981	1 084	705	288	1 084	705	288	986	564	319	241	436	278	68 900	42.0
1982	1 062	663	320	1 062	663	320	1 001	546	366	240	412	255	69 300	43.0
1983	1 703	1 068	522	1 703	1 068	522	1 605	902	570	296	623	304	75 300	43.9
1984	1 750	1 084	544	1 750	1 084	544	1 682	922	617	295	639	358	79 900	45.7
1985	1 742	1 072	576	1 742	1 072	576	1 733	957	657	284	688	350	84 300	46.2
1986	1 805	1 179	542	1 805	1 179	542	1 769	1 078	584	244	750	361	92 000	48.0
1987	1 621	1 146	409	1 621	1 146	409	1 535	1 024	421	233	671	370	104 500	50.6
1988	1 488	1 081	348	1 488	1 081	348	1 456	994	386	218	676	371	112 500	52.5
1989	1 376	1 003	318	1 376	1 003	318	1 338	932	340	198	650	366	120 000	54.6
1990	1 193	895	260	1 193	895	260	1 111	794	263	188	534	321	122 900	55.7
1991	1 014	840	138	1 014	840	138	949	754	152	171	509	284	120 000	56.4
1992	1 200	1 030	139	1 200	1 030	139	1 095	911	138	211	610	267	121 500	57.2
1993	1 288	1 126	133	1 288	1 126	133	1 199	987	160	254	666	295	126 500	59.4
1994	1 457	1 198	224	1 457	1 198	224	1 372	1 069	241	304	670	340	130 000	62.9
1995	1 354	1 076	244	1 354	1 076	244	1 333	997	272	340	667	374	133 900	64.3
1996	1 477	1 161	271	1 477	1 161	271	1 426	1 070	290	363	757	326	140 000	66.0
1997	1 474	1 134	296	1 474	1 134	296	1 441	1 062	310	354	804	287	146 000	67.5
1998	1 617	1 271	303	1 617	1 271	303	1 612	1 188	356	373	886	300	152 500	69.2
1999	1 641	1 302	307	1 641	1 302	307	1 664	1 247	351	348	880	315	161 000	72.8
2000	1 569	1 231	299	1 569	1 231	299	1 592	1 198	329	250	877	301	169 000	75.6
2001	1 603	1 273	293	1 603	1 273	293	1 637	1 236	335	193	908	310	175 200	77.9
2002	1 705	1 359	308	1 705	1 359	308	1 748	1 333	341	169	973	344	187 600	81.4
2003	1 848	1 499	315	1 848	1 499	315	1 889	1 461	346	131	1 086	377	195 000	86.0
2004	1 956	1 611	303	1 956	1 611	303	2 070	1 613	366	131	1 203	431	221 000	92.8
2005	2 068	1 716	311	2 068	1 716	311	2 155	1 682	389	147	1 283	515	240 900	100.0
2006	1 801	1 465	293	1 801	1 465	293	1 839	1 378	384	117	1 051	537	246 500	104.8
2007	1 355	1 046	277	1 355	1 046	277	1 398	980	359	96	776	496	247 900	104.9
2008	906	622	266	906	622	266	905	576	295	82	485	352	232 100	99.5
2009	554	445	97	554	445	97	583	441	121	50	375	232	216 700	95.1
2007														
January	95	75	18	1 409	1 130	256	1 626	1 174	382	97	891	538	254 400	. . .
February	103	83	18	1 480	1 189	262	1 598	1 136	392	97	828	544	250 800	. . .
March	124	101	20	1 495	1 202	256	1 596	1 147	380	98	833	545	262 600	107.2
April	136	111	21	1 490	1 197	256	1 470	1 058	352	98	887	548	242 500	. . .
May	137	111	22	1 415	1 130	252	1 493	1 042	387	97	842	545	245 000	. . .
June	138	110	24	1 448	1 131	279	1 407	995	355	98	793	542	235 500	105.9
July	128	100	24	1 354	1 042	273	1 361	978	326	96	778	537	246 200	. . .
August	121	87	31	1 330	957	336	1 321	916	348	94	699	533	236 500	. . .
September	102	79	20	1 183	935	219	1 261	855	356	93	686	527	240 300	103.0
October	115	77	34	1 264	878	347	1 192	821	321	94	727	514	234 300	. . .
November	89	59	28	1 197	833	343	1 224	795	377	93	641	503	249 100	. . .
December	69	52	16	1 037	805	221	1 149	742	350	92	619	497	227 700	102.1
2008														
January	71	49	20	1 084	773	285	1 094	708	344	94	608	486	232 400	. . .
February	78	52	25	1 103	724	350	1 014	664	309	97	576	477	245 300	. . .
March	82	62	20	1 005	728	261	967	642	287	93	509	471	229 300	98.8
April	90	63	26	1 013	682	316	1 008	661	306	91	533	460	246 400	. . .
May	92	66	24	973	679	275	995	633	326	87	509	453	229 300	. . .
June	103	65	35	1 046	647	378	1 180	605	540	83	488	436	234 300	102.2
July	87	60	26	923	615	294	921	571	316	82	500	419	237 300	. . .
August	76	54	21	844	607	222	858	543	282	79	444	412	221 000	. . .
September	74	49	23	820	537	263	797	529	232	75	436	395	225 200	100.2
October	68	46	21	777	542	225	736	469	234	69	409	380	213 200	. . .
November	48	31	15	652	459	175	626	420	186	66	390	370	221 600	. . .
December	38	26	11	560	403	149	554	364	169	63	374	350	229 600	95.7
2009														
January	32	23	8	488	360	115	549	343	184	54	329	340	208 600	. . .
February	40	25	14	581	362	205	566	386	159	52	354	328	209 700	. . .
March	43	31	10	520	363	126	522	371	130	51	332	313	205 100	92.7
April	43	35	7	477	386	80	523	395	108	49	345	300	219 200	. . .
May	52	40	12	550	406	135	550	425	103	50	371	293	222 300	. . .
June	59	49	9	583	476	96	600	451	124	48	399	280	214 700	96.2
July	57	49	6	587	500	72	587	479	89	51	419	270	214 200	. . .
August	53	43	9	585	482	96	610	482	108	48	408	262	207 100	. . .
September	53	46	6	586	507	70	605	473	112	48	391	252	216 600	94.3
October	45	39	5	529	475	49	576	468	92	48	400	242	215 100	. . .
November	42	35	6	589	504	76	621	489	106	49	362	236	218 800	. . .
December	37	30	6	576	486	78	681	517	145	49	353	231	222 600	96.2

[1] Includes structures with 2 to 4 units, not shown separately.
[2] Data beginning with 2004 cover 20,000 permit-issuing places; 1994 through 2003: 19,000 places; 1984 through 1993: 17,000 places; 1978 through 1983: 16,000 places; 1972 through 1977: 14,000 places; 1971: 13,000 places.
. . . = Not available.

Table 17-4. Manufacturers' Shipments

(Millions of dollars, seasonally adjusted.)

Year and month	Total	Total durable goods [1]	Total nondurable goods [1]	By topical categories								
				Construction materials and supplies	Information technology industries	Capital goods				Consumer goods		
						Total	Nondefense		Defense	Total	Durable	Nondurable
							Total	Excluding aircraft and parts				
1992	2 904 024	1 518 862	1 385 162	281 232	236 015	566 268	471 485	435 696	94 783	1 098 480	253 111	845 369
1993	3 020 497	1 604 544	1 415 953	303 391	241 680	580 859	493 875	463 753	86 984	1 127 629	274 813	852 816
1994	3 238 112	1 764 061	1 474 051	332 734	264 092	616 435	538 203	512 327	78 232	1 192 098	314 931	877 167
1995	3 479 677	1 902 815	1 576 862	353 198	291 885	666 167	590 578	565 729	75 589	1 256 611	324 036	932 575
1996	3 597 188	1 978 597	1 618 591	371 401	311 028	704 635	630 932	605 295	73 703	1 292 955	328 402	964 553
1997	3 834 699	2 147 384	1 687 315	399 880	349 846	779 232	702 971	665 074	76 261	1 358 516	360 193	998 323
1998	3 899 813	2 231 588	1 668 225	418 756	362 564	821 736	747 046	695 717	74 690	1 351 812	373 404	978 408
1999	4 031 887	2 326 736	1 705 151	434 138	374 384	839 754	768 799	713 042	70 955	1 424 828	412 646	1 012 182
2000	4 208 584	2 373 688	1 834 896	444 812	399 751	875 396	808 345	757 617	67 051	1 500 532	391 463	1 109 069
2001	3 970 499	2 174 406	1 796 093	424 517	353 237	801 999	728 466	678 229	73 533	1 480 495	367 522	1 112 973
2002	3 914 723	2 123 621	1 791 102	424 008	284 799	728 585	652 500	609 654	76 085	1 494 575	395 953	1 098 622
2003	4 015 388	2 142 589	1 872 799	429 183	274 829	719 602	633 878	600 699	85 724	1 584 329	418 821	1 165 508
2004	4 308 970	2 264 667	2 044 303	463 148	287 837	752 905	661 217	629 207	91 688	1 700 835	419 182	1 281 653
2005	4 742 077	2 424 844	2 317 233	509 865	295 447	821 906	729 862	686 827	92 044	1 895 119	422 555	1 472 564
2006	5 019 962	2 560 891	2 459 071	545 973	320 307	885 526	795 525	745 209	90 001	1 988 697	421 854	1 566 843
2007	5 081 075	2 562 863	2 518 212	533 380	322 058	889 599	796 439	739 632	93 160	2 037 553	418 456	1 619 097
2008	5 183 142	2 493 610	2 689 532	520 076	320 586	907 439	800 133	748 842	107 306	2 120 604	354 114	1 766 490
2009	4 375 395	2 095 220	2 280 175	455 094	297 448	813 083	687 842	636 823	125 241	1 747 958	263 156	1 484 802
2006												
January	419 915	211 758	208 157	46 666	26 281	71 657	64 023	60 394	7 634	168 651	36 246	132 405
February	417 408	214 994	202 414	46 997	26 519	72 771	65 695	60 928	7 076	163 530	35 844	127 686
March	422 496	215 752	206 744	46 682	26 726	74 203	66 660	62 348	7 543	168 833	36 403	132 430
April	418 061	210 843	207 218	45 561	26 934	73 090	65 448	62 137	7 642	168 353	35 645	132 708
May	427 467	217 287	210 180	45 899	27 110	74 489	67 024	62 749	7 465	171 590	36 903	134 687
June	425 586	216 957	208 629	45 789	27 090	74 345	66 768	62 546	7 577	169 836	36 537	133 299
July	416 620	207 165	209 455	44 546	26 631	73 118	65 931	62 105	7 187	166 506	31 604	134 902
August	423 869	214 447	209 422	45 230	27 165	74 937	67 388	63 250	7 549	167 805	33 950	133 855
September	410 395	211 742	198 653	44 703	26 902	74 540	67 180	62 443	7 360	158 516	33 433	125 083
October	406 762	209 855	196 907	44 397	25 708	73 403	65 744	61 482	7 659	157 402	33 378	124 024
November	410 229	211 387	198 842	44 203	26 954	74 405	66 790	62 463	7 615	159 813	33 536	126 277
December	421 917	218 144	203 773	46 068	26 421	74 545	66 805	62 827	7 740	166 443	36 722	129 721
2007												
January	410 507	210 801	199 706	44 853	26 064	71 820	64 072	59 204	7 748	160 721	33 732	126 989
February	414 107	211 583	202 524	44 668	27 299	72 613	64 783	60 427	7 830	163 679	34 464	129 215
March	421 793	214 722	207 071	45 206	26 747	73 310	65 788	61 423	7 522	168 069	35 208	132 861
April	423 940	215 725	208 215	45 355	26 772	73 833	66 213	61 588	7 620	168 906	35 598	133 308
May	427 839	217 610	210 229	45 661	26 926	74 194	66 464	61 943	7 730	170 295	35 786	134 509
June	422 345	214 854	207 491	44 838	26 973	74 073	66 592	61 869	7 481	168 706	35 776	132 930
July	423 309	214 302	209 007	44 721	25 708	73 251	65 167	60 212	8 084	169 663	35 685	133 978
August	422 170	215 676	206 494	44 315	26 858	75 967	68 080	62 531	7 887	166 990	35 605	131 385
September	420 192	211 234	208 958	43 487	27 309	75 388	67 652	62 969	7 681	172 295	34 271	134 248
October	425 742	211 466	214 276	43 713	26 889	75 050	67 369	62 020	7 681	172 295	34 441	137 854
November	435 012	212 164	222 848	43 636	26 858	74 826	66 860	61 941	7 966	179 813	33 848	145 965
December	435 601	213 247	222 354	42 823	27 559	76 207	68 187	63 739	8 020	180 340	33 841	146 499
2008												
January	439 923	215 887	224 036	43 442	27 779	77 280	68 622	62 655	8 658	180 767	34 027	146 740
February	434 265	212 974	221 291	44 189	26 711	74 546	66 242	61 700	8 304	178 507	33 193	145 314
March	439 275	212 170	227 105	44 000	27 189	75 959	67 297	63 223	8 662	180 674	31 051	149 623
April	448 658	214 371	234 287	44 230	27 353	77 082	67 790	63 112	9 292	186 465	30 622	155 843
May	449 729	213 192	236 537	43 994	27 814	77 151	68 085	63 582	9 066	187 466	30 220	157 246
June	452 979	212 691	240 288	44 369	27 183	77 172	68 183	63 645	8 989	189 244	29 878	159 366
July	457 116	214 430	242 686	44 304	27 013	77 441	68 364	63 125	9 077	190 666	29 519	161 147
August	440 921	206 941	233 980	43 742	26 460	75 668	66 686	62 419	8 982	182 075	28 444	153 631
September	429 156	206 450	222 706	43 071	26 657	76 692	67 515	63 510	9 177	175 011	28 769	146 242
October	412 885	198 521	214 364	42 455	25 716	73 227	63 958	60 576	9 269	165 294	27 164	138 130
November	384 413	190 015	194 398	40 588	25 380	71 476	62 355	59 745	9 121	151 189	26 017	125 172
December	373 446	189 253	184 193	39 319	25 042	73 079	64 563	60 238	8 516	143 312	25 033	118 279
2009												
January	363 750	177 696	186 054	38 676	24 125	68 344	59 680	53 995	8 664	144 354	23 265	121 089
February	362 685	176 094	186 591	39 167	24 558	68 001	57 710	53 822	10 291	143 038	22 817	120 221
March	357 240	173 884	183 356	37 752	24 372	67 585	57 490	53 265	10 095	140 584	22 557	118 027
April	357 324	173 480	183 844	37 866	24 220	66 673	56 395	52 163	10 278	141 450	22 951	118 499
May	354 190	169 440	184 750	37 531	24 059	66 151	55 799	51 908	10 352	141 125	21 512	119 613
June	360 117	169 672	190 445	37 618	24 588	67 418	56 560	52 778	10 858	145 881	21 028	124 853
July	362 611	174 982	187 629	38 202	25 405	67 560	57 143	53 100	10 417	143 215	21 910	121 305
August	362 269	172 366	189 903	37 852	25 039	66 395	55 676	52 168	10 719	144 662	21 394	123 268
September	366 882	174 914	191 968	37 870	24 756	68 840	57 510	52 444	11 330	146 199	21 144	125 055
October	370 294	175 345	194 949	37 724	25 554	67 780	56 817	52 693	10 963	149 527	21 263	128 264
November	376 048	176 772	199 276	37 812	25 691	68 155	57 427	53 547	10 728	152 835	21 665	131 170
December	382 727	180 942	201 785	37 227	25 186	70 121	59 784	54 783	10 337	155 668	22 087	133 581

[1] Includes categories not shown separately.

Table 17-5. Manufacturers' Inventories

(Current cost basis, end of period; seasonally adjusted, millions of dollars.)

Year and month	Total	Total durable goods [1]	Durables total by stage of fabrication			Total nondurable goods [1]	Nondurables total by stage of fabrication		
			Materials and supplies	Work in process	Finished goods		Materials and supplies	Work in process	Finished goods
1992	378 709	238 102	69 737	104 211	64 154	140 607	53 179	23 304	64 124
1993	379 660	238 737	72 657	101 999	64 081	140 923	54 289	23 305	63 329
1994	399 910	253 141	78 573	106 556	68 012	146 769	57 161	24 383	65 225
1995	424 772	267 358	85 473	106 658	75 227	157 414	60 725	25 755	70 934
1996	430 446	272 495	86 226	110 563	75 706	157 951	59 101	26 438	72 412
1997	443 566	281 074	92 292	109 960	78 822	162 492	60 160	28 478	73 854
1998	449 065	290 700	93 629	115 235	81 836	158 365	58 223	27 044	73 098
1999	463 625	296 553	97 959	114 111	84 483	167 072	61 098	28 741	77 233
2000	481 673	306 727	106 214	111 196	89 317	174 946	61 509	30 015	83 422
2001	427 720	267 533	91 194	93 776	82 563	160 187	55 798	27 056	77 333
2002	422 724	260 265	88 512	92 231	79 522	162 459	56 593	27 793	78 073
2003	407 967	246 712	82 301	88 499	75 912	161 255	56 899	26 965	77 391
2004	440 330	264 794	92 129	90 932	81 733	175 536	61 760	29 821	83 955
2005	472 398	283 220	98 134	98 590	86 496	189 178	66 502	32 668	90 008
2006	510 865	309 320	108 592	104 910	95 818	201 545	69 816	35 968	95 761
2007	529 957	319 923	109 057	113 569	97 297	210 034	73 222	38 106	98 706
2008	541 767	342 699	115 800	130 373	96 526	199 068	68 138	36 423	94 507
2009	494 435	302 714	99 974	121 716	81 024	191 721	66 938	38 615	86 168
2006									
January	478 174	284 901	97 877	99 334	87 690	193 273	66 816	34 653	91 804
February	478 685	285 283	98 541	98 551	88 191	193 402	67 409	33 099	92 894
March	483 277	288 359	100 173	99 932	88 254	194 918	68 270	33 117	93 531
April	488 469	291 664	101 296	101 076	89 292	196 805	68 775	34 348	93 682
May	492 450	294 557	102 749	101 539	90 269	197 893	70 340	33 357	94 196
June	496 725	297 126	103 498	102 323	91 305	199 599	69 730	35 658	94 211
July	500 894	300 675	105 283	103 141	92 251	200 219	69 783	36 005	94 431
August	503 117	302 233	106 538	101 609	94 086	200 884	70 002	36 411	94 471
September	507 461	305 663	107 613	103 425	94 625	201 798	70 668	36 014	95 116
October	509 790	307 956	108 719	104 252	94 985	201 834	69 541	36 164	96 129
November	510 893	308 576	108 626	103 846	96 104	202 317	69 907	36 512	95 898
December	510 865	309 320	108 592	104 910	95 818	201 545	69 816	35 968	95 761
2007									
January	511 628	310 934	108 798	105 956	96 180	200 694	69 795	35 850	95 049
February	512 891	311 921	108 391	106 305	97 225	200 970	70 325	35 987	94 658
March	513 228	312 258	108 448	106 437	97 373	200 970	70 392	36 157	94 421
April	516 116	313 328	109 144	107 127	97 057	202 788	71 210	36 112	95 466
May	518 552	314 552	109 652	108 122	96 778	204 000	71 390	36 402	96 208
June	518 355	314 362	109 392	108 204	96 766	203 993	71 232	36 290	96 471
July	518 531	314 038	109 137	108 597	96 304	204 493	71 272	35 843	97 378
August	517 048	313 651	108 835	109 094	95 722	203 397	71 443	35 192	96 762
September	521 748	314 948	108 180	110 012	96 756	206 800	73 341	35 664	97 795
October	522 632	315 359	108 558	110 827	95 974	207 273	73 273	36 328	97 672
November	525 515	316 612	108 728	111 491	96 393	208 903	73 045	37 231	98 627
December	529 957	319 923	109 057	113 569	97 297	210 034	73 222	38 106	98 706
2008									
January	537 072	321 132	109 728	114 690	96 714	215 940	75 588	40 448	99 904
February	541 454	323 203	110 129	116 281	96 793	218 251	75 794	41 745	100 712
March	546 023	326 847	111 359	118 462	97 026	219 176	75 691	41 634	101 851
April	547 716	329 380	112 303	120 140	96 937	218 336	75 688	40 883	101 765
May	550 178	331 525	112 846	121 409	97 270	218 653	76 358	42 147	100 148
June	554 737	333 786	113 958	122 319	97 509	220 951	76 274	41 114	103 563
July	558 252	336 804	115 823	123 246	97 735	221 448	76 073	42 417	102 958
August	561 150	339 813	116 182	124 636	98 995	221 337	75 837	42 223	103 277
September	559 091	340 723	116 712	125 223	98 788	218 368	76 113	41 480	100 775
October	556 012	341 408	116 664	126 525	98 219	214 604	74 097	39 533	100 974
November	551 297	341 207	116 702	127 358	97 147	210 090	71 562	38 404	100 124
December	541 767	342 699	115 800	130 373	96 526	199 068	68 138	36 423	94 507
2009									
January	535 486	338 475	115 240	129 265	93 970	197 011	66 897	37 221	92 893
February	527 872	334 112	114 345	127 694	92 073	193 760	65 599	36 648	91 513
March	521 501	328 422	112 272	125 769	90 381	193 079	64 949	37 122	91 008
April	515 642	324 569	110 135	125 256	89 178	191 073	64 050	37 212	89 811
May	511 305	320 714	108 234	124 856	87 624	190 591	64 106	37 160	89 325
June	505 009	315 984	106 139	124 091	85 754	189 025	63 838	36 685	88 502
July	500 593	312 367	103 840	123 880	84 647	188 226	64 118	36 454	87 654
August	496 549	308 133	102 920	121 442	83 771	188 416	63 832	36 872	87 712
September	492 559	305 056	102 367	120 306	82 383	187 503	63 632	37 166	86 705
October	494 397	304 023	101 161	120 971	81 891	190 374	64 548	38 065	87 761
November	495 268	303 298	100 059	121 704	81 535	191 970	66 087	38 442	87 441
December	494 435	302 714	99 974	121 716	81 024	191 721	66 938	38 615	86 168

[1] Includes categories not shown separately.

Table 17-5. Manufacturers' Inventories—Continued

(Current cost basis, end of period; seasonally adjusted, millions of dollars.)

Year and month	Construction materials and supplies	Information technology industries	Capital goods Total	Nondefense Total	Nondefense Excluding aircraft and parts	Defense	Consumer goods Total	Durable	Nondurable
1992	36 729	40 236	120 589	97 442	78 978	23 147	103 237	20 892	82 345
1993	38 275	39 180	118 499	97 175	79 595	21 324	104 761	21 868	82 893
1994	40 894	41 551	123 438	103 396	85 733	20 042	109 516	23 980	85 536
1995	43 444	46 832	129 674	111 508	94 556	18 166	116 392	25 283	91 109
1996	44 149	43 530	132 808	115 225	93 383	17 583	116 378	24 788	91 590
1997	45 740	48 112	137 621	122 593	98 784	15 028	119 680	24 936	94 744
1998	46 506	45 384	145 203	127 187	97 386	18 016	117 437	24 928	92 509
1999	48 508	46 178	146 439	126 353	99 634	20 086	124 285	26 097	98 188
2000	50 526	52 735	149 298	131 850	110 244	17 448	130 943	27 225	103 718
2001	46 346	42 928	128 653	114 964	93 237	13 689	121 599	25 381	96 218
2002	46 572	38 977	122 429	108 280	88 466	14 149	124 705	25 671	99 034
2003	45 327	35 170	114 994	99 733	81 991	15 261	124 872	24 996	99 876
2004	51 158	33 133	117 829	99 586	84 021	18 243	133 688	26 224	107 464
2005	54 568	39 134	127 343	111 268	93 181	16 075	144 443	28 090	116 353
2006	59 843	39 853	137 555	120 899	100 298	16 656	152 698	29 157	123 541
2007	59 398	40 316	146 653	128 083	103 385	18 570	158 660	29 376	129 284
2008	59 922	42 797	166 866	147 361	109 264	19 505	148 541	28 124	120 417
2009	50 617	38 661	151 378	131 455	95 953	19 923	144 876	23 259	121 617
2006									
January	55 069	39 539	127 735	112 204	93 733	15 531	147 288	28 154	119 134
February	55 546	39 677	128 008	112 290	94 035	15 718	147 034	28 253	118 781
March	55 890	39 715	128 916	112 898	94 671	16 018	147 570	28 144	119 426
April	56 712	39 856	130 100	114 075	95 414	16 025	149 578	28 362	121 216
May	57 459	39 572	130 381	114 151	95 644	16 230	150 572	28 584	121 988
June	58 128	39 266	131 500	115 301	96 354	16 199	151 261	28 491	122 770
July	58 615	39 772	133 336	116 746	97 367	16 590	152 013	28 966	123 047
August	59 483	40 072	133 184	116 422	98 116	16 762	152 116	29 356	122 760
September	59 919	40 308	135 806	118 877	99 316	16 929	151 934	28 900	123 034
October	60 094	40 142	136 695	119 749	99 789	16 946	152 108	29 247	122 861
November	60 142	40 378	136 436	119 436	99 663	17 000	152 793	29 471	123 322
December	59 843	39 853	137 555	120 899	100 298	16 656	152 698	29 157	123 541
2007									
January	59 900	40 621	137 837	120 785	100 899	17 052	151 801	29 204	122 597
February	60 044	40 410	138 343	121 366	101 113	16 977	152 605	29 421	123 184
March	59 917	40 165	138 732	121 842	100 837	16 890	152 176	29 348	122 828
April	60 052	39 843	139 197	121 885	100 535	17 312	153 568	29 225	124 343
May	60 022	40 272	140 707	123 568	101 635	17 139	154 470	29 491	124 979
June	59 828	40 114	140 740	123 433	101 493	17 307	154 163	29 353	124 810
July	59 700	39 235	140 641	123 226	101 310	17 415	154 574	29 470	125 104
August	59 489	39 444	141 418	124 061	101 556	17 357	152 665	28 902	123 763
September	59 375	40 237	143 040	125 375	102 271	17 665	156 385	28 976	127 409
October	59 315	40 330	143 756	125 899	102 938	17 857	156 956	29 092	127 864
November	59 160	40 463	144 921	126 943	103 251	17 978	157 995	29 052	128 943
December	59 398	40 316	146 653	128 083	103 385	18 570	158 660	29 376	129 284
2008									
January	59 437	40 433	148 103	129 654	103 820	18 449	164 112	29 103	135 009
February	59 458	40 728	149 584	130 745	104 632	18 839	165 416	29 039	136 377
March	59 113	41 554	152 267	133 319	105 875	18 948	166 100	29 130	136 970
April	59 641	41 728	153 739	134 377	106 522	19 362	164 278	28 605	135 673
May	59 824	41 703	154 833	135 486	106 731	19 347	164 254	28 578	135 676
June	60 053	41 793	155 623	136 347	107 165	19 276	166 786	28 701	138 085
July	60 757	41 886	157 631	138 280	108 139	19 351	165 982	28 573	137 409
August	61 154	42 267	159 508	140 335	108 808	19 173	164 854	28 556	136 298
September	61 356	42 460	160 381	141 437	109 044	18 944	163 415	28 746	134 669
October	60 950	42 493	161 826	142 576	109 238	19 250	159 811	28 758	131 053
November	60 335	42 097	163 019	143 493	108 804	19 526	155 797	28 467	127 330
December	59 922	42 797	166 866	147 361	109 264	19 505	148 541	28 124	120 417
2009									
January	59 021	42 210	165 665	145 493	108 266	20 172	147 362	27 448	119 914
February	57 474	42 009	164 743	144 872	107 349	19 871	144 778	26 743	118 035
March	56 454	41 707	162 722	142 660	105 657	20 062	144 780	26 292	118 488
April	55 149	41 525	162 132	141 862	104 517	20 270	143 848	25 865	117 983
May	54 254	41 265	160 787	140 507	103 301	20 280	143 693	25 327	118 366
June	53 361	40 043	158 684	138 617	101 053	20 067	141 914	24 804	117 110
July	52 480	39 638	156 943	136 683	99 150	20 260	141 411	24 382	117 029
August	51 911	39 524	154 872	134 710	98 326	20 162	141 625	24 156	117 469
September	51 482	39 131	152 520	132 722	97 332	19 798	140 296	23 680	116 616
October	51 161	38 822	152 813	132 496	96 475	20 317	142 805	23 288	119 517
November	51 050	38 617	152 505	132 266	96 137	20 239	144 195	23 166	121 029
December	50 617	38 661	151 378	131 455	95 953	19 923	144 876	23 259	121 617

Table 17-6. Manufacturers' New Orders

(Net, millions of dollars, seasonally adjusted.)

Year and month	Total [1]	Total durable goods [1]	By topical categories								
					Capital goods				Consumer goods		
			Construction materials and supplies	Information technology industries	Total	Nondefense		Defense	Total	Durable	Nondurable
						Total	Excluding aircraft and parts				
1993	2 960 015	1 544 062	304 264	239 387	561 097	488 166	466 433	72 931	1 128 447	275 631	852 816
1994	3 199 686	1 725 635	335 962	265 010	616 252	542 094	523 461	74 158	1 192 584	315 417	877 167
1995	3 426 503	1 849 641	355 161	297 605	680 857	612 132	576 769	68 725	1 256 721	324 146	932 575
1996	3 567 384	1 948 793	373 536	310 074	737 268	648 797	607 174	88 471	1 293 537	328 984	964 553
1997	3 779 835	2 092 520	403 860	352 700	792 859	728 362	676 119	64 497	1 360 010	361 687	998 323
1998	3 808 143	2 139 918	419 330	365 723	809 727	745 600	698 279	64 127	1 352 708	374 300	978 408
1999	3 957 242	2 252 091	435 034	389 160	840 603	772 703	728 089	67 900	1 425 617	413 435	1 012 182
2000	4 161 472	2 326 576	446 792	409 500	910 933	831 335	767 754	79 598	1 501 810	392 741	1 109 069
2001	3 872 952	2 076 859	419 920	344 402	782 700	698 956	665 460	83 744	1 478 648	365 675	1 112 973
2002	3 801 705	2 010 603	422 093	265 375	692 742	621 805	582 747	70 937	1 494 706	396 084	1 098 622
2003	3 964 425	2 091 626	429 286	276 833	731 556	634 722	609 135	96 834	1 585 289	419 781	1 165 508
2004	4 255 431	2 211 128	466 369	293 621	765 326	673 126	630 522	92 200	1 701 298	419 645	1 281 653
2005	4 744 813	2 427 580	517 655	296 540	882 158	789 245	702 052	92 913	1 893 962	421 398	1 472 564
2006	5 037 520	2 578 449	549 140	337 686	948 873	860 705	775 897	88 168	1 988 746	421 903	1 566 843
2007	5 131 164	2 612 952	540 104	327 798	988 684	891 459	755 394	97 225	2 037 940	418 843	1 619 097
2008	5 152 120	2 462 588	519 892	323 407	945 917	829 588	753 240	116 329	2 119 437	352 947	1 766 490
2009	4 247 055	1 966 880	453 036	294 235	743 029	630 413	615 716	112 616	1 748 063	263 261	1 484 802
2006											
January	411 396	203 239	47 153	26 290	66 270	65 799	62 755	471	168 567	36 162	132 405
February	416 124	213 710	47 120	27 146	76 008	68 312	63 055	7 696	163 732	36 046	127 686
March	429 319	222 575	47 628	29 978	84 061	75 510	65 652	8 551	168 387	35 957	132 430
April	420 800	213 582	46 228	27 838	77 234	70 173	63 337	7 061	168 493	35 785	132 708
May	423 988	213 808	46 944	27 472	75 742	69 947	64 535	5 795	171 711	37 024	134 687
June	427 018	218 389	45 609	28 260	80 549	71 290	64 860	9 259	169 694	36 395	133 299
July	417 356	207 901	45 016	28 751	76 588	69 269	64 172	7 319	166 907	32 005	134 902
August	416 427	207 005	44 846	28 170	74 036	66 154	64 477	7 882	167 574	33 719	133 855
September	427 728	229 075	44 708	28 943	96 158	82 907	67 405	13 251	158 360	33 277	125 083
October	406 791	209 884	44 477	26 586	77 890	72 367	65 304	5 523	157 738	33 714	124 024
November	416 142	217 300	43 994	29 818	82 678	72 777	65 639	9 901	160 116	33 839	126 277
December	424 441	220 668	46 138	28 582	81 476	75 858	65 508	5 618	166 024	36 303	129 721
2007											
January	410 541	210 835	45 577	26 178	74 432	66 694	61 788	7 738	161 013	34 024	126 989
February	415 578	213 054	45 698	27 842	78 563	69 885	61 096	8 678	163 514	34 299	129 215
March	426 332	219 261	45 162	25 742	83 755	77 640	63 527	6 115	167 921	35 060	132 861
April	431 114	222 899	45 222	27 188	85 804	78 088	64 445	7 716	169 256	35 948	133 308
May	427 851	217 622	46 023	28 376	80 351	72 411	63 200	7 940	170 574	36 065	134 509
June	424 799	217 308	45 285	26 426	82 287	76 012	62 538	6 275	168 621	35 691	132 930
July	432 473	223 466	44 901	27 204	87 040	77 821	62 071	9 219	169 863	35 885	133 978
August	423 597	217 103	44 545	27 620	80 365	70 436	63 428	9 929	166 797	35 412	131 385
September	421 995	213 037	44 697	28 510	80 983	73 883	62 905	7 100	168 507	34 259	134 248
October	428 809	214 533	44 199	26 957	80 878	72 200	62 516	8 678	172 283	34 429	137 854
November	438 770	215 922	44 308	27 003	82 535	75 894	62 325	6 641	179 798	33 833	145 965
December	449 407	227 053	44 425	28 420	91 196	79 952	65 893	11 244	180 228	33 729	146 499
2008											
January	442 055	218 019	44 462	27 689	84 145	75 327	64 992	8 818	180 489	33 749	146 740
February	438 780	217 489	43 280	27 105	84 314	74 657	64 079	9 657	178 195	32 881	145 314
March	445 319	218 214	44 266	27 171	84 352	75 574	63 844	8 778	180 640	31 017	149 623
April	449 119	214 832	45 501	27 426	82 037	73 624	65 467	8 413	186 567	30 724	155 843
May	450 956	214 419	44 253	28 537	83 193	73 707	65 278	9 486	187 202	29 956	157 246
June	454 835	214 547	45 201	28 182	82 301	70 983	65 327	11 318	189 274	29 908	159 366
July	455 354	212 668	45 322	26 895	81 281	72 441	65 115	8 840	190 729	29 582	161 147
August	436 596	202 616	43 636	26 872	76 981	67 788	64 174	9 193	181 710	28 079	153 631
September	425 853	203 147	42 415	26 488	79 207	66 885	61 636	12 322	175 014	28 772	146 242
October	400 753	186 389	41 835	25 374	70 874	62 576	57 898	8 298	165 012	26 882	138 130
November	374 334	179 936	39 530	26 587	69 007	60 071	58 684	8 936	151 220	26 048	125 172
December	357 472	173 279	37 673	24 646	67 035	54 895	55 339	12 140	143 326	25 047	118 279
2009											
January	345 563	159 509	37 180	23 314	57 064	49 783	48 550	7 281	144 201	23 112	121 089
February	347 187	160 596	38 467	24 247	59 793	49 733	49 729	10 060	142 578	22 357	120 221
March	341 319	157 963	36 530	24 497	58 598	49 773	49 773	8 825	140 648	22 621	118 027
April	343 818	159 974	37 562	23 746	59 023	48 324	48 302	10 699	141 385	22 886	118 499
May	348 109	163 359	37 084	24 415	65 091	52 945	50 150	12 116	140 877	21 264	119 613
June	350 431	159 986	37 513	24 542	60 764	52 369	52 207	8 395	145 850	20 997	124 853
July	356 836	169 207	37 921	25 198	66 739	57 030	51 799	9 709	143 416	22 111	121 305
August	353 923	164 020	37 813	24 725	61 877	52 185	51 054	9 692	144 730	21 462	123 268
September	360 153	168 185	38 480	24 633	65 113	54 383	52 865	10 730	146 256	21 201	125 055
October	363 047	168 098	38 056	24 904	64 128	55 458	51 920	8 670	149 574	21 310	128 264
November	366 688	167 412	38 682	24 986	62 093	53 808	53 579	8 285	153 145	21 975	131 170
December	372 285	170 500	37 683	25 121	63 332	55 000	55 212	8 332	155 990	22 409	133 581

[1]Includes categories not shown separately.

Table 17-7. Manufacturers' Unfilled Orders, Durable Goods Industries

(End of period, millions of dollars, seasonally adjusted.)

Year and month	Total [1]	Transportation equipment		Construction materials and supplies	Information technology industries	By topical categories				Consumer durable goods
		Nondefense aircraft and parts	Defense aircraft and parts			Capital goods				
						Total	Nondefense		Defense	
							Total	Excluding aircraft and parts		
1992	451 273	127 556	49 508	20 951	80 429	318 867	179 562	92 692	139 305	3 868
1993	425 979	110 908	46 574	21 843	78 157	299 168	173 915	95 478	125 253	4 706
1994	434 979	101 069	44 570	25 177	79 170	299 111	177 963	106 847	121 148	5 256
1995	447 411	109 318	42 222	27 226	84 979	313 830	199 565	118 050	114 265	5 354
1996	488 726	130 420	45 093	29 466	84 135	346 373	217 425	120 101	128 948	5 892
1997	512 916	143 330	40 811	33 590	87 260	360 246	242 973	131 551	117 273	7 428
1998	496 083	137 436	37 667	34 219	90 634	348 173	241 333	134 087	106 840	8 334
1999	505 498	126 443	35 541	35 174	105 748	349 430	245 578	149 553	103 852	9 166
2000	549 445	138 296	42 385	37 271	115 762	384 973	268 541	159 929	116 432	10 498
2001	514 262	122 051	50 810	32 581	106 836	365 301	238 573	146 719	126 728	8 573
2002	462 056	111 062	55 750	30 662	87 277	329 156	207 508	119 601	121 648	8 693
2003	477 557	102 474	61 082	30 787	89 403	340 951	208 359	128 078	132 592	9 689
2004	496 395	111 073	51 176	34 115	95 090	353 299	220 224	129 579	133 075	10 222
2005	572 827	152 946	43 021	42 092	96 092	412 388	278 714	144 658	133 674	9 120
2006	660 243	194 719	42 328	45 212	113 492	475 575	343 621	175 685	131 954	9 145
2007	772 982	276 672	43 441	51 978	118 996	573 232	437 310	191 551	135 922	9 524
2008	798 967	303 711	48 442	51 649	121 671	611 186	466 178	195 854	145 008	8 232
2009	717 672	270 568	45 471	49 323	118 446	541 778	408 978	174 328	132 800	8 344
2006										
January	569 348	152 577	43 291	42 579	96 101	407 001	280 490	147 019	126 511	9 036
February	575 643	154 479	43 477	42 702	96 728	410 238	283 107	149 146	127 131	9 238
March	589 248	162 432	43 436	43 648	99 980	420 096	291 957	152 450	128 139	8 792
April	596 568	166 840	42 703	44 315	100 884	424 240	296 682	153 650	127 558	8 932
May	599 364	168 399	41 978	45 360	101 253	425 493	299 605	155 436	125 888	9 053
June	607 206	171 056	41 511	45 180	102 423	431 697	304 127	157 750	127 570	8 911
July	613 165	172 670	40 743	45 650	104 543	435 167	307 465	159 817	127 702	9 312
August	611 585	170 307	40 108	45 266	105 548	434 266	306 231	161 044	128 035	9 081
September	634 897	181 892	39 558	45 271	107 589	455 884	321 958	166 006	133 926	8 925
October	640 492	185 261	38 895	45 351	108 467	460 371	328 581	169 828	131 790	9 261
November	652 221	188 817	40 125	45 142	111 331	468 644	334 568	173 004	134 076	9 564
December	660 243	194 719	42 328	45 212	113 492	475 575	343 621	175 685	131 954	9 145
2007										
January	666 069	195 205	41 243	45 936	113 606	478 187	346 243	178 269	131 944	9 437
February	673 057	200 011	41 016	46 966	114 149	484 137	351 345	178 938	132 792	9 272
March	683 049	210 327	40 004	46 922	113 144	494 582	363 197	181 042	131 385	9 124
April	695 765	219 222	39 329	46 789	113 560	506 553	375 072	183 899	131 481	9 474
May	701 487	223 941	38 630	47 151	115 010	512 710	381 019	185 156	131 691	9 753
June	709 237	233 391	38 552	47 598	114 463	520 924	390 439	185 825	130 485	9 668
July	723 376	244 010	37 972	47 778	115 959	534 713	403 093	187 684	131 620	9 868
August	730 011	246 067	40 330	48 008	116 721	539 111	405 449	188 581	133 662	9 675
September	736 849	252 814	41 008	49 218	117 922	544 706	411 680	188 517	133 026	9 663
October	744 254	257 354	40 939	49 704	117 990	550 534	416 511	189 013	134 023	9 651
November	753 532	265 973	40 327	50 376	118 135	558 243	425 545	189 397	132 698	9 636
December	772 982	276 672	43 441	51 978	118 996	573 232	437 310	191 551	135 922	9 524
2008										
January	780 822	281 440	43 773	52 998	118 906	580 097	444 015	193 888	136 082	9 246
February	790 370	287 849	43 571	52 089	119 300	589 865	452 430	196 267	137 435	8 934
March	801 204	295 703	44 127	52 355	119 282	598 258	460 707	196 888	137 551	8 900
April	807 250	298 935	44 091	53 626	119 355	603 213	466 541	199 243	136 672	9 002
May	813 304	303 227	44 788	53 885	120 078	609 255	472 163	200 939	137 092	8 738
June	819 087	304 617	44 848	54 717	121 077	614 384	474 963	202 621	139 421	8 768
July	822 963	306 895	45 269	55 735	120 959	618 224	479 040	204 611	139 184	8 831
August	823 183	306 046	45 585	55 629	121 371	619 537	480 142	206 366	139 395	8 466
September	823 768	308 149	46 355	54 973	121 202	622 052	479 512	204 492	142 540	8 469
October	816 392	309 741	46 930	54 353	120 860	619 699	478 130	201 814	141 569	8 187
November	810 059	308 808	47 440	53 295	122 067	617 230	475 846	200 753	141 384	8 218
December	798 967	303 711	48 442	51 649	121 671	611 186	466 178	195 854	145 008	8 232
2009										
January	784 714	301 180	47 823	50 153	120 860	599 906	456 281	190 409	143 625	8 079
February	772 059	296 889	47 658	49 453	120 549	591 698	448 304	186 316	143 394	7 619
March	759 101	292 592	47 749	48 231	120 674	582 711	440 587	182 824	142 124	7 683
April	749 752	288 370	47 819	47 927	120 200	575 061	432 516	178 963	142 545	7 618
May	747 473	287 557	47 346	47 480	120 556	574 001	429 662	177 205	144 339	7 370
June	740 349	284 080	48 111	47 375	120 510	567 347	425 471	176 634	141 876	7 339
July	739 445	285 332	48 165	47 094	120 303	566 526	425 358	175 333	141 168	7 540
August	735 313	283 197	47 450	47 055	119 989	562 008	421 867	174 219	140 141	7 608
September	732 138	279 559	46 581	47 665	119 866	558 281	418 740	174 640	139 541	7 665
October	729 336	279 245	46 271	47 997	119 216	554 629	417 381	173 867	137 248	7 712
November	724 054	276 178	45 350	48 867	118 511	548 567	413 762	173 899	134 805	8 022
December	717 672	270 568	45 471	49 323	118 446	541 778	408 978	174 328	132 800	8 344

[1] Includes categories not shown separately.

Table 17-8. Motor Vehicle Sales and Inventories

(Units.)

Year and month	Retail sales of new passenger cars						Retail inventories of new domestic passenger cars (thousands of units, end of period)		
	Thousands of units, not seasonally adjusted			Millions of units, seasonally adjusted annual rate			Not seasonally adjusted	Seasonally adjusted	Inventory to sales ratio
	Total	Domestic	Foreign	Total	Domestic	Foreign			
1970	8 402.6	7 119.4	1 283.2	8.402	7.119	1.283	...	...	...
1971	10 227.9	8 661.9	1 566.0	10.228	8.662	1.566	...	...	...
1972	10 873.4	9 252.7	1 620.7	10.874	9.253	1.621	1 311.0	1 379.0	1.700
1973	11 350.2	9 588.7	1 761.5	11.351	9.589	1.762	1 600.0	1 654.0	2.500
1974	8 773.7	7 361.8	1 411.9	8.774	7.362	1.412	1 672.0	1 730.0	3.400
1975	8 537.9	6 951.0	1 586.9	8.538	6.951	1.587	1 419.0	1 468.0	2.200
1976	9 994.3	8 492.3	1 502.0	9.994	8.492	1.502	1 465.0	1 494.0	1.900
1977	11 046.0	8 971.2	2 074.8	11.046	8.971	2.075	1 731.0	1 743.0	2.300
1978	11 163.9	9 163.8	2 000.1	11.164	9.164	2.000	1 729.0	1 731.0	2.300
1979	10 558.8	8 230.1	2 328.7	10.559	8.230	2.329	1 691.0	1 667.0	2.400
1980	8 981.7	6 581.3	2 400.4	8.982	6.581	2.401	1 448.0	1 440.0	2.600
1981	8 534.3	6 208.8	2 325.5	8.535	6.209	2.326	1 471.0	1 495.0	3.600
1982	7 979.4	5 758.2	2 221.2	7.979	5.758	2.221	1 126.0	1 127.0	2.200
1983	9 178.8	6 793.2	2 385.6	9.179	6.793	2.386	1 352.0	1 350.0	2.000
1984	10 390.0	7 951.5	2 438.5	10.391	7.952	2.439	1 415.0	1 411.0	2.100
1985	10 978.3	8 204.6	2 773.7	10.979	8.205	2.774	1 630.0	1 619.0	2.500
1986	11 405.6	8 214.9	3 190.7	11.406	8.215	3.191	1 499.0	1 515.0	2.000
1987	10 170.8	7 080.8	3 090.0	10.171	7.081	3.090	1 680.0	1 716.0	2.800
1988	10 545.5	7 539.3	3 006.2	10.545	7.539	3.006	1 601.0	1 601.0	2.300
1989	9 776.8	7 078.1	2 698.7	9.777	7.078	2.699	1 669.0	1 687.0	3.100
1990	9 300.2	6 896.9	2 403.3	9.300	6.897	2.403	1 408.0	1 418.0	2.600
1991	8 174.9	6 136.8	2 038.1	8.175	6.137	2.038	1 283.0	1 296.0	2.600
1992	8 214.3	6 276.5	1 937.8	8.215	6.277	1.938	1 276.0	1 288.0	2.300
1993	8 517.9	6 734.2	1 783.7	8.518	6.734	1.784	1 345.5	1 392.3	2.489
1994	8 990.5	7 255.3	1 735.2	8.990	7.255	1.735	1 378.6	1 409.6	2.335
1995	8 636.5	7 129.1	1 507.4	8.637	7.129	1.508	1 639.2	1 665.9	2.810
1996	8 526.9	7 253.8	1 273.1	8.527	7.254	1.273	1 441.4	1 485.4	2.463
1997	8 272.8	6 906.5	1 366.3	8.273	6.907	1.366	1 316.8	1 356.4	2.360
1998	8 142.5	6 764.3	1 378.2	8.142	6.764	1.378	1 270.5	1 344.2	2.394
1999	8 696.6	6 981.8	1 714.8	8.697	6.982	1.715	1 318.1	1 398.3	2.405
2000	8 852.1	6 832.8	2 019.3	8.852	6.833	2.019	1 330.5	1 372.4	2.421
2001	8 422.1	6 322.7	2 099.4	8.422	6.323	2.099	1 108.2	1 157.1	2.217
2002	8 108.7	5 877.6	2 231.1	8.102	5.871	2.231	1 105.6	1 031.0	2.383
2003	7 610.5	5 527.5	2 083.0	7.614	5.527	2.087	1 143.6	1 264.2	2.747
2004	7 545.1	5 396.2	2 148.9	7.545	5.396	2.149	1 096.2	1 232.0	2.745
2005	7 719.8	5 533.0	2 186.8	7.720	5.533	2.187	947.8	1 066.3	2.315
2006	7 820.7	5 476.1	2 344.6	7.821	5.476	2.345	971.3	1 072.7	2.362
2007	7 618.4	5 253.4	2 365.0	7.618	5.253	2.365	991.1	1 085.6	2.483
2008	6 813.5	4 535.3	2 278.2	6.814	4.535	2.278	921.4	1 006.9	2.762
2009	5 456.2	3 619.1	1 837.1	5.422	3.595	1.827	787.5	900.7	3.148
2007									
January	510.3	348.9	161.4	7.777	5.298	2.479	1 101.9	1 127.2	2.553
February	564.9	393.8	171.1	7.615	5.213	2.402	1 114.9	1 113.2	2.563
March	723.9	493.3	230.6	7.542	5.156	2.386	1 119.1	1 109.3	2.582
April	626.8	429.8	197.0	7.368	5.068	2.300	1 071.5	1 105.4	2.618
May	781.3	541.4	239.9	7.835	5.428	2.407	988.3	1 089.4	2.409
June	721.8	500.8	221.0	7.586	5.278	2.308	981.4	1 091.9	2.483
July	621.8	419.5	202.3	7.313	5.038	2.275	884.4	1 116.9	2.661
August	683.5	476.1	207.4	7.397	5.161	2.236	871.6	1 104.6	2.568
September	616.3	431.7	184.6	7.566	5.216	2.350	866.8	1 081.3	2.487
October	564.4	387.9	176.5	7.645	5.246	2.399	960.5	1 068.7	2.444
November	568.8	392.6	176.2	8.009	5.590	2.419	1 012.6	1 028.9	2.209
December	634.6	437.6	197.0	7.768	5.348	2.420	920.1	989.8	2.221
2008									
January	499.2	350.1	149.1	7.535	5.220	2.315	948.5	964.9	2.218
February	559.3	391.1	168.2	7.527	5.159	2.368	979.8	952.5	2.216
March	683.8	452.5	231.3	7.571	4.998	2.573	931.6	923.5	2.217
April	661.0	426.5	234.5	7.498	4.872	2.626	911.9	912.2	2.247
May	799.0	524.1	274.9	7.846	5.146	2.700	795.7	882.6	2.058
June	664.4	427.9	236.5	7.548	4.858	2.690	791.2	875.6	2.163
July	622.6	391.8	230.8	6.976	4.511	2.465	738.7	962.0	2.559
August	631.2	418.6	212.6	6.800	4.514	2.286	758.1	997.0	2.650
September	481.0	338.2	142.8	6.315	4.336	1.979	853.5	1 040.7	2.880
October	429.5	289.3	140.2	5.729	3.838	1.891	1 042.8	1 137.3	3.556
November	359.8	235.8	124.0	5.157	3.389	1.768	1 149.5	1 207.2	4.275
December	422.7	289.4	133.3	5.260	3.582	1.678	1 154.9	1 226.9	4.110
2009									
January	315.2	202.4	112.8	4.673	2.970	1.703	1 083.5	1 134.1	4.582
February	340.8	219.9	120.9	4.654	2.933	1.721	1 026.5	1 067.7	4.369
March	445.6	286.8	158.8	5.038	3.258	1.780	1 002.4	1 037.2	3.820
April	429.7	282.8	146.9	4.737	3.140	1.597	940.3	1 017.1	3.887
May	484.1	319.4	164.7	4.855	3.211	1.644	843.5	981.5	3.668
June	456.2	300.1	156.1	5.003	3.312	1.691	785.5	933.3	3.382
July	550.3	360.4	189.9	6.158	4.159	1.999	637.2	857.2	2.473
August	721.5	477.6	243.9	7.985	5.266	2.719	466.8	705.4	1.608
September	398.2	267.7	130.5	4.968	3.268	1.700	564.9	757.9	2.783
October	427.3	288.0	139.3	5.448	3.654	1.794	671.6	785.4	2.579
November	374.7	255.2	119.5	5.595	3.815	1.780	734.5	777.9	2.447
December	512.6	358.8	153.8	5.947	4.148	1.799	693.6	754.1	2.181

. . . = Not available.

Table 17-8. Motor Vehicle Sales and Inventories—*Continued*

(Units.)

Year and month	Retail sales of new trucks and buses								Unit sales of cars and light trucks (millions of units, seasonally adjusted annual rate)		
	Thousands of units, not seasonally adjusted				Millions of units, seasonally adjusted annual rate						
	Total	0–14,000 pounds		14,001 pounds and over	Total	0–14,000 pounds		14,001 pounds and over	Total	Domestic	Foreign
		Domestic	Foreign			Domestic	Foreign				
1970	...	1 408.5	...	337.3	...	1.408	...	0.335	...	8.527	...
1971	...	1 693.0	...	338.9	...	1.700	...	0.339	...	10.362	...
1972	...	2 122.5	...	437.4	...	2.116	...	0.437	...	11.369	...
1973	...	2 509.4	...	495.7	...	2.513	...	0.495	...	12.102	...
1974	...	2 180.1	...	423.9	...	2.176	...	0.424	...	9.538	...
1975	...	2 052.6	...	298.3	...	2.055	...	0.298	...	9.006	...
1976	3 300.5	2 738.3	237.5	324.7	3.296	2.733	0.239	0.324	12.966	11.225	1.741
1977	3 813.0	3 112.8	323.1	377.1	3.818	3.116	0.324	0.378	14.486	12.087	2.399
1978	4 256.8	3 481.1	335.9	439.8	4.249	3.469	0.340	0.440	14.973	12.633	2.340
1979	3 589.7	2 730.2	469.4	390.1	3.599	2.740	0.469	0.390	13.768	10.970	2.798
1980	2 487.4	1 731.1	484.6	271.7	2.482	1.731	0.480	0.271	11.193	8.312	2.881
1981	2 255.6	1 581.7	447.6	226.3	2.255	1.585	0.444	0.226	10.565	7.794	2.770
1982	2 562.8	1 967.5	410.4	184.9	2.569	1.971	0.413	0.185	10.363	7.729	2.634
1983	3 117.3	2 465.2	463.3	188.8	3.130	2.480	0.461	0.189	12.120	9.273	2.847
1984	4 093.1	3 207.2	607.7	278.2	4.085	3.199	0.609	0.278	14.198	11.151	3.048
1985	4 741.7	3 618.4	828.3	295.0	4.759	3.634	0.831	0.295	15.443	11.839	3.605
1986	4 912.1	3 671.4	967.2	273.5	4.918	3.676	0.969	0.273	16.051	11.891	4.160
1987	4 991.5	3 792.0	912.2	287.3	4.977	3.783	0.907	0.288	14.861	10.864	3.997
1988	5 231.9	4 199.7	697.9	334.3	5.225	4.194	0.697	0.334	15.436	11.733	3.703
1989	5 055.9	4 113.6	630.3	312.0	5.065	4.123	0.629	0.313	14.529	11.201	3.328
1990	4 837.0	3 956.8	602.7	277.5	4.841	3.960	0.602	0.278	13.863	10.857	3.005
1991	4 355.4	3 605.6	528.8	221.0	4.360	3.612	0.528	0.221	12.314	9.749	2.566
1992	4 892.2	4 247.0	395.9	249.3	4.894	4.247	0.398	0.248	12.861	10.524	2.336
1993	5 667.8	5 000.5	364.5	302.8	5.658	4.991	0.365	0.302	13.874	11.725	2.149
1994	6 407.3	5 658.2	396.3	352.8	6.408	5.659	0.395	0.354	15.044	12.914	2.130
1995	6 469.8	5 690.9	390.5	388.4	6.486	5.703	0.393	0.390	14.733	12.832	1.901
1996	6 921.8	6 131.8	430.9	359.1	6.914	6.127	0.429	0.357	15.083	13.381	1.702
1997	7 217.8	6 270.4	571.2	376.2	7.229	6.283	0.570	0.376	15.126	13.190	1.936
1998	7 815.8	6 745.3	646.2	424.3	7.788	6.720	0.644	0.425	15.506	13.484	2.022
1999	8 704.2	7 420.0	762.9	521.3	8.713	7.429	0.763	0.521	16.889	14.411	2.478
2000	8 953.5	7 650.8	840.8	461.9	8.951	7.649	0.841	0.461	17.342	14.482	2.860
2001	9 046.3	7 718.4	977.8	350.1	9.043	7.715	0.978	0.350	17.115	14.038	3.077
2002	9 035.6	7 646.9	1 066.3	322.4	9.035	7.647	1.066	0.322	16.815	13.518	3.297
2003	9 357.0	7 801.4	1 227.2	328.4	9.356	7.802	1.227	0.328	16.643	13.329	3.314
2004	9 753.3	8 075.5	1 246.2	431.6	9.751	8.076	1.246	0.429	16.867	13.472	3.395
2005	9 724.9	8 012.9	1 215.5	496.5	9.724	8.012	1.215	0.497	16.947	13.545	3.402
2006	9 227.8	7 336.8	1 346.6	544.4	9.229	7.337	1.347	0.545	16.505	12.813	3.692
2007	8 841.8	7 082.6	1 388.1	371.1	8.844	7.083	1.388	0.373	16.089	12.336	3.753
2008	6 680.0	5 285.0	1 096.5	298.5	6.679	5.285	1.097	0.298	13.195	9.820	3.375
2009	5 145.1	4 061.1	884.2	199.8	5.123	4.043	0.880	0.199	10.345	7.638	2.708
2007											
January	613.9	473.5	103.6	36.8	9.122	7.195	1.435	0.492	16.407	12.493	3.914
February	720.2	582.3	103.9	34.0	9.398	7.548	1.388	0.462	16.551	12.761	3.790
March	851.0	677.7	135.3	38.0	8.972	7.147	1.398	0.427	16.087	12.303	3.784
April	739.2	596.3	109.3	33.6	9.174	7.394	1.389	0.391	16.151	12.462	3.689
May	808.9	656.6	120.8	31.5	8.756	7.048	1.351	0.357	16.234	12.476	3.758
June	759.5	607.5	120.9	31.1	8.540	6.800	1.388	0.352	15.774	12.078	3.696
July	709.4	569.0	113.6	26.8	8.517	6.816	1.357	0.344	15.486	11.854	3.632
August	817.0	663.8	124.0	29.2	8.961	7.304	1.317	0.340	16.018	12.465	3.553
September	719.5	584.2	109.9	25.4	8.868	7.135	1.398	0.335	16.099	12.351	3.748
October	692.1	549.3	112.9	29.9	8.859	7.087	1.445	0.327	16.177	12.333	3.844
November	631.6	496.3	110.2	25.1	8.511	6.785	1.405	0.321	16.199	12.375	3.824
December	779.5	626.1	123.7	29.7	8.444	6.735	1.385	0.324	15.888	12.083	3.805
2008											
January	564.2	444.1	95.8	24.3	8.222	6.588	1.308	0.326	15.431	11.808	3.623
February	637.2	511.2	101.2	24.8	8.207	6.586	1.300	0.321	15.413	11.745	3.668
March	694.8	553.5	114.2	27.1	7.728	6.134	1.276	0.318	14.981	11.132	3.849
April	612.1	480.5	102.1	29.5	7.190	5.635	1.228	0.327	14.361	10.507	3.854
May	621.6	486.7	107.2	27.7	6.708	5.226	1.160	0.322	14.232	10.372	3.860
June	548.2	438.4	82.5	27.3	6.532	5.168	1.048	0.316	13.764	10.026	3.738
July	533.4	421.1	88.6	23.7	5.963	4.667	1.002	0.294	12.645	9.178	3.467
August	637.9	518.8	96.8	22.3	7.014	5.721	1.012	0.281	13.533	10.235	3.298
September	503.6	404.1	77.2	22.3	6.485	5.168	1.042	0.275	12.525	9.504	3.021
October	429.5	330.1	75.0	24.4	5.318	4.131	0.920	0.267	10.780	7.969	2.811
November	404.1	313.2	70.6	20.3	5.491	4.290	0.925	0.276	10.372	7.679	2.693
December	493.4	383.3	85.3	24.8	5.289	4.103	0.938	0.248	10.301	7.685	2.616
2009											
January	355.1	266.6	72.9	15.6	5.131	3.942	0.974	0.215	9.589	6.912	2.677
February	360.8	271.3	75.0	14.5	4.686	3.497	0.992	0.197	9.143	6.430	2.713
March	427.2	327.0	82.5	17.7	4.855	3.715	0.937	0.203	9.690	6.973	2.717
April	402.9	322.5	65.1	15.3	4.636	3.693	0.773	0.170	9.203	6.833	2.370
May	454.3	364.7	75.1	14.5	5.168	4.148	0.845	0.175	9.848	7.359	2.489
June	418.6	337.3	63.9	17.4	4.863	3.881	0.788	0.194	9.672	7.193	2.479
July	461.5	366.0	79.4	16.1	5.263	4.169	0.896	0.198	11.223	8.328	2.895
August	553.1	432.5	106.0	14.6	6.272	4.896	1.191	0.185	14.072	10.162	3.910
September	361.3	287.6	58.3	15.4	4.406	3.477	0.740	0.189	9.185	6.745	2.440
October	426.6	343.8	64.5	18.3	5.187	4.220	0.761	0.206	10.429	7.874	2.555
November	387.0	310.1	59.5	17.4	5.523	4.475	0.819	0.229	10.889	8.290	2.599
December	536.7	431.7	82.0	23.0	5.486	4.405	0.849	0.232	11.201	8.553	2.648

. . . = Not available.

Table 17-9. Retail and Food Services Sales

(All retail establishments and food services; millions of dollars; not seasonally adjusted.)

Year and month	Retail and food services, total [1]	GAFO (department store type goods), total [2]	Motor vehicles and parts	Furniture and home furnishings	Electronics and appliances	Building materials and garden	Food and beverages	Health and personal care	Gasoline	Clothing and accessories	General merchandise	Nonstore retailers	Food services and drinking places
					Retail (NAICS industry categories)								
1992	2 019 131	534 367	419 353	52 467	42 763	131 244	371 451	89 782	156 556	120 346	247 968	78 657	203 415
1993	2 158 299	571 790	473 948	55 587	48 760	141 220	375 440	92 671	162 587	125 001	266 088	85 977	216 051
1994	2 335 650	617 379	542 235	60 551	57 413	157 497	385 265	96 442	171 416	129 341	285 278	96 460	225 629
1995	2 456 129	651 071	580 842	63 601	64 919	164 831	391 312	101 719	181 294	131 593	300 589	103 705	233 625
1996	2 609 561	683 678	628 687	67 848	68 515	176 972	402 020	109 646	194 601	136 851	315 398	117 963	242 896
1997	2 732 043	714 453	655 013	72 863	70 211	191 345	410 288	118 769	199 856	140 565	331 454	126 397	258 040
1998	2 859 332	759 063	689 679	77 569	74 686	202 724	417 433	129 699	191 887	149 433	351 186	134 113	272 227
1999	3 093 569	816 827	765 549	84 451	79 138	218 611	434 599	142 829	212 682	160 043	380 291	152 022	285 013
2000	3 294 217	863 903	797 568	91 328	82 363	229 320	445 666	155 372	249 975	167 968	404 344	180 688	305 461
2001	3 385 577	883 866	816 941	91 644	80 395	239 707	463 330	166 678	251 537	167 583	427 586	180 805	317 852
2002	3 466 136	913 925	820 269	94 610	83 897	248 888	465 794	180 143	250 770	172 617	446 648	189 535	331 814
2003	3 618 859	947 355	842 882	96 853	86 816	263 833	475 174	192 630	275 287	178 819	468 990	206 187	351 027
2004	3 854 598	1 005 434	867 789	103 918	94 566	296 249	491 007	199 802	324 530	190 152	497 684	228 794	374 804
2005	4 095 471	1 061 518	889 984	109 235	101 501	321 770	509 026	210 646	379 641	201 668	527 887	256 065	397 841
2006	4 305 813	1 114 024	901 262	112 819	107 954	334 926	526 333	223 968	422 885	213 615	554 637	284 186	424 241
2007	4 451 521	1 148 762	911 165	111 152	110 706	322 005	548 934	237 798	451 364	221 622	578 920	308 441	446 273
2008	4 417 318	1 147 269	788 657	101 059	109 086	306 667	573 619	247 308	499 366	216 584	596 935	319 938	458 161
2009	4 130 678	1 113 375	690 437	89 522	100 102	271 292	575 778	254 579	373 089	208 617	592 859	318 865	459 493
2007													
January	329 736	82 149	66 740	8 779	8 715	21 997	43 611	19 662	30 933	13 926	40 873	25 376	33 722
February	324 287	81 481	69 535	8 405	8 346	20 854	41 143	18 482	29 753	15 167	41 050	24 350	33 216
March	375 294	92 350	84 027	9 399	8 574	27 382	45 362	20 285	35 561	18 044	46 490	25 723	38 382
April	359 619	87 360	77 417	8 542	7 709	29 008	43 635	19 312	36 637	17 117	45 079	23 557	36 711
May	392 640	93 931	85 331	9 258	8 450	34 364	47 100	20 260	41 336	18 498	47 930	24 352	38 481
June	377 695	92 065	79 954	9 163	8 433	30 342	46 231	19 553	40 449	17 314	47 157	23 137	38 626
July	373 405	90 342	79 198	9 194	8 456	28 623	46 459	19 492	40 653	16 904	45 879	23 397	38 736
August	388 846	98 335	84 725	9 873	9 188	28 365	46 692	20 172	40 322	18 874	48 393	24 842	38 995
September	354 721	87 933	73 497	8 895	8 287	25 331	44 807	18 851	37 635	16 798	43 976	23 470	36 929
October	369 434	91 174	74 453	9 085	8 311	27 472	45 657	20 200	39 373	17 658	46 300	26 926	37 730
November	378 619	107 281	67 292	10 043	11 026	25 933	46 952	19 650	39 739	20 588	54 320	29 437	36 045
December	427 225	144 361	68 996	10 516	15 211	22 334	51 285	21 879	38 973	30 734	71 473	33 874	38 700
2008													
January	343 616	83 534	65 730	8 228	8 731	20 673	45 952	20 304	38 581	14 238	42 247	27 666	35 129
February	345 010	86 145	68 946	8 191	8 752	20 517	44 293	20 134	37 465	15 916	44 334	25 926	35 778
March	374 208	92 461	76 517	8 497	8 548	24 175	47 296	20 836	42 052	17 873	48 094	26 263	38 569
April	370 352	88 110	73 676	8 169	8 005	29 075	45 639	20 133	43 468	17 136	45 715	26 047	37 998
May	399 773	98 324	76 131	8 778	8 870	32 325	49 978	20 974	48 318	19 132	51 587	25 716	40 773
June	380 389	93 052	69 505	8 305	8 664	29 717	47 487	20 098	49 872	17 080	49 448	24 888	38 824
July	385 985	93 368	69 903	8 714	8 823	29 104	49 591	20 474	51 415	17 434	48 543	25 476	39 730
August	385 211	99 276	70 003	8 715	9 035	25 905	49 441	20 290	48 649	19 097	50 491	24 938	40 610
September	353 128	85 898	60 945	7 927	8 068	25 619	46 447	20 064	44 667	15 975	44 269	25 744	37 433
October	352 847	89 731	55 591	7 970	7 822	26 328	48 208	20 945	40 010	16 905	47 803	26 891	38 665
November	338 774	102 305	48 516	8 394	10 129	22 134	48 165	19 883	29 284	18 865	54 818	26 074	36 590
December	388 025	135 065	53 194	9 171	13 639	21 095	51 122	23 173	25 585	26 933	69 586	34 309	38 062
2009													
January	313 864	82 838	51 066	7 075	8 475	18 020	47 536	20 779	25 604	13 651	43 661	26 366	36 588
February	303 504	82 035	51 121	6 885	8 317	17 527	43 049	19 934	24 633	14 928	43 493	24 332	35 393
March	333 230	86 438	58 594	7 234	7 759	22 148	46 224	21 647	27 204	15 794	46 607	25 930	38 992
April	334 767	86 369	57 579	6 933	7 093	25 730	46 975	21 174	28 066	16 498	46 880	24 320	38 412
May	353 263	92 417	59 392	7 331	7 523	27 838	49 831	21 198	31 384	17 602	50 371	23 687	40 910
June	349 960	87 636	61 467	7 317	7 631	27 271	47 621	21 131	34 232	15 746	47 400	24 813	39 022
July	353 617	88 559	64 219	7 614	7 583	24 867	49 570	20 973	34 558	16 334	47 434	24 635	39 948
August	359 221	94 276	68 141	7 599	7 969	22 337	48 521	20 728	35 153	17 995	49 192	24 593	39 601
September	330 260	85 240	53 712	7 397	7 400	22 171	46 887	20 814	32 673	15 964	44 535	25 417	37 284
October	344 716	90 466	56 422	7 289	7 346	22 240	48 566	21 556	33 276	17 400	48 896	26 929	38 958
November	345 700	100 355	51 424	7 862	9 754	20 915	48 092	20 825	32 707	18 750	53 915	29 205	36 154
December	408 576	136 746	57 300	8 986	13 252	20 228	52 906	23 820	33 599	27 955	70 475	38 638	38 231

[1]Includes store categories not shown separately.
[2]Includes furniture, home furnishings, electronics, appliances, clothing, sporting goods, hobby, book, music, general merchandise, office supplies, stationery, and gifts.

Table 17-9. Retail and Food Services Sales—Continued

(All retail establishments and food services; millions of dollars; seasonally adjusted.)

Year and month	Total	Retail and food services											
		Retail (NAICS industry categories)											
		Total	GAFO (department store type goods) [2]	Motor vehicles and parts	Furniture and home furnishings	Electronics and appliances	Building materials and garden	Food and beverages				Health and personal care	Gasoline
								Total [1]	Groceries	Beer, wine, and liquor		
1992	2 019 131	1 815 716	534 367	419 353	52 467	42 763	131 244	371 451	337 925	21 825	89 782	156 556
1993	2 158 299	1 942 248	571 790	473 948	55 587	48 760	141 220	375 440	341 855	21 675	92 671	162 587
1994	2 335 650	2 110 021	617 379	542 235	60 551	57 413	157 497	385 265	351 056	22 240	96 442	171 416
1995	2 456 129	2 222 504	651 071	580 842	63 601	64 919	164 831	391 312	356 932	22 145	101 719	181 294
1996	2 609 561	2 366 665	683 678	628 687	67 848	68 515	176 972	402 020	366 075	23 300	109 646	194 601
1997	2 732 043	2 474 003	714 453	655 013	72 863	70 211	191 345	410 288	373 072	24 222	118 769	199 856
1998	2 859 332	2 587 105	759 063	689 679	77 569	74 686	202 724	417 433	378 675	25 533	129 699	191 887
1999	3 093 569	2 808 556	816 827	765 549	84 451	79 138	218 611	434 599	394 724	26 635	142 829	212 682
2000	3 294 217	2 988 756	863 903	797 568	91 328	82 363	229 320	445 666	402 988	28 668	155 372	249 975
2001	3 385 577	3 067 725	883 866	816 941	91 644	80 395	239 707	463 330	418 596	29 783	166 678	251 537
2002	3 466 136	3 134 322	913 925	820 269	94 610	83 897	248 888	465 794	420 288	30 061	180 143	250 770
2003	3 618 859	3 267 832	947 355	842 882	96 853	86 816	263 833	475 174	428 294	30 628	192 630	275 287
2004	3 854 598	3 479 794	1 005 434	867 789	103 918	94 566	296 249	491 007	441 269	32 336	199 802	324 530
2005	4 095 471	3 697 630	1 061 518	889 984	109 235	101 501	321 770	509 026	457 614	33 751	210 646	379 641
2006	4 305 813	3 881 572	1 114 024	901 262	112 819	107 954	334 926	526 333	472 094	36 256	223 968	422 885
2007	4 451 521	4 005 248	1 148 762	911 165	111 152	110 706	322 005	548 934	491 841	38 209	237 798	451 364
2008	4 417 318	3 959 157	1 147 269	788 657	101 059	109 086	306 667	573 619	513 847	40 085	247 308	499 366
2009	4 130 678	3 671 185	1 113 375	690 437	89 522	100 102	271 292	575 778	513 814	40 368	254 579	373 089
2007												
January	364 654	328 158	95 558	75 963	9 553	9 253	27 300	45 024	40 366	3 090	19 487	34 218
February	365 796	329 494	94 403	76 338	9 381	9 111	27 118	45 342	40 664	3 135	19 455	35 128
March	369 515	332 680	96 268	76 250	9 446	9 062	27 856	45 166	40 433	3 162	19 599	36 103
April	367 394	330 646	94 875	76 099	9 397	9 061	26 634	45 218	40 570	3 123	19 666	36 564
May	372 224	335 294	95 541	76 794	9 314	9 126	27 394	45 467	40 708	3 216	19 747	38 524
June	368 149	331 009	95 270	74 341	9 200	9 006	26 698	45 569	40 789	3 244	19 770	37 212
July	370 082	332 656	96 173	74 174	9 268	9 125	26 818	45 932	41 161	3 238	19 992	37 365
August	370 183	332 867	96 000	75 766	9 279	9 244	26 749	45 615	40 884	3 186	20 072	36 557
September	373 510	335 942	95 874	77 191	9 161	9 288	26 546	45 980	41 171	3 201	20 012	37 824
October	375 199	337 355	96 186	77 760	9 177	9 364	26 278	46 396	41 594	3 178	20 020	38 189
November	379 960	342 295	97 145	76 035	9 180	9 600	26 660	46 680	41 868	3 189	19 949	42 547
December	377 616	339 185	97 016	75 050	9 042	9 395	25 926	46 956	42 080	3 235	20 054	41 417
2008												
January	377 407	339 552	96 417	74 600	8 943	9 287	25 790	47 039	42 257	3 234	20 243	42 490
February	373 295	335 831	95 407	72 687	8 714	9 097	25 798	46 922	42 139	3 245	20 317	42 381
March	374 688	337 096	96 221	71 815	8 796	9 163	25 505	47 218	42 396	3 273	20 288	43 263
April	376 064	338 104	96 876	70 045	8 746	9 305	25 882	47 651	42 744	3 295	20 398	43 425
May	377 272	339 095	97 900	68 962	8 760	9 500	26 042	47 480	42 577	3 296	20 502	44 451
June	377 687	339 437	98 011	66 601	8 588	9 393	26 134	47 968	42 939	3 372	20 592	46 135
July	376 056	337 707	97 960	63 401	8 543	9 438	26 270	48 177	43 090	3 404	20 681	46 911
August	373 158	334 847	96 807	64 772	8 348	9 199	25 789	48 460	43 382	3 393	20 683	44 838
September	366 950	328 439	94 439	61 490	8 015	9 007	25 587	48 225	43 140	3 377	20 685	44 712
October	355 484	317 126	93 438	57 900	8 026	8 867	25 455	48 211	43 084	3 409	20 717	38 620
November	345 704	307 309	94 143	56 920	7 897	8 865	23 914	48 157	43 076	3 395	20 755	31 900
December	335 614	297 322	92 007	55 932	7 733	8 401	23 366	47 092	42 128	3 330	20 764	27 017
2009												
January	341 617	303 063	93 791	58 176	7 674	8 954	23 271	47 931	42 830	3 403	20 821	27 770
February	341 390	302 751	94 022	56 303	7 642	8 902	23 078	47 365	42 256	3 363	20 983	28 946
March	336 801	298 498	92 206	54 589	7 458	8 304	22 869	47 699	42 539	3 378	21 223	28 161
April	336 833	298 459	92 355	54 730	7 423	8 219	22 790	47 691	42 534	3 361	21 153	27 871
May	339 232	300 855	92 343	55 661	7 428	8 141	22 991	47 892	42 702	3 377	21 093	29 140
June	343 108	304 851	92 008	56 943	7 398	8 175	22 853	47 934	42 811	3 321	21 216	31 550
July	343 490	305 299	91 870	58 339	7 399	8 086	22 523	47 772	42 650	3 326	21 121	31 190
August	350 727	312 576	92 855	62 865	7 363	8 186	22 310	47 994	42 788	3 389	21 173	32 609
September	343 050	304 888	93 146	53 987	7 464	8 289	22 242	48 330	43 146	3 374	21 458	32 837
October	348 321	310 202	93 604	59 366	7 370	8 340	21 967	48 215	43 071	3 370	21 427	32 275
November	353 863	315 401	93 421	60 189	7 445	8 494	22 204	48 750	43 504	3 366	21 513	35 359
December	354 098	315 752	93 284	60 307	7 558	8 221	22 274	48 372	43 149	3 375	21 459	35 442

[1]Includes store categories not shown separately.
[2]Includes furniture, home furnishings, electronics, appliances, clothing, sporting goods, hobby, book, music, general merchandise, office supplies, stationery, and gifts.

Table 17-9. Retail and Food Services Sales—Continued

(All retail establishments and food services; millions of dollars; seasonally adjusted, except as noted.)

Classification basis, year, and month	Retail and food services—Continued												Food services and drinking places
	Retail (NAICS industry categories)—Continued												
	Clothing and accessories					Sporting goods, hobby, book, and music	General merchandise			Miscellaneous store retailers	Nonstore retailers		
	Total[1]	Men's clothing[3]	Women's clothing	Family clothing[3]	Shoes		Total	Department stores[4]	Other general merchandise		Total[1]	Electronic shopping and mail order	
1992	120 346	10 185	31 840	33 159	18 630	49 296	247 968	177 089	70 879	55 833	78 657	35 252	203 415
1993	125 001	9 968	32 377	35 311	19 042	52 368	266 088	187 685	78 403	62 601	85 977	40 725	216 051
1994	129 341	10 039	30 611	38 118	19 921	57 538	285 278	198 945	86 333	70 585	96 460	47 093	225 629
1995	131 593	9 322	28 723	40 014	20 354	60 922	300 589	205 920	94 669	77 177	103 705	52 741	233 625
1996	136 851	9 554	28 266	42 275	21 248	64 055	315 398	212 203	103 195	84 109	117 963	61 174	242 896
1997	140 565	10 077	27 851	45 259	21 463	65 573	331 454	220 108	111 346	91 669	126 397	70 136	258 040
1998	149 433	10 204	28 363	50 169	22 251	68 939	351 186	223 290	127 896	99 757	134 113	80 366	272 227
1999	160 043	9 675	29 581	55 333	22 704	72 764	380 291	230 304	149 987	105 577	152 022	94 361	285 013
2000	167 968	9 515	31 480	58 928	22 888	76 112	404 344	232 475	171 869	108 052	180 688	113 877	305 461
2001	167 583	8 632	31 487	60 165	22 897	77 138	427 586	228 377	199 209	104 381	180 805	114 844	317 852
2002	172 617	8 119	31 280	64 305	23 215	76 988	446 648	220 743	225 905	104 163	189 535	122 313	331 814
2003	178 819	8 258	32 599	67 322	23 199	77 070	468 990	214 522	254 468	103 291	206 187	133 950	351 027
2004	190 152	8 577	34 888	72 068	23 701	79 559	497 684	215 812	281 872	105 744	228 794	153 223	374 804
2005	201 668	8 750	37 056	77 618	25 303	81 123	527 887	214 516	313 371	109 084	256 065	175 577	397 841
2006	213 615	8 858	38 791	81 820	26 731	83 518	554 637	213 202	341 435	115 469	284 186	201 375	424 241
2007	221 622	8 788	40 538	84 429	26 867	84 994	578 920	209 368	369 552	118 147	308 441	222 464	446 273
2008	216 584	8 630	38 574	82 373	27 064	84 067	596 935	199 586	397 349	115 871	319 938	227 084	458 161
2009	208 617	8 070	35 646	80 494	26 089	83 603	592 859	188 101	404 758	112 442	318 865	235 173	459 493
2007													
January	18 494	626	3 382	5 158	2 266	6 892	47 890	17 875	30 015	9 700	24 384	17 582	36 496
February	18 274	601	3 335	5 356	2 173	6 863	47 355	17 662	29 693	9 610	25 519	17 901	36 302
March	18 813	680	3 386	7 110	2 274	7 089	48 272	17 848	30 424	9 920	25 104	18 159	36 835
April	18 310	732	3 307	6 498	2 206	6 981	47 647	17 387	30 260	9 695	25 374	18 072	36 748
May	18 618	741	3 446	6 875	2 217	7 171	47 864	17 557	30 307	9 960	25 315	18 353	36 930
June	18 468	719	3 351	6 614	2 229	7 134	48 007	17 365	30 642	10 171	25 433	18 453	37 140
July	18 609	630	3 378	6 718	2 268	7 270	48 427	17 542	30 885	9 884	25 792	18 838	37 426
August	18 431	637	3 370	7 460	2 274	7 101	48 511	17 458	31 053	9 920	25 622	18 630	37 316
September	18 405	658	3 366	6 419	2 225	7 122	48 443	17 320	31 123	10 006	25 964	18 841	37 568
October	18 453	719	3 410	6 862	2 211	7 215	48 543	17 273	31 270	9 789	26 171	19 078	37 844
November	18 646	805	3 401	8 252	2 257	7 264	48 991	17 325	31 666	9 822	26 921	19 475	37 665
December	18 545	1 240	3 414	11 107	2 258	7 137	49 498	17 193	32 305	9 765	26 400	18 840	38 431
2008													
January	18 617	617	3 361	5 213	2 269	7 135	48 974	16 934	32 040	10 208	26 226	18 683	37 855
February	18 313	595	3 352	5 562	2 231	7 002	48 969	16 905	32 064	9 649	25 982	18 406	37 464
March	18 649	693	3 310	6 612	2 203	7 023	49 196	16 786	32 410	9 680	26 500	18 706	37 592
April	18 761	725	3 355	6 253	2 317	7 049	49 625	16 799	32 826	9 704	27 513	19 390	37 960
May	18 704	775	3 305	7 007	2 343	7 204	50 371	16 936	33 435	9 717	27 402	19 216	38 177
June	18 797	736	3 297	6 425	2 332	7 169	50 747	17 140	33 607	9 776	27 537	19 315	38 250
July	18 761	644	3 286	6 952	2 327	7 129	50 705	16 952	33 753	9 998	27 693	19 333	38 349
August	18 599	680	3 235	7 484	2 344	7 114	50 273	16 675	33 598	9 636	27 136	19 041	38 311
September	17 574	663	3 176	6 032	2 170	6 872	49 743	16 295	33 448	9 572	26 957	19 017	38 511
October	17 303	695	3 050	6 582	2 177	6 801	49 302	16 102	33 200	9 539	26 385	18 761	38 358
November	17 289	745	3 052	7 764	2 191	6 883	50 074	16 578	33 496	9 232	25 423	18 146	38 395
December	16 814	1 062	2 957	10 487	2 137	6 763	49 136	15 977	33 159	8 982	25 322	18 531	38 292
2009													
January	17 335	563	2 956	5 315	2 137	6 979	49 530	15 966	33 564	9 067	25 555	18 623	38 554
February	17 721	536	2 987	5 561	2 190	6 957	49 525	15 802	33 723	9 491	25 838	18 738	38 639
March	17 217	588	2 952	6 032	2 145	6 841	49 176	15 717	33 459	9 431	25 530	18 718	38 303
April	17 290	728	2 981	6 097	2 119	6 992	49 170	15 710	33 460	9 482	25 648	18 858	38 374
May	17 446	710	2 983	6 472	2 140	6 863	49 157	15 717	33 440	9 331	25 712	19 039	38 377
June	17 231	665	2 958	5 946	2 150	6 944	49 008	15 590	33 418	9 308	26 291	19 269	38 257
July	17 322	633	2 924	6 546	2 164	6 914	48 947	15 509	33 438	9 269	26 417	19 473	38 191
August	17 594	608	2 989	7 179	2 237	7 058	49 428	15 679	33 749	9 371	26 625	19 841	38 151
September	17 491	640	2 983	6 067	2 206	7 070	49 618	15 640	33 978	9 368	26 734	19 981	38 162
October	17 538	677	3 007	7 036	2 168	6 993	50 111	15 682	34 429	9 426	27 174	20 124	38 119
November	17 483	689	3 005	7 661	2 191	6 983	49 864	15 681	34 183	9 468	27 649	20 586	38 462
December	17 319	1 033	2 957	10 582	2 237	7 120	49 945	15 677	34 268	9 474	28 261	20 975	38 346

[1]Includes store categories not shown separately.
[3]Not seasonally adjusted.
[4]Excluding leased departments.

Table 17-10. Quarterly U.S. Retail Sales: Total and E-Commerce

Year and quarter	Retail sales (millions of dollars)		E-commerce as a percent of total sales	Percent change from prior quarter		Percent change from same quarter a year ago	
	Total	E-commerce		Total sales	E-commerce sales	Total sales	E-commerce sales
NOT SEASONALLY ADJUSTED							
2005							
1st quarter	834 847	19 408	2.3	-10.8	-11.2	5.0	22.0
2nd quarter	930 532	20 075	2.2	11.5	3.4	6.9	24.3
3rd quarter	938 131	21 196	2.3	0.8	5.6	7.5	24.6
4th quarter	984 549	26 718	2.7	4.9	26.1	5.1	22.2
2006							
1st quarter	896 182	24 131	2.7	-9.0	-9.7	7.3	24.3
2nd quarter	988 830	24 448	2.5	10.3	1.3	6.3	21.8
3rd quarter	980 553	25 233	2.6	-0.8	3.2	4.5	19.0
4th quarter	1 021 798	32 771	3.2	4.2	29.9	3.8	22.7
2007							
1st quarter	930 677	28 594	3.1	-8.9	-12.7	3.8	18.5
2nd quarter	1 025 517	29 894	2.9	10.2	4.5	3.7	22.3
3rd quarter	1 012 064	30 210	3.0	-1.3	1.1	3.2	19.7
4th quarter	1 072 153	38 992	3.6	5.9	29.1	4.9	19.0
2008							
1st quarter	952 071	32 011	3.4	10.1	-17.1	3.3	12.5
2nd quarter	1 034 377	32 233	3.1	8.6	0.7	2.0	8.6
3rd quarter	1 066 578	31 351	3.1	-2.7	-2.7	0.7	4.6
4th quarter	966 931	36 662	3.8	-3.9	16.9	-8.7	-5.0
2009							
1st quarter	839 625	32 125	3.8	-13.1	-18.3	-11.9	-7.0
2nd quarter	919 646	32 769	3.6	9.5	2.0	-11.0	-5.2
3rd quarter	926 265	34 031	3.7	0.7	3.9	-8.0	1.6
4th quarter	985 649	45 199	4.6	6.4	32.8	2.0	15.0
SEASONALLY ADJUSTED							
1999							
4th quarter	724 737	4 600	0.6	2.2	. . .	9.0	. . .
2000							
1st quarter	742 622	5 795	0.8	2.5	26.0	9.3	. . .
2nd quarter	741 410	6 454	0.9	-0.2	11.4	7.0	. . .
3rd quarter	748 083	7 362	1.0	0.9	14.1	5.5	. . .
4th quarter	753 134	7 856	1.0	0.7	6.7	3.9	70.8
2001							
1st quarter	756 971	8 209	1.1	0.5	4.5	1.9	41.7
2nd quarter	765 448	8 340	1.1	1.1	1.6	3.2	29.2
3rd quarter	759 291	8 300	1.1	-0.8	-0.5	1.5	12.7
4th quarter	786 127	9 354	1.2	3.5	12.7	4.4	19.1
2002							
1st quarter	773 200	10 050	1.3	-1.6	7.4	2.1	22.4
2nd quarter	779 478	10 785	1.4	0.8	7.3	1.8	29.3
3rd quarter	789 941	11 543	1.5	1.3	7.0	4.0	39.1
4th quarter	792 471	12 274	1.5	0.3	6.3	0.8	31.2
2003							
1st quarter	799 911	12 764	1.6	0.9	4.0	3.5	27.0
2nd quarter	805 286	13 665	1.7	0.7	7.1	3.3	26.7
3rd quarter	828 124	14 631	1.8	2.8	7.1	4.8	26.8
4th quarter	830 826	15 361	1.8	0.3	5.0	4.8	25.2
2004							
1st quarter	847 184	16 462	1.9	2.0	7.2	5.9	29.0
2nd quarter	856 086	17 129	2.0	1.1	4.1	6.3	25.3
3rd quarter	868 399	18 052	2.1	1.4	5.4	4.9	23.4
4th quarter	890 268	19 088	2.1	2.5	5.7	7.2	24.3
2005							
1st quarter	898 783	20 083	2.2	1.0	5.2	6.1	22.0
2nd quarter	917 012	21 253	2.3	2.0	5.8	7.1	24.1
3rd quarter	932 108	22 580	2.4	1.6	6.2	7.3	25.1
4th quarter	937 149	23 236	2.5	0.5	2.9	5.3	21.7
2006							
1st quarter	966 276	25 012	2.6	3.1	7.6	7.5	24.5
2nd quarter	971 912	25 824	2.7	0.6	3.2	6.0	21.5
3rd quarter	976 919	26 989	2.8	0.5	4.5	4.8	19.5
4th quarter	977 869	28 311	2.9	0.1	4.9	4.3	21.8
2007							
1st quarter	996 673	29 758	3.0	1.9	5.1	3.1	19.0
2nd quarter	1 009 517	31 602	3.1	1.3	6.2	3.9	22.4
3rd quarter	1 015 408	32 504	3.2	0.6	2.9	3.9	20.4
4th quarter	1 032 040	33 793	3.3	1.6	4.0	5.5	19.4
2008							
1st quarter	1 012 727	33 543	3.3	-0.6	0.6	2.5	12.9
2nd quarter	1 015 423	33 897	3.3	0.3	1.1	2.3	8.8
3rd quarter	997 086	33 426	3.4	-1.8	-1.4	-0.1	4.5
4th quarter	921 637	31 339	3.4	-7.6	-6.2	-9.5	-6.0
2009							
1st quarter	903 718	33 865	3.7	-2.0	1.7	-10.7	-6.6
2nd quarter	904 045	34 827	3.9	0.0	2.8	-11.1	-4.8
3rd quarter	922 763	36 587	4.0	2.1	5.1	-7.8	1.7
4th quarter	941 355	38 141	4.1	2.0	4.2	2.1	14.6

. . . = Not available.

Table 17-11. Retail Inventories

(All retail stores; end of period, millions of dollars.)

Year and month	Not seasonally adjusted			Seasonally adjusted								
	Total	Excluding motor vehicles and parts	Motor vehicles and parts	Total	Excluding motor vehicles and parts	Motor vehicles and parts	Furniture, home furnishings, electronics, and appliances	Building materials and garden	Food and beverages	Clothing and accessories	General merchandise Total	Department stores [1]
1992	256 810	185 195	71 615	261 369	192 066	69 303	16 208	21 144	27 467	27 467	49 783	38 333
1993	274 748	196 932	77 816	279 526	204 233	75 293	18 138	22 667	27 558	28 193	53 700	40 854
1994	300 517	211 758	88 759	305 442	219 514	85 928	20 421	24 905	28 171	29 602	56 830	42 136
1995	318 021	221 462	96 559	322 925	229 379	93 546	21 839	26 384	28 776	29 382	59 550	43 455
1996	328 912	228 456	100 456	333 926	236 601	97 325	22 300	27 497	29 718	29 864	60 611	44 124
1997	339 565	234 858	104 707	344 609	243 120	101 489	22 157	28 947	29 949	31 167	60 735	44 309
1998	351 996	245 964	106 032	357 269	254 466	102 803	22 705	30 966	30 901	32 383	61 566	43 438
1999	379 581	260 438	119 143	384 963	269 135	115 828	24 135	33 072	32 700	33 817	64 296	43 808
2000	401 209	269 557	131 652	406 730	278 392	128 338	25 655	34 355	32 174	36 845	64 899	42 612
2001	388 668	266 910	121 758	394 554	275 343	119 211	24 523	34 340	33 228	35 719	64 735	40 384
2002	410 169	272 295	137 874	415 977	280 659	135 318	25 878	36 214	32 944	37 501	65 899	38 646
2003	426 490	277 915	148 575	432 084	286 128	145 956	27 202	37 545	32 556	38 576	66 576	36 712
2004	455 639	298 043	157 596	461 253	306 414	154 839	30 155	41 767	33 478	41 466	70 887	37 110
2005	466 476	310 450	156 026	472 038	318 966	153 072	30 713	45 094	33 795	43 238	74 095	37 844
2006	480 957	324 033	156 924	486 502	332 789	153 713	31 279	46 854	34 673	47 638	75 407	36 851
2007	493 208	332 622	160 586	498 302	341 265	157 037	32 041	47 415	36 437	47 850	75 924	36 665
2008	474 040	324 582	149 458	478 823	332 706	146 117	28 864	46 540	37 296	46 779	73 564	33 553
2009	424 281	309 227	115 054	428 946	316 511	112 435	27 338	43 471	37 054	41 862	70 790	31 348
2006												
January	465 827	309 401	156 426	474 584	320 625	153 959	30 958	45 813	33 982	42 999	73 447	37 063
February	468 471	310 886	157 585	473 540	320 177	153 363	31 220	45 271	34 135	43 468	72 758	36 515
March	483 104	319 582	163 522	479 874	323 647	156 227	31 474	46 388	34 199	44 239	73 251	36 562
April	482 544	319 426	163 118	478 269	323 063	155 206	31 555	46 564	34 222	44 620	71 729	36 138
May	483 255	318 963	164 292	485 142	325 263	159 879	31 813	46 802	34 451	45 021	72 380	35 995
June	483 765	318 976	164 789	488 532	326 765	161 767	31 903	47 179	34 529	45 242	72 537	35 677
July	472 140	319 898	152 242	487 423	327 001	160 422	31 772	47 741	34 627	45 244	73 287	35 840
August	473 870	326 234	147 636	489 070	329 717	159 353	31 718	48 393	34 685	45 428	73 967	36 047
September	484 302	337 532	146 770	487 393	329 821	157 572	31 565	47 823	34 758	45 820	73 987	36 092
October	507 525	355 532	151 993	485 925	330 086	155 839	31 081	47 506	34 728	46 107	74 597	36 183
November	516 616	361 085	155 531	484 728	331 432	153 296	31 274	47 370	34 707	46 755	75 101	36 703
December	480 957	324 033	156 924	486 502	332 789	153 713	31 279	46 854	34 673	47 638	75 407	36 851
2007												
January	478 611	321 413	157 198	487 689	332 942	154 747	31 630	46 487	34 661	47 730	75 769	37 030
February	483 440	325 772	157 668	488 903	335 445	153 458	31 948	46 806	34 605	48 492	76 219	37 105
March	489 011	330 425	158 586	487 052	335 238	151 814	31 868	46 262	34 846	48 104	76 181	36 872
April	492 286	331 582	160 704	488 879	335 701	153 178	31 701	47 662	34 520	47 848	76 414	37 100
May	489 261	331 371	157 890	492 477	338 263	154 214	31 616	47 554	34 955	48 177	76 723	36 981
June	488 934	330 575	158 359	494 756	338 719	156 037	31 772	47 816	35 207	48 012	76 613	37 141
July	482 556	331 174	151 382	497 575	338 243	159 332	31 859	47 682	35 311	47 878	76 039	36 938
August	485 276	335 135	150 141	500 789	338 759	162 030	31 785	47 541	35 683	47 905	76 023	36 766
September	496 953	346 406	150 547	499 707	338 249	161 458	31 931	46 933	35 767	48 072	75 809	36 641
October	522 626	366 684	155 942	499 272	339 994	159 278	32 313	47 397	36 109	47 809	75 992	36 907
November	530 984	368 612	162 372	498 330	338 566	159 764	32 308	47 330	36 183	47 684	74 942	36 080
December	493 208	332 622	160 586	498 302	341 265	157 037	32 041	47 415	36 437	47 850	75 924	36 665
2008												
January	491 926	331 032	160 894	500 987	342 739	158 248	31 955	47 673	36 487	47 782	76 699	36 440
February	495 604	332 636	162 968	500 947	342 460	158 487	31 875	47 315	36 655	47 640	76 791	36 563
March	498 702	335 178	163 524	497 062	340 342	156 720	31 605	47 712	36 717	47 258	75 310	36 044
April	501 801	337 553	164 248	498 714	342 123	156 591	31 816	47 220	37 000	47 442	76 149	35 983
May	494 247	334 729	159 518	498 139	341 905	156 234	31 490	47 224	37 041	47 115	76 024	35 954
June	490 723	333 598	157 125	496 980	341 594	155 386	31 540	47 352	37 165	47 142	75 502	35 382
July	488 398	336 674	151 724	503 246	343 479	159 767	31 914	47 620	37 217	47 458	75 584	35 273
August	484 208	338 879	145 329	499 565	342 604	156 961	31 764	47 975	37 324	47 348	74 923	34 771
September	496 853	351 527	145 326	499 041	343 368	155 673	31 699	48 122	37 519	47 614	75 335	34 923
October	520 340	369 332	151 008	496 383	342 488	153 895	31 454	47 916	37 674	47 595	75 207	34 916
November	518 755	367 082	151 673	486 476	337 464	149 012	29 557	47 731	37 526	47 277	74 561	34 144
December	474 040	324 582	149 458	478 823	332 706	146 117	28 864	46 540	37 296	46 779	73 564	33 553
2009												
January	461 119	319 357	141 762	469 891	330 383	139 508	28 512	46 208	37 697	46 275	72 875	32 987
February	458 008	319 486	138 522	463 369	328 878	134 491	28 145	46 265	37 720	46 305	72 019	32 532
March	459 596	322 777	136 819	458 816	327 655	131 161	27 938	46 677	37 847	45 395	72 497	32 884
April	454 912	321 203	133 709	453 141	325 475	127 666	27 868	45 788	37 824	44 686	71 941	32 618
May	440 790	316 334	124 456	445 255	323 183	122 072	27 739	45 114	37 900	44 402	71 512	32 383
June	434 159	314 607	119 552	440 798	322 132	118 666	27 631	44 365	37 681	44 085	71 790	32 550
July	424 660	314 338	110 322	436 520	320 499	116 021	27 355	43 876	37 749	43 515	71 435	32 257
August	415 150	315 445	99 705	426 344	318 919	107 425	27 340	43 623	37 551	43 185	70 933	32 112
September	429 027	324 533	104 494	428 757	317 116	111 641	27 368	43 614	37 678	42 477	70 599	31 956
October	451 662	340 910	110 752	428 774	316 240	112 534	27 626	43 317	37 673	42 205	70 524	31 756
November	457 792	342 855	114 937	428 102	315 192	112 910	27 306	42 688	37 722	42 002	70 229	31 360
December	424 281	309 227	115 054	428 946	316 511	112 435	27 338	43 471	37 054	41 862	70 790	31 348

[1] Excluding leased departments.

Table 17-12. Merchant Wholesalers—Sales and Inventories

(Millions of dollars.)

Classification basis, year, and month	Not seasonally adjusted						Seasonally adjusted					
	Sales			Inventories (current cost, end of period)			Sales			Inventories (current cost, end of period)		
	Total	Durable goods establishments	Nondurable goods establishments	Total	Durable goods establishments	Nondurable goods establishments	Total	Durable goods establishments	Nondurable goods establishments	Total	Durable goods establishments	Nondurable goods establishments
1992	1 767 130	861 182	905 948	197 793	121 809	75 984	1 767 130	861 182	905 948	196 914	123 435	73 479
1993	1 848 215	939 945	908 270	205 815	127 094	78 721	1 848 215	939 945	908 270	204 842	128 851	75 991
1994	1 974 899	1 037 638	937 261	222 826	139 941	82 885	1 974 899	1 037 638	937 261	221 978	141 975	80 003
1995	2 158 980	1 141 701	1 017 279	239 275	151 709	87 566	2 158 980	1 141 701	1 017 279	238 392	154 089	84 303
1996	2 284 343	1 190 342	1 094 001	241 396	154 207	87 189	2 284 343	1 190 342	1 094 001	241 050	156 664	84 386
1997	2 377 845	1 256 384	1 121 461	258 900	165 371	93 529	2 377 845	1 256 384	1 121 461	258 575	168 079	90 496
1998	2 427 120	1 306 545	1 120 575	272 575	175 994	96 581	2 427 120	1 306 545	1 120 575	272 449	178 945	93 504
1999	2 599 159	1 406 371	1 192 788	290 207	187 750	102 457	2 599 159	1 406 371	1 192 788	290 077	190 912	99 165
2000	2 814 554	1 486 673	1 327 881	309 413	198 557	110 856	2 814 554	1 486 673	1 327 881	308 906	201 835	107 071
2001	2 785 152	1 422 195	1 362 957	298 169	182 532	115 637	2 785 152	1 422 195	1 362 957	297 135	185 565	111 570
2002	2 835 528	1 421 503	1 414 025	182 158	182 158	120 080	2 835 528	1 421 503	1 414 025	300 813	185 096	115 717
2003	2 971 488	1 464 088	1 507 400	309 384	182 158	122 996	2 971 488	1 464 088	1 507 400	307 550	189 340	118 210
2004	3 314 559	1 685 729	1 628 830	339 868	213 062	126 806	3 314 559	1 685 729	1 628 830	338 542	216 161	122 381
2005	3 595 563	1 811 065	1 784 498	366 553	231 519	135 034	3 595 563	1 811 065	1 784 498	365 037	234 579	130 458
2006	3 889 699	1 983 574	1 906 125	397 773	252 550	145 223	3 889 699	1 983 574	1 906 125	395 634	255 404	140 230
2007	4 153 429	2 065 939	2 087 490	424 177	258 834	165 343	4 153 429	2 065 939	2 087 490	420 779	261 466	159 313
2008	4 410 763	2 069 702	2 341 061	438 730	273 532	165 198	4 410 763	2 069 702	2 341 061	436 423	275 982	160 441
2009	3 758 089	1 713 723	2 044 366	394 105	229 889	164 216	3 758 089	1 713 723	2 044 366	390 453	232 064	158 389
2006												
January	295 218	147 048	148 170	368 933	234 616	134 317	315 741	160 599	155 142	365 993	235 280	130 713
February	287 028	145 189	141 839	371 944	238 616	133 328	317 379	162 123	155 256	369 672	237 578	132 094
March	340 237	175 272	164 965	372 664	239 103	133 561	318 577	161 836	156 741	371 620	239 347	132 273
April	308 581	154 107	154 474	375 939	244 595	131 344	321 039	161 250	159 789	376 646	243 997	132 649
May	338 143	171 241	166 902	375 605	245 570	130 035	324 543	165 367	159 176	379 884	245 738	134 146
June	343 147	176 628	166 519	380 974	247 780	133 194	326 702	165 274	161 428	382 524	247 336	135 188
July	316 100	158 615	157 485	385 425	252 051	133 374	328 233	166 006	162 227	386 149	250 292	135 857
August	350 191	177 237	172 954	386 731	251 503	135 228	330 004	166 946	163 058	389 807	251 700	138 107
September	326 374	169 506	156 868	391 447	254 431	137 016	326 085	167 590	158 495	392 126	254 349	137 777
October	339 953	177 045	162 908	395 392	257 435	137 957	324 557	167 972	156 585	393 749	256 543	137 206
November	324 958	167 899	157 059	399 516	257 100	142 416	328 042	169 796	158 246	397 455	256 831	140 624
December	319 769	163 787	155 982	397 773	252 550	145 223	333 886	171 561	162 325	395 634	255 404	140 230
2007												
January	316 806	161 039	155 767	400 476	256 175	144 301	329 225	170 448	158 777	397 066	256 746	140 320
February	301 295	151 181	150 114	402 124	258 646	143 478	334 242	169 149	165 093	399 289	257 527	141 762
March	351 230	180 539	170 691	402 433	257 787	144 646	339 274	171 940	167 334	401 472	258 395	143 077
April	338 775	170 098	168 677	401 802	257 581	144 221	343 983	173 233	170 750	402 791	257 521	145 270
May	360 973	177 311	183 662	399 587	258 182	141 405	346 090	171 327	174 763	404 368	258 795	145 573
June	353 891	178 110	175 781	403 426	258 480	144 946	345 419	171 658	173 761	405 623	258 589	147 034
July	341 462	168 394	173 068	405 631	259 076	146 555	343 214	170 367	172 847	407 118	257 697	149 421
August	365 468	183 014	182 454	404 358	257 734	146 624	344 120	172 347	171 773	408 457	258 062	150 395
September	339 569	169 124	170 445	410 408	259 636	150 772	349 595	172 551	177 044	412 243	259 032	153 211
October	380 121	188 903	191 218	414 490	260 097	154 393	352 817	173 768	179 049	412 672	258 567	154 105
November	360 341	175 033	185 308	418 881	260 359	158 522	363 189	176 399	186 790	415 913	259 442	156 471
December	343 498	163 193	180 305	424 177	258 834	165 343	359 261	171 156	188 105	420 779	261 466	159 313
2008												
January	354 691	165 888	188 803	431 620	264 432	167 188	367 675	175 553	192 122	426 435	264 936	161 499
February	342 874	159 622	183 252	435 645	267 888	167 757	364 842	171 022	193 820	430 885	266 617	164 268
March	372 056	177 918	194 138	432 827	267 267	165 560	372 691	175 354	197 337	431 009	268 054	162 955
April	383 942	183 007	200 935	437 094	271 913	165 181	379 477	180 623	198 854	437 891	272 224	165 667
May	389 939	180 453	209 486	435 140	273 173	161 967	383 937	179 865	204 072	440 930	274 235	166 695
June	400 182	187 270	212 912	441 842	275 282	166 560	391 108	181 094	210 014	445 292	275 773	169 519
July	398 090	183 555	214 535	449 057	280 414	168 643	387 723	179 916	207 807	451 805	279 459	172 346
August	382 049	176 047	206 002	450 156	282 158	167 998	378 780	175 635	203 145	455 636	282 782	172 854
September	382 055	180 766	201 289	452 549	285 234	167 315	370 554	172 508	198 046	454 573	284 395	170 178
October	378 763	178 903	199 860	449 883	284 067	165 816	352 534	164 761	187 773	447 953	282 010	165 943
November	306 661	143 931	162 730	445 979	281 548	164 431	328 152	155 127	173 025	442 951	280 089	162 862
December	319 461	152 342	167 119	438 730	273 532	165 198	314 603	150 008	164 595	436 423	275 982	160 441
2009												
January	286 915	128 755	158 160	436 599	272 647	163 952	305 636	140 328	165 308	432 529	272 953	159 576
February	277 745	127 358	150 387	428 793	267 067	161 726	308 505	143 165	165 340	425 041	265 488	159 553
March	310 657	144 576	166 081	418 560	258 414	160 146	300 489	137 409	163 080	416 943	258 748	158 195
April	306 237	137 985	168 252	410 988	253 430	157 558	303 700	137 262	166 438	411 710	253 696	158 014
May	301 467	132 642	168 825	402 507	248 223	154 284	305 446	137 041	168 405	407 542	249 321	158 221
June	325 311	149 002	176 309	398 176	245 039	153 137	308 123	139 205	168 918	400 535	245 671	154 864
July	318 031	144 040	173 991	393 999	242 743	151 256	310 491	141 351	169 140	395 608	242 121	153 487
August	314 604	143 146	171 458	386 564	237 679	148 885	313 562	143 266	170 296	390 396	238 206	152 190
September	326 085	151 433	174 652	385 975	236 724	149 251	315 975	144 360	171 615	387 349	235 956	151 393
October	333 961	154 569	179 392	390 888	237 615	153 273	319 030	146 136	172 894	389 434	235 739	153 695
November	318 817	143 868	174 949	396 711	236 426	160 285	330 869	149 620	181 249	393 627	235 060	158 567
December	338 259	156 349	181 910	394 105	229 889	164 216	332 897	153 185	179 712	390 453	232 064	158 389

. . . = Not available.

Table 17-13. Selected Services—Quarterly Estimated Revenue for Employer Firms

(Millions of dollars.)

2002 NAICS code	Kind of business	2003 4th quarter	2004 1st quarter	2nd quarter	3rd quarter	4th quarter	2005 1st quarter	2nd quarter	3rd quarter	4th quarter
SEASONALLY ADJUSTED										
51	**Information**	234 329	234 129	237 974	239 841	243 128	246 610	248 631	251 507	253 072
5112	Software publishers	28 769	27 817	27 614	28 347	28 526	28 872	29 846	30 394	30 783
512	Motion picture and sound recording industries	22 348	21 829	22 103	21 781	22 538	23 674	22 806	23 934	23 444
54 pt	**Professional, Scientific, and Technical Services (Except Landscape Architectural Services and Veterinary Services)**	225 736	232 241	239 189	244 402	250 055	254 242	259 689	265 976	271 901
5411	Legal services	49 712	50 245	52 376	54 023	54 903	56 483	56 089	55 539	56 260
5412	Accounting, tax preparation, bookkeeping, and payroll services	23 490	22 672	23 036	23 544	23 927	25 478	25 244	24 985	25 215
56 pt	**Administrative and Support and Waste Management and Remediation Services (Except Landscaping Services)**	100 519	105 135	109 307	112 505	116 816	116 180	119 901	121 521	124 561
5613	Employment services	32 041	33 609	36 180	37 170	38 633	38 963	39 218	40 576	40 283
5615	Travel arrangement and reservation services	6 597	6 864	7 051	7 137	7 134	7 245	7 265	7 134	7 325
562	Waste management and remediation services	13 130	14 176	14 268	15 019	15 156	14 878	15 166	16 080	16 951
622	**Hospitals**	. . .	. . .	. . .	. . .	148 527	150 098	151 313	154 975	155 361
NOT SEASONALLY ADJUSTED										
51	**Information**	242 296	228 276	237 974	237 682	251 151	240 445	248 631	249 495	261 170
511	Publishing industries (except Internet)	. . .	. . .	. . .	. . .	. . .	. . .	. . .	. . .	. . .
51111	Newspaper publishers	. . .	. . .	. . .	. . .	. . .	. . .	. . .	. . .	. . .
51112	Periodical publishers	. . .	. . .	. . .	. . .	. . .	. . .	. . .	. . .	. . .
5111 pt	Book, directory and mailing list, and other publishers	. . .	. . .	. . .	. . .	. . .	. . .	. . .	. . .	. . .
5112	Software publishers	31 214	26 899	27 227	27 270	30 865	28 006	29 488	29 178	33 184
512	Motion picture and sound recording industries	24 963	20 934	22 214	20 126	24 995	22 727	22 920	22 354	25 718
515	Broadcasting (except Internet)	. . .	. . .	. . .	. . .	. . .	. . .	. . .	. . .	. . .
5151	Radio and television broadcasting	12 787	11 522	13 484	12 900	14 187	12 547	13 252	12 240	14 270
5152	Cable and other subscription programming	. . .	. . .	. . .	. . .	. . .	. . .	. . .	. . .	. . .
516, 5181, 519	Internet publishing and broadcasting, Internet service providers and web search portals, and other information services	. . .	. . .	. . .	. . .	. . .	. . .	. . .	. . .	. . .
517	Telecommunications [1]	. . .	. . .	. . .	. . .	. . .	. . .	. . .	. . .	. . .
5171	Wired telecommunications carriers	53 937	53 233	52 853	52 466	52 624	51 966	51 688	51 192	50 806
5172	Wireless telecommunications carriers (except satellite)	29 383	29 920	31 496	33 063	33 123	33 209	34 691	35 720	36 410
5175	Cable and other program distribution	. . .	. . .	. . .	. . .	. . .	. . .	. . .	. . .	. . .
5182	Data processing, hosting, and related services	15 049	13 838	14 507	14 393	14 592	14 465	15 269	16 035	16 602
54	**Professional, Scientific, and Technical Services** [1]	. . .	. . .	. . .	. . .	. . .	. . .	. . .	. . .	. . .
54 pt	Professional, scientific, and technical services (except landscape architectural services and veterinary services)	230 928	230 615	243 734	235 604	256 056	252 717	263 584	257 199	278 699
5411	Legal services	55 379	46 276	52 428	51 970	61 217	52 134	56 033	53 373	62 842
5412	Accounting, tax preparation, bookkeeping, and payroll services	21 235	27 569	23 980	19 777	21 558	31 007	26 329	20 962	22 744
5413	Architectural, engineering, and related services	. . .	. . .	. . .	. . .	. . .	. . .	. . .	. . .	. . .
5415	Computer systems design and related services	41 691	43 083	42 444	43 103	44 895	45 168	47 556	47 280	48 262
5416	Management, scientific, and technical consulting services	28 146	28 041	30 676	30 562	32 430	32 470	34 177	34 057	36 600
5417	Scientific research and development services	. . .	. . .	. . .	. . .	. . .	. . .	. . .	. . .	. . .
5418	Advertising and related services	15 652	14 873	15 737	15 742	17 233	15 456	16 962	16 642	17 978
56	**Administrative and Support and Waste Management and Remediation Services** [1]	. . .	. . .	. . .	. . .	. . .	. . .	. . .	. . .	. . .
56 pt	Administrative and support and waste management and remediation services (except landscaping services)	101 867	103 088	109 448	112 965	118 425	113 955	120 065	121 982	126 171
561	Administrative and support services	. . .	. . .	. . .	. . .	. . .	. . .	. . .	. . .	. . .
5613	Employment services	33 226	32 634	35 963	37 058	40 062	37 872	38 943	40 495	41 733
5615	Travel arrangement and reservation services	6 261	6 713	7 580	7 108	6 799	7 078	7 795	7 113	7 010
562	Waste management and remediation services	13 629	13 255	14 097	15 620	15 671	13 911	15 075	16 643	17 426
62 pt	**Selected Health Care Services**	. . .	. . .	. . .	. . .	183 719	187 136	188 373	190 104	191 346
622	Hospitals	. . .	. . .	. . .	. . .	147 636	151 599	152 070	153 580	154 273
623	Nursing and residential care facilities	. . .	. . .	. . .	. . .	36 083	35 537	36 303	36 524	37 073

. . . = Not available.
[1]Includes components not shown separately.

Table 17-13. Selected Services—Quarterly Estimated Revenue for Employer Firms—*Continued*

(Millions of dollars.)

2002 NAICS code	Kind of business	2006 1st quarter	2006 2nd quarter	2006 3rd quarter	2006 4th quarter	2007 1st quarter	2007 2nd quarter	2007 3rd quarter	2007 4th quarter
SEASONALLY ADJUSTED									
51	**Information**	256 658	261 094	264 575	269 591	272 741	276 680	280 917	283 513
5112	Software publishers	31 442	32 208	33 378	33 672	36 277	35 199	35 077	36 184
512	Motion picture and sound recording industries	23 597	24 067	24 317	25 212	24 966	25 013	25 427	25 208
54 pt	**Professional, Scientific, and Technical Services (Except Landscape Architectural Services and Veterinary Services)**	277 184	280 772	285 888	292 549	303 504	309 651	313 544	318 796
5411	Legal services	56 648	58 603	60 304	62 413	65 160	62 163	62 325	64 040
5412	Accounting, tax preparation, bookkeeping, and payroll services	27 324	26 306	27 243	28 277	28 608	30 436	31 290	32 327
56 pt	**Administrative and Support and Waste Management and Remediation Services (Except Landscaping Services)**	126 039	127 513	128 761	130 309	131 462	135 202	136 571	135 530
5613	Employment services	42 113	42 339	42 878	43 541	43 873	44 712	44 386	44 850
5615	Travel arrangement and reservation services	7 084	7 305	7 654	8 144	8 250	8 198	8 103	8 023
562	Waste management and remediation services	17 003	17 330	17 086	17 100	17 739	17 606	17 701	17 725
622	**Hospitals**	157 180	159 721	162 206	165 579	167 861	169 889	172 549	175 211
NOT SEASONALLY ADJUSTED									
51	**Information**	250 498	261 094	262 194	278 488	266 468	276 403	278 389	292 869
511	Publishing industries (except Internet)	. . .	. . .	70 498	75 703	70 385	72 528	73 538	79 317
51111	Newspaper publishers	. . .	. . .	11 667	13 177	11 367	12 208	11 837	12 502
51112	Periodical publishers	. . .	. . .	12 084	12 507	11 232	12 281	12 434	12 745
5111 pt	Book, directory and mailing list, and other publishers	. . .	. . .	14 838	13 788	12 343	13 051	15 944	15 028
5112	Software publishers	30 656	31 886	31 909	36 231	35 443	34 988	33 323	39 042
512	Motion picture and sound recording industries	22 653	24 284	22 907	27 355	23 967	25 338	24 156	27 073
515	Broadcasting (except Internet)	. . .	. . .	22 201	24 942	22 811	24 289	23 753	25 600
5151	Radio and television broadcasting	13 438	13 854	12 853	14 933	13 485	14 137	13 296	14 628
5152	Cable and other subscription programming	. . .	. . .	9 348	10 009	9 326	10 152	10 457	10 972
516, 5181, 519	Internet publishing and broadcasting, Internet service providers and web search portals, and other information services	. . .	. . .	11 948	12 922	13 000	13 112	13 717	15 348
517	Telecommunications [1]	. . .	. . .	116 853	119 326	119 062	122 630	124 954	126 963
5171	Wired telecommunications carriers	48 965	48 553	48 885	49 229	48 209	49 239	49 948	49 585
5172	Wireless telecommunications carriers (except satellite)	37 393	38 704	40 275	41 119	41 854	42 740	44 192	45 047
5175	Cable and other program distribution	. . .	. . .	22 597	23 871	23 886	25 481	25 626	27 171
5182	Data processing, hosting, and related services	16 444	17 610	17 787	18 240	17 243	18 506	18 271	18 568
54	**Professional, Scientific, and Technical Services [1]**	. . .	. . .	285 854	307 644	308 281	319 618	313 691	334 987
54 pt	Professional, scientific, and technical services (except landscape architectural services and veterinary services)	275 244	283 860	277 883	300 155	300 772	311 819	306 332	327 722
5411	Legal services	52 286	58 486	58 133	69 590	60 143	61 852	60 580	71 084
5412	Accounting, tax preparation, bookkeeping, and payroll services	33 089	27 542	22 911	25 619	34 301	32 049	26 409	29 353
5413	Architectural, engineering, and related services	. . .	. . .	56 753	58 151	58 572	59 473	61 760	64 002
5415	Computer systems design and related services	48 701	50 245	49 962	53 448	53 933	57 375	58 107	59 564
5416	Management, scientific, and technical consulting services	37 486	37 549	37 068	37 084	38 988	41 924	41 204	42 328
5417	Scientific research and development services	. . .	. . .	. . .	. . .	24 043	25 229	25 379	26 854
5418	Advertising and related services	17 219	18 018	17 926	19 785	18 492	19 917	19 705	20 831
56	**Administrative and Support and Waste Management and Remediation Services [1]**	. . .	. . .	144 851	146 710	140 687	149 735	150 640	150 474
56 pt	Administrative and support and waste management and remediation services (except landscaping services)	123 806	127 664	129 135	131 988	129 193	135 394	136 963	137 324
561	Administrative and support services	. . .	. . .	127 270	129 200	123 941	132 006	132 479	132 359
5613	Employment services	41 060	41 958	42 749	45 152	42 820	44 265	44 253	46 599
5615	Travel arrangement and reservation services	6 907	7 802	7 662	7 802	8 027	8 714	8 168	7 678
562	Waste management and remediation services	16 000	17 365	17 581	17 510	16 746	17 729	18 161	18 115
62 pt	**Selected Health Care Services**	196 300	198 132	197 943	202 615	208 796	210 554	211 099	214 962
622	Hospitals	158 909	160 679	160 584	164 420	169 707	170 908	170 824	173 985
623	Nursing and residential care facilities	37 391	37 453	37 359	38 195	39 089	39 646	40 275	40 977

. . . = Not available.
[1] Includes components not shown separately.

Table 17-13. Selected Services—Quarterly Estimated Revenue for Employer Firms—*Continued*

(Millions of dollars.)

2002 NAICS code	Kind of business	2008				2009			
		1st quarter	2nd quarter	3rd quarter	4th quarter	1st quarter	2nd quarter	3rd quarter	4th quarter
SEASONALLY ADJUSTED									
51	**Information**	288 556	290 562	292 485	284 746	282 578	283 059	283 845	286 174
5112	Software publishers	38 180	38 597	38 388	36 576	34 672	35 621	35 919	38 061
512	Motion picture and sound recording industries	25 920	26 166	25 680	24 204	25 165	25 113	25 246	25 714
54 pt	**Professional, Scientific, and Technical Services (Except Landscape Architectural Services and Veterinary Services)**	325 155	333 302	333 324	326 071	320 798	318 676	318 980	315 869
5411	Legal services	64 105	65 890	65 358	63 940	64 484	64 703	66 124	65 154
5412	Accounting, tax preparation, bookkeeping, and payroll services	32 703	32 625	31 727	31 054	30 108	29 931	30 233	29 452
56 pt	**Administrative and Support and Waste Management and Remediation Services (Except Landscaping Services)**	139 305	140 230	139 210	135 912	130 817	129 903	130 955	132 822
5613	Employment services	45 887	45 920	44 998	42 627	39 867	38 905	39 900	42 155
5615	Travel arrangement and reservation services	8 378	8 224	8 284	7 796	7 476	7 417	7 430	7 553
562	Waste management and remediation services	18 525	18 995	18 364	17 996	16 905	16 512	16 685	16 637
622	**Hospitals**	178 944	179 411	180 432	182 482	184 258	187 990	190 293	192 047
NOT SEASONALLY ADJUSTED									
51	**Information**	281 919	290 271	289 853	294 712	275 796	282 776	281 290	296 190
511	Publishing industries (except Internet)	73 230	75 132	75 313	76 690	65 570	68 287	68 105	74 771
51111	Newspaper publishers	10 958	11 100	10 861	10 999	9 108	9 631	9 424	9 984
51112	Periodical publishers	11 664	11 760	12 267	11 814	9 851	9 691	9 407	10 344
5111 pt	Book, directory and mailing list, and other publishers	13 344	13 829	15 832	14 229	12 910	13 451	15 295	13 071
5112	Software publishers	37 264	38 443	36 353	39 648	33 701	35 514	33 979	41 372
512	Motion picture and sound recording industries	24 883	26 637	24 422	25 850	24 209	25 590	24 034	27 411
515	Broadcasting (except Internet)	24 358	25 241	25 081	25 618	22 832	23 479	23 433	25 481
5151	Radio and television broadcasting	13 959	14 067	13 806	13 415	11 547	11 961	11 771	13 630
5152	Cable and other subscription programming	10 399	11 174	11 275	12 203	11 285	11 518	11 662	11 851
516, 5181, 519	Internet publishing and broadcasting, Internet service providers and web search portals, and other information services	15 018	15 185	15 363	15 556	14 778	14 929	15 117	16 589
517	Telecommunications [1]	125 997	128 356	130 410	130 752	128 683	130 464	130 594	131 545
5171	Wired telecommunications carriers	48 642	48 736	49 134	48 253	46 714	47 204	46 328	46 047
5172	Wireless telecommunications carriers (except satellite)	44 964	45 720	46 841	47 279	46 719	47 363	48 270	48 580
5175	Cable and other program distribution	27 438	28 585	29 119	30 042	30 133	30 822	30 880	31 783
5182	Data processing, hosting, and related services	18 433	19 720	19 264	20 246	19 724	20 027	20 007	20 393
54	**Professional, Scientific, and Technical Services** [1]	328 565	342 107	335 492	343 720	323 462	326 263	322 559	334 065
54 pt	Professional, scientific, and technical services (except landscape architectural services and veterinary services)	321 253	333 969	327 324	336 179	315 986	317 720	314 514	326 609
5411	Legal services	58 977	65 561	64 116	70 398	59 390	64 379	65 264	71 409
5412	Accounting, tax preparation, bookkeeping, and payroll services	38 949	34 419	26 936	28 135	35 768	31 577	25 789	26 566
5413	Architectural, engineering, and related services	62 461	66 322	68 227	69 096	62 586	60 526	59 704	58 531
5415	Computer systems design and related services	60 519	61 740	61 739	62 639	60 099	62 437	63 092	66 838
5416	Management, scientific, and technical consulting services	41 238	43 465	43 505	43 989	39 428	39 711	40 732	40 659
5417	Scientific research and development services	26 201	28 352	29 033	28 254	28 124	29 365	30 146	30 857
5418	Advertising and related services	19 554	19 783	20 097	19 989	17 730	17 297	17 313	19 283
56	**Administrative and Support and Waste Management and Remediation Services** [1]	147 819	153 841	154 097	150 857	139 838	142 880	143 445	146 909
56 pt	Administrative and support and waste management and remediation services (except landscaping services)	136 969	140 289	139 587	137 834	128 572	129 889	131 373	134 869
561	Administrative and support services	130 294	134 675	135 292	132 429	123 964	126 236	126 293	129 790
5613	Employment services	44 786	45 323	44 818	44 460	38 870	38 321	39 740	44 052
5615	Travel arrangement and reservation services	8 143	8 709	8 400	7 453	7 259	7 855	7 541	7 221
562	Waste management and remediation services	17 525	19 166	18 805	18 428	15 874	16 644	17 152	17 119
62 pt	**Selected Health Care Services**	222 467	223 051	220 364	223 272	228 482	232 583	231 896	234 754
622	Hospitals	180 912	180 667	178 447	181 022	186 285	189 306	188 390	190 511
623	Nursing and residential care facilities	41 555	42 384	41 917	42 250	42 197	43 277	43 506	44 243

[1] Includes components not shown separately.

NOTES AND DEFINITIONS, CHAPTER 17

TABLE 17-1
PETROLEUM AND PETROLEUM PRODUCTS—PRICES, IMPORTS, DOMESTIC PRODUCTION, AND STOCKS

SOURCES: FUTURES PRICES—U.S. DEPARTMENT OF ENERGY, ENERGY INFORMATION ADMINISTRATION (EIA), AND U.S. DEPARTMENT OF COMMERCE, BUREAU OF ECONOMIC ANALYSIS; IMPORTS—U.S. DEPARTMENT OF COMMERCE, CENSUS BUREAU (SEE NOTES AND DEFINITIONS FOR TABLES 7-9 THROUGH 7-14); SUPPLY (NET IMPORTS AND DOMESTIC PRODUCTION) AND STOCKS—EIA.

Definitions and notes on the data

The *crude oil futures price* in *current dollars per barrel* is the price for next-month delivery in Cushing, Oklahoma (a pipeline hub), of light, sweet crude oil, as determined by trading on the New York Mercantile Exchange (NYMEX). Official daily closing prices are reported each day at 2:30 p.m., and are tabulated weekly in Table 16 of *EIA's Weekly Petroleum Status Report*. (Beginning with the reports for 2010, they appear in Table 13.) The monthly averages shown in this volume are the average prices for the nearest future from each trading day of the month. For example, for most days in January, the futures contract priced will be for February; for the last few days in January, the February contract will have expired and the March contract will be quoted. The annual averages are averages of the monthly averages.

The *crude oil futures price* in *2005 dollars* is calculated by the editor, by dividing each month's current-dollar price by that month's chain price index for total personal consumption expenditures (PCE), with the price index average for the year 2005 set at 1.0000. The PCE chain price index is compiled by the Bureau of Economic Analysis (BEA). It is described in the notes and definitions for Chapter 1 and is also presented in Chapter 8, Table 8-2, and discussed in its notes and definitions.

The import data in Columns 3 through 6 of this table are those published as Exhibit 17, "Imports of Energy-related Petroleum Products, including Crude Petroleum," in the monthly Census-BEA foreign trade press release, FT900. *Total energy-related petroleum products* includes the following Standard International Trade Classification (SITC) commodity groupings: crude oil, petroleum preparations, and liquefied propane and butane gas.

The data in Columns 7 through 11, on exports, imports, and net imports (imports minus exports) of petroleum and products and domestic production of crude oil and natural gas plant liquids (all expressed as thousands of barrels per day), and in Columns 12 through 14, depicting stocks of crude oil in millions of barrels, are derived from the Department of Energy's weekly petroleum supply reporting system. They are published in EIA's *Monthly Energy Review*, which is classified under Reports and Products/Multifuel Energy Overview on the Web site, and can be found in Tables 3.1 and 3.4. Stock totals are as of the end of the period. Geographic coverage includes the 50 states and the District of Columbia.

Data availability

Data on futures prices, petroleum supply and stocks are available from the EIA Web site at <http://www.eia.doe.gov>, under the categories "Publications and Reports/Monthly Energy Review" and "Petroleum/Weekly Petroleum Status Report." The *Monthly Energy Review* is no longer published in printed form.

See the notes and definitions for Tables 7-9 through 7-14 for information about the availability of import data.

TABLE 17-2
CONSTRUCTION PUT IN PLACE

SOURCE: U.S. DEPARTMENT OF COMMERCE, CENSUS BUREAU

The Census Bureau's estimates of the value of new construction put in place are intended to provide monthly estimates of the total dollar value of construction work done in the United States.

Definitions and notes on the data

The estimates cover all construction work done each month on new private residential and nonresidential buildings and structures, public construction, and improvements to existing buildings and structures. Included are the cost of labor, materials, and equipment rental; cost of architectural and engineering work; overhead costs assigned to the project; interest and taxes paid during construction; and contractor's profits.

The total value put in place for a given period is the sum of the value of work done on all projects underway during this period, regardless of when work on each individual project was started or when payment was made to the contractors. For some categories, estimates are derived by distributing the total construction cost of the project by means of historic construction progress patterns. Published estimates represent payments made during a period for some categories.

The statistics on the value of construction put in place result from direct measurement and indirect estimation. A series results from direct measurement when it is based on reports of the actual value of construction progress or construction expenditures obtained in a complete census or a sample survey. All other series are developed by indirect estimation using related construction statistics. On an annual basis, estimates for series directly measured monthly, quarterly, or annually accounted for about 71 percent of total construction in 1998 (private multifamily residential, private residential improvements, private nonresidential buildings, farm nonresidential construction, public utility construction, all other private construction, and virtually all of public construction). On a monthly basis, directly measured data are available for about 55 percent of the value in place estimates.

Beginning in 1993, the Construction Expenditures Branch of the Census Bureau's Manufacturing and Construction Division began collecting these data using a new classification system, which bases project types on their end usage instead of on building/nonbuilding types. Data collection on this system for federal construction began in January 2002.

With the changes in project classifications, data presented in these tables for 1993 to date are not directly comparable with data for previous years, except at aggregate levels. For that reason, *Business Statistics* shows earlier historical data only at these aggregate levels. Although some categories, such as lodging, office, education, and religion, have the same names as categories in previously published data, there have been changes within the classifications that make these values noncomparable. For example, private medical office buildings were classified as "office" buildings previously, but are categorized as "health care" under the new classification.

The seasonally adjusted data are obtained by removing normal seasonal movement from the unadjusted data to bring out underlying trends and business cycles, which is accomplished by using the Census X-12-ARIMA method. Seasonal adjustment accounts for month-to-month variations resulting from normal or average changes in any phenomena affecting the data, such as weather conditions, the differing lengths of months, and the varying number of holidays, weekdays, and weekends within each month. It does not adjust for abnormal conditions within each month or for year-to-year variations in weather. The seasonally adjusted annual rate is the seasonally adjusted monthly rate multiplied by 12.

Residential consists of new houses, town houses, apartments, and condominiums for sale or rent; these dwellings are built by the owner or for the owner on contract. It includes improvements inside and outside residential structures, such as remodeling, additions, major replacements, and additions of swimming pools and garages. Manufactured housing, houseboats, and maintenance and repair work are not included.

Office includes general office buildings, administration buildings, professional buildings, and financial institution buildings. Office buildings at manufacturing sites are classified as *manufacturing*, but office buildings owned by manufacturing companies but not at such a site are included in the *office* category. In the state and local government category, *office* includes capitols, city halls, courthouses, and similar buildings.

Commercial includes buildings and structures used by the retail, wholesale, farm, and selected service industries. One of the subgroups of this category is *multi-retail*, which consists of department and variety stores, shopping centers and malls, and warehouse-type retail stores.

Health care includes hospitals, medical buildings, nursing homes, adult day-care centers, and similar institutions.

Educational includes schools at all levels, higher education facilities, trade schools, libraries, museums, and similar institutions.

Amusement and recreation includes theme and amusement parks, sports structures not located at educational institutions, fitness centers and health clubs, neighborhood centers, camps, movie theaters, and similar establishments.

Transportation includes airport facilities; rail facilities, track, and bridges; bus, rail, maritime, and air terminals; and docks, marinas, and similar structures.

Communication includes telephone, television, and radio distribution and maintenance structures.

Power includes electricity production and distribution and gas and crude oil transmission, storage, and distribution.

Manufacturing includes all buildings and structures at manufacturing sites but not the installation of production machinery or special-purpose equipment.

Included in *total private construction*, but not shown separately in these pages, are lodging facilities (hotels and motels), religious structures, and private public safety, sewage and waste disposal, water supply, highway and street, and conservation and development spending.

Included in *total state and local construction,* but not shown separately in these pages, are state and local construction of commercial buildings, conservation and development (dams, levees, jetties, and dredging), lodging, religious facilities, and communication structures.

Public safety includes correctional facilities, police and sheriffs' stations, fire stations, and similar establishments.

Highway and street includes pavement, lighting, retaining walls, bridges, tunnels, toll facilities, and maintenance and rest facilities.

Sewage and waste disposal includes sewage systems, solid waste disposal, and recycling.

Water supply includes water supply, transmission, and storage facilities.

Among the data sources for construction expenditures are the Census Bureau's Survey of Construction, Building Permits Survey, Consumer Expenditure Survey (conducted for the Bureau of Labor Statistics), Annual Capital Expenditures Survey, and Construction Progress Reporting Survey; also included are data from the F.W. Dodge Division of the McGraw-Hill Information Systems Company, the U.S. Department of Agriculture, and utility regulatory agencies.

Data availability

Each month's "Construction Spending" press release is released on the last workday of the following month. The release, more detailed data, and a discussion of methodologies can be found on the Census Bureau's Web site at <http://www.census.gov/constructionspending>.

TABLE 17-3
HOUSING STARTS AND BUILDING PERMITS; NEW HOUSE SALES AND PRICES

SOURCES: U.S. DEPARTMENT OF COMMERCE, CENSUS BUREAU

These data are mainly found in two major Census Bureau reports, "New Residential Construction" and "New Residential Sales." They cover new housing units intended for occupancy and maintained by the occupants, excluding hotels, motels, and group residential structures. Manufactured home units are reported in a separate survey.

Definitions

A *housing unit* is a house, an apartment, or a group of rooms or single room intended for occupancy as separate living quarters. Occupants must live separately from other individuals in the building and have direct access to the housing unit from the outside of the building or through a common hall. Each apartment unit in an apartment building is counted as one housing unit. As of January 2000, a previous requirement for residents to have the capability to eat separately has been eliminated. (Based on the old definition, some senior housing projects were excluded from the multifamily housing statistics because individual units did not have their own eating facilities.) Housing starts exclude group quarters such as dormitories or rooming houses, transient accommodations such as motels, and manufactured homes. Publicly owned housing units are excluded, but units in structures built by private developers with subsidies or for sale to local public housing authorities are both classified as private housing.

The *start* of construction of a privately owned housing unit is when excavation begins for the footings or foundation of a building primarily intended as a housekeeping residential structure and designed for nontransient occupancy. All housing units in a multifamily building are defined as being started when excavation for the building begins.

One-family structures includes fully detached, semi-detached, row houses, and townhouses. In the case of attached units, each must be separated from the adjacent unit by a ground-to-roof wall to be classified as a one-unit structure and must not share facilities such as heating or water supply. Units built one on top of another and those built side-by-side without a ground-to-roof wall and/or with common facilities are classified by the number of units in the structure.

Apartment buildings are defined as buildings containing *five units or more*. The type of ownership is not the criterion—a condominium apartment building is not classified as one-family structures but as a multifamily structure.

A *manufactured* home is a moveable dwelling, 8 feet or more wide and 40 feet or more long, designed to be towed on its own chassis with transportation gear integral to the unit when it leaves the factory, and without need of a permanent foundation. Multiwides and expandable manufactured homes are included. Excluded are travel trailers, motor homes, and modular housing. The shipments figures are based on reports submitted by manufacturers on the number of homes actually shipped during the survey month. Shipments to dealers may not necessarily be placed for residential use in the same month as they are shipped. The number of manufactured "homes" used for nonresidential purposes (for example, those used for offices) is not known.

Units authorized by building permits represents the approximately 97 percent of housing in permit-requiring areas.

The *start* occurs when excavation begins for the footing or foundation. Starts are estimated for all areas, regardless of whether permits are required.

New house *sales* are reported only for new single-family residential structures. The sales transaction must intend to include both house and land. Excluded are houses built for rent, houses built by the owner, and houses built by a contractor on the owner's land. A sale is reported when a deposit is taken or a sales agreement is signed; this can occur prior to a permit being issued.

Once the sale is reported, the sold housing unit drops out of the survey. Consequently the Census Bureau does not find out if the sales contract is cancelled or if the house is ever resold. As a result, if conditions are worsening and cancellations are high, sales are temporarily overestimated. When conditions improve and the cancelled sales materialize as actual sales, the Census sales estimates are then underestimated because the case did not re-enter the survey. In the long run, cancellations do not cause the survey to overestimate or underestimate sales; but in the short run, cancellations and ultimate resales are not reflected in this survey, and fluctuations can appear less severe than in reality.

A house is *for sale* when a permit to build has been issued (or work begun in non-permit areas) and a sales contract has not been signed nor a deposit accepted.

The *sales price* used in this survey is the price agreed upon between the purchaser and the seller at the time the first sales contract is signed or deposit made. It includes the price of the improved lot. The *median sales price* is the sales price of the house that falls on the middle point of a distribution by price of the total number of houses sold. Half of the houses sold have a sales lower than the median; half have a price higher than the median. Changes in the *sales price* data reflect changes in the distribution of houses by region, size, and the like, as well as changes in the prices of houses with identical characteristics.

The *price index* measures the change in price of a new single-family house of constant physical characteristics, using the characteristics of houses built in 1996. Characteristics held constant include floor area, whether inside or outside a metropolitan area, number of bedrooms, number of bathrooms, number of fireplaces, type of parking facility, type of foundation, presence of a deck, construction method, exterior wall material, type of heating, and presence of air-conditioning. The indexes are calculated separately for attached and detached houses and combined with base period weights. The price measured includes the value of the lot.

See the notes and definitions to Table 12-10 for a discussion of the characteristics of the various price indexes for single-family houses.

Notes on the data

Monthly permit authorizations are based on data collected by a mail survey from a sample of about 9,000 permit-issuing places, selected from and representing a universe of 20,000 such places in the United States. The remaining places are surveyed annually. Data for 1994 through 2003 represented 19,000 places; data for 1984 through 1993 represented 17,000 places; data for 1978 through 1983 represented 16,000 places; data for 1972 through 1977 represented 14,000 places; data for 1967 through 1971 represented 13,000 places; data for 1963 through 1966 represented 12,000 places; and data for 1959 through 1962 represented 10,000 places.

Housing starts and sales data are obtained from the Survey of Construction, for which Census Bureau field representatives sample both permit-issuing and non-permit-issuing places.

Effective with the January 2005 data release, the Survey of Construction implemented a new sample of building permit offices, replacing a previous sample selected in 1985. As a result, writes the Census Bureau, "Data users should uses caution when analyzing year over year changes in housing prices and characteristics between 2004 and 2005." In the newer sample, land may be more abundant, lot sizes larger, and sales prices lower.

For 2004, the permit data were compiled for both the new 20,000 place universe and the old 19,000 place universe. Ratios of the new estimates to the old were calculated by state for total housing units, structures by number of units, and valuation. For the United States as a whole, the new estimate was 100.9 percent of the old estimate. The complete table of ratios can be found on the Census Bureau Web site at <http://www.census.gov/const/www/permitsindex>.

Effective with the data for April 2001, the Census Bureau made changes to the methodology used for new house sales, including discontinuing an adjustment for construction in areas in which building permits are required without a permit being issued. It was believed that such unauthorized construction has virtually ceased. The upward adjustment was not phased out but dropped completely in revised estimates as of January 1999. The total effect of these changes was to lower the number of sales by about 2.9 percent relative to those published for earlier years.

The data used in the price index are collected in the Survey of Construction, through monthly interviews with the builders or owners. The size of the sample is currently about 20,000 observations per year.

Data availability and references

Housing starts and building permit data have been collected monthly by the Bureau of the Census since 1959.

The monthly report for "New Residential Construction" (permits, starts, and completions) is issued in the middle of the following month. The monthly report and associated descriptions and historical data can be found at <http://www.census.gov/newresconst>.

The monthly report for "New Residential Sales" (sales, houses for sale, and prices) is issued toward the end of the following month. The monthly report and associated descriptions and historical data can be found at <http://www.census.gov/newhomesales>.

The manufactured housing data (not seasonally adjusted) and background information can be found at <http://www.manufacturedhousing.org/statistics>. Data with and without seasonal adjustment can be found at <http://www.census.gov/const/mhs/shiphist>.

Data and background on the price index for new one-family houses can be found at <http://www.census/gov>, in the alphabetical index under the category "Construction price indexes."

TABLES 17-4 THROUGH 17-7
MANUFACTURERS' SHIPMENTS, INVENTORIES, AND ORDERS

SOURCE: U.S. DEPARTMENT OF COMMERCE, CENSUS BUREAU

These data are from the Census Bureau's monthly M3 survey, a sample-based survey that provides measures of changes in the value of domestic manufacturing activity and indications of future production commitments. The sample is not a probability sample. It includes approximately 4,300 reporting units, including most companies with $500 million or more in annual shipments and a selection of smaller companies. Currently, reported monthly data represent approximately 60 percent of shipments at the total manufacturing level.

One important technology industry, semiconductors, is represented in the shipments and inventories data in this report but not in new or unfilled orders. This affects the new and unfilled orders totals for computers and electronic products, durable goods industries, and total manufacturing. Based on shipments data, semiconductors accounted for about 15 percent of computers and electronic products, 3 percent of durable goods industries, and 1.5 percent of total manufacturing. Since semiconductors are intermediate materials and components rather than finished final products, the absence of these data does not distort new and unfilled orders data for important final demand categories, such as capital goods and information technology.

Definitions and notes on the data

Shipments. The value of shipments data represent net selling values, f.o.b. (free on board) plant, after discounts and allowances and excluding freight charges and excise taxes. For multi-establishment companies, the M3 reports are typically company- or division-level reports that encompass groups of plants or products. The data reported are usually net sales and receipts from customers and do not include the value of interplant transfers. The reported sales are used to calculate month-to-month changes that bring forward the estimates for the entire industry (that is, estimates of the statistical "universe") that have been developed from the Annual Survey of Manufactures (ASM). The value of products made elsewhere under contract from materials owned by the plant is also included in shipments, along with receipts for contract work performed for others, resales, miscellaneous activities such as the sale of scrap and refuse, and installation and repair work performed by employees of the plant.

Inventories. Inventories in the M3 survey are collected on a current cost or pre-LIFO (last in, first out) basis. As different inventory valuation methods are reflected in the reported data, the estimates differ slightly from replacement cost estimates. Companies using the LIFO method for valuing inventories report their pre-LIFO value; the adjustment to their base-period prices is excluded. In the ASM, inventories are collected according to this same definition. However, there are discontinuities in the historical data in both surveys. Inventory data prior to 1982 are not comparable to later years because of changes in valuation methods. Until 1982, respondents were asked in the ASM to report their inventories at book values—that is, according to whatever method they used for tax purposes (LIFO, FIFO [first in, first out], and so forth). Because of this, the value of aggregate inventories for an industry was not precise. The change in instructions for reporting current cost inventories was carried to the monthly survey beginning in January 1987. The data for 1982 to 1987 were redefined (but not re-collected by survey) on a pre-LIFO, or current cost, basis.

Inventory data are requested from respondents by three stages of fabrication: finished goods, work in process, and raw materials and supplies. Response to the stage of fabrication inquiries is lower than for total inventories; not all companies keep their monthly data at this level of detail. It should be noted that a product considered to be a finished good in one industry, such as steel mill shapes, may be reported as a raw material in another industry, such as stamping plants. For some purposes, this difference in definitions is an advantage. When a factory accumulates inventory that it considers to be raw materials, it can be expected that that accumulation is intentional. But when a factory—whether a materials-making or a final-product producer—has a buildup of finished goods inventories, it may indicate involuntary accumulation as a result of sales falling short of expectations. Hence, the two types of accumulation can have different economic interpretations, even if they represent identical types of goods.

Like total inventories, stage of fabrication inventories are benchmarked to the ASM data. Stage of fabrication data are benchmarked at the major group level, as opposed to the level of total inventories, which is benchmarked at the individual industry level.

New orders, as reported in the monthly survey, are net of order cancellations and include orders received and filled during the month as well as orders received for future delivery. They also include the value of contract changes that increase or decrease the value of the unfilled orders to which they relate. Orders are defined to include those supported by binding legal documents such as signed contracts, letters of award, or letters of intent, although this definition may not be strictly applicable in some industries.

Unfilled orders includes new orders (as defined above) that have not been reflected as shipments. Generally, unfilled orders at the end of the reporting period are equal to unfilled orders at the beginning of the period plus net new orders received less net shipments.

Series are adjusted for seasonal variation and variation in the number of trading days in the month using the X-12-ARIMA version of the Census Bureau's seasonal adjustment program.

Benchmarking and revisions

The data shown in the volume have been benchmarked to the 2006 Annual Survey of Manufactures (ASM). In May 2010, too late for inclusion in this volume, revised data were issued incorporating benchmarking of shipments and inventories to the 2007 Economic Census and the 2008 ASM. In each benchmark revision, new and unfilled orders are adjusted to be consistent with the benchmarked shipments and inventory data, seasonal adjustment factors are revised and updated, and other corrections are made.

Data availability and references

Data have been collected monthly since 1958.

The "Advance Report on Durable Goods Manufacturers' Shipments, Inventories and Orders" is available as a press release about 18 working days after the end of each month.

It includes seasonally adjusted and not seasonally adjusted estimates of shipments, new orders, unfilled orders, and inventories for durable goods industries.

The monthly "Manufacturers' Shipments, Inventories, and Orders" report is released on the 23rd working day after the end of the month. Content includes revisions to the advance durable goods data, estimates for nondurable goods industries, tabulations by market category, and ratios of shipments to inventories and to unfilled orders. Revisions may affect selected data for the two previous months.

Press releases, historical data, descriptions of the survey, and documentation are available on the Census Bureau Web site at <http://www.census.gov>, under the category "Economic Indicators".

TABLE 17-8
MOTOR VEHICLE SALES AND INVENTORIES

SOURCE: U.S. DEPARTMENT OF COMMERCE, BUREAU OF ECONOMIC ANALYSIS

Retail sales and *inventories of cars, trucks, and buses.* These estimates are prepared by the Bureau of Economic Analysis (BEA), based on data from the American Automobile Manufacturers Association, Ward's Automotive Reports, and other sources. Seasonal adjustments are recalculated annually. Data are available on the BEA Web site at <http://www.bea.gov> as a part of the national income and product accounts data set; they are found under the "Supplemental Estimates" heading. They are also available on the STAT-USA subscription Web site at <http://www.stat-usa.gov>.

In this table, unlike in most other tables that include inventories in *Business Statistics,* the yearly values shown for inventories and the inventory to sales ratio are annual averages of monthly figures, not year-end values.

TABLES 17-9 AND 17-11
RETAIL AND FOOD SERVICES SALES; RETAIL INVENTORIES

SOURCE: U.S. DEPARTMENT OF COMMERCE, CENSUS BUREAU

Every month, the Census Bureau prepares estimates of retail sales and inventories by kind of business, based on a mail-out/mail-back survey of about 12,500 retail businesses with paid employees.

Retail sales and inventories are now compiled using the new NAICS classification system, which replaced the old SIC system. Historical data have been restated on the NAICS basis back to January 1992. In NAICS, Eating and drinking places and Mobile food services have been reclassified out of retail trade and into sector 72, Accommodation and food services, which also includes Hotels. The retail sales survey still collects and publishes sales data for Food services and drinking places. It no longer includes them in

the Retail total, but they are included in a new Retail and food services total.

Subtotals of durable and nondurable goods are no longer published. They were always imprecise for retail sales, since general merchandise stores (including department stores) were included in nondurable goods, yet obviously sold substantial quantities of durable goods.

For further information about SIC and NAICS, see Chapter 14.

Definitions

Sales is the value of merchandise sold for cash or credit at retail or wholesale. Services that are incidental to the sale of merchandise, and excise taxes that are paid by the manufacturer or wholesaler and passed along to the retailer, are also included. Sales are net, after deductions for refunds and merchandise returns. They exclude sales taxes collected directly from customers and paid directly to a local, state, or federal tax agency. The sales estimates include only sales by establishments primarily engaged in retail trade, and are not intended to measure the total sales for a given commodity or merchandise line.

Inventories is the value of stocks of goods held for sale through retail stores, valued at cost, as of the last day of the report period. Stocks may be held either at the store or at warehouses that maintain supplies primarily intended for distribution to retail stores within the organization.

Inventory data prior to 1980 are not comparable to later years, due to changes in valuation methods. Prior to 1980, inventories are the book values of merchandise on hand at the end of the period. They are valued according to the valuation method used by each respondent. Thus the aggregates are a mixture of LIFO (last in, first out) and non-LIFO values. Beginning with 1980, inventories are valued using methods other than LIFO in order to better reflect the current costs of goods held as inventory.

Leased departments consists of the operations of one company conducted within the establishment of another company, such as jewelry counters or optical centers within department stores. The values for sales and inventories at department stores in Tables 17-9 and 17-10 exclude sales of leased departments.

GAFO (department store type goods) is a special aggregate grouping of sales at general merchandise stores and at other stores that sell merchandise normally sold in department stores—clothing and accessories, furniture and home furnishings, electronics, appliances, sporting goods, hobby, book, music, office supplies, stationery, and gifts.

Notes on the data

The data published here have been benchmarked to the 2007 (preliminary), 2002, 1997, and 1992 Economic Censuses and the Annual Retail Trade Surveys for 2008 and previous years. Each year, the monthly series are benchmarked to the latest annual survey and new factors are incorporated to adjust for seasonal, trading-day, and holiday variations, using the Census Bureau's X-12-ARIMA program.

The survey sample is stratified by kind of business and estimated sales. All firms with sales above applicable size cutoffs are included. Firms are selected randomly from the remaining strata. The sample used for the end-of-month inventory estimates is a sub-sample of the monthly sales sample, about one-third of the size of the whole sample.

New samples, designed to produce NAICS estimates, were introduced with the 1999 Annual Retail Trade Survey and the March 2001 Monthly Retail Trade Survey. On November 30, 2006, another new sample was introduced, affecting the data for September 2006 and the following months. The sample is updated quarterly to take account of business births and deaths.

Data availability and references

An "Advance Monthly Retail Sales" report is released about nine working days after the close of the reference month, based on responses from a sub-sample of the complete retail sample.

The revised and more complete monthly "Retail Trade, Sales, and Inventories" reports are released six weeks after the close of the reference month. They contain preliminary figures for the current month and final figures for the prior 12 months. Statistics include retail sales, inventories, and ratios of inventories to sales. Data are both seasonally adjusted and unadjusted.

The "Annual Benchmark Report for Retail Trade" is released each spring. It includes updated seasonal adjustment factors; revised and benchmarked monthly estimates of sales and inventories; monthly data for the most recent 10 or more years; detailed annual estimates and ratios for the United States by kind of business; and comparable prior-year statistics and year-to-year changes. The latest such report available when *Business Statistics* was compiled was U.S. Census Bureau, *Annual Revision of Monthly Retail and Food Services: Sales and inventories—January 1992 through March 2010,* available on the Census Bureau Web site at <http://www.census.gov/retail/mrts>, along with the latest data releases and complete historical data.

TABLE 17-10
QUARTERLY RETAIL SALES: TOTAL AND E-COMMERCE

SOURCE: U.S. DEPARTMENT OF COMMERCE, CENSUS BUREAU

Beginning with the fourth quarter of 1999, the Census Bureau has conducted a quarterly survey of retail e-commerce sales from the Monthly Retail Trade Survey sample. (The monthly survey does not report electronic shopping separately; it is combined with mail order.) E-commerce sales are the sales of goods and services in which an order is placed by the buyer or the price and terms of sale are negotiated over the Internet or an extranet, Electronic Data Interchange (EDI) network, electronic mail, or other online system. Payment may or may not be made online. The quarterly release is issued around the 20th of February, May, August, and November, and is available along with full historical data on the Census Bureau Web site at <http://www.census.gov>. It can be located under the heading "Retail" in the alphabetical Web site index, under "E" for "Economic data and information."

These estimates reflect the NAICS definition of retail sales, which excludes food service. Online travel services, financial brokers and dealers, and ticket sales agencies are not classified as retail and are not included in these estimates; they are, however, included in the annual survey of selected services. See Table 17-16 for more information.

TABLE 17-12
MERCHANT WHOLESALERS—SALES AND INVENTORIES

SOURCE: U.S. DEPARTMENT OF COMMERCE, CENSUS BUREAU

These data are based on a monthly mail-out/mail-back sample survey conducted by the Census Bureau. The sample consists of about 4,500 establishments, with a response rate of about 75 percent; missing reports are imputed based on reports of similar reporters.

These data are now based on the new NAICS classification system, which replaced the old SIC system. Historical data have been restated on the NAICS basis back to January 1992.

Classification changes in NAICS

NAICS shifts a significant number of businesses from the Wholesale to the Retail sector. An important new criterion for classification concerns whether or not the establishment is intended to solicit walk-in traffic. If it is, and if it uses mass-media advertising, it is now classified as Retail, even if it also serves business and institutional clients. (See Chapter 14 for the major categories involved in this shift.)

Definitions

Merchant wholesalers includes merchant wholesalers that take title of the goods they sell, as well as jobbers, industrial distributors, exporters, and importers. The survey does not cover marketing sales offices and branches of manufacturing, refining, and mining firms, nor does it include NAICS 4251: Wholesale Electronic Markets and Agents and Brokers.

Notes on the data

Inventories are valued using methods other than LIFO (last in, first out) in order to better reflect the current costs of goods held as inventory.

A survey has been conducted monthly since 1946. New samples are drawn every 5 years, most recently in 2006. The samples are updated every quarter to add new businesses and to drop companies that are no longer active.

Data availability and references

"Monthly Wholesale Trade, Sales and Inventories" reports are released six weeks after the close of the reference month. They contain preliminary current-month figures and final figures for the previous month. Statistics include sales, inventories, and stock/sale ratios, along with standard errors. Data are both seasonally adjusted and unadjusted.

The "Annual Benchmark Report for Wholesale Trade" is released each spring. It contains estimated annual sales, monthly and year-end inventories, inventory/sales ratios, purchases, gross margins, and gross margin/sales ratios by kind of business. Annual estimates are benchmarked to annual surveys and the most recent census of wholesale trade. Monthly sales and inventories estimates are revised consistent with the annual data, seasonal adjustment factors are updated, and revised data for both seasonally adjusted and unadjusted values are published.

Data and documentation are available on the Census Bureau Web site at <http://www.census.gov>, under "Eco-nomic Indicators" and in the alphabetic index under "E" for economic data.

TABLE 17-13
SELECTED SERVICES, QUARTERLY: ESTIMATED REVENUE FOR EMPLOYER FIRMS

SOURCE: U.S. DEPARTMENT OF COMMERCE, CENSUS BUREAU

Census data on quarterly revenue for selected service industries are based on information collected from a probability sample of approximately 13,000 employer firms (firms with employees) chosen from the sample for the larger Service Annual Survey and expanded to represent totals—for employer firms only—for the selected industries. Industries are defined according to the 2002 NAICS. The scope of the survey and the size of the sample have increased several times since the inception of this survey in 2004.

Data for selected industry groups are adjusted for seasonal variation using the X-12 ARIMA program.

Data availability and references

The quarterly release "U.S. Government Estimates of Quarterly Revenue for Selected Services" is available on the Census Web site at <http://www.census.gov/>, under the general category of "Economic Indicators", around the middle of the third month following the end of the quarter. In the alphabetic index it appears under "Q". Information about the survey and its reliability is included in this release. Also available on the Web site are historical data benchmarked to the results of the latest Service Annual Survey.

PART C

HISTORICAL DATA

CHAPTER 18: THE U.S. ECONOMY 1929–1948

- In this chapter, summary annual statistics for the years 1929 through 1948 are presented, depicting the economy during two of its most tumultuous decades. This period encompasses the "great contraction," the economic collapse that began in August 1929 and lasted until March 1933; a subsequent period of recovery, which failed to return many important economic indicators to their expected trend levels and was interrupted by a new, though less severe, recession; apprehension of coming war, then the outbreak of war in Europe in September 1939, leading to increased war-related production; United States participation in all-out war, beginning with the Japanese attack on Pearl Harbor on December 7, 1941, and ending in 1945, with supercharged production and employment rates; then, rapid demobilization, and return to a high peacetime rate of economic activity by 1948.

- For a first overall view of the economy during these decades, Figure 18-1 shows total U.S. employment as calculated by the Bureau of Economic Analysis, including all private and government jobs, both civilian and military. In this graph a "trend" line is shown connecting the two peacetime high employment levels of 1929 and 1948.

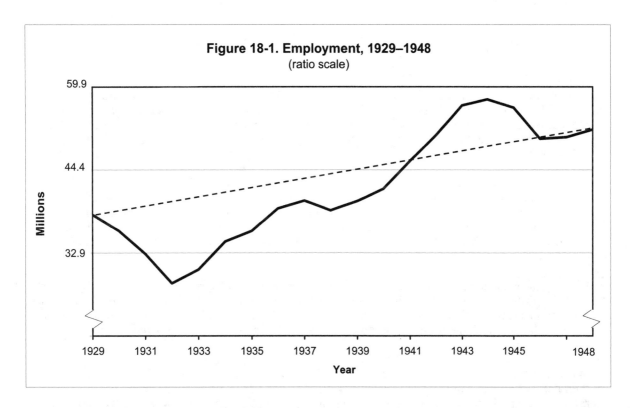

Figure 18-1. Employment, 1929–1948
(ratio scale)

- More than one-fifth of all the jobs held in the U.S. economy in 1929 were gone by 1932. In the subsequent recovery, total employment was back at the 1929 level by 1936, but only because of government employment, including over 3 ½ million work relief jobs; private industry employment would not recover to its 1929 level until 1941. (Table 18-2)

- Because the recovery was incomplete and economic activity did not recover to a trend level until after the decade's end, the entire decade of the 1930s is often described as "The Great Depression."

- During the war, men were drafted into the armed forces, practically all of the unemployed were put back to work, and women were drawn into the labor force, resulting in a period of what might be called "super-employment." After the war, employment fell back to a more normal trend level. (Tables 18-2 and 18-4)

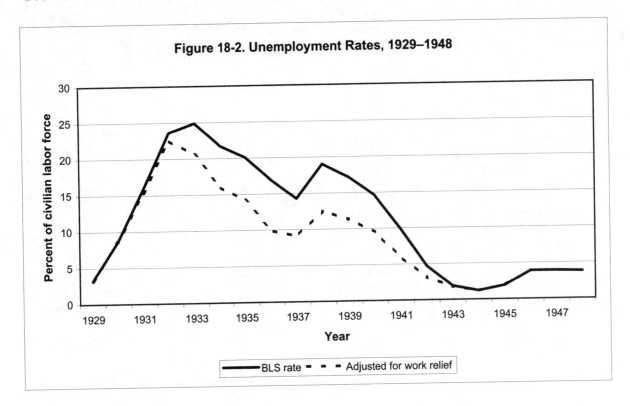

Figure 18-2. Unemployment Rates, 1929–1948

- The unemployment rates for the prewar period calculated by the Bureau of Labor Statistics, unlike the employment data used in Figure 18-1, count people on government work relief programs as unemployed. By this reckoning, unemployment rose from 3.2 percent of the civilian labor force in 1929 to a peak of 24.9 percent in 1933, and got no lower than 14.3 percent for the rest of the 1930s, as shown in Figure 18-2. (Table 18-4.)

- State and local governments started hiring people for work relief in 1930. The Federal government's programs began in 1933, and in 1936 and 1938 agencies such as the WPA and the CCC employed over 3 ½ million people. When workers in these programs are counted as employed rather than unemployed, the high point for unemployment was 22.5 percent in 1932, and it was reduced to 9.1 percent in 1937, as shown by the dashed line in Figure 18-2. (Table 18-4; see Notes and Definitions for further explanation.)

- By 1943, the economy reached a state of over-full employment, which would have been associated with runaway inflation if not for comprehensive price, wage, and production controls; the years of full wartime production, 1943 through 1945, all saw unemployment rates below 2 percent. After demobilization, the unemployment rate returned to just under 4 percent. (Tables 18-4 and 20-3)

- Real GDP declined 26.7 percent from 1929 to 1933—28.9 percent on a per capita basis. Per capita output recovered almost to the 1929 level in 1937 but fell back 4.1 percent in the 1938 recession. Output then nearly doubled from 1939 to the peak war production year, 1944; the per capita annual growth rate was 12.4 percent. Output fell back during the demobilization, but in 1948 was still at a per capita level representing a 4.9 percent growth rate since 1939. (Figure 18-3; Table 18-2)

- Per capita personal consumption expenditures fell 20.9 percent from 1929 to 1933. The decline would have been greater if consumers had not dipped into their assets to keep their living standards from declining as steeply as their incomes; the personal saving rate was negative in 1932 and 1933. Real per capita consumption recovered to the 1929 level by 1937. Despite rationing and shortages, real per capita consumption spending declined little during the war years. In 1948, it was 29.3 percent above the 1939 level. (Figure 18-3; Tables 18-1 and 18-2)

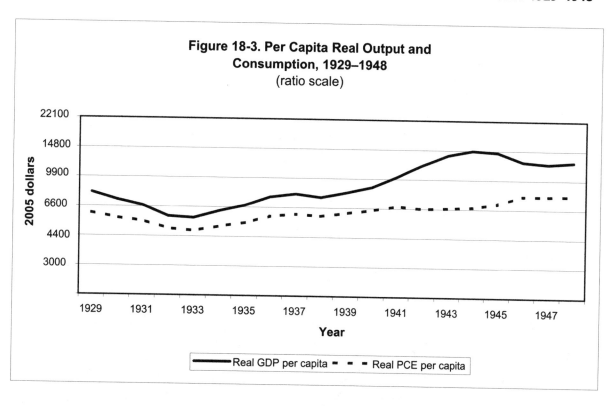

Figure 18-3. Per Capita Real Output and Consumption, 1929–1948
(ratio scale)

- Why was the 1929–1933 contraction so deep and long-lasting? Often, blame is placed on U.S. government tax increases and imposition of new trade barriers (the Smoot-Hawley Tariff), which undoubtedly made their contribution. A substantial number of well-regarded economists, however, point primarily to deflation and its interaction with debt. The price index for personal consumption expenditures, whose rate of change is shown in Figure 18-4, declined 27.2 percent from 1929 to 1933, for an annual average <u>deflation</u> rate of 7.6 percent. Current and prospective price declines make debt more burdensome and debtors more likely to default, as interest payments remain fixed while incomes and asset values decline. (Table 18-2)

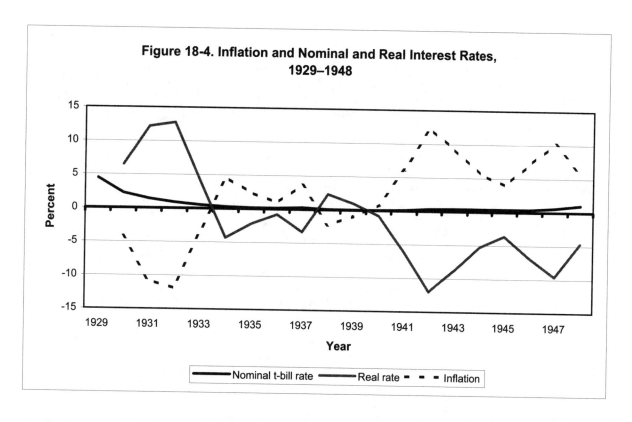

Figure 18-4. Inflation and Nominal and Real Interest Rates, 1929–1948

- Current and prospective price declines also make borrowing prohibitively expensive; a low nominal interest rate becomes high in real terms (since the real rate is the nominal rate <u>minus</u> the inflation rate, and subtraction means changing the sign and adding). A dollar in the hands of a prospective lender will be worth more in terms of purchasing power if he simply holds on to it than if he invests it in some real economic asset or activity whose price will be lower at the end of the year. There is no feasible way for a central bank to lower interest rates below zero in order to reduce real rates in the presence of deflation. As Table 18-5 and Figure 18-4 show, real rates were high from 1930 through 1933 despite near-zero market nominal rates on Treasury bills. (Table 18-5)

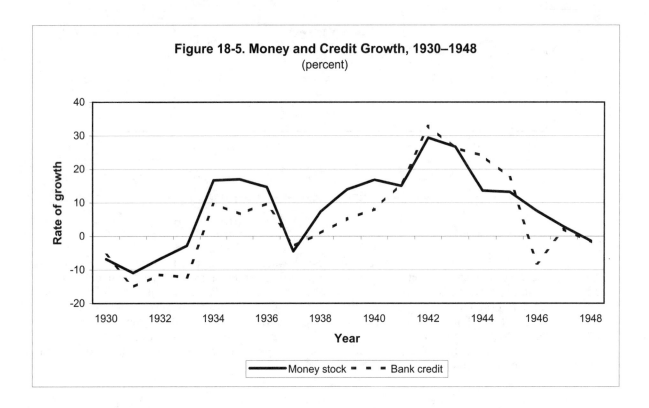

Figure 18-5. Money and Credit Growth, 1930–1948
(percent)

- Deflation was rooted in deep and sustained declines in the dollar volume of money and credit, as shown in Table 18-3 and illustrated in Figure 18-5. The money stock (currency and demand deposits) declined 27 percent from June 30, 1929, to June 30, 1933. Loans and investments at all commercial banks declined 29 percent over the same period. Commercial paper outstanding plunged 76 percent between December 1929 and December 1932, and bankers' acceptances were down 59 percent. (Table 18-3)

- Positive money and credit growth after 1933 was reflected in moderate rates of price increase and moderately negative—which means stimulative—real interest rates. As can be seen in Figures 18-4 and 18-5, there was a monetary component to the 1937–1938 recession (Tables 18-3 and 18-5). There was also a premature federal budget retrenchment at that time (Table 18-6).

- During the war, monetary policy was pre-empted by wartime needs. Interest rates were held low to facilitate the financing of huge federal deficits (Tables 18-3 and 18-6).

- Worker incomes increased during the wartime boom as employment, average hours, and hourly wages all rose. But inflation and consumer spending were held down by price and production controls and rationing. Personal saving rates soared when there was little to buy and the government emphasized the sale of "war bonds"; the saving rate reached 26 percent in 1943 and 1944, then fell back to 4.2 percent in 1947, almost equal to its 1929 level. (Tables 18-1 and 18-4)

Table 18-1. National Income and Product Accounts, 1929–1948

(Billions of current dollars, except as noted.)

Classification	1929	1930	1931	1932	1933	1934	1935	1936	1937	1938
Gross domestic product, total	103.6	91.2	76.5	58.7	56.4	66.0	73.3	83.8	91.9	86.1
Personal consumption expenditures, total	77.4	70.1	60.7	48.7	45.9	51.5	55.9	62.2	66.8	64.3
Durable goods	9.8	7.7	5.9	4.0	3.8	4.6	5.5	6.7	7.4	6.1
Nondurable goods	33.9	30.5	25.8	20.2	20.0	23.9	26.1	29.2	31.0	29.9
Services	33.6	32.0	29.0	24.6	22.2	23.0	24.3	26.2	28.5	28.3
Gross private domestic fixed investment, total	14.9	11.0	7.0	3.6	3.1	4.3	5.6	7.5	9.5	7.7
Nonresidential, total	11.0	8.6	5.3	2.9	2.5	3.3	4.3	5.8	7.5	5.5
Structures	5.5	4.4	2.6	1.4	1.1	1.2	1.4	1.9	2.7	2.1
Equipment and software	5.5	4.2	2.6	1.5	1.4	2.1	2.8	3.9	4.8	3.4
Residential	4.0	2.4	1.8	0.8	0.6	0.9	1.3	1.7	2.1	2.1
Change in private inventories	1.5	-0.2	-1.1	-2.4	-1.4	-0.6	1.1	1.2	2.6	-0.6
Net exports of goods and services	0.4	0.3	0.0	0.0	0.1	0.3	-0.2	-0.1	0.1	1.0
Exports	5.9	4.4	2.9	2.0	2.0	2.6	2.8	3.0	4.0	3.8
Imports	5.6	4.1	2.9	1.9	1.9	2.2	3.0	3.2	4.0	2.8
Government consumption expenditures and gross investment, total	9.4	10.0	9.9	8.7	8.7	10.5	10.9	13.1	12.8	13.8
Federal	1.7	1.8	1.9	1.8	2.3	3.3	3.4	5.6	5.1	5.7
National defense	0.9	0.9	0.9	0.9	0.9	0.8	1.0	1.2	1.3	1.4
State and local	7.6	8.2	8.0	6.9	6.4	7.2	7.5	7.5	7.7	8.1
Gross national product	104.4	91.9	77.0	59.1	56.7	66.3	73.6	84.0	92.2	86.5
National income, total	93.9	82.9	67.4	51.1	48.8	58.1	66.0	74.7	83.3	76.6
Compensation of employees	51.1	46.9	39.8	31.1	29.6	34.3	37.4	42.9	48.0	45.0
Proprietors' income with IVA and CCAdj	14.1	10.9	8.4	5.1	5.3	7.0	10.1	10.4	12.5	10.6
Farm	5.7	3.9	3.0	1.8	2.2	2.6	4.9	3.9	5.6	4.0
Nonfarm	8.4	7.0	5.3	3.3	3.1	4.5	5.2	6.4	6.9	6.6
Rental income of persons with CCAdj	6.2	5.5	4.5	3.6	2.9	2.6	2.6	2.7	3.0	3.6
Corporate profits with IVA and CCAdj	10.7	7.4	2.8	-0.3	-0.3	2.4	3.9	6.0	6.9	4.8
Net interest and miscellaneous payments	4.6	4.8	4.8	4.5	4.0	4.0	4.1	3.8	3.7	3.6
Taxes on production and imports	6.8	7.0	6.7	6.6	6.9	7.6	8.0	8.5	8.9	8.9
Less: Subsidies less current surplus of government enterprises	0.0	0.0	0.1	0.1	0.1	0.4	0.5	0.2	0.2	0.4
Business current transfer payments (net)	0.5	0.5	0.5	0.6	0.5	0.5	0.5	0.5	0.5	0.4
Personal income, total	84.9	76.1	65.2	49.9	46.8	53.7	60.3	68.6	74.1	68.4
Less: Personal current taxes	1.7	1.6	1.0	0.7	0.8	0.9	1.1	1.3	1.9	1.9
Equals: Disposable personal income (DPI)	83.2	74.6	64.2	49.1	46.0	52.8	59.3	67.3	72.2	66.5
Less: Personal outlays	79.6	71.6	61.8	49.7	46.8	52.3	56.7	63.1	67.9	65.2
Equals: Personal saving	3.6	2.9	2.4	-0.5	-0.8	0.5	2.5	4.2	4.3	1.3
As a percentage of DPI	4.3	4.0	3.7	-1.1	-1.7	0.9	4.2	6.2	5.9	1.9
Gross saving	19.3	15.0	8.3	3.3	3.3	6.4	9.6	11.5	16.2	11.7
Net saving	9.7	5.6	-0.5	-4.4	-4.1	-1.4	1.8	3.4	7.2	2.5
Net private saving	7.1	4.0	0.7	-3.7	-3.6	-0.4	2.6	4.3	5.0	1.9
Net government saving, federal	1.0	0.2	-2.1	-1.3	-0.9	-2.2	-1.9	-3.2	0.2	-1.3
Net government saving, state and local	1.5	1.3	1.0	0.7	0.4	1.2	1.1	2.3	2.0	2.0
Consumption of fixed capital, private	8.7	8.5	7.9	6.9	6.5	6.7	6.7	6.9	7.7	7.8
Consumption of fixed capital, government	1.0	1.0	0.9	0.8	0.9	1.1	1.1	1.2	1.3	1.4
Gross domestic investment, total	19.3	13.9	8.9	3.4	3.7	6.4	9.5	12.8	15.9	11.3
Private	16.5	10.8	5.9	1.3	1.7	3.7	6.7	8.6	12.2	7.1
Government	2.8	3.2	3.0	2.1	1.9	2.7	2.8	4.1	3.8	4.2
Net lending or net borrowing (-), NIPAs	0.8	0.7	0.2	0.2	0.2	0.4	-0.1	-0.1	0.2	1.2
Net domestic investment	9.6	4.5	0.1	-4.3	-3.7	-1.4	1.7	4.7	7.0	2.0
Gross saving as a percentage of gross national income	18.6	16.3	10.9	5.6	5.8	9.7	13.0	13.9	17.5	13.7
Net saving as a percentage of gross national income	9.3	6.0	-0.6	-7.5	-7.4	-2.1	2.5	4.1	7.8	2.9

Table 18-1. National Income and Product Accounts, 1929–1948—*Continued*

(Billions of current dollars, except as noted.)

Classification	1939	1940	1941	1942	1943	1944	1945	1946	1947	1948
Gross domestic product, total	92.2	101.4	126.7	161.9	198.6	219.8	223.0	222.2	244.1	269.1
Personal consumption expenditures, total	67.2	71.3	81.1	89.0	99.9	108.7	120.0	144.3	162.0	175.0
Durable goods	7.2	8.3	10.3	7.6	7.5	7.7	9.1	17.1	21.8	24.5
Nondurable goods	30.8	32.3	37.2	43.4	48.9	52.8	58.5	69.1	77.6	83.0
Services	29.3	30.7	33.6	38.0	43.6	48.1	52.4	58.1	62.6	67.6
Gross private domestic fixed investment, total	9.1	11.2	13.8	8.5	6.9	8.7	12.3	25.1	35.5	42.4
Nonresidential, total	6.1	7.7	9.7	6.3	5.4	7.4	10.6	17.3	23.5	26.8
Structures	2.2	2.6	3.3	2.2	1.8	2.4	3.3	7.4	8.1	9.5
Equipment and software	3.9	5.2	6.4	4.1	3.7	5.0	7.3	9.9	15.3	17.3
Residential	3.0	3.5	4.1	2.2	1.4	1.4	1.7	7.8	12.1	15.6
Change in private inventories	0.2	2.4	4.3	1.9	-0.7	-0.9	-1.5	6.0	-0.6	5.7
Net exports of goods and services	0.8	1.5	1.0	-0.3	-2.2	-2.0	-0.8	7.2	10.8	5.5
Exports	4.0	4.9	5.5	4.4	4.0	4.9	6.8	14.2	18.7	15.5
Imports	3.1	3.4	4.4	4.6	6.3	6.9	7.5	7.0	7.9	10.1
Government consumption expenditures and gross investment, total	14.8	15.0	26.5	62.7	94.8	105.3	93.0	39.6	36.3	40.5
Federal	6.0	6.5	18.0	54.1	86.5	96.9	84.0	28.8	22.6	24.2
National defense	1.5	2.5	14.3	51.1	84.2	94.5	81.9	25.1	18.2	18.2
State and local	8.8	8.6	8.6	8.6	8.4	8.4	9.0	10.8	13.7	16.3
Gross national product	92.5	101.7	127.2	162.3	198.9	220.1	223.3	222.9	245.2	270.6
National income, total	82.0	90.9	115.8	149.5	184.2	198.0	198.3	198.6	216.3	242.6
Compensation of employees	48.1	52.2	64.8	85.3	109.6	121.3	123.3	119.6	130.1	142.0
Proprietors' income with IVA and CCAdj	11.1	12.3	16.6	23.4	28.3	29.4	30.8	35.7	34.5	39.2
Farm	4.0	4.1	6.0	9.7	11.5	11.4	11.8	14.2	14.3	16.7
Nonfarm	7.1	8.2	10.6	13.7	16.7	18.0	19.0	21.5	20.1	22.5
Rental income of persons with CCAdj	3.8	3.9	4.5	5.5	6.1	6.4	6.7	7.1	7.2	7.8
Corporate profits with IVA and CCAdj	6.4	9.6	15.3	20.4	24.7	24.8	20.2	17.9	23.5	30.9
Net interest and miscellaneous payments	3.6	3.3	3.3	3.2	2.9	2.4	2.3	1.9	2.5	2.6
Taxes on production and imports	9.1	9.8	11.1	11.5	12.4	13.7	15.1	16.8	18.1	19.7
Less: Subsidies less current surplus of government enterprises	0.7	0.6	0.3	0.4	0.4	0.9	1.0	1.2	0.2	0.3
Business current transfer payments (net)	0.4	0.5	0.5	0.5	0.6	0.8	0.9	0.7	0.7	0.7
Personal income, total	72.9	78.4	96.0	123.4	152.1	166.0	171.6	178.6	190.9	209.7
Less: Personal current taxes	1.5	1.7	2.3	4.9	16.7	17.7	19.4	17.2	19.8	19.2
Equals: Disposable personal income (DPI)	71.4	76.8	93.7	118.5	135.4	148.3	152.2	161.4	171.1	190.5
Less: Personal outlays	68.2	72.4	82.3	90.0	100.8	109.7	121.2	145.9	163.8	177.3
Equals: Personal saving	3.2	4.3	11.4	28.6	34.6	38.6	31.0	15.5	7.3	13.2
As a percentage of DPI	4.4	5.7	12.2	24.1	25.5	26.0	20.4	9.6	4.2	6.9
Gross saving	13.6	18.5	29.9	39.8	44.9	39.9	29.8	38.4	46.6	58.0
Net saving	4.3	8.8	18.8	26.1	28.4	20.4	8.7	15.3	19.9	29.6
Net private saving	4.4	7.1	14.7	33.3	41.0	45.6	36.0	18.8	13.2	24.7
Net government saving, federal	-2.1	-0.3	2.2	-8.7	-14.1	-26.9	-28.9	-5.0	5.3	3.7
Net government saving, state and local	2.0	2.0	1.9	1.5	1.5	1.6	1.6	1.5	1.4	1.2
Consumption of fixed capital, private	7.8	8.1	9.0	10.1	10.3	10.7	11.0	12.3	16.1	18.9
Consumption of fixed capital, government	1.4	1.5	2.0	3.5	6.2	8.9	10.1	10.8	10.6	9.6
Gross domestic investment, total	13.8	18.0	28.9	39.0	45.2	44.4	35.0	34.6	39.6	55.1
Private	9.3	13.6	18.1	10.4	6.1	7.8	10.8	31.1	35.0	48.1
Government	4.5	4.4	10.8	28.5	39.1	36.6	24.1	3.5	4.6	7.0
Net lending or net borrowing (-), NIPAs	1.0	1.5	1.3	-0.1	-2.1	-2.0	-1.3	4.9	9.3	2.4
Net domestic investment	4.6	8.3	17.9	25.3	28.7	24.9	13.8	11.5	12.9	26.7
Gross saving as a percentage of gross national income	14.9	18.4	23.5	24.4	22.4	18.3	13.6	17.3	19.2	21.4
Net saving as a percentage of gross national income	4.7	8.7	14.8	16.0	14.1	9.4	3.9	6.9	8.2	10.9

Table 18-2. NIPA Data on Real Output, Prices, and Employment, 1929–1948

Classification	1929	1930	1931	1932	1933	1934	1935	1936	1937	1938
POPULATION										
Population (midperiod, thousands)	121 878	123 188	124 149	124 949	125 690	126 485	127 362	128 181	128 961	129 969
BILLIONS OF CHAINED (2005) DOLLARS (except as noted)										
Real gross domestic product, total	977.0	892.8	834.9	725.8	716.4	794.4	865.0	977.9	1 028.0	992.6
Per capita (2005 dollars)	8 016	7 247	6 725	5 809	5 700	6 280	6 791	7 629	7 971	7 638
Personal consumption expenditures	736.6	697.1	675.2	614.7	601.1	644.0	683.3	752.9	780.7	768.2
Per capita (2005 dollars)	6 044	5 659	5 439	4 920	4 782	5 092	5 365	5 873	6 054	5 910
Gross private domestic investment	101.7	67.9	42.6	12.9	18.9	34.2	63.4	81.2	101.5	67.1
Exports	38.0	31.4	26.1	20.4	20.6	22.8	24.1	25.3	31.9	31.5
Imports	49.1	42.7	37.3	30.9	32.2	32.9	43.1	42.6	48.0	37.3
Government	146.5	161.4	168.2	162.6	157.2	177.3	182.2	212.6	203.6	219.3
Disposable personal income	792.0	741.1	714.9	619.9	601.6	660.3	723.9	815.1	842.8	795.1
Per capita (2005 dollars)	6 498	6 016	5 759	4 961	4 786	5 220	5 684	6 359	6 535	6 118
CHAIN-TYPE PRICE INDEXES, 2005 = 100										
Gross domestic product	10.58	10.18	9.16	8.12	7.91	8.30	8.46	8.55	8.87	8.70
Percent change	. . .	-3.9	-9.9	-11.4	-2.6	4.9	2.0	1.1	3.7	-1.9
Personal consumption expenditures	10.51	10.07	8.99	7.93	7.65	8.00	8.19	8.26	8.57	8.37
Percent change	. . .	-4.2	-10.7	-11.8	-3.5	4.5	2.4	0.9	3.6	-2.3
EMPLOYMENT (THOUSANDS)										
Total	37 699	35 590	32 724	29 445	30 940	34 238	35 577	38 599	39 701	38 322
Domestic industries	37 699	35 590	32 723	29 444	30 939	34 237	35 576	38 598	39 700	38 321
Private industries	34 088	31 811	28 590	25 071	25 038	27 417	28 426	30 548	32 508	30 124
Agriculture, forestry, and fisheries	3 556	3 337	3 252	3 028	2 995	2 986	3 013	3 106	3 083	2 949
Mining	993	932	813	672	693	822	840	897	955	859
Contract construction	1 484	1 366	1 198	907	703	806	866	1 104	1 082	1 055
Manufacturing	10 428	9 309	7 895	6 678	7 204	8 364	8 904	9 645	10 591	9 131
Durable goods	5 238	4 457	3 497	2 724	2 893	3 587	3 941	4 460	5 130	4 085
Nondurable goods	5 190	4 852	4 398	3 954	4 311	4 777	4 963	5 185	5 461	5 046
Transportation and public utilities	3 989	3 742	3 282	2 826	2 684	2 774	2 808	2 973	3 140	2 837
Wholesale trade	1 757	1 693	1 530	1 380	1 377	1 492	1 507	1 612	1 770	1 767
Retail trade and automobile services	4 684	4 469	4 148	3 688	3 699	4 075	4 200	4 543	4 904	4 780
Finance, insurance, and real estate	1 520	1 491	1 423	1 358	1 309	1 332	1 352	1 401	1 445	1 436
Services	5 677	5 472	5 049	4 534	4 374	4 766	4 936	5 267	5 538	5 310
Government	3 611	3 779	4 133	4 373	5 901	6 820	7 150	8 050	7 192	8 197
Federal	981	1 034	1 019	1 006	1 470	2 227	2 209	4 993	4 085	4 987
General government	644	695	683	673	1 135	1 868	1 835	4 612	3 698	4 583
Civilian, except work relief	267	310	296	290	294	357	449	521	517	507
Military[1]	377	385	387	383	370	371	396	438	474	504
Work relief	. . .	. . .	. . .	. . .	471	1 140	990	3 653	2 707	3 572
Government enterprises	337	339	336	333	335	359	374	381	387	404
State and local	2 630	2 745	3 114	3 367	4 431	4 593	4 941	3 057	3 107	3 210
General government	2 509	2 618	2 984	3 249	4 317	4 473	4 815	2 922	2 967	3 070
Public education	1 067	1 095	1 105	1 093	1 069	1 069	1 097	1 118	1 149	1 180
Nonschool, except work relief	1 442	1 503	1 580	1 564	1 524	1 570	1 621	1 713	1 762	1 871
Work relief	. . .	20	299	592	1 724	1 834	2 097	91	56	19
Government enterprises	121	127	130	118	114	120	126	135	140	140
Rest of the world	0	0	1	1	1	1	1	1	1	1

[1] Includes Coast Guard.
. . . = Not available.

Table 18-2. NIPA Data on Real Output, Prices, and Employment, 1929–1948—*Continued*

Classification	1939	1940	1941	1942	1943	1944	1945	1946	1947	1948
POPULATION										
Population (midperiod, thousands)	131 028	132 122	133 402	134 860	136 739	138 397	139 928	141 389	144 126	146 631
BILLIONS OF CHAINED (2005) DOLLARS (except as noted)										
Real gross domestic product, total	1 072.8	1 166.9	1 366.1	1 618.2	1 883.1	2 035.2	2 012.4	1 792.2	1 776.1	1 854.2
Per capita (2005 dollars)	8 188	8 832	10 241	11 999	13 772	14 705	14 382	12 676	12 324	12 646
Personal consumption expenditures	811.1	853.1	913.6	892.0	916.9	943.0	1 001.4	1 125.9	1 147.5	1 173.4
Per capita (2005 dollars)	6 190	6 457	6 848	6 614	6 706	6 814	7 156	7 963	7 962	8 002
Gross private domestic investment	86.2	120.1	146.7	77.5	45.8	56.5	74.7	191.4	183.9	234.9
Exports	33.3	37.9	38.8	25.6	21.6	23.2	32.5	70.3	80.1	63.1
Imports	39.2	40.1	49.3	44.8	56.5	59.1	62.8	52.1	49.4	57.7
Government	238.6	245.3	407.7	959.4	1 427.2	1 606.1	1 402.2	482.1	409.5	439.4
Disposable personal income	861.4	918.6	1 056.3	1 187.8	1 242.6	1 287.2	1 270.2	1 259.4	1 211.9	1 277.0
Per capita (2005 dollars)	6 574	6 953	7 918	8 808	9 087	9 301	9 078	8 907	8 409	8 709
CHAIN-TYPE PRICE INDEXES, 2005 = 100										
Gross domestic product	8.59	8.67	9.23	9.99	10.55	10.81	11.08	12.36	13.73	14.51
Percent change	-1.3	0.9	6.5	8.2	5.6	2.4	2.6	11.5	11.1	5.7
Personal consumption expenditures	8.29	8.36	8.88	9.98	10.90	11.53	11.99	12.82	14.13	14.92
Percent change	-1.0	0.8	6.2	12.4	9.2	5.8	4.0	7.0	10.1	5.7
EMPLOYMENT (THOUSANDS)										
Total	39 633	41 437	45 785	50 219	55 995	57 221	55 548	49 643	49 936	51 332
Domestic industries	39 632	41 435	45 782	50 214	56 016	57 276	55 614	49 690	49 941	51 325
Private industries	31 612	33 518	37 210	39 728	40 723	39 749	38 183	40 379	42 458	43 431
Agriculture, forestry, and fisheries	2 859	2 809	2 779	2 692	2 563	2 372	2 259	2 343	2 427	2 498
Mining	832	927	975	985	917	879	829	871	933	981
Contract construction	1 219	1 285	1 774	2 131	1 566	1 110	1 135	1 739	2 062	2 278
Manufacturing	9 967	10 882	13 137	15 284	17 402	17 050	15 186	14 493	15 205	15 276
Durable goods	4 609	5 367	6 999	8 846	10 924	10 722	8 933	7 742	8 330	8 309
Nondurable goods	5 358	5 515	6 138	6 438	6 478	6 328	6 253	6 751	6 875	6 967
Transportation and public utilities	2 943	3 064	3 311	3 458	3 652	3 822	3 926	4 113	4 173	4 212
Wholesale trade	1 833	1 899	2 014	1 916	1 808	1 828	1 927	2 286	2 480	2 573
Retail trade and automobile services	4 992	5 321	5 754	5 623	5 570	5 529	5 717	6 769	7 061	7 223
Finance, insurance, and real estate	1 470	1 518	1 559	1 531	1 475	1 447	1 477	1 692	1 744	1 811
Services	5 497	5 813	5 907	6 108	5 770	5 712	5 727	6 073	6 373	6 579
Government	8 020	7 917	8 572	10 486	15 293	17 527	17 431	9 311	7 483	7 894
Federal	4 754	4 652	5 281	7 252	12 155	14 405	14 258	5 902	3 808	4 007
General government	4 342	4 227	4 829	6 765	11 611	13 885	13 722	5 294	3 268	3 437
Civilian, except work relief	560	642	944	1 702	2 497	2 520	2 420	1 822	1 436	1 428
Military[1]	566	793	1 693	4 154	9 029	11 365	11 302	3 472	1 832	2 009
Work relief	3 216	2 792	2 192	909	85	. . .	. . .	. . .	. . .	. . .
Government enterprises	412	425	452	487	544	520	536	608	540	570
State and local	3 266	3 265	3 291	3 234	3 138	3 122	3 173	3 409	3 675	3 887
General government	3 123	3 104	3 119	3 063	2 965	2 956	3 007	3 236	3 481	3 657
Public education	1 207	1 194	1 256	1 264	1 256	1 256	1 273	1 347	1 445	1 504
Nonschool, except work relief	1 877	1 872	1 846	1 794	1 709	1 700	1 734	1 889	2 036	2 153
Work relief	39	38	17	5	. . .	. . .	. . .	. . .	. . .	230
Government enterprises	143	161	172	171	173	166	166	173	194	230
Rest of the world	1	2	3	5	-21	-55	-66	-47	-5	7

[1]Includes Coast Guard.
. . . = Not available.

Table 18-3. Fixed Assets, Money and Credit, and Interest Rates, 1929–1948

Classification	1929	1930	1931	1932	1933	1934	1935	1936	1937	1938
CURRENT-COST NET STOCK OF FIXED ASSETS (billions of dollars, year end)										
Total fixed assets	294.6	281.0	242.8	224.3	239.8	246.0	249.9	276.6	291.1	293.3
Private, total	253.9	241.4	206.7	188.6	198.0	200.2	201.2	222.5	233.9	234.1
Nonresidential										
Equipment and software	34.7	33.0	30.0	27.0	26.7	26.7	26.2	28.2	30.3	30.3
Structures	99.4	94.1	83.2	77.7	79.6	80.7	80.8	89.6	92.2	90.6
Residential	119.8	114.3	93.5	84.0	91.8	92.7	94.2	104.7	111.4	113.2
Government, total	40.8	39.6	36.1	35.6	41.8	45.8	48.7	54.1	57.2	59.2
Nonresidential										
Equipment and software	2.4	2.3	2.3	2.3	2.3	2.6	2.8	2.9	3.2	3.3
Structures	38.4	37.3	33.7	33.3	39.4	43.2	45.8	51.1	53.8	55.6
Residential	0.0	0.0	0.0	0.0	0.0	0.0	0.0	0.1	0.2	0.2
Private and government fixed assets, total	294.6	281.0	242.8	224.3	239.8	246.0	249.9	276.6	291.1	293.3
Nonresidential										
Equipment and software	37.1	35.3	32.3	29.2	29.0	29.4	29.0	31.1	33.5	33.6
Structures	137.8	131.4	116.9	111.0	119.0	124.0	126.7	140.7	146.0	146.3
Residential	119.8	114.3	93.6	84.0	91.8	92.7	94.2	104.8	111.6	113.4
Government, by level										
Federal	7.9	7.4	6.8	6.7	7.6	8.7	9.9	11.4	12.6	13.3
State and local	32.9	32.2	29.2	29.0	34.2	37.2	38.8	42.7	44.6	45.9
CHAIN-TYPE QUANTITY INDEXES FOR NET STOCK OF FIXED ASSETS (index numbers, 2005 = 100)										
Total fixed assets	13.46	13.70	13.79	13.72	13.61	13.58	13.63	13.83	14.06	14.21
Private, total	15.03	15.21	15.19	14.98	14.76	14.61	14.56	14.62	14.76	14.78
Nonresidential										
Equipment and software	6.15	6.17	5.97	5.62	5.32	5.14	5.09	5.21	5.43	5.41
Structures	23.47	23.99	24.09	23.92	23.65	23.43	23.25	23.20	23.28	23.24
Residential	15.18	15.29	15.34	15.27	15.18	15.13	15.14	15.21	15.30	15.39
Government, total	8.83	9.32	9.84	10.25	10.53	10.90	11.30	11.95	12.49	13.10
Nonresidential										
Equipment and software	2.22	2.23	2.26	2.25	2.24	2.38	2.55	2.65	2.76	2.93
Structures	11.54	12.23	12.94	13.52	13.92	14.38	14.88	15.73	16.41	17.19
Residential	0.03	0.05	0.08	0.10	0.13	0.15	0.22	0.63	1.19	1.41
Private and government fixed assets, total	13.46	13.70	13.79	13.72	13.61	13.58	13.63	13.83	14.06	14.21
Nonresidential										
Equipment and software	5.14	5.16	5.00	4.73	4.50	4.38	4.37	4.48	4.67	4.68
Structures	18.10	18.69	19.05	19.20	19.22	19.32	19.46	19.83	20.18	20.51
Residential	14.89	14.99	15.04	14.98	14.89	14.84	14.86	14.93	15.03	15.12
Government, by level										
Federal	6.85	6.90	7.04	7.27	7.72	8.35	9.21	10.03	10.77	11.49
State and local	9.64	10.29	10.95	11.43	11.65	11.94	12.20	12.80	13.27	13.86
MONEY STOCK AND BANK CREDIT (millions of dollars)										
June 30										
Currency outside banks	3 639	3 369	3 651	4 616	4 761	4 659	4 783	5 222	5 489	5 417
Demand deposits adjusted	22 540	21 706	19 832	15 625	14 411	16 694	20 433	23 780	25 198	24 313
Total	26 179	25 075	23 483	20 241	19 172	21 353	25 216	29 002	30 687	29 730
Time deposits	28 611	28 992	28 961	24 756	21 656	22 875	23 854	24 908	25 905	26 236
Loans and investments, all commercial banks	49 424	48 892	44 853	36 091	30 357	32 742	34 588	38 540	39 472	37 109
December 31										
Currency outside banks	3 557	3 605	4 470	4 669	4 782	4 655	4 917	5 516	5 638	5 775
Demand deposits adjusted	22 809	20 967	17 412	15 728	15 035	18 459	22 115	25 483	23 959	25 986
Total	26 366	24 572	21 882	20 397	19 817	23 114	27 032	30 999	29 597	31 761
Time deposits	28 189	28 676	25 979	24 457	21 715	23 156	24 241	25 361	26 218	26 305
Loans and investments, all commercial banks	49 467	46 700	39 653	35 083	30 789	33 735	35 982	39 472	38 333	38 669
COMMERCIAL PAPER AND BANKERS' ACCEPTANCES (millions of dollars outstanding, year end)										
Commercial paper	334	358	120	81	109	166	171	215	279	187
Bankers' acceptances	1 732	1 556	974	710	764	543	397	373	343	270
INTEREST RATES AND YIELDS										
Federal Reserve discount rate	5.17	3.04	2.11	2.82	2.56	1.54	1.50	1.50	1.33	1.00
U.S. Treasury 3-month bills	4.42	2.23	1.40	0.88	0.52	0.28	0.17	0.17	0.28	0.07
Bank prime rate	5.5–6	3.5–6	2.75–5	3.25–4	1.5–4	1.50	1.50	1.50	1.50	1.50
Prime commercial paper, 4- to 6-months	5.85	3.59	2.64	2.73	1.73	1.02	0.76	0.75	0.94	0.81
Bond yields:										
United States government, long-term	3.60	3.29	3.34	3.68	3.31	3.12	2.79	2.65	2.68	2.56
Corporate:										
Moodys Aaa	4.73	4.55	4.58	5.01	4.49	4.00	3.60	3.24	3.26	3.19
Moodys Baa	5.90	5.90	7.62	9.30	7.76	6.32	5.75	4.77	5.03	5.80
State and local	4.27	4.07	4.01	4.65	4.71	4.03	3.41	3.07	3.10	2.91

Table 18-3. Fixed Assets, Money and Credit, and Interest Rates, 1929–1948—*Continued*

Classification	1939	1940	1941	1942	1943	1944	1945	1946	1947	1948
CURRENT-COST NET STOCK OF FIXED ASSETS (billions of dollars, year end)										
Total fixed assets	299.5	324.2	369.2	421.6	468.7	501.5	543.9	638.5	735.6	781.1
Private, total	238.0	256.7	284.7	304.6	319.5	331.9	356.0	439.1	522.5	567.8
Nonresidential										
Equipment and software	30.9	33.2	38.3	39.2	39.6	39.5	44.7	54.5	66.6	81.3
Structures	90.3	95.3	106.5	114.7	116.3	117.5	126.8	157.4	188.3	198.3
Residential	116.8	128.2	139.9	150.7	163.6	174.9	184.5	227.3	267.6	288.3
Government, total	61.5	67.5	84.5	117.0	149.2	169.6	187.9	199.3	213.1	213.3
Nonresidential										
Equipment and software	3.6	4.0	7.7	20.9	45.3	65.2	75.4	70.2	61.7	51.9
Structures	57.7	63.0	75.8	94.4	101.3	101.5	109.5	125.2	145.8	156.5
Residential	0.3	0.5	1.0	1.7	2.6	2.8	3.0	4.0	5.6	5.0
Private and government fixed assets, total	299.5	324.2	369.2	421.6	468.7	501.5	543.9	638.5	735.6	781.1
Nonresidential										
Equipment and software	34.5	37.2	45.9	60.1	84.9	104.7	120.1	124.7	128.3	133.1
Structures	148.0	158.3	182.3	209.1	217.6	219.1	236.3	282.5	334.1	354.7
Residential	117.1	128.7	141.0	152.4	166.2	177.7	187.5	231.3	273.2	293.2
Government, by level										
Federal	13.9	15.7	24.3	49.6	80.7	102.7	118.5	121.6	119.8	111.8
State and local	47.6	51.8	60.1	67.4	68.4	66.9	69.4	77.8	93.3	101.5
CHAIN-TYPE QUANTITY INDEXES FOR NET STOCK OF FIXED ASSETS (index numbers, 2005 = 100)										
Total fixed assets	14.44	14.73	15.31	16.26	17.32	18.20	18.57	18.50	18.62	18.90
Private, total	14.89	15.09	15.35	15.31	15.18	15.12	15.20	15.71	16.35	17.06
Nonresidential										
Equipment and software	5.45	5.66	5.95	5.86	5.73	5.76	6.10	6.70	7.54	8.33
Structures	23.22	23.27	23.39	23.24	22.97	22.81	22.82	23.31	23.72	24.23
Residential	15.59	15.85	16.13	16.18	16.13	16.07	16.02	16.45	17.06	17.80
Government, total	13.79	14.43	16.15	20.65	26.08	30.50	32.03	29.62	27.57	26.07
Nonresidential										
Equipment and software	3.12	3.30	6.14	17.96	40.88	62.85	70.52	57.86	46.06	36.24
Structures	18.07	18.83	20.12	22.56	23.53	23.82	23.95	23.73	23.76	24.00
Residential	1.83	3.06	5.56	8.30	11.80	12.64	12.84	14.24	14.68	14.95
Private and government fixed assets, total	14.44	14.73	15.31	16.26	17.32	18.20	18.57	18.50	18.62	18.90
Nonresidential										
Equipment and software	4.74	4.93	5.61	7.27	10.30	13.25	14.55	13.43	12.61	12.02
Structures	20.90	21.27	21.92	22.95	23.25	23.29	23.36	23.53	23.77	24.16
Residential	15.34	15.61	15.94	16.04	16.07	16.03	15.98	16.43	17.04	17.78
Government, by level										
Federal	12.14	13.13	19.20	38.15	62.38	82.62	89.91	79.20	69.52	61.67
State and local	14.58	15.10	15.38	15.41	15.28	15.11	14.98	14.99	15.17	15.47
MONEY STOCK AND BANK CREDIT (millions of dollars)										
June 30										
Currency outside banks	6 005	6 699	8 204	10 936	15 814	20 881	25 097	26 516	. . .	. . .
Demand deposits adjusted	27 355	31 962	37 317	41 870	56 039	60 065	69 053	79 476	. . .	. . .
Total	33 360	38 661	45 521	52 806	71 853	80 946	94 150	105 992	. . .	. . .
Time deposits	26 791	27 463	27 879	27 320	30 260	35 720	44 253	51 829	. . .	. . .
Loans and investments, all commercial banks	39 367	41 148	47 627	53 652	76 633	95 731	114 505	119 448	112 756	113 855
December 31										
Currency outside banks	6 401	7 325	9 615	13 946	18 837	23 505	26 490	26 730	. . .	. . .
Demand deposits adjusted	29 793	34 945	38 992	48 922	60 803	66 930	75 851	83 814	. . .	. . .
Total	36 194	42 270	48 607	62 868	79 640	90 435	102 341	110 044	. . .	. . .
Time deposits	27 059	27 738	27 729	28 431	32 748	39 790	48 452	53 960	. . .	. . .
Loans and investments, all commercial banks	40 667	43 922	50 746	67 393	85 095	105 530	124 019	113 993	116 284	114 298
COMMERCIAL PAPER AND BANKERS' ACCEPTANCES (millions of dollars outstanding, year end)										
Commercial paper	210	218	375	230	202	166	159	228	287	269
Bankers' acceptances	233	209	194	118	117	129	154	227	261	259
INTEREST RATES AND YIELDS										
Federal Reserve discount rate	1.00	1.00	1.00	1.00	1.00	1.00	1.00	1.00	1.00	1.34
U.S. Treasury 3-month bills	0.05	0.04	0.13	0.34	0.38	0.38	0.38	0.38	0.61	1.05
Bank prime rate	1.50	1.50	1.50	1.50	1.50	1.50	1.50	1.50	1.63	1.88
Prime commercial paper, 4- to 6-months	0.59	0.56	0.53	0.66	0.69	0.73	0.75	0.81	1.03	1.44
Bond yields:										
United States government, long-term	2.36	2.21	2.12	2.46	2.47	2.48	2.37	2.19	2.25	2.44
Corporate:										
Moodys Aaa	3.01	2.84	2.77	2.83	2.73	2.72	2.62	2.53	2.61	2.82
Moodys Baa	4.96	4.75	4.33	4.28	3.91	3.61	3.29	3.05	3.24	3.47
State and local	2.76	2.50	2.10	2.36	2.06	1.86	1.67	1.64	2.01	2.40

. . . = Not available.

Table 18-4. Price and Production Indexes, Labor Force Data, and Stock Prices and Yields, 1929–1948

Classification	1929	1930	1931	1932	1933	1934	1935	1936	1937	1938
CONSUMER AND PRODUCER PRICE INDEXES										
Consumer prices, all items; 1982–1984 = 100:										
All urban consumers (CPI-U)	17.1	16.7	15.2	13.7	13.0	13.4	13.7	13.9	14.4	14.1
Percent change	0.0	-2.3	-9.0	-9.9	-5.1	3.1	2.2	1.5	3.6	-2.1
Urban wage earners and clerical workers (CPI-W)	17.2	16.8	15.3	13.7	13.0	13.5	13.8	13.9	14.4	14.2
Producer prices, 1982 = 100:										
All commodities	16.4	14.9	12.6	11.2	11.4	12.9	13.8	13.9	14.9	13.5
Farm products	26.4	22.4	16.4	12.2	13.0	16.5	19.8	20.4	21.8	17.3
Industrial commodities	15.6	14.5	12.8	11.9	12.1	13.3	13.3	13.5	14.5	13.9
INDEXES OF INDUSTRIAL PRODUCTION (2002 = 100)										
Total	8.5	7.1	5.8	4.6	5.4	5.9	6.8	8.0	8.8	6.9
Products	...	...	...	...	...	...	...	...	...	...
Consumer goods	...	...	...	...	...	...	...	...	...	...
Materials	...	...	...	...	...	...	...	...	...	...
Manufacturing (SIC)	8.2	6.8	5.5	4.3	5.1	5.6	6.5	7.8	8.5	6.5
EMPLOYMENT STATUS OF THE CIVILIAN NONINSTITUTIONAL POPULATION, 14 YEARS AND OVER (Thousands of persons, except as noted)										
Civilian noninstitutional population	...	...	...	...	...	...	...	...	...	...
Civilian labor force	49 180	49 820	50 420	51 000	51 590	52 230	52 870	53 440	54 000	54 610
Participation rate, percent	...	...	...	...	...	...	...	...	...	...
Employment, total	47 630	45 480	42 400	38 940	38 760	40 890	42 260	44 410	46 300	44 220
Ratio, employment to population, percent	...	...	...	...	...	...	...	...	...	...
Agricultural	10 450	10 340	10 290	10 170	10 090	9 900	10 110	10 000	9 820	9 690
Nonagricultural	37 180	35 140	32 110	28 770	28 670	30 990	32 150	34 410	36 480	34 530
Unemployment	1 550	4 340	8 020	12 060	12 830	11 340	10 610	9 030	7 700	10 390
Percent of civilian labor force	3.2	8.7	15.9	23.6	24.9	21.7	20.1	16.9	14.3	19.0
Unemployment rate counting persons on work relief as employed, percent of civilian labor force [1]	3.2	8.7	15.3	22.5	20.6	16.0	14.2	9.9	9.1	12.5
NONFARM PAYROLL EMPLOYMENT (NAICS) (Thousands of persons, except as noted)										
Total	...	...	...	...	...	...	...	...	...	...
Private, total	...	...	...	...	...	...	...	...	...	...
Goods-producing, total	...	...	...	...	...	...	...	...	...	...
Natural resources and mining	...	...	...	...	...	...	...	...	...	...
Construction	...	...	...	...	...	...	...	...	...	...
Manufacturing, total	...	...	...	...	...	...	...	...	...	...
Durable goods	...	...	...	...	...	...	...	...	...	...
Nondurable goods, total	...	...	...	...	...	...	...	...	...	...
Private service-providing, total	...	...	...	...	...	...	...	...	...	...
Trade, transportation, and utilities, total	...	...	...	...	...	...	...	...	...	...
Wholesale trade	...	...	...	...	...	...	...	...	...	...
Retail trade	...	...	...	...	...	...	...	...	...	...
Information	...	...	...	...	...	...	...	...	...	...
Financial activities	...	...	...	...	...	...	...	...	...	...
Professional and business services	...	...	...	...	...	...	...	...	...	...
Education and health services	...	...	...	...	...	...	...	...	...	...
Leisure and hospitality	...	...	...	...	...	...	...	...	...	...
Other services	...	...	...	...	...	...	...	...	...	...
Government, total	...	...	...	...	...	...	...	...	...	...
Federal, total	...	...	...	...	...	...	...	...	...	...
Department of Defense, total	...	...	...	...	...	...	...	...	...	...
Service-providing	...	...	...	...	...	...	...	...	...	...
Manufacturing, production workers:										
Total (thousands)	...	...	...	...	...	...	...	...	...	...
Average weekly hours (number of hours per week)	...	...	...	...	...	...	...	...	...	...
Index of aggregate weekly hours (2002 = 100)	...	...	...	...	...	...	...	...	...	...
Average hourly earnings (dollars)	...	...	...	...	...	...	...	...	...	...
Average weekly earnings (dollars)	...	...	...	...	...	...	...	...	...	...
CORPORATE COMMON STOCKS (STANDARD AND POOR'S CORPORATION)										
Price index, 500 stocks, 1941–1943 = 10	26.02	21.03	13.66	6.93	8.96	9.84	10.60	15.47	15.41	11.49
Dividend-price ratio	3.47	4.51	6.15	7.43	4.21	3.72	3.82	3.44	4.86	5.18
Earnings-price ratio	7.51	6.33	7.51	5.95	4.36	5.16	7.23	6.57	8.25	5.55

[1]Michael Darby, "Three-and-a-Half Million U.S. Employees Have Been Mislaid." *Journal of Political Economy*, February 1976, v. 84, no. 1
. . . = Not available.

Table 18-4. Price and Production Indexes, Labor Force Data, and Stock Prices and Yields, 1929–1948
—Continued

Classification	1939	1940	1941	1942	1943	1944	1945	1946	1947	1948
CONSUMER AND PRODUCER PRICE INDEXES										
Consumer prices, all items; 1982–1984 = 100:										
All urban consumers (CPI-U)	13.9	14.0	14.7	16.3	17.3	17.6	18.0	19.5	22.3	24.1
Percent change	-1.4	0.7	5.0	10.9	6.1	1.7	2.3	8.3	14.4	8.1
Urban wage earners and clerical workers (CPI-W)	14.0	14.1	14.8	16.4	17.4	17.7	18.1	19.6	22.5	24.2
Producer prices, 1982 = 100:										
All commodities	13.3	13.5	15.1	17.0	17.8	17.9	18.2	20.8	25.6	27.7
Farm products	16.5	17.1	20.8	26.7	30.9	31.2	32.4	37.5	45.1	48.5
Industrial commodities	13.9	14.1	15.1	16.2	16.5	16.7	17.0	18.6	22.7	24.6
INDEXES OF INDUSTRIAL PRODUCTION (2002 = 100)										
Total	8.5	9.8	12.4	14.2	17.3	18.6	16.0	13.8	15.5	16.1
Products	8.5	9.6	12.1	13.8	17.1	18.7	15.8	13.8	15.4	16.1
Consumer goods	11.6	12.3	14.8	13.7	13.9	14.6	15.0	18.0	19.1	19.7
Materials	8.3	10.0	12.5	14.5	17.1	18.0	15.8	13.4	15.2	15.8
Manufacturing (SIC)	7.8	9.2	11.7	13.7	17.0	18.4	15.4	12.8	14.3	14.8
EMPLOYMENT STATUS OF THE CIVILIAN NONINSTITUTIONAL POPULATION, 14 YEARS AND OVER (Thousands of persons, except as noted)										
Civilian noninstitutional population	...	99 840	99 900	98 640	94 640	93 220	94 090	103 070	106 018	...
Civilian labor force	55 230	55 640	55 910	56 410	55 540	54 630	53 860	57 520	60 168	...
Participation rate, percent	...	55.7	56.0	57.2	58.7	58.6	57.2	55.8	56.8	...
Employment, total	45 750	47 520	50 350	53 750	54 470	53 960	52 820	55 250	57 812	...
Ratio, employment to population, percent	...	47.6	50.4	54.5	57.6	57.9	56.1	53.6	54.5	...
Agricultural	9 610	9 540	9 100	9 250	9 080	8 950	8 580	8 320	8 256	...
Nonagricultural	36 140	37 980	41 250	44 500	45 390	45 010	44 240	46 930	49 557	...
Unemployment	9 480	8 120	5 560	2 660	1 070	670	1 040	2 270	2 356	...
Percent of civilian labor force	17.2	14.6	9.9	4.7	1.9	1.2	1.9	3.9	3.9	...
Unemployment rate counting persons on work relief as employed, percent of civilian labor force [1]	11.3	9.5	6.0	3.1	1.8	...	...	...	...	...
NONFARM PAYROLL EMPLOYMENT (NAICS) (Thousands of persons, except as noted)										
Total	30 645	32 407	36 600	40 213	42 574	42 006	40 510	41 759	43 945	44 954
Private, total	26 606	28 156	31 874	34 621	36 353	35 819	34 428	36 054	38 379	39 213
Goods-producing, total	11 511	12 378	14 940	17 275	18 738	17 981	16 308	16 122	17 314	17 579
Natural resources and mining	856	927	967	1 010	958	864	885	976	1 014	
Construction	1 205	1 352	1 852	2 234	1 627	1 152	1 190	1 724	2 051	2 241
Manufacturing, total	9 450	10 099	12 121	14 030	16 153	15 903	14 255	13 513	14 287	14 324
Durable goods	4 654	5 261	6 778	8 502	10 583	10 372	8 732	7 535	8 079	8 028
Nondurable goods, total	4 796	4 839	5 343	5 528	5 570	5 531	5 523	5 978	6 208	6 296
Private service-providing, total	15 094	15 778	16 934	17 347	17 615	17 839	18 121	19 932	21 064	21 634
Trade, transportation, and utilities, total	6 739	7 043	7 550	7 607	7 628	7 805	8 048	8 945	9 452	9 716
Wholesale trade	1 507.6	1 570.9	1 678.7	1 635.0	1 565.8	1 585.0	1 671.9	1 962.4	2 115.7	2 229.7
Retail trade	3 157.5	3 324.4	3 551.7	3 521.5	3 479.2	3 515.5	3 623.5	4 118.3	4 392.7	4 523.6
Information	1 141	1 196	1 342	1 470	1 605	1 635	1 581	1 594	1 658	1 669
Financial activities	1 386	1 424	1 466	1 455	1 431	1 414	1 435	1 619	1 674	1 742
Professional and business services	1 976	2 073	2 265	2 410	2 518	2 523	2 495	2 666	2 828	2 893
Education and health services	1 405	1 470	1 566	1 632	1 660	1 667	1 698	1 885	2 015	2 077
Leisure and hospitality	1 896	1 995	2 130	2 133	2 122	2 142	2 200	2 485	2 650	2 726
Other services	553	578	616	641	652	654	664	737	788	812
Government, total	4 040	4 251	4 726	5 592	6 222	6 187	6 082	5 705	5 567	5 742
Federal, total	950	1 045	1 406	2 322	3 047	3 071	2 945	2 365	1 985	1 954
Department of Defense, total	132.5	181.6	374.9	920.4	1 361.2	1 352.3	1 233.8	745.8	498.6	511.4
Service-providing	19 134	20 029	21 660	22 938	23 837	24 026	24 203	25 637	26 631	27 376
Manufacturing, production workers:										
Total (thousands)	8 163	8 737	10 641	12 447	14 407	14 031	12 445	11 781	12 453	12 383
Average weekly hours (number of hours per week)	37.7	38.2	40.7	43.2	45.1	45.4	43.6	40.4	40.5	40.1
Index of aggregate weekly hours (2002 = 100)	70.5	76.4	99.2	123.1	148.8	145.6	124.3	108.9	115.7	114.0
Average hourly earnings (dollars)	0.49	0.53	0.61	0.74	0.86	0.91	0.90	0.95	1.10	1.20
Average weekly earnings (dollars)	18.47	20.25	24.83	31.97	38.79	41.31	39.24	38.38	44.55	48.12
CORPORATE COMMON STOCKS (STANDARD AND POOR'S CORPORATION)										
Price index, 500 stocks, 1941–1943 = 10	12.06	11.02	9.82	8.67	11.50	12.47	15.16	17.08	15.17	15.53
Dividend-price ratio	4.05	5.59	6.82	7.24	4.93	4.86	4.17	3.85	4.93	5.54
Earnings-price ratio	7.34	9.80	12.14	11.42	7.82	7.34	6.39	6.31	10.69	14.60

[1]Michael Darby, "Three-and-a-Half Million U.S. Employees Have Been Mislaid." *Journal of Political Economy*, February 1976, v. 84, no. 1
. . . = Not available.

Table 18-5. Money, Credit, and Real Interest Rates, 1930–1948

(Percent.)

Classification	1930	1931	1932	1933	1934	1935	1936	1937	1938	1939
Change in money stock, December 31 from year earlier	-6.8	-10.9	-6.8	-2.8	16.6	17.0	14.7	-4.5	7.3	14.0
Change in bank credit (loans and investments), December 31 from year earlier	-5.6	-15.1	-11.5	-12.2	9.6	6.7	9.7	-2.9	0.9	5.2
Nominal Treasury bill rate	2.23	1.40	0.88	0.52	0.28	0.17	0.17	0.28	0.07	0.05
Inflation (PCE price index)	-4.2	-10.8	-11.9	-3.6	4.6	2.4	1.0	3.6	-2.3	-0.9
Real treasury bill rate	6.5	12.2	12.8	4.1	-4.3	-2.2	-0.8	-3.4	2.3	1.0

Classification	1940	1941	1942	1943	1944	1945	1946	1947	1948
Change in money stock, December 31 from year earlier	16.8	15.0	29.3	26.7	13.6	13.2	7.5	2.8	-1.4
Change in bank credit (loans and investments), December 31 from year earlier	8.0	15.5	32.8	26.3	24.0	17.5	-8.1	2.0	-1.7
Nominal Treasury bill rate	0.04	0.13	0.34	0.38	0.38	0.38	0.38	0.61	1.05
Inflation (PCE price index)	0.8	6.1	12.3	9.1	5.7	4.0	7.2	10.2	5.7
Real treasury bill rate	-0.8	-6.0	-12.0	-8.8	-5.3	-3.6	-6.8	-9.6	-4.7

Table 18-6. Federal Budget, 1929–1948

(Fiscal years, billions of dollars, percent.)

Classification	1929	1930	1931	1932	1933	1934	1935	1936	1937	1938
Receipts	3.9	4.1	3.1	1.9	2.0	3.0	3.6	3.9	5.4	6.8
Outlays	3.1	3.3	3.6	4.7	4.6	6.5	6.4	8.2	7.6	6.8
National defense	. . .	. . .	. . .	. . .	. . .	. . .	. . .	. . .	. . .	. . .
Surplus or deficit (-)	0.7	0.7	-0.5	-2.7	-2.6	-3.6	-2.8	-4.3	-2.2	-0.1
Fiscal year GDP	. . .	97.4	83.9	67.6	57.6	61.2	69.6	78.5	87.8	89.0
As percent of GDP:										
Receipts	. . .	4.2	3.7	2.8	3.5	4.8	5.2	5.0	6.1	7.6
Outlays	. . .	3.4	4.3	6.9	8.0	10.7	9.2	10.5	8.6	7.7
National defense	. . .	1.7	5.6	17.8	37.0	37.8	37.5	19.2	5.5	3.5
Surplus or deficit (-)	. . .	0.8	-0.6	-4.0	-4.5	-5.9	-4.0	-5.5	-2.5	-0.1
Debt held by the public, end of year:										
Billions of dollars	. . .	. . .	. . .	. . .	. . .	. . .	. . .	. . .	. . .	. . .
Percent of GDP	. . .	. . .	. . .	. . .	. . .	. . .	. . .	. . .	. . .	. . .

Classification	1939	1940	1941	1942	1943	1944	1945	1946	1947	1948
Receipts	6.3	6.5	8.7	14.6	24.0	43.7	45.2	39.3	38.5	41.6
Outlays	9.1	9.5	13.7	35.1	78.6	91.3	92.7	55.2	34.5	29.8
National defense	. . .	1.7	6.4	25.7	66.7	79.1	83.0	42.7	12.8	9.1
Surplus or deficit (-)	-2.8	-2.9	-4.9	-20.5	-54.6	-47.6	-47.6	-15.9	4.0	11.8
Fiscal year GDP	89.1	96.8	114.1	144.3	180.3	209.2	221.4	222.6	233.2	256.6
As percent of GDP:										
Receipts	7.1	6.8	7.6	10.1	13.3	20.9	20.4	17.7	16.5	16.2
Outlays	10.3	9.8	12.0	24.3	43.6	43.6	41.9	24.8	14.8	11.6
National defense	. . .	1.7	5.6	17.8	37.0	37.8	37.5	19.2	5.5	3.6
Surplus or deficit (-)	-3.2	-3.0	-4.3	-14.2	-30.3	-22.7	-21.5	-7.2	1.7	4.6
Debt held by the public, end of year:										
Billions of dollars	. . .	42.8	48.2	67.8	127.8	184.8	235.2	241.9	224.3	216.3
Percent of GDP	. . .	44.2	42.3	47.0	70.9	88.3	106.2	108.7	96.2	84.5

. . . = Not available.

NOTES AND DEFINITIONS, CHAPTER 18

General note on the chronology of the 1930s and 1940s

See the article at the beginning of this book, "Business Statistics in the Great Recession," for the business cycle peaks and troughs occurring in this period, as determined by the National Bureau of Economic Research (NBER).

The NBER chronology may surprise readers who are looking for "The Great Depression" and are not familiar with the NBER approach to business cycles. As NBER perceives it, a downtrend in economic activity began in August 1929 (before the stock market crash) and lasted until March 1933. This 43-month period has been called the "Great Contraction": it was the longest period of economic decline since the 1870s, and nearly three times as long as the longest recession identified and completed since that time (16 months). For the rest of the 1930s—except a 13-month recession in 1937–1938—the economy is viewed by the NBER as being in an expansion phase. The NBER chronology does not use the term "depression."

However, the term "Great Depression" is often colloquially used for the entire 1929–1939 period, even though the economy was expanding for most of the period following March 1933. This is because economic activity during that time, though increasing, remained below the likely capacity of the economy, as is indicated in Figures 18-1 and 18-2.

It should also be noted that NBER construes the entire period from June 1938 through February 1945 as a business cycle expansion. The recovery from the 1937–1938 recession merged into a further, continued rise in activity that reflected the outbreak of war in Europe in September 1939, a consequent preparedness effort in the United States, and an increase in demand from abroad for U.S. output. The United States entered the war after being attacked by Japan in December 1941, launching an all-out war production effort at that time.

The February 1945 end of the "wartime expansion" (as NBER terms the period June 1938–February 1945) preceded the end of the war, as the European war ended in May 1945 and the Pacific war concluded in August 1945. A brief demobilization recession occurred from February to October 1945, followed by the first postwar expansion, which lasted from October 1945 to November 1948.

TABLES 18-1 AND 18-2
NATIONAL INCOME AND PRODUCT ACCOUNTS (NIPAS) AND RELATED DATA, 1929–1948

For most of these data, the sources, definitions, and availability are the same as for the identically titled series in Part A. Specific references to the appropriate chapter's notes and definitions are given below.

Gross domestic product and its components in current and constant dollars, gross national product, national income and

its components, population and per capita data, and chain-type price indexes: See the notes and definitions for Chapter 1.

Personal income and its disposition and disposable personal income: See the notes and definitions for Chapter 4.

Saving and investment: See the notes and definitions for Chapter 5.

Employment, NIPA data, full-time and part-time employees: As is evident in Table 18-4, payroll employment data from the Bureau of Labor Statistics (BLS) are not available for the years before 1939, and the BLS civilian employment estimates do not include work-relief employees. In order to provide more complete information on employment, this table presents NIPA estimates for the total number of full-time and part-time employees. Like the BLS payroll data, these estimates are a count of jobs rather than of persons employed, and persons with two jobs will appear as two persons employed in these data. These estimates include members of the armed forces and employees of Depression-era work-relief programs in the total, and also show them as separate categories. The issue of counting work-relief jobs is discussed below.

References

The data published here have been calculated after the fact and differ from what was actually available during the 1930s and 1940s. For an article on what was available at that time and the history of the NIPAs during that period, see Rosemary D. Marcuss and Richard E. Kane, "U.S. National Income and Product Statistics: Born of the Great Depression and World War II," *Survey of Current Business,* February 2007, pp. 32-46.

TABLE 18-3
FIXED ASSETS, MONEY AND CREDIT, AND INTEREST RATES, 1929–1948

For the data on the *net stock of fixed assets,* see the notes and definitions for Tables 5-5 and 5-6.

All of the other data in this table are taken from two volumes of statistical data issued by the Board of Governors of the Federal Reserve System: *Banking and Monetary Statistics,* Washington, D.C., Board of Governors of the Federal Reserve System, 1943, and *Banking and Monetary Statistics, 1941–1970,* Washington: Board of Governors of the Federal Reserve System, 1976. None of these data are included in the online data banks made available by the Federal Reserve on its Web site.

Federal Reserve *money stock* data for the years presented here pertain only to the last day of June and the last day of December. These are the "call dates" on which banks report to the federal government. For more data and analysis covering monetary developments in this period, including monthly money supply estimates, see Milton Friedman and Anna Jacobson Schwartz, *A Monetary History of the*

United States, 1867-1960, Princeton, Princeton University Press, 1963.

Federal Reserve calculation of money stock data based on monthly averages of daily figures begins with the data for January 1947, shown in Table 20-5A and described in its notes and definitions. The definitions for the money stock data in Table 18-3 are the same as for the data in 20-5A, although the terms used in the source documents are slightly different.

Currency outside banks is defined the same as the *currency component* of Table 20-5A: currency in circulation outside the Treasury and Federal Reserve Banks less vault cash held by commercial banks.

Demand deposits adjusted is defined the same as the *demand deposit component* of Table 20-5A: demand deposits at commercial banks in the continental United States except interbank and U.S. Government deposits, less cash items in process of collection. The term "adjusted" in this context refers to the elimination of these three items, which represent double counting—not to seasonal adjustment, which is not applicable to call report data.

The *total* of currency outside banks and demand deposits adjusted is the concept labeled *money stock, total* in Table 20-5A, and corresponds to M1.

Time deposits are the same as *time deposits adjusted* in Table 20-5A: they include time deposits at commercial banks, mutual savings banks, and the Postal Savings System, except interbank deposits, postal savings redeposited in banks, and U.S. Government time deposits. This item could be added to the money stock total to yield an approximation of the current concept of M2.

Bank credit. Loans and investments, all commercial banks is the sum of these items from commercial bank balance sheets, including total loans, holdings of U.S. Government securities, and holdings of other securities, which according to the 1976 Federal Reserve source book "consist mainly of State and municipal issues."

Data are also shown for the outstanding values of two forms of securities used by businesses for short-term borrowing, *commercial paper* and *bankers' acceptances.* Figures for bankers' acceptances represent amounts reported by banks and dealers in the United States as well as by agencies of foreign banks located in the United States. From 1929 through 1934, acceptances includes acceptances held by Federal Reserve Banks, both for their own account ($391 million in December 1929) and for account of foreign correspondent banks ($548 million in December 1929). These Federal Reserve holdings declined rapidly after 1931 and amounted to zero by December 1934. By then, most of the outstanding acceptances were held by banks.

Federal Reserve discount rate is the rate set by the New York Federal Reserve Bank for bank borrowing secured by eligible paper, in percent per annum. Annual averages calculated by editor.

U.S. Treasury 3-month bills, yield in percent per annum, based on dealers' quotations from 1934 through 1948. For 1931 through 1933, the average rate on new issues of bills offered within the period. For 1929 and 1930, the rate on 3- to 6-month Treasury notes and certificates.

Bank prime rate is the rate that banks charge their most creditworthy business customers on short-term loans. According to the 1976 source document cited above, "A nationally publicized and uniform prime rate did not emerge until the depression of the 1930's. The rate in that period—1 ½ percent—represented a floor below which banks were said to regard lending as unprofitable…The date shown [for the beginning of a changed rate] is that on which the new rate was put into effect by the first bank to make the change. The table shows a range of rates for 1929–1933 because no information is available to indicate when the rate changed in that period." For further information, the source document cites "The Prime Rate," *Monthly Review,* Federal Reserve Bank of New York, April and May 1962, pp. 54-59 and 70-73, respectively.

Prime commercial paper, 4- to 6-months. Prevailing rate in New York City, percent per annum.

U.S. government bond yields, long-term. Yield in percent per annum. Before 1941, yields on bonds that were partly tax-exempt. The 1941 yield for the partly tax-exempt series was 1.95 percent.

Corporate bond yields, Moody's Investors Service. See Notes and Definitions for Table 12-9.

State and local bond yields on high-grade municipal bonds were provided by Standard and Poor's.

TABLE 18-4
PRICE AND PRODUCTION INDEXES, LABOR FORCE DATA, AND STOCK PRICES AND YIELDS, 1929–1948

Consumer and producer price indexes: See the notes and definitions for Chapter 8.

Indexes of industrial production: See the notes and definitions for Chapter 2.

Civilian noninstitutional population, labor force, employment, and unemployment are as defined in the notes and definitions to Chapter 10 with the following exceptions:

- The data for 1929 to 1947 in Chapter 18 pertain to persons 14 years of age and over. The data in Chapter 10 and Table 20-3 from 1947 to the present are for persons 16 years of age and over. The differences made by this change in definitions can be observed in the two different sets of data—one from this table, the other from Table 20-3—for the overlap year, 1947. In that year, the unemployment rates are the same (3.9 percent) for both age definitions. However, the labor force participation rate and the employment/population ratio are higher when the 14- and 15-year-olds are excluded.

- The Census Bureau began the monthly survey of households that provides labor force data in 1942, and the Census of Population supplied data for 1940. For earlier years, data for the labor force, employment, and unemployment are retrospective estimates made by BLS.

- The 1940 Census and the BLS data for 1931 through 1942 did not treat government work relief employment as employment; persons engaged in such work were counted as unemployed. In the labor force survey used today, anyone who worked for pay or profit is counted as employed (see the notes and definitions for Chapter 10). Therefore, today's survey would count work relief as employment and not unemployment, and the BLS figures for the period before 1942 are not consistent with today's unemployment rates. Michael Darby calculated an alternative unemployment rate in which such workers are counted as employed, and this rate is also shown in Table 18-4. It would appear that the Darby rate is more consistent with the NIPA total employment data. Furthermore, the NIPA data on GDP include, as output, the work done by relief workers, and the buildings they constructed are included in investment and capital stock.

BLS data for 1940 through 1947 are published on their Web site at <http://www.bls.gov>. The data for 1929 through 1939 were published in *Employment and Earnings*, May 1972, and in U.S. Commerce Department, Bureau of Economic Analysis, *Long-Term Economic Growth, 1860–1970*, June 1973, p. 163.

The Darby alternative unemployment rate is found in Michael Darby, "Three-and-a-Half Million U.S. Employees Have Been Mislaid," *Journal of Political Economy*, February 1976, v. 84, no. 1. It is also displayed and discussed in Robert A. Margo, "Employment and Unemployment in the 1930s," *Journal of Economic Perspectives*, v. 7, no. 2, Spring 1993.

Nonfarm employment and its components, and number, hours, and earnings for manufacturing production workers:

See the notes and definitions for Chapter 10. Note that because age is not specified in the Current Employment Survey that is the source of these data, this measure of employment includes any payroll workers that are under 16 years of age and has always done so.

Corporate common stock price index, dividend-price ratio, and earnings-price ratio (Standard and Poor's Corporation). See Notes and Definitions for Table 12-9. Before 1957, these measures represent a conversion of an earlier 90-stock index to the current 500-stock index. They are obtained from the Federal Reserve volumes of *Banking and Monetary Statistics* cited above in the notes to Table 18-3.

TABLE 18-5
MONEY, CREDIT, AND REAL INTEREST RATES, 1930–1948

These data are derived from data in preceding tables.

Change in money stock is the percent change from a year earlier in the December 31 value of the total of currency outside banks and demand deposits adjusted, usually known as M1, from Table 18-3.

Change in bank credit is the percent change from a year earlier in the December 31 value of loans and investments at all commercial banks, from Table 18-3.

The *nominal Treasury bill rate* is the interest rate on U.S. Treasury 3-month bills from Table 18-3.

Inflation is the percent change in the chain-type price index for personal consumption expenditures (PCE) from Table 18-2.

The *real Treasury bill rate* is the nominal rate minus the inflation rate. Note that subtraction means changing the sign and adding—hence negative inflation (deflation, price decline) contributes to large positive real rates.

TABLE 18-6
FEDERAL BUDGET, 1929–1948

See notes and definitions for Tables 6-14 and 6-15.

Table 19-1. Gross Domestic Product

(Billions of dollars, quarterly data are at seasonally adjusted annual rates.)

NIPA Tables 1.1.5, 1.4.5

Year and quarter	Gross domestic product	Personal consumption expenditures	Gross private domestic investment — Total	Fixed investment — Nonresidential	Fixed investment — Residential	Change in private inventories	Net exports	Exports	Imports	Government — Total	Government — Federal	State and local	Addendum: Final sales of domestic product
1946	222.2	144.3	31.1	17.3	7.8	6.0	7.2	14.2	7.0	39.6	28.8	10.8	216.2
1947	244.1	162.0	35.0	23.5	12.1	-0.6	10.8	18.7	7.9	36.3	22.6	13.7	244.6
1948	269.1	175.0	48.1	26.8	15.6	5.7	5.5	15.5	10.1	40.5	24.2	16.3	263.5
1949	267.2	178.5	36.9	24.9	14.6	-2.7	5.2	14.5	9.2	46.6	27.6	19.0	269.9
1947													
1st quarter	237.2	156.3	33.7	22.8	10.4	0.5	10.9	18.4	7.5	36.3	23.3	13.0	236.7
2nd quarter	240.4	160.2	32.4	23.2	10.4	-1.2	11.3	19.5	8.2	36.6	23.2	13.4	241.6
3rd quarter	244.5	163.7	32.7	23.3	12.3	-2.9	11.8	19.4	7.7	36.3	22.3	14.0	247.4
4th quarter	254.3	167.8	41.0	24.5	15.1	1.5	9.3	17.6	8.3	36.2	21.5	14.7	252.9
1948													
1st quarter	260.3	170.5	45.0	26.2	15.2	3.6	7.3	16.9	9.6	37.5	22.4	15.2	256.7
2nd quarter	267.3	174.3	48.1	26.0	16.3	5.9	5.2	15.2	10.0	39.7	23.7	15.9	261.4
3rd quarter	273.8	177.2	50.2	27.0	16.1	7.2	4.9	15.4	10.5	41.4	24.6	16.8	266.6
4th quarter	275.1	178.1	49.1	28.1	15.0	6.0	4.5	14.6	10.1	43.4	26.0	17.5	269.1
1949													
1st quarter	269.9	177.0	40.9	26.6	14.0	0.4	6.5	16.1	9.6	45.5	27.5	18.0	269.6
2nd quarter	266.2	178.6	34.0	25.5	13.7	-5.1	6.3	15.6	9.4	47.3	28.5	18.7	271.3
3rd quarter	267.6	178.0	37.3	24.1	14.5	-1.3	5.2	14.1	8.9	47.1	27.7	19.5	268.9
4th quarter	265.2	180.4	35.2	23.5	16.3	-4.7	3.0	12.1	9.1	46.6	26.9	19.7	269.9
1950													
1st quarter	275.2	183.1	44.4	24.2	18.1	2.0	2.2	11.7	9.5	45.5	25.5	20.0	273.2
2nd quarter	284.5	187.0	49.9	26.6	20.4	2.8	1.6	11.9	10.2	46.0	25.7	20.4	281.7
3rd quarter	301.9	200.7	56.1	29.6	22.3	4.2	-0.7	12.3	13.0	45.8	24.9	21.0	297.8
4th quarter	313.3	198.1	65.9	30.6	21.3	14.0	-0.2	13.5	13.7	49.5	27.8	21.6	299.3
1951													
1st quarter	329.0	209.4	62.1	30.9	20.8	10.4	0.2	15.0	14.9	57.3	35.2	22.1	318.6
2nd quarter	336.6	205.1	64.8	31.8	18.2	14.8	1.9	17.1	15.2	64.7	41.8	22.9	321.8
3rd quarter	343.5	207.8	59.4	32.5	17.2	9.7	3.7	18.1	14.3	72.6	49.1	23.4	333.8
4th quarter	347.9	211.8	54.4	32.2	17.5	4.7	4.2	18.2	14.0	77.6	53.9	23.7	343.2
1952													
1st quarter	351.2	213.1	55.2	32.4	18.0	4.7	3.7	18.7	15.0	79.1	55.3	23.8	346.5
2nd quarter	352.1	217.3	49.9	32.9	18.5	-1.5	2.0	16.6	14.6	83.0	58.4	24.6	353.7
3rd quarter	358.5	219.8	53.9	29.8	18.5	5.6	0.0	15.2	15.3	84.8	60.4	24.4	352.9
4th quarter	371.4	227.9	57.1	32.5	19.4	5.3	-1.0	15.3	16.3	87.3	62.4	25.0	366.1
1953													
1st quarter	378.4	231.5	57.9	34.3	19.7	3.9	-0.7	15.1	15.8	89.6	63.9	25.8	374.5
2nd quarter	382.0	233.3	58.1	34.8	19.8	3.6	-1.3	15.2	16.4	91.8	66.2	25.6	378.4
3rd quarter	381.1	234.0	57.4	35.9	19.2	2.3	-0.6	15.8	16.3	90.2	63.9	26.3	378.8
4th quarter	375.9	233.5	52.3	35.4	18.9	-2.0	-0.3	15.2	15.5	90.4	63.5	26.9	377.9
1954													
1st quarter	375.2	235.5	51.5	34.5	19.0	-2.0	-0.4	14.4	14.8	88.5	60.8	27.8	377.2
2nd quarter	376.0	238.3	51.2	34.3	20.3	-3.4	0.3	16.4	16.2	86.2	57.7	28.5	379.3
3rd quarter	380.8	240.7	54.7	35.0	21.8	-2.1	0.6	15.9	15.3	84.8	55.3	29.5	382.9
4th quarter	389.4	245.5	57.8	34.9	23.2	-0.3	1.1	16.6	15.5	85.0	55.2	29.8	389.7
1955													
1st quarter	402.6	251.8	64.2	35.4	25.0	3.8	1.1	17.3	16.2	85.4	54.6	30.8	398.8
2nd quarter	410.9	256.9	68.1	37.9	25.6	4.6	-0.2	16.9	17.1	86.0	54.7	31.3	406.3
3rd quarter	419.4	261.1	70.0	40.4	25.2	4.3	0.7	18.1	17.4	87.6	55.8	31.8	415.2
4th quarter	426.0	265.1	73.9	42.5	24.2	7.2	0.2	18.3	18.1	86.7	54.3	32.4	418.8
1956													
1st quarter	428.3	266.7	73.0	42.9	23.7	6.4	0.4	19.4	18.9	88.2	54.7	33.5	421.9
2nd quarter	434.2	269.4	71.4	43.9	23.9	3.6	1.9	20.9	19.0	91.4	57.1	34.4	430.6
3rd quarter	439.2	272.6	72.5	45.4	23.5	3.6	2.6	21.8	19.3	91.5	56.4	35.1	435.6
4th quarter	448.1	278.0	71.2	45.9	23.0	2.2	4.5	23.1	18.5	94.3	58.5	35.8	445.8
1957													
1st quarter	457.2	282.4	71.8	47.0	22.6	2.2	4.8	24.9	20.1	98.1	61.0	37.1	455.0
2nd quarter	459.2	284.7	71.9	47.1	22.2	2.7	4.1	24.4	20.3	98.4	60.4	38.0	456.5
3rd quarter	466.4	289.3	73.2	48.4	22.0	2.8	4.0	23.8	19.8	99.8	61.2	38.7	463.6
4th quarter	461.5	291.0	64.9	47.5	21.9	-4.5	3.4	23.0	19.6	102.3	62.7	39.6	466.0
1958													
1st quarter	453.9	290.5	60.5	43.6	20.9	-4.0	1.1	20.5	19.5	101.8	61.2	40.6	457.9
2nd quarter	458.0	293.4	58.7	42.0	21.0	-4.2	0.5	20.5	20.1	105.4	63.8	41.6	462.3
3rd quarter	471.7	298.5	65.5	41.4	22.5	1.5	0.9	20.6	19.7	106.9	64.2	42.7	470.2
4th quarter	485.0	302.3	73.2	43.1	24.9	5.2	-0.3	20.6	20.8	109.7	66.0	43.7	479.7
1959													
1st quarter	495.5	310.1	76.2	44.5	27.8	3.9	0.4	21.8	21.4	108.8	64.3	44.5	491.6
2nd quarter	508.5	316.1	82.2	46.1	28.8	7.3	0.0	22.6	22.5	110.2	65.4	44.7	501.2
3rd quarter	509.3	321.3	76.4	47.8	28.3	0.4	0.6	23.5	22.9	111.0	66.2	44.8	508.9
4th quarter	513.2	323.4	79.3	47.7	27.5	4.1	0.6	23.1	22.5	110.0	65.4	44.6	509.1
1960													
1st quarter	527.0	326.9	89.1	49.5	28.4	11.2	2.7	26.0	23.3	108.2	62.4	45.8	515.8
2nd quarter	526.2	332.8	79.7	50.3	26.1	3.2	4.2	27.6	23.5	109.5	62.4	47.2	522.9
3rd quarter	529.0	332.8	78.7	49.0	25.3	4.3	4.2	27.0	22.9	113.3	65.3	48.1	524.6
4th quarter	523.7	334.7	68.1	48.6	25.3	-5.8	5.8	27.5	21.7	115.1	66.3	48.8	529.5
1961													
1st quarter	528.0	335.2	70.3	47.5	25.3	-2.5	5.8	27.5	21.7	116.7	66.0	50.7	530.5
2nd quarter	539.0	340.2	75.8	48.4	25.5	1.8	5.5	27.4	21.9	117.6	66.8	50.8	537.2
3rd quarter	549.5	343.1	82.4	48.8	26.9	6.7	3.9	27.2	23.3	120.1	68.6	51.6	542.8
4th quarter	562.6	350.3	84.2	50.4	27.8	6.0	4.4	28.3	23.9	123.6	70.2	53.4	556.6

Table 19-1. Gross Domestic Product—*Continued*

(Billions of dollars, quarterly data are at seasonally adjusted annual rates.)   **NIPA Tables 1.1.5, 1.4.5**

| Year and quarter | Gross domestic product | Personal consumption expenditures | Gross private domestic investment | | | | Exports and imports of goods and services | | | Government consumption expenditures and gross investment | | | Addendum: Final sales of domestic product |
| | | | Total | Fixed investment | | Change in private inventories | Net exports | Exports | Imports | Total | Federal | State and local | |
				Nonresidential	Residential								
1962													
1st quarter	576.1	355.6	89.4	51.6	28.4	9.4	4.0	28.3	24.3	127.1	73.4	53.7	566.6
2nd quarter	583.2	361.2	87.9	53.2	29.2	5.4	5.8	30.7	24.9	128.3	73.9	54.4	577.8
3rd quarter	590.0	365.1	89.3	53.9	29.2	6.2	3.8	29.0	25.1	131.8	76.6	55.2	583.8
4th quarter	593.3	371.4	86.0	53.5	29.1	3.4	2.8	28.4	25.6	133.2	77.0	56.1	590.0
1963													
1st quarter	602.5	375.0	90.5	53.4	30.2	6.9	3.9	29.1	25.2	133.1	75.5	57.6	595.6
2nd quarter	611.2	379.1	92.2	55.1	32.2	4.8	6.5	32.4	25.9	133.4	74.9	58.5	606.3
3rd quarter	623.9	386.1	95.0	56.8	32.5	5.7	3.9	30.6	26.7	139.0	78.8	60.2	618.2
4th quarter	633.5	390.7	97.4	58.7	33.7	5.1	5.4	32.2	26.8	139.9	78.4	61.5	628.4
1964													
1st quarter	649.6	400.4	100.7	60.1	35.4	5.1	7.3	34.2	27.0	141.3	78.6	62.7	644.5
2nd quarter	658.9	408.4	100.6	61.9	34.2	4.5	7.1	34.8	27.7	142.9	78.4	64.5	654.4
3rd quarter	670.5	417.3	102.5	64.1	33.7	4.7	6.4	34.8	28.4	144.4	78.9	65.5	665.8
4th quarter	675.6	419.8	104.6	65.7	33.8	5.0	6.9	36.2	29.3	144.3	77.8	66.5	670.6
1965													
1st quarter	695.7	430.5	115.7	70.3	33.9	11.5	4.6	33.1	28.5	144.9	77.1	67.8	684.1
2nd quarter	708.1	437.5	115.8	73.1	34.2	8.6	7.5	39.1	31.7	147.4	77.5	69.9	699.6
3rd quarter	725.2	446.6	119.7	76.1	34.3	9.3	4.9	36.9	32.0	154.0	81.5	72.5	715.9
4th quarter	747.5	460.6	121.8	79.7	34.5	7.6	5.5	39.5	33.9	159.6	85.5	74.1	739.9
1966													
1st quarter	770.8	471.0	131.7	83.0	34.8	13.9	4.4	39.4	35.0	163.6	87.6	76.0	756.9
2nd quarter	779.9	476.1	130.7	85.2	33.2	12.3	5.2	41.5	36.2	167.9	90.0	77.9	767.6
3rd quarter	793.1	485.3	130.2	86.4	31.9	11.9	2.2	40.4	38.2	175.5	95.6	79.9	781.3
4th quarter	806.9	491.1	132.7	87.0	29.2	16.5	3.6	42.4	38.8	179.6	96.5	83.0	790.4
1967													
1st quarter	817.8	495.4	129.3	85.6	28.3	15.4	4.6	44.0	39.4	188.5	103.0	85.4	802.3
2nd quarter	822.3	504.6	123.7	85.7	31.6	6.3	4.5	43.5	39.0	189.6	102.7	86.8	816.0
3rd quarter	837.0	511.8	128.5	85.8	33.4	9.3	2.9	42.4	39.5	193.8	105.4	88.3	827.7
4th quarter	852.7	519.4	132.9	88.4	36.0	8.4	2.2	43.9	41.7	198.2	107.3	90.9	844.3
1968													
1st quarter	879.8	537.3	137.2	91.9	36.9	8.4	1.1	45.5	44.4	204.1	110.1	94.0	871.3
2nd quarter	904.1	551.1	143.4	91.2	38.2	14.1	1.9	47.4	45.4	207.6	110.6	97.0	890.0
3rd quarter	919.3	567.3	139.7	93.2	38.9	7.7	1.3	49.5	48.2	210.9	111.7	99.2	911.6
4th quarter	936.2	576.2	144.4	97.4	40.9	6.0	1.1	49.2	48.2	214.6	112.6	102.0	930.2
1969													
1st quarter	960.9	588.4	155.7	101.0	43.2	11.5	0.2	44.0	43.8	216.5	112.1	104.4	949.4
2nd quarter	976.1	599.8	155.7	103.0	43.4	9.2	1.2	53.9	52.7	219.4	112.0	107.4	966.9
3rd quarter	996.3	610.1	160.3	106.9	43.2	10.2	1.0	53.3	52.4	224.9	115.4	109.5	986.1
4th quarter	1 004.5	622.1	154.1	107.6	40.7	5.8	3.3	56.5	53.1	224.9	113.6	111.3	998.7
1970													
1st quarter	1 017.1	633.2	150.7	108.1	40.7	1.8	3.4	56.9	53.5	229.8	115.0	114.9	1 015.3
2nd quarter	1 033.1	643.1	153.9	109.4	39.4	5.1	5.4	60.6	55.2	230.6	112.7	118.0	1 028.0
3rd quarter	1 050.5	655.1	156.1	110.6	40.4	5.1	3.8	60.3	56.4	235.5	112.7	122.7	1 045.4
4th quarter	1 052.7	661.8	148.9	107.9	45.0	-4.0	3.2	61.1	57.9	238.8	113.3	125.6	1 056.7
1971													
1st quarter	1 098.1	680.8	171.3	110.4	48.6	12.3	4.4	63.1	58.7	241.6	112.8	128.7	1 085.8
2nd quarter	1 118.8	694.9	178.8	113.4	54.6	10.9	-0.2	63.1	63.3	245.3	113.5	131.8	1 107.9
3rd quarter	1 139.1	707.3	183.4	114.8	58.3	10.2	-0.1	65.4	65.5	248.5	114.7	133.8	1 128.9
4th quarter	1 151.4	723.5	179.2	118.0	61.5	-0.3	-1.7	60.3	61.9	250.3	113.6	136.8	1 151.7
1972													
1st quarter	1 190.1	740.9	193.2	123.3	66.6	3.2	-3.5	68.6	72.2	259.6	119.7	139.9	1 186.9
2nd quarter	1 225.6	759.4	206.5	126.3	68.2	12.0	-4.3	67.2	71.4	263.9	122.6	141.3	1 213.6
3rd quarter	1 249.3	777.9	212.4	129.1	69.6	13.7	-2.6	71.5	74.1	261.6	116.8	144.8	1 235.6
4th quarter	1 286.6	802.7	218.4	136.6	74.3	7.5	-3.1	76.1	79.2	268.6	119.4	149.2	1 279.1
1973													
1st quarter	1 335.1	827.3	232.5	144.1	77.9	10.6	-1.4	84.0	85.4	276.7	123.3	153.4	1 324.5
2nd quarter	1 371.5	842.9	246.0	152.1	75.8	18.2	2.5	91.9	89.5	280.0	123.3	156.8	1 353.3
3rd quarter	1 390.7	861.4	241.8	157.0	75.0	9.8	6.4	97.6	91.1	281.1	120.3	160.8	1 380.9
4th quarter	1 431.8	876.5	257.6	159.9	72.7	25.0	9.0	107.6	98.7	288.8	122.8	165.9	1 406.8
1974													
1st quarter	1 446.5	894.7	244.1	162.6	69.0	12.5	6.4	116.7	110.3	301.4	128.6	172.8	1 434.0
2nd quarter	1 484.8	923.2	252.3	167.4	67.5	17.4	-2.7	126.7	129.4	312.0	131.1	181.0	1 467.4
3rd quarter	1 513.7	952.0	245.4	172.5	67.4	5.6	-7.0	126.6	133.6	323.2	136.1	187.1	1 508.1
4th quarter	1 552.8	961.8	255.8	175.4	60.0	20.4	0.0	136.6	136.6	335.1	142.5	192.6	1 532.3
1975													
1st quarter	1 569.4	988.1	218.7	171.0	57.7	-10.0	16.5	141.4	124.9	346.2	144.0	202.2	1 579.5
2nd quarter	1 605.0	1 016.8	216.8	170.8	59.9	-14.0	21.6	136.8	115.2	349.8	144.9	204.9	1 618.9
3rd quarter	1 662.4	1 050.6	237.8	174.6	64.6	-1.4	12.0	134.1	122.1	362.0	151.3	210.7	1 663.8
4th quarter	1 713.9	1 079.6	247.6	178.6	68.7	0.3	13.8	142.5	128.7	372.9	156.0	216.9	1 713.6
1976													
1st quarter	1 771.9	1 113.4	274.8	183.9	76.2	14.7	4.7	143.6	138.9	379.1	156.3	222.8	1 757.2
2nd quarter	1 804.2	1 133.0	291.6	188.5	80.7	22.4	-0.5	146.6	147.1	380.1	157.8	222.3	1 781.8
3rd quarter	1 837.7	1 162.4	296.5	195.1	80.6	20.8	-4.1	151.8	155.8	382.8	159.8	223.0	1 816.9
4th quarter	1 884.5	1 196.2	304.9	201.9	92.5	10.5	-6.6	156.1	162.7	390.0	164.8	225.2	1 874.0

Table 19-1. Gross Domestic Product—*Continued*

(Billions of dollars, quarterly data are at seasonally adjusted annual rates.)   **NIPA Tables 1.1.5, 1.4.5**

Year and quarter	Gross domestic product	Personal consumption expenditures	Gross private domestic investment				Exports and imports of goods and services			Government consumption expenditures and gross investment			Addendum: Final sales of domestic product
			Total	Fixed investment		Change in private inventories	Net exports	Exports	Imports	Total	Federal	State and local	
				Nonresidential	Residential								
1977													
1st quarter	1 938.5	1 231.7	326.6	214.2	97.6	14.8	-21.1	155.4	176.4	401.3	169.8	231.5	1 923.7
2nd quarter	2 005.2	1 259.7	354.9	223.8	111.7	19.5	-21.1	161.9	183.0	411.8	174.8	237.0	1 985.8
3rd quarter	2 066.0	1 290.9	378.4	232.5	115.0	30.9	-20.6	162.3	182.9	417.3	176.5	240.8	2 035.1
4th quarter	2 110.8	1 329.1	385.5	244.5	116.9	24.1	-29.6	157.8	187.4	425.8	180.5	245.3	2 086.7
1978													
1st quarter	2 149.1	1 359.1	396.8	250.4	121.0	25.5	-38.7	164.6	203.3	431.9	182.9	249.0	2 123.6
2nd quarter	2 274.7	1 416.7	430.9	276.0	130.6	24.3	-22.6	186.2	208.8	449.7	189.2	260.6	2 250.5
3rd quarter	2 335.2	1 447.7	451.4	290.6	135.8	25.0	-23.8	191.3	215.1	459.9	192.4	267.4	2 310.3
4th quarter	2 416.0	1 487.0	472.8	305.3	139.0	28.5	-16.4	205.4	221.8	472.7	199.1	273.6	2 387.6
1979													
1st quarter	2 463.3	1 522.6	481.1	318.8	138.5	23.9	-18.2	211.7	229.8	477.8	202.2	275.5	2 439.5
2nd quarter	2 526.4	1 563.2	493.0	324.9	140.6	27.4	-22.2	220.9	243.1	492.5	207.9	284.6	2 499.0
3rd quarter	2 599.7	1 617.7	497.9	342.3	143.5	12.1	-23.0	234.3	257.3	507.2	211.7	295.5	2 587.6
4th quarter	2 659.4	1 661.2	499.5	349.6	141.4	8.6	-26.8	253.7	280.5	525.5	220.4	305.0	2 650.8
1980													
1st quarter	2 724.1	1 708.0	505.2	361.3	134.0	9.9	-35.8	268.5	304.3	546.7	231.6	315.1	2 714.2
2nd quarter	2 728.0	1 710.0	470.4	350.9	111.7	7.8	-15.2	277.4	292.6	562.7	243.0	319.8	2 720.3
3rd quarter	2 785.2	1 768.7	443.5	361.1	116.3	-33.9	5.5	284.7	279.2	567.5	243.6	324.0	2 819.0
4th quarter	2 915.3	1 836.6	497.9	376.2	130.8	-9.1	-6.7	292.5	299.2	587.5	256.7	330.7	2 924.4
1981													
1st quarter	3 051.4	1 892.4	563.1	393.1	131.3	38.8	-14.3	305.5	319.7	610.1	266.5	343.6	3 012.6
2nd quarter	3 084.3	1 924.0	551.4	410.8	128.9	11.7	-13.5	308.4	322.0	622.4	278.7	343.8	3 072.6
3rd quarter	3 177.0	1 963.4	592.8	428.4	120.4	44.0	-7.6	302.3	309.9	628.4	281.4	347.0	3 133.1
4th quarter	3 194.7	1 978.2	582.2	447.8	109.6	24.8	-14.8	304.7	319.4	649.0	294.1	354.8	3 169.9
1982													
1st quarter	3 184.9	2 016.2	526.5	443.2	104.8	-21.5	-16.3	293.2	309.5	658.5	298.7	359.9	3 206.4
2nd quarter	3 240.9	2 042.7	530.8	432.0	102.9	-4.2	-4.4	294.7	299.1	671.9	305.1	366.8	3 245.1
3rd quarter	3 274.4	2 090.7	528.7	419.4	103.5	5.8	-29.7	279.6	309.3	684.7	312.3	372.4	3 268.6
4th quarter	3 312.5	2 152.4	482.9	411.2	111.5	-39.8	-29.6	265.3	294.9	706.7	327.0	379.7	3 352.3
1983													
1st quarter	3 381.0	2 192.2	496.6	400.5	131.2	-35.1	-24.6	270.7	295.3	716.7	332.8	383.9	3 416.0
2nd quarter	3 482.2	2 256.4	542.2	402.9	147.0	-7.7	-45.4	272.5	318.0	729.1	342.1	387.0	3 489.9
3rd quarter	3 587.1	2 326.5	577.7	419.5	162.4	-4.2	-65.2	278.2	343.4	748.1	354.1	394.0	3 591.3
4th quarter	3 688.1	2 379.2	640.7	446.0	170.8	23.9	-71.4	286.6	358.0	739.7	342.4	397.3	3 664.2
1984													
1st quarter	3 807.4	2 425.5	709.7	460.1	176.6	73.0	-95.0	293.0	388.0	767.2	359.2	408.0	3 734.4
2nd quarter	3 906.3	2 484.1	735.1	484.4	181.4	69.3	-104.3	302.2	406.5	791.4	373.9	417.4	3 837.0
3rd quarter	3 976.0	2 522.8	753.5	500.7	181.4	71.3	-103.9	305.7	409.6	803.6	375.2	428.4	3 904.6
4th quarter	4 034.0	2 572.0	744.3	513.3	183.0	48.0	-107.8	308.6	416.4	825.5	388.8	436.7	3 986.0
1985													
1st quarter	4 117.2	2 643.4	720.0	520.5	183.3	16.2	-91.9	305.4	397.3	845.6	398.0	447.6	4 101.0
2nd quarter	4 175.7	2 687.4	735.3	528.5	185.1	21.6	-115.4	303.1	418.6	868.4	407.6	460.7	4 154.0
3rd quarter	4 258.3	2 755.9	727.2	522.2	188.8	16.3	-118.6	295.6	414.2	893.9	420.7	473.2	4 242.0
4th quarter	4 318.7	2 783.7	762.2	533.6	195.5	33.1	-134.9	304.0	438.9	907.7	424.6	483.0	4 285.6
1986													
1st quarter	4 382.4	2 827.2	763.8	527.2	206.3	30.3	-127.4	312.0	439.4	918.8	421.3	497.5	4 352.1
2nd quarter	4 423.2	2 859.2	753.0	517.5	219.8	15.7	-129.8	314.2	444.0	940.9	434.7	506.2	4 407.6
3rd quarter	4 491.3	2 930.6	732.5	513.5	226.1	-7.0	-139.3	320.2	459.4	967.4	451.9	515.5	4 498.3
4th quarter	4 543.3	2 969.9	736.7	521.2	228.3	-12.7	-133.6	335.0	468.6	970.2	445.8	524.4	4 556.0
1987													
1st quarter	4 611.1	3 004.8	765.0	506.8	230.1	28.0	-141.0	336.7	477.7	982.4	451.6	530.9	4 583.1
2nd quarter	4 686.7	3 071.9	767.6	518.2	232.9	16.5	-147.3	355.0	502.3	994.6	458.6	536.0	4 670.2
3rd quarter	4 764.5	3 138.3	769.5	534.2	234.2	1.0	-145.7	371.6	517.3	1 002.5	460.5	542.0	4 763.5
4th quarter	4 883.1	3 173.0	837.8	537.2	237.5	63.1	-145.7	391.8	537.5	1 018.1	467.5	550.6	4 820.0
1988													
1st quarter	4 948.6	3 253.5	797.6	546.2	234.4	17.0	-124.4	418.4	542.7	1 021.9	460.1	561.8	4 931.6
2nd quarter	5 059.3	3 313.0	820.4	562.3	238.4	19.7	-107.2	438.9	546.1	1 033.0	459.0	574.0	5 039.6
3rd quarter	5 142.8	3 380.4	825.7	567.5	240.0	18.2	-100.2	452.7	552.8	1 036.9	456.1	580.8	5 124.6
4th quarter	5 251.0	3 453.3	842.6	579.1	244.4	19.1	-108.7	465.6	574.3	1 063.8	471.1	592.7	5 231.9
1989													
1st quarter	5 360.3	3 507.7	884.1	591.3	244.6	48.2	-102.1	484.0	586.2	1 070.7	469.3	601.4	5 312.2
2nd quarter	5 453.6	3 570.0	878.2	601.9	240.2	36.0	-89.5	505.8	595.4	1 095.0	481.4	613.6	5 417.5
3rd quarter	5 532.9	3 626.8	870.3	621.9	238.4	10.0	-76.3	508.2	584.4	1 112.1	489.0	623.2	5 523.0
4th quarter	5 581.7	3 673.5	867.3	615.8	234.8	16.6	-83.6	514.5	598.2	1 124.6	486.1	638.5	5 565.1
1990													
1st quarter	5 708.1	3 758.7	880.0	626.9	239.2	13.9	-89.2	537.6	626.8	1 158.6	500.8	657.8	5 694.2
2nd quarter	5 797.4	3 811.8	882.5	617.9	230.9	33.7	-68.4	546.4	614.8	1 171.4	506.0	665.4	5 763.7
3rd quarter	5 850.6	3 875.2	866.8	626.1	218.8	21.9	-74.4	555.7	630.1	1 183.0	505.0	678.0	5 828.8
4th quarter	5 846.0	3 896.0	814.6	618.9	207.0	-11.3	-78.5	568.8	647.3	1 213.8	518.2	695.6	5 857.3
1991													
1st quarter	5 880.2	3 909.7	787.9	608.2	195.2	-15.5	-45.6	574.7	620.3	1 228.1	529.2	698.9	5 895.7
2nd quarter	5 962.0	3 963.3	784.1	601.4	200.7	-18.0	-21.6	592.3	613.9	1 236.2	531.7	704.5	5 980.0
3rd quarter	6 033.7	4 008.7	805.3	594.1	210.3	0.8	-19.5	602.2	621.7	1 239.2	526.0	713.2	6 032.8
4th quarter	6 092.5	4 038.6	834.3	589.0	214.2	31.1	-21.2	617.1	638.3	1 240.8	519.2	721.5	6 061.4

Table 19-1. Gross Domestic Product—*Continued*

(Billions of dollars, quarterly data are at seasonally adjusted annual rates.)   NIPA Tables 1.1.5, 1.4.5

Year and quarter	Gross domestic product	Personal consumption expenditures	Gross private domestic investment				Exports and imports of goods and services			Government consumption expenditures and gross investment			Addendum: Final sales of domestic product
			Total	Fixed investment		Change in private inventories	Net exports	Exports	Imports	Total	Federal	State and local	
				Nonresidential	Residential								
1992													
1st quarter	6 190.7	4 140.1	810.2	585.6	224.4	0.2	-18.5	627.3	645.8	1 258.8	525.7	733.1	6 190.5
2nd quarter	6 295.2	4 193.5	865.4	607.1	235.1	23.2	-31.1	627.9	659.0	1 267.3	528.9	738.4	6 272.0
3rd quarter	6 389.7	4 267.7	876.8	619.0	237.3	20.5	-36.5	641.4	677.9	1 281.7	538.6	743.1	6 369.2
4th quarter	6 493.6	4 346.2	906.7	636.7	248.6	21.4	-45.3	643.2	688.5	1 286.0	538.4	747.7	6 472.2
1993													
1st quarter	6 544.5	4 384.9	931.3	642.8	252.6	35.9	-54.3	645.0	699.3	1 282.6	526.8	755.8	6 508.6
2nd quarter	6 622.7	4 452.1	942.3	660.3	257.9	24.1	-62.0	654.3	716.3	1 290.3	522.9	767.4	6 598.6
3rd quarter	6 688.3	4 516.3	943.4	667.5	269.3	6.6	-67.9	651.4	719.3	1 296.6	522.4	774.2	6 681.7
4th quarter	6 813.8	4 581.1	996.4	695.7	284.1	16.6	-73.4	671.7	745.0	1 309.7	527.9	781.9	6 797.2
1994													
1st quarter	6 916.3	4 650.4	1 043.6	704.8	293.5	45.3	-80.7	681.2	761.8	1 302.9	512.0	791.0	6 871.0
2nd quarter	7 044.3	4 709.8	1 106.9	720.5	305.0	81.4	-91.3	706.3	797.6	1 318.8	515.0	803.7	6 962.9
3rd quarter	7 131.8	4 786.3	1 092.9	734.7	304.9	53.2	-96.7	737.1	833.8	1 349.3	529.1	820.2	7 078.6
4th quarter	7 248.2	4 856.7	1 145.7	765.6	304.9	75.2	-102.3	758.3	860.6	1 348.1	518.2	829.9	7 173.0
1995													
1st quarter	7 307.7	4 888.7	1 160.6	797.7	301.8	61.1	-106.2	780.7	886.9	1 364.6	523.1	841.5	7 246.5
2nd quarter	7 355.8	4 957.5	1 132.7	805.5	293.5	33.7	-110.6	797.7	908.3	1 376.3	521.7	854.6	7 322.1
3rd quarter	7 452.5	5 022.9	1 126.2	811.2	303.8	11.3	-75.4	830.5	905.8	1 378.8	520.1	858.7	7 441.2
4th quarter	7 542.5	5 080.1	1 156.7	825.8	312.4	18.5	-70.6	838.6	909.2	1 376.4	510.2	866.2	7 524.1
1996													
1st quarter	7 638.2	5 156.5	1 170.0	841.4	321.8	6.9	-89.1	847.6	936.7	1 400.7	527.9	872.8	7 631.3
2nd quarter	7 800.0	5 248.8	1 227.8	860.5	336.9	30.5	-93.8	859.0	952.8	1 417.1	530.9	886.2	7 769.5
3rd quarter	7 892.7	5 304.4	1 279.8	889.0	339.7	51.1	-114.0	859.7	973.8	1 422.6	523.6	898.9	7 841.6
4th quarter	8 023.0	5 384.7	1 283.1	910.6	337.9	34.6	-88.3	904.3	992.6	1 443.5	525.5	918.0	7 988.3
1997													
1st quarter	8 137.0	5 467.1	1 320.6	930.1	340.7	49.8	-108.1	919.1	1 027.2	1 457.4	523.6	933.7	8 087.2
2nd quarter	8 276.8	5 504.0	1 385.0	949.9	346.7	88.4	-84.7	955.0	1 039.7	1 472.4	533.5	939.0	8 188.4
3rd quarter	8 409.9	5 613.3	1 414.9	995.6	351.3	68.0	-96.2	974.7	1 070.9	1 477.9	532.4	945.6	8 341.9
4th quarter	8 505.7	5 698.1	1 434.1	998.8	357.5	77.8	-116.5	968.9	1 085.3	1 490.0	534.4	955.6	8 428.0
1998													
1st quarter	8 600.6	5 757.5	1 494.9	1 025.0	364.9	105.1	-134.5	963.8	1 098.2	1 482.6	519.5	963.1	8 495.5
2nd quarter	8 698.6	5 870.2	1 471.5	1 055.8	378.4	37.3	-161.8	947.8	1 109.6	1 518.7	534.8	983.9	8 661.3
3rd quarter	8 847.2	5 968.0	1 512.7	1 066.7	393.6	52.4	-173.9	936.0	1 109.9	1 540.4	531.8	1 008.6	8 794.8
4th quarter	9 027.5	6 078.2	1 564.0	1 097.1	406.8	60.0	-177.1	967.9	1 145.0	1 562.5	537.9	1 024.6	8 967.5
1999													
1st quarter	9 148.6	6 157.4	1 617.3	1 120.7	413.3	83.3	-212.0	958.7	1 170.6	1 585.8	541.2	1 044.6	9 065.3
2nd quarter	9 252.6	6 290.0	1 604.7	1 147.4	422.3	35.1	-250.9	971.2	1 222.2	1 608.8	544.3	1 064.5	9 217.5
3rd quarter	9 405.1	6 398.9	1 644.5	1 174.5	429.4	40.6	-282.9	998.8	1 281.7	1 644.6	558.9	1 085.7	9 364.5
4th quarter	9 607.7	6 524.9	1 699.5	1 177.0	438.1	84.3	-302.5	1 028.5	1 331.0	1 685.9	575.3	1 110.6	9 523.4
2000													
1st quarter	9 709.5	6 683.0	1 688.8	1 223.5	449.2	16.1	-357.9	1 052.8	1 410.7	1 695.6	562.4	1 133.2	9 693.5
2nd quarter	9 949.1	6 775.7	1 810.9	1 270.1	450.5	90.4	-364.4	1 089.2	1 453.6	1 726.9	583.2	1 143.7	9 858.7
3rd quarter	10 017.5	6 881.7	1 791.7	1 288.4	446.0	57.2	-395.9	1 119.1	1 515.0	1 740.0	579.4	1 160.6	9 960.2
4th quarter	10 129.8	6 981.1	1 797.4	1 292.7	450.2	54.5	-410.0	1 111.8	1 521.8	1 761.3	579.3	1 182.0	10 075.3
2001													
1st quarter	10 165.1	7 058.1	1 701.3	1 273.7	458.3	-30.7	-395.4	1 097.1	1 492.5	1 801.1	594.3	1 206.7	10 195.7
2nd quarter	10 301.3	7 118.7	1 699.4	1 240.6	470.4	-11.6	-363.8	1 056.6	1 420.3	1 846.9	608.7	1 238.2	10 312.9
3rd quarter	10 305.2	7 151.2	1 670.4	1 219.6	480.9	-30.1	-367.0	997.1	1 364.2	1 850.6	616.3	1 234.2	10 335.3
4th quarter	10 373.1	7 267.2	1 576.6	1 177.3	480.1	-80.8	-357.8	960.1	1 317.9	1 887.2	627.4	1 259.8	10 453.9
2002													
1st quarter	10 498.7	7 309.0	1 628.0	1 149.5	491.9	-13.4	-374.9	973.4	1 348.3	1 936.6	657.8	1 278.9	10 512.1
2nd quarter	10 601.9	7 403.4	1 648.1	1 128.3	506.6	13.2	-418.1	1 005.9	1 424.0	1 968.5	674.4	1 294.1	10 588.7
3rd quarter	10 701.7	7 491.2	1 650.4	1 120.6	511.5	18.3	-435.8	1 020.6	1 456.4	1 996.0	685.4	1 310.6	10 683.4
4th quarter	10 766.9	7 553.2	1 661.3	1 103.3	528.1	30.0	-479.9	1 012.2	1 492.1	2 032.3	705.0	1 327.3	10 737.0
2003													
1st quarter	10 888.4	7 646.9	1 671.5	1 097.7	545.2	28.6	-503.6	1 012.5	1 516.1	2 073.6	725.2	1 348.4	10 859.7
2nd quarter	11 008.1	7 723.8	1 678.6	1 123.8	557.9	-3.1	-504.3	1 011.6	1 515.9	2 110.0	762.1	1 347.8	11 011.2
3rd quarter	11 255.7	7 882.5	1 745.1	1 150.8	590.1	4.2	-499.5	1 041.4	1 540.8	2 127.5	765.2	1 362.3	11 251.5
4th quarter	11 416.5	7 962.8	1 823.6	1 170.4	617.4	35.8	-509.1	1 098.6	1 607.8	2 139.1	773.4	1 365.7	11 380.7
2004													
1st quarter	11 597.2	8 105.3	1 853.6	1 164.6	637.6	51.4	-546.3	1 138.8	1 685.1	2 184.5	805.1	1 379.4	11 545.8
2nd quarter	11 778.4	8 209.4	1 956.0	1 204.4	675.6	76.0	-606.1	1 170.8	1 776.9	2 219.0	819.9	1 399.2	11 702.4
3rd quarter	11 950.5	8 330.7	2 001.3	1 244.0	696.6	60.8	-635.9	1 185.4	1 821.3	2 254.4	839.1	1 415.3	11 889.8
4th quarter	12 144.9	8 494.9	2 063.2	1 279.1	712.6	71.5	-686.5	1 225.9	1 912.4	2 273.3	834.5	1 438.8	12 073.5
2005													
1st quarter	12 379.5	8 609.6	2 130.7	1 305.2	734.8	90.7	-677.4	1 262.4	1 939.8	2 316.5	862.0	1 454.6	12 288.8
2nd quarter	12 516.8	8 747.2	2 115.2	1 334.9	764.5	15.9	-690.2	1 298.5	1 988.7	2 344.6	867.2	1 477.3	12 500.9
3rd quarter	12 741.6	8 908.8	2 166.6	1 362.9	792.6	11.0	-734.0	1 308.2	2 042.1	2 400.1	894.1	1 506.0	12 730.6
4th quarter	12 915.6	9 010.3	2 276.3	1 386.3	807.9	82.2	-789.3	1 351.3	2 140.6	2 418.3	881.9	1 536.4	12 833.4
2006													
1st quarter	13 183.5	9 148.2	2 336.5	1 457.2	813.3	66.0	-775.8	1 414.0	2 189.8	2 474.5	928.5	1 546.1	13 117.5
2nd quarter	13 347.8	9 266.6	2 352.1	1 495.3	784.4	72.4	-781.4	1 456.0	2 237.4	2 510.5	930.3	1 580.2	13 275.4
3rd quarter	13 452.9	9 391.8	2 333.5	1 522.7	741.7	69.1	-805.7	1 476.0	2 281.7	2 533.3	932.2	1 601.2	13 383.8
4th quarter	13 611.5	9 484.1	2 286.5	1 546.1	708.1	32.3	-714.3	1 538.2	2 252.5	2 555.2	935.9	1 619.4	13 579.2

Table 19-2. Real Gross Domestic Product

(Billions of chained [2005] dollars, quarterly data are at seasonally adjusted annual rates.)   NIPA Tables 1.1.6, 1.4.6

| Year and quarter | Gross domestic product | Personal consumption expenditures | Gross private domestic investment | | | | Exports and imports of goods and services | | | Government consumption expenditures and gross investment | | | Addendum: Final sales of domestic product |
| | | | Total | Fixed investment | | Change in private inventories | Net exports | Exports | Imports | Total | Federal | State and local | |
				Nonresidential	Residential								
1946	1 792.2	1 125.9	191.4	...	...	...	...	70.3	52.1	482.1	...	...	1 766.2
1947	1 776.1	1 147.5	183.9	...	...	...	...	80.1	49.4	409.5	...	...	1 803.2
1948	1 854.2	1 173.4	234.9	...	...	...	...	63.1	57.7	439.4	...	...	1 837.2
1949	1 844.7	1 205.9	179.3	...	...	...	...	62.5	55.6	491.9	...	...	1 880.9
1947													
1st quarter	1 772.2	1 131.5	189.4	...	...	...	...	85.3	51.0	407.3	...	...	1 787.0
2nd quarter	1 769.5	1 150.2	174.1	...	...	...	...	84.2	52.0	409.8	...	...	1 798.7
3rd quarter	1 768.0	1 154.0	168.5	...	...	...	...	80.0	46.1	413.6	...	...	1 813.3
4th quarter	1 794.8	1 154.3	203.5	...	...	...	...	70.9	48.6	407.5	...	...	1 813.9
1948													
1st quarter	1 823.4	1 160.1	225.5	...	...	...	...	67.7	54.8	415.5	...	...	1 821.8
2nd quarter	1 856.9	1 173.6	240.4	...	...	...	...	61.3	57.0	435.5	...	...	1 835.0
3rd quarter	1 866.9	1 175.3	242.9	...	...	...	...	62.8	60.0	444.0	...	...	1 838.1
4th quarter	1 869.8	1 184.7	230.9	...	...	...	...	60.6	59.0	462.7	...	...	1 854.0
1949													
1st quarter	1 843.8	1 186.5	194.9	...	...	...	...	67.8	57.2	475.9	...	...	1 861.6
2nd quarter	1 837.1	1 204.7	167.7	...	...	...	...	67.2	56.4	497.4	...	...	1 885.6
3rd quarter	1 857.7	1 207.4	182.4	...	...	...	...	61.6	54.1	502.4	...	...	1 884.8
4th quarter	1 840.3	1 225.1	172.4	...	...	...	...	53.3	54.9	491.8	...	...	1 891.7
1950													
1st quarter	1 914.6	1 245.4	215.6	...	...	...	...	52.5	56.4	483.5	...	...	1 922.0
2nd quarter	1 972.9	1 265.9	239.8	...	...	...	...	53.1	59.5	491.4	...	...	1 973.7
3rd quarter	2 050.1	1 330.9	261.4	...	...	...	...	54.5	73.5	482.0	...	...	2 044.8
4th quarter	2 086.2	1 290.8	296.1	...	...	...	...	58.9	73.6	512.7	...	...	2 022.5
1951													
1st quarter	2 112.5	1 322.0	264.9	...	...	...	...	61.8	73.6	567.5	...	...	2 082.2
2nd quarter	2 147.6	1 284.7	271.4	...	...	...	...	67.9	71.2	645.6	...	...	2 092.1
3rd quarter	2 190.4	1 299.7	250.5	...	...	...	...	69.6	65.2	718.8	...	...	2 161.3
4th quarter	2 194.1	1 307.3	229.1	...	...	...	...	68.9	63.5	758.9	...	...	2 193.4
1952													
1st quarter	2 216.2	1 310.2	234.5	...	...	...	...	72.6	70.8	782.4	...	...	2 211.4
2nd quarter	2 218.6	1 335.9	215.0	...	...	...	...	64.6	70.5	808.9	...	...	2 247.2
3rd quarter	2 233.5	1 342.4	226.5	...	...	...	...	59.5	74.8	817.0	...	...	2 225.3
4th quarter	2 307.2	1 389.8	242.7	...	...	...	...	59.9	81.5	831.6	...	...	2 299.1
1953													
1st quarter	2 350.4	1 406.4	247.5	...	...	...	...	58.9	79.5	859.8	...	...	2 348.7
2nd quarter	2 368.2	1 414.9	248.4	...	...	...	...	59.3	83.6	878.7	...	...	2 367.3
3rd quarter	2 353.8	1 411.6	242.5	...	...	...	...	61.7	83.3	868.1	...	...	2 361.5
4th quarter	2 316.5	1 402.2	223.4	...	...	...	...	59.6	79.2	865.4	...	...	2 348.1
1954													
1st quarter	2 305.5	1 407.3	221.6	...	...	...	...	56.9	74.6	842.2	...	...	2 334.4
2nd quarter	2 308.4	1 425.7	220.8	...	...	...	...	65.1	81.3	812.5	...	...	2 343.9
3rd quarter	2 334.4	1 445.0	232.1	...	...	...	...	63.0	76.4	792.9	...	...	2 367.2
4th quarter	2 381.2	1 475.4	242.8	...	...	...	...	65.9	77.1	788.0	...	...	2 406.6
1955													
1st quarter	2 449.7	1 508.5	268.7	...	...	...	...	68.4	81.7	787.1	...	...	2 452.6
2nd quarter	2 490.3	1 537.3	285.6	...	...	...	...	66.8	86.3	779.3	...	...	2 484.8
3rd quarter	2 523.5	1 556.3	289.7	...	...	...	...	71.2	87.8	784.0	...	...	2 521.0
4th quarter	2 537.6	1 575.9	296.0	...	...	...	...	71.5	90.9	767.0	...	...	2 526.4
1956													
1st quarter	2 526.1	1 578.5	286.0	...	...	...	...	74.9	94.8	766.6	...	...	2 520.8
2nd quarter	2 545.9	1 583.7	282.8	...	...	...	...	79.9	94.3	782.7	...	...	2 548.7
3rd quarter	2 542.7	1 587.3	279.5	...	...	...	...	82.6	95.1	775.3	...	...	2 549.8
4th quarter	2 584.3	1 609.2	276.2	...	...	...	...	86.3	90.7	795.4	...	...	2 593.8
1957													
1st quarter	2 600.2	1 620.3	271.7	...	...	...	...	91.9	97.9	811.7	...	...	2 616.5
2nd quarter	2 593.9	1 623.2	271.4	...	...	...	...	89.2	98.7	806.7	...	...	2 606.9
3rd quarter	2 618.9	1 636.1	277.8	...	...	...	...	86.7	96.8	812.9	...	...	2 626.4
4th quarter	2 591.3	1 636.9	254.6	...	...	...	...	84.1	97.1	827.7	...	...	2 625.9
1958													
1st quarter	2 521.2	1 614.6	235.7	...	...	...	...	75.8	98.6	818.4	...	...	2 558.7
2nd quarter	2 536.6	1 627.9	230.1	...	...	...	...	76.1	102.8	838.9	...	...	2 572.0
3rd quarter	2 596.1	1 654.5	249.1	...	...	...	...	76.4	101.2	844.2	...	...	2 609.5
4th quarter	2 656.6	1 676.4	271.6	...	...	...	...	76.1	106.5	862.2	...	...	2 659.9
1959													
1st quarter	2 710.3	1 707.4	286.9	...	...	...	...	81.2	109.3	856.6	...	...	2 714.7
2nd quarter	2 778.8	1 733.7	310.9	...	...	...	...	83.9	114.6	869.7	...	...	2 761.5
3rd quarter	2 775.5	1 751.8	289.2	...	...	...	...	86.5	115.6	880.6	...	...	2 795.1
4th quarter	2 785.2	1 753.7	299.4	...	...	...	...	84.2	112.7	871.0	...	...	2 784.6
1960													
1st quarter	2 847.7	1 770.5	331.7	...	...	...	...	94.8	117.0	853.9	...	...	2 815.0
2nd quarter	2 834.4	1 792.9	298.2	...	...	...	...	100.8	117.8	860.8	...	...	2 841.9
3rd quarter	2 839.0	1 785.8	296.4	...	...	...	...	98.2	114.4	881.5	...	...	2 837.9
4th quarter	2 802.6	1 788.2	259.8	...	...	...	...	100.3	109.0	887.7	...	...	2 851.8
1961													
1st quarter	2 819.3	1 787.7	266.4	...	...	...	...	99.6	108.5	899.3	...	...	2 854.0
2nd quarter	2 872.0	1 814.3	286.2	...	...	...	...	98.2	109.8	901.4	...	...	2 884.6
3rd quarter	2 918.4	1 823.1	310.2	...	...	...	...	97.7	117.0	919.1	...	...	2 906.9
4th quarter	2 977.8	1 859.6	315.5	...	...	...	...	100.7	119.8	939.3	...	...	2 973.0

... = Not available.

Table 19-2. Real Gross Domestic Product—*Continued*

(Billions of chained [2005] dollars, quarterly data are at seasonally adjusted annual rates.)

NIPA Tables 1.1.6, 1.4.6

Year and quarter	Gross domestic product	Personal consumption expenditures	Gross private domestic investment				Exports and imports of goods and services			Government consumption expenditures and gross investment			Addendum: Final sales of domestic product
			Total	Fixed investment		Change in private inventories	Net exports	Exports	Imports	Total	Federal	State and local	
				Nonresidential	Residential								
1962													
1st quarter	3 031.2	1 879.4	334.3	...	...	...	...	100.4	123.5	955.9	...	...	3 009.2
2nd quarter	3 064.7	1 902.5	331.0	...	...	...	...	110.1	126.2	961.1	...	...	3 060.5
3rd quarter	3 093.0	1 917.9	337.0	...	...	...	...	103.9	127.8	983.0	...	...	3 084.3
4th quarter	3 100.6	1 945.1	325.7	...	...	...	...	101.7	129.3	984.4	...	...	3 105.6
1963													
1st quarter	3 141.1	1 958.2	343.7	...	...	...	...	104.1	126.3	978.4	...	...	3 126.2
2nd quarter	3 180.4	1 976.9	348.7	...	...	...	...	116.2	129.3	977.2	...	...	3 179.2
3rd quarter	3 240.3	2 003.8	360.1	...	...	...	...	110.0	132.6	1 019.1	...	...	3 235.7
4th quarter	3 265.0	2 020.6	364.5	...	...	...	...	115.6	132.2	1 009.8	...	...	3 269.3
1964													
1st quarter	3 338.2	2 060.5	379.5	...	...	...	...	122.6	132.0	1 013.5	...	...	3 340.8
2nd quarter	3 376.6	2 096.7	377.8	...	...	...	...	124.7	135.0	1 020.1	...	...	3 380.5
3rd quarter	3 422.5	2 135.2	386.8	...	...	...	...	123.7	138.6	1 020.7	...	...	3 422.4
4th quarter	3 432.0	2 141.2	389.9	...	...	...	...	127.4	142.4	1 017.8	...	...	3 431.3
1965													
1st quarter	3 516.3	2 188.8	429.1	...	...	...	...	113.6	137.3	1 015.3	...	...	3 485.5
2nd quarter	3 564.0	2 213.0	429.1	...	...	...	...	135.0	153.5	1 028.4	...	...	3 548.5
3rd quarter	3 636.3	2 251.0	444.4	...	...	...	...	127.2	154.1	1 064.0	...	...	3 615.2
4th quarter	3 724.0	2 314.3	446.5	...	...	...	...	136.5	161.6	1 086.9	...	...	3 713.4
1966													
1st quarter	3 815.4	2 348.5	484.2	...	...	...	...	134.1	165.8	1 106.4	...	...	3 775.3
2nd quarter	3 828.1	2 354.5	475.4	...	...	...	...	139.9	169.9	1 126.0	...	...	3 792.4
3rd quarter	3 853.3	2 381.5	470.7	...	...	...	...	134.7	179.4	1 156.5	...	...	3 824.0
4th quarter	3 884.5	2 391.4	473.0	...	...	...	...	139.1	181.4	1 175.3	...	...	3 834.8
1967													
1st quarter	3 918.7	2 405.3	460.0	...	...	...	...	141.8	184.3	1 225.2	...	...	3 873.6
2nd quarter	3 919.6	2 438.1	440.4	...	...	...	...	140.5	182.8	1 218.5	...	...	3 915.0
3rd quarter	3 950.8	2 450.6	453.0	...	...	...	...	137.1	185.2	1 231.2	...	...	3 934.9
4th quarter	3 981.0	2 465.7	462.8	...	...	...	...	141.0	195.0	1 239.6	...	...	3 969.8
1968													
1st quarter	4 063.0	2 524.6	472.9	...	...	...	...	145.1	206.5	1 261.3	...	...	4 052.9
2nd quarter	4 132.0	2 563.3	492.0	...	...	...	...	148.0	209.6	1 267.1	...	...	4 093.6
3rd quarter	4 160.3	2 611.5	476.1	...	...	...	...	156.7	222.2	1 269.7	...	...	4 152.2
4th quarter	4 178.3	2 623.5	481.0	...	...	...	...	154.7	220.3	1 270.8	...	...	4 178.6
1969													
1st quarter	4 244.1	2 652.9	512.7	...	...	...	...	136.1	199.6	1 272.0	...	...	4 221.8
2nd quarter	4 256.5	2 669.8	508.6	...	...	...	...	166.7	238.9	1 266.7	...	...	4 242.6
3rd quarter	4 283.4	2 682.7	520.4	...	...	...	...	162.7	235.8	1 268.5	...	...	4 264.6
4th quarter	4 263.3	2 704.1	492.3	...	...	...	...	168.3	233.2	1 249.8	...	...	4 265.4
1970													
1st quarter	4 256.6	2 720.7	476.9	...	...	...	...	169.8	232.5	1 243.1	...	...	4 277.0
2nd quarter	4 264.3	2 733.2	478.4	...	...	...	...	177.2	237.1	1 227.1	...	...	4 268.7
3rd quarter	4 302.3	2 757.1	486.6	...	...	...	...	176.6	236.5	1 232.4	...	...	4 307.0
4th quarter	4 256.6	2 749.6	458.4	...	...	...	...	178.3	240.2	1 232.4	...	...	4 299.0
1971													
1st quarter	4 374.0	2 802.2	517.9	...	...	...	...	178.9	237.4	1 212.4	...	...	4 352.2
2nd quarter	4 398.8	2 827.9	534.0	...	...	...	...	178.6	255.3	1 208.5	...	...	4 382.3
3rd quarter	4 433.9	2 850.4	541.0	...	...	...	...	185.9	260.9	1 207.8	...	...	4 420.9
4th quarter	4 446.3	2 897.8	524.1	...	...	...	...	170.3	243.2	1 198.8	...	...	4 474.2
1972													
1st quarter	4 525.8	2 936.5	561.1	...	...	...	...	188.4	278.8	1 203.1	...	...	4 536.3
2nd quarter	4 633.1	2 992.6	595.5	...	...	...	...	182.9	268.9	1 210.6	...	...	4 611.6
3rd quarter	4 677.5	3 038.8	604.0	...	...	...	...	193.9	274.5	1 185.6	...	...	4 653.2
4th quarter	4 754.5	3 110.1	607.1	...	...	...	...	202.2	286.8	1 193.1	...	...	4 761.4
1973													
1st quarter	4 876.2	3 167.0	645.7	...	...	...	...	217.0	300.1	1 204.8	...	...	4 865.8
2nd quarter	4 932.6	3 165.4	675.8	...	...	...	...	227.4	291.4	1 197.6	...	...	4 889.7
3rd quarter	4 906.3	3 176.7	649.4	...	...	...	...	228.2	283.4	1 182.3	...	...	4 895.7
4th quarter	4 953.1	3 167.4	674.3	...	...	...	...	239.4	285.5	1 191.0	...	...	4 901.4
1974													
1st quarter	4 909.6	3 139.7	631.2	...	...	...	...	242.5	275.8	1 215.9	...	...	4 895.4
2nd quarter	4 922.2	3 150.6	628.1	...	...	...	...	254.3	290.4	1 224.1	...	...	4 900.8
3rd quarter	4 873.5	3 163.6	592.7	...	...	...	...	240.5	285.4	1 225.9	...	...	4 885.7
4th quarter	4 854.3	3 117.3	598.3	...	...	...	...	246.8	282.5	1 230.2	...	...	4 814.7
1975													
1st quarter	4 795.3	3 143.4	493.2	...	...	...	...	248.6	254.2	1 245.2	...	...	4 852.4
2nd quarter	4 831.9	3 195.8	476.1	...	...	...	...	241.3	233.8	1 235.7	...	...	4 902.1
3rd quarter	4 913.3	3 241.4	516.4	...	...	...	...	237.3	253.3	1 257.4	...	...	4 946.2
4th quarter	4 977.5	3 275.7	530.6	...	...	...	...	250.7	266.8	1 268.0	...	...	5 004.6
1976													
1st quarter	5 090.7	3 341.2	585.5	...	...	...	...	249.0	283.5	1 271.2	...	...	5 073.8
2nd quarter	5 128.9	3 371.8	610.5	...	...	...	...	251.5	295.8	1 257.3	...	...	5 090.9
3rd quarter	5 154.1	3 407.5	611.6	...	...	...	...	258.8	307.9	1 250.7	...	...	5 122.4
4th quarter	5 191.5	3 451.8	615.9	...	...	...	...	261.4	318.0	1 249.7	...	...	5 194.0
1977													
1st quarter	5 251.8	3 491.3	646.2	...	...	...	...	257.2	333.1	1 261.0	...	...	5 242.7
2nd quarter	5 356.1	3 510.6	696.1	...	...	...	...	264.1	336.2	1 274.1	...	...	5 327.0
3rd quarter	5 451.9	3 544.1	734.1	...	...	...	...	266.2	331.5	1 276.5	...	...	5 383.0
4th quarter	5 450.8	3 597.5	713.4	...	...	...	...	257.6	336.2	1 272.3	...	...	5 426.9

. . . = Not available.

Table 19-2. Real Gross Domestic Product—*Continued*

(Billions of chained [2005] dollars, quarterly data are at seasonally adjusted annual rates.)   NIPA Tables 1.1.6, 1.4.6

| Year and quarter | Gross domestic product | Personal consumption expenditures | Gross private domestic investment | | | | Exports and imports of goods and services | | | Government consumption expenditures and gross investment | | | Addendum: Final sales of domestic product |
| | | | Total | Fixed investment | | Change in private inventories | Net exports | Exports | Imports | Total | Federal | State and local | |
				Nonresidential	Residential								
1978													
1st quarter	5 469.4	3 618.5	727.5	...	...	...	...	263.7	358.7	1 274.4	...	...	5 433.8
2nd quarter	5 684.6	3 695.9	777.5	...	...	...	...	291.2	359.9	1 308.8	...	...	5 649.4
3rd quarter	5 740.3	3 711.4	801.5	...	...	...	...	294.4	364.6	1 319.3	...	...	5 701.2
4th quarter	5 816.2	3 741.3	819.7	...	...	...	...	306.1	369.6	1 331.2	...	...	5 774.5
1979													
1st quarter	5 825.9	3 760.2	819.6	...	...	...	...	306.3	368.6	1 319.2	...	...	5 792.7
2nd quarter	5 831.4	3 758.0	817.7	...	...	...	...	307.1	370.6	1 333.2	...	...	5 792.4
3rd quarter	5 873.3	3 794.9	801.7	...	...	...	...	318.2	364.9	1 335.1	...	...	5 876.4
4th quarter	5 889.5	3 805.0	786.8	...	...	...	...	338.2	372.9	1 343.8	...	...	5 903.2
1980													
1st quarter	5 908.5	3 798.4	781.1	...	...	...	...	347.7	373.2	1 365.4	...	...	5 914.7
2nd quarter	5 787.4	3 712.2	710.6	...	...	...	...	354.2	346.1	1 369.7	...	...	5 798.8
3rd quarter	5 776.6	3 752.0	656.5	...	...	...	...	353.5	321.2	1 350.8	...	...	5 874.4
4th quarter	5 883.5	3 802.0	723.2	...	...	...	...	351.3	338.4	1 349.4	...	...	5 926.8
1981													
1st quarter	6 005.7	3 822.8	795.1	...	...	...	...	357.9	352.9	1 367.3	...	...	5 956.0
2nd quarter	5 957.8	3 822.8	757.2	...	...	...	...	359.9	353.4	1 370.4	...	...	5 967.8
3rd quarter	6 030.2	3 838.3	804.2	...	...	...	...	352.2	349.4	1 367.3	...	...	5 974.8
4th quarter	5 955.1	3 809.3	773.1	...	...	...	...	353.9	359.4	1 379.9	...	...	5 939.5
1982													
1st quarter	5 857.3	3 833.9	692.5	...	...	...	...	338.5	349.2	1 378.5	...	...	5 922.8
2nd quarter	5 889.1	3 847.7	691.9	...	...	...	...	340.6	343.4	1 386.5	...	...	5 920.3
3rd quarter	5 866.4	3 877.2	683.8	...	...	...	...	325.5	359.4	1 396.0	...	...	5 881.5
4th quarter	5 871.0	3 947.9	622.9	...	...	...	...	310.6	345.3	1 420.1	...	...	5 968.6
1983													
1st quarter	5 944.0	3 986.6	645.1	...	...	...	...	315.6	353.2	1 430.8	...	...	6 031.7
2nd quarter	6 077.6	4 065.7	707.4	...	...	...	...	316.5	380.3	1 443.0	...	...	6 117.1
3rd quarter	6 197.5	4 137.6	754.9	...	...	...	...	321.3	410.0	1 468.0	...	...	6 230.5
4th quarter	6 325.6	4 203.2	834.4	...	...	...	...	327.8	430.1	1 443.2	...	...	6 312.4
1984													
1st quarter	6 448.3	4 239.2	921.8	...	...	...	...	334.6	464.6	1 457.8	...	...	6 354.6
2nd quarter	6 559.6	4 299.9	952.8	...	...	...	...	343.0	484.1	1 489.2	...	...	6 471.1
3rd quarter	6 623.3	4 333.0	975.0	...	...	...	...	350.5	496.6	1 500.2	...	...	6 530.8
4th quarter	6 677.3	4 390.1	959.0	...	...	...	...	357.6	511.2	1 532.3	...	...	6 626.0
1985													
1st quarter	6 740.3	4 464.6	927.4	...	...	...	...	357.9	499.9	1 549.9	...	...	6 738.3
2nd quarter	6 797.3	4 505.2	943.4	...	...	...	...	356.6	524.5	1 584.7	...	...	6 789.6
3rd quarter	6 903.5	4 590.8	933.0	...	...	...	...	351.4	519.4	1 625.8	...	...	6 899.9
4th quarter	6 955.9	4 600.9	969.4	...	...	...	...	362.0	539.8	1 635.5	...	...	6 928.1
1986													
1st quarter	7 022.8	4 639.3	967.4	...	...	...	...	373.4	539.3	1 653.2	...	...	6 999.4
2nd quarter	7 051.0	4 688.7	946.0	...	...	...	...	377.5	562.2	1 688.3	...	...	7 052.2
3rd quarter	7 119.0	4 770.7	916.3	...	...	...	...	386.1	577.8	1 726.6	...	...	7 151.4
4th quarter	7 153.4	4 799.4	917.7	...	...	...	...	400.5	582.3	1 716.6	...	...	7 192.0
1987													
1st quarter	7 193.0	4 792.1	945.8	...	...	...	...	400.8	578.8	1 723.7	...	...	7 172.8
2nd quarter	7 269.5	4 856.3	947.1	...	...	...	...	416.7	593.2	1 734.6	...	...	7 268.4
3rd quarter	7 332.6	4 910.4	948.1	...	...	...	...	434.6	604.8	1 734.6	...	...	7 355.2
4th quarter	7 458.0	4 922.2	1 022.0	...	...	...	...	450.7	618.7	1 755.6	...	...	7 388.3
1988													
1st quarter	7 496.6	5 004.4	964.4	...	...	...	...	475.7	615.8	1 747.1	...	...	7 497.5
2nd quarter	7 592.9	5 040.8	987.9	...	...	...	...	488.8	608.7	1 751.7	...	...	7 587.9
3rd quarter	7 632.1	5 080.6	994.2	...	...	...	...	497.9	623.1	1 750.7	...	...	7 624.0
4th quarter	7 734.0	5 140.4	1 007.4	...	...	...	...	513.1	642.0	1 786.2	...	...	7 721.9
1989													
1st quarter	7 806.6	5 159.3	1 046.0	...	...	...	...	528.2	645.0	1 775.2	...	...	7 759.2
2nd quarter	7 865.0	5 182.4	1 033.8	...	...	...	...	551.2	648.1	1 802.8	...	...	7 834.5
3rd quarter	7 927.4	5 236.1	1 021.6	...	...	...	...	557.2	647.2	1 819.7	...	...	7 933.2
4th quarter	7 944.7	5 261.7	1 011.1	...	...	...	...	566.0	658.9	1 829.4	...	...	7 943.1
1990													
1st quarter	8 027.7	5 303.3	1 021.1	...	...	...	...	590.7	679.8	1 857.6	...	...	8 029.3
2nd quarter	8 059.6	5 320.8	1 021.4	...	...	...	...	598.7	678.7	1 860.4	...	...	8 032.8
3rd quarter	8 059.5	5 341.0	997.3	...	...	...	...	603.1	675.9	1 859.8	...	...	8 048.6
4th quarter	7 988.9	5 299.5	934.2	...	...	...	...	608.2	657.8	1 878.3	...	...	8 020.0
1991													
1st quarter	7 950.2	5 284.4	896.2	...	...	...	...	612.5	650.3	1 885.9	...	...	7 988.0
2nd quarter	8 003.8	5 324.7	891.7	...	...	...	...	634.6	661.9	1 892.5	...	...	8 045.4
3rd quarter	8 037.5	5 345.0	913.9	...	...	...	...	649.1	680.5	1 873.6	...	...	8 056.5
4th quarter	8 069.0	5 342.6	948.9	...	...	...	...	663.9	695.5	1 875.6	...	...	8 049.1
1992													
1st quarter	8 157.6	5 434.5	927.8	...	...	...	...	675.7	700.6	1 889.9	...	...	8 173.5
2nd quarter	8 244.3	5 466.7	988.9	...	...	...	...	675.8	712.1	1 887.6	...	...	8 232.0
3rd quarter	8 329.4	5 527.1	999.1	...	...	...	...	690.4	723.3	1 897.3	...	...	8 322.5
4th quarter	8 417.0	5 594.6	1 030.8	...	...	...	...	694.0	740.6	1 897.9	...	...	8 409.1
1993													
1st quarter	8 432.5	5 617.2	1 055.0	...	...	...	...	695.5	756.7	1 877.9	...	...	8 403.6
2nd quarter	8 486.4	5 671.1	1 063.3	...	...	...	...	704.1	772.3	1 876.5	...	...	8 474.1
3rd quarter	8 531.1	5 732.7	1 062.5	...	...	...	...	701.8	782.5	1 874.6	...	...	8 540.5
4th quarter	8 643.8	5 783.7	1 118.6	...	...	...	...	724.2	813.9	1 883.9	...	...	8 642.8

. . . = Not available.

Table 19-2. Real Gross Domestic Product—*Continued*

(Billions of chained [2005] dollars, quarterly data are at seasonally adjusted annual rates.)   **NIPA Tables 1.1.6, 1.4.6**

| Year and quarter | Gross domestic product | Personal consumption expenditures | Gross private domestic investment | | | | Exports and imports of goods and services | | | Government consumption expenditures and gross investment | | | Addendum: Final sales of domestic product |
| | | | Total | Fixed investment | | Change in private inventories | Net exports | Exports | Imports | Total | Federal | State and local | |
				Nonresidential	Residential								
1994													
1st quarter	8 727.9	5 848.1	1 166.8	...	...	...	...	731.1	832.9	1 859.9	...	...	8 689.0
2nd quarter	8 847.3	5 891.5	1 234.9	...	...	...	...	755.2	863.9	1 867.7	...	...	8 762.2
3rd quarter	8 904.3	5 938.7	1 212.7	...	...	...	...	784.1	888.2	1 900.5	...	...	8 857.2
4th quarter	9 003.2	5 997.3	1 269.2	...	...	...	...	801.5	913.2	1 884.1	...	...	8 928.4
1995													
1st quarter	9 025.3	6 004.3	1 282.1	781.5	457.7	65.9	-117.1	816.2	933.2	1 891.6	715.3	1 174.8	8 966.4
2nd quarter	9 044.7	6 053.5	1 247.6	787.0	443.0	37.7	-114.7	827.4	942.1	1 897.9	712.5	1 184.1	9 019.4
3rd quarter	9 120.7	6 107.6	1 235.6	792.2	456.7	8.2	-81.9	863.4	945.4	1 893.7	707.6	1 184.8	9 126.8
4th quarter	9 184.3	6 150.6	1 270.4	808.2	467.0	16.5	-81.5	875.9	957.4	1 872.5	681.1	1 190.7	9 180.1
1996													
1st quarter	9 247.2	6 206.9	1 287.1	828.2	479.3	3.2	-101.6	886.9	988.6	1 884.5	695.3	1 188.2	9 259.4
2nd quarter	9 407.1	6 277.1	1 353.8	852.1	499.5	26.8	-108.9	901.8	1 010.7	1 911.6	705.2	1 205.4	9 392.1
3rd quarter	9 488.9	6 314.6	1 422.1	880.4	498.2	62.0	-134.4	909.1	1 043.5	1 909.7	692.7	1 216.3	9 433.0
4th quarter	9 592.5	6 366.1	1 418.2	904.2	493.0	32.8	-98.0	966.1	1 064.0	1 925.9	690.7	1 234.6	9 565.4
1997													
1st quarter	9 666.2	6 430.2	1 451.3	927.3	494.7	43.2	-125.0	984.5	1 109.5	1 929.4	681.4	1 247.6	9 632.6
2nd quarter	9 809.6	6 456.2	1 544.0	950.3	500.9	103.9	-123.3	1 023.5	1 146.7	1 946.0	693.5	1 252.1	9 709.3
3rd quarter	9 932.7	6 566.0	1 571.4	998.8	503.2	75.4	-141.8	1 047.2	1 189.0	1 948.2	691.3	1 256.6	9 862.5
4th quarter	10 008.9	6 641.1	1 596.5	1 006.8	508.4	87.0	-169.3	1 045.3	1 214.7	1 951.5	690.3	1 260.9	9 925.9
1998													
1st quarter	10 103.4	6 707.2	1 672.7	1 041.6	517.5	117.2	-210.0	1 050.3	1 260.2	1 939.7	668.8	1 271.1	9 988.3
2nd quarter	10 194.3	6 822.6	1 652.7	1 079.7	533.0	43.2	-250.9	1 038.2	1 289.1	1 981.9	687.2	1 294.7	10 157.1
3rd quarter	10 328.8	6 913.1	1 700.1	1 096.0	549.0	60.6	-273.1	1 033.3	1 306.5	2 000.2	681.5	1 319.0	10 274.3
4th quarter	10 507.6	7 019.1	1 754.7	1 132.2	562.2	65.5	-276.4	1 072.3	1 348.7	2 018.1	688.1	1 330.2	10 448.5
1999													
1st quarter	10 601.2	7 088.3	1 810.0	1 158.4	565.5	89.4	-319.0	1 064.1	1 383.1	2 028.4	683.6	1 345.2	10 517.3
2nd quarter	10 684.0	7 199.9	1 803.7	1 190.9	571.6	41.1	-350.9	1 076.3	1 427.2	2 036.9	683.6	1 353.7	10 648.2
3rd quarter	10 819.9	7 286.4	1 848.9	1 225.1	576.4	44.6	-374.4	1 104.5	1 478.9	2 063.3	697.9	1 365.7	10 779.7
4th quarter	11 014.3	7 389.2	1 914.6	1 229.0	583.4	99.1	-382.2	1 132.2	1 514.4	2 095.9	713.4	1 382.7	10 917.5
2000													
1st quarter	11 043.0	7 501.3	1 887.8	1 274.7	588.0	18.7	-424.1	1 151.7	1 575.8	2 078.7	685.2	1 394.0	11 027.6
2nd quarter	11 258.5	7 571.8	2 018.5	1 321.7	584.0	101.0	-439.4	1 184.4	1 623.9	2 106.4	712.6	1 394.2	11 158.0
3rd quarter	11 267.9	7 645.9	1 987.0	1 336.3	573.7	63.1	-467.2	1 213.3	1 680.6	2 099.8	698.8	1 401.4	11 206.4
4th quarter	11 334.5	7 713.5	1 987.8	1 341.5	574.2	58.1	-475.6	1 203.8	1 679.3	2 106.2	695.6	1 411.0	11 278.1
2001													
1st quarter	11 297.2	7 744.3	1 882.7	1 328.7	576.8	-34.8	-466.8	1 188.0	1 654.8	2 137.3	710.4	1 427.3	11 335.1
2nd quarter	11 371.3	7 773.5	1 876.7	1 293.8	584.9	-10.7	-456.3	1 149.2	1 605.5	2 181.7	725.6	1 456.5	11 385.2
3rd quarter	11 340.1	7 807.7	1 837.1	1 272.5	588.1	-30.8	-476.6	1 090.1	1 566.7	2 177.8	730.5	1 447.7	11 373.8
4th quarter	11 380.1	7 930.0	1 731.2	1 232.2	583.1	-90.7	-488.7	1 059.3	1 548.0	2 216.4	739.3	1 477.6	11 472.8
2002													
1st quarter	11 477.9	7 957.3	1 789.3	1 203.4	598.7	-15.1	-510.5	1 076.2	1 586.8	2 250.4	756.9	1 494.0	11 496.4
2nd quarter	11 538.8	7 997.8	1 810.8	1 183.9	613.4	13.4	-534.9	1 105.5	1 640.4	2 272.0	774.4	1 498.1	11 528.9
3rd quarter	11 596.4	8 052.0	1 814.5	1 177.8	616.9	19.8	-554.3	1 113.2	1 667.4	2 290.4	786.7	1 504.2	11 579.7
4th quarter	11 598.8	8 080.6	1 813.2	1 155.6	626.4	32.9	-595.6	1 101.8	1 697.4	2 305.7	800.0	1 506.3	11 569.1
2003													
1st quarter	11 645.8	8 122.3	1 813.1	1 150.4	632.4	31.5	-585.3	1 091.6	1 676.9	2 300.9	800.2	1 501.2	11 616.5
2nd quarter	11 738.7	8 197.8	1 823.7	1 181.4	646.8	-3.5	-612.7	1 088.2	1 700.9	2 335.1	838.8	1 496.6	11 743.8
3rd quarter	11 935.5	8 312.1	1 889.9	1 208.3	679.8	3.0	-603.1	1 117.6	1 720.7	2 342.0	839.6	1 502.7	11 933.4
4th quarter	12 042.8	8 358.0	1 959.8	1 224.0	698.2	38.3	-614.7	1 169.7	1 784.4	2 343.7	845.7	1 498.2	12 005.3
2004													
1st quarter	12 127.6	8 437.6	1 970.0	1 214.3	704.5	52.4	-632.5	1 197.3	1 829.8	2 354.9	856.6	1 498.4	12 076.2
2nd quarter	12 213.8	8 483.2	2 055.6	1 247.0	731.0	78.7	-687.1	1 216.0	1 903.1	2 363.5	861.4	1 502.2	12 136.3
3rd quarter	12 303.5	8 555.8	2 082.2	1 281.2	738.4	62.7	-705.7	1 225.0	1 930.7	2 372.1	876.4	1 495.7	12 241.1
4th quarter	12 410.3	8 654.2	2 125.2	1 309.6	744.2	71.6	-726.7	1 252.9	1 979.7	2 357.6	865.6	1 492.0	12 339.2
2005													
1st quarter	12 534.1	8 719.0	2 170.3	1 321.5	757.7	91.4	-714.8	1 276.2	1 991.0	2 359.9	869.2	1 490.7	12 443.2
2nd quarter	12 587.5	8 802.9	2 131.5	1 340.8	775.3	15.5	-709.4	1 303.5	2 012.9	2 362.4	870.0	1 492.4	12 572.0
3rd quarter	12 683.2	8 865.6	2 154.9	1 359.7	783.3	11.8	-721.4	1 303.9	2 025.2	2 383.9	890.4	1 493.5	12 671.2
4th quarter	12 748.7	8 888.5	2 232.2	1 367.3	783.5	81.0	-745.3	1 336.7	2 082.0	2 373.4	875.6	1 497.7	12 667.2
2006													
1st quarter	12 915.9	8 986.6	2 264.7	1 424.9	775.2	65.8	-732.6	1 388.8	2 121.3	2 397.1	900.5	1 496.6	12 851.3
2nd quarter	12 962.5	9 035.0	2 261.2	1 450.3	740.1	72.5	-732.8	1 412.1	2 144.9	2 399.1	892.8	1 506.3	12 891.0
3rd quarter	12 965.9	9 090.7	2 229.6	1 466.0	697.4	67.5	-756.5	1 414.1	2 170.5	2 402.7	892.0	1 510.8	12 898.3
4th quarter	13 060.7	9 181.6	2 166.0	1 474.5	660.2	31.8	-694.9	1 473.2	2 168.1	2 409.4	894.4	1 515.0	13 027.8

. . . = Not available.

Table 19-3. Contributions to Percent Change in Real Gross Domestic Product

(Percent; percentage points.)   NIPA Table 1.1.2

Year and quarter	Percent change at seasonally adjusted annual rate, real GDP	Personal consumption expenditures	Gross private domestic investment				Exports and imports of goods and services			Government consumption expenditures and gross investment		
			Total	Fixed investment		Change in private inventories	Net exports	Exports	Imports	Total	Federal	State and local
				Nonresidential	Residential							
1946	-10.9	6.48	7.45	2.24	2.37	2.84	3.82	3.25	0.57	-28.69	-29.08	0.39
1947	-0.9	1.24	-0.57	1.31	1.06	-2.94	1.08	0.91	0.17	-2.65	-3.32	0.67
1948	4.4	1.50	4.00	0.51	0.98	2.51	-2.18	-1.63	-0.55	1.08	0.71	0.37
1949	-0.5	1.80	-4.22	-0.93	-0.44	-2.85	0.08	-0.05	0.13	1.83	0.90	0.93
1947												
1st quarter	. . .	. . .	. . .	. . .	. . .	. . .	. . .	. . .	. . .	. . .	. . .	. . .
2nd quarter	-0.6	4.40	-4.78	-0.56	-0.88	-3.34	-0.71	-0.44	-0.27	0.47	0.16	0.31
3rd quarter	-0.3	0.96	-1.90	-0.67	2.71	-3.94	-0.17	-1.73	1.56	0.78	0.25	0.53
4th quarter	6.2	0.25	10.97	1.44	4.03	5.50	-4.33	-3.62	-0.72	-0.68	-1.07	0.39
1948												
1st quarter	6.5	1.55	6.45	2.65	-0.29	4.08	-3.06	-1.36	-1.70	1.57	1.56	0.01
2nd quarter	7.6	3.19	4.49	-1.23	1.41	4.31	-3.07	-2.43	-0.64	2.96	2.25	0.71
3rd quarter	2.2	0.38	0.93	0.20	-0.76	1.49	-0.33	0.49	-0.82	1.19	0.76	0.43
4th quarter	0.6	1.86	-3.09	1.04	-1.77	-2.35	-0.60	-0.81	0.21	2.44	1.86	0.58
1949												
1st quarter	-5.4	0.17	-10.06	-1.98	-1.68	-6.40	2.91	2.49	0.42	1.55	0.55	1.00
2nd quarter	-1.4	3.64	-8.00	-1.56	-0.34	-6.10	0.03	-0.16	0.19	2.88	1.41	1.47
3rd quarter	4.6	0.15	5.04	-1.82	1.76	5.10	-1.34	-1.90	0.56	0.70	-0.46	1.17
4th quarter	-3.7	3.34	-2.72	-0.50	2.71	-4.92	-2.92	-2.71	-0.20	-1.41	-1.98	0.57
1950												
1st quarter	17.2	4.11	14.27	1.26	2.95	10.06	-0.58	-0.21	-0.37	-0.62	-1.43	0.81
2nd quarter	12.7	4.11	7.70	3.34	2.68	1.69	-0.50	0.24	-0.75	1.43	1.15	0.28
3rd quarter	16.6	13.70	6.55	3.51	1.63	1.41	-2.83	0.45	-3.29	-0.83	-0.87	0.04
4th quarter	7.2	-7.89	9.83	-0.06	-1.38	11.27	1.27	1.31	-0.04	4.01	3.99	0.02
1951												
1st quarter	5.1	6.46	-9.01	-1.10	-1.45	-6.46	0.82	0.84	-0.01	6.88	7.16	-0.28
2nd quarter	6.8	-7.03	1.74	0.51	-3.44	4.66	2.38	1.82	0.57	9.72	9.25	0.46
3rd quarter	8.2	2.95	-5.75	0.48	-1.39	-4.85	2.00	0.51	1.49	9.02	8.88	0.14
4th quarter	0.7	1.34	-5.67	-0.68	0.17	-5.16	0.15	-0.18	0.33	4.85	4.89	-0.04
1952												
1st quarter	4.1	0.33	1.49	0.30	0.52	0.67	-0.78	1.16	-1.94	3.04	2.93	0.11
2nd quarter	0.4	4.59	-5.06	0.54	0.37	-5.97	-2.28	-2.25	-0.03	3.19	2.59	0.60
3rd quarter	2.7	1.10	3.13	-3.24	-0.22	6.59	-2.47	-1.39	-1.08	0.94	1.69	-0.74
4th quarter	13.9	8.84	4.49	3.16	1.14	0.19	-1.31	0.20	-1.52	1.86	1.19	0.67
1953												
1st quarter	7.7	2.94	1.20	1.94	0.34	-1.08	0.25	-0.18	0.43	3.32	2.72	0.59
2nd quarter	3.1	1.37	0.25	0.27	0.06	-0.09	-0.72	0.16	-0.88	2.16	2.20	-0.04
3rd quarter	-2.4	-0.72	-1.30	0.87	-0.78	-1.39	0.69	0.67	0.03	-1.09	-1.81	0.73
4th quarter	-6.2	-1.82	-4.44	-0.37	-0.17	-3.90	0.25	-0.54	0.79	-0.18	-0.87	0.69
1954												
1st quarter	-1.9	0.66	-0.21	-1.02	0.22	0.60	0.14	-0.75	0.88	-2.48	-3.52	1.03
2nd quarter	0.5	3.06	0.02	-0.30	1.33	-1.01	0.69	2.17	-1.49	-3.25	-3.38	0.12
3rd quarter	4.6	3.28	3.04	1.08	1.34	0.62	0.37	-0.60	0.97	-2.10	-2.96	0.86
4th quarter	8.3	5.24	2.89	-0.02	1.46	1.45	0.49	0.72	-0.23	-0.36	-0.52	0.16
1955												
1st quarter	12.0	5.71	6.51	0.74	1.80	3.97	-0.41	0.58	-0.98	0.22	-1.11	1.32
2nd quarter	6.8	4.76	4.05	2.26	0.35	1.45	-1.42	-0.45	-0.97	-0.61	-1.03	0.41
3rd quarter	5.4	3.04	0.94	1.90	-0.56	-0.41	0.71	1.06	-0.34	0.76	0.79	-0.03
4th quarter	2.3	3.16	1.37	1.03	-1.03	1.37	-0.58	0.05	-0.63	-1.70	-1.89	0.19
1956												
1st quarter	-1.8	0.39	-2.40	-0.84	-0.63	-0.93	0.07	0.82	-0.75	0.12	-0.23	0.35
2nd quarter	3.2	0.81	-0.79	0.57	-0.16	-1.20	1.28	1.23	0.05	1.88	1.48	0.40
3rd quarter	-0.5	0.53	-0.77	0.27	-0.45	-0.59	0.44	0.64	-0.20	-0.70	-0.86	0.16
4th quarter	6.7	3.43	-0.68	-0.11	-0.35	-0.22	1.68	0.91	0.77	2.27	1.93	0.34
1957												
1st quarter	2.5	1.69	-0.94	0.28	-0.30	-0.92	-0.01	1.36	-1.36	1.74	0.93	0.81
2nd quarter	-1.0	0.43	-0.08	-0.10	-0.48	0.51	-0.82	-0.63	-0.19	-0.49	-0.77	0.28
3rd quarter	3.9	2.00	1.41	0.90	-0.26	0.77	-0.26	-0.57	0.31	0.77	0.29	0.48
4th quarter	-4.1	0.14	-5.35	-1.03	-0.03	-4.28	-0.63	-0.57	-0.07	1.69	0.86	0.84
1958												
1st quarter	-10.4	-3.31	-4.27	-2.82	-0.72	-0.72	-2.11	-1.89	-0.22	-0.71	-1.70	0.99
2nd quarter	2.5	2.18	-1.35	-1.63	0.05	0.24	-0.65	0.12	-0.77	2.30	1.78	0.52
3rd quarter	9.7	4.37	4.43	-0.53	1.34	3.62	0.29	0.10	0.19	0.63	-0.18	0.80
4th quarter	9.7	3.56	5.24	1.30	2.03	1.90	-1.00	-0.01	-0.99	1.86	1.19	0.67
1959												
1st quarter	8.3	4.86	3.78	1.07	2.33	0.38	0.55	1.16	-0.61	-0.84	-1.14	0.30
2nd quarter	10.5	4.08	5.47	1.09	0.80	3.59	-0.32	0.63	-0.94	1.25	1.15	0.11
3rd quarter	-0.5	2.69	-4.52	1.13	-0.43	-5.22	0.35	0.58	-0.23	1.00	0.97	0.03
4th quarter	1.4	0.33	2.06	-0.15	-0.64	2.85	-0.03	-0.48	0.45	-0.95	-0.77	-0.18
1960												
1st quarter	9.3	2.45	6.67	1.46	0.63	4.58	1.69	2.29	-0.60	-1.53	-2.15	0.62
2nd quarter	-1.9	3.14	-6.86	0.60	-1.76	-5.70	1.17	1.26	-0.09	0.70	-0.15	0.86
3rd quarter	0.7	-1.01	-0.40	-0.94	-0.60	1.14	0.02	-0.53	0.55	2.04	1.50	0.54
4th quarter	-5.0	0.36	-7.26	-0.18	-0.02	-7.06	1.25	0.43	0.82	0.62	0.20	0.42
1961												
1st quarter	2.4	-0.05	1.40	-0.76	0.07	2.08	-0.07	-0.14	0.07	1.12	-0.09	1.21
2nd quarter	7.7	3.82	4.12	0.76	0.07	3.29	-0.48	-0.28	-0.20	0.23	0.49	-0.25
3rd quarter	6.6	1.26	4.83	0.30	1.02	3.50	-1.18	-0.10	-1.07	1.72	1.39	0.32
4th quarter	8.4	5.05	1.17	1.20	0.66	-0.69	0.22	0.62	-0.40	1.95	0.89	1.05

. . . = Not available.

Table 19-3. Contributions to Percent Change in Real Gross Domestic Product—*Continued*

(Percent; percentage points.)   NIPA Table 1.1.2

Year and quarter	Percent change at seasonally adjusted annual rate, real GDP	Personal consump-tion expen-ditures	Gross private domestic investment				Exports and imports of goods and services			Government consumption expenditures and gross investment		
			Total	Fixed investment		Change in private inventories	Net exports	Exports	Imports	Total	Federal	State and local
				Nonresi-dential	Residential							
1962												
1st quarter	7.4	2.67	3.67	0.82	0.36	2.49	-0.56	-0.05	-0.51	1.59	1.86	-0.27
2nd quarter	4.5	3.05	-0.54	1.06	0.62	-2.22	1.51	1.87	-0.37	0.48	0.21	0.27
3rd quarter	3.7	2.02	1.11	0.46	-0.02	0.66	-1.39	-1.17	-0.21	2.01	1.53	0.48
4th quarter	1.0	3.52	-2.04	-0.25	-0.03	-1.76	-0.63	-0.42	-0.21	0.13	-0.28	0.41
1963												
1st quarter	5.3	1.72	3.26	-0.04	0.71	2.59	0.86	0.45	0.40	-0.50	-1.23	0.72
2nd quarter	5.1	2.40	0.92	1.14	1.44	-1.66	1.88	2.26	-0.39	-0.09	-0.44	0.35
3rd quarter	7.7	3.42	2.08	1.10	0.39	0.58	-1.53	-1.11	-0.42	3.78	2.75	1.03
4th quarter	3.1	2.06	0.79	1.19	0.63	-1.03	1.04	0.98	0.06	-0.81	-1.35	0.54
1964												
1st quarter	9.3	4.94	2.68	0.93	1.31	0.44	1.29	1.26	0.03	0.38	-0.21	0.59
2nd quarter	4.7	4.35	-0.24	0.94	-1.10	-0.08	-0.02	0.35	-0.37	0.58	-0.31	0.89
3rd quarter	5.5	4.58	1.48	1.28	-0.34	0.54	-0.60	-0.16	-0.44	0.08	-0.35	0.43
4th quarter	1.1	0.71	0.47	0.81	-0.37	0.03	0.17	0.62	-0.45	-0.23	-0.65	0.42
1965												
1st quarter	10.2	5.63	6.32	2.68	0.08	3.57	-1.65	-2.29	0.65	-0.12	-0.51	0.39
2nd quarter	5.5	2.78	-0.02	1.54	0.15	-1.72	1.67	3.58	-1.91	1.12	0.12	1.00
3rd quarter	8.4	4.32	2.41	1.58	0.08	0.74	-1.31	-1.25	-0.07	2.95	1.82	1.13
4th quarter	10.0	7.03	0.45	1.80	-0.41	-0.94	0.64	1.49	-0.85	1.88	1.29	0.59
1966												
1st quarter	10.2	3.72	5.68	1.86	0.42	3.40	-0.82	-0.36	-0.45	1.61	1.10	0.51
2nd quarter	1.3	0.63	-1.22	0.65	-1.47	-0.40	0.44	0.89	-0.45	1.49	1.18	0.31
3rd quarter	2.7	2.79	-0.63	0.52	-0.55	-0.60	-1.82	-0.80	-1.02	2.33	1.86	0.46
4th quarter	3.3	1.02	0.35	-0.11	-1.70	2.16	0.48	0.67	-0.20	1.43	0.39	1.04
1967												
1st quarter	3.6	1.42	-1.77	-0.91	-0.43	-0.43	0.13	0.41	-0.28	3.78	3.27	0.52
2nd quarter	0.1	3.30	-2.68	-0.15	1.57	-4.11	-0.03	-0.20	0.17	-0.51	-0.74	0.23
3rd quarter	3.2	1.27	1.74	-0.21	0.77	1.18	-0.75	-0.51	-0.24	0.97	0.80	0.17
4th quarter	3.1	1.52	1.32	0.84	0.93	-0.45	-0.41	0.58	-0.99	0.65	-0.09	0.74
1968												
1st quarter	8.5	5.90	1.44	1.32	0.11	0.01	-0.54	0.60	-1.14	1.70	0.94	0.76
2nd quarter	7.0	3.80	2.57	-0.72	0.43	2.87	0.12	0.42	-0.31	0.48	-0.36	0.84
3rd quarter	2.8	4.60	-2.06	0.52	0.30	-2.88	0.01	1.22	-1.21	0.21	-0.41	0.62
4th quarter	1.7	1.13	0.63	1.18	0.21	-0.76	-0.10	-0.27	0.17	0.09	-0.29	0.37
1969												
1st quarter	6.5	2.77	4.13	1.22	0.64	2.28	-0.57	-2.52	1.95	0.12	-0.24	0.36
2nd quarter	1.2	1.56	-0.50	0.44	-0.19	-0.75	0.50	4.08	-3.58	-0.38	-0.74	0.36
3rd quarter	2.6	1.18	1.50	1.13	-0.14	0.51	-0.25	-0.53	0.28	0.12	0.03	0.09
4th quarter	-1.9	1.94	-3.45	-0.25	-1.27	-1.93	0.98	0.74	0.24	-1.34	-1.25	-0.10
1970												
1st quarter	-0.6	1.51	-1.89	-0.23	0.03	-1.68	0.26	0.19	0.07	-0.51	-0.92	0.41
2nd quarter	0.7	1.15	0.19	-0.24	-1.08	1.50	0.57	0.98	-0.41	-1.18	-1.42	0.24
3rd quarter	3.6	2.22	1.01	0.20	0.80	0.01	-0.02	-0.07	0.05	0.40	-0.64	1.04
4th quarter	-4.2	-0.61	-3.47	-1.60	1.62	-3.49	-0.12	0.22	-0.33	0.02	-0.23	0.24
1971												
1st quarter	11.5	4.97	7.51	0.36	0.94	6.22	0.39	0.12	0.27	-1.38	-1.63	0.24
2nd quarter	2.3	2.32	1.89	0.57	1.80	-0.48	-1.65	-0.04	-1.60	-0.28	-0.60	0.32
3rd quarter	3.2	2.01	0.85	0.18	0.97	-0.30	0.43	0.92	-0.49	-0.06	-0.18	0.12
4th quarter	1.1	4.13	-1.98	0.92	0.79	-3.70	-0.36	-1.93	1.57	-0.67	-1.27	0.60
1972												
1st quarter	7.3	3.36	4.54	1.49	1.43	1.63	-0.88	2.24	-3.12	0.32	0.16	0.16
2nd quarter	9.8	4.80	4.21	0.78	0.45	2.98	0.23	-0.67	0.90	0.59	0.68	-0.09
3rd quarter	3.9	3.81	1.04	0.69	0.05	0.30	0.82	1.30	-0.48	-1.78	-2.16	0.38
4th quarter	6.8	5.84	0.47	2.18	0.80	-2.52	-0.11	0.96	-1.07	0.56	-0.10	0.66
1973												
1st quarter	10.6	4.63	4.48	1.99	0.79	1.69	0.61	1.74	-1.13	0.91	0.69	0.22
2nd quarter	4.7	-0.13	3.35	1.75	-1.19	2.80	1.96	1.20	0.75	-0.47	-0.55	0.08
3rd quarter	-2.1	0.87	-2.73	0.73	-0.95	-2.51	0.78	0.06	0.71	-1.04	-1.52	0.48
4th quarter	3.9	-0.71	2.83	0.34	-1.03	3.52	1.16	1.38	-0.22	0.60	0.03	0.57
1974												
1st quarter	-3.5	-2.13	-4.40	-0.06	-1.50	-2.84	1.39	0.38	1.01	1.68	1.07	0.61
2nd quarter	1.0	0.89	-0.29	-0.10	-0.83	0.64	-0.14	1.56	-1.70	0.57	-0.05	0.62
3rd quarter	-3.9	1.07	-3.88	-0.50	-0.59	-2.78	-1.26	-1.87	0.61	0.17	0.21	-0.05
4th quarter	-1.6	-3.61	0.48	-1.25	-2.31	4.04	1.23	0.87	0.36	0.33	0.29	0.04
1975												
1st quarter	-4.8	2.13	-11.84	-2.73	-0.94	-8.17	3.81	0.25	3.56	1.12	-0.36	1.49
2nd quarter	3.1	4.24	-2.03	-1.13	0.33	-1.23	1.52	-1.04	2.56	-0.63	-0.26	-0.37
3rd quarter	6.9	3.67	4.53	0.40	1.05	3.09	-2.88	-0.56	-2.32	1.60	0.95	0.65
4th quarter	5.3	2.69	1.62	0.37	0.68	0.57	0.26	1.81	-1.56	0.76	0.11	0.66
1976												
1st quarter	9.4	5.07	6.20	0.72	1.64	3.84	-2.11	-0.23	-1.89	0.25	-0.32	0.57
2nd quarter	3.0	2.29	2.74	0.47	0.49	1.77	-1.05	0.32	-1.37	-0.94	-0.08	-0.86
3rd quarter	2.0	2.66	0.14	0.90	-0.29	-0.47	-0.39	0.94	-1.33	-0.43	-0.09	-0.34
4th quarter	2.9	3.32	0.42	0.85	2.25	-2.68	-0.77	0.34	-1.11	-0.04	0.11	-0.15

Table 19-3. Contributions to Percent Change in Real Gross Domestic Product—*Continued*

(Percent; percentage points.)

NIPA Table 1.1.2

Year and quarter	Percent change at seasonally adjusted annual rate, real GDP	Personal consumption expenditures	Gross private domestic investment				Exports and imports of goods and services			Government consumption expenditures and gross investment		
			Total	Fixed investment		Change in private inventories	Net exports	Exports	Imports	Total	Federal	State and local
				Nonresidential	Residential							
1977												
1st quarter	4.7	2.98	3.09	1.70	0.61	0.78	-2.13	-0.52	-1.62	0.79	0.32	0.46
2nd quarter	8.2	1.49	5.23	1.32	2.34	1.57	0.57	0.88	-0.30	0.89	0.61	0.29
3rd quarter	7.3	2.44	3.97	1.00	-0.07	3.04	0.77	0.25	0.52	0.17	0.22	-0.05
4th quarter	-0.1	3.73	-1.99	1.56	-0.30	-3.25	-1.53	-1.03	-0.51	-0.29	-0.36	0.07
1978												
1st quarter	1.4	1.41	1.62	0.54	0.10	0.98	-1.75	0.67	-2.42	0.08	0.09	-0.01
2nd quarter	16.7	5.60	5.63	4.09	1.11	0.42	3.20	3.27	-0.07	2.25	0.86	1.39
3rd quarter	4.0	1.03	2.47	1.75	0.32	0.40	-0.14	0.34	-0.48	0.62	0.11	0.51
4th quarter	5.4	1.99	1.88	1.63	-0.08	0.33	0.81	1.31	-0.50	0.72	0.29	0.43
1979												
1st quarter	0.7	1.24	-0.01	1.04	-0.54	-0.51	0.14	0.03	0.10	-0.70	0.04	-0.74
2nd quarter	0.4	-0.16	-0.18	-0.21	-0.42	0.46	-0.10	0.09	-0.19	0.82	0.40	0.41
3rd quarter	2.9	2.41	-1.51	1.56	-0.27	-2.80	1.89	1.25	0.64	0.12	-0.05	0.16
4th quarter	1.1	0.62	-1.43	0.08	-0.84	-0.67	1.41	2.24	-0.83	0.50	-0.01	0.51
1980												
1st quarter	1.3	-0.48	-0.55	0.54	-1.65	0.56	1.07	1.03	0.04	1.26	1.06	0.20
2nd quarter	-7.9	-5.68	-6.63	-2.69	-3.63	-0.31	4.08	0.75	3.33	0.27	0.88	-0.61
3rd quarter	-0.7	2.67	-5.31	0.37	0.28	-5.96	3.04	-0.07	3.11	-1.14	-0.48	-0.67
4th quarter	7.6	3.43	6.55	1.09	1.64	3.82	-2.31	-0.19	-2.12	-0.06	0.14	-0.20
1981												
1st quarter	8.6	1.45	6.93	0.87	-0.30	6.37	-0.91	0.84	-1.75	1.09	0.74	0.36
2nd quarter	-3.2	0.02	-3.55	1.06	-0.58	-4.03	0.19	0.26	-0.07	0.19	1.04	-0.86
3rd quarter	4.9	1.04	4.42	1.33	-1.28	4.37	-0.35	-0.82	0.47	-0.16	-0.02	-0.14
4th quarter	-4.9	-1.85	-2.88	1.36	-1.55	-2.70	-0.92	0.18	-1.10	0.76	0.41	0.35
1982												
1st quarter	-6.4	1.62	-7.50	-1.25	-0.79	-5.47	-0.49	-1.65	1.16	-0.03	0.10	-0.13
2nd quarter	2.2	0.90	-0.05	-1.98	-0.42	2.35	0.84	0.20	0.63	0.50	0.36	0.14
3rd quarter	-1.5	1.92	-0.72	-1.82	-0.04	1.15	-3.31	-1.61	-1.69	0.57	0.57	0.00
4th quarter	0.3	4.64	-5.66	-1.09	0.92	-5.48	-0.10	-1.57	1.47	1.44	1.13	0.31
1983												
1st quarter	5.1	2.54	2.20	-1.02	2.28	0.94	-0.30	0.51	-0.81	0.63	0.47	0.15
2nd quarter	9.3	5.22	5.87	0.52	1.84	3.51	-2.54	0.11	-2.65	0.75	0.86	-0.11
3rd quarter	8.1	4.66	4.30	2.02	1.68	0.60	-2.32	0.48	-2.80	1.48	1.12	0.36
4th quarter	8.5	4.20	6.84	2.98	0.77	3.09	-1.17	0.65	-1.82	-1.35	-1.34	-0.02
1984												
1st quarter	8.0	2.35	7.15	1.55	0.52	5.07	-2.37	0.67	-3.04	0.86	0.35	0.51
2nd quarter	7.1	3.75	2.44	2.39	0.35	-0.30	-0.89	0.78	-1.67	1.79	1.22	0.56
3rd quarter	3.9	2.02	1.67	1.62	-0.17	0.21	-0.36	0.68	-1.05	0.62	-0.13	0.75
4th quarter	3.3	3.38	-1.26	1.22	0.02	-2.50	-0.58	0.62	-1.19	1.75	1.27	0.48
1985												
1st quarter	3.8	4.34	-2.38	0.62	-0.06	-2.94	0.91	0.01	0.90	0.95	0.43	0.52
2nd quarter	3.4	2.35	1.24	0.74	0.14	0.35	-2.01	-0.12	-1.88	1.85	0.95	0.90
3rd quarter	6.4	4.91	-0.68	-0.75	0.23	-0.16	-0.01	-0.44	0.43	2.18	1.32	0.85
4th quarter	3.1	0.54	2.72	0.85	0.42	1.45	-0.68	0.81	-1.49	0.50	-0.02	0.51
1986												
1st quarter	3.9	2.12	-0.08	-0.68	0.78	-0.17	0.95	0.85	0.10	0.90	-0.21	1.11
2nd quarter	1.6	2.72	-1.51	-1.22	1.04	-1.34	-1.37	0.28	-1.65	1.78	1.22	0.55
3rd quarter	3.9	4.52	-2.08	-0.70	0.31	-1.69	-0.47	0.63	-1.10	1.94	1.50	0.44
4th quarter	1.9	1.58	0.12	0.44	-0.04	-0.29	0.72	1.06	-0.33	-0.48	-0.60	0.13
1987												
1st quarter	2.2	-0.37	2.00	-1.29	-0.06	3.34	0.23	0.03	0.20	0.38	0.26	0.12
2nd quarter	4.3	3.52	0.12	1.03	0.09	-1.00	0.10	1.17	-1.08	0.58	0.58	0.00
3rd quarter	3.5	2.94	0.08	1.41	-0.06	-1.27	0.45	1.31	-0.86	0.04	0.08	-0.04
4th quarter	7.0	0.67	5.10	-0.09	0.10	5.09	0.18	1.18	-1.00	1.08	0.63	0.45
1988												
1st quarter	2.1	4.34	-3.87	0.35	-0.42	-3.80	1.99	1.78	0.20	-0.37	-1.01	0.64
2nd quarter	5.2	1.92	1.59	1.10	0.15	0.34	1.47	0.95	0.52	0.26	-0.34	0.60
3rd quarter	2.1	2.06	0.40	0.24	0.01	0.15	-0.36	0.64	-1.00	-0.02	-0.25	0.23
4th quarter	5.5	3.11	0.88	0.48	0.16	0.24	-0.21	1.07	-1.29	1.67	1.09	0.58
1989												
1st quarter	3.8	0.96	2.46	0.75	-0.12	1.84	0.86	1.04	-0.18	-0.48	-0.72	0.24
2nd quarter	3.0	1.18	-0.78	0.63	-0.54	-0.86	1.38	1.56	-0.19	1.25	0.80	0.45
3rd quarter	3.2	2.72	-0.76	1.26	-0.19	-1.83	0.48	0.41	0.07	0.77	0.35	0.42
4th quarter	0.9	1.29	-0.67	-0.67	-0.36	0.37	-0.18	0.58	-0.76	0.43	-0.17	0.60
1990												
1st quarter	4.2	2.11	0.62	0.58	0.17	-0.13	0.26	1.61	-1.35	1.26	0.53	0.73
2nd quarter	1.6	0.87	0.03	-0.77	-0.64	1.44	0.58	0.51	0.07	0.12	0.04	0.08
3rd quarter	0.0	0.99	-1.41	0.26	-0.91	-0.76	0.44	0.28	0.16	-0.03	-0.31	0.29
4th quarter	-3.5	-2.08	-3.68	-0.83	-0.83	-2.02	1.50	0.33	1.17	0.81	0.31	0.50
1991												
1st quarter	-1.9	-0.79	-2.21	-1.11	-0.84	-0.26	0.75	0.28	0.46	0.33	0.27	0.06
2nd quarter	2.7	2.01	-0.23	-0.41	0.31	-0.12	0.65	1.40	-0.75	0.29	0.10	0.19
3rd quarter	1.7	1.01	1.32	-0.40	0.56	1.16	-0.25	0.91	-1.16	-0.39	-0.66	0.27
4th quarter	1.6	-0.11	2.02	-0.23	0.30	1.95	0.00	0.91	-0.91	-0.33	-0.67	0.34

Table 19-3. Contributions to Percent Change in Real Gross Domestic Product—*Continued*

(Percent; percentage points.)

NIPA Table 1.1.2

Year and quarter	Percent change at seasonally adjusted annual rate, real GDP	Personal consump-tion expen-ditures	Gross private domestic investment				Exports and imports of goods and services			Government consumption expenditures and gross investment		
			Total	Fixed investment		Change in private inventories	Net exports	Exports	Imports	Total	Federal	State and local
				Nonresi-dential	Residential							
1992												
1st quarter	4.5	4.61	-1.24	-0.20	0.72	-1.77	0.45	0.74	-0.29	0.65	0.03	0.62
2nd quarter	4.3	1.61	3.45	1.48	0.56	1.40	-0.67	0.01	-0.68	-0.07	-0.02	-0.05
3rd quarter	4.2	2.96	0.59	0.77	0.04	-0.22	0.21	0.87	-0.66	0.43	0.39	0.03
4th quarter	4.3	3.26	1.78	1.16	0.51	0.12	-0.80	0.21	-1.01	0.03	0.02	0.01
1993												
1st quarter	0.7	1.06	1.36	0.25	0.07	1.05	-0.83	0.08	-0.92	-0.85	-1.03	0.18
2nd quarter	2.6	2.56	0.48	1.04	0.18	-0.73	-0.40	0.48	-0.88	-0.06	-0.46	0.40
3rd quarter	2.1	2.92	-0.03	0.43	0.54	-1.00	-0.69	-0.13	-0.57	-0.07	-0.33	0.26
4th quarter	5.4	2.44	3.00	1.66	0.82	0.52	-0.45	1.26	-1.71	0.41	0.18	0.22
1994												
1st quarter	4.0	3.04	2.49	0.39	0.36	1.75	-0.62	0.39	-1.02	-0.96	-1.09	0.14
2nd quarter	5.6	2.04	3.53	0.81	0.57	2.16	-0.32	1.31	-1.63	0.34	-0.15	0.49
3rd quarter	2.6	2.16	-1.13	0.74	-0.19	-1.68	0.26	1.53	-1.27	1.32	0.80	0.51
4th quarter	4.5	2.66	2.89	1.80	-0.23	1.32	-0.39	0.91	-1.29	-0.65	-0.81	0.16
1995												
1st quarter	1.0	0.29	0.69	1.69	-0.38	-0.62	-0.28	0.74	-1.02	0.28	-0.08	0.36
2nd quarter	0.9	2.19	-1.69	0.27	-0.53	-1.43	0.12	0.58	-0.45	0.25	-0.12	0.36
3rd quarter	3.4	2.42	-0.59	0.27	0.49	-1.35	1.72	1.88	-0.16	-0.15	-0.18	0.03
4th quarter	2.8	1.91	1.68	0.85	0.37	0.45	0.03	0.65	-0.62	-0.81	-1.04	0.24
1996												
1st quarter	2.8	2.49	0.76	1.07	0.44	-0.74	-0.99	0.58	-1.57	0.50	0.59	-0.08
2nd quarter	7.1	3.13	3.18	1.26	0.72	1.20	-0.30	0.78	-1.08	1.09	0.42	0.67
3rd quarter	3.5	1.64	3.13	1.46	-0.05	1.72	-1.18	0.38	-1.56	-0.07	-0.47	0.40
4th quarter	4.4	2.22	-0.19	1.21	-0.18	-1.22	1.80	2.74	-0.94	0.60	-0.06	0.66
1997												
1st quarter	3.1	2.73	1.47	1.15	0.06	0.25	-1.19	0.87	-2.05	0.10	-0.35	0.45
2nd quarter	6.1	1.13	4.14	1.13	0.21	2.80	0.18	1.81	-1.63	0.61	0.47	0.15
3rd quarter	5.1	4.56	1.21	2.32	0.08	-1.19	-0.72	1.09	-1.81	0.08	-0.08	0.16
4th quarter	3.1	3.06	1.07	0.34	0.17	0.56	-1.16	-0.07	-1.08	0.12	-0.03	0.15
1998												
1st quarter	3.8	2.67	3.22	1.57	0.30	1.36	-1.66	0.22	-1.89	-0.40	-0.78	0.38
2nd quarter	3.6	4.62	-0.82	1.68	0.51	-3.02	-1.66	-0.51	-1.16	1.51	0.67	0.85
3rd quarter	5.4	3.61	1.96	0.69	0.53	0.75	-0.86	-0.19	-0.67	0.67	-0.19	0.86
4th quarter	7.1	4.19	2.24	1.56	0.43	0.25	0.02	1.61	-1.59	0.65	0.25	0.40
1999												
1st quarter	3.6	2.67	2.16	1.08	0.11	0.98	-1.59	-0.33	-1.27	0.36	-0.15	0.52
2nd quarter	3.2	4.26	-0.26	1.33	0.20	-1.79	-1.14	0.48	-1.62	0.30	0.01	0.29
3rd quarter	5.2	3.31	1.76	1.41	0.15	0.19	-0.80	1.11	-1.91	0.92	0.50	0.41
4th quarter	7.4	3.93	2.53	0.17	0.23	2.14	-0.22	1.08	-1.30	1.14	0.55	0.59
2000												
1st quarter	1.1	4.16	-0.99	1.83	0.14	-2.97	-1.53	0.74	-2.27	-0.58	-0.95	0.38
2nd quarter	8.0	2.67	4.91	1.89	-0.12	3.14	-0.50	1.26	-1.75	0.96	0.94	0.02
3rd quarter	0.3	2.67	-1.14	0.55	-0.32	-1.37	-0.98	1.07	-2.05	-0.22	-0.46	0.24
4th quarter	2.4	2.43	0.04	0.17	0.02	-0.14	-0.30	-0.34	0.04	0.22	-0.10	0.32
2001												
1st quarter	-1.3	1.08	-3.73	-0.52	0.08	-3.28	0.30	-0.56	0.86	1.04	0.49	0.55
2nd quarter	2.6	1.03	-0.19	-1.33	0.25	0.89	0.33	-1.39	1.72	1.48	0.50	0.97
3rd quarter	-1.1	1.20	-1.37	-0.80	0.10	-0.67	-0.79	-2.10	1.31	-0.13	0.16	-0.29
4th quarter	1.4	4.33	-3.71	-1.49	-0.16	-2.06	-0.48	-1.09	0.61	1.27	0.29	0.99
2002												
1st quarter	3.5	0.97	2.09	-1.03	0.49	2.63	-0.70	0.58	-1.28	1.12	0.58	0.54
2nd quarter	2.1	1.41	0.77	-0.69	0.46	1.01	-0.76	1.00	-1.76	0.71	0.58	0.13
3rd quarter	2.0	1.89	0.15	-0.21	0.11	0.26	-0.63	0.26	-0.89	0.60	0.40	0.20
4th quarter	0.1	0.98	-0.03	-0.79	0.29	0.47	-1.37	-0.39	-0.97	0.50	0.43	0.07
2003												
1st quarter	1.6	1.43	0.01	-0.19	0.19	0.01	0.34	-0.35	0.69	-0.16	0.01	-0.17
2nd quarter	3.2	2.61	0.38	1.08	0.46	-1.16	-0.90	-0.12	-0.78	1.14	1.29	-0.15
3rd quarter	6.9	3.96	2.28	0.95	1.04	0.29	0.39	1.00	-0.62	0.25	0.04	0.20
4th quarter	3.6	1.56	2.32	0.54	0.57	1.20	-0.29	1.73	-2.02	0.06	0.20	-0.14
2004												
1st quarter	2.8	2.68	0.35	-0.31	0.19	0.46	-0.54	0.91	-1.45	0.36	0.35	0.01
2nd quarter	2.9	1.53	2.79	1.09	0.83	0.87	-1.73	0.61	-2.34	0.28	0.16	0.12
3rd quarter	3.0	2.40	0.88	1.12	0.24	-0.48	-0.59	0.29	-0.88	0.28	0.48	-0.20
4th quarter	3.5	3.23	1.40	0.92	0.18	0.30	-0.65	0.90	-1.56	-0.46	-0.34	-0.11
2005												
1st quarter	4.1	2.11	1.47	0.38	0.43	0.66	0.39	0.75	-0.36	0.08	0.12	-0.04
2nd quarter	1.7	2.68	-1.23	0.61	0.56	-2.39	0.19	0.87	-0.68	0.08	0.02	0.06
3rd quarter	3.1	1.99	0.76	0.61	0.25	-0.09	-0.36	0.01	-0.37	0.68	0.65	0.04
4th quarter	2.1	0.71	2.46	0.25	0.01	2.21	-0.74	1.03	-1.78	-0.34	-0.47	0.13
2006												
1st quarter	5.4	3.08	1.08	1.84	-0.27	-0.49	0.44	1.64	-1.20	0.75	0.79	-0.03
2nd quarter	1.4	1.48	-0.11	0.80	-1.12	0.22	0.02	0.72	-0.70	0.06	-0.24	0.30
3rd quarter	0.1	1.70	-0.99	0.49	-1.36	-0.13	-0.71	0.06	-0.78	0.11	-0.03	0.14
4th quarter	3.0	2.79	-1.99	0.27	-1.18	-1.08	1.94	1.84	0.10	0.21	0.08	0.14

Table 19-4. Chain-Type Quantity Indexes for Gross Domestic Product and Domestic Purchases

(Index numbers, 2005 = 100.)

NIPA Tables 1.1.3, 1.4.3, 2.3.3

Year and quarter	Gross domestic product, total	Personal consumption expenditures		Private fixed investment			Exports and imports of goods and services		Government consumption expenditures and gross investment			Gross domestic purchases
		Total	Excluding food and energy	Total	Nonresidential	Residential	Exports	Imports	Total	Federal	State and local	
1946	14.2	12.8	10.3	7.9	6.7	12.3	5.4	2.6	20.3	34.3	10.8	13.3
1947	14.1	13.0	10.5	9.5	7.8	15.9	6.1	2.4	17.3	25.4	12.3	13.0
1948	14.7	13.3	10.8	10.5	8.2	19.0	4.8	2.8	18.5	27.4	13.1	13.9
1949	14.6	13.7	11.2	9.6	7.5	17.6	4.8	2.7	20.8	30.0	15.1	13.8
1947												
1st quarter	14.0	12.8	. . .	9.3	7.9	14.6	6.5	2.5	17.2	25.5	12.0	12.9
2nd quarter	14.0	13.0	. . .	9.1	7.8	13.9	6.5	2.6	17.3	25.6	12.2	12.9
3rd quarter	14.0	13.1	. . .	9.4	7.6	16.0	6.1	2.3	17.5	25.6	12.5	12.9
4th quarter	14.2	13.1	. . .	10.2	7.9	19.1	5.4	2.4	17.2	24.7	12.7	13.3
1948												
1st quarter	14.4	13.2	. . .	10.6	8.4	18.9	5.2	2.7	17.5	25.6	12.6	13.6
2nd quarter	14.7	13.3	. . .	10.6	8.1	20.0	4.7	2.8	18.4	27.1	13.0	13.9
3rd quarter	14.8	13.3	. . .	10.4	8.1	19.3	4.8	3.0	18.7	27.7	13.2	14.0
4th quarter	14.8	13.4	. . .	10.3	8.3	17.9	4.6	2.9	19.5	29.2	13.6	14.1
1949												
1st quarter	14.6	13.5	. . .	9.7	7.9	16.6	5.2	2.8	20.1	29.8	14.1	13.8
2nd quarter	14.5	13.7	. . .	9.4	7.6	16.3	5.2	2.8	21.0	30.9	14.9	13.7
3rd quarter	14.7	13.7	. . .	9.4	7.2	17.7	4.7	2.7	21.2	30.5	15.5	13.9
4th quarter	14.6	13.9	. . .	9.7	7.1	19.8	4.1	2.7	20.8	29.0	15.8	13.9
1950												
1st quarter	15.1	14.1	. . .	10.3	7.3	22.1	4.0	2.8	20.4	27.6	16.2	14.5
2nd quarter	15.6	14.4	. . .	11.3	8.0	24.2	4.1	2.9	20.7	28.3	16.4	15.0
3rd quarter	16.2	15.1	. . .	12.2	8.7	25.6	4.2	3.6	20.3	27.3	16.4	15.7
4th quarter	16.5	14.6	. . .	11.9	8.7	24.4	4.5	3.6	21.6	30.5	16.4	15.9
1951												
1st quarter	16.7	15.0	. . .	11.5	8.4	23.1	4.7	3.6	23.9	36.4	16.2	16.0
2nd quarter	17.0	14.6	. . .	10.9	8.6	20.0	5.2	3.5	27.2	44.2	16.5	16.2
3rd quarter	17.3	14.7	. . .	10.8	8.6	18.7	5.3	3.2	30.3	51.8	16.6	16.5
4th quarter	17.4	14.8	. . .	10.6	8.5	18.9	5.3	3.1	32.0	56.2	16.6	16.5
1952												
1st quarter	17.5	14.9	. . .	10.8	8.5	19.4	5.6	3.5	33.0	58.6	16.6	16.7
2nd quarter	17.6	15.1	. . .	10.9	8.6	19.7	5.0	3.5	34.1	60.9	17.0	16.8
3rd quarter	17.7	15.2	. . .	10.2	7.8	19.5	4.6	3.7	34.5	62.5	16.5	17.0
4th quarter	18.3	15.8	. . .	11.0	8.5	20.6	4.6	4.0	35.1	63.5	16.9	17.6
1953												
1st quarter	18.6	15.9	. . .	11.5	9.0	20.9	4.5	3.9	36.3	65.9	17.3	17.9
2nd quarter	18.7	16.0	. . .	11.5	9.1	20.9	4.5	4.1	37.1	68.0	17.2	18.1
3rd quarter	18.6	16.0	. . .	11.5	9.3	20.1	4.7	4.1	36.6	66.2	17.7	18.0
4th quarter	18.3	15.9	. . .	11.4	9.1	20.0	4.6	3.9	36.5	65.2	18.1	17.7
1954												
1st quarter	18.2	16.0	. . .	11.2	8.9	20.2	4.4	3.7	35.5	61.7	18.8	17.6
2nd quarter	18.3	16.2	. . .	11.4	8.8	21.5	5.0	4.0	34.3	58.4	18.8	17.6
3rd quarter	18.5	16.4	. . .	11.9	9.0	22.8	4.8	3.8	33.5	55.5	19.4	17.7
4th quarter	18.8	16.7	. . .	12.1	9.0	24.2	5.1	3.8	33.3	54.9	19.5	18.1
1955												
1st quarter	19.4	17.1	. . .	12.6	9.2	26.0	5.2	4.0	33.2	53.6	20.3	18.6
2nd quarter	19.7	17.4	. . .	13.2	9.7	26.4	5.1	4.3	32.9	52.3	20.5	19.0
3rd quarter	20.0	17.6	. . .	13.5	10.2	25.9	5.5	4.3	33.1	52.9	20.5	19.2
4th quarter	20.1	17.9	. . .	13.5	10.5	24.8	5.5	4.5	32.4	50.9	20.6	19.3
1956												
1st quarter	20.0	17.9	. . .	13.2	10.3	24.1	5.7	4.7	32.3	50.5	20.9	19.2
2nd quarter	20.1	18.0	. . .	13.3	10.5	24.0	6.1	4.6	33.0	51.9	21.1	19.3
3rd quarter	20.1	18.0	. . .	13.3	10.6	23.5	6.3	4.7	32.7	50.9	21.2	19.3
4th quarter	20.4	18.2	. . .	13.2	10.5	23.1	6.6	4.5	33.6	52.7	21.4	19.5
1957												
1st quarter	20.6	18.4	. . .	13.2	10.6	22.8	7.0	4.8	34.3	53.7	22.0	19.6
2nd quarter	20.5	18.4	. . .	13.1	10.6	22.3	6.8	4.9	34.0	52.9	22.2	19.6
3rd quarter	20.7	18.6	. . .	13.2	10.8	22.0	6.6	4.8	34.3	53.1	22.5	19.8
4th quarter	20.5	18.6	. . .	13.0	10.5	21.9	6.4	4.8	34.9	53.8	23.0	19.6
1958												
1st quarter	19.9	18.3	. . .	12.1	9.8	21.1	5.8	4.9	34.5	51.9	23.7	19.2
2nd quarter	20.1	18.5	. . .	11.8	9.3	21.1	5.8	5.1	35.4	53.5	24.0	19.4
3rd quarter	20.5	18.8	. . .	12.0	9.2	22.6	5.9	5.0	35.6	53.3	24.5	19.8
4th quarter	21.0	19.0	. . .	12.7	9.5	25.1	5.8	5.3	36.4	54.6	25.0	20.3
1959												
1st quarter	21.4	19.4	15.9	13.5	9.8	27.9	6.2	5.4	36.1	53.7	25.2	20.7
2nd quarter	22.0	19.7	16.3	13.9	10.1	28.9	6.4	5.6	36.7	55.0	25.3	21.2
3rd quarter	22.0	19.9	16.5	14.1	10.5	28.4	6.6	5.7	37.2	56.1	25.3	21.2
4th quarter	22.0	19.9	16.5	13.9	10.4	27.5	6.5	5.6	36.8	55.3	25.2	21.3
1960												
1st quarter	22.5	20.1	16.7	14.4	10.8	28.3	7.3	5.8	36.0	52.8	25.6	21.7
2nd quarter	22.4	20.3	16.9	14.1	11.0	26.0	7.7	5.8	36.3	52.6	26.2	21.5
3rd quarter	22.5	20.3	16.9	13.7	10.7	25.2	7.5	5.6	37.2	54.2	26.6	21.5
4th quarter	22.2	20.3	16.9	13.7	10.7	25.2	7.7	5.4	37.5	54.4	26.9	21.2
1961												
1st quarter	22.3	20.3	16.9	13.5	10.4	25.3	7.6	5.3	37.9	54.3	27.8	21.3
2nd quarter	22.7	20.6	17.1	13.7	10.6	25.4	7.5	5.4	38.0	54.8	27.6	21.7
3rd quarter	23.1	20.7	17.2	14.0	10.7	26.7	7.5	5.8	38.8	56.4	27.8	22.2
4th quarter	23.6	21.1	17.7	14.5	11.1	27.6	7.7	5.9	39.6	57.4	28.6	22.6

. . . = Not available.

Table 19-4. Chain-Type Quantity Indexes for Gross Domestic Product and Domestic Purchases—*Continued*

(Index numbers, 2005 = 100.)

NIPA Tables 1.1.3, 1.4.3, 2.3.3

Year and quarter	Gross domestic product, total	Personal consumption expenditures		Private fixed investment			Exports and imports of goods and services		Government consumption expenditures and gross investment			Gross domestic purchases
		Total	Excluding food and energy	Total	Nonresidential	Residential	Exports	Imports	Total	Federal	State and local	
1962												
1st quarter	24.0	21.3	17.9	14.8	11.4	28.1	7.7	6.1	40.3	59.5	28.4	23.0
2nd quarter	24.2	21.6	18.2	15.3	11.7	29.0	8.4	6.2	40.6	59.7	28.6	23.2
3rd quarter	24.5	21.7	18.3	15.4	11.8	29.0	8.0	6.3	41.5	61.5	29.0	23.5
4th quarter	24.5	22.1	18.7	15.3	11.8	28.9	7.8	6.4	41.5	61.2	29.3	23.6
1963												
1st quarter	24.9	22.2	18.8	15.5	11.7	30.0	8.0	6.2	41.3	59.7	29.8	23.9
2nd quarter	25.2	22.4	19.0	16.2	12.1	32.1	8.9	6.4	41.2	59.2	30.1	24.1
3rd quarter	25.6	22.7	19.3	16.6	12.5	32.7	8.4	6.5	43.0	62.4	30.9	24.6
4th quarter	25.8	22.9	19.5	17.2	12.9	33.7	8.9	6.5	42.6	60.8	31.3	24.7
1964												
1st quarter	26.4	23.4	20.0	17.8	13.2	35.8	9.4	6.5	42.8	60.5	31.8	25.2
2nd quarter	26.7	23.8	20.3	17.8	13.6	34.0	9.6	6.7	43.0	60.1	32.5	25.5
3rd quarter	27.1	24.2	20.7	18.0	14.0	33.4	9.5	6.8	43.1	59.6	32.9	25.9
4th quarter	27.2	24.3	20.7	18.2	14.3	32.8	9.8	7.0	42.9	58.8	33.2	26.0
1965												
1st quarter	27.8	24.8	21.3	19.0	15.3	32.9	8.7	6.8	42.8	58.0	33.6	26.7
2nd quarter	28.2	25.1	21.5	19.5	15.8	33.2	10.3	7.6	43.4	58.1	34.4	27.0
3rd quarter	28.8	25.5	21.9	20.1	16.4	33.3	9.8	7.6	44.9	60.5	35.4	27.6
4th quarter	29.5	26.2	22.5	20.5	17.1	32.6	10.5	8.0	45.9	62.2	35.9	28.2
1966												
1st quarter	30.2	26.6	22.9	21.3	17.9	33.3	10.3	8.2	46.7	63.6	36.3	29.0
2nd quarter	30.3	26.7	22.9	21.0	18.2	30.7	10.7	8.4	47.5	65.3	36.6	29.1
3rd quarter	30.5	27.0	23.2	21.0	18.4	29.7	10.3	8.8	48.8	67.9	37.0	29.4
4th quarter	30.7	27.1	23.4	20.4	18.3	26.6	10.7	8.9	49.6	68.5	38.0	29.6
1967												
1st quarter	31.0	27.3	23.5	19.9	18.0	25.8	10.9	9.1	51.7	73.2	38.5	29.9
2nd quarter	31.0	27.6	23.8	20.4	17.9	28.7	10.8	9.0	51.4	72.1	38.7	29.9
3rd quarter	31.3	27.8	24.0	20.6	17.8	30.1	10.5	9.1	52.0	73.2	38.8	30.2
4th quarter	31.5	28.0	24.1	21.2	18.2	31.9	10.8	9.6	52.3	73.1	39.5	30.4
1968												
1st quarter	32.1	28.6	24.7	21.8	18.7	32.1	11.1	10.2	53.2	74.4	40.2	31.1
2nd quarter	32.7	29.1	25.1	21.6	18.4	32.9	11.3	10.3	53.5	73.8	41.0	31.6
3rd quarter	32.9	29.6	25.6	22.0	18.7	33.5	12.0	11.0	53.6	73.1	41.6	31.8
4th quarter	33.1	29.7	25.7	22.5	19.2	33.9	11.9	10.9	53.6	72.7	41.9	32.0
1969												
1st quarter	33.6	30.1	26.0	23.2	19.8	35.1	10.4	9.8	53.7	72.3	42.3	32.5
2nd quarter	33.7	30.3	26.2	23.3	20.0	34.7	12.8	11.8	53.5	71.1	42.6	32.6
3rd quarter	33.9	30.4	26.4	23.7	20.5	34.5	12.5	11.6	53.5	71.2	42.7	32.8
4th quarter	33.7	30.7	26.5	23.1	20.4	31.9	12.9	11.5	52.7	69.3	42.6	32.6
1970												
1st quarter	33.7	30.9	26.6	23.0	20.3	32.0	13.0	11.5	52.5	67.9	43.0	32.5
2nd quarter	33.7	31.0	26.8	22.5	20.2	29.9	13.6	11.7	51.8	65.8	43.3	32.5
3rd quarter	34.0	31.3	27.0	22.9	20.3	31.5	13.5	11.7	52.0	64.8	44.2	32.8
4th quarter	33.7	31.2	26.9	22.9	19.5	34.8	13.7	11.8	52.0	64.5	44.5	32.5
1971												
1st quarter	34.6	31.8	27.5	23.4	19.7	36.6	13.7	11.7	51.2	61.9	44.7	33.3
2nd quarter	34.8	32.1	27.8	24.4	20.0	40.3	13.7	12.6	51.0	61.1	45.0	33.7
3rd quarter	35.1	32.3	28.1	24.9	20.1	42.3	14.2	12.9	51.0	60.8	45.1	33.9
4th quarter	35.2	32.9	28.7	25.6	20.5	44.0	13.1	12.0	50.6	58.9	45.6	34.0
1972												
1st quarter	35.8	33.3	29.2	26.7	21.2	46.9	14.4	13.7	50.8	59.2	45.8	34.7
2nd quarter	36.7	33.9	29.7	27.2	21.6	47.8	14.0	13.3	51.1	60.1	45.7	35.5
3rd quarter	37.0	34.5	30.2	27.5	21.9	47.9	14.9	13.5	50.0	56.9	46.1	35.8
4th quarter	37.6	35.3	30.9	28.7	23.0	49.6	15.5	14.1	50.3	56.7	46.7	36.4
1973												
1st quarter	38.6	35.9	31.7	30.0	24.1	51.3	16.6	14.8	50.8	57.6	46.9	37.3
2nd quarter	39.0	35.9	31.9	30.2	25.1	48.7	17.4	14.4	50.5	56.7	47.0	37.5
3rd quarter	38.8	36.0	32.0	30.1	25.5	46.6	17.5	14.0	49.9	54.3	47.5	37.2
4th quarter	39.2	35.9	32.0	29.8	25.7	44.4	18.3	14.1	50.3	54.4	48.1	37.5
1974												
1st quarter	38.8	35.6	31.9	29.1	25.7	41.1	18.6	13.6	51.3	56.1	48.7	37.0
2nd quarter	38.9	35.7	32.0	28.7	25.6	39.3	19.5	14.3	51.7	56.0	49.3	37.1
3rd quarter	38.6	35.9	32.0	28.2	25.3	38.1	18.4	14.1	51.7	56.3	49.3	36.8
4th quarter	38.4	35.3	31.4	26.6	24.6	33.0	18.9	13.9	51.9	56.7	49.3	36.6
1975												
1st quarter	37.9	35.6	31.8	25.0	23.1	31.0	19.0	12.5	52.5	56.0	50.8	35.8
2nd quarter	38.2	36.2	32.2	24.6	22.5	31.7	18.5	11.5	52.1	55.6	50.4	35.9
3rd quarter	38.9	36.8	32.8	25.2	22.7	33.9	18.2	12.5	53.1	57.0	51.0	36.8
4th quarter	39.4	37.1	33.3	25.7	22.9	35.4	19.2	13.2	53.5	57.1	51.7	37.3
1976												
1st quarter	40.3	37.9	34.0	26.8	23.3	39.0	19.1	14.0	53.6	56.6	52.2	38.3
2nd quarter	40.6	38.2	34.2	27.2	23.6	40.1	19.3	14.6	53.1	56.5	51.3	38.7
3rd quarter	40.8	38.6	34.5	27.5	24.1	39.4	19.8	15.2	52.8	56.3	51.0	39.0
4th quarter	41.1	39.1	34.9	28.9	24.6	44.5	20.0	15.7	52.7	56.5	50.8	39.3

Table 19-4. Chain-Type Quantity Indexes for Gross Domestic Product and Domestic Purchases—*Continued*

(Index numbers, 2005 = 100.)

NIPA Tables 1.1.3, 1.4.3, 2.3.3

Year and quarter	Gross domestic product											Gross domestic purchases
	Gross domestic product, total	Personal consumption expenditures		Private fixed investment			Exports and imports of goods and services		Government consumption expenditures and gross investment			
		Total	Excluding food and energy	Total	Nonresi-dential	Residential	Exports	Imports	Total	Federal	State and local	
1977												
1st quarter	41.6	39.6	35.5	30.0	25.6	45.8	19.7	16.4	53.2	56.9	51.3	40.0
2nd quarter	42.4	39.8	35.8	31.7	26.3	51.0	20.2	16.6	53.8	57.9	51.6	40.7
3rd quarter	43.1	40.2	36.2	32.1	26.9	50.9	20.4	16.3	53.9	58.2	51.6	41.4
4th quarter	43.1	40.8	36.8	32.6	27.8	50.2	19.7	16.6	53.7	57.6	51.6	41.5
1978												
1st quarter	43.3	41.0	37.0	32.9	28.0	50.5	20.2	17.7	53.8	57.8	51.7	41.8
2nd quarter	45.0	41.9	38.1	35.3	30.4	52.9	22.3	17.7	55.2	59.2	53.2	43.1
3rd quarter	45.4	42.1	38.3	36.3	31.5	53.6	22.6	18.0	55.7	59.4	53.8	43.6
4th quarter	46.0	42.4	38.7	37.1	32.5	53.4	23.5	18.2	56.2	59.9	54.3	44.0
1979												
1st quarter	46.1	42.6	38.8	37.4	33.2	52.2	23.5	18.2	55.7	60.0	53.4	44.1
2nd quarter	46.1	42.6	38.9	37.1	33.1	51.2	23.5	18.3	56.3	60.8	53.9	44.1
3rd quarter	46.5	43.0	39.4	37.8	34.2	50.6	24.4	18.0	56.3	60.7	54.1	44.3
4th quarter	46.6	43.1	39.5	37.4	34.3	48.7	25.9	18.4	56.7	60.6	54.7	44.2
1980												
1st quarter	46.8	43.1	39.4	36.9	34.6	45.0	26.6	18.4	57.6	62.6	54.9	44.3
2nd quarter	45.8	42.1	38.4	33.7	32.9	36.6	27.1	17.1	57.8	64.2	54.2	42.9
3rd quarter	45.7	42.5	39.0	34.0	33.1	37.3	27.1	15.8	57.0	63.3	53.5	42.5
4th quarter	46.6	43.1	39.7	35.4	33.8	40.9	26.9	16.7	56.9	63.5	53.2	43.6
1981												
1st quarter	47.5	43.3	40.1	35.6	34.4	40.2	27.4	17.4	57.7	64.8	53.6	44.6
2nd quarter	47.1	43.3	39.9	35.8	35.1	38.8	27.6	17.4	57.8	66.8	52.6	44.2
3rd quarter	47.7	43.5	40.2	35.8	35.9	35.8	27.0	17.2	57.7	66.7	52.4	44.8
4th quarter	47.1	43.2	39.7	35.7	36.8	32.2	27.1	17.7	58.2	67.4	52.8	44.3
1982												
1st quarter	46.3	43.5	40.0	34.6	35.9	30.3	25.9	17.2	58.2	67.5	52.7	43.7
2nd quarter	46.6	43.6	40.2	33.4	34.6	29.3	26.1	16.9	58.5	68.1	52.8	43.8
3rd quarter	46.4	44.0	40.6	32.5	33.5	29.3	24.9	17.7	58.9	69.1	52.9	44.0
4th quarter	46.5	44.8	41.4	32.4	32.8	31.4	23.8	17.0	59.9	71.2	53.2	44.1
1983												
1st quarter	47.0	45.2	41.9	33.2	32.2	36.7	24.2	17.4	60.4	72.0	53.4	44.6
2nd quarter	48.1	46.1	42.9	34.4	32.6	41.1	24.3	18.8	60.9	73.6	53.3	45.9
3rd quarter	49.0	46.9	43.6	36.5	34.0	45.2	24.6	20.2	61.9	75.6	53.7	47.1
4th quarter	50.1	47.7	44.4	38.6	36.2	47.1	25.1	21.2	60.9	73.0	53.7	48.2
1984												
1st quarter	51.0	48.1	45.0	39.8	37.4	48.4	25.6	22.9	61.5	73.6	54.3	49.4
2nd quarter	51.9	48.8	45.6	41.5	39.3	49.3	26.3	23.9	62.8	75.9	55.0	50.3
3rd quarter	52.4	49.1	46.1	42.4	40.6	48.8	26.9	24.5	63.3	75.6	55.9	50.9
4th quarter	52.8	49.8	46.8	43.1	41.6	48.9	27.4	25.2	64.7	78.1	56.6	51.3
1985												
1st quarter	53.3	50.6	47.6	43.5	42.0	48.7	27.4	24.7	65.4	79.0	57.3	51.7
2nd quarter	53.8	51.1	48.2	44.0	42.6	49.1	27.3	25.9	66.9	80.9	58.4	52.4
3rd quarter	54.6	52.1	49.2	43.6	42.0	49.7	26.9	25.6	68.6	83.6	59.6	53.2
4th quarter	55.0	52.2	49.2	44.5	42.7	50.9	27.7	26.6	69.0	83.6	60.3	53.7
1986												
1st quarter	55.6	52.6	49.7	44.5	42.1	53.1	28.6	26.6	69.8	83.1	61.8	54.0
2nd quarter	55.8	53.2	50.3	44.4	41.1	56.0	28.9	27.7	71.2	85.8	62.5	54.4
3rd quarter	56.3	54.1	51.3	44.2	40.5	56.9	29.6	28.5	72.9	89.0	63.1	55.0
4th quarter	56.6	54.4	51.6	44.5	40.9	56.8	30.7	28.7	72.4	87.7	63.3	55.2
1987												
1st quarter	56.9	54.3	51.6	43.6	39.8	56.6	30.7	28.5	72.7	88.2	63.4	55.4
2nd quarter	57.5	55.1	52.3	44.4	40.7	56.9	31.9	29.3	73.2	89.4	63.4	56.0
3rd quarter	58.0	55.7	53.1	45.3	42.0	56.7	33.3	29.8	73.2	89.5	63.4	56.4
4th quarter	59.0	55.8	53.2	45.3	41.9	57.0	34.5	30.5	74.1	90.8	64.0	57.3
1988												
1st quarter	59.3	56.7	54.1	45.2	42.2	55.8	36.4	30.4	73.7	88.4	64.9	57.3
2nd quarter	60.1	57.2	54.4	46.1	43.3	56.2	37.5	30.0	73.9	87.5	65.8	57.8
3rd quarter	60.4	57.6	54.9	46.3	43.5	56.2	38.2	30.7	73.9	86.8	66.1	58.2
4th quarter	61.2	58.3	55.6	46.8	44.0	56.7	39.3	31.7	75.4	89.4	66.9	59.0
1989												
1st quarter	61.8	58.5	55.8	47.2	44.7	56.4	40.5	31.8	74.9	87.6	67.3	59.4
2nd quarter	62.2	58.8	56.2	47.3	45.3	54.7	42.2	32.0	76.1	89.6	68.0	59.6
3rd quarter	62.7	59.4	56.8	48.1	46.6	54.1	42.7	31.9	76.8	90.4	68.6	60.0
4th quarter	62.9	59.7	56.9	47.3	46.0	53.0	43.4	32.5	77.2	90.0	69.5	60.2
1990												
1st quarter	63.5	60.1	57.7	47.9	46.6	53.5	45.3	33.5	78.4	91.3	70.6	60.8
2nd quarter	63.8	60.3	57.7	46.8	45.8	51.4	45.9	33.5	78.5	91.4	70.7	60.9
3rd quarter	63.8	60.6	58.0	46.3	46.1	48.5	46.2	33.3	78.5	90.6	71.2	60.8
4th quarter	63.2	60.1	57.6	45.0	45.2	45.8	46.6	32.4	79.3	91.4	71.9	60.1
1991												
1st quarter	62.9	59.9	57.4	43.5	44.0	43.1	46.9	32.1	79.6	92.1	72.0	59.7
2nd quarter	63.3	60.4	57.7	43.4	43.6	44.1	48.6	32.6	79.9	92.4	72.3	60.0
3rd quarter	63.6	60.6	58.0	43.5	43.2	46.0	49.7	33.6	79.5	90.7	72.7	60.3
4th quarter	63.8	60.6	58.1	43.6	42.9	47.0	50.9	34.3	79.1	88.9	73.3	60.5

Table 19-4. Chain-Type Quantity Indexes for Gross Domestic Product and Domestic Purchases—*Continued*

(Index numbers, 2005 = 100.)

NIPA Tables 1.1.3, 1.4.3, 2.3.3

Year and quarter	Gross domestic product, total	Personal consumption expenditures		Private fixed investment			Exports and imports of goods and services		Government consumption expenditures and gross investment			Gross domestic purchases
		Total	Excluding food and energy	Total	Nonresidential	Residential	Exports	Imports	Total	Federal	State and local	
1992												
1st quarter	64.5	61.6	59.3	44.1	42.7	49.4	51.8	34.5	79.7	88.9	74.2	61.1
2nd quarter	65.2	62.0	59.6	45.8	44.4	51.2	51.8	35.1	79.7	88.8	74.1	61.9
3rd quarter	65.9	62.7	60.4	46.5	45.3	51.4	52.9	35.7	80.1	89.8	74.2	62.5
4th quarter	66.6	63.4	61.1	47.9	46.7	53.1	53.2	36.5	80.1	89.9	74.2	63.3
1993												
1st quarter	66.7	63.7	61.4	48.2	47.0	53.3	53.3	37.3	79.2	87.1	74.5	63.5
2nd quarter	67.1	64.3	62.1	49.3	48.3	54.0	53.9	38.1	79.2	85.9	75.1	64.0
3rd quarter	67.5	65.0	62.8	50.2	48.8	55.8	53.8	38.6	79.1	85.0	75.5	64.4
4th quarter	68.4	65.6	63.4	52.4	50.8	58.7	55.5	40.1	79.5	85.4	75.9	65.3
1994												
1st quarter	69.1	66.3	64.1	53.1	51.3	59.9	56.0	41.1	78.5	82.4	76.1	66.1
2nd quarter	70.0	66.8	64.6	54.4	52.4	61.9	57.9	42.6	78.8	81.9	76.9	67.0
3rd quarter	70.5	67.3	65.2	54.9	53.4	61.2	60.1	43.8	80.2	84.1	77.8	67.4
4th quarter	71.2	68.0	66.0	56.4	55.7	60.4	61.4	45.0	79.5	81.8	78.0	68.2
1995												
1st quarter	71.4	68.1	66.1	57.7	58.0	59.1	62.5	46.0	79.8	81.6	78.7	68.4
2nd quarter	71.6	68.6	66.6	57.5	58.4	57.2	63.4	46.5	80.1	81.3	79.3	68.5
3rd quarter	72.2	69.3	67.3	58.2	58.8	58.9	66.2	46.6	79.9	80.8	79.3	68.8
4th quarter	72.7	69.7	67.8	59.5	60.0	60.3	67.1	47.2	79.0	77.7	79.7	69.3
1996												
1st quarter	73.2	70.4	68.4	61.0	61.5	61.9	68.0	48.8	79.5	79.3	79.6	69.9
2nd quarter	74.4	71.2	69.3	62.9	63.2	64.5	69.1	49.8	80.7	80.5	80.7	71.2
3rd quarter	75.1	71.6	69.9	64.4	65.3	64.3	69.7	51.5	80.6	79.1	81.4	72.0
4th quarter	75.9	72.2	70.4	65.5	67.1	63.6	74.0	52.5	81.3	78.8	82.7	72.5
1997												
1st quarter	76.5	72.9	71.2	66.8	68.8	63.8	75.4	54.7	81.4	77.8	83.5	73.3
2nd quarter	77.6	73.2	71.6	68.2	70.5	64.6	78.4	56.6	82.1	79.1	83.8	74.3
3rd quarter	78.6	74.5	72.9	70.8	74.1	64.9	80.2	58.6	82.2	78.9	84.1	75.4
4th quarter	79.2	75.3	73.8	71.4	74.7	65.6	80.1	59.9	82.3	78.8	84.4	76.2
1998												
1st quarter	79.9	76.1	74.7	73.6	77.3	66.8	80.5	62.1	81.8	76.3	85.1	77.2
2nd quarter	80.7	77.4	76.0	76.1	80.1	68.8	79.5	63.6	83.6	78.4	86.7	78.2
3rd quarter	81.7	78.4	77.1	77.6	81.3	70.8	79.2	64.4	84.4	77.8	88.3	79.4
4th quarter	83.1	79.6	78.5	80.0	84.0	72.5	82.2	66.5	85.2	78.5	89.1	80.7
1999												
1st quarter	83.9	80.4	79.2	81.4	86.0	73.0	81.5	68.2	85.6	78.0	90.1	81.8
2nd quarter	84.5	81.6	80.5	83.4	88.4	73.8	82.5	70.4	86.0	78.0	90.6	82.6
3rd quarter	85.6	82.6	81.5	85.3	90.9	74.4	84.6	72.9	87.1	79.6	91.4	83.8
4th quarter	87.1	83.8	82.8	85.8	91.2	75.3	86.8	74.7	88.4	81.4	92.6	85.3
2000												
1st quarter	87.4	85.1	84.4	88.3	94.6	75.9	88.3	77.7	87.7	78.2	93.3	85.9
2nd quarter	89.1	85.9	85.0	90.5	98.1	75.4	90.8	80.1	88.9	81.3	93.3	87.6
3rd quarter	89.2	86.7	85.9	90.8	99.2	74.0	93.0	82.9	88.6	79.7	93.8	87.9
4th quarter	89.7	87.5	86.6	91.1	99.6	74.1	92.2	82.8	88.9	79.4	94.5	88.4
2001												
1st quarter	89.4	87.8	87.1	90.6	98.6	74.4	91.0	81.6	90.2	81.1	95.6	88.1
2nd quarter	90.0	88.1	87.6	89.1	96.0	75.5	88.1	79.2	92.1	82.8	97.5	88.6
3rd quarter	89.7	88.5	88.0	88.2	94.4	75.9	83.5	77.3	91.9	83.4	96.9	88.5
4th quarter	90.0	89.9	89.6	86.0	91.5	75.2	81.2	76.3	93.5	84.4	98.9	88.9
2002												
1st quarter	90.8	90.2	90.0	85.2	89.3	77.3	82.5	78.3	95.0	86.4	100.0	89.8
2nd quarter	91.3	90.7	90.4	84.9	87.9	79.1	84.7	80.9	95.9	88.4	100.3	90.4
3rd quarter	91.8	91.3	91.0	84.7	87.4	79.6	85.3	82.2	96.6	89.8	100.7	91.0
4th quarter	91.8	91.6	91.2	84.1	85.8	80.8	84.4	83.7	97.3	91.3	100.8	91.3
2003												
1st quarter	92.1	92.1	91.7	84.1	85.4	81.6	83.6	82.7	97.1	91.3	100.5	91.6
2nd quarter	92.9	93.0	92.7	86.2	87.7	83.5	83.4	83.9	98.5	95.7	100.2	92.5
3rd quarter	94.4	94.3	94.1	89.0	89.7	87.7	85.6	84.9	98.8	95.8	100.6	93.9
4th quarter	95.3	94.8	94.6	90.6	90.8	90.1	89.6	88.0	98.9	96.5	100.3	94.8
2004												
1st quarter	96.0	95.7	95.5	90.4	90.1	90.9	91.7	90.2	99.4	97.7	100.3	95.5
2nd quarter	96.6	96.2	96.0	93.2	92.6	94.3	93.2	93.8	99.7	98.3	100.6	96.6
3rd quarter	97.4	97.0	97.0	95.2	95.1	95.3	93.9	95.2	100.1	100.0	100.1	97.4
4th quarter	98.2	98.1	98.1	96.8	97.2	96.0	96.0	97.6	99.5	98.8	99.9	98.3
2005												
1st quarter	99.2	98.9	98.8	98.0	98.1	97.8	97.8	98.2	99.6	99.2	99.8	99.2
2nd quarter	99.6	99.8	99.9	99.7	99.5	100.0	99.9	99.3	99.7	99.3	99.9	99.5
3rd quarter	100.4	100.5	100.5	101.0	100.9	101.1	99.9	99.9	100.6	101.6	100.0	100.3
4th quarter	100.9	100.8	100.8	101.4	101.5	101.1	102.4	102.7	100.1	99.9	100.3	101.0
2006												
1st quarter	102.2	101.9	102.3	103.7	105.8	100.0	106.4	104.6	101.1	102.8	100.2	102.2
2nd quarter	102.6	102.5	102.7	103.2	107.6	95.5	108.2	105.8	101.2	101.9	100.9	102.5
3rd quarter	102.6	103.1	103.3	101.9	108.8	90.0	108.4	107.0	101.4	101.8	101.1	102.7
4th quarter	103.3	104.1	104.5	100.5	109.4	85.2	112.9	106.9	101.7	102.1	101.4	103.0

Table 19-5. Chain-Type Price Indexes for Gross Domestic Product and Domestic Purchases

(Index numbers, 2005 = 100.)

NIPA Tables 1.1.4, 1.6.4, 2.3.4

Year and quarter	Gross domestic product											Gross domestic purchases
	Gross domestic product, total	Personal consumption expenditures		Private fixed investment			Exports and imports of goods and services		Government consumption expenditures and gross investment			
		Total	Excluding food and energy	Total	Nonresidential	Residential	Exports	Imports	Total	Federal	State and local	
1946	12.4	12.8	12.9	15.0	19.2	8.2	20.1	13.4	8.2	9.6	6.7	12.1
1947	13.7	14.1	14.0	17.6	22.3	9.8	23.4	16.0	8.9	10.2	7.5	13.4
1948	14.5	14.9	14.8	19.1	24.2	10.6	24.6	17.4	9.2	10.1	8.3	14.2
1949	14.5	14.8	14.8	19.5	24.8	10.7	23.2	16.6	9.5	10.5	8.4	14.2
1947												
1st quarter	13.4	13.8	. . .	16.8	21.4	9.2	21.5	14.7	8.9	10.4	7.2	13.1
2nd quarter	13.6	13.9	. . .	17.5	22.1	9.7	23.1	15.7	8.9	10.3	7.4	13.3
3rd quarter	13.8	14.2	. . .	17.9	22.7	10.0	24.2	16.6	8.8	10.0	7.5	13.5
4th quarter	14.1	14.5	. . .	18.3	23.1	10.2	24.8	17.2	8.9	9.9	7.8	13.8
1948												
1st quarter	14.3	14.7	. . .	18.5	23.2	10.4	25.0	17.6	9.0	10.0	8.0	13.9
2nd quarter	14.4	14.9	. . .	18.9	23.9	10.5	24.9	17.6	9.1	10.0	8.2	14.1
3rd quarter	14.7	15.1	. . .	19.5	24.8	10.7	24.6	17.4	9.3	10.1	8.5	14.4
4th quarter	14.7	15.0	. . .	19.7	25.1	10.8	24.2	17.2	9.4	10.2	8.6	14.4
1949												
1st quarter	14.6	14.9	. . .	19.7	24.9	10.9	23.7	16.8	9.6	10.6	8.5	14.3
2nd quarter	14.5	14.8	. . .	19.6	24.9	10.9	23.3	16.6	9.5	10.5	8.4	14.2
3rd quarter	14.4	14.7	. . .	19.4	24.8	10.6	22.9	16.5	9.4	10.3	8.4	14.1
4th quarter	14.4	14.7	. . .	19.3	24.6	10.6	22.7	16.6	9.5	10.6	8.3	14.1
1950												
1st quarter	14.4	14.7	. . .	19.3	24.7	10.6	22.3	16.9	9.4	10.5	8.3	14.1
2nd quarter	14.4	14.8	. . .	19.6	24.9	10.9	22.4	17.3	9.4	10.4	8.3	14.2
3rd quarter	14.7	15.1	. . .	20.2	25.4	11.3	22.6	17.8	9.5	10.4	8.6	14.5
4th quarter	15.0	15.4	. . .	20.6	26.3	11.3	23.0	18.6	9.7	10.4	8.8	14.7
1951												
1st quarter	15.5	15.9	. . .	21.3	27.2	11.6	24.4	20.2	10.1	11.0	9.1	15.2
2nd quarter	15.6	16.0	. . .	21.6	27.7	11.8	25.2	21.3	10.0	10.8	9.3	15.3
3rd quarter	15.6	16.0	. . .	21.8	27.9	11.8	26.0	21.9	10.1	10.8	9.5	15.4
4th quarter	15.8	16.2	. . .	22.0	28.2	11.9	26.4	22.0	10.2	11.0	9.6	15.6
1952												
1st quarter	15.8	16.3	. . .	22.1	28.4	12.0	25.7	21.1	10.1	10.8	9.6	15.6
2nd quarter	15.9	16.3	. . .	22.2	28.4	12.1	25.7	20.7	10.3	11.0	9.7	15.6
3rd quarter	16.0	16.4	. . .	22.2	28.3	12.2	25.6	20.4	10.4	11.1	9.9	15.8
4th quarter	16.1	16.4	. . .	22.2	28.4	12.2	25.6	20.0	10.5	11.2	9.9	15.8
1953												
1st quarter	16.1	16.5	. . .	22.2	28.4	12.2	25.7	19.9	10.4	11.1	10.0	15.8
2nd quarter	16.1	16.5	. . .	22.3	28.6	12.2	25.6	19.7	10.4	11.1	10.0	15.8
3rd quarter	16.2	16.6	. . .	22.5	28.8	12.3	25.6	19.6	10.4	11.0	10.0	15.9
4th quarter	16.2	16.7	. . .	22.5	28.8	12.2	25.4	19.6	10.4	11.1	9.9	15.9
1954												
1st quarter	16.3	16.7	. . .	22.5	28.9	12.2	25.3	19.8	10.5	11.2	9.9	16.0
2nd quarter	16.3	16.7	. . .	22.6	29.0	12.2	25.2	19.9	10.6	11.3	10.1	16.1
3rd quarter	16.3	16.7	. . .	22.6	28.8	12.3	25.2	20.0	10.7	11.4	10.2	16.0
4th quarter	16.3	16.7	. . .	22.6	28.9	12.3	25.2	20.0	10.8	11.5	10.3	16.1
1955												
1st quarter	16.4	16.7	. . .	22.6	28.8	12.4	25.3	19.8	10.8	11.6	10.2	16.1
2nd quarter	16.5	16.7	. . .	22.7	29.0	12.5	25.4	19.8	11.0	11.9	10.2	16.2
3rd quarter	16.6	16.8	. . .	23.0	29.4	12.6	25.5	19.9	11.2	12.0	10.4	16.3
4th quarter	16.7	16.8	. . .	23.3	30.0	12.6	25.7	19.9	11.3	12.2	10.5	16.4
1956												
1st quarter	16.9	16.9	. . .	23.8	30.9	12.7	25.9	20.0	11.5	12.4	10.8	16.6
2nd quarter	17.1	17.0	. . .	24.1	31.2	12.9	26.1	20.1	11.7	12.6	10.9	16.7
3rd quarter	17.2	17.2	. . .	24.5	32.0	12.9	26.4	20.2	11.8	12.6	11.1	16.9
4th quarter	17.3	17.3	. . .	24.7	32.4	12.9	26.7	20.4	11.9	12.7	11.2	17.0
1957												
1st quarter	17.6	17.4	. . .	24.9	32.9	12.8	27.1	20.5	12.1	13.0	11.3	17.2
2nd quarter	17.7	17.6	. . .	25.0	33.1	12.8	27.3	20.5	12.2	13.1	11.5	17.3
3rd quarter	17.8	17.7	. . .	25.2	33.3	12.9	27.4	20.4	12.3	13.2	11.5	17.5
4th quarter	17.9	17.8	. . .	25.3	33.6	12.9	27.4	20.2	12.4	13.3	11.5	17.5
1958												
1st quarter	18.1	18.0	. . .	25.1	33.2	12.8	27.1	19.7	12.4	13.5	11.5	17.7
2nd quarter	18.1	18.0	. . .	25.2	33.4	12.8	27.0	19.5	12.6	13.6	11.6	17.8
3rd quarter	18.2	18.1	. . .	25.2	33.4	12.8	27.0	19.5	12.7	13.7	11.7	17.8
4th quarter	18.2	18.0	. . .	25.2	33.5	12.8	27.0	19.6	12.7	13.8	11.7	17.8
1959												
1st quarter	18.3	18.2	18.5	25.3	33.6	12.9	26.9	19.6	12.7	13.7	11.8	17.9
2nd quarter	18.3	18.2	18.6	25.4	33.8	12.9	26.9	19.7	12.7	13.6	11.9	17.9
3rd quarter	18.4	18.4	18.7	25.4	33.9	12.9	27.1	19.8	12.6	13.5	11.9	18.0
4th quarter	18.4	18.5	18.9	25.5	34.0	12.9	27.4	20.0	12.6	13.5	11.9	18.1
1960												
1st quarter	18.5	18.5	18.9	25.5	34.0	12.9	27.4	19.9	12.7	13.5	12.0	18.1
2nd quarter	18.6	18.6	19.0	25.6	34.0	13.0	27.4	19.9	12.7	13.5	12.0	18.2
3rd quarter	18.6	18.6	19.1	25.5	34.0	13.0	27.5	20.0	12.9	13.8	12.1	18.3
4th quarter	18.7	18.7	19.1	25.5	33.9	13.0	27.4	19.9	13.0	13.9	12.1	18.3
1961												
1st quarter	18.8	18.8	19.2	25.4	33.8	12.9	27.6	20.0	13.0	13.9	12.2	18.4
2nd quarter	18.8	18.8	19.2	25.5	33.8	13.0	27.9	19.9	13.0	13.9	12.3	18.4
3rd quarter	18.8	18.8	19.3	25.4	33.8	13.0	27.9	19.9	13.1	13.9	12.4	18.4
4th quarter	18.9	18.9	19.4	25.4	33.8	13.0	28.1	19.9	13.2	14.0	12.5	18.5

. . . = Not available.

Table 19-5. Chain-Type Price Indexes for Gross Domestic Product and Domestic Purchases—*Continued*

(Index numbers, 2005 = 100.)

NIPA Tables 1.1.4, 1.6.4, 2.3.4

Year and quarter	Gross domestic product											Gross domestic purchases
	Gross domestic product, total	Personal consumption expenditures		Private fixed investment			Exports and imports of goods and services		Government consumption expenditures and gross investment			
		Total	Excluding food and energy	Total	Nonresidential	Residential	Exports	Imports	Total	Federal	State and local	
1962												
1st quarter	19.0	18.9	19.4	25.5	33.8	13.0	28.1	19.7	13.3	14.1	12.7	18.6
2nd quarter	19.0	19.0	19.5	25.5	33.8	13.0	27.9	19.7	13.4	14.1	12.7	18.6
3rd quarter	19.1	19.1	19.6	25.5	33.8	13.0	27.9	19.7	13.4	14.2	12.8	18.7
4th quarter	19.2	19.1	19.6	25.4	33.8	13.0	27.9	19.8	13.5	14.4	12.8	18.7
1963												
1st quarter	19.2	19.2	19.7	25.5	33.8	13.0	27.9	19.9	13.6	14.4	12.9	18.8
2nd quarter	19.2	19.2	19.7	25.4	33.8	12.9	27.9	20.0	13.7	14.5	13.0	18.8
3rd quarter	19.3	19.3	19.8	25.3	33.8	12.8	27.8	20.1	13.6	14.4	13.0	18.9
4th quarter	19.4	19.4	19.9	25.4	33.8	12.9	27.9	20.3	13.9	14.7	13.1	19.0
1964												
1st quarter	19.5	19.4	20.0	25.3	33.8	12.8	27.9	20.4	13.9	14.8	13.2	19.1
2nd quarter	19.5	19.5	20.1	25.5	33.9	13.0	27.9	20.5	14.0	14.9	13.3	19.1
3rd quarter	19.6	19.6	20.1	25.5	34.0	13.0	28.1	20.5	14.1	15.1	13.3	19.2
4th quarter	19.7	19.6	20.2	25.8	34.1	13.3	28.4	20.6	14.2	15.1	13.4	19.3
1965												
1st quarter	19.8	19.7	20.2	25.8	34.2	13.3	29.1	20.7	14.3	15.2	13.5	19.4
2nd quarter	19.9	19.8	20.3	25.9	34.3	13.3	29.0	20.6	14.3	15.2	13.6	19.5
3rd quarter	20.0	19.9	20.4	25.9	34.4	13.3	29.0	20.8	14.5	15.4	13.7	19.5
4th quarter	20.1	19.9	20.4	26.2	34.5	13.6	28.9	21.0	14.7	15.7	13.8	19.7
1966												
1st quarter	20.2	20.1	20.5	26.1	34.5	13.5	29.4	21.1	14.8	15.7	14.0	19.8
2nd quarter	20.4	20.2	20.7	26.6	34.8	13.9	29.6	21.3	14.9	15.7	14.2	20.0
3rd quarter	20.6	20.4	20.9	26.6	34.9	13.9	30.0	21.3	15.2	16.1	14.4	20.1
4th quarter	20.8	20.6	21.1	26.9	35.2	14.2	30.5	21.4	15.3	16.1	14.6	20.3
1967												
1st quarter	20.9	20.6	21.2	27.0	35.4	14.2	31.0	21.4	15.4	16.1	14.9	20.4
2nd quarter	21.0	20.7	21.3	27.1	35.6	14.2	31.0	21.3	15.6	16.3	15.0	20.5
3rd quarter	21.2	20.9	21.5	27.3	35.8	14.3	31.0	21.4	15.7	16.4	15.2	20.7
4th quarter	21.4	21.1	21.7	27.6	36.2	14.6	31.1	21.4	16.0	16.8	15.4	20.9
1968												
1st quarter	21.7	21.3	22.0	27.9	36.4	14.8	31.4	21.5	16.2	16.9	15.7	21.2
2nd quarter	21.9	21.5	22.2	28.2	36.8	15.0	32.0	21.7	16.4	17.1	15.8	21.4
3rd quarter	22.1	21.7	22.5	28.4	37.1	15.0	31.6	21.7	16.6	17.4	16.0	21.6
4th quarter	22.4	22.0	22.7	29.0	37.7	15.6	31.8	21.9	16.9	17.7	16.3	21.9
1969												
1st quarter	22.6	22.2	23.0	29.3	37.9	15.9	32.3	22.0	17.0	17.7	16.5	22.1
2nd quarter	22.9	22.5	23.3	29.6	38.3	16.1	32.4	22.1	17.3	18.0	16.9	22.4
3rd quarter	23.3	22.8	23.5	29.9	38.7	16.2	32.8	22.2	17.7	18.5	17.2	22.7
4th quarter	23.6	23.0	23.8	30.3	39.2	16.4	33.6	22.8	18.0	18.7	17.5	23.0
1970												
1st quarter	23.9	23.3	24.1	30.5	39.6	16.4	33.5	23.0	18.5	19.3	17.9	23.3
2nd quarter	24.2	23.5	24.3	31.2	40.3	17.0	34.2	23.3	18.8	19.6	18.3	23.7
3rd quarter	24.4	23.8	24.6	31.1	40.5	16.6	34.1	23.9	19.1	19.9	18.6	23.9
4th quarter	24.7	24.1	25.0	31.4	41.0	16.7	34.3	24.1	19.4	20.1	18.9	24.2
1971												
1st quarter	25.1	24.3	25.3	32.0	41.6	17.1	35.2	24.7	19.9	20.8	19.3	24.6
2nd quarter	25.5	24.6	25.6	32.5	42.1	17.5	35.3	24.8	20.3	21.2	19.6	24.9
3rd quarter	25.7	24.8	25.8	32.8	42.5	17.8	35.2	25.1	20.6	21.5	19.9	25.2
4th quarter	25.9	25.0	26.0	33.1	42.8	18.1	35.4	25.5	20.9	22.0	20.1	25.4
1972												
1st quarter	26.3	25.3	26.2	33.6	43.2	18.3	36.4	25.9	21.6	23.1	20.5	25.8
2nd quarter	26.5	25.4	26.4	33.8	43.6	18.4	36.7	26.6	21.8	23.3	20.7	26.0
3rd quarter	26.7	25.6	26.6	34.1	43.8	18.7	36.9	27.0	22.1	23.5	21.0	26.2
4th quarter	27.0	25.8	26.8	34.6	44.1	19.3	37.7	27.6	22.5	24.0	21.4	26.5
1973												
1st quarter	27.4	26.1	26.9	34.9	44.4	19.6	38.8	28.4	23.0	24.4	21.9	26.9
2nd quarter	27.9	26.6	27.3	35.6	45.1	20.0	40.5	30.6	23.4	24.8	22.3	27.4
3rd quarter	28.4	27.1	27.7	36.3	45.7	20.7	42.8	32.1	23.8	25.3	22.7	27.9
4th quarter	28.9	27.7	28.1	36.8	46.2	21.1	45.0	34.5	24.2	25.8	23.1	28.4
1974												
1st quarter	29.5	28.5	28.5	37.4	47.0	21.6	48.2	40.0	24.8	26.2	23.8	29.1
2nd quarter	30.1	29.3	29.2	38.5	48.5	22.1	49.8	44.6	25.5	26.7	24.6	30.0
3rd quarter	31.1	30.1	30.1	40.0	50.6	22.8	52.6	46.9	26.4	27.6	25.4	30.9
4th quarter	32.0	30.9	30.8	41.7	52.9	23.4	55.3	48.4	27.2	28.7	26.1	31.8
1975												
1st quarter	32.8	31.5	31.4	43.2	54.9	24.0	56.9	49.1	27.8	29.4	26.7	32.5
2nd quarter	33.2	31.8	31.9	44.2	56.4	24.4	56.7	49.3	28.3	29.8	27.2	33.0
3rd quarter	33.9	32.4	32.4	44.7	57.1	24.7	56.5	48.2	28.8	30.3	27.6	33.6
4th quarter	34.5	33.0	32.9	45.4	57.9	25.1	56.9	48.2	29.4	31.2	28.1	34.1
1976												
1st quarter	34.8	33.4	33.4	45.8	58.6	25.2	57.7	49.0	29.8	31.5	28.5	34.5
2nd quarter	35.2	33.6	33.8	46.6	59.3	26.0	58.3	49.8	30.2	31.9	29.0	34.9
3rd quarter	35.7	34.1	34.3	47.3	60.1	26.4	58.7	50.7	30.6	32.4	29.3	35.4
4th quarter	36.3	34.7	34.9	48.0	61.0	26.9	59.7	51.2	31.2	33.3	29.7	36.0

Table 19-5. Chain-Type Price Indexes for Gross Domestic Product and Domestic Purchases—*Continued*

(Index numbers, 2005 = 100.)   **NIPA Tables 1.1.4, 1.6.4, 2.3.4**

Year and quarter	Gross domestic product, total	Personal consumption expenditures — Total	Personal consumption expenditures — Excluding food and energy	Private fixed investment — Total	Private fixed investment — Nonresidential	Private fixed investment — Residential	Exports and imports of goods and services — Exports	Exports and imports of goods and services — Imports	Government consumption expenditures and gross investment — Total	Government consumption expenditures and gross investment — Federal	Government consumption expenditures and gross investment — State and local	Gross domestic purchases
1977												
1st quarter	36.9	35.3	35.5	49.1	62.2	27.5	60.4	53.0	31.8	34.1	30.2	36.7
2nd quarter	37.5	35.9	36.0	50.0	63.2	28.3	61.3	54.5	32.3	34.5	30.7	37.3
3rd quarter	38.0	36.4	36.6	51.1	64.3	29.2	61.0	55.2	32.7	34.6	31.3	37.9
4th quarter	38.7	37.0	37.1	52.3	65.5	30.1	61.3	55.7	33.5	35.8	31.8	38.5
1978												
1st quarter	39.3	37.6	37.7	53.3	66.4	31.0	62.5	56.7	33.9	36.1	32.3	39.1
2nd quarter	40.0	38.4	38.4	54.4	67.5	31.9	64.0	58.0	34.4	36.5	32.8	39.9
3rd quarter	40.7	39.0	39.1	55.4	68.6	32.7	65.1	59.0	34.9	37.0	33.3	40.6
4th quarter	41.6	39.8	39.8	56.5	69.8	33.6	67.2	60.0	35.5	37.9	33.8	41.4
1979												
1st quarter	42.3	40.5	40.3	57.7	71.3	34.2	69.2	62.4	36.2	38.5	34.6	42.2
2nd quarter	43.4	41.6	41.2	59.2	72.9	35.4	72.0	65.6	37.0	39.1	35.4	43.2
3rd quarter	44.3	42.7	41.9	60.7	74.4	36.5	73.7	70.5	38.0	39.9	36.6	44.3
4th quarter	45.1	43.7	42.8	61.9	75.8	37.4	75.1	75.2	39.1	41.5	37.3	45.4
1980												
1st quarter	46.1	45.0	43.8	63.3	77.5	38.4	77.3	81.5	40.0	42.3	38.4	46.7
2nd quarter	47.2	46.1	44.8	64.8	79.3	39.3	78.3	84.4	41.1	43.2	39.5	47.8
3rd quarter	48.2	47.2	45.8	66.2	81.0	40.2	80.5	86.8	42.0	43.9	40.6	48.9
4th quarter	49.6	48.3	46.9	67.6	82.7	41.2	83.3	88.3	43.5	46.2	41.6	50.2
1981												
1st quarter	50.9	49.6	48.0	69.4	85.0	42.1	85.3	90.6	44.6	47.0	42.9	51.5
2nd quarter	51.8	50.4	48.9	71.0	87.1	42.8	85.7	91.1	45.4	47.7	43.8	52.5
3rd quarter	52.8	51.2	49.8	72.2	88.7	43.3	85.8	88.7	46.0	48.2	44.3	53.3
4th quarter	53.7	52.0	50.7	73.6	90.5	44.0	86.1	88.9	47.0	49.8	45.0	54.2
1982												
1st quarter	54.4	52.7	51.4	74.6	91.7	44.6	86.6	88.6	47.8	50.5	45.7	54.9
2nd quarter	55.1	53.2	52.1	75.5	92.7	45.3	86.6	87.1	48.5	51.2	46.5	55.5
3rd quarter	55.9	54.0	52.9	75.9	93.1	45.6	85.9	86.1	49.1	51.6	47.2	56.2
4th quarter	56.5	54.6	53.6	76.0	93.2	45.9	85.4	85.4	49.8	52.5	47.8	56.8
1983												
1st quarter	56.9	55.1	54.4	75.6	92.5	46.1	85.8	83.6	50.1	52.8	48.1	57.2
2nd quarter	57.4	55.6	54.8	75.3	91.9	46.2	86.1	83.6	50.5	53.1	48.6	57.6
3rd quarter	57.9	56.3	55.6	75.2	91.6	46.4	86.6	83.8	51.0	53.5	49.1	58.1
4th quarter	58.4	56.7	56.1	75.3	91.4	46.8	87.4	83.2	51.3	53.6	49.6	58.4
1984												
1st quarter	59.1	57.3	56.6	75.4	91.3	47.1	87.5	83.5	52.6	55.7	50.3	59.2
2nd quarter	59.6	57.9	57.3	75.7	91.6	47.5	88.1	83.9	53.2	56.2	50.8	59.7
3rd quarter	60.1	58.3	57.8	75.9	91.7	47.9	87.2	82.4	53.6	56.7	51.3	60.1
4th quarter	60.5	58.7	58.3	76.1	91.8	48.3	86.3	81.4	53.9	56.8	51.7	60.4
1985												
1st quarter	61.2	59.3	59.0	76.4	92.0	48.6	85.3	79.5	54.6	57.6	52.3	61.0
2nd quarter	61.5	59.7	59.4	76.5	92.1	48.7	85.0	79.8	54.8	57.5	52.8	61.4
3rd quarter	61.8	60.1	59.9	76.8	92.4	49.0	84.1	79.8	55.0	57.4	53.2	61.7
4th quarter	62.1	60.6	60.4	77.3	92.8	49.6	84.0	81.3	55.5	58.0	53.7	62.2
1986												
1st quarter	62.5	61.0	61.1	77.7	93.0	50.2	83.5	81.5	55.6	57.9	53.9	62.5
2nd quarter	62.8	61.1	61.6	78.3	93.6	50.6	83.2	78.9	55.7	57.9	54.2	62.6
3rd quarter	63.2	61.5	62.2	78.9	94.3	51.3	82.9	79.5	56.0	58.0	54.7	63.1
4th quarter	63.6	62.0	62.8	79.5	94.7	51.9	83.7	80.5	56.5	58.1	55.5	63.6
1987												
1st quarter	64.1	62.7	63.4	79.7	94.7	52.4	84.0	82.6	57.0	58.5	56.0	64.2
2nd quarter	64.5	63.3	64.0	79.8	94.6	52.8	85.2	84.7	57.4	58.6	56.6	64.6
3rd quarter	65.0	63.9	64.6	80.0	94.5	53.3	85.5	85.6	57.8	58.8	57.2	65.2
4th quarter	65.5	64.5	65.2	80.6	95.2	53.8	87.0	86.9	58.0	58.8	57.6	65.7
1988												
1st quarter	66.0	65.0	65.9	81.3	96.1	54.2	88.0	88.2	58.5	59.5	57.9	66.2
2nd quarter	66.6	65.7	66.7	81.8	96.5	54.7	89.8	89.7	59.0	59.9	58.4	66.9
3rd quarter	67.4	66.5	67.5	82.2	96.9	55.1	90.9	88.7	59.2	60.0	58.8	67.5
4th quarter	68.0	67.2	68.2	83.0	97.9	55.6	90.8	89.4	59.6	60.2	59.3	68.1
1989												
1st quarter	68.7	68.0	69.0	83.4	98.3	56.0	91.6	90.9	60.3	61.2	59.8	68.8
2nd quarter	69.3	68.9	69.6	83.9	98.6	56.7	91.8	91.9	60.8	61.4	60.4	69.6
3rd quarter	69.8	69.3	70.1	84.3	99.1	56.9	91.2	90.3	61.1	61.8	60.8	70.0
4th quarter	70.3	69.8	70.7	84.7	99.6	57.2	90.9	90.8	61.5	61.7	61.5	70.5
1990												
1st quarter	71.1	70.9	71.6	85.2	100.0	57.7	91.0	92.2	62.4	62.6	62.4	71.4
2nd quarter	71.9	71.6	72.5	85.5	100.3	57.9	91.3	90.6	63.0	63.2	63.0	72.1
3rd quarter	72.6	72.6	73.3	86.0	101.0	58.2	92.2	93.2	63.6	63.6	63.8	72.9
4th quarter	73.2	73.5	73.9	86.5	101.8	58.3	93.5	98.4	64.6	64.7	64.7	73.8
1991												
1st quarter	74.0	74.0	74.7	87.2	102.7	58.4	93.8	95.3	65.1	65.6	65.0	74.3
2nd quarter	74.5	74.4	75.3	87.2	102.5	58.7	93.3	92.7	65.3	65.7	65.2	74.6
3rd quarter	75.1	75.0	76.0	87.1	102.2	59.1	92.8	91.3	65.8	66.3	65.6	75.1
4th quarter	75.5	75.6	76.7	86.8	101.9	58.9	92.9	91.8	66.2	66.7	65.9	75.6

Table 19-5. Chain-Type Price Indexes for Gross Domestic Product and Domestic Purchases—*Continued*

(Index numbers, 2005 = 100.)   **NIPA Tables 1.1.4, 1.6.4, 2.3.4**

Year and quarter	Gross domestic product, total	Personal consumption expenditures		Private fixed investment			Exports and imports of goods and services		Government consumption expenditures and gross investment			Gross domestic purchases
		Total	Excluding food and energy	Total	Nonresidential	Residential	Exports	Imports	Total	Federal	State and local	
1992												
1st quarter	75.9	76.2	77.4	86.7	101.8	58.7	92.8	92.2	66.6	67.5	66.1	76.1
2nd quarter	76.4	76.7	78.0	86.7	101.5	59.2	92.9	92.5	67.1	68.0	66.7	76.5
3rd quarter	76.7	77.2	78.5	86.9	101.4	59.6	92.9	93.7	67.6	68.5	67.1	77.0
4th quarter	77.1	77.7	79.0	87.1	101.2	60.4	92.7	93.0	67.8	68.4	67.5	77.4
1993												
1st quarter	77.6	78.1	79.4	87.5	101.5	61.1	92.7	92.4	68.3	69.0	68.0	77.8
2nd quarter	78.0	78.5	79.9	87.8	101.6	61.7	92.9	92.7	68.8	69.5	68.4	78.2
3rd quarter	78.4	78.8	80.3	88.0	101.5	62.2	92.8	91.9	69.2	70.2	68.6	78.5
4th quarter	78.8	79.2	80.7	88.1	101.5	62.5	92.8	91.5	69.5	70.6	69.0	78.9
1994												
1st quarter	79.3	79.5	81.1	88.6	101.9	63.2	93.2	91.5	70.1	71.0	69.6	79.3
2nd quarter	79.6	79.9	81.6	88.9	102.1	63.6	93.5	92.4	70.6	71.8	70.0	79.7
3rd quarter	80.1	80.6	82.1	89.2	102.2	64.3	94.0	93.9	71.0	71.8	70.6	80.2
4th quarter	80.5	81.0	82.6	89.4	102.0	65.1	94.6	94.3	71.6	72.3	71.2	80.6
1995												
1st quarter	81.0	81.4	83.0	89.8	102.1	65.9	95.7	95.1	72.2	73.2	71.6	81.1
2nd quarter	81.3	81.9	83.5	90.1	102.4	66.3	96.4	96.4	72.5	73.3	72.2	81.5
3rd quarter	81.7	82.2	83.9	90.2	102.4	66.5	96.2	95.8	72.8	73.5	72.5	81.8
4th quarter	82.1	82.6	84.4	90.2	102.2	66.9	95.7	95.0	73.5	74.9	72.7	82.2
1996												
1st quarter	82.6	83.1	84.7	89.9	101.6	67.1	95.5	94.7	74.3	76.0	73.4	82.6
2nd quarter	82.9	83.6	85.1	89.6	101.0	67.4	95.2	94.3	74.1	75.3	73.5	82.9
3rd quarter	83.3	84.0	85.5	89.9	101.0	68.2	94.5	93.3	74.5	75.6	73.9	83.3
4th quarter	83.7	84.6	86.0	89.8	100.7	68.5	93.6	93.3	75.0	76.1	74.4	83.8
1997												
1st quarter	84.1	85.0	86.4	89.7	100.3	68.9	93.4	92.5	75.5	76.8	74.8	84.1
2nd quarter	84.5	85.3	86.9	89.6	99.9	69.2	93.3	90.6	75.7	76.9	75.0	84.3
3rd quarter	84.7	85.5	87.1	89.6	99.7	69.8	93.1	90.0	75.9	77.0	75.3	84.5
4th quarter	85.0	85.8	87.5	89.5	99.2	70.3	92.7	89.3	76.4	77.4	75.8	84.7
1998												
1st quarter	85.1	85.8	87.7	89.0	98.4	70.5	91.8	87.1	76.4	77.7	75.8	84.7
2nd quarter	85.3	86.0	88.1	88.7	97.8	71.0	91.3	86.0	76.6	77.8	76.0	84.8
3rd quarter	85.7	86.3	88.4	88.7	97.3	71.7	90.6	84.9	77.0	78.0	76.5	85.1
4th quarter	85.9	86.6	88.7	88.6	96.9	72.4	90.3	84.9	77.4	78.2	77.0	85.3
1999												
1st quarter	86.3	86.9	89.1	88.7	96.7	73.1	90.1	84.7	78.2	79.2	77.7	85.6
2nd quarter	86.6	87.4	89.4	88.7	96.3	73.9	90.2	85.7	79.0	79.6	78.6	86.1
3rd quarter	86.9	87.8	89.7	88.6	95.9	74.5	90.4	86.7	79.7	80.1	79.5	86.5
4th quarter	87.3	88.3	90.1	88.7	95.8	75.1	90.9	87.9	80.4	80.6	80.3	87.0
2000												
1st quarter	87.9	89.1	90.6	89.3	96.0	76.4	91.4	89.5	81.6	82.1	81.3	87.8
2nd quarter	88.4	89.5	90.9	89.6	96.1	77.1	92.0	89.5	82.0	81.8	82.0	88.2
3rd quarter	88.9	90.0	91.3	90.0	96.4	77.7	92.2	90.2	82.9	82.9	82.8	88.7
4th quarter	89.4	90.5	91.7	90.2	96.4	78.4	92.4	90.6	83.6	83.3	83.8	89.2
2001												
1st quarter	90.0	91.1	92.3	90.1	95.9	79.4	92.4	90.2	84.3	83.7	84.5	89.7
2nd quarter	90.6	91.6	92.6	90.4	95.9	80.4	92.0	88.5	84.7	83.9	85.0	90.1
3rd quarter	90.9	91.6	92.8	90.8	95.9	81.8	91.5	87.1	85.0	84.4	85.3	90.3
4th quarter	91.1	91.6	93.3	90.8	95.5	82.3	90.7	85.2	85.2	84.9	85.3	90.3
2002												
1st quarter	91.5	91.9	93.6	90.7	95.5	82.2	90.5	85.0	86.1	86.9	85.6	90.6
2nd quarter	91.9	92.6	94.2	90.7	95.3	82.6	91.0	86.8	86.6	87.1	86.4	91.2
3rd quarter	92.3	93.0	94.6	90.8	95.1	82.9	91.7	87.4	87.2	87.1	87.1	91.6
4th quarter	92.8	93.5	95.0	91.5	95.5	84.3	91.9	87.9	88.1	88.1	88.1	92.2
2003												
1st quarter	93.5	94.2	95.2	92.1	95.4	86.2	92.8	90.4	90.1	90.6	89.8	93.1
2nd quarter	93.8	94.2	95.6	91.9	95.1	86.3	93.0	89.1	90.4	90.9	90.1	93.2
3rd quarter	94.3	94.8	96.0	92.2	95.2	86.8	93.2	89.5	90.8	91.1	90.7	93.7
4th quarter	94.8	95.3	96.4	93.0	95.6	88.5	93.9	90.1	91.3	91.5	91.2	94.2
2004												
1st quarter	95.6	96.1	97.0	94.0	95.9	90.5	95.1	92.1	92.8	94.0	92.1	95.2
2nd quarter	96.4	96.8	97.6	95.1	96.6	92.5	96.3	93.4	93.9	95.2	93.1	96.0
3rd quarter	97.1	97.4	98.1	96.1	97.1	94.4	96.8	94.4	95.0	95.8	94.6	96.8
4th quarter	97.9	98.2	98.5	97.0	97.7	95.8	97.9	96.7	96.4	96.4	96.4	97.7
2005												
1st quarter	98.8	98.8	99.2	98.1	98.8	97.0	98.9	97.5	98.2	99.2	97.6	98.6
2nd quarter	99.4	99.4	99.8	99.2	99.6	98.6	99.6	98.8	99.2	99.7	99.0	99.3
3rd quarter	100.5	100.5	100.2	100.6	100.2	101.2	100.3	100.9	100.7	100.4	100.8	100.5
4th quarter	101.3	101.4	100.8	102.0	101.4	103.1	101.1	102.8	101.9	100.7	102.6	101.6
2006												
1st quarter	102.1	101.8	101.3	103.2	102.3	104.9	101.8	103.2	103.2	103.1	103.3	102.3
2nd quarter	103.0	102.6	102.1	104.1	103.1	105.9	103.1	104.3	104.6	104.2	104.9	103.2
3rd quarter	103.8	103.3	102.6	104.7	103.9	106.3	104.4	105.1	105.4	104.5	106.0	103.9
4th quarter	104.2	103.3	103.2	105.7	104.9	107.2	104.4	103.9	106.1	104.6	106.9	104.2

Table 19-6. Personal Income and Its Disposition

(Billions of current dollars, except as noted; quarterly data are at seasonally adjusted annual rates.)   **NIPA Table 2.1**

| Year and quarter | Personal income | | | | | | | Less: Personal current taxes | Equals: Disposable personal income | Less: Personal outlays | Equals: Personal saving | | Billions of chained (2005) dollars | |
	Total	Compensation of employees, received	Proprietors' income with IVA and CCAdj	Rental income of persons with CCAdj	Personal income receipts on assets	Personal current transfer receipts	Less: Contributions for government social insurance, domestic				Billions of dollars	Percent of disposable personal income	Personal income excluding current transfers	Disposable personal income
1946	178.6	119.6	35.6	7.1	12.3	10.6	6.6	17.2	161.4	145.9	15.5	9.6	1 311.4	1 259.4
1947	191.0	130.1	34.5	7.2	13.9	10.8	5.6	19.8	171.2	163.8	7.4	4.3	1 275.4	1 211.9
1948	209.8	141.9	39.3	7.9	15.1	10.3	4.6	19.2	190.6	177.3	13.4	7.0	1 337.0	1 277.0
1949	207.1	141.9	34.7	8.2	16.0	11.2	4.9	16.7	190.4	180.9	9.5	5.0	1 322.5	1 285.2
1947														
1st quarter	187.5	127.2	36.6	6.9	13.4	9.7	6.3	19.2	168.3	158.1	10.2	6.1	1 287.0	1 218.6
2nd quarter	185.5	128.7	32.3	7.1	13.8	9.6	6.0	19.5	166.1	161.9	4.2	2.5	1 263.6	1 192.6
3rd quarter	193.6	130.0	33.8	7.3	14.2	13.5	5.2	19.7	173.8	165.6	8.3	4.8	1 269.7	1 225.6
4th quarter	196.9	134.3	35.2	7.5	14.2	10.5	4.8	20.8	176.1	169.7	6.4	3.6	1 282.0	1 211.3
1948														
1st quarter	202.1	137.8	36.0	7.6	14.9	10.7	4.8	21.2	180.9	172.7	8.3	4.6	1 302.6	1 231.1
2nd quarter	208.1	139.4	40.4	7.8	14.7	10.4	4.6	18.9	189.2	176.5	12.7	6.7	1 331.3	1 274.0
3rd quarter	214.2	144.6	40.9	7.9	15.2	10.1	4.6	18.2	195.9	179.5	16.5	8.4	1 353.3	1 299.3
4th quarter	214.3	145.8	39.6	7.9	15.6	9.8	4.5	18.4	195.9	180.4	15.5	7.9	1 360.6	1 302.9
1949														
1st quarter	208.2	143.9	35.4	7.8	15.7	10.5	5.2	17.8	190.4	179.2	11.1	5.8	1 325.4	1 276.2
2nd quarter	206.8	142.2	34.8	7.9	15.9	11.0	5.1	17.0	189.8	181.0	8.8	4.7	1 320.3	1 280.1
3rd quarter	206.1	141.0	34.2	8.2	16.0	11.5	4.8	16.3	189.8	180.4	9.4	5.0	1 320.0	1 287.7
4th quarter	206.8	140.5	34.2	8.4	16.5	11.8	4.5	15.8	191.0	183.0	8.0	4.2	1 324.4	1 297.0
1950														
1st quarter	221.5	144.6	35.6	8.7	17.7	20.2	5.3	16.6	204.9	185.7	19.1	9.3	1 369.0	1 393.4
2nd quarter	222.3	150.6	36.3	9.0	18.0	13.8	5.3	17.6	204.7	189.7	15.0	7.3	1 411.7	1 385.9
3rd quarter	231.1	159.0	38.7	9.1	19.0	10.8	5.5	18.9	212.2	203.6	8.7	4.1	1 461.2	1 407.4
4th quarter	240.5	166.8	39.4	9.4	19.6	11.1	5.8	22.5	218.0	201.1	16.9	7.8	1 494.8	1 420.3
1951														
1st quarter	249.5	174.8	42.0	9.6	18.6	11.1	6.6	24.4	225.1	212.4	12.7	5.6	1 505.1	1 420.9
2nd quarter	256.8	180.7	42.4	9.9	19.1	11.4	6.7	26.4	230.4	208.1	22.3	9.7	1 536.7	1 443.0
3rd quarter	260.0	183.0	42.6	10.2	19.2	11.6	6.6	27.8	232.2	210.8	21.4	9.2	1 553.6	1 452.3
4th quarter	265.3	187.0	43.5	10.5	19.5	11.6	6.7	29.6	235.7	214.8	20.9	8.9	1 566.5	1 454.9
1952														
1st quarter	267.4	191.3	41.8	10.7	19.1	11.4	6.9	30.9	236.5	216.2	20.3	8.6	1 573.6	1 453.9
2nd quarter	271.3	192.7	43.1	11.0	19.8	11.5	6.8	31.8	239.4	220.5	19.0	7.9	1 596.9	1 472.2
3rd quarter	278.1	196.6	44.8	11.3	20.0	12.3	6.9	32.3	245.8	223.2	22.6	9.2	1 623.6	1 501.4
4th quarter	284.1	204.1	42.6	11.6	20.5	12.3	7.1	33.1	251.1	231.5	19.5	7.8	1 657.3	1 530.9
1953														
1st quarter	288.8	208.0	43.0	11.9	20.6	12.4	7.1	33.4	255.4	235.3	20.1	7.9	1 679.4	1 551.5
2nd quarter	292.8	211.4	42.3	12.2	21.7	12.3	7.1	33.4	259.3	237.3	22.0	8.5	1 701.0	1 572.9
3rd quarter	292.9	211.6	41.5	12.5	21.9	12.5	7.2	33.2	259.7	238.2	21.5	8.3	1 691.3	1 566.6
4th quarter	292.1	210.1	41.3	12.8	22.1	12.9	7.1	32.9	259.2	237.7	21.5	8.3	1 677.0	1 556.7
1954														
1st quarter	292.2	208.1	42.6	13.1	23.0	13.5	8.1	30.2	262.0	239.7	22.3	8.5	1 665.4	1 565.6
2nd quarter	291.8	207.7	42.0	13.3	22.7	14.1	8.0	30.0	261.8	242.5	19.3	7.4	1 661.5	1 566.5
3rd quarter	293.9	208.3	42.3	13.5	23.4	14.5	8.1	30.0	263.9	245.2	18.7	7.1	1 677.3	1 584.1
4th quarter	299.3	212.6	42.2	13.6	23.9	15.2	8.1	30.5	268.9	249.9	19.0	7.1	1 707.5	1 615.6
1955														
1st quarter	305.1	216.9	43.4	13.7	24.7	15.3	8.9	31.4	273.7	256.3	17.4	6.4	1 736.2	1 639.6
2nd quarter	313.0	223.1	44.5	13.7	25.2	15.6	9.0	32.4	280.6	261.7	19.0	6.8	1 779.7	1 679.1
3rd quarter	320.4	229.1	44.7	13.8	26.1	15.9	9.2	33.4	287.0	266.1	20.9	7.3	1 815.0	1 710.7
4th quarter	325.4	233.6	44.5	13.9	26.7	16.0	9.3	34.2	291.2	270.3	20.9	7.2	1 839.2	1 730.6
1956														
1st quarter	330.8	238.0	44.9	14.0	27.4	16.3	9.9	35.4	295.4	272.1	23.3	7.9	1 861.1	1 748.4
2nd quarter	336.6	242.6	45.5	14.0	27.9	16.6	10.0	36.2	300.3	274.9	25.4	8.5	1 881.3	1 765.7
3rd quarter	341.5	245.7	46.2	14.1	28.3	17.1	10.0	36.9	304.6	278.2	26.3	8.6	1 888.7	1 773.2
4th quarter	349.1	251.6	46.9	14.2	29.2	17.3	10.1	37.9	311.2	283.7	27.5	8.9	1 920.3	1 801.5
1957														
1st quarter	353.1	255.3	46.9	14.3	29.8	18.2	11.4	38.6	314.6	288.3	26.3	8.4	1 921.4	1 804.6
2nd quarter	357.6	257.0	47.8	14.4	30.5	19.4	11.4	39.0	318.7	290.6	28.0	8.8	1 928.0	1 816.7
3rd quarter	362.0	259.7	48.7	14.5	31.0	19.6	11.5	39.2	322.8	295.3	27.5	8.5	1 935.9	1 825.3
4th quarter	361.4	258.1	47.9	14.7	31.1	20.8	11.3	38.8	322.6	297.0	25.6	7.9	1 916.1	1 814.9
1958														
1st quarter	362.0	254.6	50.3	15.0	31.3	22.1	11.3	38.2	323.8	296.6	27.2	8.4	1 888.9	1 799.6
2nd quarter	364.2	254.2	50.4	15.2	31.8	23.9	11.3	37.7	326.5	299.4	27.1	8.3	1 887.9	1 811.5
3rd quarter	372.5	262.2	50.1	15.3	32.1	24.2	11.4	38.9	333.5	304.4	29.1	8.7	1 930.6	1 848.8
4th quarter	377.0	267.2	50.0	15.4	32.2	23.7	11.5	39.4	337.6	308.3	29.3	8.7	1 959.4	1 872.2
1959														
1st quarter	383.4	274.5	50.2	15.4	33.0	24.0	13.7	40.8	342.6	316.0	26.7	7.8	1 979.1	1 886.9
2nd quarter	392.0	281.6	50.4	15.9	34.0	23.9	13.9	42.0	350.0	322.2	27.8	7.9	2 018.7	1 919.7
3rd quarter	394.1	282.3	50.2	16.3	35.1	24.2	13.9	42.7	351.5	327.6	23.8	6.8	2 017.2	1 916.4
4th quarter	399.9	285.5	50.6	16.5	36.3	24.8	13.9	43.7	356.1	330.0	26.1	7.3	2 033.8	1 931.3
1960														
1st quarter	406.4	294.0	50.0	16.7	37.4	24.6	16.4	45.3	361.1	333.7	27.4	7.6	2 067.3	1 955.5
2nd quarter	411.0	296.9	50.8	16.9	37.5	25.3	16.5	46.0	364.9	339.8	25.2	6.9	2 077.9	1 966.1
3rd quarter	413.2	297.6	50.9	17.0	38.1	26.0	16.5	46.5	366.7	339.9	26.7	7.3	2 077.7	1 967.8
4th quarter	414.5	297.1	51.1	17.2	38.5	27.0	16.4	46.4	368.1	342.0	26.1	7.1	2 070.4	1 966.6
1961														
1st quarter	418.6	298.0	52.4	17.4	38.7	28.8	16.7	46.5	372.1	342.6	29.5	7.9	2 078.8	1 984.5
2nd quarter	424.6	302.2	52.6	17.6	39.5	29.7	16.9	46.9	377.7	347.6	30.1	8.0	2 106.4	2 014.4
3rd quarter	431.6	307.2	53.3	17.8	40.5	29.9	17.1	47.4	384.2	350.6	33.7	8.8	2 135.0	2 041.9
4th quarter	440.4	313.8	54.5	18.1	41.9	29.4	17.3	48.1	392.2	358.0	34.3	8.7	2 181.5	2 082.0

Table 19-6. Personal Income and Its Disposition—*Continued*

(Billions of current dollars, except as noted; quarterly data are at seasonally adjusted annual rates.)   **NIPA Table 2.1**

| Year and quarter | Personal income | | | | | | | Less: Personal current taxes | Equals: Disposable personal income | Less: Personal outlays | Equals: Personal saving | | Billions of chained (2005) dollars | |
	Total	Compensation of employees, received	Proprietors' income with IVA and CCAdj	Rental income of persons with CCAdj	Personal income receipts on assets	Personal current transfer receipts	Less: Contributions for government social insurance, domestic				Billions of dollars	Percent of disposable personal income	Personal income excluding current transfers	Disposable personal income
1962														
1st quarter	447.1	320.4	55.3	18.3	42.0	30.0	18.9	49.4	397.7	363.3	34.4	8.6	2 204.2	2 101.7
2nd quarter ...	454.5	326.4	55.1	18.5	43.6	30.0	19.1	50.9	403.5	369.2	34.4	8.5	2 235.5	2 125.2
3rd quarter ...	459.1	329.2	55.1	18.7	44.9	30.4	19.2	52.3	406.8	373.3	33.5	8.2	2 252.0	2 137.0
4th quarter ...	465.0	332.6	55.7	18.9	45.9	31.2	19.3	53.6	411.4	379.8	31.6	7.7	2 272.0	2 154.6
1963														
1st quarter	470.1	337.5	56.0	19.1	46.1	32.6	21.3	54.1	416.0	383.6	32.4	7.8	2 284.5	2 172.5
2nd quarter ...	474.8	342.4	55.9	19.3	47.1	31.7	21.5	54.3	420.5	388.0	32.5	7.7	2 311.1	2 193.1
3rd quarter ...	481.9	347.4	56.4	19.5	48.4	32.0	21.8	54.6	427.3	395.4	31.9	7.5	2 335.3	2 217.9
4th quarter ...	491.2	353.6	57.8	19.4	49.9	32.5	22.0	55.2	436.0	400.3	35.7	8.2	2 371.8	2 254.6
1964														
1st quarter	500.6	360.0	58.1	19.4	51.5	33.6	22.0	53.8	446.8	410.1	36.7	8.2	2 403.5	2 299.6
2nd quarter ...	509.8	367.4	59.0	19.4	53.1	33.2	22.3	49.7	460.0	418.4	41.6	9.0	2 446.9	2 362.1
3rd quarter ...	519.1	374.6	59.6	19.5	54.6	33.5	22.5	51.6	467.6	427.7	39.8	8.5	2 485.2	2 392.7
4th quarter ...	527.8	380.8	60.7	19.4	55.8	33.7	22.7	53.2	474.6	430.5	44.0	9.3	2 519.8	2 420.4
1965														
1st quarter	538.4	387.3	62.2	19.7	57.1	35.0	22.9	57.0	481.4	441.3	40.1	8.3	2 558.9	2 447.4
2nd quarter ...	547.6	394.1	63.4	19.9	58.8	34.6	23.2	58.4	489.2	448.8	40.4	8.3	2 594.8	2 474.5
3rd quarter ...	561.5	402.3	64.2	20.1	60.3	38.1	23.6	57.0	504.5	458.2	46.3	9.2	2 637.7	2 542.6
4th quarter ...	574.6	414.3	65.9	20.1	61.4	36.9	24.0	58.3	516.3	472.3	44.0	8.5	2 701.5	2 594.1
1966														
1st quarter	586.7	426.7	69.4	20.5	62.6	37.8	30.4	61.5	525.2	482.9	42.3	8.1	2 736.5	2 618.4
2nd quarter ...	596.3	437.8	67.5	20.4	63.6	37.9	30.8	65.6	530.8	488.3	42.5	8.0	2 761.6	2 624.7
3rd quarter ...	609.5	449.0	67.7	20.6	64.5	39.6	31.9	67.9	541.6	497.7	43.9	8.1	2 796.4	2 657.8
4th quarter ...	622.6	457.2	68.4	20.6	65.5	43.1	32.2	70.6	552.1	503.7	48.4	8.8	2 821.8	2 688.2
1967														
1st quarter	633.1	463.3	69.1	20.8	67.5	46.1	33.6	71.2	562.0	508.3	53.7	9.6	2 850.2	2 728.4
2nd quarter ...	640.2	469.0	68.9	20.9	68.7	47.2	34.6	70.9	569.2	517.9	51.3	9.0	2 865.4	2 750.8
3rd quarter ...	653.8	478.7	71.0	21.0	69.8	48.7	35.2	73.8	580.0	525.0	55.0	9.5	2 897.4	2 777.1
4th quarter ...	665.1	489.7	70.4	20.9	70.1	50.0	36.0	75.9	589.2	532.6	56.6	9.6	2 920.1	2 797.4
1968														
1st quarter	684.3	504.5	72.1	20.6	72.4	52.4	37.6	78.6	605.8	550.9	54.9	9.1	2 969.0	2 846.2
2nd quarter ...	703.8	517.6	73.4	20.6	74.7	55.9	38.4	81.7	622.1	565.1	57.0	9.2	3 013.3	2 893.5
3rd quarter ...	721.7	531.4	75.3	20.7	76.0	57.3	39.1	91.9	629.8	581.8	48.0	7.6	3 058.2	2 899.3
4th quarter ...	736.9	543.8	76.0	20.6	77.6	58.7	39.7	95.9	641.0	591.1	49.9	7.8	3 087.6	2 918.4
1969														
1st quarter	751.0	555.9	76.3	20.8	80.5	60.4	42.9	102.6	648.4	603.8	44.6	6.9	3 113.5	2 923.4
2nd quarter ...	769.1	569.8	77.6	20.9	83.0	61.5	43.7	105.7	663.4	615.9	47.5	7.2	3 149.3	2 952.9
3rd quarter ...	789.4	586.6	78.2	21.0	85.3	62.9	44.6	104.1	685.2	626.6	58.6	8.6	3 194.2	3 012.9
4th quarter ...	803.9	598.2	78.0	20.9	87.7	64.3	45.3	105.6	698.2	639.1	59.1	8.5	3 214.3	3 034.9
1970														
1st quarter ...	814.4	606.1	77.6	20.9	89.6	66.1	46.0	104.6	709.8	650.5	59.3	8.4	3 215.4	3 050.1
2nd quarter ...	835.8	616.3	77.1	20.6	91.9	76.1	46.3	105.5	730.3	660.8	69.5	9.5	3 228.6	3 103.5
3rd quarter ...	848.0	622.5	79.2	21.2	95.4	76.3	46.7	100.7	747.4	673.0	74.4	9.9	3 247.7	3 145.4
4th quarter ...	856.1	623.9	79.9	21.5	97.1	80.1	46.5	101.5	754.6	680.0	74.6	9.9	3 224.1	3 135.1
1971														
1st quarter	875.2	641.6	81.1	21.5	99.5	82.0	50.5	98.3	776.8	699.4	77.4	10.0	3 264.4	3 197.3
2nd quarter ...	898.2	653.5	83.7	22.0	100.3	89.6	51.0	100.7	797.4	713.9	83.5	10.5	3 290.6	3 245.3
3rd quarter ...	911.5	663.5	85.3	22.4	101.7	89.6	51.3	102.3	808.8	726.9	81.9	10.1	3 311.1	3 259.7
4th quarter ...	927.9	674.8	88.6	22.8	102.4	91.3	51.9	105.5	822.5	743.7	78.8	9.6	3 351.1	3 294.2
1972														
1st quarter	956.1	702.6	88.7	23.5	105.2	94.3	58.1	119.8	836.4	761.5	74.9	9.0	3 415.8	3 314.9
2nd quarter ...	972.5	716.2	92.2	20.5	107.6	94.9	58.8	123.4	849.1	780.6	68.5	8.1	3 458.3	3 346.1
3rd quarter ...	998.4	729.9	96.5	24.3	111.1	96.0	59.5	124.3	874.1	799.5	74.7	8.5	3 524.9	3 414.6
4th quarter ...	1 043.5	751.9	106.7	24.3	114.6	106.4	60.4	127.1	916.4	824.6	91.8	10.0	3 630.8	3 550.5
1973														
1st quarter	1 064.4	781.6	105.9	24.2	117.2	109.1	73.6	126.4	938.0	849.5	88.5	9.4	3 657.1	3 590.7
2nd quarter ...	1 094.8	801.1	111.7	24.1	121.1	111.5	74.7	129.2	965.6	865.6	100.0	10.4	3 692.7	3 626.2
3rd quarter ...	1 122.3	819.9	114.4	23.1	127.6	113.3	76.1	134.1	988.2	884.5	103.7	10.5	3 721.0	3 644.4
4th quarter ...	1 160.7	842.5	122.5	24.1	132.6	116.5	77.6	140.0	1 020.8	901.2	119.5	11.7	3 773.8	3 688.9
1974														
1st quarter	1 177.8	860.7	116.2	24.4	137.7	121.9	83.1	142.8	1 035.0	918.3	116.7	11.3	3 705.7	3 632.3
2nd quarter ...	1 204.1	881.9	109.3	23.8	144.0	129.9	84.7	148.9	1 055.2	947.3	107.8	10.2	3 666.0	3 601.1
3rd quarter ...	1 241.9	904.6	113.3	24.1	149.1	137.1	86.4	154.9	1 087.0	976.9	110.1	10.1	3 671.5	3 612.4
4th quarter ...	1 267.1	915.7	115.1	23.9	154.7	144.3	86.6	157.6	1 109.6	987.5	122.1	11.0	3 639.1	3 596.0
1975														
1st quarter	1 283.9	919.4	113.5	23.7	159.0	155.9	87.6	158.0	1 125.9	1 015.0	110.9	9.8	3 588.6	3 581.9
2nd quarter ...	1 314.0	931.7	115.5	23.5	159.9	171.5	88.0	121.1	1 193.0	1 044.0	149.0	12.5	3 590.7	3 749.3
3rd quarter ...	1 351.7	957.6	122.5	23.3	163.1	174.8	89.8	152.8	1 198.8	1 078.5	120.3	10.0	3 630.8	3 698.6
4th quarter ...	1 389.9	987.5	126.9	22.9	166.7	177.6	91.8	158.5	1 231.3	1 107.7	123.6	10.0	3 678.1	3 736.0
1976														
1st quarter	1 425.4	1 022.3	127.6	22.6	170.4	181.4	98.9	162.1	1 263.3	1 141.2	122.1	9.7	3 733.1	3 791.0
2nd quarter ...	1 453.4	1 046.0	130.0	21.7	176.3	179.7	100.4	169.0	1 284.4	1 161.0	123.4	9.6	3 790.4	3 822.2
3rd quarter ...	1 491.4	1 070.7	133.8	21.9	180.8	186.4	102.2	175.8	1 315.7	1 190.8	124.9	9.5	3 825.6	3 856.7
4th quarter ...	1 528.4	1 098.0	137.5	22.0	186.2	188.5	103.8	182.4	1 346.1	1 225.2	120.9	9.0	3 866.8	3 884.4

Table 19-6. Personal Income and Its Disposition—*Continued*

(Billions of current dollars, except as noted; quarterly data are at seasonally adjusted annual rates.)   NIPA Table 2.1

Year and quarter	Personal income							Less: Personal current taxes	Equals: Disposable personal income	Less: Personal outlays	Equals: Personal saving		Billions of chained (2005) dollars	
	Total	Compensation of employees, received	Proprietors' income with IVA and CCAdj	Rental income of persons with CCAdj	Personal income receipts on assets	Personal current transfer receipts	Less: Contributions for government social insurance, domestic				Billions of dollars	Percent of disposable personal income	Personal income excluding current transfers	Disposable personal income
1977														
1st quarter	1 559.9	1 126.9	140.5	20.9	190.2	190.6	109.3	188.4	1 371.4	1 262.0	109.5	8.0	3 881.4	3 887.5
2nd quarter	1 606.1	1 164.3	141.9	19.9	201.0	191.1	112.1	195.3	1 410.8	1 291.0	119.8	8.5	3 943.7	3 931.8
3rd quarter	1 651.8	1 196.8	143.6	19.0	210.5	196.2	114.3	198.2	1 453.6	1 323.2	130.4	9.0	3 996.3	3 990.8
4th quarter	1 712.2	1 233.7	158.0	18.7	219.5	199.0	116.7	208.1	1 504.1	1 362.5	141.6	9.4	4 095.9	4 071.2
1978														
1st quarter	1 750.3	1 269.6	158.4	20.4	224.9	203.1	126.2	211.7	1 538.6	1 394.1	144.4	9.4	4 119.4	4 096.4
2nd quarter	1 811.1	1 317.8	168.1	19.8	230.6	204.9	130.1	222.8	1 588.2	1 453.4	134.9	8.5	4 190.2	4 143.4
3rd quarter	1 865.4	1 354.3	171.3	21.4	237.4	213.6	132.8	236.0	1 629.3	1 485.9	143.5	8.8	4 234.5	4 177.1
4th quarter	1 920.1	1 398.9	172.2	21.9	246.2	216.9	136.0	247.0	1 673.2	1 526.4	146.8	8.8	4 285.3	4 209.8
1979														
1st quarter	1 976.7	1 443.3	179.2	23.4	257.1	222.5	148.8	253.4	1 723.3	1 562.8	160.5	9.3	4 332.2	4 255.9
2nd quarter	2 019.7	1 476.1	179.3	21.1	267.0	227.1	150.9	261.8	1 757.9	1 604.5	153.4	8.7	4 309.3	4 226.1
3rd quarter	2 086.4	1 516.4	182.5	21.2	277.7	242.7	154.2	274.6	1 811.8	1 660.5	151.3	8.4	4 325.0	4 250.3
4th quarter	2 155.4	1 558.1	183.5	24.8	297.2	248.9	157.1	285.0	1 870.4	1 705.8	164.6	8.8	4 366.9	4 284.3
1980														
1st quarter	2 216.0	1 599.2	168.5	28.6	324.0	258.7	163.1	284.2	1 931.8	1 758.2	173.6	9.0	4 352.7	4 296.2
2nd quarter	2 242.9	1 621.3	162.2	24.1	334.6	263.9	163.2	291.5	1 951.4	1 760.1	191.3	9.8	4 296.1	4 236.1
3rd quarter	2 319.0	1 652.9	175.8	25.0	336.0	295.9	166.6	301.5	2 017.5	1 818.4	199.1	9.9	4 291.6	4 279.7
4th quarter	2 428.2	1 717.0	187.3	36.3	360.1	299.3	171.8	318.2	2 110.0	1 888.7	221.3	10.5	4 407.1	4 368.1
1981														
1st quarter	2 487.6	1 768.9	190.1	36.2	378.2	305.9	191.6	330.3	2 157.4	1 949.0	208.3	9.7	4 407.5	4 358.1
2nd quarter	2 535.7	1 801.9	177.9	35.1	405.6	309.3	194.1	342.1	2 193.6	1 983.1	210.5	9.6	4 423.7	4 358.6
3rd quarter	2 635.3	1 839.8	184.2	35.7	445.5	327.9	197.7	356.3	2 279.1	2 025.9	253.2	11.1	4 510.9	4 455.4
4th quarter	2 670.4	1 867.9	174.2	38.8	458.5	330.4	199.4	352.0	2 318.4	2 043.4	275.0	11.9	4 506.0	4 464.4
1982														
1st quarter	2 702.3	1 892.0	167.6	39.5	474.7	335.7	207.2	351.9	2 350.4	2 084.9	265.6	11.3	4 500.4	4 469.6
2nd quarter	2 748.5	1 911.1	173.0	36.2	491.7	344.9	208.4	359.1	2 389.4	2 114.8	274.6	11.5	4 527.6	4 500.8
3rd quarter	2 787.1	1 930.8	174.4	38.0	492.3	361.5	209.8	349.5	2 437.6	2 165.5	272.1	11.2	4 498.3	4 520.6
4th quarter	2 829.2	1 944.7	184.2	38.5	494.7	377.3	210.2	355.9	2 473.3	2 229.9	243.4	9.8	4 497.3	4 536.4
1983														
1st quarter	2 864.6	1 972.8	188.0	37.6	506.4	380.2	220.4	350.3	2 514.3	2 272.3	242.0	9.6	4 517.9	4 572.2
2nd quarter	2 914.9	2 011.8	188.2	37.8	514.4	386.4	223.6	359.0	2 555.9	2 339.3	216.7	8.5	4 556.2	4 605.5
3rd quarter	2 973.4	2 052.8	188.4	38.2	539.3	381.9	227.2	344.9	2 628.5	2 412.6	216.0	8.2	4 608.8	4 674.7
4th quarter	3 055.7	2 106.6	198.0	39.1	558.2	386.5	232.6	355.1	2 700.6	2 467.5	233.1	8.6	4 715.7	4 771.1
1984														
1st quarter	3 150.2	2 175.8	224.2	38.1	569.7	393.4	251.0	360.7	2 789.5	2 515.2	274.3	9.8	4 818.2	4 875.4
2nd quarter	3 235.1	2 225.5	234.9	36.7	596.0	397.8	255.8	369.9	2 865.1	2 576.8	288.3	10.1	4 911.2	4 959.4
3rd quarter	3 316.0	2 270.9	237.1	40.4	627.1	400.5	259.9	383.6	2 932.4	2 618.5	313.9	10.7	5 007.6	5 036.6
4th quarter	3 374.2	2 308.7	236.0	44.8	638.9	408.9	263.1	395.4	2 978.8	2 670.3	308.5	10.4	5 061.6	5 084.5
1985														
1st quarter	3 434.9	2 353.6	248.2	42.9	646.0	419.6	275.4	431.8	3 003.1	2 746.1	257.0	8.6	5 092.7	5 072.0
2nd quarter	3 473.6	2 390.2	244.6	41.7	653.7	422.1	278.8	388.1	3 085.6	2 795.2	290.3	9.4	5 115.6	5 172.7
3rd quarter	3 507.0	2 427.9	244.6	42.2	647.6	427.5	282.8	421.1	3 086.0	2 865.6	220.4	7.1	5 130.1	5 140.7
4th quarter	3 571.0	2 476.1	246.9	40.5	665.5	430.4	288.4	428.4	3 142.6	2 896.1	246.5	7.8	5 190.7	5 193.9
1986														
1st quarter	3 628.6	2 510.0	249.5	36.8	687.7	442.6	297.9	425.7	3 202.9	2 941.6	261.3	8.2	5 228.0	5 255.8
2nd quarter	3 670.2	2 533.3	257.2	35.6	694.4	448.5	300.7	428.8	3 241.4	2 974.5	266.8	8.2	5 283.2	5 315.5
3rd quarter	3 721.3	2 569.2	271.5	32.5	697.7	455.5	305.1	438.9	3 282.4	3 046.4	236.0	7.2	5 316.3	5 343.3
4th quarter	3 763.9	2 618.2	272.1	30.4	696.1	457.2	310.1	455.4	3 308.5	3 086.9	221.6	6.7	5 343.6	5 346.5
1987														
1st quarter	3 823.2	2 664.5	282.7	31.6	698.3	462.6	316.5	450.2	3 373.0	3 119.5	253.5	7.5	5 359.6	5 379.4
2nd quarter	3 877.0	2 706.2	289.7	30.5	703.3	467.6	320.2	511.1	3 365.9	3 186.1	179.7	5.3	5 389.9	5 321.0
3rd quarter	3 949.9	2 752.4	297.2	35.3	720.9	468.6	324.5	488.4	3 461.5	3 253.6	207.9	6.0	5 447.1	5 416.2
4th quarter	4 047.4	2 819.5	307.4	39.4	740.7	471.6	331.2	506.4	3 540.9	3 288.3	252.6	7.1	5 547.1	5 493.1
1988														
1st quarter	4 117.1	2 869.1	327.5	38.4	745.3	488.9	352.1	501.1	3 616.1	3 370.8	245.3	6.8	5 580.8	5 562.1
2nd quarter	4 186.8	2 932.3	333.8	36.9	750.4	492.5	359.1	496.8	3 690.0	3 431.8	258.1	7.0	5 620.8	5 614.3
3rd quarter	4 269.9	2 981.0	343.0	38.8	773.0	498.6	364.4	505.7	3 764.3	3 500.4	263.9	7.0	5 668.1	5 657.5
4th quarter	4 351.1	3 034.2	335.1	46.8	799.5	505.8	370.3	516.2	3 834.9	3 575.8	259.2	6.8	5 724.1	5 708.5
1989														
1st quarter	4 476.5	3 078.5	357.0	44.2	846.9	529.8	379.8	551.3	3 925.3	3 634.4	290.9	7.4	5 804.9	5 773.4
2nd quarter	4 525.9	3 107.8	348.4	43.5	871.8	537.2	382.8	565.0	3 960.8	3 700.3	260.5	6.6	5 790.2	5 749.8
3rd quarter	4 578.2	3 144.4	347.8	41.1	885.0	546.2	386.4	569.9	4 008.3	3 760.2	248.1	6.2	5 821.2	5 787.0
4th quarter	4 649.3	3 194.6	353.2	40.8	895.4	557.2	391.8	578.2	4 071.1	3 810.8	260.4	6.4	5 861.3	5 831.3
1990														
1st quarter	4 744.5	3 259.0	360.6	43.3	908.3	577.5	404.1	580.5	4 164.0	3 897.4	266.6	6.4	5 879.4	5 875.1
2nd quarter	4 829.3	3 317.4	364.3	48.2	919.3	588.5	408.3	592.6	4 236.7	3 952.1	284.6	6.7	5 919.6	5 913.9
3rd quarter	4 892.6	3 358.5	369.2	53.3	927.7	598.0	414.1	598.8	4 293.9	4 018.7	275.2	6.4	5 919.1	5 918.1
4th quarter	4 920.4	3 370.0	366.6	54.4	927.9	615.5	413.9	598.9	4 321.5	4 041.1	280.4	6.5	5 855.5	5 878.2
1991														
1st quarter	4 941.0	3 384.8	357.8	56.1	927.3	639.4	424.5	578.5	4 362.5	4 059.2	303.3	7.0	5 814.0	5 896.3
2nd quarter	5 005.8	3 419.8	365.2	58.1	931.3	659.1	427.7	583.7	4 422.1	4 114.3	307.8	7.0	5 839.7	5 941.1
3rd quarter	5 053.1	3 455.3	367.7	62.7	931.5	668.5	432.6	588.0	4 465.1	4 160.8	304.4	6.8	5 846.2	5 953.6
4th quarter	5 126.1	3 493.6	378.4	69.4	924.2	696.5	435.9	596.4	4 529.8	4 192.4	337.3	7.4	5 859.9	5 992.4

Table 19-6. Personal Income and Its Disposition—*Continued*

(Billions of current dollars, except as noted; quarterly data are at seasonally adjusted annual rates.)   **NIPA Table 2.1**

| Year and quarter | Personal income | | | | | | Less: Contributions for government social insurance, domestic | Less: Personal current taxes | Equals: Disposable personal income | Less: Personal outlays | Equals: Personal saving | | Billions of chained (2005) dollars | |
	Total	Compensation of employees, received	Proprietors' income with IVA and CCAdj	Rental income of persons with CCAdj	Personal income receipts on assets	Personal current transfer receipts					Billions of dollars	Percent of disposable personal income	Personal income excluding current transfers	Disposable personal income
1992														
1st quarter	5 220.7	3 561.1	396.4	71.6	915.5	724.7	448.7	586.5	4 634.1	4 290.6	343.5	7.4	5 901.5	6 082.9
2nd quarter	5 306.8	3 612.7	410.4	81.3	912.8	743.3	453.7	604.9	4 701.9	4 344.2	357.7	7.6	5 949.0	6 129.5
3rd quarter	5 370.7	3 656.6	420.9	89.3	906.3	755.3	457.8	613.9	4 756.8	4 423.8	333.0	7.0	5 977.4	6 160.6
4th quarter	5 490.9	3 758.4	431.9	96.3	904.3	759.7	459.6	636.9	4 854.1	4 496.0	358.1	7.4	6 090.1	6 248.2
1993														
1st quarter	5 420.5	3 660.1	435.8	105.5	907.2	779.4	467.5	614.6	4 805.9	4 537.3	268.6	5.6	5 945.4	6 156.5
2nd quarter	5 549.7	3 775.3	450.1	113.5	902.5	783.8	475.6	641.3	4 908.4	4 604.9	303.4	6.2	6 070.8	6 252.3
3rd quarter	5 593.1	3 817.8	447.0	115.4	895.3	797.7	480.1	657.0	4 936.2	4 668.1	268.1	5.4	6 087.0	6 265.7
4th quarter	5 709.2	3 909.3	465.5	122.0	896.8	802.1	486.6	673.3	5 036.0	4 734.6	301.4	6.0	6 195.4	6 358.1
1994														
1st quarter	5 706.7	3 870.5	476.7	133.1	909.2	815.6	498.4	671.1	5 035.7	4 806.2	229.5	4.6	6 150.9	6 332.6
2nd quarter	5 844.1	3 973.9	481.8	141.6	932.8	820.3	506.4	695.3	5 148.8	4 870.1	278.7	5.4	6 284.2	6 440.6
3rd quarter	5 921.8	4 011.8	485.8	148.5	962.0	824.3	510.6	692.8	5 229.0	4 952.8	276.2	5.3	6 324.8	6 487.9
4th quarter	6 026.6	4 067.5	496.1	148.4	986.6	845.4	517.4	702.9	5 323.7	5 025.4	298.3	5.6	6 398.1	6 574.0
1995														
1st quarter	6 107.2	4 119.1	500.4	151.0	993.0	869.4	525.7	720.0	5 387.2	5 059.9	327.3	6.1	6 433.1	6 616.6
2nd quarter	6 161.3	4 155.0	506.3	153.0	998.3	879.0	530.1	742.2	5 419.1	5 138.1	281.0	5.2	6 450.3	6 617.2
3rd quarter	6 230.4	4 200.0	520.0	152.8	1 007.0	885.9	535.3	747.7	5 482.7	5 209.4	273.3	5.0	6 498.7	6 666.8
4th quarter	6 304.7	4 241.1	537.4	161.5	1 023.1	881.5	540.0	765.7	5 539.0	5 275.6	263.4	4.8	6 566.0	6 706.2
1996														
1st quarter	6 427.3	4 291.9	560.2	166.7	1 041.7	910.9	544.2	796.5	5 630.8	5 353.6	277.2	4.9	6 640.0	6 777.7
2nd quarter	6 562.7	4 360.6	586.5	168.4	1 067.9	931.3	552.1	834.4	5 728.3	5 451.3	277.0	4.8	6 734.7	6 850.6
3rd quarter	6 642.0	4 419.8	588.6	172.1	1 093.6	926.7	558.7	838.4	5 803.6	5 512.0	291.5	5.0	6 803.8	6 908.9
4th quarter	6 734.3	4 478.6	599.4	174.5	1 119.7	927.5	565.4	858.4	5 875.9	5 597.0	278.9	4.7	6 865.1	6 946.8
1997														
1st quarter	6 855.6	4 557.6	619.6	174.9	1 134.3	944.6	575.5	896.4	5 959.1	5 682.8	276.3	4.6	6 952.3	7 008.9
2nd quarter	6 930.4	4 620.9	619.4	175.9	1 152.2	944.3	582.2	910.5	6 019.9	5 725.2	294.7	4.9	7 021.8	7 061.5
3rd quarter	7 041.5	4 698.2	632.8	176.4	1 173.8	950.5	590.2	935.4	6 106.1	5 839.8	266.3	4.4	7 124.8	7 142.4
4th quarter	7 175.5	4 797.6	641.1	178.9	1 201.5	957.4	601.0	962.2	6 213.2	5 928.9	284.4	4.6	7 247.2	7 241.5
1998														
1st quarter	7 347.7	4 899.1	663.6	182.7	1 245.4	968.7	611.8	990.1	6 357.6	5 987.2	370.4	5.8	7 431.2	7 406.2
2nd quarter	7 479.8	4 982.7	677.0	188.6	1 276.8	975.1	620.4	1 016.4	6 463.4	6 108.1	355.4	5.5	7 560.0	7 512.0
3rd quarter	7 590.4	5 066.1	692.9	195.7	1 286.2	978.5	629.0	1 037.2	6 553.2	6 210.3	342.9	5.2	7 659.0	7 591.0
4th quarter	7 683.6	5 147.8	716.6	198.8	1 268.3	989.4	637.4	1 062.0	6 621.6	6 324.3	297.2	4.5	7 730.4	7 646.5
1999														
1st quarter	7 760.9	5 241.3	729.6	203.0	1 229.5	1 010.0	652.5	1 073.5	6 687.4	6 400.9	286.5	4.3	7 771.6	7 698.4
2nd quarter	7 831.6	5 292.7	738.9	206.9	1 236.2	1 013.2	656.4	1 090.8	6 740.8	6 540.9	199.9	3.0	7 804.7	7 716.0
3rd quarter	7 936.2	5 366.9	750.6	209.2	1 245.4	1 026.3	662.2	1 116.2	6 819.9	6 653.9	166.0	2.4	7 868.3	7 765.9
4th quarter	8 114.7	5 494.3	768.1	213.5	1 276.0	1 036.8	674.1	1 149.6	6 965.1	6 786.4	178.7	2.6	8 015.4	7 887.7
2000														
1st quarter	8 379.6	5 692.1	783.7	214.6	1 334.3	1 052.4	697.5	1 204.7	7 174.9	6 955.1	219.9	3.1	8 224.3	8 053.4
2nd quarter	8 506.6	5 731.4	819.4	212.1	1 363.1	1 079.4	698.9	1 226.1	7 280.5	7 054.0	226.5	3.1	8 299.8	8 135.9
3rd quarter	8 644.2	5 845.8	826.7	213.3	1 375.9	1 093.7	711.2	1 243.6	7 400.6	7 171.5	229.0	3.1	8 388.9	8 222.3
4th quarter	8 707.3	5 886.1	840.1	221.1	1 369.4	1 106.5	715.8	1 254.6	7 452.7	7 275.7	177.0	2.4	8 398.3	8 234.6
2001														
1st quarter	8 859.0	5 993.9	867.4	225.3	1 357.8	1 150.0	735.5	1 297.6	7 561.4	7 353.2	208.2	2.8	8 458.5	8 296.5
2nd quarter	8 881.2	5 979.9	871.6	230.6	1 350.6	1 182.6	734.0	1 304.5	7 576.8	7 414.9	161.9	2.1	8 406.8	8 273.7
3rd quarter	8 880.6	5 965.8	878.1	239.5	1 340.6	1 188.2	731.5	1 109.5	7 771.1	7 448.1	323.0	4.2	8 398.6	8 484.5
4th quarter	8 912.3	5 977.7	865.8	234.1	1 334.8	1 231.7	731.7	1 227.7	7 684.6	7 557.9	126.7	1.6	8 381.1	8 385.5
2002														
1st quarter	8 978.3	6 038.4	880.5	229.2	1 319.1	1 257.7	746.6	1 068.4	7 909.9	7 596.2	313.7	4.0	8 405.5	8 611.6
2nd quarter	9 060.7	6 101.3	884.2	231.7	1 315.4	1 280.4	752.3	1 045.3	8 015.4	7 694.0	321.4	4.0	8 405.0	8 658.9
3rd quarter	9 074.6	6 128.8	893.3	212.7	1 303.8	1 288.6	752.7	1 046.3	8 028.3	7 781.3	247.0	3.1	8 368.8	8 629.2
4th quarter	9 126.8	6 174.7	903.2	201.4	1 300.0	1 301.9	754.2	1 041.7	8 085.1	7 838.5	246.7	3.1	8 371.3	8 649.6
2003														
1st quarter	9 194.5	6 244.4	889.6	209.7	1 299.2	1 318.1	766.7	1 021.3	8 173.2	7 923.3	249.9	3.1	8 366.0	8 681.3
2nd quarter	9 321.1	6 332.7	919.1	204.2	1 306.2	1 333.7	774.9	1 018.1	8 303.0	8 008.5	294.5	3.5	8 477.5	8 812.5
3rd quarter	9 418.7	6 400.6	945.8	186.2	1 312.4	1 355.6	781.8	945.2	8 473.5	8 167.2	306.3	3.6	8 502.6	8 935.4
4th quarter	9 578.3	6 492.6	968.1	216.6	1 333.8	1 359.6	792.3	1 016.8	8 561.5	8 253.2	308.3	3.6	8 626.6	8 986.4
2004														
1st quarter	9 679.8	6 543.3	1 002.1	204.2	1 350.0	1 392.5	812.3	1 009.3	8 670.5	8 394.9	275.5	3.2	8 627.1	9 025.9
2nd quarter	9 847.1	6 657.9	1 029.8	197.1	1 372.9	1 411.0	821.6	1 026.4	8 820.7	8 505.4	315.4	3.6	8 717.5	9 115.0
3rd quarter	9 999.1	6 781.3	1 040.1	196.8	1 395.5	1 418.5	833.1	1 064.7	8 934.4	8 635.3	299.1	3.3	8 812.5	9 175.9
4th quarter	10 223.1	6 851.2	1 063.1	195.4	1 515.5	1 440.1	842.2	1 090.9	9 132.1	8 807.1	325.0	3.6	8 947.7	9 303.4
2005														
1st quarter	10 238.6	6 921.1	1 046.8	190.7	1 459.7	1 481.3	861.0	1 164.2	9 074.3	8 932.5	141.8	1.6	8 868.4	9 189.6
2nd quarter	10 386.7	7 003.6	1 054.0	181.5	1 507.1	1 506.4	865.8	1 192.3	9 194.4	9 077.4	117.0	1.3	8 936.9	9 253.0
3rd quarter	10 577.5	7 128.4	1 082.6	168.4	1 560.4	1 516.7	879.0	1 224.0	9 353.5	9 243.2	110.2	1.2	9 016.7	9 308.0
4th quarter	10 740.8	7 187.1	1 095.8	172.3	1 640.8	1 529.8	885.0	1 253.8	9 487.1	9 345.2	141.8	1.5	9 086.4	9 358.7
2006														
1st quarter	11 026.7	7 373.7	1 126.9	161.3	1 711.1	1 569.0	915.4	1 321.5	9 705.2	9 493.5	211.7	2.2	9 290.6	9 533.8
2nd quarter	11 204.0	7 419.9	1 133.2	153.2	1 817.2	1 597.9	917.4	1 340.2	9 863.8	9 618.2	245.6	2.5	9 366.1	9 617.3
3rd quarter	11 336.9	7 484.1	1 131.2	140.3	1 881.3	1 620.7	920.8	1 354.3	9 982.5	9 754.9	227.7	2.3	9 404.7	9 662.5
4th quarter	11 504.8	7 625.3	1 140.6	131.2	1 909.0	1 632.4	933.8	1 393.5	10 111.2	9 856.4	254.8	2.5	9 557.5	9 788.8

Table 19-7. Per Capita Product and Income, Population, and Inventories to Sales Ratios

(Seasonally adjusted.)   NIPA Tables 5.7.5A, 5.7.5B, 5.7.6A, 5.7.6B, 7.1

Year and quarter	Chained (2005) dollars per capita		Population (mid-period, thousands)	Ratio, inventories at end of quarter to monthly rate of sales during the quarter					
				Total private inventories to final sales of domestic business		Nonfarm inventories to final sales of domestic business		Nonfarm inventories to final sales of goods and structures	
	Gross domestic product	Disposable personal income		Current dollars	Chained (2005) dollars	Current dollars	Chained (2005) dollars	Current dollars	Chained (2005) dollars
1946	12 676	8 907	141 389	. . .	. . .	2.81	. . .	3.65	. . .
1947	12 324	8 409	144 126	6.30	3.74	3.00	2.25	3.90	3.92
1948	12 646	8 709	146 631	5.74	3.91	2.77	2.36	3.61	4.12
1949	12 365	8 615	149 188	5.23	3.73		2.23		3.86
1947									
1st quarter	12 380	8 512	143 156	5.93	3.87	2.82	2.27	3.71	3.98
2nd quarter	12 305	8 293	143 803	5.89	3.83	2.82	2.26	3.69	3.99
3rd quarter	12 239	8 484	144 462	6.02	3.76	2.76	2.23	3.61	3.92
4th quarter	12 367	8 346	145 135	6.30	3.74	2.81	2.25	3.65	3.92
1948									
1st quarter	12 509	8 446	145 761	6.00	3.76	2.87	2.27	3.71	3.95
2nd quarter	12 689	8 705	146 341	6.02	3.80	2.89	2.30	3.76	4.02
3rd quarter	12 702	8 841	146 973	5.88	3.87	2.97	2.34	3.85	4.09
4th quarter	12 663	8 824	147 659	5.74	3.91	3.00	2.36	3.90	4.12
1949									
1st quarter	12 433	8 606	148 298	5.66	3.90	2.97	2.35	3.88	4.13
2nd quarter	12 338	8 598	148 891	5.38	3.81	2.83	2.29	3.70	4.01
3rd quarter	12 424	8 612	149 529	5.39	3.80	2.82	2.29	3.69	3.99
4th quarter	12 251	8 634	150 211	5.23	3.73	2.77	2.23	3.61	3.86
1950									
1st quarter	12 692	9 237	150 852	5.26	3.69	2.76	2.21	3.61	3.83
2nd quarter	13 032	9 155	151 385	5.27	3.62	2.75	2.19	3.57	3.78
3rd quarter	13 484	9 257	152 039	5.21	3.46	2.72	2.12	3.50	3.62
4th quarter	13 660	9 300	152 724	5.81	3.66	3.04	2.29	3.94	3.96
1951									
1st quarter	13 777	9 266	153 336	5.94	3.67	3.12	2.33	4.01	4.00
2nd quarter	13 950	9 373	153 947	5.99	3.80	3.25	2.45	4.23	4.27
3rd quarter	14 163	9 390	154 655	5.89	3.78	3.20	2.46	4.16	4.28
4th quarter	14 120	9 363	155 389	5.85	3.75	3.15	2.45	4.07	4.23
1952									
1st quarter	14 203	9 318	156 033	5.77	3.79	3.16	2.48	4.11	4.30
2nd quarter	14 163	9 398	156 644	5.63	3.75	3.08	2.44	4.01	4.23
3rd quarter	14 197	9 543	157 324	5.63	3.85	3.15	2.50	4.13	4.37
4th quarter	14 599	9 687	158 043	5.24	3.73	3.06	2.44	3.98	4.22
1953									
1st quarter	14 815	9 779	158 648	5.06	3.68	3.02	2.42	3.93	4.16
2nd quarter	14 872	9 878	159 234	5.00	3.69	3.06	2.43	3.99	4.19
3rd quarter	14 715	9 793	159 963	4.99	3.71	3.09	2.45	4.05	4.22
4th quarter	14 414	9 686	160 713	5.04	3.74	3.08	2.45	4.04	4.21
1954									
1st quarter	14 285	9 701	161 389	5.02	3.72	3.04	2.42	4.01	4.19
2nd quarter	14 245	9 667	162 044	4.91	3.66	2.98	2.37	3.93	4.10
3rd quarter	14 340	9 731	162 792	4.85	3.59	2.93	2.32	3.89	4.03
4th quarter	14 556	9 876	163 585	4.74	3.51	2.88	2.27	3.81	3.93
1955									
1st quarter	14 913	9 981	164 266	4.68	3.46	2.86	2.25	3.77	3.87
2nd quarter	15 099	10 181	164 926	4.57	3.44	2.87	2.26	3.73	3.82
3rd quarter	15 232	10 326	165 674	4.47	3.41	2.89	2.26	3.77	3.84
4th quarter	15 243	10 395	166 481	4.43	3.44	2.95	2.29	3.87	3.93
1956									
1st quarter	15 109	10 458	167 190	4.50	3.48	3.00	2.33	3.96	4.01
2nd quarter	15 166	10 518	167 869	4.57	3.48	3.03	2.35	3.99	4.03
3rd quarter	15 077	10 514	168 654	4.50	3.47	3.02	2.36	3.98	4.06
4th quarter	15 247	10 629	169 497	4.47	3.44	3.03	2.35	4.00	4.06
1957									
1st quarter	15 275	10 601	170 218	4.44	3.44	3.02	2.35	3.97	4.04
2nd quarter	15 176	10 629	170 915	4.48	3.47	3.04	2.38	4.00	4.10
3rd quarter	15 254	10 632	171 684	4.46	3.46	3.03	2.37	3.99	4.10
4th quarter	15 025	10 524	172 463	4.46	3.47	3.01	2.37	4.01	4.13
1958									
1st quarter	14 563	10 395	173 116	4.67	3.56	3.04	2.40	4.06	4.19
2nd quarter	14 597	10 424	173 781	4.65	3.56	3.00	2.38	4.00	4.16
3rd quarter	14 874	10 593	174 535	4.58	3.48	2.92	2.32	3.92	4.06
4th quarter	15 151	10 678	175 340	4.50	3.44	2.90	2.30	3.88	3.99
1959									
1st quarter	15 396	10 718	176 045	4.37	3.34	2.83	2.24	3.79	3.92
2nd quarter	15 724	10 863	176 727	4.33	3.34	2.86	2.27	3.85	3.97
3rd quarter	15 638	10 798	177 481	4.25	3.31	2.84	2.26	3.82	3.95
4th quarter	15 624	10 834	178 268	4.26	3.36	2.90	2.32	3.94	4.07
1960									
1st quarter	15 847	10 882	179 694	4.29	3.37	2.93	2.34	3.96	4.09
2nd quarter	15 717	10 903	180 335	4.21	3.36	2.91	2.34	3.95	4.10
3rd quarter	15 677	10 866	181 094	4.27	3.41	2.95	2.38	3.99	4.15
4th quarter	15 406	10 811	181 915	4.22	3.37	2.89	2.34	3.93	4.09
1961									
1st quarter	15 437	10 866	182 634	4.19	3.35	2.86	2.31	3.90	4.06
2nd quarter	15 665	10 987	183 337	4.12	3.33	2.83	2.30	3.89	4.06
3rd quarter	15 852	11 091	184 103	4.17	3.35	2.85	2.32	3.89	4.08
4th quarter	16 106	11 261	184 894	4.12	3.30	2.81	2.29	3.84	4.02

. . . = Not available.

Table 19-7. Per Capita Product and Income, Population, and Inventories to Sales Ratios—*Continued*

(Seasonally adjusted.) NIPA Tables 5.7.5A, 5.7.5B, 5.7.6A, 5.7.6B, 7.1

Year and quarter	Chained (2005) dollars per capita		Population (mid-period, thousands)	Ratio, inventories at end of quarter to monthly rate of sales during the quarter					
	Gross domestic product	Disposable personal income		Total private inventories to final sales of domestic business		Nonfarm inventories to final sales of domestic business		Nonfarm inventories to final sales of goods and structures	
				Current dollars	Chained (2005) dollars	Current dollars	Chained (2005) dollars	Current dollars	Chained (2005) dollars
1962									
1st quarter	16 336	11 327	185 553	4.15	3.32	2.82	2.31	3.85	4.06
2nd quarter	16 459	11 413	186 203	4.09	3.29	2.80	2.30	3.84	4.05
3rd quarter	16 547	11 432	186 926	4.17	3.31	2.83	2.33	3.87	4.08
4th quarter	16 520	11 480	187 680	4.14	3.31	2.82	2.33	3.87	4.10
1963									
1st quarter	16 681	11 537	188 299	4.12	3.33	2.83	2.35	3.87	4.11
2nd quarter	16 836	11 610	188 906	4.04	3.28	2.79	2.32	3.83	4.08
3rd quarter	17 088	11 696	189 631	4.00	3.27	2.79	2.32	3.81	4.06
4th quarter	17 151	11 844	190 362	3.95	3.25	2.78	2.32	3.81	4.06
1964									
1st quarter	17 482	12 043	190 954	3.85	3.19	2.74	2.29	3.75	4.00
2nd quarter	17 627	12 331	191 560	3.79	3.17	2.73	2.29	3.75	4.01
3rd quarter	17 802	12 445	192 256	3.78	3.15	2.73	2.29	3.74	3.99
4th quarter	17 788	12 545	192 938	3.79	3.16	2.75	2.31	3.79	4.06
1965									
1st quarter	18 175	12 650	193 467	3.81	3.16	2.76	2.32	3.79	4.07
2nd quarter	18 371	12 755	193 994	3.82	3.14	2.75	2.31	3.79	4.07
3rd quarter	18 681	13 063	194 647	3.78	3.14	2.76	2.32	3.78	4.05
4th quarter	19 070	13 284	195 279	3.77	3.08	2.72	2.29	3.71	3.98
1966									
1st quarter	19 490	13 376	195 763	3.80	3.09	2.73	2.30	3.71	3.99
2nd quarter	19 504	13 372	196 277	3.86	3.15	2.80	2.37	3.83	4.15
3rd quarter	19 572	13 500	196 877	3.91	3.19	2.84	2.42	3.88	4.21
4th quarter	19 670	13 613	197 481	3.92	3.26	2.92	2.49	4.01	4.37
1967									
1st quarter	19 795	13 782	197 967	3.94	3.32	2.98	2.55	4.11	4.49
2nd quarter	19 750	13 861	198 455	3.92	3.31	2.95	2.54	4.07	4.45
3rd quarter	19 852	13 954	199 012	3.92	3.34	2.97	2.57	4.10	4.51
4th quarter	19 948	14 017	199 572	3.90	3.35	2.99	2.59	4.14	4.55
1968									
1st quarter	20 316	14 231	199 995	3.87	3.32	2.94	2.56	4.08	4.50
2nd quarter	20 613	14 435	200 452	3.87	3.34	2.93	2.57	4.07	4.54
3rd quarter	20 698	14 425	200 997	3.81	3.31	2.90	2.56	4.03	4.50
4th quarter	20 732	14 481	201 538	3.79	3.32	2.90	2.58	4.03	4.55
1969									
1st quarter	21 015	14 476	201 955	3.79	3.32	2.90	2.58	4.02	4.53
2nd quarter	21 028	14 588	202 419	3.83	3.35	2.91	2.61	4.06	4.60
3rd quarter	21 102	14 843	202 986	3.83	3.37	2.94	2.64	4.10	4.66
4th quarter	20 941	14 907	203 584	3.88	3.40	2.98	2.67	4.18	4.75
1970									
1st quarter	20 857	14 945	204 086	3.86	3.38	2.96	2.66	4.18	4.73
2nd quarter	20 830	15 160	204 721	3.85	3.40	2.96	2.67	4.20	4.79
3rd quarter	20 944	15 312	205 419	3.84	3.38	2.97	2.67	4.22	4.78
4th quarter	20 650	15 209	206 130	3.81	3.38	2.96	2.68	4.23	4.82
1971									
1st quarter	21 155	15 464	206 763	3.83	3.37	2.95	2.67	4.21	4.80
2nd quarter	21 213	15 651	207 362	3.81	3.38	2.94	2.68	4.20	4.80
3rd quarter	21 317	15 672	208 000	3.80	3.38	2.93	2.67	4.18	4.78
4th quarter	21 310	15 789	208 642	3.76	3.33	2.88	2.64	4.12	4.74
1972									
1st quarter	21 640	15 850	209 142	3.72	3.29	2.84	2.62	4.06	4.68
2nd quarter	22 101	15 962	209 637	3.75	3.27	2.83	2.60	4.03	4.63
3rd quarter	22 255	16 246	210 181	3.77	3.26	2.83	2.60	4.05	4.65
4th quarter	22 562	16 848	210 737	3.74	3.17	2.77	2.54	3.94	4.52
1973									
1st quarter	23 089	17 002	211 192	3.86	3.10	2.79	2.51	3.92	4.44
2nd quarter	23 304	17 132	211 663	4.03	3.14	2.86	2.54	4.02	4.50
3rd quarter	23 122	17 175	212 191	4.11	3.16	2.87	2.55	4.05	4.54
4th quarter	23 286	17 343	212 708	4.20	3.22	2.98	2.62	4.22	4.66
1974									
1st quarter	23 034	17 041	213 144	4.26	3.27	3.13	2.68	4.42	4.75
2nd quarter	23 044	16 859	213 602	4.29	3.30	3.28	2.71	4.67	4.85
3rd quarter	22 758	16 869	214 147	4.45	3.34	3.40	2.74	4.84	4.92
4th quarter	22 610	16 749	214 700	4.52	3.46	3.54	2.87	5.11	5.24
1975									
1st quarter	22 290	16 650	215 135	4.32	3.42	3.41	2.81	4.94	5.15
2nd quarter	22 406	17 386	215 652	4.26	3.35	3.30	2.74	4.81	5.05
3rd quarter	22 716	17 100	216 289	4.18	3.30	3.24	2.71	4.69	4.94
4th quarter	22 954	17 229	216 848	4.04	3.25	3.16	2.66	4.59	4.87
1976									
1st quarter	23 425	17 445	217 314	4.00	3.22	3.14	2.64	4.56	4.82
2nd quarter	23 551	17 551	217 776	4.07	3.26	3.21	2.68	4.67	4.90
3rd quarter	23 606	17 664	218 338	4.04	3.27	3.23	2.70	4.74	4.95
4th quarter	23 714	17 744	218 917	3.95	3.23	3.19	2.67	4.68	4.91

Table 19-7. Per Capita Product and Income, Population, and Inventories to Sales Ratios—*Continued*

(Seasonally adjusted.)

NIPA Tables 5.7.5A, 5.7.5B, 5.7.6A, 5.7.6B, 7.1

Year and quarter	Chained (2005) dollars per capita		Population (mid-period, thousands)	Ratio, inventories at end of quarter to monthly rate of sales during the quarter					
	Gross domestic product	Disposable personal income		Total private inventories to final sales of domestic business		Nonfarm inventories to final sales of domestic business		Nonfarm inventories to final sales of goods and structures	
				Current dollars	Chained (2005) dollars	Current dollars	Chained (2005) dollars	Current dollars	Chained (2005) dollars
1977									
1st quarter	23 934	17 717	219 427	3.96	3.22	3.21	2.68	4.72	4.91
2nd quarter	24 351	17 875	219 956	3.88	3.19	3.16	2.65	4.62	4.83
3rd quarter	24 717	18 093	220 573	3.86	3.22	3.16	2.67	4.63	4.87
4th quarter	24 642	18 405	221 201	3.89	3.21	3.16	2.67	4.63	4.86
1978									
1st quarter	24 668	18 476	221 719	4.02	3.26	3.21	2.71	4.78	4.99
2nd quarter	25 574	18 640	222 281	3.92	3.13	3.12	2.62	4.55	4.73
3rd quarter	25 749	18 737	222 933	3.95	3.14	3.13	2.62	4.54	4.73
4th quarter	26 014	18 829	223 583	3.98	3.14	3.15	2.63	4.54	4.71
1979									
1st quarter	25 991	18 987	224 152	4.15	3.16	3.22	2.65	4.66	4.77
2nd quarter	25 948	18 805	224 737	4.19	3.21	3.29	2.69	4.78	4.85
3rd quarter	26 055	18 855	225 418	4.16	3.15	3.28	2.64	4.74	4.72
4th quarter	26 046	18 947	226 117	4.19	3.16	3.34	2.64	4.85	4.74
1980									
1st quarter	26 057	18 947	226 754	4.25	3.17	3.45	2.65	5.02	4.77
2nd quarter	25 451	18 629	227 389	4.40	3.28	3.57	2.76	5.26	5.00
3rd quarter	25 328	18 765	228 070	4.34	3.18	3.50	2.68	5.15	4.86
4th quarter	25 727	19 101	228 689	4.24	3.13	3.44	2.64	5.08	4.80
1981									
1st quarter	26 208	19 018	229 155	4.26	3.16	3.48	2.67	5.13	4.83
2nd quarter	25 940	18 978	229 674	4.24	3.17	3.47	2.67	5.15	4.86
3rd quarter	26 184	19 346	230 301	4.20	3.22	3.48	2.70	5.16	4.92
4th quarter	25 790	19 334	230 903	4.17	3.28	3.49	2.75	5.20	5.02
1982									
1st quarter	25 313	19 316	231 395	4.19	3.28	3.46	2.74	5.20	5.02
2nd quarter	25 394	19 408	231 906	4.15	3.28	3.42	2.73	5.17	5.02
3rd quarter	25 232	19 443	232 498	4.12	3.32	3.43	2.77	5.26	5.14
4th quarter	25 189	19 463	233 074	3.97	3.23	3.30	2.67	5.10	4.98
1983									
1st quarter	25 451	19 577	233 546	3.89	3.15	3.19	2.61	4.98	4.88
2nd quarter	25 970	19 679	234 028	3.81	3.09	3.14	2.57	4.89	4.79
3rd quarter	26 417	19 926	234 603	3.73	3.02	3.12	2.55	4.86	4.72
4th quarter	26 900	20 289	235 153	3.69	2.98	3.08	2.52	4.77	4.63
1984									
1st quarter	27 369	20 693	235 605	3.78	3.02	3.15	2.56	4.87	4.70
2nd quarter	27 785	21 007	236 082	3.76	3.02	3.16	2.57	4.88	4.68
3rd quarter	27 987	21 282	236 657	3.75	3.05	3.18	2.60	4.93	4.74
4th quarter	28 147	21 433	237 232	3.72	3.04	3.16	2.59	4.89	4.71
1985									
1st quarter	28 359	21 340	237 673	3.60	2.99	3.06	2.54	4.77	4.64
2nd quarter	28 539	21 718	238 176	3.55	2.99	3.04	2.54	4.76	4.65
3rd quarter	28 911	21 528	238 789	3.47	2.96	2.98	2.51	4.67	4.59
4th quarter	29 057	21 697	239 387	3.51	2.98	3.01	2.53	4.74	4.64
1986									
1st quarter	29 278	21 912	239 861	3.42	2.97	2.94	2.52	4.65	4.62
2nd quarter	29 334	22 114	240 368	3.37	2.97	2.92	2.53	4.63	4.64
3rd quarter	29 544	22 175	240 962	3.29	2.92	2.85	2.48	4.52	4.54
4th quarter	29 616	22 135	241 539	3.25	2.89	2.82	2.46	4.49	4.52
1987									
1st quarter	29 722	22 228	242 009	3.31	2.93	2.86	2.51	4.62	4.65
2nd quarter	29 975	21 940	242 520	3.30	2.90	2.86	2.49	4.60	4.59
3rd quarter	30 160	22 278	243 120	3.25	2.85	2.82	2.45	4.52	4.50
4th quarter	30 601	22 538	243 721	3.33	2.90	2.90	2.50	4.65	4.61
1988									
1st quarter	30 698	22 776	244 208	3.30	2.86	2.86	2.47	4.61	4.55
2nd quarter	31 027	22 942	244 716	3.29	2.82	2.85	2.45	4.60	4.51
3rd quarter	31 106	23 059	245 354	3.30	2.83	2.85	2.46	4.63	4.56
4th quarter	31 443	23 209	245 966	3.29	2.81	2.86	2.46	4.63	4.54
1989									
1st quarter	31 675	23 425	246 460	3.32	2.82	2.89	2.48	4.70	4.56
2nd quarter	31 840	23 277	247 017	3.28	2.82	2.87	2.48	4.65	4.55
3rd quarter	32 004	23 363	247 698	3.21	2.79	2.82	2.45	4.55	4.48
4th quarter	31 987	23 478	248 374	3.23	2.80	2.83	2.47	4.63	4.55
1990									
1st quarter	32 248	23 601	248 936	3.18	2.78	2.78	2.45	4.53	4.49
2nd quarter	32 276	23 683	249 711	3.17	2.80	2.78	2.47	4.58	4.59
3rd quarter	32 161	23 616	250 595	3.20	2.81	2.82	2.48	4.67	4.62
4th quarter	31 767	23 374	251 482	3.22	2.83	2.82	2.49	4.71	4.65
1991									
1st quarter	31 516	23 374	252 258	3.18	2.85	2.78	2.50	4.65	4.70
2nd quarter	31 628	23 477	253 063	3.08	2.81	2.70	2.47	4.55	4.65
3rd quarter	31 648	23 443	253 965	3.04	2.81	2.69	2.47	4.54	4.66
4th quarter	31 664	23 515	254 835	3.06	2.83	2.70	2.49	4.62	4.73

Table 19-7. Per Capita Product and Income, Population, and Inventories to Sales Ratios—*Continued*

(Seasonally adjusted.)   **NIPA Tables 5.7.5A, 5.7.5B, 5.7.6A, 5.7.6B, 7.1**

Year and quarter	Chained (2005) dollars per capita		Population (mid-period, thousands)	Ratio, inventories at end of quarter to monthly rate of sales during the quarter					
	Gross domestic product	Disposable personal income		Total private inventories to final sales of domestic business		Nonfarm inventories to final sales of domestic business		Nonfarm inventories to final sales of goods and structures	
				Current dollars	Chained (2005) dollars	Current dollars	Chained (2005) dollars	Current dollars	Chained (2005) dollars
1992									
1st quarter	31 917	23 800	255 585	3.00	2.78	2.63	2.44	4.52	4.63
2nd quarter	32 149	23 902	256 439	2.99	2.77	2.62	2.43	4.50	4.59
3rd quarter	32 361	23 935	257 386	2.96	2.75	2.60	2.41	4.47	4.56
4th quarter	32 589	24 192	258 277	2.92	2.72	2.56	2.39	4.41	4.52
1993									
1st quarter	32 553	23 767	259 039	2.95	2.75	2.58	2.42	4.47	4.59
2nd quarter	32 662	24 063	259 826	2.92	2.73	2.57	2.41	4.44	4.55
3rd quarter	32 722	24 033	260 714	2.89	2.71	2.54	2.40	4.42	4.54
4th quarter	33 049	24 310	261 547	2.85	2.68	2.51	2.37	4.33	4.46
1994									
1st quarter	33 281	24 147	262 250	2.87	2.69	2.51	2.37	4.33	4.46
2nd quarter	33 637	24 487	263 020	2.86	2.71	2.53	2.39	4.37	4.48
3rd quarter	33 745	24 588	263 870	2.86	2.71	2.53	2.38	4.36	4.47
4th quarter	34 016	24 838	264 678	2.89	2.72	2.56	2.40	4.39	4.46
1995									
1st quarter	34 008	24 932	265 388	2.93	2.74	2.62	2.42	4.49	4.51
2nd quarter	33 984	24 864	266 142	2.94	2.74	2.64	2.43	4.55	4.54
3rd quarter	34 160	24 969	267 000	2.90	2.70	2.60	2.41	4.49	4.49
4th quarter	34 293	25 040	267 820	2.88	2.69	2.58	2.40	4.45	4.45
1996									
1st quarter	34 442	25 244	268 487	2.84	2.66	2.55	2.38	4.39	4.41
2nd quarter	34 938	25 443	269 251	2.81	2.63	2.51	2.35	4.30	4.34
3rd quarter	35 127	25 576	270 128	2.81	2.64	2.50	2.35	4.29	4.33
4th quarter	35 398	25 635	270 991	2.76	2.61	2.47	2.33	4.24	4.27
1997									
1st quarter	35 576	25 796	271 709	2.74	2.61	2.45	2.33	4.21	4.27
2nd quarter	36 000	25 915	272 487	2.73	2.64	2.44	2.36	4.21	4.32
3rd quarter	36 331	26 125	273 391	2.69	2.62	2.41	2.34	4.14	4.26
4th quarter	36 496	26 405	274 246	2.70	2.65	2.42	2.37	4.17	4.31
1998									
1st quarter	36 746	26 937	274 950	2.69	2.68	2.42	2.40	4.20	4.37
2nd quarter	36 976	27 247	275 703	2.64	2.65	2.38	2.37	4.13	4.31
3rd quarter	37 347	27 447	276 564	2.59	2.64	2.36	2.37	4.06	4.28
4th quarter	37 879	27 565	277 400	2.55	2.61	2.32	2.34	3.98	4.21
1999									
1st quarter	38 120	27 682	278 103	2.56	2.63	2.33	2.36	4.01	4.26
2nd quarter	38 313	27 669	278 864	2.54	2.61	2.32	2.34	3.98	4.22
3rd quarter	38 677	27 760	279 751	2.55	2.59	2.32	2.34	4.01	4.20
4th quarter	39 254	28 111	280 592	2.57	2.60	2.35	2.34	4.06	4.22
2000									
1st quarter	39 257	28 629	281 304	2.56	2.57	2.34	2.33	4.05	4.18
2nd quarter	39 923	28 850	282 007	2.56	2.58	2.35	2.34	4.07	4.21
3rd quarter	39 845	29 075	282 792	2.57	2.59	2.36	2.35	4.10	4.23
4th quarter	39 971	29 039	283 570	2.59	2.60	2.37	2.36	4.13	4.25
2001									
1st quarter	39 744	29 188	284 246	2.57	2.58	2.34	2.34	4.10	4.21
2nd quarter	39 908	29 037	284 939	2.52	2.57	2.30	2.33	4.02	4.19
3rd quarter	39 691	29 696	285 706	2.49	2.57	2.27	2.33	3.98	4.21
4th quarter	39 728	29 274	286 451	2.40	2.51	2.19	2.27	3.83	4.09
2002									
1st quarter	39 980	29 996	287 092	2.40	2.51	2.19	2.26	3.87	4.11
2nd quarter	40 101	30 092	287 746	2.40	2.51	2.19	2.27	3.91	4.15
3rd quarter	40 197	29 912	288 488	2.41	2.51	2.20	2.27	3.94	4.14
4th quarter	40 106	29 908	289 204	2.45	2.53	2.22	2.29	4.01	4.21
2003									
1st quarter	40 184	29 955	289 815	2.47	2.53	2.24	2.29	4.04	4.19
2nd quarter	40 413	30 339	290 467	2.42	2.50	2.20	2.26	3.97	4.13
3rd quarter	40 988	30 685	291 197	2.38	2.44	2.14	2.21	3.83	3.99
4th quarter	41 257	30 786	291 899	2.39	2.44	2.16	2.21	3.86	3.99
2004									
1st quarter	41 466	30 861	292 471	2.42	2.44	2.18	2.22	3.92	4.02
2nd quarter	41 669	31 097	293 114	2.45	2.46	2.20	2.23	3.96	4.04
3rd quarter	41 871	31 227	293 845	2.45	2.46	2.22	2.23	3.98	4.02
4th quarter	42 129	31 582	294 577	2.45	2.46	2.22	2.23	4.01	4.04
2005									
1st quarter	42 460	31 130	295 198	2.47	2.47	2.25	2.24	4.05	4.05
2nd quarter	42 550	31 278	295 826	2.43	2.44	2.21	2.22	3.97	3.98
3rd quarter	42 765	31 385	296 575	2.43	2.43	2.21	2.20	3.97	3.96
4th quarter	42 879	31 477	297 316	2.48	2.45	2.25	2.23	4.07	4.02
2006									
1st quarter	43 348	31 997	297 959	2.44	2.43	2.23	2.21	4.01	3.96
2nd quarter	43 407	32 205	298 625	2.47	2.45	2.26	2.23	4.07	4.01
3rd quarter	43 305	32 272	299 411	2.50	2.47	2.28	2.26	4.14	4.08
4th quarter	43 505	32 606	300 213	2.48	2.45	2.27	2.24	4.13	4.06

Table 19-8. National Income by Type of Income

(Billions of dollars, quarterly data are at seasonally adjusted annual rates.)   NIPA Tables 1.7.5, 1.12

Year and quarter	National income, total	Compensation of employees			Proprietors' income with IVA and CCAdj		Rental income of persons with CCAdj	Corporate profits with IVA and CCAdj	Net interest and miscellaneous payments	Taxes on production and imports	Less: Subsidies	Business current transfer payments, net	Addendum: Net national factor income
		Total	Wage and salary accruals	Supplements to wages and salaries	Farm	Nonfarm							
1946	198.6	119.6	112.0	7.6	14.2	21.5	7.1	17.9	1.9	16.8	1.2	0.7	182.2
1947	216.3	130.1	123.1	7.0	14.3	20.1	7.2	23.5	2.5	18.1	0.2	0.7	197.7
1948	242.6	142.0	135.6	6.4	16.7	22.5	7.8	30.9	2.6	19.7	0.3	0.7	222.4
1949	237.5	141.9	134.7	7.1	12.0	22.6	8.1	28.7	2.9	20.9	0.3	0.7	216.1
1947													
1st quarter	211.8	127.2	119.7	7.5	16.0	20.6	6.9	20.7	2.3	17.7	0.3	0.7	193.7
2nd quarter	212.7	128.7	121.5	7.2	12.4	20.0	7.1	23.9	2.4	17.7	0.2	0.7	194.4
3rd quarter	216.1	130.1	123.4	6.6	14.1	19.7	7.3	23.8	2.6	18.0	0.2	0.7	197.5
4th quarter	224.6	134.3	127.8	6.5	14.9	20.3	7.5	25.5	2.6	19.0	0.1	0.7	205.0
1948													
1st quarter	233.0	137.9	131.4	6.5	14.5	21.5	7.6	29.4	2.5	19.0	0.2	0.7	213.5
2nd quarter	241.8	139.6	133.2	6.4	18.0	22.4	7.8	31.2	2.6	19.7	0.1	0.7	221.5
3rd quarter	246.9	144.5	138.1	6.4	17.9	23.0	7.9	30.7	2.6	20.0	0.4	0.7	226.5
4th quarter	248.7	145.9	139.5	6.4	16.4	23.2	7.9	32.3	2.6	20.3	0.6	0.7	228.3
1949													
1st quarter	241.5	144.1	137.0	7.1	12.7	22.7	7.8	30.7	2.7	20.4	0.3	0.7	220.8
2nd quarter	237.1	141.9	134.6	7.2	12.1	22.7	7.9	28.3	2.8	20.8	0.2	0.7	215.8
3rd quarter	237.5	141.0	133.9	7.1	11.6	22.5	8.2	29.5	2.9	21.3	0.3	0.7	215.8
4th quarter	233.9	140.5	133.4	7.0	11.5	22.7	8.4	26.2	3.0	21.2	0.2	0.8	212.2
1950													
1st quarter	243.6	144.6	137.1	7.5	12.2	23.4	8.7	29.8	3.1	21.6	0.4	0.7	221.8
2nd quarter	255.2	150.6	142.9	7.8	12.2	24.0	9.0	33.4	3.2	22.5	0.6	0.8	232.4
3rd quarter	272.8	159.0	150.8	8.2	13.1	25.6	9.1	38.1	3.2	24.4	0.5	0.9	248.1
4th quarter	283.8	166.9	158.3	8.6	13.9	25.5	9.4	41.3	3.2	23.4	0.8	1.0	260.3
1951													
1st quarter	295.5	175.0	165.5	9.4	15.0	27.0	9.6	40.2	3.4	25.1	0.9	1.1	270.2
2nd quarter	301.1	180.6	170.8	9.7	15.4	27.0	9.9	40.2	3.6	24.1	0.8	1.2	276.7
3rd quarter	306.2	183.7	173.8	9.9	15.1	27.5	10.2	40.7	3.8	24.5	0.6	1.2	281.1
4th quarter	312.3	186.5	176.2	10.2	15.7	27.9	10.5	42.1	3.8	25.3	0.7	1.3	286.4
1952													
1st quarter	314.3	191.5	181.2	10.3	13.7	28.1	10.7	39.5	3.9	26.1	0.5	1.3	287.4
2nd quarter	316.0	192.8	182.4	10.4	14.5	28.5	11.0	37.4	4.0	26.9	0.4	1.3	288.3
3rd quarter	321.7	196.3	185.7	10.6	16.0	28.8	11.3	37.1	4.1	27.3	0.4	1.2	293.6
4th quarter	332.9	204.1	193.3	10.8	13.0	29.5	11.6	41.3	4.2	28.1	0.3	1.2	303.8
1953													
1st quarter	339.0	208.0	196.9	11.1	13.0	30.0	11.9	42.0	4.5	28.7	0.3	1.3	309.3
2nd quarter	342.0	211.3	200.1	11.3	12.4	29.9	12.2	41.2	4.6	29.2	0.1	1.3	311.7
3rd quarter	340.8	211.5	200.3	11.2	11.7	29.8	12.5	40.2	4.8	29.3	0.3	1.2	310.5
4th quarter	332.7	210.0	198.7	11.3	11.5	29.8	12.8	33.1	5.0	29.2	-0.2	1.1	302.2
1954													
1st quarter	334.5	208.1	196.4	11.7	12.9	29.7	13.1	35.5	5.2	28.7	-0.3	1.0	304.5
2nd quarter	334.8	207.7	196.0	11.7	11.7	30.3	13.3	36.8	5.5	28.8	0.3	1.0	305.3
3rd quarter	338.3	208.3	196.3	11.9	11.8	30.5	13.5	38.7	5.7	28.7	-0.1	1.0	308.5
4th quarter	347.3	212.6	200.4	12.2	10.7	31.5	13.6	42.4	6.0	29.3	-0.3	1.0	316.7
1955													
1st quarter	359.3	217.1	204.2	12.9	10.9	32.5	13.7	47.5	6.1	30.2	-0.2	1.2	327.8
2nd quarter	369.4	223.6	210.3	13.3	11.3	33.2	13.7	48.7	6.3	31.2	-0.1	1.3	336.8
3rd quarter	376.4	228.6	214.7	13.9	10.7	34.0	13.8	49.4	6.2	31.9	-0.4	1.5	342.6
4th quarter	382.9	233.6	219.5	14.1	10.0	34.6	13.9	50.4	6.3	32.5	-0.2	1.6	348.7
1956													
1st quarter	386.6	238.0	223.3	14.8	10.2	34.7	14.0	48.4	6.6	33.0	-0.1	1.7	351.9
2nd quarter	392.1	242.6	227.5	15.1	10.4	35.1	14.0	48.2	6.8	33.6	0.2	1.7	357.0
3rd quarter	396.3	245.7	230.0	15.8	10.9	35.3	14.1	47.4	7.1	34.6	0.5	1.8	360.5
4th quarter	404.5	251.6	235.4	16.2	10.9	36.0	14.2	48.1	7.0	35.7	0.8	1.8	367.7
1957													
1st quarter	411.1	255.3	238.1	17.1	9.9	37.0	14.3	49.7	7.7	36.1	0.9	1.9	373.9
2nd quarter	413.4	257.0	239.6	17.4	10.5	37.3	14.4	48.5	8.0	36.6	0.8	1.9	375.7
3rd quarter	417.4	259.7	241.8	17.8	11.0	37.6	14.5	48.0	8.2	37.0	0.6	1.9	379.1
4th quarter	411.5	258.1	240.1	18.1	10.7	37.2	14.7	44.3	8.2	36.7	0.5	1.9	373.3
1958													
1st quarter	406.0	255.2	237.4	17.9	13.3	37.0	15.0	38.4	9.0	36.8	0.6	1.9	367.9
2nd quarter	407.5	254.8	236.9	17.9	13.0	37.4	15.2	39.2	9.5	37.3	0.8	1.8	369.1
3rd quarter	417.9	260.9	242.6	18.3	12.1	37.9	15.3	43.3	9.8	37.8	1.0	1.8	379.3
4th quarter	431.0	267.2	248.4	18.8	11.2	38.8	15.4	49.0	9.9	38.9	1.2	1.7	391.5
1959													
1st quarter	442.7	274.5	254.0	20.5	10.9	39.3	15.4	52.6	8.8	39.8	1.1	1.7	401.4
2nd quarter	457.3	281.6	260.6	21.1	9.9	40.5	15.9	57.6	9.8	40.3	0.9	1.8	415.3
3rd quarter	454.2	282.3	260.9	21.4	9.4	40.8	16.3	52.3	9.8	41.7	1.1	1.8	410.8
4th quarter	459.8	285.5	263.9	21.6	10.1	40.5	16.5	52.8	10.1	42.4	1.1	1.8	415.5
1960													
1st quarter	473.5	294.1	270.8	23.3	9.6	40.3	16.7	57.0	10.2	43.7	1.0	1.8	428.0
2nd quarter	473.8	296.9	273.4	23.5	10.6	40.2	16.9	53.2	10.1	44.3	1.3	1.8	427.9
3rd quarter	475.1	297.6	274.0	23.7	11.0	39.9	17.0	52.3	10.7	44.9	1.0	1.9	428.5
4th quarter	473.3	297.1	273.3	23.8	11.3	39.8	17.2	49.9	11.2	45.3	1.2	1.9	426.5
1961													
1st quarter	475.3	298.0	273.8	24.2	11.5	40.8	17.4	48.9	11.6	45.8	1.6	2.0	428.3
2nd quarter	484.9	302.2	277.6	24.6	10.9	41.7	17.6	53.2	12.2	46.5	2.0	2.0	437.7
3rd quarter	494.3	307.2	282.3	24.9	11.0	42.3	17.8	55.4	12.6	47.3	2.2	2.0	446.4
4th quarter	508.2	313.8	288.4	25.4	11.5	43.0	18.1	59.3	13.4	48.4	2.3	2.1	459.0

Table 19-8. National Income by Type of Income—*Continued*

(Billions of dollars, quarterly data are at seasonally adjusted annual rates.) NIPA Tables 1.7.5, 1.12

Year and quarter	National income, total	Compensation of employees Total	Wage and salary accruals	Supplements to wages and salaries	Proprietors' income with IVA and CCAdj Farm	Nonfarm	Rental income of persons with CCAdj	Corporate profits with IVA and CCAdj	Net interest and miscellaneous payments	Taxes on production and imports	Less: Subsidies	Business current transfer payments, net	Addendum: Net national factor income
1962													
1st quarter	519.0	320.4	293.3	27.2	11.9	43.4	18.3	61.7	13.1	49.4	2.3	2.2	468.8
2nd quarter	525.6	326.4	298.7	27.6	11.1	44.0	18.5	61.0	14.1	49.9	2.4	2.2	475.0
3rd quarter	531.7	329.2	301.2	28.0	10.7	44.5	18.7	62.2	14.6	50.9	2.2	2.3	479.9
4th quarter	539.2	332.6	304.2	28.4	11.3	44.4	18.9	64.5	15.0	51.3	2.2	2.3	486.8
1963													
1st quarter	545.8	337.5	308.0	29.5	11.4	44.6	19.1	64.7	14.6	52.0	2.0	2.6	492.0
2nd quarter	555.3	342.4	312.4	30.0	10.8	45.1	19.3	68.1	14.8	52.9	2.2	2.6	500.6
3rd quarter	563.8	347.4	316.8	30.6	10.7	45.7	19.5	69.5	15.3	53.9	2.3	2.7	508.1
4th quarter	574.1	353.6	322.2	31.3	11.1	46.6	19.4	71.0	15.8	54.7	2.4	2.8	517.6
1964													
1st quarter	586.5	360.0	328.2	31.8	9.9	48.2	19.4	75.2	16.6	55.7	2.7	2.9	529.3
2nd quarter	596.2	367.4	334.8	32.5	9.5	49.5	19.4	75.1	17.1	56.7	2.9	2.9	538.0
3rd quarter	607.6	374.7	341.4	33.3	9.3	50.3	19.5	76.3	17.9	57.9	2.6	3.3	547.9
4th quarter	615.5	380.7	346.7	34.0	10.4	50.3	19.4	75.4	18.1	58.8	2.7	3.4	554.4
1965													
1st quarter	633.8	387.3	352.8	34.5	11.4	50.7	19.7	83.3	19.0	60.2	2.9	3.6	571.5
2nd quarter	644.8	394.1	358.9	35.2	12.0	51.4	19.9	85.4	19.5	60.3	3.0	3.6	582.3
3rd quarter	655.8	402.3	366.2	36.1	12.2	52.0	20.1	86.7	20.0	60.5	3.0	3.6	593.3
4th quarter	674.4	414.3	377.1	37.2	12.5	53.4	20.1	90.7	20.0	61.8	3.1	3.6	611.0
1966													
1st quarter	694.1	426.7	385.8	40.9	14.9	54.6	20.5	93.9	21.1	61.4	3.6	3.6	631.6
2nd quarter	703.8	437.8	395.9	41.9	12.7	54.9	20.4	92.8	21.9	62.8	3.9	3.5	640.3
3rd quarter	715.1	449.0	406.1	42.8	12.3	55.4	20.6	91.1	22.7	63.7	4.1	3.5	651.1
4th quarter	727.5	457.1	413.5	43.7	12.2	56.1	20.6	92.4	23.8	64.9	4.2	3.5	662.4
1967													
1st quarter	733.6	463.3	418.8	44.4	11.9	57.2	20.8	89.6	24.7	65.6	4.0	3.6	667.5
2nd quarter	740.5	469.0	423.6	45.4	11.1	57.7	20.9	88.5	25.5	66.8	3.9	3.7	672.7
3rd quarter	755.9	478.7	432.0	46.6	12.0	59.0	21.0	89.7	25.8	68.7	3.7	3.8	686.1
4th quarter	771.6	489.7	441.6	48.1	11.5	58.9	20.9	92.9	26.2	70.6	3.7	3.9	700.0
1968													
1st quarter	792.2	504.5	454.2	50.3	11.6	60.5	20.6	93.9	26.6	73.4	4.0	4.1	717.6
2nd quarter	813.0	517.6	465.9	51.7	11.2	62.2	20.6	97.7	27.0	75.4	4.2	4.3	736.3
3rd quarter	831.6	531.4	478.3	53.1	11.8	63.5	20.7	97.9	27.1	77.7	4.2	4.4	752.5
4th quarter	848.0	543.8	489.4	54.4	12.0	64.0	20.6	99.4	27.7	79.1	4.2	4.6	767.4
1969													
1st quarter	864.9	555.9	499.1	56.8	11.6	64.7	20.8	99.4	30.5	80.6	4.3	4.9	782.9
2nd quarter	881.0	569.8	511.4	58.4	12.5	65.0	20.9	96.4	32.1	82.9	4.5	5.0	796.6
3rd quarter	899.6	586.6	526.4	60.1	13.1	65.1	21.0	93.6	33.7	85.2	4.7	5.0	813.0
4th quarter	908.4	598.2	536.5	61.8	14.1	63.9	20.9	88.5	34.6	86.7	4.7	5.0	820.2
1970													
1st quarter	912.7	608.6	545.1	63.5	13.5	64.1	20.9	80.6	36.0	88.5	4.7	4.8	823.7
2nd quarter	924.4	614.2	549.1	65.1	12.4	64.7	20.6	84.4	38.1	90.5	4.8	4.6	834.4
3rd quarter	939.8	622.2	555.7	66.4	13.2	66.0	21.2	84.6	40.5	92.5	4.7	4.4	847.7
4th quarter	941.1	623.9	556.3	67.6	12.5	67.4	21.5	80.4	41.9	94.1	4.8	4.3	847.8
1971													
1st quarter	976.6	641.6	570.2	71.4	13.1	68.0	21.5	92.7	43.1	97.7	4.8	4.3	880.0
2nd quarter	996.4	653.7	580.3	73.4	13.3	70.5	22.0	94.6	44.0	98.9	4.8	4.3	898.0
3rd quarter	1 013.9	664.1	588.8	75.3	13.0	72.4	22.4	96.7	44.1	101.7	4.5	4.3	912.7
4th quarter	1 035.6	676.3	599.0	77.3	14.2	74.3	22.8	100.2	44.3	103.7	4.6	4.4	932.2
1972													
1st quarter	1 067.8	701.1	618.0	83.2	13.1	75.6	23.5	106.2	45.2	104.6	6.1	4.7	964.7
2nd quarter	1 088.6	715.8	630.5	85.3	15.4	76.7	20.5	107.9	46.5	106.8	6.2	4.8	982.8
3rd quarter	1 118.8	729.7	642.4	87.3	17.2	79.4	24.3	112.1	48.9	108.9	7.2	5.0	1 011.6
4th quarter	1 166.1	753.9	664.3	89.7	22.4	84.3	24.3	119.5	51.1	111.5	7.1	5.2	1 055.5
1973													
1st quarter	1 203.6	781.7	683.4	98.3	21.8	84.2	24.2	126.0	51.3	114.6	5.9	5.7	1 089.1
2nd quarter	1 228.6	800.8	700.1	100.7	27.6	84.1	24.1	122.8	52.8	116.2	5.7	6.1	1 112.3
3rd quarter	1 256.5	819.9	716.2	103.7	29.5	84.9	23.1	123.2	56.8	118.4	4.7	5.9	1 137.4
4th quarter	1 295.6	842.5	735.4	107.1	37.5	85.0	24.1	126.0	60.0	119.7	4.6	6.1	1 175.2
1974													
1st quarter	1 307.6	860.7	748.2	112.5	28.6	87.6	24.4	118.8	64.4	120.8	3.6	6.6	1 184.5
2nd quarter	1 328.7	881.4	765.3	116.1	20.1	89.2	23.8	117.4	69.1	124.1	2.9	6.9	1 200.8
3rd quarter	1 357.2	903.1	783.1	120.0	21.5	91.9	24.1	114.1	72.4	127.1	3.2	7.3	1 227.1
4th quarter	1 372.3	915.8	792.5	123.3	23.7	91.4	23.9	110.3	77.3	127.7	3.6	7.7	1 242.3
1975													
1st quarter	1 379.7	919.5	791.9	127.6	19.7	93.7	23.7	111.8	80.7	128.8	4.2	8.7	1 249.2
2nd quarter	1 411.2	931.7	800.4	131.4	20.1	95.4	23.5	124.5	80.8	133.0	4.3	9.5	1 276.0
3rd quarter	1 470.3	957.7	821.3	136.4	23.8	98.7	23.3	144.8	82.2	138.2	4.6	9.7	1 330.6
4th quarter	1 514.9	987.6	845.8	141.9	24.3	102.6	22.9	152.2	82.8	141.1	4.9	9.8	1 372.4
1976													
1st quarter	1 564.8	1 022.4	871.2	151.1	19.4	108.2	22.6	164.9	82.5	141.7	5.1	9.9	1 420.0
2nd quarter	1 591.4	1 046.1	889.4	156.8	17.0	113.0	21.7	160.3	85.2	144.9	4.8	9.8	1 443.4
3rd quarter	1 624.2	1 070.8	908.4	162.4	16.1	117.7	21.9	160.9	86.6	147.7	5.1	9.4	1 474.0
4th quarter	1 658.7	1 098.1	929.9	168.1	16.3	121.2	22.0	160.4	87.9	151.3	5.5	8.9	1 505.9

Table 19-8. National Income by Type of Income—*Continued*

(Billions of dollars, quarterly data are at seasonally adjusted annual rates.)

NIPA Tables 1.7.5, 1.12

Year and quarter	National income, total	Compensation of employees			Proprietors' income with IVA and CCAdj		Rental income of persons with CCAdj	Corporate profits with IVA and CCAdj	Net interest and miscellaneous payments	Taxes on production and imports	Less: Subsidies	Business current transfer payments, net	Addendum: Net national factor income
		Total	Wage and salary accruals	Supplements to wages and salaries	Farm	Nonfarm							
1977													
1st quarter	1 704.4	1 127.0	950.0	177.0	16.0	124.6	20.9	170.3	90.5	154.8	5.8	8.5	1 549.1
2nd quarter	1 774.2	1 164.4	980.9	183.5	14.1	127.9	19.9	191.5	98.6	158.0	5.9	8.2	1 616.3
3rd quarter	1 831.4	1 196.9	1 007.5	189.4	11.8	131.9	19.0	206.2	105.1	161.5	6.4	8.4	1 670.8
4th quarter	1 879.7	1 233.7	1 038.2	195.6	22.0	136.0	18.7	199.5	110.1	164.3	10.3	8.7	1 720.1
1978													
1st quarter	1 917.4	1 269.7	1 064.2	205.5	18.5	139.9	20.4	192.5	111.3	166.9	8.7	9.8	1 752.3
2nd quarter	2 012.6	1 317.9	1 106.0	212.0	20.9	147.2	19.8	220.2	113.9	173.1	8.4	10.5	1 839.9
3rd quarter	2 059.0	1 354.8	1 137.1	217.7	20.8	150.5	21.4	225.1	115.3	169.7	8.3	11.2	1 888.0
4th quarter	2 122.6	1 399.3	1 175.0	224.3	19.5	152.7	21.9	235.9	119.6	173.9	10.4	11.8	1 949.0
1979													
1st quarter	2 177.4	1 443.5	1 208.4	235.1	23.8	155.4	23.4	226.1	126.6	176.4	8.4	12.8	1 998.7
2nd quarter	2 216.8	1 475.2	1 234.0	241.2	21.8	157.4	21.1	228.0	132.8	178.5	8.8	13.2	2 036.4
3rd quarter	2 270.1	1 516.2	1 268.2	248.1	22.3	160.3	21.2	226.2	140.8	180.9	8.1	13.6	2 087.0
4th quarter	2 328.8	1 558.2	1 302.7	255.5	20.8	162.8	24.8	221.1	155.4	184.6	8.9	13.7	2 143.1
1980													
1st quarter	2 374.1	1 599.0	1 334.9	264.1	13.3	155.2	28.6	216.5	171.3	189.5	9.2	13.9	2 184.0
2nd quarter	2 367.7	1 621.3	1 351.0	270.3	3.1	159.1	24.1	186.3	176.9	196.9	9.6	14.1	2 170.9
3rd quarter	2 430.2	1 653.5	1 376.6	276.9	11.7	164.0	25.0	192.6	180.1	204.3	10.1	14.5	2 227.0
4th quarter	2 559.9	1 716.5	1 431.2	285.3	18.7	168.7	36.3	210.2	199.0	210.6	10.3	16.5	2 349.3
1981													
1st quarter	2 649.0	1 768.9	1 469.1	299.8	17.6	172.5	36.2	221.0	201.9	230.8	10.6	17.2	2 418.0
2nd quarter	2 690.8	1 801.9	1 496.2	305.7	18.2	159.7	35.1	217.2	221.4	235.5	10.7	17.4	2 453.4
3rd quarter	2 784.2	1 840.0	1 528.7	311.3	23.3	160.9	35.7	235.4	251.0	237.5	11.1	18.2	2 546.2
4th quarter	2 795.4	1 867.9	1 551.5	316.4	17.0	157.2	38.8	219.6	255.1	238.8	13.5	18.8	2 555.6
1982													
1st quarter	2 801.9	1 891.8	1 567.2	324.6	14.4	153.2	39.5	197.3	266.4	237.4	14.0	20.0	2 562.6
2nd quarter	2 851.2	1 911.1	1 580.9	330.2	12.8	160.3	36.2	211.6	278.3	238.3	13.6	20.6	2 610.2
3rd quarter	2 869.1	1 930.8	1 596.1	334.8	11.9	162.5	38.0	210.1	271.4	241.8	13.0	20.8	2 624.8
4th quarter	2 883.4	1 944.8	1 605.9	338.9	14.2	170.1	38.5	203.9	268.4	246.3	19.4	21.0	2 639.8
1983													
1st quarter	2 946.6	1 972.7	1 623.1	349.7	12.9	175.1	37.6	225.2	274.8	250.7	19.9	21.2	2 698.3
2nd quarter	3 026.5	2 010.5	1 655.1	355.4	7.9	180.3	37.8	256.1	275.6	261.2	21.6	21.8	2 768.2
3rd quarter	3 106.9	2 052.4	1 691.8	360.6	0.2	188.2	38.2	273.3	290.0	267.5	22.2	22.8	2 842.3
4th quarter	3 203.6	2 106.5	1 740.1	366.4	3.8	194.3	39.1	284.6	300.8	273.7	21.5	24.6	2 929.1
1984													
1st quarter	3 339.2	2 176.0	1 785.2	390.8	19.5	204.7	38.1	311.5	303.3	281.6	21.2	27.7	3 053.1
2nd quarter	3 436.9	2 225.7	1 828.2	397.5	21.3	213.7	36.7	323.2	321.7	287.7	21.0	29.8	3 142.3
3rd quarter	3 505.5	2 270.9	1 866.7	404.1	20.4	216.6	40.4	316.6	340.0	292.2	20.9	31.3	3 205.0
4th quarter	3 563.6	2 309.3	1 899.5	409.7	22.5	213.5	44.8	323.1	343.2	297.5	21.2	32.4	3 256.5
1985													
1st quarter	3 626.2	2 353.7	1 933.8	419.9	22.8	225.4	42.9	325.6	343.0	301.0	21.1	33.4	3 313.5
2nd quarter	3 669.2	2 389.2	1 963.2	426.0	20.4	224.2	41.7	327.4	341.3	305.7	21.0	39.3	3 344.2
3rd quarter	3 721.1	2 427.9	1 996.1	431.8	19.3	225.3	42.2	346.0	334.8	311.9	21.3	33.9	3 395.6
4th quarter	3 768.5	2 476.1	2 037.1	439.1	21.4	225.5	40.5	331.2	346.7	313.9	22.0	34.2	3 441.4
1986													
1st quarter	3 824.0	2 510.0	2 063.5	446.4	18.2	231.3	36.8	324.4	365.0	317.5	23.1	43.0	3 485.6
2nd quarter	3 841.8	2 533.3	2 081.8	451.5	19.7	237.5	35.6	315.1	368.9	319.5	24.2	35.4	3 510.0
3rd quarter	3 886.7	2 569.2	2 111.7	457.4	26.7	244.8	32.5	307.5	370.5	326.2	25.5	34.1	3 551.2
4th quarter	3 933.3	2 618.2	2 152.2	465.9	26.7	245.4	30.4	309.5	364.0	330.4	26.8	34.8	3 594.2
1987													
1st quarter	4 007.1	2 664.5	2 193.7	470.8	27.3	255.4	31.6	323.3	362.1	336.0	28.3	34.8	3 664.1
2nd quarter	4 100.7	2 706.2	2 230.1	476.1	29.1	260.7	30.5	363.1	361.9	344.4	30.4	35.1	3 751.4
3rd quarter	4 197.8	2 752.7	2 270.6	482.1	28.9	268.3	35.3	389.7	368.6	352.4	31.3	33.2	3 843.5
4th quarter	4 294.6	2 819.2	2 330.7	488.5	30.4	277.0	39.4	395.2	374.0	357.4	31.1	33.1	3 935.2
1988													
1st quarter	4 385.5	2 869.1	2 367.2	501.9	33.4	294.2	38.4	405.1	379.4	365.1	30.4	31.9	4 019.5
2nd quarter	4 476.5	2 932.3	2 422.2	510.1	27.4	306.3	36.9	421.4	373.6	372.6	29.8	32.5	4 097.9
3rd quarter	4 562.7	2 981.0	2 462.7	518.3	28.8	314.2	38.8	428.3	385.6	377.6	29.2	34.0	4 176.7
4th quarter	4 664.5	3 034.2	2 507.1	527.2	17.6	317.5	46.8	451.7	402.6	382.5	28.6	36.0	4 270.5
1989													
1st quarter	4 743.4	3 078.5	2 542.0	536.5	36.7	320.2	44.2	431.4	426.5	391.1	28.0	38.2	4 337.6
2nd quarter	4 771.9	3 107.8	2 563.3	544.5	32.4	316.0	43.5	423.9	434.7	397.4	27.4	38.6	4 358.3
3rd quarter	4 823.5	3 144.4	2 591.6	552.8	30.4	317.4	41.1	428.6	439.7	403.8	27.1	40.0	4 401.6
4th quarter	4 863.2	3 194.6	2 635.3	559.3	32.5	320.6	40.8	418.4	435.4	403.2	27.3	39.9	4 442.3
1990													
1st quarter	4 964.4	3 259.0	2 686.8	572.2	34.4	326.2	43.3	427.3	438.8	419.4	27.1	40.2	4 528.9
2nd quarter	5 059.7	3 317.4	2 735.9	581.5	32.7	331.6	48.2	452.4	443.5	419.5	26.9	39.9	4 625.7
3rd quarter	5 091.7	3 358.5	2 768.7	589.8	31.8	337.4	53.3	426.9	442.8	426.9	26.9	39.8	4 650.8
4th quarter	5 122.5	3 370.1	2 773.4	596.7	29.8	336.8	54.4	431.2	451.7	434.2	27.0	40.5	4 674.0
1991													
1st quarter	5 151.6	3 385.0	2 776.0	609.0	26.7	331.2	56.1	462.4	429.0	444.3	27.1	40.8	4 690.3
2nd quarter	5 190.0	3 419.4	2 801.2	618.2	28.5	336.6	58.1	455.8	421.5	451.6	27.2	39.7	4 720.0
3rd quarter	5 236.9	3 455.3	2 826.5	628.8	25.3	342.5	62.7	453.2	418.6	461.2	27.5	39.5	4 757.5
4th quarter	5 293.1	3 493.6	2 854.2	639.4	29.5	348.9	69.4	457.7	403.9	471.3	28.1	39.7	4 803.0

Table 19-8. National Income by Type of Income—*Continued*

(Billions of dollars, quarterly data are at seasonally adjusted annual rates.)   **NIPA Tables 1.7.5, 1.12**

Year and quarter	National income, total	Compensation of employees Total	Wage and salary accruals	Supplements to wages and salaries	Proprietors' income with IVA and CCAdj Farm	Nonfarm	Rental income of persons with CCAdj	Corporate profits with IVA and CCAdj	Net interest and miscellaneous payments	Taxes on production and imports	Less: Subsidies	Business current transfer payments, net	Addendum: Net national factor income
1992													
1st quarter	5 411.3	3 561.1	2 903.4	657.7	33.9	362.5	71.6	491.0	396.3	476.2	28.6	39.6	4 916.4
2nd quarter	5 492.0	3 612.7	2 942.8	669.9	36.4	374.0	81.3	498.7	389.6	481.1	29.2	39.3	4 992.6
3rd quarter	5 533.7	3 656.6	2 976.1	680.5	37.8	383.1	89.3	480.5	382.1	485.9	30.4	39.8	5 029.4
4th quarter	5 631.4	3 695.4	3 008.8	686.5	35.1	396.9	96.3	514.7	382.9	490.3	32.2	44.0	5 121.2
1993													
1st quarter	5 666.2	3 732.2	3 034.6	697.6	29.3	406.5	105.5	509.3	380.2	489.8	35.5	41.2	5 163.0
2nd quarter	5 755.2	3 777.3	3 067.4	709.8	35.6	414.5	113.5	533.6	370.5	497.9	37.6	40.4	5 245.1
3rd quarter	5 799.4	3 819.8	3 100.3	719.5	26.7	420.3	115.4	543.4	357.9	505.0	37.7	39.8	5 283.4
4th quarter	5 918.2	3 859.2	3 129.9	729.3	36.5	429.1	122.0	588.4	349.8	519.8	36.0	40.5	5 384.9
1994													
1st quarter	6 028.1	3 926.9	3 186.2	740.7	42.6	434.1	133.1	590.5	351.0	531.9	33.6	41.9	5 478.2
2nd quarter	6 129.3	3 978.6	3 229.3	749.3	37.5	444.3	141.6	610.0	354.7	544.2	32.4	40.9	5 566.8
3rd quarter	6 230.2	4 016.4	3 262.7	753.7	33.1	452.7	148.5	643.2	366.1	550.2	31.9	42.4	5 660.0
4th quarter	6 337.3	4 072.2	3 315.6	756.5	29.2	467.0	148.4	669.2	377.1	554.7	32.2	42.4	5 763.0
1995													
1st quarter	6 411.5	4 135.5	3 377.0	758.5	21.6	478.8	151.0	674.8	371.0	554.9	34.0	44.7	5 832.7
2nd quarter	6 468.6	4 171.3	3 411.6	759.7	19.8	486.5	153.0	702.2	358.1	553.7	34.6	45.7	5 890.9
3rd quarter	6 562.7	4 216.4	3 454.6	761.8	22.8	497.2	152.8	737.7	351.9	559.2	35.1	46.8	5 978.8
4th quarter	6 646.5	4 257.5	3 494.4	763.1	29.5	507.9	161.5	750.0	352.3	563.9	35.5	46.2	6 058.7
1996													
1st quarter	6 757.1	4 295.5	3 529.5	766.1	38.2	522.0	166.7	783.2	354.1	570.8	35.5	48.1	6 159.8
2nd quarter	6 886.9	4 364.3	3 594.2	770.1	45.4	541.1	168.4	795.9	366.4	577.7	35.4	49.2	6 281.4
3rd quarter	6 972.4	4 423.4	3 650.2	773.2	34.6	554.0	172.1	802.1	375.3	581.6	35.2	49.9	6 361.5
4th quarter	7 110.3	4 482.2	3 706.2	776.1	35.6	563.8	174.5	824.8	388.6	592.9	34.8	67.8	6 469.5
1997													
1st quarter	7 225.8	4 554.7	3 774.2	780.5	38.2	581.5	174.9	855.7	397.3	595.6	34.4	48.4	6 602.2
2nd quarter	7 333.4	4 617.9	3 832.3	785.6	28.3	591.1	175.9	878.8	401.6	610.3	33.6	48.6	6 693.6
3rd quarter	7 476.6	4 695.2	3 900.5	794.8	32.5	600.3	176.4	912.0	408.5	616.6	33.4	54.5	6 825.0
4th quarter	7 588.1	4 794.7	3 987.6	807.1	31.4	609.7	178.9	892.9	422.8	624.0	33.8	53.7	6 930.4
1998													
1st quarter	7 689.5	4 898.4	4 075.2	823.2	28.2	635.5	182.7	817.7	458.5	629.1	33.8	60.3	7 021.0
2nd quarter	7 815.4	4 982.0	4 145.2	836.8	26.8	650.2	188.6	811.5	480.8	635.5	35.0	61.4	7 140.0
3rd quarter	7 949.0	5 065.4	4 216.2	849.2	27.1	665.8	195.7	820.1	491.2	643.0	36.8	63.8	7 265.3
4th quarter	8 048.4	5 147.1	4 287.1	860.1	33.4	683.1	198.8	800.3	486.8	650.3	39.9	75.3	7 349.7
1999													
1st quarter	8 204.2	5 246.4	4 375.5	870.9	34.3	695.3	203.0	859.7	469.0	657.5	42.4	66.3	7 507.8
2nd quarter	8 284.0	5 297.9	4 417.9	880.0	28.7	710.1	206.9	859.4	477.0	667.1	45.0	67.2	7 580.1
3rd quarter	8 379.7	5 372.0	4 479.5	892.5	26.6	724.1	209.2	848.4	483.6	679.0	46.4	69.1	7 663.8
4th quarter	8 563.9	5 499.4	4 587.8	911.6	24.3	743.7	213.5	857.6	495.9	690.8	46.9	73.2	7 834.5
2000													
1st quarter	8 809.8	5 692.1	4 755.0	937.0	25.8	758.0	214.6	840.5	532.1	698.6	45.1	80.8	8 062.9
2nd quarter	8 896.0	5 731.4	4 781.4	949.5	31.6	787.8	212.1	831.7	543.9	707.3	45.5	84.6	8 138.5
3rd quarter	9 005.7	5 845.8	4 874.4	971.5	29.7	796.9	213.3	814.7	543.2	711.3	45.8	88.9	8 243.7
4th quarter	9 044.0	5 886.1	4 899.5	986.6	31.5	808.6	221.1	790.0	537.8	717.1	47.0	93.5	8 275.1
2001													
1st quarter	9 184.4	5 993.9	4 988.1	1 005.8	32.1	835.4	225.3	782.8	541.8	724.1	55.2	99.9	8 411.3
2nd quarter	9 209.9	5 979.9	4 961.4	1 018.5	30.8	840.8	230.6	812.3	547.7	724.1	62.0	102.8	8 442.1
3rd quarter	9 157.3	5 965.8	4 932.4	1 033.3	31.1	846.9	239.5	765.0	544.3	725.4	71.2	102.6	8 392.6
4th quarter	9 189.2	5 977.7	4 926.8	1 050.8	28.1	837.7	234.1	776.6	543.6	737.2	46.4	99.8	8 397.8
2002													
1st quarter	9 304.7	6 038.4	4 963.6	1 074.9	16.3	864.3	229.2	830.3	529.1	745.2	42.6	90.3	8 507.6
2nd quarter	9 380.5	6 101.3	5 003.0	1 098.2	11.6	872.6	231.7	852.0	505.7	756.9	39.8	84.2	8 574.9
3rd quarter	9 418.0	6 128.8	5 006.3	1 122.6	20.1	873.2	212.7	869.8	494.2	772.1	41.4	79.4	8 598.8
4th quarter	9 530.9	6 174.7	5 016.4	1 158.3	25.8	877.4	201.4	936.7	496.5	777.0	41.7	75.6	8 712.4
2003													
1st quarter	9 614.2	6 255.8	5 061.0	1 194.9	29.9	859.7	209.7	917.5	511.9	787.9	44.9	77.3	8 784.6
2nd quarter	9 757.3	6 346.3	5 123.5	1 222.9	37.5	881.6	204.2	950.1	511.5	799.5	57.1	75.8	8 931.2
3rd quarter	9 899.4	6 425.6	5 184.6	1 241.0	38.3	907.4	186.2	992.7	501.0	813.0	47.0	75.8	9 051.2
4th quarter	10 089.8	6 502.6	5 249.4	1 253.2	40.4	927.7	216.6	1 050.9	492.1	826.9	47.3	75.7	9 230.2
2004													
1st quarter	10 281.2	6 539.8	5 275.9	1 263.9	54.2	947.9	204.2	1 187.2	467.7	843.5	44.8	77.8	9 401.1
2nd quarter	10 444.7	6 636.4	5 363.6	1 272.8	52.0	977.8	197.1	1 226.9	460.6	855.7	43.6	80.0	9 550.7
3rd quarter	10 641.6	6 756.3	5 468.9	1 287.4	44.0	996.1	196.8	1 292.2	454.0	867.9	44.9	79.0	9 739.4
4th quarter	10 768.7	6 841.2	5 534.4	1 306.8	48.5	1 014.6	195.4	1 281.4	464.2	886.5	52.2	89.9	9 845.3
2005													
1st quarter	11 019.6	6 921.1	5 584.2	1 336.9	43.7	1 003.1	190.7	1 408.2	509.4	905.6	56.9	96.5	10 076.1
2nd quarter	11 156.6	7 003.6	5 651.7	1 351.9	46.4	1 007.6	181.5	1 429.0	528.0	925.1	61.0	99.6	10 196.0
3rd quarter	11 360.2	7 128.4	5 758.3	1 370.1	45.6	1 037.0	168.4	1 454.7	558.0	939.6	62.1	95.2	10 392.0
4th quarter	11 559.0	7 207.1	5 829.7	1 377.4	39.9	1 055.9	172.3	1 532.5	576.9	950.3	63.7	92.3	10 584.6
2006													
1st quarter	11 838.2	7 353.7	5 958.9	1 394.8	28.4	1 098.5	161.3	1 590.9	608.9	971.5	55.6	82.8	10 841.8
2nd quarter	11 965.9	7 419.9	6 018.6	1 401.3	28.4	1 104.8	153.2	1 597.7	654.4	983.3	51.4	79.3	10 958.4
3rd quarter	12 009.3	7 484.1	6 075.4	1 408.7	28.4	1 102.8	140.3	1 655.1	661.6	991.6	49.8	83.6	11 072.2
4th quarter	12 227.9	7 650.3	6 227.6	1 422.6	32.2	1 108.4	131.2	1 589.6	684.0	1 000.7	48.7	86.1	11 195.7

Table 19-9. Saving and Investment

(Billions of dollars, except as noted; quarterly data are at seasonally adjusted annual rates.)   **NIPA Tables 1.7.5, 5.1**

Year and quarter	Gross saving — Total	Net saving — Private	Net saving — Government — Federal	Net saving — Government — State and local	Consumption of fixed capital — Total	Consumption of fixed capital — Private	Consumption of fixed capital — Government — Federal	Consumption of fixed capital — Government — State and local	Gross domestic investment — Total	Gross domestic investment — Private	Gross domestic investment — Government	Net lending or net borrowing (-), NIPAs	Net domestic investment	Gross national income	Net saving as a percentage of gross national income
1946	38.4	18.8	-5.0	1.5	23.1	12.3	9.3	1.5	34.6	31.1	3.5	4.9	11.5	221.7	6.9
1947	46.6	13.2	5.3	1.4	26.6	16.1	8.8	1.8	39.6	35.0	4.6	9.3	12.9	242.9	8.2
1948	58.0	24.7	3.7	1.2	28.5	18.9	7.5	2.1	55.1	48.1	7.0	2.4	26.7	271.1	10.9
1949	45.6	20.6	-5.6	1.5	29.2	20.5	6.6	2.1	46.6	36.9	9.7	0.9	17.4	266.7	6.2
1947															
1st quarter	46.6	13.4	6.0	1.6	25.6	14.6	9.3	1.7	38.0	33.7	4.3	9.4	12.4	237.3	8.8
2nd quarter	44.0	10.9	5.2	1.6	26.3	15.7	8.8	1.8	36.7	32.4	4.3	9.9	10.4	238.9	7.4
3rd quarter	45.1	14.8	2.0	1.1	27.1	16.6	8.6	1.9	37.4	32.7	4.7	10.1	10.3	243.2	7.4
4th quarter	50.6	13.7	8.0	1.3	27.6	17.4	8.3	1.9	46.2	41.0	5.1	7.8	18.5	252.3	9.1
1948															
1st quarter	55.4	18.6	7.8	1.0	27.9	18.0	7.9	2.0	51.2	45.0	6.2	4.9	23.3	261.0	10.5
2nd quarter	59.1	24.5	5.1	1.2	28.3	18.6	7.6	2.1	54.8	48.1	6.7	3.0	26.5	270.1	11.4
3rd quarter	58.7	27.3	1.4	1.2	28.7	19.1	7.4	2.1	57.4	50.2	7.1	0.9	28.6	275.6	10.9
4th quarter	58.9	28.3	0.2	1.5	28.9	19.6	7.2	2.2	57.1	49.1	8.0	0.8	28.1	277.6	10.8
1949															
1st quarter	51.1	23.7	-3.4	1.5	29.2	20.0	7.1	2.2	49.5	40.9	8.6	2.2	20.3	270.7	8.1
2nd quarter	44.1	19.9	-6.5	1.4	29.2	20.4	6.7	2.1	43.6	34.0	9.5	1.7	14.4	266.3	5.6
3rd quarter	46.0	21.7	-6.5	1.6	29.1	20.7	6.3	2.1	47.6	37.3	10.3	0.6	18.5	266.6	6.3
4th quarter	41.3	16.9	-6.1	1.3	29.2	21.0	6.1	2.1	45.5	35.2	10.4	-1.0	16.4	263.1	4.6
1950															
1st quarter	48.7	27.0	-8.3	1.0	29.1	21.2	5.9	2.0	53.4	44.4	9.0	-1.0	24.3	272.7	7.2
2nd quarter	56.7	23.8	2.8	0.7	29.4	21.6	5.7	2.0	59.2	49.9	9.4	-1.3	29.8	284.5	9.6
3rd quarter	63.1	17.7	13.6	1.8	30.1	22.2	5.7	2.1	66.4	56.1	10.2	-2.7	36.3	302.9	10.9
4th quarter	74.1	26.9	14.2	1.8	31.2	23.1	5.9	2.3	76.5	65.9	10.6	-2.5	45.3	315.1	13.6
1951															
1st quarter	70.8	18.4	17.3	2.7	32.5	24.1	6.0	2.4	75.0	62.1	13.0	-1.7	42.5	328.0	11.7
2nd quarter	77.5	31.5	10.1	2.5	33.5	24.9	6.0	2.5	81.1	64.8	16.2	0.3	47.6	334.6	13.2
3rd quarter	75.6	33.5	5.4	2.4	34.3	25.6	6.1	2.6	78.4	59.4	19.0	2.2	44.1	340.5	12.1
4th quarter	76.5	32.8	6.0	2.7	34.9	26.0	6.3	2.7	76.7	54.4	22.3	2.7	41.7	347.2	12.0
1952															
1st quarter	77.1	31.9	6.9	2.9	35.4	26.3	6.5	2.6	77.1	55.2	21.9	3.5	41.7	349.7	11.9
2nd quarter	70.8	29.1	3.4	2.4	35.9	26.6	6.7	2.7	71.8	49.9	22.0	1.1	35.9	352.0	9.9
3rd quarter	73.2	32.1	1.1	3.3	36.6	26.9	6.9	2.8	76.4	53.9	22.5	-1.1	39.7	358.3	10.2
4th quarter	75.7	31.5	3.5	3.4	37.2	27.3	7.2	2.8	80.1	57.1	22.9	-1.2	42.9	370.1	10.4
1953															
1st quarter	77.0	32.0	4.3	2.9	37.9	27.7	7.4	2.8	81.8	57.9	23.9	-1.4	43.9	376.9	10.4
2nd quarter	77.4	32.3	2.6	4.0	38.5	28.0	7.6	2.8	82.8	58.1	24.6	-1.8	44.3	380.5	10.2
3rd quarter	77.2	31.4	3.5	3.5	38.9	28.4	7.6	2.8	81.7	57.4	24.3	-1.2	42.8	379.6	10.1
4th quarter	68.9	29.1	-3.2	3.6	39.3	28.7	7.8	2.8	75.4	52.3	23.1	-0.9	36.1	372.1	7.9
1954															
1st quarter	71.9	31.9	-3.4	3.6	39.8	29.0	8.0	2.8	75.3	51.5	23.8	-0.5	35.5	374.3	8.6
2nd quarter	72.0	30.3	-2.0	3.3	40.4	29.3	8.2	2.9	74.4	51.2	23.2	0.3	34.1	375.2	8.4
3rd quarter	72.6	30.2	-1.4	3.0	40.8	29.6	8.3	2.9	76.4	54.7	21.7	-0.1	35.5	379.1	8.4
4th quarter	77.0	32.6	0.0	3.1	41.4	29.9	8.5	3.0	79.2	57.8	21.4	0.9	37.8	388.7	9.2
1955															
1st quarter	81.7	33.5	3.5	3.0	41.7	30.2	8.5	2.9	85.2	64.2	21.0	0.5	43.6	401.0	10.0
2nd quarter	88.1	35.9	6.7	3.3	42.2	30.7	8.5	3.0	90.0	68.1	21.9	-0.2	47.8	411.6	11.1
3rd quarter	89.1	37.4	4.8	3.8	43.1	31.3	8.7	3.2	90.7	70.0	20.7	0.8	47.6	419.5	11.0
4th quarter	93.1	37.3	7.7	3.9	44.2	32.1	8.8	3.2	94.1	73.9	20.3	0.4	49.9	427.1	11.5
1956															
1st quarter	96.7	38.4	8.5	4.3	45.5	33.0	9.1	3.4	94.7	73.0	21.8	0.9	49.3	432.1	11.8
2nd quarter	97.7	39.9	6.6	4.5	46.6	34.0	9.2	3.5	93.7	71.4	22.2	2.2	47.0	438.8	11.6
3rd quarter	101.3	41.4	7.7	4.5	47.7	34.8	9.3	3.6	96.4	72.5	23.9	3.0	48.7	444.0	12.1
4th quarter	101.9	41.7	7.2	4.3	48.6	35.6	9.4	3.7	94.9	71.2	23.7	4.5	46.3	453.1	11.8
1957															
1st quarter	102.1	41.5	6.1	4.8	49.6	36.3	9.6	3.7	96.0	71.8	24.2	5.5	46.4	460.7	11.4
2nd quarter	102.0	42.9	4.3	4.3	50.5	37.0	9.7	3.9	95.8	71.9	23.9	4.8	45.3	463.9	11.1
3rd quarter	101.8	42.2	4.3	4.1	51.3	37.6	9.8	3.9	97.9	73.2	24.6	4.9	46.6	468.7	10.8
4th quarter	92.6	38.7	-1.6	3.6	51.9	38.2	9.9	3.9	89.6	64.9	24.7	3.6	37.7	463.4	8.8
1958															
1st quarter	88.8	37.2	-3.3	2.7	52.3	38.7	9.7	3.9	85.6	60.5	25.1	1.5	33.4	458.3	8.0
2nd quarter	84.4	37.3	-8.4	2.6	52.9	39.2	9.8	4.0	84.0	58.7	25.3	0.8	31.1	460.3	6.8
3rd quarter	91.0	41.3	-6.5	2.6	53.6	39.6	9.9	4.1	92.8	65.5	27.3	1.0	39.2	471.5	7.9
4th quarter	99.0	44.6	-3.6	3.6	54.2	40.1	10.0	4.1	101.5	73.2	28.2	-0.2	47.2	485.2	9.2
1959															
1st quarter	104.6	43.7	3.1	3.1	54.8	40.5	10.1	4.2	106.7	76.2	30.5	-1.5	51.9	497.5	10.0
2nd quarter	111.1	47.2	5.1	3.6	55.3	40.9	10.2	4.2	111.7	82.2	29.5	-2.1	56.5	512.6	10.9
3rd quarter	102.9	40.3	2.8	4.2	55.6	41.1	10.3	4.3	105.8	76.4	29.3	-0.6	50.1	509.9	9.3
4th quarter	105.7	43.4	2.0	4.3	55.9	41.3	10.4	4.3	107.1	79.3	27.8	-0.9	51.2	515.7	9.6
1960															
1st quarter	118.2	46.1	11.6	4.3	56.2	41.4	10.5	4.3	116.8	89.1	27.7	1.7	60.6	529.6	11.7
2nd quarter	110.8	42.0	8.2	4.2	56.4	41.5	10.5	4.4	107.2	79.7	27.5	2.5	50.8	530.2	10.3
3rd quarter	111.0	43.4	6.6	4.3	56.7	41.6	10.6	4.5	107.7	78.7	29.0	3.7	51.0	531.8	10.2
4th quarter	105.1	41.6	2.1	4.4	57.1	41.9	10.7	4.5	97.0	68.1	28.9	4.8	39.9	530.4	9.1
1961															
1st quarter	108.2	44.2	2.4	4.1	57.5	42.2	10.7	4.6	101.7	70.3	31.4	5.3	44.2	532.7	9.5
2nd quarter	110.2	47.5	0.7	4.0	57.9	42.5	10.8	4.6	105.7	75.8	30.0	4.0	47.8	542.9	9.6
3rd quarter	117.1	51.8	2.4	4.5	58.4	42.8	10.9	4.7	113.5	82.4	31.2	3.8	55.1	552.7	10.6
4th quarter	121.8	53.6	4.6	4.6	58.9	43.1	11.0	4.8	117.0	84.2	32.8	3.7	58.1	567.2	11.1

Table 19-9. Saving and Investment—*Continued*

(Billions of dollars, except as noted; quarterly data are at seasonally adjusted annual rates.)   **NIPA Tables 1.7.5, 5.1**

Year and quarter	Gross saving Total	Net saving Private	Net saving Government Federal	Net saving Government State and local	Consumption of fixed capital Total	Consumption of fixed capital Private	Consumption of fixed capital Government Federal	Consumption of fixed capital Government State and local	Gross domestic investment Total	Gross domestic investment Private	Gross domestic investment Government	Net lending or net borrowing (-), NIPAs	Net domestic investment	Gross national income	Net saving as a percentage of gross national income
1962															
1st quarter	124.4	57.6	2.3	4.9	59.6	43.5	11.2	4.9	122.4	89.4	33.0	3.1	62.8	578.6	11.2
2nd quarter	123.9	56.7	2.1	5.0	60.1	43.9	11.3	5.0	120.6	87.9	32.7	4.8	60.4	585.8	10.9
3rd quarter	125.6	56.2	3.0	5.5	60.9	44.3	11.5	5.1	123.0	89.3	33.7	4.1	62.2	592.6	10.9
4th quarter	125.7	56.3	2.3	5.5	61.7	44.7	11.8	5.1	119.7	86.0	33.7	3.2	58.0	600.8	10.7
1963															
1st quarter	128.5	56.7	4.0	5.4	62.3	45.1	11.9	5.2	123.5	90.5	33.0	3.9	61.2	608.1	10.9
2nd quarter	133.1	58.3	6.2	5.5	63.0	45.6	12.1	5.3	125.0	92.2	32.8	5.3	62.0	618.3	11.3
3rd quarter	133.5	58.1	5.8	6.1	63.7	46.1	12.1	5.4	129.8	95.0	34.8	4.6	66.2	627.5	11.1
4th quarter	137.6	62.3	5.1	5.9	64.4	46.7	12.2	5.5	131.3	97.4	33.9	6.0	67.0	638.4	11.5
1964															
1st quarter	140.0	66.6	1.9	6.4	65.1	47.2	12.3	5.6	134.9	100.7	34.2	8.2	69.8	651.6	11.5
2nd quarter	140.3	70.8	-2.7	6.3	65.9	47.9	12.3	5.7	135.2	100.6	34.6	6.7	69.3	662.1	11.2
3rd quarter	143.6	69.1	1.2	6.5	66.8	48.6	12.3	5.8	137.2	102.5	34.8	7.6	70.5	674.3	11.4
4th quarter	149.7	72.4	3.1	6.4	67.7	49.4	12.4	5.9	139.5	104.6	34.9	7.3	71.7	683.2	12.0
1965															
1st quarter	157.2	74.6	7.5	6.2	68.8	50.3	12.5	6.0	149.9	115.7	34.2	5.7	81.1	702.6	12.6
2nd quarter	158.7	75.4	6.7	6.5	70.1	51.3	12.6	6.2	150.6	115.8	34.8	7.0	80.6	714.8	12.4
3rd quarter	158.8	81.4	-0.5	6.6	71.3	52.3	12.7	6.3	156.1	119.7	36.5	6.0	84.8	727.1	12.0
4th quarter	159.2	80.5	-0.7	6.8	72.7	53.5	12.7	6.4	158.5	121.8	36.7	5.9	85.9	747.1	11.6
1966															
1st quarter	167.5	80.8	4.9	7.7	74.1	54.7	12.8	6.6	170.4	131.7	38.7	4.7	96.3	768.2	12.2
2nd quarter	167.3	80.2	3.4	8.0	75.7	55.9	13.0	6.8	168.9	130.7	38.2	3.9	93.2	779.5	11.8
3rd quarter	167.3	80.6	1.5	8.0	77.2	57.1	13.2	7.0	170.4	130.2	40.3	2.7	93.2	792.3	11.4
4th quarter	172.8	87.5	-0.8	7.3	78.8	58.3	13.4	7.1	174.7	132.7	42.0	3.9	95.9	806.3	11.6
1967															
1st quarter	168.1	89.8	-9.6	7.5	80.4	59.6	13.5	7.3	172.8	129.3	43.4	4.4	92.4	814.0	10.8
2nd quarter	164.4	85.9	-10.4	6.9	82.0	60.9	13.7	7.4	165.7	123.7	42.0	3.6	83.7	822.5	10.0
3rd quarter	171.9	90.2	-8.5	6.4	83.8	62.2	14.0	7.6	171.7	128.5	43.2	3.2	87.9	839.7	10.5
4th quarter	177.9	93.9	-8.9	7.2	85.6	63.6	14.2	7.8	176.2	132.9	43.3	2.8	90.5	857.2	10.8
1968															
1st quarter	176.2	87.5	-6.0	7.2	87.5	65.1	14.4	8.1	180.3	137.2	43.1	1.7	92.8	879.8	10.1
2nd quarter	181.9	91.9	-7.5	8.2	89.4	66.6	14.6	8.2	187.4	143.4	44.0	2.2	98.1	902.4	10.3
3rd quarter	182.4	82.3	1.4	7.4	91.3	68.2	14.8	8.3	183.6	139.7	43.8	1.5	92.3	922.9	9.9
4th quarter	187.6	84.5	2.4	7.2	93.5	69.8	15.0	8.6	187.9	144.4	43.6	0.8	94.5	941.4	10.0
1969															
1st quarter	196.0	78.6	14.4	7.4	95.6	71.6	15.2	8.9	201.1	155.7	45.4	1.6	105.4	960.6	10.5
2nd quarter	196.4	79.3	11.4	7.8	98.0	73.4	15.3	9.2	199.1	155.7	43.4	0.6	101.1	979.0	10.1
3rd quarter	203.0	88.8	5.5	8.5	100.3	75.4	15.4	9.4	203.9	160.3	43.6	1.5	103.7	999.9	10.3
4th quarter	198.3	84.2	3.0	8.2	102.9	77.5	15.6	9.7	194.8	154.1	40.7	2.7	91.9	1 011.3	9.4
1970															
1st quarter	192.2	80.9	-2.5	8.2	105.6	79.8	15.8	10.0	193.5	150.7	42.8	3.8	87.9	1 018.3	8.5
2nd quarter	194.3	95.0	-16.2	7.7	107.8	81.4	16.0	10.4	196.5	153.9	42.6	5.2	88.7	1 032.2	8.4
3rd quarter	195.8	99.0	-19.7	7.1	109.4	82.5	16.2	10.7	200.1	156.1	44.1	3.5	90.7	1 049.2	8.2
4th quarter	189.0	96.6	-23.5	5.4	110.5	83.1	16.3	11.1	193.7	148.9	44.8	2.4	83.2	1 051.6	7.5
1971															
1st quarter	202.2	107.3	-23.9	5.0	113.8	86.0	16.5	11.4	212.9	171.3	41.7	4.3	99.1	1 090.4	8.1
2nd quarter	207.1	114.7	-30.4	6.0	116.7	88.5	16.5	11.7	220.6	178.8	41.8	0.1	103.9	1 113.1	8.1
3rd quarter	212.1	115.9	-29.5	6.5	119.2	90.8	16.5	11.9	225.7	183.4	42.3	-0.3	106.5	1 133.1	8.2
4th quarter	215.5	116.7	-31.0	8.4	121.3	92.8	16.4	12.2	220.5	179.2	41.3	-2.8	99.2	1 156.9	8.1
1972															
1st quarter	223.4	113.8	-22.9	9.1	123.5	94.5	16.6	12.4	235.5	193.2	42.3	-5.0	112.0	1 191.3	8.4
2nd quarter	225.2	109.1	-28.2	18.7	125.6	96.4	16.5	12.7	249.4	206.5	42.9	-4.8	123.8	1 214.2	8.2
3rd quarter	238.7	117.5	-17.1	10.1	128.2	98.7	16.6	12.9	253.5	212.4	41.1	-3.6	125.2	1 247.1	8.9
4th quarter	261.7	137.1	-31.4	24.6	131.3	101.3	16.8	13.3	262.7	218.4	44.3	-2.8	131.4	1 297.4	10.0
1973															
1st quarter	274.7	136.4	-15.2	18.9	134.6	104.1	16.8	13.7	280.0	232.5	47.5	2.2	145.4	1 338.2	10.5
2nd quarter	282.1	143.2	-15.2	15.7	138.4	107.4	17.0	14.1	292.8	246.0	46.7	5.4	154.3	1 367.0	10.5
3rd quarter	294.5	147.9	-10.6	14.6	142.7	111.1	17.1	14.5	287.4	241.8	45.6	12.5	144.7	1 399.2	10.8
4th quarter	317.4	162.7	-6.2	13.6	147.4	115.2	17.2	15.0	305.1	257.6	47.5	15.4	157.7	1 443.0	11.8
1974															
1st quarter	309.2	153.2	-8.9	11.8	153.1	119.8	17.4	15.9	295.6	244.1	51.5	16.5	142.5	1 460.7	10.7
2nd quarter	298.7	139.7	-11.4	10.6	159.7	124.8	17.8	17.1	308.8	252.3	56.5	2.7	149.1	1 488.4	9.3
3rd quarter	299.2	133.3	-11.3	10.0	167.2	130.4	18.5	18.4	303.4	245.4	58.0	0.3	136.2	1 524.4	8.7
4th quarter	300.2	147.0	-26.4	4.9	174.7	136.4	19.0	19.3	314.9	255.8	59.0	4.4	140.2	1 547.0	8.1
1975															
1st quarter	280.1	145.9	-48.5	0.6	182.1	143.0	19.2	19.9	281.3	218.7	62.6	17.9	99.2	1 561.8	6.3
2nd quarter	279.0	194.0	-105.7	2.6	188.1	148.6	19.4	20.1	274.8	216.8	58.1	21.5	86.7	1 599.3	5.7
3rd quarter	308.4	175.1	-63.7	3.6	193.4	153.3	19.9	20.3	301.7	237.8	63.9	18.4	108.3	1 663.7	6.9
4th quarter	320.0	183.6	-64.6	3.1	197.9	157.0	20.3	20.6	315.5	247.6	67.8	21.6	117.6	1 712.8	7.1
1976															
1st quarter	337.0	184.2	-54.3	5.7	201.4	159.7	20.8	20.9	345.2	274.8	70.4	13.2	143.8	1 766.2	7.7
2nd quarter	342.4	180.4	-50.0	6.5	205.5	163.2	21.1	21.2	357.4	291.6	65.8	9.0	151.9	1 796.9	7.6
3rd quarter	343.8	180.9	-53.6	6.3	210.2	167.3	21.6	21.3	361.8	296.5	65.3	2.4	151.7	1 834.4	7.3
4th quarter	344.7	174.9	-56.8	11.0	215.6	172.0	22.0	21.6	368.9	304.9	64.0	3.8	153.3	1 874.3	6.9

Table 19-9. Saving and Investment—*Continued*

(Billions of dollars, except as noted; quarterly data are at seasonally adjusted annual rates.)   **NIPA Tables 1.7.5, 5.1**

Year and quarter	Gross saving Total	Net saving Private	Net saving Government Federal	Net saving Government State and local	Consumption of fixed capital Total	Consumption of fixed capital Private	Consumption of fixed capital Government Federal	Consumption of fixed capital Government State and local	Gross domestic investment Total	Gross domestic investment Private	Gross domestic investment Government	Net lending or net borrow-ing (-), NIPAs	Net domestic invest-ment	Gross national income	Net saving as a percent-age of gross national income
1977															
1st quarter	352.7	168.2	-47.2	9.6	222.1	177.5	22.6	22.0	393.5	326.6	66.9	-8.0	171.4	1 926.5	6.8
2nd quarter	391.8	192.9	-41.3	11.8	228.4	183.1	22.9	22.4	424.0	354.9	69.1	-8.8	195.6	2 002.6	8.2
3rd quarter	417.4	214.2	-47.3	15.7	234.8	189.0	23.0	22.8	446.0	378.4	67.6	-7.9	211.2	2 066.2	8.8
4th quarter	425.0	216.4	-48.7	15.5	241.8	195.0	23.6	23.2	452.0	385.5	66.5	-18.9	210.1	2 121.6	8.6
1978															
1st quarter	433.6	216.1	-48.6	16.9	249.2	201.3	24.3	23.6	463.2	396.8	66.4	-25.0	214.0	2 166.6	8.5
2nd quarter	471.2	219.0	-27.9	23.0	257.0	208.1	24.8	24.2	507.9	430.9	77.0	-12.9	250.8	2 269.6	9.4
3rd quarter	488.9	229.3	-21.9	16.1	265.4	215.3	25.3	24.8	532.0	451.4	80.7	-11.4	266.6	2 324.4	9.6
4th quarter	511.6	236.1	-17.2	18.7	274.0	223.1	25.6	25.4	557.0	472.8	84.2	-1.3	282.9	2 396.6	9.9
1979															
1st quarter	530.2	241.0	-8.7	14.5	283.3	231.3	25.9	26.1	560.2	481.1	79.1	-1.8	276.9	2 460.7	10.0
2nd quarter	530.0	233.6	-8.9	11.9	293.4	239.9	26.6	27.0	578.4	493.0	85.4	-2.7	285.0	2 510.2	9.4
3rd quarter	532.3	228.9	-14.6	13.9	304.0	248.7	27.4	27.9	591.6	497.9	93.7	2.4	287.5	2 574.1	8.9
4th quarter	540.4	237.6	-23.6	11.6	314.8	257.9	28.0	28.9	595.2	499.5	95.7	-2.6	280.4	2 643.7	8.5
1980															
1st quarter	534.2	231.3	-33.7	10.6	326.0	267.4	28.6	30.0	606.9	505.2	101.7	-10.7	281.0	2 700.0	7.7
2nd quarter	522.0	236.1	-57.6	5.5	337.9	277.1	29.7	31.1	570.3	470.4	99.9	9.8	232.4	2 705.6	6.8
3rd quarter	530.0	244.4	-71.8	7.5	349.9	287.2	30.4	32.4	541.3	443.5	97.9	28.2	191.4	2 780.1	6.5
4th quarter	584.7	274.1	-63.4	11.5	362.5	297.5	31.4	33.6	599.4	497.9	101.5	6.7	236.9	2 922.4	7.6
1981															
1st quarter	614.0	269.5	-42.6	11.7	375.3	308.1	32.4	34.8	670.7	563.1	107.6	1.7	295.4	3 024.4	7.9
2nd quarter	621.2	272.3	-46.9	8.0	387.7	318.4	33.4	35.9	656.9	551.4	105.5	0.2	269.2	3 078.4	7.6
3rd quarter	679.0	326.5	-54.6	7.7	399.5	328.4	34.3	36.8	698.0	592.8	105.2	7.1	298.5	3 183.7	8.8
4th quarter	670.1	339.4	-83.0	2.8	410.9	338.0	35.2	37.7	691.5	582.2	109.3	4.6	280.6	3 206.3	8.1
1982															
1st quarter	636.9	319.4	-103.9	-0.7	422.1	347.3	36.3	38.5	633.3	526.5	106.7	0.7	211.2	3 223.9	6.7
2nd quarter	661.7	341.2	-109.4	-1.4	431.3	354.7	37.3	39.3	643.6	530.8	112.8	17.5	212.3	3 282.5	7.0
3rd quarter	624.8	336.4	-147.2	-2.6	438.2	360.1	38.1	40.0	640.9	528.7	112.3	-14.0	202.8	3 307.3	5.6
4th quarter	562.5	304.6	-180.6	-4.0	442.6	363.6	38.7	40.3	600.4	482.9	117.4	-17.2	157.7	3 326.1	3.6
1983															
1st quarter	583.3	322.0	-176.4	-7.4	445.1	365.2	39.4	40.6	614.5	496.6	117.9	-7.8	169.3	3 391.8	4.1
2nd quarter	590.2	311.5	-172.6	3.0	448.4	367.6	40.1	40.7	662.0	542.2	119.7	-27.5	213.6	3 474.9	4.1
3rd quarter	590.5	316.7	-188.9	9.8	453.0	370.7	41.3	41.0	703.5	577.7	125.8	-47.8	250.5	3 559.9	3.9
4th quarter	645.5	340.5	-167.0	14.2	457.9	374.6	42.0	41.3	768.7	640.7	128.0	-56.7	310.8	3 661.5	5.1
1984															
1st quarter	722.9	393.3	-157.0	22.5	464.0	379.3	43.1	41.6	842.6	709.7	133.0	-78.4	378.6	3 803.2	6.8
2nd quarter	747.9	417.8	-167.3	26.7	470.6	384.4	44.1	42.1	872.2	735.1	137.1	-87.8	401.6	3 907.5	7.1
3rd quarter	771.9	448.4	-175.2	21.1	477.5	390.0	44.9	42.6	892.6	753.5	139.1	-90.3	415.0	3 983.1	7.4
4th quarter	770.8	446.6	-186.4	25.4	485.2	396.2	46.0	43.0	892.5	744.3	148.3	-103.3	407.3	4 048.9	7.1
1985															
1st quarter	755.8	388.5	-150.7	24.7	493.3	402.8	46.8	43.7	869.2	720.0	149.1	-89.3	375.9	4 119.5	6.4
2nd quarter	747.8	423.7	-201.0	24.0	501.1	409.4	47.4	44.3	893.3	735.3	157.9	-111.2	392.2	4 170.2	5.9
3rd quarter	719.0	365.8	-178.0	21.7	509.5	416.1	48.5	44.9	892.2	727.2	165.0	-121.1	382.7	4 230.6	5.0
4th quarter	730.8	378.6	-184.7	19.0	517.9	422.8	49.4	45.7	925.3	762.2	163.1	-135.0	407.4	4 286.5	5.0
1986															
1st quarter	744.5	375.9	-184.2	26.9	525.9	429.6	49.9	46.4	928.9	763.8	165.1	-128.1	403.0	4 349.9	5.0
2nd quarter	718.3	369.2	-205.7	20.2	534.5	436.1	51.1	47.4	923.5	753.0	170.5	-141.7	389.0	4 376.3	4.2
3rd quarter	683.1	328.7	-210.9	22.5	542.7	442.3	52.2	48.3	913.6	732.5	181.1	-150.1	370.9	4 429.5	3.2
4th quarter	691.4	305.0	-177.7	13.3	550.7	448.3	53.1	49.3	913.0	736.7	176.2	-150.1	362.3	4 484.0	3.1
1987															
1st quarter	733.2	349.3	-181.9	7.4	558.4	454.0	54.2	50.1	943.8	765.0	178.9	-150.7	385.4	4 565.5	3.8
2nd quarter	758.5	300.2	-127.8	19.9	566.2	460.5	54.7	51.0	951.3	767.6	183.7	-154.2	385.1	4 666.9	4.1
3rd quarter	793.7	346.3	-139.0	11.2	575.1	467.7	55.5	51.9	957.4	769.5	187.9	-153.8	382.2	4 772.9	4.6
4th quarter	843.6	398.3	-148.7	9.4	584.6	475.7	56.3	52.6	1 024.4	837.8	186.7	-156.8	439.8	4 879.2	5.3
1988															
1st quarter	859.2	399.3	-147.9	12.3	595.5	484.4	57.5	53.5	979.1	797.6	181.5	-126.6	383.6	4 980.9	5.3
2nd quarter	896.6	416.4	-137.9	12.1	605.9	493.0	58.6	54.3	1 006.7	820.4	186.3	-109.6	400.8	5 082.4	5.7
3rd quarter	920.5	412.8	-130.0	21.6	616.2	501.4	59.5	55.2	1 012.0	825.7	186.3	-106.1	395.8	5 178.9	5.9
4th quarter	929.7	418.2	-137.8	22.9	626.5	509.6	60.8	56.1	1 033.1	842.6	190.4	-119.2	406.5	5 291.0	5.7
1989															
1st quarter	964.4	415.9	-115.4	27.4	636.4	517.6	61.8	57.0	1 075.2	884.1	191.1	-106.3	438.8	5 379.8	6.1
2nd quarter	921.3	383.6	-134.9	26.1	646.4	525.6	62.7	58.0	1 073.2	878.2	195.1	-93.2	426.9	5 418.3	5.1
3rd quarter	912.4	375.2	-140.8	21.6	656.5	533.6	63.8	59.1	1 072.5	870.3	202.2	-81.3	416.0	5 480.0	4.7
4th quarter	898.5	371.2	-144.7	5.4	666.6	541.6	64.9	60.1	1 069.6	867.3	202.3	-87.9	403.0	5 529.8	4.2
1990															
1st quarter	905.3	384.5	-171.3	15.3	676.8	549.5	66.1	61.2	1 092.4	880.0	212.4	-90.3	415.6	5 641.2	4.1
2nd quarter	941.1	422.2	-176.7	9.0	686.6	557.0	67.1	62.5	1 096.2	882.5	213.7	-72.4	409.7	5 746.2	4.4
3rd quarter	910.9	382.3	-172.0	4.4	696.1	564.2	68.2	63.8	1 082.6	866.8	215.8	-81.9	386.5	5 787.8	3.7
4th quarter	913.2	397.6	-185.8	-3.9	705.3	571.0	69.6	64.7	1 035.6	814.6	221.0	-82.0	330.3	5 827.7	3.6
1991															
1st quarter	998.2	448.5	-157.4	-6.6	713.8	577.4	70.8	65.6	1 004.4	787.9	216.4	42.6	290.5	5 865.4	4.8
2nd quarter	942.5	446.3	-217.1	-8.1	721.3	583.2	71.5	66.6	1 005.3	784.1	221.3	14.9	284.0	5 911.4	3.7
3rd quarter	922.1	436.8	-240.5	-2.4	728.3	588.3	72.6	67.4	1 027.2	805.3	222.0	-28.4	299.0	5 965.1	3.3
4th quarter	942.4	473.1	-258.7	-6.1	734.1	592.8	73.3	68.0	1 055.8	834.3	221.5	-16.3	321.8	6 027.1	3.5

Table 19-9. Saving and Investment—*Continued*

(Billions of dollars, except as noted; quarterly data are at seasonally adjusted annual rates.)   **NIPA Tables 1.7.5, 5.1**

Year and quarter	Gross saving									Gross domestic investment and net lending, NIPAs				Net domestic invest-ment	Gross national income	Net saving as a percent-age of gross national income
	Total	Net saving			Consumption of fixed capital				Gross domestic investment			Net lending or net borrow-ing (-), NIPAs			
		Private	Government		Total	Private	Government		Total	Private	Govern-ment				
			Federal	State and local			Federal	State and local							
1992															
1st quarter	944.1	501.9	-296.0	-0.5	738.7	596.6	73.6	68.5	1 037.3	810.2	227.1	-22.5	298.6	6 150.0	3.3
2nd quarter	960.3	519.7	-302.2	-0.4	743.2	599.4	74.3	69.5	1 090.0	865.4	224.6	-40.3	346.8	6 235.2	3.5
3rd quarter	908.6	480.2	-313.2	-4.8	746.3	601.3	74.8	70.2	1 098.1	876.8	221.3	-47.3	351.8	6 280.0	2.6
4th quarter	916.1	465.5	-298.6	0.1	749.2	602.3	75.7	71.2	1 126.1	906.7	219.4	-69.1	376.9	6 380.6	2.6
1993															
1st quarter	937.7	498.0	-312.1	-10.2	762.0	612.7	77.0	72.3	1 147.2	931.3	215.9	-59.7	385.3	6 428.1	2.7
2nd quarter	965.0	470.6	-275.3	-3.6	773.3	622.3	77.5	73.4	1 163.2	942.3	220.9	-74.5	390.0	6 528.4	2.9
3rd quarter	944.0	446.2	-282.2	-3.7	783.6	631.2	78.2	74.2	1 162.4	943.4	219.0	-77.7	378.8	6 583.0	2.4
4th quarter	987.0	431.4	-251.3	13.7	793.2	639.4	78.7	75.2	1 218.3	996.4	221.8	-108.2	425.0	6 711.4	2.9
1994															
1st quarter	1 047.8	476.6	-236.4	5.4	802.2	646.8	79.0	76.4	1 254.2	1 043.6	210.6	-92.9	452.0	6 830.4	3.6
2nd quarter	1 089.3	475.7	-202.9	3.7	812.7	655.4	79.9	77.4	1 324.3	1 106.9	217.3	-112.5	511.5	6 942.1	4.0
3rd quarter	1 101.7	482.8	-220.6	15.2	824.3	665.3	80.2	78.7	1 321.8	1 092.9	229.0	-122.6	497.6	7 054.5	3.9
4th quarter	1 139.8	515.5	-221.7	8.6	837.5	676.3	81.2	79.9	1 372.5	1 145.7	226.8	-138.5	535.1	7 174.8	4.2
1995															
1st quarter	1 196.8	556.0	-221.4	10.9	851.4	688.6	81.5	81.3	1 391.6	1 160.6	231.0	-119.3	540.2	7 262.9	4.8
2nd quarter	1 191.5	535.9	-206.2	-2.3	864.1	699.9	81.6	82.6	1 367.7	1 132.7	235.1	-119.0	503.6	7 332.8	4.5
3rd quarter	1 223.9	549.3	-210.3	9.3	875.7	710.3	81.7	83.7	1 357.6	1 126.2	231.4	-101.8	482.0	7 438.3	4.7
4th quarter	1 263.9	545.1	-186.7	18.9	886.7	719.8	82.0	84.9	1 389.6	1 156.7	233.0	-84.7	503.0	7 533.2	5.0
1996															
1st quarter	1 284.0	561.6	-194.3	20.5	896.2	728.3	82.0	85.9	1 409.3	1 170.0	239.3	-103.0	513.1	7 653.3	5.1
2nd quarter	1 325.0	549.7	-149.5	18.6	906.3	737.8	81.9	86.7	1 470.2	1 227.8	242.4	-109.4	563.9	7 793.2	5.4
3rd quarter	1 363.9	559.5	-138.3	25.1	917.7	748.1	81.9	87.7	1 525.7	1 279.8	245.9	-133.6	608.0	7 890.1	5.7
4th quarter	1 404.5	557.6	-110.8	27.8	929.9	759.3	81.9	88.7	1 532.4	1 283.1	249.3	-114.4	602.6	8 040.2	5.9
1997															
1st quarter	1 452.4	571.3	-92.4	30.0	943.5	771.4	82.4	89.8	1 574.4	1 320.6	253.8	-132.2	630.9	8 169.3	6.2
2nd quarter	1 519.8	600.6	-71.0	33.1	957.1	783.5	82.5	91.0	1 638.0	1 385.0	253.0	-102.5	680.9	8 290.6	6.8
3rd quarter	1 560.5	585.4	-35.6	40.4	970.3	795.8	82.5	92.0	1 668.8	1 414.9	253.9	-123.5	698.5	8 446.9	7.0
4th quarter	1 570.0	585.5	-41.5	41.7	984.3	808.1	82.7	93.5	1 682.9	1 434.1	248.8	-164.1	698.6	8 572.4	6.8
1998															
1st quarter	1 638.3	587.5	7.9	45.6	997.3	820.6	82.3	94.4	1 741.6	1 494.9	246.6	-165.1	744.3	8 686.8	7.4
2nd quarter	1 640.8	565.6	20.7	42.5	1 011.9	834.0	82.7	95.3	1 730.1	1 471.5	258.6	-196.3	718.2	8 827.4	7.1
3rd quarter	1 682.1	556.8	52.3	45.0	1 027.9	848.3	82.9	96.8	1 785.8	1 512.7	273.0	-224.8	757.8	8 977.0	7.3
4th quarter	1 656.4	503.6	53.4	54.4	1 045.0	863.5	83.3	98.2	1 837.1	1 564.0	273.2	-236.0	792.1	9 093.4	6.7
1999															
1st quarter	1 746.1	559.8	79.1	44.1	1 063.2	879.6	84.0	99.5	1 893.8	1 617.3	276.5	-244.7	830.7	9 267.3	7.4
2nd quarter	1 696.1	479.4	96.1	37.4	1 083.2	897.1	84.7	101.3	1 888.4	1 604.7	283.7	-280.0	805.2	9 367.2	6.5
3rd quarter	1 674.3	425.1	103.5	41.6	1 104.2	916.0	85.4	102.8	1 933.6	1 644.5	289.1	-314.1	829.4	9 483.9	6.0
4th quarter	1 715.6	427.8	116.6	44.2	1 127.1	936.2	86.1	104.8	1 999.6	1 699.5	300.2	-349.7	872.6	9 691.0	6.1
2000															
1st quarter	1 827.5	419.4	205.3	51.2	1 151.6	957.7	87.2	106.7	1 992.2	1 688.8	303.4	-386.9	840.6	9 961.4	6.8
2nd quarter	1 807.8	405.6	175.0	52.8	1 174.4	978.0	87.5	109.0	2 111.8	1 810.9	300.9	-392.3	937.4	10 070.5	6.3
3rd quarter	1 820.9	404.8	181.8	38.6	1 195.8	997.0	88.1	110.8	2 097.0	1 791.7	305.3	-431.1	901.1	10 201.6	6.1
4th quarter	1 744.5	327.6	178.8	22.6	1 215.4	1 014.7	88.3	112.4	2 105.1	1 797.4	307.8	-436.6	889.7	10 259.5	5.2
2001															
1st quarter	1 802.4	394.6	159.4	15.0	1 233.5	1 031.2	88.3	114.0	2 013.7	1 701.3	312.4	-424.3	780.3	10 417.8	5.5
2nd quarter	1 753.9	390.6	119.0	-5.7	1 250.0	1 045.9	88.7	115.4	2 030.3	1 699.4	330.9	-386.9	780.3	10 459.9	4.8
3rd quarter	1 661.5	524.4	-104.4	-22.9	1 264.4	1 059.0	88.8	116.6	1 984.7	1 670.4	314.2	-361.5	720.3	10 421.7	3.8
4th quarter	1 564.9	349.8	-12.0	-50.0	1 277.1	1 070.3	88.7	118.1	1 907.2	1 576.6	330.6	-347.2	630.1	10 466.3	2.7
2002															
1st quarter	1 602.6	575.6	-205.4	-55.9	1 288.3	1 079.8	88.8	119.6	1 965.8	1 628.0	337.7	-408.2	677.6	10 593.0	3.0
2nd quarter	1 580.3	588.4	-249.7	-57.9	1 299.5	1 089.4	88.9	121.2	1 988.9	1 648.1	340.7	-455.6	689.4	10 680.0	2.6
3rd quarter	1 519.4	518.8	-262.9	-47.0	1 310.5	1 098.8	89.1	122.6	1 997.2	1 650.4	346.8	-459.1	686.7	10 728.5	1.9
4th quarter	1 541.5	568.4	-293.0	-55.6	1 321.7	1 108.1	89.8	123.7	2 009.8	1 661.3	348.5	-490.7	688.2	10 852.6	2.0
2003															
1st quarter	1 494.3	543.0	-300.6	-81.3	1 333.2	1 117.4	90.2	125.5	2 020.4	1 671.5	349.0	-535.5	687.3	10 947.3	1.5
2nd quarter	1 541.4	622.8	-375.0	-52.3	1 345.9	1 128.6	90.7	126.6	2 030.2	1 678.6	351.6	-525.3	684.3	11 103.2	1.8
3rd quarter	1 531.8	648.4	-451.4	-25.5	1 360.4	1 141.5	91.1	127.8	2 106.9	1 745.1	361.8	-517.6	746.5	11 259.8	1.5
4th quarter	1 643.5	641.5	-378.5	3.8	1 376.8	1 156.2	91.4	129.1	2 184.4	1 823.6	360.8	-501.2	807.7	11 466.6	2.3
2004															
1st quarter	1 648.7	684.0	-409.3	-22.7	1 396.7	1 172.8	92.6	131.3	2 214.9	1 853.6	361.3	-538.5	818.3	11 677.9	2.2
2nd quarter	1 713.8	699.6	-384.4	-21.0	1 419.5	1 190.7	94.1	134.7	2 328.2	1 956.0	372.2	-616.4	908.7	11 864.2	2.5
3rd quarter	1 785.5	706.4	-361.6	-3.6	1 444.4	1 209.8	95.5	139.1	2 379.3	2 001.3	377.9	-621.7	934.9	12 086.1	2.8
4th quarter	1 748.7	627.0	-362.5	13.8	1 470.4	1 230.2	97.1	143.2	2 441.2	2 063.2	378.0	-717.4	970.8	12 239.1	2.3
2005															
1st quarter	1 842.8	610.8	-288.9	25.2	1 495.7	1 251.9	98.8	145.0	2 508.4	2 130.7	377.6	-705.2	1 012.7	12 515.3	2.8
2nd quarter	1 866.4	611.5	-288.1	18.9	1 524.2	1 276.1	99.7	148.3	2 502.6	2 115.2	387.4	-706.2	978.5	12 680.7	2.7
3rd quarter	1 896.1	602.2	-287.4	25.3	1 556.0	1 302.9	100.9	152.2	2 563.3	2 166.6	396.6	-675.3	1 007.2	12 916.2	2.6
4th quarter	2 008.2	651.9	-267.7	34.4	1 589.6	1 332.3	102.4	154.9	2 682.7	2 276.3	406.4	-831.1	1 093.1	13 148.6	3.2
2006															
1st quarter	2 148.9	675.6	-207.3	62.6	1 618.0	1 357.4	103.8	156.8	2 746.2	2 336.5	409.7	-796.7	1 128.2	13 456.2	3.9
2nd quarter	2 159.2	677.2	-229.4	63.2	1 648.2	1 381.4	106.0	161.2	2 779.5	2 352.1	427.4	-815.4	1 131.3	13 614.0	3.8
3rd quarter	2 161.2	659.0	-215.5	42.4	1 675.2	1 403.2	107.8	164.2	2 761.1	2 333.5	427.6	-855.8	1 085.8	13 768.2	3.5
4th quarter	2 228.4	654.1	-163.0	35.9	1 701.3	1 423.9	108.7	168.7	2 722.1	2 286.5	435.6	-742.5	1 020.8	13 929.2	3.8

Table 19-10. U.S. International Transactions

(Millions of dollars, seasonally adjusted.)

Year and quarter	Exports of goods, services, and income				Imports of goods, services, and income [1]				Unilateral current transfers, net [2]	U.S.-owned assets abroad, net, excluding financial derivatives [3]					
										Total	U.S. official reserve assets, net	U.S. government assets other than official reserve assets, net	U.S. private assets, net		
	Total	Goods	Services	Income receipts	Total	Goods	Services	Income payments					Total	Direct investment	Foreign securities
1960															
1st quarter	7 355	4 685	1 543	1 127	-6 050	-3 812	-1 907	-331	-955	-1 066	159	-237	-988	-664	-266
2nd quarter	7 762	4 916	1 715	1 131	-6 078	-3 858	-1 906	-314	-1 154	-1 156	175	-339	-992	-586	-166
3rd quarter	7 650	5 031	1 453	1 166	-5 925	-3 648	-1 970	-307	-889	-956	740	-160	-1 536	-754	-111
4th quarter	7 791	5 018	1 580	1 193	-5 619	-3 440	-1 892	-287	-1 064	-923	1 071	-365	-1 629	-936	-120
1961															
1st quarter	7 827	5 095	1 481	1 251	-5 599	-3 394	-1 912	-293	-989	-1 320	371	-381	-1 310	-774	-135
2nd quarter	7 773	4 806	1 758	1 209	-5 659	-3 438	-1 922	-299	-1 208	-1 029	-320	471	-1 180	-551	-246
3rd quarter	7 757	5 038	1 468	1 251	-6 026	-3 809	-1 900	-317	-887	-1 928	-212	-486	-1 230	-737	-124
4th quarter	8 047	5 169	1 590	1 288	-6 171	-3 896	-1 939	-336	-1 043	-1 260	768	-513	-1 515	-592	-257
1962															
1st quarter	8 015	5 077	1 666	1 272	-6 256	-3 966	-1 971	-319	-1 113	-1 301	427	-406	-1 322	-545	-196
2nd quarter	8 719	5 336	2 004	1 379	-6 402	-4 080	-1 992	-330	-1 272	-1 461	-163	-381	-917	-716	-308
3rd quarter	8 295	5 331	1 567	1 397	-6 455	-4 116	-2 005	-334	-879	-279	881	8	-1 168	-811	-87
4th quarter	8 315	5 037	1 709	1 569	-6 567	-4 098	-2 126	-343	-1 016	-1 134	390	-306	-1 218	-779	-378
1963															
1st quarter	8 428	5 063	1 849	1 516	-6 478	-4 064	-2 057	-357	-1 107	-1 922	32	-482	-1 472	-980	-522
2nd quarter	9 244	5 599	2 150	1 495	-6 674	-4 226	-2 066	-382	-1 371	-2 631	124	-654	-2 101	-874	-536
3rd quarter	8 832	5 671	1 620	1 541	-6 893	-4 372	-2 122	-399	-918	-887	227	-86	-1 028	-721	-100
4th quarter	9 275	5 939	1 731	1 605	-6 926	-4 386	-2 118	-422	-999	-1 831	-5	-440	-1 386	-908	53
1964															
1st quarter	9 885	6 242	1 922	1 721	-6 982	-4 416	-2 140	-426	-993	-2 086	-51	-288	-1 747	-822	20
2nd quarter	9 975	6 199	2 088	1 688	-7 179	-4 598	-2 142	-439	-1 269	-2 018	303	-386	-1 935	-970	-206
3rd quarter	10 009	6 423	1 851	1 735	-7 349	-4 756	-2 153	-440	-935	-2 255	70	-414	-1 911	-1 018	2
4th quarter	10 299	6 637	1 982	1 680	-7 594	-4 930	-2 186	-478	-1 043	-3 200	-151	-592	-2 457	-949	-494
1965															
1st quarter	9 689	5 768	2 047	1 874	-7 395	-4 711	-2 187	-497	-1 037	-1 576	843	-374	-2 045	-1 606	-198
2nd quarter	11 263	6 876	2 448	1 939	-8 208	-5 428	-2 269	-511	-1 478	-1 270	69	-536	-803	-1 250	-147
3rd quarter	10 625	6 643	2 120	1 862	-8 307	-5 516	-2 263	-528	-1 013	-1 454	42	-254	-1 242	-1 030	-209
4th quarter	11 149	7 174	2 212	1 763	-8 802	-5 855	-2 393	-554	-1 058	-1 416	271	-441	-1 246	-1 125	-205
1966															
1st quarter	11 190	7 242	2 124	1 824	-9 068	-6 012	-2 483	-573	-1 140	-1 465	424	-321	-1 568	-1 115	-437
2nd quarter	11 726	7 169	2 705	1 852	-9 390	-6 195	-2 601	-594	-1 547	-1 967	68	-504	-1 531	-1 373	-115
3rd quarter	11 470	7 290	2 301	1 879	-9 912	-6 576	-2 693	-643	-1 073	-1 681	83	-339	-1 425	-1 314	-115
4th quarter	12 068	7 609	2 487	1 972	-10 098	-6 710	-2 717	-671	-1 194	-2 208	-5	-380	-1 823	-1 616	-53
1967															
1st quarter	12 439	7 751	2 731	1 957	-10 248	-6 708	-2 866	-674	-1 315	-1 203	1 027	-643	-1 587	-1 186	-265
2nd quarter	12 275	7 693	2 666	1 916	-10 136	-6 475	-2 986	-675	-1 472	-2 339	-419	-543	-1 377	-964	-261
3rd quarter	12 134	7 530	2 540	2 064	-10 262	-6 526	-3 059	-677	-1 309	-3 155	-375	-551	-2 229	-1 359	-419
4th quarter	12 506	7 692	2 731	2 083	-10 833	-7 157	-2 955	-721	-1 199	-3 060	-180	-685	-2 195	-1 297	-363
1968															
1st quarter	13 016	7 998	2 816	2 202	-11 571	-7 796	-2 997	-778	-1 249	-1 299	912	-706	-1 505	-981	-449
2nd quarter	13 577	8 324	2 936	2 317	-11 885	-8 051	-2 990	-844	-1 363	-2 427	-135	-632	-1 660	-1 172	-283
3rd quarter	14 195	8 745	3 039	2 411	-12 611	-8 612	-3 129	-870	-1 445	-3 447	-572	-568	-2 307	-1 573	-318
4th quarter	14 126	8 559	3 129	2 438	-12 604	-8 532	-3 185	-887	-1 573	-3 803	-1 075	-368	-2 360	-1 568	-519
1969															
1st quarter	12 921	7 468	2 884	2 569	-11 622	-7 444	-3 174	-1 004	-1 177	-2 595	-45	-406	-2 144	-1 556	-366
2nd quarter	15 492	9 536	3 283	2 673	-13 978	-9 527	-3 303	-1 148	-1 645	-3 428	-298	-632	-2 498	-1 663	-498
3rd quarter	15 439	9 400	3 245	2 794	-14 072	-9 380	-3 368	-1 324	-1 319	-3 361	-685	-703	-1 973	-1 548	-546
4th quarter	16 279	10 010	3 394	2 875	-14 329	-9 456	-3 481	-1 392	-1 593	-2 199	-151	-459	-1 589	-1 192	-139
1970															
1st quarter	16 461	10 258	3 235	2 968	-14 458	-9 587	-3 449	-1 422	-1 383	-3 478	-386	-399	-2 693	-1 958	-306
2nd quarter	17 419	10 744	3 645	3 030	-14 861	-9 766	-3 690	-1 405	-1 586	-1 725	1 025	-348	-2 402	-2 144	80
3rd quarter	17 267	10 665	3 625	2 977	-15 141	-10 049	-3 715	-1 377	-1 611	-2 146	802	-423	-2 525	-1 718	-517
4th quarter	17 241	10 802	3 666	2 773	-15 443	-10 464	-3 668	-1 311	-1 576	-1 989	1 040	-419	-2 610	-1 771	-333
1971															
1st quarter	17 980	10 920	4 048	3 012	-15 551	-10 600	-3 724	-1 227	-1 746	-3 464	151	-573	-3 042	-2 033	-408
2nd quarter	18 163	10 878	4 087	3 198	-16 764	-11 614	-3 867	-1 283	-1 808	-2 534	839	-567	-2 806	-1 949	-368
3rd quarter	18 676	11 548	3 972	3 156	-17 460	-12 171	-3 861	-1 428	-1 752	-3 390	1 377	-387	-4 380	-2 308	-346
4th quarter	17 564	9 973	4 251	3 340	-16 639	-11 194	-3 948	-1 497	-2 098	-3 084	-18	-355	-2 711	-1 327	9
1972															
1st quarter	19 757	11 833	4 473	3 451	-19 153	-13 501	-4 173	-1 479	-2 297	-4 295	-90	-212	-3 993	-2 187	-476
2nd quarter	19 427	11 618	4 233	3 576	-19 105	-13 254	-4 228	-1 623	-2 011	-2 125	-60	-271	-1 794	-1 481	-318
3rd quarter	20 788	12 351	4 634	3 803	-19 767	-14 022	-4 095	-1 650	-2 306	-3 952	96	-518	-3 530	-2 435	203
4th quarter	22 015	13 579	4 503	3 933	-21 212	-15 020	-4 371	-1 821	-1 933	-4 125	50	-566	-3 609	-1 644	-28
1973															
1st quarter	24 681	15 474	4 579	4 628	-23 000	-16 285	-4 613	-2 102	-1 536	-7 886	213	-572	-7 527	-3 785	55
2nd quarter	27 127	17 112	4 828	5 187	-24 301	-17 168	-4 741	-2 392	-1 953	-4 154	11	-423	-3 742	-2 691	-86
3rd quarter	29 329	18 271	5 145	5 913	-24 841	-17 683	-4 640	-2 518	-1 751	-3 189	-23	-608	-2 558	-2 159	-196
4th quarter	31 912	20 553	5 279	6 080	-26 855	-19 363	-4 849	-2 643	-1 674	-7 646	-43	-1 042	-6 561	-2 718	-445

[1] A minus sign indicates imports of goods or services or income payments.
[2] A minus sign indicates net unilateral transfers to foreigners.
[3] A minus sign indicates financial outflows or increases in U.S. official assets.

Table 19-10. U.S. International Transactions—Continued

(Millions of dollars, seasonally adjusted.)

Year and quarter	U.S.-owned assets abroad, net³ —Continued / U.S. private assets, net—Continued / U.S. claims		Foreign-owned assets in the United States, net, excluding financial derivatives⁴								Statistical discrep-ancy⁵	Balance on goods and services	Balance on current account
			Total	Foreign official assets in the United States, net	Other foreign assets in the United States, net				U.S. liabilities				
	On unaffiliated foreigners reported by U.S. nonbanking concerns	Reported by U.S. banks and securities brokers			Total	Direct invest-ment	U.S. Treasury securities and U.S. currency flows	U.S. securities other than U.S. Treasury securities	To unaffiliated foreigners reported by U.S. nonbanking concerns	Reported by U.S. banks and securities brokers			
1960													
1st quarter	38	-96	926	380	546	89	-100	170	-1	388	-210	509	350
2nd quarter	-100	-140	912	435	477	102	-143	118	-50	450	-286	867	530
3rd quarter	-51	-620	381	283	98	93	-99	5	-11	110	-261	866	836
4th quarter	-281	-292	77	377	-300	31	-22	-11	-28	-270	-262	1 266	1 108
1961													
1st quarter	-117	-284	435	438	-3	68	-82	104	73	-166	-354	1 270	1 239
2nd quarter	-164	-219	620	-307	927	86	-38	152	72	655	-497	1 204	906
3rd quarter	-149	-220	934	673	261	58	83	3	14	103	150	797	844
4th quarter	-128	-538	715	-41	756	99	188	66	67	336	-288	924	833
1962													
1st quarter	-186	-395	737	...	737	89	193	145	-14	324	-82	806	646
2nd quarter	-5	112	675	503	172	130	-51	7	-64	150	-259	1 268	1 045
3rd quarter	-181	-89	-277	178	-455	59	-109	-23	16	-398	-405	777	961
4th quarter	17	-78	779	591	188	68	-99	6	-47	260	-377	522	732
1963													
1st quarter	-27	57	1 191	946	245	40	25	14	-36	202	-112	791	843
2nd quarter	-108	-583	1 527	910	617	108	-109	119	69	430	-95	1 457	1 199
3rd quarter	47	-254	205	56	149	105	1	52	11	-20	-339	797	1 021
4th quarter	245	-776	295	75	220	-22	-66	102	-80	286	186	1 166	1 350
1964													
1st quarter	-206	-739	462	393	69	87	32	-42	...	-8	-286	1 608	1 910
2nd quarter	-166	-593	630	227	403	109	-108	14	19	369	-139	1 547	1 527
3rd quarter	-532	-363	769	275	494	56	-65	-30	37	496	-239	1 365	1 725
4th quarter	-204	-810	1 781	763	1 018	70	-5	-27	19	961	-243	1 503	1 662
1965													
1st quarter	286	-527	208	-202	410	184	60	57	3	106	111	917	1 257
2nd quarter	165	429	-330	-194	-136	-21	64	-243	63	1	23	1 627	1 577
3rd quarter	-19	16	587	115	472	147	-149	-227	49	652	-438	984	1 305
4th quarter	-91	175	280	421	-141	104	-106	54	63	-256	-153	1 138	1 289
1966													
1st quarter	-159	143	458	-164	622	143	-102	173	68	340	25	871	982
2nd quarter	-68	25	961	-57	1 018	133	-316	518	78	605	217	1 078	789
3rd quarter	-105	109	909	-342	1 251	-37	66	107	195	920	287	322	485
4th quarter	-110	-44	1 332	-111	1 443	187	-4	108	135	1 017	100	669	776
1967													
1st quarter	-107	-29	401	708	-307	169	-6	133	219	-822	-74	908	876
2nd quarter	-69	-83	1 884	1 100	784	174	-61	329	66	276	-212	898	667
3rd quarter	-40	-411	2 513	548	1 965	127	-36	520	164	1 190	79	485	563
4th quarter	-563	28	2 584	1 098	1 486	228	-32	34	135	1 121	2	311	474
1968													
1st quarter	-231	156	1 374	-533	1 907	367	22	855	207	456	-271	21	196
2nd quarter	-567	362	2 192	-2 007	4 199	133	86	1 122	478	2 380	-94	219	329
3rd quarter	-213	-203	2 809	442	2 367	148	-8	1 124	315	788	499	43	139
4th quarter	-191	-82	3 550	1 321	2 229	160	36	1 312	474	247	304	-29	-51
1969													
1st quarter	-132	-90	3 664	-1 117	4 781	359	-125	1 388	90	3 069	-1 191	-266	122
2nd quarter	-21	-316	3 896	-766	4 662	267	-35	365	181	3 884	-337	-11	-131
3rd quarter	141	-20	3 833	1 256	2 577	261	79	396	345	1 496	-520	-103	48
4th quarter	-114	-144	1 311	-672	1 983	376	13	981	176	437	531	467	357
1970													
1st quarter	-366	-63	3 027	3 697	-670	592	16	304	222	-1 804	-169	457	620
2nd quarter	-73	-265	848	694	154	212	-35	374	534	-931	-95	933	972
3rd quarter	-157	-133	1 940	1 411	529	357	1	720	510	-1 059	-309	526	515
4th quarter	0	-506	1 413	1 975	-562	303	99	792	748	-2 504	354	336	222
1971													
1st quarter	-355	-246	3 809	5 895	-2 086	196	179	559	-62	-2 958	-1 028	644	683
2nd quarter	-131	-358	5 154	5 630	-476	140	1 862	196	-34	-2 640	-2 211	-516	-409
3rd quarter	-337	-1 389	8 726	10 367	-1 641	-293	-795	626	79	-1 258	-4 800	-512	-536
4th quarter	-406	-987	5 997	5 704	293	324	-1 270	908	386	-55	-1 740	-918	-1 173
1972													
1st quarter	-248	-1 082	5 077	3 472	1 605	-136	-3	1 059	-14	699	911	-1 368	-1 693
2nd quarter	-185	190	4 277	1 103	3 174	373	-83	961	250	1 673	-463	-1 631	-1 689
3rd quarter	-241	-1 057	6 382	4 740	1 642	310	-12	718	216	410	-1 145	-1 132	-1 285
4th quarter	-380	-1 557	6 437	1 871	4 566	403	59	1 769	363	1 972	-1 182	-1 309	-1 130
1973													
1st quarter	-809	-2 988	10 743	9 937	806	631	-119	1 718	246	-1 670	-3 002	-845	145
2nd quarter	-202	-763	3 056	-403	3 458	835	-185	489	54	2 265	225	31	873
3rd quarter	-502	299	2 168	-772	2 940	539	-205	1 173	454	979	-1 716	1 093	2 737
4th quarter	-870	-2 528	2 423	-2 736	5 159	795	293	662	281	3 128	1 840	1 620	3 383

³A minus sign indicates financial outflows or increases in U.S. official assets.
⁴A minus sign indicates financial outflows or decreases in foreign official assets in the United States.
⁵Sum of credits and debits with the sign reversed.
. . . = Not available.

Table 19-10. U.S. International Transactions—Continued

(Millions of dollars, seasonally adjusted.)

| Year and quarter | Exports of goods, services, and income | | | | Imports of goods, services, and income [1] | | | | Unilateral current transfers, net [2] | U.S.-owned assets abroad, net, excluding financial derivatives [3] | | | U.S. private assets, net | | |
	Total	Goods	Services	Income receipts	Total	Goods	Services	Income payments		Total	U.S. official reserve assets, net	U.S. government assets other than official reserve assets, net	Total	Direct investment	Foreign securities
1974															
1st quarter	34 698	22 614	5 189	6 895	-29 643	-21 952	-4 985	-2 706	-3 443	-5 914	-246	1 389	-7 057	900	-600
2nd quarter	37 295	24 500	5 691	7 104	-34 710	-26 346	-5 359	-3 005	-2 475	-10 318	-358	267	-10 227	-1 790	-272
3rd quarter	37 385	24 629	5 633	7 123	-36 004	-27 368	-5 360	-3 276	-1 676	-7 694	-1 002	-354	-6 338	-4 385	-282
4th quarter	39 105	26 563	6 078	6 464	-36 918	-28 145	-5 675	-3 098	-1 656	-10 818	139	-938	-10 019	-3 776	-699
1975															
1st quarter	40 047	27 480	6 454	6 113	-33 797	-24 980	-5 580	-3 237	-2 043	-10 576	-327	-877	-9 372	-4 022	-1 931
2nd quarter	38 675	25 866	6 807	6 002	-31 284	-22 832	-5 309	-3 143	-2 377	-9 591	-28	-875	-8 688	-3 990	-985
3rd quarter	38 347	26 109	5 886	6 352	-33 078	-24 487	-5 379	-3 212	-1 189	-5 099	-333	-745	-4 021	-1 495	-938
4th quarter	40 868	27 633	6 351	6 884	-34 588	-25 886	-5 729	-2 973	-1 467	-14 436	-161	-977	-13 298	-4 736	-2 393
1976															
1st quarter	41 183	27 575	6 556	7 052	-37 464	-28 176	-5 883	-3 405	-1 153	-12 364	-777	-749	-10 838	-3 923	-2 467
2nd quarter	42 309	28 256	6 660	7 393	-39 494	-30 182	-5 980	-3 332	-1 167	-11 701	-1 580	-914	-9 207	-2 017	-1 405
3rd quarter	43 818	29 056	7 311	7 451	-41 737	-32 213	-6 231	-3 293	-2 165	-10 618	-408	-1 428	-8 782	-3 327	-2 751
4th quarter	44 780	29 858	7 444	7 478	-43 416	-33 657	-6 478	-3 281	-1 201	-16 588	207	-1 124	-15 671	-2 682	-2 262
1977															
1st quarter	44 916	29 668	7 494	7 754	-46 360	-36 585	-6 676	-3 099	-1 243	-1 198	-420	-1 062	284	-1 880	-749
2nd quarter	46 796	30 852	7 901	8 043	-48 401	-38 063	-6 940	-3 398	-1 426	-12 182	-24	-885	-11 273	-3 783	-1 784
3rd quarter	47 125	30 752	7 991	8 382	-48 511	-38 005	-6 894	-3 612	-1 371	-6 297	112	-1 001	-5 408	-2 762	-2 177
4th quarter	45 818	29 544	8 098	8 176	-50 495	-39 254	-7 133	-4 108	-1 185	-15 109	-43	-746	-14 320	-3 466	-749
1978															
1st quarter	48 847	30 470	8 704	9 673	-54 471	-42 487	-7 612	-4 372	-1 396	-15 219	187	-1 009	-14 397	-4 771	-1 115
2nd quarter	54 213	35 674	8 772	9 767	-56 513	-43 419	-7 768	-5 326	-1 477	-5 606	248	-1 257	-4 597	-3 720	-1 094
3rd quarter	56 058	36 523	9 203	10 332	-58 300	-44 422	-8 248	-5 630	-1 425	-9 703	115	-1 394	-8 424	-2 753	-510
4th quarter	61 399	39 408	9 673	12 318	-60 587	-45 674	-8 561	-6 352	-1 491	-30 601	182	-999	-29 784	-4 812	-907
1979															
1st quarter	64 530	41 475	9 664	13 391	-63 492	-47 582	-8 649	-7 261	-1 462	-8 980	-3 585	-1 094	-4 301	-5 465	-908
2nd quarter	68 445	43 885	9 713	14 847	-67 584	-50 778	-8 960	-7 846	-1 552	-15 565	322	-970	-14 917	-7 220	-492
3rd quarter	74 411	47 104	9 936	17 371	-71 856	-54 002	-9 329	-8 525	-1 632	-27 156	2 779	-779	-29 156	-7 166	-2 331
4th quarter	80 577	51 975	10 378	18 224	-78 726	-59 645	-9 751	-9 330	-1 949	-14 353	-649	-904	-12 800	-5 370	-995
1980															
1st quarter	85 274	54 237	10 997	20 040	-86 559	-65 815	-10 335	-10 409	-2 174	-13 814	-3 268	-1 441	-9 105	-5 188	-787
2nd quarter	83 441	55 967	11 491	15 983	-82 734	-62 274	-10 106	-10 354	-1 648	-24 724	502	-1 159	-24 067	-2 659	-1 387
3rd quarter	86 148	55 830	12 543	17 775	-79 906	-59 010	-10 292	-10 604	-1 909	-19 666	-1 109	-1 382	-17 175	-4 156	-944
4th quarter	89 578	58 216	12 554	18 808	-84 577	-62 651	-10 760	-11 166	-2 618	-28 761	-4 279	-1 178	-23 304	-7 219	-450
1981															
1st quarter	94 665	60 317	13 684	20 664	-91 024	-67 004	-11 360	-12 660	-2 678	-23 015	-4 529	-1 361	-17 125	-2 044	-473
2nd quarter	96 294	60 141	14 392	21 761	-92 303	-67 181	-11 447	-13 675	-2 763	-24 158	-905	-1 491	-21 762	-5 709	-1 564
3rd quarter	95 013	58 031	14 835	22 147	-89 787	-64 407	-11 236	-14 144	-3 145	-17 945	-4	-1 268	-16 673	-1 124	-697
4th quarter	94 958	58 555	14 446	21 957	-91 082	-66 475	-11 460	-13 147	-3 117	-49 028	262	-976	-48 314	-745	-2 966
1982															
1st quarter	94 006	55 163	16 032	22 811	-90 336	-63 502	-12 749	-14 085	-3 955	-36 335	-1 089	-800	-34 446	-2 695	-628
2nd quarter	96 060	55 344	16 187	24 529	-88 318	-60 580	-13 096	-14 642	-3 953	-42 754	-1 132	-1 727	-39 895	1 074	-471
3rd quarter	90 925	52 089	16 003	22 833	-90 938	-63 696	-12 794	-14 448	-4 027	-23 547	-794	-2 524	-20 229	903	-3 397
4th quarter	85 993	48 561	15 857	21 575	-86 379	-59 864	-13 109	-13 406	-4 611	-25 246	-1 950	-1 080	-22 217	-3 838	-3 488
1983															
1st quarter	86 146	49 198	16 239	20 709	-85 097	-59 757	-12 951	-12 389	-3 566	-28 890	-787	-1 136	-26 967	-862	-1 549
2nd quarter	87 214	49 340	16 093	21 781	-91 096	-64 783	-13 557	-12 756	-3 951	-2 974	16	-1 263	-1 727	-1 842	-2 813
3rd quarter	89 919	50 324	16 308	23 287	-98 481	-70 370	-14 133	-13 978	-4 339	-12 191	529	-1 171	-11 549	-4 861	-1 308
4th quarter	92 831	52 937	15 671	24 223	-102 822	-73 991	-14 337	-14 494	-5 453	-22 318	-953	-1 436	-19 929	-4 962	-1 093
1984															
1st quarter	96 000	52 991	17 353	25 656	-112 576	-79 740	-16 131	-16 705	-4 354	-8 338	-657	-2 033	-5 648	-1 837	758
2nd quarter	100 257	54 626	18 045	27 586	-119 220	-83 798	-16 885	-18 537	-4 476	-25 718	-566	-1 342	-23 811	-1 967	-764
3rd quarter	102 296	55 893	17 936	28 467	-120 533	-83 918	-17 168	-19 447	-5 147	15 298	-799	-1 392	17 489	-3 209	-1 106
4th quarter	101 361	56 416	17 834	27 111	-121 591	-84 962	-17 564	-19 065	-6 359	-21 618	-1 110	-720	-19 789	-9 396	-3 644
1985															
1st quarter	97 794	54 866	18 227	24 701	-116 249	-80 319	-17 707	-18 223	-5 064	-5 491	-233	-760	-4 498	-2 783	-2 474
2nd quarter	97 437	54 154	18 214	25 069	-120 891	-84 565	-18 276	-18 050	-5 235	-2 340	-356	-1 053	-931	-4 374	-2 219
3rd quarter	94 771	52 836	17 961	23 974	-120 285	-83 909	-18 151	-18 225	-5 789	-5 776	-121	-453	-5 202	-4 698	-1 572
4th quarter	97 612	54 059	18 756	24 797	-126 349	-89 295	-18 732	-18 322	-5 911	-31 146	-3 148	-555	-27 444	-7 073	-1 217
1986															
1st quarter	100 332	53 536	21 052	25 744	-129 342	-89 220	-19 855	-20 267	-5 199	-17 406	-115	-266	-17 025	-9 781	-5 930
2nd quarter	102 206	56 828	20 912	24 466	-131 690	-91 743	-19 066	-20 881	-6 208	-24 945	16	-230	-24 731	-7 298	-1 051
3rd quarter	101 288	55 645	21 969	23 674	-132 879	-92 801	-20 448	-19 630	-6 458	-32 615	280	-1 554	-31 341	-4 975	181
4th quarter	103 275	57 335	22 761	23 179	-136 232	-94 661	-20 778	-20 793	-6 269	-36 753	132	29	-36 914	-1 938	2 529
1987															
1st quarter	104 750	56 696	23 602	24 452	-138 887	-96 023	-21 273	-21 591	-5 128	8 177	1 956	-5	6 226	-6 547	-1 749
2nd quarter	111 642	60 202	24 740	26 700	-146 125	-100 648	-22 537	-22 940	-5 502	-26 738	3 419	-168	-29 989	-7 541	-287
3rd quarter	116 688	64 217	24 986	27 485	-151 111	-104 412	-22 833	-23 866	-5 706	-27 791	32	310	-28 133	-8 795	-1 159
4th quarter	123 968	69 093	25 329	29 546	-158 324	-108 682	-24 146	-25 496	-6 926	-32 943	3 742	868	-37 553	-12 150	-2 056

[1] A minus sign indicates imports of goods or services or income payments.
[2] A minus sign indicates net unilateral transfers to foreigners.
[3] A minus sign indicates financial outflows or increases in U.S. official assets.

Table 19-10. U.S. International Transactions—Continued

(Millions of dollars, seasonally adjusted.)

Year and quarter	U.S.-owned assets abroad, net [3] —Continued		Foreign-owned assets in the United States, net, excluding financial derivatives [4]								Statistical discrep-ancy [5]	Balance on goods and services	Balance on current account
	U.S. private assets, net—Continued		Total	Foreign official assets in the United States, net	Other foreign assets in the United States, net								
	U.S. claims								U.S. liabilities				
	On unaffiliated foreigners reported by U.S. nonbanking concerns	Reported by U.S. banks and securities brokers			Total	Direct invest-ment	U.S. Treasury securities and U.S. currency flows	U.S. securities other than U.S. Treasury securities	To unaffiliated foreigners reported by U.S. nonbanking concerns	Reported by U.S. banks and securities brokers			
1974													
1st quarter	-2 113	-5 244	6 444	-1 138	7 582	1 784	266	712	354	4 466	-2 142	866	1 612
2nd quarter	-588	-7 577	9 897	4 434	5 463	539	-5	363	390	4 176	311	-1 514	110
3rd quarter	273	-1 944	9 310	3 062	6 248	1 610	407	227	239	3 765	-1 321	-2 466	-295
4th quarter	-793	-4 751	9 577	4 188	5 389	828	1 015	-925	861	3 610	710	-1 179	531
1975													
1st quarter	353	-3 772	2 701	3 419	-718	278	805	344	359	-2 504	3 668	3 374	4 207
2nd quarter	112	-3 825	4 307	2 244	2 063	870	-54	385	55	807	270	4 532	5 014
3rd quarter	-939	-649	2 934	-1 731	4 665	86	2 367	737	-163	1 638	-1 915	2 129	4 080
4th quarter	-883	-5 286	6 929	3 095	3 834	1 369	672	1 038	68	687	2 694	2 369	4 813
1976													
1st quarter	-747	-3 701	7 709	3 699	4 010	1 471	677	1 036	154	672	2 089	72	2 566
2nd quarter	-999	-4 786	8 425	4 039	4 386	1 086	-119	134	-231	3 516	1 628	-1 246	1 648
3rd quarter	616	-3 320	9 062	2 958	6 104	999	3 267	64	-184	1 958	1 640	-2 077	-84
4th quarter	-1 166	-9 561	12 644	6 997	5 647	790	279	51	-317	4 844	3 781	-2 833	163
1977													
1st quarter	-771	3 684	2 968	5 554	-2 586	980	1 087	749	-98	-5 304	917	-6 099	-2 687
2nd quarter	-1 124	-4 582	14 673	7 888	6 785	965	-907	589	-102	6 240	540	-6 250	-3 031
3rd quarter	1 310	-1 779	14 585	8 257	6 328	1 023	1 560	337	768	2 640	-5 531	-6 156	-2 757
4th quarter	-1 355	-8 750	20 547	15 117	5 430	761	245	763	518	3 143	424	-8 745	-5 862
1978													
1st quarter	-2 241	-6 270	18 461	15 448	3 013	1 356	1 158	396	507	-404	3 778	-10 925	-7 020
2nd quarter	315	-98	1 412	-5 113	6 525	2 313	1 354	1 082	304	1 472	7 971	-6 741	-3 777
3rd quarter	-29	-5 132	17 390	4 903	12 487	2 620	-560	296	912	9 219	-4 020	-6 944	-3 667
4th quarter	-1 898	-22 167	29 013	18 440	10 573	1 608	2 465	480	166	5 854	2 267	-5 154	-679
1979													
1st quarter	-3 854	5 926	3 472	-7 558	11 030	1 554	2 590	409	-296	6 773	5 932	-5 092	-424
2nd quarter	716	-7 921	7 379	-9 775	17 154	3 354	459	524	799	12 018	8 877	-6 140	-691
3rd quarter	-1 826	-17 833	25 063	6 036	19 027	3 382	2 116	166	210	13 153	1 170	-6 291	923
4th quarter	-50	-6 385	4 780	-1 228	6 008	3 588	597	252	908	663	9 671	-7 043	-98
1980													
1st quarter	-1 927	-1 203	10 180	-6 261	16 441	3 321	3 746	2 435	340	6 599	7 093	-10 916	-3 459
2nd quarter	144	-20 165	10 994	7 731	3 264	5 756	-150	496	1 671	-4 509	14 671	-4 922	-941
3rd quarter	365	-12 440	14 599	7 564	7 035	4 713	-109	263	1 252	916	734	-929	4 333
4th quarter	-2 605	-13 030	26 263	7 614	18 649	3 128	1 931	2 263	3 590	7 737	115	-2 641	2 383
1981													
1st quarter	-2 944	-11 664	10 303	6 595	3 708	3 146	1 877	2 357	121	-3 793	11 749	-4 363	963
2nd quarter	513	-15 002	14 906	-3 159	18 065	5 294	1 183	3 512	13	8 063	8 024	-4 095	1 228
3rd quarter	458	-15 310	17 212	-5 992	23 204	5 505	-567	704	1 084	16 478	-1 348	-2 777	2 081
4th quarter	-2 404	-42 199	43 264	8 609	34 655	11 251	1 993	332	-301	21 380	5 005	-4 934	759
1982													
1st quarter	2 220	-33 343	26 797	-3 265	30 062	2 154	854	1 263	-65	25 856	9 768	-5 056	-285
2nd quarter	-1 095	-39 403	34 995	1 534	33 461	2 945	3 928	2 486	-2 023	26 125	3 918	-2 145	3 789
3rd quarter	3 670	-21 405	18 267	2 694	15 573	2 849	1 695	555	-282	10 756	9 272	-8 398	-4 040
4th quarter	2 028	-16 919	14 995	2 629	12 366	4 685	3 017	1 781	-13	2 896	15 204	-8 555	-4 997
1983													
1st quarter	-4 253	-20 303	15 870	-38	15 908	1 254	3 317	2 873	-2 763	11 227	15 486	-7 271	-2 517
2nd quarter	-590	3 518	16 049	1 612	14 437	3 287	4 340	2 470	-64	4 404	-5 294	-12 907	-7 833
3rd quarter	-1 764	-3 616	20 106	-2 689	22 795	4 059	1 994	1 777	1 311	13 654	4 933	-17 871	-12 901
4th quarter	-4 347	-9 527	35 373	6 960	28 413	1 771	3 143	1 044	1 398	21 057	2 336	-19 720	-15 444
1984													
1st quarter	-3 012	-1 557	22 780	-2 956	25 736	4 858	1 928	1 333	6 092	11 525	6 432	-25 527	-20 930
2nd quarter	-934	-20 146	42 415	-156	42 571	8 625	7 762	362	4 232	21 590	6 685	-28 012	-23 439
3rd quarter	3 987	17 817	7 158	-884	8 042	4 432	5 693	1 447	1 662	-5 192	868	-27 257	-23 384
4th quarter	492	-7 241	43 694	7 136	36 558	6 552	10 014	9 426	4 640	5 926	4 451	-28 276	-26 589
1985													
1st quarter	475	284	17 783	-10 962	28 745	4 913	2 831	9 615	-720	12 106	11 156	-24 933	-23 519
2nd quarter	2 337	3 325	28 903	8 502	20 401	4 376	6 457	7 194	1 724	650	2 050	-30 473	-28 689
3rd quarter	-2 779	3 847	37 802	2 506	35 296	4 839	8 675	11 669	2 801	7 312	-804	-31 263	-31 303
4th quarter	-10 375	-8 779	59 746	-1 165	60 911	5 618	5 786	22 484	6 046	20 977	5 961	-35 212	-34 648
1986													
1st quarter	-6 230	4 916	40 898	2 712	38 186	3 431	5 829	18 730	696	9 500	10 633	-34 487	-34 209
2nd quarter	-2 722	-13 660	53 279	15 918	37 361	5 520	4 189	22 752	1 635	3 265	7 282	-33 069	-35 692
3rd quarter	-7 638	-18 909	70 490	15 789	54 701	8 746	-1 240	17 107	1 947	28 141	104	-35 635	-38 049
4th quarter	-5 183	-32 322	63 662	1 229	62 433	17 723	-2 548	12 380	-953	35 831	12 246	-35 343	-39 226
1987													
1st quarter	-5 715	20 237	41 667	14 199	27 468	12 883	-2 906	18 372	6 151	-7 032	-10 666	-36 998	-39 265
2nd quarter	712	-22 873	57 020	10 444	46 576	8 593	-1 042	15 960	5 595	17 470	9 612	-38 243	-39 985
3rd quarter	-1 319	-16 860	82 791	764	82 027	20 763	-2 189	12 676	6 656	44 121	-14 965	-38 042	-40 129
4th quarter	-724	-22 623	65 621	19 980	45 641	16 230	2 360	-4 888	-39	31 978	8 511	-38 406	-41 282

3A minus sign indicates financial outflows or increases in U.S. official assets.
4A minus sign indicates financial outflows or decreases in foreign official assets in the United States.
5Sum of credits and debits with the sign reversed.

Table 19-10. U.S. International Transactions—*Continued*

(Millions of dollars, seasonally adjusted.)

Year and quarter	Exports of goods, services, and income				Imports of goods, services, and income [1]				Unilateral current transfers, net [2]	U.S.-owned assets abroad, net, excluding financial derivatives [3]					
										Total	U.S. official reserve assets, net	U.S. government assets other than official reserve assets, net	U.S. private assets, net		
	Total	Goods	Services	Income receipts	Total	Goods	Services	Income payments					Total	Direct investment	Foreign securities
1988															
1st quarter	134 932	75 655	26 598	32 679	-161 810	-109 963	-24 503	-27 344	-6 074	2 892	1 502	-1 597	2 987	-5 037	-4 504
2nd quarter	139 984	79 542	27 567	32 875	-163 265	-110 836	-24 282	-28 147	-5 615	-23 428	39	-854	-22 613	-2 594	1 318
3rd quarter	143 879	80 941	28 453	34 485	-165 901	-110 901	-24 588	-30 412	-5 902	-49 965	-7 380	1 960	-44 545	-7 791	-1 500
4th quarter	149 068	84 092	28 302	36 674	-172 770	-115 489	-25 157	-32 124	-7 685	-36 074	1 925	3 457	-41 456	-7 105	-3 294
1989															
1st quarter	155 853	86 322	30 576	38 955	-178 297	-118 709	-25 140	-34 448	-6 048	-53 703	-4 000	961	-50 664	-12 136	-2 225
2nd quarter	163 435	91 482	31 110	40 843	-182 850	-121 012	-25 241	-36 597	-5 753	-8 202	-12 095	-306	4 199	-7 686	-6 192
3rd quarter	163 560	90 743	32 316	40 501	-178 980	-117 459	-25 792	-35 729	-6 630	-51 678	-5 996	489	-46 171	-8 704	-9 149
4th quarter	165 444	91 369	33 087	40 988	-181 480	-120 485	-26 306	-34 689	-7 739	-61 803	-3 202	87	-58 688	-14 922	-4 504
1990															
1st quarter	171 856	95 070	35 016	41 770	-188 962	-124 947	-28 173	-35 842	-6 540	37 828	-3 177	-756	41 761	-10 391	8 580
2nd quarter	174 266	96 273	35 988	42 005	-186 146	-121 782	-28 764	-35 600	-7 644	-37 204	371	-796	-36 779	-4 651	-11 037
3rd quarter	176 466	97 227	37 402	41 837	-190 664	-124 132	-29 923	-36 609	-7 339	-43 716	1 739	-338	-45 117	-17 898	-1 037
4th quarter	184 389	98 831	39 428	46 130	-193 514	-127 577	-30 795	-35 142	-5 133	-38 142	-1 092	4 205	-41 255	-4 240	-8 111
1991															
1st quarter	181 296	101 258	37 891	42 147	-186 167	-122 326	-29 801	-34 040	14 828	-10 570	-353	549	-10 766	-14 318	-9 960
2nd quarter	180 627	102 674	40 745	37 208	-181 695	-120 103	-29 660	-31 932	3 593	745	1 014	-423	154	-1 230	-12 021
3rd quarter	181 647	104 238	41 860	35 549	-182 800	-122 448	-29 200	-31 152	-3 033	-15 900	3 878	3 256	-23 034	-9 356	-12 550
4th quarter	183 993	105 913	43 766	34 314	-183 906	-126 143	-29 799	-27 964	-5 488	-38 664	1 226	-459	-39 431	-12 987	-11 142
1992															
1st quarter	186 444	108 062	44 164	34 218	-185 468	-127 962	-29 762	-27 744	-7 210	-11 428	-1 057	-259	-10 112	-20 695	-8 668
2nd quarter	186 873	107 941	44 133	34 799	-190 414	-132 484	-29 443	-28 487	-8 349	-16 235	1 464	-302	-17 397	-10 268	-8 196
3rd quarter	188 127	110 847	44 609	32 671	-193 313	-136 048	-30 175	-27 090	-9 517	-13 570	1 952	-392	-15 130	-5 157	-13 059
4th quarter	189 201	112 781	44 343	32 077	-196 427	-140 034	-30 182	-26 211	-11 561	-33 177	1 542	-715	-34 004	-12 145	-19 243
1993															
1st quarter	191 422	112 099	45 984	33 339	-197 860	-142 331	-29 996	-25 533	-8 339	-21 491	-983	487	-20 995	-14 982	-28 208
2nd quarter	193 169	113 257	46 457	33 455	-204 737	-146 800	-30 661	-27 276	-9 111	-45 843	822	-304	-46 361	-23 264	-29 833
3rd quarter	194 153	112 982	46 707	34 464	-205 549	-147 763	-30 922	-26 864	-9 906	-52 975	-544	-194	-52 237	-13 155	-51 940
4th quarter	200 170	118 605	46 766	34 799	-215 772	-152 500	-32 202	-31 070	-12 456	-80 243	-673	-340	-79 230	-32 550	-36 272
1994															
1st quarter	204 240	118 833	48 362	37 045	-220 726	-156 303	-32 809	-31 614	-8 495	-39 740	-59	399	-40 080	-28 554	-19 540
2nd quarter	211 812	122 251	49 978	39 583	-231 476	-163 200	-33 023	-35 253	-8 914	-45 677	3 537	477	-49 691	-14 932	-11 834
3rd quarter	222 795	128 947	50 667	43 181	-244 319	-171 342	-33 624	-39 353	-10 084	-31 948	-165	-323	-31 460	-17 316	-13 368
4th quarter	230 930	132 828	51 391	46 711	-254 602	-177 845	-33 603	-43 154	-12 773	-61 574	2 033	-943	-62 664	-19 367	-18 448
1995															
1st quarter	241 117	138 370	52 173	50 574	-263 108	-183 966	-34 426	-44 716	-9 443	-64 771	-5 318	-553	-58 900	-19 325	-8 596
2nd quarter	248 705	142 520	53 163	53 022	-271 587	-189 910	-35 094	-46 580	-9 131	-118 089	-2 722	-225	-115 142	-15 078	-27 964
3rd quarter	255 495	146 536	56 436	52 523	-272 929	-187 685	-35 604	-49 640	-9 543	-47 311	-1 893	252	-45 670	-21 772	-42 116
4th quarter	259 310	147 778	57 408	54 124	-272 501	-187 813	-36 272	-48 416	-9 956	-122 091	191	-458	-121 824	-42 573	-43 718
1996															
1st quarter	263 221	150 552	57 442	55 227	-279 419	-194 445	-37 090	-47 884	-11 242	-80 431	17	-210	-80 238	-23 759	-43 538
2nd quarter	266 995	152 861	59 350	54 784	-287 312	-200 070	-37 606	-49 636	-9 523	-68 123	-523	-568	-67 032	-15 096	-30 579
3rd quarter	266 854	151 856	58 664	56 334	-293 261	-202 367	-38 836	-52 058	-9 651	-91 580	7 489	105	-99 174	-23 129	-33 178
4th quarter	280 655	156 844	64 029	59 782	-299 487	-206 231	-39 023	-54 233	-12 603	-173 272	-315	-316	-172 641	-29 898	-42 020
1997															
1st quarter	287 279	162 670	62 515	62 094	-313 391	-214 209	-40 405	-58 777	-9 967	-152 729	4 480	-76	-157 133	-29 544	-24 352
2nd quarter	299 679	170 249	64 292	65 138	-318 210	-217 296	-40 879	-60 035	-10 267	-93 152	-236	-298	-92 618	-24 883	-31 275
3rd quarter	303 542	173 155	64 855	65 532	-325 593	-220 974	-42 078	-62 541	-10 666	-119 387	-730	377	-119 034	-21 217	-51 401
4th quarter	300 762	172 292	64 429	64 041	-329 728	-224 315	-42 571	-62 842	-14 160	-120 209	-4 524	65	-115 750	-29 161	-9 824
1998															
1st quarter	302 195	171 060	64 690	66 445	-334 146	-227 667	-43 304	-63 175	-12 053	-74 438	-444	-80	-73 914	-41 844	-19 451
2nd quarter	298 846	165 559	66 174	67 113	-337 834	-228 497	-44 627	-64 710	-12 361	-138 628	-1 945	-483	-136 200	-44 689	-42 961
3rd quarter	293 115	164 054	64 786	64 275	-338 864	-227 854	-45 784	-65 226	-13 140	-58 520	-2 025	188	-56 683	-20 479	7 783
4th quarter	300 835	169 743	67 106	63 986	-346 026	-234 619	-46 965	-64 442	-15 633	-82 245	-2 369	-47	-79 829	-35 634	-75 575
1999															
1st quarter	300 183	164 302	68 755	67 126	-351 564	-239 080	-47 703	-64 781	-11 885	-84 623	4 068	118	-88 809	-68 498	2 696
2nd quarter	307 288	166 144	70 138	71 006	-367 128	-250 480	-49 234	-67 414	-12 260	-182 426	1 159	-392	-183 193	-50 190	-69 682
3rd quarter	319 936	172 989	71 185	75 762	-388 656	-264 829	-50 818	-73 009	-11 987	-123 490	1 951	-686	-124 755	-64 062	-39 790
4th quarter	332 407	180 530	71 842	80 035	-403 662	-277 395	-51 435	-74 832	-14 295	-113 524	1 569	3 710	-118 803	-42 185	-15 460
2000															
1st quarter	341 683	185 253	73 127	83 303	-427 646	-294 137	-54 240	-79 269	-12 859	-207 606	-554	-127	-206 925	-34 934	-32 542
2nd quarter	355 307	191 227	75 335	88 745	-441 576	-302 219	-55 245	-84 112	-13 368	-107 301	2 020	-570	-108 751	-52 029	-38 171
3rd quarter	360 295	198 811	74 662	86 822	-454 243	-313 330	-57 353	-83 560	-14 208	-84 847	-346	114	-84 615	-39 618	-32 363
4th quarter	364 231	196 703	75 479	92 049	-456 835	-316 998	-56 914	-82 923	-18 212	-160 771	-1 410	-358	-159 003	-32 633	-24 832
2001															
1st quarter	350 489	193 976	74 564	81 949	-442 884	-309 943	-56 420	-76 521	-15 171	-216 194	190	77	-216 461	-35 381	-25 355
2nd quarter	334 968	185 030	74 110	75 828	-416 828	-290 851	-57 578	-68 399	-15 802	-86 702	-1 343	-783	-84 576	-26 783	-50 200
3rd quarter	312 093	172 647	70 579	68 867	-400 716	-278 585	-54 863	-67 268	-16 134	32 858	-3 559	77	36 340	-44 327	11 639
4th quarter	298 144	167 058	66 932	64 154	-369 050	-269 229	-52 930	-46 891	-17 374	-112 577	-199	143	-112 521	-35 857	-26 728

[1]A minus sign indicates imports of goods or services or income payments.
[2]A minus sign indicates net unilateral transfers to foreigners.
[3]A minus sign indicates financial outflows or increases in U.S. official assets.

Table 19-10. U.S. International Transactions—*Continued*

(Millions of dollars, seasonally adjusted.)

Year and quarter	U.S.-owned assets abroad, net [3] —Continued / U.S. private assets, net—Continued / U.S. claims		Foreign-owned assets in the United States, net, excluding financial derivatives [4]								Statistical discrepancy [5]	Balance on goods and services	Balance on current account
						Other foreign assets in the United States, net							
									U.S. liabilities				
	On unaffiliated foreigners reported by U.S. nonbanking concerns	Reported by U.S. banks and securities brokers	Total	Foreign official assets in the United States, net	Total	Direct investment	U.S. Treasury securities and U.S. currency flows	U.S. securities other than U.S. Treasury securities	To unaffiliated foreigners reported by U.S. nonbanking concerns	Reported by U.S. banks and securities brokers			
1988													
1st quarter	-3 454	15 982	31 524	24 925	6 599	8 425	6 007	2 423	12 593	-22 849	-1 573	-32 213	-32 952
2nd quarter	-9 954	-11 383	74 187	6 006	68 181	13 717	7 329	9 702	6 742	30 691	-21 981	-28 009	-28 896
3rd quarter	-5 217	-30 037	52 329	-1 974	54 303	13 778	4 275	7 464	6 399	22 387	25 430	-26 095	-27 924
4th quarter	-2 568	-28 489	86 793	10 801	75 992	21 815	6 739	6 764	7 159	33 515	-19 468	-28 252	-31 387
1989													
1st quarter	-9 293	-27 010	66 021	7 700	58 321	18 584	10 316	8 544	6 637	14 240	16 046	-26 951	-28 492
2nd quarter	-5 767	23 844	10 571	-5 114	15 685	15 325	4 380	9 365	12 000	-25 385	22 666	-23 661	-25 168
3rd quarter	-5 924	-22 394	73 526	13 060	60 466	11 519	12 202	10 270	-1 121	27 596	63	-20 192	-22 050
4th quarter	-6 662	-32 600	72 660	-7 142	79 802	22 846	6 469	10 588	4 570	35 329	12 982	-22 335	-23 775
1990													
1st quarter	3 019	57 713	-23 477	-6 421	-17 056	15 774	1 056	1 311	12 904	-48 101	9 314	-23 034	-23 646
2nd quarter	-5 069	-16 022	40 868	6 207	34 661	13 773	5 910	2 114	6 713	6 151	15 703	-18 285	-19 524
3rd quarter	-15 514	-10 668	62 621	13 937	48 684	8 313	5 434	-2 874	16 838	20 973	2 467	-19 426	-21 537
4th quarter	-10 260	-18 644	59 345	20 186	39 159	10 635	1 652	1 041	8 678	17 153	-63	-20 113	-14 258
1991													
1st quarter	-40	13 552	7 590	5 569	2 021	4 076	8 782	5 023	-586	-15 274	-6 036	-12 978	9 957
2nd quarter	7 902	5 503	12 016	-4 913	16 929	13 378	14 999	14 872	-2 549	-23 771	-15 359	-6 344	2 525
3rd quarter	3 341	-4 469	32 574	3 854	28 720	-1 354	2 342	10 310	4 761	12 661	-8 702	-5 550	-4 186
4th quarter	-106	-15 196	56 043	12 879	43 164	7 072	5 516	4 939	-4 741	30 378	-12 153	-6 263	-5 401
1992													
1st quarter	7 562	11 689	30 212	20 988	9 224	2 086	1 119	4 569	5 689	-4 239	-12 413	-5 498	-6 234
2nd quarter	-6 620	7 687	49 732	20 879	28 853	5 916	10 759	10 467	3 954	-2 243	-21 432	-9 853	-11 890
3rd quarter	-3 737	6 823	34 931	-7 524	42 455	2 898	10 470	2 531	4 854	21 702	-8 062	-10 767	-14 703
4th quarter	2 408	-5 024	53 472	6 133	47 339	8 922	25 869	12 476	-924	996	-1 394	-13 092	-18 787
1993													
1st quarter	-6 130	28 325	24 531	10 937	13 594	8 060	15 795	9 694	-215	-19 740	12 495	-14 244	-14 777
2nd quarter	-725	7 461	58 599	17 466	41 133	11 386	5 169	15 205	6 531	2 842	8 073	-17 747	-20 679
3rd quarter	5 896	6 962	84 967	19 073	65 894	11 688	8 931	17 782	288	27 205	-10 458	-18 996	-21 302
4th quarter	1 725	-12 133	111 662	24 277	87 385	20 229	11 104	37 411	3 885	14 756	-3 202	-19 331	-28 058
1994													
1st quarter	-2 215	10 229	89 488	10 568	78 920	5 883	14 620	21 070	5 856	31 491	-24 609	-21 917	-24 981
2nd quarter	-20 966	-1 959	56 279	9 455	46 824	5 767	-1 361	12 352	4 269	25 797	18 987	-23 994	-28 578
3rd quarter	-960	184	81 239	19 358	61 881	13 709	9 666	13 389	-1 620	26 737	-17 287	-25 352	-31 608
4th quarter	-12 195	-12 654	76 168	202	75 966	20 762	31 934	10 160	-7 203	20 313	22 009	-27 229	-36 445
1995													
1st quarter	-2 631	-28 348	96 842	21 956	74 886	9 924	33 337	12 400	17 764	1 461	-462	-27 849	-31 434
2nd quarter	-24 580	-47 520	121 385	37 072	84 313	11 888	29 574	15 851	11 864	28 763	29 324	-32 013	-32 013
3rd quarter	13 729	4 489	115 499	39 302	76 197	16 764	36 327	26 218	13 493	-16 605	-40 574	-20 317	-26 977
4th quarter	-31 804	-3 729	101 376	11 550	89 826	19 200	1 146	22 780	16 516	30 184	43 931	-18 899	-23 147
1996													
1st quarter	-15 210	2 269	84 335	51 771	32 564	28 518	12 726	20 356	4 350	-33 386	23 714	-23 541	-27 440
2nd quarter	-22 000	643	100 610	13 503	87 107	16 184	28 719	24 686	15 259	2 259	-2 469	-25 465	-29 840
3rd quarter	-9 090	-33 777	143 269	23 020	120 249	15 257	43 276	29 719	28 925	3 072	-15 445	-30 683	-36 058
4th quarter	-40 033	-60 690	219 670	38 430	181 240	26 542	76 452	28 511	5 202	44 533	-14 770	-24 381	-31 435
1997													
1st quarter	-38 112	-65 125	172 247	27 763	144 484	28 626	31 779	38 490	25 055	20 534	16 776	-29 429	-36 079
2nd quarter	-9 885	-26 575	140 222	-6 019	146 241	23 150	38 253	45 651	6 461	32 726	-17 992	-23 634	-28 798
3rd quarter	-22 173	-24 243	166 609	23 474	143 135	17 865	42 095	52 544	25 550	5 081	-14 205	-25 042	-32 717
4th quarter	-51 590	-25 175	225 372	-26 182	251 554	35 960	40 733	24 724	59 452	90 685	-61 805	-30 165	-43 126
1998													
1st quarter	-7 822	-4 797	78 365	11 072	67 293	19 759	-6 594	63 237	39 833	-48 942	40 271	-35 221	-44 004
2nd quarter	-20 363	-28 187	154 539	-10 235	164 774	20 391	23 647	56 146	30 722	33 868	35 629	-41 391	-51 349
3rd quarter	-15 658	-28 329	75 193	-46 640	121 833	23 490	1 425	6 628	14 976	75 314	42 413	-44 798	-58 889
4th quarter	5 639	25 741	112 697	25 900	86 797	115 405	23 950	30 304	-62 391	-20 471	30 556	-44 735	-60 824
1999													
1st quarter	-47 211	24 204	108 317	4 381	103 936	28 759	-11 853	49 157	51 307	-13 434	39 768	-53 726	-63 266
2nd quarter	-27 021	-36 300	247 211	-757	247 968	140 759	-9 004	70 205	16 928	29 080	7 506	-63 432	-72 100
3rd quarter	-13 663	-7 240	156 060	12 625	143 435	50 758	7 584	86 202	-8 777	7 668	48 326	-71 473	-80 707
4th quarter	-9 809	-51 349	230 623	27 294	203 329	69 169	-6 817	93 270	16 789	30 918	-27 186	-76 458	-85 550
2000													
1st quarter	-79 800	-59 649	242 782	22 542	220 240	52 094	-23 776	129 306	72 433	-9 817	63 869	-89 997	-98 822
2nd quarter	-25 287	6 736	246 564	6 952	239 612	91 669	22 889	88 189	28 796	53 847	-39 388	-90 902	-99 637
3rd quarter	-14 121	1 487	245 064	11 354	233 710	79 979	-13 777	122 138	16 914	28 456	-51 791	-97 210	-108 156
4th quarter	-19 582	-81 956	303 816	1 910	301 906	97 534	-12 898	120 256	52 529	44 485	-31 950	-101 730	-110 816
2001													
1st quarter	-46 769	-108 956	330 767	21 333	309 434	59 145	-16 736	129 474	112 097	25 454	-6 705	-97 824	-107 567
2nd quarter	-7 507	-86	206 867	-19 965	226 832	59 338	-10 143	108 537	-173	69 273	-22 190	-89 289	-97 662
3rd quarter	1 824	67 204	24 246	15 653	8 573	13 783	1 495	60 748	-23 171	-44 282	34 814	-90 222	-104 757
4th quarter	43 932	-93 868	221 010	11 038	209 972	34 755	34 800	95 126	-22 643	67 934	-19 830	-88 169	-88 280

[3]A minus sign indicates financial outflows or increases in U.S. official assets.
[4]A minus sign indicates financial outflows or decreases in foreign official assets in the United States.
[5]Sum of credits and debits with the sign reversed.

Table 19-10. U.S. International Transactions—*Continued*

(Millions of dollars, seasonally adjusted.)

| Year and quarter | Exports of goods, services, and income | | | | Imports of goods, services, and income [1] | | | | Unilateral current transfers, net [2] | U.S.-owned assets abroad, net, excluding financial derivatives [3] | | | U.S. private assets, net | | |
	Total	Goods	Services	Income receipts	Total	Goods	Services	Income payments		Total	U.S. official reserve assets, net	U.S. government assets other than official reserve assets, net	Total	Direct investment	Foreign securities
2002															
1st quarter	303 113	165 855	70 799	66 459	-388 736	-273 800	-55 981	-58 955	-18 542	-84 841	390	133	-85 364	-48 155	-9 012
2nd quarter	314 893	172 850	72 292	69 751	-415 445	-291 968	-56 586	-66 891	-15 007	-139 712	-1 843	42	-137 911	-36 163	-20 735
3rd quarter	322 397	174 895	73 650	73 852	-423 480	-298 023	-57 979	-67 478	-15 005	892	-1 416	-27	2 335	-33 165	4 884
4th quarter	318 013	171 571	75 558	70 884	-424 949	-304 211	-60 522	-60 216	-16 394	-70 987	-812	197	-70 372	-36 979	-23 705
2003															
1st quarter	322 280	174 077	73 417	74 786	-439 190	-310 903	-60 683	-67 604	-18 219	-82 315	83	53	-82 451	-22 656	-31 947
2nd quarter	325 332	175 025	72 781	77 526	-438 044	-311 215	-59 848	-66 981	-17 600	-157 427	-170	310	-157 567	-46 512	-32 734
3rd quarter	335 764	178 377	76 996	80 391	-448 175	-314 878	-63 417	-69 880	-17 707	-755	-611	483	-627	-40 597	-27 677
4th quarter	357 265	188 369	81 147	87 749	-464 962	-327 864	-66 416	-70 682	-18 269	-84 924	2 221	-309	-86 836	-39 796	-54 364
2004															
1st quarter	375 738	194 136	85 435	96 167	-489 332	-345 330	-69 528	-74 474	-22 987	-353 976	557	727	-355 260	-77 283	-36 045
2nd quarter	387 174	199 838	87 323	100 014	-521 845	-365 340	-71 973	-84 532	-21 385	-170 502	1 122	-2	-171 622	-75 377	-44 702
3rd quarter	396 473	203 351	87 759	105 363	-534 397	-373 762	-73 461	-87 175	-21 141	-169 462	429	484	-170 375	-51 998	-53 988
4th quarter	413 584	208 836	92 555	112 194	-570 166	-393 564	-76 262	-100 339	-22 850	-306 929	697	501	-308 127	-111 564	-35 814
2005															
1st quarter	434 626	214 782	95 191	124 653	-580 374	-400 122	-76 183	-104 069	-28 723	-129 175	5 331	2 591	-137 097	-58 799	-59 599
2nd quarter	447 206	223 086	95 633	128 487	-601 069	-412 775	-77 679	-110 615	-25 196	-222 397	-797	989	-222 589	-41 548	-57 317
3rd quarter	456 955	223 049	97 767	136 138	-617 635	-423 077	-78 963	-115 595	-24 658	-204 361	4 766	1 501	-210 628	12 163	-66 383
4th quarter	477 936	231 420	100 530	145 986	-660 557	-447 214	-80 715	-132 627	-27 194	9 302	4 796	459	4 047	51 948	-67 900
2006															
1st quarter	503 350	243 445	104 692	155 212	-681 005	-454 618	-85 141	-141 245	-20 995	-387 689	513	1 049	-389 251	-58 801	-75 689
2nd quarter	528 763	252 086	107 217	169 459	-707 132	-463 797	-86 679	-156 657	-23 708	-223 953	-560	1 765	-225 158	-35 160	-80 203
3rd quarter	540 184	255 925	108 687	175 572	-730 097	-476 361	-87 542	-166 195	-24 876	-295 389	1 006	1 570	-297 965	-72 149	-72 552
4th quarter	561 608	264 355	115 276	181 978	-727 946	-468 296	-89 610	-170 039	-21 693	-378 698	1 415	962	-381 075	-78 812	-136 685
2007															
1st quarter	574 689	269 538	118 170	186 981	-742 980	-475 571	-90 175	-177 234	-30 807	-485 867	-72	445	-486 240	-99 975	-122 024
2nd quarter	600 300	277 655	120 333	202 312	-765 079	-483 294	-92 253	-189 531	-25 752	-545 158	26	-596	-544 588	-94 415	-107 064
3rd quarter	631 854	289 160	129 189	213 505	-774 912	-494 075	-95 739	-185 098	-28 557	-192 530	-54	623	-193 099	-65 800	-113 826
4th quarter	655 255	302 031	137 092	216 132	-789 703	-516 435	-97 048	-176 220	-30 883	-248 571	-22	-22 744	-225 805	-138 408	-23 610
2008															
1st quarter	654 217	315 637	135 653	202 927	-800 185	-534 482	-99 461	-166 241	-33 330	-251 501	-276	3 268	-254 493	-89 792	-47 870
2nd quarter	671 886	332 876	140 214	198 796	-828 458	-554 372	-101 565	-172 521	-31 147	107 343	-1 267	-41 592	150 202	-103 619	-40 566
3rd quarter	673 383	337 912	140 152	195 319	-825 200	-559 002	-105 004	-161 194	-32 361	29 322	-179	-225 997	255 498	-54 115	79 182
4th quarter	591 747	290 569	133 583	167 596	-715 096	-469 389	-99 257	-146 450	-31 527	114 730	-3 126	-265 293	383 150	-84 486	70 015
2009															
1st quarter	507 291	249 108	122 917	135 267	-581 287	-373 107	-91 137	-117 044	-30 185	94 092	-982	244 102	-149 028	-40 903	-36 201
2nd quarter	506 204	245 868	125 349	134 987	-570 691	-361 318	-90 975	-118 399	-33 256	36 762	-3 632	193 750	-153 356	-48 078	-92 589
3rd quarter	535 114	263 645	129 155	142 315	-602 438	-395 746	-93 437	-113 255	-35 025	-269 192	-49 021	57 736	-277 907	-68 537	-46 967
4th quarter	567 322	286 923	131 756	148 642	-651 138	-432 418	-95 209	-123 511	-31 777	-99 116	1 379	46 187	-146 682	-63 453	-45 782

[1] A minus sign indicates imports of goods or services or income payments.
[2] A minus sign indicates net unilateral transfers to foreigners.
[3] A minus sign indicates financial outflows or increases in U.S. official assets.

Table 19-10. U.S. International Transactions—*Continued*

(Millions of dollars, seasonally adjusted.)

Year and quarter	U.S.-owned assets abroad, net [3] —Continued / U.S. private assets, net—Continued / U.S. claims / On unaffiliated foreigners reported by U.S. nonbanking concerns	Reported by U.S. banks and securities brokers	Foreign-owned assets in the United States, net, excluding financial derivatives [4] / Total	Foreign official assets in the United States, net	Other foreign assets in the United States, net / Total	Direct invest-ment	U.S. Treasury securities and U.S. currency flows	U.S. securities other than U.S. Treasury securities	U.S. liabilities / To unaffiliated foreigners reported by U.S. nonbanking concerns	Reported by U.S. banks and securities brokers	Statistical discrep-ancy [5]	Balance on goods and services	Balance on current account
2002													
1st quarter	-27 798	-399	173 225	12 801	160 424	24 485	13 964	73 750	57 788	-9 563	16 103	-93 128	-104 166
2nd quarter	-13 680	-67 333	231 325	53 312	178 013	7 194	26 042	99 689	17 805	27 283	24 279	-103 412	-115 559
3rd quarter	-7 443	38 059	160 335	18 328	142 007	13 929	55 166	43 282	7 515	22 115	-44 740	-107 457	-116 088
4th quarter	-1 101	-8 587	230 275	31 504	198 771	38 763	24 092	66 578	12 763	56 575	-35 542	-117 603	-123 329
2003													
1st quarter	1 757	-29 605	240 908	50 531	190 377	37 169	10 894	52 209	68 460	21 645	-22 975	-124 092	-135 129
2nd quarter	-15 089	-63 232	217 732	66 877	150 855	-5 460	48 179	81 187	15 129	11 820	71 670	-123 257	-130 312
3rd quarter	21 261	46 386	129 177	64 397	64 780	-1 574	36 749	15 354	9 137	5 114	2 605	-122 922	-130 118
4th quarter	-26 113	33 437	270 487	96 264	174 223	33 616	6 224	71 955	3 800	58 628	-59 178	-124 764	-125 966
2004													
1st quarter	-67 088	-174 844	459 483	147 636	311 847	26 000	29 034	47 862	61 265	147 686	31 561	-135 287	-136 581
2nd quarter	-11 754	-39 789	331 630	79 949	251 681	32 658	73 376	87 270	21 013	37 364	-4 646	-150 152	-156 055
3rd quarter	-9 235	-55 154	274 147	76 120	198 027	34 113	-3 198	86 577	29 957	50 578	51 641	-156 113	-159 066
4th quarter	-64 489	-96 260	467 941	94 050	373 891	53 195	7 697	159 784	53 637	99 578	18 923	-168 436	-179 432
2005													
1st quarter	-64 051	45 352	234 182	25 052	209 130	38 871	76 819	75 631	86 298	-68 489	72 057	-166 332	-174 471
2nd quarter	59 260	-182 984	304 880	81 292	223 588	-9 004	-13 197	107 694	-26 159	164 254	97 086	-171 735	-179 059
3rd quarter	-69 527	-86 881	425 404	54 736	370 668	38 016	26 597	141 900	51 727	112 428	-50 616	-181 223	-185 339
4th quarter	3 111	16 888	282 881	98 188	184 693	44 755	50 528	125 161	-42 294	6 543	-81 904	-195 979	-209 815
2006													
1st quarter	-41 792	-212 969	545 648	130 427	415 221	44 357	-25 884	167 589	66 064	163 095	40 780	-191 622	-198 651
2nd quarter	-48 226	-61 569	407 652	127 303	280 349	65 611	-26 369	139 681	59 820	41 606	5 305	-191 172	-202 078
3rd quarter	-57 478	-95 786	525 441	121 843	403 598	55 495	-23 914	197 877	69 975	104 165	-29 858	-199 290	-214 789
4th quarter	-33 803	-131 775	586 428	108 366	478 062	77 688	20 165	178 098	48 934	153 177	-17 924	-178 276	-188 031
2007													
1st quarter	-42 947	-221 294	700 961	165 837	535 124	21 016	35 962	183 460	91 302	203 384	-30 242	-178 038	-199 098
2nd quarter	-133 201	-209 908	737 457	88 331	649 126	83 683	-15 102	310 303	127 498	142 744	-637	-177 560	-190 531
3rd quarter	75 747	-89 220	278 424	47 674	230 750	97 944	17 520	-9 829	75 447	49 668	80 403	-171 465	-171 614
4th quarter	59 884	-123 671	412 618	179 107	233 511	73 115	17 752	121 718	-92 566	113 492	15 388	-174 360	-165 330
2008													
1st quarter	116 232	-233 063	426 058	208 646	217 412	59 473	9 377	-15 179	73 211	90 530	13 344	-182 653	-179 298
2nd quarter	64 906	229 481	2 003	178 826	-176 823	100 706	19 177	19 983	-54 996	-261 693	81 410	-182 847	-187 719
3rd quarter	87 352	143 079	117 897	115 573	2 324	62 755	85 894	-102 512	76 442	-120 255	38 067	-185 942	-184 178
4th quarter	103 739	293 882	-11 888	-16 024	4 136	96 802	111 358	-29 029	-139 824	-35 171	67 236	-144 495	-154 875
2009													
1st quarter	17 477	-89 401	-67 583	70 892	-138 475	24 025	65 532	-55 992	-8 270	-163 770	69 976	-92 219	-104 182
2nd quarter	14 519	-27 208	14 648	124 299	-109 651	37 009	-24 690	13 917	43 003	-178 890	35 787	-81 076	-97 743
3rd quarter	81 700	-244 103	343 388	123 786	219 602	47 472	-4 717	28 732	13 880	134 235	17 373	-96 383	-102 348
4th quarter	22 140	-59 587	144 782	128 598	16 184	43 579	14 127	6 729	-21 648	-26 603	70 640	-108 948	-115 593

[3]A minus sign indicates financial outflows or increases in U.S. official assets.
[4]A minus sign indicates financial outflows or decreases in foreign official assets in the United States.
[5]Sum of credits and debits with the sign reversed.

Table 19-11. Productivity and Related Data

(1992 = 100, seasonally adjusted.)

Year and quarter	Business sector								Nonfarm business sector							
	Output per hour of all persons	Output	Hours of all persons	Compensation per hour	Real compensation per hour	Unit labor costs	Unit nonlabor payments	Implicit price deflator	Output per hour of all persons	Output	Hours of all persons	Compensation per hour	Real compensation per hour	Unit labor costs	Unit nonlabor payments	Implicit price deflator
1947	32.2	20.4	63.4	7.0	41.2	21.8	18.5	20.6	37.0	20.1	54.2	7.5	43.8	20.2	17.8	19.3
1948	33.7	21.5	63.8	7.6	41.3	22.6	20.6	21.9	38.1	21.0	55.1	8.1	44.0	21.3	19.4	20.6
1949	34.5	21.3	61.8	7.7	42.4	22.4	20.4	21.6	39.3	20.8	53.0	8.4	45.9	21.3	19.9	20.8
1947																
1st quarter	32.1	20.3	63.1	6.8	41.0	21.2	17.9	20.0	36.5	19.7	54.0	7.3	43.7	19.9	16.7	18.7
2nd quarter	32.3	20.3	63.0	7.0	41.4	21.6	18.0	20.2	37.4	20.2	54.0	7.4	43.8	19.7	17.7	19.0
3rd quarter	32.1	20.3	63.5	7.0	40.8	21.9	18.8	20.8	36.3	19.7	54.2	7.5	43.8	20.7	18.2	19.8
4th quarter	32.5	20.8	63.9	7.3	41.2	22.5	19.4	21.3	37.8	20.7	54.7	7.7	43.6	20.4	18.6	19.7
1948																
1st quarter	33.2	21.1	63.6	7.4	40.9	22.3	20.2	21.5	38.0	20.9	55.0	7.9	43.8	20.8	18.8	20.1
2nd quarter	34.0	21.6	63.6	7.5	40.8	22.1	21.0	21.7	38.0	20.9	55.0	8.0	43.7	21.2	19.1	20.4
3rd quarter	33.8	21.7	64.2	7.7	41.3	22.8	20.8	22.1	38.0	21.1	55.4	8.2	44.0	21.6	19.5	20.8
4th quarter	34.0	21.7	63.8	7.9	42.6	23.2	20.3	22.1	38.2	21.0	54.9	8.3	44.9	21.8	20.0	21.1
1949																
1st quarter	33.9	21.3	62.9	7.7	42.1	22.8	20.5	21.9	38.6	20.8	54.0	8.4	45.6	21.6	19.8	21.0
2nd quarter	34.0	21.2	62.4	7.6	41.6	22.4	20.5	21.7	39.0	20.7	53.1	8.3	45.5	21.4	19.7	20.8
3rd quarter	35.0	21.5	61.3	7.7	42.6	22.1	20.6	21.5	40.0	21.0	52.5	8.4	46.1	20.9	20.3	20.7
4th quarter	35.1	21.3	60.6	7.8	43.2	22.3	20.1	21.5	39.7	20.8	52.3	8.4	46.2	21.1	19.9	20.6
1950																
1st quarter	36.7	22.3	60.7	8.1	44.9	22.1	20.3	21.4	41.1	21.7	52.7	8.6	47.5	20.9	20.4	20.7
2nd quarter	37.1	23.0	62.1	8.2	44.9	22.0	20.7	21.5	41.6	22.4	54.0	8.7	48.0	21.0	20.4	20.8
3rd quarter	37.7	24.0	63.7	8.3	44.9	22.1	22.0	22.0	42.5	23.7	55.7	8.9	48.1	21.0	21.1	21.0
4th quarter	37.9	24.3	64.1	8.5	44.9	22.4	22.7	22.5	42.6	23.9	56.2	9.2	48.4	21.5	21.3	21.4
1951																
1st quarter	37.9	24.5	64.7	8.8	44.7	23.2	23.6	23.3	42.7	24.4	57.2	9.4	47.7	22.0	22.1	22.0
2nd quarter	38.1	24.8	65.1	9.0	45.4	23.7	23.4	23.6	42.5	24.5	57.6	9.6	48.1	22.5	22.1	22.3
3rd quarter	39.2	25.2	64.3	9.2	46.2	23.4	23.8	23.6	43.5	24.8	57.0	9.7	48.9	22.3	22.8	22.5
4th quarter	39.0	25.2	64.5	9.3	45.9	23.7	24.0	23.8	43.6	24.9	57.1	9.8	48.8	22.6	22.7	22.6
1952																
1st quarter	39.2	25.4	64.8	9.4	46.3	23.9	23.5	23.7	43.8	25.2	57.4	10.0	49.3	22.8	22.4	22.6
2nd quarter	39.5	25.3	64.1	9.5	47.1	24.2	23.0	23.7	43.7	25.0	57.2	10.1	49.6	23.0	22.0	22.7
3rd quarter	39.6	25.5	64.3	9.7	47.4	24.4	23.2	24.0	43.5	25.1	57.6	10.2	49.7	23.3	22.1	22.9
4th quarter	40.2	26.5	65.9	9.9	48.4	24.6	22.9	24.0	44.4	26.2	59.2	10.4	50.9	23.5	22.4	23.1
1953																
1st quarter	40.8	27.0	66.2	10.1	49.4	24.7	22.8	24.0	44.7	26.7	59.8	10.5	51.7	23.6	22.3	23.1
2nd quarter	41.2	27.2	66.1	10.2	49.8	24.7	22.7	24.0	44.8	26.8	59.9	10.7	52.2	23.8	22.3	23.2
3rd quarter	41.2	27.0	65.6	10.3	50.3	25.1	22.3	24.1	45.0	26.7	59.3	10.8	52.5	24.0	22.2	23.3
4th quarter	41.0	26.5	64.5	10.3	50.2	25.2	22.4	24.1	44.8	26.2	58.3	10.9	52.9	24.3	21.8	23.4
1954																
1st quarter	41.0	26.3	64.1	10.4	50.4	25.3	22.2	24.2	44.9	25.9	57.6	11.0	53.2	24.4	21.7	23.4
2nd quarter	41.6	26.3	63.2	10.5	51.2	25.3	22.1	24.1	45.3	25.9	57.1	11.0	53.3	24.3	22.0	23.5
3rd quarter	42.3	26.6	63.0	10.6	51.4	25.0	22.7	24.1	46.1	26.2	56.9	11.1	53.9	24.0	22.4	23.4
4th quarter	42.9	27.2	63.4	10.7	52.3	25.0	22.7	24.1	46.6	26.9	57.6	11.2	54.6	24.0	22.7	23.5
1955																
1st quarter	43.5	28.1	64.6	10.7	52.1	24.5	23.9	24.3	47.5	27.8	58.5	11.3	54.9	23.7	23.5	23.6
2nd quarter	43.9	28.7	65.2	10.8	52.9	24.7	23.7	24.3	47.6	28.3	59.3	11.4	55.6	23.9	23.5	23.7
3rd quarter	43.9	29.0	66.2	10.8	52.8	24.7	24.1	24.5	47.8	28.7	59.9	11.5	56.2	24.1	23.7	24.0
4th quarter	43.6	29.2	67.0	11.0	53.3	25.2	24.0	24.7	47.7	28.9	60.7	11.7	56.8	24.5	23.7	24.2
1956																
1st quarter	43.4	29.0	66.8	11.2	54.7	25.9	23.4	25.0	47.0	28.7	61.0	11.9	57.6	25.2	23.1	24.4
2nd quarter	43.6	29.2	67.0	11.5	55.4	26.3	23.0	25.1	47.2	28.9	61.2	12.1	58.4	25.6	22.9	24.6
3rd quarter	43.6	29.1	66.7	11.6	55.4	26.6	23.5	25.4	47.2	28.8	60.9	12.3	58.7	26.0	23.0	24.9
4th quarter	44.5	29.6	66.5	11.9	56.2	26.6	23.6	25.5	47.7	29.2	61.2	12.5	59.1	26.1	23.1	25.0
1957																
1st quarter	44.8	29.8	66.5	12.1	56.9	27.0	24.0	25.9	48.3	29.6	61.3	12.7	59.5	26.2	23.8	25.3
2nd quarter	44.8	29.6	66.1	12.2	56.9	27.3	24.0	26.0	48.1	29.4	61.2	12.8	59.6	26.6	23.6	25.5
3rd quarter	45.3	29.9	66.1	12.3	57.0	27.2	24.4	26.2	48.8	29.7	60.9	12.9	59.8	26.5	24.0	25.6
4th quarter	45.7	29.5	64.5	12.5	57.7	27.4	24.0	26.1	48.9	29.2	59.6	13.1	60.3	26.8	23.7	25.7
1958																
1st quarter	45.4	28.5	62.8	12.7	57.6	27.9	23.9	26.4	48.2	28.1	58.3	13.2	59.9	27.3	23.1	25.8
2nd quarter	46.0	28.6	62.2	12.7	57.3	27.6	24.4	26.4	49.1	28.2	57.4	13.3	60.0	27.0	23.7	25.8
3rd quarter	46.9	29.4	62.7	12.9	58.4	27.6	24.9	26.6	50.1	29.1	58.1	13.5	60.8	26.9	24.3	25.9
4th quarter	47.4	30.2	63.7	13.0	58.9	27.5	25.4	26.7	50.9	30.0	59.0	13.6	61.4	26.7	24.9	26.0
1959																
1st quarter	47.9	30.9	64.7	13.2	59.5	27.6	25.1	26.7	51.1	30.7	60.1	13.7	61.8	26.9	24.8	26.1
2nd quarter	48.1	31.9	66.2	13.2	59.5	27.5	25.3	26.7	51.7	31.7	61.3	13.9	62.3	26.8	25.0	26.1
3rd quarter	48.4	31.7	65.6	13.4	60.0	27.7	25.1	26.7	51.7	31.6	61.1	13.9	62.4	27.0	24.9	26.2
4th quarter	48.5	31.8	65.5	13.6	60.5	28.0	24.9	26.8	51.6	31.5	61.1	14.1	62.6	27.3	24.7	26.4
1960																
1st quarter	49.8	32.6	65.3	13.9	62.0	28.0	25.2	26.9	52.8	32.4	61.5	14.4	63.9	27.3	24.9	26.4
2nd quarter	48.9	32.2	66.0	13.9	61.3	28.4	24.6	27.0	52.0	32.0	61.6	14.5	63.9	27.8	24.1	26.5
3rd quarter	48.9	32.3	65.9	13.9	61.2	28.3	24.9	27.1	52.1	31.9	61.2	14.5	64.2	27.9	24.3	26.6
4th quarter	48.6	31.7	65.1	14.0	61.4	28.8	24.2	27.1	51.5	31.2	60.7	14.6	64.1	28.4	23.6	26.6

Table 19-11. Productivity and Related Data—*Continued*

(1992 = 100, seasonally adjusted.)

Year and quarter	Business sector								Nonfarm business sector							
	Output per hour of all persons	Output	Hours of all persons	Compensation per hour	Real compensation per hour	Unit labor costs	Unit nonlabor payments	Implicit price deflator	Output per hour of all persons	Output	Hours of all persons	Compensation per hour	Real compensation per hour	Unit labor costs	Unit nonlabor payments	Implicit price deflator
1961																
1st quarter	49.1	31.8	64.8	14.1	61.9	28.8	24.4	27.2	52.1	31.4	60.3	14.7	64.5	28.3	23.9	26.7
2nd quarter	50.8	32.5	64.0	14.4	63.3	28.4	25.1	27.2	53.6	32.3	60.2	15.0	65.5	27.9	24.7	26.7
3rd quarter	51.3	33.1	64.5	14.5	63.5	28.3	25.4	27.3	54.3	32.9	60.5	15.1	65.7	27.7	25.1	26.8
4th quarter	51.9	33.8	65.1	14.7	64.1	28.4	25.6	27.3	54.8	33.6	61.3	15.2	66.1	27.7	25.2	26.8
1962																
1st quarter	52.4	34.5	65.8	14.9	64.5	28.4	25.9	27.5	55.8	34.3	61.5	15.4	66.9	27.6	25.6	26.9
2nd quarter	52.7	34.9	66.1	15.0	65.0	28.5	25.7	27.5	55.7	34.7	62.3	15.5	67.1	27.9	25.5	27.0
3rd quarter	53.5	35.2	65.8	15.2	65.3	28.4	26.1	27.5	56.4	35.0	62.1	15.6	67.3	27.7	25.8	27.0
4th quarter	53.9	35.2	65.3	15.3	66.0	28.5	26.0	27.6	56.8	35.1	61.7	15.8	67.8	27.8	25.8	27.0
1963																
1st quarter	54.3	35.7	65.8	15.4	66.1	28.4	26.1	27.6	57.1	35.5	62.1	15.9	68.2	27.9	25.8	27.1
2nd quarter	54.7	36.2	66.2	15.5	66.3	28.4	26.3	27.6	57.7	36.0	62.5	16.0	68.5	27.8	26.0	27.1
3rd quarter	55.8	37.0	66.2	15.7	66.9	28.2	26.8	27.7	58.8	36.9	62.7	16.2	68.8	27.5	26.5	27.1
4th quarter	56.0	37.3	66.6	15.9	67.4	28.4	26.8	27.8	58.9	37.2	63.2	16.4	69.4	27.8	26.4	27.3
1964																
1st quarter	56.7	38.2	67.4	16.0	67.6	28.2	27.3	27.8	59.5	38.3	64.3	16.3	69.0	27.5	27.1	27.3
2nd quarter	56.9	38.7	68.0	16.1	68.0	28.3	27.2	27.9	59.8	38.7	64.6	16.5	69.7	27.6	27.2	27.4
3rd quarter	57.4	39.2	68.4	16.3	68.7	28.4	27.3	28.0	60.3	39.2	65.0	16.7	70.4	27.8	27.3	27.6
4th quarter	57.1	39.3	68.8	16.5	69.0	28.8	26.9	28.1	59.7	39.2	65.7	16.9	70.6	28.2	26.7	27.7
1965																
1st quarter	58.1	40.4	69.6	16.6	69.4	28.6	27.7	28.3	60.6	40.4	66.7	16.9	70.7	28.0	27.5	27.8
2nd quarter	58.1	41.0	70.5	16.7	69.3	28.7	27.8	28.4	60.9	41.0	67.4	17.0	70.7	28.0	27.5	27.8
3rd quarter	59.5	41.9	70.4	16.9	69.9	28.4	28.5	28.4	62.0	41.9	67.5	17.2	71.2	27.8	28.2	27.9
4th quarter	60.5	43.0	71.2	17.1	70.4	28.3	29.0	28.6	63.2	43.1	68.2	17.5	71.9	27.7	28.6	28.0
1966																
1st quarter	61.5	44.2	71.9	17.5	71.4	28.5	29.2	28.7	64.0	44.3	69.1	17.8	72.5	27.8	28.7	28.1
2nd quarter	61.2	44.3	72.4	17.8	72.0	29.1	28.7	29.0	63.6	44.4	69.8	18.1	73.0	28.4	28.4	28.4
3rd quarter	61.3	44.4	72.5	18.1	72.5	29.6	28.7	29.2	63.7	44.7	70.1	18.3	73.4	28.8	28.4	28.6
4th quarter	61.8	44.7	72.3	18.4	73.1	29.8	29.0	29.5	64.1	44.9	70.0	18.6	73.8	29.0	29.0	29.0
1967																
1st quarter	62.4	45.1	72.3	18.6	73.5	29.8	29.3	29.6	64.6	45.2	69.9	18.8	74.5	29.1	29.1	29.1
2nd quarter	62.9	45.0	71.6	18.9	74.4	30.1	29.1	29.7	64.9	45.1	69.4	19.1	75.3	29.5	28.9	29.3
3rd quarter	62.9	45.3	72.0	19.1	74.6	30.4	29.4	30.0	65.1	45.4	69.7	19.4	75.6	29.8	29.1	29.5
4th quarter	63.1	45.6	72.4	19.4	74.7	30.7	29.6	30.3	65.3	45.7	70.0	19.7	75.9	30.1	29.3	29.8
1968																
1st quarter	64.4	46.7	72.4	20.0	76.2	31.0	30.1	30.6	66.8	46.8	70.1	20.2	77.2	30.3	29.9	30.1
2nd quarter	65.1	47.5	73.0	20.3	76.8	31.2	30.5	30.9	67.4	47.7	70.8	20.6	77.8	30.5	30.4	30.5
3rd quarter	65.2	47.8	73.4	20.7	77.2	31.8	30.2	31.2	67.4	48.0	71.3	20.9	78.0	31.0	30.0	30.7
4th quarter	65.1	48.0	73.8	21.1	77.8	32.4	30.2	31.6	67.3	48.2	71.7	21.3	78.6	31.7	30.0	31.1
1969																
1st quarter	65.3	48.9	74.9	21.2	77.2	32.5	31.1	32.0	67.8	49.1	72.4	21.6	78.7	31.9	30.8	31.5
2nd quarter	65.2	48.9	75.0	21.7	78.0	33.3	30.7	32.4	67.2	49.1	73.1	22.0	78.7	32.6	30.4	31.8
3rd quarter	65.4	49.2	75.3	22.2	78.6	34.0	30.6	32.7	67.3	49.4	73.4	22.3	79.0	33.2	30.3	32.1
4th quarter	65.2	48.9	74.9	22.7	79.0	34.8	30.2	33.1	67.0	49.0	73.2	22.8	79.4	34.0	29.8	32.5
1970																
1st quarter	65.5	48.8	74.5	23.1	79.3	35.3	30.2	33.4	67.2	49.0	72.9	23.2	79.6	34.5	29.8	32.8
2nd quarter	66.3	48.9	73.8	23.4	79.2	35.3	31.3	33.8	68.2	49.1	71.9	23.6	79.8	34.6	31.1	33.3
3rd quarter	67.5	49.4	73.3	23.9	79.8	35.4	31.8	34.0	69.3	49.6	71.6	24.0	80.3	34.6	31.5	33.5
4th quarter	67.1	48.7	72.6	24.2	79.7	36.0	31.8	34.5	68.7	48.8	71.0	24.3	80.0	35.3	31.6	34.0
1971																
1st quarter	69.0	50.3	72.9	24.6	80.5	35.7	33.4	34.8	70.7	50.5	71.4	24.8	81.0	35.0	33.1	34.3
2nd quarter	69.1	50.7	73.4	24.9	80.8	36.1	33.9	35.3	71.0	50.8	71.6	25.1	81.5	35.4	33.5	34.7
3rd quarter	69.9	51.1	73.2	25.4	81.4	36.3	34.4	35.6	71.6	51.3	71.6	25.5	81.8	35.6	34.1	35.1
4th quarter	69.3	51.2	73.9	25.6	81.5	36.9	33.9	35.8	71.0	51.4	72.4	25.7	81.9	36.2	33.5	35.2
1972																
1st quarter	69.9	52.4	74.9	26.2	82.7	37.4	34.3	36.2	71.9	52.7	73.2	26.3	83.2	36.6	34.0	35.7
2nd quarter	71.7	53.9	75.3	26.5	83.2	37.0	35.4	36.4	73.4	54.2	73.8	26.7	83.7	36.3	34.9	35.8
3rd quarter	71.9	54.5	75.8	26.8	83.5	37.3	35.6	36.7	73.9	54.8	74.2	27.0	84.2	36.6	35.0	36.0
4th quarter	72.6	55.6	76.5	27.4	84.4	37.7	36.2	37.1	74.5	55.8	75.0	27.6	85.1	37.1	34.8	36.2
1973																
1st quarter	74.0	57.4	77.5	28.2	85.6	38.1	36.5	37.5	76.2	58.0	76.1	28.3	86.0	37.2	35.1	36.4
2nd quarter	74.2	58.2	78.4	28.6	85.1	38.6	37.3	38.1	76.2	58.6	76.9	28.8	85.6	37.7	35.3	36.8
3rd quarter	73.2	57.7	78.8	29.2	85.2	39.9	37.1	38.9	75.5	58.5	77.4	29.3	85.5	38.8	34.7	37.3
4th quarter	73.5	58.3	79.3	29.8	84.8	40.5	38.2	39.7	75.0	58.4	77.8	30.0	85.2	39.9	35.2	38.2
1974																
1st quarter	72.5	57.5	79.3	30.4	83.9	41.9	38.1	40.5	74.9	58.0	77.5	30.7	84.7	41.0	35.7	39.0
2nd quarter	72.7	57.6	79.1	31.3	84.3	43.1	39.0	41.5	74.7	58.0	77.7	31.5	84.7	42.2	37.5	40.5
3rd quarter	72.1	56.8	78.7	32.3	84.5	44.8	39.7	42.9	73.9	57.2	77.4	32.4	84.8	43.8	38.0	41.7
4th quarter	72.7	56.4	77.5	33.1	83.9	45.5	42.1	44.2	74.6	56.8	76.1	33.2	84.3	44.6	40.3	43.0
1975																
1st quarter	73.7	55.3	75.1	34.1	84.6	46.2	43.8	45.3	75.2	55.4	73.7	34.2	84.9	45.4	42.6	44.4
2nd quarter	75.0	55.8	74.5	34.7	85.3	46.3	45.9	45.9	76.4	55.8	73.0	34.9	85.6	45.6	44.1	45.1
3rd quarter	75.7	57.0	75.2	35.2	84.8	46.5	47.2	46.8	77.3	57.0	73.7	35.5	85.4	45.9	45.6	45.8
4th quarter	75.9	57.9	76.3	36.0	85.1	47.4	47.7	47.5	77.3	58.0	75.0	36.1	85.4	46.7	46.0	46.5

Table 19-11. Productivity and Related Data—*Continued*

(1992 = 100, seasonally adjusted.)

Year and quarter	Business sector								Nonfarm business sector							
	Output per hour of all persons	Output	Hours of all persons	Compensation per hour	Real compensation per hour	Unit labor costs	Unit nonlabor payments	Implicit price deflator	Output per hour of all persons	Output	Hours of all persons	Compensation per hour	Real compensation per hour	Unit labor costs	Unit nonlabor payments	Implicit price deflator
1976																
1st quarter	77.0	59.6	77.4	36.9	86.2	47.9	48.0	48.0	78.5	59.8	76.2	36.9	86.3	47.1	46.9	47.0
2nd quarter	77.5	60.1	77.6	37.6	87.1	48.5	48.2	48.4	79.2	60.4	76.2	37.7	87.3	47.6	47.3	47.5
3rd quarter	77.5	60.4	77.9	38.3	87.4	49.5	48.3	49.1	79.3	60.7	76.5	38.5	87.8	48.6	47.5	48.2
4th quarter	78.0	60.9	78.1	39.3	88.2	50.4	49.1	49.9	79.5	61.2	77.0	39.3	88.4	49.5	48.3	49.0
1977																
1st quarter	78.3	61.8	78.9	40.0	88.2	51.0	50.2	50.7	79.9	62.2	77.8	40.0	88.3	50.1	49.3	49.8
2nd quarter	78.5	63.3	80.7	40.6	88.0	51.7	50.8	51.4	80.3	63.7	79.3	40.8	88.5	50.8	50.2	50.6
3rd quarter	79.5	64.7	81.3	41.4	88.7	52.1	51.7	51.9	81.1	65.0	80.1	41.6	89.0	51.3	51.2	51.3
4th quarter	78.6	64.6	82.1	42.2	88.9	53.6	52.0	53.0	80.0	64.8	80.9	42.4	89.4	53.0	50.9	52.2
1978																
1st quarter	78.3	64.6	82.5	43.6	90.6	55.7	51.2	54.0	80.1	65.1	81.3	43.9	91.1	54.8	49.9	53.0
2nd quarter	79.9	67.8	84.9	44.1	89.6	55.2	54.4	54.9	81.7	68.3	83.6	44.4	90.1	54.3	52.9	53.8
3rd quarter	80.0	68.5	85.6	44.8	89.4	56.0	55.4	55.7	81.7	68.9	84.3	45.1	89.9	55.2	54.0	54.7
4th quarter	80.3	69.5	86.5	45.9	89.7	57.1	56.7	56.9	82.1	70.1	85.4	46.1	90.2	56.1	55.4	55.8
1979																
1st quarter	79.8	69.5	87.1	47.2	90.4	59.2	56.0	58.0	81.3	69.9	86.0	47.4	90.8	58.3	54.2	56.8
2nd quarter	79.6	69.6	87.4	48.3	90.0	60.7	57.8	59.6	81.1	70.0	86.3	48.5	90.4	59.8	56.2	58.5
3rd quarter	79.6	70.1	88.1	49.4	89.7	62.1	58.9	60.9	81.0	70.5	87.0	49.6	90.0	61.2	57.2	59.8
4th quarter	79.4	70.2	88.4	50.6	89.5	63.7	59.2	62.0	80.9	70.6	87.2	50.8	90.0	62.8	57.7	60.9
1980																
1st quarter	79.9	70.3	88.0	52.1	89.4	65.2	60.2	63.4	81.2	70.7	87.0	52.3	89.7	64.4	59.3	62.5
2nd quarter	78.9	68.2	86.5	53.4	89.5	67.7	59.8	64.8	80.3	68.6	85.5	53.6	89.8	66.8	59.9	64.3
3rd quarter	79.0	68.1	86.2	54.7	89.6	69.3	61.1	66.2	80.6	68.6	85.1	55.0	90.0	68.3	60.1	65.3
4th quarter	79.8	69.7	87.3	56.1	89.6	70.3	63.9	67.9	81.4	70.2	86.2	56.5	90.2	69.3	62.2	66.7
1981																
1st quarter	81.4	71.4	87.7	57.6	89.4	70.7	67.9	69.7	82.7	71.7	86.6	58.0	90.1	70.0	66.6	68.8
2nd quarter	80.6	70.6	87.6	58.6	89.5	72.7	68.1	71.0	81.6	70.7	86.7	59.0	90.0	72.2	66.6	70.2
3rd quarter	81.7	71.6	87.6	59.9	89.6	73.3	70.6	72.3	82.3	71.3	86.6	60.3	90.2	73.2	69.0	71.7
4th quarter	80.5	70.3	87.3	60.8	89.4	75.5	70.0	73.5	81.3	70.2	86.3	61.2	89.9	75.2	69.1	73.0
1982																
1st quarter	80.0	68.7	85.9	62.4	90.6	78.0	68.3	74.4	80.8	68.6	84.9	62.7	91.1	77.7	67.5	73.9
2nd quarter	80.3	69.1	86.1	63.0	90.5	78.5	69.7	75.2	80.9	69.0	85.2	63.3	90.9	78.2	69.0	74.8
3rd quarter	80.3	68.7	85.6	63.9	90.3	79.6	70.6	76.2	81.1	68.6	84.6	64.2	90.8	79.3	69.7	75.7
4th quarter	81.1	68.7	84.8	64.7	90.5	79.8	71.9	76.9	81.8	68.6	83.9	65.1	91.0	79.6	71.3	76.5
1983																
1st quarter	81.8	69.7	85.2	65.3	90.7	79.8	73.4	77.4	82.8	69.8	84.4	65.7	91.3	79.4	72.7	76.9
2nd quarter	83.3	71.7	86.1	65.9	90.5	79.1	75.7	77.8	84.7	72.2	85.3	66.3	91.0	78.3	75.4	77.2
3rd quarter	83.6	73.4	87.8	66.2	90.0	79.1	77.7	78.6	85.4	74.3	87.0	66.6	90.6	78.0	78.0	78.0
4th quarter	84.3	75.2	89.2	67.1	90.3	79.5	78.4	79.1	85.8	76.0	88.6	67.3	90.7	78.4	78.5	78.5
1984																
1st quarter	84.7	77.0	91.0	67.8	90.2	80.1	79.2	79.8	85.8	77.5	90.3	68.1	90.5	79.4	78.1	79.0
2nd quarter	85.4	78.7	92.1	68.5	90.1	80.1	80.6	80.3	86.3	79.0	91.5	68.8	90.6	79.7	79.6	79.6
3rd quarter	85.8	79.5	92.6	69.4	90.6	80.8	80.8	80.8	86.7	79.7	91.9	69.7	91.1	80.4	80.0	80.3
4th quarter	86.1	80.1	93.1	69.9	90.6	81.2	81.2	81.2	86.8	80.3	92.5	70.2	91.0	80.9	80.2	80.7
1985																
1st quarter	86.4	81.0	93.8	70.8	90.9	82.0	82.0	82.0	87.0	81.1	93.3	71.1	91.2	81.7	81.2	81.5
2nd quarter	86.7	81.8	94.3	71.4	90.9	82.3	82.3	82.3	87.2	81.9	93.9	71.6	91.2	82.1	81.7	82.0
3rd quarter	88.2	83.3	94.4	72.5	91.7	82.2	83.0	82.5	88.3	83.2	94.1	72.6	91.8	82.2	82.9	82.5
4th quarter	88.5	83.9	94.8	73.8	92.5	83.4	82.2	82.9	88.8	83.9	94.6	73.9	92.6	83.3	81.8	82.7
1986																
1st quarter	89.4	84.8	94.8	74.7	93.1	83.5	82.8	83.2	89.9	84.9	94.5	74.9	93.3	83.3	82.9	83.2
2nd quarter	90.0	85.1	94.6	75.4	94.4	83.8	83.2	83.6	90.6	85.3	94.2	75.6	94.7	83.5	83.2	83.4
3rd quarter	90.4	86.0	95.1	76.2	94.9	84.2	83.4	83.9	90.9	86.1	94.7	76.5	95.3	84.1	82.9	83.7
4th quarter	90.2	86.4	95.8	77.1	95.5	85.6	82.3	84.4	90.7	86.6	95.4	77.4	95.8	85.4	81.9	84.1
1987																
1st quarter	89.6	86.8	96.9	77.5	94.9	86.5	82.6	85.1	90.1	87.0	96.6	77.8	95.2	86.3	82.3	84.8
2nd quarter	90.1	87.9	97.5	78.1	94.5	86.6	83.5	85.4	90.7	88.1	97.1	78.3	94.9	86.3	83.3	85.2
3rd quarter	90.3	88.6	98.1	78.9	94.6	87.4	84.0	86.1	90.7	88.7	97.8	79.1	94.9	87.2	83.8	86.0
4th quarter	91.1	90.2	99.1	79.8	95.0	87.7	84.5	86.5	91.6	90.5	98.8	80.1	95.2	87.4	84.3	86.3
1988																
1st quarter	91.3	90.6	99.2	81.3	96.0	89.0	84.4	87.3	91.8	90.8	98.9	81.5	96.3	88.8	84.0	87.0
2nd quarter	91.5	92.0	100.6	82.3	96.2	90.0	84.7	88.0	92.1	92.4	100.3	82.4	96.4	89.5	84.7	87.7
3rd quarter	91.7	92.4	100.7	83.3	96.4	90.9	86.0	89.1	92.3	92.9	100.6	83.4	96.4	90.3	85.8	88.7
4th quarter	91.9	93.7	101.9	83.8	96.0	91.1	87.2	89.7	92.9	94.4	101.7	83.9	96.2	90.4	87.6	89.4
1989																
1st quarter	92.0	94.6	102.9	84.0	95.3	91.3	89.6	90.7	92.4	94.9	102.7	84.1	95.5	91.0	88.9	90.2
2nd quarter	92.4	95.3	103.1	84.4	94.3	91.3	92.1	91.6	92.8	95.7	103.1	84.4	94.3	90.9	91.8	91.3
3rd quarter	92.9	96.1	103.5	85.0	94.3	91.5	93.0	92.1	93.3	96.4	103.3	85.0	94.3	91.1	93.0	91.8
4th quarter	93.0	96.2	103.5	86.1	94.7	92.6	92.6	92.6	93.4	96.5	103.4	86.2	94.8	92.3	92.2	92.2
1990																
1st quarter	93.9	97.2	103.6	88.0	95.2	93.7	93.7	93.7	94.1	97.5	103.6	87.9	95.1	93.3	93.3	93.3
2nd quarter	94.7	97.5	103.0	90.0	96.5	95.0	94.3	94.7	94.9	97.8	103.1	89.7	96.3	94.6	94.1	94.4
3rd quarter	95.2	97.3	102.2	91.4	96.5	95.9	94.7	95.5	95.3	97.6	102.4	91.2	96.2	95.7	94.4	95.2
4th quarter	94.3	96.1	101.9	92.1	95.7	97.6	93.8	96.2	94.5	96.2	101.9	92.0	95.6	97.4	93.8	96.1

Table 19-11. Productivity and Related Data—*Continued*

(1992 = 100, seasonally adjusted.)

Year and quarter	Business sector								Nonfarm business sector							
	Output per hour of all persons	Output	Hours of all persons	Compensation per hour	Real compensation per hour	Unit labor costs	Unit nonlabor payments	Implicit price deflator	Output per hour of all persons	Output	Hours of all persons	Compensation per hour	Real compensation per hour	Unit labor costs	Unit nonlabor payments	Implicit price deflator
1991																
1st quarter	94.5	95.3	100.8	92.9	96.0	98.3	95.3	97.2	94.7	95.4	100.8	92.8	95.9	98.0	95.6	97.1
2nd quarter	95.9	96.1	100.2	94.6	97.4	98.6	96.3	97.8	96.1	96.3	100.2	94.6	97.3	98.4	96.4	97.7
3rd quarter	96.5	96.5	100.1	95.6	97.8	99.2	97.5	98.5	96.7	96.7	100.0	95.6	97.8	98.9	97.9	98.5
4th quarter	97.0	96.9	99.9	96.7	98.3	99.7	97.7	99.0	97.1	97.1	99.9	96.7	98.2	99.5	97.8	98.9
1992																
1st quarter	98.8	98.2	99.4	98.7	99.6	99.8	98.4	99.3	98.8	98.2	99.4	98.6	99.6	99.8	98.4	99.3
2nd quarter	99.5	99.4	99.9	99.3	99.6	99.8	99.6	99.7	99.5	99.3	99.8	99.3	99.7	99.9	99.6	99.7
3rd quarter	100.5	100.5	100.0	100.8	100.6	100.3	100.0	100.2	100.5	100.5	100.0	100.9	100.6	100.4	99.9	100.2
4th quarter	101.2	101.9	100.7	101.2	100.2	100.1	101.9	100.8	101.2	102.0	100.7	101.2	100.2	100.0	102.1	100.8
1993																
1st quarter	100.4	101.8	101.4	101.6	100.0	101.1	101.5	101.3	100.5	102.1	101.6	101.4	99.8	100.9	102.2	101.4
2nd quarter	100.1	102.6	102.5	102.0	99.8	101.9	101.6	101.8	100.1	102.8	102.8	101.8	99.5	101.7	101.9	101.8
3rd quarter	100.3	103.3	103.0	102.5	99.8	102.2	102.1	102.2	100.5	103.7	103.2	102.2	99.5	101.8	103.0	102.2
4th quarter	101.2	105.1	103.8	102.9	99.5	101.7	104.4	102.7	101.2	105.3	104.1	102.6	99.3	101.5	104.6	102.6
1994																
1st quarter	101.6	106.3	104.6	103.9	100.2	102.2	104.4	103.0	101.7	106.3	104.5	103.8	100.1	102.1	104.5	103.0
2nd quarter	101.4	108.0	106.5	103.6	99.4	102.1	105.6	103.4	101.6	108.0	106.3	103.7	99.4	102.0	106.0	103.5
3rd quarter	100.9	108.7	107.7	103.6	98.6	102.7	106.4	104.0	101.0	108.7	107.5	103.6	98.6	102.6	107.1	104.2
4th quarter	101.7	110.2	108.4	104.1	98.6	102.4	108.0	104.5	102.0	110.3	108.2	104.2	98.7	102.2	108.8	104.6
1995																
1st quarter	101.1	110.3	109.1	105.0	98.9	103.8	106.9	105.0	101.6	110.7	108.9	105.0	98.9	103.3	108.2	105.1
2nd quarter	101.1	110.5	109.3	105.4	98.5	104.3	107.3	105.4	101.8	110.9	109.0	105.6	98.7	103.8	108.7	105.6
3rd quarter	101.3	111.7	110.2	106.1	98.7	104.7	107.7	105.9	101.9	112.2	110.1	106.2	98.8	104.2	108.7	105.9
4th quarter	102.3	112.8	110.3	107.1	99.2	104.8	108.6	106.2	102.7	113.2	110.2	107.2	99.3	104.4	109.1	106.1
1996																
1st quarter	103.2	113.7	110.1	108.1	99.3	104.7	109.9	106.6	103.6	114.0	110.1	108.2	99.4	104.5	110.0	106.5
2nd quarter	104.5	116.0	111.0	109.2	99.5	104.5	111.7	107.1	104.7	116.2	111.0	109.2	99.5	104.3	111.3	106.9
3rd quarter	104.9	117.2	111.7	110.2	99.8	105.0	111.3	107.4	105.1	117.5	111.8	110.0	99.7	104.7	111.7	107.3
4th quarter	105.0	118.7	113.1	110.6	99.4	105.3	112.3	107.9	105.1	119.0	113.2	110.5	99.3	105.1	112.6	107.9
1997																
1st quarter	104.7	119.7	114.4	111.2	99.4	106.3	112.5	108.6	104.8	119.9	114.5	111.2	99.4	106.1	112.7	108.5
2nd quarter	106.0	121.8	115.0	112.1	100.0	105.8	113.7	108.8	106.0	122.0	115.1	112.0	100.0	105.7	114.6	109.0
3rd quarter	107.0	123.6	115.5	113.4	100.7	106.0	114.3	109.1	106.9	123.7	115.8	113.2	100.5	105.9	115.2	109.3
4th quarter	107.5	124.6	116.0	115.6	102.1	107.6	112.6	109.4	107.3	124.8	116.3	115.2	101.8	107.4	113.6	109.7
1998																
1st quarter	108.0	125.9	116.6	117.7	103.9	109.0	110.4	109.5	107.9	126.3	117.0	117.4	103.6	108.8	111.3	109.7
2nd quarter	108.6	127.2	117.2	119.3	104.9	109.9	109.1	109.6	108.6	127.6	117.5	119.0	104.7	109.6	110.2	109.8
3rd quarter	110.1	129.1	117.3	121.1	106.1	110.0	109.5	109.8	110.0	129.5	117.7	120.9	105.9	109.9	110.6	110.1
4th quarter	111.0	131.9	118.8	121.7	106.1	109.6	110.4	109.9	110.9	132.3	119.3	121.3	105.8	109.4	111.3	110.1
1999																
1st quarter	112.3	133.2	118.7	124.1	107.8	110.5	109.8	110.2	112.0	133.6	119.4	123.4	107.2	110.2	110.9	110.5
2nd quarter	112.4	134.3	119.5	124.3	107.2	110.6	110.1	110.4	112.1	134.7	120.2	123.7	106.7	110.4	111.7	110.9
3rd quarter	113.3	136.3	120.3	125.3	107.3	110.6	111.0	110.8	113.0	136.7	121.0	124.7	106.8	110.4	112.7	111.2
4th quarter	115.2	139.1	120.8	127.8	108.6	111.0	110.9	111.0	114.9	139.5	121.4	127.4	108.2	110.8	112.8	111.5
2000																
1st quarter	114.8	139.3	121.3	132.4	111.5	115.3	105.8	111.8	114.5	139.5	121.9	132.1	111.2	115.3	107.4	112.4
2nd quarter	117.5	142.5	121.3	133.0	111.1	113.2	110.9	112.3	117.1	142.8	121.9	132.5	110.7	113.2	112.4	112.9
3rd quarter	117.5	142.5	121.3	135.8	112.4	115.5	108.4	112.9	117.1	142.8	121.9	135.3	112.0	115.5	110.0	113.5
4th quarter	118.8	143.3	120.6	136.8	112.4	115.1	110.5	113.4	118.3	143.6	121.4	136.1	111.8	115.1	112.1	114.0
2001																
1st quarter	118.4	142.5	120.4	139.9	113.9	118.2	106.8	114.0	117.9	142.9	121.2	139.2	113.3	118.1	108.2	114.5
2nd quarter	120.4	143.5	119.1	140.5	113.6	116.6	111.5	114.7	120.0	144.0	120.0	139.6	112.9	116.3	113.1	115.2
3rd quarter	121.2	142.7	117.7	141.0	113.7	116.3	112.2	114.8	120.7	143.2	118.6	140.1	112.9	116.0	113.8	115.2
4th quarter	123.0	143.3	116.5	142.3	114.8	115.7	113.5	114.9	122.5	143.6	117.2	141.5	114.2	115.5	115.4	115.5
2002																
1st quarter	125.2	144.7	115.6	143.6	115.5	114.7	115.2	114.9	125.1	145.4	116.2	142.9	115.0	114.3	117.2	115.4
2nd quarter	125.6	145.4	115.8	145.0	115.7	115.5	115.1	115.3	125.2	145.8	116.5	144.3	115.1	115.3	117.3	116.0
3rd quarter	127.0	146.5	115.3	145.9	115.8	114.9	117.0	115.7	126.4	146.7	116.1	145.1	115.2	114.8	118.9	116.3
4th quarter	126.9	146.6	115.6	146.5	115.6	115.5	117.2	116.1	126.3	146.8	116.3	145.8	115.0	115.4	119.0	116.7
2003																
1st quarter	128.1	147.1	114.9	148.9	116.3	116.3	117.2	116.6	127.4	147.3	115.6	148.2	115.7	116.3	118.9	117.2
2nd quarter	130.1	148.6	114.2	151.8	118.7	116.6	117.0	116.8	129.1	148.7	115.2	150.7	117.9	116.7	118.4	117.4
3rd quarter	132.8	152.2	114.6	153.6	119.3	115.7	120.2	117.3	132.1	152.5	115.4	152.8	118.6	115.7	121.5	117.8
4th quarter	133.1	153.3	115.2	154.8	119.7	116.3	120.4	117.8	132.6	153.8	115.9	154.1	119.2	116.2	121.4	118.1
2004																
1st quarter	133.8	154.6	115.6	154.3	118.4	115.3	124.7	118.8	132.9	154.7	116.4	153.4	117.6	115.4	125.4	119.1
2nd quarter	134.8	155.9	115.7	156.4	119.1	116.1	126.0	119.8	134.1	156.2	116.5	155.5	118.4	116.0	126.7	119.9
3rd quarter	135.0	157.1	116.3	158.9	120.2	117.7	125.4	120.5	134.4	157.4	117.1	158.0	119.5	117.6	126.5	120.9
4th quarter	135.8	158.6	116.7	160.7	120.2	118.3	127.0	121.5	134.6	158.7	117.9	159.3	119.2	118.3	128.1	121.9
2005																
1st quarter	137.0	160.3	117.1	161.8	120.4	118.1	129.9	122.5	136.0	160.6	118.1	160.6	119.5	118.1	131.5	123.0
2nd quarter	136.4	161.0	118.0	162.5	120.2	119.1	130.5	123.3	135.7	161.2	118.8	161.6	119.6	119.1	132.1	123.9
3rd quarter	137.6	162.5	118.1	164.9	120.2	119.9	132.7	124.7	136.7	162.7	119.0	164.0	119.5	120.0	134.6	125.3
4th quarter	137.7	163.4	118.7	166.2	119.8	120.7	134.3	125.8	136.6	163.6	119.7	165.0	119.0	120.7	136.2	126.4

Table 19-11. Productivity and Related Data—*Continued*

(1992 = 100, seasonally adjusted.)

Year and quarter	Business sector								Nonfarm business sector							
	Output per hour of all persons	Output	Hours of all persons	Compensation per hour	Real compensation per hour	Unit labor costs	Unit nonlabor payments	Implicit price deflator	Output per hour of all persons	Output	Hours of all persons	Compensation per hour	Real compensation per hour	Unit labor costs	Unit nonlabor payments	Implicit price deflator
2006																
1st quarter	138.6	166.0	119.8	168.4	120.8	121.5	134.5	126.4	137.5	166.4	120.9	167.1	119.9	121.5	136.8	127.1
2nd quarter	138.7	166.6	120.1	169.0	120.3	121.8	136.7	127.4	137.7	166.8	121.1	167.9	119.5	122.0	139.1	128.3
3rd quarter	137.9	166.4	120.6	169.7	119.6	123.0	137.3	128.3	137.0	166.7	121.7	168.6	118.9	123.0	139.5	129.1
4th quarter	138.8	168.1	121.1	173.5	122.7	125.0	135.1	128.7	138.0	168.4	122.1	172.5	122.0	125.0	136.8	129.3
2007																
1st quarter	139.0	168.4	121.1	175.2	122.7	126.0	136.7	130.0	138.3	168.8	122.1	174.3	122.1	126.0	138.2	130.5
2nd quarter	140.0	169.8	121.3	176.3	122.2	125.9	139.4	130.9	139.0	170.3	122.5	174.9	121.3	125.8	141.0	131.4
3rd quarter	142.0	171.4	120.7	177.7	122.5	125.1	141.9	131.4	141.0	172.0	122.0	176.2	121.5	125.0	143.3	131.7
4th quarter	142.8	172.3	120.6	179.9	122.3	126.0	141.9	131.9	142.0	172.8	121.7	178.8	121.5	125.9	142.9	132.2
2008																
1st quarter	142.8	171.7	120.3	180.3	121.2	126.3	141.7	132.1	141.8	172.0	121.3	179.3	120.5	126.4	142.5	132.3
2nd quarter	143.8	172.2	119.8	181.0	120.3	125.8	143.8	132.5	142.8	172.6	120.8	179.7	119.5	125.9	144.9	132.9
3rd quarter	144.3	170.6	118.2	183.6	120.3	127.2	145.3	134.0	143.2	170.8	119.3	182.4	119.5	127.4	146.5	134.4
4th quarter	145.0	167.4	115.4	185.4	124.1	127.8	143.4	133.6	144.0	167.5	116.3	184.4	123.5	128.1	145.1	134.3
2009																
1st quarter	145.3	163.6	112.6	183.5	123.6	126.2	148.0	134.3	144.3	163.7	113.4	182.5	122.9	126.4	150.3	135.2
2nd quarter	148.0	163.2	110.3	186.8	125.4	126.2	147.7	134.2	147.0	163.2	111.1	185.9	124.8	126.4	150.0	135.1
3rd quarter	150.9	164.1	108.7	186.8	124.3	123.8	151.9	134.3	149.8	164.1	109.6	185.7	123.6	124.0	154.6	135.2
4th quarter	153.6	167.1	108.8	187.1	123.4	121.8	155.3	134.3	152.3	167.2	109.7	186.0	122.7	122.1	157.5	135.1

NOTES AND DEFINITIONS, CHAPTER 19

TABLES 19-1 THROUGH 19-9
SELECTED NATIONAL INCOME AND PRODUCT ACCOUNT DATA

See the notes and definitions for Chapter 1.

For *personal income and its disposition* (Table 19-6), see the notes and definitions for Table 4-1.

For *inventories to sales ratios* (Table 19-7), see the notes and definitions for Table 5-7.

For *saving and investment* (Table 19-9), see the notes and definitions for Table 5-1.

TABLE 19-10
U.S. INTERNATIONAL TRANSACTIONS

See the notes and definitions for Table 7-6.

For space reasons, the amounts for *U.S. Treasury securities and U.S. currency flows* under the heading *Other foreign assets in the United States, net*, which are separate columns in Table 7-6, are combined in Table 19-10.

The *Balance on current account* as shown in the final column of Table 19-10 includes some items not shown separately, which are displayed in Table 7-6. They are *Capital account transactions, net* and *Financial derivatives, net*.

TABLE 19-11
PRODUCTIVITY AND RELATED DATA

See the notes and definitions for Table 9-3.

CHAPTER 20: SELECTED HISTORICAL DATA FOR MONTHLY SERIES

Table 20-1. Industrial Production and Capacity Utilization

(Seasonally adjusted; 2002 = 100, except as noted.)

Year and month	Total industry	Manufac- turing (SIC)	Market groups								Capacity utilization (output as percentage of capacity)	
			Consumer goods			Business equipment	Defense and space equipment	Construction supplies	Business supplies	Materials	Total industry	Manufac- turing (SIC)
			Total	Durable	Nondurable							
1947	15.5	14.3	19.1	12.5	22.6	7.8	9.1	23.1	12.8	15.5	. . .	82.5
1948	16.1	14.8	19.7	13.1	23.2	8.1	10.7	24.7	13.3	16.2	. . .	74.2
1949	15.2	14.0	19.6	12.4	23.4	7.1	11.1	22.7	13.2	14.7	. . .	82.8
1950	17.6	16.3	22.4	16.6	25.4	7.6	13.1	27.2	14.7	17.7	. . .	85.8
1951	19.1	17.6	22.2	14.4	26.3	9.2	32.2	28.4	15.6	19.5	. . .	85.4
1952	19.9	18.3	22.7	13.9	27.3	10.5	45.3	28.2	15.5	19.8	. . .	89.3
1953	21.5	19.9	24.0	16.3	28.1	10.9	54.2	30.3	16.5	22.0	. . .	80.1
1954	20.3	18.6	23.8	15.1	28.4	9.6	47.7	29.8	16.7	20.3	. . .	87.0
1955	22.9	21.0	26.6	18.6	30.6	10.4	43.6	34.2	18.7	24.0	. . .	86.1
1956	23.9	21.8	27.6	18.0	32.5	12.0	42.7	35.3	19.8	24.6	. . .	83.6
1957	24.3	22.1	28.3	18.0	33.6	12.5	44.6	34.8	20.1	24.6	. . .	75.0
1958	22.7	20.6	28.0	15.9	34.6	10.5	44.8	33.5	19.9	22.2	. . .	81.6
1959	25.4	23.1	30.7	19.0	37.0	11.8	47.2	37.6	21.7	25.5	. . .	80.1
1960	26.0	23.6	31.9	20.0	38.2	12.2	48.5	36.8	22.4	25.9	. . .	77.3
1961	26.1	23.7	32.6	19.7	39.4	11.8	49.2	37.0	23.1	25.9	. . .	81.4
1962	28.3	25.8	34.8	22.3	41.3	12.8	57.0	39.3	24.5	28.2	. . .	83.5
1963	30.1	27.4	36.7	24.3	43.2	13.5	61.5	41.1	26.1	30.1	. . .	85.6
1964	32.1	29.3	38.8	26.1	45.3	15.1	59.6	43.6	28.0	32.5	. . .	89.5
1965	35.3	32.4	41.8	30.5	47.2	17.3	65.9	46.3	29.8	36.2	. . .	91.1
1966	38.4	35.4	43.9	32.2	49.5	20.0	77.5	48.3	32.2	39.5	. . .	87.2
1967	39.2	36.1	45.1	31.0	52.1	20.4	88.4	49.5	33.8	39.1	87.0	87.1
1947												
January	15.3	14.1	19.0	11.9	22.8	7.5	9.4	21.9	12.7	15.2	. . .	. . .
February	15.4	14.2	18.9	12.2	22.5	7.6	9.2	22.6	12.7	15.4	. . .	. . .
March	15.4	14.2	19.0	12.5	22.4	7.6	9.0	22.8	12.7	15.9	. . .	. . .
April	15.3	14.3	18.9	12.6	22.3	7.7	9.1	23.0	12.9	15.5	. . .	. . .
May	15.4	14.1	18.8	12.5	22.1	7.8	9.0	23.3	12.8	15.5	. . .	. . .
June	15.4	14.1	18.8	12.6	22.1	7.8	8.9	23.4	12.7	15.4	. . .	. . .
July	15.3	14.1	18.9	12.3	22.3	7.7	8.9	22.8	12.8	15.2	. . .	. . .
August	15.4	14.1	19.0	12.2	22.6	7.8	8.8	23.1	12.6	15.2	. . .	. . .
September	15.5	14.2	19.2	12.6	22.7	7.9	8.8	23.3	12.7	15.4	. . .	. . .
October	15.7	14.4	19.5	12.8	23.0	8.0	9.1	23.3	12.7	15.5	. . .	. . .
November	15.9	14.6	19.8	13.2	23.3	8.0	9.2	23.7	13.0	15.9	. . .	. . .
December	15.9	14.6	19.8	13.3	23.2	8.0	9.4	23.8	13.2	15.7	. . .	. . .
1948												
January	16.0	14.7	19.7	13.2	23.1	8.1	9.5	24.9	13.2	15.8	. . .	84.4
February	16.1	14.7	19.8	13.0	23.4	8.1	9.9	24.6	13.3	15.9	. . .	84.0
March	15.9	14.7	19.6	13.1	23.0	8.1	10.1	24.7	13.3	15.7	. . .	83.4
April	15.9	14.7	19.7	13.0	23.3	8.1	10.3	24.5	13.2	15.6	. . .	82.8
May	16.2	14.8	19.6	12.7	23.3	8.0	10.1	24.7	13.3	16.4	. . .	83.3
June	16.4	15.0	20.0	13.3	23.5	8.1	10.5	24.4	13.4	16.4	. . .	83.6
July	16.4	15.0	19.9	13.6	23.2	8.2	10.7	25.1	13.3	16.6	. . .	83.4
August	16.3	14.9	19.8	13.4	23.1	8.2	10.9	25.0	13.5	16.4	. . .	82.7
September	16.2	14.8	19.6	13.0	23.1	8.1	11.2	24.7	13.3	16.4	. . .	81.5
October	16.3	14.9	19.9	13.4	23.2	8.0	11.4	25.2	13.4	16.4	. . .	81.7
November	16.1	14.7	19.6	12.9	23.3	8.0	11.6	24.5	13.4	16.3	. . .	80.2
December	16.0	14.6	19.4	12.4	23.1	7.9	11.6	24.3	13.4	16.2	. . .	79.3
1949												
January	15.8	14.4	19.2	12.0	23.0	7.7	11.4	23.6	13.2	15.9	. . .	77.9
February	15.7	14.3	19.1	11.9	23.1	7.7	11.4	23.1	13.0	15.8	. . .	76.9
March	15.4	14.1	19.3	11.9	23.3	7.5	11.4	22.8	13.0	15.2	. . .	75.9
April	15.3	13.9	19.2	11.9	23.2	7.4	11.2	22.5	13.0	14.9	. . .	74.2
May	15.1	13.7	19.2	11.8	23.3	7.2	11.4	22.2	13.1	14.5	. . .	73.2
June	15.0	13.8	19.5	12.1	23.3	7.1	11.4	22.2	13.1	14.3	. . .	73.1
July	15.0	13.8	19.6	12.5	23.4	7.0	11.4	21.9	13.0	14.2	. . .	73.1
August	15.1	13.9	19.8	12.7	23.7	6.9	11.2	22.1	13.1	14.5	. . .	73.6
September	15.3	14.2	20.1	13.1	23.7	6.9	11.0	22.8	13.3	14.7	. . .	74.8
October	14.7	13.7	20.2	13.3	23.8	6.6	10.7	22.1	13.5	13.2	. . .	71.7
November	15.1	13.8	19.9	12.6	23.7	6.4	10.6	22.8	13.4	14.5	. . .	72.0
December	15.4	14.1	19.7	12.5	23.6	6.4	10.5	23.8	13.5	15.1	. . .	73.6
1950												
January	15.7	14.4	20.5	13.9	24.0	6.5	10.5	23.5	13.6	15.3	. . .	74.9
February	15.7	14.6	20.5	13.9	24.0	6.7	10.5	24.4	14.0	15.0	. . .	75.4
March	16.2	14.8	21.0	14.5	24.3	6.8	10.6	25.0	14.0	16.0	. . .	76.4
April	16.8	15.4	21.6	15.5	24.7	7.0	10.8	26.3	14.3	16.7	. . .	79.2
May	17.2	15.8	22.0	16.3	24.9	7.3	11.2	26.6	14.4	17.2	. . .	81.0
June	17.7	16.3	22.6	17.7	25.1	7.6	11.6	27.5	14.5	17.8	. . .	83.1
July	18.2	16.8	23.3	18.4	25.6	7.8	12.2	28.2	14.9	18.3	. . .	85.5
August	18.8	17.5	24.1	19.0	26.6	8.3	13.4	28.8	15.2	18.8	. . .	88.4
September	18.7	17.3	23.5	18.1	26.2	8.1	14.8	28.8	15.1	19.1	. . .	87.2
October	18.8	17.4	23.3	17.7	26.0	8.2	15.9	29.1	15.3	19.3	. . .	87.5
November	18.8	17.4	23.2	17.4	26.1	8.3	17.0	29.1	15.4	19.1	. . .	87.0
December	19.1	17.6	23.5	17.2	26.8	8.4	18.5	29.2	15.6	19.4	. . .	88.1
1951												
January	19.2	17.8	23.7	16.9	27.2	8.5	20.5	29.4	15.8	19.2	. . .	88.3
February	19.3	17.8	23.7	16.9	27.2	8.6	23.7	29.1	15.6	19.3	. . .	88.3
March	19.4	17.9	23.3	16.8	26.6	8.8	26.9	29.3	15.9	19.7	. . .	88.4
April	19.4	17.9	22.9	16.0	26.5	9.0	29.5	29.1	16.2	19.8	. . .	88.2
May	19.4	17.8	22.5	15.2	26.2	9.1	30.5	28.9	16.0	20.0	. . .	87.4
June	19.3	17.7	22.2	14.5	26.2	9.2	32.1	28.7	15.8	20.1	. . .	86.6
July	19.0	17.4	21.4	13.0	26.0	9.2	33.9	28.0	15.6	19.7	. . .	84.9
August	18.8	17.2	21.0	12.1	25.7	9.4	35.0	27.9	15.4	19.4	. . .	83.6
September	18.9	17.3	21.2	12.6	25.7	9.6	36.1	27.9	15.3	19.5	. . .	83.7
October	18.9	17.2	21.0	12.5	25.7	9.7	37.7	27.6	15.0	19.2	. . .	83.1
November	19.0	17.4	21.4	12.8	26.0	9.9	39.8	27.4	15.1	19.3	. . .	83.6
December	19.1	17.5	21.6	12.9	26.2	10.0	40.7	27.4	15.1	19.3	. . .	83.9

. . . = Not available.

Table 20-1. Industrial Production and Capacity Utilization—*Continued*

(Seasonally adjusted; 2002 = 100, except as noted.)

Year and month	Total industry	Manufac-turing (SIC)	Market groups								Capacity utilization (output as percentage of capacity)	
			Consumer goods			Business equipment	Defense and space equipment	Construction supplies	Business supplies	Materials	Total industry	Manufac-turing (SIC)
			Total	Durable	Nondurable							
1952												
January	19.4	17.7	21.7	12.9	26.5	10.3	41.4	27.8	15.2	19.8	. . .	84.4
February	19.5	17.8	21.9	12.8	26.8	10.4	41.8	28.0	15.2	19.6	. . .	84.6
March	19.5	17.9	22.0	13.1	26.8	10.5	41.9	27.9	15.2	19.6	. . .	84.7
April	19.4	17.7	22.0	13.0	26.8	10.5	42.4	27.4	15.1	19.2	. . .	83.6
May	19.2	17.7	22.0	13.4	26.5	10.5	43.8	27.0	15.0	19.0	. . .	83.1
June	19.0	17.5	22.6	13.5	27.5	10.6	45.1	26.8	15.3	17.9	. . .	81.9
July	18.7	17.1	22.2	12.2	27.6	10.1	45.4	26.8	15.5	17.5	. . .	79.8
August	19.9	18.3	22.6	13.4	27.7	10.2	46.1	28.6	15.6	19.7	. . .	85.1
September	20.6	19.0	23.2	14.8	27.7	10.5	46.8	28.9	15.8	21.0	. . .	87.7
October	20.8	19.3	23.6	15.3	27.9	10.6	48.4	29.3	16.0	20.9	. . .	88.8
November	21.3	19.7	24.1	16.3	28.2	10.7	49.4	29.8	16.2	21.5	. . .	90.2
December	21.4	19.8	24.1	16.3	28.1	10.8	50.9	29.9	16.1	21.6	. . .	90.5
1953												
January	21.4	19.9	24.3	17.0	28.1	10.9	51.6	30.4	15.9	21.5	. . .	90.5
February	21.6	20.1	24.5	17.1	28.3	11.0	52.7	30.9	16.2	22.0	. . .	91.1
March	21.7	20.2	24.5	17.3	28.1	11.0	53.7	30.9	16.5	22.2	. . .	91.4
April	21.8	20.3	24.4	17.1	28.3	11.1	54.5	31.1	16.6	22.4	. . .	91.5
May	21.9	20.4	24.5	17.2	28.4	11.0	55.4	30.4	16.7	22.9	. . .	91.7
June	21.9	20.2	24.2	16.6	28.3	10.9	55.8	30.2	16.7	22.9	. . .	90.7
July	22.1	20.4	24.2	16.5	28.2	11.1	56.2	30.6	16.8	23.2	. . .	91.0
August	22.0	20.3	24.1	16.3	28.1	11.0	55.8	30.5	16.8	22.6	. . .	90.6
September	21.6	19.9	23.7	15.7	27.9	10.9	55.8	29.9	16.7	22.0	. . .	88.3
October	21.4	19.7	23.7	15.5	28.1	10.9	55.2	30.0	16.5	21.3	. . .	87.2
November	20.9	19.2	23.4	15.0	27.8	10.5	51.6	29.5	16.5	20.8	. . .	84.7
December	20.3	18.7	23.0	14.4	27.5	10.4	52.1	28.8	16.2	20.3	. . .	82.3
1954												
January	20.2	18.6	23.1	14.2	27.9	10.1	51.0	29.3	16.2	20.0	. . .	81.3
February	20.3	18.5	23.4	14.6	28.1	9.9	50.6	29.4	16.4	20.0	. . .	80.8
March	20.1	18.4	23.4	14.6	28.1	9.8	50.0	29.2	16.4	19.8	. . .	80.2
April	20.0	18.3	23.4	14.7	27.9	9.6	49.1	29.2	16.4	19.8	. . .	79.4
May	20.1	18.4	23.5	15.0	28.0	9.6	48.4	29.6	16.4	20.0	. . .	79.8
June	20.2	18.5	23.7	15.1	28.1	9.5	47.6	28.9	16.6	20.3	. . .	79.9
July	20.2	18.4	23.8	15.0	28.4	9.5	47.4	28.8	16.4	20.4	. . .	79.4
August	20.2	18.4	23.8	15.1	28.4	9.4	46.5	28.7	16.5	20.3	. . .	78.8
September	20.2	18.5	24.0	15.2	28.7	9.3	46.0	30.1	17.0	20.1	. . .	79.2
October	20.5	18.7	24.1	15.4	28.7	9.3	45.5	31.1	17.1	20.5	. . .	79.7
November	20.8	19.0	24.6	15.8	29.2	9.4	45.3	31.4	17.4	20.9	. . .	80.9
December	21.1	19.3	25.0	16.4	29.5	9.5	44.6	31.7	17.6	21.3	. . .	81.8
1955												
January	21.6	19.8	25.6	17.6	29.6	9.5	44.3	32.1	17.7	22.0	. . .	83.5
February	21.8	20.0	25.7	17.8	29.6	9.7	44.3	32.6	18.0	22.6	. . .	84.1
March	22.3	20.4	26.2	18.3	30.1	9.8	44.1	33.7	18.5	23.2	. . .	85.8
April	22.6	20.7	26.4	18.6	30.3	10.1	44.0	33.9	18.4	23.6	. . .	86.7
May	23.0	21.1	26.7	19.1	30.5	10.3	44.0	34.0	18.7	24.1	. . .	87.9
June	23.0	21.1	26.5	18.7	30.4	10.4	43.6	34.6	18.8	24.1	. . .	87.6
July	23.2	21.2	26.6	18.9	30.4	10.4	43.5	34.7	18.8	24.4	. . .	87.7
August	23.1	21.2	26.7	18.9	30.4	10.5	43.2	34.7	18.6	24.4	. . .	87.3
September	23.3	21.3	26.8	19.0	30.7	10.5	43.3	34.9	19.1	24.7	. . .	87.5
October	23.7	21.6	27.3	19.1	31.5	11.0	43.1	34.9	19.2	24.9	. . .	88.4
November	23.7	21.7	27.4	18.9	31.7	11.1	43.1	35.3	19.5	24.8	. . .	88.3
December	23.8	22.0	27.5	18.8	32.0	11.3	43.2	35.5	19.4	25.0	. . .	89.0
1956												
January	24.0	21.8	27.6	18.6	32.2	11.3	42.7	36.1	19.6	25.1	. . .	88.2
February	23.8	21.7	27.5	18.3	32.2	11.5	42.3	36.0	19.6	24.6	. . .	87.4
March	23.8	21.7	27.5	18.3	32.2	11.6	41.4	35.9	19.7	24.6	. . .	87.0
April	24.0	22.0	27.6	18.6	32.2	12.0	41.7	35.7	19.9	24.7	. . .	87.8
May	23.7	21.7	27.4	18.2	32.3	11.9	41.8	35.2	19.8	24.3	. . .	86.3
June	23.5	21.6	27.4	17.7	32.4	12.0	41.8	34.8	19.7	24.0	. . .	85.3
July	22.8	20.7	27.4	17.8	32.5	12.0	41.8	33.0	19.8	22.0	. . .	81.5
August	23.7	21.7	27.6	17.8	32.8	12.1	42.3	34.7	19.9	24.0	. . .	84.9
September	24.3	22.0	27.5	17.5	32.8	12.2	42.7	35.6	19.8	25.3	. . .	86.0
October	24.5	22.2	27.8	17.7	33.0	12.3	43.8	35.3	20.0	25.7	. . .	86.5
November	24.3	22.1	27.6	17.5	32.9	12.5	44.5	35.1	20.0	25.2	. . .	85.8
December	24.6	22.5	27.8	18.2	32.8	12.6	45.5	35.7	20.1	25.6	. . .	86.8
1957												
January	24.6	22.4	28.0	18.3	33.0	12.8	45.7	35.2	20.2	25.1	. . .	86.2
February	24.8	22.7	28.4	18.6	33.4	13.1	45.9	36.3	20.2	25.3	. . .	87.0
March	24.8	22.6	28.4	18.5	33.6	13.0	45.8	35.7	20.1	25.2	. . .	86.4
April	24.4	22.3	28.1	18.0	33.5	12.8	46.0	34.9	20.2	24.9	. . .	85.0
May	24.3	22.2	28.2	17.9	33.5	12.5	45.3	34.7	20.3	24.7	. . .	84.2
June	24.4	22.3	28.3	18.2	33.6	12.6	45.5	35.0	20.1	24.9	. . .	84.6
July	24.6	22.3	28.4	18.0	33.9	12.6	45.0	35.1	20.2	25.0	. . .	84.3
August	24.6	22.4	28.6	18.5	33.8	12.6	45.1	34.8	20.2	25.1	. . .	84.2
September	24.3	22.2	28.6	18.4	33.9	12.5	44.2	34.6	20.2	24.7	. . .	83.2
October	24.0	21.8	28.1	17.7	33.6	12.1	43.1	34.2	20.0	24.3	. . .	81.4
November	23.4	21.3	28.1	17.7	33.5	11.8	41.7	33.7	19.8	23.5	. . .	79.4
December	23.0	20.9	27.9	16.9	33.8	11.4	41.4	33.2	19.7	22.7	. . .	77.5

. . . = Not available.

Table 20-1. Industrial Production and Capacity Utilization—*Continued*

(Seasonally adjusted; 2002 = 100, except as noted.)

Year and month	Total industry	Manufac-turing (SIC)	Market groups — Consumer goods Total	Durable	Nondurable	Business equipment	Defense and space equipment	Construction supplies	Business supplies	Materials	Capacity utilization — Total industry	Manufac-turing (SIC)
1958												
January	22.5	20.4	27.5	16.2	33.7	11.2	41.8	32.8	19.6	22.0	. . .	75.7
February	22.1	20.0	27.3	15.7	33.7	10.8	42.2	31.7	19.6	21.3	. . .	73.8
March	21.8	19.7	27.1	15.1	33.7	10.6	43.0	31.6	19.6	20.8	. . .	72.7
April	21.4	19.4	26.8	14.5	33.7	10.4	43.7	31.2	19.5	20.3	. . .	71.3
May	21.6	19.6	27.2	15.1	34.0	10.1	44.2	32.2	19.4	20.5	. . .	71.9
June	22.2	20.2	27.8	15.5	34.5	10.1	45.4	33.5	19.7	21.4	. . .	73.9
July	22.5	20.4	28.2	15.7	35.0	10.2	45.5	33.3	19.7	21.9	. . .	74.3
August	23.0	20.8	28.3	16.0	35.0	10.4	45.9	34.8	19.9	22.6	. . .	75.7
September	23.2	21.0	27.9	14.9	35.2	10.4	46.2	34.9	20.2	23.1	. . .	76.2
October	23.5	21.1	28.2	15.7	35.2	10.6	46.2	34.8	20.5	23.5	. . .	76.4
November	24.2	21.9	29.6	18.3	35.6	10.8	46.5	36.2	20.7	24.2	. . .	79.1
December	24.2	22.0	29.7	18.4	35.7	10.9	46.6	35.7	20.5	24.3	. . .	79.0
1959												
January	24.6	22.4	30.0	18.5	36.1	11.1	46.8	36.4	21.0	24.7	. . .	80.2
February	25.0	22.8	30.3	18.6	36.5	11.2	46.3	37.4	21.2	25.5	. . .	81.4
March	25.4	23.1	30.3	18.9	36.3	11.3	46.5	38.4	21.4	26.1	. . .	82.5
April	25.9	23.6	30.7	19.1	36.9	11.6	46.8	39.5	21.4	26.8	. . .	84.0
May	26.3	24.0	30.9	19.4	36.9	12.0	47.2	39.8	21.5	27.5	. . .	84.9
June	26.4	24.0	30.7	19.6	36.6	12.3	47.3	39.6	21.7	27.4	. . .	84.8
July	25.7	23.5	31.1	20.0	37.0	12.3	47.5	38.1	21.9	25.7	. . .	83.0
August	24.9	22.6	31.2	19.4	37.4	12.2	47.3	35.7	21.9	23.8	. . .	79.5
September	24.8	22.6	31.1	18.8	37.6	12.1	47.5	35.3	22.0	23.7	. . .	79.0
October	24.6	22.4	30.9	19.3	37.1	12.0	47.4	35.4	21.9	23.5	. . .	78.2
November	24.8	22.5	30.3	16.9	37.6	11.8	47.4	36.6	21.9	24.4	. . .	78.5
December	26.3	24.1	31.3	19.1	37.8	12.0	47.8	39.5	22.1	27.1	. . .	83.6
1960												
January	27.0	24.7	32.2	21.1	37.9	12.5	48.1	39.2	22.4	27.8	. . .	85.6
February	26.8	24.5	31.9	20.8	37.6	12.5	48.4	38.8	22.4	27.5	. . .	84.6
March	26.5	24.2	31.9	20.4	37.9	12.6	48.6	37.6	22.3	27.0	. . .	83.2
April	26.3	24.0	32.1	20.4	38.3	12.4	48.3	37.6	22.7	26.4	. . .	82.3
May	26.3	23.9	32.3	20.6	38.4	12.5	48.9	37.2	22.8	26.2	. . .	81.5
June	26.0	23.6	32.1	20.4	38.2	12.3	47.6	36.5	22.6	25.7	. . .	80.2
July	25.9	23.6	31.8	19.6	38.3	12.2	48.8	36.9	22.6	25.8	. . .	79.7
August	25.8	23.5	31.9	19.8	38.3	12.0	49.0	36.0	22.4	25.6	. . .	79.1
September	25.6	23.2	31.7	19.6	38.2	11.9	48.9	35.6	22.3	25.2	. . .	77.9
October	25.5	23.2	32.1	19.8	38.5	11.8	48.4	35.7	22.4	25.1	. . .	77.5
November	25.2	22.7	31.5	19.1	38.2	11.8	48.6	35.3	22.4	24.5	. . .	75.8
December	24.7	22.4	31.3	18.5	38.1	11.5	47.9	34.9	22.0	23.8	. . .	74.3
1961												
January	24.7	22.4	31.0	17.8	38.2	11.6	48.4	34.5	22.3	24.0	. . .	74.1
February	24.7	22.3	31.2	17.7	38.5	11.5	48.0	34.5	22.4	23.8	. . .	73.5
March	24.9	22.4	31.2	17.7	38.5	11.5	47.9	35.3	22.6	24.0	. . .	73.9
April	25.4	23.0	31.9	19.0	38.8	11.6	48.1	36.2	22.7	24.8	. . .	75.4
May	25.8	23.3	32.3	19.6	39.1	11.6	48.1	36.3	22.8	25.5	. . .	76.4
June	26.1	23.7	32.6	20.3	39.3	11.7	48.1	37.1	23.0	25.9	. . .	77.3
July	26.4	24.0	32.9	20.6	39.5	11.8	48.4	37.7	23.2	26.3	. . .	78.1
August	26.7	24.3	33.2	20.7	39.8	11.8	48.6	38.1	23.4	26.8	. . .	79.0
September	26.6	24.1	32.6	19.5	39.6	12.0	49.7	38.4	23.3	26.8	. . .	78.2
October	27.1	24.6	33.5	20.6	40.3	12.0	50.8	38.7	23.6	27.3	. . .	79.6
November	27.6	25.0	34.1	21.5	40.7	12.3	52.0	38.4	23.8	27.7	. . .	80.8
December	27.8	25.4	34.2	21.9	40.7	12.3	52.9	38.7	24.0	28.1	. . .	81.6
1962												
January	27.6	25.0	33.9	21.4	40.5	12.3	53.5	36.9	24.0	27.9	. . .	80.2
February	28.0	25.5	34.1	21.5	40.7	12.5	54.5	39.1	24.3	28.3	. . .	81.4
March	28.2	25.7	34.4	21.9	41.0	12.6	55.2	39.5	24.2	28.3	. . .	81.9
April	28.2	25.7	34.7	22.4	41.1	12.7	55.7	39.0	24.2	28.3	. . .	81.7
May	28.2	25.7	34.9	22.6	41.3	12.7	56.1	39.0	24.6	27.9	. . .	81.3
June	28.1	25.6	34.6	22.2	41.2	12.8	56.6	39.3	24.5	27.8	. . .	80.9
July	28.4	25.8	35.2	22.6	41.7	12.9	57.7	39.1	24.5	28.1	. . .	81.5
August	28.4	25.9	34.8	22.3	41.3	13.1	58.5	39.8	24.6	28.1	. . .	81.4
September	28.6	26.1	35.0	22.6	41.6	13.1	58.6	40.2	24.9	28.4	. . .	81.8
October	28.6	26.0	35.0	22.7	41.4	13.1	58.8	39.6	24.9	28.4	. . .	81.4
November	28.8	26.3	35.2	22.7	41.6	13.1	59.4	39.8	25.0	28.6	. . .	81.8
December	28.8	26.3	35.3	22.9	41.8	13.0	59.7	40.1	24.9	28.5	. . .	81.7
1963												
January	29.0	26.4	35.8	23.1	42.3	13.0	62.5	39.1	25.1	28.6	. . .	81.9
February	29.3	26.7	36.2	23.4	42.8	13.2	62.0	39.2	25.3	29.0	. . .	82.4
March	29.5	26.8	36.3	23.4	43.0	13.1	61.7	39.6	25.1	29.4	. . .	82.6
April	29.8	27.2	36.5	23.6	43.2	13.2	61.6	41.0	25.9	29.7	. . .	83.5
May	30.1	27.4	36.5	24.0	43.0	13.2	61.6	41.9	26.1	30.4	. . .	84.0
June	30.2	27.5	36.8	24.4	43.1	13.2	61.5	41.7	26.0	30.5	. . .	83.9
July	30.1	27.4	36.7	24.4	42.9	13.4	60.9	41.6	26.2	30.2	. . .	83.3
August	30.1	27.5	36.9	24.5	43.4	13.7	61.2	41.7	26.3	29.9	. . .	83.5
September	30.4	27.7	37.1	24.9	43.3	13.7	61.4	41.4	26.6	30.5	. . .	83.8
October	30.7	28.0	37.3	24.9	43.6	13.9	61.4	42.0	26.8	30.7	. . .	84.3
November	30.8	28.1	37.3	25.2	43.6	14.0	61.2	42.5	27.1	30.9	. . .	84.3
December	30.7	28.1	37.6	25.2	43.9	14.0	61.4	41.9	26.9	30.7	. . .	84.0

. . . = Not available.

Table 20-1. Industrial Production and Capacity Utilization—*Continued*

(Seasonally adjusted; 2002 = 100, except as noted.)

Year and month	Total industry	Manufac-turing (SIC)	Market groups								Capacity utilization (output as percentage of capacity)	
			Consumer goods			Business equipment	Defense and space equipment	Construction supplies	Business supplies	Materials	Total industry	Manufac-turing (SIC)
			Total	Durable	Nondurable							
1964												
January	31.0	28.3	37.9	25.3	44.4	14.4	60.7	42.1	27.2	31.0	. . .	84.5
February	31.2	28.5	37.9	25.4	44.2	14.3	60.2	43.3	27.3	31.4	. . .	84.7
March	31.2	28.5	37.7	25.2	44.1	14.5	60.1	43.4	27.5	31.4	. . .	84.4
April	31.7	29.0	38.6	25.9	45.1	14.8	59.9	43.5	27.9	31.8	. . .	85.6
May	31.9	29.1	38.9	26.1	45.5	15.0	58.9	43.7	28.1	32.1	. . .	85.6
June	32.0	29.2	38.9	26.3	45.2	15.0	58.5	43.5	28.2	32.3	. . .	85.4
July	32.2	29.4	39.4	26.8	45.8	15.2	58.4	44.3	28.2	32.3	. . .	85.9
August	32.4	29.6	39.3	27.0	45.5	15.2	58.7	43.8	28.1	33.0	. . .	86.1
September	32.6	29.7	38.9	26.3	45.3	15.4	59.1	43.5	28.1	33.5	. . .	86.2
October	32.1	29.3	38.1	23.6	45.9	15.2	59.5	43.7	28.1	32.9	. . .	84.6
November	33.1	30.2	39.6	26.8	46.0	15.8	60.1	44.7	28.4	33.9	. . .	86.8
December	33.5	30.7	40.4	28.4	46.3	16.0	60.6	44.1	28.6	34.3	. . .	88.0
1965												
January	33.8	31.1	40.9	28.9	46.9	16.0	61.2	44.4	28.9	34.7	. . .	88.6
February	34.1	31.3	41.1	29.3	46.8	16.3	61.9	45.6	29.0	34.8	. . .	88.7
March	34.5	31.7	41.4	30.1	46.9	16.5	63.0	46.0	29.3	35.4	. . .	89.3
April	34.7	31.8	41.3	30.0	46.7	16.6	63.8	45.3	29.3	35.7	. . .	89.3
May	34.9	32.1	41.6	30.2	47.0	16.9	65.2	45.8	29.6	35.9	. . .	89.4
June	35.2	32.3	41.7	30.5	47.1	17.1	66.0	45.8	29.8	36.3	. . .	89.5
July	35.5	32.8	41.7	30.7	46.9	17.4	67.0	47.1	29.8	36.6	. . .	90.3
August	35.7	32.8	41.6	30.4	47.1	17.4	67.6	46.6	30.0	37.0	. . .	89.9
September	35.8	32.9	42.3	31.0	47.7	17.8	67.7	46.2	30.1	36.7	. . .	89.6
October	36.1	33.2	42.5	31.2	47.8	18.0	68.6	46.9	30.4	37.1	. . .	89.8
November	36.3	33.3	42.7	31.5	48.1	18.3	69.2	47.6	30.6	36.9	. . .	89.6
December	36.7	33.8	43.0	32.1	48.0	18.7	69.8	48.6	31.1	37.4	. . .	90.5
1966												
January	37.1	34.1	43.2	32.2	48.3	19.1	71.3	48.5	31.0	37.9	. . .	90.9
February	37.3	34.4	43.3	32.2	48.6	19.1	72.4	48.1	31.4	38.3	. . .	90.9
March	37.8	34.8	43.6	32.4	48.9	19.4	73.0	49.0	31.7	39.0	. . .	91.6
April	37.9	35.0	43.8	33.0	48.8	19.6	74.6	49.0	31.4	38.9	. . .	91.5
May	38.3	35.3	43.8	32.5	49.1	19.8	75.9	49.3	31.9	39.3	. . .	91.6
June	38.4	35.4	44.0	32.5	49.4	20.0	77.0	48.6	32.3	39.6	. . .	91.5
July	38.7	35.6	43.9	31.9	49.7	20.4	78.1	49.0	32.6	39.7	. . .	91.4
August	38.7	35.7	43.7	31.4	49.8	20.4	79.1	47.6	32.5	40.0	. . .	91.1
September	39.0	36.0	43.9	31.6	49.9	20.7	80.2	47.6	32.7	40.4	. . .	91.2
October	39.3	36.3	44.8	33.2	50.3	20.6	81.4	47.6	32.7	40.6	. . .	91.6
November	39.0	35.9	44.6	32.2	50.6	20.3	82.9	47.7	32.8	40.0	. . .	90.1
December	39.1	36.1	44.5	31.8	50.6	20.6	83.7	47.6	32.9	40.0	. . .	90.0
1967												
January	39.3	36.2	44.9	31.1	51.8	20.4	85.2	48.9	33.5	39.8	89.4	89.8
February	38.9	35.8	44.3	30.2	51.4	20.5	86.2	48.4	33.3	39.1	88.0	88.4
March	38.7	35.6	44.4	30.5	51.4	20.4	87.1	48.5	33.3	38.3	87.1	87.5
April	39.0	35.8	45.2	30.7	52.5	20.4	87.9	48.4	33.6	38.7	87.5	87.7
May	38.7	35.6	44.3	30.3	51.4	20.5	88.5	49.1	33.1	38.3	86.4	86.6
June	38.7	35.5	44.4	29.9	51.8	20.4	88.3	49.4	33.3	38.2	86.0	86.1
July	38.6	35.4	44.4	30.3	51.4	20.0	88.8	49.6	33.4	38.2	85.4	85.3
August	39.3	36.1	44.8	30.7	51.9	20.3	89.0	50.1	34.3	39.3	86.6	86.5
September	39.3	36.1	44.9	30.6	52.1	20.2	89.3	50.6	34.4	39.1	86.1	86.1
October	39.6	36.4	45.5	31.2	52.7	20.1	90.0	50.3	34.6	39.6	86.4	86.4
November	40.1	37.0	46.5	32.9	53.1	20.6	90.1	50.6	34.7	40.0	87.3	87.5
December	40.6	37.4	47.2	34.2	53.5	20.8	90.1	50.6	34.6	40.5	87.8	88.0
1968												
January	40.5	37.3	46.6	33.2	53.1	20.9	89.7	50.9	34.8	40.7	87.4	87.4
February	40.7	37.5	46.8	33.7	53.2	20.9	90.8	51.4	35.0	40.7	87.4	87.4
March	40.8	37.5	47.1	33.7	53.7	21.1	89.0	51.5	35.1	40.9	87.3	87.2
April	40.9	37.6	47.0	33.7	53.6	21.0	87.2	51.8	35.4	41.2	87.1	86.9
May	41.3	38.0	47.3	34.1	53.7	21.3	88.4	52.0	35.7	41.8	87.7	87.6
June	41.5	38.1	47.6	34.5	54.0	21.3	88.9	52.1	35.9	42.0	87.7	87.4
July	41.4	38.0	47.5	34.2	54.0	21.0	88.9	52.1	35.8	42.0	87.2	86.8
August	41.5	38.2	48.0	34.6	54.6	21.2	89.1	52.3	36.2	41.7	87.1	86.8
September	41.7	38.2	48.2	35.0	54.6	21.5	89.1	51.9	36.4	41.9	87.1	86.5
October	41.8	38.5	48.5	35.4	54.8	21.6	86.7	51.9	36.6	41.9	86.9	86.7
November	42.3	39.0	49.2	36.2	55.3	21.7	87.6	53.1	37.0	42.6	87.7	87.5
December	42.4	39.0	48.9	36.6	54.6	21.9	87.1	54.1	37.2	42.8	87.7	87.2
1969												
January	42.7	39.2	49.1	36.5	55.1	22.2	87.3	54.5	37.3	43.0	87.9	87.3
February	43.0	39.6	49.5	36.5	55.7	22.2	86.7	55.0	37.2	43.5	88.1	87.7
March	43.3	39.9	49.9	36.7	56.1	22.4	87.0	55.2	38.4	43.7	88.5	88.0
April	43.2	39.7	49.2	35.7	55.6	22.6	86.3	54.7	37.9	43.8	87.9	87.3
May	43.0	39.5	48.8	35.2	55.3	22.5	86.1	54.3	38.2	43.7	87.2	86.7
June	43.4	39.8	49.3	36.4	55.4	22.7	84.9	54.6	38.5	44.3	87.8	86.8
July	43.6	40.1	50.2	36.4	56.8	22.9	84.6	54.1	38.3	44.3	87.9	87.2
August	43.7	40.1	50.1	36.8	56.4	22.9	83.4	54.0	38.5	44.8	87.8	86.9
September	43.7	40.1	49.7	36.4	56.0	23.1	82.9	54.1	38.4	44.9	87.5	86.5
October	43.7	40.1	49.8	36.6	55.9	23.1	82.1	54.2	38.5	44.9	87.2	86.3
November	43.3	39.7	49.3	35.1	56.2	22.6	80.6	53.9	38.3	44.6	86.1	85.1
December	43.2	39.5	49.4	34.9	56.5	22.5	79.6	53.6	38.7	44.4	85.5	84.3

. . . = Not available.

Table 20-1. Industrial Production and Capacity Utilization—*Continued*

(Seasonally adjusted; 2002 = 100, except as noted.)

Year and month	Total industry	Manufac-turing (SIC)	Market groups								Capacity utilization (output as percentage of capacity)	
			Consumer goods			Business equipment	Defense and space equipment	Construction supplies	Business supplies	Materials	Total industry	Manufac-turing (SIC)
			Total	Durable	Nondurable							
1970												
January	42.4	38.6	48.6	33.1	56.4	22.2	78.5	51.9	38.7	43.4	83.7	82.2
February	42.4	38.6	49.0	33.6	56.8	22.3	77.2	51.8	38.4	43.1	83.4	82.0
March	42.3	38.5	49.0	33.9	56.5	22.4	75.5	52.2	38.6	43.0	83.0	81.5
April	42.2	38.4	49.2	33.9	56.8	22.3	73.8	52.7	38.4	42.7	82.5	80.9
May	42.2	38.3	49.5	33.9	57.2	22.3	72.2	52.8	38.3	42.6	82.2	80.5
June	42.0	38.2	49.6	34.6	57.0	22.2	71.0	52.6	38.3	42.4	81.7	80.0
July	42.1	38.3	49.7	34.6	57.2	22.1	69.8	53.2	38.4	42.6	81.6	80.0
August	42.1	38.1	48.9	33.6	56.5	22.1	69.2	52.9	38.1	43.1	81.2	79.2
September	41.8	37.7	48.7	32.7	56.8	21.6	68.5	52.8	38.4	42.8	80.4	78.3
October	40.9	36.9	48.1	30.7	57.1	20.9	67.6	52.3	38.2	41.7	78.6	76.3
November	40.7	36.7	47.7	30.8	56.6	20.8	67.1	51.6	38.3	41.4	77.9	75.6
December	41.6	37.6	49.8	34.4	57.5	21.0	66.3	52.2	38.3	42.4	79.4	77.4
1971												
January	41.9	37.9	50.5	35.8	57.8	20.6	66.8	52.3	38.5	43.0	79.8	77.8
February	41.9	38.0	50.5	36.6	57.2	20.7	65.2	52.6	38.9	42.7	79.4	77.7
March	41.8	37.9	50.7	36.6	57.4	20.5	64.7	52.4	38.6	42.8	79.1	77.3
April	42.1	38.1	51.1	36.9	57.9	20.4	64.7	52.9	39.0	43.1	79.4	77.5
May	42.3	38.3	51.1	37.4	57.6	20.2	65.5	53.1	39.0	43.6	79.6	77.8
June	42.4	38.4	51.5	37.7	58.0	20.3	64.5	53.7	38.9	43.8	79.7	77.8
July	42.3	38.5	52.3	38.4	58.8	20.4	64.0	54.2	39.9	42.7	79.3	77.8
August	42.1	38.0	51.7	38.1	58.1	20.7	64.0	53.3	39.4	42.5	78.6	76.7
September	42.8	38.8	52.2	38.0	58.9	21.1	63.4	55.2	40.0	43.3	79.7	78.0
October	43.1	39.4	52.9	38.7	59.6	21.4	63.0	56.0	40.3	43.4	80.1	79.0
November	43.3	39.5	53.3	39.1	60.1	21.5	62.5	56.2	40.7	43.5	80.3	79.1
December	43.8	39.9	53.7	39.2	60.5	21.6	61.5	57.2	40.9	44.4	81.0	79.6
1972												
January	44.8	40.9	54.5	40.4	61.1	22.3	61.3	58.7	41.6	45.8	82.7	81.4
February	45.2	41.2	54.8	40.6	61.4	22.6	61.6	58.9	42.3	46.2	83.3	81.8
March	45.6	41.5	54.8	40.3	61.7	22.9	62.1	59.4	42.8	46.7	83.7	82.2
April	46.0	42.0	55.4	41.5	61.9	23.3	62.4	60.0	42.8	47.1	84.3	82.9
May	46.0	42.1	55.2	41.1	61.7	23.3	61.9	60.3	43.0	47.2	84.1	82.8
June	46.2	42.2	55.2	41.1	61.7	23.4	61.9	60.9	43.4	47.3	84.2	82.9
July	46.2	42.3	55.6	42.0	61.8	23.5	61.9	61.7	43.4	47.0	83.9	82.7
August	46.8	42.8	56.2	42.4	62.6	23.9	61.9	62.2	44.0	47.7	84.8	83.6
September	47.1	43.1	56.5	42.8	62.7	24.1	62.2	62.7	43.9	48.2	85.2	83.9
October	47.7	43.7	57.3	43.8	63.4	24.5	62.4	63.6	44.7	48.7	86.0	84.9
November	48.3	44.3	57.8	44.8	63.4	24.9	64.1	64.1	44.8	49.4	86.8	85.7
December	48.8	44.9	58.2	45.7	63.5	25.2	65.2	63.9	44.9	50.2	87.5	86.6
1973												
January	49.2	45.2	58.1	45.5	63.4	25.8	66.0	64.7	45.3	50.6	87.8	86.9
February	49.9	46.0	58.8	46.4	64.0	26.3	67.6	65.9	45.7	51.4	88.8	88.1
March	49.9	46.0	59.0	46.4	64.3	26.4	67.2	66.3	45.8	51.2	88.5	87.9
April	49.8	45.9	58.4	45.7	63.8	26.6	66.7	66.0	45.7	51.3	88.1	87.4
May	50.2	46.2	58.8	45.6	64.5	26.9	67.1	66.4	46.0	51.6	88.4	87.7
June	50.2	46.2	58.4	45.5	63.9	27.2	67.7	66.5	46.1	51.7	88.1	87.4
July	50.4	46.4	58.3	45.5	63.7	27.6	69.2	67.0	46.3	51.9	88.2	87.5
August	50.3	46.3	57.7	44.1	63.8	27.6	69.2	67.1	46.3	52.0	87.8	87.0
September	50.8	46.7	58.7	45.6	64.3	28.1	69.2	67.0	46.4	52.2	88.2	87.4
October	51.1	47.1	58.9	45.3	64.9	28.5	70.7	66.9	46.9	52.6	88.6	87.9
November	51.4	47.5	59.1	45.3	65.2	28.7	70.1	67.4	46.9	52.9	88.7	88.3
December	51.3	47.5	58.0	44.3	64.0	28.9	69.6	68.0	46.5	53.2	88.3	88.1
1974												
January	50.9	47.1	57.2	42.1	64.3	28.9	69.2	68.1	46.5	52.8	87.4	87.1
February	50.7	46.9	57.0	41.9	64.1	28.6	70.1	67.3	46.3	52.7	86.8	86.4
March	50.7	46.9	57.1	42.0	64.2	29.0	69.9	67.4	46.4	52.5	86.6	86.1
April	50.6	46.7	56.9	41.7	64.1	28.7	69.7	66.8	46.4	52.5	86.2	85.6
May	51.0	47.0	57.4	41.8	64.8	29.1	70.1	67.1	46.7	52.7	86.6	85.9
June	50.9	47.1	57.7	42.4	64.9	29.1	69.2	66.8	46.9	52.5	86.3	85.7
July	50.9	47.0	57.5	42.2	64.8	29.1	70.0	65.5	46.5	52.8	86.1	85.3
August	50.4	46.6	57.5	42.2	64.7	29.1	71.4	64.7	46.3	51.8	85.1	84.5
September	50.5	46.7	57.0	42.1	64.0	29.6	71.6	64.3	46.1	52.0	85.0	84.4
October	50.3	46.3	57.1	41.6	64.4	29.6	72.6	63.2	45.9	51.7	84.5	83.5
November	48.7	44.9	55.4	39.6	63.1	29.3	72.2	61.1	44.9	49.5	81.6	80.9
December	46.9	42.9	53.7	36.3	62.5	28.0	71.6	58.3	44.0	47.6	78.6	77.1
1975												
January	46.3	42.1	52.5	34.8	61.5	27.5	72.1	58.1	43.3	47.2	77.4	75.4
February	45.2	40.9	51.7	33.8	61.0	26.6	68.4	56.2	42.4	46.0	75.4	73.1
March	44.8	40.3	51.9	34.3	61.0	26.1	69.0	54.1	41.8	45.3	74.5	72.0
April	44.8	40.3	53.0	35.5	61.8	25.8	68.5	53.6	41.9	45.0	74.4	71.7
May	44.7	40.3	53.2	36.5	61.6	25.6	71.7	53.7	41.7	44.8	74.1	71.6
June	45.0	40.6	54.0	36.9	62.7	25.3	72.8	53.4	41.9	45.1	74.5	72.1
July	45.5	41.2	55.4	38.7	63.6	25.5	71.8	54.2	42.3	45.3	75.1	73.0
August	45.9	41.6	55.7	39.3	63.8	25.3	71.2	54.7	42.7	46.1	75.7	73.6
September	46.5	42.3	56.5	40.1	64.5	25.7	73.3	55.4	42.8	46.7	76.5	74.6
October	46.7	42.5	56.6	39.9	64.7	25.7	73.2	55.7	43.0	46.9	76.6	74.8
November	46.8	42.6	56.8	40.0	65.1	25.7	70.2	56.0	43.1	47.1	76.7	74.9
December	47.4	43.2	57.3	40.7	65.4	26.1	72.2	56.0	43.6	47.8	77.5	75.7

Table 20-1. Industrial Production and Capacity Utilization—*Continued*

(Seasonally adjusted; 2002 = 100, except as noted.)

Year and month	Total industry	Manufac-turing (SIC)	Consumer goods Total	Consumer goods Durable	Consumer goods Nondurable	Business equipment	Defense and space equipment	Construction supplies	Business supplies	Materials	Capacity utilization Total industry	Capacity utilization Manufac-turing (SIC)
1976												
January	48.1	43.8	58.1	41.4	66.2	26.4	72.3	57.5	44.0	48.6	78.5	76.6
February	48.5	44.4	58.2	41.8	66.1	26.6	72.2	58.3	44.2	49.3	79.0	77.5
March	48.6	44.5	58.1	41.8	65.9	26.7	72.2	57.4	44.4	49.5	78.9	77.5
April	48.9	44.8	58.2	41.8	66.2	27.0	70.8	58.2	44.6	49.8	79.3	77.9
May	49.1	45.0	58.7	41.9	66.9	27.3	70.1	58.9	44.8	49.9	79.5	78.1
June	49.1	45.0	58.5	41.7	66.7	27.3	69.3	59.3	44.5	50.0	79.3	77.9
July	49.3	45.3	58.9	41.9	67.1	27.5	67.5	60.6	45.2	50.1	79.6	78.3
August	49.7	45.6	59.0	42.5	66.9	28.0	67.6	59.9	45.3	50.6	80.0	78.7
September	49.8	45.7	59.0	42.2	67.1	27.9	67.3	60.3	46.2	50.7	80.0	78.6
October	49.8	45.7	59.5	42.7	67.6	28.0	67.1	60.3	46.5	50.5	79.9	78.5
November	50.6	46.3	60.6	44.1	68.4	28.9	66.8	60.6	46.7	51.1	80.9	79.3
December	51.1	46.8	61.2	45.2	68.7	29.4	65.4	60.9	47.2	51.6	81.5	79.9
1977												
January	50.8	46.7	61.0	45.1	68.5	29.5	64.5	60.0	47.0	51.2	80.9	79.5
February	51.6	47.5	61.8	45.6	69.4	30.2	64.3	61.3	47.6	52.0	82.0	80.8
March	52.2	48.2	61.8	46.9	68.6	30.6	63.0	62.7	47.9	53.0	82.8	81.7
April	52.7	48.7	62.2	47.2	69.0	31.0	63.4	64.2	48.5	53.5	83.3	82.4
May	53.1	49.1	62.3	47.4	68.9	31.5	63.3	65.1	49.0	53.9	83.8	82.8
June	53.5	49.5	62.7	48.3	69.1	32.1	63.2	65.6	49.4	54.1	84.1	83.2
July	53.6	49.5	62.8	48.3	69.3	32.5	63.0	65.6	49.5	54.1	84.1	83.0
August	53.7	49.8	62.9	48.3	69.4	32.7	62.5	66.1	49.8	54.0	83.9	83.3
September	53.9	49.9	63.0	48.6	69.4	33.0	62.6	65.9	50.0	54.4	84.1	83.1
October	54.1	50.0	63.6	48.6	70.3	32.9	57.0	65.9	50.0	54.6	84.1	83.1
November	54.1	50.0	63.5	48.5	70.3	32.8	56.5	66.2	50.0	54.7	83.8	82.9
December	54.1	50.6	64.1	48.7	71.0	33.4	60.2	66.8	50.4	54.1	83.7	83.5
1978												
January	53.4	49.9	62.5	46.2	70.1	32.9	61.0	65.5	50.3	53.6	82.3	82.1
February	53.7	50.0	63.5	47.3	71.0	33.5	57.9	65.4	50.4	53.5	82.5	82.1
March	54.7	50.9	64.8	48.8	72.0	34.3	63.1	66.5	51.1	54.3	83.7	83.2
April	55.8	51.7	65.3	49.7	72.3	34.9	62.7	68.1	51.3	56.0	85.2	84.2
May	56.0	51.9	64.8	49.0	71.9	35.2	63.0	68.0	51.6	56.5	85.3	84.3
June	56.4	52.3	65.2	49.3	72.4	35.8	63.7	68.6	52.0	56.8	85.7	84.8
July	56.4	52.3	64.9	49.4	71.8	36.2	63.6	68.6	52.0	56.8	85.4	84.5
August	56.6	52.5	64.8	49.2	71.9	36.8	64.4	68.7	52.0	56.9	85.5	84.6
September	56.8	52.8	64.9	48.9	72.2	37.0	64.6	69.0	52.1	57.0	85.5	84.7
October	57.2	53.2	64.9	49.0	72.1	37.7	64.0	69.6	52.4	57.7	85.9	85.1
November	57.6	53.6	65.1	49.2	72.3	38.4	63.7	70.1	52.7	58.1	86.3	85.6
December	58.0	54.1	65.2	49.3	72.4	38.9	64.6	71.3	53.1	58.4	86.6	86.1
1979												
January	57.6	53.6	65.0	49.7	71.9	39.3	64.7	69.5	53.1	57.6	85.8	85.0
February	57.9	53.9	64.6	49.1	71.6	39.9	66.1	70.0	53.6	58.1	86.1	85.2
March	58.1	54.1	64.9	49.0	72.1	40.1	65.5	70.8	53.8	58.2	86.1	85.3
April	57.5	53.3	63.7	46.6	71.8	39.3	63.9	69.6	53.5	57.8	85.0	83.8
May	57.9	53.9	64.1	47.9	71.5	40.4	65.1	70.0	53.7	58.1	85.5	84.6
June	57.9	54.0	63.8	47.4	71.5	40.6	65.7	70.3	53.4	58.2	85.3	84.5
July	57.8	54.0	63.3	46.7	71.0	41.0	66.9	70.3	53.5	58.0	84.9	84.4
August	57.4	53.3	62.6	44.7	71.2	40.4	67.7	69.5	53.7	57.6	84.1	83.1
September	57.5	53.5	63.0	46.3	70.8	41.6	68.4	69.7	53.0	57.3	84.1	83.1
October	57.8	53.7	63.1	46.0	71.2	41.1	70.4	70.2	53.6	57.8	84.4	83.2
November	57.8	53.5	62.9	45.2	71.4	41.2	72.0	70.0	53.8	57.7	84.1	82.8
December	57.8	53.7	62.9	44.9	71.6	41.4	73.7	70.3	53.8	57.6	84.0	82.8
1980												
January	58.0	53.9	62.6	44.1	71.7	42.0	74.7	70.1	53.4	58.1	84.2	83.0
February	58.1	53.9	62.9	43.9	72.3	42.3	77.9	69.1	53.5	58.0	84.1	82.8
March	57.9	53.5	62.5	43.1	72.1	42.0	78.6	68.2	53.4	57.9	83.7	82.0
April	56.8	52.4	61.5	41.3	71.7	41.6	79.2	65.0	52.5	56.5	81.9	80.1
May	55.3	50.8	60.2	38.6	71.2	40.9	79.4	62.4	51.4	54.8	79.7	77.5
June	54.6	50.0	59.9	38.1	71.2	40.3	80.1	61.1	50.8	53.9	78.5	76.1
July	54.3	49.5	60.0	38.0	71.3	40.4	80.8	60.7	51.0	53.0	77.8	75.1
August	54.5	49.9	60.2	38.3	71.5	40.4	81.0	61.5	51.3	53.2	77.9	75.5
September	55.3	50.7	60.8	40.2	71.2	41.1	81.2	63.1	52.0	54.2	79.0	76.5
October	56.1	51.6	61.2	40.9	71.5	41.9	82.5	64.4	52.1	55.0	79.8	77.7
November	57.0	52.6	61.6	41.9	71.3	42.6	83.5	65.8	52.7	56.3	81.0	78.9
December	57.3	52.7	61.5	41.3	71.6	42.7	83.6	65.8	53.2	56.9	81.3	78.9
1981												
January	57.0	52.6	61.5	41.1	71.8	42.9	83.0	65.6	53.4	56.2	80.7	78.4
February	56.7	52.3	61.3	40.9	71.6	42.4	82.6	64.9	52.8	56.0	80.1	77.8
March	57.1	52.5	61.3	41.5	71.2	42.9	82.8	65.1	52.8	56.3	80.3	77.8
April	56.7	52.6	61.5	42.0	71.2	42.9	83.0	65.2	53.1	55.5	79.7	77.9
May	57.1	52.9	62.2	42.7	71.8	43.0	83.9	65.1	53.8	55.9	80.0	78.1
June	57.4	52.7	61.7	42.4	71.3	42.8	84.7	64.1	54.0	56.6	80.2	77.6
July	57.8	52.8	62.1	42.6	71.8	43.0	86.0	64.2	54.3	57.0	80.6	77.5
August	57.8	52.9	62.2	42.3	72.1	43.1	87.2	64.1	54.0	57.0	80.4	77.5
September	57.4	52.6	61.6	41.3	71.7	43.0	89.0	63.7	54.0	56.6	79.7	76.9
October	57.0	52.1	61.9	41.1	72.5	42.9	91.0	61.7	53.6	55.8	79.0	76.0
November	56.4	51.5	61.9	40.3	72.8	42.4	93.3	60.8	53.4	54.8	77.9	74.9
December	55.8	50.7	61.3	38.6	73.0	41.7	95.9	59.7	53.3	54.1	76.9	73.5

Table 20-1. Industrial Production and Capacity Utilization—*Continued*

(Seasonally adjusted; 2002 = 100, except as noted.)

Year and month	Total industry	Manufac-turing (SIC)	Market groups								Capacity utilization (output as percentage of capacity)	
			Consumer goods			Business equipment	Defense and space equipment	Construction supplies	Business supplies	Materials	Total industry	Manufac-turing (SIC)
			Total	Durable	Nondurable							
1982												
January	54.7	49.5	60.3	37.6	72.1	40.0	95.5	57.8	52.6	53.2	75.2	71.6
February	55.8	50.8	61.9	39.0	73.7	41.4	100.7	59.7	53.6	53.8	76.5	73.4
March	55.4	50.4	61.5	38.8	73.1	40.8	102.1	58.5	53.4	53.4	75.8	72.7
April	54.9	50.1	61.4	39.6	72.6	40.4	103.0	58.1	53.2	52.7	75.0	72.0
May	54.5	50.0	61.5	39.6	72.7	40.1	104.5	58.4	52.8	52.1	74.4	71.7
June	54.3	49.8	61.8	39.9	73.0	39.3	104.4	57.8	52.8	51.9	73.9	71.4
July	54.1	49.8	61.9	40.1	73.0	39.1	105.8	57.7	52.8	51.5	73.6	71.2
August	53.6	49.3	61.8	39.6	73.2	38.2	105.5	57.7	52.8	51.0	72.8	70.5
September	53.4	49.2	61.7	39.0	73.4	37.9	106.7	57.8	52.9	50.7	72.5	70.1
October	53.0	48.7	61.8	38.5	74.0	37.2	106.1	57.0	52.7	50.2	71.8	69.3
November	52.8	48.4	61.7	38.5	73.7	37.1	106.6	56.7	52.7	49.9	71.5	68.8
December	52.4	48.2	60.9	38.4	72.4	37.7	105.5	56.2	52.4	49.5	70.9	68.6
1983												
January	53.4	49.4	62.2	40.1	73.4	37.7	4.8	58.3	53.1	50.6	72.2	70.2
February	53.1	49.3	61.4	40.0	72.3	37.5	103.0	58.0	53.0	50.5	71.8	70.1
March	53.6	49.8	61.7	40.6	72.4	37.9	103.3	58.8	53.9	50.9	72.3	70.7
April	54.2	50.4	62.9	41.4	73.8	37.9	102.6	59.6	54.5	51.5	73.2	71.5
May	54.6	51.0	63.2	42.3	73.7	38.3	102.6	60.7	54.5	52.0	73.7	72.4
June	54.9	51.4	63.4	43.0	73.6	38.5	102.1	61.8	54.8	52.3	74.1	72.8
July	55.7	52.1	64.3	44.0	74.4	39.2	103.6	63.1	55.5	53.2	75.2	73.9
August	56.4	52.6	64.9	44.8	74.8	39.6	104.4	63.3	56.1	53.9	76.0	74.4
September	57.2	53.5	65.7	45.6	75.6	40.7	105.6	64.1	57.1	54.6	77.1	75.8
October	57.7	54.2	65.3	46.2	74.7	41.3	106.8	65.1	57.3	55.4	77.7	76.6
November	57.9	54.3	65.3	46.1	74.7	41.5	107.5	64.9	57.5	55.7	77.9	76.8
December	58.1	54.5	65.4	47.2	74.2	41.9	108.4	65.0	57.6	55.9	78.2	76.9
1984												
January	59.3	55.5	66.7	48.3	75.6	42.9	11.7	65.5	58.7	57.0	79.7	78.2
February	59.6	56.1	66.6	48.5	75.2	43.3	114.2	67.1	58.9	57.4	80.0	79.0
March	59.9	56.4	66.9	48.6	75.6	43.7	114.6	66.6	59.4	57.6	80.2	79.2
April	60.3	56.6	67.0	48.5	75.9	44.1	117.3	67.0	59.4	58.0	80.6	79.5
May	60.6	56.8	66.8	48.1	75.8	44.3	118.2	67.2	60.2	58.4	80.8	79.5
June	60.8	57.0	66.7	48.2	75.6	44.9	119.4	67.7	60.6	58.6	81.0	79.7
July	60.9	57.3	66.7	48.7	75.3	45.6	118.1	67.5	60.7	58.7	81.0	79.9
August	61.0	57.4	66.3	49.1	74.5	45.9	121.9	67.7	60.8	58.7	80.9	79.8
September	60.9	57.3	66.2	48.4	74.6	46.4	124.7	68.0	60.8	58.4	80.6	79.4
October	60.8	57.5	66.7	48.0	75.7	46.7	125.5	67.7	61.1	57.9	80.3	79.5
November	61.1	57.7	66.9	48.8	75.6	47.0	124.7	67.6	61.3	58.1	80.4	79.5
December	61.1	57.9	67.3	49.3	75.8	47.3	127.1	68.3	60.9	58.0	80.3	79.6
1985												
January	60.9	57.7	66.8	48.6	75.5	47.1	27.5	67.0	61.0	58.0	79.9	79.0
February	61.2	57.5	67.3	48.2	76.5	46.8	128.9	67.2	61.6	58.2	80.0	78.6
March	61.3	58.0	67.2	48.7	76.1	47.3	130.9	69.0	61.5	58.1	79.9	79.0
April	61.2	57.8	66.9	48.1	75.9	46.8	131.3	69.0	61.8	58.1	79.6	78.5
May	61.2	57.8	66.9	48.1	75.9	46.9	132.2	69.2	62.0	58.1	79.5	78.3
June	61.3	57.9	67.2	48.1	76.4	47.0	134.2	69.7	61.7	58.0	79.3	78.3
July	60.9	57.6	66.9	48.1	76.0	46.7	133.1	69.3	61.2	57.6	78.7	77.7
August	61.1	57.9	67.2	48.6	76.1	46.7	135.4	69.5	61.8	57.7	78.8	77.9
September	61.4	58.0	67.6	48.5	76.8	46.6	136.4	69.5	62.3	58.0	79.0	77.8
October	61.1	57.8	67.5	48.3	76.8	46.5	137.9	69.6	61.7	57.6	78.5	77.5
November	61.3	58.2	67.9	49.5	76.7	46.9	139.7	69.6	61.9	57.7	78.7	77.8
December	62.0	58.4	68.6	49.6	77.8	46.9	141.0	69.3	62.9	58.5	79.4	78.0
1986												
January	62.3	59.1	69.4	50.9	78.2	46.9	142.1	70.9	63.2	58.6	79.6	78.8
February	61.8	58.7	68.8	50.6	77.4	46.4	139.8	70.1	62.7	58.4	79.0	78.3
March	61.4	58.6	68.5	50.6	77.1	46.4	141.0	70.4	62.4	57.7	78.4	78.0
April	61.5	58.8	68.9	50.5	77.7	46.1	141.2	71.1	62.9	57.6	78.3	78.2
May	61.6	58.9	69.3	50.6	78.2	46.0	141.7	71.5	63.4	57.6	78.4	78.2
June	61.4	58.7	69.4	51.1	78.1	45.5	142.2	70.7	64.0	57.3	78.1	77.9
July	61.7	59.0	69.9	51.8	78.4	45.8	143.3	71.2	63.9	57.7	78.4	78.2
August	61.6	59.2	69.8	52.0	78.2	45.9	143.2	71.9	64.0	57.5	78.2	78.3
September	61.8	59.3	69.8	52.4	78.1	45.9	142.7	71.9	64.2	57.6	78.3	78.4
October	62.0	59.5	70.1	52.4	78.5	45.9	143.3	71.9	64.6	58.0	78.6	78.6
November	62.3	59.8	70.6	53.1	78.9	46.0	144.0	72.1	64.7	58.3	78.8	78.8
December	62.9	60.3	71.3	54.1	79.4	46.5	144.0	72.6	65.5	58.7	79.4	79.4
1987												
January	62.7	60.2	70.6	53.8	78.4	46.6	144.7	73.4	65.1	58.6	79.0	79.0
February	63.5	61.1	71.5	54.6	79.3	47.7	145.2	74.7	65.6	59.3	79.9	79.9
March	63.6	61.1	71.7	54.4	79.8	47.5	144.9	74.3	66.0	59.5	79.9	79.8
April	64.0	61.4	71.6	54.0	79.9	47.9	145.2	74.7	66.7	59.9	80.2	80.0
May	64.4	61.9	72.1	54.4	80.5	48.3	144.8	75.3	67.5	60.3	80.6	80.4
June	64.7	62.1	72.2	53.8	81.0	48.7	144.3	75.5	67.8	60.6	80.8	80.5
July	65.1	62.5	72.7	53.7	81.7	48.9	144.0	75.7	68.2	61.1	81.2	80.8
August	65.6	62.8	73.1	54.2	82.1	49.5	145.6	76.3	68.4	61.5	81.6	81.1
September	65.8	63.2	72.8	54.7	81.3	50.4	146.1	76.6	68.6	61.8	81.7	81.4
October	66.8	64.2	74.1	56.5	82.3	51.5	145.7	77.7	69.1	62.6	82.8	82.5
November	67.1	64.6	74.1	56.5	82.4	52.0	146.5	77.8	69.1	63.2	83.1	82.9
December	67.4	65.0	74.3	56.0	82.8	52.5	147.7	78.4	69.3	63.5	83.4	83.3

Table 20-1. Industrial Production and Capacity Utilization—Continued

(Seasonally adjusted; 2002 = 100, except as noted.)

Year and month	Total industry	Manufac-turing (SIC)	Consumer goods Total	Consumer goods Durable	Consumer goods Nondurable	Business equipment	Defense and space equipment	Construction supplies	Business supplies	Materials	Capacity utilization Total industry	Capacity utilization Manufac-turing (SIC)
1988												
January	67.5	64.9	74.6	55.8	83.5	52.5	151.1	77.2	69.6	63.3	83.4	83.0
February	67.7	65.0	75.0	55.8	84.1	52.8	148.6	77.7	70.1	63.5	83.6	83.1
March	67.9	65.2	75.0	56.3	83.7	53.3	147.6	78.1	70.0	63.8	83.8	83.3
April	68.3	65.8	75.4	57.6	83.7	53.9	146.2	77.8	70.1	64.1	84.2	84.0
May	68.2	65.7	75.2	57.7	83.3	54.3	146.1	78.0	69.5	64.2	84.1	83.8
June	68.4	65.8	75.2	57.9	83.2	54.8	144.9	77.5	69.8	64.4	84.2	83.9
July	68.5	65.9	75.1	56.5	83.9	54.5	146.3	77.6	70.1	64.6	84.3	84.0
August	68.8	65.9	75.7	57.1	84.5	54.7	146.1	77.1	70.7	64.9	84.7	84.0
September	68.6	66.2	75.2	58.3	83.0	55.2	146.2	77.4	70.2	64.6	84.3	84.2
October	69.0	66.5	75.9	58.8	83.7	55.4	146.5	77.7	70.5	64.9	84.7	84.6
November	69.1	66.7	75.9	59.5	83.5	55.6	146.3	78.1	70.5	65.1	84.8	84.7
December	69.4	67.0	76.3	60.2	83.6	55.7	146.7	78.2	70.7	65.4	85.0	84.9
1989												
January	69.6	67.5	76.3	61.6	82.9	56.3	147.1	79.5	70.7	65.5	85.1	85.4
February	69.3	66.8	76.3	60.9	83.3	56.1	147.4	77.6	71.0	65.0	84.6	84.5
March	69.4	66.8	76.5	60.0	84.1	55.9	146.1	77.7	71.7	65.3	84.7	84.3
April	69.4	66.8	76.3	60.4	83.6	56.5	148.2	77.7	71.2	65.2	84.6	84.2
May	68.9	66.3	75.6	59.1	83.1	55.4	148.9	77.0	70.8	65.0	83.8	83.3
June	69.0	66.4	75.6	58.3	83.6	56.2	148.6	77.2	71.1	64.7	83.7	83.3
July	68.3	65.7	74.0	56.5	82.2	55.8	149.2	77.2	70.5	64.4	82.8	82.2
August	69.0	66.3	75.2	58.6	82.9	56.8	150.2	77.2	70.9	64.7	83.3	82.7
September	68.8	66.1	74.9	58.5	82.5	56.8	149.1	77.0	71.1	64.5	83.0	82.3
October	68.7	66.0	75.1	57.5	83.4	55.9	143.9	77.3	71.1	64.6	82.7	82.0
November	68.9	66.1	75.4	57.9	83.6	56.3	141.8	77.3	71.5	64.8	82.8	82.0
December	69.4	66.2	76.7	58.5	85.2	57.2	145.0	76.4	71.9	64.7	83.1	81.9
1990												
January	69.0	66.1	75.0	55.2	84.4	57.2	145.4	78.1	72.4	64.5	82.5	81.6
February	69.6	67.1	75.9	58.8	83.9	57.9	145.4	78.5	72.3	65.2	83.1	82.6
March	70.0	67.4	76.5	59.9	84.2	58.6	144.3	78.3	72.8	65.3	83.3	82.8
April	69.9	67.2	76.2	58.6	84.4	58.5	143.5	77.5	72.8	65.4	83.0	82.4
May	70.0	67.3	76.1	59.0	84.1	58.9	142.2	77.0	73.1	65.5	83.0	82.3
June	70.2	67.4	76.9	59.8	84.8	58.9	141.6	77.3	73.0	65.6	83.1	82.3
July	70.1	67.3	76.3	58.2	84.8	59.0	142.6	76.6	73.2	65.6	82.8	82.0
August	70.2	67.5	76.4	57.9	85.0	59.1	140.7	76.6	73.1	66.0	82.9	82.0
September	70.4	67.5	77.2	58.3	86.0	59.1	139.8	76.3	73.2	65.9	82.9	81.8
October	69.9	66.9	76.0	56.4	85.2	58.9	140.6	75.4	73.1	65.6	82.2	81.0
November	69.0	66.2	75.1	53.3	85.5	57.6	138.2	75.4	72.7	64.8	81.0	80.0
December	68.6	65.7	74.6	52.5	85.2	57.1	139.7	74.9	72.3	64.3	80.3	79.2
1991												
January	68.2	65.1	75.0	52.6	85.6	56.8	137.9	72.1	72.0	63.8	79.9	78.5
February	67.8	64.8	74.3	51.4	85.2	56.6	136.9	71.9	71.4	63.5	79.2	77.9
March	67.5	64.3	74.4	51.6	85.2	56.7	135.9	71.0	70.5	63.0	78.7	77.2
April	67.6	64.5	74.3	52.7	84.6	56.7	132.4	71.5	71.0	63.3	78.8	77.4
May	68.3	65.0	75.6	53.7	86.1	57.1	129.6	71.6	71.6	63.8	79.5	77.8
June	68.9	65.7	76.7	55.1	87.0	57.8	130.4	72.9	72.2	64.3	80.1	78.5
July	68.9	65.9	76.3	56.0	85.9	57.7	129.1	72.6	71.6	64.8	80.0	78.6
August	69.0	66.0	76.3	55.2	86.3	57.6	129.9	73.4	72.1	64.8	80.0	78.7
September	69.6	66.7	77.5	57.5	86.9	58.4	129.3	73.8	72.5	65.1	80.6	79.4
October	69.5	66.6	77.2	57.2	86.6	57.9	129.8	73.0	72.2	65.2	80.4	79.2
November	69.4	66.4	77.3	57.3	86.7	57.9	128.7	73.6	72.4	65.0	80.2	78.9
December	69.1	66.4	76.3	56.9	85.5	57.9	127.9	73.7	72.3	65.0	79.8	78.7
1992												
January	68.7	65.9	75.5	54.4	85.6	56.7	126.2	73.9	72.2	65.0	79.1	78.0
February	69.2	66.6	76.3	56.7	85.6	58.1	125.4	74.4	72.2	65.3	79.6	78.6
March	69.8	67.2	77.1	58.0	86.0	58.5	124.9	74.8	72.7	65.8	80.1	79.2
April	70.3	67.5	77.8	59.1	86.5	59.1	122.8	75.4	73.2	66.2	80.5	79.4
May	70.6	68.0	78.3	61.0	86.3	59.7	122.0	76.1	73.4	66.3	80.6	79.7
June	70.6	68.2	77.9	60.2	86.1	59.9	121.9	75.7	73.4	66.6	80.5	79.8
July	71.2	68.7	78.9	61.9	86.8	60.3	120.5	76.1	73.8	67.0	81.0	80.2
August	70.8	68.4	79.0	61.3	87.2	60.0	120.4	76.4	73.7	66.3	80.4	79.7
September	71.0	68.5	78.6	61.0	86.7	60.3	120.3	76.2	73.9	66.8	80.5	79.6
October	71.5	68.9	79.6	62.2	87.7	60.7	119.9	76.4	74.2	67.1	80.9	79.9
November	71.8	69.2	79.8	62.7	87.7	61.1	119.7	76.2	74.4	67.5	81.1	80.0
December	71.8	69.0	79.9	63.4	87.5	61.3	119.7	76.4	74.7	67.3	80.9	79.7
1993												
January	72.2	69.8	80.2	64.4	87.5	62.0	119.0	76.8	74.8	67.7	81.2	80.4
February	72.4	69.9	80.3	64.1	87.8	61.6	118.0	77.9	75.2	68.1	81.4	80.3
March	72.4	69.8	80.4	64.6	87.7	61.9	116.7	77.3	75.8	68.0	81.3	80.1
April	72.6	70.1	80.5	64.9	87.7	62.4	116.9	77.7	75.8	68.2	81.4	80.4
May	72.3	70.0	79.9	65.0	86.7	62.1	115.6	78.6	75.5	68.0	81.0	80.2
June	72.5	69.9	80.1	64.4	87.2	61.7	114.8	78.5	75.5	68.4	81.1	80.0
July	72.8	70.2	80.8	64.4	88.4	61.8	115.8	79.0	75.7	68.4	81.3	80.1
August	72.8	70.1	80.8	63.7	88.6	61.4	113.9	79.3	75.8	68.5	81.2	79.9
September	73.1	70.5	81.0	65.1	88.3	62.2	114.2	79.7	76.1	68.8	81.4	80.3
October	73.6	71.1	81.4	66.8	88.1	63.3	113.5	80.4	76.2	69.4	81.9	80.8
November	73.9	71.4	81.5	67.4	87.9	63.6	113.2	81.1	76.3	69.8	82.1	81.0
December	74.3	71.8	81.7	67.8	88.1	63.9	111.9	82.0	76.7	70.3	82.3	81.2

Table 20-1. Industrial Production and Capacity Utilization—*Continued*

(Seasonally adjusted; 2002 = 100, except as noted.)

Year and month	Total industry	Manufac-turing (SIC)	Market groups								Capacity utilization (output as percentage of capacity)	
			Consumer goods			Business equipment	Defense and space equipment	Construction supplies	Business supplies	Materials	Total industry	Manufac-turing (SIC)
			Total	Durable	Nondurable							
1994												
January	74.6	71.9	82.4	69.0	88.5	64.3	110.9	81.7	77.3	70.4	82.5	81.2
February	74.6	72.0	82.6	68.9	88.8	63.6	109.1	81.1	77.3	70.7	82.3	81.1
March	75.4	73.0	83.2	69.7	89.4	64.4	110.4	82.6	77.9	71.5	83.0	82.0
April	75.8	73.6	83.3	70.4	89.2	64.8	110.6	83.9	78.1	71.9	83.2	82.4
May	76.2	74.1	83.9	70.8	89.9	65.0	109.0	84.5	78.3	72.5	83.4	82.7
June	76.7	74.3	84.6	71.5	90.6	65.5	107.6	84.6	79.0	72.9	83.7	82.7
July	76.9	74.6	84.3	71.6	90.0	66.2	107.0	85.5	78.8	73.3	83.6	82.7
August	77.3	75.1	85.2	73.0	90.7	66.2	105.8	85.4	78.8	73.7	83.7	83.0
September	77.4	75.4	84.7	73.1	89.9	66.7	106.7	86.2	79.2	74.0	83.6	83.0
October	78.1	76.1	85.5	73.9	90.8	67.7	106.7	86.6	79.8	74.5	84.1	83.5
November	78.6	76.7	85.5	73.7	90.8	68.4	108.0	86.7	80.1	75.3	84.3	83.8
December	79.4	77.6	86.2	74.6	91.4	69.0	108.1	87.6	80.6	76.3	84.9	84.5
1995												
January	79.7	77.8	86.2	75.3	91.2	69.7	108.2	87.6	80.9	76.6	84.9	84.4
February	79.7	77.8	86.5	75.1	91.6	69.9	107.0	86.6	81.0	76.5	84.6	84.0
March	79.8	77.9	86.5	75.1	91.6	70.3	107.1	86.5	81.2	76.6	84.4	83.9
April	79.7	77.8	86.1	74.8	91.2	70.4	106.6	86.0	81.2	76.7	84.1	83.5
May	79.9	77.9	86.3	74.1	91.9	70.6	106.3	85.4	81.6	76.9	84.0	83.2
June	80.1	78.2	86.8	74.6	92.3	71.2	106.7	85.6	81.8	76.9	83.9	83.2
July	79.9	77.7	86.3	73.0	92.3	71.2	105.6	85.5	81.8	76.6	83.3	82.4
August	80.9	78.7	87.7	75.5	93.2	72.8	105.5	86.2	82.8	77.5	84.2	83.0
September	81.3	79.4	87.7	76.3	92.9	73.7	104.4	87.6	82.8	77.8	84.2	83.4
October	81.1	79.3	87.0	75.4	92.3	73.3	103.1	87.4	83.0	78.0	83.7	82.9
November	81.3	79.3	87.3	75.5	92.7	73.4	100.7	87.5	83.3	78.2	83.6	82.5
December	81.7	79.7	87.6	76.1	92.8	74.4	100.7	88.0	83.3	78.5	83.6	82.5
1996												
January	81.1	79.0	86.5	74.0	92.2	73.8	99.1	86.3	82.9	78.4	82.6	81.4
February	82.4	80.3	88.1	76.3	93.4	75.7	102.3	87.6	83.9	79.5	83.6	82.3
March	82.3	80.2	87.4	73.7	93.7	75.6	102.4	88.6	84.0	79.5	83.1	81.7
April	83.0	81.0	88.4	77.5	93.2	76.5	102.1	89.1	83.9	80.1	83.4	82.1
May	83.5	81.5	88.5	77.9	93.2	77.3	102.2	90.0	84.7	80.7	83.5	82.2
June	84.2	82.4	89.3	79.8	93.6	78.3	101.7	91.5	85.0	81.4	83.9	82.6
July	84.2	82.6	88.7	80.3	92.4	79.2	102.3	91.0	85.0	81.4	83.4	82.4
August	84.7	83.1	88.5	79.5	92.5	80.0	102.6	91.9	85.8	82.1	83.5	82.5
September	85.1	83.7	89.3	79.6	93.6	80.6	103.0	92.2	86.3	82.4	83.6	82.6
October	85.2	83.6	88.8	78.1	93.6	80.5	102.6	92.4	86.5	82.7	83.2	82.1
November	85.9	84.3	89.9	79.2	94.6	81.7	102.1	93.1	87.2	83.1	83.5	82.3
December	86.4	85.0	90.1	80.4	94.4	83.3	102.2	92.7	87.7	83.7	83.7	82.5
1997												
January	86.5	85.1	89.8	80.0	94.2	83.5	100.6	91.8	88.2	84.0	83.3	82.1
February	87.6	86.3	90.3	81.2	94.3	85.2	101.0	93.5	89.1	85.2	83.9	82.8
March	88.3	87.3	91.0	82.3	94.9	86.8	100.5	94.5	89.4	85.7	84.2	83.3
April	88.3	87.1	90.0	79.8	94.5	87.3	100.6	94.2	89.8	86.2	83.8	82.6
May	88.9	87.9	90.6	80.8	94.9	88.5	100.2	94.8	90.3	86.6	83.9	82.9
June	89.3	88.5	90.7	82.6	94.2	89.9	100.2	94.6	90.7	87.1	83.8	82.9
July	89.8	88.8	90.8	80.8	95.3	90.1	100.3	94.7	91.3	87.8	83.8	82.7
August	91.0	90.4	92.3	84.7	95.7	92.7	100.6	95.3	91.6	88.9	84.4	83.5
September	91.9	91.2	93.2	85.9	96.3	93.2	100.7	95.8	92.7	89.8	84.7	83.7
October	92.5	91.7	94.4	86.2	98.0	94.2	101.1	96.3	93.6	89.9	84.7	83.6
November	93.3	92.7	94.7	88.5	97.4	96.0	100.6	96.7	94.0	91.0	85.0	83.9
December	93.7	93.2	94.3	88.3	96.9	96.6	102.4	97.9	94.4	91.6	84.7	83.7
1998												
January	94.1	93.9	94.7	88.7	97.3	97.9	103.1	98.6	94.3	92.0	84.6	83.8
February	94.2	93.9	94.5	88.4	97.1	98.0	103.8	99.0	94.5	92.0	84.1	83.2
March	94.2	93.8	94.7	88.8	97.2	98.2	103.2	98.4	95.1	91.9	83.6	82.5
April	94.6	94.4	95.3	89.2	97.9	98.5	103.3	98.8	95.4	92.3	83.5	82.4
May	95.3	94.9	95.7	89.7	98.2	100.0	104.3	100.0	96.2	92.9	83.6	82.3
June	94.8	94.3	94.5	85.2	98.5	100.4	104.5	99.7	96.3	92.3	82.6	81.2
July	94.4	93.8	93.4	81.3	98.7	99.6	105.8	100.2	96.9	92.0	81.8	80.3
August	96.3	96.1	96.6	92.1	98.6	102.2	106.4	100.6	97.6	93.6	83.1	81.8
September	96.1	95.8	95.7	91.5	97.6	102.0	105.4	100.2	97.5	93.7	82.4	81.0
October	96.7	96.6	96.2	93.4	97.4	103.1	107.6	101.4	97.8	94.3	82.6	81.3
November	96.6	96.8	95.5	93.0	96.7	103.1	107.2	101.5	98.1	94.5	82.1	81.0
December	97.0	97.3	95.4	93.6	96.2	103.5	106.3	102.7	98.1	95.2	82.0	81.0
1999												
January	97.5	97.7	96.5	93.8	97.7	103.8	106.1	102.2	98.8	95.5	82.1	80.9
February	97.9	98.4	96.7	94.3	97.7	104.6	106.9	102.1	99.0	96.0	82.1	81.1
March	98.1	98.3	96.5	93.9	97.7	104.4	106.2	101.2	99.4	96.7	81.9	80.6
April	98.3	98.6	96.4	94.9	97.0	104.8	105.3	101.5	99.6	97.1	81.7	80.5
May	99.0	99.5	97.4	95.8	98.0	106.1	103.9	101.8	100.2	97.7	82.0	80.9
June	98.8	99.2	96.4	95.2	96.9	105.7	102.7	101.8	100.1	98.1	81.5	80.3
July	99.5	99.6	95.9	95.1	96.2	106.9	102.4	102.6	100.9	99.4	81.8	80.3
August	100.0	100.4	97.3	97.5	97.2	107.4	102.3	102.5	101.0	99.5	81.9	80.5
September	99.7	100.1	96.6	96.2	96.7	107.1	99.3	102.6	101.0	99.3	81.3	79.9
October	101.0	101.7	98.4	99.1	98.1	108.2	99.1	103.9	102.0	100.6	82.1	80.8
November	101.6	102.4	98.3	98.4	98.3	108.3	97.0	104.5	102.6	101.8	82.2	81.0
December	102.4	103.1	99.3	98.4	99.7	109.4	95.2	105.5	103.3	102.5	82.6	81.3

Table 20-1. Industrial Production and Capacity Utilization—*Continued*

(Seasonally adjusted; 2002 = 100, except as noted.)

Year and month	Total industry	Manufac-turing (SIC)	Consumer goods Total	Consumer goods Durable	Consumer goods Nondurable	Business equipment	Defense and space equipment	Construction supplies	Business supplies	Materials	Capacity utilization Total industry	Capacity utilization Manufac-turing (SIC)
2000												
January	102.4	103.3	98.2	100.5	97.3	110.3	95.3	106.0	103.8	103.0	82.3	81.0
February	102.9	103.6	98.8	100.2	98.3	111.3	93.0	106.3	104.0	103.3	82.4	80.9
March	103.3	104.3	98.5	99.9	98.0	112.7	92.1	106.4	104.7	103.9	82.4	81.1
April	103.9	104.9	99.4	101.2	98.8	114.0	90.4	106.7	105.8	104.3	82.6	81.3
May	104.1	104.8	99.6	100.9	99.1	114.7	89.5	105.1	106.0	104.6	82.5	80.8
June	104.3	105.0	99.7	100.6	99.4	114.9	90.3	104.7	105.8	104.8	82.3	80.7
July	104.0	105.0	98.9	97.9	99.4	116.1	92.0	105.3	105.9	104.3	81.8	80.3
August	103.8	104.5	98.8	98.8	98.9	115.7	90.0	104.6	105.7	104.1	81.4	79.6
September	104.3	104.9	99.9	99.8	100.0	116.9	85.9	104.7	105.5	104.4	81.5	79.6
October	103.9	104.5	98.8	98.1	99.1	117.1	90.2	104.3	105.2	104.1	80.9	79.0
November	103.9	104.2	99.2	96.1	100.4	116.8	93.1	104.0	105.4	103.8	80.7	78.5
December	103.5	103.5	99.6	94.5	101.6	115.8	93.8	102.5	105.1	103.1	80.1	77.7
2001												
January	102.7	102.8	98.8	93.0	101.1	115.5	96.7	102.7	104.7	101.8	79.3	76.9
February	102.1	102.2	98.2	92.8	100.2	114.9	96.6	101.7	103.4	101.5	78.6	76.2
March	101.8	101.9	98.1	95.2	99.3	114.1	99.0	101.9	102.7	101.0	78.1	75.7
April	101.5	101.6	98.6	95.2	99.8	111.8	100.0	101.5	102.1	100.7	77.7	75.3
May	100.8	100.8	98.4	96.1	99.4	109.7	100.0	101.0	101.3	99.8	76.9	74.5
June	100.1	100.1	98.3	95.4	99.4	108.6	101.2	100.3	100.7	98.9	76.2	73.8
July	99.7	99.8	98.0	96.2	98.7	107.6	102.3	100.3	100.6	98.3	75.7	73.4
August	99.3	99.1	97.9	94.8	99.1	105.5	101.0	99.1	100.2	98.3	75.2	72.7
September	99.0	98.8	97.4	94.0	98.7	104.1	101.7	99.1	100.1	98.2	74.7	72.3
October	98.4	98.1	97.6	92.7	99.5	102.2	101.3	97.9	99.3	97.6	74.1	71.7
November	97.9	97.9	97.7	94.6	98.9	101.4	100.4	97.8	98.4	96.9	73.6	71.4
December	97.9	98.1	98.1	96.6	98.8	100.6	100.1	98.6	98.5	96.6	73.5	71.5
2002												
January	98.4	98.5	99.2	96.8	100.2	100.3	99.1	98.3	98.2	97.3	73.7	71.7
February	98.4	98.5	98.7	97.1	99.3	100.3	98.6	98.9	98.1	97.8	73.6	71.7
March	99.2	99.2	99.6	97.8	100.3	100.8	98.4	100.2	99.1	98.5	74.1	72.1
April	99.5	99.2	99.4	99.2	99.5	99.5	98.1	100.1	99.6	99.5	74.2	72.1
May	100.0	99.9	99.7	99.5	99.7	100.1	98.3	100.6	100.1	100.1	74.5	72.5
June	100.9	100.9	100.8	100.8	100.9	100.8	99.2	101.3	100.5	101.0	75.2	73.3
July	100.6	100.5	100.5	101.1	100.2	100.0	99.1	99.7	100.5	101.0	74.9	73.0
August	100.6	100.8	100.2	101.2	99.8	100.4	99.5	100.2	100.5	101.2	75.0	73.2
September	100.7	100.9	100.6	101.2	100.3	100.0	101.2	100.7	100.8	101.0	75.0	73.3
October	100.4	100.4	100.2	100.4	100.1	99.5	102.0	100.3	101.2	100.6	74.9	72.9
November	100.9	100.8	101.1	103.2	100.2	99.6	101.1	100.3	100.8	101.1	75.2	73.2
December	100.4	100.3	100.0	101.5	99.4	98.7	105.4	99.5	100.5	100.9	74.9	72.9
2003												
January	101.1	100.9	100.9	103.6	99.8	98.7	105.8	99.8	102.3	101.5	75.5	73.3
February	101.4	101.1	101.8	102.0	101.7	99.2	106.9	99.3	102.1	101.6	75.8	73.5
March	101.3	101.3	101.8	102.1	101.7	99.7	106.8	99.1	102.4	101.1	75.7	73.7
April	100.5	100.4	100.8	101.1	100.6	98.6	106.4	97.9	100.9	100.6	75.1	73.0
May	100.5	100.5	100.5	100.9	100.4	98.7	107.2	99.2	101.4	100.5	75.2	73.1
June	100.6	101.0	100.7	101.9	100.2	99.2	107.3	99.6	100.9	100.6	75.3	73.5
July	101.0	101.1	101.5	103.9	100.5	99.2	106.8	99.2	101.6	100.8	75.6	73.6
August	100.9	100.8	101.1	102.6	100.4	100.0	107.0	99.9	101.4	100.7	75.6	73.4
September	101.5	101.6	102.0	106.1	100.4	100.8	107.6	99.6	101.3	101.4	76.0	74.0
October	101.6	101.7	101.4	104.7	100.0	100.6	107.5	100.2	101.6	101.9	76.1	74.1
November	102.5	102.8	102.2	106.0	100.7	102.5	106.5	101.5	102.6	102.6	76.8	74.9
December	102.4	102.5	102.3	105.9	100.8	102.0	104.0	101.2	102.2	102.7	76.7	74.8
2004												
January	102.7	102.6	102.8	107.4	101.0	102.8	101.4	101.2	102.6	102.9	77.0	74.8
February	103.3	103.3	103.2	106.9	101.8	104.0	102.6	101.1	103.5	103.3	77.4	75.4
March	102.7	103.0	101.9	105.5	100.6	103.6	103.0	101.1	102.5	103.1	76.9	75.2
April	103.1	103.5	102.5	105.5	101.4	103.8	103.3	101.1	103.3	103.6	77.3	75.6
May	103.9	104.2	103.1	104.8	102.4	104.6	103.8	102.1	104.1	104.4	77.9	76.1
June	103.0	103.4	101.5	102.5	101.1	104.5	102.8	101.4	103.4	103.7	77.2	75.5
July	103.7	104.3	101.6	102.8	101.0	106.5	104.5	102.6	104.0	104.5	77.7	76.2
August	103.9	104.9	102.4	104.5	101.6	106.0	105.0	102.7	104.0	104.6	77.9	76.6
September	103.9	104.7	102.2	103.3	101.7	106.2	106.7	101.6	103.7	104.7	77.9	76.5
October	104.8	105.8	103.3	105.7	102.4	107.1	106.7	103.2	104.4	105.6	78.7	77.2
November	105.1	105.7	103.2	104.4	102.8	106.7	107.6	103.0	104.8	106.2	78.8	77.2
December	105.8	106.4	104.0	105.1	103.5	107.6	109.0	102.6	105.9	106.9	79.4	77.6
2005												
January	106.3	107.2	104.5	104.5	104.4	109.2	109.5	103.7	106.6	106.9	79.7	78.1
February	107.0	108.0	105.1	107.4	104.2	110.4	113.2	104.7	106.4	107.7	80.2	78.7
March	106.9	107.6	104.5	104.8	104.3	110.2	115.4	103.9	106.6	107.8	80.1	78.3
April	106.8	107.7	104.2	103.8	104.2	110.9	117.5	105.6	106.9	107.5	80.0	78.3
May	107.1	108.2	105.0	104.1	105.2	111.9	117.0	105.8	107.0	107.4	80.2	78.5
June	107.5	108.4	105.8	104.6	106.1	112.2	117.7	104.7	107.5	107.6	80.4	78.6
July	107.5	108.3	105.5	103.4	106.0	112.7	116.9	105.7	107.1	107.6	80.3	78.4
August	107.7	108.7	105.7	105.4	105.7	113.2	118.8	106.0	107.3	107.6	80.4	78.6
September	105.8	107.6	106.0	107.5	105.4	109.9	114.4	107.6	107.3	103.8	78.9	77.7
October	107.0	109.3	106.0	108.1	105.2	115.8	115.9	110.0	107.8	104.8	79.7	78.8
November	108.2	110.2	105.8	106.4	105.5	117.6	116.5	110.6	108.1	107.1	80.5	79.4
December	108.9	110.3	106.5	104.5	107.0	117.5	116.8	110.8	108.6	108.1	80.9	79.4

Table 20-1. Industrial Production and Capacity Utilization—*Continued*

(Seasonally adjusted; 2002 = 100, except as noted.)

Year and month	Total industry	Manufac-turing (SIC)	Consumer goods Total	Consumer goods Durable	Consumer goods Nondurable	Business equipment	Defense and space equipment	Construction supplies	Business supplies	Materials	Capacity utilization Total industry	Capacity utilization Manufac-turing (SIC)
2006												
January	108.9	111.1	105.3	106.2	104.9	119.0	115.1	111.5	108.4	108.8	80.9	79.8
February	108.9	110.8	105.1	105.5	104.9	119.3	115.2	111.0	108.1	108.9	80.8	79.5
March	109.1	110.6	105.9	105.8	105.8	119.9	112.6	110.8	108.4	108.7	80.8	79.3
April	109.5	111.2	105.7	105.4	105.7	122.1	112.9	110.3	108.7	109.2	81.0	79.6
May	109.4	110.9	105.6	104.7	105.7	122.0	112.0	109.4	108.5	109.3	80.8	79.3
June	109.9	111.3	106.1	105.2	106.2	123.1	112.0	108.9	108.7	109.8	81.1	79.5
July	110.1	111.3	105.4	102.4	106.2	125.2	113.4	109.5	108.9	110.2	81.1	79.5
August	110.3	111.7	106.2	104.4	106.7	125.4	112.4	108.5	108.7	110.3	81.2	79.6
September	110.0	111.5	105.9	103.6	106.5	125.2	112.7	107.9	108.1	110.0	80.8	79.4
October	109.8	110.9	106.0	101.8	107.2	125.2	113.4	106.8	108.6	109.5	80.6	78.9
November	109.6	110.8	106.1	102.6	107.1	125.1	113.9	105.8	108.2	109.1	80.3	78.7
December	110.5	112.1	106.5	104.6	107.0	126.8	115.1	107.8	108.9	110.1	80.9	79.5
2007												
January	109.9	111.4	106.1	102.3	107.3	124.4	116.6	106.1	109.2	109.6	80.3	78.8
February	110.8	111.7	107.7	103.9	108.8	124.4	115.8	106.2	110.1	110.4	80.8	78.9
March	110.6	112.2	106.7	104.0	107.4	124.9	112.8	107.5	109.8	110.6	80.6	79.1
April	111.1	112.5	107.1	105.7	107.4	124.8	114.4	107.6	110.1	111.2	80.7	79.2
May	111.1	112.5	106.9	105.4	107.3	124.9	115.9	107.7	109.8	111.5	80.7	79.1
June	111.2	112.9	106.9	106.3	107.0	125.7	117.4	108.1	109.7	111.3	80.6	79.1
July	111.5	113.5	107.1	106.8	107.1	127.3	118.1	108.0	109.5	111.7	80.7	79.4
August	111.6	113.0	107.0	105.5	107.4	126.8	118.5	107.1	109.9	112.1	80.6	78.9
September	112.0	113.4	107.2	104.5	108.0	128.5	120.1	107.0	110.3	112.4	80.7	79.1
October	111.4	112.9	106.1	104.0	106.7	128.1	119.4	106.0	109.8	112.2	80.2	78.6
November	112.1	113.3	106.3	104.2	106.9	128.3	121.1	105.7	110.1	113.3	80.5	78.7
December	112.4	113.7	106.6	104.2	107.3	129.4	121.4	105.6	110.1	113.7	80.6	78.8
2008												
January	112.3	113.4	106.9	102.7	108.2	130.2	122.3	105.0	110.2	113.2	80.5	78.5
February	112.0	112.8	106.7	101.6	108.2	129.8	120.5	104.0	109.9	113.1	80.2	78.0
March	111.6	112.7	105.6	98.7	107.6	130.8	120.7	103.3	109.4	112.9	79.8	77.8
April	111.0	111.7	105.0	96.0	107.7	128.4	120.8	102.1	109.1	112.4	79.2	77.0
May	110.7	111.5	104.7	96.0	107.3	128.4	120.2	102.2	108.3	112.1	78.9	76.7
June	110.4	111.0	104.8	97.1	107.1	128.2	121.9	101.7	107.6	111.7	78.7	76.3
July	110.4	110.8	104.5	97.8	106.6	127.4	120.2	102.4	107.3	111.9	78.6	76.1
August	109.2	109.7	102.7	92.2	105.9	126.2	120.8	101.2	106.6	110.9	77.6	75.3
September	104.8	105.7	101.4	91.5	104.3	117.7	118.9	99.1	104.3	104.3	74.5	72.5
October	106.2	106.0	103.0	89.5	107.0	114.8	120.4	97.8	104.3	106.9	75.4	72.7
November	104.8	103.6	102.0	86.4	106.7	117.6	120.0	93.6	102.8	104.7	74.4	71.1
December	102.4	100.6	100.6	82.6	106.0	120.8	119.9	89.1	100.1	101.0	72.7	69.0
2009												
January	100.1	97.8	98.6	74.6	105.9	115.7	120.5	85.8	98.9	99.0	71.1	67.1
February	99.3	97.7	98.7	76.1	105.5	113.6	118.4	84.6	97.3	98.5	70.6	67.1
March	97.7	96.1	98.3	76.1	105.0	110.6	119.2	82.7	95.6	96.5	69.5	66.0
April	97.2	95.7	97.9	76.2	104.4	108.5	119.0	82.0	95.5	96.2	69.2	65.8
May	96.2	94.8	96.9	74.1	103.8	106.2	119.7	82.1	94.5	95.2	68.5	65.3
June	95.8	94.4	96.3	72.7	103.5	105.8	119.8	82.1	94.6	94.7	68.3	65.1
July	96.9	95.9	97.3	78.8	102.8	107.3	122.0	82.5	94.7	96.4	69.2	66.2
August	98.1	97.1	98.5	80.4	103.8	108.8	123.1	82.9	94.9	97.9	70.1	67.1
September	98.7	97.7	99.4	83.0	104.3	108.8	124.8	81.7	95.1	98.5	70.6	67.6
October	98.9	97.6	100.3	82.1	105.7	109.6	123.6	80.2	95.3	98.3	70.8	67.6
November	99.6	98.6	100.3	83.6	105.2	109.3	122.6	81.4	95.5	99.8	71.4	68.4
December	100.3	98.5	100.9	83.0	106.2	110.6	121.4	79.6	97.3	100.4	72.0	68.4

Table 20-2. Summary Consumer and Producer Price Indexes

(Seasonally adjusted.)

Year and month	Consumer Price Index, all urban consumers, 1982–1984 = 100							Producer Price Index, 1982 = 100					
								Finished goods		Intermediate materials, supplies, and components		Crude materials for further processing	
	All items	All items less food and energy	Food	Energy	Apparel	Transportation	Medical care	Total	Less food and energy	Total	Less food and energy	Total	Crude nonfood less energy
1946	19.5	...	19.8	...	34.4	16.7	12.5	...	...	...	...	...	...
1947	22.3	...	24.1	...	39.9	18.5	13.5	26.4	...	23.3	...	31.7	...
1948	24.1	...	26.1	...	42.5	20.6	14.4	28.5	...	25.2	...	34.7	...
1949	23.8	...	25.0	...	40.8	22.1	14.8	27.7	...	24.2	...	30.1	...
1950	24.1	...	25.4	...	40.3	22.7	15.1	28.2	...	25.3	...	32.7	...
1951	26.0	...	28.2	...	43.9	24.1	15.9	30.8	...	28.4	...	37.6	...
1952	26.5	...	28.7	...	43.5	25.7	16.7	30.6	...	27.5	...	34.5	...
1953	26.7	...	28.3	...	43.1	26.5	17.3	30.3	...	27.7	...	31.9	...
1954	26.9	...	28.2	...	43.1	26.1	17.8	30.4	...	27.9	...	31.6	...
1955	26.8	...	27.8	...	42.9	25.8	18.2	30.5	...	28.4	...	30.4	...
1956	27.2	...	28.0	...	43.7	26.2	18.9	31.3	...	29.6	...	30.6	...
1957	28.1	28.9	28.9	21.5	44.5	27.7	19.7	32.5	...	30.3	...	31.2	...
1958	28.9	29.6	30.2	21.5	44.6	28.6	20.6	33.2	...	30.4	...	31.9	...
1959	29.1	30.2	29.7	21.9	45.0	29.8	21.5	33.1	...	30.8	...	31.1	...
1960	29.6	30.6	30.0	22.4	45.7	29.8	22.3	33.4	...	30.8	...	30.4	...
1961	29.9	31.0	30.4	22.5	46.1	30.1	22.9	33.4	...	30.6	...	30.2	...
1962	30.2	31.4	30.6	22.6	46.3	30.8	23.5	33.5	...	30.6	...	30.5	...
1963	30.6	31.8	31.1	22.6	46.9	30.9	24.1	33.4	...	30.7	...	29.9	...
1964	31.0	32.3	31.5	22.5	47.3	31.4	24.6	33.5	...	30.8	...	29.6	...
1947													
January	21.5	...	22.8	...	38.4	17.9	13.2	...	...	...	...	...	...
February	21.6	...	23.1	...	38.8	17.9	13.3	...	...	...	...	...	...
March	22.0	...	23.8	...	39.4	18.1	13.3	...	...	...	...	...	...
April	22.0	...	23.5	...	39.7	18.3	13.4	26.0	...	23.1	...	30.7	...
May	22.0	...	23.4	...	39.8	18.3	13.5	26.1	...	23.0	...	30.4	...
June	22.1	...	23.5	...	40.0	18.4	13.5	26.2	...	23.2	...	30.6	...
July	22.2	...	23.8	...	40.0	18.5	13.5	26.2	...	23.2	...	31.0	...
August	22.4	...	24.1	...	40.1	18.5	13.6	26.3	...	23.3	...	31.6	...
September	22.8	...	24.8	...	40.2	18.7	13.7	26.7	...	23.7	...	32.4	...
October	22.9	...	24.9	...	40.4	18.8	13.8	26.8	...	24.0	...	33.7	...
November	23.1	...	25.2	...	40.6	19.0	13.8	27.1	...	24.3	...	33.9	...
December	23.4	...	25.7	...	41.0	19.1	13.9	27.7	...	24.5	...	35.3	...
1948													
January	23.7	...	26.1	...	41.3	19.6	14.0	28.1	...	25.0	...	36.2	...
February	23.7	...	25.9	...	41.8	19.5	14.0	27.9	...	24.7	...	34.4	...
March	23.5	...	25.3	...	42.0	19.6	14.1	28.0	...	24.8	...	33.5	...
April	23.8	...	26.0	...	42.1	19.9	14.3	28.1	...	25.1	...	34.2	...
May	24.0	...	26.3	...	42.5	19.9	14.3	28.4	...	25.1	...	35.3	...
June	24.2	...	26.5	...	42.4	20.0	14.4	28.6	...	25.4	...	36.2	...
July	24.4	...	26.7	...	42.7	21.0	14.5	28.8	...	25.4	...	36.1	...
August	24.4	...	26.5	...	43.1	21.3	14.6	28.9	...	25.5	...	35.5	...
September	24.4	...	26.3	...	43.1	21.4	14.5	28.8	...	25.5	...	34.9	...
October	24.3	...	26.1	...	43.1	21.5	14.6	28.7	...	25.5	...	33.8	...
November	24.2	...	25.7	...	43.0	21.6	14.7	28.5	...	25.4	...	33.5	...
December	24.1	...	25.5	...	43.0	21.6	14.7	28.5	...	25.2	...	33.0	...
1949													
January	24.0	...	25.4	...	42.2	21.6	14.7	28.3	...	25.2	...	32.0	...
February	23.9	...	25.3	...	41.8	21.8	14.8	28.0	...	24.8	...	30.9	...
March	23.9	...	25.3	...	41.6	21.9	14.8	28.0	...	24.7	...	30.8	...
April	23.9	...	25.3	...	41.3	22.0	14.8	27.9	...	24.5	...	30.2	...
May	23.9	...	25.2	...	41.1	22.2	14.8	27.8	...	24.3	...	30.1	...
June	23.9	...	25.3	...	41.0	22.1	14.8	27.7	...	24.1	...	29.7	...
July	23.7	...	24.8	...	40.8	22.2	14.8	27.5	...	24.1	...	29.2	...
August	23.7	...	24.8	...	40.5	22.3	14.9	27.4	...	23.9	...	29.2	...
September	23.8	...	25.0	...	40.2	22.2	14.9	27.4	...	23.9	...	29.5	...
October	23.7	...	24.8	...	39.9	22.3	14.9	27.3	...	23.8	...	29.5	...
November	23.7	...	24.8	...	39.8	22.3	14.9	27.2	...	23.7	...	29.6	...
December	23.6	...	24.5	...	39.8	22.5	14.9	27.2	...	23.8	...	29.6	...
1950													
January	23.5	...	24.3	...	39.7	22.4	14.9	27.2	...	23.8	...	29.6	...
February	23.6	...	24.7	...	39.7	22.4	15.0	27.2	...	23.9	...	30.5	...
March	23.6	...	24.6	...	39.7	22.4	14.9	27.3	...	24.1	...	30.3	...
April	23.7	...	24.6	...	39.7	22.4	15.0	27.3	...	24.2	...	30.5	...
May	23.8	...	24.8	...	39.7	22.5	15.0	27.5	...	24.6	...	31.6	...
June	23.9	...	25.1	...	39.7	22.5	15.0	27.6	...	24.7	...	32.1	...
July	24.1	...	25.6	...	39.9	22.7	15.1	28.0	...	25.3	...	33.3	...
August	24.2	...	25.8	...	40.1	22.9	15.1	28.6	...	25.6	...	34.0	...
September	24.3	...	25.8	...	40.6	22.9	15.2	28.9	...	26.2	...	34.5	...
October	24.5	...	26.0	...	41.2	22.9	15.3	29.0	...	26.7	...	34.5	...
November	24.6	...	26.1	...	41.5	23.0	15.3	29.4	...	26.9	...	35.4	...
December	25.0	...	26.9	...	41.9	23.2	15.4	30.0	...	27.8	...	36.7	...

. . . = Not available.

Table 20-2. Summary Consumer and Producer Price Indexes—Continued

(Seasonally adjusted.)

Year and month	Consumer Price Index, all urban consumers, 1982–1984 = 100							Producer Price Index, 1982 = 100					
								Finished goods		Intermediate materials, supplies, and components		Crude materials for further processing	
	All items	All items less food and energy	Food	Energy	Apparel	Transportation	Medical care	Total	Less food and energy	Total	Less food and energy	Total	Crude nonfood less energy
1951													
January	25.4	...	27.6	...	42.6	23.3	15.4	30.5	...	28.5	...	38.2	...
February	25.8	...	28.5	...	43.3	23.6	15.5	30.8	...	28.7	...	39.6	...
March	25.9	...	28.4	...	43.5	23.8	15.7	30.9	...	28.8	...	39.1	...
April	25.9	...	28.2	...	43.8	23.9	15.7	30.9	...	28.8	...	39.1	...
May	26.0	...	28.3	...	43.9	24.0	15.8	31.1	...	28.8	...	38.4	...
June	25.9	...	28.0	...	43.9	24.1	15.8	31.0	...	28.7	...	38.1	...
July	25.9	...	27.9	...	44.0	24.1	15.8	30.8	...	28.4	...	36.8	...
August	25.9	...	27.8	...	44.0	24.2	15.9	30.7	...	28.0	...	36.2	...
September	26.0	...	27.9	...	44.8	24.4	15.9	30.6	...	28.0	...	35.9	...
October	26.2	...	28.4	...	44.7	24.5	16.0	30.8	...	27.9	...	36.7	...
November	26.3	...	28.6	...	44.4	24.8	16.1	30.9	...	27.9	...	36.4	...
December	26.5	...	28.9	...	44.3	24.9	16.3	30.9	...	27.8	...	36.6	...
1952													
January	26.5	...	28.9	...	43.9	25.0	16.3	30.8	...	27.8	...	35.8	...
February	26.4	...	28.6	...	43.9	25.2	16.4	30.7	...	27.7	...	35.5	...
March	26.4	...	28.5	...	43.7	25.3	16.5	30.9	...	27.6	...	35.0	...
April	26.5	...	28.7	...	43.6	25.5	16.5	30.7	...	27.5	...	34.9	...
May	26.5	...	28.7	...	43.6	25.6	16.5	30.7	...	27.5	...	34.8	...
June	26.5	...	28.6	...	43.5	25.8	16.8	30.7	...	27.6	...	34.6	...
July	26.7	...	28.9	...	43.5	26.0	16.9	30.8	...	27.5	...	34.6	...
August	26.7	...	28.9	...	43.4	25.9	16.9	30.7	...	27.6	...	34.7	...
September	26.6	...	28.7	...	43.3	26.0	16.9	30.6	...	27.6	...	33.8	...
October	26.7	...	28.8	...	43.1	26.1	16.9	30.5	...	27.5	...	33.8	...
November	26.7	...	28.8	...	43.0	26.2	16.9	30.4	...	27.4	...	33.7	...
December	26.7	...	28.6	...	43.0	26.2	17.0	30.2	...	27.3	...	32.9	...
1953													
January	26.6	...	28.4	...	43.0	26.3	17.0	30.3	...	27.4	...	32.5	...
February	26.6	...	28.3	...	43.0	26.2	17.0	30.2	...	27.4	...	32.4	...
March	26.6	...	28.3	...	43.0	26.3	17.0	30.3	...	27.5	...	32.4	...
April	26.7	...	28.1	...	43.1	26.4	17.1	30.2	...	27.5	...	31.6	...
May	26.7	...	28.2	...	43.2	26.4	17.2	30.3	...	27.6	...	31.8	...
June	26.8	...	28.4	...	43.3	26.5	17.3	30.4	...	27.7	...	31.4	...
July	26.8	...	28.2	...	43.3	26.6	17.3	30.5	...	28.0	...	32.3	...
August	26.9	...	28.3	...	43.2	26.7	17.4	30.4	...	27.9	...	31.8	...
September	26.9	...	28.4	...	43.2	26.7	17.5	30.4	...	27.9	...	32.0	...
October	27.0	...	28.4	...	43.2	26.6	17.5	30.4	...	27.9	...	31.4	...
November	26.9	...	28.1	...	43.3	26.3	17.6	30.3	...	27.8	...	31.2	...
December	26.9	...	28.3	...	43.2	26.2	17.6	30.4	...	27.8	...	31.7	...
1954													
January	26.9	...	28.5	...	43.3	26.5	17.6	30.5	...	27.9	...	32.0	...
February	27.0	...	28.5	...	43.2	26.3	17.7	30.4	...	27.9	...	32.0	...
March	26.9	...	28.4	...	43.0	26.3	17.7	30.4	...	27.9	...	32.1	...
April	26.9	...	28.4	...	43.0	26.4	17.8	30.6	...	27.9	...	32.2	...
May	26.9	...	28.4	...	43.1	26.4	17.8	30.6	...	27.9	...	32.1	...
June	26.9	...	28.4	...	43.2	26.4	17.8	30.4	...	27.8	...	31.5	...
July	26.9	...	28.4	...	43.1	26.0	17.8	30.5	...	27.9	...	31.4	...
August	26.9	...	28.3	...	43.0	25.9	17.9	30.4	...	27.9	...	31.3	...
September	26.8	...	28.0	...	42.9	25.9	17.9	30.3	...	27.8	...	31.5	...
October	26.7	...	27.9	...	42.9	25.4	17.9	30.2	...	27.8	...	31.2	...
November	26.8	...	27.9	...	42.9	25.8	18.0	30.3	...	27.9	...	31.4	...
December	26.8	...	27.8	...	42.9	25.8	18.0	30.3	...	27.9	...	30.8	...
1955													
January	26.8	...	27.8	...	42.8	25.9	18.0	30.4	...	27.9	...	31.1	...
February	26.8	...	28.0	...	42.8	25.9	18.1	30.5	...	28.0	...	31.0	...
March	26.8	...	28.0	...	42.7	25.9	18.1	30.3	...	28.0	...	30.7	...
April	26.8	...	28.0	...	42.8	25.6	18.1	30.4	...	28.1	...	31.0	...
May	26.8	...	27.9	...	42.8	25.7	18.2	30.4	...	28.1	...	30.2	...
June	26.7	...	27.7	...	42.8	25.8	18.2	30.5	...	28.2	...	30.7	...
July	26.8	...	27.7	...	42.8	25.7	18.2	30.4	...	28.4	...	30.4	...
August	26.7	...	27.6	...	42.9	25.6	18.3	30.4	...	28.5	...	30.1	...
September	26.9	...	27.8	...	43.0	25.7	18.3	30.5	...	28.8	...	30.4	...
October	26.8	...	27.7	...	43.0	25.8	18.4	30.6	...	28.9	...	30.4	...
November	26.9	...	27.6	...	43.0	26.0	18.5	30.6	...	28.9	...	29.4	...
December	26.9	...	27.6	...	43.1	25.8	18.6	30.7	...	29.0	...	29.5	...
1956													
January	26.8	...	27.5	...	43.2	25.8	18.6	30.7	...	29.1	...	29.4	...
February	26.9	...	27.5	...	43.5	25.8	18.7	30.8	...	29.2	...	29.9	...
March	26.9	...	27.5	...	43.5	25.8	18.7	30.9	...	29.4	...	29.8	...
April	26.9	...	27.6	...	43.6	25.8	18.8	31.0	...	29.5	...	30.3	...
May	27.0	...	27.8	...	43.6	26.0	18.8	31.2	...	29.6	...	30.7	...
June	27.2	...	28.1	...	43.6	26.0	18.8	31.4	...	29.6	...	30.5	...
July	27.3	...	28.4	...	43.8	26.2	18.9	31.3	...	29.4	...	30.5	...
August	27.3	...	28.2	...	43.9	26.3	19.0	31.4	...	29.7	...	31.0	...
September	27.4	...	28.2	...	44.0	26.4	19.1	31.6	...	29.8	...	31.0	...
October	27.5	...	28.3	...	44.0	27.0	19.1	31.8	...	30.0	...	31.0	...
November	27.5	...	28.4	...	44.1	26.9	19.1	31.9	...	30.0	...	31.1	...
December	27.6	...	28.5	...	44.3	27.0	19.2	31.9	...	30.1	...	31.7	...

... = Not available.

Table 20-2. Summary Consumer and Producer Price Indexes—*Continued*

(Seasonally adjusted.)

Year and month	Consumer Price Index, all urban consumers, 1982–1984 = 100							Producer Price Index, 1982 = 100					
								Finished goods		Intermediate materials, supplies, and components		Crude materials for further processing	
	All items	All items less food and energy	Food	Energy	Apparel	Transpor-tation	Medical care	Total	Less food and energy	Total	Less food and energy	Total	Crude nonfood less energy
1957													
January	27.7	28.5	28.4	21.3	44.3	27.2	19.3	32.1	...	30.3	...	31.3	...
February	27.8	28.6	28.7	21.4	44.3	27.4	19.3	32.2	...	30.3	...	31.0	...
March	27.9	28.7	28.6	21.5	44.5	27.5	19.4	32.1	...	30.3	...	30.9	...
April	27.9	28.8	28.6	21.6	44.4	27.7	19.5	32.3	...	30.2	...	30.8	...
May	28.0	28.8	28.7	21.6	44.5	27.6	19.6	32.3	...	30.2	...	30.7	...
June	28.1	28.9	28.9	21.6	44.5	27.7	19.7	32.5	...	30.3	...	31.5	...
July	28.2	29.0	29.1	21.5	44.5	27.8	19.7	32.6	...	30.3	...	32.0	...
August	28.3	29.0	29.4	21.4	44.6	27.8	19.8	32.6	...	30.4	...	32.0	...
September	28.3	29.1	29.2	21.4	44.5	27.9	19.8	32.6	...	30.4	...	31.2	...
October	28.3	29.2	29.2	21.4	44.6	27.5	19.9	32.7	...	30.3	...	31.0	...
November	28.4	29.3	29.2	21.5	44.7	28.3	20.0	32.9	...	30.4	...	31.1	...
December	28.5	29.3	29.2	21.5	44.6	28.1	20.1	33.0	...	30.4	...	31.5	...
1958													
January	28.6	29.3	29.8	21.6	44.8	28.1	20.2	33.2	...	30.4	...	31.4	...
February	28.7	29.4	29.9	21.3	44.7	28.2	20.2	33.2	...	30.3	...	31.9	...
March	28.9	29.5	30.5	21.4	44.7	28.3	20.3	33.4	...	30.3	...	32.3	...
April	28.9	29.5	30.6	21.4	44.7	28.3	20.4	33.2	...	30.2	...	31.8	...
May	28.9	29.5	30.5	21.5	44.7	28.4	20.5	33.2	...	30.3	...	32.4	...
June	28.9	29.6	30.3	21.5	44.8	28.4	20.6	33.3	...	30.3	...	32.0	...
July	28.9	29.6	30.2	21.6	44.7	28.7	20.7	33.2	...	30.3	...	32.1	...
August	28.9	29.6	30.1	21.7	44.7	28.8	20.7	33.2	...	30.4	...	31.9	...
September	28.9	29.7	30.0	21.7	44.5	28.9	20.9	33.2	...	30.4	...	31.6	...
October	28.9	29.7	30.0	21.7	44.5	28.9	21.0	33.2	...	30.4	...	31.9	...
November	29.0	29.8	30.0	21.4	44.7	29.1	21.0	33.2	...	30.5	...	32.1	...
December	29.0	29.9	29.9	21.4	44.7	29.2	21.1	33.1	...	30.6	...	31.6	...
1959													
January	29.0	29.9	30.0	21.4	44.8	29.3	21.1	33.1	...	30.6	...	31.6	...
February	29.0	29.9	29.8	21.6	44.7	29.4	21.2	33.2	...	30.7	...	31.4	...
March	29.0	30.0	29.7	21.7	44.7	29.6	21.3	33.2	...	30.7	...	31.5	...
April	29.0	30.0	29.5	21.8	44.8	29.7	21.3	33.2	...	30.7	...	31.7	...
May	29.0	30.1	29.5	21.8	44.9	29.7	21.4	33.3	...	30.9	...	31.5	...
June	29.1	30.2	29.7	21.9	45.0	29.8	21.5	33.2	...	30.9	...	31.3	...
July	29.2	30.2	29.6	21.8	45.1	29.9	21.5	33.1	...	30.8	...	31.0	...
August	29.2	30.2	29.6	21.9	45.2	29.9	21.6	33.0	...	30.8	...	30.7	...
September	29.3	30.3	29.7	21.9	45.3	30.0	21.7	33.4	...	30.8	...	30.9	...
October	29.4	30.4	29.7	22.2	45.3	30.1	21.7	33.1	...	30.8	...	30.7	...
November	29.4	30.4	29.7	22.2	45.3	30.1	21.8	33.0	...	30.9	...	30.5	...
December	29.4	30.5	29.6	22.3	45.3	30.1	21.8	33.0	...	30.9	...	30.3	...
1960													
January	29.4	30.5	29.6	22.3	45.3	30.0	21.9	33.1	...	30.8	...	30.4	...
February	29.4	30.6	29.5	22.2	45.5	30.0	22.0	33.1	...	30.9	...	30.4	...
March	29.4	30.6	29.6	22.3	45.5	29.9	22.1	33.4	...	30.9	...	30.7	...
April	29.5	30.6	30.0	22.4	45.6	29.9	22.2	33.4	...	30.8	...	30.8	...
May	29.6	30.6	30.0	22.3	45.7	29.8	22.2	33.4	...	30.8	...	30.8	...
June	29.6	30.7	30.0	22.4	45.7	29.8	22.2	33.4	...	30.9	...	30.4	...
July	29.6	30.6	29.9	22.5	45.8	29.8	22.3	33.5	...	30.8	...	30.4	...
August	29.6	30.6	30.0	22.5	45.8	29.8	22.3	33.4	...	30.8	...	29.8	...
September	29.6	30.6	30.1	22.6	45.9	29.6	22.4	33.4	...	30.8	...	30.0	...
October	29.8	30.8	30.3	22.5	46.0	29.6	22.4	33.7	...	30.8	...	30.2	...
November	29.8	30.8	30.5	22.7	45.9	29.6	22.5	33.7	...	30.7	...	30.2	...
December	29.8	30.7	30.5	22.6	45.9	29.7	22.6	33.6	...	30.7	...	30.3	...
1961													
January	29.8	30.8	30.5	22.7	46.0	29.7	22.6	33.6	...	30.6	...	30.4	...
February	29.8	30.8	30.5	22.6	46.0	29.8	22.7	33.7	...	30.7	...	30.5	...
March	29.8	30.9	30.5	22.6	46.0	29.8	22.7	33.6	...	30.8	...	30.3	...
April	29.8	30.9	30.4	22.2	45.9	29.8	22.8	33.4	...	30.7	...	30.2	...
May	29.8	30.9	30.3	22.4	46.0	30.0	22.8	33.3	...	30.6	...	29.9	...
June	29.8	31.0	30.2	22.5	46.0	30.1	22.9	33.3	...	30.5	...	29.5	...
July	29.9	31.0	30.3	22.5	46.1	30.3	22.9	33.3	...	30.5	...	29.7	...
August	29.9	31.1	30.3	22.5	46.1	30.4	23.0	33.4	...	30.5	...	30.5	...
September	30.0	31.1	30.3	22.6	46.2	30.5	23.1	33.3	...	30.5	...	30.3	...
October	30.0	31.1	30.3	22.4	46.2	30.5	23.1	33.3	...	30.4	...	30.3	...
November	30.0	31.2	30.3	22.5	46.1	30.4	23.1	33.4	...	30.5	...	30.2	...
December	30.0	31.2	30.3	22.4	46.1	30.3	23.2	33.4	...	30.6	...	30.6	...
1962													
January	30.0	31.2	30.4	22.4	46.0	30.4	23.2	33.5	...	30.5	...	30.6	...
February	30.1	31.2	30.5	22.6	46.1	30.5	23.3	33.6	...	30.6	...	30.5	...
March	30.2	31.3	30.6	22.4	46.2	30.5	23.4	33.5	...	30.6	...	30.5	...
April	30.2	31.3	30.7	22.7	46.2	30.9	23.4	33.5	...	30.6	...	30.1	...
May	30.2	31.4	30.6	22.7	46.2	30.9	23.5	33.4	...	30.6	...	30.1	...
June	30.2	31.4	30.5	22.5	46.3	30.9	23.5	33.4	...	30.6	...	29.9	...
July	30.2	31.4	30.4	22.3	46.4	30.6	23.6	33.4	...	30.6	...	30.2	...
August	30.3	31.5	30.6	22.4	46.2	30.8	23.6	33.5	...	30.6	...	30.5	...
September	30.4	31.5	30.9	22.8	46.6	31.0	23.6	33.8	...	30.6	...	31.2	...
October	30.4	31.5	30.8	22.7	46.7	30.9	23.7	33.6	...	30.5	...	30.8	...
November	30.4	31.5	30.9	22.7	46.5	30.9	23.7	33.5	...	30.5	...	31.0	...
December	30.4	31.6	30.7	22.8	46.4	30.9	23.8	33.5	...	30.5	...	30.6	...

. . . = Not available.

Table 20-2. Summary Consumer and Producer Price Indexes—*Continued*

(Seasonally adjusted.)

Year and month	Consumer Price Index, all urban consumers, 1982–1984 = 100							Producer Price Index, 1982 = 100					
								Finished goods		Intermediate materials, supplies, and components		Crude materials for further processing	
	All items	All items less food and energy	Food	Energy	Apparel	Transportation	Medical care	Total	Less food and energy	Total	Less food and energy	Total	Crude nonfood less energy
1963													
January	30.4	31.5	31.0	22.8	46.6	30.6	23.9	33.4	...	30.5	...	30.3	...
February	30.5	31.6	31.1	22.7	46.7	30.7	23.9	33.4	...	30.5	...	30.0	...
March	30.5	31.7	31.0	22.7	46.7	30.8	23.9	33.3	...	30.5	...	29.6	...
April	30.5	31.7	30.9	22.6	46.8	30.8	23.9	33.3	...	30.5	...	29.8	...
May	30.5	31.7	30.9	22.6	46.7	30.9	24.0	33.4	...	30.7	...	29.6	...
June	30.6	31.8	31.0	22.5	46.8	30.9	24.1	33.5	...	30.7	...	29.9	...
July	30.7	31.8	31.2	22.7	46.9	30.9	24.1	33.4	...	30.7	...	30.0	...
August	30.8	31.9	31.2	22.6	47.0	31.0	24.2	33.4	...	30.7	...	29.9	...
September	30.7	31.9	31.1	22.5	47.0	31.0	24.2	33.4	...	30.7	...	29.8	...
October	30.8	32.0	31.0	22.7	47.1	31.2	24.2	33.5	...	30.8	...	29.9	...
November	30.8	32.0	31.2	22.6	47.2	31.1	24.3	33.5	...	30.8	...	30.2	...
December	30.9	32.1	31.3	22.6	47.2	31.2	24.3	33.4	...	30.8	...	29.4	...
1964													
January	30.9	32.2	31.4	22.8	47.2	31.4	24.4	33.5	...	30.8	...	29.8	...
February	30.9	32.2	31.4	22.2	47.2	31.3	24.4	33.5	...	30.8	...	29.4	...
March	30.9	32.2	31.4	22.6	47.2	31.4	24.4	33.4	...	30.8	...	29.5	...
April	31.0	32.2	31.4	22.5	47.3	31.3	24.5	33.5	...	30.8	...	29.5	...
May	31.0	32.2	31.4	22.5	47.3	31.3	24.5	33.5	...	30.8	...	29.4	...
June	31.0	32.3	31.4	22.6	47.3	31.4	24.6	33.5	...	30.7	...	29.0	...
July	31.0	32.3	31.5	22.5	47.4	31.3	24.6	33.5	...	30.7	...	29.2	...
August	31.1	32.3	31.4	22.6	47.4	31.4	24.7	33.6	...	30.6	...	29.4	...
September	31.1	32.3	31.6	22.5	47.2	31.3	24.7	33.6	...	30.7	...	30.1	...
October	31.1	32.4	31.6	22.5	47.2	31.3	24.7	33.6	...	30.7	...	29.8	...
November	31.2	32.5	31.7	22.5	47.3	31.4	24.8	33.6	...	30.8	...	29.9	...
December	31.3	32.5	31.7	22.6	47.4	31.7	24.8	33.6	...	30.9	...	29.8	...
1965													
January	31.3	32.6	31.6	22.8	47.5	31.9	24.8	33.6	...	30.9	...	29.5	...
February	31.3	32.6	31.5	22.7	47.5	31.8	24.9	33.7	...	30.9	...	29.9	...
March	31.3	32.6	31.7	22.6	47.5	31.8	25.0	33.7	...	31.0	...	30.0	...
April	31.4	32.7	31.8	22.9	47.6	31.9	25.0	34.0	...	31.1	...	30.4	...
May	31.5	32.7	32.1	23.0	47.7	32.0	25.1	34.1	...	31.1	...	30.8	...
June	31.6	32.7	32.6	23.1	47.8	31.9	25.1	34.2	...	31.2	...	31.6	...
July	31.6	32.7	32.5	23.0	47.7	31.9	25.3	34.1	...	31.2	...	31.2	...
August	31.6	32.7	32.4	23.0	47.8	31.9	25.3	34.2	...	31.3	...	31.5	...
September	31.6	32.8	32.3	23.1	47.8	31.9	25.3	34.3	...	31.3	...	31.4	...
October	31.7	32.8	32.5	23.0	47.9	31.8	25.4	34.4	...	31.3	...	31.8	...
November	31.8	32.9	32.6	23.1	48.0	31.9	25.5	34.5	...	31.4	...	32.1	...
December	31.9	33.0	32.8	23.1	48.1	32.0	25.5	34.7	...	31.4	...	32.7	...
1966													
January	31.9	33.0	33.0	23.1	48.3	31.9	25.6	34.7	...	31.4	...	33.1	...
February	32.1	33.1	33.5	23.2	48.4	32.0	25.6	35.0	...	31.6	...	33.7	...
March	32.2	33.1	33.8	23.2	48.5	32.1	25.8	35.0	...	31.7	...	33.5	...
April	32.3	33.3	33.8	23.2	48.7	32.2	25.9	35.1	...	31.8	...	33.3	...
May	32.4	33.4	33.7	23.2	48.8	32.1	26.0	35.1	...	32.0	...	33.0	...
June	32.4	33.5	33.7	23.3	48.9	32.2	26.1	34.9	...	32.0	...	33.0	...
July	32.5	33.6	33.5	23.4	49.1	32.5	26.3	35.1	...	32.2	...	33.4	...
August	32.7	33.7	34.0	23.3	49.1	32.6	26.4	35.4	...	32.3	...	33.5	...
September	32.8	33.8	34.1	23.4	49.4	32.6	26.7	35.6	...	32.2	...	33.4	...
October	32.9	34.0	34.2	23.4	49.6	32.7	26.9	35.5	...	32.1	...	32.9	...
November	32.9	34.0	34.1	23.5	49.7	32.8	27.1	35.5	...	32.2	...	32.3	...
December	32.9	34.1	34.0	23.5	49.9	32.6	27.2	35.4	...	32.2	...	32.1	...
1967													
January	32.9	34.2	33.9	23.6	50.1	32.6	27.4	35.4	...	32.2	...	32.2	...
February	33.0	34.2	33.8	23.7	50.3	32.8	27.5	35.3	...	32.1	...	31.5	...
March	33.0	34.3	33.8	23.6	50.4	32.8	27.6	35.3	...	32.1	...	31.1	...
April	33.1	34.4	33.7	23.9	50.6	33.0	27.8	35.3	...	32.1	...	30.7	...
May	33.1	34.5	33.7	23.9	50.7	33.1	27.9	35.4	...	32.1	...	31.1	...
June	33.3	34.6	34.0	23.8	50.9	33.1	28.1	35.7	...	32.2	...	31.4	...
July	33.4	34.7	34.1	23.8	51.1	33.3	28.2	35.7	...	32.2	...	31.3	...
August	33.5	34.9	34.3	23.9	51.3	33.4	28.3	35.8	...	32.2	...	31.3	...
September	33.6	35.0	34.3	24.0	51.3	33.7	28.5	35.8	...	32.3	...	31.2	...
October	33.7	35.1	34.4	23.9	51.5	33.6	28.7	35.9	...	32.3	...	31.3	...
November	33.9	35.2	34.5	24.0	51.6	33.9	28.8	35.9	...	32.4	...	31.1	...
December	34.0	35.4	34.6	23.9	51.9	33.9	29.0	36.0	...	32.6	...	31.5	...
1968													
January	34.1	35.5	34.6	24.0	52.1	34.1	29.1	36.1	...	32.6	...	31.4	...
February	34.2	35.7	34.8	24.1	52.4	34.2	29.2	36.2	...	32.7	...	31.5	...
March	34.3	35.8	34.9	24.1	52.7	34.2	29.4	36.3	...	32.8	...	31.6	...
April	34.4	35.9	35.0	24.0	53.0	34.1	29.5	36.5	...	32.8	...	31.7	...
May	34.5	36.0	35.1	24.1	53.3	34.1	29.6	36.5	...	32.8	...	31.5	...
June	34.7	36.2	35.2	24.2	53.5	34.3	29.7	36.6	...	32.9	...	31.3	...
July	34.9	36.4	35.3	24.2	53.9	34.3	29.9	36.7	...	33.0	...	31.6	...
August	35.0	36.5	35.4	24.3	54.2	34.4	30.0	36.8	...	33.0	...	31.7	...
September	35.1	36.7	35.6	24.3	54.5	34.4	30.2	37.0	...	33.1	...	31.9	...
October	35.3	36.9	35.9	24.3	54.8	34.5	30.4	37.0	...	33.2	...	32.1	...
November	35.4	37.1	35.9	24.4	54.9	34.7	30.6	37.1	...	33.2	...	32.8	...
December	35.6	37.2	36.0	24.3	55.2	34.5	30.8	37.1	...	33.4	...	32.4	...

. . . = Not available.

Table 20-2. Summary Consumer and Producer Price Indexes—*Continued*

(Seasonally adjusted.)

Year and month	Consumer Price Index, all urban consumers, 1982–1984 = 100							Producer Price Index, 1982 = 100					
								Finished goods		Intermediate materials, supplies, and components		Crude materials for further processing	
	All items	All items less food and energy	Food	Energy	Apparel	Transportation	Medical care	Total	Less food and energy	Total	Less food and energy	Total	Crude nonfood less energy
1969													
January	35.7	37.3	36.1	24.4	55.5	34.7	30.9	37.2	...	33.6	...	32.6	...
February	35.8	37.6	36.1	24.4	55.7	35.2	31.2	37.2	...	33.7	...	32.3	...
March	36.1	37.8	36.2	24.7	55.9	35.8	31.4	37.4	...	33.9	...	32.7	...
April	36.3	38.1	36.4	24.9	56.2	35.8	31.6	37.6	...	33.8	...	33.1	...
May	36.4	38.1	36.6	24.8	56.4	35.5	31.8	37.8	...	33.9	...	34.0	...
June	36.6	38.3	37.0	25.0	56.7	35.6	31.9	38.0	...	34.0	...	34.5	...
July	36.8	38.5	37.3	24.9	57.0	35.6	32.1	38.1	...	34.0	...	34.1	...
August	36.9	38.7	37.5	24.9	57.0	35.7	32.2	38.2	...	34.2	...	34.4	...
September	37.1	38.9	37.7	25.0	57.4	35.6	32.5	38.3	...	34.2	...	34.4	...
October	37.3	39.1	37.8	25.0	57.6	35.9	32.3	38.5	...	34.4	...	34.8	...
November	37.5	39.2	38.2	25.0	57.9	36.0	32.5	38.8	...	34.6	...	35.2	...
December	37.7	39.4	38.6	25.1	58.0	36.2	32.6	38.9	...	34.7	...	35.1	...
1970													
January	37.9	39.6	38.7	25.1	58.2	36.6	32.8	39.1	...	35.0	...	35.1	...
February	38.1	39.8	38.9	25.1	58.5	36.7	33.0	39.0	...	35.0	...	35.2	...
March	38.3	40.1	38.9	25.0	58.5	36.6	33.2	39.1	...	34.9	...	35.6	...
April	38.5	40.4	39.0	25.5	58.7	37.1	33.5	39.1	...	35.1	...	35.5	...
May	38.6	40.5	39.2	25.4	58.8	37.2	33.7	39.1	...	35.2	...	35.0	...
June	38.8	40.8	39.2	25.3	59.0	37.4	33.9	39.2	...	35.3	...	35.0	...
July	38.9	40.9	39.2	25.5	59.1	37.6	34.1	39.2	...	35.5	...	35.1	...
August	39.0	41.1	39.2	25.4	59.3	37.5	34.3	39.2	...	35.5	...	34.7	...
September	39.2	41.3	39.4	25.6	59.6	37.7	34.5	39.6	...	35.6	...	35.5	...
October	39.4	41.5	39.5	25.9	59.8	38.1	34.6	39.6	...	35.8	...	35.5	...
November	39.6	41.8	39.5	26.0	60.1	38.5	34.8	39.8	...	35.9	...	35.1	...
December	39.8	42.0	39.5	26.2	60.3	38.9	35.1	39.8	...	35.9	...	34.5	...
1971													
January	39.9	42.1	39.4	26.3	60.4	39.2	35.2	39.9	...	36.0	...	34.8	...
February	39.9	42.2	39.5	26.2	60.6	39.4	35.4	40.1	...	36.1	...	35.9	...
March	40.0	42.2	39.8	26.2	60.6	39.4	35.6	40.2	...	36.3	...	35.4	...
April	40.1	42.4	40.1	26.1	60.7	39.4	35.8	40.3	...	36.3	...	36.0	...
May	40.3	42.6	40.3	26.2	61.1	39.4	36.0	40.5	...	36.5	...	36.0	...
June	40.5	42.8	40.5	26.3	61.2	39.6	36.2	40.6	...	36.7	...	36.2	...
July	40.6	42.9	40.6	26.3	61.3	39.6	36.4	40.4	...	36.9	...	35.9	...
August	40.7	43.0	40.6	26.8	61.1	39.7	36.5	40.7	...	37.2	...	35.8	...
September	40.8	43.0	40.6	26.9	61.3	39.5	36.7	40.7	...	37.2	...	35.7	...
October	40.9	43.1	40.7	27.0	61.4	39.5	36.5	40.7	...	37.1	...	36.4	...
November	41.0	43.2	40.9	26.9	61.5	39.4	36.6	40.8	...	37.2	...	37.0	...
December	41.1	43.3	41.3	27.0	61.6	39.4	36.7	41.1	...	37.4	...	37.2	...
1972													
January	41.2	43.5	41.1	27.0	61.7	39.7	36.8	41.0	...	37.5	...	37.8	...
February	41.4	43.6	41.7	26.8	61.9	39.6	36.9	41.3	...	37.7	...	38.1	...
March	41.4	43.6	41.6	26.9	61.9	39.6	37.0	41.3	...	37.8	...	38.1	...
April	41.5	43.8	41.6	26.9	62.1	39.6	37.1	41.3	...	37.9	...	38.7	...
May	41.6	43.9	41.7	27.0	62.2	39.7	37.2	41.5	...	38.0	...	39.3	...
June	41.7	44.0	41.9	27.0	62.2	39.7	37.3	41.7	...	38.0	...	39.4	...
July	41.8	44.1	42.1	27.1	62.2	39.8	37.3	41.8	...	38.1	...	40.0	...
August	41.9	44.3	42.2	27.3	62.0	40.0	37.4	42.0	...	38.2	...	40.3	...
September	42.1	44.3	42.5	27.6	62.5	40.2	37.4	42.2	...	38.5	...	40.5	...
October	42.2	44.4	42.8	27.7	62.8	40.1	37.8	42.0	...	38.7	...	40.9	...
November	42.4	44.4	43.0	27.9	63.0	40.3	37.8	42.3	...	39.0	...	42.0	...
December	42.5	44.6	43.2	27.8	63.2	40.4	37.9	42.7	...	39.6	...	43.8	...
1973													
January	42.7	44.6	44.0	27.9	63.2	40.4	38.0	43.0	...	39.8	...	45.0	...
February	43.0	44.8	44.6	28.2	63.4	40.6	38.1	43.5	...	40.4	...	47.1	...
March	43.4	45.0	45.8	28.3	63.8	40.7	38.2	44.4	...	41.1	...	49.3	...
April	43.7	45.1	46.5	28.6	64.2	41.0	38.3	44.7	...	41.3	...	50.1	...
May	43.9	45.3	47.1	28.8	64.4	41.0	38.5	45.0	...	42.2	...	52.5	...
June	44.2	45.4	47.6	29.2	64.6	41.2	38.6	45.5	...	43.0	...	55.0	...
July	44.2	45.5	47.7	29.2	64.6	41.2	38.6	45.4	...	42.3	...	52.5	...
August	45.0	45.7	50.5	29.4	64.9	41.2	38.7	47.0	...	43.5	...	64.1	...
September	45.2	46.0	50.4	29.4	65.2	41.1	38.9	46.9	...	43.0	...	60.9	...
October	45.6	46.3	50.7	30.3	65.4	41.4	39.6	46.8	...	43.4	...	58.5	...
November	45.9	46.5	51.4	31.5	65.7	41.8	39.7	47.2	...	43.8	...	59.0	...
December	46.3	46.7	51.9	32.5	66.0	42.2	39.9	47.6	...	44.8	...	59.1	...
1974													
January	46.8	46.9	52.5	34.1	66.3	42.8	40.1	48.8	49.7	45.9	47.5	63.3	86.3
February	47.3	47.2	53.6	35.4	67.0	43.4	40.3	49.7	50.0	46.8	48.1	64.3	86.5
March	47.8	47.6	54.2	36.9	67.5	44.2	40.7	50.2	50.5	48.1	49.5	62.3	88.3
April	48.1	47.9	54.1	37.6	68.2	44.7	41.0	50.7	51.1	49.0	50.9	60.6	89.7
May	48.6	48.5	54.5	38.3	68.7	45.3	41.4	51.3	52.2	50.6	52.5	58.3	83.8
June	49.0	49.0	54.5	38.6	69.2	45.9	42.1	51.3	53.1	51.5	53.7	55.4	82.9
July	49.3	49.5	54.3	38.9	69.5	46.4	42.6	52.7	54.0	53.4	55.2	59.8	84.2
August	49.9	50.2	55.1	39.2	70.8	46.6	43.2	53.7	55.0	55.8	57.0	62.9	85.5
September	50.6	50.7	56.2	39.3	71.0	47.0	43.7	54.3	55.7	55.9	57.6	60.9	82.5
October	51.0	51.2	56.8	39.2	71.2	47.3	44.1	55.3	56.7	57.2	58.2	63.2	80.6
November	51.5	51.6	57.5	39.4	71.7	47.6	44.4	56.4	57.4	57.8	58.8	64.2	77.6
December	51.9	52.0	58.2	39.6	71.7	47.9	44.8	56.4	57.9	57.8	59.1	61.5	71.6

. . . = Not available.

Table 20-2. Summary Consumer and Producer Price Indexes—*Continued*

(Seasonally adjusted.)

Year and month	Consumer Price Index, all urban consumers, 1982–1984 = 100							Producer Price Index, 1982 = 100					
								Finished goods		Intermediate materials, supplies, and components		Crude materials for further processing	
	All items	All items less food and energy	Food	Energy	Apparel	Transportation	Medical care	Total	Less food and energy	Total	Less food and energy	Total	Crude nonfood less energy
1975													
January	52.3	52.3	58.4	40.0	71.8	48.0	45.3	56.7	58.3	58.0	59.6	59.6	69.8
February	52.6	52.8	58.5	40.3	72.0	48.3	45.8	56.6	58.7	57.8	59.8	57.9	69.2
March	52.8	53.0	58.4	40.6	72.1	48.7	46.3	56.6	59.0	57.4	59.7	57.1	68.2
April	53.0	53.3	58.3	41.0	72.1	48.8	46.7	57.1	59.2	57.5	59.7	59.5	67.7
May	53.1	53.5	58.6	41.3	72.2	48.9	47.0	57.4	59.3	57.3	59.7	61.2	68.8
June	53.5	53.8	59.2	41.7	72.2	49.4	47.4	57.9	59.5	57.3	59.8	61.5	66.5
July	54.0	54.0	60.3	42.5	72.6	50.2	47.8	58.4	59.8	57.5	59.9	62.4	66.5
August	54.2	54.2	60.3	42.8	72.6	50.6	48.1	58.9	59.9	58.0	60.1	63.0	67.7
September	54.6	54.5	60.7	43.2	72.7	51.4	48.5	59.3	60.2	58.2	60.3	64.5	71.2
October	54.9	54.8	61.3	43.5	73.0	51.7	48.9	59.8	60.6	58.8	61.0	65.1	71.5
November	55.3	55.2	61.7	43.9	73.2	52.4	48.8	60.0	61.0	59.0	61.4	64.4	71.9
December	55.6	55.5	62.1	44.1	73.4	52.6	49.3	60.1	61.4	59.2	61.8	64.0	73.1
1976													
January	55.8	55.9	61.9	44.5	73.7	53.0	49.7	60.0	61.7	59.4	62.1	63.0	72.4
February	55.9	56.2	61.3	44.4	74.0	53.3	50.2	59.9	61.9	59.6	62.3	62.1	73.8
March	56.0	56.5	60.9	44.1	74.2	53.8	50.7	60.0	62.2	59.8	62.6	61.5	74.5
April	56.1	56.7	60.9	43.9	74.3	54.0	51.0	60.3	62.3	60.0	62.8	63.9	78.1
May	56.4	57.0	61.1	44.1	74.6	54.3	51.4	60.4	62.4	60.3	63.2	63.6	80.6
June	56.7	57.2	61.3	44.4	74.9	54.8	51.8	60.5	62.8	60.8	63.6	65.2	82.8
July	57.0	57.6	61.6	44.8	75.3	55.1	52.3	60.7	63.1	61.1	63.9	64.8	87.3
August	57.3	57.9	61.8	45.2	75.8	55.4	52.6	60.9	63.5	61.3	64.3	63.6	84.1
September	57.6	58.2	62.1	45.7	76.1	56.0	53.0	61.1	63.9	61.9	64.7	63.4	84.4
October	57.9	58.5	62.4	46.1	76.2	56.6	53.2	61.4	64.1	62.0	65.0	63.0	82.2
November	58.1	58.7	62.3	46.8	76.5	57.0	53.9	61.9	64.6	62.4	65.3	63.4	81.8
December	58.4	58.9	62.5	47.5	76.8	57.3	54.2	62.4	64.9	62.8	65.6	64.5	81.1
1977													
January	58.7	59.3	62.7	48.1	77.2	57.8	54.6	62.5	65.1	63.0	65.8	64.3	78.7
February	59.3	59.7	63.9	48.1	77.6	58.2	54.9	63.2	65.4	63.3	65.9	65.7	79.7
March	59.6	60.0	64.2	48.4	77.5	58.7	55.5	63.7	65.7	63.9	66.4	66.6	81.5
April	60.0	60.3	65.0	48.6	77.6	59.0	56.0	64.0	65.9	64.4	66.7	68.3	82.1
May	60.2	60.6	65.3	48.9	78.1	59.1	56.5	64.4	66.1	64.9	67.1	67.6	82.5
June	60.5	61.0	65.7	48.9	78.5	59.1	57.0	64.6	66.5	64.9	67.4	65.5	79.7
July	60.8	61.2	65.9	49.1	79.1	59.0	57.3	64.8	66.8	65.1	67.9	64.7	78.8
August	61.1	61.5	66.2	49.5	79.2	58.9	57.7	65.2	67.3	65.4	68.2	63.9	79.2
September	61.3	61.8	66.4	49.8	79.1	59.1	58.2	65.5	67.8	65.7	68.7	63.7	79.2
October	61.6	62.0	66.6	50.5	79.3	59.3	58.4	65.9	68.2	65.8	68.8	64.0	78.5
November	62.0	62.3	67.1	51.3	79.8	59.5	58.6	66.4	68.8	66.3	69.1	65.4	78.4
December	62.3	62.7	67.4	51.6	80.1	59.8	59.0	66.7	69.0	66.6	69.4	66.4	80.1
1978													
January	62.7	63.1	67.9	51.1	80.1	60.1	59.3	67.0	69.2	66.9	69.8	67.3	80.3
February	63.0	63.4	68.6	50.6	79.5	60.2	59.9	67.5	69.5	67.4	70.3	68.4	80.6
March	63.4	63.8	69.5	51.0	79.9	60.3	60.2	67.8	69.9	67.8	70.6	69.8	80.3
April	63.9	64.3	70.6	51.4	80.7	60.4	60.7	68.6	70.6	68.1	71.1	72.1	82.2
May	64.5	64.7	71.6	51.7	81.3	60.7	61.1	69.1	71.1	68.7	71.6	72.8	84.6
June	65.0	65.2	72.7	51.9	81.6	61.1	61.5	69.7	71.7	69.2	72.2	74.6	87.4
July	65.5	65.6	73.0	52.1	81.5	61.6	61.9	70.3	72.3	69.4	72.5	74.2	89.6
August	65.9	66.1	73.3	52.6	81.7	62.0	62.4	70.4	72.8	69.9	73.2	73.7	90.4
September	66.5	66.7	73.6	53.2	81.9	62.6	62.8	71.1	73.5	70.5	73.7	75.1	92.3
October	67.1	67.2	74.2	54.1	82.4	63.3	63.3	71.4	73.4	71.3	74.5	77.0	94.7
November	67.5	67.6	74.7	54.9	82.6	63.9	63.8	72.0	74.1	71.9	75.2	77.4	96.3
December	67.9	68.0	75.1	55.9	82.6	64.5	64.1	72.8	74.7	72.4	75.6	78.0	96.8
1979													
January	68.5	68.5	76.4	55.8	83.0	64.6	64.8	73.7	75.3	73.1	76.3	80.1	96.4
February	69.2	69.2	77.7	55.9	83.3	65.2	65.2	74.4	75.9	73.7	77.0	82.1	99.6
March	69.9	69.8	78.4	57.4	83.6	66.4	65.7	75.0	76.4	74.6	77.8	83.8	104.2
April	70.6	70.3	79.0	59.5	84.0	67.8	66.1	75.8	77.0	75.7	78.9	84.4	105.1
May	71.4	70.8	79.7	62.0	84.5	69.1	66.6	76.2	77.4	76.6	79.6	84.7	106.7
June	72.2	71.3	80.0	64.7	84.7	70.5	67.1	76.6	78.0	77.5	80.1	85.6	111.6
July	73.0	71.9	80.5	67.3	84.8	71.7	67.7	77.4	78.5	78.7	81.1	86.5	109.4
August	73.7	72.7	80.4	69.7	85.0	72.7	68.2	78.2	78.8	79.8	81.8	85.5	106.4
September	74.4	73.3	80.9	71.9	85.6	73.5	68.7	79.5	79.7	81.1	82.7	87.9	106.5
October	75.2	74.0	81.5	73.5	86.1	74.0	69.2	80.4	80.4	82.4	83.9	88.8	108.9
November	76.0	74.8	82.0	74.8	86.6	74.7	69.8	81.4	81.0	83.2	84.5	90.0	111.3
December	76.9	75.7	82.8	76.8	87.3	75.8	70.6	82.2	81.7	84.0	85.2	91.2	111.3
1980													
January	78.0	76.7	83.3	79.1	88.1	78.0	71.4	83.4	83.3	86.0	87.2	90.9	112.6
February	79.0	77.5	83.4	81.9	88.7	79.8	72.3	84.6	84.2	87.6	88.2	92.6	115.3
March	80.1	78.6	84.1	84.5	89.7	81.8	73.0	85.5	84.7	88.2	88.6	90.8	111.7
April	80.9	79.5	84.7	85.4	90.1	82.2	73.6	86.2	85.5	88.5	88.8	88.3	109.9
May	81.7	80.1	85.2	86.4	90.3	82.8	74.2	86.6	85.7	89.0	89.1	89.5	107.2
June	82.5	81.0	85.7	86.5	90.6	82.7	74.7	87.3	86.6	89.8	89.8	90.1	106.1
July	82.6	80.8	86.6	86.7	90.9	83.1	75.2	88.7	87.7	90.5	90.3	94.6	109.6
August	83.2	81.3	88.0	87.2	91.4	83.7	75.6	89.7	88.4	91.5	91.1	99.0	112.4
September	83.9	82.1	89.1	87.5	92.0	84.6	76.3	90.1	88.8	91.9	91.4	100.4	116.2
October	84.7	83.0	89.8	88.0	92.7	85.3	76.9	90.8	89.6	92.8	92.1	102.2	118.2
November	85.6	83.9	90.8	88.8	93.1	86.1	77.3	91.4	90.1	93.5	92.6	103.5	119.8
December	86.4	84.9	91.3	90.7	93.3	86.8	77.8	91.8	90.4	94.4	93.7	102.7	119.3

Table 20-2. Summary Consumer and Producer Price Indexes—*Continued*

(Seasonally adjusted.)

Year and month	Consumer Price Index, all urban consumers, 1982–1984 = 100							Producer Price Index, 1982 = 100					
								Finished goods		Intermediate materials, supplies, and components		Crude materials for further processing	
	All items	All items less food and energy	Food	Energy	Apparel	Transportation	Medical care	Total	Less food and energy	Total	Less food and energy	Total	Crude nonfood less energy
1981													
January	87.2	85.4	91.6	92.1	93.4	88.5	78.6	92.8	91.4	95.6	94.7	103.4	113.3
February	88.0	85.9	92.1	95.2	93.9	90.7	79.2	93.6	92.0	96.1	94.9	104.2	106.2
March	88.6	86.4	92.6	97.4	94.3	91.8	79.9	94.7	92.6	97.1	95.6	103.8	108.9
April	89.1	87.0	92.8	97.6	94.7	91.7	80.7	95.7	93.5	98.3	96.6	104.2	111.9
May	89.7	87.8	92.8	97.9	94.8	92.2	81.4	96.0	94.0	98.7	97.1	103.8	113.7
June	90.5	88.6	93.2	97.3	95.0	92.7	82.3	96.5	94.6	99.0	97.7	104.9	115.5
July	91.5	89.8	93.9	97.3	95.4	93.5	83.4	96.7	94.8	99.2	98.4	105.0	116.4
August	92.2	90.7	94.4	97.8	95.9	93.9	84.3	96.8	95.3	99.7	98.9	104.0	115.5
September	93.1	91.8	94.8	98.6	96.1	94.6	85.1	97.2	95.9	99.7	99.3	102.7	112.6
October	93.4	92.1	95.0	99.2	96.4	95.5	85.9	97.6	96.5	99.8	99.5	101.2	110.8
November	93.8	92.5	95.1	100.5	96.4	96.2	86.8	97.9	97.0	99.9	99.7	99.7	107.5
December	94.1	93.0	95.3	101.5	96.7	96.4	87.5	98.3	97.6	100.0	99.8	98.8	106.0
1982													
January	94.4	93.3	95.6	100.6	96.7	96.7	88.2	98.9	98.1	100.4	99.9	99.7	101.2
February	94.7	93.8	96.3	98.0	97.0	96.2	88.8	98.8	98.1	100.3	100.0	100.0	100.7
March	94.7	93.9	96.2	96.6	97.3	95.8	89.6	98.8	98.7	99.9	99.9	99.7	100.0
April	95.0	94.7	96.4	94.2	97.5	94.5	90.5	99.0	99.0	99.7	99.8	100.2	101.1
May	95.9	95.4	97.2	95.7	97.6	95.1	91.3	99.0	99.4	99.7	100.1	101.9	102.2
June	97.0	96.1	98.1	98.4	97.7	97.2	92.2	99.8	99.9	99.8	100.0	101.8	101.0
July	97.5	96.7	98.2	99.3	98.1	98.1	93.0	100.2	100.1	100.0	99.8	100.7	101.4
August	97.7	97.1	98.0	99.8	98.1	98.2	93.9	100.6	100.6	99.9	99.7	99.8	100.0
September	97.7	97.2	98.2	100.3	98.1	98.0	94.7	100.7	100.8	100.0	100.2	99.2	98.9
October	98.1	97.5	98.2	101.7	98.3	98.2	95.5	101.0	101.3	99.9	100.2	98.7	97.7
November	98.0	97.3	98.2	102.5	98.3	98.2	96.5	101.4	101.6	100.1	100.2	99.2	96.3
December	97.7	97.2	98.2	102.8	98.2	97.7	97.2	101.8	102.2	100.1	100.3	98.8	95.9
1983													
January	97.9	97.6	98.1	99.6	98.6	97.6	97.9	101.0	101.8	99.8	100.3	98.8	97.3
February	98.0	98.0	98.2	97.7	99.1	96.9	98.8	101.1	102.2	100.0	100.8	100.0	99.8
March	98.1	98.2	98.8	96.8	99.1	96.5	99.0	101.0	102.5	99.7	100.8	100.5	102.2
April	98.8	98.6	99.2	98.9	99.3	97.8	99.4	101.1	102.4	99.5	100.9	101.2	102.1
May	99.2	98.9	99.5	100.4	99.9	98.6	99.9	101.4	102.6	99.8	101.0	100.9	103.4
June	99.4	99.2	99.6	100.6	100.3	99.0	100.4	101.6	102.8	100.2	101.3	100.5	104.8
July	99.8	99.8	99.6	100.9	100.9	99.6	100.8	101.6	103.1	100.5	101.8	99.5	106.2
August	100.1	100.1	99.7	101.2	101.0	100.4	101.4	101.9	103.5	100.9	102.0	102.2	108.4
September	100.4	100.5	100.0	101.0	100.8	100.7	101.8	102.2	103.5	101.6	102.3	103.3	109.0
October	100.8	101.0	100.3	100.8	100.6	101.1	102.3	102.2	103.6	101.7	102.5	103.2	109.1
November	101.1	101.5	100.3	100.5	100.9	101.5	102.8	102.0	103.8	101.8	102.8	102.3	109.9
December	101.4	101.8	100.6	100.0	101.1	101.5	103.4	102.3	104.1	101.9	103.1	103.5	111.2
1984													
January	102.1	102.5	102.0	100.2	101.5	102.0	104.0	103.0	104.5	102.1	103.4	104.6	111.5
February	102.6	102.8	102.7	101.4	101.2	102.2	105.0	103.4	104.7	102.5	103.8	103.8	113.8
March	102.9	103.2	102.9	101.4	101.3	102.9	105.2	103.8	105.2	103.0	104.4	105.7	114.8
April	103.3	103.7	102.9	101.7	101.2	103.3	105.8	103.9	105.3	103.2	104.5	105.2	115.1
May	103.5	104.1	102.7	101.6	101.4	103.7	106.2	103.8	105.3	103.4	104.6	104.5	115.7
June	103.7	104.5	103.1	100.8	101.3	103.9	106.7	103.8	105.5	103.6	104.8	103.3	114.1
July	104.1	105.0	103.3	100.5	101.9	103.7	107.2	104.0	105.7	103.4	104.9	104.0	112.0
August	104.4	105.4	103.9	100.1	102.5	103.8	107.7	103.8	105.9	103.2	105.1	103.3	109.6
September	104.7	105.8	103.8	100.6	102.7	104.1	108.1	103.8	106.2	103.1	105.0	102.8	110.5
October	105.1	106.2	104.0	101.1	103.0	104.8	108.7	103.6	105.9	103.2	105.1	101.5	108.5
November	105.3	106.4	104.1	100.8	103.0	104.9	109.3	104.0	106.2	103.3	105.3	101.9	107.7
December	105.5	106.8	104.5	100.1	103.1	104.7	109.8	104.0	106.3	103.2	105.3	101.4	107.3
1985													
January	105.7	107.1	104.7	100.3	103.2	105.1	110.2	104.0	106.9	103.1	105.3	99.9	107.4
February	106.3	107.7	105.2	100.3	104.1	105.6	110.8	104.1	107.3	102.8	105.3	99.4	107.2
March	106.8	108.1	105.5	101.3	104.5	106.3	111.4	104.1	107.6	102.7	105.2	97.6	107.0
April	107.0	108.4	105.4	102.3	104.5	106.8	112.0	104.6	107.6	102.9	105.2	96.7	107.4
May	107.2	108.8	105.2	102.2	104.4	106.5	112.6	104.9	107.8	103.2	105.3	95.8	105.3
June	107.5	109.1	105.5	102.2	105.1	106.5	113.3	104.6	108.2	102.6	105.5	95.2	103.6
July	107.7	109.4	105.5	102.2	105.2	106.6	113.9	104.7	108.4	102.3	105.3	94.9	104.3
August	107.9	109.8	105.6	101.2	105.3	106.2	114.6	104.5	108.5	102.3	105.3	92.9	103.6
September	108.1	110.0	105.8	101.2	105.5	106.2	115.2	103.8	107.9	102.2	105.2	91.8	103.3
October	108.5	110.5	105.8	101.2	105.7	106.5	115.8	104.9	108.9	102.3	105.1	94.1	103.7
November	109.0	111.1	106.5	101.8	106.0	107.0	116.5	105.5	109.1	102.5	105.1	95.7	103.0
December	109.5	111.4	107.3	102.4	106.1	107.5	117.1	106.0	109.1	102.9	105.1	95.5	102.4
1986													
January	109.9	111.9	107.5	102.6	106.1	108.0	118.0	105.5	109.3	102.4	105.0	94.2	103.6
February	109.7	112.2	107.3	99.5	105.4	107.0	118.8	104.1	109.5	101.2	104.9	90.5	103.5
March	109.1	112.5	107.5	92.6	105.0	103.6	119.7	102.8	109.6	99.9	105.0	88.2	103.8
April	108.7	112.9	107.7	87.2	105.0	101.0	120.4	102.3	110.1	98.9	104.7	85.6	103.9
May	109.0	113.1	108.2	87.2	104.9	101.4	121.2	102.8	110.2	98.7	104.6	86.5	104.1
June	109.4	113.4	108.3	88.8	104.9	102.3	121.8	103.1	110.5	98.6	104.7	86.2	104.7
July	109.5	113.8	109.1	85.6	105.5	101.1	122.5	102.3	110.7	98.0	104.8	86.4	105.3
August	109.6	114.2	110.1	83.6	106.4	100.1	123.2	102.7	110.8	98.0	104.9	86.7	99.7
September	110.0	114.6	110.2	84.4	106.9	100.6	124.0	102.9	110.7	98.5	105.1	86.6	100.3
October	110.2	115.0	110.5	82.8	106.6	100.5	124.7	103.5	111.8	98.3	105.1	87.4	102.0
November	110.4	115.3	111.1	82.1	106.9	100.8	125.5	103.4	112.0	98.3	105.2	87.6	102.8
December	110.8	115.6	111.4	82.5	107.2	101.1	126.2	103.6	112.1	98.5	105.3	86.9	104.1

Table 20-2. Summary Consumer and Producer Price Indexes—*Continued*

(Seasonally adjusted.)

Year and month	Consumer Price Index, all urban consumers, 1982–1984 = 100							Producer Price Index, 1982 = 100					
								Finished goods		Intermediate materials, supplies, and components		Crude materials for further processing	
	All items	All items less food and energy	Food	Energy	Apparel	Transportation	Medical care	Total	Less food and energy	Total	Less food and energy	Total	Crude nonfood less energy
1987													
January	111.4	115.9	111.8	85.4	108.0	102.6	126.7	104.1	112.5	99.0	105.6	89.3	105.4
February	111.8	116.2	112.2	87.4	108.6	103.5	127.2	104.4	112.3	99.8	105.9	90.2	106.2
March	112.2	116.6	112.4	87.6	109.2	103.8	127.8	104.5	112.4	99.9	106.2	90.5	106.5
April	112.7	117.3	112.6	87.6	109.8	104.3	128.6	105.1	112.9	100.3	106.5	92.5	107.5
May	113.0	117.7	113.2	87.1	110.3	104.4	129.2	105.2	113.0	100.8	107.0	93.8	110.0
June	113.5	117.9	113.9	88.5	110.3	105.1	130.0	105.5	113.1	101.4	107.5	94.5	113.2
July	113.8	118.3	113.7	89.2	110.3	105.9	130.6	105.7	113.3	101.9	107.9	95.6	115.9
August	114.3	118.7	113.9	90.5	111.0	106.6	131.2	105.9	113.6	102.4	108.3	96.5	119.1
September	114.7	119.2	114.3	90.3	111.6	106.9	131.9	106.2	113.9	102.6	108.9	96.0	122.8
October	115.0	119.8	114.5	89.6	112.3	107.0	132.4	106.0	114.0	103.1	109.6	95.8	126.6
November	115.4	120.1	114.5	90.0	113.0	107.3	133.0	106.0	114.2	103.5	110.1	95.1	127.5
December	115.6	120.4	115.1	89.5	112.7	107.2	133.5	105.8	114.3	103.8	110.7	94.9	127.9
1988													
January	116.0	120.9	115.6	88.8	113.2	107.0	134.4	106.4	115.0	104.1	111.8	94.2	129.4
February	116.2	121.2	115.6	88.7	112.1	107.0	135.2	106.3	115.3	104.4	112.2	95.2	131.7
March	116.5	121.7	115.8	88.4	113.4	107.0	135.8	106.6	115.6	104.8	112.8	94.1	133.0
April	117.2	122.3	116.4	88.8	115.1	107.5	136.7	107.0	115.9	105.5	113.6	95.4	132.1
May	117.5	122.7	116.9	88.5	115.1	107.9	137.6	107.2	116.2	106.2	114.3	95.8	130.7
June	118.0	123.2	117.6	88.9	115.5	108.3	138.3	107.5	116.6	107.4	114.9	97.0	131.1
July	118.5	123.6	118.8	89.4	115.9	108.8	139.1	108.4	117.2	108.3	115.8	96.7	133.2
August	119.0	124.0	119.4	90.1	114.5	109.7	139.8	108.8	117.7	108.5	116.3	97.0	134.3
September	119.5	124.7	120.1	89.8	116.3	109.9	140.5	109.0	118.1	108.7	116.8	97.0	133.3
October	119.9	125.2	120.3	89.8	117.5	110.0	141.4	109.2	118.4	108.6	117.3	96.6	133.6
November	120.3	125.6	120.5	89.8	117.7	110.2	142.0	109.6	118.7	108.8	118.0	95.2	136.0
December	120.7	126.0	121.1	89.6	118.2	110.4	142.7	110.0	119.2	109.4	118.6	98.1	137.6
1989													
January	121.2	126.5	121.6	90.3	118.4	110.9	143.8	111.1	119.9	110.8	119.5	102.0	140.6
February	121.6	126.9	122.5	90.8	117.1	111.7	144.9	111.9	120.5	111.3	119.9	101.7	140.3
March	122.2	127.4	123.2	91.8	118.1	112.4	145.8	112.3	120.7	111.9	120.2	102.9	140.6
April	123.1	127.8	123.9	96.6	118.6	115.0	146.6	113.1	120.8	112.5	120.5	104.1	140.3
May	123.7	128.3	124.7	97.4	118.9	115.8	147.5	114.0	121.6	112.6	120.6	104.5	139.8
June	124.1	128.8	125.1	96.9	118.7	115.7	148.6	114.0	122.2	112.5	120.6	103.2	137.9
July	124.5	129.2	125.6	96.7	118.3	115.4	149.6	113.8	122.1	112.2	120.3	103.5	135.9
August	124.5	129.5	125.9	94.9	117.1	114.5	150.6	113.4	122.7	111.8	120.2	101.2	136.8
September	124.8	129.9	126.3	93.8	118.7	113.9	151.8	114.0	123.1	112.1	120.2	102.5	137.5
October	125.4	130.6	126.8	94.4	119.6	114.5	152.8	114.6	123.5	112.2	120.3	102.7	137.9
November	125.9	131.1	127.4	93.9	120.0	114.4	154.1	114.8	123.9	112.0	120.0	103.5	134.9
December	126.3	131.6	127.8	94.2	119.8	114.7	154.9	115.5	124.2	112.2	119.8	105.1	132.8
1990													
January	127.5	132.1	129.7	98.9	119.9	117.0	156.0	117.7	124.5	113.7	120.0	106.7	132.7
February	128.0	132.7	130.8	98.2	122.0	117.2	157.1	117.6	124.9	112.8	119.9	106.8	131.6
March	128.6	133.5	131.0	97.6	123.8	117.3	158.3	117.5	125.3	112.9	120.2	105.1	133.9
April	128.9	134.0	130.8	97.5	124.1	117.7	159.6	117.4	125.5	113.1	120.5	102.7	137.0
May	129.1	134.4	131.1	96.7	124.0	117.5	160.8	117.5	126.0	113.1	120.6	103.1	138.0
June	129.9	135.1	132.1	97.3	124.2	118.0	162.0	117.6	126.4	112.9	120.4	100.6	137.3
July	130.5	135.8	132.8	97.1	124.2	118.5	163.4	117.9	126.6	112.8	120.6	101.0	138.0
August	131.6	136.6	133.2	101.6	124.5	120.7	164.8	119.2	127.1	114.0	120.8	110.5	140.1
September	132.5	137.1	133.6	106.5	125.4	123.2	165.9	120.7	127.7	115.8	121.5	115.8	139.9
October	133.4	137.6	134.1	110.8	125.4	125.6	167.3	121.9	128.0	117.4	122.1	125.8	138.4
November	133.7	138.0	134.5	111.2	125.4	126.1	168.7	122.6	128.4	117.7	122.3	117.8	135.7
December	134.2	138.6	134.6	111.0	126.2	126.9	169.8	122.0	128.6	116.9	122.1	110.8	133.8
1991													
January	134.7	139.5	135.0	108.5	126.9	125.5	171.0	122.6	129.5	116.9	122.4	113.3	134.2
February	134.8	140.2	135.1	104.5	127.3	123.9	172.1	121.8	129.8	115.9	122.1	104.1	133.7
March	134.8	140.5	135.3	101.9	127.0	122.7	173.2	121.3	130.1	114.7	121.7	100.5	131.8
April	135.1	140.9	136.1	101.2	127.5	122.5	174.3	121.3	130.4	114.2	121.5	100.2	131.7
May	135.6	141.3	136.6	102.1	128.0	123.2	175.2	121.6	130.6	114.1	121.3	100.9	130.4
June	136.0	141.8	137.4	101.1	127.9	123.4	176.4	121.4	130.7	113.9	121.3	99.2	126.1
July	136.2	142.3	136.7	100.7	128.7	123.3	177.4	121.1	131.0	113.6	121.1	99.4	125.4
August	136.6	142.9	136.2	101.1	129.9	124.0	178.8	121.3	131.3	113.8	121.0	99.1	125.8
September	137.0	143.4	136.4	101.5	130.0	124.1	179.9	121.5	131.8	114.0	121.0	98.4	125.7
October	137.2	143.7	136.2	101.6	130.1	123.9	180.9	121.9	132.3	114.0	121.1	100.8	125.4
November	137.8	144.2	136.7	102.4	131.0	124.5	181.9	122.4	132.5	114.1	121.1	100.7	124.4
December	138.2	144.7	137.0	103.1	130.7	125.1	183.1	122.3	132.6	114.0	121.1	98.2	123.4
1992													
January	138.3	145.1	136.6	101.5	130.9	124.6	184.3	122.0	133.0	113.4	121.0	97.2	123.4
February	138.6	145.4	137.1	101.2	131.0	124.5	185.6	122.3	133.1	113.8	121.3	98.6	125.2
March	139.1	145.9	137.6	101.2	131.3	125.0	186.8	122.4	133.4	113.9	121.5	97.1	127.7
April	139.4	146.3	137.5	101.4	130.7	125.6	187.9	122.5	133.8	114.1	121.7	98.1	128.4
May	139.7	146.8	137.2	102.0	131.6	125.9	188.7	122.9	134.3	114.5	121.8	100.3	129.1
June	140.1	147.1	137.6	103.3	132.1	126.4	189.6	123.4	134.1	115.1	122.0	101.6	128.8
July	140.5	147.6	137.4	103.7	132.7	126.9	190.6	123.3	134.3	115.2	122.1	101.6	129.6
August	140.8	147.9	138.4	103.5	132.3	127.0	191.5	123.4	134.3	115.1	122.3	100.7	130.4
September	141.1	148.1	138.9	103.6	132.2	127.0	192.4	123.7	134.6	115.3	122.4	102.8	130.4
October	141.7	148.8	138.9	104.3	132.5	128.1	193.5	124.2	134.9	115.3	122.4	102.8	128.9
November	142.1	149.2	138.7	105.1	132.7	128.7	194.5	124.1	135.1	115.1	122.4	102.5	128.2
December	142.3	149.6	138.8	105.3	132.8	128.9	195.3	124.2	135.2	115.1	122.5	101.3	130.5

Table 20-2. Summary Consumer and Producer Price Indexes—*Continued*

(Seasonally adjusted.)

Year and month	Consumer Price Index, all urban consumers, 1982–1984 = 100							Producer Price Index, 1982 = 100					
								Finished goods		Intermediate materials, supplies, and components		Crude materials for further processing	
	All items	All items less food and energy	Food	Energy	Apparel	Transpor-tation	Medical care	Total	Less food and energy	Total	Less food and energy	Total	Crude nonfood less energy
1993													
January	142.8	150.1	139.1	105.0	132.8	129.2	196.4	124.4	135.6	115.4	122.9	101.7	135.0
February	143.1	150.6	139.6	104.3	134.0	129.6	197.4	124.7	135.9	115.9	123.5	101.2	136.8
March	143.3	150.8	139.6	104.9	134.0	129.4	198.1	125.0	136.1	116.3	123.8	101.7	137.0
April	143.8	151.4	140.0	104.9	134.0	129.6	199.1	125.7	136.5	116.6	124.0	103.2	138.4
May	144.2	151.8	141.0	104.3	133.5	129.9	200.5	125.7	136.6	116.3	123.7	105.6	140.3
June	144.3	152.1	140.6	103.9	133.0	129.9	201.3	125.2	136.4	116.3	123.7	103.8	140.3
July	144.5	152.3	140.6	103.4	132.8	130.1	202.2	125.1	136.6	116.3	123.7	101.6	142.1
August	144.8	152.8	141.1	103.4	134.0	130.5	202.8	123.9	134.9	116.2	123.9	100.8	140.4
September	145.0	152.9	141.4	103.0	133.7	130.4	203.6	124.1	134.9	116.3	124.0	101.2	140.7
October	145.6	153.4	142.0	105.3	133.8	132.0	204.5	124.2	135.0	116.4	124.0	103.7	142.6
November	146.0	153.9	142.3	104.4	134.4	132.2	205.1	124.4	135.3	116.5	124.3	103.0	144.1
December	146.3	154.3	142.8	103.7	134.1	132.1	205.8	124.4	135.7	116.2	124.5	101.7	145.3
1994													
January	146.3	154.5	142.9	102.8	133.3	131.7	206.4	124.8	136.3	116.5	124.7	103.8	148.3
February	146.7	154.8	142.7	104.1	133.2	132.3	207.2	125.0	136.3	116.9	124.9	102.1	151.0
March	147.1	155.3	142.7	104.3	133.8	132.6	207.9	125.1	136.4	117.1	125.1	103.8	151.5
April	147.2	155.5	143.0	103.7	133.5	132.8	209.0	125.1	136.6	117.1	125.3	103.8	150.7
May	147.5	155.9	143.3	102.8	134.0	132.4	209.7	125.1	137.0	117.2	125.6	102.2	149.7
June	147.9	156.4	143.8	103.1	134.8	133.2	210.5	125.2	137.2	117.8	126.3	102.7	151.2
July	148.4	156.7	144.6	104.5	134.2	134.4	211.3	125.7	137.3	118.3	126.7	101.7	155.5
August	149.0	157.1	145.1	106.7	133.2	136.0	212.2	126.2	137.6	119.1	127.4	101.6	158.8
September	149.3	157.5	145.3	106.1	133.6	136.1	213.1	125.9	137.7	119.6	128.4	99.7	160.5
October	149.4	157.8	145.3	105.7	133.0	136.2	214.1	125.5	137.4	120.1	129.3	98.6	161.3
November	149.8	158.2	145.6	106.1	132.5	136.7	215.0	126.1	137.6	121.0	130.3	99.8	166.6
December	150.1	158.3	146.8	105.9	132.1	137.1	215.9	126.6	137.9	121.5	131.0	101.1	169.9
1995													
January	150.5	159.0	146.7	105.7	132.2	137.4	216.6	126.9	138.4	122.8	132.6	102.1	174.5
February	150.9	159.4	147.3	105.8	131.9	137.9	217.4	127.2	138.7	123.7	133.7	102.9	176.5
March	151.2	159.9	147.1	105.5	132.2	138.4	218.1	127.4	139.0	124.3	134.3	102.3	177.8
April	151.8	160.4	148.1	105.6	131.9	139.2	218.6	127.7	139.3	125.0	135.2	103.7	180.2
May	152.1	160.7	148.2	105.8	131.6	139.7	219.2	127.8	139.7	125.2	135.5	102.4	179.6
June	152.4	161.1	148.3	106.7	131.3	140.6	219.9	127.8	139.8	125.5	135.7	103.0	179.5
July	152.6	161.4	148.5	105.8	131.4	139.9	220.6	128.0	140.2	125.6	136.1	101.6	176.4
August	152.9	161.8	148.6	105.6	132.5	139.4	221.6	127.9	140.2	125.6	136.1	99.7	173.4
September	153.1	162.2	149.1	104.1	132.3	139.1	222.4	128.1	140.2	125.5	136.2	102.0	170.9
October	153.5	162.7	149.5	104.4	132.4	139.5	223.0	128.4	141.0	125.4	135.8	101.9	166.6
November	153.7	163.0	149.6	103.4	132.0	139.1	223.7	128.7	141.3	125.2	135.5	104.1	163.6
December	153.9	163.1	149.9	104.4	132.2	139.1	224.3	129.3	141.5	125.4	135.2	106.5	162.3
1996													
January	154.7	163.7	150.4	106.9	132.7	140.4	225.2	129.7	141.5	125.5	134.8	109.8	162.6
February	155.0	164.0	150.8	107.1	132.2	140.9	225.7	129.7	141.6	125.0	134.4	111.6	162.1
March	155.5	164.4	151.4	108.3	132.6	141.5	226.2	130.5	141.6	125.3	134.1	109.8	158.2
April	156.1	164.6	152.0	111.2	131.8	142.9	226.8	130.9	141.6	125.7	133.8	114.2	156.7
May	156.4	165.0	151.9	112.0	131.8	143.5	227.4	130.9	142.0	126.2	134.0	114.6	157.6
June	156.7	165.4	152.9	110.3	131.6	143.4	228.0	131.3	142.2	125.8	133.9	112.2	154.6
July	157.0	165.7	153.4	110.1	131.3	143.0	228.6	131.2	142.2	125.5	133.6	114.6	152.2
August	157.2	166.0	153.9	109.7	130.6	143.0	229.1	131.6	142.3	125.6	133.6	115.3	152.5
September	157.7	166.5	154.6	109.8	131.3	143.6	229.7	131.7	142.2	126.1	134.0	112.7	153.5
October	158.2	166.8	155.5	110.5	131.3	143.9	230.3	132.4	142.3	126.0	133.7	111.9	153.3
November	158.7	167.2	156.1	111.8	131.6	144.6	231.0	132.5	142.1	125.8	133.7	115.7	153.0
December	159.1	167.4	156.3	113.9	131.9	145.7	231.2	132.9	142.3	126.4	133.9	122.5	153.6
1997													
January	159.4	167.8	155.9	115.2	132.3	145.6	231.8	133.0	142.5	126.6	134.1	127.5	156.2
February	159.7	168.1	156.5	115.0	133.0	145.2	232.2	132.7	142.4	126.5	134.1	116.6	157.6
March	159.8	168.4	156.6	113.0	132.4	145.0	233.0	132.6	142.6	126.1	134.2	107.5	158.7
April	159.9	168.9	156.5	111.0	133.0	144.3	233.5	131.8	142.6	125.6	134.1	107.8	155.8
May	159.9	169.2	156.6	108.8	133.3	143.3	234.1	131.5	142.4	125.4	134.2	109.1	157.0
June	160.2	169.4	156.9	110.0	133.1	143.6	234.4	131.3	142.4	125.4	134.2	106.2	156.9
July	160.4	169.7	157.2	109.1	133.3	143.3	234.7	130.9	142.2	125.1	134.2	106.2	155.7
August	160.8	169.8	157.7	110.9	132.7	144.1	235.1	131.4	142.3	125.3	134.3	106.8	156.8
September	161.2	170.2	158.0	112.4	132.9	144.8	235.5	131.6	142.6	125.5	134.3	108.4	155.8
October	161.5	170.6	158.3	111.8	132.7	144.7	236.1	131.9	142.6	125.4	134.3	113.4	156.7
November	161.7	170.8	158.6	111.4	132.7	143.9	236.9	131.6	142.4	125.6	134.4	115.8	156.5
December	161.8	171.2	158.7	109.8	133.0	143.7	237.8	131.4	142.3	125.4	134.4	108.8	154.2
1998													
January	162.0	171.6	159.5	107.5	133.1	143.0	238.1	130.7	142.4	124.6	134.3	102.8	150.4
February	162.0	171.9	159.4	105.1	133.0	142.4	238.8	130.6	142.6	124.2	134.2	100.8	150.1
March	162.0	172.2	159.7	103.3	132.7	141.5	239.4	130.5	143.3	123.7	134.1	99.5	148.7
April	162.2	172.5	159.7	102.4	132.3	140.9	240.3	130.7	143.4	123.6	134.0	100.6	147.3
May	162.6	172.9	160.3	103.2	132.7	141.2	241.2	130.5	143.5	123.5	133.9	99.6	146.2
June	162.8	173.2	160.2	103.6	133.3	141.4	241.8	130.4	143.5	123.1	133.6	97.1	145.9
July	163.2	173.5	160.6	103.3	133.5	141.7	242.5	130.7	143.8	123.0	133.5	97.4	143.4
August	163.4	174.0	161.0	102.1	135.1	141.6	243.3	130.4	143.8	122.7	133.4	93.6	139.4
September	163.5	174.2	161.1	101.3	133.1	141.2	244.1	130.4	144.0	122.3	133.1	91.4	137.6
October	163.9	174.4	162.0	101.5	132.7	141.4	244.8	130.9	144.2	122.2	132.7	93.9	134.0
November	164.1	174.8	162.2	101.1	132.7	141.3	245.3	130.8	144.3	122.0	132.5	93.6	131.6
December	164.4	175.4	162.4	100.1	132.0	140.9	245.9	131.3	145.8	121.3	132.2	90.2	129.4

Table 20-2. Summary Consumer and Producer Price Indexes—*Continued*

(Seasonally adjusted.)

Year and month	Consumer Price Index, all urban consumers, 1982–1984 = 100							Producer Price Index, 1982 = 100					
								Finished goods		Intermediate materials, supplies, and components		Crude materials for further processing	
	All items	All items less food and energy	Food	Energy	Apparel	Transportation	Medical care	Total	Less food and energy	Total	Less food and energy	Total	Crude nonfood less energy
1999													
January	164.7	175.6	163.0	99.7	131.5	140.8	246.5	. . .	. . .	121.2	132.0	91.0	128.7
February	164.7	175.6	163.3	99.2	130.8	140.0	247.3	. . .	. . .	120.8	131.8	89.0	130.5
March	164.8	175.7	163.3	100.4	130.4	140.7	247.9	. . .	. . .	121.1	131.9	89.6	129.6
April	165.9	176.3	163.5	105.5	131.7	143.6	248.7	. . .	. . .	121.9	132.0	91.3	128.7
May	166.0	176.5	163.8	104.9	131.7	143.4	249.3	. . .	. . .	122.2	132.4	96.8	130.5
June	166.0	176.6	163.7	104.5	131.7	143.0	250.0	. . .	. . .	122.6	132.8	97.0	131.6
July	166.7	177.1	163.9	106.7	131.5	144.6	250.9	. . .	. . .	123.4	133.3	97.3	133.6
August	167.1	177.3	164.2	109.5	130.9	144.9	251.7	. . .	. . .	124.1	133.6	102.4	136.3
September	167.8	177.8	164.6	111.8	131.2	147.0	252.5	. . .	. . .	124.6	133.9	106.4	138.8
October	168.1	178.1	165.0	112.0	131.4	147.6	253.1	. . .	. . .	124.9	134.3	103.8	142.5
November	168.4	178.4	165.3	111.5	131.0	147.5	253.9	. . .	. . .	125.4	134.5	109.7	144.4
December	168.8	178.7	165.5	113.8	131.3	148.8	254.9	. . .	. . .	125.8	134.7	104.4	147.6
2000													
January	169.3	179.3	165.6	115.0	130.7	149.1	255.6	135.2	146.8	126.4	135.1	106.8	150.5
February	170.0	179.4	166.2	118.8	130.4	150.0	256.5	136.6	147.3	127.5	135.5	111.0	151.3
March	171.0	180.0	166.5	124.3	130.3	153.6	257.7	137.3	147.4	128.4	136.0	113.2	150.5
April	170.9	180.3	166.7	120.9	129.8	152.1	258.4	136.9	147.4	128.3	136.5	111.3	148.8
May	171.2	180.7	167.3	120.0	129.7	152.0	259.2	137.0	147.8	128.2	136.6	115.1	147.8
June	172.2	181.1	167.4	126.8	129.3	155.0	260.3	138.1	147.8	129.3	136.9	124.8	145.1
July	172.7	181.5	168.3	127.3	128.9	154.6	261.2	138.2	148.1	129.6	137.1	122.1	142.8
August	172.7	181.9	168.7	123.8	128.9	153.2	262.4	137.9	148.2	129.3	136.9	117.6	141.2
September	173.6	182.3	168.9	129.2	129.5	155.2	263.3	139.0	148.6	130.3	137.0	125.6	142.9
October	173.9	182.6	169.0	129.6	129.2	154.7	264.1	139.5	148.5	130.7	137.1	130.2	142.1
November	174.2	183.1	169.2	129.2	129.2	155.0	264.7	140.2	148.7	130.7	136.9	129.1	139.6
December	174.6	183.3	170.0	130.1	129.1	155.1	265.6	140.5	148.9	131.3	136.9	141.1	139.5
2001													
January	175.6	183.9	170.3	135.0	129.4	155.4	267.2	141.7	149.5	132.1	137.1	165.6	138.7
February	176.0	184.4	171.2	134.1	129.6	155.2	268.3	141.9	149.2	131.8	137.3	141.7	136.5
March	176.1	184.7	171.7	131.7	129.5	154.2	269.4	141.2	149.5	131.0	137.4	132.4	135.0
April	176.4	185.1	172.1	132.3	128.2	154.8	270.4	142.0	149.8	130.9	137.3	133.0	131.3
May	177.3	185.3	172.4	138.4	127.4	157.6	271.3	142.3	150.1	131.1	137.3	130.5	130.9
June	177.7	186.0	173.1	136.9	127.4	157.3	272.4	141.8	150.2	130.9	137.1	119.9	129.7
July	177.4	186.4	173.6	129.6	127.3	154.0	272.8	140.1	150.5	129.4	136.4	113.3	130.6
August	177.4	186.7	174.0	127.3	126.4	153.4	274.3	140.7	150.5	129.1	135.9	112.3	128.4
September	178.1	187.1	174.2	130.9	125.8	156.0	275.2	141.3	150.7	129.3	135.9	107.2	128.8
October	177.6	187.4	174.8	122.9	125.8	152.9	276.3	139.0	149.8	127.6	135.4	97.4	126.5
November	177.5	188.1	174.9	116.9	125.4	150.2	277.4	138.5	150.2	127.0	135.1	102.7	126.2
December	177.4	188.4	174.7	113.9	124.9	149.2	278.2	138.0	150.4	126.1	134.8	95.5	125.7
2002													
January	177.7	188.7	175.3	114.2	124.4	149.3	279.8	137.7	150.0	125.7	134.7	99.8	126.2
February	178.0	189.1	175.7	113.5	124.6	148.7	280.4	138.0	150.1	125.5	134.6	98.4	127.5
March	178.5	189.2	176.1	117.6	125.3	150.5	281.4	138.8	150.0	126.4	135.0	103.8	128.1
April	179.3	189.7	176.4	121.5	125.1	152.5	282.7	138.7	150.3	127.2	135.3	108.1	130.8
May	179.5	190.0	175.8	121.9	124.6	152.8	283.9	138.4	150.2	127.1	135.3	109.0	134.2
June	179.6	190.2	175.9	121.6	123.9	152.8	284.6	138.8	150.5	127.3	135.6	105.1	138.2
July	180.0	190.5	176.1	122.4	123.5	153.3	286.4	138.6	150.0	127.7	136.0	106.5	140.8
August	180.5	191.1	176.1	123.1	124.3	154.0	287.2	138.7	149.9	128.0	136.2	108.3	140.0
September	180.8	191.3	176.5	123.7	123.4	154.2	288.1	139.2	150.3	128.9	136.5	110.8	140.2
October	181.2	191.5	176.4	126.9	123.0	155.5	289.8	140.0	150.5	129.8	136.7	112.6	140.0
November	181.5	191.9	176.9	126.7	123.1	155.4	291.2	140.0	150.3	129.9	136.8	116.6	141.0
December	181.8	192.1	177.1	127.1	122.7	155.3	292.1	139.7	149.5	130.0	136.7	118.9	141.3
2003													
January	182.6	192.4	177.1	133.5	122.1	158.0	292.7	141.1	149.8	131.4	137.2	128.0	143.3
February	183.6	192.5	178.1	140.8	121.8	160.8	293.0	142.7	149.9	133.8	138.1	134.3	148.1
March	183.9	192.5	178.4	143.9	120.7	160.8	293.4	144.0	150.7	136.3	138.6	152.2	147.5
April	183.2	192.5	178.5	136.5	120.3	157.7	294.0	142.2	149.9	133.1	138.3	128.2	145.9
May	182.9	192.9	178.8	129.4	120.0	154.4	295.2	141.9	150.1	132.4	138.4	129.9	146.0
June	183.1	193.0	179.7	129.8	120.6	154.6	296.1	142.7	150.1	133.1	138.4	135.5	145.7
July	183.7	193.4	179.8	132.2	121.1	155.7	297.4	142.8	150.3	133.3	138.2	131.9	148.5
August	184.5	193.6	180.5	137.8	120.8	158.2	298.3	143.7	150.5	133.9	138.4	130.8	152.1
September	185.1	193.7	180.9	142.9	120.9	159.9	299.8	144.0	150.4	133.8	138.8	134.4	156.2
October	184.9	194.0	181.6	137.8	121.1	157.5	300.4	144.8	151.1	134.2	139.1	138.2	160.2
November	185.0	194.0	182.6	136.9	120.8	156.9	301.4	144.6	151.0	134.2	139.3	137.9	165.6
December	185.5	194.2	183.5	138.8	120.2	157.4	303.0	145.1	151.0	135.0	139.6	142.4	171.0
2004													
January	186.3	194.6	183.4	143.9	120.1	159.8	303.8	145.9	151.4	136.6	140.5	148.7	179.7
February	186.7	194.9	183.9	145.8	120.1	160.7	305.2	145.8	151.3	137.8	141.8	150.8	190.0
March	187.1	195.5	184.2	145.1	120.4	160.8	306.5	146.2	151.8	138.4	142.9	153.2	195.0
April	187.4	195.9	184.6	143.4	120.6	159.8	307.8	147.2	151.9	140.1	144.6	156.2	187.1
May	188.2	196.2	186.1	147.6	120.9	161.6	308.6	148.4	152.3	141.7	145.7	160.6	177.6
June	188.9	196.6	186.4	151.5	121.2	162.8	309.8	148.4	152.8	142.2	146.2	161.5	176.3
July	189.1	196.8	186.8	151.1	121.0	162.3	310.8	148.2	152.5	142.9	146.9	161.3	195.7
August	189.2	196.9	187.0	151.5	120.3	162.1	311.8	148.6	152.9	144.4	148.4	161.7	201.6
September	189.8	197.5	186.9	152.9	120.0	163.4	312.9	148.8	153.2	144.8	149.6	154.0	198.3
October	190.8	197.9	187.8	158.6	120.3	166.7	314.0	151.2	153.7	146.6	150.2	161.0	204.6
November	191.7	198.3	188.4	163.8	120.6	169.1	314.7	152.1	154.1	147.9	150.7	172.7	208.9
December	191.7	198.6	188.4	162.3	119.8	168.5	315.8	151.4	154.5	147.7	151.3	167.2	206.0

. . . = Not available.

Table 20-2. Summary Consumer and Producer Price Indexes—*Continued*

(Seasonally adjusted.)

Year and month	Consumer Price Index, all urban consumers, 1982–1984 = 100							Producer Price Index, 1982 = 100					
								Finished goods		Intermediate materials, supplies, and components		Crude materials for further processing	
	All items	All items less food and energy	Food	Energy	Apparel	Transportation	Medical care	Total	Less food and energy	Total	Less food and energy	Total	Crude nonfood less energy
2005													
January	191.6	199.0	188.7	157.2	120.3	166.5	316.9	151.9	155.4	148.5	152.4	164.2	203.7
February	192.4	199.4	188.6	161.8	120.0	168.4	318.4	152.7	155.3	149.5	153.2	162.9	200.2
March	193.1	200.1	189.1	163.5	120.5	169.2	319.7	153.7	155.6	150.7	153.8	170.5	199.6
April	193.7	200.2	190.4	166.7	119.9	170.3	320.7	154.2	156.0	151.3	153.9	175.0	203.5
May	193.6	200.5	190.6	163.3	119.9	168.7	321.8	153.9	156.4	150.6	153.5	169.1	196.6
June	193.7	200.6	190.5	163.7	119.4	169.1	322.8	153.9	156.2	151.1	153.3	165.5	188.9
July	194.9	200.9	190.9	172.8	119.0	172.8	324.1	155.0	156.8	152.3	153.5	174.4	190.5
August	196.1	201.1	191.1	183.5	119.5	177.3	324.2	156.3	156.9	153.2	153.4	181.5	200.9
September	198.8	201.3	191.5	208.2	119.1	187.7	325.3	158.8	157.1	157.2	155.0	200.3	211.3
October	199.1	202.0	192.0	205.9	119.0	184.5	326.9	160.5	156.8	162.3	157.2	212.7	207.7
November	198.1	202.5	192.6	191.0	119.2	176.8	328.7	158.7	156.8	160.3	157.9	209.9	214.0
December	198.1	202.8	192.9	187.6	118.6	176.0	329.2	159.6	156.8	160.2	158.5	202.0	216.7
2006													
January	199.2	203.2	193.6	196.0	119.1	178.7	329.6	160.6	157.5	162.4	159.8	200.2	216.5
February	199.4	203.6	193.7	194.8	117.9	178.7	331.2	158.8	158.0	161.6	160.3	183.3	224.0
March	199.7	204.3	194.0	192.2	119.0	178.0	332.7	159.4	158.3	161.6	161.1	178.5	227.4
April	200.6	204.9	193.8	197.4	119.6	181.1	334.0	160.4	158.5	162.9	162.0	182.9	238.6
May	201.4	205.5	194.1	200.6	119.9	183.0	335.1	160.5	158.9	164.4	163.8	185.5	259.0
June	201.9	206.0	194.7	200.5	120.1	183.4	336.1	161.3	159.0	165.3	164.7	180.0	255.2
July	202.9	206.3	195.1	207.5	119.0	186.8	336.9	160.9	158.1	165.5	165.6	185.0	259.7
August	203.7	206.8	195.7	211.2	119.8	188.3	338.0	162.1	158.7	166.6	166.3	190.8	251.8
September	202.9	207.2	196.3	198.9	120.2	181.9	339.0	160.1	159.2	164.6	166.2	183.9	255.1
October	201.8	207.6	196.9	183.5	119.8	175.7	339.9	158.6	158.4	162.8	166.1	168.5	249.5
November	202.0	207.8	197.0	183.8	119.4	174.7	340.7	160.1	159.9	163.7	165.4	188.4	249.5
December	203.1	208.1	197.1	192.7	119.8	178.4	341.1	161.2	160.0	164.7	165.6	192.6	253.6
2007													
January	203.4	208.6	198.3	189.9	120.1	177.1	343.6	160.8	160.2	164.0	165.6	181.4	256.0
February	204.3	209.1	199.8	193.0	120.2	177.9	345.4	162.7	160.9	165.4	165.6	197.5	265.6
March	205.3	209.3	200.4	201.2	119.7	181.3	346.0	164.4	160.9	166.9	166.3	202.2	284.3
April	206.0	209.7	201.0	204.0	119.1	182.7	347.4	165.7	161.1	168.7	167.7	204.4	287.7
May	206.9	210.1	201.8	209.4	119.0	184.9	348.5	166.5	161.5	170.1	168.7	206.1	282.2
June	207.2	210.4	202.6	209.0	118.4	184.7	349.5	166.4	161.8	170.6	169.0	207.0	281.2
July	207.7	210.9	203.2	209.2	118.6	185.3	351.7	167.4	162.2	171.9	169.6	208.2	284.2
August	207.7	211.2	204.0	205.9	118.0	184.2	353.3	165.9	162.3	170.2	168.9	201.9	285.7
September	208.5	211.6	205.0	210.0	118.1	186.1	354.5	167.2	162.4	170.7	169.0	204.3	291.5
October	209.1	212.1	205.6	211.2	118.4	186.5	356.3	168.4	162.6	171.7	169.6	212.9	294.9
November	210.7	212.6	206.4	223.1	119.0	191.9	357.7	172.0	163.2	176.4	170.9	226.5	291.9
December	211.4	213.1	206.8	225.9	119.5	193.3	358.8	171.5	163.3	176.5	171.1	229.8	293.4
2008													
January	212.2	213.7	208.1	227.9	119.7	194.4	360.5	173.3	164.1	179.1	172.6	236.3	308.1
February	212.7	213.9	208.9	230.6	118.8	194.9	361.1	173.9	164.9	180.9	173.8	245.3	319.9
March	213.5	214.3	209.4	235.4	118.1	196.4	361.9	175.8	165.1	185.1	175.9	261.3	332.0
April	214.1	214.5	211.3	236.8	118.4	196.0	362.4	176.5	165.9	187.0	178.4	273.6	366.0
May	215.3	214.9	212.1	244.5	118.4	198.8	362.8	178.8	166.4	191.7	181.3	289.5	371.8
June	217.3	215.5	213.4	259.3	118.3	205.5	363.7	181.5	166.6	195.5	183.8	296.1	373.4
July	219.1	216.2	215.4	270.4	119.4	209.3	364.0	183.7	167.6	200.8	187.5	309.4	386.3
August	218.8	216.5	216.5	262.2	119.9	206.2	364.8	181.9	168.4	197.8	188.6	273.5	375.7
September	218.8	216.8	217.8	259.2	119.6	205.9	365.7	182.0	169.1	196.8	188.8	254.5	339.6
October	216.8	216.8	218.6	236.7	118.9	194.9	366.4	177.3	170.1	188.3	184.8	213.9	278.8
November	212.9	216.9	219.0	193.4	119.1	174.5	367.2	172.3	170.2	179.2	180.4	185.0	226.6
December	211.3	216.9	219.0	176.6	118.3	166.5	368.3	169.4	170.6	172.1	176.1	174.0	222.7
2009													
January	212.0	217.2	219.1	179.8	118.6	168.7	369.9	171.2	171.0	172.1	174.7	171.2	225.6
February	212.9	217.7	218.9	186.5	119.8	172.2	371.3	170.9	171.2	170.7	173.5	160.7	224.5
March	212.6	218.1	218.6	181.2	119.8	170.3	372.1	169.6	171.5	168.4	172.7	159.7	221.7
April	212.8	218.6	218.3	179.1	119.5	170.7	373.4	170.6	171.6	168.6	171.9	163.5	223.0
May	213.1	218.9	217.9	179.9	119.5	172.3	374.4	170.6	171.5	169.4	171.6	168.7	232.8
June	214.6	219.3	217.9	193.2	120.2	179.5	375.1	173.7	172.0	171.3	172.0	175.9	239.9
July	214.8	219.5	217.4	194.1	120.7	180.6	375.8	171.6	171.8	170.4	172.3	170.1	246.6
August	215.6	219.7	217.4	201.3	120.6	184.0	376.9	174.1	172.3	173.3	173.3	177.8	264.9
September	215.9	220.0	217.3	202.4	120.9	185.5	378.4	173.3	172.1	173.3	174.2	173.9	270.3
October	216.4	220.5	217.3	203.6	120.6	187.3	379.2	173.6	171.3	174.0	174.4	186.1	274.6
November	216.9	220.5	217.5	208.0	120.2	189.6	380.2	176.3	172.1	176.8	175.9	193.9	273.9
December	217.2	220.8	217.8	209.7	120.7	191.0	380.7	177.3	172.1	177.4	175.8	195.4	285.9

Table 20-3. Summary Labor Force, Employment, and Unemployment

(Thousands of persons, percent, seasonally adjusted, except as noted.)

Year and month	Civilian noninstitutional population [1]	Civilian labor force Thousands of persons	Participation rate (percent)	Men, 20 years and over	Women, 20 years and over	Both sexes, 16 to 19 years	Agricultural	Nonagricultural	Employment-population ratio, percent	Total	Unemployed 15 weeks and over	Rate (percent)
1947	101 827	59 350	58.3			57 038	7 890	49 148	56.0	2 311	...	3.9
1948	103 068	60 621	58.8	39 382	14 936	4 026	7 629	50 714	56.6	2 276	309	3.8
1949	103 994	61 286	58.9	38 803	15 137	3 712	7 658	49 993	55.4	3 637	684	5.9
1950	104 995	62 208	59.2	39 394	15 824	3 703	7 160	51 758	56.1	3 288	782	5.3
1951	104 621	62 017	59.2	39 626	16 570	3 767	6 726	53 235	57.3	2 055	303	3.3
1952	105 231	62 138	59.0	39 578	16 958	3 719	6 500	53 749	57.3	1 883	232	3.0
1953	107 056	63 015	58.9	40 296	17 164	3 720	6 260	54 919	57.1	1 834	210	2.9
1954	108 321	63 643	58.8	39 634	17 000	3 475	6 205	53 904	55.5	3 532	812	5.5
1955	109 683	65 023	59.3	40 526	18 002	3 642	6 450	55 722	56.7	2 852	702	4.4
1956	110 954	66 552	60.0	41 216	18 767	3 818	6 283	57 514	57.5	2 750	533	4.1
1957	112 265	66 929	59.6	41 239	19 052	3 778	5 947	58 123	57.1	2 859	560	4.3
1958	113 727	67 639	59.5	40 411	19 043	3 582	5 586	57 450	55.4	4 602	1 452	6.8
1959	115 329	68 369	59.3	41 267	19 524	3 838	5 565	59 065	56.0	3 740	1 040	5.5
1960	117 245	69 628	59.4	41 543	20 105	4 129	5 458	60 318	56.1	3 852	957	5.5
1961	118 771	70 459	59.3	41 342	20 296	4 108	5 200	60 546	55.4	4 714	1 532	6.7
1962	120 153	70 614	58.8	41 815	20 693	4 195	4 944	61 759	55.5	3 911	1 119	5.5
1963	122 416	71 833	58.7	42 251	21 257	4 255	4 687	63 076	55.4	4 070	1 088	5.7
1964	124 485	73 091	58.7	42 886	21 903	4 516	4 523	64 782	55.7	3 786	973	5.2
1948												
January	102 603	60 095	58.6	39 386	14 556	4 119	8 077	49 984	56.6	2 034	311	3.4
February	102 698	60 524	58.9	39 480	14 621	4 095	7 696	50 500	56.7	2 328	283	3.8
March	102 771	60 070	58.5	39 098	14 481	4 092	7 333	50 338	56.1	2 399	292	4.0
April	102 831	60 677	59.0	39 157	15 001	4 133	7 557	50 734	56.7	2 386	324	3.9
May	102 923	59 972	58.3	39 139	14 712	4 003	7 141	50 713	56.2	2 118	329	3.5
June	102 992	60 957	59.2	39 392	15 213	4 138	7 591	51 152	57.0	2 214	322	3.6
July	103 216	61 181	59.3	39 607	15 348	4 013	7 602	51 366	57.1	2 213	295	3.6
August	103 240	60 806	58.9	39 510	14 994	3 952	7 562	50 894	56.6	2 350	332	3.9
September	103 291	60 815	58.9	39 324	15 207	3 982	7 865	50 648	56.6	2 302	298	3.8
October	103 361	60 646	58.7	39 522	14 956	3 909	7 626	50 761	56.5	2 259	324	3.7
November	103 424	60 702	58.7	39 459	15 054	3 904	7 624	50 793	56.5	2 285	282	3.8
December	103 468	61 169	59.1	39 539	15 137	4 064	7 984	50 756	56.8	2 429	305	4.0
1949												
January	103 529	60 771	58.7	39 233	14 991	3 951	7 790	50 385	56.2	2 596	315	4.3
February	103 559	61 057	59.0	39 117	15 117	3 974	8 022	50 186	56.2	2 849	374	4.7
March	103 665	61 073	58.9	39 015	15 069	3 959	8 008	50 035	56.0	3 030	414	5.0
April	103 739	61 007	58.8	38 993	14 978	3 776	7 911	49 836	55.7	3 260	483	5.3
May	103 845	61 259	59.0	38 701	15 066	3 785	8 067	49 485	55.4	3 707	602	6.1
June	103 930	60 948	58.6	38 632	15 003	3 537	7 802	49 370	55.0	3 776	705	6.2
July	104 042	61 301	58.9	38 405	15 244	3 541	8 021	49 169	55.0	4 111	848	6.7
August	104 121	61 590	59.2	38 610	15 181	3 606	7 604	49 793	55.1	4 193	917	6.8
September	104 219	61 633	59.1	38 744	15 129	3 711	7 297	50 287	55.3	4 049	973	6.6
October	104 338	62 185	59.6	38 394	15 260	3 615	6 814	50 455	54.9	4 916	1 000	7.9
November	104 421	62 005	59.4	38 860	15 422	3 727	7 497	50 512	55.6	3 996	1 056	6.4
December	104 524	61 908	59.2	38 908	15 300	3 637	7 379	50 466	55.3	4 063	961	6.6
1950												
January	104 619	61 661	58.9	38 780	15 255	3 600	7 065	50 570	55.1	4 026	947	6.5
February	104 737	61 687	58.9	38 818	15 339	3 594	7 057	50 694	55.1	3 936	947	6.4
March	104 844	61 604	58.8	38 851	15 366	3 511	7 116	50 612	55.1	3 876	912	6.3
April	104 943	62 158	59.2	39 100	15 831	3 652	7 264	51 319	55.8	3 575	920	5.8
May	105 014	62 083	59.1	39 416	15 628	3 605	7 277	51 372	55.8	3 434	890	5.5
June	105 104	62 419	59.4	39 476	15 953	3 623	7 285	51 767	56.2	3 367	868	5.4
July	105 194	62 121	59.1	39 517	15 793	3 691	7 126	51 875	56.1	3 120	769	5.0
August	105 282	62 596	59.5	39 879	16 124	3 794	7 248	52 549	56.8	2 799	633	4.5
September	105 269	62 349	59.2	39 865	15 902	3 808	6 992	52 583	56.6	2 774	648	4.4
October	105 096	62 428	59.4	39 737	16 175	3 891	7 371	52 432	56.9	2 625	545	4.2
November	104 979	62 286	59.3	39 668	16 195	3 834	7 163	52 534	56.9	2 589	507	4.2
December	104 872	62 068	59.2	39 536	16 149	3 744	6 760	52 669	56.7	2 639	482	4.3
1951												
January	104 844	61 941	59.1	39 595	16 279	3 762	6 828	52 808	56.9	2 305	438	3.7
February	104 604	61 778	59.1	39 695	16 257	3 709	6 738	52 923	57.0	2 117	386	3.4
March	104 629	62 526	59.8	40 013	16 557	3 831	6 858	53 543	57.7	2 125	355	3.4
April	104 541	61 808	59.1	39 804	16 426	3 659	6 722	53 167	57.3	1 919	294	3.1
May	104 491	62 044	59.4	39 752	16 581	3 855	6 752	53 436	57.6	1 856	269	3.0
June	104 488	61 615	59.0	39 538	16 368	3 714	6 529	53 091	57.1	1 995	258	3.2
July	104 504	62 106	59.4	39 483	16 898	3 775	6 601	53 555	57.6	1 950	260	3.1
August	104 536	61 927	59.2	39 508	16 665	3 821	6 790	53 204	57.4	1 933	249	3.1
September	104 588	61 780	59.1	39 416	16 504	3 793	6 558	53 155	57.1	2 067	223	3.3
October	104 690	62 204	59.4	39 555	16 674	3 781	6 636	53 374	57.3	2 194	269	3.5
November	104 740	62 014	59.2	39 504	16 669	3 663	6 699	53 137	57.1	2 178	316	3.5
December	104 810	62 457	59.6	39 691	16 946	3 860	7 065	53 432	57.7	1 960	269	3.1

[1] Not seasonally adjusted.
. . . = Not available.

Table 20-3. Summary Labor Force, Employment, and Unemployment—*Continued*

(Thousands of persons, percent, seasonally adjusted, except as noted.)

Year and month	Civilian noninsti- tutional population [1]	Civilian labor force		Employment, thousands of persons					Employ- ment- population ratio, percent	Unemployment		
				By age and sex			By industry			Thousands of persons		
		Thousands of persons	Participa- tion rate (percent)	Men, 20 years and over	Women, 20 years and over	Both sexes, 16 to 19 years	Agricultural	Nonagri- cultural		Total	Unem- ployed 15 weeks and over	Rate (percent)
1952												
January	104 862	62 432	59.5	39 714	17 001	3 745	7 148	53 312	57.7	1 972	282	3.2
February	104 868	62 419	59.5	39 772	16 935	3 755	7 020	53 442	57.7	1 957	248	3.1
March	104 860	61 721	58.9	39 580	16 627	3 701	6 468	53 440	57.1	1 813	234	2.9
April	104 906	61 720	58.8	39 542	16 659	3 708	6 525	53 384	57.1	1 811	242	2.9
May	104 996	62 058	59.1	39 588	16 844	3 763	6 334	53 861	57.3	1 863	219	3.0
June	105 118	62 103	59.1	39 558	16 837	3 824	6 529	53 690	57.3	1 884	210	3.0
July	105 246	61 962	58.9	39 496	16 778	3 697	6 334	53 637	57.0	1 991	194	3.2
August	105 346	61 877	58.7	39 289	16 867	3 634	6 174	53 616	56.8	2 087	211	3.4
September	105 436	62 457	59.2	39 386	17 477	3 658	6 537	53 984	57.4	1 936	249	3.1
October	105 591	61 971	58.7	39 451	17 032	3 649	6 363	53 769	56.9	1 839	230	3.0
November	105 706	62 491	59.1	39 549	17 450	3 749	6 509	54 239	57.5	1 743	216	2.8
December	105 812	62 621	59.2	40 011	17 181	3 762	6 361	54 593	57.6	1 667	238	2.7
1953												
January	106 594	63 439	59.5	40 256	17 482	3 862	6 642	54 958	57.8	1 839	268	2.9
February	106 678	63 520	59.5	40 546	17 321	4 017	6 463	55 421	58.0	1 636	208	2.6
March	106 744	63 657	59.6	40 648	17 397	3 965	6 420	55 590	58.1	1 647	213	2.6
April	106 826	63 167	59.1	40 346	17 242	3 856	6 362	55 082	57.5	1 723	180	2.7
May	106 910	62 615	58.6	40 323	16 983	3 713	5 937	55 082	57.1	1 596	176	2.5
June	106 978	63 063	58.9	40 358	17 301	3 797	6 361	55 095	57.4	1 607	213	2.5
July	107 034	63 057	58.9	40 378	17 341	3 678	6 267	55 130	57.4	1 660	168	2.6
August	107 132	62 816	58.6	40 352	17 108	3 691	6 319	54 832	57.1	1 665	177	2.7
September	107 253	62 727	58.5	40 192	17 063	3 651	6 198	54 708	56.8	1 821	178	2.9
October	107 383	62 867	58.5	40 155	17 236	3 502	6 096	54 797	56.7	1 974	190	3.1
November	107 504	62 949	58.6	40 163	16 974	3 601	6 345	54 393	56.5	2 211	259	3.5
December	107 623	62 795	58.3	39 885	16 599	3 493	5 929	54 048	55.7	2 818	309	4.5
1954												
January	107 763	63 101	58.6	39 834	16 574	3 616	6 073	53 951	55.7	3 077	372	4.9
February	107 880	63 994	59.3	39 899	17 162	3 602	6 590	54 073	56.2	3 331	532	5.2
March	107 987	63 793	59.1	39 497	17 022	3 667	6 395	53 791	55.7	3 607	765	5.7
April	108 080	63 934	59.2	39 613	17 015	3 557	6 142	54 043	55.7	3 749	774	5.9
May	108 184	63 675	58.9	39 467	16 975	3 466	6 210	53 698	55.4	3 767	879	5.9
June	108 267	63 343	58.5	39 476	16 894	3 422	6 162	53 630	55.2	3 551	880	5.6
July	108 344	63 302	58.4	39 467	16 777	3 399	6 222	53 421	55.0	3 659	932	5.8
August	108 440	63 707	58.7	39 582	16 868	3 403	6 087	53 766	55.2	3 854	1 002	6.0
September	108 546	64 209	59.2	39 702	17 133	3 447	6 453	53 829	55.5	3 927	1 017	6.1
October	108 668	63 936	58.8	39 618	17 209	3 443	6 242	54 028	55.5	3 666	1 009	5.7
November	108 798	63 759	58.6	39 745	17 213	3 399	5 934	54 423	55.5	3 402	975	5.3
December	108 892	63 312	58.1	39 763	17 121	3 232	5 848	54 268	55.2	3 196	827	5.0
1955												
January	109 059	63 910	58.6	39 937	17 375	3 441	6 113	54 640	55.7	3 157	882	4.9
February	109 078	63 696	58.4	39 964	17 413	3 350	5 854	54 873	55.7	2 969	826	4.7
March	109 254	63 882	58.5	40 111	17 415	3 438	6 242	54 722	55.8	2 918	816	4.6
April	109 377	64 564	59.0	40 120	17 867	3 528	6 363	55 152	56.2	3 049	811	4.7
May	109 544	64 381	58.8	40 410	17 665	3 559	6 327	55 307	56.3	2 747	734	4.3
June	109 680	64 482	58.8	40 444	17 837	3 500	6 243	55 538	56.3	2 701	668	4.2
July	109 792	65 145	59.3	40 751	18 123	3 639	6 438	56 075	56.9	2 632	640	4.0
August	109 882	65 581	59.7	40 747	18 377	3 673	6 575	56 222	57.1	2 784	535	4.2
September	109 977	65 628	59.7	40 920	18 285	3 745	6 819	56 131	57.2	2 678	558	4.1
October	110 085	65 821	59.8	40 858	18 327	3 806	6 728	56 263	57.2	2 830	572	4.3
November	110 177	66 037	59.9	40 936	18 422	3 899	6 655	56 602	57.4	2 780	564	4.2
December	110 296	66 445	60.2	41 063	18 630	3 991	6 653	57 031	57.7	2 761	581	4.2
1956												
January	110 390	66 419	60.2	41 203	18 691	3 859	6 590	57 163	57.8	2 666	561	4.0
February	110 478	66 124	59.9	41 175	18 582	3 761	6 457	57 061	57.5	2 606	545	3.9
March	110 582	66 175	59.8	41 199	18 496	3 716	6 221	57 190	57.3	2 764	521	4.2
April	110 650	66 264	59.9	41 289	18 629	3 696	6 460	57 154	57.5	2 650	476	4.0
May	110 810	66 722	60.2	41 166	18 844	3 851	6 375	57 486	57.6	2 861	506	4.3
June	110 903	66 702	60.1	41 196	18 748	3 876	6 335	57 485	57.5	2 882	516	4.3
July	111 019	66 752	60.1	41 216	18 718	3 866	6 320	57 480	57.5	2 952	523	4.4
August	111 099	66 673	60.0	41 265	18 864	3 843	6 280	57 692	57.6	2 701	543	4.1
September	111 222	66 714	60.0	41 221	19 019	3 839	6 375	57 704	57.6	2 635	577	3.9
October	111 335	66 546	59.8	41 261	18 928	3 786	6 137	57 838	57.5	2 571	530	3.9
November	111 432	66 657	59.8	41 208	18 846	3 742	5 997	57 799	57.3	2 861	575	4.3
December	111 526	66 700	59.8	41 192	18 859	3 859	5 806	58 104	57.3	2 790	567	4.2
1957												
January	111 626	66 428	59.5	41 168	18 740	3 724	5 790	57 842	57.0	2 796	509	4.2
February	111 711	66 879	59.9	41 341	19 115	3 801	6 125	58 132	57.5	2 622	530	3.9
March	111 824	66 913	59.8	41 500	19 066	3 838	5 963	58 441	57.6	2 509	514	3.7
April	111 933	66 647	59.5	41 345	18 937	3 765	5 836	58 211	57.2	2 600	516	3.9
May	112 031	66 695	59.5	41 334	18 897	3 754	5 999	57 986	57.1	2 710	538	4.1
June	112 172	67 052	59.8	41 411	18 973	3 812	6 002	58 194	57.2	2 856	526	4.3
July	112 317	67 336	60.0	41 472	19 262	3 806	6 401	58 139	57.5	2 796	535	4.2
August	112 421	66 706	59.3	41 243	19 020	3 696	5 898	58 061	56.9	2 747	542	4.1
September	112 554	67 064	59.6	41 213	19 116	3 792	5 728	58 393	57.0	2 943	559	4.4
October	112 710	67 066	59.5	41 069	19 160	3 817	5 875	58 171	56.8	3 020	650	4.5
November	112 874	67 123	59.5	40 853	19 082	3 734	5 686	57 983	56.4	3 454	674	5.1
December	113 013	67 398	59.6	40 884	19 285	3 753	6 037	57 885	56.6	3 476	731	5.2

[1] Not seasonally adjusted.

Table 20-3. Summary Labor Force, Employment, and Unemployment—*Continued*

(Thousands of persons, percent, seasonally adjusted, except as noted.)

Year and month	Civilian noninstitutional population [1]	Civilian labor force — Thousands of persons	Civilian labor force — Participation rate (percent)	Men, 20 years and over	Women, 20 years and over	Both sexes, 16 to 19 years	Agricultural	Nonagricultural	Employment-population ratio, percent	Total	Unemployed 15 weeks and over	Rate (percent)
1958												
January	113 138	67 095	59.3	40 617	19 035	3 568	5 831	57 389	55.9	3 875	879	5.8
February	113 234	67 201	59.3	40 336	18 951	3 611	5 654	57 244	55.5	4 303	1 005	6.4
March	113 337	67 223	59.3	40 180	18 968	3 583	5 561	57 170	55.3	4 492	1 128	6.7
April	113 415	67 647	59.6	40 129	18 969	3 533	5 602	57 029	55.2	5 016	1 387	7.4
May	113 534	67 895	59.8	40 253	18 978	3 643	5 647	57 227	55.4	5 021	1 493	7.4
June	113 647	67 674	59.5	40 208	19 008	3 514	5 510	57 220	55.2	4 944	1 677	7.3
July	113 727	67 824	59.6	40 270	19 039	3 436	5 525	57 220	55.2	5 079	1 796	7.5
August	113 835	68 037	59.8	40 343	19 103	3 566	5 673	57 339	55.4	5 025	1 888	7.4
September	113 977	68 002	59.7	40 564	19 033	3 584	5 453	57 728	55.4	4 821	1 795	7.1
October	114 138	68 045	59.6	40 699	19 091	3 685	5 563	57 912	55.6	4 570	1 708	6.7
November	114 283	67 658	59.2	40 684	19 157	3 629	5 571	57 899	55.5	4 188	1 570	6.2
December	114 429	67 740	59.2	40 666	19 170	3 713	5 521	58 028	55.5	4 191	1 490	6.2
1959												
January	114 582	67 936	59.3	40 769	19 292	3 807	5 481	58 387	55.7	4 068	1 396	6.0
February	114 712	67 649	59.0	40 699	19 167	3 818	5 429	58 255	55.5	3 965	1 277	5.9
March	114 849	68 068	59.3	41 079	19 379	3 809	5 677	58 590	56.0	3 801	1 210	5.6
April	114 986	68 339	59.4	41 419	19 498	3 851	5 893	58 875	56.3	3 571	1 039	5.2
May	115 144	68 178	59.2	41 355	19 565	3 779	5 792	58 907	56.2	3 479	965	5.1
June	115 287	68 278	59.2	41 387	19 658	3 804	5 712	59 137	56.3	3 429	963	5.0
July	115 429	68 539	59.4	41 596	19 595	3 820	5 564	59 447	56.3	3 528	889	5.1
August	115 555	68 432	59.2	41 485	19 568	3 791	5 442	59 402	56.1	3 588	889	5.2
September	115 668	68 545	59.3	41 351	19 531	3 888	5 447	59 323	56.0	3 775	895	5.5
October	115 798	68 821	59.4	41 362	19 702	3 847	5 355	59 556	56.1	3 910	883	5.7
November	115 916	68 533	59.1	41 062	19 594	3 874	5 480	59 050	55.7	4 003	982	5.8
December	116 040	68 994	59.5	41 651	19 717	3 973	5 458	59 883	56.3	3 653	920	5.3
1960												
January	116 594	68 962	59.1	41 637	19 686	4 024	5 458	59 889	56.0	3 615	915	5.2
February	116 702	68 949	59.1	41 729	19 765	4 126	5 443	60 177	56.2	3 329	841	4.8
March	116 827	68 399	58.5	41 320	19 388	3 965	4 959	59 714	55.4	3 726	959	5.4
April	116 910	69 579	59.5	41 641	20 110	4 208	5 471	60 488	56.4	3 620	896	5.2
May	117 033	69 626	59.5	41 668	20 186	4 203	5 359	60 698	56.4	3 569	797	5.1
June	117 167	69 934	59.7	41 553	20 290	4 325	5 416	60 752	56.5	3 766	854	5.4
July	117 281	69 745	59.5	41 490	20 257	4 162	5 542	60 367	56.2	3 836	921	5.5
August	117 431	69 841	59.5	41 503	20 316	4 076	5 520	60 375	56.1	3 946	927	5.6
September	117 521	70 151	59.7	41 604	20 493	4 170	5 755	60 512	56.4	3 884	982	5.5
October	117 643	69 884	59.4	41 464	20 076	4 092	5 436	60 196	55.8	4 252	1 189	6.1
November	117 829	70 439	59.8	41 543	20 384	4 182	5 513	60 596	56.1	4 330	1 223	6.1
December	118 001	70 395	59.7	41 416	20 332	4 030	5 622	60 156	55.7	4 617	1 142	6.6
1961												
January	118 155	70 447	59.6	41 363	20 325	4 088	5 422	60 354	55.7	4 671	1 328	6.6
February	118 250	70 420	59.6	41 177	20 392	4 019	5 472	60 116	55.5	4 832	1 416	6.9
March	118 358	70 703	59.7	41 273	20 459	4 118	5 406	60 444	55.6	4 853	1 463	6.9
April	118 503	70 267	59.3	41 206	20 145	4 023	5 037	60 337	55.2	4 893	1 598	7.0
May	118 638	70 452	59.4	41 139	20 261	4 049	5 099	60 350	55.2	5 003	1 686	7.1
June	118 767	70 878	59.7	41 349	20 446	4 198	5 220	60 773	55.6	4 885	1 651	6.9
July	118 889	70 536	59.3	41 245	20 252	4 111	5 153	60 455	55.2	4 928	1 830	7.0
August	119 006	70 534	59.3	41 362	20 279	4 211	5 366	60 486	55.3	4 682	1 649	6.6
September	119 107	70 217	59.0	41 400	20 112	4 029	5 021	60 520	55.0	4 676	1 531	6.7
October	119 202	70 492	59.1	41 509	20 338	4 072	5 203	60 716	55.3	4 573	1 481	6.5
November	119 153	70 376	59.1	41 556	20 330	4 195	5 090	60 991	55.5	4 295	1 388	6.1
December	119 214	70 077	58.8	41 534	20 287	4 079	4 992	60 908	55.3	4 177	1 361	6.0
1962												
January	119 300	70 189	58.8	41 547	20 501	4 060	5 094	61 014	55.4	4 081	1 235	5.8
February	119 360	70 409	59.0	41 745	20 693	4 100	5 289	61 249	55.7	3 871	1 244	5.5
March	119 476	70 414	58.9	41 696	20 567	4 230	5 157	61 336	55.7	3 921	1 162	5.6
April	119 702	70 278	58.7	41 647	20 567	4 158	5 009	61 363	55.4	3 906	1 122	5.6
May	119 813	70 551	58.9	41 847	20 558	4 283	4 964	61 724	55.7	3 863	1 134	5.5
June	119 943	70 514	58.8	41 761	20 547	4 362	4 943	61 727	55.6	3 844	1 079	5.5
July	120 128	70 302	58.5	41 671	20 592	4 220	4 840	61 643	55.3	3 819	1 049	5.4
August	120 323	70 981	59.0	41 900	20 841	4 227	4 866	62 102	55.7	4 013	1 081	5.7
September	120 653	71 153	59.0	42 020	20 982	4 190	4 867	62 325	55.7	3 961	1 096	5.6
October	120 856	70 917	58.7	42 086	20 856	4 172	4 816	62 298	55.5	3 803	1 022	5.4
November	121 045	70 871	58.5	41 985	20 794	4 068	4 831	62 016	55.2	4 024	1 051	5.7
December	121 236	70 854	58.4	41 934	20 831	4 182	4 647	62 300	55.2	3 907	1 068	5.5
1963												
January	121 463	71 146	58.6	41 938	20 933	4 201	4 882	62 190	55.2	4 074	1 122	5.7
February	121 633	71 262	58.6	41 876	21 046	4 102	4 652	62 372	55.1	4 238	1 137	5.9
March	121 824	71 423	58.6	42 047	21 162	4 142	4 696	62 655	55.3	4 072	1 087	5.7
April	121 986	71 697	58.8	42 131	21 281	4 230	4 670	62 972	55.5	4 055	1 071	5.7
May	122 162	71 832	58.8	42 145	21 225	4 245	4 729	62 886	55.3	4 217	1 157	5.9
June	122 352	71 626	58.5	42 268	21 185	4 196	4 642	63 007	55.3	3 977	1 067	5.6
July	122 521	71 956	58.7	42 427	21 268	4 210	4 694	63 211	55.4	4 051	1 070	5.6
August	122 667	71 786	58.5	42 400	21 185	4 323	4 604	63 304	55.4	3 878	1 114	5.4
September	122 821	72 131	58.7	42 500	21 317	4 357	4 650	63 524	55.5	3 957	1 069	5.5
October	123 014	72 281	58.8	42 437	21 456	4 401	4 702	63 592	55.5	3 987	1 071	5.5
November	123 192	72 418	58.8	42 415	21 553	4 299	4 694	63 573	55.4	4 151	1 054	5.7
December	123 360	72 188	58.5	42 427	21 481	4 305	4 629	63 584	55.3	3 975	1 007	5.5

[1] Not seasonally adjusted.

Table 20-3. Summary Labor Force, Employment, and Unemployment—*Continued*

(Thousands of persons, percent, seasonally adjusted, except as noted.)

Year and month	Civilian noninsti-tutional population [1]	Civilian labor force		Employment, thousands of persons					Employ-ment-population ratio, percent	Unemployment		
		Thousands of persons	Participa-tion rate (percent)	By age and sex			By industry			Thousands of persons		Rate (percent)
				Men, 20 years and over	Women, 20 years and over	Both sexes, 16 to 19 years	Agricultural	Nonagri-cultural		Total	Unem-ployed 15 weeks and over	
1964												
January	123 560	72 356	58.6	42 510	21 462	4 355	4 603	63 724	55.3	4 029	1 057	5.6
February	123 707	72 683	58.8	42 579	21 652	4 520	4 563	64 188	55.6	3 932	1 015	5.4
March	123 857	72 713	58.7	42 600	21 685	4 478	4 366	64 397	55.5	3 950	1 039	5.4
April	124 019	73 274	59.1	42 885	22 110	4 361	4 414	64 942	55.9	3 918	934	5.3
May	124 204	73 395	59.1	43 025	22 103	4 503	4 603	65 028	56.1	3 764	975	5.1
June	124 386	73 032	58.7	42 760	21 995	4 463	4 556	64 662	55.6	3 814	1 047	5.2
July	124 567	73 007	58.6	42 998	21 846	4 555	4 591	64 808	55.7	3 608	1 002	4.9
August	124 731	73 118	58.6	42 963	22 002	4 498	4 573	64 890	55.7	3 655	934	5.0
September	124 920	73 290	58.7	43 009	21 863	4 706	4 619	64 959	55.7	3 712	917	5.1
October	125 108	73 308	58.6	43 023	21 984	4 575	4 550	65 032	55.6	3 726	903	5.1
November	125 291	73 286	58.5	43 171	21 954	4 610	4 496	65 239	55.7	3 551	922	4.8
December	125 468	73 465	58.6	43 109	22 136	4 569	4 322	65 492	55.6	3 651	873	5.0
1965												
January	125 647	73 569	58.6	43 237	22 282	4 478	4 271	65 726	55.7	3 572	793	4.9
February	125 810	73 857	58.7	43 279	22 276	4 572	4 322	65 805	55.7	3 730	919	5.1
March	125 985	73 949	58.7	43 370	22 373	4 696	4 318	66 121	55.9	3 510	796	4.7
April	126 155	74 228	58.8	43 397	22 416	4 820	4 424	66 209	56.0	3 595	796	4.8
May	126 320	74 466	59.0	43 579	22 494	4 961	4 724	66 310	56.2	3 432	736	4.6
June	126 499	74 412	58.8	43 487	22 759	4 779	4 444	66 581	56.1	3 387	786	4.6
July	126 573	74 761	59.1	43 489	22 841	5 130	4 390	67 070	56.5	3 301	683	4.4
August	126 756	74 616	58.9	43 447	22 783	5 132	4 355	67 007	56.3	3 254	733	4.4
September	126 906	74 502	58.7	43 371	22 684	5 231	4 271	67 015	56.2	3 216	732	4.3
October	127 043	74 838	58.9	43 461	22 819	5 415	4 418	67 277	56.4	3 143	672	4.2
November	127 171	74 797	58.8	43 447	22 829	5 448	4 093	67 631	56.4	3 073	645	4.1
December	127 294	75 093	59.0	43 513	22 983	5 566	4 159	67 903	56.6	3 031	659	4.0
1966												
January	127 394	75 186	59.0	43 495	23 098	5 605	4 077	68 121	56.7	2 988	623	4.0
February	127 514	74 954	58.8	43 528	23 089	5 517	4 078	68 056	56.6	2 820	594	3.8
March	127 626	75 075	58.8	43 576	23 109	5 503	4 069	68 119	56.6	2 887	583	3.8
April	127 744	75 338	59.0	43 679	23 227	5 604	4 108	68 402	56.8	2 828	575	3.8
May	127 879	75 447	59.0	43 710	23 282	5 505	3 930	68 567	56.7	2 950	534	3.9
June	127 983	75 647	59.1	43 662	23 359	5 754	3 967	68 808	56.9	2 872	475	3.8
July	128 102	75 736	59.1	43 574	23 422	5 864	3 920	68 940	56.9	2 876	427	3.8
August	128 240	76 046	59.3	43 636	23 605	5 905	3 921	69 225	57.0	2 900	464	3.8
September	128 359	76 056	59.3	43 718	23 881	5 659	3 952	69 306	57.1	2 798	488	3.7
October	128 494	76 199	59.3	43 776	23 881	5 744	3 912	69 489	57.1	2 798	494	3.7
November	128 627	76 610	59.6	43 804	24 130	5 906	3 945	69 895	57.4	2 770	464	3.6
December	128 730	76 641	59.5	43 820	24 025	5 884	3 906	69 823	57.3	2 912	488	3.8
1967												
January	128 909	76 639	59.5	44 029	23 872	5 770	3 890	69 781	57.1	2 968	489	3.9
February	129 032	76 521	59.3	43 997	23 919	5 690	3 723	69 883	57.0	2 915	459	3.8
March	129 190	76 328	59.1	43 922	23 832	5 685	3 757	69 682	56.8	2 889	436	3.8
April	129 344	76 777	59.4	44 061	24 161	5 660	3 748	70 134	57.1	2 895	428	3.8
May	129 515	76 773	59.3	44 100	24 172	5 572	3 658	70 186	57.0	2 929	417	3.8
June	129 722	77 270	59.6	44 230	24 303	5 745	3 689	70 589	57.3	2 992	422	3.9
July	129 918	77 464	59.6	44 364	24 416	5 740	3 833	70 687	57.4	2 944	412	3.8
August	130 187	77 712	59.7	44 410	24 600	5 757	3 963	70 804	57.4	2 945	441	3.8
September	130 392	77 812	59.7	44 535	24 683	5 636	3 851	71 003	57.4	2 958	448	3.8
October	130 582	78 194	59.9	44 610	24 802	5 639	4 008	71 043	57.5	3 143	472	4.0
November	130 754	78 191	59.8	44 625	24 914	5 586	3 933	71 192	57.5	3 066	490	3.9
December	130 936	78 491	59.9	44 719	25 104	5 650	4 076	71 397	57.6	3 018	485	3.8
1968												
January	131 112	77 578	59.2	44 606	24 581	5 513	3 908	70 792	57.0	2 878	503	3.7
February	131 277	78 230	59.6	44 659	24 881	5 689	3 959	71 270	57.3	3 001	468	3.8
March	131 412	78 256	59.6	44 663	25 019	5 697	3 904	71 475	57.4	2 877	447	3.7
April	131 553	78 270	59.5	44 753	25 072	5 736	3 875	71 686	57.4	2 709	393	3.5
May	131 712	78 847	59.9	44 841	25 513	5 753	3 814	72 293	57.8	2 740	395	3.5
June	131 872	79 120	60.0	44 914	25 466	5 802	3 806	72 376	57.8	2 938	405	3.7
July	132 053	78 970	59.8	44 935	25 347	5 805	3 820	72 267	57.6	2 883	426	3.7
August	132 251	78 811	59.6	44 897	25 201	5 945	3 736	72 307	57.5	2 768	393	3.5
September	132 446	78 858	59.5	44 893	25 445	5 834	3 758	72 414	57.5	2 686	375	3.4
October	132 617	78 913	59.5	44 884	25 475	5 865	3 741	72 483	57.5	2 689	386	3.4
November	132 903	79 209	59.6	44 996	25 674	5 824	3 758	72 736	57.6	2 715	357	3.4
December	133 120	79 463	59.7	45 262	25 712	5 804	3 746	73 032	57.7	2 685	351	3.4
1969												
January	133 324	79 523	59.6	45 154	25 777	5 874	3 704	73 101	57.6	2 718	339	3.4
February	133 465	80 019	60.0	45 339	26 092	5 896	3 770	73 557	57.9	2 692	358	3.4
March	133 639	80 079	59.9	45 305	26 115	5 947	3 668	73 699	57.9	2 712	353	3.4
April	133 821	80 281	60.0	45 262	26 233	6 028	3 629	73 894	57.9	2 758	386	3.4
May	134 027	80 125	59.8	45 278	26 283	5 851	3 706	73 706	57.8	2 713	387	3.4
June	134 213	80 696	60.1	45 313	26 429	6 138	3 663	74 217	58.0	2 816	368	3.5
July	134 414	80 827	60.1	45 305	26 516	6 138	3 548	74 411	58.0	2 868	377	3.5
August	134 597	81 106	60.3	45 513	26 556	6 181	3 613	74 637	58.1	2 856	373	3.5
September	134 774	81 290	60.3	45 447	26 572	6 231	3 551	74 699	58.1	3 040	391	3.7
October	135 012	81 494	60.4	45 488	26 658	6 299	3 517	74 928	58.1	3 049	374	3.7
November	135 239	81 397	60.2	45 505	26 652	6 384	3 477	75 064	58.1	2 856	392	3.5
December	135 489	81 624	60.2	45 577	26 832	6 331	3 409	75 331	58.1	2 884	413	3.5

[1]Not seasonally adjusted.

Table 20-3. Summary Labor Force, Employment, and Unemployment—*Continued*

(Thousands of persons, percent, seasonally adjusted, except as noted.)

Year and month	Civilian noninstitutional population [1]	Civilian labor force		Employment, thousands of persons					Employment-population ratio, percent	Unemployment		
		Thousands of persons	Participation rate (percent)	By age and sex			By industry			Thousands of persons		Rate (percent)
				Men, 20 years and over	Women, 20 years and over	Both sexes, 16 to 19 years	Agricultural	Nonagricultural		Total	Unemployed 15 weeks and over	
1970												
January	135 713	81 981	60.4	45 654	26 908	6 218	3 422	75 358	58.0	3 201	431	3.9
February	135 957	82 151	60.4	45 627	26 828	6 243	3 439	75 259	57.9	3 453	470	4.2
March	136 179	82 498	60.6	45 668	26 933	6 262	3 499	75 364	57.9	3 635	534	4.4
April	136 416	82 727	60.6	45 679	27 114	6 137	3 568	75 362	57.9	3 797	602	4.6
May	136 686	82 483	60.3	45 666	26 739	6 159	3 547	75 017	57.5	3 919	591	4.8
June	136 928	82 484	60.2	45 554	26 904	5 955	3 555	74 858	57.3	4 071	657	4.9
July	137 196	82 901	60.4	45 516	27 083	6 127	3 517	75 209	57.4	4 175	662	5.0
August	137 455	82 880	60.3	45 495	27 011	6 118	3 418	75 206	57.2	4 256	705	5.1
September	137 717	82 954	60.2	45 535	26 784	6 179	3 451	75 047	57.0	4 456	788	5.4
October	137 988	83 276	60.4	45 508	27 058	6 119	3 337	75 348	57.0	4 591	771	5.5
November	138 264	83 548	60.4	45 540	27 020	6 090	3 372	75 278	56.9	4 898	871	5.9
December	138 529	83 670	60.4	45 466	27 038	6 090	3 380	75 214	56.7	5 076	1 102	6.1
1971												
January	138 795	83 850	60.4	45 527	27 173	6 164	3 393	75 471	56.8	4 986	1 113	5.9
February	139 021	83 603	60.1	45 455	27 040	6 205	3 288	75 412	56.6	4 903	1 068	5.9
March	139 285	83 575	60.0	45 520	26 967	6 101	3 356	75 232	56.4	4 987	1 098	6.0
April	139 566	83 946	60.1	45 789	26 984	6 214	3 574	75 413	56.6	4 959	1 149	5.9
May	139 826	84 135	60.2	45 917	27 056	6 166	3 449	75 690	56.6	4 996	1 173	5.9
June	140 090	83 706	59.8	45 879	27 013	5 865	3 334	75 423	56.2	4 949	1 167	5.9
July	140 343	84 340	60.1	46 000	27 054	6 251	3 386	75 919	56.5	5 035	1 251	6.0
August	140 596	84 673	60.2	46 041	27 171	6 327	3 395	76 144	56.6	5 134	1 261	6.1
September	140 869	84 731	60.1	46 090	27 390	6 209	3 367	76 322	56.6	5 042	1 239	6.0
October	141 146	84 872	60.1	46 132	27 538	6 248	3 405	76 513	56.6	4 954	1 268	5.8
November	141 393	85 458	60.4	46 209	27 721	6 367	3 410	76 887	56.8	5 161	1 277	6.0
December	141 666	85 625	60.4	46 280	27 791	6 400	3 371	77 100	56.8	5 154	1 283	6.0
1972												
January	142 736	85 978	60.2	46 471	27 956	6 532	3 366	77 593	56.7	5 019	1 257	5.8
February	143 017	86 036	60.2	46 600	28 016	6 492	3 358	77 750	56.7	4 928	1 292	5.7
March	143 263	86 611	60.5	46 821	28 126	6 626	3 438	78 135	56.9	5 038	1 232	5.8
April	143 483	86 614	60.4	46 863	28 114	6 678	3 382	78 273	56.9	4 959	1 203	5.7
May	143 760	86 809	60.4	46 950	28 184	6 753	3 412	78 475	57.0	4 922	1 168	5.7
June	144 033	87 006	60.4	47 147	28 175	6 761	3 402	78 681	57.0	4 923	1 141	5.7
July	144 285	87 143	60.4	47 244	28 225	6 761	3 461	78 769	57.0	4 913	1 154	5.6
August	144 522	87 517	60.6	47 321	28 382	6 875	3 603	78 975	57.1	4 939	1 156	5.6
September	144 761	87 392	60.4	47 394	28 417	6 732	3 568	78 975	57.0	4 849	1 131	5.5
October	144 988	87 491	60.3	47 354	28 438	6 824	3 634	78 982	57.0	4 875	1 123	5.6
November	145 211	87 592	60.3	47 529	28 567	6 894	3 517	79 473	57.2	4 602	1 040	5.3
December	145 446	87 943	60.5	47 747	28 698	6 955	3 596	79 804	57.3	4 543	1 006	5.2
1973												
January	145 720	87 487	60.0	47 701	28 596	6 864	3 456	79 705	57.1	4 326	947	4.9
February	145 943	88 364	60.5	47 884	28 995	7 033	3 415	80 497	57.5	4 452	894	5.0
March	146 230	88 846	60.8	48 117	29 110	7 225	3 469	80 983	57.8	4 394	889	4.9
April	146 459	89 018	60.8	48 098	29 304	7 157	3 407	81 152	57.7	4 459	809	5.0
May	146 719	88 977	60.6	48 068	29 432	7 148	3 376	81 272	57.7	4 329	816	4.9
June	146 981	89 548	60.9	48 244	29 505	7 436	3 509	81 676	58.0	4 363	779	4.9
July	147 233	89 604	60.9	48 452	29 592	7 255	3 540	81 759	57.9	4 305	756	4.8
August	147 471	89 509	60.7	48 353	29 578	7 273	3 425	81 779	57.8	4 305	788	4.8
September	147 731	89 838	60.8	48 408	29 710	7 370	3 342	82 146	57.9	4 350	785	4.8
October	147 980	90 131	60.9	48 631	29 885	7 471	3 424	82 563	58.1	4 144	793	4.6
November	148 219	90 716	61.2	48 764	30 071	7 485	3 593	82 727	58.2	4 396	832	4.8
December	148 479	90 890	61.2	48 902	29 991	7 508	3 658	82 743	58.2	4 489	767	4.9
1974												
January	148 753	91 199	61.3	49 107	29 893	7 555	3 756	82 799	58.2	4 644	799	5.1
February	148 982	91 485	61.4	49 057	30 146	7 551	3 824	82 930	58.2	4 731	829	5.2
March	149 225	91 453	61.3	48 986	30 293	7 540	3 726	83 093	58.2	4 634	849	5.1
April	149 478	91 287	61.1	48 853	30 376	7 440	3 582	83 087	58.0	4 618	889	5.1
May	149 750	91 596	61.2	49 039	30 424	7 428	3 529	83 362	58.0	4 705	880	5.1
June	150 012	91 868	61.2	48 946	30 512	7 483	3 386	83 555	58.0	4 927	926	5.4
July	150 248	92 212	61.4	48 883	30 869	7 397	3 436	83 713	58.0	5 063	924	5.5
August	150 493	92 059	61.2	48 950	30 662	7 425	3 429	83 608	57.8	5 022	960	5.5
September	150 753	92 488	61.4	48 978	30 569	7 504	3 460	83 591	57.7	5 437	1 021	5.9
October	151 009	92 518	61.3	48 959	30 570	7 466	3 431	83 564	57.6	5 523	1 072	6.0
November	151 256	92 766	61.3	48 833	30 424	7 369	3 405	83 221	57.3	6 140	1 128	6.6
December	151 494	92 780	61.2	48 458	30 431	7 255	3 361	82 783	56.9	6 636	1 326	7.2
1975												
January	151 755	93 128	61.4	48 086	30 343	7 198	3 401	82 226	56.4	7 501	1 555	8.1
February	151 990	92 776	61.0	47 927	30 215	7 114	3 361	81 895	56.1	7 520	1 841	8.1
March	152 217	93 165	61.2	47 776	30 334	7 077	3 358	81 829	56.0	7 978	2 074	8.6
April	152 443	93 399	61.3	47 759	30 410	7 020	3 315	81 874	55.9	8 210	2 442	8.8
May	152 704	93 884	61.5	47 835	30 483	7 133	3 560	81 891	56.0	8 433	2 643	9.0
June	152 976	93 575	61.2	47 754	30 618	6 983	3 368	81 987	55.8	8 220	2 843	8.8
July	153 309	94 021	61.3	48 050	30 794	7 050	3 457	82 437	56.0	8 127	2 943	8.6
August	153 580	94 162	61.3	48 239	30 966	7 029	3 429	82 805	56.1	7 928	2 862	8.4
September	153 848	94 202	61.2	48 126	30 979	7 174	3 508	82 771	56.1	7 923	2 906	8.4
October	154 082	94 267	61.2	48 165	31 121	7 084	3 397	82 973	56.1	7 897	2 689	8.4
November	154 338	94 250	61.1	48 203	31 135	7 118	3 331	83 125	56.0	7 794	2 789	8.3
December	154 589	94 409	61.1	48 266	31 268	7 131	3 259	83 406	56.1	7 744	2 868	8.2

[1]Not seasonally adjusted.

Table 20-3. Summary Labor Force, Employment, and Unemployment—*Continued*

(Thousands of persons, percent, seasonally adjusted, except as noted.)

Year and month	Civilian noninsti-tutional population [1]	Civilian labor force		Employment, thousands of persons					Employ-ment-population ratio, percent	Unemployment		
				By age and sex			By industry			Thousands of persons		
		Thousands of persons	Participa-tion rate (percent)	Men, 20 years and over	Women, 20 years and over	Both sexes, 16 to 19 years	Agricultural	Nonagri-cultural		Total	Unem-ployed 15 weeks and over	Rate (percent)
1976												
January	154 853	94 934	61.3	48 592	31 595	7 213	3 387	84 013	56.4	7 534	2 713	7.9
February	155 066	94 998	61.3	48 721	31 680	7 271	3 304	84 368	56.5	7 326	2 519	7.7
March	155 306	95 215	61.3	48 836	31 842	7 307	3 296	84 689	56.7	7 230	2 441	7.6
April	155 529	95 746	61.6	49 097	31 951	7 368	3 438	84 978	56.8	7 330	2 210	7.7
May	155 765	95 847	61.5	49 193	32 147	7 454	3 367	85 427	57.0	7 053	2 115	7.4
June	156 026	95 885	61.5	49 010	32 267	7 286	3 310	85 253	56.8	7 322	2 332	7.6
July	156 276	96 583	61.8	49 236	32 334	7 523	3 358	85 735	57.0	7 490	2 316	7.8
August	156 525	96 741	61.8	49 417	32 437	7 369	3 380	85 843	57.0	7 518	2 378	7.8
September	156 779	96 553	61.6	49 485	32 390	7 298	3 278	85 895	56.9	7 380	2 296	7.6
October	156 993	96 704	61.6	49 524	32 412	7 338	3 316	85 958	56.9	7 430	2 292	7.7
November	157 235	97 254	61.9	49 561	32 753	7 320	3 263	86 371	57.0	7 620	2 354	7.8
December	157 438	97 348	61.8	49 599	32 914	7 290	3 251	86 552	57.0	7 545	2 375	7.8
1977												
January	157 688	97 208	61.6	49 738	32 872	7 318	3 185	86 743	57.0	7 280	2 200	7.5
February	157 913	97 785	61.9	49 838	32 997	7 507	3 222	87 120	57.2	7 443	2 174	7.6
March	158 131	98 115	62.0	50 031	33 246	7 531	3 212	87 596	57.4	7 307	2 057	7.4
April	158 371	98 330	62.1	50 185	33 470	7 616	3 313	87 958	57.6	7 059	1 936	7.2
May	158 657	98 665	62.2	50 280	33 851	7 623	3 432	88 322	57.8	6 911	1 928	7.0
June	158 928	99 093	62.4	50 544	33 678	7 737	3 340	88 619	57.9	7 134	1 918	7.2
July	159 185	98 913	62.1	50 597	33 749	7 738	3 247	88 837	57.8	6 829	1 907	6.9
August	159 430	99 366	62.3	50 745	33 809	7 887	3 260	89 181	58.0	6 925	1 836	7.0
September	159 674	99 453	62.3	50 825	34 218	7 659	3 201	89 501	58.1	6 751	1 853	6.8
October	159 915	99 815	62.4	51 046	34 187	7 819	3 272	89 780	58.2	6 763	1 789	6.8
November	160 129	100 576	62.8	51 316	34 536	7 909	3 375	90 386	58.6	6 815	1 804	6.8
December	160 376	100 491	62.7	51 492	34 668	7 945	3 320	90 785	58.7	6 386	1 717	6.4
1978												
January	160 617	100 873	62.8	51 542	34 948	7 894	3 434	90 950	58.8	6 489	1 643	6.4
February	160 831	100 837	62.7	51 578	35 118	7 823	3 320	91 199	58.8	6 318	1 584	6.3
March	161 038	101 092	62.8	51 635	35 310	7 810	3 351	91 404	58.8	6 337	1 531	6.3
April	161 263	101 574	63.0	51 912	35 546	7 936	3 349	92 045	59.2	6 180	1 502	6.1
May	161 518	101 896	63.1	52 050	35 597	8 122	3 325	92 444	59.3	6 127	1 420	6.0
June	161 794	102 371	63.3	52 240	35 828	8 275	3 483	92 860	59.5	6 028	1 352	5.9
July	162 034	102 399	63.2	52 190	35 764	8 136	3 441	92 649	59.3	6 309	1 373	6.2
August	162 259	102 511	63.2	52 228	35 856	8 347	3 401	93 030	59.4	6 080	1 242	5.9
September	162 502	102 795	63.3	52 284	36 274	8 112	3 400	93 270	59.5	6 125	1 308	6.0
October	162 783	103 080	63.3	52 448	36 525	8 160	3 409	93 724	59.7	5 947	1 319	5.8
November	163 017	103 562	63.5	52 802	36 559	8 124	3 284	94 201	59.8	6 077	1 242	5.9
December	163 272	103 809	63.6	52 807	36 686	8 088	3 396	94 185	59.8	6 228	1 269	6.0
1979												
January	163 516	104 057	63.6	53 072	36 697	8 179	3 305	94 643	59.9	6 109	1 250	5.9
February	163 726	104 502	63.8	53 233	36 904	8 192	3 373	94 956	60.1	6 173	1 297	5.9
March	164 027	104 589	63.8	53 120	37 159	8 201	3 368	95 112	60.0	6 109	1 365	5.8
April	164 162	104 172	63.5	53 085	36 944	8 074	3 291	94 812	59.8	6 069	1 272	5.8
May	164 459	104 171	63.3	53 178	37 134	8 019	3 272	95 059	59.8	5 840	1 239	5.6
June	164 720	104 638	63.5	53 309	37 221	8 149	3 331	95 348	59.9	5 959	1 171	5.7
July	164 970	105 002	63.6	53 384	37 514	8 108	3 335	95 671	60.0	5 996	1 123	5.7
August	165 198	105 096	63.6	53 336	37 548	7 892	3 374	95 402	59.8	6 320	1 203	6.0
September	165 431	105 530	63.8	53 510	37 798	8 032	3 371	95 969	60.0	6 190	1 172	5.9
October	165 813	105 700	63.7	53 478	37 931	7 995	3 325	96 079	59.9	6 296	1 219	6.0
November	166 051	105 812	63.7	53 435	38 065	8 074	3 436	96 138	60.0	6 238	1 239	5.9
December	166 300	106 258	63.9	53 555	38 259	8 119	3 400	96 533	60.1	6 325	1 277	6.0
1980												
January	166 544	106 562	64.0	53 501	38 367	8 011	3 316	96 563	60.0	6 683	1 353	6.3
February	166 759	106 697	64.0	53 686	38 389	7 920	3 397	96 598	60.0	6 702	1 358	6.3
March	166 984	106 442	63.7	53 353	38 406	7 954	3 418	96 295	59.7	6 729	1 457	6.3
April	167 197	106 591	63.8	53 035	38 427	7 771	3 326	95 907	59.4	7 358	1 694	6.9
May	167 407	106 929	63.9	52 915	38 335	7 695	3 382	95 563	59.1	7 984	1 740	7.5
June	167 643	106 780	63.7	52 712	38 312	7 658	3 296	95 386	58.9	8 098	1 760	7.6
July	167 932	107 159	63.8	52 733	38 374	7 689	3 319	95 477	58.8	8 363	1 995	7.8
August	168 103	107 105	63.7	52 815	38 511	7 498	3 234	95 590	58.8	8 281	2 162	7.7
September	168 297	107 098	63.6	52 866	38 595	7 616	3 443	95 634	58.9	8 021	2 309	7.5
October	168 503	107 405	63.7	53 094	38 620	7 603	3 372	95 945	58.9	8 088	2 306	7.5
November	168 695	107 568	63.8	53 210	38 795	7 540	3 396	96 149	59.0	8 023	2 329	7.5
December	168 883	107 352	63.6	53 333	38 737	7 564	3 492	96 142	59.0	7 718	2 406	7.2
1981												
January	169 104	108 026	63.9	53 392	39 042	7 521	3 429	96 526	59.1	8 071	2 389	7.5
February	169 280	108 242	63.9	53 445	39 280	7 466	3 345	96 846	59.2	8 051	2 344	7.4
March	169 453	108 553	64.1	53 662	39 464	7 445	3 365	97 206	59.4	7 982	2 276	7.4
April	169 641	108 925	64.2	53 886	39 628	7 542	3 529	97 527	59.6	7 869	2 231	7.2
May	169 829	109 222	64.3	53 879	39 759	7 410	3 369	97 679	59.5	8 174	2 221	7.5
June	170 042	108 396	63.7	53 576	39 682	7 040	3 334	96 964	59.0	8 098	2 250	7.5
July	170 246	108 556	63.8	53 814	39 683	7 196	3 296	97 397	59.1	7 863	2 166	7.2
August	170 399	108 725	63.8	53 718	39 723	7 248	3 379	97 310	59.1	8 036	2 241	7.4
September	170 593	108 294	63.5	53 625	39 342	7 097	3 361	96 703	58.7	8 230	2 261	7.6
October	170 809	109 024	63.8	53 482	39 843	7 053	3 412	96 966	58.8	8 646	2 303	7.9
November	170 996	109 236	63.9	53 335	39 908	6 964	3 415	96 792	58.6	9 029	2 345	8.3
December	171 166	108 912	63.6	53 149	39 708	6 788	3 227	96 418	58.2	9 267	2 374	8.5

[1]Not seasonally adjusted.

Table 20-3. Summary Labor Force, Employment, and Unemployment—*Continued*

(Thousands of persons, percent, seasonally adjusted, except as noted.)

Year and month	Civilian noninsti-tutional population [1]	Civilian labor force Thousands of persons	Civilian labor force Participa-tion rate (percent)	Men, 20 years and over	Women, 20 years and over	Both sexes, 16 to 19 years	Agricultural	Nonagri-cultural	Employ-ment-population ratio, percent	Total	Unem-ployed 15 weeks and over	Rate (percent)
1982												
January	171 335	109 089	63.7	53 103	39 821	6 768	3 393	96 299	58.2	9 397	2 409	8.6
February	171 489	109 467	63.8	53 172	39 859	6 731	3 375	96 387	58.2	9 705	2 758	8.9
March	171 667	109 567	63.8	53 054	39 936	6 682	3 372	96 300	58.1	9 895	2 965	9.0
April	171 844	109 820	63.9	53 081	39 848	6 647	3 351	96 225	57.9	10 244	3 086	9.3
May	172 026	110 451	64.2	53 234	40 121	6 761	3 434	96 682	58.2	10 335	3 276	9.4
June	172 190	110 081	63.9	52 933	40 219	6 391	3 331	96 212	57.8	10 538	3 451	9.6
July	172 364	110 342	64.0	52 896	40 228	6 369	3 402	96 091	57.7	10 849	3 555	9.8
August	172 511	110 514	64.1	52 797	40 336	6 500	3 408	96 225	57.8	10 881	3 696	9.8
September	172 690	110 721	64.1	52 760	40 275	6 469	3 385	96 119	57.6	11 217	3 889	10.1
October	172 881	110 744	64.1	52 624	40 105	6 486	3 489	95 726	57.4	11 529	4 185	10.4
November	173 058	111 050	64.2	52 537	40 111	6 464	3 510	95 602	57.3	11 938	4 485	10.8
December	173 199	111 083	64.1	52 497	40 164	6 371	3 414	95 618	57.2	12 051	4 662	10.8
1983												
January	173 354	110 695	63.9	52 487	40 268	6 406	3 439	95 722	57.2	11 534	4 668	10.4
February	173 505	110 634	63.8	52 453	40 336	6 300	3 382	95 707	57.1	11 545	4 641	10.4
March	173 656	110 587	63.7	52 615	40 368	6 196	3 360	95 819	57.1	11 408	4 612	10.3
April	173 794	110 828	63.8	52 814	40 542	6 204	3 341	96 219	57.3	11 268	4 370	10.2
May	173 953	110 796	63.7	52 922	40 538	6 182	3 328	96 314	57.3	11 154	4 538	10.1
June	174 125	111 879	64.3	53 515	40 695	6 423	3 462	97 171	57.8	11 246	4 470	10.1
July	174 306	111 756	64.1	53 835	41 041	6 332	3 481	97 727	58.1	10 548	4 329	9.4
August	174 440	112 231	64.3	53 837	41 314	6 457	3 502	98 106	58.2	10 623	4 070	9.5
September	174 602	112 298	64.3	53 983	41 650	6 383	3 347	98 669	58.4	10 282	3 854	9.2
October	174 779	111 926	64.0	54 146	41 597	6 296	3 303	98 736	58.4	9 887	3 648	8.8
November	174 951	112 228	64.1	54 499	41 788	6 442	3 291	99 438	58.7	9 499	3 535	8.5
December	175 121	112 327	64.1	54 662	41 852	6 482	3 332	99 664	58.8	9 331	3 379	8.3
1984												
January	175 533	112 209	63.9	54 975	41 812	6 414	3 293	99 908	58.8	9 008	3 254	8.0
February	175 679	112 615	64.1	55 213	42 196	6 415	3 353	100 471	59.1	8 791	2 991	7.8
March	175 824	112 713	64.1	55 281	42 328	6 358	3 233	100 734	59.1	8 746	2 881	7.8
April	175 969	113 098	64.3	55 373	42 512	6 451	3 291	101 045	59.3	8 762	2 858	7.7
May	176 123	113 649	64.5	55 661	43 071	6 461	3 343	101 850	59.7	8 456	2 884	7.4
June	176 284	113 817	64.6	55 996	42 944	6 651	3 383	102 208	59.9	8 226	2 612	7.2
July	176 440	113 972	64.6	55 921	42 979	6 535	3 344	102 091	59.8	8 537	2 638	7.5
August	176 583	113 682	64.4	55 930	42 885	6 348	3 286	101 877	59.6	8 519	2 604	7.5
September	176 763	113 857	64.4	56 095	42 967	6 428	3 393	102 097	59.7	8 367	2 538	7.3
October	176 956	114 019	64.4	56 183	43 052	6 403	3 194	102 444	59.7	8 381	2 526	7.4
November	177 135	114 170	64.5	56 274	43 244	6 454	3 394	102 578	59.8	8 198	2 438	7.2
December	177 306	114 581	64.6	56 313	43 472	6 438	3 385	102 838	59.9	8 358	2 401	7.3
1985												
January	177 384	114 725	64.7	56 184	43 589	6 529	3 317	102 985	59.9	8 423	2 284	7.3
February	177 516	114 876	64.7	56 216	43 787	6 552	3 317	103 238	60.0	8 321	2 389	7.2
March	177 667	115 328	64.9	56 356	44 035	6 598	3 250	103 739	60.2	8 339	2 394	7.2
April	177 799	115 331	64.9	56 374	44 000	6 562	3 306	103 630	60.1	8 395	2 393	7.3
May	177 944	115 234	64.8	56 531	43 905	6 496	3 280	103 652	60.1	8 302	2 292	7.2
June	178 096	114 965	64.6	56 288	43 958	6 259	3 161	103 344	59.8	8 460	2 310	7.4
July	178 263	115 320	64.7	56 435	43 975	6 397	3 143	103 664	59.9	8 513	2 329	7.4
August	178 405	115 291	64.6	56 655	44 103	6 337	3 121	103 974	60.0	8 196	2 258	7.1
September	178 572	115 905	64.9	56 845	44 395	6 417	3 064	104 593	60.3	8 248	2 242	7.1
October	178 770	116 145	65.0	56 969	44 565	6 313	3 051	104 796	60.3	8 298	2 295	7.1
November	178 940	116 135	64.9	56 972	44 617	6 418	3 062	104 945	60.4	8 128	2 207	7.0
December	179 112	116 354	65.0	56 995	44 889	6 332	3 141	105 075	60.4	8 138	2 208	7.0
1986												
January	179 670	116 682	64.9	57 637	44 944	6 306	3 287	105 600	60.6	7 795	2 089	6.7
February	179 821	116 882	65.0	57 269	44 804	6 407	3 083	105 397	60.3	8 402	2 308	7.2
March	179 985	117 220	65.1	57 353	44 960	6 524	3 200	105 637	60.5	8 383	2 261	7.2
April	180 148	117 316	65.1	57 358	45 081	6 513	3 153	105 799	60.5	8 364	2 162	7.1
May	180 311	117 528	65.2	57 287	45 289	6 513	3 150	105 939	60.5	8 439	2 232	7.2
June	180 503	118 084	65.4	57 471	45 621	6 484	3 193	106 383	60.7	8 508	2 320	7.2
July	180 682	118 129	65.4	57 514	45 837	6 459	3 141	106 669	60.8	8 319	2 269	7.0
August	180 828	118 150	65.3	57 597	45 926	6 492	3 082	106 933	60.8	8 135	2 276	6.9
September	180 997	118 395	65.4	57 630	45 972	6 483	3 171	106 914	60.8	8 310	2 318	7.0
October	181 186	118 516	65.4	57 660	46 046	6 567	3 128	107 145	60.9	8 243	2 188	7.0
November	181 363	118 634	65.4	57 941	46 070	6 464	3 220	107 255	60.9	8 159	2 202	6.9
December	181 547	118 611	65.3	58 185	46 132	6 411	3 148	107 580	61.0	7 883	2 161	6.6
1987												
January	181 827	118 845	65.4	58 264	46 219	6 470	3 143	107 810	61.0	7 892	2 168	6.6
February	181 998	119 122	65.5	58 279	46 444	6 534	3 208	108 049	61.1	7 865	2 117	6.6
March	182 179	119 270	65.5	58 362	46 549	6 497	3 214	108 194	61.2	7 862	2 070	6.6
April	182 344	119 336	65.4	58 503	46 746	6 545	3 246	108 548	61.3	7 542	2 091	6.3
May	182 533	120 008	65.7	58 713	47 052	6 669	3 345	109 089	61.6	7 574	2 104	6.3
June	182 703	119 644	65.5	58 581	47 102	6 563	3 216	109 030	61.4	7 398	2 087	6.2
July	182 885	119 902	65.6	58 740	47 229	6 665	3 235	109 399	61.6	7 268	1 921	6.1
August	183 002	120 318	65.7	58 810	47 322	6 925	3 112	109 945	61.8	7 261	1 878	6.0
September	183 161	120 011	65.5	58 964	47 285	6 660	3 189	109 720	61.6	7 102	1 866	5.9
October	183 311	120 509	65.7	59 073	47 533	6 676	3 219	110 063	61.8	7 227	1 794	6.0
November	183 470	120 540	65.7	59 210	47 622	6 673	3 145	110 360	61.9	7 035	1 797	5.8
December	183 620	120 729	65.7	59 217	47 781	6 795	3 213	110 580	62.0	6 936	1 767	5.7

[1]Not seasonally adjusted.

Table 20-3. Summary Labor Force, Employment, and Unemployment—*Continued*

(Thousands of persons, percent, seasonally adjusted, except as noted.)

Year and month	Civilian noninstitutional population [1]	Civilian labor force Thousands of persons	Participation rate (percent)	Men, 20 years and over	Women, 20 years and over	Both sexes, 16 to 19 years	Agricultural	Nonagricultural	Employment-population ratio, percent	Total	Unemployed 15 weeks and over	Rate (percent)
1988												
January	183 822	120 969	65.8	59 346	47 862	6 808	3 247	110 769	62.0	6 953	1 714	5.7
February	183 969	121 156	65.9	59 535	47 919	6 773	3 201	111 026	62.1	6 929	1 738	5.7
March	184 111	120 913	65.7	59 393	48 090	6 554	3 169	110 868	61.9	6 876	1 744	5.7
April	184 232	121 251	65.8	59 832	48 147	6 671	3 224	111 426	62.2	6 601	1 563	5.4
May	184 374	121 071	65.7	59 644	47 946	6 702	3 121	111 171	62.0	6 779	1 647	5.6
June	184 562	121 473	65.8	59 751	48 146	7 030	3 111	111 816	62.3	6 546	1 531	5.4
July	184 729	121 665	65.9	59 888	48 186	6 986	3 060	112 000	62.3	6 605	1 601	5.4
August	184 830	122 125	66.1	59 877	48 467	6 938	3 119	112 163	62.4	6 843	1 639	5.6
September	184 962	121 960	65.9	59 980	48 511	6 865	3 165	112 191	62.4	6 604	1 569	5.4
October	185 114	122 206	66.0	60 023	48 859	6 756	3 231	112 407	62.5	6 568	1 562	5.4
November	185 244	122 637	66.2	60 042	49 254	6 804	3 241	112 859	62.7	6 537	1 468	5.3
December	185 402	122 622	66.1	60 059	49 257	6 788	3 194	112 910	62.6	6 518	1 490	5.3
1989												
January	185 644	123 390	66.5	60 477	49 529	6 702	3 287	113 421	62.9	6 682	1 480	5.4
February	185 777	123 135	66.3	60 588	49 497	6 691	3 234	113 542	62.9	6 359	1 304	5.2
March	185 897	123 227	66.3	60 795	49 503	6 724	3 198	113 824	62.9	6 205	1 353	5.0
April	186 024	123 565	66.4	60 764	49 565	6 768	3 162	113 935	62.9	6 468	1 397	5.2
May	186 181	123 474	66.3	60 795	49 583	6 721	3 125	113 974	62.9	6 375	1 348	5.2
June	186 329	123 995	66.5	61 054	49 542	6 822	3 068	114 350	63.0	6 577	1 300	5.3
July	186 483	123 967	66.5	60 947	49 693	6 832	3 227	114 245	63.0	6 495	1 435	5.2
August	186 598	124 166	66.5	60 915	49 804	6 936	3 284	114 371	63.1	6 511	1 302	5.2
September	186 726	123 944	66.4	60 668	50 015	6 671	3 219	114 135	62.8	6 590	1 360	5.3
October	186 871	124 211	66.5	60 958	49 871	6 752	3 215	114 366	62.9	6 630	1 392	5.3
November	187 017	124 637	66.6	60 958	50 221	6 733	3 132	114 780	63.0	6 725	1 418	5.4
December	187 165	124 497	66.5	61 068	50 116	6 646	3 188	114 642	63.0	6 667	1 375	5.4
1990												
January	188 413	125 833	66.8	61 742	50 436	6 903	3 210	115 871	63.2	6 752	1 412	5.4
February	188 516	125 710	66.7	61 805	50 438	6 816	3 188	115 871	63.2	6 651	1 350	5.3
March	188 630	125 801	66.7	61 832	50 463	6 908	3 260	115 943	63.2	6 598	1 331	5.2
April	188 778	125 649	66.6	61 579	50 457	6 816	3 231	115 621	63.0	6 797	1 376	5.4
May	188 913	125 893	66.6	61 778	50 646	6 727	3 266	115 885	63.1	6 742	1 415	5.4
June	189 058	125 573	66.4	61 762	50 550	6 671	3 245	115 738	62.9	6 590	1 436	5.2
July	189 188	125 732	66.5	61 683	50 514	6 613	3 192	115 618	62.8	6 922	1 534	5.5
August	189 342	125 990	66.5	61 715	50 635	6 452	3 197	115 605	62.7	7 188	1 607	5.7
September	189 528	125 892	66.4	61 608	50 587	6 329	3 206	115 318	62.5	7 368	1 695	5.9
October	189 710	125 995	66.4	61 606	50 616	6 314	3 270	115 266	62.5	7 459	1 689	5.9
November	189 872	126 070	66.4	61 545	50 541	6 220	3 189	115 117	62.3	7 764	1 831	6.2
December	190 017	126 142	66.4	61 506	50 530	6 205	3 245	114 996	62.2	7 901	1 804	6.3
1991												
January	190 163	125 955	66.2	61 383	50 472	6 085	3 208	114 732	62.0	8 015	1 866	6.4
February	190 271	126 020	66.2	61 117	50 523	6 115	3 270	114 485	61.9	8 265	1 955	6.6
March	190 381	126 238	66.3	61 144	50 422	6 086	3 177	114 475	61.8	8 586	2 137	6.8
April	190 517	126 548	66.4	61 280	50 760	6 069	3 241	114 868	62.0	8 439	2 206	6.7
May	190 650	126 176	66.2	61 052	50 457	5 931	3 275	114 165	61.6	8 736	2 252	6.9
June	190 800	126 331	66.2	61 147	50 585	5 907	3 300	114 339	61.7	8 692	2 533	6.9
July	190 946	126 154	66.1	61 179	50 636	5 753	3 319	114 249	61.6	8 586	2 388	6.8
August	191 116	126 150	66.0	61 122	50 601	5 761	3 313	114 171	61.5	8 666	2 460	6.9
September	191 302	126 650	66.2	61 279	50 864	5 785	3 319	114 609	61.6	8 722	2 497	6.9
October	191 497	126 642	66.1	61 174	50 811	5 815	3 289	114 511	61.5	8 842	2 638	7.0
November	191 657	126 701	66.1	61 201	50 759	5 810	3 296	114 474	61.4	8 931	2 718	7.0
December	191 798	126 664	66.0	61 074	50 728	5 664	3 146	114 320	61.2	9 198	2 892	7.3
1992												
January	191 953	127 261	66.3	61 116	51 095	5 767	3 155	114 823	61.5	9 283	3 060	7.3
February	192 067	127 207	66.2	61 062	51 033	5 658	3 239	114 514	61.3	9 454	3 182	7.4
March	192 204	127 604	66.4	61 363	51 204	5 577	3 236	114 908	61.5	9 460	3 196	7.4
April	192 354	127 841	66.5	61 468	51 323	5 635	3 245	115 181	61.6	9 415	3 130	7.4
May	192 503	128 119	66.6	61 513	51 245	5 617	3 213	115 162	61.5	9 744	3 444	7.6
June	192 663	128 459	66.7	61 537	51 383	5 499	3 297	115 122	61.5	10 040	3 758	7.8
July	192 826	128 563	66.7	61 641	51 458	5 614	3 285	115 428	61.6	9 850	3 614	7.7
August	193 018	128 613	66.6	61 681	51 386	5 759	3 279	115 547	61.6	9 787	3 579	7.6
September	193 229	128 501	66.5	61 663	51 359	5 698	3 274	115 446	61.4	9 781	3 504	7.6
October	193 442	128 026	66.2	61 550	51 373	5 705	3 254	115 374	61.3	9 398	3 505	7.3
November	193 621	128 441	66.3	61 644	51 535	5 697	3 207	115 669	61.4	9 565	3 397	7.4
December	193 784	128 554	66.3	61 721	51 524	5 752	3 259	115 738	61.4	9 557	3 651	7.4
1993												
January	193 962	128 400	66.2	61 895	51 505	5 675	3 222	115 853	61.4	9 325	3 346	7.3
February	194 108	128 458	66.2	61 963	51 573	5 739	3 125	116 150	61.4	9 183	3 190	7.1
March	194 248	128 598	66.2	62 007	51 808	5 727	3 119	116 423	61.5	9 056	3 115	7.0
April	194 398	128 584	66.1	62 032	51 732	5 710	3 074	116 400	61.5	9 110	3 014	7.1
May	194 549	129 264	66.4	62 309	51 996	5 810	3 100	117 015	61.7	9 149	3 101	7.1
June	194 719	129 411	66.5	62 409	52 183	5 698	3 108	117 182	61.8	9 121	3 141	7.0
July	194 882	129 397	66.4	62 497	52 088	5 882	3 126	117 341	61.8	8 930	3 046	6.9
August	195 063	129 619	66.4	62 634	52 294	5 928	3 026	117 830	62.0	8 763	3 026	6.8
September	195 259	129 268	66.2	62 437	52 241	5 876	3 174	117 380	61.7	8 714	3 042	6.7
October	195 444	129 573	66.3	62 614	52 379	5 830	3 084	117 739	61.8	8 750	3 029	6.8
November	195 625	129 711	66.3	62 732	52 531	5 906	3 157	118 012	61.9	8 542	2 986	6.6
December	195 794	129 941	66.4	62 760	52 813	5 891	3 116	118 348	62.0	8 477	2 968	6.5

[1] Not seasonally adjusted.

Table 20-3. Summary Labor Force, Employment, and Unemployment—Continued

(Thousands of persons, percent, seasonally adjusted, except as noted.)

Year and month	Civilian noninsti-tutional population [1]	Civilian labor force		Employment, thousands of persons					Employ-ment-population ratio, percent	Unemployment		Rate (percent)
				By age and sex			By industry			Thousands of persons		
		Thousands of persons	Participa-tion rate (percent)	Men, 20 years and over	Women, 20 years and over	Both sexes, 16 to 19 years	Agricultural	Nonagri-cultural		Total	Unem-ployed 15 weeks and over	
1994												
January	195 953	130 596	66.6	62 798	53 052	6 116	3 302	118 664	62.2	8 630	3 060	6.6
February	196 090	130 669	66.6	62 708	53 266	6 112	3 339	118 747	62.3	8 583	3 118	6.6
March	196 213	130 400	66.5	62 780	53 099	6 051	3 354	118 576	62.1	8 470	3 055	6.5
April	196 363	130 621	66.5	62 906	53 274	6 110	3 428	118 862	62.3	8 331	2 921	6.4
May	196 510	130 779	66.6	63 116	53 624	6 124	3 409	119 455	62.5	7 915	2 836	6.1
June	196 693	130 561	66.4	63 041	53 393	6 200	3 299	119 335	62.3	7 927	2 735	6.1
July	196 859	130 652	66.4	63 034	53 531	6 141	3 333	119 373	62.3	7 946	2 822	6.1
August	197 043	131 275	66.6	63 294	53 744	6 304	3 451	119 891	62.6	7 933	2 750	6.0
September	197 248	131 421	66.6	63 631	53 991	6 065	3 430	120 257	62.7	7 734	2 746	5.9
October	197 430	131 744	66.7	63 818	54 071	6 223	3 490	120 622	62.9	7 632	2 955	5.8
November	197 607	131 891	66.7	64 080	54 168	6 268	3 574	120 942	63.0	7 375	2 666	5.6
December	197 765	131 951	66.7	64 359	54 054	6 308	3 577	121 144	63.1	7 230	2 488	5.5
1995												
January	197 753	132 038	66.8	64 185	54 087	6 391	3 519	121 144	63.0	7 375	2 396	5.6
February	197 886	132 115	66.8	64 378	54 226	6 324	3 620	121 308	63.1	7 187	2 345	5.4
March	198 007	132 108	66.7	64 321	54 141	6 493	3 634	121 321	63.1	7 153	2 287	5.4
April	198 148	132 590	66.9	64 165	54 366	6 414	3 566	121 379	63.1	7 645	2 473	5.8
May	198 286	131 851	66.5	63 829	54 272	6 320	3 349	121 072	62.7	7 430	2 577	5.6
June	198 452	131 949	66.5	63 992	54 020	6 510	3 461	121 061	62.7	7 427	2 266	5.6
July	198 615	132 343	66.6	63 962	54 476	6 378	3 379	121 437	62.8	7 527	2 311	5.7
August	198 801	132 336	66.6	63 875	54 434	6 543	3 374	121 478	62.8	7 484	2 391	5.7
September	199 005	132 611	66.6	64 179	54 507	6 447	3 285	121 848	62.9	7 478	2 306	5.6
October	199 192	132 716	66.6	64 272	54 692	6 424	3 438	121 950	62.9	7 328	2 272	5.5
November	199 355	132 614	66.5	63 931	54 850	6 407	3 338	121 850	62.8	7 426	2 339	5.6
December	199 508	132 511	66.4	64 041	54 674	6 373	3 352	121 736	62.7	7 423	2 331	5.6
1996												
January	199 634	132 616	66.4	64 180	54 580	6 365	3 483	121 642	62.7	7 491	2 371	5.6
February	199 772	132 952	66.6	64 398	54 844	6 397	3 547	122 092	62.9	7 313	2 307	5.5
March	199 921	133 180	66.6	64 506	54 994	6 362	3 489	122 373	63.0	7 318	2 454	5.5
April	200 101	133 409	66.7	64 481	55 067	6 446	3 406	122 588	63.0	7 415	2 455	5.6
May	200 278	133 667	66.7	64 683	55 034	6 527	3 473	122 771	63.0	7 423	2 403	5.6
June	200 459	133 697	66.7	64 940	55 177	6 485	3 424	123 178	63.2	7 095	2 355	5.3
July	200 641	134 284	66.9	65 068	55 362	6 517	3 433	123 514	63.3	7 337	2 297	5.5
August	200 847	134 054	66.7	65 216	55 525	6 431	3 395	123 777	63.3	6 882	2 267	5.1
September	201 060	134 515	66.9	65 169	55 669	6 698	3 448	124 088	63.4	6 979	2 220	5.2
October	201 273	134 921	67.0	65 460	55 750	6 680	3 463	124 427	63.5	7 031	2 268	5.2
November	201 463	135 007	67.0	65 320	55 896	6 555	3 356	124 415	63.4	7 236	2 159	5.4
December	201 636	135 113	67.0	65 435	55 849	6 576	3 445	124 415	63.4	7 253	2 124	5.4
1997												
January	202 285	135 456	67.0	65 679	56 024	6 595	3 449	124 849	63.4	7 158	2 162	5.3
February	202 388	135 400	66.9	65 758	55 955	6 585	3 353	124 945	63.4	7 102	2 140	5.2
March	202 513	135 891	67.1	65 974	56 270	6 647	3 419	125 472	63.6	7 000	2 110	5.2
April	202 674	136 016	67.1	66 092	56 347	6 704	3 462	125 681	63.7	6 873	2 176	5.1
May	202 832	136 119	67.1	66 328	56 446	6 690	3 437	126 027	63.8	6 655	2 121	4.9
June	203 000	136 211	67.1	66 308	56 573	6 531	3 409	126 003	63.7	6 799	2 085	5.0
July	203 166	136 477	67.2	66 422	56 785	6 615	3 422	126 400	63.9	6 655	2 119	4.9
August	203 364	136 618	67.2	66 508	56 852	6 650	3 359	126 651	63.9	6 608	2 004	4.8
September	203 570	136 675	67.1	66 483	56 931	6 605	3 392	126 627	63.9	6 656	2 074	4.9
October	203 767	136 633	67.1	66 511	56 982	6 686	3 312	126 867	63.9	6 454	1 950	4.7
November	203 941	136 961	67.2	66 765	57 039	6 849	3 386	127 267	64.1	6 308	1 817	4.6
December	204 098	137 155	67.2	66 643	57 219	6 817	3 405	127 274	64.0	6 476	1 901	4.7
1998												
January	204 238	137 095	67.1	66 750	56 941	7 035	3 299	127 389	64.0	6 368	1 833	4.6
February	204 400	137 112	67.1	66 856	56 992	6 959	3 284	127 522	64.0	6 306	1 809	4.6
March	204 546	137 236	67.1	66 721	57 080	7 014	3 146	127 650	64.0	6 422	1 772	4.7
April	204 731	137 150	67.0	67 151	57 074	6 985	3 334	127 852	64.1	5 941	1 476	4.3
May	204 899	137 372	67.0	67 164	57 155	7 007	3 360	127 959	64.1	6 047	1 490	4.4
June	205 085	137 455	67.0	67 054	57 156	7 033	3 380	127 874	64.0	6 212	1 613	4.5
July	205 270	137 588	67.0	67 119	57 192	7 018	3 455	127 913	64.0	6 259	1 577	4.5
August	205 479	137 570	67.0	66 985	57 332	7 074	3 509	127 970	63.9	6 179	1 626	4.5
September	205 699	138 286	67.2	67 254	57 520	7 212	3 500	128 399	64.2	6 300	1 688	4.6
October	205 919	138 279	67.2	67 433	57 529	7 036	3 593	128 389	64.1	6 280	1 582	4.5
November	206 104	138 381	67.1	67 591	57 638	7 052	3 375	128 897	64.2	6 100	1 590	4.4
December	206 270	138 634	67.2	67 548	57 840	7 214	3 246	129 320	64.3	6 032	1 559	4.4
1999												
January	206 719	139 003	67.2	67 679	58 256	7 092	3 233	129 802	64.4	5 976	1 490	4.3
February	206 873	138 967	67.2	67 498	58 129	7 229	3 246	129 647	64.2	6 111	1 551	4.4
March	207 036	138 730	67.0	67 660	58 132	7 155	3 238	129 656	64.2	5 783	1 472	4.2
April	207 236	138 959	67.1	67 542	58 260	7 153	3 336	129 615	64.2	6 004	1 480	4.3
May	207 427	139 107	67.1	67 539	58 440	7 331	3 335	129 937	64.3	5 796	1 505	4.2
June	207 632	139 329	67.1	67 700	58 641	7 037	3 386	129 982	64.2	5 951	1 624	4.3
July	207 828	139 439	67.1	67 731	58 490	7 193	3 346	130 146	64.2	6 025	1 513	4.3
August	208 038	139 430	67.0	67 768	58 707	7 117	3 234	130 366	64.2	5 838	1 455	4.2
September	208 265	139 622	67.0	67 882	58 735	7 090	3 173	130 434	64.2	5 915	1 449	4.2
October	208 483	139 771	67.0	67 840	58 921	7 232	3 229	130 758	64.3	5 778	1 438	4.1
November	208 666	140 025	67.1	68 094	59 018	7 198	3 343	130 989	64.4	5 716	1 378	4.1
December	208 832	140 177	67.1	68 217	59 056	7 251	3 260	131 257	64.4	5 653	1 375	4.0

[1]Not seasonally adjusted.

Table 20-3. Summary Labor Force, Employment, and Unemployment—*Continued*

(Thousands of persons, percent, seasonally adjusted, except as noted.)

Year and month	Civilian noninstitutional population [1]	Civilian labor force		Employment, thousands of persons					Employment-population ratio, percent	Unemployment		
		Thousands of persons	Participation rate (percent)	By age and sex			By industry			Thousands of persons		Rate (percent)
				Men, 20 years and over	Women, 20 years and over	Both sexes, 16 to 19 years	Agricultural	Nonagricultural		Total	Unemployed 15 weeks and over	
2000												
January	211 410	142 267	67.3	69 419	59 842	7 298	2 613	133 863	64.6	5 708	1 380	4.0
February	211 576	142 456	67.3	69 505	59 887	7 206	2 731	133 912	64.6	5 858	1 300	4.1
March	211 772	142 434	67.3	69 482	59 977	7 241	2 579	134 022	64.6	5 733	1 312	4.0
April	212 018	142 751	67.3	69 519	60 358	7 393	2 505	134 806	64.7	5 481	1 261	3.8
May	212 242	142 388	67.1	69 399	59 951	7 280	2 480	134 144	64.4	5 758	1 325	4.0
June	212 466	142 591	67.1	69 629	60 027	7 284	2 445	134 528	64.5	5 651	1 242	4.0
July	212 677	142 278	66.9	69 525	60 011	6 995	2 408	134 196	64.2	5 747	1 343	4.0
August	212 916	142 514	66.9	69 823	59 719	7 120	2 433	134 311	64.2	5 853	1 394	4.1
September	213 163	142 518	66.9	69 700	60 083	7 110	2 384	134 489	64.2	5 625	1 290	3.9
October	213 405	142 622	66.8	69 762	60 238	7 088	2 319	134 808	64.2	5 534	1 337	3.9
November	213 540	142 962	66.9	69 910	60 269	7 143	2 330	134 921	64.3	5 639	1 315	3.9
December	213 736	143 248	67.0	69 939	60 503	7 172	2 389	135 194	64.4	5 634	1 329	3.9
2001												
January	213 888	143 800	67.2	70 064	60 609	7 104	2 360	135 304	64.4	6 023	1 372	4.2
February	214 110	143 701	67.1	69 959	60 615	7 038	2 370	135 291	64.3	6 089	1 491	4.2
March	214 305	143 924	67.2	69 881	60 902	7 001	2 350	135 372	64.3	6 141	1 521	4.3
April	214 525	143 569	66.9	69 916	60 523	6 860	2 336	135 036	64.0	6 271	1 499	4.4
May	214 732	143 318	66.7	69 865	60 509	6 717	2 353	134 735	63.8	6 226	1 502	4.3
June	214 950	143 357	66.7	69 690	60 371	6 812	2 082	134 755	63.7	6 484	1 532	4.5
July	215 180	143 654	66.8	69 808	60 480	6 784	2 295	134 858	63.7	6 583	1 653	4.6
August	215 420	143 284	66.5	69 585	60 301	6 356	2 305	133 944	63.2	7 042	1 861	4.9
September	215 665	143 989	66.8	69 933	60 265	6 649	2 322	134 558	63.5	7 142	1 950	5.0
October	215 903	144 086	66.7	69 621	60 168	6 602	2 327	134 098	63.2	7 694	2 082	5.3
November	216 117	144 240	66.7	69 444	60 174	6 620	2 203	133 955	63.0	8 003	2 318	5.5
December	216 315	144 305	66.7	69 551	60 095	6 400	2 293	133 751	62.9	8 258	2 444	5.7
2002												
January	216 506	143 883	66.5	69 308	60 032	6 361	2 385	133 233	62.7	8 182	2 578	5.7
February	216 663	144 653	66.8	69 534	60 479	6 425	2 397	134 127	63.0	8 215	2 608	5.7
March	216 823	144 481	66.6	69 480	60 190	6 507	2 368	133 816	62.8	8 304	2 719	5.7
April	217 006	144 725	66.7	69 574	60 204	6 349	2 371	133 833	62.7	8 599	2 852	5.9
May	217 198	144 938	66.7	69 981	60 226	6 332	2 260	134 278	62.9	8 399	2 967	5.8
June	217 407	144 808	66.6	69 769	60 297	6 348	2 161	134 135	62.7	8 393	3 023	5.8
July	217 630	144 803	66.5	69 806	60 290	6 317	2 324	134 107	62.7	8 390	2 966	5.8
August	217 866	145 009	66.6	69 937	60 560	6 208	2 127	134 593	62.7	8 304	2 887	5.7
September	218 107	145 552	66.7	70 207	60 679	6 416	2 285	135 102	63.0	8 251	2 971	5.7
October	218 340	145 314	66.6	69 948	60 663	6 397	2 471	134 580	62.7	8 307	3 042	5.7
November	218 548	145 041	66.4	69 615	60 697	6 209	2 261	134 171	62.5	8 520	3 062	5.9
December	218 741	145 066	66.3	69 620	60 667	6 139	2 352	134 071	62.4	8 640	3 271	6.0
2003												
January	219 897	145 937	66.4	69 919	61 406	6 091	2 337	135 045	62.5	8 520	3 166	5.8
February	220 114	146 100	66.4	70 262	61 159	6 060	2 234	135 306	62.5	8 618	3 161	5.9
March	220 317	146 022	66.3	70 243	61 317	5 874	2 263	135 232	62.4	8 588	3 161	5.9
April	220 540	146 474	66.4	70 311	61 374	5 948	2 150	135 561	62.4	8 842	3 348	6.0
May	220 768	146 500	66.4	70 215	61 393	5 936	2 183	135 370	62.3	8 957	3 318	6.1
June	221 014	147 056	66.5	70 159	61 747	5 884	2 185	135 419	62.3	9 266	3 552	6.3
July	221 252	146 485	66.2	70 190	61 437	5 847	2 187	135 242	62.1	9 011	3 633	6.2
August	221 507	146 445	66.1	70 237	61 442	5 870	2 313	135 200	62.1	8 896	3 557	6.1
September	221 779	146 530	66.1	70 631	61 119	5 860	2 349	135 355	62.0	8 921	3 486	6.1
October	222 039	146 716	66.1	70 685	61 451	5 848	2 479	135 571	62.1	8 732	3 451	6.0
November	222 279	147 000	66.1	70 935	61 494	5 995	2 373	136 003	62.3	8 576	3 420	5.8
December	222 509	146 729	65.9	71 170	61 396	5 845	2 243	136 145	62.2	8 317	3 366	5.7
2004												
January	222 161	146 842	66.1	71 318	61 183	5 971	2 196	136 228	62.3	8 370	3 364	5.7
February	222 357	146 709	66.0	71 122	61 514	5 906	2 210	136 362	62.3	8 167	3 248	5.6
March	222 550	146 944	66.0	71 155	61 534	5 764	2 180	136 302	62.2	8 491	3 314	5.8
April	222 757	146 850	65.9	71 121	61 647	5 912	2 241	136 474	62.3	8 170	2 971	5.6
May	222 967	147 065	66.0	71 180	61 762	5 911	2 300	136 556	62.3	8 212	3 103	5.6
June	223 196	147 460	66.1	71 562	61 793	5 819	2 237	136 748	62.4	8 286	3 130	5.6
July	223 422	147 692	66.1	71 780	61 884	5 891	2 222	137 354	62.5	8 136	2 918	5.5
August	223 677	147 564	66.0	71 808	61 836	5 930	2 333	137 230	62.4	7 990	2 846	5.4
September	223 941	147 415	65.8	71 744	61 859	5 884	2 251	137 323	62.3	7 927	2 910	5.4
October	224 192	147 793	65.9	71 860	61 942	5 931	2 216	137 598	62.3	8 061	3 041	5.5
November	224 422	148 162	66.0	72 110	62 088	6 033	2 206	137 978	62.5	7 932	2 960	5.4
December	224 640	148 059	65.9	72 058	62 136	5 931	2 171	137 947	62.4	7 934	2 927	5.4
2005												
January	224 837	148 029	65.8	72 063	62 260	5 922	2 112	138 111	62.4	7 784	2 851	5.3
February	225 041	148 364	65.9	72 299	62 253	5 832	2 129	138 267	62.4	7 980	2 896	5.4
March	225 236	148 391	65.9	72 478	62 222	5 954	2 180	138 462	62.4	7 737	2 817	5.2
April	225 441	148 926	66.1	72 860	62 483	5 912	2 248	138 992	62.7	7 672	2 678	5.2
May	225 670	149 261	66.1	73 133	62 557	5 920	2 225	139 379	62.8	7 651	2 683	5.1
June	225 911	149 238	66.1	73 223	62 516	5 975	2 302	139 276	62.7	7 524	2 405	5.0
July	226 153	149 432	66.1	73 337	62 691	5 999	2 308	139 789	62.8	7 406	2 449	5.0
August	226 421	149 779	66.2	73 513	62 844	6 077	2 183	140 277	62.9	7 345	2 569	4.9
September	226 693	149 954	66.1	73 333	63 035	6 033	2 181	140 276	62.8	7 553	2 537	5.0
October	226 959	150 001	66.1	73 445	63 127	5 976	2 191	140 435	62.8	7 453	2 492	5.0
November	227 204	150 065	66.0	73 341	63 127	6 031	2 174	140 299	62.7	7 566	2 486	5.0
December	227 425	150 030	66.0	73 467	63 209	6 076	2 094	140 635	62.8	7 279	2 429	4.9

[1]Not seasonally adjusted.

Table 20-3. Summary Labor Force, Employment, and Unemployment—*Continued*

(Thousands of persons, percent, seasonally adjusted, except as noted.)

| Year and month | Civilian noninsti-tutional population [1] | Civilian labor force | | Employment, thousands of persons | | | | | Employ-ment-population ratio, percent | Unemployment | | |
| | | Thousands of persons | Participa-tion rate (percent) | By age and sex | | | By industry | | | Thousands of persons | | Rate (percent) |
				Men, 20 years and over	Women, 20 years and over	Both sexes, 16 to 19 years	Agricultural	Nonagri-cultural		Total	Unem-ployed 15 weeks and over	
2006												
January	227 553	150 201	66.0	73 868	63 166	6 107	2 163	140 932	62.9	7 059	2 269	4.7
February	227 763	150 629	66.1	73 960	63 305	6 179	2 180	141 251	63.0	7 185	2 542	4.8
March	227 975	150 839	66.2	74 225	63 377	6 163	2 157	141 573	63.1	7 075	2 371	4.7
April	228 199	150 915	66.1	74 214	63 421	6 159	2 253	141 461	63.0	7 122	2 352	4.7
May	228 428	151 085	66.1	74 246	63 657	6 205	2 198	141 889	63.1	6 977	2 302	4.6
June	228 671	151 368	66.2	74 280	63 866	6 224	2 258	142 065	63.1	6 998	2 125	4.6
July	228 912	151 383	66.1	74 039	64 025	6 166	2 280	142 083	63.0	7 154	2 285	4.7
August	229 167	151 729	66.2	74 399	64 129	6 103	2 237	142 442	63.1	7 097	2 294	4.7
September	229 420	151 650	66.1	74 881	63 893	6 022	2 176	142 640	63.1	6 853	2 230	4.5
October	229 675	152 020	66.2	74 834	64 282	6 176	2 179	143 188	63.3	6 728	2 067	4.4
November	229 905	152 360	66.3	74 921	64 315	6 241	2 159	143 280	63.3	6 883	2 165	4.5
December	230 108	152 698	66.4	75 198	64 511	6 204	2 226	143 661	63.4	6 784	2 089	4.4
2007												
January	230 650	153 117	66.4	75 194	64 671	6 167	2 214	143 757	63.3	7 085	2 155	4.6
February	230 834	152 941	66.3	75 223	64 752	6 069	2 302	143 738	63.3	6 898	2 198	4.5
March	231 034	153 093	66.3	75 389	64 962	6 017	2 188	144 155	63.4	6 725	2 246	4.4
April	231 253	152 531	66.0	75 371	64 396	5 918	2 077	143 545	63.0	6 845	2 275	4.5
May	231 480	152 717	66.0	75 429	64 729	5 794	2 088	143 843	63.1	6 765	2 226	4.4
June	231 713	153 045	66.0	75 349	64 788	5 942	1 951	144 137	63.0	6 966	2 275	4.6
July	231 958	153 039	66.0	75 276	64 756	5 895	2 017	144 033	62.9	7 113	2 359	4.6
August	232 211	152 781	65.8	75 224	64 816	5 645	1 861	143 856	62.7	7 096	2 336	4.6
September	232 461	153 393	66.0	75 289	65 026	5 877	2 077	144 117	62.9	7 200	2 356	4.7
October	232 715	153 158	65.8	75 134	64 800	5 951	2 113	143 846	62.7	7 273	2 324	4.7
November	232 939	153 767	66.0	75 625	64 952	5 906	2 138	144 347	62.9	7 284	2 390	4.7
December	233 156	153 869	66.0	75 451	64 893	5 829	2 207	143 926	62.7	7 696	2 519	5.0
2008												
January	232 616	154 048	66.2	75 477	65 181	5 763	2 205	144 146	62.9	7 628	2 540	5.0
February	232 809	153 600	66.0	75 439	65 041	5 685	2 202	143 965	62.8	7 435	2 419	4.8
March	232 995	153 966	66.1	75 306	65 127	5 740	2 190	143 976	62.7	7 793	2 472	5.1
April	233 198	153 936	66.0	75 232	65 178	5 896	2 122	144 129	62.7	7 631	2 668	5.0
May	233 405	154 420	66.2	75 044	65 152	5 827	2 125	143 888	62.6	8 397	2 773	5.4
June	233 627	154 327	66.1	75 000	65 178	5 590	2 126	143 639	62.4	8 560	2 911	5.5
July	233 864	154 410	66.0	74 964	65 067	5 483	2 141	143 422	62.2	8 895	3 107	5.8
August	234 107	154 696	66.1	74 698	64 956	5 533	2 148	143 045	62.0	9 509	3 430	6.1
September	234 360	154 590	66.0	74 480	65 015	5 526	2 207	142 793	61.9	9 569	3 627	6.2
October	234 612	154 849	66.0	74 241	65 003	5 433	2 192	142 576	61.7	10 172	4 040	6.6
November	234 828	154 524	65.8	73 850	64 806	5 251	2 195	141 742	61.3	10 617	3 990	6.9
December	235 035	154 587	65.8	73 237	64 744	5 207	2 185	140 975	60.9	11 400	4 599	7.4
2009												
January	234 739	154 140	65.7	72 625	64 391	5 205	2 147	140 014	60.6	11 919	4 762	7.7
February	234 913	154 401	65.7	72 266	64 238	5 183	2 148	139 559	60.3	12 714	5 369	8.2
March	235 086	154 164	65.6	71 667	64 110	5 077	2 051	138 830	59.9	13 310	5 815	8.6
April	235 271	154 718	65.8	71 665	64 147	5 089	2 143	138 762	59.9	13 816	6 296	8.9
May	235 452	154 956	65.8	71 552	63 847	5 039	2 166	138 287	59.6	14 518	7 013	9.4
June	235 655	154 759	65.7	71 354	63 741	4 943	2 154	137 825	59.4	14 721	7 844	9.5
July	235 870	154 351	65.4	71 255	63 685	4 877	2 138	137 629	59.3	14 534	7 819	9.4
August	236 087	154 426	65.4	71 142	63 552	4 740	2 095	137 285	59.1	14 993	7 849	9.7
September	236 322	153 927	65.1	70 861	63 280	4 627	2 009	136 752	58.7	15 159	8 405	9.8
October	236 550	153 854	65.0	70 662	63 133	4 448	2 041	136 311	58.4	15 612	8 804	10.1
November	236 743	153 720	64.9	70 662	63 269	4 450	2 086	136 357	58.5	15 340	8 976	10.0
December	236 924	153 059	64.6	70 391	62 998	4 403	2 056	135 717	58.2	15 267	8 969	10.0

[1]Not seasonally adjusted.

Table 20-3A. Labor Force and Employment Estimates Smoothed for Population Adjustments

(Thousands of persons, seasonally adjusted.)

Year	January	February	March	April	May	June	July	August	September	October	November	December
CIVILIAN LABOR FORCE												
1990	125 845	125 734	125 837	125 697	125 953	125 645	125 816	126 087	126 001	126 116	126 203	126 287
1991	126 112	126 189	126 420	126 742	126 382	126 549	126 384	126 392	126 905	126 909	126 981	126 956
1992	127 566	127 524	127 934	128 184	128 475	128 829	128 945	129 008	128 908	128 444	128 872	128 998
1993	128 856	128 926	129 079	129 077	129 772	129 932	129 931	130 166	129 826	130 145	130 296	130 539
1994	131 210	131 296	131 038	131 272	131 444	131 237	131 341	131 980	132 139	132 477	132 637	132 710
1995	132 811	132 901	132 906	133 404	132 673	132 784	133 193	133 199	133 489	133 607	133 517	133 426
1996	133 545	133 896	134 138	134 381	134 654	134 697	135 302	135 083	135 560	135 982	136 082	136 202
1997	136 560	136 517	137 025	137 164	137 281	137 387	137 668	137 824	137 894	137 865	138 209	138 418
1998	138 370	138 401	138 539	138 465	138 703	138 800	138 947	138 942	139 679	139 685	139 801	140 070
1999	140 456	140 433	140 207	140 452	140 615	140 852	140 977	140 981	141 189	141 353	141 623	141 790
2000	142 262	142 447	142 420	142 732	142 364	142 563	142 245	142 476	142 475	142 574	142 910	143 191
2001	143 738	143 634	143 852	143 492	143 237	143 271	143 563	143 188	143 888	143 980	144 129	144 189
2002	143 763	144 527	144 350	144 589	144 797	144 662	144 653	144 853	145 391	145 148	144 871	144 891
2003	145 126	145 266	145 166	145 594	145 598	146 128	145 539	145 477	145 540	145 702	145 962	145 671
2004	146 206	146 060	146 281	146 175	146 376	146 756	146 974	146 833	146 672	147 035	147 389	147 274
2005	147 280	147 601	147 616	148 136	148 457	148 421	148 602	148 935	149 096	149 131	149 182	149 135
2006	149 424	149 839	150 037	150 102	150 260	150 531	150 535	150 868	150 779	151 136	151 464	151 789
2007	152 030	151 843	151 981	151 410	151 582	151 895	151 876	151 607	152 202	151 956	152 547	152 636
2008	153 443	152 991	153 349	153 313	153 789	153 690	153 766	154 045	153 933	154 184	153 855	153 911
2009	153 912	154 170	153 931	154 483	154 718	154 519	154 110	154 183	153 682	153 607	153 471	152 809
CIVILIAN EMPLOYMENT, TOTAL												
1990	119 093	119 082	119 238	118 898	119 209	119 052	118 891	118 894	118 628	118 651	118 432	118 379
1991	118 089	117 915	117 823	118 293	117 634	117 845	117 785	117 712	118 169	118 052	118 033	117 740
1992	118 265	118 050	118 454	118 748	118 709	118 764	119 071	119 195	119 101	119 020	119 280	119 413
1993	119 503	119 715	119 995	119 938	120 594	120 781	120 970	121 373	121 081	121 363	121 722	122 031
1994	122 547	122 679	122 534	122 908	123 497	123 277	123 362	124 013	124 372	124 811	125 230	125 448
1995	125 402	125 681	125 720	125 722	125 207	125 321	125 629	125 677	125 972	126 241	126 052	125 963
1996	126 013	126 542	126 779	126 924	127 189	127 562	127 922	128 161	128 540	128 909	128 801	128 904
1997	129 358	129 370	129 981	130 247	130 584	130 544	130 970	131 172	131 194	131 368	131 859	131 898
1998	131 958	132 053	132 072	132 484	132 614	132 545	132 643	132 718	133 333	133 359	133 655	133 994
1999	134 436	134 276	134 381	134 402	134 775	134 855	134 905	135 097	135 227	135 529	135 862	136 092
2000	136 554	136 589	136 687	137 252	136 607	136 913	136 499	136 626	136 852	137 042	137 272	137 559
2001	137 718	137 548	137 714	137 226	137 014	136 791	136 984	136 150	136 750	136 292	136 133	135 938
2002	135 587	136 319	136 054	135 998	136 406	136 278	136 271	136 558	137 150	136 851	136 360	136 261
2003	136 656	136 700	136 632	136 809	136 700	136 924	136 590	136 644	136 683	137 035	137 451	137 417
2004	137 873	137 930	137 829	138 043	138 202	138 510	138 878	138 883	138 785	139 016	139 501	139 383
2005	139 535	139 663	139 919	140 504	140 845	140 938	141 237	141 631	141 586	141 720	141 660	141 900
2006	142 400	142 690	142 999	143 018	143 320	143 570	143 420	143 809	143 964	144 446	144 619	145 043
2007	144 997	144 995	145 306	144 617	144 869	144 982	144 818	144 567	145 059	144 741	145 323	145 003
2008	145 839	145 578	145 580	145 706	145 418	145 159	144 901	144 568	144 397	144 048	143 276	142 554
2009	141 993	141 457	140 624	140 669	140 204	139 803	139 580	139 195	138 529	138 002	138 138	137 548

Table 20-4. Nonfarm Payroll Employment, Hours, and Earnings

(Wage and salary workers on nonfarm payrolls, seasonally adjusted.)

Year and month	All wage and salary workers (thousands)					Production or nonsupervisory workers on private payrolls								
		Private			Service-providing	Number (thousands)		Average hours per week		Average hourly earnings, dollars		Average weekly earnings, dollars		
	Total	Total	Goods-producing			Total private	Manufac-turing	Total private	Manufac-turing	Total private	Manufac-turing	Total private	Manufac-turing	
			Total	Manufac-turing										
1946	41 759	36 054	16 122	13 513	25 637	. . .	11 781	. . .	40.4	. . .	0.95	. . .	38.38	
1947	43 945	38 379	17 314	14 287	26 631	. . .	12 453	. . .	40.5	. . .	1.10	. . .	44.55	
1948	44 954	39 213	17 579	14 324	27 376	. . .	12 383	. . .	40.1	. . .	1.20	. . .	48.12	
1949	43 843	37 893	16 464	13 281	27 379	. . .	11 355	. . .	39.2	. . .	1.25	. . .	49.00	
1950	45 287	39 167	17 343	14 013	27 945	. . .	12 032	. . .	40.6	. . .	1.32	. . .	53.59	
1951	47 930	41 427	18 703	15 070	29 227	. . .	12 808	. . .	40.7	. . .	1.45	. . .	59.02	
1952	48 909	42 182	18 928	15 291	29 981	. . .	12 797	. . .	40.8	. . .	1.53	. . .	62.42	
1953	50 310	43 552	19 733	16 131	30 577	. . .	13 437	. . .	40.6	. . .	1.63	. . .	66.18	
1954	49 093	42 235	18 515	15 002	30 578	. . .	12 300	. . .	39.7	. . .	1.66	. . .	65.90	
1955	50 744	43 722	19 234	15 524	31 510	. . .	12 735	. . .	40.8	. . .	1.74	. . .	70.99	
1956	52 473	45 087	19 799	15 858	32 674	. . .	12 869	. . .	40.5	. . .	1.84	. . .	74.52	
1957	52 959	45 235	19 669	15 798	33 290	. . .	12 640	. . .	39.9	. . .	1.93	. . .	77.01	
1958	51 426	43 480	18 319	14 656	33 107	. . .	11 532	. . .	39.2	. . .	1.99	. . .	78.01	
1959	53 374	45 182	19 163	15 325	34 211	. . .	12 089	. . .	40.3	. . .	2.08	. . .	83.82	
1960	54 296	45 832	19 182	15 438	35 114	. . .	12 074	. . .	39.8	. . .	2.15	. . .	85.57	
1961	54 105	45 399	18 647	15 011	35 458	. . .	11 612	. . .	39.9	. . .	2.20	. . .	87.78	
1962	55 659	46 655	19 203	15 498	36 455	. . .	11 986	. . .	40.5	. . .	2.27	. . .	91.94	
1963	56 764	47 423	19 385	15 631	37 379	. . .	12 051	. . .	40.6	. . .	2.34	. . .	95.00	
1964	58 391	48 680	19 733	15 888	38 658	40 575	12 298	38.5	40.8	2.53	2.41	97.41	98.33	
1946														
January	39 839	34 054	15 031	12 719	24 808	. . .	10 990	. . .	40.9	. . .	0.86	. . .	35.17	
February	39 250	33 472	14 308	11 922	24 942	. . .	10 292	. . .	40.4	. . .	0.85	. . .	34.34	
March	40 192	34 434	15 017	12 545	25 175	. . .	10 989	. . .	40.6	. . .	0.89	. . .	36.13	
April	40 908	35 147	15 439	13 200	25 469	. . .	11 616	. . .	40.4	. . .	0.92	. . .	37.17	
May	41 348	35 616	15 875	13 389	25 473	. . .	11 758	. . .	39.8	. . .	0.93	. . .	37.01	
June	41 732	36 052	16 206	13 598	25 526	. . .	11 905	. . .	40.0	. . .	0.94	. . .	37.60	
July	42 153	36 471	16 461	13 771	25 692	. . .	12 065	. . .	40.2	. . .	0.96	. . .	38.59	
August	42 642	36 961	16 728	13 981	25 914	. . .	12 241	. . .	40.6	. . .	0.98	. . .	39.79	
September	42 908	37 239	16 912	14 135	25 996	. . .	12 311	. . .	40.4	. . .	0.99	. . .	40.00	
October	43 094	37 430	17 002	14 182	26 092	. . .	12 302	. . .	40.4	. . .	1.00	. . .	40.40	
November	43 396	37 757	17 157	14 310	26 239	. . .	12 421	. . .	40.3	. . .	1.02	. . .	41.11	
December	43 379	37 751	17 164	14 301	26 215	. . .	12 419	. . .	40.5	. . .	1.02	. . .	41.31	
1947														
January	43 545	37 926	17 213	14 328	26 332	. . .	12 445	. . .	40.5	. . .	1.03	. . .	41.72	
February	43 563	37 957	17 200	14 278	26 363	. . .	12 487	. . .	40.4	. . .	1.04	. . .	42.02	
March	43 605	38 017	17 196	14 259	26 409	. . .	12 518	. . .	40.3	. . .	1.06	. . .	42.72	
April	43 491	37 933	17 178	14 240	26 313	. . .	12 531	. . .	40.5	. . .	1.06	. . .	42.93	
May	43 637	38 086	17 176	14 189	26 461	. . .	12 449	. . .	40.4	. . .	1.08	. . .	43.63	
June	43 808	38 284	17 253	14 200	26 555	. . .	12 389	. . .	40.4	. . .	1.10	. . .	44.44	
July	43 742	38 218	17 106	14 076	26 636	. . .	12 265	. . .	40.4	. . .	1.10	. . .	44.44	
August	43 958	38 439	17 280	14 200	26 678	. . .	12 370	. . .	40.0	. . .	1.11	. . .	44.40	
September	44 201	38 662	17 398	14 315	26 803	. . .	12 430	. . .	40.5	. . .	1.11	. . .	44.96	
October	44 415	38 849	17 499	14 393	26 916	. . .	12 464	. . .	40.5	. . .	1.13	. . .	45.77	
November	44 486	38 901	17 517	14 414	26 969	. . .	12 494	. . .	40.5	. . .	1.14	. . .	46.17	
December	44 578	38 973	17 563	14 428	27 015	. . .	12 526	. . .	40.8	. . .	1.16	. . .	47.33	
1948														
January	44 686	39 062	17 625	14 438	27 061	. . .	12 520	. . .	40.5	. . .	1.16	. . .	46.98	
February	44 537	38 922	17 447	14 339	27 090	. . .	12 437	. . .	40.2	. . .	1.16	. . .	46.63	
March	44 680	39 057	17 544	14 364	27 136	. . .	12 489	. . .	40.4	. . .	1.16	. . .	46.86	
April	44 369	38 726	17 302	14 183	27 067	. . .	12 304	. . .	40.1	. . .	1.17	. . .	46.92	
May	44 795	39 114	17 508	14 235	27 287	. . .	12 344	. . .	40.2	. . .	1.18	. . .	47.44	
June	45 032	39 296	17 633	14 318	27 399	. . .	12 402	. . .	40.3	. . .	1.19	. . .	47.96	
July	45 160	39 386	17 649	14 359	27 511	. . .	12 417	. . .	40.2	. . .	1.21	. . .	48.64	
August	45 175	39 384	17 655	14 353	27 520	. . .	12 397	. . .	40.2	. . .	1.23	. . .	49.45	
September	45 294	39 489	17 741	14 441	27 553	. . .	12 450	. . .	40.1	. . .	1.24	. . .	49.72	
October	45 250	39 421	17 683	14 390	27 567	. . .	12 364	. . .	39.8	. . .	1.25	. . .	49.75	
November	45 194	39 325	17 599	14 292	27 595	. . .	12 302	. . .	39.8	. . .	1.26	. . .	50.15	
December	45 028	39 140	17 417	14 086	27 611	. . .	12 127	. . .	39.6	. . .	1.26	. . .	49.90	
1949														
January	44 675	38 781	17 170	13 867	27 505	. . .	11 905	. . .	39.4	. . .	1.26	. . .	49.64	
February	44 500	38 607	17 019	13 734	27 481	. . .	11 792	. . .	39.4	. . .	1.26	. . .	49.64	
March	44 238	38 323	16 848	13 581	27 390	. . .	11 654	. . .	39.1	. . .	1.26	. . .	49.27	
April	44 230	38 282	16 685	13 439	27 545	. . .	11 517	. . .	38.8	. . .	1.25	. . .	48.50	
May	43 982	38 020	16 492	13 269	27 490	. . .	11 352	. . .	38.9	. . .	1.25	. . .	48.63	
June	43 739	37 783	16 351	13 178	27 388	. . .	11 266	. . .	39.0	. . .	1.26	. . .	49.14	
July	43 530	37 568	16 222	13 067	27 308	. . .	11 168	. . .	39.2	. . .	1.26	. . .	49.39	
August	43 621	37 636	16 327	13 158	27 294	. . .	11 251	. . .	39.2	. . .	1.25	. . .	49.00	
September	43 784	37 794	16 403	13 225	27 381	. . .	11 284	. . .	39.4	. . .	1.25	. . .	49.25	
October	42 950	36 980	15 739	12 891	27 211	. . .	10 940	. . .	39.6	. . .	1.24	. . .	49.10	
November	43 244	37 294	16 040	12 882	27 204	. . .	10 964	. . .	39.1	. . .	1.24	. . .	48.48	
December	43 516	37 564	16 217	13 062	27 299	. . .	11 173	. . .	39.4	. . .	1.25	. . .	49.25	

. . . = Not available.

Table 20-4. Nonfarm Payroll Employment, Hours, and Earnings—*Continued*

(Wage and salary workers on nonfarm payrolls, seasonally adjusted.)

Year and month	All wage and salary workers (thousands)					Production or nonsupervisory workers on private payrolls							
	Total	Private				Number (thousands)		Average hours per week		Average hourly earnings, dollars		Average weekly earnings, dollars	
		Total	Goods-producing		Service-providing	Total private	Manufac-turing	Total private	Manufac-turing	Total private	Manufac-turing	Total private	Manufac-turing
			Total	Manufac-turing									
1950													
January	43 530	37 596	16 255	13 161	27 275	. . .	11 258	. . .	39.6	. . .	1.27	. . .	50.29
February	43 298	37 372	16 035	13 169	27 263	. . .	11 262	. . .	39.7	. . .	1.26	. . .	50.02
March	43 952	37 874	16 482	13 290	27 470	. . .	11 362	. . .	39.7	. . .	1.28	. . .	50.82
April	44 376	38 282	16 718	13 471	27 658	. . .	11 528	. . .	40.3	. . .	1.29	. . .	51.99
May	44 717	38 674	17 080	13 780	27 637	. . .	11 855	. . .	40.3	. . .	1.30	. . .	52.39
June	45 084	39 062	17 288	13 923	27 796	. . .	11 979	. . .	40.6	. . .	1.30	. . .	52.78
July	45 453	39 363	17 464	14 072	27 989	. . .	12 107	. . .	40.9	. . .	1.31	. . .	53.58
August	46 187	40 000	17 917	14 461	28 270	. . .	12 476	. . .	41.3	. . .	1.33	. . .	54.93
September	46 442	40 214	18 040	14 561	28 402	. . .	12 519	. . .	40.8	. . .	1.33	. . .	54.26
October	46 712	40 463	18 249	14 737	28 463	. . .	12 659	. . .	41.1	. . .	1.36	. . .	55.90
November	46 778	40 516	18 288	14 762	28 490	. . .	12 682	. . .	41.0	. . .	1.37	. . .	56.17
December	46 855	40 541	18 283	14 782	28 572	. . .	12 710	. . .	40.9	. . .	1.39	. . .	56.85
1951													
January	47 289	40 937	18 518	14 950	28 771	. . .	12 816	. . .	41.0	. . .	1.40	. . .	57.40
February	47 577	41 195	18 666	15 076	28 911	. . .	12 929	. . .	40.9	. . .	1.41	. . .	57.67
March	47 871	41 461	18 754	15 125	29 117	. . .	12 936	. . .	41.0	. . .	1.42	. . .	58.22
April	47 856	41 405	18 810	15 166	29 046	. . .	12 960	. . .	41.0	. . .	1.43	. . .	58.63
May	47 952	41 535	18 829	15 164	29 123	. . .	12 941	. . .	41.0	. . .	1.44	. . .	59.04
June	48 067	41 568	18 826	15 176	29 241	. . .	12 934	. . .	40.9	. . .	1.45	. . .	59.31
July	48 061	41 523	18 747	15 110	29 314	. . .	12 848	. . .	40.6	. . .	1.45	. . .	58.87
August	48 008	41 489	18 709	15 061	29 299	. . .	12 772	. . .	40.4	. . .	1.46	. . .	58.98
September	47 955	41 403	18 622	14 996	29 333	. . .	12 659	. . .	40.4	. . .	1.46	. . .	58.98
October	48 009	41 432	18 630	14 973	29 379	. . .	12 615	. . .	40.3	. . .	1.47	. . .	59.24
November	48 149	41 523	18 617	14 999	29 532	. . .	12 628	. . .	40.4	. . .	1.48	. . .	59.79
December	48 308	41 620	18 698	15 045	29 610	. . .	12 667	. . .	40.7	. . .	1.49	. . .	60.64
1952													
January	48 299	41 710	18 719	15 067	29 580	. . .	12 675	. . .	40.8	. . .	1.49	. . .	60.79
February	48 522	41 872	18 813	15 105	29 709	. . .	12 689	. . .	40.8	. . .	1.49	. . .	60.79
March	48 504	41 842	18 775	15 127	29 729	. . .	12 695	. . .	40.6	. . .	1.51	. . .	61.31
April	48 616	41 954	18 806	15 162	29 810	. . .	12 713	. . .	40.3	. . .	1.51	. . .	60.85
May	48 645	41 951	18 784	15 143	29 861	. . .	12 676	. . .	40.5	. . .	1.51	. . .	61.16
June	48 286	41 574	18 419	14 828	29 867	. . .	12 353	. . .	40.6	. . .	1.51	. . .	61.31
July	48 144	41 407	18 268	14 707	29 876	. . .	12 233	. . .	40.2	. . .	1.50	. . .	60.30
August	48 922	42 204	18 908	15 279	29 994	. . .	12 764	. . .	40.7	. . .	1.53	. . .	62.27
September	49 319	42 585	19 206	15 553	30 113	. . .	13 007	. . .	41.1	. . .	1.55	. . .	63.71
October	49 598	42 782	19 312	15 690	30 286	. . .	13 122	. . .	41.2	. . .	1.56	. . .	64.27
November	49 816	43 015	19 473	15 843	30 343	. . .	13 262	. . .	41.2	. . .	1.58	. . .	65.10
December	50 164	43 229	19 610	15 973	30 554	. . .	13 375	. . .	41.2	. . .	1.58	. . .	65.10
1953													
January	50 145	43 351	19 721	16 067	30 424	. . .	13 447	. . .	41.1	. . .	1.59	. . .	65.35
February	50 339	43 542	19 841	16 158	30 498	. . .	13 529	. . .	41.0	. . .	1.61	. . .	66.01
March	50 474	43 690	19 909	16 270	30 565	. . .	13 620	. . .	41.2	. . .	1.61	. . .	66.33
April	50 432	43 662	19 908	16 293	30 524	. . .	13 629	. . .	40.9	. . .	1.62	. . .	66.26
May	50 491	43 774	19 930	16 341	30 561	. . .	13 645	. . .	41.0	. . .	1.62	. . .	66.42
June	50 522	43 788	19 909	16 343	30 613	. . .	13 636	. . .	40.9	. . .	1.63	. . .	66.67
July	50 536	43 813	19 910	16 353	30 626	. . .	13 653	. . .	40.7	. . .	1.64	. . .	66.75
August	50 487	43 733	19 834	16 278	30 653	. . .	13 564	. . .	40.7	. . .	1.64	. . .	66.75
September	50 365	43 616	19 726	16 151	30 639	. . .	13 419	. . .	40.1	. . .	1.65	. . .	66.17
October	50 242	43 478	19 578	15 981	30 664	. . .	13 244	. . .	40.1	. . .	1.65	. . .	66.17
November	49 906	43 157	19 315	15 728	30 591	. . .	12 990	. . .	40.0	. . .	1.65	. . .	66.00
December	49 702	42 959	19 173	15 581	30 529	. . .	12 847	. . .	39.7	. . .	1.65	. . .	65.51
1954													
January	49 467	42 707	18 963	15 440	30 504	. . .	12 706	. . .	39.5	. . .	1.65	. . .	65.18
February	49 381	42 598	18 880	15 307	30 501	. . .	12 593	. . .	39.7	. . .	1.65	. . .	65.51
March	49 158	42 362	18 748	15 197	30 410	. . .	12 493	. . .	39.6	. . .	1.65	. . .	65.34
April	49 177	42 371	18 602	15 065	30 575	. . .	12 361	. . .	39.7	. . .	1.65	. . .	65.51
May	48 965	42 136	18 476	14 974	30 489	. . .	12 282	. . .	39.7	. . .	1.67	. . .	66.30
June	48 896	42 050	18 400	14 910	30 496	. . .	12 220	. . .	39.7	. . .	1.67	. . .	66.30
July	48 834	41 966	18 280	14 799	30 554	. . .	12 121	. . .	39.7	. . .	1.66	. . .	65.90
August	48 825	41 933	18 251	14 772	30 574	. . .	12 089	. . .	39.8	. . .	1.66	. . .	66.07
September	48 881	41 987	18 261	14 805	30 620	. . .	12 104	. . .	39.9	. . .	1.66	. . .	66.23
October	48 944	42 044	18 321	14 841	30 623	. . .	12 142	. . .	39.7	. . .	1.67	. . .	66.30
November	49 179	42 215	18 438	14 913	30 741	. . .	12 206	. . .	40.1	. . .	1.68	. . .	67.37
December	49 331	42 374	18 508	14 967	30 823	. . .	12 254	. . .	40.1	. . .	1.68	. . .	67.37
1955													
January	49 497	42 544	18 609	15 034	30 888	. . .	12 309	. . .	40.4	. . .	1.69	. . .	68.28
February	49 644	42 721	18 726	15 138	30 918	. . .	12 408	. . .	40.6	. . .	1.70	. . .	69.02
March	49 963	43 025	18 910	15 258	31 053	. . .	12 524	. . .	40.7	. . .	1.71	. . .	69.60
April	50 246	43 287	19 067	15 375	31 179	. . .	12 626	. . .	40.8	. . .	1.71	. . .	69.77
May	50 512	43 521	19 223	15 493	31 289	. . .	12 731	. . .	41.1	. . .	1.73	. . .	71.10
June	50 790	43 770	19 331	15 585	31 459	. . .	12 810	. . .	40.8	. . .	1.73	. . .	70.58
July	50 985	43 936	19 376	15 614	31 609	. . .	12 818	. . .	40.7	. . .	1.75	. . .	71.23
August	51 112	44 089	19 432	15 679	31 680	. . .	12 866	. . .	40.7	. . .	1.76	. . .	71.63
September	51 262	44 195	19 427	15 668	31 835	. . .	12 830	. . .	40.7	. . .	1.77	. . .	72.04
October	51 431	44 313	19 482	15 740	31 949	. . .	12 896	. . .	41.0	. . .	1.77	. . .	72.57
November	51 592	44 509	19 554	15 813	32 038	. . .	12 967	. . .	41.1	. . .	1.78	. . .	73.16
December	51 805	44 673	19 608	15 859	32 197	. . .	13 009	. . .	40.9	. . .	1.78	. . .	72.80

. . . = Not available.

Table 20-4. Nonfarm Payroll Employment, Hours, and Earnings—Continued

(Wage and salary workers on nonfarm payrolls, seasonally adjusted.)

Year and month	All wage and salary workers (thousands)					Production or nonsupervisory workers on private payrolls							
	Total	Private			Service-providing	Number (thousands)		Average hours per week		Average hourly earnings, dollars		Average weekly earnings, dollars	
		Total	Goods-producing			Total private	Manufac-turing	Total private	Manufac-turing	Total private	Manufac-turing	Total private	Manufac-turing
			Total	Manufac-turing									
1956													
January	51 975	44 808	19 665	15 882	32 310	...	13 011	...	40.8	...	1.78	...	72.62
February	52 167	44 955	19 731	15 889	32 436	...	12 986	...	40.7	...	1.79	...	72.85
March	52 295	45 043	19 691	15 829	32 604	...	12 905	...	40.6	...	1.80	...	73.08
April	52 375	45 099	19 811	15 909	32 564	...	12 970	...	40.5	...	1.82	...	73.71
May	52 506	45 139	19 825	15 893	32 681	...	12 925	...	40.4	...	1.83	...	73.93
June	52 583	45 216	19 905	15 835	32 678	...	12 836	...	40.3	...	1.83	...	73.75
July	51 954	44 549	19 390	15 468	32 564	...	12 435	...	40.3	...	1.82	...	73.35
August	52 632	45 181	19 922	15 893	32 710	...	12 860	...	40.3	...	1.85	...	74.56
September	52 600	45 119	19 860	15 863	32 740	...	12 822	...	40.5	...	1.87	...	75.74
October	52 781	45 262	19 918	15 937	32 863	...	12 908	...	40.6	...	1.88	...	76.33
November	52 822	45 269	19 886	15 916	32 936	...	12 864	...	40.4	...	1.88	...	75.95
December	52 930	45 346	19 926	15 957	33 004	...	12 882	...	40.6	...	1.91	...	77.55
1957													
January	52 888	45 268	19 833	15 970	33 055	...	12 881	...	40.4	...	1.90	...	76.76
February	53 098	45 452	19 933	15 998	33 165	...	12 885	...	40.5	...	1.91	...	77.36
March	53 156	45 484	19 936	15 994	33 220	...	12 855	...	40.4	...	1.92	...	77.57
April	53 238	45 537	19 887	15 970	33 351	...	12 811	...	40.0	...	1.91	...	76.40
May	53 149	45 436	19 834	15 931	33 315	...	12 762	...	40.0	...	1.92	...	76.80
June	53 066	45 364	19 777	15 873	33 289	...	12 697	...	40.0	...	1.92	...	76.80
July	53 122	45 368	19 735	15 854	33 387	...	12 669	...	40.0	...	1.93	...	77.20
August	53 128	45 371	19 728	15 867	33 400	...	12 673	...	40.0	...	1.94	...	77.60
September	52 932	45 183	19 545	15 710	33 387	...	12 528	...	39.7	...	1.95	...	77.42
October	52 765	44 997	19 421	15 599	33 344	...	12 437	...	39.4	...	1.96	...	77.22
November	52 557	44 788	19 260	15 466	33 297	...	12 301	...	39.2	...	1.96	...	76.83
December	52 385	44 539	19 111	15 332	33 274	...	12 170	...	39.1	...	1.95	...	76.25
1958													
January	52 077	44 256	18 902	15 130	33 175	...	11 969	...	38.9	...	1.95	...	75.86
February	51 576	43 744	18 529	14 908	33 047	...	11 757	...	38.7	...	1.95	...	75.47
March	51 300	43 452	18 335	14 670	32 965	...	11 532	...	38.8	...	1.96	...	76.05
April	51 026	43 158	18 120	14 506	32 906	...	11 373	...	38.9	...	1.96	...	76.24
May	50 913	43 019	18 008	14 414	32 905	...	11 294	...	38.9	...	1.97	...	76.63
June	50 912	42 986	17 984	14 408	32 928	...	11 300	...	39.1	...	1.98	...	77.42
July	51 037	43 065	18 038	14 450	32 999	...	11 349	...	39.3	...	1.98	...	77.81
August	51 233	43 221	18 147	14 524	33 086	...	11 412	...	39.5	...	2.01	...	79.40
September	51 506	43 490	18 331	14 658	33 175	...	11 556	...	39.5	...	2.00	...	79.00
October	51 485	43 454	18 218	14 503	33 267	...	11 394	...	39.6	...	2.00	...	79.20
November	51 943	43 915	18 610	14 827	33 333	...	11 702	...	39.9	...	2.03	...	81.00
December	52 088	43 988	18 592	14 877	33 496	...	11 743	...	39.9	...	2.04	...	81.40
1959													
January	52 481	44 376	18 796	14 998	33 685	...	11 849	...	40.2	...	2.04	...	82.01
February	52 687	44 571	18 890	15 115	33 797	...	11 950	...	40.3	...	2.05	...	82.62
March	53 016	44 884	19 069	15 259	33 947	...	12 078	...	40.4	...	2.07	...	83.63
April	53 320	45 178	19 269	15 385	34 051	...	12 185	...	40.5	...	2.08	...	84.24
May	53 549	45 396	19 378	15 487	34 171	...	12 277	...	40.7	...	2.08	...	84.66
June	53 678	45 535	19 462	15 554	34 216	...	12 330	...	40.6	...	2.09	...	84.85
July	53 803	45 630	19 529	15 623	34 274	...	12 366	...	40.3	...	2.09	...	84.23
August	53 337	45 156	19 049	15 202	34 288	...	11 936	...	40.4	...	2.07	...	83.63
September	53 428	45 189	19 052	15 254	34 376	...	11 984	...	40.4	...	2.08	...	84.03
October	53 359	45 094	18 925	15 158	34 434	...	11 864	...	40.1	...	2.07	...	83.01
November	53 635	45 351	19 108	15 300	34 527	...	11 991	...	39.9	...	2.07	...	82.59
December	54 175	45 807	19 425	15 573	34 750	...	12 254	...	40.3	...	2.11	...	85.03
1960													
January	54 274	45 967	19 491	15 687	34 783	...	12 362	...	40.6	...	2.13	...	86.48
February	54 513	46 187	19 605	15 765	34 908	...	12 434	...	40.3	...	2.14	...	86.24
March	54 458	45 933	19 373	15 707	35 085	...	12 362	...	40.0	...	2.14	...	85.60
April	54 812	46 278	19 446	15 654	35 366	...	12 299	...	40.0	...	2.14	...	85.60
May	54 472	46 040	19 374	15 575	35 098	...	12 218	...	40.1	...	2.14	...	85.81
June	54 347	45 915	19 240	15 466	35 107	...	12 102	...	39.9	...	2.14	...	85.39
July	54 303	45 861	19 170	15 413	35 133	...	12 047	...	39.9	...	2.14	...	85.39
August	54 272	45 800	19 105	15 360	35 167	...	11 986	...	39.7	...	2.15	...	85.36
September	54 228	45 734	19 057	15 330	35 171	...	11 956	...	39.4	...	2.16	...	85.10
October	54 144	45 642	18 952	15 231	35 192	...	11 846	...	39.7	...	2.16	...	85.75
November	53 962	45 446	18 799	15 112	35 163	...	11 726	...	39.3	...	2.15	...	84.50
December	53 743	45 146	18 548	14 947	35 195	...	11 556	...	38.4	...	2.16	...	82.94
1961													
January	53 683	45 119	18 508	14 863	35 175	...	11 473	...	39.3	...	2.16	...	84.89
February	53 556	44 969	18 418	14 801	35 138	...	11 414	...	39.4	...	2.16	...	85.10
March	53 662	45 051	18 438	14 802	35 224	...	11 410	...	39.5	...	2.16	...	85.32
April	53 626	44 997	18 432	14 825	35 194	...	11 444	...	39.5	...	2.18	...	86.11
May	53 783	45 119	18 523	14 932	35 260	...	11 544	...	39.7	...	2.19	...	86.94
June	53 977	45 289	18 618	14 981	35 359	...	11 593	...	40.0	...	2.20	...	88.00
July	54 124	45 400	18 640	15 029	35 484	...	11 639	...	40.0	...	2.21	...	88.40
August	54 299	45 535	18 725	15 093	35 574	...	11 701	...	40.1	...	2.22	...	89.02
September	54 387	45 591	18 730	15 080	35 657	...	11 679	...	39.5	...	2.20	...	86.90
October	54 521	45 716	18 805	15 143	35 716	...	11 731	...	40.3	...	2.23	...	89.87
November	54 743	45 931	18 927	15 259	35 816	...	11 842	...	40.7	...	2.23	...	90.76
December	54 871	46 035	18 981	15 309	35 890	...	11 872	...	40.4	...	2.24	...	90.50

... = Not available.

Table 20-4. Nonfarm Payroll Employment, Hours, and Earnings—*Continued*

(Wage and salary workers on nonfarm payrolls, seasonally adjusted.)

Year and month	All wage and salary workers (thousands)					Production or nonsupervisory workers on private payrolls							
	Total	Private			Service-providing	Number (thousands)		Average hours per week		Average hourly earnings, dollars		Average weekly earnings, dollars	
		Total	Goods-producing			Total private	Manufac-turing	Total private	Manufac-turing	Total private	Manufac-turing	Total private	Manufac-turing
			Total	Manufac-turing									
1962													
January	54 891	46 040	18 936	15 322	35 955	. . .	11 865	. . .	40.0	. . .	2.25	. . .	90.00
February	55 187	46 309	19 109	15 411	36 078	. . .	11 950	. . .	40.4	. . .	2.26	. . .	91.30
March	55 276	46 375	19 109	15 451	36 167	. . .	11 970	. . .	40.6	. . .	2.26	. . .	91.76
April	55 601	46 679	19 258	15 524	36 343	. . .	12 034	. . .	40.6	. . .	2.26	. . .	91.76
May	55 626	46 668	19 253	15 513	36 373	. . .	12 011	. . .	40.6	. . .	2.27	. . .	92.16
June	55 644	46 644	19 186	15 518	36 458	. . .	12 006	. . .	40.5	. . .	2.26	. . .	91.53
July	55 746	46 720	19 248	15 522	36 498	. . .	12 004	. . .	40.5	. . .	2.27	. . .	91.94
August	55 838	46 775	19 251	15 517	36 587	. . .	11 990	. . .	40.5	. . .	2.28	. . .	92.34
September	55 977	46 888	19 305	15 568	36 672	. . .	12 033	. . .	40.5	. . .	2.28	. . .	92.34
October	56 041	46 927	19 301	15 569	36 740	. . .	12 034	. . .	40.3	. . .	2.29	. . .	92.29
November	56 055	46 910	19 260	15 530	36 795	. . .	11 977	. . .	40.5	. . .	2.29	. . .	92.75
December	56 027	46 901	19 219	15 520	36 808	. . .	11 961	. . .	40.3	. . .	2.29	. . .	92.29
1963													
January	56 116	46 912	19 257	15 545	36 859	. . .	11 974	. . .	40.5	. . .	2.30	. . .	93.15
February	56 231	47 000	19 228	15 542	37 003	. . .	11 965	. . .	40.5	. . .	2.31	. . .	93.56
March	56 322	47 077	19 233	15 564	37 089	. . .	11 990	. . .	40.5	. . .	2.32	. . .	93.96
April	56 580	47 316	19 343	15 602	37 237	. . .	12 029	. . .	40.5	. . .	2.32	. . .	93.96
May	56 616	47 328	19 399	15 641	37 217	. . .	12 066	. . .	40.5	. . .	2.33	. . .	94.37
June	56 658	47 356	19 371	15 624	37 287	. . .	12 050	. . .	40.7	. . .	2.34	. . .	95.24
July	56 795	47 461	19 423	15 646	37 372	. . .	12 080	. . .	40.6	. . .	2.35	. . .	95.41
August	56 910	47 542	19 437	15 644	37 473	. . .	12 060	. . .	40.6	. . .	2.34	. . .	95.00
September	57 078	47 661	19 483	15 674	37 595	. . .	12 088	. . .	40.6	. . .	2.36	. . .	95.82
October	57 284	47 805	19 517	15 714	37 767	. . .	12 131	. . .	40.7	. . .	2.36	. . .	96.05
November	57 255	47 771	19 456	15 675	37 799	. . .	12 072	. . .	40.7	. . .	2.37	. . .	96.46
December	57 360	47 863	19 493	15 712	37 867	. . .	12 108	. . .	40.6	. . .	2.38	. . .	96.63
1964													
January	57 487	47 925	19 406	15 715	38 081	39 914	12 132	38.2	40.1	2.50	2.38	95.50	95.44
February	57 752	48 171	19 530	15 742	38 182	40 123	12 165	38.5	40.7	2.50	2.38	96.25	96.87
March	57 898	48 287	19 587	15 770	38 311	40 171	12 190	38.5	40.6	2.50	2.38	96.25	96.63
April	57 923	48 279	19 593	15 785	38 330	40 208	12 211	38.6	40.7	2.52	2.40	97.27	97.68
May	58 089	48 419	19 630	15 812	38 459	40 332	12 231	38.6	40.8	2.52	2.40	97.27	97.92
June	58 221	48 552	19 682	15 839	38 539	40 448	12 255	38.6	40.8	2.53	2.41	97.66	98.33
July	58 412	48 735	19 740	15 887	38 672	40 624	12 309	38.5	40.8	2.53	2.41	97.41	98.33
August	58 620	48 888	19 810	15 948	38 810	40 770	12 354	38.5	40.9	2.55	2.42	98.18	98.98
September	58 903	49 117	19 943	16 073	38 960	41 026	12 479	38.5	40.9	2.55	2.44	98.18	99.80
October	58 794	48 949	19 723	15 821	39 071	40 827	12 224	38.5	40.7	2.55	2.40	98.18	97.68
November	59 217	49 338	20 026	16 096	39 191	41 157	12 477	38.6	41.0	2.56	2.42	98.82	99.22
December	59 420	49 523	20 111	16 176	39 309	41 308	12 551	38.7	41.2	2.58	2.44	99.85	100.53
1965													
January	59 583	49 646	20 173	16 245	39 410	41 453	12 603	38.7	41.3	2.58	2.45	99.85	101.19
February	59 800	49 826	20 216	16 291	39 584	41 583	12 644	38.7	41.3	2.59	2.46	100.23	101.60
March	60 003	49 993	20 292	16 353	39 711	41 675	12 701	38.7	41.3	2.60	2.47	100.62	102.01
April	60 258	50 207	20 317	16 418	39 941	41 886	12 752	38.7	41.2	2.60	2.47	100.62	101.76
May	60 492	50 398	20 444	16 477	40 048	42 044	12 792	38.8	41.3	2.62	2.49	101.66	102.84
June	60 690	50 562	20 522	16 554	40 168	42 183	12 854	38.6	41.2	2.62	2.49	101.13	102.59
July	60 963	50 762	20 611	16 669	40 352	42 364	12 962	38.6	41.2	2.63	2.49	101.52	102.59
August	61 228	50 957	20 726	16 732	40 502	42 537	12 994	38.5	41.1	2.64	2.50	101.64	102.75
September	61 490	51 152	20 808	16 802	40 682	42 726	13 046	38.6	41.1	2.65	2.51	102.29	103.16
October	61 718	51 340	20 895	16 864	40 823	42 870	13 100	38.5	41.2	2.66	2.52	102.41	103.82
November	61 997	51 561	21 021	16 962	40 976	43 045	13 175	38.6	41.3	2.67	2.52	103.06	104.08
December	62 321	51 822	21 151	17 051	41 170	43 270	13 243	38.6	41.3	2.68	2.53	103.45	104.49
1966													
January	62 528	51 987	21 214	17 143	41 314	43 401	13 301	38.6	41.5	2.68	2.54	103.45	105.41
February	62 796	52 185	21 315	17 288	41 481	43 552	13 426	38.7	41.7	2.69	2.56	104.10	106.75
March	63 191	52 499	21 515	17 400	41 676	43 801	13 508	38.7	41.6	2.70	2.56	104.49	106.50
April	63 436	52 677	21 568	17 517	41 868	43 959	13 598	38.7	41.8	2.71	2.58	104.88	107.84
May	63 711	52 890	21 675	17 625	42 036	44 138	13 678	38.5	41.5	2.72	2.58	104.72	107.07
June	64 110	53 208	21 846	17 733	42 264	44 390	13 753	38.5	41.4	2.72	2.58	104.72	106.81
July	64 301	53 327	21 872	17 760	42 429	44 484	13 758	38.4	41.2	2.74	2.60	105.22	107.12
August	64 507	53 501	21 972	17 882	42 535	44 596	13 843	38.4	41.4	2.75	2.61	105.60	108.05
September	64 645	53 582	21 948	17 886	42 697	44 659	13 841	38.3	41.2	2.76	2.63	105.71	108.36
October	64 854	53 727	21 991	17 956	42 863	44 789	13 906	38.4	41.3	2.77	2.64	106.37	109.03
November	65 019	53 816	21 988	17 981	43 031	44 834	13 918	38.3	41.2	2.78	2.65	106.47	109.18
December	65 199	53 943	22 008	17 998	43 191	44 916	13 906	38.2	40.9	2.78	2.64	106.20	107.98
1967													
January	65 407	54 092	22 057	18 033	43 350	45 050	13 925	38.3	41.1	2.79	2.65	106.86	108.92
February	65 427	54 074	21 987	17 978	43 440	44 967	13 853	37.9	40.4	2.81	2.67	106.50	107.87
March	65 530	54 133	21 919	17 940	43 611	44 991	13 797	37.9	40.5	2.81	2.67	106.50	108.14
April	65 467	54 032	21 842	17 878	43 625	44 871	13 712	37.8	40.4	2.82	2.68	106.60	108.27
May	65 618	54 144	21 779	17 832	43 839	44 961	13 664	37.8	40.4	2.83	2.69	106.97	108.68
June	65 750	54 216	21 761	17 812	43 989	45 004	13 632	37.8	40.4	2.84	2.69	107.35	108.68
July	65 887	54 343	21 772	17 784	44 115	45 105	13 602	37.8	40.5	2.86	2.71	108.11	109.76
August	66 142	54 552	21 887	17 905	44 255	45 267	13 681	37.8	40.6	2.87	2.73	108.49	110.84
September	66 163	54 540	21 775	17 794	44 388	45 236	13 559	37.8	40.6	2.88	2.73	108.86	110.84
October	66 225	54 583	21 779	17 800	44 446	45 278	13 587	37.8	40.6	2.89	2.74	109.24	111.24
November	66 703	55 008	21 996	17 985	44 707	45 701	13 777	37.9	40.6	2.91	2.75	110.29	111.65
December	66 900	55 165	22 037	18 025	44 863	45 800	13 782	37.7	40.7	2.92	2.77	110.08	112.74

. . . = Not available.

Table 20-4. Nonfarm Payroll Employment, Hours, and Earnings—*Continued*

(Wage and salary workers on nonfarm payrolls, seasonally adjusted.)

Year and month	All wage and salary workers (thousands)					Production or nonsupervisory workers on private payrolls							
	Total	Private			Service-providing	Number (thousands)		Average hours per week		Average hourly earnings, dollars		Average weekly earnings, dollars	
		Total	Goods-producing			Total private	Manufac-turing	Total private	Manufac-turing	Total private	Manufac-turing	Total private	Manufac-turing
			Total	Manufac-turing									
1968													
January	66 805	55 011	21 917	18 040	44 888	45 655	13 798	37.6	40.4	2.94	2.81	110.54	113.52
February	67 214	55 395	22 117	18 054	45 097	45 980	13 793	37.8	40.8	2.95	2.82	111.51	115.06
March	67 296	55 454	22 119	18 067	45 177	46 041	13 803	37.7	40.8	2.97	2.84	111.97	115.87
April	67 555	55 677	22 207	18 131	45 348	46 239	13 858	37.6	40.3	2.98	2.85	112.05	114.86
May	67 652	55 747	22 255	18 190	45 397	46 267	13 900	37.7	40.9	3.00	2.87	113.10	117.38
June	67 904	55 917	22 264	18 228	45 640	46 402	13 921	37.8	40.9	3.01	2.88	113.78	117.79
July	68 126	56 108	22 329	18 265	45 797	46 562	13 953	37.7	40.8	3.03	2.89	114.23	117.91
August	68 328	56 286	22 350	18 254	45 978	46 669	13 903	37.7	40.7	3.03	2.89	114.23	117.62
September	68 487	56 420	22 390	18 252	46 097	46 792	13 914	37.7	40.9	3.06	2.92	115.36	119.43
October	68 720	56 619	22 419	18 293	46 301	46 989	13 974	37.7	41.0	3.07	2.94	115.74	120.54
November	68 985	56 878	22 512	18 346	46 473	47 244	14 028	37.5	40.9	3.09	2.96	115.88	121.06
December	69 245	57 100	22 617	18 410	46 628	47 384	14 044	37.5	40.7	3.11	2.97	116.63	120.88
1969													
January	69 438	57 229	22 644	18 432	46 794	47 528	14 086	37.7	40.8	3.12	2.99	117.62	121.99
February	69 698	57 474	22 755	18 502	46 943	47 697	14 134	37.5	40.4	3.14	3.00	117.75	121.20
March	69 906	57 677	22 813	18 558	47 093	47 852	14 169	37.6	40.8	3.15	3.01	118.44	122.81
April	70 072	57 827	22 815	18 554	47 257	47 959	14 144	37.7	41.0	3.17	3.03	119.51	124.23
May	70 328	58 044	22 899	18 588	47 429	48 122	14 161	37.6	40.7	3.19	3.04	119.94	123.73
June	70 636	58 277	22 981	18 640	47 655	48 330	14 206	37.5	40.7	3.20	3.05	120.00	124.14
July	70 730	58 390	22 990	18 642	47 740	48 434	14 194	37.5	40.6	3.22	3.08	120.75	125.05
August	71 005	58 632	23 111	18 767	47 894	48 616	14 287	37.5	40.6	3.24	3.10	121.50	125.86
September	70 918	58 539	22 988	18 620	47 930	48 524	14 159	37.5	40.6	3.26	3.12	122.25	126.67
October	71 119	58 689	22 976	18 613	48 143	48 669	14 174	37.4	40.5	3.28	3.13	122.67	126.77
November	71 088	58 640	22 840	18 467	48 248	48 589	14 035	37.5	40.5	3.29	3.14	123.38	127.17
December	71 240	58 763	22 884	18 485	48 356	48 638	14 013	37.5	40.6	3.30	3.15	123.75	127.89
1970													
January	71 176	58 680	22 726	18 424	48 450	48 564	13 964	37.3	40.4	3.31	3.16	123.46	127.66
February	71 302	58 784	22 747	18 361	48 555	48 600	13 897	37.3	40.2	3.33	3.17	124.21	127.43
March	71 453	58 850	22 738	18 360	48 715	48 690	13 917	37.2	40.1	3.35	3.19	124.62	127.92
April	71 348	58 643	22 552	18 207	48 796	48 479	13 785	37.0	39.8	3.36	3.19	124.32	126.96
May	71 122	58 454	22 336	18 029	48 786	48 287	13 616	37.0	39.8	3.38	3.22	125.06	128.16
June	71 028	58 361	22 241	17 930	48 787	48 226	13 554	36.9	39.8	3.39	3.24	125.09	128.95
July	71 055	58 358	22 195	17 877	48 860	48 242	13 527	37.0	40.0	3.41	3.25	126.17	130.00
August	70 932	58 221	22 105	17 779	48 827	48 089	13 449	37.0	39.8	3.43	3.26	126.91	129.75
September	70 949	58 208	21 988	17 692	48 961	48 101	13 401	36.8	39.6	3.45	3.29	126.96	130.28
October	70 519	57 726	21 477	17 173	49 042	47 619	12 905	36.8	39.5	3.46	3.26	127.33	128.77
November	70 409	57 579	21 345	17 024	49 064	47 466	12 781	36.7	39.5	3.47	3.26	127.35	128.77
December	70 790	57 945	21 673	17 309	49 117	47 778	13 062	36.8	39.5	3.50	3.32	128.80	131.14
1971													
January	70 866	57 988	21 594	17 280	49 272	47 859	13 069	36.8	39.9	3.52	3.36	129.54	134.06
February	70 805	57 928	21 514	17 216	49 291	47 779	13 033	36.7	39.7	3.54	3.39	129.92	134.58
March	70 859	57 951	21 491	17 154	49 368	47 819	12 984	36.7	39.8	3.56	3.39	130.65	134.92
April	71 037	58 092	21 552	17 149	49 485	47 966	12 993	36.8	39.9	3.57	3.41	131.38	136.06
May	71 247	58 277	21 645	17 225	49 602	48 153	13 081	36.7	40.0	3.60	3.43	132.12	137.20
June	71 253	58 245	21 568	17 139	49 685	48 109	13 012	36.8	39.9	3.62	3.45	133.22	137.66
July	71 316	58 305	21 564	17 126	49 752	48 167	13 001	36.7	40.0	3.63	3.46	133.22	138.40
August	71 368	58 327	21 570	17 115	49 798	48 164	12 993	36.7	39.8	3.66	3.48	134.32	138.50
September	71 620	58 552	21 650	17 154	49 970	48 362	13 038	36.7	39.7	3.67	3.48	134.69	138.16
October	71 642	58 527	21 604	17 126	50 038	48 305	13 027	36.8	39.9	3.68	3.50	135.42	139.65
November	71 844	58 696	21 684	17 166	50 160	48 442	13 064	36.9	40.0	3.69	3.49	136.16	139.60
December	72 108	58 918	21 741	17 202	50 367	48 613	13 078	36.9	40.2	3.73	3.55	137.64	142.71
1972													
January	72 445	59 179	21 865	17 283	50 580	49 035	13 173	36.9	40.2	3.80	3.57	140.22	143.51
February	72 652	59 354	21 915	17 361	50 737	49 143	13 235	36.9	40.4	3.82	3.61	140.96	145.84
March	72 945	59 616	22 036	17 447	50 909	49 437	13 316	36.9	40.4	3.84	3.63	141.70	146.65
April	73 163	59 805	22 099	17 508	51 064	49 561	13 373	36.9	40.5	3.86	3.65	142.43	147.83
May	73 467	60 051	22 222	17 602	51 245	49 745	13 451	36.8	40.5	3.87	3.67	142.42	148.64
June	73 760	60 355	22 282	17 641	51 478	49 997	13 475	36.9	40.6	3.88	3.68	143.17	149.41
July	73 709	60 227	22 162	17 556	51 547	49 842	13 387	36.8	40.5	3.90	3.69	143.52	149.45
August	74 137	60 607	22 400	17 741	51 737	50 156	13 562	36.8	40.6	3.92	3.73	144.26	151.44
September	74 268	60 693	22 456	17 774	51 812	50 224	13 572	36.9	40.6	3.94	3.75	145.39	152.25
October	74 672	61 066	22 613	17 893	52 059	50 552	13 681	37.0	40.7	3.97	3.78	146.89	153.85
November	74 965	61 322	22 688	18 005	52 277	50 790	13 783	36.9	40.7	3.98	3.79	146.86	154.25
December	75 270	61 586	22 772	18 158	52 498	51 054	13 902	36.8	40.6	4.01	3.83	147.57	155.50
1973													
January	75 620	61 930	22 955	18 276	52 665	51 349	14 006	36.8	40.4	4.03	3.86	148.30	155.94
February	76 017	62 306	23 160	18 410	52 857	51 686	14 127	36.9	40.9	4.04	3.87	149.08	158.28
March	76 286	62 541	23 262	18 493	53 024	51 901	14 181	37.0	40.9	4.06	3.88	150.22	158.69
April	76 456	62 679	23 316	18 530	53 140	51 982	14 192	36.9	40.8	4.08	3.91	150.55	159.53
May	76 646	62 829	23 382	18 564	53 264	52 082	14 217	36.9	40.7	4.10	3.93	151.29	159.95
June	76 886	63 014	23 485	18 606	53 401	52 234	14 253	36.9	40.7	4.12	3.95	152.03	160.77
July	76 911	63 046	23 522	18 598	53 389	52 238	14 232	36.9	40.7	4.15	3.98	153.14	161.99
August	77 166	63 262	23 559	18 629	53 607	52 393	14 251	36.9	40.6	4.16	4.00	153.50	162.40
September	77 281	63 389	23 548	18 609	53 733	52 410	14 213	36.8	40.7	4.19	4.03	154.19	164.02
October	77 605	63 628	23 641	18 702	53 964	52 655	14 289	36.7	40.6	4.21	4.05	154.51	164.43
November	77 909	63 874	23 719	18 773	54 190	52 847	14 342	36.9	40.6	4.23	4.07	156.09	165.24
December	78 035	63 965	23 779	18 820	54 256	52 954	14 386	36.7	40.6	4.25	4.09	155.98	166.05

Table 20-4. Nonfarm Payroll Employment, Hours, and Earnings—*Continued*

(Wage and salary workers on nonfarm payrolls, seasonally adjusted.)

Year and month	All wage and salary workers (thousands)					Production or nonsupervisory workers on private payrolls							
	Total	Private Total	Goods-producing Total	Manufac-turing	Service-providing	Number (thousands) Total private	Manufac-turing	Average hours per week Total private	Manufac-turing	Average hourly earnings, dollars Total private	Manufac-turing	Average weekly earnings, dollars Total private	Manufac-turing
1974													
January	78 104	64 014	23 709	18 788	54 395	52 896	14 340	36.6	40.5	4.26	4.10	155.92	166.05
February	78 253	64 118	23 718	18 727	54 535	52 971	14 269	36.6	40.4	4.29	4.13	157.01	166.85
March	78 295	64 143	23 687	18 700	54 608	52 951	14 223	36.6	40.4	4.31	4.15	157.75	167.66
April	78 384	64 193	23 670	18 702	54 714	53 003	14 225	36.4	39.5	4.34	4.16	157.98	164.32
May	78 547	64 326	23 635	18 688	54 912	53 095	14 199	36.5	40.3	4.39	4.25	160.24	171.28
June	78 602	64 363	23 591	18 690	55 011	53 107	14 197	36.5	40.2	4.43	4.30	161.70	172.86
July	78 634	64 346	23 462	18 656	55 172	53 044	14 152	36.5	40.1	4.45	4.33	162.43	173.63
August	78 619	64 291	23 396	18 570	55 223	53 025	14 089	36.5	40.2	4.49	4.38	163.89	176.08
September	78 614	64 192	23 274	18 492	55 340	52 915	14 025	36.4	40.0	4.53	4.42	164.89	176.80
October	78 627	64 143	23 118	18 364	55 509	52 836	13 884	36.3	40.0	4.56	4.48	165.53	179.20
November	78 259	63 727	22 773	18 077	55 486	52 413	13 607	36.1	39.5	4.57	4.49	164.98	177.36
December	77 657	63 098	22 303	17 693	55 354	51 856	13 259	36.1	39.3	4.61	4.52	166.42	177.64
1975													
January	77 297	62 673	21 974	17 344	55 323	51 439	12 933	36.1	39.2	4.61	4.54	166.42	177.97
February	76 919	62 172	21 512	17 004	55 407	50 934	12 622	35.9	38.9	4.63	4.58	166.22	178.16
March	76 649	61 895	21 274	16 853	55 375	50 666	12 483	35.7	38.8	4.66	4.63	166.36	179.64
April	76 463	61 668	21 109	16 759	55 354	50 439	12 407	35.8	39.0	4.66	4.63	166.83	180.57
May	76 623	61 796	21 097	16 746	55 526	50 558	12 406	35.9	39.0	4.68	4.65	168.01	181.35
June	76 519	61 735	21 018	16 690	55 501	50 537	12 371	35.9	39.2	4.72	4.68	169.45	183.46
July	76 768	61 907	20 981	16 678	55 787	50 726	12 374	35.9	39.4	4.73	4.71	169.81	185.57
August	77 154	62 284	21 176	16 824	55 978	51 070	12 538	36.1	39.7	4.77	4.75	172.20	188.58
September	77 232	62 408	21 284	16 904	55 948	51 183	12 617	36.1	39.8	4.79	4.78	172.92	190.24
October	77 535	62 635	21 384	16 984	56 151	51 376	12 687	36.1	39.9	4.81	4.80	173.64	191.52
November	77 679	62 776	21 442	17 025	56 237	51 458	12 700	36.1	39.9	4.85	4.83	175.09	192.72
December	78 017	63 071	21 602	17 140	56 415	51 759	12 811	36.2	40.2	4.87	4.86	176.29	195.37
1976													
January	78 506	63 537	21 799	17 287	56 707	52 182	12 945	36.3	40.3	4.90	4.90	177.87	197.47
February	78 817	63 836	21 893	17 384	56 924	52 430	13 030	36.3	40.4	4.94	4.94	179.32	199.58
March	79 049	64 062	21 980	17 470	57 069	52 615	13 092	36.0	40.2	4.96	4.98	178.56	200.20
April	79 293	64 308	22 050	17 541	57 243	52 810	13 160	36.0	39.6	4.98	4.98	179.28	197.21
May	79 311	64 340	21 988	17 513	57 323	52 802	13 130	36.1	40.3	5.02	5.04	181.22	203.11
June	79 376	64 413	21 982	17 521	57 394	52 830	13 121	36.1	40.2	5.04	5.07	181.94	203.81
July	79 546	64 553	21 988	17 524	57 558	52 973	13 124	36.1	40.3	5.07	5.11	183.03	205.93
August	79 704	64 697	22 038	17 596	57 666	53 072	13 195	36.0	40.2	5.12	5.16	184.32	207.43
September	79 892	64 921	22 142	17 665	57 750	53 268	13 253	36.0	40.2	5.15	5.20	185.40	209.04
October	79 905	64 877	22 037	17 548	57 868	53 165	13 109	35.9	40.0	5.17	5.19	185.60	207.60
November	80 237	65 164	22 207	17 682	58 030	53 362	13 199	35.9	40.1	5.21	5.25	187.04	210.53
December	80 448	65 373	22 261	17 719	58 187	53 543	13 230	35.9	39.9	5.23	5.29	187.76	211.07
1977													
January	80 692	65 636	22 320	17 803	58 372	53 756	13 305	35.6	39.4	5.26	5.35	187.26	210.79
February	80 987	65 931	22 478	17 843	58 509	54 016	13 331	36.0	40.2	5.30	5.36	190.80	215.47
March	81 391	66 341	22 672	17 941	58 719	54 390	13 424	35.9	40.3	5.33	5.40	191.35	217.62
April	81 730	66 655	22 807	18 024	58 923	54 670	13 490	36.0	40.4	5.37	5.45	193.32	220.18
May	82 089	66 957	22 919	18 107	59 170	54 940	13 567	36.0	40.5	5.40	5.49	194.40	222.35
June	82 488	67 281	23 046	18 192	59 442	55 195	13 622	36.0	40.5	5.43	5.54	195.48	224.37
July	82 836	67 537	23 106	18 259	59 730	55 395	13 670	35.9	40.4	5.46	5.58	196.01	225.43
August	83 074	67 746	23 124	18 276	59 950	55 543	13 679	35.9	40.4	5.48	5.61	196.73	226.64
September	83 532	68 129	23 244	18 334	60 288	55 859	13 714	35.9	40.4	5.51	5.65	197.81	228.26
October	83 794	68 331	23 279	18 356	60 515	56 004	13 722	36.0	40.6	5.56	5.69	200.16	231.01
November	84 173	68 658	23 371	18 419	60 802	56 281	13 771	35.9	40.5	5.59	5.72	200.68	231.66
December	84 408	68 870	23 371	18 531	61 037	56 466	13 861	35.8	40.4	5.61	5.75	200.84	232.30
1978													
January	84 595	68 984	23 374	18 593	61 221	56 547	13 917	35.3	39.5	5.66	5.83	199.80	230.29
February	84 948	69 277	23 453	18 639	61 495	56 768	13 950	35.6	39.9	5.69	5.86	202.56	233.81
March	85 461	69 730	23 649	18 699	61 812	57 176	13 992	35.8	40.5	5.73	5.88	205.13	238.14
April	86 163	70 366	24 008	18 772	62 155	57 709	14 037	35.8	40.4	5.79	5.93	207.28	239.57
May	86 509	70 675	24 082	18 848	62 427	57 941	14 096	35.8	40.4	5.82	5.96	208.36	240.78
June	86 951	71 099	24 238	18 919	62 713	58 263	14 129	35.9	40.6	5.87	6.01	210.73	244.01
July	87 205	71 304	24 300	18 951	62 905	58 422	14 152	35.9	40.6	5.90	6.06	211.81	246.04
August	87 481	71 590	24 374	19 006	63 107	58 626	14 187	35.8	40.5	5.93	6.09	212.29	246.65
September	87 618	71 799	24 444	19 068	63 174	58 819	14 241	35.8	40.5	5.97	6.15	213.73	249.08
October	87 954	72 096	24 548	19 142	63 406	59 017	14 291	35.8	40.5	6.03	6.20	215.87	251.10
November	88 391	72 497	24 678	19 257	63 713	59 377	14 388	35.7	40.6	6.06	6.26	216.34	254.16
December	88 674	72 763	24 758	19 334	63 916	59 599	14 459	35.7	40.5	6.10	6.31	217.77	255.56
1979													
January	88 811	72 874	24 740	19 388	64 071	59 659	14 497	35.6	40.4	6.14	6.36	218.58	256.94
February	89 054	73 107	24 784	19 409	64 270	59 840	14 501	35.7	40.5	6.18	6.40	220.63	259.20
March	89 480	73 524	24 998	19 453	64 482	60 216	14 526	35.8	40.6	6.22	6.45	222.68	261.87
April	89 418	73 441	24 958	19 450	64 460	60 067	14 515	35.3	39.3	6.22	6.43	219.57	252.70
May	89 790	73 800	25 071	19 509	64 719	60 368	14 551	35.6	40.2	6.28	6.52	223.57	262.10
June	90 108	74 063	25 161	19 553	64 947	60 583	14 566	35.6	40.2	6.32	6.56	224.99	263.71
July	90 214	74 064	25 163	19 531	65 051	60 558	14 536	35.6	40.2	6.36	6.59	226.42	264.92
August	90 296	74 067	25 059	19 406	65 237	60 516	14 397	35.6	40.1	6.40	6.63	227.84	265.86
September	90 323	74 195	25 088	19 442	65 235	60 629	14 440	35.6	40.1	6.45	6.67	229.62	267.47
October	90 480	74 344	25 038	19 390	65 442	60 746	14 384	35.6	40.2	6.47	6.71	230.33	269.74
November	90 574	74 401	24 947	19 299	65 627	60 778	14 295	35.6	40.1	6.51	6.74	231.76	270.27
December	90 669	74 489	24 970	19 301	65 699	60 860	14 300	35.5	40.1	6.57	6.80	233.24	272.68

Table 20-4. Nonfarm Payroll Employment, Hours, and Earnings—*Continued*

(Wage and salary workers on nonfarm payrolls, seasonally adjusted.)

Year and month	All wage and salary workers (thousands)					Production or nonsupervisory workers on private payrolls							
	Total	Private			Service-providing	Number (thousands)		Average hours per week		Average hourly earnings, dollars		Average weekly earnings, dollars	
		Total	Goods-producing			Total private	Manufac-turing	Total private	Manufac-turing	Total private	Manufac-turing	Total private	Manufac-turing
			Total	Manufac-turing									
1980													
January	90 800	74 599	24 949	19 282	65 851	60 896	14 241	35.4	40.0	6.57	6.82	232.58	272.80
February	90 879	74 653	24 874	19 219	66 005	60 964	14 170	35.4	40.1	6.63	6.88	234.70	275.89
March	90 991	74 695	24 818	19 217	66 173	60 987	14 165	35.3	39.9	6.70	6.95	236.51	277.31
April	90 846	74 263	24 507	18 973	66 339	60 540	13 914	35.2	39.8	6.72	6.97	236.54	277.41
May	90 415	73 961	24 234	18 726	66 181	60 194	13 632	35.1	39.3	6.76	7.02	237.28	275.89
June	90 095	73 654	23 968	18 490	66 127	59 892	13 405	35.0	39.2	6.82	7.10	238.70	278.32
July	89 832	73 414	23 698	18 276	66 134	59 693	13 227	34.9	39.1	6.86	7.16	239.41	279.96
August	90 092	73 682	23 860	18 414	66 232	59 908	13 349	35.1	39.5	6.91	7.24	242.54	285.98
September	90 205	73 875	23 931	18 445	66 274	60 075	13 396	35.1	39.6	6.95	7.30	243.95	289.08
October	90 485	74 099	24 012	18 506	66 473	60 239	13 437	35.2	39.8	7.02	7.38	247.10	293.72
November	90 741	74 350	24 123	18 601	66 618	60 449	13 528	35.3	39.9	7.09	7.47	250.28	298.05
December	90 936	74 563	24 182	18 640	66 754	60 606	13 550	35.3	40.1	7.13	7.52	251.69	301.55
1981													
January	91 031	74 671	24 152	18 639	66 879	60 710	13 545	35.4	40.1	7.19	7.58	254.53	303.96
February	91 098	74 752	24 118	18 613	66 980	60 736	13 518	35.2	39.8	7.23	7.62	254.50	303.28
March	91 202	74 910	24 203	18 647	66 999	60 875	13 550	35.3	40.0	7.29	7.68	257.34	307.20
April	91 276	75 016	24 151	18 711	67 125	60 973	13 594	35.3	40.1	7.33	7.76	258.75	311.18
May	91 286	75 088	24 148	18 766	67 138	60 973	13 633	35.3	40.2	7.37	7.81	260.16	313.96
June	91 482	75 323	24 290	18 789	67 192	61 134	13 632	35.2	40.0	7.42	7.85	261.18	314.00
July	91 594	75 419	24 302	18 785	67 292	61 222	13 629	35.2	39.9	7.46	7.89	262.59	314.81
August	91 558	75 448	24 258	18 748	67 300	61 216	13 573	35.2	40.0	7.53	7.97	265.06	318.80
September	91 471	75 440	24 210	18 712	67 261	61 235	13 565	35.0	39.6	7.57	8.03	264.95	317.99
October	91 371	75 302	24 051	18 566	67 320	61 066	13 399	35.1	39.6	7.59	8.06	266.41	319.18
November	91 162	75 084	23 875	18 409	67 287	60 817	13 235	35.1	39.4	7.64	8.08	268.16	318.35
December	90 884	74 811	23 656	18 223	67 228	60 511	13 033	34.9	39.2	7.64	8.09	266.64	317.13
1982													
January	90 557	74 516	23 362	18 047	67 195	60 206	12 874	34.1	37.3	7.72	8.26	263.25	308.10
February	90 551	74 540	23 361	17 981	67 190	60 277	12 831	35.1	39.6	7.73	8.21	271.32	325.12
March	90 422	74 398	23 214	17 857	67 208	60 140	12 727	34.9	39.1	7.76	8.24	270.82	322.18
April	90 141	74 131	22 996	17 683	67 145	59 867	12 566	34.8	39.1	7.77	8.28	270.40	323.75
May	90 096	74 093	22 884	17 588	67 212	59 840	12 506	34.8	39.1	7.83	8.33	272.48	325.70
June	89 853	73 837	22 643	17 430	67 210	59 589	12 365	34.8	39.2	7.85	8.37	273.18	328.10
July	89 510	73 620	22 434	17 278	67 076	59 411	12 261	34.8	39.2	7.89	8.40	274.57	329.28
August	89 352	73 422	22 268	17 160	67 084	59 203	12 153	34.7	39.0	7.94	8.43	275.52	328.77
September	89 171	73 248	22 146	17 074	67 025	59 069	12 104	34.8	39.0	7.94	8.45	276.31	329.55
October	88 894	72 938	21 879	16 853	67 015	58 750	11 880	34.6	38.9	7.96	8.44	275.42	328.32
November	88 770	72 793	21 736	16 722	67 048	58 613	11 766	34.6	39.0	7.98	8.46	276.11	329.94
December	88 756	72 775	21 688	16 690	67 068	58 585	11 746	34.7	39.0	8.02	8.49	278.29	331.11
1983													
January	88 981	72 958	21 757	16 705	67 224	58 813	11 783	34.8	39.3	8.06	8.52	280.49	334.84
February	88 903	72 899	21 676	16 706	67 227	58 792	11 794	34.5	39.3	8.10	8.59	279.45	337.59
March	89 076	73 071	21 649	16 711	67 427	58 958	11 817	34.7	39.6	8.10	8.59	281.07	340.16
April	89 352	73 362	21 729	16 794	67 623	59 201	11 894	34.8	39.7	8.13	8.61	282.92	341.82
May	89 629	73 624	21 829	16 885	67 800	59 444	11 987	34.9	40.0	8.17	8.64	285.13	345.60
June	90 007	73 987	21 949	16 960	68 058	59 806	12 054	34.9	40.1	8.19	8.66	285.83	347.27
July	90 425	74 414	22 103	17 059	68 322	60 189	12 155	34.9	40.3	8.23	8.71	287.23	351.01
August	90 717	74 101	22 207	17 118	67 910	59 820	12 200	34.9	40.3	8.20	8.71	286.18	351.01
September	91 231	75 189	22 381	17 255	68 850	60 849	12 318	35.0	40.6	8.26	8.76	289.10	355.66
October	91 502	75 516	22 546	17 367	68 956	61 095	12 408	35.2	40.6	8.31	8.80	292.51	357.28
November	91 854	75 857	22 698	17 479	69 156	61 378	12 503	35.1	40.6	8.32	8.84	292.03	358.90
December	92 210	76 202	22 803	17 551	69 407	61 664	12 553	35.1	40.5	8.33	8.87	292.38	359.24
1984													
January	92 657	76 647	22 942	17 630	69 715	61 906	12 617	35.1	40.6	8.38	8.91	294.14	361.75
February	93 136	77 111	23 146	17 728	69 990	62 329	12 703	35.3	41.1	8.37	8.92	295.46	366.61
March	93 411	77 381	23 209	17 806	70 202	62 516	12 768	35.1	40.7	8.41	8.96	295.19	364.67
April	93 774	77 699	23 305	17 872	70 469	62 801	12 814	35.2	40.8	8.45	8.98	297.44	366.38
May	94 082	77 979	23 389	17 916	70 693	63 012	12 840	35.1	40.7	8.44	8.99	296.24	365.89
June	94 461	78 334	23 497	17 967	70 964	63 296	12 871	35.1	40.6	8.48	9.03	297.65	366.62
July	94 773	78 601	23 571	18 013	71 202	63 517	12 901	35.1	40.6	8.52	9.05	299.05	367.43
August	95 014	78 790	23 608	18 034	71 406	63 654	12 906	35.0	40.5	8.52	9.09	298.20	368.15
September	95 325	79 070	23 617	18 019	71 708	63 874	12 880	35.1	40.5	8.56	9.12	300.46	369.36
October	95 611	79 337	23 626	18 024	71 985	64 083	12 868	34.9	40.5	8.55	9.15	298.40	370.58
November	95 960	79 649	23 639	18 016	72 321	64 325	12 846	35.0	40.4	8.57	9.19	299.95	371.28
December	96 087	79 805	23 673	18 023	72 414	64 441	12 848	35.1	40.5	8.61	9.22	302.21	373.41
1985													
January	96 353	80 017	23 672	18 009	72 681	64 657	12 833	34.9	40.3	8.61	9.27	300.49	373.58
February	96 477	80 128	23 621	17 966	72 856	64 758	12 784	34.8	40.1	8.64	9.29	300.67	372.53
March	96 823	80 428	23 661	17 939	73 162	65 007	12 758	34.9	40.4	8.67	9.32	302.58	376.53
April	97 018	80 588	23 644	17 886	73 374	65 113	12 701	34.9	40.5	8.69	9.35	303.28	378.68
May	97 292	80 818	23 632	17 855	73 660	65 307	12 673	34.9	40.4	8.70	9.37	303.63	378.55
June	97 437	80 939	23 592	17 819	73 845	65 382	12 635	34.9	40.5	8.74	9.39	305.03	380.30
July	97 626	81 006	23 549	17 776	74 077	65 432	12 596	34.8	40.4	8.74	9.42	304.15	380.57
August	97 819	81 200	23 546	17 756	74 273	65 615	12 593	34.8	40.6	8.77	9.43	305.20	382.86
September	98 023	81 385	23 528	17 718	74 495	65 750	12 556	34.8	40.6	8.80	9.44	306.24	383.26
October	98 210	81 556	23 529	17 708	74 681	65 917	12 556	34.8	40.7	8.79	9.46	305.89	385.02
November	98 419	81 745	23 520	17 697	74 899	66 069	12 545	34.8	40.7	8.82	9.49	306.94	386.24
December	98 587	81 893	23 518	17 693	75 069	66 197	12 550	34.9	40.9	8.87	9.55	309.56	390.60

Table 20-4. Nonfarm Payroll Employment, Hours, and Earnings—*Continued*

(Wage and salary workers on nonfarm payrolls, seasonally adjusted.)

Year and month	All wage and salary workers (thousands)					Production or nonsupervisory workers on private payrolls							
	Total	Private			Service-providing	Number (thousands)		Average hours per week		Average hourly earnings, dollars		Average weekly earnings, dollars	
		Total	Goods-producing			Total private	Manufac-turing	Total private	Manufac-turing	Total private	Manufac-turing	Total private	Manufac-turing
			Total	Manufac-turing									
1986													
January	98 710	81 995	23 530	17 686	75 180	66 293	12 546	35.0	40.7	8.85	9.53	309.75	387.87
February	98 817	82 058	23 485	17 663	75 332	66 365	12 530	34.8	40.7	8.88	9.56	309.02	389.09
March	98 910	82 155	23 428	17 624	75 482	66 403	12 498	34.8	40.7	8.89	9.58	309.37	389.91
April	99 098	82 333	23 427	17 616	75 671	66 531	12 495	34.7	40.5	8.89	9.56	308.48	387.18
May	99 223	82 433	23 349	17 593	75 874	66 606	12 474	34.8	40.7	8.90	9.59	309.72	390.31
June	99 130	82 351	23 263	17 530	75 867	66 533	12 424	34.7	40.7	8.91	9.58	309.18	389.91
July	99 448	82 669	23 235	17 497	76 213	66 810	12 389	34.6	40.6	8.92	9.60	308.63	389.76
August	99 561	82 761	23 225	17 489	76 336	66 909	12 399	34.7	40.7	8.94	9.61	310.22	391.13
September	99 907	82 997	23 216	17 498	76 691	67 108	12 411	34.6	40.7	8.94	9.60	309.32	390.72
October	100 094	83 125	23 208	17 477	76 886	67 206	12 396	34.6	40.6	8.96	9.62	310.02	390.57
November	100 280	83 275	23 204	17 472	77 076	67 344	12 407	34.7	40.7	9.00	9.64	312.30	392.35
December	100 484	83 463	23 237	17 478	77 247	67 493	12 425	34.6	40.8	9.01	9.66	311.75	394.13
1987													
January	100 655	83 610	23 232	17 465	77 423	67 614	12 405	34.7	40.8	9.02	9.67	312.99	394.54
February	100 887	83 851	23 296	17 499	77 591	67 845	12 438	34.9	41.2	9.05	9.69	315.85	399.23
March	101 136	84 072	23 307	17 507	77 829	67 991	12 446	34.7	41.0	9.07	9.71	314.73	398.11
April	101 474	84 365	23 342	17 525	78 132	68 237	12 465	34.7	40.8	9.08	9.71	315.08	396.17
May	101 701	84 589	23 390	17 542	78 311	68 426	12 481	34.8	41.0	9.11	9.73	317.03	398.93
June	101 872	84 748	23 390	17 537	78 482	68 552	12 482	34.7	40.9	9.11	9.74	316.12	398.37
July	102 218	85 058	23 455	17 593	78 763	68 798	12 521	34.7	41.0	9.12	9.74	316.46	399.34
August	102 388	85 216	23 506	17 630	78 882	68 926	12 560	34.9	40.9	9.18	9.80	320.38	400.82
September	102 617	85 482	23 566	17 691	79 051	69 139	12 614	34.7	40.8	9.19	9.85	318.89	401.88
October	103 109	85 840	23 655	17 729	79 454	69 416	12 637	34.8	41.1	9.22	9.84	320.86	404.42
November	103 340	86 041	23 711	17 775	79 629	69 594	12 678	34.8	41.0	9.27	9.87	322.60	404.67
December	103 634	86 287	23 772	17 809	79 862	69 826	12 707	34.6	41.0	9.28	9.89	321.09	405.49
1988													
January	103 728	86 363	23 668	17 790	80 060	69 833	12 684	34.6	41.1	9.29	9.91	321.43	407.30
February	104 180	86 791	23 769	17 823	80 411	70 228	12 706	34.7	41.1	9.29	9.92	322.36	407.71
March	104 456	87 009	23 824	17 844	80 632	70 371	12 712	34.5	40.9	9.31	9.94	321.20	406.55
April	104 701	87 249	23 880	17 874	80 821	70 578	12 733	34.6	41.0	9.36	9.99	323.86	409.59
May	104 928	87 447	23 896	17 892	81 032	70 693	12 747	34.6	41.0	9.41	10.02	325.59	410.82
June	105 291	87 776	23 951	17 916	81 340	71 000	12 767	34.6	41.1	9.42	10.04	325.93	412.64
July	105 514	88 020	23 966	17 926	81 548	71 210	12 774	34.7	41.1	9.45	10.05	327.92	413.06
August	105 635	88 091	23 926	17 891	81 709	71 273	12 752	34.5	40.9	9.46	10.07	326.37	411.86
September	105 975	88 341	23 942	17 914	82 033	71 456	12 764	34.5	41.0	9.51	10.12	328.10	414.92
October	106 243	88 573	23 987	17 966	82 256	71 649	12 812	34.7	41.1	9.56	10.16	331.73	417.58
November	106 582	88 836	24 030	18 003	82 552	71 872	12 851	34.5	41.1	9.58	10.19	330.51	418.81
December	106 871	89 135	24 054	18 025	82 817	72 144	12 864	34.6	40.9	9.60	10.20	332.16	417.18
1989													
January	107 133	89 359	24 097	18 057	83 036	72 361	12 882	34.7	41.1	9.65	10.23	334.86	420.45
February	107 391	89 579	24 080	18 055	83 311	72 545	12 880	34.5	41.2	9.68	10.26	333.96	422.71
March	107 583	89 761	24 069	18 060	83 514	72 663	12 878	34.5	41.1	9.70	10.29	334.65	422.92
April	107 756	89 916	24 100	18 055	83 656	72 788	12 867	34.4	41.1	9.75	10.28	337.35	422.51
May	107 874	89 998	24 089	18 040	83 785	72 826	12 852	34.4	41.0	9.73	10.30	334.71	422.30
June	107 991	90 079	24 052	18 013	83 939	72 906	12 822	34.4	40.9	9.77	10.33	336.09	422.50
July	108 030	90 125	24 027	17 980	84 003	72 943	12 790	34.5	40.9	9.82	10.36	338.79	423.72
August	108 077	90 088	24 048	17 964	84 029	72 931	12 790	34.5	40.9	9.83	10.39	339.14	424.95
September	108 326	90 299	24 000	17 922	84 326	73 080	12 745	34.4	40.8	9.87	10.41	339.53	424.73
October	108 437	90 404	23 997	17 895	84 440	73 176	12 723	34.6	40.8	9.93	10.43	343.58	425.54
November	108 714	90 657	24 009	17 886	84 705	73 392	12 713	34.4	40.7	9.93	10.44	341.59	424.91
December	108 809	90 734	23 949	17 881	84 860	73 468	12 705	34.3	40.5	9.98	10.49	342.31	424.85
1990													
January	109 151	91 000	23 984	17 799	85 167	73 700	12 741	34.4	40.5	10.01	10.51	344.34	425.66
February	109 396	91 219	24 074	17 896	85 322	73 901	12 850	34.3	40.6	10.08	10.64	345.74	431.98
March	109 611	91 317	24 025	17 870	85 586	73 964	12 823	34.4	40.7	10.11	10.70	347.78	435.49
April	109 651	91 274	23 968	17 847	85 683	73 928	12 805	34.3	40.6	10.13	10.68	347.46	433.61
May	109 800	91 201	23 887	17 796	85 913	73 840	12 755	34.3	40.6	10.16	10.74	348.49	436.04
June	109 817	91 261	23 848	17 775	85 969	73 823	12 738	34.4	40.7	10.20	10.77	350.88	438.34
July	109 775	91 215	23 745	17 703	86 030	73 773	12 674	34.3	40.6	10.22	10.81	350.55	438.89
August	109 567	91 110	23 647	17 648	85 920	73 707	12 624	34.2	40.5	10.24	10.80	350.21	437.40
September	109 485	91 048	23 572	17 610	85 913	73 602	12 597	34.2	40.5	10.28	10.86	351.58	439.83
October	109 324	90 881	23 471	17 575	85 853	73 466	12 576	34.1	40.4	10.30	10.92	351.23	441.17
November	109 180	90 730	23 283	17 428	85 897	73 315	12 437	34.2	40.2	10.32	10.89	352.94	437.78
December	109 120	90 652	23 202	17 394	85 918	73 248	12 413	34.2	40.3	10.35	10.93	353.97	440.48
1991													
January	109 001	90 527	23 062	17 331	85 939	73 101	12 352	34.1	40.2	10.37	10.97	353.62	440.99
February	108 695	90 213	22 903	17 214	85 792	72 816	12 245	34.1	40.1	10.39	10.98	354.30	440.30
March	108 535	90 047	22 780	17 141	85 755	72 665	12 191	34.0	40.0	10.41	11.00	353.94	440.00
April	108 324	89 839	22 689	17 095	85 635	72 495	12 157	34.0	40.1	10.45	11.04	355.30	442.70
May	108 196	89 698	22 617	17 069	85 579	72 401	12 147	34.0	40.1	10.49	11.08	356.66	444.31
June	108 283	89 722	22 569	17 042	85 714	72 418	12 135	34.1	40.5	10.52	11.13	358.73	450.77
July	108 236	89 638	22 508	17 016	85 728	72 382	12 130	34.1	40.5	10.55	11.17	359.76	452.39
August	108 251	89 684	22 493	17 025	85 758	72 439	12 154	34.1	40.6	10.56	11.18	360.10	453.91
September	108 286	89 743	22 467	17 011	85 819	72 451	12 140	34.1	40.6	10.58	11.22	360.78	455.53
October	108 298	89 705	22 417	16 998	85 881	72 422	12 138	34.2	40.6	10.59	11.25	362.18	456.75
November	108 240	89 613	22 315	16 960	85 925	72 348	12 101	34.1	40.6	10.61	11.26	361.80	457.16
December	108 263	89 622	22 274	16 916	85 989	72 393	12 074	34.1	40.7	10.64	11.26	362.82	458.28

Table 20-4. Nonfarm Payroll Employment, Hours, and Earnings—*Continued*

(Wage and salary workers on nonfarm payrolls, seasonally adjusted.)

Year and month	All wage and salary workers (thousands)					Production or nonsupervisory workers on private payrolls								
	Total	Private			Service-providing	Number (thousands)		Average hours per week		Average hourly earnings, dollars		Average weekly earnings, dollars	
		Total	Goods-producing			Total private	Manufac-turing	Total private	Manufac-turing	Total private	Manufac-turing	Total private	Manufac-turing
			Total	Manufac-turing									
1992													
January	108 312	89 624	22 214	16 840	86 098	72 429	12 011	34.1	40.6	10.65	11.24	363.17	456.34
February	108 246	89 557	22 144	16 831	86 102	72 407	12 018	34.1	40.7	10.67	11.30	363.85	459.91
March	108 296	89 581	22 127	16 805	86 169	72 422	12 007	34.1	40.7	10.70	11.33	364.87	461.13
April	108 454	89 715	22 131	16 830	86 323	72 570	12 029	34.3	41.0	10.72	11.36	367.70	465.76
May	108 580	89 827	22 134	16 834	86 446	72 684	12 045	34.2	40.9	10.74	11.39	367.31	465.85
June	108 640	89 878	22 096	16 825	86 544	72 726	12 042	34.1	40.8	10.77	11.41	367.26	465.53
July	108 711	89 894	22 075	16 820	86 636	72 734	12 047	34.2	40.8	10.79	11.43	369.02	466.34
August	108 852	89 969	22 045	16 783	86 807	72 815	12 020	34.2	40.8	10.82	11.47	370.04	467.98
September	108 887	90 058	22 020	16 761	86 867	72 919	12 002	34.3	40.8	10.82	11.46	371.13	467.57
October	109 064	90 236	22 028	16 750	87 036	73 074	12 000	34.2	40.8	10.86	11.47	371.41	467.98
November	109 204	90 363	22 042	16 758	87 162	73 221	12 010	34.2	40.9	10.88	11.49	372.10	469.94
December	109 415	90 537	22 074	16 767	87 341	73 411	12 031	34.2	40.9	10.89	11.51	372.44	470.76
1993													
January	109 725	90 824	22 133	16 791	87 592	73 683	12 058	34.3	41.1	10.93	11.55	374.90	474.71
February	109 967	91 065	22 189	16 806	87 778	73 941	12 075	34.3	41.1	10.95	11.58	375.59	475.94
March	109 916	91 009	22 142	16 795	87 774	73 855	12 074	34.1	40.8	10.99	11.58	374.76	472.46
April	110 225	91 287	22 130	16 771	88 095	74 079	12 056	34.4	41.5	10.99	11.63	378.06	482.65
May	110 490	91 539	22 189	16 766	88 301	74 331	12 055	34.3	41.1	11.02	11.66	377.99	479.23
June	110 663	91 694	22 165	16 742	88 498	74 440	12 039	34.3	40.9	11.03	11.67	378.33	477.30
July	110 958	91 898	22 184	16 740	88 774	74 618	12 042	34.4	41.1	11.05	11.69	380.12	480.46
August	111 119	92 091	22 203	16 741	88 916	74 793	12 049	34.3	41.2	11.08	11.72	380.04	482.86
September	111 360	92 319	22 252	16 769	89 108	74 981	12 080	34.4	41.3	11.10	11.77	381.84	486.10
October	111 637	92 595	22 305	16 777	89 332	75 227	12 092	34.4	41.3	11.13	11.79	382.87	486.93
November	111 898	92 830	22 347	16 800	89 551	75 443	12 118	34.4	41.3	11.15	11.83	383.56	488.58
December	112 206	93 097	22 413	16 815	89 793	75 662	12 141	34.4	41.4	11.18	11.88	384.59	491.83
1994													
January	112 474	93 327	22 464	16 854	90 010	75 871	12 181	34.4	41.4	11.21	11.89	385.62	492.25
February	112 675	93 525	22 452	16 863	90 223	76 076	12 199	34.2	40.9	11.25	11.98	384.75	489.98
March	113 137	93 947	22 549	16 896	90 588	76 436	12 234	34.5	41.7	11.25	11.95	388.13	498.32
April	113 490	94 267	22 640	16 932	90 850	76 734	12 276	34.5	41.7	11.27	11.96	388.82	498.73
May	113 821	94 557	22 703	16 961	91 118	77 012	12 304	34.5	41.8	11.30	11.98	389.85	500.76
June	114 136	94 862	22 765	17 011	91 371	77 262	12 352	34.5	41.8	11.31	12.00	390.20	501.60
July	114 499	95 198	22 807	17 026	91 692	77 566	12 369	34.6	41.8	11.34	12.02	392.36	502.44
August	114 799	95 493	22 877	17 082	91 922	77 801	12 427	34.5	41.7	11.36	12.06	391.92	502.90
September	115 153	95 816	22 946	17 113	92 207	78 067	12 458	34.4	41.6	11.39	12.09	391.82	502.94
October	115 360	96 016	22 973	17 143	92 387	78 252	12 489	34.5	41.8	11.43	12.12	394.34	506.62
November	115 783	96 416	23 051	17 187	92 732	78 601	12 528	34.5	41.8	11.45	12.16	395.03	508.29
December	116 057	96 669	23 096	17 218	92 961	78 840	12 559	34.5	41.8	11.48	12.17	396.06	508.71
1995													
January	116 378	96 981	23 146	17 261	93 232	79 085	12 594	34.5	41.8	11.49	12.19	396.41	509.54
February	116 587	97 180	23 103	17 265	93 484	79 239	12 602	34.4	41.7	11.53	12.25	396.63	510.83
March	116 809	97 382	23 150	17 262	93 659	79 423	12 600	34.4	41.5	11.55	12.24	397.32	507.96
April	116 971	97 537	23 174	17 278	93 797	79 559	12 608	34.3	41.2	11.57	12.26	396.85	505.11
May	116 955	97 537	23 120	17 259	93 835	79 573	12 589	34.2	41.2	11.59	12.28	396.38	505.94
June	117 186	97 741	23 139	17 249	94 047	79 739	12 575	34.3	41.2	11.63	12.31	398.91	507.17
July	117 265	97 828	23 119	17 239	94 146	79 813	12 539	34.3	41.1	11.68	12.38	400.62	508.82
August	117 536	98 107	23 163	17 239	94 373	80 058	12 566	34.3	41.2	11.69	12.39	400.97	510.47
September	117 781	98 351	23 207	17 246	94 574	80 252	12 565	34.3	41.2	11.72	12.41	402.00	511.29
October	117 928	98 464	23 205	17 215	94 723	80 373	12 535	34.3	41.2	11.76	12.44	403.37	512.53
November	118 076	98 613	23 198	17 207	94 878	80 449	12 514	34.3	41.3	11.78	12.45	404.05	514.19
December	118 207	98 741	23 207	17 229	95 000	80 604	12 550	34.2	40.9	11.81	12.49	403.90	510.84
1996													
January	118 188	98 738	23 196	17 208	94 992	80 525	12 519	33.8	39.7	11.86	12.60	400.87	500.22
February	118 622	99 137	23 281	17 230	95 341	80 912	12 532	34.3	41.3	11.87	12.56	407.14	518.73
March	118 885	99 353	23 275	17 192	95 610	81 092	12 489	34.3	41.1	11.89	12.50	407.83	513.75
April	119 046	99 531	23 316	17 204	95 730	81 258	12 504	34.2	41.2	11.95	12.69	408.69	522.83
May	119 369	99 840	23 358	17 222	96 011	81 518	12 517	34.3	41.4	11.98	12.70	410.91	525.78
June	119 647	100 119	23 400	17 227	96 247	81 731	12 523	34.4	41.5	12.04	12.76	414.18	529.54
July	119 879	100 332	23 417	17 222	96 462	81 922	12 517	34.3	41.4	12.06	12.78	413.66	529.09
August	120 075	100 571	23 479	17 255	96 596	82 121	12 545	34.4	41.5	12.09	12.82	415.90	532.03
September	120 295	100 728	23 497	17 252	96 798	82 243	12 543	34.4	41.6	12.14	12.84	417.62	534.14
October	120 538	100 984	23 546	17 268	96 992	82 476	12 558	34.4	41.4	12.16	12.84	418.30	531.58
November	120 834	101 269	23 583	17 276	97 251	82 662	12 558	34.4	41.5	12.21	12.89	420.02	534.94
December	121 001	101 430	23 597	17 283	97 404	82 832	12 571	34.4	41.7	12.25	12.95	421.40	540.02
1997													
January	121 231	101 638	23 620	17 299	97 611	82 978	12 581	34.3	41.4	12.29	13.00	421.55	538.20
February	121 532	101 934	23 687	17 317	97 845	83 252	12 592	34.5	41.6	12.32	13.00	425.04	540.80
March	121 844	102 236	23 738	17 339	98 106	83 478	12 613	34.5	41.8	12.37	13.03	426.77	544.65
April	122 135	102 532	23 767	17 351	98 368	83 727	12 618	34.6	41.8	12.38	13.04	428.35	545.07
May	122 391	102 790	23 810	17 363	98 581	83 947	12 633	34.6	41.7	12.43	13.06	430.08	544.60
June	122 644	102 984	23 835	17 388	98 809	84 080	12 648	34.4	41.6	12.47	13.08	428.97	544.13
July	122 927	103 241	23 861	17 388	99 066	84 319	12 644	34.5	41.6	12.50	13.09	431.25	544.54
August	122 909	103 292	23 951	17 451	98 958	84 266	12 699	34.6	41.6	12.57	13.17	434.92	547.87
September	123 417	103 738	23 996	17 465	99 421	84 661	12 711	34.6	41.6	12.59	13.17	435.61	547.87
October	123 756	104 018	24 053	17 513	99 703	84 866	12 745	34.5	41.8	12.67	13.28	437.12	555.10
November	124 059	104 298	24 112	17 556	99 947	85 055	12 776	34.6	41.8	12.72	13.33	440.11	557.19
December	124 358	104 592	24 183	17 587	100 175	85 289	12 800	34.6	42.0	12.75	13.35	441.15	560.70

Table 20-4. Nonfarm Payroll Employment, Hours, and Earnings—Continued

(Wage and salary workers on nonfarm payrolls, seasonally adjusted.)

Year and month	All wage and salary workers (thousands)					Production or nonsupervisory workers on private payrolls							
	Total	Private				Number (thousands)		Average hours per week		Average hourly earnings, dollars		Average weekly earnings, dollars	
		Total	Goods-producing		Service-providing	Total private	Manufac-turing	Total private	Manufac-turing	Total private	Manufac-turing	Total private	Manufac-turing
			Total	Manufac-turing									
1998													
January	124 628	104 858	24 266	17 623	100 362	85 442	12 820	34.6	41.9	12.79	13.35	442.53	559.37
February	124 817	105 031	24 283	17 627	100 534	85 606	12 828	34.6	41.7	12.84	13.39	444.26	558.36
March	124 961	105 169	24 264	17 637	100 697	85 630	12 823	34.5	41.6	12.88	13.44	444.36	559.10
April	125 238	105 422	24 338	17 635	100 900	85 846	12 814	34.5	41.3	12.92	13.41	445.74	553.83
May	125 639	105 764	24 360	17 623	101 279	86 124	12 789	34.5	41.5	12.96	13.46	447.12	558.59
June	125 851	105 972	24 388	17 609	101 463	86 272	12 770	34.4	41.4	12.99	13.43	446.86	556.00
July	125 970	106 040	24 237	17 421	101 733	86 278	12 557	34.5	41.4	13.01	13.34	448.85	552.28
August	126 322	106 363	24 420	17 563	101 902	86 571	12 702	34.5	41.4	13.09	13.47	451.61	557.66
September	126 540	106 555	24 419	17 557	102 121	86 737	12 714	34.4	41.3	13.11	13.53	450.98	558.79
October	126 733	106 732	24 405	17 511	102 328	86 879	12 673	34.5	41.4	13.14	13.52	453.33	559.73
November	127 017	106 973	24 394	17 465	102 623	87 041	12 634	34.5	41.4	13.18	13.54	454.71	560.56
December	127 359	107 280	24 452	17 447	102 907	87 307	12 624	34.5	41.5	13.21	13.56	455.75	562.74
1999													
January	127 480	107 396	24 406	17 432	103 074	87 359	12 607	34.4	41.3	13.27	13.60	456.49	561.68
February	127 890	107 746	24 434	17 395	103 456	87 680	12 575	34.4	41.4	13.30	13.63	457.52	564.28
March	127 996	107 828	24 378	17 368	103 618	87 732	12 562	34.3	41.3	13.34	13.69	457.56	565.40
April	128 372	108 135	24 424	17 343	103 948	87 961	12 540	34.4	41.3	13.38	13.75	460.27	567.88
May	128 585	108 356	24 445	17 333	104 140	88 154	12 533	34.4	41.4	13.43	13.80	461.99	571.32
June	128 851	108 579	24 435	17 296	104 416	88 331	12 503	34.4	41.3	13.47	13.86	463.37	572.42
July	129 142	108 803	24 474	17 308	104 668	88 520	12 526	34.4	41.4	13.52	13.91	465.09	575.87
August	129 334	108 959	24 466	17 286	104 868	88 642	12 502	34.4	41.5	13.55	13.93	466.12	578.10
September	129 536	109 132	24 483	17 279	105 053	88 766	12 494	34.4	41.5	13.61	13.99	468.18	580.59
October	129 944	109 487	24 506	17 273	105 438	89 084	12 483	34.4	41.4	13.64	13.99	469.22	579.19
November	130 238	109 742	24 560	17 281	105 678	89 310	12 488	34.4	41.4	13.66	14.00	469.90	579.60
December	130 532	109 992	24 579	17 277	105 953	89 525	12 491	34.4	41.4	13.70	14.06	471.28	582.08
2000													
January	130 781	110 210	24 636	17 292	106 145	89 685	12 496	34.4	41.5	13.75	14.13	473.00	586.40
February	130 902	110 303	24 608	17 284	106 294	89 770	12 482	34.4	41.6	13.80	14.15	474.72	588.64
March	131 374	110 641	24 705	17 302	106 669	90 037	12 490	34.3	41.4	13.85	14.18	475.06	587.05
April	131 660	110 858	24 688	17 298	106 972	90 260	12 477	34.4	41.5	13.91	14.24	478.50	590.96
May	131 885	110 738	24 647	17 279	107 238	90 165	12 463	34.3	41.3	13.94	14.22	478.14	587.29
June	131 839	110 952	24 674	17 298	107 165	90 329	12 468	34.3	41.3	13.98	14.29	479.51	590.18
July	132 002	111 135	24 716	17 321	107 286	90 482	12 475	34.3	41.5	14.03	14.31	481.23	593.87
August	132 005	111 168	24 682	17 286	107 323	90 498	12 431	34.2	41.0	14.07	14.36	481.19	588.76
September	132 127	111 392	24 638	17 226	107 489	90 650	12 381	34.2	41.0	14.12	14.40	482.90	590.40
October	132 116	111 373	24 636	17 215	107 480	90 631	12 356	34.3	41.1	14.18	14.48	486.37	595.13
November	132 347	111 587	24 623	17 202	107 724	90 760	12 337	34.2	41.1	14.23	14.52	486.67	596.77
December	132 485	111 681	24 572	17 178	107 913	90 805	12 306	34.0	40.4	14.28	14.51	485.52	586.20
2001													
January	132 469	111 634	24 543	17 114	107 926	90 759	12 236	34.2	40.7	14.29	14.48	488.72	589.34
February	132 530	111 624	24 475	17 029	108 055	90 688	12 156	34.0	40.5	14.38	14.56	488.92	589.68
March	132 500	111 555	24 410	16 939	108 090	90 655	12 084	34.1	40.5	14.42	14.58	491.72	590.49
April	132 219	111 227	24 255	16 803	107 964	90 432	11 980	34.0	40.5	14.45	14.64	491.30	592.92
May	132 175	111 146	24 120	16 662	108 055	90 344	11 858	34.0	40.4	14.50	14.69	493.00	593.48
June	132 047	110 910	23 966	16 516	108 081	90 148	11 737	34.0	40.3	14.55	14.74	494.70	594.02
July	131 922	110 737	23 833	16 378	108 089	90 042	11 631	34.0	40.6	14.56	14.80	495.04	600.88
August	131 762	110 544	23 660	16 225	108 102	89 886	11 493	33.9	40.3	14.60	14.85	494.94	598.46
September	131 518	110 276	23 533	16 113	107 985	89 618	11 398	33.8	40.2	14.64	14.90	494.83	598.98
October	131 193	109 918	23 377	15 971	107 816	89 329	11 286	33.7	40.1	14.66	14.88	494.04	596.69
November	130 901	109 575	23 209	15 825	107 692	88 999	11 175	33.8	40.1	14.72	14.96	497.54	599.90
December	130 723	109 368	23 093	15 710	107 630	88 898	11 079	33.9	40.3	14.75	15.02	500.03	605.31
2002													
January	130 591	109 214	22 972	15 598	107 619	88 857	11 004	33.8	40.2	14.76	15.06	498.89	605.41
February	130 444	109 054	22 879	15 518	107 565	88 799	10 953	33.8	40.3	14.79	15.12	499.90	609.34
March	130 420	108 989	22 789	15 446	107 631	88 756	10 900	33.9	40.5	14.82	15.15	502.40	613.58
April	130 335	108 892	22 691	15 394	107 644	88 601	10 859	33.9	40.5	14.83	15.17	502.74	614.39
May	130 328	108 814	22 605	15 338	107 723	88 475	10 822	33.9	40.6	14.88	15.23	504.43	618.34
June	130 373	108 824	22 577	15 297	107 796	88 387	10 795	33.9	40.7	14.95	15.26	506.81	621.08
July	130 276	108 732	22 515	15 250	107 761	88 240	10 760	33.8	40.4	14.98	15.27	506.32	616.91
August	130 260	108 671	22 442	15 164	107 818	88 163	10 696	33.9	40.5	15.02	15.34	509.18	621.27
September	130 205	108 659	22 393	15 115	107 812	88 141	10 666	33.9	40.5	15.07	15.38	510.87	622.89
October	130 331	108 772	22 324	15 059	108 007	88 217	10 630	33.8	40.3	15.12	15.45	511.06	622.64
November	130 339	108 758	22 282	14 992	108 057	88 167	10 581	33.8	40.4	15.15	15.48	512.07	625.39
December	130 183	108 595	22 187	14 910	107 996	87 973	10 522	33.8	40.5	15.21	15.54	514.10	629.37
2003													
January	130 266	108 640	22 147	14 867	108 119	88 020	10 483	33.8	40.3	15.22	15.59	514.44	628.28
February	130 108	108 484	22 022	14 780	108 086	87 873	10 417	33.6	40.2	15.29	15.62	513.74	627.92
March	129 896	108 286	21 946	14 722	107 950	87 572	10 355	33.8	40.4	15.29	15.64	516.80	631.86
April	129 847	108 252	21 863	14 608	107 984	87 539	10 255	33.6	40.0	15.28	15.63	513.41	625.20
May	129 841	108 274	21 831	14 556	108 010	87 506	10 220	33.7	40.2	15.34	15.67	516.96	629.93
June	129 839	108 233	21 788	14 493	108 051	87 478	10 166	33.6	40.3	15.36	15.72	516.10	633.52
July	129 864	108 231	21 707	14 401	108 157	87 462	10 093	33.6	40.0	15.40	15.74	517.44	629.60
August	129 822	108 266	21 708	14 378	108 114	87 524	10 085	33.7	40.2	15.42	15.78	519.65	634.36
September	129 925	108 421	21 700	14 347	108 225	87 635	10 058	33.6	40.5	15.42	15.82	518.11	640.71
October	130 128	108 570	21 691	14 334	108 437	87 721	10 055	33.7	40.6	15.43	15.83	519.99	642.70
November	130 146	108 611	21 687	14 315	108 459	87 778	10 040	33.7	40.9	15.47	15.90	521.34	650.31
December	130 270	108 724	21 703	14 300	108 567	87 859	10 029	33.6	40.7	15.48	15.92	520.13	647.94

Table 20-4. Nonfarm Payroll Employment, Hours, and Earnings—*Continued*

(Wage and salary workers on nonfarm payrolls, seasonally adjusted.)

Year and month	All wage and salary workers (thousands)					Production or nonsupervisory workers on private payrolls							
	Total	Private			Service-providing	Number (thousands)		Average hours per week		Average hourly earnings, dollars		Average weekly earnings, dollars	
		Total	Goods-producing			Total private	Manufac-turing	Total private	Manufac-turing	Total private	Manufac-turing	Total private	Manufac-turing
			Total	Manufac-turing									
2004													
January	130 420	108 882	21 717	14 292	108 703	87 940	10 029	33.7	40.9	15.52	15.94	523.02	651.95
February	130 463	108 913	21 691	14 277	108 772	87 958	10 014	33.8	41.0	15.52	15.97	524.58	654.77
March	130 801	109 213	21 759	14 288	109 042	88 217	10 025	33.7	40.9	15.57	16.02	524.71	655.22
April	131 051	109 437	21 803	14 316	109 248	88 465	10 058	33.7	40.8	15.60	16.07	525.72	655.66
May	131 361	109 747	21 881	14 342	109 480	88 780	10 091	33.8	41.0	15.64	16.06	528.63	658.46
June	131 442	109 841	21 884	14 331	109 558	88 927	10 085	33.6	40.7	15.67	16.11	526.51	655.68
July	131 489	109 883	21 903	14 333	109 586	89 034	10 100	33.7	40.8	15.71	16.18	529.43	660.14
August	131 610	109 984	21 942	14 343	109 668	89 170	10 115	33.7	40.9	15.75	16.20	530.78	662.58
September	131 770	110 135	21 956	14 334	109 814	89 363	10 103	33.7	40.7	15.79	16.29	532.12	663.00
October	132 121	110 465	22 006	14 334	110 115	89 678	10 104	33.7	40.6	15.82	16.26	533.13	660.16
November	132 185	110 493	21 995	14 305	110 190	89 707	10 077	33.7	40.5	15.85	16.30	534.15	660.15
December	132 317	110 624	22 003	14 285	110 314	89 877	10 063	33.8	40.6	15.87	16.35	536.41	663.81
2005													
January	132 453	110 718	21 962	14 261	110 491	89 965	10 044	33.7	40.7	15.91	16.38	536.17	666.67
February	132 693	110 949	22 037	14 274	110 656	90 187	10 054	33.8	40.6	15.94	16.44	538.77	667.46
March	132 835	111 095	22 068	14 271	110 767	90 371	10 057	33.7	40.5	15.98	16.44	538.53	665.82
April	133 195	111 441	22 139	14 253	111 056	90 717	10 049	33.8	40.5	16.02	16.46	541.48	666.63
May	133 364	111 583	22 174	14 258	111 190	90 825	10 061	33.7	40.4	16.05	16.53	540.89	667.81
June	133 610	111 847	22 185	14 227	111 425	91 093	10 047	33.7	40.4	16.08	16.54	541.90	668.22
July	133 979	112 122	22 202	14 223	111 777	91 321	10 041	33.7	40.4	16.16	16.56	544.59	669.02
August	134 174	112 311	22 226	14 201	111 948	91 505	10 043	33.7	40.5	16.18	16.63	545.27	673.52
September	134 237	112 392	22 225	14 174	112 012	91 588	10 045	33.8	40.7	16.21	16.60	547.90	675.62
October	134 321	112 492	22 291	14 191	112 030	91 694	10 071	33.8	41.0	16.30	16.69	550.94	684.29
November	134 655	112 796	22 351	14 181	112 304	92 039	10 088	33.8	40.9	16.32	16.68	551.62	682.21
December	134 813	112 934	22 372	14 189	112 441	92 222	10 110	33.8	40.8	16.37	16.69	553.31	680.95
2006													
January	135 075	113 232	22 470	14 210	112 605	92 537	10 150	33.9	41.1	16.43	16.70	556.98	686.37
February	135 401	113 531	22 554	14 215	112 847	92 824	10 166	33.9	41.2	16.50	16.71	559.35	688.45
March	135 705	113 803	22 579	14 220	113 126	93 130	10 179	33.8	41.1	16.55	16.72	559.39	687.19
April	135 879	113 956	22 635	14 232	113 244	93 311	10 194	33.9	41.2	16.65	16.74	564.44	689.69
May	135 910	113 988	22 609	14 209	113 301	93 375	10 184	33.8	41.2	16.66	16.76	563.11	690.51
June	135 979	114 065	22 606	14 217	113 373	93 447	10 193	33.9	41.2	16.73	16.78	567.15	691.34
July	136 211	114 223	22 593	14 190	113 618	93 570	10 179	33.9	41.4	16.79	16.79	569.18	695.11
August	136 352	114 344	22 577	14 159	113 775	93 708	10 160	33.9	41.1	16.83	16.83	570.54	691.71
September	136 452	114 401	22 533	14 125	113 919	93 715	10 119	33.8	41.1	16.88	16.83	570.54	691.71
October	136 495	114 428	22 448	14 070	114 047	93 737	10 068	33.9	41.1	16.95	16.90	574.61	694.59
November	136 696	114 616	22 398	14 030	114 298	93 946	10 037	33.9	41.0	16.99	16.91	575.96	693.31
December	136 873	114 785	22 394	14 001	114 479	94 163	10 033	34.0	41.1	17.06	17.00	580.04	698.70
2007													
January	137 067	114 971	22 431	14 007	114 636	94 349	10 030	33.8	41.0	17.11	17.02	578.32	697.82
February	137 171	115 050	22 341	13 998	114 830	94 392	10 033	33.8	41.0	17.17	17.05	580.35	699.05
March	137 410	115 263	22 398	13 973	115 012	94 644	10 014	33.9	41.3	17.23	17.10	584.10	706.23
April	137 502	115 328	22 365	13 949	115 137	94 737	10 010	33.9	41.3	17.28	17.20	585.79	710.36
May	137 651	115 455	22 344	13 939	115 307	94 909	10 016	33.9	41.2	17.34	17.23	587.83	709.88
June	137 706	115 497	22 335	13 916	115 371	95 003	10 001	33.9	41.4	17.43	17.30	590.88	716.22
July	137 686	115 512	22 290	13 898	115 396	95 080	9 998	33.8	41.3	17.48	17.31	590.82	714.90
August	137 615	115 403	22 169	13 833	115 446	94 998	9 951	33.8	41.2	17.52	17.35	592.18	714.82
September	137 667	115 389	22 090	13 788	115 577	95 038	9 931	33.8	41.3	17.58	17.36	594.20	716.97
October	137 753	115 454	22 037	13 753	115 716	95 123	9 902	33.8	41.2	17.60	17.36	594.88	715.23
November	137 881	115 551	22 015	13 745	115 866	95 224	9 907	33.8	41.3	17.65	17.41	596.57	719.03
December	137 951	115 574	21 956	13 726	115 995	95 321	9 909	33.8	41.1	17.70	17.42	598.26	715.96
2008													
January	137 941	115 562	21 932	13 721	116 009	95 342	9 909	33.7	41.1	17.76	17.51	598.51	719.66
February	137 891	115 477	21 877	13 691	116 014	95 261	9 882	33.7	41.2	17.82	17.57	600.53	723.88
March	137 858	115 419	21 815	13 654	116 043	95 262	9 863	33.8	41.3	17.89	17.64	604.68	728.53
April	137 709	115 258	21 707	13 604	116 002	95 115	9 810	33.8	41.2	17.93	17.64	606.03	726.77
May	137 478	115 005	21 626	13 577	115 852	94 909	9 791	33.7	41.0	18.00	17.69	606.60	725.29
June	137 285	114 775	21 511	13 528	115 774	94 703	9 740	33.7	41.0	18.06	17.76	608.62	728.16
July	137 075	114 518	21 392	13 456	115 683	94 483	9 676	33.6	40.9	18.12	17.82	608.83	728.84
August	136 741	114 171	21 254	13 363	115 487	94 196	9 592	33.7	40.8	18.19	17.79	613.00	725.83
September	136 283	113 715	21 092	13 270	115 191	93 815	9 503	33.5	40.4	18.22	17.80	610.37	719.12
October	135 729	113 168	20 856	13 129	114 873	93 345	9 367	33.5	40.3	18.28	17.95	612.38	723.39
November	135 001	112 434	20 573	12 999	114 428	92 686	9 265	33.4	40.2	18.32	17.95	611.89	721.59
December	134 328	111 767	20 294	12 822	114 034	92 138	9 112	33.3	39.8	18.39	17.97	612.39	715.21
2009													
January	133 549	110 961	19 855	12 543	113 694	91 458	8 882	33.3	39.8	18.43	18.01	613.72	716.80
February	132 823	110 254	19 559	12 377	113 264	90 847	8 734	33.2	39.5	18.47	18.09	613.20	714.56
March	132 070	109 510	19 233	12 212	112 837	90 247	8 593	33.1	39.4	18.52	18.14	613.01	714.72
April	131 542	108 861	18 956	12 063	112 586	89 676	8 478	33.1	39.6	18.53	18.15	613.34	718.74
May	131 155	108 527	18 731	11 911	112 424	89 401	8 349	33.1	39.5	18.55	18.15	614.01	716.93
June	130 640	108 075	18 503	11 782	112 137	88 984	8 244	33.0	39.5	18.57	18.17	612.81	717.72
July	130 294	107 778	18 375	11 739	111 919	88 760	8 230	33.1	39.9	18.62	18.26	616.32	728.57
August	130 082	107 563	18 245	11 682	111 837	88 575	8 192	33.1	40.0	18.69	18.31	618.64	732.40
September	129 857	107 377	18 124	11 634	111 733	88 418	8 166	33.1	39.9	18.71	18.39	619.30	733.76
October	129 633	107 115	17 993	11 577	111 640	88 194	8 124	33.0	40.0	18.78	18.41	619.74	736.40
November	129 697	107 190	17 960	11 552	111 737	88 302	8 108	33.2	40.5	18.80	18.38	624.16	744.39
December	129 588	107 107	17 906	11 534	111 682	88 239	8 089	33.2	40.5	18.85	18.38	625.82	744.39

Table 20-5A. Money Stock and Related Data, January 1947–January 1959

(Averages of daily figures; seasonally adjusted, billions of dollars.)

Year and month	Money stock			Time deposits adjusted
	Total	Currency component	Demand deposit component	
1947				
January	109.5	26.7	82.8	33.3
February	109.7	26.7	83.0	33.5
March	110.3	26.7	83.7	33.6
April	111.1	26.6	84.5	33.7
May	111.7	26.6	85.1	33.8
June	112.1	26.6	85.5	33.9
July	112.2	26.5	85.7	34.0
August	112.6	26.5	86.1	34.4
September	113.0	26.7	86.3	34.7
October	112.9	26.5	86.4	35.0
November	113.3	26.5	86.8	35.2
December	113.1	26.4	86.7	35.4
1948				
January	113.4	26.4	87.0	35.5
February	113.2	26.3	86.8	35.7
March	112.6	26.2	86.4	35.7
April	112.3	26.1	86.3	35.7
May	112.1	26.0	86.0	35.7
June	112.0	26.0	86.0	35.8
July	112.2	26.0	86.2	35.8
August	112.3	26.0	86.2	35.9
September	112.2	26.0	86.2	35.9
October	112.1	26.0	86.1	35.9
November	111.8	26.0	85.9	36.0
December	111.5	25.8	85.8	36.0
1949				
January	111.2	25.7	85.5	36.1
February	111.2	25.7	85.5	36.1
March	111.2	25.7	85.6	36.1
April	111.3	25.7	85.6	36.2
May	111.5	25.7	85.8	36.3
June	111.3	25.6	85.7	36.4
July	111.2	25.5	85.7	36.4
August	111.0	25.5	85.6	36.4
September	110.9	25.3	85.6	36.4
October	110.9	25.3	85.6	36.4
November	111.0	25.2	85.8	36.4
December	111.2	25.1	86.0	36.4
1950				
January	111.5	25.1	86.4	36.4
February	112.1	25.1	86.9	36.6
March	112.5	25.2	87.3	36.6
April	113.2	25.3	88.0	36.7
May	113.7	25.2	88.5	36.9
June	114.1	25.1	89.0	36.9
July	114.6	25.0	89.6	36.8
August	115.0	24.9	90.1	36.7
September	115.2	24.9	90.3	36.6
October	115.7	24.9	90.8	36.5
November	115.9	24.9	90.9	36.6
December	116.2	25.0	91.2	36.7
1951				
January	116.7	25.0	91.7	36.7
February	117.1	25.1	92.0	36.6
March	117.6	25.2	92.4	36.6
April	117.8	25.2	92.6	36.7
May	118.2	25.3	92.8	36.8
June	118.6	25.4	93.2	36.9
July	119.1	25.6	93.4	37.2
August	119.6	25.7	93.8	37.4
September	120.4	25.8	94.5	37.7
October	121.0	26.0	95.1	37.8
November	122.0	26.0	96.0	38.0
December	122.7	26.1	96.5	38.2
1952				
January	123.1	26.2	96.9	38.4
February	123.6	26.3	97.3	38.7
March	123.8	26.4	97.5	38.9
April	124.1	26.4	97.6	39.1
May	124.5	26.5	98.0	39.3
June	125.0	26.7	98.4	39.5
July	125.3	26.7	98.6	39.7
August	125.7	26.8	98.9	40.0
September	126.4	26.9	99.4	40.3
October	126.7	27.0	99.7	40.5
November	127.1	27.2	99.9	40.9
December	127.4	27.3	100.1	41.1

Table 20-5A. Money Stock and Related Data, January 1947–January 1959—*Continued*

(Averages of daily figures; seasonally adjusted, billions of dollars.)

Year and month	Money stock			Time deposits adjusted
	Total	Currency component	Demand deposit component	
1953				
January	127.3	27.4	99.9	41.4
February	127.4	27.5	99.9	41.6
March	128.0	27.6	100.4	41.9
April	128.3	27.7	100.7	42.1
May	128.5	27.7	100.7	42.4
June	128.5	27.7	100.7	42.6
July	128.6	27.8	100.8	42.9
August	128.7	27.8	100.9	43.2
September	128.6	27.8	100.8	43.5
October	128.7	27.8	100.9	43.9
November	128.7	27.8	100.9	44.2
December	128.8	27.7	101.1	44.5
1954				
January	129.0	27.7	101.3	44.8
February	129.1	27.7	101.5	45.2
March	129.2	27.6	101.6	45.6
April	128.6	27.6	101.0	46.1
May	129.7	27.6	102.1	46.5
June	129.9	27.5	102.3	46.8
July	130.3	27.5	102.8	47.3
August	130.7	27.5	103.2	47.8
September	130.9	27.4	103.5	47.9
October	131.5	27.4	104.1	48.1
November	132.1	27.4	104.7	48.2
December	132.3	27.4	104.9	48.3
1955				
January	133.0	27.4	105.6	48.5
February	133.9	27.5	106.4	48.7
March	133.6	27.5	106.0	48.8
April	133.9	27.5	106.3	49.0
May	134.6	27.6	107.0	49.0
June	134.4	27.6	106.8	49.2
July	134.8	27.7	107.2	49.3
August	134.8	27.7	107.0	49.3
September	135.0	27.7	107.3	49.6
October	135.2	27.8	107.4	49.7
November	134.9	27.8	107.1	49.9
December	135.2	27.8	107.4	50.0
1956				
January	135.5	27.9	107.7	49.9
February	135.5	27.9	107.7	49.9
March	135.7	27.9	107.8	50.1
April	136.0	27.9	108.1	50.3
May	135.8	27.9	107.9	50.4
June	136.0	27.9	108.1	50.7
July	136.0	28.0	108.0	50.9
August	135.7	28.0	107.8	51.2
September	136.2	28.0	108.2	51.5
October	136.3	28.0	108.2	51.6
November	136.6	28.1	108.4	51.8
December	136.9	28.2	108.7	51.9
1957				
January	136.9	28.2	108.6	52.6
February	136.8	28.2	108.6	53.1
March	136.9	28.2	108.7	53.7
April	136.9	28.2	108.7	54.0
May	137.0	28.2	108.8	54.5
June	136.9	28.3	108.6	54.8
July	137.0	28.3	108.7	55.3
August	137.1	28.3	108.8	55.7
September	136.8	28.3	108.4	56.1
October	136.5	28.3	108.2	56.6
November	136.3	28.3	108.0	57.0
December	135.9	28.3	107.6	57.4
1958				
January	135.5	28.3	107.2	57.6
February	136.2	28.2	107.9	59.2
March	136.5	28.2	108.3	60.5
April	137.0	28.2	108.7	61.5
May	137.5	28.3	109.2	62.3
June	138.4	28.3	110.1	63.2
July	138.4	28.4	110.0	64.0
August	139.1	28.4	110.7	64.6
September	139.5	28.5	111.1	64.8
October	140.1	28.5	111.6	64.9
November	140.9	28.5	112.4	65.2
December	141.1	28.6	112.6	65.4
1959				
January	142.2	28.7	113.5	66.3

Table 20-5B. Money Stock, Reserves, and Monetary Base

(Averages of daily figures; seasonally adjusted, except as noted.)

Year and month	Money stock measures, billions of dollars		Reserves and monetary base, adjusted for change in reserve requirements, millions of dollars					
	M1	M2	Total reserves	Nonborrowed reserves	Nonborrowed reserves plus extended credit [1]	Required reserves	Excess reserves, not seasonally adjusted	Monetary base
1959								
January	138.9	286.6	11 112	10 560	10 560	10 614	498	40 425
February	139.4	287.7	11 129	10 624	10 624	10 675	454	40 605
March	139.7	289.2	11 081	10 482	10 482	10 621	460	40 615
April	139.7	290.1	11 116	10 424	10 424	10 684	431	40 694
May	140.7	292.2	11 058	10 317	10 317	10 637	421	40 731
June	141.2	294.1	10 972	10 043	10 043	10 566	407	40 750
July	141.7	295.2	11 109	10 148	10 148	10 693	416	40 896
August	141.9	296.4	11 168	10 177	10 177	10 720	448	40 992
September	141.0	296.7	11 128	10 202	10 202	10 686	443	41 034
October	140.5	296.5	11 057	10 150	10 150	10 616	441	40 903
November	140.4	297.1	11 052	10 194	10 194	10 609	444	40 822
December	140.0	297.8	11 109	10 168	10 168	10 603	506	40 880
1960								
January	140.0	298.2	11 081	10 194	10 194	10 567	514	40 794
February	139.9	298.5	10 884	10 074	10 074	10 430	454	40 666
March	139.8	299.4	10 796	10 155	10 155	10 373	423	40 616
April	139.6	300.1	10 767	10 161	10 161	10 341	426	40 621
May	139.6	300.9	10 840	10 344	10 344	10 396	445	40 639
June	139.6	302.3	10 885	10 451	10 451	10 406	479	40 689
July	140.2	304.1	10 994	10 615	10 615	10 493	501	40 794
August	141.3	306.9	11 078	10 782	10 782	10 536	542	40 895
September	141.2	308.4	11 147	10 932	10 932	10 520	627	41 040
October	140.9	309.5	11 216	11 049	11 049	10 554	662	41 097
November	140.9	310.9	11 299	11 166	11 166	10 556	743	41 130
December	140.7	312.4	11 247	11 172	11 172	10 503	743	40 977
1961								
January	141.1	314.1	11 324	11 259	11 259	10 553	772	40 960
February	141.6	316.5	11 229	11 096	11 096	10 580	649	40 945
March	141.9	318.3	11 108	11 038	11 038	10 563	546	40 851
April	142.1	319.9	11 123	11 066	11 066	10 507	616	40 823
May	142.7	322.2	11 035	10 940	10 940	10 480	556	40 791
June	142.9	324.3	11 087	11 024	11 024	10 497	590	40 902
July	142.9	325.6	11 124	11 070	11 070	10 508	616	40 980
August	143.5	327.6	11 234	11 169	11 169	10 655	579	41 227
September	143.8	329.5	11 289	11 251	11 251	10 709	580	41 417
October	144.1	331.1	11 413	11 342	11 342	10 881	532	41 651
November	144.8	333.4	11 482	11 384	11 384	10 891	591	41 782
December	145.2	335.5	11 499	11 366	11 366	10 915	584	41 853
1962								
January	145.2	337.5	11 490	11 403	11 403	10 867	623	41 864
February	145.7	340.1	11 301	11 233	11 233	10 799	502	41 810
March	146.0	343.1	11 259	11 170	11 170	10 788	472	41 923
April	146.4	345.5	11 330	11 258	11 258	10 838	492	42 096
May	146.8	347.5	11 384	11 323	11 323	10 867	517	42 194
June	146.6	349.3	11 328	11 226	11 226	10 855	473	42 259
July	146.5	350.8	11 394	11 302	11 302	10 860	534	42 398
August	146.6	352.8	11 355	11 231	11 231	10 826	530	42 491
September	146.3	354.9	11 383	11 303	11 303	10 893	490	42 537
October	146.7	357.2	11 450	11 387	11 387	10 972	477	42 700
November	147.3	359.8	11 492	11 372	11 372	10 936	557	42 861
December	147.8	362.7	11 604	11 344	11 344	11 033	572	42 957
1963								
January	148.3	365.2	11 567	11 421	11 421	11 062	505	43 008
February	148.9	367.9	11 456	11 290	11 290	10 995	461	43 155
March	149.2	370.7	11 404	11 255	11 255	10 970	434	43 289
April	149.7	373.3	11 449	11 319	11 319	10 992	457	43 444
May	150.4	376.1	11 426	11 216	11 216	10 996	430	43 586
June	150.4	378.4	11 398	11 139	11 139	10 981	417	43 780
July	151.3	381.1	11 530	11 232	11 232	11 075	454	44 058
August	151.8	383.6	11 484	11 155	11 155	11 039	445	44 149
September	152.0	386.0	11 503	11 184	11 184	11 075	428	44 339
October	152.6	388.3	11 457	11 137	11 137	11 060	397	44 444
November	153.7	391.5	11 547	11 198	11 198	11 106	441	44 744
December	153.3	393.2	11 730	11 397	11 397	11 239	490	45 003
1964								
January	153.7	395.2	11 643	11 369	11 369	11 204	440	45 042
February	154.3	397.6	11 547	11 261	11 261	11 150	397	45 112
March	154.5	399.8	11 563	11 285	11 285	11 177	386	45 371
April	154.8	401.7	11 537	11 326	11 326	11 185	352	45 470
May	155.3	404.2	11 523	11 263	11 263	11 169	354	45 651
June	155.6	407.1	11 595	11 326	11 326	11 220	375	45 959
July	156.8	410.1	11 651	11 387	11 387	11 275	376	46 143
August	157.8	413.4	11 795	11 480	11 480	11 374	421	46 410
September	158.7	416.9	11 863	11 518	11 518	11 432	431	46 714
October	159.2	419.1	11 888	11 567	11 567	11 490	398	46 823
November	160.0	422.1	11 998	11 598	11 598	11 591	408	47 106
December	160.3	424.7	12 011	11 747	11 747	11 605	406	47 161

[1]Extended credit program discontinued January 9, 2003. See notes and definitions for more information.

Table 20-5B. Money Stock, Reserves, and Monetary Base—Continued

(Averages of daily figures; seasonally adjusted, except as noted.)

Year and month	Money stock measures, billions of dollars		Reserves and monetary base, adjusted for change in reserve requirements, millions of dollars					
	M1	M2	Total reserves	Nonborrowed reserves	Nonborrowed reserves plus extended credit [1]	Required reserves	Excess reserves, not seasonally adjusted	Monetary base
1965								
January	160.7	427.5	11 952	11 653	11 653	11 537	415	47 281
February	160.9	430.4	11 883	11 479	11 479	11 472	412	47 500
March	161.5	433.2	11 884	11 472	11 472	11 518	366	47 584
April	162.0	435.4	12 043	11 571	11 571	11 701	341	47 721
May	161.7	437.1	11 912	11 417	11 417	11 578	334	47 799
June	162.2	440.1	12 005	11 467	11 467	11 643	362	48 061
July	163.1	442.9	12 073	11 544	11 544	11 720	353	48 281
August	163.7	445.8	12 079	11 531	11 531	11 682	396	48 453
September	164.9	449.5	12 071	11 517	11 517	11 662	410	48 712
October	166.0	452.6	12 118	11 630	11 630	11 759	358	49 029
November	166.7	455.7	12 087	11 655	11 655	11 735	352	49 234
December	167.8	459.2	12 316	11 872	11 872	11 892	423	49 620
1966								
January	169.1	462.0	12 295	11 875	11 875	11 916	379	49 850
February	169.6	464.6	12 193	11 711	11 711	11 846	347	50 054
March	170.5	467.2	12 164	11 604	11 604	11 822	342	50 171
April	171.8	469.3	12 258	11 621	11 621	11 903	355	50 439
May	171.3	470.1	12 263	11 575	11 575	11 922	341	50 591
June	171.6	471.2	12 256	11 549	11 549	11 901	356	50 754
July	170.3	470.9	12 371	11 629	11 629	11 993	378	51 019
August	170.8	472.6	12 165	11 430	11 430	11 798	367	50 989
September	172.0	475.4	12 229	11 460	11 460	11 858	371	51 154
October	171.2	475.7	12 199	11 465	11 465	11 867	333	51 200
November	171.4	477.3	12 205	11 598	11 598	11 820	385	51 422
December	172.0	480.2	12 223	11 690	11 690	11 884	339	51 565
1967								
January	171.9	481.6	12 334	11 924	11 924	11 931	403	51 876
February	173.0	485.1	12 280	11 916	11 916	11 911	369	52 173
March	174.8	489.7	12 438	12 237	12 237	12 024	414	52 494
April	174.2	492.1	12 488	12 342	12 342	12 138	350	52 517
May	175.7	497.2	12 418	12 329	12 329	12 053	365	52 682
June	177.0	502.0	12 457	12 351	12 351	12 104	352	52 867
July	178.1	506.3	12 722	12 607	12 607	12 304	418	53 165
August	179.7	510.8	12 678	12 598	12 598	12 313	365	53 347
September	180.7	514.7	12 846	12 758	12 758	12 504	342	53 670
October	181.6	518.2	13 088	12 959	12 959	12 752	335	54 044
November	182.4	521.2	13 131	12 999	12 999	12 773	358	54 241
December	183.3	524.8	13 180	12 952	12 952	12 805	375	54 579
1968								
January	184.3	527.4	13 239	12 993	12 993	12 852	387	54 892
February	184.7	530.4	13 188	12 815	12 815	12 801	386	55 171
March	185.5	533.2	13 186	12 527	12 527	12 849	337	55 436
April	186.6	535.7	13 117	12 432	12 432	12 782	335	55 692
May	188.0	538.9	13 130	12 389	12 389	12 771	360	55 872
June	189.4	542.6	13 251	12 557	12 557	12 923	328	56 323
July	190.5	545.6	13 455	12 928	12 928	13 105	351	56 626
August	191.8	549.4	13 440	12 875	12 875	13 110	329	56 976
September	192.7	553.6	13 435	12 931	12 931	13 074	361	57 160
October	194.0	557.6	13 529	13 086	13 086	13 283	245	57 477
November	196.0	562.4	13 649	13 104	13 104	13 340	308	57 887
December	197.4	566.8	13 767	13 021	13 021	13 341	426	58 357
1969								
January	198.7	569.3	13 629	12 893	12 893	13 383	246	58 597
February	199.3	571.9	13 714	12 879	12 879	13 460	254	58 917
March	200.0	574.4	13 653	12 751	12 751	13 434	219	58 999
April	200.7	575.7	13 471	12 468	12 468	13 304	167	59 062
May	200.8	576.5	13 844	12 470	12 470	13 589	255	59 552
June	201.3	578.5	13 795	12 410	12 410	13 491	304	59 794
July	201.7	579.5	13 491	12 239	12 239	13 266	225	59 713
August	201.7	580.1	13 784	12 565	12 565	13 547	237	60 137
September	202.1	582.1	13 822	12 743	12 743	13 549	274	60 357
October	202.9	583.4	13 904	12 754	12 754	13 741	163	60 633
November	203.6	585.4	14 172	12 969	12 969	13 943	229	61 229
December	203.9	587.9	14 168	13 049	13 049	13 882	286	61 569
1970								
January	206.2	589.6	14 087	13 128	13 128	13 914	174	61 792
February	205.0	586.3	14 099	13 019	13 019	13 891	208	61 931
March	205.7	587.3	14 071	13 173	13 173	13 908	163	62 205
April	206.7	588.4	14 209	13 364	13 364	14 057	152	62 653
May	207.2	591.5	14 007	13 040	13 040	13 850	157	62 977
June	207.6	595.2	14 078	13 197	13 197	13 888	190	63 189
July	208.0	599.1	14 159	12 799	12 799	13 993	166	63 444
August	209.9	604.9	14 282	13 445	13 445	14 108	174	63 725
September	211.8	611.2	14 447	13 847	13 847	14 203	244	64 087
October	212.9	616.4	14 480	14 017	14 017	14 274	205	64 303
November	213.7	621.1	14 470	14 055	14 055	14 236	234	64 574
December	214.4	626.5	14 558	14 225	14 225	14 309	249	65 013

[1] Extended credit program discontinued January 9, 2003. See notes and definitions for more information.

Table 20-5B. Money Stock, Reserves, and Monetary Base—*Continued*

(Averages of daily figures; seasonally adjusted, except as noted.)

Year and month	Money stock measures, billions of dollars		Reserves and monetary base, adjusted for change in reserve requirements, millions of dollars					
	M1	M2	Total reserves	Nonborrowed reserves	Nonborrowed reserves plus extended credit [1]	Required reserves	Excess reserves, not seasonally adjusted	Monetary base
1971								
January	215.5	633.0	14 604	14 240	14 240	14 371	234	65 545
February	217.4	641.0	14 819	14 488	14 488	14 565	254	66 037
March	218.8	649.9	14 798	14 479	14 479	14 603	195	66 378
April	220.0	658.4	14 759	14 606	14 606	14 591	168	66 731
May	222.0	666.7	14 982	14 698	14 698	14 763	219	67 315
June	223.5	673.0	15 057	14 564	14 564	14 855	201	67 678
July	224.9	679.6	15 125	14 302	14 302	14 941	184	68 155
August	225.6	685.5	15 190	14 380	14 380	14 994	196	68 413
September	226.5	692.5	15 423	14 928	14 928	15 234	189	68 751
October	227.2	698.4	15 211	14 854	14 854	15 049	163	68 603
November	227.8	704.6	15 247	14 864	14 864	15 010	237	68 894
December	228.3	710.3	15 230	15 104	15 104	15 049	182	69 108
1972								
January	230.1	717.7	15 369	15 347	15 347	15 163	206	69 853
February	232.3	725.7	15 363	15 331	15 331	15 211	152	70 368
March	234.3	733.5	15 480	15 382	15 382	15 291	190	70 820
April	235.6	738.4	15 651	15 534	15 534	15 495	156	71 031
May	235.9	743.4	15 739	15 628	15 628	15 600	139	71 525
June	236.6	749.7	15 909	15 809	15 809	15 706	203	71 817
July	238.8	759.5	15 835	15 597	15 597	15 642	193	72 173
August	240.9	768.7	16 010	15 623	15 623	15 822	188	72 623
September	243.2	778.3	16 000	15 459	15 459	15 788	212	72 984
October	245.0	786.9	16 193	15 637	15 637	15 981	211	73 644
November	246.4	793.9	16 441	15 833	15 833	16 088	354	74 370
December	249.2	802.3	16 645	15 595	15 595	16 361	284	75 167
1973								
January	251.5	810.3	16 708	15 548	15 548	16 450	258	75 925
February	252.2	814.1	16 714	15 120	15 120	16 516	197	76 160
March	251.7	815.3	16 923	15 099	15 099	16 714	209	76 663
April	252.7	819.7	16 731	15 020	15 020	16 508	223	76 962
May	254.9	826.8	16 672	14 829	14 830	16 533	138	77 393
June	256.7	833.3	16 746	14 895	14 903	16 528	217	77 842
July	257.5	836.5	16 988	15 035	15 067	16 705	283	78 531
August	257.7	838.8	16 796	14 631	14 657	16 624	172	78 781
September	257.9	839.3	16 735	14 883	14 909	16 505	231	79 316
October	259.0	842.6	16 924	15 448	15 464	16 672	252	80 173
November	261.0	848.9	16 978	15 585	15 585	16 753	225	80 479
December	262.9	855.5	17 021	15 723	15 723	16 717	304	81 073
1974								
January	263.8	859.7	17 222	16 171	16 174	17 060	162	81 850
February	265.3	864.2	17 125	15 933	15 933	16 941	184	82 341
March	266.7	870.1	17 131	15 817	15 817	16 997	134	82 835
April	267.2	872.9	17 298	15 561	15 561	17 116	182	83 621
May	267.6	874.6	17 423	14 833	15 491	17 263	160	84 432
June	268.5	877.8	17 367	14 361	15 587	17 169	198	84 895
July	269.3	881.4	17 486	14 185	15 615	17 323	162	85 439
August	270.1	884.1	17 391	14 055	15 592	17 203	188	85 974
September	271.0	887.9	17 385	14 102	15 731	17 204	181	86 377
October	272.3	893.3	17 349	15 536	16 021	17 228	120	86 513
November	273.7	898.6	17 453	16 201	16 361	17 248	205	87 043
December	274.2	902.1	17 550	16 823	16 970	17 292	258	87 535
1975								
January	273.9	906.3	17 273	16 874	17 010	17 126	147	87 756
February	275.0	914.1	17 271	17 123	17 176	17 077	194	88 192
March	276.4	925.0	17 439	17 333	17 370	17 239	200	88 916
April	276.2	935.1	17 498	17 387	17 398	17 340	158	89 116
May	279.2	947.9	17 353	17 288	17 291	17 198	155	89 610
June	282.4	963.0	17 715	17 488	17 504	17 513	201	90 817
July	283.7	975.1	17 632	17 331	17 351	17 445	188	91 373
August	284.1	983.1	17 660	17 449	17 461	17 465	195	91 700
September	285.7	991.5	17 834	17 438	17 452	17 643	191	92 119
October	285.4	997.8	17 587	17 397	17 408	17 380	207	92 448
November	286.8	1 006.9	17 849	17 789	17 794	17 566	283	93 373
December	287.1	1 016.2	17 822	17 692	17 704	17 556	266	93 887
1976								
January	288.4	1 026.6	17 616	17 537	17 549	17 376	240	94 281
February	290.8	1 040.3	17 806	17 725	17 734	17 587	219	95 039
March	292.7	1 050.0	17 875	17 821	17 824	17 651	223	95 786
April	294.7	1 060.8	17 719	17 675	17 675	17 564	155	96 479
May	295.9	1 072.1	17 940	17 826	17 826	17 731	210	97 251
June	296.2	1 077.6	17 946	17 820	17 820	17 732	214	97 732
July	297.2	1 086.3	17 846	17 714	17 714	17 612	234	98 234
August	299.0	1 098.7	18 053	17 953	17 953	17 846	207	98 888
September	299.6	1 110.8	18 009	17 948	17 948	17 808	201	99 446
October	302.0	1 125.0	18 077	17 983	17 983	17 858	219	100 066
November	303.6	1 138.2	18 340	18 268	18 268	18 083	257	100 892
December	306.2	1 152.0	18 388	18 335	18 335	18 115	274	101 515

[1]Extended credit program discontinued January 9, 2003. See notes and definitions for more information.

Table 20-5B. Money Stock, Reserves, and Monetary Base—*Continued*

(Averages of daily figures; seasonally adjusted, except as noted.)

Year and month	Money stock measures, billions of dollars		Reserves and monetary base, adjusted for change in reserve requirements, millions of dollars					
	M1	M2	Total reserves	Nonborrowed reserves	Nonborrowed reserves plus extended credit [1]	Required reserves	Excess reserves, not seasonally adjusted	Monetary base
1977								
January	308.3	1 165.2	18 421	18 353	18 353	18 156	266	102 237
February	311.5	1 177.6	18 299	18 227	18 227	18 100	198	102 654
March	313.9	1 188.5	18 405	18 301	18 301	18 190	215	103 337
April	316.0	1 199.6	18 479	18 406	18 406	18 287	192	104 076
May	317.2	1 209.0	18 585	18 379	18 379	18 377	208	104 630
June	318.8	1 217.8	18 471	18 208	18 208	18 324	147	105 186
July	320.2	1 226.7	18 748	18 425	18 425	18 473	275	106 394
August	322.3	1 237.0	18 919	17 858	17 858	18 719	200	107 185
September	324.5	1 246.2	18 873	18 247	18 247	18 664	209	107 923
October	326.4	1 254.0	18 963	17 658	17 658	18 753	210	108 750
November	328.6	1 262.4	19 012	18 150	18 150	18 761	251	109 560
December	330.9	1 270.3	18 990	18 420	18 420	18 800	190	110 324
1978								
January	334.4	1 279.7	19 290	18 806	18 806	19 023	267	111 449
February	335.3	1 285.5	19 561	19 155	19 155	19 319	241	112 450
March	337.0	1 292.2	19 286	18 958	18 958	19 087	199	112 778
April	339.9	1 300.4	19 408	18 851	18 851	19 260	148	113 377
May	344.9	1 310.5	19 655	18 443	18 443	19 436	219	114 418
June	346.9	1 318.5	19 868	18 774	18 774	19 691	178	115 376
July	347.6	1 324.1	20 118	18 801	18 801	19 921	197	116 273
August	349.6	1 333.5	19 912	18 772	18 772	19 744	168	116 904
September	352.2	1 345.0	19 994	18 934	18 934	19 801	193	118 112
October	353.3	1 352.3	20 109	18 832	18 832	19 947	162	119 044
November	355.4	1 359.1	19 872	19 169	19 169	19 650	222	119 733
December	357.3	1 366.0	19 753	18 885	18 885	19 521	232	120 445
1979								
January	358.6	1 371.6	19 821	18 818	18 818	19 606	214	121 272
February	359.9	1 377.8	19 396	18 423	18 423	19 187	209	121 504
March	362.5	1 387.8	19 429	18 439	18 439	19 271	158	122 065
April	368.0	1 402.1	19 504	18 587	18 587	19 328	176	122 819
May	369.6	1 410.2	19 553	17 788	17 788	19 412	141	123 487
June	373.4	1 423.0	19 808	18 390	18 390	19 587	221	124 635
July	377.2	1 434.8	19 992	18 822	18 822	19 782	211	125 810
August	378.8	1 446.6	20 008	18 923	18 923	19 786	222	127 079
September	379.3	1 454.1	20 007	18 667	18 667	19 816	191	128 309
October	380.8	1 460.4	20 375	18 353	18 353	20 103	272	129 458
November	380.8	1 465.9	20 398	18 492	18 492	20 153	245	130 369
December	381.8	1 473.7	20 720	19 248	19 248	20 279	442	131 143
1980								
January	385.8	1 482.7	20 693	19 452	19 452	20 442	251	131 998
February	390.1	1 494.6	20 682	19 027	19 027	20 471	211	132 785
March	388.4	1 499.8	20 703	17 879	17 978	20 517	186	133 607
April	383.8	1 502.2	20 629	18 174	18 726	20 432	197	134 740
May	384.8	1 512.3	20 440	19 421	20 164	20 262	178	134 998
June	389.1	1 529.2	20 575	20 196	20 503	20 372	203	135 679
July	394.0	1 545.5	20 796	20 401	20 654	20 511	284	136 637
August	399.2	1 561.5	21 011	20 352	20 594	20 709	302	137 977
September	404.8	1 574.0	21 232	19 921	20 011	20 977	256	139 220
October	409.0	1 584.8	21 147	19 837	19 837	20 941	206	140 150
November	410.7	1 595.8	22 150	20 091	20 091	21 629	521	141 566
December	408.5	1 599.8	22 015	20 325	20 328	21 501	514	142 004
1981								
January	411.3	1 606.9	21 673	20 278	20 348	21 298	374	141 462
February	414.8	1 618.7	21 840	20 536	20 557	21 489	350	142 270
March	419.0	1 636.6	22 072	21 072	21 086	21 791	280	143 029
April	427.4	1 659.2	22 187	20 849	20 857	22 018	169	143 917
May	424.7	1 664.2	22 442	20 219	20 224	22 184	257	144 587
June	425.2	1 670.3	22 326	20 289	20 295	21 988	338	145 001
July	426.9	1 681.9	22 329	20 650	20 653	21 989	340	145 839
August	426.9	1 694.3	22 356	20 936	21 017	22 064	292	146 467
September	427.0	1 706.0	22 487	21 031	21 332	22 073	414	146 941
October	428.4	1 721.8	22 296	21 115	21 553	22 018	278	147 062
November	431.3	1 736.1	22 338	21 675	21 840	21 993	344	147 749
December	436.7	1 755.5	22 443	21 807	21 956	22 124	319	149 021
1982								
January	442.7	1 770.4	22 669	21 152	21 349	22 251	418	149 991
February	441.9	1 774.5	22 551	20 762	20 994	22 248	304	150 459
March	442.7	1 786.5	22 452	20 898	21 206	22 091	361	150 660
April	447.1	1 803.9	22 337	20 769	21 014	22 064	273	151 606
May	446.7	1 815.4	22 402	21 285	21 461	22 043	359	152 868
June	447.5	1 826.0	22 368	21 164	21 268	22 060	308	153 861
July	448.0	1 833.7	22 182	21 490	21 541	21 868	314	154 385
August	451.4	1 848.5	22 348	21 833	21 926	22 036	312	155 470
September	456.9	1 862.4	22 686	21 752	21 871	22 302	384	156 629
October	464.5	1 873.7	22 889	22 412	22 553	22 485	404	157 716
November	471.5	1 887.3	23 354	22 733	22 921	22 952	402	158 667
December	474.8	1 909.3	23 600	22 966	23 152	23 100	500	160 127

[1] Extended credit program discontinued January 9, 2003. See notes and definitions for more information.

Table 20-5B. Money Stock, Reserves, and Monetary Base—*Continued*

(Averages of daily figures; seasonally adjusted, except as noted.)

Year and month	Money stock measures, billions of dollars		Reserves and monetary base, adjusted for change in reserve requirements, millions of dollars					
	M1	M2	Total reserves	Nonborrowed reserves	Nonborrowed reserves plus extended credit [1]	Required reserves	Excess reserves, not seasonally adjusted	Monetary base
1983								
January	477.2	1 962.4	23 226	22 697	22 854	22 678	548	161 136
February	484.3	1 999.6	23 901	23 319	23 597	23 466	435	163 170
March	490.6	2 017.8	24 414	23 621	23 939	23 981	433	165 052
April	493.2	2 031.1	24 900	23 890	24 295	24 424	476	166 549
May	500.0	2 045.5	24 860	23 907	24 420	24 411	449	167 842
June	504.0	2 055.8	25 277	23 641	24 599	24 797	480	169 393
July	507.8	2 067.1	25 356	23 903	24 480	24 848	507	170 129
August	510.5	2 076.2	25 376	23 830	24 320	24 929	446	171 208
September	512.8	2 085.3	25 435	23 994	24 509	24 937	498	172 411
October	517.2	2 101.5	25 454	24 610	24 866	24 949	505	173 584
November	519.0	2 114.6	25 396	24 491	24 497	24 867	529	174 605
December	521.4	2 125.7	25 367	24 593	24 595	24 806	561	175 467
1984								
January	525.1	2 140.4	25 451	24 736	24 740	24 838	613	176 896
February	527.5	2 160.5	25 829	25 262	25 266	24 923	906	177 838
March	531.4	2 177.5	25 763	24 811	24 838	25 095	668	178 872
April	535.0	2 193.9	25 691	24 457	24 501	25 218	473	179 898
May	536.7	2 206.4	25 882	22 894	22 931	25 313	569	180 722
June	540.2	2 217.4	26 094	22 793	24 666	25 334	759	181 995
July	540.9	2 225.8	25 980	20 056	25 064	25 351	630	182 991
August	541.0	2 232.5	26 039	18 023	25 066	25 359	680	183 754
September	543.1	2 246.5	26 089	18 847	25 306	25 440	649	184 661
October	543.7	2 261.1	26 259	20 242	25 299	25 641	618	185 219
November	547.5	2 283.6	26 518	21 901	25 738	25 820	698	186 104
December	551.6	2 308.8	26 913	23 727	26 331	26 078	835	187 252
1985								
January	557.0	2 334.9	27 077	25 682	26 732	26 334	742	188 080
February	563.6	2 356.4	27 596	26 307	27 110	26 746	850	189 636
March	566.6	2 368.5	27 590	25 997	27 056	26 916	675	190 320
April	570.4	2 377.8	27 870	26 548	27 416	27 134	736	191 353
May	575.1	2 392.1	28 155	26 821	27 355	27 402	753	192 689
June	582.3	2 415.2	28 848	27 644	28 309	27 926	922	194 762
July	589.1	2 432.0	29 141	28 034	28 541	28 301	840	195 946
August	596.2	2 446.5	29 652	28 580	29 149	28 818	834	198 013
September	603.3	2 458.8	30 030	28 741	29 397	29 333	697	199 306
October	607.8	2 470.6	30 490	29 303	29 932	29 746	744	200 739
November	612.2	2 480.2	30 916	29 175	29 706	29 998	918	202 120
December	619.8	2 494.6	31 569	30 250	30 749	30 505	1 063	203 555
1986								
January	621.4	2 504.8	31 563	30 793	31 290	30 481	1 082	204 221
February	625.2	2 515.3	31 658	30 775	31 267	30 645	1 014	205 314
March	633.5	2 535.6	32 090	31 330	31 848	31 207	883	206 929
April	641.0	2 560.3	32 517	31 625	32 259	31 745	772	208 125
May	652.0	2 587.8	33 265	32 389	32 974	32 387	878	210 154
June	660.6	2 608.0	33 947	33 144	33 674	33 028	919	211 794
July	670.3	2 629.8	34 657	33 916	34 294	33 784	873	213 406
August	678.7	2 649.7	35 191	34 319	34 784	34 451	740	215 273
September	687.4	2 671.2	35 621	34 613	35 183	34 932	690	216 763
October	694.9	2 691.1	36 262	35 420	35 917	35 545	717	218 635
November	705.4	2 704.9	37 270	36 519	36 937	36 369	901	220 714
December	724.7	2 731.6	38 840	38 014	38 317	37 667	1 173	223 416
1987								
January	730.2	2 747.3	39 244	38 664	38 889	38 173	1 070	225 346
February	730.7	2 751.1	39 006	38 450	38 733	37 813	1 193	226 567
March	733.8	2 757.0	38 827	38 300	38 564	37 907	921	227 083
April	743.9	2 771.3	39 533	38 540	38 811	38 677	857	228 964
May	745.8	2 776.6	39 812	38 776	39 064	38 744	1 067	230 521
June	743.2	2 778.2	39 462	38 685	38 958	38 228	1 234	231 302
July	743.0	2 782.7	39 080	38 408	38 602	38 221	859	231 973
August	744.9	2 791.8	39 208	38 561	38 693	38 157	1 051	233 529
September	747.6	2 803.2	39 118	38 178	38 586	38 333	784	234 708
October	756.2	2 818.8	39 826	38 883	39 333	38 737	1 089	237 110
November	753.2	2 823.5	39 334	38 709	39 103	38 394	940	238 807
December	750.2	2 831.0	38 913	38 135	38 618	37 893	1 019	239 829
1988								
January	756.2	2 852.0	39 464	38 383	38 754	38 213	1 252	241 825
February	757.7	2 875.0	39 406	39 010	39 215	38 268	1 138	242 804
March	761.8	2 895.3	39 266	37 514	38 993	38 321	945	243 750
April	768.1	2 915.4	39 622	36 628	39 252	38 737	885	245 760
May	771.7	2 930.8	39 958	37 380	39 487	38 911	1 047	247 434
June	778.3	2 942.9	40 277	37 195	39 748	39 382	895	249 160
July	781.4	2 952.7	40 514	37 075	39 613	39 623	891	251 001
August	783.3	2 957.8	40 470	37 229	39 882	39 500	970	252 064
September	783.7	2 962.7	40 343	37 503	39 562	39 326	1 017	253 358
October	783.3	2 971.1	40 422	38 123	39 904	39 370	1 053	254 579
November	784.9	2 986.1	40 548	37 687	40 009	39 374	1 174	255 675
December	786.7	2 994.1	40 453	38 738	39 982	39 392	1 061	256 897

[1]Extended credit program discontinued January 9, 2003. See notes and definitions for more information.

Table 20-5B. Money Stock, Reserves, and Monetary Base—*Continued*

(Averages of daily figures; seasonally adjusted, except as noted.)

Year and month	Money stock measures, billions of dollars		Reserves and monetary base, adjusted for change in reserve requirements, millions of dollars					
	M1	M2	Total reserves	Nonborrowed reserves	Nonborrowed reserves plus extended credit [1]	Required reserves	Excess reserves, not seasonally adjusted	Monetary base
1989								
January	785.7	2 997.4	40 422	38 773	39 811	39 278	1 144	257 914
February	783.8	2 997.8	40 339	38 852	39 901	39 184	1 154	258 308
March	783.0	3 005.5	39 844	38 032	39 366	38 926	918	259 160
April	779.2	3 011.7	39 533	37 244	38 950	38 719	813	259 559
May	775.0	3 017.4	39 301	37 580	38 778	38 258	1 042	260 264
June	773.5	3 033.6	39 085	37 595	38 512	38 177	908	261 107
July	777.8	3 058.3	39 438	38 744	38 850	38 455	982	262 225
August	779.4	3 080.3	39 397	38 722	38 764	38 505	892	262 843
September	781.0	3 098.7	39 673	38 980	39 002	38 728	945	263 759
October	786.6	3 120.6	40 163	39 607	39 629	39 123	1 040	264 899
November	787.9	3 139.4	40 170	39 820	39 841	39 221	948	265 614
December	792.9	3 158.5	40 486	40 221	40 241	39 545	941	267 774
1990								
January	795.4	3 172.6	40 731	40 291	40 317	39 688	1 042	269 568
February	798.1	3 185.0	40 743	39 295	39 830	39 743	1 000	271 141
March	801.6	3 195.9	40 650	38 526	40 477	39 769	881	273 063
April	806.2	3 207.5	40 845	39 236	40 621	39 974	871	275 233
May	804.3	3 206.3	40 750	39 419	40 291	39 796	954	276 739
June	808.9	3 219.0	40 666	39 785	40 131	39 879	787	278 974
July	810.1	3 229.4	40 575	39 818	40 098	39 707	868	281 000
August	815.7	3 246.9	40 873	39 946	40 074	39 997	876	284 104
September	820.1	3 259.5	41 090	40 466	40 472	40 177	913	287 272
October	819.8	3 264.2	40 808	40 398	40 416	39 968	840	289 202
November	822.1	3 267.9	40 970	40 740	40 765	40 043	928	291 105
December	824.7	3 277.0	41 766	41 440	41 463	40 101	1 665	293 278
1991								
January	827.1	3 292.9	42 293	41 759	41 786	40 153	2 140	297 757
February	832.7	3 309.8	42 071	41 819	41 853	40 267	1 804	300 911
March	838.8	3 327.2	41 804	41 563	41 616	40 623	1 182	302 771
April	843.2	3 338.1	41 862	41 630	41 716	40 833	1 029	303 025
May	848.8	3 348.7	42 411	42 108	42 196	41 376	1 035	304 205
June	856.7	3 357.5	42 712	42 372	42 379	41 716	996	305 498
July	861.5	3 361.1	42 984	42 377	42 423	42 080	904	307 245
August	866.7	3 359.9	43 392	42 628	42 908	42 308	1 085	309 305
September	870.2	3 359.7	43 558	42 912	43 214	42 625	933	310 674
October	878.0	3 365.1	44 007	43 746	43 758	42 950	1 057	312 682
November	887.6	3 370.6	44 614	44 506	44 508	43 722	893	314 941
December	897.0	3 377.3	45 516	45 324	45 325	44 526	990	317 543
1992								
January	910.4	3 385.9	46 373	46 140	46 141	45 381	993	319 643
February	925.3	3 404.9	47 602	47 524	47 526	46 557	1 045	322 566
March	936.7	3 408.7	48 274	48 183	48 185	47 249	1 025	324 383
April	943.7	3 404.4	49 041	48 951	48 953	47 908	1 133	326 698
May	950.5	3 403.2	49 336	49 182	49 182	48 333	1 004	328 786
June	954.3	3 398.1	49 270	49 041	49 041	48 346	924	330 177
July	963.2	3 398.3	49 755	49 471	49 471	48 780	975	333 268
August	973.7	3 403.1	50 479	50 228	50 228	49 540	939	336 915
September	988.1	3 414.8	51 394	51 107	51 107	50 380	1 015	340 757
October	1 003.8	3 428.4	52 767	52 624	52 624	51 704	1 063	344 561
November	1 015.7	3 430.9	53 750	53 646	53 646	52 707	1 043	347 636
December	1 024.9	3 429.7	54 421	54 298	54 298	53 267	1 154	350 882
1993								
January	1 030.4	3 424.0	54 970	54 805	54 806	53 708	1 262	353 717
February	1 033.5	3 419.7	54 686	54 641	54 641	53 593	1 093	355 376
March	1 038.5	3 417.1	54 970	54 879	54 879	53 737	1 233	357 882
April	1 047.6	3 416.4	55 358	55 285	55 285	54 255	1 103	360 902
May	1 065.9	3 441.7	56 655	56 533	56 533	55 656	999	364 919
June	1 075.1	3 447.6	57 086	56 905	56 905	56 191	895	367 904
July	1 084.5	3 447.1	57 729	57 485	57 485	56 662	1 068	371 491
August	1 094.2	3 450.9	58 183	57 831	57 831	57 231	952	374 562
September	1 104.2	3 457.7	58 871	58 443	58 443	57 784	1 086	378 243
October	1 113.0	3 462.0	59 594	59 309	59 309	58 517	1 077	381 579
November	1 124.2	3 475.6	60 304	60 214	60 214	59 184	1 120	384 054
December	1 129.6	3 479.9	60 566	60 484	60 484	59 497	1 069	386 586
1994								
January	1 131.6	3 480.7	60 895	60 822	60 822	59 436	1 459	390 196
February	1 136.3	3 481.5	60 515	60 445	60 445	59 367	1 149	393 224
March	1 140.2	3 487.0	60 299	60 244	60 244	59 315	984	396 054
April	1 141.1	3 490.5	60 503	60 379	60 379	59 361	1 142	398 949
May	1 143.3	3 500.0	59 972	59 772	59 772	59 103	869	401 453
June	1 145.1	3 488.5	60 048	59 715	59 715	58 931	1 117	404 400
July	1 150.6	3 496.9	60 321	59 863	59 863	59 205	1 116	407 894
August	1 150.6	3 494.0	59 959	59 490	59 490	58 949	1 010	409 595
September	1 151.9	3 494.2	59 800	59 313	59 313	58 751	1 048	411 771
October	1 150.1	3 492.6	59 374	58 993	58 993	58 576	797	413 992
November	1 151.0	3 495.7	59 412	59 163	59 163	58 415	996	416 777
December	1 150.6	3 494.6	59 466	59 257	59 257	58 295	1 171	418 313

[1] Extended credit program discontinued January 9, 2003. See notes and definitions for more information.

Table 20-5B. Money Stock, Reserves, and Monetary Base—*Continued*

(Averages of daily figures; seasonally adjusted, except as noted.)

Year and month	Money stock measures, billions of dollars		Reserves and monetary base, adjusted for change in reserve requirements, millions of dollars					
	M1	M2	Total reserves	Nonborrowed reserves	Nonborrowed reserves plus extended credit [1]	Required reserves	Excess reserves, not seasonally adjusted	Monetary base
1995								
January	1 151.4	3 500.0	59 404	59 268	59 272	58 071	1 332	421 060
February	1 147.4	3 497.2	58 652	58 593	58 593	57 683	970	421 595
March	1 146.7	3 498.4	58 209	58 140	58 140	57 386	823	424 722
April	1 149.3	3 506.4	57 973	57 862	57 862	57 216	757	427 902
May	1 145.4	3 531.5	57 641	57 491	57 491	56 768	873	430 544
June	1 144.2	3 556.8	57 376	57 104	57 104	56 393	983	430 142
July	1 145.4	3 575.1	57 817	57 446	57 446	56 711	1 106	430 775
August	1 145.5	3 597.1	57 538	57 256	57 256	56 532	1 006	431 242
September	1 141.9	3 609.6	57 310	57 032	57 032	56 338	971	431 921
October	1 137.3	3 620.8	56 719	56 474	56 474	55 640	1 079	432 642
November	1 134.0	3 627.9	56 305	56 101	56 101	55 360	946	432 937
December	1 127.5	3 637.4	56 483	56 226	56 226	55 193	1 290	434 610
1996								
January	1 123.5	3 655.5	55 884	55 846	55 846	54 417	1 467	434 905
February	1 118.5	3 669.5	54 622	54 587	54 587	53 761	861	432 510
March	1 122.5	3 695.4	55 294	55 273	55 273	54 153	1 142	435 925
April	1 124.8	3 706.2	55 178	55 088	55 088	54 052	1 126	436 933
May	1 116.5	3 717.2	54 041	53 913	53 913	53 130	911	437 458
June	1 115.1	3 730.7	54 145	53 758	53 758	53 031	1 114	439 999
July	1 112.5	3 745.3	53 377	53 009	53 009	52 356	1 021	442 625
August	1 101.6	3 752.2	52 162	51 828	51 828	51 201	961	444 650
September	1 096.1	3 760.9	51 312	50 945	50 945	50 262	1 050	446 041
October	1 086.1	3 777.2	50 037	49 750	49 750	49 030	1 007	446 858
November	1 083.6	3 794.6	49 779	49 565	49 565	48 724	1 055	448 849
December	1 081.6	3 815.8	50 185	50 030	50 030	48 766	1 418	452 088
1997								
January	1 081.5	3 829.3	49 683	49 639	49 639	48 456	1 228	453 647
February	1 078.8	3 840.8	48 715	48 673	48 673	47 681	1 035	454 488
March	1 071.8	3 854.2	47 850	47 694	47 694	46 681	1 169	456 221
April	1 064.0	3 873.0	47 353	47 093	47 093	46 339	1 015	457 856
May	1 063.9	3 883.3	46 657	46 414	46 414	45 374	1 283	459 446
June	1 065.7	3 898.7	46 937	46 570	46 570	45 593	1 344	462 092
July	1 066.2	3 920.3	46 755	46 346	46 346	45 518	1 237	464 693
August	1 074.4	3 949.5	46 913	46 315	46 315	45 653	1 260	467 024
September	1 067.6	3 969.0	46 247	45 809	45 809	44 950	1 297	469 228
October	1 065.5	3 985.2	45 959	45 690	45 690	44 544	1 416	471 873
November	1 070.1	4 007.9	46 411	46 258	46 258	44 742	1 668	475 999
December	1 072.8	4 029.7	46 875	46 551	46 551	45 189	1 687	479 996
1998								
January	1 074.3	4 052.0	46 658	46 448	46 448	44 894	1 764	482 183
February	1 077.9	4 083.9	45 742	45 684	45 684	44 208	1 535	483 203
March	1 077.5	4 109.2	45 854	45 812	45 812	44 503	1 350	484 903
April	1 076.2	4 132.0	46 130	46 058	46 058	44 739	1 391	486 780
May	1 078.4	4 155.5	45 531	45 379	45 379	44 241	1 290	488 797
June	1 077.0	4 180.1	45 417	45 166	45 166	43 798	1 619	491 748
July	1 075.1	4 196.2	44 893	44 635	44 635	43 519	1 374	494 640
August	1 074.8	4 220.4	44 956	44 685	44 685	43 423	1 532	497 888
September	1 080.2	4 264.4	44 850	44 599	44 599	43 152	1 697	502 687
October	1 085.9	4 301.3	44 887	44 714	44 714	43 312	1 575	506 911
November	1 094.6	4 338.8	44 815	44 732	44 732	43 205	1 611	510 422
December	1 095.8	4 372.2	45 172	45 055	45 055	43 659	1 512	513 954
1999								
January	1 097.8	4 394.6	45 005	44 799	44 799	43 516	1 489	516 847
February	1 097.0	4 420.1	44 901	44 786	44 786	43 708	1 194	520 766
March	1 097.8	4 431.2	44 538	44 474	44 474	43 270	1 268	525 084
April	1 101.9	4 458.0	43 742	43 576	43 576	42 587	1 155	528 490
May	1 102.6	4 477.3	43 965	43 838	43 838	42 744	1 221	533 264
June	1 099.7	4 502.1	42 973	42 828	42 828	41 675	1 297	536 817
July	1 098.6	4 525.3	41 811	41 502	41 502	40 847	964	540 057
August	1 099.1	4 546.5	42 127	41 783	41 783	40 966	1 161	544 666
September	1 096.3	4 560.3	41 917	41 578	41 578	40 703	1 213	549 964
October	1 102.3	4 581.0	41 530	41 249	41 249	40 382	1 148	557 423
November	1 111.7	4 606.4	41 741	41 506	41 506	40 413	1 328	571 203
December	1 122.7	4 630.5	42 173	41 852	41 852	40 879	1 294	593 740
2000								
January	1 121.9	4 657.3	42 522	42 148	42 148	40 508	2 013	591 013
February	1 109.3	4 674.4	41 439	41 331	41 331	40 326	1 113	573 073
March	1 108.3	4 702.3	40 807	40 627	40 627	39 599	1 208	571 831
April	1 113.5	4 754.1	40 580	40 276	40 276	39 414	1 166	572 338
May	1 105.8	4 747.8	40 657	40 295	40 295	39 687	970	573 707
June	1 103.3	4 760.9	40 089	39 610	39 610	38 974	1 115	575 666
July	1 103.0	4 776.0	39 934	39 364	39 364	38 791	1 143	576 880
August	1 100.4	4 810.3	39 665	39 086	39 086	38 611	1 054	577 693
September	1 099.1	4 841.5	39 530	39 052	39 052	38 384	1 146	578 308
October	1 098.7	4 859.9	39 333	38 915	38 915	38 185	1 148	580 313
November	1 092.4	4 869.0	39 359	39 076	39 076	38 156	1 203	582 051
December	1 087.7	4 912.6	38 724	38 515	38 515	37 399	1 325	584 984

[1] Extended credit program discontinued January 9, 2003. See notes and definitions for more information.

Table 20-5B. Money Stock, Reserves, and Monetary Base—*Continued*

(Averages of daily figures; seasonally adjusted, except as noted.)

Year and month	Money stock measures, billions of dollars		Reserves and monetary base, adjusted for change in reserve requirements, millions of dollars					
	M1	M2	Total reserves	Nonborrowed reserves	Nonborrowed reserves plus extended credit [1]	Required reserves	Excess reserves, not seasonally adjusted	Monetary base
2001								
January	1 097.5	4 967.2	37 891	37 818	37 818	36 628	1 263	588 059
February	1 101.5	5 004.4	38 601	38 550	38 550	37 257	1 345	589 758
March	1 109.9	5 063.4	38 508	38 450	38 450	37 258	1 251	592 386
April	1 115.0	5 125.0	38 495	38 444	38 444	37 238	1 257	595 614
May	1 119.6	5 128.6	38 614	38 401	38 401	37 596	1 019	598 793
June	1 126.4	5 167.3	38 770	38 540	38 540	37 521	1 249	601 890
July	1 139.8	5 201.0	39 337	39 054	39 054	37 935	1 401	607 781
August	1 149.8	5 232.4	39 828	39 645	39 645	38 625	1 203	615 420
September	1 204.0	5 342.7	57 903	54 518	54 518	38 888	19 015	639 549
October	1 165.9	5 334.9	45 405	45 278	45 278	44 079	1 326	630 184
November	1 171.6	5 376.9	40 923	40 839	40 839	39 485	1 439	629 834
December	1 182.2	5 427.8	41 428	41 361	41 361	39 785	1 643	635 567
2002								
January	1 190.4	5 457.2	41 682	41 632	41 632	40 276	1 405	641 320
February	1 190.7	5 485.0	41 853	41 823	41 823	40 481	1 373	646 112
March	1 193.2	5 494.4	41 196	41 117	41 117	39 793	1 403	649 922
April	1 185.8	5 497.8	40 697	40 627	40 627	39 493	1 205	653 780
May	1 189.3	5 520.7	39 500	39 388	39 388	38 242	1 259	657 728
June	1 192.2	5 543.9	39 069	38 927	38 927	37 832	1 238	662 760
July	1 199.6	5 592.9	39 160	38 968	38 968	37 784	1 376	668 368
August	1 185.9	5 629.4	39 764	39 431	39 431	38 158	1 607	670 155
September	1 194.6	5 653.3	38 900	38 671	38 671	37 416	1 484	671 352
October	1 203.8	5 705.3	39 090	38 947	38 947	37 557	1 533	673 810
November	1 209.4	5 749.9	39 772	39 501	39 501	38 135	1 637	677 008
December	1 220.4	5 776.6	40 339	40 259	40 259	38 331	2 008	681 648
2003								
January	1 226.3	5 802.1	40 741	40 714	10 361	39 033	1 708	685 258
February	1 238.6	5 839.8	41 288	41 263	. . .	39 323	1 965	690 362
March	1 239.2	5 855.5	41 363	41 342	. . .	39 734	1 630	694 663
April	1 248.3	5 899.9	40 769	40 740	. . .	39 230	1 539	698 036
May	1 268.1	5 953.1	40 911	40 855	. . .	39 293	1 618	701 096
June	1 280.3	5 991.6	42 215	42 053	. . .	40 174	2 040	703 451
July	1 287.9	6 046.0	42 972	42 842	. . .	41 038	1 935	705 296
August	1 294.1	6 092.7	45 707	45 378	. . .	41 942	3 764	709 643
September	1 296.8	6 072.6	44 222	44 042	. . .	42 713	1 509	711 093
October	1 297.3	6 058.2	43 387	43 279	. . .	41 920	1 467	715 086
November	1 298.2	6 059.3	42 870	42 802	. . .	41 388	1 483	717 780
December	1 306.9	6 065.5	42 630	42 585	. . .	41 583	1 047	720 391
2004								
January	1 305.3	6 066.2	43 006	42 900	. . .	42 119	888	721 826
February	1 321.9	6 107.5	43 080	43 038	. . .	41 888	1 192	723 649
March	1 330.5	6 147.4	45 109	45 058	. . .	43 302	1 808	726 544
April	1 332.0	6 185.6	45 841	45 755	. . .	44 036	1 805	730 163
May	1 331.7	6 254.8	45 413	45 301	. . .	43 729	1 684	733 353
June	1 342.6	6 267.3	45 810	45 630	. . .	43 879	1 931	738 499
July	1 340.3	6 272.4	46 005	45 760	. . .	44 283	1 722	746 124
August	1 353.2	6 297.5	45 481	45 230	. . .	43 899	1 582	747 831
September	1 361.2	6 332.2	46 617	46 282	. . .	44 963	1 654	752 622
October	1 360.9	6 356.9	46 292	46 113	. . .	44 536	1 756	755 329
November	1 376.5	6 392.2	46 024	45 841	. . .	44 239	1 785	759 284
December	1 377.1	6 407.1	46 540	46 477	. . .	44 631	1 909	759 378
2005								
January	1 365.8	6 405.5	47 453	47 391	. . .	45 714	1 738	760 403
February	1 372.9	6 423.1	45 973	45 931	. . .	44 484	1 489	762 842
March	1 373.0	6 438.9	47 067	47 017	. . .	45 287	1 780	765 253
April	1 357.6	6 444.0	46 345	46 214	. . .	44 682	1 664	766 243
May	1 365.4	6 461.1	45 401	45 262	. . .	43 876	1 525	766 744
June	1 378.5	6 493.9	46 008	45 759	. . .	44 269	1 739	770 427
July	1 366.5	6 521.7	46 246	45 821	. . .	44 455	1 791	773 423
August	1 376.1	6 553.9	45 267	44 905	. . .	43 648	1 619	775 731
September	1 377.5	6 589.1	46 573	46 241	. . .	44 579	1 994	779 965
October	1 374.7	6 620.1	45 492	45 208	. . .	43 609	1 883	781 559
November	1 377.9	6 647.0	45 099	44 973	. . .	43 319	1 780	784 201
December	1 375.3	6 671.6	45 088	44 919	. . .	43 188	1 900	787 578
2006								
January	1 380.2	6 711.8	44 271	44 161	. . .	42 696	1 575	791 496
February	1 380.6	6 739.3	44 110	44 057	. . .	42 561	1 549	795 647
March	1 384.5	6 755.2	44 062	43 893	. . .	42 556	1 506	798 002
April	1 380.0	6 780.3	44 676	44 429	. . .	42 852	1 824	800 853
May	1 386.3	6 798.0	44 757	44 582	. . .	42 960	1 797	805 037
June	1 372.8	6 832.8	45 325	45 072	. . .	43 544	1 781	804 887
July	1 368.5	6 868.4	44 305	43 955	. . .	42 753	1 553	804 093
August	1 368.8	6 898.3	43 043	42 674	. . .	41 524	1 519	804 671
September	1 361.5	6 928.2	43 507	43 104	. . .	41 747	1 760	805 934
October	1 369.1	6 987.3	42 826	42 597	. . .	41 134	1 692	806 278
November	1 372.4	7 023.5	42 910	42 750	. . .	41 221	1 688	808 789
December	1 367.9	7 071.7	43 219	43 028	. . .	41 357	1 862	812 410

[1]Extended credit program discontinued January 9, 2003. See notes and definitions for more information.
. . . = Not available.

Table 20-5B. Money Stock, Reserves, and Monetary Base—*Continued*

(Averages of daily figures; seasonally adjusted, except as noted.)

Year and month	Money stock measures, billions of dollars		Reserves and monetary base, adjusted for change in reserve requirements, millions of dollars					
	M1	M2	Total reserves	Nonborrowed reserves	Nonborrowed reserves plus extended credit [1]	Required reserves	Excess reserves, not seasonally adjusted	Monetary base
2007								
January	1 374.0	7 107.8	41 857	41 646	. . .	40 313	1 544	812 963
February	1 367.1	7 126.9	42 109	42 080	. . .	40 657	1 453	811 856
March	1 369.1	7 160.1	42 122	42 068	. . .	40 505	1 617	812 895
April	1 379.2	7 212.0	42 416	42 337	. . .	40 829	1 587	816 198
May	1 380.8	7 245.5	43 224	43 121	. . .	41 770	1 455	818 581
June	1 364.6	7 271.1	43 922	43 735	. . .	42 169	1 753	819 627
July	1 368.6	7 303.8	42 210	41 949	. . .	40 577	1 634	821 298
August	1 371.8	7 363.5	45 401	44 426	. . .	40 575	4 826	824 868
September	1 372.4	7 403.2	43 502	41 935	. . .	41 770	1 732	823 262
October	1 379.0	7 436.1	43 042	42 788	. . .	41 583	1 459	826 238
November	1 375.5	7 464.4	43 180	42 814	. . .	41 487	1 693	826 722
December	1 375.8	7 501.4	43 214	27 783	. . .	41 429	1 784	824 373
2008								
January	1 381.1	7 534.3	42 288	-3 371	. . .	40 641	1 647	820 299
February	1 387.0	7 623.6	43 396	-16 761	. . .	41 782	1 614	820 953
March	1 389.7	7 684.3	45 118	-49 405	. . .	42 474	2 644	824 824
April	1 392.1	7 709.3	44 789	-90 621	. . .	43 052	1 737	823 692
May	1 391.5	7 732.8	45 707	-110 074	. . .	43 869	1 837	827 434
June	1 398.1	7 745.2	45 673	-125 605	. . .	43 449	2 224	833 058
July	1 415.1	7 797.0	45 273	-120 391	. . .	43 361	1 912	839 686
August	1 400.0	7 785.0	46 257	-121 822	. . .	44 382	1 875	843 235
September	1 459.5	7 892.0	103 583	-186 523	. . .	44 101	59 482	905 224
October	1 472.7	8 007.1	315 457	-332 862	. . .	48 299	267 159	1 130 443
November	1 518.1	8 058.7	609 304	-89 481	. . .	50 484	558 821	1 435 012
December	1 594.7	8 239.7	820 304	166 739	. . .	52 972	767 332	1 654 067
2009								
January	1 573.8	8 300.7	856 991	293 495	. . .	58 812	798 179	1 702 464
February	1 562.0	8 338.4	699 934	117 437	. . .	56 486	643 448	1 555 038
March	1 564.2	8 390.4	779 496	167 385	. . .	54 891	724 604	1 640 731
April	1 592.7	8 342.5	881 019	322 825	. . .	56 657	824 361	1 747 297
May	1 593.0	8 415.4	900 865	375 417	. . .	56 798	844 067	1 768 831
June	1 641.0	8 442.1	809 196	370 473	. . .	57 841	751 355	1 679 686
July	1 649.9	8 437.7	794 994	428 033	. . .	62 015	732 979	1 666 475
August	1 648.3	8 414.5	828 466	497 017	. . .	62 639	765 827	1 703 378
September	1 660.9	8 455.2	922 473	615 646	. . .	62 408	860 065	1 800 960
October	1 674.6	8 487.8	1 056 405	791 347	. . .	61 673	994 732	1 936 564
November	1 687.6	8 522.7	1 140 488	923 181	. . .	63 200	1 077 288	2 018 817
December	1 696.4	8 543.9	1 138 597	968 670	. . .	63 187	1 075 410	2 017 692

[1] Extended credit program discontinued January 9, 2003. See notes and definitions for more information.
. . . = Not available.

Table 20-6. Interest Rates, Bond Yields, and Stock Price Indexes

(Not seasonally adjusted.)

Year and month	Percent per annum											Stock price indexes		
	Short-term rates					U.S. Treasury securities		Bond yields						
								Domestic corporate (Moody's)		State and local bonds (Bond Buyer)	Fixed-rate first mortgages	Dow Jones industrials (30 stocks)	Standard and Poor's composite (500 stocks)[2]	Nasdaq composite[3]
	Federal funds	Federal Reserve discount rate[1]	U.S. Treasury bills, 3-month	U.S. Treasury bills, 6-month	Bank prime rate	1-year	10-year	Aaa	Baa					
1945	...	1.00	0.38	...	1.50	...	...	2.62	3.29	...	...	169.82	15.16	...
1946	...	1.00	0.38	...	1.50	...	...	2.53	3.05	...	...	191.65	17.08	...
1947	...	1.00	0.60	...	1.63	...	...	2.61	3.24	...	...	177.58	15.17	...
1948	...	1.34	1.04	...	1.88	...	...	2.82	3.47	...	...	179.95	15.53	...
1949	...	1.50	1.10	...	2.00	...	...	2.66	3.42	...	...	179.48	15.23	...
1950	...	1.59	1.22	...	2.07	...	...	2.62	3.24	...	...	216.31	18.40	...
1951	...	1.75	1.55	...	2.56	...	...	2.86	3.41	...	...	257.64	22.34	...
1952	...	1.75	1.77	...	3.00	...	...	2.96	3.52	...	...	270.76	24.50	...
1953	...	1.99	1.94	...	3.17	...	...	3.20	3.73	2.74	...	275.97	24.73	...
1954	...	1.60	0.95	...	3.05	1.05	2.40	2.90	3.51	2.39	...	333.94	29.69	...
1955	1.79	1.89	1.72	...	3.16	2.04	2.82	3.05	3.53	2.48	...	442.72	40.49	...
1956	2.73	2.77	2.62	...	3.77	2.99	3.18	3.36	3.88	2.76	...	493.01	46.62	...
1957	3.11	3.12	3.22	...	4.20	3.62	3.65	3.89	4.71	3.28	...	475.71	44.38	...
1958	1.57	2.15	1.77	3.01	3.83	2.27	3.32	3.79	4.73	3.16	...	491.66	46.24	...
1959	3.31	3.36	3.39	3.81	4.48	4.24	4.33	4.38	5.05	3.56	...	632.12	57.38	...
1945														
January	...	1.00	0.38	...	1.50	...	...	2.69	3.46	...	...	153.95	13.49	...
February	...	1.00	0.38	...	1.50	...	...	2.65	3.41	...	...	157.24	13.94	...
March	...	1.00	0.38	...	1.50	...	...	2.62	3.38	...	...	157.31	13.93	...
April	...	1.00	0.38	...	1.50	...	...	2.61	3.36	...	...	160.34	14.28	...
May	...	1.00	0.38	...	1.50	...	...	2.62	3.32	...	...	165.52	14.82	...
June	...	1.00	0.38	...	1.50	...	...	2.61	3.29	...	...	167.37	15.09	...
July	...	1.00	0.38	...	1.50	...	...	2.60	3.26	...	...	163.92	14.78	...
August	...	1.00	0.38	...	1.50	...	...	2.61	3.26	...	...	166.17	14.83	...
September	...	1.00	0.38	...	1.50	...	...	2.62	3.24	...	...	177.85	15.84	...
October	...	1.00	0.38	...	1.50	...	...	2.62	3.20	...	...	185.06	16.50	...
November	...	1.00	0.38	...	1.50	...	...	2.62	3.15	...	...	190.34	17.04	...
December	...	1.00	0.38	...	1.50	...	...	2.61	3.10	...	...	192.68	17.33	...
1946														
January	...	1.00	0.38	...	1.50	...	...	2.54	3.01	...	...	199.23	18.02	...
February	...	1.00	0.38	...	1.50	...	...	2.48	2.95	...	...	198.56	18.07	...
March	...	1.00	0.38	...	1.50	...	...	2.47	2.94	...	...	194.23	17.53	...
April	...	1.00	0.38	...	1.50	...	...	2.46	2.96	...	...	205.71	18.66	...
May	...	1.00	0.38	...	1.50	...	...	2.51	3.02	...	...	206.80	18.70	...
June	...	1.00	0.38	...	1.50	...	...	2.49	3.03	...	...	207.32	18.58	...
July	...	1.00	0.38	...	1.50	...	...	2.48	3.03	...	...	202.28	18.05	...
August	...	1.00	0.38	...	1.50	...	...	2.51	3.03	...	...	199.45	17.70	...
September	...	1.00	0.38	...	1.50	...	...	2.58	3.10	...	...	172.74	15.09	...
October	...	1.00	0.38	...	1.50	...	...	2.60	3.15	...	...	169.47	14.75	...
November	...	1.00	0.38	...	1.50	...	...	2.59	3.17	...	...	168.74	14.69	...
December	...	1.00	0.38	...	1.50	...	...	2.61	3.17	...	...	174.29	15.13	...
1947														
January	...	1.00	0.38	...	1.50	...	...	2.57	3.13	...	...	176.15	15.21	...
February	...	1.00	0.38	...	1.50	...	...	2.55	3.12	...	...	181.43	15.80	...
March	...	1.00	0.38	...	1.50	...	...	2.55	3.15	...	...	176.69	15.16	...
April	...	1.00	0.38	...	1.50	...	...	2.53	3.16	...	...	171.23	14.60	...
May	...	1.00	0.38	...	1.50	...	...	2.53	3.17	...	...	168.63	14.34	...
June	...	1.00	0.38	...	1.50	...	...	2.55	3.21	...	...	173.76	14.84	...
July	...	1.00	0.66	...	1.50	...	...	2.55	3.18	...	...	183.53	15.77	...
August	...	1.00	0.75	...	1.50	...	...	2.56	3.17	...	...	180.08	15.46	...
September	...	1.00	0.80	...	1.50	...	...	2.61	3.23	...	...	176.81	15.06	...
October	...	1.00	0.85	...	1.50	...	...	2.70	3.35	...	...	181.95	15.45	...
November	...	1.00	0.92	...	1.50	...	...	2.77	3.44	...	...	181.52	15.27	...
December	...	1.00	0.95	...	1.75	...	...	2.86	3.52	...	...	179.24	15.03	...
1948														
January	...	1.25	0.97	...	1.75	...	...	2.86	3.52	...	...	176.30	14.83	...
February	...	1.25	1.00	...	1.75	...	...	2.85	3.53	...	...	168.64	14.10	...
March	...	1.25	1.00	...	1.75	...	...	2.83	3.53	...	...	169.77	14.30	...
April	...	1.25	1.00	...	1.75	...	...	2.78	3.47	...	...	180.05	15.40	...
May	...	1.25	1.00	...	1.75	...	...	2.76	3.38	...	...	186.51	16.15	...
June	...	1.25	1.00	...	1.75	...	...	2.76	3.34	...	...	191.06	16.82	...
July	...	1.25	1.00	...	1.75	...	...	2.81	3.37	...	...	187.07	16.42	...
August	...	1.50	1.06	...	2.00	...	...	2.84	3.44	...	...	181.77	15.94	...
September	...	1.50	1.09	...	2.00	...	...	2.84	3.45	...	...	180.34	15.76	...
October	...	1.50	1.12	...	2.00	...	...	2.84	3.50	...	...	185.16	16.19	...
November	...	1.50	1.14	...	2.00	...	...	2.84	3.53	...	...	176.76	15.29	...
December	...	1.50	1.16	...	2.00	...	...	2.79	3.53	...	...	176.30	15.19	...

[1]Federal Reserve Bank of New York. Through 2002, represents the rate for adjustment credit. Beginning in 2003, represents the rate for primary credit. See notes and definitions for more information.
[2]1941–1943 = 10.
[3]February 5, 1971 = 100.
. . . = Not available.

Table 20-6. Interest Rates, Bond Yields, and Stock Price Indexes—*Continued*

(Not seasonally adjusted.)

Year and month	Percent per annum											Stock price indexes		
	Short-term rates					U.S. Treasury securities		Bond yields				Dow Jones industrials (30 stocks)	Standard and Poor's composite (500 stocks) [2]	Nasdaq composite [3]
								Domestic corporate (Moody's)		State and local bonds (Bond Buyer)	Fixed-rate first mortgages			
	Federal funds	Federal Reserve discount rate [1]	U.S. Treasury bills, 3-month	U.S. Treasury bills, 6-month	Bank prime rate	1-year	10-year	Aaa	Baa					
1949														
January	...	1.50	1.17	...	2.00	...	...	2.71	3.46	...	...	179.63	15.36	...
February	...	1.50	1.17	...	2.00	...	...	2.71	3.45	...	...	174.54	14.77	...
March	...	1.50	1.17	...	2.00	...	...	2.70	3.47	...	...	175.87	14.91	...
April	...	1.50	1.17	...	2.00	...	...	2.70	3.45	...	...	175.62	14.89	...
May	...	1.50	1.17	...	2.00	...	...	2.71	3.45	...	...	173.93	14.78	...
June	...	1.50	1.17	...	2.00	...	...	2.71	3.47	...	...	165.60	13.97	...
July	...	1.50	1.02	...	2.00	...	...	2.67	3.46	...	...	173.34	14.76	...
August	...	1.50	1.04	...	2.00	...	...	2.62	3.40	...	...	179.25	15.29	...
September	...	1.50	1.07	...	2.00	...	...	2.60	3.37	...	...	180.92	15.49	...
October	...	1.50	1.05	...	2.00	...	...	2.61	3.36	...	...	186.57	15.89	...
November	...	1.50	1.08	...	2.00	...	...	2.60	3.35	...	...	191.49	16.11	...
December	...	1.50	1.10	...	2.00	...	...	2.58	3.31	...	...	196.78	16.54	...
1950														
January	...	1.50	1.07	...	2.00	...	...	2.57	3.24	...	...	199.75	16.88	...
February	...	1.50	1.12	...	2.00	...	...	2.58	3.24	...	...	203.31	17.21	...
March	...	1.50	1.12	...	2.00	...	...	2.58	3.24	...	...	206.25	17.35	...
April	...	1.50	1.15	...	2.00	...	...	2.60	3.23	...	...	212.76	17.84	...
May	...	1.50	1.16	...	2.00	...	...	2.61	3.25	...	...	219.30	18.44	...
June	...	1.50	1.15	...	2.00	...	...	2.62	3.28	...	...	221.02	18.74	...
July	...	1.50	1.16	...	2.00	...	...	2.65	3.32	...	...	205.31	17.38	...
August	...	1.59	1.20	...	2.00	...	...	2.61	3.23	...	...	216.61	18.43	...
September	...	1.75	1.30	...	2.08	...	...	2.64	3.21	...	...	223.20	19.08	...
October	...	1.75	1.31	...	2.25	...	...	2.67	3.22	...	...	229.24	19.87	...
November	...	1.75	1.36	...	2.25	...	...	2.67	3.22	...	...	229.08	19.83	...
December	...	1.75	1.34	...	2.25	...	...	2.67	3.20	...	...	229.18	19.75	...
1951														
January	...	1.75	1.34	...	2.44	...	...	2.66	3.17	...	...	244.41	21.21	...
February	...	1.75	1.36	...	2.50	...	...	2.66	3.16	...	...	253.16	22.00	...
March	...	1.75	1.40	...	2.50	...	...	2.78	3.23	...	...	249.36	21.63	...
April	...	1.75	1.47	...	2.50	...	...	2.87	3.35	...	...	253.02	21.92	...
May	...	1.75	1.55	...	2.50	...	...	2.89	3.40	...	...	254.45	21.93	...
June	...	1.75	1.45	...	2.50	...	...	2.94	3.49	...	...	249.32	21.55	...
July	...	1.75	1.56	...	2.50	...	...	2.94	3.53	...	...	253.61	21.93	...
August	...	1.75	1.62	...	2.50	...	...	2.88	3.50	...	...	264.93	22.89	...
September	...	1.75	1.63	...	2.50	...	...	2.84	3.46	...	...	273.37	23.48	...
October	...	1.75	1.54	...	2.62	...	...	2.89	3.50	...	...	269.85	23.36	...
November	...	1.75	1.56	...	2.75	...	...	2.96	3.56	...	...	259.65	22.71	...
December	...	1.75	1.73	...	2.85	...	...	3.01	3.61	...	...	266.15	23.41	...
1952														
January	...	1.75	1.57	...	3.00	...	...	2.98	3.59	...	...	271.64	24.19	...
February	...	1.75	1.54	...	3.00	...	...	2.93	3.53	...	...	264.72	23.75	...
March	...	1.75	1.59	...	3.00	...	...	2.96	3.51	...	...	264.45	23.81	...
April	...	1.75	1.57	...	3.00	...	...	2.93	3.50	...	...	262.46	23.74	...
May	...	1.75	1.67	...	3.00	...	...	2.93	3.49	...	...	261.63	23.73	...
June	...	1.75	1.70	...	3.00	...	...	2.94	3.50	...	...	268.39	24.38	...
July	...	1.75	1.81	...	3.00	...	...	2.95	3.50	...	...	276.05	25.08	...
August	...	1.75	1.83	...	3.00	...	...	2.94	3.51	...	...	276.70	25.18	...
September	...	1.75	1.71	...	3.00	...	...	2.95	3.52	...	...	272.41	24.78	...
October	...	1.75	1.74	...	3.00	...	...	3.01	3.54	...	...	267.78	24.26	...
November	...	1.75	1.85	...	3.00	...	...	2.98	3.53	...	...	276.38	25.03	...
December	...	1.75	2.09	...	3.00	...	...	2.97	3.51	...	...	285.96	26.04	...
1953														
January	...	1.88	1.96	...	3.00	...	...	3.02	3.51	2.44	...	288.45	26.18	...
February	...	2.00	1.97	...	3.00	...	...	3.07	3.53	2.59	...	283.96	25.86	...
March	...	2.00	2.01	...	3.00	...	...	3.12	3.57	2.65	...	286.79	25.99	...
April	...	2.00	2.19	...	3.03	2.36	2.83	3.23	3.65	2.67	...	275.29	24.71	...
May	...	2.00	2.16	...	3.25	2.48	3.05	3.34	3.78	2.82	...	276.84	24.84	...
June	...	2.00	2.11	...	3.25	2.45	3.11	3.40	3.86	3.03	...	266.89	23.95	...
July	...	2.00	2.04	...	3.25	2.38	2.93	3.28	3.86	2.95	...	270.33	24.29	...
August	...	2.00	2.04	...	3.25	2.28	2.95	3.24	3.85	2.90	...	272.20	24.39	...
September	...	2.00	1.79	...	3.25	2.20	2.87	3.29	3.88	2.87	...	261.90	23.27	...
October	...	2.00	1.38	...	3.25	1.79	2.66	3.16	3.82	2.71	...	270.72	23.97	...
November	...	2.00	1.44	...	3.25	1.67	2.68	3.11	3.75	2.60	...	277.09	24.50	...
December	...	2.00	1.60	...	3.25	1.66	2.59	3.13	3.74	2.59	...	281.15	24.83	...
1954														
January	...	2.00	1.18	...	3.25	1.41	2.48	3.06	3.71	2.50	...	286.64	25.46	...
February	...	1.79	0.97	...	3.25	1.14	2.47	2.95	3.61	2.42	...	292.13	26.02	...
March	...	1.75	1.03	...	3.13	1.13	2.37	2.86	3.51	2.39	...	299.16	26.57	...
April	...	1.63	0.97	...	3.00	0.96	2.29	2.85	3.47	2.47	...	310.93	27.63	...
May	...	1.50	0.76	...	3.00	0.85	2.37	2.88	3.47	2.49	...	322.85	28.73	...
June	...	1.50	0.64	...	3.00	0.82	2.38	2.90	3.49	2.47	...	327.91	28.96	...
July	0.80	1.50	0.72	...	3.00	0.84	2.30	2.89	3.50	2.32	...	341.27	30.13	...
August	1.22	1.50	0.92	...	3.00	0.88	2.36	2.87	3.49	2.26	...	346.06	30.73	...
September	1.06	1.50	1.01	...	3.00	1.03	2.38	2.89	3.47	2.31	...	352.71	31.45	...
October	0.85	1.50	0.98	...	3.00	1.17	2.43	2.87	3.46	2.34	...	358.29	32.18	...
November	0.83	1.50	0.93	...	3.00	1.14	2.48	2.89	3.45	2.32	...	375.70	33.44	...
December	1.28	1.50	1.15	...	3.00	1.21	2.51	2.90	3.45	2.36	...	393.84	34.97	...

[1]Federal Reserve Bank of New York. Through 2002, represents the rate for adjustment credit. Beginning in 2003, represents the rate for primary credit. See notes and definitions for more information.
[2]1941–1943 = 10.
[3]February 5, 1971 = 100.
. . . = Not available.

Table 20-6. Interest Rates, Bond Yields, and Stock Price Indexes—Continued

(Not seasonally adjusted.)

Year and month	Percent per annum											Stock price indexes		
	Short-term rates					U.S. Treasury securities		Bond yields				Dow Jones industrials (30 stocks)	Standard and Poor's composite (500 stocks) [2]	Nasdaq composite [3]
								Domestic corporate (Moody's)		State and local bonds (Bond Buyer)	Fixed-rate first mortgages			
	Federal funds	Federal Reserve discount rate [1]	U.S. Treasury bills, 3-month	U.S. Treasury bills, 6-month	Bank prime rate	1-year	10-year	Aaa	Baa					
1955														
January	1.39	1.50	1.22	...	3.00	1.39	2.61	2.93	3.45	2.40	...	398.43	35.60	...
February	1.29	1.50	1.17	...	3.00	1.57	2.65	2.93	3.47	2.43	...	410.26	36.79	...
March	1.35	1.50	1.28	...	3.00	1.59	2.68	3.02	3.48	2.44	...	408.91	36.50	...
April	1.43	1.63	1.59	...	3.00	1.75	2.75	3.01	3.49	2.41	...	423.00	37.76	...
May	1.43	1.75	1.45	...	3.00	1.90	2.76	3.04	3.50	2.38	...	421.55	37.60	...
June	1.64	1.75	1.41	...	3.00	1.91	2.78	3.05	3.51	2.41	...	440.83	39.78	...
July	1.68	1.75	1.60	...	3.00	2.02	2.90	3.06	3.52	2.54	...	462.16	42.69	...
August	1.96	1.97	1.90	...	3.23	2.37	2.97	3.11	3.56	2.60	...	457.31	42.43	...
September	2.18	2.18	2.07	...	3.25	2.36	2.97	3.13	3.59	2.58	...	476.44	44.34	...
October	2.24	2.25	2.23	...	3.40	2.39	2.88	3.10	3.59	2.51	...	452.65	42.11	...
November	2.35	2.36	2.24	...	3.50	2.48	2.89	3.10	3.58	2.45	...	476.60	44.95	...
December	2.48	2.50	2.54	...	3.50	2.73	2.96	3.15	3.62	2.57	...	484.58	45.37	...
1956														
January	2.45	2.50	2.41	...	3.50	2.58	2.90	3.11	3.60	2.50	...	474.75	44.15	...
February	2.50	2.50	2.32	...	3.50	2.49	2.84	3.08	3.58	2.44	...	475.53	44.43	...
March	2.50	2.50	2.25	...	3.50	2.61	2.96	3.10	3.60	2.57	...	502.67	47.49	...
April	2.62	2.65	2.60	...	3.65	2.92	3.18	3.24	3.68	2.70	...	511.05	48.05	...
May	2.75	2.75	2.61	...	3.75	2.94	3.07	3.28	3.73	2.68	...	495.21	46.54	...
June	2.71	2.75	2.49	...	3.75	2.74	3.00	3.26	3.76	2.54	...	485.33	46.27	...
July	2.75	2.75	2.31	...	3.75	2.76	3.11	3.28	3.80	2.65	...	509.75	48.78	...
August	2.73	2.81	2.60	...	3.84	3.10	3.33	3.43	3.93	2.80	...	511.69	48.49	...
September	2.95	3.00	2.84	...	4.00	3.35	3.38	3.56	4.07	2.93	...	495.03	46.84	...
October	2.96	3.00	2.90	...	4.00	3.28	3.34	3.59	4.17	2.95	...	483.81	46.24	...
November	2.88	3.00	2.99	...	4.00	3.44	3.49	3.69	4.24	3.16	...	479.36	45.76	...
December	2.94	3.00	3.21	...	4.00	3.68	3.59	3.75	4.37	3.22	...	492.02	46.44	...
1957														
January	2.84	3.00	3.11	...	4.00	3.37	3.46	3.77	4.49	3.18	...	485.90	45.43	...
February	3.00	3.00	3.10	...	4.00	3.38	3.34	3.67	4.47	3.00	...	466.83	43.47	...
March	2.96	3.00	3.08	...	4.00	3.42	3.41	3.66	4.43	3.09	...	472.77	44.03	...
April	3.00	3.00	3.07	...	4.00	3.49	3.48	3.67	4.44	3.13	...	485.42	45.05	...
May	3.00	3.00	3.06	...	4.00	3.48	3.60	3.74	4.52	3.27	...	500.83	46.78	...
June	3.00	3.00	3.29	...	4.00	3.65	3.80	3.91	4.63	3.41	...	505.28	47.55	...
July	2.99	3.00	3.16	...	4.00	3.81	3.93	3.99	4.73	3.39	...	514.65	48.51	...
August	3.24	3.15	3.37	...	4.42	4.01	3.93	4.10	4.82	3.54	...	487.97	45.84	...
September	3.47	3.50	3.53	...	4.50	4.07	3.92	4.12	4.93	3.53	...	471.80	43.98	...
October	3.50	3.50	3.58	...	4.50	4.01	3.97	4.10	4.99	3.42	...	443.38	41.24	...
November	3.28	3.23	3.31	...	4.50	3.57	3.72	4.08	5.09	3.37	...	436.73	40.35	...
December	2.98	3.00	3.04	...	4.50	3.18	3.21	3.81	5.03	3.04	...	436.96	40.33	...
1958														
January	2.72	2.94	2.44	...	4.34	2.65	3.09	3.60	4.83	2.91	...	445.69	41.12	...
February	1.67	2.75	1.53	...	4.00	1.99	3.05	3.59	4.66	3.02	...	444.16	41.26	...
March	1.20	2.35	1.30	...	4.00	1.84	2.98	3.63	4.68	3.06	...	450.15	42.11	...
April	1.26	2.03	1.13	...	3.83	1.45	2.88	3.60	4.67	2.96	...	446.91	42.34	...
May	0.63	1.75	0.91	...	3.50	1.37	2.92	3.57	4.62	2.92	...	460.04	43.70	...
June	0.93	1.75	0.83	...	3.50	1.23	2.97	3.57	4.55	2.97	...	471.98	44.75	...
July	0.68	1.75	0.91	...	3.50	1.61	3.20	3.67	4.53	3.09	...	488.30	45.98	...
August	1.53	1.75	1.69	...	3.50	2.50	3.54	3.85	4.67	3.35	...	507.55	47.70	...
September	1.76	1.91	2.44	...	3.83	3.05	3.76	4.09	4.87	3.54	...	521.81	48.96	...
October	1.80	2.00	2.63	...	4.00	3.19	3.80	4.11	4.92	3.45	...	539.85	50.95	...
November	2.27	2.40	2.67	...	4.00	3.10	3.74	4.09	4.87	3.32	...	557.11	52.50	...
December	2.42	2.50	2.77	3.01	4.00	3.29	3.86	4.08	4.85	3.33	...	566.44	53.49	...
1959														
January	2.48	2.50	2.82	3.09	4.00	3.36	4.02	4.12	4.87	3.42	...	592.30	55.62	...
February	2.43	2.50	2.70	3.13	4.00	3.54	3.96	4.14	4.89	3.36	...	590.72	54.77	...
March	2.80	2.92	2.80	3.13	4.00	3.61	3.99	4.13	4.85	3.30	...	609.13	56.15	...
April	2.96	3.00	2.95	3.27	4.00	3.72	4.12	4.23	4.86	3.39	...	617.00	57.10	...
May	2.90	3.05	2.84	3.33	4.23	3.96	4.31	4.37	4.96	3.57	...	630.80	57.96	...
June	3.39	3.50	3.21	3.52	4.50	4.07	4.34	4.46	5.04	3.71	...	631.52	57.46	...
July	3.47	3.50	3.20	3.82	4.50	4.39	4.40	4.47	5.08	3.71	...	662.81	59.74	...
August	3.50	3.50	3.38	3.87	4.50	4.42	4.43	4.43	5.09	3.58	...	660.58	59.40	...
September	3.76	3.83	4.04	4.70	5.00	5.00	4.68	4.52	5.18	3.78	...	635.49	57.05	...
October	3.98	4.00	4.05	4.53	5.00	4.80	4.53	4.57	5.28	3.62	...	637.35	57.00	...
November	4.00	4.00	4.15	4.54	5.00	4.81	4.53	4.56	5.26	3.55	...	646.43	57.23	...
December	3.99	4.00	4.49	4.85	5.00	5.14	4.69	4.58	5.28	3.70	...	671.36	59.06	...
1960														
January	3.99	4.00	4.35	4.74	5.00	5.03	4.72	4.61	5.34	3.72	...	655.39	58.03	...
February	3.97	4.00	3.96	4.30	5.00	4.66	4.49	4.56	5.34	3.60	...	624.89	55.78	...
March	3.84	4.00	3.31	3.61	5.00	4.02	4.25	4.49	5.25	3.57	...	614.70	55.02	...
April	3.92	4.00	3.23	3.55	5.00	4.04	4.28	4.45	5.20	3.56	...	619.98	55.73	...
May	3.85	4.00	3.29	3.58	5.00	4.21	4.35	4.46	5.28	3.60	...	615.63	55.22	...
June	3.32	3.65	2.46	2.74	5.00	3.36	4.15	4.45	5.26	3.55	...	644.39	57.26	...
July	3.23	3.50	2.30	2.71	5.00	3.20	3.90	4.41	5.22	3.50	...	625.83	55.84	...
August	2.98	3.18	2.30	2.59	4.85	2.95	3.80	4.28	5.08	3.33	...	624.47	56.51	...
September	2.60	3.00	2.48	2.83	4.50	3.07	3.80	4.25	5.01	3.42	...	598.10	54.81	...
October	2.47	3.00	2.30	2.73	4.50	3.04	3.89	4.30	5.11	3.53	...	582.47	53.73	...
November	2.44	3.00	2.37	2.66	4.50	3.08	3.93	4.31	5.08	3.40	...	601.14	55.47	...
December	1.98	3.00	2.25	2.50	4.50	2.86	3.84	4.35	5.10	3.40	...	609.54	56.80	...

[1]Federal Reserve Bank of New York. Through 2002, represents the rate for adjustment credit. Beginning in 2003, represents the rate for primary credit. See notes and definitions for more information.
[2]1941–1943 = 10.
[3]February 5, 1971 = 100.
... = Not available.

Table 20-6. Interest Rates, Bond Yields, and Stock Price Indexes—Continued

(Not seasonally adjusted.)

Year and month	Percent per annum											Stock price indexes		
	Short-term rates					U.S. Treasury securities		Bond yields				Dow Jones industrials (30 stocks)	Standard and Poor's composite (500 stocks) [2]	Nasdaq composite [3]
	Federal funds	Federal Reserve discount rate [1]	U.S. Treasury bills, 3-month	U.S. Treasury bills, 6-month	Bank prime rate	1-year	10-year	Domestic corporate (Moody's)		State and local bonds (Bond Buyer)	Fixed-rate first mortgages			
								Aaa	Baa					
1961														
January	1.45	3.00	2.24	2.47	4.50	2.81	3.84	4.32	5.10	3.39	...	632.20	59.72	...
February	2.54	3.00	2.42	2.60	4.50	2.93	3.78	4.27	5.07	3.31	...	650.02	62.17	...
March	2.02	3.00	2.39	2.54	4.50	2.88	3.74	4.22	5.02	3.45	...	670.57	64.12	...
April	1.49	3.00	2.29	2.47	4.50	2.88	3.78	4.25	5.01	3.48	...	684.90	65.83	...
May	1.98	3.00	2.29	2.45	4.50	2.87	3.71	4.27	5.01	3.43	...	693.03	66.50	...
June	1.73	3.00	2.33	2.54	4.50	3.06	3.88	4.33	5.03	3.52	...	691.46	65.62	...
July	1.17	3.00	2.24	2.45	4.50	2.92	3.92	4.41	5.09	3.51	...	690.67	65.44	...
August	2.00	3.00	2.39	2.66	4.50	3.06	4.04	4.45	5.11	3.52	...	718.64	67.79	...
September	1.88	3.00	2.28	2.68	4.50	3.06	3.98	4.45	5.12	3.53	...	711.02	67.26	...
October	2.26	3.00	2.30	2.66	4.50	3.05	3.92	4.42	5.13	3.42	...	703.01	68.00	...
November	2.61	3.00	2.48	2.70	4.50	3.07	3.94	4.39	5.11	3.41	...	724.74	71.08	...
December	2.33	3.00	2.60	2.88	4.50	3.18	4.06	4.42	5.10	3.47	...	728.44	71.74	...
1962														
January	2.15	3.00	2.72	2.94	4.50	3.28	4.08	4.42	5.08	3.34	...	705.15	69.07	...
February	2.37	3.00	2.73	2.93	4.50	3.28	4.04	4.42	5.07	3.21	...	711.95	70.22	...
March	2.85	3.00	2.72	2.87	4.50	3.06	3.93	4.39	5.04	3.14	...	714.20	70.29	...
April	2.78	3.00	2.73	2.83	4.50	2.99	3.84	4.33	5.02	3.06	...	690.28	68.05	...
May	2.36	3.00	2.69	2.78	4.50	3.03	3.87	4.28	5.00	3.11	...	643.71	62.99	...
June	2.68	3.00	2.73	2.80	4.50	3.03	3.91	4.28	5.02	3.25	...	572.65	55.63	...
July	2.71	3.00	2.92	3.08	4.50	3.29	4.01	4.34	5.05	3.27	...	581.79	56.97	...
August	2.93	3.00	2.82	2.99	4.50	3.20	3.98	4.35	5.06	3.23	...	602.50	58.52	...
September	2.90	3.00	2.78	2.93	4.50	3.06	3.98	4.32	5.03	3.11	...	597.02	58.00	...
October	2.90	3.00	2.74	2.84	4.50	2.98	3.93	4.28	4.99	3.02	...	580.67	56.17	...
November	2.94	3.00	2.83	2.89	4.50	3.00	3.92	4.25	4.96	3.04	...	628.83	60.04	...
December	2.93	3.00	2.87	2.91	4.50	3.01	3.86	4.24	4.92	3.07	...	648.38	62.64	...
1963														
January	2.92	3.00	2.91	2.96	4.50	3.04	3.83	4.21	4.91	3.10	...	672.10	65.06	...
February	3.00	3.00	2.92	2.98	4.50	3.01	3.92	4.19	4.89	3.15	...	679.74	65.92	...
March	2.98	3.00	2.89	2.95	4.50	3.03	3.93	4.19	4.88	3.05	...	674.63	65.67	...
April	2.90	3.00	2.90	2.98	4.50	3.11	3.97	4.21	4.87	3.10	...	707.12	68.76	...
May	3.00	3.00	2.93	3.01	4.50	3.12	3.93	4.22	4.85	3.11	...	720.84	70.14	...
June	2.99	3.00	2.99	3.08	4.50	3.20	3.99	4.23	4.84	3.21	...	719.14	70.11	...
July	3.02	3.24	3.18	3.31	4.50	3.48	4.02	4.26	4.84	3.22	...	700.75	69.07	...
August	3.49	3.50	3.32	3.44	4.50	3.53	4.00	4.29	4.83	3.13	...	714.16	70.98	...
September	3.48	3.50	3.38	3.50	4.50	3.57	4.08	4.31	4.84	3.20	...	738.52	72.85	...
October	3.50	3.50	3.45	3.58	4.50	3.64	4.11	4.32	4.83	3.20	...	747.53	73.03	...
November	3.48	3.50	3.52	3.65	4.50	3.74	4.12	4.33	4.84	3.30	...	743.24	72.62	...
December	3.38	3.50	3.52	3.66	4.50	3.81	4.13	4.35	4.85	3.27	...	759.96	74.17	...
1964														
January	3.48	3.50	3.52	3.64	4.50	3.79	4.17	4.39	4.83	3.22	...	777.07	76.45	...
February	3.48	3.50	3.53	3.67	4.50	3.78	4.15	4.36	4.83	3.14	...	793.02	77.39	...
March	3.43	3.50	3.54	3.72	4.50	3.91	4.22	4.38	4.83	3.28	...	812.19	78.80	...
April	3.47	3.50	3.47	3.66	4.50	3.91	4.23	4.40	4.85	3.28	...	820.96	79.94	...
May	3.50	3.50	3.48	3.60	4.50	3.84	4.20	4.41	4.85	3.20	...	823.13	80.72	...
June	3.50	3.50	3.48	3.56	4.50	3.83	4.17	4.41	4.85	3.20	...	817.65	80.24	...
July	3.42	3.50	3.46	3.56	4.50	3.72	4.19	4.40	4.83	3.18	...	844.25	83.22	...
August	3.50	3.50	3.50	3.61	4.50	3.74	4.19	4.41	4.82	3.19	...	835.31	82.00	...
September	3.45	3.50	3.53	3.68	4.50	3.84	4.20	4.42	4.82	3.23	...	863.55	83.41	...
October	3.36	3.50	3.57	3.72	4.50	3.86	4.19	4.42	4.81	3.25	...	875.27	84.85	...
November	3.52	3.62	3.64	3.81	4.50	3.91	4.15	4.43	4.81	3.18	...	880.03	85.44	...
December	3.85	4.00	3.84	3.95	4.50	4.02	4.18	4.44	4.81	3.13	...	866.73	83.96	...
1965														
January	3.90	4.00	3.81	3.94	4.50	3.94	4.19	4.43	4.80	3.06	...	889.91	86.12	...
February	3.98	4.00	3.93	4.00	4.50	4.03	4.21	4.41	4.78	3.09	...	894.42	86.75	...
March	4.04	4.00	3.93	4.00	4.50	4.06	4.21	4.42	4.78	3.17	...	896.45	86.83	...
April	4.09	4.00	3.93	3.99	4.50	4.04	4.20	4.43	4.80	3.15	...	907.72	87.97	...
May	4.10	4.00	3.89	3.95	4.50	4.03	4.21	4.44	4.81	3.17	...	927.50	89.28	...
June	4.04	4.00	3.80	3.86	4.50	3.99	4.21	4.46	4.85	3.24	...	878.07	85.04	...
July	4.09	4.00	3.84	3.90	4.50	3.98	4.20	4.48	4.88	3.27	...	873.44	84.91	...
August	4.12	4.00	3.84	3.95	4.50	4.07	4.25	4.49	4.88	3.24	...	887.71	86.49	...
September	4.01	4.00	3.92	4.07	4.50	4.20	4.29	4.52	4.91	3.35	...	922.20	89.38	...
October	4.08	4.00	4.03	4.19	4.50	4.30	4.35	4.56	4.93	3.40	...	944.78	91.39	...
November	4.10	4.00	4.09	4.24	4.50	4.37	4.45	4.60	4.95	3.45	...	953.31	92.15	...
December	4.32	4.42	4.38	4.55	4.92	4.72	4.62	4.68	5.02	3.54	...	955.20	91.73	...
1966														
January	4.42	4.50	4.59	4.71	5.00	4.88	4.61	4.74	5.06	3.52	...	985.93	93.32	...
February	4.60	4.50	4.65	4.82	5.00	4.94	4.83	4.78	5.12	3.64	...	977.15	92.69	...
March	4.65	4.50	4.59	4.78	5.35	4.97	4.87	4.92	5.32	3.72	...	926.43	88.88	...
April	4.67	4.50	4.62	4.74	5.50	4.90	4.75	4.96	5.41	3.56	...	943.46	91.60	...
May	4.90	4.50	4.64	4.81	5.50	4.93	4.78	4.98	5.48	3.65	...	890.71	86.78	...
June	5.17	4.50	4.50	4.65	5.52	4.97	4.81	5.07	5.58	3.77	...	888.83	86.06	...
July	5.30	4.50	4.80	4.93	5.75	5.17	5.02	5.16	5.68	3.95	...	875.88	85.84	...
August	5.53	4.50	4.96	5.27	5.88	5.54	5.22	5.31	5.83	4.12	...	817.55	80.65	...
September	5.40	4.50	5.37	5.79	6.00	5.82	5.18	5.49	6.09	4.12	...	791.66	77.81	...
October	5.53	4.50	5.35	5.62	6.00	5.58	5.01	5.41	6.10	3.93	...	778.11	77.13	...
November	5.76	4.50	5.32	5.54	6.00	5.54	5.16	5.35	6.13	3.86	...	806.56	80.99	...
December	5.40	4.50	4.96	5.07	6.00	5.20	4.84	5.39	6.18	3.86	...	800.88	81.33	...

[1]Federal Reserve Bank of New York. Through 2002, represents the rate for adjustment credit. Beginning in 2003, represents the rate for primary credit. See notes and definitions for more information.
[2]1941–1943 = 10.
[3]February 5, 1971 = 100.
. . . = Not available.

Table 20-6. Interest Rates, Bond Yields, and Stock Price Indexes—*Continued*

(Not seasonally adjusted.)

| Year and month | Percent per annum | | | | | | | | | | | Stock price indexes | | |
| | Short-term rates | | | | | U.S. Treasury securities | | Bond yields | | | | Dow Jones industrials (30 stocks) | Standard and Poor's composite (500 stocks)[2] | Nasdaq composite[3] |
	Federal funds	Federal Reserve discount rate[1]	U.S. Treasury bills, 3-month	U.S. Treasury bills, 6-month	Bank prime rate	1-year	10-year	Domestic corporate (Moody's) Aaa	Baa	State and local bonds (Bond Buyer)	Fixed-rate first mortgages			
1967														
January	4.94	4.50	4.72	4.74	5.96	4.75	4.58	5.20	5.97	3.54	...	830.55	84.45	...
February	5.00	4.50	4.56	4.59	5.75	4.71	4.63	5.03	5.82	3.52	...	851.12	87.36	...
March	4.53	4.50	4.26	4.22	5.71	4.35	4.54	5.13	5.85	3.55	...	858.12	89.42	...
April	4.05	4.10	3.84	3.89	5.50	4.11	4.59	5.11	5.83	3.60	...	883.74	90.96	...
May	3.94	4.00	3.60	3.80	5.50	4.15	4.85	5.24	5.96	3.89	...	892.59	92.59	...
June	3.98	4.00	3.54	3.89	5.50	4.48	5.02	5.44	6.15	3.96	...	872.66	91.43	...
July	3.79	4.00	4.21	4.72	5.50	5.01	5.16	5.58	6.26	4.02	...	888.50	93.01	...
August	3.90	4.00	4.27	4.83	5.50	5.13	5.28	5.62	6.33	3.99	...	912.48	94.49	...
September	3.99	4.00	4.42	4.96	5.50	5.24	5.30	5.65	6.40	4.12	...	923.46	95.81	...
October	3.88	4.00	4.56	5.07	5.50	5.37	5.48	5.82	6.52	4.29	...	907.55	95.66	...
November	4.13	4.18	4.73	5.25	5.68	5.61	5.75	6.07	6.72	4.34	...	865.44	92.66	...
December	4.51	4.50	4.97	5.49	6.00	5.71	5.70	6.19	6.93	4.43	...	887.20	95.30	...
1968														
January	4.60	4.50	5.00	5.24	6.00	5.43	5.53	6.17	6.84	4.29	...	884.78	95.04	...
February	4.71	4.50	4.98	5.17	6.00	5.41	5.56	6.10	6.80	4.31	...	847.20	90.75	...
March	5.05	4.66	5.17	5.33	6.00	5.58	5.74	6.11	6.85	4.54	...	834.76	89.09	...
April	5.76	5.20	5.38	5.49	6.20	5.71	5.64	6.21	6.97	4.34	...	893.38	95.67	...
May	6.11	5.50	5.66	5.83	6.50	6.14	5.87	6.27	7.03	4.54	...	905.23	97.87	...
June	6.07	5.50	5.52	5.64	6.50	5.98	5.72	6.28	7.07	4.49	...	906.82	100.53	...
July	6.02	5.50	5.31	5.41	6.50	5.65	5.50	6.24	6.98	4.33	...	905.33	100.30	...
August	6.03	5.48	5.09	5.23	6.50	5.43	5.42	6.02	6.82	4.21	...	883.73	98.11	...
September	5.78	5.25	5.19	5.25	6.45	5.45	5.46	5.97	6.79	4.38	...	922.82	101.34	...
October	5.91	5.25	5.35	5.41	6.25	5.57	5.58	6.09	6.84	4.49	...	955.48	103.76	...
November	5.82	5.25	5.45	5.60	6.25	5.75	5.70	6.19	7.01	4.60	...	964.13	105.40	...
December	6.02	5.36	5.96	6.06	6.60	6.19	6.03	6.45	7.23	4.82	...	968.39	106.48	...
1969														
January	6.30	5.50	6.14	6.28	6.95	6.34	6.04	6.59	7.32	4.85	...	935.00	102.04	...
February	6.61	5.50	6.12	6.30	7.00	6.41	6.19	6.66	7.30	4.98	...	931.31	101.46	...
March	6.79	5.50	6.02	6.16	7.24	6.34	6.30	6.85	7.51	5.26	...	916.52	99.30	...
April	7.41	5.95	6.11	6.13	7.50	6.26	6.17	6.89	7.54	5.19	...	927.38	101.26	...
May	8.67	6.00	6.04	6.15	7.50	6.42	6.32	6.79	7.52	5.33	...	954.88	104.62	...
June	8.90	6.00	6.44	6.75	8.23	7.04	6.57	6.98	7.70	5.75	...	896.62	99.14	...
July	8.61	6.00	7.00	7.24	8.50	7.60	6.72	7.08	7.84	5.75	...	844.02	94.71	...
August	9.19	6.00	6.98	7.19	8.50	7.54	6.69	6.97	7.86	6.00	...	825.46	94.18	...
September	9.15	6.00	7.09	7.32	8.50	7.82	7.16	7.14	8.05	6.26	...	826.72	94.51	...
October	9.00	6.00	7.00	7.29	8.50	7.64	7.10	7.33	8.22	6.09	...	832.52	95.52	...
November	8.85	6.00	7.24	7.62	8.50	7.89	7.14	7.35	8.25	6.30	...	841.10	96.21	...
December	8.97	6.00	7.82	7.90	8.50	8.17	7.65	7.72	8.65	6.82	...	789.23	91.11	...
1970														
January	8.98	6.00	7.87	7.78	8.50	8.10	7.79	7.91	8.86	6.63	...	782.93	90.31	...
February	8.98	6.00	7.13	7.22	8.50	7.59	7.24	7.93	8.78	6.22	...	756.22	87.16	...
March	7.76	6.00	6.63	6.58	8.39	6.97	7.07	7.84	8.63	6.05	...	777.63	88.65	...
April	8.10	6.00	6.51	6.60	8.00	7.06	7.39	7.83	8.70	6.65	...	771.65	85.95	...
May	7.94	6.00	6.84	7.02	8.00	7.75	7.91	8.11	8.98	7.00	...	691.97	76.06	...
June	7.60	6.00	6.68	6.86	8.00	7.55	7.84	8.48	9.25	6.93	...	699.30	75.59	...
July	7.21	6.00	6.45	6.51	8.00	7.10	7.46	8.44	9.40	6.42	...	712.81	75.72	...
August	6.61	6.00	6.41	6.55	8.00	6.98	7.53	8.13	9.44	6.17	...	731.98	77.92	...
September	6.29	6.00	6.12	6.46	7.83	6.73	7.39	8.09	9.39	6.31	...	759.39	82.58	...
October	6.20	6.00	5.91	6.21	7.50	6.43	7.33	8.03	9.33	6.37	...	763.74	84.37	...
November	5.60	5.85	5.28	5.42	7.28	5.51	6.84	8.05	9.38	5.71	...	769.28	84.28	...
December	4.90	5.52	4.87	4.89	6.92	5.00	6.39	7.64	9.12	5.47	...	821.51	90.05	...
1971														
January	4.14	5.23	4.44	4.47	6.29	4.57	6.24	7.36	8.74	5.35	...	849.04	93.49	...
February	3.72	4.91	3.70	3.78	5.88	3.89	6.11	7.08	8.39	5.23	...	879.69	97.11	...
March	3.71	4.75	3.38	3.50	5.44	3.69	5.70	7.21	8.46	5.17	...	901.29	99.60	...
April	4.15	4.75	3.86	4.03	5.28	4.30	5.83	7.25	8.45	5.37	7.31	932.54	103.04	...
May	4.63	4.75	4.14	4.36	5.46	5.04	6.39	7.53	8.62	5.90	7.43	925.50	101.64	...
June	4.91	4.75	4.75	4.97	5.50	5.64	6.52	7.64	8.75	5.95	7.53	900.45	99.72	...
July	5.31	4.88	5.40	5.63	5.91	6.04	6.73	7.64	8.76	6.06	7.60	887.81	99.00	...
August	5.56	5.00	4.94	5.22	6.00	5.80	6.58	7.59	8.76	5.82	7.70	875.41	97.24	...
September	5.55	5.00	4.69	4.97	6.00	5.41	6.14	7.44	8.59	5.37	7.69	901.22	99.40	...
October	5.20	5.00	4.46	4.60	5.90	4.91	5.93	7.39	8.48	5.06	7.63	872.15	97.29	...
November	4.91	4.90	4.22	4.38	5.53	4.67	5.81	7.26	8.38	5.20	7.55	822.11	92.78	...
December	4.14	4.63	4.01	4.23	5.49	4.60	5.93	7.25	8.38	5.21	7.48	869.92	99.17	...
1972														
January	3.50	4.50	3.38	3.66	5.18	4.28	5.95	7.19	8.23	5.12	7.44	904.65	103.30	...
February	3.29	4.50	3.20	3.63	4.75	4.27	6.08	7.27	8.23	5.28	7.33	914.37	105.24	...
March	3.83	4.50	3.73	4.12	4.75	4.67	6.07	7.24	8.24	5.31	7.30	939.23	107.69	...
April	4.17	4.50	3.71	4.23	4.97	4.96	6.19	7.30	8.24	5.43	7.29	958.16	108.81	...
May	4.27	4.50	3.69	4.12	5.00	4.64	6.13	7.30	8.23	5.30	7.37	948.22	107.65	...
June	4.46	4.50	3.91	4.35	5.04	4.93	6.11	7.23	8.20	5.33	7.37	943.44	108.01	...
July	4.55	4.50	3.98	4.50	5.25	4.96	6.11	7.21	8.23	5.41	7.40	925.94	107.21	...
August	4.80	4.50	4.02	4.55	5.27	4.98	6.21	7.19	8.19	5.30	7.40	958.36	111.01	...
September	4.87	4.50	4.66	5.13	5.50	5.52	6.55	7.22	8.09	5.36	7.42	950.60	109.39	...
October	5.04	4.50	4.74	5.13	5.73	5.52	6.48	7.21	8.06	5.18	7.42	944.10	109.56	...
November	5.06	4.50	4.78	5.09	5.75	5.27	6.28	7.12	7.99	5.02	7.43	1 001.20	115.05	...
December	5.33	4.50	5.07	5.30	5.79	5.52	6.36	7.08	7.93	5.05	7.44	1 020.32	117.50	...

[1]Federal Reserve Bank of New York. Through 2002, represents the rate for adjustment credit. Beginning in 2003, represents the rate for primary credit. See notes and definitions for more information.
[2]1941–1943 = 10.
[3]February 5, 1971 = 100.
... = Not available.

Table 20-6. Interest Rates, Bond Yields, and Stock Price Indexes—*Continued*

(Not seasonally adjusted.)

| Year and month | Percent per annum | | | | | | | | | | | Stock price indexes | | |
| | Short-term rates | | | | | U.S. Treasury securities | | Bond yields | | | | Dow Jones industrials (30 stocks) | Standard and Poor's composite (500 stocks) [2] | Nasdaq composite [3] |
	Federal funds	Federal Reserve discount rate [1]	U.S. Treasury bills, 3-month	U.S. Treasury bills, 6-month	Bank prime rate	1-year	10-year	Domestic corporate (Moody's) Aaa	Domestic corporate (Moody's) Baa	State and local bonds (Bond Buyer)	Fixed-rate first mortgages			
1973														
January	5.94	4.77	5.41	5.62	6.00	5.89	6.46	7.15	7.90	5.05	7.44	1 026.82	118.42	...
February	6.58	5.05	5.60	5.83	6.02	6.19	6.64	7.22	7.97	5.13	7.44	974.05	114.16	...
March	7.09	5.50	6.09	6.51	6.30	6.85	6.71	7.29	8.03	5.29	7.46	957.36	112.42	...
April	7.12	5.50	6.26	6.52	6.61	6.85	6.67	7.26	8.09	5.15	7.54	944.12	110.27	...
May	7.84	5.90	6.36	6.62	7.01	6.89	6.85	7.29	8.06	5.15	7.65	922.41	107.22	...
June	8.49	6.33	7.19	7.23	7.49	7.31	6.90	7.37	8.13	5.17	7.73	893.90	104.75	...
July	10.40	6.98	8.01	8.12	8.30	8.39	7.13	7.45	8.24	5.40	8.05	903.61	105.83	...
August	10.50	7.29	8.67	8.65	9.23	8.82	7.40	7.68	8.53	5.48	8.50	883.73	103.80	...
September	10.78	7.50	8.29	8.45	9.86	8.31	7.09	7.63	8.63	5.10	8.82	909.99	105.61	...
October	10.01	7.50	7.22	7.32	9.94	7.40	6.79	7.60	8.41	5.05	8.77	967.63	109.84	...
November	10.03	7.50	7.83	7.96	9.75	7.57	6.73	7.67	8.42	5.18	8.58	878.99	102.03	...
December	9.95	7.50	7.45	7.56	9.75	7.27	6.74	7.68	8.48	5.12	8.54	824.08	94.78	...
1974														
January	9.65	7.50	7.77	7.65	9.73	7.42	6.99	7.83	8.48	5.22	8.54	857.25	96.11	...
February	8.97	7.50	7.12	6.96	9.21	6.88	6.96	7.85	8.53	5.20	8.46	831.33	93.45	...
March	9.35	7.50	7.96	7.83	8.85	7.76	7.21	8.01	8.62	5.40	8.41	874.01	97.44	...
April	10.51	7.60	8.33	8.32	10.02	8.62	7.51	8.25	8.87	5.73	8.58	847.79	92.46	...
May	11.31	8.00	8.23	8.40	11.25	8.78	7.58	8.37	9.05	6.02	8.97	830.26	89.67	...
June	11.93	8.00	7.90	8.12	11.54	8.67	7.54	8.47	9.27	6.13	9.09	831.45	89.79	...
July	12.92	8.00	7.55	7.94	11.97	8.80	7.81	8.72	9.48	6.68	9.28	783.01	82.82	...
August	12.01	8.00	8.96	9.11	12.00	9.36	8.04	9.00	9.77	6.71	9.59	729.30	76.03	...
September	11.34	8.00	8.06	8.53	12.00	8.87	8.04	9.24	10.18	6.76	9.96	651.29	68.12	...
October	10.06	8.00	7.46	7.74	11.68	8.05	7.90	9.27	10.48	6.57	9.98	638.62	69.44	...
November	9.45	8.00	7.47	7.52	10.83	7.66	7.68	8.89	10.60	6.61	9.79	642.11	71.74	...
December	8.53	7.81	7.15	7.11	10.50	7.31	7.43	8.89	10.63	7.05	9.62	596.50	67.07	...
1975														
January	7.13	7.40	6.26	6.36	10.05	6.83	7.50	8.83	10.81	6.82	9.43	659.09	72.56	...
February	6.24	6.82	5.50	5.62	8.96	5.98	7.39	8.62	10.65	6.39	9.11	724.89	80.10	...
March	5.54	6.40	5.49	5.62	7.93	6.11	7.73	8.67	10.48	6.73	8.90	765.06	83.78	...
April	5.49	6.25	5.61	6.00	7.50	6.90	8.23	8.95	10.58	6.95	8.82	790.94	84.72	...
May	5.22	6.12	5.23	5.59	7.40	6.39	8.06	8.90	10.69	6.97	8.91	836.55	90.10	...
June	5.55	6.00	5.34	5.61	7.07	6.29	7.86	8.77	10.62	6.94	8.89	845.70	92.40	...
July	6.10	6.00	6.13	6.50	7.15	7.11	8.06	8.84	10.55	7.07	8.89	856.29	92.49	...
August	6.14	6.00	6.44	6.94	7.66	7.70	8.40	8.95	10.59	7.17	8.94	815.52	85.71	...
September	6.24	6.00	6.42	6.92	7.88	7.75	8.43	8.95	10.61	7.44	9.13	818.29	84.67	...
October	5.82	6.00	5.96	6.25	7.96	6.95	8.14	8.86	10.62	7.39	9.22	831.27	88.57	...
November	5.22	6.00	5.48	5.80	7.53	6.49	8.05	8.78	10.56	7.43	9.15	845.52	90.07	...
December	5.20	6.00	5.44	5.85	7.26	6.60	8.00	8.79	10.56	7.31	9.10	840.80	88.70	...
1976														
January	4.87	5.79	4.87	5.14	7.00	5.81	7.74	8.60	10.41	7.07	9.02	929.34	96.86	...
February	4.77	5.50	4.88	5.20	6.75	5.91	7.79	8.55	10.24	6.94	8.81	971.72	100.64	...
March	4.84	5.50	5.00	5.44	6.75	6.21	7.73	8.52	10.12	6.91	8.76	988.55	101.08	...
April	4.82	5.50	4.86	5.18	6.75	5.92	7.56	8.40	9.94	6.60	8.73	992.52	101.93	...
May	5.29	5.50	5.20	5.62	6.75	6.40	7.90	8.58	9.86	6.87	8.77	988.82	101.16	...
June	5.48	5.50	5.41	5.77	7.20	6.52	7.86	8.62	9.89	6.87	8.85	985.60	101.77	...
July	5.31	5.50	5.23	5.53	7.25	6.20	7.83	8.56	9.82	6.79	8.93	993.20	104.20	...
August	5.29	5.50	5.14	5.40	7.01	6.00	7.77	8.45	9.64	6.61	9.00	981.63	103.29	...
September	5.25	5.50	5.08	5.30	7.00	5.84	7.59	8.38	9.40	6.51	8.98	994.38	105.45	...
October	5.02	5.50	4.92	5.06	6.77	5.50	7.41	8.32	9.29	6.30	8.93	951.96	101.89	...
November	4.95	5.43	4.75	4.88	6.50	5.29	7.29	8.25	9.23	6.29	8.81	944.58	101.19	...
December	4.65	5.25	4.35	4.51	6.35	4.89	6.87	7.98	9.12	5.94	8.79	976.87	104.66	...
1977														
January	4.61	5.25	4.62	4.83	6.25	5.29	7.21	7.96	9.08	5.87	8.72	970.63	103.81	...
February	4.68	5.25	4.67	4.90	6.25	5.47	7.39	8.04	9.12	5.88	8.67	941.75	100.96	...
March	4.69	5.25	4.60	4.88	6.25	5.50	7.46	8.10	9.12	5.89	8.69	946.10	100.57	...
April	4.73	5.25	4.54	4.80	6.25	5.44	7.37	8.04	9.07	5.72	8.75	929.12	99.05	...
May	5.35	5.25	4.96	5.20	6.41	5.84	7.46	8.05	9.01	5.75	8.82	926.30	98.76	...
June	5.39	5.25	5.02	5.21	6.75	5.80	7.28	7.95	8.91	5.62	8.86	916.57	99.29	...
July	5.42	5.25	5.19	5.40	6.75	5.94	7.33	7.94	8.87	5.63	8.94	908.21	100.18	...
August	5.90	5.27	5.49	5.83	6.83	6.37	7.40	7.98	8.82	5.62	8.94	872.27	97.75	...
September	6.14	5.75	5.81	6.04	7.13	6.53	7.34	7.92	8.80	5.51	8.90	853.37	96.23	...
October	6.47	5.80	6.16	6.43	7.52	6.97	7.52	8.04	8.89	5.64	8.92	823.96	93.74	...
November	6.51	6.00	6.10	6.41	7.75	6.95	7.58	8.08	8.95	5.49	8.92	828.52	94.28	...
December	6.56	6.00	6.07	6.40	7.75	6.96	7.69	8.19	8.99	5.57	8.96	818.80	93.82	...
1978														
January	6.70	6.37	6.44	6.70	7.93	7.28	7.96	8.41	9.17	5.71	9.02	781.08	90.25	...
February	6.78	6.50	6.45	6.74	8.00	7.34	8.03	8.47	9.20	5.62	9.16	763.58	88.98	...
March	6.79	6.50	6.29	6.63	8.00	7.31	8.04	8.47	9.22	5.61	9.20	756.37	88.82	...
April	6.89	6.50	6.29	6.73	8.00	7.45	8.15	8.56	9.32	5.79	9.36	794.66	92.71	...
May	7.36	6.84	6.41	7.02	8.27	7.82	8.35	8.69	9.49	6.03	9.58	838.56	97.41	...
June	7.60	7.00	6.73	7.23	8.63	8.09	8.46	8.76	9.60	6.22	9.71	840.25	97.66	...
July	7.81	7.23	7.01	7.44	9.00	8.39	8.64	8.88	9.60	6.28	9.74	831.72	97.19	...
August	8.04	7.43	7.08	7.37	9.01	8.31	8.41	8.69	9.48	6.12	9.79	887.93	103.92	...
September	8.45	7.83	7.85	7.99	9.41	8.64	8.42	8.69	9.42	6.09	9.76	878.64	103.86	...
October	8.96	8.26	7.99	8.55	9.94	9.14	8.64	8.89	9.59	6.13	9.86	857.70	100.58	...
November	9.76	9.50	8.64	9.24	10.94	10.01	8.81	9.03	9.83	6.19	10.11	804.30	94.71	...
December	10.03	9.50	9.08	9.36	11.55	10.30	9.01	9.16	9.94	6.50	10.35	807.96	96.11	...

[1]Federal Reserve Bank of New York. Through 2002, represents the rate for adjustment credit. Beginning in 2003, represents the rate for primary credit. See notes and definitions for more information.
[2]1941–1943 = 10.
[3]February 5, 1971 = 100.
. . . = Not available.

Table 20-6. Interest Rates, Bond Yields, and Stock Price Indexes—*Continued*

(Not seasonally adjusted.)

| | Percent per annum | | | | | | | | | | | Stock price indexes | | |
| | Short-term rates | | | | | U.S. Treasury securities | | Bond yields | | | | Dow Jones industrials (30 stocks) | Standard and Poor's composite (500 stocks) [2] | Nasdaq composite [3] |
Year and month	Federal funds	Federal Reserve discount rate [1]	U.S. Treasury bills, 3-month	U.S. Treasury bills, 6-month	Bank prime rate	1-year	10-year	Domestic corporate (Moody's) Aaa	Domestic corporate (Moody's) Baa	State and local bonds (Bond Buyer)	Fixed-rate first mortgages			
1979														
January	10.07	9.50	9.35	9.47	11.75	10.41	9.10	9.25	10.13	6.46	10.39	837.39	99.71	...
February	10.06	9.50	9.32	9.41	11.75	10.24	9.10	9.26	10.08	6.31	10.41	825.18	98.23	...
March	10.09	9.50	9.48	9.47	11.75	10.25	9.12	9.37	10.26	6.33	10.43	847.85	100.11	...
April	10.01	9.50	9.46	9.49	11.75	10.12	9.18	9.38	10.33	6.28	10.50	864.96	102.07	...
May	10.24	9.50	9.61	9.54	11.75	10.12	9.25	9.50	10.47	6.25	10.69	837.41	99.73	...
June	10.29	9.50	9.06	9.06	11.65	9.57	8.91	9.29	10.38	6.12	11.04	838.65	101.73	...
July	10.47	9.69	9.24	9.24	11.54	9.64	8.95	9.20	10.29	6.13	11.09	836.96	102.71	...
August	10.94	10.24	9.52	9.49	11.91	9.98	9.03	9.23	10.35	6.20	11.09	873.55	107.36	...
September	11.43	10.70	10.26	10.20	12.90	10.84	9.33	9.44	10.54	6.52	11.30	878.51	108.60	...
October	13.77	11.77	11.70	11.66	14.39	12.44	10.30	10.13	11.40	7.08	11.64	840.52	104.47	...
November	13.18	12.00	11.79	11.82	15.55	12.39	10.65	10.76	11.99	7.30	12.83	815.79	103.66	...
December	13.78	12.00	12.04	11.84	15.30	11.98	10.39	10.74	12.06	7.22	12.90	836.14	107.78	...
1980														
January	13.82	12.00	12.00	11.84	15.25	12.06	10.80	11.09	12.42	7.35	12.88	860.75	110.87	...
February	14.13	12.52	12.86	12.86	15.63	13.92	12.41	12.38	13.57	8.16	13.04	878.22	115.34	...
March	17.19	13.00	15.20	15.03	18.31	15.82	12.75	12.96	14.45	9.16	15.28	803.57	104.69	...
April	17.61	13.00	13.20	12.88	19.77	13.30	11.47	12.04	14.19	8.63	16.33	786.35	102.97	...
May	10.98	12.94	8.58	8.65	16.57	9.39	10.18	10.99	13.17	7.59	14.26	828.20	107.69	...
June	9.47	11.40	7.07	7.30	12.63	8.16	9.78	10.58	12.71	7.63	12.71	869.86	114.55	...
July	9.03	10.87	8.06	8.06	11.48	8.65	10.25	11.07	12.65	8.13	12.19	909.79	119.83	...
August	9.61	10.00	9.13	9.41	11.12	10.24	11.10	11.64	13.15	8.67	12.56	947.33	123.50	...
September	10.87	10.17	10.27	10.57	12.23	11.52	11.51	12.02	13.70	8.94	13.20	946.68	126.51	...
October	12.81	11.00	11.62	11.63	13.79	12.49	11.75	12.31	14.23	9.11	13.79	949.17	130.22	...
November	15.85	11.47	13.73	13.50	16.06	14.15	12.68	12.97	14.64	9.56	14.21	971.09	135.65	...
December	18.90	12.87	15.49	14.64	20.35	14.88	12.84	13.21	15.14	10.20	14.79	945.97	133.48	...
1981														
January	19.08	13.00	15.02	14.08	20.16	14.08	12.57	12.81	15.03	9.66	14.90	962.14	132.97	...
February	15.93	13.00	14.79	14.05	19.43	14.57	13.19	13.35	15.37	10.09	15.13	945.51	128.40	...
March	14.70	13.00	13.36	12.81	18.05	13.71	13.12	13.33	15.34	10.16	15.40	987.18	133.19	...
April	15.72	13.00	13.69	13.45	17.15	14.32	13.68	13.88	15.56	10.62	15.58	1 004.86	134.43	...
May	18.52	13.87	16.30	15.29	19.61	16.20	14.10	14.32	15.95	10.77	16.40	979.52	131.73	...
June	19.10	14.00	14.73	14.09	20.03	14.86	13.47	13.75	15.80	10.67	16.70	996.27	132.28	...
July	19.04	14.00	14.95	14.74	20.39	15.72	14.28	14.38	16.17	11.14	16.83	947.95	129.13	...
August	17.82	14.00	15.51	15.52	20.50	16.72	14.94	14.89	16.34	12.26	17.29	926.26	129.63	...
September	15.87	14.00	14.70	14.92	20.08	16.52	15.32	15.49	16.92	12.92	18.16	853.39	118.27	...
October	15.08	14.00	13.54	13.82	18.45	15.38	15.15	15.40	17.11	12.83	18.45	853.26	119.80	...
November	13.31	13.03	10.86	11.30	16.84	12.41	13.39	14.22	16.39	11.89	17.83	860.43	122.92	...
December	12.37	12.10	10.85	11.52	15.75	12.85	13.72	14.23	16.55	12.91	16.92	878.29	123.79	...
1982														
January	13.22	12.00	12.28	12.83	15.75	14.32	14.59	15.18	17.10	13.28	17.40	853.42	117.28	...
February	14.78	12.00	13.48	13.61	16.56	14.73	14.43	15.27	17.18	12.97	17.60	833.16	114.50	...
March	14.68	12.00	12.68	12.77	16.50	13.95	13.86	14.58	16.82	12.82	17.16	812.34	110.84	...
April	14.94	12.00	12.70	12.80	16.50	13.98	13.87	14.46	16.78	12.58	16.89	844.93	116.31	...
May	14.45	12.00	12.09	12.16	16.50	13.34	13.62	14.26	16.64	11.95	16.68	846.74	116.35	...
June	14.15	12.00	12.47	12.70	16.50	14.07	14.30	14.81	16.92	12.44	16.70	804.37	109.70	...
July	12.59	11.81	11.35	11.88	16.26	13.24	13.95	14.61	16.80	12.28	16.82	818.41	109.38	...
August	10.12	10.68	8.68	9.88	14.39	11.43	13.06	13.71	16.32	11.23	16.27	832.11	109.65	...
September	10.31	10.00	7.92	9.37	13.50	10.85	12.34	12.94	15.63	10.66	15.43	917.27	122.43	...
October	9.71	9.68	7.71	8.29	12.52	9.32	10.91	12.12	14.73	9.68	14.61	988.73	132.66	...
November	9.20	9.35	8.07	8.34	11.85	9.16	10.55	11.68	14.30	10.06	13.83	1 027.76	138.10	...
December	8.95	8.73	7.94	8.16	11.50	8.91	10.54	11.83	14.14	9.96	13.62	1 033.10	139.37	...
1983														
January	8.68	8.50	7.86	7.93	11.16	8.62	10.46	11.79	13.94	9.50	13.25	1 064.31	144.27	...
February	8.51	8.50	8.11	8.23	10.98	8.92	10.72	12.01	13.95	9.58	13.04	1 087.40	146.80	...
March	8.77	8.50	8.35	8.37	10.50	9.04	10.51	11.73	13.61	9.20	12.80	1 129.58	151.88	...
April	8.80	8.50	8.21	8.30	10.50	8.98	10.40	11.51	13.29	9.04	12.78	1 168.43	157.71	...
May	8.63	8.50	8.19	8.22	10.50	8.90	10.38	11.46	13.09	9.11	12.63	1 212.86	164.10	...
June	8.98	8.50	8.79	8.89	10.50	9.66	10.85	11.74	13.37	9.52	12.87	1 221.47	166.39	...
July	9.37	8.50	9.08	9.26	10.50	10.20	11.38	12.15	13.39	9.53	13.42	1 213.94	166.96	...
August	9.56	8.50	9.34	9.51	10.89	10.53	11.85	12.51	13.64	9.72	13.81	1 189.22	162.42	...
September	9.45	8.50	9.00	9.15	11.00	10.16	11.65	12.37	13.55	9.58	13.73	1 237.04	167.16	...
October	9.48	8.50	8.64	8.83	11.00	9.81	11.54	12.25	13.46	9.66	13.54	1 252.20	167.65	...
November	9.34	8.50	8.76	8.93	11.00	9.94	11.69	12.41	13.61	9.74	13.44	1 250.00	165.23	...
December	9.47	8.50	9.00	9.17	11.00	10.11	11.83	12.57	13.75	9.89	13.42	1 257.65	164.36	...
1984														
January	9.56	8.50	8.90	9.01	11.00	9.90	11.67	12.20	13.65	9.63	13.37	1 258.89	166.39	...
February	9.59	8.50	9.09	9.18	11.00	10.04	11.84	12.08	13.59	9.64	13.23	1 164.45	157.25	...
March	9.91	8.50	9.52	9.66	11.21	10.59	12.32	12.57	13.99	9.94	13.39	1 161.98	157.44	...
April	10.29	8.87	9.69	9.84	11.93	10.90	12.63	12.81	14.31	9.96	13.65	1 152.72	157.60	...
May	10.32	9.00	9.83	10.31	12.39	11.66	13.41	13.28	14.74	10.49	13.94	1 143.42	156.55	...
June	11.06	9.00	9.87	10.51	12.60	12.08	13.56	13.55	15.05	10.67	14.42	1 121.14	153.12	...
July	11.23	9.00	10.12	10.52	13.00	12.03	13.36	13.44	15.15	10.42	14.67	1 113.29	151.08	...
August	11.64	9.00	10.47	10.61	13.00	11.82	12.72	12.87	14.63	9.99	14.47	1 212.82	164.42	...
September	11.30	9.00	10.37	10.47	12.97	11.58	12.52	12.66	14.35	10.10	14.35	1 213.52	166.11	...
October	9.99	9.00	9.74	9.87	12.58	10.90	12.16	12.63	13.94	10.25	14.13	1 199.30	164.82	...
November	9.43	8.83	8.61	8.81	11.77	9.82	11.57	12.29	13.48	10.17	13.64	1 211.31	166.27	247.00
December	8.38	8.37	8.06	8.28	11.06	9.33	11.50	12.13	13.40	9.95	13.18	1 188.96	164.48	242.52

[1]Federal Reserve Bank of New York. Through 2002, represents the rate for adjustment credit. Beginning in 2003, represents the rate for primary credit. See notes and definitions for more information.
[2]1941–1943 = 10.
[3]February 5, 1971 = 100.
. . . = Not available.

Table 20-6. Interest Rates, Bond Yields, and Stock Price Indexes—*Continued*

(Not seasonally adjusted.)

Year and month	Percent per annum											Stock price indexes		
	Short-term rates					U.S. Treasury securities		Bond yields						
								Domestic corporate (Moody's)		State and local bonds (Bond Buyer)	Fixed-rate first mortgages	Dow Jones industrials (30 stocks)	Standard and Poor's composite (500 stocks) [2]	Nasdaq composite [3]
	Federal funds	Federal Reserve discount rate [1]	U.S. Treasury bills, 3-month	U.S. Treasury bills, 6-month	Bank prime rate	1-year	10-year	Aaa	Baa					
1985														
January	8.35	8.00	7.76	8.00	10.61	9.02	11.38	12.08	13.26	9.51	13.08	1 238.16	171.61	260.85
February	8.50	8.00	8.27	8.39	10.50	9.29	11.51	12.13	13.23	9.65	12.92	1 283.23	180.88	285.52
March	8.58	8.00	8.52	8.90	10.50	9.86	11.86	12.56	13.69	9.77	13.17	1 268.84	179.42	280.43
April	8.27	8.00	7.95	8.23	10.50	9.14	11.43	12.23	13.51	9.42	13.20	1 266.38	180.62	280.90
May	7.97	7.81	7.48	7.65	10.31	8.46	10.85	11.72	13.15	9.01	12.91	1 279.41	184.90	287.51
June	7.53	7.50	6.95	7.09	9.78	7.80	10.16	10.94	12.40	8.69	12.22	1 314.00	188.89	290.44
July	7.88	7.50	7.08	7.20	9.50	7.86	10.31	10.97	12.43	8.81	12.03	1 343.17	192.54	302.04
August	7.90	7.50	7.14	7.32	9.50	8.05	10.33	11.05	12.50	9.08	12.19	1 326.19	188.31	298.25
September	7.92	7.50	7.10	7.27	9.50	8.07	10.37	11.07	12.48	9.27	12.19	1 317.95	184.06	287.94
October	7.99	7.50	7.16	7.33	9.50	8.01	10.24	11.02	12.36	9.08	12.14	1 351.58	186.18	285.37
November	8.05	7.50	7.24	7.30	9.50	7.88	9.78	10.55	11.99	8.54	11.78	1 432.88	197.45	304.36
December	8.27	7.50	7.10	7.14	9.50	7.67	9.26	10.16	11.58	8.42	11.26	1 517.02	207.26	320.24
1986														
January	8.14	7.50	7.07	7.16	9.50	7.73	9.19	10.05	11.44	8.08	10.88	1 534.85	208.19	328.54
February	7.86	7.50	7.06	7.11	9.50	7.61	8.70	9.67	11.11	7.44	10.71	1 652.74	219.37	348.79
March	7.48	7.10	6.56	6.57	9.10	7.03	7.78	9.00	10.50	7.08	10.08	1 757.36	232.33	368.28
April	6.99	6.83	6.06	6.08	8.83	6.44	7.30	8.79	10.19	7.19	9.94	1 807.06	237.98	382.54
May	6.85	6.50	6.15	6.19	8.50	6.65	7.71	9.09	10.29	7.54	10.14	1 801.81	238.46	388.49
June	6.92	6.50	6.21	6.27	8.50	6.73	7.80	9.13	10.34	7.87	10.68	1 867.71	245.30	398.60
July	6.56	6.16	5.83	5.86	8.16	6.27	7.30	8.88	10.16	7.51	10.51	1 809.92	240.18	385.90
August	6.17	5.82	5.53	5.55	7.90	5.93	7.17	8.72	10.18	7.21	10.20	1 843.45	245.00	375.62
September	5.89	5.50	5.21	5.35	7.50	5.77	7.45	8.89	10.20	7.11	10.01	1 813.48	238.27	358.26
October	5.85	5.50	5.18	5.26	7.50	5.72	7.43	8.86	10.24	7.08	9.97	1 817.06	237.36	355.05
November	6.04	5.50	5.35	5.41	7.50	5.80	7.25	8.68	10.07	6.84	9.70	1 883.65	245.09	358.08
December	6.91	5.50	5.53	5.55	7.50	5.87	7.11	8.49	9.97	6.87	9.31	1 924.09	248.61	354.90
1987														
January	6.43	5.50	5.43	5.44	7.50	5.78	7.08	8.36	9.72	6.66	9.20	2 065.13	264.51	384.24
February	6.10	5.50	5.59	5.59	7.50	5.96	7.25	8.38	9.65	6.61	9.08	2 202.34	280.93	411.71
March	6.13	5.50	5.59	5.60	7.50	6.03	7.25	8.36	9.61	6.65	9.04	2 292.61	292.47	432.19
April	6.37	5.50	5.64	5.90	7.75	6.50	8.02	8.85	10.04	7.55	9.83	2 302.66	289.32	422.75
May	6.85	5.50	5.66	6.05	8.14	7.00	8.61	9.33	10.51	8.00	10.60	2 291.12	289.12	416.64
June	6.73	5.50	5.67	5.99	8.25	6.80	8.40	9.32	10.52	7.79	10.54	2 384.02	301.38	423.70
July	6.58	5.50	5.69	5.76	8.25	6.68	8.45	9.42	10.61	7.72	10.28	2 481.73	310.09	429.01
August	6.73	5.50	6.04	6.15	8.25	7.03	8.76	9.67	10.80	7.82	10.33	2 655.02	329.36	448.45
September	7.22	5.95	6.40	6.64	8.70	7.67	9.42	10.18	11.31	8.26	10.89	2 570.81	318.66	442.82
October	7.29	6.00	6.13	6.69	9.07	7.59	9.52	10.52	11.62	8.70	11.26	2 224.58	280.16	385.05
November	6.69	6.00	5.69	6.19	8.78	6.96	8.86	10.01	11.23	7.95	10.65	1 931.88	245.01	318.76
December	6.77	6.00	5.77	6.36	8.75	7.17	8.99	10.11	11.29	7.96	10.65	1 910.07	240.96	314.55
1988														
January	6.83	6.00	5.81	6.25	8.75	6.99	8.67	9.88	11.07	7.69	10.43	1 947.34	250.48	339.29
February	6.58	6.00	5.66	5.93	8.51	6.64	8.21	9.40	10.62	7.49	9.89	1 980.65	258.13	353.58
March	6.58	6.00	5.70	5.91	8.50	6.71	8.37	9.39	10.57	7.74	9.93	2 044.32	265.74	375.55
April	6.87	6.00	5.91	6.21	8.50	7.01	8.72	9.67	10.90	7.81	10.20	2 036.14	262.61	377.23
May	7.09	6.00	6.26	6.56	8.84	7.40	9.09	9.90	11.04	7.91	10.46	1 988.91	256.12	371.88
June	7.51	6.00	6.46	6.71	9.00	7.49	8.92	9.86	11.00	7.78	10.46	2 104.95	270.68	385.99
July	7.75	6.00	6.73	6.99	9.29	7.75	9.06	9.96	11.11	7.76	10.43	2 104.23	269.05	391.43
August	8.01	6.37	7.06	7.39	9.84	8.17	9.26	10.11	11.21	7.79	10.60	2 051.28	263.73	379.60
September	8.19	6.50	7.24	7.43	10.00	8.09	8.98	9.82	10.90	7.66	10.48	2 080.07	267.97	382.17
October	8.30	6.50	7.35	7.50	10.00	8.11	8.80	9.51	10.41	7.46	10.30	2 144.33	277.40	385.02
November	8.35	6.50	7.76	7.86	10.05	8.48	8.96	9.45	10.48	7.46	10.27	2 099.04	271.02	372.90
December	8.76	6.50	8.07	8.22	10.50	8.99	9.11	9.57	10.65	7.61	10.61	2 148.59	276.51	375.80
1989														
January	9.12	6.50	8.27	8.36	10.50	9.05	9.09	9.62	10.65	7.35	10.73	2 234.68	285.41	389.33
February	9.36	6.59	8.53	8.55	10.93	9.25	9.17	9.64	10.61	7.44	10.65	2 304.31	294.01	404.09
March	9.85	7.00	8.82	8.85	11.50	9.57	9.36	9.80	10.67	7.59	11.03	2 283.10	292.71	404.00
April	9.84	7.00	8.65	8.65	11.50	9.36	9.18	9.79	10.61	7.49	11.05	2 348.92	302.25	417.14
May	9.81	7.00	8.43	8.41	11.50	8.98	8.86	9.57	10.46	7.25	10.77	2 439.57	313.93	435.99
June	9.53	7.00	8.15	7.93	11.07	8.44	8.28	9.10	10.03	7.02	10.20	2 494.89	323.73	447.63
July	9.24	7.00	7.88	7.61	10.98	7.89	8.02	8.93	9.87	6.96	9.88	2 554.04	331.93	446.70
August	8.99	7.00	7.90	7.74	10.50	8.18	8.11	8.96	9.88	7.06	9.99	2 691.12	346.61	461.83
September	9.02	7.00	7.75	7.74	10.50	8.22	8.19	9.01	9.91	7.26	10.13	2 693.41	347.33	469.28
October	8.84	7.00	7.64	7.62	10.50	7.99	8.01	8.92	9.81	7.22	9.95	2 692.01	347.40	469.69
November	8.55	7.00	7.69	7.49	10.50	7.77	7.87	8.89	9.81	7.14	9.77	2 642.50	340.22	454.69
December	8.45	7.00	7.63	7.42	10.50	7.72	7.84	8.86	9.82	6.98	9.74	2 728.46	348.57	449.02
1990														
January	8.23	7.00	7.64	7.55	10.11	7.92	8.21	8.99	9.94	7.10	9.90	2 679.24	339.97	439.35
February	8.24	7.00	7.74	7.70	10.00	8.11	8.47	9.22	10.14	7.22	10.20	2 614.19	330.45	424.53
March	8.28	7.00	7.90	7.85	10.00	8.35	8.59	9.37	10.21	7.29	10.27	2 700.13	338.47	436.10
April	8.26	7.00	7.77	7.84	10.00	8.40	8.79	9.46	10.30	7.39	10.37	2 708.27	338.18	429.00
May	8.18	7.00	7.74	7.76	10.00	8.32	8.76	9.47	10.41	7.35	10.48	2 793.82	350.25	442.60
June	8.29	7.00	7.73	7.63	10.00	8.10	8.48	9.26	10.22	7.24	10.16	2 894.84	360.39	462.31
July	8.15	7.00	7.62	7.52	10.00	7.94	8.47	9.24	10.20	7.19	10.04	2 934.23	360.03	455.83
August	8.13	7.00	7.45	7.38	10.00	7.78	8.75	9.41	10.41	7.32	10.10	2 681.89	330.75	396.33
September	8.20	7.00	7.36	7.32	10.00	7.76	8.89	9.56	10.64	7.43	10.18	2 550.69	315.41	368.57
October	8.11	7.00	7.17	7.16	10.00	7.55	8.72	9.53	10.74	7.49	10.18	2 460.54	307.12	338.02
November	7.81	7.00	7.06	7.03	10.00	7.31	8.39	9.30	10.62	7.18	10.01	2 518.58	315.29	347.72
December	7.31	6.79	6.74	6.70	10.00	7.05	8.08	9.05	10.43	7.09	9.67	2 610.92	328.75	370.21

[1]Federal Reserve Bank of New York. Through 2002, represents the rate for adjustment credit. Beginning in 2003, represents the rate for primary credit. See notes and definitions for more information.
[2]1941–1943 = 10.
[3]February 5, 1971 = 100.

Table 20-6. Interest Rates, Bond Yields, and Stock Price Indexes—*Continued*

(Not seasonally adjusted.)

Year and month	Percent per annum											Stock price indexes		
	Short-term rates					U.S. Treasury securities		Bond yields			Fixed-rate first mortgages	Dow Jones industrials (30 stocks)	Standard and Poor's composite (500 stocks) [2]	Nasdaq composite [3]
	Federal funds	Federal Reserve discount rate [1]	U.S. Treasury bills, 3-month	U.S. Treasury bills, 6-month	Bank prime rate	1-year	10-year	Domestic corporate (Moody's)		State and local bonds (Bond Buyer)				
								Aaa	Baa					
1991														
January	6.91	6.50	6.22	6.28	9.52	6.64	8.09	9.04	10.45	7.08	9.64	2 587.60	325.49	376.67
February	6.25	6.00	5.94	5.93	9.05	6.27	7.85	8.83	10.07	6.91	9.37	2 863.05	362.26	442.59
March	6.12	6.00	5.91	5.92	9.00	6.40	8.11	8.93	10.09	7.10	9.50	2 920.12	372.28	469.10
April	5.91	5.98	5.65	5.71	9.00	6.24	8.04	8.86	9.94	7.02	9.49	2 925.55	379.68	496.32
May	5.78	5.50	5.46	5.61	8.50	6.13	8.07	8.86	9.86	6.95	9.47	2 928.43	377.99	490.93
June	5.90	5.50	5.57	5.75	8.50	6.36	8.28	9.01	9.96	7.13	9.62	2 968.14	378.29	490.38
July	5.82	5.50	5.58	5.70	8.50	6.31	8.27	9.00	9.89	7.05	9.58	2 978.19	380.23	489.37
August	5.66	5.50	5.33	5.39	8.50	5.78	7.90	8.75	9.65	6.90	9.24	3 006.09	389.40	513.25
September	5.45	5.20	5.22	5.25	8.20	5.57	7.65	8.61	9.51	6.80	9.01	3 010.36	387.20	520.56
October	5.21	5.00	4.99	5.04	8.00	5.33	7.53	8.55	9.49	6.68	8.86	3 019.74	386.88	528.92
November	4.81	4.58	4.56	4.61	7.58	4.89	7.42	8.48	9.45	6.73	8.71	2 986.12	385.92	536.58
December	4.43	4.11	4.07	4.10	7.21	4.38	7.09	8.31	9.26	6.69	8.50	2 958.66	388.51	544.10
1992														
January	4.03	3.50	3.80	3.87	6.50	4.15	7.03	8.20	9.13	6.54	8.43	3 227.06	416.08	615.73
February	4.06	3.50	3.84	3.93	6.50	4.29	7.34	8.29	9.23	6.74	8.76	3 257.27	412.56	632.05
March	3.98	3.50	4.04	4.18	6.50	4.63	7.54	8.35	9.25	6.76	8.94	3 247.42	407.36	619.60
April	3.73	3.50	3.75	3.87	6.50	4.30	7.48	8.33	9.21	6.67	8.85	3 294.10	407.41	582.79
May	3.82	3.50	3.63	3.75	6.50	4.19	7.39	8.28	9.13	6.57	8.67	3 376.78	414.81	581.47
June	3.76	3.50	3.66	3.77	6.50	4.17	7.26	8.22	9.05	6.49	8.51	3 337.79	408.27	566.66
July	3.25	3.02	3.21	3.28	6.02	3.60	6.84	8.07	8.84	6.13	8.13	3 329.41	415.05	568.72
August	3.30	3.00	3.13	3.21	6.00	3.47	6.59	7.95	8.65	6.16	7.98	3 307.46	417.93	569.00
September	3.22	3.00	2.91	2.96	6.00	3.18	6.42	7.92	8.62	6.25	7.92	3 293.93	418.48	580.68
October	3.10	3.00	2.86	3.04	6.00	3.30	6.59	7.99	8.84	6.41	8.09	3 198.70	412.50	585.01
November	3.09	3.00	3.13	3.34	6.00	3.68	6.87	8.10	8.96	6.36	8.31	3 238.49	422.84	630.86
December	2.92	3.00	3.22	3.36	6.00	3.71	6.77	7.98	8.81	6.22	8.22	3 303.15	435.64	661.28
1993														
January	3.02	3.00	3.00	3.14	6.00	3.50	6.60	7.91	8.67	6.16	8.02	3 277.73	435.23	691.13
February	3.03	3.00	2.93	3.07	6.00	3.39	6.26	7.71	8.39	5.87	7.68	3 367.26	441.70	681.71
March	3.07	3.00	2.95	3.05	6.00	3.33	5.98	7.58	8.15	5.64	7.50	3 440.73	450.16	684.49
April	2.96	3.00	2.87	2.97	6.00	3.24	5.97	7.46	8.14	5.76	7.47	3 423.62	443.08	665.33
May	3.00	3.00	2.96	3.07	6.00	3.36	6.04	7.43	8.21	5.73	7.47	3 478.18	445.25	686.45
June	3.04	3.00	3.07	3.20	6.00	3.54	5.96	7.33	8.07	5.63	7.42	3 513.81	448.06	695.38
July	3.06	3.00	3.04	3.16	6.00	3.47	5.81	7.17	7.93	5.57	7.21	3 529.44	447.29	703.40
August	3.03	3.00	3.02	3.14	6.00	3.44	5.68	6.85	7.60	5.45	7.11	3 597.03	454.13	725.15
September	3.09	3.00	2.95	3.06	6.00	3.36	5.36	6.66	7.34	5.29	6.92	3 592.29	459.24	745.94
October	2.99	3.00	3.02	3.12	6.00	3.39	5.33	6.67	7.31	5.25	6.83	3 625.81	463.90	771.31
November	3.02	3.00	3.10	3.26	6.00	3.58	5.72	6.93	7.66	5.47	7.16	3 674.71	462.89	764.04
December	2.96	3.00	3.06	3.23	6.00	3.61	5.77	6.93	7.69	5.35	7.17	3 744.10	465.95	762.94
1994														
January	3.05	3.00	2.98	3.15	6.00	3.54	5.75	6.92	7.65	5.31	7.06	3 868.37	472.99	787.77
February	3.25	3.00	3.25	3.43	6.00	3.87	5.97	7.08	7.76	5.40	7.15	3 905.62	471.58	787.81
March	3.34	3.00	3.50	3.78	6.06	4.32	6.48	7.48	8.13	5.91	7.68	3 816.99	463.81	785.93
April	3.56	3.00	3.68	4.09	6.45	4.82	6.97	7.88	8.52	6.23	8.32	3 661.49	447.23	732.30
May	4.01	3.24	4.14	4.60	6.99	5.31	7.18	7.99	8.62	6.19	8.60	3 708.00	450.90	727.76
June	4.25	3.50	4.14	4.55	7.25	5.27	7.10	7.97	8.65	6.11	8.40	3 737.58	454.83	723.21
July	4.26	3.50	4.33	4.75	7.25	5.48	7.30	8.11	8.80	6.23	8.61	3 718.30	451.40	713.49
August	4.47	3.76	4.48	4.88	7.51	5.56	7.24	8.07	8.74	6.21	8.51	3 797.48	464.24	738.87
September	4.73	4.00	4.62	5.04	7.75	5.76	7.46	8.34	8.98	6.28	8.64	3 880.60	466.96	763.94
October	4.76	4.00	4.95	5.39	7.75	6.11	7.74	8.57	9.20	6.52	8.93	3 868.10	463.81	762.46
November	5.29	4.40	5.29	5.72	8.15	6.54	7.96	8.68	9.32	6.97	9.17	3 792.44	461.01	760.42
December	5.45	4.75	5.60	6.21	8.50	7.14	7.81	8.46	9.10	6.80	9.20	3 770.30	455.19	734.96
1995														
January	5.53	4.75	5.71	6.21	8.50	7.05	7.78	8.46	9.08	6.53	9.15	3 872.46	465.25	758.01
February	5.92	5.25	5.77	6.03	9.00	6.70	7.47	8.26	8.85	6.22	8.83	3 953.73	481.92	784.24
March	5.98	5.25	5.73	5.89	9.00	6.43	7.20	8.12	8.70	6.10	8.46	4 062.78	493.15	807.16
April	6.05	5.25	5.65	5.77	9.00	6.27	7.06	8.03	8.60	6.02	8.32	4 230.67	507.91	825.34
May	6.01	5.25	5.67	5.67	9.00	6.00	6.63	7.65	8.20	5.95	7.96	4 391.58	523.81	859.77
June	6.00	5.25	5.47	5.42	9.00	5.64	6.17	7.30	7.90	5.84	7.57	4 510.77	539.35	906.04
July	5.85	5.25	5.42	5.37	8.80	5.59	6.28	7.41	8.04	5.92	7.61	4 684.78	557.37	979.36
August	5.74	5.25	5.40	5.41	8.75	5.75	6.49	7.57	8.19	6.06	7.86	4 639.27	559.11	1 009.59
September	5.80	5.25	5.28	5.30	8.75	5.62	6.20	7.32	7.93	5.91	7.64	4 746.76	578.77	1 051.00
October	5.76	5.25	5.28	5.32	8.75	5.59	6.04	7.12	7.75	5.80	7.48	4 760.48	582.92	1 022.15
November	5.80	5.25	5.36	5.27	8.75	5.43	5.93	7.02	7.68	5.64	7.38	4 935.82	595.53	1 046.64
December	5.60	5.25	5.14	5.13	8.65	5.31	5.71	6.82	7.49	5.45	7.20	5 136.10	614.57	1 047.04
1996														
January	5.56	5.24	5.00	4.92	8.50	5.09	5.65	6.81	7.47	5.43	7.03	5 179.38	614.42	1 024.95
February	5.22	5.00	4.83	4.77	8.25	4.94	5.81	6.99	7.63	5.43	7.08	5 518.74	649.54	1 094.02
March	5.31	5.00	4.96	4.96	8.25	5.34	6.27	7.35	8.03	5.79	7.62	5 612.25	647.07	1 092.65
April	5.22	5.00	4.95	5.06	8.25	5.54	6.51	7.50	8.19	5.94	7.93	5 579.86	647.17	1 135.63
May	5.24	5.00	5.02	5.12	8.25	5.64	6.74	7.62	8.30	5.98	8.07	5 616.71	661.23	1 220.54
June	5.27	5.00	5.09	5.25	8.25	5.81	6.91	7.71	8.40	6.02	8.32	5 671.52	668.50	1 205.00
July	5.40	5.00	5.15	5.30	8.25	5.85	6.87	7.65	8.35	5.92	8.25	5 496.27	644.07	1 105.61
August	5.22	5.00	5.05	5.13	8.25	5.67	6.64	7.46	8.18	5.76	8.00	5 685.51	662.68	1 134.25
September	5.30	5.00	5.09	5.24	8.25	5.83	6.83	7.66	8.35	5.87	8.23	5 804.01	674.88	1 186.44
October	5.24	5.00	4.99	5.11	8.25	5.55	6.53	7.39	8.07	5.72	7.92	5 996.22	701.45	1 234.04
November	5.31	5.00	5.03	5.07	8.25	5.42	6.20	7.10	7.79	5.59	7.62	6 318.36	735.67	1 259.83
December	5.29	5.00	4.91	5.04	8.25	5.47	6.30	7.20	7.89	5.64	7.60	6 435.87	743.25	1 292.15

[1]Federal Reserve Bank of New York. Through 2002, represents the rate for adjustment credit. Beginning in 2003, represents the rate for primary credit. See notes and definitions for more information.
[2]1941–1943 = 10.
[3]February 5, 1971 = 100.

Table 20-6. Interest Rates, Bond Yields, and Stock Price Indexes—*Continued*

(Not seasonally adjusted.)

Year and month	Percent per annum											Stock price indexes		
	Short-term rates					U.S. Treasury securities		Bond yields			Fixed-rate first mortgages	Dow Jones industrials (30 stocks)	Standard and Poor's composite (500 stocks)[2]	Nasdaq composite[3]
	Federal funds	Federal Reserve discount rate[1]	U.S. Treasury bills, 3-month	U.S. Treasury bills, 6-month	Bank prime rate	1-year	10-year	Domestic corporate (Moody's)		State and local bonds (Bond Buyer)				
								Aaa	Baa					
1997														
January	5.25	5.00	5.03	5.10	8.25	5.61	6.58	7.42	8.09	5.72	7.82	6 707.05	766.22	1 345.41
February	5.19	5.00	5.01	5.06	8.25	5.53	6.42	7.31	7.94	5.63	7.65	6 917.46	798.39	1 349.17
March	5.39	5.00	5.14	5.26	8.30	5.80	6.69	7.55	8.18	5.76	7.90	6 901.14	792.16	1 282.86
April	5.51	5.00	5.16	5.37	8.50	5.99	6.89	7.73	8.34	5.88	8.14	6 657.51	763.93	1 225.00
May	5.50	5.00	5.05	5.30	8.50	5.87	6.71	7.58	8.20	5.70	7.94	7 242.33	833.09	1 352.56
June	5.56	5.00	4.93	5.13	8.50	5.69	6.49	7.41	8.02	5.53	7.69	7 599.61	·876.29	1 422.45
July	5.52	5.00	5.05	5.12	8.50	5.54	6.22	7.14	7.75	5.35	7.50	7 990.65	925.29	1 531.14
August	5.54	5.00	5.14	5.19	8.50	5.56	6.30	7.22	7.82	5.41	7.48	7 948.42	927.74	1 596.74
September	5.54	5.00	4.95	5.09	8.50	5.52	6.21	7.15	7.70	5.39	7.43	7 866.59	937.02	1 660.15
October	5.50	5.00	4.97	5.09	8.50	5.46	6.03	7.00	7.57	5.38	7.29	7 875.82	951.16	1 682.17
November	5.52	5.00	5.14	5.17	8.50	5.46	5.88	6.87	7.42	5.33	7.21	7 677.35	938.92	1 600.97
December	5.50	5.00	5.16	5.24	8.50	5.53	5.81	6.76	7.32	5.19	7.10	7 909.82	962.37	1 567.00
1998														
January	5.56	5.00	5.04	5.03	8.50	5.24	5.54	6.61	7.19	5.06	6.99	7 808.36	963.36	1 570.23
February	5.51	5.00	5.09	5.07	8.50	5.31	5.57	6.67	7.25	5.10	7.04	8 323.62	1 023.74	1 714.87
March	5.49	5.00	5.03	5.04	8.50	5.39	5.65	6.72	7.32	5.21	7.13	8 709.48	1 076.83	1 781.27
April	5.45	5.00	4.95	5.06	8.50	5.38	5.64	6.69	7.33	5.23	7.14	9 037.43	1 112.20	1 852.30
May	5.49	5.00	5.00	5.14	8.50	5.44	5.65	6.69	7.30	5.20	7.14	9 080.08	1 108.42	1 836.39
June	5.56	5.00	4.98	5.12	8.50	5.41	5.50	6.53	7.13	5.12	7.00	8 872.96	1 108.39	1 795.74
July	5.54	5.00	4.96	5.03	8.50	5.36	5.46	6.55	7.15	5.14	6.95	9 097.15	1 156.58	1 941.58
August	5.55	5.00	4.90	4.95	8.50	5.21	5.34	6.52	7.14	5.10	6.92	8 478.54	1 074.63	1 784.75
September	5.51	5.00	4.61	4.63	8.49	4.71	4.81	6.40	7.09	4.99	6.72	7 909.80	1 020.64	1 663.43
October	5.07	4.86	3.96	4.05	8.12	4.12	4.53	6.37	7.18	4.93	6.71	8 164.47	1 032.47	1 615.69
November	4.83	4.63	4.41	4.42	7.89	4.53	4.83	6.41	7.34	5.03	6.87	9 005.78	1 144.43	1 888.72
December	4.68	4.50	4.39	4.40	7.75	4.52	4.65	6.22	7.23	4.98	6.72	9 018.68	1 190.05	2 071.03
1999														
January	4.63	4.50	4.34	4.33	7.75	4.51	4.72	6.24	7.29	5.01	6.79	9 345.86	1 248.77	2 357.80
February	4.76	4.50	4.44	4.44	7.75	4.70	5.00	6.40	7.39	5.03	6.81	9 322.94	1 246.58	2 356.99
March	4.81	4.50	4.44	4.47	7.75	4.78	5.23	6.62	7.53	5.10	7.04	9 753.64	1 281.66	2 391.14
April	4.74	4.50	4.29	4.37	7.75	4.69	5.18	6.64	7.48	5.08	6.92	10 443.50	1 334.76	2 537.89
May	4.74	4.50	4.50	4.56	7.75	4.85	5.54	6.93	7.72	5.18	7.15	10 853.88	1 332.07	2 512.60
June	4.76	4.50	4.57	4.82	7.75	5.10	5.90	7.23	8.02	5.37	7.55	10 704.03	1 322.55	2 520.96
July	4.99	4.50	4.55	4.58	8.00	5.03	5.79	7.19	7.95	5.36	7.63	11 052.22	1 380.99	2 741.26
August	5.07	4.56	4.72	4.87	8.06	5.20	5.94	7.40	8.15	5.58	7.94	10 935.48	1 327.49	2 642.45
September	5.22	4.75	4.68	4.88	8.25	5.25	5.92	7.39	8.20	5.69	7.82	10 714.03	1 318.17	2 807.95
October	5.20	4.75	4.86	4.98	8.25	5.43	6.11	7.55	8.38	5.92	7.85	10 396.89	1 300.01	2 815.28
November	5.42	4.86	5.07	5.20	8.37	5.55	6.03	7.36	8.15	5.86	7.74	10 809.80	1 391.00	3 230.55
December	5.30	5.00	5.20	5.44	8.50	5.84	6.28	7.55	8.19	5.95	7.91	11 246.37	1 428.68	3 739.88
2000														
January	5.45	5.00	5.32	5.50	8.50	6.12	6.66	7.78	8.33	6.08	8.21	11 281.27	1 425.59	4 013.49
February	5.73	5.24	5.55	5.72	8.73	6.22	6.52	7.68	8.29	6.00	8.33	10 541.92	1 388.87	4 410.87
March	5.85	5.34	5.69	5.85	8.83	6.22	6.26	7.68	8.37	5.83	8.24	10 483.38	1 442.21	4 802.99
April	6.02	5.50	5.66	5.81	9.00	6.15	5.99	7.64	8.40	5.75	8.15	10 944.32	1 461.36	3 863.64
May	6.27	5.71	5.79	6.10	9.24	6.33	6.44	7.99	8.90	6.00	8.52	10 580.28	1 418.48	3 528.42
June	6.53	6.00	5.69	5.97	9.50	6.17	6.10	7.67	8.48	5.80	8.29	10 582.93	1 461.96	3 865.48
July	6.54	6.00	5.96	6.00	9.50	6.08	6.05	7.65	8.35	5.63	8.15	10 662.98	1 473.00	4 017.68
August	6.50	6.00	6.09	6.07	9.50	6.18	5.83	7.55	8.26	5.51	8.03	11 014.51	1 485.46	3 909.60
September	6.52	6.00	6.00	5.98	9.50	6.13	5.80	7.62	8.35	5.56	7.91	10 967.68	1 468.05	3 875.82
October	6.51	6.00	6.11	6.04	9.50	6.01	5.74	7.55	8.34	5.59	7.80	10 440.96	1 390.14	3 333.82
November	6.51	6.00	6.17	6.06	9.50	6.09	5.72	7.45	8.28	5.54	7.75	10 666.08	1 375.04	3 055.42
December	6.40	6.00	5.77	5.68	9.50	5.60	5.24	7.21	8.02	5.22	7.38	10 652.52	1 330.93	2 657.81
2001														
January	5.98	5.52	5.15	4.95	9.05	4.81	5.16	7.15	7.93	5.10	7.03	10 682.76	1 335.63	2 656.86
February	5.49	5.00	4.88	4.71	8.50	4.68	5.10	7.10	7.87	5.18	7.05	10 774.58	1 305.75	2 449.57
March	5.31	4.81	4.42	4.28	8.32	4.30	4.89	6.98	7.84	5.13	6.95	10 081.33	1 185.85	1 986.66
April	4.80	4.28	3.87	3.85	7.80	3.98	5.14	7.20	8.07	5.27	7.08	10 234.52	1 189.84	1 933.93
May	4.21	3.73	3.62	3.62	7.24	3.78	5.39	7.29	8.07	5.29	7.15	11 004.95	1 270.37	2 181.13
June	3.97	3.47	3.49	3.45	6.98	3.58	5.28	7.18	7.97	5.20	7.16	10 767.19	1 238.71	2 112.05
July	3.77	3.25	3.51	3.45	6.75	3.62	5.24	7.13	7.97	5.20	7.13	10 444.50	1 204.45	2 033.98
August	3.65	3.16	3.36	3.29	6.67	3.47	4.97	7.02	7.85	5.03	6.95	10 314.70	1 178.50	1 929.71
September	3.07	2.77	2.64	2.63	6.28	2.82	4.73	7.17	8.03	5.09	6.82	9 042.57	1 044.64	1 573.31
October	2.49	2.02	2.16	2.12	5.53	2.33	4.57	7.03	7.91	5.05	6.62	9 220.75	1 076.59	1 656.43
November	2.09	1.58	1.87	1.88	5.10	2.18	4.65	6.97	7.81	5.04	6.66	9 721.83	1 129.68	1 870.06
December	1.82	1.33	1.69	1.78	4.84	2.22	5.09	6.77	8.05	5.25	7.07	9 979.89	1 144.93	1 977.71
2002														
January	1.73	1.25	1.65	1.73	4.75	2.16	5.04	6.55	7.87	5.16	7.00	9 923.81	1 140.21	1 976.77
February	1.74	1.25	1.73	1.82	4.75	2.23	4.91	6.51	7.89	5.11	6.89	9 891.05	1 100.67	1 799.72
March	1.73	1.25	1.79	2.01	4.75	2.57	5.28	6.81	8.11	5.29	7.01	10 500.96	1 153.79	1 863.05
April	1.75	1.25	1.72	1.93	4.75	2.48	5.21	6.76	8.03	5.22	6.99	10 165.18	1 112.03	1 758.80
May	1.75	1.25	1.73	1.86	4.75	2.35	5.16	6.75	8.09	5.19	6.81	10 080.49	1 079.27	1 660.31
June	1.75	1.25	1.70	1.79	4.75	2.20	4.93	6.63	7.95	5.09	6.65	9 492.44	1 014.05	1 505.49
July	1.73	1.25	1.68	1.70	4.75	1.96	4.65	6.53	7.90	5.02	6.49	8 616.53	903.59	1 346.09
August	1.74	1.25	1.62	1.60	4.75	1.76	4.26	6.37	7.58	4.95	6.29	8 685.48	912.55	1 327.36
September	1.75	1.25	1.63	1.60	4.75	1.72	3.87	6.15	7.40	4.74	6.09	8 160.78	867.81	1 251.07
October	1.75	1.25	1.58	1.56	4.75	1.65	3.94	6.32	7.73	4.88	6.11	8 048.12	854.63	1 241.91
November	1.34	0.83	1.23	1.27	4.35	1.49	4.05	6.31	7.62	4.95	6.07	8 625.72	909.93	1 409.16
December	1.24	0.75	1.19	1.24	4.25	1.45	4.03	6.21	7.45	4.85	6.05	8 526.67	899.18	1 387.15

[1]Federal Reserve Bank of New York. Through 2002, represents the rate for adjustment credit. Beginning in 2003, represents the rate for primary credit. See notes and definitions for more information.
[2]1941–1943 = 10.
[3]February 5, 1971 = 100.

Table 20-6. Interest Rates, Bond Yields, and Stock Price Indexes—*Continued*

(Not seasonally adjusted.)

Year and month	Percent per annum											Stock price indexes		
	Short-term rates					U.S. Treasury securities		Bond yields				Dow Jones industrials (30 stocks)	Standard and Poor's composite (500 stocks) [2]	Nasdaq composite [3]
	Federal funds	Federal Reserve discount rate [1]	U.S. Treasury bills, 3-month	U.S. Treasury bills, 6-month	Bank prime rate	1-year	10-year	Domestic corporate (Moody's)		State and local bonds (Bond Buyer)	Fixed-rate first mortgages			
								Aaa	Baa					
2003														
January	1.24	. . .	1.17	1.20	4.25	1.36	4.05	6.17	7.35	4.90	5.92	8 474.59	895.84	1 389.56
February	1.26	2.25	1.17	1.18	4.25	1.30	3.90	5.95	7.06	4.81	5.84	7 916.18	837.62	1 313.26
March	1.25	2.25	1.13	1.13	4.25	1.24	3.81	5.89	6.95	4.76	5.75	7 977.73	846.62	1 348.50
April	1.26	2.25	1.13	1.14	4.25	1.27	3.96	5.74	6.85	4.74	5.81	8 332.09	890.03	1 409.83
May	1.26	2.25	1.07	1.08	4.25	1.18	3.57	5.22	6.38	4.41	5.48	8 623.41	935.96	1 524.18
June	1.22	2.20	0.92	0.92	4.22	1.01	3.33	4.97	6.19	4.33	5.23	9 098.07	988.00	1 631.75
July	1.01	2.00	0.90	0.95	4.00	1.12	3.98	5.49	6.62	4.74	5.63	9 154.39	992.54	1 716.85
August	1.03	2.00	0.95	1.03	4.00	1.31	4.45	5.88	7.01	5.10	6.26	9 284.78	989.53	1 724.82
September	1.01	2.00	0.94	1.01	4.00	1.24	4.27	5.72	6.79	4.92	6.15	9 492.54	1 019.44	1 856.22
October	1.01	2.00	0.92	1.00	4.00	1.25	4.29	5.70	6.73	4.89	5.95	9 682.46	1 038.73	1 907.89
November	1.00	2.00	0.93	1.02	4.00	1.34	4.30	5.65	6.66	4.73	5.93	9 762.20	1 049.90	1 939.25
December	0.98	2.00	0.90	0.99	4.00	1.31	4.27	5.62	6.60	4.65	5.88	10 124.66	1 080.64	1 956.98
2004														
January	1.00	2.00	0.88	0.97	4.00	1.24	4.15	5.54	6.44	4.61	5.74	10 540.05	1 132.52	2 098.00
February	1.01	2.00	0.93	0.99	4.00	1.24	4.08	5.50	6.27	4.55	5.64	10 601.50	1 143.36	2 048.36
March	1.00	2.00	0.94	0.99	4.00	1.19	3.83	5.33	6.11	4.41	5.45	10 323.73	1 123.98	1 979.48
April	1.00	2.00	0.94	1.09	4.00	1.43	4.35	5.73	6.46	4.82	5.83	10 418.40	1 133.08	2 021.32
May	1.00	2.00	1.02	1.31	4.00	1.78	4.72	6.04	6.75	5.07	6.27	10 083.81	1 102.78	1 930.09
June	1.03	2.01	1.27	1.60	4.01	2.12	4.73	6.01	6.78	5.05	6.29	10 364.90	1 132.76	2 000.98
July	1.26	2.25	1.33	1.66	4.25	2.10	4.50	5.82	6.62	4.87	6.06	10 152.09	1 105.85	1 912.42
August	1.43	2.43	1.48	1.72	4.43	2.02	4.28	5.65	6.46	4.70	5.87	10 032.80	1 088.94	1 821.54
September	1.61	2.58	1.65	1.87	4.58	2.12	4.13	5.46	6.27	4.56	5.75	10 204.67	1 117.66	1 884.73
October	1.76	2.75	1.76	2.00	4.75	2.23	4.10	5.47	6.21	4.49	5.72	10 001.60	1 118.07	1 938.25
November	1.93	2.93	2.07	2.27	4.93	2.50	4.19	5.52	6.20	4.52	5.73	10 411.76	1 168.94	2 062.87
December	2.16	3.15	2.19	2.43	5.15	2.67	4.23	5.47	6.15	4.48	5.75	10 673.38	1 199.21	2 149.53
2005														
January	2.28	3.25	2.33	2.61	5.25	2.86	4.22	5.36	6.02	4.41	5.71	10 539.51	1 181.41	2 071.87
February	2.50	3.49	2.54	2.77	5.49	3.03	4.17	5.20	5.82	4.35	5.63	10 723.82	1 199.63	2 065.74
March	2.63	3.58	2.74	3.00	5.58	3.30	4.50	5.40	6.06	4.57	5.93	10 682.09	1 194.90	2 030.43
April	2.79	3.75	2.78	3.05	5.75	3.32	4.34	5.33	6.05	4.46	5.86	10 283.19	1 164.42	1 957.49
May	3.00	3.98	2.84	3.08	5.98	3.33	4.14	5.15	6.01	4.31	5.72	10 377.18	1 178.28	2 005.22
June	3.04	4.01	2.97	3.13	6.01	3.36	4.00	4.96	5.86	4.23	5.58	10 486.68	1 202.26	2 074.02
July	3.26	4.25	3.22	3.42	6.25	3.64	4.18	5.06	5.95	4.31	5.70	10 545.38	1 222.24	2 145.14
August	3.50	4.44	3.44	3.66	6.44	3.87	4.26	5.09	5.96	4.32	5.82	10 554.27	1 224.27	2 157.85
September	3.62	4.59	3.42	3.67	6.59	3.85	4.20	5.13	6.03	4.29	5.77	10 532.54	1 225.91	2 144.61
October	3.78	4.75	3.71	3.99	6.75	4.18	4.46	5.35	6.30	4.49	6.07	10 324.31	1 191.96	2 087.09
November	4.00	5.00	3.88	4.15	7.00	4.33	4.54	5.42	6.39	4.57	6.33	10 695.25	1 237.37	2 202.84
December	4.16	5.15	3.89	4.18	7.15	4.35	4.47	5.37	6.32	4.46	6.27	10 827.79	1 262.07	2 246.09
2006														
January	4.29	5.26	4.24	4.31	7.26	4.45	4.42	5.29	6.24	4.37	6.15	10 872.48	1 278.72	2 289.99
February	4.49	5.50	4.43	4.52	7.50	4.68	4.57	5.35	6.27	4.41	6.25	10 971.19	1 276.65	2 273.67
March	4.59	5.53	4.51	4.62	7.53	4.77	4.72	5.53	6.41	4.44	6.32	11 144.45	1 293.74	2 300.26
April	4.79	5.75	4.60	4.72	7.75	4.90	4.99	5.84	6.68	4.58	6.51	11 234.68	1 302.18	2 338.68
May	4.94	5.93	4.72	4.82	7.93	5.00	5.11	5.95	6.75	4.59	6.60	11 333.88	1 290.00	2 245.28
June	4.99	6.02	4.79	4.97	8.02	5.16	5.11	5.89	6.78	4.60	6.68	10 997.97	1 253.12	2 137.41
July	5.24	6.25	4.95	5.06	8.25	5.22	5.09	5.85	6.76	4.61	6.76	11 032.53	1 260.24	2 086.21
August	5.25	6.25	4.96	4.97	8.25	5.08	4.88	5.68	6.59	4.39	6.52	11 257.35	1 287.15	2 117.77
September	5.25	6.25	4.81	4.89	8.25	4.97	4.72	5.51	6.43	4.27	6.40	11 533.60	1 317.81	2 221.94
October	5.25	6.25	4.92	4.92	8.25	5.01	4.73	5.51	6.42	4.30	6.36	11 963.12	1 363.38	2 330.17
November	5.25	6.25	4.94	4.95	8.25	5.01	4.60	5.33	6.20	4.14	6.24	12 185.15	1 388.63	2 408.70
December	5.24	6.25	4.85	4.88	8.25	4.94	4.56	5.32	6.22	4.11	6.14	12 377.62	1 416.42	2 431.91
2007														
January	5.25	6.25	4.98	4.95	8.25	5.06	4.76	5.40	6.34	4.23	6.22	12 512.89	1 424.16	2 453.19
February	5.26	6.25	5.03	4.96	8.25	5.05	4.72	5.39	6.28	4.22	6.29	12 631.48	1 444.79	2 479.86
March	5.26	6.25	4.94	4.89	8.25	4.92	4.56	5.30	6.27	4.15	6.16	12 268.53	1 406.95	2 401.49
April	5.25	6.25	4.87	4.86	8.25	4.93	4.69	5.47	6.39	4.26	6.18	12 754.80	1 463.65	2 499.57
May	5.25	6.25	4.73	4.78	8.25	4.91	4.75	5.47	6.39	4.31	6.26	13 407.76	1 511.14	2 562.14
June	5.25	6.25	4.61	4.76	8.25	4.96	5.10	5.79	6.70	4.60	6.66	13 480.21	1 514.49	2 595.40
July	5.26	6.25	4.82	4.83	8.25	4.96	5.00	5.73	6.65	4.56	6.70	13 677.89	1 520.70	2 655.08
August	5.02	6.01	4.20	4.38	8.25	4.47	4.67	5.79	6.65	4.64	6.57	13 239.71	1 454.62	2 539.50
September	4.94	5.53	3.89	4.05	8.03	4.14	4.52	5.74	6.59	4.51	6.38	13 557.69	1 497.12	2 634.47
October	4.76	5.24	3.90	4.01	7.74	4.10	4.53	5.66	6.48	4.39	6.38	13 901.28	1 539.66	2 780.42
November	4.49	5.00	3.27	3.46	7.50	3.50	4.15	5.44	6.40	4.46	6.21	13 200.58	1 463.39	2 662.80
December	4.24	4.83	3.00	3.23	7.33	3.26	4.10	5.49	6.65	4.42	6.10	13 406.99	1 479.23	2 661.55
2008														
January	3.94	4.48	2.75	2.75	6.98	2.71	3.74	5.33	6.54	4.27	5.76	12 538.12	1 378.76	2 418.09
February	2.98	3.50	2.12	2.04	6.00	2.05	3.74	5.53	6.82	4.64	5.92	12 419.57	1 354.87	2 325.83
March	2.61	3.04	1.26	1.48	5.66	1.54	3.51	5.51	6.89	4.93	5.97	12 193.88	1 316.94	2 254.82
April	2.28	2.49	1.29	1.55	5.24	1.74	3.68	5.55	6.97	4.70	5.92	12 656.63	1 370.47	2 368.10
May	1.98	2.25	1.73	1.82	5.00	2.06	3.88	5.57	6.93	4.58	6.04	12 812.48	1 403.22	2 483.24
June	2.00	2.25	1.86	2.13	5.00	2.42	4.10	5.68	7.07	4.69	6.32	12 056.67	1 341.25	2 427.45
July	2.01	2.25	1.63	1.93	5.00	2.28	4.01	5.67	7.16	4.68	6.43	11 322.38	1 257.33	2 278.14
August	2.00	2.25	1.72	1.92	5.00	2.18	3.89	5.64	7.15	4.69	6.48	11 530.75	1 281.47	2 389.27
September	1.81	2.25	1.13	1.61	5.00	1.91	3.69	5.65	7.31	4.86	6.04	11 114.08	1 217.01	2 205.20
October	0.97	1.81	0.67	1.20	4.56	1.42	3.81	6.28	8.88	5.50	6.20	9 176.71	968.80	1 730.32
November	0.39	1.25	0.19	0.73	4.00	1.07	3.53	6.12	9.21	5.23	6.09	8 614.55	883.04	1 542.70
December	0.16	0.86	0.03	0.26	3.61	0.49	2.42	5.05	8.43	5.56	5.33	8 595.56	877.56	1 525.89

[1] Federal Reserve Bank of New York. Through 2002, represents the rate for adjustment credit. Beginning in 2003, represents the rate for primary credit. See notes and definitions for more information.
[2] 1941–1943 = 10.
[3] February 5, 1971 = 100.
. . . = Not available.

NOTES AND DEFINITIONS, CHAPTER 20

TABLE 20-1
INDUSTRIAL PRODUCTION AND CAPACITY UTILIZATION

See the notes and definitions for Tables 2-1 through 2-3.

TABLE 20-2
SUMMARY CONSUMER AND PRODUCER PRICE INDEXES

See the notes and definitions for Tables 8-1 through 8-6.

TABLE 20-3
SUMMARY LABOR FORCE, EMPLOYMENT, AND UNEMPLOYMENT

See the notes and definitions for Tables 10-1 through 10-5.

TABLE 20-3A
LABOR FORCE AND EMPLOYMENT ESTIMATES SMOOTHED FOR POPULATION ADJUSTMENTS

SOURCE: U.S. DEPARTMENT OF LABOR, BUREAU OF LABOR STATISTICS

This table presents seasonally adjusted monthly estimates of total civilian labor force and total civilian employment in which discontinuities caused by the introduction of new population controls in the official series—as described in the notes and definitions for Tables 10-1 through 10-5—have been smoothed. They are taken from the article "Labor force and employment estimates smoothed for population adjustments, 1990–2009," which was posted on the Bureau of Labor Statistics (BLS) Web site on February 5, 2010. The method of smoothing is described in Marisa L. Di Natale, "Creating Comparability in CPS Employment Series," on the BLS Web site at <http://www.bls.gov/cps/cpscomp.pdf>. BLS notes that these series do not match the official estimates in BLS publications, which are also the data shown in all other tables in this volume.

TABLE 20-4
NONFARM PAYROLL EMPLOYMENT, HOURS, AND EARNINGS

See the notes and definitions for Tables 10-7 and 10-12 through 10-16.

TABLE 20-5A
MONEY STOCK AND RELATED DATA, 1947–1958

SOURCE: BOARD OF GOVERNORS OF THE FEDERAL RESERVE SYSTEM

This table extends monthly data on money supply back to 1947. These figures are not currently maintained online by the Federal Reserve and are found in *Banking and Monetary Statistics, 1941–1970*, Washington: Board of Governors

of the Federal Reserve System, 1976. They are not continuous with the currently maintained data for January 1959 forward that are shown in Table 20-5B. For that reason, the data on the 1976 basis for January 1959 are shown in Table 20-5A, for users who might need to calculate a factor to link the two sets of data.

Definitions and notes on the data

Money stock is the sum of the *currency component* and the *demand deposit component*. This is the narrowly defined money stock, best known as M1. As noted above, however, it is not continuous with the measure of M1 shown in Table 20-5B.

Currency component is all currency and coin outside the Treasury, Federal Reserve Banks, and commercial banks. Currency in circulation was reported by the U.S. Treasury Department. Member bank currency holdings were reported to the Federal Reserve, and nonmember bank holdings were estimated by the Federal Reserve.

Demand deposit component includes demand deposits held in commercial banks by individuals, partnerships, and corporations both domestic and foreign and demand deposits held by nonbank financial institutions and foreign banks. This measure also includes demand deposit liabilities to foreign governments, central banks, and international institutions—said to be "relatively small" in the source document. (Deposits held by foreign banks and official institutions are excluded from the current measure of M1 shown in Tables 20-5B and 12-1.) U.S. government deposits are excluded but deposits of state and local governments are included. To eliminate double counting, the following are also excluded: domestic commercial interbank deposits, cash items in the process of collection, and Federal Reserve float. (See the notes and definitions to Chapter 12 for explanation.)

Time deposits adjusted is time and savings deposits at commercial banks, other than large negotiable certificates of deposit (CDs), and excluding all deposits due to the U.S. government and domestic commercial banks. This can be added to M1 to yield a measure of M2, although the source document does not publish such a measure for the years shown here.

TABLE 20-5B
MONEY STOCK, RESERVES, AND MONETARY BASE

See the notes and definitions for Tables 12-1 through 12-3. Note that these data are not precisely continuous with the data for earlier years in Table 20-5A; see notes above.

TABLE 20-6
INTEREST RATES, BOND YIELDS, AND STOCK PRICE INDEXES

See the notes and definitions for Tables 12-9 and 12-10.

PART D

REGIONAL AND STATE DATA

CHAPTER 21: REGIONAL AND STATE DATA

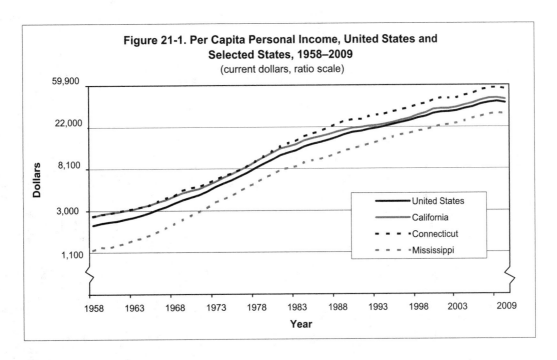

Figure 21-1. Per Capita Personal Income, United States and Selected States, 1958–2009
(current dollars, ratio scale)

- Per capita personal income (total personal income divided by the size of the population) provides one measure of the affluence of states and regions and how it has changed over time. To provide examples, Figure 21-1 shows the time path since 1958 for the U.S. total; for the largest state in terms of both population and total income (California); for the state with the highest per capita income in 2009 (Connecticut); and for the state with the lowest per capita income in 2009 (Mississippi). (The District of Columbia, which is shown in Tables 21-1 and 21-2 in order to complete the coverage of the United States, has even higher per capita income than Connecticut. However, DC data are not really comparable with state data, since DC consists entirely of a central city area, but one with a large proportion of high-earning residents.)

- The severity of the recession that began in December 2007 can be seen in the fact that in 2009, the current-dollar value of personal income per capita declined. For the U.S. total and for California, this was the first year-over-year decline in 51 years. The U.S. percentage decline was 2.6 percent, California saw a 3.5 percent drop, and Connecticut a 3.3 percent drop. (Table 21-2)

- These data are not adjusted to remove the effects of inflation or the effects of different costs of living in different states or regions. In addition, they are averages ("means") and—due to the skewed distribution of income—do not necessarily approximate the income of the typical, or "median," person in the state. Inflation-adjusted state median household income data are shown in Table 3-6 of this volume. (See the article at the beginning of this volume for a discussion of means and medians, under the heading "Whose Standard of Living?" The District of Columbia provides an extreme example of the difference. Despite its high per capita income, the District's <u>median</u> income is low and its poverty rate is high.) However, per capita income data can be useful for assessing and comparing the economic and fiscal capacities of the states.

Table 21-1. Gross Domestic Product by Region and State

(Billions of dollars; index numbers, 2000 = 100.)

Year	United States (sum of states) [1]	New England							Mideast						
		Total	Connecticut	Maine	Massachusetts	New Hampshire	Rhode Island	Vermont	Total	Delaware	District of Columbia	Maryland	New Jersey	New York	Pennsylvania
VALUE															
1977	1 986.1	103.4	29.3	7.6	49.6	6.3	7.3	3.4	402.8	6.0	15.1	35.4	66.6	179.2	100.4
1978	2 243.6	116.0	32.8	8.3	55.5	7.5	8.0	4.0	446.4	6.7	16.5	39.3	73.8	198.5	111.7
1979	2 491.4	128.7	36.4	9.2	61.4	8.4	8.9	4.5	488.6	7.3	18.0	43.2	82.1	215.7	122.3
1980	2 719.1	142.4	40.3	10.1	68.0	9.4	9.7	4.9	528.6	7.9	19.5	47.0	89.7	235.0	129.6
1981	3 064.6	159.3	45.1	11.1	76.2	10.6	10.8	5.5	585.6	8.9	21.4	52.7	99.9	261.3	141.4
1982	3 217.6	172.5	49.4	12.0	82.3	11.5	11.5	5.8	623.0	9.6	22.8	55.9	106.8	282.6	145.2
1983	3 451.3	190.4	54.4	13.1	91.4	12.7	12.4	6.4	676.2	10.7	24.3	61.8	119.0	305.2	155.2
1984	3 872.8	217.7	62.1	14.9	104.9	14.9	13.9	7.0	756.6	12.0	26.4	69.9	134.9	342.1	171.2
1985	4 155.0	239.0	67.4	16.1	115.6	16.9	15.3	7.7	814.6	13.2	28.5	77.3	147.6	366.8	181.2
1986	4 364.3	261.2	73.5	17.5	126.4	18.8	16.7	8.3	874.9	14.2	30.1	84.4	160.5	394.1	191.7
1987	4 663.3	287.7	81.3	19.3	138.5	21.5	17.9	9.3	945.8	15.6	32.2	92.1	175.7	423.8	206.5
1988	5 067.5	315.3	89.3	21.6	151.2	23.2	19.7	10.4	1 037.3	17.0	35.3	102.0	196.4	462.8	223.8
1989	5 385.8	331.2	94.6	22.8	157.7	23.9	20.9	11.3	1 089.7	19.0	37.7	108.5	206.4	481.3	236.7
1990	5 674.0	338.3	99.0	23.3	158.9	23.8	21.5	11.7	1 140.7	20.1	40.1	113.7	214.8	503.6	248.3
1991	5 857.3	341.9	100.2	23.4	160.2	24.8	21.6	11.7	1 168.7	21.9	41.8	116.2	221.7	508.9	258.1
1992	6 174.4	356.8	104.2	24.2	166.6	26.6	22.6	12.6	1 225.5	23.0	43.8	119.5	233.2	532.6	273.5
1993	6 453.5	368.8	106.3	25.0	173.2	27.6	23.6	13.1	1 271.7	23.6	45.7	124.7	243.4	549.2	285.0
1994	6 865.5	390.3	111.2	26.2	185.3	29.5	24.4	13.7	1 326.3	25.1	46.8	132.1	254.5	569.4	298.3
1995	7 232.7	415.4	120.8	27.6	195.3	32.1	25.7	13.9	1 387.7	27.5	47.1	137.4	266.7	594.4	314.5
1996	7 659.7	439.8	126.7	28.6	208.3	34.8	26.7	14.6	1 456.7	28.9	47.6	142.9	281.8	630.0	325.5
1997	8 171.0	472.0	137.5	29.9	223.0	37.1	29.0	15.5	1 539.2	31.3	49.4	152.3	296.1	668.1	342.0
1997 [2]	8 238.0	470.6	137.7	30.9	221.8	36.6	28.5	15.2	1 539.0	35.5	50.4	154.1	300.9	654.8	343.4
1998 [2]	8 679.7	497.8	145.4	31.7	236.1	39.1	29.5	15.9	1 613.3	36.8	51.7	162.0	314.1	686.9	361.8
1999 [2]	9 201.1	524.1	150.3	33.4	252.6	40.2	30.8	16.8	1 700.9	39.4	56.4	171.4	327.3	730.3	376.1
2000 [2]	9 749.1	565.8	160.4	35.5	274.9	43.5	33.6	17.8	1 792.1	41.5	58.7	180.4	344.8	777.2	389.6
2001 [2]	10 058.2	580.9	165.0	37.1	280.5	44.3	35.1	18.8	1 878.8	44.2	63.7	192.7	363.0	808.5	406.7
2002 [2]	10 398.4	591.7	166.1	38.6	284.4	46.2	36.9	19.6	1 934.6	45.3	67.7	204.1	372.8	821.6	423.1
2003 [2]	10 886.2	612.0	169.9	40.2	293.8	48.2	39.4	20.6	2 013.6	48.6	71.7	213.3	389.1	850.2	440.7
2004 [2]	11 607.0	647.5	182.1	43.2	306.8	51.4	42.1	21.8	2 124.9	52.3	77.9	228.2	410.1	896.4	459.9
2005 [2]	12 339.0	671.8	190.5	44.5	317.4	53.5	43.1	22.8	2 246.3	57.6	83.4	241.5	425.5	956.4	482.0
2006 [2]	13 090.8	707.7	201.6	46.3	334.5	56.1	45.5	23.7	2 389.1	59.2	88.1	253.0	445.7	1 034.1	509.0
2007 [2]	13 715.7	741.6	212.3	48.0	352.2	57.8	46.7	24.6	2 518.0	61.5	92.5	264.4	461.3	1 105.0	533.2
2008 [2]	14 165.6	763.7	216.2	49.7	365.0	60.0	47.4	25.4	2 605.1	61.8	97.2	273.3	474.9	1 144.5	553.3
QUANTITY INDEX															
1977	47.7	42.3	43.6	51.4	41.7	29.4	51.0	41.3	54.2	44.3	80.8	49.4	45.7	54.9	59.9
1978	50.3	44.6	45.9	52.9	44.0	32.5	52.5	45.5	56.4	46.2	83.2	51.4	47.6	57.1	62.2
1979	51.8	46.3	47.7	54.3	45.6	34.4	54.2	47.5	57.7	46.5	84.3	52.7	49.5	58.2	63.4
1980	51.8	47.2	48.6	55.3	46.5	35.4	54.2	49.0	57.4	45.7	83.9	52.9	49.6	58.3	62.2
1981	53.2	48.4	49.7	55.9	47.8	36.7	55.5	50.6	58.3	46.6	82.7	54.1	50.7	59.3	62.4
1982	52.5	49.0	50.8	56.8	48.2	37.3	55.2	50.2	58.0	47.5	80.8	53.7	50.8	60.0	60.1
1983	54.0	51.6	53.2	59.2	51.1	39.7	56.7	52.3	60.0	51.0	81.4	56.3	54.2	61.4	60.1
1984	58.1	56.4	57.9	63.7	56.1	44.9	61.0	55.1	64.1	55.0	83.5	60.6	58.7	65.7	65.2
1985	60.6	59.9	60.9	67.0	59.8	49.2	64.8	58.7	66.3	58.7	85.1	64.5	61.9	67.5	66.9
1986	61.8	63.1	63.9	70.2	63.0	52.8	67.9	61.2	68.4	60.1	85.8	67.7	64.8	69.5	68.1
1987	64.4	67.8	69.1	74.9	67.3	58.9	70.6	66.3	72.0	64.4	88.6	71.4	69.0	72.9	71.7
1988	67.7	72.0	73.6	80.5	71.3	61.8	75.3	72.1	76.2	67.3	92.3	76.2	74.2	77.0	74.8
1989	69.2	72.7	74.7	82.0	71.6	61.3	77.1	75.1	77.0	72.2	94.4	78.0	75.1	77.2	76.1
1990	70.3	71.4	75.1	81.0	69.4	58.9	76.4	75.8	77.7	73.8	96.5	78.8	75.3	77.7	77.1
1991	70.0	69.5	73.2	78.4	67.3	59.2	73.6	73.4	76.5	76.3	94.6	77.3	74.8	75.4	77.3
1992	72.0	70.6	74.0	79.1	68.1	62.0	74.9	77.2	77.9	76.7	95.7	77.3	76.9	76.4	79.9
1993	73.3	71.0	73.3	79.3	68.9	62.9	76.0	78.2	78.7	76.7	96.7	78.4	78.0	76.7	81.0
1994	76.3	73.4	74.7	80.9	72.1	65.5	76.6	80.3	80.2	79.2	96.1	80.8	79.6	78.0	82.7
1995	78.8	76.4	79.2	82.5	74.4	70.5	78.9	80.2	81.9	83.5	93.2	81.8	81.5	79.6	85.3
1996	82.1	79.6	81.5	84.7	78.1	75.8	80.5	83.6	84.6	85.1	91.5	83.6	85.0	82.8	87.2
1997	86.3	84.0	86.7	87.5	82.2	80.1	85.6	87.3	87.7	88.6	92.4	87.3	87.7	86.3	90.2
1997 [2]	88.4	86.2	90.3	93.8	82.6	84.1	90.6	87.2	89.6	92.3	93.2	90.2	91.7	86.3	93.1
1998 [2]	92.4	90.4	94.0	93.9	87.5	90.9	92.0	91.1	92.8	93.7	93.9	93.7	94.5	89.9	96.6
1999 [2]	96.5	94.0	95.6	96.4	92.8	93.3	94.0	95.3	96.5	98.3	99.4	97.2	96.9	94.8	98.7
2000 [2]	100.0	100.0	100.0	100.0	100.0	100.0	100.0	100.0	100.0	100.0	100.0	100.0	100.0	100.0	100.0
2001 [2]	100.9	100.8	100.5	101.8	100.6	100.2	101.7	104.3	102.5	103.6	104.9	103.9	103.0	100.2	101.5
2002 [2]	102.4	100.5	98.9	103.3	100.0	102.4	103.9	106.3	103.3	103.5	107.0	107.3	103.8	101.9	103.4
2003 [2]	104.9	102.4	99.4	105.1	102.2	105.4	108.6	110.2	105.7	108.2	110.2	109.8	106.3	104.0	105.6
2004 [2]	108.5	105.5	103.4	109.5	104.2	109.7	112.6	114.0	108.4	112.5	115.1	114.0	109.0	106.8	106.8
2005 [2]	111.9	106.9	105.4	109.8	105.4	111.5	112.3	116.5	111.5	120.3	119.3	117.2	109.9	111.4	108.4
2006 [2]	115.1	109.6	108.6	110.8	108.3	113.2	114.5	118.1	115.1	119.7	121.7	118.8	111.5	117.5	110.6
2007 [2]	117.3	112.1	111.2	111.9	111.5	114.1	114.4	120.0	118.1	120.7	123.8	120.8	112.5	122.2	112.6
2008 [2]	118.2	113.2	110.8	113.5	113.6	116.2	113.4	122.0	119.6	118.7	127.5	122.5	113.2	124.1	113.9

[1]See notes and definitions for explanation.
[2]NAICS basis, not continuous with previous years, which are based on the SIC.

Table 21-1. Gross Domestic Product by Region and State—*Continued*

(Billions of dollars; index numbers, 2000 = 100.)

Year	Great Lakes						Plains							
	Total	Illinois	Indiana	Michigan	Ohio	Wisconsin	Total	Iowa	Kansas	Minnesota	Missouri	Nebraska	North Dakota	South Dakota
VALUE														
1977	390.7	115.7	47.8	88.3	97.9	41.0	149.1	26.4	20.5	36.4	41.7	13.7	5.3	5.2
1978	434.9	128.8	53.7	98.0	108.6	45.8	169.1	30.1	22.8	41.1	46.9	15.7	6.5	6.0
1979	470.5	139.9	57.8	103.8	118.3	50.6	188.2	32.8	26.3	46.4	51.4	17.3	7.3	6.8
1980	483.6	146.4	58.7	102.4	122.7	53.4	198.1	34.0	28.2	49.7	53.4	18.1	7.7	6.9
1981	530.7	160.8	64.6	113.0	134.2	58.0	222.1	37.9	32.0	55.0	58.7	20.8	10.0	7.8
1982	539.2	165.2	64.7	113.4	135.9	60.0	228.0	36.9	33.5	57.0	61.6	21.2	10.0	7.8
1983	577.7	173.5	69.0	125.5	146.1	63.7	239.7	37.0	35.2	61.0	66.5	21.7	10.1	8.2
1984	650.8	194.7	78.6	141.5	165.4	70.7	270.3	41.0	38.4	70.3	75.9	24.6	10.7	9.3
1985	690.7	206.5	81.8	151.8	176.0	74.6	283.6	42.4	40.8	74.8	79.4	25.8	10.7	9.7
1986	729.2	218.5	86.1	161.5	184.5	78.5	293.8	43.1	41.7	78.2	84.7	26.1	9.8	10.2
1987	763.8	230.6	91.2	166.9	192.8	82.4	310.6	45.1	43.9	83.9	89.8	26.8	10.3	10.7
1988	823.4	251.1	98.7	177.4	206.3	89.9	331.9	48.9	46.3	90.0	96.5	29.3	9.7	11.2
1989	872.2	265.2	106.5	186.7	218.5	95.4	353.2	52.8	48.3	96.2	102.0	31.4	10.7	11.9
1990	905.7	277.2	110.1	189.7	228.3	100.3	369.7	55.9	51.3	100.3	104.1	33.8	11.5	12.8
1991	934.3	286.6	113.8	194.3	234.7	104.9	385.5	57.7	53.3	103.8	109.5	35.6	11.7	13.8
1992	997.9	304.0	123.6	207.4	250.2	112.8	410.2	61.3	56.1	111.9	115.2	38.0	12.8	14.9
1993	1 046.9	317.2	130.6	221.3	258.3	119.6	421.9	62.7	57.9	114.9	118.3	39.1	12.9	16.0
1994	1 137.5	343.4	141.2	246.1	278.5	128.4	458.0	69.2	61.8	124.7	128.5	42.8	14.0	17.0
1995	1 186.1	359.7	148.0	251.0	293.3	134.1	481.3	71.9	63.7	131.4	137.5	44.5	14.5	17.8
1996	1 243.8	377.3	155.5	263.9	305.4	141.8	515.4	77.2	68.0	141.7	145.0	48.3	16.1	19.1
1997	1 318.3	401.1	164.2	278.8	325.4	148.8	546.5	81.9	72.5	152.2	154.5	49.8	16.1	19.5
1997 [2]	1 354.8	404.0	168.1	299.0	332.1	151.5	554.8	81.9	72.1	155.9	158.2	50.5	16.3	19.8
1998 [2]	1 421.6	423.9	178.9	309.4	348.7	160.7	578.6	83.7	76.0	164.9	164.3	52.1	16.9	20.8
1999 [2]	1 485.3	443.8	185.7	326.2	360.6	169.0	598.5	86.1	78.7	172.9	169.0	53.4	16.9	21.6
2000 [2]	1 543.6	464.2	194.4	337.2	372.0	175.7	631.1	90.2	82.8	185.1	176.7	55.5	17.8	23.1
2001 [2]	1 562.7	476.5	195.2	334.4	374.7	181.9	650.8	91.9	86.4	190.2	182.4	57.4	18.5	23.9
2002 [2]	1 620.4	487.1	205.0	349.8	389.8	188.6	680.1	97.4	89.6	198.6	188.4	59.9	19.9	26.4
2003 [2]	1 683.1	510.3	215.4	359.0	402.4	195.9	713.2	102.2	93.6	208.2	195.5	64.6	21.7	27.4
2004 [2]	1 755.5	534.4	228.3	363.1	423.7	205.9	759.4	111.9	98.4	223.5	204.9	68.4	22.7	29.5
2005 [2]	1 811.5	553.0	232.9	372.0	438.8	214.8	790.6	115.8	102.9	232.8	213.2	71.0	24.3	30.7
2006 [2]	1 877.8	588.9	239.9	375.1	449.0	224.9	823.1	121.1	109.9	240.9	219.7	75.0	25.4	31.2
2007 [2]	1 942.5	617.4	249.2	379.9	462.5	233.4	872.5	129.9	117.0	252.5	229.0	80.4	28.5	35.2
2008 [2]	1 983.0	633.7	254.9	382.5	471.5	240.4	910.5	135.7	122.7	262.8	237.8	83.3	31.2	37.0
QUANTITY INDEX														
1977	57.7	56.7	54.5	63.7	58.9	50.8	52.3	58.6	56.7	43.4	55.6	52.5	62.3	48.1
1978	60.1	59.2	57.1	66.1	61.1	53.2	55.1	62.0	58.2	45.7	58.4	55.7	69.8	51.5
1979	60.7	60.0	57.3	65.3	62.1	54.9	57.0	63.2	61.8	47.8	59.8	57.2	71.8	53.8
1980	57.8	58.1	54.2	59.4	59.6	54.1	55.8	62.0	61.0	47.7	57.6	56.6	69.0	51.6
1981	58.2	58.8	54.9	59.6	60.1	54.3	57.7	64.2	62.9	49.1	58.1	60.0	79.4	54.6
1982	55.6	56.7	51.8	55.8	57.0	53.1	56.3	60.0	62.3	48.3	57.4	58.7	76.4	53.0
1983	57.3	57.2	52.9	59.5	59.2	54.0	56.5	57.2	62.4	49.6	59.1	57.0	74.5	52.2
1984	62.0	61.5	57.9	64.6	64.5	57.5	61.1	61.0	65.4	54.9	64.5	61.6	76.6	56.5
1985	64.1	63.2	59.1	67.6	66.9	59.6	63.0	62.6	68.2	57.3	65.5	64.3	77.2	58.9
1986	65.1	64.5	60.1	68.9	67.6	60.5	63.2	61.8	68.2	57.7	67.2	63.0	71.6	59.5
1987	66.8	66.6	62.3	69.5	69.3	61.9	65.2	63.1	70.3	60.5	69.5	63.2	73.3	60.8
1988	69.8	70.1	65.2	72.1	71.7	65.6	67.4	66.4	71.8	62.6	72.2	66.6	67.3	61.2
1989	71.2	71.4	67.7	73.0	73.1	66.9	69.1	68.9	72.3	64.4	73.6	68.7	71.2	62.2
1990	71.5	72.1	67.9	71.8	73.9	68.0	69.9	70.8	73.8	65.0	72.6	71.6	73.5	65.4
1991	71.1	71.9	67.9	70.6	73.3	68.9	70.7	71.1	74.5	65.0	73.6	73.7	73.3	68.7
1992	74.1	74.5	72.1	73.2	76.3	72.6	73.5	74.2	76.5	68.6	75.5	76.8	78.7	72.1
1993	75.8	75.7	74.3	75.9	76.8	75.3	73.7	74.2	76.8	68.6	75.8	77.1	77.5	75.8
1994	80.3	80.1	78.4	82.2	80.8	78.9	78.1	80.0	80.2	72.6	79.9	82.6	82.7	78.8
1995	82.2	82.3	80.8	82.3	83.5	80.4	80.4	82.1	81.1	74.6	83.8	84.1	84.0	80.9
1996	85.1	85.2	84.0	85.1	85.9	84.1	84.5	86.5	84.5	79.3	87.0	88.9	90.1	84.4
1997	89.0	89.2	87.7	88.9	90.4	87.6	88.8	91.6	89.2	84.3	91.3	91.2	90.0	86.3
1997 [2]	92.6	91.6	91.0	94.1	94.2	91.2	92.4	95.0	91.9	88.1	95.2	95.1	95.9	87.3
1998 [2]	95.7	94.8	95.2	95.8	97.5	95.0	95.1	95.8	95.9	92.2	97.1	96.8	98.7	91.2
1999 [2]	98.2	97.6	97.4	98.7	99.1	98.1	96.8	97.1	97.6	95.2	97.9	98.0	97.1	94.5
2000 [2]	100.0	100.0	100.0	100.0	100.0	100.0	100.0	100.0	100.0	100.0	100.0	100.0	100.0	100.0
2001 [2]	98.8	100.2	97.9	96.9	98.3	101.0	100.5	99.1	101.3	100.7	100.6	100.6	100.9	101.1
2002 [2]	100.7	100.4	101.2	99.9	100.4	102.6	103.0	102.9	103.0	103.3	101.8	102.6	106.0	109.6
2003 [2]	102.8	103.3	104.7	101.1	101.8	104.8	105.7	105.6	104.7	106.3	103.7	107.9	111.8	111.2
2004 [2]	104.3	105.0	107.8	100.2	104.1	107.0	109.0	111.9	106.6	110.8	105.5	109.8	112.5	115.0
2005 [2]	105.0	105.6	107.0	100.8	105.0	109.1	111.0	113.8	108.7	112.6	107.0	112.1	117.5	118.6
2006 [2]	105.7	108.9	107.1	99.3	104.1	110.9	112.2	115.9	112.5	113.1	106.9	115.0	119.0	117.2
2007 [2]	106.4	110.9	108.6	98.2	104.4	112.1	115.0	119.9	115.9	115.0	108.2	118.4	127.4	126.7
2008 [2]	106.0	111.2	108.0	96.7	103.6	112.9	117.4	122.4	118.5	117.3	109.7	120.0	136.7	131.2

[2]NAICS basis, not continuous with previous years, which are based on the SIC.

Table 21-1. Gross Domestic Product by Region and State—*Continued*

(Billions of dollars; index numbers, 2000 = 100.)

Year	Southeast												
	Total	Alabama	Arkansas	Florida	Georgia	Kentucky	Louisiana	Mississippi	North Carolina	South Carolina	Tennessee	Virginia	West Virginia
VALUE													
1977	389.5	26.5	15.0	66.3	40.9	28.6	39.6	16.0	44.0	20.3	33.7	44.0	14.7
1978	443.5	30.4	17.3	77.1	46.3	32.1	45.2	17.9	50.2	23.2	38.4	49.2	16.3
1979	494.8	33.5	18.9	88.2	51.6	35.2	51.8	20.2	54.9	25.8	42.4	54.4	17.7
1980	546.9	36.0	20.1	100.6	56.3	36.6	64.0	21.5	59.3	28.0	45.4	60.0	19.0
1981	621.0	40.1	22.7	115.3	63.7	40.7	77.6	24.3	66.4	31.5	50.7	67.6	20.5
1982	651.7	41.5	23.3	124.8	68.3	41.7	78.5	24.9	69.4	32.8	52.4	72.9	21.3
1983	707.2	45.2	25.0	139.5	76.6	43.4	77.3	26.2	78.2	36.3	57.5	81.0	21.0
1984	796.8	49.7	28.2	158.8	88.6	48.8	83.0	29.1	89.3	41.9	64.6	91.8	22.8
1985	858.2	53.7	29.1	173.8	98.7	51.5	84.8	30.6	98.0	44.9	69.3	100.4	23.6
1986	906.3	56.0	30.4	188.1	108.4	53.3	75.9	31.3	106.2	48.5	74.1	110.0	24.0
1987	976.6	60.6	32.2	206.9	116.8	56.6	76.5	33.6	114.1	53.2	81.2	120.1	24.7
1988	1 058.7	65.4	34.5	226.6	126.1	60.7	82.3	35.7	125.2	58.0	87.5	130.4	26.2
1989	1 125.2	67.9	36.6	243.3	133.1	64.7	86.2	37.3	134.6	62.0	91.9	140.2	27.3
1990	1 181.7	71.1	38.1	257.2	139.5	67.5	93.6	38.8	140.3	65.7	94.6	147.0	28.3
1991	1 234.4	75.3	41.0	267.9	146.3	70.5	94.3	40.8	146.5	68.4	101.4	152.7	29.4
1992	1 309.7	80.5	44.3	283.8	158.3	76.6	88.9	43.7	159.2	71.6	111.3	160.5	31.0
1993	1 384.0	83.5	46.6	302.1	169.0	80.4	93.2	46.7	167.2	75.5	118.9	168.6	32.4
1994	1 485.3	88.6	50.2	322.1	184.3	86.3	101.9	50.6	179.6	81.0	128.9	177.0	34.9
1995	1 575.5	94.0	53.3	340.5	199.1	90.5	109.2	53.8	191.6	86.1	135.7	185.5	36.4
1996	1 664.3	97.9	56.5	363.0	215.1	95.0	115.0	56.0	201.3	89.3	141.3	196.6	37.3
1997	1 768.9	102.5	58.7	384.0	230.4	101.8	121.7	58.3	218.4	94.9	151.0	208.6	38.5
1997 [2]	1 797.9	102.4	59.2	391.5	237.5	105.7	113.3	58.0	228.9	97.4	153.4	211.9	38.8
1998 [2]	1 901.5	106.7	61.9	417.2	255.6	108.8	118.1	60.5	242.9	102.9	160.9	226.6	39.5
1999 [2]	2 022.5	111.9	65.6	442.6	277.1	113.5	124.0	63.0	262.7	108.7	169.6	242.7	41.1
2000 [2]	2 114.5	114.6	66.8	471.3	290.9	111.9	131.5	64.3	273.7	112.5	174.9	260.7	41.5
2001 [2]	2 202.9	118.7	68.9	497.4	299.4	115.1	133.7	66.0	285.7	117.3	180.6	276.8	43.4
2002 [2]	2 288.9	123.8	72.2	522.7	306.7	120.7	134.3	68.1	296.4	121.6	191.5	285.8	45.0
2003 [2]	2 409.9	130.2	75.7	559.0	317.9	124.9	146.7	72.3	306.0	127.9	200.3	302.5	46.5
2004 [2]	2 586.7	141.5	82.1	607.3	338.5	131.7	163.4	76.5	324.4	131.9	214.8	324.9	49.7
2005 [2]	2 782.4	150.6	86.5	670.0	359.5	138.6	183.0	79.5	348.4	138.6	223.8	350.9	52.9
2006 [2]	2 959.2	158.9	90.7	721.4	375.6	146.4	197.6	83.8	378.6	146.5	236.1	368.0	55.8
2007 [2]	3 069.2	164.5	95.1	741.9	391.2	152.1	207.4	87.7	390.5	151.7	245.2	384.1	57.9
2008 [2]	3 148.0	170.0	98.3	744.1	397.8	156.4	222.2	91.8	400.2	156.4	252.1	397.0	61.7
QUANTITY INDEX													
1977	44.2	52.2	49.3	35.2	33.3	53.1	73.1	54.4	40.2	40.5	43.9	44.8	73.7
1978	46.9	55.6	52.9	38.3	35.3	55.5	76.6	56.2	42.7	43.5	46.9	46.9	75.2
1979	48.4	57.1	53.6	40.9	37.0	56.9	75.7	58.3	44.0	45.4	48.4	48.5	76.0
1980	49.0	56.8	52.8	43.1	37.4	55.3	78.0	57.3	44.2	45.7	47.9	49.3	75.8
1981	50.6	57.8	54.7	45.1	38.8	56.9	80.5	59.3	45.7	47.3	49.1	50.7	74.8
1982	50.0	56.3	53.2	45.8	39.3	54.9	77.4	57.4	44.7	46.4	48.0	50.9	72.9
1983	51.9	58.9	54.9	48.5	41.9	54.7	76.5	58.5	47.0	49.3	50.6	53.2	70.1
1984	56.1	62.0	59.3	52.6	46.2	59.3	81.1	62.7	51.3	54.3	54.5	57.1	74.1
1985	58.7	65.2	60.1	55.4	49.8	61.4	82.5	64.7	54.7	56.4	56.7	60.0	74.8
1986	60.4	65.9	61.1	57.6	52.7	61.2	80.5	64.5	56.8	58.9	58.5	63.1	75.3
1987	63.3	69.5	63.1	61.3	55.1	63.7	80.2	68.3	59.1	62.9	62.4	66.7	76.1
1988	66.4	72.4	65.5	64.8	57.4	66.3	84.3	70.0	62.5	66.1	64.9	69.9	78.5
1989	67.9	72.4	66.9	67.1	58.5	68.2	83.8	70.6	64.4	68.3	65.7	72.3	79.3
1990	68.8	73.6	67.5	68.4	59.3	69.0	85.3	70.7	64.7	70.3	65.3	73.1	80.5
1991	69.3	75.5	70.5	68.6	60.0	69.4	85.0	72.1	64.6	70.7	67.5	72.6	81.1
1992	71.7	78.8	74.6	70.9	63.3	73.4	79.2	75.5	68.1	72.4	72.4	74.0	84.1
1993	73.9	79.7	76.6	73.3	65.9	75.4	80.6	78.4	70.0	74.7	75.3	75.8	86.4
1994	77.9	82.6	80.6	76.3	70.4	80.0	87.1	83.2	74.9	78.5	79.7	78.4	91.0
1995	80.9	85.2	83.9	78.9	74.3	82.8	91.5	87.1	78.6	81.3	82.2	80.4	93.3
1996	84.1	87.8	87.5	82.7	79.2	85.7	92.3	89.3	81.4	83.5	84.6	83.7	95.2
1997	88.0	90.8	90.5	86.1	83.5	90.9	95.6	91.7	87.1	87.9	89.1	87.1	96.9
1997 [2]	90.3	93.9	93.5	88.0	86.2	99.7	98.0	95.9	87.6	91.8	93.2	86.7	97.9
1998 [2]	94.2	96.6	96.2	92.4	91.5	101.1	102.4	98.5	91.7	95.2	96.2	91.1	98.4
1999 [2]	98.2	99.9	100.4	96.2	97.2	103.4	104.2	100.6	97.6	98.6	99.3	95.4	101.3
2000 [2]	100.0	100.0	100.0	100.0	100.0	100.0	100.0	100.0	100.0	100.0	100.0	100.0	100.0
2001 [2]	101.5	100.9	100.3	102.9	100.7	100.2	98.3	99.5	101.7	101.4	100.8	103.4	101.1
2002 [2]	103.2	103.2	103.1	105.5	101.1	103.2	98.6	100.5	103.2	102.8	104.7	104.0	102.4
2003 [2]	106.3	106.1	105.9	110.4	103.0	104.8	100.3	103.6	104.6	106.3	107.8	107.9	102.8
2004 [2]	110.6	111.6	111.1	116.4	106.8	107.2	105.9	105.7	108.0	106.5	112.8	112.8	105.7
2005 [2]	115.4	115.4	114.5	125.0	110.9	109.9	106.7	106.5	113.2	109.1	114.9	118.6	107.7
2006 [2]	118.6	117.8	116.1	130.2	112.2	112.4	108.8	108.3	119.4	111.3	118.0	120.6	108.3
2007 [2]	119.7	118.8	117.8	130.1	113.9	113.5	109.8	109.8	120.2	112.3	119.6	122.9	109.0
2008 [2]	119.6	119.7	118.6	128.0	113.3	113.5	110.1	111.6	120.4	112.9	120.2	124.5	111.7

[2]NAICS basis, not continuous with previous years, which are based on the SIC.

Table 21-1. Gross Domestic Product by Region and State—*Continued*

(Billions of dollars; index numbers, 2000 = 100.)

Year	Southwest					Rocky Mountain					
	Total	Arizona	New Mexico	Oklahoma	Texas	Total	Colorado	Idaho	Montana	Utah	Wyoming
VALUE											
1977	184.5	19.4	10.3	24.0	130.8	54.6	25.1	7.1	6.4	10.4	5.5
1978	211.6	23.0	11.7	27.2	149.7	63.9	29.2	8.4	7.5	12.1	6.7
1979	245.0	27.3	13.4	31.7	172.6	73.1	33.7	9.2	8.3	13.8	8.2
1980	288.9	30.4	16.0	37.8	204.6	83.1	38.2	9.8	9.0	15.4	10.6
1981	345.7	33.7	18.9	45.8	247.3	95.2	43.8	10.6	10.3	17.5	13.0
1982	367.0	35.0	19.7	49.8	262.5	99.8	47.4	10.6	10.4	18.5	12.9
1983	375.7	38.8	20.4	48.3	268.2	104.8	50.4	11.7	10.7	19.9	12.0
1984	412.8	45.2	22.1	52.0	293.5	114.7	55.9	12.5	11.2	22.4	12.7
1985	439.5	50.1	23.3	53.6	312.6	120.7	59.3	13.0	11.2	24.4	12.8
1986	425.6	55.2	22.4	49.2	298.8	120.1	60.1	13.1	11.2	24.6	11.1
1987	433.4	59.2	23.0	48.9	302.4	124.6	62.9	13.8	11.7	25.3	11.0
1988	471.7	63.6	23.8	52.7	331.6	132.0	66.3	15.1	11.9	27.4	11.3
1989	501.2	66.4	25.3	54.8	354.7	140.0	69.6	16.8	12.8	28.9	11.9
1990	538.0	69.3	26.9	57.7	384.1	150.0	74.2	17.8	13.4	31.4	13.2
1991	561.1	72.3	30.5	59.5	398.9	158.2	78.6	18.6	14.1	33.7	13.3
1992	596.3	79.7	32.6	62.0	422.1	169.5	85.1	20.3	15.0	35.7	13.3
1993	635.9	85.2	36.5	65.0	449.2	183.6	92.5	22.7	16.1	38.4	13.9
1994	681.7	95.3	41.1	67.1	478.1	198.5	100.4	24.8	17.0	42.2	14.1
1995	722.5	104.0	41.5	69.6	507.4	213.4	108.0	27.1	17.4	46.3	14.6
1996	781.7	113.1	43.7	74.9	550.0	229.4	116.0	28.2	18.0	51.4	15.7
1997	855.2	122.9	47.6	79.5	605.3	246.7	127.9	29.4	18.8	54.6	16.0
1997 [2]	852.3	127.4	47.4	78.0	599.5	252.0	132.9	28.5	19.1	56.6	14.9
1998 [2]	892.0	137.6	45.9	79.3	629.2	267.9	143.2	29.8	19.9	60.2	14.9
1999 [2]	949.7	148.5	49.0	83.2	669.0	289.1	156.3	32.7	20.4	63.8	15.9
2000 [2]	1 026.2	158.5	50.7	89.8	727.2	313.1	171.9	35.0	21.4	67.6	17.3
2001 [2]	1 073.3	165.4	51.4	94.3	762.2	325.2	178.1	35.6	22.5	70.1	18.9
2002 [2]	1 105.1	171.9	52.5	97.2	783.5	334.6	182.2	36.7	23.6	72.7	19.6
2003 [2]	1 171.7	182.0	57.5	103.5	828.8	348.2	187.4	38.1	25.5	75.4	21.7
2004 [2]	1 270.1	193.4	63.5	111.5	901.7	371.7	197.3	42.6	27.5	80.9	23.4
2005 [2]	1 385.9	215.2	68.0	120.6	982.1	404.5	212.6	46.6	29.8	89.1	26.4
2006 [2]	1 508.1	236.4	71.8	129.6	1 070.3	433.8	225.1	48.6	31.8	98.3	30.1
2007 [2]	1 606.0	246.0	75.2	136.4	1 148.5	459.3	235.8	52.1	34.3	105.6	31.5
2008 [2]	1 698.7	248.9	79.9	146.4	1 223.5	482.3	248.6	52.7	35.9	109.8	35.3
QUANTITY INDEX											
1977	42.3	28.7	43.0	62.0	42.8	40.9	36.6	38.6	68.3	36.7	63.2
1978	44.8	31.7	45.4	64.8	45.2	44.2	39.6	41.9	73.3	39.6	69.3
1979	46.7	34.8	45.9	67.9	46.7	46.3	42.3	42.6	73.4	41.6	72.2
1980	48.5	35.7	47.5	71.2	48.5	47.8	43.7	43.0	73.7	42.6	79.5
1981	51.1	36.5	48.2	75.4	51.4	49.6	45.6	43.2	76.7	44.2	82.7
1982	51.3	35.5	47.6	77.7	51.7	49.2	46.6	41.4	73.6	43.9	78.0
1983	51.3	37.5	48.4	74.1	51.7	49.6	47.2	43.1	73.1	45.3	73.6
1984	54.7	41.8	51.0	77.8	55.0	52.4	50.0	44.2	74.1	49.0	77.6
1985	57.1	44.8	53.0	79.1	57.4	53.8	51.2	45.6	72.7	52.0	78.8
1986	55.8	47.5	52.1	74.0	55.6	52.8	50.5	44.5	71.9	51.2	74.9
1987	55.6	49.3	52.0	72.3	55.2	53.4	51.4	45.5	72.6	51.3	73.5
1988	58.8	51.2	52.4	76.0	58.8	54.9	52.6	48.0	71.4	53.8	76.1
1989	60.0	51.6	53.6	75.9	60.4	56.1	53.2	51.1	74.4	54.6	76.6
1990	61.5	52.1	54.6	76.4	62.3	57.9	54.6	52.7	75.4	57.5	80.3
1991	62.6	52.5	60.5	76.7	63.3	59.4	55.9	53.8	77.3	59.7	81.8
1992	65.4	56.6	63.7	78.4	65.8	62.3	59.1	57.5	81.0	61.8	82.0
1993	67.9	58.9	70.0	80.1	68.2	65.8	62.6	62.4	84.2	64.8	84.2
1994	71.6	64.4	78.2	81.3	71.5	69.7	66.5	66.8	86.6	69.5	85.5
1995	74.8	69.1	79.3	82.8	74.8	73.5	70.1	72.5	86.9	74.4	87.8
1996	79.2	74.6	82.5	86.9	79.0	77.5	73.8	74.7	88.4	81.5	90.3
1997	85.4	80.2	89.8	90.8	85.5	82.2	80.0	78.0	91.1	85.0	90.9
1997 [2]	86.1	80.4	90.2	92.3	86.3	83.9	80.2	82.3	94.1	88.9	92.3
1998 [2]	91.2	87.5	91.2	94.1	91.7	88.6	86.1	85.8	96.6	93.2	92.9
1999 [2]	96.0	94.4	98.7	96.8	96.1	94.4	92.7	93.6	97.9	97.1	98.0
2000 [2]	100.0	100.0	100.0	100.0	100.0	100.0	100.0	100.0	100.0	100.0	100.0
2001 [2]	102.5	103.1	100.4	102.3	102.5	101.6	101.7	100.7	101.4	101.0	104.5
2002 [2]	104.5	105.3	101.8	103.5	104.6	102.5	102.1	102.0	104.1	102.3	106.1
2003 [2]	106.5	109.9	105.8	105.1	106.0	103.9	102.7	104.2	109.1	103.8	108.8
2004 [2]	111.2	113.9	112.2	108.4	110.8	107.4	105.1	113.2	112.4	108.0	109.9
2005 [2]	115.1	123.7	113.6	110.5	113.9	112.9	109.6	122.6	118.0	115.2	111.5
2006 [2]	120.7	131.6	116.2	113.8	119.5	117.0	112.5	125.1	120.9	122.4	119.4
2007 [2]	125.0	133.5	118.6	116.0	124.8	120.4	114.8	130.2	125.3	128.0	120.2
2008 [2]	127.1	132.6	121.0	119.1	127.3	123.1	118.1	130.2	127.6	129.8	125.5

[2] NAICS basis, not continuous with previous years, which are based on the SIC.

Table 21-1. Gross Domestic Product by Region and State—*Continued*

(Billions of dollars; index numbers, 2000 = 100.)

Year	Far West						
	Total	Alaska	California	Hawaii	Nevada	Oregon	Washington
VALUE							
1977	311.5	7.5	228.5	9.4	7.5	22.3	36.3
1978	358.2	9.1	261.5	10.5	9.1	25.9	42.2
1979	402.6	10.9	291.9	11.9	10.6	29.0	48.4
1980	447.6	15.1	324.4	13.3	12.0	30.5	52.2
1981	504.9	21.7	365.2	14.5	13.6	32.0	58.0
1982	536.4	23.3	389.9	15.4	14.3	31.9	61.6
1983	579.5	22.5	423.9	16.8	15.4	34.0	66.8
1984	653.1	23.8	483.2	18.6	17.0	37.9	72.6
1985	708.7	26.2	528.0	20.0	18.5	40.1	75.9
1986	753.2	18.8	568.4	21.5	20.2	42.3	81.9
1987	820.8	22.3	620.2	23.3	22.4	45.0	87.7
1988	897.2	21.3	678.8	25.7	25.5	49.6	96.2
1989	973.1	23.4	734.4	28.4	28.6	53.3	105.1
1990	1 050.0	25.0	788.3	31.9	31.8	57.3	115.7
1991	1 073.3	22.2	801.2	33.6	33.6	60.1	122.7
1992	1 108.5	22.6	819.4	35.2	36.5	63.7	131.1
1993	1 140.6	23.0	833.7	35.9	40.0	69.2	138.8
1994	1 187.9	23.1	862.5	36.3	44.9	74.4	146.7
1995	1 250.8	24.8	909.0	36.6	49.0	80.1	151.3
1996	1 328.5	26.1	958.5	37.0	54.1	91.2	161.8
1997	1 424.3	26.9	1 028.6	37.9	58.9	97.5	174.4
1997 [2]	1 416.6	25.0	1 019.2	37.5	59.9	96.6	178.3
1998 [2]	1 507.0	23.2	1 085.9	37.5	63.6	101.0	195.8
1999 [2]	1 631.0	24.3	1 180.6	38.6	68.8	104.3	214.4
2000 [2]	1 762.5	27.0	1 287.1	40.2	73.7	112.4	222.0
2001 [2]	1 783.5	26.6	1 301.1	41.8	77.3	110.9	225.8
2002 [2]	1 843.0	29.2	1 340.4	43.5	81.3	117.1	231.5
2003 [2]	1 934.5	31.2	1 406.5	46.4	87.8	121.6	240.8
2004 [2]	2 091.3	35.1	1 519.4	50.4	100.2	132.8	253.2
2005 [2]	2 246.0	39.4	1 628.6	54.9	112.4	138.0	272.7
2006 [2]	2 392.0	43.3	1 727.6	59.1	121.7	151.2	289.1
2007 [2]	2 506.5	44.9	1 801.8	62.0	129.3	158.3	310.3
2008 [2]	2 574.1	47.9	1 846.8	63.8	131.2	161.6	322.8
QUANTITY INDEX							
1977	40.9	66.3	40.8	61.4	26.7	38.7	41.3
1978	43.8	72.4	43.6	64.0	30.0	41.2	44.7
1979	45.7	76.0	45.2	67.6	32.2	42.9	47.6
1980	46.8	87.3	46.3	69.3	33.2	42.5	47.7
1981	48.2	100.6	47.9	68.0	34.4	41.2	48.9
1982	48.1	103.6	47.9	68.0	33.9	38.9	48.9
1983	49.7	101.0	49.8	70.4	34.9	39.2	49.9
1984	53.6	105.5	54.3	72.9	36.8	41.8	51.6
1985	56.3	117.3	57.4	74.9	38.4	43.0	52.2
1986	58.1	96.0	59.7	77.2	40.3	43.7	54.3
1987	61.5	112.2	63.3	80.8	42.7	45.0	56.4
1988	65.0	109.0	67.1	85.7	46.4	47.9	59.6
1989	67.9	112.7	69.9	91.3	50.3	49.4	62.7
1990	70.5	112.0	72.2	98.9	54.4	51.4	66.6
1991	69.6	100.2	70.8	99.8	55.5	52.2	68.1
1992	70.2	101.3	70.7	101.9	59.0	53.9	70.8
1993	70.2	100.3	70.0	101.1	63.2	56.6	72.7
1994	71.5	100.1	70.8	99.6	68.9	59.5	74.9
1995	73.9	105.0	73.4	98.3	73.1	63.1	75.3
1996	77.2	103.6	76.1	97.4	79.7	71.7	79.1
1997	81.5	104.8	80.5	97.6	84.8	76.5	84.0
1997 [2]	82.8	104.0	81.1	100.5	87.5	85.0	84.9
1998 [2]	87.8	99.0	86.1	98.4	90.7	89.7	92.0
1999 [2]	94.1	100.1	93.0	98.9	95.8	92.8	98.9
2000 [2]	100.0	100.0	100.0	100.0	100.0	100.0	100.0
2001 [2]	99.5	95.3	99.6	101.1	101.9	98.3	99.2
2002 [2]	101.1	103.7	100.9	102.2	104.6	102.3	99.6
2003 [2]	104.0	101.4	103.9	105.9	110.7	104.9	101.4
2004 [2]	109.3	107.0	109.3	111.0	121.9	111.9	103.6
2005 [2]	114.2	108.4	114.0	116.7	131.9	115.1	108.9
2006 [2]	118.1	113.2	117.5	121.2	137.2	124.1	112.0
2007 [2]	120.7	113.0	119.6	122.9	140.9	128.7	116.9
2008 [2]	121.4	110.8	120.1	123.8	140.0	130.8	119.2

[2] NAICS basis, not continuous with previous years, which are based on the SIC.

Table 21-2. Personal Income and Employment by Region and State

(Millions of dollars, except as noted.)

Region or state and year	Personal income, total	Earnings by place of work			Less: Contributions for government social insurance	Plus: Adjustment for residence	Equals: Net earnings by place of residence	Plus: Dividends, interest, and rent	Plus: Personal current transfer receipts	Per capita (dollars)		Population (thousands)	Total employment (thousands)
		Nonfarm	Farm	Total						Personal income	Disposable personal income		
UNITED STATES (sum of states)[1]													
1958	367 249	292 629	15 252	307 881	11 371	-204	296 306	47 413	23 529	2 109	1 888	174 153	...
1959	391 286	317 047	13 034	330 081	13 824	-217	316 040	50 939	24 306	2 209	1 970	177 136	...
1960	408 376	330 712	13 561	344 273	16 349	-285	327 639	54 997	25 740	2 269	2 014	179 972	...
1961	425 829	341 270	14 265	355 535	16 905	-279	338 351	58 028	29 450	2 327	2 070	182 976	...
1962	453 276	364 933	14 329	379 262	19 011	-233	360 018	62 866	30 392	2 440	2 164	185 739	...
1963	476 109	384 082	14 167	398 249	21 548	-208	376 493	67 407	32 209	2 527	2 238	188 434	...
1964	510 599	413 156	13 017	426 173	22 247	-207	403 719	73 376	33 504	2 672	2 400	191 085	...
1965	551 432	443 773	15 369	459 142	23 268	-152	435 722	79 532	36 178	2 850	2 553	193 457	...
1966	598 615	489 059	16 397	505 456	31 127	-143	474 186	84 812	39 617	3 062	2 723	195 499	...
1967	642 212	523 648	15 077	538 725	34 558	-143	504 024	90 174	48 014	3 254	2 885	197 375	...
1968	705 105	576 211	15 276	591 487	38 338	-170	552 979	96 032	56 094	3 538	3 104	199 312	...
1969	772 084	631 215	17 433	648 648	43 792	-107	604 749	105 013	62 322	3 836	3 320	201 298	91 053
1970	832 238	671 411	17 660	689 071	46 012	-112	642 947	114 558	74 733	4 084	3 581	203 799	91 278
1971	897 559	719 019	18 141	737 160	50 859	-122	686 179	123 132	88 248	4 340	3 851	206 818	91 581
1972	987 073	793 307	21 949	815 256	58 897	-145	756 214	132 729	98 130	4 717	4 128	209 275	94 312
1973	1 105 426	884 499	34 874	919 373	75 183	-153	844 037	148 541	112 848	5 230	4 606	211 349	98 428
1974	1 217 673	968 581	30 099	998 680	84 873	-163	913 644	170 390	133 639	5 708	5 002	213 334	100 112
1975	1 329 714	1 033 803	29 152	1 062 955	88 975	-199	973 781	185 509	170 424	6 172	5 489	215 457	98 901
1976	1 469 355	1 160 337	25 236	1 185 573	100 987	-211	1 084 375	200 498	184 482	6 754	5 964	217 554	101 591
1977	1 626 621	1 295 401	24 510	1 319 911	112 699	-235	1 206 977	224 893	194 751	7 402	6 506	219 761	105 042
1978	1 830 836	1 467 571	28 424	1 495 995	130 827	-257	1 364 911	255 616	210 309	8 243	7 213	222 098	109 687
1979	2 052 037	1 640 850	30 233	1 671 083	152 274	-231	1 518 578	297 330	236 129	9 138	7 944	224 569	113 147
1980	2 292 903	1 790 748	20 755	1 811 503	165 669	-255	1 645 579	367 107	280 217	10 091	8 779	227 225	113 983
1981	2 572 070	1 962 327	27 547	1 989 874	195 066	-208	1 794 600	458 323	319 147	11 209	9 709	229 466	114 914
1982	2 757 048	2 058 870	24 786	2 083 656	208 173	-255	1 875 228	526 312	355 508	11 901	10 377	231 664	114 163
1983	2 941 857	2 198 024	17 432	2 215 456	225 147	-212	1 990 097	567 643	384 117	12 583	11 080	233 792	115 646
1984	3 256 048	2 432 295	32 118	2 464 413	256 554	-254	2 207 605	647 715	400 728	13 807	12 211	235 825	120 528
1985	3 482 520	2 610 934	32 182	2 643 116	280 384	-257	2 362 475	694 758	425 287	14 637	12 887	237 924	123 797
1986	3 683 091	2 772 954	33 350	2 806 304	302 394	228	2 504 138	727 831	451 122	15 338	13 521	240 133	126 232
1987	3 909 771	2 974 891	39 704	3 014 595	322 011	259	2 692 843	749 363	467 565	16 137	14 123	242 289	129 548
1988	4 216 123	3 233 770	39 454	3 273 224	360 256	226	2 913 194	806 520	496 409	17 244	15 184	244 499	133 564
1989	4 541 996	3 420 658	46 164	3 466 822	383 937	236	3 083 121	916 328	542 547	18 402	16 114	246 819	136 178
1990	4 831 282	3 627 230	47 623	3 674 853	408 655	313	3 266 511	969 500	595 271	19 354	16 985	249 623	138 331
1991	5 013 484	3 744 437	42 500	3 786 937	428 559	367	3 358 745	988 967	665 772	19 818	17 504	252 981	137 613
1992	5 335 268	3 998 738	50 774	4 049 512	453 762	478	3 596 228	993 372	745 668	20 799	18 423	256 514	138 166
1993	5 558 374	4 182 270	47 658	4 229 928	476 378	493	3 754 043	1 013 647	790 684	21 385	18 901	259 919	140 774
1994	5 866 796	4 406 376	51 053	4 457 429	507 203	533	3 950 759	1 089 725	826 312	22 297	19 676	263 126	144 197
1995	6 194 245	4 647 549	39 899	4 687 448	531 890	703	4 156 261	1 159 118	878 866	23 262	20 472	266 278	147 916
1996	6 584 404	4 908 173	55 382	4 963 555	554 164	675	4 410 066	1 250 337	924 001	24 442	21 357	269 394	151 056
1997	6 994 388	5 238 319	51 440	5 289 759	586 311	672	4 704 120	1 341 139	949 129	25 654	22 260	272 647	154 541
1998	7 519 327	5 655 589	49 079	5 704 668	623 701	755	5 081 722	1 459 720	977 885	27 258	23 541	275 854	158 481
1999	7 906 131	6 040 317	49 572	6 089 889	660 324	1 017	5 430 582	1 453 995	1 021 554	28 333	24 368	279 040	161 531
2000	8 554 866	6 548 165	52 468	6 600 633	704 861	1 122	5 896 894	1 574 990	1 082 982	30 318	25 955	282 172	165 371
2001	8 878 830	6 789 672	54 779	6 844 451	732 130	1 058	6 113 379	1 577 379	1 188 072	31 145	26 817	285 082	165 510
2002	9 054 781	6 951 836	65 468	6 994 620	750 231	977	6 245 366	1 527 299	1 282 116	31 462	27 816	287 804	165 063
2003	9 369 072	7 228 400	59 770	7 288 170	777 575	819	6 511 414	1 515 977	1 341 681	32 271	28 829	290 326	166 020
2004	9 928 790	7 656 172	76 295	7 732 467	825 892	762	6 907 337	1 605 771	1 415 682	33 881	30 309	293 046	169 027
2005	10 476 669	8 048 405	71 394	8 119 799	871 241	738	7 249 296	1 718 902	1 508 471	35 424	31 342	295 753	172 551
2006	11 256 516	8 539 008	57 333	8 596 341	920 430	646	7 676 557	1 975 147	1 604 812	37 698	33 174	298 593	176 125
2007	11 879 836	8 879 019	65 468	8 944 487	957 971	537	7 987 053	2 175 274	1 717 509	39 392	34 453	301 580	179 872
2008	12 225 589	9 058 491	76 343	9 134 834	989 195	588	8 146 227	2 203 774	1 875 588	40 166	35 464	304 375	181 755
2009	12 015 535	8 755 030	57 475	8 812 505	965 585	675	7 847 596	2 059 324	2 108 616	39 138	35 553	307 007	...

[1]See notes and definitions for explanation.
. . . = Not available.

Table 21-2. Personal Income and Employment by Region and State—*Continued*

(Millions of dollars, except as noted.)

Region or state and year	Personal income, total	Derivation of personal income								Per capita (dollars)		Population (thousands)	Total employment (thousands)
		Earnings by place of work			Less: Contributions for government social insurance	Plus: Adjustment for residence	Equals: Net earnings by place of residence	Plus: Dividends, interest, and rent	Plus: Personal current transfer receipts	Personal income	Disposable personal income		
		Nonfarm	Farm	Total									
NEW ENGLAND													
1958	23 237	18 684	317	19 002	722	18	18 297	3 250	1 690	2 274	2 019	10 219	...
1959	24 798	20 248	248	20 496	872	20	19 644	3 468	1 686	2 376	2 103	10 437	...
1960	25 854	21 094	315	21 408	1 025	27	20 411	3 682	1 761	2 455	2 154	10 532	...
1961	27 111	21 999	266	22 265	1 073	28	21 220	3 914	1 977	2 542	2 241	10 666	...
1962	28 786	23 401	256	23 657	1 215	31	22 473	4 306	2 007	2 665	2 344	10 800	...
1963	30 043	24 325	248	24 573	1 357	36	23 252	4 665	2 126	2 735	2 400	10 986	...
1964	32 186	25 882	286	26 168	1 400	42	24 810	5 170	2 207	2 877	2 568	11 186	...
1965	34 527	27 608	337	27 945	1 450	44	26 539	5 658	2 330	3 048	2 712	11 329	...
1966	37 550	30 471	341	30 812	1 937	51	28 926	6 113	2 512	3 285	2 899	11 430	...
1967	40 858	32 904	237	33 141	2 133	58	31 066	6 710	3 082	3 534	3 107	11 562	...
1968	44 339	35 781	264	36 045	2 367	71	33 748	6 908	3 682	3 810	3 300	11 637	...
1969	48 997	38 949	294	39 243	2 634	850	37 458	7 428	4 111	4 175	3 570	11 735	5 516
1970	52 711	41 501	306	41 807	2 769	856	39 894	7 914	4 903	4 438	3 860	11 878	5 518
1971	56 072	43 667	283	43 950	3 008	884	41 825	8 371	5 876	4 674	4 124	11 996	5 454
1972	60 743	47 661	288	47 949	3 449	941	45 440	8 896	6 408	5 025	4 367	12 088	5 573
1973	66 530	52 615	398	53 013	4 355	997	49 656	9 678	7 196	5 477	4 790	12 148	5 783
1974	72 384	56 318	430	56 748	4 823	1 084	53 008	10 846	8 531	5 954	5 200	12 157	5 843
1975	77 634	58 557	313	58 871	4 913	1 171	55 128	11 370	11 136	6 376	5 653	12 176	5 685
1976	84 888	64 835	428	65 264	5 515	1 300	61 048	12 171	11 669	6 954	6 116	12 207	5 811
1977	92 982	71 653	384	72 037	6 127	1 453	67 363	13 509	12 110	7 586	6 656	12 257	6 007
1978	103 424	80 707	397	81 104	7 097	1 638	75 645	14 973	12 806	8 407	7 327	12 303	6 276
1979	115 808	90 538	380	90 917	8 287	1 867	84 497	17 046	14 265	9 381	8 111	12 345	6 503
1980	131 114	100 302	368	100 671	9 186	2 180	93 665	21 043	16 406	10 598	9 133	12 372	6 623
1981	146 743	109 612	472	110 084	10 785	2 347	101 646	26 323	18 773	11 800	10 105	12 436	6 666
1982	159 995	117 383	513	117 896	11 773	2 523	108 646	30 826	20 523	12 833	11 057	12 468	6 667
1983	172 736	128 327	479	128 806	13 048	2 654	118 413	32 403	21 920	13 770	11 991	12 544	6 799
1984	193 957	144 853	567	145 420	15 177	2 830	133 073	37 913	22 972	15 342	13 427	12 642	7 159
1985	209 448	158 528	556	159 084	16 771	2 984	145 297	39 984	24 167	16 440	14 290	12 741	7 400
1986	225 755	172 283	574	172 857	18 496	3 153	157 514	42 867	25 374	17 592	15 207	12 833	7 638
1987	245 535	190 119	641	190 760	20 167	3 311	173 904	45 538	26 094	18 958	16 271	12 951	7 771
1988	269 692	209 695	658	210 353	22 618	3 512	191 247	50 400	28 045	20 612	17 891	13 085	8 018
1989	287 995	219 275	608	219 883	23 601	3 437	199 718	56 965	31 311	21 848	18 923	13 182	8 005
1990	297 157	223 120	701	223 820	24 072	3 445	203 193	58 954	35 010	22 462	19 499	13 230	7 853
1991	302 930	224 009	645	224 654	24 508	3 444	203 589	58 866	40 475	22 867	19 966	13 248	7 526
1992	319 527	236 653	794	237 447	25 687	4 665	216 425	59 212	43 889	24 077	20 997	13 271	7 566
1993	330 333	246 297	731	247 028	26 867	4 104	224 265	60 599	45 469	24 773	21 531	13 334	7 689
1994	345 678	258 129	678	258 808	28 422	3 915	234 300	63 608	47 769	25 804	22 396	13 396	7 782
1995	364 408	271 573	603	272 176	29 927	4 705	246 953	66 694	50 761	27 048	23 352	13 473	7 875
1996	386 599	286 953	688	287 641	31 309	5 527	261 859	72 516	52 225	28 521	24 353	13 555	8 004
1997	410 458	307 252	594	307 846	33 366	5 156	279 636	76 652	54 170	30 087	25 408	13 642	8 165
1998	441 242	330 873	657	331 530	35 427	6 615	302 717	83 637	54 887	32 128	26 906	13 734	8 336
1999	464 677	354 940	702	355 641	37 624	6 507	324 525	83 425	56 727	33 581	27 964	13 838	8 481
2000	510 702	391 907	775	392 682	40 848	6 816	358 650	92 155	59 896	36 601	30 022	13 953	8 697
2001	533 483	408 792	710	409 502	42 131	6 243	373 614	94 883	64 987	37 965	31 465	14 052	8 770
2002	538 406	412 971	653	413 625	42 834	5 570	376 361	92 022	70 023	38 089	32 895	14 135	8 710
2003	550 071	423 962	704	424 667	43 762	5 224	386 129	90 790	73 152	38 758	33 808	14 192	8 697
2004	580 052	449 405	816	450 221	46 778	5 928	409 371	93 653	77 028	40 801	35 610	14 216	8 789
2005	602 313	466 629	788	467 417	48 776	6 005	424 647	95 837	81 830	42 335	36 480	14 227	8 885
2006	649 754	491 345	662	492 007	50 753	6 400	447 654	116 167	85 934	45 569	39 125	14 259	9 004
2007	684 836	512 030	792	512 822	52 875	6 557	466 505	126 679	91 653	47 897	40 526	14 298	9 150
2008	702 966	521 067	764	521 831	54 713	6 675	473 793	128 573	100 601	48 944	41 861	14 363	9 275
2009	692 541	503 246	748	503 994	53 458	6 086	456 622	121 458	114 461	47 994	42 643	14 430	...

. . . = Not available.

Table 21-2. Personal Income and Employment by Region and State—*Continued*

(Millions of dollars, except as noted.)

| Region or state and year | Personal income, total | Earnings by place of work | | | Less: Contributions for government social insurance | Plus: Adjustment for residence | Equals: Net earnings by place of residence | Plus: Dividends, interest, and rent | Plus: Personal current transfer receipts | Per capita (dollars) | | Population (thousands) | Total employment (thousands) |
		Nonfarm	Farm	Total						Personal income	Disposable personal income		
MIDEAST													
1958	90 864	75 901	985	76 886	3 047	-582	73 256	11 892	5 715	2 409	2 124	37 721	...
1959	96 289	81 169	787	81 955	3 679	-623	77 653	12 702	5 935	2 521	2 212	38 202	...
1960	100 494	84 920	890	85 810	4 353	-749	80 708	13 666	6 119	2 604	2 279	38 597	...
1961	104 502	87 673	893	88 565	4 580	-780	83 205	14 303	6 994	2 670	2 338	39 133	...
1962	110 533	92 962	721	93 683	5 116	-792	87 775	15 607	7 150	2 795	2 440	39 552	...
1963	115 398	96 647	783	97 431	5 641	-828	90 962	16 844	7 593	2 879	2 512	40 083	...
1964	123 680	103 129	790	103 919	5 691	-887	97 341	18 478	7 861	3 050	2 701	40 555	...
1965	132 265	109 860	884	110 743	5 938	-926	103 879	19 981	8 405	3 224	2 844	41 025	...
1966	142 545	120 014	903	120 916	7 889	-1 004	112 023	21 121	9 401	3 446	3 021	41 360	...
1967	153 635	128 437	961	129 398	8 607	-1 171	119 620	22 413	11 602	3 692	3 220	41 617	...
1968	168 522	140 404	912	141 316	9 391	-1 292	130 633	24 017	13 872	4 020	3 474	41 924	...
1969	181 420	152 275	1 105	153 379	11 063	-1 711	140 606	25 557	15 257	4 308	3 670	42 111	19 432
1970	195 852	162 604	1 063	163 667	11 648	-1 618	150 402	27 345	18 105	4 606	3 981	42 517	19 465
1971	209 590	172 466	970	173 436	12 763	-1 687	158 986	28 866	21 738	4 889	4 281	42 870	19 299
1972	226 658	187 087	966	188 053	14 524	-1 850	171 679	30 560	24 419	5 272	4 551	42 992	19 521
1973	245 956	204 116	1 387	205 503	18 181	-1 983	185 339	33 316	27 301	5 742	4 986	42 837	19 968
1974	267 917	219 698	1 293	220 991	20 147	-2 211	198 633	37 477	31 808	6 273	5 426	42 709	19 954
1975	289 318	231 247	1 199	232 446	20 828	-2 527	209 092	39 760	40 467	6 771	5 946	42 728	19 480
1976	313 453	251 669	1 280	252 948	22 884	-2 869	227 195	42 574	43 684	7 346	6 421	42 667	19 563
1977	341 482	275 126	1 099	276 225	24 856	-3 266	248 103	47 364	46 014	8 026	6 976	42 547	19 848
1978	375 220	304 691	1 314	306 005	28 197	-3 788	274 021	52 383	48 816	8 845	7 660	42 421	20 411
1979	413 320	335 407	1 524	336 931	32 242	-4 438	300 251	59 494	53 575	9 758	8 389	42 358	20 871
1980	459 655	365 079	1 141	366 220	35 077	-5 273	325 870	72 162	61 623	10 874	9 340	42 272	20 911
1981	511 352	397 747	1 504	399 251	40 961	-5 833	352 457	89 386	69 509	12 081	10 295	42 329	20 978
1982	552 995	420 856	1 459	422 315	43 975	-6 062	372 278	103 523	77 194	13 048	11 150	42 382	20 858
1983	591 398	450 322	1 090	451 412	47 845	-6 163	397 404	110 517	83 477	13 901	12 048	42 544	21 045
1984	650 569	494 561	1 901	496 462	54 377	-6 474	435 611	128 083	86 875	15 241	13 236	42 687	21 766
1985	695 700	531 785	2 010	533 795	59 560	-6 760	467 476	136 914	91 310	16 257	14 053	42 794	22 333
1986	739 831	569 596	2 196	571 791	64 792	-6 744	500 255	143 097	96 478	17 209	14 870	42 991	22 837
1987	790 486	617 843	2 295	620 139	69 475	-7 161	543 503	147 850	99 134	18 303	15 672	43 190	23 321
1988	863 253	680 069	2 205	682 274	77 994	-7 846	596 433	161 608	105 212	19 874	17 181	43 435	23 927
1989	928 403	717 061	2 578	719 639	82 250	-8 087	629 302	185 350	113 751	21 301	18 330	43 585	24 201
1990	986 464	758 301	2 519	760 820	85 066	-8 768	666 986	194 855	124 623	22 542	19 511	43 762	24 260
1991	1 009 194	763 739	2 053	765 792	87 865	-9 240	668 687	199 485	141 022	22 899	19 947	44 071	23 703
1992	1 062 717	810 248	2 650	812 899	92 357	-10 887	709 655	196 623	156 439	23 939	20 871	44 392	23 597
1993	1 093 766	836 997	2 520	839 517	95 837	-10 788	732 892	195 665	165 209	24 460	21 266	44 717	23 714
1994	1 133 990	866 167	2 308	868 476	100 829	-10 523	757 124	205 767	171 100	25 217	21 884	44 970	23 879
1995	1 190 946	906 695	1 765	908 460	104 512	-11 482	792 466	217 816	180 664	26 357	22 834	45 186	24 157
1996	1 256 732	951 858	2 698	954 556	107 626	-11 977	834 952	232 104	189 676	27 691	23 820	45 384	24 387
1997	1 327 517	1 009 331	1 852	1 011 183	112 202	-12 347	886 635	248 915	191 967	29 125	24 847	45 580	24 763
1998	1 410 199	1 075 279	2 318	1 077 598	117 980	-13 491	946 127	265 990	198 082	30 776	26 096	45 822	25 194
1999	1 472 262	1 138 405	2 304	1 140 708	123 962	-14 699	1 002 048	264 313	205 901	31 932	26 913	46 106	25 631
2000	1 585 504	1 225 157	2 772	1 227 929	132 242	-13 374	1 082 313	285 899	217 292	34 183	28 694	46 383	26 277
2001	1 637 586	1 269 388	2 828	1 272 215	138 230	-12 901	1 121 085	282 783	233 719	35 122	29 431	46 626	26 446
2002	1 662 885	1 294 151	1 934	1 296 085	141 971	-13 810	1 140 305	270 424	252 156	35 489	30 688	46 856	26 423
2003	1 707 811	1 335 820	2 859	1 338 679	145 566	-13 886	1 179 228	266 371	262 212	36 289	31 718	47 061	26 529
2004	1 808 646	1 417 790	3 600	1 421 391	153 264	-14 882	1 253 245	278 989	276 413	38 281	33 461	47 247	26 916
2005	1 899 255	1 487 030	3 453	1 490 483	160 827	-15 196	1 314 460	299 397	285 398	40 090	34 635	47 375	27 334
2006	2 047 042	1 582 511	2 884	1 585 395	169 143	-16 451	1 399 801	344 900	302 341	43 095	36 970	47 501	27 733
2007	2 181 571	1 660 634	3 351	1 663 985	178 389	-17 457	1 468 139	394 552	318 881	45 767	38 859	47 667	28 301
2008	2 242 857	1 699 281	3 213	1 702 494	185 336	-18 095	1 499 062	400 350	343 445	46 900	40 192	47 822	28 712
2009	2 204 611	1 648 412	2 318	1 650 731	181 945	-18 262	1 450 524	372 414	381 673	45 893	40 772	48 038	...

. . . = Not available.

Table 21-2. Personal Income and Employment by Region and State—*Continued*

(Millions of dollars, except as noted.)

Region or state and year	Personal income, total	Earnings by place of work — Nonfarm	Farm	Total	Less: Contributions for government social insurance	Plus: Adjustment for residence	Equals: Net earnings by place of residence	Plus: Dividends, interest, and rent	Plus: Personal current transfer receipts	Per capita (dollars) — Personal income	Disposable personal income	Population (thousands)	Total employment (thousands)
GREAT LAKES													
1958	79 768	64 987	2 400	67 388	2 492	-112	64 784	9 925	5 059	2 242	2 008	35 578	. . .
1959	85 126	70 816	1 903	72 719	3 045	-126	69 547	10 636	4 943	2 369	2 115	35 928	. . .
1960	88 445	73 432	1 976	75 408	3 656	-124	71 629	11 559	5 257	2 437	2 159	36 290	. . .
1961	90 551	73 553	2 402	75 954	3 617	-112	72 226	12 195	6 130	2 473	2 204	36 616	. . .
1962	96 107	78 602	2 309	80 911	4 043	-116	76 753	13 201	6 154	2 603	2 308	36 927	. . .
1963	100 629	82 530	2 311	84 842	4 561	-114	80 166	14 119	6 343	2 694	2 385	37 357	. . .
1964	108 246	89 273	1 999	91 273	4 762	-122	86 389	15 383	6 474	2 859	2 564	37 868	. . .
1965	118 260	97 093	2 587	99 680	4 946	-134	94 600	16 725	6 935	3 079	2 752	38 405	. . .
1966	128 663	107 168	2 921	110 089	6 742	-147	103 201	17 933	7 529	3 303	2 932	38 951	. . .
1967	135 549	112 492	2 495	114 987	7 271	-136	107 581	18 959	9 009	3 445	3 049	39 347	. . .
1968	147 984	123 164	2 399	125 563	7 985	-146	117 432	20 140	10 413	3 733	3 265	39 645	. . .
1969	160 960	134 751	2 871	137 622	9 310	288	128 599	21 027	11 334	4 034	3 469	39 904	17 785
1970	169 128	139 807	2 518	142 325	9 504	263	133 085	22 495	13 548	4 195	3 649	40 320	17 630
1971	181 688	149 025	2 900	151 925	10 425	335	141 835	23 752	16 102	4 473	3 943	40 622	17 549
1972	198 678	163 784	3 169	166 954	12 096	384	155 242	25 463	17 972	4 867	4 230	40 824	17 933
1973	223 058	183 715	5 214	188 930	15 629	436	173 736	28 384	20 938	5 447	4 761	40 947	18 710
1974	242 856	197 752	4 663	202 415	17 400	537	185 552	32 373	24 932	5 918	5 155	41 037	18 911
1975	261 450	205 382	5 824	211 206	17 671	630	194 165	35 254	32 031	6 360	5 614	41 105	18 399
1976	289 369	232 028	4 821	236 849	20 243	778	217 384	37 792	34 193	7 026	6 144	41 187	18 891
1977	321 738	260 962	4 823	265 785	22 759	962	243 989	42 032	35 717	7 780	6 769	41 353	19 508
1978	357 351	292 740	4 516	297 256	26 310	1 188	272 133	46 813	38 405	8 609	7 452	41 510	20 190
1979	394 609	321 099	5 227	326 327	29 955	1 406	297 778	53 403	43 429	9 483	8 176	41 611	20 491
1980	427 919	334 101	3 321	337 423	30 983	1 680	308 120	65 287	54 512	10 263	8 910	41 694	19 978
1981	467 100	356 142	3 697	359 839	35 398	1 438	325 880	80 610	60 610	11 215	9 696	41 648	19 795
1982	488 502	360 110	2 933	363 042	36 329	1 338	328 051	92 433	68 017	11 773	10 313	41 492	19 248
1983	512 689	379 282	-121	379 161	38 845	1 323	341 639	98 367	72 683	12 394	10 894	41 366	19 265
1984	565 479	418 399	4 404	422 803	44 261	1 426	379 968	111 055	74 456	13 661	12 061	41 393	20 028
1985	599 673	446 337	4 953	451 290	48 194	1 465	404 561	116 927	78 186	14 479	12 732	41 418	20 492
1986	630 428	471 888	4 486	476 373	51 649	1 538	426 263	122 313	81 851	15 208	13 391	41 455	20 934
1987	662 129	500 824	5 030	505 855	54 321	1 605	453 139	124 877	84 112	15 921	13 922	41 590	21 516
1988	707 371	542 892	3 394	546 286	60 500	1 728	487 514	132 106	87 750	16 955	14 887	41 721	22 070
1989	758 613	572 979	7 031	580 010	64 370	1 764	517 404	147 135	94 074	18 117	15 824	41 873	22 556
1990	800 635	603 474	6 007	609 481	68 628	1 961	542 815	155 036	102 784	19 021	16 641	42 091	22 928
1991	824 736	622 072	3 611	625 683	71 893	2 008	555 799	156 986	111 951	19 407	17 063	42 496	22 845
1992	883 129	667 538	6 137	673 675	76 360	2 236	599 552	159 902	123 675	20 585	18 176	42 903	22 971
1993	920 576	700 555	5 218	705 772	80 852	2 319	627 240	163 325	130 011	21 273	18 696	43 275	23 359
1994	980 371	747 541	6 094	753 635	87 256	2 523	668 902	177 448	134 021	22 491	19 714	43 590	24 060
1995	1 027 993	785 247	3 358	788 606	91 794	2 662	699 474	187 456	141 063	23 404	20 448	43 924	24 713
1996	1 082 802	818 105	6 939	825 045	94 889	2 963	733 118	202 226	147 458	24 476	21 247	44 239	25 105
1997	1 143 441	863 648	6 619	870 267	99 402	3 310	774 175	216 981	152 284	25 699	22 193	44 494	25 513
1998	1 220 815	925 461	5 589	931 050	104 514	3 441	829 977	236 091	154 747	27 294	23 479	44 728	25 957
1999	1 267 538	976 031	4 540	980 571	109 871	3 870	874 570	231 895	161 073	28 187	24 232	44 969	26 329
2000	1 348 478	1 033 685	5 339	1 039 024	114 327	4 211	928 908	248 859	170 710	29 819	25 665	45 223	26 775
2001	1 383 178	1 059 180	5 562	1 064 742	115 982	4 426	953 186	242 672	187 320	30 437	26 354	45 445	26 493
2002	1 410 207	1 087 294	3 620	1 090 914	117 466	4 455	977 903	233 202	199 103	30 916	27 307	45 614	26 257
2003	1 457 148	1 132 890	6 343	1 139 233	121 024	4 587	1 022 796	226 566	207 786	31 838	28 460	45 768	26 221
2004	1 507 294	1 171 944	10 282	1 182 226	127 254	4 900	1 059 872	230 682	216 740	32 821	29 415	45 925	26 437
2005	1 552 167	1 204 650	7 093	1 211 743	132 564	5 245	1 084 423	235 074	232 669	33 717	29 985	46 035	26 675
2006	1 635 601	1 249 381	6 897	1 256 278	138 498	5 520	1 123 300	267 598	244 702	35 428	31 360	46 166	26 897
2007	1 703 059	1 279 255	9 213	1 288 468	142 607	5 915	1 151 775	287 469	263 815	36 784	32 366	46 299	27 148
2008	1 742 912	1 293 299	12 869	1 306 168	145 435	6 310	1 167 043	291 070	284 799	37 571	33 348	46 389	27 212
2009	1 707 090	1 229 710	8 823	1 238 533	139 102	6 345	1 105 777	277 615	323 699	36 711	33 491	46 501	. . .

. . . = Not available.

Table 21-2. Personal Income and Employment by Region and State—*Continued*

(Millions of dollars, except as noted.)

Region or state and year	Personal income, total	Earnings by place of work			Less: Contributions for government social insurance	Plus: Adjustment for residence	Equals: Net earnings by place of residence	Plus: Dividends, interest, and rent	Plus: Personal current transfer receipts	Per capita (dollars)		Population (thousands)	Total employment (thousands)
		Nonfarm	Farm	Total						Personal income	Disposable personal income		
PLAINS													
1958	30 375	21 265	3 831	25 097	826	7	24 278	4 140	1 957	2 026	1 830	14 994	...
1959	31 179	22 993	2 664	25 657	1 000	8	24 665	4 417	2 097	2 052	1 852	15 195	...
1960	32 729	23 903	3 071	26 974	1 156	7	25 825	4 687	2 218	2 122	1 902	15 424	...
1961	33 917	24 786	2 983	27 769	1 211	6	26 564	4 888	2 464	2 178	1 953	15 570	...
1962	36 235	26 311	3 484	29 795	1 317	7	28 485	5 191	2 560	2 314	2 073	15 657	...
1963	37 686	27 544	3 414	30 959	1 493	3	29 469	5 521	2 696	2 398	2 145	15 715	...
1964	39 277	29 455	2 733	32 187	1 554	5	30 638	5 851	2 788	2 488	2 254	15 787	...
1965	43 108	31 395	4 048	35 443	1 632	4	33 815	6 272	3 021	2 725	2 463	15 819	...
1966	46 359	34 470	4 240	38 710	2 197	0	36 513	6 583	3 263	2 918	2 617	15 888	...
1967	48 663	36 961	3 623	40 583	2 549	-5	38 030	6 739	3 894	3 053	2 730	15 942	...
1968	53 037	40 516	3 625	44 141	2 837	-14	41 291	7 241	4 505	3 305	2 934	16 047	...
1969	58 190	44 462	4 221	48 683	3 164	-414	45 105	8 144	4 940	3 592	3 140	16 202	7 506
1970	62 923	47 457	4 444	51 901	3 342	-358	48 201	8 930	5 792	3 849	3 403	16 350	7 516
1971	67 617	50 789	4 611	55 400	3 697	-355	51 348	9 617	6 653	4 104	3 672	16 475	7 544
1972	74 763	55 475	6 163	61 638	4 228	-361	57 050	10 460	7 252	4 514	3 987	16 563	7 731
1973	87 540	61 766	11 295	73 061	5 405	-399	67 257	11 833	8 450	5 265	4 687	16 628	8 065
1974	92 793	68 202	7 689	75 891	6 194	-432	69 265	13 677	9 850	5 566	4 874	16 672	8 219
1975	101 673	73 756	7 507	81 263	6 600	-423	74 239	15 311	12 122	6 073	5 387	16 743	8 181
1976	109 482	83 432	4 415	87 847	7 518	-521	79 808	16 507	13 167	6 492	5 724	16 864	8 438
1977	121 261	92 407	5 201	97 607	8 276	-659	88 671	18 673	13 916	7 154	6 296	16 950	8 657
1978	137 489	104 033	7 851	111 884	9 619	-818	101 447	20 884	15 158	8 074	7 085	17 028	8 953
1979	151 931	116 631	6 621	123 251	11 228	-986	111 037	23 916	16 978	8 886	7 732	17 097	9 232
1980	164 154	125 656	1 886	127 541	12 066	-1 142	114 333	29 543	20 277	9 540	8 296	17 208	9 227
1981	185 705	135 419	5 464	140 883	13 959	-1 335	125 589	37 001	23 115	10 757	9 334	17 264	9 180
1982	198 011	140 443	4 013	144 456	14 744	-1 341	128 371	43 885	25 755	11 451	9 957	17 292	9 050
1983	207 462	149 060	1 575	150 635	15 669	-1 432	133 533	46 222	27 707	11 975	10 566	17 325	9 163
1984	230 818	163 945	6 540	170 485	17 709	-1 601	151 176	50 771	28 872	13 279	11 824	17 382	9 470
1985	243 340	173 151	7 454	180 605	19 110	-1 709	159 786	52 975	30 578	13 984	12 426	17 402	9 612
1986	254 419	181 808	8 063	189 871	20 471	-1 826	167 574	54 797	32 048	14 628	13 034	17 393	9 701
1987	267 958	193 695	9 793	203 488	21 693	-1 935	179 859	55 126	32 973	15 375	13 612	17 428	9 949
1988	280 290	207 116	7 413	214 528	24 098	-2 100	188 330	57 375	34 585	15 986	14 158	17 533	10 156
1989	301 245	219 611	9 208	228 819	25 708	-2 181	200 931	62 866	37 448	17 121	15 100	17 595	10 357
1990	319 413	232 056	10 549	242 605	27 940	-2 419	212 246	66 680	40 487	18 048	15 906	17 698	10 544
1991	331 694	241 854	8 125	249 979	29 494	-2 474	218 010	69 039	44 645	18 589	16 470	17 843	10 597
1992	354 655	259 682	10 656	270 338	31 356	-2 714	236 268	70 016	48 372	19 674	17 464	18 026	10 708
1993	365 479	272 335	6 256	278 591	33 015	-2 800	242 776	71 371	51 331	20 071	17 760	18 210	10 934
1994	391 974	289 744	10 497	300 241	35 465	-3 019	261 758	76 608	53 608	21 325	18 868	18 381	11 230
1995	410 298	306 779	5 768	312 547	37 359	-3 162	272 026	81 519	56 753	22 119	19 484	18 550	11 537
1996	442 590	324 116	13 578	337 694	38 964	-3 382	295 348	87 880	59 362	23 661	20 752	18 705	11 761
1997	465 474	344 711	9 926	354 637	41 483	-3 794	309 361	94 865	61 249	24 692	21 527	18 851	11 980
1998	499 369	371 987	9 215	381 202	44 126	-4 056	333 021	103 135	63 213	26 299	22 893	18 988	12 238
1999	520 948	395 534	7 917	403 451	46 513	-4 387	352 551	102 154	66 243	27 231	23 744	19 131	12 411
2000	559 195	422 645	9 532	432 177	49 047	-4 681	378 449	109 822	70 924	29 017	25 265	19 271	12 601
2001	579 008	438 441	8 939	447 380	50 770	-4 830	391 780	109 253	77 975	29 891	26 110	19 371	12 589
2002	593 251	453 497	6 046	459 543	51 949	-4 944	402 650	106 663	83 938	30 484	27 160	19 461	12 502
2003	618 738	471 677	12 741	484 418	53 863	-5 028	425 527	106 255	86 955	31 648	28 513	19 551	12 515
2004	651 327	495 879	16 950	512 829	56 461	-5 187	451 180	108 983	91 164	33 125	29 934	19 663	12 664
2005	673 380	515 134	16 299	531 433	59 190	-5 516	466 727	110 099	96 555	34 058	30 473	19 772	12 861
2006	714 335	540 898	11 510	552 408	62 659	-5 717	484 032	126 066	104 236	35 868	31 903	19 916	13 058
2007	753 857	563 053	15 783	578 835	65 153	-6 043	507 639	135 198	111 021	37 579	33 195	20 060	13 281
2008	788 786	582 617	23 830	606 446	68 018	-6 333	532 096	136 498	120 192	39 037	34 761	20 206	13 459
2009	773 842	566 525	16 164	582 689	66 893	-6 070	509 727	129 111	135 005	38 052	34 704	20 336	...

... = Not available.

Table 21-2. Personal Income and Employment by Region and State—*Continued*

(Millions of dollars, except as noted.)

Region or state and year	Personal income, total	Earnings by place of work			Less: Contributions for government social insurance	Plus: Adjustment for residence	Equals: Net earnings by place of residence	Plus: Dividends, interest, and rent	Plus: Personal current transfer receipts	Per capita (dollars)		Population (thousands)	Total employment (thousands)
		Nonfarm	Farm	Total						Personal income	Disposable personal income		
SOUTHEAST													
1958	58 253	45 299	3 569	48 868	1 738	465	47 595	6 595	4 063	1 556	1 423	37 435	. . .
1959	62 411	49 084	3 459	52 543	2 106	505	50 942	7 122	4 347	1 637	1 489	38 115	. . .
1960	64 713	50 920	3 318	54 238	2 445	552	52 345	7 765	4 603	1 664	1 508	38 885	. . .
1961	68 143	52 712	3 735	56 446	2 510	578	54 514	8 334	5 295	1 723	1 565	39 544	. . .
1962	72 754	56 795	3 495	60 290	2 803	634	58 122	9 076	5 556	1 811	1 634	40 179	. . .
1963	77 570	60 759	3 716	64 475	3 284	691	61 881	9 788	5 901	1 904	1 717	40 742	. . .
1964	83 864	66 215	3 584	69 798	3 441	752	67 109	10 598	6 158	2 028	1 848	41 349	. . .
1965	91 117	72 211	3 464	75 675	3 675	854	72 854	11 540	6 723	2 177	1 976	41 857	. . .
1966	99 915	80 502	3 667	84 170	4 912	951	80 209	12 366	7 340	2 364	2 130	42 257	. . .
1967	108 436	87 252	3 664	90 916	5 655	1 104	86 365	13 325	8 746	2 545	2 291	42 611	. . .
1968	120 221	97 328	3 544	100 871	6 394	1 202	95 679	14 442	10 100	2 793	2 489	43 042	. . .
1969	133 687	107 855	4 061	111 916	7 217	1 135	105 834	16 464	11 390	3 078	2 705	43 440	19 085
1970	146 233	116 480	4 050	120 529	7 781	1 015	113 763	18 691	13 778	3 325	2 952	43 974	19 254
1971	161 167	127 757	4 261	132 018	8 838	989	124 169	20 718	16 279	3 580	3 202	45 013	19 635
1972	181 372	144 512	4 964	149 476	10 454	1 050	140 072	22 880	18 420	3 941	3 484	46 019	20 523
1973	207 034	164 053	7 277	171 330	13 505	1 120	158 945	26 259	21 829	4 406	3 915	46 992	21 636
1974	231 390	181 855	6 661	188 516	15 476	1 238	174 278	30 721	26 391	4 825	4 271	47 955	22 069
1975	252 983	193 662	5 997	199 660	16 283	1 480	184 856	33 874	34 253	5 185	4 674	48 788	21 642
1976	282 893	219 111	6 366	225 477	18 670	1 669	208 476	37 082	37 335	5 713	5 111	49 514	22 351
1977	314 718	246 148	5 766	251 914	20 907	1 902	232 910	42 048	39 761	6 255	5 578	50 312	23 208
1978	358 233	281 116	6 935	288 051	24 367	2 208	265 892	48 772	43 570	7 009	6 218	51 113	24 305
1979	404 260	315 265	6 843	322 108	28 409	2 571	296 270	57 733	50 256	7 778	6 859	51 977	24 987
1980	456 292	348 102	4 174	352 277	31 472	3 114	323 919	72 487	59 886	8 629	7 603	52 881	25 324
1981	516 878	384 200	6 648	390 849	37 410	3 533	356 972	91 371	68 536	9 638	8 462	53 627	25 594
1982	554 972	404 263	6 758	411 021	40 103	3 746	374 664	104 253	76 055	10 230	9 028	54 249	25 499
1983	598 916	436 431	4 892	441 324	43 702	3 811	401 433	114 607	82 876	10 918	9 714	54 856	26 030
1984	667 490	486 815	8 386	495 201	49 939	3 992	449 254	130 885	87 351	12 024	10 768	55 515	27 280
1985	719 023	525 299	7 425	532 724	54 905	4 187	482 005	143 747	93 270	12 794	11 391	56 199	28 090
1986	764 145	560 657	6 939	567 596	60 004	4 412	512 003	152 720	99 421	13 439	11 971	56 861	28 826
1987	816 018	604 764	8 319	613 083	64 257	4 702	553 528	158 940	103 550	14 183	12 574	57 536	29 529
1988	885 115	656 505	10 926	667 431	72 111	5 146	600 466	173 649	111 000	15 229	13 569	58 120	30 527
1989	960 489	696 013	11 410	707 423	77 506	5 494	635 411	201 853	123 225	16 353	14 507	58 733	31 251
1990	1 022 843	739 128	10 880	750 008	83 412	6 263	672 859	214 764	135 220	17 186	15 284	59 516	31 840
1991	1 074 282	770 520	12 426	782 947	87 924	6 804	701 826	219 553	152 902	17 757	15 887	60 501	31 724
1992	1 150 752	830 362	13 222	843 585	93 957	7 262	756 889	221 200	172 664	18 709	16 767	61 508	32 180
1993	1 213 303	879 265	12 820	892 085	100 011	7 649	799 723	228 547	185 034	19 403	17 356	62 531	33 186
1994	1 290 878	933 787	14 017	947 805	107 423	7 577	847 959	246 410	196 508	20 305	18 121	63 574	34 135
1995	1 371 695	991 028	12 448	1 003 476	113 622	7 910	897 765	262 560	211 370	21 233	18 908	64 602	35 254
1996	1 458 514	1 047 906	14 189	1 062 094	119 023	7 469	950 540	284 364	223 610	22 230	19 679	65 611	36 087
1997	1 547 392	1 113 691	13 888	1 127 579	126 536	8 282	1 009 325	305 983	232 084	23 215	20 432	66 655	37 050
1998	1 660 978	1 200 512	12 954	1 213 465	135 291	8 159	1 086 334	335 754	238 890	24 561	21 520	67 627	38 044
1999	1 747 241	1 283 773	13 084	1 296 856	143 524	9 562	1 162 894	334 510	249 838	25 481	22 302	68 569	38 847
2000	1 879 680	1 381 140	14 372	1 395 512	151 979	7 960	1 251 493	361 127	267 059	27 049	23 665	69 491	39 656
2001	1 967 929	1 441 106	16 199	1 457 305	158 756	7 867	1 306 416	366 794	294 719	27 984	24 579	70 323	39 545
2002	2 024 875	1 491 170	10 238	1 501 408	163 625	9 435	1 347 218	358 131	319 526	28 453	25 484	71 166	39 737
2003	2 103 264	1 562 505	13 764	1 576 269	170 222	9 632	1 415 680	353 246	334 338	29 218	26 442	71 986	40 167
2004	2 248 429	1 663 383	16 849	1 680 233	181 261	9 733	1 508 704	382 186	357 539	30 804	27 891	72 992	41 219
2005	2 403 019	1 765 407	17 866	1 783 273	192 609	9 992	1 600 656	415 267	387 096	32 442	29 074	74 072	42 308
2006	2 579 839	1 874 373	13 232	1 887 605	205 828	10 798	1 692 575	477 100	410 164	34 426	30 715	74 938	43 341
2007	2 714 177	1 944 194	11 640	1 955 834	213 795	11 707	1 753 746	521 214	439 217	35 695	31 752	76 038	44 308
2008	2 785 178	1 972 536	13 615	1 986 150	219 823	12 210	1 778 538	522 709	483 931	36 196	32 496	76 948	44 501
2009	2 753 858	1 920 408	13 320	1 933 728	216 298	12 700	1 730 130	484 921	538 807	35 458	32 617	77 664	. . .

. . . = Not available.

Table 21-2. Personal Income and Employment by Region and State—*Continued*

(Millions of dollars, except as noted.)

Region or state and year	Personal income, total	Derivation of personal income								Per capita (dollars)		Population (thousands)	Total employment (thousands)
		Earnings by place of work			Less: Contributions for government social insurance	Plus: Adjustment for residence	Equals: Net earnings by place of residence	Plus: Dividends, interest, and rent	Plus: Personal current transfer receipts	Personal income	Disposable personal income		
		Nonfarm	Farm	Total									
SOUTHWEST													
1958	25 372	19 745	1 627	21 372	708	3	20 666	3 267	1 438	1 866	1 686	13 598	. . .
1959	26 926	21 132	1 477	22 608	847	4	21 766	3 604	1 556	1 941	1 750	13 874	. . .
1960	27 935	21 939	1 458	23 397	1 005	5	22 397	3 894	1 645	1 962	1 764	14 235	. . .
1961	29 462	22 931	1 610	24 541	1 039	6	23 508	4 103	1 851	2 022	1 817	14 572	. . .
1962	30 964	24 374	1 393	25 767	1 131	9	24 645	4 324	1 995	2 074	1 858	14 930	. . .
1963	32 317	25 667	1 175	26 842	1 276	12	25 579	4 586	2 152	2 139	1 916	15 108	. . .
1964	34 600	27 667	1 113	28 781	1 329	14	27 465	4 889	2 247	2 265	2 059	15 278	. . .
1965	37 086	29 492	1 330	30 821	1 399	16	29 438	5 197	2 451	2 406	2 182	15 414	. . .
1966	40 256	32 568	1 389	33 957	1 881	17	32 093	5 489	2 674	2 586	2 327	15 567	. . .
1967	43 804	35 693	1 278	36 971	2 180	19	34 809	5 752	3 242	2 784	2 499	15 734	. . .
1968	48 805	39 886	1 410	41 296	2 450	24	38 869	6 123	3 812	3 051	2 710	15 998	. . .
1969	54 295	44 498	1 513	46 011	2 889	-70	43 052	6 992	4 252	3 325	2 917	16 328	7 219
1970	59 826	48 234	1 837	50 071	3 105	-83	46 883	7 904	5 039	3 599	3 193	16 621	7 311
1971	65 344	52 645	1 680	54 325	3 502	-87	50 736	8 723	5 886	3 826	3 436	17 077	7 457
1972	72 786	58 798	2 017	60 814	4 087	-105	56 622	9 569	6 595	4 159	3 692	17 503	7 807
1973	83 134	66 437	3 298	69 734	5 309	-118	64 307	10 987	7 840	4 633	4 133	17 943	8 215
1974	93 954	75 797	2 139	77 936	6 216	-79	71 641	12 956	9 358	5 119	4 523	18 354	8 511
1975	105 874	84 516	2 113	86 629	6 833	-46	79 750	14 292	11 832	5 635	5 052	18 789	8 633
1976	119 588	96 937	2 084	99 021	7 905	26	91 141	15 500	12 947	6 206	5 529	19 270	9 001
1977	133 904	110 118	1 865	111 983	9 030	-220	102 733	17 424	13 747	6 794	6 007	19 710	9 466
1978	154 903	128 445	1 693	130 138	10 769	-358	119 012	20 651	15 241	7 676	6 774	20 180	10 046
1979	179 695	147 993	2 983	150 975	12 999	-349	137 627	24 656	17 412	8 649	7 560	20 777	10 528
1980	207 235	169 458	1 543	171 001	14 993	-454	155 555	31 265	20 416	9 672	8 428	21 426	10 923
1981	242 928	195 600	2 843	198 443	18 576	-188	179 678	39 922	23 327	11 050	9 525	21 985	11 449
1982	266 303	210 968	2 354	213 322	20 466	-249	192 606	47 317	26 380	11 684	10 146	22 791	11 682
1983	282 202	220 036	2 408	222 444	21 391	-177	200 877	51 863	29 462	12 057	10 678	23 405	11 712
1984	310 770	241 779	2 673	244 452	24 041	-177	220 234	59 283	31 253	13 070	11 642	23 776	12 259
1985	333 306	257 948	2 575	260 523	26 112	-144	234 267	65 559	33 480	13 792	12 275	24 166	12 617
1986	343 473	264 028	2 582	266 610	26 716	-24	239 869	67 120	36 484	13 971	12 570	24 585	12 483
1987	353 317	271 004	3 531	274 535	27 117	67	247 486	67 294	38 537	14 277	12 782	24 748	12 785
1988	373 756	287 487	4 177	291 664	29 853	166	261 976	70 923	40 856	15 035	13 521	24 860	13 055
1989	399 573	303 394	4 119	307 513	31 824	247	275 936	78 518	45 119	15 930	14 248	25 083	13 241
1990	429 496	325 832	4 970	330 802	34 104	346	297 044	82 435	50 017	16 902	15 097	25 411	13 553
1991	450 815	343 145	4 539	347 684	36 671	308	311 321	84 032	55 462	17 394	15 622	25 917	13 759
1992	484 363	368 911	5 379	374 290	39 031	351	335 611	84 259	64 493	18 284	16 492	26 491	13 885
1993	512 943	393 111	6 187	399 298	41 542	401	358 157	85 777	69 009	18 917	17 042	27 116	14 332
1994	546 930	418 610	5 310	423 920	44 685	424	379 659	93 302	73 969	19 693	17 725	27 772	14 845
1995	583 637	446 897	4 289	451 186	47 393	406	404 199	99 568	79 870	20 536	18 458	28 420	15 396
1996	627 956	481 649	3 911	485 560	50 616	407	435 351	107 441	85 164	21 639	19 321	29 020	15 883
1997	681 302	526 884	5 014	531 899	54 693	398	477 604	115 018	88 680	22 997	20 407	29 625	16 482
1998	739 859	577 172	4 817	581 990	59 237	408	523 161	125 724	90 975	24 467	21 626	30 240	17 066
1999	783 243	617 856	6 646	624 502	62 760	504	562 245	126 242	94 755	25 407	22 466	30 827	17 402
2000	859 138	681 392	5 510	686 902	67 507	570	619 965	138 756	100 418	27 372	24 133	31 387	17 915
2001	901 256	716 156	6 305	722 461	71 081	442	651 822	138 450	110 984	28 225	24 994	31 931	18 013
2002	914 157	725 100	6 223	731 323	72 422	457	659 359	132 595	122 203	28 130	25 459	32 498	18 064
2003	950 506	753 255	7 294	760 549	75 633	538	685 454	134 291	130 762	28 788	26 302	33 017	18 238
2004	1 019 583	810 133	8 419	818 552	79 947	584	739 190	141 505	138 888	30 359	27 829	33 584	18 668
2005	1 107 823	869 625	8 127	877 752	85 653	559	792 658	162 595	152 570	32 368	29 320	34 226	19 299
2006	1 209 260	947 462	5 240	952 702	92 073	469	861 098	183 946	164 215	34 473	31 010	35 078	20 037
2007	1 283 849	990 717	5 743	996 461	97 741	265	898 984	205 711	179 154	35 881	32 191	35 781	20 719
2008	1 339 513	1 031 745	4 465	1 036 210	102 150	176	934 236	207 219	198 058	36 765	33 269	36 434	21 231
2009	1 317 742	1 004 516	2 443	1 006 959	100 330	160	906 789	189 482	221 472	35 543	32 901	37 075	. . .

. . . = Not available.

Table 21-2. Personal Income and Employment by Region and State—*Continued*

(Millions of dollars, except as noted.)

Region or state and year	Personal income, total	Earnings by place of work			Less: Contributions for government social insurance	Plus: Adjustment for residence	Equals: Net earnings by place of residence	Plus: Dividends, interest, and rent	Plus: Personal current transfer receipts	Per capita (dollars)		Population (thousands)	Total employment (thousands)
		Nonfarm	Farm	Total						Personal income	Disposable personal income		
ROCKY MOUNTAIN													
1958	8 406	6 292	704	6 995	252	-3	6 741	1 134	531	2 031	1 829	4 139	...
1959	8 885	6 793	578	7 372	291	-3	7 078	1 214	594	2 103	1 885	4 226	...
1960	9 390	7 247	580	7 827	354	-3	7 471	1 295	624	2 159	1 923	4 350	...
1961	9 938	7 744	525	8 269	382	-3	7 885	1 363	690	2 210	1 968	4 497	...
1962	10 720	8 224	711	8 935	412	-3	8 520	1 479	721	2 341	2 092	4 580	...
1963	11 050	8 605	623	9 228	478	-2	8 748	1 545	758	2 386	2 126	4 632	...
1964	11 554	9 109	509	9 617	491	-2	9 125	1 652	777	2 473	2 243	4 673	...
1965	12 423	9 584	726	10 310	499	-2	9 810	1 773	840	2 643	2 395	4 700	...
1966	13 175	10 328	693	11 022	646	-1	10 375	1 898	902	2 782	2 506	4 735	...
1967	14 009	10 942	707	11 650	720	-1	10 928	2 011	1 069	2 929	2 628	4 783	...
1968	15 230	11 979	747	12 726	803	-1	11 922	2 093	1 215	3 128	2 783	4 868	...
1969	17 010	13 222	889	14 111	884	15	13 242	2 423	1 345	3 441	3 016	4 943	2 216
1970	18 966	14 577	1 003	15 580	965	16	14 631	2 733	1 601	3 765	3 338	5 038	2 271
1971	21 054	16 284	966	17 250	1 105	19	16 165	3 018	1 871	4 053	3 617	5 194	2 343
1972	23 895	18 533	1 269	19 802	1 323	22	18 500	3 305	2 090	4 451	3 943	5 368	2 482
1973	27 437	21 161	1 751	22 913	1 732	22	21 203	3 792	2 442	4 964	4 395	5 527	2 646
1974	31 039	23 921	1 837	25 757	2 006	25	23 776	4 425	2 838	5 494	4 839	5 650	2 740
1975	34 283	26 563	1 386	27 949	2 181	37	25 804	4 949	3 530	5 930	5 290	5 782	2 778
1976	38 222	30 304	1 027	31 330	2 515	42	28 858	5 484	3 880	6 461	5 729	5 916	2 912
1977	42 852	34 586	686	35 272	2 873	44	32 442	6 264	4 146	7 049	6 221	6 079	3 060
1978	49 745	40 305	958	41 263	3 414	54	37 904	7 305	4 536	7 950	7 005	6 257	3 257
1979	56 593	46 011	749	46 759	4 095	54	42 718	8 724	5 151	8 789	7 691	6 439	3 402
1980	64 520	51 189	965	52 153	4 581	78	47 650	10 829	6 041	9 787	8 579	6 592	3 474
1981	73 555	57 455	1 057	58 511	5 550	49	53 010	13 486	7 059	10 909	9 513	6 743	3 559
1982	79 688	61 086	826	61 911	6 016	51	55 946	15 710	8 032	11 542	10 096	6 904	3 596
1983	84 804	64 328	1 143	65 471	6 398	53	59 126	16 847	8 831	12 055	10 727	7 035	3 642
1984	92 144	70 204	1 041	71 245	7 176	72	64 141	18 785	9 218	12 962	11 584	7 109	3 801
1985	96 745	73 807	841	74 647	7 732	89	67 004	19 963	9 777	13 497	12 030	7 168	3 861
1986	100 127	75 835	1 240	77 074	8 020	111	69 165	20 469	10 493	13 907	12 446	7 200	3 854
1987	103 466	78 239	1 584	79 823	8 211	135	71 748	20 587	11 132	14 359	12 798	7 206	3 885
1988	108 663	82 921	1 637	84 558	9 072	171	75 657	21 292	11 714	15 087	13 452	7 203	4 021
1989	117 760	87 996	2 217	90 213	9 762	206	80 657	24 185	12 918	16 278	14 431	7 234	4 114
1990	125 998	94 567	2 515	97 083	10 828	241	86 496	25 533	13 969	17 248	15 230	7 305	4 230
1991	134 080	101 365	2 467	103 832	11 850	272	92 253	26 420	15 406	17 932	15 892	7 477	4 335
1992	144 634	110 354	2 547	112 901	12 836	303	100 368	27 112	17 154	18 792	16 637	7 696	4 434
1993	156 627	119 846	3 224	123 069	14 026	334	109 378	28 779	18 470	19 729	17 440	7 939	4 626
1994	168 444	129 383	2 097	131 480	15 217	384	116 647	32 382	19 415	20 614	18 176	8 171	4 886
1995	181 605	138 693	2 000	140 692	16 206	449	124 935	35 343	21 327	21 672	19 091	8 380	5 046
1996	195 544	148 806	2 191	150 997	17 085	520	134 432	38 808	22 305	22 829	19 987	8 565	5 249
1997	209 840	160 612	2 059	162 671	18 215	591	145 047	41 941	22 853	23 993	20 881	8 746	5 440
1998	227 665	174 045	2 398	176 443	19 145	686	157 984	46 108	23 572	25 528	22 128	8 918	5 625
1999	244 060	189 563	2 741	192 303	20 458	788	172 634	46 597	24 828	26 836	23 192	9 094	5 767
2000	269 821	211 101	2 372	213 473	22 307	855	192 020	51 143	26 657	29 109	25 069	9 269	5 966
2001	287 228	224 761	3 038	227 799	23 435	923	205 286	52 745	29 196	30 413	26 474	9 444	5 999
2002	291 857	229 293	2 284	231 576	24 214	925	208 288	51 471	32 098	30 440	27 152	9 588	5 993
2003	299 172	235 239	2 345	237 583	25 042	976	213 518	51 932	33 722	30 815	27 755	9 709	6 021
2004	318 334	250 215	3 361	253 576	26 709	1 043	227 911	54 849	35 574	32 288	29 133	9 859	6 167
2005	341 594	266 481	3 467	269 948	28 671	1 084	242 360	60 975	38 259	34 066	30 350	10 027	6 368
2006	372 407	288 564	2 432	290 996	31 267	1 143	260 871	70 274	41 263	36 296	32 055	10 260	6 597
2007	396 421	302 431	3 225	305 656	33 047	1 217	273 826	78 369	44 226	37 805	33 180	10 486	6 844
2008	409 538	310 852	3 474	314 326	34 339	1 258	281 245	79 429	48 864	38 307	33 939	10 691	6 984
2009	400 643	301 554	2 265	303 819	33 602	1 228	271 446	73 185	56 012	36 843	33 513	10 874	...

. . . = Not available.

Table 21-2. Personal Income and Employment by Region and State—*Continued*

(Millions of dollars, except as noted.)

Region or state and year	Personal income, total	Earnings by place of work			Less: Contributions for government social insurance	Plus: Adjustment for residence	Equals: Net earnings by place of residence	Plus: Dividends, interest, and rent	Plus: Personal current transfer receipts	Per capita (dollars)		Population (thousands)	Total employment (thousands)
		Nonfarm	Farm	Total						Personal income	Disposable personal income		
FAR WEST													
1958	50 973	40 455	1 819	42 274	1 584	-1	40 689	7 209	3 076	2 490	2 229	20 469	. . .
1959	55 671	44 813	1 917	46 730	1 984	-1	44 745	7 777	3 148	2 631	2 349	21 159	. . .
1960	58 816	47 258	1 953	49 211	2 356	-2	46 854	8 449	3 513	2 716	2 400	21 659	. . .
1961	62 206	49 873	1 852	51 725	2 494	-2	49 229	8 928	4 049	2 780	2 460	22 378	. . .
1962	67 177	54 264	1 961	56 225	2 976	-4	53 245	9 682	4 250	2 906	2 569	23 114	. . .
1963	71 416	58 004	1 897	59 900	3 458	-6	56 436	10 340	4 640	2 999	2 649	23 811	. . .
1964	77 190	62 426	2 004	64 430	3 580	-7	60 843	11 355	4 992	3 165	2 844	24 389	. . .
1965	82 647	66 529	1 995	68 524	3 730	-8	64 786	12 387	5 474	3 318	2 982	24 908	. . .
1966	90 151	73 538	2 243	75 781	4 925	-10	70 846	13 309	5 996	3 562	3 180	25 311	. . .
1967	97 258	78 966	2 113	81 078	5 443	-11	75 624	14 264	7 370	3 773	3 357	25 779	. . .
1968	106 969	87 154	2 375	89 529	6 111	-14	83 404	15 068	8 496	4 090	3 600	26 151	. . .
1969	117 525	95 203	2 480	97 683	6 630	-199	90 854	16 978	9 694	4 412	3 848	26 635	12 295
1970	126 599	100 751	2 439	103 190	6 899	-203	96 088	18 544	11 967	4 671	4 143	27 101	12 313
1971	135 027	106 387	2 469	108 856	7 521	-220	101 115	20 068	13 844	4 898	4 393	27 570	12 300
1972	148 178	117 457	3 113	120 570	8 736	-225	111 609	21 596	14 972	5 308	4 683	27 918	12 742
1973	164 737	130 637	4 253	134 890	11 068	-228	123 594	24 291	16 852	5 815	5 170	28 328	13 405
1974	185 339	145 038	5 388	150 427	12 611	-324	137 491	27 915	19 933	6 435	5 703	28 801	13 865
1975	206 499	160 120	4 812	164 933	13 666	-521	150 747	30 698	25 054	7 037	6 311	29 346	14 103
1976	231 461	182 022	4 815	186 836	15 736	-635	170 465	33 389	27 607	7 734	6 877	29 929	14 625
1977	257 684	204 402	4 685	209 087	17 871	-449	190 767	37 579	29 339	8 434	7 455	30 553	15 287
1978	294 470	235 533	4 760	240 293	21 055	-381	218 858	43 836	31 776	9 412	8 266	31 285	16 248
1979	335 820	267 907	5 907	273 814	25 059	-355	248 401	52 358	35 061	10 506	9 167	31 965	17 133
1980	382 014	296 861	7 356	304 217	27 313	-437	276 467	64 491	41 056	11 654	10 176	32 780	17 523
1981	427 810	326 152	5 862	332 014	32 427	-219	299 368	80 225	48 217	12 796	11 186	33 434	17 693
1982	456 582	343 762	5 930	349 692	34 767	-261	314 665	88 365	53 553	13 395	11 814	34 086	17 564
1983	491 650	370 238	5 966	376 204	38 250	-281	337 673	96 816	57 162	14 162	12 544	34 716	17 989
1984	544 820	411 739	6 605	418 345	43 874	-322	374 149	110 939	59 732	15 425	13 678	35 321	18 767
1985	585 286	444 079	6 368	450 447	48 001	-368	402 078	118 689	64 519	16 241	14 324	36 037	19 392
1986	624 913	476 861	7 271	484 132	52 245	-392	431 494	124 448	68 972	16 974	14 978	36 815	19 959
1987	670 862	518 402	8 511	526 913	56 770	-466	469 676	129 152	72 033	17 823	15 571	37 641	20 793
1988	727 983	567 087	9 045	576 131	64 009	-552	511 570	139 167	77 246	18 888	16 631	38 542	21 790
1989	787 918	604 330	8 993	613 323	68 917	-643	543 762	159 455	84 700	19 930	17 370	39 534	22 453
1990	849 277	650 752	9 482	660 234	74 606	-757	584 871	171 243	93 162	20 913	18 263	40 610	23 122
1991	885 753	677 733	8 634	686 368	78 354	-754	607 259	174 585	103 908	21 381	18 848	41 428	23 124
1992	935 491	714 989	9 389	724 378	82 179	-738	641 460	175 048	118 982	22 154	19 652	42 226	22 825
1993	965 348	733 865	10 703	744 568	84 229	-726	659 613	179 584	126 151	22 556	20 011	42 798	22 934
1994	1 008 531	763 013	10 052	773 065	87 907	-749	684 410	194 200	129 922	23 307	20 661	43 271	23 380
1995	1 063 662	800 637	9 668	810 305	91 077	-785	718 443	208 161	137 058	24 315	21 470	43 745	23 938
1996	1 133 666	848 781	11 188	859 969	94 652	-852	764 466	224 998	144 202	25 582	22 363	44 314	24 580
1997	1 208 963	912 189	11 487	923 677	100 414	-925	822 337	240 784	145 842	26 834	23 254	45 054	25 149
1998	1 319 200	1 000 260	11 130	1 011 390	107 982	-1 007	902 401	263 280	153 519	28 805	24 829	45 798	26 021
1999	1 406 162	1 084 216	11 640	1 095 855	115 613	-1 128	979 115	264 859	162 189	30 236	25 699	46 506	26 663
2000	1 542 349	1 201 138	11 796	1 212 934	126 603	-1 235	1 085 095	287 229	170 024	32 681	27 376	47 194	27 484
2001	1 589 162	1 231 849	11 197	1 243 046	131 744	-1 112	1 110 189	289 800	189 173	33 184	28 204	47 890	27 656
2002	1 619 143	1 258 360	11 786	1 270 146	135 751	-1 111	1 133 284	282 792	203 068	33 394	29 433	48 486	27 378
2003	1 682 361	1 313 051	13 721	1 326 772	142 462	-1 227	1 183 083	286 524	212 754	34 305	30 503	49 042	27 632
2004	1 795 124	1 397 422	16 017	1 413 439	154 218	-1 357	1 257 864	314 924	222 336	36 222	32 240	49 559	28 167
2005	1 897 118	1 473 450	14 301	1 487 751	162 951	-1 435	1 323 365	339 658	234 095	37 928	33 293	50 019	28 822
2006	2 048 279	1 564 474	14 475	1 578 950	170 209	-1 515	1 407 226	389 095	251 957	40 580	35 461	50 475	29 458
2007	2 162 066	1 626 705	15 722	1 642 427	174 364	-1 625	1 466 439	426 083	269 543	42 434	36 899	50 951	30 121
2008	2 213 838	1 647 095	14 114	1 661 208	179 380	-1 613	1 480 215	437 926	295 697	42 970	37 776	51 521	30 380
2009	2 165 207	1 580 658	11 395	1 592 053	173 958	-1 513	1 416 582	411 138	337 488	41 568	37 641	52 088	. . .

. . . = Not available.

Table 21-2. Personal Income and Employment by Region and State—*Continued*

(Millions of dollars, except as noted.)

Region or state and year	Personal income, total	Derivation of personal income								Per capita (dollars)		Population (thousands)	Total employment (thousands)
		Earnings by place of work			Less: Contributions for government social insurance	Plus: Adjustment for residence	Equals: Net earnings by place of residence	Plus: Dividends, interest, and rent	Plus: Personal current transfer receipts	Personal income	Disposable personal income		
		Nonfarm	Farm	Total									
ALABAMA													
1958	4 595	3 670	304	3 974	135	1	3 839	412	344	1 453	1 331	3 163	. . .
1959	4 837	3 934	248	4 181	159	1	4 024	451	363	1 510	1 382	3 204	. . .
1960	5 042	4 091	255	4 346	187	2	4 161	496	385	1 540	1 404	3 274	. . .
1961	5 199	4 193	245	4 438	194	2	4 247	523	429	1 568	1 435	3 316	. . .
1962	5 465	4 425	224	4 649	219	4	4 434	564	468	1 645	1 494	3 323	. . .
1963	5 821	4 695	271	4 966	259	6	4 713	613	496	1 734	1 577	3 358	. . .
1964	6 327	5 159	245	5 404	265	8	5 146	668	513	1 864	1 705	3 395	. . .
1965	6 884	5 625	254	5 879	273	10	5 616	718	551	1 999	1 825	3 443	. . .
1966	7 384	6 157	241	6 398	376	15	6 038	747	599	2 132	1 929	3 464	. . .
1967	7 801	6 524	206	6 730	429	21	6 323	787	690	2 256	2 040	3 458	. . .
1968	8 526	7 103	227	7 330	472	24	6 882	843	801	2 474	2 221	3 446	. . .
1969	9 405	7 733	280	8 013	551	137	7 599	914	892	2 734	2 418	3 440	1 411
1970	10 219	8 282	250	8 533	590	136	8 078	1 044	1 097	2 962	2 662	3 450	1 413
1971	11 212	9 010	279	9 289	655	144	8 778	1 150	1 285	3 206	2 892	3 497	1 423
1972	12 483	10 050	348	10 398	765	171	9 804	1 249	1 431	3 526	3 157	3 540	1 471
1973	14 118	11 284	535	11 818	983	188	11 024	1 413	1 681	3 943	3 531	3 581	1 526
1974	15 731	12 657	340	12 997	1 136	198	12 059	1 661	2 011	4 336	3 878	3 628	1 552
1975	17 543	13 667	414	14 081	1 221	204	13 063	1 879	2 600	4 766	4 308	3 681	1 543
1976	19 857	15 670	479	16 149	1 421	218	14 946	2 071	2 840	5 313	4 774	3 737	1 594
1977	21 918	17 572	383	17 955	1 595	247	16 607	2 315	2 996	5 794	5 201	3 783	1 651
1978	24 783	19 940	509	20 449	1 840	270	18 880	2 640	3 263	6 464	5 785	3 834	1 713
1979	27 625	22 021	521	22 542	2 102	297	20 737	3 086	3 802	7 139	6 357	3 869	1 736
1980	30 522	23 890	211	24 101	2 281	327	22 147	3 913	4 461	7 825	6 955	3 900	1 732
1981	33 931	25 739	491	26 229	2 655	426	24 000	4 922	5 009	8 659	7 679	3 919	1 719
1982	35 926	26 641	411	27 052	2 795	447	24 705	5 684	5 537	9 152	8 200	3 925	1 687
1983	38 443	28 668	292	28 960	3 053	440	26 347	6 098	5 997	9 772	8 754	3 934	1 717
1984	42 488	31 580	481	32 061	3 428	491	29 123	7 026	6 339	10 752	9 679	3 952	1 780
1985	45 699	34 049	466	34 515	3 740	501	31 276	7 729	6 695	11 504	10 291	3 973	1 822
1986	48 219	36 094	458	36 552	3 973	525	33 104	8 151	6 964	12 080	10 806	3 992	1 858
1987	51 136	38 517	542	39 059	4 195	534	35 397	8 618	7 120	12 735	11 328	4 015	1 912
1988	54 881	41 352	806	42 158	4 680	531	38 009	9 446	7 426	13 639	12 228	4 024	1 970
1989	59 549	43 676	941	44 617	5 001	551	40 167	10 992	8 390	14 776	13 176	4 030	2 006
1990	63 254	46 554	849	47 403	5 410	529	42 523	11 496	9 235	15 618	13 943	4 050	2 048
1991	66 969	48 990	1 124	50 114	5 766	562	44 910	11 855	10 204	16 337	14 645	4 099	2 060
1992	71 714	52 675	1 004	53 679	6 163	620	48 135	11 977	11 602	17 264	15 514	4 154	2 097
1993	74 871	55 130	1 019	56 149	6 541	671	50 278	12 274	12 318	17 766	15 943	4 214	2 159
1994	79 481	58 121	1 070	59 190	7 010	766	52 946	13 469	13 065	18 656	16 688	4 260	2 180
1995	84 005	61 095	790	61 885	7 396	844	55 332	14 579	14 094	19 551	17 454	4 297	2 242
1996	87 682	63 569	918	64 487	7 649	854	57 692	15 124	14 865	20 245	18 006	4 331	2 275
1997	92 243	66 520	956	67 476	8 024	956	60 408	16 295	15 540	21 118	18 717	4 368	2 321
1998	97 858	70 428	1 078	71 506	8 426	1 069	64 148	17 854	15 857	22 217	19 693	4 405	2 371
1999	101 719	73 932	1 244	75 176	8 808	1 136	67 505	17 653	16 562	22 961	20 333	4 430	2 388
2000	107 151	77 199	957	78 156	9 084	1 264	70 337	19 140	17 674	24 069	21 357	4 452	2 400
2001	112 003	80 508	1 385	81 893	9 422	1 282	73 753	19 128	19 123	25 090	22 369	4 464	2 370
2002	115 397	83 837	977	84 814	9 713	1 298	76 399	18 439	20 559	25 802	23 321	4 472	2 369
2003	120 030	87 294	1 364	88 658	10 070	1 344	79 932	18 341	21 757	26 729	24 368	4 491	2 380
2004	128 009	92 380	1 794	94 175	10 525	1 414	85 064	19 878	23 067	28 370	25 919	4 512	2 441
2005	135 617	97 687	1 775	99 463	11 191	1 473	89 745	20 997	24 875	29 838	27 027	4 545	2 505
2006	144 437	103 836	1 079	104 916	11 879	1 534	94 571	23 075	26 791	31 415	28 239	4 598	2 565
2007	152 136	107 708	847	108 555	12 454	1 639	97 741	25 743	28 652	32 803	29 426	4 638	2 628
2008	157 422	110 199	1 050	111 249	12 890	1 641	100 000	26 112	31 310	33 655	30 438	4 677	2 641
2009	155 840	107 382	922	108 304	12 694	1 586	97 196	24 334	34 309	33 096	30 597	4 709	. . .

. . . = Not available.

Table 21-2. Personal Income and Employment by Region and State—*Continued*

(Millions of dollars, except as noted.)

Region or state and year	Personal income, total	Derivation of personal income									Per capita (dollars)		Population (thousands)	Total employment (thousands)
		Earnings by place of work			Less: Contributions for government social insurance	Plus: Adjustment for residence	Equals: Net earnings by place of residence	Plus: Dividends, interest, and rent	Plus: Personal current transfer receipts		Personal income	Disposable personal income		
		Nonfarm	Farm	Total										
ALASKA														
1958	559	533	2	535	22	0	513	25	21		2 494	. . .	224	. . .
1959	592	566	1	567	24	0	544	27	21		2 645	. . .	224	. . .
1960	701	673	2	675	28	-2	646	33	22		3 062	2 703	229	. . .
1961	698	664	2	666	28	-3	635	36	27		2 931	2 611	238	. . .
1962	731	697	1	698	29	-5	665	40	26		2 970	2 622	246	. . .
1963	790	758	1	758	33	-8	717	45	27		3 086	2 714	256	. . .
1964	890	855	1	856	37	-13	806	55	29		3 385	3 047	263	. . .
1965	963	926	1	927	41	-18	869	63	31		3 554	3 149	271	. . .
1966	1 034	995	1	997	48	-23	926	74	34		3 814	3 392	271	. . .
1967	1 133	1 095	1	1 096	53	-30	1 012	82	39		4 075	3 620	278	. . .
1968	1 231	1 199	2	1 201	67	-38	1 096	87	48		4 319	3 822	285	. . .
1969	1 412	1 376	1	1 378	94	-26	1 258	100	54		4 769	4 071	296	144
1970	1 597	1 564	2	1 566	105	-47	1 414	111	72		5 248	4 559	304	149
1971	1 767	1 728	2	1 730	118	-61	1 551	125	91		5 583	4 883	316	153
1972	1 939	1 903	2	1 905	134	-76	1 695	141	103		5 940	5 125	326	158
1973	2 268	2 113	2	2 115	165	-94	1 856	165	246		6 805	5 960	333	167
1974	2 802	2 840	2	2 842	241	-210	2 391	203	208		8 130	6 946	345	189
1975	3 957	4 478	4	4 482	407	-614	3 461	258	237		10 666	9 038	371	227
1976	4 760	5 630	4	5 634	526	-885	4 224	303	233		12 109	10 263	393	243
1977	4 922	5 213	5	5 218	463	-454	4 302	343	278		12 388	10 536	397	237
1978	5 025	5 083	5	5 088	434	-326	4 328	399	299		12 495	10 812	402	238
1979	5 327	5 316	4	5 319	467	-289	4 563	471	293		13 199	11 271	404	241
1980	6 070	6 013	3	6 016	527	-329	5 161	566	343		14 975	13 057	405	244
1981	6 917	6 970	2	6 972	686	-470	5 816	694	406		16 528	14 086	418	252
1982	8 461	8 069	3	8 071	798	-562	6 712	886	864		18 819	16 331	450	277
1983	9 203	8 984	2	8 986	852	-622	7 512	1 058	633		18 843	16 537	488	297
1984	9 963	9 623	2	9 625	948	-637	8 040	1 241	682		19 395	17 267	514	309
1985	10 705	10 023	2	10 025	970	-629	8 426	1 393	886		20 104	17 966	532	316
1986	10 707	9 757	7	9 764	916	-569	8 279	1 432	997		19 673	17 805	544	310
1987	10 379	9 233	9	9 242	858	-532	7 853	1 487	1 039		19 244	17 260	539	310
1988	10 757	9 553	11	9 564	929	-556	8 079	1 560	1 117		19 848	17 913	542	317
1989	11 778	10 395	6	10 400	1 026	-618	8 756	1 784	1 238		21 525	19 129	547	329
1990	12 501	10 977	8	10 986	1 145	-652	9 189	1 943	1 369		22 594	19 937	553	339
1991	13 167	11 589	9	11 598	1 214	-699	9 686	2 012	1 469		23 092	20 597	570	347
1992	13 957	12 228	9	12 237	1 283	-735	10 220	2 106	1 631		23 706	21 240	589	351
1993	14 673	12 683	11	12 695	1 364	-753	10 578	2 278	1 817		24 478	21 963	599	358
1994	15 195	12 985	12	12 997	1 418	-772	10 808	2 526	1 861		25 186	22 538	603	363
1995	15 580	13 166	13	13 179	1 428	-778	10 974	2 659	1 948		25 778	23 096	604	365
1996	15 931	13 262	14	13 276	1 430	-791	11 055	2 781	2 096		26 179	23 377	609	369
1997	16 671	13 656	16	13 673	1 471	-781	11 421	2 987	2 263		27 197	24 204	613	374
1998	17 323	14 103	17	14 120	1 522	-832	11 766	3 096	2 460		27 943	24 786	620	381
1999	17 830	14 421	20	14 441	1 543	-834	12 064	3 059	2 707		28 538	25 368	625	381
2000	19 158	15 298	21	15 319	1 616	-887	12 815	3 273	3 069		30 531	27 101	627	392
2001	20 434	16 658	20	16 677	1 724	-940	14 014	3 212	3 209		32 266	28 723	633	401
2002	21 302	17 705	19	17 724	1 802	-1 000	14 921	3 072	3 308		33 144	29 980	643	405
2003	21 817	18 454	12	18 466	1 873	-1 022	15 571	3 017	3 229		33 519	30 577	651	409
2004	23 067	19 756	15	19 770	1 993	-1 077	16 700	3 179	3 188		34 867	32 029	662	417
2005	24 613	21 056	14	21 070	2 131	-1 143	17 795	3 442	3 375		36 764	33 567	669	425
2006	26 307	22 464	10	22 474	2 298	-1 265	18 911	3 796	3 600		38 839	35 279	677	434
2007	28 030	23 362	7	23 369	2 384	-1 370	19 616	4 343	4 071		41 081	36 988	682	443
2008	30 224	24 413	4	24 417	2 485	-1 449	20 482	4 414	5 327		43 922	39 945	688	453
2009	29 757	25 229	5	25 234	2 585	-1 473	21 176	4 089	4 492		42 603	39 416	698	. . .

. . . = Not available.

Table 21-2. Personal Income and Employment by Region and State—*Continued*

(Millions of dollars, except as noted.)

Region or state and year	Personal income, total	Derivation of personal income								Per capita (dollars)		Population (thousands)	Total employment (thousands)
		Earnings by place of work			Less: Contributions for government social insurance	Plus: Adjustment for residence	Equals: Net earnings by place of residence	Plus: Dividends, interest, and rent	Plus: Personal current transfer receipts	Personal income	Disposable personal income		
		Nonfarm	Farm	Total									
ARIZONA													
1958	2 258	1 771	130	1 901	79	-2	1 820	303	135	1 893	1 710	1 193	...
1959	2 496	1 975	124	2 099	95	-2	2 001	342	153	1 979	1 776	1 261	...
1960	2 728	2 165	127	2 293	117	-2	2 173	389	166	2 065	1 843	1 321	...
1961	2 970	2 329	134	2 462	125	-2	2 335	440	194	2 111	1 895	1 407	...
1962	3 198	2 527	136	2 664	139	-2	2 523	463	212	2 174	1 943	1 471	...
1963	3 358	2 680	111	2 790	162	0	2 628	499	231	2 208	1 974	1 521	...
1964	3 600	2 853	129	2 981	167	*	2 814	536	250	2 314	2 105	1 556	...
1965	3 816	3 008	127	3 134	174	1	2 961	572	282	2 409	2 191	1 584	...
1966	4 161	3 369	120	3 489	232	0	3 257	600	305	2 578	2 333	1 614	...
1967	4 524	3 620	148	3 767	265	0	3 502	644	377	2 748	2 473	1 646	...
1968	5 188	4 101	191	4 292	312	2	3 982	770	435	3 084	2 754	1 682	...
1969	6 071	4 714	203	4 918	322	-26	4 570	1 009	492	3 495	3 071	1 737	711
1970	6 873	5 319	180	5 499	362	-29	5 108	1 173	593	3 829	3 379	1 795	747
1971	7 832	6 067	201	6 268	430	-28	5 809	1 312	711	4 131	3 689	1 896	786
1972	8 986	7 060	205	7 265	525	-32	6 708	1 461	817	4 473	3 953	2 009	850
1973	10 423	8 236	240	8 476	695	-31	7 750	1 689	984	4 904	4 384	2 125	925
1974	11 791	9 077	384	9 461	791	-41	8 629	1 973	1 189	5 301	4 711	2 224	955
1975	12 654	9 472	218	9 690	816	-47	8 827	2 166	1 662	5 535	5 034	2 286	935
1976	14 231	10 662	330	10 992	916	-47	10 029	2 377	1 825	6 061	5 478	2 348	976
1977	16 055	12 261	267	12 527	1 061	-56	11 410	2 721	1 925	6 615	5 935	2 427	1 048
1978	18 963	14 565	318	14 884	1 292	-69	13 523	3 269	2 171	7 532	6 700	2 518	1 150
1979	22 451	17 290	399	17 689	1 606	-71	16 012	3 968	2 471	8 509	7 521	2 639	1 240
1980	25 964	19 374	477	19 851	1 810	-80	17 962	5 033	2 970	9 484	8 418	2 738	1 283
1981	29 737	21 649	415	22 064	2 177	-14	19 873	6 374	3 490	10 582	9 311	2 810	1 313
1982	31 447	22 444	396	22 841	2 299	-6	20 535	7 018	3 894	10 882	9 616	2 890	1 315
1983	34 529	24 631	327	24 958	2 580	4	22 382	7 883	4 264	11 630	10 371	2 969	1 379
1984	39 268	28 111	526	28 637	3 018	8	25 626	9 070	4 571	12 803	11 442	3 067	1 504
1985	43 410	31 296	491	31 787	3 435	20	28 372	10 076	4 962	13 636	12 117	3 184	1 622
1986	47 424	34 332	471	34 803	3 805	40	31 038	10 944	5 443	14 335	12 759	3 308	1 701
1987	51 201	37 040	635	37 675	4 075	66	33 665	11 588	5 947	14 896	13 235	3 437	1 765
1988	55 088	40 051	762	40 813	4 557	107	36 363	12 203	6 522	15 583	13 926	3 535	1 833
1989	58 971	41 429	690	42 119	4 852	164	37 432	13 984	7 555	16 281	14 476	3 622	1 865
1990	61 916	43 483	642	44 125	5 222	225	39 129	14 420	8 367	16 806	14 932	3 684	1 894
1991	65 364	46 156	739	46 895	5 566	222	41 551	14 462	9 351	17 253	15 372	3 789	1 903
1992	69 550	49 626	673	50 299	5 940	248	44 607	14 290	10 653	17 762	15 891	3 916	1 925
1993	74 686	53 432	789	54 221	6 408	266	48 080	15 111	11 496	18 371	16 403	4 065	2 011
1994	82 292	59 086	577	59 663	7 093	277	52 847	17 173	12 272	19 385	17 277	4 245	2 141
1995	89 378	64 438	824	65 262	7 404	296	58 154	18 178	13 046	20 164	17 953	4 432	2 258
1996	97 054	70 679	737	71 416	8 317	324	63 423	19 743	13 888	21 159	18 642	4 587	2 388
1997	105 307	76 875	740	77 616	8 945	358	69 029	21 800	14 477	22 231	19 527	4 737	2 497
1998	115 841	85 315	872	86 187	9 699	404	76 892	23 920	15 030	23 722	20 758	4 883	2 611
1999	123 500	92 501	849	93 350	10 418	462	83 394	24 066	16 040	24 583	21 492	5 024	2 697
2000	135 687	102 646	807	103 453	11 338	516	92 631	26 098	16 958	26 262	22 939	5 167	2 796
2001	142 863	108 173	747	108 920	11 880	562	97 603	26 026	19 235	26 933	23 676	5 304	2 823
2002	148 174	111 705	764	112 469	12 262	548	100 755	25 968	21 452	27 177	24 455	5 452	2 842
2003	155 607	117 206	732	117 937	12 731	576	105 783	26 521	23 303	27 831	25 231	5 591	2 914
2004	170 027	127 372	1 006	128 378	13 774	632	115 236	29 288	25 503	29 522	26 728	5 759	3 040
2005	188 153	139 700	967	140 666	15 127	656	126 195	33 608	28 350	31 491	28 159	5 975	3 208
2006	206 957	153 362	692	154 054	16 613	677	138 118	37 951	30 888	33 423	29 753	6 192	3 370
2007	218 639	159 243	804	160 047	17 459	720	143 309	41 991	33 340	34 365	30 629	6 362	3 455
2008	223 184	159 197	619	159 816	17 733	749	142 832	42 941	37 412	34 339	30 964	6 499	3 437
2009	217 235	150 621	409	151 031	16 934	700	134 797	39 659	42 779	32 935	30 456	6 596	...

. . . = Not available.
* = Less than $50,000, but the estimates for this item are included in the total.

Table 21-2. Personal Income and Employment by Region and State—*Continued*

(Millions of dollars, except as noted.)

Region or state and year	Personal income, total	Earnings by place of work			Less: Contributions for government social insurance	Plus: Adjustment for residence	Equals: Net earnings by place of residence	Plus: Dividends, interest, and rent	Plus: Personal current transfer receipts	Per capita (dollars)		Population (thousands)	Total employment (thousands)
		Nonfarm	Farm	Total						Personal income	Disposable personal income		
ARKANSAS													
1958	2 254	1 606	283	1 889	66	-1	1 823	222	209	1 306	1 209	1 726	. . .
1959	2 476	1 727	364	2 091	79	-1	2 011	240	225	1 410	1 302	1 756	. . .
1960	2 503	1 785	310	2 095	92	-2	2 001	262	240	1 399	1 289	1 789	. . .
1961	2 715	1 894	365	2 258	95	-2	2 161	286	269	1 504	1 387	1 806	. . .
1962	2 893	2 082	320	2 402	109	-3	2 290	315	288	1 561	1 424	1 853	. . .
1963	3 073	2 228	318	2 546	126	-4	2 415	348	310	1 639	1 496	1 875	. . .
1964	3 338	2 416	356	2 772	137	-5	2 631	381	326	1 760	1 629	1 897	. . .
1965	3 525	2 598	283	2 881	147	-6	2 728	440	357	1 861	1 714	1 894	. . .
1966	3 920	2 849	388	3 238	191	-5	3 042	487	391	2 064	1 880	1 899	. . .
1967	4 158	3 097	297	3 394	221	-5	3 168	523	468	2 188	1 992	1 901	. . .
1968	4 512	3 413	334	3 747	251	-7	3 488	499	525	2 372	2 137	1 902	. . .
1969	5 005	3 744	346	4 090	279	30	3 840	581	584	2 616	2 334	1 913	800
1970	5 482	3 997	415	4 412	297	20	4 135	664	684	2 840	2 548	1 930	805
1971	6 090	4 468	407	4 875	341	19	4 553	735	802	3 088	2 805	1 972	831
1972	6 881	5 089	482	5 571	406	18	5 183	804	893	3 409	3 083	2 018	867
1973	8 189	5 769	913	6 683	526	14	6 171	935	1 083	3 978	3 585	2 058	902
1974	9 174	6 493	833	7 326	610	7	6 723	1 136	1 315	4 368	3 908	2 100	927
1975	10 075	6 942	795	7 737	640	6	7 103	1 302	1 669	4 668	4 254	2 158	905
1976	11 185	8 050	641	8 691	746	-4	7 941	1 421	1 823	5 157	4 640	2 169	941
1977	12 486	9 058	725	9 784	849	-8	8 927	1 624	1 936	5 657	5 106	2 207	981
1978	14 496	10 329	1 176	11 506	990	-13	10 502	1 866	2 128	6 469	5 837	2 241	1 021
1979	15 930	11 467	995	12 462	1 137	-15	11 310	2 180	2 440	7 020	6 287	2 269	1 031
1980	17 214	12 454	372	12 826	1 227	-3	11 597	2 728	2 889	7 521	6 701	2 289	1 032
1981	19 510	13 388	852	14 240	1 428	-21	12 791	3 448	3 271	8 508	7 589	2 293	1 026
1982	20 526	13 853	642	14 495	1 504	-18	12 973	3 996	3 557	8 947	7 933	2 294	1 011
1983	21 819	15 022	417	15 438	1 639	-48	13 752	4 216	3 850	9 463	8 491	2 306	1 039
1984	24 325	16 655	882	17 537	1 869	-67	15 601	4 689	4 036	10 486	9 479	2 320	1 079
1985	25 896	17 646	863	18 509	2 006	-72	16 431	5 191	4 274	11 128	10 031	2 327	1 098
1986	27 108	18 686	804	19 490	2 141	-95	17 253	5 352	4 503	11 625	10 508	2 332	1 110
1987	28 161	19 714	937	20 651	2 252	-114	18 285	5 241	4 635	12 023	10 819	2 342	1 137
1988	30 114	20 981	1 349	22 331	2 508	-148	19 675	5 576	4 863	12 855	11 592	2 343	1 170
1989	32 208	22 192	1 238	23 431	2 678	-149	20 604	6 233	5 370	13 727	12 341	2 346	1 189
1990	33 939	23 708	1 048	24 756	2 977	-211	21 568	6 557	5 814	14 402	12 928	2 357	1 204
1991	35 994	25 242	1 129	26 370	3 182	-239	22 949	6 593	6 452	15 103	13 605	2 383	1 230
1992	39 149	27 511	1 432	28 943	3 467	-264	25 212	6 778	7 158	16 204	14 616	2 416	1 255
1993	41 002	29 063	1 338	30 401	3 688	-295	26 418	7 028	7 555	16 692	15 050	2 456	1 301
1994	43 634	31 042	1 467	32 510	3 993	-320	28 197	7 509	7 928	17 496	15 708	2 494	1 329
1995	46 297	32 894	1 484	34 378	4 210	-291	29 877	7 889	8 531	18 260	16 355	2 535	1 382
1996	49 309	34 338	1 924	36 262	4 369	-281	31 612	8 671	9 025	19 170	17 165	2 572	1 405
1997	51 621	36 015	1 814	37 829	4 583	-280	32 965	9 235	9 421	19 846	17 680	2 601	1 427
1998	54 623	38 414	1 597	40 012	4 863	-284	34 865	10 019	9 739	20 798	18 456	2 626	1 453
1999	57 164	40 755	1 807	42 562	5 090	-316	37 156	9 943	10 066	21 556	19 168	2 652	1 471
2000	60 468	43 185	1 699	44 884	5 321	-362	39 201	10 574	10 693	22 577	20 034	2 678	1 493
2001	64 236	45 530	2 001	47 531	5 498	-360	41 672	10 706	11 858	23 870	21 296	2 691	1 483
2002	65 652	47 292	1 260	48 552	5 660	-389	42 503	10 336	12 813	24 273	21 942	2 705	1 478
2003	69 239	49 499	2 512	52 011	5 834	-394	45 783	10 124	13 332	25 434	23 242	2 722	1 480
2004	73 725	52 571	2 757	55 328	6 135	-407	48 786	10 660	14 278	26 846	24 573	2 746	1 501
2005	77 478	55 292	1 883	57 175	6 492	-397	50 286	11 845	15 347	27 908	25 344	2 776	1 531
2006	82 929	58 571	1 508	60 079	6 964	-388	52 726	13 445	16 759	29 459	26 694	2 815	1 565
2007	89 576	60 990	1 912	62 902	7 237	-320	55 344	16 191	18 041	31 517	28 399	2 842	1 583
2008	92 505	62 180	2 286	64 466	7 566	-306	56 594	16 172	19 740	32 257	29 239	2 868	1 599
2009	92 307	61 846	1 916	63 763	7 653	-341	55 768	14 421	22 118	31 946	29 536	2 889	. . .

. . . = Not available.

Table 21-2. Personal Income and Employment by Region and State—*Continued*

(Millions of dollars, except as noted.)

Region or state and year	Personal income, total	Earnings by place of work			Less: Contributions for government social insurance	Plus: Adjustment for residence	Equals: Net earnings by place of residence	Plus: Dividends, interest, and rent	Plus: Personal current transfer receipts	Per capita (dollars)		Population (thousands)	Total employment (thousands)
		Nonfarm	Farm	Total						Personal income	Disposable personal income		
CALIFORNIA													
1958	38 676	30 512	1 335	31 847	1 112	-4	30 731	5 721	2 223	2 599	2 312	14 880	...
1959	42 432	34 008	1 413	35 421	1 423	-5	33 992	6 167	2 273	2 743	2 432	15 467	...
1960	44 846	35 878	1 430	37 308	1 719	-6	35 583	6 679	2 584	2 826	2 497	15 870	...
1961	47 529	37 964	1 361	39 325	1 830	-6	37 488	7 042	2 999	2 881	2 549	16 497	...
1962	51 304	41 321	1 425	42 746	2 247	-7	40 492	7 633	3 179	3 005	2 655	17 072	...
1963	54 800	44 377	1 357	45 734	2 623	-7	43 104	8 179	3 517	3 102	2 740	17 668	...
1964	59 452	47 837	1 508	49 345	2 729	-8	46 608	9 031	3 812	3 275	2 945	18 151	...
1965	63 434	50 792	1 456	52 248	2 845	-10	49 393	9 829	4 213	3 413	3 069	18 585	...
1966	68 937	55 942	1 574	57 516	3 739	-12	53 765	10 519	4 653	3 656	3 268	18 858	...
1967	74 287	59 941	1 489	61 430	4 094	-14	57 323	11 210	5 755	3 874	3 450	19 176	...
1968	81 475	65 966	1 716	67 682	4 579	-16	63 087	11 744	6 643	4 201	3 699	19 394	...
1969	89 337	71 809	1 704	73 513	4 830	-130	68 553	13 168	7 616	4 532	3 962	19 711	9 033
1970	96 133	75 949	1 708	77 657	5 020	-114	72 523	14 309	9 301	4 801	4 266	20 023	9 057
1971	102 282	80 005	1 707	81 711	5 452	-124	76 135	15 451	10 695	5 027	4 519	20 346	9 036
1972	112 207	88 379	2 172	90 550	6 337	-127	84 087	16 599	11 522	5 451	4 812	20 585	9 368
1973	124 033	97 799	2 930	100 730	7 979	-113	92 638	18 638	12 758	5 944	5 298	20 868	9 844
1974	138 832	107 860	3 644	111 504	9 020	-127	102 357	21 358	15 117	6 557	5 825	21 173	10 163
1975	153 687	117 666	3 273	120 939	9 606	-17	111 316	23 377	18 994	7 136	6 419	21 537	10 286
1976	171 862	132 964	3 478	136 442	10 984	86	125 544	25 332	20 986	7 835	6 982	21 935	10 633
1977	191 580	149 944	3 544	153 488	12 566	-65	140 857	28 442	22 280	8 572	7 591	22 350	11 119
1978	218 613	172 805	3 491	176 296	14 800	-76	161 421	33 103	24 089	9 572	8 421	22 839	11 816
1979	249 280	196 439	4 572	201 011	17 658	-52	183 301	39 510	26 469	10 719	9 372	23 255	12 461
1980	283 904	218 286	5 583	223 868	19 245	-85	204 539	48 634	30 731	11 928	10 420	23 801	12 762
1981	319 204	240 879	4 362	245 240	23 003	247	222 484	60 558	36 162	13 144	11 506	24 286	12 935
1982	341 069	255 162	4 600	259 761	24 901	253	235 113	66 322	39 634	13 742	12 116	24 820	12 863
1983	368 163	276 298	4 233	280 531	27 639	266	253 158	72 676	42 329	14 517	12 833	25 360	13 182
1984	411 268	310 260	4 904	315 164	32 061	240	283 344	83 751	44 174	15 913	14 066	25 844	13 797
1985	443 596	336 304	4 939	341 243	35 322	187	306 108	89 728	47 760	16 777	14 738	26 441	14 285
1986	474 995	362 877	5 376	368 253	38 689	143	329 707	93 989	51 299	17 526	15 407	27 102	14 710
1987	512 411	396 911	6 608	403 519	42 356	63	361 226	97 660	53 524	18 447	16 040	27 777	15 300
1988	555 467	433 471	6 968	440 439	47 655	23	392 807	105 399	57 260	19 515	17 118	28 464	16 022
1989	597 464	458 611	6 829	465 440	50 960	8	414 488	120 359	62 617	20 448	17 763	29 218	16 426
1990	640 548	489 727	7 206	496 933	54 185	-50	442 699	128 969	68 880	21 380	18 614	29 960	16 835
1991	662 252	505 684	6 309	511 993	56 329	-37	455 627	130 151	76 473	21 734	19 139	30 471	16 750
1992	695 028	528 831	6 815	535 646	58 339	-37	477 270	129 349	88 408	22 439	19 904	30 975	16 391
1993	711 327	537 929	7 760	545 689	59 105	31	486 615	131 356	93 356	22 744	20 176	31 275	16 367
1994	738 250	555 748	7 541	563 289	61 142	47	502 194	140 544	95 511	23 448	20 790	31 484	16 541
1995	776 490	582 427	7 226	589 652	62 901	37	526 788	149 931	99 771	24 498	21 600	31 697	16 940
1996	825 689	615 673	8 124	623 797	64 880	25	558 942	161 860	104 887	25 788	22 487	32 019	17 342
1997	879 160	661 589	8 685	670 274	69 059	-70	601 145	172 947	105 068	27 063	23 367	32 486	17 667
1998	963 067	728 714	8 205	736 920	74 352	-76	662 492	189 612	110 964	29 195	25 081	32 988	18 371
1999	1 027 715	791 305	8 966	800 271	80 470	-128	719 674	191 287	116 754	30 679	25 937	33 499	18 860
2000	1 135 342	887 048	8 872	895 920	89 266	-296	806 358	207 463	121 521	33 398	27 664	33 995	19 466
2001	1 168 733	908 405	8 428	916 833	94 003	-303	822 528	211 202	135 003	33 890	28 521	34 486	19 610
2002	1 187 360	925 832	8 956	934 788	97 031	-256	837 501	204 840	145 019	34 045	29 852	34 876	19 374
2003	1 232 991	966 250	10 150	976 401	102 270	-273	873 857	206 644	152 490	34 977	30 940	35 251	19 506
2004	1 312 244	1 029 164	12 281	1 041 445	111 248	-287	929 909	222 128	160 207	36 904	32 667	35 558	19 795
2005	1 387 682	1 082 552	10 768	1 093 320	117 096	-239	975 984	243 777	167 921	38 767	33 811	35 795	20 161
2006	1 495 560	1 144 440	10 718	1 155 158	120 647	-211	1 034 300	280 234	181 026	41 567	36 084	35 979	20 514
2007	1 572 271	1 184 118	11 921	1 196 039	122 462	-147	1 073 430	305 889	192 951	43 402	37 449	36 226	20 920
2008	1 604 113	1 194 906	9 994	1 204 900	126 462	-76	1 078 362	315 328	210 423	43 852	38 307	36 580	21 063
2009	1 564 389	1 141 728	8 256	1 149 984	122 349	-42	1 027 593	297 438	239 358	42 325	38 127	36 962	...

. . . = Not available.

Table 21-2. Personal Income and Employment by Region and State—*Continued*

(Millions of dollars, except as noted.)

| Region or state and year | Personal income, total | Earnings by place of work | | | Less: Contributions for government social insurance | Plus: Adjustment for residence | Equals: Net earnings by place of residence | Plus: Dividends, interest, and rent | Plus: Personal current transfer receipts | Per capita (dollars) | | Population (thousands) | Total employment (thousands) |
		Nonfarm	Farm	Total						Personal income	Disposable personal income		
COLORADO													
1958	3 583	2 756	177	2 932	95	1	2 839	524	220	2 149	1 917	1 667	. . .
1959	3 857	2 992	156	3 148	109	1	3 040	558	259	2 256	2 016	1 710	. . .
1960	4 130	3 226	171	3 397	133	1	3 266	589	275	2 335	2 058	1 769	. . .
1961	4 446	3 492	172	3 665	150	1	3 516	629	302	2 411	2 126	1 844	. . .
1962	4 680	3 686	153	3 839	163	1	3 676	685	319	2 465	2 176	1 899	. . .
1963	4 899	3 885	137	4 022	191	0	3 832	728	339	2 530	2 235	1 936	. . .
1964	5 186	4 129	135	4 264	197	*	4 066	776	343	2 632	2 374	1 970	. . .
1965	5 541	4 323	210	4 534	197	0	4 336	830	375	2 791	2 513	1 985	. . .
1966	5 960	4 735	188	4 924	263	-1	4 660	893	407	2 970	2 655	2 007	. . .
1967	6 431	5 089	184	5 272	294	-1	4 977	970	483	3 132	2 789	2 053	. . .
1968	7 147	5 658	242	5 900	333	-2	5 565	1 033	549	3 371	2 969	2 120	. . .
1969	7 985	6 339	251	6 590	388	2	6 204	1 176	605	3 687	3 199	2 166	1 001
1970	8 985	7 072	289	7 361	427	2	6 935	1 319	730	4 040	3 550	2 224	1 032
1971	10 133	8 027	301	8 328	499	3	7 833	1 450	850	4 399	3 888	2 304	1 072
1972	11 481	9 225	333	9 558	606	4	8 957	1 581	943	4 774	4 162	2 405	1 149
1973	13 186	10 612	440	11 052	797	3	10 257	1 821	1 108	5 283	4 628	2 496	1 243
1974	14 835	11 794	535	12 330	905	4	11 429	2 122	1 283	5 837	5 091	2 541	1 276
1975	16 350	12 904	464	13 368	966	8	12 410	2 329	1 610	6 322	5 591	2 586	1 285
1976	18 111	14 574	336	14 911	1 104	9	13 816	2 537	1 758	6 880	6 056	2 632	1 340
1977	20 314	16 563	266	16 829	1 260	12	15 581	2 868	1 865	7 535	6 587	2 696	1 411
1978	23 476	19 376	209	19 585	1 505	20	18 101	3 344	2 031	8 485	7 395	2 767	1 506
1979	27 073	22 418	218	22 636	1 837	20	20 819	3 971	2 282	9 502	8 232	2 849	1 593
1980	31 165	25 327	290	25 617	2 101	28	23 544	4 975	2 646	10 714	9 288	2 909	1 651
1981	35 968	28 868	307	29 175	2 586	5	26 594	6 266	3 108	12 078	10 409	2 978	1 717
1982	39 505	31 556	185	31 741	2 895	2	28 848	7 135	3 522	12 904	11 105	3 062	1 760
1983	42 423	33 487	360	33 848	3 130	0	30 717	7 808	3 898	13 538	11 950	3 134	1 788
1984	46 499	36 746	425	37 171	3 539	8	33 640	8 751	4 108	14 669	13 002	3 170	1 883
1985	48 988	38 716	394	39 111	3 835	17	35 292	9 394	4 301	15 267	13 490	3 209	1 915
1986	50 869	40 118	397	40 515	4 021	22	36 516	9 739	4 615	15 713	13 936	3 237	1 914
1987	52 836	41 516	479	41 995	4 122	34	37 907	9 954	4 975	16 205	14 323	3 260	1 903
1988	55 695	43 829	581	44 411	4 501	49	39 959	10 505	5 231	17 072	15 127	3 262	1 968
1989	60 269	46 338	621	46 959	4 829	66	42 196	12 244	5 829	18 398	16 190	3 276	2 003
1990	64 093	49 416	713	50 129	5 245	91	44 975	12 872	6 247	19 377	17 003	3 308	2 040
1991	68 160	52 971	640	53 610	5 748	102	47 965	13 260	6 935	20 123	17 704	3 387	2 087
1992	73 772	57 785	679	58 465	6 233	117	52 348	13 634	7 790	21 102	18 563	3 496	2 135
1993	80 051	62 965	815	63 781	6 841	129	57 069	14 631	8 352	22 152	19 443	3 614	2 234
1994	86 537	67 700	584	68 285	7 392	146	61 039	16 640	8 858	23 237	20 353	3 724	2 345
1995	94 039	73 040	545	73 585	7 897	167	65 855	18 269	9 915	24 575	21 524	3 827	2 425
1996	101 777	78 993	671	79 664	8 437	185	71 413	20 102	10 262	25 964	22 569	3 920	2 519
1997	110 110	86 220	677	86 897	9 118	206	77 985	21 704	10 421	27 402	23 625	4 018	2 629
1998	120 100	93 981	807	94 788	9 529	232	85 491	23 970	10 639	29 174	24 958	4 117	2 732
1999	130 663	104 224	938	105 162	10 384	262	95 040	24 283	11 340	30 919	26 374	4 226	2 816
2000	147 056	118 625	775	119 401	11 536	289	108 154	26 914	11 988	33 977	28 857	4 328	2 926
2001	156 469	126 234	1 069	127 304	12 146	340	115 498	27 881	13 091	35 296	30 404	4 433	2 941
2002	157 753	127 678	705	128 384	12 560	347	116 170	26 793	14 789	35 023	30 959	4 504	2 910
2003	159 919	129 770	749	130 518	12 848	363	118 033	26 465	15 421	35 156	31 434	4 549	2 906
2004	168 588	137 268	951	138 219	13 669	384	124 934	27 554	16 100	36 652	32 831	4 600	2 954
2005	179 698	145 296	1 140	146 437	14 536	400	132 301	30 072	17 326	38 555	34 161	4 661	3 031
2006	194 393	155 073	845	155 918	15 430	420	140 909	34 887	18 598	40 899	35 947	4 753	3 101
2007	205 548	160 983	1 030	162 012	16 173	448	146 287	39 293	19 968	42 449	37 001	4 842	3 208
2008	212 320	166 016	1 005	167 021	16 929	454	150 546	39 672	22 102	43 021	37 828	4 935	3 285
2009	207 742	161 152	765	161 917	16 577	440	145 780	36 580	25 381	41 344	37 418	5 025	. . .

. . . = Not available.
* = Less than $50,000, but the estimates for this item are included in the total.

Table 21-2. Personal Income and Employment by Region and State—*Continued*

(Millions of dollars, except as noted.)

Region or state and year	Personal income, total	Derivation of personal income									Per capita (dollars)		Population (thousands)	Total employment (thousands)
		Earnings by place of work			Less: Contributions for government social insurance	Plus: Adjustment for residence	Equals: Net earnings by place of residence	Plus: Dividends, interest, and rent	Plus: Personal current transfer receipts		Personal income	Disposable personal income		
		Nonfarm	Farm	Total										
CONNECTICUT														
1958	6 396	5 121	67	5 188	184	-2	5 003	1 003	390		2 615	2 302	2 446	...
1959	6 839	5 552	58	5 610	230	-2	5 378	1 084	376		2 711	2 381	2 523	...
1960	7 117	5 787	63	5 849	278	3	5 575	1 154	389		2 798	2 437	2 544	...
1961	7 524	6 049	58	6 106	290	3	5 819	1 257	448		2 910	2 543	2 586	...
1962	8 042	6 479	59	6 538	320	3	6 221	1 381	441		3 038	2 652	2 647	...
1963	8 485	6 825	63	6 888	369	4	6 523	1 493	469		3 111	2 701	2 727	...
1964	9 112	7 299	61	7 360	379	5	6 985	1 632	495		3 257	2 883	2 798	...
1965	9 791	7 815	71	7 885	395	2	7 492	1 776	523		3 427	3 013	2 857	...
1966	10 753	8 747	73	8 820	553	0	8 267	1 923	564		3 704	3 230	2 903	...
1967	11 791	9 464	57	9 521	602	2	8 921	2 168	701		4 017	3 474	2 935	...
1968	12 576	10 196	67	10 264	671	7	9 600	2 122	854		4 243	3 604	2 964	...
1969	14 464	11 125	67	11 192	752	728	11 168	2 348	947		4 821	4 068	3 000	1 417
1970	15 410	11 724	72	11 795	783	722	11 733	2 531	1 146		5 071	4 398	3 039	1 414
1971	16 211	12 140	69	12 209	840	746	12 115	2 672	1 424		5 295	4 665	3 061	1 388
1972	17 474	13 231	68	13 299	968	785	13 115	2 854	1 505		5 692	4 942	3 070	1 416
1973	19 109	14 721	81	14 802	1 234	808	14 376	3 103	1 630		6 226	5 444	3 069	1 480
1974	20 896	15 987	84	16 071	1 395	841	15 517	3 461	1 918		6 794	5 939	3 076	1 511
1975	22 371	16 627	75	16 703	1 423	916	16 196	3 629	2 546		7 252	6 432	3 085	1 468
1976	24 311	18 204	83	18 287	1 577	1 011	17 721	3 881	2 709		7 878	6 903	3 086	1 493
1977	26 824	20 257	84	20 340	1 778	1 121	19 684	4 308	2 832		8 684	7 612	3 089	1 546
1978	29 884	22 837	80	22 917	2 062	1 275	22 130	4 834	2 920		9 656	8 379	3 095	1 615
1979	33 650	25 742	79	25 821	2 421	1 448	24 848	5 551	3 251		10 855	9 345	3 100	1 673
1980	38 357	28 675	84	28 759	2 682	1 691	27 768	6 852	3 738		12 321	10 551	3 113	1 705
1981	43 117	31 424	82	31 506	3 140	1 865	30 231	8 572	4 314		13 780	11 749	3 129	1 727
1982	46 612	33 554	108	33 662	3 413	2 020	32 269	9 546	4 796		14 849	12 645	3 139	1 726
1983	49 765	36 170	105	36 275	3 737	2 140	34 679	9 906	5 181		15 737	13 740	3 162	1 743
1984	55 639	40 603	129	40 732	4 306	2 288	38 714	11 509	5 416		17 496	15 361	3 180	1 823
1985	59 652	44 243	127	44 370	4 742	2 424	42 052	11 856	5 745		18 635	16 211	3 201	1 879
1986	64 135	47 887	140	48 027	5 166	2 576	45 437	12 622	6 076		19 895	17 206	3 224	1 937
1987	70 053	53 184	143	53 327	5 654	2 696	50 369	13 404	6 281		21 573	18 474	3 247	1 984
1988	77 079	58 784	157	58 941	6 347	2 884	55 477	14 827	6 775		23 557	20 434	3 272	2 039
1989	83 387	61 842	140	61 982	6 655	2 777	58 104	17 694	7 590		25 397	22 041	3 283	2 032
1990	86 244	63 468	185	63 653	6 748	2 757	59 662	18 094	8 487		26 198	22 815	3 292	2 003
1991	87 296	64 315	165	64 480	6 940	2 724	60 265	17 528	9 504		26 430	23 046	3 303	1 923
1992	93 367	67 452	188	67 640	7 155	3 924	64 408	17 777	11 182		28 287	24 396	3 301	1 904
1993	96 134	70 092	210	70 302	7 415	3 342	66 229	18 238	11 666		29 051	24 935	3 309	1 925
1994	99 121	72 643	186	72 829	7 766	3 116	68 178	18 863	12 080		29 891	25 666	3 316	1 906
1995	104 266	76 184	173	76 357	8 131	3 869	72 095	19 249	12 923		31 366	26 740	3 324	1 944
1996	109 560	79 620	161	79 780	8 472	4 648	75 957	20 345	13 259		32 835	27 517	3 337	1 975
1997	116 817	86 129	158	86 287	8 991	4 192	81 487	21 703	13 626		34 877	28 852	3 349	2 000
1998	125 278	91 735	180	91 915	9 435	5 578	88 058	23 422	13 798		37 226	30 476	3 365	2 028
1999	131 113	97 667	193	97 859	9 885	5 403	93 377	23 597	14 140		38 718	31 533	3 386	2 057
2000	143 021	106 837	226	107 063	10 515	5 631	102 178	25 953	14 890		41 920	33 837	3 412	2 096
2001	149 518	112 830	200	113 030	10 818	4 997	107 210	26 506	15 802		43 611	35 306	3 428	2 108
2002	149 467	113 681	189	113 870	11 324	4 327	106 874	25 629	16 964		43 344	36 633	3 448	2 117
2003	151 653	116 568	195	116 763	11 583	3 950	109 130	25 263	17 261		43 733	37 368	3 468	2 113
2004	161 314	123 216	209	123 425	12 198	4 550	115 777	27 233	18 304		46 427	39 630	3 475	2 139
2005	168 666	128 726	200	128 926	12 617	4 545	120 855	28 830	18 981		48 503	40 649	3 477	2 169
2006	183 820	135 634	180	135 814	13 102	4 876	127 589	35 988	20 243		52 744	44 068	3 485	2 200
2007	194 068	141 579	189	141 768	13 624	4 937	133 082	39 693	21 294		55 629	45 474	3 489	2 242
2008	197 024	142 304	201	142 505	14 108	5 083	133 480	40 156	23 388		56 245	46 592	3 503	2 279
2009	191 385	136 483	218	136 700	13 768	4 586	127 518	37 201	26 665		54 397	47 154	3 518	...

. . . = Not available.

Table 21-2. Personal Income and Employment by Region and State—*Continued*

(Millions of dollars, except as noted.)

Region or state and year	Personal income, total	Derivation of personal income								Per capita (dollars)		Population (thousands)	Total employment (thousands)
		Earnings by place of work			Less: Contributions for government social insurance	Plus: Adjustment for residence	Equals: Net earnings by place of residence	Plus: Dividends, interest, and rent	Plus: Personal current transfer receipts	Personal income	Disposable personal income		
		Nonfarm	Farm	Total									
DELAWARE													
1958	1 156	917	35	952	32	-49	871	234	52	2 671	2 248	433	...
1959	1 207	974	30	1 004	42	-50	912	243	52	2 738	2 288	441	...
1960	1 264	1 023	34	1 057	53	-51	953	257	54	2 816	2 356	449	...
1961	1 300	1 049	29	1 079	51	-51	976	259	65	2 821	2 375	461	...
1962	1 377	1 114	32	1 147	58	-52	1 037	273	67	2 936	2 440	469	...
1963	1 475	1 209	26	1 234	69	-56	1 109	296	70	3 053	2 560	483	...
1964	1 598	1 308	26	1 333	68	-58	1 207	317	74	3 215	2 702	497	...
1965	1 762	1 444	35	1 478	69	-65	1 345	338	80	3 475	2 917	507	...
1966	1 860	1 584	26	1 609	99	-69	1 441	330	88	3 604	3 039	516	...
1967	1 983	1 683	32	1 715	117	-69	1 530	345	108	3 777	3 199	525	...
1968	2 173	1 848	29	1 878	119	-71	1 688	358	127	4 070	3 424	534	...
1969	2 379	1 992	55	2 048	139	-43	1 865	378	139	4 411	3 638	540	271
1970	2 528	1 992	35	2 167	147	-43	1 865	376	139	4 406	3 819	550	275
1971	2 763	2 132	38	2 387	168	-48	1 971	392	165	4 594	4 104	565	280
1972	3 040	2 348	49	2 655	196	-60	2 158	410	194	4 888	4 435	574	293
1973	3 392	2 606	96	3 023	253	-68	2 392	433	215	5 297	4 899	579	305
1974	3 695	2 927	82	3 253	282	-97	2 674	470	248	5 858	5 322	583	302
1975	3 968	3 171	92	3 432	293	-108	2 864	528	303	6 336	5 745	589	292
1976	4 354	3 340	84	3 776	325	-110	3 029	532	408	6 740	6 175	593	296
1977	4 694	3 692	56	4 046	352	-121	3 330	586	438	7 345	6 644	595	296
1978	5 159	3 990	61	4 497	402	-133	3 561	657	477	7 892	7 265	598	304
1979	5 678	4 436	54	4 931	460	-163	3 933	727	499	8 624	7 919	599	312
1980	6 399	4 876	13	5 430	512	-184	4 286	819	572	9 482	8 977	595	312
1981	7 049	5 418	43	5 859	594	-231	4 688	1 017	694	10 756	9 795	596	314
1982	7 599	5 816	66	6 308	651	-249	5 015	1 253	781	11 827	10 655	599	317
1983	8 154	6 242	78	6 786	704	-270	5 387	1 384	829	12 684	11 470	605	325
1984	9 019	6 707	96	7 471	780	-317	5 765	1 505	884	13 468	12 648	612	340
1985	9 831	7 375	104	8 153	865	-357	6 335	1 737	948	14 748	13 648	618	357
1986	10 411	8 049	144	8 606	934	-399	6 889	1 945	997	15 900	14 201	628	370
1987	11 213	8 463	114	9 392	1 017	-398	7 275	2 057	1 078	16 589	15 137	637	387
1988	12 187	9 277	182	10 282	1 154	-452	7 923	2 166	1 124	17 604	16 256	648	403
1989	13 533	10 100	192	11 238	1 267	-496	8 632	2 317	1 238	18 819	17 727	658	415
1990	14 201	11 046	141	11 822	1 318	-604	9 367	2 826	1 340	20 559	18 262	670	420
1991	15 077	12 249	133	12 382	1 388	-688	10 307	3 102	1 669	22 073	19 208	683	414
1992	15 636	13 003	117	13 120	1 428	-969	10 723	3 097	1 817	22 500	19 598	695	413
1993	16 165	13 344	108	13 453	1 488	-916	11 049	3 174	1 942	22 885	19 890	706	421
1994	16 853	14 064	122	14 186	1 588	-1 072	11 526	3 263	2 064	23 487	20 300	718	424
1995	17 812	14 594	87	14 682	1 677	-912	12 092	3 468	2 251	24 409	21 107	730	442
1996	19 123	15 392	121	15 512	1 763	-936	12 813	3 818	2 492	25 808	22 153	741	453
1997	19 970	16 415	95	16 510	1 868	-1 209	13 433	4 017	2 519	26 574	22 527	751	464
1998	21 676	17 744	142	17 886	1 986	-1 383	14 517	4 475	2 684	28 397	24 080	763	481
1999	22 530	19 048	140	19 187	2 131	-1 650	15 406	4 320	2 804	29 072	24 665	775	493
2000	24 384	20 292	148	20 440	2 232	-1 707	16 500	4 823	3 061	31 007	26 427	786	504
2001	25 750	21 696	212	21 908	2 331	-1 835	17 741	4 651	3 358	32 405	27 569	795	500
2002	26 695	22 490	87	22 577	2 394	-1 872	18 311	4 763	3 621	33 197	29 040	804	501
2003	27 586	23 324	174	23 498	2 485	-1 986	19 027	4 680	3 879	33 852	29 915	815	506
2004	29 521	24 830	257	25 086	2 668	-2 045	20 373	4 973	4 174	35 712	31 555	827	520
2005	31 077	26 391	292	26 683	2 797	-2 227	21 659	4 889	4 529	37 001	32 252	840	530
2006	33 307	27 814	207	28 021	3 019	-2 399	22 603	5 778	4 925	39 046	34 073	853	540
2007	34 537	28 347	197	28 543	3 110	-2 206	23 227	6 000	5 309	39 932	34 801	865	549
2008	35 377	28 560	181	28 742	3 210	-2 136	23 396	6 107	5 874	40 375	35 580	876	553
2009	35 243	27 591	199	27 789	3 146	-1 976	22 668	5 930	6 645	39 817	36 097	885	...

. . . = Not available.

Table 21-2. Personal Income and Employment by Region and State—*Continued*

(Millions of dollars, except as noted.)

Region or state and year	Personal income, total	Earnings by place of work			Less: Contributions for government social insurance	Plus: Adjustment for residence	Equals: Net earnings by place of residence	Plus: Dividends, interest, and rent	Plus: Personal current transfer receipts	Per capita (dollars)		Population (thousands)	Total employment (thousands)
		Nonfarm	Farm	Total						Personal income	Disposable personal income		
DISTRICT OF COLUMBIA													
1958	2 057	2 751	0	2 751	79	-1 049	1 623	327	106	2 717	2 360	757	. . .
1959	2 123	2 902	0	2 902	89	-1 139	1 673	340	109	2 789	2 383	761	. . .
1960	2 147	3 088	0	3 088	101	-1 321	1 666	369	112	2 806	2 384	765	. . .
1961	2 265	3 281	0	3 281	107	-1 410	1 765	376	123	2 911	2 513	778	. . .
1962	2 445	3 536	0	3 536	114	-1 496	1 926	393	127	3 103	2 668	788	. . .
1963	2 601	3 805	0	3 805	138	-1 612	2 055	411	135	3 259	2 828	798	. . .
1964	2 765	4 086	0	4 086	135	-1 749	2 202	423	140	3 465	3 055	798	. . .
1965	2 995	4 443	0	4 443	140	-1 903	2 399	446	150	3 758	3 335	797	. . .
1966	3 126	4 792	0	4 792	186	-2 090	2 516	449	160	3 952	3 467	791	. . .
1967	3 349	5 418	0	5 418	213	-2 498	2 706	450	192	4 234	3 739	791	. . .
1968	3 524	5 840	0	5 840	234	-2 767	2 839	456	230	4 530	3 991	778	. . .
1969	3 416	6 140	0	6 140	252	-3 181	2 708	474	234	4 483	3 833	762	676
1970	3 753	6 688	0	6 688	274	-3 481	2 933	518	302	4 970	4 273	755	672
1971	4 126	7 270	0	7 270	299	-3 791	3 180	571	375	5 497	4 788	751	666
1972	4 482	7 877	0	7 877	343	-4 120	3 414	621	447	6 026	5 218	744	668
1973	4 747	8 396	0	8 396	414	-4 404	3 578	657	512	6 470	5 586	734	662
1974	5 227	9 236	0	9 236	472	-4 861	3 904	728	595	7 252	6 289	721	673
1975	5 707	10 213	0	10 213	521	-5 468	4 224	741	741	8 034	7 003	710	677
1976	6 077	11 123	0	11 123	573	-6 033	4 518	792	768	8 728	7 489	696	674
1977	6 572	12 200	0	12 200	609	-6 672	4 919	865	787	9 639	8 363	682	680
1978	6 946	13 296	0	13 296	668	-7 451	5 177	959	810	10 367	8 899	670	693
1979	7 358	14 532	0	14 532	770	-8 391	5 371	1 083	904	11 224	9 500	656	704
1980	7 799	15 962	0	15 962	859	-9 605	5 497	1 276	1 026	12 218	10 378	638	701
1981	8 522	17 308	0	17 308	1 040	-10 485	5 783	1 606	1 133	13 381	11 210	637	689
1982	9 240	18 366	0	18 366	1 115	-11 111	6 140	1 832	1 267	14 570	12 275	634	673
1983	9 726	19 308	0	19 308	1 294	-11 492	6 521	1 879	1 326	15 379	13 094	632	667
1984	10 759	21 017	0	21 017	1 465	-12 388	7 164	2 181	1 414	16 986	14 485	633	689
1985	11 454	22 476	0	22 476	1 681	-13 157	7 638	2 401	1 416	18 051	15 378	635	703
1986	12 084	23 736	0	23 736	1 859	-13 760	8 118	2 497	1 470	18 932	16 165	638	721
1987	12 768	25 497	0	25 497	2 023	-14 750	8 723	2 530	1 515	20 046	16 972	637	733
1988	13 969	28 129	0	28 129	2 318	-16 248	9 562	2 780	1 627	22 157	18 945	630	756
1989	14 882	29 739	0	29 739	2 556	-17 320	9 862	3 395	1 625	23 843	20 378	624	763
1990	15 748	31 850	0	31 850	2 758	-18 457	10 634	3 379	1 734	26 015	22 400	605	773
1991	16 423	33 666	0	33 666	2 938	-19 611	11 117	3 369	1 938	27 333	23 792	601	759
1992	17 147	35 604	0	35 604	3 124	-20 914	11 566	3 404	2 177	28 694	25 092	598	752
1993	17 789	37 045	0	37 045	3 273	-21 773	11 999	3 400	2 391	29 883	26 243	595	750
1994	18 151	37 940	0	37 940	3 419	-22 284	12 237	3 483	2 431	30 804	26 843	589	730
1995	18 165	38 367	0	38 367	3 475	-22 512	12 379	3 429	2 357	31 291	27 268	581	718
1996	18 878	38 817	0	38 817	3 509	-22 411	12 897	3 420	2 561	32 981	28 467	572	704
1997	19 761	40 093	0	40 093	3 626	-23 091	13 375	3 830	2 556	34 807	29 697	568	699
1998	20 633	41 682	0	41 682	3 759	-24 089	13 833	4 075	2 724	36 503	30 732	565	702
1999	21 151	44 918	0	44 918	4 104	-26 344	14 471	3 954	2 726	37 093	30 783	570	715
2000	23 146	47 411	0	47 411	4 336	-26 939	16 135	4 204	2 807	40 484	33 459	572	737
2001	25 920	51 203	0	51 203	4 944	-27 402	18 858	4 161	2 901	44 841	37 806	578	748
2002	26 316	54 116	0	54 116	5 261	-29 775	19 080	4 026	3 211	45 405	39 359	580	759
2003	27 442	56 570	0	56 570	5 496	-30 918	20 157	4 019	3 266	47 495	41 531	578	763
2004	29 821	61 331	0	61 331	5 920	-33 091	22 319	4 190	3 312	51 433	44 926	580	774
2005	32 169	64 853	0	64 853	6 252	-34 479	24 123	4 449	3 597	55 268	47 829	582	782
2006	35 172	68 636	0	68 636	6 586	-35 843	26 207	5 262	3 703	60 229	52 227	584	791
2007	37 554	72 017	0	72 017	6 943	-37 426	27 648	5 923	3 983	64 040	54 989	586	803
2008	39 131	75 403	0	75 403	7 505	-39 056	28 842	5 939	4 351	66 316	57 471	590	814
2009	39 578	77 958	0	77 958	7 874	-40 899	29 185	5 560	4 832	66 000	59 056	600	. . .

. . . = Not available.

Table 21-2. Personal Income and Employment by Region and State—*Continued*

(Millions of dollars, except as noted.)

Region or state and year	Personal income, total	Earnings by place of work			Less: Contributions for government social insurance	Plus: Adjustment for residence	Equals: Net earnings by place of residence	Plus: Dividends, interest, and rent	Plus: Personal current transfer receipts	Per capita (dollars)		Population (thousands)	Total employment (thousands)
		Nonfarm	Farm	Total						Personal income	Disposable personal income		
FLORIDA													
1958	8 710	6 449	368	6 817	216	-1	6 600	1 531	580	1 881	1 708	4 630	...
1959	9 626	7 144	441	7 586	282	-1	7 302	1 668	655	2 002	1 811	4 808	...
1960	10 088	7 507	379	7 886	329	-1	7 556	1 817	715	2 016	1 822	5 004	...
1961	10 666	7 784	437	8 222	343	-1	7 877	1 959	829	2 034	1 839	5 243	...
1962	11 524	8 412	451	8 863	389	-1	8 474	2 122	928	2 111	1 907	5 458	...
1963	12 368	9 071	433	9 504	449	-1	9 055	2 302	1 011	2 198	1 985	5 628	...
1964	13 571	10 000	490	10 490	481	-1	10 008	2 508	1 055	2 347	2 137	5 781	...
1965	14 854	10 948	463	11 411	516	-1	10 894	2 788	1 171	2 495	2 265	5 954	...
1966	16 344	12 175	473	12 648	679	-1	11 967	3 071	1 306	2 678	2 426	6 104	...
1967	18 129	13 376	512	13 889	808	-2	13 079	3 422	1 628	2 904	2 608	6 242	...
1968	20 850	15 267	526	15 793	963	-4	14 826	4 089	1 936	3 241	2 875	6 433	...
1969	3 416	17 585	636	18 221	1 132	-22	17 067	5 028	2 195	3 658	3 218	6 641	2 857
1970	3 753	19 645	546	20 191	1 272	-19	18 899	5 824	2 646	3 998	3 559	6 845	2 966
1971	4 126	21 796	639	22 435	1 472	-13	20 949	6 532	3 188	4 282	3 835	7 163	3 082
1972	4 482	25 327	738	26 066	1 796	-11	24 259	7 302	3 755	4 696	4 138	7 520	3 338
1973	4 747	29 860	836	30 696	2 420	-9	28 267	8 525	4 561	5 217	4 623	7 927	3 666
1974	5 227	32 992	908	33 900	2 780	0	31 119	9 885	5 497	5 591	4 973	8 317	3 766
1975	5 707	34 390	998	35 388	2 859	-9	32 520	10 706	7 183	5 901	5 352	8 542	3 676
1976	6 077	37 736	1 035	38 771	3 168	11	35 613	11 728	7 962	6 360	5 730	8 695	3 730
1977	6 572	42 322	1 033	43 355	3 570	23	39 807	13 450	8 713	6 972	6 263	8 889	3 929
1978	6 946	49 054	1 234	50 288	4 245	26	46 069	15 845	9 686	7 841	6 995	9 132	4 239
1979	7 358	56 196	1 311	57 507	5 105	22	52 424	19 037	11 225	8 731	7 735	9 471	4 454
1980	7 799	64 477	1 667	66 144	5 915	16	60 246	24 032	13 346	9 921	8 752	9 840	4 688
1981	8 522	72 762	1 403	74 166	7 230	114	67 049	30 500	15 599	11 101	9 773	10 193	4 865
1982	9 240	77 618	1 776	79 394	7 942	137	71 589	33 082	17 657	11 682	10 204	10 471	4 954
1983	9 726	85 793	2 465	88 258	8 777	160	79 641	36 925	19 313	12 640	11 317	10 750	5 167
1984	10 759	96 825	1 826	98 651	10 141	210	88 720	42 154	20 571	13 718	12 391	11 040	5 502
1985	11 454	106 444	1 831	108 276	11 348	255	97 182	46 833	22 198	14 643	13 075	11 351	5 772
1986	12 084	115 679	1 967	117 646	12 681	315	105 279	50 381	23 912	15 391	13 693	11 668	6 015
1987	12 768	127 280	2 140	129 420	13 790	376	116 005	52 916	25 355	16 193	14 380	11 997	6 094
1988	13 969	139 638	2 699	142 336	15 642	452	127 147	57 894	27 755	17 291	15 420	12 306	6 390
1989	14 882	148 959	2 482	151 441	16 954	531	135 018	70 482	31 260	18 734	16 690	12 638	6 596
1990	253 324	159 096	2 082	161 178	17 989	638	143 827	75 257	34 240	19 437	17 398	13 033	6 740
1991	264 396	165 659	2 457	168 116	18 866	684	149 935	75 967	38 494	19 776	17 838	13 370	6 718
1992	279 479	177 448	2 458	179 906	20 059	750	160 596	74 679	44 203	20 474	18 468	13 651	6 763
1993	295 218	189 387	2 534	191 921	21 342	803	171 382	76 493	47 343	21 197	19 089	13 927	7 002
1994	312 116	200 468	2 164	202 632	22 867	864	180 629	81 032	50 455	21 919	19 703	14 239	7 234
1995	334 574	214 448	2 209	216 656	24 231	932	193 357	86 836	54 381	23 014	20 644	14 538	7 494
1996	357 219	228 904	1 951	230 855	25 535	1 003	206 323	93 434	57 462	24 050	21 357	14 853	7 740
1997	378 429	242 337	2 163	244 500	27 120	1 098	218 478	100 351	59 600	24 919	21 931	15 186	8 005
1998	409 670	263 112	2 648	265 760	29 065	1 221	237 915	110 701	61 055	26 453	23 196	15 487	8 298
1999	430 694	284 057	2 710	286 767	30 988	1 344	257 123	110 085	63 486	27 329	23 944	15 759	8 567
2000	466 644	309 556	2 589	312 145	33 237	1 505	280 413	118 514	67 717	29 080	25 392	16 047	8 842
2001	487 504	322 437	2 582	325 019	35 611	1 578	290 986	122 703	73 815	29 810	26 163	16 354	8 917
2002	508 402	337 843	2 517	340 361	37 165	1 539	304 735	123 831	79 836	30 479	27 361	16 680	9 056
2003	531 216	358 925	2 167	361 092	39 039	1 535	323 587	122 754	84 875	31 283	28 489	16 981	9 286
2004	582 767	387 219	2 283	389 503	42 313	1 594	348 784	142 663	91 320	33 540	30 367	17 375	9 662
2005	633 198	420 631	2 701	423 332	46 199	1 642	378 774	156 369	98 055	35 605	31 726	17 784	10 088
2006	690 273	449 676	2 678	452 354	49 909	1 725	404 170	181 692	104 412	38 161	33 994	18 089	10 407
2007	713 490	458 278	2 088	460 366	51 127	1 895	411 134	190 852	111 504	39 036	34 739	18 278	10 553
2008	719 708	453 138	2 039	455 176	51 225	1 975	405 926	191 210	122 572	39 064	35 172	18 424	10 424
2009	700 361	433 480	1 968	435 448	49 530	1 901	387 819	176 160	136 381	37 780	34 880	18 538	...

. . . = Not available.

Table 21-2. Personal Income and Employment by Region and State—*Continued*

(Millions of dollars, except as noted.)

Region or state and year	Personal income, total	Earnings by place of work — Nonfarm	Earnings — Farm	Earnings — Total	Less: Contributions for government social insurance	Plus: Adjustment for residence	Equals: Net earnings by place of residence	Plus: Dividends, interest, and rent	Plus: Personal current transfer receipts	Per capita — Personal income	Per capita — Disposable personal income	Population (thousands)	Total employment (thousands)
GEORGIA													
1958	5 974	4 845	359	5 204	186	-11	5 007	589	379	1 570	1 436	3 804	. . .
1959	6 378	5 261	310	5 571	224	-13	5 334	644	401	1 649	1 503	3 868	. . .
1960	6 670	5 485	323	5 808	261	-15	5 532	721	417	1 686	1 525	3 956	. . .
1961	6 954	5 641	343	5 985	266	-16	5 703	777	473	1 732	1 569	4 015	. . .
1962	7 475	6 150	309	6 459	297	-20	6 142	846	488	1 830	1 647	4 086	. . .
1963	8 123	6 655	395	7 051	349	-24	6 678	924	522	1 947	1 752	4 172	. . .
1964	8 808	7 316	330	7 647	376	-29	7 242	1 019	547	2 069	1 875	4 258	. . .
1965	9 713	8 051	374	8 425	407	-35	7 983	1 129	601	2 242	2 027	4 332	. . .
1966	10 695	9 023	385	9 408	545	-43	8 820	1 219	656	2 442	2 193	4 379	. . .
1967	11 625	9 829	383	10 212	624	-52	9 535	1 309	781	2 637	2 378	4 408	. . .
1968	12 873	11 011	341	11 352	682	-62	10 608	1 334	930	2 872	2 558	4 482	. . .
1969	14 332	12 273	420	12 692	786	-76	11 830	1 439	1 063	3 149	2 746	4 551	2 119
1970	15 560	13 138	398	13 536	836	-69	12 631	1 630	1 299	3 379	2 990	4 605	2 121
1971	17 193	14 392	456	14 849	951	-65	13 833	1 814	1 546	3 650	3 265	4 710	2 167
1972	19 341	16 304	471	16 775	1 127	-57	15 591	2 009	1 741	4 023	3 550	4 807	2 253
1973	21 986	18 368	788	19 156	1 444	-55	17 657	2 319	2 010	4 481	3 983	4 907	2 356
1974	24 244	20 006	672	20 678	1 626	-55	18 997	2 736	2 511	4 854	4 314	4 995	2 374
1975	26 089	20 920	638	21 558	1 679	-45	19 834	2 928	3 327	5 157	4 673	5 059	2 313
1976	29 153	23 885	630	24 514	1 945	-77	22 493	3 112	3 548	5 687	5 107	5 126	2 400
1977	32 313	27 069	365	27 434	2 188	-97	25 149	3 483	3 681	6 200	5 534	5 212	2 503
1978	36 742	30 785	568	31 353	2 550	-79	28 724	4 014	4 004	6 951	6 163	5 286	2 621
1979	41 274	34 501	597	35 099	2 972	-96	32 031	4 681	4 562	7 656	6 707	5 391	2 700
1980	46 128	38 164	40	38 204	3 309	-113	34 781	5 891	5 456	8 408	7 397	5 486	2 741
1981	52 303	42 101	524	42 625	3 928	-29	38 668	7 415	6 220	9 393	8 229	5 568	2 776
1982	56 728	44 992	683	45 674	4 282	-69	41 323	8 611	6 794	10 041	8 854	5 650	2 793
1983	62 193	49 613	475	50 088	4 793	-111	45 184	9 631	7 378	10 857	9 558	5 728	2 877
1984	70 881	56 593	955	57 548	5 612	-176	51 761	11 237	7 883	12 148	10 753	5 835	3 068
1985	77 822	62 656	785	63 441	6 362	-192	56 887	12 480	8 455	13 052	11 475	5 963	3 207
1986	84 679	68 697	826	69 524	7 086	-241	62 197	13 477	9 005	13 917	12 252	6 085	3 335
1987	91 136	74 328	897	75 225	7 618	-242	67 365	14 322	9 449	14 679	12 853	6 208	3 433
1988	99 295	80 753	1 158	81 911	8 517	-237	73 156	15 942	10 197	15 721	13 844	6 316	3 545
1989	106 798	84 971	1 358	86 328	9 063	-198	77 067	18 420	11 311	16 658	14 606	6 411	3 608
1990	114 382	90 510	1 262	91 772	9 680	-121	81 971	19 837	12 574	17 563	15 424	6 513	3 664
1991	120 488	94 149	1 566	95 716	10 145	-139	85 432	20 509	14 547	18 110	16 025	6 653	3 622
1992	130 474	102 442	1 642	104 084	10 866	-191	93 027	21 201	16 245	19 139	16 973	6 817	3 698
1993	138 629	109 317	1 477	110 793	11 615	-180	98 998	22 242	17 388	19 866	17 548	6 978	3 866
1994	149 907	117 330	1 942	119 272	12 568	-234	106 470	24 698	18 739	20 945	18 486	7 157	4 020
1995	161 393	126 724	1 766	128 490	13 504	-321	114 664	26 534	20 195	22 023	19 389	7 328	4 188
1996	175 077	137 075	1 858	138 934	14 432	-375	124 127	29 499	21 451	23 340	20 425	7 501	4 333
1997	186 651	146 827	1 816	148 643	15 463	-462	132 719	31 988	21 944	24 287	21 123	7 685	4 449
1998	201 938	159 603	1 806	161 409	16 779	-583	144 047	35 442	22 449	25 680	22 195	7 864	4 610
1999	215 405	173 098	1 945	175 043	18 118	-613	156 312	35 336	23 757	26 772	23 108	8 046	4 739
2000	234 814	188 577	1 842	190 419	19 381	-766	170 272	38 750	25 792	28 531	24 606	8 230	4 854
2001	245 864	196 185	2 212	198 397	20 098	-815	177 484	39 914	28 465	29 201	25 314	8 420	4 856
2002	251 264	200 462	1 636	202 098	20 457	-848	180 793	38 129	32 341	29 266	25 955	8 586	4 879
2003	259 217	208 171	2 147	210 318	21 081	-867	188 369	38 079	32 769	29 675	26 592	8 735	4 918
2004	273 016	220 124	2 163	222 287	22 805	-918	198 564	39 328	35 125	30 629	27 517	8 914	5 058
2005	292 611	232 786	2 478	235 264	23 920	-939	210 405	43 856	38 351	32 164	28 660	9 097	5 234
2006	311 927	245 700	1 589	247 289	25 322	-944	221 022	50 072	40 832	33 432	29 588	9 330	5 393
2007	329 983	256 219	1 745	257 964	26 246	-1 003	230 715	55 069	44 200	34 612	30 582	9 534	5 535
2008	337 961	258 272	2 258	260 531	26 971	-979	232 581	55 935	49 445	34 849	31 093	9 698	5 572
2009	332 091	249 990	1 964	251 954	26 458	-998	224 498	51 875	55 717	33 786	30 926	9 829	. . .

. . . = Not available.

Table 21-2. Personal Income and Employment by Region and State—*Continued*

(Millions of dollars, except as noted.)

Region or state and year	Personal income, total	Earnings by place of work			Less: Contributions for government social insurance	Plus: Adjustment for residence	Equals: Net earnings by place of residence	Plus: Dividends, interest, and rent	Plus: Personal current transfer receipts	Per capita (dollars)		Population (thousands)	Total employment (thousands)
		Nonfarm	Farm	Total						Personal income	Disposable personal income		
HAWAII													
1958	1 168	963	64	1 027	40	0	986	140	42	1 931	. . .	605	. . .
1959	1 306	1 077	73	1 151	45	0	1 106	155	46	2 100	. . .	622	. . .
1960	1 496	1 216	81	1 297	52	0	1 245	203	48	2 330	2 005	642	. . .
1961	1 619	1 316	75	1 391	57	0	1 334	227	59	2 457	2 112	659	. . .
1962	1 736	1 403	78	1 481	61	0	1 421	248	67	2 538	2 222	684	. . .
1963	1 850	1 505	87	1 592	76	0	1 516	264	70	2 712	2 377	682	. . .
1964	2 013	1 647	88	1 735	82	0	1 653	289	70	2 876	2 556	700	. . .
1965	2 205	1 795	91	1 885	85	0	1 800	323	81	3 132	2 796	704	. . .
1966	2 410	1 983	95	2 077	113	0	1 964	351	95	3 394	2 982	710	. . .
1967	2 620	2 145	98	2 243	130	0	2 112	387	121	3 623	3 176	723	. . .
1968	2 949	2 442	117	2 559	152	0	2 407	402	140	4 018	3 495	734	. . .
1969	3 367	2 826	119	2 945	183	0	2 763	445	160	4 532	3 882	743	416
1970	3 873	3 238	133	3 371	212	0	3 159	507	207	5 077	4 372	763	434
1971	4 210	3 475	131	3 605	236	0	3 369	571	270	5 319	4 658	792	437
1972	4 640	3 839	131	3 971	274	0	3 697	621	323	5 671	4 902	818	453
1973	5 159	4 297	138	4 435	349	0	4 086	703	370	6 128	5 312	842	473
1974	5 931	4 741	340	5 081	401	0	4 680	806	444	6 911	6 024	858	485
1975	6 472	5 251	202	5 453	443	0	5 010	885	577	7 396	6 600	875	499
1976	7 032	5 735	173	5 909	485	0	5 424	934	674	7 880	6 981	892	505
1977	7 636	6 244	185	6 428	523	0	5 905	1 024	707	8 338	7 352	916	509
1978	8 462	6 943	168	7 111	597	0	6 514	1 188	760	9 111	7 973	929	528
1979	9 594	7 839	194	8 033	701	0	7 332	1 423	839	10 098	8 810	950	556
1980	11 026	8 750	374	9 124	781	0	8 343	1 720	963	11 394	9 959	968	575
1981	11 968	9 450	199	9 650	902	0	8 747	2 089	1 132	12 235	10 701	978	568
1982	12 700	10 058	235	10 292	954	0	9 338	2 135	1 227	12 780	11 394	994	567
1983	14 059	10 839	338	11 177	1 037	0	10 140	2 569	1 350	13 883	12 384	1 013	577
1984	15 325	11 873	239	12 112	1 136	0	10 976	2 925	1 424	14 909	13 348	1 028	582
1985	16 210	12 653	221	12 875	1 238	0	11 637	3 064	1 509	15 591	13 893	1 040	598
1986	17 131	13 457	255	13 712	1 352	0	12 361	3 198	1 572	16 288	14 479	1 052	612
1987	18 281	14 582	240	14 822	1 477	0	13 345	3 309	1 628	17 118	15 007	1 068	643
1988	19 972	16 069	263	16 332	1 700	0	14 632	3 600	1 739	18 496	16 183	1 080	669
1989	22 203	17 715	247	17 962	1 894	0	16 068	4 209	1 926	20 285	17 553	1 095	696
1990	24 294	19 653	260	19 913	2 188	0	17 725	4 481	2 088	21 818	18 901	1 113	724
1991	25 876	21 006	231	21 237	2 358	0	18 879	4 701	2 296	22 763	19 636	1 137	745
1992	27 823	22 489	218	22 707	2 513	0	20 195	4 961	2 667	24 014	21 148	1 159	746
1993	28 811	23 071	215	23 287	2 556	0	20 730	5 159	2 922	24 566	21 665	1 173	742
1994	29 507	23 240	209	23 449	2 588	0	20 861	5 484	3 163	24 847	21 939	1 188	737
1995	30 112	23 295	199	23 494	2 566	0	20 928	5 612	3 572	25 160	22 346	1 197	734
1996	30 399	23 402	195	23 597	2 545	0	21 051	5 687	3 661	25 253	22 316	1 204	733
1997	31 372	23 955	205	24 160	2 550	0	21 610	6 088	3 674	25 892	22 871	1 212	734
1998	32 259	24 464	218	24 681	2 575	0	22 107	6 405	3 747	26 546	23 382	1 215	736
1999	33 244	25 232	245	25 477	2 651	0	22 826	6 511	3 907	27 467	24 145	1 210	735
2000	35 222	26 765	241	27 005	2 785	0	24 221	6 885	4 116	29 071	25 495	1 212	757
2001	35 937	27 357	237	27 594	2 937	0	24 657	6 869	4 411	29 497	25 867	1 218	766
2002	37 475	29 184	250	29 434	3 136	0	26 298	6 412	4 765	30 516	27 214	1 228	758
2003	39 032	31 043	248	31 291	3 363	0	27 928	6 195	4 909	31 495	28 268	1 239	775
2004	42 285	33 560	249	33 809	3 529	0	30 280	6 738	5 267	33 753	30 302	1 253	797
2005	45 332	35 914	259	36 173	3 782	0	32 391	7 243	5 698	35 804	31 764	1 266	822
2006	49 124	38 324	256	38 580	4 055	0	34 525	8 586	6 013	38 510	34 138	1 276	843
2007	52 253	40 091	228	40 319	4 208	0	36 111	9 547	6 595	40 924	36 276	1 277	868
2008	54 175	41 064	220	41 284	4 293	0	36 991	9 924	7 260	42 078	37 647	1 287	874
2009	54 409	40 849	232	41 081	4 277	0	36 804	9 340	8 266	42 009	38 614	1 295	. . .

. . . = Not available.

Table 21-2. Personal Income and Employment by Region and State—*Continued*

(Millions of dollars, except as noted.)

Region or state and year	Personal income, total	Earnings by place of work			Less: Contributions for government social insurance	Plus: Adjustment for residence	Equals: Net earnings by place of residence	Plus: Dividends, interest, and rent	Plus: Personal current transfer receipts	Per capita (dollars)		Population (thousands)	Total employment (thousands)
		Nonfarm	Farm	Total						Personal income	Disposable personal income		
IDAHO													
1958	1 165	824	164	988	37	-3	948	139	78	1 804	1 627	646	. . .
1959	1 236	884	164	1 048	43	-3	1 002	149	85	1 881	1 693	657	. . .
1960	1 263	913	156	1 069	50	-3	1 016	156	90	1 882	1 683	671	. . .
1961	1 336	971	156	1 127	56	-3	1 068	166	102	1 954	1 760	684	. . .
1962	1 430	1 046	165	1 210	62	-3	1 145	179	106	2 067	1 866	692	. . .
1963	1 459	1 062	171	1 233	69	-2	1 162	188	109	2 137	1 920	683	. . .
1964	1 507	1 141	132	1 273	70	-2	1 201	194	112	2 215	2 017	680	. . .
1965	1 728	1 247	229	1 477	76	-2	1 399	209	120	2 519	2 296	686	. . .
1966	1 753	1 322	177	1 499	93	-1	1 405	219	129	2 544	2 308	689	. . .
1967	1 865	1 387	204	1 591	107	-1	1 484	226	155	2 711	2 450	688	. . .
1968	1 989	1 515	184	1 698	121	-1	1 576	239	174	2 862	2 573	695	. . .
1969	2 307	1 675	253	1 927	127	12	1 812	301	194	3 264	2 912	707	315
1970	2 538	1 828	267	2 094	137	14	1 971	338	229	3 539	3 183	717	324
1971	2 762	1 999	249	2 249	154	15	2 109	384	269	3 739	3 363	739	332
1972	3 154	2 278	321	2 599	183	16	2 432	416	306	4 133	3 741	763	347
1973	3 664	2 588	453	3 041	240	18	2 819	495	351	4 686	4 208	782	365
1974	4 325	2 964	628	3 592	282	22	3 332	572	421	5 353	4 770	808	381
1975	4 636	3 366	387	3 754	316	28	3 466	647	524	5 573	5 011	832	393
1976	5 228	3 916	343	4 259	370	35	3 924	712	591	6 100	5 478	857	419
1977	5 724	4 417	240	4 658	418	35	4 275	822	627	6 479	5 803	883	435
1978	6 607	5 123	309	5 431	487	42	4 986	951	669	7 253	6 478	911	460
1979	7 271	5 658	233	5 891	567	48	5 372	1 118	782	7 796	6 950	933	469
1980	8 187	6 022	408	6 430	605	61	5 886	1 367	935	8 637	7 708	948	464
1981	9 023	6 480	428	6 908	700	52	6 260	1 692	1 071	9 378	8 288	962	462
1982	9 369	6 471	394	6 865	717	62	6 210	1 929	1 230	9 622	8 591	974	452
1983	10 144	6 993	583	7 576	779	63	6 861	1 983	1 301	10 331	9 294	982	463
1984	10 887	7 614	500	8 115	870	77	7 321	2 220	1 346	10 988	9 916	991	472
1985	11 428	8 012	457	8 470	930	83	7 623	2 362	1 443	11 497	10 346	994	474
1986	11 659	8 122	479	8 601	955	99	7 745	2 392	1 522	11 774	10 651	990	474
1987	12 241	8 564	596	9 160	988	108	8 279	2 395	1 567	12 428	11 221	985	487
1988	13 245	9 375	674	10 049	1 121	123	9 051	2 512	1 682	13 437	12 116	986	508
1989	14 550	10 090	881	10 971	1 229	138	9 880	2 845	1 824	14 632	13 045	994	525
1990	15 796	11 028	1 001	12 029	1 417	151	10 764	3 065	1 968	15 603	13 868	1 012	548
1991	16 676	11 819	829	12 648	1 548	173	11 273	3 199	2 204	16 015	14 264	1 041	566
1992	18 286	13 092	876	13 969	1 686	190	12 472	3 346	2 467	17 063	15 106	1 072	586
1993	20 080	14 350	1 086	15 435	1 844	208	13 799	3 625	2 656	18 110	16 073	1 109	612
1994	21 603	15 780	780	16 560	2 032	235	14 764	4 023	2 817	18 865	16 751	1 145	647
1995	23 152	16 673	845	17 518	2 163	279	15 634	4 425	3 093	19 665	17 446	1 177	667
1996	24 693	17 509	953	18 462	2 228	324	16 558	4 829	3 306	20 525	18 175	1 203	689
1997	25 751	18 339	758	19 097	2 324	368	17 141	5 183	3 426	20 961	18 486	1 229	708
1998	27 844	19 655	958	20 613	2 464	436	18 585	5 689	3 570	22 234	19 638	1 252	734
1999	29 684	21 264	1 006	22 271	2 594	503	20 180	5 704	3 800	23 269	20 470	1 276	752
2000	32 076	23 167	1 012	24 179	2 819	525	21 885	6 070	4 122	24 683	21 575	1 300	781
2001	33 885	24 213	1 122	25 334	2 869	530	22 995	6 280	4 609	25 647	22 543	1 321	786
2002	34 916	25 048	1 094	26 142	2 947	534	23 729	6 194	4 993	26 015	23 533	1 342	791
2003	36 082	26 046	853	26 900	3 065	567	24 402	6 387	5 293	26 451	24 097	1 364	802
2004	39 559	27 965	1 370	29 335	3 266	602	26 670	7 217	5 672	28 425	25 932	1 392	826
2005	42 215	29 853	1 209	31 062	3 548	615	28 129	7 971	6 115	29 606	26 585	1 426	862
2006	46 273	32 832	1 130	33 962	3 955	648	30 655	9 002	6 616	31 598	28 140	1 464	905
2007	49 231	34 087	1 579	35 666	4 110	704	32 260	9 811	7 159	32 837	29 250	1 499	932
2008	50 399	34 095	1 710	35 805	4 182	744	32 366	10 057	7 976	32 994	29 670	1 528	940
2009	48 898	32 612	1 045	33 658	4 053	733	30 338	9 311	9 249	31 632	29 148	1 546	. . .

. . . = Not available.

Table 21-2. Personal Income and Employment by Region and State—*Continued*

(Millions of dollars, except as noted.)

Region or state and year	Personal income, total	Earnings by place of work			Less: Contributions for government social insurance	Plus: Adjustment for residence	Equals: Net earnings by place of residence	Plus: Dividends, interest, and rent	Plus: Personal current transfer receipts	Per capita (dollars)		Population (thousands)	Total employment (thousands)
		Nonfarm	Farm	Total						Personal income	Disposable personal income		
ILLINOIS													
1958	24 601	20 156	856	21 012	704	-111	20 198	3 052	1 350	2 488	2 208	9 886	. . .
1959	26 130	21 778	657	22 435	852	-127	21 456	3 267	1 407	2 617	2 321	9 986	. . .
1960	26 950	22 507	636	23 143	1 073	-133	21 937	3 540	1 472	2 672	2 352	10 086	. . .
1961	27 971	22 922	800	23 723	1 088	-138	22 496	3 775	1 699	2 761	2 439	10 130	. . .
1962	29 527	24 220	785	25 004	1 195	-154	23 655	4 108	1 763	2 872	2 528	10 280	. . .
1963	30 678	25 126	805	25 931	1 329	-159	24 443	4 419	1 815	2 949	2 602	10 402	. . .
1964	32 775	26 982	651	27 633	1 337	-175	26 122	4 806	1 847	3 098	2 772	10 580	. . .
1965	35 524	28 969	888	29 857	1 356	-194	28 307	5 237	1 981	3 322	2 965	10 693	. . .
1966	38 473	31 888	960	32 848	1 820	-222	30 806	5 523	2 145	3 551	3 142	10 836	. . .
1967	40 917	33 884	922	34 806	1 986	-239	32 581	5 781	2 555	3 738	3 295	10 947	. . .
1968	43 848	36 625	680	37 306	2 192	-265	34 849	6 006	2 993	3 988	3 476	10 995	. . .
1969	47 837	39 953	913	40 866	2 717	94	38 243	6 357	3 236	4 333	3 706	11 039	5 179
1970	50 816	42 169	723	42 892	2 811	19	40 100	6 879	3 837	4 568	3 928	11 125	5 144
1971	54 544	44 867	885	45 752	3 075	-22	42 655	7 298	4 590	4 867	4 252	11 206	5 104
1972	59 242	48 790	1 000	49 790	3 518	-41	46 231	7 844	5 167	5 262	4 538	11 258	5 155
1973	66 343	54 066	1 842	55 907	4 491	-58	51 359	8 837	6 147	5 892	5 117	11 260	5 351
1974	72 735	59 106	1 674	60 780	5 079	-69	55 632	10 095	7 008	6 452	5 579	11 274	5 441
1975	79 233	62 176	2 465	64 641	5 196	-95	59 350	10 899	8 984	7 008	6 146	11 306	5 342
1976	86 566	69 296	1 715	71 011	5 882	-74	65 054	11 598	9 914	7 620	6 620	11 360	5 458
1977	95 351	76 899	1 718	78 617	6 516	-8	72 094	12 886	10 371	8 359	7 243	11 406	5 587
1978	105 450	85 878	1 514	87 392	7 467	80	80 005	14 407	11 038	9 222	7 968	11 434	5 748
1979	115 824	93 867	1 839	95 707	8 483	165	87 388	16 413	12 023	10 140	8 697	11 423	5 803
1980	125 551	99 252	383	99 635	8 955	266	90 946	20 021	14 584	10 980	9 439	11 435	5 675
1981	139 036	106 001	1 526	107 528	10 260	204	97 471	24 808	16 756	12 150	10 424	11 443	5 664
1982	147 000	108 791	917	109 707	10 701	133	99 139	29 460	18 400	12 868	11 231	11 423	5 563
1983	153 106	113 692	-486	113 206	11 259	99	102 046	31 357	19 702	13 420	11 790	11 409	5 520
1984	168 437	124 773	1 226	126 000	12 810	-6	113 184	35 183	20 071	14 760	13 036	11 412	5 718
1985	176 973	131 686	1 716	133 402	13 763	-74	119 565	36 463	20 946	15 524	13 665	11 400	5 780
1986	185 656	139 605	1 426	141 031	14 681	-125	126 224	37 728	21 703	16 304	14 367	11 387	5 892
1987	196 340	150 002	1 435	151 437	15 563	-212	135 662	38 522	22 156	17 236	15 034	11 391	6 031
1988	211 302	164 263	862	165 125	17 350	-340	147 435	40 956	22 912	18 551	16 284	11 390	6 187
1989	224 449	172 359	2 173	174 532	18 409	-354	155 769	44 347	24 333	19 672	17 149	11 410	6 294
1990	238 635	182 888	1 764	184 652	19 126	-272	165 253	46 826	26 556	20 835	18 180	11 453	6 390
1991	244 660	187 235	978	188 214	20 062	-285	167 867	48 199	28 594	21 148	18 568	11 569	6 369
1992	263 740	200 813	2 060	202 872	21 162	-331	181 379	49 624	32 737	22 553	19 908	11 694	6 351
1993	272 422	209 273	1 715	210 988	22 340	-492	188 156	49 923	34 344	23 068	20 269	11 810	6 441
1994	288 060	220 653	2 309	222 962	23 829	-513	198 620	53 856	35 583	24 181	21 176	11 913	6 611
1995	304 796	233 873	610	234 482	25 100	-772	208 610	58 300	37 887	25 382	22 179	12 008	6 773
1996	324 408	245 850	2 501	248 351	26 167	-823	221 361	63 219	39 827	26 806	23 282	12 102	6 875
1997	342 789	261 285	2 144	263 428	27 611	-868	234 948	67 300	40 541	28 130	24 251	12 186	6 981
1998	365 040	278 941	1 539	280 480	29 288	-847	250 345	73 364	41 331	29 746	25 509	12 272	7 133
1999	378 415	295 252	1 078	296 330	30 701	-1 045	264 584	71 795	42 037	30 619	26 170	12 359	7 218
2000	405 919	314 541	1 794	316 335	32 402	-1 344	282 590	78 603	44 726	32 636	27 877	12 438	7 355
2001	415 145	322 460	1 662	324 122	33 177	-1 527	289 418	77 482	48 244	33 191	28 530	12 508	7 317
2002	423 393	330 799	956	331 755	33 600	-1 504	296 651	74 798	51 945	33 714	29 665	12 558	7 220
2003	435 952	343 833	1 949	345 782	34 500	-1 521	309 761	72 032	54 160	34 605	30 870	12 598	7 198
2004	455 416	359 386	3 740	363 127	36 705	-1 604	324 817	74 416	56 182	36 015	32 227	12 645	7 250
2005	472 185	371 380	1 830	373 210	38 861	-1 589	332 760	77 896	61 528	37 255	32 981	12 674	7 336
2006	504 628	391 781	2 078	393 859	40 815	-1 759	351 286	90 967	62 375	39 678	34 888	12 718	7 448
2007	533 162	405 925	3 176	409 101	42 908	-1 989	364 204	99 377	69 581	41 720	36 360	12 779	7 590
2008	546 344	412 441	5 188	417 629	43 746	-1 841	372 042	100 730	73 572	42 540	37 425	12 843	7 657
2009	534 638	394 916	4 378	399 293	42 033	-1 687	355 574	95 036	84 028	41 411	37 539	12 910	. . .

. . . = Not available.

Table 21-2. Personal Income and Employment by Region and State—*Continued*

(Millions of dollars, except as noted.)

Region or state and year	Personal income, total	Earnings by place of work			Less: Contributions for government social insurance	Plus: Adjustment for residence	Equals: Net earnings by place of residence	Plus: Dividends, interest, and rent	Plus: Personal current transfer receipts	Per capita (dollars)		Population (thousands)	Total employment (thousands)
		Nonfarm	Farm	Total						Personal income	Disposable personal income		
INDIANA													
1958	9 197	7 480	420	7 900	295	35	7 640	986	570	2 007	1 816	4 583	. . .
1959	9 790	8 186	294	8 479	356	41	8 164	1 055	571	2 122	1 908	4 613	. . .
1960	10 286	8 534	359	8 893	415	40	8 518	1 164	604	2 201	1 964	4 674	. . .
1961	10 590	8 584	455	9 039	411	43	8 671	1 227	692	2 239	2 010	4 730	. . .
1962	11 343	9 289	444	9 733	461	48	9 320	1 326	697	2 395	2 137	4 736	. . .
1963	11 909	9 775	460	10 236	526	48	9 757	1 428	724	2 482	2 201	4 799	. . .
1964	12 684	10 603	293	10 896	545	46	10 397	1 538	749	2 612	2 341	4 856	. . .
1965	14 029	11 559	544	12 103	581	49	11 571	1 653	806	2 850	2 551	4 922	. . .
1966	15 137	12 807	470	13 277	818	55	12 515	1 756	866	3 028	2 684	4 999	. . .
1967	15 860	13 426	423	13 849	916	59	12 992	1 856	1 011	3 139	2 775	5 053	. . .
1968	17 245	14 664	373	15 037	992	69	14 113	1 951	1 180	3 386	2 968	5 093	. . .
1969	18 990	16 012	550	16 563	1 097	25	15 491	2 220	1 279	3 692	3 193	5 143	2 327
1970	19 730	16 470	381	16 850	1 116	58	15 792	2 437	1 501	3 791	3 319	5 204	2 291
1971	21 453	17 524	596	18 120	1 229	118	17 009	2 653	1 790	4 086	3 616	5 250	2 290
1972	23 510	19 483	507	19 990	1 442	151	18 698	2 841	1 970	4 439	3 887	5 296	2 367
1973	27 088	21 953	1 228	23 182	1 865	195	21 512	3 241	2 335	5 083	4 494	5 329	2 483
1974	29 014	23 617	735	24 352	2 091	256	22 516	3 741	2 757	5 423	4 720	5 350	2 493
1975	31 235	24 288	1 098	25 386	2 122	301	23 565	4 159	3 512	5 837	5 175	5 351	2 405
1976	34 939	27 777	1 077	28 854	2 440	351	26 765	4 509	3 665	6 504	5 709	5 372	2 489
1977	38 740	31 431	725	32 156	2 757	413	29 812	5 079	3 849	7 167	6 267	5 405	2 578
1978	43 299	35 399	732	36 132	3 196	467	33 403	5 661	4 236	7 950	6 921	5 446	2 670
1979	47 774	38 892	673	39 565	3 636	543	36 472	6 435	4 867	8 726	7 563	5 475	2 708
1980	51 357	40 023	380	40 403	3 725	666	37 344	7 928	6 085	9 353	8 168	5 491	2 626
1981	56 380	42 996	309	43 305	4 286	712	39 730	9 849	6 801	10 287	8 941	5 480	2 603
1982	58 360	43 033	309	43 342	4 378	776	39 739	11 043	7 578	10 673	9 360	5 468	2 522
1983	60 957	45 301	-260	45 041	4 660	827	41 208	11 590	8 159	11 184	9 872	5 450	2 542
1984	67 695	49 743	752	50 495	5 258	989	46 227	12 910	8 558	12 402	10 994	5 458	2 642
1985	71 327	52 601	680	53 281	5 686	1 075	48 669	13 649	9 008	13 065	11 538	5 459	2 695
1986	74 932	55 494	578	56 071	6 056	1 169	51 184	14 235	9 512	13 739	12 161	5 454	2 755
1987	79 482	59 691	766	60 457	6 435	1 238	55 260	14 523	9 698	14 522	12 805	5 473	2 849
1988	84 704	64 611	289	64 900	7 220	1 362	59 043	15 390	10 271	15 424	13 606	5 492	2 935
1989	92 067	68 799	965	69 764	7 738	1 428	63 454	17 465	11 148	16 668	14 629	5 524	3 010
1990	97 005	72 470	864	73 334	8 410	1 503	66 427	18 463	12 114	17 454	15 331	5 558	3 070
1991	100 334	75 774	243	76 018	8 899	1 527	68 646	18 357	13 331	17 865	15 747	5 616	3 072
1992	108 377	81 376	853	82 228	9 475	1 740	74 493	18 646	15 238	19 099	16 906	5 675	3 121
1993	114 121	86 101	869	86 970	10 081	1 927	78 815	19 212	16 094	19 885	17 552	5 739	3 197
1994	121 510	91 945	831	92 776	10 920	2 076	83 932	20 790	16 788	20 973	18 438	5 794	3 287
1995	126 651	96 177	353	96 531	11 441	2 329	87 419	22 167	17 065	21 644	18 994	5 851	3 379
1996	133 798	100 178	1 197	101 375	11 831	2 470	92 014	23 784	18 001	22 655	19 815	5 906	3 418
1997	140 588	105 447	1 167	106 614	12 429	2 633	96 819	25 295	18 474	23 607	20 548	5 955	3 476
1998	150 987	113 416	771	114 188	13 214	2 665	103 639	28 158	19 191	25 169	21 848	5 999	3 546
1999	156 559	119 284	471	119 756	13 857	3 017	108 916	27 522	20 121	25 899	22 490	6 045	3 599
2000	167 276	126 035	864	126 899	14 435	3 356	115 820	29 788	21 668	27 460	23 983	6 092	3 647
2001	171 799	128 731	1 051	129 782	14 624	3 468	118 626	29 220	23 953	28 049	24 579	6 125	3 588
2002	175 398	133 050	451	133 501	15 007	3 427	121 921	28 048	25 429	28 525	25 359	6 149	3 547
2003	182 817	140 127	1 297	141 424	15 544	3 480	129 360	27 009	26 448	29 573	26 600	6 182	3 548
2004	190 329	145 308	2 062	147 370	16 284	3 662	134 748	27 540	28 040	30 627	27 633	6 214	3 586
2005	195 590	149 729	1 386	151 115	17 029	3 850	137 937	27 158	30 495	31 279	28 026	6 253	3 626
2006	206 959	155 673	1 228	156 901	17 931	4 140	143 109	30 964	32 886	32 842	29 303	6 302	3 666
2007	213 875	159 262	1 621	160 883	18 390	4 549	147 042	32 328	34 504	33 702	29 883	6 346	3 714
2008	220 670	161 589	2 509	164 098	18 843	4 619	149 874	32 714	38 082	34 543	30 875	6 388	3 718
2009	216 618	153 525	1 794	155 320	18 073	4 484	141 730	31 500	43 388	33 725	30 998	6 423	. . .

. . . = Not available.

Table 21-2. Personal Income and Employment by Region and State—*Continued*

(Millions of dollars, except as noted.)

| Region or state and year | Personal income, total | Earnings by place of work | | | Less: Contributions for government social insurance | Plus: Adjustment for residence | Equals: Net earnings by place of residence | Plus: Dividends, interest, and rent | Plus: Personal current transfer receipts | Per capita (dollars) | | Population (thousands) | Total employment (thousands) |
		Nonfarm	Farm	Total						Personal income	Disposable personal income		
IOWA													
1958	5 394	3 437	1 005	4 442	135	27	4 335	729	331	1 992	1 803	2 708	. . .
1959	5 540	3 775	741	4 516	166	29	4 379	799	362	2 030	1 841	2 729	. . .
1960	5 674	3 889	720	4 609	186	33	4 457	833	385	2 059	1 850	2 756	. . .
1961	6 007	4 000	838	4 838	189	36	4 685	898	424	2 180	1 969	2 756	. . .
1962	6 271	4 184	870	5 054	203	39	4 890	938	444	2 281	2 060	2 750	. . .
1963	6 667	4 407	983	5 390	233	41	5 198	1 005	464	2 427	2 194	2 747	. . .
1964	6 984	4 727	905	5 633	247	44	5 430	1 075	479	2 543	2 318	2 746	. . .
1965	7 744	5 060	1 232	6 292	261	48	6 080	1 143	522	2 824	2 569	2 742	. . .
1966	8 428	5 626	1 328	6 955	352	52	6 655	1 207	566	3 051	2 746	2 762	. . .
1967	8 589	6 020	1 066	7 086	418	56	6 725	1 189	675	3 075	2 760	2 793	. . .
1968	9 226	6 491	1 009	7 500	457	60	7 103	1 340	782	3 292	2 931	2 803	. . .
1969	10 280	7 108	1 239	8 347	544	82	7 885	1 540	856	3 665	3 233	2 805	1 289
1970	10 968	7 539	1 216	8 754	568	89	8 275	1 701	992	3 878	3 448	2 829	1 295
1971	11 480	8 041	1 013	9 054	627	88	8 515	1 838	1 127	4 025	3 620	2 852	1 297
1972	12 867	8 773	1 485	10 258	720	94	9 632	2 019	1 216	4 498	3 979	2 861	1 316
1973	15 492	9 873	2 732	12 605	931	88	11 761	2 327	1 404	5 409	4 824	2 864	1 374
1974	16 069	11 080	1 722	12 801	1 094	84	11 792	2 652	1 626	5 603	4 865	2 868	1 407
1975	17 954	12 049	1 972	14 021	1 169	100	12 952	2 986	2 017	6 231	5 500	2 881	1 407
1976	19 152	13 715	1 229	14 944	1 324	92	13 712	3 225	2 215	6 596	5 772	2 904	1 455
1977	21 177	15 320	1 228	16 548	1 461	65	15 152	3 684	2 341	7 267	6 363	2 914	1 488
1978	24 460	16 943	2 444	19 387	1 675	62	17 774	4 105	2 581	8 379	7 361	2 919	1 513
1979	26 233	18 970	1 577	20 547	1 960	71	18 659	4 682	2 892	8 994	7 820	2 917	1 554
1980	27 894	20 091	719	20 811	2 067	92	18 836	5 653	3 405	9 573	8 307	2 914	1 537
1981	31 521	21 234	1 643	22 878	2 329	117	20 666	6 980	3 876	10 840	9 413	2 908	1 507
1982	32 452	21 253	818	22 071	2 357	190	19 904	8 129	4 419	11 236	9 861	2 888	1 471
1983	33 094	22 096	6	22 101	2 426	205	19 880	8 477	4 736	11 529	10 205	2 871	1 474
1984	36 633	23 715	1 462	25 177	2 684	238	22 731	9 050	4 852	12 815	11 508	2 859	1 499
1985	37 832	24 338	1 750	26 088	2 810	278	23 555	9 127	5 150	13 370	12 002	2 830	1 495
1986	39 067	25 059	2 129	27 188	2 967	271	24 492	9 231	5 344	13 993	12 591	2 792	1 494
1987	40 912	26 871	2 463	29 333	3 174	268	26 427	9 025	5 459	14 786	13 178	2 767	1 514
1988	42 096	28 858	1 653	30 511	3 544	310	27 277	9 125	5 694	15 206	13 519	2 768	1 557
1989	45 670	30 720	2 400	33 120	3 789	319	29 650	9 949	6 071	16 484	14 595	2 771	1 600
1990	48 250	32 468	2 505	34 973	4 105	328	31 196	10 456	6 598	17 350	15 330	2 781	1 635
1991	49 518	33 932	1 782	35 714	4 325	381	31 770	10 643	7 105	17 700	15 681	2 798	1 654
1992	52 954	36 156	2 705	38 861	4 578	407	34 691	10 590	7 674	18 789	16 723	2 818	1 669
1993	53 053	37 989	893	38 882	4 831	391	34 442	10 576	8 034	18 700	16 573	2 837	1 692
1994	58 062	40 511	2 865	43 375	5 204	404	38 575	11 137	8 349	20 367	18 108	2 851	1 725
1995	60 232	42 641	1 824	44 465	5 473	467	39 459	11 992	8 781	21 006	18 636	2 867	1 785
1996	65 627	44 647	3 725	48 372	5 468	521	43 425	12 981	9 221	22 787	20 228	2 880	1 815
1997	68 655	47 210	3 407	50 618	5 996	604	45 226	13 951	9 478	23 747	20 918	2 891	1 841
1998	72 276	50 985	2 164	53 149	6 369	692	47 472	15 086	9 718	24 898	21 923	2 903	1 883
1999	74 512	54 093	1 595	55 688	6 639	768	49 817	14 602	10 093	25 539	22 497	2 918	1 899
2000	79 920	57 007	2 443	59 449	6 886	873	53 436	15 667	10 816	27 293	24 136	2 928	1 921
2001	81 726	58 325	2 238	60 564	7 097	838	54 305	15 721	11 701	27 898	24 723	2 929	1 901
2002	84 461	60 264	2 098	62 362	7 223	880	56 019	15 555	12 887	28 834	26 026	2 929	1 878
2003	86 372	62 968	2 396	65 364	7 560	920	58 724	14 824	12 824	29 450	26 785	2 933	1 874
2004	93 209	66 705	4 847	71 552	7 943	963	64 572	15 337	13 299	31 689	28 933	2 941	1 904
2005	95 359	69 695	3 982	73 677	8 360	910	66 227	15 012	14 119	32 331	29 261	2 949	1 937
2006	100 450	73 126	3 064	76 190	8 824	916	68 282	16 654	15 514	33 885	30 465	2 964	1 966
2007	106 504	76 107	4 187	80 295	9 282	1 073	72 086	18 100	16 318	35 755	31 912	2 979	1 996
2008	112 302	78 790	5 972	84 761	9 711	1 078	76 128	18 435	17 738	37 509	33 752	2 994	2 025
2009	110 541	77 347	3 976	81 323	9 644	1 073	72 752	17 630	20 159	36 751	33 734	3 008	. . .

. . . = Not available.

Table 21-2. Personal Income and Employment by Region and State—*Continued*

(Millions of dollars, except as noted.)

Region or state and year	Personal income, total	Earnings by place of work			Less: Contributions for government social insurance	Plus: Adjustment for residence	Equals: Net earnings by place of residence	Plus: Dividends, interest, and rent	Plus: Personal current transfer receipts	Per capita (dollars)		Population (thousands)	Total employment (thousands)
		Nonfarm	Farm	Total						Personal income	Disposable personal income		
KANSAS													
1958	4 469	3 025	524	3 548	121	147	3 575	636	258	2 086	1 889	2 142	. . .
1959	4 514	3 180	365	3 545	142	163	3 567	667	280	2 090	1 892	2 160	. . .
1960	4 693	3 241	435	3 676	161	173	3 688	703	302	2 150	1 930	2 183	. . .
1961	4 895	3 394	442	3 836	177	176	3 835	725	335	2 210	1 986	2 215	. . .
1962	5 101	3 579	414	3 993	183	192	4 002	754	345	2 286	2 046	2 231	. . .
1963	5 226	3 683	394	4 077	206	212	4 083	777	366	2 357	2 100	2 217	. . .
1964	5 494	3 928	360	4 288	213	234	4 309	806	379	2 487	2 260	2 209	. . .
1965	5 855	4 100	454	4 554	222	257	4 589	853	413	2 654	2 410	2 206	. . .
1966	6 277	4 496	469	4 966	293	292	4 965	869	444	2 853	2 554	2 200	. . .
1967	6 573	4 791	400	5 191	339	322	5 174	868	532	2 992	2 672	2 197	. . .
1968	7 143	5 257	395	5 651	376	353	5 628	899	616	3 223	2 850	2 216	. . .
1969	7 950	5 720	465	6 185	423	441	6 203	1 058	689	3 555	3 117	2 236	1 029
1970	8 596	6 033	606	6 639	444	439	6 634	1 158	803	3 824	3 377	2 248	1 017
1971	9 326	6 506	706	7 212	494	430	7 148	1 261	916	4 152	3 720	2 246	1 022
1972	10 418	7 207	963	8 170	575	453	8 047	1 386	985	4 619	4 099	2 256	1 048
1973	11 944	8 099	1 386	9 485	737	468	9 216	1 577	1 151	5 275	4 672	2 264	1 090
1974	12 949	9 080	1 060	10 140	856	483	9 767	1 858	1 324	5 710	5 000	2 268	1 122
1975	14 140	10 057	807	10 865	938	497	10 423	2 104	1 613	6 206	5 503	2 279	1 133
1976	15 438	11 386	585	11 971	1 070	514	11 414	2 243	1 781	6 716	5 950	2 299	1 169
1977	16 871	12 552	499	13 050	1 176	559	12 434	2 511	1 927	7 279	6 404	2 318	1 208
1978	18 709	14 255	287	14 542	1 375	604	13 771	2 836	2 102	8 020	7 032	2 333	1 252
1979	21 406	16 088	706	16 794	1 617	651	15 829	3 258	2 319	9 119	7 917	2 347	1 296
1980	23 546	17 644	101	17 744	1 760	727	16 711	4 078	2 756	9 939	8 616	2 369	1 309
1981	26 704	19 307	347	19 654	2 066	752	18 341	5 187	3 177	11 197	9 613	2 385	1 322
1982	28 948	20 021	577	20 598	2 191	775	19 182	6 201	3 564	12 056	10 397	2 401	1 306
1983	30 134	21 024	383	21 407	2 288	749	19 869	6 465	3 800	12 475	10 983	2 416	1 323
1984	33 037	23 055	750	23 805	2 567	792	22 030	7 089	3 918	13 629	12 118	2 424	1 365
1985	34 742	24 138	809	24 948	2 733	837	23 052	7 558	4 132	14 312	12 672	2 427	1 368
1986	36 385	25 451	938	26 389	2 885	821	24 324	7 726	4 335	14 957	13 352	2 433	1 368
1987	38 068	26 764	1 175	27 939	3 003	894	25 829	7 782	4 457	15 567	13 787	2 445	1 421
1988	39 901	28 250	1 145	29 396	3 310	905	26 990	8 234	4 676	16 207	14 353	2 462	1 432
1989	42 059	29 956	831	30 787	3 497	954	28 244	8 685	5 130	17 008	14 949	2 473	1 454
1990	44 750	31 531	1 383	32 915	3 858	972	30 029	9 152	5 569	18 034	15 921	2 481	1 474
1991	46 489	32 913	1 036	33 949	4 087	951	30 814	9 632	6 044	18 605	16 497	2 499	1 489
1992	49 914	35 530	1 410	36 941	4 349	962	33 554	9 657	6 702	19 710	17 573	2 532	1 502
1993	52 079	37 327	1 348	38 676	4 559	1 056	35 173	9 804	7 101	20 371	18 109	2 557	1 525
1994	54 796	39 435	1 437	40 872	4 859	929	36 942	10 520	7 334	21 235	18 854	2 581	1 551
1995	56 883	41 438	797	42 235	5 049	1 096	38 282	10 887	7 714	21 870	19 307	2 601	1 600
1996	60 802	43 666	1 509	45 175	5 279	1 150	41 046	11 787	7 969	23 255	20 446	2 615	1 632
1997	64 576	46 718	1 425	48 143	5 630	1 057	43 570	12 646	8 360	24 504	21 387	2 635	1 677
1998	69 261	50 498	1 312	51 810	6 024	1 082	46 868	13 897	8 496	26 032	22 722	2 661	1 724
1999	71 848	53 356	1 402	54 758	6 294	971	49 435	13 548	8 865	26 826	23 406	2 678	1 739
2000	76 684	56 935	1 007	57 942	6 599	1 078	52 420	14 647	9 617	28 477	24 841	2 693	1 758
2001	80 148	59 866	1 151	61 017	6 849	974	55 142	14 501	10 505	29 668	26 017	2 701	1 771
2002	80 722	61 007	476	61 483	6 972	1 019	55 530	14 007	11 184	29 758	26 609	2 713	1 748
2003	83 901	63 523	1 649	65 173	7 146	884	58 911	13 341	11 649	30 824	27 880	2 722	1 737
2004	87 171	66 652	1 608	68 261	7 495	817	61 582	13 611	11 978	31 922	28 935	2 731	1 747
2005	90 850	69 275	1 943	71 219	7 844	887	64 262	13 952	12 636	33 136	29 705	2 742	1 761
2006	98 554	74 081	1 170	75 252	8 350	866	67 768	17 170	13 617	35 764	31 836	2 756	1 794
2007	103 845	77 263	1 452	78 715	8 674	971	71 012	18 433	14 401	37 414	32 977	2 776	1 843
2008	108 779	80 113	2 696	82 809	9 082	1 070	74 797	18 442	15 539	38 886	34 555	2 797	1 875
2009	106 875	78 412	1 820	80 232	8 987	965	72 209	17 104	17 562	37 916	34 528	2 819	. . .

. . . = Not available.

Table 21-2. Personal Income and Employment by Region and State—*Continued*

(Millions of dollars, except as noted.)

| Region or state and year | Personal income, total | Earnings by place of work | | | Less: Contributions for government social insurance | Plus: Adjustment for residence | Equals: Net earnings by place of residence | Plus: Dividends, interest, and rent | Plus: Personal current transfer receipts | Per capita (dollars) | | Population (thousands) | Total employment (thousands) |
		Nonfarm	Farm	Total						Personal income	Disposable personal income		
KENTUCKY													
1958	4 532	3 344	361	3 705	142	83	3 646	507	379	1 531	1 385	2 961	...
1959	4 769	3 575	336	3 911	169	97	3 839	537	393	1 590	1 438	2 999	...
1960	4 921	3 675	319	3 994	184	97	3 907	585	429	1 618	1 461	3 041	...
1961	5 238	3 770	392	4 162	184	89	4 066	618	555	1 715	1 558	3 054	...
1962	5 563	4 108	391	4 500	209	92	4 383	676	504	1 807	1 628	3 079	...
1963	5 848	4 374	400	4 774	240	92	4 625	719	504	1 889	1 706	3 096	...
1964	6 112	4 670	293	4 963	245	99	4 817	765	530	1 953	1 775	3 129	...
1965	6 631	5 044	361	5 405	258	107	5 255	798	579	2 112	1 915	3 140	...
1966	7 243	5 621	377	5 997	339	116	5 775	842	627	2 302	2 064	3 147	...
1967	7 840	6 117	378	6 495	399	95	6 191	903	746	2 472	2 227	3 172	...
1968	8 577	6 777	369	7 146	445	104	6 805	929	843	2 684	2 395	3 195	...
1969	9 478	7 416	428	7 843	511	174	7 507	1 027	944	2 964	2 596	3 198	1 332
1970	10 260	7 991	393	8 385	549	164	8 000	1 155	1 105	3 176	2 811	3 231	1 336
1971	11 157	8 704	408	9 111	616	107	8 602	1 257	1 298	3 383	3 022	3 298	1 360
1972	12 360	9 651	507	10 158	716	101	9 543	1 376	1 441	3 705	3 266	3 336	1 392
1973	13 931	10 964	579	11 543	922	59	10 680	1 532	1 720	4 132	3 685	3 372	1 461
1974	15 700	12 265	665	12 931	1 063	26	11 893	1 756	2 051	4 595	4 018	3 417	1 496
1975	17 137	13 216	483	13 699	1 124	11	12 586	1 968	2 584	4 940	4 419	3 469	1 465
1976	19 266	15 043	557	15 600	1 293	-23	14 284	2 160	2 823	5 457	4 862	3 530	1 523
1977	21 718	17 052	683	17 736	1 454	1	16 282	2 477	2 959	6 075	5 367	3 575	1 579
1978	24 406	19 343	605	19 948	1 690	13	18 271	2 963	3 172	6 758	5 953	3 611	1 645
1979	27 703	21 619	679	22 299	1 950	4	20 353	3 652	3 698	7 603	6 701	3 644	1 665
1980	29 727	22 679	561	23 241	2 064	28	21 205	4 067	4 454	8 113	7 173	3 664	1 642
1981	33 005	24 426	941	25 366	2 407	-7	22 952	5 027	5 026	8 992	7 901	3 670	1 634
1982	35 183	25 327	903	26 230	2 539	-16	23 675	6 022	5 486	9 552	8 419	3 683	1 616
1983	36 432	26 505	232	26 737	2 654	11	24 094	6 397	5 942	9 861	8 743	3 694	1 624
1984	40 781	29 267	1 120	30 388	3 000	-66	27 322	7 242	6 218	11 035	9 881	3 695	1 676
1985	42 503	30 693	875	31 568	3 218	-77	28 272	7 723	6 507	11 503	10 252	3 695	1 698
1986	43 584	31 576	648	32 224	3 453	-47	28 723	8 049	6 812	11 819	10 529	3 688	1 733
1987	45 987	33 793	734	34 527	3 682	-76	30 768	8 173	7 045	12 485	11 066	3 683	1 765
1988	49 877	37 036	783	37 819	4 089	-88	33 642	8 766	7 469	13 553	12 062	3 680	1 816
1989	53 430	38 953	1 142	40 095	4 383	-133	35 579	9 657	8 193	14 530	12 838	3 677	1 865
1990	56 741	41 191	1 124	42 315	4 789	-94	37 432	10 342	8 967	15 360	13 544	3 694	1 906
1991	60 088	43 165	1 125	44 290	5 079	-131	39 080	10 802	10 205	16 142	14 328	3 722	1 903
1992	64 578	46 972	1 312	48 283	5 513	-398	42 372	10 998	11 208	17 150	15 226	3 765	1 949
1993	66 918	49 241	1 118	50 359	5 866	-406	44 087	11 166	11 666	17 554	15 560	3 812	1 993
1994	70 469	51 923	1 168	53 092	6 306	-511	46 275	11 961	12 233	18 308	16 193	3 849	2 035
1995	73 774	54 326	712	55 038	6 619	-542	47 877	12 766	13 132	18 978	16 724	3 887	2 110
1996	78 319	56 888	1 139	58 026	6 887	-602	50 537	13 886	13 896	19 982	17 571	3 920	2 141
1997	83 089	60 404	1 146	61 550	7 290	-616	53 644	14 760	14 684	21 021	18 383	3 953	2 189
1998	88 652	64 647	1 014	65 661	7 736	-552	57 373	16 199	15 080	22 244	19 420	3 985	2 228
1999	92 545	69 034	783	69 817	8 252	-641	60 923	15 953	15 668	23 032	20 103	4 018	2 271
2000	100 354	73 684	1 485	75 169	8 517	-655	65 998	17 508	16 849	24 786	21 726	4 049	2 314
2001	103 029	75 720	1 067	76 787	8 748	-897	67 142	17 500	18 386	25 319	22 178	4 069	2 282
2002	105 593	78 504	655	79 159	9 031	-977	69 151	16 704	19 738	25 809	22 979	4 091	2 270
2003	108 314	82 009	699	82 708	9 253	-1 207	72 248	15 787	20 279	26 299	23 593	4 119	2 281
2004	113 803	85 808	1 248	87 057	9 665	-1 377	76 014	15 988	21 800	27 436	24 738	4 148	2 310
2005	118 968	89 815	1 580	91 395	10 150	-1 774	79 470	16 439	23 059	28 446	25 468	4 182	2 343
2006	126 525	94 178	1 248	95 426	10 670	-2 054	82 703	19 001	24 821	29 987	26 848	4 219	2 381
2007	132 198	97 671	776	98 447	11 126	-2 227	85 094	20 486	26 617	31 060	27 651	4 256	2 425
2008	136 940	100 209	1 094	101 303	11 605	-2 454	87 244	20 734	28 962	31 936	28 558	4 288	2 442
2009	137 546	98 430	1 364	99 794	11 524	-2 828	85 443	19 654	32 449	31 883	29 204	4 314	...

. . . = Not available.

Table 21-2. Personal Income and Employment by Region and State—*Continued*

(Millions of dollars, except as noted.)

Region or state and year	Personal income, total	Derivation of personal income								Per capita (dollars)		Population (thousands)	Total employment (thousands)
		Earnings by place of work			Less: Contributions for government social insurance	Plus: Adjustment for residence	Equals: Net earnings by place of residence	Plus: Dividends, interest, and rent	Plus: Personal current transfer receipts	Personal income	Disposable personal income		
		Nonfarm	Farm	Total									
LOUISIANA													
1958	5 162	4 114	187	4 301	140	-3	4 159	625	378	1 636	1 496	3 155	. . .
1959	5 412	4 279	203	4 482	159	-2	4 321	679	411	1 687	1 524	3 208	. . .
1960	5 510	4 356	183	4 539	185	-2	4 353	721	436	1 690	1 541	3 260	. . .
1961	5 723	4 464	215	4 679	187	-1	4 491	747	486	1 741	1 587	3 287	. . .
1962	6 038	4 747	202	4 949	208	0	4 740	794	504	1 805	1 641	3 345	. . .
1963	6 441	5 042	257	5 300	246	-1	5 054	852	535	1 907	1 726	3 377	. . .
1964	6 894	5 494	223	5 717	262	-1	5 455	885	554	2 001	1 830	3 446	. . .
1965	7 456	6 007	195	6 202	285	-1	5 915	943	598	2 133	1 952	3 496	. . .
1966	8 242	6 763	236	6 999	389	2	6 613	987	642	2 322	2 093	3 550	. . .
1967	9 024	7 405	265	7 670	432	4	7 242	1 030	752	2 520	2 278	3 581	. . .
1968	9 880	8 159	297	8 455	489	4	7 970	1 059	850	2 742	2 458	3 603	. . .
1969	10 446	8 654	241	8 895	568	4	8 330	1 154	961	2 886	2 567	3 619	1 440
1970	11 276	9 158	283	9 441	591	4	8 854	1 268	1 154	3 089	2 787	3 650	1 429
1971	12 284	9 926	320	10 246	657	-9	9 580	1 385	1 318	3 310	2 991	3 711	1 445
1972	13 453	10 933	349	11 281	756	-21	10 504	1 499	1 450	3 576	3 208	3 762	1 488
1973	15 067	12 123	579	12 702	960	-37	11 705	1 676	1 686	3 977	3 580	3 789	1 550
1974	17 166	13 723	614	14 336	1 117	-54	13 165	2 026	1 975	4 493	4 008	3 821	1 598
1975	19 271	15 502	419	15 921	1 242	-83	14 596	2 234	2 440	4 958	4 471	3 887	1 641
1976	21 926	17 916	455	18 371	1 453	-113	16 806	2 430	2 690	5 549	4 955	3 952	1 702
1977	24 525	20 222	454	20 676	1 625	-139	18 911	2 719	2 895	6 107	5 439	4 016	1 756
1978	28 155	23 568	374	23 942	1 929	-187	21 826	3 177	3 152	6 912	6 111	4 073	1 849
1979	32 055	26 737	503	27 240	2 273	-233	24 734	3 735	3 587	7 744	6 795	4 139	1 897
1980	37 022	30 688	175	30 863	2 595	-337	27 931	4 814	4 277	8 767	7 669	4 223	1 964
1981	42 794	35 084	267	35 351	3 173	-363	31 815	6 202	4 777	9 991	8 671	4 283	2 030
1982	45 970	36 670	263	36 934	3 374	-342	33 217	7 241	5 511	10 561	9 309	4 353	2 023
1983	47 781	37 059	231	37 290	3 378	-321	33 591	7 917	6 273	10 871	9 691	4 395	1 984
1984	51 025	39 234	322	39 556	3 664	-313	35 579	8 915	6 532	11 595	10 393	4 400	2 023
1985	53 004	40 068	230	40 298	3 775	-282	36 241	9 728	7 036	12 024	10 763	4 408	2 009
1986	52 874	39 159	235	39 394	3 647	-224	35 523	9 629	7 721	11 998	10 880	4 407	1 928
1987	53 080	39 256	397	39 654	3 609	-188	35 857	9 403	7 820	12 219	11 058	4 344	1 904
1988	55 880	41 414	632	42 045	3 983	-169	37 894	9 792	8 194	13 029	11 838	4 289	1 935
1989	59 385	43 487	468	43 955	4 214	-136	39 606	10 817	8 962	13 963	12 608	4 253	1 953
1990	64 046	47 141	404	47 545	4 674	-111	42 760	11 415	9 871	15 171	13 687	4 222	2 005
1991	67 759	49 636	469	50 106	5 028	-129	44 949	11 537	11 274	15 931	14 412	4 253	2 030
1992	72 366	52 631	578	53 209	5 256	-128	47 824	11 593	12 948	16 857	15 319	4 293	2 038
1993	75 792	54 691	590	55 281	5 493	-132	49 656	11 872	14 264	17 559	15 935	4 316	2 086
1994	81 042	57 975	679	58 654	5 925	-157	52 573	12 696	15 773	18 641	16 897	4 347	2 126
1995	84 804	60 908	674	61 581	6 213	-183	55 185	13 712	15 907	19 367	17 518	4 379	2 194
1996	88 662	63 616	884	64 501	6 507	-206	57 788	14 714	16 160	20 155	18 059	4 399	2 239
1997	93 229	67 548	644	68 193	6 906	-221	61 066	15 712	16 451	21 088	18 780	4 421	2 290
1998	98 217	71 582	466	72 047	7 336	-241	64 470	17 064	16 683	22 119	19 733	4 440	2 339
1999	100 180	73 380	636	74 016	7 437	-233	66 345	16 667	17 168	22 458	20 094	4 461	2 355
2000	105 332	76 921	619	77 540	7 683	-245	69 613	18 102	17 617	23 570	21 073	4 469	2 385
2001	113 172	82 655	654	83 309	8 145	-127	75 038	17 746	20 388	25 370	22 720	4 461	2 382
2002	115 863	85 576	424	86 000	8 397	-122	77 481	16 806	21 575	25 943	23 573	4 466	2 404
2003	119 481	89 718	861	90 579	8 699	-173	81 707	16 161	21 613	26 701	24 526	4 475	2 427
2004	125 957	94 189	822	95 011	8 961	-169	85 881	16 486	23 589	28 057	25 807	4 489	2 443
2005	135 317	97 967	714	98 681	9 185	-147	89 349	18 529	27 439	30 086	27 557	4 498	2 415
2006	143 222	104 161	721	104 882	9 904	-163	94 815	22 674	25 733	33 776	30 560	4 240	2 432
2007	154 652	109 764	808	110 572	10 450	-161	99 961	27 890	26 801	35 340	31 995	4 376	2 521
2008	160 659	116 327	737	117 065	11 041	-194	105 830	24 961	29 868	36 091	32 894	4 452	2 577
2009	159 499	116 006	868	116 874	11 097	-225	105 552	21 736	32 212	35 507	32 953	4 492	. . .

. . . = Not available.

Table 21-2. Personal Income and Employment by Region and State—*Continued*

(Millions of dollars, except as noted.)

Region or state and year	Personal income, total	Earnings by place of work			Less: Contributions for government social insurance	Plus: Adjustment for residence	Equals: Net earnings by place of residence	Plus: Dividends, interest, and rent	Plus: Personal current transfer receipts	Per capita (dollars)		Population (thousands)	Total employment (thousands)
		Nonfarm	Farm	Total						Personal income	Disposable personal income		
MAINE													
1958	1 678	1 294	100	1 395	52	-20	1 322	215	141	1 778	1 626	944	. . .
1959	1 749	1 409	59	1 468	60	-24	1 383	219	148	1 828	1 674	957	. . .
1960	1 854	1 473	102	1 575	70	-28	1 477	224	152	1 901	1 724	975	. . .
1961	1 872	1 513	66	1 579	73	-29	1 477	228	167	1 882	1 707	995	. . .
1962	1 950	1 576	65	1 641	78	-30	1 533	245	172	1 962	1 773	994	. . .
1963	2 014	1 626	58	1 684	87	-30	1 566	267	181	2 028	1 843	993	. . .
1964	2 179	1 734	88	1 823	92	-31	1 700	295	184	2 195	2 011	993	. . .
1965	2 357	1 832	125	1 957	92	-30	1 834	331	192	2 364	2 168	997	. . .
1966	2 510	1 998	106	2 104	118	-33	1 953	347	210	2 513	2 300	999	. . .
1967	2 641	2 145	54	2 199	137	-35	2 027	365	248	2 630	2 396	1 004	. . .
1968	2 824	2 326	54	2 381	157	-38	2 185	360	279	2 841	2 557	994	. . .
1969	3 113	2 504	74	2 579	181	-23	2 375	425	312	3 138	2 789	992	443
1970	3 402	2 704	78	2 782	193	-18	2 571	460	371	3 413	3 069	997	446
1971	3 646	2 870	66	2 937	211	-17	2 709	499	438	3 590	3 276	1 016	443
1972	3 993	3 159	65	3 224	241	-20	2 963	539	490	3 858	3 502	1 035	453
1973	4 508	3 497	148	3 645	301	-11	3 333	591	584	4 308	3 874	1 046	470
1974	5 032	3 799	195	3 995	337	-6	3 651	678	703	4 747	4 276	1 060	478
1975	5 394	4 062	82	4 144	357	-19	3 767	728	899	5 026	4 575	1 073	475
1976	6 211	4 722	163	4 885	422	-23	4 440	796	975	5 698	5 167	1 090	498
1977	6 761	5 178	129	5 306	461	-25	4 820	903	1 038	6 116	5 552	1 105	513
1978	7 474	5 814	90	5 904	531	-23	5 350	1 010	1 115	6 700	6 045	1 115	531
1979	8 338	6 466	76	6 542	607	-16	5 919	1 159	1 260	7 412	6 647	1 125	545
1980	9 391	7 130	49	7 179	670	-14	6 494	1 426	1 471	8 333	7 450	1 127	553
1981	10 384	7 637	118	7 755	773	-51	6 931	1 776	1 677	9 164	8 125	1 133	551
1982	11 254	8 113	104	8 217	834	-50	7 332	2 083	1 839	9 901	8 715	1 137	553
1983	12 075	8 808	72	8 881	910	-41	7 930	2 156	1 989	10 548	9 403	1 145	565
1984	13 438	9 764	118	9 882	1 043	-31	8 808	2 532	2 098	11 628	10 421	1 156	587
1985	14 492	10 624	102	10 726	1 132	-11	9 584	2 688	2 220	12 462	11 114	1 163	606
1986	15 687	11 555	93	11 648	1 239	28	10 437	2 947	2 303	13 406	11 889	1 170	630
1987	17 098	12 713	136	12 848	1 356	46	11 538	3 203	2 357	14 434	12 677	1 185	653
1988	18 772	14 138	118	14 256	1 543	59	12 772	3 500	2 500	15 593	13 735	1 204	686
1989	20 352	15 164	125	15 289	1 651	57	13 695	3 966	2 691	16 683	14 707	1 220	702
1990	21 199	15 641	173	15 814	1 791	56	14 079	4 116	3 005	17 211	15 222	1 232	701
1991	21 596	15 607	127	15 734	1 808	73	13 999	4 139	3 459	17 457	15 558	1 237	678
1992	22 558	16 245	178	16 423	1 910	116	14 629	4 110	3 819	18 214	16 305	1 239	681
1993	23 218	16 755	156	16 911	2 018	175	15 068	4 121	4 029	18 690	16 738	1 242	692
1994	24 297	17 457	148	17 606	2 132	235	15 708	4 373	4 215	19 552	17 457	1 243	703
1995	25 332	17 991	123	18 114	2 214	305	16 206	4 688	4 439	20 372	18 197	1 243	705
1996	26 864	18 793	151	18 943	2 280	358	17 022	5 096	4 746	21 507	19 105	1 249	714
1997	28 315	19 839	104	19 943	2 406	431	17 969	5 382	4 964	22 566	19 896	1 255	727
1998	30 434	21 322	178	21 500	2 557	505	19 448	5 874	5 112	24 171	21 153	1 259	747
1999	31 862	22 776	194	22 970	2 705	573	20 839	5 755	5 268	25 151	22 010	1 267	763
2000	34 097	24 140	207	24 347	2 839	692	22 200	6 295	5 601	26 696	23 227	1 277	785
2001	36 232	25 802	193	25 995	2 972	723	23 747	6 452	6 034	28 201	24 627	1 285	790
2002	37 385	26 827	156	26 982	3 004	701	24 680	6 261	6 443	28 892	25 794	1 294	789
2003	39 002	28 040	159	28 199	3 115	693	25 777	6 230	6 995	29 930	27 001	1 303	794
2004	41 165	29 680	187	29 866	3 255	731	27 342	6 372	7 451	31 466	28 455	1 308	808
2005	41 983	30 269	187	30 457	3 363	759	27 853	6 026	8 104	32 008	28 676	1 312	810
2006	44 306	31 696	168	31 864	3 593	808	29 079	6 962	8 265	33 694	30 111	1 315	819
2007	46 142	32 701	175	32 876	3 750	840	29 966	7 442	8 734	35 028	31 209	1 317	830
2008	47 994	33 509	158	33 668	3 882	856	30 642	7 587	9 765	36 368	32 665	1 320	841
2009	48 441	32 883	201	33 084	3 847	804	30 041	7 384	11 016	36 745	33 859	1 318	. . .

. . . = Not available.

Table 21-2. Personal Income and Employment by Region and State—*Continued*

(Millions of dollars, except as noted.)

Region or state and year	Personal income, total	Earnings by place of work			Less: Contributions for government social insurance	Plus: Adjustment for residence	Equals: Net earnings by place of residence	Plus: Dividends, interest, and rent	Plus: Personal current transfer receipts	Per capita (dollars)		Population (thousands)	Total employment (thousands)
		Nonfarm	Farm	Total						Personal income	Disposable personal income		
MARYLAND													
1958	6 580	5 040	103	5 143	188	466	5 422	848	311	2 207	1 940	2 982	. . .
1959	6 954	5 365	85	5 450	239	516	5 727	901	327	2 268	1 976	3 066	. . .
1960	7 312	5 622	93	5 715	289	582	6 008	964	340	2 349	2 041	3 113	. . .
1961	7 771	5 941	88	6 029	312	641	6 359	1 021	391	2 447	2 141	3 176	. . .
1962	8 403	6 417	84	6 500	350	720	6 870	1 117	416	2 575	2 226	3 263	. . .
1963	8 997	6 848	66	6 913	380	804	7 337	1 225	436	2 657	2 288	3 386	. . .
1964	9 822	7 435	85	7 520	396	886	8 010	1 352	460	2 813	2 460	3 492	. . .
1965	10 727	8 035	96	8 131	398	1 003	8 735	1 488	504	2 980	2 598	3 600	. . .
1966	11 841	9 015	77	9 093	526	1 117	9 684	1 600	557	3 205	2 754	3 695	. . .
1967	12 913	9 601	94	9 694	585	1 366	10 476	1 746	691	3 437	2 948	3 757	. . .
1968	14 305	10 668	86	10 755	641	1 528	11 641	1 837	826	3 750	3 128	3 815	. . .
1969	16 243	11 865	133	11 997	750	2 154	13 401	1 897	944	4 199	3 486	3 868	1 679
1970	17 951	12 942	122	13 064	815	2 512	14 761	2 063	1 126	4 558	3 857	3 938	1 702
1971	19 633	14 074	94	14 168	916	2 764	16 016	2 245	1 373	4 881	4 188	4 023	1 729
1972	21 552	15 480	128	15 608	1 059	3 000	17 550	2 429	1 574	5 281	4 456	4 081	1 781
1973	23 853	17 259	209	17 468	1 353	3 203	19 319	2 718	1 816	5 805	4 927	4 109	1 846
1974	26 322	18 951	165	19 116	1 531	3 478	21 063	3 155	2 105	6 368	5 367	4 133	1 868
1975	28 641	20 107	204	20 311	1 622	3 864	22 553	3 442	2 647	6 890	5 914	4 157	1 846
1976	31 431	22 278	175	22 453	1 806	4 179	24 826	3 754	2 851	7 534	6 470	4 172	1 866
1977	34 287	24 339	130	24 468	1 972	4 586	27 083	4 167	3 037	8 174	6 960	4 195	1 919
1978	38 033	27 095	184	27 279	2 258	4 952	29 973	4 709	3 351	9 030	7 674	4 212	2 004
1979	42 112	29 929	160	30 089	2 607	5 381	32 863	5 448	3 802	9 971	8 424	4 223	2 059
1980	47 197	32 775	58	32 833	2 861	5 947	35 919	6 751	4 527	11 164	9 488	4 228	2 070
1981	52 571	35 975	130	36 105	3 381	6 395	39 120	8 264	5 187	12 335	10 362	4 262	2 095
1982	57 107	37 856	145	38 001	3 617	6 964	41 347	9 987	5 774	13 334	11 284	4 283	2 084
1983	61 600	41 324	90	41 414	4 072	7 347	44 690	10 614	6 295	14 281	12 257	4 313	2 151
1984	68 537	46 014	266	46 280	4 673	8 033	49 640	12 261	6 636	15 701	13 456	4 365	2 243
1985	74 736	50 418	277	50 695	5 285	8 674	54 084	13 636	7 015	16 935	14 587	4 413	2 342
1986	80 460	54 752	287	55 039	5 838	9 291	58 491	14 484	7 485	17 932	15 457	4 487	2 428
1987	87 052	60 047	301	60 347	6 332	10 049	64 064	15 216	7 772	19 067	16 239	4 566	2 553
1988	95 337	66 080	367	66 446	7 259	11 132	70 319	16 732	8 286	20 468	17 651	4 658	2 647
1989	102 738	70 445	366	70 810	7 847	11 964	74 927	18 789	9 022	21 733	18 557	4 727	2 704
1990	108 865	74 709	357	75 066	8 522	12 450	78 993	19 988	9 883	22 681	19 420	4 800	2 737
1991	113 329	76 672	310	76 982	8 828	13 122	81 276	20 931	11 122	23 282	20 114	4 868	2 662
1992	118 713	79 991	343	80 334	9 136	13 957	85 155	21 086	12 472	24 112	20 923	4 923	2 636
1993	123 328	83 217	321	83 538	9 479	14 351	88 410	21 902	13 016	24 805	21 490	4 972	2 659
1994	129 493	87 434	309	87 743	10 046	14 822	92 519	23 378	13 597	25 780	22 278	5 023	2 706
1995	134 952	91 432	215	91 647	10 443	14 863	96 067	24 659	14 226	26 618	22 900	5 070	2 765
1996	141 548	95 144	395	95 539	10 805	15 225	99 959	26 404	15 185	27 689	23 692	5 112	2 806
1997	149 563	101 576	281	101 858	11 464	15 201	105 594	28 467	15 501	29 000	24 424	5 157	2 870
1998	159 994	108 459	326	108 785	12 142	16 522	113 166	30 646	16 183	30 742	26 036	5 204	2 925
1999	169 278	115 873	350	116 223	12 884	17 414	120 754	31 339	17 186	32 216	27 232	5 255	2 990
2000	184 174	125 534	415	125 949	13 768	19 706	131 888	34 111	18 175	34 681	29 231	5 311	3 065
2001	194 986	134 592	416	135 008	14 840	20 101	140 269	34 904	19 813	36 276	30 714	5 375	3 106
2002	202 148	140 919	223	141 142	15 548	20 790	146 384	34 473	21 290	37 160	32 121	5 440	3 142
2003	209 974	147 586	321	147 907	16 221	21 495	153 181	33 964	22 828	38 200	33 328	5 497	3 181
2004	225 023	158 520	452	158 972	17 427	23 376	164 921	36 235	23 866	40 598	35 498	5 543	3 240
2005	237 522	167 442	408	167 850	18 354	24 523	174 019	37 730	25 773	42 547	36 854	5 583	3 309
2006	252 781	176 743	320	177 063	19 584	25 094	182 573	43 240	26 967	45 041	38 853	5 612	3 368
2007	264 367	183 301	295	183 595	20 528	26 043	189 110	46 240	29 017	46 922	40 234	5 634	3 434
2008	272 542	187 322	367	187 688	21 439	27 136	193 385	47 423	31 734	48 164	41 642	5 659	3 472
2009	275 201	188 196	342	188 537	21 844	28 015	194 709	45 383	35 109	48 285	43 125	5 699	. . .

. . . = Not available.

Table 21-2. Personal Income and Employment by Region and State—*Continued*

(Millions of dollars, except as noted.)

Region or state and year	Personal income, total	Earnings by place of work Nonfarm	Farm	Total	Less: Contributions for government social insurance	Plus: Adjustment for residence	Equals: Net earnings by place of residence	Plus: Dividends, interest, and rent	Plus: Personal current transfer receipts	Per capita Personal income	Disposable personal income	Population (thousands)	Total employment (thousands)
MASSACHUSETTS													
1958	11 553	9 446	67	9 513	353	-56	9 104	1 574	874	2 306	2 041	5 010	...
1959	12 350	10 226	59	10 285	427	-69	9 788	1 687	874	2 413	2 124	5 117	...
1960	12 869	10 657	68	10 725	499	-75	10 150	1 798	921	2 494	2 175	5 160	...
1961	13 510	11 151	60	11 211	528	-83	10 600	1 883	1 027	2 589	2 276	5 219	...
1962	14 303	11 829	60	11 889	617	-93	11 180	2 072	1 051	2 718	2 379	5 263	...
1963	14 866	12 229	60	12 289	679	-99	11 511	2 245	1 110	2 782	2 434	5 344	...
1964	15 890	12 952	62	13 014	697	-109	12 208	2 531	1 151	2 917	2 595	5 448	...
1965	16 966	13 749	68	13 818	714	-122	12 982	2 772	1 212	3 084	2 740	5 502	...
1966	18 318	15 028	71	15 099	942	-141	14 015	3 002	1 300	3 309	2 914	5 535	...
1967	19 937	16 197	56	16 252	1 032	-158	15 062	3 270	1 605	3 564	3 132	5 594	...
1968	21 805	17 670	64	17 735	1 138	-176	16 421	3 449	1 936	3 881	3 359	5 618	...
1969	23 646	19 260	66	19 327	1 259	-126	17 942	3 548	2 157	4 185	3 557	5 650	2 679
1970	25 505	20 587	69	20 656	1 323	-108	19 225	3 729	2 550	4 472	3 861	5 704	2 679
1971	27 218	21 775	63	21 839	1 443	-111	20 284	3 914	3 020	4 743	4 152	5 739	2 644
1972	29 397	23 665	63	23 728	1 647	-110	21 971	4 111	3 314	5 102	4 391	5 762	2 697
1973	32 047	26 016	71	26 087	2 069	-134	23 884	4 447	3 716	5 541	4 805	5 784	2 787
1974	34 725	27 703	70	27 772	2 269	-150	25 353	4 967	4 405	6 011	5 200	5 777	2 811
1975	37 186	28 665	69	28 734	2 290	-155	26 289	5 165	5 732	6 453	5 672	5 762	2 728
1976	40 201	31 437	76	31 513	2 550	-182	28 781	5 483	5 937	6 993	6 102	5 749	2 756
1977	43 720	34 559	79	34 638	2 811	-224	31 602	6 019	6 099	7 611	6 611	5 744	2 833
1978	48 369	38 734	104	38 837	3 242	-287	35 308	6 591	6 469	8 422	7 290	5 743	2 958
1979	53 849	43 324	90	43 414	3 788	-360	39 266	7 421	7 163	9 371	8 037	5 746	3 074
1980	60 736	48 049	106	48 155	4 217	-482	43 456	9 106	8 173	10 570	9 021	5 746	3 134
1981	67 749	52 583	116	52 700	4 993	-596	47 110	11 348	9 291	11 744	9 933	5 769	3 142
1982	74 405	56 618	131	56 749	5 497	-725	50 527	13 835	10 043	12 892	11 034	5 771	3 143
1983	80 858	62 388	164	62 552	6 141	-902	55 509	14 705	10 644	13 942	11 990	5 799	3 215
1984	91 342	71 082	182	71 264	7 225	-1 175	62 863	17 284	11 195	15 639	13 519	5 841	3 402
1985	98 786	77 860	160	78 020	8 002	-1 360	68 658	18 413	11 714	16 798	14 432	5 881	3 510
1986	106 265	84 478	175	84 653	8 883	-1 489	74 281	19 661	12 323	18 003	15 387	5 903	3 605
1987	115 125	92 812	154	92 966	9 651	-1 665	81 651	20 803	12 672	19 397	16 483	5 935	3 632
1988	126 339	102 171	174	102 345	10 771	-1 898	89 675	23 021	13 643	21 127	18 198	5 980	3 739
1989	132 913	105 859	153	106 012	11 133	-2 019	92 860	24 675	15 379	22 095	18 931	6 015	3 710
1990	137 300	107 176	153	107 330	11 135	-2 076	94 119	25 950	17 231	22 797	19 549	6 023	3 615
1991	140 313	107 427	172	107 599	11 310	-2 280	94 010	26 542	19 761	23 314	20 154	6 018	3 451
1992	147 235	113 898	171	114 070	11 893	-2 383	99 793	26 822	20 620	24 422	21 166	6 029	3 482
1993	152 619	118 702	165	118 867	12 487	-2 592	103 788	27 610	21 221	25 182	21 752	6 061	3 548
1994	160 869	125 228	150	125 378	13 273	-2 799	109 306	29 117	22 446	26 393	22 729	6 095	3 616
1995	169 886	132 266	146	132 412	14 054	-2 865	115 493	30 635	23 758	27 662	23 664	6 141	3 649
1996	180 938	141 071	166	141 238	14 818	-3 126	123 294	33 159	24 485	29 279	24 786	6 180	3 713
1997	192 455	150 627	168	150 795	15 892	-3 406	131 497	35 617	25 341	30 911	25 914	6 226	3 802
1998	207 008	162 903	108	163 010	16 937	-3 636	142 438	39 106	25 464	33 006	27 400	6 272	3 885
1999	219 031	175 908	109	176 018	18 170	-4 209	153 639	39 000	26 391	34 671	28 570	6 317	3 949
2000	243 132	196 896	131	197 027	20 076	-5 082	171 869	43 440	27 823	38 210	30 786	6 363	4 058
2001	253 085	203 068	110	203 177	20 591	-5 025	177 561	45 151	30 373	39 472	32 355	6 412	4 096
2002	254 183	202 848	131	202 979	20 488	-4 774	177 717	43 469	32 997	39 463	33 937	6 441	4 026
2003	258 696	206 242	132	206 374	20 714	-4 668	180 992	42 840	34 863	40 098	34 781	6 452	3 993
2004	271 160	218 974	146	219 120	22 496	-4 851	191 773	43 161	36 225	42 032	36 472	6 451	4 016
2005	282 447	227 030	126	227 157	23 564	-4 825	198 767	44 749	38 931	43 770	37 559	6 453	4 056
2006	304 970	239 339	131	239 470	24 383	-4 968	210 119	54 193	40 659	47 162	40 327	6 466	4 117
2007	322 652	251 050	138	251 189	25 503	-5 580	220 105	59 027	43 520	49 644	41 804	6 499	4 187
2008	333 046	257 234	179	257 414	26 414	-5 759	225 241	59 936	47 870	50 897	43 306	6 544	4 251
2009	328 858	248 419	184	248 603	25 709	-5 552	217 342	56 670	54 846	49 875	44 163	6 594	...

. . . = Not available.

Table 21-2. Personal Income and Employment by Region and State—*Continued*

(Millions of dollars, except as noted.)

Region or state and year	Personal income, total	Derivation of personal income								Per capita (dollars)		Population (thousands)	Total employment (thousands)
		Earnings by place of work			Less: Contributions for government social insurance	Plus: Adjustment for residence	Equals: Net earnings by place of residence	Plus: Dividends, interest, and rent	Plus: Personal current transfer receipts	Personal income	Disposable personal income		
		Nonfarm	Farm	Total									
MICHIGAN													
1958	17 188	13 954	295	14 249	560	30	13 719	2 286	1 183	2 242	2 025	7 667	. . .
1959	18 278	15 158	220	15 378	695	34	14 717	2 488	1 073	2 353	2 115	7 767	. . .
1960	19 088	15 800	234	16 034	824	37	15 246	2 730	1 112	2 437	2 174	7 834	. . .
1961	19 156	15 411	293	15 704	786	38	14 956	2 868	1 332	2 427	2 183	7 893	. . .
1962	20 582	16 724	269	16 993	888	41	16 146	3 131	1 304	2 595	2 314	7 933	. . .
1963	22 021	18 018	292	18 310	1 038	44	17 317	3 377	1 327	2 733	2 429	8 058	. . .
1964	24 210	19 813	289	20 101	1 077	49	19 074	3 771	1 366	2 957	2 662	8 187	. . .
1965	26 937	22 103	268	22 371	1 122	54	21 303	4 158	1 476	3 223	2 890	8 357	. . .
1966	29 419	24 418	342	24 760	1 571	63	23 252	4 550	1 617	3 456	3 083	8 512	. . .
1967	30 765	25 205	271	25 476	1 652	68	23 892	4 871	2 002	3 565	3 175	8 630	. . .
1968	34 072	28 062	300	28 362	1 853	76	26 585	5 175	2 312	3 918	3 429	8 696	. . .
1969	36 414	30 767	351	31 118	2 203	107	29 023	4 832	2 559	4 147	3 559	8 781	3 640
1970	37 347	31 035	341	31 376	2 193	112	29 295	4 837	3 216	4 198	3 654	8 897	3 558
1971	40 385	33 733	310	34 043	2 446	104	31 700	4 846	3 838	4 501	3 953	8 972	3 571
1972	44 849	37 703	427	38 129	2 901	112	35 341	5 191	4 318	4 970	4 288	9 025	3 687
1973	50 370	42 827	561	43 389	3 794	138	39 733	5 712	4 925	5 552	4 826	9 072	3 858
1974	53 986	44 633	649	45 283	4 077	140	41 346	6 487	6 153	5 926	5 178	9 109	3 854
1975	57 440	45 629	578	46 207	4 087	154	42 274	7 090	8 075	6 307	5 595	9 108	3 695
1976	64 657	52 801	478	53 279	4 789	197	48 687	7 659	8 311	7 092	6 200	9 117	3 844
1977	72 803	60 451	560	61 011	5 485	223	55 748	8 521	8 534	7 950	6 886	9 157	4 016
1978	80 979	68 216	511	68 728	6 394	270	62 603	9 300	9 076	8 800	7 550	9 202	4 186
1979	89 056	74 423	546	74 968	7 197	310	68 081	10 509	10 466	9 629	8 263	9 249	4 228
1980	95 248	75 135	537	75 672	7 181	354	68 845	12 595	13 808	10 291	8 961	9 256	4 030
1981	101 992	79 184	517	79 701	8 141	382	71 942	15 424	14 626	11 075	9 611	9 209	3 978
1982	105 030	78 429	410	78 840	8 195	391	71 036	17 665	16 329	11 522	10 130	9 115	3 823
1983	111 142	83 354	221	83 575	8 954	426	75 047	18 813	17 282	12 284	10 761	9 048	3 866
1984	122 968	92 827	550	93 377	10 357	489	83 509	21 983	17 476	13 588	11 937	9 049	4 040
1985	133 283	101 881	661	102 542	11 666	509	91 385	23 861	18 038	14 685	12 807	9 076	4 233
1986	141 659	108 700	492	109 192	12 551	492	97 133	25 612	18 914	15 520	13 555	9 128	4 349
1987	146 669	112 768	669	113 437	12 897	511	101 050	26 169	19 450	15 964	13 895	9 187	4 483
1988	155 728	121 107	592	121 699	14 304	522	107 917	27 546	20 264	16 894	14 768	9 218	4 582
1989	167 227	128 111	980	129 092	15 164	517	114 445	30 874	21 908	18 072	15 726	9 253	4 709
1990	174 296	133 015	777	133 792	16 100	459	118 150	32 408	23 738	18 719	16 368	9 311	4 791
1991	179 824	136 499	667	137 166	16 638	476	121 004	32 400	26 420	19 129	16 833	9 400	4 721
1992	191 274	146 728	758	147 487	17 675	605	130 416	32 869	27 988	20 179	17 880	9 479	4 751
1993	200 784	154 530	738	155 268	18 756	671	137 183	33 674	29 926	21 046	18 484	9 540	4 812
1994	216 842	167 972	564	168 537	20 565	775	148 747	37 883	30 212	22 593	19 787	9 598	4 985
1995	226 693	176 339	698	177 036	21 663	751	156 125	38 729	31 839	23 428	20 407	9 676	5 142
1996	236 927	182 461	618	183 078	22 197	776	161 658	41 854	33 415	24 279	21 013	9 759	5 247
1997	248 650	190 515	612	191 127	23 286	870	168 710	44 615	35 325	25 349	21 840	9 809	5 330
1998	264 936	204 615	631	205 246	24 457	917	181 706	48 141	35 089	26 903	23 062	9 848	5 381
1999	275 718	214 540	820	215 360	25 873	1 033	190 520	47 544	37 655	27 858	23 861	9 897	5 475
2000	292 606	228 046	602	228 648	27 085	1 048	202 611	51 054	38 941	29 392	25 285	9 955	5 587
2001	299 903	232 778	556	233 334	26 864	1 100	207 570	48 984	43 349	29 972	26 034	10 006	5 490
2002	303 009	236 506	589	237 095	27 194	1 113	211 014	47 085	44 911	30 184	26 775	10 039	5 454
2003	314 192	245 978	704	246 682	27 688	1 180	220 174	46 894	47 125	31 212	28 014	10 066	5 430
2004	319 358	248 478	1 141	249 619	28 493	1 284	222 410	47 793	49 154	31 653	28 516	10 089	5 454
2005	325 664	252 992	1 060	254 052	29 404	1 354	226 002	47 456	52 206	32 274	28 916	10 091	5 480
2006	334 769	254 780	1 165	255 945	30 177	1 457	227 226	51 644	55 900	33 203	29 684	10 082	5 468
2007	343 585	256 141	1 137	257 279	30 458	1 522	228 342	55 240	60 003	34 185	30 370	10 051	5 440
2008	349 612	255 141	1 683	256 824	30 627	1 562	227 759	55 956	65 897	34 953	31 343	10 002	5 398
2009	339 219	235 794	1 038	236 833	28 484	1 547	209 895	53 935	75 389	34 025	31 309	9 970	. . .

. . . = Not available.

Table 21-2. Personal Income and Employment by Region and State—*Continued*

(Millions of dollars, except as noted.)

Region or state and year	Personal income, total	Earnings by place of work			Less: Contributions for government social insurance	Plus: Adjustment for residence	Equals: Net earnings by place of residence	Plus: Dividends, interest, and rent	Plus: Personal current transfer receipts	Per capita (dollars)		Population (thousands)	Total employment (thousands)
		Nonfarm	Farm	Total						Personal income	Disposable personal income		
MINNESOTA													
1958	6 645	4 886	594	5 480	179	1	5 302	879	464	2 006	1 800	3 313	. . .
1959	6 905	5 287	409	5 695	220	0	5 475	942	488	2 052	1 836	3 366	. . .
1960	7 332	5 575	505	6 080	260	-1	5 819	1 006	507	2 141	1 907	3 425	. . .
1961	7 706	5 818	529	6 347	269	-3	6 075	1 061	571	2 221	1 980	3 470	. . .
1962	8 129	6 263	456	6 719	303	-3	6 414	1 125	590	2 314	2 054	3 513	. . .
1963	8 620	6 521	608	7 128	339	-4	6 785	1 210	625	2 441	2 175	3 531	. . .
1964	8 968	6 979	390	7 370	348	-4	7 018	1 299	651	2 520	2 271	3 558	. . .
1965	9 914	7 531	641	8 172	372	-7	7 793	1 413	708	2 760	2 478	3 592	. . .
1966	10 749	8 308	721	9 028	522	-13	8 493	1 495	761	2 972	2 650	3 617	. . .
1967	11 562	9 035	633	9 668	601	-17	9 050	1 587	925	3 160	2 808	3 659	. . .
1968	12 731	10 001	672	10 673	683	-24	9 966	1 707	1 058	3 438	3 038	3 703	. . .
1969	14 186	11 176	721	11 897	782	-33	11 082	1 943	1 162	3 775	3 277	3 758	1 691
1970	15 451	11 946	876	12 822	826	-29	11 967	2 111	1 373	4 050	3 565	3 815	1 699
1971	16 447	12 731	796	13 527	911	-28	12 588	2 265	1 594	4 270	3 797	3 852	1 706
1972	17 887	13 820	960	14 779	1 038	-30	13 711	2 414	1 762	4 626	4 051	3 867	1 780
1973	21 061	15 461	2 179	17 640	1 336	-38	16 267	2 729	2 066	5 421	4 812	3 885	1 878
1974	22 705	17 047	1 644	18 691	1 528	-34	17 130	3 152	2 423	5 824	5 067	3 898	1 921
1975	24 462	18 410	1 266	19 676	1 615	-34	18 027	3 512	2 924	6 231	5 462	3 926	1 920
1976	26 609	20 694	784	21 477	1 847	-43	19 588	3 813	3 209	6 725	5 861	3 957	1 977
1977	30 000	22 915	1 503	24 418	2 045	-55	22 318	4 307	3 375	7 538	6 557	3 980	2 034
1978	33 720	26 150	1 627	27 777	2 412	-70	25 295	4 801	3 623	8 420	7 288	4 005	2 122
1979	37 603	29 736	1 247	30 983	2 858	-88	28 037	5 514	4 052	9 312	7 983	4 038	2 218
1980	41 786	32 353	960	33 313	3 111	-92	30 110	6 818	4 857	10 229	8 810	4 085	2 248
1981	46 288	34 956	1 044	36 000	3 620	-130	32 250	8 464	5 575	11 258	9 663	4 112	2 233
1982	49 639	36 508	821	37 329	3 853	-153	33 323	10 047	6 268	12 015	10 380	4 131	2 192
1983	52 385	39 025	119	39 143	4 161	-182	34 800	10 827	6 758	12 649	10 975	4 141	2 219
1984	59 249	43 734	1 444	45 178	4 796	-238	40 144	12 015	7 090	14 250	12 487	4 158	2 324
1985	62 859	46 810	1 340	48 150	5 234	-286	42 630	12 695	7 534	15 023	13 164	4 184	2 385
1986	66 483	49 586	1 641	51 227	5 702	-325	45 201	13 411	7 871	15 810	13 900	4 205	2 417
1987	70 885	53 362	2 142	55 504	6 107	-375	49 022	13 742	8 121	16 737	14 590	4 235	2 509
1988	74 544	57 667	1 259	58 926	6 854	-455	51 617	14 356	8 571	17 351	15 151	4 296	2 580
1989	81 313	61 472	2 051	63 523	7 339	-438	55 746	16 251	9 316	18 744	16 341	4 338	2 634
1990	86 524	65 450	1 956	67 406	7 901	-467	59 039	17 472	10 014	19 710	17 123	4 390	2 692
1991	89 389	68 391	1 208	69 599	8 381	-474	60 744	17 869	10 776	20 129	17 591	4 441	2 717
1992	95 784	74 215	1 404	75 620	9 019	-509	66 091	17 978	11 714	21 306	18 570	4 496	2 762
1993	98 414	77 496	190	77 685	9 497	-514	67 674	18 377	12 363	21 601	18 755	4 556	2 817
1994	106 052	82 161	1 342	83 503	10 218	-559	72 726	20 326	13 001	23 003	19 982	4 610	2 904
1995	112 515	87 062	524	87 586	10 799	-604	76 183	22 575	13 757	24 144	20 880	4 660	2 995
1996	121 927	92 960	1 922	94 882	11 455	-672	82 755	24 776	14 397	25 871	22 141	4 713	3 056
1997	129 062	99 293	907	100 200	12 128	-764	87 307	27 138	14 617	27 095	23 136	4 763	3 109
1998	140 904	108 495	1 399	109 894	13 052	-822	96 021	29 750	15 133	29 273	24 932	4 813	3 181
1999	148 942	116 497	1 257	117 753	13 933	-930	102 890	30 123	15 930	30 562	26 239	4 873	3 248
2000	160 833	126 083	1 437	127 520	14 914	-1 023	111 583	32 175	17 075	32 597	27 780	4 934	3 317
2001	166 136	130 838	1 004	131 842	15 459	-1 118	115 266	31 717	19 153	33 342	28 564	4 983	3 333
2002	170 949	135 443	981	136 423	15 844	-1 148	119 431	30 741	20 777	34 071	29 747	5 017	3 327
2003	178 095	140 495	1 891	142 386	16 489	-1 189	124 708	31 602	21 785	35 281	31 163	5 048	3 340
2004	188 285	148 515	2 467	150 981	17 410	-1 245	132 326	33 034	22 925	37 069	32 871	5 079	3 384
2005	193 938	152 742	3 089	155 831	18 172	-1 260	136 400	33 623	23 915	37 978	33 291	5 107	3 446
2006	205 803	159 137	2 680	161 817	19 003	-1 242	141 572	37 923	26 308	39 975	34 923	5 148	3 492
2007	216 436	166 089	2 641	168 730	19 679	-1 364	147 688	40 434	28 315	41 693	36 202	5 191	3 537
2008	224 671	170 481	4 330	174 811	20 332	-1 350	153 129	40 915	30 627	42 953	37 599	5 231	3 567
2009	218 823	162 650	2 870	165 520	19 617	-1 154	144 749	38 880	35 193	41 552	37 493	5 266	. . .

. . . = Not available.

Table 21-2. Personal Income and Employment by Region and State—*Continued*

(Millions of dollars, except as noted.)

Region or state and year	Personal income, total	Earnings by place of work			Less: Contributions for government social insurance	Plus: Adjustment for residence	Equals: Net earnings by place of residence	Plus: Dividends, interest, and rent	Plus: Personal current transfer receipts	Per capita (dollars)		Population (thousands)	Total employment (thousands)
		Nonfarm	Farm	Total						Personal income	Disposable personal income		
MISSISSIPPI													
1958	2 396	1 758	271	2 029	72	9	1 966	226	204	1 149	1 076	2 086	. . .
1959	2 651	1 922	333	2 255	87	10	2 178	254	219	1 240	1 155	2 138	. . .
1960	2 680	1 990	278	2 268	101	12	2 179	268	233	1 228	1 136	2 182	. . .
1961	2 895	2 074	350	2 423	104	13	2 332	301	262	1 312	1 223	2 206	. . .
1962	3 023	2 228	294	2 522	115	15	2 422	328	273	1 348	1 245	2 243	. . .
1963	3 331	2 374	428	2 801	136	17	2 682	359	290	1 484	1 370	2 244	. . .
1964	3 454	2 543	366	2 909	143	20	2 785	366	303	1 541	1 434	2 241	. . .
1965	3 749	2 823	348	3 171	152	22	3 041	380	328	1 669	1 547	2 246	. . .
1966	4 078	3 158	343	3 501	197	23	3 327	391	360	1 816	1 670	2 245	. . .
1967	4 417	3 384	383	3 767	226	25	3 565	421	431	1 983	1 825	2 228	. . .
1968	4 834	3 768	361	4 129	252	32	3 908	437	489	2 179	1 994	2 219	. . .
1969	5 334	4 159	349	4 508	291	35	4 251	531	552	2 403	2 186	2 220	909
1970	5 838	4 431	394	4 826	311	36	4 551	598	689	2 628	2 381	2 221	917
1971	6 467	4 858	436	5 293	351	58	5 000	654	814	2 855	2 627	2 266	939
1972	7 370	5 594	494	6 087	422	73	5 738	713	918	3 194	2 896	2 307	979
1973	8 453	6 321	692	7 013	539	93	6 567	821	1 065	3 597	3 282	2 350	1 019
1974	9 323	7 014	515	7 528	616	123	7 035	976	1 312	3 920	3 541	2 379	1 031
1975	10 096	7 508	377	7 885	654	150	7 381	1 083	1 631	4 207	3 862	2 400	1 001
1976	11 535	8 586	576	9 162	757	182	8 586	1 171	1 778	4 746	4 323	2 430	1 039
1977	12 873	9 679	610	10 288	851	223	9 660	1 311	1 902	5 233	4 781	2 460	1 071
1978	14 352	10 989	455	11 445	984	279	10 740	1 518	2 094	5 768	5 209	2 488	1 101
1979	16 280	12 190	704	12 895	1 131	337	12 101	1 789	2 391	6 491	5 841	2 508	1 114
1980	17 690	13 153	186	13 339	1 216	425	12 547	2 278	2 864	7 005	6 303	2 525	1 111
1981	19 911	14 387	335	14 722	1 425	454	13 751	2 911	3 250	7 004	7 004	2 539	1 107
1982	21 046	14 775	425	15 200	1 500	472	14 171	3 301	3 574	8 231	7 487	2 557	1 079
1983	22 006	15 526	101	15 627	1 594	529	14 562	3 506	3 938	8 570	7 762	2 568	1 088
1984	24 174	16 860	479	17 339	1 774	592	16 157	3 943	4 074	9 377	8 540	2 578	1 117
1985	25 512	17 802	437	18 239	1 914	621	16 946	4 298	4 268	9 857	8 975	2 588	1 124
1986	26 388	18 684	203	18 887	2 032	606	17 460	4 407	4 521	10 174	9 303	2 594	1 131
1987	27 953	19 637	589	20 225	2 125	643	18 743	4 500	4 710	10 799	9 841	2 589	1 141
1988	29 844	20 972	737	21 709	2 379	683	20 013	4 812	5 019	11 566	10 581	2 580	1 169
1989	32 176	22 284	569	22 853	2 558	725	21 020	5 659	5 496	12 499	11 379	2 574	1 189
1990	33 826	23 691	494	24 184	2 812	749	22 122	5 746	5 958	13 117	11 938	2 579	1 203
1991	35 731	24 794	589	25 383	2 990	809	23 202	5 859	6 669	13 749	12 573	2 599	1 211
1992	38 441	26 712	672	27 385	3 189	827	25 023	5 938	7 480	14 651	13 411	2 624	1 234
1993	40 957	28 853	586	29 439	3 452	846	26 832	6 147	7 979	15 426	14 077	2 655	1 287
1994	44 399	31 349	845	32 195	3 797	843	29 241	6 698	8 460	16 512	15 022	2 689	1 335
1995	46 764	32 913	680	33 594	3 985	930	30 539	7 010	9 216	17 176	15 605	2 723	1 365
1996	49 683	34 317	1 079	35 396	4 115	972	32 254	7 571	9 858	18 079	16 381	2 748	1 389
1997	52 429	36 254	994	37 247	4 333	1 110	34 024	8 174	10 230	18 880	17 063	2 777	1 415
1998	55 949	39 010	968	39 978	4 617	1 188	36 549	9 082	10 318	19 947	17 997	2 805	1 453
1999	58 137	41 065	946	42 011	4 827	1 285	38 469	9 002	10 666	20 555	18 539	2 828	1 477
2000	61 396	42 857	788	43 644	4 963	1 479	40 160	9 765	11 472	21 555	19 491	2 848	1 482
2001	65 104	44 151	1 577	45 728	5 054	1 633	42 307	9 961	12 836	22 817	20 702	2 853	1 449
2002	66 158	45 928	633	46 562	5 251	1 677	42 988	9 349	13 821	23 143	21 244	2 859	1 455
2003	68 798	47 949	1 350	49 299	5 419	1 764	45 644	8 721	14 433	23 991	22 170	2 868	1 453
2004	72 602	50 393	1 810	52 204	5 719	1 902	48 387	8 670	15 545	25 157	23 357	2 886	1 471
2005	77 777	52 622	1 785	54 408	5 937	2 052	50 523	9 828	17 426	26 819	24 806	2 900	1 485
2006	81 136	55 485	848	56 333	6 429	2 249	52 153	11 307	17 676	28 006	25 764	2 897	1 512
2007	86 314	57 317	1 127	58 444	6 669	2 506	54 281	13 568	18 465	29 542	27 099	2 922	1 543
2008	89 331	59 202	1 098	60 301	6 909	2 574	55 965	12 758	20 608	30 383	27 994	2 940	1 558
2009	88 864	57 788	1 202	58 989	6 811	2 455	54 634	11 901	22 329	30 103	28 221	2 952	. . .

. . . = Not available.

Table 21-2. Personal Income and Employment by Region and State—*Continued*

(Millions of dollars, except as noted.)

Region or state and year	Personal income, total	Earnings by place of work			Less: Contributions for government social insurance	Plus: Adjustment for residence	Equals: Net earnings by place of residence	Plus: Dividends, interest, and rent	Plus: Personal current transfer receipts	Per capita (dollars)		Population (thousands)	Total employment (thousands)
		Nonfarm	Farm	Total						Personal income	Disposable personal income		
MISSOURI													
1958	8 692	8 692	6 822	7 381	260	-149	6 971	1 122	598	2 076	1 864	4 186	. . .
1959	9 211	9 211	7 372	7 840	311	-165	7 363	1 215	633	2 163	1 938	4 258	. . .
1960	9 483	9 483	7 623	8 060	358	-176	7 526	1 286	671	2 192	1 950	4 326	. . .
1961	9 796	9 796	7 793	8 269	375	-182	7 713	1 338	745	2 252	2 004	4 349	. . .
1962	10 325	10 325	8 265	8 743	408	-198	8 137	1 417	771	2 370	2 100	4 357	. . .
1963	10 840	10 840	8 771	9 202	469	-222	8 511	1 521	808	2 468	2 182	4 392	. . .
1964	11 452	11 452	9 403	9 730	491	-246	8 993	1 628	830	2 578	2 316	4 442	. . .
1965	12 449	12 449	10 084	10 609	517	-271	9 820	1 741	888	2 787	2 486	4 467	. . .
1966	13 314	13 314	11 094	11 502	695	-310	10 497	1 857	960	2 944	2 617	4 523	. . .
1967	14 170	14 170	11 852	12 249	796	-346	11 107	1 943	1 120	3 122	2 773	4 539	. . .
1968	15 683	15 683	13 052	13 524	898	-382	12 244	2 127	1 313	3 433	3 028	4 568	. . .
1969	16 561	14 160	450	14 611	954	-758	12 899	2 233	1 428	3 569	3 087	4 640	2 216
1970	18 059	15 082	525	15 607	1 004	-702	13 902	2 465	1 692	3 855	3 381	4 685	2 203
1971	19 448	16 079	571	16 651	1 108	-683	14 860	2 638	1 951	4 118	3 646	4 723	2 200
1972	21 167	17 455	714	18 170	1 261	-703	16 206	2 849	2 112	4 453	3 895	4 753	2 242
1973	23 565	19 088	1 216	20 303	1 584	-737	17 983	3 132	2 450	4 935	4 363	4 775	2 325
1974	25 266	20 653	640	21 293	1 766	-763	18 764	3 610	2 892	5 280	4 631	4 785	2 341
1975	27 619	21 917	699	22 616	1 841	-773	20 002	3 962	3 655	5 759	5 124	4 795	2 291
1976	30 450	24 744	472	25 216	2 095	-850	22 271	4 285	3 895	6 313	5 574	4 824	2 365
1977	33 848	27 559	718	28 277	2 330	-990	24 957	4 825	4 066	6 986	6 169	4 845	2 424
1978	37 767	30 824	922	31 746	2 695	-1 142	27 909	5 436	4 422	7 753	6 796	4 871	2 512
1979	42 203	34 163	1 180	35 343	3 087	-1 305	30 951	6 250	5 002	8 632	7 530	4 889	2 576
1980	45 802	36 497	243	36 741	3 284	-1 520	31 936	7 782	6 084	9 306	8 124	4 922	2 549
1981	51 211	39 306	775	40 081	3 793	-1 660	34 628	9 746	6 838	10 383	9 024	4 932	2 540
1982	54 769	41 164	348	41 512	4 049	-1 727	35 736	11 577	7 456	11 110	9 611	4 929	2 516
1983	58 376	44 268	-104	44 164	4 389	-1 752	38 022	12 344	8 010	11 808	10 436	4 944	2 562
1984	64 732	48 883	425	49 307	4 997	-1 878	42 433	13 938	8 361	13 011	11 556	4 975	2 667
1985	69 181	52 299	796	53 096	5 479	-1 994	45 623	14 738	8 820	13 836	12 238	5 000	2 738
1986	72 691	55 328	584	55 913	5 879	-2 048	47 986	15 420	9 285	14 471	12 814	5 023	2 801
1987	76 552	58 885	741	59 626	6 196	-2 171	51 259	15 732	9 562	15 139	13 366	5 057	2 836
1988	80 930	62 768	662	63 430	6 824	-2 262	54 344	16 498	10 088	15 926	14 099	5 082	2 885
1989	86 263	66 177	913	67 090	7 268	-2 391	57 430	17 904	10 929	16 928	14 915	5 096	2 938
1990	90 177	69 116	709	69 825	7 828	-2 622	59 375	18 960	11 842	17 582	15 492	5 129	2 972
1991	94 731	71 261	591	71 852	8 163	-2 641	61 049	19 836	13 846	18 320	16 280	5 171	2 942
1992	100 829	76 005	865	76 870	8 603	-2 809	65 458	20 583	14 787	19 327	17 218	5 217	2 957
1993	105 164	79 538	503	80 042	9 024	-2 918	68 100	21 185	15 879	19 951	17 742	5 271	3 041
1994	112 001	84 782	728	85 510	9 707	-2 922	72 881	22 472	16 648	21 035	18 653	5 324	3 113
1995	117 418	89 978	222	90 201	10 299	-3 155	76 746	22 960	17 712	21 832	19 287	5 378	3 196
1996	124 385	94 591	1 054	95 645	10 737	-3 283	81 625	24 271	18 490	22 901	20 130	5 432	3 255
1997	132 117	100 544	1 065	101 610	11 378	-3 493	86 739	26 195	19 183	24 104	21 089	5 481	3 328
1998	140 360	107 607	548	108 155	11 938	-3 699	92 519	28 023	19 818	25 419	22 181	5 522	3 383
1999	145 826	113 714	239	113 953	12 574	-3 758	97 620	27 418	20 788	26 218	22 866	5 562	3 423
2000	156 359	121 114	778	121 893	13 233	-4 054	104 606	29 535	22 219	27 891	24 335	5 606	3 470
2001	161 496	124 629	818	125 448	13 645	-3 962	107 841	29 148	24 507	28 614	24 989	5 644	3 454
2002	166 103	129 239	378	129 617	13 952	-4 099	111 566	28 314	26 222	29 239	26 107	5 681	3 429
2003	172 505	133 985	1 094	135 079	14 396	-3 967	116 716	28 411	27 378	30 185	27 268	5 715	3 438
2004	180 518	139 409	2 250	141 659	14 922	-3 963	122 773	28 793	28 953	31 348	28 429	5 758	3 473
2005	186 732	145 608	1 419	147 027	15 689	-4 247	127 091	28 642	30 999	32 158	28 880	5 807	3 526
2006	198 683	152 529	1 276	153 805	16 706	-4 436	132 663	33 172	32 849	33 896	30 288	5 862	3 579
2007	207 552	157 847	1 369	159 217	17 355	-4 748	137 114	35 433	35 006	35 120	31 162	5 910	3 633
2008	216 547	163 877	2 243	166 120	18 267	-5 052	142 801	35 723	38 022	36 356	32 487	5 956	3 673
2009	213 610	158 567	1 660	160 228	17 870	-4 777	137 581	33 876	42 154	35 676	32 623	5 988	. . .

. . . = Not available.

Table 21-2. Personal Income and Employment by Region and State—*Continued*

(Millions of dollars, except as noted.)

| Region or state and year | Personal income, total | Earnings by place of work | | | Less: Contributions for government social insurance | Plus: Adjustment for residence | Equals: Net earnings by place of residence | Plus: Dividends, interest, and rent | Plus: Personal current transfer receipts | Per capita (dollars) | | Population (thousands) | Total employment (thousands) |
		Nonfarm	Farm	Total						Personal income	Disposable personal income		
MONTANA													
1958	1 380	906	235	1 142	44	0	1 098	182	100	2 072	1 891	666	...
1959	1 352	956	146	1 102	51	0	1 052	193	107	2 021	1 806	669	...
1960	1 405	996	160	1 156	62	0	1 094	203	108	2 069	1 864	679	...
1961	1 402	1 041	107	1 149	62	*	1 086	198	117	2 014	1 801	696	...
1962	1 646	1 104	274	1 378	64	0	1 314	213	119	2 358	2 144	698	...
1963	1 631	1 153	209	1 362	72	0	1 290	220	121	2 319	2 094	703	...
1964	1 662	1 206	166	1 373	74	0	1 298	238	126	2 355	2 153	706	...
1965	1 787	1 282	187	1 470	76	0	1 394	259	134	2 531	2 300	706	...
1966	1 915	1 367	223	1 590	99	0	1 491	282	143	2 709	2 451	707	...
1967	1 952	1 408	188	1 596	108	0	1 487	296	169	2 785	2 510	701	...
1968	2 052	1 487	194	1 680	115	-1	1 565	296	191	2 932	2 642	700	...
1969	2 286	1 613	242	1 855	127	-1	1 726	350	210	3 294	2 888	694	298
1970	2 527	1 736	291	2 027	137	-1	1 888	397	241	3 624	3 228	697	301
1971	2 695	1 895	251	2 146	152	-1	1 993	421	280	3 790	3 419	711	307
1972	3 128	2 132	401	2 534	179	0	2 355	464	310	4 350	3 880	719	319
1973	3 637	2 389	575	2 964	229	0	2 736	541	360	5 000	4 444	727	333
1974	3 957	2 701	466	3 166	264	1	2 903	631	423	5 367	4 756	737	344
1975	4 356	3 011	401	3 412	285	3	3 130	712	514	5 814	5 202	749	344
1976	4 704	3 446	226	3 671	326	3	3 349	786	569	6 202	5 506	759	359
1977	5 108	3 886	71	3 957	371	4	3 591	904	613	6 622	5 841	771	372
1978	6 002	4 427	303	4 731	435	3	4 299	1 029	674	7 655	6 795	784	390
1979	6 465	4 881	119	5 000	500	6	4 507	1 199	759	8 192	7 170	789	396
1980	7 129	5 187	121	5 308	537	14	4 785	1 452	893	9 038	7 936	789	393
1981	8 102	5 639	228	5 867	631	25	5 262	1 808	1 032	10 187	8 980	795	395
1982	8 545	5 791	172	5 964	661	18	5 320	2 069	1 155	10 628	9 476	804	391
1983	8 998	6 119	127	6 246	700	9	5 555	2 177	1 266	11 054	9 899	814	398
1984	9 537	6 488	44	6 532	758	6	5 779	2 407	1 351	11 617	10 440	821	408
1985	9 672	6 621	-85	6 536	790	3	5 749	2 494	1 429	11 762	10 571	822	406
1986	10 049	6 597	238	6 835	805	-2	6 028	2 496	1 525	12 350	11 211	814	402
1987	10 343	6 789	318	7 107	828	-3	6 277	2 468	1 598	12 848	11 570	805	406
1988	10 595	7 207	112	7 319	926	-1	6 392	2 517	1 686	13 241	11 862	800	416
1989	11 650	7 582	420	8 002	992	-3	7 008	2 795	1 847	14 569	12 972	800	424
1990	12 280	8 042	396	8 438	1 114	-4	7 321	2 935	2 024	15 346	13 693	800	433
1991	13 157	8 666	552	9 218	1 222	-12	7 984	3 042	2 132	16 250	14 588	810	444
1992	13 922	9 360	490	9 849	1 335	-2	8 513	3 096	2 312	16 859	15 107	826	456
1993	15 025	10 088	774	10 862	1 477	1	9 386	3 155	2 484	17 787	15 955	845	470
1994	15 494	10 695	390	11 085	1 566	6	9 525	3 391	2 578	17 989	16 068	861	494
1995	16 256	11 091	340	11 431	1 586	9	9 854	3 647	2 756	18 546	16 599	877	504
1996	17 070	11 584	310	11 894	1 595	13	10 311	3 900	2 859	19 261	17 198	886	519
1997	17 826	12 042	240	12 282	1 617	14	10 679	4 229	2 918	20 033	17 815	890	526
1998	19 151	12 910	301	13 210	1 670	19	11 559	4 562	3 031	21 459	19 069	892	537
1999	19 786	13 582	389	13 971	1 722	22	12 271	4 502	3 013	22 045	19 547	898	544
2000	21 200	14 546	256	14 802	1 820	27	13 009	4 818	3 374	23 470	20 781	903	555
2001	22 931	15 839	342	16 181	1 956	34	14 260	5 019	3 653	25 314	22 536	906	560
2002	23 370	16 395	187	16 582	2 054	33	14 561	5 014	3 795	25 685	23 220	910	568
2003	24 752	17 247	337	17 583	2 175	32	15 440	5 367	3 945	27 000	24 607	917	575
2004	26 495	18 491	544	19 035	2 296	35	16 774	5 494	4 226	28 616	26 103	926	589
2005	28 179	19 733	599	20 332	2 490	35	17 876	5 797	4 506	30 144	27 192	935	603
2006	30 447	21 267	190	21 457	2 694	33	18 796	6 753	4 897	32 177	28 850	946	623
2007	32 475	22 280	387	22 667	2 903	37	19 802	7 441	5 233	33 927	30 163	957	641
2008	33 516	22 862	445	23 306	3 015	41	20 333	7 447	5 736	34 622	31 035	968	651
2009	33 154	22 500	250	22 750	2 991	41	19 800	6 892	6 462	34 004	31 123	975	...

. . . = Not available.
* = Less than $50,000, but the estimates for this item are included in the total.

Table 21-2. Personal Income and Employment by Region and State—*Continued*

(Millions of dollars, except as noted.)

Region or state and year	Personal income, total	Earnings by place of work			Less: Contributions for government social insurance	Plus: Adjustment for residence	Equals: Net earnings by place of residence	Plus: Dividends, interest, and rent	Plus: Personal current transfer receipts	Per capita (dollars)		Population (thousands)	Total employment (thousands)
		Nonfarm	Farm	Total						Personal income	Disposable personal income		
NEBRASKA													
1958	2 863	1 824	521	2 345	75	-9	2 261	442	160	2 070	1 891	1 383	. . .
1959	2 892	1 992	357	2 349	93	-9	2 247	471	174	2 070	1 885	1 397	. . .
1960	3 072	2 129	385	2 514	116	-11	2 387	500	185	2 168	1 957	1 417	. . .
1961	3 138	2 235	312	2 547	119	-11	2 417	516	205	2 170	1 943	1 446	. . .
1962	3 411	2 359	430	2 789	128	-10	2 652	544	216	2 330	2 109	1 464	. . .
1963	3 502	2 441	384	2 825	140	-9	2 676	597	229	2 373	2 140	1 476	. . .
1964	3 592	2 586	304	2 891	146	-8	2 736	619	236	2 423	2 214	1 482	. . .
1965	3 951	2 701	490	3 191	148	-8	3 035	659	258	2 686	2 462	1 471	. . .
1966	4 252	2 908	583	3 490	196	-8	3 287	685	280	2 920	2 655	1 456	. . .
1967	4 403	3 141	481	3 622	228	-8	3 386	676	341	3 022	2 734	1 457	. . .
1968	4 692	3 433	438	3 871	245	-8	3 618	679	394	3 198	2 868	1 467	. . .
1969	5 264	3 800	604	4 404	269	-100	4 035	799	429	3 571	3 142	1 474	704
1970	5 644	4 120	542	4 662	289	-107	4 266	880	498	3 793	3 364	1 488	715
1971	6 196	4 436	688	5 124	320	-110	4 693	941	562	4 119	3 718	1 504	728
1972	6 870	4 878	809	5 687	364	-119	5 204	1 046	620	4 525	4 011	1 518	748
1973	8 039	5 466	1 227	6 693	467	-123	6 103	1 196	741	5 259	4 676	1 529	775
1974	8 384	6 079	771	6 850	541	-133	6 177	1 361	847	5 452	4 788	1 538	793
1975	9 529	6 577	1 110	7 687	579	-140	6 969	1 524	1 036	6 182	5 539	1 541	790
1976	9 982	7 476	589	8 066	661	-147	7 257	1 622	1 103	6 445	5 751	1 549	811
1977	10 820	8 152	533	8 685	723	-146	7 817	1 830	1 174	6 961	6 130	1 554	831
1978	12 533	9 126	1 087	10 212	832	-169	9 211	2 019	1 303	8 030	7 111	1 561	854
1979	13 526	10 191	755	10 947	970	-197	9 779	2 294	1 452	8 646	7 554	1 564	876
1980	14 395	11 041	107	11 148	1 051	-214	9 883	2 818	1 694	9 155	8 010	1 572	877
1981	16 699	11 866	836	12 702	1 228	-253	11 221	3 526	1 952	10 579	9 337	1 579	871
1982	17 970	12 342	768	13 110	1 307	-260	11 542	4 277	2 151	11 361	9 880	1 582	861
1983	18 614	12 949	549	13 498	1 351	-276	11 871	4 416	2 328	11 749	10 489	1 584	867
1984	20 716	14 198	1 160	15 358	1 520	-327	13 511	4 764	2 441	13 040	11 777	1 589	886
1985	21 799	14 903	1 449	16 352	1 646	-352	14 354	4 852	2 593	13 756	12 414	1 585	898
1986	22 406	15 459	1 414	16 873	1 766	-350	14 757	4 938	2 711	14 232	12 841	1 574	898
1987	23 415	16 325	1 638	17 963	1 867	-347	15 749	4 894	2 773	14 947	13 436	1 567	925
1988	25 011	17 404	2 035	19 440	2 080	-381	16 979	5 139	2 893	15 915	14 302	1 571	947
1989	26 443	18 493	1 847	20 340	2 222	-390	17 727	5 613	3 103	16 790	14 987	1 575	965
1990	28 388	19 761	2 200	21 961	2 460	-383	19 118	5 905	3 365	17 948	15 996	1 582	988
1991	29 562	20 752	1 998	22 749	2 605	-422	19 722	6 214	3 626	18 523	16 565	1 596	992
1992	31 272	22 084	2 119	24 203	2 735	-462	21 006	6 329	3 937	19 403	17 384	1 612	999
1993	32 246	23 219	1 748	24 968	2 876	-477	21 615	6 426	4 205	19 836	17 742	1 626	1 021
1994	34 459	24 920	1 852	26 772	3 079	-489	23 204	6 869	4 386	21 024	18 788	1 639	1 061
1995	36 468	26 788	1 327	28 115	3 230	-536	24 349	7 457	4 661	22 008	19 569	1 657	1 071
1996	39 923	28 408	2 596	31 004	3 404	-591	27 009	7 956	4 958	23 853	21 203	1 674	1 097
1997	41 080	30 068	1 762	31 830	3 615	-667	27 548	8 394	5 138	24 359	21 430	1 686	1 111
1998	43 852	32 018	1 649	33 667	3 848	-701	29 118	9 255	5 479	25 859	22 711	1 696	1 138
1999	46 057	34 219	1 573	35 792	4 043	-783	30 967	9 288	5 802	27 017	23 727	1 705	1 158
2000	48 998	36 439	1 441	37 880	4 225	-854	32 801	10 108	6 088	28 598	25 070	1 713	1 176
2001	51 371	38 072	1 801	39 874	4 411	-871	34 592	10 086	6 693	29 902	26 342	1 718	1 175
2002	52 294	39 480	1 047	40 527	4 553	-902	35 072	10 095	7 127	30 314	27 266	1 725	1 167
2003	55 696	41 218	2 625	43 843	4 716	-956	38 171	10 101	7 424	32 126	29 252	1 734	1 171
2004	57 953	43 254	2 885	46 139	4 924	-971	40 244	9 926	7 783	33 265	30 287	1 742	1 184
2005	60 116	44 981	2 926	47 907	5 187	-991	41 729	10 177	8 210	34 318	30 997	1 752	1 198
2006	62 871	47 376	1 745	49 121	5 595	-960	42 566	11 471	8 833	35 713	31 971	1 760	1 213
2007	67 078	49 410	2 789	52 198	5 793	-1 064	45 341	12 354	9 382	37 899	33 711	1 770	1 234
2008	69 821	50 947	3 437	54 385	5 984	-1 081	47 319	12 426	10 076	39 182	35 159	1 782	1 254
2009	68 417	50 507	2 368	52 875	5 998	-1 090	45 787	11 691	10 940	38 081	34 824	1 797	. . .

. . . = Not available.

Table 21-2. Personal Income and Employment by Region and State—*Continued*

(Millions of dollars, except as noted.)

Region or state and year	Personal income, total	Earnings by place of work			Less: Contributions for government social insurance	Plus: Adjustment for residence	Equals: Net earnings by place of residence	Plus: Dividends, interest, and rent	Plus: Personal current transfer receipts	Per capita (dollars)		Population (thousands)	Total employment (thousands)
		Nonfarm	Farm	Total						Personal income	Disposable personal income		
NEVADA													
1958	705	595	22	617	26	-2	589	79	37	2 622	2 309	269	...
1959	776	663	19	682	30	-2	650	88	38	2 780	2 470	279	...
1960	851	730	14	744	36	-2	706	104	41	2 923	2 573	291	...
1961	941	805	13	817	40	-3	775	117	49	2 988	2 606	315	...
1962	1 134	985	18	1 004	50	-4	950	133	51	3 222	2 829	352	...
1963	1 276	1 127	20	1 147	66	-6	1 075	143	58	3 213	2 804	397	...
1964	1 387	1 222	11	1 234	67	-5	1 161	161	65	3 257	2 909	426	...
1965	1 487	1 285	13	1 299	66	-5	1 228	187	72	3 348	2 999	444	...
1966	1 570	1 359	18	1 377	80	-4	1 294	199	78	3 521	3 144	446	...
1967	1 668	1 429	17	1 446	86	-3	1 356	217	95	3 715	3 309	449	...
1968	1 935	1 642	19	1 661	100	-4	1 557	265	113	4 170	3 632	464	...
1969	2 174	1 888	32	1 921	132	-34	1 754	295	125	4 530	3 851	480	244
1970	2 432	2 096	34	2 130	144	-39	1 947	338	148	4 932	4 356	493	256
1971	2 713	2 322	35	2 356	165	-42	2 150	379	184	5 218	4 662	520	267
1972	3 036	2 589	42	2 631	194	-45	2 393	425	218	5 553	4 931	547	280
1973	3 466	2 976	56	3 032	256	-55	2 721	491	254	6 093	5 415	569	304
1974	3 866	3 277	35	3 312	287	-57	2 968	583	315	6 479	5 740	597	317
1975	4 357	3 621	33	3 654	312	-58	3 284	636	438	7 029	6 390	620	326
1976	5 000	4 190	36	4 226	367	-68	3 791	721	489	7 731	6 924	647	349
1977	5 777	4 919	27	4 946	438	-84	4 425	819	534	8 519	7 580	678	384
1978	6 990	6 032	23	6 055	552	-117	5 386	1 001	603	9 718	8 558	719	432
1979	8 140	6 995	9	7 004	678	-132	6 194	1 235	712	10 639	9 292	765	468
1980	9 463	7 957	57	8 014	775	-159	7 080	1 519	863	11 679	10 279	810	489
1981	10 774	8 909	28	8 937	940	-165	7 831	1 890	1 053	12 711	11 151	848	500
1982	11 551	9 199	33	9 232	964	-166	8 102	2 276	1 173	13 104	11 603	882	494
1983	12 267	9 727	26	9 753	1 049	-177	8 528	2 456	1 283	13 600	12 137	902	499
1984	13 413	10 606	36	10 641	1 191	-187	9 263	2 775	1 375	14 501	12 963	925	523
1985	14 561	11 442	29	11 471	1 313	-195	9 963	3 087	1 510	15 310	13 605	951	545
1986	15 682	12 350	28	12 378	1 452	-212	10 713	3 286	1 683	15 992	14 169	981	570
1987	17 103	13 645	49	13 694	1 615	-236	11 843	3 464	1 796	16 713	14 728	1 023	616
1988	19 406	15 676	65	15 742	1 872	-276	13 593	3 838	1 975	18 052	15 850	1 075	662
1989	21 798	17 420	79	17 499	2 118	-321	15 060	4 457	2 281	19 165	16 818	1 137	710
1990	24 465	19 576	83	19 659	2 494	-374	16 792	5 065	2 608	20 042	17 562	1 221	756
1991	26 930	21 047	76	21 123	2 662	-346	18 115	5 606	3 209	20 777	18 399	1 296	769
1992	29 864	23 170	73	23 243	2 895	-308	20 041	6 191	3 633	22 099	19 541	1 351	776
1993	32 222	25 145	119	25 264	3 170	-347	21 747	6 636	3 838	22 833	20 109	1 411	819
1994	35 821	27 885	82	27 967	3 543	-358	24 067	7 731	4 024	23 892	21 136	1 499	898
1995	39 403	30 728	70	30 798	3 893	-354	26 552	8 497	4 355	24 914	22 038	1 582	953
1996	43 722	33 996	70	34 067	4 217	-374	29 476	9 565	4 681	26 239	22 957	1 666	1 024
1997	47 838	37 108	71	37 179	4 501	-329	32 349	10 502	4 988	27 118	23 787	1 764	1 089
1998	53 046	41 020	93	41 113	4 809	-339	35 965	11 768	5 313	28 624	24 943	1 853	1 131
1999	57 363	45 130	85	45 216	5 109	-373	39 734	12 074	5 555	29 650	25 814	1 935	1 196
2000	62 535	48 550	104	48 654	5 010	-333	43 311	13 250	5 974	30 986	26 882	2 018	1 251
2001	65 303	50 539	118	50 657	5 306	-304	45 047	13 476	6 780	31 178	27 245	2 095	1 270
2002	67 827	52 154	90	52 244	5 555	-309	46 380	13 791	7 656	31 311	27 885	2 166	1 296
2003	73 068	55 980	90	56 071	5 633	-367	50 071	14 810	8 187	32 664	29 372	2 237	1 350
2004	82 149	62 161	124	62 285	6 178	-446	55 661	17 673	8 815	35 277	31 580	2 329	1 438
2005	91 817	68 563	135	68 698	6 785	-536	61 377	20 925	9 515	38 117	33 735	2 409	1 530
2006	97 818	73 985	131	74 116	7 825	-553	65 738	21 745	10 335	39 231	34 706	2 493	1 606
2007	105 099	77 826	98	77 924	8 204	-633	69 087	24 783	11 229	40 930	36 353	2 568	1 644
2008	107 079	77 626	143	77 769	7 758	-613	69 397	25 062	12 620	40 936	36 804	2 616	1 638
2009	101 966	71 544	100	71 644	7 025	-506	64 114	22 738	15 114	38 578	35 611	2 643	...

. . . = Not available.

Table 21-2. Personal Income and Employment by Region and State—*Continued*

(Millions of dollars, except as noted.)

Region or state and year	Personal income, total	Earnings by place of work			Less: Contributions for government social insurance	Plus: Adjustment for residence	Equals: Net earnings by place of residence	Plus: Dividends, interest, and rent	Plus: Personal current transfer receipts	Per capita (dollars)		Population (thousands)	Total employment (thousands)
		Nonfarm	Farm	Total						Personal income	Disposable personal income		
NEW HAMPSHIRE													
1958	1 163	887	21	908	39	57	926	155	83	2 002	1 807	581	. . .
1959	1 265	976	16	992	46	70	1 016	163	86	2 122	1 912	596	. . .
1960	1 336	1 025	19	1 044	55	79	1 068	178	90	2 194	1 959	609	. . .
1961	1 407	1 068	20	1 089	56	85	1 118	188	102	2 277	2 040	618	. . .
1962	1 509	1 142	19	1 160	62	94	1 193	211	105	2 387	2 134	632	. . .
1963	1 569	1 185	17	1 202	68	100	1 234	223	113	2 418	2 150	649	. . .
1964	1 686	1 271	18	1 289	71	108	1 326	244	116	2 543	2 309	663	. . .
1965	1 822	1 365	21	1 386	75	119	1 430	268	123	2 695	2 435	676	. . .
1966	2 005	1 519	24	1 543	103	139	1 579	294	132	2 945	2 630	681	. . .
1967	2 191	1 668	17	1 685	116	154	1 723	313	155	3 143	2 805	697	. . .
1968	2 424	1 838	20	1 858	128	173	1 902	342	180	3 418	3 029	709	. . .
1969	2 712	1 991	21	2 012	129	232	2 116	393	203	3 745	3 305	724	334
1970	2 881	2 113	17	2 130	135	220	2 215	424	241	3 883	3 406	742	334
1971	3 118	2 269	15	2 283	150	230	2 363	463	292	4 091	3 655	762	336
1972	3 448	2 525	16	2 541	176	252	2 617	508	322	4 411	3 880	782	350
1973	3 899	2 882	21	2 903	229	284	2 957	562	380	4 863	4 333	802	374
1974	4 299	3 119	14	3 133	257	329	3 205	639	455	5 262	4 667	817	381
1975	4 649	3 265	17	3 283	266	359	3 375	688	586	5 602	5 043	830	370
1976	5 293	3 786	19	3 805	310	411	3 906	763	624	6 249	5 582	847	394
1977	5 986	4 304	18	4 322	353	480	4 449	876	660	6 866	6 102	872	418
1978	6 910	5 029	19	5 048	420	572	5 200	987	723	7 730	6 807	894	446
1979	7 921	5 754	22	5 775	503	680	5 952	1 141	828	8 686	7 639	912	468
1980	9 072	6 374	14	6 388	560	847	6 675	1 428	969	9 816	8 664	924	482
1981	10 289	7 036	23	7 059	665	956	7 350	1 803	1 136	10 985	9 667	937	492
1982	11 353	7 605	19	7 624	737	1 047	7 934	2 172	1 246	11 979	10 667	948	498
1983	12 470	8 521	17	8 538	841	1 171	8 869	2 270	1 331	13 015	11 582	958	518
1984	14 121	9 613	22	9 635	977	1 386	10 043	2 669	1 408	14 455	12 906	977	553
1985	15 612	10 794	24	10 818	1 126	1 508	11 201	2 937	1 474	15 663	13 867	997	586
1986	17 240	12 093	25	12 117	1 276	1 589	12 431	3 263	1 546	16 819	14 795	1 025	617
1987	19 070	13 650	43	13 693	1 420	1 712	13 985	3 505	1 579	18 088	15 894	1 054	635
1988	20 960	15 053	46	15 099	1 611	1 865	15 353	3 893	1 714	19 361	17 133	1 083	660
1989	22 350	15 643	35	15 678	1 689	1 955	15 944	4 489	1 917	20 235	17 917	1 105	660
1990	22 510	15 505	44	15 549	1 723	1 995	15 821	4 542	2 147	20 236	18 016	1 112	643
1991	23 370	15 474	45	15 519	1 746	2 181	15 955	4 542	2 874	21 056	18 898	1 110	616
1992	24 435	16 534	51	16 586	1 854	2 238	16 969	4 405	3 061	21 861	19 636	1 118	629
1993	25 200	17 285	42	17 328	1 931	2 358	17 754	4 481	2 964	22 311	19 951	1 129	642
1994	27 012	18 434	40	18 474	2 087	2 457	18 843	4 802	3 367	23 642	21 176	1 143	666
1995	28 760	19 643	35	19 679	2 232	2 446	19 893	5 242	3 626	24 845	22 192	1 158	679
1996	31 305	20 977	41	21 017	2 355	2 613	21 276	6 450	3 580	26 649	23 656	1 175	696
1997	32 764	22 739	38	22 777	2 531	2 821	23 068	5 976	3 720	27 546	24 059	1 189	717
1998	35 773	25 134	40	25 174	2 745	2 942	25 370	6 543	3 860	29 664	25 923	1 206	739
1999	37 926	27 014	44	27 059	2 914	3 400	27 545	6 439	3 942	31 036	26 934	1 222	756
2000	42 283	30 008	44	30 052	3 203	4 037	30 886	7 151	4 246	34 087	29 273	1 240	778
2001	43 625	31 097	42	31 139	3 326	4 014	31 827	7 164	4 634	34 709	30 066	1 257	789
2002	44 635	32 099	42	32 141	3 416	3 833	32 558	7 026	5 051	35 113	31 436	1 271	787
2003	45 739	33 513	49	33 562	3 562	3 773	33 774	6 795	5 170	35 682	32 293	1 282	796
2004	48 597	35 801	58	35 859	3 820	3 911	35 950	6 997	5 650	37 591	34 157	1 293	811
2005	49 956	37 369	51	37 420	3 993	3 901	37 327	6 747	5 882	38 386	34 536	1 301	825
2006	53 661	39 451	41	39 492	4 173	3 977	39 296	8 099	6 266	40 903	36 645	1 312	835
2007	56 205	40 348	44	40 392	4 325	4 517	40 584	8 845	6 777	42 665	37 981	1 317	847
2008	57 399	40 853	46	40 900	4 486	4 612	41 026	9 031	7 343	43 423	38 988	1 322	857
2009	56 732	39 655	46	39 701	4 424	4 458	39 735	8 705	8 292	42 831	39 436	1 325	. . .

. . . = Not available.

Table 21-2. Personal Income and Employment by Region and State—*Continued*

(Millions of dollars, except as noted.)

Region or state and year	Personal income, total	Earnings by place of work			Less: Contributions for government social insurance	Plus: Adjustment for residence	Equals: Net earnings by place of residence	Plus: Dividends, interest, and rent	Plus: Personal current transfer receipts	Per capita (dollars)		Population (thousands)	Total employment (thousands)
		Nonfarm	Farm	Total						Personal income	Disposable personal income		
NEW JERSEY													
1958	14 369	11 477	133	11 610	469	684	11 825	1 698	847	2 440	2 160	5 890	...
1959	15 456	12 474	105	12 580	557	769	12 792	1 809	855	2 570	2 279	6 015	...
1960	16 288	13 087	120	13 207	660	855	13 403	1 989	896	2 669	2 357	6 103	...
1961	17 112	13 633	119	13 752	694	912	13 970	2 118	1 024	2 731	2 411	6 265	...
1962	18 410	14 592	108	14 700	771	1 013	14 943	2 389	1 079	2 887	2 545	6 376	...
1963	19 320	15 227	106	15 333	869	1 088	15 552	2 608	1 159	2 958	2 605	6 531	...
1964	20 731	16 175	102	16 277	881	1 205	16 601	2 925	1 205	3 113	2 793	6 660	...
1965	22 283	17 303	118	17 421	934	1 317	17 804	3 194	1 285	3 293	2 932	6 767	...
1966	24 138	18 890	118	19 008	1 212	1 514	19 310	3 442	1 385	3 523	3 135	6 851	...
1967	26 025	20 250	104	20 354	1 345	1 680	20 689	3 694	1 642	3 757	3 319	6 928	...
1968	28 601	22 151	102	22 253	1 533	1 888	22 608	4 030	1 964	4 083	3 575	7 005	...
1969	31 930	24 079	105	24 184	1 827	3 117	25 474	4 243	2 212	4 500	3 901	7 095	3 061
1970	34 610	26 046	100	26 146	1 957	3 071	27 260	4 660	2 689	4 813	4 218	7 190	3 125
1971	37 230	27 819	93	27 912	2 168	3 155	28 899	5 054	3 277	5 113	4 542	7 282	3 119
1972	40 446	30 382	89	30 471	2 482	3 354	31 343	5 440	3 663	5 513	4 829	7 337	3 184
1973	44 208	33 597	127	33 724	3 128	3 511	34 108	5 969	4 131	6 027	5 325	7 335	3 288
1974	48 130	36 187	138	36 325	3 458	3 701	36 569	6 713	4 847	6 561	5 775	7 335	3 301
1975	51 776	37 719	97	37 816	3 541	3 983	38 258	7 180	6 338	7 053	6 295	7 341	3 191
1976	56 546	41 563	102	41 665	3 930	4 326	42 061	7 642	6 842	7 699	6 805	7 344	3 248
1977	61 957	45 750	112	45 862	4 313	4 720	46 269	8 471	7 217	8 439	7 376	7 342	3 325
1978	68 849	51 327	127	51 454	4 985	5 305	51 774	9 394	7 681	9 359	8 159	7 356	3 465
1979	76 470	56 830	127	56 957	5 744	6 052	57 265	10 663	8 542	10 372	8 948	7 373	3 552
1980	86 123	62 265	116	62 381	6 325	7 144	63 200	13 162	9 761	11 676	10 053	7 376	3 601
1981	96 195	68 068	150	68 218	7 346	7 755	68 628	16 606	10 961	12 986	11 149	7 407	3 631
1982	104 010	72 797	166	72 962	7 972	8 290	73 281	18 713	12 016	13 997	12 029	7 431	3 639
1983	112 222	79 397	191	79 589	8 983	8 519	79 125	20 121	12 976	15 027	13 059	7 468	3 739
1984	124 048	88 235	200	88 435	10 427	8 903	86 911	23 604	13 533	16 506	14 408	7 515	3 914
1985	132 934	95 574	226	95 800	11 396	9 266	93 670	25 079	14 186	17 571	15 192	7 566	4 026
1986	141 913	103 145	228	103 373	12 409	9 833	100 797	26 264	14 851	18 618	16 067	7 622	4 122
1987	153 050	113 016	259	113 275	13 525	10 350	110 100	27 602	15 347	19 952	17 056	7 671	4 220
1988	167 840	125 244	255	125 498	15 240	10 689	120 947	30 554	16 339	21 763	18 816	7 712	4 317
1989	179 512	131 690	246	131 937	15 883	10 198	126 251	35 765	17 496	23 235	20 102	7 726	4 351
1990	189 061	137 643	243	137 886	16 036	10 440	132 290	37 465	19 305	24 354	21 163	7 763	4 310
1991	193 443	139 420	228	139 649	16 560	10 535	133 623	37 630	22 190	24 754	21 607	7 815	4 172
1992	207 020	148 454	237	148 691	17 565	12 510	143 636	37 680	25 704	26 270	22 974	7 881	4 170
1993	213 023	154 252	265	154 517	18 224	12 918	149 211	36 943	26 869	26 799	23 335	7 949	4 197
1994	221 140	160 825	283	161 107	19 274	13 028	154 862	39 040	27 238	27 593	23 935	8 014	4 232
1995	234 591	169 382	277	169 659	20 033	14 090	163 717	41 817	29 058	29 022	25 242	8 083	4 296
1996	249 483	179 232	297	179 529	20 869	15 513	174 173	45 346	29 963	30 613	26 445	8 150	4 352
1997	265 679	189 423	247	189 670	21 590	18 319	186 400	48 559	30 720	32 326	27 690	8 219	4 412
1998	283 528	201 239	264	201 503	22 796	20 648	199 355	52 598	31 574	34 212	29 017	8 287	4 489
1999	295 592	211 813	232	212 044	23 866	22 283	210 461	52 196	32 935	35 360	29 748	8 360	4 551
2000	325 986	232 754	338	233 092	25 647	25 447	232 892	57 929	35 165	38 666	32 333	8 431	4 713
2001	336 916	239 093	284	239 376	26 615	27 067	239 828	58 064	39 025	39 686	33 367	8 489	4 741
2002	341 590	246 188	303	246 491	27 390	23 896	242 997	56 350	42 242	39 980	34 648	8 544	4 777
2003	347 910	253 799	307	254 106	27 764	23 968	250 310	54 549	43 051	40 532	35 504	8 583	4 815
2004	365 571	266 819	336	267 155	29 017	26 910	265 048	56 817	43 706	42 451	37 278	8 612	4 894
2005	379 876	277 551	346	277 896	30 577	29 550	276 869	57 097	45 910	44 060	38 153	8 622	4 980
2006	411 746	293 143	384	293 527	31 695	33 561	295 392	66 687	49 666	47 746	41 264	8 624	5 059
2007	434 948	304 335	380	304 715	33 349	38 747	310 114	73 024	51 810	50 364	42 951	8 636	5 128
2008	445 928	309 730	383	310 113	34 482	39 176	314 807	74 772	56 349	51 473	44 397	8 663	5 176
2009	438 111	299 122	404	299 526	33 625	36 594	302 495	71 612	64 004	50 313	44 893	8 708	...

. . . = Not available.

Table 21-2. Personal Income and Employment by Region and State—*Continued*

(Millions of dollars, except as noted.)

Region or state and year	Personal income, total	Earnings by place of work			Less: Contributions for government social insurance	Plus: Adjustment for residence	Equals: Net earnings by place of residence	Plus: Dividends, interest, and rent	Plus: Personal current transfer receipts	Per capita (dollars)		Population (thousands)	Total employment (thousands)
		Nonfarm	Farm	Total						Personal income	Disposable personal income		
NEW MEXICO													
1958	1 630	1 322	113	1 435	45	-13	1 377	168	84	1 840	1 672	886	. . .
1959	1 754	1 448	99	1 546	54	-14	1 478	184	93	1 909	1 728	919	. . .
1960	1 807	1 494	86	1 580	61	-14	1 505	200	102	1 894	1 719	954	. . .
1961	1 891	1 533	101	1 634	61	-14	1 558	214	118	1 959	1 778	965	. . .
1962	1 965	1 622	82	1 703	66	-15	1 623	223	120	2 008	1 816	979	. . .
1963	2 029	1 672	85	1 757	74	-16	1 667	233	129	2 052	1 857	989	. . .
1964	2 144	1 785	65	1 850	78	-17	1 755	254	135	2 131	1 955	1 006	. . .
1965	2 272	1 877	77	1 954	81	-19	1 854	272	145	2 245	2 041	1 012	. . .
1966	2 393	1 967	99	2 066	104	-19	1 943	294	156	2 376	2 161	1 007	. . .
1967	2 481	2 040	89	2 129	121	-20	1 989	297	195	2 481	2 257	1 000	. . .
1968	2 683	2 182	101	2 284	124	-21	2 138	316	228	2 699	2 443	994	. . .
1969	2 952	2 399	107	2 506	152	-22	2 332	359	261	2 920	2 598	1 011	395
1970	3 263	2 592	131	2 723	163	-22	2 538	399	325	3 189	2 849	1 023	399
1971	3 598	2 855	130	2 985	188	-22	2 774	446	378	3 416	3 103	1 053	416
1972	4 040	3 225	137	3 362	221	-20	3 121	496	422	3 748	3 376	1 078	440
1973	4 548	3 610	180	3 790	283	-17	3 490	559	500	4 119	3 714	1 104	461
1974	5 141	4 079	147	4 226	328	-15	3 882	658	601	4 551	4 084	1 130	478
1975	5 872	4 595	177	4 772	367	-13	4 393	741	738	5 050	4 614	1 163	491
1976	6 597	5 262	124	5 386	421	-12	4 953	818	826	5 520	4 999	1 195	512
1977	7 423	5 981	135	6 116	481	-11	5 624	930	870	6 059	5 481	1 225	539
1978	8 516	6 878	168	7 046	565	-11	6 470	1 091	954	6 802	6 092	1 252	568
1979	9 662	7 744	207	7 951	667	-9	7 274	1 287	1 101	7 545	6 747	1 281	592
1980	10 908	8 545	180	8 725	740	-4	7 982	1 617	1 310	8 331	7 467	1 309	597
1981	12 376	9 603	130	9 733	895	-14	8 824	2 055	1 497	9 286	8 226	1 333	611
1982	13 524	10 250	116	10 366	973	-17	9 376	2 502	1 647	9 916	8 764	1 364	619
1983	14 549	10 872	127	10 998	1 035	-14	9 950	2 799	1 800	10 434	9 443	1 394	631
1984	15 914	11 912	146	12 058	1 165	-6	10 888	3 103	1 923	11 233	10 204	1 417	655
1985	17 201	12 760	208	12 968	1 272	1	11 697	3 443	2 061	11 959	10 837	1 438	674
1986	17 870	13 143	194	13 337	1 328	8	12 017	3 635	2 218	12 217	11 128	1 463	680
1987	18 685	13 708	241	13 949	1 371	23	12 601	3 738	2 346	12 638	11 386	1 479	699
1988	19 713	14 441	321	14 761	1 510	35	13 286	3 916	2 512	13 227	11 926	1 490	733
1989	21 069	15 237	383	15 620	1 611	42	14 051	4 223	2 795	14 009	12 568	1 504	749
1990	22 555	16 354	417	16 771	1 823	51	14 999	4 511	3 045	14 823	13 313	1 522	761
1991	24 228	17 577	403	17 980	1 976	64	16 068	4 761	3 399	15 577	14 040	1 555	784
1992	25 942	18 854	485	19 339	2 102	80	17 318	4 843	3 781	16 260	14 674	1 595	797
1993	27 883	20 381	531	20 912	2 270	99	18 741	5 041	4 101	17 039	15 334	1 636	825
1994	29 900	21 807	458	22 264	2 470	116	19 910	5 580	4 410	17 772	15 973	1 682	857
1995	32 029	23 306	391	23 697	2 646	128	21 179	6 008	4 841	18 617	16 757	1 720	898
1996	33 801	24 105	402	24 508	2 726	148	21 930	6 596	5 275	19 289	17 294	1 752	909
1997	35 440	25 264	544	25 808	2 859	171	23 121	6 933	5 387	19 968	17 799	1 775	923
1998	37 769	26 893	586	27 479	2 999	193	24 673	7 427	5 669	21 059	18 786	1 793	939
1999	38 803	27 766	680	28 446	3 112	221	25 555	7 234	6 015	21 461	19 100	1 808	943
2000	41 425	29 817	541	30 358	3 287	246	27 318	7 718	6 390	22 751	20 200	1 821	965
2001	45 336	32 465	787	33 251	3 531	249	29 970	8 237	7 129	24 790	22 197	1 829	969
2002	46 342	33 905	545	34 451	3 693	252	31 010	7 483	7 849	25 049	22 699	1 850	980
2003	48 141	35 653	562	36 215	3 862	258	32 612	7 155	8 374	25 748	23 526	1 870	999
2004	51 576	37 939	864	38 802	4 069	260	34 993	7 646	8 938	27 263	24 981	1 892	1 023
2005	55 342	40 367	834	41 201	4 320	275	37 155	8 563	9 624	28 876	26 242	1 917	1 047
2006	59 274	43 297	602	43 899	4 727	293	39 465	9 328	10 482	30 513	27 515	1 943	1 076
2007	63 182	44 894	835	45 729	4 981	327	41 075	10 832	11 275	32 093	28 881	1 969	1 100
2008	66 337	46 693	812	47 505	5 270	344	42 579	11 130	12 628	33 389	30 299	1 987	1 117
2009	66 304	46 154	405	46 558	5 267	339	41 630	10 437	14 236	32 992	30 604	2 010	. . .

. . . = Not available.

Table 21-2. Personal Income and Employment by Region and State—*Continued*

(Millions of dollars, except as noted.)

Region or state and year	Personal income, total	Derivation of personal income								Per capita (dollars)		Population (thousands)	Total employment (thousands)
		Earnings by place of work			Less: Contributions for government social insurance	Plus: Adjustment for residence	Equals: Net earnings by place of residence	Plus: Dividends, interest, and rent	Plus: Personal current transfer receipts	Personal income	Disposable personal income		
		Nonfarm	Farm	Total									
NEW YORK													
1958	42 844	35 970	374	36 344	1 434	-589	34 321	5 925	2 597	2 581	2 263	16 601	...
1959	45 478	38 431	314	38 745	1 711	-663	36 371	6 385	2 721	2 726	2 373	16 685	...
1960	47 504	40 258	348	40 607	2 040	-738	37 828	6 882	2 794	2 821	2 452	16 838	...
1961	49 537	41 747	359	42 106	2 191	-792	39 123	7 207	3 207	2 904	2 511	17 061	...
1962	52 265	44 181	282	44 463	2 489	-879	41 095	7 875	3 295	3 021	2 615	17 301	...
1963	54 369	45 662	330	45 992	2 712	-945	42 335	8 485	3 549	3 114	2 696	17 461	...
1964	58 119	48 468	313	48 781	2 681	-1 042	45 058	9 338	3 723	3 304	2 902	17 589	...
1965	61 648	51 125	361	51 486	2 803	-1 129	47 554	10 079	4 016	3 476	3 042	17 734	...
1966	66 196	55 520	421	55 941	3 719	-1 284	50 938	10 623	4 636	3 710	3 226	17 843	...
1967	71 480	59 466	376	59 842	4 031	-1 429	54 382	11 198	5 900	3 985	3 437	17 935	...
1968	78 777	65 221	385	65 606	4 444	-1 611	59 551	12 012	7 213	4 364	3 736	18 051	...
1969	82 789	70 343	440	70 783	5 283	-3 346	62 154	12 900	7 735	4 573	3 850	18 105	8 494
1970	88 953	74 832	420	75 252	5 525	-3 292	66 434	13 610	8 909	4 868	4 177	18 272	8 466
1971	94 869	79 029	410	79 438	6 021	-3 394	70 023	14 102	10 744	5 166	4 495	18 365	8 345
1972	101 448	84 811	353	85 164	6 786	-3 646	74 732	14 722	11 993	5 528	4 757	18 352	8 348
1973	108 487	91 136	470	91 606	8 402	-3 861	79 343	15 855	13 288	5 963	5 157	18 195	8 465
1974	117 010	96 729	444	97 173	9 177	-4 081	83 916	17 677	15 418	6 474	5 582	18 073	8 392
1975	125 678	101 166	380	101 546	9 443	-4 422	87 681	18 492	19 506	6 970	6 098	18 032	8 172
1976	134 260	108 567	402	108 969	10 240	-4 860	93 870	19 619	20 772	7 469	6 511	17 975	8 125
1977	145 174	117 731	332	118 063	11 004	-5 407	101 652	21 792	21 730	8 132	7 063	17 852	8 199
1978	158 209	129 508	434	129 942	12 359	-6 062	111 521	23 923	22 765	8 928	7 721	17 720	8 384
1979	173 149	142 215	540	142 755	14 064	-6 902	121 788	27 046	24 315	9 819	8 430	17 634	8 581
1980	192 979	155 974	531	156 504	15 326	-8 101	133 078	31 968	27 933	10 985	9 395	17 567	8 602
1981	215 380	171 059	544	171 604	18 051	-8 838	144 715	39 130	31 536	12 260	10 385	17 568	8 666
1982	234 315	183 691	519	184 210	19 659	-9 692	154 859	44 953	34 503	13 321	11 264	17 590	8 673
1983	252 337	197 670	370	198 040	21 222	-10 140	166 679	48 327	37 332	14 267	12 272	17 687	8 730
1984	279 079	217 192	493	217 685	23 937	-10 775	182 974	56 587	39 518	15 727	13 566	17 746	9 003
1985	298 210	234 166	559	234 725	26 271	-11 401	197 053	59 442	41 715	16 761	14 357	17 792	9 227
1986	318 024	252 356	653	253 009	28 844	-12 068	212 096	61 728	44 200	17 833	15 258	17 833	9 424
1987	339 123	272 932	735	273 667	30 681	-12 814	230 173	63 599	45 351	18 978	16 076	17 869	9 472
1988	371 746	300 828	652	301 480	34 313	-13 610	253 557	69 967	48 222	20 720	17 762	17 941	9 684
1989	399 258	314 933	777	315 710	36 040	-13 203	266 466	79 904	52 887	22 202	18 903	17 983	9 752
1990	427 268	334 411	775	335 186	36 559	-13 503	285 124	84 128	58 015	23 710	20 371	18 021	9 727
1991	429 233	328 531	647	329 179	37 425	-13 531	278 222	86 423	64 588	23 685	20 471	18 123	9 483
1992	450 562	349 488	750	350 238	39 094	-16 710	294 433	83 919	72 209	24 693	21 351	18 247	9 410
1993	461 006	358 069	795	358 864	40 118	-16 624	302 122	82 180	76 705	25 089	21 595	18 375	9 431
1994	476 377	367 512	673	368 185	41 885	-16 637	309 663	86 283	80 431	25 807	22 218	18 459	9 465
1995	502 113	386 451	541	386 991	43 395	-18 905	324 691	91 942	85 480	27 106	23 292	18 524	9 511
1996	529 721	408 631	767	409 398	44 681	-21 642	343 075	97 365	89 281	28 497	24 285	18 588	9 595
1997	559 927	435 613	459	436 072	46 509	-24 148	365 415	105 128	89 384	30 012	25 401	18 657	9 732
1998	589 236	461 474	690	462 164	48 905	-27 694	385 565	110 775	92 896	31 416	26 324	18 756	9 923
1999	616 057	489 836	768	490 603	51 340	-29 301	409 962	110 278	95 816	32 625	27 104	18 883	10 109
2000	657 894	527 931	774	528 705	55 178	-33 281	440 245	117 346	100 304	34 630	28 623	18 998	10 346
2001	676 825	545 924	919	546 843	57 401	-34 318	455 125	114 776	106 923	35 456	29 013	19 089	10 422
2002	678 647	544 557	699	545 256	58 458	-30 349	456 448	105 929	116 269	35 417	30 169	19 162	10 334
2003	695 479	557 819	845	558 664	59 804	-30 126	468 734	105 714	121 031	36 164	31 177	19 231	10 361
2004	741 124	593 956	1 071	595 027	62 802	-33 982	498 243	112 434	130 446	38 404	33 020	19 298	10 509
2005	786 571	626 401	1 066	627 467	65 613	-36 926	524 928	132 054	129 589	40 690	34 601	19 331	10 649
2006	851 635	675 261	920	676 181	69 240	-41 631	565 310	148 932	137 392	43 997	36 940	19 357	10 788
2007	925 063	718 512	1 230	719 742	74 104	-47 299	598 339	182 689	144 036	47 628	39 545	19 423	11 072
2008	950 210	735 524	1 179	736 703	76 965	-47 810	611 927	184 379	153 903	48 809	40 909	19 468	11 289
2009	917 610	700 447	806	701 253	74 139	-44 216	582 897	165 804	168 909	46 957	41 068	19 541	...

. . . = Not available.

Table 21-2. Personal Income and Employment by Region and State—*Continued*

(Millions of dollars, except as noted.)

Region or state and year	Personal income, total	Earnings by place of work			Less: Contributions for government social insurance	Plus: Adjustment for residence	Equals: Net earnings by place of residence	Plus: Dividends, interest, and rent	Plus: Personal current transfer receipts	Per capita (dollars)		Population (thousands)	Total employment (thousands)
		Nonfarm	Farm	Total						Personal income	Disposable personal income		
NORTH CAROLINA													
1958	6 552	5 065	625	5 690	214	9	5 485	666	400	1 497	1 383	4 376	. . .
1959	7 014	5 609	518	6 127	257	9	5 879	705	430	1 573	1 435	4 458	. . .
1960	7 414	5 879	600	6 478	306	9	6 181	776	457	1 621	1 473	4 573	. . .
1961	7 834	6 140	639	6 779	314	10	6 474	836	524	1 680	1 526	4 663	. . .
1962	8 416	6 653	621	7 275	346	10	6 939	924	552	1 788	1 615	4 707	. . .
1963	8 849	7 072	599	7 670	412	11	7 270	985	595	1 866	1 682	4 742	. . .
1964	9 596	7 687	628	8 316	435	11	7 892	1 081	623	1 998	1 823	4 802	. . .
1965	10 349	8 440	526	8 966	467	11	8 510	1 160	679	2 128	1 922	4 863	. . .
1966	11 484	9 499	611	10 110	617	10	9 504	1 243	738	2 346	2 107	4 896	. . .
1967	12 429	10 362	602	10 964	714	10	10 259	1 311	859	2 510	2 257	4 952	. . .
1968	13 702	11 642	514	12 156	825	12	11 343	1 377	981	2 738	2 429	5 004	. . .
1969	15 322	12 884	673	13 557	899	16	12 674	1 540	1 107	3 046	2 665	5 031	2 458
1970	16 688	13 879	672	14 551	971	13	13 594	1 757	1 338	3 273	2 884	5 099	2 469
1971	18 205	15 178	627	15 805	1 101	10	14 714	1 922	1 569	3 500	3 113	5 201	2 490
1972	20 600	17 279	750	18 029	1 308	4	16 725	2 118	1 757	3 890	3 414	5 296	2 602
1973	23 428	19 491	1 161	20 652	1 677	2	18 977	2 412	2 038	4 353	3 848	5 382	2 720
1974	25 851	21 306	1 109	22 416	1 900	8	20 524	2 793	2 533	4 734	4 159	5 461	2 743
1975	27 942	22 236	1 066	23 302	1 977	14	21 339	3 080	3 522	5 048	4 542	5 535	2 647
1976	31 216	25 128	1 147	26 275	2 271	15	24 019	3 414	3 783	5 581	4 968	5 593	2 754
1977	34 242	28 007	856	28 863	2 512	22	26 373	3 876	3 993	6 041	5 353	5 668	2 851
1978	38 713	31 742	1 142	32 885	2 922	21	29 984	4 425	4 304	6 744	5 949	5 740	2 946
1979	42 937	35 473	756	36 229	3 390	19	32 858	5 157	4 923	7 401	6 473	5 802	3 046
1980	48 272	38 859	651	39 509	3 727	23	35 805	6 595	5 872	8 183	7 160	5 899	3 052
1981	54 457	42 716	1 051	43 767	4 390	-20	39 356	8 327	6 774	9 142	7 984	5 957	3 072
1982	58 450	44 828	1 063	45 892	4 645	-30	41 217	9 690	7 544	9 711	8 605	6 019	3 042
1983	63 810	49 482	633	50 115	5 173	-48	44 894	10 781	8 134	10 500	9 277	6 077	3 129
1984	72 559	56 063	1 290	57 353	5 970	-82	51 301	12 661	8 597	11 771	10 446	6 164	3 292
1985	78 747	61 043	1 157	62 200	6 590	-145	55 465	14 062	9 220	12 592	11 138	6 254	3 392
1986	84 667	65 994	1 143	67 137	7 295	-209	59 633	15 229	9 805	13 393	11 840	6 322	3 494
1987	91 198	72 061	1 144	73 205	7 871	-290	65 044	15 953	10 201	14 241	12 488	6 404	3 610
1988	99 420	78 418	1 486	79 904	8 850	-350	70 704	17 687	11 029	15 341	13 533	6 481	3 751
1989	108 027	83 763	1 723	85 485	9 515	-402	75 568	20 183	12 277	16 454	14 417	6 565	3 838
1990	114 583	88 092	2 136	90 228	10 306	-446	79 476	21 536	13 571	17 194	15 145	6 664	3 902
1991	120 020	91 023	2 396	93 418	10 794	-431	82 193	22 189	15 638	17 691	15 662	6 784	3 866
1992	130 259	99 974	2 343	102 317	11 701	-454	90 162	22 773	17 324	18 886	16 764	6 897	3 964
1993	138 771	106 118	2 615	108 733	12 502	-470	95 761	23 956	19 054	19 704	17 454	7 043	4 087
1994	148 277	113 284	2 827	116 111	13 461	-528	102 122	26 341	19 814	20 630	18 213	7 187	4 201
1995	158 756	120 613	2 711	123 324	14 300	-602	108 422	28 184	22 150	21 615	19 036	7 345	4 355
1996	170 369	127 575	2 998	130 573	14 999	-659	114 914	31 439	24 015	22 714	19 941	7 501	4 459
1997	183 344	137 045	3 067	140 111	16 118	-727	123 267	34 867	25 210	23 945	20 924	7 657	4 603
1998	197 581	148 572	2 412	150 984	17 264	-717	133 003	38 357	26 222	25 301	21 960	7 809	4 716
1999	209 278	159 714	2 242	161 956	18 411	-786	142 759	38 597	27 923	26 326	22 902	7 949	4 812
2000	225 528	172 451	2 965	175 416	19 521	-904	154 991	40 635	29 902	27 914	24 253	8 079	4 887
2001	232 832	177 386	3 118	180 504	20 226	-809	159 469	40 022	33 340	28 382	24 735	8 203	4 841
2002	236 694	182 100	1 505	183 605	20 511	-813	162 281	38 215	36 198	28 460	25 287	8 317	4 834
2003	243 701	188 388	1 597	189 985	21 417	-748	167 821	38 000	37 880	28 955	25 972	8 416	4 849
2004	260 694	199 305	2 372	201 677	22 472	-791	178 414	41 561	40 719	30 557	27 499	8 531	4 963
2005	277 729	210 438	3 148	213 586	23 978	-908	188 699	44 981	44 049	32 035	28 545	8 669	5 093
2006	297 558	224 941	2 550	227 491	25 756	-1 090	200 645	49 208	47 705	33 558	29 716	8 867	5 251
2007	316 023	237 152	2 070	239 221	27 527	-1 264	210 431	54 078	51 514	34 865	30 654	9 064	5 440
2008	325 954	241 642	2 225	243 866	28 498	-1 272	214 096	55 008	56 850	35 249	31 258	9 247	5 498
2009	323 204	233 707	2 213	235 920	27 799	-1 144	206 977	51 579	64 648	34 453	31 443	9 381	. . .

. . . = Not available.

Table 21-2. Personal Income and Employment by Region and State—*Continued*

(Millions of dollars, except as noted.)

Region or state and year	Personal income, total	Earnings by place of work			Less: Contributions for government social insurance	Plus: Adjustment for residence	Equals: Net earnings by place of residence	Plus: Dividends, interest, and rent	Plus: Personal current transfer receipts	Per capita (dollars)		Population (thousands)	Total employment (thousands)
		Nonfarm	Farm	Total						Personal income	Disposable personal income		
NORTH DAKOTA													
1958	1 156	624	321	945	31	-10	904	179	73	1 908	1 766	606	...
1959	1 069	680	185	865	34	-11	820	170	78	1 729	1 594	618	...
1960	1 185	706	269	974	41	-11	922	180	83	1 869	1 724	634	...
1961	1 077	735	140	875	43	-11	820	166	90	1 680	1 543	641	...
1962	1 516	796	472	1 268	47	-14	1 207	215	94	2 379	2 206	637	...
1963	1 401	847	321	1 168	56	-14	1 097	206	98	2 176	2 000	644	...
1964	1 392	913	235	1 148	59	-17	1 072	215	104	2 145	1 976	649	...
1965	1 621	971	376	1 347	62	-17	1 268	238	114	2 497	2 315	649	...
1966	1 638	1 023	343	1 366	74	-16	1 276	239	123	2 531	2 330	647	...
1967	1 640	1 052	305	1 357	89	-16	1 252	241	147	2 620	2 395	626	...
1968	1 708	1 121	280	1 402	95	-16	1 291	252	164	2 750	2 510	621	...
1969	1 924	1 226	385	1 611	103	-52	1 456	286	183	3 099	2 783	621	274
1970	2 016	1 367	306	1 673	115	-55	1 502	302	212	3 257	2 948	619	281
1971	2 328	1 499	434	1 933	130	-58	1 745	335	248	3 715	3 420	627	284
1972	2 784	1 680	668	2 348	148	-62	2 139	369	276	4 412	4 051	631	288
1973	3 925	1 901	1 529	3 430	190	-65	3 174	441	310	6 207	5 704	632	300
1974	3 891	2 155	1 164	3 319	225	-78	3 016	520	356	6 136	5 466	634	308
1975	4 080	2 442	946	3 388	257	-84	3 048	612	420	6 390	5 721	638	314
1976	4 005	2 796	479	3 274	295	-99	2 881	660	464	6 206	5 554	645	326
1977	4 168	3 038	275	3 313	304	-106	2 903	759	506	6 421	5 776	649	331
1978	5 267	3 470	867	4 337	355	-118	3 864	851	553	8 095	7 260	651	345
1979	5 407	3 885	503	4 388	414	-136	3 838	956	613	8 290	7 412	652	353
1980	5 166	4 215	-383	3 832	448	-153	3 231	1 211	723	7 894	6 920	654	355
1981	6 793	4 705	374	5 079	531	-175	4 372	1 591	830	10 300	9 058	660	359
1982	7 365	4 985	307	5 292	575	-178	4 539	1 896	930	11 009	9 902	669	360
1983	7 726	5 232	366	5 599	613	-182	4 804	1 888	1 035	11 417	10 349	677	365
1984	8 349	5 476	612	6 088	652	-187	5 248	1 991	1 109	12 268	11 163	680	366
1985	8 616	5 577	698	6 275	678	-187	5 410	2 027	1 179	12 728	11 592	677	364
1986	8 720	5 611	694	6 305	698	-184	5 423	2 012	1 285	13 025	11 920	670	357
1987	8 984	5 844	790	6 634	727	-185	5 722	1 918	1 344	13 589	12 379	661	363
1988	8 292	6 078	-59	6 020	794	-191	5 035	1 909	1 348	12 653	11 407	655	366
1989	9 289	6 307	442	6 749	842	-197	5 710	2 110	1 468	14 371	12 999	646	370
1990	10 117	6 670	773	7 444	936	-192	6 316	2 229	1 573	15 866	14 380	638	374
1991	10 278	7 029	615	7 644	1 009	-201	6 434	2 245	1 599	16 167	14 632	636	382
1992	11 258	7 492	1 076	8 569	1 079	-220	7 270	2 222	1 765	17 639	16 055	638	388
1993	11 347	7 993	627	8 620	1 166	-240	7 214	2 272	1 861	17 696	15 999	641	397
1994	12 352	8 499	1 061	9 560	1 246	-256	8 059	2 398	1 895	19 156	17 394	645	411
1995	12 311	8 945	432	9 377	1 298	-281	7 798	2 514	1 999	19 004	17 147	648	418
1996	13 840	9 458	1 309	10 767	1 360	-316	9 091	2 669	2 081	21 279	19 296	650	426
1997	13 549	9 928	310	10 238	1 409	-341	8 487	2 893	2 169	20 854	18 728	650	430
1998	15 008	10 574	973	11 548	1 475	-368	9 705	3 106	2 197	23 177	20 925	648	436
1999	15 141	11 044	688	11 732	1 513	-399	9 820	3 027	2 295	23 502	21 185	644	439
2000	16 430	11 618	1 090	12 708	1 584	-424	10 701	3 266	2 464	25 624	23 121	641	443
2001	16 987	12 374	785	13 158	1 638	-459	11 062	3 371	2 553	26 697	24 027	636	445
2002	17 339	12 957	579	13 536	1 681	-480	11 375	3 280	2 684	27 364	25 037	634	443
2003	18 830	13 683	1 492	15 175	1 770	-511	12 894	3 184	2 752	29 755	27 490	633	444
2004	19 302	14 638	953	15 591	1 876	-562	13 153	3 235	2 913	30 334	28 010	636	454
2005	20 551	15 439	1 208	16 646	1 957	-613	14 076	3 349	3 127	32 346	29 681	635	463
2006	21 386	16 371	787	17 157	2 055	-670	14 433	3 676	3 277	33 585	30 501	637	472
2007	23 408	17 193	1 532	18 726	2 146	-705	15 875	4 011	3 522	36 678	33 069	638	484
2008	25 576	18 442	2 347	20 789	2 304	-778	17 707	4 119	3 749	39 874	36 272	641	499
2009	25 570	18 998	1 752	20 749	2 398	-854	17 497	3 971	4 102	39 530	36 496	647	...

. . . = Not available.

Table 21-2. Personal Income and Employment by Region and State—*Continued*

(Millions of dollars, except as noted.)

Region or state and year	Personal income, total	Earnings by place of work			Less: Contributions for government social insurance	Plus: Adjustment for residence	Equals: Net earnings by place of residence	Plus: Dividends, interest, and rent	Plus: Personal current transfer receipts	Per capita (dollars)		Population (thousands)	Total employment (thousands)
		Nonfarm	Farm	Total						Personal income	Disposable personal income		
OHIO													
1958	20 843	17 271	378	17 649	700	-119	16 830	2 567	1 446	2 171	1 945	9 599	. . .
1959	22 308	18 960	261	19 221	860	-133	18 228	2 712	1 368	2 307	2 059	9 671	. . .
1960	23 209	19 579	327	19 906	1 002	-131	18 772	2 925	1 512	2 384	2 114	9 734	. . .
1961	23 635	19 548	365	19 914	984	-121	18 809	3 066	1 760	2 398	2 139	9 854	. . .
1962	24 920	20 810	328	21 138	1 125	-126	19 888	3 302	1 731	2 510	2 229	9 929	. . .
1963	25 946	21 726	325	22 051	1 236	-129	20 686	3 477	1 782	2 598	2 304	9 986	. . .
1964	27 708	23 369	297	23 666	1 354	-134	22 178	3 742	1 789	2 749	2 474	10 080	. . .
1965	30 005	25 317	350	25 667	1 408	-147	24 112	4 000	1 893	2 941	2 630	10 201	. . .
1966	32 757	27 971	487	28 458	1 864	-166	26 428	4 290	2 038	3 171	2 821	10 330	. . .
1967	34 362	29 268	322	29 590	1 957	-161	27 472	4 512	2 379	3 300	2 933	10 414	. . .
1968	37 916	32 238	407	32 645	2 133	-184	30 328	4 899	2 690	3 606	3 167	10 516	. . .
1969	41 316	35 344	418	35 762	2 360	-187	33 215	5 201	2 900	3 911	3 386	10 563	4 695
1970	43 614	36 737	435	37 171	2 409	-178	34 584	5 634	3 395	4 088	3 591	10 669	4 683
1971	46 395	38 655	415	39 070	2 605	-128	36 337	6 044	4 014	4 322	3 857	10 735	4 627
1972	50 378	42 093	506	42 599	2 987	-125	39 487	6 453	4 438	4 688	4 118	10 747	4 710
1973	56 089	47 153	667	47 820	3 865	-153	43 802	7 121	5 166	5 209	4 583	10 767	4 902
1974	61 623	50 973	798	51 771	4 312	-129	47 330	8 090	6 203	5 724	5 023	10 766	4 964
1975	65 713	52 659	815	53 474	4 338	-75	49 062	8 719	7 933	6 101	5 402	10 770	4 809
1976	72 586	58 959	789	59 747	4 944	-85	54 718	9 383	8 486	6 751	5 946	10 753	4 889
1977	80 693	66 241	676	66 917	5 557	-98	61 262	10 516	8 915	7 492	6 560	10 771	5 034
1978	89 424	73 907	630	74 536	6 407	-116	68 014	11 826	9 584	8 283	7 234	10 795	5 206
1979	99 044	81 237	763	82 000	7 332	-137	74 531	13 569	10 943	9 172	7 956	10 799	5 291
1980	108 244	84 953	576	85 528	7 615	-153	77 761	16 697	13 786	10 022	8 746	10 801	5 204
1981	117 830	90 936	169	91 105	8 719	-460	81 927	20 582	15 320	10 922	9 476	10 788	5 135
1982	123 385	91 776	271	92 047	8 904	-582	82 560	23 042	17 783	11 470	10 075	10 757	4 967
1983	130 705	96 885	-69	96 816	9 613	-704	86 499	25 185	19 021	12 173	10 709	10 738	4 960
1984	144 285	107 136	874	108 010	10 933	-838	96 239	28 417	19 628	13 437	11 891	10 738	5 160
1985	152 957	114 033	868	114 902	11 870	-925	102 107	29 925	20 926	14 249	12 567	10 735	5 287
1986	159 588	119 415	684	120 099	12 856	-957	106 285	31 140	22 162	14 873	13 138	10 730	5 401
1987	167 097	126 210	737	126 947	13 615	-996	112 337	31 728	23 033	15 529	13 606	10 760	5 548
1988	178 707	136 353	789	137 142	15 095	-1 049	120 998	33 533	24 177	16 549	14 563	10 799	5 682
1989	191 375	143 753	1 172	144 925	16 102	-1 091	127 732	37 869	25 774	17 672	15 469	10 829	5 803
1990	202 486	151 020	1 206	152 226	17 256	-1 081	133 889	39 922	28 676	18 638	16 341	10 864	5 863
1991	208 109	155 467	704	156 171	18 100	-1 088	136 983	40 222	30 904	19 013	16 737	10 946	5 842
1992	220 866	165 836	1 188	167 023	19 214	-1 290	146 519	40 400	33 948	20 025	17 672	11 029	5 854
1993	229 527	173 338	937	174 275	20 295	-1 357	152 623	41 603	35 301	20 676	18 191	11 101	5 960
1994	243 329	184 483	1 164	185 647	21 829	-1 504	162 313	44 368	36 647	21 818	19 173	11 152	6 136
1995	253 778	192 242	895	193 138	22 967	-1 433	168 738	46 425	38 615	22 653	19 833	11 203	6 300
1996	264 716	199 030	1 251	200 281	23 637	-1 396	175 248	49 459	40 009	23 545	20 441	11 243	6 395
1997	280 936	209 992	1 691	211 683	24 347	-1 481	185 855	53 870	41 211	24 912	21 564	11 277	6 500
1998	298 833	224 563	1 274	225 836	25 112	-1 596	199 128	57 734	41 971	26 418	22 808	11 312	6 616
1999	309 384	236 268	849	237 117	26 243	-1 621	209 253	56 763	43 368	27 293	23 597	11 335	6 691
2000	326 075	248 042	1 199	249 241	26 568	-1 569	221 103	58 836	46 135	28 694	24 757	11 364	6 782
2001	333 539	253 621	1 121	254 742	27 174	-1 472	226 096	57 136	50 306	29 266	25 355	11 397	6 711
2002	340 664	260 530	559	261 088	27 160	-1 517	232 411	54 539	53 715	29 828	26 272	11 421	6 641
2003	350 893	270 964	850	271 814	28 296	-1 553	241 965	52 651	56 277	30 659	27 323	11 445	6 630
2004	361 854	280 832	1 457	282 289	29 969	-1 576	250 745	52 238	58 872	31 563	28 148	11 465	6 678
2005	372 133	287 846	1 145	288 990	30 816	-1 652	256 523	53 374	62 236	32 429	28 738	11 475	6 723
2006	390 645	297 803	1 041	298 844	32 209	-1 754	264 881	59 978	65 786	33 991	30 014	11 492	6 762
2007	405 236	304 706	1 175	305 881	33 055	-1 906	270 920	64 451	69 865	35 174	30 954	11 521	6 813
2008	413 732	307 567	1 316	308 883	33 821	-1 828	273 235	65 041	75 456	35 889	31 875	11 528	6 819
2009	408 395	295 125	898	296 023	32 649	-1 599	261 775	62 070	84 550	35 381	32 255	11 543	. . .

. . . = Not available.

Table 21-2. Personal Income and Employment by Region and State—*Continued*

(Millions of dollars, except as noted.)

| Region or state and year | Personal income, total | Earnings by place of work | | | Less: Contributions for government social insurance | Plus: Adjustment for residence | Equals: Net earnings by place of residence | Plus: Dividends, interest, and rent | Plus: Personal current transfer receipts | Per capita (dollars) | | Population (thousands) | Total employment (thousands) |
		Nonfarm	Farm	Total						Personal income	Disposable personal income		
OKLAHOMA													
1958	4 085	3 022	326	3 348	113	4	3 239	514	331	1 802	1 636	2 267	...
1959	4 265	3 207	262	3 469	130	5	3 344	562	359	1 863	1 685	2 289	...
1960	4 488	3 303	331	3 634	150	7	3 491	619	378	1 921	1 736	2 336	...
1961	4 638	3 432	297	3 728	159	8	3 578	644	416	1 949	1 754	2 380	...
1962	4 836	3 659	236	3 895	178	11	3 728	668	441	1 993	1 791	2 427	...
1963	4 997	3 825	209	4 035	208	12	3 839	688	471	2 049	1 844	2 439	...
1964	5 355	4 116	204	4 320	207	14	4 127	737	491	2 189	1 989	2 446	...
1965	5 736	4 347	273	4 620	216	17	4 422	788	526	2 351	2 136	2 440	...
1966	6 142	4 734	263	4 996	286	21	4 731	827	584	2 503	2 261	2 454	...
1967	6 695	5 188	273	5 461	336	25	5 150	845	700	2 690	2 425	2 489	...
1968	7 341	5 777	216	5 993	384	31	5 640	912	789	2 933	2 626	2 503	...
1969	8 121	6 304	276	6 579	402	63	6 240	1 026	855	3 204	2 822	2 535	1 107
1970	8 919	6 801	359	7 159	431	65	6 793	1 145	981	3 475	3 098	2 566	1 120
1971	9 712	7 387	335	7 721	484	64	7 302	1 280	1 131	3 710	3 349	2 618	1 132
1972	10 672	8 154	417	8 572	558	73	8 087	1 344	1 240	4 016	3 573	2 657	1 183
1973	12 164	9 095	734	9 828	720	83	9 191	1 567	1 406	4 515	4 056	2 694	1 221
1974	13 597	10 389	452	10 841	846	107	10 102	1 831	1 664	4 976	4 399	2 732	1 256
1975	15 227	11 527	404	11 931	928	142	11 145	2 030	2 052	5 493	4 932	2 772	1 269
1976	16 868	12 957	338	13 295	1 054	177	12 418	2 204	2 245	5 974	5 335	2 823	1 305
1977	18 829	14 809	183	14 992	1 198	153	13 947	2 494	2 388	6 570	5 833	2 866	1 359
1978	21 391	17 019	175	17 194	1 417	149	15 926	2 893	2 571	7 343	6 451	2 913	1 428
1979	24 933	19 478	635	20 113	1 687	163	18 589	3 391	2 952	8 395	7 356	2 970	1 481
1980	28 847	22 612	265	22 877	1 964	171	21 084	4 353	3 410	9 487	8 260	3 041	1 547
1981	33 881	26 295	332	26 627	2 444	195	24 378	5 629	3 874	10 943	9 391	3 096	1 625
1982	37 885	28 841	487	29 329	2 743	200	26 786	6 731	4 368	11 816	10 070	3 206	1 673
1983	38 619	28 855	214	29 069	2 740	238	26 567	7 258	4 794	11 737	10 333	3 290	1 638
1984	41 456	30 716	376	31 092	2 969	287	28 409	8 072	4 975	12 618	11 213	3 286	1 665
1985	43 085	31 516	381	31 897	3 109	328	29 115	8 655	5 315	13 171	11 713	3 271	1 648
1986	43 301	31 404	645	32 049	3 162	378	29 265	8 388	5 649	13 312	12 103	3 253	1 588
1987	43 194	31 410	566	31 976	3 182	425	29 219	8 099	5 877	13 455	12 070	3 210	1 599
1988	44 864	32 511	767	33 278	3 500	473	30 251	8 400	6 213	14 166	12 702	3 167	1 608
1989	47 860	34 380	802	35 181	3 742	497	31 937	9 305	6 619	15 192	13 552	3 150	1 623
1990	50 623	36 419	862	37 281	4 086	559	33 755	9 747	7 122	16 077	14 170	3 149	1 655
1991	52 187	37 741	624	38 365	4 369	590	34 587	9 830	7 770	16 434	14 630	3 175	1 668
1992	55 614	40 172	846	41 017	4 607	611	37 021	9 897	8 696	17 269	15 447	3 221	1 680
1993	57 801	42 097	869	42 966	4 865	647	38 747	9 907	9 147	17 772	15 905	3 252	1 716
1994	60 458	43 736	827	44 563	5 139	703	40 127	10 616	9 715	18 427	16 463	3 281	1 748
1995	62 768	45 362	289	45 651	5 363	741	41 028	11 273	10 467	18 973	16 939	3 308	1 800
1996	66 590	47 970	360	48 330	5 564	768	43 534	12 088	10 968	19 936	17 717	3 340	1 850
1997	70 491	50 955	665	51 620	5 810	841	46 652	12 570	11 269	20 899	18 442	3 373	1 897
1998	74 741	54 274	519	54 794	6 116	875	49 553	13 687	11 501	21 949	19 345	3 405	1 947
1999	78 220	56 865	838	57 703	6 302	928	52 329	13 852	12 038	22 757	20 077	3 437	1 962
2000	84 985	61 556	827	62 383	6 684	1 011	56 710	15 538	12 737	24 605	21 723	3 454	2 003
2001	90 838	66 383	807	67 190	7 141	1 014	61 063	15 698	14 077	26 218	23 214	3 465	2 010
2002	91 364	66 444	968	67 412	7 346	1 038	61 105	15 104	15 155	26 218	23 613	3 485	1 979
2003	94 148	69 112	954	70 066	7 578	1 074	63 562	14 696	15 890	26 909	24 444	3 499	1 966
2004	101 179	74 312	1 234	75 546	8 056	1 115	68 605	15 682	16 892	28 789	26 216	3 514	1 989
2005	107 641	78 350	1 322	79 672	8 534	1 160	72 298	17 126	18 217	30 469	27 435	3 533	2 032
2006	118 747	86 343	690	87 033	9 200	1 212	79 045	19 859	19 843	33 222	29 718	3 574	2 091
2007	123 889	88 771	544	89 315	9 714	1 207	80 808	21 752	21 329	34 298	30 503	3 612	2 145
2008	131 070	93 894	828	94 723	10 218	1 222	85 727	22 101	23 243	35 969	32 248	3 644	2 206
2009	130 037	92 039	468	92 508	10 076	1 202	83 634	20 430	25 973	35 268	32 370	3 687	...

. . . = Not available.

Table 21-2. Personal Income and Employment by Region and State—*Continued*

(Millions of dollars, except as noted.)

Region or state and year	Personal income, total	Nonfarm	Farm	Total	Less: Contributions for government social insurance	Plus: Adjustment for residence	Equals: Net earnings by place of residence	Plus: Dividends, interest, and rent	Plus: Personal current transfer receipts	Personal income	Disposable personal income	Population (thousands)	Total employment (thousands)
OREGON													
1958	3 596	2 826	175	3 001	145	-11	2 846	467	283	2 093	1 834	1 718	...
1959	3 896	3 120	178	3 297	180	-14	3 103	507	286	2 232	1 957	1 746	...
1960	4 021	3 238	172	3 410	207	-17	3 185	532	304	2 269	1 987	1 772	...
1961	4 170	3 321	159	3 480	211	-19	3 250	568	352	2 333	2 061	1 787	...
1962	4 441	3 554	170	3 724	232	-22	3 470	612	359	2 443	2 150	1 818	...
1963	4 678	3 792	161	3 953	266	-27	3 660	647	371	2 524	2 202	1 853	...
1964	5 041	4 123	148	4 270	271	-32	3 967	690	384	2 670	2 348	1 888	...
1965	5 492	4 484	166	4 650	276	-38	4 337	741	414	2 835	2 512	1 937	...
1966	5 929	4 883	193	5 076	352	-42	4 681	800	447	3 011	2 650	1 969	...
1967	6 296	5 141	183	5 324	392	-46	4 886	877	533	3 181	2 802	1 979	...
1968	6 864	5 632	182	5 814	444	-54	5 315	948	600	3 425	2 986	2 004	...
1969	7 578	6 144	226	6 370	483	-91	5 796	1 120	662	3 675	3 149	2 062	920
1970	8 248	6 541	216	6 757	506	-67	6 184	1 259	805	3 927	3 427	2 100	926
1971	9 023	7 139	204	7 343	569	-56	6 717	1 374	932	4 197	3 694	2 150	951
1972	10 109	8 062	259	8 321	680	-50	7 591	1 496	1 022	4 605	4 014	2 195	1 001
1973	11 437	9 111	371	9 482	881	-56	8 546	1 679	1 213	5 109	4 471	2 239	1 058
1974	13 003	10 142	477	10 619	1 004	-63	9 553	1 955	1 496	5 701	4 956	2 281	1 089
1975	14 378	10 973	394	11 367	1 057	-31	10 278	2 199	1 901	6 185	5 466	2 325	1 105
1976	16 364	12 733	370	13 102	1 235	-16	11 852	2 445	2 067	6 898	6 042	2 372	1 156
1977	18 358	14 488	320	14 808	1 421	-74	13 314	2 809	2 235	7 526	6 499	2 439	1 223
1978	21 103	16 867	318	17 184	1 694	-131	15 359	3 303	2 441	8 409	7 236	2 510	1 296
1979	23 966	19 075	390	19 465	1 989	-203	17 273	3 956	2 738	9 295	7 971	2 578	1 350
1980	26 640	20 385	477	20 863	2 125	-252	18 486	4 905	3 249	10 086	8 705	2 641	1 350
1981	28 820	21 218	407	21 625	2 365	-262	18 997	6 062	3 761	10 802	9 365	2 668	1 319
1982	29 623	21 094	294	21 388	2 398	-249	18 741	6 642	4 240	11 116	9 668	2 665	1 270
1983	31 437	22 210	301	22 511	2 558	-232	19 720	7 159	4 558	11 849	10 411	2 653	1 295
1984	34 161	24 271	402	24 673	2 890	-278	21 504	7 949	4 707	12 811	11 310	2 667	1 342
1985	35 890	25 624	426	26 050	3 070	-315	22 665	8 299	4 926	13 429	11 808	2 673	1 370
1986	37 728	27 012	548	27 560	3 251	-361	23 949	8 766	5 014	14 059	12 298	2 684	1 406
1987	39 770	28 937	517	29 455	3 438	-420	25 596	8 983	5 191	14 724	12 882	2 701	1 455
1988	43 248	31 887	708	32 594	3 924	-493	28 178	9 548	5 522	15 776	13 972	2 741	1 522
1989	47 318	34 424	674	35 099	4 254	-546	30 298	10 959	6 060	16 956	14 739	2 791	1 574
1990	51 187	37 640	713	38 352	4 766	-608	32 979	11 617	6 591	17 895	15 709	2 860	1 626
1991	54 088	39 671	727	40 398	5 091	-666	34 641	12 145	7 302	18 469	16 157	2 929	1 636
1992	57 446	42 507	730	43 238	5 457	-753	37 028	12 292	8 126	19 201	16 780	2 992	1 654
1993	61 444	45 435	851	46 286	5 833	-844	39 609	13 156	8 680	20 077	17 502	3 060	1 698
1994	66 231	49 051	776	49 827	6 318	-898	42 611	14 609	9 010	21 219	18 443	3 121	1 781
1995	71 747	52 510	689	53 199	6 793	-1 072	45 334	16 448	9 965	22 531	19 631	3 184	1 845
1996	77 121	56 949	841	57 790	7 469	-1 294	49 026	17 495	10 600	23 751	20 585	3 247	1 920
1997	82 127	61 139	958	62 097	7 940	-1 478	52 678	18 548	10 900	24 854	21 372	3 304	1 986
1998	87 218	65 187	862	66 049	8 386	-1 600	56 062	19 820	11 336	26 016	22 427	3 352	2 024
1999	91 691	69 539	823	70 362	8 746	-1 749	59 867	19 470	12 355	27 016	23 192	3 394	2 049
2000	98 530	75 260	822	76 082	9 426	-1 918	64 737	20 789	13 003	28 718	24 536	3 431	2 095
2001	101 476	77 047	828	77 875	9 474	-1 924	66 476	20 305	14 695	29 241	25 245	3 470	2 089
2002	104 697	79 786	829	80 615	9 619	-1 991	69 005	19 999	15 694	29 768	26 340	3 517	2 065
2003	108 506	82 796	1 133	83 929	9 913	-2 045	71 971	20 386	16 149	30 564	27 247	3 550	2 084
2004	113 001	86 132	1 267	87 399	10 604	-2 058	74 737	21 634	16 630	31 622	28 149	3 574	2 137
2005	117 671	89 988	1 251	91 239	11 193	-2 147	77 900	21 989	17 782	32 525	28 503	3 618	2 200
2006	127 448	96 033	1 396	97 429	12 059	-2 281	83 089	25 406	18 953	34 656	30 256	3 678	2 264
2007	133 405	99 951	1 203	101 153	12 592	-2 551	86 011	26 997	20 397	35 737	31 362	3 733	2 320
2008	137 570	101 535	1 198	102 734	12 874	-2 547	87 313	27 649	22 608	36 365	31 798	3 783	2 339
2009	136 449	97 245	1 068	98 312	12 417	-2 404	83 491	26 373	26 586	35 667	32 246	3 826	...

. . . = Not available.

Table 21-2. Personal Income and Employment by Region and State—*Continued*

(Millions of dollars, except as noted.)

Region or state and year	Personal income, total	Derivation of personal income								Per capita (dollars)		Population (thousands)	Total employment (thousands)
		Earnings by place of work			Less: Contributions for government social insurance	Plus: Adjustment for residence	Equals: Net earnings by place of residence	Plus: Dividends, interest, and rent	Plus: Personal current transfer receipts	Personal income	Disposable personal income		
		Nonfarm	Farm	Total									

PENNSYLVANIA

1958	23 858	19 746	339	20 086	846	-45	19 195	2 861	1 803	2 158	1 925	11 058	. . .
1959	25 072	21 023	252	21 275	1 042	-57	20 177	3 024	1 871	2 232	1 986	11 234	. . .
1960	25 978	21 843	294	22 137	1 211	-75	20 851	3 205	1 922	2 293	2 036	11 329	. . .
1961	26 517	22 021	297	22 318	1 225	-81	21 012	3 322	2 183	2 328	2 080	11 392	. . .
1962	27 632	23 123	214	23 337	1 334	-97	21 905	3 560	2 167	2 433	2 161	11 355	. . .
1963	28 637	23 897	255	24 153	1 473	-106	22 573	3 818	2 245	2 507	2 222	11 424	. . .
1964	30 646	25 658	264	25 922	1 530	-129	24 264	4 124	2 259	2 660	2 388	11 519	. . .
1965	32 850	27 511	273	27 785	1 593	-149	26 043	4 438	2 370	2 827	2 530	11 620	. . .
1966	35 384	30 213	260	30 473	2 147	-193	28 133	4 676	2 575	3 034	2 694	11 664	. . .
1967	37 885	32 020	355	32 375	2 316	-222	29 837	4 980	3 068	3 243	2 883	11 681	. . .
1968	41 142	34 675	310	34 985	2 420	-258	32 307	5 323	3 512	3 504	3 089	11 741	. . .
1969	44 663	37 856	372	38 227	483	-413	35 004	5 667	3 992	3 804	3 306	11 741	5 250
1970	48 058	39 964	387	40 351	506	-379	37 042	6 101	4 914	4 069	3 563	11 812	5 226
1971	50 968	41 926	335	42 261	569	-361	38 709	6 484	5 775	4 289	3 799	11 884	5 159
1972	55 691	45 931	347	46 278	680	-371	42 249	6 915	6 527	4 678	4 057	11 905	5 247
1973	61 269	50 800	485	51 284	881	-335	46 317	7 647	7 305	5 155	4 501	11 885	5 402
1974	67 533	55 423	463	55 886	1 004	-341	50 317	8 677	8 539	5 692	4 946	11 864	5 419
1975	73 548	58 703	426	59 128	1 057	-374	53 347	9 373	10 827	6 182	5 457	11 898	5 302
1976	80 786	64 444	517	64 962	1 235	-362	58 590	10 182	12 013	6 796	5 981	11 887	5 353
1977	88 798	71 116	469	71 586	1 421	-360	64 618	11 414	12 766	7 473	6 541	11 882	5 429
1978	98 024	79 030	508	79 537	1 694	-369	71 642	12 672	13 710	8 262	7 204	11 865	5 562
1979	108 552	87 024	642	87 666	1 989	-393	78 677	14 435	15 440	9 142	7 930	11 874	5 664
1980	119 159	92 686	424	93 110	2 125	-428	83 488	17 988	17 683	10 040	8 725	11 868	5 624
1981	131 635	99 520	637	100 157	2 365	-411	89 196	22 528	19 911	11 100	9 581	11 859	5 584
1982	140 723	101 904	564	102 469	2 398	-243	91 264	26 655	22 804	11 880	10 346	11 845	5 474
1983	147 359	105 915	360	106 275	2 558	-80	94 624	28 071	24 664	12 448	10 973	11 838	5 433
1984	159 128	114 728	847	115 575	2 890	109	102 589	31 714	24 825	13 468	11 876	11 815	5 577
1985	168 534	121 102	844	121 947	3 070	257	108 142	34 411	25 981	14 318	12 610	11 771	5 679
1986	176 939	127 144	884	128 028	3 251	358	113 478	36 067	27 395	15 017	13 248	11 783	5 772
1987	187 282	137 075	887	137 961	3 438	456	122 520	36 737	28 025	15 857	13 902	11 811	5 957
1988	202 175	149 689	749	150 438	3 924	686	133 415	39 258	29 502	17 067	15 009	11 846	6 120
1989	218 480	159 209	997	160 205	4 254	879	142 429	44 671	31 381	18 412	16 143	11 866	6 216
1990	231 322	168 008	1 002	169 010	19 872	980	150 118	46 959	34 245	19 433	17 091	11 903	6 293
1991	241 689	173 201	734	173 935	20 727	934	154 142	48 031	39 516	20 171	17 854	11 982	6 212
1992	253 640	183 710	1 203	184 913	22 009	1 239	164 143	47 437	42 060	21 050	18 611	12 049	6 216
1993	262 454	191 070	1 031	192 101	23 255	1 256	170 102	48 066	44 286	21 655	19 152	12 120	6 256
1994	271 976	198 393	922	199 316	24 618	1 619	176 317	50 320	45 339	22 355	19 717	12 166	6 323
1995	283 314	206 470	645	207 114	25 489	1 895	183 520	52 501	47 292	23 226	20 406	12 198	6 423
1996	297 979	214 642	1 118	215 760	25 998	2 274	192 035	55 750	50 194	24 384	21 298	12 220	6 477
1997	312 618	226 210	770	226 980	27 144	2 581	202 417	58 913	51 287	25 566	22 187	12 228	6 585
1998	335 132	244 681	896	245 577	28 392	2 504	219 690	63 421	52 021	27 367	23 709	12 246	6 674
1999	347 654	256 918	814	257 732	29 637	2 899	230 994	62 226	54 434	28 348	24 511	12 264	6 774
2000	369 919	271 236	1 097	272 333	31 081	3 401	244 652	67 486	57 781	30 110	25 999	12 286	6 912
2001	377 189	276 879	997	277 877	32 099	3 486	249 264	66 226	61 698	30 667	26 530	12 300	6 927
2002	387 491	285 881	622	286 503	32 919	3 500	257 084	64 883	65 524	31 436	27 818	12 326	6 909
2003	399 420	296 721	1 213	297 933	33 796	3 681	267 819	63 445	68 157	32 322	28 874	12 358	6 904
2004	417 588	312 334	1 484	313 819	35 428	3 950	282 340	64 339	70 909	33 708	30 174	12 388	6 979
2005	432 040	324 392	1 342	325 734	37 234	4 364	292 863	63 177	76 000	34 791	30 792	12 418	7 084
2006	462 402	340 914	1 053	341 967	39 020	4 767	307 715	74 999	79 688	37 078	32 683	12 471	7 186
2007	485 103	354 122	1 250	355 371	40 355	4 685	319 701	80 677	84 725	38 738	33 878	12 523	7 316
2008	499 669	362 742	1 103	363 845	41 734	4 595	326 706	81 730	91 234	39 762	35 041	12 566	7 407
2009	498 868	355 099	568	355 668	41 316	4 220	318 571	78 124	102 173	39 578	35 861	12 605	. . .

. . . = Not available.

Table 21-2. Personal Income and Employment by Region and State—*Continued*

(Millions of dollars, except as noted.)

Region or state and year	Personal income, total	Derivation of personal income								Per capita (dollars)		Population (thousands)	Total employment (thousands)
		Earnings by place of work			Less: Contributions for government social insurance	Plus: Adjustment for residence	Equals: Net earnings by place of residence	Plus: Dividends, interest, and rent	Plus: Personal current transfer receipts	Personal income	Disposable personal income		
		Nonfarm	Farm	Total									
RHODE ISLAND													
1958	1 793	1 443	8	1 450	75	44	1 418	225	149	2 090	1 865	858	. . .
1959	1 893	1 543	6	1 550	86	51	1 514	232	146	2 209	1 978	857	. . .
1960	1 934	1 581	7	1 589	96	54	1 547	237	150	2 262	2 012	855	. . .
1961	2 023	1 634	7	1 641	98	57	1 601	256	166	2 358	2 090	858	. . .
1962	2 169	1 751	7	1 758	108	63	1 713	287	169	2 490	2 215	871	. . .
1963	2 265	1 807	7	1 814	117	67	1 764	323	179	2 586	2 299	876	. . .
1964	2 416	1 933	8	1 940	122	73	1 892	340	184	2 729	2 459	885	. . .
1965	2 600	2 078	8	2 086	133	82	2 035	367	198	2 912	2 617	893	. . .
1966	2 840	2 296	9	2 305	162	96	2 239	383	218	3 159	2 818	899	. . .
1967	3 082	2 468	7	2 474	174	105	2 405	411	265	3 390	3 038	909	. . .
1968	3 367	2 700	8	2 708	200	116	2 625	434	308	3 652	3 235	922	. . .
1969	3 586	2 901	8	2 909	230	65	2 744	495	347	3 847	3 386	932	440
1970	3 895	3 117	9	3 126	245	66	2 948	525	423	4 098	3 647	951	440
1971	4 131	3 277	8	3 285	267	61	3 079	555	497	4 285	3 817	964	436
1972	4 504	3 614	8	3 621	306	56	3 371	588	546	4 613	4 060	976	447
1973	4 846	3 873	6	3 879	381	71	3 569	652	625	4 955	4 366	978	452
1974	5 135	3 973	9	3 982	410	88	3 660	741	734	5 385	4 737	954	439
1975	5 537	4 112	9	4 121	415	82	3 788	778	972	5 851	5 251	946	424
1976	6 084	4 631	9	4 640	472	89	4 256	835	993	6 402	5 693	950	442
1977	6 662	5 096	8	5 104	520	103	4 688	935	1 040	6 975	6 216	955	459
1978	7 309	5 659	9	5 668	597	102	5 174	1 025	1 111	7 636	6 706	957	474
1979	8 128	6 297	8	6 304	684	110	5 730	1 164	1 235	8 497	7 388	957	483
1980	9 151	6 861	8	6 868	746	124	6 247	1 476	1 428	9 645	8 445	949	484
1981	10 229	7 405	9	7 414	849	155	6 720	1 875	1 634	10 733	9 405	953	484
1982	11 011	7 785	27	7 812	900	209	7 121	2 097	1 793	11 540	10 170	954	475
1983	11 849	8 389	37	8 426	988	265	7 703	2 234	1 912	12 389	10 956	956	480
1984	13 110	9 315	32	9 348	1 136	335	8 547	2 598	1 965	13 629	12 107	962	504
1985	14 086	10 087	42	10 129	1 220	394	9 302	2 698	2 086	14 538	12 891	969	519
1986	15 095	10 914	43	10 957	1 330	417	10 043	2 881	2 170	15 445	13 616	977	537
1987	16 217	11 835	41	11 875	1 430	483	10 928	3 053	2 236	16 387	14 299	990	546
1988	17 845	13 042	42	13 084	1 599	558	12 043	3 412	2 390	17 909	15 729	996	560
1989	19 402	13 747	32	13 780	1 664	619	12 734	4 058	2 609	19 389	17 028	1 001	560
1990	19 940	14 054	31	14 085	1 792	664	12 957	4 098	2 884	19 821	17 453	1 006	550
1991	20 194	13 822	32	13 853	1 798	691	12 746	3 945	3 504	19 981	17 674	1 011	524
1992	21 082	14 681	29	14 710	1 916	708	13 502	3 926	3 654	20 820	18 495	1 013	529
1993	21 927	15 217	30	15 247	2 007	748	13 989	3 972	3 965	21 600	19 155	1 015	533
1994	22 553	15 756	25	15 782	2 098	820	14 504	4 106	3 943	22 199	19 655	1 016	533
1995	23 761	16 541	25	16 566	2 172	850	15 244	4 360	4 157	23 364	20 683	1 017	536
1996	24 807	17 080	23	17 103	2 213	917	15 808	4 765	4 235	24 299	21 407	1 021	540
1997	26 271	18 017	16	18 032	2 321	978	16 690	5 083	4 499	25 621	22 361	1 025	546
1998	27 784	19 133	15	19 148	2 458	1 060	17 750	5 486	4 548	26 945	23 388	1 031	554
1999	28 861	20 126	15	20 142	2 575	1 154	18 720	5 410	4 731	27 741	24 038	1 040	565
2000	30 980	21 609	17	21 626	2 745	1 319	20 200	5 873	4 908	29 484	25 340	1 051	578
2001	32 976	22 949	18	22 966	2 865	1 302	21 403	6 089	5 483	31 166	26 891	1 058	581
2002	34 278	24 023	22	24 045	2 993	1 244	22 296	6 260	5 722	32 155	28 418	1 066	585
2003	35 855	25 580	24	25 604	3 132	1 207	23 680	6 292	5 883	33 462	29 847	1 072	591
2004	37 585	26 867	25	26 893	3 268	1 295	24 919	6 384	6 282	35 079	31 320	1 071	600
2005	38 567	27 830	23	27 853	3 409	1 303	25 747	6 284	6 536	36 214	32 137	1 065	604
2006	40 657	29 134	23	29 157	3 592	1 350	26 914	6 988	6 755	38 349	33 905	1 060	610
2007	42 356	29 807	24	29 831	3 670	1 459	27 620	7 447	7 289	40 147	35 309	1 055	616
2008	43 469	30 165	19	30 184	3 730	1 500	27 954	7 604	7 911	41 261	36 659	1 054	612
2009	43 185	29 238	24	29 262	3 646	1 434	27 050	7 410	8 726	41 003	37 460	1 053	. . .

. . . = Not available.

Table 21-2. Personal Income and Employment by Region and State—*Continued*

(Millions of dollars, except as noted.)

Region or state and year	Personal income, total	Derivation of personal income								Per capita (dollars)		Population (thousands)	Total employment (thousands)
		Earnings by place of work			Less: Contributions for government social insurance	Plus: Adjustment for residence	Equals: Net earnings by place of residence	Plus: Dividends, interest, and rent	Plus: Personal current transfer receipts	Personal income	Disposable personal income		
		Nonfarm	Farm	Total									
SOUTH CAROLINA													
1958	3 014	2 438	182	2 620	95	13	2 538	287	189	1 308	1 211	2 304	. . .
1959	3 249	2 678	164	2 842	113	15	2 745	305	199	1 384	1 267	2 348	. . .
1960	3 416	2 824	168	2 991	135	17	2 874	333	210	1 428	1 306	2 392	. . .
1961	3 585	2 913	194	3 107	138	19	2 988	359	238	1 488	1 360	2 409	. . .
1962	3 853	3 153	183	3 336	153	22	3 205	395	253	1 590	1 444	2 423	. . .
1963	4 074	3 355	186	3 541	189	25	3 377	425	272	1 656	1 505	2 460	. . .
1964	4 389	3 645	178	3 823	202	30	3 650	455	284	1 773	1 625	2 475	. . .
1965	4 839	4 030	180	4 210	221	35	4 024	506	310	1 940	1 770	2 494	. . .
1966	5 433	4 611	194	4 804	290	43	4 557	533	342	2 156	1 947	2 520	. . .
1967	5 876	4 994	196	5 190	341	49	4 898	577	401	2 320	2 096	2 533	. . .
1968	6 519	5 618	154	5 772	386	57	5 443	605	471	2 547	2 283	2 559	. . .
1969	7 249	6 158	188	6 346	416	115	6 045	667	537	2 821	2 503	2 570	1 170
1970	7 937	6 656	189	6 845	448	116	6 513	755	669	3 055	2 741	2 598	1 196
1971	8 692	7 251	204	7 455	509	128	7 074	839	779	3 265	2 936	2 662	1 215
1972	9 769	8 205	214	8 419	599	145	7 965	928	876	3 594	3 170	2 718	1 262
1973	11 147	9 348	302	9 650	773	159	9 037	1 066	1 044	4 016	3 562	2 775	1 328
1974	12 656	10 493	342	10 835	897	174	10 111	1 228	1 318	4 451	3 940	2 843	1 365
1975	13 719	10 991	277	11 268	927	185	10 526	1 379	1 814	4 730	4 296	2 900	1 326
1976	15 457	12 647	234	12 881	1 088	220	12 014	1 524	1 919	5 255	4 712	2 941	1 376
1977	16 941	13 977	188	14 165	1 198	243	13 210	1 724	2 006	5 668	5 065	2 989	1 411
1978	19 162	15 864	247	16 111	1 389	261	14 982	1 975	2 205	6 301	5 614	3 041	1 466
1979	21 572	17 785	260	18 044	1 607	285	16 722	2 306	2 544	6 988	6 158	3 087	1 507
1980	24 250	19 648	36	19 684	1 777	319	18 226	2 935	3 089	7 736	6 840	3 135	1 523
1981	27 360	21 649	173	21 822	2 097	349	20 073	3 714	3 572	8 606	7 571	3 179	1 536
1982	29 120	22 427	195	22 622	2 201	381	20 802	4 396	3 923	9 078	8 071	3 208	1 514
1983	31 662	24 534	50	24 584	2 470	394	22 508	4 969	4 185	9 790	8 701	3 234	1 547
1984	35 663	27 621	269	27 890	2 850	441	25 480	5 768	4 415	10 900	9 744	3 272	1 625
1985	38 284	29 471	196	29 667	3 097	496	27 067	6 432	4 785	11 590	10 332	3 303	1 655
1986	40 761	31 573	91	31 664	3 426	562	28 800	6 914	5 046	12 194	10 874	3 343	1 697
1987	43 740	34 081	251	34 332	3 666	605	31 271	7 280	5 189	12 939	11 489	3 381	1 738
1988	47 448	37 148	350	37 498	4 149	626	33 976	7 937	5 535	13 906	12 421	3 412	1 809
1989	51 613	39 674	367	40 041	4 506	581	36 115	9 119	6 379	14 931	13 239	3 457	1 858
1990	55 471	42 743	301	43 044	4 957	507	38 594	9 812	7 065	15 844	14 044	3 501	1 913
1991	58 039	44 035	399	44 434	5 176	494	39 753	10 172	8 114	16 256	14 537	3 570	1 886
1992	61 583	46 640	378	47 018	5 458	505	42 065	10 384	9 134	17 010	15 243	3 620	1 897
1993	64 662	48 997	338	49 336	5 799	510	44 047	10 823	9 791	17 651	15 801	3 663	1 931
1994	68 841	51 349	491	51 840	6 152	620	46 308	11 892	10 641	18 579	16 598	3 705	1 979
1995	72 664	54 227	385	54 612	6 510	744	48 846	12 472	11 346	19 384	17 241	3 749	2 038
1996	77 285	56 899	464	57 363	6 736	864	51 491	13 605	12 189	20 359	18 025	3 796	2 080
1997	82 160	60 278	474	60 751	7 162	1 014	54 603	14 784	12 772	21 287	18 772	3 860	2 141
1998	88 470	65 015	335	65 350	7 700	1 091	58 741	16 296	13 433	22 573	19 853	3 919	2 195
1999	93 605	69 642	403	70 046	8 114	1 184	63 116	16 191	14 298	23 550	20 712	3 975	2 240
2000	100 913	74 443	525	74 968	8 559	1 419	67 828	17 702	15 383	25 081	22 165	4 024	2 275
2001	104 199	76 219	647	76 865	8 827	1 407	69 446	17 598	17 155	25 648	22 731	4 063	2 244
2002	106 985	78 716	226	78 942	9 118	1 420	71 244	17 015	18 726	26 069	23 507	4 104	2 290
2003	110 644	82 382	540	82 921	9 447	1 447	74 922	16 141	19 582	26 684	24 259	4 146	2 317
2004	117 230	86 644	639	87 282	9 907	1 551	78 926	17 166	21 138	27 903	25 407	4 201	2 384
2005	124 379	91 206	649	91 855	10 375	1 716	83 196	18 454	22 729	29 223	26 365	4 256	2 428
2006	134 204	97 021	461	97 482	11 320	1 929	88 091	21 617	24 496	30 927	27 765	4 339	2 491
2007	141 244	100 938	271	101 209	11 808	2 145	91 546	23 471	26 226	31 925	28 534	4 424	2 559
2008	146 335	102 703	471	103 174	12 171	2 165	93 168	23 796	29 371	32 495	29 312	4 503	2 579
2009	145 041	99 392	469	99 861	11 891	2 056	90 026	22 182	32 834	31 799	29 386	4 561	. . .

. . . = Not available.

Table 21-2. Personal Income and Employment by Region and State—*Continued*

(Millions of dollars, except as noted.)

Region or state and year	Personal income, total	Earnings by place of work			Less: Contributions for government social insurance	Plus: Adjustment for residence	Equals: Net earnings by place of residence	Plus: Dividends, interest, and rent	Plus: Personal current transfer receipts	Per capita (dollars)		Population (thousands)	Total employment (thousands)
		Nonfarm	Farm	Total						Personal income	Disposable personal income		
SOUTH DAKOTA													
1958	1 156	648	308	956	26	0	930	153	73	1 762	1 620	656	. . .
1959	1 048	707	140	847	34	0	814	153	82	1 571	1 454	667	. . .
1960	1 290	740	320	1 060	35	0	1 026	179	86	1 889	1 752	683	. . .
1961	1 297	811	246	1 057	39	0	1 019	184	94	1 872	1 723	693	. . .
1962	1 482	865	364	1 229	45	1	1 184	198	100	2 102	1 941	705	. . .
1963	1 429	875	293	1 168	51	1	1 118	205	106	2 018	1 853	708	. . .
1964	1 397	918	211	1 129	50	1	1 080	208	109	1 993	1 853	701	. . .
1965	1 574	950	330	1 279	51	2	1 230	226	119	2 275	2 124	692	. . .
1966	1 701	1 016	388	1 404	64	2	1 342	230	129	2 491	2 311	683	. . .
1967	1 726	1 070	340	1 411	77	3	1 336	236	154	2 573	2 383	671	. . .
1968	1 853	1 162	359	1 521	83	3	1 440	236	177	2 770	2 542	669	. . .
1969	2 024	1 272	357	1 629	90	6	1 546	284	194	3 030	2 760	668	303
1970	2 190	1 371	373	1 744	96	6	1 654	314	222	3 286	3 025	667	305
1971	2 393	1 496	404	1 900	107	6	1 799	338	255	3 564	3 322	671	306
1972	2 770	1 662	564	2 226	121	7	2 111	376	282	4 089	3 813	677	309
1973	3 514	1 878	1 027	2 905	159	7	2 753	433	327	5 175	4 794	679	323
1974	3 527	2 108	688	2 795	184	8	2 620	524	383	5 187	4 735	680	326
1975	3 888	2 302	708	3 010	201	10	2 819	612	456	5 706	5 288	681	326
1976	3 846	2 621	278	2 899	225	12	2 686	659	501	5 600	5 122	687	336
1977	4 376	2 871	445	3 316	238	13	3 091	757	529	6 352	5 887	689	342
1978	5 033	3 266	617	3 883	275	15	3 623	836	574	7 302	6 722	689	355
1979	5 553	3 598	652	4 251	323	16	3 944	961	648	8 059	7 398	689	359
1980	5 564	3 814	137	3 951	344	18	3 625	1 181	758	8 054	7 298	691	353
1981	6 489	4 044	445	4 489	392	14	4 111	1 508	869	9 410	8 556	690	348
1982	6 869	4 171	374	4 545	412	12	4 144	1 758	966	9 946	8 996	691	344
1983	7 133	4 467	255	4 723	441	5	4 287	1 806	1 040	10 293	9 473	693	353
1984	8 103	4 884	689	5 572	491	-2	5 079	1 924	1 100	11 621	10 807	697	362
1985	8 309	5 085	611	5 697	530	-5	5 162	1 978	1 170	11 898	11 040	698	365
1986	8 667	5 312	663	5 976	574	-11	5 390	2 060	1 217	12 452	11 566	696	366
1987	9 141	5 644	844	6 488	618	-19	5 851	2 033	1 257	13 133	12 133	696	381
1988	9 517	6 090	716	6 807	692	-26	6 089	2 114	1 314	13 631	12 583	698	388
1989	10 209	6 486	724	7 210	751	-36	6 423	2 355	1 431	14 653	13 465	697	396
1990	11 206	7 060	1 022	8 082	852	-55	7 175	2 506	1 525	16 075	14 725	697	409
1991	11 727	7 576	895	8 471	924	-68	7 478	2 600	1 649	16 666	15 288	704	420
1992	12 645	8 199	1 076	9 275	994	-84	8 197	2 656	1 792	17 740	16 270	713	431
1993	13 178	8 772	947	9 719	1 062	-98	8 559	2 732	1 887	18 248	16 641	722	442
1994	14 252	9 437	1 212	10 649	1 152	-127	9 371	2 885	1 996	19 503	17 886	731	464
1995	14 471	9 927	642	10 569	1 210	-150	9 209	3 134	2 128	19 610	17 886	738	472
1996	16 085	10 387	1 462	11 849	1 261	-190	10 397	3 441	2 247	21 672	19 845	742	479
1997	16 436	10 950	1 050	12 000	1 327	-189	10 484	3 648	2 305	22 085	19 984	744	485
1998	17 708	11 809	1 169	12 978	1 420	-240	11 318	4 018	2 373	23 736	21 501	746	494
1999	18 622	12 612	1 164	13 775	1 518	-256	12 002	4 149	2 471	24 816	22 359	750	505
2000	19 970	13 449	1 336	14 785	1 606	-277	12 902	4 422	2 646	26 427	23 881	756	516
2001	21 145	14 337	1 141	15 478	1 671	-234	13 573	4 710	2 862	27 860	25 251	759	512
2002	21 383	15 107	487	15 594	1 723	-215	13 656	4 670	3 057	28 058	25 811	762	510
2003	23 340	15 804	1 595	17 399	1 786	-208	15 404	4 793	3 142	30 431	28 389	767	510
2004	24 888	16 706	1 941	18 646	1 891	-225	16 531	5 046	3 312	32 144	29 971	774	519
2005	25 834	17 394	1 731	19 125	1 981	-202	16 942	5 344	3 548	33 117	30 619	780	529
2006	26 587	18 278	788	19 065	2 125	-191	16 750	6 000	3 838	33 718	30 815	789	540
2007	29 034	19 143	1 812	20 955	2 225	-206	18 524	6 432	4 078	36 428	33 189	797	554
2008	31 091	19 966	2 805	22 771	2 338	-219	20 213	6 437	4 440	38 644	35 527	805	566
2009	30 006	20 044	1 718	21 762	2 377	-232	19 152	5 959	4 895	36 935	34 483	812	. . .

. . . = Not available.

Table 21-2. Personal Income and Employment by Region and State—*Continued*

(Millions of dollars, except as noted.)

Region or state and year	Personal income, total	Earnings by place of work			Less: Contributions for government social insurance	Plus: Adjustment for residence	Equals: Net earnings by place of residence	Plus: Dividends, interest, and rent	Plus: Personal current transfer receipts	Per capita (dollars)		Population (thousands)	Total employment (thousands)
		Nonfarm	Farm	Total						Personal income	Disposable personal income		
TENNESSEE													
1958	5 272	4 206	313	4 520	175	27	4 372	531	370	1 519	1 393	3 471	. . .
1959	5 657	4 589	305	4 893	207	23	4 709	562	386	1 606	1 471	3 522	. . .
1960	5 808	4 771	243	5 014	242	23	4 794	610	404	1 625	1 478	3 575	. . .
1961	6 144	4 966	290	5 256	247	22	5 031	654	459	1 696	1 547	3 622	. . .
1962	6 525	5 336	250	5 586	273	22	5 335	713	477	1 777	1 595	3 673	. . .
1963	6 912	5 687	273	5 959	323	22	5 658	751	502	1 859	1 687	3 718	. . .
1964	7 436	6 188	234	6 422	339	21	6 104	807	525	1 972	1 808	3 771	. . .
1965	8 109	6 756	250	7 006	363	21	6 664	867	578	2 135	1 949	3 798	. . .
1966	8 935	7 605	253	7 858	502	21	7 377	922	636	2 338	2 115	3 822	. . .
1967	9 577	8 150	215	8 366	564	35	7 836	978	763	2 482	2 252	3 859	. . .
1968	10 675	9 077	222	9 299	634	33	8 697	1 103	875	2 753	2 467	3 878	. . .
1969	11 524	9 904	256	10 160	659	-155	9 345	1 201	978	2 957	2 617	3 897	1 789
1970	12 505	10 537	269	10 806	695	-155	9 956	1 352	1 197	3 176	2 833	3 937	1 785
1971	13 791	11 586	267	11 853	789	-165	10 899	1 496	1 397	3 439	3 091	4 010	1 817
1972	15 538	13 152	326	13 478	937	-192	12 349	1 650	1 539	3 800	3 412	4 088	1 924
1973	17 731	14 915	493	15 407	1 211	-181	14 015	1 899	1 817	4 284	3 846	4 138	2 025
1974	19 685	16 479	318	16 797	1 383	-191	15 222	2 242	2 221	4 685	4 207	4 202	2 055
1975	21 414	17 341	251	17 591	1 430	-190	15 971	2 509	2 934	5 026	4 559	4 261	1 983
1976	24 115	19 652	372	20 023	1 639	-184	18 199	2 721	3 195	5 570	5 033	4 329	2 052
1977	26 805	22 170	300	22 470	1 846	-241	20 383	3 067	3 355	6 089	5 505	4 402	2 135
1978	30 615	25 574	320	25 893	2 151	-308	23 435	3 515	3 665	6 862	6 169	4 462	2 227
1979	34 248	28 369	342	28 711	2 480	-358	25 874	4 106	4 268	7 555	6 780	4 533	2 279
1980	37 847	30 453	197	30 650	2 675	-424	27 551	5 158	5 138	8 227	7 374	4 600	2 259
1981	42 205	33 181	361	33 542	3 155	-457	29 930	6 448	5 827	9 120	8 173	4 628	2 255
1982	45 048	34 472	303	34 775	3 352	-414	31 009	7 645	6 395	9 696	8 736	4 646	2 217
1983	47 964	37 162	-34	37 129	3 652	-428	33 049	8 044	6 871	10 293	9 296	4 660	2 239
1984	53 490	41 276	412	41 688	4 190	-427	37 070	9 223	7 197	11 413	10 367	4 687	2 344
1985	57 302	44 415	334	44 750	4 590	-444	39 716	9 936	7 650	12 152	10 995	4 715	2 399
1986	61 105	47 717	241	47 958	5 066	-481	42 410	10 484	8 211	12 895	11 679	4 739	2 477
1987	65 786	51 953	307	52 259	5 474	-512	46 273	10 860	8 652	13 754	12 400	4 783	2 578
1988	71 289	56 326	392	56 719	6 097	-525	50 097	11 898	9 295	14 783	13 391	4 822	2 663
1989	76 300	59 467	443	59 911	6 543	-549	52 819	13 257	10 224	15 718	14 183	4 854	2 735
1990	81 121	62 784	444	63 228	6 958	-585	55 685	14 119	11 317	16 574	15 004	4 894	2 777
1991	85 632	65 893	511	66 404	7 394	-582	58 428	14 352	12 853	17 242	15 671	4 967	2 778
1992	93 558	72 238	668	72 906	7 997	-423	64 486	14 605	14 467	18 527	16 844	5 050	2 837
1993	99 315	77 327	595	77 923	8 604	-549	68 770	15 024	15 521	19 331	17 551	5 138	2 943
1994	106 112	83 038	657	83 695	9 380	-644	73 670	16 163	16 278	20 283	18 369	5 231	3 061
1995	113 671	88 794	444	89 238	10 006	-733	78 500	17 360	17 812	21 339	19 297	5 327	3 145
1996	119 901	93 153	394	93 548	10 369	-708	82 471	18 704	18 726	22 136	19 910	5 417	3 195
1997	126 654	98 877	385	99 262	11 016	-912	87 334	19 853	19 467	23 031	20 646	5 499	3 269
1998	136 253	106 829	207	107 036	11 710	-1 067	94 260	21 657	20 337	24 462	21 927	5 570	3 353
1999	143 053	113 453	56	113 509	12 358	-1 247	99 904	21 884	21 265	25 370	22 764	5 639	3 409
2000	152 224	119 802	321	120 123	12 918	-1 416	105 789	23 342	23 093	26 691	24 011	5 703	3 471
2001	158 421	124 317	448	124 765	13 323	-1 472	109 970	23 279	25 172	27 525	24 821	5 755	3 434
2002	163 204	129 802	74	129 876	13 872	-1 444	114 560	21 578	27 066	28 123	25 780	5 803	3 425
2003	169 791	135 537	255	135 793	14 433	-1 404	119 956	21 164	28 672	28 992	26 783	5 857	3 450
2004	178 961	143 788	385	144 173	15 198	-1 494	127 481	21 010	30 469	30 246	28 017	5 917	3 530
2005	187 633	149 716	546	150 262	15 842	-1 242	133 179	21 879	32 575	31 294	28 802	5 996	3 597
2006	200 169	158 423	275	158 697	16 684	-1 138	140 876	25 249	34 043	32 871	30 013	6 089	3 666
2007	210 838	163 830	-167	163 663	17 335	-1 309	145 019	28 556	37 263	34 156	31 100	6 173	3 733
2008	217 373	166 258	143	166 400	17 887	-1 121	147 392	29 342	40 639	34 833	31 976	6 240	3 760
2009	214 633	159 335	202	159 537	17 315	-649	141 573	27 882	45 178	34 089	31 964	6 296	. . .

. . . = Not available.

Table 21-2. Personal Income and Employment by Region and State—*Continued*

(Millions of dollars, except as noted.)

Region or state and year	Personal income, total	Derivation of personal income								Per capita (dollars)		Population (thousands)	Total employment (thousands)
		Earnings by place of work			Less: Contributions for government social insurance	Plus: Adjustment for residence	Equals: Net earnings by place of residence	Plus: Dividends, interest, and rent	Plus: Personal current transfer receipts	Personal income	Disposable personal income		
		Nonfarm	Farm	Total									
TEXAS													
1958	17 399	13 629	1 058	14 687	472	14	14 229	2 282	888	1 881	1 697	9 252	. . .
1959	18 411	14 502	992	15 495	567	14	14 942	2 517	951	1 958	1 765	9 405	. . .
1960	18 913	14 976	914	15 890	677	15	15 228	2 687	998	1 965	1 764	9 624	. . .
1961	19 964	15 638	1 078	16 716	695	15	16 036	2 806	1 122	2 033	1 824	9 820	. . .
1962	20 965	16 567	938	17 505	748	15	16 772	2 971	1 222	2 085	1 866	10 053	. . .
1963	21 932	17 491	769	18 260	831	16	17 444	3 166	1 321	2 159	1 930	10 159	. . .
1964	23 502	18 914	716	19 630	877	16	18 770	3 361	1 371	2 288	2 079	10 270	. . .
1965	25 263	20 260	853	21 113	929	18	20 201	3 564	1 498	2 434	2 206	10 378	. . .
1966	27 561	22 499	907	23 406	1 259	15	22 162	3 769	1 630	2 627	2 358	10 492	. . .
1967	30 103	24 846	768	25 614	1 458	13	24 169	3 966	1 969	2 840	2 543	10 599	. . .
1968	33 593	27 825	901	28 726	1 630	12	27 108	4 124	2 360	3 105	2 747	10 819	. . .
1969	37 151	31 081	927	32 008	2 013	-85	29 910	4 597	2 644	3 364	2 944	11 045	5 005
1970	40 772	33 523	1 168	34 690	2 150	-96	32 445	5 187	3 139	3 628	3 216	11 237	5 045
1971	44 202	36 336	1 015	37 351	2 400	-101	34 850	5 685	3 667	3 840	3 444	11 510	5 123
1972	49 088	40 359	1 257	41 616	2 784	-127	38 705	6 267	4 116	4 175	3 703	11 759	5 334
1973	55 998	45 496	2 144	47 641	3 610	-154	43 876	7 172	4 950	4 659	4 144	12 019	5 608
1974	63 426	52 252	1 156	53 408	4 251	-131	49 027	8 494	5 904	5 170	4 556	12 268	5 822
1975	72 121	58 921	1 314	60 236	4 722	-128	55 385	9 356	7 380	5 738	5 123	12 568	5 938
1976	81 892	68 055	1 292	69 347	5 514	-93	63 741	10 100	8 051	6 347	5 630	12 903	6 207
1977	91 596	77 067	1 280	78 347	6 290	-306	71 751	11 279	8 565	6 943	6 107	13 192	6 521
1978	106 034	89 983	1 032	91 015	7 495	-427	83 093	13 396	9 545	7 856	6 920	13 498	6 900
1979	122 649	103 481	1 741	105 222	9 039	-432	95 751	16 010	10 888	8 832	7 686	13 887	7 215
1980	141 516	118 927	621	119 548	10 479	-541	108 527	20 263	12 726	9 870	8 553	14 338	7 496
1981	166 934	138 053	1 966	140 019	13 060	-355	126 604	25 864	14 466	11 320	9 712	14 746	7 900
1982	183 447	149 432	1 354	150 786	14 451	-426	135 910	31 065	16 472	11 965	10 384	15 331	8 074
1983	194 505	155 679	1 740	157 418	15 035	-406	141 977	33 923	18 604	12 348	10 917	15 752	8 064
1984	214 133	171 040	1 625	172 665	16 889	-466	155 311	39 038	19 784	13 377	11 896	16 007	8 434
1985	229 610	182 376	1 495	183 871	18 296	-493	165 082	43 384	21 143	14 110	12 546	16 273	8 674
1986	234 878	185 148	1 272	186 421	18 421	-450	167 550	44 154	23 174	14 182	12 752	16 561	8 514
1987	240 237	188 846	2 089	190 935	18 488	-446	172 001	43 868	24 368	14 453	12 950	16 622	8 723
1988	254 091	200 484	2 327	202 811	20 286	-449	182 076	46 405	25 609	15 245	13 733	16 667	8 880
1989	271 673	212 348	2 244	214 592	21 619	-457	192 517	51 006	28 150	16 165	14 479	16 807	9 005
1990	294 401	229 576	3 049	232 625	22 974	-490	209 162	53 757	31 482	17 260	15 463	17 057	9 243
1991	309 037	241 671	2 773	244 444	24 760	-568	219 116	54 978	34 943	17 763	15 999	17 398	9 404
1992	333 257	260 259	3 376	263 635	26 382	-588	236 665	55 229	41 363	18 765	16 977	17 760	9 483
1993	352 573	277 201	3 999	281 200	28 000	-610	252 590	55 718	44 265	19 413	17 542	18 162	9 781
1994	374 279	293 981	3 448	297 429	29 983	-671	266 775	59 933	47 572	20 161	18 209	18 564	10 098
1995	399 463	313 792	2 784	316 576	31 979	-759	283 838	64 109	51 516	21 070	18 995	18 959	10 440
1996	430 511	338 895	2 412	341 307	34 009	-833	306 465	69 014	55 032	22 260	19 942	19 340	10 738
1997	470 065	373 789	3 065	376 855	37 080	-972	338 803	73 715	57 547	23 812	21 188	19 740	11 165
1998	511 509	410 690	2 840	413 531	40 424	-1 064	372 043	80 691	58 775	25 376	22 474	20 158	11 570
1999	542 720	440 724	4 279	445 002	42 928	-1 107	400 968	81 090	60 662	26 399	23 400	20 558	11 800
2000	597 041	487 373	3 335	490 708	46 198	-1 203	443 307	89 401	64 333	28 504	25 166	20 946	12 151
2001	622 219	509 134	3 965	513 100	48 530	-1 383	463 187	88 489	70 543	29 167	25 851	21 333	12 211
2002	628 277	513 046	3 945	516 991	49 122	-1 381	466 489	84 040	77 747	28 938	26 243	21 711	12 263
2003	652 610	531 284	5 046	536 331	51 463	-1 370	483 497	85 919	83 194	29 586	27 104	22 058	12 358
2004	696 800	570 510	5 316	575 826	54 048	-1 423	520 355	88 889	87 556	31 082	28 605	22 418	12 617
2005	756 686	611 207	5 005	616 212	57 671	-1 532	557 009	103 299	96 378	33 185	30 175	22 802	13 012
2006	824 281	664 459	3 256	667 715	61 533	-1 712	604 471	116 808	103 002	35 272	31 832	23 369	13 500
2007	878 139	697 809	3 560	701 369	65 588	-1 989	633 793	131 136	113 210	36 838	33 138	23 838	14 019
2008	918 921	731 961	2 205	734 166	68 929	-2 138	663 099	131 047	124 775	37 809	34 281	24 304	14 470
2009	904 166	715 701	1 161	716 862	68 054	-2 081	646 728	118 955	138 484	36 484	33 818	24 782	. . .

. . . = Not available.

Table 21-2. Personal Income and Employment by Region and State—*Continued*

(Millions of dollars, except as noted.)

Region or state and year	Personal income, total	Derivation of personal income								Per capita (dollars)		Population (thousands)	Total employment (thousands)
		Earnings by place of work			Less: Contributions for government social insurance	Plus: Adjustment for residence	Equals: Net earnings by place of residence	Plus: Dividends, interest, and rent	Plus: Personal current transfer receipts	Personal income	Disposable personal income		
		Nonfarm	Farm	Total									
UTAH													
1958	1 591	1 308	53	1 360	54	0	1 307	189	95	1 883	1 708	845	...
1959	1 710	1 415	49	1 464	62	1	1 402	207	101	1 965	1 770	870	...
1960	1 827	1 514	43	1 557	75	1	1 483	239	105	2 030	1 826	900	...
1961	1 951	1 628	34	1 662	79	1	1 583	250	117	2 084	1 869	936	...
1962	2 131	1 770	53	1 822	87	1	1 736	273	122	2 225	2 002	958	...
1963	2 214	1 867	40	1 907	105	1	1 803	279	132	2 273	2 041	974	...
1964	2 326	1 952	29	1 982	106	1	1 876	309	141	2 378	2 167	978	...
1965	2 462	2 043	46	2 089	109	1	1 982	329	152	2 485	2 266	991	...
1966	2 615	2 199	48	2 247	144	1	2 105	349	162	2 592	2 353	1 009	...
1967	2 763	2 311	62	2 373	159	1	2 216	356	191	2 711	2 454	1 019	...
1968	2 974	2 497	66	2 563	175	1	2 390	364	220	2 890	2 587	1 029	444
1969	3 251	2 693	74	2 767	176	2	2 594	410	248	3 105	2 746	1 047	455
1970	3 611	2 959	78	3 037	191	2	2 848	465	299	3 389	3 032	1 066	455
1971	4 016	3 279	77	3 356	218	3	3 140	523	352	3 649	3 289	1 101	467
1972	4 505	3 682	88	3 770	260	5	3 515	588	402	3 971	3 560	1 135	494
1973	5 045	4 137	130	4 267	339	8	3 936	637	472	4 316	3 866	1 169	523
1974	5 680	4 688	96	4 784	396	11	4 400	743	538	4 738	4 238	1 199	545
1975	6 384	5 210	67	5 278	433	14	4 859	851	673	5 173	4 686	1 234	553
1976	7 322	6 012	74	6 086	502	17	5 601	990	730	5 755	5 152	1 272	580
1977	8 351	6 910	64	6 974	575	22	6 420	1 144	787	6 344	5 667	1 316	613
1978	9 625	7 973	72	8 045	678	27	7 395	1 354	876	7 055	6 292	1 364	651
1979	11 034	9 041	82	9 124	810	36	8 349	1 686	998	7 792	6 922	1 416	678
1980	12 506	9 997	60	10 057	897	52	9 212	2 118	1 176	8 492	7 575	1 473	687
1981	14 165	11 196	42	11 238	1 087	53	10 204	2 583	1 377	9 347	8 298	1 515	697
1982	15 510	11 898	46	11 944	1 175	53	10 822	3 104	1 584	9 953	8 832	1 558	707
1983	16 756	12 647	36	12 684	1 267	42	11 459	3 571	1 726	10 506	9 440	1 595	719
1984	18 448	14 056	57	14 112	1 448	38	12 702	3 966	1 779	11 371	10 264	1 622	761
1985	19 593	14 929	57	14 985	1 578	39	13 446	4 213	1 933	11 926	10 726	1 643	789
1986	20 490	15 558	87	15 645	1 658	34	14 021	4 378	2 091	12 322	11 072	1 663	801
1987	21 231	16 243	131	16 374	1 723	24	14 675	4 315	2 241	12 652	11 315	1 678	830
1988	22 236	17 339	210	17 549	1 926	23	15 646	4 256	2 334	13 162	11 772	1 689	865
1989	23 782	18 481	205	18 686	2 092	21	16 615	4 592	2 575	13 941	12 482	1 706	897
1990	25 704	20 190	253	20 443	2 363	16	18 096	4 783	2 825	14 847	13 131	1 731	938
1991	27 549	21 841	233	22 074	2 595	11	19 489	4 936	3 124	15 479	13 772	1 780	961
1992	29 636	23 697	280	23 976	2 812	6	21 170	4 999	3 466	16 135	14 350	1 837	979
1993	31 978	25 634	301	25 935	3 056	7	22 886	5 333	3 759	16 845	14 945	1 898	1 026
1994	34 848	28 027	220	28 247	3 371	6	24 883	6 092	3 873	17 775	15 691	1 960	1 102
1995	37 795	30 504	166	30 670	3 680	0	26 991	6 614	4 191	18 765	16 497	2 014	1 150
1996	41 151	33 089	173	33 263	3 926	0	29 337	7 381	4 433	19 899	17 455	2 068	1 218
1997	44 518	35 950	198	36 148	4 222	0	31 926	7 986	4 606	21 001	18 379	2 120	1 270
1998	48 057	38 877	233	39 110	4 491	-6	34 613	8 635	4 810	22 188	19 418	2 166	1 309
1999	50 555	41 301	240	41 541	4 719	-2	36 820	8 648	5 087	22 943	20 038	2 203	1 338
2000	55 025	44 774	205	44 980	5 031	2	39 950	9 610	5 465	24 517	21 454	2 244	1 378
2001	58 505	47 623	315	47 938	5 285	15	42 668	9 837	6 000	25 534	22 502	2 291	1 380
2002	59 874	48 842	197	49 039	5 419	9	43 629	9 708	6 537	25 648	23 061	2 334	1 390
2003	61 487	50 325	226	50 551	5 661	15	44 905	9 649	6 933	25 835	23 384	2 380	1 401
2004	65 453	53 760	317	54 077	6 100	23	48 000	10 130	7 323	26 837	24 325	2 439	1 453
2005	71 533	57 905	287	58 192	6 609	34	51 618	11 979	7 937	28 617	25 555	2 500	1 517
2006	78 382	63 581	167	63 748	7 271	47	56 524	13 227	8 631	30 337	26 850	2 584	1 597
2007	84 709	68 173	203	68 376	7 767	36	60 645	14 880	9 184	31 800	28 020	2 664	1 674
2008	87 411	69 699	233	69 933	7 974	41	62 000	15 288	10 124	32 050	28 585	2 727	1 702
2009	85 975	67 859	150	68 009	7 826	31	60 214	14 175	11 586	30 875	28 188	2 785	...

. . . = Not available.

Table 21-2. Personal Income and Employment by Region and State—*Continued*

(Millions of dollars, except as noted.)

Region or state and year	Personal income, total	Earnings by place of work			Less: Contributions for government social insurance	Plus: Adjustment for residence	Equals: Net earnings by place of residence	Plus: Dividends, interest, and rent	Plus: Personal current transfer receipts	Per capita (dollars)		Population (thousands)	Total employment (thousands)
		Nonfarm	Farm	Total						Personal income	Disposable personal income		
VERMONT													
1958	653	493	54	547	19	-5	523	77	52	1 718	1 553	380	. . .
1959	703	542	50	592	22	-5	564	83	55	1 816	1 634	387	. . .
1960	744	571	56	626	27	-5	594	90	59	1 912	1 718	389	. . .
1961	774	584	55	639	28	-5	606	101	67	1 985	1 787	390	. . .
1962	813	624	46	670	31	-5	634	109	70	2 068	1 863	393	. . .
1963	843	653	43	696	36	-5	655	114	74	2 124	1 893	397	. . .
1964	903	693	49	742	38	-5	698	128	77	2 264	2 034	399	. . .
1965	990	770	45	814	41	-7	765	144	81	2 451	2 218	404	. . .
1966	1 124	883	58	941	58	-10	873	164	87	2 722	2 426	413	. . .
1967	1 217	962	46	1 008	71	-10	927	183	107	2 878	2 562	423	. . .
1968	1 342	1 050	50	1 100	74	-11	1 015	201	126	3 121	2 750	430	. . .
1969	1 477	1 167	58	1 224	83	-27	1 114	219	144	3 380	2 931	437	203
1970	1 618	1 256	62	1 318	89	-27	1 202	244	172	3 625	3 162	446	205
1971	1 748	1 336	61	1 397	98	-24	1 275	268	205	3 848	3 451	454	206
1972	1 928	1 467	68	1 535	111	-21	1 403	295	230	4 163	3 666	463	211
1973	2 122	1 626	72	1 697	141	-20	1 537	323	262	4 528	4 035	469	220
1974	2 297	1 736	59	1 795	155	-17	1 623	359	315	4 855	4 327	473	222
1975	2 497	1 825	61	1 887	162	-11	1 713	383	401	5 203	4 659	480	220
1976	2 788	2 055	78	2 133	184	-6	1 944	413	431	5 747	5 176	485	228
1977	3 028	2 259	66	2 326	203	-2	2 120	467	441	6 153	5 495	492	236
1978	3 478	2 635	95	2 730	244	-2	2 484	527	467	6 979	6 227	498	252
1979	3 922	2 955	105	3 060	284	5	2 782	610	530	7 756	6 874	506	261
1980	4 407	3 213	108	3 321	310	14	3 025	755	627	8 599	7 593	513	266
1981	4 975	3 527	124	3 651	365	17	3 303	949	723	9 650	8 491	516	270
1982	5 359	3 708	123	3 831	392	23	3 462	1 092	805	10 324	9 175	519	271
1983	5 719	4 050	83	4 133	431	21	3 724	1 132	863	10 930	9 734	523	277
1984	6 308	4 476	84	4 560	490	27	4 098	1 321	889	11 977	10 697	527	289
1985	6 820	4 920	101	5 020	548	29	4 500	1 392	927	12 867	11 426	530	300
1986	7 333	5 356	99	5 455	602	32	4 886	1 493	955	13 731	12 135	534	311
1987	7 972	5 925	124	6 049	656	39	5 433	1 569	970	14 755	12 933	540	320
1988	8 698	6 507	122	6 629	747	45	5 927	1 747	1 024	15 822	13 939	550	334
1989	9 590	7 019	123	7 141	808	48	6 381	2 083	1 125	17 195	15 097	558	341
1990	9 965	7 275	115	7 390	883	48	6 555	2 155	1 255	17 643	15 527	565	341
1991	10 161	7 363	104	7 467	907	55	6 615	2 172	1 373	17 869	15 835	569	334
1992	10 849	7 842	177	8 019	959	63	7 123	2 172	1 554	18 941	16 841	573	342
1993	11 235	8 245	128	8 373	1 008	72	7 437	2 175	1 623	19 446	17 272	578	349
1994	11 826	8 611	129	8 740	1 066	86	7 760	2 347	1 718	20 255	18 028	584	359
1995	12 403	8 948	100	9 048	1 125	100	8 023	2 520	1 859	21 057	18 752	589	362
1996	13 124	9 412	147	9 559	1 171	116	8 503	2 701	1 920	22 106	19 561	594	367
1997	13 837	9 902	110	10 012	1 225	139	8 926	2 891	2 021	23 168	20 326	597	373
1998	14 963	10 646	136	10 782	1 294	165	9 653	3 206	2 104	24 921	21 808	600	383
1999	15 884	11 448	146	11 594	1 375	186	10 405	3 225	2 253	26 268	22 964	605	391
2000	17 189	12 417	150	12 567	1 469	219	11 317	3 445	2 427	28 183	24 523	610	401
2001	18 047	13 047	148	13 194	1 561	232	11 865	3 520	2 661	29 481	25 757	612	405
2002	18 458	13 494	113	13 607	1 610	238	12 236	3 377	2 846	30 016	26 744	615	407
2003	19 126	14 019	145	14 164	1 657	268	12 776	3 370	2 979	31 020	28 015	617	409
2004	20 231	14 868	190	15 058	1 741	292	13 609	3 505	3 117	32 729	29 623	618	415
2005	20 694	15 404	200	15 604	1 829	321	14 097	3 201	3 396	33 441	29 910	619	420
2006	22 340	16 091	119	16 210	1 910	357	14 657	3 937	3 746	36 033	32 094	620	424
2007	23 413	16 546	221	16 768	2 002	383	15 149	4 225	4 039	37 735	33 385	620	429
2008	24 034	17 001	161	17 161	2 093	382	15 450	4 260	4 324	38 700	34 443	621	435
2009	23 939	16 568	75	16 643	2 063	356	14 937	4 088	4 915	38 503	35 232	622	. . .

. . . = Not available.

Table 21-2. Personal Income and Employment by Region and State—Continued

(Millions of dollars, except as noted.)

Region or state and year	Personal income, total	Earnings by place of work			Less: Contributions for government social insurance	Plus: Adjustment for residence	Equals: Net earnings by place of residence	Plus: Dividends, interest, and rent	Plus: Personal current transfer receipts	Per capita (dollars)		Population (thousands)	Total employment (thousands)
		Nonfarm	Farm	Total						Personal income	Disposable personal income		
VIRGINIA													
1958	6 872	5 383	258	5 641	184	361	5 818	723	331	1 756	1 579	3 914	...
1959	7 327	5 840	192	6 033	234	386	6 185	781	361	1 854	1 662	3 951	...
1960	7 598	5 992	212	6 203	268	432	6 367	859	373	1 906	1 693	3 986	...
1961	8 089	6 317	222	6 538	284	463	6 717	944	428	1 975	1 760	4 095	...
1962	8 741	6 829	219	7 047	317	512	7 242	1 046	452	2 091	1 853	4 180	...
1963	9 353	7 409	133	7 542	369	565	7 738	1 130	485	2 187	1 921	4 276	...
1964	10 338	8 118	219	8 337	383	615	8 569	1 258	512	2 373	2 126	4 357	...
1965	11 158	8 710	205	8 915	402	704	9 217	1 381	560	2 529	2 254	4 411	...
1966	12 078	9 592	153	9 745	544	779	9 981	1 486	610	2 710	2 395	4 456	...
1967	13 230	10 380	199	10 579	630	933	10 882	1 614	734	2 935	2 589	4 508	...
1968	14 683	11 639	176	11 816	696	1 008	12 128	1 701	855	3 221	2 819	4 558	...
1969	16 428	13 208	213	13 421	800	956	13 577	1 872	979	3 560	3 053	4 614	2 148
1970	17 669	14 218	213	14 431	871	851	14 412	2 078	1 180	3 792	3 267	4 660	2 158
1971	19 443	15 646	193	15 839	1 000	877	15 716	2 314	1 413	4 091	3 561	4 753	2 196
1972	21 661	17 463	254	17 717	1 167	933	17 483	2 556	1 622	4 486	3 850	4 828	2 263
1973	24 393	19 682	355	20 037	1 484	1 005	19 557	2 898	1 938	4 971	4 300	4 907	2 384
1974	27 306	21 865	316	22 181	1 701	1 134	21 615	3 390	2 301	5 485	4 711	4 978	2 451
1975	30 136	23 552	266	23 818	1 821	1 394	23 391	3 797	2 948	5 960	5 244	5 056	2 425
1976	33 614	26 391	237	26 628	2 071	1 617	26 174	4 220	3 220	6 549	5 729	5 133	2 501
1977	37 443	29 522	169	29 691	2 302	1 857	29 246	4 744	3 454	7 193	6 256	5 206	2 585
1978	42 408	33 303	291	33 594	2 621	2 189	33 162	5 428	3 817	8 025	6 940	5 284	2 698
1979	47 654	37 198	157	37 355	3 050	2 582	36 887	6 385	4 382	8 950	7 730	5 325	2 767
1980	54 258	41 172	69	41 241	3 388	3 154	41 007	8 041	5 209	10 107	8 732	5 368	2 797
1981	61 121	45 598	272	45 870	4 045	3 367	45 192	9 915	6 014	11 227	9 636	5 444	2 812
1982	66 437	49 082	122	49 204	4 406	3 431	48 229	11 636	6 572	12 095	10 463	5 493	2 824
1983	72 304	53 697	44	53 742	4 947	3 424	52 219	12 976	7 109	12 993	11 367	5 565	2 897
1984	80 697	60 541	327	60 868	5 704	3 529	58 694	14 483	7 521	14 298	12 590	5 644	3 041
1985	87 350	66 282	229	66 511	6 438	3 645	63 718	15 594	8 038	15 284	13 376	5 715	3 181
1986	94 082	71 980	276	72 256	7 281	3 792	68 768	16 796	8 519	16 188	14 172	5 812	3 316
1987	101 980	78 939	373	79 312	7 982	3 993	75 323	17 809	8 848	17 191	14 933	5 932	3 480
1988	111 336	86 190	527	86 717	9 038	4 364	82 044	19 843	9 448	18 442	16 118	6 037	3 558
1989	120 041	91 757	644	92 400	9 809	4 587	87 178	22 523	10 339	19 614	17 059	6 120	3 655
1990	126 278	95 518	688	96 206	10 388	5 338	91 156	23 901	11 221	20 312	17 735	6 217	3 700
1991	132 030	99 083	623	99 706	10 867	5 859	94 698	24 942	12 390	20 953	18 403	6 301	3 642
1992	140 101	105 197	674	105 871	11 472	6 308	100 707	25 454	13 940	21 842	19 232	6 414	3 657
1993	147 091	110 419	546	110 965	12 070	6 737	105 632	26 708	14 751	22 596	19 852	6 510	3 730
1994	155 163	116 047	645	116 692	12 781	6 719	110 629	28 918	15 616	23 534	20 618	6 593	3 813
1995	162 498	121 488	569	122 057	13 319	6 926	115 665	29 958	16 876	24 360	21 312	6 671	3 903
1996	171 165	128 368	571	128 939	13 998	6 386	121 327	32 022	17 816	25 354	22 081	6 751	3 983
1997	182 303	137 508	429	137 937	14 999	6 947	129 885	33 982	18 435	26 695	23 134	6 829	4 082
1998	194 597	147 961	422	148 383	16 087	6 618	138 914	36 599	19 084	28 199	24 083	6 901	4 156
1999	207 326	159 334	326	159 659	17 312	7 986	150 334	36 839	20 153	29 617	25 054	7 000	4 247
2000	224 788	174 946	564	175 510	18 671	6 050	162 888	40 295	21 604	31 640	26 780	7 105	4 374
2001	239 103	187 091	480	187 572	19 703	5 758	173 627	41 440	24 036	33 249	28 301	7 191	4 410
2002	245 782	191 552	366	191 918	20 326	7 350	178 942	41 227	25 613	33 745	29 451	7 284	4 403
2003	257 927	202 136	288	202 424	21 273	7 504	188 655	41 965	27 308	34 979	30 793	7 374	4 453
2004	275 167	218 707	545	219 252	23 184	7 551	203 618	42 742	28 807	36 842	32 506	7 469	4 575
2005	294 173	233 538	594	234 131	24 771	7 532	216 892	46 016	31 266	38 892	33 965	7 564	4 693
2006	315 565	246 380	298	246 679	26 362	8 112	228 429	53 067	34 069	41 267	35 887	7 647	4 772
2007	333 167	257 125	210	257 335	27 333	8 653	238 655	58 014	36 498	43 158	37 359	7 720	4 866
2008	343 580	263 168	277	263 445	28 342	9 116	244 219	59 198	40 163	44 075	38 596	7 795	4 916
2009	345 841	263 410	277	263 688	28 721	9 901	244 867	55 977	44 996	43 874	39 502	7 883	...

. . . = Not available.

Table 21-2. Personal Income and Employment by Region and State—*Continued*

(Millions of dollars, except as noted.)

Region or state and year	Personal income, total	Earnings by place of work			Less: Contributions for government social insurance	Plus: Adjustment for residence	Equals: Net earnings by place of residence	Plus: Dividends, interest, and rent	Plus: Personal current transfer receipts	Per capita (dollars)		Population (thousands)	Total employment (thousands)
		Nonfarm	Farm	Total						Personal income	Disposable personal income		
WASHINGTON													
1958	6 270	5 026	221	5 246	239	16	5 023	778	469	2 261	2 019	2 773	. . .
1959	6 668	5 380	232	5 612	281	21	5 351	833	484	2 364	2 122	2 821	. . .
1960	6 901	5 523	253	5 777	313	25	5 489	898	514	2 417	2 163	2 855	. . .
1961	7 248	5 802	244	6 046	327	29	5 747	938	563	2 515	2 248	2 882	. . .
1962	7 832	6 304	268	6 572	357	34	6 248	1 017	567	2 662	2 375	2 942	. . .
1963	8 024	6 445	271	6 716	395	42	6 363	1 063	598	2 715	2 419	2 955	. . .
1964	8 406	6 742	248	6 990	394	51	6 647	1 128	631	2 839	2 582	2 961	. . .
1965	9 066	7 247	268	7 515	417	62	7 159	1 244	663	3 056	2 770	2 967	. . .
1966	10 272	8 376	362	8 738	593	71	8 216	1 367	689	3 360	3 011	3 057	. . .
1967	11 255	9 215	325	9 540	687	82	8 935	1 491	829	3 546	3 163	3 174	. . .
1968	12 515	10 273	339	10 612	769	99	9 942	1 622	951	3 827	3 390	3 270	. . .
1969	13 657	11 159	398	11 557	910	83	10 730	1 850	1 077	4 085	3 582	3 343	1 539
1970	14 316	11 363	346	11 709	913	65	10 861	2 020	1 435	4 189	3 746	3 417	1 491
1971	15 031	11 719	391	12 110	981	63	11 193	2 167	1 671	4 361	3 937	3 447	1 457
1972	16 246	12 684	506	13 191	1 117	73	12 147	2 315	1 784	4 713	4 210	3 447	1 481
1973	18 374	14 340	756	15 095	1 438	90	13 747	2 616	2 011	5 284	4 705	3 477	1 558
1974	20 905	16 179	890	17 069	1 659	133	15 543	3 010	2 352	5 892	5 253	3 548	1 622
1975	23 648	18 131	906	19 037	1 840	200	17 397	3 343	2 907	6 535	5 849	3 619	1 659
1976	26 441	20 770	754	21 523	2 140	247	19 631	3 654	3 157	7 165	6 397	3 691	1 739
1977	29 412	23 593	605	24 197	2 459	227	21 965	4 143	3 304	7 797	6 943	3 772	1 815
1978	34 276	27 805	754	28 559	2 977	269	25 851	4 841	3 584	8 820	7 772	3 886	1 939
1979	39 514	32 244	739	32 983	3 567	322	29 738	5 764	4 011	9 847	8 601	4 013	2 058
1980	44 912	35 472	861	36 333	3 862	387	32 858	7 147	4 907	10 810	9 464	4 155	2 105
1981	50 126	38 727	864	39 591	4 531	431	35 491	8 932	5 703	11 834	10 333	4 236	2 119
1982	53 177	40 181	766	40 947	4 752	463	36 658	10 103	6 416	12 435	11 071	4 277	2 094
1983	56 522	42 181	1 065	43 246	5 114	484	38 615	10 897	7 010	13 144	11 826	4 300	2 140
1984	60 690	45 107	1 023	46 129	5 648	541	41 022	12 298	7 370	13 972	12 629	4 344	2 214
1985	64 324	48 033	750	48 783	6 088	584	43 279	13 118	7 927	14 619	13 180	4 400	2 277
1986	68 669	51 408	1 057	52 465	6 586	607	46 486	13 777	8 407	15 422	13 933	4 453	2 351
1987	72 918	55 094	1 088	56 182	7 026	658	49 814	14 249	8 855	16 090	14 426	4 532	2 470
1988	79 133	60 430	1 030	61 460	7 929	749	54 280	15 220	9 633	17 055	15 351	4 640	2 600
1989	87 357	65 765	1 157	66 922	8 665	834	59 091	17 687	10 579	18 405	16 389	4 746	2 718
1990	96 282	73 179	1 211	74 390	9 829	927	65 488	19 167	11 626	19 637	17 449	4 903	2 842
1991	103 441	78 736	1 283	80 019	10 701	994	70 312	19 970	13 159	20 583	18 396	5 026	2 877
1992	111 373	85 762	1 544	87 306	11 692	1 093	76 707	20 149	14 517	21 581	19 313	5 161	2 907
1993	116 871	89 601	1 746	91 347	12 200	1 187	80 334	20 998	15 538	22 139	19 871	5 279	2 951
1994	123 528	94 104	1 431	95 535	12 897	1 232	83 869	23 306	16 353	22 981	20 572	5 375	3 060
1995	130 328	98 512	1 470	99 982	13 497	1 382	87 867	25 013	17 448	23 778	21 252	5 481	3 101
1996	140 803	105 499	1 945	107 444	14 110	1 582	94 916	27 611	18 277	25 280	22 410	5 570	3 192
1997	151 795	114 742	1 553	116 295	14 894	1 734	103 134	29 713	18 948	26 749	23 519	5 675	3 298
1998	166 287	126 773	1 734	128 507	16 338	1 840	114 009	32 579	19 699	28 821	25 055	5 770	3 379
1999	178 319	138 589	1 501	140 089	17 094	1 955	124 950	32 459	20 911	30 521	26 111	5 843	3 442
2000	191 562	148 218	1 736	149 954	18 500	2 199	133 653	35 568	22 341	32 407	27 951	5 911	3 523
2001	197 279	151 843	1 566	153 410	18 301	2 359	137 467	34 737	25 075	32 947	28 850	5 988	3 520
2002	200 482	153 700	1 642	155 342	18 609	2 446	139 178	34 678	26 626	33 104	29 759	6 056	3 479
2003	206 947	158 527	2 087	160 615	19 411	2 481	143 684	35 473	27 790	33 852	30 730	6 113	3 509
2004	222 379	166 648	2 082	168 730	20 666	2 512	150 576	43 572	28 230	35 959	32 811	6 184	3 582
2005	230 002	175 377	1 875	177 252	21 963	2 630	157 918	42 281	29 803	36 734	33 207	6 261	3 684
2006	252 023	189 228	1 965	191 194	23 325	2 796	170 664	49 329	32 030	39 550	35 526	6 372	3 796
2007	271 008	201 357	2 264	203 622	24 515	3 076	182 183	54 525	34 300	41 919	37 343	6 465	3 926
2008	280 678	207 550	2 554	210 104	25 507	3 073	187 669	55 549	37 459	42 747	38 447	6 566	4 012
2009	278 236	204 063	1 734	205 798	25 305	2 911	183 404	51 160	43 673	41 751	38 472	6 664	. . .

. . . = Not available.

Table 21-2. Personal Income and Employment by Region and State—*Continued*

(Millions of dollars, except as noted.)

Region or state and year	Personal income, total	Derivation of personal income								Per capita (dollars)		Population (thousands)	Total employment (thousands)
		Earnings by place of work			Less: Contributions for government social insurance	Plus: Adjustment for residence	Equals: Net earnings by place of residence	Plus: Dividends, interest, and rent	Plus: Personal current transfer receipts	Personal income	Disposable personal income		
		Nonfarm	Farm	Total									
WEST VIRGINIA													
1958	2 921	2 421	58	2 479	114	-21	2 344	275	301	1 583	1 444	1 845	...
1959	3 014	2 526	45	2 571	135	-20	2 415	296	303	1 625	1 470	1 855	...
1960	3 062	2 566	49	2 615	155	-20	2 440	318	304	1 653	1 484	1 853	...
1961	3 101	2 557	42	2 599	153	-20	2 426	331	344	1 696	1 524	1 828	...
1962	3 238	2 673	31	2 703	168	-19	2 517	354	367	1 790	1 609	1 809	...
1963	3 378	2 798	24	2 821	186	-18	2 618	381	379	1 881	1 684	1 796	...
1964	3 601	2 977	23	2 999	173	-17	2 809	407	385	2 004	1 816	1 797	...
1965	3 850	3 180	24	3 205	184	-13	3 008	431	411	2 155	1 957	1 786	...
1966	4 080	3 450	14	3 463	244	-10	3 209	437	434	2 298	2 072	1 775	...
1967	4 329	3 634	28	3 662	268	-8	3 386	451	492	2 447	2 210	1 769	...
1968	4 590	3 854	22	3 876	298	2	3 579	467	544	2 603	2 325	1 763	...
1969	4 875	4 138	31	4 169	324	-79	3 766	510	599	2 792	2 447	1 746	652
1970	5 430	4 547	26	4 573	350	-82	4 141	568	722	3 109	2 753	1 747	660
1971	5 963	4 943	26	4 969	395	-100	4 473	620	871	3 369	2 999	1 770	670
1972	6 601	5 464	31	5 496	455	-114	4 927	676	997	3 673	3 256	1 797	684
1973	7 238	5 929	45	5 973	567	-117	5 289	763	1 186	4 009	3 579	1 805	700
1974	8 051	6 563	29	6 592	647	-131	5 814	894	1 344	4 438	3 916	1 814	711
1975	9 153	7 398	15	7 412	709	-158	6 545	1 008	1 601	4 973	4 405	1 841	717
1976	10 265	8 407	4	8 411	817	-195	7 400	1 111	1 754	5 468	4 820	1 877	739
1977	11 484	9 498	-1	9 497	915	-226	8 355	1 257	1 872	6 026	5 322	1 906	758
1978	12 803	10 624	13	10 637	1 056	-263	9 317	1 406	2 080	6 667	5 907	1 920	781
1979	14 297	11 708	18	11 726	1 211	-273	10 242	1 620	2 435	7 373	6 490	1 939	790
1980	15 739	12 464	9	12 474	1 297	-301	10 876	2 033	2 830	8 066	7 077	1 951	782
1981	17 132	13 171	-22	13 149	1 477	-279	11 394	2 542	3 197	8 767	7 705	1 954	762
1982	18 209	13 578	-28	13 550	1 563	-233	11 754	2 949	3 506	9 340	8 259	1 950	740
1983	18 625	13 370	-15	13 355	1 571	-192	11 592	3 147	3 886	9 575	8 516	1 945	722
1984	19 961	14 300	24	14 324	1 737	-140	12 447	3 546	3 969	10 355	9 250	1 928	732
1985	20 690	14 730	22	14 752	1 828	-119	12 805	3 742	4 143	10 851	9 684	1 907	732
1986	21 105	14 818	48	14 866	1 922	-92	12 852	3 852	4 401	11 212	10 041	1 882	731
1987	21 584	15 206	8	15 214	1 992	-26	13 195	3 865	4 524	11 619	10 395	1 858	738
1988	22 935	16 277	6	16 283	2 180	6	14 109	4 056	4 770	12 532	11 290	1 830	751
1989	24 204	16 831	34	16 866	2 282	86	14 670	4 511	5 024	13 398	11 978	1 807	757
1990	25 878	18 101	47	18 148	2 472	71	15 747	4 744	5 387	14 436	12 908	1 793	778
1991	27 135	18 851	38	18 889	2 637	45	16 297	4 775	6 063	15 086	13 544	1 799	779
1992	29 050	19 922	63	19 985	2 817	110	17 278	4 819	6 953	16 081	14 513	1 806	789
1993	30 078	20 721	65	20 786	3 039	114	17 862	4 812	7 405	16 549	14 937	1 818	801
1994	31 436	21 861	61	21 922	3 184	161	18 899	5 031	7 507	17 269	15 538	1 820	822
1995	32 493	22 598	24	22 622	3 328	207	19 501	5 262	7 730	17 817	16 015	1 824	838
1996	33 845	23 203	9	23 212	3 428	221	20 005	5 695	8 145	18 567	16 662	1 823	847
1997	35 242	24 079	0	24 080	3 522	374	20 931	5 981	8 329	19 373	17 330	1 819	858
1998	37 168	25 337	1	25 339	3 707	416	22 048	6 486	8 635	20 472	18 315	1 816	873
1999	38 136	26 309	-14	26 295	3 810	465	22 950	6 361	8 826	21 049	18 829	1 812	872
2000	40 067	27 519	18	27 537	4 124	591	24 004	6 801	9 263	22 174	19 815	1 807	880
2001	42 463	28 908	28	28 936	4 102	688	25 522	6 796	10 145	23 609	21 125	1 799	878
2002	43 884	29 557	-35	29 522	4 125	743	26 141	6 502	11 241	24 388	22 129	1 799	873
2003	44 906	30 497	-16	30 481	4 255	831	27 057	6 011	11 838	24 917	22 788	1 802	871
2004	46 497	32 255	29	32 284	4 377	877	28 784	6 033	11 680	25 785	23 667	1 803	881
2005	48 139	33 708	13	33 722	4 567	984	30 138	6 076	11 924	26 686	24 249	1 804	894
2006	51 894	36 001	-23	35 977	4 630	1 026	32 374	6 692	12 828	28 714	26 059	1 807	907
2007	54 555	37 203	-47	37 156	4 483	1 152	33 825	7 294	13 436	30 121	27 214	1 811	922
2008	57 411	39 237	-63	39 174	4 716	1 065	35 523	7 484	14 403	31 634	28 703	1 815	935
2009	58 631	39 644	-47	39 597	4 805	985	35 777	7 220	15 635	32 219	29 790	1 820	...

. . . = Not available.

Table 21-2. Personal Income and Employment by Region and State—*Continued*

(Millions of dollars, except as noted.)

| Region or state and year | Personal income, total | Earnings by place of work | | | Less: Contributions for government social insurance | Plus: Adjustment for residence | Equals: Net earnings by place of residence | Plus: Dividends, interest, and rent | Plus: Personal current transfer receipts | Per capita (dollars) | | Population (thousands) | Total employment (thousands) |
		Nonfarm	Farm	Total						Personal income	Disposable personal income		
WISCONSIN													
1958	7 940	6 126	451	6 578	233	52	6 397	1 033	510	2 066	1 843	3 843	. . .
1959	8 620	6 733	472	7 205	282	59	6 982	1 113	524	2 215	1 969	3 891	. . .
1960	8 911	7 012	421	7 432	341	63	7 155	1 199	557	2 249	1 982	3 962	. . .
1961	9 199	7 087	487	7 575	348	67	7 294	1 260	646	2 295	2 040	4 009	. . .
1962	9 735	7 559	484	8 043	374	74	7 743	1 334	658	2 404	2 127	4 049	. . .
1963	10 074	7 884	430	8 314	433	81	7 962	1 417	695	2 450	2 159	4 112	. . .
1964	10 869	8 506	470	8 976	449	91	8 618	1 527	724	2 610	2 327	4 165	. . .
1965	11 765	9 146	537	9 683	479	104	9 307	1 678	779	2 780	2 469	4 232	. . .
1966	12 877	10 084	661	10 745	668	123	10 200	1 815	862	3 013	2 652	4 274	. . .
1967	13 645	10 709	557	11 266	759	137	10 644	1 938	1 063	3 171	2 769	4 303	. . .
1968	14 904	11 574	640	12 214	815	158	11 557	2 109	1 237	3 430	2 992	4 345	. . .
1969	16 404	12 675	638	13 313	934	249	12 628	2 417	1 359	3 747	3 213	4 378	1 944
1970	17 621	13 396	639	14 036	974	253	13 314	2 708	1 599	3 981	3 463	4 426	1 954
1971	18 913	14 246	693	14 939	1 070	264	14 133	2 910	1 870	4 241	3 738	4 460	1 957
1972	20 698	15 716	729	16 445	1 248	287	15 485	3 134	2 079	4 601	4 011	4 498	2 014
1973	23 168	17 716	916	18 632	1 615	313	17 330	3 473	2 365	5 127	4 480	4 518	2 116
1974	25 499	19 423	806	20 229	1 841	339	18 728	3 960	2 811	5 619	4 884	4 538	2 159
1975	27 830	20 630	867	21 497	1 928	345	19 914	4 388	3 528	6 090	5 349	4 570	2 148
1976	30 620	23 196	763	23 958	2 188	390	22 161	4 643	3 817	6 679	5 832	4 585	2 211
1977	34 151	25 940	1 145	27 085	2 444	432	25 073	5 029	4 048	7 403	6 440	4 613	2 293
1978	38 199	29 340	1 129	30 469	2 847	487	28 109	5 619	4 471	8 247	7 115	4 632	2 380
1979	42 911	32 680	1 407	34 087	3 307	525	31 305	6 476	5 130	9 197	7 956	4 666	2 460
1980	47 519	34 738	1 446	36 184	3 507	548	33 225	8 045	6 248	10 085	8 764	4 712	2 443
1981	51 862	37 025	1 175	38 201	3 992	601	34 810	9 946	7 106	10 973	9 478	4 726	2 415
1982	54 727	38 081	1 025	39 106	4 150	620	35 576	11 223	7 927	11 573	10 092	4 729	2 373
1983	56 779	40 051	472	40 523	4 360	675	36 839	11 421	8 519	12 026	10 584	4 721	2 376
1984	62 094	43 919	1 002	44 921	4 905	792	40 808	12 561	8 724	13 112	11 567	4 736	2 467
1985	65 132	46 135	1 028	47 163	5 209	880	42 835	13 030	9 268	13 719	12 098	4 748	2 495
1986	68 594	48 674	1 306	49 980	5 504	961	45 437	13 598	9 560	14 424	12 718	4 756	2 537
1987	72 541	52 154	1 423	53 577	5 811	1 065	48 830	13 935	9 776	15 182	13 309	4 778	2 605
1988	76 929	56 557	863	57 420	6 531	1 233	52 121	14 682	10 126	15 953	13 998	4 822	2 684
1989	83 494	59 956	1 740	61 697	6 956	1 264	56 004	16 580	10 911	17 192	15 049	4 857	2 740
1990	88 213	64 081	1 397	65 479	7 735	1 352	59 095	17 418	11 700	17 986	15 716	4 905	2 814
1991	91 809	67 096	1 019	68 115	8 194	1 378	61 299	17 809	12 702	18 494	16 197	4 964	2 840
1992	98 872	72 786	1 279	74 065	8 832	1 513	66 745	18 363	13 765	19 674	17 244	5 025	2 894
1993	103 722	77 314	959	78 272	9 381	1 571	70 462	18 914	14 346	20 398	17 836	5 085	2 950
1994	110 630	82 488	1 226	83 714	10 113	1 689	75 289	20 550	14 791	21 550	18 803	5 134	3 040
1995	116 074	86 616	802	87 418	10 623	1 787	78 582	21 835	15 657	22 387	19 483	5 185	3 120
1996	122 953	90 586	1 372	91 958	11 058	1 936	82 837	23 911	16 206	23 509	20 327	5 230	3 171
1997	130 478	96 410	1 005	97 415	11 729	2 157	87 843	25 902	16 734	24 777	21 296	5 266	3 226
1998	141 019	103 926	1 374	105 300	12 443	2 303	95 159	28 696	17 165	26 619	22 827	5 298	3 282
1999	147 462	110 686	1 322	112 008	13 196	2 486	101 298	28 271	17 893	27 652	23 753	5 333	3 346
2000	156 603	117 022	880	117 901	13 837	2 720	106 784	30 579	19 240	29 139	25 078	5 374	3 405
2001	162 792	121 590	1 171	122 761	14 143	2 858	111 476	29 849	21 467	30 098	26 032	5 409	3 387
2002	167 742	126 410	1 066	127 475	14 504	2 935	115 906	28 732	23 104	30 797	27 216	5 447	3 395
2003	173 295	131 989	1 542	133 531	14 996	3 001	121 536	27 981	23 777	31 642	28 215	5 477	3 415
2004	180 338	137 939	1 881	139 821	15 803	3 134	127 152	28 695	24 491	32 721	29 257	5 511	3 469
2005	186 595	142 703	1 671	144 375	16 455	3 281	131 201	29 190	26 204	33 673	29 873	5 541	3 510
2006	198 598	149 342	1 386	150 728	17 366	3 436	136 798	34 046	27 755	35 644	31 445	5 572	3 552
2007	207 201	153 221	2 103	155 324	17 796	3 739	141 267	36 073	29 861	36 990	32 554	5 602	3 591
2008	212 553	156 561	2 172	158 733	18 398	3 799	144 134	36 628	31 791	37 770	33 433	5 628	3 620
2009	208 220	150 350	715	151 065	17 863	3 600	136 802	35 074	36 344	36 822	33 452	5 655	. . .

. . . = Not available.

Table 21-2. Personal Income and Employment by Region and State—*Continued*

(Millions of dollars, except as noted.)

Region or state and year	Personal income, total	Earnings by place of work			Less: Contributions for government social insurance	Plus: Adjustment for residence	Equals: Net earnings by place of residence	Plus: Dividends, interest, and rent	Plus: Personal current transfer receipts	Per capita (dollars)		Population (thousands)	Total employment (thousands)
		Nonfarm	Farm	Total						Personal income	Disposable personal income		
WYOMING													
1958	687	498	75	573	23	-1	549	100	38	2 182	1 973	315	...
1959	730	546	64	610	27	-1	582	107	42	2 282	2 053	320	...
1960	765	597	50	647	34	-1	611	109	45	2 312	2 068	331	...
1961	803	611	56	667	34	-1	632	119	53	2 384	2 146	337	...
1962	832	619	66	685	35	-1	649	128	54	2 498	2 238	333	...
1963	848	638	66	703	40	-1	662	130	56	2 524	2 235	336	...
1964	874	681	46	727	43	-1	684	135	55	2 577	2 348	339	...
1965	904	688	52	741	41	-1	700	147	58	2 724	2 479	332	...
1966	931	705	57	762	48	0	714	155	61	2 882	2 606	323	...
1967	999	748	70	818	53	0	764	163	71	3 101	2 787	322	...
1968	1 066	822	62	884	59	0	825	161	81	3 291	2 946	324	...
1969	1 180	901	70	971	66	*	905	186	89	3 587	3 169	329	158
1970	1 305	982	79	1 061	72	0	989	213	103	3 910	3 472	334	159
1971	1 447	1 084	88	1 172	81	-1	1 090	239	119	4 257	3 807	340	165
1972	1 628	1 215	126	1 341	96	-3	1 242	256	129	4 692	4 243	347	172
1973	1 904	1 436	153	1 589	128	-7	1 454	298	152	5 389	4 806	353	182
1974	2 242	1 774	111	1 885	159	-14	1 712	358	172	6 150	5 387	365	194
1975	2 557	2 071	67	2 138	182	-16	1 940	410	208	6 721	5 986	380	203
1976	2 857	2 355	48	2 403	213	-23	2 167	458	232	7 224	6 382	395	214
1977	3 355	2 809	45	2 854	249	-30	2 575	526	254	8 152	7 205	412	231
1978	4 036	3 405	65	3 471	309	-39	3 123	627	286	9 366	8 259	431	250
1979	4 751	4 012	96	4 108	381	-56	3 671	749	330	10 515	9 133	452	266
1980	5 533	4 656	86	4 742	442	-77	4 224	917	392	11 668	10 167	474	279
1981	6 298	5 272	52	5 324	546	-87	4 691	1 136	471	12 808	11 085	492	289
1982	6 760	5 369	29	5 398	569	-84	4 745	1 473	541	13 349	11 763	506	287
1983	6 483	5 082	36	5 118	522	-62	4 534	1 309	640	12 703	11 321	510	274
1984	6 773	5 301	14	5 315	560	-56	4 699	1 442	633	13 416	12 048	505	276
1985	7 064	5 529	17	5 546	599	-54	4 893	1 500	672	14 137	12 691	500	277
1986	7 060	5 440	39	5 479	581	-43	4 856	1 465	740	14 244	12 935	496	264
1987	6 814	5 128	60	5 188	550	-28	4 610	1 454	750	14 287	12 911	477	258
1988	6 893	5 171	60	5 231	598	-23	4 609	1 503	781	14 821	13 367	465	264
1989	7 509	5 504	90	5 594	621	-16	4 958	1 709	842	16 382	14 671	458	265
1990	8 125	5 890	153	6 043	690	-12	5 341	1 879	905	17 910	16 056	454	271
1991	8 537	6 068	213	6 281	737	-2	5 542	1 984	1 011	18 589	16 725	459	277
1992	9 019	6 420	222	6 642	770	-8	5 864	2 036	1 119	19 344	17 428	466	280
1993	9 492	6 809	248	7 057	809	-10	6 238	2 035	1 219	20 065	18 013	473	285
1994	9 962	7 180	122	7 302	857	-9	6 436	2 237	1 288	20 741	18 607	480	298
1995	10 362	7 386	103	7 488	880	-7	6 601	2 389	1 372	21 358	19 167	485	301
1996	10 853	7 631	83	7 714	899	-2	6 813	2 596	1 444	22 233	19 517	488	304
1997	11 636	8 062	185	8 247	935	3	7 316	2 839	1 482	23 774	20 776	489	307
1998	12 513	8 623	99	8 722	991	5	7 737	3 253	1 524	25 496	22 275	491	313
1999	13 372	9 191	168	9 359	1 039	4	8 324	3 460	1 588	27 192	23 700	492	316
2000	14 463	9 989	123	10 112	1 101	12	9 022	3 732	1 709	29 281	25 330	494	326
2001	15 438	10 851	190	11 041	1 180	4	9 866	3 728	1 844	31 315	27 364	493	331
2002	15 944	11 330	100	11 429	1 233	2	10 198	3 762	1 984	32 075	28 837	497	334
2003	16 933	11 851	180	12 031	1 294	1	10 738	4 065	2 129	33 920	30 854	499	337
2004	18 239	12 732	179	12 910	1 378	0	11 532	4 454	2 253	36 261	33 060	503	344
2005	19 969	13 694	232	13 925	1 488	-1	12 437	5 157	2 376	39 446	35 371	506	355
2006	22 912	15 810	100	15 910	1 917	-6	13 987	6 405	2 520	44 677	39 292	513	371
2007	24 457	16 909	26	16 935	2 094	-9	14 832	6 944	2 681	46 726	40 864	523	389
2008	25 892	18 180	82	18 261	2 239	-22	16 000	6 966	2 926	48 580	42 827	533	405
2009	24 876	17 431	55	17 485	2 155	-17	15 314	6 227	3 335	45 705	41 382	544	...

. . . = Not available.
* = Less than $50,000, but the estimates for this item are included in the total.

NOTES AND DEFINITIONS, CHAPTER 21

TABLE 21-1
GROSS DOMESTIC PRODUCT BY REGION AND STATE

SOURCE: U.S. DEPARTMENT OF COMMERCE, BUREAU OF ECONOMIC ANALYSIS (BEA)

A state's gross domestic product (GDP) is the sum of the value added or GDP originating in all the industries in a state. For explanation of GDP, see the notes and definitions to Tables 1-1 through 1-15. In concept, the sum of state GDPs, including the District of Columbia, is identical with national GDP except for Federal military and civilian activity located overseas, which cannot be attributed to a particular state. But because of that definitional difference, the "sum of states" GDP will differ from the national values shown in Chapter 1. GDP by state is only calculated on an annual basis.

Definitions and notes on the data

The value of an industry's GDP is equal to the market value of its gross output (which consists of sales or receipts and other operating income, taxes on production and imports, and inventory change) minus the value of its intermediate inputs (which consist of energy, raw materials, semifinished goods, and services that are purchased from domestic industries or foreign sources). In concept, this definition is equal to the sum of labor and property-type income earned in that industry in the production of GDP, plus commodity taxes. Property-type income is the sum of corporate profits, proprietors' income, rental income of persons, net interest, capital consumption allowances, business transfer payments, and the current surplus of government enterprises less subsidies.

In practice, GDP by state, like GDP by industry, is measured using the incomes data rather than data on gross output and intermediate inputs, which are not available on a sufficiently detailed and timely basis.

Therefore, the *value* of *GDP by state* is defined as the sum of labor and property-type incomes originating in each of 63 industries in that state, plus commodity taxes, and plus the allocated value of the statistical discrepancy between national GDP and national gross national income. Starting with the 2004 comprehensive revision of the data from 1997 forward, the annual industry accounts and the GDP-by-state accounts allocate the statistical discrepancy across all private-sector industries, making the GDP by state estimates more similar to GDP estimates than they had been in the past. In the SIC-based measures for 1977 through 1997, the statistical discrepancy has not been allocated to industries and states.

The *quantity indexes* of state GDP are aggregates of the real output of each industry in the state, net of intermediate inputs, based on chained constant-dollar estimates and

expressed as index numbers, 2000 = 100. They are derived by applying national implicit deflators calculated for each industry group to the current-dollar GDP estimates for that industry group in each state, and then applying the chain-type index formula used in the national accounts to aggregate the industry groups to the state total.

To the extent that a state's output is produced and sold in national markets at relatively uniform output and input prices, or sold locally at national prices, GDP by state captures the differences across states that reflect the relative differences in the mix of goods and services produced by the states. However, real GDP by state does not capture geographic differences in the output and input prices of goods and services produced and sold locally.

Estimates for the latest year (2008) are made using more limited source data and an abbreviated estimation methodology.

GDP by state is now calculated on a North American Industry Classification System (NAICS) basis back through 1997. Data for earlier years, beginning with 1977, were calculated on the Standard Industrial Classification (SIC) basis. According to BEA (in a "Cautionary note" on the Web site, dated June 7, 2007), "There is a discontinuity in the GDP by state time series at 1997, where the data change from SIC industry definitions to NAICS industry definitions. This discontinuity results from many sources, including differences in source data and different estimation methodologies. In addition, the NAICS-based GDP by state estimates are consistent with U.S. gross domestic product (GDP) while the SIC-based GDP by state estimates are consistent with U.S. gross domestic income (GDI). This data discontinuity may affect both the levels and the growth rates of the GDP by state estimates. Users of the GDP by state estimates are strongly cautioned against appending the two data series in an attempt to construct a single time series of GDP by state estimates for 1963 to 2006."

Business Statistics provides SIC-based data for 1977 to 1997 for those who require information about economic growth before 1997 by state. If a continuous series spanning the two time periods is needed despite the cautions just quoted, the earlier data can be linked to the later data using the values of the two series in the overlap year 1997.

Data availability and references

The estimates published here were presented and explained in "Gross Domestic Product by State: Advance Statistics for 2008 and Revised Statistics for 2005–2007" in the *Survey of Current Business,* June 2009. In addition to the data reproduced here, this article includes per capita real GDP by state and the contributions of the major industry sectors to economic growth in each state. This article and all historical data can be found on the Bureau of Economic Analysis (BEA) Web site <http://www.bea.gov>. The next release is scheduled for November 18, 2010.

TABLE 21-2
PERSONAL INCOME AND EMPLOYMENT BY REGION AND STATE

SOURCE: U.S. DEPARTMENT OF COMMERCE, BUREAU OF ECONOMIC ANALYSIS (BEA)

This table presents annual time-series data on personal income and employment for the United States as a whole, each individual state, the District of Columbia, and eight geographic regions for 1958 through 2009. In almost all respects, the data are consistent with the national personal income data as defined and presented in Chapters 1 and 4. BEA also publishes quarterly estimates of state personal income, which are not shown here.

The sum of state personal incomes for the United States shown in this table (which includes the District of Columbia) is somewhat smaller than U.S. personal income as shown in the national income and product accounts (NIPAs) in Chapters 1 and 4, due to slightly different definitions. The national total of the state estimates consists only of the income earned by persons who live in the United States and of foreign residents who work in the United States. The measure of personal income in the NIPAs is broader. It includes the earnings of federal civilian and military personnel stationed abroad (see below for a change in the definition of "stationed abroad") and of U.S. residents on foreign assignment for less than a year. It also includes the investment income received by federal retirement plans for federal workers stationed abroad. NIPA personal income includes all income earned by U.S. citizens living abroad for less than a year; state personal excludes the portion earned while the individual lives abroad. Earnings of foreign residents are included in the NIPAs only if they live and work in the United States for a year or more; state personal income, on the other hand, includes income paid to foreign nationals working in the United States regardless of length of residency. There are also statistical differences that reflect different timing of the availability of source data.

In an article entitled "State Personal Income: Second Quarter of 2005 and Revised Estimates for 2002–2005:I" in the October 2005 *Survey of Current Business*, BEA announced "New Treatment of State Estimates of Military Compensation." This announcement says, "BEA's state estimates of military compensation are based on troop data by base and national estimates of average pay from the Department of Defense (DOD). For 2001–2004, the DOD estimates of troops stationed at U.S. bases do not show a large decrease for troops sent to Afghanistan and Iraq. Those estimates reflect the DOD's new method of reporting active duty military personnel for the Army and the Air Force. The DOD now reports active duty regular military personnel according to the troops' home bases and reserve personnel according to the state of the reservists' bases. However, for the Marines, DOD continues to use an approach that reduces domestic base personnel figures when troops are sent overseas. Since BEA's state estimates of military earnings reflect

the geographic distribution of military personnel as reported by the DOD, the surge in military earnings due to the activation of reservists and the special pay associated with the war is recorded in the states from which the forces were deployed. This practice is consistent with the pay being received by family members at home and with news reports of strong retail sales at affected military bases.... Since the Persian Gulf war, the demographics of the armed forces have evolved, and BEA has changed its military residency definition accordingly. The current Army has a larger proportion of mature troops with families to support, in contrast to the typical young, single soldiers of the past."

Definitions

A state's *personal income* is the sum of earnings, dividends, interest, rental income, and current transfer receipts, net of government contributions for social insurance, of persons resident in that state, not persons working in that state. Its derivation from source data on earnings by place of work is shown in Table 21-2 and is explained below.

Earnings by place of work consists of payments to persons working in the state of wage and salary disbursements, all supplements to wages and salaries (including employer contributions for government social insurance and all other benefits), and farm and nonfarm proprietors' income.

Contributions for government social insurance, which is subtracted from total earnings, includes both the employer and the employee contributions for persons working in the state. Personal income is defined as net of all contributions for government social insurance, though not net of other taxes on wages or other income.

Adjustment for residence. BEA adjusts earnings by place of work to a place-of-residence basis, to account for interstate and international commuting. The difference between earnings by place of residence and earnings by place of work is shown in the "Adjustment for residence" column. This adjustment is a net figure, equaling income received by state (or area) residents from employment outside the state minus income paid to persons residing outside the state but working in the state. The treatment of wages earned by U.S. residents from employment at international organizations and foreign embassies and consulates was changed in the 2009 comprehensive revision, shifting those wages from state wages and salaries to the adjustment for residence category.

The effect of interstate commuting can be seen in its most extreme form by comparing 2009 data for the District of Columbia, with its adjustment for residence of negative $41 billion—representing net payments to persons living outside D.C.—with Maryland, which has an adjustment for residence of positive $28 billion net, from the District of Columbia and other employment sources outside the state.

Dividends, interest, and rent are aggregates for state residents of these categories as defined in U.S. personal income. The rental income component of personal income, which includes the imputed rent on owner-occupied homes, is net of capital consumption with capital consumption adjustment. The revised treatment of disaster losses in the NIPAs (see notes and definitions to Chapter 1, Tables 1-10 through 1-12) means that the estimates of state rental incomes are no longer offset, or even completely wiped out, by extreme events such as Hurricane Katrina, which had been the case in the pre-2009 estimates; now, only normal depreciation enters into rental income calculations.

Personal current transfer receipts are aggregates for state residents of such receipts as defined in U.S. personal income.

Population is the U.S. Census Bureau estimate for the <u>middle</u> of the year. Note that because Hurricane Katrina occurred in September of 2005, the population decline in Louisiana caused by that event does not appear until the entry for 2006.

Total employment is the total number of jobs, full-time plus part-time; each job that any person holds is counted at full weight. The employment estimates are on a place-of-work basis. Both wage and salary employment and self-employment are included. The main source for the wage and salary employment estimates is the Bureau of Labor Statistics estimates from unemployment insurance data (the ES-202 data), which also provides benchmarks for the payroll employment measures (see Table 10-7 and its notes and definitions). Self-employment is estimated mainly from individual and partnership federal income tax returns.

This concept of employment differs from the concept of employment in the Current Population Survey (CPS), which is derived from a monthly count of persons employed; any individual will appear only once in the CPS in a given month, no matter how many different jobs he or she might hold. (See the notes and definitions to Tables 10-1 through 10-5.) In addition, a self-employed individual who files more than one Schedule C income-tax filing will be counted more than once in the state figures. Finally, the state figures include members of the armed forces, who are not covered in the CPS. Due to these differences and other possible reporting inconsistencies, the BEA employment estimates are different from, and usually larger than, state employment estimates from the CPS.

The employment estimates correspond closely in coverage to the earnings estimates by place of work. However, the earnings estimates include the income of limited partnerships and of tax-exempt cooperatives, for which there are no corresponding employment estimates.

Per capita income is total income divided by the state's midyear population. It is therefore an average or "mean,"

subject to the qualifications discussed in the article at the beginning of this volume, under the "Whose Standard of Living?" heading. For recent data on median household income by state, which give a better idea of the income received by typical residents of the state, see Table 3-6 in Chapter 3.

The states and the District of Columbia are divided into regions by BEA as follows:

- **New England:** Connecticut, Maine, Massachusetts, New Hampshire, Rhode Island, and Vermont
- **Mideast:** Delaware, District of Columbia, Maryland, New Jersey, New York, and Pennsylvania
- **Great Lakes:** Illinois, Indiana, Michigan, Ohio, and Wisconsin
- **Plains:** Iowa, Kansas, Minnesota, Missouri, Nebraska, North Dakota, and South Dakota
- **Southeast:** Alabama, Arkansas, Florida, Georgia, Kentucky, Louisiana, Mississippi, North Carolina, South Carolina, Tennessee, Virginia, and West Virginia
- **Southwest:** Arizona, New Mexico, Oklahoma, and Texas
- **Rocky Mountain:** Colorado, Idaho, Montana, Utah, and Wyoming
- **Far West:** Alaska, California, Hawaii, Nevada, Oregon, and Washington

These BEA regional groupings differ from the region and division definitions used by the Census Bureau.

Data availability and references

The 2009 comprehensive revision of state personal incomes is presented and described in the November 2009 *Survey of Current Business*, which can be found in the publications section of the general BEA web site. Detailed data on the revised basis back to 1969 are available at <http://www.bea.gov/bea/regional/spi>. Additional revisions for 1929 through 1968 are scheduled to be released in 2010. The 1958-1968 data shown here in *Business Statistics* are unrevised data from the 2003 comprehensive revision of the NIPAs, described in the *Survey of Current Business* for May 2004.

Also on the BEA Web site are some annual state data that go back even farther than shown here. Included are data on personal income, per capita personal income, and population back to 1929; disposable personal income and per capita disposable personal income back to 1948; and various levels of industry detail for income and wages and salaries within the state data back to 1929. For a complete listing, see the article "State Personal Income: Second Quarter of 2005 and Revised Estimates for 2002–2005:I" in the October 2005 issue of the *Survey of Current Business*.

INDEX